OXFORD PAPERBAC

The Concise Oxford Dictionary of

Music

Michael Kennedy was chief music critic of the *Sunday Telegraph* from 1989 to 2005. Before that he was a staff music critic on the *Daily Telegraph* from 1950 and its Northern Editor from 1960 to 1986. He is an authority on English music of the twentieth century and has written books on Elgar, Vaughan Williams, Britten, and Walton as well as on Mahler, Strauss, Barbirolli, Boult, and the Hallé Orchestra. He was awarded the OBE in 1981 and the CBE in 1997. He was a member of the Board of Governors of the Royal Northern College of Music, Manchester from 1971 to 2006. The honorary degree of Doctor of Music was conferred on him in 2003 by the University of Manchester and he became an honorary member of the Royal Philharmonic Society in 2005.

Joyce Bourne Kennedy practised for almost 30 years as an anaesthetist and general practitioner until her retirement in 1990. She has a lifelong interest in and love of music. She is married to Michael Kennedy and has assisted him with his works since 1978. Her book *Who's Who in Opera* was published in 1998.

Oxford Paperback Reference

The most authoritative and up-to-date reference books for both students and the general reader.

ABC of Music
Accounting
Allusions
Animal Behaviour
Archaeology
Architecture and Landscape Architecture
Art and Artists
Art Terms
Arthurian Legend and Literature*
Astronomy
Battles*
Better Wordpower
Bible
Biology
British History
British Place-Names
Buddhism
Business and Management
Card Games
Catchphrases
Celtic Mythology
Chemistry
Christian Art
Christian Church
Chronology of English Literature
Century of New Words
Classical Literature
Classical Myth and Religion
Classical World*
Computing
Contemporary World History
Countries of the World
Dance
Dynasties of the World
Earth Sciences
Ecology
Economics
Encyclopedia
Engineering*
English Etymology
English Folklore
English Grammar
English Language
English Literature
English Surnames
Euphemisms
Everyday Grammar
Finance and Banking
First Names
Food and Drink
Food and Nutrition
Foreign Words and Phrases
Geography
Humorous Quotations
Idioms
Internet

Islam
Kings and Queens of Britain
Language Toolkit
Law
Law Enforcement*
Linguistics
Literary Terms
Local and Family History
London Place-Names
Mathematics
Medical
Medicinal Drugs
Modern Design
Modern Quotations
Modern Slang
Music
Musical Terms
Musical Works
Nicknames
Nursing
Ologies and Isms
Philosophy
Phrase and Fable
Physics
Plant Sciences
Plays*
Pocket Fowler's Modern English Usage
Political Quotations
Politics
Popes
Proverbs
Psychology
Quotations
Quotations by Subject
Reverse Dictionary
Rhymes*
Rhyming Slang
Saints
Science
Scientific Quotations
Shakespeare
Ships and the Sea
Slang
Sociology
Space Exploration
Statistics
Superstitions
Synonyms and Antonyms
Weather
Weights, Measures, and Units
Word Histories
World History
World Mythology
World Place-Names
World Religions
Zoology

forthcoming

The Concise
Oxford Dictionary of

Music

FIFTH EDITION

MICHAEL KENNEDY
and JOYCE BOURNE KENNEDY

UNIVERSITY PRESS

OXFORD
UNIVERSITY PRESS

Great Clarendon Street, Oxford OX2 6DP

Oxford University Press is a department of the University of Oxford.
It furthers the University's objective of excellence in research, scholarship,
and education by publishing worldwide in

Oxford New York

Auckland Cape Town Dar es Salaam Hong Kong Karachi
Kuala Lumpur Madrid Melbourne Mexico City Nairobi
New Delhi Shanghai Taipei Toronto

With offices in

Argentina Austria Brazil Chile Czech Republic France Greece
Guatemala Hungary Italy Japan Poland Portugal Singapore
South Korea Switzerland Thailand Turkey Ukraine Vietnam

Oxford is a registered trade mark of Oxford University Press
in the UK and in certain other countries

Published in the United States
by Oxford University Press Inc., New York

First edition (edited by Percy A. Scholes) 1952
Second edition (edited by John Owen Ward) 1964
Third edition (edited by Michael Kennedy) 1980
Fourth edition 1996
Reissued with new covers 2004
Fifth edition 2007

British Library Cataloguing in Publication Data

Data available

Library of Congress Cataloging in Publication Data

Data available

Typeset by SPI Publisher Services, Pondicherry, India
Printed in Great Britain by
Clays Ltd, St Ives plc

ISBN-13: 978-0-19-920383-3

1

Contents

FOR EMILY, JENNIFER, REBEKAH,
DANIEL, AND ALISTAIR

Preface to Fifth Edition

For this latest edition, a substantial revision of many entries has been undertaken. We have updated many contemporary composers' work-lists and have also corrected and updated, wherever possible, musicians' appointments. We have also added a considerable number of new entries. We are extremely grateful to agents and to press officers of many organizations all over the world for their help in ascertaining dates and facts. We are also grateful to Google! No dictionary can claim to be error-free and we would be happy to hear from readers who notice mistakes.

MICHAEL AND JOYCE KENNEDY

Manchester 2006

Preface to Fourth Edition

This new edition of the *Concise Oxford Dictionary of Music* is based on the extensive revision of the *Oxford Dictionary of Music* which was published towards the end of 1994. It incorporates various additions, updatings of work-lists, corrections, and also several extra entries. As this is the Concise version, a number of entries have been deleted, details compressed, and some of the work-lists of lesser-known composers abbreviated. But none of the entries for major composers has been shortened in any way. For this work of reduction, I am greatly indebted to my associate editor, Joyce Bourne, but the responsibility for errors and omissions is mine.

Asterisks (indicating a separate entry) occur against compositions only in the work-list, not in the biographical essay. Asterisks occur against individuals where I think a cross-reference could be useful. If an asterisk was used *every* time the name of a separate entry occurs, the book would look like the Milky Way. Dates of works are those of composition whenever that has accurately been ascertained; otherwise the date given is that of first performance or publication, whichever is the earlier.

The American nomenclature of whole-note, quarter-note, measure, etc. has been preferred to the English semibreve, crotchet, bar, etc. Place names generally are given their modern spelling, and I have differentiated between St Petersburg, Petrograd, Leningrad, and now St Petersburg again, and between Christiania and Oslo, etc. For titles of foreign works, my policy is usually to give the chief entry under the name by which the work is familiarly known, with a leaning towards the original-language title. This leaves a broad band of disputable decisions. For some opera titles I have given no English title cross-reference, for example *Der Rosenkavalier, La traviata, Così fan tutte*, and *Der Freischütz*. Border-line cases such as *Le nozze di Figaro* and *Die Soldaten* are listed under their original titles.

In the contentious matter of transliteration of Russian names, I prefer Rachmaninov, Scriabin, Chaliapin, Diaghilev, and Tchaikovsky to Rakhmaninov, Skryabin, Shalyapin, Dyaghilev, and Chaykovsky, on the grounds that most books and record-labels still favour the former spellings.

I repeat here the thanks I offered in the preface to the *Oxford Dictionary of Music*: to Joyce Bourne, who in addition to editorial work has typed all the new material and corrections on a word-processor; to Mr Lee Charin, for transferring the first edition from magnetic tape to computer disks; to Mr David Cummings of Harrow for suggestions, corrections, provision of dates, and much support; to Mr Dennis K. McIntire of Indianapolis and Mr Paul E. Morrison of Rochester, Michigan, for their invaluable help. Thanks, too, to many others who have made suggestions and sent corrections.

MICHAEL KENNEDY

Manchester 1995

Abbreviations

AAM	Academy of Ancient Music	ch.	chorus
ABC	Australian Broadcasting Commission	Ch. Ch.	Christ Church, Oxford
acad.	academy	choreog.	choreography/choreographed (by)/
acc.	accompanying/accompanied (by)/		choreographer
	accompanist/accordion	cit.	citizen
adv.	adviser	cl.	clarinet
Amer.	America(n)	CMG	Companion of the Order of St
AMF	Academy of St Martin-in-the-Fields		Michael and St George
amp.	amplified	CO	Chamber Orchestra
arr.	arranged (by, for)/arrangement	coll.	college/collection
	(by, of)	collab.	collaboration/collaborated (with)
art. dir.	artistic director	comp.	composer/composed (by, in)/
ass.	assistant (to)/assisted (by)		composition/competition
assoc.	associate/association	conc.	concerto
attrib.	attributed (to)	cond.	conductor (of)/conducted (by)
		Conn.	Connecticut
b	born	cons.	conservatory
b	bass (vocal or as in bcl, bass clari-	cont.	contralto/contribution
	net)	counterten.	countertenor
bar.	baritone	CVO	Commander of the Royal Victorian
bass-bar.	bass-baritone		Order
BBC	British Broadcasting Corporation	Cz.	Czechoslovakia(n)
BBCPO	BBC Philharmonic Orchestra		
BBCSO	BBC Symphony Orchestra	*d*	died
bc	basso continuo	D	Deutsch catalogue number
BC	Before Christ/British Columbia		(Schubert works)
Belg.	Belgium/Belgian	db.	double bass
bn.	bassoon	DBE	Dame Commander of the Order of
BNOC	British National Opera Company		the British Empire
Braz.	Brazil/Brazilian	ded.	dedicated (to)
Brit.	Britain/British	Del.	Delaware
BWV	Bach Werke-Verzeichnis	dept.	department
		dir.	director (of)
c.	*circa* (Latin = about)	DMus	Doctor of Music
ca.	cor anglais		
Calif.	California	E.	East
Cath.	Cathedral	ECO	English Chamber Orchestra
CB	Companion of the Order of	ed.	editor/edited (by)
	the Bath	edn.	edition
CBE	Commander of the Order of the	elec.	electronic
	British Empire	EMS	Electronic Music Studio(s)
CBS	Columbia Broadcasting System	EMT	English Music Theatre
CBSO	City of Birmingham Symphony	Eng.	England/English
	Orchestra	ENO	English National Opera
CBTO	City of Birmingham Touring Opera	ens.	ensemble
cel.	celesta	ENSA	Entertainments National Service
CEMA	Council for the Encouragement of		Association
	Music and the Arts	EOG	English Opera Group
cent.	century	esp.	especially
cf.	*conferatur* (Latin = compare)	est.	established (in, by)/establishment
CG	Covent Garden (Royal Opera	ETO	English Touring Opera
	House), London	euph.	euphonium
CH	Companion of Honour	Eur.	Europe(an)

fest.	festival	La.	Louisiana
Finn.	Finnish	Lat.	Latin
fl.	*floruit* (Latin = flourished)	ldr.	leader
fl.	flute	lect.	lecturer/lectured
Fla.	Florida	lib.	libretto/library
f.p., f.ps.	first performance(s)/first	LPO	London Philharmonic Orchestra
	performed (by, in)	LSO	London Symphony Orchestra
Fr.	France/French		
		man.	manager
GBE	Knight or Dame Grand Cross of the	mand.	mandolin
	Order of the British Empire	man. dir.	managing director
GCVO	Knight or Dame Grand Cross of the	mar.	marimba
	Royal Victorian Order	Mass.	Massachusetts
gen.	general	MBE	Member of the Order of the British
gen. man.	general manager		Empire
Ger.	German(y)	Md.	Maryland
glock.	glockenspiel	Me.	Maine
Gr.	Greece/Greek	Met	Metropolitan Opera House, New
GSMD	Guildhall School of Music and		York
	Drama, London	mez.	mezzo-soprano
GTO	Glyndebourne Touring Opera	Mich.	Michigan
	(now known as Glyndebourne	Miss.	Missouri
	on Tour)	movt(s).	movement(s)
gui.	guitar	MS(S)	manuscript(s)
		mus.	music/musical
hn.	horn (French)	mus. adv.	musical adviser
hon.	honorary	mus. dir.	musical director
hp.	harp		
hpd.	harpsichord	N.	North
Hung.	Hungary/Hungarian	narr.	narrator
		nat.	national
Ill.	Illinois	NBC	National Broadcasting Company of
incid.	incidental (music)		America
incl.	include(d)/including	NH	New Hampshire
Ind.	Indiana	NHKSO	Nippon Hōsō Kyōkai Symphony
insp.	inspector		Orchestra
inst.	institute	NJ	New Jersey
instr(s).	instrument(s)/instrumental	Norweg.	Norwegian
int.	international	nr.	near
IoW	Isle of Wight	NSM	Northern School of Music,
IRCAM	Institut de Recherche et de		Manchester
	Co-ordination Acoustique-Musique,	NSW	New South Wales, Australia
	Paris	NY	New York
ISCM	International Society for	NY Met	Metropolitan Opera House (or
	Contemporary Music		Company), New York
ISM	Incorporated Society of Musicians	NYPO	New York Philharmonic Orchestra
	(Britain)	NYSO	New York Symphony Orchestra
It.	Italy/Italian	NZ	New Zealand
K	Köchel catalogue number (Mozart	OAE	Orchestra of the Age of
	works)		Enlightenment
kbd.	keyboard	ob.	oboe
KBE	Knight Commander of the Order of	obbl.	obbligato
	the British Empire	OBE	Officer of the Order of the British
KCVO	Knight Commander of the Royal		Empire
	Victorian Order	OC	Opera Company

OM	Order of Merit (Member of)
Op.	Opus
opt.	optional
orch.	orchestra/orchestral/orchestrated (by, for)
ORF	Österreichische Rundfunk (Austrian Radio)
org.	organ/organist
ov.	overture
Pa.	Pennsylvania
perc.	percussion(ist)
perf.	performer/performed (by)
pf.	pianoforte
Phil.	Philharmonic
picc.	piccolo
PO	Philharmonic Orchestra
posth.	posthumous(ly)
pres.	president
prin.	principal
prod.	produced (by, in)/producer/ production
prof.	professor/profession(al)
prog.	programme
prol.	prologue
pub.	publication
pubd.	published (by, in)
QEH	Queen Elizabeth Hall, London
RADA	Royal Academy of Dramatic Art
RAH	Royal Albert Hall
RAI	Italian Radio
RAM	Royal Academy of Music, London
RC	Roman Catholic
RCCO	Royal Canadian College of Organists
RCM	Royal College of Music, London
RCO	Royal College of Organists, London
rec.	recorder
recit.	reciter
reh.	rehearsal/rehearsed (by)
res.	residence/resident
rev.	revised/revision (by, in, for)
RFH	Royal Festival Hall, London
RI	Rhode Island
RLPO	Royal Liverpool Philharmonic Orchestra
RMA	Royal Musical Association (Britain)
RMCM	Royal Manchester College of Music
RNCM	Royal Northern College of Music, Manchester
ROH	Royal Opera House, Covent Garden
RPO	Royal Philharmonic Orchestra
RPS	Royal Philharmonic Society
RSAMD	Royal Scottish Academy of Music and Drama

RSC	Royal Shakespeare Company
RSCM	Royal School of Church Music, London
RSM	Royal Schools of Music (Britain)
RSNO	Royal Scottish National Orchestra (previously SNO)
RTE	Radio Telefís Éireann, Dublin
Russ.	Russia(n)
S.	South
S./San/St/Ste	Saint
SATB	soprano, alto (contralto), tenor, bass
sax.	saxophone
S.C.	South Carolina
sch.	school
schol.	scholarship
SCO	Scottish Chamber Orchestra
sec.	secretary
SNO	Scottish National Orchestra (see RSNO)
SO	Symphony Orchestra
soc.	society
sop.	soprano
Sp.	Spain/Spanish
spkr.	speaker
SPNM	Society for the Promotion of New Music
str(s).	string(s)
str. qt(s).	string quartet(s)
suppl.	supplement
SW	Sadler's Wells (Theatre, Opera, Ballet), London
Swed.	Sweden/Swedish
sym(s).	symphony, symphonies
synth.	synthesizer
tb.	trombone
TCL	Trinity College of Music, London
tech.	technical/technician
ten.	tenor
Tenn.	Tennessee
th.	theatre
timp.	timpani
tpt.	trumpet
trans.	translated (by, for)/translation
transcr.	transcribed (by, for)/transcription
TV	television
UCLA	University of California at Los Angeles, USA
unacc.	unaccompanied
univ.	university
USA	United States of America
v., vv.	voice, voices
Va.	Virginia

va.	viola(s)	WoO	Werk ohne Opuszahl (work without opus number)
var.	various/variation(s)		
vc.	cello(s)	ww.	woodwind
vers.	version		
vib.	vibraphone	xyl.	xylophone
vn.	violin(s)	*	See separate entry for further information
W.	West		
WNO	Welsh National Opera		

Designation of Notes by Letters

 c''' to c''''

 c'' to b''

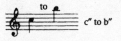 c' to b'

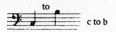 c to b

 C to B

 C, to B,

A

A. Note of the scale (6th degree of natural scale of C). Hence A♭, A♭♭, A♮, A♯, A♯♯, A major, A minor, etc. A is note commonly used for tuning instr. (orchs. tune to the ob. A). a′ = 440 vibrations per second, internationally accepted since 1939, although some orchs. still accept a′ = 435 and (in USA) a′ = 445.

a (It.), **à** (Fr.). At, by, for, with, in, to, in the manner of, etc. For expressions beginning with 'a' or 'à', e.g. *a cappella*, *a tempo*, see under their own entries.
  'A 2' in orch. scores and parts directs (a) 2 instr. that normally play separate parts (e.g. the 2 ob. or 2 fl.) to play in unison, or (b) 2 or more instr. that normally play in unison (e.g. 1st vns.) to divide to play the separate parts provided for them.

a. Abbreviation for *accelerando* found particularly in Elgar's scores.

AAGO. Associate of the *American Guild of Organists.

ab (Ger.). Off. In org. mus., applied to a stop no longer required.

ABA. Term of analysis to describe form of a piece of mus., i.e. 1st section (A) followed by different section (B) followed by repeat of 1st section (A). Many permutations possible.

abandonné (Fr.). Negligent (in such an expression as *Un rhythme un peu abandonné*—rhythm rather free-and-easy).

a battuta (It.). With the beat, indicating return to strict tempo.

Abbà-Cornaglia, Pietro (*b* Alessandria, Piedmont, 1851; *d* Alessandria, 1894). It. composer and organist. Operas incl. *Isabella Spinola* (1877) and *Una partita di scacchi* (1892). Also wrote a requiem and chamber mus.

Abbado, Claudio (*b* Milan, 1933). It. conductor. Cond. début, Trieste 1958. Won Koussevitzky Award at Berkshire Music Center, 1958, Mitropoulos prize (jointly), 1963. Débuts: Salzburg Fest. 1965; NY Met 1968; CG 1968; Vienna Opera 1984. Prin. cond., La Scala 1968, mus. dir. 1972, art. dir. 1976–86; regular cond., Vienna PO 1971–82. Eng. début Manchester 1965 (Hallé Orch.). Prin. cond. LSO 1979, mus. dir. 1983–8. Mus. dir., Vienna Opera 1986–91, Berlin PO from 1989. Founded European Community Youth Orch. 1978; prin. cond. of Europe from 1981; founded Gustav Mahler Youth Orch., Vienna, 1986. In USA, worked with Chicago SO 1982–5. Art. dir. Salzburg Easter Fest. 1994–2002.

abbandono (It.). Abandon. Free, impassioned style.

abbassare (It.). To lower, e.g. to tune down a str. of an instr. of the vn. family to obtain a note normally outside its compass.

Abbatini, Antonio Maria (*b* Città di Castello, *c*.1609; *d* Città di Castello, 1677). It. church musician and composer. Choirmaster at St John Lateran and other Roman churches. Helped to prepare new edn. of Gregorian hymns. Wrote sacred canzonas, a 16-part mass, cantatas, and operas.

abbellimenti (It.). Ornaments, embellishments.

abbreviations. Signs whereby writing-out of phrases or groups of notes may be abbreviated. For example, continued repetition of a note is indicated by crossing its stem with one or more strokes to show the required sub-division into smaller values (for triplets or groups of 6 the figures 3 or 6 are added above the notes); and a passage to be played in octaves may be written asa single line, with the words *con ottave* or *con 8ve*.

abdämpfen (Ger.). To damp off. To mute, especially in connection with timp.

Abduction from the Seraglio, The (Mozart). See *Entführung aus dem Serail, Die*.

Abe, Komei (*b* Hiroshima, 1911). Japanese composer and conductor. Prof. of comp., Kyoto Univ. of Arts 1969–74. Works incl.: *Theme and Variations*, orch. (1936); vc. conc. (1942); pf. conc. (1945); sym. No.1 (1957), No.2 (1960); *Serenade* (1963); Sinfonietta (1965); *Variations on a Subject by Grieg*, brass ens. (1972); 14 str. qts. (1935–92); 2 fl. sonatas (1948, 1949); cl. quintet (1942); pf. sextet (1964); pf. sonatina (1970); 3 sonatas for children, pf. (1972); *Kaze No Yukue*, sop., pf. (1993); *Kareno Komachi*, mez., pf. (1994); choral mus.; songs; film mus.

Abegg Variations. Schumann's Op.1, for solo pf., comp. 1830. Written on a theme made out of the notes A–B(Ger. B = Eng. B♭)–E–G–G, and ded. to his friend Meta Abegg.

Abel, Karl Friedrich (*b* Cöthen, 1723; *d* London, 1787). Ger. composer and player of viola da gamba. Pupil of J. S. Bach at Leipzig; orch. player under Hasse at Dresden 1748–58. Settled in London 1759, becoming chamber musician to Queen Charlotte. Associated with J. C. *Bach in promoting and directing Bach–Abel subscription concerts 1765–82. Comps. incl. ov. to T. Arne's pasticcio *Love in a village* (1762), syms., ovs., sonatas, etc.

Abencérages, Les. Opera in 3 acts by Cherubini to lib. by V. J. E. de Jouy, based on Florian's novel

(1791) *Gonzalve de Cordove* (f.p. Paris, 1813; revived Florence, 1957). Title refers to Moorish Abenceragi warriors.

Abend (Ger.). Evening; **Abendlied**. Evening Song; **Abendmusik**. Evening mus. perfs., usually religious and specifically those by *Buxtehude at Lübeck on the five Sundays before Christmas, started in 1673. Continued after his death until 1810.

Abendroth, Hermann (*b* Frankfurt am Main, 1883; *d* Jena, 1956). Ger. conductor. Chief cond. Lübeck Opera 1907–11 and mus. dir. at Essen 1911–15. Dir. of Cologne Cons. 1915, becoming gen. mus. dir. of Gürzenich Orch. 1918–34. Guest cond. of LSO 1927–37. Cond. Leipzig Gewandhaus Orch., 1934–45. Mus. dir., Weimar Nat. Th. 1945, Weimar SO from 1946. Chief cond. Leipzig Radio SO from 1949. Chief cond. Berlin (East) Radio SO 1953. Bayreuth 1943–4.

Abercrombie, (John Ralph) **Alexander** (Giles) (*b* London, 1949). Eng. pianist and composer. Début London 1972. Gave f.ps. of pf. works by Finnissy, Xenakis, Skalkottas, etc.

Abert, Hermann (*b* Stuttgart, 1871; *d* Stuttgart, 1927). Ger. mus. scholar. His recasting (1919–21) of *Jahn's standard life of Mozart was very important. Prof. at Univs. of Leipzig (1920), Berlin (1923).

Aberystwyth. Hymn-tune by Joseph *Parry to which words 'Jesu, lover of my soul' are sung. Tune pubd. 1879. Words, by Charles Wesley, written in 1740 for his *Hymns and Sacred Poems*.

Abide With Me. Hymn, words written by Rev. Henry Francis Lyte (1793–1847) in 1820 after attending death-bed of friend at Pole Hore, near Wexford, and first pubd. in Lyte's *Remains* (1850). Tune, 'Eventide', comp. by org. William Henry Monk (1823–89) for these words for *Hymns Ancient and Modern* (1861). Descant by Vaughan Williams in *Songs of Praise* (1925). Among most popular hymns, nowadays particularly assoc. with FA Cup Final at Wembley where crowd sing it, movingly if incongruously, before teams come on to the pitch.

ablösen (Ger.). To loosen from one another. There are various applications, e.g. to separate the notes (i.e. to play *staccato).

abnehmend (Ger.). Off-taking, i.e. *diminuendo.

Abraham, Gerald (Ernest Heal) (*b* Newport, IoW, 1904; *d* Midhurst, 1988). Eng. mus. critic and scholar, authority on Russ. mus.; ed. of *Monthly Musical Record* 1945–60. On BBC staff 1935–47, again 1962–7; first Prof. of Mus., Liverpool Univ. 1947–62. Author of *Concise Oxford History of Music* (1979). CBE 1974.

Abraham and Isaac. (1) Britten's Canticle II for alto, ten., and pf., text from Chester miracle play, comp. 1952 for Kathleen *Ferrier and Peter *Pears.

(2) Sacred ballad for bar. and chamber orch. by Stravinsky to Hebrew text. Comp. 1962–3 and ded. to 'people of the State of Israel'. F.p. Jerusalem 1964.

Abram, Jacques (*b* Lufkin, Texas, 1915). Amer. pianist and teacher. Schubert memorial award, 1938. Professional début Philadelphia 1938. Toured Eur. 1951. Taught at Juilliard Sch. 1934–8, at Oklahoma Coll. for Women, Chickasha, 1955–60, and at Toronto Royal Cons. of Mus. from 1960.

Abravanel, Maurice (*b* Salonika, 1903; *d* Salt Lake City, 1993). Gr.-born Amer. conductor. Début Berlin 1924. Cond. at Zwickau and in opera houses in Berlin and Rome. Toured Australia 1934–6. Cond. at NY Met 1936–8 (début *Samson et Dalila*). Cond. on Broadway and at Chicago Opera 1940–1. Cond., Utah SO 1947–79. Special sympathy for Eng. mus., notably that of Vaughan Williams.

abruzzese (It.). A song or dance in the style of the Abruzzi district, to the E. of Rome. 3rd movt. of Berlioz's *Harold en Italie* is called 'Serenade of an Abruzzi mountaineer to his mistress'.

Abschied (Ger.). Farewell. Hence *Abschiedsymphonie* (No.45 in F♯ minor) by Haydn. 6th and last movt. of Mahler's *Das *Lied von der Erde* is named 'Der Abschied'.

Abschiedsymphonie (Farewell Symphony). Nickname of Haydn's Sym. No.45 in F♯ minor, 1772 (Hob. I:45) because of the following incident: Prince Nikolaus, Haydn's employer, became so attracted to his lonely Eszterháza Castle that he spent longer there each year. Except for Haydn, the court musicians could not have their families with them and grew depressed. Haydn comp. this sym. with a final *adagio* during which one player after another blew out the candle on his mus.-stand and crept away, leaving only 2 vns., Tomasini and Haydn. As they too were about to leave, the Prince is supposed to have taken the hint by saying: 'Well, if they all leave, we might as well go too'—and next day the court returned to Vienna.

Absil, Jean (*b* Bonsecours, Belgium, 1893; *d* Brussels, 1974). Belg. composer. Prof. of harmony, Brussels Cons. 1939–59. Many comps., incl. 5 syms., 3 pf. concs., 4 vn. concs., 4 str. qts., and many instr. and choral works.

ABSM; ABSM (TTD). Associate of the Birmingham School of Music (Teachers' Training Diploma).

absolute music. Instr. mus. which exists simply as such, i.e. not *'programme music', or in any way illustrative.

absolute pitch (sense of). That sense which some people possess of the actual pitch of any note heard, as distinct from relative pitch, which implies the recognition of a note as being a certain degree of the scale or as lying at a certain interval above or below another note heard. The sense of relative pitch may readily be acquired by practice, but the sense of absolute pitch much less easily.

Absolute pitch is really an innate form of memory: the possessor retains in his or her mind (consciously or unconsciously) the pitch of some instr. to which he or she has been accustomed and instinctively relates to that pitch every sound heard. Many good musicians possess this faculty; as many others do not. The possession of this sense is sometimes extremely useful, but may also prove an embarrassment, as, for instance, when a singer with absolute pitch is called upon to read mus. accompanied by an instr. tuned to what is to him or her 'the wrong pitch', necessitating a conscious transposition of the vocal line.

abstossen (Ger.). (1) To detach notes from one another, i.e. to play *staccato.

(2) In org. playing, to cease to use a stop. (The past participle is *abgestossen*.)

abstract music. Same as *absolute music. As used by Ger. writers (*Abstrakte Musik*), the term has a different meaning—mus. lacking in sensitivity, 'dry' or 'academic'.

Abu Hassan. *Singspiel in 1 act by Weber to lib. by F. K. Hiemer after tale in *1001 Nights*. Comp. 1810–11. Prod. Munich 1811; London (with mus. adapted) 1825; NY 1827.

abwechseln, abzuwechseln (Ger.). To change. Used of orch. instr. alternating with another in the hands of the same player, etc.

Abyngdon [Abingdon, Habyngton, etc.], **Henry** (*b* c.1418; *d* 1497). Eng. singer, organist, and composer (none of whose works has yet been found). Precentor of Wells Cath. First person known to have taken a mus. degree at Cambridge (B.Mus., 1464).

Academic Festival Overture (*Akademische Festouvertüre*). Brahms's Op.80, f.p. 1881 at Breslau Univ. in acknowledgement of an honorary Ph.D. degree conferred on him there in 1879. Makes fantasia-like use of 4 Ger. student songs, *Wir hatten gebauet ein stattliches Haus* (We have built a stately house), *Der Landesvater* (The Land Father), *Was kommt dort von der Höhe* (What comes from afar), and *Gaudeamus igitur* (Therefore let us rejoice).

Academy of Ancient Music. London Soc. formed 1726 for perf. and study of vocal and instr. works. For some time dir. was *Pepusch. Survived until 1792. Title revived in 1973 for early mus. ens. dir. by Christopher *Hogwood until 2006, succeeded by Richard Eggar.

Academy of St Martin-in-the-Fields. Chamber orch. founded 1958 and so called because it gave concerts in the London church of that name. Dir. Neville *Marriner until 1978, then Iona Brown until 2004. Kenneth Sillito art. dir. from 2004. Salzburg Fest. 1982 (cond. Marriner).

Academy of Vocal Music. Founded at St Clement Dane's, Strand, in 1725/6 and met fortnightly. Members incl. Pepusch, Greene, Bononcini, Geminiani, etc.

a cappella (It.). In the chapel style, which in choral singing has come to mean unaccompanied. See *cappella*.

Accardo, Salvatore (*b* Turin, 1941). It. violinist and conductor. Gave concerts as child, professional début Naples, aged 13. First winner, Paganini Comp., 1958. Dir., I Musici in Rome, 1972–7. Wide repertory, but particularly assoc. with mus. of Paganini, of whose long-lost E minor conc. he gave first modern perf. Author of *L'arte del violino* (Milan, 1987).

accarezzevole,   accarezzevolmente   (It.). Caressing, caressingly.

accelerando, accelerato (It.). Accelerating, accelerated; i.e. getting gradually quicker.

accent. (1) An emphasis on a particular note, giving a regular or irregular rhythmic pattern. For more detail, see *rhythm*.

(2) The name is also applied to the simplest forms of plainsong tones (see *plainsong*), i.e. very slightly inflected monotones.

accento (It.). Accent; hence *accentato*, accented.

accentuation. Emphasizing certain notes. In setting words to mus., coincidence of natural accents in text with mus. results in good accentuation.

Accentus (Lat.). (1) The part of the RC liturgy chanted only by the priest or his representative, as distinct from the *Concentus*, chanted by the congregation or choir.

(2) See *accent* 2.

acciaccato (It.). Broken down, crushed. The sounding of the notes of a chord not quite simultaneously, but from bottom to top.

acciaccatura. A species of *grace note, indicated by a small note with its stem crossed through, viz.,

The prin. note retains its accent and almost all its time-value. The auxiliary note is theoretically timeless; it is just 'crushed' in as quickly as possible before the prin. note is heard. Some renowned pianists even play the 2 notes simultaneously, immediately releasing the acciaccatura and retaining the prin. note.

Sometimes 2 or more small notes are shown before the prin. notes, and then they generally amount to acciaccature (being in most cases perf. on the 'crushed-in', or timeless and accentless, principle), although they have no strokes through their tails, and although the names *double* or *triple appoggiatura* are often given them.

Note a combination of acciaccatura with spread chord:

perf. as though notated—

Although the acciaccatura is theoretically timeless, it nevertheless must take a fragment of time from somewhere. In the cases shown above (which may be considered the normal ones) it takes it from the following note. In 2 other cases, however, time is taken from the preceding note: (1) when harmonically and in context it is clearly attached to that note rather than the following note; (2) when, in pf. mus., it appears in the bass followed by a chord in the left hand or in both hands—the composer's intention being to increase harmonic richness by sounding the bass note in a lower octave and then holding it by the pedal whilst the chord is played; in this case the chord (as a whole) is to be heard on the beat, the acciaccatura slightly preceding it. See also *mordent*.

accidental. The sign indicating momentary departure from the key signature by the raising or lowering of a note by means of a sharp, flat, natural, etc. It holds good throughout the measure (bar) unless contradicted, and where it occurs attached to the last note of the measure and this note is tied to a note in the next measure, it holds good for that latter note also. In some 20th-cent. mus. any accidental which occurs is understood to affect only the note before which it is placed, as was also often the case with mus. from the medieval period to the 17th cent.

accompagnato (It.). Accompanied. In It. opera, from about the time of Cavalli, *recitativo accompagnato* meant a dramatic type of recit., fully written-out with ens. acc., as opposed to *recitativo secco*, notated with figured bass acc. only. In 18th-cent. opera, *acc. recit.* was normally reserved for the most important dramatic scenes and introduced the most brilliant arias.

accompaniment. The term as sometimes used today implies the presence of a prin. perf. (singer, violinist, etc.) more or less subserviently supplied with a background by another perf. or perfs. (pianist, orch., etc.). This is not the original use of the word, which carried no suggestion of subservience, 'Sonata for Harpsichord with Violin Accompaniment' being a common 18th-cent. term. However, to describe the orch. part of a Brahms conc. as a subservient acc. is obviously ridiculous. Equally, the pf. part of songs by such

composers as Schubert, Wolf, Strauss, Fauré, and others is often of equal importance with the v. Thus, in the 20th cent., the art of pf. acc. has become highly developed, e.g. by Gerald *Moore, Benjamin *Britten, and many others.

Accompaniment to a Film Scene (*Begleitungsmusik zu einer Lichtspielszene*). Orch. work by Schoenberg, Op.34, comp. Berlin 1929–30. F.p. Berlin 1930 cond. Klemperer; f.Eng.p. BBC broadcast 1931 cond. Webern. 3 movts. are: *Drohende Gefahr* (Danger threatens), *Angst* (Anguish), *Katastrophe*. No specific film was in Schoenberg's mind, this being an example of 'pure' film mus.

accoppiare (It.). To couple (org.). Hence *accoppiato*, coupled; *accoppiamento*, coupling (the noun).

accord (Fr.). (1) Chord.
   (2) 'Tuning'.

accordare (It.). To tune.

accordato, accordati, accordata, accordate (It.). Tuned. (The word is sometimes used in a phrase indicating a particular instr. tuning, e.g. of the timps.) Hence *accordatura* (It.), tuning.

accorder (Fr.). To tune. Hence *accordé*, tuned.

accordion (accordeon). Small portable instr., shaped like a box, with metal reeds which are vibrated by air from bellows. The accordion is similar in principle to the mouth org. but is provided with bellows and studs for producing the required notes (or, in the *piano-accordion*, a small kbd. of up to 3½ octaves). It is designed to be held in both hands, the one approaching and separating from the other, so expanding and contracting the bellows section, while melody studs or keys are operated by the fingers of the right hand and studs providing simple chords by those of the left hand. Invention credited to Damian of Vienna, 1829.

accordo (It.). Chord.

accoupler (Fr.). To couple (org.). So *accouplé*, coupled; *accouplement*, coupling, coupler (nouns); *accouplez*, couple (imperative).

Accursed Hunter, The (Franck). See *Chasseur maudit, Le*.

acht (Ger.). (1) Eight.
   (2) Care.

Achtel, Achtelnote (Ger.). Eighth, eighth-note, i.e. quaver; hence *Achtelpause*, a quaver rest. *Achtstimmig*, in 8 vv. (or parts).

Achucarro, Joaquin (*b* Bilbao, 1936). Sp. pianist. Début Bilbao aged 12, and in Masaveu, Spain, 1950. Won Liverpool Int. pf. comp., 1959, making London début same year.

Acis and Galatea. Masque, serenata, or pastoral in 2 acts by Handel to text by John Gay with additions by Pope, Dryden, and Hughes, based on

Ovid's *Metamorphoses XIII*. Written and f.p. at Cannons, Edgware, seat of Earl of Carnarvon, later Duke of Chandos, May 1718; London f.p. 1732, when part of *Aci, Galatea e Polifemo*, comp. Naples, 1708, was incorporated. Rev. for larger forces and pubd. 1743. Contains bass aria *O ruddier than the cherry*. Lully, Haydn, and Hatton were among other composers of dramatic works on this subject.

Ackermann, Otto (*b* Bucharest, 1909; *d* Wabern, 1960). Romanian-born conductor (Swiss cit.) who worked in most leading opera houses. Cond. Düsseldorf Opera 1928–32, Brno Opera 1932–5, Berne Opera 1935–47, Theater an der Wien 1947–53, Cologne 1953–8, Zurich 1958–60. Noted for interpretation of J. Strauss II and Lehár.

Ackté, Aïno (*b* Helsinki, Finland, 1876; *d* Nummela, 1944). Finn. soprano. Début Paris Opéra 1897 as Marguérite in *Faust*. NY Met 1904; London 1907. First London Salome (1910), a role in which she won special acclaim. Dir., Finn. Nat. Opera, 1938–9.

acoustic bass. Org. stop with 2 rows of pipes, those mentioned under **quint*.

acoustics. In its true sense, anything pertaining to the sense of hearing, but, as commonly used, firstly, the branch of physics concerned with the properties, production, and transmission of sound; and secondly, the quality of a building as regards its suitability for the clear hearing of speech or mus.

Sound is due to the vibrations of a source, such as a mus. instr., which are transmitted through the air to the ear-drum where they set up vibrations at the same rate. The *pitch* of a sound depends on the speed of those vibrations, which if rapid produce a 'high' pitch and if slow a 'low' pitch. The rate of vibration per second is known as the 'frequency' of the note.

The *loudness* of a sound depends on the 'amplitude' of the vibrations; for instance, a vn. str. violently bowed will oscillate for a considerable distance on either side of its line of repose, thereby producing strong vibrations and a loud sound, whereas one gently bowed will only oscillate a short distance on each side and so produce small vibrations and a soft sound.

Smaller instr. produce more rapid vibrations and larger ones slower vibrations: thus the ob. is pitched higher than its relative the bn., likewise a vn. than a vc., a stopped str. than an 'open' str., a boy's v. than a man's v., etc. But other factors enter into the control of pitch. For instance, *mass* (the thinner str. of a vn. vibrate more quickly than the thicker ones and so possess a higher general pitch) and *tension* (a vn. str. tightened by turning the peg rises in pitch).

The varying *quality* of the sound produced by different instr. and vv. is explained as follows. Almost all vibrations are compound. Thus a sounding vn. str. may be vibrating not only as a whole but also at the same time in various fractions which produce notes according to their varying

lengths. These notes are not easily identifiable by the ear but are nevertheless present as factors in the tonal ens. Taking any particular note of the harmonic series (as G, D, or B), the numbers of its harmonics double with each octave as the series ascends. The numbers attached to the harmonics represent also the ratios of the frequencies of the various harmonics to the fundamental. Thus if the frequency of the low G is 96 vibrations per second, that of the B in the treble stave (5th harmonic) is $5 \times 96 = 480$ vibrations per second.

Whilst these harmonics are normally heard in combination some of them may, on some instr., be separately obtained. By a certain method of blowing, a brass tube, instead of producing its first harmonic, or fundamental, can be made to produce other harmonics. By lightly touching a str. (i.e. a stopped str.), at its centre and then bowing it, it can be made to produce (in a peculiar silvery tone-quality) its 2nd harmonic; by touching it at a 3rd of its length it will similarly produce its 3rd harmonic, etc. (Harmonics are notated in str. parts as an 'o' above the note. 'Natural' harmonics are those produced from an open str.; 'artificial' harmonics those produced from a stopped str.)

The normal *transmission of sound* is through the air. The vibrations of a str., a drum-head, the vocal cords, etc. set up similar vibrations in the nearest particles of air; these communicate them to other particles, and so on, until the initial energy is gradually exhausted. This process of transmission of pressure to adjacent particles of air creates what are known as *sound waves*: unlike waves created by water-motion, there is no forward movement, but each particle of air oscillates, setting up alternate pressure and relaxation of pressure which in turn produce similar effects on the human or animal ear-drum (= vibrations), so causing the subjective effect of 'sound'.

To judge pitch differences, or intervals, the human ear obeys a law of perception called the Weber–Fechner law, which states that equal increments of perception are associated with equal ratios of stimulus. Perception of the octave pitch is a 2:1 frequency ratio. In judging the loudness of sound there are 2 'thresholds', those of hearing and of pain. If the intensity of sound at the threshold of hearing is regarded as 1, the intensity at the pain threshold is 1 million million. Acousticians' scale of loudness, following the Weber-Fechner law, is logarithmic and based on a ratio of intensities 10:1. This is known as a *bel*. The range of loudness perception is divided into 12 large units. Each increment of a *bel* is divided into 10 smaller increments known as *decibels*, i.e. 1 bel = 10 decibels. A difference in loudness of 1 decibel in the middle range of hearing is about the smallest increment of change which the ear can gauge.

When 2 notes near to one another in vibration frequency are heard together their vibrations necessarily coincide at regular intervals and thus reinforce one another in the effect produced.

This is called a *beat*. When the pf. tuner is tuning a str. of a certain note to another str. of the same note the beat may be heard to diminish in frequency until it gradually disappears with correct adjustment. When the rate of beating exceeds 20 per second, the sensation of a low bass note is perceived.

When 2 loud notes are heard together they give rise to a 3rd sound, a *combination* or *resultant tone*, corresponding to the difference between the 2 vibration numbers: this low-pitched note is called a *difference tone*. They also give rise to a 4th sound (another *combination tone*—high and faint) corresponding to the sum of the 2 vibration numbers: this is called a *summation tone*.

There is *reflection of sound*, as of light, as we experience on hearing an echo. Similarly there are *sound shadows*, caused by some obstruction which impedes the passage of vibrations which reach it. However, unlike light vibrations, sound vibrations tend to 'diffract' round an obstruction, and not every solid object will create a complete 'shadow': most solids will transmit sound vibrations to a greater or lesser extent, whereas only a few (e.g. glass) will transmit light vibrations.

The term *resonance* is applied to the response of an object to the sound of a given note, i.e. its taking up the vibrations of that note. Thus if 2 identical tuning-forks are placed in close proximity and one is sounded, the other will set up sympathetic vibrations and will also produce the note. The 1st fork is then a *generator* of sound and the 2nd a *resonator*. It is often found that a particular church window will vibrate in response to a particular organ note, and that a metal or glass object in a room will similarly respond to a certain vocal or instr. note.

This phenomenon is true resonance ('re-sounding') in the strict scientific sense of the word. There is also a less strict use of the word, which is sometimes applied to the vibration of floor, walls, and ceiling of a hall, not limited to a particular note, but in response to any note played or sung. A hall may either be too resonant for the comfort of performers and audience, or too little so—too 'dead' (a hall with echo is often described as 'too resonant', but there is an obvious clear distinction to be made between the mere reflection of sounds and the sympathetic reinforcements of them). Reverberation time is defined as the time it takes for sound to fall 60 decibels (1 millionth of original intensity).

Materials of walls and ceiling should be neither too reverberatory nor too absorbent ('dead'). Acoustical engineers have worked out co-efficients of absorption for building materials, but absorption is rarely uniform throughout the whole spectrum of pitch. Only wood and certain special acoustic materials show nearly even absorption in the total frequency range. Amplifiers and loudspeakers can be used (as they nowadays often are) to overcome difficulties caused by original faulty design. Most modern halls can be electronically 'tuned' and have movable panels, canopies, and reverberation chambers which can be adapted to whatever type of music is being performed.

action. The mechanism of a pf., org., or similar instr. which connects the kbd. and str., or the pipes and stops.

action, ballet d' (pas d'). A ballet with a dramatic basis.

act tune (curtain tune, curtain music). A 17th- and 18th-cent. term for mus. between the acts of a play while the curtain was down, similar to an *entr'acte* or *intermezzo*.

Actus Tragicus. Name for Bach's church cantata No.106, *Gottes Zeit ist die allerbeste Zeit* (God's Time is the best). It appears to have been written, probably in 1707, for an occasion of mourning on the death of some public personage.

adagietto (It.). (1) Slow, but less so than *adagio*.
(2) A short *adagio* comp. A famous example is the *adagietto* for str. and hp., the 4th movt. of Mahler's Sym. No.5.

adagio (It.). At ease. Slow (not so slow as *largo*, but slower than *andante*). A slow movt. is often called 'an Adagio'. *adagissimo*, extremely slow. *adagio assai*, very slow.

Adam, Adolphe (Charles) (*b* Paris, 1803; *d* Paris, 1856). Fr. composer and critic. Wrote 70 operas, mostly *opéras-comiques*, of which best-known are *Le Postillon de Longjumeau* (1836) and *Si j'étais roi* (1852). Also wrote church mus., songs, and several ballets, incl. **Giselle* (1841). Prof. of comp., Paris Cons. from 1849.

Adam, Theo (*b* Dresden, 1926). Ger. bass-baritone. Opera début Dresden 1949 (Hermit in *Der Freischütz*). Berlin Staatsoper from 1953. Débuts: Bayreuth 1952; CG 1967; NY Met 1969; Salzburg Fest. 1969. Notable in Wagner roles but also as Ochs, Pizarro, Wozzeck, and Don Giovanni. Sang in premières of Cerha's *Baal* and Berio's *Un re in ascolto*, 1984. Has also prod. operas.

Adam de la Halle [Adam de la Hale, Adam le Bossu] (*b* Arras, *c*.1245; *d* Naples, ?1288 or in England after 1306). Fr. trouvère, poet, and composer. Wrote in all genres current in 13th cent., both monophonic *chansons* and polyphonic motets. Few biographical facts known. Probably studied in Paris, returning to Arras *c*.1270. His *Le jeu de Robin et de Marion*, probably written for Fr. court at Naples, anticipated the genre of *opéra-comique*.

Adam le Bossu (Adam the Hunchback). Identical with **Adam de la Halle.

Adams, Byron (*b* Atlanta, Ga., 1955). Amer. composer, conductor, and teacher. Ass. Prof., Univ. of Calif., Riverside, from 1987; lect., Cornell Univ., 1985–7. Comps. incl. quintet, pf. and str. (1979); conc. for tpt. and str. (1983); sonata, tpt. and pf. (1983); vn. conc. (1984); *Go, Lovely Rose*, male vv. (1984); *Missa Brevis* (1988); *3 Epitaphs* (1988); *Introduction and Siciliana*, str. (1992); *Irises*, cl., hp., str. (1996); *Trois Illuminations*, chamber ch., hp. (1999); *Praises of Jerusalem*, ch., org. (2003); *Variationis achemisticae*, fl., va., vc., pf. (2005).

Adams, Donald (*b* Bristol, 1928; *d* Norwich, 1996). Eng. bass. Prof. début as actor 1944, as singer 1951 (D'Oyly Carte Opera). Prin. bass D'Oyly Carte Co. 1953–69. Débuts: Amer. (Chicago) 1983; CG 1983; WNO 1984; ENO 1986; Glyndebourne 1988.

Adams, John (Coolidge) (*b* Worcester, Mass., 1947). Amer. composer, conductor, and clarinettist. Head, comp. dept., S. Francisco Cons. 1972–82. Comp.-in-res., S. Francisco SO 1979–85. One of composers known as minimalists, but his style has broadened and he has deliberately forged an eclectic idiom which borrows from most of the major 20th-cent. composers and from jazz. Comps.:

OPERAS: *Nixon in China (1984–7); The *Death of Klinghoffer (1990–1); I was looking at the ceiling and then I saw the sky, mus. th. (1994–5); El Niño (1999–2000); Dr Atomic (2004–5); A Flowering Tree (2006).

ORCH.: Common Tones in Simple Time (1980); Shaker Loops, str. (1983); Harmonielehre (1984–5); Tromba lontana (1986); Short Ride in a Fast Machine (1986); The Chairman Dances (1987); Fearful Symmetries (1988); Eros Piano, pf., orch. or chamber orch. (1989); El Dorado (1991); Chamber Symphony (1991); vn. conc. (1993); Lollapalooza (1995); Century Rolls, pf., orch. (1996); Naive and Sentimental Music (1997–8); Guide to Strange Places (2001); Dharma at Big Sur, elec. vn., orch. (2003);

VOICE(S) & ORCH. OR ENS.: Christian Zeal and Activity, spkr. on tape., ens. (1973); Grounding, 3 solo vv., instr., elec. (1975); Harmonium, ch., orch. (1980); Grand Pianola Music, 2 sop., 2 pf., small orch. (1981–2); The Wound Dresser, bar., orch. or chamber orch. (1988); On the Transmigration of Souls, orch., ch., children's ch., pre-recorded soundtrack (2002).

CHAMBER MUSIC: pf. quintet (1970); American Standard, unspecified ens. (1973); Shaker Loops, str. septet (1978); Chamber Sym. (1992); Road Movies, vn., pf. (1995); Gnarly Buttons, cl., ens. (1996).

PIANO: Ragamarole (1973); China Gates (1977); Phrygian Gates (1977); Hallelujah Junction, 2 pf. (1996).

TAPE ONLY: Onyx (1975); Light Over Water (1983); Hoodoo Zephyr (1992–3).

Adams, Stephen. See *Maybrick, Michael*.

ADCM. Archbishop of Canterbury's Diploma in Church Music, awarded only after examination to Fellows of the RCO who hold the Ch.M. (Choirmaster) diploma.

added 6th, chord of. In key of C, the chord F–A–C–D and similarly in other keys, i.e. the subdominant chord plus the 6th from the bass (major 6th added to major or minor triad), or, looked at from another viewpoint, the first inversion of the (diatonic) supertonic 7th. Frequently used by Delius, Mahler, and in jazz.

Addinsell, Richard (*b* Oxford, 1904; *d* Chelsea, 1977). Eng. composer. Wrote songs and film mus., of which outstanding example is *Warsaw*

Concerto, skilful pastiche of romantic pf. conc., written for 1941 film *Dangerous Moonlight*. (See *Film Music*).

additional accompaniments. New or rev. accs. written by a later composer or ed. for mus. of the early masters, where perhaps only a figured bass is provided in the original. An extravagant example of such additions is found in the instr. parts Mozart wrote into Handel's *Messiah* for an occasion when no organ was available to provide the figured bass used in perf. of Handel's own time.

addolcendo (It.). Becoming *dolce* (gentle or sweet).

addolorato (It.). Grieved, i.e. in a saddened style.

Adelaide. Song for high v. and pf. by Beethoven, Op.46, comp. 1795/6 to poem by F. von Matthisson.

Adélaïde Concerto. Vn. conc. falsely attrib. to the 10-year-old Mozart, supposedly ded. to the Princess Adélaïde, daughter of King Louis XV of France. F.p. Paris 1931 with M. *Casadesus as soloist and accepted as genuine by many distinguished violinists. In 1977 Casadesus admitted he had written it.

Adès, Thomas (*b* London, 1971). Eng. composer, pianist, and conductor. Studied pf. at GSMD and read music at King's Coll., Cambridge. Comp.-in-assoc., Hallé Orch. 1993–5. Art. dir., Aldeburgh Fest. from 1999. Comps. incl.:

OPERAS: *Powder her Face, Op.14 (1995); The *Tempest, Op.22 (2003–4, rev. 2006).

ORCH.: . . . but all shall be well, Op.10 (1993); These premises are alarmed, Op.16 (1996); Asyla, Op.17 (1997); vn. conc., Op.23 (2005).

CHORAL: O thou who didst with pitfall and with gin, Op.3a, male vv. (1990); Gefriolsae me, Op.3b, male vv., org. (1990); Fool's Rhymes, Op.5, SATB, 4 players (1992); The Fayrfax Carol, SATB, opt. org. (1997); January Writ, SATB, org. (1999).

VOICE(S) & INSTR(S).: The Lover in Winter, 4 songs for counterten., pf (1989); Five Eliot Landscapes, Op.1, sop., pf. (1990); Life Story, Op.8, sop., 3 players (1993); Life Story, Op.8a, sop., pf. (1994); America – A Prophecy, Op.19, mez., opt. ch., orch. (1999); Brahms, Op.21, bar., orch. (2001); Scenes from The Tempest, sop., mez., ten., bar., orch. (2005).

INSTR. ENS.: Chamber Sym., Op.2 (1990); Catch, Op.4 (1991); Living Toys, Op.9 (1993); Sonata da Caccia, Op.11 (1993); The Origin of the Harp, Op.13 (1994); Concerto Conciso, Op.18 (1997); Court Studies, Op.23 (2005).

CHAMBER MUSIC: Arcadiana, Op.12, str. qt. (1994); pf. quintet, Op.20 (2000).

KEYBOARD: Still Sorrowing, Op.7, pf. (1991–2); Darknesse Visible, pf. (1992); Under Hamelin Hill, Op.6, org. (1992); Traced Overhead, Op.15, pf. (1995–6).

Adeste Fideles (O come, all ye faithful). This hymn and tune probably date from the first half of the 18th cent. The late G. E. P. Arkwright detected that the first part of the tune closely resembled a tune which appeared in a Paris *vaudeville* of 1744 (where it was described as 'Air Anglais') and suggested that it was probably an adaptation of some popular tune combined, in the hymn, with reminiscences of the air 'Pensa ad amare' from Handel's *Ottone* (1723). This view is supported by more recent researches, notably those of Dom John Stéphan, of Buckfast Abbey, Devon, who in 1947 discussed a newly discovered MS of the tune in the handwriting of John Francis Wade, a Lat. teacher and music copyist of Douai (*d* 1786). Stéphan believed this to be the 'first and original version', dating from 1740–3, and attrib. both words and mus. to Wade.

à deux cordes (Fr.). On 2 strings.

à deux mains (Fr.). For 2 hands.

à deux temps (Fr.). In 2/2 time.

Adieux Sonata. Fr. title (in full, *sonate caractéristique; les adieux, l'absence et le retour*) given by publisher to Beethoven's Pf. Sonata No.26 in E♭ major, Op.81a, comp. 1809–10. Beethoven disapproved of the title, preferring the Ger. *Das *Lebewohl* (The Farewell). Ded. to Archduke Rudolph on his departure from Vienna for 9 months.

Adler, Guido (*b* Eibenschütz, Moravia, 1855; *d* Vienna, 1941). Austrian critic and musicologist. Prof. of mus. history, Prague Univ., 1885–97. Succeeded *Hanslick as prof. of mus. history, Vienna Univ. 1898–1927. Author of books on Wagner (1904) and Mahler (1916), gen. ed. *Handbuch der Musikgeschichte* (1924).

Adler, Kurt (*b* Neuhaus, Cz., 1907; *d* Butler, NJ, 1977). Cz. conductor, pianist, and scholar. Ass. cond. Berlin State Opera 1927–9; cond. Ger. Opera, Prague, 1929–32, Kiev Opera 1933–5, Stalingrad PO 1935–7. Settled in USA 1938. Ass. cond. NY Met 1943, ch. master 1945–73 and a cond. there 1951–68.

Adler, Kurt Herbert (*b* Vienna, 1905; *d* Ross, Calif., 1988). Austrian-born conductor and impresario. Th. cond. in Vienna, Prague, etc. Ass. to Toscanini, Salzburg 1936. Went to USA as ass. cond. and ch. master Chicago Opera 1938–43. Ch. master, S. Francisco Opera 1943, art. dir. 1953, gen. dir. 1956–81. Hon. CBE 1980.

Adler, Larry [Lawrence] (Cecil) (*b* Baltimore, 1914; *d* London, 2001). Amer. virtuoso on *harmonica (mouth organ). First stage appearance, NY 1928. Toured the world as mus.-hall artist and recitalist. First solo engagement with Sydney SO, 1939. Works written for him by Vaughan Williams, Gordon Jacob, Milhaud, Arnold, etc. Settled in Eng. 1949. Also wrote for periodicals, reviews, etc., and wrote autobiography *It Ain't Necessarily So* (London, 1984).

Adler, Peter Herman (*b* Gablonz, Bohemia (now Jablonec, Cz.), 1899; *d* Ridgefield, Conn., 1990). Cz. conductor who emigrated to USA in 1939 (Amer. cit.). Held conducting posts in Bremen (1929–32) and Kiev (1933–6). Helped Fritz

*Busch to found New Opera Co., NY, 1941. Dir. NBC TV opera 1949–59. Cond., Baltimore SO 1959–68. NY Met début 1972. Dir., Amer. Opera Center, Juilliard Sch. of Mus. 1973–81.

Adler, Samuel (*b* Mannheim, 1928). Ger.-born Amer. composer, conductor, and teacher. Dir. of Mus., Temple Emanu-El, Dallas, 1953–66; cond., Dallas Lyric Th., 1955–7; prof. of comp. N. Texas State Univ., Denton, 1957–66; prof. of comp., Eastman Sch. of Mus. from 1966 (chairman, comp. dept. from 1973). Comps. incl. 4 operas (1959–72), 6 syms. (1953–85), pf. conc., fl. conc., org. conc., 8 str. qts. (1945–90), pf. pieces, and songs.

ad libitum (*ad lib.*) (Lat.). Optional or at will, with regard to (a) rhythm, tempo, etc.; (b) inclusion or omission of some v. or instr.; (c) inclusion or omission of some passage; (d) the extemporization of a cadenza.

Adni, Daniel (*b* Haifa, 1951). Israeli pianist. London début 1970. Soloist and recitalist in Israel, Holland, Finland, Germany, USA, and Japan. Recordings incl. complete Mendelssohn *Lieder ohne Worte*.

Adriana Lecouvreur. Opera in 4 acts by Cilea to lib. by Colautti from play of same name by Scribe and Legouvé (1849). Prod. Milan 1902; London 1904; New Orleans 1907. Adriana was one of greatest 18th-cent. Fr. tragic actresses, much admired by Voltaire.

a due corde (It.). On two str.

Adventures of Mr Brouček, The (Janáček). See *Excursions of Mr Brouček, The*.

Adventures of the Vixen Bystroušky (Janáček). See *Cunning Little Vixen, The*.

aeolian harp (from Aeolus, the mythological keeper of the winds). An instr. consisting of a box about 3′ long, with catgut str. of different thicknesses but tuned in unison attached to its upper surface. It could be placed along a window ledge or elsewhere where the wind could catch it and set the str. in vibration, thereby producing harmonics which varied with the thickness of the str. and the velocity of the wind to give a chordal effect. The Aeolian harp was popular from the late 16th or early 17th cents. to the late 19th cent. Now made as a toy.

aeolian mode. See *modes*.

aeolina. Mouth org. or harmonica, comprising metal plates enclosing free reeds.

aeoline. Soft org. stop of 8′ length and pitch, supposed to imitate *aeolian harp*.

aeroforo (It.). *aerophor.

aerophone. Term for mus. instrs. which produce their sound by using air as principal vibrating factor. These instrs. are subdivided according to whether air is unconfined by the instr. (bullroarer, motor horn, etc.) or enclosed within a tube (wind instrs. proper). One of 4 classifications of instr. devised by C. Sachs and E. M. von Hornbostel and pubd. in *Zeitschrift für Ethnologie*, 1914. Other categories are *chordophones, *idiophones, and *membranophones, with *electrophones recently added.

aerophor. Device (invented by Ger. flautist Bernhard Samuel and patented 1912) to help wind players. A small bellows, worked by foot, supplies wind by tube to a corner of the mouth, leaving the player free to breathe uninterruptedly through the nose. Richard Strauss called for its use in his *Festliches Präludium*, Op.61, erroneously describing it as *aerophon*, and in his *Alpensinfonie*, Op.64.

aevia. This 'word' consists of the vowels of 'Alleluia'. Used as an abbreviation in a similar way to *evovae.

Affekt (Ger. 'fervour'). *affektvoll*, full of fervour; *mit Affekt*, with warmth or passion.

affetto (It.). Affection. Hence, *affettuoso, affettuosa*, affectionate, with tenderness; *affettuosamente*, affectionately; *affezione*, affection.

affretando (It. 'hurrying', 'quickening'). Instruction to increase tempo, implying also an increase in nervous energy.

Africaine, L' (The African Woman). Opera in 5 acts by *Meyerbeer to lib. by Scribe. Begun 1837, but work on it intermittent owing to constant alterations to lib., etc. Completed 1864. Meyerbeer died in Paris while supervising rehearsals. Orig. version lasts 6 hours. Prod. Paris, London, and NY 1865; NY Met 1888 (in German).

African Sanctus. Comp. by David *Fanshawe for 2 sop., pf., org., ch., and perc. incl. rock-kit drummer, cymbals, congas, timp., bass and ten. drums, tam-tam, tom-tom, amplified lead and rhythmic guitars, and tape recordings made in Africa. F.p. London 1972. Rev. version f.p. Toronto, Jan. 1978, f.p. in England BBC TV film. F. concert p. Worcester 1978.

Afternoon of a Faun, The (Debussy). See *Après-midi d'un faune, Prélude à L'*.

Age of Anxiety, The. Sym. No.2 by Leonard *Bernstein for pf. and orch. (Title from Auden poem.) F.p. Boston, Apr. 1949 cond. Koussevitzky, soloist Bernstein. As ballet, NY Feb. 1950.

Age of Enlightenment, Orchestra of the. Self-governing orch. founded by the players in London, 1986. Uses period instrs. No permanent cond., but has worked under Sigiswald Kuijken, Gustav Leonhardt, and Charles Mackerras. Glyndebourne Fest. début 1989, cond. Rattle, in Mozart's *Le nozze di Figaro* (also 1991, and *Così fan tutte* 1991 and 1992). Salzburg Fest. début 1991. Prin. guest conds., Frans Brüggen and Simon Rattle, from 1992. First Eur. tour 1994, cond. Rattle.

Age of Gold, The (*Zolotoy vek*). Ballet in 3 acts with mus. by Shostakovich, Op.22, lib. A. Ivanovsky,

choreog. E. Kaplan and V. Vaynonen. Comp. 1927–30. Prod. Leningrad 1930. Also suite for orch., 1929–32. Some of the mus. used in ballet *The Dreamers*, 1975.

Age of Steel, The (*Stalnoy skok*; Fr. *Le Pas d'acier*). Ballet in 2 scenes with mus. by Prokofiev (Op.41, 1925–6), choreog. Massine, lib. Yakulov. Prod. Paris 1927. Symphonic suite contains 4 movts.

aggiustamente, aggiustatamente (It.). Exact (in point of rhythm).

agiatamente (It.). Comfortably, freely, i.e. with suitable liberty as regards speed, etc. (not to be confused with *agitatamente*).

agilement (Fr.), **agilmente** (It.). In an agile manner, implying speed and nimble execution. **agilité** (Fr.), **agilità** (It.). Agility.

Agincourt Song. A famous 15th-cent. Eng. song commemorating the victory at Agincourt in 1415, for 2 vv. and 3-part ch. Used by Walton in his film music for *Henry V* (1944).

agitato; agitatamente (It.), **agité** (Fr.), **agitirt, agitiert** (Ger.). Agitated, in an agitated manner. **agitazione, agitamento** (It.). Agitation. Not to be confused with *agiatamente.

Agnew, Roy (Ewing) (*b* Sydney, NSW, 1893; *d* Sydney, 1944). Australian pianist and composer of pf. sonatas and smaller pieces, also chamber and orch. mus., and songs. On staff NSW State Cons., Sydney.

Agnus Dei (Lamb of God). Part of Ordinary of the *Mass. Many settings by various composers.

agogic (from Gr. *agoge*, melody). (1) An adjective indicating a variety of accentuation demanded by the nature of a particular mus. phrase, rather than by the regular metric pulse of the mus. The first note of a phrase, for instance, may be felt to suggest a slight lingering which confers the effect of an accent: similarly, a leap to note significantly higher or lower than the preceding notes, or a strong discord resolving to a concord, may convey an effect of accentuation (by means of lingering, pressure, etc.) and there are other examples. The complementary term to 'agogic accent' (accent of movement) is 'dynamic accent' (accent of force), which implies the normal and regular rhythmic accentuation of a piece of music.

(2) In a wider sense, 'agogic' covers everything connected with 'expression', e.g. *rallentando, accelerando, rubato*, pause, accentuation as described above, etc.

Agon (Contest). Ballet for 12 dancers by Stravinsky, choreog. *Balanchine. Comp. 1953–7. F.p. as concert work Los Angeles, June 1957; as stage work by NY City Ballet, Dec. 1957.

Agrell, Johan (Joachim) (*b* Löth, 1701; *d* Nuremberg, 1765). Swed. composer, violinist, and harpsichordist. At court in Kassel 1734–46. Kapellmeister, Nuremberg, from 1746. Wrote syms., concs., and many kbd. sonatas.

agrémens (agréments) (Fr.). Grace notes or other ornaments. Can also indicate an ornamented version of a phrase or tune.

Agricola, Johann Friedrich (b Dobitschen, 1720; d Berlin, 1774). Ger. composer, organist, conductor, and singing teacher. Became court composer to Frederick the Great in 1751, year after success of his first intermezzo *Il filosofo convito in amore* in Potsdam. Mus. dir., Berlin Opera 1759–72. Besides opera in the It. style, comp. oratorios, songs, and kbd. works.

Agrippina. Opera in 3 acts by Handel to lib. by Grimani. Prod. Venice 1709, Abingdon 1963, Philadelphia 1972 (concert), Fort Worth 1985 (stage).

AGSM. Associate of *Guildhall School of Music and Drama (internal students only).

Agujari, Lucrezia (b Ferrara, 1743; d Parma, 1783). It. operatic sop., much admired by Mozart, with remarkable range and compass (3 octaves). Début Florence 1764. Sang in London 1775–6. Because she was illegitimate, was known as 'La Bastardella' or 'Bastardina'. Retired on marriage to It. composer Giuseppe Colla, 1780.

Ägyptische Helena, Die (The Egyptian Helen). Opera in 2 acts, Op.75, by R. Strauss to lib. by Hofmannsthal, comp. 1923–7, f.p. Dresden and NY Met 1928, Garsington 1997. Rev. 1933.

Ahna, Pauline de (b Ingoldstadt, 1863; d Garmisch, 1950). Ger. soprano who married Richard *Strauss in 1894 and became notable exponent of his *Lieder*, many of which were written for her. Début Weimar 1890 (Pamina). Sang at Bayreuth (1891). Created role of Freihild in *Guntram*, Weimar 1894. Christine in *Intermezzo* is a portrait of her, as (less directly) are several other of Strauss's operatic heroines. Known for her waspish tongue and massive (probably calculated) indiscretions; her coquettish nature is instrumentally portrayed in her husband's *Ein Heldenleben* and *Symphonia Domestica*.

Aho, Kalevi (b Forssa, 1949). Finnish composer. Lect. on mus., Helsinki Univ. 1974–88. Works, influenced by Mahler and Shostakovich, incl. opera *Insect Life (Hyönteiselämää)*; 13 syms. (1969–2003); vn. conc.; vc. conc.; 2 pf. concs.; cl. conc.; 3 str. qts. (No.1 withdrawn); and other chamber mus. and pf. pieces.

Ahronovitch, Yuri (Mikhailovich) (b Leningrad, 1933; d Cologne, 2002). Israeli conductor of Russ. birth. Cond. Saratov PO 1956–7, Yaroslav SO 1957–64, Moscow Radio SO 1964–72. Settled in Israel 1972. CG début 1974. Cond. Gürzenich Concerts, Cologne, 1975–86. Prin. cond. Stockholm PO 1982–7. Teacher at Royal Swedish Acad. of Mus. from 1984.

Aichinger, Gregor (b Regensburg, 1564; d Augsburg, 1628). Ger. organist and composer. Spent some years in It. and was influenced by Venetian sch., notably Giovanni Gabrieli whose pupil he became. His religious choral works are among the finest of their time in Ger. His *Cantiones ecclesiasticae* (1607), containing Latin motets and settings of *Magnificat*, was first Ger. publication with thoroughbass.

Aïda. Opera in 4 acts by Verdi to lib. by Ghislanzoni, being It. trans. from Fr. prose of Camille du Locle based on plot by Fr. Egyptologist Auguste Mariette Bey (Verdi had major hand in lib. and wrote words of final duet 'O terra, addio'). Metastasio's lib. *Nitteti* (1756) was major source of plot. Commissioned by Khedive of Egypt (but not, as is often said, for opening of either Suez Canal or Cairo Opera House). Comp. 1870. F.p. Cairo 1871, La Scala 1872 (with extra aria for Aïda), NY 1873, Met 1886 (in German), London 1876. Spelling Aïda, with diaeresis, is incorrect in It.

Aiglon, L' (Fr. 'The Eaglet'). Rare example of opera by two composers, *Ibert writing the 1st and 5th acts and *Honegger the middle 3. Text by Cain after Rostand. Comp. 1935. (Prod. Monte Carlo 1937, rev. Paris 1952.)

Ainsley, John Mark (b Crewe, 1962). Eng. tenor. Début London 1984. From 1985 with Taverner Consort, New London Consort, and London Baroque. Amer. début NY; ENO 1989; GTO 1991; Glyndebourne 1992; WNO 1991. CG début 2002 (Don Ottavio); created Der Daemon in Henze's *L'Upupa*, Salzburg 2003.

air. (1) Melody.
(2) Comp. of melodious character. See also *aria* and *ayre*.

Airborne Symphony. Sym. for narrator, ten., bar., ch., and orch. by *Blitzstein to composer's text on evolution of flying. Comp. 1945, f.p. NY 1946 cond. *Bernstein.

air de caractère (Fr.). In ballet, mus. for 'characteristic' occasions, such as an entry of warriors.

Air on the G String. The name given to an arr. for vn. and pf. by *Wilhelmj in 1871 of the 2nd movement (Air) of J. S. Bach's Suite No.3 in D, in which the melody is transposed from D to C, the violinist playing on his lowest (G) str. Also heard in arr. for full str. orch., and for various other instr.

Ais (Ger.). A♯. **Aisis**, A♯♯.

Aix-en-Provence Festival. Mus. fest. founded by Gabriel Dusserget in 1948 and held annually in the summer. Perfs. take place in the courtyard of the Archbishop's Palace and in a small th. Dusserget's 1948 prod. of *Don Giovanni* was in the repertoire for 20 years. Bernard Lefort became dir. in 1974, Louis Erlo in 1980, and Stéphane Lissner in 1998. Operas range from the baroque to the present cent. Int. singers, conds., and dirs.

work at Aix each year. Its first Wagner, *Das Rheingold*, 2006, cond. Rattle, began the building of a complete *Ring* for 2009.

Ajmone-Marsan, Guido (*b* Turin, 1947). It.-born Amer. conductor (Amer. cit. 1962). Won Rupert Foundation cond. comp. 1973, Solti comp., Chicago, 1973. Cond. Gelders Orch., Arnhem, 1982–6; prin. cond. Orch. of Illinois, Chicago, 1982–7; mus. dir. Essen opera 1986–90.

Akademische Festouvertüre (Brahms). See *Academic Festival Overture*.

Akhnaten. Opera in 3 acts by *Glass to lib. by composer, S. Goldman, R. Israel, and R. Riddell. Comp. 1980–3. F.p. Stuttgart 1984, Houston 1984, London (ENO) 1985.

Akkord (Ger.). Chord. Also a set of several different-sized instr. of one type.

akkordieren (Ger.). To tune.

al (It.). At the, to the, in the, in the style of, etc., i.e. the same as *a* with the article added.

Ala and Lolly (Prokofiev). See *Scythian Suite*.

à la corde (Fr.). At the string. In str. playing, indication that the bow should be kept on the str., to ensure *legato* movement from note to note.

Alagna, Roberto (*b* Clichy-sous-Bois, 1964). Fr.-born tenor of Sicilian parentage. Won Pavarotti int. comp., Philadelphia 1988. Opera début GTO (Alfredo in *La traviata*). La Scala début 1990; CG 1992; NY Met 1992.

Alain, Jehan (*b* St Germain-en-Laye, 1911; killed Petit-Puis, nr. Saumur, 1940). Fr. organist and composer for org., pf., chamber combinations, etc. Org. of St Nicolas de Maisons Lafitte, Paris, 1935–9. Brother of Marie-Claire *Alain.

Alain, Marie-Claire (*b* St Germain-en-Laye, 1926). Fr. organist. Début St Germain-en-Laye 1937 (aged 11). Org. prize, Geneva Comp. 1950. Paris début 1950. Worldwide tours as recitalist. Recorded complete org. works of Bach and of her brother Jehan *Alain.

alalà. Plainsong-like type of Sp. folksong, in 4-line verses. The singer is at liberty to add melodic decorations to the vocal line.

ALAM. Associate of the London Academy of Music.

Alan, Hervey (*b* Whitstable, 1910; *d* Croydon, 1982). Eng. bass-baritone in opera and oratorio. First sang with Glyndebourne co. at Edinburgh Fest. 1949, then regularly to 1960. Prof. of singing, RCM. Pres. ISM 1969. OBE 1974.

à la pointe d'archet (Fr.). At the point of the bow.

Alard, (Jean-)**Delphin** (*b* Bayonne, 1815; *d* Paris, 1888). Fr. violinist and violin teacher, author of a standard violin method, *École du violin: méthode*

complete *et progressive* (Paris, 1844) and ed. and comp. of vn. works. Among pupils was *Sarasate. Prof. of vn., Paris Cons., 1843–75.

Alban Berg Quartet. Austrian str. qt. founded in 1971. Gives annual series of concerts in Vienna. Salzburg Fest. début 1978. Present membership Gunter Pichler (vn.), Gerhard Schulz (vn.), Thomas Kakuda (va.), Valentin Erben (vc.).

Albanese, Licia (*b* Bari, 1913). It.-born soprano (Amer. cit. 1945). Début Milan 1934 (Madama Butterfly). La Scala 1935; CG 1937; NY Met 1940–63 and 1964–6. Recorded Mimì and Violetta with Toscanini.

Albani, (Dame) **Emma** (*b* Chambly, nr. Montreal, 1847; *d* London, 1930). Fr.-Canadian soprano, born Marie Louise Cécilie Emma Lajeunesse, taking professional name from Albany, NY, where she spent early life. Début Messina 1870 in *La sonnambula* (Amina). CG début 1872. First CG Senta (*Der fliegende Holländer*), 1877. NY Met début 1891; first Desdemona at NY Met 1894. Sang Isolde, CG 1896, retiring from stage a month later, but continuing to sing in oratorio. Retired to teach in 1911. DBE 1925. Wrote autobiography, *Forty Years of Song* (London, 1911).

Albéniz, Isaac (Manuel Francisco) (*b* Camprodón, Catalonia, 1860; *d* Cambô-les-Bains, France, 1909). Sp. pianist and composer. From 1880 toured widely, playing many of own pf. works, of which he comp. 250 between 1880 and 1892, most of them employing Sp. rhythmic and melodic idioms. For his Eng. banker patron F. Money-Coutts (Lord Latymer) he set 3 opera libs., *Henry Clifford* (Barcelona 1895), *Merlin*, and *Pepita Jiménez* (Barcelona 1896). Settled in Paris 1893, being influenced by Fauré and Dukas. His *Iberia, 12 pf. pieces, was pubd. in 4 vols., 1906–9. Also wrote operettas, songs, orch. rhapsody *Catalonia*, pf. conc., and 5 pf. sonatas. *Iberia* was orch. by *Arbós, and *Suite española* by R.*Frühbeck de Burgos.

Alberni Quartet. Brit. string quartet founded in 1962 by students of RAM (Dennis Simons, Howard Davis, John White, and Gregory Baron). From 1975 Davis became 1st vn., with Peter Pople, Roger Best, and David Smith. First Western quartet to visit China (1987). Resident quartet RSAMD 1981–8.

Albert, Eugen d' [Eugène Francis Charles] (*b* Glasgow, 1864; *d* Riga, 1932). Scottish-born pianist and composer of Anglo-Fr. parentage, Ger. by adoption. Début London 1881; in same year won Mendelssohn Scholarship. Gave f.p. of Strauss's *Burleske* (Eisenach, 1890). Added fresh reputation as composer of operas, and wrote 2 pf. concs., vc. conc., sym., chamber mus., also ed. of pf. classics. Succeeded Joachim as dir., Berlin Hochschule für Musik, 1907. Of his 20 operas comp. 1893–1932, most successful were *Die Abreise* (Frankfurt 1898), *Tiefland* (Prague 1903), and *Die toten Augen* (Dresden 1916). 2nd of 6 wives was pianist Teresa *Carreño.

Albert, Heinrich (*b* Lobenstein, Saxony, 1604; *d* Königsberg, 1651). Ger. organist, poet, and composer. Cousin and pupil of *Schütz, whom he assisted at Dresden. Org., Königsberg Cath. Comp. 8 vols. of sacred and secular *Arien* (1638–50). Pioneer of *basso continuo. His *Comödien-Musik* (1644) is early example of Ger. opera.

Albert, Prince, Consort of Queen Victoria (*b* Rosenau, Ger., 1819; *d* Windsor, 1861). Trained in mus. by his father Ernest, Duke of Saxe-Coburg, who himself comp. opera. Patron of many Eng. mus. enterprises and friend of Mendelssohn. Wrote church mus. and some pleasant *Lieder* in style of Schubert and Mendelssohn.

Albert, Stephen (Joel) (*b* NY, 1941; *d* Truro, Mass., 1992). Amer. composer. Won Amer. *Prix de Rome* 1965–6, 1966–7. Teacher at Stanford Univ. 1970–1, Smith Coll., Northampton, Mass., 1974–6. Comp.-in-res. Seattle SO 1985–7. Won Pulitzer Prize 1985 for *RiverRun*. Several of his works are based on, or are settings of, James Joyce's novel *Finnegans Wake*. Works incl. *Illuminations*, brass, pf., hps., perc. (1962); *Imitations*, str. qt. (1964); *Bacchae*, narr., ch., orch. (1967–8); *Letters from the Golden Notebooks*, orch. (1971); *Cathedral Music*, elec. and traditional instrs. (1972); *To Wake the Dead*, sop., 5 instr. (1977); *Music from the Stone Harp*, 8 players (1980); Sym., *RiverRun*, orch. (1983–4); *Flower on the Mountain*, sop., chamber orch. (1985); vn. conc. (*In Concordiam*) (1988); vc. conc. (1990); *Wind Canticle*, cl., orch. (1992).

Albert Hall, Royal (London). See *Royal Albert Hall*.

Albert Herring. Comic chamber opera in 3 acts, Op.39, by Britten to lib. by Eric Crozier freely adapted from short story by Maupassant. Prod. Glyndebourne 1947, Tanglewood, Mass., 1949, London (CG, by Glyndebourne co.) 1989.

Alberti, Domenico (*b* Venice, *c.*1710; *d* Rome, 1746). It. composer of operas, songs, and of 36 hpd. sonatas in which his use of the formula known as *Alberti bass occurs frequently. Was also a singer, accompanying himself on the hpd. Was heard by *Farinelli in Spain, 1736.

Alberti bass. Simple (and often commonplace) acc. to a melody, consisting of 'broken chords', i.e. broken triads of which the notes are played in the order: lowest, highest, middle, highest. It takes its name from the It. composer who favoured it, Domenico *Alberti.

Albery, Tim (*b* Harpenden, 1952). Eng. theatre and opera producer. Début in opera Batignano Fest. 1983 (*The Turn of the Screw*). Prod. *The Trojans* 1986–90 (Opera North, Scottish Opera, WNO, CG). Has prod. for all the major Brit. cos. CG début 1994. For Scottish Opera, *The Ring* (2000–3).

Albinoni, Tomaso (*b* Venice, 1671; *d* Venice, 1751). It. composer of 81 operas, 99 sonatas, 59 concs., and 9 sinfonias. J. S. Bach made use of several of his themes and used Albinoni

bass parts for practice in thoroughbass. In recent years there has been keen interest in his concs. for str., *concerti grossi*, ob. and tpt. concs. Credited with being first It. composer of ob. concs. and first to employ 3 movts. in concs. (Op.2). The popular *Adagio* for org. and str. in G minor owes very little to Albinoni, having been constructed from a MS fragment by the 20th-cent. It. musicologist Remo Giazotto, whose copyright it is.

Alboni, Marietta (Maria Anna Marzia) (*b* Città di Castello, 1823; *d* Villa d'Avray, France, 1894). It. contralto. So impressed Rossini that he taught her the cont. roles in his operas. Début Bologna and La Scala 1842. Leading cont. CG 1847, becoming rival attraction to Jenny Lind, her salary being voluntarily raised overnight from £500 to £2,000 for the season. Sang in Paris and toured USA 1852. Sang with *Patti at Rossini's funeral, 1868. Retired from opera 1872 (because of obesity) but continued to give concerts seated in a chair.

alborada (Sp.). Dawn. Morning music (see also *aubade*). This word has special application to a type of instr. mus. with a good deal of rhythmic freedom and often played on bagpipe (or rustic ob.) and small drum.

Alborado del gracioso (Aubade of the Clown). 4th of Ravel's pf. pieces entitled *Miroirs* (1905). Orch. 1918.

Albrecht, Gerd (*b* Essen, 1935). Ger. conductor, pianist, and violinist. Début Hamburg 1956. Won Hilversum Cond. Competition 1958. Coach and cond., Stuttgart Opera 1958–61. Opera cond. Mainz 1961–3, Lübeck 1963–6, Kassel 1966–72, Berlin (Deutsche Oper) 1972–9. Cond. Tonhalle Orch., Zurich, 1975–80. Chief cond. Hamburg State Opera and PO from 1988. Prin. cond. Czech PO 1992–6. Cond. f.ps. of operas by Henze, Fortner, and Reimann (*Lear*, Munich, 1978). Salzburg Fest. début 1977; CG début 1986.

Albrechtsberger, Johann Georg (*b* Klosterneuberg, nr. Vienna, 1736; *d* Vienna, 1809). Austrian organist at Viennese court (1772) and cath. (1791); composer, but best remembered as comp. teacher (pupils incl. Beethoven) and as author of many theoretical works, incl. important textbook of comp. (1790, widely used in Eng. trans.).

Albright, William (*b* Gary, Indiana, 1944; *d* Ann Arbor, MI, 1998). Amer. composer. Ass. dir. of EMS, Michigan Univ. 1970. Many comps. for org. and for jazz ens.

Albumblatt (Ger.). Album Leaf. Fanciful title for a brief instr. comp., usually for pf., and of a personal character (like an autograph in an album).

Albumblätter (Album-leaves). Title of 20 pf. pieces by Schumann (Op.124, 1832–45, pubd. 1854).

Alceste (Gr. *Alkestis*). Opera in 3 acts by Gluck, lib. by Calzabigi, after Euripides. Prod. Vienna

1767, London 1795; Wellesley Coll., Mass., 1938, NY Met 1941 (in Fr.). Fr. version rev. by Gluck with text by Du Roullet, prod. Paris 1776. Preface to score contains Gluck's famous declaration on the nature of opera, which adumbrates mus.-drama. Other operas on this subject by Lully (1674), Schweitzer (1773), Boughton (1922), and Wellesz (1923), among others. Handel wrote a masque, *Alceste*, to a lib. by T. Smollett.

Alcina. Opera in 3 acts by Handel to lib. by Marchi after Ariosto's *Orlando furioso* (1516). Prod. CG 1735, revived London 1957, Dallas 1960 (with Sutherland, prod. Zeffirelli).

Alcock, (Sir) **Walter** (Galpin) (*b* Edenbridge, Kent, 1861; *d* Salisbury, 1947). Eng. organist. Ass. org. Westminster Abbey; org. of Chapels Royal (1902), and Salisbury Cath. from 1916 to death; comp. of church mus. Played org. at coronations of Edward VII (1902) and George V (1911). Knighted 1933.

alcuno, alcuna, alcun' (plurals *alcuni, alcune*) (It.). Some.

Alda (née Davis), **Frances** (Jean) (*b* Christchurch, NZ, 1883; *d* Venice, 1952). NZ-born soprano (Amer. cit. 1939). Début Paris 1904 (Massenet's Manon). CG début 1906, La Scala and NY Met 1908. From 1908 to 1929 sang at NY Met, to whose dir., Gatti-Casazza, she was married 1910–28. Much given to litigation. A fine Desdemona. Autobiography, *Men, Women and Tenors* (Boston, 1937).

Aldeburgh Festival. Annual fest. at Aldeburgh, Suffolk, since 1948, revolving largely round mus. and personality of Benjamin *Britten and his circle. Has superb concert-hall, The Maltings, at nearby Snape. Several Britten works had first perf. at Fest., incl. *Let's Make an Opera!* (1949), *Noye's Fludde* (1958), *A Midsummer Night's Dream* (1960), the three church parables (1964, 1966, 1968), and *Death in Venice* (1973). Berkeley's *A Dinner Engagement* (1954), Walton's *The Bear* (1967), and Birtwistle's *Punch and Judy* (1968) were also f.p. at Aldeburgh. After Britten's death, *Rostropovich became one of art. dirs., as did Murray Perahia, Oliver Knussen, and (from 1999) Thomas Adès.

Alden, David (*b* NY, 1949). Amer. opera producer. Brit. début Glasgow (Scottish Opera) 1979, NY Met début 1980, Santa Fe 1983, Los Angeles 1988. Some of his prods. are controversially radical, e.g. *Mazeppa* (1984), *Simon Boccanegra* (1987), *A Masked Ball* (1989), and *Ariodante* (1993), all for ENO.

Aldrich, Richard (*b* Providence, RI, 1863; *d* Rome, 1937). Amer. music critic. On *NY Tribune* 1891–1902, mus. critic of *NY Times* 1902–24. Books incl. *Guide to Parsifal* (1904) and *Guide to The Ring* (1905).

aleatory music (from Lat. *alea*, dice; hence the throw of the dice for chance). Synonym for *in-

determinacy, i.e. mus. that cannot be predicted before perf. or mus. which was comp. through chance procedures (statistical or computerized). The adjective 'aleatoric' is a bastard word, to be avoided by those who care for language.

Aleko. Opera in 1 act by Rachmaninov, lib. by V. Nemirovich-Danchenko, based on Pushkin's 1824 poem *Tsygany* (*Gipsies*). Comp. 1892. Prod. Moscow 1893, London 1915, NY 1926.

Aler, John (*b* Baltimore, Md., 1949). Amer. tenor. Opera début 1977, as Ernesto in *Don Pasquale* at Amer. Opera Center. Eur. début, Brussels 1979; Glyndebourne 1979; CG 1986; Salzburg Fest. 1988.

Alessandro (Alexander). Opera in 3 acts by Handel to lib. by Paolo Rolli (prod. London 1726). Revived as *Roxana*, with additions probably by Lampugnani, London 1743.

Alessandro Stradella. Opera in 3 acts by Flotow to lib. by W. Friedrich [F. W. Riese] after play *Stradella* (1837) by P. Dupont and P. A. P. Deforges. Comp. 1843. Prod. Hamburg 1844, London 1846, Hoboken, NJ, 1853, NY Met 1910.

Alexander, John (*b* Meridian, Miss., 1923; *d* Meridian, 1990). Amer. tenor. Début 1952, Cincinnati Opera (Faust). Débuts: NY City Opera 1957; NY Met 1961; Vienna Opera 1968; CG 1970. Sang title-role in f. Amer. p. of orig. Fr. vers. of *Don Carlos*, Boston 1973.

Alexander, Roberta (*b* Lynchburg, Va., 1949). Amer. soprano. Eur. début Netherlands Opera 1979. CG début 1980; NY Met début 1983; Salzburg Fest. 1986; Glyndebourne début 1989. Concert repertoire incl. Strauss, Mahler, and Ives.

Alexander Balus. Oratorio by Handel, text by Dr Thomas Morell. Comp. 1747. F.p. CG 1748.

Alexander Nevsky. Mus. by *Prokofiev for film dir. by S. Eisenstein (1938), later developed into cantata, Op.78, with text by V. Lugovskoy and Prokofiev, for mez., ch., and orch. (f.p. Moscow 1939). Film mus. in adaptation for broadcast, f.p. Eng. 1941.

Alexander's Feast. Setting by Handel of Dryden's ode, with some changes and additions by Newburgh Hamilton, f.p. London 1736. Re-orch. by Mozart. Orig. setting for St Cecilia's Day, 1697, by Jeremiah Clarke.

Alexandre, Jacob (*b* Paris, 1804; *d* Paris, 1876). Fr. founder of Paris firm of harmonium makers. In 1874 introduced the *Alexandre Organ*.

Alexandrov, Alexander (Vasilyevich) (*b* Plakhino, 1883; *d* Berlin, 1946). Russ. composer. Cond. from 1928 of Red Army Song and Dance Ens. Comp. *Hymn of the Bolshevik Party*, adapted as Russ. nat. anthem, 1943.

Alexandrov, Anatoly (*b* Moscow, 1888; *d* Moscow, 1982). Russ. pianist and composer. Composer of operas, syms., 14 pf. sonatas, and incidental mus. for many plays. Taught at Moscow Cons. from 1923.

Alexeev, Dimitri (*b* Moscow, 1947). Russ. pianist. Entered Cent. Mus. Sch., Moscow Cons., aged 6. Winner, Leeds int. pf. comp. 1975. Amer. début Chicago 1976. Soloist with world's leading orchs.

Alfano, Franco (*b* Posilippo, Naples, 1875; *d* San Remo, 1954). It. composer. Dir. of Bologna Cons. 1919–23, Turin 1924–39. Operas incl. *Risurrezione* (1902–3) and *Sakùntala* (1914–20; rewritten 1952). Completed Puccini's *Turandot* (1926) from composer's sketches, but his ending was severely cut by Toscanini and was not heard complete until 1982. Also wrote syms., str. qts., sonatas, etc.

Alfonso und Estrella. Opera in 3 acts (1821–2, D732) by Schubert to lib. by F. von Schober. Its ov., possibly revised, was used by Schubert as the ov. to *Rosamunde* at the latter's f.p. in Dec. 1823. Prod. Weimar 1854, Vienna 1882, Edinburgh 1968 (concert), Reading 1977 (stage), Detroit 1978 (concert).

Alford, Kenneth J. [Ricketts, Frederick Joseph] (*b* Ratcliff, London, 1881; *d* Reigate, 1945). Eng. composer and bandmaster. Student bandmaster at Kneller Hall 1904–8, bandmaster Argyll and Sutherland Highlanders 1908. Dir. of mus., Royal Marines 1927–40. His march comps. incl. *Colonel Bogey* (1914) and *Eagle Squadron* (1942).

Alfred. Masque orig. in 2 acts about King Alfred by Thomas *Arne, with words by J. Thomson and D. Mallet, prod. Cliveden, Bucks., 1740. Contains song *'Rule, Britannia!' Later revised extensively both as oratorio and opera in 3 acts, with much new material. Perfs. in Dublin 1744, 1756; London 1751, 1753, 1754, 1755, 1759, 1762, and 1773.

Alfvén, Hugo (Emil) (*b* Stockholm, 1872; *d* Falun, 1960). Swed. composer and violinist. Dir. of mus. at Univ. of Uppsala (1910–39). Comp. 5 syms., choral works, and 3 Swed. Rhapsodies of which the first, *Midsummer's Vigil* (*Midsommarvaka*), comp. 1904, is well known.

aliquot scaling. Arr., devised by the Blüthner firm, whereby the weak upper notes of a pf. are provided with sympathetic str. tuned an octave higher, thus increasing vol. of tone.

Alkan [Morhange, Charles-Valentin] (*b* Paris, 1813; *d* Paris, 1888). Fr. pianist, composer, and teacher. His comps. for pf. (and for pedal-pf.) incl. chromatic harmonies well in advance of their time and are extremely difficult to perform. Among best known are the *Grande Sonate*, Op.33, and the conc. for pf. solo, Op.39.

Alkestis. Gr. tragedy by Euripides which has been the basis of many operas. See *Alceste*.

all', alla (It.). To the, at the, on the, with the, in the manner of.

alla breve (It.). Indicates 2/2 time when, in a measure of 4 beats, the tempo is so fast that the measure may be considered to have 2 beats. See also *breve*.

allant (Fr.). (1) Going, i.e. active, brisk.
(2) Going on, in sense of continuing, e.g. Debussy's *allant grandissant*—going on growing, continuing to grow (i.e. getting louder).

allargando (It.). Enlarging. Getting slower and broadening, without loss of fullness in tone.

Alldis, John (*b* London, 1929). Eng. conductor and chorusmaster. Founder and cond. John Alldis Choir, 1962. Prof., GSMD 1966–77. Founder and cond., London Symphony Chorus 1966–9; cond., London Phil. Choir, 1969–82, Danish Radio Choir 1972–7. Mus. dir. Groupe Vocal de France 1978–83.

alle (Ger.). All. Thus if 1 vn. has been playing alone all are now to enter. *alle ersten* means all the first vns. and *alle zweiten* all the 2nd.

allegramente (It.). **allègrement** (Fr.). Brightly.

allegretto (It.). Moderately quick, pretty lively (but not so much as *allegro*). **allegrezza**. Mirth, cheerfulness.

Allegri, Gregorio (*b* Rome, 1582; *d* Rome, 1652). It. priest, tenor, and composer of a celebrated *Miserere* in 9 parts, long kept as exclusive possession of Sistine Chapel, where he served for the last part of his life. Mozart at the age of 14 secretly wrote out this work after 1 or 2 hearings. Also comp. several concertini, 2 books of motets, and 4-part sonata for str.

Allegri Quartet. Brit. string quartet founded 1953 with Eli Goren (vn.), James Barton (vn.), Patrick Ireland (va.), William Pleeth (vc.). Various changes in personnel. Since 1989: Peter Carter and David Roth (vns.), Roger Tapping (va.), and Bruno Schrecker (vc.). In addition to classics, the Allegri has specialized in works by Brit. composers, e.g. Britten, Maconchy, LeFanu, and Tippett.

allegro (It.). Merry, i.e. quick, lively, bright. Often used as the title of a comp. or movement in that style. The superlative is *allegrissimo*.

Allegro Barbaro. Work for solo pf. by Bartók, comp. 1911 and f.p. by him in Budapest on 27 Feb. 1921. Orch. transcr. by Kenessey, 1946.

Alleluia. This Lat. form of Hebrew exclamation, meaning 'Praise Jehovah', was added to certain of the responds of the RC Church, suitably joyful mus. to be grafted on to traditional plainsong and, in time, itself becoming traditional.

Alleluiasymphonie. Title given to Haydn's Sym. No.30 in C (Hob. I:30), 1765. Incorporates part of a plainsong alleluia.

Allemand (Fr.). German.

Allemande (Almand, Almayne, Almain, etc.) (Fr.). The name of 2 distinct types of comp., both probably of Ger. origin.

(1) Dance, usually in 4/4, but sometimes in duple time, much used by 17th- and earlier 18th-cent. composers as the first movement of the suite, or the first after a prelude. It is serious in character but not heavy, and of moderate speed: it is in simple *binary form.

(2) Peasant dance still in use in parts of Germany and Switzerland. It is in triple time, and of waltz-like character. Occasionally composers have called a comp. of this type a *Deutscher Tanz* (plural *Deutsche Tänze*), or simply *Deutsch* (plural *Deutsche*).

Allen, (Sir) **Hugh** (Percy) (*b* Reading, 1869; *d* Oxford, 1946). Eng. organist, conductor, and teacher. Org. scholar Christ's College, Cambridge, org. at caths. of St Asaph (1897) and Ely (1898); then of New College, Oxford (1901–18). Prof. of mus., Oxford Univ. (1918–46), and general inspirer of Oxford mus. activities. Dir. RCM (1918–37). Cond., Bach Choir 1907–20. Knighted 1920, GCVO 1935.

Allen, (Sir) **Thomas** (Boaz) (*b* Seaham Harbour, 1944). Eng. baritone. Opera début with WNO 1969 (Figaro in *Il barbiere di Siviglia*). CG début 1971; Glyndebourne 1973; NY Met 1981; La Scala 1987. Fine interpreter of Billy Budd and of Don Giovanni. Sang Ulisse in Henze's realization of Monteverdi's *Il *Ritorno d'Ulisse in Patria*, Salzburg 1985 and title-role in f. Brit. stage p. of *Doktor Faust*, London (ENO) 1986. Also concert career. CBE 1989. Knighted 1999.

allentamento, allentando (It.). Slowing down.

Allin, Norman (*b* Ashton-under-Lyne, 1884; *d* Hereford, 1973). Eng. bass. Became member of Beecham Opera Co. in 1916. Début CG 1919. Leading bass and dir. BNOC 1922–9. Member, Carl Rosa Co. 1942–9. Sang Bartolo in first Glyndebourne *Figaro*, 1934. One of orig. singers in *Serenade to Music* (1938). On staff RAM 1935–60, RMCM 1938–42. CBE 1958.

Allison, John (*b* Cape Town, 1965). S. African-born Brit. critic, organist, and author. Studied at Cape Town Univ. Ass. org., Cape Town Cath. 1985–9. Settled in Eng. 1989. Contributed mus. criticism to *Financial Times* 1993–5 before joining *The Times* 1995–2005. Mus. critic *Sunday Telegraph* from 2005. Ass. ed. *Opera* 1991–7, co-ed. 1998–9, ed. from 2000. Wrote *Edward Elgar: Sacred Music* (1994); *Pocket Companion to Opera* (1994).

All through the Night. The tune usually known outside Wales by this title is that of the Welsh folk-song *Ar Hyd y Nos*. Pubd. London 1784.

Alma redemptoris mater (Lat.: 'Sweet Mother of the Redeemer'). See *Antiphons of the Blessed Virgin Mary*.

Almeida, Antonio (Jacques) **de** (*b* Neuilly-sur-Seine, 1928; *d* Pittsburgh, 1997). Fr. conductor. Was cond. with Portuguese Radio 1957–60. Prin.

cond. Stuttgart PO 1960–4. Prin. guest cond. Houston SO 1969–71. Mus. dir. and cond. Moscow SO from 1993.

Almira. Opera in 3 acts (his first) by Handel to lib. by Feustking after It. text by G. Pancieri. Contains 41 Ger. and 15 It. airs. Prod. Hamburg 1705. Revived Leipzig 1985.

Alpaerts, Flor (*b* Antwerp, 1876; *d* Antwerp, 1954). Belg. composer and conductor. Prof. at Antwerp Cons. Wrote opera *Shylock* (1913), sym.-poems, and cantatas.

Alpensinfonie, Eine (An Alpine Symphony). Orch. comp. by Richard Strauss (Op.64, 1911–15). 10th and last of his tone-poems. In 22 sections, it describes 24 hours in the mountains. Scored for very large orch. incl. wind and thunder machines. F.p. Berlin 1915, London 1923.

Alphorn, Alpenhorn (Ger.), **cor des Alpes** (Fr.). The Alpine horn, a Swiss peasant instr. used for the evening calling of the cattle scattered over the summer pastures of the mountains (see also *Ranz des vaches*). It is made of wood and varies in length from about 7' to 12'. It has a similar mouthpiece to that of the *cornet, and is restricted to notes of the harmonic series. Strauss wrote a part for Alphorn in *Daphne*, but it is usually played by tb. (except in Haitink's recording).

Alpine Symphony, An. See *Alpensinfonie, Eine*.

als (Ger.). As, like, when, than.

Alsager, Thomas Massa (*b* 1779; *d* 1846). Eng. newspaper manager and amateur musician particularly devoted to furtherance of Beethoven's chamber music. At his prompting *The Times* became first newspaper to employ professional mus. critics.

al segno (It.). To the sign, meaning 'Go to the sign 𝄋'. This may mean '*go back* to the sign', i.e. the same as *dal segno*, or it may mean '*continue* until you reach the sign'.

Alsop, Marin (*b* NY, 1956). Amer. conductor. Studied Yale Univ. and Juilliard Sch. Prizewinner Stokowski int. cond. comp. 1989, Koussevitzky cond. prize, Tanglewood 1989. Pupil of Bernstein and Ozawa. Mus. dir. Cabrillo Fest. of Contemporary Mus., Calif., from 1991. Cond. Colorado SO 1993–2005. Prin. cond. Bournemouth SO from 2002. Mus. dir. Baltimore SO from 2007.

Also sprach Zarathustra (Thus spake Zoroaster). Tone-poem by Richard Strauss, Op.30, comp. 1895–6 and f.p. Frankfurt 1896. Freely based on Nietzsche's epic prose poem of same name. Delius set 11 sections of poem in his *Mass of Life*.

alt. (1) High. The note g'' marks the beginning of the range of vocal notes spoken of as *in alt*, and from g''' as *in altissimo*.

(2) (Ger.). The alto (contralto) v.: prefixed to the

name of an instr. (e.g. *Althorn*), it implies an alto pitch.

(3) (Ger.). Old.

alta (It.). High, e.g. *ottava alta*, high octave, i.e. one octave higher than written. Not to be confused with **alto*.

Altenberglieder (Songs by Altenberg). 5 songs to picture-postcard texts by Peter Altenberg (pseudonym of Richard Englander, 1862–1919), comp. by *Berg for v. and orch. (Op.4). At f.p. in Vienna of 2 of the songs on 31 Mar. 1913, a riot seriously disrupted the concert. Not perf. complete until 1953 (Rome, cond. Horenstein).

altered chord. Amer. synonym for chromatic chord.

alternativo (It.). Name applied in early 18th-cent. mus. in dance style to a contrasting middle section (later called **trio*). Sometimes used of a whole comp., apparently implying that the 2 sections may be alternated at will.

Altflügelhorn (Ger.). Another name for the **Flügelhorn* in E♭.

Altgeige (Ger.). Alto fiddle, i.e. the **viola*.

Althorn (Ger.). The alto *saxhorn in E♭ and the *Flügelhorn* in E♭ are sometimes referred to as *Althorns*.

altissimo. See *alt*.

altiste (Fr.). (1) a player of the *alto*, i.e. of the *viola.

(2) An *alto singer.

Altmeyer, Jeannine (Theresa) (*b* La Habra, Calif., 1948). Amer. soprano of Ger. parentage. Début, NY Met 1971 (Heavenly Voice in *Don Carlos*), Chicago 1972, European début 1973 (Salzburg Easter Fest.). Zurich Opera 1973–5, CG début 1975, Stuttgart Opera 1975–9. Bayreuth début 1976. Sang Isolde at Bayreuth 1986. Sang Brünnhilde in *Janowski recording of *The Ring*.

alto (It.). High. (1) Usually high type of falsetto male v., much used in Eng. church mus.; thus in SATB, A stands for alto.

(2) Low-register female v., usually referred to as *contralto.

(3) Applied to instr., the 2nd or 3rd highest of the family.

(4) (Fr.). *Viola.

alto clarinet. The *clarinet in E♭ and in F.

alto clef. Formerly used for alto v., now mainly used for viola. See *clefs*.

alto Flügelhorn. The B♭ *Flügelhorn*, also in E♭.

alto flute. The fl. in G, transposing instr. notated 4th above actual sound.

alto moderne. Also called *viole-ténor*. A large viola, played like the vc. and introduced in the 1930s by R. Parramon of Barcelona.

alto oboe. The Eng. hn. (**cor anglais*), pitched in F, a 5th below the *oboe.

Alto Rhapsody. Name by which Brahms's Rhapsody for cont. solo, male ch., and orch. (Op.53, 1869) is known in Eng. Text taken from Goethe's poem *Harzreise im Winter*. Ger. title of comp. is *Rhapsodie aus Goethes Harzreise im Winter*.

alto saxhorn. The sop. *saxhorn in B♭ (or C), differing little from the B♭ cornet.

alto saxophone. The E♭ sax., usually played in jazz (especially beautifully by Johnny Hodges of Duke Ellington's orch.).

alto staff. See *great staff*.

alto trombone. Obsolete type of *trombone, written for by Mozart, later replaced by ten. tb.

altposaune (Ger.). *alto trombone.

altra, altre. See *altro*.

altra volta (It.). *Encore.

altro, altri; altra, altre (It.). Another, others.

Alva, Luigi [Alva Talledo, Luis Ernesto] (*b* Lima, 1927). Peruvian tenor. Début Lima 1949. Milan 1954 and at opening of Piccola Scala 1955 (Paolini in *Il matrimonio segreto*). Débuts at La Scala 1956; Salzburg Fest. 1957; CG 1960, NY Met 1964. Specialist in light, lyrical Mozart and Rossini roles. Retired 1989.

Álvarez, Marcelo (*b* Córdoba, 1962). Argentinian tenor. Worked in furniture factory until aged 30, then studied singing. Prof. début La Fenice 1995 (*La sonnambula*). London début 1997 (concert perf. of *Linda di Chamounix*) and with Royal Opera (Alfredo in *La traviata* at RAH). Vienna, Paris, and NY Met débuts 1998 (all as Alfredo). USA recital début 2001 (Kansas City).

Alvary, Max [Achenbach, Maximilian] (*b* Düsseldorf, 1856; *d* Gross-Tabarz, Thuringia, 1898). Ger. tenor. Début Weimar 1879 (*Alessandro Stradella*). NY Met début 1885. Specialist in Wagnerian roles (Loge, Siegfried, Tristan, Tannhäuser). Bayreuth début 1891. Siegfried in first CG *Ring* under Mahler, 1892.

Alwin, Carl [Alwin, Oskar Pinkus] (*b* Königsberg, 1891; *d* Mexico City, 1945). Ger. pianist, conductor, and composer. Held various operatic posts before going to Vienna State Opera 1920–8. Married to the sop. Elisabeth *Schumann 1920–36. Arr. certain items by R. Strauss. Salzburg Fest. 1922. Cond. first London perf. (1924) of 2nd version (1916) of *Ariadne auf Naxos*. Cond., Nat. Opera, Mexico City, from 1941.

Alwyn [Wetherall], **Kenneth** (*b* Croydon, 1925). Eng. conductor and composer. Prin. cond. BBC

Northern Ireland Orch. Assoc. cond. SW Th. Ballet 1952–6, Royal Ballet 1956–9. Comp. film and TV mus.

Alwyn, William (*b* Northampton, 1905; *d* Southwold, 1985). Eng. composer, pianist, flautist, poet, translator, and painter. Began career as orch. flautist with LSO. Prof. of comp., RAM, 1926–56. First orch. work (*5 Preludes for Orch.*) played at a Promenade Concert, 1927. Three times chairman, Composers' Guild. Wrote much mus. for films, incl. wartime documentaries *Desert Victory* and *The Way Ahead*. Wrote several vols. of poetry and trans. Fr. poets. CBE 1978. Prin. comps.:

OPERA: **Miss Julie* (1961–76).

ORCH.: syms. No.1 (1950), No.2 (1954), No.3 (1956), No.4 (1960), No.5 (1973); symphonic prelude *The Magic Island* (1953); *Festival March* (1952); *Conc. grosso* No.1 (1952), No.2, str. (1951), No.3 (1964); *Elizabethan Dances* (1957); ob. conc. (1951); *Lyra Angelica*, conc. for harp and str. (1955); *Autumn Legend*, ca. and str. (1956); *Derby Day* (1962); *Sinfonietta* for str. (1970), No.2 (1976).

CHAMBER MUSIC: str. trio (1963); str. qts. No.1 in D minor (1955), No.2 (*Spring Waters*) (1976); cl. sonata (1962); *Naiades*, fl. and hp. sonata (1972); *Divertimento*, fl. (1940).

PIANO: *Fantasy Waltzes* (1956); *Sonata alla toccata* (1951); *12 Preludes* (1959).

SONG-CYCLES (all with pf.): *Mirages*, bar. (1974); *6 Nocturnes*, bar. (1976); *A Leavetaking*, ten. (1977); *Invocations*, sop. (1978).

Alyabyev, Alexander (*b* Tobolsk, 1787; *d* Moscow, 1851). Russ. composer and precursor of national school. Wrote famous song *The Nightingale* (1823), utilized by Patti and others for lesson scene of Rossini's *Il barbiere di Siviglia*, and transcr. for pf. by Liszt.

alzato, alzati; alzata, alzate (It.). Raised, lifted off (of a mute or mutes, etc.).

Alzira. Opera in prol. and 2 acts by Verdi to lib. by Cammarano based on Voltaire's play *Alzire* (1736). Comp. 1845. Prod. Naples 1845; revived Rome 1967, NY (concert) 1968, London (stage) 1970.

am (Ger.). At the, on the, to the, by the, near the. As in *Am Meer*, by the sea.

amabile (It.). Lovable, hence *amabilità*, lovableness.

Amadeus Quartet. Highly successful and admired Brit. str. qt. which gave its first London concert in Jan. 1948, though it had played, under various different titles, for a year before then. Its membership remained constant, viz., Norbert **Brainin, Sigmund Nissel (vns.), Peter Schidlof (va.), Martin Lovett (vc.). Salzburg Fest. 1956. Britten's 3rd str. qt. (1975) comp. for them. After Schidlof's death in 1987, continued playing as Amadeus Trio. Brainin OBE 1960, his three colleagues 1973.

Amahl and the Night Visitors. Opera in 1 act by **Menotti to his own lib. First TV opera (NBC

NY 1951). First stage perf. Indiana Univ., Bloomington, 1952, NY 1952, BBC TV 1967. The Night Visitors are the Magi.

Amati. It. family of vn.-makers (also vas., vcs., and dbs.) at Cremona. Comprised Andrea (*c*.1505–*c*.1580) whose sons Antonio (*c*.1538–*c*.1595) and Girolamo (Geronimus) (1561–1630) made many changes. Nicola (1596–1684), son of Girolamo, is reckoned the greatest of the Amatis. Among his pupils were Stradivari and Guarneri. The last of the line was Nicola's son Girolamo (1649–1740).

Amberley Wild Brooks. No.2 of *2 Pf. Pieces* by **Ireland, comp. 1921.

Ambrosian chant. Type of plainsong now lost, assoc. with St Ambrose, Bishop of Milan 374–97, who reorganized singing and tonality in the Christian church. See under *modes* and *plainsong*.

âme (Fr.). Soul. The **sound-post of the vn., etc. The fanciful name doubtless comes from its importance to the whole tone-quality of the instr., which depends much on its correct position. The Italians call it *anima*, which also means 'soul'.

Amelia goes to the Ball (*Amelia al ballo*). Comic opera in 1 act by **Menotti to It. lib. by composer (Eng. trans. by George Meade). Comp. 1934–7. Prod. Berlin and Philadelphia 1937, NY Met 1938, San Remo 1938, Liverpool 1956.

Ameling, Elly [Elisabeth] (Sara) (*b* Rotterdam, 1934). Dutch soprano. Début Amsterdam 1961. London début 1966, Amer. (NY) 1968. Specialist in *Lieder* and oratorio, being particularly fine in Bach cantatas and Passions, and Schubert songs. Rare opera appearances, e.g. Madama Butterfly (Dutch TV 1970), and with Netherlands Opera 1973; Washington DC Opera 1974.

amen. So be it. The Hebrew terminal word of prayer in Jewish, Christian, and Mohammedan worship. It has been extended by composers, many times, into a long comp., e.g. the 'Amen Chorus' of Handel's *Messiah*. Shorter settings have been made for liturgical use, such as Gibbons's Threefold Amen and Stainer's Sevenfold Amen. The **Dresden Amen comes from the Threefold Amen of the Royal Chapel of Dresden (common also throughout Saxony); its composer was J. G. **Naumann.

amen cadence. See *cadence*.

America ('My Country, 'tis of thee'). Patriotic hymn with words of Rev. Samuel Francis Smith (1832) sung to tune of 'God save the King'. Also title of symphonic rhapsody (1928) by E.**Bloch.

American Academy (Rome). Building in Rome, formerly Amer. Sch. of Architecture, where winners of Amer. Rome Prize live. See *Prix de Rome*.

American Federation of Musicians. Trade-union organization for professional musicians in USA and Canada; founded 1895 and very active under the presidency (1942–58) of James C. Petrillo.

American Guild of Organists. Nat. assoc. of Amer. church orgs., founded 1896.

American in Paris, An. Orch. piece by *Gershwin, score of which incl. parts for 4 taxi-horns. F.p. NY 1928.

American musical terminology (compared with Brit.). Certain divergences between Amer. and Brit. mus. terminology sometimes cause confusion:

(1) NOTE and TONE. Such expressions as '3 tones lower', or 'the scale of 5 tones' have different meanings to the Amer. and the Brit. reader. A Brit. reader, finding these expressions in an Amer. book or journal, must be careful to understand by them '3 notes lower' and 'scale of 5 notes', while an Amer. reader finding such expressions in a Brit. book must interpret them as '3 whole-steps lower' or 'a scale of 5 whole-steps'.

(2) Eng. BAR = Amer. MEASURE, the former term being often reserved in Amer. for the actual bar-line.

(3) Eng. SEMIBREVE, MINIM, etc.= Amer. WHOLE-NOTE, HALF-NOTE, etc.

(4) Eng. NATURALS, e.g. the white keys of a pf., etc.= Amer. LONG-KEYS.

(5) Eng. NATURAL NOTES (of brass instr.) = Amer. PRIMARY TONES.

(6) Eng. TO FLATTEN and TO SHARPEN = Amer. TO FLAT and TO SHARP.

(7) Eng. ORGAN (generally) = Amer. PIPE ORGAN (to distinguish from the various reed organs).

(8) Eng. GRAMOPHONE = Amer. PHONOGRAPH.

(9) Eng. CONCERT-GIVING = Amer. CONCERTIZING.

(10) Amer. APPLIED MUSIC means perf. mus.; hence univ. courses in Applied Music are courses in instr. or vocal technique and interpretation.

(11) The Eng. term FOLK SONG is often used in the USA in a loose way, covering not only trad. peasant songs but also any songs which have become widely known by people in general.

(12) Eng. FIRST VIOLIN or *leader* (of orch.) = Amer. CONCERT MASTER.

(13) Eng. CONDUCTOR (of orch.) = (often) Amer. LEADER (and Eng. *to conduct* = Amer. *to lead*).

(14) Eng. PART-WRITING = Amer. VOICE-LEADING.

(15) Eng. RECORD SLEEVE (container) = Amer. DISC (DISK) LINER.

American organ. Called in USA the 'cabinet org.', this is a type of reed org. like the *harmonium in which air is sucked through reeds. Invented by workman in *Alexandre's factory but developed in Boston, Mass.

'American' Quartet. Name by which Dvořák's str. qt. in F, Op.96, is generally known. Comp. in USA, 1893 and partly inspired by Negro melodies, hence its former names, now frowned on, of 'Negro' or 'Nigger' Qt.

American Society of Composers, Authors and Publishers (ASCAP). Founded 1914 to protect copyrights, perf. rights, etc. Headquarters in NY.

America the Beautiful. Patriotic Amer. hymn, words by Katharine Lee Bates (1859–1929) pubd. 1895. Set to mus. (1913) of Samuel Augustus Ward (1848–1903) taken from his hymn *Materna* (1882).

Amériques (New Worlds). Comp. for large orch. by *Varèse, instr. incl. cyclone whistle, fire siren, crow-call, etc. Comp. 1918–21. F.p. Philadelphia 1926.

Amfiparnaso L'. *Comedia harmonica* by Orazio Vecchi. A string of pieces in madrigal style, in 3 acts with a prol.; not intended to be staged. Prod. Modena 1594; pubd. 1597; revived Florence 1933, NY (concert) 1933, London 1946.

Amico Fritz, L' (Friend Fritz). Opera in 3 acts by Mascagni, lib. by P. Suardon (N. Daspuro), based on novel by Erckmann-Chatrian (1864). Prod. Rome 1891; London and Philadelphia 1892; NY Met 1894.

Amid Nature (or *In Nature's Realm*, Cz. *Vpřírodě*). Ov. for orch., Op.91, by Dvořák, comp. 1891, as first of cycle of 3 ovs. called *Nature, Life, and Love*, the others being *Carneval and *Othello. Also title of Dvořák's 5 chs. for mixed vv., Op.63, to words by Hálek, comp. 1882.

Amis, John (*b* London, 1922). Eng. critic and administrator, with prin. reputation as presenter of music programmes on radio and TV. Studied to be professional singer and recorded ten. solo in Bernard Herrmann's *Moby Dick*. Secretary of Dartington Summer School 1948–79.

Amor brujo, El (Love, the Magician). Ballet in 1 act by Falla, based on Andalusian gipsy tale. Requires ballerina to sing as well as dance. Also exists as orch. suite (with cont.). The famous 'Ritual Fire Dance' occurs in it. *Brujo* means 'male witch' and the title is best trans. as 'Wedded by Witchcraft'. F.p. Madrid 1915; London in concert version 1921, as ballet 1931.

amore (It.), **amour** (Fr.). Love. A word often found in the names of certain forms of old instr., generally implying a lower pitch than the ordinary and a claim to sweeter tone, e.g. *va. d'amore*, *ob. d'amore*. In bowed instr. it also indicates the possession of *sympathetic strings.

Amore dei tre re, L' (The Love of the Three Kings). Opera in 3 acts by *Montemezzi to lib. adapted by Sem Benelli from his verse tragedy (1910). Prod. La Scala 1913; NY Met and London CG 1914.

amoroso (It.). Loving, affectionate. Fourth movt. of Mahler's 7th Sym. is *andante amoroso*.

Amoyal, Pierre (*b* Paris, 1949). Fr. violinist. Won Ginette Neveu Prize 1963, Paganini Prize 1964, Enescu Prize 1970. Gave 4 perfs. of Berg conc.

with *Solti and Orchestre de Paris, 1971. NY début 1985. World-wide tours. Prof. of vn., Paris Cons. 1977–86 and at Lausanne Cons.

amplifier. A piece of electrical equipment which 'amplifies', i.e. increases, the vol. of sound. Voltage-controlled amplifiers alter the vol. of the input signal. They can be used in *electronic music in conjunction with voltage-controlled oscillators and filters and a kbd. to function as a monophonic mus. instr.

Amram, David (b Philadelphia, 1930). Amer. horn-player and composer. Played in jazz groups and sym. orchs. First comp.-in-residence with NYPO. Mus. dir. Lincoln Center Theater 1963–5. Works incl.: incid. mus. for chamber orch. for nearly 20 Shakespeare prods.; opera *Twelfth Night* (1968); *Shakespearean Concerto*; *King Lear Variations*; incid. mus. to *Peer Gynt*; triple conc.; vn. conc.; cantata *A Year in our Land*; vn. sonata; str. qt.; and songs. Published autobiography (NY, 1968).

AMusLCM. Associate in Music [i.e. theory of mus.] of London College of Music.

AMusTCL. Associate in Music, Trinity College of Music, London.

Amy, Gilbert (b Paris, 1936). Fr. composer and conductor. Strongly influenced by Boulez and for 3 years attended Darmstadt summer courses. Succeeded Boulez as cond. of *Domaine Musical*, Paris, 1967–73. Founder and cond. French Radio New PO 1976–81. Dir., Lyons Cons. from 1984. His comps. have moved from strict serialism to a more flexible use of the system and his later works, some employing tape, are of considerable poetic refinement. Works incl.:

OPERA: *Le premier cercle* (1996–9).

ORCH.: *Inventions* (1959–61); *Triade* (1965/1971); *Trajectoires*, vn., orch. (1966); *Chant pour orchestre* (1969–72, 1980); *Adagio et Stretto* (1977–8); *Orchestrahl* (1986–7); *17 Juillet* (1994); *3 Scènes* (1995).

INSTR. ENS.: *Mouvements*, 17 instr. (1958); *Jeux et formes*, ob., ens. (1971); *7 Sites*, 14 players (1975); *Echos XIII*, ens. (1976); *La Variation ajoutée*, elec. tape (IRCAM) and 17 instr. (1984–6); *D'Après 'Ecrits sur Toiles'*, chamber orch. (1984); *en trio*, cl., pf., vn. (1985); *Un saison enfer*, instrs., vv., tape (1992); 2 str. qts. (1990–2, 1995).

UNACC. CHORUS: *Récitatif, air et variation* (1970). Also much vocal, chamber, and kbd. mus.

an (Ger.). On, by, to, at, as in *An die Musík*, 'To Music'. In org. mus. it signifies that the stop in question is to be drawn.

Anacréon, ou L'amour fugitif. Opera-ballet in 2 acts by Cherubini, text by Mendouze. Prod. Paris 1803, Siena 1971.

Anacreontic Society. Aristocratic mus. soc. in London 1766–94, meeting fortnightly during the season. Haydn attended a meeting. At each meeting, pres. sang constitutional song 'To Anacreon in Heaven'. See *Star-Spangled Banner*.

anacrusis (plural *anacruses*). Unstressed syllable at the beginning of a line of poetry or an unstressed note or group of notes at the beginning of a mus. phrase. See also *up-beat*.

analytical notes. Another name for 'programme-notes', the descriptions of comps. which appear in annotated programmes. Possibly the earliest example is the programme of a Concert of Catches and Glees, given by Arne at Drury Lane Th. in 1768. It has a preface explaining the nature of the catch and the glee, and the various items are provided with historical interest. 15 years later (1783) Frederick the Great's Kapellmeister, J. F. Reichardt, founded in Potsdam a regular Tuesday perf. and provided in his programmes both the words of the songs and 'historical and aesthetic explanations enabling the audience to gain a more immediate understanding'. John Ella, prominent in London mus. life as dir. of a chamber mus. organization, the Musical Union (1845–80), is often spoken of in Britain as the introducer of annotated programmes: he had been anticipated, but it was probably the utility of his analytical notes over a long period that formally est. the practice which from then on became widespread. Some programme-notes have had a value beyond the occasion for which they were written, notably those by Sir George Grove for August Manns's orch. concerts at the Crystal Palace and those by Sir Donald *Tovey for the Reid concerts in Edinburgh.

Ančerl, Karel (b Tučapy, Bohemia, 1908; d Toronto, 1973). Cz. conductor. Ass. cond. in Königsberg to H. Scherchen (1929–31). Cond. for Prague radio 1933–9. Sent to concentration camp by Nazis in 1942. Cond. Cz. Radio Orch. 1947–50, Cz. PO, 1950–68 (Salzburg Fest. début 1963); Toronto SO, 1969–73.

Ancient Concert (Concert of Ancient Music). Important London subscription series (1776–1848). The royal and noble 'Directors' (e.g. George III, Prince Albert, Duke of Wellington) took turns to choose programmes. Another name was 'King's Concert' or, in Victorian times, 'Queen's Concert'. (Sometimes confused with *Academy of Ancient Music, 1726–92.) From 1804 the concerts were given in Hanover Sq. Rooms.

ancora (It.). Still, yet; i.e. *ancora forte*, still loud; *ancora più forte*, even louder. Also used to mean 'again', i.e. repeat. See also *encore*.

Anda, Géza (b Budapest, 1921; d Zurich, 1976). Hung.-born pianist and conductor (Swiss cit. 1952). Won Liszt Prize (1940). Escaped from Hung. to Switzerland in 1942. Salzburg Fest. début 1952. World-wide reputation as interpreter of Mozart, Brahms, Beethoven, and especially Bartók.

andaluz, andaluza (Sp.), **andalouse** (Fr.). Vaguely applied to several Sp. dances common in Andalusia, e.g. *fandango, *malagueña, and *polo.

andamento (It.). Going (i.e. running). A fugue subject of above average length, often of a running character. See also *attacco*.

andante (It., from *andare*, to go). Moving along, flowing (slowish but not slow). The word is often used for the title of a comp. *andantino*. A diminution of *andante*. Some composers use it to mean a little slower than *andante*, but the commonly accepted modern usage means a little quicker.

andante cantabile (It.). Flowing and songlike. A direction often used by composers. To a large section of the public, however, it means one work, the 2nd movt., *andante cantabile*, of Tchaikovsky's str. qt. No.1 in D (1871), Op.11.

Andante favori. Publisher's title for Andante in F, pf. solo by Beethoven comp. 1804 and intended for the Sonata in C (*Waldstein*), Op.53, but discarded and pubd. separately in 1806.

Andante spianato (It.). Flowing and smooth. The title of Chopin's. Op.22 for pf. and orch., 1834. Linked by Chopin to a Polonaise in E♭ major.

An den Baum Daphne (To the Daphne Tree). Epilogue by R. Strauss to his opera **Daphne* (1936–7) for unacc. 9-part mixed ch., to words by J. Gregor, comp. 1943. This was the lib. for a choral finale to the opera which Strauss discarded in favour of an orch. transformation scene. He set the words later as this motet.

Anders, Peter (*b* Essen, 1908; *d* in car crash, Hamburg, 1954). Ger. tenor. Début Hamburg 1931 (*La Belle Hélène*). Bavarian State Opera in Munich 1938–40; Berlin State Opera 1940–8; Hamburg Opera 1948–54. Specialized in lighter Mozart roles, though later he sang Otello. Salzburg Fest. début 1941, Brit. début in Edinburgh, 1950, CG début 1951. Distinguished concert singer.

Andersen, Karsten (*b* Oslo, 1920). Norweg. conductor and violinist. Cond. and mus. dir. Stavanger SO 1945–65, Bergen SO 1965–85. Chief cond. Iceland SO 1973–80. Guest cond. of leading European orchs.

Anderson, Emily (*b* Galway, Ireland, 1891; *d* London, 1962). Eng. translator of the letters of Mozart and his family (1938) and of the letters of Beethoven (1961). Worked in Brit. Foreign Office, being seconded to War Office 1940–3. OBE 1944.

Anderson, Julian (David) (*b* London, 1967). Eng. composer. Studied at RCM with John Lambert, privately in Paris with Tristan Murail, and at Cambridge with Alexander Goehr. Advice and guidance from Oliver Knussen. Britten Memorial Fellow, Tanglewood 1993. Head of comp., RCM 2000–4, comp.-in-assoc., CBSO 2001–4, prof. of comp., Harvard Univ. from 2005. Works incl.:

ORCH.: *Diptych* (1992); *Pavillons en l'air* (1992); *Khorovod* (1994); *The Crazed Moon* (1997); *The*

Stations of the Sun (1997); *Alhambra Fantasy* (2000); *Imagin'd Corners* (2002); sym. (2003); *Book of Hours*, ens., elec. (2004); *Eden* (2005).
CHORAL: *Heaven is shy of earth*, mez., ch., orch. (2006).
VOCAL: *I'm nobody, who are you?*, song-cycle, bar., pf. (1995).

Anderson, June (*b* Boston, Mass., 1952). Amer. soprano. Won schol. to study at NY Met, 1970. NY City Opera 1978–82 (début as Queen of Night in *Die Zauberflöte*). Débuts: Eur. (Rome) 1982; Paris 1985, CG début 1986, La Scala 1986, Vienna 1987, NY Met 1989. Sings coloratura roles.

Anderson, Leroy (*b* Cambridge, Mass., 1908; *d* Woodbury, Conn., 1975). Amer. composer of light music, notably *Sleigh Ride* and *Blue Tango*, but also wrote more extended works.

Anderson, Marian (*b* Philadelphia, 1897; *d* Portland, Oregon, 1993). Amer. contralto. Won comp. to appear with NYPO 1925. First NY recital 1929. London début 1930. Sang mainly in concert repertory but became first black singer at NY Met 1955 (Ulrica in *Un ballo in maschera*). Delegate to United Nations 1958. Sang at Inauguration of Pres. D. Eisenhower (1953) and at Inauguration Ball of Pres. J. F. Kennedy, 1961. Retired 1965. Autobiography *My Lord, What a Morning* (NY, 1956).

Anderszewski, Piotr (*b* Warsaw, 1969). Polish pianist. Studied in Warsaw, Strasbourg, Lyons, and Los Angeles. Prof. début London 1990. Duo with violinist Victoria Mullova, touring Japan and Europe. Notable interpreter of Beethoven, Mozart, and Szymanowski.

An die ferne Geliebte (To the Distant Beloved). Song-cycle by Beethoven, with pf. acc. (Op.98, 1816), of 6 poems by Alois Jeitteles. Not to be confused with Beethoven's songs *An die fernen Geliebten* (1809, words by Reissig) and *An die Geliebte* (1811, words by J. L. Stoll, re-comp. 1814).

André, Franz (*b* Brussels, 1893; *d* Brussels, 1975). Belg. violinist, conductor and composer. Played vn. in Belgian Radio Orch. 1923, then became its cond. Founder and mus. dir. Belg. Radio SO 1935–58. On staff Brussels Cons. 1920–44. Cond. f.ps. of several modern works, incl. 7th Sym. of Milhaud, 1955.

André, Johann (*b* Offenbach-am-Main, 1741; *d* Offenbach-am-Main, 1799). Ger. composer, but best known for publishing firm he founded in 1774. Among his own operas was the 4-act *Belmonte und Constanze, oder die Entführung aus dem Serail*, prod. Berlin 1781, the year before Mozart's setting of the same opera. His son, Johann Anton (1775–1842), in 1799 acquired entire mus. relicta of Mozart from the composer's widow and also pubd. Mozart's own thematic catalogue of his works from 1784 to 1791.

Andre, Martin (*b* West Wickham, 1960). Eng. conductor. Percussionist, Nat. Youth Orch. of Great Britain from 1970. Cond. his edn. of Purcell's *King Arthur*, Cambridge 1982. WNO from

1982, Vancouver Opera 1986–7. London concert début 1987 (ECO). Scottish Opera début 1989, ENO 1990. Cond. f.p. of Buller's *The Bacchae* (London, ENO, 1992). Cond. ETO from 1993.

André, Maurice (*b* Alès, Gard, 1933). Fr. trumpeter. Début 1954. Won Geneva Int. Comp. 1955, Munich Int. Comp. 1963. Prof. of tpt., Paris Cons., 1967–78. Soloist with leading orchs. Salzburg Fest. début 1966. Specialist in baroque and contemporary mus. Plays over 30 concs., incl. several written for him, e.g. by Blacher.

Andrea Chénier. Fr. Revolution opera in 4 acts by Giordano to lib. by Illica. Prod. Milan (La Scala) 1896; NY 1896, Met 1921; London 1903.

Andreae, Volkmar (*b* Berne, 1879; *d* Zurich, 1962). Swiss conductor and composer. Dir. Tonhalle Orch., Zurich, 1906–49, Dir. of Zurich Cons. 1914–41. Cond. f.p. of Walton's *Portsmouth Point*, 1926. Comp. 2 operas, 2 syms., chamber mus.

Andreozzi, Gaetano (*b* Aversa, 1755; *d* Paris, 1826). It. composer. Wrote 43 operas and 6 str. qts.

Andrews, Hilda [Mrs. G. M. Lees] (*b* Birmingham, 1900; *d* Louth, Lincs., 1983). Eng. musicologist. Ed. of Byrd's *My Ladye Nevells Booke*, North's *Musicall Grammarian* (part of his *Memoires of Musick*), biography of Sir Richard *Terry (1948), etc. Compiler of Catalogue of misc. MS Mus. in King's (now Royal) Music Library.

Andriessen, Hendrik (*b* Haarlem, 1892; *d* Heemstede, 1981). Dutch composer and organist. Org. at Haarlem and Utrecht between 1916 and 1938. Dir., Utrecht Cons. 1937–49, and Royal Cons., The Hague, 1949–57. Comp. principally org. and choral mus. but also operas, syms., and sonatas.

Andriessen, Jurriaan (*b* Haarlem, 1925; *d* The Hague, 1996). Dutch composer, son of Hendrik *Andriessen. Works incl. operas, 5 syms. (1949–70), *Serenade* for hn. (1985), and many chamber works involving hpd. and elec.

Andriessen, Louis (*b* Utrecht, 1939). Dutch composer, son of Hendrik *Andriessen. Comps. incl. th. and film scores and reflect influences of Cage, Stockhausen, and Stravinsky. Has made special critical study of Stravinsky. Comps. incl. mus., th. pieces *Matthew Passion* (1976), *Orpheus* (1977), and *George Sand* (1980); *Rosa*, opera (1994); *Trilogie van de laatste dag*, soli, children's ch., large ens. (1996–7); *Writing to Vermeer*, opera (1997–9); *La passione*, sop., vn., ens. (2002); *Inanna*, opera (2003); *Haags Hakkuh*, 2 pfs. (2003); *De Opening*, 3 ens. (2005); *Xenia*, vn., v. (2005); *Commedia*, opera (2006–7); much orch. mus., choral works, chamber mus., and works involving amp. and elec.

Andsnes, Leif Ove (*b* Karmoy, Norway, 1970). Norweg. pianist. Studied at Bergen Cons. with Jiří Hlinka. Won Hindemith Prize, Frankfurt 1987, and Grieg Prize, Bergen 1990. Int. career and many recordings. Co-art. dir. Riser Fest. Directs many works from kbd. Specialist in Grieg, Janáček, Rachmaninov, Brahms, Schumann.

Anfang (Ger.). Beginning. *anfangs*, at the beginning. *wie anfänglich*, as at the beginning. *vom Anfang* is Ger. equivalent of *da capo*.

Anfossi, Pasquale (*b* Taggia, nr. Naples, 1727; *d* Rome, 1797). It. composer. Comp. of over 70 operas, and then of church mus. when he became maestro di capella of St John Lateran (Rome) in 1792. For Vienna prod. (1783) of his opera *Il curioso indiscreto*, Mozart comp. 3 additional arias. Mus. dir., King's Th., London, 1782–6.

Angeles, Victoria de los. See *Los Angeles, Victoria de*.

angelica (It.), **angélique** (Fr.), **angel-lute** (Eng.). Instr. of the lute type popular *c*.1700. An archlute with long neck, 16 or 17 gut str. and 2 peg-boxes. Tuned diatonically.

Angelus. Prayer to the Virgin Mary offered at morning, noon, and evening at the sound of the angelus bell. Also title of opera by Edward Naylor (1867–1934) which won Ricordi Prize and was prod. CG 1909.

Angerer, Paul (*b* Vienna, 1927). Austrian conductor and composer. Began career as orchestral violist in Vienna SO, Tonhalle Orch., Zurich, and Suisse Romande; first va., Vienna SO 1953–7. Chief cond. Vienna Chamber Orch. 1956–63; Kapellmeister, Bonn State Theatre 1964–6; mus. dir. Ulm Th. 1966–8; Salzburg Fest. début 1961, chief cond. Salzburg Landestheater 1967–72. Harpsichordist and recorder-player in various baroque ens. Dir., SW Ger. CO, Pforzheim, 1972–82. Prof., Vienna Hochschule für Musik from 1983. Comps. incl. va. conc., fl. conc., chamber works, and setting of Whitman's *Song of Myself*.

anglais, anglaise (Fr.). English. Term of variable meaning sometimes used by 18th-cent. composers as the title of a hornpipe or country dance; or of anything else thought to be Eng. in character.

Anglican chant. Simple type of harmonized melody used in the Anglican Church (and nowadays often in other Eng.-speaking Protestant churches) for singing unmetrical texts, principally the Psalms and the canticles (when these latter are not sung in a more elaborate setting). The main principle is that of the trad. *Gregorian tones, i.e. a short melody is repeated to each verse of the text (or sometimes to 2 or more verses; see below), the varying numbers of syllables in the different lines of the words being accommodated by the flexible device of a *reciting note* at the opening of each line—this being treated as timeless and so capable of serving as the vehicle for many or few syllables, while succeeding notes are sung in time and (normally) take one syllable each. The 1st part of the chant has 3 measures and the 2nd part 4.

Anhalt, István (*b* Budapest, 1919). Hung.-born Canadian composer and teacher. Went to Canada 1949 to join faculty of McGill Univ. Founder-dir. EMS 1964–71. Head of mus. dept., Queen's Univ., Kingston, Ontario, 1971–81 (prof. emeritus 1984). Comps. use synthetic sounds and incl. ballet *Arc en Ciel* for 2 pf.

Anhang (Ger.). A supplement, i.e. a coda in the mus. sense, or in musicological terminology a section appended to a critical edn. of a work and containing variant readings, material of doubtful attribution, etc.

Aniara. Opera in 2 acts by Blomdahl. Lib. by E. Lindegren based on H. Martinson's fantasy poem about space travel (1956). Prod. Stockholm and Edinburgh Fest. 1959.

Anievas, Agustin (*b* NY, 1934). Amer. pianist of Sp.-Mexican descent. Début NY 1952. Winner of Queen Elisabeth of the Belgians and Mitropoulos Int. prizes (1961). Prof. of pf., Brooklyn Coll. of City Univ. of NY, 1974.

anima (It.). Soul, i.e. the sound-post of a vn., etc. (See also *âme, sound-post.*) *con anima*, with feeling.

animando (It.). Animating. *animandosi*, becoming animated, *animato* (It.)., *animé* (Fr.), animated.

animo, animoso (It.). Spirit, spirited; *animosamente*, (1) spiritedly, (2) malevolently.

Animuccia, Giovanni (*b* Florence, *c*.1500; *d* Rome, 1571). It. composer. Predecessor of Palestrina as maestro of the Vatican and regarded as extraordinarily fertile innovator. Comp. *Laudi*, some of which were pubd. in 1563 and 1570.

Anna Bolena. Opera in 2 acts by Donizetti to lib. by Romani. Inaccurate but moving dramatization of life of Henry VIII's 2nd wife Anne Boleyn. Prod. Milan 1830; London 1831; New Orleans 1839. Revived for Maria *Callas at La Scala 1957, and at Glyndebourne 1965.

Anna Magdalena Books (J. S. Bach). 2nd and 3rd of the 3 colls. of kbd. pieces by J. S. Bach, C. Petzold, and anon. comp., known as *Klavierbüchlein*. They were for the instruction of Bach's 2nd wife Anna Magdalena and were pubd. 1722 and 1725.

Années de pèlerinage (Years of Pilgrimage). 23 pf. pieces by Liszt issued in 3 books as follows: Book 1 (1st Année, Switzerland, incl. *Vallée d'Obermann*); comp. 1848–54, pubd. 1855 (some items based on *Album d'un Voyageur*, 1835–6). Book 2 (2nd Année, Italy); comp. 1837–49, pubd. 1858. Book 3 (3rd Année); comp. 1867–77, pubd. 1883.

Annie Laurie. The poem is by William Douglas of Fingland (*c*.1780), but has been much altered by

various people, especially Lady John Douglas Scott (1810–1900), who said she also wrote the air. First pubd. 1838.

Annunzio, Gabriele d' (*b* Pescara, 1863; *d* Vittoriale, 1938). It. poet and dramatist who was keen student of music. Worked in Rome as mus. critic; in 1917 ed. *National Collection of Italian Music* with help of Pizzetti and Malipiero, among others. Debussy comp. incid. mus. for his play *Le Martyre de Saint-Sébastien* (1911) and Zandonai's *Francesca da Rimini* is based on another of his plays.

Anon in Love. Sequence of 6 love poems, anonymous 16th- and 17th-cent. lyrics, set for ten. and guitar in 1959 by Walton. F.p. Aldeburgh 1960 (Peter Pears and Julian Bream). Version for ten. and small orch. 1971.

anreissen (Ger.). To tear at. Use a very forceful *pizzicato*.

Anschlag (Ger.). (1) Sometimes called a 'double appoggiatura' but consisting of the notes immediately below and above the prin. note.
(2) Touch (pertaining to a kbd. instr.).
(3) 'Attack', etc.

Ansermet, Ernest (*b* Vevey, Switzerland, 1883; *d* Geneva, 1969). Swiss conductor. Taught mathematics at a Lausanne school, not (as is often stated) at the Univ. Became cond. at Kursaal, Montreux, 1911. Cond. for Diaghilev's Russian Ballet 1915–23, touring widely. Cond. Buenos Aires SO, 1924–7. In 1918 founded L'Orchestre de la Suisse Romande, of which he remained cond. until 1967. Noted as interpreter of Stravinsky (cond. several f.ps.), Ravel, and Debussy. Salzburg Fest. début 1942 (Vienna PO). Cond. f.p. of *The Rape of Lucretia*, Glyndebourne 1946. Début NY Met 1962.

anstimmen (Ger.). To tune.

Anstrich (Ger.). Bow 'stroke'. (See also *Strich*).

answer in fugue. The 2nd entry of the main theme (subject) of a *fugue a 5th higher (or 4th lower) than the 1st is called the answer. If subject and answer are identical it is a real answer; if the intervals are changed in the answer it is a tonal answer.

Antar. (1) Orch. work by Rimsky-Korsakov, Op.9, first described as his Sym. No.2 when it appeared in 1868. Rev. and re-orch. 1876 and 1897 and again in 1903 when it was designated 'oriental suite'. Based on an oriental tale by Sennkovsky.
(2) Opera by Gabriel *Dupont (1912–13).

Antarctic Symphony (Vaughan Williams). See *Sinfonia Antartica*. See also *Maxwell Davies, (Sir) Peter*.

antecedent. In a *canon the v. which first enters with the tune to be imitated is called the dux or antecedent.

Antechrist. Work for chamber ens. (incl. cowbell) by *Maxwell Davies. Comp. and f.p. 1967 (London, Pierrot Players, cond. composer).

Antheil, George (*b* Trenton, NJ, 1900; *d* NY, 1959). Amer. composer of Polish descent. Caused furore in Europe in 1920s at his pf. recitals with his comps. called *Airplane Sonata* and *Mechanisms*. His *Ballet méchanique*, comp. 1923–4 and f.p. Paris 1926, was designed as film mus. but was rev. for the concert hall (scored for 8 pf., pianola, 8 xyls., 2 doorbells, and sound of aeroplane propeller). For NY première in 1927 he doubled the pfs., added car-horns and anvils, and used a real propeller. A final rev. (1953) reduced the pfs. to 4 but incl. tape of a jet engine. Returned to USA 1933 and wrote Hollywood film scores from 1936. Became more conservative. Works incl. 6 syms., ballets, 3-act opera *Volpone* (1950–2), and 2 earlier 3-act operas, pf. conc., vn. conc., str. qts., and vn. sonatas. Also wrote detective stories, a study of the glandular abnormalities of criminals, and a daily column of advice to the lovelorn. Autobiography *Bad Boy of Music* (NY, 1945).

anthem. The English-speaking Protestant Churches' equivalent of the Latin motet, from which it sprang. An Anglican creation, with a place in the C of E liturgy. It constitutes in ordinary churches the one great occasion when the choir alone undertakes the duty of song, and when an elaborate vocal setting impossible and unsuitable in other parts of the service becomes proper and effective. It is usually but not necessarily acc. by organ, and frequently incl. passages for solo vv., individually or in combination. The anthems of Purcell and Blow are like cantatas. S. S. *Wesley was prolific composer of anthems nearer to the style favoured today. The term is also less strictly used, as in the phrase 'National Anthem', to denote a solemn, hymn-like song.

anticipation. The sounding of a note of a chord before the rest of the chord.

Antill, John (*b* Sydney, NSW, 1904; *d* Sydney, 1986). Australian composer and administrator on staff of Australian Broadcasting Commission 1934–71. Comp. operas and orch. works, and ballet *Corroboree* (1946) (based on aboriginal dances). CMG 1981.

antiphon (from Gr., 'sounding across'). (1) A versicle or phrase sung by one choir in reply to another.

(2) In the RC Church the antiphon is intoned or sung during the recitation of Divine Office, before and after the psalm or canticle, which is itself responsively sung by the singers divided into two bodies. The antiphon may serve to reinforce the meaning of the psalm, or to introduce a Christian application of the orig. Jewish text. The plainsong tune of the antiphon, though not the same as the 'tone' of the psalm, is in keeping with it as to mode, etc.

(3) Many antiphons now exist without psalms and are sometimes sung to comp. settings, rather than to the orig. plainsong, hence the Eng. word *'anthem', derived from 'antiphona'. Several composers have given the title *Antiphon* to a comp., e.g. Vaughan Williams in *5 Mystical Songs*.

Antiphonal, Antiphonary, Antiphoner. Properly, the RC Church's coll. of trad. plainsong *antiphons, but the word has come to be more comprehensively used as meaning the book containing all plainsong for the Divine Office, as distinct from the *Gradual, which contains the plainsong for the Mass.

antiphonal singing. When 2 parts of a choir (*decani* and *cantoris*) sing alternately, one answering the other. (Alternation between officiant and choir is 'responsorial'.) The term 'antiphonal' is generally used of the mus. effects drawn from groups of singers or instrumentalists stationed apart.

Antiphons of the Blessed Virgin Mary. There are 4, each with its season: (*a*) during Advent and until the Purification of the Virgin Mary, *Alma redemptoris mater*; (*b*) from then until Wednesday in Holy Week, *Ave regina coelorum*; (*c*) from then until Whitsun, *Regina coeli laetare*; (*d*) from the Octave of Whitsun until Advent, *Salve regina, mater misericordiae*.

Antony and Cleopatra. Opera in 3 acts by *Barber to lib. by comp. and F. Zeffirelli based on Shakespeare's play (1606–7). Comp. 1966, rev. 1974. Prod. NY Met 1966 (opening night of new theatre in Lincoln Center, 16 Sept.).

anvil. Perc. instr., imitating real anvil, used in many works, usually operas. In *Das Rheingold* Wagner uses 18 in 3 sizes to depict the activity in Nibelheim. In *Siegfried* Act I, Siegfried splits an anvil with the sword Nothung. Real anvils are used in *Il trovatore* (Verdi), *Benvenuto Cellini* (Berlioz), Mahler's 6th sym., Bax's 3rd sym., Walton's *Belshazzar's Feast*, and Britten's *The Burning Fiery Furnace*.

anwachsend (Ger.). Growing. Swelling out in tone.

Apel, Willi (*b* Konitz, 1893; *d* Bloomington, Ind., 1988). Amer. (Ger.-born) musicologist. Taught at various Ger. univs. and in 1936 settled in USA, joining staff of Harvard Univ. 1938–42 and becoming prof. of musicology, Indiana Univ., 1950–70. Pubd. many works, incl. *Harvard Dictionary of Music* (1944, rev. 1969). Wrote books on fugue, medieval harmony, and Gregorian chant.

aperto (It.). Open. (1) Clear, distinct.
(2) Broad in style.

Apivor, Denis (*b* Collinstown, Eire, 1916; *d* Robertsbridge, E. Sussex, 2004). Irish-born composer of Welsh parentage. Works incl. 2 syms.; operas *She Stoops to Conquer* (1943–7), *Yerma* (1959), *Ubu Roi* (1966); ballets *A Mirror for Witches* (1952), *Blood Wedding* (1953), and *Saudades* (1955); cantata *The Hollow Men* (T. S. Eliot, 1939–46) for bar., male ch., and orch.; concs. for cl., pf., and vn.; cl. concertante (1981); cl. quintet (1981); wind quintet (1981). Was qualified doctor of medicine.

Apollo Musagetes (Apollo, Leader of the Muses; Fr. *Apollon Musagète*). Ballet in 2 scenes by

Stravinsky, scored for str. (1927–8). (Prod. Washington, Paris, London, 1928.) Choreog. Adolph Bolm for Washington, Balanchine for Paris (Diaghilev).

Apostles, The. Oratorio by Elgar, Op.49, text compiled by Elgar from the Bible and other sources. Comp. 1901–3. For 6 soloists, ch., and orch. (F.p. Birmingham 1903, NY, London, and Cologne 1904.) See *Kingdom, The*.

Appalachia. 'Variations on an Old Slave Song' by Delius, for orch. with bar. solo and ch. First version, for orch. only, *American Rhapsody*, comp. 1896, re-worked and lengthened 1902–3. (F.p. Elberfeld 1904, London 1907.)

Appalachian Spring. Ballet by Copland, comp. 1943–4, choreog. Martha Graham, 1944. Scored for fl., cl., bn., 4 vn., 2 va., 2 vc., db., pf. Prod. Washington DC 1944. Fuller orch. version of suite and of ballet 1945.

Appassionata Sonata. Publisher's apt title for Beethoven's Pf. Sonata No.23 in F minor, Op.57, comp. 1804–5.

appassionato, appassionata (It.). Impassioned; so *appassionatamente*, passionately; *appassionamento*, passion.

Appenzeller, Benedictus (*b* Oudenaarde, *c*.1480–8; *d* after 1558). Flemish composer. Wrote a 4-part *Nenia in memory of Josquin Desprès. Choirmaster to Netherlands regent (Mary of Hungary) 1537–after 1551. Composed nearly 50 *chansons*.

Appia, Adolphe (François) (*b* Geneva, 1862; *d* Nyon, 1928). Swiss scenic artist. Pioneered modern operatic trend for imaginative lighting and minimum of scenery. Designed *Tristan und Isolde* for La Scala (Toscanini, 1923), and *Das Rheingold* and *Die Walküre* for Basle (1924–5). Never employed at Bayreuth but his ideas were an influence on Wieland and Wolfgang Wagner.

applied music. Amer. term for a study course in perf. as opposed to theory.

appoggiando; appoggiato (It.). Leaning; leaned. (1) Each note passing very smoothly to the next (i.e. *portamento*).
(2) Stressed.

appoggiatura (It.). Leaning note. A grace note or species of ornament of which the exact interpretation has differed in various periods. In the 18th cent. the appoggiatura was often unwritten and left, e.g. in Handel and Mozart, to be inserted by the singer. Operatic appoggiatura was regarded as obsolete until its revival in certain operatic productions *c*.1960. Its harmonic application may be described as follows: Properly an unprepared suspension (if such a contradictory term may be allowed) whether it be shown in full-sized type as a part of the chord in which it momentarily appears, or as a small note printed just before that chord. Having a harmonic status it is not an 'ornament' in the same sense as, for instance, the *acciaccatura.

(a) With ordinary and dotted notes.

The appoggiatura is as important melodically as the note on which it 'leans', from which it takes normally half the time-value (two-thirds the time-value if the supporting note is dotted).

(b) With tied notes.

When the appoggiatura 'leans upon' two tied notes, it normally takes the whole of the time-value of the first of these to itself.

(c) With a chord.

As the appoggiatura leans only upon one note of the chord the other notes are unaffected.

Apprenti Sorcier, L' (The Sorcerer's Apprentice). Symphonic poem ('Scherzo') by Dukas, f.p. Paris 1897, London and NY 1899. 'The Apprentice Sorcerer' would be a more accurate trans. Based on a poem by Goethe which, in turn, is based on a dialogue in Lucian (2nd cent. AD). The apprentice, in his master's absence, tries one of his spells and, to his consternation, cannot countermand it. In Disney film *Fantasia*, the apprentice was represented by Mickey Mouse.

Aprahamian, Felix (*b* London, 1914; *d* London, 2005). Eng. music critic and organist of Armenian descent. On staff of *Sunday Times* 1948–89. Authority on org. mus., Fr. mus., and works of Delius (mus. adviser, Delius Trust from 1961).

Après-midi d'un faune, Prélude à L' (Prelude to 'The afternoon of a faun'). Tone-poem by Debussy, comp. 1892–4 and f.p. Paris 23 Dec. 1894 (London 1904), being an orch. 'impression' of the poem by Mallarmé. He intended a set of 3 pieces, *Prélude, Interlude*, and *Paraphrase finale*, but only the first was written. It was the subject of a ballet by Nijinsky, Paris 1912, for Diaghilev.

a punta d'arco (It.). At the point of the bow (in str. playing).

aquarelle (Fr.). Water-colour; sometimes musically applied to a piece of delicate texture, as in

Eric *Fenby's arr. for str. (1938), as *Aquarelles*, of Delius's 2 wordless chs. 'To be sung of a summer night on the water' (1917).

Arabella. Opera in 3 acts by R. Strauss to lib. by Hofmannsthal based on a combination of his short story *Lucidor* (1909) and his play *Der Fiaker als Graf* (The Cabby as Count) (1925). Their last collaboration. Comp. 1930–2. Prod. Dresden 1933, CG 1934, NY Met 1955. Rev. 1939 (Munich).

arabesque (Fr., Eng.), **Arabeske** (Ger.). A florid element in Arabian architecture, hence a florid melodic section. The term is sometimes applied to a piece of instr. mus. (not always in an appropriate manner) as by Schumann for his pf. piece, Op.18, or by Debussy to his 2 *Arabesques* for pf.

arada (Sp.). Ploughed land. A type of folk-song assoc. with ploughing.

Aragall (y Garriga), Giacomo [Jaime] (b Barcelona, 1939). Sp. tenor. Début Venice 1963, La Scala 1963. CG début 1966, NY Met 1968.

aragonesa (Sp.), **aragonaise** (Fr.). Sp. dance deriving from Aragon.

Araiza, Francisco (b Mexico City, 1950). Mexican tenor. Début Mexico City 1969 (concert), opera début 1970 (1st Prisoner in *Fidelio*). Eur. début Karlsruhe 1974; Bayreuth début 1978; NY Met 1984; Salzburg Fest. 1981; CG 1983.

ARAM, ARCM, ARCO, ARMCM. Assoc. of, respectively, *Royal Academy of Music, *Royal College of Music, *Royal College of Organists, *Royal Manchester College of Music.

Arányi, Jelly (Eva) **d'** (b Budapest, 1893; d Florence, 1966). Hung.-born violinist, great-niece of *Joachim. Début Vienna 1908 in duo with her sister, Adila *Fachiri. Settled in London and became Brit. subject. Gave f. London ps. with Bartók of his 2-vn. sonatas (1922 and 1923) both of which were ded. to her, as were Vaughan Williams's vn. conc. (1925) and Ravel's *Tzigane* (1924), in both of which she was also first soloist. Gave f. Brit. p. of Szymanowski 1st vn. conc. (1930) and of Schumann vn. conc. (1938). CBE 1946.

Arban, (Joseph) **Jean-Baptiste** (Laurent) (b Lyons, 1825; d Paris, 1889). Fr. cornet-player and conductor. Prof. of saxhorn, École Militaire from 1857. Established cornet class at Paris Cons. 1869–74, returning 1880–9. Founded modern sch. of trumpet-playing and wrote standard treatise in 1864. His *Theme and Variations on the Carnival of Venice* remains a cornet-player's showpiece.

Arbeau, Thoinot [Tabourot, Jehan] (b Dijon, 1520; d Langres, 1595). Fr. priest. Author of famous book on the dance, *Orchésographie* (1588–9), which also contained mus. illustrations. See *Capriol Suite*.

Arbós, Enrique (Fernández) (b Madrid, 1863; d San Sebastián, 1939). Sp. conductor, composer, and violinist. Leader of Berlin PO and Boston SO.

Cond., Madrid SO 1904–36. Settled in Eng. and on staff of RCM 1894–1916. Comp. opera and chamber mus. but best known for his orch. of several pieces from *Albéniz's *Iberia*: those he left unfinished were completed in 1954 by *Surinach.

Arcadelt [Arkadelt, Arcadet, Arcadente, etc.], **Jacob** (b c.1505; d Paris, 1568). Flemish composer. Probably singer at Medici court in Florence after 1532. In Venice after 1537. Singing-master to boys of St Peter's, Rome, 1540–51, then in Paris until 1562 at court of Charles of Lorraine. Wrote church mus. but is chiefly remembered for secular madrigals (over 200), *chansons* (126), and motets, of which 5 books were pubd. before 1544.

arcata (It.). Stroke of bow (in str. playing), often followed by the words *in giù* (down), or *in su* (up).

arcato (It.). Bowed (after a passage of *pizzicato).

ARCCO. Assoc. of the Royal Canadian College of Organists.

Archbishop of Canterbury's Degrees. By a custom begun in 13th cent. the Archbishop of Canterbury may confer degrees, among them a doctorate of mus., known as 'Canterbury' or 'Lambeth' degrees (Lambeth being site of the Archbishop's London palace). In 1936 he instituted a diploma in church mus. granted on examination to FRCOs who hold a choirmaster's diploma. Those who pass become *ADCMs.

Archduke Trio. Beethoven's pf. trio in B♭, Op.97 (1811). So nicknamed from ded. to Archduke Rudolph of Austria, who was pf. and comp. pupil of Beethoven.

arched viall. Instr. similar to a *Geigenwerk, a kind of hurdy-gurdy, mentioned by Pepys in 1664 ('It will never do', he said).

archet (Fr.). Bow (of a str. instr.).

archi (It.). Bows (of str. instr.); the singular is *arco.

archlute. Large double-necked lute with 2 pegboxes, one of which contains unstopped bass strings. Had 14 single or double courses. In use as continuo instr. from end of 16th cent. to 1730. In Eng. at end of 17th cent. was used as alternative to *theorbo.

arco (plural *archi) (It.). Bow. Used alone or as *coll' arco* (with the bow) after a passage marked *pizzicato* (plucked).

Arden muss Sterben (Arden must die). Opera in 3 acts by A. Goehr to Ger. lib. by Erich Fried based on anonymous play *Arden of Feversham* (1592). Comp. 1966. Prod. Hamburg 1967, London 1974 (in Eng. trans. by G. Skelton).

Arditi, Luigi (b Crescentino, 1822; d Hove, 1903). It. composer and conductor. Toured widely as cond. of opera cos., e.g. Mapleson's. Settled in Eng. in 1858, conducting regularly at

CG. Cond. f.p. in London of *Cavalleria rusticana*. Remembered as composer for his waltz-song *Il bacio* (The Kiss).

Arditti Quartet. Brit. string quartet founded 1974 and specializing in contemp. mus. Orig. members were Irvine Arditti, Lennox Mackenzie (succeeded by Alexander Balanescu and then David Alberman 1987) (vns.), Levine Andrade (va.), and John Senter (vc.) (succeeded by Rohan de Saram 1985).

Arensky, Anton (Stepanovich) (*b* Novgorod, 1861; *d* Terijoki, Finland, 1906). Russ. composer. Prof. of harmony and counterpoint, Moscow Cons. 1882. Comp. 3 operas, 2 str. qts., and 2 syms., but best-known works are the pf. conc., vn. conc. in A minor, pf. trio in D minor (in memory of the cellist Davidov), *Variations on a Theme of Tchaikovsky* for str., and many pf. pieces.

Aretino, Guido. See *Guido d'Arezzo*.

Arezzo, Guido d'. See *Guido d'Arezzo*.

Argento, Dominick (*b* York, Penn., 1927). Amer. composer. Mus. dir., Hilltop Opera, Baltimore, 1958. Member of Dept. of Mus., Minnesota Univ., from 1958 (Regents Prof. from 1980). Co-founder, 1963, of Center Opera Co. (now Minnesota Opera). Pulitzer Prize 1975 for *From the Diary of Virginia Woolf*, commissioned by Janet Baker. Primarily interested in opera. Works incl.:

OPERAS: *The Boor* (1957); *Colonel Jonathan the Saint* (1958–60); *Christopher Sly* (1962); *The Masque of Angels* (1963); *The Shoemaker's Holiday* (1967); *Postcard from Morocco* (1971); *The Voyage of Edgar Allan Poe* (1975–6); *Miss Havisham's Fire* (1978–9, rev. 2000); *Casanova's Homecoming* (1980–4); *The Aspern Papers* (1986–8); *The Dream of Valentino* (1993).

MONODRAMAS: *A Waterbird Talk* (1974); *Miss Havisham's Wedding Night* (1980).

BALLET: *The Resurrection of Don Juan* (1955).

ORCH.: *Divertimento*, pf., str. (1955); *Ode to the West Wind*, conc. for sop., orch. (1956); *Suite, Resurrection of Don Juan* (1956); *Songs About Spring*, 5 songs for high v., orch. (1960); *From the Album of Allegra Harper, 1867* (suite from opera *Colonel Jonathan*) (1961); *Royal Invitation, or Homage to the Queen of Tonga* (1964); *Suite, Royal Invitation* (1964); *Variations (The Mask of Night)* (1965); *Bravo Mozart!*, vn., ob., hn., chamber orch. (1969); *A Ring of Time* (1972); *In Praise of Music* (1977); *Fire Variations* (1981–2); *Casa Guidi*, 5 songs for mez., orch. (1983); *Le Tombeau d'Edgar Poe* (1985); *Capriccio: Rossini in Paris*, cl., orch. (1985); *Reverie (Reflections on a Hymn Tune)*, orch. (1997–8).

CHAMBER MUSIC: str. qt. (1956).

CHORAL: *Gloria*, mixed ch., pf. (1963); *Revelation of St John the Divine*, ten., male ch., brass, perc. (1966); *A Nation of Cowslips*, 7 Keats songs for unacc. ch. (1968); *Tria Carmina Paschalia*, women's vv., harp, guitar (1970); *Jonah and the Whale*, oratorio, ten., bass, narrator, ch., chamber ens. (1973); *Peter Quince at the Clavier*, ch., pf. (1981); *Te Deum*, ch., orch. (1987); *Easter Day*, unacc. mixed ch. (1989); *Four Seascapes*, ch., orch. (2004).

SONG-CYCLES: *Songs About Spring*, sop., pf. (1950 and 1955, with orch. 1960); *6 Elizabethan Songs*, ten. (or sop.), pf. (1957), high v., baroque ens. (1960); *Letters from Composers*, 7 songs, high v., gui. (1968); *To be Sung Upon the Water*, high v., pf., cl., bcl. (1973); **From the Diary of Virginia Woolf*, medium v., pf. (1974); *I Hate and I Love*, ch., perc. (1981); *The Andree Expedition*, bar., pf. (1982); *A Few Words about Chekhov*, sop., bar., pf. (1994); *Miss Manners on Music*, mez., pf. (1998).

Argerich, Martha (*b* Buenos Aires, 1941). Argentinian pianist. Soloist with orch. in Buenos Aires at age of 8. First prize, Busoni Contest and Geneva international mus. comp., 1957. First prize international Chopin comp., Warsaw, 1965. Soloist with world's leading orchs. London début 1964. Salzburg Fest. début 1971. Remarkable vitality and power in her performances.

aria (It.). Air. From the time of A. Scarlatti in the 18th cent. onwards this has had the definite implication of a more or less lengthy and well-developed solo vocal piece in ABA form normally called a *da capo* aria. The singer was expected to add ornaments in the repeated A section. The 19th-cent. operatic aria became more elaborate and complex. Arias used to be rather minutely classified as (a) *aria cantabile*, slow and smooth; (b) *aria di portamento*, in long notes and dignified, to be sung in *legato style; (c) *aria di mezzo carattere*, more passionate and with often elaborate orch. acc.; (d) *aria parlante*, declamatory; (e) *aria di bravura* (or *d'agilità*, or *d'abilità*), requiring great v.-control; (f) *aria all'unisono*, with acc. in unison or octaves with the vocal part; (g) *aria d'imitazione*, imitative of bird-song, hunting hns., etc.; (h) *aria concertata* with elaborate acc.; and so on.

Ariadne. (1) Setting of poem by C. Day Lewis for sop. and orch. (1970) by **Maconchy (f.p. King's Lynn Fest. 1971.

(2) *Concertante* for ob. and 12 instrumentalists by **Crosse (f.p. Cheltenham Fest. 1972.

Ariadne auf Naxos (Ariadne on Naxos). Opera in prol. and 1 act by R. Strauss to lib. by Hofmannsthal. There are 2 versions. No.1 was designed for perf. after Molière's play *Le* **bourgeois Gentilhomme* (with incidental mus. by Strauss). Comp. 1911–12. F.p. Stuttgart 1912, London 1913. Perfs. at Salzburg Landesth. 1991–2 were the first in which the score was perf. without cuts. 2nd version substituted an operatic prol. for the play, comp. 1916, f.p. Vienna 1916, London 1924, Philadelphia 1928, NY 1934, Met 1962. Many other composers have based operas on the Ariadne legend. Naxos is the island on which Ariadne, awaiting death, is consoled by Bacchus.

Ariane et Barbe-bleue (Ariadne and Bluebeard). Fantasy-opera in 3 acts by Dukas to lib. by Maeterlinck based on his play. Comp. 1899–1906. Prod. Paris 1907; NY Met 1911; London 1937.

Arianna (Ariadne). Opera in prol. and 8 scenes by *Monteverdi to lib. by Rinuccini. Prod. Mantua 1608. Score now lost, only surviving part being *Lamento d'Arianna*.

Arianna a Naxos (Ariadne on Naxos). Dramatic cantata by Haydn, for sop./mez. and hpd. or pf. (Hob. XXVIb:2), comp. 1790.

arietta (It.). A shorter and simpler *aria. Usually lacks a middle section. Term sometimes applied to a piece of instr. mus.

Ariettes oubliées (Forgotten ariettas). Debussy's settings of 6 poems by Verlaine (1888). The songs' titles are: *C'est l'Extase langoureuse*; *Il Pleure dans mon coeur*; *L'Ombre des arbres*; *Chevaux de bois*; *Green*; *Spleen*.

Ariodante. Opera in 3 acts by Handel to It. lib. anonymously adapted from *Ginevra, Principessa di Scozia* by Antonio Salvi (Pratolino, 1705) based on Ariosto's *Orlando furioso* (1516), canti V and VI. F.p. London (CG) 1735, NY 1971.

arioso. (1) A recitative of the more melodious type.
(2) A short melodious passage at the beginning or end of an aria.
(3) A short air in an opera or oratorio.
(4) In instr. mus., a *cantabile passage.

Ariosti, Attilio (b Bologna, 1666; d ?England, 1729). It. composer, formerly monk who obtained dispensation to devote himself to music. Comp. oratorio *La Passione* (1693) which contained mad scene. Wrote first operas 1696–7 in Mantua, then worked in Berlin and Vienna. Returned to It. as agent of Austrian Emperor Joseph I. Colleague in London from 1716 of Bononcini and Handel as dir. of opera enterprise (Royal Academy of Music, 1719–27), and composer of 20 operas etc.

Arkadelt, Jacob. See *Arcadelt, Jacob*.

Arkhipova, Irina (Konstantinova) (b Moscow, 1925). Russian mezzo-soprano. Member of Bolshoy Opera, Moscow, from 1956 and sang in Moscow premières of Prokofiev's *War and Peace* and *The Story of a Real Man*. La Scala début 1965; S. Francisco 1972; CG début 1975.

arlecchinesco (It.). In the spirit of a harlequinade.

Arlecchino (Harlequin). Opera in 1 act by Busoni, Op.50, to his own lib. A 'theatrical capriccio', comp. 1914–16, prod. Zurich 1917, London (radio and TV) 1939, NY (Carnegie Hall) 1951 (concert), Glyndebourne (stage) 1954.

Arlésienne, L' (The Maid of Arles). Daudet's play, for which Bizet composed 27 items of incidental mus., Paris 1872 (later incorporating some of it into the ballet of *Carmen*). There are 2 orch. suites, the first arr. Bizet, the 2nd *Guiraud.

Armide. Opera in 5 acts by Gluck. Lib. by Quinault, based on Tasso's *Jerusalem Delivered* (1575). Prod. Paris 1777; Manchester, in concert version, 1860; CG 1906; NY Met 1910. Among 40 operas based on Tasso's story are those by Lully, Handel, Jommelli, Salieri, Haydn, Rossini, and Dvořák.

armonia, armonica (It.). (1) 'Harmony'.
(2) 'Wind band'.
(3) One of several names for the *hurdy-gurdy (also *armonie*).

Armstrong, Karan (b Horne, Montana, 1941). Amer. soprano. Début S. Francisco Opera 1966. NY Met 1969. NY City Opera 1975–8. Eur. début Strasbourg 1976, Bayreuth 1979, CG 1981. Sang in f.ps. of several contemp. operas, incl. Berio's *Un re in ascolto* (Salzburg 1984, her début). Roles incl. Tosca, Butterfly, Alice Ford, Mélisande, Minnie, and Adina.

Armstrong, Louis ('Satchmo') (b New Orleans, 1901; d NY, 1971). Amer. jazz trumpeter and singer. From 1917 played on Miss. river boats. Joined King Oliver's Creole Jazz Band 1922. Played often with Fletcher Henderson's orch. 1924–5, then formed own band. Became world-famous as result of recordings in 1920s in which his virtuoso trumpet-playing and his idiosyncratic singing had enormous influence on jazz scene. Nickname 'Satchmo' a diminutive of 'Satchelmouth'. Visited Eng. and Eur. 1932 and 1934. Made many films and appeared with big bands in 'swing' era. Formed his All Stars 1947. Appeared with Bing Crosby and Frank Sinatra in film *High Society* (1956).

Armstrong, (Sir) **Richard** (b Leicester, 1943). Eng. conductor. Mus. staff CG 1966–8. Ass. cond. WNO 1968–73, mus. dir. 1973–86. Mus. dir. Scottish Opera 1993–2005. Janáček Medal 1979. CG début 1982 (*Billy Budd*). Cond. WNO in *Der Ring* at CG, 1986. ENO début 1991, NY Met 2007. CBE 1992. Knighted 2004.

Armstrong, Sheila (Ann) (b Ashington, 1942). Eng. soprano. Opera début SW 1965. Glyndebourne 1966; NY 1971; CG 1973. Sang in f.p. of McCabe's *Notturni ed Alba*, 1970. Notable exponent of Elgar oratorios, Vaughan Williams's *Sea Symphony*, etc. Retired 1993.

Armstrong, (Sir) **Thomas** (Henry Wait) (b Peterborough, 1898; d Milton Keynes, 1994). Eng. organist and teacher. Org., Exeter Cath. 1928–33, Christ Church Cath., Oxford, 1933–55. Choragus and lect. in mus., Oxford Univ., 1937–54. Prin., RAM, 1955–68. Comp. choral works, church mus., chamber mus., etc. Knighted 1957.

Arne, Michael (b London, c.1740; d London, 1786). Eng. composer, illegitimate son of Thomas *Arne. Lived for a time in Hamburg. Comp. stage mus., etc.; his song *The Lass with a delicate air* is still heard.

Arne, Thomas (Augustine) (b London, 1710; d London, 1778). The leading Brit. composer of his day, notable for incidental music to plays, incl. Shakespeare's. His masque *Alfred* (1740) incl. song 'Rule, Britannia!' Operas incl. *Artaxerxes

(1761), *Love in a Village* (1762), *The Guardian Outwitted* (1764), *The Fairy Prince* (1771), and *The Cooper* (1772). Wrote 2 oratorios, *The Death of Abel* (1743) and **Judith* (1764); 6 cantatas (1755); several kbd. concs. (1750–70); syms.; sonatas for 2 vns. and continuo (1757); 8 kbd. sonatas (1756); and many songs incl. *The British Grenadiers*.

Arnell, Richard (Anthony Sayer) (*b* London, 1917). Eng. composer. Lived in USA 1939–47. Comps. incl. 7 syms., ballet *Punch and the Child* (1947), symphonic portrait *Lord Byron*, pf. conc., vn. conc., str. qts., and 3 operas. On staff TCL 1948–64.

Arnim, Achim [Joachim] (Ludwig) **von** (*b* Berlin, 1781; *d* Wiepersdorf, 1831). Ger. poet who can claim inclusion in a music dictionary because of his co-editorship with his future brother-in-law Clemens Brentano of the anthology of German folk poetry *Des Knaben Wunderhorn* (Youth's Magic Horn), 1805–8, extracts from which have been set by several composers, notably Mahler. In 1811 he married Elisabeth (Bettina) **Brentano, a friend of Beethoven.

Arnold, Denis (Midgley) (*b* Sheffield, 1926; *d* Budapest, 1986). Eng. critic and teacher. Senior lect., Hull Univ., 1964–9; Prof. of Mus., Nottingham Univ. 1969–75 and Oxford Univ. from 1975. Author of books on Monteverdi and G. Gabrieli. Specialist on 16th- and 17th-cent. It. mus. Joint ed. *Music and Letters* 1976–80. Ed., *New Oxford Companion to Music*, 1983. CBE 1983.

Arnold, (Sir) **Malcolm** (Henry) (*b* Northampton, 1921; *d* Norwich, 2006). Eng. composer, trumpeter, and conductor. Trumpeter in LPO 1941–2, BBCSO 1945, LPO (prin.) 1946–8. Works, in many genres, notable for melodic invention, colour, exuberance, and craftsmanship. One of post-1950 Eng. composers who kept in touch with his audience without debasing his style or lowering his standards. Several film scores, incl. *The Bridge on the River Kwai*, 1957. CBE 1970. Knighted 1992. Prin. works:

BALLETS: **Homage to the Queen*, Op.42 (1953); *Rinaldo and Armida*, Op.49 (1955); *Electra*, Op.79 (1963).

ORCH.: syms: No.1, Op.22 (1951), No.2, Op.40 (1953), No.3, Op.63 (1954), No.4, Op.71 (1960), No.5, Op.74 (1961), No.6, Op.95 (1967), No.7, Op.113 (1973), No.8, Op.124 (1979), No.9 (1987); **Toy Symphony*, Op.62 (1957); Sym. for Brass, Op.123 (1979); concs.: cl., No.1, Op.20 (1951), No.2, Op.115 (1974); fl., No.1, with str., Op.45 (1954), No.2, Op.111 (1972); gui., Op.67 (1961); harmonica, Op.46 (1954); hn., No.1, with str., Op.11 (1947), No.2, with str., Op.58 (1956); ob., str., Op.39 (1952); org., Op.47 (1954); pf. duet, str., Op.32 (1950); 2 pf. (3 hands), Op.104 (1969); va., Op.108 (1971), 2 vn., str., Op.77 (1962); recorder (1988); vc. (1989); *Fantasy on Theme of John Field*, pf., Op.116 (1975); *Serenade*, gui., str., Op.50 (1957); *Serenade*, Op.26 (1950); *Symphony for Str.*, Op.13 (1947); *Sinfonietta* No.1, Op.48 (1956), No.2, Op.65 (1958), No.3, Op.81 (1964); *A Grand Grand Ov.* (3 vacuum cleaners, floor polisher, 4 rifles, orch.), Op.57 (1956); *Anniversary Ov.*, Op.99

(1968); **Beckus the Dandipratt*, Op.5 (1948); *The Fair Field Ov.*, Op.110 (1972); *Ov., Peterloo*, Op.97 (1968); **Tam O'Shanter*, Op.51 (1955); *Divertimento* No.2, Op.24 (1952); *English Dances*, Set I, Op.27 (1951), Set II, Op.33 (1951); *A Sussex Ov.*, Op.31 (1951); *Ov., The Smoke*, Op.21 (1948); *4 Scottish Dances*, Op.59 (1957); *Suite, Homage to the Queen*, Op.42 (1953); *Little Suite* No.1, Op.53 (1956), No.2, Op.78 (1963), *Little Suite* for brass band, No.1, Op.80 (1963), No.2, Op.93 (1966); *Water Music*, Op.82b (1965); *Concerto for 28 Players*, Op.105 (1970); *Flourish*, Op.112 (1973); *4 Cornish Dances*, Op.91 (1966); *Philharmonic Conc.*, Op.120 (1976); *6 Variations on a Theme of Ruth Gipps*, Op.122 (1977); *4 Welsh Dances* (1989); *Manx Suite* (1990).

CHORAL: Psalm 150, ch., org., Op.25 (1950); *A John Clare Cantata*, Op.52 (1956); *The Return of Odysseus*, cantata, ch., orch. (text by P. Dickinson), Op.119 (1976).

CHAMBER MUSIC: *Divertimento*, fl., ob., cl., Op.37 (1952); vn. sonatas No.1, Op.15 (1947), No.2, Op.43 (1953); quintet, fl., vn., va., hn., bn., Op.7 (1944); quintet, 2 tpts., hn., tb., tuba, Op.73 (1963); *Sonatina*, recorder, pf., Op.41 (1953); *3 Shanties*, wind quintet, Op.4 (1943); trio, fl., va., bn., Op.6 (1943); pf. trio, Op.54 (1956); str. qts., No.1, Op.23 (1951), No.2, Op.118 (1975); ob. qt., Op.61 (1957); *Trevelyan Suite*, wind ens., Op.93 (1967); *Fantasies*, solo wind, brass (1965–7); *Fantasy*, gui., Op.107 (1970); *Fantasy*, hp., Op.117 (1975); va. sonata, Op.17 (1948); fl. sonatina, Op.19 (1948); fl. sonata, Op.121 (1977); ob. sonatina, Op.28 (1951); cl. sonatina, Op.29 (1951); wind octet (1989); *Fantasy*, rec., str.qt. (1991).

PIANO: *Five by Ten*, Books I-V (1952); *Variations on a Ukrainian Folk Song*, Op.9 (1948); *Children's Suite*, Op.16 (1948).

Arnold, Samuel (*b* London, 1740; *d* London, 1802). Eng. composer, conductor, and organist. Comp. of Chapel Royal from 1783; cond. Academy of Ancient Mus. from 1789; org. Westminster Abbey from 1793; composer to CG Th., proprietor of Marylebone Gardens. Comp. many popular operas, church mus., etc.; ed. Handel's works in 36 vols. and a supplement to Boyce's *Cathedral Music* in 4 vols. Comp. 4 numbers in pasticcio *The Maid of the Mill* (London, 1765) (based on Richardson's *Pamela* (1740–1)).

Arnold Schoenberg Choir. Austrian mixed-voice choir founded in Vienna 1972 by Erwin Ortner. Comprises students and former students of Vienna Acad. of Mus.

Aroldo (Harold). Opera in 4 acts by Verdi to lib. by Piave. Comp. 1856–7. Most of mus. is same as that for **Stiffelio* (1850), though Act 4 was newly composed and lib. is new. Prod. Rimini 1857, NY 1863, Wexford 1959, London (Camden Fest.) 1964.

Aronowitz, Cecil (Solomon) (*b* King William's Town, S. Africa, 1916; *d* Ipswich, 1978). Eng. viola-player of Russo-Lithuanian parentage. Trained as vn. player but changed to va. Played in all London professional orchs. and was prin.

violist of Boyd Neel Orch., London Mozart Players, and ECO. Founder member, Melos Ens. Frequent chamber mus. player. Prof. of va., RCM 1950–75; Head of Str. Sch., RNCM, 1975–7; dir. of str. studies, Snape Maltings Sch. 1977–8. Salzburg Fest. 1978 (with *Amadeus Qt.).

arpa (It.). Harp.

arpa doppia (It. 'double harp'). Name given in 16th-cent. Italy to both double-strung and triple-strung harp, probably because of increased range and size. Incl. in Monteverdi's *Orfeo* (1607).

arpège (Fr., from *arpe*, 'harp'), **arpeggio** (It., plural *arpeggi*). A chord 'spread', i.e. the notes heard one after the other from the bottom upwards, or sometimes from the top downwards, as on the hp.

arpeggiare (It.). To play chords as arpeggios. (Present and past participles, *arpeggiando, arpeggiato*.)

arpeggione (*guitare d'amour*). Type of guitar-shaped 6-str. vc. with fretted fingerboard, played with a bow. Invented 1823 by G. Staufer. Schubert wrote a sonata for it in 1824 which is normally played on the vc. (also transcr. for va.).

arraché (Fr.). Torn. Extreme form of *pizzicato*.

arrangement or **transcription**. Adaptation of a piece of mus. for a medium other than that for which it was orig. comp. Sometimes 'transcription' means a rewriting for the same medium but in a style easier to play. (In the USA there appears to be a tendency to use 'arrangement' for a free treatment of the material and 'transcription' for a more faithful treatment. In jazz 'arrangement' tends to signify 'orchestration'.)

Arrau, Claudio (*b* Chillán, Chile, 1903; *d* Mürzzuschlag, Austria, 1991). Chilean pianist (Amer. cit. 1979). Début Chillán 1908 (aged 5). Début Berlin 1914. Prof. of pf., Stern Cons., Berlin, 1924–40. Won Grand Prix de Genève 1927. London début 1922, USA 1923. Salzburg Fest. début 1938. Founded own pf. sch. in Santiago 1940. Settled in USA 1941. Superb interpreter of Chopin, Liszt, Beethoven, Mozart, Schumann, and Brahms. Played all Bach's kbd. mus. in 12 recitals in Berlin, 1935–6.

Arroyo, Martina (*b* NY, 1936). Amer. soprano. Début NY 1958 then sang at Vienna State Opera and Deutsche Oper, Berlin. NY Met début 1959. Zurich Opera 1963–8. Substituted for *Nilsson as Aida at NY Met 1965. CG début 1968. Noted Verdi singer.

ars antiqua (Lat.). Old art. The medieval W. European mus. style, based on plainsong and organum, employed by composers (notably Leonin and Pérotin) of the Notre Dame or Parisian sch. in the 12th and 13th cents. See *ars nova*.

arsin et thesin, per. See *canon*.

ars nova (Lat.). New art. The new style of mus. comp. in Fr. and It. in 14th cent. Name derived from tract (*c*.1320) by Philippe de Vitry. Restrictions of *ars antiqua* were replaced by greater variety of rhythm, duple instead of triple time, and increased independence in part-writing. In Fr. *Machaut was finest exponent of *ars nova* and in Italy G. da Cascia, J. da Bologna, and Landini. The It. madrigal was a later flowering of *ars nova*.

Artaxerxes. Thomas *Arne's most successful opera, in 3 acts. Lib. is Eng. trans. by the composer of Metastasio. Prod. London 1762; Dublin 1765; NY 1828. Many operas on this subject, e.g. by Hasse (1730), Galuppi (1749), Gluck (1741), Paisiello (1771), Piccinni (1762), Sacchini (1768), Cimarosa (1784), and Isouard (1794).

Art de toucher le clavecin, L' (The Art of playing the Harpsichord). Method by F. *Couperin (1716), with instructions and 8 illustrative comps. Known to have influenced Bach.

articolato (It.), **articulé** (Fr.). Well-articulated; so *articolazione* (It.). Articulation.

Art of Fugue, The (J. S. Bach). See *Kunst der Fuge, Die*.

Art of Playing the Harpsichord (Couperin). See *Art de toucher le clavecin, L'*.

Artôt, Alexandre-Joseph (Montagney) (*b* Brussels, 1815; *d* Ville d'Avray, Paris, 1845). Belg. violinist. Made many world tours. London début 1893 at RPS concert, playing his own *Fantaisie* for vn. and orch. Composer for vn. and for chamber combinations. Uncle of Désirée *Artôt.

Artôt, (Marguerite-Joséphine) **Désirée** (*b* Paris, 1835; *d* Berlin, 1907). Belg. mez., later sop. Opera début Paris Opéra, 1858. Sang in concerts and opera in London 1859–66. In 1869 married Spanish bar. Mariano Padilla y Ramos, with whom she often sang. Their daughter Lola Artôt de Padilla (*b* Sèvres, 1876; *d* Berlin, 1933) was member of the Berlin Hofoper company from 1909 and sang the role of Oktavian at the first Berlin perf. of *Der Rosenkavalier*. Created Vreli in *A Village Romeo and Juliet*, Berlin 1907.

Arts Council of England (formerly of Great Britain). Independent body est. 1945 as successor to wartime Council for the Encouragement of Music and the Arts. Incorporated by Royal Charter 1946 'to preserve and improve standards of performance in the various arts'. New charter granted 1967. Annual grant-in-aid is provided by the Government. Professional staff, under secretary-general, incl. mus. dir. Specialist advisory panels incl. one for mus. Subsidies are disbursed to many organizations, being channelled through certain independent bodies and regional arts assoc. Headquarters in London. In 1994 the Arts Council of Great Britain was divided to form the Arts Council of England, Scottish Arts Council, and Arts Council of Wales.

Arts Florissants, Les. Ensemble (vocal and instrumental) devoted to baroque mus., founded in Paris 1978 by William *Christie. Has performed revivals of operas by Lully and Hasse and revived works by M.-A. Charpentier, Monteverdi, Purcell, etc. London début 1990. Christie continues as their director.

Artyomov, Vyacheslav (*b* Moscow, 1940). Russ. composer. With *Gubaidulina and Suslin, formed folk-instr. improvisatory ens. Astrea, 1975. Works incl. 3 syms.; pf. conc.; vn. conc.; accordeon conc.; *Requiem* (1988); 2 cl. sonatas; and ballet *By Faith Alone* (1987).

Arundell, Dennis (Drew) (*b* London, 1898; *d* London, 1988). Eng. actor, author, translator, and comp. but best known as opera producer. Prod. first stage perf. of Handel's *Semele*, Cambridge 1925. Also Stravinsky's *The Soldier's Tale* (Cambridge, 1928), Honegger's *King David* (Cambridge, 1929), Purcell's *Fairy Queen* (1931), and Vaughan Williams's *The Pilgrim's Progress* (Cambridge 1954). Many prods. for SW Opera. Radio prods. of *The Rake's Progress* and Benjamin's *Tale of Two Cities*. Eng. trans. of *L'Enfant et les sortilèges* and Honegger's *Jeanne d'Arc au bûcher*. OBE 1978.

A.S. *Al segno.

As (Ger.). The note A♭.

Asas (Ases) (Ger.). The note A♭♭.

Ascanio in Alba. *Serenata teatrale* in 2 acts by boy Mozart to lib. by Parini (Milan, 17 Oct. 1771).

ASCAP. American Society of Composers, Authors and Publishers. Founded 1914.

Ascension, L' (The Ascension). Comp. in 4 movements by *Messiaen, for orch. (1933) and for org. (1934). The movements are 1. *Majesté du Christ demandant sa gloire à son Père*. 2. *Alléluias sereins d'une âme qui désire le ciel*. 3. *Alléluia sur la trompette, alléluia sur la cymbale*. 4. *Prière du Christ montant vers son Père*. 3rd movement of orch. version differs from that in the organ version, which is entitled *Transports de Joie d'une âme devant la gloire du Christ*. F.p. orch. version, Paris 1935.

Ashdown Ltd, Edwin. London mus. publishing firm (founded 1860), successors to Wessel and Stodart (dating from 1825).

Ashkenazy, Vladimir (Davidovich) (*b* Gorky, 1937). Russ.-born pianist and conductor. Winner Queen Elisabeth Prize, Brussels, 1956; joint winner (with John *Ogdon) Tchaikovsky comp., Moscow 1962. Toured USA 1958. London début 1963. Settled in Eng., but in 1968 went to Iceland (became cit. 1972). One of finest pianists of post-1950 generation. Salzburg Fest. début 1981. Made cond. début 1969, Brit. cond. début 1977. Mus. dir. RPO 1987–94, prin. cond. Berlin Radio SO 1988–96, chief cond. Czech PO 1998–2003. Pubd. (with J. Parrott) *Ashkenazy: Beyond Frontiers* (London, 1984). Prin. cond. *NHKSO from 2004.

Ashton, (Sir) **Frederick** (William) (*b* Guayaquil, Ecuador, 1904; *d* Eye, Suffolk, 1988). Eng. choreographer. Associated with SW (now Royal) Ballet from 1936. Ballets incl. *Symphonic Variations*, *La Fille mal gardée*, *Façade*, *Horoscope*, *Ondine*, *Sylvia*, *Romeo and Juliet*, *Cinderella* (first 3-act ballet choreog. by Englishman), *Enigma Variations*, *A Month in the Country*. CBE 1950. Knighted 1962. CH 1970. OM 1977.

Askenase, Stefan (*b* Lemberg, Poland, 1896; *d* Bonn, 1985). Polish-born pianist (Belg. cit. 1950). Début Vienna 1919. Salzburg Fest. 1929. Teacher at Rotterdam Cons. 1937–40. Prof. of pf., Royal Cons., Brussels 1954–61. Noted Chopin player.

Asrael. Title of sym. in C minor, Op.27, by *Suk, comp. 1906. Asrael is the Angel of Death. Begun as memorial to Dvořák, Suk's father-in-law, in 1904, became memorial also to Suk's wife who died 18 months after her father. Contains quotation from Dvořák's *Requiem*.

assai (It.). Very, extremely (formerly synonymous with Fr. *assez*, but respective meanings have changed).

Assassinio nella cattedrale, L' (Murder in the Cathedral). Opera in 2 acts by Pizzetti to his own lib. after A. Castelli's trans. of play by T. S. Eliot (1935). Prod. Milan 1958, NY 1958 (concert), Coventry 1962.

Assemble All Ye Maidens. No.7 of Holst's 7 *Partsongs* Op.44 for female vv. and str. to words by Robert Bridges, and often perf. separately. Has part for solo sop. Comp. 1925–6. F.p. London 1927.

assez (Fr.). Enough, but the usual and best translation is 'fairly', e.g. *assez vite*, fairly quick.

Associated Board of the Royal Schools of Music. Founded 1889, partly to combat effect of numerous spurious examining bodies, being a combination, for the conduct of local and sch. examinations, of the RAM, RCM, and also (since 1972) the RNCM, Manchester, and the RSAMD.

assoluto (It.). Absolute, free, alone. As in *prima donna (ballerina) assoluta*.

Aston [Ashton, Aystoun, etc.], **Hugh** (*b c.*1485; *d* 1558). Eng. composer of church and virginal mus., and pioneer of true instr. style. Master of choristers, St Mary Newarke Coll., Leicester, 1525–48. Kbd. writing well in advance of his time.

Aston, Peter (George) (*b* Edgbaston, 1938). Eng. composer, conductor, and teacher. Lect., York Univ. 1964–74. Prof. of music, Univ. of E. Anglia, 1974–99. Cond. Aldeburgh Fest. Singers from 1975. Ed. complete works of George *Jeffreys. Works incl. *Sacrapane the Sorcerer*, children's opera (1969); *My Dancing Day*, cantata (1969); 5 *Songs of Crazy Jane* (Yeats), for sop. solo (1960); *Haec Dies*, mixed vv. and org. (1971); 3 *Pieces* for ob. (1968); and many choral works and part-songs.

Atalanta in Calydon. 'Choral sym.' for vv. only by Bantock (Manchester 1912), poem by Swinburne (1865). Comp. 1911.

ATCL. Associate of *Trinity College of Music, London.

Atempause (Ger.). Breath pause. Very slight pause on a weak beat in order to give greater effect to the following strong beat.

a tempo (It.). In time. Denotes reversion to speed at beginning of piece or movement after a deviation.

Athalia. Oratorio by Handel to lib. by S. Humphreys, after Racine. Rev. 1735 and 1756. (F.p. Oxford 1733).

Athalie. Mendelssohn's incidental mus. to Racine's drama (Op.74; 1843–5). Ov. and *War March of the Priests* are the parts usually heard today.

Atherton, David (*b* Blackpool, 1944). Eng. conductor. Début at CG 1968 (res. cond. 1968–80), La Scala 1976, San Francisco 1978. Joint founder, and mus. dir. London Sinfonietta 1968–73 and 1989–91. Youngest ever cond. at Henry Wood Proms and at CG début. Prin. cond. RLPO 1980–3. Mus. dir. San Diego SO 1981–7, Hong Kong PO 1989–2000. Cond. f.ps. of *Punch and Judy* (Aldeburgh 1968) and *We Come to the River* (CG 1976). OBE 1999.

Atkins, (Sir) **Ivor** (Algernon) (*b* Llandaff, 1869; *d* Worcester, 1953). Eng. organist, composer, and conductor. Org., Worcester Cath. 1897–1950. Cond. Worcester Fests. for 50 years; composer of choral works, e.g. *Hymn of Faith*. Ed. with Elgar of Bach's *St Matthew Passion* (1911). Knighted 1921.

Atlántida (Atlantis). *Cantata escénica* by *Falla in prol. and 3 parts, text being poem (1877) by Jacinto Verdaguer adapted by Falla. Begun 1926 and left unfinished in 1946. Rev. and completed in first version by Ernesto *Halffter, Barcelona 1961 (staged Milan 1962), Edinburgh 1962. Halffter's 2nd (concert) version f.p. Lucerne 1976.

Atlantov, Vladimir (Andreyevich) (*b* Leningrad, 1939). Russ. tenor. Sang at Kirov Th., Leningrad, from 1963, Bolshoy Th., Moscow, from 1967. Vienna début 1971; Milan 1973; Berlin 1974; NY 1975 (with Bolshoy co.); CG 1987 (Otello). From 1977 has also sung bar. roles.

Atlas, Dalia (*b* Haifa, 1933). Israeli conductor and pianist. Cond. Haifa Chamber Orch. from 1963. Guest cond. BBC Northern SO from 1964, RLPO 1964, Houston SO 1976, and other leading orchs.

Atmosphères (Atmosphere). Work for orch. by *Ligeti, comp. 1961, f.p. Donaueschingen, cond. Rosbaud, 1961.

atonal. Not in any key, hence atonality. *Schoenberg preferred the term pantonal, denoting synthesis of all keys. Atonality is usually applied where there is no tonal centre and the notes of the chromatic scale are used impartially: the 12 notes of the octave function independently, unrelated to a key centre. Atonality is foreshadowed in the mus. of Debussy and Scriabin, even Liszt, but can perhaps be dated from the finale of Schoenberg's 2nd str. qt. (1908). From atonality there developed the *twelve-note system. With atonality, consonances and dissonances of trad. harmony no longer apply.

ATSC. Associate, Tonic Sol-fa College of Music.

attacca (It.). Attack! (imperative). Used at the end of a movement to mean 'start the next movement without a break'.

attacco. Very short *motif* used as material for imitation or as fugue subject (see *andamento*).

Attaignant, Pierre (*b* ?Donai, *c.*1494; *d* Paris, 1552). Fr. music printer and publisher. Experimented for years with music types. In 1527–8 produced *Chansons nouvelles* in a diamond-shaped notation, with staff segments attached, which required only one impression. This halved the printing time and led to cheap printed mus. From 1537 was official printer of the King's mus. First publisher to achieve a European distribution.

attaque (Fr.). Attack. The *chef d'attaque* in an orch. is the leader (Amer. 'concert-master').

Atterberg, Kurt (*b* Gothenburg, 1887; *d* Stockholm, 1974). Swed. composer and writer on music, subsidized by the Swed. Govt. Mus. critic, *Stockholms Tidningen* 1919–57. Comp. 5 operas, 5 concs., and 9 syms. of which the 6th won the £2,000 prize offered by Columbia Graphophone Co. in the centenary year of Schubert's death (1928). Sec. RAM, Stockholm, 1940–53.

At The Boar's Head. Opera in 1 act about Falstaff by Holst to lib. adapted by composer from Shakespeare's *Henry IV Parts 1 and 2* (1597–8). Music based largely on folk tunes. Comp. 1924. Prod. BNOC, Manchester, 1925; NY 1935.

Attila. Opera in 3 acts with prol., by Verdi to lib. by Solera. Verdi's 9th opera. Comp. 1845–6. Prod. Venice 1846; London 1848; NY 1850. Revived in 1951 (concert perf.) after long neglect; staged Florence 1962; SW 1963.

Attwood, Thomas (*b* London, 1765; *d* London, 1838). Eng. composer and organist. Boy chorister in Chapel Royal; host and friend in London of Mendelssohn; org. St Paul's Cath., 1796–1838 and of Chapel Royal from 1836; composer of th. and church mus. One of first profs. at RAM, 1823. Founder-member of Philharmonic Soc., 1813.

Atzmon [Groszberger], **Moshe** (*b* Budapest, 1931). Hung.-born conductor. Played hn. in Israel PO and cond. Tel Aviv municipal orch. First prize, Liverpool Int. Cond. Competition, 1964. Chief cond. Sydney SO 1969–71. Cond. N. Ger. Radio SO 1972–6. Salzburg Fest. 1967. Chief cond. Basle SO 1972–7, Tokyo Metropolitan SO 1978–82, co.-prin. cond. American SO of NY 1982–4. Opera début, Berlin 1969. Mus. dir. Dortmund Opera 1991–2001.

aubade (Fr., from *aube*, dawn). Early morning music, likewise *serenade*—evening music.

Aubade Héroïque (Heroic dawn). Orch. work by *Lambert, f.p. 1942, inspired by composer's witnessing dawn invasion of The Hague by Ger. parachutists in 1940.

Auber, Daniel (François Esprit) (*b* Caen, 1782; *d* Paris, 1871). Fr. composer. Pupil of Cherubini. In youth, in business in London; then prominent in Paris as composer of instr. mus., and later of operas in which he collab. with the dramatist Scribe. Wrote in all 49 operas, of which the best known are *La Bergère châtelaine* (1820), *La Muette de Portici* (*Masaniello*) (1828), *Fra Diavolo* (1830), *Le Cheval de bronze* (1835), *Le Domino noir* (1837), *Les Diamants de la couronne* (1841), and *Manon Lescaut* (1856). From 1842 to 1870 was head of Paris Cons. and in 1852 mus. dir. to Napoleon III.

Aubert, Jacques (*b* Paris, 1689; *d* Belleville, 1753). Fr. violinist and composer of music for violin and for the stage. Started career as dancing-master and violinist in cabarets. Wrote incid. mus. Entered Duke of Bourbon's service 1719. Member of 24 Violins du Roy 1727–46. Led orch. at Opéra 1728–52 and played at Concert Spirituel 1729–40. Wrote several vn. sonatas with bass, 10 concs. for 4 vn. and bass, operas, and short pieces.

Aubin, Tony (Louis Alexandre) (*b* Paris, 1907; *d* Paris, 1981). Fr. composer and conductor. Won *Prix de Rome* 1930. Prof. of comp., Paris Cons., 1945. Works incl. opera *Goya* (1973), ballet *Au fil de l'eau* (1964), orch., vocal, and piano works.

Auden, W(ystan) **H**(ugh) (*b* York, 1907; *d* Vienna, 1973). Eng.-born poet (Amer. cit.) and librettist. Wrote lib. for Britten's first opera *Paul Bunyan* (1941) and, with Chester Kallman, for Stravinsky's The *Rake's Progress* (1951), and Henze's *Elegy for Young Lovers* (1961) and The *Bassarids* (1966).

Auer, Leopold (*b* Veszprém, Hung., 1845; *d* Loschwitz, Dresden, 1930). Hung. violinist and teacher. Played in Ger. orchs. until in 1868 he became head of the vn. dept. of St Petersburg Cons., a post he held until 1917. Tchaikovsky dedicated his vn. conc. to him, but he refused it, saying the work was unplayable in its orig. form. Taught at Inst. of Mus. Art., NY (1926–8), and at Curtis Inst. from 1928. Among his pupils were Heifetz, Zimbalist, and Elman. Wrote 2 manuals on vn. playing and autobiography, *My Long Life in Music* (NY, 1923). Great-uncle of György *Ligeti.

auf (Ger.). On, etc., e.g. *auf der G* (like It. *sul G*), means on the G (str.).

Auf einer Gondel (On a gondola). Title given by *Mendelssohn to 3 of his *Lieder ohne Worte*: Op.19, No.6 in G minor, Book I (1834); Op.30, No.12 in F♯ minor, Book II (1835); and Op.62, No.29 in A minor, Book VI (1843).

Aufforderung zum Tanz (Weber). See *Invitation to the Dance*.

Aufführung (Ger., from *aufführen*, to perform). Performance. *Aufführungspraxis* is the practicalities of perf., particularly in relation to old mus. where a composer's directions were often lacking in explicit detail.

Auflage (Ger.). Edition.

auflösen (Ger.). To loosen, release, etc. (1) To resolve a discord.
(2) In harp playing, to lower again a str. which has been raised in pitch. (Hence the noun *Auflösung*, *Auflösungszeichen*, release-sign).
(3) The sign for the natural (♮).

Aufschlag (Ger.). Up-beat (down-beat being *Niederschlag*).

Aufschnitt (Ger.). Slit, i.e. portion omitted, a cut (in a score, etc.).

aufschwung (Ger.). Up-soaring, flight, e.g. *mit aufschwung*, in a lofty (impassioned) spirit.

Aufstieg und Fall der Stadt Mahagonny (Weill). See *Rise and Fall of the City of Mahagonny*.

Aufstrich (Ger.). Up-bow (in str. playing; down-bow being *Niederstrich*).

Auftakt (Ger.). Up-beat (down-beat being *Niederschlag*).

Aufzug (Ger.). Raising (of curtain). Act (of stage work).

Augengläser (Ger.). Eye-glasses. Word used by Beethoven on title-page of his duet for vn. and vc.—'mit 2 Augengläser obbligato', being a jocular reference to the 2 spectacled players for whom it was comp.

Augenlicht, Das (Eyesight). Setting by *Webern, Op.26, for mixed ch. and orch. of text by Hildegard Jone. Comp. 1935. Pubd. 1938. F.p. London 1938, cond. Scherchen.

Augér, Arleen (Joyce) (*b* Los Angeles, Calif., 1939; *d* Leusden, Holland, 1993). Amer. soprano. Début 1967, Vienna State Opera; Salzburg Fest. début 1970, Met 1978. Specialist in Bach cantatas, many of which she recorded. Prof. of mus. for v., Frankfurt Univ., 1975–87. Sang at wedding of Prince Andrew and Sarah Ferguson, Westminster Abbey, 23 July 1986.

augmentation, canon by. When the imitating vv. in a *canon are in longer notes than that which they are imitating. Canon by diminution is the reverse process.

augmentation and diminution. In melodic parts, the respective lengthening and shortening of the time-values of the notes. Thus, in a fugue, the subject may (especially towards the end) appear in longer notes, a device which adds dignity and impressiveness.

augmented intervals. If any perfect or major *interval is increased by a semitone it becomes augmented. Thus:

Augmented 1st: C up to C♯
Augmented 2nd: C up to D♯
Augmented 4th: C up to F♯
Augmented 5th: C up to G♯, with harmonic
                 implication of major 3rd,
                 e.g. augmented 5th chord on
                 C = C–E–G♯
Augmented 6th: C up to A♯.

Chords of augmented 6th are chromatic. The 3 most common are as follows (e.g. in key of C):

(a) Chord of the Italian 6th: A♭–C–F♯
(b) Chord of French 6th: A♭–C–D–F♯
(c) Chord of the German 6th: A♭–C–E♭–F♯

The Ger. 6th is the commonest and serves as a convenient pivot for modulation, since it may be approached as based on the flattened submediant in one key, and quitted as based on the flattened supertonic in another (or vice versa); also, by enharmonic change (see *Interval*), it can be transformed into the chord of the dominant 7th of another key, and so quitted (e.g. the Ger. 6th in key C (A♭–C–E♭–F♯) can be treated as the chord of the dominant 7th in key D♭ (A♭–C–E♭–G♭)).

There are other possibilities.
Augmented 8th: C up to next C♯ but one.

augmented triad. A triad of which the 5th is augmented (and so in a diminished triad, the 5th is diminished).

Augusteo. Rome concert-hall, opened in 1908, built on the ruins of the mausoleum of Augustus.

Auld Lang Syne. The poem is a re-casting by Robert Burns (pubd. in final form 1794) of a popular song (probably orig. a folk-song) then current in various versions. The tune now current is sometimes stated to be by *Shield; something like it appeared in his opera *Rosina*, as a part of the ov. (CG 1783), where it is treated to imitate Scottish bagpipe mus. Sir Alexr. *Don's Strathspey* (issued possibly a year later than the perf. of Shield's opera) seems to have strong claim to be the orig.; it may have already been known to Shield, who was brought up at Durham, not far from the Scottish border. The air, like many Scots tunes, is based on the pentatonic scale. It has been proposed as the 'hidden theme' in Elgar's *Enigma Variations*, but the composer denied it.

aulos. Ancient Gr. wind instr. with double reed, used to accompany the dithyramb in the orgiastic rites of Dionysus.

Auric, Georges (*b* Lodève, Hérault, Fr., 1899; *d* Paris, 1983). Fr. composer. Youngest member of *Les *Six*. Wrote for Diaghilev ballet in 1920s and worked as mus. critic. Gen. admin., Paris Opéra

and Opéra-Comique 1962–8. Works incl. operas, ballets (notably *Les Matelots*, 1925), film mus., orch. works, pf. sonata, songs, etc.

Aurora's Wedding. The divertissement of the last act, perf. separately, of ballet *The Sleeping Beauty* (mus. by Tchaikovsky) supplemented by extra numbers based on Diaghilev's London prod. 1921. F.p. Paris 1922.

aurresku. A type of Basque folk dance. The *zortziko forms part of it.

Aus den Sieben Tagen (From the Seven Days). 15 comps. by *Stockhausen (1968) for varying ens. for upwards of 3 musicians. Each piece has a verse or text to suggest a mood the players must create, a way of playing, combinations of both, etc., e.g. No.14 *Goldstaub* (Gold Dust) for small ens.: 'Live completely alone for 4 days without food in complete silence, without much movement. Sleep as little as necessary, think as little as possible. After 4 days, late at night, without talking beforehand, play single sounds WITHOUT THINKING what you are playing. Close your eyes. Just listen.' The 15 items are 1. *Richtige Dauern* (Right Durations), about 4 players; 2. *Unbegrenzt* (Unlimited), ens.; 3. *Verbindung* (Union), ens.; 4. *Treffpunkt* (Rendezvous), ens.; 5. *Nachtmusik* (Night Music), ens.; 6. *Abwärts* (Downwards), ens.; 7. *Aufwärts* (Upwards), ens.; 8. *Oben und Unten* (High and Low), th. piece for man, woman, child, 4 instr.; 9. *Intensität* (Intensity), ens.; 10. *Setz die Segel zur Sonne* (Set sail for the Sun), ens.; 11. *Kommunion* (Communion), ens.; 12. *Litanei* (Litany), speaker or ch.; 13. *Es* (It.), ens.; 14. *Goldstaub* (Gold Dust), small ens.; 15. *Ankunft* (Arrival), speaker or speaking ch.

Ausdruck (Ger.). Expression. Hence *ausdrucksvoll*, expressively.

Ausfüllgeiger (Ger.). Filling-out fiddler. A *ripieno violinist.

Ausgabe (Ger.). Out-giving. Edition.

ausgehalten (Ger.). Held out, i.e. sustained.

aushalten (Ger.). To hold out, i.e. to sustain; so *Aushaltungszeichen*, holding-out sign, i.e. pause.

Aus Italien (From Italy). Symphonic Fantasia in 4 movements by Richard Strauss, Op.16, his first orch. work with pictorial background. Comp. 1886. F.p. Munich 1887. Finale quotes Denza's *Funiculì, Funiculà*.

Aus meinem Leben (From my Life; Cz. *Z méhoživota*). Sub-title of Smetana's str. qt. No.1 in E minor (1876), an avowedly autobiographical work.

Austin, Frederic (*b* London, 1872; *d* London, 1952). Eng. baritone and composer. Opera début CG 1908 as Gunther in *The Ring* under Richter. Prin. bar., Beecham Opera. Sang Peachum in his own highly successful version of *The *Beggar's Opera*, 1920. Art dir., BNOC, 1924–9. Comp. sym., sym.-poem, choral works.

Austin, Richard (*b* Birkenhead, 1903; *d* Reading, 1989). Eng. conductor. Cond. Carl Rosa Opera and then Bournemouth Municipal Orch. 1934–40. Mus. dir. New Era Concert Soc. 1947–57. Prof. RCM 1946–76. Son of Frederic *Austin.

Austin, Sumner (Francis) (*b* Anerley, Kent, 1888; *d* Oxford, 1981). Eng. baritone and opera producer. Carl Rosa 1919, then with O'Mara Opera Co. Sang at Old Vic and SW from 1920s to 1940. Prod. many SW operas, also first Eng. prod. of *Wozzeck at CG 1952.

Austral (*née* Wilson), **Florence** (*b* Richmond, Melbourne, 1894; *d* Newcastle, NSW, 1968). Australian soprano. Début as Brünnhilde for BNOC in *Die Walküre*, CG 1922, and later in complete *Ring* cycles in London and on tour. Also a fine Isolde and Aida.

Austria. Name under which the Austrian 'Emperor's Hymn', comp. by Haydn, is found in many hymnals.

Auszug (Ger.). (1) Extract.
(2) Arrangement.

authentic cadence. See *cadence*.

authentic modes. See *modes*.

autoharp. Type of easily-played *zither, played with the fingers or a plectrum. Chords are prod. by depressing keys.

auxiliary note. This may be described as a variety of *passing-note which, instead of passing *on* to another note, passes *back* to the note it has just left. Such a note may, like a passing note, be either diatonic or chromatic. Shakes, *mordents, and turns offer examples of the auxiliary note applied decoratively.

avant-garde (Fr. 'vanguard'). Term used in the arts to denote those who make a radical departure from tradition. In 20th-cent. mus., Stockhausen may be regarded as *avant-garde*, but not Shostakovich.

Aveling, Valda (*b* Sydney, NSW, 1920). Australian pianist, harpsichordist, and teacher. Settled in Eng. Duo with Evelyn *Barbirolli, co-recitalist with Menuhin, Joan Sutherland, etc. OBE 1982.

Ave Maria (Hail Mary). Prayer consisting partly of the biblical salutations of the Archangel Gabriel and Elizabeth to the Virgin Mary, and partly of matter added in the 15th cent. Many settings, that by Schubert being to a Ger. trans. of Walter Scott's poem from 'The Lady of the Lake' (1810). That known as by 'Bach–Gounod' is the first prelude from Bach's *Wohltemperierte Klavier* with Gounod's *Méditation* as counterpoint, the words having been added by someone else.

Ave maris stella (Hail, Star of the Sea). Hymn of RC Church.

Ave regina coelorum. See *Antiphons of the Blessed Virgin Mary*.

Ave verum corpus (Hail, true body). Hymn (anonymous and of unknown date) possessing its own plainsong and also frequently set by composers (Desprès, Byrd, Mozart, Cherubini, S. Wesley, Gounod, Elgar, etc.), such motet settings being frequently sung in the Roman office of Benediction. Translations sometimes begin *Jesu, Word of God Incarnate, Jesu, Blessed Word of God Incarnate*, or *Word of God Incarnate*.

Avison, Charles (*b* Newcastle upon Tyne, 1709; *d* Newcastle upon Tyne, 1770). Eng. organist and composer. Org., St John's Church in his native town from 1736 and then at St Nicholas from 1736 to his death. Composer of 60 concs. for str. orch. (pubd. between 1740 and 1760), 3 vols. of sonatas for hpd. and vn., and author of much-discussed *Essay on Musical Expression* (1752), in which he compared Handel unfavourably with Geminiani and Benedetto Marcello. In 1743 pubd. 12 hpd. sonatas by D. Scarlatti as concerti grossi.

Avison Edition. Edn. of works by Brit. composers, prod. by certain publishers under the auspices of Soc. of Brit. Composers between 1905 and 1918.

Avni, Tzvi (Jacob) (*b* Saarbrücken, 1927). Ger.-born Israeli composer, teacher, and writer. Emigrated to Palestine 1935. Dir., AMLI Cent. Mus. Library, Tel Aviv, 1961–75, EMS, Rubin Acad., Jerusalem, from 1970 (prof. from 1976 and head of dept. of theory and comp.). Awarded prize for life's work 1986. Works incl. 7 ballets (1969–78); orch. and chamber works; 2 str. qts. (1962, 1969); pf. sonatas (1961, 1979); and unacc. choral works.

avoided cadence. See *cadence*.

Ax, Emanuel (*b* Lwów, 1949). Polish-born Amer. pianist. Lived in USA from 1961 (cit. 1970). NY début 1973. 1st prize, first Rubinstein comp., Israel, 1974. London 1977. Noted Chopin-player, also interpreter of Ravel, Bartók, and Schoenberg.

ayre. Medieval spelling of 'air', a type of Eng. song written by *Dowland and others, less contrapuntal than a madrigal, being more like a strophic song, with vocal or instr. (usually lute) acc., pubd. in a large book around which the performers could gather.

Ayrton, Edmund (*b* Ripon, 1734; *d* Westminster, 1808). Eng. organist and composer. Master of Children of Chapel Royal 1780–1805. His son William (*b* London, 1777; *d* London, 1858) was a mus. critic and a founder of the Philharmonic Soc. As dir. of It. opera at King's Th., London, was first to stage *Don Giovanni* in Britain (1817).

B

B. 7th degree of natural scale of C. So B♭, B♭♭, B♮, B♯, B♯♯, B major, B minor etc. In Ger., B=B♭ and B♭=B♭♭. The Eng. note B is represented in Ger. by H (hence composers can write fantasias on the name BACH, the notes being B♭–A–C–B♮. J. S. Bach himself used these notes in the unfinished final fugue of *The Art of Fugue*).

Baal Shem. Suite for vn. and pf. by Bloch, comp. 1923, subtitled '3 pictures of Chassidic Life'. Baal Shem Tov (Master of the Good Name) founded the Jewish sect of Chassidism in 17th cent. Movements are *Vidui* (Contrition), *Nigun* (Improvisation), and *Simchas Torah* (Rejoicing of the Law). Version with orch., 1939, f.p. NY 1941.

Babar le petit éléphant, Histoire de (Story of Babar the little elephant). Narration for v. and pf. by Poulenc to text by Jean de Brunhoff (1899–1937). Comp. 1940–5. Version with orch. by *Françaix, 1962.

Babbitt, Milton (*b* Philadelphia, 1916). Amer. composer and mathematician. On staff at Princeton since 1938, becoming Conant Prof. of Mus. His comps. developed from the 12-note system of Schoenberg and Webern, later employing elec. devices such as synthesizers and tape. Author of articles and monographs on Bartók and elec. mus., Varèse, and Schoenberg. Works incl.:

ORCH.: *Relata I* (1965), *II* (1968); *Concerti*, vn., orch., tape (1974–6); pf. conc. No. 1 (1985), No. 2 (1998).
CHAMBER MUSIC: *Composition for 4 instruments* (1948); str. qts.: No.1 (1950), No.2 (1954), No.3 (1969–70), No.4 (1970), No.5 (1982), No. 6 (1993); ww. qt. (1953); *Groupwise*, 7 instrs. (1983); *Sheer Pluck*, gui. (1984); *The Joy of More Sextets* (1986); *Beaten Paths*, marimba (1988); *The Crowded Air*, 11 instrs. (1988); pf. qt. (1995); cl. quintet (1996); *Swan Song*, 6 instrs. (2002).
CHORAL: *Music for the Mass* (1941); 4 *Canons* (1969); *More Phonemena* (1977); *Glosses*, boys' choir (1988).
PIANO: 3 *Compositions* (1947); *Partitions* (1957); *Post-Partitions* (1966); *Reflections*, with tape (1974); *Playing for Time* (1983); *Envoi*, pf. 4 hands (1990); *Tutte le corde* (1994).
ELECTRONIC: *Composition for Synthesizer* (1961); *Philomel*, sop., recorded sop., and syn. (1964); *Correspondences*, string orch. and syn. (1967); *Phonemena*, sop. and tape (1974); *Images*, sax., tape (1979).

Babin, Victor (*b* Moscow, 1908; *d* Cleveland, Ohio, 1972). Russ.-born pianist and composer. Settled in USA 1937. Dir., Cleveland Institute of Mus. from 1961. Famous pf. duo with his wife, Vitya *Vronsky, whom he married 1933. Works incl. 2-pf. conc., *Konzertstück* for vn. and orch., str. qt., songs, etc.

Babi-Yar. Sub-title of Shostakovich's Sym. No.13 in B minor, Op.113, for bass, bass ch., and orch.,

to poems by Yevtushenko. Comp. and f.p. 1962. Babi-Yar was site of grave of thousands of Russ. Jews, murdered by Germans in World War II.

Baccaloni, Salvatore (*b* Rome, 1900; *d* NY, 1969). It. operatic bass. Début Rome 1922; La Scala 1926; CG 1928; Amer. (Chicago) 1930; Glyndebourne 1936–9; Salzburg Fest. début 1939; NY Met 1940. Outstanding as Leporello, Don Pasquale, Osmin, and similar comic roles.

bacchanale (Fr., from Lat. *bacchanalia*, a feast of dancing and singing in honour of Bacchus, god of wine). An orgiastic comp., as in the Venusberg scene of *Tannhäuser* and in *Samson et Dalila*.

bacchetta (It.). Stick. (1) Drumstick. (2) Baton. The plural is *bacchette*—e.g. *bacchette di legno*, wooden drumsticks; *bacchette di spugna*, sponge-headed drumsticks.

Bacchus et Ariane (Bacchus and Ariadne). Ballet in 2 acts with mus. by *Roussel, choreog. Lifar, comp. 1930 and prod. Paris 1931. 2 orch. suites were extracted, the 2nd being the more popular.

Bacewicz, Grażyna (*b* Łódź, 1909; *d* Warsaw, 1969). Polish violinist and composer. Vn. pupil of Flesch. Taught at Łódź Cons. 1934–5, 1945; Warsaw Acad. of Mus. 1966–9. Wrote 4 syms., 7 vn. concs., 7 str. qts., 2 vc. concs., va. conc., pf. conc., 5 vn. sonatas, 2 pf. quintets, etc.

Bach (Family). The Bach family lived from the early 16th cent. in the Thuringian duchies of Saxe-Weimar-Eisenach, Saxe-Coburg-Gotha, and Saxe-Meiningen and the principality of Schwarzburg-Arnstadt. Their profession was mus.—there are records that 53 Bachs held posts as organists, cantors, or town musicians over a span of 300 years. J. S. Bach himself compiled a genealogy of his family, which began, as far as his own line was concerned, with Veit Bach (*d* 1619), a miller with a passion for lute-playing. Other prin. members of the family up to J. S. Bach's time were:

Hans Bach (*b* c.1550; *d* 1626). Violinist, son of Veit, and known as *Der Spielmann* (The Player). Carpet-weaver by trade. Johann Bach (*b* 1604; *d* 1673). Eldest son of Hans. Organist at Schweinfurt and Erfurt. Christoph Bach (*b* 1613; *d* 1661). 2nd son of Hans. Organist and composer. Town-musician at Eisenach. Heinrich Bach (*b* Wechmar, 1615; *d* Arnstadt, 1692). 3rd son of Hans. Arnstadt church organist for 51 years. Johann Christian Bach (*b* Erfurt, 1640; *d* Erfurt, 1682). Eldest son of Johann. Served under his father among town musicians of Erfurt but became first of family to settle at Eisenach where he married. Returned to Erfurt to succeed his father 1671. Johann Egidius Bach (*b* 1645; *d* 1716). 2nd son of Johann. Organist at Erfurt and composer of church mus., also va.-player. Georg Christoph Bach (b Eisenach, 1642; d 1697). Eldest son of Christoph. Cantor at Schweinfurt. Composer. Johann Christoph Bach (1) (b Arnstadt, 1642; d Eisenach, 1703). Eldest son of Heinrich. Became organist at Eisenach at age 23 in 1665. Considered by C. P. E. Bach as 'great and expressive' composer. Many elaborate and progressive vocal works, also instr. comps. 2 motets for double ch., *Herr nun Lassest* and *Ich lasse dich nicht* are extremely fine. Johann Michael Bach (b Arnstadt, 1648; d Gehren, 1694). Brother of preceding. Organist and parish clerk of Gehren from 1673 until his death. Maker of vns. and hpds. His motets have high merit. The youngest of his 5 daughters, Maria Barbara (b 20 Oct. 1684), became J. S. Bach's first wife. Johann Ambrosius Bach (b Erfurt, 1645; d Eisenach, 1695). 2nd (twin) son of Christoph. Played vn. and va. in addition to org. One of Erfurt *compagnie* of musicians from 1667 until Oct. 1671 when he succeeded his cousin, Johann Christian, at Eisenach. There the youngest of his 8 children, Johann Sebastian, was born on 21 Mar. 1685. Johann Christoph Bach (2) (b Erfurt, 1645; d Arnstadt, 1693). Twin brother of Johann Ambrosius. Court violinist at Arnstadt, where he was *Hofmusikus* and *Stadtpfeifer*. Johann Jakob Bach (b Wolfsbehringen, 1655; d Ruhla, 1718). Org. in Thal, cantor in Steinbach. Johann Bernard Bach (b Erfurt, 1676; d Eisenach, 1749). Son of Johann Egidius. Organist at Erfurt and Magdeburg. In 1703 succeeded cousin Johann Christoph (1) at Eisenach and became *Kammermusikus* in court orch. of Duke of Saxe-Eisenach. Instr. comps. admired and perf. at Leipzig by Johann Sebastian. Johann Nikolaus Bach (b Eisenach, 1669; d Eisenach, 1753). Eldest son of Johann Christoph (1). University and town organist at Jena from 1695 until death. Org.-builder and maker of hpds., to which he contributed some improvements. Comp. orch. suites, church mus. and opera. Johann Ludwig Bach (b Thal, 1677; d Meiningen, 1731). Son of Johann Jakob. Composer and Kapellmeister at Saxe-Meiningen. Johann Christoph Bach (3) (b Erfurt, 1671; d Ohrdruf, 1721). Eldest son of Johann Ambrosius, and brother of Johann Sebastian. Pupil of Pachelbel at Erfurt. Organist at Ohrdruf. Taught his brother the klavier. Johann Jakob Bach (b Eisenach, 1682; d Stockholm, 1722). Son of Johann Ambrosius and brother of Johann Sebastian. Town musician at Eisenach. Entered Swed. army service in 1704 as oboist and in 1713 became *Hofmusikus* at Stockholm. It was for his joining the army that Johann Sebastian comp. the *Capriccio on the departure of his beloved brother* (BWV 992).

Bach, Carl [Karl] **Philipp Emanuel** (b Weimar, 1714; d Hamburg, 1788). Ger. composer. 5th child and 3rd son of J. S. *Bach. Intended for legal career but turned to mus. while at Frankfurt Univ. In 1738 became cembalist in Berlin at court of Frederick the Great, holding this post until 1767, when he succeeded *Telemann as dir. of church mus. at Hamburg. Applied unsuc-

cessfully in 1750 to succeed his father at Leipzig. His achievement was to develop sonata-form and invest it with weight and imaginative quality, most evidently in his kbd. sonatas, of which there are over 200, but also in his sinfonias, concs. (over 50), vn. sonatas, and the masterly solo fl. sonata in A minor. Also comp. 22 Passions, *Magnificat* (1749), the oratorios *Die Israeliten in der Wusten* (1769) and *Die Auferstehung und Himmelfahrt Jesu* (1780), and many songs. Wrote celebrated treatise on klavier-playing.

Bach, Johann Christian (b Leipzig, 1735; d London, 1782). Ger. composer. 18th child and 11th (youngest) son of J. S. *Bach. Known as 'the English Bach'. Learned klavier-playing from his half-brother C. P. E. *Bach in Berlin. Went to Bologna in 1754 to study counterpoint with Padre *Martini. After becoming a Roman Catholic was appointed organist Milan Cath. in 1760. His 3-act opera *Artaserse* was prod. at Turin in 1760, followed by *Catone in Utica* in Naples the same year and *Alessandro nell'Indie* in 1762. These events were regarded in Milan as unduly frivolous, and Bach accepted offer from Signora Mattei, dir., King's Th., London, to succeed Cocchi as composer to the opera. His first London opera, *Orione*, prod. 1763. On this occasion cls. were first used in an Eng. orch. Later the same year his *Zanaida* was an equal success, and he was appointed music-master to Queen Charlotte. In 1764, when the boy Mozart visited London, Bach perf. a sonata with him. Also in 1764 he inaugurated a series of concerts with Karl Friedrich *Abel, who had been a pupil of J. S. Bach. These continued until 1782. His later operas met with less success. One of them, *Carattaco*, was on an Eng. subject which later attracted Elgar. On visits to Ger., Bach prod. his *Temistocle* in 1772 at Mannheim and his *Lucio Silla*, which Mozart had already set, in 1774. Comp. an opera for Paris, *Amadis de Gaule*, in 1779, and his last London opera, *La Clemenza di Scipione*, was successfully perf. in 1778. He died in debt, and was buried in a mass grave in St Pancras churchyard. Queen Charlotte helped to meet expenses arising from his debts and enabled his widow to return to Italy. His death went almost unnoticed by Londoners. There is a fine portrait of him by Gainsborough. Besides 11 operas, Bach wrote many instr. works—sinfonias, ovs., nearly 40 pf. concs., sonatas, qts., trios, marches, etc. Their felicitous scoring and melodic charm leave no doubt why Mozart admired Bach so much and why not only Mozart but also Haydn and Beethoven were fruitfully influenced by his work. Most of his church mus. was written before he left Italy.

Bach, Johann Christoph Friedrich (b Leipzig, 1732; d Bückeburg, 1795). Ger. composer. 16th child and 9th son of J. S. *Bach. Attended Leipzig Univ. and in 1750 appointed *Kammermusikus* to the court at Bückeburg; Konzertmeister 1756. In 1778 visited his half-brother Emmanuel in

Hamburg and his brother Johann Christian in London. Comps. incl. 14 syms., 8 kbd. concs., sonatas, trios, oratorios, cantatas, secular songs.

Bach, Johann Sebastian (*b* Eisenach, 1685; *d* Leipzig, 1750). Ger. composer and organist. Son of Johann Ambrosius Bach, organist and town musician, J. S. Bach was orphaned at the age of 10 and went to live with his elder brother Johann Christoph at Ohrdruf where he had klavier and org. lessons. In 1700 was a chorister at St Michael's Church, Lüneburg, staying for 3 years, learning much from the organist-composer Georg Böhm. Organist at Arnstadt, 1703, and then Mühlhausen, 1707, when he married his cousin Maria Barbara Bach. In 1708 became organist in the Kapelle of the Duke of Saxe-Weimar, where he remained for 9 years, leaving in disappointment at not being appointed Kapellmeister in 1717. By this time he had comp. some of his finest org. works and church cantatas.

In 1717 appointed Kapellmeister at the court of Anhalt-Cöthen where the prince's interest was not in religious works but in instr. comps. From this period date his vn. concs., sonatas, suites, and Brandenburg concs. Also comp. many of his best klavier works at Cöthen, probably for his children's instruction. In 1720 his wife died and in Dec. 1721 he married Anna Magdalena Wilcken, 20-year-old daughter of the court trumpeter. Now dissatisfied with life at Cöthen, where the ruler's new wife showed little interest in mus., Bach applied for the cantorship at St Thomas's, Leipzig, in Dec. 1722. He was not selected, but the chosen candidate, Graupner, withdrew and Bach was appointed in May 1723, having in the meantime cond. his *St John Passion* in St Thomas's as evidence of his fitness for the post. Remained at St Thomas's for the rest of his life, not without several disputes with the authorities. During time there, comp. more than 250 church cantatas, the *St Matthew Passion*, Mass in B minor, *Christmas Oratorio*, *Goldberg Variations*, and many other works incl. his last, the unfinished *Die Kunst der Fuge* (Art of Fugue). In 1740 began to have trouble with his eyesight and in the last year of his life was almost totally blind.

Bach was famous as an org. virtuoso. As a composer his reputation in his lifetime was restricted to a fairly narrow circle and his mus. was regarded by many as old-fashioned. His fame in no way approached that of, e.g., Telemann. His pubd. works today fill many vols., but in his lifetime fewer than a dozen of his comps. were printed, and for half a century after his death this position was only slightly improved until in 1801 the *Well-Tempered Klavier* was issued. The revival of interest in Bach's mus. may be dated from the Berlin perf. of the *St Matthew Passion* on 11 Mar. 1829, cond. Mendelssohn. Systematic publication of his works by the *Bach Gesellschaft began in 1850 to mark the centenary of his death. (See *Bach Revival*.)

Bach's supreme achievement was as a polyphonist. His N. Ger. Protestant religion was the root of all his art, allied to a tireless industry in the pursuit of every kind of refinement of his skill and technique. Sonata form was not yet developed enough for him to be interested in it, and he had no leaning towards the (to him) frivolities of opera. Although some of the forms in which he wrote—the church cantata, for example—were outdated before he died, he poured into them all the resources of his genius so that they have outlived most other examples. The dramatic and emotional force of his mus., as evidenced in the Passions, was remarkable in its day and has spoken to succeeding generations with increasing power. Suffice it to say that for many composers and for countless listeners, Bach's mus. is supreme—to quote Wagner: 'the most stupendous miracle in all music'. Prin. works:

ORCH.: *Brandenburg Concertos Nos. 1–6 (*BWV1046–51); 7 *Concertos* for hpd. and str. (BWV1052–8), No.1 in D minor, No.2 in E, No.3 in D, No.4 in A, No.5 in F minor, No.6 in F, No.7 in G minor; 3 concs. for 2 hpd. and str. (BWV1060–2), No.1 in C minor, No.2 in C, No.3 in C minor; 2 concs. for 3 hpd. and str. (BWV1063–4), No.1 in D minor, No.2 in C (No.1 arr. for vn., fl., ob., No.2 for 3 vn. or fl., ob., vn.); conc. for 4 hpd. and str. in A minor (BWV1065, transcr. of Vivaldi conc. Op.3 No.10); conc. for fl., vn., hpd., str. (BWV1044), hpd., ob., str. (BWV1059), vn., str. in A minor (BWV1041, same work as BWV1058), vn., str. in E (BWV1042, same work as BWV1054), 2 vn., str. in D minor (BWV1043, same work as BWV1062), vn., ob., str., in D minor (BWV1060, reconstr. of hpd. conc.); 4 *Suites* (BWV1066–9), No.1 in C, No.2 in B minor, No.3 in D, No.4 in D.

CHAMBER MUSIC: *Die *Kunst der Fuge* (The Art of Fugue) (BWV1080); *Das Musikalische Opfer* (The *Musical Offering*) (BWV1079); 3 *Partitas*, solo vn. (BWV1002, 1004, 1006), No.1 in B minor, No.2 in D minor, No.3 in E; 3 *Sonatas*, solo vn. (BWV1001, 1003, 1005), No.1 in G minor, No.2 in A minor, No.3 in C; 6 *Sonatas*, vn., klavier (BWV1014–9), No.1 in B minor, No.2 in A, No.3 in E, No.4 in C minor, No.5 in F minor, No.6 in G; 6 *Sonatas*, vn./fl., klavier (BWV1020–5), No.1 in G minor, No.2 in G, No.3 in F, No.4 in E minor, No.5 in C minor, No.6 in A; 4 *Sonatas*, 2 vn./2 fl./2 ob., hpd. (BWV1036–9), No.1 in D minor, No.2 in C, Nos.3 and 4 in G; 6 *Sonatas*, fl., hpd. (BWV1030–5), No.1 in B minor, No.2 in Eb, No.3 in A, No.4 in C, No.5 in E minor, No.6 in E; 3 *Sonatas*, viola da gamba (vc.), klavier (BWV1027–9), No.1 in G (same as BWV1039), No.2 in D, No.3 in G minor; sonata, fl. in A minor (BWV1013); 6 *Suites*, vc. (BWV1007–12), No.1 in G, No.2 in D minor, No.3 in C, No.4 in Eb, No.5 in C minor, No.6 in D.

KEYBOARD: *Capriccio* in Bb (on the departure of a beloved brother) (BWV992); *Chromatic Fantasia and Fugue* in D minor (BWV903); 16 concs., solo hpd. (BWV972–87), Nos. 1, 2, 4, 5, 7, and 9 transcr. of Vivaldi, No.3 of Marcello, Nos. 14 and 15 of Telemann; 6 *English Suites* (BWV806–11), No.1 in A, No.2 in A minor, No.3 in G minor, No.4 in F, No.5 in E minor, No.6 in D minor;

Fantasia in A minor (BWV922); *Fantasia and Fugue* in A minor (BWV904); 6 **French Suites* (BWV812-17), No.1 in D minor, No.2 in C minor, No.3 in B minor, No.4 in E♭, No.5 in G, No.6 in E; *Fugue in C* (BWV952); **'Goldberg' Variations* (BWV988); *15 Inventions* (2-part) (BWV772-86); *15 Inventions* (3-part) (BWV787-801); **Italian Concerto* (BWV971); *6 Partitas* (BWV825-30); *9 Preludes for W. F. Bach* (BWV924-32); *6 Preludes* (BWV933-8); *7 Toccatas* (BWV910-16), No.1 in F♯ minor, No.2 in C minor, No.3 in D, No.4 in D minor, No.5 in E minor, No.6 in G minor, No.7 in G; *Variations in the Italian Style* (BWV989); *Das *Wohltemperierte Klavier* (The Well-Tempered Klavier), 48 preludes and fugues (BWV846-93).

LUTE: *Suites:* in A (BWV1007), in E minor (BWV996), in E (BWV1006a, transcr. from BWV1006, vn. Partita No.3), in C minor (BWV997), in G minor (BWV995).

ORGAN: 6 concs. (BWV592-7), all transcr. from other composers, incl. Vivaldi); *4 Duets* (BWV802-5); *Fantasia and Fugue* in C minor (BWV537), in G minor (BWV542); *Fantasias,* in C (BWV573), in C minor (BWV562), in G (BWV572); *Fugues,* in C minor (BWV574), in C minor (BWV575), in G (BWV577), in G minor (BWV578); *Passacaglia and Fugue* in C minor (BWV582); *Prelude and Fugue:* in A (BWV536), in A minor (BWV543), in A minor (BWV551), in B minor (BWV544), in C (BWV531), in C (BWV545), in C (BWV547), in C minor (BWV546), in C minor (BWV549), in D (BWV532), in D minor (BWV538), in D minor (BWV539), in E minor (BWV533), in E minor (**'Wedge'*) (BWV548), in E♭ (BWV552), in F minor (BWV534), in G (BWV541), in G (BWV550), in G minor (BWV535), in G minor (BWV542); *8 Preludes and Fugues* (BWV553-60), No.1 in C, No.2 in D minor, No.3 in E minor, No.4 in F, No.5 in G, No.6 in G minor, No.7 in A minor, No.8 in B♭; *6 Sonatas* (BWV525-30), No.1 in E♭, No.2 in C minor, No.3 in D minor, No.4 in E minor, No.5 in C, No.6 in G; *Toccata, Adagio, and Fugue* in C (BWV564); *Toccata and Fugue* in D minor (*Dorian*) (BWV538), in D minor (BWV565), in E (BWV566), in F (BWV540); *Trio* in D minor (BWV583), in G (BWV586).

CHORALE PRELUDES: *Orgelbüchlein* (Little Organ Book) (BWV599-644), containing 46 items; also many others of which only a brief selection is given here: *Ach, bleib bei uns* (BWV649), *Allein Gott in der Höh' sei Ehr* (BWV711), *An Wasserflüssen Babylon* (BWV653b), *Christum wir sollen Loben schon* (BWV696), *Ein' feste Burg* (BWV720), *Herr Jesu Christ, dich zu uns wend* (BWV709), *In dulci jubilo* (BWV729), *Jesu, meine Freude* (BWV713), *Jesus Christus, unser Heiland* (BWV688), *Komm, Gott Schöpfer* (BWV667), *Komm, heiliger Geist* (BWV652), *Kommst du nun, Jesu* (BWV650), *Liebster Jesu, wir sind hier* (BWV706), *Meine Seele erhebet den Herren* (BWV648), *Nun danket alle Gott* (BWV657), *Nun komm, der Heiden Heiland* (BWV659), *O Gott, du frommer Gott* (BWV767), *O Lamm Gottes unschuldig* (BWV656), *Schmücke dich, O liebe Seele* (BWV654), *Vater unser in Himmelreich* (BWV682/3, 737), *Vom Himmel hoch* (BWV700, 701 fughetta, 738, 769

canonic variations), **Wachet auf* (BWV645), *Wer nur den lieben Gott* (BWV647, 690, 691), *Wo soll ich fliehen hin* (BWV646).

CANTATAS: Merely a selection of these is given here, with dates of comp. where known: No.4 *Christ lag in Todesbanden* (c.1707), No.6 *Bleib bei uns* (1725), No.10 *Meine Seele' erhebt den Herren* (1724, rev. 1744-50), No.11 *Lobet Gott* (c.1735), No.12 *Weinen, Klagen, Sorgen, Zagen* (1714), No.20 *O Ewigkeit, du Donnerwort* (1724), No.23 *Du wahrer Gott und Davids Sohn* (1723), No.28 *Gottlob Nun geht das Jahr zu Ende* (1725), No.29 *Wir danken dir, Gott* (1731), No.34 *O ewiger Feuer* (? after 1742), No.40 *Dazu ist erschiene der Sohn Gottes* (1723), No.45 *Est ist dir gesagt* (1726), No.51 *Jauchzet Gott* (1730), No.60 *O Ewigkeit, du Donnerwort* (1723), No.61 *Nun komm, der Heiden Heiland* (1714), No.68 *Also hat Gott die Welt geliebt* (1725), No.78 *Jesu, der du meine Seele* (1724), No.80 *Ein' feste Burg ist unser Gott* (1724), No.82 *Ich habe genug* (1727), No.93 *Wer nur den lieben Gott* (1724), No.95 *Christus der ist mein Leben* (1723), No.106 *Gottes Zeit ist die allerbeste Zeit* (c.1707), No.140 **Wachet auf* (1731), No.143 *Lobe den herrn* (1735), No.147 *Herz und Mund* (10th movement is *Jesu, bleibet meine Freude, Jesu, joy of man's desiring*) (1723), No.197 *Gott ist unser Zuversicht* (c.1728), No.201 *Der Streit zwischen *Phoebus und Pan* (?1729), No.202 *Weichet nur, betrübte Schatten* (?1718-23), No.208 *Was mir behagt* (?1713), No.209 *Non sa che sia dolore* (after 1740), No.211 *Schweigt stille, plaudert nicht* (**Coffee cantata, 1732*), No.212 *Mer hahn en neue Oberkeet* (**Peasant cantata, 1742*). *Canons* for 2, 3, 4, and 7 voices (BWV1075, 1077, 1073, and 1078 respectively).

ORATORIOS, etc: **Christmas Oratorio* in 6 parts (Weihnachtsoratorium) (BWV248, 1734); *Easter Oratorio* (BWV249, 1736); *Magnificat* in E♭ (BWV 243a, perf. Christmas Day 1723 incl. 4 Christmas texts), *Magnificat* in D (BWV243, rev. of *Magnificat* in E♭, c.1728-31, omitting Christmas texts); *Mass in B minor* (BWV232, 1724-49); *Mass* in G (BWV236, c.1738); *Mass* in G minor (BWV235, c.1737); *6 Motets* (BWV225-230) 1. *Singet dem Herrn ein neues Lied*, 2. *Der Geist hilft*, 3. *Jesu meine Freude*, 4. *Fürchte dich nicht*, 5. *Komm, Jesu, komm*, 6. *Lobet den Herrn*; **St John Passion* (*Johannespassion*) (BWV245, 1723); **St Matthew Passion* (*Matthäuspassion*) (BWV244, 1727).

SONGS AND ARIAS: *Notebook (No.2) of *Anna Magdalena Bach* (BWV508-18), contains 11 songs, the first being **Bist du bei mir* (but not by Bach); *Aria, Gott lebet noch* (BWV461); *Jesus ist das schönste Licht* (BWV474); *Aria, Komm, süsser Tod* (BWV478); *O Jesulein süss* (BWV493); *Song, Vergiss mein nicht, mein allerliebst Gott* (BWV505).

Bach, Wilhelm Friedemann (*b* Weimar, 1710; *d* Berlin, 1784). Ger. composer. 2nd child and eldest son of J. S.*Bach. Possibly also favourite son, but one who sadly failed to justify parental hopes. First part of *The Well-Tempered Clavier* was written for his instruction. After Leipzig Univ., became a church org. in Dresden (he was regarded as one of the greatest organists of his day, and comp. many instr. works, such as kbd. concs. and sonatas. In 1746 resigned to become organist of the Liebfrauenkirche at Halle. In 1762 was invited to succeed Graupner at Darmstadt but does not seem to have taken up his duties. Left Halle in 1764. For the last 20 years of his life held no regular post, giving occasional org. recitals in Brunswick, Göttingen, and Berlin, and teaching. Befriended by his father's biographer, J. N. Forkel. Poverty led him to sell several of his father's MSS and also to pass off some of his father's works as his own. In fact his own comps. have character and are today often played.

Bachauer, Gina (*b* Athens, 1913; *d* Athens, 1976). Gr. pianist of Austrian parentage. Début Athens 1935. Recitalist and soloist at orch. concerts in Athens, Middle-Eastern centres, and Paris. London début 1947; NY 1950.

Bach bow. A curved (convex) vn. bow invented by the violinist Emil *Telmányi as particularly suitable for performing the contrapuntal solo vn. mus. of J. S. Bach.

Bach Choir. Formed permanently in London in 1876 following success of first 2 complete Brit. perfs. in Apr. and May 1876 of Bach's Mass in B minor by group of amateurs assembled in 1875 under the choral direction of Otto *Goldschmidt, who remained cond. until 1885. His successors have been *Stanford, Walford *Davies, Hugh *Allen, *Vaughan Williams, *Boult, Reginald *Jacques, David *Willcocks, and David Hill. Gives annual perfs. of *St Matthew Passion*; many modern works in its repertory. Choirs in several other cities and towns use the title preceded by their name, e.g. Oxford Bach Choir, Newcastle Bach Choir.

Bache, Walter (*b* Birmingham, 1842; *d* London, 1888). Eng. pianist and conductor. For many years dir. concerts devoted to Liszt's mus. at which several of Liszt's works (*Faust Symphony*, both pf. concs., *St Elizabeth*, etc.) were f.p. in London. Prof. of pf. RAM. His brother Francis Edward (*b* Birmingham, 1833; *d* Birmingham, 1858) was a composer and pianist of exceptional promise. Their sister Constance (*b* Birmingham, 1846; *d* Montreux, 1903) trans. Bülow's letters (1896).

Bach Gesellschaft (Bach Society). Ger. soc. founded 1850 to commemorate the centenary of the death of J. S. Bach by publishing complete critical edn. of his works based mainly on the coll. of his MSS in Berlin. The project, urged by Robert Schumann in an article in the *Neue Zeitschrift für Musik* (xix, 87), was executed by Otto Jahn in assoc. with Schumann, Carl Friedrich Becker, Moritz Hauptmann, and the publishing firm of Breitkopf and Härtel. Issued 46 annual publications in 59 vols. between 1850 and 1900. The achievement was a vast feat of scholarship but, understandably, not without error. Some works definitely or probably not by Bach were incl.

With publication of the concluding volume on 27 Jan. 1900 the Society was wound up and the

Neue Bach Gesellschaft founded under the presidency of Herman Kretzschmar, Prof. at Leipzig Univ. Its objective was to publish Bach's mus. in practicable performing scores and to popularize it throughout Ger. by Bach fests. In 1904 the soc. began issue of a *Jahrbuch* (Yearbook), in which the latest Bach research is pubd., and in 1907 bought Bach's birthplace at Eisenach and made it a museum.

A Bach Soc. was founded in London 1849 to collect a library of Bach's comps. either printed or in MS. Under its auspices took place the first Eng. perfs. of *St Matthew Passion* (Hanover Sq. Rooms, London, 6 Apr. 1854) and *Christmas Oratorio* (London, 13 June 1864). 11 movements from the Mass in B minor were perf. on 24 July 1860. Soc. dissolved in Mar. 1870 and library given to RAM.

Bachianas Brasileiras. 9 pieces by *Villa-Lobos combining native Brazilian elements with the contrapuntal spirit of J. S. Bach's mus. They are: 1. for 8 vc. (1930); 2. for small orch. (1930); 3. for pf. and orch. (1938); 4. for pf. (1930–6) orch. 1941; 5. for v. and vcs. (1938); 6. for fl. and bn. (1938); 7. for orch. (1942); 8. for orch. (1945); 9. for str. or unacc. ch. (1944).

Bach revival. In the half-century after J. S. Bach's death only a handful of his works were pubd., though these incl. C. P. E. Bach's edn. of the complete coll. of *Vierstimmige Choralgesänge* (Choral Songs for 4 Voices), issued by Breitkopf & Härtel (1784–7). Nevertheless, Mozart at the end of his life was a profound admirer of Bach, and at Bonn in 1780 Beethoven was instructed in the '48' preludes and fugues, then still in MS. The revival gathered momentum with publication in 1801 in 4 centres (Bonn, Zurich, Vienna, and Leipzig, with a London reprint of the Bonn edn.) of the *Well-Tempered Klavier* (*Wohltemperierte Klavier*) and the appearance in 1802 of Forkel's biography *Über Johann Sebastian Bachs Leben*. The *Magnificat* was pubd. in 1811, the *St Matthew Passion* in 1830, the Mass in B minor partially in 1833, fully in 1845, the *St John Passion* in 1830 (pf. score), vocal parts 1834; many cantatas, all the org. works, many works for klavier, and much besides appeared between 1803 and 1850. In the matter of perf., the critic Johann Friedrich Rochlitz (1769–1842) stimulated interest by his articles in the *Allgemeine musikalische Zeitung*, which he founded in 1798, remaining ed. until 1818. Publication of the motets led to their perf. in the 1820s by the Berlin Singakademie under Carl Friedrich *Zelter. At his house Mendelssohn and the Devrients met to study Bach's mus. On 11 Mar. 1829 Mendelssohn cond. the first perf. since Bach's day of the *St Matthew Passion* with the Singakademie. Two further perfs. followed within 5 weeks. In 1833 the Singakademie perf. the *St John Passion* and a much-cut Mass in B minor. Other leading Ger. mus. centres, incl. Leipzig, followed Berlin's lead.

In Eng., where it might have been thought that J. C. Bach would have encouraged study of his father's work, little was done until Samuel

*Wesley's concerts of J. S. Bach's mus. in 1808 and 1809. William *Crotch also helped, but the main stimulus came from Mendelssohn's visits in 1829 and 1832, when he played Bach's org. works in St Paul's Cath. and elsewhere. In 1837 he had a section of the *St Matthew Passion* incl. in the Birmingham Fest. But it was not until the later 19th cent. that regular perfs. of Bach's mus. in Eng. began. Sterndale Bennett cond. first complete Eng. perf. of *St Matthew Passion* (in English) on 6 April 1854, in London. It was f.p. at Three Choirs Fest. 1871.

Bach trumpet. High-pitched natural (i.e. unvalved) tpt. used in late 17th and 18th cents. J. S. Bach and Handel wrote ornate passages for it in certain comps. In the late 1880s valved versions were prod. on which such passages could be played, but virtuoso players today have recovered the art of playing the natural tpt. and need no such aids.

back. The lower or rear part of the resonant box of str. instr. The strings are extended across the upper part, the belly or 'table'. The back has no sound holes; its primary function is to be reverberated by the air waves generated by the belly as it vibrates under the str. Usually made of maple, pear, or other hard wood.

Bäck, Sven-Erik (*b* Stockholm, 1919; *d* Stockholm, 1994). Swed. composer, conductor, and violinist. Member of several str. qts. Comp. 2 chamber operas, 3 str. qts., orch. works, elec. works.

Backer-Gröndahl, Agathe Ursula (*b* Holmestrand, Norway, 1847; *d* Ormoen, 1907). Norweg. pianist. Popular composer of songs and pf. mus.

backfall. (1) Part of an org., being the lever which connects the rods (stickers) to the kbd.
 (2) 17th-cent. Eng. term for a type of upper *appoggiatura in lute and hpd. mus.

Backhaus [Bachaus], **Wilhelm** (*b* Leipzig, 1884; *d* Villach, Austria, 1969). Ger. pianist. Made first concert tour age 16; later toured world. Prof. of pf., RMCM in 1905. Salzburg Fest. début 1953. Noted Beethoven interpreter, recording most of the sonatas after his 80th birthday.

Bacon, Ernst (*b* Chicago, 1898; *d* Orinda, Cal., 1990). Amer. composer, conductor, and critic. Works are mainly for v. with various accs. and incl. settings of Walt Whitman and Emily Dickinson. Also 4 syms., incl. one with narrator (No.3, 1956), and 2-act 'music play' *A Tree on the Plains* (1940, rev. 1962); 2 pf. concs. (1963, 1982); *Remembering Ansel Adams*, elegy, cl., str. (1986); *A Life*, vc. (1986); pf. trio (1987). Wrote over 250 songs.

Badarczewska, Tekla (*b* Warsaw, 1834; *d* Warsaw, 1861). Polish composer of pf. pieces, among them *The Maiden's Prayer*, pubd. Warsaw 1856 and Paris 1859.

badinage, badinerie (Fr.). Playfulness. Used as title of movement in 18th-cent. suite, e.g. *Badinerie* of J. S. Bach's Suite in B minor.

Badings, Henk (*b* Bandoeng, Java, 1907; *d* Vijlen, 1987). Dutch composer. Taught at Rotterdam Cons. from 1934; co-dir. Amsterdam Lyceum 1937–41; dir. Hague Cons. 1941–5; dir. EMS, Utrecht Univ., 1960–4; Prof. of comp. Musikhochschule, Stuttgart, 1962–72. Comps. incl. several operas and 14 syms., 25 concs., chamber mus., and elec. works. His sonata No.2 for 2 vn. (1963) is in 31-note scale and his ballet *Genesis* (1968) for 5 tone-generators.

Badura-Skoda (*née* Halfar), **Eva** (*b* Munich, 1929). Austrian musicologist. Authority on Scarlattis, Haydn operas, and Mozart. Has written on comic opera developments, incl. *Singspiele* and *opera buffa*.

Badura-Skoda, Paul (*b* Vienna, 1927). Austrian pianist. Début Vienna 1948. Salzburg Fest. début 1950. Many recordings; specialist in Mozart and with musicologist wife, Eva *Badura-Skoda, author of book on interpretation of his pf. mus. Also wrote, jointly with Jörg *Demus, *Beethoven Piano Sonatas* (1970).

bagatelle (Fr., Ger.). Trifle. So a short unpretentious instr. comp., esp. for pf. (Beethoven wrote 26 bagatelles, of which *Für Elise* is one). Dvořák's *Bagatelles* Op.47 (1878) are for 2 vn., vc., and harmonium (or pf.).

bagpipe family. Forms of the bagpipe have existed for at least 3,000 years and it is known to many races in Europe and Asia. *Machaut (1300–77) mentions bagpipes in a description of one of his own polyphonic works. Its essentials are that (*a*) It is a reed-pipe instr. and (*b*) Interposed between the medium supplying the wind and the reed-pipe is a bag serving as a reservoir and so preventing any undesired breaking of the flow of sound by the player's necessity to take breath.

Variable characteristics are: (*c*) The source of the wind-supply to the reservoir may be either by mouth or by a small bellows held under the arm. (*d*) The reed-pipe (*chanter*) from which the various notes of the tune are obtained by means of a series of holes or keys may, or may not, be acc. by 1 or more other reed-pipes each confined to a single note (*drones*), these being tuned to the Tonic or Tonic and Dominant of the key of the instr. (*e*) The reed may be either single, like that of the cl. family, or double like that of the ob. family; in practice the chanter reed is usually (perhaps always) double, while the drone reeds vary in different types of instr.

The compass of nearly all bagpipes is limited to an octave but on some few types a 2nd octave can be obtained.

Brit. forms of the instr. are: 1. *Scottish highland bagpipe*, or *great pipe*, mouth-blown and possessing a conical-bore chanter and 3 drones (2 tuned to a' and 1 to a). The tone is penetrating and best heard in the open air; the chanter scale is of D major but extends from a′ with a G and with the C and F pitched between sharp and natural. 2. *Scottish lowland bagpipe* is much the same as the foregoing but bellows-blown. 3. *Northumbrian bagpipe* is also bellows-blown but sweet and gentle in tone and normal as to scale (G major); it has usually 4 drones; its chanter pipes are end-stopped, so that when the player closes all the finger-holes at once sound from them ceases, making possible a characteristic crisp staccato. 4. *Irish 'Union' bagpipe* (the assertion that the word is a corruption of *villean* is unfounded). This is bellows-blown and sweet in tone; it has 3 drones. Its scale is nearly chromatic. Foreign terms for the bagpipe are: Fr. *musette*; Ger. *Dudelsack, Sackpfeife*; It. *piva, zampogna*; Sp. *gaita*.

baguette (Fr.). Stick. In mus. usage (1) drumstick (*baguettes de bois*, wooden drumsticks; *baguettes d'éponge*, sponge-headed drumsticks).
(2) Stick of bow of vn., etc.
(3) Conductor's baton.

Bahr-Mildenburg, Anna von. See *Mildenburg, Anna von*.

Bailey, Norman (*b* Birmingham, 1933). Eng. bass-baritone. Made early reputation in Austria and Ger. Début Vienna Chamber Opera 1959. SW début 1967 (on tour), 1968 (London). Débuts: CG 1969; Bayreuth 1969; NY 1975; NY City Opera 1975; Met 1976. Specialist in Wagner roles, e.g. Sachs, Dutchman, Wotan, Kurwenal. Has appeared with ENO, WNO, and Scottish Opera. CBE 1977.

Baillie, Alexander (*b* Stockport, 1956). Eng. cellist. Gave f.p. of Colin Matthew's conc., London Proms 1984. Has given f.ps. of works by Lutosławski, Schnittke, Crosse, and Takemitsu. Prof. of vc., RAM from 1992.

Baillie, (Dame) **Isobel** [Isabella] (*b* Hawick, Scotland, 1895; *d* Manchester, 1983). Scot.-born soprano, noted for singing of oratorio (especially *Messiah*) and *Lieder*. Début, Hallé Concert, Manchester 1921 (as Bella Baillie), then at chief Eng. Fests. Chosen by Toscanini for perfs. of Brahms's *Requiem*. One of orig. singers in Vaughan Williams's *Serenade to Music* 1938. Amer. début 1933. Taught at RCM 1955–7, Cornell Univ. 1960–1, Manchester Sch. of Mus. from 1970. Autobiography, *Never Sing Louder Than Lovely* (London, 1982). CBE 1951, DBE 1978.

Baillot, Pierre (Marie François de Sales) (*b* Passy, nr. Paris, 1771; *d* Paris, 1842). Fr. violin virtuoso and composer of 9 vn. concs. Member of Napoleon's private band 1802. Prof., Paris Cons. from 1795. Leader of Paris Opéra Orch. in 1820s. Wrote vn. method (1803) and *L'Art du violon* (1834).

Bainbridge, Simon (*b* London, 1952). Eng. composer. Works incl. *Music to Oedipus Rex* (1969); *3 Pieces for Chamber Ensembles* (*Spirogyra*) (1970); str. qt. (1972); *Interlude Music* (1973); *Flugal* (1973);

People of the Dawn, sop., ens. (1975); va. conc. (1976); *Path to Othona* (1982); *Fantasia for Double Orch.* (1983–4); *Ceremony and Fanfare*, 11 brass (1985); *A Capella*, 6 solo vv. (1985); *Metamorphosis* (1988); *Cantus contra cantum* (1989, rev., with elec., 1990); Double Concerto, ob., cl. in A, chamber orch. (1990); *Marimolin Inventions*, vn., marimba (1990); *Caliban Fragments and Aria*, with mez. (1991); cl. quintet (1992–3); *Ad oro incerta*, 4 songs from Primo Levi, mez., bn., orch. (1995); *Eichá*, ens. (1997); *Three Pieces for Orch.* (1998); gui. conc. (1998); *Chant*, amp. vv., orch. (1999); *Scherzi*, orch. (2000); *Paths and Labyrinths*, ens. (2001); *Voiles*, bn., 12 str. (2002).

Baines, William (*b* Horbury, Yorks., 1899; *d* York, 1922). Eng. composer and pianist. Worked as cinema pianist. Few works pubd. in his lifetime, but his mother gave his musical effects to Brit. Mus. in 1960. Wrote sym. (1917); vn. sonata (1917); str. qt. (1917–18); songs; and a large number of piano pieces, incl. sonatas, *Paradise Gardens* (1918–19), *Coloured Leaves* (1918–21), *7 Preludes* (1918–19), *Twilight Pieces* (1921), and *8 Preludes* (1921).

Bainton, Edgar (Leslie) (*b* London, 1880; *d* Sydney, NSW, 1956). Eng. composer. Pianist and dir. of Cons. in Newcastle upon Tyne 1912–34, having been prof. of pf. and comp. there from 1901. Dir., State Cons., Sydney, NSW (1934–47). Comps. in many genres.

Baird, Tadeusz (*b* Grodzisk Mazowiecki, Poland, 1928; *d* Warsaw, 1981). Polish composer. Several of post–1956 works use 12-note procedures. Works incl.:

OPERA: *Tomorrow* (*Jutro*) (after J. Conrad) (1966).

ORCH.: syms.: No.1 (1950), No.2 (1952), No.3 (1968–9); *Sinfonietta* (1949); pf. conc. (1949); *Concerto for Orchestra* (1953); *Cassation* (1956); *4 Essays* (1958); *Espressioni varianti*, vn. and orch. (1959); *Variations without a Theme* (1962); *Epiphany Music* (1963); *Sinfonia brevis* (1968); *Psychodram* (1972); ob. conc. (1973).

INSTR.: *Colas Breugnon*, fl., chamber orch. (1951); *4 Dialogues*, ob., chamber orch. (1964); *4 Novelettes*, chamber orch. (1967).

VOCAL: *4 Shakespeare Love Sonnets*, bar., chamber orch. (1956); *Exhortation*, narr., ch., orch. (1960); *Erotica*, sop., orch. (1961); *Songs of Trouvères*, mez., fl., vc. (1964); *5 Songs*, mez., chamber orch. (1967–8); *Goethe Letters*, bar., ch., orch. (1970).

Bairstow, (Sir) **Edward** (Cuthbert) (*b* Huddersfield, 1874; *d* York, 1946). Eng. organist and composer. Held various organist's positions, incl. Leeds Parish Church (1906) and York Minster (1913 to death). V. trainer and choral cond. Wrote church mus. Prof. of mus., Durham Univ. from 1929. Knighted 1932.

Baiser de la fée, Le (The Fairy's Kiss). Ballet in 1 act by Stravinsky, mus. based on pf. pieces and songs by Tchaikovsky with linking passages by Stravinsky in Tchaikovsky's vein. Orch. 1928, rev. 1950. Scenario based on Andersen's *Ice Maiden*.

Choreog. Nijinskaya. Prod. Paris 1928; London with choreog. by Ashton 1935. A *Divertimento* arr. from *Le Baiser de la Fée* was comp. 1934, rev. 1949.

Baker, George (*b* Birkenhead, 1885; *d* Hereford, 1976). Eng. baritone, especially but not exclusively associated with the Gilbert and Sullivan operettas. Also writer and adjudicator. BBC Overseas Music Dir. 1944–7. 2nd wife was sop. Olive Groves (*d* 1974). CBE 1971.

Baker, (Dame) **Janet** (Abbott) (*b* Hatfield, Doncaster, 1933). Eng. mezzo-soprano. Sang in Leeds Phil. Choir (soloist in Haydn's *Nelson Mass* 1953). Joined Ambrosian Singers 1955; 2nd prize Kathleen Ferrier Comp. 1956; opera début 1956 (Roza in Smetana's *The Secret*) with Oxford Univ. Opera Club. Glyndebourne Ch. 1956. Queen's Prize 1959. Wexford Fest. 1959. Sang leading roles with Handel Opera Soc. 1959; Aldeburgh Fest. with Britten from 1962, giving f.p. of *Phaedra*, 1976. Sang Lucretia in EOG's Russ. tour 1964. Recorded Angel in Elgar's *The Dream of Gerontius* (1964, cond. Barbirolli). NY début 1966 (concert); CG 1966; Glyndebourne 1970; ENO 1971. Created Kate in *Owen Wingrave* (TV 1971, CG 1973). Salzburg Fest. 1973 (concert). Retired from opera 1982, last appearance being as Orpheus in Gluck's opera at Glyndebourne (but sang Orpheus in NY concert 1989). One of most intense and intelligent of contemp. singers, as impressive in operatic parts as in the realm of *Lieder*, Eng. and Fr. song, oratorio, and Mahler. Hamburg Shakespeare Prize 1971. Autobiography *Full Circle* (London, 1982). CBE 1970. DBE 1976. CH 1994.

Baker, Richard (Douglas James) (*b* London, 1925). Eng. broadcaster and music presenter. Professional appearances on concert-platform as narrator in *King David* (Honegger), *Façade* (Walton), *Peter and the Wolf* (Prokofiev), *Survivor from Warsaw* (Schoenberg), etc. OBE 1976.

Baker, Theodore (*b* NY, 1851; *d* Dresden, 1934). Amer. music scholar. Literary ed. (1892–1926) for G. Schirmer; books incl. *Biographical Dictionary of Musicians* (1900; 6th edn. 1978, 7th edn. 1984, 8th edn. 1992, all ed. N. Slonimsky).

Bakst, Ryszard (*b* Warsaw, 1926; *d* Manchester, 1999). Polish pianist and teacher. Taught at Warsaw State Acad. of Mus. 1953–68; RMCM 1969–72; RNCM 1972–91. Exponent of Chopin and Szymanowski.

Balakirev, Mily (Alexeyevich) (*b* Nizhny-Novgorod, 1837 (old style 1836); *d* St Petersburg, 1910). Russ. composer who made major contribution to development of nationalist school. Spent his formative years in the country home of Oulibichev, biographer of Mozart, where he studied in the library and had practical instruction with private orch. At 18 went to St Petersburg, where *Glinka, impressed by his nationalist ideals, encouraged him to continue his own work. From 1861 Balakirev became centre of a group of nationalistically inclined composers known as 'the *Five' (the others being Cui, Borodin, Mussorgsky, and Rimsky-Korsakov). In 1862 founded Free Sch. of Mus. At its sym. concerts Balakirev introduced many of the new works by his colleagues of 'the Five' and later those by Lyadov and Glazunov. Nervous breakdown led to his retirement from music 1871–6, during which period he worked as a railway official. From 1883 was mus. dir. to the Russ. court. Himself a fine pianist, his *Islamey*, like his other pf. works, is a brilliant virtuoso showpiece. Prin. works:

ORCH.: syms. No.1 in C (1893–7), No.2 in D minor (1900–08); pf. concs. No.1 in F♯ minor (1855), No.2 in E♭ (1861, completed 1911 by Lyapunov); *Overture on Spanish Themes* (1857, rev. 1886), *Overture on 3 Russian Themes* (1863–4, rev. 1884), *Overture on Czech Themes* (1867, rev. 1905); sym.-poem *Tamara* (1867–82).

PIANO: Oriental fantasy *Islamey* (1869, rev. 1902), 6 mazurkas, 3 scherzos, 3 nocturnes, 4 waltzes, *Spanish Serenade*.

Also many songs.

balalaika. Russ. guitar, triangular in shape with (normally) 3 str., and a fretted fingerboard. Exists in various sizes. Assoc. with it, in balalaika bands, are the *domra*, a somewhat similar instr., and the *gusli*.

Balanchine [Balanchivadze], **George** (*b* St Petersburg, 1904; *d* NY, 1983). Russ.-Amer. choreographer. Thorough mus. training. Imperial Sch. of Ballet 1914–21. Left Russ. 1924. After an appearance in Paris, was engaged by *Diaghilev as choreographer. Stravinsky's *Apollo Musagetes* had Balanchine choreog. for its first Paris perf. (1928). (Other Stravinsky works were later choreog. by Balanchine, incl. *Orpheus, Jeu de Cartes, Baiser de la fée, Danses concertantes, Movements*, and *Agon*.) In 1932 became choreog. for Col. de Basil's Ballets Russes de Monte Carlo. In 1934 went to USA to create Amer. Ballet Co., début 1935. This was resident ballet at NY Met 1935–8, when it was disbanded. Balanchine then worked as teacher and free-lance choreog. (incl. Hollywood films). Co-founder Ballet Soc. (1946) which became celebrated NY City Ballet, 1948, with Balanchine as art. dir. From this period dates his great and influential work for modern dance. Among ballets he choreog. were: *The Prodigal Son* (Prokofiev) 1929, *Ballet Imperial* (Tchaikovsky) 1941, *Night Shadow* (Bellini–Rieti) 1946, *La Valse* (Ravel) 1951, *Ivesiana* (Ives) 1954, *7 Deadly Sins* (Weill) 1958, *Slaughter on 10th Avenue* (Rodgers) 1968, *Duo Concertante* (Stravinsky) 1970. Among musicals he choreographed were: *On your Toes* (1936), *The Boys from Syracuse* (1938). Also worked as opera producer (Stravinsky's *Rake's Progress*, NY 1953; Tchaikovsky's *Eugene Onegin*, Hamburg 1962).

Balassa, Sándor (*b* Budapest, 1935). Hung. composer. Mus. dir. Hung. Radio. Comps. incl. *Beyond the Threshold*, opera (1976); vn. conc. (1964); *The Golden Age*, cantata (1965); *Requiem for Lajos Kassák*

(1969); *Xenia*, nonet (1970); *Iris* (1971), orch.; wind quintet; *Legend*, ch.; *Tabulae*, chamber orch. (1973); *Calls and Cries*, orch. (1982); 3 *Fantasies*, orch. (1984); *The Third Planet*, opera-oratorio (1987); *Bölcskei Concerto*, str. (1994); *Damjanich's Prayer*, ch. (1996); *Sons of the Sun*, orch. (1998); str. qt. (2002).

Balbi, Lodovico (*b* Venice, *c.*1545; *d* Venice, *c.*1604). It. church musician and composer. Cath. choirmaster in Padua (1585–91), Feltra (1593–7), and Treviso (1597–8). Also comp. madrigals.

Baldi, Antonio (*fl.* 1722–35). It. counter-tenor. Sang in London 1725–8 in operas by Handel (*Alessandro, Ottone, Scipione, Radamisto*, and *Serse*).

Baldwin Company. Pf. makers of Cincinatti. Founded 1862 by Dwight Hamilton Baldwin (1821–99). Factories also in Canada, Eng., and Ger. Developed electronic org. 1947. Acquired Bechstein co., 1963. Introduced new concert grand 1965.

Balfe, Michael (William) (*b* Dublin, 1808; *d* Rowney Abbey, Herts., 1870). Irish composer, violinist, and baritone. Lived for a time in Paris and Berlin and prod. his operas there and in St Petersburg. Sang Figaro in *Il barbiere di Siviglia* in Paris, 1827, and sang at La Scala with *Malibran in 1830s. Sang Papageno in *The Magic Flute* in Eng. at Drury Lane, 1838. First opera, *I rivali di se stessi*, was prod. Palermo 1829. He followed this with *The Siege of Rochelle* (1835), *The Maid of Artois* (1836), *Catherine Grey* (1837, the first Eng. Romantic opera without spoken dialogue), and *Falstaff* (1838), all except the last (Her Majesty's) prod. Drury Lane. His greatest success was *The *Bohemian Girl* in 1843. It contains the songs 'I dreamt that I dwelt in marble halls' and 'When other lips'. Cond. of opera at Her Majesty's, London, 1845–52.

Ball, Eric (Walter John) (*b* Kingswood, Glos., 1903; *d* Bournemouth, 1989). Eng. composer, conductor, and arranger, principally of works for brass band. Also adjudicator of band competitions. Ed. of *The British Bandsman*. Cond. Brighouse & Rastrick Band, later CWS (Manchester), Ransome & Marles, and City of Coventry Bands. Arr. Elgar's *Enigma Variations* for brass band and wrote many test-pieces.

Ball, Ernest R. (*b* Cleveland, Ohio, 1878; *d* Santa Ana, Calif., 1927). Amer. popular composer, 3 of whose songs were in the regular repertory of John *McCormack, namely *Mother Machree* (1910), *When Irish Eyes are Smiling* (1913), and *A Little Bit of Heaven* (1915). Wrote *Let the Rest of the World go by* in 1919.

Ball, (Sir) **George Thomas Thalben**. See *Thalben-Ball, George Thomas*.

Ball, Michael (*b* Manchester, 1946). Eng. composer. Works incl. *Resurrection Symphonies* (1982); org. conc. (1987); *Midsummer Music*, brass band (1991); also choral, chamber, piano mus., and songs.

ballabile (It.). In a dance style.

ballad. (1) Properly a song to be danced to (It. *ballare*, to dance) but from the 16th cent. or earlier the term has been applied to anything singable, simple, popular in style, and for solo v.

(2) The word 'ballad' was in the 19th cent. also attached to the simpler type of 'drawing-room song'—sometimes called 'Shop Ballad', possibly to distinguish it from those hawked by the ballad-seller on broadsheets. Hence the Eng. 'Ballad Concerts' inaugurated by the mus. publisher, John Boosey, in 1867.

(3) Self-contained narrative song, such as Loewe's *Edward* or Schubert's *Erlkönig*. Also applied to certain narrative operatic arias, e.g. Senta's ballad in Wagner's *Der fliegende Holländer*.

(4) Term applied in jazz to sentimental song.

ballade (Fr.). Ballad. A term given by *Chopin to a long, dramatic type of pf. piece, the mus. equivalent of a poetical ballad of the heroic type. He wrote 4—G minor, Op.23; F major, Op.38; A♭ major, Op.47; and F minor, Op.52. Brahms, Liszt, Grieg, Fauré, and others later used the title.

ballad horn. Type of saxhorn invented *c.*1870. Different makers apply the name to different varieties, but generally understood as alto hn. in E♭ or C with cup mouthpiece and 3 piston valves.

ballad opera. Opera with spoken dialogue and using popular tunes of the day provided with new words. Form originated in England with Allan Ramsay's *The Gentle Shepherd* (1725), but the success in 1728 of Gay's *The *Beggar's Opera* started the vogue for this type of entertainment which lasted for nearly 30 years. Charles Coffey's *The Devil to pay* (1731) was adapted in Ger. in 1743 as *Der Teufel ist los* and est. the *Singspiel* tradition which culminated in Mozart's *Die Entführung aus dem Serail*. There are also wider definitions of the genre; and in the 20th cent. Vaughan Williams's *Hugh the Drover* (1914) is described as a 'romantic ballad opera' by the composer although it has no spoken dialogue and does not exclusively comprise traditional tunes.

ballata (It.). One of poetic forms in It. secular songs of 14th and early 15th cents., the others being madrigal and caccia.

ballerina, ballerino (It.). Ballet dancer—female and male respectively, hence *prima ballerina*, the leading female dancer of the co., and *prima ballerina assoluta*, the undisputed leading female dancer of the co.

ballet. Entertainment in which dancers, by use of mime, etc., perform to mus. to tell a story or to express a mood. The ballet was largely developed in the courts of Fr. and It. during the 16th and 17th cents. and especially in that of Louis XIV (reigned 1643–1715), where *Lully was in charge of the mus. The ballets of this period were danced by the court itself and were very formal (gavottes, minuets, chaconnes, etc.), heavy dresses being worn, with wigs, high heels, and other trappings of court life. But the first ballet is generally held to have been the *Balet comique de la Royne* given in Paris in 1581.

Even in the days of the ballerina Camargo (1710–70), who introduced many innovations, dress was ample, skirts still falling below the knees; however, she introduced a more vigorous style involving high jumps. J. G. Noverre (1727–1810) banished the conventions hitherto ruling as to the use of mythological subjects, set order of dances, elaborate dresses, etc., and thus made himself the founder of the dramatic ballet, or *ballet d'action*. He est. the 5-act ballet as an entertainment in its own right; collab. with Gluck and Mozart on operatic ballets, and wrote an important treatise on the ballet. Other great masters of this period were Dauberval (1742–1806), Gaetano Vestris (1729–1808), and Pierre Gardel (1758–1840). Vestris was the founder of a family of *maîtres de ballet*, active in 3 generations (1747–1825), and of several important ballerinas. The Italian choreographer Salvatore Vigano (1769–1819), for whom Beethoven wrote *Die Geschöpfe des Prometheus*, continued Noverre's work. By the end of the 18th cent. the ballet had almost discarded the last of its stately court influences and had developed gymnastic virtuosity, although movement was still mainly confined to the legs and feet. Dancing on the *pointe* (on the tips of the toes) came in only about 1814; it calls for arduous practice, requires special shoes, and carries a danger of dislocation; Marie Taglioni (career from 1822 to 1847) was its first notable exponent. The Romantic Movement introduced into the ballet an attempt at ethereal informality. Costumes grew shorter and the skin-tight *Maillot*, named after its Parisian inventor, was daringly introduced.

From the mid-19th cent., spectacular ballets, of a realistic and topical character, became common, and much effective ballet mus. was written, esp. by Fr. composers: Adam's **Giselle* (1841) has remained a classic and the appearance of Delibes's **Coppélia* (1870) marks an epoch.

Ballet as an integral part of opera was at its height of popularity in the first half of the 19th cent. Some of the operas of Rossini and Donizetti incl. ballets, and Verdi, bowing to the demands of Paris, where a ballet was *de rigueur* in opera, incl. ballets in many of his operas for that capital, even writing ballet mus. for *Otello* for its Paris prod. (1894). The high priest of ballet-in-opera was Meyerbeer, and even Wagner had to introduce ballet into *Tannhäuser* to placate his Paris audiences (but enraged the blades of the Jockey Club by refusing to place it, as was customary, in the 2nd act, by which time they would have finished their coffee and cigars). The extent of the Parisian 'craze' can be judged from the fact that Berlioz's orchestration of Weber's *Invitation to the Dance* (*Aufforderung zum Tanz*, 1819) was commissioned for the 1841 prod. of *Der Freischütz*, and dances from Bizet's incidental mus. to *L'Arlésienne* were interpolated into *Carmen*.

Fr. influence on the Russ. Imperial court ths. also created a tradition of ballet in St Petersburg and Moscow to which national traditions were added. Both cities had long had their royal schs. of ballet where technique was highly polished but there was little of mus. worth for them to dance until the masterpieces of Tchaikovsky: **Swan Lake* (1876), *The *Sleeping Beauty* (1889), and **Nutcracker* (1892). The outstanding choreog. was Marius Petipa (b Marseilles, 1818; d Gurzuf, Crimea, 1910) who was principal ballet master in St Petersburg from 1862 to 1903.

The 20th cent. saw reforms and revolutionary tendencies in the development of ballet which may be identified principally but not wholly with two individuals. The Amer. Isadora Duncan (1878–1927) was inspired by Gr. classicism and by the natural movements of the birds, the waves, etc., thereby rejecting many conventional choreographical formulae. She toured Russ. and was seen by the young dancer Mikhail *Fokine (1880–1942) who was also working to free ballet from its 19th-cent. conventions, having been deeply impressed by the visit of Siamese dancers to Russ. in 1900. He achieved his ambition in collab. with the impresario and opera producer Serge *Diaghilev (1872–1929). Taking advantage of the Franco-Russ. entente and realizing that radical reforms would not be allowed in the imperial ths., Diaghilev est. his Russian Ballet (Ballets Russes) in Paris, 1909, bringing together choreogs. such as Fokine, and dancers such as *Nijinsky, Pavlova, and Karsavina. Ballet scores were commissioned from 'progressive' contemporary composers, e.g. Ravel (**Daphnis et Chloé*), Stravinsky (**Firebird*, **Petrushka*, *The *Rite of Spring*), Strauss (**Josephslegende*), and Debussy (**Jeux*). The artists Bakst and Picasso were among those commissioned to design scenery. Ballet mus. ceased to be wholly subservient to the dancers' demands. The impact of these Diaghilev prods. on Paris, London, Berlin, and other cities was electrifying and exercised considerable influence on all the arts. Diaghilev introduced 1-act ballets, making an evening from 2 or 3 short ballets. In this way there came about the ballet based on the Polovtsian Dances from Borodin's *Prince Igor*, the famous *Spectre de la rose* (to the Weber–Berlioz *Invitation to the Dance*) and, as a vehicle for Nijinsky, a ballet to the mus. of Debussy's *Prélude à L'après-midi d'un faune*. Diaghilev frequently used re-workings of mus. not comp. for dancing as the basis of successful ballets, the most famous being *Les *Sylphides* (1909), from Chopin pieces. Other composers treated in this way were Rossini, Cimarosa, Scarlatti, and Handel. Stravinsky was adept at these re-workings, as can be heard from *Pulcinella (Pergolesi and others) and *Le *Baiser de la fée* (Tchaikovsky). After the 1914–18 war, Stravinsky continued for a time to collaborate with Diaghilev but other composers who wrote ballets for him were Satie (**Parade*), Falla (**Three-Cornered Hat*) and Prokofiev (**Chout, Le Pas d'acier*, and *L'*Enfant prodigue*). Most of the outstanding figures of ballet between 1918 and 1939 came from the Diaghilev co., Serge Lifar, Léonide Massine and George *Balanchine among them. The virtuosity of dancers and the constantly developing art of choreogs. has successfully brought a vast range of non-ballet mus. into the ballet th. Examples of scores to which ballets have been devised incl. Strauss's *Till Eulenspiegel*, Tchaikovsky's 5th Sym., Brahms's 4th Sym., Berlioz's *Symphonie fantastique*, Elgar's *Enigma Variations* and Mahler's *Das Lied von der Erde*. Nevertheless the comp. of orig. ballet scores has prospered. Tchaikovsky's heir was undoubtedly Prokofiev, whose *Cinderella* and *Romeo and Juliet*, for the Bolshoy Ballet, are superb, and distinguished scores have been written for ballet by Bartók, Copland, Shostakovich, Henze, Hindemith, Britten, and others.

In Brit. ballet was imported after the days of the masque, but the impetus provided by the Diaghilev co. led to the formation of the Camargo Soc. in 1930, of whom the leading lights were the economist Maynard Keynes (married to Lydia Lopokova), his doctor brother Geoffrey Keynes, and Ninette de *Valois. Among its first prods. was Vaughan Williams's *Job*, the first large-scale modern ballet score (though it is designated 'a masque for dancing') by a Brit. composer. The Camargo Soc. became the Vic-Wells Ballet, under the aegis of Lilian *Baylis at the Old Vic and SW, later the SW Ballet, and eventually the Royal Ballet (based on CG). Leading figures assoc. with Brit. ballet have incl. Constant *Lambert, Frederick *Ashton, John Cranko, Antony Tudor, Anton Dolin, Alicia Markova, Robert Helpmann, Marie Rambert, Margot Fonteyn, Rudolf Nureyev, and Kenneth MacMillan. Beside the Royal Ballet, leading cos. working regularly in Brit. are Birmingham Royal Ballet, Ballet Rambert, and Northern Ballet. Orig. ballet scores by Brit. composers incl. Bliss's *Checkmate* and *Miracle in the Gorbals*, Britten's *Prince of the Pagodas*, Walton's *The Quest*, Arnold's *Homage to the Queen* and *Solitaire*, and Maxwell Davies's *Salome*.

In Europe after Diaghilev, and contemporary with him, leading influences in varying degrees were the Paris-based Ballets Suédois, under Rolf de Maré (1886–1964), the Ger. choreog. Kurt Jooss's Ballets Jooss, for which the mus. was written by one composer, Frederick Cohen (1904- 67), Rudolf von Laban (1879–1958), Mary Wigman (1886–1973), Ida Rubinstein (c.1885–1960), Emile Jaques-Dalcroze (1865–1950) and Maud Allan (1883–1956). There has been a vigorous expansion of ballet and ballet potentialities in the USA. Ex-Diaghilev associates such as Balanchine worked there and other pioneers of ballet there incl. Ruth St Denis (1877–1968), Ted Shawn (1891–1972), and Adolph Bolm (1884–1951). Later the chief figures were Mary Wigman and especially Martha Graham (1894–1991), Paul Taylor (*b* 1930), and Louis Horst (1884–1964) who was director of the Denishawn Sch. 1915–25 and mus. dir. for the Graham co. 1926–48. Amer. composers have been prolific in writing mus. specifically for dancing and while ballet has invaded the popular Broadway musicals such as *On Your Toes*, *Oklahoma!*, and *Kiss Me, Kate*, avant-garde ballet developments have kept pace with those in music. The collab. between the composer John *Cage and the choreog.

Merce Cunningham (*b* 1919) pioneered new forms of presenting ballet as, to quote Cage, 'an activity of movement, sound, and light', using non-sequential, non-mimetic movement. The aleatory trend in mus. has had its parallel in ballet, where all formal organization has been thrown overboard. Elec. scores have become commonplace, and slide and film projections are used. As mus. is now prod. without instr. or performers, ballet can be prod. without dancers, by means of electro-cybernetic devices. Mention should also be made, if briefly, of the influence on ballet of jazz, Latin-Amer. mus., African tribal dances, and the stylized ballets of China and Japan.

ballet de cour (Fr.). Fr. court ballet of the 17th cent. The *Balet comique de la royne*, comp. for the marriage festivities of the Duc de Joyeuse and the sister of the queen of Fr. in 1581 is considered the first of its kind. Numerous other ballets were comp. for the Fr. court up to the 1670s, when they were gradually superseded by Lully's operas.

balletomane. 20th-cent. term meaning one who is extremely enthusiastic about ballet, hence also 'balletomania'.

Ballet Russe de Monte Carlo. Ballet co. formed in 1932, and orig. called Ballets Russes de Monte Carlo, in effort to continue *Diaghilev's work. It was headed by Colonel Wassili de Basil and René Blum, with Fokine, Massine, and Balanchine as choreogs. Later de Basil split away from Blum and Massine and his co. disbanded in Paris in 1947, though it was revived for a year in London, 1951. The Blum-Massine co., under the name Ballet Russe de Monte Carlo, went to USA at outbreak of World War II where it toured N. Amer. until disbandment in 1962.

Ballets Russes (Russian Ballet). See under *Ballet* and *Diaghilev*.

ballett [ballet]. A form of *madrigal orig. so called because the performers also danced to the tune. Thought to have been invented by the It. 16th-cent. composer Gastoldi who in 1591 pubd. *balletti a cinque voci* with instructions for dancing and instr. accs. In Eng. the ballett was popularized by *Morley and *Weelkes, whose first colls. were pubd. respectively in 1595 and 1598. Balletts differ from madrigals in their regular rhythm and (an indispensable feature) the singing of 'fal-lal-la' between the clauses.

Ballif, Claude (André François) (*b* Paris, 1924; *d* Poisson, 2004). Fr. composer and teacher. Studied at Bordeaux 1942–51, Paris Cons. (under Messiaen), and Berlin Hochschule (with Blacher). Taught in Berlin and Hamburg 1955–8. Worked at Fr. radio's *Groupe de Recherches Musicales* 1959–61. Teacher at Reims Cons. 1965–8; prof. of analysis Paris Cons. 1971–90, and assoc. prof. of comp. 1982–90. Author of a book on Berlioz (1968).
Works incl.:

ORCH.: *La Vie du mond qui vient*, sym., ch., orch.
(1953, rev. 1972–3); *Voyage de mon oreille* (1957);

Fantasio (1957, rev. 1976); *Ceci et cela* (1959–65); *A cor et à cri* (1962); *Poème de la félicité* (1978); *Conc. Symphonique I* (1976), *II* (1984), *III* (1988), *IV* (1999); *Au clair de la lune bleue* (2000–1).

INSTR(S).: *Antienne No.1 à la Ste. Vierge*, 6 singers, 8 instr. (1952, rev. 1956); 5 str. qts. (1955, 1958, 1959, 1987, 1989); 4 str. trios (1956, 1959, 1969, 1992); vn. sonata (1957); 4 quintets (1952–60); *Phrases sur le souffle*, alto, 8 instr. (1958); quintet, fl., ob., str. trio (1958); fl. sonata (1958); *Mouvement pour 2*, fl., pf. (1959); double trio, fl., ob., vc., and vn., cl., hn. (1961); *Solfeggietto*, Nos. 1–19, various solo instr. (1961–99); *Imaginaire I*, fl., cl., tpt., tb., vn., vc., hp. (1963); sax. qt. (1995).

CHORAL: *Requiem*, 8 solo vv., 5 ch., orch. (1953–68); *Prières*, ch. (1971); *Chapelet*, ch. (1971); *Le Livre du serviteur*, ten., ch., orch. (1984).

KEYBOARD: 4 sonatas, org. (1956); sonatas: Nos. 1–6, pf. (1957–94).

Balling, Michael (*b* Heidingsfeld-am-Main, 1866; *d* Darmstadt, 1925). Ger. conductor who began as violist. Founded mus. sch. in NZ, 1892. Violist in Mainz, Schwerin, and Bayreuth. Ass. cond. at Bayreuth, 1896–1902, and cond. *Der Ring*, *Tristan und Isolde*, and *Parsifal* (his début) 1904–25. Cond. Karlsruhe Opera 1903–9. Cond. *The Ring* in Eng. with Denhof Co., Edinburgh, 1910. Cond. Hallé Orch., 1912–14; mus. dir. Darmstadt from 1919. Ed. of Breitkopf & Härtel Wagner Edition from 1912.

ballo (It.). Ball, dance; so *tempo di ballo*, which can mean (*a*) at a dancing speed, or (*b*) a dance-style movement.

Ballo in Maschera, Un (A Masked Ball). Opera in 3 acts by Verdi to lib. by Somma based on Scribe's lib. for Auber's *Gustave III ou Le Bal masqué*. Comp. 1857–8. Prod. Rome 1859, NY and London 1861, NY Met 1869. Events of the opera are based on assassination of King Gustavus III of Sweden in 1792. The Naples censor forbade regicide on the opera stage and ordered Verdi to adapt his mus. to a new lib. He refused, but Rome agreed to stage the opera if the locale was moved outside Europe. Verdi and Somma thereupon changed Sweden to Boston, Mass., before the War of Independence. In Copenhagen 1935 (and at CG 1952) the action was replaced in Sweden and the characters resumed their orig. (and historical) names. These, with the Boston version equivalents in brackets, are: Gustavus (Riccardo, Earl of Warwick); Count Anckarstroem (Renato); Mme Arvidson (Ulrica); Count Ribbing (Samuel); Count Horn (Tom). Only the heroine, Amelia, and the page Oscar were unaffected by the change. Other operas on this subject are *Auber's *Gustave III* (Paris 1833), *Gabussi's *Clemenza di Valois* (Venice 1841), and *Mercadante's *Il reggente* (Turin 1843).

Balsam, Artur (*b* Warsaw, 1906; *d* NY, 1994). Polish-born pianist. Début Łódź 1918. Settled in USA and taught at various academies. Distinguished chamber-mus. player. Comp. cadenzas for about 12 of Mozart's concs.

Baltsa, Agnes (*b* Lefkas, 1944). Greek mezzo-soprano. Won first Callas Scholarship. Frankfurt Opera 1968–71, making début as Cherubino (*Le nozze di Figaro*). Débuts: Vienna 1970; Deutsche Oper, Berlin, 1970; Salzburg Fest. 1970; Amer. (Houston) 1971; La Scala 1976; CG 1976; NY Met 1979. Outstanding Carmen, Composer, Dorabella, and Dido in *Les Troyens*.

Bamberger, Carl (*b* Vienna, 1902; *d* NY, 1987). Austrian-born conductor and teacher. Cond. opera in Danzig, Darmstadt, and Russia 1924–31, before settling in USA in 1937. Mus. dir., spring fest., Columbia, S.Car., 1942–50. Cond. Montreal Chamber Concerts 1950–2. Founder-cond. Mannes Coll. Orch. 1938–75. Author of *The Conductor's Art* (1965).

Bamberg Symphony Orchestra. Orch. based in Bamberg, Bavaria, founded 1946 from the Prague Deutsche Philharmonie. Prin. conds. have incl. Herbert Albert (1947–8); Eugen Jochum (1948–9); Joseph Keilberth (1949–68); Jochum (1969–78); James Loughran (1978–83); Witold Rowicki (1983–6); Horst Stein 1986–96; Jonathan Nott from 2000. Resident orch. Edinburgh Fest. 2005.

bamboo pipe. Simple instr. of the *recorder type, introduced into Amer. schs. in the 1920s and later into those of Brit., the players usually making their own instr. Vaughan Williams wrote a *Suite* (1939) for treble, alto, ten., and bass pipes.

bamboula. (1) Primitive Negro tambourine in use in the West Indies.
(2) Dance to which this is the acc.

Bamert, Matthias (*b* Ersigen, Switz., 1942). Swiss conductor, oboist, and composer. Was prin. oboist, Salzburg Mozarteum Orch. 1965–9. Salzburg Fest. début 1966 (as oboist). Ass. cond. Amer. SO, NY, 1970–1, with *Stokowski. On cond. staff Cleveland Orch. 1971. Mus. dir. Basle Radio SO 1977–83. Prin. cond. London Mozart Players 1993–2000. Comps. incl. cor ang. concertino (1966).

Bampton, Rose (*b* Lakewood, Ohio, 1907). Amer. soprano (at first mezzo-soprano). Début Chautauqua 1928. Début NY Met 1932, member of Met 1932–50. CG début 1937. Buenos Aires 1942–50. Taught at Juilliard Sch. from 1974.

Banalités (Banalities). Song-cycle by Poulenc to 5 poems by Guillaume Appollinaire, comp. 1940. Titles are: *Chanson d'Orkenise, Hôtel, Fagnes de Wallonie, Voyage à Paris, Sanglots*.

Banchieri, Adriano (*b* Bologna, 1568; *d* Bologna, 1634). It. composer, organist, and theorist. Org., S. Michele, Bosco, and of Monte Oliveto, where in 1613 he became abbot. His *L'organo suonarino*, pubd. Venice 1605, contains first precise rules for accompanying from a figured bass. In *Moderna practica musicale* (Venice 1613) he discusses alterations necessary because of the influence of figured bass on ornaments in singing. Comp. much church mus., also 'Intermedi' for comedies. His *La pazzia senile* (1598), based on the *commedia dell'arte* character Pantaloon, is regarded as almost the first comic opera. He was pioneer of fantasies for instr. ens.

band. A numerous body of instr. players, e.g. brass, dance, military, steel, and perc. bands. Rarely now applied to full sym. orch except affectionately (Hallé Band). Also applied to sections of the orch., e.g. str. band and, particularly, wind band. Thus when Berlioz in his *Requiem* and Walton in *Belshazzar's Feast* require extra brass 'bands', they mean brass sections, not a full complement à la Black Dyke Mills.

bandoneon. Argentinian type of *accordion. Instead of a kbd. it has buttons producing single notes.

bandora. Eng. wire-str. mus. instr. similar to lute invented by John Rose of Bridewell in 1561. A bass instr. with sonorous quality of sound, it was used to acc. the v. by such composers as J. *Mundy and *Peerson and works for solo bandora survive. Orig. had 6 courses but a 7th was added in 17th cent. Name possibly derived from Sp. *bandurria*.

bandurria. Sp. type of flat-backed guitar, known as early as 14th cent. as *mandurria*. 3-course (sometimes 4 or 5) instr. shaped like *rebec and played with plectrum.

banjo. Instr. of the same general type as the *guitar, but the resonating body is of parchment strained over a metal hoop and it has an open back. There are from 4 to 9 str. (usually 5 or 6), passing over a low bridge and 'stopped' against a fingerboard, which is often without *frets; one is a *melody string* (thumb string, or *chanterelle*), the others providing a simple chordal acc. Some examples have gut str. (played with the finger-tips) and others wire str. (played with a plectrum). Used by Gershwin in *Porgy and Bess* and by Delius in *Koanga. The origin of this instr. is supposed to be Africa, and it was in use among the slaves of S. USA; then, in the 19th cent., it became the accepted instr. of 'Negro *Minstrels' and in the 20th found a place in jazz bands. These last sometimes used a *Tenor Banjo*, with a different scheme of tuning (resembling that of the vn. family). The *Zither Banjo* is of small size and has wire str.

banjolin. Instrument of the banjo type, but with a short, fretted neck, like that of a mandoline. It has 4 single (or pairs of) str., played with a plectrum.

Banks, Don (Donald Oscar) (*b* Melbourne, 1923; *d* Sydney, NSW, 1980). Australian composer. Worked in Australia as jazz pianist and arranger. Several film scores. Met Milton *Babbitt in 1952 and followed his excursions into elec. mus. Mus. dir., Goldsmiths' College, London Univ., 1969–71. Head of comp. and elec. mus. studies, Canberra Sch. of Mus. from 1974. Prin. works incl. concs. for vn. (1968), hn. (1965); *Settings from Roget*, jazz singer, jazz qt. (1966); *Assemblies*, orch. (1966); *Tirade*, mez., pf., harp, perc. (1968); Psalm 70, sop., chamber orch.; *Divisions*, orch.; *Nexus*, orch., jazz quintet; *Commentary*, pf., tape; *Prospects* (1973).

Banner of St George, The. Ballad for ch. and orch., Op.33, by Elgar. Text by Shapcott Wensley. Comp. 1896–7. F.p. London 1897.

Bantock, (Sir) **Granville** (*b* Westbourne Park, London, 1868; *d* London, 1946). Eng. composer, cond., and educationist. Toured as cond. of a theatrical co. and became mus. dir. at New Brighton, nr. Liverpool, where he gave remarkable concerts of mus. by contemp. Brit. composers. Among first Eng. champions of mus. of Sibelius, whose 3rd sym. is ded. to him. From 1900 Prin. of Sch. of Mus. in Birmingham and from 1908 Prof. of Mus., Birmingham Univ.; in 1934 became Chairman of Corporation of TCL. Knighted 1930.

His orch. mus. is extremely brilliantly scored in a romantic manner but has not held its place in the repertory apart from occasional perfs. of his ov. *Pierrot of the Minute* and his tone-poem after Browning *Fifine at the Fair*. Prolific composer of part-songs for competitive fests., and his most ambitious works were 2 unacc. choral syms., *Atalanta in Calydon* (Manchester 1912) and *Vanity of Vanities* (Liverpool 1914) and a 3-part setting for cont., ten., and bass soloists, ch., and orch. of *Omar Khayyám* (1906, 1907, 1909). Other comps. incl.:

STAGE: *Caedmar*, opera (1893); *The Pearl of Iran*, opera (1894); *Eugene Aram*, unfinished opera (1896); *Hippolytus*, incid. mus. (1908); *Electra*, incid. mus. (1909); *The Great God Pan*, ballet (1915); *Salome*, incid. mus. (1918); *The Seal-Woman*, opera (1924); *Macbeth*, incid. mus. (1926).

ORCH.: *Elegiac Poem*, vc., orch. (1898); *Helena Variations* (1899); *English Scenes* (1900); Tone-poems: *Dante* (1901, rev. as *Dante and Beatrice*, 1910); *Fifine at the Fair* (1901); *Hudibras* (1902); *The Witch of Atlas* (1902); *Lalla Rookh* (1902); *Sapphic Poem*, vc., orch. (1906); ov. *The Pierrot of the Minute* (1908); *From the Scottish Highlands*, str. (1913); *Dramatic Poem*, vc., orch. (1914); *Hebridean Symphony* (1915); *Pagan Symphony* (1923–8); *Celtic Symphony*, str., 6 hps. (1940); *Overture to a Greek Comedy* (1941); *The Funeral* (1946).

CHORUS AND ORCH.: *The Fire Worshippers*, soloists, ch., orch. (1892); *The Blessed Damozel*, reciter, orch. (1892); *The Time Spirit*, ch., orch. (1902); *Ferishtah's Fancies*, v., orch. (1905); *Sappho*, v., orch. (1906); *Sea Wanderers*, ch., orch. (1906); *Omar Khayyám*, cont., ten., bass, ch., orch. (1906–9); *Song of Liberty*, ch., orch. (1914); *Song of Songs*, soloists, ch., orch. (1922); *Pagan Chants*, v., orch. (1917–26); *The *Pilgrim's Progress*, soloists, ch., orch. (1928); *Prometheus Unbound*, ch., orch. (1936); *Thomas the Rhymer*, v., orch. (1946).

UNACC. VOICES: Mass in B♭, male vv. (1903); *Atalanta in Calydon*, sym. for ch. (1911); *Vanity of Vanities*, sym. for ch. (1913); *A Pageant of Human

Life, sym. for ch. (1913); *7 Burdens of Isaiah*, male vv. (1927); *5 Choral Songs and Dances from The Bacchae*, female vv. (1945).

CHAMBER MUSIC: str. qt. (*c*.1899); *Pibroch*, vc., hp. (1917); va. sonata (1919); vc. sonata (1924); 3 vn. sonatas (1929, 1932, 1940); 2 vc. sonatas (1940, 1945).

Also many pf. pieces, 40 song-cycles, nearly 50 solo songs, works for brass band.

Bär, Olaf (*b* Dresden, 1957). Ger. baritone. Member, Dresden Kreuzchor 1966–75. Prin. bar. Dresden State Opera. Emerged in 1970s as one of finest *Lieder* singers. Opera début Dresden 1981. Brit. recital début, 1983; CG 1986; Glyndebourne 1987; Amer. 1987; Salzburg Fest. 1990.

bar, bar line. The vertical line marked on a stave to denote the point of metrical division is actually the bar but in modern usage has come to be called the bar line, while the space between such lines is the bar itself. Thus, '3 beats to the bar'. In Amer. parlance, a bar is called a measure, and a bar means a bar line. 2 vertical lines close together are, in Eng., a double bar, not double bar line.

Barbarie, orgue de. Small mechanical org. played by turning a handle, at one time commonly found in Eng. streets.

Barber, Samuel (*b* West Chester, Penn., 1910; *d* NY, 1981). Amer. composer. Played pf. at age 6 and composed when 7. At 14 entered Curtis Inst. as one of first charter students, studying comp. under Scalero 1925–34, pf. under Isabelle Vengerova 1926–31, and singing under Emilio de Gogorza 1926–30. In 1928 formed a lasting and fruitful friendship with Gian Carlo *Menotti. From 1933 his comps. began to be played, notably his setting of Arnold's *Dover Beach*, in which he sang the bar. part, and his Vc. Sonata, in which he played the pf. In 1935 won a Pulitzer scholarship and in 1936 the Amer. Academy's *Prix de Rome*. His first sym. was given its f.p. in Rome that year, cond. Molinari. Toscanini cond. f.ps. of his *Adagio for Strings* (orig. the slow movement of his str. qt.) and the first *Essay for Orchestra* in 1938 and in subsequent years f.ps. of his works were given in NY, Boston, and Philadelphia under Walter, Koussevitzsky, Leinsdorf, Mitropoulos, Ormandy, and Mehta. His 4-act opera *Vanessa*, to lib. by Menotti, was perf. at the NY Met in 1958 and another opera *Antony and Cleopatra*, to lib. by Zeffirelli, was commissioned for the opening of the new Metropolitan in the Lincoln Center, NY, in Sept. 1966.

Barber's mus. is in the European traditional line rather than specifically 'American'. Conservative in idiom, it is melodic, elegant, and brilliant. His lyricism is best heard in *Vanessa* and in *Knoxville: Summer of 1915*, and the *Vc.* Sonata, and his romanticism in *Dover Beach*, the Vc. Sonata, and the Sym. No.1. His Pf. Sonata, first played by Horowitz, is a bravura work. The operas met with a poor initial response which is in process of being reversed, and the concs. and songs are highly effective. Prin. works:

OPERAS: **Vanessa*, Op.32 (1957, rev. 1964); *A Hand of Bridge*, Op.35 (1959); *Antony and Cleopatra*, Op.40 (1966, rev. 1974).

BALLETS: *Medea*, Op.23 (1946, rev. as *Cave of the Heart*, 1947); *Souvenirs*, Op.28 (1952).

ORCH.: sym. No.1, Op.9 (1936), No.2, Op.19 (1944); *Overture to School for Scandal*, Op.5 (1931); *Music for a Scene from Shelley*, Op.7 (1933); *Essay No.1*, Op.12 (1937), *No.2*, Op.17 (1942), *No.3*, Op.47 (1978); *Adagio for Strings*, Op.11 (1938) (orch. from str. qt. Op.11); *Mutations from Bach*, brass, timp. (1967); *Fadograph of a Yestern Scene*, Op.44 (1971).

CONCERTOS: vn., Op.14 (1939); vc., Op.22 (1945); pf., Op.38 (1962); *Capricorn Concerto*, Op.21 (for chamber orch.) (1944); *Canzonetta*, ob., str., Op.48 (1977–8).

VOCAL AND CHORAL: *Dover Beach*, Op.3 (bar. or cont. with str. qt. or str. orch.) (1931); *A Stopwatch and an Ordnance Map*, Op.15, male vv., timp. (1939); **Knoxville: Summer of 1915*, Op.24, sop., orch. (1947, arr. for sop. and chamber orch. 1950); *Prayers of Kierkegaard*, Op.30, sop., orch. (1954); *Andromache's Farewell*, Op.39, sop., orch. (1962); *Agnus Dei* (1967, choral vers. of *Adagio for Strings*).

CHAMBER MUSIC: *Serenade*, Op.1, str. qt. (1928, arr. for str. orch. 1944); vc. sonata, Op.6 (1932); str. qt., Op.11 (1936); *Excursions*, Op.20, pf. (1942–4); pf. sonata, Op.26 (1949); *Souvenirs*, Op.28, pf., 4 hands (1951, arr. for pf. solo, for 2 pfs. and for orch., 1952); *Summer Music*, Op.31 (woodwind quintet) (1955); *Canzone (Elegy)*, Op.38a, fl. or vn., pf. (1958).

He also comp. many songs, incl. *10 Hermit Songs*, Op.29 to Irish texts (1952–3).

Barber of Bagdad, The (Cornelius). See *Barbier von Bagdad, Der*.

Barber of Seville, The (Rossini; also Paisiello). See *Barbiere di Siviglia, Il*.

Barber's Shop Music. One of the regular haunts of mus. in the 16th and 17th cents. was the barber's shop. Here customers awaiting their turn found some simple instr. on which they could strum. The barbers themselves, waiting between customers, took up the instr. and thus came to possess some repute as performers. In Eng. lit. of the 16th and 17th cents. allusions to barbers as musicians are numerous. The mus. proclivities of barbers ceased in Eng. in the earlier part of the 18th cent. The tradition was maintained longer in Amer. where 'barber-shop harmony', implying a rather banal style of close harmony singing, has enjoyed a 20th-cent. revival.

Barbican. District in City of London where arts and conference centre is situated. Arts centre, opened in 1982 at a cost of £143 million, includes concert-hall, theatre and studios, lending and reference library, art gallery, sculpture court, and cinema. *Guildhall School of Music and Drama housed on the site since 1977.

Barbiere di Siviglia, Il (The Barber of Seville). (1) opera buffa in 2 acts by Rossini, to lib. by Sterbini based on Beaumarchais's comedy (1775). To differentiate it from Paisiello's opera of the same name it was called *Almaviva, ossia L'inutile precauzione* (Almaviva, or the Useless Precaution) at its f.p. (Rome 1816). Perf. London 1818, NY 1819. The famous ov. had already been used by Rossini for 2 other operas (*Aureliano in Palmira* and *Elisabetta, Regina d'Inghilterra*).

(2) Paisiello's opera is in 4 acts to a lib. by Petrosellini. Prod. St Petersburg 1782, London 1789, New Orleans 1805. Several modern revivals.

(3) Operas on this subject were also comp. by Elsperger (1783), Benda (1785), Schulz (1786), Morlacchi (1816), and Graffigna (1879).

Barbieri, Fedora (*b* Trieste, 1920; *d* Florence, 2003). It. mezzo-soprano. Operatic débuts in Trieste and Florence, 1940. Sang in opera cos. at Rome 1941–2, Milan (La Scala) 1943, Florence 1945. CG 1950 (with La Scala co.), and 1957–8. NY Met 1950–4 and 1956–75. Salzburg Fest. 1952.

Barbier von Bagdad, Der (The Barber of Bagdad). Comedy-opera in 2 acts by Cornelius to his own lib. based on *The Tale of the Tailor* from *1001 Nights*. Prod. Weimar, under Liszt, 1 perf. 1858; NY and Chicago 1890; London 1891 (RCM students). Most perfs. since 1884 have been of a rev. and re-orchestration by *Mottl which he made that year for Karlsruhe.

Barbirolli (Lady) (*née* Rothwell), **Evelyn** (*b* Wallingford, 1911). Eng. oboist and teacher. 2nd wife of Sir John *Barbirolli whom she married 1939. Oboist, CG Touring Orch. 1931–2, Scottish Orch. 1933–7, Glyndebourne Opera Orch. 1934–8, LSO 1935–9. Thereafter soloist and recitalist, member of various ens. Gave f.p. in modern times of Mozart's oboe concerto (K314), Salzburg, 1948. Author of several books on ob. technique. Prof. of ob., RAM, 1971–87. OBE 1984.

Barbirolli, (Sir) **John** (Giovanni Battista) (*b* London, 1899; *d* London, 1970). Eng. cond., of It.-Fr. parentage. First public appearance as solo cellist, London 1911. Member of Queen's Hall Orch. 1916. Served in army 1918. After war, free-lance cellist and member of str. qt. Formed own str. orch. to conduct, 1924. Appointed staff cond., BNOC, 1926. Cond at CG 1929 and became prin. cond. CG touring co. 1929–33. Cond., Scottish Orch., Glasgow 1933–6, NY Phil.-Sym. Orch. 1936–42. Returned to Eng. 1943 as cond., Hallé Orch., Manchester, where he remained until his death, lifting the orch. to new heights and taking it on several foreign tours. Salzburg Fest. début 1946 (Vienna PO). Prin. cond. Houston SO 1961–7. Guest cond. of orchs. throughout the world, esp. Berlin PO, Boston SO, and Chicago SO, etc. Famed interpretations of Mahler, Elgar,

Vaughan Williams, Sibelius, Puccini, and Verdi, but successful in remarkably wide repertory. Cond. f. Eng. p. of Berg's *Chamber Concerto* (London 1931); f.ps. of Warlock's *Serenade* (London 1925); Britten's Violin Concerto (NY 1940) and *Sinfonia da Requiem* (NY 1941); Vaughan Williams's *Sinfonia Antartica* (Manchester 1953) and 8th Sym., dedicated to him (Manchester 1956); Fricker's 1st Sym. (Cheltenham 1950); and several other Eng. syms. and concs. at Cheltenham Fest. 1950–9. Cond. opera at CG 1951–4, incl. *Aida* with Callas, *Tristan und Isolde* with Sylvia Fisher and Ludwig Suthaus, and *Orfeo* with Kathleen Ferrier (1953, her last public appearances). Cond. *Aida* (Rome 1969). Also arr. mus. by Purcell, Corelli, Pergolesi, and Elizabethan composers for orch. and as ob. concs. for his wife Evelyn *Barbirolli whom he married 1939. Knighted 1949, CH 1969. Hon. Freeman of Manchester, 1958.

barcarolle (Fr. from It.; Ger. *Barkarole*). Boat song or an instr. comp. with a steady rhythm (in compound duple or compound quadruple time) reminiscent of songs of the Venetian gondoliers or *barcaruoli*.

Barcarolle from *Les contes d'Hoffmann*. Retrieved by Offenbach from his much earlier opera, *Die Rheinnixen*, 1864 (a failure). In this it figured as a Goblin's Song.

Bard, The (Barden). Tone-poem for orch., Op.64, by *Sibelius, comp. 1913, rev. 1914. F.p. Helsinki 1913, cond. Sibelius. F.p. in England 1935 (broadcast, cond. Boult, public 1938, cond. Beecham).

Bardi, Giovanni de', Count of Vernio (*b* Florence, 1534; *d* Rome, 1612). It. nobleman and soldier in whose palace in Florence a group of poets and musicians met regularly in the later years of the 16th cent., this giving rise to what are considered to have been the first operatic perfs. He wrote at least 2 libs. and comp. madrigals. See *Camerata*.

Bárdos, Lajos (*b* Budapest, 1899; *d* Budapest, 1986). Hung. composer, conductor, and scholar. His work as choral cond. raised Hung. standards to world-class. Toured abroad with choirs. Wrote major studies of Gregorian chant and of Liszt, Bartók, and Kodály. Comp. mainly choral works and made many folk-song arrs.

Barenboim, Daniel (*b* Buenos Aires, 1942). Israeli pianist and conductor. Taught pf. by his mother, then his father. Début Buenos Aires 1949. Family moved to Israel 1952. Début as conc. soloist, Paris 1955. Brit. début, Bournemouth 1955, London Jan. 1956, and NY 1957. Has several times given recital series of all Beethoven pf. sonatas (Israel, S. Amer. 1960, London 1967, 1970, NY 1970). Cond. début in Israel 1962. Salzburg Fest. début (as pianist) 1965 (Mozart conc. K491, Vienna PO cond. Mehta); (as cond.) 1990 (Berlin PO). Worked as cond.-soloist with ECO 1965 and cond. New Philharmonia

Orch. 1967, Hallé and LSO (US tour) 1968, Berlin Phil. Orch. 1969, NYPO 1970. Mus. dir. Orchestre de Paris 1975–88, Chicago SO 1991–2006. Cond., Deutsche Staatsoper, Berlin, 1992–2002 (début *Parsifal*). Début in opera, Edinburgh Fest. 1973 (*Don Giovanni*). Cond. *Tristan und Isolde*, Bayreuth, 1981, *Der Ring des Nibelungen*, 1988. Married cellist Jacqueline *du Pré, 1967, and settled in Eng., pursuing highly successful career both as pianist and cond. Acc. Janet Baker and Fischer-Dieskau in recitals and chamber-mus. player with Zukerman, Perlman, and (until 1976) Piatigorsky. Awarded Bruckner Medal. Founded West-Eastern Divan Workshop and Orchestra 1999, based in Seville since 2002. Autobiography, *A Life in Music* (1991, rev. 2002). First musician to give annual BBC Reith Lectures, 2006.

Bärenhäuter, Der (The Bear Skinner). Opera in 3 acts by Siegfried *Wagner to his own lib. Prod. Munich, 1899.

Bärenreiter-Verlag (Kassel). Ger. publishers. Founded Augsburg 1924 by Karl Vötterle. Emphasis on early mus.; many musicological publications including the monumental encyclo- pedia, *Die Musik in Geschichte und Gegenwart* ed. *Blume (17 vols., 1949–87). Moved to Kassel, 1927.

Baring-Gould, Sabine (*b* Exeter, 1834; *d* Lew Trenchard, Devon, 1924). Eng. author, folk-song collector, and rector. Compiled (with Rev. H. Fleetwood Shephard) *Songs and Ballads of the West* (1889–91). Wrote words of popular hymns (e.g. *Onward, Christian Soldiers*, 1865).

bariolage (Fr.). Rapid alternation of open and stopped str. in vn.-playing. The word means 'odd mixture of colours'.

baritone. Male v. roughly midway in compass between ten. and bass and sometimes combining elements of both. Normal range from A to f♯'. But in It. and Fr. opera bars. are sometimes required to sing up to a♭'. The bass-bar. (e.g. Wagner's Wotan and Hans Sachs) has a range A♭–f'.

baritone horn. See *saxhorn*.

Barlow, David (Frederick) (*b* Rothwell, Northants., 1927; *d* Newcastle upon Tyne, 1975). Eng. composer and teacher. Senior lect. Newcastle upon Tyne Univ. from 1968. Comps. include 2 syms., prelude *The Tempest*, church operas *David and Bathsheba* (1969) and *Judas* (1974), and chamber mus.

Barlow, Wayne (*b* Elyria, Ohio, 1912; *d* Rochester, NY, 1995). Amer. composer and author. Taught at Eastman 1937–78, becoming dir. of EMS. Comps. incl. religious choral works (*7 Seals of Revelation*, cantata, SATB, ch., orch., 1989), orch. works (*Sinfonietta*, sax. conc.), *Frontiers* for band (1982), works incorporating pre-recorded tape (*Sonic Pictures*, 1971; Psalm 97, 1971; *Dialogues*, 1969; *Moonflight*, 1970; *Soundscapes*, 1972), and instr. works (4 *Chorale Voluntaries*, org., 1979–80; *Sonatina*, fl., cl., vc., hp., 1984).

Bärmann, Heinrich Joseph (*b* Potsdam, 1784; *d* Munich, 1847). Ger. clarinettist for whom Weber's cl. works were comp. Prin. cl. of Munich Court Orch. Comp. especially for combinations incl. his instr. His son Karl (*b* Munich, 1811; *d* Munich, 1885), composer and clarinettist, toured with him and succeeded him in court orch. Wrote *Clarinet Method*. Karl's son, also Karl (*b* Munich, 1839; *d* Boston, Mass., 1913) was pianist and pupil of Liszt. Settled Boston 1881.

Barnard's Collection. Valuable and distinguished coll. of mus. in use in Brit. cath. services in the 17th cent., made by the Rev. John Barnard, a canon of St Paul's Cath. during Charles I's reign. Mus. is in 10 parts for each side of the ch., and incl. works by Tallis, Byrd, Gibbons, Morley, Weelkes, and others.

Barnby, (Sir) **Joseph** (*b* York, 1838; *d* London, 1896). Eng. organist, conductor, and composer. His finest service to mus. was during his period as organist at St Anne's, Soho, 1863–71, when he gave yearly perfs. of Bach's *St John Passion*. Cond. f.ps. in England of Dvořák's *Stabat Mater* (1883) and Wagner's *Parsifal* (in concert version, 1884). Precentor, Eton College, 1875. Prin., GSMD, 1892–6. Knighted 1892. Among his many comps., sacred and secular, the chief survivor has been the part-song *Sweet and Low*.

barn dance. Amer. rural meeting where dances are performed, perhaps taking its name from the festivities usual in the building of a new barn. But in Britain the name was applied in the late 1880s to a particular dance also known as the Military Schottische.

Barnett, John (*b* Bedford, 1802; *d* Leckhampton, 1890). Eng. composer of Prussian and Hung. parentage. Sang as alto in London theatres until age 16. Mus. dir. Olympia Th. 1832. Attempted to establish permanent Eng. opera house but after quarrels with managements and promoters, retired to Cheltenham in 1841 as singing teacher. Said to have written 2,000 songs.

Barnett, John Francis (*b* London, 1837; *d* London, 1916). Eng. composer, conductor, and pianist. Nephew of John *Barnett. Studied pf. from age 6. Won Queen's Scholarship, RAM, 1849. Soloist in Mendelssohn's D minor pf. conc., cond. Spohr, London 1853. Later became pf. teacher at RCM and GSMD. Comp. several choral works, incl. *The Ancient Mariner* (Birmingham, 1867), *The Triumph of Labour* (London, 1888), and *The Eve of St Agnes* (London, 1913). Also sym., pf. conc., and part-songs. In 1883 completed Schubert's Sym. in E from sketches.

Baroque (Fr.). Bizarre. Term applied to the ornate architecture of Ger. and Austria during the 17th and 18th cents. and borrowed to describe comparable mus. developments from about 1600 to the deaths of Bach and Handel in 1750 and 1759 respectively. It was a period in which harmonic complexity grew alongside emphasis on contrast. So, in opera, interest was transferred from recit. to aria, and in church mus. the contrasts of solo vv., ch., and orch. were developed to a high degree. In instr. mus. the period saw the emergence of the sonata, the suite, and particularly the concerto grosso, as in the mus. of Corelli, Vivaldi, Handel, and Bach. Most baroque mus. uses *basso continuo. By 'baroque organ' is meant the 18th-cent. type of instr., more brilliant in tone and flexible than its 19th-cent. counterpart. Note that 18th-cent. writers used 'baroque' in a pejorative sense to mean 'coarse' or 'old-fashioned in taste'.

Barraqué, Jean (*b* Puteaux, Seine, 1928; *d* Paris, 1973). Fr. composer. Member of French Radio's *Groupe de Recherches musicales* 1951–3. Serialist composer, developing 'proliferating series' (e.g. 2 series producing a 3rd). Complex polyphonic writing is combined with irregular rhythms. Opposed to aleatory methods. Works incl. pf. sonata (1952), cl. conc. (1968), and group of works comp. after 1956 part of, or related to, large-scale dramatic cycle *The Death of Virgil*.

Barraud, Henry (*b* Bordeaux, 1900; *d* Paris, 1997). Fr. composer. Expelled from Paris Cons. because his comps. were considered 'a bad influence' and worked under Dukas, Aubert, etc. In charge organization of mus., Paris Int. Exposition, 1937. Mus. dir., Paris Radio, 1948–65. Comps. incl. syms.; opera; oratorio *Le Mystère des Saints Innocents* (1946–7); pf. conc. (1939); fl. conc. (1962); *Rapsodie dionysienne*, orch. (1962), *Symphonie concertante* for tpt. (1966); *Études* for orch. (1967); *Une saison en enfer*, orch. (1969); saxophone qt. (1972); *Te Deum*, ch., 16 winds (1955); and *La Divine Comédie* (Dante), 5 solo vv., orch. (1972).

barré (Fr.). Barred. Method of playing a chord on the guitar, etc., with one finger laid rigidly (like a bar) across all the str. raising their pitch equally.

barrel organ. Popular misusage has conferred this term on the *street piano. The real barrel org., formerly used in churches, was a genuine automatic pipe-org. in which projections on a hand-rotated barrel brought the required notes into play. It was restricted to a no. of predetermined tunes, like a musical box.

Barrett, Richard (*b* Swansea, 1959). Brit. composer and guitarist. Took up composing 1980. Took part in comp. course at Darmstadt 1984, returning as member of staff in 1986 and 1988. Also writer on mus. and co-dir. of Ensemble Exposé. Works incl. *Essay in Radiance*, ens. (1981–3); *Invention 6*, pf. (1982); *Principia*, bar., pf. (1982–4); *Coïgitum*, mez., ens. (1983–5); *I open and close*, amp. str. qt. (1983–8); *Illuminer le temps*, amp. ens. (1984–7); *Tract*, pf. (1984–9); *Ne songe plus à fuir*, amp. vc. (1985–6); *Anatomy*, amp. ens. (1985–6); *Temptation*, ens., elec. (1986); *Alba*, bn., elec. (1986–7); *Nothing elsewhere*, va. (1987); *EARTH*, tb., perc. (1987–8); *Dark Ages*, vc. (1987–90); *Reticule*, vn. (1988); *The Unthinkable*, elec. tape (1988–9);

colloid, gui. (1988–91); *another heavenly day*, Eb cl., elec. gui., db., live elec. (1989–90); *lieder vom wasser*, sop., bcl., db., perc. (1989–90); *what remains*, fl., bcl., pf. (1990–1); *basalt*, tb. (1990–1); *praha*, vc. (1991); *negatives*, gui., tb., fl., perc., mandolins, vn., va., vc., db. (1992); *knospend-gespaltener*, cl. (1993); *vanity*, orch. (1994); *Liebestod*, 4 rec., elec. (1995–7); *Stress*, str. qt. (1997); *13 Self-Portraits*, str. qt. (2002); *No*, orch. (1999–2004).

Barrett, Thomas A. See *Stuart, Leslie*.

Barri, Odoardo [Slater, Edward] (*b* Dublin, 1844; *d* London, 1920). Irish composer of Eng. drawing-room songs (e.g. *The Boys of the Old Brigade*, 1874).

Barrington, Daines (*b* London, 1727; *d* London, 1800). Eng. lawyer who wrote essays and books on mus. and musicians incl. *Crotch, Mornington, Mozart, The Wesleys*; in 1773 pubd. *Experiments and Observations on the Singing of Birds*.

Barrios, Angel (*b* Granada, 1882; *d* Madrid, 1964). Sp. violinist; composer for orch. and the stage, also of gui. mus.

Barry, Gerald (*b* Ennid, Co. Clare, 1952). Irish composer. Lived in Ger. for 5 yrs. Taught at Univ. Coll., Cork, 1982–3. Works incl. operas *The Intelligence Park* (1982–7), *The Bitter Tears of Petra von Kant* (2002–4), and TV opera *The Triumph of Beauty and Deceit* (1994). Also much orch., chamber, and vocal mus.

Barry, John (*b* York, 1933). Eng. composer of film mus. Has had much success with scores for films and TV.

Barshay, Rudolf (*b* Labinskaya, 1924). Russ. conductor. Founder and cond. Moscow Chamber Orch. 1956–76. Left Russia 1976 and settled in Israel. Salzburg Fest. 1980. Arr. Shostakovich's 8th str. qt. for str. orch. Prin. cond. Bournemouth SO 1983–8. Mus. dir. Vancouver SO 1985–8.

Barstow, (Dame) **Josephine** (Clare) (*b* Sheffield, 1940). Eng. soprano. Début Opera for All, 1964. ENO (SW) début 1967; CG début 1969; NY Met début 1977. Created Denise in *The Knot Garden* (CG 1970) and Gayle in *The Ice Break* (CG 1977), Young Woman in *We Come to the River* (CG 1976), and Benigna in Penderecki's *Die schwarze Maske* (Salzburg, 1986, her début). Fine Salome, Jenůfa, Katerina Ismailova, etc. Sang Gutrune in *Ring*, Bayreuth 1983. Outstanding as title-role in *Gloriana*, Opera North (Leeds 1993 and CG 1994). CBE 1985. DBE 1995.

Bartered Bride, The (*Prodaná Nevěstá*; Ger. *Die verkaufte Braut*). Opera in 3 acts by Smetana to lib. by Karel Sabina. Prod. Prague 1866; Chicago 1893 (amateur); London 1895; NY Met 1909. 1st version was in 2 acts, with ov. and 20 nos. (1863–6), rev. with ballet added 1866; further rev. 1869, and 1869–70; 3 acts, with additions, 1870; fifth and final vers., with recitatives replacing spoken dialogue, 1870.

Barth, Hans (*b* Leipzig, 1897; *d* Jacksonville, Fla., 1956). Ger.-born pianist and composer. Taken to USA at age 10. Became known as recitalist, etc., and held various teaching positions. Comps. incl. opera, 2 syms., etc., some employing microtones. Invented quarter-tone pf. for which he wrote 2 concs., 10 *études*, and quintet.

Barthélemon, François Hippolyte (*b* Bordeaux, 1741; *d* London, 1808). Fr. violinist and composer. Settled London 1764 as orch. leader at the opera and remained there with exception of continental tours and residence in Dublin 1771–3. Comps. incl. 6 syms., concs., and several operas (*The Judgment of Paris* 1768, *Belphegor* 1778, etc.), and ballets. Also wrote well-known tune to Bishop Ken's Morning Hymn ('Awake my soul and with the sun'). Became close friend of Haydn during his two visits to London.

Bartlett, Ethel (*b* Epping Forest, 1896; *d* S. Barbara, Calif., 1978). Eng. pianist. Married fellow-student Rae *Robertson and with him est. int. reputation in interpretation of mus. for 2 pf. Settled in USA and in later years was teacher. Pianist with *Barbirolli (vc.) in his recitals in 1920s.

Bartók, Béla (*b* Nagyszentmiklós, Hungary (now Romania), 1881; *d* NY, 1945). Hung. composer, pianist, and folklorist. Parents were musical and mother gave him his first pf. lessons. In 1894 at Bratislava (then Pozsony) studied with the cond. Laszlo Erkel until 1899 when he entered Budapest Royal Acad. In 1902 heard a perf. of Strauss's *Also sprach Zarathustra* which stimulated his powers of comp. to such a degree that he wrote his nationalistic tone-poem *Kossuth* in 1903. By this time was travelling abroad as solo pianist in mus. by Liszt and other kbd. virtuosi. In 1905 began systematic exploration of Hungarian peasant mus. and in 1906, with his fellow-composer Kodály, pubd. a coll. of 20 folk-songs. In 1907 became prof. of pf. at the Budapest RAM. For the next decade, while his mus. was badly received in his own country, continued systematic coll. of Magyár folk-songs. In 1917 his ballet *The Wooden Prince* was successfully prod. in Budapest and led to the staging in the following year of his 1-act opera *Duke Bluebeard's Castle* (1911). In 1922 and 1923 his first 2 vn. sonatas had their f.ps. in London, and in 1923 comp. the *Dance Suite* to celebrate the 50th anniv. of the union of Buda and Pest. During the 1920s resumed career as pianist, composing several works for his own use. In 1934 was given a salaried post in the Hung. Acad. of Sciences in order that he could prepare his folk-song coll. for publication. In the spring of 1940, in view of political developments in Hungary, emigrated to USA. This was not a happy time for him; his health began to fail, his mus. was infrequently perf., and there was little demand for his services as a pianist. Nevertheless the Koussevitzky Foundation commissioned the *Concerto for Orchestra*, Yehudi Menuhin a solo vn. sonata, and William Primrose a va. conc. (left unfinished but completed by Tibór *Sérly). He

died from leukaemia.

Bartók's mus. is a highly individual blend of elements transformed from his own admirations: Liszt, Strauss, Debussy, folk-mus., and Stravinsky. Perhaps his greatest achievement lies in his 6 str. qts. in which formal symmetry and thematic unity were successfully related. But the melodic fertility and rhythmical vitality of all his mus. have ensured its consistent success since his death. Prin. comps.:

STAGE: *Duke Bluebeard's Castle (A kékszakállú herceg vára)*, Op.11, 1-act opera (1911, rev. 1912, 1918); The *Wooden Prince (A fából faragott királyfi), Op.13, 1-act ballet (1914–17); The *Miraculous Mandarin (A csodálatos mandarin), Op.19, 1-act pantomime (1918–19, orch. 1923, rev. 1924, 1926–31).

ORCH.: *Kossuth, sym.-poem (1903); Rhapsody, pf., orch., Op.1 (1904); Suite No.1, Op.3 (1905, rev. c.1920), No.2 (small orch.), Op.4 (1905–7, rev. 1920, 1943); vn. conc. No.1. (1907–8; 1st movt. rev. as No.1 of 2 Portraits), No.2 (1937- 8); 2 Portraits, Op.5 (No.1 1907–8, No.2 orch. 1911); 2 Pictures, Op.10 (1910); Romanian Dance, Op.11 (1911); 4 Pieces, Op.12 (1912, orch. 1921); Suite (3 dances), The Wooden Prince (1921–4); Suite, The Miraculous Mandarin (1919, 1927); *Dance Suite (1923); pf. conc. No.1 (1926), No.2 (1930–1), No.3 (1945); Rhapsody, vn., orch., No.1 (1928), No.2 (1928, rev. 1944); Transylvanian Dances (1931); Hungarian Sketches (1931); Hungarian Peasant Songs (1933); Music for Strings, Percussion and Celesta (1936); Divertimento, str. (1939); 2-pf. conc. (arr. of sonata for 2 pf. and perc.) (1940); Concerto for Orchestra (1942–3, rev. 1945); va. conc. (completed from draft by Sérly) (1945).

VOICE(S) & ORCH.: 3 Village Scenes, women's vv. (1926); *Cantata Profana (The 9 Enchanted Stags), ten., bar., double ch., orch. (1930); 5 Hungarian Folk Songs, low v. (1933).

CHORUS: Evening, male vv. (1903); 4 Old Hungarian Folk Songs, male vv. (1910, rev. 1912); 5 Slovak Folk Songs, male vv. (1917); 5 Hungarian Folk Songs (1930); 5 Székely Songs, male vv. (1932); 27 Traditional Choruses, children's and women's vv. (1935); From Olden Times, male vv. (1935).

CHAMBER MUSIC: pf. qt. (1898); pf. quintet (1903–4, rev. ?1920); str. qt. No.1, Op.7 (1908), No.2, Op.17 (1915–17), No.3 (1927), No.4 (1928), No.5 (1934), No.6 (1939); vn. sonatas, No.1 (1921), No.2 (1922); Rhapsody No.1, vn., pf. (1928, also orch. vers.), No.2 (1928, rev. 1945, also orch. vers.); Rhapsody, vc., pf. (1928); 44 Duos, 2 vn. (1931); sonata, 2 pf., 2 perc. (1937, orch. 1940); sonata, unacc. vn. (1944); *Contrasts, vn., cl., pf. (1938).

PIANO: 3 Klavierstücke, Op.13 (1897); Scherzo (Fantasie), Op.18 (1897); Scherzo in B minor (1900); 12 Variations (1900–1); 4 Pieces (1903); Rhapsody, Op.1 (1904, also orch. vers.); 14 Bagatelles, Op.6 (1908); 10 Easy Pieces (1908); 85 Pieces for Children (1908–9, rev. 1945); 2 Romanian Dances, Op.8a (1909–10, No.1 orch. 1911); 7 Sketches, Op.9b (1908–10); 4 Dirges, Op.9a (1909–10, No.2 orch. as No.3 of Hungarian Sketches, 1931); 3 Burlesques, Op.8c (1908–11, No.2 orch. as No.4 of Hungarian Sketches, 1931); *Allegro barbaro (1911); sonatina (1915, orch. as Transylvanian Dances, 1931);

Romanian Dances (1915, orch. 1917); *Suite*, Op.14 (1916); *3 Hungarian Folk Tunes* (c.1914–18); *15 Hungarian Peasant Songs* (1914–18, Nos. 6–12, 14–15 orch. 1933); *3 Studies*, Op.18 (1918); *8 Improvisations on Hungarian Peasant Songs*, Op.20 (1920); *Dance Suite* (1925, arr. of orch. work); sonata (1926); *Out of Doors* (1926); *9 Little Pieces* (1926); **Mikrokosmos*, 6 vols. containing 153 'progressive pieces' (1926, 1932–9).

Also many solo songs, editions of Italian kbd. mus., etc.

Bartoletti, Bruno (*b* Sesto Fiorentino, 1926). It. flautist and conductor, particularly of opera. Début Florence 1953. Mus. dir. Rome Opera 1965–73, cond. Maggio Musicale Orch. 1957–64. Introduced several 20th cent. operas to It. repertory. Amer. début Chicago 1956. Prin. cond. Chicago Lyric Opera from 1964 (art. dir. from 1975).

Bartoli, Cecilia (*b* Rome, 1966). Italian mezzosoprano. Début Rome, aged 19 (Shepherd Boy in *Tosca*). Sang in Callas memorial concert 1985. Stage début Verona 1987. Salzburg début 1993; USA 1993 (Houston). CG début 2001 (Haydn's *L'anima del filosofo*). Particularly assoc. with Rossini's music.

Bartolozzi, Bruno (*b* Florence, 1911; *d* Fiesole, 1980). It. violinist and composer. Taught at Cherubini Cons., Florence, from 1965. Comps. incl. Conc. for Orch., vn. conc., str. qt., and vocal works. Author of book *New Sounds for Woodwind*.

Bartós, Jan Zdeněk (*b* Dvůr Králové nad Labem, Cz., 1908; *d* Prague, 1981). Cz. composer and violinist. Violinist in orchs. and as soloist 1929–31. Teacher of comp. and theory, Prague Cons., from 1958. Works incl. 2 operas, va. conc., hn. conc., 4 syms., ballets, choral works, and chamber mus.

baryton. Str. instr. rather like viola da gamba but with sympathetic str. There are many works by Haydn for it, because his patron, Prince Nikolaus Esterházy, played it. Use revived in 2nd half of 20th cent.

Barzun, Jacques (*b* Créteil, Val-de-Marne, 1907). Fr.-born historian, critic, and musicologist. Settled in USA 1919. Lect. at Columbia Univ., NY, 1927, Prof. 1945, Provost 1958–67. Authority on Berlioz, about whom he has written extensively.

Bashmet, Yuri (*b* Rostov, 1953). Russ. violist and conductor. Won Munich int. va. comp. 1976. Soon became soloist with leading European orchs. Formed chamber orch., Moscow Soloists, 1986, with which he toured Europe (Eng. 1988, Salzburg Fest. début 1989). Gave f.p. of Schnittke va. conc., Amsterdam 1986. London recital début 1989.

Baskische Trommel (Ger.). Basque drum, i.e. tambourine.

Basques. Various Basque dances. *Pas de Basque* (Fr.) is sometimes a general term with the same

meaning, but it may indicate a particular dance of the Basque peasantry—one with very varied rhythms.

bass. (1) Lowest male voice—see *basso*.
(2) Lowest note or part in a chord.
(3) Lowest regions of mus. pitch.
(4) Lowest of a family of instr., as shown in entries below.
(5) Colloquialism for (in sym. orchs.) the db., and (in military and brass bands) the bombardon.

bassanello. Obsolete woodwind instr., first mentioned in 1577, related to *shawm. Made in 3 sizes, bass, tenor, and alto. 7 finger-holes and reed set on a crook. Legend that it was invented by the composer Giovanni Bassano or Bassani is suspect.

Bassani, Giovanni Battista (*b* Padua, c.1657; *d* Bergamo, 1716). It. violinist, composer, and organist. Choirmaster, Modena, 1677–80; Ferrara Cath. from 1686, later at Bergamo, 1712. Wrote 15 oratorios, masses, 9 operas, and trio sonatas for strings.

Bassano [Bassani], **Giovanni** (*b* c.1558; *d* Venice, ?1617). It. composer and cornett player. Member of instr. ens. at St Mark's, Venice, from 1576. Publication in 1585 of his book on ornamentation (*Ricercate passaggi et cadentie*) led to appt. as singing teacher at St Mark's seminary. Became head of the instr. ens 1601. G. Gabrieli's *Canzona in echo* (1599) were probably written for Bassano to perform. Comp. motets, canzonettas, etc.

Bassarids, The. Opera seria with intermezzo in 1 act by Henze to lib. by W. H. Auden and Chester Kallman based on *The Bacchae* of Euripides. Comp. 1965. Prod. Salzburg 1966 in Ger. trans. by M. Bosse-Sporleder; Santa Fe 1968 (in orig. Eng.); London (broadcast) 1968; ENO 1974 (cond. and prod. Henze).

bass-bar. In a bowed instr. the strip of wood glued under the belly along the line of the lowest str. and supporting one foot of the bridge.

bass-baritone. See *baritone*.

bass clarinet. One of cl. family, pitched in B♭, an octave below the B♭ sop. (treble) cl. In Eng. and Fr. instrs. its range extends to E♭ (sounding D♭). Earliest extant examples made in 1793. Meyerbeer wrote for it, later Wagner, Mahler, Schoenberg, and Stravinsky. See *clarinet*.

bass clef. Sometimes called the F clef: the F below middle C as the top line but one of the staff.

bass drum. Large drum of indefinite low pitch. In most orchs. is mounted on a large, wheeled rack so that drum can be tilted at any desired angle.

basse chantante (Fr.). basso cantante (It.). Lyric bass, sometimes of bar. quality.

basse chiffrée, basse continue (Fr.). Figured bass. See *basso continuo*.

basse d'harmonie (Fr.). *Ophicleide.

basset horn. Alto cl. in F (occasionally in G), whole tone higher than Eb alto cl., with a total possible compass of 4 complete octaves. Invented *c.*1765 and used by Mozart in *Requiem, Die Zauberflöte, La Clemenza di Tito* and his masonic pieces. He first used it 1781 in the *Serenade* in Bb (K361). Beethoven (*Prometheus*) and Mendelssohn (*Scottish Symphony*) wrote for it, but after 1850 it was replaced by the Eb alto cl. Richard Strauss revived it in his operas *Elektra* (1906–8) and *Daphne* (1936–7), and for his 2 wind sonatinas comp. 1943 and 1945. A transposing instr., its name is said to derive from a Bavarian term for small bass, and the basset-hound was named after the sound it makes. The It. term *corno di bassetto* was adopted by Bernard *Shaw as his pseudonym when writing mus. criticism.

Bassettflöte (Ger.). A 17th- and 18th-cent. name for a recorder of low pitch. Sometimes called *Bassflöte*.

bassett nicolo. An alto reed-cap shawm in F with extension keys and a 9-note range.

bassflicorno (flicorno basso). Large size of It. variety of saxhorn or Flügelhorn called *flicorno*. Others are *flicorno basso grave* and *flicorno contrabasso*.

Bassflöte. See *Bassettflöte*.

bass flute. Fl. in C, pitched one octave below the ordinary fl. (not, as sometimes miscalled, the *alto fl. in G). Also an org.-stop, 8′ length and pitch. See *flute*.

bass horn. Obsolete brass instr. made in 3 sizes, alto, bass, and db., but only the bass was much used; now supplanted by bass tuba.

bass oboe. Term used to denote baritone oboe.

Bass-Saite (Ger.). Bass string. Lowest str. on any (bowed or plucked) instr.

bass saxhorn. One of brass wind instr. made by *Sax. In Bb, Eb, and double Bb.

bass staff. See *great staff*.

bass trombone (Ger. *Bassposaune*). Brass instr. with a range to For E below the ten. tb. Bb. See *trombone*.

bass trumpet (Ger. *Basstrompete*). Wind instr., made of brass. Really a valve tb. Pitched in C, therefore not a transposing instr. See *trumpet*.

bass tuba. Brass instr. of the *tuba family of which there are the following: Eb bass tuba or Eb bombardon; F bass tuba; and Bb bass tuba or Bb bombardon. Vaughan Williams wrote a conc. for bass tuba. See *tuba*.

bass viol. Member of the *viol group of str.

instr. Often called *viola da gamba, 'leg viol', because it is held as the vc. is. Also an old-fashioned name for the double bass.

basso (It.; plural *bassi*). Low male v., bass, normally ranging from E to e′/f′.

basso continuo (It.). Continuous bass. Figured bass from which in concerted mus. of the 17th and 18th cents. the cembalist or organist played. Doubled the lowest v. part. Term often shortened to *continuo*. To 'play the *continuo*' does not mean to play a particular instr., but to play this variety of bass.

basson (Fr.). *Bassoon.

basson russe (Fr.). Russian bassoon, a variety of *bass horn.

bassoon (It. *fagotto*). Bass member of the double reed (ob.) family, pitched in C, with range from Bb′ upwards for about 3$\frac{1}{2}$ octaves. Made of wood and with conical bore. Dates from 1660s. Came to prominence as solo instr. in 18th cent. Vivaldi comp. 39 concerti for it. Others to use it as solo instr. incl. J. C. Bach, Telemann, and Boismortier. In 1774 Mozart wrote his concerto (K191). Modern instrs. made by Heckel (Ger.), Buffet-Crampon (Fr.), and Fox (Amer.). Often used for comic effect but its capacity for melancholy has not been overlooked by composers. Also an org. reed stop of 8′ length and pitch.

bassoon, double. See *double bassoon*.

bassoon, Russian. See *basson russe*.

basso ostinato (It.). Obstinate bass, i.e. *ground bass.

basso profondo. Bass v. of exceptionally low range.

Bastardella, La. See *Agujari, Lucrezia*.

Bastianini, Ettore (*b* Siena, 1922; *d* Sirmione, 1967). It. baritone, outstanding in Verdi. Began career as bass at Ravenna 1945. La Scala début 1948. Raised voice to bar., making 2nd début Bologna 1951. NY Met 1953–66. Sang Prince Andrey in Eur. première of *War and Peace*, Florence 1953. La Scala début as bar. 1954, singing there regularly until 1964. Salzburg Fest. début 1958. CG 1962.

Bastien und Bastienne. *Singspiel* in 1 act, K50, by the 12-year-old Mozart to lib. by Friedrich Wilhelm Weiskern, after Favart's parody on Rousseau's *Le *Devin du village* (1752). Prod. in the garden th. of Mesmer, the introducer of mesmerism, Vienna, 1768; not again perf. until Berlin 1890; London 1894; NY 1916.

Bastin, Jules (*b* Pont, 1933; *d* Brussels, 1996). Belg. bass-baritone. Début Brussels 1960. Member of Belg. Nat. Opera from 1960. Salzburg Fest. début 1976, CG début 1972. Sang the Banker in f. complete p. of *Lulu* (Paris 1979).

Bat, The (Strauss). See *Fledermaus, Die*.

Bate, Jennifer (Lucy) (b London, 1944). Eng. organist and composer. Repertory of 60 concs. and hundreds of solo works. Gave f. Brit. p. of Messiaen's *Livre du Saint Sacrement* (London 1986). Comps. incl. *Variations on an Old French Carol* and *Homage to 1685*.

Bateson, Thomas (b c.1570; d Dublin, 1630). Eng. organist and composer of madrigals. Org., Chester Cath. and Christ Church Cath., Dublin. Pubd. 2 sets of madrigals, 1604 (29 items) and 1618 (30). Contrib. to *The *Triumphs of Oriana*.

Batka, Richard (b Prague, 1868; d Vienna, 1922). Austrian critic and music scholar of Cz. ancestry. Ed. (with Richard Specht) periodical *Der Merker* and the *Notebooks of Anna Magdalena Bach*. Admirer of Mahler and Strauss. Taught history of opera at Vienna Acad. 1909–14. Trans. Czech, It., and Fr. opera libretti into Ger. and wrote several himself.

baton (Fr.). The stick used by conds. for beating time and securing expressive playing. The accurate orig. of its use is undiscoverable, but it is said that in the 15th cent. in the Sistine Choir at Rome the maestro di cappella beat time with a roll of paper called 'sol-fa'. Lully's death is alleged to have been the result of an injury to his foot caused by accidentally striking it with a heavier-than-usual cane he was using to thump out the beat on the floor. During the 18th cent. perfs. were dir. from the kbd. and early in the 19th cent. by the first violinist waving his bow at his colleagues when he was not playing. The use of a baton began in Ger. in the 19th cent. Beethoven appears to have cond. with a baton and so did Mendelssohn. Then followed the virtuoso conds. such as Wagner and Bülow. The length of the stick varies, some conds. (e.g. Richter and Boult) using a long baton. Generally, however, a light, short baton is preferred with which the cond. can indicate more than merely the beats of the bar; hence 'stick technique'. Some conds. abjure the baton and use their hands only (and, of course, their eyes).

Battaglia di Legnano, La (The Battle of Legnano). Opera in 3 acts by Verdi, his 13th, to lib. by S. Cammarano after Joseph Méry's drama *La bataille de Toulouse* (1828). Comp. 1848–9. Prod. Rome 1849; Cardiff 1960; NY 1976.

Batten, Adrian (b Salisbury, 1591; d London, 1637). Eng. composer. Chorister at Winchester Cath., then sang in choirs of Westminster Abbey 1614–26, St Paul's Cath. 1626–37. Wrote services and over 40 anthems. Collected 16th-cent. church mus. in *Batten Organ Book*.

batterie (Fr.). Battery. (1) The perc. instr.
(2) Any rhythmic formula for the drums such as those used in the army for signalling.
(3) Striking instead of plucking str. of guitar.

Battishill, Jonathan (b London, 1738; d Islington, 1801). Eng. organist, theatre musician, and composer for church, stage, and glee clubs. His anthem, *O Lord, look down from Heaven*, still often sung. (Elgar provided an orch. accompaniment for it, Worcester Fest. 1923).

Battistini, Mattia (b Rome, 1856; d Rieti, 1928). It. *bel canto* baritone of great dramatic force and vocal agility. His v. could encompass a high A and Massenet re-wrote the ten. role in *Werther* for him. Début Rome 1878, London 1883. Repertory of over 80 roles. Sang in S. America 1881, but never sang in USA. Kept his vocal powers till he was over 70. Much admired as Don Giovanni and Germont *père*.

Battle, Kathleen (Deanna) (b Portsmouth, Ohio, 1948). Amer. soprano. Prof. début Spoleto Fest. 1972 (Brahms's *Requiem*). Opera début, Detroit 1975; NY Met 1978; Glyndebourne 1979; Salzburg 1982; CG 1985.

Battle Hymn of the Republic. Poem by Julia Ward Howe (1819–1910) written 1862, first line being 'Mine eyes have seen the glory of the coming of the Lord', sung to the tune of *John Brown's Body*. Last verse beginning 'He is coming like the glory of the morning on the wave' is not in orig., authorship being unknown.

Battle of Prague. Pf. piece, with *ad lib* vn., vc., and drum, by Franz *Kotzwara. Comp. 1788, it was long a favourite in Eng.

Battle of the Huns (Ger. *Hunnenschlacht*). Symphonic poem for orch. by Liszt, 1856–7, inspired by a fresco by Kaulbach.

Battle Symphony (or Battle of Victoria, or Wellington's Victory). Eng. title for Beethoven's *Wellingtons Sieg, oder die Schlacht bei Vittoria*, Op.91, a piece of programme-mus. illustrating the Eng. defeat of Napoleon's troops at Vitoria in Sp. in 1812. Comp. 1813 for perf. by Beethoven's friend Maelzel's panharmonicon but actually perf. by a live orch. at 2 Viennese concerts in Dec. 1813 in aid of Austrian soldiers wounded in the Battle of Hanau. The tunes *Rule, Britannia!*, *Malbrouck s'en va-t-en guerre*, and *God Save the King* are incorporated, and the work was ded. to the Prince Regent. 'Vittoria' in the title was Beethoven's mistake for *Vitoria*. The work was the cause of a rift with Maelzel.

battre (Fr.). To beat: *battre à deux temps*, to beat 2 in a measure.

battuta, a (It.). To the beat—same as *a tempo*, i.e. return to normal speed (after a *rallentando* or *accelerando*).

Baudo, Serge (b Marseilles, 1927). Fr. conductor. Début 1950 at Concerts Lamoureux. Cond. Orch. Nationale and radio orch. Cond. Nice-Côte d'Azur Orch. 1959–62, Paris Opéra 1962–5. La Scala début 1970, NY Met 1971. Cond. Orchestre de Paris, 1968–70 (Salzburg Fest. début 1969), art. dir. Rhône-Alpes PO 1969. Mus. dir. Opéra de Lyon, 1969–71, prin. cond. Orch. de Lyon, 1971–89. Cond. f.ps. of Messiaen's *Et exspecto* *resurrectionem mortuorum* (Chartres, 1965), Milhaud's *La Mère coupable* (Geneva, 1966), and Dutilleux's vc. conc. (Aix, 1970). Art. dir. Berlioz Fest., Lyons, from 1979. Mus. dir. and chief cond. Prague SO from 2001.

Baudrier, Yves (*b* Paris, 1906; *d* Paris, 1988). Fr. composer; co-founder of group '*Jeune France*', formed 1936. Works incl. *Le Musicien dans la cité* for orch. (1937).

Bauer, Harold (*b* New Malden, Surrey, 1873; *d* Miami, 1951). Eng.-born pianist. From age 9 made frequent public appearances as violinist; then, 1892, as pianist (London newspaper notices show him within 3 weeks in that year as leader of str. qt., solo violinist, and pf. recitalist). After study with Paderewski appeared as pianist throughout Europe and USA, settling in NY. US début Boston 1900. Known principally as Beethoven interpreter, but did much for Fr. pf. mus. (Debussy, Ravel, Franck). Gave f.p. of Debussy's *Children's Corner*, 1908.

Bauerncantate (Bach). See *Peasant Cantata*.

Bauernleier (Ger.). *hurdy-gurdy.

Bauernlied (Ger.). Peasant song or ballad.

Bauld, Alison (*b* Sydney, NSW, 1944). Australian composer and writer. Mus. dir., Laban Centre for Dance, London Univ., 1975–8. Works incl. *Exiles*, mus.-th. (1974); *Inanna*, tape for ballet (1975); *In a Dead Brown Land*, mus.-th. (1971, rev. 1972); *Mad Moll*, sop. (1973); *I Loved Miss Watson*, sop., pf., with tape (1977); *One Pearl II*, sop., alto fl., str. (1976, rev. of *One Pearl*, 1973); *Van Diemen's Land*, unacc. ch. (1976); *The Busker's Story*, alto sax., bn., tpt., vn., db. (1978); *Banquo's Buried*, sop., pf. (1982); *Monody*, fl. (1985); *Copy Cats*, vn., vc., pf., chamber ens. (1986); *Nell*, ballad opera, sop., mez., ten., bar., ch., small orch. (1988); *My own Island*, cl., pf. (1989); *Play your Way*, pf. (1992); *Farewell Already*, sop., str. qt. (1993); *Where Should Othello Go?*, bar., pf. (1998). Wrote novel *Mozart's Sister* (1997).

Baumann, Hermann (Rudolf Konrad) (*b* Hamburg, 1934). Ger. horn-player. Prin. hn., Dortmund orch. 1957–61, Stuttgart Radio Orch. 1961–7. Teacher in Essen (prof. from 1969). Int. career as soloist. Salzburg Fest. début 1977. Uses natural hn. in Baroque mus., hand horn for Mozart, and varying modern instrs.

Baumgartner, Rudolf (*b* Zurich, 1917; *d* Siena, 2002). Swiss violinist and conductor. Became member of Stefi Geyer Quartet and of Zurich String Trio. With Schneiderhan, founded Lucerne Festival Strings 1956, which he cond. on many tours and in many recordings (Salzburg Fest. début 1957, as soloist and cond.). Cond. f.ps. of Penderecki's *Capriccio*, 1965, and Ligeti's *Ramifications*, 1970. Arr. J. S. Bach's *Art of Fugue* and *Musical Offering*. Taught vn. Lucerne Cons. from 1954, dir. from 1960. Dir., Lucerne Fest., 1968–80.

Bavarian Highlands, Scenes from the. 6 choral songs by Elgar, Op.27. Texts, in style of Bavarian folk-songs, by C. A. Elgar. Pf. acc. 1895, orch. 1896. Three (*The Dance, Lullaby*, and *The Marksmen*) arr. for orch. alone by Elgar.

Bavarian Radio Symphony Orchestra. Founded in Munich 1949, with Eugen Jochum as cond. until 1961. Rafael Kubelik 1961–79; Colin Davis 1983–92; Lorin Maazel 1993–2002; Mariss Jansons from 2003. Has toured frequently and made many recordings.

Bawden, Rupert (*b* London, 1958). Eng. composer and conductor. Played vn. and va. in London Sinfonietta and English Concert. Cond. début, Aldeburgh Fest. 1986. Works incl.: *The Angel and the Ship of Death*, for 13 players (1983, rev. 1987); 7 *Songs from the House of Sand*, brass quintet (1985); *Le Livre de Fauvel*, sop., mez., and 18 players (1986); *Dramatic Cantata on Legend of Apollo and Daphne*, for vn., vc., and 13 players (1989); *Ultima Scena*, for chamber ens. (1989); *Wanderjahr*, ens. (1990); *Three Pictures*, sop., 2 cl./vn., va., vc., db. (1992); *Two Studies*, orch. (1994); *The Sailor's Tale*, chamber opera (2002).

Bax, (Sir) Arnold (Edward Trevor) (*b* Streatham, London, 1883; *d* Cork, 1953). Eng. composer who was Master of the King's (Queen's) Musick 1942–53. Studied RAM, 1900–5. Was himself a brilliant pianist and wrote fluently and perceptively for the kbd. Felt a special sympathy with Irish subjects, particularly Yeats's poetry, and with the Irish land and seascapes, hence the intensely picturesque and romantic flavour of his mus. Also much influenced by Russ. mus. after his visit to Russ. in 1910. Only stage works involved ballet, incl. *The Truth About the Russian Dancers* (1919), a play by Barrie in which the central non-speaking part of the ballerina was created and choreog. by Karsavina when prod. 1920 by Gerald du Maurier, with Paul Nash décor.

Although a prolific composer, Bax's mus. has never est. itself in the forefront. His 7 syms., luxuriantly scored and full of romantic melody, contain too much good mus. ever to deserve total neglect, but are only intermittently perf. in the concert-hall, the public seeming to prefer the more concise tone-poems. The chamber mus. is less diffuse in form and is beautifully written for the instr., while there are also some exquisite short choral pieces. Bax's autobiography, *Farewell, My Youth* (1943), is one of the best books by a composer. Knighted 1937. Prin. works:

BALLET: *Between Dusk and Dawn* (1917).

ORCH.: syms.: No.1 in E♭ (1921–2), No.2 in E minor and C (1924–5), No.3 in C (1929), No.4 in E♭ (1930–1), No.5 in E minor (1931–2), No.6 in C minor (1934), No.7 in A♭ (1939); *Into the Twilight* (1908); *In the Faery Hills* (1909); *Roscatha* (1910); *Festival Overture* (1911, rev. 1918); *Christmas Eve on the Mountains* (1911, rev. as *Christmas Eve c.*1933); 4 *Orchestral Sketches* (1912–13); *Irish Landscape* (1912–13, rev. 1928); *Nympholept* (1912–15); *Spring Fire* (1913); *The *Garden of Fand* (1913–16); *The Happy Forest* (1914, orch. 1921); *November Woods* (1917);

Summer Music (1917–20, rev. 1932); *Symphonic Scherzo* (1917, rev. 1933); *Symphonic Variations*, pf., orch. (1917, orch. 1918); **Tintagel* (1917–19); *Russian Suite* (1919); *The Truth about the Russian Dancers* (incid. mus., 1919, rev. 1926); *Paean* (1920, orch. 1938); *Phantasy*, va., orch. (1920); *Mediterranean* (1922, orch. of pf. piece 1920); *Cortège* (1925); *Romantic Overture*, chamber orch. (1926); *Overture, Elegy and Rondo* (1927); *Northern Ballad* No.1 (1927), No.2 (1934); *Prelude for a Solemn Occasion* (1927–33); *Evening Piece* (1928); *Dance in the Sunlight* (1928); *Winter Legends*, pf., orch. (1929–30); *Overture to a Picaresque Comedy* (1930); *The Tale the Pine Trees Knew* (1931); *Sinfonietta* (1932); vc. conc. (1932); *Saga Fragment*, pf., chamber orch. (1932); *Rogue's Comedy Overture* (1936); *Overture to Adventure* (1936); *London Pageant* (1937); vn. conc. (1938); *Legend* (1943); *Morning Song (Maytime in Sussex)*, pf., orch. (1946); *Golden Eagle* (incid. mus., 1946); concertante for orch. and pf. (left hand) (1948–9); *Coronation March* (1952).

VOICE(S) & INSTR(S).: *Fatherland*, ten., ch., orch. (1907, rev. 1934); *Enchanted Summer*, 2 sops., ch., orch. (1910); *6 Songs from The Bard of the Dimbovitza*, mez., orch. (1914); *Of a Rose I Sing*, ch., hp., vc., db. (1920); *To The Name Above Every Name*, sop., ch., orch. (1923); *St Patrick's Breastplate*, ch., orch. (1923); *Walsinghame*, ten., ch., orch. (1926); *The Morning Watch*, ch., orch. (1935–6); *5 Fantasies on Polish Christmas Carols*, children's ch., orch. (1942); *Nunc Dimittis*, ch., org. (1945); *Te Deum*, ch., org. (1945); *Magnificat*, ch., org. (1948).

UNACC. VOICES: *Mater Ora Filium* (1921); *This Worlde's Joie* (1922); *The Boar's Head* (1923); *I sing of a maiden* (1923); *5 Greek Folk Songs* (1944); *What is it like to be young and fair?* (**Garland for the Queen*) (1953).

CHAMBER MUSIC: str. qts.: No.1 in G (1918), No.2 (1924–5), No.3 in F (1936); pf. trio (1906); str. quintet in G (1908); *Legend*, vn., pf. (1915); pf. quintet in G minor (1915); *Ballad*, vn., pf. (1916); *Elegiac Trio*, fl., va., hp. (1916); *Folk Tale*, vc., pf. (1918); hp. quintet (1919); va. sonata (1921–2); ob. quintet (1922); vc. sonata (1923); *Legend*, va., pf. (1929); *Nonett*, fl., ob., cl., hp., str. quintet (1929); str. quintet (1932); vc. sonatina (1933); cl. sonata (1934); octet, hn., pf., str. sextet (1934); conc., fl., ob., hp., str. qt. ('Septet') (1936); *Legend-sonata*, vc., pf. (1943); Trio, pf., vn., va. (1946); Vn. sonatas: No.1 (1910, rev. 1915), No.2 in D (1915, rev. 1921).

PIANO: sonatas: No.1 in F♯ minor (1910, rev. 1917–21), No.2 in G (1919), No.3 (1926), No.4 (1932); *Valse de Concert* (1904); *2 Russian Tone-Pictures* (1911); *Toccata* (1913); *The Maiden with the Daffodil* (1915); *The Princess's Rose Garden* (1915); *In a Vodka Shop* (1915); *A Mountain Mood* (1915); *Dream in Exile* (1916); *Romance* (1918); *On a May Evening* (1918); *What the Minstrel told us* (1919); *Lullaby, A Hill Tune, Country Tune* (1920); *Mediterranean* (1920, orch. 1922); *Suite for Fauré* (1945).

2 PIANOS: *Moy Mell* (1916); *Hardanger* (1927); *The Devil that Tempted St Anthony* (1928); sonata (1929); *Red Autumn* (1931) .

SONGS: *A Celtic Song-Cycle* (1904); *A Christmas Carol* (1909); *3 Chaucer Roundels* (1914); *Parting* (1916); *5 Traditional French Songs* (1920); *5 Irish Songs* (1921); *3 Irish Songs* (incl. *Rann of Exile*) (1922).

FILM MUSIC: *Malta GC* (1942); *Oliver Twist* (1948).

Baylis, Lilian (*b* London, 1874; *d* London, 1937). Eng. theatre manager and impresario. From 1898 until her death was man. of the *Old Vic, of which her aunt, Emma Cons, was lessee. Staged Shakespeare there, also opera and ballet (with Ninette de *Valois). In 1931 re-opened SW Th., to which she transferred the opera and ballet cos. CH 1929.

Baynes, Sydney (*b* Sudbury, 1879; *d* Willesden, 1938). Eng. composer and conductor. Church organist and pf. acc. to Edward *Lloyd and Ben Davies. Mus. dir. Drury Lane Th. 1910–14. Wrote popular waltzes, notably *Destiny* (1912), songs, and religious mus. Cond. revue orchs. and, from 1928, his broadcasting orch.

Bayreuth. Town in Bavaria, Ger., where Wagner built his home, *Wahnfried, and also his long-planned fest. th. to house perfs. of *Der *Ring des Nibelungen*. First fest. 1876, cond. Hans Richter. Th. holds *c*.1,800 and has wonderful acoustics. Innovation was covered orch. pit. *Parsifal* f.p. there, 1882. Fests. of Wagner's operas held regularly (with wartime interruptions) since 1892, the successive dirs. having been members of the Wagner family—his wife Cosima (1883–1908), son Siegfried (1908–30), Siegfried's widow Winifred (1931–44), their sons Wieland and Wolfgang jointly (1951–66), and Wolfgang (from 1966). In 1945, under Amer. occupation, operas by composers other than Wagner were perf. in the Festspielhaus. Concerts were also given there.

Bazelon, Irwin (Allen) (*b* Evanston, Ill., 1922; *d* NY, 1995). Amer. composer. Has written much incid. mus. for th., cinema, and TV. Author of book on film mus. Works incl. *De-Tonations*, brass quintet and orch. (1978); woodwind quintet (1975); *Concatenations*, perc. qt. and va. (1976); *Sound Dreams*, fl., cl., va., vc., pf., solo perc. (1977); *Imprints*, pf. (1978); *Junctures for Orchestra*, with sop. (1979); *Sym.* No.7, 'ballet for orch.' (1980); *Spires*, tpt. and orch. (1981); *Suite*, marimba (1983); *Quintessentials*, wind quintet (1983); *Trajectories*, pf., orch. (1984); *Motivations*, tb., orch. (1985); *Legends and Love Letters*, sop., chamber orch. (1987); *Fourscore 2*, perc. qt., orch. (1988); *Sym.* No.8, str. (1986); *Sym.* No.8½ (1989); *Sym.* No.9 (*Sunday Silence*) (1992); *Prelude to Hart Crane's 'The Bridge'*, str. ens. (1991); *Fire and Smoke*, timp., band (1994).

Bazzini, Antonio (*b* Brescia, 1818; *d* Milan, 1897). It. violinist and composer. Lived in Ger. 1841–5, becoming friend of Schumann and Mendelssohn. Gave first private perf. of Mendelssohn vn. conc. Retired from concert career 1864. Became prof. of comp., Milan Cons., 1873 and dir., 1882. One of leaders of It. non-operatic revival.

Comp. 4 vn. concs., 6 str. qts., 2 quintets, tone-poem *Francesca da Rimini*, also celebrated vn. solo, *Ronde des lutins* (Dance of the Elves) (1852).

BBC (British Broadcasting Corporation). The first Brit. broadcasting station was opened at Writtle, Chelmsford, in 1920 by the Marconi Co. In 1922 four Brit. electrical manufacturers formed the Brit. Broadcasting Co. which began transmitting from 2LO at Savoy Hill on 15 Nov. of that year. The first mus. broadcast, by an orch. of 9 players, was on 25 Nov. 1922. In Jan. 1923 relays of *Hänsel und Gretel* and Act I of *Die Zauberflöte* (from CG) proved so successful that 20 other operatic relays followed shortly, incl. those of *Siegfried* and *Le nozze di Figaro*. The first studio opera prod. was of Gounod's *Roméo et Juliette* in Oct. 1923. The importance of mus. as a staple element of broadcasting was recognized by the appointment in May 1923 of a Mus. Controller, the first being Percy *Pitt. In 1924 the BBC, amid opposition and controversy, sponsored 6 public sym. concerts in London. On 1 Jan. 1927 the private co. became a public monopoly with the issue of a Royal charter constituting the British Broadcasting Corporation, its revenue coming from licence-holders. In the same year the BBC assumed financial responsibility for the London Promenade Concerts and its mus. patronage extended to the commissioning of new works and the sponsorship of important perfs. of contemporary mus. A logical outcome was the formation in 1930 of the BBC SO, offering permanent contracts to over 110 players. Adrian *Boult, who had succeeded Pitt as controller of mus. in 1929, was appointed cond. in 1931, a post he held until 1950. Regional sym. orchs. were later formed in Glasgow, Manchester, Birmingham, Cardiff, and Belfast.

With the inauguration of a TV service on 2 Nov. 1936 the BBC quickly seized the chance to televise opera, and in the three years 1936–9 nearly 30 operas were prod. for TV, incl. *La serva padrona*, *Pagliacci*, *Gianni Schicchi*, and the first perf. in Britain of Busoni's *Arlecchino*. During the war the BBC's role as a dispenser of mus. of all kinds intensified. Arthur *Bliss succeeded Boult in 1942 as mus. dir., and was himself succeeded in 1944 by Victor *Hely-Hutchinson. Successive dirs. (or controllers) have been Steuart *Wilson 1947–50, Herbert Murrill 1950–2, R. J. F. Howgill 1952–9, William *Glock 1959–73, Robert Ponsonby 1973–85, John Drummond 1985–92, Nicholas Kenyon 1992–8, Roger Wright from 1998.

A major broadcasting development was the formation in Sept. 1946 of the Third Programme, designed for 'cultivated tastes and interests'. Music made up 50 per cent of its output and the opportunities for broadcasting a wide range of mus. were almost limitless. In Mar. 1965 the 3rd Programme underwent changes, incl. the emergence of the Mus. Programme which ran continuously for nearly 12 hours a day. In 1970 the 3rd Programme and Mus. Programme became Radio 3. TV has also developed mus. series of its own, reaching enormous audi-

ences. Among operas specially commissioned by BBC TV were Bliss's *Tobias and the Angel* (1960), and Britten's *Owen Wingrave* (1971).

BBC Philharmonic Orchestra. Regional symphony orchestra based in Manchester which adopted this name in 1983 having previously been BBC Northern SO. Developed from Northern Wireless Orchestra, founded 1931, and renamed BBC Northern Orch. 1934. Chief conds. have incl. Charles Groves (1944–51); John Hopkins (1952–7); George Hurst (1958–68); Bryden Thomson (1968–73); Raymond Leppard (1973–80); Edward Downes (1980–91); Yan Pascal Tortelier 1991–2002, Gianandrea Noseda from 2002.

BBC Singers. Unacc. ch. (present strength 28 full-time professional singers) formed 1924 as Wireless Chorus. Changed name to BBC Chorus 1935, present title 1973. First cond. was Stanford *Robinson. Cond. 1934–61 was Leslie Woodgate. Other conds. Peter Gellhorn and John Poole.

BBC Symphony Orchestra. Chief orch. of the BBC, formed 1930 with 114 (later 119) players on permanent contract. Has given f.ps. of many works by Brit. composers. Guest conds. have incl. the world's leading exponents, notably *Toscanini. Chief conds. since inception: Adrian *Boult 1931–50; Malcolm *Sargent 1950–7; Rudolf *Schwarz 1957–62; Antal *Dorati 1962–6; Colin *Davis 1967–71; Pierre *Boulez 1971–5; Rudolf *Kempe 1975–6; Gennady *Rozhdestvensky 1978–81; John *Pritchard 1981–9; Andrew *Davis 1989–2000; Leonard *Slatkin 2000–5; Jiří *Bělohlávek from 2006. Other BBC sym. orchs. are the Philharmonic (based in Manchester), Scottish (based in Glasgow), and Welsh (based in Cardiff and known from 1993 as BBC National Orchestra of Wales). The BBC Symphony Chorus was formed 1928 as National Chorus (at its 1st concert, 23 Nov. 1928, *Bantock cond. f.p. of his *Pilgrim's Progress*). Name changed to BBC Chorus 1932, to BBC Choral Society 1935, to present title 1977. Up to 1976, ch. master was dir. of *BBC Singers, but in that year separate appointment (Brian Wright) was made.

B Dur (Ger.). The key of B♭ major (not B major). See *B*.

Be (Ger.). The flat sign (♭).

Beach (*née* Cheney), **Amy Marcy** (*b* Henniker, New Hampshire, 1867; *d* NY, 1944). Amer. pianist and composer. Her performing career was cut short by her marriage in 1885, after which she concentrated on comp., but she resumed it in 1910 when her husband died. Toured Europe playing her own conc. Wrote numerous songs; Mass in E♭ (1891); *Gaelic Symphony* (1896); vn. sonata (1896); pf. conc. (1899); pf. quintet (1908); *The Canticle of the Sun* (1925); *Christ in the Universe* (1931); pf. trio (1938); and opera *Cabildo* (1932).

Beach, John Parsons (*b* Gloversville, NY, 1877; *d* Pasadena, Calif., 1953). Amer. composer, regarded as one of the first modernists. Spent 7 years in Paris from 1910. Comps. incl. 2 short stage works, 2 ballets, orch. and chamber mus.

Beamish, Sally (*b* London, 1956). Eng. composer and violist. Spent 10 years as violist but continued composing. Moved to Scotland 1989. Founded Chamber Group of Scotland, with James *MacMillan as co-dir. Comps. for orch. and various instr. and vocal ens, and opera *Monster* (2000).

Bean, Hugh (Cecil) (*b* Beckenham, 1929; *d* Sydenham, 2003). Eng. violinist. Leader, Philharmonia and New Philharmonia Orch. 1957–67. Ass. leader, BBC SO 1967–9. Active in chamber mus. (Music Group of London) and as conc. soloist. Prof. of vn., RCM from 1954. CBE 1970.

Bear, The. Comic opera in 1 act—extravaganza by *Walton to lib. by Paul Dehn adapted from play (vaudeville) by Chekhov (1888). Comp. 1965–7. Prod. Aldeburgh 1967, Aspen, Colorado, 1968. Also set by Jacobo *Ficher, 1952.

bearbeitet (Ger.). Worked-over, i.e. arranged. *Bearbeitung*, *arrangement.

Beard, John (*b* 1716; *d* Hampton, 1791). Eng. tenor assoc. with Handel operas and oratorios. Début CG 1734 (Silvio in Handel's *Il pastor fido*). Ten. parts of his *Israel in Egypt*, *Messiah*, *Samson*, *Judas Maccabaeus*, and *Jephtha* were written with Beard in mind. Also sang Macheath in The *Beggar's Opera*. Manager, CG Th., 1761–7, resigning due to deafness.

Beard, Paul (*b* Birmingham, 1901; *d* Epsom, 1989). Eng. violinist. Taught by father and played in public 1907. Spa orch., Scarborough, 1920; Leader, CBSO 1922–32, LPO 1932–6, BBC SO 1936–62. Prof. of vn. GSMD and also taught at RAM. OBE 1952.

Beare. Eng. family of vn. restorers and dealers. Founded by John Beare (1847–1928), a dealer from 1865, when in 1892 he split his business into Beare & Son and Beare, Goodwin & Co. (J. and A. Beare Ltd. from 1954). Former concentrated on new instrs., latter on early examples.

'Bear' Symphony (*L'Ours*). Nickname for Haydn's sym. No.82 in C (Hob. I:82), 1786, first of Paris syms., because the bagpipe-like theme of the finale suggests the perf. of a bear-leader, or because of a 'growling' theme in the same movement.

beat. (1) Unit of measurement of rhythmic pulse of mus. (i.e. waltz has 3 beats to the measure), as indicated in time signature. In 4/4 time each quarter-note (crotchet) is one beat, but in more complicated signatures much depends on the tempo selected. E.g. in 12/8 time there are 12 beats to a measure if taken very slowly, or else one for each dotted crotchet.
(2) The cond.'s action corresponding to the required rhythmic pulse.
(3) When 2 notes near to each other in vibration frequency are heard together their vibra-

tions necessarily coincide at regular intervals and thus reinforce each other. This periodical reinforcement is known as a beat and is made use of in pf.-tuning.
(4) Name given variously to ornament in early mus., sometimes applied to a *mordent and sometimes to *acciaccatura. Still other references imply a 'reversed shake' by this term.
(5) Term in jazz, basically meaning the rhythmical pulse of the mus., but also meaning jazz in a generic sense, e.g. 'the beat is black' = Negro jazz.

Béatitudes, Les (The Beatitudes). Oratorio by Franck, comp. 1869–79, based on Sermon on the Mount, for sop., mez., cont., 2 tens., bar., 2 basses, ch., and orch. (F.p. Paris 1879, privately; first complete public perf. Paris 1893. Glasgow 1900; Cardiff 1902.)

Beatitudes, The. Cantata by *Bliss, 1961, for sop., ten., ch., org., and orch., biblical text being interspersed with poems. F.p. Coventry Cath. 1962.

Beatles, The. Vocal and instr. Eng. pop group (guitars and drums) who attained worldwide popularity and critical acclaim during 1960s, chiefly in songs by 2 of the members, John Lennon (*b* Liverpool, 1940; *d* NY, 1980) and Paul *McCartney (*b* Liverpool, 1942). Formed and named in Liverpool *c*.1957 by Lennon, with McCartney and George Harrison (*b* Liverpool, 1943; *d* Los Angeles, 2001). Played at Casbah and Cavern Clubs, Liverpool, until invited to Hamburg, 1960, where 2 extra members were Stuart Sutcliffe (electric bass guitar) and Pete Best (drums). Sutcliffe died 1962. Best was replaced by Ringo Starr (orig. Richard Starkey, *b* Liverpool, 1940). Group's nat. popularity as qt. (Lennon, McCartney, Harrison, and Starr) began 1962 under management of Brian Epstein (*b* Liverpool, 1935; *d* London, 1967), followed by highly successful tours of USA and elsewhere. Term 'Beatlemania' coined to describe adulation accorded them, not only by the young. Among songs written by Lennon and McCartney were *Please, please me*, *She loves you*, *Yesterday*, *Eleanor Rigby*, *Yellow submarine*, and *Hey Jude*. Each of group became MBE, 1965. Group made several films; record sales were phenomenal. Ceased performing together 1969, partnership being later legally dissolved. McCartney formed new group called 'Wings', Lennon settled in USA where he was shot dead, Harrison continued to record, performing only rarely, and Starr continued to record and to perform in films.

Beatrice di Tenda. Opera in 2 acts by Bellini, lib. by Romani. Prod. Venice 1833; London 1836; Paris 1841; New Orleans 1842. Revived Catania 1935.

Béatrice et Bénédict (Beatrice and Benedick). Opera in 2 acts by Berlioz, with lib. considerably adapted by the composer from Shakespeare's comedy *Much Ado about Nothing* (1599–1600). Comp. 1860–2. Prod. Baden-Baden 1862; Glasgow 1936; Washington, DC, 1964. His last work.

Beaumarchais, Pierre-Augustin Caron de (*b* Paris, 1732; *d* Paris, 1799). Fr. playwright and musician. An accomplished flautist and harpist, his mus. fame rests, however, on his authorship of the plays *Le Barbier de Séville* (1772, perf. 1775) and its sequels *La Folle Journée, ou Le Mariage de Figaro* (1781, perf. 1784), and *La Mère Coupable* (perf. 1792). The first play was originally intended as a comic opera, with mus. by Beaumarchais adapted from Sp. airs. Librettist of *Tarare*, opera in 5 acts by Salieri (1787). *The Barber of Seville* was set as an opera by Paisiello (1782) and Rossini (1816) and also by F. L. Benda (1776) and Isouard (c.1796), *The Marriage of Figaro* by Mozart (1786), and *La Mère Coupable* by Milhaud (1964–5). Appears as character in Corigliano's *The *Ghosts of Versailles*.

Beautiful Galathea, The (*Die schöne Galatea*). Operetta by Suppé, prod. Vienna 1865, of which ov. is still often heard. Libretto by P. Henrion.

Beaux Arts Trio. Amer. pf. trio who gave their f.p. at Berkshire Mus. Fest., 1955. International reputation, esp. in Haydn, Beethoven, and Schubert. Original members were Menahem Pressler, pf. (*b* Magdeburg, 1923), Daniel Guilet, vn., and Bernard Greenhouse, vc. (*b* Newark, NJ, 1916). Guilet was succeeded in 1968 by Isadore Cohen (*b* NY, 1922). Salzburg Fest. début 1979.

bebend (Ger.). Trembling, i.e. *tremolo.

be-bop. Jazz development of the 1940s, primarily for small groups of instrumentalists, such as a rhythm section of 4 or 5 players with some solo instr. Scat singing was a feature. Be-bop used highly complex chord sequences often at very fast tempi. Specially assoc. with the alto saxophonist Charlie Parker. It had a marked effect on the jazz techniques of drumming and pf.-playing.

bebung (Ger.). Trembling. A tremolo effect obtained by a rapid shaking movement of the finger on a str. of a bowed instr. or on a key of a clavichord (see also *bebend*).

bec (Fr.), **becco** (It.). Mouthpiece of cl. *flûte à bec* is Fr. for recorder.

bécarre (Fr.). The natural sign (♮).

Bechstein, Friedrich Wilhelm Carl (*b* Gotha, 1826; *d* Berlin, 1900). Ger. pf. manufacturer. After working in pf. factories in Ger., Fr., and Eng., founded his own firm in Berlin, 1853. His first grand pf., 1856, was inaugurated by Hans von Bülow with perf. of Liszt B minor sonata. Branches were est. in Fr., London (1879), and Russ. London recital hall built in 1901 was named Bechstein Hall, though re-named Wigmore Hall in 1917 after the street in which it stands. Production of pfs. reached 5,000 a year in

years preceding First World War. Factory almost entirely destroyed in Second World War, but production resumed in 1951, reaching 1,000 instr. after a year.

Beck. Short for *Becken*, cymbals.

Beck, Conrad (*b* Lohn, Schaffhausen, Switz., 1901; *d* Basle, 1990). Swiss composer. Lived in Paris 1923–32. Mus. dir. Basle Radio, 1938–66. Works incl. syms.; concs. for str. qt. and orch., vn. and chamber orch., fl., va., cl.; concertinos for pf., for cl., bn., and orch., ob. and orch.; 5 str. qts.; cantatas, *La Mort d'Œdipe* (1928), *Die Sonnen-finsternis* (1967); chamber cantata on sonnets of Louiza Labé (1937); and ballet *Der Bär* (1937).

Becken (Ger.). *Cymbals.

Becker, Günther Hugo (*b* Forbach, Ger., 1924). Ger. composer and teacher. Taught in Gr. 1956–68. In 1969 in Essen founded elec. instr. ens. *Gruppe MHz*, re-named (1971) Live-Electronic Ensemble Folkwang, Essen. Prof. of comp., Düsseldorf Cons. from 1973. Works incl. *Meteoren* for org., perc., tape (1969), and Scenic oratorio *Magnum Mysterium—Zeugenaussagen zur Aufersteheung* (1979–80).

Becker, Hugo (*b* Strasbourg, 1863; *d* Geiselgasteig, 1941). Ger. cellist. Member of Heermann Qt. 1890–1906. Taught during that time at Frankfurt Cons. From 1910 prin. vc. teacher, Berlin Hochschule. Cellist in trios with Schnabel and Flesch, and Ysaÿe and Busoni. Comp. vc. conc. (1898) and short pieces.

Becker, John Joseph (*b* Henderson, Ky., 1886; *d* Wilmette, Ill., 1961). Amer. composer. Prof. of comp., North Texas College, 1906–14; dir. of mus., Univ. of Notre Dame, 1918–28; chairman of fine arts dept., St Thomas College, St Paul, 1928–33. While at St Paul his romantic-impressionist style as composer changed into more radical and dissonant idiom after assoc. with Cowell, Ives, Ruggles, and Riegger. Several of his later works carry message of social protest. From 1943, dir. of mus. and composer in residence, Barat College, Lake Forest, Ill. Comp. 7 syms. between 1915 and 1954, the last being unfinished; 2 pf. concs., va. conc., hn. conc.; 7 *Soundpieces* for various chamber combinations; *The Snow Goose* (orch.); 1-act opera *Deirdre of the Sorrows* (1945).

Beckus the Dandipratt. Concert-ov. by Malcolm *Arnold, pubd. 1948. A dandipratt is an urchin.

Beckwith, John (*b* Victoria, B.C., 1927). Canadian composer. Instructor in mus. theory, Toronto Royal Cons. 1955–65. Member of mus. faculty, Toronto Univ. since 1952, dean 1970–7, prof. 1977–90; dir., Inst. for Canadian Mus., 1984–90. Works incl. 1-act opera *The Night Blooming Cereus* (1953–8); *A Message to Winnipeg* (1960); *Wednesday's Child* (1962); *Circle, With Tangents*, for hpd. and 13 str. (1967); *The Sun Dance* (1968);

Musical Chairs (1973); *The Shivaree* (1978); *A Concert of Myths* (1983); *Crazy to Kill* (1988); *Round and Round*, for orch. (1991–2); *March! March!*, for pf. (2001); and *A New Pibroch*, for Highland pipes, 7 str., perc. (2002). Several of his works are described as 'collages' and employ narrators.

Bedford, David (Vickerman) (*b* London, 1937). Eng. composer and teacher. Was member of pop group 'The Whole World'. Worked as mus. teacher 1968–80. Comp.-in-residence Queen's Coll., London, 1969–81. Prin. works:

MUSIC THEATRE: *The Rime of the Ancient Mariner* (school opera, 1975–6); *The Ragnarok* (1982–3) (school opera, part of trilogy with *The Death of Baldur* (1979) and *Indiof's Saga* (1980)); *The Camlann Game* (school opera) (1987); *The Return of Odysseus* (children's opera) (1988); *Anna* (children's opera) (1992–3).

ORCH.: *This One for You* (1965); *Gastrula* (1968); *Star's End*, rock instr. and orch. (1974); sym. for 12 mus. (1981); *Sun Paints Rainbows on the Vast Waves* (1982); *The Valley-Sleeper, The Children, Snakes and the Giant* (1982); Sym. No.1 (1984), No.2, sym. wind band (1985); *Seascapes* (1986); *The Transfiguration* (1988); *Frameworks* (1989–90); *In Plymouth Town* (1992); *Allison's Overture* (1992); *Allison's Concerto*, tpt., orch. (1993); *The Goddess of Mahi River* (1994); *Colchester Variations* (1995); *Levels* (1995); *At the Sign of the Crumhorn* (1998); ob. conc. (1998); *The Sultan's Turret* (1998); *Hetty Pegler's Tump* (1999); *Like a Strand of Scarlet* (1999); *Odyssey 3000* (2000).

CHORUS & ORCH.: *Dream of the 7 Lost Stars* (1964–5); *Star Clusters, Nebulae, and Places in Devon* (1971); *12 Hours of Sunset* (1974); *The Odyssey*, sop., girls' vv., instr., elec. (1976); *Song of the White Horse* (1977); *The Way of Truth*, ch., elec. (1978); *Into Thy Wondrous House*, sop., ch., children's ch., orch. (1987); *Gere curam mei finis*, ch., elec. (1987); *I am going home with thee*, 6 solo women's vv., str. (1993); *A Charm of Joy*, ch., str. tune tubes (1996); *A Charm of Blessings*, soloists, ch. children's ch. (1996–7); *From Clocks to Stars*, ch., children's ch., soloists, org., perc. (1999–2000); *The City and the Stars*, ch. (2000).

WIND BAND: *Sun Paints Rainbow on the Vast Waves*, arr. for wind (1984); *Sea and Sky and Golden Hill* (1985); *Ronde for Isolde* (1986); *Symphony 2* (1987); *Canons and Cadenzas* (1995–6); *Sprites, Elves and Blue Jets*, wind, str. (2000); *Saturday Night at the Dinosaur Stomp*, wind band (2001).

BRASS: *Pancakes, with Butter, Maple Syrup and Bacon and the TV Weatherman*, brass quintet (1973); *For Tess*, brass quintet (1985); *Toccata for Tristan* (1989); *Canzona* (1992); *Requiem* (1998).

UNACC. CHORUS: *2 Poems* (Patchen) (1963); *The Golden Wine is Drunk* (Dowson) (1974); *The Way of Truth*, ch., elec. (1977–8); *Of Stars, Dreams and Cymbals*, ch. (1982); *An Island in the Moon*, ch. (1985–6); *Gere curam mei finis*, 4 soloists, elec. (1987); *A Charm of Grace*, 24 vv. (1994); *Lift up your Heads*, ch. (1997); *The Grace of Love*, ch. (1999).

INSTR. ENSEMBLE: *Piece for Mo* (1963); *Five* (1967); *Pentomino*, wind quintet (1968); *The Garden of Love* (1970); *The Sword of Orion* (1970); *With 100 Kazoos* (1971); *Nurse's Song with Elephants* (1971); *Jack of Shadows*, va., small orch. (1973); *A Horse, His Name was Hunry Fencewaver Walkins*, acoustic gui., chamber ens. (1973); *Variations on a Rhythm by Mike Oldfield*, perc. (3 players, 84 instr.) (1973); *Erkenne mich* (1988); *Susato Variations*, pf., wind, perc. (1992); *Cadenzas and Interludes* (1992); rec. conc., rec., str. (1994); str. qt. No.1 (1981), No.2 (1997–8); ob. conc., ob./ca., str. (1998); *Cisac Fanfare*, 3 cl., 3 tpt., 3 tb., perc. (2002).

VOICE AND INSTRS. (all with various ens.): *Music for Albion Moonlight*, sop. (1965); *That White and Radiant Legend*, sop., spkr. (1966); *The Tentacles of the Dark Nebula*, ten. (1969); *When I Heard the Learn'd Astronomer*, ten. (1972); *Holy Thursday with Squeekers*, sop. (1972); *The OCD Band and the Minotaur*, sop. (1990); *Even Now*, sop. (1990); *Maggie's Farewell*, sop. (1991); *The Bird of the Mountain*, sop. (1991); *Touristen Dachau*, sop., male vv., instr. (1992); *My Mother, my Sister and I*, 3 sop., tape (1994); *Inventress of the Vocal Frame*, counterten., hpd., 2 vn., vc. (1997); *Magnificat and Nunc dimittis*, ch., org. (1999).

INSTR(S).: *18 Bricks Left on April 21st*, 2 electric guitars (1967); *Piano Piece I* (1966), *II* (1968); *You Asked for It'*, acoustic guitar (1969); *Spillihpernak*, va. (1972); wind sextet (1981); *SPNM Birthday Piece*, str. qt. (1983); *Diafone*, fl., vib. (1985); *Memories of Ullapool*, fl., gui. or hp. (1988); *Backings*, sop. sax., tape (1990); *Say Not the Struggle Naught Availeth*, org. (1991); *Hey Presto*, cl. (1994); *Piers de résistance*, rec. (1995); *Oh Eva, Hear my Lament*, fl., pf. (1997); *The Fragrance of your Hair*, ob., pf. (1998); *Like as the Waves Make Towards the Pebbled Shore*, rec., gui., vc., db. (1999); *McSax*, sop. sax. (1999); *Dreams of Stac Pollaidh*, bn. (1999); *To Ullapool and Beyond*, vib. (2001).

VOICE AND ACCOMP.: *O Now the Drenched Land Wakes*, bar., pf. duet; *Come In Here, Child*, sop., amplified pf. (1968); *Because He Liked to be at Home*, ten. (also plays recorder), hp. (1974); *On the Beach at Night*, 2 ten., pf., chamber org. (1978); *Be Music Night*, sop., pf. (1986); *Epitaphs*, bar., pf. (1995); *Found in a Country Churchyard*, sop., pf., or 2 sop., 2 cl., va., db., cel. (1995); *I Thirst for Shadows*, counterten. (1998).

PIANO: *Ma non sempre* (1987); *Hoquetus David*, 2 pf. (1987).

Bedford, Luke (*b* Wokingham, 1978). Eng. composer. Studied at RCM with E. Roxburgh and S. Bainbridge 1996–2000 and with Bainbridge at RAM 2000–2. Won RPS comp. prize 2000 and BBC3 Listeners' Award 2004. Works incl. *Broken Neon Arabesque*, orch. (1999); *5 Pieces*, orch. (2000); *5 Abstracts*, orch. (2000); *Catafalque*, orch. (2002); *Rode with Darkness*, orch. (2003); hn. trio (2004).

Bedford, Steuart (John Rudolf) (*b* London, 1939). Eng. conductor and pianist, particularly assoc. with EMT and Aldeburgh Fest. Début, Oxford Chamber Orch., 1964. On Glyndebourne mus. staff 1965–7. Professional cond. début SW 1967. Prof. at RAM from 1965. Cond. f.p. of

Britten's *Death in Venice*, 1973, and *Phaedra*, 1976. Arr. orch. suite from *Death in Venice* (Aldeburgh 1984). Art. dir. Aldeburgh Fest. 1973–98.

Bédos de Celles, Dom Francis (*b* Caux, 1709; *d* Saint-Denis, 1779). Fr. Benedictine, organ builder and author of important book, *L'Art du facteur d'orgues* (The Art of the Organ-builder, 1766–78).

Beecham, (Sir) **Thomas** (*b* St Helens, 1879; *d* London, 1961). Eng. conductor and impresario. First appearance was as cond. of Hallé Orch. at St Helens, 1899. Educated Rossall School and Wadham College, Oxford. Studied comp. with Charles Wood. Early ambition to be composer, but took up cond. instead. Came to the fore about 1905 when he founded New Sym. Orch. In 1910, with backing of his father, the industrialist Sir Joseph Beecham, staged season of opera at CG at which **Elektra* had first Eng. perf., also *A *Village Romeo and Juliet* and *The *Wreckers*. Cond. f. Eng. ps. of *Der Rosenkavalier* (CG 1913) and *Ariadne auf Naxos* (1st vers.) (London 1913). Brought Diaghilev's Ballets Russes to London 1913–14. Thereafter there was hardly a feature of Eng. mus. life with which Beecham was not closely, often controversially, and always artistically involved. Assoc. with most leading Brit. orchs. Founded Beecham SO 1909, Beecham Opera Co. 1915, LPO 1932, and RPO 1946. Salzburg Fest. 1931 (Vienna PO). NY Met début 1942 (*Phoebus and Pan* (Bach)/*The Golden Cockerel*). In decade preceding Second World War was art. dir. of Royal Opera House, CG. Cond. many Amer. orchs. Ardent champion of Delius, about whom he wrote a book, and cond. f.ps. of his *A Mass of Life* (1909), *Songs of Sunset* (1911), *North Country Sketches* (1915), *Cynara* (1929), *Koanga* (CG 1935), *Florida Suite* (1937), and *Irmelin* (Oxford 1953). Notable interpreter of Mozart, Haydn, Sibelius, Strauss, and Fr. composers of 19th cent. Thrice married. Knighted 1915, 2nd baronet 1916, CH 1957. Autobiography *A Mingled Chime* (London, 1944).

Beer, Jakob Liebmann. Real name of Giacomo *Meyerbeer.

Beer Barrel Polka ('Roll out the barrel'). Tune composed by Jaromir Vejvoda (*b* 1902) and pubd. in Prague, 1934, as *Lost Love* (*Škoda Lásky*). Acquired Eng. title when pubd. in NY, 1939. Became very popular with Servicemen in 2nd World War.

Beeson, Jack (Hamilton) (*b* Muncie, Ind., 1921). Amer. composer and conductor. Taught at Columbia Univ. Taught at Juilliard Sch. 1961–3. MacDowell prof. of mus., Columbia Univ. 1965–88 (chairman of mus. dept., 1969–72). Works incl. operas (incl. *Jonah* (1948–50), *Lizzie Borden* (1965), *Cyrano* (1990), *Sorry, Wrong Number* (1996), and *Practice in the Art of Elocution* (1998)); orch. works incl. a sym. (1959); *The Daring Young Man on the Flying Trapeze*, ten., ens. (1999); *Ophelia Sings*, mez., ens. (2000); *A Rupert Brooke Cycle*, bar./bass, pf. (2002); *Summer Rounds and Canons*, unacc. ch. (2002); choral and vocal works; chamber mus.; and pf. and org. pieces.

Bee's Wedding, The. Fanciful name for Mendelssohn's *Lieder ohne Worte* No.34 in C for solo pf. (Book VI, Op.67, No.4, *Spinnerlied*). Sometimes known as *Spinning Song*. Comp. 1845.

Beethoven, Ludwig van (*b* Bonn, 1770; *d* Vienna, 1827). Ger. composer and pianist who radically transformed every mus. form in which he worked. His paternal family were of Flemish stock, his grandfather having emigrated to Bonn where he became Court Singer to the Elector. Beethoven's father also became Court Singer, but was a coarse, drunken man, hopeful of exploiting his 2nd child Ludwig's mus. talents. Beethoven's early mus. education came from his father and several mediocre teachers. In 1779 he became a pupil of Christian Gottlob Neefe and his ass. as court organist in 1784. In 1786 he visited Vienna and may have extemporized for Mozart. On return to Bonn he found an understanding patron in Count Waldstein. For 4 years he was a violist in the court th. orch. in addition to other duties. In 1792 Haydn, visiting Bonn, saw some of Beethoven's early comps. and invited him to study with him in Vienna. There, despite his brusque and often uncouth manner, he was patronized by the aristocracy and lived for 2 years (1794–6) in the home of Prince Lichnowsky. His fame was entirely that of a virtuoso improviser at the kbd. Lessons from Haydn proved unsatisfactory and Beethoven went for theory to Schenk and later to Albrechtsberger and Salieri. His Op.1, 3 pf. trios, was pubd. 1795 and had immediate success.

Apart from occasional visits to the countryside Beethoven passed the rest of his life in Vienna. For 30 years he prod. mus. of all kinds in a steady flow. His first public appearance in Vienna was as soloist in his B♭ major pf. conc. in 1795. His 3rd Symphony (the *Eroica*), besides being a work of revolutionary import because it greatly extended the possibilities of symphonic form, was significant because it was originally ded. to Napoleon Bonaparte. Beethoven erased the dedication when he heard that Napoleon had proclaimed himself emperor. His 1805 his only opera *Fidelio*, originally called *Leonore*, was performed but withdrawn for rev. after 3 perfs. and given the following year in a 2-act version. His 5th and 6th (*Pastoral*) Syms. were f.p. at the same concert in 1808 and the 7th appeared in 1813, the year before the successful prod. of the further rev. *Fidelio*. In 1817 and 1818 he began work on his 9th Sym., which departed from all precedent by including a choral finale for solo vv., ch., and orch., and the *Missa Solemnis*. These were perf. in 1824. From 1824 to 1826 he comp. the last 5 of his 17 str. qts.

Beethoven's mus. may have sometimes been misunderstood in his lifetime but it was never neglected. However, his personal eccentricities and unpredictability were to grow, principally because of his discovery in 1798 that he was going deaf. It was not until 1819 that conversation with him was possible only by writing in a notebook, but in the intervening 20 years his affliction, though it varied in intensity, steadily worsened. Perhaps this is also why he never married, though he loved several women, and one in particular, the still unidentified 'Immortal Beloved' (Maynard Solomon, in his *Beethoven*, 1977, gives convincing but not incontrovertible reasons for believing that she was Antonie Brentano, wife of a Frankfurt merchant. She lived from 1780 to 1869. Beethoven dedicated the *Diabelli Variations* to her.) An indication of the esteem in which Beethoven was held is that in 1815 Vienna conferred its honorary freedom on him. When he died, his funeral at Währing was a nat. occasion. His grave is now in the Central Friedhof, Vienna.

Beethoven's significance in the history and development of mus. is immense. He emancipated and democratized the art, composing out of spiritual inner necessity rather than as provider of virtuoso display material. He was not a quick or facile worker—his sketchbooks show how he laboriously developed an idea from sometimes banal beginnings to the final version. His mastery of structure and of key relationships was the basis on which he worked a revolution in the handling of sonata-form. It is to Beethoven that we owe the full emergence of the symphony as a repository for a composer's most important ideas. He expanded the coda from a formal conclusion to a climactic splendour; he transformed the minuet into the tempestuous, exultant scherzo; he was the first to use 'motto-themes' as a consistent formal device. In his slow movements, mus. expressed a mystical exaltation which even Mozart had never approached. In the str. qt. and the pf. sonata also, Beethoven extended the medium to a vastly increased technical and expressive degree (though in the case of the pf. it was not until his last sonatas that his technical use of the instr. went beyond that of his predecessors). It is probably true to say that today his mus. is the most frequently performed of any composer's.

Among the most important of his many comps. are:

OPERA: **Fidelio*, Op.72 (1805, rev. 1806 and 1814).

SYMPHONIES: No.1 in C, Op.21, comp. 1799–1800, f.p. Vienna, 2 April 1800, cond. P. Wranitzky; pubd. 1801. No.2 in D, Op.36, comp. 1801–2, f.p. Vienna, 5 Apr. 1803, cond. Beethoven; pubd. 1804. No.3 in E♭ (**Eroica*), Op.55, comp. 1803–4, f.pub.p.Vienna, 7 Apr. 1805; pubd. 1806. No.4 in B♭, Op.60, comp. 1806, f.pub.p. Vienna, 15 Nov. 1807, cond. Clement; pubd. 1808. No.5 in C minor, Op. 67, comp. 1804–8, f.p. Vienna, 22 Dec. 1808, cond. Beethoven; pubd. 1809. No.6 in F (**Pastoral*), Op.68, comp. 1807–8, f.p. Vienna, 22 Dec. 1808, cond. Beethoven; pubd. 1809. No.7 in A, Op.92, comp. 1811–12, f.p. Vienna, 8 Dec. 1813, cond. Beethoven; pubd. 1816. No.8 in F, Op.93, comp. 1812, f.p. Vienna, 27 Feb. 1814, cond. Beethoven; pubd. 1816. No.9 in D minor (**Choral*), Op.125, comp. 1817–23, f.p. Vienna, 7 May 1824, cond. Beethoven; pubd. 1826. **Battle Symphony*, Op.91, comp. 1813, f.p. Vienna, 8 Dec. 1813, cond. Beethoven; pubd. 1816.

CONCERTOS: *Piano*: E♭ (1783); No.1 in C, Op.15 (really No.2 in order of comp.), comp. 1795–8, f.p. (presumed) Vienna, 2 April 1800, soloist Beethoven, cond. Wranitzky; pubd. March 1801. No.2 in B♭, Op.19 (really No.1 in order of comp.), comp. 1794–5, f.p. Vienna, 29 Mar. 1795, soloist Beethoven; pubd. Dec. 1801. No.3 in C minor, Op.37, comp. 1800–1, f.p. Vienna, 5 Apr. 1803, soloist Beethoven; pubd. 1804. No.4 in G, Op. 58, comp. 1805–6, f.p. Vienna, 22 Dec. 1808, soloist Beethoven; pubd. 1808. No.5 in E♭ (nicknamed **'Emperor'* but not by Beethoven), Op.73, comp. 1809, f.p. Leipzig, Dec. 1810, soloist F. Schneider, f. Vienna p. 12 Feb. 1812, soloist Czerny; pubd. 1811. Vn. conc., Op.61, arr. for pf. by Beethoven in 1807 and pubd. 1808. *Violin*: vn. conc. in D, Op.61, comp. 1806, f.p. Vienna, 23 Dec. 1806, soloist Franz Clement; pub. 1809. *Piano, violin, and cello*: triple conc. in C, Op.56, comp. 1804, f.p. 1808; pubd. 1807.

ORCHESTRAL (excl. Syms. & Concs.): *Overtures*: **Coriolan*, Op.62 (1807); *Die Weihe des Hauses* (**Consecration of the House*), Op.124 (1822); *Leonora No.1*, Op.138 (1805), *Leonora No.2* (1805), *Leonora No.3* (1806); *Fidelio* (1814). For details see under *Fidelio*; *Overture* and 9 items of incidental mus. for **Egmont* (Goethe), Op.84 (1809–10); *Overture* and 8 items of incidental mus. for *Die *Ruinen von Athen* (Kotzebue), Op.113 (1811); *Overture* and 9 items of incidental mus. for **König Stephan* (Kotzebue), Op.117 (1811); Ov. in C (**Namensfeier*), Op.115 (1814–15); Ov., introduction, and 16 Nos. for ballet *Die Geschöpfe des *Prometheus*, *Op.43 (1800–1)*.

PIANO SONATAS (32 in number): Nos. 1, 2 and 3, Op.2, No.1 in F minor, No.2 in A major, No.3 in C major (1794–5); No.4, Op.7, in E♭ (1796); Nos. 5, 6 and 7, Op.10, No.1 in C minor, No.2 in F major, No.3 in D major (1798); No.8, Op.13, **Pathétique* in C minor (1799); Nos. 9 and 10, Op.14, No.1 in E major, No.2 in G major (1799); No.11, Op.22, in B♭ (1800); No.12, Op.26, in A♭ (1800–1); Nos. 13 and 14, Op.27, No.1 in E♭, No.2 in C♯ minor (**Moonlight*), both described as *quasi una fantasia* (1800–1); No.15, Op.28, in D major (**Pastoral*) (1801); Nos. 16, 17 and 18, Op.31, No.1 in G major, No.2 in D minor, No.3 in E♭ (1801–2); Nos. 19 and 20, Op.49, No.1 in G minor, No.2 in G major (1802); No.21, Op.53, in C major (**Waldstein*) (1804); No.22, Op.54, in F major (1804); No.23, Op.57, in F minor (**Appassionata*) (1804–5); No.24, Op.78, in F♯ major (1809); No. 25, Op.79, *Sonatina* in G major (1809); No.26, Op.81a, in E♭ (**Lebewohl*, usually known as *Les *Adieux*) (1809–10); No.27, Op.90, in E minor (1814); No.28, Op.101, in A major (1816); No.29, Op.106, in B♭ (**Hammerklavier*) (1817–18); No.30, Op.109, in E major (1820); No.31, Op.110, in A♭ (1821); No.32, Op.111, in C minor (1821–2).

OTHER PIANO WORKS: sonata in D for 4 hands, Op.6 (1797); 7 *Bagatelles*, Op.33 (1782–1802); 6 variations in F major on orig. theme, Op.34 (1802); 15 variations in E♭ and fugue on theme from *Prometheus* (known as **Eroica Variations*) Op.35 (1802); 32 variations in C minor (1806–7); 6 variations in D, Op.76 (1810); fantaisie in G minor, Op.77 (1810); 11 *Bagatelles*, Op.119 (1821); 33 *Variations on a Waltz by* *Diabelli, Op.120 (1819–23); 6 *Bagatelles*, Op.126 (1823–4); *Grosse Fuge* in B♭, Op.133 (arr. Beethoven for pf. duet, Op.134) (1826); *Rondo a capriccio* in G ('Rage over a lost Groschen'), Op.129 (1825–6).

CHAMBER MUSIC: str. qts: Op.18, Nos. 1–6 in F major, G major, D major, C minor, A major, B♭ (1798–1800); Nos. 7, 8 and 9, Op.59, Nos. 1–3 in F major, E minor, C major (the *Rasoumovsky qts., ded. to Count *Rasoumovsky, Russian ambassador in Vienna, a keen qt. player) (comp. 1806); No.10, Op.74, in E♭ (known as *Harp; 1809); No.11, Op.95, in F minor (1810); No.12, Op.127, in E♭ (1822–5); No.13, Op.130, in B♭ (1825–6; present finale replaces *Grosse Fuge, Op.133); No.14, Op.131, in C♯ minor (1825–6); No.15, Op.132, in A minor (1825); No.16, Op.135, in F major (1826); Op.133, in B♭ (*Grosse Fuge), orig. finale of Op.130 (1825). Str. quintets: Op.4, in E♭ (1795–6), arr. of Octet for wind instr. (comp. 1792–3, pubd. 1830 as Op.103); Op.29 in C major (1800–1); Op.104, in C minor, arr. by Beethoven in 1817 of his pf. trio, Op.1, No.3 (1792–4). Pf. trios: Op.1, Nos. 1–3, in E♭, G major, and C minor (1792–4); Op.38, in E♭ (with vn. or cl.), arr. by Beethoven of his Septet, Op.20 (1820–3); 14 Variations in E♭, Op.44 (1802–3); Op.70, Nos. 1–2, in D major and E♭ (1808); Op.97, in B♭ (*Archduke) (1810–11); Variations on 'Ich bin der Schneider *Kakadu', Op.121a (Kakadu) (c.1798). String Trios: Op.3 in E♭ (pre–1794) transcribed for vc. and pf., Op.64; Op.8, *Serenade* in D major (1796–7); Op.9, Nos. 1–3, in G major, D major, and C minor (1797–8); Pf. quintet (pf., ob., cl., hn., bn.), in E♭ (1796), arr. for pf. qt. (1796, pubd. 1801); *Septet* (vn., va., vc., cl., hn., bn., and db.), Op.20 in E♭ (1799–1800). Vn. sonatas (but note that Beethoven described them as sonatas for pf. and vn.): Op.12, Nos. 1–3, in D major, A major and E♭ (1797–8); Op.23, in A minor (1800); Op.24, in F major (*Spring) (1800–1); Op.30, Nos. 1–3, in A major, C minor, and G major (1801–2); Op.47, in A major (*Kreutzer) (1802–3); Op.96, in G major (1812, rev. 1815). Vc. sonatas: Op.5, Nos. 1–2, in F major and G minor (1796); Op.69, in A major (1807–8); Op.102, Nos. 1–2, in C major and D major (1815). Miscellaneous: *Serenade* in D major, Op.25, fl., vn., va. (1801); *Sextet* in E♭, Op.81b, 2 hn., str. (?1795); *Trio* in B♭, Op.11, pf., cl. or vn., vc. (1797); *Sonata* in F major, Op.17, hn., pf. (1800); *Variations* for vc. and pf.: in G major, WoO 45, on 'See the conqu'ring hero comes' from *Judas Maccabaeus* (1796), in F major, Op.66, on 'Ein Mädchen oder Weibchen' from *Die Zauberflöte* (1796), and in E♭, WoO 46, on 'Bei Männern, welche Liebe fühlen' from *Die Zauberflöte* (1801).

CHORAL: *Cantata on the death of the Emperor Joseph II* (1790); *Cantata on the accession of Emperor Leopold II* (1790); *Christus am Ölberge, oratorio, Op.85 (1803); Mass in C major, Op.86 (1807); *Mass in D major (*Missa Solemnis*), Op.123 (1819–22); *Choral Fantasia (pf., ch., and orch.), Op.80 (1808); *Meeresstille und glückliche Fahrt* (*Calm Sea

and Prosperous Voyage), Op.112 (1814–15); *Der glorreiche Augenblick* (The Glorious Moment), cantata, Op.136 (1814).

SOLO VOICE (Songs, etc.): scena and aria *'Ah! Perfido!'*, sop. and orch., Op.65 (comp. 1796); *Adelaide, Op.46 (1795); *An die Hoffnung*, Op.32 (1805); *An die ferne Geliebte (To the distant beloved), song-cyle for ten. and pf. (words by A. Jeitteles), Op.98 (1816); 25 Scot. songs, with acc. for pf. trio, Op.108 (1815–16); 12 Scot. songs, with acc. for pf. trio, Op.108 (1815–16); 12 Scottish songs (pubd. 1841).

Beggar's Opera, The. First and most popular of ballad operas. In 3 acts, arr. and adapted by Christoph Pepusch to a lib. by John Gay. Prod. London, Jan. 1728; NY Dec. 1750. Its 69 tunes are mostly derived from popular ballads of the day. The plot deals with London low life, the 'hero' being the highwayman Macheath and the heroine Polly, and is a satire on contemporary politics and on It. operatic conventions. 20th-cent. vogue dates from London revival at Lyric, Hammersmith, in version re-orchestrated and re-harmonized by Frederic *Austin which ran from June 1920 for 1,463 perfs. Other versions by E. J. *Dent (Birmingham 1944), *Britten (Cambridge 1948), *Bliss (film, 1953), Jeremy Barlow (1980), and Muldowney (1982). Milhaud's 3-act *L'Opéra des gueux* (1937) is an arr. of *The Beggar's Opera*. The Gay-Pepusch sequel *Polly, dating from 1729, was banned by the Lord Chamberlain for nearly 50 years. See also *Weill, Kurt*.

Beggar Student, The (Millöcker). See *Bettelstudent, Der*.

Beglarian, Grant (b Tiflis, 1927; d White Plains, NY, 2002). Russ.-born Amer. composer. Went to USA in 1947. Founded Music Book Associates in NY, 1961. Dir. young composers' project, Ford Foundation 1961–9. Dean and prof. of mus., sch. of performing arts, Univ. of S. California, Los Angeles, 1969–82. Comps. incl. vn. sonata; vc. sonata; Sym.; *Divertimento for orchestra* (1957–8); cantata '. . . *And All the Hills Echoed*' (1968); *Fables, Foibles, and Fancies* (1971); *Diversions*, va., vc., orch. (1972); Sinfonia for str. (1974); *To Manitou*, sop., orch. (1976); and *Partita for Orch.* (1986).

begleiten (Ger.). To accompany. Hence *Begleitung*, accompaniment; *begleitend*, accompanying.

Begley, Kim (b Birkenhead, 1955). Eng. tenor. CG début 1983. Has sung many contemp. operatic roles, incl. Achilles in Tippett's *King Priam* and Pellegrin in his *New Year* (Glyndebourne 1990). Sang Fritz in Opera North revival of Schreker's *Der ferne Klang* (1992). Bayreuth début 2000 (Loge in *Ring*); NY Met début 2003 (Laca in *Jenůfa*). Created Samuel Griffiths in Picker's *An American Tragedy*, NY Met 2005.

Beherrscher der Geister, Der (Weber). See *Ruler of the Spirits, The*.

Behrens, Hildegard (b Land Oldenburg, 1937). Ger. soprano. Opera début Freiburg, 1971. At

Deutsche Oper am Rhein, Düsseldorf, she sang wide variety of roles incl. title-role of *Káťa Kabanová*. Sang Leonore in *Fidelio*, Zurich 1975. CG début 1976; NY Met 1976; Salzburg Fest. 1977; Bayreuth 1983 (Brünnhilde).

Beiderbecke, Bix [Leon Bismarck] (*b* Davenport, Iowa, 1903; *d* NY, 1931). Amer. jazz cornet player, pianist, and composer. Went to Lake Forest Acad., 1921, whence he was expelled for persistently visiting Chicago to hear and play jazz. Made records in Chicago with the Wolverines, 1924. Formed mus. partnership 1925 with Frank Trumbauer, saxophonist, both joining Jean Goldkette's dance band until it was disbanded in 1927. Joined Paul Whiteman band 1927–9. Alcoholism ruined his health, although he worked in NY with Tommy Dorsey and Benny Goodman. His tone was highly individual and unmistakable, as can be heard in two 1927 recordings, *Singin' the Blues* and *I'm coming Virginia*.

Beinum, Eduard van. See *Van Beinum, Eduard.*

Beisser (Ger.). Biter i.e. *mordent.

beklemmt, beklommen (Ger.). Oppressed, heavy of heart. Most famous use of this instruction is by Beethoven in middle section of cavatina of str. qt. in B♭ major, Op.130, where mus. modulates into C♭.

Belaieff, Mitrofan. See *Belyayev, Mitrofan.*

bel canto (It.). Beautiful singing, beautiful song. A term covering the remarkable qualities of the great 18th-cent. and early 19th-cent. It. singers, and suggesting rather perf. in the lyrical style, in which tone is made to tell, than in the declamatory style. Vocal agility, beauty of tone, and legato phrasing, with faultless technique, were the prin. ingredients.

Belcea Quartet. Brit. string quartet. Formed as students at RCM in 1994. 1st prize at Osaka and Bordeaux Int. Str. Qt. Comps. 1999; RPS Chamber Mus. Award 2002 and 2003. Resident qt., Wigmore Hall, London, from 2001. USA début 2004–5 (incl. NY and Boston), Carnegie Hall 2006. Tours to Eur., Australia, NZ, Japan. Salzburg Fest. début 2005. Noted recordings of Britten qts.

Belfagor. Lyric comedy in prol., 2 acts, and epilogue by *Respighi to lib. by C. Guastalla after Marselli's comedy (1920). Comp. 1921–2. Prod. Milan 1923, NY (concert) 1971.

Belisario. Opera in 3 acts by Donizetti, to lib. by Cammarano after Marmontel's drama *Bélisaire* (1776). Prod. Venice 1836, London 1837, New Orleans 1842, Paris 1843.

Belkin, Boris (*b* Sverdlovsk, 1948). Russian violinist. Made first public appearances at age of 6. Won first prize, 1973, in Soviet nat. comp. Emigrated to Israel 1974. Soloist with leading Amer. and European orchs.

bell. (1) This popular and ubiquitous mus. instr. varies in weight from over 100 tons to a fraction of an ounce. For public bells the most usual bell metal is a bronze of 13 parts copper to 4 parts tin: the shape and proportions are the result of very intricate calculations in order to secure good tone and tuning—the latter not only of the *strike note* with its attendant overtones but also of the deep tone which persists after these have died away, i.e. the *hum note*, which should be an octave below the strike note.

There are 2 chief ways of sounding ordinary church bells, *chiming* (the clapper moved mechanically just sufficiently to strike the side of the bell) and *ringing* (in which the bell is swung round full circle).

A *ring* of church bells may consist of any number from 5 to 12. With 5 bells 120 variations of order, or *changes*, are possible; with 12 bells they number almost 480 millions. *Change ringing* by hand-ropes, a characteristic British practice, is a still popular hobby. Various standard changes are described by various traditional names, as 'Grandsire Triples', 'Bob Major', or 'Oxford Treble Bob'. Dorothy L. Sayers's detective story *The Nine Tailors* (1934) hinges on bell-ringing most ingeniously.

On the continent of Europe 'rings' are unknown but the *carillon* is there an ancient institution—esp. in Belgium and Holland. This consists of a series of anything up to 77 bells played by skilful artists from a manual and pedal console somewhat similar to that of an organ but more cumbrous. Tunes and simple accompanying harmonies can be perf. At the hours and their halves and quarters the carillon is set in operation by clockwork. There are now some carillons in Britain and in the USA.

(2) *Tubular bells* are often used in the orch. and are also now used (electrically operated from a kbd.) in church towers. They are cylindrical metal tubes of different lengths, suspended in a frame and played by being struck with a hammer.

(3) *Handbells* are small bells with handles: they are arr. in pitch order on a table and played by several performers, each in charge of several bells. They are used for the practice of change ringers and also as an entertainment.

(4) A term to describe the open end of a wind instr. from which the sound comes.

Bell, Joshua (*b* Indianapolis, 1967). Amer. violinist. When 14 was soloist with Philadelphia Orch., cond. Muti. NY début 1985 with St Louis Symphony. Toured Ger. with Indianapolis SO 1987. London début 1987 (with RPO). NY recital début 1988. Gave f.p. of Maw's vn. conc., NY 1993.

Bell, William Henry (*b* St Albans, 1873; *d* Gordon's Bay, Cape Province, 1946). Eng. composer, organist, and violinist. Prof. of harmony, RAM, 1903–12. Went to Capetown 1912 to become prin., S. African College of Mus. in 1919, becoming dean of faculty of mus., Capetown Univ., until retirement 1935. Comp. operas, syms., hymns, va. conc., chamber mus.

Bellaigue, Camille (*b* Paris, 1858; *d* Paris, 1930). Fr. music critic, 1885–1930 for *Revue des deux mondes*. Biographer of Mendelssohn, Gounod, Mozart, and Verdi.

Bell Anthem. Purcell's *Rejoice in the Lord alway* (1684–5). The name (which dates from the composer's lifetime) alludes to the pealing scale passages of the instr. introduction.

Belle Hélène, La (Beautiful Helen). Opéra-bouffe in 3 acts by Offenbach to lib. by Meilhac and Halévy. Prod. Paris 1864; London 1866; Chicago 1867. Successfully revived in Paris 1960 and later in London by SW Opera (now ENO).

Belletti, Giovanni Battista (*b* Sarzana, 1813; *d* Sarzana, 1890). It. baritone assoc. with Jenny *Lind. Début in Stockholm 1839 in *Il barbiere di Siviglia*. Sang with Lind in Donizetti, Meyerbeer, and Rossini operas in Sweden, Eng. (1848 début), and USA. In the USA his tours with Lind were arr. by Barnum. Retired 1862.

Bellezza, Vincenzo (*b* Bitonto, Bari, 1888; *d* Rome, 1964). It. conductor. Début San Carlo, Naples, 1908, in *Aida*. Cond. at NY Met 1926–35, CG 1926–30 and 1935–6. At CG cond. at Melba's farewell (1926), and at first London perf. of *Turandot* (1927). Rome Opera after 1935. Re-visited London 1957 (Stoll Th.) and 1958 (Drury Lane).

Bellincioni, Gemma (Cesira Matilda) (*b* Como, 1864; *d* Naples, 1950). It. soprano. Début in Naples, 1879. Created Santuzza in *Cavalleria rusticana* (1890) and title-role in *Fedora* (1898). Was first It. Salome (Turin 1906) and sang role over 100 times. Wife of ten. Roberto Stagno, the first Turiddù, who was also her teacher.

Bellini, Vincenzo (*b* Catania, Sicily, 1801; *d* Puteaux, nr. Paris, 1835). It. composer. Educated San Sebastiano Cons., Naples, where he studied under *Zingarelli. Perf. of his first opera, *Adelson e Salvini*, at cons. in 1825 led to commission for opera for San Carlo, Naples; and this in its turn led to a commission from La Scala which resulted in *Il pirata*, a vehicle for the expressive lyrical style of the ten.*Rubini. This opera was then prod. in Paris and initiated Bellini's fame outside It. Another success was his setting of Vaccai's version of the Romeo and Juliet story, *I Capuleti e i Montecchi*, prod. Venice 1830 with Pasta in the *travesti* role of Romeo. Recent revivals have shown this to be one of Bellini's masterpieces. However, its popularity was eclipsed by *La sonnambula* (Milan 1831), in which *Malibran appeared throughout Europe. Less than a year later came *Norma*; its sop. title-role was first sung by Pasta and succeeding exponents have included Grisi, Tietjens, Lilli Lehmann, Ponselle, Callas, and Sutherland. His last opera, *I Puritani*, was written for Paris (on the advice of Rossini) where its first cast in 1835 was led by Grisi, Rubini, Tamburini, and Lablache. Seven of his operas have libretti by Felice Romani.

Bellini's vocal style requires superb legato allied to great florid agility. His long elegant me-

lodies, of which *Casta diva* from *Norma* is a supreme example, were admired by, and influenced, Berlioz. Wagner, too, was attracted by Bellini's operas and noted the close alliance between mus. and lib. For a period, Bellini was out of fashion, being regarded as merely a composer of display pieces, but a new generation of great singers has restored them to favour, revealing their dramatic force and melodic beauty.

OPERAS: *Adelson e Salvini* (Naples 1825); *Bianca e Gernando* (Naples 1826; rev. as *Bianca e Fernando*, Genoa 1828); *Il *pirata* (Milan 1827); *La straniera* (Milan 1829); *Zaira* (Parma 1829); *I *Capuleti e i Montecchi* (Venice 1830); *La *sonnambula* (Milan 1831); *Norma* (Milan 1831); *Beatrice di Tenda* (Venice 1833); *I *Puritani* (Paris 1835).

Also comp. songs and instr. works, incl. an ob. conc.

bell lyra. Portable form of glockenspiel. It is mounted on a rod held perpendicularly in the left hand whilst the right hand holds the beater.

bellows and tongs. One of the burlesque means of mus.-making common in the 18th cent. Presumably the sound evoked was merely that of adroit rhythmic tapping.

Bell Rondo (It. *Rondo alla campanella*). Finale of vn. conc. in B minor by Paganini, containing bell-like effect. Liszt twice used same theme, in his *Grande Fantaisie de bravoure sur 'La Clochette'* (1832) and in *La campanella* (from the 6 *Transcendental studies based on Paganini*, 1838).

Bells, The (*Kolokola*). Choral sym., Op.35, by Rachmaninov for sop., ten., and bar. soloists, ch., and orch. Comp. 1913, f.p. St Petersburg 1913, cond. Rachmaninov; f.Eng.p. Liverpool 1921, cond. Wood. Rev. version 1936, f.p. Sheffield 1936, cond. Wood. Text is adaptation by Konstantin Balmont of E. A. Poe's poem.

Bells of Aberdovey. This is not a Welsh folk-song, as claimed in many books of such songs, but appears to be the comp. of *Dibdin. He pubd. it in 1785, when it was sung in his Drury Lane opera *Liberty Hall*, and it appeared many times subsequently in vols. of his songs, not figuring in any of the numerous Welsh colls. before 1844.

Bells of Corneville (Planquette). See *Cloches de Corneville*.

Bells of Zlonice, The. A sym. in C minor by Dvořák, comp. 1865. Orig. his Op.3, it was lost and not recovered until 1923. Pubd. 1961, it is the longest of his orch. works (c.55 mins.).

belly. The upper surface of a str. instr., over which the str. are stretched. Also the sound-board of pf.

Bělohlávek, Jiří (*b* Prague, 1946). Cz. conductor. Finalist in 1971 Karajan int. cond. comp. After spell as ass. cond. Czech PO became cond. Brno State PO 1971–7; chief cond. Prague SO 1977–90;

prin. cond. Czech PO 1990–2; prin. cond. BBCSO from 2006. Guest cond. of leading Amer., Brit., and Russ. orchs. Took Prague SO to Edinburgh Fest. 1990.

Belshazzar. Oratorio by Handel. (F.p. London 1745.) Text by Charles Jennens.

Belshazzar's Feast. (1) Cantata by *Walton for bar., ch., and orch. to text compiled from biblical sources by O. Sitwell, comp. 1930–1, rev. 1931, 1948, 1957; f.p. Leeds Fest., 1931, cond. Sargent.

(2) Incidental mus. by Sibelius for play by Hjalmar Procopé, from which he provided 4-movement suite for small orch. (1906).

Belyayev, Mitrofan (Petrovich) (*b* St Petersburg, 1836; *d* St Petersburg, 1904). Russ. music publisher. Enthusiastic sponsor of 'new' nationalist school of Russian composers. Founded his publishing house at Leipzig, 1885, and sponsored concerts in St Petersburg. Russian composers gathered at his St Petersburg house every Friday from 1891, hence 16 pieces for str. qt. known as 'Les Vendredis' (Fridays) written in his honour in collab. by Borodin, Rimsky-Korsakov, Glazunov, Lyadov, and others. Firm moved to Bonn, then to Frankfurt. Absorbed by C. F. Peters, 1971.

bémol (Fr.), **bemolle** (It.). Flat (♭).

Beňačková, Gabriela (*b* Bratislava, 1944). Cz. soprano. Won Dvořák comp., Karlovy Vary, 1963. Opera début Prague 1970. Member Prague Nat. Th., but guest artist at world's leading opera houses, particularly in Janáček operas. Débuts: Dublin 1975, Moscow 1977, Vienna 1978, CG 1979; Salzburg Fest. 1984.

Benatzky, Ralph [Rudolf] (Josef Frantisek) (*b* Maravaské-Budejovice, 1884; *d* Zurich, 1957). Cz. composer of nearly 100 operettas, 250 film scores, and 5,000 songs. Wrote title-song and much of the score of *White Horse Inn* (*Im weissen Rössl*, Berlin 1930). Left Austria for USA in 1938, settling in Switzerland after Second World War.

Benda. Bohem. mus. family active in the 18th cent., 4 of them being the sons of a weaver and peripatetic musician. Three of these were:

(1) František (Franz) (*b* Staré-Benátky, 1709; *d* Potsdam, 1786). Chorister in Prague, then became violinist and moved to Dresden. In 1732 obtained a place at the Berlin court of Crown Prince of Prussia, later Frederick the Great. In 1771 became Frederick's Konzertmeister, accompanying him in fl. conc. Works incl. trio sonatas, vn. concs., 6 vn. sonatas, and 2 books of vn. *Études*.

(2) Jiří Antonin (Georg) (*b* Jungbunzlau, 1722; *d* Köstritz, Thuringia, 1795). Skilled oboist and kbd.-player. Went to Berlin in 1740 for lessons from his brother ((1) above). Violinist in royal band from 1742. Became Kapellmeister to Duke of Gotha in 1748. Spent 2 years in It. after 1764; on return wrote his *Ariadne auf Naxos* (1774) which earned him the claim to have invented *melodrama. Another melodrama, *Medea*, followed, also *Romeo und Julie* (1776). Retired 1778.

(3) Josef (*b* Staré-Benátky, 1724; *d* Berlin, 1804). Violinist, succeeded his brother František as leader of Frederick the Great's orch.

Several sons of the above also achieved mus. distinction, usually in Prussian court bands. Jiři's son, Friedrich Ludwig (*b* Gotha, 1752; *d* Königsberg, 1792) comp. an oratorio, church cantatas, 3 operas incl. *Der Barbier von Sevilla* (1776) and 3 vn. concs. František's eldest son, Friedrich Wilhelm Heinrich (*b* Potsdam, 1745; *d* Potsdam, 1814) was a fine violinist, playing in the Berlin court band from 1782, and comp. 2 operas, *Alceste* (1786) and *Orpheus* (1785), an operetta, *Das Blumenmädchen*, a cantata *Pygmalion*, and instr. works.

Bender, Paul (*b* Driedorf, 1875; *d* Munich, 1947). Ger. bass. Début Breslau 1900 (Sarastro in *Die Zauberflöte*); closely assoc. with Munich Opera until 1933 after his début there 1903. CG début 1914 (Amfortas in f. Eng. stage p. of *Parsifal*). NY Met 1922–7; Salzburg Fest. début 1926. Distinguished exponent of roles of Wotan, Sachs, Osmin, and Baron Ochs and of ballads of J. Loewe. Became teacher at Munich Mus. Sch.

Benedicite. (1) *The Song of the Three Holy Children* (Shadrach, Meshach, and Abednego) while in Nebuchadnezzar's fiery furnace. It is not in the Hebrew version of the book of Daniel, but comes from the Septuagint, or early Gr. translation of the Old Testament. It is one of the canticles of the Anglican service.

(2) Work by Vaughan Williams, for sop., ch., and orch. Comp. 1929 (prod. Leith Hill Fest. 1930); combines text of the canticle with a poem by J. Austin (1613–69).

Benedict, (Sir) **Julius** (*b* Stuttgart, 1804; *d* London, 1885). Ger.-born composer and conductor, naturalized Eng. Son of a banker, he had lessons in Weimar from Hummel who introduced him to Weber, in whose house in Dresden he lived as pupil and protégé 1821–4 and by whom he was taken to meet Beethoven in 1823. Appointed cond., Vienna Kärntnerthor Th. 1823–5. Went to work at San Carlo, Naples, 1825, where several of his operas were perf., and to Paris in 1834, where the singer *Malibran suggested he should visit London. From 1835 lived in Eng. He cond. opera seasons at Lyceum (1836–7), Drury Lane (1838–48), and Her Majesty's Th. from 1852. In 1848 cond. *Elijah* when Jenny Lind first sang in oratorio and later dir. most of her Amer. concerts. Cond., Norwich Fest., 1845–78, Liverpool Phil. Soc. 1867–79. Of his operas, oratorios, cantatas, syms., and concs., only the opera *The Lily of Killarney* (1862) is still occasionally perf. Wrote important biog. of Weber (London, 1881). Knighted 1871.

Benedictus. (1) In the RC Mass, the *Benedictus qui venit*, i.e. simply the words 'Blessed is he that cometh in the name of the Lord', which complete the *Sanctus* section of the *Mass.

(2) The song of Zacharias (Luke I. 68 et seq.). 'Blessed be the Lord God of Israel', which is sung

daily at *Lauds in RC churches and in the Eng. Prayer Book occurs in the Order for Morning Prayer.

beneplacito, beneplacimento (It.). Good pleasure. Preceded by the words *a suo* (at one's) this has the same sense as *ad libitum*.

Benet, John (*fl.* ?c.1420–50). Eng. composer of sacred mus. in style of Dunstable. Not to be confused with John *Bennet.

Ben-Haim [Frankenburger], **Paul** (*b* Munich, 1897; *d* Tel Aviv, 1984). Israeli composer and conductor. Ass. cond. at State Opera, Munich, 1920–4. Cond. at Augsburg opera 1924–31. Emigrated to Tel Aviv 1933. After formation of State of Israel in 1948 became Pres., Israeli Composers' Assoc., Dir., Jerusalem Acad. of Mus. 1949–54. Traditional Jewish and Arab melodies of the Near East flavour his works, which incl. 2 syms.; vn. conc.; vc. conc. (1962); pf. sonatina; pf. conc.; str. qt.; and oratorio *Thanksgiving from the Desert*.

Beni Mora. Oriental Suite in E minor, Op.29 No.1 for orch. by Holst in 3 movements. Comp. 1909–10 after visit to Algeria and rev. 1912. F.p. London 1912.

Benjamin, Arthur (*b* Sydney, NSW, 1893; *d* London, 1960). Australian composer and pianist. Prof. of pf. at Sydney Cons. 1919–21, then returned to Eng. in similar post at RCM from 1926. Pupils incl. Britten. Cond. Vancouver SO 1940–6. As pianist gave f.p. of Howells's 1st pf. conc., London 1914, and of Lambert's pf. conc., London 1931. Works incl. operas (incl. The *Devil Take Her* (1931) and A *Tale of Two Cities* (1949–50); ballet *Orlando's Silver Wedding* (1951); sym. (1941–5); pf. concertino (1927–8); vn. conc. (1932); harmonica conc. (1953); chamber mus. and pf. pieces. Also film mus. and songs.

Benjamin, George (*b* London, 1960). Eng. composer, pianist, and conductor. Began pf. lessons at 7 and comp. when he was 9. Gave f.p. of Britten's *Sonatina Romantica*, Aldeburgh Fest. 1983. Research at IRCAM, Paris, 1984–7. Guest cond., Hallé Orch. Teacher at RCM. Prof. of comp., King's Coll., London, from 2001. Works incl.:

ORCH.: *Altitude*, brass band (1977); *Ringed by the Flat Horizon* (1979–80); *At First Light*, chamber orch. (1982); *Fanfare for Aquarius*, chamber orch. (1983); *Antara* (with electronics) (1985–7, rev. 1989); *Cascade* (1990); *Helix* (1992); *Sudden Time* (1993); *Inventions*, chamber orch. (1995); *Dance Figures* (2004).

VOCAL: *A Mind of Winter*, sop. and small orch. (1981); *Jubilation*, orch. and mixed children's groups (1985); *Upon Silence*, mez., 5 viols (1990), mez., 2 va., 3 vc., 2 db. (1991); *Sometime Voices*, bar., ch., orch. (1996).

TAPE: *Panorama* (1985).

CHAMBER MUSIC: vn. sonata (1976–7); octet, fl. (picc.), cl., perc., celesta, str. (1978); *Flight*, fl.

(1979); *Duo*, vc. and pf. (1980); *Viola, Violo*, 2 va. (1997); *3 Miniatures*, vn. (2001); *Olicantus*, ens. (2002).

PIANO: pf. sonata (1977–8); *Sortilèges* (1981); *3 Studies (Iambic Rhythm, Meditation on Haydn's Name, Relativity Rag)* (1982–5); *Shadowlines* (2001).

Benjamin Cosyn's Virginal Book. A MS coll. of mus., chiefly for virginals, made 1622–43 by Benjamin *Cosyn. It is now in the Brit. Library. Pubd. 1923.

Bennet, John (*b* c.1575; *fl.*1599–1614). Eng. (probably Lancastrian) composer of madrigals, whose first book, for 44 vv., pubd. 1599, refers in preface to his youth. Remembered for *All creatures now are merry-minded*, his contribution to The *Triumphs of Oriana*, in which it is No.4, and *Weep, O mine eyes*. Not to be confused with John *Benet.

Bennett, (Sir) **Richard Rodney** (*b* Broadstairs, 1936). Eng. composer and pianist. A fluent composer, absorbing influences of jazz, atonality, and traditional harmony and structures, he has had success in many spheres incl. films, for which he has comp. over 35 scores (*Far From the Madding Crowd* a notable example). Prof. of comp., RAM, 1963–5. Settled in NY, 1979. CBE 1977. Knighted 1998. Prin. works incl.:

OPERAS: *The Ledge* (1961); The *Mines of Sulphur* (1963–5); *Penny for a Song* (1966); *Victory* (1968–9).

BALLET: *Jazz Calendar*, for chamber ens. (1963–4); *Isadora* (1981).

ORCH.: *Nocturnes* (1962); *Aubade* (1964); syms.: No.1 (1965), No.2 (1967), No.3 (1987); *Suite* for small orch. (1966); *Concerto for Orchestra* (1973); *Zodiac* (1976); *Serenade* (1976); *Commedia III*, 10 instr. (1973); *Music for Strings* (1977); *Anniversaries* (1982); *Sinfonietta* (1984); *Moving into Aquarius* (with T. Musgrave, 1984); *Reflections on a Theme of William Walton*, 11 solo str. (1985); *Dream Dancing* (1986); *Diversions* (1989); *Celebration* (1991); *Variations on a Nursery Tune* (1992); *Partita for Orch.* (1995); *Reflections on a 16th century Tune*, str. (1999); *Rondel for Large Jazz Ens.* (1999); *Country Dances (Book I)* (2001).

CONCERTOS: pf. (1968); ob. and str. (1969–70); guitar (1970); va. (1973); vn. (1975); *Actaeon (Metamorphosis I)*, hn. (1977); db. (1978); *Sonnets to Orpheus*, vc. (1979); hpd. (1980); *Memento*, fl., str. (1983); cl. (1987); marimba (1988); sax. (1988); perc. (1990); *Concerto for Stan Getz*, sax. (1990); tpt., wind band (1993); bn. conc., str. (1994); 7 *Country Dances*, ob./sax. (2000); *Suite française*, vers. for fl., orch. (2002, see also CHAMBER MUSIC).

VOICE(S) AND ORCH.: *The Approaches of Sleep* (1960); *London Pastoral*, ten., chamber orch. (1962); *Jazz Pastoral*, v., jazz orch. (1969); *Sonnet Sequence*, ten., str. (1974); *Spells*, sop., ch., orch. (1974); *Love Spells* (2nd and 5th movements from preceding), sop., orch. (1974); 5 *Sonnets of Louise Labé*, sop., ens. (1984); *Lovesongs*, ten., orch. (1984); *Ophelia*, counterten., ondes martenot, hp., 9 str. (1987).

CHAMBER MUSIC: *Winter Music*, fl., pf. (1960); ob. sonata (1962); solo vn. sonatas: No.1 (1955), No.2 (1964); str. qts.: No.1 (1952), No.2 (1953), No.3 (1960), No.4 (1964); wind quintet (1967–8); 5

Impromptus, gui. (1968); *Commedia II*, fl., vc., pf. (1972); *IV*, brass quintet (1973); *Scena II*, vc. (1973), *III*, cl. (1977); ob. qt. (1975); *Travel Notes, 1*, str. qt. (1975); *2*, wind qt. (1976); hn. sonata (1978); vn. sonata (1978); *Up Bow, Down Bow I*, vn., pf. (1979), *II*, va., pf. (1979); *Metamorphoses*, str. octet (1980); *6 Tunes for the Instruction of Singing Birds*, fl. (1981); *Music for String Quartet* (1981); sonatina for cl. (1981); *After Syrinx I*, ob., pf. (1982), *II*, marimba (1984); *Summer Music*, fl., pf. (1982); conc., wind quintet (1983); gui. sonata (1983); *Serenade No.2*, ondes martenot, pf. (1984); *Romances*, hn., pf. (1985); *Duo concertante*, cl., pf. (1985); *Sonata After Syrinx*, fl., va., hp. (1985); *Sounds and Sweet Aires*, fl., ob., pf. (1985); sonata, wind quintet, pf. (1986); *Lamento d'Arianna*, str. qt. (1986); sonata, sop. sax., pf. (1986); *After Ariadne*, va., pf. (1986); *Tender is the Night: Suite*, ondes martenot, str. qt. (1986); *Arethusa*, ob., str. trio (1989); *Capriccio*, vc., pf. (1990); vc. sonata (1991); bn. sonata (1991); *Arabesque*, ob. (1992); cl. quintet (1992); sax. qt. (1994); *Rondel*, va. (1997); *4 Country Dances*, ob./sop. sax., pf. (2000); *Suite française*, fl., pf. (2002); *Ballad in Memory of Shirley Horn*, cl., pf. (2005).

VOICE AND PF. (or other instr.): *The Music that her Echo is*, ten., pf. (1967); *Crazy Jane*, sop., cl., vc., pf. (1968–9); *A Garland for Marjory Fleming*, sop., pf. (1969); *Time's Whiter Series*, counterten., lute (1974); *The Little Ghost Who Died for Love*, sop., pf. (1976); *Just Friends in Print*, v., pf. (1979); *Vocalise*, sop., pf. (1981); *This is the Garden*, high v., pf. (1984); *Dream Songs*, sop. (or unison high vv.), pf. (1986); *A History of Thé dansant*, mez., pf. (1994); *The Glory and the Dream*, ch., org. (2000); *A Farewell to Arms*, female ch., vc. (2001); *Ballad of Sweet William*, female ch., pf. (2003).

PIANO: sonata (1954); *Fantasy* (1962); *5 Studies* (1962–4); *Capriccio*, 4 hands (1968); *Scena I* (1973); *4-Piece Suite*, 2 pf. (1974); *Kandinsky Variations*, 2 pf. (1977); *Eustace and Hilda* (1977); *Impromptu on the Name of Haydn* (1981); *Noctuary (Variations on a Theme of Joplin)* (1981); *Tango after Syrinx* (1985); *Tender is the Night*, 2 themes (1985); *Suite for Skip and Sadie*, pf. duet (1986); *3 Romantic Pieces* (1988); *Partridge Pie* (1990); *Over the Hills and Far Away*, pf. duet (1991); *Impromptu on a Theme of Henri Dutilleux* (1994).

FILM SCORES: *Billy Liar* (1963); *Far from the Madding Crowd* (1967); *Billion Dollar Brain* (1967); *Murder on the Orient Express* (1974); *Equus* (1977); *Four Weddings and a Funeral* (1994); *Sweeney Todd* (1997); *Gormenghast* (1999).

Bennett, Robert Russell (*b* Kansas City, 1894; *d* NY, 1981). Amer. composer and arranger. At 16 began to earn living by orchestrating and arranging scores for Broadway mus. comedies and the list of works to which he has applied his talent proves his success. It incl. *Rose-Marie* (1924), *Show Boat* (1927), *On Your Toes* (1936), *Oklahoma!* (1943), *Carmen Jones* (1943), *Carousel* (1945), *Annie Get Your Gun* (1946), *South Pacific* (1948), *Kiss Me Kate* (1948), *The King and I* (1951), *My Fair Lady* (1956), and *The Sound of Music* (1959). But perhaps his most famous arr. is the symphonic suite from Gershwin's

Porgy and Bess. His own comps. incl. *Abraham Lincoln Symphony* (1931); *Hollywood* for orch. (1937); *Concerto Grosso* for wind (1957); and sym. (1963). In 1935 he comp. a 3-act opera, *Maria Malibran*.

Bennett, (Sir) **William Sterndale** (*b* Sheffield, 1816; *d* London, 1875). Eng. composer, pianist, and teacher. Chorister at King's, Cambridge, at 7 and went 2 years later to newly founded RAM in London. Learned vn., pf., and comp. (with *Crotch). Later was taught by Cipriani *Potter. A pf. conc. written when he was 16 was heard a year later by Mendelssohn, who invited him to Ger. For 3 more years stayed at the RAM, composing 5 syms. and 3 more pf. concs. In one of these was soloist at a Phil. Soc. concert at the age of 19. In 1836 visited Leipzig where he became a friend of Schumann, who praised his work highly. Played his own concs. at Gewandhaus concerts. After marriage in 1844, career restricted to Eng., where he took on several demanding executive and admin. duties such as cond. of Phil. Soc. (1856–66), founder of Bach Soc., and, also in 1856, prof. of mus., Cambridge Univ. Cond. f. Eng. p. of J. S. Bach's *St Matthew Passion*, 1854. In 1866 became prin., RAM. Knighted 1871.

The reasons for Schumann's perhaps extravagant praise are now a little easier to judge, since some of Sterndale Bennett's music has been recorded. Undoubtedly his powers as a composer were lessened by the load of official work he undertook. In his lifetime his most popular works were the pastoral cantata *The May Queen* (Leeds Fest. 1858) and the oratorio *The Woman of Samaria* (Birmingham Fest. 1867). Other works incl. ov. *The Naiads*. Schumann's *Symphonic Studies* are ded. to him.

Bent, Ian (David) (*b* Birmingham, 1938). Eng. musicologist and university lecturer specializing in medieval mus. Lect. in mus., King's College, London Univ. 1965–75. Prof. of mus., Nottingham Univ. 1975–87. Visiting prof., Harvard Univ. 1982–3, Columbia Univ. 1986–7. Prof., Columbia Univ. 1987–2003.

Bentzon, Niels (Viggo) (*b* Copenhagen, 1919; *d* Fredericksberg, 2000). Danish composer. Comp. several ballets; an opera *Faust III* (1964); 8 pf. concs.; over 20 pf. sonatas; 15 syms.; 4 vn. concs.; 3 vc. concs.; 12 str. qts.; *Symphonic Variations*; 2 fl. concs.; ob. conc.; cl. conc. Some of works use 12-note system, and he is also influenced by jazz.

Benvenuto Cellini. Opera in 2 acts by Berlioz (Op.23) to lib. by Léon de Wailly and A. Barbier, loosely based on Cellini's autobiography (1728). Comp. 1834–7. Prod. Paris 1838, London 1853 (cond. Berlioz). Revived London 1966, Boston 1975. Rev. in 3 acts after Weimar perfs. in 1852. Berlioz withdrew the opera because of its failure. Some of the mus. is used in the ov. *Carnaval romain*. Cellini is subject of operas by Schlösser, Lachner, Diaz, and Saint-Saëns, among others.

bequadro (It.). The natural sign (♮).

Berberian, Cathy (*b* Attleboro, Mass., 1925; *d* Rome, 1983). Amer. soprano and singer-actress. Specialized in *avant-garde* works, notably those of her husband (from 1950 to 1966) Luciano *Berio. Salzburg Fest. 1974. Also teacher, composer, and writer.

berceuse (from Fr. *bercer*, to rock to sleep). A lullaby or an instr. comp. (in compound duple time) suggesting such. The popular pf. piece of this name, and in this style, by Chopin, is his Op.57 in D major (1844).

Berceuse de Jocelyn. See *Godard, Benjamin*.

Berceuse élégiaque. Piano piece by Busoni, comp. 1909 and added to *Elegien* (1907). Orch. version, Op.42, comp. 1909, sub-titled 'The man's lullaby at his mother's coffin'. F.p. NY 1911.

bereite vor (Ger.). Make ready, prepare (an organ stop).

Berenice. Opera in 3 acts by Handel to lib. by Antonio Salvi already used by Perti in 1709. Prod. London 1737. Well-known minuet occurs in the ov.

Berezovsky, Boris (*b* Moscow, 1969). Russ. pianist. Studied at Moscow Cons. with Eliso Virsaladze and privately with Alexander Satz. Won Gold Medal at Int. Tchaikovsky Comp., Moscow, 1990 and won John Ogdon Prize. Brit. début 1988 (Wigmore Hall recital). Noted duo with Vadim Repin; formed his own pf. trio. Concerto soloist with leading orchs. and conds. throughout Eur. and Asia.

Berezovsky [Berezowsky], **Nikolay** (*b* St Petersburg, 1900; *d* NY, 1953). Russ.-born violinist in Moscow and then in NYPO 1923–9. Cond., composer of 4 syms., concs. for vn., va., and vc., and chamber mus.

Berg, Alban (Maria Johannes) (*b* Vienna, 1885; *d* Vienna, 1935). Austrian composer whose output, though small, is among the most influential and important of the 20th cent. One of four children of a well-to-do family, had little formal mus. education but comp. romantic songs when he was 15. In 1904 began private comp. lessons with *Schoenberg and decided to devote his life to mus., giving up a job in the Civil Service. With his friend and fellow-pupil *Webern, entered the *avant-garde* artistic life of Vienna—the Sezession artists, the poet Peter Altenberg, the painter Kokoschka—but the dominating figure was *Mahler. Some of his songs were perf. at a concert by Schoenberg pupils in Vienna, Nov. 1907, the pf. variations a year later, and the str. qt. in 1911. When 2 of the 5 *Altenberglieder* with orch. were perf. in Vienna in Mar. 1913, cond. Schoenberg, the concert was continually interrupted and eventually abandoned. In May 1914 Berg attended a perf. of Büchner's play *Woyzeck* and determined to make an opera of it. Military service delayed work, but the mus. was eventually

finished in 1922 and was perf. in Berlin, Dec. 1925. It caused a furore but its success with the public was never in doubt, despite critical polemics. In the next decade Berg's powers were at their height and he comp. the Chamber Conc. (1925), the *Lyric Suite* for str. qt. (1926), and the concert aria *Der Wein* (1929). In 1929 began adaptation of 2 Wedekind plays as an opera lib. called *Lulu*. By 1934 he had completed the mus. in short score and begun full instrumentation. In the spring of 1935 began vn. conc. commissioned by Louis *Krasner. Impelled by news of the death of the beautiful 18-year-old Manon Gropius, daughter of Mahler's widow by her 2nd marriage, worked unwontedly quickly and finished the conc. in Aug. 1935, dedicating it 'to the memory of an angel'. Four months later he too died, through blood poisoning from an insect-bite. It has recently been established that several of Berg's works, incl. the *Lyric Suite, Lulu,* and the Violin Concerto, contain mus. cryptograms referring to his love for Frau Hanna Fuchs-Robettin (and others).

Berg has become, to the general public, the most acceptable of the so-called '12-note' or 'dodecaphonic' composers, probably because he never was an orthodox atonalist. His work is nearer to the Mahler idiom than to the Schoenbergian. In *Wozzeck* atonality is very freely used and applied to a highly formal structure, each scene being in a particular mus. form (variations, passacaglia, fugue, etc.). From the *Lyric Suite* onwards, Berg used 12-note procedures nearer to, but still significantly different from, the Schoenberg method. Technical methods notwithstanding, however, it is the emotional content of Berg's mus. which has awoken a ready response in listeners, particularly the Vn. Conc., which quotes the Bach chorale *Es ist genug* at its climax. Prin. comps.:

OPERAS: *Wozzeck* (1914–22); *Lulu* (1929–35), Act 3 realized from short score by *Cerha (1978–9).

ORCH.: *Three Pieces*, Op.6 (1913–14); 3 movements from *Lyric Suite* arr. for str. orch. (1928); *Chamber Concerto* for pf., vn., and 14 wind instr. (1923–5); vn. conc. (1935).

VOICE AND ORCH.: 7 *Early Songs* (1905–8, orch. 1928); 5 *Altenberglieder* (1912); 3 *Fragments from Wozzeck*, Op.7 (f.p. Frankfurt 1924); *Der *Wein* (1929); *Lulu-Symphonie* (1934).

CHAMBER MUSIC: *Variations on an Original Theme* for pf. (1908); pf. sonata (1907–8); str. qt., Op.3 (1910); 4 *Pieces* for cl. and pf. (1913); *Lyric Suite* for str. qt. (1925–6); *Adagio* from *Chamber Concerto* arr. for vn., cl., and pf. (1935).

SONGS: 7 *Early Songs* (1905–8); 4 *Songs*, Op.2 (1909–10); and about 70 early songs.

Berg, Natanaël (*b* Stockholm, 1879; *d* Stockholm, 1957). Swed. composer, mainly self-taught. Comp. 5 operas (*Leila* (1912), *Engelbrekt* (1929), *Judith* (1936), *Birgitta* (1942), and *Genoveva* (1947)); concs.; symphonic poems; ballets; and chamber mus. By profession an army veterinary surgeon.

bergamasque (Fr.), **bergamasca** (It.), **bergomask** (Eng.). Tune and chord sequence from Bergamo, It., found as ground bass in 16th and 17th cents. Also a peasant's dance from Bergamo. Composers have used the term with little significance, e.g. Debussy's *Suite Bergamasque* (1890, rev. 1905) for pf.

Berganza [Vargas], **Teresa** (*b* Madrid, 1935). Sp. mezzo-soprano. Début Madrid 1955. Sang at Aix-en-Provence 1957, La Scala 1957. Notable for her singing of Rossini, as in *La Cenerentola*. Débuts: Glyndebourne 1958; CG 1960; NY Met 1967; Salzburg Fest. 1972.

Berger, Erna (*b* Dresden, 1900; *d* Essen, 1990). Ger. soprano. Début Dresden 1925. Bayreuth 1929–33. Salzburg début 1932 and in 1953 and 1954. Member of Berlin State Opera from 1934. CG début 1934; NY Met 1949–51. Notable Mozart singer, esp. of Queen of Night. Sang in opera until 1955, when became teacher. Retired 1968.

Berger, Jean (*b* Hamm, 1909; *d* Aurora, Col., 2002). Ger.-born composer long resident in Fr., then in USA (Amer. cit.). From 1932 to 1946 was choral cond. and accompanist. Works incl. *Brazilian Psalm*, ch. (1941); *Vision of Peace*, ch. (1948); *The Pied Piper*, play with mus. (1968). Ed. of Bolognese 17th-cent. mus., e.g. by Torelli, Perti, etc.

Berger, Theodor (*b* Traismauer, Austria, 1905; *d* Vienna, 1992). Austrian composer. Works incl. *Homeric Symphony* (1948); vn. conc. (1954); and *Concerto-manuale* for 2 pf., metallophone, marimbaphone, perc., str. (1951).

bergerette (from Fr. *berger*, shepherd). A shepherd's song or dance or simple comp. supposed to be in the style of such. Popular in Fr. in 18th cent.

Berghaus, Ruth (*b* Dresden, 1927; *d* Berlin, 1996). Ger. theatre director. One of team of radical producers at Frankfurt Opera 1980–7. In *Parsifal* (1982) she represented the Grail knights as a depraved group with bald heads. Brit. début Cardiff (WNO) 1984 (*Don Giovanni*).

Berglund, Paavo (Allan Engelbert) (*b* Helsinki, 1929). Finn. conductor. Violinist in Finn. Radio SO 1949–56, ass. cond. 1956–62, prin. cond. 1967–71. Brit. début 1965, with Bournemouth SO. Prin. cond. Bournemouth SO 1972–9, Helsinki PO 1975–9, Stockholm PO 1987–92, Royal Danish Orch. from 1993. Cond. f.p. outside Finland (in Bournemouth and London) of Sibelius's *Kullervo* sym., 1970. OBE 1977.

Bergman, Erik (Valdemar) (*b* Uusikaarlepyy, Finland, 1911; *d* Helsinki, 2006). Finn. composer and conductor. Worked as mus. critic and cond. choirs 1950–78. Prof. of comp., Helsinki Acad., 1963–76. Works incl. setting of Rubaiyat of Omar Khayyám for bar., male ch., orch. (1953); *Aubade*, orch. (1958); concertino da camera (1961); *The Birds* (*Fåglarna*), vocal soloists, perc., cel. (1962); *Noa*, bar., vv., orch. (1976); *Arctica*, orch. (1979);

pf. conc. (1981); vn. conc. (1982); str. qt. (1982); *Lemminkäinen*, spkr., mez., bar., mixed ch. (1984); *Poseidon*, orch. (1993); and many smaller choral works.

Bergmann, Walter (George) (*b* Hamburg, 1902; *d* London, 1988). Ger.-born continuo player, recorder virtuoso, and musicologist. Settled in Eng. (1939). On staff Morley Coll, where he played major role in revival of recorder and counterten. voice. Acc. Alfred *Deller in perf. of Purcell, etc.

Bergonzi, Carlo (*b* Cremona, *c*.1683; *d* Cremona, 1747). It. maker of vns. in style of his master, Stradivarius. Finest period 1730–40. His instrs. look as beautiful as they sound. Succeeded by his son and nephews.

Bergonzi, Carlo (*b* Polisene, Parma, 1924). It. tenor. Began career as bar. at Lecce 1948 as Figaro in *Il barbiere di Siviglia*. Second début, as ten., at Bari 1951 (Andrea Chénier). London (Stoll Th.) 1953; La Scala 1953; US (Chicago) début 1955; NY Met 1956; CG 1962; Salzburg Fest. 1970. CG farewell recital 1991.

Bergsma, William (Laurence) (*b* Oakland, Calif., 1921; *d* Seattle, 1994). Amer. composer. On staff Juilliard Sch. 1946–63; Prof. Washington Univ., Seattle, from 1963, dir. 1963–71. Comps. incl. opera, *The Wife of Martin Guerre* (1955); ballet *Paul Bunyan* (1937); vn. conc. (1966); 2 syms.; *The Voice of the Coelacanth* (1980); and chamber mus.

Beringer, Oscar (*b* Furtwangen, Baden, 1844; *d* London, 1922). Ger.-born pianist. Spent childhood in Eng. to which his father fled 1849. Appointed prof. at Tausig's Berlin Sch. for pianists, 1869. In 1873 returned to London, founding pf. sch. which survived until 1897. Gave f. Eng. p. Brahms's 2nd conc., London, 14 Oct. 1882. Prof. RAM from 1885. Composer of pf. pieces.

Berio, Luciano (*b* Oneglia, now Imperia, It., 1925; *d* Rome, 2003). It. composer. In 1955 with *Maderna founded EMS at It. Radio, remaining until 1961. Went to USA 1963, teaching in Calif. and from 1965 at Juilliard Sch., returning to It. in 1972. Collab. with Boulez at IRCAM, Paris, 1974–9. Comps. are influenced by serialism, elec. devices, and indeterminacy. Has developed individually the 'collage' technique, borrowing extracts from other composers or imitating stylistic characteristics. Examples are *Sinfonia*, in which Berio quotes material from Mahler's 2nd Sym., Wagner's *Das Rheingold*, Ravel's *La Valse*, and Strauss's *Der Rosenkavalier*, and *Laborintus II*, where street cries and interjections are blended with references to madrigals and to jazz. Another collage is *Recital I* (*for Cathy*), one of several works (e.g. *Epifanie* and *Sequenza 3*) written for his former wife, the sop. Cathy *Berberian. His *Sequenza* series for various instr. is largely aleatory. In *Circles* the singer may perform either the notated pitches or the approximations: the choice is hers. While in Milan in his youth

Berio cond. a small touring opera co. and has remained enthusiastic about the th., though his works for it have so far been extremely unconventional. In 1986 and 1987 he transcr. 11 of Mahler's early songs for male v. and orch. and he has also re-worked mus. by Brahms and Schubert. At Salzburg Fest. in 1989 he cond. a prog. of his own works. Wrote ending for Puccini's *Turandot* (f.p. Los Angeles 2002). Prin. works:

THEATRE: *Passaggio, messa in scena* for sop., 2 ch., and orch. (1962–3); *Opera* (3 acts), 10 actors, sop., ten., bar., orch. (1960–70, rev. 1977); *Allez Hop*, mimed tale, mez., 8 mimes, dancers, orch. (1952–9, 1968); *I trionfi del Petrarca*, ballet (1974); *La vera storia*, sop., mez., ten., bar., bass, vocal ens., ch., orch. (1977–8); *Un *Re in Ascolto*, 2-act opera (1979–83); *Duo*, bar., 2 vns., ch., orch. (1982); *Naturale*, ballet, va., tam-tam, vv. (tape) (1985–6).

ORCH.: *Nones* (1954–5); *Allelujah I* (1955–7), *II* (1956–8); *Divertimento* (collab. *Maderna) (1957); *Différences*, 5 instr., tape (1958–9); *Quaderni I–III* from *Epifanie* (1959–63); *Chemins IIB* (1969); *Bewegung I* (1971); *Still* (1973); *Eindrücke* (1973–4); *Encore* (1978); *Entrata* (1980); *Suite da 'La vera storia'* (1981); *Accordo*, for 4 wind bands (1981); *Fanfara* (1982); *Requies* (1983–4); *Formazioni* (1986); *Continuo* (1989); *Festum* (1989); *Schubert/Berio: Rendering* (1989); *Compass* (1994).

SOLO INSTR(S). & ORCH.: *Concertino*, cl., vn., harp, celesta, str. (1950); *Variazioni*, 2 bassethorns, str. (1954–5); *Serenata*, fl., 14 instr. (1957); *Tempi Concertati*, fls., vn., 2 pf., ens. (1958–9); *Chemins I* (from *Sequenza II*), hp., orch. (1965); *Chemins II* (from *Sequenza VI*), va., 9 instr. (1967–8); *Chemins III* (from *Chemins II*), va., orch. (1968–9); *Chemins IIC*, bcl., orch. (1972); 2-pf. conc. (1972–3); *'Points on the Curve to Find . . .'*, pf., 23 instr. (1973–4); *Linea*, 2 pf., vib., marimbaphone (1973–4); *Chemins IV* (from *Sequenza VII*), ob., str. (1975); *Il Ritorno degli Snovidenia*, vc., 30 instr. (1976–7); pf. conc. (1977); *Corale on Sequenza VIII*, vn., 2 hns., str. (1981); *Voci*, va., orch. (1984); *Brahms/Berio: Opus 120, No.1*, cl. or va., orch. (1984–6); *Concerto II (Echoing Curves)*, pf., 2 groups of instr. (1988); *Alternatim*, cl., va., orch. (1997); *SOLO*, tb., orch. (1999).

VOICE(S) & ORCH. OR ENS.: *Magnificat*, 2 sop., mystic ch., ens. (1949); *El mar la mar*, mez., 7 players (1952); *Chamber Music*, female v., cl., vc., hp. (1953); *Epifanie*, sop. or mez., orch. (1959–61, rev. 1965); **Circles*, female v., hp., 2 perc. (1960); *Laborintus II*, vv., instr., reciter, tape (1965); *O King*, mez., 5 players (1967); *Sinfonia*, 8 vv., orch. (1968–9); *Air*, sop., orch. (1969); *Air*, sop., 4 instr. (1970); *Agnus*, 2 sop., 3 cl. (1970); *Bewegung II*, bar., orch. (1971); *Ora*, sop., mez., chamber ens. (1971); *Recital I (for Cathy)*, mez., 17 instr. (1972); *Cries of London*, 6 vv. (1973–4), 8 vv. (1975); *Calmo (in memoriam Bruno Maderna)*, mez., ens. (1974, rev. 1988–9); *A-Ronne*, radiophonic documentary for 8 actors (1974), version for 8 vv. and tape (1975); *Coro*, 40 vv., instr. (1974–6); 11 *Folk Songs*, mez., orch. (1975), from version for mez. and 7 players (1964); *Ofanim*, 2 instr. groups, 2 children's ch., women's vv., and Real Time Computer Mus. System, or for female singer, children's ch. (or tape), orch. (or tape), live ens. (1988); *Epiphanies*, female v., orch. (1991); *Rage and Outrage*, vv., orch. (1993); *Stanza*, bar., ch., orch. (2003).

INSTR(S).: *Opus Number Zoo*, 5 wind instr. (1950–1, rev. 1970); 2 *Pieces*, vn., pf. (1951); str. qt. (1956); *Sincronie*, str. qt. (1963–4); *Gesti*, fl. (1966); *Autre Fois*, lullaby canon for Stravinsky, fl., cl., hp. (1971); *Les mots sont allés*, vc. (1978); *Duetti per due violini* (1979–82, arr. for 2 gui. by E. Kanthou, 1987); *Lied*, cl. (1983); *Call (St Louis Fanfare)* (1985); *Riccorenze*, wind quintet (1985–7); str. qt. (1986–90); *Psy*, db. (1989); *Notturno*, str. qt. (1993); *Glosse*, str. qt. (1997); *Korót*, 8 vc. (1998).

PIANO: *Petite Suite* (1947); 5 *Variations* (1952–3); *Rounds* (1967), hpd. (1965); *Wasserklavier* (1965); *Erdenklavier* (1969); *Memory*, 2 pf. (1970); *Luftklavier* (1985); *Feuerklavier* (1989); *Brin* (1990); sonata (2001).

*SEQUENZA SERIES I, fl. solo (1958); II, hp. solo (1963); III, female v. (1965); IV, pf. (1966); V, tb. (1967); VI, va. (1967); VII, ob. (1969); VIII, vn. (1975–7); IX, perc. (1978–9); IX A, cl. (1980); IX B, alto-sax. (1981); X, tpt., pf. (1985); XI, gui. (1987–8); XII, bn. (1995); XIII, acc. (1995); XIV, vc. (2002), db. (2004); II arr. with orch. as *Chemins I* (1965); VI arr. for va. and 9 instr. as *Chemins II* (1967), for orch. as *Chemins IIB* (1969), and for bcl. and orch. as *Chemins IIC* (1972); VII arr. for ob., str. as *Chemins IV* (1975); X arr. with ens. as *Chemins VI (Chol Od)* (1996); XI arr. with chamber orch. as *Chemins V* (1992).

ELECTRONIC: *Mutations* (1954); *Perspectives* (1956); *Momenti* (1957); *Theme* (homage to Joyce) with v. of C. Berberian (1958); *Visage*, with v. of C. Berberian (1961); *Chants parallèles* (1975); *Diario imaginario* (1975); *Altra voce*, fl., mez., elec. (1999).

Bériot, Charles-Auguste de (*b* Louvain, 1802; *d* Brussels, 1870). Belg. violinist and composer, also mechanic, landscape painter, and sculptor. Married the singer *Malibran in 1836. Prof., Brussels Cons. 1843, retiring 1852 when sight failed. Wrote 10 vn. concs., a no. of pieces for 2 vn., etc., and also a *Violin School* which enjoyed much popularity.

Bériot, Charles Wilfrid de (*b* Paris, 1833; *d* Sceaux-en-Gatinais, 1914). Son of C.-A. de *Bériot. Pianist and, as Prof., Paris Cons., teacher of Granados, Ravel, and others. Comp. 4 pf. concs.

Berkeley, (Sir) **Lennox** (Randall Francis) (*b* Boar's Hill, Oxford, 1903; *d* London, 1989). Eng. composer. Studied mus. in Paris with Nadia Boulanger 1927–32. On BBC mus. staff 1942–5. Prof. of comp., RAM, 1946–68. His works are outstanding in quality and fastidious of workmanship. CBE 1957. Knighted 1974. Prin. comps.:

OPERAS: *Nelson (1953); A *Dinner Engagement (1954); *Ruth (1956); Castaway (1966).

ORCH.: *Mont Juic (suite in collab. with *Britten, 1937); Serenade for Strings (1939); syms., No.1

(1940), No.2 (1956–8, rev. 1976), No.3 (1969), No.4 (1976–8); *Divertimento* (1943); *Nocturne* (1946); *Sinfonietta* (1950); *Suite from Nelson* (1955); *Suite, A Winter's Tale* (1960); *Partita* (1965); *Windsor Variations* (1969); *Antiphon*, str. (1973); *Voices of the Night* (1973); *Suite for Strings* (1974).

CONCERTOS: *Introduction and Allegro*, 2 pf. (1938); vc. (1939, f.p. 1983); pf. (1947); 2 pf. (1948); fl. (1952); 5 *Pieces*, vn., orch. (1961); vn., chamber orch. (1961); *Dialogue*, vc., chamber orch. (1970); *Sinfonia concertante*, ob. (1973); guitar (1974).

VOICE(S) AND ORCH.: *Domini est Terra* (1937); 4 *Poems of St Teresa of Avila*, cont., str. (1947); *Stabat Mater* (1947); *Colonus' Praise* (1949); *Batter my Heart* (1962); *Signs in the Dark*, ch., str. (1967); *Magnificat* (1968); 4 *Ronsard Sonnets*, Set 2, ten., orch. (1963, also with chamber orch.).

CHORAL: *Gibbons Variations* (1951); *Crux fidelis* (1955); *Salve Regina* (1955); *Missa brevis* (1960); *Justorum Animae* (1963); Mass for 5 vv. (1964); 3 *Latin Motets* (1972); *Hymn for Shakespeare's Birthday* (1972); *Herrick Songs* (1974); *The Lord is My Shepherd* (1975); *The Hill of the Graces* (1975); *Judica Me* (1978); *Ubi Caritas* (1978); *Magnificat and Nunc Dimittis* (1980).

VOICE AND PIANO (or other instr.): *How Love Came In* (1935); 5 *Songs* (1939–40); 5 *De La Mare Songs* (1946); *The Lowlands of Holland* (1947); 3 *Greek Songs* (1951); 4 *Ronsard Sonnets* Set 1, 2 ten. (1952, rev. 1977); 5 *Poems of W. H. Auden* (1958); *Autumn's Legacy* (1962); *Songs of the Half Light* (with guitar) (1964); *Chinese Songs* (1971); 5 *Housman Songs* (1978); *Una and the Lion*, cantata, sop., recorders, hpd., viola da gamba (1979); *Sonnet*, high v., pf. (1982).

CHAMBER MUSIC: str. qts., No.1 (1935), No.2 (1942), No.3 (1970); recorder sonatina (1940); vn. sonatina (1942); str. trio (1943); va. sonata (1945); *Elegy* and *Toccata*, vn., pf. (1950); hn. trio (1954); sextet, cl., hns., str. (1955); gui. sonatina (1957); ob. sonatina (1962); *Diversions*, ob., cl., bn., hn., vn., va., vc., pf. (1964); ob. qt. (1967); *Introduction and Allegro*, db., pf. (1971); *Duo*, vc., pf. (1971); *In Memoriam Igor Stravinsky*, str. qt. (1971); pf., wind quintet (1975); fl. sonata (1978).

PIANO: 5 *Short Pieces* (1936); 3 *Pieces*, 2 pf. (1938–40); 3 *Impromptus* (1935); 4 *Concert Studies, Set 1* (1940); sonata (1945); 6 *Preludes* (1945); 3 *Mazurkas* and *Scherzo* (1949); sonatina, pf. duet (1954); *Concert Study* in E (1955); sonatina, 2 pf. (1959); *Improvisation on a theme of Falla* (1960); 4 *Concert Studies, Set 2* (1972); *Prelude and Capriccio* (1978); *Bagatelle*, 2 pf. (1981); *Mazurka* (1982).

Berkeley, Michael (*b* London, 1948). Eng. composer; son of Lennox *Berkeley. BBC Radio 3 announcer 1976–9. Prog. dir., Cheltenham Fest. 1995–2004. Works incl.: operas *Baa Baa Black Sheep* (1991–3); *Jane Eyre* (2000); oratorio *Or Shall We Die?*, sop., bar., ch., orch. (1982); *Meditations*, str. (1976); ob. conc. (1977); *Fantasia Concertante*, chamber orch. (1977); *Chamber Sym.*, orch. (1980); Suite, *Vision of Piers the Ploughman*, orch. (1981); vc. conc. (1982); cl. conc. (1991); *Elegy*, fl., str. (1993); *Gethsemane Fragment*, str. (1990); *Concerto for Orch.* (2005); also vocal works, 4 str. qts., and works for kbd.

Berlin, Irving [Baline, Israel] (*b* Tyumen, Russia, 1888; *d* NY, 1989). Russ.-born Amer. composer of highly successful popular music. He was a thoroughly professional musician, at the start of his career, between 1907 and 1914, composing over 200 songs. Wrote the lyrics for almost all his songs. Wrote the musicals *Annie Get Your Gun* (1946) and *Call Me Madam* (1950). Among his songs, many for films and mus. comedies, are *Alexander's Ragtime Band* (1911), *God Bless America*, *Easter Parade, White Christmas, Putting on my Top Hat, This is the Army, What'll I do?*, and *Always* (1925).

Berlin Philharmonic Orchestra. One of the world's major orchs., founded 1882. Among prin. conds. have been Franz Wüllner; Karl Klindworth; Hans von Bülow; Richard Strauss; Arthur Nikisch (1895–1922); Wilhelm Furtwängler (1922–45); Leo Borchard (1945); Sergiù Celibidache (1945–51); Herbert von Karajan 1954–89, Salzburg Fest. début 1975); Claudio Abbado 1989–2002; Simon *Rattle from 2002. The Philharmonic Hall was destroyed during 1939–45 war and replaced by a fine modern hall in 1963.

Berlinski, Herman (*b* Leipzig, 1910; *d* Washington, DC, 2001). Ger. composer and organist. Escaped to USA, 1940, and entered Seminary College of Jewish Mus., NY, 1953–60. Org., Temple Emmanu-El, NY, 1954–63; Minister of Mus., Washington Hebrew Congregation 1963–77. Early works influenced by Schoenberg and Hindemith but experiences as a refugee from Nazis led to his concentration on Jewish sacred and secular mus.

Berlioz, (Louis) **Hector** (*b* La Côte-St André, Grenoble, 1803; *d* Paris, 1869). Fr. composer, cond., and critic. His life, especially as related by himself in his marvellous *Memoirs*, reads like a novel. Son of a provincial doctor, he showed early liking for mus., learning the fl. and flageolet, and later the guitar, but never the pf. Intended for a medical career, in 1821 went to Paris medical sch. In 1822 applied for mus. lessons and began to compose an opera. In 1823 he became a private pupil of *Le Sueur and in 1824 comp. his *Messe solennelle*. This was perf. in Paris 1825 and 1827. Berlioz said he destroyed the score, but in fact he gave it to his friend Antoine Bessems in 1835 and this was found in Antwerp in 1991 by Frans Moors, an organist, and received its f. modern. ps. 1993 in Paris, Bremen, and London, all cond. John Eliot *Gardiner.

In 1826 entered Paris Cons. to study with Reicha and Le Sueur, 1826–8. In 1827 saw Kemble's co. in *Hamlet* at the Odéon and was stricken 'like a thunderbolt' with a passion both for Shakespeare and for the Irish actress who played Ophelia, Harriet Smithson. In the first 5 months of 1830, comp. the *Symphonie fantastique*, subtitled 'Episodes in the life of an artist' and dealing autobiographically with his passion for Miss Smithson. It was perf. on 5 Dec. In Dec. 1832 at last met Miss Smithson and married her 10 months later. Over the next decade some of his greatest works were comp., incl. *Harold in Italy*, the *Symphonie funèbre et triomphale*, the dramatic sym. *Roméo et Juliette*, the *Grand' Messe des morts* (*Requiem*), and the opera *Benvenuto Cellini*. Though some of these works were commissions (and Paganini gave him 20,000 francs for *Harold in Italy*, although he never played the va. solo), Berlioz supplemented his income by writing mus. criticism, a chore he detested but accomplished brilliantly. In 1841 his marriage broke up and he formed a liaison with the singer Marie Recio. They toured Ger. in 1843, and in the ensuing years he travelled frequently, visiting Russia and also paying 4 visits to London. Dramatic cantata *La Damnation de Faust* was a failure in Paris, 1846, and *Te Deum*, comp. 1849–50, was not perf. until 1855. From 1856 to 1858 engaged on enormous opera *Les Troyens*, for which he wrote the lib., basing it on Virgil's *Aeneid*. This work, Berlioz's masterpiece, was on too large a scale and efforts to have it staged at the Opéra failed. Eventually, having divided it into 2 parts, *La Prise de Troie* and *Les Troyens à Carthage*, he saw the 2nd part prod. at the Théâtre-Lyrique, Paris, in Nov. 1863. It was withdrawn after 22 perfs., a failure which broke Berlioz's spirit. In 1860–2 completed his last work, the comic opera *Béatrice et Bénédict*, based on Shakespeare. For nearly 100 years after his death, Berlioz's true qualities were obscured by his image as the 'Romantic artist' *par excellence*. His extravagances in his scores, no longer very remarkable but ahead of their time, diverted critical attention, even among his admirers, from the classical purity of his melody and the Beethovenian grandeur of his command of dramatic contrasts. Today, the opera *Les Troyens*, the *Grand' Messe des morts* and the *Nuits d'été* (forerunner of Mahler's song-cycles with orch.) are recognized for their poetry and originality. Prin. comps.:

STAGE: *Les Francs Juges*, Op.3 (1826, rev. 1829, 1833); **Benvenuto Cellini*, Op.23 (1834–7); *Les *Troyens* (1856–8); **Béatrice et Bénédict* (1860–2); **Lélio* (monodrama, 1831).

ORCH.: OVS.: *Waverley*, Op.1 bis (1827–8); *Les *Francs Juges*, Op.3 (1826); *Le Roi Lear*, Op.4 (1831); *Le *Corsaire*, Op.21 (1831); *Rob Roy* (1832); *Le *Carnaval romain*, Op.9 (1844); **Harold en Italie*, va., orch., Op.16 (1834); **Symphonie fantastique*, Op.14 (1830); *Rêverie et caprice*, vn., orch., Op.8 (1839); **Symphonie funèbre et triomphale* (ch. ad lib.), Op.15 (1840).

VOICES & ORCH.: *Messe solennelle* (1824); **Grand' Messe des morts* (*Requiem*), Op.5 (1837); *La *Mort de Cléopâtre* (1829); **Roméo et Juliette*, dramatic sym., Op.17 (1838–9); *La *Damnation de Faust*, Op.24 (1828–46); *L'*Enfance du Christ*, oratorio, Op.25 (1850–4); *Te Deum*, Op.22 (1849–50); *Les *Nuits d'été* (with pf. or orch.), Op.7 (1840–1, pf.; 1843–56, orch.).

Berman, Lazar (Naumovich) (*b* Leningrad, 1930; *d* Florence, 2005). Russ. pianist. Début Leningrad 1934. Played Mozart conc. (K503) with Moscow PO, 1940. Professional career began 1957. London début 1958, NY 1976. Specialist in 19th-cent. composers.

Bernac, Pierre [Bertin, Pierre] (*b* Paris, 1899; *d* Avignon, 1979). Fr. baritone, distinguished as recitalist and teacher (Gérard **Souzay* among his pupils). Gave first recital 1925. Frequently assoc. with composer **Poulenc*, his accompanist in concerts throughout Eur. and USA. Several Poulenc song-cycles written for him, incl. *Tel jour telle nuit*.

Bernacchi, Antonio Maria (*b* Bologna, 1685; *d* Bologna, 1756). It. alto castrato. Sang in Ger. and studied counterpoint in Munich. It. opera début Genoa 1703. From 1709 to 1736 sang in most It. cities, and regularly in Munich 1720–7. London début 1716. Engaged as prin. singer by Handel for London season 1729–30. Retired 1736 and founded singing sch. in Bologna.

Bernard, Anthony (*b* London, 1891; *d* London, 1963). Eng. conductor, pianist, and composer. Cond. with BNOC. Org., pf. accompanist, and cond. at Shakespeare Memorial Th., Stratford-on-Avon (1932–42), of London Chamber Singers and of London Chamber Orch., which he founded in 1921, reviving much old mus. Cond. of Dutch Chamber Orch., The Hague, 1922–6.

Bernardi, Mario (*b* Kirkland, Ontario, 1930). Canadian-It. conductor and pianist. At SW 1963–9 (mus. dir. 1966–9). Cond. Nat. Arts Centre Orch., Ottawa, 1969–82. Cond. S. Francisco Opera, NY City Opera 1970–86. NY Met début 1984; CG 1994.

Bernas, Richard (*b* NY, 1950). Amer. conductor and pianist. Début as pianist, Kent Univ. 1966, as cond. London 1976. Cond., Music Projects, London, 1978. Cond.-in-residence, Sussex Univ. 1979–82. CG début as cond. 1988. Writer of books on Verdi's *La forza del destino*, Rossini's *Mosè*, and on the vn.

Bernasconi [Wagele], **Antonia** (*b* Stuttgart, ?1741; *d* ?Vienna, ?1803). Ger. soprano for whom Gluck is said to have written *Alceste*, in which she sang in Vienna 1767. Sang Aspasia in the child Mozart's *Mitridate, Rè di Ponto* in Milan 1770–1. Also sang in London as member of King's Th. co. 1778–80 and returned to Vienna 1781. Step-daughter of It. composer Andrea Bernasconi (?1706–?1784), in whose opera *Temistocle* she made her début in Munich, 1762.

Bernauerin, Die (The Wife of Bernauer). A 'Bavarian piece' by **Orff*, to his own lib., for spkr., sop., ten., ch., and orch. Comp. 1944–5. Prod. Stuttgart 1947, Kansas City 1968.

Berners, Lord (Gerald Hugh Tyrwhitt-Wilson) (*b* Apley Park, Bridgnorth, Shropshire, 1883; *d* Faringdon, Berks., 1950). Eng. composer, also painter, author, and diplomat. Career as diplomat 1909–20, mainly in Rome. Early works pubd. under name Gerald Tyrwhitt. Had advice and lessons in Rome from Casella and Stravinsky. Marked gift for mus. satire and parody, as exemplified in his *Fragments psychologiques*, pf. (1915); *3 Little Funeral Marches*, pf. (1916); *3 Orchestral Pieces*

(1918); *Fantaisie espagnole*, orch. (1918–19); *Valses bourgeoises*, 2 pf. (1919); and Fugue in C minor for orch. (1924). Set Mérimée's *Le Carrosse du Saint-Sacrement* as 1-act opera (prod. Paris 1924). His best-known work is the ballet *The *Triumph of Neptune* (London, 3 Dec. 1926). Other ballets were *Luna Park* (1930 Cochran revue); *A Wedding Bouquet* (London 1936), which has choral parts to words by Gertrude Stein; *Cupid and Psyche* (1938); and *Les Sirènes* (1946). Also wrote *L'Uomo dai Baffi*, solo woodwind, pf., str. (1918); 3 *Songs in the German manner* (1913–19); 3 *Chansons* (1919–20); 3 *Sea Shanties* (1921); and pf. piece *Portsmouth Point* (1920). Succeeded to barony 1918. Autobiography, *First Childhood* (1934) and *A Distant Prospect* (1945), highly recommended. Comp. mus. for film *Nicholas Nickleby* (1946), and other film scores. Also wrote novel *Far from the Madding War* (1941).

Bernstein, Leonard [Louis] (*b* Lawrence, Mass., 1918; *d* NY, 1990). Amer. composer, conductor, and pianist. Educated Boston Latin Sch. and at Harvard Univ. (with Piston) 1935–9. In 1939 entered Curtis Inst., studying cond. with *Reiner. Already his outstanding talent had led a friend to say 'Lenny is doomed to success'. In summers of 1940–3 studied at Tanglewood summer sch., Lenox, becoming ass. to *Koussevitzky and was also noticed by *Rodzinski, who invited him to become ass. cond. of NY Phil. Sym. Orch. 1943–4; début Nov. 1943, deputizing for Bruno Walter. Cond. NY City Center Orch., 1945–8, presenting adventurous programmes. Cond. f.p. of Messiaen's *Turangalîla-symphonie*, Boston, 1949. Taught at Tanglewood 1951–5 in orch. and cond. dept.; part-time prof. of mus., Brandeis Univ. 1951–5.

Career as opera cond. began at Tanglewood, 1946, in Amer. première of *Peter Grimes*. Cond. his own *Trouble in Tahiti* at Brandeis, 1952, and Cherubini's *Medea* (with Callas) at La Scala 1953 (the first Amer. to conduct there), returning to cond. *La sonnambula* for *Callas. Salzburg Fest. début 1959 (NYPO). Début NY Met 1964 (*Falstaff*), Vienna 1966. In 1957–8 appointed joint prin. cond. (with *Mitropoulos) of NYPO, becoming sole cond. 1958–69, the first Amer.-born holder of the post. Guest cond. many of world's leading orchs., notably Vienna PO, Israel PO, and LSO. In 1969 was made 'laureate conductor for life' of NYPO. Bernstein's outstanding quality as a musician was his catholic taste. Hence his comps. are markedly eclectic, bearing influences of Gershwin, Jewish ritual mus., Mahler, Stravinsky, Villa-Lobos, and Copland. (In 1941 he worked for a popular mus. publisher, making arrs. and jazz transcrs.) His first sym., *Jeremiah* (1941–4), won 1944 NY Music Critics' Award and in that year his ballet *Fancy Free*, with choreog. by Jerome Robbins, was perf. in NY. Later the same year his musical *On the Town* began a Broadway run of 463 perfs. He made a comic operetta from Voltaire's novel *Candide* (1954–6) and adapted Shakespeare's *Romeo and Juliet* to a New York gang warfare setting as the highly successful *West Side Story* (1957). As a conductor, he was a notable interpreter of Mahler, Copland, Brahms, Shostakovich, and his own music. Brilliant pianist, often directing Mozart concertos from the keyboard. Influential as teacher and television lecturer. Books include *The Joy of Music* (1959), *The Infinite Variety of Music* (1966), *The Unanswered Question* (1976), and *Findings* (1982). Works incl.:

OPERAS & MUSICALS: *On the Town* (1944); *Trouble in Tahiti* (1951); *Wonderful Town* (1952); *Candide* (1954–6, rev., not by composer, 1957, 1959, 1966, 1967, 1968, 1971, 1973, 1982; by Mauceri with composer, 1987 and 1989); *West Side Story* (1957); *1600 Pennsylvania Avenue* (1976); *A *Quiet Place* (incorp. *Trouble in Tahiti*) (1983, rev. 1984).

THEATRE PIECE: *Mass*, for singers, players, and dancers (1971, chamber version 1972).

BALLETS: *Fancy Free* (1943–4); *Facsimile* (1946); *Prelude, Fugue and Riffs* (1949); *The *Age of Anxiety* (1949); *Serenade* (after Plato's *Symposium*), for 7 dancers (1954); *Dybbuk* (1974).

INCIDENTAL MUSIC: *Peter Pan* (Barrie), 4 songs and 2 choruses (1950); *The Lark* (Anouilh) (1955); *The Firstborn* (Fry) (1958).

FILM: *On the Waterfront* (1954).

ORCH.: syms.: No.1 (*Jeremiah*), mez., orch. (1942), No.2 (*The Age of Anxiety*) (after Auden), pf., orch. (1949), No.3 (*Kaddish*), orch., mixed ch., boys' ch., spkr., sop. (1963, rev. 1977); suite, *Fancy Free* (1944); 3 *Dance Episodes* from *On the Town* (1945); *Facsimile* (1946); *Prelude, Fugue and Riffs*, cl., jazz ens. (1949); *Serenade*, vn., str., hp., perc. (1954); Symphonic Suite, *On the Waterfront* (1955); ov., *Candide* (1956); Symphonic Dances, *West Side Story* (1960); *Fanfares* (1961); 2 *Meditations* from *Mass* (1971), *Meditation 3* from *Mass* (1972), 3 *Meditations* from *Mass*, arr. for vc., orch. (1977); *Dybbuk*, Suites Nos. 1 and 2 (1974); *Slava!* (1977); *CBS Music* (1977); *Divertimento* (1980); *A Musical Toast* (1980); *Halil*, fl., str., perc. (1981); *Jubilee Games* (1982); *Concerto for Orchestra* (incorp. *Jubilee Games*) (1988).

CHORUS & ORCH.: *Kaddish* (sym. No.3), mixed ch., boys' ch., spkr., sop., orch. (1963, rev. 1977); *Chichester Psalms*, mixed ch., boy soloist, orch. (1965); 'If you can't eat you got to', ten., male ch., ens. (1973, rev. 1977).

VOICE(S) & INSTR(S).: *Hashkivenu*, ten., ch., org. (1945); *Simchu Na*, ch., pf. (1947); Suite from *Candide*, soloists, ch., orch. (1956); *Glitter and be Gay*, from *Candide*, v., orch. (1956); *Take Care of this House*, from *1600 Pennsylvania Avenue*, v., orch. (1976); *Songfest*, sop., 2 mez., ten., bar., bass., orch. (1976).

VOICE & PIANO: *I Hate Music*, sop. (1943); *La bonne cuisine*, sop. (1947); 2 *Love Songs* (on poems of Rilke), sop. (1949); *Silhouette*, sop. (1951); *So Pretty*, v. (1968); *My New Friends*, v. (1979); *Piccola Serenata* ('for Karl Böhm on his 85th birthday'), v. (1979).

CHAMBER MUSIC: pf. trio (1937); cl. sonata (1941–2), also transcr. for va. and pf. by R. Hillyer; *Brass Music* (1948); *Shivaree*, double brass ens., perc. (1969); 3 *Meditations* from *Mass*, vc., pf. (1971).

PIANO: sonata (1938); 7 *Anniversaries* (1943); 4 *Anniversaries* (1948); 5 *Anniversaries* (1954); *Moby Diptych* (1981).

Béroff, Michel (*b* Epinal, Vosges, 1950). Fr. pianist. Début Paris 1966, London 1968. Won int. Messiaen comp. 1967. Salzburg Fest. début 1977. Specialist in works of Messiaen.

Berry, Walter (*b* Vienna, 1929; *d* Vienna, 2000). Austrian bass-baritone. Début at Vienna Opera 1950. Sang regularly at Salzburg Fest. after 1953, creating roles in 20th cent. works. London début (RFH) 1954; CG 1976; NY Met 1966. Fine exponent of Figaro, Ochs, Wozzeck, and Wotan. Distinguished concert-hall career.

Bersag horn or **Bersaglieri bugle**. Bugle with a single valve, lowering the pitch by a 4th. Made in different sizes: sop. in B♭, cont. in E♭, ten. in B♭, bar. in B♭, and bass in F. Became popular with bugle bands during 1914–18 war. Presumably of It. origin (*Bersaglieri* = a sharpshooter corps of It. army).

Berté, Heinrich [Harry] (*b* Galgócz, 1857; *d* Perchtoldsdorf, 1924). Austro-Hung. composér of ballets, notably *Der Karneval in Venedig* (Vienna, 1900), and operettas of which the best-known is *Das Dreimäderlhaus* (1916, Vienna) based on Schubert melodies and depicting (mainly fictitious) scenes from Schubert's life. Amer. version arr. Romberg prod. in 1921 as **Blossom Time* and Eng. version arr. G. H. Clutsam as *Lilac Time* (1922).

Bertini, Gary (*b* Brichevo, Bessarabia, 1927; *d* Tel Hashomir, Israel, 2005). Israeli conductor and composer. Founder and cond. Israel CO from 1965. Brit. début 1965 with ECO. Prin. guest cond. SNO 1970s. Cond. Detroit SO 1981–3; Cologne Radio SO from 1983. Head, cond. class, Israel Acad. of Mus. from 1958. Mus. dir. Jerusalem SO from 1977; cond. Frankfurt Opera 1987–91; mus. dir. New Israeli Opera 1994–5. Comps. incl. incidental mus., ballets, vn. sonata, hn. conc.w

Bertini, Henri Jérôme (*b* London, 1798; *d* Meylan, Grenoble, 1876). Fr. pianist and composer for pf., especially of pf. studies which have long been used by teachers. Worked in Paris 1821–59. Wrote many chamber works.

Berton, Henri-Montan (*b* Paris, 1767; *d* Paris, 1844). Fr. violinist, composer, and teacher. Violinist in Opéra orch. from 1782. Prof. of harmony Paris Cons., 1795–1818, then prof. of comp. Cond. Opéra-Comique 1807–9. Besides sacred mus. and instr. works, comp. over 40 operas (some in cooperation with Méhul, Spontini, Paër, and Boieldieu) of which best-known were *Les Rigueurs du cloître* (1790), a 'rescue opera' which was an exemplar for *Fidelio*, and *Montano et Stéphanie* (1799). Wrote pamphlets attacking Rossini.

Bertoni, Ferdinando Gasparo (*b* Saló, Brescia, 1725; *d* Desenzano, Brescia, 1813). It. composer. Org. St Mark's Venice, 1752–85. Comp. *Orfeo* (1776) to same lib. as Gluck, also using some of Gluck's mus. Two visits to London (1778–80 and 1781–3) to conduct his own operas (of which he wrote about 50) at King's Th. Became choirmaster at St Mark's 1785 on death of *Galuppi, retiring in 1808. Most successful works were *Le pescatrici* (1751) and *Artaserse* (1785).

Bertrand, Anthoine de (*b* Fontanges, Auvergne, *c*.1540; *d* Toulouse, *c*.1580). Fr. composer. Comp. notable 4-part settings of Ronsard Sonnets, using half-modal, half-tonal harmonic idiom.

Berwald, Franz (Adolf) (*b* Stockholm, 1796; *d* Stockholm, 1868). Swed. composer (mainly self-taught) and violinist. Violinist in Stockholm court orch. 1812–18 and 1820–8. Won scholarship in Berlin 1829, where he comp. opera *Der Verräter*. Lived for time in Vienna, where opera *Estrella di Soria* was comp., also orch. works. Returned to Sweden, where his work was unfavourably received, so went back to Vienna, where Jenny Lind sang in his opera *Ein Ländlisches Verlobungsfest in Schweden* (A Swedish country betrothal, 1847). Berwald opened an orthopaedic institute in Berlin in 1835, running it successfully for 6 years. From 1850 to 1859 he was manager for a glass works in Sandö, N. Sweden, and wrote on social issues of the day. Prof. of comp. Swedish Royal Academy of Mus. from 1867. His comps. were neglected until the 20th cent. His chamber mus. is rewarding, also his 4 syms., of which only No.1 in G minor (*Sérieuse*) (1842) was perf. in his lifetime. No.3 in C major (*Singulière*) (1845) has become relatively popular. The best-known of his 11 operas (several lost) is the last, *Queen of Golconda*, 1864. Also wrote vn. conc.; pf. conc.; 3 str. qts.; 2 pf. quintets; and Septet in B.

Bes (Ger.). The note B♭♭.

Besch, Anthony (John Elwyn) (*d* London, 1924; *d* London, 2002). Eng. opera producer for Glyndebourne, ENO, Scottish Opera, NY City Opera, S. Francisco Opera, and others. Head of opera studies, GSMD, 1986–9. Prod. f.p. of *Birtwistle's *Punch and Judy* (1968) and Brit. première of Shostakovich's *The Nose* (London, SW, 1973).

Besozzi. It. family of orch. musicians specializing in woodwind, particularly ob. Headed by Alessandro (*b* Parma, 1702; *d* Turin, 1793) who comp. several trio sonatas, etc. Second generation settled in Paris where the last member, Louis-Désiré (*b* Versailles, 1814), died in 1879.

Besson, Gustave Auguste (*b* Paris, 1820; *d* Paris, 1875). Fr. maker of musical instr. Prod. a new cornet when only 18. Many inventions to improve valve-mechanism of cornet, most successful being 'prototype system' of construction with conical steel mandrels. Also invented db. cl., and family of 'cornophones' to reinforce orch. hns. Branch factory opened London 1851.

Best, Matthew (*b* Sevenoaks, 1957). Eng. conductor and bass. Opera début Cambridge 1978. Won Decca Kathleen Ferrier Prize 1982. Prin. bass, CG, 1980–6. Founder-dir., Corydon Singers from 1973. Guest cond. of ECO, London Mozart Players, etc.

Best, William Thomas (*b* Carlisle, 1826; *d* Liverpool, 1897). Eng. organist, recognized as the greatest concert organist of his time, the centre of his activities being St George's Hall, Liverpool, where he was city organist 1855–94. Org., Liverpool Philharmonic Soc. 1848–52 and from 1872. Assoc. with Handel fests. in London 1871–91. Arr. many works for his instr. Ed. org. works of Bach, Handel, and Mendelssohn, and wrote books on organ-playing. Gave first recital on Royal Albert Hall organ, 1871, and on Sydney (NSW) Town Hall organ, 1890.

bestimmt (Ger.). (1) Decided (in style). (2) (applied to a particular line in the score) Prominent.

Besuch der alten Dame, Der (Einem). See *Visit of the Old Lady, The.*

Bethlehem. Choral-drama by *Boughton. Lib. based on medieval Coventry Play. (Prod. Street, Somerset, 1915).

Betonung (Ger.). Accentuation.

Betrothal in a Monastery (Prokofiev). See *Duenna, The.*

Bettelstudent, Der (The Beggar Student). Operetta in 3 acts by *Millöcker to lib. by F. Zell and R. Genée based on books by Sardou (*Fernande*) and Bulwer-Lytton (*Lady of Lyons*). Prod. Vienna 1882, NY 1883, London 1884.

Betz, Franz (*b* Mainz, 1835; *d* Berlin, 1900). Ger. bass-baritone. Début Hanover 1856. Created role of Hans Sachs in *Die Meistersinger*, Munich 1868, and sang Wotan at first Bayreuth Fest. 1876.

Bevignani, Enrico (*b* Naples, 1841; *d* Naples, 1903). It. conductor and composer. Spent much of his career in London. Répétiteur at Her Majesty's Th. 1863–9. Cond., CG 1869–87 and 1890–6, NY Met 1894–1900. Cond. first London perfs. of *Aida* (1876), *La Gioconda* (1883), *L'Amico Fritz* (1892), and *Pagliacci* (1893). Patti insisted on his conducting for her whenever possible, and he cond. her CG farewell in 1895. Cond. f. Bolshoy p. of Tchaikovsky's *Eugene Onegin*, Moscow 1881. Wrote opera *Caterina Blum* (Naples, 1863).

Bevington and Sons. Eng. firm of organ-builders founded in London 1794 by Henry Bevington. Built orgs. of St Martin-in-the-Fields, London (1854), and St Patrick's Cath., Dublin.

beweglich (Ger.). Agile. So *beweglichkeit*, agility.

bewegt. (1) Moved, i.e. speeded. (2) Moved, i.e. emotionally. **bewegter**. Quicker. **Bewegung**. (1) Rate of motion, speed. (2) Emotion. (3) Commotion.

bianca (It.). White. Half-note or minim.

Bianca und Giuseppe. Opera in 4 acts by Kittl (prod. Prague 1848) memorable only because lib. is by Wagner, who adapted König's novel for his own use in 1836 but did not set it.

Bianchi, Francesco (*b* Cremona, *c.*1752; *d* Hammersmith, 1810). It. composer of over 80 operas and oratorios. Worked at It. Opera in Paris under Piccinni, 1775. From 1785 to 1797 was 2nd org. at St Mark's, Venice. Went to London 1794. Wrote opera *Ines de Castro* for It. début of Elizabeth *Billington, 1794. Cond. in Dublin, 1797–1801. Among operas are *Semiramide* (1790), *Acis and Galatea* (1792), and *Alzira* (1801). Took own life.

Biancolli, Louis (Leopold) (*b* NY, 1907; *d* New Milford, Conn., 1992). Amer. mus. critic, chiefly for *World-Telegram and Sun* 1928–66. Programme annotator NY Phil. 1941–9. Author of several books, incl. biography of Kirsten Flagstad (1952).

Bibalo, Antonio (*b* Trieste, 1922). It. composer who settled in Norway. Concentrated principally on opera. Comps. in this genre incl. *The Smile at the foot of the ladder* (based on story by Henry Miller, comp. 1958–62), *Miss Julie* (based on Strindberg's play, comp. 1973), *Ghosts* (based on Ibsen's play, comp. 1981), *Macbeth* (1989), and *The Glass Menagerie* (1996).

Bibelorgel, Bibelregal (Ger.). A type of Regal, a reed org. which came into use in the 15th cent. and remained popular into the 17th. In appearance it was a small, portable, single-manual org. of small compass, but the pipes (all short) were at first all reed-pipes, the reeds being of that type called 'beating reeds' (see *reed*): later flue pipes were sometimes added. The Bible Regal folded in two like a book.

Biber, Heinrich Ignaz Franz von (*b* Wartenberg, Bohemia, 1644; *d* Salzburg, 1704). Ger.-Bohemian violinist and composer, becoming Kapellmeister at Salzburg, 1684. Prolific composer for vn. Also wrote 2 operas, a Requiem, chamber mus., tpt. conc., and 'Nightwatchman' Serenade (for 2 vn., 2 va., and continuo). His 8 vn. sonatas with continuo (1681) demand a virtuoso's technique, as do the 15 *Mystery* (or *Rosary*) sonatas (*c.*1678) for vn. and bass. His *Battalia* is an early example of programme mus.

Biblical Songs. 10 settings for v. and pf. by Dvořák, comp. 1894 as his Op.99, of passages from the Psalms. Nos.1 and 5 orch. Dvořák.

Biches, Les. (The Hinds; colloq. The Little Darlings). Ballet in 1 act with ch., incorporating 17th-cent. texts, comp. by Poulenc in 1923 and prod. Monte Carlo 1924. Scenario by composer, choreog. Nijinskaya. Suite (re-scored) 1940.

bicinium (Lat.). A 2-v. song.

Biene, August van (*b* Holland, 1850; *d* Eng., 1913). Dutch cellist. Went to London as child and played in streets; discovered by *Costa. Comp. popular *The Broken Melody* and played it (in mus. halls, etc.) over 6,000 times.

Biggs, E(dward George) **Power** (*b* Westcliff-on-Sea, 1906; *d* Boston, Mass., 1977). Eng.-born concert organist (Amer. cit. 1937). Played in USA from 1930. Specialized in reviving neglected classical works, often on reconstructions of old instr. Commissioned works from Amer. composers.

bigophone, bigotphone: Improved *mirliton introduced by Bigot, a Frenchman, in the 1880s. Often made up to resemble the various brass instr.

Bihári, János (b Nagyabony, 1764; d Pest, 1827). Hung. violinist and composer credited with composing the *Rákóczy March, although version of the tune already existed.

Bilitis, Chansons de (Debussy). See Chansons de Bilitis.

Billings, William (b Boston, Mass., 1746; d Boston, 1800). One of first Amer.-born composers, he abandoned tanning for mus. Wrote over 340 pieces, mostly between 1770 and 1794, including much church mus., 'fuguing tunes' (essays in imitative counterpoint). Comp. patriotic songs. Among his printed songbooks were The New-England Psalm-Singer (1770) and The Continental Harmony (1794). Wrote popular Christmas carol Shiloh and choral pieces.

Billington, Elizabeth (b London, 1765; d Venice, 1818). Eng. soprano with European reputation. Daughter of Carl Weichsel, Ger.-born oboist at King's Th., London. Child prodigy as pianist and composer. Studied with J. C. Bach. In 1783 married James Billington, db. player, with whom she also studied. Began opera career in Dublin, 1783, as Polly in The Beggar's Opera. Sang in Naples 1794 in Bianchi's Ines di Castro. Paisiello, Paër, and Himmel wrote operas for her. First Eng. Vitellia in La clemenza di Tito, London 1806. Retired 1817, living in Venice from 1817. Painted by Reynolds.

Billy Budd. Opera, orig. in 4 acts, by Britten, Op.50, to lib. by E. M. Forster and Eric Crozier from Melville's story of 1891. Comp. 1950–1, prod. CG, London, 1951, NY (TV) 1952. Rev. in 2 acts for BBC radio Nov. 1960. F. stage p. of this vers., CG 1964, Chicago 1970. 4-act vers. revived St Louis 1993 and CG 1995. Subject also of opera by *Ghedini (Venice 1949).

Billy the Kid. Ballet in 1 act, mus. by Copland, to lib. by Kirstein, choreog. Loring; comp. for Ballet Caravan 1938 (Chicago). Subject was 'Wild West' gunman (William Bonney). Concert Suite for orch., and pf. suite, 1938.

Bilson, Malcolm (b Los Angeles, 1935). Amer. pianist. Has given many recitals of late 18th-cent. kbd. mus. on 5-octave fortepiano and of late 19th-cent. repertoire on 6 and 6½-octave Viennese pfs. Toured Eur. with Eng. Baroque Soloists, cond. John Eliot Gardiner. Ass. prof., Cornell Univ. 1968, assoc. 1970, prof. 1975, prof. of mus. 1990.

binary form. Literally, a form in 2 sections. Simple binary form, as in an 18th-cent. kbd. suite, has no strong contrast of material. The first sec-

tion opens in the tonic key and then (subject to an exception shortly to be mentioned) modulates, as it ends, into the key of the dominant. The 2nd section then opens in that 2nd key and, before it ends, modulates back to the 1st. There are, then, 2 distinct main cadences, or points of rest, the 1st in the dominant and the 2nd in the tonic. The exception just referred to occurs if the piece is in a minor key, when the 1st section sometimes ends in the relative major. This form is unsuitable for very long pieces, since the variety offered to the listener is almost entirely confined to details of treatment and the element of key, the thematic material employed throughout being the same. Since the deaths of Bach and Handel, this form has been little used. It developed into compound binary form, another name for *sonata form.

Binchois, Gilles de Bins dit (b ?Mons, c.1400; d Soignies, 1460). Franco-Flemish composer and organist. Regarded as one of major composers of early part of 15th cent. Probably trained as chorister. Org. at Mons, 1419–23 after which he is thought to have been soldier in service of Earl of Suffolk in Eng. occupation army in France. In 1420s joined Burgundian court chapel. Most of his surviving secular songs are rondeaux. Church mus. incl. a Te Deum, settings of the Magnificat, Credo, and Gloria, but no complete Mass survives.

bind. See tie (or bind).

Bing, (Sir) **Rudolf** (Franz Joseph) (b Vienna, 1902; d NY. 1997). Austrian-born impresario. Worked in concert agency 1923–7. At Darmstadt State Th., 1928–30, and Charlottenburg-Berlin Opera 1930–3, under Carl *Ebert. Went to Eng. (cit. 1946) and was manager, *Glyndebourne Opera 1935–9 and 1946–9. First dir., *Edinburgh Festival, 1947–9. Gen. man. NY Met, 1950–72. CBE 1956. KBE 1971. Autobiography 5,000 Nights at the Opera (London, 1972).

Binge, Ronald (b Derby, 1910; d Ringwood, Hants, 1979). Eng. composer of light orch. works such as Elizabethan Serenade, Spitfire, Thames Rhapsody, also alto sax. conc. and film mus. Began career as cinema organist. Became arr. in 1935 for Mantovani, whose post-1945 'singing strings' style was his creation.

biniou (Fr.). Bagpipe.

Binns, Malcolm (b Gedling, Nottingham, 1936). Eng. pianist. London début 1957. Prof. of pf., RCM, 1962–9. Specialist in playing instr. of the period in which works were composed. Gave f. Brit. p. of Prokofiev's 4th conc., London 1961.

bird organ (or serinette). Simple form of the *'orgue de Barbarie', intended by reiteration of a short tune to teach captive birds to sing. (serin, Fr. = the domestic canary).

Birds, The (Gli uccelli). Suite for small orch. by *Respighi. Based on 17th- and 18th-cent.

bird-pieces for lute and for hpd. In 5 movements: *Prelude, Dove, Hen, Nightingale,* and *Cuckoo*. (F.p. São Paulo, Brazil, 1927.)

Birmingham. City in West Midlands, Eng., with splendid mus. tradition. Fest. was held there triennially, with occasional breaks, from 1768 to 1912. *Costa cond., 1849–82; Mendelssohn's *Elijah* f.p. 1846 and Gounod's *Rédemption* 1882. *Richter became cond. 1885. Byrd's Mass in 5 parts was revived 1900. Most significant fest. f.ps. were of Elgar works: *The Dream of Gerontius* (1900), *The Apostles* (1903), *The Kingdom* (1906), *The Music Makers* (1912). Sibelius cond. f.p. in England of his 4th sym., 1912. CBSO was founded 1920 with Appleby Matthews as cond. (though first concert cond. Elgar). Conds. since then have been *Boult 1924–30; *Heward 1930–43; *Weldon 1943–51; *Schwarz 1951–7; *Panufnik 1957–9; *Rignold 1960–8; *Frémaux 1969–78; *Rattle 1980–98, Sakari Oramo from 1998. New concert-hall, Symphony Hall, opened 1991. At univ., Peyton Chair of Mus. was founded 1905 with Elgar as first prof. Succeeded by Bantock (1908), other incumbents being V. Hely-Hutchinson, J. A. Westrup, A. Lewis, I. Keys, and C. Timms. New Elgar Chair, S. Banfield from 1993.

Birmingham Conservatoire. College of mus. Orig. part of Birmingham and Midland Inst. and formally constituted in 1886 as Birmingham Sch. of Mus. In new building since 1973. Title changed to Birmingham Conservatoire 1989, as part of Univ. of Central Eng. in Birmingham. Granville *Bantock was appointed Principal 1900, followed by A. K. Blackall (1934–45); Christopher Edmunds (1945–57); Steuart *Wilson (1957–60); Gordon Clinton (1960–73); Louis Carus (1975–87); Roy Wales (1987–8); Kevin Thompson (1988–93); George Caird from 1993.

Birtwistle, (Sir) **Harrison** (Paul) (*b* Accrington, 1934). Eng. composer. As clarinettist, entered RMCM 1952, studying comp. with Richard *Hall. While still a student was one of Manchester New Music Group (with A. *Goehr, P. *Maxwell Davies and J. *Ogdon), performing *avant-garde* works. Leaving RMCM in 1960, spent a year at RAM. From 1962 to 1965 dir. of mus., Cranborne Chase Sch. In USA 1966–8, first year as visiting fellow, Princeton Univ. Ass. dir. Nat. Th. 1975–83. Prof. of comp., King's Coll., London, 1995–2001. With Maxwell Davies formed *Pierrot Players in London for perf. of new chamber mus. involving theatrical elements (named after *Pierrot Lunaire*). Received commissions for works from many organizations and rapidly moved into forefront of Eng. composers of his generation. His first opera, *Punch and Judy*, is a compelling study in violence and was followed by *The Mask of Orpheus* for ENO and *Gawain* for CG. Music marked by genuine lyrical impulse built on dramatic use of ostinato and repeated thematic fragments. A strong poetic feeling pervades all his work. Knighted 1988. CH 2001. Prin. comps.:

OPERA AND MUSIC THEATRE: *Punch and Judy* (1966–7);

Down by the Greenwood Side (1968–9); *The* *Mask of Orpheus* (1973–5, 1981–4); *Bow Down* (1977); *Yan Tan Tethera*, TV opera (1983–4); *Gawain* (1987–90, rev. 1994); *The Second Mrs Kong* (1993–4); *The Last Supper* (1998–9); *The Io Passion* (2003).

BALLET: *Pulse Field (Frames, Pulses and Interruptions)* (1977).

INCIDENTAL MUSIC: *Hamlet* (1975); *The Oresteia* (1981).

ORCH.: *Chorales* (1960–3); *3 Movements with Fanfares* (1964); *Nomos* (1967–8); *An Imaginary Landscape* (1971); *The Triumph of Time* (1972); *Melencolia I* (1976); *Still Movement*, 13 solo str. (1984); *Earth Dances* (1985–6); *Endless Parade*, tpt., vib., str. (1986–7); *Machaut à ma manière* (1988); *Ritual Fragment* (1990); *Gawain's Journey* (1991); *Antiphonies*, pf., orch. (1992); *The Cry of Anubis*, tuba, orch. (1994); *Night's Blackbird* (2004).

INSTRUMENTAL (without v.): *Refrains and Choruses*, wind quintet (1957); *The World is Discovered*, chamber ens. (1960); *Tragoedia*, wind quintet, hp., str. qt. (1965); *Chorale from a Toy Shop*, 1st vers. for fl, ob. or cl., cl. or ca., hn. or tb., bn. or tuba (1967), 2nd vers. for 2 tpt., hn., tb., tuba (1978); *Three Lessons in a Frame*, pf., fl., cl., vn., vc., perc. (1967); *Verses for Ensembles*, wind quintet, brass, perc. (1968–9); *Some Petals from my Twickenham Herbarium*, chamber ens. (1969); *Medusa*, ens. (1969–70, rev. 1980); *Dinah and Nick's Love Song*, 3 sop. sax., hp., or 3 cor. ang., hp. (1970); *Tombeau, in mem. Igor Stravinsky*, fl., cl., hp., str. qt. (1971); *Silbury Air*, chamber ens. (1977); *Carmen Arcadiae Mechanicae Perpetuum*, chamber ens. (1977); *For O, For O, the Hobby Horse is Forgot*, 6 perc. players (1976); *Pulse Sampler*, ob., claves (1981); *Secret Theatre*, fl., ob., cl., bn., tpt., hn., tb., perc., pf., str. qt. (1984); *Slow Frieze*, pf., ens. (1996); *Cantus Iambeus*, 13 players (2005).

INSTRUMENTAL (with vv.): *Monody for Corpus Christi* (1959); *Entr'actes and Sappho Fragments*, sop., ens. (1964); *Ring a Dumb Carillon*, sop. (doubling suspended cymbals), cl., perc. (1964–5); *Monodrama*, sop., narr., fl., cl., vn., vc., perc. (1967); *Cantata*, sop., ens. (1969); *Nenia: the Death of Orpheus*, sop., ens. (1970); *Prologue*, ten., ens. (1970); *Meridian*, mez., ch., ens. (1970–1); *The Fields of Sorrow*, 2 sop., ch., ens. (1971, rev. 1972); *Epilogue*, bar., hn., 4 tb., 6 tam-tams (1972); *La Plage*, sop., 3 cl., pf., marimba (1972); . . . agm . . . , 16 solo vv., 3 instr. ens. (1978–90); *Songs by Myself*, sop., fl., vn., va., vc., db., pf., vib. (1984); *Words Overheard*, sop., fl., ob., str. (1985); *4 Songs of Autumn*, sop., str. qt. (1987); *An die Musik*, sop., fl., ob., cl., bn., vib., str. qt., db. (1988); *4 Poems by Jaan Kaplinski*, sop., fl., ob., cl., bn., hn., tpt., pf., hp., str. quintet (1991); *9 Settings of Celan*, sop., ens. (1989–96); *Pulse Shadows*, sop., str. qt., ens. (1989–96); *Neruda madrigales*, vv., ens. (2004–5).

UNACC. VOICES: *Description of the Passing of a Year*, ch. (1963); *On the Sheer Threshold of the Night*, 4 solo vv., 12-part ch. (1980).

CHAMBER MUSIC: *Verses*, cl., pf. (1965); *Linoi*, 1st vers., cl., pf. (1968), cl., pf., tape, dancer (1969), 3rd vers., cl., pf., vc. (1973); cl. quintet (1980); *Deowa*, sop., cl. (1983); *Duets for Storab*, 2 fl. (1983); *An Interrupted Endless Melody*, ob., pf. (1991); *Five*

Distances for Five Instruments, fl., ob., cl., bn., hn. (1992); *Nine Movements for String Quartet*, str. qt. (1991–6).

BRASS BAND: *Grimethorpe Aria* (1973); *Fanfare for Will*, 3 tpt., 4 hn., 3 tb., tuba (1987); *Salford Toccata* (1989); *Tenebrae David* (2001).

PIANO: *Précis* (1960); *Hector's Dawn* (1987).

ELECTRONIC: *4 Interludes for a Tragedy*, basset cl., tape (1968–9); *Chronometer*, 8-track tape (1971–2).

bis (Fr.). Twice. (1) (at a concert) 'Encore!'. (2) (in a score) Repeat the passage.

bisbigliando (It. 'whispering'). Effect used on harp. Constantly repeated notes are played *pianissimo* in upper and middle registers. Involves both hands playing adjacent strings set to same pitch with the pedals.

biscroma (It.). The 32nd note or demisemiquaver.

Bishop, (Sir) **Henry** (Rowley) (*b* London, 1786; *d* London, 1855). Eng. composer and conductor. Went to Newmarket to train as a jockey but was physically unsuitable. His patron paid for his musical education in London. Engaged in 1810 as mus. dir., CG. Founder member and dir., London Phil. Soc., 1813. Left CG 1824, becoming mus. dir. Drury Lane. In 1831 married his pupil the soprano Anna Riviere, touring the provinces with her and the harpist Nicolas *Bochsa, with whom she eloped to the Continent in 1839. 'Adapted' other composers' operas for Eng. stage, incl. Mozart's *Figaro* and *Don Giovanni*. Prof. of mus. Edinburgh Univ. 1841–3, Oxford Univ. 1848–55. Knighted 1842. Of his large output only 2 songs effectively survive, **Home, Sweet Home* and *Lo, Here the Gentle Lark*.

Bishop-Kovacevich, Stephen. See *Kovacevich, Stephen*.

Bispham, David (Scull) (*b* Philadelphia, 1857; *d* NY, 1921). Amer. baritone. Eng. début 1891 (Longueville in Messager's *La Basoche*); CG début 1892; sang Kurwenal in *Tristan* under Mahler, Drury Lane, 1892; NY Met début 1896. Determined advocate of opera in English.

bissex. 12-str. guitar, invented 1770 by Vanhecke, with 6 str. over the finger-board and the rest sympathetic.

Bist du bei mir (With you beside me). Aria for long attrib. J. S. Bach from Anna Magdalena Bach notebook (1725) written on 2 staves only, with v. part and unfigured bass. Now ascribed to the Ger. composer Gottfried Heinrich Stölzel (1690–1749).

bitonality. The use of 2 keys simultaneously, as in the works of Stravinsky, Vaughan Williams, Holst, and many other 20th-cent. composers. See *tonality* and *polytonality*.

Bizet, [Alexandre Césare Léopold], known as **Georges** (*b* Paris, 1838; *d* Bougival, 1875). Fr. composer. Studied Paris Cons., pupil of Zimmerman

and then of Halévy (whose daughter he married). Won *Grand Prix de Rome* 1857, in which year his *Docteur Miracle* was perf. In Rome comp. an *opéra-bouffe Don Procopio* (prod. Monte Carlo 1906) and a choral sym. *Vasco da Gama*, also his *Te Deum* (1858). On return to Paris comp. several operas, none of which had much success. They were *Les Pêcheurs de perles* (The Pearl Fishers) (1863), *La Jolie Fille de Perth* (The Fair Maid of Perth) (1866), and *Djamileh* (1871). In the early 1860s, comp. a 5-act opera *Ivan IV* which he later abandoned, using some of the mus. in other works, but which was prod. in a mutilated edn. after World War II as *Ivan le Terrible*. Other operas which exist either in incomplete or fragmentary form are *La Coupe du Roi de Thule* (1868), *Grisélidis* (1870–1) which incl. mus. later used in *L'Arlésienne* and *Carmen* (Flower Song), and *Don Rodrigue* (1873). Had more success in his lifetime with non-operatic works such as *Souvenirs de Rome* (perf. 1869, pubd. 1880 as suite *Roma*), the *Petite Suite*, *Jeux d'enfants* (1871), and incidental music to *L'Arlésienne* (1872). In 1873 began work on an *opéra-comique Carmen*, prod. Paris 1875 and coolly received, though it has since become one of the most popular operas ever written.

A brilliant pianist, Bizet also comp. for that instr. and his songs and church mus. are of high quality. A Sym. in C, 1855, of felicitous youthful charm, was disinterred in 1933 and f.p. in Basle cond. Weingartner, 26 Feb. 1935. If Bizet's fame rests largely on *Carmen*, all his pubd. work has colour, melody, and brilliant aptness of orchestration. But in practically all of Bizet's work, incl. *Carmen*, there are musicological pitfalls for the unwary writer who has not consulted the work of authorities such as Winton *Dean concerning spurious edns., additions, and interpolations. Prin. works:

OPERAS: *Le *Docteur Miracle* (1856); *Don Procopio* (1858–9); *La Prêtesse* (?1861); **Ivan IV* (?1862–3, rev. 1864–5); *Les *Pêcheurs de perles* (The Pearl Fishers) (1863); *La *Jolie Fille de Perth* (The Fair Maid of Perth) (1866); **Djamileh* (1871); **Carmen* (1873–4).

INCIDENTAL MUSIC: *L'*Arlésienne* (play by A. Daudet) (1872).

ORCH.: *Overture* (c.1855); sym. in C (1855); *Scherzo et Marche funèbre* (1860–1); *Roma*, sym. (1860–8, rev. 1871); *Marche funèbre* (1868–9); *Petite Suite* (1871, orch. of Nos. 2, 3, 6, 11, and 12 from **Jeux d'enfants*, pf. duet 1871); *L'*Arlésienne*, suite No.1 (1872; suite No.2 is by **Guiraud*); *Patrie*, ov. (1873).

CHORAL: *Valse in G*, 4 vv., orch. (1855); *La Chanson du Rouet*, solo v., 4 vv., pf. (1857); *Clovis et Clotilde*, cantata (1857); *Te Deum*, sop., ten., 4 vv., orch. (1858); *Vasco da Gama*, ode-symphony (1859–60); *La Mort s'avance*, 4 vv., orch. (1869).

PIANO: *Grande Valse de Concert in E♭*, *Nocturne in F* (1854); *3 Esquisses Musicales* (1858); *Chants du Rhin* (1865); *Variations Chromatiques de Concert* (1868); *Nocturne in D* (1868); **Jeux d'enfants* (Children's Games), 12 pieces, pf. duet (1871).

SONGS: *Vieille Chanson* (1865); *Après l'hiver* (1866);

Feuilles d'Album, 6 songs (1866); *Chants des Pyrénées*, 6 folk-songs (1867); *Berceuse* (1868); *La Coccinelle* (1868); *Absence* (1872); *Chant d'Amour* (1872); *Sérénade: O, quand je dors* (1870); 12 extracts from unperf. stage works all fitted with new words (pubd. 1886).

Bizony, Celia (*b* Berlin, 1904; *d* London, 1987). Ger.-born voice teacher, composer, and harpsichordist. Co-founder Musica Antica e Nuova, Cambridge, 1942–8. Lect. and teacher in Canada 1949–55. Prof., GSMD and lecturer, Morley College, London, 1956–69. Mus. dir., Musica Antica e Nuova, London, from 1956. Comp. part-songs, str. qt., hpd. pieces. Wrote short history of Bach family.

Björling, Jussi (Johan) (*b* Stora Tuna, Sweden, 1911; *d* Island of Siar Oe, 1960). Swed. tenor, taught by father, a professional tenor. Early public appearances in male v. qt. with father and 2 brothers. Studied in Gothenburg and Stockholm, 1928, with Joseph *Hislop. Official début Stockholm 1930 as Don Ottavio in *Don Giovanni* (had already sung Lamplighter in *Manon Lescaut* there a month earlier). Débuts Vienna 1936; Chicago 1937; CG 1939—did not sing again at CG until 1960; NY Met 1938–59 (excluding war years).

Blacher, Boris (*b* Niu-chang, China, 1903; *d* Berlin, 1975). Ger. composer. Worked in the opera house in China, 1919. Moving to Berlin 1922, studied architecture and mathematics, and comp., after 1924, with Friedrich Koch. Taught at Dresden Cons. 1938–9. Prof. of comp. Berlin Hochschule, from 1945; dir. 1953–1970. Prolific composer in many forms, Blacher's mus. is basically tonal, though he has used the 12-note method, and he developed (in *Ornamente*, Op.37, for pf., 1950) a rhythmical process called 'variable metres' whereby systematic changes of metre are planned according to mathematical relationships. Employed jazz styles in early works and elec. devices in later ones (after 1962). Works incl.:

OPERAS: *Fürstin Tarakanowa* (1940; also orch. suite); *Romeo und Julia* (1943); *Die Flut* (1946); *Die Nachtschwalbe* (1947); *Preussisches Märchen* (1949); *Abstrakte Oper No.1* (1953); *Rosamunde Floris* (1960); *Zwischenfälle bei einer Notlandung*, 'reportage' for elec. instr. and singers (1965); *200,000 Taler* (1969); *Yvonne, Prinzessin von Bergund* (1972); *Das Geheimnis des entwendeten Briefes* (1974).

BALLETS: *Harlekinade* (1939); *Das Zauberbuch von Erzerum* (on themes of Flotow) (1941; rev. as *Der erste Ball*, 1950); *Chiarina* (1946); *Lysistrata* (1950; also orch. suite); *Hamlet* (1949; also orch. suite); *Der Mohr von Venedig* (based on *Othello*) (1955); *Demeter* (1963); *Tristan* (1965; also orch. suite).

ORCH.: *Kleine Marschmusik* (1932); *Kurmusik* (1933); *Divertimento*, str. (1935); *Divertimento*, wind (1936); *Geigenmusik*, vn., orch. (1936); *Concertante Musik* (1937); sym. (1938); *Hamlet*, sym.-poem (1940); conc., str. (1940); *Partita*, str., perc. (1945); *Variations on a Theme of Paganini* (1947); pf. conc. No.1 (1947), No.2 (1952); vn. conc. (1948);

conc. for cl., bn., hn., tpt., hp., str. (1950); *2 Inventions* (1954); va. conc. (1954); *Fantasy* (1955); *Homage to Mozart* (1956); *Music for Cleveland* (1957); *Variations on a Theme of Clementi*, pf., orch. (1961); *Konzertstück*, wind quintet, str. (1963); vc. conc. (1964); *Collage* (1968); conc., tpt., str. (1970); cl. conc. (1971); *Stars and Strings*, jazz ens., str. (1972); *Poème* (1974); *Pentagramm*, str. (1974).

CHORAL: *Der Grossinquisitor*, oratorio after Dostoyevsky (1942); *Träume vom Tod und vom Leben*, cantata, ten., ch., orch. (1955); *Die Gesänge des Seeräubers O'Rourke und seiner Geliebten Sally Brown*, sop., female cabaret singer, bar., speaker, speaking ch., orch. (1958); *Requiem*, sop., bar., ch., orch. (1958).

VOICE(S) & INSTR(S).: *Jazz-Koloraturen*, sop., alto sax., bn. (1929); *Francesca da Rimini*, sop., vn. (1954); *13 Ways of Looking at a Blackbird*, sop. or ten., str. (1957); *3(6 + x) oder For Seven*, sop., perc., db. (1973).

CHAMBER MUSIC: str. qts., No.1 (1930), No.2 (1940), No.3 (1944), No.4 (*Epitaph*) (1951), No. 5 (*Variationem über einem divergierenden c-moll-Dreiklang*) (1967); vc. sonata (1940); vn. sonata (1941); solo vn. sonata (1951); *4 Studies*, hpd. (1967); pf. trio (1970); quintet, fl., ob., str. trio (1973); *Tchaikovsky-Variations*, vc., pf. (1974).

PIANO: 2 sonatinas (1940); *3 Pieces* (1943); *Ornamente* (1950); sonata (1951); 24 Preludes (1974).

ELEC.: *Multiple Raumperspektiven*, pf., elec. (1962); *Glissierende Deviationen*, tape (1962); *Der Astronaut*, tape (1963); *Elektronisches Scherzo*, tape (1965); *Ariadne*, duodrama, 2 speakers, elec. (1971).

Blachut, Beno (*b* Ostrava-Vitkovice, 1913; *d* Prague, 1985). Cz. tenor. Opera début Olomouc 1939 (Jenik in *The Bartered Bride*). Member, Prague Nat. Th. from 1941. One of finest singers of Janáček and Smetana operatic roles. Rarely sang in West, but appeared with Prague Nat. Th. at Edinburgh Fest., 1970.

Black, Neil (Cathcart) (*b* Birmingham, 1932). Eng. oboist. Prin. oboe, LPO 1958–60. Prof., RAM, 1960–70. Has been prin. ob. of ECO, Academy of St Martin-in-the-Fields, London Mozart Players, and Monteverdi Orch. Frequent soloist with chamber orchs. Specialist in Baroque and pre-classical repertoire.

Black, Stanley (*b* London, 1913; *d* London, 2002). Eng. composer, pianist, and conductor, esp. of film mus. Cond. BBC Dance Orch. 1944–52; mus. dir. ABC Pictures, 1958–63; prin. cond. BBC Northern Ireland Orch., 1968–9; ass. cond. Osaka PO 1971; NZ Proms 1972. Comp. of over 100 film scores. OBE 1986.

Black Dyke Mills Band. Brass band, founded 1855, in connection with mills of same name in village of Queensbury, Yorkshire. Has always held high place in band world, frequently winning Brit. nat. championships and other prizes, and touring both sides of the Atlantic.

Black Key Étude. No.5 (in G major) of Chopin's 12 *Grandes Études* for pf. (Op.10; pubd. 1833). The right hand confines itself to the black keys.

Black Knight, The. Sym. for ch. and orch. by Elgar, his Op.25. Comp. 1889–93. Setting of Long-fellow's trans. of Uhland. (F.p. Worcester Choral Soc. 1893; London, 1895).

Blackshaw, Christian (*b* Cheadle Hulme, 1949). Eng. pianist. Début, London 1969. First prize Casella Int. Pf. Comp., Naples, 1974.

bladder-pipe. Instr. similar to *bagpipe which existed from 13th to 16th cents. and was sometimes called *platerspil*. Attempted to combine bagpipe's continuous air flow with a means of stopping and starting more easily, thus making some kind of tonguing and articulation possible. This it did by using elastic animal bladder which expelled air down the pipe by its own elasticity instead of, as in the bagpipe, by arm pressure on animal skin.

Blades, James (*b* Peterborough, 1901; *d* Cheam, 1999). Eng. percussion-player. Prin. percussionist LSO 1940. Prof. of timp. and perc. RAM 1960–77. Former member, ECO, Melos Ens., and EOG. Advised Britten on special percussion effects for his church parables, etc. Author of books on perc. instr. and technique. OBE 1972.

Blagrove, Henry (Gamble) (*b* Nottingham, 1811; *d* London, 1872). Eng. violinist. On return to Eng. formed qt., establishing first regular series of chamber concerts in London, 1835. Leader of many British orchs. of his time.

Blake, David (Leonard) (*b* London, 1936). Eng. composer. Lect. in mus., York Univ., 1964–71, senior lect. from 1971, prof. 1981–94. Also cond. and pianist with his ensemble Lumina. Early works in tonal idiom influenced by Bartók and Mahler, later adopted 12-note system, but later evolved a freer, more relaxed style, the 1st vn. conc. being deeply romantic in style and spirit. Prin. works:

OPERAS: *Toussaint L'Ouverture*, 3 acts (lib. by T. Ward) (1974–6, rev. 1982); *The Plumber's Gift* (lib. by J. Birtwhistle) (1985–8); *Scoring a Century – an Entertainment* (1999).

ORCH.: *Chamber Symphony* (1966); *Metamorphoses* (1971); vn. conc. No.1 (1976), No.2 (1983); *Sonata alla marcia* (1978); *Scherzi ed Intermezzi* (1984); *Pastoral Paraphrase*, bn., orch. (1986); *Mill Music*, brass band (1986); vc. conc. (1989–93); *Nocturne*, str. (1994).

VOCAL AND CHORAL: *3 Choruses to Poems by Frost* (1964); *On Christmas Day*, ch. (1964); *Beata L'Alma*, sop., pf. (1966); *What is the Cause*, ch. (1967); *The Almanack*, ch. (1968); *Lumina*, soloist, ch., orch. (1969); *The Bones of Chuang Tzu*, bar., pf. (1972); bar., chamber orch. (1973); *In Praise of Krishna*, sop., 9 instr. (1973); *Toussaint Suite*, mez., bar., orch. (1977); *Toussaint: Song of the Common Wind*, mez., orch. (1977); *From the Mattress Grave*, 12 Heine poems, sop., 11 instr. (1978); *The Spear*, mez., speaker, ch., cl., tpt., va., pf. (1982); *Change*

is *Going to Come*, mez., bar., ch., 4 players (1982); *Rise, Dove*, bar., orch. (1982); *Three Ritsos Choruses*, ch., orch. (1993); *5 Heine Songs*, bar., ob./cl., pf. (1985); *6 Heine Songs*, bar., ob./cl., str. (1988); *The Fabulous Adventures of Alexander the Great*, bar., bass, young ch., orch. (1996).

CHAMBER MUSIC: *Variations*, pf. (1960); str. qt. No.1 (1961–2), No.2 (1973), No.3 (1982); *Sequence*, 2 fl. (1967); nonet for wind (1971, rev. 1978); *Scenes*, vc. (1972); *Arias*, cl. (1978); cl. quintet (1979–80); *Cassation*, wind octet (1979); *Capriccio*, wind, str., pf. (7 players) (1980); *Fantasia*, vn. (1984); *Seasonal Variants*, 7 players (1985); *Nightmusic*, sax. qt. (1990).

Blake, Howard (*b* London, 1938). Eng. composer. Worked in London 1960–70 as pianist, orchestrator, cond., and comp. Enjoyed immense success with mus. for children's TV film *The Snowman*. OBE 1994. Works incl. opera: *The Station* (1987); Symphony in 1 Movement (*Impressions of a City*) (1967, rev. 1990); *Heartbeat*, ten. sax., big band, str. (1982, rev. 1989); cl. conc. (1984); *The Conquest of Space* (1988); pf. conc. (1990); vn. conc. (1992–3). Also many choral and vocal works; chamber music; piano pieces; and incid. mus. for theatre, TV, and films incl. *The Avengers* (1968–9); *SOS Titanic* (1979); *The Snowman* (1982); *Henry V* (1985); *The Canterville Ghost* (1986); *A Month in the Country* (1986); *The Master Builder* (1989).

Blake Watkins, Michael. See *Watkins, Michael Blake*.

blanche (Fr.). White. The half-note or minim.

Blanik (Smetana). See *Má Vlast*.

Blasinstrumente (Ger.). Blowing instruments, i.e. wind instr.

Blasis, Carlo de (*b* Naples, 1797; *d* Cernobbio, L. Como, 1878). It. ballet dancer and choreographer on whose system classical training is still based. Dir., Royal Acad. of Dance, Milan, 1837–53. Worked in London and Paris. Created 90 ballets, some with own mus. Father was composer and sister operatic sop.

Blasmusik (Ger.). Blowing mus., i.e. mus. of wind instr.

Blaukopf, Kurt (*b* Czernowitz [now Chernovtsy, Ukraine], 1914; *d* Vienna, 1999). Austrian musicologist and writer. Prof. of mus. sociology, Vienna Hochschule für Musik from 1963. Ed., *Phono*, 1954–65. Author of two books on Mahler (1969, Eng. trans. 1973, and 1976, Eng. trans. 1976, rev. with Herta Blaukopf, 1991).

Blech (Ger.). Sheet metal, i.e. the brass. *Blechmusik*, brass band.

Blech, Harry (*b* London, 1909; *d* Wimbledon, 1999). Eng. violinist and conductor. Member Hallé Orch. 1929–30, BBC SO 1930–6. Founder and leader, Blech Str. Qt. 1933–50. Founded London Wind Players 1942, London Symphonic Players 1946, London Mozart Players 1949 (mus. dir. until 1984). OBE 1962, CBE 1984.

Blech, Leo (*b* Aachen, 1871; *d* Berlin, 1958). Ger. conductor and composer. First cond. posts in Aachen (1893–6) and Prague (1899–1906); from 1906 Kapellmeister, Royal Berlin Opera, becoming Generalmusikdirektor 1913–23, working for much of that period with R. Strauss, of whose operas he cond. several f.ps. in Berlin. Brief spell in Vienna, then cond. (jointly with *Kleiber) Berlin State Opera 1926–37, until removal by Nazis. Cond. Riga 1937–41 and Stockholm 1941–6. Returned to Berlin Städtische Oper 1949–53. Composer of 5 operas, sym.-poems, and other works.

'bleeding chunks'. Phrase sometimes used by writers on mus. when referring to operatic extracts played out of context in the concert-hall. It is a quotation from a programme-note by Sir Donald *Tovey on Bruckner's 4th Sym. in his *Essays in Musical Analysis*, Vol.II (1935), p.71. Tovey wrote: 'Defects of form are not a justifiable ground for criticism from listeners who profess to enjoy the bleeding chunks of butcher's meat chopped from Wagner's operas and served up on Wagner nights as *Waldweben* and *Walkürenritt*.'

Blegen, Judith (*b* Missoula, Montana, 1941). Amer. soprano. Nuremberg Opera 1965–8. State Opera 1968–70. Salzburg Fest. début 1967; NY Met 1970; CG 1975. Frequent duettist with Frederica von Stade.

bleiben (Ger.). To remain. In org. mus., *bleibt* (remains) means that the stop in question is to remain in use.

Blessed Damozel, The (*La Damoiselle élue*). Cantata (*poème lyrique*) by Debussy for sop., women's ch., and orch., comp. 1887–8 on G. Sarrazin's trans. of D. G. Rossetti's poem (1850). Re-orchestrated 1902.

Blessed Virgin's Expostulation, The. Song for sop. or treble by *Purcell, comp. 1693 to text by Nahum Tate beginning 'Tell me some pitying angel'.

Blest Pair of Sirens. Ode for ch. and orch. by Parry, f.p. 1887. Words from Milton's *At a Solemn Musick*.

Blind Man's Buff. Th. piece by *Maxwell Davies, masque for sop. (or treble), mez., and mime, and stage band. Text by composer from Büchner's *Leonce und Lena*, and other sources. F.p. London 1972 (Josephine Barstow, Mary Thomas, Mark Fourneaux, BBC SO, cond. *Boulez).

Bliss, (Sir) **Arthur** (Drummond) (*b* London, 1891; *d* London, 1975). Eng. composer, conductor, and administrator. Served in Royal Fusiliers 1914–17, Grenadier Guards 1917–18. From 1919 earned reputation of being *enfant terrible*, influenced in such works as *Madame Noy* and *Rout* by Stravinsky, Satie, etc. Wrote incid. mus. for Nigel Playfair, 1919. Cond. Portsmouth Philharmonic Soc. 1921. His *Colour Symphony* was commissioned for the 1922 Three Choirs Fest. on Elgar's sugges-

tion. Went to Santa Barbara, Calif., 1923–5, working as cond. Returned to Eng. 1925, writing a series of chamber works for virtuosi soloists and ensembles. His *Morning Heroes* (1930) was perf. at 1930 Norwich Fest., one of its movts. being a setting of a war poem by Wilfred Owen. *Music for Strings* followed in 1935. In 1934–5 he wrote the mus. for Korda's H. G. Wells film *Things to Come* and in 1937 his ballet *Checkmate* was produced at SW. Two other important ballet scores, *Miracle in the Gorbals* (1944) and *Adam Zero* (1946), followed. His piano concerto was first performed at the 1939 New York World Fair. From 1939 to 1941 he taught at Berkeley in California, but on return to Eng. became BBC dir. of mus., 1942–4. An opera, *The Olympians*, to a lib. by J. B. Priestley, failed to win approval at its 1949 CG première, but he wrote an opera for television, *Tobias and the Angel*, in 1960 to a lib. by Christopher Hassall. Among the best of his later works were the vn. conc. (for Campoli) and the orch. *Meditations on a Theme by John Blow* (both 1955) and the vc. conc. (1970). Bliss's early Stravinskyan phase gave way to works in a bold, post-Elgarian style, vigorous and rich in texture but lacking the inner poetry of his model. Some of his best music is to be found in his chamber works, notably the cl. quintet, written for Frederick Thurston, and the ob. quintet, for Léon Goossens. His sense of drama and of vivid musical imagery found their truest outlet in his ballet scores and in the excellent *Things to Come* suite. In 1950 he was knighted and in 1953 became Master of the Queen's Music, a post he filled with flair and energy. KCVO 1969. CH 1971. Prin. works:

OPERAS: *The *Olympians* (1948–9); *The *Beggar's Opera* (1952–3, version of Gay–Pepusch work for film); *Tobias and the Angel* (1960).

BALLETS: *Checkmate* (1937); *Miracle in the Gorbals* (1944); *Adam Zero* (1946); *The Lady of Shalott* (1958).

ORCH.: *2 Studies* (1920); *Mêlée Fantasque* (1921, rev. 1937 and 1965); *A *Colour Symphony* (1921–2, rev. 1932); *Introduction and Allegro* (1926, rev. 1937); *Hymn to Apollo* (1926, rev. 1965); *Music for Strings* (1935); *Processional*, with org. (1953); *Meditations on a Theme by John Blow* (1955); *Edinburgh Overture* (1956); *Metamorphic Variations* (1972); *2 Contrasts*, str. (1972, arr. from str. qt. No.2).

CONCERTOS: *2 pianos* (1924, rev. 1925–9 and 1950), also arr. for 2 pianos (3 hands) in 1968; pf. (1938–9); vn. (1955); vc. (1970).

CHORAL: *Pastoral: *Lie Strewn the White Flocks*, mez., ch., orch. (1928), *Morning Heroes*, sym., orator, ch., orch. (1930); *A Song of Welcome*, sop., bar., ch., orch. (1954); *The *Beatitudes*, sop., ten., ch., orch. (1961); *Mary of Magdala*, cont., bar., ch., orch. (1962); *The Golden Cantata*, ten., ch., orch. (1963); *The World is charged with the grandeur of God*, ch., wind (1969); *2 Ballads*, women's vv., orch. (1971).

UNACC. VOICES: *Aubade for Coronation Morning* (1953); *Seek the Lord* (1956); *Birthday Song for a Royal Child* (1959); *Stand up and bless the Lord your God* (1960); *Cradle Song for a Newborn Child* (1963); *O Give

Thanks (1965); *River Music* (1967); *Lord, who shall abide in Thy Tabernacle* (1968); *A Prayer to the Infant Jesus* (1968); *Ode for Sir William Walton* (1972); *Prayer of St Francis of Assisi* (1972); *Put thou thy trust in the Lord* (1972); *Sing, Mortals!* (1974); *Shield of Faith* (1974).

VOICE(s) & ENS.: *Madam Noy*, sop. (1918); *Rhapsody*, sop., ten. (1919); *Rout*, sop. (1920); *2 Nursery Rhymes*, sop. (1920); *The Women of Yueh*, sop. (1923–4); *Serenade*, bar. (1929); *The Enchantress*, scena for cont. (1951); *Elegiac Sonnet*, ten. (1954); *A Knot of Riddles*, bar. (1963).

BRASS AND MILITARY BAND: *Kenilworth Suite* (1936); *The First Guards* (1956); *Belmont Variations* (1963); *The Linburn Air* (1965); and many ceremonial fanfares for royal and other occasions.

CHAMBER MUSIC: str. qt. (1914, withdrawn), str. qt. (1923–4? MS), No.1 in B♭ (1941), No.2 (1950); *Conversations*, fl., alto fl., ob., cor ang., vn., va., vc. (1920); pf. quintet (1919, unpubd.); ob. quintet (1927); cl. quintet (1932).

INCID. MUS. (STAGE AND RADIO) AND FILM MUSIC: *As You Like It* (1919); *King Solomon* (1924); *Things to Come* (1934–5); *Conquest of the Air* (1937); *Caesar and Cleopatra* (1944); *Men of Two Worlds* (1945); *Christopher Columbus* (1949); *Summer Day's Dream* (1949).

PIANO: *Bliss* (1923); *Masks* (1924); *Toccata* (c.1925); *Interludes* (1925); *Suite* (1926); *The Rout Trot* (1927); *Study* (1927); *Sonata* (1952); *Miniature Scherzo* (1969); *Fun and Games*, 2 pf. 3 hands (1970); *Triptych* (1970); *A Wedding Suite* (1974).

SOLO SONGS: *The Tramps* (c.1916); *3 Romantic Songs* (1921); *3 Songs* (1923, rev. 1972); *When I was One and Twenty* (1923); *Ballads of the 4 Seasons* (1923); *3 Jolly Gentlemen* (1924); *The Fallow Deer at the Lonely House* (1924); *A Child's Prayer* (1926); *Rich or Poor* (1925–6); *Simples* (1932); *7 American Poems* (1940); *Auvergnat* (1943); *Angels of the Mind*, song-cycle, 7 songs (1969); *Tulips* (1970).

Blitheman, John (*b* c.1525; *d* London, 1591). Eng. organist of Queen Elizabeth's Chapel Royal from 1553; comp. of church mus. and virginals mus.—the latter important for its influence on his successor as org., his pupil John *Bull.

Blitzstein, Marc (*b* Philadelphia, 1905; *d* Fort-de-France, Martinique, 1964). Amer. composer and pianist. Scion of a wealthy family, his work reflected his radical political outlook. During depression in USA, decided to compose for the popular th. and prod. perhaps his finest work, *The *Cradle will Rock* (1936). Never repeated its success, though his adaptation of Brecht's *Threepenny Opera* (1952) was acclaimed and his *Regina* (1949), an adaptation of Lillian Hellman's play *The Little Foxes*, has been successfully revived. Served 1942–5 with US Air Force in Eng. and comp. *Airborne Symphony* (1945). After he abandoned Parisian neo-classicism, his work was based on diatonicism laced with jazz and popular influences, in the manner made more familiar by *Bernstein. Works incl.:

OPERAS: *Triple-Sec* (1928); *The *Cradle will Rock* (1936);

No For An Answer (1940); *I've Got the Tune* (1937); *Regina* (1946–9); *The Threepenny Opera* (1952); *Reuben, Reuben* (1955); *Juno*, based on O'Casey's *Juno and the Paycock* (1958); *Sacco and Vanzetti* (1964, unfinished).

BALLETS: *Cain* (1930); *The Guests* (1949).

ORCH.: *Airborne Symphony* (1945); and other works, incl. pf. conc. and mus. for th. and films.

Bloch, Ernest (*b* Geneva, 1880; *d* Portland, Oregon, 1959). Swiss-born composer (Amer. cit. 1924). First mus. instruction from Jaques-Dalcroze in Geneva 1894–7. Comp str. qt. and sym. before age 15. Brussels Cons. 1897–9, studying vn. with Ysaÿe, followed by spells at Frankfurt with Knorr and Munich with Thuille. Went to Paris 1903. Returned to Geneva 1904, beginning comp. of opera *Macbeth* (prod. Paris 1910) in which the influence of Mussorgsky and Debussy can be detected together with Bloch's hallmarks of frequent changes of tempo and key, use of modality, cyclic form, and propensity for open 5ths and 4ths. In next few years wrote works of Jewish inspiration, this distinctive and powerful element in his mus. springing from a deep spiritual impulse and not from external application. Prof. of comp. Geneva Cons. 1915. Went to USA 1916 as cond. for the dancer Maud Allan. Returned in 1917 as teacher at Mannes Sch. of Mus., NY, until 1920. First dir., Cleveland Inst. of Mus. 1920–5, dir. S. Francisco Cons., 1925–30. From 1930 to 1939 lived principally in Geneva and Rome. Returned to USA as prof. of mus., Univ. of Calif., Berkeley, 1940–52. Among his Amer. pupils were Sessions, Antheil, Porter, and Kirchner. Prin. works:

OPERA: *Macbeth* (1904–9).

ORCH.: *Vivre-aimer*, sym.-poem (1900); sym. in C♯ minor (1901); *Hiver-Printemps*, sym.-poem (1904–5); *Israel Symphony* (1912–16); *Trois poèmes juifs* (1913); *Schelomo*, vc., orch. (1916); *Suite*, va., orch. or pf. (1919); *Concerto Grosso No.1*, str., pf. (1924–5), No.2, str. (1952); *America*, sym.-poem (1926); *Episodes*, chamber orch. (1926); *Helvetia*, sym.-poem (1928); *Voice in the Wilderness*, vc. obbl. (1936); *Evocations*, sym. suite (1937); vn. conc. (1938); *Baal Shem*, vn., orch. (1939, orch. of 1923 work with pf.); *Suite symphonique* (1945); *Concerto symphonique*, pf., orch. (1949); *Scherzo fantasque*, pf., orch. (1950); *In memoriam* (1952); *Suite hébraïque*, va., orch. (1952); *Sinfonia breve* (1952–3); sym., tb., orch. (1953–4); Sym. in E♭ (1954–5); *Proclamation*, tpt., orch. (1955); *Suite modale*, fl., str. (1957); *2 Last Poems* (*Funeral Music* and *Life Again?*), fl., chamber orch. (1958).

VOICE(s) & ORCH.: *Poèmes d'automne*, mez., orch. (1906); *Prelude and 2 Psalms* (114 and 137), sop., orch. (1912–14); *Psalm 22*, bar., orch. (1914); *Sacred Service* (*Avodath Hakodesh*), bar., ch., orch. (1930–3).

VOICE & PIANO: *Historiettes au crépuscule*, mez., pf. (1903).

CHAMBER MUSIC: str. qts.: No.1 (1916), No.2 (1946), No.3 (1951), No.4 (1954), No.5 (1956); *Suite*, va., pf. (1919, also with orch.); vn. sonatas No.1 (1920), No.2 (*Poème mystique*) (1924); *Baal Shem*, vn., pf. (1923, with orch. 1939); pf. quintets No.1 (1923), No.2 (1956); *3 Nocturnes*, pf. trio (1924); *2 Suites*, str. qt. (1925); *Méditation hébraïque* and *From Jewish Life*, vc., pf. (1925); *3 Suites*, vc. (1956); *2 Suites*, vn. (1958); *Suite*, va. (1958, last movt. incomplete).

PIANO: sonata (1935); *Poems of the Sea*; *In the Night*; *Nirvana*; *5 Sketches in Sepia*.

block flute (Ger. *Blockflöte*). Recorder or flageolet, so called after its 'block' or fipple; also an org. stop.

Blockx, Jan (b Antwerp, 1851; d Antwerp, 1912). Belg. composer. Succeeded Benoit in 1901 as dir. of Royal Flemish Cons., Antwerp. Propagandist for Flemish nat. movement. Wrote 8 operas to Fr. and Flemish texts, incl. *Thyl Uylenspiegel* (1900).

Blom, Eric (Walter) (b Berne, 1888; d London, 1959). Eng. critic and scholar. Active as writer of annotated programmes; London mus. critic *Manchester Guardian* 1923–31; *Birmingham Post* 1931–46; *Observer* 1949–59; ed. *Everyman's Dictionary of Music* (1946, rev. 1954), *Grove's Dictionary of Music and Musicians*, 5th edn. (1954); *Music and Letters*, 1937–50 and 1954–9; *Master Musicians* series. Author of book on Mozart. CBE 1955.

Blomdahl, Karl-Birger (b Växjö, Sweden, 1916; d Kungsängen, 1968). Swed. composer. Prof. of comp., Swedish Royal Acad. of Mus., 1960–4, dir. of mus., Swedish Radio, from 1965. Pioneered EMS. After a Hindemithian early phase, adopted serial techniques and, later, elecs. First opera *Aniara* (Stockholm 1959) is set in a spaceship. Prin. works incl.:

OPERAS: *Aniara* (1959); *Herr von Hancken* (1962–4).

ORCH.: Concerto Grosso (1944); sym. No.1 (1943), No.2 (1947), No.3 (*Facets*) (1948); va. conc. (1941); vn. conc. (1947); chamber conc. (1952–3); *Sisyphos*, choreographic suite (1954); *Minotauros*, choreographic suite (1957); *Altisonans*, tape (1966).

CHORAL: *In the Hall of Mirrors* (*I splegnarnes sal*) for soloists, reciter, ch., and orch. (1951–2).

CHAMBER MUSIC: trio (1938); str. qt. (1939); str. trio (1945); etc.

Blomstedt, Herbert (Thorson) (b Springfield, Mass., 1927). Amer.-born cond. who became Swed. citizen. Studied conducting Stockholm Royal Acad. of Mus., 1950–2, philosophy Uppsala Univ. 1952. Mus. dir., Nörrkoping SO 1954–61. Prof. of cond., Stockholm RAM, 1961–70. Cond., Oslo PO 1962–8; Danish Radio SO 1967–77; Dresden Staatskapelle 1975–85 (his Salzburg Fest. début 1976); Swedish Radio SO 1977–82; S. Francisco SO 1985–95, Leipzig Gewandhaus Orch. 1998–2005. Distinguished interpreter of Sibelius, Nielsen, Strauss.

Bloomfield, Theodore (Robert) (b Cleveland, Ohio, 1923). Amer. conductor. Début, NY Little SO, 1945. Apprentice cond. to *Szell, Cleveland Orch., 1946–7. Cond. Cleveland Civic Opera Workshop 1947–52. Mus. dir., Portland (Oregon) SO 1955–9, Rochester PO 1959–63. First cond. at

Hamburg Opera 1964–6; gen. mus. dir. Frankfurt-am-Main 1966–8; chief cond. (W) Berlin SO 1975–82.

Blossom Time. Amer. version of operetta *Das Dreimäderlhaus* by Berté in which Schubert's mus. is arr. by S. Romberg. F.p. NY 1921.

Blow, John (b Newark, Notts., 1649; d Westminster, 1708). Eng. composer and organist. One of first choirboys of Chapel Royal after Restoration in 1660. Organist, Westminster Abbey, 1668–79, when his pupil Purcell succeeded him, and 1695–1708. Also Master of Choristers, St Paul's Cath., 1687–1703. Wrote over 100 anthems, 13 services, many secular songs, and the masque *Venus and Adonis* (c.1682). *Bliss comp. *Meditations on a Theme by John Blow*.

Bluebeard's Castle (Bartók). See *Duke Bluebeard's Castle*.

Blue Bells of Scotland (properly 'Bell', not 'Bells'). This song, of unknown origin, first appears at the end of the 18th or beginning of the 19th cent., sung by the London actress, Mrs Jordan (an Irishwoman), at Drury Lane Th.

Blue Bird, The. Part-song for mixed ch., with sop. solo, by *Stanford, Op.119 No.4, comp. 1911, setting of poem by Mary Coleridge (1861–1907).

Blue Danube, On The Beautiful (*An der schönen blauen Donau*). Concert waltz, Op.314, by Johann *Strauss II, known in Eng. simply as *The Blue Danube*. F.p. Vienna 1867. Orig. with ch. part.

blues. Slow *jazz song of lamentation, generally for an unhappy love affair. Usually in groups of 12 bars, instead of 8 or 16, each stanza being 3 lines covering 4 bars of music. Tonality predominantly major, but with the flattened 3rd and 7th of the key (the 'blue notes'). Harmony tended towards the plagal or subdominant. The earlier (almost entirely Negro) history of the blues is traced by oral tradition as far back as the 1860s, but the form was popularized about 1911–14 by the Negro composer W. C. Handy (*St Louis Blues*, *Basin Street Blues*). Composers such as Gershwin, Ravel, Copland, and Tippett have used the term to indicate a blues-type mood rather than a strict adherence to the form. Among notable blues singers were Bessie Smith and Billie Holiday (though Holiday's main repertoire was pop music).

Blume, Friedrich (b Schlüchtern, 1893; d Schlüchtern, 1975). Ger. musicologist. Distinguished career as ed. of early mus. and writer of scholarly studies on a wide variety of mus. subjects. Reader in musicology, Kiel Univ. 1934–8, prof. 1938–58. Ed. complete works of Michael Praetorius, 1928–40. From 1943 directed the preparation of the encyclopedia *Die Musik in Geschichte und Gegenwart*, 14 vols. of which appeared between 1949 and 1968, containing 9,414 articles for all of which he was personally responsible. Authority on Bach and Mozart.

Blumenstück (Flower-piece). Pf. solo in D major, Op.19, by Schumann, comp. 1839.

Blüthner. Piano-making firm, founded Leipzig 1853 by Julius Blüthner (*b* Falkenhain, 1824; *d* Leipzig, 1910). In 1873 patented *aliquot scaling (addition of fourth, sympathetic, string to each trichord group in treble) to strengthen upper register. Factory destroyed during Second World War, re-opened 1974.

Blyth, Alan (*b* London, 1929). Eng. critic, broadcaster, and author. Contributor to *The Times* 1963–77, *Musical Times*, *Opera* (ass. ed. 1967–84), esp. on operatic subjects. Member of mus. staff of *Daily Telegraph* 1977–94. Author of monographs on Colin Davis (1969) and Janet Baker (1972). Ed. *Opera on Record* 1, 2, and 3 (1979, 1983, 1984); *Remembering Britten* (1981); *Song on Record* 1 and 2 (1986, 1988); *Choral Music on Record* (1991); *Opera on CD* (1992); *Opera on Video* (1995).

Blyton, Carey (*b* Beckenham, 1932; *d* Woodbridge, 2002). Eng. composer. Bantock comp. prize 1954. Prof. of harmony, TCL, 1963–73. Mus. ed., Faber Mus., 1963–74. Prof. of comp. for films, television, and radio, GSMD, 1972–83. Comps. incl. orch. suite *Cinque Port*; ov. *The Hobbit*; works for sax. qt. and for guitar; cantatas; song-cycles; madrigals; chamber mus.; and vocal pieces such as *Lyrics from the Chinese*, *Lachrymae*, and *Symphony in Yellow*. Nephew of writer Enid Blyton.

b moll (Ger.). The key of B♭ minor (not B minor; see B).

BNOC. See *British National Opera Company*.

Boatswain's Mate, The. Opera in 1 act by Ethel *Smyth to her lib. based on W. W. Jacobs's story. Comp. 1913–14. Prod. London 1916.

Boatwright, Howard (Leake), jr. (*b* Newport News, Virginia, 1918; *d* Syracuse, NY, 1999). Amer. composer. Teacher of mus. theory, Yale, 1948–64, dean of mus. sch., Syracuse Univ. from 1964. Works incl. *The Woman of Trachis* (1955), cl. qt. (1958), *St Matthew Passion* (1962), *Canticle of the Sun* (1963), *Ship of Death* (1966), *6 Prayers of Kierkegaard*, sop., pf. (1978), Sonata, cl., pf. (1980), *5 Poems of Sylvia Plath*, sop., pf. (1993), *Nunc dimittis and Magnificat*, SATB, org. (1997).

Bobillier, Marie. See *Brenet, Michel*.

Boccaccio. Opera in 3 acts by Suppé to lib. by F. Zell and R. Genée. Prod. Vienna 1879, Boston and NY 1880, London 1882.

bocca chiusa (It.). Closed mouth, i.e. a wordless humming (in choral mus.).

Boccherini, (Ridolfo) **Luigi** (*b* Lucca, 1743; *d* Madrid, 1805). It. cellist and composer. Famous in teens as virtuoso cellist (début at age of 13). Studied in Rome with G. B. Costanzi, 1757. Contemp. of Haydn and resembling him in ideals, methods, and general spirit. Spent much time in Vienna 1757–64. Settled in Madrid in 1770 with court post, remaining until 1787. Appointed 'composer of his Chamber' by Friedrich Wilhelm II of Prussia, but it is doubtful if he ever took up his duties at the court in Berlin. After 1798 he lacked a patron and died in poverty. Comp. opera; 30 syms.; 11 vc. concs.; 91 str. qts.; 154 quintets (various combinations); gui. qts.; 60 trios; church mus.; etc. The famous Minuet is from the string quintet in E major, Op.13, No.5. Boccherini's mus., which combines harmonic adventurousness with melodic profundity, is well worth detailed study.

bocchino (It.). Mouthpiece of a wind instr.

bocedization. 16th-cent. Flemish system of naming notes of scale (Bo–Ce–Di, etc.), somewhat on principle of tonic sol-fa. Introduced by Hubert Waelrant.

Bochsa, (Robert) **Nicolas Charles** (*b* Montmédi, 1789; *d* Sydney, NSW, 1856). Fr. composer and harpist, author of a famous harp method and leader of a colourful life. Revolutionized way of playing the hp. Harpist to Napoleon 1813 and to Louis XVIII 1816. Wrote 8 operas for Opéra-Comique between 1813 and 1816. Fled from France 1817, was tried *in absentia* for forgeries and sentenced to 12 years' imprisonment. Settled in London. Dir., Lent oratorios from 1823. First gen. sec. and prof. of hp. RAM from 1822. Dismissed 1827. Cond., King's Th., London, 1826–30. In 1839 ran away with singer Anna Bishop, wife of Henry *Bishop, after touring provinces as her accompanist. Spent rest of his life on tour abroad (except in Fr.). Composed Requiem in 15 movts., 1816, commissioned for ceremony of reinterment of the beheaded Louis XVI's remains. Contains anticipations of Berlioz's *Symphonie funèbre et triomphale*. Also comp. sym. (1821), 5 hp. concs., and many chamber works involving harp.

Bodanzky, Artur (*b* Vienna, 1877; *d* NY, 1939). Austrian conductor. Took various humble conducting posts from 1900. Ass. to Mahler at Vienna Opera 1903–4. Cond. f. Brit. stage p. of *Parsifal*, CG 1914. Then at NY Met from 1915 until his death, apart from brief break in 1928. Notorious for the cuts he made in *Ring* cycle. Had wide and catholic repertory. Cond. f. Amer. p. of Krenek's opera *Jonny spielt auf* (1929) and of Janáček's *Glagolitic Mass*.

Bode, Hannelore (*b* Berlin-Zehlendorf, 1941). Ger. soprano. Début Bonn 1964. Basle Opera 1967–8, Düsseldorf from 1968. Specialist in Wagner roles, singing at Bayreuth Fest. between 1969 and 1974. CG début 1977; S. Francisco 1981 (Eva).

Bode, Johann Joachim Christoph (*b* Barum, Brunswick, 1730; *d* Weimar, 1793). Ger. composer, bassoonist, and oboist. Mus. teacher and ed., Hamburg, 1757–78, later becoming printer and publisher. Comp. syms., bn. conc., vc. conc., vn. conc., and songs.

Boehm, Theobald (Boehm System, Boehm Flute) (*b* Munich, 1794; *d* Munich, 1881). Ger. flautist and composer, remembered principally for the system whereby he replaced the clumsily-placed holes of his instr. by keys enabling the cutting of the holes in their proper acoustical positions, yet leaving them in easy control of the fingers. He made his first 'ring key' fl. in 1832, while a player in Munich court orch., and in 1847 brought out an improved metal fl. with 15 holes and 23 levers and keys. This system has been adapted for ob., cl., and bn. Boehm was also a goldsmith and ironmaster. From 1833 to 1846 he superintended reorganization of Bavarian steel industry.

Boëllmann, Léon (*b* Ensisheim, Upper Alsace, 1862; *d* Paris, 1897). Fr. organist and composer. From 1881. org. of Paris church of St Vincent de Paul; wrote org. mus. and mus. for other instr., incl. *Symphonic Variations* for vc. and orch.

Boësset, Antoine (*b* Blois, 1586; *d* Paris, 1643). Fr. court musician, being master of royal mus. from 1613 and holding other royal posts simultaneously. Pubd. 9 vols. of airs (1617–42), also masses and motets.

Boethius, Anicius Manlius Torquatus Severinus (*b* Rome, *c*.475; *d* Pavia, *c*.525). Roman philosopher and mathematician who wrote *De institutione musica*, a 5-vol. treatise on Gr. mus.

Boettcher, Wilfried (*b* Bremen, 1929). Ger. conductor and cellist. Prin. cellist, Hanover Opera 1956–8. Prof. of vc., Vienna Acad. of Mus. 1958. Founder and dir. Vienna Soloists 1959 (Salzburg Fest. début 1964). Prof. of vc. and chamber mus., Hamburg Acad. 1965. Cond. Hamburg SO 1967–71. Guest cond. of several Brit. orchs.

Bœuf sur le toit, Le (The Ox on the Roof). Pantomimic divertissement with mus. by Milhaud to lib. by Cocteau. Comp. 1919. Prod. Paris 1920 as mus.-hall spectacle, later as ballet.

Bogen (Ger.). (1) Bow. So *Bogenstrich*, bow stroke.
(2) Short for **Krummbogen*.
(3) The **tie (or bind).
(4) *Bogen* form. The design of e.g. a movement of a sym. which can be likened to the curve of a bow.

Bohème, La (Bohemian Life). (1) Opera in 4 acts by Puccini to lib. by Giacosa and Illica, based on H. Murger's novel *Scènes de la vie de bohème* (1847–9). Comp. 1894–5. Prod. Turin 1896; Manchester (in Eng.) and Los Angeles 1897; San Francisco and NY 1898; London 1899.
(2) Opera by Leoncavallo, also founded on Murger's novel but using different episodes. Prod. Venice 1897; NY 1960; London 1970; Wexford 1994.

Bohemian Girl, The. Opera in 3 acts by Balfe to lib. by Alfred Bunn based on a ballet-pantomime *The Gipsy* by Saint-Georges (1839) and orig. from Cervantes's *La Gitanella* (1614). Prod. London

1843, NY 1844. Incl. songs *I dreamt that I dwelt in marble halls* and *When other lips*. Revived by Beecham, Liverpool and London, 1951.

Bohemian String Quartet. See *Czech Quartet*.

Bohemia's Meadows and Forests, From (Smetana). See *Má Vlast*.

Böhm, Karl (*b* Graz, 1894; *d* Salzburg, 1981). Austrian conductor. First post at Graz 1917, becoming chief cond. 1920. Munich Opera 1921–7. Generalmusikdirektor Darmstadt 1927–31, Hamburg 1931–4, Dresden 1934–42, Vienna 1943–5. Dir. of rebuilt Vienna State Opera 1955–6. Regular cond. Salzburg Fest. (début 1943), Vienna, Bayreuth (début 1962). London début, CG 1936; NY Met 1957. Specialist in mus. of R. Strauss. Cond. f.ps. of *Die schweigsame Frau* (1935) and *Daphne* (1938), both Dresden.

Böhme, Kurt (*b* Dresden, 1908; *d* Munich, 1989). Ger. bass. Début Bautzen 1929. Member of Dresden Opera 1930–50, creating roles of Dominik in *Arabella* (1933) and Vanuzzi in *Die schweigsame Frau* (1935). Sang Ochs in *Der Rosenkavalier* over 500 times, his first being at La Scala in 1942. Salzburg Fest. 1941–59. Member of Bavarian State Opera, Munich, from 1950, Vienna State Opera from 1955. CG début 1936 (with Dresden Opera), returning as guest 1956–60. Sang at CG with Bavarian State Opera 1972. NY Met début 1954; Bayreuth 1952, 1963–4.

Bohnen, Michael (*b* Cologne, 1887; *d* Berlin, 1965). Ger. bass-baritone. Début as Kaspar in *Der Freischütz*, Düsseldorf, 1910. Berlin Court Opera 1913–21. CG and Bayreuth débuts 1914. NY Met 1923–32 incl. Jonny in NY première of Krenek's *Jonny spielt auf*. Berlin Deutsches Oper 1933–45. Salzburg Fest. 1939. Intendant, Berlin Städtische Oper, 1945–7.

Boieldieu, François Adrien (*b* Rouen, 1775; *d* Jarcy, 1834). Fr. composer. First 2 operas, to libs. by his father, were prod. in Rouen in 1793 and 1795. Went to Paris in 1795, soon having operas staged there. First major success in 1800 with *Le *Calife de Bagdad*, but Cherubini asked him 'Are you not ashamed of such undeserved success?' and took him as pupil, the first result (another success) being *Ma Tante Aurore* (1803). From 1803 to 1811 cond. of Imperial Opera, St Petersburg. Returning to Paris 1811, comp. *Jean de Paris* (1812), his biggest success until *La *Dame blanche* (The White Lady) 1825, which is based on two Scott novels (*The Monastery* and *Guy Mannering*). Last years were haunted by ill-health and money troubles. Also composed chamber mus., concs. for hp. and for pf., and was prof. of pf., Paris Cons., 1798–1803, prof. of comp. 1817–26.

bois (Fr.). Wood. *avec le bois d'archet*, play with the wood of the bow, not the hair (same as **col legno*); *les bois*, the woodwind; *baguette de bois*, wooden-headed drumstick.

Boismortier, Joseph Bodin de (*b* Thionville, 1689; *d* Roissy-en-Brie, 1755). Fr. composer of pieces for the then fashionable hurdygurdy (vielle). Remembered chiefly for his many works for fl.

boîte (Fr.). Box, i.e. swell box of org.

Boîte à joujoux, La (The box of toys). Children's ballet in 4 scenes by Debussy, comp. 1913 for pf. to scenario and choreog. by André Hellé and f.p. Paris 1919. Version for orch. sketched 1914 and completed 1918–19 by *Caplet, f.p. Paris 1923.

Boito, Arrigo [Enrico] (*b* Padua, 1842; *d* Milan, 1918). It. composer and poet, son of It. painter and Polish countess. Fame chiefly rests on superb libs. for Verdi's last operas, *Otello* (1886) and *Falstaff* (1893). Studied mus. in Milan with Mazzucato, and went to Paris on a government travelling scholarship, 1862, with *Faccio. Met Hugo, Berlioz, Verdi, and Rossini there. First collab. with Verdi in 1862 on *The Hymn of the Nations*, after which there was coolness between them until he rev. the existing lib. of *Simon Boccanegra* in 1880–1. Returning to It., espoused cause of mus. reform and redress of neglect of Ger. classics. Comp. opera *Mefistofele* 1866–7. F.p. in Milan 1868 was attended by much publicity about its revolutionary nature; this led to a riot in La Scala between traditionalists and reformers and eventually to the opera's withdrawal on police orders. Rev. version, perf. Bologna 1875, was acclaimed. Wrote libs. for Faccio's *Amleto* (1865), Catalani's *La Falce* (1875), and Ponchielli's *La Gioconda* (1876, under the anagrammatic pseudonym Tobia Gorrio). Also trans. into It. the texts of Beethoven's 9th Sym. and Wagner's *Rienzi* and *Tristan*. Only other pubd. opera, *Nerone*, was begun in 1877 and left unfinished. Completed and rev. by Toscanini, Smareglia, and Tommasini, and prod. Milan 1924. Received hon. doctorates of mus. from both Cambridge and Oxford and was dir., Parma Cons. 1889–97. Correspondence with Verdi is of great interest.

Bolcom, William (Elden) (*b* Seattle, 1938). Amer. composer. Has worked as teacher (at Sch. of Mus. of Univ. of Michigan at Ann Arbor from 1973, becoming prof. 1983) and critic. Comps. admit wide range of influences, from serialism to collage. They include the operas *McTeague* (Chicago, 1992), *A View from the Bridge* (1997–9), and *A Wedding* (2004); 6 syms.; 11 str. qts. (1950–2003); *Session 2*, vn., va. (1966); *Black Host*, org., perc., tape (1967); *14 Piano Rags* (1967–70); *Dark Music*, timp., vc. (1970); *Open House*, ten., chamber orch. (1975); pf. conc. (1976); pf. qt. (1976); vn. conc. (1983); *Concertante*, va., vc., orch. (1985); *Fantasy Sonata*, pf. (1989); *Spring Concertino*, ob., chamber orch. (1989); cl. conc. (1990); fl. conc. (1993); sonata, 2 pf. (1993); *A Whitman Triptych*, mez., orch. (1995); *Concert Suite*, sax., band (1999); *Concerto Grosso*, sax. qt., orch. (2000); pf. quintet (2001); *Seventh Symphony: a Symphonic Concerto*, orch. (2002); *Medusa*, sop., chamber orch. (2003). One of his highly praised works is the *Songs of Innocence and Experi-*

ence (48 Blake poems), for 9 solo vv., 2 ch., unacc. ch., children's ch., and orch. (1956–82, f.p. Stuttgart, 1984).

bolero. Sp. dance in simple triple time, almost same as *cachucha* but danced by a couple or several couples. Acc. is of (or incl.) the dancers' own vv. and castanets, sometimes with added guitars and tambourines. Introduced *c*.1780.

Boléro. Ballet in 1 act by *Ravel, choreog. *Nijinskaya, comp. for Ida Rubinstein in 1928 (prod. Paris Opéra, Nov. 1928). Mus. consists of repetition of theme, in C major almost throughout, in unvarying rhythm and gradual crescendo. Its immense popularity made Ravel world-famous. Later also choreog. Lifar (1941), Béjart (1961), and others.

Bolet, Jorge (*b* Havana, 1914; *d* Mountainview, Calif., 1990). Cuban-born pianist (Amer. cit.). Eur. début Amsterdam 1935, Amer. début Philadelphia 1937. Mus. dir. US Army GHQ Tokyo, 1946, when he directed Japanese première of Sullivan's *The Mikado*. Prof. of mus., Indiana Univ. 1968–77, then head of piano dept., Curtis Inst. Soundtrack pianist in film biography of Liszt, *Song Without End* (1960). Outstanding player of Liszt.

Bolshoy Theatre (Russ., 'Great Theatre'), Moscow. Oldest th. in Moscow, home of the Bolshoy opera and ballet cos. Orig. named Petrovsky and built by Englishman (Maddox) in 1780. Destroyed by fire in 1805. Bolshoy Petrovsky opened 1825, but in 1853 its interior was burnt out. Restored by Cavos and reopened in 1856. Seats approx. 2,000 people. Stage is half as wide again as that of CG. There was also a Bolshoy Theatre in St Petersburg, 1783–1859.

Bolt, The (*Bolt*). Ballet (choreographic spectacle) in 3 acts, mus. by Shostakovich, Op.27, lib. by V. Smirnov, choreog. Lopokov. Comp. 1930–1. Prod. Leningrad 1931. Also orch. suite 1931.

Bolton, Ivor (*b* Blackrod, Lancs., 1958). Eng. conductor. Studied at Clare Coll., Cambridge (1976–80), RCM (1980–1), and Nat. Opera Studio (1981–2). Founded St James Baroque Players (1984). Prin. cond. ETO (1990–2), GTO (1992–7), and Scottish CO (1994–6). CG début 1995 (world première of Goehr's *Arianna*). Salzburg Fest. début 2000 (*Iphigénie en Tauride*). Has worked closely with Bayerische Staatsoper, Munich, since his début there 1994 (*Giulio Cesare*); Paris Opéra début 1997 (*Clemenza di Tito*). Chief cond. Mozarteum Orch., Salzburg, from 2004.

Bomarzo. Opera ('gothic melodrama of sex and violence') in 2 acts (15 scenes with instr. interludes) by *Ginastera, to lib. by Manuel Mujica Láinez based on his novel. Bomarzo is 16th-cent. It. nobleman. Prod. Washington and NY 1967, Buenos Aires 1972, London 1976 (Eng. trans. by Lionel Salter). Ginastera's cantata *Bomarzo* (1964) for narrator, bar., and orch. is derived from the same literary source by Láinez but is distinct musically.

bombard. A type of *shawm—but in 14th and 15th cents. was applied in Fr. and Eng. to alto-pitched shawm. Name was probably taken over from an artillery piece of the same name. (The word is derived from the Lat. *bombus*, drone or buzz). Note that the *bombardon has nothing in common with it, being a brass instr., as is the It. *bombarda*, euphonium.

bombarda (It.). Euphonium.

bombarde, bombardon. Powerful org. *reed stop*, often in pedal department and sometimes of 32′ pitch.

bombardon. (1) Form of bass tuba with 3 piston valves, in B♭, C, CC, F, or E♭. Replaced by *Sax's E♭ or BB♭ bass tubas, 1842 (double letter indicates specimens with wider bore).
(2) It. term for bass shawm.

Bonavia, Ferruccio (*b* Trieste, 1877; *d* London, 1950). It.-born violinist and music critic. For 10 years was member of Hallé Orch., Manchester, under Richter, at same time writing for *Manchester Guardian* on mus. subjects. From 1920 until death a mus. critic of London *Daily Telegraph*. Wrote book on Verdi, and comp. str. mus. (qt., octet, etc.).

Bonci, Alessandro (*b* Cesena, 1870; *d* Viserba, 1940). It. tenor. Opera début Parma 1896. La Scala 1897. CG début 1900, NY 1906, Met 1907. Especially effective in *bel canto* opera. Served in It. airforce in First World War. After war sang in Chicago until 1921. Retired 1925.

Bond (*née* Jacobs), **Carrie (Jacobs)** (*b* Janesville, Wisc., 1862; *d* Glendale, Calif., 1946). Amer. song composer, among her most popular being 'Just a-wearyin' for you' and 'The end of a perfect day' (of which over 5 million copies were sold).

Bondeville, Emmanuel (Pierre Georges) (*b* Rouen, 1898; *d* Paris, 1987). Fr. composer and administrator. Art. dir. Radiodiffusion Française 1937–45, dir., Monte Carlo Opera 1945–9, Paris Opéra-Comique 1949–52, and Paris Opéra 1952–70. Comps. incl. *Madame Bovary*, opera (1951); *L'École des Maris*, lyric comedy (1935); *Symphonie lyrique* (1957); *Symphonie choréographique* (1965); *Antoine et Cléopâtre* (1974).

Bonduca, or The British Heroine. Incidental mus. by Purcell to a play adapted from Beaumont and Fletcher on the story of Boadicea (1695).

Bondy, Luc (*b* Zurich, 1948). Swiss producer. Studied at Jacques Leqoq's Mime Sch. Ass. dir. Thalia Th., Hamburg, 1968–74, then worked in theatres in Frankfurt 1974–6, Berlin 1985–7. Opera début Hamburg 1976 (*Wozzeck*). Prod. operas in Brussels 1986 (*Così fan tutte*), Salzburg Fest. 1992 (*Salome*), CG 1996 (*Don Carlos*), Scottish Opera 1999 (Edinburgh Fest., *Macbeth*), Aix 2001 (*Turn of the Screw*).

Bonell, Carlos (Antonio) (*b* London, 1949). Eng. guitarist. Founded Carlos Bonell Ens. 1983. Comp. pieces for guitar. Concerto soloist with leading orchs. Author of books on gui. technique.

bones. Two pieces of animal rib bone held between the fingers and rhythmically clacked—the 19th-cent. 'nigger *minstrel' equivalent of the castanets.

bongos. Small Cuban drums, bucket-shaped vessels cut out of solid wood, bound with brass, and having strong vellum heads. Two of them are fixed together by a bar of metal. They are played with the thumb and fingers by dance-band musicians and have been used in comps. by John *McCabe, Varèse, Orff, and Boulez.

Bonini, Severo (*b* Florence, 1582; *d* Florence, 1663.). It. organist and composer of madrigals, motets, and a setting of Rinuccini's *Lamento d'Arianna* (1613). One of first to use monodic style. Author of important treatise *Prima parte de' discorsi e regole sovra la musica* (First part of discourses and rules about music), completed 1649–50.

Bonne Chanson, La (The Good Song). (1) Settings by *Fauré in 1892–3, Op.61, of 9 poems by Verlaine, namely *Une Sainte en son auréole; Puisque l'aube grandit; La Lune blanche luit dans les bois; J'allais par des chemins perfides; J'ai presque peur en vérité; Avant que tu ne t'en ailles; Donc ce sera par un clair jour d'été; N'est ce pas?; L'hiver a cessé*.
(2) Tone-poem by *Loeffler comp. 1901 and f.p. Boston 1902. Also inspired by Verlaine.

Bonnet, Joseph (Élie Georges Marie) (*b* Bordeaux, 1884; *d* nr. Quebec, 1944). Fr. organist and composer. Org., of St Eustache, Paris, from 1906. Toured widely in Europe and Amer. Org. comps. have wide popularity.

Bonney, Barbara (*b* New Jersey, Montreal, 1956). Canadian soprano. Opera début Darmstadt 1979. Sang in Frankfurt, Hamburg, and Munich 1983–4. CG début 1984; Milan 1985; Salzburg Fest. 1987 (concert).

Bonnie Annie. Folk tune to which words of 'John Peel' were later fitted by J. W. Graves.

Bononcini, Antonio Maria (*b* Modena, 1677; *d* Rome, 1726). It. composer. Brother of Giovanni *Bononcini and said to be the more talented. Comp. at least 17 operas and 39 cantatas. Was also cellist.

Bononcini, Giovanni (*b* Modena, 1670; *d* Vienna, 1747). It. composer and cellist. Usually spelt his name Buononcini. Elder son of G. M. *Bononcini. Studied in Bologna. Worked in Rome from 1692 and scored success throughout It. with opera *Il trionfo di Camilla* (Naples, 1696). Went to Vienna 1697 and was court composer there 1700–11, but also spent time in Rome and Berlin. Invited to London in 1720 to work at newly-founded Royal Acad. of Mus. with Handel as dir. Enjoyed great favour, esp. with the Marlborough family who, from 1724, paid him £500 p.a. Several operas prod. in London over next decade, most successful being *Astarto* (1720, rev. of 1714 Rome version). In 1721 contrib. act to *Muzio Scevola*, the other 2 being by Amadei and Handel. In 1722 wrote anthem for Duke of Marlborough's funeral in Westminster Abbey. In 1732 left Eng. for Fr., scorning to answer an accusation of plagiarism. Lived rest of his life in Paris and Vienna. Comp. nearly 50 operas, also masses, oratorios, many cantatas for solo voice, and a large amount of chamber mus.

Bononcini, Giovanni Maria (*b* Montecorone, nr. Modena, 1642; *d* Modena, 1678). It. composer. Head of family of musicians. Employed at court of Duke of Modena. Wrote masses, cantatas, sonatas, etc. Pubd. treatise on mus. 1673.

Bonporti [Buonporti], **Francesco Antonio** (*b* Trent, 1672; *d* Padua, 1749). It. violinist and composer of instr. mus. Ordained as priest 1695. Comp. 10 'Inventions' for vn. and figured bass, 1712 (Bach's use of word apparently taken from this), also vn. sonatas and minuets.

Bontempi [Angelini], **Giovanni Andrea** (*b* Perugia, 1624; *d* Brufa, nr. Perugia, 1705). It. composer, singer, and writer on music. Sang as castrato under Monteverdi and Cavalli in St Mark's, Venice, 1643–50, when he went to Dresden. Befriended by Schütz, becoming associate Kapellmeister with him in 1656. Wrote 3 operas and several theoretical treatises. Settled in It., 1680, becoming choirmaster Spello 1686.

Bonynge, Richard (Alan) (*b* Sydney, NSW, 1930). Australian conductor and pianist. Cond. début, Rome 1962. Specialist in late 18th- and early 19th-cent. *bel canto* operas, many of them vehicles for his wife, the sop. Joan *Sutherland. CG début 1964; NY Met 1970. Mus. dir., Vancouver Opera 1974–8 and Australian Opera 1975–86. CBE 1977.

boobams. Perc. instr. of definite pitch made of lengths of bamboo each having an end covered by a plastic membrane which is struck by the finger or a soft-headed hammer. Pitch determined by length of tubes. Name is an inversion of bamboos.

boogie-woogie (or boogie). Jazz style of blues pf.-playing originating in early years of 20th cent. but becoming popular from about 1928. One of first exponents was Negro jazz pianist Clarence 'Pine Top' Smith. Prin. feature is ostinato bass in broken octaves.

Boosey & Hawkes, Ltd. London mus. publishers and instr. manufacturers. Boosey founded 1816; Hawkes 1865. Amalgamation 1930. Catalogue incl. works by R. Strauss, Stravinsky, Bartók, Prokofiev, Copland, Britten, Ginastera, Maxwell Davies, and many young composers. Specialists in

brass band mus. Subsidiary cos. in USA, Fr., Ger. Major manufacturer of wind instr. Pubd. magazine *Tempo* from 1939.

Bord. Paris pf.-making firm; est. 1843 by Antoine-Jean Denis Bord (*b* Toulouse, 1814; *d* Paris, 1888) and taken over by Pleyel 1934. Mass-produced small upright pianos known as 'pianettes'.

Bordes, Charles (Marie Anne) (*b* La Roche-Corbon, Indre-et-Loire, 1863; *d* Toulon, 1909). Fr. composer. Choirmaster from 1890 of Paris church of St Gervais, where he founded a choral body for the perf. of Renaissance church mus. under the name of 'Les Chanteurs de St Gervais' (later an independent body); with Guilmant and d'Indy founded also the Société Schola Cantorum for the study of church mus. (1894), which led to est. of Schola Cantorum of Paris as mus. sch. (1896). Collected and pubd. early church mus. and Basque folk tunes, and comp. mus. for pf., orch., etc. From 1905, at Montpellier, organized perfs. of Rameau operas.

Bordoni [Hasse], **Faustina** (*b* Venice, 1700; *d* Venice, 1781). It. mezzo-soprano. Début Venice 1716. Sang in Venice until 1725 in operas by Albinoni, Lotti, etc. Ger. début Munich 1723, Vienna 1725. First sang in London 1726 in Handel's *Alessandro*. Created 4 other Handel operatic roles 1727–8. Her rivalry with Cuzzoni led to a fight between them on stage in 1727. Returned to It. 1728–32. Married comp. *Hasse in 1730 and thereafter sang chiefly in his operas after he became Kapellmeister at Dresden 1731. Retired from stage 1751.

bore. Interior of tube of wind instr. Determines length and proportions of air column and pitch of lowest note obtainable. In brass instr. length of bore is variable by use of valves, in woodwind by opening and closing sideholes.

Boréades, Les (The Sons of Boreas). Opera (his last) in 5 acts by *Rameau to lib. attrib. to L. de Cahusac. Comp. 1762–3. Unperf. in Rameau's lifetime. Extracts perf. Paris (radio) 1964; f. stage p. Aix-en-Provence 1982; London (QEH concert) 1975, RAM (stage, abridged) 1985; Birmingham (CBTO) 1993.

Borg, Kim (*b* Helsinki, 1919; *d* Copenhagen, 2000). Finn. bass and composer. Début Helsinki 1947, in opera at Åarhus 1951. NY Met début 1959. Frequent visits to USA and Eng. Roles incl. Boris Godunov, Scarpia, and Don Giovanni. Salzburg Fest. début 1956, opera 1966; Glyndebourne 1956. Recorded Elgar's *Dream of Gerontius* with Barbirolli. Prof., RAM, Denmark, from 1972. Comp. songs.

Borge, Victor (*b* Copenhagen, 1909; *d* Greenwich, Conn., 2000). Danish-born pianist and entertainer (Amer. cit. 1948). Début Copenhagen 1922. Best known as humorist, dealing amusingly with mus. quirks and oddities.

Borgioli, Dino (*b* Florence, 1891; *d* Florence, 1960). It. tenor. Also a painter. Début Milan,

1914; CG 1925; Salzburg Fest. début 1931. Often sang at CG and Glyndebourne (1937-9). NY Met début 1934. His Mozart and Rossini style was much admired. Settled in London as teacher.

Bori, Lucrezia [Borja y Gonzalez de Riancho, Lucrecia] (*b* Valencia, 1887; *d* NY, 1960). Sp. soprano. Début Rome 1908 (Micaela in *Carmen*). Sang Manon Lescaut opposite Caruso in Paris 1910 (with NY Met co.). First It. Oktavian, Milan 1911. NY Met début 1912. Career interrupted by throat operation 1915, but resumed 1919. Member of NY Met co. 1921-36 and of board of dirs. from 1935.

Boris Godunov. Opera in 4 acts, with prol., by *Mussorgsky to his own lib. based on Pushkin's poetic drama, *The Comedy of the Distress of the Muscovite State, of Tsar Boris, and of Grishka Otrepyev* (1826) and Karamzin's *History of the Russian Empire* (1829). Orig. version comp. 1868-9, rev. 1871-2, rev. 1873, 3 scenes prod. St Petersburg 1873 and complete opera 1874, but withdrawn after 25 perfs. Cut, re-orchestrated, and rev. by Rimsky-Korsakov after Mussorgsky's death and thus prod. St Petersburg 1896. This version rev., with some cuts restored, 1906, prod. NY and London 1913. Orig. versions of 1869 and 1872 pubd. Leningrad 1928 in edn. prepared by Prof. Pavel Lamm of Moscow and perf. Leningrad 1928, London (SW) and Paris 1935. The 1869 version had 7 scenes which were altered and re-arranged and an extra (Kromy Forest) scene added. Musicological controversy rages on the 'correct' version to use, but there is a growing tendency to prefer the Mussorgsky orchestration. In 1975 David Lloyd-Jones pubd. an edn., for which he had the use of MS sources unknown to Lamm, which also corrects errors of detail and transcr. in Lamm. Vol. I of Lloyd-Jones contains Mussorgsky's 1872 version of prol. and 4 acts and Vol. II the 1869 version of Act 2, the discarded 'St Basil' scene, with variants and other scenes. A re-orch. version by Shostakovich exists (1939-40, prod. Leningrad 1959). Title-role inseparably assoc. with *Chaliapin and *Christoff.

Borkh, Inge [Simon, Ingeborg] (*b* Mannheim, 1917). Ger.-born Swiss soprano. Began career as actress 1937. Début as singer Lucerne 1940. Int. career followed success in *The *Consul* in Lucerne 1952. Bayreuth début 1952; US début 1953 (S. Francisco); Salzburg Fest. 1955; London 1955 (concert); CG 1959; NY Met 1958. Renowned for dramatic Strauss roles and Verdi's Lady Macbeth, esp. as member of Stuttgart Opera.

Bořkovec, Pavel (*b* Prague, 1894; *d* Prague, 1972). Cz. composer. In 1920s was a leading figure in Czech neo-classic sch. Taught comp. Prague Acad. 1946-64. Comps. incl. 3 syms. (1926-7, 1955, 1959); 2 sinfoniettas (1947, 1969); 2 pf. concs. (1931, 1950); vn. conc. (1933); vc. conc. (1951); opera *Tom Thumb* (*Paláček*) (1945-7); *Dreams* (*Sny*), 7 songs for low v. and orch. (1962); chamber mus., etc.

Borodin, Alexander (Porfiryevich) (*b* St Petersburg, 1833; *d* St Petersburg, 1887). Russ. composer, one of the group known as 'The *Five'. Illegitimate son of Russ. prince. Showed childhood talent for mus. and science, composing pf. pieces and fl. conc. Entered medical profession, graduating in 1855, Acad. of Medicine and Surgery, St Petersburg. Studied science in Heidelberg and elsewhere 1859-62. Appointed ass. prof. of chemistry, Acad. of Medicine 1862, prof. from 1864. Meeting with *Balakirev 1862 persuaded him to devote leisure to serious study of mus. while continuing his scientific work, which incl. foundation of School of Medicine for Women, where he lectured from 1872 to his death. His first sym. was prod. 1869, but he had already tasted failure with comic opera *The Bogatyrs* in 1867. His Sym. No.2 in B minor was also a failure at f.p. 1877, the year in which he visited Liszt at Weimar. Liszt in 1880 ensured a perf. of the First Sym. at Baden-Baden which initiated Borodin's popularity outside Russia. In 1869 his friend Stasov suggested an opera on the subject of *Prince Igor*. This appealed to Borodin's nationalism, but difficulties with the lib., plus the interruptions from his scientific career, made comp. slow and the work, Borodin's masterpiece, was never finished, but was completed by Rimsky-Korsakov and Glazunov. Melodic and harmonic originality of Borodin's style are best heard in *Prince Igor*, but the second sym., the 2 str. qts., and the tone-poem *In the Steppes of Central Asia* (1880) ensure his survival. Prin. works:

OPERA: *Prince Igor* (unfinished, completed and partly orch. by *Rimsky-Korsakov and *Glazunov) (1869-70, 1874-87).

ORCH.: syms.: No.1 in E♭ (1862-7), No.2 in B minor (1869-76), No.3 in A minor (1885-6, unfinished, completed and orch. by Glazunov); tone-picture *In the Steppes of Central Asia* (V sredney Azii) (1880); *Nocturne* from 2nd str. qt., orch. Sargent.

CHAMBER MUSIC: str. qts.: No.1 in A major (1877-9), No.2 in D (1881-7); pf. quintet in C minor (1862).

PIANO: *Petite Suite* (1885), orch. Glazunov; *Scherzo* in A♭; *Polka, Requiem, Dead March,* and *Mazurka* in coll. *Paraphrases on theme of *Chopsticks* (1880).

Borodina, Olga (*b* Leningrad, 1960). Russian mezzo-soprano. Member of Kirov (Mariinsky) Opera, St Petersburg, from 1987. Toured with Kirov to Hamburg 1990, Edinburgh Fest. 1991 (and Birmingham), and Palermo, 1992. Paris début 1992; CG 1992 (with Domingo); NY Met 1992 (with Kirov); Berlin 1993.

Borodin Quartet. Russian string quartet founded Oct. 1945. From 1974 personnel has been unchanged: Mikhail Kopelman and Andrei Abramenclov (vns.), Dmitri Shebalin (va.), and Valentin Berlinsky (vc.). Recorded all Shostakovich qts. 1979-84 and gave complete cycle in 1986 in London.

Boroni [Buroni], **Antonio** (*b* Rome, 1738; *d* Rome, 1792). It. composer and choirmaster. Followed Jommelli as Kapellmeister at Stuttgart 1771-7. Choirmaster, St Peter's, Rome, 1778-92.

Comp. 16 operas, masses, motets, and contrib. with J. C. Bach to a book of odes pubd. in London 1775.

borre, borree, borry. Old Eng. spellings of *bourrée*.

Borsdorf, (Friedrich) **Adolph** (b Dittmansdorf, Saxony, 1854; d London, 1923). Ger. horn-player who in 1879 settled in Eng. where he joined CG orch. and became 1st hn. in Richter's London orch. Later with Scottish Orch., Queen's Hall Orch, and LSO. Superb technician but especially noted for beauty of phrasing in such works as Brahms's hn. trio. As a teacher at RCM (from 1882) and RAM (from 1897) trained whole generation of English hn.-players, incl. his three sons and Alfred and Aubrey Brain.

Bortnyansky, Dmitry (Stepanovich) (b Glukhov, Ukraine, 1751; d St Petersburg, 1825). Russ. composer. Followed Galuppi to Venice 1768. His operas *Creonte* and *Quinto Fabio* were performed, respectively, in Venice (1776) and Modena (1778). On return to Russia in 1779, became dir. of Empress's church choir (re-named Imperial Kapelle in 1796) which he reformed and for which he comp. large amount of mus. His sacred works were pubd. in 10 vols. in St Petersburg under editorship of Tchaikovsky (1885).

Boschi, Giuseppe Maria (fl. 1698–1744). It. bass. Venice 1707, London 1710–11, creating Argante in Handel's *Rinaldo*. Dresden 1717–20. From 1720 to 1728 sang in London in all 32 operas prod. by Handel's Royal Academy, incl. 13 by Handel. Returned to Venice 1729 and became member of choir of St Mark's. His wife was the cont. Francesca Vanini (d Venice, 1744).

Bose, Hans-Jürgen von (b Munich, 1953). Ger. composer. Comps. incl. 4 operas; sym. (1976); ob. conc. (1986–7); 3 str. qts. (1973, 1976–7, 1987); vocal works and chamber mus.

Bösendorfer. Viennese pf.-making firm, founded 1828 by Ignaz Bösendorfer (b Vienna, 1796; d Vienna, 1859) and carried on by son Ludwig (b Vienna, 1835; d Vienna, 1919) from 1859. *Bösendorfersaal* (concert-room) opened 1872, closed 1913. Between 1828 and 1975 made 33 different models. Taken over by Jasper Corp., 1966.

Boskovich, Alexander (Urijah) (b Cluj, Transylvania, 1907; d Tel Aviv, 1964). Romanian-born Israeli composer, conductor, and pianist. Cond. Cluj State Opera 1930–8. Emigrated to Palestine 1938, teaching at Tel Aviv Acad. 1945–64. Mus. critic, Israeli newspaper *Ha'aretz* 1955–64. Comps. incl. suite, *The Golden Chain* (1937); vn. conc. (1942); ob. conc. (1943, rev. 1960); *Semitic Suite*, orch. (1946–7); *Daughter of Israel*, cantata (1960); *Concerto da camera*, vn., 10 instr. (1962); and *The Hidden Light* (*Ha'or haganuz*), oratorio (1964).

Boskovsky, Willi (b Vienna, 1909; d Visp, Switz., 1991). Austrian violinist and conductor. Joined

Vienna PO, 1932, co-leader 1939–71. Salzburg Fest. début (as violinist) 1938, (as cond.) 1975 (Strauss 150th Birthday Anniversary). Cond. of celebrated New Year's Day Vienna concerts of Strauss waltzes. Cond. Vienna Strauss Orch. from 1969. Founded Vienna Octet and Vienna Philharmonic Qt.

bossa-nova. Brazilian term that first appeared in 1959 in a song 'Desafinado' by Jobim which was extremely complex in melody and harmony, but its innovation was its radical change in the rhythmic structure of the samba. In 1960 bossa-nova became associated with social protest. 'Bossa' in Rio slang means 'shrewdness'.

Bossi, Marco Enrico (b Saló, Lake Garda, 1861; d at sea, 1925). It. organist, teacher, and composer, one of chief figures in revival of non-operatic It. mus. at end of 19th cent. Org. and choirmaster, Como Cath. 1881–91; prof. of org. and theory, Naples Cons., 1891–5. Dir. Liceo Benedetto Marcello, Venice, 1896–1902, dir. Liceo Musicale, Bologna, 1902–12, dir. Academy of St Cecilia, Rome, 1916–23. Wrote large body of works, incl. 3 operas; org. conc.; and chamber mus.; but best known are 3 choral works, *Canticum Canticorum* (Leipzig 1900), *Il paradiso perduto* (Augsburg 1903), and *Giovanna d'Arco* (Cologne 1914). His son Renzo (b Como, 1883; d Milan, 1965) was also organist, composer, and cond.

Boston Symphony Orchestra. One of great orchs. of world, founded at Boston, Mass., 1881 by Henry Lee Higginson who endowed it with a million dollars. First concert 22 Oct. 1881, cond. by Sir George *Henschel who was cond. 1881–4. He was succeeded by Wilhelm *Gericke 1884–9; *Nikisch 1889–93; Emil *Paur 1893–8; Gericke 1898–1906; Karl *Muck 1906–8; Max *Fiedler 1908–12; Muck 1912–18; Henri *Rabaud 1918–19; Pierre *Monteux 1919–24; Serge *Koussevitzky 1924–49; Charles *Munch 1949–62; Erich *Leinsdorf 1962–9; William *Steinberg 1969–72; Seiji *Ozawa 1973–2004; James Levine from 2004. Salzburg Fest. début 1979. Koussevitzky's 25-year tenure was outstanding for its encouragement of new works both by Amer. composers and by est. composers such as Prokofiev, Stravinsky, and Bartók. See *Tanglewood*.

Bostridge, Ian (Charles) (b London, 1964). Eng. tenor. Studied philosophy at Cambridge Univ. and history at Oxford Univ. (doctorate 1990) before taking up music full-time in 1995. Début London 1993. Wigmore Hall début 1993; Purcell Room 1994 (*Winterreise*); Aldeburgh Fest. 1994. Opera début CG Fest. (Lysander in *A Midsummer Night's Dream*) and Edinburgh Fest. 1994 (Lysander, with Australian Opera). ENO 1996 (Tamino); CG 1997 (Quint in *The Turn of the Screw*). Created Caliban in Adès's *The Tempest* (CG 2004). Carnegie Hall début 2000 (Britten's *War Requiem*). Salzburg Fest. 2002 (recital). Has written book about witchcraft. CBE 2004.

Bote & Bock. Ger. mus. publishing firm, founded in Berlin in 1838 by Eduard Bote and

Gustav Bock. Remained in Bock family until 1935 when it was reorganized as limited co. under direction of Robert Lienau, dir. of R. & W. Lienau. Publishing house completely destroyed 1943. Wiesbaden branch, 1948. Publisher of mus. of many Ger. composers incl. Reger, Blacher, and Einem. Satirized in 1st and 2nd songs of R. Strauss's *Krämerspiegel*.

Bottesini, Giovanni (*b* Crema, Lombardy, 1821; *d* Parma, 1889). It. virtuoso of double-bass which he took up because there was a vacancy at Milan Cons. in 1835 only for a db. student. In 1849 became lifelong friend of Verdi. Settled in Havana, Cuba, as prin. db. of orch. there. First played in London 1849. Used 3-str. *basso da camera* made by Testore of Milan, with a bow more like that for a vc. Was successful opera cond. in Paris 1855–7 and in London 1871. Dir. of opera ths. at Palermo, 1861–3, Barcelona, and Cairo. Cond. f.p. of Verdi's *Aida*, Cairo, 1871. Dir. of Parma Cons. 1889. Comp. many pieces for db., 13 operas, *Requiem* (1880), and an oratorio *The Garden of Olivet* (Norwich, 1887).

bouche fermée (Fr.). Closed-mouth singing, i.e. humming.

bouchés, sons (Fr.). Stopped notes in hn. playing (see also *Gestopft* and *Schmetternd*).

Boucourechliev, André (*b* Sofia, 1925; *d* Paris, 1997). Bulg.-born composer and pianist (Fr. cit. 1956). Worked for radio in Milan and Paris. Teacher of pf., École Normale 1954–60. Mus. critic of various Fr. publications from 1957. Author of books on Schumann, Chopin, Beethoven, and Stravinsky. Comps. incl. pf. sonata (1959); *Texte I* (tape, 1959); *Texte II* (tape, 1960); *Musiques nocturnes*, cl., hp., pf. (1966); *Archipel 1*, 2 pf., 2 percussionists (1967); *Archipel 2*, str. qt. (1968); *Archipel 3*, pf., 6 percussionists (1969); *Archipel 4*, pf. (1970); *Archipel 5*, 6 instr. (1970); *Ombres*, 11 str. (1970); *Faces*, orch. (1972); pf. conc. (1974–5). The *Archipel* works are in open form, generally perf. in 2 or more versions per concert. In *open form the sequence and/or structure of some parts of a work can be varied by the performers.

bouffons (or *mattachins*, or *matassins*). Old sword dance of men wearing armour of gilded cardboard.

Bouffons, Querelle des. 'War of the Comedians' in Paris, 1752–4. A quarrel over an opera by *Destouches led to the invitation to Paris of troupe of It. comedians, who made much stir with their perf. of Pergolesi's intermezzo *La *serva padrona*. The Fr. literary and mus. world split into 2 factions, favouring, respectively, It. and Fr. opera (as exemplified by Rameau). Rousseau and Diderot joined the controversy on the It. side.

Boughton, Rutland (*b* Aylesbury, 1878; *d* London, 1960). Eng. composer. Early orch. works perf. 1901 and 1902. From 1904 to 1911 on staff of Birmingham Midland Institute of Mus. Choral work, *Midnight* (1907), perf. Birmingham Fest.

1909. Inspired by Wagner's theory of mus. drama, conceived idea of an Eng. Bayreuth at Glastonbury for perf. of series of 'choral dramas', based on the Arthurian legends, by himself, with Reginald Buckley as librettist. First fest. held 1914 when his *The *Immortal Hour* (1912–13) was perf. In 1916 his *Bethlehem* (1915) and parts of *The Birth of Arthur* (1908–9) were perf. In 1920 the Glastonbury Players perf. *The Immortal Hour* and other works at the Old Vic, London, preceding f.p. at Glastonbury in Aug. of the complete *Birth of Arthur* and *The Round Table* (1915–16). In 1922 his *Alkestis* (1920–2), a 3-act setting of Gilbert Murray's trans. of Euripides, was perf. at Glastonbury and, in 1926, *The Queen of Cornwall* (1923–4), based on Hardy's verse-play. Greatest success came in 1922 with the long London run of Birmingham Repertory Th.'s prod. of *The Immortal Hour*, with Gwen Ffrangçon-Davies. *Alkestis* was prod. CG 1924. In 1934 *The Lily Maid* (1933–4) was prod. in London. In 1943–4 Boughton wrote the mus. drama *Galahad*, followed in 1944–5 by *Avalon*. Also comp. 3 syms. (1904–5, 1926–7, 1937); 2 ob. concs. with str. (1936, 1937); fl. conc. with str. (1937); tpt. conc. (1943); vc. concertante (1955); vn. sonata (1921); 2 str. qts. (1923); 2 ob. qts. (1932, 1945); pf. trio (1948); vc. sonata (1948); and many songs and part-songs. His daughter Joy (1913–63) was a talented oboist.

Boulanger, Lili (Juliette Marie Olga) (*b* Paris, 1893; *d* Mézy, 1918). Fr. composer, sister of Nadia *Boulanger. Won 1st *Grand Prix de Rome* in 1913 (the first woman to do so) with cantata *Faust et Hélène*. Career constantly interrupted by ill-health, but comps. show exceptional gifts. They incl. mus. for Maeterlinck's *Princesse Maleine* (1918); 2 sym.-poems: *Du fond de l'abîme*, alto, ten., ch., org., orch. (1914–17), *Vielle prière bouddhique*, ten., ch., orch. (1917); 2 Psalms with orch.; vn. sonata (1916).

Boulanger, Nadia (Juliette) (*b* Paris, 1887; *d* Paris, 1979). Fr. composer and conductor but principally known as outstandingly influential teacher of comp. At Paris Cons. won 1st prizes in harmony, counterpoint, fugue, org., and acc. Awarded 2nd *Grand Prix de Rome* 1908 for cantata *La Sirène*. Teacher at Paris Cons. from 1946, at École Normale de Musique, Paris, 1920–39, in USA 1940–6, and at Amer. Cons., Fontainebleau, from 1921 (dir. 1950). The list of her pupils is long and incl. many distinguished composers, esp. Americans (Copland, Harris, Thomson, Carter, and Piston). Eng. pupils incl. Lennox Berkeley and Hugo Cole. Frequent visitor to USA, teaching at Juilliard Sch., etc. Was among first in 20th cent. to rediscover Monteverdi madrigals, making famous 78 rpm records. Noted cond. of Fauré's *Requiem*. First woman to cond. complete concert of Royal Phil. Soc., London, 4 Nov. 1937. Cond. Boston SO (1938), NYPO (1939), and Hallé Orch. (1963). Cond. f.p. of Stravinsky's *Dumbarton Oaks Concerto*, Washington DC, 1938. Hon. CBE 1977.

Boulevard Solitude. Opera in 7 scenes by *Henze to lib. by comp. G. Weil after W. Jöckisch's play, being modernized version of Prévost's *Manon Lescaut* (1731). Comp. 1951. Prod. Hanover 1952, London (SW) 1962, Santa Fe 1967.

Boulez, Pierre (*b* Montbrison, 1925). Fr. composer and conductor. Went to Paris Cons. in 1942, studying comp. with Messiaen 1944–5. Studied counterpoint with Andrée Vaurabourg-Honegger (wife of Arthur *Honegger) and 12-note technique with René Leibowitz. In 1946 became mus. dir. and cond. of Barrault-Renaud co. at Théâtre Marigny, Paris, travelling with them to N. and S. Amer. and European cities during next 10 years. In 1953, with Barrault's help, founded the Concerts Marigny, later re-named Domaine Musical when the venue was moved to the Odéon in 1959. In this series Boulez introduced to Paris audiences not only works by Schoenberg, Webern, and Berg, but mus. of his contemporaries. At this time, est. contacts with Maderna and Stockhausen and joined teaching staff at the Int. summer sch. for new mus., Darmstadt. Salzburg Fest. début 1960 (Cologne Radio SO). In early 1960s cond. engagements increased and dir. several major European orchs., incl. the Vienna PO at Salzburg, 1962. Cond. f. Fr. stage p. of *Wozzeck*, Paris 1963. In 1963 visiting prof. at Harvard Univ.; made Amer. conducting début with Cleveland Orch. 1964. In 1966 cond. *Parsifal* at Bayreuth and in same year severed connection with Paris life as a protest over a ministerial appointment. Guest cond. BBC SO in London 1964 and in USA in 1965 and on its Russ. tour in 1967. Gave up conductorship of Domaine Musical, 1967. Prin. guest cond., Cleveland Orch., 1969–70 and chief cond. of the BBC SO 1971–5 and NYPO 1971–7. His BBC period was notable for remarkable perfs. of 20th-cent. music, especially Schoenberg, Webern, and Debussy. Cond. centenary cycle of *Ring* at Bayreuth, 1976. From 1976 dir. Fr. Govt.'s research institute into techniques of modern comp. (IRCAM). Cond. first complete perf. of *Lulu*, Paris, 1979.

Boulez's importance and originality as an *avant-garde* composer were evident from the first. He came to prominence with the *Sonatine* for fl. and pf. and the pf. sonata No.1. The cantata *Le visage nuptial*, to poems by René Char, made use of choral speech, spoken glissandi, crying, and whispering. Boulez's orthodox use of serialism is found in *Structures I* for 2 pf. *Le Marteau sans maître*, to text by Char (f.p. Baden-Baden June 1955, cond. Rosbaud) made him a celebrity. His most ambitious work to date is *Pli selon pli* for sop. and orch. This 5-part portrait of Mallarmé developed from *Improvisation sur Mallarmé*. These are now flanked by 2 outer movements, *Don* and *Tombeau*, all 5 containing extracts from Mallarmé sung or declaimed in many ways. There are elements of indeterminacy in the 3 sections of the improvisations. The work has constantly been radically rev., in accordance with Boulez's view that a comp. is never finished.

Boulez experimented with *musique concrète* in early 1950s and combined it with elec. sounds in *Poésie pour pouvoir* (1958). His use of indeterminacy dates from about 1957 with the 3rd pf.

sonata, the 5 movements of which can be played in any order except for the 3rd which must be central. Like Mahler and Richard Strauss, Boulez has pursued parallel careers as cond. and composer. Hon. CBE 1979. Prin. comps.:

INCIDENTAL MUSIC: *L'Orestie* (Aeschylus/Obey) (1948); *Le Crépuscule de Yang Kouï-Feï* (Louise Fauré), for radio (1967); *Ainsi parla Zarathoustra* (Nietzsche/Barrault) (1974).

ORCH.: *Doubles* (1957–8), expanded as *Figures-Doubles-Prismes* (1963, 1968); *Tombeau* (1959–62); *Livre pour Cordes*, orch. of *Livre pour quatuor*, str. qt. (1968); *. . . explosante fixe . . .* , unspecified forces (1971), fl., cl., tpt., hp., vib., vn., va., vc., elec. (1972, unpub.), fl., elec. (1989, unpub.); *Mémoriales* (1973–5); *Rituel in memoriam Bruno Maderna* (1974–5); *Notations* (rev. of early pf. pieces) (1980); *Répons*, 24 players, 6 instr. soloists, chamber ens., computers, live elec. (1981); *Initiale*, fanfare, 7 brass instr. (1987).

ENS.: *Le Visage nuptial* (Char), sop., alto, 2 ondes Martenot, pf., perc. (1946–7), rev. sop., alto, women's ch., orch. (1951–2), third version for sop., mez., ch., and orch. (1985–9); *Éclat*, 15 instr. (1965), expanded as *Éclats/Multiples*, 27 instr. (1966, in progress); *Domaines*, cl., 21 instr. (1961–8); *Dérive*, fl., cl., vn., vc., vib., pf. (1984), *Dérive II* for 11 instr. (1988).

VOCAL: *Le *Soleil des eaux* (Char), mus. for radio play, v. and orch. (1948), rev. as cantata for sop., ten., bass, chamber orch. (1948, withdrawn), rev. sop., ten., bass, ch., orch. (1958), rev. sop., ch. and orch. (1965); *Le *Marteau sans maître* (Char), alto, alto fl., guitar, vib., xylorimba, perc., va. (1953–5, rev. 1957); *Improvisation sur Mallarmé I*, sop., hp., bells, vib., perc. (1957), alternative version, sop., orch. 1962; *II*, sop., celesta, hp., pf., bells, vib., perc. (1957); *III*, sop., orch. (1959) 2nd version (1983–4), definitive version for sop. and orch. (1983–4); *Don*, sop., pf. (1960), alternative version sop., orch. (1962), new version for sop. and orch. (1989–90); *Tombeau*, sop., orch. (1959–60); *Pli selon pli* (*Don, Improvisation sur Mallarmé I–III, Tombeau*) (1957–90); *cummings ist der dichter*, (e.e. cummings), 16 solo vv., 24 instr. (1970), rev. version (1986).

CHAMBER MUSIC: *Sonatine*, fl., pf. (1946); *Livre pour quatuor*, str. qt. (1948–9), new version (1989, unpub.); *Strophes*, fl. (1957); *Domaines*, cl. (1961–8), alternative version, cl. and 21 instr. (1961–8); *Messagesquisse*, vc. solo, 6 vc. (1976); *Dialogue de l'ombre double*, cl., elec. (1984); *Mémoriale* ('. . . explosante fixe . . .' *originel*), fl., 8 instr. (1985); *Anthems*, vn. (1991).

PIANO: *12 Notations* (1945); sonatas: No.1 (1946), No.2 (1946–8), No.3 (1955–7); *Structures*, Book I, 2 pf. (1951–2), complete (1953); Book II, 2 pf. (1956–61).

TAPE: *Etudes I, sur un son, II, sur sept sons*, 1-track tape (1951–2); *Symphonie Mécanique* (mus. for film), 1-track tape (1955).

Boult, (Sir) **Adrian** (Cedric) (*b* Chester, 1889; *d* Hampstead, 1983). Eng. conductor. Came into prominence 1918–19 with outstanding perfs. of works by Elgar, Vaughan Williams, and Holst, all of whom became close friends. Teaching staff RCM 1919–30. Cond. London season of Diaghilev ballet and operas at Empire Th., 1919. Toured Eur. introducing Brit. mus. to foreign audiences. Championship of Eng. composers was dominant but not exclusive element in his career. Cond., CBSO 1924–30. Appointed mus. dir., BBC, 1930–42, and chief cond., BBC SO, 1931–50 (cond. f. Brit. p. of Mahler's 3rd Sym., BBC studio broadcast 1947.) Prin. cond. LPO 1951–7. Guest cond. of world's leading orchs. Returned to RCM staff 1962–6. Cond. f.ps. of Holst's *The Planets* (1918); Vaughan Williams's *A Pastoral Symphony* (1922), 4th sym. (1935), and 6th sym. (1948); Bliss's *Music for Strings* (1935, his Salzburg Fest. début); Tippett's 2nd sym. (1958); and of many other works by Brit. composers. Also f. Eng. ps. of Berg's *Wozzeck* (1934, concert) and Busoni's *Dr. Faust* (1937, concert). Author of handbook on conducting and of autobiography *My Own Trumpet* (London, 1973). Knighted 1937. CH 1969. Retired 1979.

bourdon. (1) Dull-toned pedal stop found on every org., however small; end-plugged; 8′ length and 16′ pitch.
  (2) Lowest str. on the lute or vn.
  (3) Very large and deep-toned bell.
  (4) Drone str. of hurdy-gurdy.
  (5) Drone pipe of bagpipe.

Bourgault-Ducoudray, Louis Albert (*b* Nantes, 1840; *d* Vernouillet, Paris, 1910). Fr. composer and scholar. Won *Prix de Rome*. From 1868 cond. of a Paris choral body which revived comps. of Palestrina, Bach, and others. Prof. of History of Mus. at Cons., 1878–1908. In 1874 went to Greece on official mission, and studied folk mus. on which he became authority. Pubd. colls. of folk-songs from Greece, Brittany, Scotland, and the Middle East. Comp. 5 operas and choral works, incl. *Stabat Mater* (1868).

Bourgeois, Derek (David) (*b* Kingston-on-Thames, 1941). Eng. composer. Lect. in mus., Bristol Univ., 1971–84, dir. of mus. Nat. Youth Orch. of GB 1984–93. Comps. incl. opera, syms., concs., cantatas, str. qt., vn. sonatas, variations for 2 db. and orch., brass quintets, org. sym., etc.

Bourgeois, Louis (*b* Paris, *c.*1510; *d* Paris, *c.*1561). Fr. church musician. In Geneva 1541–57 where he played leading part in compiling Genevan Psalter. Developed a system of sight-reading. Pubd. settings of 83 psalms, 1561.

Bourgeois Gentilhomme, Le (The would-be gentleman). *Comédie-ballet* in 5 acts by Molière (Jean-Baptiste Poquelin), written in 1670 for court of Louis XIV. Mus. for f.p. comp. by *Lully. In 1912, for the first version of *Ariadne auf Naxos*, R. Strauss comp. incid. mus. for adaptation by Hofmannsthal (*Der Bürger als Edelmann*). Some of Lully's mus. was quoted. In 1916, for second version of *Ariadne auf Naxos*, the play was abandoned and Strauss expanded the incid. mus. in 1917 to 17 items for a further adaptation of *Le bourgeois gentilhomme* by Hofmannsthal. This was

f.p. Berlin, 9 April 1918. From this Strauss arr. a Suite for orch. comprising 9 movts., f.p. Vienna 1920; f. Eng. p. Manchester 1921.

Bournemouth Symphony Orchestra. Title adopted in 1954 by Bournemouth Municipal Orch., founded 1893, as band of 30 wind players, by Dan *Godfrey. Augmented to incl. str. players 1893–4. Weekly sym. concerts began 1896, famous for encouragement of mus. by Eng. composers. Godfrey was succeeded, 1934, by Richard Austin. Other conds.: Rudolf Schwarz 1946–51; Charles Groves 1951–61; Constantin Silvestri 1961–9; George Hurst 1969–71; Paavo Berglund 1972–9; Uri Segal 1980–3; Rudolf Barshay 1983–8; Andrew Litton 1988–95; Yakov Kreizberg 1995–2000; Marin Alsop from 2002.

bourrée (Fr.; Old Eng. *borry*, *borree*, etc.). A lively dance style very like the gavotte, in quadruple time beginning with an up-beat. It is sometimes found in the classical suite in a ternary arrangement: (a) 1st bourrée, (b) 2nd bourrée, (c) 1st bourrée again.

boutade (Fr.). Improvised dance or other comp.

Boutique fantasque, La (The Fantastic Toyshop). Ballet in 1 act with mus. arr. from Rossini's *Soirées musicales*, and other pieces, by *Respighi to lib. by Derain. Choreog. Massine. Prod. London 1919.

bow. Flexible stick with horsehair (usually) stretched across it, used to produce sound vibrations from strings of vn., va., vc., db., and other str. instr. Until 17th cent. bow was convex. As vn. technique developed, new forms of concave bow were devised, with hairs kept in place and at an even spread by means of metal ferrule through which hair passed as it left the nut, or 'frog' at one end of the bow. Prin. developer of modern bow was François *Tourte, *c.*1785.

bowed lyre. Instr. known in Middle Ages by variety of names—cruit, crot, rota, rotta, crwth, crouthe, chorus, and others—of which the Welsh *crwth has survived longest. The bowed lyre was made from one piece, the yoke's resonator and pillars being hollowed out and the soundboard added. Fitted with plain pegs which required a tuning key.

Bowen, (Edwin) York (*b* Crouch End, 1884; *d* London, 1961). Eng. composer and pianist. Taught at RAM. Best known for short pf. pieces but wrote sym. (1912), 3 pf. concs. (1904, 1906, 1908), vn. conc. (1920), and va. conc.

Bower, (Sir) John Dykes (*b* Gloucester, 1905; *d* Orpington, 1981). Eng. organist. Org. Truro Cath. 1926; New Coll., Oxford 1929; Durham Cath. 1933; St Paul's Cath., London 1936–67. Prof. of org., RCM, 1936–69. Knighted 1968.

bowing. (1) Style or method in which bow is applied to str. of instr.
  (2) Marking of score (often by cond.) to indicate to the player which notes should be played

to an up (V) or down ( ) stroke of the bow.

(3) Particular types of bowing technique incl. *spiccato*, *sautillé*, *staccato*, *ricochet*, *saltato*, *col legno*.

Bowles, Paul (Frederic) (*b* NY, 1910; *d* Tangier, Morocco, 1999). Amer. composer. Collector of folk mus. in Sp., N. Africa, C. and S. America, results influencing his exotic and colourful mus. Has comp. much chamber mus., 3 operas (2 to texts by Lorca), 5 ballets, incl. *Yankee Clipper* (1936), film mus. and much th. mus. (for plays by Tennessee Williams, Saroyan, Koestler, and Hellman). Was for 4 years mus. critic of *NY Herald Tribune*. Also successful as novelist (e.g. *The Sheltering Sky*, 1949).

Bowman, James (Thomas) (*b* Oxford, 1941). Eng. countertenor. Début London 1967 as Oberon in *A Midsummer Night's Dream*, a role he made his own. His perf. led Britten to comp. the Voice of Apollo in *Death in Venice* for him (Aldeburgh 1973). CG début 1972. Has sung with EOG, Early Music Consort, Glyndebourne, ENO, Scottish Opera, etc. and many of the castrato roles in Handel operas. CBE 1997.

Boyce, William (*b* London, 1711; *d* London, 1779). Eng. composer and organist. Org. of Earl of Oxford's Chapel, Vere Street, 1734–6, and became known as composer of masques and oratorios. Org., St Michael's, Cornhill, 1736, also becoming composer to Chapel Royal. Appointed cond., 3 Choirs Fest., 1737. Org., Allhallows the Great and Less, Thane Street, 1749. D.Mus., Oxford, 1749. Succeeded Greene as Master of the King's Musick, 1755. Org., Chapel Royal, 1758. Resigned from St Michael's 1768, dismissed from Allhallows 1769. Increasing deafness, which had first manifested itself in his youth, caused him to give up other posts *c.*1770. Retired to Kensington to edit a coll. of *English Cathedral Music*, a task projected by Greene who bequeathed to Boyce the material he had collected. Boyce's 3 vols. remained in use for almost 150 years. His comps. incl. masques, odes, ovs., church anthems and services, trio sonatas, and 8 syms. (1760), of which the modern revival is due to the researches and enthusiasm of Constant *Lambert. Their dates of comp. are not accurately known. As pubd., the first two date from *c.*1759, the last four from 1735 to 1741. The song *Heart of Oak* was comp. by Boyce in 1759, to words by David Garrick, for the pantomime *Harlequin's Invasion*.

Boyd, Anne (Elizabeth) (*b* Sydney, NSW, 1946). Australian composer. Lect. in mus. Sussex Univ. 1975–7. Head of Mus. Dept., Hong Kong Univ. 1980–8, Prof. of mus., Univ. of Sydney from 1990. Works incl.: *The Voice of the Phoenix* (1971) (orch., incl. amplified instr. and optional synthesizer); *As Far As Crawls the Toad* (1970, rev. 1972), th. piece for 5 young percussionists; 2 str. qts. (1968, rev. 1971, and 1973); *The Rose Garden* (1971), th. piece for singing actress, ch., chamber ens.; *The Metamorphoses of the Solitary Female Phoenix* (1971), wind quintet, pf., perc.; *As it leaves the Bell* (1973), pf., hp., perc.; *Summer Nights* (1976), alto,

str., perc., hp.; *As All Waters Flow* (1976), 5 female vv., chamber ens.; *As I Crossed a Bridge of Dreams* (1975), 12 unacc. vv.; *Anklung* (1974), pf.; *Bencharong* (1976), str.; *The Death of Captain Cook*, oratorio, sop., ten., bar., ch., orch. (1978); *The Little Mermaid*, children's opera (1978); *The Beginning of the Day*, children's opera (1980); *Anklung 2*, vn. (1980); *Grathawai*, orch. (1993); *Meditations on a Chinese Character*, v., chamber ens. (1996).

Boyden, David (Dodge) (*b* Westport, Conn., 1910; *d* Berkeley, Calif., 1986). Amer. musicologist and expert on string instruments. Teacher at Univ. of Calif. 1938–75 (prof. from 1955). Author of *History of Violin-playing from its Origins to 1761* (1965), the standard work on the topic.

Boyhood's End. Cantata for ten. and pf. by *Tippett on texts by W. H. Hudson. Comp. 1943.

Bozza, Eugène (*b* Nice, 1905; *d* Valenciennes, 1991). Fr. composer and cond. Won 1st *Grand Prix de Rome* 1934. Prin. cond. Opéra-Comique 1939–48. Composer of 3 operas, 4 syms., oratorio, vn. conc., pf. conc., and mus. for wind ens.

Br. Short for *Bratsche(n)* (Ger.), i.e. viola(s).

Brabançonne, La. Belg. nat. anthem. Written and comp. at time of 1830 demonstration in Brussels which led to separation of Belg. from Holland. Author of words was Fr. actor then in Brussels, named Jenneval, and composer was François van *Campenhout. Name comes from 'Brabant'.

'braccio' and 'gamba'. All *viols were held downwards and to them was given the general name of *viole da gamba*, i.e. 'leg-viols', a description afterwards restricted to latest survivor of the family, bass viol. The smaller members of the vn. family were held on the shoulder, and, by analogy, all members of this family (incl. even those which from their size had to be held downwards) came to be called *viole da braccio*, i.e. 'arm-viols'. Later this term became limited to the alto vn., i.e. the va. (still in Ger. called *Bratsche*).

brace. Perpendicular line, with bracket, joining the staves in scores, and indicating that mus. on these staves should be played simultaneously.

Bradshaw, Richard (*b* Rugby, 1944). Eng. conductor. Degree in English at London Univ. 1965. Studied cond. privately with Adrian *Boult, with Charles *Groves at the RLPO, and with John *Pritchard. Ch. master Glyndebourne Fest. 1975–7; res. cond. at S. Francisco Opera 1977–89. Chief cond. Canadian Opera Co. from 1989, art. dir. from 1994, gen. dir. from 1998. Oversaw the building of the company's new opera house, opened 2006 with a new prod. of Wagner's *Ring*. Guest cond. with leading opera comps. and orchs. throughout the world.

Bradshaw, Susan (*b* Monmouth, 1931; *d* London, 2005). Eng. pianist and critic. Specialist in contemporary works.

Braga, (Antônio) **Francisco** (*b* Rio de Janeiro, 1868; *d* Rio, 1945). Brazilian composer, cond., and teacher. Settled in Ger. 1896–1900. Prof. of comp., Brazil Nat. Inst. of Mus. 1902–38. Cond. sym. concerts in Rio 1908–33. Comp. operas *Jupira* (Rio 1900) and *Anita Garibaldi* (1901, unfinished), sym.-poems, etc.

Braga, Gaetano (*b* Giulianova, Abruzzi, 1829; *d* Milan, 1907). It. cellist and composer. After touring widely, lived mainly in Paris and London. Comp. 9 operas, 2 vc. concs., 2 syms., and a very popular song, 'Angel's Serenade'. Also wrote vc. method.

Braham [Abraham], **John** (*b* London, 1774; *d* London, 1856). Eng. tenor, pupil of Leoni in London. Début aged 13 at CG. Became pf. teacher until 1794 when he took up singing again at Bath with Rauzzini. Engaged by S. *Storace for Drury Lane 1796. Sang in oratorios and at Three Choirs Fests. Sang in Fr. and It. with Nancy (Anna) Storace. Reappeared CG 1801. Following custom of time, wrote mus. of his own part in several operas in which he appeared. For Lyceum opera *The Americans* (1811), comp. *The Death of Nelson*, which remained most popular item in his repertory. Sang Max in f. Brit. p. *Der Freischütz*, London 1824, and created role of Sir Huon in *Oberon*, 1826. His v., regarded as unequalled in It. opera and in Handel, deepened in the 1830s and he sang bar. roles of William Tell at Drury Lane in 1838 and Don Giovanni a year later. Toured America unsuccessfully in 1840. Last appearance was in London, Mar. 1852, when he was 78.

Brahms, Johannes (*b* Hamburg, 1833; *d* Vienna, 1897). Ger. composer and pianist. Son of db. player in Hamburg State Th. In childhood was taught vn. by father, pf. by Otto Cossel, and comp. by Eduard Marxsen. Public début as pianist, Hamburg, Sept. 1848. Earned living from age of 13 by teaching and by playing at theatres, for dances, and in taverns frequented by prostitutes. In 1853 engaged to acc. Hung. vn. virtuoso *Reményi on a concert tour. While in Hanover met *Joachim, who was impressed by youth's comps. and gave him letters of introduction to Liszt and Schumann. Latter hailed him as genius in an article entitled *Neue Bahnen* (New Paths) in the *Neue Zeitschrift für Musik* of 28 Oct. 1853. After Schumann's death in 1856, Brahms became pf. teacher to Princess Friederike and choral cond. at little court of Lippe-Detmold 1857–60, unexacting duties which left him time for comp. In 1860 signed famous manifesto opposing 'new music' methods adopted by Liszt and his followers and thereafter was regarded as the polar opposite to Wagnerian sch. in Ger. mus. His first pf. conc. had been a failure at its f.p. in Leipzig on 27 Jan. 1859 and it was not until nearly 10 years later, with *Ein Deutsches Requiem*, that he achieved a major success. In 1862 first visited Vienna, where he lived for most of next 35 years. Cond. Vienna Singakademie for 1863–4 season, and in 1872 succeeded Rubinstein as art. dir. of Gesellschaft der Musikfreunde, holding post until 1875. Thereafter his life was uneventful ex-

cept for comp. of major works and tours as pianist.

Brahms was a master in every form of comp. except opera, which he never attempted. He eschewed programme-mus. and wrote in the classical forms, yet his nature was essentially romantic. His 4 syms. are superb examples of his devotion to classical mus. architecture within which he introduced many novel thematic developments. In the chamber mus. practically every work is a masterpiece; his 4 concs. are indispensable features of concert life, and his songs, numbering nearly 200, are closely based on Ger. folk-songs but are polished and refined to a highly sophisticated degree. His prin. comps. are:

SYMPHONIES: No.1 in C minor, Op.68 (1855–76; f.p. Karlsruhe, 6 Nov. 1876, cond. Dessoff); No.2 in D major, Op.73 (1877; f.p. Vienna, 30 Dec. 1877, cond. Richter); No.3 in F major, Op.90 (1883; f.p. Vienna, 2 Dec. 1883, cond. Richter); No.4 in E minor, Op.98 (1884–5; f.p. Meiningen, 25 Oct. 1885, cond. Bülow).

CONCERTOS: pf., No.1 in D minor, Op.15 (1854–8; f.p. Leipzig, 27 Jan. 1859, Brahms soloist); No.2 in B♭ major, Op.83 (1878–81; f.p. Budapest, 9 Nov. 1881, Brahms soloist); vn., in D major, Op.77 (1878; f.p. Leipzig, 1 Jan. 1879, cond. Brahms, Joachim soloist); vn. and vc. in A minor, Op.102 (1887; f.p. Cologne, 15 Oct. 1887, soloists Joachim (vn.), R. Hausmann (vc.), cond. Brahms).

CHAMBER MUSIC: str. sextets No.1 in B♭ major, Op.18 (1858–60), No.2 in G major, Op.36 (1864–5); str. qts., Op.51, No.1 in C minor, No.2 in A minor (1859–73), No.3 in B♭ major, Op.67 (1876); str. quintets, No.1 in F major, Op.88 (1882), No.2 in G major, Op.111 (1890); cl. quintet in B minor, Op.115 (1891); pf. qts., No.1 in G minor, Op.25 (1861), No.2 in A major, Op.26 (1861–2), No.3 in C minor, Op.60 (1855–75); pf. quintet in F minor, Op.34 (1864); pf. trios, No.1 in B major, Op.8 (1853–4, rev. version 1889), No.2 in C major, Op.87 (1880–2), No.3 in C minor, Op.101 (1886); hn. trio in E♭ major, Op.40 (1865); vc. sonatas, No.1 in E minor, Op.38 (1862–5), No.2 in F major, Op.99 (1886); vn. sonatas, No.1 in G major, Op.78 (1878–9), No.2 in A major, Op.100 (1886), No.3 in D minor, Op.108 (1886–8); cl. (or va.) trio in A minor, Op.114 (1891); cl. (or va.) sonatas, Op.120, No.1 in F minor, No.2 in E♭ major (both 1894); Scherzo in C minor, vn., pf. (1853).

MISC. ORCH.: *Serenades*, No.1 in D, Op.11 (1857–8), No.2 in A, Op.16 (1858–9, rev. 1875); 3 *HungarianDances* (1873); *Variations on a Theme by Haydn*, Op.56a (1873); *Akademische Festouvertüre* (*Academic Festival Overture*) Op.80 (1880); *Tragic Ov.*, Op.81 (1880, rev. 1881).

CHORUS & ORCH.: *Ein *Deutsches Requiem*, sop., bar., ch., and orch., Op.45 (1857–68); *Rinaldo*, ten., male ch., and orch., Op.50 (1863–8); *Rhapsody* for cont., male ch., and orch., Op.53 (1869); *Schicksalslied*, ch. and orch., Op.54 (1871); *Triumphlied*, ch. and orch., Op.55 (1870–1); *Nänie*, ch. and orch., Op.82 (1880–1); *Gesang der Parzen*, ch. and orch., Op.89 (1882).

PIANO: sonatas, No.1 in C major, Op.1 (1852–3),

No.2 in F♯ minor, Op.2 (1852), No.3 in F minor, Op.5 (1853); Scherzo in E♭ minor, Op.4 (1851); *Variations on a Theme by R. Schumann*, in F♯ minor, Op.9 (1854); 4 Ballades (No.1 in D minor, No.2 in D, No.3 in B minor, No.4 in B), Op.10 (1854); *Variations on a Theme by R. Schumann*, in E♭, Op.23, pf. duet (1861); *Variations and Fugue on a Theme by Handel*, Op.24 (1861);*Hungarian Dances* (21 pf. duets) (1852–69); *Variations on a Theme by Paganini*, Op.35 (1862–3); 16 Waltzes, Op.39, pf. duet (1865, arr. for solo pf. 1867); *Variations on a Theme by Haydn*, Op.56b (2 pf.) (1873); *Liebesliederwalzer*, Op.52, 18 waltzes for SATB and pf. 4 hands (1868–9); Op.52a (without vocal parts) (1874); *Neue Liebesliederwalzer*, Op.65, 15 waltzes for SATB and pf. 4 hands (1874); Op.65a, without vocal parts (1875); pf. quintet in F minor, Op.34, arr. for 2 pf. as Op.34a; rhapsodies, intermezzos, and studies.

ORGAN: 11 Choral Preludes, Op.122 (pubd. 1896 in 2 books) Bk. I: 1, *Mein Jesu, der du mich*. 2, *Herzliebster Jesu*. 3, *O Welt, ich muss dich lassen*. 4, *Herzlich tut mich erfreuen*. Bk. II: 5, *Schmücke dich, O liebe Seele*. 6, *O wie selig seid ihr doch, ihr Frommen*. 7, *O Gott, du frommer Gott*. 8, *Es ist ein Ros' entsprungen*. 9, *Herzlich tut mich verlangen*. 10, *O Welt, ich muss dich lassen* (II); *Fugue in A minor* (1856); *Prelude and Fugue in A minor* (1856); *Prelude and Fugue in G minor* (1857).

PART-SONGS etc.: 4 Part-Songs, Op.17, women's vv., 2 hns., harp (1860); 7 *Marienlieder*, Op.22, mixed ch.; Ps. XIII, Op.27, women's vv., pf. (1859); 2 *Motets*, Op.29, unacc. ch. (1860); *Geistliches Lied* (*Lass dich nur nichts dauern*), Op.30, ch., org. or pf. (1856); 3 *Quartets*, Op.31, solo vv., pf. (1859–63); 3 *Sacred Ch.*, Op.37, unacc. women's vv. (1859–63); 5 *Soldatenlieder*, Op.41, unacc. male ch. (1861–2); 3 *Lieder* (incl. *Abendständchen*), Op.42, unacc. mixed ch. (1859–61); 12 *Lieder und Romanzen*, Op.44, unacc. women's vv. (1859–63); 7 *Lieder*, Op.62, unacc. (1874); 3 *Quartets*, Op.63, 4 solo vv., pf. (1862–74); 2 *Motets*, Op.74, unacc. (1863–77); 4 *Quartets*, Op.92, solo vv., pf. (1877–84); 6 *Lieder und Romanzen*, Op.93a, unacc. (1883–4); *Tagelied*, Op.93b, unacc. (1884); 11 *Zigeunerlieder*, Op.103, 4 vv., pf. (1887); 5 *Lieder*, Op.104, unacc. (1888); *Deutsche Fest- und Gedenksprüche*, Op.109, unacc. double ch. (1886–8); 3 *Motets*, Op.110, unacc. (1889); 6 *Vocal Quartets*, Op.112, unacc. (1889–91); 13 *Canons*, Op.113, women's vv., pf. (1863–90); also 14 *Ger. Folksongs*, unacc. (1864); 14 *Volks-Kinderlieder*, vv., pf. (pubd. 1858).

SONG-CYCLES: *Die schöne *Magelone*, Op.33, v. and pf., 15 *Romanzen* from *Magelone* (L. Tieck, 1773–1853): 1, *Keinen hat es noch gereut*. 2, *Traun! Bogen und Pfeil*. 3, *Sind es Schmerzen, sind es Freuden*. 4, *Liebe kam aus fernen Landen*. 5, *So willst du des Armen*. 6, *Wie soll ich die Freude*. 7, *War es dir?* 8, *Wir müssen uns trennen*. 9, *Ruhe, Süssliebchen*. 10, *So tönet denn*. 11, *Wie schnell verschwindet*. 12, *Muss es eine Trennung geben*. 13, *Geliebter, wo zaudert dein irrender Fuss*. 14, *Wie froh und frisch*. 15, *Treue Liebe dauert lange*. (1861–8); *Vier ernste Gesänge*, Op.121, low v., pf. (orch. by Sargent) (1896).

SONGS: Brahms published over 200 songs, from his Op.3 (1852–3) to his Op.107 (1886). Among the best known, with poets' names, are: *Abend-dämmerung* (Schack), Op.49, No.5 (1868); *Am Sonntag Morgen* (Heyse), Op.49, No.1 (1868); *An eine Aeolsharfe* (Mörike), Op.19, No.5 (1859); *Auf dem Kirchhofe* (Liliencron), Op.105, No.4 (1886); *Blinde Kuh* (Kopisch), Op.58, No.1 (1871); *Botschaft* (Daumer), Op.47, No.1 (c.1860); *Dein blaues Auge* (Groth), Op.59, No.8 (1873); *Es liebt sich so lieblich* (Heine), Op.71, No.1 (1877); *Feldeinsamkeit* (Allmers), Op.86, No.2 (1877–8); *Geistliches Wiegenlied* (Geibel), with va. obb., Op.91, No.2 (1884); *Gestillte Sehnsucht* (Rückert), with va. obb., Op.91, No.1 (1884); *Immer leise* (Ling), Op.105, No.2 (1886); *Der Jäger* (Halm), Op.95, No.4 (1884); *Kein Haus, keine Heimat* (Halm), Op.94, No.5 (1884); *Komm bald* (Groth), Op.97, No.5 (1884); *Der Kranz* (Schmidt), Op.84, No.2 (1881); *Lerchengesang* (Candidus), Op.70, No.2 (1877); *Liebestreu* (Reinick), Op.3, No.1 (1853); *Das Mädchen spricht* (Gruppe), Op.107, No.3 (1886); *Die Mainacht* (Hölty), Op.43, No.2 (1868); *Mein Herz ist schwer* (Geibel), Op.94, No.3 (1884); *Mit vierzig Jahren* (Rückert), Op.94, No.1 (1884); *Die Nachtigall* (Reinhold), Op.97, No.1 (1884); *Nachtigallen schwingen* (Fallersleben), Op.6, No.6 (1853); *O kühler Wald* (Brentano), Op.72, No.3 (1876–7); *Salome* (Keller), Op.69, No.8 (1877); *Sapphische Ode* (Schmidt), Op.94, No.4 (1884); *Sonntag* (Uhland), Op.47, No.3 (c.1865); *Ständchen* (Kugler), Op.106, No.1 (1886); *Steig auf, geliebter Schatten* (Halm), Op.94, No.2 (1884); *Therese* (Keller), Op.86, No.1 (1877); *Vergebliches Ständchen* (trad.), Op.84, No.4 (1881); *Verzagen* (Lemcke), Op.72, No.4 (1877); also several duets and 7 vols. containing 49 Ger. folk-song settings.

Braille, Louis (*b* Coupvray, Paris, 1809; *d* Coupvray, 1852). Fr. inventor of 'Braille'. Blind from age of 3, developed Braille system of mus. notation for blind, perfecting it by 1834. Attempts to standardize method for int. use began at Cologne in 1888 but were not finally agreed until 1929.

Brailowsky, Alexander (*b* Kiev, 1896; *d* NY, 1976). Amer. pianist of Russ. birth. Début Paris 1919; NY 1924. Specialist in Chopin.

Brain, Aubrey (Harold) (*b* London, 1893; *d* London, 1955). Eng. player of French horn. Prin. hn. from 1913 of Beecham's touring opera orch. and later at CG. Prin. hn. BBC SO 1930–45. Prof. RAM 1923–55. His brother **Alfred** (*b* London, 1885; *d* Los Angeles, 1966), regarded by some as an even finer player, was for many years first hn. of Henry Wood's Queen's Hall Orch., until in 1923 he went to USA becoming prin. hn. of Los Angeles PO and manager of Hollywood Bowl concerts. From 1943 to retirement played in MGM and 20th Century Fox film studio orchs.

Brain, Dennis (*b* London, 1921; *d* in car crash, Hatfield, 1957). Eng. player of French horn, son of Aubrey *Brain. Played 1st hn. in inaugural concert of Philharmonia Orch. 1945 and remained prin. hn. until his death although, apart from 1949–50, he was also prin. hn. of

Beecham's RPO 1946–54, touring USA with it in late 1950. Frequent conc. soloist, and founder of Dennis Brain Wind Ens. (Salzburg Fest. 1957). Regarded as finest virtuoso of his day. Britten, Hindemith, Lutyens, Malcolm Arnold, and others comp. works for him.

Brain, Leonard (b London, 1915; d London, 1975). Eng. player of oboe and cor anglais, son of Aubrey *Brain. Played in Philharmonia Orch. 1945–6, RPO 1946–73. Member, Dennis Brain Wind Ens. Prof. of oboe, RAM, from 1963.

Brainin, Norbert (b Vienna, 1923; d Harrow, Middlesex, 2005). Austrian-born violinist. Settled in London 1938. Co-founded *Amadeus Quartet 1947. OBE 1960.

Braithwaite, Nicholas (Paul Dallon) (b London, 1939). Eng. cond. Son of Warwick *Braithwaite. Prin. trombonist Nat. Youth Orch. of GB, 1955–7. Prof. début with WNO 1966, concert début 1966. Ass. cond., Bournemouth SO, 1967–70, ass. prin. cond., SW Opera, 1971–4. Cond. Brit. première of Penderecki's The Devils of Loudun, SW 1973. CG début 1973. Cond. GTO 1977–81; prin. cond. Göteborg Opera 1981–4; Manchester Camerata 1984–91. Dean of mus. faculty, Victorian Coll. of the Arts, Melbourne, from 1987. Cond. Adelaide SO from 1987.

Braithwaite, Warwick (b Dunedin, NZ, 1896; d London, 1971). NZ conductor. Cond. with *O'Mara Opera Co. 1919–22, BNOC 1922. Mus. dir. BBC Wales, 1924–32. Cond., Sadler's Wells Opera, 1932–40; Scottish Orch. 1940–6; CG 1950–2; prin. cond. SW Ballet 1948–52; cond. Nat. Orch. of NZ 1953–4; Australia Nat. Opera 1954–5; mus. dir. WNO 1956–60; SW Opera 1960–8.

Brand, Max (b Lwów, 1896; d Langenzersdorf, 1980). Austrian composer. Adopted Schoenberg's 12-note method in 1920s. Went to USA in 1940 and after 1960s experimented with elec. instr.

Brandenburg Concertos. Bach's 6 'Concerti Grossi' for various combinations. Dedicated to Christian Ludwig, Margrave of Brandenburg (1721) but it appears they were never played for him. They are as follows:

(1) F Major. 2 hn., 3 ob., and bn., str. (incl. Violino Piccolo, i.e. small vn.), hpd.

(2) †F Major. In 2 groups, plus Continuo—(a) Concertino: tpt., fl., ob., vn.; (b) Ripieno: str.; (c) hpd.

(3) G Major. 3 groups of str. (each vn., va., vc.), db., and hpd.

(4) †G Major. In 2 groups, plus Continuo—(a) Concertino: vn. and 2 fl.; (b) Ripieno: str.; (c) hpd.

(5) †D major. In 2 groups, plus Continuo—(a) Concertino: hpd., fl., vn.; (b) Ripieno: str. (no 2nd vns.); (c) hpd. for the continuo.

(6) B♭ Major. (No vns.) 2 va., 2 viole da gamba, vc., hpd.

It will be seen that the 3 marked † are true Concerti Grossi in the traditional style of contrasting groups. No.3 has only 2 movements and there is considerable scholastic speculation on the 'missing' middle movement. Presumably the works were comp. for Cöthen court orch. Bach's title for them was Concerts avec plusieurs instruments.

Brandt, Marianne [Bischoff, Marie] (b Vienna, 1842; d Vienna, 1921). Austrian mezzo-soprano with voice of exceptionally wide compass. Début Olmütz (now Olomouc) 1867. Berlin Court Opera 1868–82. CG début 1872. Sang Waltraute in Götterdämmerung, Bayreuth 1876, Kundry at second perf. of Parsifal 1882, and other Wagnerian roles. NY Met 1884–8.

Brandt, Michel (b Rennes, 1934). Fr. conductor. Début, Århus, Denmark. Cond. Biel-Solothum 1961–4, Cologne Opera 1964–71. Lect., RNCM, Manchester, from 1973. Guest cond., Manchester Camerata and other orchs.

branle (Bransle, etc.; from branler, to sway). Rustic round-dance of Fr. origin, at one time carried out to singing of dancers. Popular at court of Louis XIV but had earlier been taken up in Eng. (Shakespeare calls it 'brawl'; Pepys 'brantle'). Mus. usually in simple duple time.

Brannigan, Owen (b Annitsford, 1908; d Newcastle upon Tyne, 1973). Eng. bass. Début Newcastle 1943. Member of SW Opera 1943–8, 1952–8. Created several roles in Britten operas, i.e. Swallow (Peter Grimes), Collatinus (Rape of Lucretia), Supt. Budd (Albert Herring), Noye (Noye's Fludde), Bottom (A Midsummer Night's Dream). Also distinguished in oratorio and Gilbert and Sullivan, with special affection for and knowledge of N. Country folk-songs. Glyndebourne début 1946; CG 1948. OBE 1964.

bransle, brantle. See branle.

Brant, Henry (Dreyfuss) (b Montreal, 1913). Amer. (Canadian-born) composer, flautist, pianist, and organist. Earned living in 1930 as orchestrator for *Kostelanetz and Benny *Goodman. Later comp. and cond. for radio, films, and ballet in NY and Hollywood. Teacher at Columbia Univ. (1945–52), Juilliard (1947–54), Bennington Coll., Vermont, from 1957. Disciple of *Ives. Comps. are markedly experimental, employing spatial effects. His Antiphony 1 (1953), using 5 separated orch. groups, anticipated Stockhausen's Gruppen. Other works incl. syms.; sonatas; ballets (The Great American Goof, City Portrait); cantata December; Millennium 2, sop., bass, perc.; Kingdom Come, 2 orchs., org.; Verticals Ascending, 2 orch. groups, 2 conds.; Prisons of the Mind, spatial sym. etc.

brass. This term, technically used, covers wind instr. formerly made of that metal, some of which, however, are now sometimes made of other metals; it does not incl. instr. formerly of wood but now sometimes of metal, e.g. fl., nor does it incl. metal instr. with reed mouthpieces, e.g. sax. and sarrusophone. Each instr. possesses a mouthpiece of the nature of a cup or funnel to be pressed against the player's lips, which vibrate within it something like the double reed of the ob. family. The shape of this mouthpiece affects the quality of the tone, a deep funnel-shaped mouthpiece (e.g. hn.) giving more smoothness, and a cup-shaped mouthpiece (e.g. tpt.) more brilliance. The shape of the bell with which the tube ends also affects the character of the tone as does the nature of the tube's bore, i.e. cylindrical or conical.

'Natural' brass instr., playing merely the notes of the harmonic series of their 'fundamental' note, are no longer in artistic use, a system of valves having been introduced which makes it possible instantaneously to change the fundamental note of the instr. and so to have at command the notes of another whole harmonic series. However, composers sometimes ask for a 'natural' sound, e.g. Vaughan Williams in his *Pastoral Symphony* (2nd movement) and Britten in his *Serenade*. And the 'natural' hn. is often used today for 18th-cent. mus. The tbs. have always formed a class apart, as they possess a sliding arrangement by which the length of the tube can be changed and a fresh fundamental, with its series of harmonics, quickly obtained. Usual brass section of orch. comprises 4 hns., 3 tpts., 2 ten. and 1 bass tb., 1 tuba, with additions as specified.

brass band. This type of combination is found all over Europe and in countries settled by Europeans, but highest standard of perf. is possibly reached in N. of Eng., especially Lancashire and Yorkshire, where its popularity is great. Usual constitution in Brit. is cornets, flügelhorn, sax-horns, euphoniums, tbs., and basses (formerly *bombardons), with perc. Saxs. (not strictly a brass instr.) used to be incl.

All the wind instr. of the brass band except the bass tb. are scored for as transposing instr. Their keys being B♭ and E♭, their notation shows, respectively, 2 flats less (or 2 sharps more) than the sounding effect, or 3 flats less (or 3 sharps more). With exception of bass tbs. and perc. all are notated in treble clef: except E♭ cornet, where the sound is a minor third higher than the notation, all the sounds are lower, the intervals of the discrepancy ranging from a 2nd below (B♭ cornet) to 2 octaves and a second below (B♭ bass). Thus a brass band score is rather puzzling to an unaccustomed reader.

Many 20th-cent. Eng. composers (e.g. Elgar, Holst, Vaughan Williams, Ireland, Bliss, Bantock, Howells, Birtwistle, and Bourgeois) have written for brass bands, as has Henze. There is also a distinguished line of 'brass band composers', including Percy Fletcher, Cyril Jenkins, Hubert Bath, Denis Wright, Kenneth Wright, Eric Ball, Gilbert Vinter, and Edward Gregson. The 'brass band movement' in Brit. has a history (almost a folklore) stretching back to the start of the 19th cent. It derived partly from the old city 'waits' and partly from the military wind bands, of which there were many during the Napoleonic Wars. After Waterloo (1815) men left the army, but the musicians continued playing in civilian

life. Brass instruments were comparatively cheap, and the bands flourished as hobbies among the working-class population in the manufacturing towns of Lancs. and Yorks. (though also in Cornwall and elsewhere). Brass band competitions began *c*.1818 but developed fully *c*.1840. Among the most celebrated championships are the British Open (formerly held at Belle Vue, Manchester) and the National (held in London). It was for the latter in 1930 that Elgar comp. his *Severn Suite*. Bands are frequently named after an industrial firm or colliery as well as after a place. Among the most celebrated have been Bacup, Black Dyke Mills, Besses o' th' Barn, Wingate's Temperance, Foden's Motor Works, St Hilda Colliery (reputedly the greatest of all), Creswell Colliery, Brighouse and Rastrick, Munn and Felton's, Fairey Aviation, CWS Manchester, GUS Footwear, Grimethorpe Colliery, Cory, Carlton Main Frickley, and Hammond's Sauce Works—names of industrial poetry! Among notable band impresarios, arrangers, and conductors mention should be made of Henry Geehl, William Rimmer, William Halliwell, Eric Ball, Walter Hargreaves, Elgar Howarth, J. H. Iles, Alexander Owen, John Gladney, Edwin Swift, Roy Newsome, Maj. Peter Parkes, the Wrights (Denis, Frank, and Kenneth), and the Mortimers (Alex, Fred, Harry, and Rex).

Bratsche (Ger.). Viola (see '*braccio*' and '*gamba*'). So *Bratschist*, viola player.

Braunfels, Walter (*b* Frankfurt-am-Main, 1882; *d* Cologne, 1954). Ger. pianist and composer. First dir. of Hochschule für Musik, Cologne, 1925–33 and 1946–50. Wrote 7 operas, pf. conc., Mass, and Te Deum.

Brautlied (Ger.). Bridal song.

Brautwahl, Die (The Bridal Choice). Opera in 3 acts by Busoni, Op.45, to his own lib. based on E. T. A. Hoffmann. Comp. 1908–11. Prod. Hamburg 1912.

bravo (It.). Brave, fine. Exclamation of approval which therefore has no need to alter, though purists would insist on *brava* for a woman performer, *bravi* for male performers, and *brave* for female performers. Superlative form is *bravissimo*.

bravoure (Fr.). (1) Bravery, gallantry.
(2) Same as *bravura*.

bravura (It.). Courage, or swagger. A *bravura* passage calls for a brilliant and extrovert display of vocal or instr. technique.

brawl, brawle. Old Eng. name for *branle*. 4th movt. of Lambert's *Summer's Last Will and Testament* (1932–5) is called 'Brawles'.

break. (1) Place in the v. range where the registers change.
(2) The permanent change in the male v. which

occurs at puberty.

(3) A term in jazz meaning an improvised solo passage, in the style of a *cadenza.

Bream, Julian (Alexander) (b London, 1933). Eng. guitarist and lutenist. Début Cheltenham 1947, London 1950. Has ed. and transcr. much early mus. for both his instrs. Britten, Walton, Henze, and Tippett have comp. works for him. OBE 1964. CBE 1985.

Brecher, Gustav (b Eichwald, 1879; d aboard ship, 1940). Ger.-Boh. conductor and composer. Cond. opera in Hamburg, Leipzig, Cologne, and Frankfurt 1924–33. Comp. symphonic poem *Rosmersholm* (1895) and other works.

Brecht, Bertolt (b Augsburg, 1898; d Berlin, 1956). Ger. dramatist and theatrical producer whose radical outlook had enormous influence before and after Nazi régime in Ger. After 1948 his Berliner Ens. fathered a sch. of realistic theatrical experiment. He provided libs. (though his authorship is now being questioned) for several mus. works by Kurt *Weill, chief among them *Die *Dreigroschenoper* (Threepenny Opera) (1928) and *Aufstieg und Fall der Stadt Mahagonny* (*Rise and Fall of the City of Mahagonny) (1927–9). Also wrote libs. for Hindemith, Eisler, Wagner-Régeny, Dessau, and Sessions.

breeches part. See *travesti*.

breit (Ger.). Broad. Sometimes the equivalent of *largo*, and sometimes applied to bowing, e.g. *breit gestrichen*, broadly bowed.

Breitkopf & Härtel. Ger. firm of mus. publishers founded Leipzig 1719 by Bernhard Christoph Breitkopf (b Clausthal, 1695; d Leipzig, 1777) as book publishers. His son Johann Gottlieb (b Leipzig, 1719; d Leipzig, 1794) invented system of movable mus. type in 1750 enabling publication in 1756 of full score of an opera pseudonymously comp. by Princess of Saxony. Breitkopf family severed connection in 1800, dir. being transferred to Gottfried Christoph Härtel (b Schneeberg, 1763; d Cotta, Leipzig, 1827) who concentrated on mus. and prod. complete edns. of Mozart (17 vols., 1798–1816), Haydn (12 vols., 1800–6), Clementi, and Dussek. He also founded *Allgemeine musikalische Zeitung* (1798–1848). By 1874 firm's catalogue listed over 14,000 works, incl. complete edns. of Beethoven, Mendelssohn, Schumann, Schubert, Chopin, Liszt, Wagner, and Berlioz, and edns. of earlier composers such as Palestrina, Schütz, Victoria, Lassus, and Sweelinck. In 20th cent. many important composers have been added to their lists. A 26-vol. Brahms edn. was pub. 1926–8. Leipzig works was destroyed by bombs Dec. 1943. Rebuilt 1945–6. After 1945, firm was divided between Leipzig in E. Germany, becoming state-owned 1952, and Wiesbaden in W. Germany

Brema, Marie [Fehrman, Minny] (b Liverpool, 1856; d Manchester, 1925). Eng. mezzo-soprano (Ger. father, Amer. mother). Did not begin serious mus. study until after marriage in 1874. Sang in London 1891 under name Bremer (allusion to father's birthplace, Bremen). Later that year appeared as Lola in London at f. Eng. p. of *Cavalleria Rusticana*. Sang Ortrud in *Lohengrin* at Bayreuth début 1894. Amer. tour 1894 singing Ortrud, Brangäne, and Brünnhilde. Thereafter specialized in Wagner. Created part of Angel at f.p. of Elgar's *Dream of Gerontius* 1900. In 1910 promoted 2 seasons of opera at Savoy, London, singing title-role in Gluck's *Orpheus* and producing all the works. From 1913 until her death was prof. of singing and dir. of opera class at RMCM.

Brendel, Alfred (b Wiesenberg, Moravia, 1931). Austrian pianist. First recital, Graz 1948. Toured with Vienna Chamber Orch. 1951. Salzburg Fest. début 1960. Played all Beethoven sonatas, London 1962. Amer. début 1963. Thereafter built worldwide reputation through tours and recordings. Settled in London, 1974. Admired principally for playing of Mozart, Beethoven, Schubert, Schumann, and Liszt, but is frequent performer of Schoenberg's pf. conc. Has written essays on several composers (pubd. as *Musical Thoughts and Afterthoughts*, London 1976, and *Music Sounded Out*, London 1990) and comp. pf. mus. Hon. KBE 1989.

Brendel, Wolfgang (b Munich, 1947). Ger. baritone. Joined Bavarian Nat. Opera, Munich, 1971. Has also sung at Vienna State Opera, La Scala, and NY Met. Salzburg Fest. début 1975; CG 1985. Noted singer of Mandryka in *Arabella*.

Brenet, Michel [Bobillier, Antoinette Christine Marie] (b Lunéville, 1858; d Paris, 1918). Fr. musicologist. Wrote a history of the orchestral symphony in 1882, a biog. of Grétry (1884), and a study of Berlioz in Germany and his first opera (1889). Also biographies of Ockeghem, Rameau, Palestrina, Haydn, and Handel, an historical dictionary of mus. (pubd. posthumously), and many other works of research. Noted for accuracy and precision.

Brentano, Elisabeth (Bettina) (b Frankfurt-am-Main, 1785; d Berlin, 1859). Friend of Goethe and later of Beethoven. Her hysterical nature led her to invent letters she said she received from Goethe, and only one letter to her from Beethoven, though revealing an affectionate relationship, has been authenticated. In 1811, married poet Achim von *Arnim who had collab. with her brother Clemens (1778–1842) in editing the folk-anthology *Des Knaben Wunderhorn* (1805–8).

Brett, Philip (b Edwinstowe, Notts, 1937; d Los Angeles, 2002). Eng.-born musicologist and writer (Amer. cit. 1979). Collab. with *Dart in rev. Fellowes's *English Madrigalists*. Ass. lect. in mus., Cambridge Univ. 1963–6. Teacher at Univ. of Calif., Berkeley, from 1966 (prof. from 1978); chairman of mus. dept., Univ. of Calif., Riverside, 1988–90, prof. of mus. from 1991. Author of book on Britten's *Peter Grimes*

(1983), ed. of Byrd's *Consort Songs* for v. and viols (1970), madrigals, songs, and canons (1976), masses (1981), *Gradualia* (1990–2).

Breuning. Ger. family remembered for its connection with Beethoven who at 18 became mus. teacher in Bonn to 2 of the 4 children of a widow, Hélène Breuning. He became almost a member of the family. His closest friend was perhaps the 2nd son, Stephan (1774–1827), to whom the vn. conc. is ded. Letters from Beethoven to various members of the family are pubd.

Bréval, Jean-Baptiste Sébastien (*b* Paris, 1753; *d* Colligis, 1823). Fr. composer and cellist. Played own sonata at Concert Spirituel, Paris, 1778; became member of Concert Spirituel orch. 1781–91, orch. of Th. Feydeau 1791–1800, and Paris Opéra orch. 1801–14. Comp. 7 vc. concs. (1784–94), 8 syms., concertantes for various instr., much chamber mus., and one *opéra comique* (1788). Wrote important *Traité du violoncelle* (1804).

breve (𝄺). Double whole-note. Formerly the short note of mus., but as the longer notes have fallen into disuse and shorter ones been introduced it has become the longest (twice the length of the semibreve or whole-note). *alla breve* means (it is not clear why) 'Take the minim as your beat-unit' (the same effect may be indicated by the time-signature 2/2, or ¢, or sometimes 4/2). Still occurs in vocal mus., but rarely in instr. scores where it has been replaced by 2 tied whole-notes.

Brewer, Christine (*b* Springfield, Ill., 1956). Amer. soprano. Studied with Christine Armistead, Washington Univ., St Louis. Worked as teacher while singing in ch. at Opera Theatre of St Louis. Won NY Met auditions 1989. Opera début St Louis 1990 (Ellen Orford). CG 1994 (*Figaro* Countess), NY Met 2002 (Ariadne). Acclaimed singer of Isolde (London 2000 concert, S. Francisco 2006 stage). Other roles incl. Donna Anna, Beethoven's Leonora, Britten's Gloriana, Strauss's Helena, Chrysothemis, and Dyer's Wife. Wide concert and recital repertory.

Brewer, (Sir) (Alfred) **Herbert** (*b* Gloucester, 1865; *d* Gloucester, 1928). Eng. organist, conductor, and composer assoc. in all 3 capacities with Gloucester meeting of 3 Choirs Fest. Chorister Gloucester Cath. 1877–80. Org., St Giles, Oxford, 1882–5, org. schol. Exeter College, Oxford, 1883. Studied RCM 1883–5. Org., Bristol Cath., 1885, St Michael's, Coventry, 1886–92. Mus. master Tonbridge Sch. 1892–6. Org. and choirmaster Gloucester Cath. 1896–1928. Comps. incl. cantatas *Emmaus* (1901, some of it scored by Elgar) and *The Holy Innocents* (1904), and services and anthems, but his best mus. is in his secular comps. such as *3 Elizabethan Pastorals* for v. and orch. (1906), and *Jillian of Berry*, song-cycle (1921). Wrote *Marche héroïque* for org., 1914. Knighted 1926.

Brewer, Thomas (*b* London, 1611; *d c.*1660–70). Eng. composer of songs, glees, and music for viols. His glee *Turn, Amaryllis, to thy swain* and song *O that mine eyes* are outstanding examples of his work.

Brian, Havergal (*b* Dresden, Staffs., 1876; *d* Shoreham-by-Sea, 1972) (christened William, adopted name Havergal in 1899). Eng. composer. Mainly self-taught and did not devote himself wholly to mus. until he was 23, having left school at 12 and worked as a carpenter's apprentice and in other jobs. Was Manchester mus. critic of *Musical World* 1905, attending Richter's Hallé concerts. His *English Suite* for orch. was cond. by Wood 1907, and Beecham cond. 2 of his works at Hanley 1908. His ov. *Dr. Merryheart* was perf. at Birmingham in 1913 and taken up by Wood. Other orch. works were cond. by Ronald, Godfrey, Bantock, and others, but none est. themselves in the permanent repertory. Wrote for *Musical Opinion*, 1922–40. He comp. 32 syms. but was 78 years old before any was perf., this being No.8 in a BBC broadcast, 1954. The 18th was perf. in London in 1962 and the 32nd in Jan. 1971 on the eve of his 95th birthday. He wrote 27 syms. and 4 operas between 1948, when he was 72, and 1968. The BBC undertook to broadcast all the syms. to mark the centenary of Brian's birth, and a movement developed to try to remedy the neglect he had suffered in his life. His largest work was the *Gothic Symphony* (No.1), comp. 1919–27, for an orch. of 180 (32 woodwind, 24 brass, perc. needing 17 players, etc.) with 4 brass groups and 4 large mixed choirs. This was f.p. in London 1961 and again in 1966 to mark his 90th birthday. Several of his works outdo Strauss and Mahler in their extravagance. The Second Symphony requires 16 hns., 2 pfs., and org. Prin. works:

OPERAS: *The Tigers* (1916–18, orch. 1918–29); *Turandot* (?1949–51); *The Cenci* (1952); *Faust* (?1954–6); *Agamemnon* (1957).

ORCH.: syms.: No.1 in D minor (*The *Gothic*), SATB soloists, ch., children's ch., brass band, orch. (1919–27), No.2 in E minor (1930–1), No.3 in C♯ minor (1931–2), No.4 (*Das Siegeslied*, Ger. trans. of Ps.68), sop., ch., orch. (1932–3), No.5 (*Wine of Summer*), bar. and orch. (1937), No.6 (*Sinfonia tragica*) (1947–8), No.7 in C (1948), No.8 in B♭ minor (1949), No.9 in A minor (1951), No.10 in C minor (1953–4), No.11 (1954), No.12 (1957), No.13 in C (1959), No.14 in F minor (1960), No.15 in A (1960), No.16 (1960), No.17 (1960–1), No.18 (1961), No.19 in E minor (1961), No.20 (1962), No.21 in E♭ (1963), No.22 (*Symphonia brevis*) (1964–5), No.23 (1965), No.24 in D (1965), No.25 in A minor (1965–6), No.26 (1966), No.27 in C (1966), No.28 in C minor (1967), No.29 in E♭ (1967), No.30 in B♭ minor (1967), No.31 (1968), No 32 in A♭ (1968); *Dr Merryheart*, comedy ov. (c.1911–12); *English Suite* No.3 (1919), No.4 (1921), No.5 (1953); vn. conc. No.2 in C minor (1934–5); *The Tinker's Wedding*, comedy ov. (1948); *Elegy*, sym.-poem (1954); vc. conc. (1964); *Concerto for Orchestra* (1964); *Ave atque Vale* (1968).

CHORUS & ORCH.: *Psalm 23*, ten., ch., orch. (1901, reconstructed 1945); *Requiem for the Rose*, women's vv., orch. (or pf.) (1911); *Prometheus Unbound* (1937–44, lost).

Also many choral songs and solo songs.

bridge. (1) In str. instr., the piece of wood that supports the str. and communicates their vibrations to the belly.

(2) A term, usually 'bridge passage', in comp., meaning a short section which links together— perhaps by a key change—2 important sections of a large-scale sym. or similar work.

Bridge, Frank (b Brighton, 1879; d Eastbourne, 1941). Eng. composer, conductor, violinist, violist, and teacher. Played vn. and va. in several str. qts., incl. Joachim, Grimson, and English. Was a member of the last-named until 1915. Also cond. of New SO and of opera during Marie Brema's 1910–11 season at the Savoy. Cond. at CG 1913 and many BBC studio concerts in 1930s. Visited USA 1923, under sponsorship of Elizabeth Sprague Coolidge, to cond. own works. Was noted teacher, but his only composition pupil was Benjamin *Britten, who first went to him for lessons at the age of 14.

Bridge's early songs, chamber mus., and orch. works such as *The Sea* are in an idiom familiar to British audiences from the works of Bax, Ireland, and Delius. However, the impact of the First World War on one of deeply held pacifist convictions wrought a significant change and the piano sonata of 1921–4 showed a tougher harmonic idiom, with a more radical approach which in the 3rd and 4th str. qts. came near to the atonality of the Second Viennese School but nearer still to Scriabin. Yet Bridge never wholly severed his 'Englishness', as can be heard in the orch. tone-poem *Enter Spring* (1927). His detachment from the 'establishment' figures in the Eng. mus. of his day led to his being regarded as an outsider and to the almost complete neglect of such major works as the *Phantasm* for pf. and orch. (1931) and the vc. conc. *Oration* (1930). It was not until his works were rehabilitated by his former pupil Britten at Aldeburgh Festivals that a new generation had its interest in him stimulated, leading to many more performances and recordings. Prin. comps.:

OPERA: *The Christmas Rose* (1918–29).

ORCH.: *Coronation March* (1901); *3 Orchestral Pieces* (1902); *Isabella* (1907); *Dance Rhapsody* (1908); *Suite*, str. (1910); *The *Sea* (1910–11); *Dance Poem* (1913); *Summer* (1914); *Lament*, str. (also pf.) (1915); *Sir Roger de Coverley*, str. (also str. qt.) (1922); *Enter Spring* (1927); *There is a willow grows aslant a brook* (1928); **Oration*, concerto elegiaco, vc. and orch. (1930); *Phantasm*, pf. and orch. (1931); *2 Entr'actes* (orch. of *Rosemary*, pf. 1906 and *Canzonetta*, pf. 1926) (1936); *Vignettes de danse* (*Niccollette, Zoraida*, and *Carmelita*, pf. 1925) (1938); *Norse Legend* (vn., pf., 1905) (1938); *Rebus Overture* (1940); *Allegro Moderato*, str. (1941, unfinished, last 21 bars orch. Anthony Pople 1979).

CHAMBER MUSIC: pf. trio (1900); *Scherzo Phantastick*, str. qt. (1901); str. qt. in B♭ (1901); pf. qt. in C minor (1902); *Phantasie String Quartet* (1905); *3 Idylls*, str. qt. (1906); *Phantasie Piano Trio* (1907); *Allegro appassionato*, va. and pf. (1908); *Phantasie*

Piano Quartet (1910); *Elégie*, vc. and pf. (1911); pf. quintet (1904–7); str. sextet (1906–12); *Heartsease*, vn., pf. (arr. pf. 1921) (1912); vc. sonata (1913–17); *Amaryllis*, vn., pf. (1915); str. qt. (1915); *Sally in our Alley, Cherry Ripe*, str. qt. (1916); *Morning Song*, vn., pf. (1919); *Souvenir*, vn., pf. (1919); *Sir Roger de Coverley*, str. qt. (1922); str. qt. No.3 (1925–6, rev. 1927); trio, rhapsody, 2 vn., va. (1928); pf. trio No.2 (1929); vn. sonata (1932); str. qt. No.4 (1937); *Divertimenti*, fl., ob., cl., bn. (1934–8).

VOCAL: *Music when soft voices die*, SATB (1904); *A Prayer*, ch. and orch. (1916); *A Litany*, 3-part ch. (1918); *Evening Primrose*, 2-part ch. (1923); *Golden Slumbers*, 3-part ch. (1923).

SOLO SONGS: *Blow, blow, thou winter wind* (1903); *Tears, idle tears* (1905); *Come to me in my dreams* (1906); *Love is a rose* (1907); *Love went a-riding* (1914, also orch. acc.); *Go not, happy day* (1916); *Blow out, you bugles* (1918, also orch. acc.); *When you are old* (1919); *3 Songs of Tagore* (1922–5, also orch. acc.); *Journey's End* (1925); *Golden Hair* (1925).

PIANO: *Capriccio* Nos.1 and 2 (1905); *3 Sketches* (*April, Rosemary, Capricieuse*) (1906); *3 Pieces* (*Minuet, Columbine, Romance*) (1912); *Lament* (1915, also for str.); *4 Characteristic Pieces* (*Water Nymphs, Fragrance, Bittersweet, Fireflies*) (1915); *Sally in our Alley, Cherry Ripe*, pf. duet (1916, also for str. qt.); *Fairy Tale Suite* (1917); sonata (1921–4); *3 Lyrics* (*Heartsease*, vn., pf. 1912, *Dainty Rogue, The Hedgerow*) (1921–4); *In Autumn* (1924); *4 Pieces* (*Carmelita, Niccollette, Zoraida, En Fête*, nos.2, 3, and 1 arr. orch. 1938) (1925); *Winter Pastoral* (1925); *Berceuse* (1929).

ORGAN: *3 Pieces* (1905); *Organ Pieces*, Book 1 (1905), Book 2 (1912); *In memoriam C.H.H.P.* (1918); *Minuet* (1939); *Prelude* (1939); *Processional* (1939).

Bridge, (Sir) (John) **Frederick** (b Oldbury, Worcs., 1844; d London, 1924). Eng. composer, conductor, and organist. Boy chorister, Rochester Cath. Org., Holy Trinity Ch., Windsor, 1865– 9. Org., Manchester Cath., 1869–75, prof. of harmony, Owens College, Manchester, 1872–5. Deputy org., Westminster Abbey, 1875–82, org., 1882–1918. Presided over modernization of Abbey org., 1884–1909. Cond., Royal Choral Soc., 1896–1922. First Prof. of Mus., Univ. of London, 1903. Arr. mus. at 2 coronations (1902 and 1911) and for Queen Victoria's golden and diamond jubilee services (1887 and 1897). Comp. mainly oratorios. Knighted 1897.

Bridgetower, George Augustus Polgreen (b Biala, Poland, 1778; d Peckham, 1860). Eng. violinist (mulatto, having African father). Début Concert Spirituel, Paris, 1789. From then lived mainly in London, but also Rome and Paris. Enjoyed patronage of Prince of Wales (later George IV), who sent him for vn. lessons to Barthélemon and Jarnowick, and for comp. to Attwood. Was violinist in service of Prince at Brighton and played in Haydn-Salomon concerts, London 1791. Gave concerts in Dresden 1802 and 1803, followed by invitation to Vienna. Beethoven's 'Kreutzer' Sonata comp. for him and first played by him and composer, Vienna 1803. Quarrel caused Beethoven to transfer ded. to Fr. violinist Rodolphe *Kreutzer. Returned to London and played in Philharmonic Soc.'s first season, 1813.

Brigg Fair. 'English Rhapsody' for orch. by Delius, being variations on Lincolnshire folk-song introduced to Delius by *Grainger. Comp. 1907. (F.p. Liverpool, Jan. 1908, cond. Bantock.)

Brighenti [Brighetti], **Maria** (*b* Bologna, 1792; *d*?). It. operatic singer, début Bologna 1814. Created Rosina in *Il barbiere di Siviglia* (Rome 1816). Rossini then wrote *La Cenerentola* for her (Rome 1817). Retired 1836.

Bright, Dora Estella [Mrs. Knatchbull] (*b* Sheffield, 1863; *d* Babington, Som., 1951). Eng. pianist and composer. First woman to be invited to compose work for Phil. Soc. (*Fantasia in G* for pf. and orch. 1892) and said to be first pianist to give a recital entirely devoted to Eng. mus. Comp. 3 operas, 2 pf. concs.

brillante (It. 'glittering', 'sparkling'). Boccherini used direction *allegro brillante*. Many concert pieces, e.g. by Chopin and Weber, have *brillante* (or Fr. *brillant*) in titles.

brindisi (It.). Toast. Jovial song to acc. the drinking of a health. A famous operatic example is 'Libiamo' in Act I of Verdi's *La traviata*.

Brindle, Reginald Smith. See *Smith Brindle, Reginald*.

Brinsmead, John and Sons, Ltd. London pf.-makers. Est. 1835 by John Brinsmead (*b* Weare Giffard, Devon, 1814; *d* London, 1908). Annual output of 2,000 pianos by 1900. Manufacture continued until 1967 when firm was bought by Kemble and Co. John Brinsmead's younger son Edgar (*d* London, 1907) wrote *History of the Pianoforte* (1870; 4th ed. 1889).

brio (It.). Vigour, spirit, fire. So the adjective *brioso. con brio*, spiritedly.

brisé (Fr.). Broken. Applied (a) to a chord played in arpeggio fashion, or (b) to str. mus. played in short, detached movements of the bow. The *style brisé* was the characteristic arpeggiated style of 17th-cent. Fr. lute mus., which in turn influenced the kbd. mus. of the later clavecinistes.

British Council. Govt.-sponsored organization formed 1935 to spread in foreign countries interest in Brit. and its cultural activities. Centres in various parts of the world, with libraries, help towards perf. of Brit. plays and mus. It sponsors exhibitions and tours by Brit. artists, actors, and musicians, and occasionally sponsors recordings. It receives a considerable govt. grant.

British Federation of Music Festivals. Founded 1921 as assoc. of amateur competitive mus. fests. in Brit. and the Commonwealth. Organizes summer schs.

British Grenadiers. Orig. words date from end of 17th cent., but a later version now sung includes an allusion to Battle of Waterloo (1815). Origin of tune unknown; earliest copy dates from *c*.1740. Regimental march of the Grenadier Guards.

British Institute of Recorded Sound. See *National Sound Archive*.

British National Opera Company (BNOC). Formed 1921 by singers and instrumentalists of Sir Thomas *Beecham's opera co., disbanded when financial difficulties compelled Beecham's temporary withdrawal from mus. scene. F.p. at Bradford in Feb. 1922, opera being *Aida*. Dir. was Percy *Pitt, succeeded 1924 by Frederic *Austin. Most of its work was in the provinces, with short seasons at CG and His Majesty's Th. Repertory was wide, embracing Wagner, Debussy, the Italians and several Eng. works, e.g. Vaughan Williams's *Hugh the Drover* and Holst's *The *Perfect Fool* and *At the Boar's Head*. Co. incl. most of leading British singers and conds. of day, Barbirolli, Boult, Harty, and Sargent among the latter, and Allin, Radford, Labbette, Turner, Mullings, Heming, and Nash among former. Co. ceased to exist, crippled by entertainment tax, in 1929, but was re-named Covent Garden English Company, with Barbirolli as mus. dir., in Sept. 1929 and survived in that form for another 3 seasons.

Britten, (Edward) **Benjamin** (Lord Britten of Aldeburgh) (*b* Lowestoft, 1913; *d* Aldeburgh, 1976). Eng. composer, pianist, conductor. His birth on St Cecilia's Day, 22 Nov., was a happy augury for the career of one of Britain's greatest composers. Essentially a vocal composer, his operas and song-cycles won wide int. acceptance. He never abandoned the principles of tonality and was a 'modern' composer who reached a mass audience and a conservative whose originality no radical would sensibly deny. He shared with his predecessors Parry, Vaughan Williams, and Holst, an intense interest in the work of amateurs and children. His brilliant gifts as a pianist and cond., coupled with the virtuoso nature of his inventiveness, also led him to compose mus. for great performers such as the cellist Rostropovich and the singers Vishnevskaya, Fischer-Dieskau, and Janet Baker. The greatest personal influence on his mus. was his friendship with the tenor *Pears, for whom he comp. many operatic and vocal roles.

Britten's mus. gifts became apparent at an early stage. In sch. holidays he had lessons from Harold *Samuel (pf.) and Frank *Bridge (comp.); the influence of Bridge in particular was strong and lasting. Britten was at RCM 1930–3, but found mus. atmosphere uncongenial and resented official refusal to allow him to study with Berg in Vienna. Studied pf. with Benjamin and comp. with Ireland. His astonishing early works were pubd., incl. the *Sinfonietta* and *A Boy was Born*, and his song-cycle with orch. *Our Hunting Fathers* (text compiled and partly written by Auden) was perf. at Norwich Fest. 1936. He worked for the G.P.O. Film Unit, writing mus. for a dozen short documentaries, the best known being *Coal Face* and *Night Mail* (both 1936). In

1937, for the Boyd Neel String Orch.'s concert at the Salzburg Fest., he wrote the *Variations on a Theme by Frank Bridge*. He and Pears followed their friend the poet Auden to N. Amer. in 1939, staying until 1942. While in NY, f.ps. of his Vn. Conc. (1939) and *Sinfonia da Requiem* (1940) were given in Carnegie Hall under Barbirolli. Returning to Eng., Britten settled at Snape and Aldeburgh, Suffolk. His opera *Peter Grimes* was perf. at SW on 7 June 1945, a day of importance for Eng. mus. comparable with the f.p. of Elgar's *Enigma Variations* in June 1899. His interest in chamber opera led in 1947 to foundation of the EOG (later EMT) and his desire for a fest. rooted in Eng. village life and the work of amateurs yet capable of enticing int. performers led to the *Aldeburgh Festival, first held in 1948. Thereafter his career was uneventful outwardly except for the prolific output of works of all kinds, in many of which he took part as cond. or pianist. He excelled not only in his own mus.: as an accompanist in Schubert he was second to none (Salzburg Fest. 1952, recital with Pears), he played and cond. Mozart superbly, and cond. major works by Bach, Mahler, Elgar, Schumann, and others. The Aldeburgh Fest. also featured neglected works by composers whom Britten and his colleagues deemed to deserve reappraisal. After a major heart operation in 1973 his activities were much reduced. CH 1953, OM 1965. First composer to be created life peer (Lord Britten of Aldeburgh, 1976). (Lord Berners was a hereditary peer.)

A major strength of Britten's art, which contributes to the dramatic effectiveness of his operas, is his gift for finding the apt, simple, quickly memorable, and not thereafter easily forgotten phrase to illustrate a point or situation. Another feature is his uncanny ability to capture the imagination and interest of children. Such works as *Let's Make an Opera, Noye's Fludde*, and *Saint Nicolas* testify to this. He was much preoccupied with themes of innocence destroyed, of the persecution of the 'outsider' in society (stemming from his own pacifism and conscientious objection to war service), and of cruelty. These themes found their most impressive outlet in the operas *Billy Budd, The Turn of the Screw*, and *Owen Wingrave*, the two last being adaptations by Myfanwy Piper of Henry James. If these, and such works as the great *War Requiem*, represent the dark side of his musical personality, the 1953 Coronation opera *Gloriana* (a failure at first), his splendid *Midsummer Night's Dream*, the comedy *Albert Herring*, and a host of choral and instrumental works such as the pf. conc., the *Cantata Academica*, and the *Spring Symphony* show a capacity for joy. He invented a new genre of music theatre in the 3 church parables, the first (*Curlew River*) being an adaptation of a Japanese Noh play; his song-cycles, to Eng., Fr., It., Ger., and Russ. texts are magnificent word-settings; his 5 canticles are works of original insights; and his instrumental works, in particular the str. qts. and vc. suites, explore and stretch the players' capacities without ceasing to be musical. Few composers have caught the pub-

lic's imagination in their lifetime as vividly as did Britten; each new work was eagerly awaited and absorbed. Intensely practical, he won the devoted admiration of the artists for whom he wrote, and on his several visits to the Soviet Union formed a firm friendship with Shostakovich who ded. his 14th Sym. to him. If it is his operas, particularly *Peter Grimes*, with its evocation of early 19th-cent. Aldeburgh, which dominate his output, it is a mistake to overlook his genius in non-vocal forms. Prin. works are:

OPERAS: *Paul Bunyan, Op.17 (1940–1, rev. 1974); *Peter Grimes, Op.33 (1945); *The* *Rape of Lucretia, Op.37 (1946); *Albert Herring, Op.39 (1947); *The* **Beggar's Opera*, Op.43 (new version of Gay's opera, 1948); **Let's Make an Opera* (*The Little Sweep*), Op.45 (1949); *Billy Budd, Op.50 (1950–1, rev. 1960); *Gloriana, Op.53 (1953); *The* **Turn of the Screw*, Op.54 (1954); **Noye's Fludde*, Op.59 (1958); *A* **Midsummer Night's Dream*, Op.64 (1959–60); *Owen Wingrave, Op.85 (1971); *Death in Venice, Op.88 (1973; orch. suite arr. S. Bedford, 1984).

CHURCH PARABLES: *Curlew River, Op.71 (1964); *The* **Burning Fiery Furnace*, Op.77 (1966); *The* *Prodigal Son, Op.81 (1968).

BALLET: *The* **Prince of the Pagodas*, Op.59 (1956).

ORCH.: *Sinfonietta*, Op.1 (1932); *A* *Simple Symphony, Op.4 (1933–4); *Soirées musicales*, Op.9 (arr. of Rossini, 1936); **Variations on a Theme of Frank Bridge*, Op.10 (1937); *Mont Juic, Op.12 (suite of Catalan dances composed jointly with L. Berkeley, 1937); *Canadian Carnival*, Op.19 (1939); *Young Apollo*, Op.16, pf., str. qt., str. orch. (1939, withdrawn until 1979); *Overture, Paul Bunyan* (1940, rev. 1974, orch. C. Matthews 1977); **Sinfonia da Requiem*, Op.20 (1940); *An American Overture*, Op.27 (1941–2, f.p. 1983); *Matinées musicales*, Op.24 (arr. of Rossini, 1941); *Prelude and Fugue*, Op.29, for str. (1943); *Four* *Sea Interludes, Op.33a, *Passacaglia*, Op.33b, from *Peter Grimes* (1944); **Young Person's Guide to the Orchestra* (*Variations and Fugue on a Theme of Purcell*), Op.34 (1946); *Occasional Overture*, Op.38 (1946); *Men of Goodwill* (*Variations on a Christmas Carol*) (1947); Ov., *The Building of the House*, Op.79 (with ch. ad. lib.) (1967); *Suite on English Folk Tunes* (*A Time There Was . . .*), Op.90 (1974); *Lachrymae*, Op.48a, va. and str. (1976, arr. of 1950 work for va. and pf.); *The Prince of the Pagodas*, concert suite arr. from 1956 ballet by Lankester (1979).

CONCERTOS: pf., Op.13 (1938, rev. 1945); vn., Op.15 (1939, rev. 1950 and 1958); *Diversions on a Theme*, Op.21, pf. left-hand (1940, rev. 1954); *Scottish Ballad*, Op.26, 2 pf. (1941); vc. sym., Op.68 (1963).

BRASS: *Russian Funeral*, brass and perc. (1936).

CHORAL: *Hymn to the Virgin* (1930, rev. 1934); *A Boy Was Born*, Op.3 (1933, rev. 1955); *Friday Afternoons*, Op.7 (children's vv.) (1933–5); *Te Deum* (1934); *Advance Democracy* (1938); *Ballad of Heroes*, Op.14 (1939); *AMDG*, 4 prayers and holy songs of G. M. Hopkins, for unacc. ch. (1939); **Ceremony of Carols*, Op.28, treble vv. and hp. (1942); **Hymn to St Cecilia*, Op.27 (1942); *Rejoice in the Lamb*, Op.30 (1943); *Festival Te Deum*, Op.32 (1944); *Saint Nicolas, Op.24 (1947–8); *Spring Symphony, Op.44

(1948–9); *Five Flower Songs* (1950); *Missa Brevis*, Op.63 (boys' vv.); *Cantata Academica*, Op.62 (1959); *Jubilate Deo and Venite* (1961); *War Requiem*, Op.66 (1961); *Cantata Misericordium*, Op.69 (1963); *Voices for Today*, Op.75 (1965); *The Golden Vanity*, Op.78 (boys' vv.) (1966); *Children's Crusade*, Op.82 (1968); *Sacred and Profane*, Op.91 (1975); *Welcome Ode*, Op.95 (young people's ch. and orch.) (1976).

SOLO VOICE & ORCH.: *Quatre chansons françaises* (1928); *Our Hunting Fathers*, Op.8 (1936); *Les *Illuminations*, Op.18 (1938–9); *Serenade*, Op.31 (1943); *Nocturne*, Op.60 (1958); *Phaedra*, Op.93 (1975).

SOLO VOICE & PIANO (unless otherwise indicated): 3 *Early Songs* (1922–6); 4 *Cabaret Songs* (1937); *On This Island*, Op.11 (1937); *Seven Sonnets of Michelangelo*, Op.22 (1939–40); *Folk-Song Arrangements*, Vol. I British (1945), II French (1946), III British (1948); 9 *Holy Sonnets of John Donne*, Op.35 (1945); *Canticle I, My Beloved is Mine*, Op.40 (1947); *A *Charm of Lullabies*, Op.41 (1947); *Canticle II, *Abraham and Isaac*, Op.51 (1952); *Winter Words*, Op.52 (1953); *Canticle III, Still Falls the Rain*, Op.55 (with hn. and pf.) (1954); *Songs from the Chinese*, Op.58 (v. and guitar) (1957); 6 *Hölderlin-Fragmente*, Op.61 (1958); *Songs and Proverbs of William Blake*, Op.74 (1965); *The *Poet's Echo*, Op.76 (1965); *Who are these Children?*, Op.84 (1969); *Canticle IV, Journey of the Magi*, Op.86 (1971); *Canticle V, The Death of St Narcissus*, Op.89 (v. and hp.) (1974); *A Birthday Hansel*, Op.92 (v. and hp.) (1975); 8 *Folk Song Arrangements* (v. and harp) (1976).

CHAMBER WORKS: *Elegy*, va. (1926); *Rhapsody*, str. qt. (1929); *Quartettino*, str. qt. (1930); *Phantasy String Quintet* (1932); *Phantasy Oboe Quartet*, Op.2 (1932); *2 Insect Pieces*, ob., pf. (1935, Op. posth., f.p. 1979); *Suite*, Op.6, vn., pf. (1934–5); *3 Divertimenti*, str. qt. (1936); *Temporal Variations*, ob., pf. (1936); *Reveille*, vn., pf. (1937); str. qt. No.1, Op.25 (1941), No.2, Op.36 (1945), No.3, Op.94 (1975); str. qt. in D (1931, rev. 1974); *Lachrymae*, Op.48, va., pf. (1950); 6 *Metamorphoses after Ovid*, Op.49, ob. (1951); vc. sonata, Op.65 (1961); Suite No.1 for vc., Op.72 (1964), No.2, Op.80 (1967), No.3, Op.87 (1971); *Gemini Variations*, Op.73 (fl., vn., and pf. 4 hands) (1965); *Tema-Sacher*, vc. (1976).

PIANO: 5 *Walztes (Waltzes)* (1923–5, re-written 1969); *Holiday Diary*, Op.5 (1934); *Sonatina Romantica* (1940, f.p. Aldeburgh 1983); *Night Piece (Notturno)* (1963).

2 PIANOS: *Introduction and Rondo alla burlesca*, Op.23, No.1 (1940); *Mazurka Elegiaca*, Op.23, No.2 (1941).

ORGAN: *Prelude and Fugue on a Theme of Vittoria* (1946).

INCIDENTAL MUSIC FOR FILMS, PLAYS, AND RADIO: *Coal Face, Night Mail* (1936); *The Ascent of F6, Love from a Stranger* (1937); *Hadrian's Wall* (1938); *The Sword in the Stone* (1938; concert suite for chamber ens. ed. C. Matthews); *Johnson Over Jordan* (1939); *The Sword in the Stone* (1939); *The Rescue* (1943); *This Way to the Tomb* (1945); *The Duchess of Malfi* (1946); *The Dark Tower* (1946); *Men of Goodwill* (1947); and others.

Britten, Improvisations on an Impromptu of Benjamin. Orch. work by *Walton, comp. 1968–9, f.p. San Francisco 1970. Theme taken from slow movt. of Britten's pf. conc.

Britten, Sinfonia in Memoriam Benjamin. Work for 17 wind instr. by *Fricker, 1976–7. F.p. in England, Aldeburgh 1978.

Britton, Thomas (*b* Rushden, Northants., 1644; *d* London, 1714). Eng. coal merchant, collector of books, and organizer of concerts in London, held from 1678 in room over his shop in Clerkenwell, in which the young *Handel took part with *Pepusch and others. Attended by aristocrats and leaders of fashion. Known as 'the small-coal man'.

Brixi, František (Franz) **Xaver** (*b* Prague, 1732; *d* Prague, 1771). Cz. composer and organist of Prague Cath. from 1759. Prolific composer of masses, oratorios, and requiems, also org. concs. and other secular works.

Broadcast Music Inc. (BMI). Amer. performing right soc. owned by the broadcasting and TV industry. Founded 1940 by broadcasters in NY.

Broadwood, Rev. **John** (*b* 1798; *d* Lyne, 1864). Eng. clergyman and folklorist. Member of pf. firm family and one of earliest collectors of Eng. folk-songs. His *Old English Songs of Surrey and Sussex* was pubd. 1843.

Broadwood, John & Sons Ltd. London firm of pf. makers, orig. founded in 1728 by Burkat *Shudi, whose daughter married John Broadwood (1732–1812), joiner and cabinet maker in the firm. Broadwood became Shudi's partner 1770. Firm re-named John Broadwood & Son in 1795, & Sons 1807. Earliest Broadwood grand built 1781. Haydn visited workshop in 1794. Early square pianos were improvements on those modelled by Johannes Zumpe. Firm reached production of 2,500 instr. a year in 1850s, but declined after 1890.

Broadwood, Lucy Etheldred (*b* Melrose, 1858; *d* Canterbury, 1929). Eng. folk-song collector. Daughter of H. F. Broadwood of pf. firm and niece of Rev. John *Broadwood, whose interest in folk-song she pursued. Pubd. *Sussex Songs* 1889, being an expanded reprint of her uncle's *Old English Songs*, and *English County Songs* (with J. A. *Fuller Maitland) 1893. Founder-member of Folk Song Soc. 1898, serving as its hon. sec. 1904–8 and 1914–18. Encouraged *Vaughan Williams to collect folk-songs.

Brockway, Howard (*b* Brooklyn, 1870; *d* NY, 1951). Amer. composer and pianist. Various important educational positions Baltimore and NY. Comp. orch. and chamber works, etc., and collected Kentucky mountain tunes.

Brod, Max (*b* Prague, 1884; *d* Tel Aviv, 1968). Cz.-Israeli novelist, critic, and composer. Member of Prague group of writers which incl. Rilke,

Werfel, and Kafka. Trans. *Janáček's operas into Ger. and wrote his biography (1924). Mus. critic of *Prague Tagblatt* for many years. Went to Palestine 1939. Comp. requiem, songs, and chamber mus.

Brodsky, Adolph (*b* Taganrog, Russia, 1851; *d* Manchester, 1929). Russ. violinist and teacher. Joined staff of Moscow Cons. and later Leipzig. Gave f.p. of Tchaikovsky vn. conc., Vienna, 1881. From 1890 to 1894 was leader of NYSO. Leader of Hallé Orch., Manchester, 1895, but on Hallé's death in Oct. 1895 succeeded him as Prin., RMCM, holding this post until 1929. Brodsky Qt. concerts were notable feature of Eng. mus. life; Elgar ded. his str. qt. in E minor to the Brodsky team. Among many famous Brodsky pupils was Arthur *Catterall.

broken cadence. Interrupted *cadence.

broken chord. A chord in which the notes are played one after the other, or a group followed by another group, instead of simultaneously.

broken consort or broken music. A consort which contained both str. and woodwind instr., as opposed to a *whole consort* (all str. or all woodwind).

Broken Melody. Comp. for vc. by A. van *Biene.

broken octave. See *short octave* and *broken octave*.

Bronfman, Yefim (*b* Tashkent, 1958). Russ.-born pianist. Début with Israel PO, 1974. Appeared with most of the leading Amer. orchs. London début 1981.

Bronsart [Bronsart von Schellendorff], **Hans** (*b* Berlin, 1830; *d* Munich, 1913). Ger. pianist, composer, and opera administrator. Toured as pianist, then became Intendant, Hanover Opera 1867–87, Weimar 1887–95. Comp. pf. conc. played by *Bülow and other pf. and orch. works and chamber mus.

Bronze Horse, The (*Le Cheval de bronze*). Opera by Auber to lib. by Scribe. F.p. Paris and London 1835, NY 1837.

Brook, Barry S(helley) (*b* NY, 1918; *d* NY, 1997). Amer. musicologist. Prof. of mus., Graduate Sch. and Univ. Center, City Univ. of NY 1967–89. From 1989 dir. of univ.'s Center for Mus. Research and Documentation. Also taught in Paris, Eastman Sch., Juilliard Sch., and Univ. of Adelaide. Authority on 17th and 18th cent. mus. and on mus. bibliography. Gen. ed. with others of complete works of Pergolesi (18 vols.).

Brook, Peter (Stephen Paul) (*b* London, 1925). Eng. producer. Produced Shakespeare at Stratford, 1945. Dir. of productions CG 1948–9, an appointment ended by the furore over his 1949 prod. of *Salome*. Prod. *Faust* NY Met 1953. His 1982 'compressed' vers. of *Carmen* in Paris—*The Tragedy of Carmen*—was controversially successful as was his similar treatment of *Pelléas et Mélisande*, 1993. CBE 1967.

Brook Green Suite. Suite for str. orch. and optional woodwind, by Holst. Comp. 1933.

Brosa, Antonio (*b* Canonja, Sp., 1894; *d* Barcelona, 1979). Sp. violinist. Début Barcelona 1904. Settled in Eng., 1914. Founded Brosa Qt. 1924 (disbanded 1938). Soloist début, London 1926. In USA 1940–6. Gave f.p. of *Britten's Vn. Conc., NY 1940. Taught at RCM.

Brott, Alexander (*b* Montreal, 1915; *d* Montreal, 2005). Canadian violinist, conductor, and composer. Leader, McGill Qt., Les Concerts Symphoniques, etc. Comps. incl. vn. conc. (1950), symphonic suite *From Sea to Sea* (1947), symphonic poems, and chamber mus.

Brott, Boris (*b* Montreal, 1944). Canadian conductor. Son of Alexander *Brott. Début as violinist, Montreal 1949, as cond. Mexico 1958. Ass. cond. Toronto SO 1963–5; cond. Northern Sinfonia, Newcastle, 1964–8; mus. dir. and cond., Lakehead SO, 1968–72; BBC Welsh SO 1972–9; cond. Hamilton (Ontario) PO 1969–90.

Broucek, The Excursions of Mr (Janáček). See *Excursions of Mr Brouček, The*.

Brouwenstijn, Gré (Gerarda Benthina van Swol-Brouwenstijn) (*b* Den Helder, 1915; *d* Amsterdam, 1999). Dutch soprano. Début Amsterdam 1940, joined Netherlands Opera 1946 (début as Tosca). Sang title-role in *Jenůfa* in Eng. for BBC perf., 1951. CG début 1951; Bayreuth 1954–6; Glyndebourne 1959. Sang Elisabeth (*Don Carlos*), CG 1958. A distinguished Leonore (*Fidelio*). Retired from stage 1971.

Brouwer, Leo (*b* Havana, 1939). Cuban composer and guitarist. Taught harmony, counterpoint, and comp., Nat. Cons., Havana, 1961–7. Dir., experimental dept. of Cuban film industry since 1969. Comps. influenced by *Xenakis, *Nono, and *Henze. His *Sonograma I* was first mus. by Cuban to use *indeterminacy. Has written over 40 film scores, works for solo guitar, 3 guitar conc. (1972–86), and elec. comp. *Homenaje a Lenin*.

Brown, Christopher (Roland) (*b* Tunbridge Wells, 1943). Eng. composer. On staff RAM from 1969. Early works were mainly religious, but increasingly has developed impressive command of instr. style. Works incl.:

OPERA: *The Ram King*, for children (1982).

ORCH.: *The Sun Rising: Threnody* (1976); *Triptych* (1978); *Sonata for Strings* (1974); *Sinfonia* (1971); org. conc. (1979); *Festival Variations*, str. (1981); *Into the Sun*, str. (1984).

VOICE(S) & ORCH.: *Soliloquy* (1976); *David*, cantata for bar. soloists, ch., and orch. (1970); *3 Mediaeval Lyrics*, sop., ten., ch., and orch. (1973, rev. 1979); *The Snows of Winter* for vv. and chamber ens. (1971); *Chauntecleer*, sop., ten., bar., ch., and orch. (1980); *Magnificat*, SATB soloists, ch., orch. (1980); *Magnificat*, SATB soloists, ch., orch. (1981); *The Vision of Saul*, sop., alto/counterten., ten., bar., ch., orch. (1983); *Tres Cantus Sacri*, ch. and chamber orch. (1984); *Fair and Feast*, bar., ch., orch. (1986); *Landscapes*, sop., ch., orch. (1987); *The Circling Year*, SATB, ch., orch. (1989).

CHORAL (unaccompanied): *Hymn to the Holy Innocents*, chamber cantata (1965); *Aubade* (1968); *Gloria* (1968); *Laus Creatorum* (1969); *4 Motets* (1970); *3 Mediaeval Carols* (1969–73); *Hodie Salvator Apparuit* (1970); *Oundle Jubilate* (1972); *Even Such is Time* (1977); *I sing of a maiden* (1983); *From the Doorways of the Dawn* (1985).

CHAMBER MUSIC: *Chamber Music*, cl., hn., vn., vc., pf. (1974, rev. 1979); str. qt. No.2 (1975); trio, fl., bn., pf. (1975); *All Year Round*, ten., gui. (1976); *Festival Variations*, str. qt. (1981); *Into the Sun*, str. (1984); *Images*, brass quintet (1987).

Brown, David (Clifford) (*b* Gravesend, 1929). Eng. writer and scholar. Schoolteacher 1954–9, mus. librarian London Univ. 1959–62. On staff Southampton Univ. 1962–89 (prof. of musicology from 1983). Author of 4-vol. biog. of Tchaikovsky (Vol.I 1978, II 1982, III 1986, IV 1991) and biographies of Weelkes (1969), Glinka (1974), Wilbye (1974), and Mussorgsky (2002).

Brown, Earle (*b* Lunenburg, Mass., 1926; *d* Rye, NY, 2002). Amer. composer. Studied at Schillinger House Sch. of Mus., Boston, 1946–50. Worked with *Cage in NY 1952–5 on project for mus. for magnetic tape. Influenced by visual arts, esp. sculpture of Calder and paintings of Pollock. His *25 Pages* (1953) for 1–25 pf. uses *open form and space-time notation, e.g. pitches and durations are specified but, clefs being absent, the pages can be played either way up. On faculty Cologne Cons. 1966. His *Available Forms I* was commissioned by Darmstadt, 1961, and *Available Forms II* (1962) by Rome Radio Orch. Other works:

ORCH.: *Modules 1 and 2* (1966); *Module 3* (1969); *Time Spans* (1972); *Cross Sections and Color Fields* (1973–5); *Sounder Rounds* (1982).

CHORAL: *From Here* (1963); *New Piece: Loops* (1972).

INSTR. ENS.: *Novara* (1962); *Times Five* (1963); *Event – Synergy II* (1967–8); *Syntagm III* (1970); *Sign Sounds* (1972); *Centering* (1973); *Transients* (1976); *Tracer* (1984).

CHAMBER MUSIC: *Music*, vn., vc., pf. (1952); *Corroboree*, 3 or 2 pf. (1964); str. qt. (1965).

Brown, Howard Mayer (*b* Los Angeles, 1930; *d* Venice, 1993). Amer. musicologist. While a student at Harvard cond. and perf. both early and 20th cent. mus. in Boston and Cambridge. Instructor at Wellesley Coll. 1958–60. On staff Chicago Univ. 1960–72. Prof. of mus., King's Coll., London Univ., 1972–4. Returned to Chicago 1974. Founded Collegium Musicum at Chicago with which he perf. and recorded medieval and Renaissance works. Authority on Burgundian composers and 15th and 16th cent. *chansons*, period instr., and performing practice.

Brown, Iona (*b* Salisbury, 1941; *d* Bowerchalke, Wilts., 2004). Eng. violinist and conductor. Violinist in LPO 1963–6. Violinist/dir. with Academy

of St Martin-in-the-Fields from 1974; art. dir. Norwegian Chamber Orch. from 1981; art. dir. Los Angeles Chamber Orch. from 1987.

Brown, Maurice John Edwin (*b* London, 1906; *d* Marlborough, 1975). English writer on music. Authority on Schubert, writing critical biog. (1958, rev. 1977, Ger. trans. 1969) and collab. on research with O. E. Deutsch. Also wrote *Essays on Schubert* (1966), *Schubert Songs* (1967), and *Schubert Symphonies* (1970). Compiled thematic index of Chopin's comps. (1960).

Browne, (William Charles) **Denis** (*b* Leamington Spa, 1888; *d* Achi Baba, Turkey, death in action, 1915). Eng. composer and critic. Wrote mus. criticism for *The Times*, 1913–14, and *New Statesman*, 1914. His works incl. a ballet *The Comic Spirit; God is Our Strength*, unacc. ch. (1912); 2 Tennyson settings (*Move Eastward, Happy Earth* and *The Snowdrop*) (*c.*1909); and the songs *Diaphenia* (H. Constable) (1912), *Epitaph on Salathiel Pavy* (Jonson) (1913), *To Gratiana Dancing and Singing* (Lovelace) (1912–14), and *Arabia* (de la Mare) (1914).

Browne, John (*fl.c.*1490). Eng. composer. Eton Choirbook contained 11 antiphons and 4 Magnificats attrib. to him, of which 9 antiphons and part of a Magnificat remain. His six-voice setting of *Stabat Mater* is highly esteemed.

Browning, John (*b* Denver, Col., 1933; *d* Sister Bay, Wisc., 2003). Amer. pianist. Début Denver 1943. Won Leventritt Award 1955. Queen Elizabeth Int. Comp. Prize, 1956. Début with NYPO 1956. Gave f.p. of Barber's pf. conc., Boston, 1962. Soloist with world's leading orchs.

Brownlee, John (Donald Mackenzie) (*b* Geelong, 1901; *d* NY, 1969). Australian baritone. Début Paris 1926. CG début as Marcello in *La bohème* (sang in last two acts only) on night of *Melba's farewell, 8 June 1926; Paris Opéra, 1927–36; Glyndebourne 1935–9 (a famous Don Giovanni); NY Met 1937–56. On staff, Manhattan Sch. of Mus., NY, from 1953, dir. from 1956, pres. 1966–9.

Bruch, Max (*b* Cologne, 1838; *d* Friedenau, 1920). Ger. composer and conductor. Studied in Cologne with F. *Hiller and *Reinecke, returning as teacher 1858–61. Cond. of various concert organizations in Berlin and Bonn and of Liverpool Phil. Soc. 1880–3 (an unhappy period). Dir. Orchesterverein, Breslau, 1883–90, prof. of comp. Berlin Hochschule 1892–1910, among his pupils for a brief period being *Vaughan Williams. Cond. Scottish Orch. 1898–1900. His comps. incl. 3 operas: *Scherz, List ind Rache* (Cologne 1858), *Die Loreley* (1862, rev. 1887, f.p. Mannheim 1863), and *Hermione* (Berlin 1872), based on Shakespeare's *The Winter's Tale*; 3 syms. (1870, 1870, 1887); many choral works (by which he was best known in Ger.), incl. *Odysseus* (1872), *Das Lied von der Glocke* (1879), *Achilleus* (1885), and *Das Feuerkreuz* (after Scott's *The Lady of the Lake*) (1889); 3 vn. concs. (No.1 in G minor, 1868, No.2 in D minor, 1878, No.3 in D minor, 1891); *Scottish

Fantasy, vn., orch. (1880); **Kol Nidrei*, vc., orch. (1881); *Adagio appassionato*, vn., orch. (1891); conc., cl., vn. (1911); *Fantasy*, 2 pf., orch. (1860); conc., 2 pf. (1912); *Septet* (1849–50); 2 str. qts. (1859, 1860); str. quintet in A minor (1919); *Klavierstücke* (1860–1).

Bruckner, (Joseph) **Anton** (*b* Ansfelden, Linz, 1824; *d* Vienna, 1896). Austrian composer and organist. Son of village schoolmaster, showed precocious mus. talent but had no expert teaching until aged 11. Was choirboy at St Florian's monastery, 1837–40, and in 1840 began training in Linz as a schoolmaster, mus. remaining an absorbing sideline. Persisted with org. studies and became a virtuoso of the instr., especially in art of improvisation. In 1845 returned to St Florian as ass. teacher, but continued his mus. studies. In 1848 became 'provisional' organist. For some years had been composing org. and choral mus., but 1849 saw the first recognizably Brucknerian work, the *Requiem* in D minor. In 1851 became official organist of St Florian and in 1855 was appointed organist of Linz Cath. Also in 1855 decided to study harmony and counterpoint with Simon *Sechter in Vienna, lessons which continued until 1861. In 1862 studied orchestration in Linz with Otto Kitzler, cellist and cond., who also introduced him to Wagner's mus. From this period, 1863–9, came 3 Masses and 3 syms. In 1868 moved to Vienna, where he was to live for the next 28 years, to succeed Sechter as prof. of harmony and counterpoint at the Cons.

Continued in demand as an improviser on the org., visiting Paris in 1869 to play in Notre Dame and London in 1871 to play at the new Royal Albert Hall. In 1865 first met Wagner in Munich at the première of *Tristan* and their friendship grew. The 3rd sym. of 1873 was ded. to Wagner. Though this was a matter of personal delight to Bruckner, it made him the butt of Viennese mus. politics at the period of great hostility between the supporters of Brahms and of Wagner and ensured him the critical hostility of *Hanslick. In 1875 became lecturer in harmony and counterpoint at Vienna Univ. During 1871–6 wrote syms. Nos. 2–5, following this with a 3-year spell of rev. F.p. of 3rd sym. in 1877 was fiasco. From 1879 to 1887 worked on syms. Nos. 6–8 and *Te Deum*. F.p. of No.4 in 1881 was first considerable success with Viennese public. In 1883, while working on the Adagio of sym. No.7, heard of Wagner's death: he referred to the coda of that movement as 'funeral music for the Master'. Success of the first 2 perfs. of No.7 under *Nikisch (1884) and *Levi (1885) launched int. recognition, but Bruckner received severe blow in 1887 when Levi rejected score of No.8 with several bitter criticisms. Began another period of rev. with the advice of friends, and the 8th sym. was not played until 1892 when, under *Richter, it had a triumphant reception.

In the last 5 years of his life Bruckner enjoyed greater financial reward than before and received several state and university honours. But his health deteriorated and he worked on his 9th (actually 11th) sym. from 1891 until the day he died (11 Oct. 1896), leaving the finale in a more complete form than was at first realized.

Bruckner's personal character has for too long been misrepresented as boorish and simple-minded. He did have a child-like religious faith, which lies at the root of all his mus., and a becoming modesty. But the composer of those superbly organized and complex syms., most of them over an hour in duration, was no simpleton. He was a late starter as a composer because of his determination to master his technique, and recognition only came late in his lifetime. The 'Wagnerian' tag on his syms. led to their being regarded as elephantine monsters, but they are now widely recognized as being in the Austrian tradition of Schubert's last sym. and are admired for their combination of contrapuntal splendour with intense melodic beauty and grandeur (but not extravagance) of orchestration. His Masses, also on a symphonic scale, are equally splendid, and in all his mature church mus. there is the radiance of a devout believer and the technical dexterity of a composer whose mastery of vocal polyphony stemmed from intimate study of Palestrina and his sch.

A peculiarly complex problem exists over the various versions of Bruckner's syms. caused by his proclivity for revisions, often at the behest of well-meaning friends who urged him to cut and reorchestrate works in order to have them perf. and pubd. Since 1934, first under the editorship of Robert *Haas and later of Leopold *Nowak, the Int. Bruckner Soc. has pubd. the 'original' edns. of the syms. Even here confusion arises because there are discrepancies in some of the syms. ed. by both Haas and Nowak. The general tendency today is to return to Bruckner's first thoughts. For this reason the list of the syms. is in some detail:

SYMPHONIES: sym. in F minor. Comp. 1863.

Symphony in D minor (designated by Bruckner as 'No.0'). Comp. 1863–4, rev. 1869 (some authorities insist 'comp. 1869'). F.p. Klosterneuburg, 12 Oct. 1924. Publication: Ed. Nowak 1968.

No.1 in C minor. Comp. 1865–6, rev. 1868, 1877, 1884 (foregoing known as 'Linz Version'). Major rev. ('Vienna version') 1890–1. F.p. 9 May 1868 Linz, cond. Bruckner; 13 Dec. 1891 Vienna, cond. Richter. Publication: 1893 (Eberle); Linz and Vienna versions ed. Haas 1934, Linz version ed. Nowak 1953. (Nowak ed. mainly corrects misprints.)

No.2 in C minor. Comp. 1871–2, rev. 1873; 1876–7 version 2 (cuts and alteration). F.p. 26 Oct. 1873, Vienna, cond. Bruckner; version 2, 20 Feb. 1876, Vienna, cond. Bruckner. Publication: 1892 (Eberle), ed. Haas 1938, version 2 ed. Nowak 1965. Haas ed. restores many of Bruckner's 1876–7 cuts.

No.3 in D minor. Comp. 1873, rev. 1874; thorough rev. (excising several Wagner quotations) 1876–7 (version 2). Another thorough rev. (version 3)

1888–9. F.p. 16 Dec. 1877 (version 2) Vienna, cond. Bruckner; 21 Dec. 1890 (version 3) Vienna, cond. Richter. F.ps. of 1873 version, 1 and 2 Dec. 1946, Dresden, cond. Keilberth. Publication: 1878 (Rättig, version 2), 1890 (Rättig, version 3); ed. Nowak (version 3) 1959.

No.4 in E♭ major ('Romantic'). Comp. 1874 (version 1). Major rev. (new scherzo) 1878, new finale 1879–80, minor rev. 1881, 1886 (version 2); major cuts and alterations by F. *Löwe 1887–8 (version 3). F.p. 20 Feb. 1881, Vienna, cond. Richter (version 2); 22 Jan. 1888, Vienna, cond. Richter (version 3); f.p. version 1: 20 Sept. 1975, Linz, cond. Wöss (but scherzo alone was perf. 12 Dec. 1909, Linz, cond. A. Göllerich). Publication: 1896 (Doblinger); ed. Haas (version 2) 1936 and 1944; ed. Nowak (version 2) 1953.

No.5 in B♭ major. Comp. 1875–6, minor rev. 1877–8. F.p. 8 April 1894, Graz, cond. F. *Schalk (spurious version by Schalk); orig. version 20 Oct. 1935, Munich, cond. Hausegger. Publication: 1899 (Doblinger); ed. Haas 1936, ed. Nowak 1951 (little discrepancy).

No.6 in A major. Comp. 1879–81. F.p. 11 Feb. 1883, Vienna, cond. Jahn (2nd and 3rd movements only); 26 Feb. 1899, Vienna, cond. Mahler (with severe cuts); 14 March 1901, Stuttgart, cond. Pohlig (complete). Publication: 1899 (Doblinger); ed. Haas 1936, ed. Nowak 1952 (minor discrepancies).

No.7 in E major. Comp. 1881–3. F.p. 30 Dec. 1884, Leipzig, cond. Nikisch. Publication: 1885 (Gutmann); ed. Haas 1944, ed. Nowak 1954. (Discrepancies affect dynamic and tempo markings, deleted by Haas, restored as 'authentic' by Nowak.)

No.8 in C minor. Comp. 1884–7 (version 1). Thorough revision, inc. rev. coda of 1st movement, new trio, major cuts and changes of scoring, 1889–90 (version 2). F.p. 18 Dec. 1892, Vienna, cond. Richter (version 2). F.p. (version 1) 2 Sept. 1973 (BBC broadcast), Bournemouth SO, cond. Schönzeler. Publication: 1892 (Lienau, version 2); ed. Haas 1935 (version 2), ed. Nowak 1955 (version 2). (Haas restores several cuts.)

No.9 in D minor. First 3 movements comp. 1891–4 (sketches from 1887), sketches for finale 1894–6. F.p. 11 Feb. 1903, Vienna, cond. Löwe (in spurious Löwe version), 2 April 1932, Munich, cond. Hausegger (orig.). Publication: 1903 (Universal); ed. Orel 1934, ed. Nowak 1951 (almost identical). Completion of finale in version prepared (1979–83) by William Carragan, prof. of physics at Hudson Valley Community Coll., Troy, NY, perf. by American SO cond. Moshe Atzmon, 8 Jan. 1984. (In 1979 Carragan, assisted by Paul Nudelman, made pf. score of finale based on Orel's unreliable edn. of sketches but with coda added. This was perf. in NY 1979.)

OTHER ORCH. WORKS: *Overture* in G minor (1863); 4 *Orchestral Pieces* (1862).

CHORAL: Masses, No.1 in D minor (1864, rev. 1876, 1881–2); No.2 in E minor (wind band acc.) (1866, rev. 1869, 1876, 1882); No.3 in F minor (1867–8, rev. 1876–7, 1881, 1890–3); *Te Deum* (ch. and orch.) (1881–4); Mass in F (1844); *Requiem* in D minor (1849); *Missa solemnis* in B♭ (1854); *Ave Maria*, ch., org. (1856); *Ave Maria*, unacc. ch. (1861); *Pange lingua* (1868); *Abendzauber* (1878); *Os justi* (1879); *Ave Maria*, mez., org. (1882); *Vexilla Regis* (1892); *Germanenzug*, male ch., brass band (1863); *Helgoland*, male ch., orch. (1893).

CHAMBER: str. quintet in F major (1879); *Intermezzo*, str. quintet (1879).

KEYBOARD: *Prelude and Fugue* in C minor, org. (1847); *3 Pieces*, pf. duet (1852–4); *Klavierstuck* in E♭, pf. (c.1856); *Erinnerung*, pf. (1868); *Fantasy* in G major, pf. (1868); *Prelude* in C, org. (1884).

Brueggen, Frans (b Amsterdam, 1934). Dutch virtuoso of the flute and recorder, also conductor. Prof. of recorder and transverse fl., Hague Royal Cons. Visiting prof., Univ. of Calif., 1974. Pioneer of perf. on period instr. Formed *avant-garde* ens. Sourcream, and commissioned many works, incl. Berio's *Gesti* (1966). Has cond. Orchestra of the Age of Enlightenment. Cond. *Idomeneo* (Amsterdam 1992).

Bruhns, Nikolaus (b Schwabstedt, Schleswig, 1665; d Husum, 1697). Ger. organist and composer. Wrote choral works and org. pieces. In his 4 small-scale sacred concs. he raised It.-style solo cantatas to a new level of virtuosity.

Brüll, Ignaz (b Prossnitz, Moravia, 1846; d Vienna, 1907). Austrian pianist and composer. Close friend of Brahms. Taught at Horák pf. school, Vienna, 1872–8. Visited London 1878, playing at 20 concerts. Comp. sym., 2 pf. concs., vn. conc., sonata for 2 pf., and 10 operas, of which best known is *Das goldene Kreuz* (Berlin 1875, London 1881).

Brumby, Colin (James) (b Melbourne, 1933). Australian composer. On staff, Univ. of Queensland from 1964. Comp. opera *The Seven Deadly Sins* (1970) and several operettas for schoolchildren. Formed Queensland Opera co. to perf. for children. Orch. works incl. vn. conc. Many sacred choral works.

Brumel, Antoine (b c.1460; d c.1520). French composer. Singer at Notre Dame, Chartres, from 1483. Master of Innocents, St Peter's, Geneva, 1486–92. Became a priest and in 1497 was canon at Laon Cath. In charge of mus. training of choirboys at Notre Dame, Paris, 1498–1500. Singer, Chambéry 1501–2. Choirmaster at Ferrara, 1506–10. Wrote mainly sacred mus., incl. 15 masses and many motets. Regarded, after Desprès, as among most eminent of 15th and early 16th cent. composers.

Bruneau, (Louis Charles Bonaventure) **Alfred** (b Paris, 1857; d Paris, 1934). Fr. composer and critic. His 2nd opera *Le Rêve* (1890), in 4 acts based on Zola, was a success at the Opéra-Comique in 1891, being regarded as very 'advanced' harmonically. Followed by *L'Attaque du moulin* (1892–3) in which Zola collab. directly as librettist, as he did for *Messidor* (1894–6), *L'Ouragan*

(1897–1900), and *L'Enfant-Roi* (1902). Comp. 13 operas, several employing Wagnerian principles, also ballet, orch. works, and songs. Worked as mus. critic and wrote several books, incl. studies of Fauré (1925) and Massenet (1935), and some reminiscences of Zola (1932).

Brunelle, Philip (Charles) (*b* Faribault, Minn., 1943). Amer. conductor. Mus. dir., Minnesota Opera 1968–85. Founder and mus. dir. Plymouth Music Series from 1969. Has cond. Minnesota Orch. and Pittsburgh SO and opera at Drottningholm, Washington DC, S. Francisco, and Houston. Aldeburgh Fest. 1989 and 1990. Cond. first complete recording of Britten's *Paul Bunyan*.

Brunskill, Muriel (*b* Kendal, Cumbria, 1900; *d* Bishops Tawton, Devon, 1980). Eng. contralto. Début London 1920. In BNOC 1922–7. Noted for singing in choral works of Handel, Mendelssohn, and Elgar. One of orig. 16 soloists in **Serenade to Music* (1938). Late in career sang frequently in Gilbert and Sullivan operas.

Brunswick, Mark (*b* NY, 1902; *d* London, 1971). Amer. composer. Prof. of Mus., City College of NY, 1946–67. Comps. incl. syms., chamber mus., and unfinished opera *The Master Builder* (Ibsen).

Bruscantini, Sesto (*b* Porto Civitanova, Macerata, 1919; *d* Rome, 2003). It. baritone. Début Civitanova 1946. La Scala 1949; Glyndebourne début 1951, appearing regularly until 1956 in leading Mozart and Rossini roles, returning in 1960. Salzburg Fest. début 1952. Sang Falstaff with Scottish Opera, Glasgow 1976. Amer. début Chicago 1961. Produced Verdi's *Un giorno di regno*, Wexford 1981. Sang at Macerata Fest. 1990 (Don Alfonso).

brushes, wire. Used to produce particular effect from snare drum, cymbals, etc., esp. in jazz.

Bruson, Renato (*b* Este, nr. Padua, 1936). It. baritone. Opera début Spoleto 1961. La Scala début 1972, NY Met 1969. Brit. début Edinburgh Fest. 1972. CG 1976. Outstanding Falstaff in Giulini-Eyre prod. for S. Francisco 1982.

Brustwerk (Ger.). Small organ-chest, usually with own manual, encased above keyboards and below *Hauptwerk* in 'breast' of the organ.

Bryars, (Richard) **Gavin** (*b* Goole, 1943). Eng. composer. Played in jazz groups in 1960s. Joined group of leading experimental Eng. composers who were influenced by Cage, Satie, and others. Lect. in mus., Leicester Polytechnic 1970–85, prof. from 1985. Works incl. *Medea*, opera (1982–4); 3 str. qts. (1985, 1990, 1998); *The Black River*, sop., org. (1991); *The Green Ray*, sax., orch. (1991); *The East Coast*, bass ob., chamber orch. (1994); *Dr Ox's Experiment*, opera (1997); *Planet Earth*, cont., instr. ens. (1998); *A Time and Place*, org. (1999); vn. conc. (*The Bulls of Bashan*), vn., str. (2000); *Marconi's Madrigal*, sop., ten. (2001); *Psalm 83*, mixed ch. (2003); *Creamer Etudes*, ww., perc., pf. (2005); and various works employing *indeterminacy.

Brydon, Roderick (*b* Edinburgh, 1939). Scot. conductor. Staff cond. SW 1963–9. Assoc. cond. SNO 1965–7. Scottish Opera début 1965, staff cond. 1966–70. Art. dir. and chief cond. SCO, 1974–83; mus. dir., Opera Sch., RSAMD, 1979–84; gen. mus. dir. Lucerne Opera 1984–7; mus. dir. Berne Opera 1988–90. CG début 1984; Los Angeles 1990.

Brymer, Jack (*b* South Shields, 1915; *d* Oxted, 2003). Eng. clarinettist. Began as schoolmaster. Prin. cl. RPO 1947–63, BBC SO 1963–71, LSO 1971–87. Soloist and chamber mus. player. Prof. RAM 1950–9. Popular broadcaster. OBE 1960.

Bryn-Jones, Delme (*b* Brynamman, Wales, 1935; *d* Towy Valley, 2001). Welsh baritone. Début with New Opera Co. 1959. Début Glyndebourne 1963, CG 1963, WNO 1963, S. Francisco 1967.

Bryn-Julson, Phyllis (Mae) (*b* Bowdon, N. Dakota, 1945). Amer. soprano of Norweg. parentage. Début with Boston SO Oct. 1966, in Berg's *Lulu-Symphonie*. Eng. début, London 1975 (Boulez's *Pli selon pli*). Sang in Amer. f.p. of *Sessions opera *Montezuma* (Boston 1976). Made reputation in contemp. mus. because of her perfect pitch, range of 3 octaves, and ability to sing accurately in quarter-tones.

Bucchi, Valentino (*b* Florence, 1916; *d* Rome, 1976). It. composer. Dir., Perugia Cons. 1957–74, Florence Cons. from 1974. Also worked as critic. Comp. operas, ballets, syms., and religious choral mus.

buccina. Roman wind instr., made of metal, varying from 8′ to 12′ long. Its notes were of the natural or 'bugle' scale.

Buchbinder, Rudolf (*b* Leitmeritz, 1946). Austrian pianist. London début 1962. Toured N. and S. Amer. 1965. Won special prize, Van Cliburn comp. 1966. Salzburg Fest. début 1971. Teacher at Basle Acad. of Mus. Frequent performer in chamber mus. and with early instrs.

Buch der hängenden Gärten, Das (The Book of the Hanging Gardens). Settings for solo v. and pf. by Schoenberg of 15 poems by Stefan George (Op.15; 1908). F.p. Vienna, Jan. 1910.

Buchner, Hans ('Hans von Constanz') (*b* Ravensburg, Württemberg, 1483; *d* 1538). Ger. organist and composer for his instr. Org., Konstanz Cath. 1506–26, Überlingen from 1526. Was also organ-builder. His *Fundamentum*, *c.*1520, deals with art and technique of org.-building and incl. many of his own comps. as mus. examples.

Buckley, Richard (Edward) (*b* NY, 1953). Amer. conductor. Ass. cond. and chorusmaster Washington DC Opera Soc., 1973–4, assoc. cond. Seattle Opera 1974–5, Seattle SO 1974–84. Mus. dir. Oakland SO 1983–6. Cond. f. Amer. p. of Sallinen's *The King Goes Forth to France*, Santa Fe 1986. CG début 1992.

Budapest Quartet. Hung. string quartet founded 1917 by players from Budapest Opera

Orch. (Emil Hauser, Alfred Indig (succeeded 1920 by Imre Pogány), Istvan Ipolyi, and Harry Son). First played in London 1925. By 1936 membership was Russ. and Ukrainian (1st vn. Joseph Roisman). Under Roisman, quartet became noted for brilliance of style and made many recordings. Settled in USA 1938. Recorded all Beethoven's quartets three times. Last public appearance 1967.

Budden, Julian (Midforth) (*b* Hoylake, 1924). Eng. writer, administrator, and musicologist. BBC mus. producer 1956, chief prod. of opera 1970–6, mus. organizer, external services from 1976. Retired 1983. Wrote *The Operas of Verdi*, Vol.I 1973, II 1978, III 1981, and *Verdi* (1984) in *Master Musicians* series. OBE 1991.

buffa, buffo (It.). Gust, Puff. The term has come to mean comic, thus *basso buffo*, comic bass in opera. *opera buffa*, comic opera, is opposite of *opera seria*.

buffet d'orgue. (Fr.). Organ case.

Buffoon, The (*Prokofiev*). See *Chout*.

bugle. Valveless brass or copper instr. of treble pitch, with wide tube of conical bore, moderate-sized bell, and cup-shaped mouthpiece. Notes are merely a few of those of the harmonic series, normally in B♭, and it is mainly a means of military signalling or (in bugle bands) simple acc. of marching.

bugle à clefs. *Key (Keyed) Bugle.

Bühnenfestspiel, Bühnenweihfestspiel. Wagner's Ger. terms respectively for (a) *Der Ring des Nibelungen*, a 'stage-festival-play', and (b) *Parsifal*, a 'stage-consecrating festival-play'.

Bühnenmusik (Ger. 'stage music'). Term denoting mus. played on stage during an opera, or incid. mus. for plays.

buisine (Fr. corruption of Lat. *buccina*). Medieval straight tpt. over 6′ long, made in jointed sections often with flared bell.

Bull, John (*b* ?Old Radnor, *c*.1562; *d* Antwerp, 1628). Eng. composer and virginalist. In Hereford Cath. choir 1573. Choirboy in Queen Elizabeth I's Chapel Royal from 1574. Org., Hereford Cath. 1582–5, Gentleman of Chapel Royal 1586; D.Mus., Oxford and Cambridge, and first Gresham Public Reader in Mus., London 1597. Granted pension by James I in 1605. Active as org.-builder 1609. In 1613, accused of adultery and fornication, he fled from Eng. to Belg., becoming organist, Chapel Royal, Brussels, and of Antwerp Cath., 1615 until his death. Friend of *Sweelinck.

His importance is as a highly skilled performer on and ingenious composer for the virginals, as in his *Walsingham* (30 vars. on a theme). He ranks as one of the founders of kbd. perf. and the kbd. repertory. He contributed to *Parthenia*, 1611. One of his comps. is called *God Save the King*

but bears no resemblance to the nat. anthem; however, another untitled piece by Bull is a possible source of this melody.

Bull, Ole (Bornemann) (*b* Bergen, Norway, 1810; *d* Lysøen, Bergen, 1880). Norweg. violinist and composer. Taught by local musicians in Bergen. Went to Christiania 1828 to study theology, but failed exam. Became cond. of theatre orch. In 1831 met peasant fiddler who taught him *slåtter* (folk-dances). Went to Paris 1831, taking Hardanger fiddle (Norwegian peasant vn.). In Milan developed new method of holding vn. and made its bridge flatter and the bow longer and heavier. Created sensation with one of his concs. in Bologna, 1833. Thereafter, in emulation of Paganini, toured widely as virtuoso recitalist, having immense success in Paris, London and America. Convinced patriot, frequently played Scandinavian melodies, earning large sums and founding in USA in 1852 a Norweg. colony and in the capital of his own country a mus. conservatory (both of which schemes proved abortive). Wrote 2 vn. concs. Helped establish a nat. theatre in Bergen and to initiate careers of Ibsen, Bjørnson, and Grieg.

Buller, John (*b* London, 1927; *d* Sherborne, Dorset, 2004). Eng. composer. Worked as architectural surveyor until 1959. Came to notice in 1970s with series of works based on James Joyce's *Finnegans Wake*, incl. *2 Night Pieces* for sop., fl., cl., pf., vc. (1971) and *Finnegan's Floras* for, ch., perc., pf. (1972). Also opera *Bakxai* (1991–2) and works for various instr. ens.

Bullock, (Sir) **Ernest** (*b* Wigan, 1890; *d* Aylesbury, 1979). Eng. organist and educator. Suborganist, Manchester Cath., 1912–15. Org., Exeter Cath. 1919–27, Westminster Abbey 1928–41. Prin., RSAMD, and prof. of mus., Glasgow Univ. 1941–52; dir., RCM 1953–60. Comp. org. mus. and songs. In charge of mus., Coronation of George VI, 1937. Knighted 1951.

Bullock, Susan (*b* Davenham, Cheshire, 1958). Eng. soprano. Studied RAM and Nat. Opera Studio. Won Decca Ferrier Prize 1984. Glyndebourne ch. 1983–4. Prof. début ENO 1986 (Pamina); sang Butterfly for ENO 1990. GTO 1994 (Jenůfa). Glyndebourne Fest. 1995 (Lisa in *Queen of Spades*). Amer. début 1996, Portland Opera (Butterfly). NY City Opera 2000 (Butterfly). Brussels 2000 (Elektra). Sang Isolde for Opera North, Leeds, 2000. First Brünnhilde in *Ring* Tokyo 2002. CG début 2005 (Marie in *Wozzeck*). London recital début 2005.

bull roarer. See *thunder stick*.

Bülow, Hans (Guido) Freiherr **von** (*b* Dresden, 1830; *d* Cairo, 1894). Ger. conductor, pianist, and composer. Became law student but abandoned it for mus. under influence of f.p. of Wagner's *Lohengrin* at Weimar. Went to Zurich for instruction from Wagner. Pf. pupil of Liszt, 1851. First concert tour of Ger., 1853. Prin. pf. prof., Stern-Marx Cons., Berlin, 1855–64, during which time developed conducting potentialities in addition to making many tours as concert pianist. Married Liszt's daughter Cosima, 1857. Chief cond., Munich Royal Opera, 1864, and there cond. f.p. of *Tristan und Isolde* (1865) and *Die Meistersinger von Nürnberg* (1868) to the composer's immense satisfaction. In 1869 left Munich, partly because of Wagner's affair with Cosima; they were divorced the next year. (In 1882 he married Marie Schanzer, the actress.) First visit to London 1873, to USA 1875–6. Gave f.p. of Tchaikovsky's 1st pf. conc. (Boston, 25 Oct. 1875). In 1880 became court cond. to Duke of Meiningen and made the court orch. finest in Europe for disciplined playing. Resigned 1885, handing over to his protégé Richard *Strauss. Cond. Berlin PO 1887–93. In 1888 became cond. of opera and concerts in Hamburg. Comp. orch. and pf. works and pubd. edn. of Beethoven sonatas. Also ed. kbd. works of J. S. Bach, Chopin, D. Scarlatti, Weber, and others.

Bumbry, Grace (Melzia) (*b* St Louis, 1937). Amer. mezzo-soprano, later soprano. Début Paris Opéra 1960. Basle Opera 1960–3. Sang at Bayreuth 1961 (Venus in *Tannhäuser*), being first black singer to do so. NY début (Carnegie Hall) 1962; CG 1963; Salzburg 1964; NY Met 1965. Sang Cassandra in *Les Troyens* at opening of Opéra Bastille, Paris, 1990. Remarkable Carmen and Salome.

Bunting, Edward (*b* Armagh, 1773; *d* Dublin, 1843). Irish organist and pianist renowned for his coll. of over 300 Irish folk tunes, harp mus., etc., pubd. in 3 sections, 1796, 1809, and 1840.

buonaccordo (It.). Child's toy pf. or spinet.

Buonamente, Giovanni Battista (*b* Mantua, late 16th cent.; *d* Assisi, 1642). It. composer, choirmaster, violinist, and singer. Member of Franciscan order. Active at Gonzaga court in Mantua, possibly working under Monteverdi. Court. mus. in Vienna 1626–9. Singer and violinist in Bergamo 1631, Parma 1632. Choirmaster of Basilica of S. Francesco, Assisi, from 1633 (incapacitated by illness after 1635). One of first composers for vn., but several of his books of sonatas are lost. Also wrote over 160 sacred vocal works.

Buonamici, Giuseppe (*b* Florence, 1846; *d* Florence, 1914). It. pianist, studied Munich Cons. under Bülow, 1868–70. Prof. of pf., Istituto Musicale, Florence, from 1873. Ed. Beethoven sonatas and other classics.

Buononcini, Giovanni. See *Bononcini, Giovanni*.

Buonporti, F. A. See *Bonporti, Francesco Antonio*.

Burchuladze, Paata (*b* Tblisi, 1950). Georgian bass. Opera début Tblisi 1975. Won several comps. 1981–2. Brit. début, Lichfield 1983 (in Elgar's *Dream of Gerontius*). CG début 1984; Salzburg 1987; NY Met 1989.

burden, or burthen. (1) A recurring line after each stanza of a ballad, etc.
(2) Drone or bass of *bagpipe.

Burgess, Anthony [Wilson, John Burgess] (*b* Manchester, 1917; *d* London, 1993). Eng. novelist, essayist, and composer. Wrote 3 syms. (1937, 1956, 1975); Sinfonietta for jazz band (1941); vc. sonata (1944); 2 pf. sonatas (1945, 1951); gui. qt. (1961); pf. conc. (1976), etc. Novels incl. *A Clockwork Orange* (1962).

Burgess, Sally (*b* Durban, 1953). South African-born mezzo-soprano. Début (as sop.), Brahms's *Requiem* with Bach Choir, London 1976. Joined ENO as sop., 1977. Sang in the f. Brit. p. of Martinů's *Julietta* (New Opera Co., 1978). Changed to mez. roles 1983. Sang Nefertiti in Glass's *Akhnaten* 1985. CG début 1983, Glyndebourne 1983. An outstanding Julie La Verne in *Show Boat* (1990). Sang Fricka in Scottish Opera's *Die Walküre* (1991). Many concert appearances in oratorio, etc.

Burgmüller, Johann Friedrich (*b* Regensburg, 1806; *d* Beaulieu, Fr., 1874). Ger. composer remembered chiefly for his mus. for the ballet *La Péri* and for pf. studies for children. His father, Johann August Franz Burgmüller (1766–1824), founded the Lower Rhine Mus. Fest. in Düsseldorf in 1818.

Burgmüller, (August Joseph) **Norbert** (*b* Düsseldorf, 1810; *d* Aachen, 1836). Ger. composer and pianist. Son of J. A. F. Burgmüller and brother of J. F. *Burgmüller. Showed extreme gifts as child. Lived in poverty owing to unwillingness to pursue professional career, but was much admired by circle of artistic friends incl. Mendelssohn and Schumann. His Rhapsody in B minor for pf. and his str. qt. in A minor have been likened to Schubert. Also wrote sym. (another unfinished), pf. conc., and pf. sonatas.

Burgon, Geoffrey (*b* Hambledon, 1941). Eng. composer. Played tpt. in jazz groups and orchs. Original and imaginative user of all the influences and procedures at the disposal of the 20th-cent. composer. High reputation as composer of incid. music for television, e.g. *Brideshead Revisited* and *Tinker, Tailor, Soldier, Spy*. Works incl.:

OPERA & MUSIC THEATRE: *Epitaph for Sir Walter Raleigh* (1968); *Joan of Arc* (text by Susan Hill) (1970); *The Fall of Lucifer* (1977); *Mirandola* (1980–1); *Orpheus*, sop., ten., bar., bass, male ch., orch. (1982); *Macbeth* (1986); *Murder in the Cathedral* (1987); *Hard Times*, opera (1991); *Nicholas Nickleby* (2001).

BALLETS: *The Golden Fish* (1964); *Ophelia* (1964); *The Calm* (1974); *Running Figures/Goldberg's Dream* (1975); *Step at a Time* (1976); *Persephone* (1979); *Songs, Lamentations and Praises* (1979); *Chamber Dances* (1982); *Mass* (1984); *The Trial of Prometheus* (1988).

INCID. MUSIC.: *Blood Wedding* (Lorca) (1988).

ORCH.: conc. for str. (1963); 5 Pieces for Str. (1967); *Gending* (1968); *Alleluia Nativitas* (1970); *Cantus Alleluia* (1973); *Brideshead Variations* (1982); *The*

Chronicles of Narnia Suite, brass band (1991); tpt. conc. (*The Turning World*) (1993); *Suite from Martin Chuzzlewit*, wind, perc., str. (1994); pf. conc. (1997); *A Different Dawn*, cel., perc., str. (1999).

VOICE(S) AND ORCH.: *Acquainted with Night*, counterten., str., harp, perc. (1965); *Think on Dredful Domesday* (1969); *Magnificat* (1970); *The Golden Eternity* (1970); *Requiem*, sop., counterten., ten., ch., orch. (1976); *Veni Spiritus*, sop., bar., ch., and orch. (1978–9); *Magnificat and Nunc Dimittis*, 2 sop., tpt., org., str. (1979); *Hymn to St Thomas of Hereford*, ch., orch. (1981); *The World Again*, sop., orch. (1982–3); *Revelations*, sop., ten., bar., ch., orch. (1984); *Title Divine*, sop., orch. (1986); *A Vision*, ten., str. (1991); *Merciless Beauty*, counterten., orch. (1991); *3 Mysteries*, 6 soloists, ch., orch. (2003).

VOICE(S) & PIANO or ENSEMBLE: *Cantata on Mediaeval Latin Texts*, counterten., fl., ob., bn. (1964); *Hymn to Venus*, mez. and pf. (1966); *5 Sonnets of Donne*, sop., mez., fl., ob., cl., hn., pf., timp., vc. (1967); *Songs of Mary*, mez., va., pf. (1970); *At the Round Earth's Imagined Corners*, sop., tpt., org. (1971); *Worldës Blissë*, counterten. and ob. (1971); *Threnody*, ten., pf., hpd. (1971); *This Endris Night*, ten., female vv., brass (1972); *Dira vi amores terror*, counterten. (1973); *Canciones del Alma*, 2 counterten. and 13 solo str. (1975); *The Fall of Lucifer*, ten., bar., counterten., ch., and ens. (1977); *Lunar Beauty*, counterten., lute (1986); *Nearing the Upper Air*, counterten., rec., vc., hpd. (1988); *Heavenly Things*, bar., pf. (2001); *At Trafalgar*, bar., pf. (2005).

CHORAL: *3 Elegies* (1964); *Short Mass* (1965); *Farewell Earth's Bliss*, 6 solo vv. (1966); *5 Allelluias*, 6 solo vv. (or brass) (1970); *A Prayer to the Trinity* (1972); *The Fire of Heaven*, triple ch. (1973); *Dos Coros*, 12 solo vv. (1975); *But Have Been Found Again*, sop., alt., ch. (1983); *The Names of the Hare*, ch. (1985); *The Song of the Creatures*, ch., org. (1987); *Prayer to St Richard*, ch. (1989); *Songs of the Creation*, ch., org. (1989); *Christ's Love*, mixed ch. (2000); *Magic Words*, ch. (2000); *Te Deum*, soloists, ch., org. (2002); *Death Be Not Proud*, soloists, ch., org./tpt. (2005).

CHAMBER MUSIC: ob. qt. (1980); *Sanctus Variations*, 2 tpts., org. (1980); *Chamber Dances* (1981–2); *Little Missenden Variations*, cl., ca., hn., bn. (1984); *The Wanderer*, str. qt., cl. (1998); str. qt. (*Dancers in a Landscape*) (1999).

Burian, Emil František (*b* Pilsen, 1904; *d* Prague, 1959). Cz. composer and actor. Founded Voice Band, 1927. In 1932 formed left-wing cultural group Levá Fronta. Sometime dir., Brno Nat. Th. Comps. incl. operas, jazz opera, 8 str. qts., wind quintet, etc. Nephew of Karel *Burian.

Burian, Karel [Burrian, Carl] (*b* Rousinov, nr. Rakovnik, 1870; *d* Senomaty, nr. Prague, 1924). Czech tenor. Début Brno 1891 and sang at Brno Opera 1981–9. Sang briefly with Nat. Th., Prague, until moving to Dresden. Created role of Herod in *Salome*, 1905, and sang it in NY and Paris 1907. Noted Wagner singer, appearing at CG between

1904 and 1914 and in seven seasons at NY Met (début 1906 as Tannhäuser). Bayreuth 1908 (Parsifal).

Burkhard, Paul (*b* Zurich, 1911; *d* Tosstal, 1977). Swiss composer, pianist, and conductor. Cond. radio orch. Beromünster, 1945–57. Successful operettas incl. *Tic-Tac* (1941) and *Der schwarze Hecht* (The Black Jack) (1939) which was rev. 1948 as *Feuerwerk* (Firework) and contained the popular 'O mein Papa'.

Burkhard, Willy (*b* Évilard-sur-Bienne, Switz., 1900; *d* Zurich, 1955). Swiss composer, pianist, and conductor. Teacher of comp. and pf. in Berne. Comp. opera *Die schwarze Spinne* (The Black Spider) (Zurich 1949), 2 syms., cantatas, 2 vn. concs., oratorio *Das Gesicht Jesajahs* (The Vision of Isaiah) (Basle 1936), str. qts., vc. sonata, org. mus.

burla (It.). Jest. So *burlando*, jestingly; *burletta*, a mus. farce, etc.

burlesco, burlesca (It.). Burlesque, jocular (see also *burla*). So the adverb, *burlescamente*.

Burleske (Burlesque). Work for pf. and orch. in D minor by R. Strauss, comp. 1885–6, rev. 1890. F.p. Eisenach, 1890.

burlesque (Fr.; It. *burlesca*; Ger. *Burleske*). Humorous form of entertainment involving an element of parody or exaggeration. Applied in 18th cent. to mus. works in which comic and serious elements were contrasted. In Eng. word usually means a dramatic work ridiculing stage conventions, while in Amer. it means a variety show, often involving strippers.

burletta (It. 'little joke'). Type of Eng. mus. farce which had a vogue in late 18th/early 19th cent. First of its kind was *Midas* by Kane O'Hara, perf. Belfast 1760 and at CG 1964.

Burney, Charles (*b* Shrewsbury, 1726; *d* London, 1814). Eng. organist (London churches, King's Lynn, finally Chelsea Hospital); minor composer; author of *History of Music* (4 vols., 1776–89), of 2 books narrating his travel experiences in Fr., It., Ger., etc., also of a life of Metastasio. Friend and greatly esteemed by Johnson, Garrick, Reynolds, Burke, and other leaders of politics, science, art, literature, and social life of his period. Haydn, on his two visits to London, spent much time with him. Father of the novelists Fanny and Sarah Harriet Burney, of the writer on South Sea exploration, Rear-Admiral James Burney (one of Cook's officers in his circumnavigation), and of the Gr. scholar, Charles Burney, jun.

Burning Fiery Furnace, The. 2nd parable for church perf., Op.77, by Britten to lib. by W. Plomer based on Book of Daniel. Prod. Aldeburgh Fest. (Orford Church) 1966, Katonah, NY, 1967.

Burrell, Diana (*b* Norwich, 1948). Eng. composer. Comp.-in-residence Greenwich Fest. 1987. Programme dir. SPNM 50th anniversary season

1992–3. Came to prominence with *Missa Sancte Endeliente* at St Endellion Fest., Cornwall, 1980. Works incl. opera *The Albatross* (1987); orch. works, choral and vocal mus., chamber mus., pieces for org., and some works involving tape.

Burrell, Mary (*b* 1850; *d* 1898). Daughter of Sir John Banks, Regius Prof. of Medicine, Trinity College, Dublin; wife of Hon. Willoughby Burrell (after her death Lord Gwydyr). Amassed enormous coll. of Wagner documents of every kind; planned complete life of Wagner but only immense first vol. was pubd., covering 21 years (1898). Other material now at Philadelphia (Catalogue pubd. 1929).

Burrian, Carl. See *Burian, Karel*.

Burrowes, Norma (Elizabeth) (*b* Bangor, Co. Down, 1944). Irish soprano. Singer in opera, *Lieder*, and oratorio. Professional début as Zerlina in *Don Giovanni* with GTO, 1970. Glyndebourne début 1970; CG 1970; Salzburg and Wexford 1971; NY Met 1979. Retired 1982.

Burrows, (James) **Stuart** (*b* Cilfynydd, nr. Pontypridd, 1933). Welsh tenor. Was schoolteacher until winning tenor comp. at Royal Nat. Eisteddfod 1959. Opera début with WNO 1963; CG, S. Francisco 1967; Vienna 1970; Salzburg 1970; NY Met 1971. Particularly noted as Mozart singer (Tamino, Don Ottavio, etc.).

Burt, Francis (*b* London, 1926). Eng. composer. Lived in Vienna from 1956. Prof. of comp., Vienna Hochschule für Musik from 1973. Comps. incl. operas *Volpone* (Ben Jonson) (1952–8) and *Barnstable* (1970); *Iambics* for orch. (1953); *Espressione orchestrale* (1958–9); *Under the Moon's Shining Crescent*, bar., orch. (1974–6); *Und Gott der Herr sprach*, mez., bar., bass, ch., and orch. (1976–83); *Morgana*, orch. (1985–6); 2 str. qts. (1951–2, 1992–3); *Hommage à Jean-Henri Fabre*, 2 fl., vn., mand., perc. (1993–4); *Blind Visions*, ob., small orch. (1994–5); and many works for Ger. and Austrian ths. and TV.

burthen. See *burden*.

Busch, Adolf (Georg Wilhelm) (*b* Siegen, Westphalia, 1891; *d* Guilford, Vermont, 1952). Ger.-born violinist and composer. From 1907 played many of Reger's chamber works with composer. Leader, Vienna Konzertverein Orch., 1912. Vn. prof. Berlin Hochschule 1918. Founded qt. 1919. Settled in Basle 1927, taking Swiss nationality 1935. Founded Busch Chamber Players in Eng. in late 1930s. Went to USA 1939. His qt. made many famous recordings. Noted for sonata recitals with his son-in-law, the pianist Rudolf *Serkin. Comp. sym., concs., sonatas.

Busch, Fritz (*b* Siegen, Westphalia, 1890; *d* London, 1951). Ger. conductor, brother of A. *Busch. Opera-house appointments at Riga 1909, Aachen 1912, Stuttgart 1918, succeeding Fritz *Reiner at Dresden, 1922, remaining there until 1933. His period at Dresden revived glories of *Schuch era.

Cond. f.ps. of *Intermezzo* (1924), *Die ägyptische Helena* (1928), *Doktor Faust* (1925), and *Cardillac* (1926). Bayreuth Fest. 1924; Salzburg Fest. début 1929 (Vienna PO), opera 1932. Left Ger. 1933, working in Buenos Aires 1933–6 and 1941–5 and at NY Met 1945–9. In England best known as first cond. of *Glyndebourne Opera 1934–9, returning in 1950 and 1951. Also had long assoc. with Danish Radio SO and Stockholm PO.

Bush, Alan (Dudley) (*b* London, 1900; *d* Watford, 1995). Eng. composer, conductor, and pianist. Teacher at RAM from 1925. Many of his works reflect his Communist sympathies but are held in high esteem for their mus. qualities by listeners of all political persuasions. Major works are:

OPERAS: *The Press-Gang* (1946); *Wat Tyler* (1948–50) (Leipzig 1953, London 1974); *The Spell Unbound* (1953); *Men of Blackmoor* (1954–5) (Oxford 1960, Weimar 1965); *The Ferryman's Daughter* (1961); *The Sugar Reapers* (1961–4) (Leipzig 1966); *Joe Hill: the Man Who Never Died* (1965–8) (Berlin 1970).

ORCH.: syms., No.1 in C (1939–40), No.2 'Nottingham' (1949), No.3 'Byron' (1959–60), No.4 'Lascaux' (1982–3); pf. conc., with bar. and male ch. (1934–7); vn. conc. (1948); *Concert Suite*, vc., orch. (1952); *English Suite*, str. (1946); *Dorian Passacaglia and Fugue* (1959); *Variations, Nocturne and Finale on an English Sea Song*, pf., orch. (1960); *Time Remembered*, chamber orch. (1968); *Africa*, pf., orch. (1971–2); *Liverpool Overture* (1972).

CHAMBER WORKS: str. qt. in A minor (1923); *Dialectic*, str. qt. (1929); 3 *Concert Studies*, pf. trio (1947); *Serenade*, str. qt. (1969); pf. sonata (1971); *Suite of Six*, str. qt. (1975); 24 *Preludes*, pf. (1977).

Bush, Geoffrey (*b* London, 1920; *d* ?London, 1998). Eng. composer, teacher, and writer. Lect., Oxford Univ., Extra-Mural Dept., 1947–52, London Univ. 1952–8. Visiting prof. of mus., King's Coll., London, 1969–89. Works incl. 5 operas (incl. *Love's Labour's Lost* (1988); 2 syms. (1954, 1957); ov. *Yorick* (1949); concs. for vc. (1943) and ob. (1948); 2 concertinos for pf. (1953, 1976); choral and vocal music; piano pieces; and song-cycles incl. *2 Songs of Ben Jonson* (1952), *A Stevie Smith Cycle* (1981), and *4 Chaucer Settings* (1987).

Busnois, Antoine (*b c.*1430; *d* Bruges, 1492). Fr. composer. May have been pupil or colleague of *Ockeghem. Was for long in service of Charles the Bold (who became Duke of Burgundy in 1467) and after Charles's death in 1477 served his daughter Mary of Burgundy until her death in 1482. Moved to Bruges and became *rector cantoriae* at the church of St Sauveur. Regarded as one of leading composers of his day, ranking next to Ockeghem, with whom he shared a penchant for elaborate melody, the use of canon, and lively rhythms. His *Missa L'homme armé* is one of earliest based on this secular tune, but some of his most original work is to be found in his *chansons*, of which over 60 survive. For some of these he wrote the words. His motet *Anthoni usque limina* has a part for a tenor who sings the note D in imitation of a bell. Its text has a reference to his name in the line '. . . in omnibus noys'. His three-part setting of an It. text, the motet *Fortunata desperata*, was a model for Josquin *Desprès, and the melodies of some of his *chansons* were used in Masses by his contemporaries just as he had used *L'homme armé*.

Busoni, Ferruccio (Dante Michelangiolo Benvenuto) (*b* Empoli, 1866; *d* Berlin, 1924). It. composer, conductor, and pianist. Son of a clarinettist and a pianist, with whom he studied. First public pf. recital, Trieste, at age 7. Studied comp. at Graz, 1880–1 and Leipzig 1886. Teaching posts at Helsinki 1889, Moscow 1890, Boston, Mass., 1891–4. After 1894 settled mainly in Berlin. Although his brilliance as a pianist earned him most fame, from 1898 concentrated on comp. and also est. master classes at Weimar in 1901 and 1902 which broke new ground as meeting-places for young composers and performers. From 1902 to 1909 cond. orch. concerts in Berlin at which contemporary works were perf. From 1913 to 1915 was dir. of Liceo Rossini, Bologna, but disagreements with the municipal authorities over reforms ensured failure. Lived in Zurich from 1915, refusing to enter the belligerent countries, but returned to Berlin 1920. Resumed pianist career despite failing health.

Busoni's pf.-playing, of virtuoso quality, was also notable for its grandeur and poetry. His mus. found mixed favour in his lifetime but has become increasingly admired for its visionary nature and for its anticipation of many of the devices and styles of 'advanced' composers. Deriving from the impressionistic late works of Liszt, it ventured into harmonic and rhythmic territory that became the preserve of *Webern, *Bartók, and *Messiaen. His earlier works, in a classical-romantic style, are best represented by the vn. sonata in E minor, the vn. conc., and the pf. conc. (in 5 movts., with male ch. in finale). His change in style dates from the *Elegies* for pf. of 1907. His most elaborate work was his opera *Doktor Faust*, begun 1916 and left incomplete. His writings were both progressive and influential, particularly the *Entwurf einer neuen Ästhetik der Tonkunst* (Trieste, 1907). Prin. works:

OPERAS: *Die *Brautwahl* (The Bridal Choice) (1908–11); *Arlecchino* (1914–16); *Turandot* (1917, orig. incid. mus. 1911); *Doktor Faust* (1916–24, completed. by P. Jarnach).

ORCH.: *Symphonic Suite* (1883); *Konzertstück*, pf., orch. (1890); *Concert-Fantasy*, pf., orch. (1888–9), rev. as *Symphonisches Tongedicht*, orch. (1893); *Suite No.2* (1895, rev. 1903); vn. conc. (1896–7); *Comedy Overture* (1897, rev. 1904); pf. conc. (male ch. in finale) (1903–4); *Turandot Suite* (1904); *Berceuse élégiaque* (1909, orig. for pf.); *Symphonic Nocturne* (1912); *Indianische Fantasie*, pf., orch. (1913); *Rondò Arlecchinesco* (1915); *Indianisches Tagebuch* (Book II) (1915); cl. concertino (1918); *Divertimento*, fl., orch. (1920); *Tanzwalzer* (1920); *Romanza e Scherzosa*, pf., orch. (1921).

VOICE & ORCH.: *Ave Maria*, bar., orch. (1882); *Unter den Linden*, sop., orch. (1885, 1893); *Zigeunerlied*, bar., orch. (1923); *Schlechter Trost*, low v., orch. (1924).

CHAMBER WORKS: str. qt. No.1 in C minor (1880–1), No. 2 in D minor (1887); vn. sonata No.1 in E minor (1890), No.2 in E minor (1898); *Little Suite*, vc., pf. (1886); *Bagatelles*, vn., pf. (1888); *Serenata*, vc., pf. (c.1882); *Elegy*, cl., pf. (1920).

PIANO: *Prelude and Fugue* in C minor (1878); *24 Preludes* (1879–80); *3 Pieces* (1884); *Study in Form of Variations* (1884); *5 Pieces* (1887); *Elegien* (7 pieces) (1907–9); No.7, *Berceuse*, comp. 1909 and orch. as *Berceuse élégiaque*); *Christmas Night* (1909); sonatinas: No.1 (1910), No.2 (1912), No.3 (1916), No.4 (1917), No.5 (transcr. of Bach) (1919), No.6 (on *Carmen*) (1920); *Indianisches Tagebuch* (Book I) (1915); *Fantasia contrappuntistica* (based on Bach), 1st version (1910), 2nd version (1910), 3rd version (1912), 4th version, arr. 2 pfs. (1921); *3 Albumblätter* (1917–21); *Klavierübung* (1st edn. in 5 parts, 1917–22; 2nd edn. in 10 parts, 1925).

Also songs and many transcr. and arr. of Bach, Beethoven, Bizet, Chopin, Cornelius, Liszt, Mozart, Schoenberg, Schubert, and Wagner. His transcr. of J. S. Bach's *Chromatic Fantasia* dates from 1911.

Busser, Henri Paul (*b* Toulouse, 1872; *d* Paris 1973). Fr. composer, organist and conductor. At 21 won *Prix de Rome*. In 1902 became cond. at the Opéra-Comique, at the Opéra 1905. Prof. of comp., Paris Cons. 1931–49. Wrote several operas incl. *Jane Grey* (1891), *Colomba* (1921), *Les Noces corinthiennes* (1922), and *Le Carrosse du Saint-Sacrement* (1948). Orch. Debussy's *Petite Suite*, *Printemps*, and other works.

Bussotti, Sylvano (*b* Florence, 1931). It. composer. Prizewinner at ISCM festival and Venice Biennale. Influenced by Webern and serialism, later by John *Cage. Dir., Teatro La Fenice, Venice, 1975. Operas incl. *Lorenzaccio* (1972), *Nottetempo* (1976), *La Racine* (1980), *L'Ispirazione* (1988), and *Fedra* (1988). Other works incl.: *La Passion selon Sade*, vv., instr., narrator (1966); *5 Piano Pieces for David Tudor* (1959); *Torso*, v. and orch. (1963); *Rara Requiem* (1969); *Poesia di De Pisis*, sop., orch. (1975). Some of these are in graphic score. Also a painter.

Buths, Julius (Emil Martin) (*b* Wiesbaden, 1851; *d* Düsseldorf, 1920). Ger. cond. and pianist. After conducting at Elberfeld, 1879–90, moved to Düsseldorf, 1890–1908, where he became mus. dir., Lower Rhine Fest. and dir., Düsseldorf Cons. from 1902. Cond. several now famous contemporary works by, among others, Mahler, Delius, and Strauss, but most notably Elgar's *Dream of Gerontius*, which he trans. into Ger. and prod. at Düsseldorf in 1901 and 1902. Soloist in f.p. of Delius's pf. conc. at Elberfeld, 1904 (cond. *Haym). Wrote some songs and instr. works.

Butler, Martin (*b* Romsey, Hants, 1960). Eng. composer. Lect., Univ. of Sussex. Works incl. pf. sonata (1982); Concertino for chamber orch.

(1983); str. qt. (1984); *3 Emily Dickinson Songs*, sop., cl., pf. (1985); *The Sirens' Song*, opera (1986); *To See the Beauties of the Earth*, ch. (1987); *Songs and Dances from a Haunted Place*, str. qt. (1988); *Graffiti*, tape (1989); wind quintet (1991); *Craig's Progress*, opera (1994).

Butt, (Dame) **Clara** (Ellen) (*b* Southwick, 1872; *d* North Stoke, Oxon, 1936). Eng. contralto. Début London (RAH) 1892 (Ursula in Sullivan's *The Golden Legend*). Sang title-role of Gluck's *Orfeo* in 1892 at Lyceum with conspicuous success but thereafter pursued career on concert platform except for an *Orfeo* with Beecham at CG, 1920. Toured British Empire in ballad recitals with husband Kennerley *Rumford. First singer of Elgar's **Sea Pictures*, Norwich 1899, and of the song version of *Land of Hope and Glory*, 1902. Also sang in his *Spirit of England*, 1916. DBE 1920.

Butterley, Nigel (Henry) (*b* Sydney, NSW, 1935). Australian composer and pianist. Mus. adv. to Australian Broadcasting Commission 1955–72. Comps. incl. opera (1988); sym. (1980); vn. conc. (1970); 3 str. qts. (1965, 1974, 1979); cl. trio (1979); *From Sorrowing Earth*, orch. (1991), etc.

Butterworth, Arthur (Eckersley) (*b* Manchester, 1923). Eng. composer, conductor, and trumpeter. Trumpeter in SNO 1949–54, Hallé Orch. 1955–61. Cond., Huddersfield PO 1964–93. Works incl. 6 syms., several works for brass band, *Trains in the Distance*, ch. and orch.; *Héjnal*, tpt., pf. (1979); *Nex Vulpinus*, str. (1981); bn. conc. (*Summer Music*) (1986); *Ov.: Solent Forts*, orch., also arr. for brass band (1992); va. conc. (1993); vc. conc. (1997); *Mist on the Marshes*, sop., db., pf. (1999). Arr. Elgar's *Introduction and Allegro* (str.) for brass band (1976). MBE 1995.

Butterworth, George (Sainton Kaye-) (*b* London, 1885; *d* Pozières, Battle of Somme, 1916). Eng. composer. At Oxford influenced by H. P. *Allen and began collecting folk-songs, leading to friendship with *Vaughan Williams and Cecil *Sharp. Was excellent folk-dancer. Wrote occasional mus. criticism for *The Times*, taught at Radley Coll., and later studied at RCM. Comps., few in number, suggest he might have achieved greatness. Left several fine settings of Housman's 'Shropshire Lad' poems, with orch. rhapsody, *A Shropshire Lad* (Leeds 1913) based on theme of his song 'Loveliest of Trees'. Orch. idyll *The Banks of Green Willow* f.p. London 1914. Song-cycle *Love Blows as the Wind Blows* (W. E. Henley) was composed 1911–12, being 4 songs for voice with pf. or str. qt. but was revised in 1914 as 3 songs with orch. Awarded Military Cross a month before his death. Vaughan Williams's *A London Symphony* is ded. to his memory.

Butting, Max (*b* Berlin, 1888; *d* Berlin, 1976). Ger. composer. Early specialist in comp. for radio. Inactive 1933–45; mus. dir., E. Berlin radio 1948. Comp. opera, 10 syms., pf. conc., 10 str. qts., etc.

button. Pin at the end of a vn., etc., which bears the pull of the str.

Buxtehude, Dietrich (Diderik) (*b* Oldesloe, Holstein, *c.*1637; *d* Lübeck, 1707). Danish organist and composer. In 1668 appointed organist, Marienkirche, Lübeck, from which his fame as a player spread through Europe. In 1673 reinstated practice of giving ambitious mus. perfs. in assoc. with church services. Known as *Abendmusiken* (evening concerts), they were held annually on the 5 Sundays before Christmas. Such was Buxtehude's fame that J. S. Bach walked 200 miles from Arnstadt to hear him play. Comp. many works for org. (which influenced Bach), and trio sonatas. His vocal music, most of it to sacred texts, is as important as his organ works. He wrote 20 cantatas, of which the cycle of seven, *Membra Jesu Nostri* (1680) is highly regarded; his other vocal comps. may be categorized as concertos, chorales, and arias. His arias suggest the influence of Monteverdi, with a strong preference for strophic form over the *da capo* aria.

Buxton Festival. Held annually in July in Derbyshire spa town in opera house and other venues. Founded 1979 by Malcolm Fraser and Anthony Hose. Prog. comprises operas, concerts, recitals, church mus., children's opera, and literary talks.

buzuk. Turkish instr. resembling long-necked lute, having 4 str. passing over a movable bridge, a fingerboard twice as long as the soundboard, a small oval body, and rounded back.

BWV, *Bach Werke-Verzeichnis* (Index to Bach's Works). The initials, preceding nos., which indicate the catalogue nos. of J. S. Bach's works in the thematic index (*Thematisch-Systematisches Verzeichnis der musikalischen Werke von Johann Sebastian Bach*) compiled and ed. by Wolfgang *Schmieder (1950). Now accepted as standard means of numbering his works, e.g. *St John Passion* is BWV245.

Bychkov, Semyon (*b* Leningrad, 1952). Russian conductor. Cond. Leningrad Cons. Sym. and Opera Orch. 1972–4. Mus. dir. Mannes Coll. of Mus. Orch. 1976–80, Grand Rapids SO 1980–5, Buffalo PO 1985–9, Orch. de Paris 1989–2000, Cologne Radio SO from 1997. Brother of Yakov *Kreizberg.

Byrd, William (*b* probably Lincoln, 1543; *d* Stondon Massey, Essex, 1623). Eng. composer. Org., Lincoln Cath., 1563. From 1572 hon. org. Chapel Royal jointly with Tallis. In 1575 he and Tallis jointly pubd. a coll. of motets, *Cantiones sacrae*, dedicated to Queen Elizabeth I. From 1587 to 1596, Byrd pubd. several important collections of Eng. mus. Left London for Essex 1591, as member of household of his patrons, the Petres. Wrote some of his *Gradualia* for undercover masses held in Ingatestone Hall. Little is known of Byrd's life apart from various lawsuits over property and the fact of his Roman Catholicism, from the consequences of which he seems to have been protected at a time of anti-Papism by his fame as a composer and by friends in high places. In his motets and masses, Byrd showed himself the equal of his Fr. and It. contemporaries as a contrapuntist. He was an innovator in form and technique in his liturgical works, the finest of which is the Great Service. His madrigals are also of exceptional quality, and there is superb mus. in his solo songs and songs for the stage. In his *Fancies* and *In Nomines* for str. instr. he est. an Eng. instr. style of comp., but perhaps even more significant was his mus. for virginals, in which he developed variation form, and his series of pavans and galliards for kbd. Among his pupils were Morley and Tomkins, and probably Weelkes and Bull. Prin. comps.:

SACRED WORKS: Masses, No.1 in 3 v.-parts, No.2 in 4, No.3 in 5. Motets: *Cantiones* (with Tallis, 1575. Contains 17 items by Byrd); *Cantiones sacrae*, Book I, 1589 (29 motets), Book II, 1591 (32 motets); *Gradualia*, Book I, 1605 (63 motets),

Book II, 1607 (45 motets); *Preces, Psalms and Litany*; Short Service; Great Service; 12 verse anthems; 10 psalms.

SECULAR WORKS: Madrigals; sonnets; *Songs of sundrie natures* (1589), containing 47 songs; solo songs, canons, and rounds.

INSTRUMENTAL: 14 *Fantasies*; 8 *In Nomines*; 9 pieces in *In Nomine* style on plainsong melodies.
KEYBOARD: Over 120 pieces in various colls., incl. *My Ladye Nevells Booke*, transcr. 1591, and *Parthenia* (1611).

Byzantine Music. Christian liturgical song (often highly ornamented) of the E. Roman Empire (capital Byzantium = Constantinople = Istanbul), founded AD 330 by Constantine the Great and destroyed 1453 with the Fall of Constantinople. It appears to derive from an ancient source common to it and to the plainsong of the W. Church. The various forms of notation are also a subject for special study.

C

C. First note of the natural scale, thus C♭, C♭♭, C♮, C♯, C♯♯, C major, C minor. *In C* means either (1) in the key of C major or (2) indicates a non-transposing instr., e.g. tpts. in C. Middle C is the C in about the middle of the pf. and is notated on the line below the treble staff. C clefs indicate position of middle C, e.g. alto and ten. clefs and sop. clef (obsolete). In SCTB, C = contralto.

C.A. **coll' arco.*

cabaca. Round or pear-shaped gourd covered with beads and with a handle. Some have beads inside to rattle. Used in Lat. American dance bands and by several 20th-cent. composers.

cabaletta (cabbaletta, cavaletta) (It., from *cavata*, extraction). A term with a number of meanings: (1) Short aria of simple and much reiterated rhythm, generally with repeats. (2) Type of song in rondo form, sometimes with variations. (3) Recurring passage in a song, first appearing simply and then varied (some authorities make a triplet acc. a necessary qualification for the title). (4) Final section of elaborate operatic duet or aria in which mus. often settles down to a steady rhythm, e.g. 'Ah! non giunge' in *La *sonnambula*.

Caballé, Montserrat (*b* Barcelona, 1933). Sp. soprano. Concert début Barcelona 1954, opera début Basle 1956, First Lady in *Die Zauberflöte*. La Scala début 1960; Amer. début (Mexico City) 1962; Glyndebourne 1965; NY Met 1965; CG 1972; Salzburg Fest. 1987 (recital).

cabaret. Term applied to places of entertainment such as night clubs and to the mus. entertainment provided there. Cabaret in the modern sense began in 1881 when the 'Chat Noir' opened in Paris. From this milieu arose the great *diseuse* Yvette Guilbert (1885–1944). In Ger. the leading cabaret was the 'Überbrettl', founded by Ernst von Wolzogen (librettist of Strauss's *Feuersnot*) in 1901. Schoenberg cond. there and comp. some *Brettllieder*. Political satire was a prin. feature of the cabaret of the 1920s and 1930s in Ger., where Kurt Weill and Hanns Eisler were protagonists. This period was captured by Christopher Isherwood in his novel *Goodbye to Berlin* (1939) (re-named *Cabaret* for the stage and film). In Eng., cabaret tended to be more genteel and like an intimate revue, but something of the Ger. spirit was emulated by W. H. Auden in his *The Ascent of F6* (1936), the songs being set to mus. by Britten (e.g. 'Tell me the truth about love').

Cabezón, Antonio de (*b* Castrillo de Matajudìos, nr. Burgos, 1510; *d* Madrid, 1566). Sp. composer, blind from birth, one of first to compose for the kbd. Org. and harpsichordist to Kings of Spain. Mus. ahead of its time, as shown by variations on popular melody *El caballero*.

cabinet organ. Amer. nomenclature for what in Eng. is called Amer. org. This resembles the *harmonium, but the air is sucked through the reeds instead of being forced through them and the tone is less pungent. There is no 'Expression' device and so where other means than the player's feet can be applied for operating the bellows, a pedal-board like that of an organ can be built in as part of the instr. Invented by worker in Alexandre's Paris factory but developed in Boston, Mass.

caccia (It.). Chase, hunt, e.g. *alla caccia*, in hunting style. In **ars nova* 2 vv. 'chased' each other in strict canon, the text often dealing with hunting. See *oboe family* and *corno da caccia*.

Caccini, Giulio (*b* Rome or Tivoli, 1551; *d* Florence, 1618). It. singer, composer, and lutenist. Taken to Florence by Cosimo I de' Medici, *c*.1565. Sang in 1579 at festivities for wedding of Francesco de' Medici and Bianca Cappello. One of members of Count Giovanni de Bardi's *Camerata, some of his mus. was incl. in Peri's *Euridice* to Rinuccini's lib. which he then also set in rivalry in 1600. From 1595 to 1600 worked in Genoa, returning to Florence 1600 on receiving commission to comp. opera *Il rapimento di Cefalo*, perf. Florence 1600 for wedding of Maria de' Medici to Henri IV of France. Canzonets and madrigals published in *Le nuove musiche* (New Music) 1602, marking change to monodic style.

cachucha. Andalusian dance for a single performer in triple time. Its mus. is not unlike that of the *bolero.

cadence or close. Any melodic or harmonic progression which has come to possess a conventional association with the ending of a comp., a section, or a phrase.

The commonest harmonic cadences are: (a) Perfect cadence (or full close). Chord of the dominant followed by that of tonic. (b) Interrupted cadence. Chord of the dominant followed by that of submediant. (c) Imperfect cadence (or half close). Chord of the tonic or some other chord followed by that of dominant. (d) Plagal cadence. Chord of the subdominant followed by that of tonic.

To any of the dominant chords above mentioned the 7th may be added. Any of the chords may be taken in *inversion, but if that is done in the case of the perfect cadence its effect of finality (i.e. its 'perfection') is lost.

The term Phrygian cadence is applied by various writers to (i) in major key a cadence ending on the chord of the dominant of relative minor (e.g. in key C major E–G♯–B), or (ii) any sort of imperfect cadence (half close) in minor mode, or (iii) first inversion of subdominant chord

(a)   (b)   (c)

(d)   (i)

followed by dominant chord (e.g. in key C the chord A–C–F followed by the chord G–B–D). (It seems best to confine the name to the cadence (i) above, which is fairly common in J. S. Bach and for which no other name is available, whereas (ii) and (iii) are simply varieties of the imperfect cadence.)

For the cadence employing the *tierce de Picardie* see under that term.

Other terms are:

Abrupt cadence = interrupted cadence (see above). Amen cadence = plagal cadence (see above). Authentic cadence = perfect cadence (full close; see above). Avoided cadence = interrupted cadence (see above). Broken cadence = interrupted cadence (see above). Church cadence = plagal cadence (see above). Complete cadence = perfect cadence (full close; see above). Deceptive cadence = interrupted cadence (see above). Demi-cadence = imperfect cadence (half close; see above). Dominant cadence = imperfect cadence (half close; see above). Evaded cadence = interrupted cadence (see above). False close = interrupted cadence (see above). Greek cadence = plagal cadence (see above). Half cadence = half close (see *imperfect cadence*, above). Inverted cadence = perfect or imperfect cadence (full close or half close; see above) with its latter chord inverted. (Some confine the name to the perfect cadence thus changed; others extend it to all cadences having either chord, or both, inverted.) Irregular cadence = interrupted cadence (see above). Mixed cadence. The term is used in 2 ways—both of them superfluous. (1) A 'mixing' of the plagal and imperfect cadences, consisting of subdominant-dominant, this being merely the imperfect cadence in one of its commonest forms. (2) A mixing of the plagal and perfect cadences, consisting of the perfect cadence preceded by the subdominant—making 3 chords, instead of the usual two. This is merely the perfect cadence led up to in one of its commonest manners and should not require any special name. Radical cadence = any cadence of which the chords are in root position, i.e. the roots of the chords in the bass. Semi-perfect cadence = perfect cadence (step above) with the 3rd or 5th of the tonic in the highest part. Surprise cadence = interrupted cadence (see above). Suspended cadence = a hold-up before the final cadence of a

piece, as that in a conc. (or, in former times, an aria) for the solo performer to work in a *cadenza.

The above definitions accord with Brit. terminology. Amer. usage is different and inconsistent.

cadenza (It.). A flourish (properly, improvised) inserted into the final cadence of any section of a vocal aria or a solo instr. movement. The conventional final cadence consists, harmonically, of 3 chords, the 2nd inversion of the tonic chord, and the dominant and tonic chords in root position (i.e. 6/5 5/3 on the dominant bass, followed by 5/3 on the tonic bass). The interpolated cadenza begins on the first of these chords, the orch. joining in again only when the soloist, after a display of vocal or instr. virtuosity, indicates by a long trill that he or she is ready to be rejoined in the final chords or in any passage elaborated out of them.

In the operatic aria conventional practice admitted 3 cadenzas—one at the end of each of its sections (see *aria*), the most elaborate being reserved to the last. The term *melisma* has been used for the vocal cadenza.

From the time of Mozart and Beethoven in instr. mus. the tendency grew for the composer to write out the cadenza in full, although Mozart's and Beethoven's cadenzas are often still rejected by soloists who substitute cadenzas by other hands (e.g. by Busoni, Reinecke, etc.). In Beethoven's and Brahms's vn. concs. the cadenza was left to the performer's invention, but Joachim and Kreisler (and others) provided written-out cadenzas which are generally used. Schumann in his pf. conc. and Mendelssohn in his vn. conc. began the trend, general now, of integrating the cadenza into the comp. There are many fine examples of acc. cadenzas (e.g. Elgar's vn. conc.). Sometimes the cadenza assumes the importance of, effectively, an extra movement (e.g. Shostakovich's first vn. conc., Walton's vc. conc.). Of course, with the growth of *aleatory procedures, the improvised cadenza has come back into its own.

cadenzato (It.). Cadenced, i.e. rhythmic.

Cadman, Charles Wakefield (*b* Johnstown, Penn., 1881; *d* Los Angeles, 1946). Amer. composer, pianist, organist, and music critic. Specialist in mus. of Amer. Indians, using it in his own works which incl. several operas, orch. comps., and many songs, incl. the popular 'From the Land of the Sky-Blue Water'. Was a founder of the Hollywood Bowl.

Caetani, Oleg (*b* Lausanne, 1956). Swiss-born It. conductor. Son of Igor *Markevitch. Studied in Paris with Boulanger, in Rome with Ferrara, at Moscow Cons. with Kondrashin and Nikolaev, and at St Petersburg Cons. with Ilya Musin. Won RAI, Turin, and Karajan cond. comps. (1982). Prof. début Deutsche Oper, Berlin, 1983. Chief cond. Weimar (1984–7) and 1st cond. Frankfurt Opera (1987–92). Mus. dir. Wiesbaden Opera (1992–5), Chemnitz Opera, and Robert Schumann PO (1996–2001). La Scala début 2001

(*Turandot*); Brit. début Manchester 2002 (Hallé Orch.), London 2003 (ENO, *Khovanshchina*). Chief cond. and art. dir. Melbourne SO from 2005.

Caffarelli [Majorano, Gaetano] (*b* Bitonto, 1710; *d* Naples, 1783). It. mezzo-soprano castrato. Début Rome 1726. Sang in prin. It. opera-houses from 1729 but chiefly in Naples. Sang in London 1737–8, creating title-roles in Handel's *Faramondo* and *Serse*.

Cage, John (*b* Los Angeles, 1912; *d* NY, 1992). Amer. composer, pianist, and writer. From 1937 developed interests in dance and perc. In 1938 experimented with Cowell's invention of the 'prepared pf.' by inserting various objects, from rubber-bands to hatpins, between the str. to create new effects. Settled in NY 1942, beginning long assoc. with Merce Cunningham Dance Co. as mus. dir. 1944–68. *Theater Piece* (1952) for Cunningham is regarded as first musical 'happening' (spontaneous event). Study of oriental philosophies and Zen Buddhism and his reading of *I Ching*, the Chinese book of changes, led to his utilization of 'chance' in his mus., as in *Music of Changes* (1951). In 1952 he prod. his first piece involving tape, *Imaginary Landscape V*, and in the same year came *4'33"* in which the performer makes no sound. He was also an expert on mushrooms.

The particular elements of Cage's *avant-garde* outlook were: use of any kind of environmental sounds or noises; use of 'chance', as in *Music of Changes* where the selection process involves tossing a coin; abandonment of formal structures; use of silence; use of a wide range of elec. and visual techniques. His stated belief was that any noise constituted music. 'Nothing is accomplished by writing, hearing or playing a piece of music', he wrote (1961). He regarded *4'33"* as his most significant work: the performer or performers sit silently on the platform. The 'music' is whatever sound comes from the audience or outside the hall. Books incl. *Silence* (1961), *A Year from Monday* (1967), and *For the Birds* (1981). Works incl.:

OPERA: *Europera I/II*, for 19 soloists and orch. (1987).

BALLET: *The Seasons* (1947).

ORCH.: conc., prepared pf., chamber orch. (1951); Concert for pf., 63 pages to be played, whole or in part, in any sequence (1957–8); *Atlas Eclipticalis* (1961–2); *Cheap Imitation* (1972, orch. version of pf. solo); *Etcetera* (1973); *Score (40 drawings by Thoreau)* and *23 Parts* (any instr. and/or vv., 1974); *Quartets I–VIII* (24, 41, or 93 instrs., 1976); *Quartet*, concert band and 12 amp. vv. (1976–8); *30 Pieces for 5 Orchestras* (1981); *Etcetera 2/4 Orchestras* (1986).

PERCUSSION & ELEC.: perc. qt. (1935); *Trio*, suite for perc. (1936); **Construction I in Metal*, perc. sextet (1939), *II*, perc. qt. (1940), *III*, perc. qt. (1941); **Imaginary Landscape I*, 2 variable speed gramophone turntables, frequency recordings, muted pf., cymbal (1939), *II* (*March*), perc. quintet (1942), *III*, perc. sextet (1942), *IV* (*March No.2*), 12 radios, 24 players, cond. (1951), *V*, any 42 recordings as magnetic tape (1952); *Living Room Music*, perc. qt. (1940); *Credo in Us*, perc. qt.

incl. radio or gramophone and pf. (1942); *Speech*, 5 radios with news reader (1955); 27'10.554", percussionist (1956); *But what about the noise of crumpling paper . . .* , perc. ens. (1986).

CHAMBER MUSIC: cl. sonata (1933); 3 pieces, fl. duet (1935); *Nocturne*, vn., pf. (1947); Str. Qt. (1949–50); *6 Melodies*, vn., kbd. (1950); *4'33"* (silent, for any instr. or combination of instr.) (1952); **Variations I–VI*, any no. of players and sound-producing means (1958–66); *HPSCHD*, 7 hpd. soloists, 51 or any no. of tape machines (1967–9); *Cheap Imitation*, vn. solo (1977); *Freeman Etudes*, vn. solo (1977); *Chorals*, vn. solo (1978); *Postcard From Heaven*, 1–20 hps. (1983); *30 Pieces for Str. Qt.* (1984); *13 Harmonies*, vn., kbd. (1986).

PIANO (solo unless stated otherwise): *Music for Xenia* (1934); *Metamorphosis* (1938); *Experiences I*, pf. duet (1945); *Ophelia* (1946); *Dream* (1948); *7 Haiku* (1952); *Music of Changes* (1951, in 4 vols.); *Music for Piano* (1952–6, several works); *Winter Music*, 1–20 pianists (1957); *0'00"* (*4'33" No.2*) to be perf. in any way by anyone (1962); *Cheap Imitation* (1969, orch. version 1972, vn. solo 1977); *Études Australes*, 32 studies in 4 books (1974–5); *ASLSP* (1985); *One* (1988); *Swinging* (1989).

PREPARED PIANO: *Bacchanale* (1940); *And the Earth Shall Bear Again* (1942); *In the Name of the Holocaust* (1942); *Amores*, 2 solos for prepared pf. and 2 trios for 3 percussionists (1943); *Totem Ancestor* (1943); *Meditation* (1943); *Spontaneous Earth* (1944); *A Valentine Out of Season* (1944); *Daughters of the Lonesome Isle* (1945); *Sonatas and Interludes* (1946–8); *Music for Marcel Duchamp* (1947); *34'46.776" for a pianist* (1954); *31'57.9864" for a pianist* (1954).

MISCELLANEOUS: *Music for Carillon* Nos. 1–5 (1952–67); *Les Chants de Maldoror pulverisés par l'assistance même* (1971); *Haikai*, gamelan (1986).

VOCAL: *5 Songs*, cont., pf. (e.e. cummings) (1938); *Forever and Sunsmell* (cummings), v., perc. duo (1942); *The Wonderful Widow of Eighteen Springs*, v., closed pf. (Joyce) (1942); *Experiences 2*, solo v. (1948); *Song Books, Solos for voice 3–92* (1970); *62 Mesostics re Merce Cunningham* (1971, unacc.); *Hymns and Variations*, 12 amp. vv. (1978); *Litany for the Whale*, 2 vv. (1980); *Five*, 5 vv. or instr. (1988); *4 Solos for Voices 93–96*, sop., mez., ten., bass (1988); *Europera III*, 6 singers, 2 pf., 6 gramophone operators, lighting, tape (1989); *IV*, 2 singers, 1 record-player, pf., lighting (1989); *V*, pianist, 2 singers, lighting, tape (1991).

TAPE, AUDIO-VISUAL, etc.: **Water Music* (1952); *Fontana Mix*, tape or any instr. (1958); *Where are we going? And what are we doing?* (1960); *Rozart Mix* (1965); *Bird Cage* (12 tapes, 1972); *Lecture on the Weather* (12 perf., 1975).

Cahier, Mme Charles [*née* Layton-Walker, Sarah Jane] (*b* Nashville, Tenn., 1870; *d* Manhattan Beach, Calif., 1951). Amer. mezzo-soprano. Début in opera, Nice 1904. Vienna Opera 1907–11 under Mahler's direction, when she sang Carmen and various Wagner roles. NY Met 1912–14 (début as Azucena in *Il trovatore*). Taught at Curtis Inst. Soloist in f.p. in 1911 (Munich) of Mahler's *Das Lied von der Erde*, cond. Walter.

Cahill, Teresa (Mary) (*b* Maidenhead, 1944). Eng. soprano. Début 1967 with Phoenix Opera. Glyndebourne 1970–80. Won John Christie award 1970. Débuts: WNO 1970; CG 1970–7; Santa Fe 1973; La Scala 1976 (with CG co.); ENO 1977. Created Mad Woman/Lady in *We Come to the River* (CG 1976). Concert career in Elgar and contemp. works. Taught at RNCM.

Ça Ira! (That will succeed). This expression, many times repeated, made up about half the words of a revolutionary song (later the official song of the Revolution) said to have originated on 5 Oct. 1789 when the Fr. mob marched to Versailles to bring the King and the royal family to Paris, and which became the mus. acc. to almost every incident of the Terror. The tune adopted was that of a popular contredanse, called *Carillon national*, by a th. violinist of the day, Bécourt. See also *Carmagnole*.

Cairns, David (Adam) (*b* Loughton, Essex, 1926). Eng. critic and writer. A founder of Chelsea Opera Group, 1950. Authority on Berlioz, translating and editing the *Memoirs* (1969, rev. 1977), and writing a 2-vol. biography *Berlioz* (Vol.I, *The Making of an Artist*, London, 1989, Vol.II, *Servitude and Greatness*, London, 1999); also *Mozart and his Operas* (2006). Mus. critic *Financial Times*, 1962–7, *New Statesman*, 1967–70, *Sunday Times* from 1973 (chief critic from 1983). His brilliant essays on mus. subjects were published under title *Responses* (1973). CBE 1997.

caisse (Fr.). Box, hence drum.

caisse claire (Fr.). Clear drum, i.e. snare-drum, otherwise *side-drum*.

caisse grosse (Fr.). Large drum, i.e. *bass drum.

caisse roulante (Fr.). Rolling drum, i.e. tenor *drum.

caisse sourde (Fr.). Dull drum, i.e. *tenor drum; see also *caisse roulante*.

Caix d'Hervelois, Louis de (*b* Paris, *c*.1670; *d* Paris, 1760). Fr. performer on and composer for the viola da gamba, some of whose works are now sometimes perf. by cellists. Wrote 5 books of pieces for viola da gamba, 3 books of fl. sonatas.

cakewalk. Dance popularized in 1890s by Amer. vaudeville team of Bert Williams and George Walker and by black dancer Charles Johnson. Originated when Amer. slaves parodied the whites' manners and method of dancing—a prize (cake) was awarded to best dancers. It featured a strutting movt., with the couple arm-in-arm and performing high kicks. Debussy wrote 'Golliwogg's Cakewalk' in his *Children's Corner* (1906–8).

calando (It.). Lowering. *diminuendo*, with also *rallentando*.

calcando (It.). Trampling. Much the same as *accelerando*, i.e. quickening gradually.

Caldara, Antonio (*b* Venice, *c*.1670; *d* Vienna, 1736). It. composer, pupil of *Legrenzi. Choirboy at St Mark's, Venice. Choirmaster at Mantua court, 1699–1708. Choirmaster in Prince Ruspoli's establishment in Rome, 1709–16. Succeeded *Fux as vice-Kapellmeister, Vienna imperial court, 1716, remaining in the post until his death and becoming a favourite of Emperor Charles VI who eventually paid him a salary higher than Fux's. Comp. 87 operas, over 40 oratorios, masses, and other church mus., incl. *Christmas Cantata*, and songs, of which *Come raggio di sol* is well known. Among his many operas was the first setting of Metastasio's libretto *La Clemenza di Tito* (Vienna, 1734).

Caldwell, Sarah (*b* Maryville, Mo., 1924; *d* Portland, Me., 2006). Amer. opera producer, administrator, and conductor. Staged Vaughan Williams's *Riders to the Sea* at Tanglewood 1947. Head of Boston Univ. opera workshop 1952–60. Founded Boston Opera Co. 1957; responsible for f. Amer. stage ps. of *Intolleranza* (1965), *Moses und Aron* (1966), *War and Peace* (1974), *Die Soldaten* (1982), *Taverner* (1986). First woman cond. at NY Met., 1976. Art. dir., New Opera Co. of Israel, 1983. Cond. NYPO, Boston SO, etc.

Calife de Bagdad, Le (The Caliph of Bagdad). Opera in 1 act by Boieldieu to lib. by C. H. d'A. de Saint-Just. Prod. Paris 1800; London 1809; New Orleans 1805.

Calinda, La. Orch. dance-interlude by Delius in his second opera *Koanga* (1896–7); it is named after a Negro dance imported to Amer. by African slaves. Music originated in Delius's *Florida Suite* (1886–7). Usually perf. in orch. arr. by Eric Fenby, pubd. 1938.

Calino Castureme (*Caleno custureme*). Tune mentioned by Shakespeare in *Henry V* (Act IV, sc. 4). It is to be found in the *Fitzwilliam Virginal Book. In *A Handefull of Pleasant Delites*, 1584, the words 'Caleno Custureme' are interpolated between every 2 lines of the poem 'When as I view your comly grace'. Possibly a perversion of the Irish 'Cailin, ó cois t Suire, mé' (I am a girl from the banks of the river Suir).

Caliph of Bagdad, The (Boieldieu). See *Calife de Bagdad, Le*.

Calisto. Opera in prologue and 3 acts by *Cavalli to lib. by G. Faustini, prod. Venice 1651, and revived at Glyndebourne 1970 in a realization by Raymond *Leppard.

Callas [Kalogeropoulou], **Maria** (Anna Sophia Cecilia) (*b* Manhattan, NY, 1923; *d* Paris, 1977). Amer.-born soprano of Gr. parentage. Studied with Sp. coloratura sop. Elvira de Hidalgo from 1940. Début Athens 1940 (Beatrice in Suppé's *Boccaccio*), as Tosca (1942), and as Leonore in *Fidelio* (1944). It. début Verona, 1947, in *La gioconda*, cond. by Tullio *Serafin. Among her roles at this time were Isolde, Brünnhilde, Kundry, and Turandot. Potentialities recognized by Serafin when, in 1949, she was singing Brünnhilde in Venice. Prima donna engaged as Elvira for next opera, Bellini's *I Puritani*, fell ill and Serafin suggested Callas as substitute. Her singing of a *bel canto* role in the powerful, dramatic way the composer intended was a revelation. Not since Lilli Lehmann had a sop. encompassed Wagnerian roles and the coloratura repertory. With Serafin and de Sabata, Callas revived operas wholly or relatively neglected in It. for over a century, incl. Rossini's *Armida* and *Il turco in Italia*, Cherubini's *Médée*, Spontini's *La vestale*, Donizetti's *Anna Bolena*, and Bellini's *Il pirata*, thereby changing the face of the post–1945 opera repertory. First sang at La Scala April 1950 (*Aida*). From then until 1958 reigned supreme there, earning title *La divina* in her vivid portrayals of Norma, Lady Macbeth, and Violetta, working with de Sabata, Giulini, Bernstein, and Karajan as conds., and the producers Visconti and Zeffirelli. Voice not always beautiful but musicianship was impeccable, insight remarkable, and acting ability exceptional, so that she presented her roles as organic wholes. Her Norma, Tosca, and Violetta were unforgettable examples of dramatic opera singing-acting, linking her in this branch of her art to the legendary names of Malibran and Schröder-Devrient. Sang at CG 1952–3 (début as Norma), 1957–9, and 1964. Amer. début at Chicago, 1954, and at NY Met 1956 (both as Norma). Private life was lived in the glare of publicity inseparable from such a magnetic personality. Retired from stage 1965 (last perf. was as Tosca at CG 5 July 1965) but continued to record and gave some concerts in 1973 and 1974. Also worked as producer and teacher.

Caller Herrin'. Poem by Lady Nairne (1766–1845) written *c*.1821 to fit tune of a hpd. piece comp. *c*.1798 by Nathaniel *Gow in which he incorporated Edinburgh fishwives' traditional cry with bells of St Andrew's Church.

Calligrammes. Song-cycle by Poulenc to 7 poems by Guillaume Apollinaire, comp. 1948. Titles are: *L'Espionne, Mutation, Vers le Sud, Il pleut, La Gâce exilée, Aussi bien que les cigales, Voyage*.

calliope. Amer. term for steamblown mechanical organ.

calmato, calmando (It.). Calmed; calming.

Calm Sea and Prosperous Voyage (Meeresstille und glückliche Fahrt). Poems by Goethe set by several composers incl. (1) Beethoven, Op.112, for SATB and orch., comp. 1815, pubd. 1823. (2) Song by *Reichardt (1752–1814). (3) Song (*Meeresstille* section only) by Schubert (D216), comp. 1815. (4) Concert-ov. by Mendelssohn, Op.27, 1832, f.p. 1836. Theme from this is quoted by Elgar in 13th (*Romanza*) of his *Enigma Variations*.

calore (It.). Heat. Passion. So the adjective *caloroso*.

Calvé [Calvet de Roquer], (Rosa-Noémie) **Emma** (*b* Decazeville, 1858; *d* Millau, 1942). Fr. soprano

particularly noted for perf. as Carmen. Début Brussels 1881; La Scala 1887; CG 1892; NY Met 1893 where first sang Carmen. Created roles of Anita in *La Navarraise* and Suzel in *L'amico Fritz*. Announced retirement from opera after singing in 1,000th perf. of *Carmen* at Paris Opéra-Comique in 1904, but sang at Manhattan Opera House, NY, in 1907 and 1908. Gave concerts in USA until 1927.

Calvocoressi, Michel-Dimitri (*b* Marseilles, 1877; *d* London, 1944). Fr.-born music critic of Gr. parentage (Eng. cit.). Career in Paris as mus. critic, author, and lect. on mus.; settled in London 1914, working for Admiralty. Early student of Russ. mus. and assoc. with Diaghilev opera and ballet enterprise 1907–10. Wrote books on Schumann, Glinka, Liszt, and Mussorgsky. Leading champion of original version of *Boris Godunov*, the lib. of which he trans. into Eng. Also trans. Shostakovich's *Lady Macbeth of the Mtsensk District*. Friend of Ravel and Vaughan Williams.

calypso. W. Indian folk dance, but better known in its sung form. Began among slaves on plantations. Forbidden to talk, they chanted news and opinions to a tom-tom rhythm, using a *patois*. Today, especially in Trinidad, is used as a way of commenting on politics, scandal, and sport. Among best-known examples are the cricket calypsos, such as 'Cricket, lovely cricket'.

Calzabigi, Raniero de (*b* Leghorn, 1714; *d* Naples, 1795). It. writer of libs. for Gluck's *Orfeo, Alceste*, and *Paride ed Elena* and for operas by Salieri and Paisiello. Pubd. ed. of Metastasio's works (1755). Ran lottery in Paris in partnership with Casanova and under the protection of Mme de Pompadour. In 1784 wrote critically of Gluck's opera reforms, claiming much of the credit for himself.

Camargo. See *ballet*.

Cambert, Robert (*b* Paris, *c*.1628; *d* London, 1677). Fr. composer, harpsichordist and organist; colleague in Paris of the poet Pierre Perrin, with whom he collaborated on *Pastorale* (1659) and *Ariane, ou Le mariage de Bacchus* (1659). In 1669 Perrin was awarded monopoly for perf. of opera in Fr. language and he and Cambert founded a company. Cambert's *Pomone* (1671), regarded as the earliest true Fr. opera, ran for 8 months. On Lully taking over the monopoly in 1672, Cambert went to Eng. where Louis Grabu was Charles II's Master of the Musick. Founded a Royal Academy of Music, at which a revised edition of *Ariane* was perf. in 1674, but the enterprise soon failed. Only fragments of his compositions remain.

cambiata. See *changing note*.

Cambreling, Sylvain (*b* Amiens, 1948). Fr. conductor. Won 1974 Besançon cond. comp. Ass. to Serge *Baudo with Orch. de Lyon 1975. Opera début Lyons 1975. Prin. guest cond. with Boulez's Ensemble Intercontemporain 1976–81.

Cond. at Paris Opéra 1980. Mus. dir. Théâtre Royal de la Monnaie, Brussels, 1981–92. Mus. dir. Frankfurt Opera from 1993. Glyndebourne and London (ENO) débuts 1981. La Scala 1984, NY Met 1985, Salzburg 1986.

Cambridge University. Eng. univ. which has conferred mus. degrees (Bachelor of Music, Doctor of Music) since 1463. Formal examinations were instituted by Sterndale Bennett, 1857. The Professors of Mus. have been: Nicolas Staggins (1684–1700); Thos. Tudway (1705–26); Maurice Greene (1730–55); John Randall (from 1755); Charles Hague (from 1799); J. Clarke-Whitfield (from 1821); Thomas A. Walmisley (1836–56); W. Sterndale Bennett (1856–66); G. A. Macfarren (1875–87); C. V. Stanford (1887–1924); Charles Wood (1924–6); E. J. Dent (1926–41); Patrick Hadley (1946–62); Thurston Dart (1962–4); Robin Orr (1965–76); Alexander Goehr (1976–99); Roger Parker (from 1999).

Camden, Archie [Archibald] (Leslie) (*b* Newark, Notts., 1888; *d* Wheathampstead, Herts., 1979). Eng. bassoonist. Member Hallé Orch. 1906–33 (prin. bn. from 1914), BBCSO 1933–45, RPO 1946–7. Soloist and recitalist. Prof. of bn. RMCM 1914–33 and later at RCM. Cond. London Stock Exchange Orch. Wrote *Bassoon Technique* (1962). OBE 1969.

Camden Festival. Annual festival founded in 1954 as the St Pancras Festival (renamed 1965). Special feature was production of operas then outside standard repertory, e.g. Haydn's *Il mondo della luna* (1960), and *L'infedeltà delusa* (1964), Verdi's *Un giorno di regno* (1961), Mozart's *Lucio Silla* (1967), Donizetti's *Torquato Tasso* (1975), Delius's *Koanga* (1972), *Fennimore and Gerda* (1979) and *Margot-la-Rouge* (1984). Concert perfs. were given of Strauss's *Feuersnot* (1978), Walton's *Troilus and Cressida* (1982), Shostakovich's *Lady Macbeth of Mtsensk* (1984), Strauss's *Friedenstag* (1985), Mozart's *La finta semplice* (1985) and *La finta giardiniera* (1986), and Weill's *Protagonist* (1986) and *Der Silbersee* (1987). Discontinued after 1987.

camera (It.). Chamber—as opposed to hall, opera-house, etc. (For *cantata da camera*, see *cantata*; for *concerto da camera*, see *concerto*; for *sonata da camera*, see *sonata*.) *musica di camera* (It.). Chamber mus.

Camerata (It.). Society. Group of poets and musicians who met in houses of Florentine aristocrats *Bardi and *Corsi between 1573 and 1590 and from whose discussions opera was developed. Among them were composers Galilei, *Peri, *Caccini, and Cavalieri. Bardi wrote lib. for Peri and Caccini. The group evolved the monodic *stile rappresentativo* of which the first example (now lost) was Peri's *dramma per musica*, *Dafne*. Various modern chamber-mus. organizations use word *Camerata* in their title.

Cameron, (George) **Basil** (*b* Reading, 1884; *d* Leominster, 1975). Eng. conductor. At early stage

of his career called himself Basil Hindenburg because conds. with Eng. names then received few engagements. After some years as orch. violinist, became cond. Torquay Municipal Orch. 1913–14, Hastings 1923–30, Harrogate 1924–30, S. Francisco SO 1930–2, Seattle 1932–8. Ass. cond. Henry Wood Promenade Concerts from 1940. Cond. f. Brit. ps. of Britten's vn. conc. 1941 and *Sinfonia da Requiem* 1942. CBE 1957.

Camidge. Eng. family of organists spanning nearly 200 years. John (*b* York, 1735; *d* York, 1803), organist, York Minster 1756–99 and composer for hpd. His son Matthew (*b* York, 1764; *d* York, 1844), organist, York Minster 1799–1842, composer of org. mus. and kbd. sonatas. His son John (*b* York, 1790; *d* York, 1859), organist, York Minster 1842–8. His son Thomas Simpson (*b* York, 1828; *d* York, 1912), organist, York Minster 1848–59. His son John (*b* York, 1853; *d* York, 1939), organist, Beverley Minster 1875–1933.

Cammarano, Salvatore (*b* Naples, 1801; *d* Naples, 1852). It. poet, dramatist, painter, and librettist. Had plays staged when he was 18. Wrote first lib. in 1834. In 1835 first collab. with *Donizetti on *Lucia di Lammermoor*. Among subsequent libs. he wrote for him were those of *L'assedio di Calais*, *Belisario*, *Roberto Devereux*, *Poliuto* and others. In 1841 wrote *Alzira* for Verdi, following it with *La battaglia di Legnano*, *Luisa Miller*, and most of *Il trovatore* (he died before completing the last).

campana; campane (It.). Bell; bells, e.g. those used in the orch.

campanella (It.). Little bell. (The plural, *campanelle*, is sometimes used for *glockenspiel.)

Campanella, La. Transcr. for pf. by Liszt of the *Rondo alla campanella* (*Ronde à la clochette*; *Bell rondo) from Paganini's Vn. Conc. in B minor. Liszt first used theme in *Grand Fantaisie sur La Clochette* (*La campanella*) of 1831–2, rev. in *Six grandes études d'après les caprices de Paganini* (1838, rev. 1851).

campanetta (It.). *Glockenspiel.

Campanini, Cleofonte (*b* Parma, 1860; *d* Chicago, 1919). It. conductor and violinist. Début Parma 1880. Ass. cond. NY Met in its first season (1883–4). Cond. f.ps. of *Adriana Lecouvreur* (Milan, 1902) and *Madama Butterfly* (Milan, 1904) and f. Amer. p. of *Pelléas et Mélisande* (1908). Cond. Chicago Grand Opera Co. from 1910.

Campbells are Coming, The. This popular Scot. tune first appeared in print in 1745, at which time it was used as a country dance under the title *Hob and Nob*, but about the same period also found with its present title. Many contradictory statements about its origin.

Campenhout, François van (*b* Brussels, 1779; *d* Brussels, 1848). Belg. tenor, violinist, and composer. Comp. operas, ballets, and church mus., but remembered chiefly as composer of Belg. nat. anthem, *La *Brabançonne* (1830).

Campiello, Il (The Small Venetian Square). Opera in 3 acts by *Wolf-Ferrari to lib. by Ghisalberti based on Goldoni's comedy (1754). Comp. *c*.1934. Prod. Milan 1936.

Campion [Campian], **Thomas** (*b* London, 1567; *d* Witham, 1620). Eng. composer, poet, lawyer, and physician. Admitted to Gray's Inn 1586 and from 1588 took part in plays and masques. Pubd. first *Book of Ayres*, with a group by *Rosseter, 1601, following it with 4 more (1610–12) in which he wrote both mus. and words, with lute acc. Wrote several masques for perf. at James I's court, critique of Eng. poetry, and treatise on counterpoint (1613)—a prototype 'Elizabethan man', proficient in all the arts.

Campoli, Alfredo (*b* Rome, 1906; *d* Princes Risborough, Bucks, 1991). It.-born violinist. Settled in Eng. as a child. London début at age 11. Made reputation in light mus., running his own orch., but after 1945 devoted himself to the conc. repertory, notably in Elgar and Bliss. Amer. début 1953 (NY). Retired 1975.

Campra, André (*b* Aix-en-Provence, 1660; *d* Versailles, 1744). Fr. composer of It. descent. Dir. of mus. at several caths., incl. Arles 1681–3, Toulouse 1683–94, and Notre Dame de Paris 1694–1700. First stage work was *opéra-ballet L'Europe galante* (Paris 1697). Created the form *opéra-ballet*. Comp. many more operas and *opéra-ballets*, incl. *Le carnaval de Venise* (1698); *Tancrède* (1702); *Iphigénie en Tauride* (1704); *Alcine* (1705); *Idoménée* (1712, rev. 1731); *Camille, reine des volsques* (1717); *Achille et Deidamie* (1735). Also wrote church mus. incl. *Requiem* (*c*.1722); 3 books of *Cantates françoises* (1708, 1714, 1728); *Mass* (1700); and many motets and psalms.

canale. Another name for *psaltery.

canaries (or *canarie*, or *canary*). Old dance in rhythm something like *gigue but with all its phrases beginning on first beat of the measure with a note a beat and a half long. So called in 17th cent. because it imitated Canary Is. rituals.

can-can (or *chahut*). Boisterous (and supposedly indecorous) Parisian dance of quadrille pattern which came into vogue in 1830s, having originated in Algeria. Best-known example is Offenbach's from *Orpheus in the Underworld* (1858). Involves high kicking by a line of women in pretty dresses.

canción (Sp.). Song. There are diminutives—*cancioncica, cancioncilla, cancioncita*. The *canción danza* is a Sp. dance-song.

cancrizans. See *canon*.

Candide. Comic operetta in 2 acts by Leonard *Bernstein, based on Voltaire's novel (1759) with lib. (book) originally by Lillian Hellman and ly-

rics by Richard Wilbur, with some later additions by John La Touche, Dorothy Parker, and Bernstein. F.p. Boston, Oct. 1956. Thereafter work underwent many revisions (none involving Bernstein) being reduced to 1-act version in 1973. Book for 1973 version by Hugh Wheeler had new lyrics by Stephen Sondheim and 13-piece orchestration by Hershy Kay. Restored to 2 acts 1982 with mus. edited by John Mauceri. Further rev., 1987, by Mauceri in assoc. with composer, and final rev. by Bernstein and Mauceri for London concert perfs. Dec. 1989, cond. (for first time) by Bernstein and for definitive recording.

Caniglia, Maria (*b* Naples, 1905; *d* Rome, 1979). It. soprano. Début Turin 1930. La Scala 1930–43 and 1948–51. Salzburg Fest. 1935; CG 1937 and also sang there 1939 and 1950; NY Met 1938–9. A famous Tosca and sang other Verdi heroines.

Canino, Bruno (*b* Naples, 1935). It. pianist and composer. Specialist in contemp. mus., notably works by Donatoni and Bussotti. Often accompanied Cathy *Berberian. Member of Trio di Milano. Prof. of mus., Milan Cons. from 1961. Works incl. chamber concs. and str. qts.

Cannabich, Johann Christian (*b* Mannheim, 1731; *d* Frankfurt, 1798). Ger. violinist, composer, and conductor. In 1759 became leader of Mannheim orch., becoming dir. 1774. Dir., court mus. at Munich, 1778. Mozart praised his conducting. Wrote operas, ballets, syms., sinfonie concertanti, and chamber mus. His son Karl (*b* Mannheim, 1771; *d* Munich, 1806) succeeded him as dir. of Munich orch. 1800.

canntaireachd. Curious Scot. Highland bagpipe notation, in which syllables stand for recognized groups of notes.

canon. (1) Strictest form of contrapuntal imitation. The word means 'rule' and, musically, it is applied to *counterpoint in which one melodic strand gives the rule to another, or to all the others, which must, at an interval of time, imitate it, note for note. Simple forms of choral canon are the *catch and the *round. There are varieties of canon, as follows:

canon at the octave in which the vv. (human or instr.) are at that pitch-interval from one another. *canon at the fifth*, or at any other interval, is similarly explained.

A canon for 2 vv. is called a *canon 2 in 1* (and similarly with *canon 3 in 1*, etc.). A *canon 4 in 2* is a double canon, i.e. one in which 2 vv. are carrying on one canon whilst 2 others are engaged on another.

canon by augmentation has the imitating vv. in longer notes than the one that they are imitating. *canon by diminution* is the reverse. *canon cancrizans* is a type in which the imitating v. gives out the melody backwards ('cancrizans' from Lat. *cancer* = crab; but crabs move sideways). Other names for it are *canon per recte et retro* (or *rectus et inversus*) and *retrograde canon*.

A *perpetual canon* or *infinite canon* is a canon so arranged that each v., having arrived at the end, can begin again, and so indefinitely as in *Three blind mice*. The converse is *finite canon*.

strict canon in which the intervals of the imitating v. are exactly the same as those of the v. imitated (i.e. as regards their quality of major, minor, etc.).

In *free canon* the intervals remain the same numerically, but not necessarily as to quality (e.g. a major 3rd may become a minor 3rd).

That v. in a canon which first enters with the melody to be imitated is called *dux* (leader) or *antecedent*, and any imitating v. is called *comes* (companion) or *consequent*.

In *canon by inversion* (also styled *al rovescio*), an upward interval in the *dux* becomes a downward one in the *comes*, and vice versa. *canon per arsin et thesin* has the same meaning, but also another one, i.e. canon in which notes that fall on strong beats in the *dux* fall on weak beats in the *comes*, and vice versa.

Choral canon in which there are non-canonic instrumental parts is *accompanied canon*.

Passages of canonic writing often occur in comps. that, as wholes, are not canons. In addition to actual canonic comp. there exists a great deal of comp. with a similar effect but which is too free to come under that designation, being mere *canonic imitation*.

(2) Name for **psaltery (or *canale*).

cantabile (It.). Singable, singingly, i.e. with the melody smoothly perf. and well brought out. Critics frequently write of a performer's *cantabile* style, meaning a lyrical 'singing' style. (For aria cantabile see *aria*.) **cantando** (It.), singing.

cantata (It.). Sung. Term with different meanings according to period: (1) In early 17th cent., often a dramatic madrigal sung by one v., with lute acc. or basso continuo. The form became very popular in It. later in 17th cent., being perf. by several vv., some cantatas being comp. of recit., others of a succession of arias. The *cantata da camera* was secular, the *cantata da chiesa* (developed by **Carissimi) sacred. A prolific exponent of the cantata was A. *Scarlatti, who wrote 600 for solo v. and continuo, 60 for v. and instrs., and several chamber cantatas for 2 vv.

(2) During 18th cent., became more theatrical, comprising a *ritornello*, *aria* on two contrasted themes, and concluding *ritornello*, and acc. by str. In Ger. the form was found mainly in the church, written for soloist(s), ch., organ, and orch. on biblical text. *Telemann, *Schütz, and *Handel wrote in this style but were overshadowed by *Bach who wrote nearly 300 church cantatas as well as secular cantatas which resemble a short opera (*Coffee Cantata* and *Peasant Cantata*).

(3) From Bach's model there developed the cantata of the 19th cent. which was usually on a sacred subject and was, in effect, a short oratorio. Secular cantatas on an elaborate scale are Elgar's *King Olaf* and *Caractacus*. In the 20th

cent. the term has acquired a much looser meaning. Walton's *Belshazzar's Feast* and Vaughan Williams's *Sancta Civitas* are described by their composers as oratorios, but could equally well be classified as cantatas. Britten's *Cantata academica* is for soloists, ch., and orch., while Stravinsky's *Cantata* is for 2 soloists, women's ch., and 6 instr.

Cantata. Setting by Stravinsky for sop., ten., female ch., 2 fl., 2 ob., cor anglais, and vc. of anon. 15th- and 16th-cent. Eng. poems (incl. 'Lyke Wake Dirge' and 'Westron Wind'). Comp. 1951–2. F.p. Los Angeles 1952; London 1953.

Cantata Academica (Carmen Basiliense). Choral work, Op.62, by Britten, comp. 1959 for 500th anniv. of Basle Univ. For SATB soloists, ch., and orch. F.p. Basle 1960. Lat. text, compiled from Univ. Charter and orations in praise of Basle, by Bernhard Wyss.

Cantata Profana (*A Kilenc csodaszarvas*; The 9 Enchanted Stags). Work by Bartók for double ch., ten. and bar. soloists, and orch., comp. 1930 and f.p. London (BBC broadcast) 25 May 1934.

cante flamenco. Type of melody popular in Andalusia and used in both song and dance. A branch of **cante hondo*. The significance of the word *flamenco* (Flemish) is much disputed. See also *flamenco*.

cante hondo or **cante jondo** (Sp.). Deep song. Traditional Andalusian song, with a good deal of repetition of the note, much melodic decoration, and the use of some intervals that do not occur in the accepted European scales. The Phrygian *cadence is much used and the acc. is usually by guitar, played by another performer.

Cantelli, Guido (*b* Novara, 1920; *d* Orly, Paris, 1956). It. conductor. Début Novara (Teatro Coccia) 1943. Guest cond. La Scala after 1945. Invited by Toscanini to guest-cond. NBC Orch., NY, 1949. Edinburgh Fest. 1950. Cond. and made recordings with Philharmonia Orch. after 1951. Salzburg Fest. début 1953 (Vienna PO). Cond. and prod. *Così fan tutte* at Piccola Scala 1956. Appointed mus. dir. of La Scala a few days before death in air crash.

Canteloube (de Malaret), (Marie-) **Joseph** (*b* Annonay, 1879; *d* Paris, 1957). Fr. composer. Pupil of Schola Cantorum of *d'Indy, whose biography he wrote (1949). Wrote 2 operas (*Le Mas*, 1910–13, and *Vercingétorix*, 1930–2), but best known as collector of Fr. folk-songs, hence the **Chants d'Auvergne*, 9 songs for v. and pf. or orch. taken from the 4 vols. he pubd., 1923–30.

Canterbury Degrees. See *Archbishop's Degrees*.

Canterbury Pilgrims, The. (1) Opera in 3 acts by Stanford to lib. by G. A. A'Beckett based on Chaucer's poem. Prod. London 1884.

(2) Opera in 4 acts by *de Koven to lib. by MacKaye after Chaucer. Prod. NY Met 1917.

(3) Cantata by George Dyson based on Chaucer (modernized text) f.p. Winchester 1931 (ov. *At the Tabard Inn* 1946).

canti carnascialeschi (It.). Carnival songs (singular is *canto carnascialesco*). Processional madrigals of an early simple variety, with several stanzas to the same mus., something like the Eng. Ayre but with the tune in the ten. Part of social life of Florence in the 15th and 16th cents., being written for the carnival festivities of the Medici court.

canticle. (1) A Bible hymn (other than a psalm) used in the liturgy of a Christian church. In the RC Church the Canticles drawn from the New Testament are called the *Evangelical Canticles* or *Major Canticles*, in distinction from those drawn from the Old Testament, which are called the *Minor Canticles*.
(2) Concert work with (usually but not exclusively) religious text, particularly favoured by Britten (see below).

Canticles. Name given by Britten to 5 of his comps. I (1947) Op.40, is a setting of a poem by Francis Quarles (*My beloved is mine*) and is subtitled 'In Memory of Dick Sheppard' (a former vicar of St Martin-in-the-Fields, London); II (1952) *Abraham and Isaac*, Op.51, on a text from a Chester miracle play, for cont. (or counterten.), ten., and pf.; III (1954) *Still Falls the Rain*, Op.55, for ten., hn., and pf., poem by Edith Sitwell; IV (1971) *Journey of the Magi*, Op.86, for counterten., ten., bar., and pf., poem by T. S. Eliot; V (1974) *The Death of St Narcissus*, Op.89, for ten. and harp, poem by Eliot.

Canticum Sacrum (ad honorem Sancti Marci nominis) (Sacred song (to the honour of the name of St Mark)). Comp. by Stravinsky in 5 movts., with introductory ded., for ten., bar., ch., and orch. Comp. 1955. F.p. Venice (St Mark's) 1956.

Canti di Prigionia (Songs of Imprisonment). Work by *Dallapiccola, comp. 1938–41 as a protest against Mussolini's adoption of Hitler's racial policies (Dallapiccola's wife was Jewish), for ch., 2 pf., 2 harps, and perc. 3 movts. are: 1. *Preghiera di Maria Stuarda*, 2. *Invocazione di Boezio*, 3. *Congedo di Girolamo Savonarola*.

cantiga. Sp. or Port. folk-song; also type of medieval religious song, of which most celebrated examples are probably contained in the 420 *Cantigas de Santa Maria* (Songs of the Virgin Mary), compiled 1250–80 by Alfonso the Wise, King of Sp.

cantilena (It.; Fr. *cantilène*). Cradle song. (1) Smooth, melodious (and not rapid) vocal writing (used operatically esp. in relation to R. Strauss) or perf.
(2) (now obsolete). Short song.
(3) In choral mus., the part carrying the main tune.
(4) Type of *solfeggio in which all the notes of the scale appeared.

cantillation. Chanting in free rhythm, in plainsong style. The term is most used in connection with Jewish liturgical mus.

Cantiones sacrae (Sacred Songs). Term used by many composers, incl. (1) Motets by William *Byrd. Book I (1589) contains 29 for 5 vv., Book II (1591) 20 for 5 vv. and 12 for 6 vv. In 1575 Byrd and Tallis jointly pubd. vol. of *Cantiones sacrae* of which 17 were by Byrd.
(2) Comp. by John *Gardner for sop., ch., and orch., to biblical text, f.p. Hereford 1952.

canto (It.). Song, melody. So *col canto*, With the song, i.e. the accompanist to take his time throughout from the performer of the melody. Also *marcato il canto*, bring out the tune.

canto fermo (It.). See *cantus firmus*.

cantor. (1) The precentor or dir. of the mus. in a Ger. Protestant church (as J. S. Bach was at Thomaskirche, Leipzig).
(2) The leading singer in a synagogue.

cantoris (Lat.). Of the singer, i.e. precentor. That side of the choir on which the precentor sits but now normally the north side. Opposite of *decani.

cantus (Lat.). Song. In the 16th and 17th cents. applied to the uppermost v. in choral mus.

cantus choralis. See *chorale*. For **cantus figuratus, cantus mensuratus**, and **cantus planus**, see plainsong.

cantus firmus (Lat.). Fixed song. A melody, usually taken from plainsong, used by composers in 14th–17th cents. as the basis of a polyphonic comp. and against which other tunes are set in counterpoint. Also, in 16th cent., the upper v.-line of a choir. Sometimes referred to as *canto fermo*. See *conductus*.

Canyons aux étoiles, Des (From Canyons to the Stars). Work by *Messiaen for pf., hn., and orch., comp. 1970–4, f.p. NY, 1974. Inspired by Amer. landscape. in Utah, where Mount Messiaen was named in his honour.

canzona, canzone (It., plural *canzoni*). (1) Type of troubadour song in the characteristic form AAB (also known as *canzo* or *canso* [Provençal]).
(2) Designation for several types of 16th-cent. It. secular vocal mus., some similar to the madrigal, others to the popular *villanella*.
(3) In 18th- and 19th-cent. mus., a song or instr. piece of lyrical character, e.g. *Voi che sapete* from Mozart's *Le nozze di Figaro*.
(4) 16th- and 17th-cent. instr. comp. which developed from lute and kbd. arrs. of Fr.-Flemish *chansons* of Janequin, Sermisy, Josquin Desprès, etc. It. composers wrote orig. comps. on these models either for organ (*canzona d'organo*), or for

instr. ens. (*canzona da sonar*), which led in turn to the 17th-cent. sonata and kbd. fugue. Notable composers of the kbd. canzona, which throughout its development retained characteristic sectional form and quasi-fugal use of imitation, incl. G. Cavazzoni, A. Gabrieli, C. Merulo, Frescobaldi, Froberger, and J. S. Bach; while sectional variety and contrast of the ens. canzona exploited by G. Gabrieli and Frescobaldi.

canzonet, canzonetta. Diminutive of *canzona. In late 16th and 17th cents., a short, polyphonic, dance-like vocal piece, unacc. or (later) with instr. acc.; later applied to a light, flowing kind of simple solo song. Tchaikovsky called the slow movt. of his vn. conc. a *canzonetta*.

caoine. Irish funeral song, acc. by wailing (Eng. spelling is 'keen').

Cape, Safford (*b* Denver, Col., 1906; *d* Brussels, 1973). Amer. conductor, specialist in medieval mus. Settled in Brussels 1925. Founded Pro Musica Antiqua for perf. of early mus., 1933. Also comp. chamber mus.

Capell, Richard (*b* Northampton, 1885; *d* London, 1954). Eng. critic and author. Mus. critic of London *Daily Mail* (1911–31) and of *Daily Telegraph* (1931–54). Owner and ed. of quarterly *Music and Letters* from 1936. Wrote *Schubert's Songs* (1928) and trans. many songs by Schubert, Schumann, and Wolf, and lib. of R. Strauss's *Friedenstag* (Day of Peace) 1938. Served 1914–18 war and as war correspondent 1939–45 war, writing *Simiomata* (*Jottings*) about Greece 1944–5. OBE 1946.

capella. See *cappella*.

capelle (Fr.). Same as Ger. *Kapelle*.

Capellmeister. See *Kapellmeister*.

Capitán, El. March by *Sousa, also an operetta by him to lib. by C. Klein with lyrics by T. Frost. Prod. Boston and NY 1896, London 1899.

Caplet, André (*b* Le Havre, 1878; *d* Neuilly-sur-Seine, 1925). Fr. conductor and composer. Won *Prix de Rome* 1901. Début as cond. 1896. Became ass. to Colonne. Mus. dir. Odéon 1899–1910. Cond. Boston, Mass., Opera Co. 1910–14; CG 1912. Friend of Debussy whose *Children's Corner* and *Pagodes* he orch. and whose *Le Martyre de Saint-Sébastien* (part of which he orch.) he cond. at its f.p. 1911. Comp. orch. works incl. vc. conc., chamber mus., choral works, and songs. Health affected by gassing when serving in Fr. army 1914–18.

capo, capotasto, capo d'astro, capodastro (It.); **capodastère** (Fr.), **Kapotaster** (Ger.). Head of the touch, i.e. the 'nut', or raised portion of the top of the fingerboard of a str. instr., which 'touches' the str. and defines their length at that end. Another name is *barre* (Fr.). A movable capotasto has sometimes been used (esp. in guitar playing) which can be placed at any point on the str. (in vc. playing the thumb acts as such

and in the 18th cent. was sometimes so called). In USA the name *capotasto* is reserved for this type.

cappella. (It.). Chapel. *a cappella* or *alla cappella* (applied to choral mus.) meaning in church style, i.e. unaccompanied (like 16th-cent. and other church mus.). A rarer sense of these expressions makes them synonymous with *alla *breve*.

Cappuccilli, Piero (*b* Trieste, 1929; *d* Trieste, 2005). It. baritone. Official début Milan 1957. Débuts: NY Met 1960, La Scala 1964, CG 1967, Chicago 1969, Salzburg 1975. Outstanding in Verdi (Germont, Posa, Iago, etc.).

capriccio (It.); **caprice** (Eng. and Fr.). (1) Term applied to some 16th-cent. It. madrigals and, later, to a kind of free fugue for kbd. instr., and later to any light quick comp.

(2) In early 18th cent. sometimes used for *'cadenza'.

(3) *a capriccio* means 'according to the fancy (caprice) of the performer', hence a comp. which has unexpected and orig. effects. Stravinsky and Janáček both wrote works for pf. and orch. which they called *Capriccio*, Janáček's being for left hand only and wind ens. (comp. for the Cz. pianist Otakar Hollmann). 2nd movt. of Haydn's Sym. No.86 (Hob. I:86) is called *Capriccio*, unusual in a sym.

Capriccio. R. Strauss's last opera, comp. 1940–1, styled a 'conversation piece', written in 1 act but usually perf. in 2-act Munich version. Lib. by Clemens *Krauss and composer, incorporating elements by Hans Swarowsky, Josef Gregor, S. Zweig, and Hofmannsthal, and loosely based on Casti's comedy *Prima la musica, poi le parole* (1786). Prod. Munich 1942, London CG 1953, NY 1954 (Juilliard). F.p. of version in Eng. trans., GTO 1976.

Capriccio Burlesco. Orch. work by Walton, commissioned for 125th anniv. of NYPO and f.p. by that orch., cond. *Kostelanetz, 1968. London 1969.

Capriccio espagnol. See *Spanish Caprice*.

Capriccio italien. See *Italian Caprice*.

capriccioso (It.), **capricieux** (Fr.). Capricious, hence in a lively, informal, whimsical style. So the adverb *capricciosamente*. *La Capricieuse* is by Elgar (Op.17) for vn. and pf., comp. 1891.

caprice. See *capriccio*.

Capriol Suite. Suite for str. orch. by Peter *Warlock, comp. 1926, arr. for full orch. 1928. Its 6 movts. are based on old Fr. dances from *Arbeau's *Orchésographie* (1589), 'Capriol' being a character in the book.

Capuana, Franco (*b* Fano, 1894; *d* Naples, 1969). It. conductor. Début Brescia 1919. Cond. Turin 1929–30, San Carlo, Naples, 1930–7, La Scala 1937–40, 1946–52 (mus. dir. from 1949). First to cond. opera at CG after World War II (*La traviata*, 5 Sept. 1946). Specialist in Wagner and Strauss. Cond. first It. perf. of *Jenůfa*, Venice 1941, and revived, ahead of fashion, *I Capuleti e i Montecchi* and *Alzira*.

Capuleti e i Montecchi, I (The Capulets and the Montagues). Opera in 4 parts (2 acts) by Bellini to lib. by Romani freely adapted from the It. sources of Shakespeare's *Romeo and Juliet*. Prod. Venice 1830, London 1833, New Orleans 1837.

Caractacus. Several composers have written mus. based on the Brit. King or chieftain who put up almost the last resistance to the Romans, but the best-known work is Elgar's dramatic cantata, Op.35, for sop., ten., bar., and bass soloists, ch., and orch. to text by H. A. Acworth. F.p. Leeds 1898, London 1899.

Caradori-Allan [de Munck], **Maria** (Caterina Rosalbina) (*b* Milan, 1800; *d* Surbiton, 1865). It.-born Alsatian soprano. Settled in Eng. Début London 1822. Successful career in opera (created Giulietta in *I Capuleti e i Montecchi*, Venice 1830), but chief claims to fame are as sop. soloist in first London perf. Beethoven's 9th Sym., 1825, and in f.p. of Mendelssohn's *Elijah*, Birmingham 1846. She was duettist with *Malibran at Manchester Fest. 1836 when the latter collapsed, dying 9 days later.

Carapetian, Armen (*b* Isphahan, Persia, of Armenian parents, 1908; *d* Francestown, NH, 1992). Persian-Amer. musicologist. In 1944 founded Institute of Renaissance and Baroque Mus., Rome, superseded by the American Institute of Musicology of which he was dir. Ed works of *Brumel.

Cardew, Cornelius (*b* Winchcombe, Glos., 1936; *d* London, 1981). Eng. composer and guitarist. Chorister, Canterbury Cath. 1943–50. Prof. of comp. RAM, from 1967. His early pf. works are in the style of early Boulez and Stockhausen, but later comps. follow a *Cage-like indeterminacy, e.g. *Treatise* (1963–7), a graphic score of nearly 200 pages containing no instructions to the performer. Became radical Maoist and revolutionary Communist. Formed Scratch Orch. 1969. Works incl. Str. Trio (1957); *2 Books of Study for Pianists* (1958); *Octet '61* (1961) for unspecified instr.; *3 Winter Potatoes* (1965), pf.; *The Great Learning* (parts 1–7, 1968–70), various perf.; *The East is Red*, vn., pf. (1972); *Piano Album*, pf. (1973); *The Old and the New*, sop., ch., orch. (1973); *Thälmann Variations*, pf. (1974); *Vietnam Sonata*, pf. (1976).

Cardillac. Opera in 3 acts by Hindemith to lib. by Ferdinand Lion based on E. T. A. Hoffmann's *Das Fräulein von Scuderi* (1818). Prod. Dresden 1926. Concert perf. London (BBC) 1936. Rev. version (4 acts), with new lib. by composer after Lion, Zurich 1952. F. London stage p. 1970 (SW), Santa Fe 1967. Cardillac is name of prin. character, a goldsmith.

Cardoso, (Frei) **Manuel** (*b* Fronteira do Alemtejo, 1566; *d* Lisbon, 1650). Portuguese composer and organist who spent most of his life as org. and choirmaster in Lisbon. From 1618 to 1625 was in household of Duke of Barcelona (later King John IV) who paid for printing of his first book of masses (1625) and a book of motets (1648). Wrote masses, motets, and other church mus. influenced by Palestrina. Many of his works were destroyed in Lisbon fire, 1755.

Cardus, (Sir) (John Frederick) **Neville** (*b* Rusholme, Manchester, 1888; *d* London, 1975). Eng. critic and essayist, also writer on cricket. Ass. cricket coach Shrewsbury Sch. 1912–16. Wrote first mus. criticism for *Daily Citizen* 1913. Joined staff of *Manchester Guardian* 1917, becoming its cricket corr. 1919 and chief mus. critic 1927–40. *Sydney Morning Herald* 1941–7, rejoined *Guardian* 1951 but wrote occasionally for other newspapers. Author of book on Mahler's first 5 syms., 2 vols. of autobiography, and several colls. of mus. and cricket essays. CBE 1964. Knighted 1967.

Carestini, Giovanni (*b* Filottrano, nr. Ancona, *c*.1705; *d* Filottrano, *c*.1760). It. contralto castrato, one of the foremost of his time. Début Rome 1721. After successes in Rome, Vienna, Prague, Mantua, Naples, Venice, and Milan 1721–33, went to London where Handel engaged him for opera prods. and oratorio perfs. 1733–5. Returned to Venice 1735 and was active for another 20 years, joining Dresden court in 1747 and Frederick the Great's in Berlin 1750–4. Sang in St Petersburg 1754–6.

Carewe, John (Maurice Foxall) (*b* Derby, 1933). Eng. conductor. Founded New Mus. Ens. 1957 and cond. f.ps. of works by Birtwistle, Maxwell Davies, and Goehr, and Brit. premières of Boulez, Messiaen, and Stockhausen. Staff, Morley Coll., 1958–66. Cond. BBC Welsh SO 1966–71. Mus. dir. Brighton Phil. Soc. 1974–87. Prin. cond. *Fires of London 1980–4. Chief cond., Chemnitz Opera and Robert Schumann PO 1993–6.

Carey, Henry (*b* ?Yorkshire, *c*.1690; *d* Clerkenwell, 1743). Eng. composer, poet, and playwright. Wrote successful burlesques of It. opera and cantatas between 1729 and 1737, several being perf. at Drury Lane. His songs incl. 'Sally in our alley' *c*.1715 (of which he also wrote the words).

carezzando, carezzevole (It.). Caressing; caressingly.

carillon. (1) See *bell*.

(2) Org. stop; a *mixture* of 3 ranks (12th, 17th, 22nd); chiefly in USA.

Carillon. Recitation with orch. by Elgar, Op.75, to poem by Belg. writer E. Cammaerts, comp. Nov. 1914 as tribute to Belgium. F.p. London, 7 Dec. 1914. Can be perf. without narrator.

Carissimi, Giacomo (*b* Marini, Rome, 1605; *d* Rome, 1674). It. composer, one of early masters of oratorio form. Choirmaster Assisi 1628–9, Collegio Germanico, Rome, 1629–74. Oratorios incl.

Lucifer, Job, Baltazar, Jephte (1650), *Judicium Salomonis*; motets, and recits. (e.g. *Abraham and Isaac*). Adapted Monteverdi's operatic innovations to sacred drama. His *Missa 'L'Homme armé'* was last of its kind. In 1656 was appointed choirmaster to Queen Christina of Sweden when she established her court in Rome after her abdication.

Carl Rosa Opera Company, Royal. Eng. opera co. founded 1875 in Dublin and London by Ger. violinist Karl August Nicolaus Rose who settled in Eng. in 1866 and became known as Carl *Rosa. Rosa died in 1889, when co. became touring organization and was accorded title 'Royal' by Queen Victoria in 1893. Alfred van Noorden dir. 1900–16; Arthur Winckworth and Rosa's second wife were co-dir. 1916–23; H. B. Phillips dir. 1923–50. After various dissensions, Arts Council withdrew subsidy in 1958 and co. became defunct, and attempt to revive it failed in 1960. Last perf. (*Don Giovanni*) was at Prince's Th., London, on 17 Sept. 1960. Policy was opera in English and co. provided invaluable training-ground for many singers. Gave f.p. in England of Massenet's *Manon* (1885), Humperdinck's *Hänsel und Gretel* (1894), Puccini's *La bohème* (1897), and Giordano's *Andrea Chénier* (1903). Revived 1988 with new repertory of operettas and Gilbert and Sullivan.

Carlton, Nicholas (*fl.* early 16th cent.). Eng. composer. His 'Verse for 2 to play on one org.' (or virginals) is among earliest examples of 4-hand mus. for kbd. instr.

Carlton, Richard (*b* c.1558; *d* c.1638). Eng. composer of madrigals and contributor to *The *Triumphs of Oriana* ('Calm was the Air', in 5 parts). Vicar of Norfolk churches.

Carmagnole, La. Originally name of short coat, worn in north It. district of Carmagnola, and imported into Fr. by workmen from that district. The insurgents of Marseilles in 1792 introduced it to Paris, where it became identified with the Revolution. A round dance of the time was given the name, and a song with the refrain, 'Dansons la Carmagnole, vive le son du canon', to a very catchy air, became identified with activities during Reign of Terror. Authorship of words and mus. unknown.

Carman's Whistle. Tune to be found, with variations by Byrd, in *Fitzwilliam Virginal Book. It is that of a ballad pubd. 1592. A carman was a carter.

Carmelites, The (Poulenc). See *Dialogues des Carmélites, Les*.

carmen (Lat.). (1) Tune, song, strain, poem.

(2) (in 14th- and 15th-cent. parlance; plural *carmina*) V. part of a comp. (as distinguished from the instr. parts), or uppermost part of a choral comp.

Carmen. Opera (*opéra-comique*) in 4 acts by Bizet to libretto by Meilhac and Halévy after Mérimée *nouvelle* (1845). Comp. 1873–4. Sometimes perf. with orig. spoken dialogue replaced by recitatives composed by Ernest Guiraud. Prod. Paris 1875, Vienna (with Guiraud recit.) 1875, London and NY 1878. The famous *Habanera* may have been inspired (consciously or unconsciously) by a *chanson havanaise* by, or collected by, Sebastian *Yradier, Sp. composer (1809–65). The Fritz Oeser edn. of the score (1964), used in most modern perfs., controversially includes mus. Bizet rejected in his own edn. of vocal score pubd. by Choudens in 1875.

Carmichael, Hoagy [Hoagland] (Howard) (*b* Bloomington, Ind., 1899; *d* Rancho Mirage, Calif., 1981). Amer. composer of songs and lyrics, pianist, film actor, and singer. Songs incl. *Two Sleepy People* (1927); *Stardust* (1927); *Georgia on my Mind* (1930); *Rockin' Chair* (1930); *Little Old Lady* (1933); *Lazy Bones* (1933); *Thanks for the Memory* (1938); *The Nearness of You* (1940); and *I Get Along Without You Very Well* (1939).

Carmina Burana (cantiones profanae) (Songs of Beuren, profane songs). Scenic cantata by Carl *Orff, with optional mimed action, in 25 movts. for sop., ten., and bar. soloists, boys' choir, ch., and orch. (14 movts. for ch.). Lat. text–student songs about wine, women, and love–based on poems in Lat., Old Ger. and Old Fr. from MS dated 1280 found in Benedictine monastery of Beuren. First part of Orff's trilogy *Trionfi. Comp. 1935–6. Prod. Frankfurt 1937, S. Francisco 1958, London 1960 (concert).

Carnaval (Carnival). Schumann's pf. comp. Op.9, comp. 1834–5 and sub-titled *Scènes mignonnes sur quatre notes* (dainty scenes on 4 notes), the notes being A–S–C–H (A♭–E♭–C–B). Asch was the home-town of a girl with whom he was in love and its 4 letters were the only 'musical' letters of his name. Each of the 21 pieces has a descriptive title, e.g. *Papillons*. Orch. version by Glazunov and others used for Fokine ballet (St Petersburg 1910).

Carnaval à Paris (Carnival in Paris). 'Episode for orchestra', Op.9, by *Svendsen, pubd. 1879.

Carnaval des animaux, Le (The Carnival of Animals). 'Grand zoological fantasy' by Saint-Saëns. Orig. chamber version for 2 pf., str. quintet, fl., cl., and xylophone, but also for 2 pf. and orch. Comp. 1886 but perf. forbidden in composer's lifetime. Pubd. 1922. 14 movts., of which No.13 is the famous *Le Cygne* (The Swan).

Carnaval de Venise (Carnival in Venice). Paganini's Op.10, comp. in or before 1829, was a set of variations for unacc. vn. on *Le Carnaval de Venise*, being the popular Venetian song 'O mamma mia'. Other composers, e.g. *Benedict, have also used the theme. A. *Thomas wrote an opera *Le Carnaval de Venise*, prod. 1857.

Carnaval Romain, Le ('The Roman Carnival'). 'Ouverture caractéristique' by Berlioz, comp. and f.p. 1844, derived from material in his opera *Benvenuto Cellini* (1834–7).

Carnegie Hall. Largest concert-hall in NY, seating *c*.3,000, and, until 1962 when the Phil. (now Avery Fisher) Hall, Lincoln Center, opened, home of the city's prin. orch. concerts. Architect, W. B. Tuthill. Opened May 1891, Tchaikovsky being among guest conds. Called 'Music Hall' until 1898, when renamed in honour of industrialist Andrew Carnegie (1835–1919), who had provided most of the money to build it.

Carner, Mosco (*b* Vienna, 1904; *d* Stratton, nr. Bude, 1985). Austrian-born conductor and critic. Cond. opera at Opava, Cz., 1929–30 and Danzig 1930–3. Settled London 1933, working as cond. and as London correspondent for some continental papers. Contrib. criticism to many Eng. newspapers and periodicals. Author of several books, notably *Puccini* (1958, 2nd edn. 1974) and *Alban Berg* (1975).

Carneval (Carnival). (1) Ger. title by which Dvořák's ov. *Karneval* is usually known. His Op.92, comp. 1891, with **Amid Nature* and **Othello* it formed a cycle, **Nature, Life and Love*. F.p. in this form, Prague and NY 1892. Now usually played separately. Orig. title was *Bohemian Carnival*.
(2) Ov., Op.45, by Glazunov (1894).

carol (Fr. *noel*; Ger. *Weihnachtslied*). In medieval times a round dance with mus. acc., but soon developed into a song for 2 or 3 vv. usually (but not necessarily) to a text dealing with the birth of Christ. All Christian nations, Western and Eastern, have carols, some of them evidently of pagan origin but taken over and adapted in early days of Christianity. The nature of the carol varies: it may be dramatic, narrative, or lyrical.

One of oldest printed Eng. Christmas carols is the *Boar's Head Carol*, sung as the traditional dish is carried in on Christmas Day at Queen's College, Oxford; it was printed in 1521. This is but one of a large group of carols assoc. with good cheer as an element in Christmas joy.

With the growth of the Christmas season as a public holiday which became increasingly commercialized, the carol grew in popularity and, concomitantly, in vulgarity so that some 19th-cent. carols are of inferior standard, but the best of them have achieved a place alongside the folk-carols and 17th-cent. Ger. carols which were revived by the late 19th-cent. folk-song movement. A fine selection is sung annually in Eng. on Christmas Eve at King's College, Cambridge. Vaughan Williams wrote a **Fantasia on Christmas Carols*, **Hely-Hutchinson A Carol Symphony*, and Britten a **Ceremony of Carols*.

Carolsfeld, Ludwig Schnorr von. See *Schnorr von Carolsfeld, Ludwig*.

Carosio, Margherita (*b* Genoa, 1908; *d* Genoa, 2005). It. soprano. Début 1927 as Lucia di Lammermoor. CG début 1928. La Scala début 1929, then 1931–9 and 1946–52. Salzburg Fest. 1939. Returned to CG in 1946 with San Carlo co., as Violetta, and in 1950.

Carpenter, John Alden (*b* Park Ridge, Ill., 1876; *d* Chicago, 1951). Amer. composer who, like **Ives, combined mus. with successful business career. Made name with orch. suite *Adventures in a Perambulator* (Chicago 1915). Comp. 3 ballets: *Birthday of the Infanta* (Chicago 1919), *Krazy-Kat*, using jazz idioms (Chicago 1922), and *Skyscrapers* (NY 1926). Other works incl. 2 syms.; tone-poem *Sea Drift* (1933, rev. 1944); vn. conc.; pf. concertino (1915); str. qt.; pf. quintet; and songs. *Skyscrapers* depicts Amer. city life and its score incl. 3 saxophones, banjo, and 2 red traffic lights operated by kbd. Quotes popular songs and alludes to jazz.

Carr, Edwin (James Nairn) (*b* Auckland, 1926; *d* Waiheke Island, 2003). NZ composer. Won 1st prize at Auckland Fest. 1950 with ov. *Mardi Gras* and won Harriet **Cohen int. mus. award 1967. Became serialist after 1961 and taught in Suffolk, returning to NZ 1970. Comps. incl. opera, ballet, sym. for str., pf. conc., and chamber and vocal mus.

carrée (Fr.). Square. Double whole-note or breve.

Carreño, (Maria) **Teresa** (*b* Caracas, 1853; *d* NY, 1917). Venezuelan pianist. Début NY at age 9. Studied with **Gottschalk and Anton **Rubinstein. Toured Europe 1865–75, when she became operatic sop. and, for a brief spell, cond. Returned to pf. 1889, consolidating reputation as leading woman player of her day. Her 4 husbands incl. d'**Albert.

Carreras, José (Maria) (*b* Barcelona, 1946). Sp. tenor. Début 1956 in Falla's *Retablo de Maese Pedro*. Prof. début Barcelona 1970. Won Giuseppe Verdi comp. and sang in It. cities and Paris. London début 1971 (concert perf.), CG 1974, NY City Opera 1972, NY Met 1974, Salzburg 1976. At height of career had intensive treatment for leukaemia. Resumed career 1988. Outstanding in It. repertoire, especially Verdi. Autobiography *Singing for the Soul* (Seattle, 1991). One of Three Tenors with **Domingo and **Pavarotti.

Carrillo, Julián (*b* Ahualulco, Mexico, 1875; *d* San Angél, 1965). Mexican composer. In his teens showed exceptional interest in fractional divisions of the accepted intervals and coined term *sonido 13* (13th sound) for the first 2-octave harmonic on the vn.'s 4th str., this being for him the first pitch outside the traditional 12 semitones to the octave. Gave concerts to demonstrate potentialities of microtonal intervals and invented special instrs., incl. the *octavina* (8th-tones) and *arpa citera* (16th-tones). In 1926 his microtonal works were championed by **Stokowski, who cond. the *Sonata casi-fantasia* (in 4ths, 8ths, and 16ths), and in the 1930s Stokowski and Carrillo toured Mexico with the Sonido 13 Orch. In 1947 built a pf. tuned in 3rds of a whole tone. Comps. divide into 3 periods: traditional tuning up to 1911, atonal from 1911 to 1922, and in *sonido 13* idiom thereafter. They incl. operas, syms., str. qts., vn. conc., and pf.

mus. His *Horizontes* (1950) employs a small orch. tuned in 4ths, 8ths, and 16ths, combined with conventionally tuned orch.

Carse, Adam (von Ahn) (*b* Newcastle upon Tyne, 1878; *d* Great Missenden, 1958). Eng. composer and author. Ass. mus. master Winchester College 1909–22, then prof. of harmony, RAM, 1922–40. Comp. orch. works, chamber mus., and educational mus., and author of valuable treatises on orchestration. Made collection of 350 old wind instruments, presented to Horniman Museum, London.

Carte, Richard D'Oyly. See *D'Oyly Carte, Richard*.

Carter, Elliott (Cook) (*b* NY, 1908). Amer. composer. At 16 befriended by *Ives, who took him to concerts of mus. by Varèse, Sessions, Ruggles, and Copland. Studied pf. at Cambridge, Mass. At Harvard Univ. 1926–32, studying with *Piston and E. B. Hill and having lessons in 1931 from Holst. Continued studies at École Normale de Mus., Paris, and privately with *Boulanger. On return to USA, mus. dir. Ballet Caravan 1936–40. Taught at Peabody Cons., Baltimore, 1946–8, Columbia Univ. 1948–50, Yale Univ. 1958–62. Worked in Rome and Berlin 1963–4. Prof. of mus., Cornell Univ. 1967–8. Pulitzer Prize 1960 (2nd str. qt.) and 1973 (3rd str. qt.). His music is uncompromising and challenging, its harsh brilliance enhanced by compelling intellectual qualities. Early works were neo-classical in style but a new harmonic structure and treatment of rhythm became apparent in the *Piano Sonata* (1945–6). With the *Cello Sonata* (1948) he developed 'metric modulation' whereby a new tempo is established from development of a cross-rhythm within the old tempo. The listener has a clear impression of the simultaneous existence of 2 tempos. The 4 str. qts. have been described as the most significant comps. in the medium since Bartók, and Stravinsky described the Double Conc. as 'the first true American masterpiece'. His writings on many subjects were collected into one vol. (NY 1977). Prin. works:

OPERA: *What Next?* (1993–8).

BALLETS: *Pocahontas* (1937–9); *The Minotaur* (1947).

ORCH.: *Prelude, Fanfare, and Polka* (1938); *Sym. No.1* (1942, rev. 1954); *Holiday Overture* (1944, rev. 1961); *Elegy*, str. (1952); *Variations* (1954–5); *Double Concerto*, hpd., pf., 2 chamber orchs. (1961); pf. conc. (1964–5); Conc. for Orch. (1968–9); *Symphony of 3 Orchestras* (1976–7); *Penthode for 5 Instrumental Quartets* (1984–5); *Three Occasions* (1986–9): 1. *A Celebration of Some 100 × 150 Notes* (1986), 2. *Remembrance* (1988), 3. *Anniversary* (1989); ob. conc. (1986–7); vn. conc. (1990); cl. conc. (1996); *Symphonia: sum fluxae pretiam spei* (1998, comprising *Partita* (1992–3), *Adagio tenebroso* (1995), and *Allegro scorrevola* (1997)); *Asko Conc.*, orch. ens. (1999–2000); vc. conc. (2000); *Boston Conc.* (2001–2); *Micomicón* (2002); *Dialogues*, pf., orch. (2003); *Fons juventatis*, orch. (2004); *Soundings*, orch. (2005); *3 Illusions*, orch. (2005); hn. conc. (2007).

VOICE & ENS.: *Warble for Lilac Time*, high v., pf. or ens. (1943, rev. 1954); *A *Mirror on Which to Dwell*, sop., ens. (1975); *Syringa*, mez., bass, gui., 10 performers (1978); *In Sleep, In Thunder*, ten., 14 players (1981); *Tempo e tempi*, sop., ob., cl., vn., vc. (1998–9).

CHORAL: *Tarantella*, male ch., pf. (1936, arr. with orch. 1971); *To Music*, unacc. (1937); *Heart Not So Heavy as Mine*, unacc. (1938); *The Defense of Corinth*, spkr., male ch., pf. (1942); *The Harmony of Morning*, women's ch., small orch. (1944); *Musicians Wrestle Everywhere*, mixed ch., opt. str. (1945); *Emblems*, male ch., pf. (1947).

CHAMBER MUSIC: *Canonic Suite*, 4 alto sax. (1939, rev. 1981; arr. for 4 cl. 1955–6); *Pastorale*, ca. (or va., or cl.), pf. (1940, arr. ca., mar., str. 1988); *Elegy*, va. or vc., pf. (1943, rev. 1961; arr. str. qt. 1946, str. 1952); ww. quintet (1948); vc. sonata (1948); *8 Études and a Fantasy*, ww. qt. (1949–50); str. qts., No.1 (1950–1), No.2 (1959), No.3 (1971), No.4 (1986), No.5 (1995); *8 Pieces for 4 Kettledrums* (1950, rev. 1966); Sonata, fl., ob., vc., hpd. (1952); *Canon for 3: in memoriam Igor Stravinsky*, equal instr. (1971); *Duo*, vn., pf. (1973–4); brass quintet (1974); *A Fantasy about Purcell's Fantasia upon One Note*, 2 tpt., hn., tb., btb. (1974); *Triple Duo*, vn., vc., fl., cl., pf., perc. (1982–3); *Changes*, gui. (1983); *Esprit rude–esprit doux*, fl., cl. (1984); *Canon for 4: Homage to William*, fl., bcl., vn., vc. (1984); *Riconoscenza–per Goffredo Petrassi*, vn. (1984); *Enchanted Preludes*, fl., vc. (1988); *Birthday Flourish*, 5 tpt. or brass quintet (1988); *Con leggerezza pensosa*, cl., vn., vc. (1990); *Scrivo in Vento*, fl. (1991); Quintet, pf., ob., cl., bn., hn. (1992); *Trilogy*: 1. *Bariolage*, hp., 2. *Inner Song*, ob., 3. *Immer Neu*, ob., hp. (1992); *Gra*, cl. (1993); *Fragment for String Quartet*, str. qt. (1994); *Esprit rude/esprit doux II*, fl., cl., mar. (1995); *Figment I*, vc. (1995); *II* (2001); pf. quintet (1997); *Shard*, gui. (1997); ob. qt. (2001).

VOICE & INSTR.: *Tell me, where is fancy bred*, v., gui. (1938); *Voyage*, mez. or bar., pf. (1943, also for small orch. 1975, rev. 1979); *3 Poems of Robert Frost*, medium v., pf. (1. *Dust of Snow*, 2. *The Rose Family*, 3. *The Line Gang*) (1943); *Of Challenge and of Love: 5 Poems of John Hollander*, sop., pf. (1994–5); *In the Distance of Sleep*, mez., ens. (2006).

PIANO: sonata (1945–6); *Night Fantasies* (1980); *2 Diversions* (1999); *Intermittences* (2005).

Caruso, Enrico (*b* Naples, 1873; *d* Naples, 1921). It. tenor. Regarded as one of the greatest there has been. Début Naples 1895. Created tenor roles in *Fedora* (Milan, 1898), *Adriana Lecouvreur* (Milan, 1902) and Dick Johnson in *La *fanciulla del West* (NY Met, 1910). Buenos Aires début 1899 (*Fedora*). Int. fame after *La bohème* with Melba at Monte Carlo 1902. CG début same year as Duke in *Rigoletto*. Début NY Met 1903 (Duke). Between then and 1920 sang 36 roles and appeared over 600 times at Met (last appearance 24 Dec. 1920 in *La *juive*). First tenor to make records, his recording career extending from 1902 to 1920 and royalties in his lifetime amounting to nearly £500,000. Though not flawless stylistically, his

v. was of sumptuous resonance, mellow and almost baritonal, with an exquisite *mezza voce*. Hon. MVO 1907.

Carvalho, Eleazar de (*b* Iguatu, Ceará, Brazil, 1912; *d* São Paulo, 1996). Brazilian conductor and composer. Tuba-player 1930–40 in orch. of Teatro Municipal, Rio de Janeiro. Cond., Brazilian SO, from 1941. Went to USA 1946, studying with Koussevitzky. Guest cond. leading Amer. orchs. Cond., St Louis SO 1963–8. Returned to Brazil 1971. Taught at Juilliard Sch. 1983. Works incl. operas, symphonic poems, and chamber mus.

Carver, Robert (*b* 1484/5; *d* after 1568). Scottish composer, a monk of Scone Abbey. Comp. in melismatic style. Wrote several masses on song *'L'homme armé'*, only known use of this *cantus firmus* by a Brit. composer. Comp. many motets, incl. one, *O bone Jesu*, in 19 independent parts. Regarded by some as equal of Dunstable. Vol. I of his collected works ed. Denis Stevens 1959.

Cary, Tristram (Ogilvie) (*b* Oxford, 1925). Eng. composer and percussionist. Began interest in elec. mus. 1944 and was producing **musique concrète* by 1949. Worked in record shop 1951–4. Founded own EMS, first in Brit., and prod. scores for several films and BBC TV and radio drama. Teacher at RCM where in 1967 founded EMS. Lect., Univ. of Adelaide, 1974–82, Dean 1982–6.

Caryll, Ivan (Felix Tilkin) (*b* Liège, 1861; *d* NY, 1921). Belg.-Amer. composer of mus. comedies such as *The Duchess of Danzig* (1903) and *Our Miss Gibbs* (1909). Also had th. orch. (Elgar's *Sérénade lyrique*, 1899, is ded. 'to Ivan Caryll's Orchestra'.)

Casadesus, Jean (*b* Paris, 1927; *d* Renfrew, Ontario, 1972). Fr. pianist, son of Robert *Casadesus. Went to USA 1939. Début 1946 with Philadelphia Orch. Winner Geneva comp. 1947. Many tours. Killed in car crash.

Casadesus, Jean-Claude (*b* Paris, 1935) Fr. conductor and composer, nephew of Robert *Casadesus. Solo timpanist, Concert Colonne, 1959–68. Cond. Paris Opéra 1969–71. Cond. Lille Nat. Orch. from 1976.

Casadesus, Marius (*b* Paris, 1892; *d* Suresnes, Paris, 1981). Fr. violinist. Gave recitals with his nephew Robert *Casadesus. Founding member Société Nouvelles des Instruments Anciens (1920–40) which revived old str. instrs. In Paris 1931, he perf. the *Adelaïde Concerto*, said to have been comp. by Mozart when he was 10 and dedicated to Adelaïde, daughter of Louis XV. In 1977 Casadesus admitted he had composed it.

Casadesus, Robert (Marcel) (*b* Paris, 1899; *d* Paris, 1972). French pianist and composer. Nephew of Marius *Casadesus with whom he gave recitals. Notable Mozart player. Wrote 7 syms., 2-pf. conc., 3-pf. conc. with str., 24 pf. preludes, and chamber mus.

Casals, Pablo (Pau, in the Catalan form) (*b* Vendrell, Catalonia, 1876; *d* Rio Piedras, Puerto Rico, 1973). Sp. cellist, conductor, composer, and pianist. Began career in Barcelona cafés and Paris ths. Prof. of vc., Barcelona Cons. 1897–9. Soloist at Lamoureux Concerts, Paris, and Crystal Palace, London, 1899. First US tour 1901. Thenceforward brilliant career as world's foremost cellist. Formed notable trio with *Cortot and *Thibaud. Founded Casals Orch., Barcelona 1919. Went into voluntary exile from Sp. 1939 in protest against Franco régime, vowing never to return while Spain was under totalitarian rule (a vow he kept). In 1950 founded Prades Fest. in French Pyrenees. Settled in Puerto Rico, 1956, founding fest. there. Played in United Nations Assembly 1958 and at White House for President Kennedy 1961. In Oct. 1971 cond. his *Hymn to the United Nations* (Auden) at the U.N. headquarters, NY. Comp. vc. pieces, orch. works, and oratorio *El pessebre* (The Manger).

Casella, Alfredo (*b* Turin, 1883; *d* Rome, 1947). It. composer, conductor, pianist, and author. Visited Russia 1907 and 1909. On return to It. in 1915, as prof. of pf. at Liceo di S. Cecilia, Rome, became champion of all that was new in the arts and headed It. section of ISCM. Anticipated tastes of a later epoch by interest in It. baroque mus., particularly Vivaldi. His own mus. reflected restless and questing mind. Early works influenced by Mahler, whose mus. he cond. in Paris in the early 1900s. Tempted by atonality but after 1920 identified himself with neo-classicism. Comps. incl.:

OPERAS: *La donna serpente* (1928–31); *La favola d'Orfeo* (1932); *Il deserto tentato* (1937).

BALLETS: *Il convento veneziano* (1912); *La Giara* (1924).

ORCH.: syms.: No.1 (1905), No.2 (1908–9 unpubd.), No.3 (1940); *Italia Suite* (1909); *Pupazzetti* (1919); *Scarlattiana*, pf., orch. (1926); vn. conc. (1928); *Concerto romano* (organ) (1926); conc. for pf., vn., and vc. (1933); vc. conc. (1934–5); *Conc. for Orch.* (1937); conc. for pf., timp., perc., str. (1943); songs; and pf. pieces (incl. 2 series entitled *À la manière de . . .* (In the style of . . .) (1911 and 1913), 2nd series collab. Ravel).

Casken, John (*b* Barnsley, 1949). Eng. composer. Lect., Birmingham Univ. 1973–9, Huddersfield Polytechnic 1979–81, Durham Univ. 1981–92. Prof. of mus., Manchester Univ. from 1992. Featured composer at Bath Fest. 1980 where his mus. created a strong impression through its individuality, while suggesting to critics the influences of Debussy and Tippett. Won first Britten Award for comp., 1991. Prin. works incl.:

OPERAS: **Golem* (1988–9); *God's Liar* (1996–2000).

ORCH.: *Tableaux des Trois Ages* (1976–7); pf. conc. (1980–1); *Masque*, ob., 2 hns., str. (1982); *Erin*, db., small orch. (1982–3); *Orion over Farne* (1984); *Maharal Dreaming* (1989); vc. conc. (1991); *Darting the Skiff*, str. (1993); *Cor d'œuvre*, ov. (1993); vn. conc. (1994–5); *Sortilège* (1995–6); *Distant*

Variations, sax. qt., wind orch. (1996–7); sym. (*Broken Consort*) (2003–4); *Rest-Ringing*, str. qt., orch. (2005).

ENSEMBLE: *Kagura*, 13 wind instr. (1972–3); *Music for the Crabbing Sun*, fl., ob., vc., hpd. (1974); *Music for a Tawny-Gold Day*, va., alto sax., bass cl., pf. (1975–6); *Arenaria*, fl., ens. (1976); *Amarantos*, 9 players (1977–8); *Melanos*, tuba, 7 players (1979); *Eructavit*, 10 instr. (1982); *Fonteyn Fanfares*, 12 brass instr. (1982); *Vaganza*, ens. (1985); *Infanta Maria*, ens. (1993–4); *Après un silence*, vn., ens. or vn., chamber orch. (1998).

VOICE & INSTR(S).: *Ia Orana, Gauguin*, sop., pf. (1978); *Firewhirl*, sop., 7 players (1979–80); *To the Lovers' Well*, counterten., 2 ten., bass (2001); *Colloque sentimental*, sop., pf. (2003).

CHORAL MUS.: *To Fields We Do Not Know*, ch. (1984); *Sunrising*, unacc. ch. (1993).

CHAMBER MUSIC: str. qts. No.1 (1981–2), No.2 (1993); *Music for Cello and Piano* (1971–2); *Jadu*, 2 vc. (1973); *Fluctus*, vc., pf. (1973–4); *Thymehaze*, alto rec., pf. (1976); *À Belle Pavine*, vn., tape (1980); *Taerset*, cl., pf. (1982–3); *Clarion Sea*, brass quintet (1985); pf. qt. (1990); *A Spring Cadenza*, vc. (1995); *Après un silence*, vn., pf. (1998, see also ENSEMBLE); *Nearly Distant*, sax. qt. (2000); pf. trio (2002); *Blue Medusa*, bn., pf. (2002); *Choses en moi*, str. qt. (2003).

KEYBOARD: *Ligature*, org. (1979–80); *The Haunting Bough*, pf. (1999).

cassa (It.). Box. Any drum of a large size, hence *gran cassa*, bass drum, and *cassa rullante*, ten. drum.

Cassadó [Moreu], **Gaspar** (*b* Barcelona, 1897; *d* Madrid, 1966). Sp. cellist and composer. Int. career began in 1918. Toured extensively as solo cellist and in chamber mus. with Menuhin, Huberman, Kentner, and Rubinstein. Prof. at Siena Acad. Wrote vc. conc., str. qts., pf. trio, and *Rapsodia Catalana*.

cassation (It. *cassazione*). 18th-cent. instr. comp. (several by Mozart) similar to divertimento and serenade and often to be perf. outdoors.

Casse-noisette (Tchaikovsky). See *Nutcracker*.

cassette (Fr.). Little box. Literally the small package into which a commercial tape-recording is packed but in a wider sense the automatic-rewinding tape itself. Record-playing equipment now generally provides facilities for playing cassettes. Many disc recordings are also issued in cassette form.

Cassilly, Richard (*b* Washington DC, 1927; *d* Boston, 1998). Amer. tenor. Opera début, Broadway, NY, 1955. Member NY City Opera 1955–66. Prin. ten. Hamburg State Opera from 1967. CG début 1968; La Scala 1970; NY Met 1973. Also appeared with Vienna State Opera, S. Francisco, Scottish Opera. Roles incl. Otello, Siegmund, Tristan, Peter Grimes, Captain Vere, Troilus, Laca, Herod, Samson, and Aaron.

Cassirer, Fritz (*b* Breslau, 1871; *d* Berlin, 1926). Ger. conductor and writer. Held opera posts in Lübeck, Elberfeld (1903–5), and Berlin. Cond. f.p. of Delius's operas **Koanga* (Elberfeld 1904) and *A *Village Romeo and Juliet* (Berlin 1907) and f.p. in Eng. of Delius's *Appalachia* (London, 1907). Selected words from Nietzsche's *Also sprach Zarathustra* for Delius's **Mass of Life*, which is dedicated to him.

castanets (Fr. *castagnettes*, It. *castagnette*). Perc. instrs. consisting of 2 cup-shaped wooden clappers clicked rhythmically together by Sp. dancers, to whose hands they are attached. In orch. use, they are mounted on a handle which is shaken.

Castelnuovo-Tedesco, Mario (*b* Florence, 1895; *d* Hollywood, Calif., 1968). It. composer. Assoc. with progressive faction in It. mus. led in 1920s by **Casella. Settled in USA 1939. Devotee of Shakespeare. Operas incl. *La mandragola* (1920–3, rev. 1928); *Aucassin et Nicolette* (1919–38); *All's Well That Ends Well* (1955–8); *Il Mercanto di Venezia* (1956); and *The Importance of Being Earnest* (1961–2). Comp. ballets; oratorios (*Ruth* 1949, *Song of Songs* 1963); orch. works incl. *Concerto Italiano*, vn., orch. (1926); 2 further vn. concs. (1933, 1939); 2 pf. concs. (1928, 1939); gui. conc. (1939); conc. for 2 guitars, *American Rhapsody* (1943); ovs. to Shakespeare's plays (1931–42). Much chamber mus. incl. gui. quintet and gui. sonata. His songs incl. *33 Shakespeare Songs* (1921–5), setting in Eng. of all the song-texts in the plays.

Castiglioni, Niccoló (*b* Milan, 1932; *d* Milan, 1996). It. composer and pianist. Early influence was Mahler, later Boulez, but returned to tonality and tradition. Taught in Amer. univs. 1966–71; returned to It. 1971 to teach at Milan Cons. Comps. incl. 2 operas; *Synchromie*, orch. (1962–3); *Solemn Music II*, sop., chamber orch. (1964–5); sym. in C, ch., orch. (1968–9); *Alef*, solo ob. (1971); *Inverno in-ver*, chamber orch. (1972); *Quodlibet*, pf., chamber orch. (1976); works for th.; and a radio opera (1961) based on Carroll's *Alice* books.

castillane (Sp.). Dance of the Province of Castile.

Castor et Pollux (Castor and Pollux). Opera in prol. and 5 acts by Rameau to lib. by Pierre-Joseph Bernard. Prod. Paris 1737 (rev. without prol. and with new Act I 1754); Glasgow 1929; NY 1937. Operas on same subject by Bianchi (Florence, 1779) and Vogler (Munich, 1787).

castrato (It.). Castrated. Male sop. or cont. whose v. was preserved by castration before puberty. In great demand in It. opera in 17th and 18th cents., the voice being brilliant, flexible, and often sensuous. Giovanni Gualberto Magli, a castrato, sang Music and Proserpine (and perhaps Hope) in f.p. of Monteverdi's *Orfeo* (Mantua 1607). Other famous castrati were Senesino, Farinelli, Caffarelli, Guadagni, and Velluti. Castrati survived in Vatican chapel and Roman churches until 20th cent. Recordings exist of Alessandro

Moreschi (1858–1922), male sop. of Sistine Chapel. Wagner wanted the male soprano D. Mustafà to sing Klingsor in *Parsifal*.

Castro, Juan José (*b* Avellaneda, 1895; *d* Buenos Aires, 1968). Argentinian composer and conductor. Cond. posts in Buenos Aires, Havana, Montevideo, and Melbourne. Dean of studies, Puerto Rico Cons. 1959–64. Cosmopolitan composer with nationalistic flavour and use of serialism. His several operas incl. *Proserpina y el extranjero* (Proserpine and the Stranger) (Milan 1952) and 2 based on plays by Lorca, *La zapatera prodigiosa* (1943) and *Bodas di sangre* (Blood Wedding) (1952). Also 5 syms., pf. conc., vn. conc., orch. suites, choral works. His brother José Maria (*b* Buenos Aires, 1892; *d* Buenos Aires, 1964) was also cond. and composer.

Castrucci, Pietro (*b* Rome, 1679; *d* Dublin, 1752). It. violinist, pupil of Corelli. Settled in London 1715 becoming leader of Handel's opera orch. until 1737. Invented 'violetta Marina' for which instr. Handel wrote solos in *Orlando* and *Sosarme*. Went to Dublin 1750.

catalán (Sp.), **catalane** (Fr.). Type of Sp. dance from Catalonia.

Catalani, Alfredo (*b* Lucca, 1854; *d* Milan, 1893). It. composer. Friend of *Boito who wrote lib. for *La Falce* (Milan 1875). Operas show affinity with Ger. romantics, e.g. Weber and Marschner, and were *Elda* (1876, rev. 1889 as *Loreley*), *Dejanice* (1883), *Edmea* (1886), and *La *Wally* (1891), the last-named being the best and most popular of his works, highly esteemed by Toscanini, who named his daughter after it.

Catalani, Angelica (*b* Sinigaglia, 1780; *d* Paris, 1849). It. soprano. Début Venice 1797, Milan 1801, London 1806. First singer in London of Susanna in *Le nozze di Figaro*, 1812. Managed Paris Théâtre des Italiens 1814–17. Retired from stage 1819 but continued concert work until 1828. In her day extremely highly paid. Founded singing sch., Florence.

Catalogue Aria. Nickname for Leporello's aria in Act 1 Sc. 2 of Mozart's *Don Giovanni* in which he recounts to Donna Elvira a list of the Don's amorous conquests in various countries, ending each instalment with the words 'but in Spain, a thousand and three (*mille e tre*)'. This aria was probably modelled on a similar one in Gazzaniga's *Don Giovanni*, the rapid singing of a list of items being a popular feature of 18th-cent. comic opera.

Catalogue d'oiseaux. Work by Messiaen for solo pf. in 7 books, comp. 1956–8, based on birdsong as noted and remembered by the composer. F.p. Paris 1959 (Loriod).

catch. A type of *round; but the term is now often used in a less general sense which confines its application to such rounds as, in the singing, afford a laugh by the way the words are heard, as for instance in the one *Ah, how Sophia*, which

in the singing suggests 'Our house afire', the later line 'Go fetch the Indian's borrowed plume' similarly suggesting 'Go fetch the engines!'. Restoration specimens are more amusing and much more indecent. A Catch Club (Noblemen and Gentlemen's Catch Club) was founded in London in 1761 and still exists.

Catel, Charles-Simon (*b* Laigle, Normandy, 1773; *d* Paris, 1830). French composer. Joined band of Garde National de Paris, for which wrote new mus. Became répétiteur at Opéra until 1803. Prof. of harmony and counterpoint at new Paris Cons. from 1795. Comp. many Revolutionary marches and hymns. Best known for *Les bayardères* (1810).

Cathédrale engloutie, La (The submerged cathedral). Pf. piece by Debussy, No.10 of his *Préludes*, Book I, comp. 1910. Based on cath. of Ys, with its legend of underwater bells and chanting. F.p. Debussy, Paris 1910. Quoted by Debussy in his vc. sonata, 1915. Orch. version by Büsser, f.p. Paris 1927.

Catiline Conspiracy, The. Opera in 2 acts by *Hamilton to lib. by comp. based on Ben Jonson's *Catalina* (1611). Comp. 1972–3. Prod. Stirling 1974.

Catterall, Arthur (*b* Preston, 1883; *d* London, 1943). Eng. violinist. Played Mendelssohn conc. at Manchester th. at age 8. First played in Hallé Orch. 1900. Played in Bayreuth orch. 1902. Soloist at Hallé concert with Richter 1904. Leader of Queen's Hall Orch., 1905–14, Hallé Orch. 1914–25, BBC SO 1930–6. Prof. of vn., RMCM, 1910–29. Led own str. qt. 1911–25. Frequent conc. soloist (gave f.p. of *Moeran conc. 1942).

Catulli Carmina (Songs of Catullus). Scenic cantata by *Orff, successor to his *Carmina Burana*, and 2nd part of his trilogy *Trionfi*. 1943 rev. of much earlier work, f.ps. Leipzig 1943, Los Angeles 1955, Cambridge 1958. For soloists, ch., 4 pf., 4 timp., and up to 12 percussionists. Setting of 12 Lat. poems by Catullus, with opening and closing Lat. choruses by Orff.

Caucasian Sketches. Symphonic suite for orch., Op.10, by *Ippolitov-Ivanov. Comp. 1894, f.p. Moscow 1895. 4 movts. are: *In the Mountain Pass; In the Village; In the Mosque; March of the Sirdar*.

Caurroy, François Eustache de (*b* Gerberoy, 1549; *d* Paris, 1609). Fr. composer and canon of Saint Chapelle, Paris, becoming court composer to Fr. Kings. His *Mass for the Dead* was perf. at Fr. royal funerals until 18th cent. Wrote church and instr. mus.

Cavaillé-Col, Aristide (*b* Montpellier, 1811; *d* Paris, 1899). Fr. organ-builder, most prominent of his family. Went to Paris 1833, built organ for basilica of St Denis. Also built org. for Madeleine. His orgs. in Eng. incl. that for Manchester Town Hall. Estimated to have built nearly 500 organs.

Cavalieri, Emilio de' (*b* Rome, *c*.1550; *d* Rome, 1602). It. composer who was at the Medici Court in Florence and a member of *Camerata. One of first to use *basso continuo*. Wrote at least 4 early mus.-dramas to texts by Guidiccioni and a morality-play, forerunner of oratorio, *La *rappresentazione di anima e di corpo* (The Representation of Soul and Body) to a text by Manni, f.p. 1600.

Cavalieri, Katharina (*b* Währing, Austria, 1760; *d* Vienna, 1801). Austrian soprano who studied with *Salieri. Début Vienna 1775. Spent most of her career in Vienna. Mozart wrote Constanze in *Die Entführung* for her and the aria 'Mi tradì', added to Elvira's part in *Don Giovanni* for its Vienna première.

Cavalleria rusticana (Rustic Chivalry). Opera (*melodramma*) in 1 act by *Mascagni to lib. by Menasci and Targioni-Tozzetti based on play (1884) by Verga adapted from his short story (1880). Won prize for 1-act opera in competition organized by *Sonzogno, 1889. Prod. Rome 1890, London 1891. Usually perf. as double bill with *Leoncavallo's *Pagliacci*, hence the vernacular 'Cav. and Pag.'. Another 1-act opera with the same title was comp. in 1906 by Domenico Monleone and f.p. Amsterdam 1907.

Cavalli [Caletti-Bruni], **Pietro** [Pier] **Francesco** (*b* Crema, 1602; *d* Venice, 1676). It. composer of operas, possibly pupil of *Monteverdi. Joined choir of St Mark's, Venice, 1616, becoming second organist 1639. Monteverdi was dir. of mus. for much of this period. Début as opera composer 1639 with *Le nozze di Teti e di Peleo*. From then until 1670 about 40 of his operas were prod. in Venice. Twice visited Paris, his *Xerse* (Venice 1654) being given in the Louvre in 1660 as part of Louis XIV's marriage festivities. Operatic importance lies in enlargement of dramatic potentialities and command of comic possibilities. Operas incl. *Didone* (1641), *La virtù de'strali d'amore* (1642), *Egisto* (1643), *Ormindo* (1644), *Doriclea* (1645), *Giasone (Jason)* (1649), *Oristeo* (1651), *Calisto* (1651), *Eritrea* (1652), *Orione* (1653), *Xerse* (1654), *Erismena* (1655), *Statira, Principessa di Persia* (1655), *Ercole amante* (1662), *Scipione affricano* (1664), *Mutio Scevola* (1665), and *Pompeo magno* (1666). *Ormindo* and *Calisto* were revived successfully at Glyndebourne in realizations by Raymond *Leppard which are sometimes some way removed from the original score. Other recent eds. incl. Jane Glover and René Jacobs. Cavalli was also an org. and composer of church mus. (e.g. *Vespers of the Annunciation* (1675) and a *Requiem*) and instr. pieces.

cavatina (It.). (1) Operatic solo aria in regular form and in one section instead of the classical aria's 3, without repetition of words or phrases, e.g. *Porgi amor* from Mozart's *Le nozze di Figaro*. Also used of song-like air incl. in a long *scena. In 19th cent. opera term was applied to elaborate virtuoso aria, e.g. Rosina's *Una voce poco fà* in Rossini's *Il barbiere di Siviglia*.

(2) Song-like instr. piece, e.g. Raff's *Cavatina* and the *Cavatina* movement of Beethoven's Str. Qt. in B♭, Op.130. 3rd movement of Vaughan Williams's 8th Sym. (1955) is a *cavatina* for str.

Cavendish, Michael (*b c*.1565; *d* London, 1628). Eng. composer of madrigals and lute mus. Madrigal 'Come, gentle swains' is in *The *Triumphs of Oriana*.

CB. Short for *contrabassi*, i.e. str. dbs.

C clef. See *clef*.

C dur (Ger.). Key of C major.

cebell (cibell). Eng. dance, used by Purcell and others, similar to a fast gavotte. So called because based on an air assoc. with the goddess Cybèle in Lully's opera *Atys* (1676).

Cebotari, Maria (*b* Kishinev, Bessarabia, 1910; *d* Vienna, 1949). Austro-Russ. soprano. Actress at Moscow Art Th. 1926. Opera début Dresden 1931. In Dresden co. 1931–6, Berlin 1936–44, Vienna 1946–9. Début CG 1936 with Dresden co., sang there with Vienna Opera 1947. Created role of Aminta in *Die schweigsame Frau* (1935). Appeared in films. Outstanding singer of Mozart, Puccini, and Strauss. Sang often at Salzburg Fest.

Ceccato, Aldo (*b* Milan, 1934). It. conductor. Ass. to *Celibidache at Siena Acad. 1961–3. Début Milan 1964 (*Don Giovanni*), Wexford 1968, Chicago 1969, CG 1970, Glyndebourne 1971. Prin. cond. Detroit SO 1973–7, Hamburg State PO 1975–83, Hanover Radio Orch. and Bergen SO from 1985.

Cecilia, Saint (martyred in Sicily *c*.176AD). Patron saint of mus., commemorated annually on 22 Nov. Her assoc. with mus. is very obscure, apparently dating from 15th cent. (There is a theory that it arose from the misreading of an antiphon for her day.) First recorded mus. fest. in her honour *c*.1570 at Evreux, Normandy; earliest recorded date of a Brit. mus. celebration 1683. Innumerable paintings and stained glass windows depict her playing the org.—always one of many centuries later than 176AD. Many comps. in her honour, outstanding examples being Purcell's *Ode for St Cecilia's Day* (1692) and Britten's *Hymn to St Cecilia* (1942).

cédez (Fr.). Give way, i.e. diminish the speed (present and past participles *cédant, cédé*).

celere (It.). Quick, speedy. Hence *celerità*, speed; *celeramente*, with speed.

celesta (It., Fr. *céleste*). Small kbd. instr. not unlike glockenspiel. Patented in Paris by Auguste Mustel in 1886, his father Victor having constructed the instrument. Series of steel plates (suspended over wooden resonators) which are struck by hammers when keys are depressed, giving ethereal bell-like sound. Range of 4 octaves upwards from middle C. Possibly first used by *Widor in his ballet *La korrigane* (1880) and first used outside France in 1892 by Tchaikovsky in 'Dance of the Sugar-Plum Fairy' in *Nutcracker ballet. Many others have used it since, notably *Bartók in *Music for Strings, Percussion and Celesta*. First used in sym. by Mahler in his 6th (1903–5).

celeste (Fr.). (1) Type of soft pedal on old-fashioned pfs., interposing a strip of cloth between the hammers and strings.

(2) The *voix céleste* stop on the organ.

Celestial Railroad, The. Fantasy for pf., c.1924, by *Ives, arr. from 2nd movt. of his Sym. No.4.

Celibidache, Sergiu (*b* Iasi, Romania, 1912; *d* Paris, 1996). Romanian conductor and composer. Cond. Berlin PO 1945–51. London début 1948 with LPO. Taught cond. at Siena. Author of study of Josquin *Desprès. Comp. 4 syms. and pf. conc. Spent much time with radio orchs., e.g. S. Ger. Radio (Stuttgart) from 1959 and Stockholm 1962–71. Chief cond. Munich PO from 1979. Insisted on heavy rehearsal schedule and disliked recordings.

cello. Short for *violoncello. It used to be spelled with a preliminary apostrophe, but *cello* is now accepted as standard, like piano.

Cello Symphony. Britten's Op.68—in full, Sym. for Cello and Orch.—comp. 1963 for, and ded. to, *Rostropovich, who gave f.p. in Moscow 1964, the composer conducting. F.p. in England, Aldeburgh 1964.

Celtic harp. See *clàrsach*.

Celtic Requiem. Work by *Tavener for sop., children's ch., mixed ch., and orch., comp. 1969 and f.p. London 1969.

cembalo. See *clavicembalo*.

Cendrillon (Cinderella). (1) Opera in 4 acts by Massenet to lib. by Henri Cain after Perrault's fairy-tale (1697). Comp. 1895. Prod. Paris 1899, New Orleans 1902, London (with puppets) 1928, London (staged by Opera Viva) 1966, Manchester (RNCM) 1992, Birmingham (WNO) 1993.

(2) Opera in 3 acts by Isouard to lib. by C.-G. Etienne after Perrault. Prod. Paris 1810.

Cenerentola, La (Cinderella). Opera in 2 acts by Rossini to lib. by Ferretti. Comp. 1816. Prod. Rome 1817, London 1820, NY 1826. There are other Cinderella operas by Laruette, Steibelt, *Massenet, Isouard, and Wolf-Ferrari. Also ballets by Prokofiev and J. Strauss II.

cento, centon, centone. A medley of tunes. See *pasticcio*.

Central Park in the Dark in the Good Old Summertime (or A Contemplation of Nothing Serious). Work for chamber orch. by *Ives, comp. 1906.

ceól beag (Gaelic). Little music. That part of Scottish Highland bagpipe repertory comprising marches, *strathspeys, and *reels. (See also *ceól mor* and *ceól meadhonach*.)

ceól meadhonach (Gaelic). Middle music. That part of Scottish Highland bagpipe repertory comprising folk songs, lullabies, croons, and slow marches. (See also *ceól beag* and *ceól mor*.)

ceól mor (Gaelic). Big music. That part of Scottish Highland bagpipe repertory comprising salutes, gatherings, and laments, also tunes comp. in memory of some historical event. (See also *ceól beag* and *ceól meadhonach*.)

Ce qu'on entend sur la montagne (What one hears on the Mountain; Ger. *Bergsymphonie*, Mountain Symphony). Sym.-poem for pf. by Liszt comp. 1848–9, scored for orch. by *Raff 1849 and by Liszt 1850, rev. 1854. Based on Victor Hugo's *Feuilles d'automne*, No.5.

Ceremony of Carols, A. Settings by Britten, Op.28, of carols (in 11 movts.) for treble vv. and hp., comp. 1942 at sea on voyage back to UK. Also arr. for SATB and hp. or pf. by Julius Harrison.

Cerha, Friedrich (*b* Vienna, 1926). Austrian composer and violinist. Co-founder with *Schwertsik of instr. ens. 'Die Reihe' 1958 (Salzburg Fest. début 1965). Prof., Vienna Acad. 1969, teaching new mus. and elec. comp. Orch. Act III of Berg's *Lulu* (from composer's short score) for first complete perf., 1979. Works incl.:

OPERAS: *Netzwerk* (1962–80); *Baal* (1974–81); *Der Rattenfänger* (1984–7).

ORCH.: *Spiegel I*, for orch., *II* for 55 str., *III–VII* for orch. (1960–71); *Fasce* (1960–72); *Langegger Nachtmusik I* (1969), *II* (1971); *Intersecazioni I* for vn. and orch. (1959), *II* (1959–72); sym. (1975); conc. for vn., vc., orch. (1975); conc. for fl., bn., orch. (1982); *Monumentum für Karl Prantl* (1988); vc. conc. (1989–97); *Langegger Nachtmusik III* (1991); *Impulse* (1992–3).

CHAMBER MUSIC.: *Enjambements* (1959); *Movements I–III* (1960); *Symphonies*, wind, drums (1964); *Catalogue des objets trouvés* (1968–9); *Curriculum*, 2 each of ob., cl., bn., hn., tpt., tb., and tuba (1972–3); str. qt. No.1 (*Maqam*) (1989), No.2 (1989–90); *Quellen*, 7 instrs., perc. (1992); sax. qt. (1995).

VOICE(S) & ORCH.: *Exercises*, bar., spkr., chamber orch. (1962–8, rev. 1982); *Baal-Gesänge*, bar., orch. (1982); *Requiem für Hollensteiner*, spkr., bar., ch., orch. (1983); *Keintate*, v., 11 instr. (1983); *Eine Art Chansons*, vc., perc., pf., db. (1989); *Requiem*, mixed ch., orch. (1994); *Im Namen der Liebe*, bar., orch. (1999).

UNACC. CHORUS: *Verzeichnis*, 16 vv. (1969).

cervelat (cervelas, Fr.; It. *cervellate*). The *rackett.

Ces (Ger.). The note Cb.

Ceses (Ger.). The note Cbb.

Cesti, Antonio (Pietro) (*b* Arezzo, 1623; *d* Florence, 1669). It. composer and singer. Orig. friar, believed to have studied with *Carissimi. Released from vows, became org. Volterra Cath. 1644–51. Became more interested in opera than in sacred mus. after success of *Orontea* in Venice, 1649. In 1666 became vice-Kapellmeister at Vienna imperial court. Operas rank with Cavalli's in importance. They incl. *Orontea* (Venice 1649 or possibly Innsbruck 1656); *Alessandro vincitor di se stesso* (Venice 1651); *La Dori* (Innsbruck 1651); *Il Cesare amante* (Venice 1651); *La Cleopatra* (Innsbruck 1654); *L'Argia* (Innsbruck 1655); *La magnanimità d'Alessandro* (Innsbruck 1662); *Il Tito* (Venice 1666); *La disgrazie d'amore* (Vienna 1667); *La Semirami* (Vienna 1667); *Il pomo d'oro* (Vienna 1668).

ceterone. The bass *cittern, dating perhaps from 1524 but certainly from end of 16th cent. Monteverdi's *Orfeo* (1615 ed.) lists '2 ceteroni'. Had a number of additional unstopped bass str. and was particularly suitable for *basso continuo.

cetula. It. medieval instr. identified by scholars as ancestor of the cittern, a derivative of the lyra. Described *c.*1487 as having '4 brass or steel strings usually tuned a tone, a 4th and back again a tone, and it is played with a quill'.

Chabrier, (Alexis) **Emmanuel** (*b* Ambert, Puy-de-Dôme, 1841; *d* Paris, 1894). Fr. composer, pianist, and conductor. Studied pf., vn., and comp. in boyhood, but had general education, entered law school, and worked as civil servant in Ministry of the Interior 1861–80, during which time he became friend of Manet, who painted him twice, and Fauré, Duparc, and Chausson. Hearing Wagner's *Tristan und Isolde* in Munich determined him to resign his govt. post and concentrate wholly on mus. After visiting Sp. wrote orch. rhapsody *España*, 1883. Became ass. ch.-master to Lamoureux in Paris in 1881. Became fervent admirer of and propagandist for Wagner. Works incl. operas *L'étoile* (1877), *Une Education manquée* (1879), *Gwendoline* (1885), *Le *Roi malgré lui* (1887) and *Briséis* (1888–91, unfinished); *Suite pastorale*, orch. (1881); *Joyeuse Marche*, orch. (1888); pf. pieces and songs (incl. *Ballade des gros dindons*, 1889).

cha cha cha. Ballroom dance originating in Cuba *c.*1952. Development of mambo. Name derives from rhythm—2 crotchets, 3 quavers, quaver rest. Steps are glided, with rocking of hips as in rumba.

chaconne (Fr.; Eng. *chacony*, It. *ciaccona*, Sp. *chacona*; from Basque *chocuna* pretty). A musical form almost indistinguishable from *passacaglia*. Both were orig. dances of 3-in-a-measure rhythm, and the mus. of both was erected on a *ground bass. In some specimens this bass theme passes into an upper part. In others while there is no actual ground bass the mus. falls into a number of quite short sections similar to those written over a ground bass. Lully, Rameau, and other composers of their period and a little later, often ended an opera with a movt. of this type (e.g. Gluck's *Orfeo*). A universally known *Chaconne* is that by Bach which closes the 2nd Partita (D minor) for solo vn.—often played without its

companion movts. Purcell's aria *When I am laid in earth* (*Dido and Aeneas*) is a *chaconne*, so are Béethoven's *32 Variations in C minor* for piano, the finale of Brahms's Sym. No.4 (usually called a passacaglia), and the last movt. of Britten's str. qt. No.2 (*Chacony*).

Chadwick, George (Whitefield) (*b* Lowell, Mass., 1854; *d* Boston, 1931). Amer. composer, organist, and conductor. Teacher, org., and choral cond. in Boston. Joined staff New England Cons. 1882, becoming dir. 1897 until his death. Comp. opera *Judith* (1900), 3 syms., several symphonic poems incl. *Tam O'Shanter* (1911), 5 str. qts., and choral works.

Chagall Windows, The. Orch. work by *McCabe inspired by Marc Chagall's stained-glass windows in synagogue of Hadassah Hospital, Hebrew Univ., Jerusalem, representing 12 tribes of Israel. Comp. 1974, f.p. Manchester 1975.

Chagrin, Francis [Paucker, Alexander] (*b* Bucharest, 1905; *d* London, 1972). Rom.-born composer and conductor. Resident in Eng. for many years. Founded 1943 Committee (now Society) for the Promotion of New Mus. (SPNM). Comp. and cond. for over 200 films. Cond. for various ballet cos. Works incl. *King Stag*, *Volpone*, *Lamento appassionato*, pf. conc., and 2 syms. (3rd unfinished).

chahut. See *can-can*.

Chailly, Luciano (*b* Ferrara, 1920; *d* Milan, 2002). It. administrator, teacher, and composer, father of Riccardo *Chailly. Dir. of mus., RAI 1950–67, art. dir. La Scala 1968–71, Teatro Regio, Turin, 1972, Angelicum, Milan, 1973–5, and Verona Arena 1975–6. Returned to La Scala 1977. Art. dir. Genoa Opera 1983–5. Taught at Milan Cons. 1968–83. Comps. incl. 13 operas, 6 ballets (incl. *Anne Frank*, 1981), orch. and chamber mus.

Chailly, Riccardo (*b* Milan, 1953). Italian conductor. Son of composer Luciano *Chailly. Drummer in jazz band before becoming ass. cond. to Abbado at La Scala 1972–4 (début in *Werther*). Amer. operatic début Chicago 1974 (*Madama Butterfly*), followed by CG 1979; NY Met 1982; Salzburg 1984. Concert début in Eng. 1979 with LSO. Worked frequently with LPO 1982–5. Chief cond., Berlin Radio SO 1982–90. Mus. dir. Teatro Communale, Bologna, 1986–9. Prin. cond. Royal Concertgebouw Orch., Amsterdam, 1988–2004, Leipzig Gewandhaus Orch. from 2005.

chains, iron. Required by Schoenberg among perc. instr. in his *Gurrelieder (1900–11) and by Janáček in the prelude to *From the *House of the Dead* (1927–8).

chair organ. Term applied to small organ in Eng. in 17th and 18th cents. Used in conjunction with 'great organ'. Originally separate, they were incorporated but played on different manuals.

Chaliapin [Shalyapin], **Fyodor** (Ivanovich) (*b* Kazan, 1873; *d* Paris, 1938). Russ. bass. Of humble orig., having little mus. training before joining provincial opera co. 1890. Sang in St Petersburg Imperial Opera 1894–6, then joined Mamontov's private opera co. in Moscow, singing Ivan in Rimsky-Korsakov's *Maid of Pskov* and especially Boris Godunov in Mussorgsky's opera, role with which he became inseparably assoc. Member of Bolshoy Opera, Moscow, 1899–1914. La Scala début 1901 (Boito's *Mefistofele*), NY Met 1907 (*Mefistofele*), London 1913–14 in Beecham's Drury Lane season (début as Boris, 1913). Sang in four of Diaghilev's Paris seasons between 1908 and 1913. NY Met 1921–9. Created title-role of Massenet's *Don Quichotte* (Monte Carlo 1910). Gave frequent recitals. Superb actor-singer. Appeared in two films.

chalumeau (Fr.). Reed. Simple rustic reed-pipe, ancestor of *clarinet, with 6 to 8 finger-holes. Also applied to *shawm and to double-reed bagpipe chanter. Also wind instr. that came into use in 17th and 18th cents. Term used to describe lowest register of cl.

Chamberlain, Houston Stewart (*b* Portsmouth, 1855; *d* Bayreuth, 1927). Eng.-born writer (Ger. cit.). In 1870 went to Stettin and conceived intense admiration for Ger. culture. Lived Dresden 1885–9 and Vienna 1889–1908. Wrote *The Foundations of the 19th Century* (1899–1901, Eng. trans. 1910). Married Wagner's daughter Eva 1908 and lived at Bayreuth, publishing several books on Wagner (propagating anti-Semitic and nationalist views) and ed. of letters.

chamber music (It. *musica da camera*, Ger. *Kammermusik*). A term orig. intended (as Burney puts it *c*.1805) to cover such mus. as was not intended 'for the church, the theatre, or a public concert room'. As now used it has lost any implication as to place of perf. and excludes, on the one side, solo vocal mus. and mus. for a single instr. (or for a solo instr. acc. by another), and, on the other, orch. and choral mus., etc., incl. merely instr. mus. for 2, 3, 4, or more instr., played with a single instr. to a 'part', all the parts being an equal terms. Thus it comprises duet sonatas for vn. and pf. or vc. and pf., sonatas for a wind instr. and pf., trios for str. or for 2 str. instr. and pf., qts. for str. or for 3 str. instr. and pf., instr. qts., sextets, septets, and octets, etc. Of all these types the most important is the str. qt.: the instrs. employed in it are 2 vn., va., and vc., the db. having very rarely a place in chamber mus. (two outstanding exceptions being Schubert's 'Trout' pf. quintet and Dvořák's str. quintet, Op.77).

The modern conception of chamber mus. may be said to date from Haydn. For a century and more before his time nearly all mus. was supplied with a figured bass guided by which a harpsichordist extemporized a background: in earlier times we find something more like our idea of chamber mus. in 16th-cent. mus. for viols.

Most composers have contributed to the now abundant repertory of chamber mus., and so far have we departed from the early 19th-cent. idea

of the meaning of the term that 'chamber concerts' are common. Such concerts date effectively from the 1830s when the Müller Brothers Str. Qt. began touring Europe with a fine classical repertory. Since that period there have been many world-famous str. qts., pf. trios, and other groups. Despite much concert-room perf., however, chamber mus. still retains some right to its name, since it is often treated as 'the music of friends' and is much practised privately.

The term *Chamber Music* (*Kammermusik*) was used by *Hindemith for 7 comps. between 1921 and 1927; these incl. a pf. conc., vc. conc., va. conc., viola d'amore conc., and org. conc., the orch. in most cases comprising at least 12 players, sometimes more. His wind quintet, 1922, he called *Kleine* (Little) *Kammermusik*.

chamber opera. Term applied to operas with comparatively small no. of singers and orch. players, e.g. Britten's *The Rape of Lucretia* and *The Turn of the Screw*, but there is no question of such works being perf. in a room instead of a th. R. Strauss's *Ariadne auf Naxos* is strictly a chamber opera, but is perf. at CG, NY Met, and Vienna State Opera.

chamber orchestra. Small-sized orch. capable of playing in a room or small hall, but term is elastic and works for chamber orch. of symphonic proportions are written.

Chamber Symphony (*Kammersymphonie*). Title of 2 works by Schoenberg for small orch. No.1 in E major, Op.9, for 15 solo instr., comp. 1906, f.p. Vienna 1907. Also exists in simplified arr. by Webern (1922) and 2 orch. versions by Schoenberg (1922 and 1935). No.2, Op.38a, was begun 1906, completed 1939, f.p. NY 1940. Other composers have used this title, e.g. *Schreker, and others have preferred the term Chamber Concerto, e.g. *Berg and Hugh *Wood.

Chambonnières, Jacques Champion de (*b* Paris, *c*.1602; *d* Paris, 1672). Fr. composer and harpsichordist. His father was harpsichordist to Louis XIII as he himself became to Louis XIV, who ennobled him. Regarded as founder of Fr. hpd. sch. Pubd. 2 books of *Pièces de clavessin* (1670), ed. in modern times by T. Dart, 1969.

Chaminade, Cécile (Louise Stéphanie) (*b* Paris, 1857; *d* Monte Carlo, 1944). Fr. pianist and composer. Began composing at 8. From 1875 regularly gave pf. recitals, incl. her own comps. Eng. debut 1892. Comp. *opéra-comique*, ballet, orch. suites, *Konzertstück* for pf. and orch., *Les Amazones* for ch. and orch., many songs, and pf. pieces of graceful *salon* variety.

champêtre (Fr.). Rustic. Hence *danse champêtre*, a peasant dance in the open air; *fête champêtre*, a picnic.

chance. See *aleatory*.

Chance, Michael (*b* Buckingham, 1955). Eng. countertenor. Dealer on Stock Exchange 1977–80.

On turning to mus., sang with ECO, Acad. of Ancient Mus., English Concert, and Monteverdi Choir. Prof. opera début Buxton Fest. 1984 (Apollo in Cavalli's *Jason*). Lyons Opera 1985; Glyndebourne début 1989; GTO 1989; CG 1992; ENO 1992; Scottish Opera 1992. Created Military Governor in *A *Night at the Chinese Opera* (Cheltenham 1987).

Chandos Anthems. 12 anthems on religious texts comp. by *Handel between 1717 and 1718 when he was dir. of mus. for the Earl of Carnarvon, later the Duke of Chandos, at his palace, Cannons, near Edgware, Middlesex (not far from London). They are short cantatas for 3-part ch. acc. by obs., str., and org. In No.6 (*As pants the hart*) Handel used Ger. chorale as *cantus firmus.

Chang, Han-Na (*b* Seoul, 1983). Korean cellist. Began to study piano aged 3, cello aged 6. Won Rostropovich Int. Cello Comp., Paris, 1994 (aged 11). Has studied with Mischa Maisky and Rostropovich. Début Seoul 1995 (Dresden Staatskapelle cond. Sinopoli). Carnegie Hall 1996 (Montreal SO cond. Dutoit). NYPO début 1998, cond. Dutoit. Has toured Japan, Eur., Australia, and USA.

Chang, Sarah (*b* Philadelphia, 1980). Amer. violinist of Korean parentage. Began to study piano aged 3, violin aged 4 with her father, a prof. violinist. Début with local orchs. aged 5. Studied at Juilliard Sch. with Dorothy DeLay from age 5. Aged 8, played with NYPO cond. Mehta and Philadelphia Orch. cond. Muti. Carnegie Hall recital début 1997. Has toured Eur., N. and S. America, Asia (inc. Beijing Mus. Fest.). In June 2004 she ran with the Olympic torch in NY.

change-ringing. Practice, virtually confined to Britain, of ringing church bells by teams, each member pulling the rope controlling one bell. See *bell*.

changing note or nota cambiata (It.). Idiomatic melodic formula, salient characteristic of which is leap of a third away from an unessential note. Earliest form (in the polyphonic age) was a 3-note figure (*a*). This was soon joined and eventually superseded by a 4-note idiom (*b*). In the harmonic age of counterpoint (from Bach and Handel onwards) a variety of other changing note figures appears (*c*) (*d*) (*e*).

In USA the term *cambiata* is in common use for 'changing note'. Also when the leap of 3rd is in the dir. opposite to that of the step-wise movt. the term *échappé* is sometimes used, and, where the movt. is back to the orig. note, the term *returning tone*.

Chanot. Family of Fr. vn.-makers. François (*b* Mirecourt, 1787; *d* Brest, 1823) invented a pear-shaped vn. with flat belly and no sound-post. His brother Georges (*b* Mirecourt, 1801; *d* Courcelles, 1873) set up his business in Paris in 1823 and his son Georges (*b* Paris, 1831; *d* London, 1893) began his own business in London in 1858.

chanson (Fr.). Song set to Fr. words. A term with many applications, especially: (1) Any sort of simple verse-repeating song. (2) Type of song, for several vv. or for one v. with acc., that grew up in Fr. and north It. in 14th cent. and flourished until end of 16th—really a kind of early madrigal of the 'ayre' type. The *chanson de geste* was an heroic verse chronicle set to mus. of the 11th and 12th cents.

Chansons de Bilitis. 3 settings by Debussy, 1897–8, for v. and pf. of prose-poems by Pierre Louÿs. They are *La Flûte de Pan*, *La Chevelure*, and *Le tombeau des Naïades*. Orch. version 1926 by *Delage. Incidental mus. for 2 fl., 2 hp., and celesta to acc. recitation of poems, 1900; arr. *Boulez for reciter, 2 hp., 2 fl., and celesta 1954.

chant. See *Anglican Chant*. For Gregorian chant see *plainsong*.

chantant (Fr.). Singing. In a singing style. Sometimes the past participle is used, *chanté* (sung).

chanter. See *bagpipe*.

chanterelle (Fr.). Highest str. of vn., etc. (See *banjo*.)

Chants d'Auvergne (Songs of the Auvergne). Series of traditional dialect songs of the Auvergne collected by *Canteloube and pubd. between 1923 and 1930. Best-known is suite of 9 for sop. and orch. (or pf.) drawn from series 1 to 4, being 1. *Baïlèro*, 2. *L'Aio dè rotso* (Spring Water), 3. *Ound 'onorèn gorda?* (Where shall we go to graze?), 4. *Obal din lou Limouzi* (Down there in Limousin), 5. *La delaïssádo* (The forsaken girl), 6. *Lo Fiolairé* (The spinning girl), 7. *Passo pel prat* (Come through the meadow), 8. *Brezairola* (Cradle Song), 9. *Chut, chut* (Hush, hush).

chanty. See *shanty*.

'Chaos instead of music' (*Sumbur vmesto muzyki*). Notorious article published in *Pravda* on 28 January 1936, followed by another 10 days later, attacking Shostakovich's opera *Lady Macbeth of the Mtsensk District* and leading to its withdrawal from the stage. Believed to have been dictated by Stalin, who had left a performance of the opera in a rage over its alleged dissonance and immorality.

chapelle (Fr.). See *Kapelle*.

Chapel Royal. No one institution was more useful in fostering Eng. musicianship and promoting the development of Eng. mus. than the Chapel Royal—by which must be properly understood not a building but a body of clergy and musicians (like Ger. *Kapelle*) whose principal duty was to arrange and perform divine service in the sovereign's presence.

Existing records go back to 1135. During reign of Edward IV (1461–83) the Chapel consisted of 26 chaplains and clerks, 13 minstrels (a very wide term), 8 choirboys and their master, and a 'Wayte', or mus. night-watchmen, sounding the hours nightly. Under Richard III (1483–5) a press-gang system was authorized (though the practice of pressing seems to have existed earlier); this remained in operation for about 2 cents.; representatives of the Chapel were entitled to listen to all the best cath. choirs, and rob them of any boys whose vv. marked them out as fit to sing before the King. Under *Henry VIII (1509–47), a practical musician, the mus. staff of the Chapel rose to 44 (32 Gentlemen and 12 Children) and remained at this strength under Edward VI (1547–53) and Mary (1553–8). Under Elizabeth I (1558–1603) and James I (1603–25), the Chapel's personnel incl. Tye, Tallis, Byrd, Gibbons, Morley, Tomkins, and Bull. These brought church mus. to a level not exceeded even by the musicians of the Sistine Chapel at Rome; they developed the Eng. madrigal, and laid foundations of artistic kbd. music. The artistically-minded Charles I (1625–49) established the King's Band (6 recorders, 3 fl., 9 ob. and sackbuts, 12 vn., and 24 'lutes and voices', plus trumpets, drums and pipes). He appointed Nicholas *Lanier as 'Master of the Musick' as from 30 Nov., 1625. With the death of Charles I in 1649 the Chapel ceased. Cromwell was a lover of mus. and retained a small body of domestic musicians, but did not maintain a princely state, and, of course, did not approve of choirs as an inst. of public worship. In 1660 Charles II recalled the Chapel. A talented choirboy, Pelham Humfrey, was sent abroad to learn foreign styles; a younger boy, Purcell, without going abroad, was very apt to learn, and these youths and others, as they matured, largely trained by Captain Henry *Cooke, were quickly able to put to good use the new resources (such as the band of 24 fiddlers in church) with which the King had provided himself. Purcell, from 1677 to his death in 1695, was 'Composer in Ordinary' to the Chapel.

Under William and Mary, Anne, and the Georges, less was heard of the Chapel. George III had musicians in his employ beyond those of his Chapel; he spent little time in London, and when at Windsor had no need of his 'Chapel Royal', in the technical sense, since the Chapel of St George, in Windsor Castle, had its own distinct staff, as it still has. The great days, then, were over, but a line of orgs. continued. Some clever boys, incl. Sullivan, still received training in the Chapel.

Today the 'Chapel Royal' consists of a body of clergy, choirmen, and boys ('Priests in Ordinary', 'Gentlemen', and 'Children'), and the org. charged with the conduct of the Sunday services. Their place of duty is chiefly the chapel of St James's Palace, but they have other places of duty incl. Buckingham Palace.

By the end of George III's reign the King's Band had almost ceased to exist. George IV maintained a private wind band and so did Victoria after her accession in 1837. The Prince Consort enlarged it to a small orchestra. In 1893 the 'Queen's Band' was constituted, unifying the private band and the state band, but Edward VII (1901–10) only required the musicians for state functions and abandoned concerts. Under George V (1910–35) they were never used, though the 24 musicians nominally still belonged to the royal household. Four survivors played in the orch. at the coronation (1937) of George VI (1936–52). Today the post of *Master of the Queen's Music is an honour for a distinguished musician, with no real duties.

Chappell, William (*b* London, 1809; *d* London, 1888). Eng music-publisher. Founded Musical Antiquarian Soc. (1840) to publish works of early Eng. composers. Ed. *Popular Music of the Olden Time* (2 vols. 1855–9; new edn. by H. E. Woodridge 1893).

Chappell & Co. Ltd. London music-publishers, pf. makers, etc. Founded 1810 by Samuel Chappell (1776–1834). Firm was largely responsible for building of St James's Hall, London, ran ballad concerts, was lessee of Queen's Hall, London, and sponsor of New Queen's Hall Orch. After 1st World War, its dominant interest was light music (musicals and film music), band music, and educational, but has recently accepted work of some important composers, e.g. Sebastian Forbes and Stephen Dodgson.

Chapple, Brian (*b* London, 1945). Eng. composer. Influenced by Messiaen, has used serial technique but is one of group of Eng. composers who moved to a more tonal idiom in the 1970s. Works incl.: *Green and Pleasant*, orch. (1973); pf. conc. (1977); *Veni Sancte Spiritus*, double ch. (1974); *In ecclesiis*, sop. and ch. (1976); *Summoned by Bells*, pfs., alarm clocks (1968); *Concert Piece*, 2 pf. qts. (1969); *5 Blake Songs*, ten., pf. (1972); *Light breaks out where no sun shines*, sop., pf. (1978); *Cantica*, sop., ten., ch., orch. (1978); *Venus Fly-Trap*, chamber ens. (1980); *Delphine*, orch. (1980); *5 Shakespeare Songs*, 6 male vv. (1981); *5 Carols*, women's vv., pf. (1982); *Little Sym.*, str. (1983); *Lamentations of Jeremiah*, ch. (1984); pf. sonata (1985); *Magnificat and Nunc Dimittis* (1986); *Magnificat*, sop., ten., ch., orch. (1987); *Confetibor*, ch., org. (1988); *In Memoriam*, str. (1989); *Tribute I and II*, pf. (1990); *Requies*, pf. (1991).

characteristic piece (Ger. *Charakterstück*). Imprecise term occasionally applied by composers to shorter instr. comp. (esp. for pf.); the equivalent of *Stimmungsbild* (Ger.), Mood-picture.

charivari (Fr.). Extemporized mus. of a violent kind made with any household utensils etc., that lie to hand, generally before the house of a person who has incurred communal disapprobation. Equivalents are *rough music* (Eng.); *chiasso* (It.). uproar; or *scampanata* (It.). bell ringing;

Katzenmusik (Ger.). cat music; *shivaree, calthumpian concert* (Amer). In USA also means 'musical' teasing of newly-weds.

Charleston. A fast *fox-trot named after Charleston, S. Carolina, popularized in NY, 1922, in Negro revues, in a song by Cecil Mack and Jimmy Johnson; it then had a short but widespread vogue in ballrooms and dance-halls. The dance-step was characterized by 2 twists on each foot, with one kicked sharply backwards, and swinging of the arms.

Charm of Lullabies, A. Songs by Britten for mez. and pf., Op.41, comp. 1947. Poems by Blake, Burns, Green, Randolph, and Philip.

Charpentier, Gustave (*b* Dieuze, 1860; *d* Paris, 1956). Fr. composer. Won *Prix de Rome*. While still a student, wrote *Impressions d'Italie* for orch. (1890, arr. as ballet 1913). Had great success with opera *Louise (comp. 1889–96, prod. Paris 1900), based on his own experiences in Montmartre when he first went to Paris in 1881, but its successor *Julien* (1913) failed to become established. Wrote cantata *La Vie du poète* (1892). Founded in 1902 Conservatoire Populaire where working girls like Louise could learn mus. and dancing. After 1913 he completed nothing. Supervised film of *Louise*, 1936. Last years were spent as recluse in Montmartre.

Charpentier, Marc-Antoine (*b* Paris, ?1645; *d* Paris, 1704). Fr. composer. *Maître de musique* and court singer to Duchess of Guise until her death in 1688. In 1672 began an association with Molière's theatrical co. which lasted until 1686. Wrote prologue and *intermèdes* for *Le malade imaginaire* (1673). Never held a court post but in 1698 became master of the music of Sainte-Chapelle, for which he wrote many of his finest religious works. These incl. 10 *Magnificats*, 4 *Te Deums* (one of which, comp. *c*.1690, has become popular), 37 antiphons, 84 psalms, and over 200 motets, some of them as extensive as oratorios. His early style was Italian based, but he soon adopted a Fr. tone of voice. His mus. is noted for harmonic richness and colour contrasts, also for the vividness of his word-painting. His 17 stage works incl. *Andromède* (1682); *Actéon* (1683–5); *La descente d'Orphée aux enfers* (1685–6); *Les arts florissants* (1685–6); *David et Jonathas* (1687); *Médée* (1693); *Philomèle* (?1694). His other th. pieces (*intermèdes* and incid. mus.) are notable for lightness of texture and for wit and humour.

Chasins, Abram (*b* NY, 1903; *d* NY, 1987). Amer. pianist and composer. On staff Curtis Inst. 1926–35. Mus. dir. of NY radio station (WQXR) 1947–65. Author of several books. Comps. incl. 2 pf. concs., *Parade* (1931), *Rush Hour in Hong Kong* (pf.), etc.

chassé (Fr.). In ballet, the 'chasing' away of one foot by a touch from the other.

chasse, cor de (Fr.). Hunting horn.

Chasse, La (Fr.). The Hunt. Nickname for Haydn's Sym. in D, No.73 (Hob. I:73); reference is to the final movt. Comp. 1780–1.

Chasseur Maudit, Le (The Accursed Hunter). Symphonic poem by Franck (1881–2), based on ballad by G. A. Bürger. F.p. Paris 1883.

Chausson, (Amédée-)**Ernest** (*b* Paris, 1855; *d* Limay, 1899). Fr. composer. Qualified as barrister 1877 but never practised. Entered Paris Cons. 1879 to study with Massenet, but left to transfer to Franck. Visits to Munich in 1879 and 1880 and to Bayreuth in 1882 to hear Wagner operas exerted profound influence. Best-known works are *Poème de l'amour et de la mer*, v. and orch., Op.19 (1882–90, rev. 1893); *Viviane*, sym.-poem, Op.5 (1882, rev. 1887); *Poème*, vn. and orch., Op.25 (1896); *Chanson perpetuelle*, v. and orch., Op.37 (1898); pf. qt., Op.30 (1897); sym. in B♭, Op.20 (1889–90); Conc. for pf., vn., and str. qt., Op.21 (1889–91); *Soir de Fête*, sym.-poem, Op.32 (1897–8). Of his 3 operas, only *Le *roi Arthus* (1885–95) has been staged (Brussels 1903). Wrote incid. mus. for *The Tempest* (Op.18, 1888). Died in a cycling accident.

Chávez (y Ramírez), **Carlos** (Antonio de Padua) (*b* Mexico City, 1899; *d* Mexico City, 1978). Mex. composer and conductor. Début as composer 1921. Travelled in Eur. and USA 1922–8. Wrote for Mexico City newspaper *El Universal* 1924, contributing to it regularly for rest of his life. Lived in NY 1926–8, forming friendships with Copland, Cowell, and Varèse. Dir., Nat. Cons. of Mexico 1928–34. Cond. Mexico SO 1928–48. Founder and dir., Mexican Nat. Institute of Fine Arts 1947–52. Dir., composers' workshop, Nat. Cons. 1960–5. Cond. f.p. of Copland's *El salón Mexicó*, 1937. Comps. incl. 6 syms.; pf. conc.; vn. conc.; opera *The Visitors* (lib. by Kallman) (1953–6); ballet *Caballos de Vapor (Horse Power)* (1926–7). Nationalist style but rarely used folk material.

Chaykovsky, Pyotr. See *Tchaikovsky, Pyotr*.

che (It.). Who, which.

Checkmate. Ballet in 1 act by *Bliss to his own lib., choreog. N. de Valois. Prod. by SW co., Paris 1937; then over 100 perfs. in Britain; as Suite, NY 1939.

chef d'attaque (Fr.). Leader of the attack. Orch. leading vn. (Eng.), or concert-master (Amer.).

chef d'orchestre (Fr.). Conductor.

chekker. 14th-cent. name for an unidentified instr. which may have been a *clavichord.

Chelsea Opera Group. Opera co. founded 1950 to give concert perfs., usually in orig. language. Gave early opportunities to many young British singers, conds., and musicians who later achieved fame, e.g. Colin Davis, Thomas Hemsley, Bernard Keeffe, John Carol Case, Heather Harper, Roger Stalman, Peter Glossop, James Loughran, Alberto Remedios, Sheila Armstrong, Pauline Tinsley,

Derek Hammond-Stroud, Sarah Walker, Roger Norrington, and John Eliot Gardiner. F.p.(*Don Giovanni*) organized by Colin Davis, David Cairns, and Stephen Gray, was given in Oxford. F. London p. was at St Pancras Town Hall 1953 (*Fidelio*).

Cheltenham Festival. Annual summer mus. fest. held (usually in July) in spa of Cheltenham, Eng. Begun in 1945 as a fest. of Brit. contemporary mus. but scope widened in 1969 to embrace contemporary mus. of other nationalities. Many post–1945 Brit. chamber works, concs., and syms. (hence the expression 'a Cheltenham Symphony') received f.ps. at the fest., many of them from Hallé Orch., cond. Barbirolli, who gave bulk of orch. concerts 1947–61. Among operas premièred at the fest. was Judith Weir's *A Night at the Chinese Opera* (1987). First dir. G. A. M. Wilkinson, 1944–69. Programme dir. John *Manduell 1969–94; Michael Berkeley 1995–2004; Martyn Brabbins from 2005.

Cheminée du roi René, La (King René's Chimney). Suite by Milhaud for fl., ob., cl., bn., and hn., 1939. Title refers to street in Aix-en-Provence commemorating 15th-cent. monarch.

Chéreau, Patrice (*b* Lézigné, Maine-et-Loire, 1944). Fr. producer. Made his name as th. director. First opera prods. were *L'Italiana in Algeri* at Spoleto 1969, and *Les contes d'Hoffmann*, Paris 1974. Invited by Wolfgang Wagner to prod. *Der Ring des Nibelungen* for Bayreuth Fest. centenary in 1976. This 'deconstructionist' prod., set in mid-19th and late 20th cents. and cond. by *Boulez, proved highly controversial. In 1979 Chéreau prod. the 3-act version of *Lulu* (in *Cerha's edn. of the complete score) in Paris. Prod. *Lucio Silla* (La Scala, 1984); *Wozzeck* (Paris, 1992); *Don Giovanni* (Salzburg Fest., 1994); and *Così fan tutte* (Aix Fest., 2005).

Cherevichki (Russ. 'The Slippers'). Opera in 4 acts by Tchaikovsky to lib. by Polonsky, amplified by composer and N. Chayev, based on Gogol story *Christmas Eve*. Comp. 1885, being a revision of *Vakula the Smith*, 1876. Prod. Moscow 1887, NY 1922, London (London Univ.) 1984, Wexford 1993. Rimsky-Korsakov's *Christmas Eve* (1894–5) is based on same story.

Cherkassky, Shura (Alexander Isaakovich) (*b* Odessa, 1909; *d* London, 1995). Russ.-born pianist (Amer. cit.). Settled USA 1922. Début Baltimore 1922. Eur. tours after 1945. Salzburg Fest. début 1960. Outstanding in Russ. mus.

Cherniavsky, Mischel (*b* Uman, S. Russia, 1893; *d* Dieppe, 1982). Russ.-born cellist (Brit. cit.). Member of pf. trio 1900–23 with brothers Leo and Jan, thereafter solo performer in concs. and recitals.

Cherry Ripe. Setting by C. E. *Horn early in 19th cent. of poem by Herrick (1648).

Chérubin (Cherubino). Opera (*comédie chantée*) in 3 acts by Massenet to lib. by Henri Cain and Francis de Croisset based on latter's play. Comp. 1902–03. Prod. Monte Carlo 1905, Santa Fe 1989, London (CG) 1994.

Cherubini, Luigi (Carlo Zanobi Salvadore Maria) (*b* Florence, 1760; *d* Paris, 1842). It. composer. Comp. quantity of church mus. by age of 16. From 1778 to 1781 worked in Bologna and Milan with Sarti, contributing arias to his operas. His own *Il Quinto Fabio* was staged in 1779. Further operas were prod. in Livorno, Rome, and Venice. Visited London in 1784 producing 2 operas there. Settled in Paris 1788 where his new, Gluck-inspired operatic style revolutionized Fr. stage. Under a cloud because of Napoleon's disfavour, went in 1805 to Vienna where he met Haydn and Beethoven. The latter was strongly influenced (esp. in *Fidelio*) by Cherubini's operas, 4 of which he heard in Vienna. Visited London 1815, writing sym. while there. Became prof. of comp. Paris Cons. 1816, dir. 1821–41. His masses are deservedly famous. Among his nearly 30 operas were: *Quinto Fabio* (1779, rev. 1783, Rome), *Armida* (Florence 1782), *Adriano in Siria* (Livorno 1782), *Lo sposo di tre* (Venice 1783), *La finta principessa* (London 1785), *Giulio Sabino* (London 1786), *Ifigenia in Aulide* (Turin 1788), *Démophoön* (Paris 1788), *Lodoïska* (Paris 1791), **Médée* (Paris 1797), *Les *Deux Journées* (Ger. *Der Wasserträger*, Eng. *The Water Carrier*) (Paris 1800), **Anacréon* (1803), *Faniska* (Vienna 1806), *Les *Abencérages* (Paris 1813), *Bayard à Mezières* (1814), *Ali Baba* (1833). His *Requiem* No.2, in D minor, still frequently performed, was written in 1836 and f.p. at the Paris Cons. in 1838. His *Requiem* in C minor was comp. in 1816 and f.p. in St Denis 1817. He also wrote 6 str. qts.

Chester, J. & W., Ltd. Eng. firm of mus. publishers founded in Brighton 1874, transferred to London 1915, specializing in Russ. and contemporary foreign composers. Pubd. journal *The Chesterian* from 1915 to 1961. Since 1957 linked with Hansen and other Scandinavian publishers.

chest of viols. Any complete set of 6 viols of different sizes (so called because they were usually stored in a specially built chest or cupboard).

chest voice. Lowest register of human v., others being 'head' and 'middle', so called because the notes seem to come from singer's chest. But tenors use chest v. to produce high notes.

Chetham's School of Music. School in Manchester founded 1653 by Humphrey Chetham as charitable foundation for boys. In 1969 became first Brit. co-educational sch. basing admission solely on mus. audition. Has 275 pupils. Specialist mus. education given within framework of full academic curriculum.

chevalet (Fr.). Trestle. Bridge of bowed instr., etc.

Chevé, Emile J. M. See *Galin-Paris-Chevé*.

Chevillard, Camille (Paul Alexandre) (*b* Paris, 1859; *d* Chatou, 1923). Fr. conductor and composer, son of leading Fr. cellist. In 1886 became ass.

cond. to *Lamoureux (his father-in-law), succeeding him 1899. Prof. at Cons. 1907. Cond. Paris Opéra 1914. Wrote orch. and chamber mus.

cheville (Fr.). Peg, e.g. of str. instr. Hence cheviller, pegbox.

Chiara, Maria(-Rita) (b Oderzo, 1939). It. soprano. Opera début Venice 1965 (Desdemona in Otello). Sang leading Verdi roles throughout It., Ger., and Austria 1965–70. Débuts: La Scala 1972; CG 1973; NY Met 1977.

chiaro, chiara (It.). Clear, unconfused. Hence chiaramente, clearly, distinctly; chiarezza, clarity, distinctness.

chiave (It.). Clef.

chica (Sp.). Early form of *fandango.

Chicago Opera Company. Several cos. have used this title, the first in 1910 with Campanini as dir. Leading light was sop. Mary Garden, who was art. dir. 1921–2. Prokofiev cond. f.p. of his Love for Three Oranges Dec. 1921. Co. re-formed as Civic Opera Co. 1922–32, with Giorgio Polacco as cond. (1918–30). Singers like Frida Leider and Eva Turner in co. at this time. New opera house opened 1929, but depression closed co. 1932. Visiting cos. until 1954 when Carol Fox (b Chicago, 1926; d Chicago, 1981) formed Lyric Opera of Chicago.

Chicago Symphony Orchestra. 3rd oldest sym. orch. in USA. Founded 1891 by Theodore Thomas as the Chicago Orch. Re-named Theodore Thomas Orch. 1906, then present name 1912. Conds.: Thomas 1891–1905; Frederick Stock 1905–42; Désiré Defauw 1943–7; Artur Rodzinski 1947–8; Rafael Kubelik 1950–3; Fritz Reiner 1953–63; Jean Martinon 1963–9; Georg Solti 1969–91; Daniel Barenboim 1991–2006. First tour of Europe 1971. Salzburg Fest. début 1978 (cond. Solti).

Chichester Psalms. Choral work by Leonard Bernstein for counterten., ch., and orch. Text in Hebrew. Written for Chichester Cath., where perf. in July 1965. Orig. scoring is for organ, harp, and perc.

chiesa (It.). Church. Hence aria da chiesa (an aria for church use); cantata da chiesa (see cantata); concerto da chiesa (see concerto); sonata da chiesa (see sonata).

chifonie. Another name for *hurdy-gurdy.

Chilcot, Thomas (b ?Bath, c.1700; d Bath, 1766). Eng. composer and organist. Org., Bath Abbey 1728–66. Taught Thomas *Linley snr. Wrote settings of Shakespeare songs, and kbd. works.

Chilcott, Susan (b Bristol, 1963; d Blagdon, Somerset, 2003). Eng. soprano. Studied at GSMD with Mollie Petrie. Opera début Oviedo, Spain, 1991 (1st Lady in Die Zauberflöte). Outstanding Ellen Orford in Peter Grimes, Brussels 1994. During 5

years at La Monnaie, Brussels, roles included Composer, Governess, Alice Ford, and Desdemona. GTO début 1994 (Tatyana in Eugene Onegin), Paris Opéra 1996 (Fiordiligi in Così fan tutte), Amsterdam 2000 (Káťa Kabanová), Glyndebourne 2001 (Desdemona), CG 2002 (Lisa in Queen of Spades), NY Met 2002 (Helena in Britten's Midsummer Night's Dream). Excelled in Janáček roles. Recitalist, often accompanied by Iain Burnside.

Childhood of Christ, The (Berlioz). See Enfance du Christ, L'.

Child of our Time, A. Oratorio by *Tippett for sop., cont., ten., and bass soloists, ch. and orch. Comp. 1939–41, f.p. 1944. Lib. by composer based on persecution of Jews begun after assassination of Nazi official vom Rath by Jewish boy Grynspan at Ger. Legation, Paris, autumn 1938. Uses Negro spirituals in manner of Bach's chorales in his Passions.

Child, William (b Bristol, 1606; d Windsor, 1697). Eng. composer and organist. Org., St George's Chapel, Windsor, 1630–97 except during period of Commonwealth 1649–60. Member of Chapel Royal from 1660. Comp. hymns, anthems, church services, mus. for viols, and catches.

Children's Corner. 6 pf. pieces by Debussy (1906–8) ded. to his daughter. With Eng. titles (explained by influence of Eng. governess)—Doctor Gradus ad Parnassum (see Gradus ad Parnassum); Jimbo's Lullaby ('Jimbo' is composer's mistake for 'Jumbo'); Serenade for the Doll; Snow is Dancing; The Little Shepherd; Golliwogg's Cakewalk. Orch. by *Caplet, 1911.

Children's Overture, A. Orch. work by *Quilter, 1914, based on nursery-rhymes. Intended as ov. to play 'Where the Rainbow Ends', for which Quilter wrote incid. mus., but not used.

Childs, Barney (Sanford) (b Spokane, 1926; d Redlands, CA, 2000). Amer. composer. Taught Eng. at Univ. of Arizona 1956–65. Dean, Deep Springs Coll., Calif., 1965–9. Prof. of comp., Univ. of Redlands 1976–92. Works had strong influence on Amer. avant-garde. Comps. incl. 2 syms.; 8 str. qts.; 5 wind quartets; 2 vn. sonatas; ca. conc.; cl. conc.; When Lilacs Last in the Dooryard Bloom'd, soloists, ch., band (1971); hn. octet; timp. conc.; and works involving elec. and tape. His Couriers of the Crimson Dawn (1977) is 'for any instr.'.

Chilingirian Quartet. Formed 1971, led by L. Chilingirian (OBE 2000), coached by S. Nissel (*Amadeus Quartet) and Hans *Keller. Resident qt. Liverpool Univ. 1973–6 and later at Univ. of Sussex. Tours of Europe and Scandinavia. NY début 1977, followed by US tour.

chime bells. Small medieval bells related to modern cymbals. Had a high central dome.

Chinese crash cymbal. This differs in shape from the normal *cymbal. The cup is much shallower and its edge turns up. It is made of a special alloy peculiar to the Chinese, and when struck with a drum stick gives a brilliant crash.

Chinese temple block. See *Korean temple block*.

Chinese wood block. Oblong block of wood, 7″ or 8″ long, with slots cut in it. Struck with stick of a snare drum gives a hard, hollow tone. Other names are *clog box* and *tap box*. Used in jazz and by 20th-cent. composers, e.g. Lambert in *Rio Grande*, Walton in *Façade*, Prokofiev in 5th and 6th Syms., and Cage in *Amores*.

chiroplast. Hand-rest for pf. practice, once a part of the *Logier system's equipment.

Chisholm, Erik (*b* Glasgow, 1904; *d* Rondebosch, S. Africa, 1965). Scot. conductor, pianist, and composer. Cond. Glasgow Grand Opera Soc. (largely amateur) 1930–9, giving Brit. première of several operas, e.g. *Idomeneo* (1934), *Les Troyens* (1935), *Béatrice et Bénédict* (1936), and reviving *La Clemenza di Tito*. Dir. of mus., S. African Coll. of Mus. in Univ. of Cape Town, 1946–65, where his opera pioneering continued. Comp. 10 operas, incl. *The Canterbury Tales* (1961–2) and *The Importance of Being Earnest* (1963), ballets, 2 pf. concs., vn. conc., 2 syms., chamber mus. During tour of Brit. 1956–7, his S. African co. gave f. Brit. p. of Bartók's *Duke Bluebeard's Castle*. Wrote book on Janáček's operas, pubd. 1971.

chistu. Basque mus. instr. similar to the Renaissance *tabor pipe.

chitarra. It. name for *guitar. Hence *chitarriglia*, a smaller higher-pitched type of Sp. guitar; *chitarrino*, 17th-cent. name for small 4-course guitar; *chitarra battente*, 5-course metal-strung guitar with fixed metal frets and played with plectrum.

chittarone. Largest of the lute family, developed in It. during 16th cent. Larger than its close relative the *theorbo, both being designed as accompanying instr. and to improve on the bass register of the lute. However a solo repertory exists. Stringing was variable, 6 double courses and 8 single basses being the most usual. Mentioned by *Caccini in his *Le nuove musiche* (1602).

chiuso, chiusa (It.). Closed, stopped, with special reference to the *horn.

Chladni, Ernst (Florenz Friedrich) (*b* Wittenberg, 1756; *d* Breslau, 1827). Ger. scientist who made important acoustic researches. Invented two variants of the glass harmonica, the 'Clavicylinder' kbd. instr. with glass cylinder, worked by pedal and revolving against strips of wood, glass, or metal activated by keys, and the similar 'euphon'.

Chlubna, Osvald (*b* Brno, 1893; *d* Brno, 1971). Cz. composer. Was bank clerk until 1953, but taught harmony and theory at Brno Organ Sch. 1918–19, Brno Cons. 1919–35, 1953–9, and Janáček Acad. 1956–8. Wrote 8 operas in Romantic style, sinfonietta (1924), and tone-poems. Janáček entrusted him with orch. of last act of his first opera, *Šárka*.

CHM. Choirmaster's diploma of *Royal College of Organists.

ChM. Choirmaster's diploma of Amer. Guild of Organists or of Royal Canadian College of Organists.

Chocolate Soldier, The (*Der tapfere Soldat*, The Valiant Soldier). Operetta by O. *Straus to lib. by L. Jacobson and R. Bernauer based on G. B. Shaw's play *Arms and the Man* (1894). Prod. Vienna 1908, NY 1909, London 1910.

chœur (Fr.). Chorus, choir. But *grand chœur*, besides meaning 'large chorus' and 'full choir', means 'full organ' (or a comp. for such).

choir or **chorus**. (1) A *mixed voice choir* (or chorus) is one of both women and men.
(2) A *male voice choir* is (usually) of men only, but may be of boys and men.
(3) A *double choir* is one arr. in 2 equal and complete bodies, with a view not merely to singing in 8 parts but also to responsive effects.
(4) Architecturally, the choir is that part of a cath. which, in a church other than a cath., is called the chancel.
(5) *Chorus* tends to be used for secular bodies, but there are many exceptions.

choir organ (or choir). Division of org. consisting of soft stops suitable for acc. of choir.

choke cymbals. 2 ordinary *cymbals fixed face to face on a rod, with a device by which their pressure one on the other can be adjusted, according to the tone-quality desired. They are played with a drumstick, giving a short, sharp crash.

Chop, Max (*b* Grenszen, 1862; *d* Berlin, 1929). Ger. composer and scholar. Turned to mus. from law. Comp. 2 pf. concs., orch. suites, songs, etc. Mus. critic and ed. Analyst of Liszt sym.-poems and Wagner operas. First to write monograph on Delius (1907).

Chopin, Fryderyk (Franciszek) [Frédéric François], (*b* Zelazowa Wola, 1810; *d* Paris, 1849). Polish composer and pianist (Fr. father, Polish mother). Began pf. studies with Zywny 1816 and played conc. by *Gyrowetz in Warsaw 1818, by then being a favourite in the aristocratic salons. In 1822 began studies in harmony and counterpoint with Józef Elsner, dir. of Warsaw Cons. In 1825 his *Rondo* in C minor was pubd. as Op.1, though it was far from being his first comp. The next year, entered Warsaw Cons. as full-time mus. student, leaving in 1829. While student, wrote *Krakowiak* Rondo. In 1829 comp. his conc. in F minor and gave 2 concerts in Vienna. Played the conc. in Warsaw twice in Mar. 1830 and later in year played E minor conc. Left home late in 1830, travelling via Dresden and Prague to

Vienna and giving many concerts. In Stuttgart heard that the Russians had captured Warsaw. Arrived Paris Sept. 1831; became pf. teacher to aristocracy, gradually renouncing public career and concentrating on composing. Gave first Paris concert in Feb. 1832 and no other in which he was the principal performer until 1841—it is reckoned he gave barely 30 pub. perfs. in his whole career. Became friend of most of outstanding musicians of day. In an essay taking the form of a discussion between Florestan and Eusebius, Schumann hailed the *Là ci darem* variations, Op.2, with the words 'Hats off, gentlemen! A new genius!' In 1836 Chopin met Fr. novelist George Sand and lived with her 1838–47. From 1836 the first signs of the tuberculosis that was to kill him appeared and the rest of his life was a constant struggle with sickness. After break with George Sand, perf. his E minor conc. in Rouen in March 1848 but left for London after the revolution, in need of money. Gave concerts in Manchester, Glasgow, Edinburgh, and London and returned to Paris to die in Oct. 1849.

Although Chopin's pf. mus. is beset with romantic stories and nicknames, he himself insisted on its existence only as absolute mus., hence the literal titles which refer only to mus. forms and are never picturesque, as in Schumann and Liszt. His own playing was both powerful and rhythmically subtle, with astonishing evenness of touch. Taking the name 'nocturne' from John *Field, he transformed the form, as he did everything, by harmonic imagination and melodic distinction. There are bold, prophetic passages in his mus., ornamentation derived from his admiration for It. opera, and, in his Polish works such as the mazurkas and polonaises, a raw passion elemental in its strength. The Victorian conception of Chopin as a consumptive drawing-room balladeer of the kbd., a conception connived at by lesser pianists, has long been exposed as a false trail leading hearers away from the true, poetic, heroic Chopin. Prin. comps.:

PIANO SONATAS: C minor, Op.4 (1828); B♭ minor, Op.35 (1839, Funeral March 1837); B minor, Op.58 (1844).

PIANO & ORCH.: conc. No.1 in E minor, Op.11 (1830); No.2 in F minor, Op.21 (1829–30); *Variations on Là ci darem la mano*, Op.2 (1827); *Grande Fantaisie on Polish Airs*, Op.13 (1828); *Krakowiak Rondo*, Op.14 (1828); *Andante Spianato* (1834); *Grande Polonaise brillante* in E flat, Op.22 (1830–1).

PIANO: *Ballade* in G minor, Op.23 (1831–5), in F major/A minor, Op.38 (1836–9), in A♭, Op.47 (1840–1), in F minor, Op.52 (1842); *Scherzo* in B minor, Op.20 (1831–2), in B♭ minor/D♭, Op.31 (1837), in C♯ minor, Op.39 (1839), in E, Op.54 (1842); 12 *Études*, Op.10 (1829–32), 12 *Études*, Op.25 (1832–6); 3 *Nocturnes*, Op.9 (1830–1), 3 *Nocturnes*, Op.15 (1830–3), 2 *Nocturnes*, Op.27 (1835), 2 *Nocturnes*, Op.32 (1836–7), 2 *Nocturnes*, Op.37 (1838–9), 2 *Nocturnes*, Op.48 (1841), 2 *Nocturnes*, Op.55 (1843), 2 *Nocturnes*, Op.62 (1846), 2 *Nocturnes*, Op.72 (1827, 1830); 24 *Preludes*, Op.28 (1836–9), Prelude in C♯ minor, Op.45 (1841);

Valses, in A♭ (1827), in E (1829), in E♭ (1829–30), in E minor (1830), in E♭ (1840), in E♭, Op.18 (1831), 3 *Valses*, Op.34 (1831–8), in A♭, Op.42 (1840), 3 *Valses*, Op.64 (1846–7), 2 *Valses*, Op.69 (1835, 1829), 3 *Valses*, Op.70 (1829–41); *Polonaises*, in G minor (1817), in B♭ (1817), in A♭ (1821), in G♯ (1822), 2 *Polonaises*, Op.26 (1834–5), 2 *Polonaises*, Op.40 (1838–9), *Polonaise* in F♯, Op.44 (1840–1), *Polonaise* in A♭, Op.53 (1842), 3 *Polonaises*, Op.71 (1825–8); *Polonaise Fantaisie* in A♭, Op.61 (1845–6); 4 *Mazurkas*, Op.6 (1830), 5 *Mazurkas*, Op.7 (1831), 4 *Mazurkas*, Op.17 (1834), 4 *Mazurkas*, Op.24 (1834–5), 4 *Mazurkas*, Op.30 (1836–7), 4 *Mazurkas*, Op.33 (1837–8), 4 *Mazurkas*, Op.41 (1838–40), 3 *Mazurkas*, Op.50 (1842), 3 *Mazurkas*, Op.56 (1843), 3 *Mazurkas*, Op.59 (1845), 3 *Mazurkas*, Op.63 (1846), 4 *Mazurkas*, Op.67 (1835, 1846, 1849), 4 *Mazurkas*, Op.68 (1827–49); *Berceuse*, in D♭, Op.57 (1843–4); *Barcarolle* in F♯, Op.60 (1845–6); *Boléro*, Op.19 (1833); 3 *Écossaises*, Op.72 (1826); *Fantasie* in F minor, Op.49 (1841); *Fantasie Impromptu* in C♯ minor, Op.66 (1835); 3 *Impromptus*, A♭, Op.29 (1837), F♯, Op.36 (1839), G♭, Op.51 (1842); *Allegro de concert*, Op.46 (1832–41); *Tarantelle* in A♭, Op.43 (1841).

2 PIANOS: *Rondo* in C, Op.73 (1828).

CHAMBER MUSIC: piano trio in G minor, Op.8 (1828–9); vc. sonata in G minor, Op.65 (1845–6); *Introduction and Polonaise* in C, vc. and pf., Op.3 (1829–30); *Grand Duo* in E on themes from Meyerbeer's *Robert le Diable*, vc. and pf. (1832).

SONGS: 17 *Polish Songs* (1829–47).

Chopsticks (Fr. *Côtelettes*, cutlets; Ger. *Koteletten Walzer*). Anonymous quick waltz tune for pf. first pub. London 1877 as 'the celebrated Chop Waltz'. It is perf. with 2 outstretched forefingers or with the flat hands held perpendicularly, the notes being struck by their sides (i.e. with the outsides of the little fingers), with a tonic-dominant vamping bass part and an occasional touch of *glissando. The name therefore refers to chopping and to Chinese eating utensils. There is a coll. of comps. based on a similar tune—*Paraphrases*, by Borodin, Cui, Lyadov, Rimsky-Korsakov, and Liszt (1877).

choragus. (1) In Ancient Gr., leader of ch. (2) An official peculiar to the Univ. of Oxford. When the lectureship or professorship in Mus. was founded and endowed by William Heather in 1626, he laid it down that a subordinate official, called choragus, was to conduct practices of mus. twice a week. The office still exists (but not with that duty).

Choral (Ger.), **chorale** (Eng.). (1) Metrical hymntune characteristic of the Ger. Reformed Church and sung in unison. Martin Luther (1483–1546) wished to restore the congregation's role in church services and wrote simple devotional words to tunes familiar either as folk-songs or as old ecclesiastical melodies (i.e. plainsong chants). A famous example is *Ein' feste Burg ist unser Gott* (A Safe Stronghold our God is still). But the Ger. word *Choral* orig. belonged to the unreformed Church and means the ecclesiastical plainsong, the *cantus choralis*. Properly, the 'choral' in the Ger. RC Church is that part of the plainsong sung by more than one v. (the 'concentus' as distinguished from the 'accentus'), but this distinction of terminology is not always observed.

The first Lutheran chorales had not the regular rhythms that they later took on. They had often a mixture of duple and triple time and, indeed, a good deal of the free rhythm of plainsong. With Lutheran chorales, as with Genevan, Eng., and Scot. hymn tunes, the melody was at first in the ten. During the 17th cent. it gradually became usual to place it in the treble, as today. 4-part settings of chorales were made by many musicians in the 16th, 17th, and 18th cents.

The repertory of the Ger. chorale may be said to have been completed in Bach's day. He comp. only about 30, but he made 400 reharmonizations of existing chorale melodies and used some of them with memorable effect in his settings of the *Passions*.

(2) The term is used in USA as a synonym for choir or chorus, e.g. Robert Wagner Chorale.

Choral Fantasia. (1) Beethoven's Op.80, in C minor, for solo pf., ch., and orch., comp. 1808. Comprises variations on Beethoven's song *Gegenliebe* (1794–5), a melody which resembles that of prin. theme of finale of his 9th Sym., for which this Fantasia seems to have been a preliminary experiment. Text is poem by Christoph Kuffner.

(2) Holst's Op.51, for sop., ch., org., brass, perc., and str., to words by Robert Bridges (1844–1930), comp. 1930. F.p. Gloucester Fest. 1931.

choral prelude or **chorale prelude** (Ger. *Choral Vorspiel*). From the custom of playing org. preludes and interludes to the chorale grew the technique of 2 special forms of comp., one based upon a treatment of the chorale melody, often taken line by line and surrounded by other melodic parts woven together into elaborate *counterpoint, and the other not reproducing the chorale intact but suggesting it to the minds of the hearers by taking its first few notes as the theme to be elaborated. For a north Ger. congregation, to whom the melodies were all known from childhood, such a piece of organ mus. had great interest and significance.

Among the composers who helped to develop this form were Sweelinck (1562–1621), Scheidt (1587–1654), Pachelbel (1653–1706), Buxtehude (1637–1707), Reinken (1623–1722), and Böhm (1661–1733). Such of Bach's forebears as were orgs. also took their part in the working out of the form, and he himself crowned the labours of all his predecessors and contemporaries.

In addition to the Chorale Preludes of Bach there are certain early works which he called *Chorale Partitas*, the word partita here, as with certain other composers, having not the usual sense of a suite but of an air with variations. The no. of variations corresponds to the number of the verses of the hymns, and each variation

seems to be designed to re-express the thought of the corresponding verse. Since Bach many other Ger. composers have written chorale preludes, Brahms's last comp., Op.122, being a set of 11.

To some extent the same form was cultivated in Eng. Purcell has a Voluntary on the Old Hundredth that, in its way, is on the lines of the Bach Chorale Prelude.

Choral Symphony. A sym. in which a ch. is used at some point. By general usage *the* Choral Sym. means Beethoven's Sym. No.9 in D minor, Op.125, in which the finale is a setting for 4 soloists, ch., and orch. of Schiller's 'Ode to Joy'. But Holst wrote a *Choral Symphony* (to poems by Keats, f.p. 1925), and there are many syms. since Beethoven which use soloists and ch. in one or more movts., e.g. Vaughan Williams's *A Sea Symphony*, Britten's *Spring Symphony*, Mahler's Syms. Nos. 2, 3, and 8, and Shostakovich's 2nd and 13th Syms. Bantock's *Atalanta in Calydon* is a choral sym. for vv. alone.

Choral Vorspiel. See *choral prelude*.

chord. Any simultaneous combination of notes, but usually of not fewer than 3. The use of chords is the basic foundation of harmony.

chording. (1) A choir-trainer's term for bad and good intonation of the notes sounded together in chords.

(2) Spacing of the intervals in a chord.

(3) In USA the term means the improvised strumming of accompanimental chords on a banjo, etc.

chordophone. Term for mus. instr. which produce sound by means of str. stretched from one point to another. Simple chordophones are various types of zither; composites are lutes, lyres, rebecs, violins, guitars, harps, etc. One of 4 classifications of instr. devised by C. Sachs and E. M. von Hornbostel and pubd. in *Zeitschrift für Ethnologie*, 1914. Other categories are *membranophones, *idiophones, and *aerophones, with *electrophones added later.

choreographic poem. An orch. work designed for ballet but also self-sufficient because it has something of the quality and form of a tone-poem, e.g. Ravel's *La Valse* (1920), described on the score as *poème choréographique*.

choreography. (1) The system of describing dances, esp. in ballet, by signs for the steps, written alongside the melodies. An early method was *Arbeau's, described in his *Orchésographie* (1588–9). The term choreography was introduced by Lefeuillet in 1699. Today one speaks of a ballet having been 'choreographed' by its creator.

(2) The visual comp. of the ballet.

chorist-fagott. Name for the bass (double) curtal, forerunner of the bn., because it was often used for doubling the bass line in church mus.

Chorley, Henry Fothergill (b Blackley Hurst, Lancs., 1808; d London, 1872). English critic and author. Contributed as freelance to *The Athenaeum* weekly magazine 1830–3 and joined staff as its mus. critic 1833–68. Influential in his time. Also wrote novels, plays, and libs. for operas by Sullivan, Benedict, and Wallace.

Chôros. A sequence of 14 works by Villa-Lobos, comp. between 1920 and 1929, for various instr. ranging from solo guitar to 2 pf. and orch. and incorporating S. Amer. rhythms and popular melodic characteristics.

chorus. (1) See *choir or chorus*.
(2) Old name for *bagpipe.
(3) Old str. instr.—generally the *crwth.

chorus reed. Any org. reed stop not intended for solo use.

Chorzempa, Daniel (Walter) (b Minneapolis, 1944). Amer. organist, pianist, and composer. Org. instructor, Univ. of Minnesota, 1962–5. Eng. début as org. London 1969, as pianist Oxford 1970. Int. reputation as org. virtuoso esp. in Liszt. Authority on *Reubke. Member of EMS, Cologne, from 1970. Comp. of elec. works.

Chotzinoff, Samuel (b Vitebsk, 1889; d NY, 1964). Russ.-Amer. pianist and critic. Settled in USA at 17, becoming accompanist to Zimbalist and Heifetz. Critic for NY *World*, then for NY *Post*. Taught at Curtis Inst. Persuaded Toscanini to become cond. of NBC Sym. Orch. in 1936 and became NBC dir. of mus. and, in 1951, producer of NBC TV operas, commissioning Menotti's *Amahl and the Night Visitors*. Wrote several books incl. *Toscanini: An Intimate Portrait*, and autobiography *A Lost Paradise*.

Chout (Fr. spelling of Russ. *Shut*, buffoon). Ballet by Prokofiev (The Buffoon who out-buffooned seven buffoons), his Op.21. First version 1915, rev. 1920. Prod. *Diaghilev, Paris 1921. Based on A. Afanasyev's Russ. tales. Symphonic suite 1922.

Chou Wen-chung (b Chefoo, China, 1923). Chinese-born Amer. composer and teacher. Moved to USA 1946. From 1949 to 1954 had private lessons from *Varèse, whose musical executor he became. Completed *Nocturnal* from Varèse's sketches 1972, and has pubd. new and corrected edns. of *Amériques* 1972 and *Octandre* 1980. Has held academic posts in several Amer. univs., becoming prof. of mus. at Columbia Univ. 1972. His comps. incl. *Landscapes* for orch. (1949); *And the Fallen Petals*, orch. (1954); *Bejing in the Mist*, chamber ens. (1986); *Echoes from the Gorge*, perc. qt. (1989); *Windswept Peaks*, vn., vc., cl., pf. (1990).

Christelflein, Das (Ger. 'The Christmas Elf'). Opera in 2 acts, Op.20, by Pfitzner to his own lib. based on a play by Ilse von Stach. Comp. 1917 (re-casting of incid. mus. for play *Das Christelflein*, Munich 1906). F.p. Dresden 1917.

Christie, (Sir) **George** (William Langham) (b Glyndebourne, 1934). Eng. opera administrator. Son of John *Christie and his wife, the sop. Audrey *Mildmay. Took non-singing/speaking role of Fleance in Verdi's *Macbeth*, Glyndebourne co. (Edinburgh Fest.) 1947. Prod. ass., Glyndebourne 1953. Worked for Gulbenkian Foundation 1951–62. Chairman, Glyndebourne Productions, 1958–2001. Chairman, London Sinfonietta 1968–88. Replaced original 1934 opera house with larger th. which opened 1994. Knighted 1984. Hamburg Shakespeare Prize 1995. CH 2002.

Christie, John (b Eggesford, 1882; d Glyndebourne, 1962). Eng. schoolmaster and organ builder. Married sop. Audrey *Mildmay 1931, and founded in 1934 annual summer fest. of opera in opera house built at his home *Glyndebourne, near Lewes, Sussex. CH 1954. His son George *Christie succeeded him as chairman, Glyndebourne Fest., 1958. In John Christie's memory, the Worshipful Company of Musicians has, since 1965, enabled the award of an annual scholarship for a promising member of the Glyndebourne company to study abroad.

Christie, William (Lincoln) (b Buffalo, NY, 1944). Amer. conductor and harpsichordist. Dir. of mus., Dartmouth Coll., NH, 1970–1, then settled in Paris. Member of Five Centuries Ens. 1971–5. Founded Les Arts Florissants 1978. With his ens. he specialised in revival of operas by M.-A. Charpentier (*Médée* and *Actéon*), Lully (*Atys*), Rameau (*Pygmalion* and *Les Indes galantes*), Handel (*Alcina*), and Rossi (*Orfeo*). Prof., Paris Cons. from 1982. London début of Les Arts Florissants, Greenwich 1990. His perfs. of Fr. and It. baroque mus. set new standards.

Christmas Concerto. Name of *Corelli's Concerto Grosso in G minor, Op.6, No.8, for str. and continuo (1712). It was intended as a *concerto da chiesa* (for church use) and was inscribed *fatto per la notte di Natale* (made for Christmas Night). Torelli's 12 Concerti Grossi Op.8 (1709) for str. and continuo are entitled *con un pastorale per il Santissimo Natale*, this 'pastoral for the most holy night of Christmas' being No.6, also in G minor.

Christmas Eve (Russ. *Noch' pered rozhdestvom*). Opera in 4 acts by Rimsky-Korsakov to his own lib. after story *Christmas Eve* in Gogol's *Evenings on a Farm near Dikanka* (1932). Comp. 1894–5. Prod. St Petersburg 1895, Indiana Univ., Bloomington, 1977, BBC (studio) 1987, London (ENO) 1988. Gogol story is also basis of Tchaikovsky's *Cherevichki* (rev. of *Vakula the Smith*), comp. 1885, and of an episode in Act II of Janáček's *From the *House of the Dead*, comp. 1927–8.

Christmas Oratorio. Choral work by Bach for soloists, ch., and orch., text by Picander and Bach, being biblical story of the Nativity with commentary. Comprises 6 cantatas designed for perf. in Leipzig on 3 days of Christmas fest., New Year's Day, New Year's Sunday, and Epiphany.

Some of the mus. was comp. for secular words. Schütz also wrote a Christmas Oratorio (1664). Ger. title is *Weihnachts-Oratorium*.

Christoff, Boris (*b* Plovdiv, Bulgaria, 1914; *d* Rome, 1993). Bulgarian bass. Studied in Sofia as lawyer then singing in Rome and Salzburg. Début Reggio CG 1949 (Boris); Salzburg Fest. 1949; Amer. début (S. Francisco) 1956; Chicago Opera 1958–63. Notable interpreter of Mussorgsky's Boris and Verdi's King Philip; also sang Wagner roles of Hagen, King Marke, and Gurnemanz. Gave concert in NY 1980, but never sang at NY Met.

Christopher Columbus. (1) (*Christophe Colomb*). Opera in 2 acts (27 scenes) by Milhaud to lib. by Paul Claudel. Comp. 1928. Prod. Berlin 1930. Paris (concert version) 1936. Uses cinema screen. Operas on this subject also by Ottoboni, Morlacchi, and Egk.
    (2) Early ov. by Wagner intended for play by Apel, comp. 1834–5, f.p. Leipzig 1835.
    (3) Incidental mus. by Walton (unpubd.) for radio play by Louis MacNeice broadcast BBC Oct. 1942.
    (4) *The Voyage*. Opera in 3 acts by Glass to lib. by D. H. Hwang. F.p. NY Met 1992. Commissioned by Met to commemorate 500th anniversary of Columbus's arrival in America.
    (5) *Cristoforo Colombo*. Opera in 4 acts by Franchetti to lib. by Illica. Comp. 1891–2, rev. 1922. F.p. Genoa 1892. Commissioned by Genoa, on Verdi's recommendation, to mark 400th anniversary of discovery of America.

Christophers, Harry (*b* Goudhurst, Kent, 1953). Eng. conductor and chorusmaster. Founded The Sixteen 1977, with which he has toured Brit., Eur., Brazil, and Japan. Salzburg Fest. début 1989 (with Sixteen, Bach's *St John Passion*). Choir sang in Birtwistle's *Gawain*, CG 1991. Many recordings of Bach, Handel, Tallis, Palestrina, and Sheppard.

Christou, Jani (*b* Heliopolis, Egypt, 1926; *d* Athens, 1970). Gr. composer. Employed serialism and 12-note technique 1948–58, then became interested in elec. sounds, establishing elec. workshop in Athens. Invented form of notation to incorporate stage action. Comps. incl. 3 syms.; *Tongues of Fire* and *Mysterion* (oratorios); incid. mus. for plays by Aeschylus, Sophocles, and Aristophanes; and works involving tape and aleatory procedures.

Christus. (1) Oratorio by Liszt for soloists, ch., and orch., comp. 1862–7, f.p. Budapest 1873.
    (2) Oratorio, Op.97, by Mendelssohn, text by Chevalier Bunsen, begun 1844, unfinished. F.p. of 8 nos., Birmingham 1852.
    (3) The part of Christ in Bach's *St Matthew Passion* is often denominated thus.

Christus am Ölberge (Christ on the Mount of Olives). Oratorio by Beethoven, Op.85, for sop., ten., bass, ch., and orch., comp. 1803. Lib. by Franz Xaver Huber. F.p. Vienna 1803. English version entitled *En Gedi* changes subject to story of David.

chromatic (derived from Gr. *chromos* = colour). The chromatic was one of the 3 classifications of Gr. scales. In modern mus. it refers to notes not belonging to the diatonic scale. They are indicated by *chromatics*. The *chromatic scale* is 12 ascending or descending semitones (sharps ascending, flats descending). *chromatic chords* incl. one or more notes not in the diatonic scale of the prevailing key of the relevant passage.

Chromatic Fantasia and Fugue. Hpd. work by Bach, comp. 1720–3 at Cöthen.

chromatic harp. Harp built by Pleyel 1897 with a str. for every semitone, thus needing no pedals.

chromaticism. (1) The use of chromatic intervals and chromatic chords.
    (2) A style of composing using chromatic harmony. *Gesualdo in 16th cent. used advanced chromaticism. Bach's experiments in chromaticism were based on diatonic principles. The age of Romanticism explored chromaticism further because of need for emotional expression, hence the chromatic elements in Wagner's *Tristan und Isolde* and later works. See also *atonal*.

Chronochromie (Time-colour). Orch. work by Messiaen in 7 sections: *Introduction, Strophe I, Antistrophe I, Strophe II, Antistrophe II, Epode, Coda*. Comp. 1960. F.p. Donaueschingen, 16 Oct. 1960, cond. Rosbaud. *Epode* is written for 18 str., each playing a different birdsong.

Chrysander, (Karl Franz) **Friedrich** (*b* Lübthen, Mecklenburg, 1826; *d* Bergedorf, nr. Hamburg, 1901). Ger. critic and music historian. Authority on Handel, editing complete works for Ger. Handel Soc., some of the vols. being subsidized by sale of produce from his market garden, and writing biography (1858–67; never completed). Worked also on other musicological subjects, publishing or editing works of Palestrina, Schütz, Carissimi, Corelli, Couperin, and J. S. Bach, and discovering autograph of Bach's B minor Mass. Modern scholarship has found much fault with the Handel edn.

Chung, Kyung-Wha (*b* Seoul, Korea, 1948). Korean violinist, sister of Myung-Wha *Chung and Myung-Whun *Chung. Won Leventritt Award jointly with Pinchas Zukerman. NY début with NYPO, 1968; Eur. début with LSO, London 1970; Salzburg Fest. 1973. Brilliant int. career. Recordings of major concs.

Chung, Myung-Wha (*b* Seoul, Korea, 1944). Korean cellist, sister of Kyung-Wha *Chung and Myung-Whun *Chung. Début with Seoul PO. Soloist with leading orchs. Plays trio with sister and brother.

Chung, Myung-Whun (*b* Seoul, Korea, 1953). Korean conductor and pianist, brother of

Kyung-Wha *Chung and Myung-Wha *Chung. Début, Seoul 1960, as pianist; as cond. 1971. 2nd prize Tchaikovsky pf. competition, Moscow, 1974. Ass. cond. Los Angeles PO 1978–81; cond. Saarländischer Radio SO 1984–9. Mus. dir. Opéra de la Bastille, Paris, 1989–94. NY Met début 1986.

Church Music Society (British). Founded 1906. Its objects are the encouragement of a high standard in the choice and perf. of mus. in worship. Predominantly Anglican in membership. See also *Royal School of Church Music*.

Chute de la Maison Usher, La (The Fall of the House of Usher). Opera in 3 scenes planned by Debussy to his own lib. based on Edgar Allan Poe but left incomplete. Work on it extended from 1908 to 1917. What survives is complete text and vocal score of scene 1 (prologue) and part of scene 2. F.p. New Haven, 1977.

Cibber, Susanna (Maria) (b London, 1714; d London, 1766). Eng. mezzo-soprano and actress; sister of Thomas *Arne and 2nd wife (1734) of Theophilus Cibber. Début 1732, frequently singing Polly in *The Beggar's Opera*. Greatly admired by Handel, in whose *Messiah* she first sang the cont. arias (Dublin 1742). Gave up singing for acting 1746.

Ciccolini, Aldo (b Naples, 1925). It.-born Fr. pianist. Début 1942 in Chopin's F minor conc. Prof. of pf., Naples Cons., 1947–9. Moved to France 1949. NY début 1950. Specialized in works of Satie. Prof. of pf., Paris Cons., from 1971.

Cid, Le. Opera in 4 acts by Massenet to lib. by A. d'Ennery, L. Gallet, and E. Blau, based on play by Corneille (1637). Comp. 1884–5. Prod. Paris 1885; New Orleans 1890, NY Met 1897. Ballet mus. very popular. Operas on this subject also by Farinelli, Aiblinger, and Cornelius.

Ciesinski, Katherine (b Newark, Del., 1950). Amer. mezzo-soprano. Won comps. in Geneva and Paris. Eur. début Aix-en-Provence 1976 (Annina in *La traviata*). Amer. début (Santa Fe) 1979; NY Met début 1988.

Ciesinski, Kristine (Frances) (b Wilmington, Del., 1952). Amer. soprano. Sister of Katherine *Ciesinski. Prof. début Denver 1976 (Countess in *Capriccio*). Sang with Chesapeake Opera, 1976–85. Won int. singing comp. Geneva 1977. NY concert début in *Messiah* 1977. Salzburg Landestheater 1979–81; Salzburg Fest. 1980 (concert). Bremen opera 1985–8. Brit. début Glasgow (Scottish Opera) 1985; London (ENO) début 1989; Wexford 1988.

cigány (Hung; Ger. *Zigeuner*). Gipsy. What are called *cigány bands* consist normally of str., cl., and dulcimer.

Cigna [Sens], **Gina** [Ginetta] (b Angère, Paris, 1900; d Milan, 2001). Fr.-It. soprano. Début La Scala 1927 (under name Genoveffa Sens) as Freia in *Das Rheingold*. Returned to La Scala as Gina

Cigna in 1929, singing every season until 1943. CG début 1933; NY Met 1936–8. Famous interpreter of Turandot. Became singing teacher 1948.

Cikker, Ján (b Banská Bystrica, Cz., 1911; d Bratislava, 1989). Cz. composer. Prof. of theory Bratislava Cons. 1938–51 and comp. at Bratislava Acad. 1951. Works incl. str. qts., sym.-poems, and operas incl. *Resurrection* (*Vzkriesenie*) (Tolstoy) (1962), *Mr Scrooge* (Dickens) (1963), *Coriolanus* (1972), and *From the Life of Insects* (1987).

Cilea, Francesco (b Palmi, Calabria, 1866; d Varazza, 1950). It. composer. First opera, *Gina* (1889), prod. while he was student. Other operas incl. *La tilda* (1892), *L'Arlesiana* (1897), *Adriana Lecouvreur* (1902), and *Gloria* (1907). Prof. of pf., Naples Cons., 1894–6, of comp., Florence Mus. Inst. 1896–1904, dir. Palermo Cons. 1913–16, Naples Cons. 1916–35.

Cillario, Carlo Felice (b San Rafael, Argentina, 1915). Argentinian conductor of It. parentage. Moved to It. as child. Began career as violinist, but changed to cond. at Odessa Opera, 1942. Formed chamber orch. Bologna 1946. Cond. Orchestra Sinfonia del Estado, Buenos Aires, 1949–51. Brit. début Glyndebourne 1961; Chicago Opera 1961; CG 1964 (*Tosca*, with Callas and Gobbi); NY Met 1972. Cond. at Royal Opera, Stockholm, from 1980, Drottningholm 1982–4. Mus. dir. Elizabethan Opera Trust, Sydney, NSW, 1970–1. Prin. guest cond. and mus. dir. Australian Opera from 1988.

Cima, Giovanni Paolo (b c.1570; fl. until 1622). It. composer and organist. Mus. dir. and org. St Celso, Milan, 1610. Wrote masses, motets, and sonatas for vn., viola da gamba and org., hpd., etc. Early user of medium of trio sonata. Wrote treatise on counterpoint 1622.

Cimarosa, Domenico (b Aversa, Naples, 1749; d Venice, 1801). It. composer. Studied in Naples, where he wrote *Le stravaganze del conti*, first of his 65 operas. Worked in Rome and Naples until 1787 when he went to St Petersburg as court composer to Catherine II where his operas were less successful than those of his deputy, Soler. In 1791 succeeded Salieri as court Kapellmeister to Leopold II in Vienna, writing *Il matrimonio segreto* there. Returned to Naples 1792 as choirmaster to the king. Sentenced to death 1799 for supporting French republican army but reprieved on condition he left Naples. Wrote orch. works incl sym., ob. conc., and Sinfonia Concertante for 2 fl., and over 30 kbd. sonatas. Among his huge output of operas are: *Le stravagante del conte* (1772); *Il tre amanti* (1777); *Il matrimonio per raggio* (c.1778–9); *L'italiana in Londre* (1779); *Il pittor parigino* (1781, rev. as *Il barone burlato*, 1784, and as *Le brame delusa*, 1787); *Chi dell'altrui si veste presto si spoglio* (1783); *I due baroni di Rossi Azzurra* (1783); *Artaserse* (1784); *I due supposti conti* (1784); *L'impresario in angustie* (1786); *Il fanatico burlato* (1787); *Il *matrimonio segreto* (1792); *I traci amanti*

(1793); *Le astuzie femminili* (1794); *Penelope* (1795); *Gli Orazi ed i Curiazi* (1796); *L'apprensivo raggirato* (1798).

cimbalom (Hung.). *Dulcimer. It is a large concert instr. (horizontal str. struck with hammers) used in popular mus., by *Kodály in his opera *Háry János, and by Debussy and other composers, incl. Stravinsky (in *Renard* and *Ragtime*). First comp. to use it in symphonic mus. was *Mosonyi.

cimbasso (It.). Narrow bore tuba in B♭, used in Verdi opera scores up to *Aida* (1871).

Cincinnati Symphony Orchestra. Founded 1895. First regular cond. Frank van der Stucken, 1896–1907. Orch. suspended 1907–9 because of labour dispute. Stokowski cond. 1909–12; Ernst Kunwald 1912–17; Ysaÿe 1918–22; Fritz Reiner 1922–31; Eugene Goossens 1931–47; Thor Johnson 1947–58; Max Rudolf 1958–70; Thomas Schippers 1970–77; Michael Gielen 1980–6; Jesús Lopez-Cóbos 1982–2001; Paavo Järvi from 2001. Concerts given in Mus. Hall since 1930s (renovated 1970).

Cinderella. (1) Various operas have been written based on Perrault's fairy-tale. See *Cenerentola, La* (Rossini) and *Cendrillon* (Massenet).

(2) (*Zolushka*). Ballet, with songs, by Prokofiev, comp. 1940–4, f.p. Moscow 1945. Also ballet by J. Strauss II.

cinelli (It.). Cymbals.

Cinesi, Le (The Chinese Ladies). 'Opera serenade', or divertissement, in 1 act by Gluck, to text expanded from lib. written by Metastasio for Caldara. Comp. 1754 for visit by Maria Theresa and Francis I to court of Gluck's employer, Prince von Hildburghausen. Prod. Vienna 1754, London 1977.

cipher, ciphering. Continuous sounding of a note on the org. because of some mechanical defect.

circle of fifths (Ger. *Qintenzirkel*). An arrangement first described by Heinichen in *Der Generalbass* (1728) and used by theorists to illustrate relative harmonic remoteness of one key from another, i.e. the number of fifths by which 2 notes are separated along the circle. If arranged clockwise by ascending (or descending) perfect fifths, the tonics of the 12 major (or minor) keys make a closed circle, thus: C–G–D–A–E–B(=C♭)–F♯(=G♭)–C♯(=D♭)–A♭–E♭–B♭–F–C and so after these 12 steps the original key is reached again.

Circles. Work by *Berio for female v., harp, and 2 percussionists to text by e. e. cummings from his 'poems 1923–54'. Comp. 1960.

Circus Polka (for a young elephant). Pf. piece comp. 1942 by *Stravinsky for Barnum and Bailey Circus to be danced by troupe of young elephants who gave f.p. in 1942 to arr. for wind

band scored by David Reskin. Composer's version for sym. orch. f.p. Cambridge, Mass., 1944; f.p. in England, London 1952.

Cis (Ger.). The note C♯.

Cisis (Ger.). The note C♯♯.

citole. Scholars are still uncertain just which medieval instr. was described by this term, but it seems possible that it was a forerunner of the Renaissance *cittern, a kind of *lyra.

cittern. Renaissance instr. something between a lyre and a guitar, but with metal str., a flat back, and pear-shaped body. Played with a quill plectrum. Name derived from Gr. *kithara* (lyre), and the cittern was known as *cistra* (Fr.), *Cister* (Ger.), and *cithren* (Eng.). In It. where it was developed it was called the *cetra*. Used as a solo instr. and in *broken consort. Not to be confused with *gittern. From late 17th cent. gave way to guitar but survived into early 20th cent. as folk instr. in Switz. and Ger.

City Center, New York. Home of enterprising opera and ballet cos., the former (NY City Opera) founded 1944 to provide high-standard opera at moderate prices. Housed in Lincoln Center since 1964. First mus. dir. László Halász 1944–51, then Joseph Rosenstock 1951–6, Erich Leinsdorf 1956, Julius Rudel 1957–79, Christopher Keene from 1979–95. Co. has given premières of several Amer. operas, also f. Amer. stage ps. of *Duke Bluebeard's Castle, Orff's *Der Mond*, and Strauss's *Die schweigsame Frau*. Several fine singers have consolidated their early careers with co. incl. Beverly *Sills (dir. 1979–87) and Plácido Domingo.

Civil, Alan (*b* Northampton, 1928; *d* London, 1989). Eng. horn-player and composer. Member of RPO 1953–55, Philharmonia Orch. 1955–66, then prin. hn. BBC SO 1966–88. Prof. of hn. RCM. Member of several chamber groups. Comp. sym. for brass and perc. (1950), wind quintet (1951), wind octet (1951), hn. trio (1952). OBE 1985.

Clair de Lune (Moonlight). (1) 3rd movt. of Debussy's *Suite bergamasque* for pf.; exists in several other arrs., none by Debussy.

(2) Song by Debussy (poem by Verlaine), No.4 of his *Fêtes galantes*, in orig. version (1882).

(3) Song by Fauré, his Op.46 No.2, same poem as (2).

claque (Fr.). Smack, clap. Members of the audience at (usually) an opera-house but also in the concert-hall who are engaged by a performer, often at considerable expense, to applaud, call for encores, and generally show enthusiasm (or the reverse). Claques are highly organized, under leadership of a *chef de claque*, and exert considerable influence. The claque appears to have developed in Paris *c*.1820 and then to have spread to It. and to Vienna, and eventually to all the famous opera houses.

clarabel, clarabella, or **claribel flute**. Org. stop much the same as *Hohlflöte*.

Clarey, Cynthia (*b* Smithfield, Va., 1949). Amer. mezzo-soprano. First opera roles with Tri-Cities Opera Co., Binghamton, NY. Sang in Musgrave's *The Voice of Ariadne*, NY City Opera, 1977 and in f. Amer. p. of *The Ice Break*, Boston 1979. Shared title-role in Peter Brook's prod., *La tragédie de Carmen*, Paris 1982. Brit. début Glyndebourne 1984, sang Serena in *Porgy and Bess* there in 1986. Wexford Fest. 1985 and 1986. Sang in f.p. of *The Mask of Time*, Boston 1984.

Clari, Giovanni Carlo Maria (*b* Pisa, 1667; *d* Pisa, 1754). It. composer. Studied at Bologna. Choirmaster, Pistoia Cath., 1703–24. His madrigals are notable for their daring modulations. Comp. operas and church mus., making advanced use of fugue in the latter. Best known for secular vocal duets and trios with continuo, comp. after 1730 and mainly fugal.

claricembalo, clarichord. Misspellings (apparently) of *clavicembalo* (harpsichord) and *clavichord*.

clarinet. Single-reed woodwind instr. with cylindrical tube developed *c*.1690 by J. C. Denner of Nuremberg, who, by adding 2 keys to the *chalumeau*, increased that instr.'s range by over 2 octaves. It was not playable in all keys until 1843 when Klose adapted the Boehm fl. key system to the cl. The first composer to use the cl. in a sym. was Mozart.

As the reed blocks one end of the tube, the pipe acts as a 'stopped' one, sounding an octave lower than it would have done if left open. Like other cylindrical tubes the cl. overblows at the interval not of its first upper partial, the interval of an octave (as the fl. and ob. do), but at its 2nd (the interval of a 12th). The notes of the instr.'s first octave are obtained in the normal way and the gap of a 5th before the overblowing begins has to be filled by additional side-holes which leave the tone weaker at this point and the fingering somewhat more awkward. All members of the family have great powers of *pianissimo* and of *crescendo* and *diminuendo*—greater than those of any other wind instr. Double, triple, and flutter *tonguing* are possible.

Varieties of cl. incl.:

(a) clarinet in C, B♭, or A—the normal treble instr. The existence of these 3 pitches was to enable the composer to use any key without creating undue difficulty for the player (see *transposing instrument*). The B♭ clarinet is a transposing instr., sounding a tone lower than written. The A clarinet sounds a minor 3rd lower than written. The C instr. is now not much used, on account of inferior tone, but figures in the scores of classical composers. It is not a transposing instr. (b) bass clarinet. Its range lies an octave below that of one of the above (usually of that of the B♭ instr.). It differs somewhat in shape, its lower end being curved upwards and ending in a bell,

and its upper one continued by a tube bent downwards to reach the player's mouth. Except in military band mus. it is treated as a transposing instr., its mus. being notated either in the treble clef or in a 9th higher than the sound (Fr. method), or in the bass clef a 2nd above the sound (Ger. Method). (c) high E♭ clarinet, a 4th above the B♭ instr. It is found in all military bands and occasionally figures in orch. scores, e.g. Richard Strauss's *Alpensinfonie*. It is a transposing instr., its mus. being notated a minor 3rd lower than the sound. (d) high D clarinet. This serves the same purpose as the E♭ cl., but is much rarer. It is a transposing instr., being written for a tone lower than the sound. R. Strauss uses it in *Symphonia Domestica* and with outstanding effect in *Till Eulenspiegel*. (e) alto clarinet—in E♭ and F. The E♭ is used in symphonic wind bands, concert bands, and cl. choirs. The F instr. is practically a modernized *basset horn*. Both are written for in the treble clef and are transposing instr. (f) pedal clarinet, or contrabass clarinet, or double-bass clarinet. Almost entirely a military band instr. Its part is written 2 octaves and a tone higher than the sound. (The word 'pedal' had no reference to any part of the construction and the origin of its use is not very clear.) (g) 3 obscure modern instr. related to the cl. family by possessing a single reed are the *clarina*, the *heckelclarina* or *Heckelclarinette*, and the *Holztrompete*. All were invented to represent the shepherd-boy's pipe in Act III of Wagner's *Tristan und Isolde*, but have not displaced customary use of the *cor anglais*.

Note that the old Eng. spelling 'clarionet' is obsolete.

clarinet flute. Org. flue stop, end-plugged; 4′ length and 8′ pitch; slightly reedy in quality.

clarinet stop. Reed stop smoother than ob.; 8′ pitch or occasionally 16′.

clarino. Term applied to the high, brilliant tpt. and hn. parts in baroque mus., probably because the *clarion* was used for high-register playing.

clarion. Org. stop like *trumpet* but of 4′ pitch.

clarion (Fr. *claron*). Medieval short tpt. (2′ or 3′ long), used particularly by armies because it was easier to carry than the longer *buisine* and its high-pitched notes (hence *clarino*) could be more easily heard.

Clarissa. Opera in 2 acts, Op.30, by Robin Holloway to his own lib. based on Richardson's novel. Comp. 1968–76. F.p. London (ENO) 1990.

Clark, Edward (*b* Newcastle upon Tyne, 1888; *d* London, 1962). Eng. conductor and administrator. For some time connected with *Diaghilev. With BBC, in various capacities 1923–36. Esp. interested in contemporary developments in comp. and was responsible for the f.ps. or f.

broadcast ps. of many important works. Pres. Brit. section of ISCM from 1945. Husband of Elisabeth *Lutyens.

Clark, Graham (*b* Littleborough, 1941). Eng. tenor. Operatic début with Gemini Opera (Jeník in *The Bartered Bride*). Scottish Opera 1975, ENO from 1976. Bayreuth début 1981; NY Met début 1985. Sang in f.p. of Corigliano's *The Ghosts of Versailles*, NY Met 1991.

Clarke, Henry Leland (*b* Dover, NH, 1907). Amer. composer. Held several teaching posts, incl. Univ. of California, Vassar Coll., and Univ. of Washington (1958–71). Many comps. in wide range of fields incl. 2 operas, 3 str. qts., and *Gloria in 5 Official Languages of the United Nations* (1950) for ch. and orch.

Clarke, Jeremiah (*b* London, *c*.1674; *d* London, 1707). Eng. composer and organist. Chorister of Chapel Royal *c*.1685–90. Org., Winchester Coll. 1692–5. Vicar-choral, St Paul's Cath. 1699, master of choristers 1703 in succession to Blow. Joint org. (with Croft) of Chapel Royal 1704. Comp. setting of Dryden's *Alexander's Feast*, cantatas, anthems, odes, and hpd. pieces. In his 'Choice lessons for the Harpsichord or Spinet' (pubd. 1700) there occurs 'The Prince of Denmark's March', better known in its arr. as the **Trumpet Voluntary*. Shot himself supposedly because of unhappy love affair.

Clarke, Rebecca (*b* Harrow, 1886; *d* NY, 1979). Eng. composer, violist, and violinist. In 1908 became Stanford's first woman comp. student at RCM and was encouraged by him to take up va. From 1911 played in various chamber groups with the d'*Arányi sisters, Myra *Hess, and *Suggia. Comp. 58 songs and part-songs and 24 instr. chamber works.

clàrsach. The ancient small Celtic harp, revived in Scotland during the 20th cent. Differs from usual orch. hp. in having brass str. instead of gut or nylon, giving a bell-like sound.

classical. Term which, applied to mus., has vague rather than specific meaning: (1) mus. comp. roughly between 1750 and 1830 (i.e. post-Baroque and pre-Romantic) which covers the development of the classical sym. and conc. (2) mus. of an orderly nature, with qualities of clarity and balance, and emphasising formal beauty rather than emotional expression (which is not to say that emotion is lacking). (3) mus. generally regarded as having permanent rather than ephemeral value. (4) 'classical music' is used as a generic term meaning the opposite of light or popular mus.

Classical Symphony. Title of Prokofiev's Sym. No.1 in D, Op.25, comp. 1916–17, f.p. Petrograd 1918 cond. composer. Deliberately written in style of Haydn. The gavotte was used by Prokofiev again in his *Romeo and Juliet* ballet mus.

clausula. (1) *Cadence. Some medieval terms are *clausula vera*, perfect cadence; *clausula falsa*,

interrupted cadence; *clausula plagalis*, plagal cadence; etc.
(2) Section of medieval *organum in which textless contrapuntal parts are heard in strict rhythm with chant tune on which organum is based.

clavecin. Fr. name for hpd., shortening of *clavecinon*, first used 1611.

claves. Cuban perc. instr., being round sticks of hard wood 7″ or 8″ long. The player holds one over the upturned fingernails of his left fist and beats it with the other held lightly in the right hand. Used in dance bands but taken up by 20th-cent. composers incl. *Birtwistle, Copland, Varèse, and *McCabe.

clavicembalo (It.). Clavicymbal. The It. word for *harpsichord. It derives from *clavichordium*, found in Ger. poem of 1404 which lists the instr. of courtly love. The It. is occasionally corrupted to *gravicembalo* and regularly shortened to *cembalo*. The Fr. form is *clavecinon*, shortened to *clavecin* (1611).

clavichord. Small kbd. instr. developed in 14th cent. from the *monochord and sometimes called *clarichord* or *manichord* or **chekker*. The early clavichord used the same str. to produce 2, 3, or 4 notes by stopping the str. at different points along its length. There was a bridge for each note which was brought into contact with the str. from pressure on a key on the kbd. The bridge also sounded the str., producing a very soft attack. Because of this process of stopping the str., the early clavichord was known as *gebunden*, or fretted. (*gebunden* means 'bound', and the frets on some early instr. were cords bound round the fingerboard.) Because some notes employed the same str. they could not be played simultaneously, but by the 17th cent. the proportion of str. to keys increased until in the early 18th cent. some clavichords were unfretted (*bundfrei*). Essentially an instr. for private practice, being too soft in tone for concert use, and is used in this way by orgs. In 20th cent. *Howells has composed for it.

clavicytherium. Upright version of hpd., developed in 15th and early 16th cents. A rare surviving example is in the coll. of the RCM.

Clavier. See *Klavier*.

clavier de récit (Fr.). *swell organ.

clavier des bombardes (Fr.). That organ manual having *trumpet* and *tuba*.

Clavierübung. See *Klavierübung*.

clavicymbal. Eng. form of It. *clavicembalo*, i.e. *harpsichord.

claviorganum. Combination of org. and hpd. developed in 16th cent. and known in Fr. as *clavecin organisé* and in It. as *claviorgano*. The org. pipes were laid horizontally inside the chest.

Clay, Frederick Emes (*b* Paris, 1838; *d* Great Marlow, 1889). Eng. composer. Wrote over a dozen operettas prod. in London between 1859 and 1883. His cantata *Lalla Rookh* (1877) contains the song 'I'll sing thee songs of Araby'. Also wrote popular ballads 'She wandered down the mountainside' and 'The Sands of Dee'.

clear flute. Organ stop much like *Waldflöte*.

clef (Lat. *clavis*, Fr. *clef*, key). Symbol normally placed at the beginning of every line of mus. to indicate the exact location of a particular note on the staff; also placed at any point where new clef begins to operate. The *treble clef* places the note G above middle C on the second line (the G clef); the *bass clef* fixes the note F below middle C on the second line (descending) (F clef); the *alto clef*, on the middle line, fixes middle C and is used for the va; the *tenor clef* fixes middle C on the fourth line (ascending) and is used for vc. and bn. parts above the bass staff. The *soprano clef*, fixing middle C on the first line, is obsolete, but is found in medieval mus. and in some works well into 19th cent. In the following example middle C is represented in five different ways:

de clavecin, first of its kind. Wrote 4 stage works, some choral pieces, and many hpd. pieces, some of which are lost.

Clement, Franz (*b* Vienna, 1780; *d* Vienna, 1842). Austrian violinist. Public début 1789, followed by tours of Ger. and Eng. Played in Haydn's London concerts 1791. Cond., Theater an der Wien, Vienna, 1802–11. Soloist, f.p. of Beethoven's vn. conc. 1806; cond. f.p. of Beethoven's 4th Sym. 1807. In Russ. and Ger. 1812–18, returning to Vienna to conduct opera 1818–21. Cond. concerts for Angelica *Catalani. Died in poverty.

Clementi, Muzio (*b* Rome, 1752; *d* Evesham, 1832). Eng. pianist and composer of It. birth. Church org. at age of 13. In 1766 went to Eng. under patronage of Peter Beckford and for 7 years studied and practised hpd. at Steepleton Iwerne, Dorset. London début as pianist and composer 1775. Cond. It. opera in London 1777–8. His 6 kbd. sonatas, Op.2, were pubd. 1779 and became popular. In 1781 began his tours of Europe in which he engaged with other pianists (incl. Mozart) in public tests of skill in improvisation, sight-reading, etc. Returned to London 1783, composing several syms., pf. conc., and coll. of 100 studies, *Gradus ad Parnassum*,

G *or* Treble Clef On 2nd line up fixing that as Treble G	F *or* Bass Clef On 2nd line down, fixing that as Bass F	C (Soprano) Clef On 1st line, fixing that as middle C	C (Alto) Clef On 3rd line, fixing that as middle C	C (Tenor) Clef On 4th line, fixing that as middle C

Clemencic, René (*b* Vienna, 1928). Austrian harpsichordist, recorder-player, conductor, and composer. Founded Musica Antiqua in Vienna, 1958, with which he gave perfs. using authentic instrs. Founded Clemencic Consort 1969, cond. it in large repertory from medieval mus. to *avant-garde*.

Clemens (non Papa). Name applied to Jacob (Jacques) Clement (*b* Middelburg, *c*.1510; *d* Dixmuide, *c*.1556). Flemish composer. Succentor at Bruges Cath. 1544–5; may then have held court post with Emperor Charles V and worked in Ieper (Ypres) after 1550. Wrote masses, motets, and *chansons*, pubd. in Louvain, 1555–80, and 4 books of psalms set to popular Flemish melodies (Antwerp 1556–7). Nickname variously explained as distinguishing him from Pope Clement VII or from Flemish poet Jacobus Papa who also lived in Ypres, but the probability is that it was a joke.

Clément, Charles-François (*b* Provence, *c*.1720; *d* ?Paris, after 1782). Fr. composer and scholar. Was hpd. teacher in Paris and was jilted by one of his pupils in favour of Casanova, 1757. Arr. mus. at Comédie-Italienne 1755–6. In 1758 and 1762 pubd. two treatises on comp., the first on hpd. accompaniment and the second on figured bass. In 1762 began monthly pubn. of his *Journal*

which remains a foundation of pf. technique. Comp. over 100 piano sonatas, some of them valued highly by Beethoven, whom Clementi met in 1807. Among pupils were John Field, Moscheles, Kalkbrenner, and Cramer. Also went into the business of making pfs., becoming partner in London firm, Clementi & Co., which in 1832 became Collard & Collard. Clementi's early sonatas were written for the hpd., but after 1780 his allegiance was to the piano.

Clemenza di Tito, La (The Clemency of Titus). Opera in 2 acts by Mozart (his last, K621) to lib. by Metastasio, altered by Mazzolà. Comp. for coronation of Emperor Leopold II as King of Bohemia. Prod. Prague 1791, London 1806, Tanglewood 1952. About 20 other composers, incl. Caldara (1734) and Gluck (1752), set Metastasio's text.

Cleobury, Nicholas (Randall) (*b* Bromley, 1950). Eng. conductor, organist, pianist, and harpsichordist. Ass. org. Chichester Cath. 1971–2, Ch. Ch., Oxford, 1972–6. Chorus master, Glyndebourne, 1976–9. Ass. dir. BBC Singers 1977–80. Ass. cond. Kent Opera. Cond. Eng. Bach Fest. Ch. Cond. Opera North's revival of Delius's *A Village Romeo and Juliet*, 1984. Prin. opera cond., RAM 1980–7.

Cleobury, Stephen (John) (*b* Bromley, 1948). Eng. conductor and organist. Org., St Matthew's, Northampton, 1971–4, sub-org. Westminster Abbey 1974–8; master of mus. Westminster Cath. 1979–82; dir. of mus., King's Coll., Cambridge, from 1982.

Cleopatra. Dramatic scena for sop. (or high v.) and orch. by Iain *Hamilton. F.p. Cheltenham Fest. 1978.

Cléopâtre, La Mort de (Berlioz). See *Mort de Cléopâtre, La*.

Clérambault, Louis-Nicolas (*b* Paris, 1676; *d* Paris, 1749). Fr. organist and composer for kbd. instr. and voice. His books of Fr. cantatas are the best of their period. Held post at court of Louis XIV and became org. of Maison Royale de St Cyr, nr. Versailles, 1714–21. Org., St Sulpice, Paris, 1715 and of the Jacobins, Rue St Jacques, from 1719. Wrote 5 books of cantatas, 20 in all, pubd. 1710, 1713, 1716, 1720, and 1726. Another 5 cantatas were pubd. separately. Also comp. 3 pieces for strs. under title *Simphonie-sonata*. His *premier livre d'orgue* comprises 2 suites of 14 pieces. Wrote theatrical pieces for court, among them *Le soleil vainqueur* (1721) and *Le départ du roi* (1745).

Cleveland Orchestra. Amer. orch. founded 1918. Conds: Nikolay Sokoloff 1918–33; Artur Rodzinski 1933–43; Erich Leinsdorf 1943–4; Georg Szell 1946–70; Lorin Maazel 1972–82; Christoph von Dohnányi 1984–2002; Franz Welser-Möst from 2002. Home since 1931 Severance Hall. Salzburg Fest. début 1967, cond. Szell.

Cliburn, Van (Harvey Lavan) (*b* Shreveport, La., 1934). Amer. pianist. First recital at age 4; played Tchaikovsky 1st conc. at Houston 1946. NY début 1948. In 1958 won Tchaikovsky Comp., Moscow. Est. Cliburn Int. piano comp. at Fort Worth, Texas, 1962. Salzburg Fest. 1964.

cloches (Fr.). Bells, e.g. those used in the orch.

Cloches de Corneville, Les (The Bells of Corneville). Opera in 3 acts by Planquette to lib. by Clairville and Gabet. Prod. Paris and NY 1877, London 1878 (as *The Chimes of Normandy*).

Clock Symphony (*Die Uhr*). Nickname of Haydn's Sym. in D, No.101 (Hob. I:101), comp. 1794 in London. So called because of 'tick-tock' acc. to 1st subject of 2nd movt. This movt. was separately pubd. in Vienna 1798 in pf. arr. as 'Rondo, Die Uhr'.

clog box. See *Chinese wood block*.

close. The same as *cadence*.

close harmony. Harmony in which the notes of a chord are close together. In close harmony singing the vv. are distributed within the compass of an octave.

Cloud Messenger, The. Ode for ch. and orch., Op.30, by Holst to text by Holst founded on Sanskrit poem of *Kalidasa*. Comp. 1910, rev. 1912. F.p. London 1913.

Club Anthem. Setting of *I will always give thanks*, for 3 or 4 vv., str., and org., comp. 1664 jointly by John Blow, Pelham Humfrey, and William Turner 'as a memorial of their fraternal esteem and friendship'.

cluster. Term used in connection with chords, meaning chords of which the constituents are a major or minor 2nd apart. In US, called 'tone-cluster'. Kbd. clusters, i.e. a group of adjacent notes played together with the forearm flat, were first demonstrated by the Amer. composer *Cowell in 1913, but *Ives had also used the same idea.

Clutsam, George Howard (*b* Sydney, NSW, 1866; *d* London, 1951). Australian composer, pianist, and critic, settled in London 1889. Accompanist to Melba. Perpetrated with *Berté Eng. version of *Das Dreimäderlhaus* as *Lilac Time* (1923).

Cluytens, André (*b* Antwerp, 1905; *d* Paris, 1967). Fr. conductor of Belgian birth. Cond. Antwerp Opera 1927–32; Lyons from 1935; Paris Opéra from 1941; Opéra Comique 1947; Société des Concerts du Cons. 1949. First Gallic cond. at Bayreuth, 1955–8 and 1965. London début 1958 (with Philharmonia Orch.). Regular cond. at Vienna State Opera after 1959.

Coates, Albert (*b* St Petersburg, 1882; *d* Cape Town, 1953). Eng. conductor and composer, born in Russ. of Eng. parents (not Anglo-Russian, as often stated). Cond. opera at Leipzig, Elberfeld, and Dresden. London début 1910 (LSO), CG 1914 (*Tristan*). Cond. of opera at St Petersburg 1911–18 during which time became close friend of Scriabin. Returned to Eng. 1919, conducting opera with Beecham, BNOC, Leeds Fest., etc. Also cond. much in USA. Settled in S. Africa 1946. Comps. incl. operas *Samuel Pepys* (1929) and *Pickwick* (1936). As a cond. was at his best in Russ. mus. and Wagner, but cond. f.ps. of Vaughan Williams's rev. *London Symphony* (1920), Bax's 1st Symphony (1922), and Holst's *Choral Symphony* (1925).

Coates, Eric (*b* Hucknall, Notts., 1886; *d* Chichester, 1957). Eng. composer and violist. Member of several str. qts. Prin. va., Queen's Hall Orch. 1912. Gave up orch. playing 1919. Comps. in light vein, distinguished by finished craftsmanship, impeccable orchestration, and personal melodic flavour. They incl. several orch. suites—*From the Countryside* (1915); *Summer Days* (1919); *Cinderella* (1929); *From Meadow to Mayfair* (1929); *London* (1932); *London Again* (1936); *The Three Elizabeths* (1944); *The Three Bears* (1926). Also *Saxo-Rhapsody* (1937); *The Jester at the Wedding*; *By the Sleepy Lagoon* (1939); *Calling All Workers* (1940); *The Dam Busters March* (1942); and many songs incl. 'Bird Songs at Eventide' (1926). The *London Suite's* 3rd movement is the march 'Knightsbridge', long famous as introductory music to BBC radio feature 'In Town Tonight'. *By the Sleepy Lagoon* is the signature-tune of the BBC's 'Desert Island Discs'.

Coates, John (*b* Girlington, Yorks., 1865; *d* Northwood, 1941). Eng. tenor, originally baritone. Sang bar. roles with D'Oyly Carte Opera Co. 1894. Début as ten. 1899. Sang Faust in Gounod's opera CG 1901. Cologne Opera 1902–7. Member of Moody-Manners and Beecham opera cos., singing Tristan and Siegfried. Also achieved eminence in choral works, notably Elgar's *Dream of Gerontius*.

Cobbett, Walter Willson (*b* Blackheath, 1847; *d* London, 1937). Eng. businessman and amateur violinist whose love of chamber mus. led him to promote many chamber concerts and to institute prizes both for playing and comp. Commissioned many works by Brit. composers in the Elizabethan fantasia-form, preferring the spelling 'Phantasy', hence the 'Phantasy' qts., quintets, and trios by Bridge, Vaughan Williams, Bax, Goossens, Ireland, Britten, etc. Endowed Cobbett Medal for services to chamber mus. and ed. *Cyclopedic Survey of Chamber Music* (1929, rev. 1963). CBE 1933.

Cocardes (Cockades). 3 songs for v. and pf. by Poulenc to texts by Cocteau. Comp. 1919. Titles are: *Miel de Narbonne, Bonne d'enfant, Enfant de troupe.*

Coccia, Carlo (*b* Naples, 1782; *d* Novara, 1873). It. composer. First opera, *Il matrimonio per lettera di cambio*, failed in Rome, 1807, but he wrote 21 more between 1809 and 1817, mostly for Venice, the most successful being *Clotilde* (1815). Eclipsed in It. by Rossini, went to Lisbon 1820 and to London 1824, where he taught singing at RAM. Comp. *Maria Stuarda* for Pasta, 1827. Returned to It. 1828, but only his *Caterina di Guisa* (Milan, 1833) had any success. Wrote his 37th and last opera in 1841. Dir. of singing sch. at Turin 1836; choirmaster at Novara 1840, remaining there composing sacred mus. until his death. Contributed *Lacrymosa* for unacc. ch. to *Requiem* organized by Verdi as memorial to Rossini.

Cockaigne (In London Town). Concert-ov., Op.40, by Elgar, comp. 1900–1 and ded. to 'my many friends the members of British orchestras'. Title refers to imaginary land of idleness and luxury from which word 'Cockney' is said to be derived.

Cocteau, Jean (*b* Maisons-Laffitte, 1889; *d* Milly-la-forêt, 1963). Fr. poet, novelist, and playwright, often assoc. with mus. as librettist or propagandist. Wrote scenario for Satie's *Parade* (1917) and libs. for Honegger's *Antigone*, Stravinsky's *Oedipus Rex*, Milhaud's *Le Pauvre Matelot*, and Poulenc's *La Voix humaine*, among others.

coda (It.). Tail. Orig. a section of a movt. added at the end to clinch matters rather than to develop the mus. further. However, in the syms. of Mozart, Haydn, and especially Beethoven, the coda came to have integral formal significance, becoming at times 2nd development section and sometimes containing new material. Later composers have increased and extended this tendency.

codetta (It.). Little tail. (1) Short or less important coda, often at the end of a section of a movt.

(2) In a fugue, an episodical passage occurring in the exposition between appearances of the subject.

Coertse, Mimi (Maria Sophia) (*b* Durban, 1932). S. African soprano. Début Naples 1955 with Vienna State Opera as Flower Maiden in *Parsifal*. Vienna début 1956. Vienna Opera 1957–73. Salzburg Fest. début 1956; Glyndebourne 1957. Sang Aminta in *Die schweigsame Frau* at its f. Vienna p. 1968. Returned to S. Africa 1973 and sang Countess in *Le nozze di Figaro* in Pretoria 1989.

Coffee Cantata (*Kaffeecantate*). Nickname for humorous cantata by Bach (BWV211, 1732) sometimes perf. as opera. Lib., by Picander, refers to the growing fondness for coffee at the time it was comp.

cogli, coi (It.). See *col*.

Cohen, Harriet (*b* London, 1895; *d* London, 1967). Eng. pianist. Won reputation as advocate of early kbd. mus. and of modern Eng. composers. Bax ded. to her his *Symphonic Variations* for pf. and orch. (1917) and his *Concertante* for orch. and pf. (left hand) (f.p. 1950), the latter written for her when she had injured her right hand. The pf. concs. by Vaughan Williams (f.p. 1933) and Fricker (1952–4) were ded. to and f.p. by her. Also considerable chamber-mus. player. CBE 1938.

Cohen, Robert (*b* London, 1959). Eng. cellist, son of Raymond Cohen. Solo début, London 1971, in Boccherini conc. Recorded Elgar conc. 1978. Won Piatigorsky comp., Tanglewood, and made Amer. début 1979. Plays in trio with father Raymond (vn.) and his mother Anthya Rael (pf.).

col, coll', colla, colle, cogli, coi (It.). With the, e.g. *col basso*, with the bass; **colla voce*, with the voice.

Colas Breugnon. Name under which **Kabalev*sky's opera *The Craftsman of Clamecy* (*Master iz Clamesy*) Op.24, is usually known outside Russ. In 3 acts, to lib. by V. Bragin based on R. Rolland's novel *Colas Breugnon*. Prod. Leningrad 1938. Rev. 1953 and in 1969, final rev. being given Op.No.90.

colascione. European version of Eastern long-necked lute, first made in It. in early 16th cent. Had 2 or 3 single or double courses made of metal, though sometimes of gut, and 24 movable frets.

Colbran, Isabella (Angela) (*b* Madrid, 1785; *d* Castenaso, Bologna, 1845). Sp. soprano. Considered to be finest dramatic coloratura of her day. Débuts Paris 1801; Bologna 1807; Milan 1808. Engaged for Naples, 1811, where she became impresario's mistress but left him in 1815 to live with **Rossini*, who married her in 1822 (they separated in 1837). Rossini wrote *Elisabetta, Regina d'Inghilterra* for her and she created the leading sop. roles in his *Otello, Semiramide, Mosè, Armida, La donna del lago*, and other operas. Also comp. songs.

Cole, Hugo (*b* London, 1917; *d* London, 1995). Eng. composer and writer. Played in London orchs. as cellist. Works incl. 7 operas (4 for children), opera-cantata *Jonah*, hn. conc., str. qts. Contributed mus. criticism to *The Guardian, Country Life* and others. Author of several books incl. study and catalogue of Malcolm Arnold.

Cole, Nat King [Coles, Nathaniel Adams] (*b* Montgomery, Alabama, 1917; *d* Santa Monica, Calif., 1965). Amer. singer and jazz pianist. Had his own band in Chicago. Formed King Cole Trio 1939–51. After a best-selling record of 1947 he concentrated on singing (to the detriment of his jazz reputation). Among his most popular recordings were 'Nature Boy' and 'Answer me'. Played part of W. C. Handy in film *St Louis Blues* (1958).

Coleman, Ornette (*b* Fort Worth, Texas, 1930). Amer. jazz composer and saxophonist. Began to play alto sax. in 1944, tenor sax. in 1946. Influenced by Charlie *Parker. Played in bebop, blues, and rhythm bands in Southern States before settling in New Orleans in 1948. In 1950 joined Pee Wee Crayton band in Fort Worth. In Los Angeles studied harmony and theory and by 1958 was regarded as one of jazz's major innovators. Attended Lenox Sch. of Jazz, Mass., 1959, and led quartet in NY 1958–62, then forming trio. Caused controversy 1960 with his recording *Free Jazz* (Coleman and 7 other musicians) in which improvisation was taken almost to anarchic limits. Semi-retired 1963 to learn tpt. and vn. Reappeared in 1965 and then toured Europe. Style noted for free improvisation based on melodic shapes over a pedal-point rather than on succession of chords. Relied greatly on intuition and at times approached atonality. Gunther Schuller wrote *Abstraction*, a serial comp., for Coleman and augmented str. qt. Coleman's own mus. includes *Lonely Woman* and *Turnaround*. His major piece of symphonic mus. is *Skies of America* (1972) for jazz qt. and orch. (recorded with LSO with solo alto sax. only). This was followed in 1977 by *Dancing in Your Head* and in 1979 by *Of Human Feelings* which explored 'funk-jazz', a development dating from about 1970 features of which incl. a repetitive bass line, a hint of Latin rhythms, and complex rhythmic relationships.

Coleridge-Taylor, Samuel (*b* London, 1875; *d* Croydon, 1912). Eng. composer, son of Sierra Leone physician and Eng. mother. His cl. quintet, Op.10, was played in 1897 in Berlin by Joachim's qt. and his *Ballad* in A minor at 1898 Gloucester Fest. (thanks to Elgar's encouragement). In Nov. 1898 his cantata *Hiawatha's Wedding Feast* was perf. at RCM. This was first of 3 works based on Longfellow's poem. The *Death of Minnehaha* followed in 1899 and *Hiawatha's Departure* in 1900. Success of these works led to many demands for fest. comps. Later works were *Meg Blane* (Sheffield 1902), *The Atonement* (Hereford 1903), *Kubla Khan*

(London 1906), and *A Tale of Old Japan* (London 1911), but none achieved the success of *The Song of Hiawatha* trilogy. Also wrote sym., *Symphonic Variations on an African Air* (1906), vn. conc. (1912), chamber mus., pf. solos, and songs.

Colgrass, Michael (Charles) (*b* Chicago, 1932). Amer. composer and percussionist. Worked in NY as free-lance percussionist 1956–7, being specially concerned with th. work. Won Pulitzer 1978 with *Déjà vu*, for 4 percussionists and orch. Works incl. *Percussion Music* (1953); *Chant*, ch., vib. (1954); *Seventeen*, full orch. (1960); wind quintet (1962); *Virgil's Dream*, 4 actor-singers, 4 mime-musicians (Brighton Fest. 1967); *The Earth's a Baked Apple*, ch., orch. (Boston 1969); *Nightingale Inc.*, opera (1971); *Auras*, hp., orch. (1976–7); *Theatre of the Universe*, solo vv., ch., orch. (1976–7); *Something's gonna happen*, children's musical (1978); *Flashbacks*, 5 brass (1979); *Winds of Nagual*, wind ens. (1985); *The Schubert Birds*, orch. (1989); *Snow Walker*, org., orch. (1990); *Arctic Dreams*, sym. band (1991); *Te Tuma Te Papa*, perc. (1994); *Hammer and Bow*, vn., mar. (1997); *Dream Dancer*, solo sax., wind ens., cel., hp., perc. (2001); *Ghosts of Pangea*, orch. (2002); *Crossworlds*, fl., pf., orch. (2002); *Apache with a Dream*, school band (2003).

coll', colla, colle (It.). See *col*.

collage (Fr.). A putting-together of independent styles in juxtaposition either simultaneously or successively. The separate styles usually consist of contrasting rhythm, melody, or harmony. For a true collage the juxtaposition must be of coherent sections which are the product of separate mus. elements, e.g. the many examples in the mus. of Charles *Ives, where dissonances are not resolved but treated as a normal situation. The term is borrowed from the visual arts, and literally means 'glueing together'.

colla parte (It.). With the part.

colla punta dell' arco (It.). With the point of the bow.

coll'arco (It.). With the bow; i.e. after a passage marked *pizzicato*. (Sometimes shortened to *c.a.*).

Collard, Jean-Philippe (*b* Mareuil-sur-Ay, 1948). Fr. pianist. In 1964 began worldwide career as soloist. Specialist in Fr. mus. and also fine player of Rachmaninov.

colla voce (It.), with the voice. An indication to an accompanist carefully to take his tempos and rhythm from the soloist.

Collegium Aureum. Ger. ensemble founded 1964 by Franzjosef Maier to record baroque and early classical mus. Has toured Russia and Japan. Pioneered recordings using original and authentic instrs., incl. one of Beethoven's *Eroica* Symphony.

Collegium Musicum (Lat. 'musical guild'). In 16th cent. term applied to groups of enthusiasts concerned with perf. of mus. From these grew concert-giving societies performing under noble patronage or in the informal surroundings of a coffee-house. J. S. Bach wrote many works for perf. at a collegium musicum.

col legno (It.). With the wood. Striking the str. with the stick of the bow, instead of playing on them with the hair.

Colles, Henry Cope (*b* Bridgnorth, 1879; *d* London, 1943). Eng. music critic. Mus. critic for *The Times* 1905–43 (chief critic from 1911), ed. of 3rd and 4th edns. of *Grove's Dictionary of Music*, and author of several books incl. history of RCM (1933) of which he was member of staff, and biog. of Walford Davies (1942). His *The Growth of Music* (1912–16) was reprinted in 1978.

Collier, Marie (*b* Ballarat, 1927; *d* London, 1971). Australian soprano. Début Melbourne 1954 (Santuzza in *Cavalleria rusticana*); CG début 1956. Possessed dramatic acting powers and richly expressive v. Was notable exponent of Emilia Marty in *The Makropoulos Affair*. Created Hecuba in *King Priam* (1962). Sang Katerina Ismailova in first Brit. staging of Shostakovich's revised opera (London, CG, 1963), making S. Francisco début in same role, 1964, and Renata in first Brit. staging of *The Fiery Angel* (London (SW) 1965). NY Met début 1967.

Collingwood, Lawrance (Arthur) (*b* London, 1887; *d* Killin, Perthshire, 1982). Eng. conductor and composer. After army service, returned to St Petersburg, where he had studied, as ass. to Albert *Coates. Cond. opera in London at Old Vic, 1920–31, and SW from 1931 (mus. dir. latter 1941–7). Comps. incl. opera *Macbeth* (SW 1934) and *Death of Tintagiles* (after Maeterlinck, concert version SW 1950), also pf. conc., pf. qt., pf. sonatas. For nearly 50 years made gramophone recordings, 'producing' many of them. Cond. Elgar's last recording session, 1934. CBE 1948.

Collins, Anthony (*b* Hastings, 1893; *d* Los Angeles, 1963). Eng. viola player and then conductor and composer. Prin. va. LSO and CG orch. Left orch. playing 1936 to become cond. Founded London Mozart Orch. Worked in USA 1936–45. Highly regarded as Sibelius interpreter. Comp. operas, 2 vn. concs., syms. for str., film mus. Orch. Schubert's *Grand Duo*.

Collins, Michael (*b* London, 1962). Eng. clarinettist. Finalist in BBC TV Young Musician of the Year 1978. Played Musgrave's conc. at Proms, 1984. NY début 1984. Prof. of cl., RCM from 1985. Prin. cl., Philharmonia Orch. from 1988.

colofonia (It.). See *colophony*.

Colonel Bogey. Military march comp. by 'Kenneth *Alford' in 1914. Popularity attributable not only to splendid tune, but to improvised words and to its use (whistled) in the film *The Bridge on the River Kwai* (1957).

Colonne, Édouard (Judas) (*b* Bordeaux, 1838; *d* Paris, 1910). Fr. conductor and violinist. Leader of Paris Opéra Orch. 1858–67 and 2nd vn. in Lamoureux Qt. In 1873 founded series of orch. concerts, eventually to be known as the Concerts Colonne, at which he championed young Fr. composers and the mus. of Berlioz. Toured as cond. in Eng., Russ., and USA. Concerts continued after his death organized by the Société des Concerts Colonne.

colophony (Fr. *colophane*; It. *colofonia*; Ger. *Kolophon*). Rosin for bow of str. instr., so called after Colophon, Asia Minor, whence best rosin comes.

colorato, colorata, or **figurato, figurata** (It.). Treated in the manner of *coloratura*. See also *musica figurata*.

coloratura. Word derived from the Ger. *Koloratur*. The elaborate and agile ornamentation of a melody, either extemporized or written, with runs, cadenzas, trills, roulades, and the like. Hence a *coloratura soprano* is one whose v. is flexible enough to cope with these demands.

colour (tone-colour). It is impossible for mus. to convey colours, but it is customary to speak of 'colouring' or 'tone-colour' where variations of *timbre* or tone are prod. by different intensities of the overtones of sounds. 'Shade' is perhaps a more accurate term, since the differences are often those of 'darker' or 'lighter' sound. But in his tone-poem *Prometheus: The Poem of Fire*, Op.60, *Scriabin introduced a colour kbd. to project colours on to a screen, intended to convey the mood of the mus. The colour-organ was used for this purpose.

Colour Symphony. Orch. work by Bliss, f.p. Gloucester Fest. 1922. The movts. are entitled *Purple*, *Red*, *Blue*, and *Green*, the colours being interpreted through their heraldic assocs.

colpo (It.). Stroke, e.g. *colpo d'arco*, a stroke of the bow.

Columbia, the Gem of the Ocean. Amer. anthem written and comp. 1843 by Thomas à Becket (1808–90), Eng.-born actor and musician, for concert at museum in Philadelphia. Commissioned by singer, David T. Shaw, who falsely claimed authorship when pubd. it. Quoted by Ives in 18 works, incl. 2nd and 4th syms. Brit. vers., *Britannia, the Pride of the Ocean*, pubd. 1852. Sometimes known as *The Red, White, and Blue*.

Combattimento di Tancredi e Clorinda, Il (The combat of Tancred and Clorinda). Dramatic madrigal by Monteverdi to text by Tasso (verses 52–68 of Canto XII of *Gerusalemme liberata*). Prod. Venice (Palazza di Girolamo Mocenigo) 1624. Pub. 1638 in *Madrigali guerrieri e amorosi*. Monteverdi's description of f.p. shows that this could be claimed as early example of 'music theatre'. A narrator comments upon the action, which is acted or danced by Tancred and Clorinda. A feature of the score is the earliest-known use of the str. *tremolo*, or *stile concitato*, to express excitement, and the str. *pizzicato* (but see *pizzicato*). Scoring is for 4 viols with contrabass and hpd.

combination pedals. See *composition pedals*.

combined counterpoint. See *counterpoint*.

come (It.). As, like, as if; *come prima*, as at first; *come stà*, as it stands; *come sopra*, as above.

comédie-ballet. Fr. musico-dramatic entertainment devised by Molière and Lully in late 17th cent. Their first collab. was in *Le mariage forcé* (1664), their last *Le bourgeois gentilhomme* (1670). Mus. and dance were regarded as complementary to the main plot; the sub-plots were carried on in the *intermèdes*.

Comedy on the Bridge (*Komedie na mostě*). Opera for radio in 1 act by Martinů to his own lib. based on V. K. Klicpera. Comp. 1935, rev. 1950. Prod. Prague Radio 1937, London (stage) 1965.

comes. See *canon*.

Come ye Sons of Art. Ode by *Purcell for the birthday of Queen Mary II, wife of William III, in 1694 for sop., counterten., bass, ch., and orch. Contains aria 'Sound the trumpet'.

comic opera. An imprecise term, though by it most people today would understand an opera with a comic element. *opéra-bouffe* or *opera buffa* means comic opera but has a specific meaning, as has *opéra-comique*.

Comissiona, Sergiu (*b* Bucharest, 1928; *d* Oklahoma City, 2005). Romanian-born conductor (Amer. cit. 1976). Violinist in str. qt. and orch. 1946–8. Cond. Romanian State Ens. 1948–55. Cond. Romanian State Opera 1955–9; Haifa SO and Israeli Chamber Orch. 1960–6; Göteborg SO 1966–77; Ulster Orch. 1967–9; Baltimore SO 1969–84; American SO 1977–82; Houston SO 1984–8. Mus. dir. NY City Opera 1987–8. Cond., Helsinki PO 1990–4. London début (LSO) 1960, CG début (ballet) 1962, CG opera début 1974 (*Il barbiere di Siviglia*), NY 1977 (*La fanciulla del West*).

comma. A minute interval such as that resulting when a rising succession of untempered 5ths (see *temperament*) and a similar succession of octaves arrive at what is ostensibly the same note, but is not really quite such.

commedia per musica (It.). Comedy through Music. Term used in It. in 18th cent. for comic opera. Note that Strauss and Hofmannsthal called their 18th-cent. comedy of manners, *Der Rosenkavalier*, a 'comedy for music'.

common chord. A *triad of which the 5th is perfect. In *major common chord* the 3rd is major and in *minor common chord* it is minor.

common time. Another name for 4/4 time. The C sometimes used instead of the figures 4/4 does not stand for 'common': it dates from the period when triple time (called 'perfect') was indicated by a full circle and quadruple time (called 'imperfect') by a broken circle.

community singing. Any occasion when a number of people sing together is 'community singing', but the term today usually means a crowd's singing at a meeting or at a sporting occasion (notably the F.A. Cup Final at Wembley or a rugger int. at Cardiff Arms Park).

comodo (It.). Leisurely, convenient, i.e. without any suspicion of strain, e.g. *tempo comodo*, at a comfortable, moderate speed. So the adverb, *comodamente*.

compact discs. See *gramophone (phonograph) recordings*.

compass. The range of a v. or instr. from the highest to the lowest note obtainable; or the extreme limit of the notes obtainable. The usual classification of vv. according to compass takes account of 6 ranges, with their distinctive qualities, the average vv. in these ranges having the following compasses:

soprano	c'–c'''
mezzo-soprano	b–b''
contralto	g–g'' (male alto a note or two less)
tenor	c–c''
baritone	A–F♯
bass	E–e'/f'

competitions, musical. The urge to compete is basic to human nature and musicians are no exception. Reports of mus. contests go back to ancient times but the modern form developed in the late 18th cent. in Great Britain. Brass band contests began early in the 19th cent. but even more widespread were the choral competitions and those between individual instrumentalists. From 1904 these have been organized by what is now the Brit. Federation of Mus. Fest., apart from the Welsh *eisteddfodau*. Similar competitions, mainly involving amateurs, are firmly est. in many other countries. Other forms of mus. competition on a high professional (and commercial) level have developed, incl. competitions for composers, conds., and for instrumentalists (notably the Moscow Tchaikovsky pf. competition, the Leeds pf. competition, the Carl Flesch award for violinists, the Mitropoulos prize for conds., the Queen Elisabeth of Belgium competition, the BBC's 'Young Musician of the Year', and numerous others). Undoubtedly the most famous mus. competitions are those involving Tannhäuser and Wolfram in the Hall of Song at the Wartburg Castle in Wagner's *Tannhäuser* (Act II) and the song contest on the banks of the River Pegnitz at Nuremberg in Act III Sc.2 of Wagner's *Die Meistersinger von Nürnberg*—both events being based on reality. In lighter vein there is the annual Eurovision song contest, promoted by European TV organizations, to discover the best 'pop song' of the year according to the votes of an int. jury.

complete cadence. See *cadence*.

composer's counterpoint. See *counterpoint*.

Composers' Guild of Great Britain. Brit. organization founded 1944 and affiliated to Soc. of

Authors. Exists to protect the interests of composers. First pres. Vaughan Williams. Publishes journal *Composer* since 1958. In 1967 founded British Music Information Centre.

composition pedals (combination pedals). Organ pedals to facilitate rapid changing of tone-colour effects by means of adjustment pistons which bring instantly into action selected groups of stops instead of their having to be operated individually by hand.

compound binary form. Same as **sonata form*.

compound intervals. Those greater than an octave, e.g. C to the D a 9th above it, which may be spoken of as a major 9th or as a compound major 2nd. See *interval*.

compound time. Each beat in a measure consists of a dotted note or its equivalent (in contrast to simple time where each beat consists of a complete note). Can be duple, triple, or quadruple, each related to corresponding simple time. Thus 3/4 (simple triple) has 3 quarter-note (crotchet) beats to a measure; 9/8 (compound triple) has 3 dotted quarter-note (crotchet) beats. So called because a measure is made up of a mixture (or *compound*) of 2, 3, or 4 main beats, each beat having 3 subdivisions. See also *simple time* and *time signature*.

comprimario, comprimaria (It. 'sub-principal'). Secondary or supporting role in opera, term being extended today to cover any singing role with the slightest importance in the plot.

compter (Fr.). To count. *comptent*, count (plural), indicates in an orch. score that the instr. in question are silent for the moment and are merely 'counting their bars' until re-entry.

computers in music. Elec. computers have so far been used in two ways by composers: (a) to aid pre-compositional calculations and (b) to produce elec. sound. They have also been used to analyse works, to study comp. styles, and to prod. systems of notation. Among the first composers to use a computer was the Amer. Lejaren **Hiller*, who used the Illiac computer to 'compose' a piece of mus. by feeding into it a program comprising Fux's rules for 16th-cent. modal counterpoint and others relating to 20th-cent. serialism. The result was the *Illiac Suite for String Quartet* (1957). Excluded from the program were all notes that broke the rules, so the computer chose at random from the remaining possibilities. In later Hiller works, such as *Computer Cantata* (1963), notes and intervals were not chosen at random but according to weighted probabilities, e.g. a note was chosen according to the implications of the previously chosen note. Another composer, **Xenakis*, used the computer for sound effects rather than for comp. processes. In his *Metastaseis* for orch. (1953–4) the computer calculates glissandi at different speeds.

A computer works musically by producing 'waveforms'. Developments involving the 'digital analogue converter' meant that waveforms could be created which perfectly simulate instr. sounds. The present tendency is to use computers in assoc. with **synthesizers* as a memory bank, capable of producing any required sounds, memorizing the composer's sequence of events, and playing the finished work whenever required. This information is fed to the computer by a teletype kbd. or special manual controller, as in certain works by Stockhausen and Boulez.

Comte Ory, Le (Count Ory). *Opera buffa* in 2 acts by Rossini to lib. by Scribe and Delestre-Poirson. Prod. Paris 1828, London 1829, New Orleans 1830. One of Rossini's 2 Fr. operas. It uses much mus. comp. in 1825 for *Il viaggio a Reims*. Revived Florence 1952, Edinburgh 1954 (Glyndebourne co.), Glyndebourne 1955.

Comus. Masque by John Milton prod. at Ludlow Castle 1634 with mus. by Henry **Lawes*, who himself took the part of the Attendant Spirit. New mus. was provided for an adapted version of the poem by Thomas **Arne* in 1738. In 1942, for a ballet in which some of Milton's verse was spoken, Lambert arr. mus. by Purcell. Another ballet, with mus. by Handel and Lawes arr. E. Irving, was prod. 1946. Hugh **Wood's* *Scenes from Comus* for sop., ten., and orch. was comp. and f.p. London 1965.

concentus. See *accentus*.

concert. A perf. of mus. in public by a fairly substantial no. of performers (but not a stage performance or as part of a religious service). A perf. by 1 or 2 performers is usually called a recital. A pre-requisite of concerts, except on certain special occasions, is that people should pay to attend them, and this seems to have begun in England in the middle of the 17th cent. Historians point to the Whitefriars concerts given by John Banister in 1672 as the 'first' in Eng., but perhaps that is only because we have a printed record of them. Thomas **Britton* also financed concerts in Clerkenwell 1678–1714. More important were the Bach–Abel concerts which began in Spring Gardens, London, in 1764. With the opening of the Hanover Square Rooms in 1775 the way was open for such major events as Haydn's concerts on his 2 visits to London. Thereafter concerts became an accepted way of life. The Phil. Soc. was founded 1813, and in several provincial cities concert socs. were formed. Other developments incl. the Promenade Concerts, so called because people could stand or walk about at them, which originated in the 18th-cent. pleasure gardens, but found their most abiding form in 1895 when Henry Wood began his famous series at Queen's Hall and which, under BBC sponsorship, are still held from mid-July to mid-Sept. in the Royal Albert Hall, London.

Public concerts for an audience of subscribers began in Frankfurt, Ger., in 1712 and in Hamburg in 1721. What were to become the Leipzig Gewandhaus concerts were founded by 16 businessmen meeting in an inn in 1743 (much as Manchester's concerts began in the 1770s when a group of flautists met regularly in a tavern, hence the 'Gentlemen's Concerts'). The *Concert Spirituel* was founded in Paris, 1725, but 'progressive' works were given at the *Concert des Amateurs*, cond. *Gossec, which in 1780 became the *Concert de la Loge Olympique* (because the venue was also a Masonic Lodge). In 1786 this organization commissioned 6 syms.—the 'Paris' syms.— from Haydn. In Vienna there was so much mus. in private houses or in the ths. that no regular concerts were given until 1782 (in the open air: Mozart played at them).

concertant(e) (Fr.). In concerted form; a term preferred to sonata or suite by Stravinsky to describe the nature of his *Duo Concertant* for vn. and pf. (1932).

concertante (It.). (1) In the nature of a conc., thus a *Sinfonia Concertante* is a work for solo instr(s). and orch. in a form nearer to that of sym. than conc.

(2) The concertante instr. in the old *concerto grosso* were those which played the solos, as distinct from the *ripieno* instr., which played in the *tuttis*. Many 20th-cent. composers have used the term to indicate that while a solo instr(s). is/are used, the work is not formally organized like a conc.

concertata, aria. See *aria*.

concertato (It.). Concerted. Another name for the *concertino* or *concertante* group in baroque mus. which contained the solo instrs. or vv. to contrast with the *ripieno*.

concert band. An Amer. band, comprising woodwind, brass, and perc., similar to the Brit. military band. Schoenberg's *Theme and Variations* Op.43a (1943) is for concert band, so is Hindemith's Sym. in B♭ (1951).

concerted. A perf. of mus. by 2 or more instrumentalists on reasonably equal terms. In opera an ens. is sometimes called a 'concerted number'.

concert flute. (1) Org. stop, sometimes on principle of *harmonic flute*: usually on solo manual; generally 4′ pitch.

(2) See *flute*.

Concertgebouw Orchestra of Amsterdam. See *Royal Concertgebouw Orchestra of Amsterdam*.

concertina. Small instr. with bellows similar to *accordion but with hexagonal ends and studs (no kbd.). The bellows are opened and closed by the hands, the pressure created causing metallic reeds to vibrate when selected by operation of the studs by the player's fingers. Made in SATB sizes, each with range of approx. an octave. Said to have been invented by Charles Wheatstone (1802–75) in 1825 and patented as 'symphonium' in 1829. First to play it at a public concert was Giulio Regondi (1822–72), who lived in Eng. from 1831 and toured Europe as concertina

player 1846. He wrote 2 concs. and shorter pieces for it. Ives and Grainger have included it in their scores.

concertino. (1) (in older usage) The solo instr. group in the concerto grosso (see also *concertante*; *concerto*).

(2) (in more modern usage) A shorter and lighter conc. for solo instr. and orch., e.g. Weber's cl. concertino, Op.26.

Concertino Pastorale. Work for str. orch. in 3 movts. by John Ireland, comp. 1939 for Boyd Neel Orch. Movts. entitled *Eclogue*, *Threnody*, and *Toccata*.

concertmaster (Amer.; Ger. *Konzertmeister*). The *leader of an orch.

concerto (It.). Concert, concerted performance. A work in which a solo instr(s). is contrasted and blended with the orch. Earliest publication using name 'concerto' is *Concerti di Andrea et di Gio. Gabrieli* (Venice, 1587). Viadana's *Cento Concerti ecclesiastici*, comp. in the 1590s, developed into church concs. (*concerti da chiesa*) and there were also in the 17th cent. vocal *concerti da camera* (chamber concs.) which were adapted as purely instr. works by *Torelli. Monteverdi's Book 7 of madrigals is called *Concerto*. From Torelli came the *concerto grosso* as comp. by *Corelli and *Handel. But the conc. for an individual player as opposed to a *concertino* group was developed by J. S. Bach in his hpd. concs., but note that his *Italian Concerto* is written for a single performer (though the effect of contrast is supplied by the effective use of the 2 manuals). Handel's organ concs. were also an important development, he being among the first to provide a *cadenza in which the soloist could display his skill by extemporization. Mozart est. the style of the modern instr. conc., composing nearly 50 for various instr. combinations. Concs. are usually in 3 movts., but there are many exceptions. A significant change since the 19th cent. has been for the composer to write out the cadenzas and sometimes (e.g. Elgar's vn. conc.) to acc. them with the orch. Thus the conc. has grown according to the increasing virtuosity of soloists. See also *concerto for orchestra*.

Concert of Ancient Music, also known as 'Ancient Concert', or 'King's Concert'. London series under royal and aristocratic management, 1776–1849, with attempts at revival in 1867 and 1870. No mus. less than 20 years old in programmes. (Not to be confused with Academy of Ancient Music.)

concerto for orchestra. A comp. like a conc. but not for one particular soloist, though individual members or sections of the orch. may have important solo (concertante) roles. The form is a 20th-cent. development. Famous examples are by Bartók, Tippett, Kodály, Gerhard, Lutosławski, Petrassi, and others.

concerto grosso (It.). Great concerto. Early form of *concerto at its zenith in the 17th and 18th cents., though the term has been used by 20th-cent. composers, e.g. Bloch and Vaughan Williams, for works based on earlier models. The works were antiphonal, i.e. a small body of str. (*concertino, concertato*, or *concertante*) was heard in alternation, contrast and combination with a larger group (*ripieno*). These were in several movts., roughly similar to the 18th-cent. ov. or suite. The most celebrated early concerti grossi are those by *Corelli (1712) (*Concerti grossi con duoi violini e violoncello di concertino obbligati*) and those by Handel (1739). J. S. Bach's *Brandenburg Concertos* Nos. 2, 4, 5, and 6 are traditional concerti grossi.

concert overture. An independent one-movement orch. work to open a concert, but not the ov. to an opera. Many concert ovs. are in sonata-form, others are practically symphonic-poems, e.g. one of the first of the genre, Mendelssohn's *The Hebrides*, and among later examples, Elgar's *Cockaigne* and *In the South*.

concert pitch. (1) The *pitch internationally agreed in 1960 by which the note a' has 440 vibrations per second, but see *A*.
(2) One speaks of someone being at 'concert pitch', meaning keyed-up and alert, on top form.

Concert Spirituel (Fr. 'Sacred concert'). Series of concerts founded in Paris in 1725 by A. D. Philidor, the oboist, to perform sacred works and instrumental mus. Later, secular works with Fr. texts were permitted. Twenty-four concerts a year were given during periods, e.g. Lent, when other perfs. were forbidden. Ended in 1790.

Concertstück. See *Konzertstück*.

Concierto de Aranjuez (Aranjuez Concerto). Conc. for guitar and orch. by Rodrigo, comp. 1939, f.p. Barcelona 1940. Arr. for harp and orch. by composer.

concord (consonance). Chord which seems satisfactory in itself, or an interval that can be so described, or a note which is part of such a chord or interval. The opposite is *discord (dissonance). What constitutes a concord is not strictly laid down and must often depend on individual assessment. However, concordant intervals comprise all perfect intervals and all major and minor 3rds and 6ths.

concordant intervals. See *interval*.

Concord Sonata. Work for pf., with solos for va. and fl., by *Ives, full title *Sonata No.2 (Concord Mass., 1840–1860)*. Comp. 1911–15. F.p. New Orleans 1920. Movts. are entitled 1. *Emerson*, 2. *Hawthorne*, 3. *The Alcotts*, 4. *Thoreau*, in honour of the Concord group of writers whom Ives admired. Early example of use of *clusters.

concrete music. See *musique concrète*.

conducting. The art (or method) of controlling an orch. or operatic perf. by means of gestures, this control involving the beating of time, ensuring of correct entries, and the 'shaping' of individual phrasing. (For a discussion of the history of the use of the baton see under that entry.) The advance of the cond. as one of the most important and idolized of musicians dates from early in the 19th cent. and is parallel with (and perhaps a consequence of) the development of the expressive, Romantic elements in mus. François *Habeneck, conductor at Paris Opéra 1824–47, also founded in 1828 the Société des Concerts du Conservatoire at which he introduced Beethoven's syms. to Paris and cond. Berlioz's works, but he never used a full score, conducting from a copy of the first vn. part (and presumably from a memory of the full score). Berlioz himself was one of the first to conduct from a full score, and Spohr, one of the best of the early 'modern' conds., probably used a pf. reduction since he is credited with the invention of 'cue' letters and nos. in scores as aids to rehearsal. Mendelssohn was an excellent cond., not only of his own mus. Perhaps the first virtuoso cond. as the term is now understood was Wagner. From him stems the great tradition of 'interpretation', whereby a cond. is not merely responsible for the technical excellence of the perf. but also for projecting his personal attitude to the composer's intentions. He was followed by *Bülow, Anton Seidl, Hermann Levi, Hans Richter, Franz Wüllner, Felix Mottl, and others. After Wagner came a trio of composer-conds., Mahler, R. Strauss, and Weingartner, who dominated European mus. until the coming of Furtwängler, Walter, Klemperer, Kleiber, Krauss, and many besides, the most illustrious being Toscanini. The first English conds. to win wide acceptance were Frederic Cowen, Henry Wood, and Thomas Beecham. With the development of recording, conducting ceased to be an ephemeral calling—the interpretations were preserved and can be studied and compared. There is no explanation, beyond the obvious one of psychological personality, for the way in which a cond. can, often with a minimum of rehearsal, impose his own style on an orch. he may not have encountered before, often completely changing the quality of sound or tone-colour even when the orch. is used to regular perf. under another permanent cond. Nor is there an explanation why some (not all) conds. differ vastly in their artistic approach to the recording-studio and the public hall.

There are many examples of long assoc. between a cond. and an orch., e.g. Amsterdam Concertgebouw (Mengelberg and Haitink), Suisse Romande (Ansermet), Boston SO (Koussevitzky and Ozawa), Philadelphia (Ormandy), Chicago (Stock and Solti), Hallé (Barbirolli), Cleveland (Szell), NBC (Toscanini), Berlin Phil. (Furtwängler and Karajan).

conductus. Metrical Latin song, sacred or secular, originating in France in 12th cent. Superseded in 13th cent. by motet. Usually for 2 or 3 vv.

Confessions of a Justified Sinner. Opera in 3 acts by Thomas *Wilson to lib. by John Currie, after novel by James Hogg (1824). Comp. 1974. Prod. York (Scot. Opera) 1976, cond. Norman Del Mar.

conjunct motion. See *motion*.

Conlon, James (*b* NY, 1950). Amer. conductor. Cond. *Boris Godunov* at Spoleto Fest., Italy, 1971 while a student. Cond. f.p. of rev. version of Barber's *Antony and Cleopatra* at Juilliard, 1975. Début NY Met 1976; Brit. début 1976; CG 1979. Cond. Rotterdam PO 1983–91; chief cond., Cologne Opera from 1989; mus. dir. Opéra de la Bastille from 1996.

Connell, Elizabeth (*b* Port Elizabeth, 1946). Irish soprano of S. African birth. Won Maggie Teyte prize 1972. Début (as mez.) Wexford Fest. 1972 (Varvara in *Kátá Kabanová*). Australian Opera 1973–5; ENO 1975–80; CG début 1976; Bayreuth 1980–2; La Scala 1981. Sop. roles from 1983. Salzburg début 1983; NY Met 1985; Glyndebourne 1985.

Connolly, Justin (Riveagh) (*b* London, 1933). Eng. composer. Prof. of theory and comp. RCM 1966–89. Taught at Yale Univ. 1963–6. Comps. incl. *The Marriage of Heaven and Hell* (Blake) for soloists, ch., and orch.; *Antiphonies* for 36 players; *Cinque-paces* (brass quintet); *Poems of Wallace Stevens I* for sop. and 7 players (1967), *II* for sop., cl., and pf. (1970); *Rebus* for orch. (1970); *Anima*, va. and orch. (1974); *Diaphony*, org. and orch. (1977); various chamber works under titles *Triad* and *Tesserae*; *Ceilidh*, for 4 vn. (1976); *Regeneration*, ch. and brass (1977); *Sestina B*, hpd., fl., ob., cl., vn., and vc. (1972, rev. 1978); *Sentences* (Traherne), ch., brass, org. (1979); *Chimaera*, dancer, alto, bar., ch., pf., perc., and vc. (1979, rev. 1981); *Obbligati V*, vn., va., vc., str. (1981); *Tesserae F*, solo bass cl. (1981); *Fourfold from the Garden Forking Path*, 2 pf. (1983); *Annead*, *Night Thoughts*, pf. (1983); Brahms's *Variations on a Theme of R. Schumann*, Op.23, arr. for 9 wind instr. (1983); *Spelt from Sibyl's Leaves*, 6 solo vv., ens. (1989); *Nocturnal*, fl., pf., perc., db. (1990); *Cantata*, sop., pf. (1991); sym. (1991); *Gymel A*, fl., cl. (1993); *Gymel B*, cl., vc. (1995); *Scardanelli Dreams*, mez., pf. (1997–8); pf. trio (1999); pf. conc. (2001–3); str. trio (2004).

Consecration of the House, The (*Die Weihe des Hauses*). Title of Ger. play by C. Meisl perf. at the opening of the Josephstadt Th., Vienna, 1822. Beethoven comp. an ov. in C major, Op.124, and an item of incidental mus. Since the play was an adaptation of Kotzebue's play *Die *Ruinen von Athen* for which he had comp. incidental mus. in 1811, Beethoven rearr. his mus. for that for *Die Weihe des Hauses*, but wrote a new ov.

consecutive. Applied to harmonic intervals of the same size which succeed one another in the same parts or vv. Academic condemnation was reserved for *consecutive fifths* and *consecutive octaves*. In both intervals, the component notes are in the closest relationship to each other so that if they are used consecutively, they may both sound as one. Many 20th-cent. composers use consecutive 5ths to splendid effect. *Hidden fifths* are consecutive 5ths believed to be implied, i.e. the progression in similar *motion of two parts

to a perfect 5th (or octave) from such an interval in the same 2 parts in the previous chord, so that it may be imagined there is also an intermediate 5th (or octave).

conservatory (Fr. *conservatoire*, Ger. *Konservatorium*). School of mus. training and instruction. Name derived from It. *conservatorio*, a sch. in Naples, Venice, and elsewhere where children were 'conserved' and educated in mus. and other matters.

Consolations. 6 pieces (nocturnes) for solo pf. by Liszt, comp. 1849–50. The best-known is No.3.

console. All that part of the machinery of an org. which is in front of and on each side of the player and by which he operates, i.e. the manuals, pedal board, mus. stand, stop handles, swell pedals, composition pedals, pistons, and levers, etc.

con sordino (It.). With *mute.

consort. An old spelling of 'concert', meaning a concerted perf. by any body of performers. A *whole consort* was one in which all the instr. were of one family; a *broken consort* one in which there was a mixture.

Constant, Marius (*b* Bucharest, 1925; *d* Paris, 2004). Romanian-born composer and conductor living in France. Pres. and mus. dir. Ars Nova 1963–71, a Paris orch. for perf. of modern mus. Mus. dir., Fr. Radio, 1953, 1963–7. Mus. dir. Roland Petit Ballet and Paris Opéra Ballet, 1973–8. Comps. incl. 24 *Preludes*, orch. (1958); *Turner*, 3 *Portraits* for orch. (1961); *Chants de Maldoror* (1962), dancer-cond., narr., 23 improvisers, 10 vc.; *Paradise Lost* (ballet by Roland Petit) (1967); *Chaconne et Marche Militaire*, orch. (1968); 14 *Stations*, perc. (1970); *Equal*, 5 percussionists (1970); *Strings*, 12 str., elec. gui. (1972); *Faciebat anno 1972*, 24 vn., orch. (1972); *Piano personnage*, ens. (1973); *For Clarinet* (1974); *Le jeu de Ste Agnes*, opera (1974); *Concerto Gli Elementi*, tb., orch. (1977); *Symphony for Winds* (1978); *Concertante*, alto sax., orch. (1979); *Nana-Symphonie* (1980); *La tragédie de Carmen*, opera (1981); 103 *Regards dans l'eau* (1981); *Pelléas et Mélisande-Symphonie* (1983); *L'Inauguration de la Maison*, wind band (1985); *Des droits de l'homme*, oratorio (1989).

Construction in Metal. 3 works by *Cage for perc. instr., No.1 for sextet (1939), Nos. 2 and 3 (1940 and 1941) for qt.

Consul, The. Opera in 3 acts by Menotti to his own lib. Comp. 1949. Prod. Philadelphia 1950, London 1951. Deals with plight of refugees in modern totalitarian state. The consul, who never appears, represents bureaucratic red tape.

conte (Fr.). Tale. Sometimes used as title for picturesque piece of instr. mus.

Contes d'Hoffmann, Les (Offenbach). See *Tales of Hoffmann, The*.

continuo. See *basso continuo*.

contra- (*Kontra-*, *contre-*). Respectively, It., Ger., and Fr. prefixes to names of instr. signifying lower in pitch (by about an octave). Thus *contrebasse* is Fr. for db., *contrebasson* Fr. for double-bn. In mus. It. these are *contrabasso* and *contrafagotto*, though in correct modern It. they should be *contrabbasso* and *controfagotto*. The Eng. *contrabass* is another name for a bass viol. To use it as the trans. of *contrabasso* is not strictly correct since the correct counterpart of the prefix is 'counter-'. But no one would know what you were talking about if you said 'counterbassoon', since the Eng. term is 'double-bassoon' and the Amer. 'contrabassoon'.

contradanza. See *country dance*.

contraltist. A *castrato with a v. of cont. range.

contralto (It.). The lowest of the ranges of female v., with a normal range g–g″. Originally term meant a male singer, falsetto or castrato, being derived from 'contr' alto', abbrev. of contratenor altus.

contrapunctus. Made-up Latin for *counterpoint and used by J. S. Bach instead of 'fugue' as a heading for the movts. of his *Die *Kunst der Fuge*.

contrapuntal. The adjective of *counterpoint.

contrary motion. See *motion*.

Contrasts. Work for vn., cl., and pf. in 2 movts. by Bartók, comp. 1938 for jazz clarinettist Benny Goodman who, with Szigeti and Endre Petri, gave f.p. NY 9 Jan. 1939. The violinist uses 2 instr., the 2nd being tuned G♯–D–A–E♭ (*scordatura*) for 30 bars.

contredanse. See *country dance*.

Converse, Frederick Shepherd (*b* Newton, Mass., 1871; *d* Westwood, Mass., 1940). Amer. composer. Studied mus. at Harvard Coll. 1889–93. Began business career but turned to mus. and studied in Munich, a Sym. in D minor being played at his graduation. Taught at Harvard Coll. 1903–7. Involved in organization of Boston Opera Co. 1908–14. His 1-act opera *The Pipe of Desire* (Boston 1906) was first Amer. opera to be staged at NY Met (1910). Wrote several more operas; 5 syms.; orch. pieces incl. The *Mystic Trumpeter (1904), and *Flivver Ten Million* (1926), a fantasy to celebrate the manufacture of the 10 millionth Ford car; vn. conc. (1902); choral works; chamber mus.; and pf. works.

Conyngham, Barry (*b* Sydney, NSW, 1944). Australian composer. Began as jazz player. In San Diego 1972–4 and France 1974–5. Returned to Amer. 1982 as visiting scholar, Minnesota Univ. and Pennsylvania State Univ. Served on various Australian artistic boards and committees. Works incl.:

OPERA & MUS. THEATRE: *Edward John Eyre*, narr., ch. (1973); *Mirror Images*, 4 actors, ens. (1974–5); *Ned*, opera (1975–8); *The Apology of Bony Anderson*, 1-act opera (1978); *Bony Anderson*, bar., ens. (1978); *Fly*,

opera (1981–4); *The Oath of Bad Brown Bill*, children's opera (1985); *Bennelong*, puppet opera (1988).

ORCH.: *Crisis: Thoughts in a City*, 2 str. orch., perc. (1968); *Five Windows* (1969); *Water . . . Footsteps . . . Time* (1970–1); *Six*, 6 perc. players, orch. (1971); *Without Gesture*, solo perc., hp., pf., orch. (1973); *Sky*, str. (1977); *Mirages* (1978); *Concerto for Orchestra: Horizons* (1981); *Recurrences*, org., cel., 2 pf., elec. pf., orch. (1986); *Vast: I, The Sea, II, The Coast, III, The Centre* (III for vn., va., vc., db., orch.), *IV, The Cities* (1987); *Decades* (1993); *Nostalgia*, str. (1997); *Passing* (1998); *Dreams Go Wandering Still* (2004); *Now That Darkness* (2004); *Again* (2005).

CONCERTOS: *Ice Carving*, vn., 4 str. orch. (1970); db. conc. *Shadows of Nōh* (1978); *Southern Cross*, vn., pf., orch. (1981); vc. conc. (1984); *Waterways*, va., orch. (1990); *Cloudlines*, hp., orch. (1991); *Bundanon*, pf., orch. (1994).

CHAMBER MUSIC: *Five*, wind quintet (1970–1); str. qt. (1979); *Voicings*, fl., tb., perc., pf., tape (1983); *Streams*, hp., fl., va. (1989); *Awakening*, hp. (1991); str. qt. No.2 (1999); *Flute*, fl. (2001); *Crux Australis*, vn., pf. (2002); *Silhouette*, hp. (2004).

VOICE(S) & INSTRS.: *From Voss*, female v., hp., perc. (1973); *Bashō*, sop., ens. (1981); *Antipodes*, sop., ten., bar., didjeridu, ch., orch. (1984–5); *Fix*, bar., orch. (2004).

Cook, Brian Rayner (*b* London, 1945). Eng. baritone. Glyndebourne chorus 1968. First major London concert 1969. Sang in McCabe's *Voyage*, Worcester Fest. 1972. Concerts in It. and Belg. 1972. Proms début 1973; opera début 1974. Outstanding interpreter of Brit. choral works, esp. Elgar and Vaughan Williams.

Cook, (Alfred) Melville (*b* Gloucester, 1912; *d* Cheltenham, 1993). Eng. organist. Ass. org., Gloucester Cath. 1932; org., Leeds Parish Church 1937–56, Hereford Cath. 1956–66; cond. Winnipeg Phil. Choir 1966–7; org. and choirmaster, United Metropolitan Church, Toronto 1967–86. On mus. staff McMaster Univ., Hamilton, Ont., 1973–86.

Cooke, Arnold (Atkinson) (*b* Gomersal, Yorks., 1906; *d* Five Oak Green, Kent, 2005). Eng. composer. Prof. of harmony and comp. RMCM 1933–8 and at TCL 1947–78. Comps. incl.:

OPERAS: *Mary Barton* (1949–54); *The Invisible Duke* (1 act) (1975–6).

BALLET: *Jabez and the Devil* (1959–60).

ORCH.: 6 syms. (1946–7, 1963, 1967–8, 1973–4, 1978–9, 1983–4); ob. conc. (1954); 2 cl. concs. (1955, 1981–2); vn. conc. (1958); vc. conc. (1974).

CHAMBER MUSIC: 4 str. qts.; 2 vc. sonatas (1941, 1979–80); ob. qt. (1948); str. trio (1950); vn. sonata No.1 (1938), No.2 (1951); ob. sonata (1957); cl. sonata (1959); hn. quintet (also exists as hn. trio) (1956); *Concertante Quartet*, 4 cl. (1976).

VOCAL: 5 *Part-Songs* (1959); *Song on May Morning* (1966); *The Sea Mew*, song-cycle for bar., fl., ob., str. qt. (1980).

ORGAN: sonata No.1 (1971), No.2 (1980).

Cooke, Deryck (Victor) (*b* Leicester, 1919; *d* Croydon, 1976). Eng. critic, broadcaster, and musicologist. On BBC staff 1947–59 and after 1965. Wrote important book, *The Language of Music*. Made perf. version from chaotic MS score of *Mahler's 10th Sym. (f.p. 1964, rev. 1972). Authority on Bruckner, Delius, and Wagner (esp. *The Ring*, first part of his projected study of which was posthumously pubd. in 1979, as *I Saw the World End*).

Cooke, Henry (*b* c.1616; *d* Hampton Court, 1672). Eng. bass and choirmaster. Choirboy in Chapel Royal; later joined the royalist forces and became captain; at Restoration, 1660, returned to Chapel Royal as Master of the Children, among whom were Pelham Humfrey, John Blow, and Henry Purcell. Introduced It. style of singing and technique of comp. Was favourably known not only as their teacher but as composer for stage and church, as actor and as singer.

Coolidge, Elizabeth Sprague (*b* Chicago, 1864; *d* Cambridge, Mass., 1953). Amer. pianist, composer, and patron of music. Founder of chamber mus. fests. (Pitsfield, Mass.; then Washington DC). Coolidge Foundation (1925) was founded to sponsor the fests. and to commission works from leading 20th-cent. composers (e.g. Stravinsky, Bartók, Pizzetti, Prokofiev, Britten, Dallapiccola, Crumb). Gave generous private sponsorship to Schoenberg and Frank Bridge. Instituted Elizabeth Sprague Coolidge Medal in 1932 to be awarded annually 'for eminent services to chamber mus.'.

Cooper, Emil (Albertovich) (*b* Kherson, Russia, 1877; *d* NY, 1960). Russ.-born conductor. Début Odessa 1896, Kiev Opera 1900–4. Cond. f.p. of *The *Golden Cockerel*, Moscow 1909, and its f.p. in London 1914. Cond. first prods. by Russ. cos. of the *Ring* and *Die Meistersinger*. Cond. for Diaghilev operas, Paris 1908 and 1909, incl. *Boris Godunov* with Chaliapin. London début 1913. Cond. Leningrad PO 1921–2. Left Russia 1922. Mus. dir. Riga Opera 1925–8. Cond. Chicago Opera 1929–32, NY Met 1944–50, where he introduced *Peter Grimes* (1948). Cond. Montreal Opera Guild from 1950.

Cooper, Imogen (*b* London, 1949). Eng. pianist, daughter of Martin *Cooper. Won a *Premier Prix* 1967. Won Mozart Prize 1969. Many solo recitals and concs. with leading orchs. Amer. début Los Angeles, 1984.

Cooper, John. See *Coprario, Giovanni*.

Cooper, Joseph (Elliott Needham) (*b* Bristol, 1912; *d* 2001). Eng. pianist. London début 1947. Lect.- recitalist, also chairman of popular TV mus. quiz. Assisted Vaughan Williams in adapting pf. conc. to double pf. conc., 1946. OBE 1982.

Cooper, Martin (Du Pré) (*b* Winchester, 1910; *d* Richmond-on-Thames, 1986). Eng. critic. Mus. critic of *Daily Telegraph* 1950–76 (chief critic from 1954). Mus. critic *London Mercury* 1935–9, *Daily Herald* 1946–50, *Spectator* 1947–54. Ed., *Musical Times* 1952–5. Author of books on Gluck, Bizet, French music, and Beethoven (*The Last Decade*, London, 1970). CBE 1972.

coperti (It.). Covered. Term used of drums muted by being covered with a cloth.

copla. (1) Sp. popular poem and song in short stanzas (see *seguidilla*), sometimes extemporized. (2) A solo movt. in a *villancico*.

Copland, Aaron (*b* Brooklyn, NY, 1900; *d* NY, 1990). Amer. composer, pianist, and conductor, of Russ. parentage (name was originally Kaplan). First Amer. composer whose mus. was recognized outside USA as distinctively nat. Studied mus. theory in 1917 with Rubin *Goldmark but in 1921 went to Paris as Nadia *Boulanger's first full-time Amer. student, staying until 1924. On return to USA, wrote Sym. for Organ and Orch. (1923–4) for Mlle Boulanger's Amer. début as organist. F.p. in 1925 gained him notoriety as apostle of dissonance, the cond. (Damrosch) remarking: 'If he can write like that at 23, in 5 years he'll be ready to commit murder'. Led to a Boston commission (*Music for the Theater*, for orch., 1925) from Koussevitzky, who also cond. f.p. of pf. conc., 1927. In both works jazz elements were introduced to purge what Copland felt was the 'too European' flavour of his mus. Abandoned jazz in 1930, adopting a more austere style in the Pf. Variations (1930) and *Short Symphony* (1932–3). At the same time, concerned with widening gap between public and contemporary composers, wrote some works in a more accessible, popular style. Visited Mexico several times in the 1930s and in 1936 prod. his highly successful *El salón México*, orch. fantasy on popular Mexican tunes. Other works in this style incl. ballets *Billy the Kid* (1938), *Rodeo* (1942), and *Appalachian Spring* (1944). In later years Copland prod. little mus., preferring to conduct.

Copland always worked hard on the promotional side of Amer. mus. as lecturer and teacher (head of the comp. faculty at Berkshire Mus. Center 1940–65). He toured the world as cond. and ambassador for his country's mus.; co-founded (with *Sessions) a series of NY concerts of new Amer. works 1928–31, founded a publishing press, and was active with the League of Composers. In 1937 he founded the Amer. Composers' Alliance. He received Pulitzer Prize for Mus. 1944, Gold Medal of Amer. Acad. 1956, and the Presidential Medal of Freedom 1964. He wrote several books. Prin. comps.:

OPERA: *The *Tender Land* (1952–4, rev. 1955).

BALLETS: *Grohg* (1922–5); *Billy the Kid* (1938); *Rodeo* (1942); *Appalachian Spring* (1943–4).

ORCH.: Sym. for Organ (1924) (version without organ is Sym. No.1, 1928); *Music for the Theater* (1925); pf. conc. (1926); *Symphonic Ode* (1928–9, rev. 1955); *A Dance Symphony* (1930, based on ballet *Grohg*); *Short Symphony* (sym. No.2) (1932–3); *Statements* (1932–5); suite: *Billy the Kid* (1938); *El salón México* (1933–6); *An Outdoor Ov.* (1938, arr. for band 1941); *Quiet City* (1939); suite from film mus. *Our Town* (1940); *A *Lincoln Portrait* for speaker, orch. (1942); *Fanfare for the Common Man* (1942); *Music for the Movies* (1942); suite, *Rodeo* (1943); suite, *Appalachian Spring* (1945); Sym.

No.3 (1944–6); cl. conc. (1947–8); *Orchestral Variations* (1957, orch. version of pf. variations); *Connotations* (1962); *Music for a Great City* (1964); *3 Latin-American Sketches* (1972); *Inscape* (1967).

CHORAL: *The House on the Hill* (1925); *In the Beginning*, mez. and unacc. ch. (1947); *Canticle of Freedom* (1955, rev. 1965).

CHAMBER MUSIC: *As it fell upon a day*, for sop., fl., and cl. (1923); 2 pieces for str. qt. (1923 and 1928, also for str. orch.); *Vitebsk* (Study on a Jewish Theme), pf. trio (1928); vn. sonata (1943); pf. qt. (1950); nonet for str. (1960); *Duo* for fl. and pf. (1971); *Threnody* (in memoriam Stravinsky), fl. qt. (1971).

PIANO: *The Cat and the Mouse* (1920); *Piano Variations* (1930, orch. version 1957); Sonata (1939–41); *Fantasy* (1952–7). Also pf. suites from *Billy the Kid* and *Our Town*.

Also songs, incl. *12 Poems of Emily Dickinson* (1950) and *Old American Songs* (1950–2), and film mus. incl. *Of Mice and Men* (1939), *Our Town* (1940), *The Red Pony* (1948) and *The Heiress* (1949) (Hollywood 'Oscar').

Copley, John (Michael Harold) (*b* Birmingham, 1933). Eng. director. Trained at Sadler's Wells Ballet Sch. and Nat. Sch. of Opera with Joan Cross. Appeared as Apprentice in *Peter Grimes*, CG 1950. Joined SW as stage manager 1953. First opera prod. at SW 1957 (*Il tabarro*). At CG 1960–88, progressing from deputy stage man. to prin. res. dir. First CG prod. 1965 (*Suor Angelica*). Major CG prods. incl. Mozart's da Ponte operas, *Benvenuto Cellini* and *Ariadne auf Naxos* both 1976, and Handel's *Semele* 1982. For ENO prod. *Carmen* (1969), *Der Rosenkavalier* (1975), Handel's *Julius Caesar* (1979), and many others. Lavish settings preferred.

Coppel (Ger.). Coupler (organ).

Coppélia, ou La Fille aux yeux d'émail (*Coppelia, or The Girl with enamel eyes*). Ballet in 3 acts with mus. by Delibes to lib. by Nuitter and Saint-Léon, choreog. Saint-Léon, prod. Paris 1870. Based on story by E. T. A. Hoffmann (*Der Sandmann*). Many other choreographic versions.

Coprario, Giovanni (John Cooper) (*b c.*1575; *d* London, 1626). Eng. composer and viol player. Visited It. *c.*1600, changing name to Giovanni Coprario (or Coperario) and retaining this on return. Comp. well over 100 str. fantasias, also masques, anthems, dances, suites and songs. Taught mus. to Charles I and to the *Lawes brothers. His *Funeral Teares* (1606) and *Songs of Mourning* (1613), 7 songs written at death of James I's eldest son, Henry, are among earliest Eng. song-cycles. Some time before 1617 he wrote his *Rules How to Compose*. Was in service of Cecil family at Hatfield House, Herts., and of Earl of Hertford in Wiltshire.

coprifuoco, coprifoco (It.). Curfew. Occasional title for instr. comp., sometimes with bell effect.

Coq d'Or, Le (Rimsky-Korsakov). See *Golden Cockerel, The*.

cor (Fr.). Properly *horn but the term forms a part of the name of several instr. which are not hns., e.g. *cor anglais.

cor anglais (Fr.). English horn. Neither Eng., nor a hn., but an alto ob. pitched a 5th below oboe. Name possibly a corruption of *cor anglé*. A transposing instr., being written a 5th higher than it sounds. Compass from e upwards for about 2½ octaves. The reed is inserted in a metal tube which is bent back. Invented by Ferlandis of Bergamo in 1760. Not much used before 19th-cent. Romantic composers, but there are several famous solos for it, e.g. Wagner's *Tristan und Isolde*, Act III, in slow movement of Franck's Sym., and in Sibelius's *The Swan of Tuonela*. Also organ reed stop of 8' pitch but sometimes 16'.

corant, coranto. See *courante*.

corda, corde (It.). String, strings. (1, pf. mus.) *una corda*, one string, i.e. use the 'soft' pedal which causes the hammers (on a pf.) to strike only one str. per note instead of three. Cancelled by term *tre corde* (3 str.) or *tutte le corde* (all the str.). (2, vn. mus., etc.) *corda vuota*, empty string, i.e. *open string.

corde (Fr.). String.

corde à jour, corde à vide (Fr.). *Open string.

cor de chasse (Fr.). Hunting horn. 17th-cent brass instr. developed from combination of tightly-coiled helical hn. and crescent-shaped hn.

cor de nuit (Fr.). Night-horn, i.e. watchman's horn. Org. flue stop, end-plugged, of 4' length and 8' pitch; of very characteristic tone quality.

Corder, Frederick (*b* London, 1852; *d* London, 1932). Eng. composer and teacher. Opera *Le morte d'Arthur* prod. Brighton 1879. Founded Soc. of Brit. Composers (1905–18) to promote Brit. mus. Prof. of comp. RAM from 1888. Opera *Nordisa* prod. Liverpool 1887. Trans. into Eng. libs. of *Ring, Tristan, Lohengrin, Die Meistersinger* and *Parsifal* (helped by his wife).

cor des alpes. See *Alphorn*.

cor d'harmonie (Fr.). Horn, with or without valves.

Corelli, Arcangelo (*b* Fusignano, nr. Milan, 1653; *d* Rome, 1713). It. violinist and composer. By 1675 was in Rome, where he became one of leading violinists. Joined court of Queen Christina 1679–86. From 1687 was under patronage of Cardinal Pamphili, and from 1690 under that of Cardinal Ottoboni. Lived in cardinal's palace and died a rich man with a fine art coll. His importance as a composer lies in his sonatas da camera and concerti grossi from which the solo sonata and the orch. concs. of Handel and Bach evolved. They are beautiful in themselves, notably the *Christmas Concerto. His works are grouped under 6 opus nos.

1. *12 Sonatas a tre*; 2. *12 Sonatas da camera a tre*; 3. *12 Sonatas a tre*; 4. *12 Sonatas da camera a tre*; 5. *12 Sonatas for vn. or vn. and cembalo* (also arr. as *concerti grossi* by *Geminiani*). 6. *12 Concerti grossi*.

Corelli, Franco (*b* Ancona, 1921; *d* Milan, 2003). It. tenor. Début Spoleto 1951 (Don José in *Carmen*); La Scala 1954; CG 1957; NY Met début 1961; Salzburg Fest. 1962. V. of heroic quality in roles such as Manrico and Calaf (*Turandot*).

Corelli, Variations on a Theme of. Work for solo pf. by Rachmaninov, Op.42, comp. and f.p. 1931 (Montreal). Theme is 'La folia'.

Corena, Fernando (*b* Geneva, 1916; *d* Lugano, 1984). Swiss-It. bass. Début Milan 1937. Returned to Zurich 1939–45. Post-war opera début Trieste 1947 (Varlaam in *Boris Godunov*). NY Met 1954; Salzburg Fest. 1956; Brit. début Edin. Fest. 1956; CG 1960.

Corigliano, John (Paul) (*b* NY, 1938). Amer. composer. Studied Columbia Univ., then with Luening and Giannini, and privately with Creston. Worked for NY radio station 1959–64. Mus. dir. Morris Th., NJ, 1962–4. Mus. producer CBS TV 1961–72. Teacher at Lehman Coll., NY, from 1972 (prof. from 1986). Comp.-in-res. with Chicago SO 1987–9. Works incl. 2 operas (*The Naked Carmen* (1970), and *The *Ghosts of Versailles* (1980–91)); sym. No.1 (1989–90), No.2, str. (2000), No.3 (*Circus Maximus*), large wind ens. (2004); concs. for pf. (1968), ob. (1975), cl. (1977), fl. (1981), vn. (2003); vn. sonata (1963); *Poem in October*, ten., orch. (1970); *Dodecaphonia*, mez., pf. (1997); *Vocalise*, sop., orch. (1999); *Forever Young*, sop., unacc. ch. (2000); *One Sweet Morning*, female ch., pf. (2005); *Kaleidoscope*, 2 pf. (1959); *Etude Fantasy*, pf. (1976); *The Red Violin Caprices*, vn. (1999); *Snapshot: Circa 1909*, str. qt. (2003).

Coriolan (Coriolanus). Ov., Op.62, by Beethoven comp. in 1807 for revival in Vienna of H. von Collin's play *Coriolan* (not Shakespeare's).

cori spezzati (It. 'divided choirs'). Singers placed in different parts of a building; also the mus. written for them.

cor mixte. See *corno alto* and *corno basso*.

cornamuse. Obsolete instr. extant during 16th cent. Term frequently means bagpipe (Fr. *cornemuse*) but It. *cornamusa* sometimes refers to a *crumhorn and sometimes to a different instr., like a soft crumhorn.

Cornelius, Peter (*b* Mainz, 1824; *d* Mainz, 1874). Ger. composer and writer. His delightful comic opera *Der Barbier von Bagdad* was produced by Liszt at Weimar, 1858, but controversy caused by Cornelius's advocacy of the Liszt–Wagner 'New Music' led to its withdrawal and to Liszt's resignation as court cond. Trans. some Berlioz libs., incl. *Benvenuto Cellini*, into Ger. Lived in Vienna 1859–65, meeting Wagner in 1861. Prof. of harmony, Munich Cons., 1867, and became one of Wagner's inner circle. Wrote 2 other operas, *Der Cid* (Weimar 1865) and *Gunlöd* (unfin-ished, completed by Bausznern, prod. 1891). Wrote many beautiful vocal works incl. *Stabat Mater* (1849) and *Requiem* (1863–72), and songs incl. the Christmas hymn known in Eng. as 'Three Kings from Persian Lands afar' but orig. *Die Könige* from the *Weihnachtslieder* (1856).

cornemuse (Fr.). Type of bagpipe.

cornet or **cornet à pistons** (Fr.). An instr. of brass (or other metal), of partly cylindrical and partly conical bore, with a cup-shaped mouthpiece. Like both tpt. and hn. it operates on the harmonic series filling in the gaps by the use of 3 valves which, singly or in combination, lengthen the tube so giving new fundamentals of a semitone to 6 lower, and consequently as many new harmonic series. Its tone is of a quality between that of the hn. and that of the tpt. Owing to the width of its bore it has great flexibility. Double and triple tonguing are possible. Like the tpt. as found in most Brit. orchs. it is constructed so that its primary key can be either B♭ or A, as desired: this removes some of the difficulties of playing in the extreme flat and sharp keys, as in the one case the player is eased of 2 flats and in the other 3 sharps. There is also a cornet in E♭, almost exclusively for wind-band use. In all these 3 keys the cornet is a *transposing instr., its mus. being written respectively a tone or minor 3rd higher, or a minor 3rd lower.

The cornet's first orch. appearance seems to have been in Rossini's opera *William Tell*, in 1829, and cornets are used by Berlioz in several works, incl. the *Symphonie Fantastique*, by Bizet, and by Tchaikovsky in *Francesca da Rimini*. By the 1890s it had almost displaced the tpt. in the orch., but is now seldom found in the orch. or in dance bands, and is now chiefly used in brass and military bands where a sop. cornet in E♭ is also used. But some 20th-cent. composers specify its use where they want its particular tone-quality, e.g. Vaughan Williams in *London Symphony*, Lambert in *Rio Grande*, and Arnold in *Beckus the Dandipratt*.

cornet stop. Org. stop of *mixture type: usually of 4 or 5 ranks. *mounted cornet* is one placed high on its own sound-board so as to be well heard.

cornett. Renaissance wind instr., spelt usually with double 't' to avoid confusion with the band *cornet. Name means 'little horn'. Heyday approx. 1500–1600. Hybrid form, combining brass cup-mouthpiece technique with woodwind finger technique, and was admired for its versatility of tone: as loud as a tpt., agile as a vn., and flexible as a v. Three varieties, curved, straight, and mute, all in different sizes. Mute prod. an exquisitely soft tone. Curved was most popular form and was used as a virtuoso instr., particularly by Monteverdi in his *Vespers* and *Orfeo*. All cornetts were in G with a range of 2 octaves. *Cornettino* developed for very high parts, pitched in C or D, and there were alto cornetts in F and the large ten. cornett in C. The cornett was displaced by baroque tpt. and baroque ob. See also *serpent* and *ophicleide*.

Cornish, William. See *Cornyshe, William*.

corno (It.). Properly *horn, but the term forms a part of the name of several instr. that are not hns. (e.g. *corno inglese*, *cor anglais*).

corno alto and **corno basso** (It.). High horn and low horn. (1) Old names for hn. players who specialized in the high and low registers respectively. (In early 19th-cent. Fr. there was a middle category, *cor mixte*.)
(2) In modern scores the terms are used to distinguish, e.g. the horn in B♭ which transposes down one tone, and that which transposes down a 9th.

corno a macchina (It.). Valve horn.

corno a mano (It.). Hand horn. The natural Fr. hn.

corno a pistoni (It.). Valve hn.

corno basso. See *corno alto*.

corno cromatico (It.). Chromatic hn., i.e. valve hn.

corno da caccia. Hunting hn.

corno di bassetto (It.). (1) The *basset horn.
(2) Pseudonym of Bernard Shaw for his mus. criticisms in *The Star* 1889–90; he used it again in articles he contrib. to the same paper in 1896 and 1897.
(3) Org. stop much like cl. stop.

corno dolce. Soft org. stop generally of fl. (not hn.) type; 8′ length and pitch (occasionally 16′).

corno inglese (It.). *Cor anglais.

cornopean. Organ stop like *trumpet* but softer.

corno ventile (It.). Valve hn.

Cornyshe [Cornish], **William** (*b* E. Greenwich, *c*.1465; *d* Hylden, Kent, 1523). Eng. composer and actor. Member of Chapel Royal 1496. Master of children, Chapel Royal, 1509–23. Organized mus. at masques, pageants, and banquets for Henry VIII and supervised mus. at Field of Cloth of Gold 1520. Wrote part-songs, notable for inventiveness and jovial humour, church mus., and several plays.

coro (It.). Choir, chorus. *gran coro*, in org. mus., means 'full org'.

cor-oboe. Org. flue stop of 8′ length and pitch, and somewhat reedy quality.

Coronation Concerto. Nickname of Mozart's pf. conc. No.26 in D, K537, perf. Frankfurt, 1790, on occasion of coronation of Leopold II but probably begun 1787 and previously perf. by Mozart in Dresden in April 1789.

Coronation Mass. Mozart's Mass in C, K317, comp. 1779 in Salzburg. So nicknamed because Salieri directed a perf. at the coronation of Leopold II in 1791 in Prague.

Coronation Ode. Choral work, Op.44, for 4 soloists, ch., and orch. by Elgar to words by A. C. Benson. Commissioned for CG gala perf. for Coronation of Edward VII, June 1902 (cancelled because of King's illness). F.p. Sheffield Fest. Oct. 1902. Finale is *'Land of Hope and Glory', to melody from trio of *Pomp and Circumstance March No.1, but with words differing from the song version.

Coronation of Poppea, The (Monteverdi). See *Incoronazione di Poppea, L'*.

corps de ballet (Fr.). The ballet troupe (excluding principals) of any particular th.

corps de réchange (Fr.). *Crook of a brass instr.

Corps glorieux, Les (The Glorious Hosts). Work for org. by *Messiaen, comp. 1939, in 7 movts.:
1. *Subtilité des corps glorieux*. 2. *Les Eaux de la grace*. 3. *L'Ange aux parfums*. 4. *Combat de la mort et de la vie*. 5. *Force et agilité des corps glorieux*. 6. *Joie et clarté des corps glorieux*. 7. *Mystère de la Sainte Trinité*.

corranach (also coronach). (1) Highland Scot. and Irish funeral dirge.
(2) Person performing such a dirge.

Corregidor, Der (The Magistrate). Opera in 4 acts by Hugo Wolf to lib. by Rosa Mayreder based on story by Alarcón, *El sombrero de tres picos* (The Three-Cornered Hat) 1874, on which *Falla's ballet was also to be based. Comp. 1895. Prod. Mannheim 1896, London 1934, NY (concert) 1959. Eng. trans. by Gerald *Larner, Manchester 1966.

corrente. See *courante*.

Corsaire, Le (The Corsair). Concert-ov., Op.21, by Berlioz, based on Byron's poem. First drafted in 1831, then rev. Nice 1844 under title *The Tower at Nice*. Perf. thus in Jan. 1845 and again rev. 1855. At one point called *Le Corsaire rouge*, Fr. title of Fenimore Cooper's *The Red Rover*.

Corsaro, Il (The Corsair). Opera in 3 acts by Verdi to lib. by Piave based on Byron's poem. Comp. 1847–8. Prod. Trieste 1848. Revived London 1966, NY 1981.

Corsi, Jacopo (*b* Florence, 1561; *d* Florence, 1602). It. nobleman in whose house in Florence the *Camerata met, as also in *Bardi's. Comp. 2 songs (the only surviving part) in Peri's *Dafne*, perf. in Corsi's house, in 1598. In 1600 was responsible for prod. of Peri's *Euridice*. Wealth came from banking, wool, and silk. When Bardi left Florence in 1592, Corsi was leading artistic patron and befriended Torquato Tasso, Carlo Gesualdo, Ottavio Rinuccini, and Jacoppo Peri.

cor simple (Fr.). Natural hn.

corta, corte, corti. See *corto*.

Corteccia, (Pier) **Francesco** (*b* Florence, 1502; *d* Florence, 1571). It. organist and composer. Choirboy in St Giovanni Ballista, Florence, 1515–22, where he became org. 1535–9. Choirmaster at ducal court in Florence 1540–71. Wrote madrigals, etc. Joint composer with Striggio of wedding mus. (lost) for Franceso de' Medici and Joanna of Austria, 1565.

Cortèges (*Funeral processions*). Fantasy ov. for orch. by *Rawsthorne, f.p. London 1945.

corto, corta, corti, corte (It.). Short.

Cortot, Alfred (Denis) (*b* Nyon, Switz., 1877; *d* Lausanne, 1962). Swiss-born pianist and conductor, long resident in Fr. Début as pianist Paris 1896. Keen Wagnerian, went to Bayreuth and became ass. cond. to Richter and Mottl 1898–1901. Cond. first Paris perf. of *Götterdämmerung* 1902. Became cond. of orch. concerts of Société Nationale 1904. Cond. f.ps. in Fr. of *Parsifal* (concert perf.), Beethoven's Mass in D, and Brahms's *Requiem*. From 1905 played in celebrated pf. trio with *Thibaud and *Casals. Prof. of pf., Paris Cons. 1907–17, succeeding *Pugno. In 1919 founded École Normale de Musique, where he gave interpretation courses. One of 3 conds. of Orchestre Symphonique de Paris, founded 1928. Ed. pf. works of Chopin, Schumann, and Liszt and wrote several books. Salzburg Fest. 1933 (Saint-Saëns conc. No.4 and Franck *Sym.-Var.*, Vienna PO cond. Krauss). Arrested 1944 on charges of collab. with Nazi occupation forces but released.

cosaque (Fr.). Cossack dance in simple duple time with continual *accelerando*.

Così fan tutte, ossia la scuola degli amanti (Women are all the same, or The School for Lovers). Opera in 2 acts by Mozart (K588, 1789) to lib. by da Ponte. Prod. Vienna 1790, London 1811, NY 1922. History of this opera is of special interest. Today it is regarded by many critics as Mozart's greatest and was a success at its first appearance, being repeated 10 times in 1790 and perf. at Prague, Dresden, Leipzig, and Frankfurt before Mozart died. After about 1830 it became a rarity for about 60 years, when it was re-est. through the advocacy of R. Strauss, Mahler, and, later, Beecham. This neglect may have been because the plot was considered (by Beethoven among others) to be immoral, but a mus. reason may have been that the chief sop. role of Fiordiligi was long regarded as unsingable: it was written for Adriana del Bene who was a brilliant high coloratura but also commanded a very low register. The opera requires carefully rehearsed ens. work.

Cosma, Edgar (*b* Bucharest, 1925). Romanian conductor and composer. Cond. Romanian film mus. orch. 1950–8; Ulster Orch. 1969–74. Comps. incl. str. qt., pf. trio, pf. sonata.

Cossotto, Fiorenza (*b* Crescentino di Vercelli, 1935). It. mezzo-soprano. Début La Scala 1957 in f.p. of *Les dialogues des Carmélites*. Wexford Fest. 1958; Milan 1961, and sang regularly at La Scala until 1972–3; CG 1959 (Neris in *Médée*, with Callas); NY Met 1968. Also recitalist, and distinguished exponent of Verdi *Requiem*, in which she sang on her Salzburg Fest. début 1975; opera début there 1976.

Cossutta, Carlo (*b* Trieste, 1932; *d* Udine, 2000). It. tenor. Début Buenos Aires 1956 (in *La traviata*), and created title-role in Ginastera's *Don Rodrigo* there, 1964. CG début 1964; NY Met from 1973; Milan etc. Noted Otello, Manrico, and Turiddù.

Costa, Mary (*b* Knoxville, Tenn., 1930). Amer. soprano. Made TV commercials. Deputized for Schwarzkopf, Hollywood Bowl 1958. Sang at Glyndebourne, S. Francisco, and Cincinnati Opera Houses. NY Met début 1964. Founded Knoxville Opera Co. 1978.

Costa, (Sir) **Michael** (Andrew Agnus) [Michele Andrea Agniello] (*b* Naples, 1808; *d* Hove, 1884). It.-born conductor and composer (Brit. cit.). Wrote 4 operas for Naples 1826–9. Went to Birmingham 1829 to conduct *Zingarelli cantata (but only sang in it), and settled in London, taking leading part in many mus. activities. *Maestro al piano* King's (later Her Majesty's) Th. 1830, cond. and mus. dir. 1833–46 and 1871–81. Cond. Phil. Soc. 1846–54, Birmingham Fest. 1849–82, Handel Fest. 1857–80, Royal It. Opera, CG 1847–68 and 1871–9. Comp. 3 syms., cantatas, operas incl. *Don Carlos* (London 1844), and oratorios *Eli* (Birmingham 1855) and *Naaman* (Birmingham 1864). Opinions differ on Costa's merits as a cond., but he was certainly a superb orch. trainer. Of his comps., Rossini's remark is perhaps pertinent: 'Good old Costa has sent me an oratorio score and a Stilton cheese; the cheese was very fine'. Knighted 1869.

Costeley, Guillaume (*b* Fontanges, *c*.1530; *d* Évreux, 1606). Fr. composer of *Chansons*, repubd. 1896. Was writing in Paris by 1554. Pres. of soc. in honour of St. Cecilia, formed 1570, which est. a mus. contest at Évreux. Experimented with microtonal comp. in *chanson* for 4 vv., *Seigneur Dieu ta pitié*. First comp. to call a work an 'air'. Court org. to Charles IX of Fr. from *c*.1560. Retired *c*.1584.

Cosyn, Benjamin (*b c*.1570; *d* ?London, after 1652). Eng. organist and composer. Org., Dulwich Coll. 1622–4 and Charterhouse 1626–43. Compiled Virginal Book of 90 pieces, incl. 32 of his own and others by Bull, Gibbons, Tallis, and Byrd. Influenced by Bull.

Côtelettes. See *Chopsticks*.

cotillon (Fr. 'under-petticoat'). Elaborate ballroom dance popular in 19th cent. as final dance of the evening. It was a type of *country dance, perf. by any no., all imitating the leading couple, who chose their figures out of a large number available. The mus. was simply that of various waltzes, mazurkas, etc. In earlier centuries was akin to quadrille.

Cotrubas, Ileana (*b* Galati, Romania, 1939). Romanian soprano. Début Bucharest Opera 1964 (Yniold in *Pelléas et Mélisande*). Salzburg Fest. début 1967; Frankfurt Opera 1968–71; Vienna Opera 1969, thereafter regular appearances there; Glyndebourne 1969 and 1970; CG 1971; Chicago from 1973; Milan 1974; NY Met 1977. Farewell recital CG 1989.

Cottrau, Teodoro (*b* Naples, 1827; *d* Naples, 1879). It. composer and publisher. Wrote 50 Neapolitan melodies, most famous being *Santa Lucia* (1850). In 1848 became joint owner of his father's publishing firm Girard's. Close friend of Bellini and Donizetti.

coulisse (Fr.). Groove, sliding-piece, etc. (1) slide of tb. and slide tpt. (2) (followed by the words *à accorder*) tuning slide of a wind instr.

Coulthard, Jean (*b* Vancouver, 1908; *d* Vancouver, 2000). Canadian composer and pianist. She taught at Univ. of British Columbia 1947–73. Works incl. pf. quintet (1932); vc. sonata (1947); ob. sonata (1947); 3 syms. (1950–1, 1966–7, 1974–5); vn. conc. (1955–9); pf. qt. (1957); pf. conc. (1963, rev. 1967); *Symphonic Ode*, vc., orch. (1965); 4 *Prophetic Songs*, cont., fl., vc., pf. (1975); *Shizen: Three Nature Sketches from Japan*, ob., pf. (1979); *Image Astrale*, pf. (1981); Duo Sonata, vn., vc. (1989).

counterpoint. The ability, unique to mus., to say two things at once comprehensibly. The term derives from the expression *punctus contra punctum*, i.e. 'point against point' or 'note against note'. A single 'part' or 'voice' added to another is called 'a counterpoint' to that other, but the more common use of the word is that of the combination of simultaneous parts or vv., each of significance in itself and the whole resulting in a coherent texture. In this sense counterpoint is the same as *polyphony.

The art of counterpoint developed gradually from the 9th cent. onwards and reached its highest point at the end of the 16th cent. and beginning of the 17th cent. When, at a later date, attempts were made to formulate rules for students of the art they were based on the practice of that period of culmination. The chief theorist responsible for the formulation of those rules was *Fux whose *Gradus ad Parnassum* of 1725 is a book which still shows its influence in modern textbooks of *strict counterpoint* (or student's counterpoint), a form of training intended to be preparatory to the practice of free counterpoint (or composer's counterpoint).

In strict counterpoint the processes are studied under 5 heads, the result of an analysis which dissects the practice of the art into 5 *species*. Following the practice of early composers a *cantus firmus* (fixed song) is employed, i.e. a short melody, set by the master, against which another melody is to be written by the student—

or, it may be, several such melodies. It is usually set out with one note to a measure (bar).

The species are as follows:

I. The added v. proceeds at the same pace as the *cantus firmus*, i.e. with one note to a measure.

II. The added v. proceeds at twice (or 3 times) the pace of the *cantus firmus*, i.e. with 2 or 3 notes to a measure.

III. The added v. proceeds at 4 (or 6) times the pace of the *cantus firmus*, i.e. with 4 notes to a measure.

IV. The added v. proceeds (as in Species II) at the rate of 2 notes to 1, i.e. 2 to a measure; but the second note is tied over to the first note of the following measure, i.e. *syncopation is introduced.

V. (Sometimes called *florid counterpoint*.) The added v. employs a mixture of the processes of the other 4 species and also introduces shorter notes (quavers).

The use of strict counterpoint as a method of study has tended to decline, its 'rules' being felt to be too rigid.

Combined counterpoint (strict or free) is that in which the added vv. are different species. *Invertible counterpoint* is such as permits of vv. changing places (the higher becoming the lower, and vice versa). *Double counterpoint* is invertible counterpoint as concerns 2 vv. *Triple counterpoint* is that in which 3 vv. are concerned, which are capable of changing places with one another, so making 6 positions of the v. parts possible. *Quadruple and quintuple counterpoint* are similarly explained, the first allowing of 24 positions and the second of 120.

Imitation is common in contrapuntal comp.— one v. entering with a phrase which is then more or less exactly copied by another v. When the imitation is strict it becomes *canon.

In the 20th cent. there have been no new contrapuntal procedures but composers have made much freer and more daring use of traditional forms. In particular they have concentrated on what is known as *linear counterpoint*, i.e. on the individual strands of the texture and on thematic and rhythmic relationships rather than on harmonic implications. *Linear* harmony is the opposite of *vertical* harmony, i.e. confluences. With the blurring or virtual elimination of the boundaries between consonance and dissonance a much wider range of confluences is open to the composer.

countersubject. In *fugue, in addition to the subject, there is often a *countersubject* appearing in the exposition and probably later also. This is a melodic acc. to the answer and subject and is generally in double counterpoint. The v. which has just given out the subject or answer then proceeds to the countersubject while the next v. gives out the answer or subject, and so on.

countertenor. High male v. not to be confused with male alto, falsetto, or *castrato and with a strong, almost instr. purity of tone. Was popular in Handel's and Purcell's lifetimes and has been revived in 20th cent. largely thanks to artistry of Alfred *Deller. Several modern composers, incl. Britten in his opera *A Midsummer Night's Dream*, have written parts for counterten. With the search for authenticity in perf. of early mus., it has reclaimed many roles in baroque works long since assigned to conts. or tens.

Count of Luxemburg, The (Der Graf von Luxemburg). Operetta in 3 acts by Lehár (1909) to libretto by A. M. Wilner and R. Bodanzky. F.p. Vienna 1909.

country dance (Eng.), **contredanse** (Fr.), **contradanza** (It.), **Kontretanz** (Ger.). This type of dance is of Brit. origin. Its various foreign names have come about from a plausible false etymology ('counter-dance'—one in which the performers stand opposite to one another—as distinguished from a round dance). Both Mozart and Beethoven wrote *Kontretänze*. No.7 of Beethoven's 12 *Kontretänze* contains the theme used also in the finale of the *Eroica* Sym. and other works. The term is generic and covers a whole series of figure dances deriving from the amusements of the Eng. village green. Such dances became popular at the court of Queen Elizabeth I, and during the Commonwealth were systematically described by *Playford in his *English Dancing Master*. In early years of the 19th cent. the waltz and quadrille drove the country dance out of the English ballroom (with the exception of the popular example known as *Sir Roger de Coverley*); the folk-dance movt. of the 20th cent., however, brought it into considerable use again. Scotland has throughout retained a number of its country dances.

Country Gardens. Eng. country dance-tune to which *The Vicar of Bray* is nowadays sung, but perhaps best known in *Grainger's arr. for pf. (1908–18) and 2 pf. (1918) orch. by L. Artok.

coup d'archet (Fr.). Bow-stroke or bowing.

coup de glotte (Fr.). Blow of the glottis. In v. prod., a method, thought by many to be harmful, of attacking a note by closing the false vocal cords (2 membranes above the true vocal cords) and quickly opening them to release the tone. If the release is too abrupt, a cough will be the result.

coupé (Fr.). In ballet, a step like the *chassé but the displaced foot goes into the air.

Couperin, François (*b* Paris, 1668; *d* Paris, 1733). Fr. composer, harpsichordist, and organist, the most distinguished of his family, known as 'Couperin le Grand' because of his prowess as an organist. Taught by his father Charles and by Jacques Thomelin. Became org. of St Gervais, Paris, in 1685, holding post until his death. In 1693 succeeded Thomelin as org. of Royal chapel, with the title 'organiste du Roi' (Louis XIV). In 1717 became 'ordinaire de la musique de la chambre du Roi', acknowledgement of his special position in the court. On almost every Sun-

day Couperin and colleagues gave chamber concerts for the king, for which he comp. what he called 'Concerts'. These are in the form of suites and may have been intended for the hpd., of which he was a virtuoso, but were probably perf. on vn., viol, ob., bn., and hpd. (*clavecin*). Couperin was greatly influenced by *Corelli and introduced into Fr. the Italian's trio-sonata form, himself publishing in 1726 *Les Nations*, a set of 4 Suites (*Ordres*) for 2 vn. and hpd. Also comp. 'grand trio sonata' sub-titled *Le Parnasse, ou l'Apothéose de Corelli*. In 1716 pubd. famous book *L'*Art de toucher le clavecin*, containing instructions for fingering, methods of touch, and execution of *agréments* (ornamentation) in performing his hpd. pieces. This had strong influence on Bach. His 4 pubd. vols. of hpd. works contain over 230 pieces which proclaim him a supreme master of the kbd. Most have picturesque or descriptive titles and are like miniature tone-poems. This perhaps is a clue to their appeal to Richard Strauss, who orchestrated several Couperin pieces. First complete edn. of Couperin's hpd. mus. was prepared by Brahms and Chrysander, 1871–88. Ravel comp. a 20th-cent. tribute to him in *Le tombeau de Couperin* (1914–17). Prin. works:

CHAMBER MUSIC: *Quatre Concerts Royaux* (1722); *Les Goûts-Réunis ou Nouveaux Concerts* (10 *Concerts* incl. the 'Corelli' Grand Trio, 1724); *Les Nations* (4 *Ordres* for 2 str. and hpd. 1726); *Concert instrumental* ('in memory of the immortal Lully', 1725).

HARPSICHORD: *Pièces de Clavecin*, Book 1 (5 *Ordres*, 1713), Book 2 (7 *Ordres*, 1717), Book 3 (7 *Ordres*, 1722), Book 4 (8 *Ordres*, 1730).

ORGAN: 42 *Pièces d'orgue consistantes en deux Messes* (1690). Also songs and religious works.

Couperin, Louis (*b* Chaumes, *c.*1626; *d* Paris, 1661). Fr. composer and organist, first of his family to be organist at St Gervais (from *c.*1650). Also played vn. and comp. instr. works, incl. 132 pieces for hpd. Uncle of F. *Couperin.

The Couperin family were professional musicians in Paris from late in the 16th cent. to the middle of the 19th. Members were organists at St Gervais for over 170 years. François (*le Grand*) and Louis were the most illustrious of the clan, but others deserving mention were: Margaret-Louise Couperin (*b* Paris, 1676 or 1679; *d* Versailles, 1728), singer and harpsichordist, who is known to have sung mus. by her cousin François; Armand-Louis Couperin (*b* Paris, 1727; *d* Paris, 1789), composer, organist, and harpsichordist. Org. at St Gervais. Well known for his gifts in improvisation and for some pleasant hpd. pieces. Gervais-François Couperin (*b* Paris, 1759; *d* Paris, 1826), son of Armand-Louis, composer and organist. By 1790 was org. of several Paris churches, incl. St Gervais. Played for Napoleon, but comp. a work called *Louis XVIII ou le retour du bonheur en France*.

couple. To arrange, by means of a mechanism called a coupler, that the pedal org. can have one or more of the manuals connected with it so that the effect of its stops is reinforced. Two manuals can be connected in the same way (e.g. the swell may be joined with the great). There are 'super-octave' and 'sub-octave' couplers which duplicate the notes played, an octave higher or lower (on the same stop). Couplers are 4', 8', and 16'.

couplet. (1) Episode in the early Fr. rondo (e.g. by Couperin).

(2) Same as *duplet, i.e. 2 in the time of 3.

(3) The 2-note slur 𝄞 —the 2nd note of which should be slightly curtailed 𝄞.

(4) Stanza of a poem, the mus. being repeated for each stanza.

coupure (Fr.). Cut. Portion omitted, e.g. in orch. score.

courante (Fr.), **corrente** (It.), **coranto, corant**. Running. Fr. dance, at height of popularity in 17th cent., which spread to It. The mus. based on it falls into 2 classifications.

(a) It. variety, in a rapid tempo and in simple triple time. (b) Fr. variety, similar to the above, but with a mixture of simple triple and compound duple rhythms, the latter pertaining especially to the end of each of the 2 sections. Occasionally in Bach's kbd. examples the conflicting rhythms are found together, one in each hand.

In classical suite the courante followed the allemande (see *pavan* and *galliard*). Occasionally it was, in turn, followed by 'Doubles', i.e. variations on itself.

course. Term used of str. instrs., particularly lute family, guitar, etc., meaning a group of strs. tuned in unison or in the octave and plucked simultaneously so as to give extra loudness. In 16th cent., lutes had double-courses on lower strs. The single str. g″ is called a course, thus lutes had 11 strs. in 6 courses. Bass-course is single or double str. running alongside fingerboard without crossing the frets and does not vary in pitch.

Covent Garden. Generally used name for London theatre of which full title is Royal Opera House, Covent Garden (since 1892). So called because site in Bow Street was orig. church property, a convent garden. First th. built there 1732 by John *Gay and used mainly for plays, though 3 of Handel's operas were given there for the first time. Destroyed by fire 1808. Second theatre opened 1809, still mixing plays and opera, but became Royal Italian Opera 1847, retaining title until 1892. Destroyed by fire 1856. Third and present building opened 1858. During 1939–45 was used as dance hall but re-opened 1946 with resident opera and ballet cos. which were renamed Royal Ballet in 1957 and Royal Opera 1969. Between 1924 and 1939 prin. opera conds. at CG were Bruno Walter and Beecham. From 1946 to 1951 Karl *Rankl was mus. dir., being

succeeded by Rafael *Kubelik 1955–8, Georg *Solti 1961–71, Colin *Davis 1971–86, Bernard *Haitink 1987–2002, Antonio Pappano from 2002. Gen. Administrators: David *Webster 1944–70, John Tooley 1970–87, Jeremy Isaacs 1988–97, Genista McIntosh 1997 (resigned), Mary Allen 1997–8, Michael Kaiser 1998–2000, Tony Hall from 2000. Famous manager-impresarios of the past incl. Frederick Gye 1849–77, and Sir Augustus Harris 1888–96.

Coward, (Sir) **Henry** (b Liverpool, 1849; d Sheffield, 1944). Eng. choral conductor. Founded Sheffield Musical Union 1876. Est. of Sheffield Fest. 1895 enabled him to set new standards of choral singing in works of Handel, Bach, and Elgar. Cond. choirs at Leeds, Glasgow, Preston, and Newcastle upon Tyne. Toured N. Amer. 1908 and 1911, also Australia and S. Africa. Advocate of *tonic sol-fa system. Knighted 1926.

Coward, (Sir) **Noël** (Pierce) (b Teddington, 1899; d Blue Harbour, Jamaica, 1973). Eng. actor, playwright, and composer. No formal mus. training. Author and composer of several successful mus. shows and plays with mus., e.g. *This Year of Grace* (1928); *Bitter-Sweet* (1929); *Private Lives* (1930); *Conversation Piece* (1934); *Operette* (1938); *Sail Away* (1961); and several revues in which his songs such as 'Mad Dogs and Englishmen' were perf. (most effectively in his own light bar.). Knighted 1970. Wrote two books of autobiography.

cowbell. As perc. instr., this is the ordinary Central European cowbell with the clapper removed. It is fixed to a drum and struck with the stick of a snare drum. Used by R. Strauss in *Eine Alpensinfonie*, by Mahler in his 6th Sym., and by Elgar in *The *Starlight Express*.

Cowell, Henry (Dixon) (b Menlo Park, Calif., 1897; d Shady, NY, 1965). Amer. composer and pianist, one of those remarkable pioneering figures who belong naturally to the *avant-garde*. Began to play vn. at age 3 and to compose at 11. In 1912 devised pf. technique known as *clusters (tone-clusters) in which adjacent notes are played simultaneously with the forearm or flat of the hand. Also altered sound of pf. by placing objects on the strs. Demonstrated this '*prepared pf.' in S. Francisco, 5 Mar. 1914. Had 100 comps. to his credit when he began formal training in 1914 at Univ. of Calif. with Charles Seeger, who encouraged him to codify the unorthodox rules he was making for himself. This resulted in his book *New Musical Resources* (1919). In the 1920s his recitals attracted notoriety among the public not only because of clusters but because he pioneered other unusual uses of the piano such as plucking the strings or muting them with cardboard or metal. Made 5 tours of Europe between 1923 and 1933, earning friendship of Bartók, Berg, and Schnabel, and studied in Berlin with Schoenberg. In 1922, 17 of his cluster pieces were pubd. Cowell also invented new methods of notation to indicate his intentions and was co- inventor with Theremin in

1931 of early elec. instrument called the *rhythmicon*, which could reproduce exactly the complicated rhythmic combinations in his work. Cowell was also one of the first composers—in the 1930s—to bring an element of indeterminacy into his works, suggesting that parts of them could be assembled by the performers in any order and repeated at will, with some measures to be improvised.

Deeply interested in mus. of other cultures, introducing Eastern instr. in combination with conventional Western ones, e.g. Indian jalatarang and tablas. Studied Persian folk mus. and in his *Ongaku* reproduced Japanese quarter-notes and third-notes. At the other extreme, explored early Amer. mus. culture in a series of works called *Hymn-and-Fuguing-Tunes*. It is not surprising that such an original man should have been friend, companion, and biographer of Charles *Ives or that he should have devoted so much time and energy to lecturing, teaching, writing, publishing, and generally promoting new Amer. mus. Most of his teaching was done as dir. of mus. at the New School for Social Research, NY 1928–63, and at Columbia Univ. 1949–65. Among his pupils were *Gershwin and *Cage. In 1936 was sentenced to 15 years' imprisonment in San Quentin for homosexual offences, but was paroled in 1940 and given a full pardon in 1942 when the evidence against him was found to be false. His list of comps. is very long. Among them are:

OPERA: *O'Higgins of Chile* (1949, unfinished).

ORCH.: 21 syms., incl. No.3 (*Gaelic*, 1942), No.11 (*Seven Rituals of Music*, 1953), No.13 (*Madras*, 1957–8), No.16 (*Icelandic*, 1963); *Synchrony* (1931); *American Melting Pot* (1939); *Shoonthree* (1941); *Hymn-and-Fuguing Tunes* Nos. 2, 3, 5, 10, and 16; 2 Concs. for Koto and orch. (2nd, 1964); *Ongaku* (1957); *Variations for Orch.* (1956), conc. for perc.

Also chamber mus. (5 str. qts.), songs, pf. solos, band works, choral, and org. pieces.

Cowen, (Sir) **Frederic** (Hymen) (*b* Kingston, Jamaica, 1852; *d* London, 1935). Eng. composer and conductor. Comp. operetta at age 8, becoming pupil of Goss and Benedict in same year. Pf. recitalist at 11. Studied Leipzig Cons. with Reinecke and Moscheles 1865–6, and, in 1867, at Stern Cons., Berlin, where he concentrated on cond. Cond. Phil. Soc., London, 1888–92 and 1900–7, Hallé Orch. 1896–9, Liverpool PO 1895–1913, Scottish Orch. 1900–10, Handel Triennial Fests. 1902–23 and several other choral socs. Comp. several operas; 6 syms.; orch. works incl. *The Butterfly's Ball* (1901); 3 oratorios; 9 cantatas; and various other works. Today best remembered by his setting of Longfellow's 'Onaway, awake beloved' (*Hiawatha*). Knighted 1911.

cowhorn. Ancient signalling instrument for calling cattle which by 10th cent. had 2 or 3 fingerholes so that simple melodies could be played. Specially constructed modern versions (*Stierhörner*) were made for Wagner in *Die Walküre*, *Götterdämmerung*, and *Die Meistersinger von Nürnberg*, and for Britten in *Spring Symphony* (1949).

Cowie, Edward (*b* Birmingham, 1943). Eng. composer and painter. Began to compose at age of 11. Chorister, Gloucester Cath. 1955–7. Worked in Poland 1971, being encouraged by Lutosławski. Lect., Lancaster Univ. 1973. Visited USA 1977. Guest prof. of mus., Kassel Univ. 1979, prof. of creative arts, Univ. of Wollongong, NSW, 1983, composer-in-residence RLPO 1983–6. Settled in Australia, where he founded Australian Composers' Ensemble 1988 and became dir., Australian Sinfonietta 1989. Deeply interested in ornithology. Has painted oils and watercolours; his Choral Sym. (1981–2) was inspired by paintings by Turner. Also fascinated by Australian criminal Ned Kelly, making him the basis of several works, incl. an opera. Prin. works:

STAGE WORKS: *Commedia*, Op.12, opera (1976–8); *Kelly*, Op.23, opera (1980–2); *Kate Kelly's Roadshow*, Op.27, mez., ens. (1982).

ORCH.: *Concerto for Orchestra*, Op.19 (1979–80); *Leonardo*, Op.20, chamber orch. (1980–1); sym. No.1 (*The American*), Op.21 (1980–1), No.2 (*The Australian*), Op.28 (1982–3); concs.: bcl. and tape, Op.1b (1969), cl. No.2, Op.5 (1975), pf., Op.8 (1976–7), hp., Op.26 (1981–2), vc. (1993), ob. (1998–9); *Four Orchestral Songs* (1991); *Denge Wood Wind Music*, ww., brass (1995); *From Moment to Moment*, chamber orch. (1999).

CHAMBER MUSIC: str. qts.: No.1 (1973), No.2, Op.11 (1977), No.3, Op.31 No.1 (1983), No.4 (*Australia II*), Op.31 No.2 (1983), No.5 (1994); *Kelly Passacaglia*, str. qt. (1980); *Harlequin*, Op.15, hp. (1980); *Commedia Lazzis*, Op.17, guitar (1980); *Kelly-Nolan-Kelly*, Op.22, cl. in A (1980); fl. qt. (1991); vn. sonata (1991); . . . *with angels and delight* . . ., vc. (1994); *Skanagoah*, gui., db. (1994); *Kandinsky*, 4 gui. (1995); *Dartmoor Etudes*, ob., cl., hp. (1999); *Several Charms*, vn., pf. (2000).

Also many choral and vocal works, comps. for brass, and for solo pf.

'cowpat music'. Derogatory term coined by Elisabeth *Lutyens to describe Eng. pastoral school of composers—e.g. Vaughan Williams, Holst, Ireland, and Bax. First used (as 'the cowpat school') in a lecture she gave at Dartington summer sch. of mus. in 1950s, referring to 'folky-wolky melodies on the cor anglais'.

Cox, David Harold (*b* Southsea, Hants, 1945). Eng. composer and teacher. On mus. staff, Sheffield Univ. from 1970. Works incl. opera *Disappearing Act* (1968); *Orpheus in the Underworld*, female v., pf. (1976); hn. trio (1978); ob. sonata (1975); cl. trio (1972); 2-pf. sonata (1974); pf. sonata (1970); *Variations on a Theme by Mozart*, solo cl. (1978); *The Presage*, unacc. ch., elec. tape (1977).

Cox, David (Vassall) (*b* Broadstairs, 1916; *d* Pratt's Bottom, London, 1997). Eng. composer, pianist, and critic. Mus. organizer, BBC External

Services 1956–76. Comps. incl. many choral and vocal works, opera *The Children in the Forest*. Author of book on Debussy (1974) and history of the Henry Wood Promenade Concerts (1980).

Cox, Frederic (Robert) (*b* London, 1905; *d* Altrincham, 1985). Eng. singing teacher, singer, and composer. London début as ten. and composer 1938. Served in Home Office 1939–45 (OBE). Worked in London 1946–9 with Joseph Hislop. Prof. of singing, RMCM, 1949–53, Prin. 1953–70 (Prin. Emeritus 1970). Head of Vocal Dept., TCL 1970–5. Chairman, London Orchestras Concert Board, 1970–5. Singing teacher at RNCM, Manchester, 1975–84. One of most distinguished singing teachers of his time. Pupils incl. John Mitchinson, Joseph Ward, Ryland Davies, Anne Howells, Elizabeth Harwood, Sandra Browne, Ann Murray, and many more. During his 17 years as Prin., opera prods. at RMCM achieved a standard which attracted int. attention and admiration.

Cox, Jean (*b* Gadsden, Alabama, 1922). Amer. tenor. Début New Eng. Opera Th. 1953 (Lensky in *Eugene Onegin*). Sang in Kiel 1953–4; Brunswick 1955–9; Mannheim Opera from 1959. Bayreuth début 1956; CG 1975; NY Met 1976.

Cox, John (*b* Bristol, 1935). Eng. opera producer. Opera début as producer 1965, SW, *L'Enfant et les sortilèges* (Ravel). Dir., Music Th. Ens. 1967–70. Glyndebourne 1970–83, dir. of prods. 1971–81 (six Strauss prods. in that time), working with such designers as Erté, Hugh Casson, and David Hockney, and incl. f. Brit. p. of *The *Visit of the Old Lady*. Gen. admin. Scottish Opera 1981–6, art. dir. 1985–6, incl. f. Brit. p. of Cavalli's *Egisto*. Dir. of Prod., CG, from 1988. Notable Strauss, Mozart, and Stravinsky prods. NY Met début 1982 (*Il barbiere di Siviglia*). Has worked in world's leading opera houses, producing *Daphne* in Munich (1986), and the 1st vers. of *Ariadne auf Naxos* in Salzburg (1991). Prod. Rossini's *Il viaggio a Reims* and Strauss's *Die Frau ohne Schatten* (both CG 1992).

Cox and Box. Operetta in 1 act by *Sullivan to lib. by F. C. Burnand after farce *Box and Cox* by Maddison Morton. Prod. London 1867, NY 1875.

cracovienne. See *krakowiak*.

Cradle will Rock, The. Opera-musical in 1 act by *Blitzstein (1936) to his own lib. on conflict between steel magnate and trade union. Prod. NY 1937.

Craft, Robert (Lawson) (*b* Kingston, NY, 1923). Amer. conductor, musicologist, and author. Skilled interpreter of mus. of Webern, Schoenberg, Berg, and especially of Stravinsky with whom he was on terms of intimate friendship, collaborating with him in recordings and in 6 vols. of conversations and memoirs. Encouraged Stravinsky to compose in serial method. Has also written *Stravinsky: Chronicle of a Friendship* (1972), and several other Stravinsky vols. Conducted

Amer. première of Berg's *Lulu* (3-act version), Santa Fe 1979, having cond. the 2-act version there in 1963.

Craig, Charles (James) (*b* London, 1920; *d* Banbury, 1997). Eng. tenor. Concert début with Beecham 1952. Opera début 1953 with Carl Rosa (*La bohème*). Prin. tenor SW 1956–9. CG début 1959; ENO 1980; Salzburg Fest. 1970. Sang nearly 50 roles at all leading opera houses. Noted for his interpretation of title-role in *Otello* and of Siegmund in *Die Walküre*.

Cramer, Johann Baptist (*b* Mannheim, 1771; *d* London, 1858). Ger.-born pianist, composer, and teacher, descendant of distinguished mus. family, most of whom worked in Eng. Came to London when 3 years old and became pupil of *Clementi 1783–4, having made début as pianist in London, Apr. 1781. Toured Europe 1788–91 and 1799–1800, meeting Haydn and Beethoven. High reputation in London as pf. teacher; pubd. first book of *Studies* (eventually composing 84) in 1804. These *Studies* are still in use, having survived his 105 sonatas and 9 concs. In 1824, with 2 partners, founded publishing firm of J. B. Cramer and Co., remaining until 1842. (After Cramer's death this firm added manufacture of pfs. to its activities.) Founder-member and dir., Phil. Soc. 1813, and one of orig. partners of *Chappell & Co., who issued his *Studies* from 1812.

Cranmer, Philip (*b* Birmingham, 1918; *d* Balcombe, W. Sussex, 2006). Eng. teacher and composer. BBC staff accompanist, Birmingham 1948–50, Lect., Birmingham Univ. 1950–4; Prof. of Mus., Queen's Univ., Belfast, 1954–70, Manchester Univ. 1970–5. Secretary, Associated Board, Royal Schs. of Mus. 1974–83.

crash cymbal. See *Chinese crash cymbal*.

Crawford [Seeger], **Ruth** (Porter) (*b* East Liverpool, Ohio, 1901; *d* Chevy Chase, Md., 1953). Amer. composer. Taught at Sch. of Mus. Arts, Jacksonville, Fla., 1918–21. At Amer. Cons., Chicago, 1920–9 as student and teacher. Studied comp. NY 1929 with Charles Seeger, whom she married. Transcr. several thousand Amer. folksongs from recordings in Library of Congress and wrote pf. acc. for over 300. Her comps., atonal and often dissonant, anticipated many *avant-garde* procedures. They incl. 9 pf. preludes (1924–8), vn. sonata (1927), str. qt. (1931), some songs, and other works.

Craxton, (Thomas) **Harold** (*b* London, 1885; *d* London, 1971). Eng. pianist and teacher. Taught at Matthay's Pf. Sch. 1914–40 and at RAM 1919–61. Noted accompanist. Ed. Beethoven sonatas (with Tovey) and Chopin for Associated Board of RSM. OBE 1960.

Craxton, Janet (*b* London, 1929; *d* London, 1981). Eng. oboist. Daughter of Harold *Craxton. Prin. ob. Hallé Orch. 1949–52, London Mozart Players 1952–4, BBC SO 1954–63, London Sinfonietta from 1969. Prin. oboe, Royal Opera

Orch., 1980–1. Also frequent soloist and recitalist. Gave f.p., with Wilfred Brown (ten.), of Vaughan Williams's 10 Blake Songs, 1958. Prof. of ob. RAM.

Crazy Jane. Work for sop., cl., vc., and pf. by Richard Rodney Bennett, comp. 1968–9, f.p. (TV) 1970.

Creation, The (Die Schöpfung). Oratorio for sop., ten., bass, ch., and orch. by Haydn, comp. 1796–8, at suggestion of *Salomon to text by unknown Eng. author trans. into Ger. by Baron Gottfried van Swieten who also provided a re-trans. into Eng. (later modified). F.p. Vienna 1798, London 1800, Boston, Mass. (complete) 1819. Contains famous sop. aria 'With verdure clad' and ch. 'The heavens are telling the glory of God'. A trans. by Haydn's London friend Mrs. Anne Hunter has recently been discovered and used in perf.

Création du monde, La (The Creation of the World). Ballet in 1 act, mus. *Milhaud, lib. Cendrars, choreog. Börlin. Prod. Paris 1923. Later choreog. de Valois, MacMillan, and others.

Creation Mass (Schöpfungsmesse). Name for Haydn's Mass No.11 in B♭, comp. 1801, because there is a quotation from The Creation in the Qui tollis.

Creatures of Prometheus, The (Beethoven). See Prometheus, Die Geschöpfe des.

crécelle (Fr.). Rattle.

Crécquillon, Thomas (b c.1490; d ?Béthune, 1557). Fr.-Flemish composer. Probably choirmaster to Emperor Charles V. Wrote over 200 chansons, over 100 motets, 12 masses, and other church mus. Regarded as one of leading composers of post-Josquin Després generation.

Credo (I believe). Section of the Proper of the *Mass frequently set by composers. Operatically speaking, the 'Credo' refers to Iago's aria in Act II of Verdi's Otello in which he states his belief in a cruel god.

Creighton, Robert. See Creyghton, Robert.

crembalum. *Jew's harp.

Cremona. (1) Org. stop much like *clarinet.
(2) It. town where lived several famous makers of str. instr., e.g. *Stradivarius, *Guarneri, and *Amati.

Creole music. Indigenous mus. of Lat. Amer. Has distinctive rhythms, and melodies often acc. by a short bass phrase much repeated with slight changes. The *castanets are used.

crescendo (<) (It., abbreviation cresc.). Growing. Directive used by composers to indicate that a passage should gradually increase in loudness. Sometimes the direction is crescendo poco a poco, meaning to increase the loudness by degrees (little by little) or subito crescendo (suddenly increasing in loudness). One also speaks of 'a crescendo', meaning a striking example of this

feature such as is found frequently in the mus. of Rossini. According to Dr *Burney, the device was first used in Terradellas's opera Bellerofonte (London 1747): it was much exploited in the orch. mus. of J. *Stamitz and his colleagues at the Mannheim court as the celebrated 'Mannheim crescendo'. (Some writers betray their lack of mus. knowledge by using the phrase 'rising to a crescendo', which is obvious nonsense.) The opposite is *diminuendo. See hairpins.

crescendo pedal. An org. device which gradually brings into action all the stops.

crescent. Turkish instr. comprising small bells hung from an inverted crescent. Also known as *'Jingling Johnny'.

Crescentini, Girolamo (b Urbania, 1762; d Naples, 1846). It. mezzo-soprano castrato. Sang in Sarti opera in Padua 1782. Visited London 1785, being coolly received, and spent next 10 years in major Eur. opera houses, his repertory being chiefly operas by Zingarelli, Mayr, Cimarosa, and Gazzaniga. Sang at Teatro São Carlos, Lisbon, 1799–1803, and was also its manager. Lived in Paris 1806–12 as singing teacher to Napoleon's family. Retired 1812 and returned to It., teaching at Naples Cons. Isabella *Colbran was one of his pupils. Also a composer.

Crespin, Régine (b Marseilles, 1927). Fr. soprano. Début Mulhouse 1950 as Elsa in Lohengrin, Paris Opéra later in 1950 in same role. Bayreuth 1958–60; Glyndebourne 1959–60; CG 1960; Amer. début Chicago 1962; NY Met 1962; Salzburg Easter Fest. 1967; mez. roles from 1971. Last appearance Paris 1989 as Countess in The Queen of Spades. Retired 1989, taught at Paris Cons. Distinguished concert career, esp. in Berlioz Les Nuits d'été.

Cresswell, Lyell (b Wellington, NZ, 1944). NZ composer. Settled in Brit. 1972. Taught at Aberdeen Univ. 1973–4, Glasgow Univ. 1976–7. Mus. organizer, Chapter Arts Centre, Cardiff, 1978–80. Works incl. vn. conc.; conc. for 2 orchs.; Translations, sop., ch., orch., tape; 4 Sentimental Songs, sop., pf., bamboo chimes, bag of wooden clothes pegs; Wagner is a Fink, brass band; Music for Skinheads, 4 percussionists; 3 str. qts.; Salm, orch; O! for Orchestra, orch.; Taking a Line for a Walk, elec. tape; vc. conc.; Passacagli, orch.; Speak for us, great sea, orch.; A Modern Ecstasy, mez., bar., orch.

Creston, Paul [Guttoveggio, Giuseppe] (b NY, 1906; d San Diego, 1985). Amer. composer and organist of It. origin. Org., St Malachy's, NY, 1934–67. Prof. of mus., Cent. Washington State Coll., 1968–75. Comps. incl.:

ORCH: Partita, fl., vn., str. (1937); A Rumor, str. (1941); 6 syms. (1941–82); Walt Whitman (1952); Invocation and Dance (1953); Corinthians: XIII (1963); Pavane Variations (1966); Jubilee, band, (1971); concertos: marimba (1940), sax. (1941), harp

(*Poem*) (1945), tb. (*Fantasy*) (1947), pf. (No.1 1949, No.2 1962), 2 pf. (No.1 1951, No.2 1968), vn. (No.1 1956, No.2 1960), accordion (1958). Also choral works, chamber mus., songs, pf. pieces.

Creyghton [Creighton], **Robert** (*b* c.1636; *d* Wells, 1734). Eng. composer. Canon and precentor of Wells Cath. 1674–1734. Wrote anthems and settings of church services. Prof. of Greek, Cambridge Univ., 1666–72.

Creyghtonian Seventh. Mannerism of *Creyghton, i.e. preceding final perfect cadence by subdominant chord with added 7th (e.g. in key C, F–A–C–E).

Cries of London. Orig. the calls of street salesmen (hawkers) in selling their wares; over 150 have been collected. Some Eng. composers, e.g. Gibbons and Weelkes, incorporated these mus. cries into their works. The 20th-cent. composer *Berio has written a work called *Cries of London* and Vaughan Williams incorporates a reminiscence of the lavender-seller's cry into his *London Symphony*.

Cristofori, Bartolomeo (*b* Padua, 1655; *d* Florence, 1731). It. harpsichord-maker and regarded as inventor of the pianoforte. Served at Medici court in Florence from 1690. In 1700 constructed a *gravicembalo col piano e forte* (hpd. with softness and loudness). This was a forerunner of the modern pf.: he substituted the blows of a series of hammers for the hpd. plucking of the str. By 1720 he improved it by graduating the force of the fall of the hammers and by putting a damper above instead of under the str. The compass was over 4 octaves. Only 3 Cristofori pfs. survive, so far as is known (in NY, Leipzig, and Rome).

Critic, The, or An Opera Rehearsal. Opera in 2 acts by Stanford, his Op.144, to lib. by L. C. James based on Sheridan's comedy (1779). Comp. 1915. Prod. London 1916.

criticism, musical. The profession of writing about the aesthetics, history, and evolution of mus. and of reviewing mus. comps. and perfs. in newspapers, periodicals, books, and on the radio and TV. No one can say exactly when criticism began, but in the sense understood today it developed parallel with the spread of the printed word. By its nature, criticism is controversial and often resented, but there are several examples of a critic's, or group of critics', championship of a composer or a branch of comp. which has had beneficial results (e.g. the revival of interest in Mahler since c.1950). The first periodical devoted to mus. was Mattheson's *Critica musica*, founded in Hamburg 1722. In Fr. the first was *Journal de musique française et italienne* in 1764, though the pamphlets written during the *Querelle des *Bouffons* 1752–4 perhaps count as criticism. In Eng. the *New Musical and Universal Magazine* was founded in 1774. The last vol. of *Burney's *History of Music*, 1789, abounds in candid criticism of composers and performers of his day.

The first professional critic was probably J. F. Rochlitz (1769–1842), ed. of the *Allgemeine Musikalische Zeitung* in Leipzig, and champion of Bach. Journalism in Ger. daily papers began with F. Rellstate, who wrote for the Berlin *Vossische Zeitung* 1803–13, but the first newspaper to appoint a professionally-trained musician as critic was *The Times* of London, through the influence of one of its managers, Thomas Alsager, a musical enthusiast. Eng. criticism in the 19th cent. was dominated by J. W. *Davison of *The Times* (1846–79) and H. F. *Chorley, of the *Athenaeum* (weekly) from 1833 to 1868. One of the first men to write about mus. and musicians not as an expert but as a fine journalist was Heinrich Heine in the 19th-cent. *Allgemeine Zeitung* of Augsburg. There have been many examples of composers who wrote criticism, notably Robert Schumann in the *Neue Zeitschrift für Musik* (in which he advanced the causes of Chopin, Berlioz, and Brahms), Berlioz in the *Journal des Débats* from 1835 to 1863 (although the outstanding critic of the day in Fr. was F. J. *Fétis, who founded the *Revue musicale*), Wolf (in the *Wiener Salon-Blatt*), Weber, Wagner, and Debussy (under the pseudonym *Monsieur Croche*), and Robin Holloway. In Vienna, where critical polemics reach a high voltage, the most illustrious and historically significant critic was Eduard *Hanslick, the 'Bismarck of music criticism' (Verdi), known for his extreme partisanship in the divergence of views on Wagner and Brahms. This resulted in his being immortalized by his opponent Wagner as Beckmesser in *Die Meistersinger* (Wagner originally called the character Hanslich). Nevertheless Hanslick is still highly readable.

In the USA several critics have achieved a reputation beyond the local sphere of their activities, notably Philip Hale of Boston, and (from NY) Lawrence Gilman, H. E. Krehbiel, Olin Downes, and Richard Aldrich. Outstanding among Brit. mus. critics of the past have been Bernard Shaw (the most entertaining of all), Ernest *Newman, a Wagner authority, Neville *Cardus, and H. C. *Colles.

Croce, Giovanni (*b* Chioggia, c.1558; *d* Venice, 1609). It. composer and priest. Choirmaster St Mark's, Venice, from 1603, having been deputy for 12 years. Wrote masses and motets (pubd. in Venice between 1594 and 1601), and other church mus. His secular madrigals were pubd. between 1590 and 1595. In one of his 'caprices' in Venetian dialect, he anticipated Mahler by setting a text about a song-contest between the cuckoo and the nightingale judged by a parrot (in Mahler's case, a donkey).

croche (Fr.). Hook. The 8th-note or quaver (not the crotchet).

Croche, Monsieur. Pseudonym under which *Debussy wrote some of his mus. criticisms, himself making a selection in 1917 called *Monsieur Croche anti-dilettante* (pubd. 1921).

Croft, William (*b* Nether Ettington, Warwicks., 1677 or 1678; *d* Bath, 1727). Eng. composer and organist. By 1700 had collab. with Blow and others in *Ayres for the Harpsichord or Spinet*. Org., St Anne, Soho, 1700–12. Joint org., Chapel Royal 1704, org. 1707, and master of the children and composer to Chapel Royal from 1708. Org., Westminster Abbey from 1708. D.Mus., Oxford Univ., 1713, submitting two odes for soloists, ch., and orch. Comp. many fine anthems and a Burial Service, also hpd. works, cantatas, vn. sonatas, and songs. Also wrote hymn-tune 'St Anne' to which is sung 'O God, our Help in Ages Past'.

Croiza [Conelly], **Claire** (*b* Paris, 1882; *d* Paris, 1946). Fr. mezzo-soprano. Opera début Nancy 1905. Sang for many years at Th. de la Monnaie, Brussels. Paris Opéra début 1908 as Dalila in *Samson et Dalila*. Taught at École Normale, Paris, from 1922 and at Paris Cons. from 1934, her pupils incl. Souzay and Micheau. Greatly admired by Fr. composers for her sensitive artistry. Sang Angel in Elgar's *Dream of Gerontius* at f. Paris p. 1906.

croma (It.). 8th-note or quaver.

cromatico, cromatica, cromatici, cromatice (It.). Chromatic. The *corno cromatico* is the valve hn.

cromorne. (1) On Fr. org. a delicate type of cl. stop.
(2) Fr. name for the *crumhorn (not encountered until 17th cent.).

crook. Detachable accessory section of tubing applied to the mouthpiece of brass instr. such as hns. and tpts. to lengthen the instr.'s tube and thus to give it a different basic key. (Players generally carried 10 or 12 crooks.) Natural tpts. or hns., without valves or slides, could play only the notes of the harmonic series, the crook enabling the player to transpose the fundamental note. Thus for a hn.-player, with all parts written in C, to play in D, he would fit a D crook. The introduction of *valves from *c*.1850 almost eliminated the need for crooks. The term is applied also to the bent metal tube connecting the body of the bn. with the reed, and to comparable detachable bent tubes at mouthpieces of cls. and saxs.

croon. To sing softly to a baby, but the wider usage since 1930s means to sing softly, and often sentimentally, with a dance band. Practitioners are known as 'crooners', the most eminent being Bing Crosby, though he was preceded by 'Whispering' Jack Smith and Rudy Vallee.

Crosby, Bing [Lillis, Harry] (*b* Tacoma, 1904; *d* La Moraleja golf course, Madrid, 1977). Amer. singer and actor. Drummer in school bands and in jazz groups in Spokane. One of Rhythm Boys who sang with Paul Whiteman Orch. 1926–30 and appeared in film *The King of Jazz* (1930). Successful radio career as solo singer from 1931, with '*signature-tune' *Where the blue of the night*. Made many other films, incl. *Holiday Inn* (1942), in which he sang Irving Berlin's 'White Christmas', and those in which he had a comedy part-

nership with Bob Hope and Dorothy Lamour. For his part as priest in *Going My Way* (1944) he won a Motion Picture Academy Award. Influenced by Al Jolson and developed a very personal intimate style of crooning.

Crosby, John (O'Hea) (*b* NY, 1926; *d* NY, 2002). Amer. conductor and administrator. Accompanist, coach, and cond., NY City Opera 1951–6. Built outdoor opera house at *Santa Fe, New Mexico, 1956 (burned down and rebuilt 1967), and founded Santa Fe Fest. 1957. Specialized in Strauss. Pres., Opera America 1975–80; pres., Manhattan Sch. of Mus. 1976–86.

Cross, Joan (*b* London, 1900; *d* Aldeburgh, 1993). Eng. soprano and opera producer. Joined Lilian *Baylis's Old Vic opera ch. 1924, graduating to leading roles. Prin. sop., SW Opera 1931–46, and dir. 1943–5. Début CG 1931 (Mimì) and sang there 1947–54. Founder member EOG 1946–54. With Anne Wood, est. Opera School in 1948 (which in 1955 became Nat. Sch. of Opera), being dir. 1948–64. Prod. operas at SW, CG, Oslo, Amsterdam, and Toronto. Dir., Phoenix Opera Co. Joint translator (with E. *Crozier) of Smetana's *The Bartered Bride*. Created five roles in Britten operas: Ellen Orford in *Peter Grimes* (1945), Female Chorus in *The Rape of Lucretia* (1946), Lady Billows in *Albert Herring* (1947), Elizabeth I in *Gloriana* (1953), and Mrs Grose in *The Turn of the Screw* (1954). CBE 1951.

cross-accent. Variation of expected accentuation of notes by shifting beat to a point ahead of or behind its normal point in a rhythmic pattern. If this is maintained for some time it becomes *syncopation.

Crosse, Gordon (*b* Bury, 1937). Eng. composer. Tutor, extra-mural dept., Birmingham Univ. 1964–6 and in mus. dept. 1966–9. Fellow in Mus., Essex Univ., 1969–76. Works incl.:

OPERAS: *Purgatory* (1965); *The Grace of Todd* (1969); *The Story of Vasco* (1974).

MUSIC DRAMA: *Wheel of the World* (1972); *World Within*, speaker, sop., chamber ens. (1977).

BALLET: *Young Apollo* (1984).

ORCH.: *Elegy* (1959); Concerto da camera (vn. conc. No.1) (1962); sym. No.1 (1964), No.2 (1975); *Ceremony*, vc., orch. (1966); vc. conc. (1979); vn. conc. No.2 (1969); *Some Marches on a Ground* (1970); *Ariadne*, ob. and 12 players (1972); *Epiphany Variations* (1975–6); *Play Ground* (1977); *Wildboy*, concertante, cl. and 8 players (1977); *Thel*, fl., 2 str. septets, 2 hns. (1978); Studies for str. qt., set 2 (1977); sym. No.1 for chamber orch. (1976 rev. of Sinfonia Concertante, 1965); *Dreamsongs*, small orch. (1979); *Elegy and Scherzo alla marcia* (adapted from str. qt.) (1981); *Peace for Brass*, brass band (1981); *Array*, tpt., str. (1986); *Quiet*, wind band (1987).

CHORAL: *Changes*, sop., bar., ch., orch. (1965); *The Covenant of the Rainbow*, ch., org. (1968); *Harvest Songs*, ch., orch. (1980); *Dreamcanon I*, ch., 2 pf., perc. (1981); *Sea Psalms*, ch., children's vv., orch. (1989–90).

VOCAL: *For the Unfallen*, ten., hn., str. (1968); *Memories of Morning, Night*, mez., orch. (1971); *The New World*, 6 poems by Ted Hughes, v., pf. (1978); *Wintersong*, 6 soloists, opt. perc. (1986).

CHAMBER MUSIC: str. qt. (1980); *Wave Songs*, vc., pf. (1983); *Fear No More*, ob., ob. d'amore, ca. (1981); *Chime*, brass quintet (1983); pf. trio (1986).

FOR CHILDREN: **Meet My Folks!* (poems by Ted Hughes), spkr., children's ch., instr. (1964); *Potter Thompson* (A. Garner), mus. drama, solo vv., children's ch., orch. (1974); *Holly from the Bongs* (A. Garner), Nativity opera (1974).

cross-fingering. On woodwind instr., fingering the ascending or descending scale in a manner contrary to the normal order of lifting or lowering successive fingers.

Crossley, Ada (*b* Tarraville, Gippsland, Australia, 1874; *d* London, 1929). Australian contralto. Melbourne début 1892; London 1895. Reputation chiefly in oratorio.

Crossley, Paul (Christopher Richard) (*b* Dewsbury, 1944). Eng. pianist. Studied Oxford Univ. Won Messiaen pf. comp., Royaun, 1968. Début Tours 1968. Specialist in Romantics (Liszt, Brahms, etc.) and in sonatas of Tippett whose 3rd sonata (Bath Fest. 1973) and 4th sonata (Los Angeles 1985) were comp. for him. Joint art. dir., London Sinfonietta, 1988–94.

Crossley-Holland, Peter (Charles) (*b* London, 1916; *d* London, 2001). Eng. musicologist, composer, and writer on music. BBC mus. staff 1948–63. Special study of Welsh folk mus. and authority on oriental mus. Comps. incl. cantata *The Sacred Dance*. Prof. of mus., UCLA from 1972, having joined faculty in 1969.

cross-rhythm. Regular shift of some beats in a metric pattern to points ahead of or behind their normal positions, e.g. division of 9/8 into 2 + 2 + 2 + 3 quavers.

crotales (Fr.). Perc. instr. Ancient Gr. *crotalum* was rattle or clapper similar to castanets, consisting of wooden or metal shells struck together. The modern version, employed by Ravel and others, consists of small cymbals of thick metal tuned to a definite pitch.

Crotch, William (*b* Norwich, 1775; *d* Taunton, 1847). Eng. organist, teacher, and composer. Child prodigy, giving org. recitals in London when 4, a pupil-ass. org. of King's and Trinity Colleges, Cambridge, at 11, wrote oratorio *The Captivity of Judah* at 14; org., Ch. Ch. Cath., Oxford, at 15, took B.Mus. at 19, became Oxford prof. of mus. (and org. St John's Coll.) at 22 (1797) and D.Mus. 1799. Left Oxford for London 1807 (but remained prof. of mus.) and gave org. and pf. recitals. His sym. was perf. at Philharmonic Soc. concert 1814. First Prin., RAM, 1822–32. Comp. prolifically in many genres. His ch. *Lo, star-led chiefs* from the oratorio *Palestine* (1812) is still heard as an anthem. Retired 1834.

crotchet (♩) (Fr. *noire*; Ger. *Viertelnote*; It. *semiminima*). The 'quarter-note', i.e. a quarter the time-value of the whole-note or semibreve.

Crown Imperial. March by Walton comp. for coronation of George VI in 1937. Score is headed by line from poem 'In Honour of the City' by Dunbar (1465–1520) 'In beautie beryng the crone imperiall'. F. public p. Westminster Abbey, 12 May 1937, cond. Boult (it had already been recorded and broadcast). Rev. 1963. Also arr. for military band, pf., and organ. See also *Orb and Sceptre*.

Crown of India, The. Masque, Op.66, by Elgar, for cont. and bass soloists, ch., and orch. to words by H. Hamilton. Written to celebrate Delhi Durbar 1911 and f.p. London 1912. Also orch. suite, 1912.

Crozier, Eric (John) (*b* London, 1914; *d* Granville, Normandy, 1994). Eng. writer and opera producer. BBC TV producer 1936–9. Closely assoc. with **Britten, being co-founder of EOG 1946, and of Aldeburgh Fest. 1948. Librettist of Britten's cantata *St Nicolas*, and operas *Albert Herring*, *Let's Make an Opera*, and (with E. M. Forster) **Billy Budd*, and of Berkeley's **Ruth*. Also wrote commentary for concert vers. of *The Young Person's Guide to the Orchestra* (1946). Trans. many operas. Prod. f.p. of *Peter Grimes* in London 1945 and in Tanglewood 1946, and of *Rape of Lucretia*, Glyndebourne 1946. Taught at Britten-Pears Sch., Snape. OBE 1991.

Crucifixion, The. Oratorio for ten. and bass soloists, ch., org., and orch. by **Stainer, comp. 1887 to text written by J. S. Simpson, with selections from the Bible. Congregation may join in 5 hymns (omitted in some perfs.).

Crucifixus. See *Mass*.

Cruft, Adrian (Francis) (*b* Mitcham, 1921; *d* London, 1987). Eng. composer, conductor, and teacher. Played db. in London orchs. 1947–69. Prof., RCM, from 1962. Chairman, Composers' Guild 1966. Comps. incl. *Partita* for orch.; *Divertimento* for str.; *Prospero's Island*; cantata *Alma Redemptoris Mater*; other choral works; and songs. See below.

Cruft, Eugene (John) (*b* London, 1887; *d* London, 1976). Eng. double-bass player. In Beecham Orch. 1909, prin. db. BBC SO 1929–49, CG Orch. 1949–52, Bath Fest. Orch. 1959–65. Prof. of db. RCM 1946–57. Organized coronation orchs. 1937 and 1953. Assoc. with many chamber orchs. Father of John and Adrian **Cruft. OBE 1953.

Cruft, John (Herbert) (*b* London, 1914). Eng. oboist and administrator. Mus. dir., Arts Council 1965–78. Oboist LPO 1937–9, Orchestre de la Suisse Romande 1939–40, LSO 1946–9, prof. of ob. RCM 1947–9, Secretary, LSO 1949–59, dir. of mus., Brit. Council 1959–61, of drama and mus. 1961–5. Son of Eugene **Cruft.

Crüger, Johannes (*b* Gross-Breesen, Prussia, 1598; *d* Berlin, 1662). Ger. composer and cantor.

Became tutor to army captain's family 1616 and entered Univ. of Wittenberg as theology student 1620. Cantor and org., St Nicholas, Berlin, from 1622 till death. Wrote text-book on thoroughbass. Comp. masses, motets, concs., and hymntunes. In vol. of hymn-tunes pubd. 1644 occur the famous chorales *Nun danket alle Gott, Schmücke dich, o liebe Seele,* and *Jesu, meine Freude,* all used later by Bach.

Crumb, George (Henry) (*b* Charleston, West Virginia, 1929). Amer. composer. Taught pf. and comp. at Univ. of Colorado at Boulder, 1959–64. Joined mus. dept., Univ. of Pa., 1965, becoming prof. of humanities 1983. His mus. is highly individual. Early influence was Webern, and has developed interest in new sonorities combined with a comp. technique which is sometimes fragmented and sometimes aleatory. This is not employed for freakish effect and his presentation of his ideas remains comprehensible, as in his 1972 fantasy-pieces for amplified pf. called *Makrokosmos* which employ many unusual pf. methods with poetic results. His other works incl.:

ORCH.: *Variazioni* (1959); *Echoes of time and the River* (1967, also as mus. th. 1970); *A Haunted Landscape* (1984).

VOICE(s) & INSTR(s).: *Night Music I,* sop., pf. or cel., perc. (1963); *Madrigals, Book I,* sop., vib., db. (1965); *Book II,* sop., fl., perc. (1965); *Book III,* sop., hp., 1 perc. (1969); *Book IV,* sop., fl., hp., db., 1 perc. (1969); *Songs, Drones, and Refrains of Death,* bar., elec. gui., elec. db., amp. pf., amp. hpd., 2 perc. (1968); *Night of the 4 Moons,* alt., alto fl., banjo., elec. vc., 1 perc. (1969); *Ancient Voices of Children,* sop., boy sop., ob., mandolin., hp., elec. pf., 3 perc. (1970); *Lux aeterna for 5 Masked Players,* sop., bfl., sitar, 2 perc. (1971); *Star-Child,* sop., children's vv., male spkrs., bellringers, orch. (1977); *Apparition,* sop., amp. pf. (1979); *Federico's Little Songs,* sop., fl., perc. (1986); *Unto the Hills,* sop., pf., perc. qt. (2001); *Winds of Destiny,* sop., pf., perc. qt. (2004).

INSTRUMENTAL: str. qt. (1954); vc. sonata (1955); 5 pieces, pf. (1962); *4 Nocturnes (Night Music II),* vn., pf. (1963); *Eleven Echoes of Autumn,* vn., fl., cl., pf. (1965); *Black Angels (Images I),* 'electric' str. qt. (1970); *Vox balaenae (Voice of the Whale),* 3 masked players, elec. fl., elec. vc., amp. pf. (1971); *Dream Sequence (Images II),* vn., vc., pf., perc. (1976); *A Little Suite for Christmas,* AD *1979,* pf. (1979); *Gnomic Variations,* pf. (1981); *Pastoral Drone,* org. (1982); *Processional,* pf. (1983); *An Idyll for the Misbegotten,* amp. fl., 3 perc. (1985); *Zeitgeist,* 2 amp. pf. (1987); *Easter Dawning,* carillon (1991); *Quest,* gui., sax., hp., db., perc. (1994); *Mundus canis,* gui., perc. (1998); *Eine kleine Mitternachtmusik,* pf. (2002); *Otherworldly Resonances,* 2 pf. (2003).

Several of Crumb's works are settings of the poems of Lorca.

crumhorn (Old Eng. *crump*; Fr. *cromorne*; Ger. *Krummhorn*). Earliest and most common of Renaissance *reed-cap instr., the name meaning 'curved horn'. Characteristic shape is like a fishhook. Name first occurred in 1489 describing an org.-stop in Dresden, and this implied that the instr. had been in use for some time. Survived in Fr. until the middle of the 17th cent. Standard consort of crumhorns was alto (in G), 2 tens., and bass. Sop. crumhorn (*stortina*) was a rarity but occurs in music by *Corteccia. Crumhorns had 7 finger-holes with 3 extension keys for low notes. With revival of interest in early music, crumhorns have been manufactured since the 1950s.

Crusell, Bernhard Henrik (*b* Uusikaupunki, Finland, 1775; *d* Stockholm, 1838). Finnish composer, conductor, teacher, and virtuoso player of clarinet for which he wrote 3 concs. (1811, 1818, 1828) and 3 qts. (1811, 1817, 1823). Was clarinettist in military band at age of 12. Visited Weber in Dresden 1822. Also comp. opera and translated Fr., Ger., and It. operas for the Swed. stage. Deputy chief cond. Royal Stockholm Opera 1822 until retirement in 1829.

Crwth. Welsh medieval instr., the most developed form of *bowed lyre, with 6 str., a central fingerboard, and the bridge acting as a soundpost.

Crystal Palace. Glass building designed by J. Paxton to house Great Exhibition of 1851 in Hyde Park, London. Later removed to S. London suburb of Sydenham and became home of Crystal Palace concerts cond. *Manns, 1855–1901, notable for adventurous nature of programmes, also of triennial Handel Fests. from 1857. Destroyed by fire 1936.

csárdás (Hung. *csárda,* a country inn). Hungarian dance, often misspelt *czardas,* in 2 parts; slow introductory *lassù* followed by excited main section in duple time, *friss.* The mus. has a wild, gipsy flavour, but its origin among peasants in country inns is dubious, since the dance was almost certainly invented by aristocrats in the 1830s, and popularized at fashionable balls. Liszt was one of first composers to use the *csárdás* as the basis for comps. The form of the *csárdás* is also used vocally, a famous example being sung by Rosalinde at Orlofsky's party in Act II of *Die *Fledermaus.*

Csárdásfürstin, Die (The Csárdás Princess; usually known in Eng. as *The Gipsy Princess*). Operetta in 3 acts by Kálmán to lib. by L. Stein and B. Jenbach, comp. 1915, prod. Vienna 1915.

Cuberli [Tervell], **Lella Alice** (*b* Austin, Texas, 1945). Amer. soprano. Opera début, Budapest 1975 (Violetta in *La traviata*). Sang at Spoleto Fest. 1977. Débuts: La Scala 1978; Salzburg Fest. 1986; Vienna 1988; CG début 1990; NY Met 1990.

cuckoo. Simple 2-note wind instr., imitating call of the bird, used in Toy Syms.

Cuckoo, The (Le Coucou). Hpd. piece by *Daquin, comp. 1735.

Cuckston, Alan (George) (*b* Horsforth, Leeds, 1940). Eng. harpsichordist, pianist, conductor, and lecturer. Studied privately with Fanny Waterman and Lamar Crowson and at King's Coll., Cambridge, 1959–63. Frequent broadcasts for BBC as soloist, esp. on historical kbd. instrs. Commissioned works for hpd. by Elizabeth Maconchy, Ronald Stevenson, David Wooldridge, and Phillip Ramey. Recorded extensively with Pro Cantione Antiqua and the Academy of St Martin-in-the-Fields as org. and hpd. player. Cond. Orch. of Opera North in 20th cent. Eng. mus. Has revived solo pf. music by Georgian, Victorian, and later Eng. comps. from Pinto to Rawsthorne.

Cudworth, Charles (*b* Cambridge, 1908; *d* Cambridge, 1977). Eng. musicologist, teacher, and critic. Protégé of E. J. Dent. Ass. in mus. section of Univ. Library, Cambridge, 1943–6; librarian, Pendlebury Library at Cambridge Univ. Mus. Sch. 1946–57, curator 1957–73. Authority on baroque and pre-classical mus. First to establish that the 'Trumpet Voluntary' was by Jeremiah Clarke, not Purcell. Wrote libs. for Patrick *Hadley and novels and plays.

cue. (1) Last few notes of another instr. part which immediately precede entrance or re-entrance after a lengthy rest of the instr. (or v.) on whose mus. the cue is written.

(2) When instrumentation is condensed, orch. parts of eliminated instrs. are 'cued' in with the parts of suitable alternative instrs.

(3) Cue nos.: the system of letters and/or nos. in a score which enable cond. to rehearse certain sections by indicating exact place in the score, e.g. '3 bars before letter D'.

Cuenod, Hugues(-Adhémar) (*b* Corseaux-sur-Vevey, 1902). Swiss tenor. Taught at Geneva Cons. then began concert career, later entering opera. Début Paris 1928 in Fr. première of Krenek's *Jonny spielt auf*. Sang in Geneva 1930–3, Paris 1934–7. Prof. of singing, Geneva Cons., 1940–6. Specialized in character roles, creating Sellem in *The Rake's Progress*, Venice 1951. CG début 1954 as Astrologer in Rimsky-Korsakov's *The Golden Cockerel*. Glyndebourne début 1954 as Sellem, the first of over 470 perfs. in many roles there, memorably as Don Basilio in *Le nozze di Figaro*. Sang Don Curzio in *Figaro* in Glyndebourne's 50th anniversary season, 1984, made NY Met début 1987 as Emperor in *Turandot*, and sang Monsieur Taupe in *Capriccio* at Glyndebourne 1987 and Geneva 1989.

Cui, César [Kyui, Tsezar Antonovich] (*b* Vilna (now Vilnius), 1835; *d* Petrograd, 1918). Russ. composer. Son of Fr. army officer. Studied mus. with *Moniuszko in 1850 but concentrated on military engineering at univ., becoming Lieut.-Gen. of engineers and authority on fortifications (prof. of engineering, St Petersburg Acad. of Military Engineering from 1878). On meeting *Balakirev in 1856, found he shared his nationalist mus. ideals and with him joined group known as 'the Five' or the 'Mighty Handful' (the others were Borodin, Mussorgsky, and Rimsky-Korsa-

kov). Although a prolific composer, his biggest contribution to the cause of the Five was through his excellent and witty (and sometimes caustic) writings. Comp. ov. for *Dargomyzhsky's *The Stone Guest* and made a version of Mussorgsky's incomplete *Sorochintsy Fair* (prod. Petrograd, 1917). Prin. comps.: 15 operas (incl. *William Ratcliffe*, 1861–8), 2 scherzos for orch., 3 str. qts., vn. sonata, choral mus., many songs, and pf. pieces.

cuivre (Fr.). Copper, brass. *Les cuivres* are the brass instr. of the orch.

cuivré (Fr.). Brassy, i.e. (in hn. mus., etc.) the tones are to be forced, with a harsh, ringing timbre.

Cullis, Rita (*b* Ellesmere Port, 1949). Eng. soprano. Prof. début, WNO chorus 1973. WNO 1973–6 (solo début 1974, 2nd Boy in *Die Zauberflöte*), prin. sop. 1976–84. Scottish Opera 1979; GTO 1984; Opera North 1985; ENO 1987; CG 1993.

Culshaw, John (Royds) (*b* Southport, 1924; *d* London, 1980). Eng. recording and television producer and writer. Worked for Decca Records 1946–54, Capitol Records, USA, 1954–5, Decca 1955–67, being assoc. with stereophonic developments. Prod. first complete recording of Wagner's *Ring* (with Solti conducting), 1958–65, and wrote book about it, *Ring Resounding* (1967). Supervised over 30 opera recordings, incl. Solti's of *Salome* and *Elektra*, and Britten's. Head of Mus. BBC TV 1967–75, during which period several of Britten's operas were televised. Author of book on Rachmaninov and an autobiography, *Putting the Record Straight*, pubd. posthumously 1981. OBE 1966.

Cummings, William Hayman (*b* Sidbury, Devon, 1831; *d* London, 1915). Eng. organist, tenor, and musicologist. Chorister at St Paul's Cath., London, and Temple Church. Org. Waltham Abbey 1847. Sang at Birmingham Fest. 1864 and became noted for perf. in Bach Passions. Prof. of singing RAM 1879–96, Prin., GSMD 1896–1910. Ed. 3 vols. of Purcell Soc. of which he was a founder. Wrote biographies of Purcell (1881) and Handel (1904) and monographs on national anthem, *Rule! Britannia*, and Blow. Comp. cantata *The Fairy Ring*. While at Waltham, adapted theme from second number of Mendelssohn's *Festgesang* to hymn 'Hark! the herald angels sing' (pubd. 1856). Formed magnificent mus. library, beginning when he was 19. By 1900 it comprised 4,500 items, incl. autograph letters and MSS. It was dispersed by auction after his death.

Cum sancto Spiritu. See *Mass*.

Cunitz, Maud (*b* London, 1911; *d* Baldham, nr. Munich, 1987). Ger. soprano. Début Gotha, 1934, thereafter singing in Coburg, Lübeck, and Stuttgart. Salzburg Fest. début 1943 (First Lady in *Die Zauberflöte* and Zdenka in *Arabella*). Created role of Semele in *Die Liebe der Danae* (Salzburg dress rehearsal 1944). Joined Bavarian State Opera,

Munich, 1946, with whom she made her CG début in 1953 as the Countess in *Capriccio*, its first London perf.

Cunning Little Vixen, The (*Příhody lišky Bystroušky*—The Adventures of the Vixen Bystrouška). Opera in 3 acts by Janáček to his own lib. based on novelette by Rudolf Těsnohlídek (1882–1928) orig. written as captions for drawings by Stanislav Lolek (1873–1936). Comp. 1921–3. Prod. Brno 1924, London 1961; NY 1964.

Cupid and Death. Masque by James Shirley prod. 1653 with mus. by, probably, Christopher *Gibbons; rev. 1659 with mus. by C. Gibbons and Matthew *Locke.

cupo (It.). Dark, sombre.

Cura, José (*b* Rosario, Argentina, 1962). Argentinian tenor and conductor. Had gui. lessons and at 15 was choral cond. Studied cond. and comp. at Sch. of Arts, Nat. Univ. of Rosario, 1982–5, and at Mus. Sch. of Teatro Colón, 1985–91. Went to Italy for vocal coaching and made stage début Verona 1992 in Henze's *Pollicino*. 1st prize int. Domingo comp., 1994. Amer. début Chicago 1994 (Loris in *Fedora*). CG 1995 (Stiffelio), Vienna 1996 (Cavaradossi in *Tosca*), Milan 1997 (Enzo in *La gioconda*). First sang Verdi's Otello with Berlin PO cond. Abbado 1997, then on stage Turin 1997. NY Met 1999 (*Cavalleria rusticana*). At Hamburg 2003 cond. *Cavalleria rusticana* and after interval sang Canio in *Pagliacci*.

Curlew, The. Song-cycle by *Warlock, on 4 poems by Yeats, for ten., fl., cor anglais, and str. qt., comp. 1920–1, f.p. London 1921, rev. 1922.

Curlew River. Parable for church perf., Op.71, by Britten to text by W. Plomer after a Japanese Noh play *Sumidagawa*, by Juro Motomasa (1395–1431). Prod. Aldeburgh Fest. (Orford Church) 1964, Katonah, NY, 1966.

curlew sign. Pause mark invented by *Britten for his church parable *Curlew River* (1964) where there is no cond. This sign, when placed over a note or rest, indicates that the singer or instrumentalist must listen and wait until the other performers have reached the next barline or meeting-point. Thus the note or rest may be longer or shorter than its written value.

curtain music or **curtain tune**. See *act tune*.

curtal (curtall). Renaissance wind instr., ancestor of the bn., developed in mid-16th cent. Had double reeds, single U-tube, and conical bore. Name comes from Lat. *curtus*, short, and, like *bombard*, was borrowed from artillery, the curtal being a variety of short-barrelled cannon. Bass curtal was known in Eng. as double curtal and had 2 keys (little finger and thumb). There were also the great bass curtal (an octave below the bass), and sop., alto, and ten. sizes.

Curtin, Phyllis (*b* Clarksburg, West Virginia, 1921). Amer. soprano. Début with New England Opera Th. 1946 (Lisa in *Queen of Spades*). Joined NY City Opera 1953; Glyndebourne 1959; Vienna 1960; NY Met 1961. Sang Walton's Cressida in NY 1955–6. Retired 1984. Taught at Aspen, Tanglewood, and Boston Univ. Sch. of Arts.

Curtis, Alan (Stanley) (*b* Mason, Mich., 1934). Amer. musicologist, harpsichordist, and conductor. On staff Univ. of Calif., Berkeley, from 1960, becoming prof. 1970. Authority on Sweelinck and on period-style interpretation of mus. of 16th–18th cents. Has cond. several baroque operas (some in his own edns.), e.g. Rameau's *Dardanus* (Basle, 1981), Landi's *Il Sant'Alessio* (Rome, 1981), *Cesti's *Il Tito* (Innsbruck, 1983), Gluck's *Armide* (Bologna, 1984) and *Paride ed Elena* (Vicenza, 1988), Handel's *Floridante* (Toronto, 1990), and Traetta's *Buovo d'Antonio* (Venice, 1993).

Curtis Institute, Philadelphia. Sch. of mus. founded and endowed in 1924 by Mrs Mary Louise Bok (later Mrs. Zimbalist) in memory of her father Cyrus H. K. Curtis. Tuition fees abolished 1928. Dir. from 1926 was the pianist Josef *Hofmann, who retired 1938, followed by Randall *Thompson 1938–40, Efrem *Zimbalist 1941–68, Rudolf *Serkin 1968–76; John de Lancie 1977–85; Gary Graffman from 1986. Long list of distinguished teachers and visiting professors.

Curtis-Smith, Curtis (Otto) (*b* Walla Walla, Wash., 1941). Amer. composer, pianist, and teacher. Began career as recitalist and soloist with orchs. 1968. Koussevitzky Prize 1972. Invented 'piano bowing', i.e. drawing fishing-line across str. of pf. to produce single and clustered pitches. Works incl. fl. sonata (1963); 3 str. qt. (1964, 1965, 1980); *Pianacaglia*, pf. (1967); *Rhapsodies*, pf. (1973); *Winter Pieces*, chamber orch. (1974); *(Bells) Belle de Jour*, pf., orch. (1974–5); *Unisonics*, alt. sax., pf. (1976); *Music for Handbells*, 10 players (1976–7); *Tonalities*, cl., perc. (1978); *Plays and Rimes*, brass quintet (1979); *The Great American Symphony* (GAS!), orch. (1981); *The Great American Guitar Solo* (GAGS!) (1982); *Ragmala (a Garland of Ragas)*, gui., str. qt. (1983); *Songs and Cantillations*, gui., orch. (1983); *Chaconne à son goût*, orch. (1984); *Sardonic Sketches*, ww. quintet (1986); '. . . Float Wild Birds, Sleeping', orch. (1988); and some vocal pieces.

curved line, various uses of (see p. 182).

Curwen. Eng. family of mus. publishers and educationists. John Curwen (*b* Heckmondwike, 1816; *d* Manchester, 1880) was a Congregational minister. Adopted *tonic sol-fa system propounded by Sarah Glover, a Norwich schoolmistress, in her *Scheme to Render Psalmody Congregational* (1835), and resigned his ministry in 1864 to promote tonic sol-fa movement. Founded pub. firm J. Curwen and Sons in 1863. His son John Spencer Curwen (*b* London, 1847; *d* London, 1916) continued the tonic sol-fa work. J. S. Curwen's nephew, John Kenneth Curwen (*b* London, 1881; *d* Gerrards Cross, 1935) supervised

Curved Line, Various uses of

The Tie or Bind

The 2 notes become 1 (see *Tie or Bind*).

The Slur, or Legato (or Bowing Mark)

All the notes affected by the curve are to be played smoothly. In str. mus. they are to be played in a single bow movement.

The Phrase Mark
See *Phrase*.

The Syllable Mark

The mark is to make clearer the fitting of the notes to the syllables.

The sun — sinks to rest

The *Portamento Mark

Instead of jumping cleanly the singer is to slide from the one note to the other, taking all intervening pitches en route. The same effect is possible on bowed instr., but here a wavy line is sometimes the indication.

for ev — er — more

the pub. firm and added to its catalogue Holst's *Planets*, Vaughan Williams's *Pastoral Symphony* and *Hugh the Drover*, and works by Bantock, Smyth, and Varèse. Published journal *The Sackbut* (1920–34), at one time edited by Philip Heseltine. In 1971 catalogue was divided between Faber Music and Roberton Publications.

Curzon, (Sir) **Clifford** (Michael) (*b* London, 1907; *d* London, 1982). Eng. pianist. In 1923 was a soloist in Bach triple concerto at Prom. Concert cond. by Wood. In 1931 married Amer. harpsichordist Lucille *Wallace. Amer. début, NY, 1939. Salzburg Fest. début 1955. Though often playing Romantics such as Liszt and Tchaikovsky, increasingly concentrated on Schubert, Beethoven, and especially Mozart. Played pf. duets with Britten. CBE 1958. Knighted 1977.

cushion dance (Ger. *Kissentanz*, or *Polstertanz*). An old dance in which a participant chose a partner by dropping a cushion before him or her, who then knelt on it and bestowed a kiss on the cushion-bearer.

Cusins, (Sir) **William** (George) (*b* London, 1833; *d* Remouchamps, Ardennes, 1893). Eng. conductor, organist, pianist, and composer. Début 1849 as pianist, then org. of Queen's private chapel, and violinist in CG orch. On staff RAM 1851–85, GSMD from 1885. Cond., Phil Soc. 1867–83, continuing to tour widely as pianist. Comp. oratorio, pf. conc., and ovs. Knighted 1892. Master of the Queen's Musick 1870–93.

Cutner, Solomon. See *Solomon*.

Cuzzoni, Francesca (*b* Parma, 1696; *d* Bologna, 1778). It. soprano, pupil of Lanzi. Probable début Parma 1714. Venice début 1718 as Dalinda in Pollarolo's *Ariodante*. London début, King's Th.

1723 in Handel's *Ottone*. Remained in Handel's opera co. (Royal Academy) until 1728, singing a leading role in all his operas. Her rivalry with Faustina Bordoni led to their fighting on the stage in 1727 during Bononcini's *Astianatte*. Cuzzoni was dismissed, but reinstated when the King threatened to end his subsidy. (Polly and Lucy in *The Beggar's Opera* are satirical portraits of Cuzzoni and Bordoni.) Sang in Vienna 1728–9, but not engaged by opera because of her exorbitant salary demands. Returned to It., where she sang in several of Hasse's operas, and to London (for the Opera of the Nobility) 1734. In 1739 returned to Vienna, moving to Hamburg and Amsterdam, and in 1750–1 to London, where she was arrested for debt. Farewell appearance London 1751. Last years spent in prison and in poverty, supporting herself by making buttons. Contemp. accounts leave no doubt of her greatness as an artist, especially in Handel.

cycle. (1) Name for series of items written to be perf. as a group and sometimes linked thematically either musically or by subject, esp. song-cycle (Ger. *Liedercyclus*). In opera the greatest cycle (4 operas) is Wagner's *Der Ring des Nibelungen*.

(2) A complete vibration in mus. acoustics.

(3) Any of systems of equal temperament in which tonal material is obtained by dividing octave into number of equal intervals.

cyclic form. Formal structure of a comp. in which one mus. theme is heard, sometimes in a varied form, in more than 1 movt. Early examples occur in Handel, Vivaldi, Mozart, and Haydn, but it was developed by Beethoven e.g. in his *Pathétique* Sonata and 5th Sym. The *idée fixe* of Berlioz and *Leitmotiv* of Wagner are akin to cyclic form, as are the thematic transformations of Liszt and R. Strauss. But the most emphatic uses of cyclic form occur in the works of Franck and in the sym. No.1 of Elgar.

cylinder or rotary valve. A special type of valve in brass instr., in much use in some European countries but in Brit. and USA applied only to the Fr. hn. The term is sometimes used for any kind of valve, e.g. It. *trombone a cilindri* (valve tb.).

cymbalon. See *cimbalom*.

cymbals. Perc. instrs. consisting of plate-shaped discs made of brass or other metal with leather handles. Played by being held one in each hand and clashed together; or fixed on a stand enabling the foot to do the clashing; or one can be fixed to the side of a big drum and the other clashed on to it; or they can be rattled at their edges; or one cymbal can be struck with a drumstick (or wire brush) or a roll perf. on it with drumsticks. *Antique cymbals*, specified in some scores (e.g. Debussy's *L'Après-midi d'un faune*), are tuned to a definite pitch. Ordinary cymbals have no definite pitch but one may sound higher than another. See *choke cymbals, Chinese crash cymbals,* and *sizzle cymbals.*

cymbel. Org. stop; a brilliant type of *mixture.*

Cymbelstern. See *Zimbelstern*.

czárdás. See *csárdás.*

Czar und Zimmermann (Lortzing). See *Zar und Zimmermann.*

Czech Philharmonic Orchestra. Founded as independent body in 1901 having previously been orch. of Prague Nat. Opera. Achieved worldwide reputation through tours and recordings during conductorship of Václav *Talich 1919–31, 1933–41. Among his successors have been Rafael *Kubelik 1941–8, Karel *Ančerl 1950–68, Václav *Neumann 1968–89, Jiří *Bělohlávek 1990–2, Gerd *Albrecht 1992–6, Vladimir *Ashkenazy 1998–2003, and Zdeněk Macal from 2003. Salzburg Fest. début 1963, cond. Ančerl.

Czech Quartet. Cz. string quartet formed in 1891 by pupils of Hanuš *Wihan at Prague Cons. First concert 1892. Visited Russ. 1895 and Brit. 1896. Last tour Holland 1931. Disbanded 1933. Orig. members were Karel Hoffmann (1872–1936), Josef *Suk (1874–1935), Oskar Nedbal (1874–1930), and Otto Berger (1873–97). Nedbal was replaced 1906 by Jiří Herold (1875–1934) and Berger in 1894 by Wihan (1855–1920). Wihan was replaced 1914 by Ladislav Zelenka

(1881–1957). Gave 1,000th concert in 1902. Specialized in Smetana, Dvořák, and Beethoven, but played many modern qts. incl. those by Reger, Pfitzner, Schoenberg, Ravel, etc.

Czerny, Karl (*b* Vienna, 1791; *d* Vienna, 1857). Austrian pianist, teacher, and composer. Pf. pupil 1800–3 and friend of Beethoven, who admired him. Début Vienna 1800 in Mozart C minor conc. (K491). Later was soloist in Beethoven's C minor conc. and, at its f. Vienna p. in 1812, E♭ conc. Also influenced by *Hummel and *Clementi. Was popular teacher at age 15. Pupils incl. Beethoven's nephew Karl, and 9-year-old Liszt. Indefatigable composer and arranger, works numbering more than 1,000 and incl. examples of every form from operas to pf. solos, but best known for his instructive studies. Arr. operas, oratorios, and syms. for pf(s). (incl. arrs. of Rossini's *Semiramide* and *William Tell* ovs. for 8 pf., 4 hands each). Contrib. to *Hexaméron.*

Czerwenka, Oskar (*b* Vöcklabruck bei Linz, Austria, 1924). Austrian bass. Opera début Graz 1947 (Hermit in *Der Freischütz*); joined Vienna Opera 1951, remaining for 30 years and singing roles such as Osmin and Ochs. NY Met 1960; Salzburg 1953; Glyndebourne 1959. Repertory of over 70 roles.

Cziffra, György (*b* Budapest, 1921; *d* Morsang-sur-Orge, 1994). Hung.-born pianist (French cit.). First public perf. at 5 in circus, playing improvisations. Had successful career in Hung. and Europe 1933–41. Prisoner of war and again imprisoned for political beliefs 1950–3. Won Liszt Prize 1955 (first non-composer to do so). Escaped from Hung. during 1956 uprising, settling in Fr. Virtuoso interpreter of 19th cent. repertory. Founded Concours International de Piano, Versailles, 1968, for young pianists.

czimbal, czimbalom, czimbalon. See *cimbalom.*

Czyz, Henryk (*b* Grudziadz, Poland, 1923; *d* Warsaw, 2003). Polish conductor and composer. Cond. début 1948, Polish Nat. Radio Orch. Cond. f.p. of Penderecki's *St Luke Passion* (Munster, 1966) and *The Devils of Loudun* (Hamburg 1969). Cond. Poznań Opera 1952–3, Polish Radio and TV SO, Katowice, 1953–6, Łódź PO 1957–60, Krakow PO 1964–8, Düsseldorf SO 1971–4, Łódź PO 1972–80. Prof., Warsaw Acad. of Mus. from 1980. Amer. début, Minnesota Orch., 1973. Comp. syms., opera, and film mus.

D

D. The name of the 2nd degree of natural scale of C. Thus D♭, D♭♭, D♮, D♯, D♯♯, D major, D minor. *In D* indicates either 'in the key of D major' or, of transposing instr., that the written note C sounds D.

D. Abbreviated prefix to nos. in the O. E. *Deutsch thematic catalogue of Schubert's works, and now generally used to identify them; e.g. the str. quintet in C major (D956).

d. tonic sol-fa symbol for first degree (tonic) of scale, pronounced *doh*.

da (It.). Of, from.

da capo (It., abbreviates to D.C.). From the head. A term meaning 'Repeat from the beginning until you come to the word *fine* (end), or the pause mark (⌢).' Sometimes the expressions *da capo al segno* (From the beginning to the sign) or *da capo al fine* (From the beginning to the word *fine*) are encountered; these are occasionally followed by *e poi la coda*, meaning that having arrived at the place indicated, the coda should immediately follow.

A *da capo* aria is one in which the first part is repeated, the singer being expected to add ornamentation in the repeated section.

Dafne. Opera in prol. and 6 scenes by *Peri to lib. by Ottavio Rinuccini. Comp. 1594–8. Generally supposed to be the earliest opera, but the mus. is lost. Prod. in *Corsi's house, Florence, 1598. (See *Camerata*.) The same lib. was also set by Corsi himself (2 fragments survive), *Gagliano (1607), and Schütz (lost, 1627). Operas on the same theme were comp. by A. Scarlatti (1700), *Astorga (1709), Mulè (1928), and R. Strauss (1936–7, see under *Daphne*).

Dahlhaus, Carl (*b* Hanover, 1928; *d* Berlin, 1989). Ger. musicologist and editor. Dramatic adviser, Deutsches Th., Göttingen, 1950–8; mus. critic, *Stuttgarter Zeitung*, 1960–2; on staff Univ. of Kiel mus. dept., 1962–6; prof. of mus. history, Berlin Technical Univ. from 1967. Scholar with range of interests from Josquin to present-day. Author of several books on Wagner, incl. *Richard Wagner's Music Dramas* (1979), ed.-in-chief, complete edn. of Wagner's works (pubn. begun 1970), contributor to several mus. encyclopaedias, and co-ed. of 4 mus. periodicals. Also wrote *Schoenberg and the New Music* (1978, Eng. trans. 1988), and *Beethoven and his Time* (1987, Eng. trans. 1991).

d'Albert, Eugen. See *Albert, Eugen d'*.

Dalberto, Michel (*b* Paris, 1955). Fr. pianist. Winner, first Mozart comp., Salzburg 1975; winner Leeds pf. comp. 1978. Recitalist and concert soloist.

Dalby, (John) **Martin** (*b* Aberdeen, 1942). Scottish composer. Violist in Nat. Youth Orch. On BBC mus. staff in London 1965–71, Glasgow Univ. 1971–2. Head of Mus. BBC Scotland from 1972. Compositions incl.:

ORCH.: *Waltz Overture* (1965); sym. (1970); *Concerto Martin Pescatore*, strings (1971); *The Tower of Victory* (1973); va. conc. (1974); *El Ruisenor* (1979); *Chamber Sym.* (1982); *Nozze di Primavera* (1984); *The Mary Bean* (1991); *Adagio for Strings*, str. (1997); *The Cabrach* (1999); *Fyvie Castle* (2000).

CHAMBER & INSTR.: ob. sonatina (1969); *Commedia*, cl., vn., vc., pf. (1969); *Whisper Music* (1971); *Cancionero para una Mariposa*, 9 instr. (1971); str. quintet (1972); *Yet Still She is the Moon*, brass septet (1973); *Unicorn*, vn. and pf. (1975); *Aleph*, 8 instr. (1975); *Almost a Madrigal*, wind and perc. (1977); *Man Walking*, octet for wind and str. (1980); *A Plain Man's Hammer*, sym. wind ens. (1984); *De Patre ex Filio*, octet for wind and str. (1988); *Butterfly Music*, brass quintet (1995); str. qt. (1995); *Bandit*, cl., pf. (2001).

VOCAL & CHORAL: *The Fiddler*, sop. or ten., vn. (1967); *Cantica*, sop. or ten., cl., va., pf. (1969); *The Keeper of the Pass*, sop., instr. (1971); *Orpheus*, ch., narr., 11 instr. (1972); *Cantigas del Cancionero*, 5 solo vv. (1972); *El Remenso del Pitido*, 12 solo vv. (1974); *Ad Flumina Babyloniae*, motet (1975); *Call for the Hazel Tree*, ch., elec. (1979); *Antoinette Alone*, mez., pf. (1980); *My Heart Aflame*, unacc. ch. (1983); *Five Sonnets from Scotland*, sop., ten., pf. (1985); *Et resurrexit*, ch., org. (1990); *Cantata: John Clare's Vision*, sop./ten., str. (1993); *The Loch Ness Monster's Song*, mez./bar., sax., mar., vc., pf. (1994); *Sunbeam for Sheba*, sop./ten., pf. (2002).

PIANO: sonatas, No.1 (1985), No.2 (1989), No.3 (1997).

Dalcroze, Émile J. See *Jaques-Dalcroze, Émile*.

Dalibor. Opera in 3 acts by Smetana to E. Spindler's Cz. trans. of Ger. text by Joseph Wenzig. Comp. 1865–7, rev. 1870. Prod. Prague 1868, Chicago 1924, Edinburgh 1964, London (King George's Hall) 1969, (ENO) 1976.

Dall'Abaco, Evaristo Felice (*b* Verona, 1675; *d* Munich, 1742). It. composer. In Modena 1696–1701. Was at Bavarian court in Munich as cellist in 1704, and followed defeated Elector, Maximilian II, to Netherlands and then to France, where court was est. in 1709. Returned to Munich with Elector 1715, became leader of court orch. until retirement 1740. His mus. showed Fr. influence. Comp. 12 vn. sonatas (1706); 12 *concerti da chiesa* for 4 str. (1714); 6 *concerti da chiesa* and 6 *concerti da camera* for 3 str. (1715); 12 *sonate da camera*, vn. and vc. (1716); and a vn. conc. (1730).

Dallapiccola, Luigi (*b* Pisino d'Istria, 1904; *d* Florence, 1975). It. composer and pianist. At the time of his birth, Pisino was in the Austro-Hungarian empire, being transferred to It. in 1918 (later part of Yugoslavia). Because Dallapiccola's father was suspected in 1917 of It. nationalism, the family was forcibly moved to Graz where Dallapiccola learned to admire opera and where he conceived the passionate love of liberty which inspires several of his works. In 1922 he entered the Cons. Cherubini, Florence, studying comp. under Frazzi. In 1924 a perf. of Schoenberg's *Pierrot Lunaire* made a deep impression on him, in addition to his existing passion for Debussy, Monteverdi, and Gesualdo. In the late 1920s he taught, gave pf. recitals, and in 1934 joined the pf. staff of the Cons. Cherubini. Travelling abroad he met Berg, Malipiero, and Casella. He fell out of favour with the authorities because of his opposition to Fascism, but after 1945 he spent a considerable time in the USA.

Known as the principal (and probably the first) It. composer to adopt 12-note methods, Dallapiccola also remained a lyrical, thoroughly It. composer. But he did not adopt *dodecaphony until he was nearly 40. His early works, such as the first pair of *Cori di Michelangelo Buonarroti il Giovane* (1933), reflect his interest in the Italian madrigalists. The later pairs (1934–6) combine the influence of Busoni with his own typically sensuous warmth. The culmination of this period of his work was the *Canti di prigionia* (1938–41).

In 1942 he adopted serialism, but never the purely academic variety. His natural It. aptitude for elaborate polyphony led him, in such works as *Piccola musica notturna* (1954), to use the all-interval row. His opera *Il prigioniero* (1944–8) exemplifies his unorthodoxy in using several different note-rows and ignoring other standard serial procedures. From about 1956 his music showed a Webernian intricacy in its textures and angularity, yet was never wholly devoid of the lyricism and colour of his earlier phases. Prin. comps.:

OPERAS: *Volo di notte* (Night Flight) 1 act, lib. by composer after Saint-Exupéry (comp. 1937–9, prod. 1940); *Il *prigioniero* (The Prisoner) (1944–8); **Job* (1950); *Ulisse* (prol. and 2 acts, lib. by composer after Homer, comp. 1959–68, prod. 1968). (See *Ulysses*.)

BALLET: *Marsia* (comp. 1942–3, prod. Venice 1948).

ORCH.: *Piccolo Concerto per Muriel Couvreux*, pf., chamber orch. (1939–41); *Variations* (1954) (adapted from *Quaderno musicale di Annalibera*, pf. 1952); *Tartiniana*, divertimento, vn., chamber orch. (1951); *Piccola musica notturna* (1954) (also arr. for chamber ens., 1961); *Dialoghi*, vc., orch. (1960).

CHORUS & ORCH.: 6 *Cori di Michelangelo Buonarroti il Giovane* in 3 pairs: 1 (1933), unacc. mixed ch., 2 (1934–5), women's vv., 17 instr., 3 (1935–6), ch., orch.; 3 **Canti di prigionia* (Songs of Imprisonment) (1938–41); *Requiescant* (1957–8); *Canti di Liberazione* (1951–5).

SOLO VOICE & ORCH.: *Partita*, orch. (sop. solo in finale) (1930–2); 3 *Laudi*, high v., 13 instr. (1936–7); *Liriche Greche* (Greek Lyrics): I, *Five Sappho Fragments*, v., 15 instr. (1942), II, *Two Anacreonte Lyrics*, v., E♭ cl., cl. in A, va., pf. (1944–5), III, *6 Songs of Alcaeus*, v., 11 instr. (1943): *An Mathilde*, sop., orch. (1955); *Concerto per la notte di Natale dell'anno 1956*, chamber orch., sop. (1957): 4 *liriche di Antonio Machado*, sop., chamber orch. (orig. version for sop. and pf., 1948) (1964); *Commiato*, sop., chamber orch. (1972).

INSTR.: *Ciacona, Intermezzo e Adagio*, vc. (1945).

SONGS: *Rencesval*, bar. (1946); 4 *Liriche di Antonio Machado*, sop. (1948).

Dal Monte, Toti [Meneghelli, Antonietta] (*b* Mogliano Veneto, 1893; *d* Treviso, 1975). It. soprano. Début Milan 1916 (Biancafiore in Zandonai's *Francesca da Rimini*). Sang Gilda in *Rigoletto* cond. Toscanini, Milan 1922. Regular operatic appearances in It., also Chicago 1924–8; NY Met 1924–5; CG 1925. Farewell appearance Verona 1949. Became teacher.

dal segno (It.). From the sign, i.e. return to the sign $ and repeat thence to the word *fine* (end), or to a double bar with a pause sign (⌒) above it.

Dame blanche, La (The White Lady). Opera in 3 acts by Boieldieu, to lib. by Scribe, based on Scott's *The Monastery* (1820) and *Guy Mannering* (1815). Prod. Paris 1825, London 1826, New Orleans 1827, Wexford 1990.

Damnation de Faust, La (The Damnation of Faust). Dramatic cantata (*légende dramatique*) in 4 parts for sop., ten., and bass soloists, ch. and orch., Op.24, by Berlioz, sometimes perf. in operatic form. Text by Berlioz and A. Gandonnière after G. de Nerval's Fr. version of Goethe. F.p. Paris, Opéra-Comique, 6 Dec. 1846. F.p. in England, Manchester, 5 Feb. 1880 cond. Hallé; f. Amer. p. NY 1880 (concert), Met 1906 (stage). Adapted as staged opera in 5 acts by Raoul Gunsbourg, Monte Carlo, 1893. Comp. was completed 1846, incorporating earlier *Huit Scènes de Faust* (1828). See also *Rákóczy March*.

damp. To check the vibrations of an instr. (e.g. kettledrum) by touching it in some way. See also *piano*.

dampers. See *piano*.

Dämpfer (Ger.). *Mute. mit Dämpfern*, with mutes.

dämpfung. Muting, or (pf.) soft-pedalling.

Damrosch, Frank (Heino) (*b* Breslau, 1859; *d* NY, 1937). Ger.-born Amer. conductor. Went to USA with father, Leopold *Damrosch, in 1871. Chorusmaster NY Met 1885–91. Cond. and founder of several NY choral socs. Founded Inst. of Musical Art, NY, 1905, remaining dir. until it was merged with *Juilliard Sch., 1926.

Damrosch, Leopold (*b* Posen, 1832; *d* NY, 1885). Ger. conductor, composer, and violinist. Violinist in Weimar court orch. under Liszt 1855–9, cond. Breslau PO 1859–60. Dir., Breslau Orchestverein 1862–71. Went to NY 1871 and played increasingly important role in US mus. life. Co-founder and first cond. NY Oratorio Soc. (1873) and NY Sym. Soc. (1878). Organized and cond. Ger. opera season at NY Met 1884–5 which incl. f. complete US p. of *Die Walküre*.

Damrosch, Walter (Johannes) (*b* Breslau, 1862; *d* NY, 1950). Ger.-born Amer. conductor and composer, younger son of Leopold *Damrosch. Succeeded father as cond. NY Oratorio Soc. 1885–98 and ass. cond. Ger. opera, NY Met 1885–91. Cond. first concert perf. in USA of *Parsifal*, 1886. Formed and cond. Damrosch Opera Co. in NY 1894–9 when it disbanded. Toured USA performing mainly Wagner's operas. Returned to Met 1900–3. In 1903 reorganized NY Sym. Soc. as permanent orch., remaining cond. until merger with NYPO in 1928. Introduced many 20th-cent. works to USA and cond. f.ps. in USA of Bruckner's 3rd and Mahler's 4th syms. Comp. 4 operas, incl. *The Scarlet Letter* (1896) and *Cyrano de Bergerac* (1913); choral works incl. *The Canterbury Pilgrims*, and *Dunkirk*, bar., male ch., orch. (1943).

dance. In every age and among every race dancing has existed either as recreation or as a religious manifestation or as both.

In Europe all countries have their traditional ('folk') dances. Those of England are numerous, falling into three classes—for men alone the Sword Dance and the Morris Dances and for men and women together the Country Dances.

There has always been a tendency for some peasant dances to pass into wider use, their steps and music then becoming sophisticated. Some typical examples are *allemande, bergomask, bourrée, branle, canaries, chaconne and passacaglia, courante, dump, gavotte, hay, jig, minuet, passamezzo, passepied, pavan and galliard, rigaudon, sarabande, volta*. The rhythms and styles of some of the above, from the 16th cent. onwards, supplied conventional models for instrumental compositions (see *suite*). The Dances later popular in social circles (some of them of rustic origin) were the *minuet* and the Eng. *country dance* (17th cent.); *cotillon* and *écossaise* (18th cent.); *waltz, quadrille, polka, schottische, mazurka, barn dance* (19th cent.); and some of these also were taken as models by instrumental composers.

In the 20th cent. the dance has become synonymous with ballet, but the pattern of previous centuries has continued and modern dances such as the foxtrot, quickstep, and rumba have influenced composers. Dance companies such as those of Merce Cunningham and Martha Graham in the USA have been of significant importance. Dance has also been harnessed to electronic mus. See *ballet*.

Dance before the Golden Calf. Climax (mainly orch.) of Act 2 of Schoenberg's opera *Moses und Aron*.

Dance of Death. See (1) *Danse macabre*; (2) *Totentanz*.

Dance of the Blessed Spirits. A slow dance episode in Act 2 of Gluck's *Orfeo ed Euridice*, characterized by a beautiful fl. solo.

Dance of the Comedians. Dance episode in Act 3 of Smetana's *The Bartered Bride* featuring the clowns and tumblers of the travelling circus.

Dance of the Hours. Episode, frequently played as separate orch. piece, in Act 3 of Ponchielli's *La *Gioconda*. It is an entertainment staged by one of the characters for his guests and symbolizes the conflict between darkness and light.

Dance of the Seven Veils. Popular title for Salome's dance before Herod in Strauss's *Salome*. For orch. alone, and often perf. as concert item.

Dance of the Sylphs. Orch. episode, often played separately, in Berlioz's La *Damnation de Faust* where it forms part of Faust's dream on the banks of the Elbe.

Dance of the Tumblers. Episode in Act 3 of Rimsky-Korsakov's *The *Snow Maiden* in which acrobats dance for the Tsar Berenday.

Dance Rhapsody. Name given by Delius to 2 orch. works. No.1, comp. 1908, was f.p. at Hereford Fest. 8 Sept. 1909, cond. composer. No.2, comp. 1916, was f.p. London, 23 Oct. 1923, cond. Wood. Also title of orch. work by Bridge (1908).

Dances of Galánta. Orch. suite by *Kodály comp. 1933 for 80th anniv. of Budapest Phil. Soc. Based on gipsy tunes collected in Hung. market town of Galánta.

Dance Suite (*Táncszvit*). Orch. work by Bartók comp. 1923 to celebrate 50th anniv. of merging of Buda and Pest. F.p. Budapest 19 Nov. 1923, cond. Dohnányi. Also pf. version.

Danco, Suzanne (*b* Brussels, 1911; *d* Fiesole, 2000). Belg. soprano. Début Genoa 1941 as Fiordiligi in *Così fan tutte*. Sang Ellen Orford in Britten's *Peter Grimes* at first Milan perf. 1947. Edinburgh Fest. 1948; CG 1951. A noted Mélisande, recording the role with Ansermet. Also exponent of *Lieder* and Fr. songs.

Dandelot, Georges (Edouard) (*b* Paris, 1895; *d* St Georges de Didon, 1975). Fr. composer. Teacher, École Normale de Musique, Paris, from 1919 and prof. at Paris Cons. 1942. Works incl. operas, ballets, oratorio *Pax* (1937), sym. (1941), pf. conc. (1934), *concerto romantique* for vn. and orch. (1944).

Danican. See *Philidor*.

Daniel, John. See *Danyel(l)*, John.

Daniel, Paul (*b* Birmingham, 1958). Eng. conductor. Guest cond. of various Eng. and Amer. orchs. Opera début 1982 (Opera Factory, *The Beggar's Opera*). On staff ENO 1980–5; Opera Factory from 1985, mus. dir. 1987–90. For ENO cond. Brit. premières of Glass's *Akhnaten* (1985), Reimann's *Lear* (1989), and Brit. stage première of *The *Stone Guest* (1987). Amer. début 1988 with

London Sinfonietta in NY. Mus. dir. Opera North and Eng. Northern Philharmonia 1990–7, ENO 1997–2005. Cond. Brit. stage première of Verdi's *Jérusalem* (Leeds 1990) and f. Brit. p. of Schreker's *Der ferne Klang* (Leeds 1992). CG début 1993. CBE 2000.

Daniel, The Play of. See *Play of Daniel, The*.

Daniel-Lesur, (Jean) **Yves** (*b* Paris, 1908; *d* Paris, 2002). Fr. composer and organist. Ass. org. Ste Clotilde 1927–37. In 1937 founded *Jeune France* group with Messiaen, Jolivet, and Baudrier. Prof. of counterpoint Schola Cantorum 1935–64, dir. 1957–64. On mus. staff Fr. radio from 1939, mus. dir. Fr. TV (ORTF) from 1968. Many comps. incl. *La vie intérieure*, org. (1932); ballet (with Jolivet), *L'Infante et le monstre* (1938); operas *Andrea del Sarto* (1968), *Ondine* (1982), and *La reine morte* (1987); dialogue *Dans la nuit*, sop., bar., orch. (1988); *Le voyage d'automne*, vv., orch. (1990); and *Permis de séjour*, vv., orch. (1990).

Daniels, Barbara (*b* Grenville, Ohio, 1946). Amer. soprano. Début West Palm Beach, Fla., 1973 (Susanna in *Le nozze di Figaro*). From 1974 sang in Innsbruck, Kassel, and Cologne. CG début 1978; S. Francisco 1980; NY Met 1983. Roles incl. Jenůfa, Violetta, and Minnie in *La fanciulla del West*.

Daniels, David (*b* Spartanburg, S.C., 1966). Amer. countertenor. Studied as ten. at Cincinnati Coll. Cons. of Mus. Switched to counterten. at Univ. of Michigan with George Shirley. Prof. début 1992. Has sung Handel roles at CG, Glyndebourne, Munich, San Francisco etc. NY Met 2002 (Oberon in Britten's *Midsummer Night's Dream*). NY Carnegie Hall recital 2002.

Dankworth, (Sir) **John** (Philip William) (*b* London, 1927). Eng. jazz musician and composer. Played alto sax. and cl. in jazz groups. Formed jazz orch. 1953. Comp. much film mus. and works combining jazz and symphonic musicians, e.g. *Improvisations*, with *Seiber 1959, str. qt. (1971), pf. conc. (1972), *Grace Abounding* (1980), *Reconciliation* (1987). Frequent appearances as acc. to wife, Cleo Laine. CBE 1974. Knighted 2006.

Dannreuther, Edward (George) (*b* Strasbourg, 1844; *d* Hastings, 1905). Alsatian-born English pianist and writer. At age 5 went to Cincinnati. Début as pianist in London 1863 (f. complete p. in Eng. of Chopin's F minor conc.), then settled there. Ardent Wagner enthusiast; founded Wagner Soc. 1872, was host to Wagner on his visit to London 1877 to conduct several concerts. Wrote several books on Wagner and his theories. Promoted chamber concerts in his home 1874–93. Gave f. Eng. ps. of pf. concs. by Grieg, Liszt (A major), and Tchaikovsky (No.1).

Danon, Oskar (*b* Sarajevo, 1913). Serbian conductor and composer. Cond. Sarajevo Opera and PO 1938–41. Dir. Belgrade Opera and PO 1945–60. Chicago 1962; Edinburgh Fest. 1962 (f. Brit. ps. of Prokofiev's *The Gambler* and *Love for Three Oranges*). Cond. f.p. in restored Nat. Th., Belgrade, 1990 (Konjović's *The Prince of Zeta*). Comp. choral works, ballet, symphonic scherzo, etc.

Danse macabre (Dance of Death). Symphonic poem by Saint-Saëns, Op.40, comp. 1874 (pf. transcr. by Liszt 1877). Based on poem by Henri Cazalis in which Death the Fiddler summons skeletons from their graves at midnight to dance. Orig. conceived as a song, in which form it exists. See also *Totentanz*.

Dante Sonata. Pf. comp. by Liszt, No.7 of the *seconde année* of the *Années de pèlerinage*, its full title being *Fantaisie, quasi Sonate: 'D'Après une lecture de Dante'*. First played by Liszt 1839, rev. 1849. Version by *Lambert for pf. and orch. 1940 as basis for ballet *Dante Sonata*.

Dante Symphony. Orch. work by Liszt (*Symphony to Dante's Divina Commedia*) comp. 1855–6 and f.p. 1857. Last movt. is Magnificat sung by women's ch. (of which there are 2 versions).

Dantons Tod (Danton's Death). Opera in 2 parts by *Einem, Op.6, to lib. by *Blacher and composer, after Büchner's drama (1835). Comp. 1944–6. Prod. Salzburg 1947, NY City Opera 1966.

Danyel(l) [Daniel], **John** (*b* Wellow, Som., 1564; *d* c.1626). Eng. lutenist and member of Queen Elizabeth's Chapel Royal. B.Mus., Oxford, 1603. His fancies and galliards for lute show advanced use of chromaticism for his time. His 20 songs for lute, viol, and v. were pubd. 1606.

danza (It.). *Dance.

danza española (Sp.). Spanish dance (in some parts of S. America applied to a particular type, generally in simple duple rhythm).

Danzi, Franz (Ignaz) (*b* Schwetzingen, 1763; *d* Karlsruhe, 1826). Ger. composer and cellist. Cellist in Mannheim Orch. 1778–83, in Munich 1783–90. Kapellmeister, Stuttgart 1807–12, Karlsruhe from 1812. Friend and patron of *Weber, putting several of his operas into production. One of first opera conds. to cond. from rostrum rather than from kbd. Comp. 15 operas, incl. one on subject of *Turandot* (1816), vc. conc., 4 fl. concs., hn. conc., and several works for wind quintet.

Daphne. Opera (bucolic tragedy) in 1 act by R. Strauss to lib. by Gregor. Comp. 1936–7. Prod. Dresden 1938, Santa Fe 1964, Leeds (Opera North) 1987, London (concert) 1990, Garsington 1995.

Daphnis et Chloé. Ballet (choreographic sym.) by Ravel in 3 scenes, choreog. Fokine, comp. 1909–12 to commission from *Diaghilev, prod. Paris 1912, London 1914. Two concert suites arr. Ravel, No.1, 1911, No.2, 1913. Score incl. part for wordless ch.

Da Ponte, Lorenzo (Emmanuele Conegliano) (*b* Ceneda, nr. Venice, 1749; *d* NY, 1838). It. poet and librettist for many composers but especially for Mozart's *Le nozze di Figaro*, *Don Giovanni*, and *Così fan tutte*. Educated at Ceneda Seminary. Prof. of literature, Portogruaro Seminary 1770–3. Ordained priest 1773. Prof. of humanities, Treviso, 1773–6, being dismissed for his views on natural laws. Went to Venice, from where he was banned for 15 years in 1779 because of adultery. Settled in Vienna 1782; was poet to the court opera but left in 1791. Worked in London 1792–1804 teaching It. and acting as poet to It. Opera. Went to NY 1805, working as tobacco dealer and grocer. Worked with Manuel García 1825 to institute It. opera season in USA and with Montressor on similar venture 1832–3. Teacher of It., Columbia Univ. 1826–37. Other libs. incl. *Una cosa rara* and *L'arbore di Dina* (both for Soler), *Gli equivoci* (Storace), and *Axur* (Salieri). Wrote entertaining memoirs (1823–7).

Daquin [d'Aquin] (*b* Paris, 1694; *d* Paris, 1772). Fr. organist and composer. Child prodigy, playing before Louis XIV at age of 6. Org., Petit St Antoine 1706–27, St Paul 1727–32, Cordeliers 1732–9. Org., Fr. Chapel Royal, 1739. Comp. many hpd. works, best-known being *Le Coucou* (The *Cuckoo*) (1735), and solo works for org., also church mus.

D'Arányi, Jelly. See *Arányi, Jelly d'*.

Dardanus. Opera in prologue and 5 acts by Rameau to lib. by de la Bruère. Comp. 1739, rev. 1744 and 1760. Prod. Paris 1739, 2nd version 1744, 3rd version 1760; London (concert) 1973. Opera on same subject by Sacchini (1784).

dargason. Eng. folk-tune, used from the 16th cent. onwards for a country dance or as a ballad tune. Also used for the folk-song *It was a maid of my country*. Tune is 8-bar 'circular' melody lending itself easily to combination with others. *Holst, in his *Suite No.2* for military band (1911), combines the Dargason with *Greensleeves* in the finale, later transposing the movt. for strings in his *St Paul's Suite* (1912–13). Name possibly derives from Anglo-Saxon word for dwarf or fairy. Also known as Sedany, meaning a woman dressed in silks.

Dargomyzhsky, Alexander (*b* Troitskoye, Tula, 1813; *d* St Petersburg, 1869). Russ. composer and pianist. His first opera *Esmeralda* (based on Hugo) was completed 1840 but not prod. until 1847, when it failed. *Rusalka* (based on Pushkin) was prod. with success in 1856. He wrote several orch. works, incl. *Baba Yaga*, and in 1864–5 visited Fr., Eng., and Belgium. Inspired by the nationalist ideals of 'the Five', he began another Pushkin opera, *The *Stone Guest*, on the Don Juan legend, making use of declamatory 'mezzo-recitative'. This was left unscored and unfinished. *Cui completed 2 scenes and the opera was scored by Rimsky-Korsakov and prod. St Petersburg 1872. Also wrote nearly 100 songs.

Darke, Harold (Edwin) (*b* London, 1888; *d* Cambridge, 1976). Eng. organist, conductor, and composer. Org. of St Michael's, Cornhill, 1916–66, with wartime break as org. King's Coll., Cambridge, 1941–5. Org. prof. RCM 1919–69. D.Mus., Oxford. Founded St Michael's Singers to perform Bach cantatas, Byrd's Great Service and works by Parry, Vaughan Williams, Howells, etc. Comp. cantatas (*Ring Out, Ye Crystal Spheres*, *An Hymn of Heavenly Beauty*, etc.), org. works, songs, pf. pieces, and notable setting of carol *In the Bleak Midwinter*. CBE 1966.

Darmstadt. City in Ger. with musical tradition dating from 17th cent. Operatic activity was especially vital under Grand Duke Ludwig I (1790–1830), when the court conductor was *Vogler. Later *Rinck was organist for 41 years. Among 20th-cent. opera conds. at Darmstadt have been Weingartner, Balling, Böhm, E. Kleiber, Schmidt-Isserstedt, and Szell. But the most significant development has been the city's association with *avant-garde* contemporary mus. The International Summer Courses for New Music were instituted in 1946 by Wolfgang Steinecke, who directed them until his death in 1961. The courses were held annually up to 1970, and now every two years.

Dart, (Robert) **Thurston** (*b* Kingston-upon-Thames, 1921; *d* London, 1971). Eng. organist, harpsichordist, and musicologist. After war service, studied in Belgium, 1945. Ass. lect. in mus., Cambridge Univ. from 1947, prof. 1962–4. Prof. of mus., London Univ., from 1964, establishing faculty of mus. at King's Coll., London. Undertook research into early mus., publishing many articles on subject and making many fine recordings as solo kbd. player and continuo player for firm of Oiseau-Lyre. Played with Boyd Neel Orch. from 1948; art. dir. Philomusica of London 1955–9. Influential teacher. Ed., *Galpin Society Journal* 1947–54; secretary *Musica Britannica*, 1950–65. Authority on J. S. Bach, kbd. and consort mus. of 16th, 17th, and 18th cents., and John Bull.

Dartington Summer School. Annual combination of coaching, festival, and holiday lasting five weeks from late July at Dartington Hall, arts and education college near Totnes, Devon. Began in 1948 at Bryanston Sch., Dorset, moving to Dartington 1953. Dir. William *Glock 1948–79, Peter *Maxwell Davies 1979–84, Gavin Henderson from 1985. Leading composers and performers instruct and lecture students, who vary from the professional to the enthusiastic amateur. Duration was four weeks up to 1993.

das (Ger.). The.

Daughter of the Regiment, The (Donizetti). See *Fille du régiment, La*.

David. Opera in 5 acts and 12 scenes by *Milhaud to lib. by Lunel, commissioned by Koussevitzky Foundation to mark 3,000th anniv. of

Jerusalem. Comp. 1952. Prod. Jerusalem, concert version, 1954, Milan, stage, 1955, Hollywood Bowl 1956.

David, Félicien (César) (*b* Cadenet, 1810; *d* St Germain-en-Laye, 1876). Fr. composer. Chorister in Aix Cath. and at 18 2nd cond. of th. there. In 1831 joined Saint-Simonist movt. and travelled in Middle East, where he collected oriental melodies which later influenced his mus. Paris success with symphonic ode *Le Désert*, 1844, which in its exotic oriental tone-colours influenced Bizet, Gounod, and Delibes. His operas incl. *La Perle du Brésil* (1851), *Lalla Roukh* (1862), and *Le Saphir* (1865). Also wrote oratorios, chamber mus., 4 syms., pf. pieces, and songs.

David, Ferdinand (*b* Hamburg, 1810; *d* nr. Klosters, Switz., 1873). Ger. violinist and composer. Début at 15 with Leipzig Gewandhaus Orch. Leader of nobleman's private str. qt. in Estonia 1829–35. Appointed leader, Leipzig Gewandhaus Orch. 1836, when Mendelssohn was cond. Prof. of vn. Leipzig Cons. 1843. Visited Eng. 1839 and 1841. Advised Mendelssohn on technicalities for his vn. conc. and was soloist at f.p. (Leipzig, 13 March 1845). Taught Joachim and Wilhelmj. Took up cond. in last decade of his life. Wrote opera (withdrawn), 5 vn. concs., str. qt., and songs.

David, Johann Nepomuk (*b* Eferding, 1895; *d* Stuttgart, 1977). Austrian composer, organist and teacher. Held many academic posts incl. Leipzig Hochschule für Musik 1934–45 (dir. from 1942); dir. of Mozarteum, Salzburg, 1945–8; and prof. of comp., Stuttgart Hochschule für Musik 1948–63. Ed. works by J. S. Bach and Mozart. Own works influenced by Baroque composers until he turned to serialism in 1953. Many choral works and org. pieces; sonata for 3 vc.; conc. for vn., vc., and orch.; 8 syms.; org. conc.; 2 vn. concs.; and 3 concs. for str.

Davidde Penitente (David the Penitent). Oratorio (K469) by Mozart for 2 sop., ten., ch., and orch. Comp. 1785 with material borrowed from unfinished Mass in C minor (K427) (1782–3), except for 2 arias (Nos. 6 and 8). Text is attrib. da Ponte. F.p. Vienna, March 1785.

Davidoff, Karl (*b* Goldingen, 1838; *d* Moscow, 1889). Russ. cellist and composer. Prin. cellist Leipzig Gewandhaus Orch. 1859–62, St Petersburg Opera Orch. from 1862. Prof. of vc. St Petersburg Cons. from 1863, becoming dir. 1876–87. Comps. incl. 4 vc. concs.

Davidovich, Bella (*b* Baku, 1928). Russ.-born Amer. pianist (Amer. cit. 1984). Lessons at age of 6 and was soloist in Beethoven's C major conc. in Baku 1937. Joint 1st prize, Chopin comp., Warsaw, 1949. Soloist each season with Leningrad PO 1950–78. Prof. of pf., Moscow Cons. 1962–78. Eur. début Amsterdam 1967; toured It. 1971. Emigrated to USA 1978. NY début 1979. On staff of Juilliard Sch. from 1982. Mother of violinist Dmitri *Sitkovetsky.

Davidovsky, Mario (*b* Medanos, Buenos Aires, 1934). Argentinian composer who settled in NY 1960. Associate dir. Columbia-Princeton elec. mus. centre, from 1964, dir. from 1981. Also held teaching posts in NY (incl. City Coll. of City Univ., 1968–80). Comps. incl. orch. works, chamber mus., and elec. works. His *Synchronism No.6* (from Nos. 1 to 8) for pf. and elec. sound won *Pulitzer Prize 1971.

Davidsbündler (Ger.). Adherents of the League of David. The *Davidsbund* was an imaginary soc. of artists invented by Robert Schumann to fight the philistines of art in the pages of his magazine *Neue Zeitschrift für Musik*. Some members represented Schumann's friends under fanciful names, e.g. Wieck (Master Raro), Mendelssohn (Felix Meritis), Stephen Heller (Jeanquirit), Clara Schumann (Chiara, Chiarina, Zilia), and Schumann himself (Florestan and Eusebius, representing the two sides of his nature, fiery and gentle). Other names were taken from the writings of Jean Paul Richter. The *Davidsbündlertänze* (Dances of the Adherents of the League of David) are 18 'characteristic pieces' for pf. by Schumann, Op.6, comp. 1837, rev. 1850.

Davie, Cedric Thorpe (*b* London, 1913; *d* Dalry, Kirkcudbrightshire, 1983). Scottish composer, organist, and pianist. Joined staff, RSAMD then Master of Mus., St Andrews Univ., 1945–73, Prof. of Mus., 1973–8. Comp. opera *Gammer Gurton's Needle*; sym.; *Fantasy on Scottish Tunes*; str. qt.; vc. sonatina; incidental mus. for *The Thrie Estaites*; films, and TV. OBE 1955.

Davies, Arthur (*b* Wrexham, 1941). Welsh tenor. Was factory draughtsman and already married before taking up singing. Solo début as Squeak in *Billy Budd*, WNO (Cardiff) 1972. Over next 12 years sang over 30 prin. roles incl. Nemorino, Nadir, Nero, the Fox (*The Cunning Little Vixen*), Števa, Lensky, Rodolfo, Pinkerton, and Don José. CG début 1976. Has sung with ENO, Scottish Opera, Opera North (Gaston in Brit. stage première of Verdi's *Jérusalem*), and Eur. and Amer. companies. In concert-hall is notable singer of Elgar oratorios.

Davies, Ben [Benjamin] (Grey) (*b* Pontardawe, 1858; *d* Bath, 1943). Welsh tenor. Won prize at Swansea Eisteddfod, 1877. Début Birmingham 1881 in *The Bohemian Girl*. Sang with Carl Rosa and other opera cos. but after 1894 was chiefly to be heard in concerts and oratorio, particularly Handel Fests. at which he last sang in 1926.

Davies, David Ffrangçon. See *Ffrangçon-Davies, David*.

Davies, Dennis Russell (*b* Toledo, Ohio, 1944). Amer. conductor. Début as pianist Toledo 1961. Taught at Juilliard Sch. 1968–71. Début as cond. with Juilliard Ens. which he co-founded with Berio and cond. 1968–74. Cond. f.p. of Berio's *Opera* in Santa Fe 1970. Mus. dir., Norwalk (Conn.) SO 1968–73, St Paul Chamber Orch.

1973–80. Bayreuth début 1978. Mus. dir., Württemberg State Opera, Stuttgart, 1980–7, Bonn Opera from 1987. Chicago début 1987. Prin. cond. and dir. of classical mus. programming, Saratoga Performing Arts Center 1985–8. Mus. dir. Brooklyn Acad. of Mus. and prin. cond. Brooklyn SO from 1991. Has cond. f.ps. of works by Cage, Carter, Feldman, Berio, etc., in NY. Chief cond. Stuttgart CO from 1995, Vienna Radio SO 1996–2000, Linz Opera from 2000.

Davies, Fanny (*b* Guernsey, 1861; *d* London, 1934). Eng. pianist. Début London 1885 (Beethoven's G major conc.), thereafter assoc. in chamber mus. with musicians such as Joachim, Casals, and Piatti. Had repertory of 30 concs. High Ger. reputation as interpreter of Brahms and Schumann. First to play Debussy preludes in Eng. Elgar's *Concert Allegro* was written for her. Pianist in chamber concert of works by Janáček during his visit to London, May 1926.

Davies, Hugh (Seymour) (*b* Exmouth, 1943; *d* London, 2005). Eng. composer. Ass. to Stockhausen 1964–6 and member of his EMS. Dir., EMS, Goldsmiths' Coll., London Univ. 1967–86; consultant, mus. dept. Gemeentemuseum, The Hague, from 1986. Comps. are mainly elec., e.g. *Quintet* (1967–8) for 5 performers, 5 microphones, sine/square wave generator, 4-channel switching unit, potentiometers, 6 loudspeakers. Other works incl. *Shozyg I and II* (1968); *Shozyg Sequence* No.1 (1971), No. 2 (1977), No.3 (1990–1); *Natural Images* (1976); *Four Songs* (1979–81); *I Have a Dream* (1984–5); *Strata* (1987); *Fanfare*, 5 tpt. (1991); *Inventio*, ens. (1994); *Three Beginnings in the Form of a Leek*, pf. (1995); *From Trees and Rocks*, elec. (2000).

Davies, (Albert) **Meredith** (*b* Birkenhead, 1922; *d* New Alresford, Hants, 2005). Eng. conductor and organist. Cond. Bach Choir 1947, org. and master of choristers St Albans Cath. 1947–9, org., Hereford Cath. 1949–56, assoc. cond. CBSO 1957–60, mus. dir. EOG 1963–5, cond. Vancouver SO 1964–71, BBC Training Orch. 1969–72. Prin., TCL 1979–88. Shared, with composer, conducting of f.p. of Britten's *War Requiem* (Coventry, 1962). Guest cond. leading Brit. orchs., also at CG, SW, Aldeburgh, and other fests. CBE 1982.

Davies, Peter Maxwell. See *Maxwell Davies, Peter*.

Davies, Ryland (*b* Cwm, Ebbw Vale, 1943). Welsh tenor. Ricordi opera prize; sang in Glyndebourne ch. and won John Christie Scholarship 1965. Début WNO 1964 as Almaviva in *Il barbiere di Siviglia*. Glyndebourne for 25 years from 1965; Scottish Opera from 1966; CG from 1969; Salzburg Fest. 1970; S. Francisco 1970; NY Met 1975. Taught at RNCM.

Davies, Tudor (*b* Cymmer, S. Wales, 1892; *d* Penault, Mon., 1958). Welsh tenor. CG début as Rodolfo in *La bohème* with BNOC 1921, singing role with Melba, 1922. First professional singer of title-role in Vaughan Williams's *Hugh the Drover*. Prin. ten. Old Vic and SW, 1931–41; Carl Rosa 1941–6. Also sang at Paris Opéra and in USA.

Davies, (Sir) (Henry) **Walford** (*b* Oswestry, 1869; *d* Wrington, 1941). Welsh composer and organist. Taught counterpoint RCM 1895–1903. Org., Temple Church, London, 1898–1918. Cond. Bach Choir 1903–7. Mus. dir. RAF 1917 (comp. its march). Prof. of mus., Univ. of Wales 1919–26. Org., St George's Chapel, Windsor, 1927–32. One of first popular broadcasters on mus., serving in advisory capacity at BBC 1927–39. Apart from RAF march, best-known comps. are *Solemn Melody*, org., str. (1908) and hymn *God be in my head*. Comps. incl. cantatas *The Temple* (1902) and *Everyman* (1904), sym. (1911), church mus., and songs. Master of the King's Musick 1934–41. OBE 1919. Knighted 1922. KCVO 1937.

Davis, (Sir) **Andrew** (Frank) (*b* Ashridge, 1944). Eng. conductor, organist, and harpsichordist. Pianist, harpsichordist, and org., Academy of St Martin-in-the-Fields, 1966–70. Assoc. cond. BBC Scottish SO 1970–2, New Philharmonia Orch. 1974, RLPO 1974–6; prin. cond. and mus. dir. Toronto SO 1975–88; prin. cond. BBC SO 1989–2000; mus. dir. Glyndebourne Opera 1989–2000. Mus. dir. Chicago Lyric Opera from 2000. Opera début Glyndebourne, 1973 (*Capriccio*). Amer. début 1974 (NYPO). Cond. f. Brit. p. of Tippett's *The Mask of Time*, 1986, and his *New Year*, 1990. CBE 1991. Knighted 1999.

Davis, Carl (*b* NY, 1936). Amer. composer and conductor. Cond. NY City Opera and Robert Shaw Chorale. Revue of which he was co-author was perf. at Edinburgh Fest. 1961, after which he was invited to write mus. for Brit. radio and TV. Has written incid. mus. for Royal Shakespeare Co. and Nat. Th., and ballets for London Contemporary Dance Th. and Northern Ballet. Has also provided scores for silent films, incl. *Napoleon* and *Ben Hur*. Collab. with Paul McCartney on *Liverpool Oratorio*, 1991. Hon. CBE 2005. Works incl.:

BALLETS: *A Simple Man* (1987); *Lippizaner* (1989); *Liaisons amoureuses* (Offenbach, arr. Davis) (1989); *A Christmas Carol* (1992); *Alice in Wonderland* (after Tchaikovsky) (1995); *Aladdin* (2001).

ORCH.: *Symphony—Lines on London* (1980); *Ov. on Australian Themes* (1981); cl. conc. (1984); *Fantasy*, fl., str., hpd. (1985); *Glenlivet Fireworks Music* (1987); *The Pigeon's Progress*, narr., orch. (1988); *A Duck's Diary*, narr., orch. (1990); *The Town Fox*, narr., orch. (1990); Suite, *The Raft of the Medusa* (1992); *Corsican Suite* (1996); *The Nativity Story* (from *Ben Hur*), narr., orch. (2005).

VOICE(S) & ORCH.: *The Most Wonderful Birthday of All*, sop., orch. (1985); *Liverpool Oratorio* (with McCartney) (1991); *Three Spirituals*, bar./mez., pf./orch. (1998); *On the Beach at Night Alone*, bar., ch., orch. (1999).

FILMS & TV: *The World at War* (1974); Suite, *The Mayor of Casterbridge* (1978); *Champions*, suite (1983); Suite, *The French Lieutenant's Woman* (1985); *The Far Pavilions—Theme* (arr. Palmer) (1986); *Scandal—Theme* (1988); *Anne Frank Remembered* (1995); *Phantom of the Opera* (1996); *A Dance to the Music of Time* (1997); *The Iron Mask* (1999); *The Adventurer* (2000); *The Freshman* (2002).

Davis, (Sir) **Colin** (Rex) (*b* Weybridge, 1927). Eng. conductor. Prof. début 1948 as clarinettist in Kalmar Orch. and as cond. with same orch. 1949. Founder (1950) and prin. cond. with Chelsea Opera Group. Assoc. cond. BBC Scottish SO 1957–9; début Glyndebourne 1960 (*Die Zauberflöte*). CG début with Royal Ballet 1960, with opera co. 1965. SW début 1958, cond. SW Opera 1959–65, mus. dir. from 1961. At SW cond. f. Brit. ps. of *The Cunning Little Vixen* (1961), *Rise and Fall of the City of Mahagonny (1963). Cond. BBCSO 1967–71; chief cond. and mus. dir. Royal Opera, CG, 1971–86; cond. Bavarian Radio SO 1983–92. Prin. cond. LSO 1995–2006. Début NY Met 1967. Notable exponent of Berlioz, Mozart, Stravinsky, Tippett, and Sibelius. Cond. f.ps. of *The Mines of Sulphur* (SW 1965), *The Knot Garden* (CG 1970) and *The Ice Break* (CG 1977). Cond. f. Brit. p. of 3-act *Lulu* (CG 1981). Salzburg Fest. début 1976. First Briton to cond. at Bayreuth Fest. (*Tannhäuser*, 1977). CBE 1965. Knighted 1980. Hamburg Shakespeare Prize 1984. CH 2001.

Davis, Miles (Dewey) (*b* Alton, Ill., 1926; *d* Santa Monica, Calif., 1991). Amer. jazz trumpeter and flügel horn player. Began playing at 13. Went to NY, playing with Charlie Parker, Coleman Hawkins, and Billy Eckstine. After success at Newport Jazz Fest. 1955 formed own quintet which lasted until 1957. In 1960s and 1970s led series of small groups. Noted for restraint and lyricism of his playing and for his consistently progressive approach, leading him to electronics and hard rock.

Davison, James William (*b* London, 1813; *d* Margate, 1885). Eng. music critic on *The Times* 1846–79. Friend of Mendelssohn and antipathetic to Wagner. Husband of pianist Arabella *Goddard. Founded *Musical Examiner* 1842.

Dawson, Anne (*b* Stoke-on-Trent, 1952). Eng. soprano. Kathleen Ferrier memorial schol. 1982. Sang Angelica in Handel's *Orlando*, Bath Festival 1978. Grenoble Fest. 1979. Prof. opera début, ENO 1981 (Xenia in *Boris Godunov*); Glyndebourne 1984; CG début 1988. Has sung with WNO, GTO, Opera North, and throughout Eur.

Dawson, Lynne (*b* York, 1953). Eng. soprano. Opera début 1986 as Countess in *Le nozze di Figaro* (Kent Opera). Scottish Opera début 1988; Paris 1988. From 1985 specialized in Eng. Baroque operas, singing with ens. cond. by John Eliot Gardiner, Trevor Pinnock, and Christopher Hogwood. Salzburg Fest. début 1990.

Dawson, Peter (*b* Adelaide, 1882; *d* Sydney, NSW, 1961). Australian bass-baritone. Début CG 1909 but became better known for singing of popular ballads, e.g. Kipling's *The Road to Mandalay* and *Boots*, which he comp. under pseudonym J. P. McCall. These overshadowed his excellent ability in operatic arias and *Lieder*, always sung in Eng. and preserved by recordings. Began recording 1904; sold 13 million records.

dazu (Ger.). Thereto, i.e. (in org. playing) the stops mentioned are now to be added to the others.

D.C. Abbreviation for *da capo.

Dead March in Saul. Popular name for the funeral march from Handel's oratorio *Saul* (1739) which is used on state occasions such as the funeral of a sovereign. See also *funeral marches*.

Dean, Stafford (Roderick) (*b* Kingswood, Surrey, 1937). Eng. bass. Toured with Opera for All 1962–3, 1963–4. Glyndebourne début 1964 (Lictor in *L'incoronazione di Poppea*). Sang with SW co. 1964–70. CG début 1969; NY Met 1976. Bass soloist in f.p. of Penderecki's *Requiem*, Stuttgart 1984. Has sung Leporello well over 300 times.

Dean, Winton (Basil) (*b* Birkenhead, 1916). Eng. music scholar and writer. Son of Basil Dean, theatrical director. Authority and author of books on Bizet, Handel, and other composers. His *Handel's Dramatic Oratorios and Masques* (1959) and *Handel's Operas 1704–26* (1987) are major works of scholarship. Has prepared several Handel edns. His *Essays on Opera* was pubd. 1990. Prof. of mus., Univ. of Calif., Berkeley, 1964–5.

Dean Paul, Lady. See *Poldowski*.

Dearnley, Christopher (Hugh) (*b* Wolverhampton, 1930). Eng. organist. Ass. org. Salisbury Cath. 1954, org. 1957–68. Org. and dir. of mus., St Paul's Cath. 1968–90. Authority on church mus. of late 17th and early 18th cents.

Death and the Maiden (Der Tod und das Mädchen). Song (D531) comp. by Schubert in Feb. 1817, a setting of poem by Matthias Claudius (1740–1815). The theme of the pf. introduction to the song was used again by Schubert in 1824 in his Str. Qt. No.14 in D minor (D810) where it is the theme for the 2nd movement set of variations.

Death and Transfiguration (Strauss). See *Tod und Verklärung*.

Death in Venice. Opera in 2 acts (17 scenes) by Britten, Op.88, to lib. by Myfanwy Piper based on Thomas Mann's novella, *Der Tod in Venedig* (1912). F.p. Aldeburgh 16 June 1973, CG 18 Oct. 1973. NY Met 1974. Orch. suite arr. S. *Bedford, Aldeburgh 1984.

Death of Klinghoffer, The. Opera in 2 acts by John *Adams to lib. by Alice Goodman. Comp. 1990–1. Prod. Brussels 1991, Brooklyn Acad. of Mus., NY, 1991, Edinburgh Fest. 2005. Plot based on events following hijacking by four Palestinian terrorists of Ital. cruise liner *Achille Lauro* in Alexandria in Oct. 1985 when Amer. passenger, Leon Klinghoffer, was shot and thrown overboard in his wheelchair.

Death of Moses, The. Choral work by Alexander *Goehr, to text by John Hollander, for sop., cont. (or male alto), ten., bar., and bass soloists, mixed ch., mixed children's ch. (or semi-ch. of sop. and alt.), and 13 instrumentalists. Comp. 1991–2. F.p. 1992, Seville Cath., Spain., cond. John Eliot Gardiner.

Debain, Alexandre François (*b* Paris, 1809; *d* Paris, 1877). Fr. manufacturer of kbd. instr. Est. factory 1834. Invented *harmonium (c.1842), antiphonel (1846), and harmonicorde (1851).

De Bériot, Charles-Auguste. See *Bériot, Charles-Auguste de*.

Deborah. Oratorio by Handel to lib. by S. Humphreys, after *Judges V*. Mus. taken partly from earlier works. F.p. London 1733.

De Burgos, Rafael Frühbeck. See *Frühbeck de Burgos, Rafael*.

Debussy, Achille-Claude (*b* St Germain-en-Laye, 1862; *d* Paris, 1918). Fr. composer and critic. As a child he had little formal education but his mus. tendencies were channelled into pf. lessons, those with Verlaine's mother-in-law, Mme Mauté de Fleurville, leading to his entry into the Paris Cons. in 1872. His reputation there was that of an erratic pianist and a recalcitrant in matters of harmony and theory. In 1880 and 1881 he went for summer employment to Russia as pianist to Tchaikovsky's patron, Mme von Meck. Failing to win the *Prix de Rome* in 1883, he succeeded in 1884 with the cantata *L'Enfant prodigue*. He spent 2 years at the Villa Medici, Rome, where he met Liszt, Verdi, and Boito, and heard *Lohengrin*. He went to the Bayreuth fests. of 1888 and 1889, but an even greater mus. influence was that of hearing the Javanese *gamelan at the 1889 Paris Exposition. Other influences of these years were his friendship with the painters of what became known as the 'Impressionist' movt. and, even more important, with writers and poets such as Mallarmé and the 'symbolists'. But after 1889 he could not share the symbolists' idolatry of Wagner, recognizing his greatness but also the fact that he represented a 'dead end' for other composers. He cultivated a distinctively Fr. mus. outlook, eventually styling himself 'musicien français'. Other significant events in his life were his study in 1889 of the score of *Boris Godunov and his acquaintance from 1891 with Erik *Satie.

In 1893 Debussy began work on an opera based on Maeterlinck's play *Pelléas et Mélisande*, a task that was to occupy him for nearly 10 years. In 1893 his str. qt. was perf., and in 1894 his orch. *Prélude à l'Après-midi d'un Faune* upset certain critics with its alleged 'formlessness'. He followed this with his 3 *Nocturnes*, orig. planned for solo vn. and orch., perf. 1900 and 1901. They are ded. to Rosalie (Lily) Texier, whom he married in 1899 but deserted 5 years later for Mme Emma Bardac, a singer and wife of a banker, whom he married in 1908. Their child was born in 1905, the year in which the symphonic sketches *La Mer* were f.p. *Pelléas* had been successfully prod. at the Opéra-Comique in 1902, to the fury of Maeter-

linck who publicly wished it 'emphatic failure'. Debussy's remaining orch. works were the set of 3 *Images* comp. between 1905 and 1912, and the ballet *Jeux* for Diaghilev (1913). In 1910 he developed cancer and was a semi-invalid when war broke out in 1914. He wrote some mus. inspired by patriotic sentiments and completed 3 sonatas before his death. He wrote mus. criticism under the pseudonym of M. Croche. A collection, *Monsieur Croche antidilettante*, was pubd. in Paris 1921 (Eng. trans. 1962).

Debussy was among the greatest and most important of 20th-cent. composers both by reason of his own achievement and by the paths he opened for others to explore, hence the homage to him paid by later composers such as Boulez, Messiaen, Webern, Bartók, Stravinsky, and many others. His use of block chords, of harmony with a modal flavour and based on the whole-tone scale, the delicate colours of his orchestration, his technique of 'layering' sounds, the declamatory yet wholly lyrical style of his vocal writing, especially in *Pelléas*, all proclaim him an innovator of the first degree who revolutionized comp. for the pf. and for the orch. In general Debussy's effects are understated, his aim being for a 'sonorous halo' of sound. But the label of 'impressionist', while accurate, has tended to obscure the strong sense of form which underlies all his works. Prin. comps.:

STAGE: *Rodrigue et Chimène* (opera, 1888–92, unfinished. Vers. by Richard Langham-Smith perf. Paris 1987 and Lyons 1993); *Pelléas et Mélisande* (opera, 1893–5, 1901–2); *Le diable le beffroi* (2 tableaux after Poe, 1902–11, incomplete); *Jeux* (ballet, 1912–13); *Khamma* (ballet, 1911–12, orch. *Koechlin, 1912–13); *La *boîte à joujoux* (children's ballet, 1913, orch. completed 1918–19, Caplet); incidental mus. to *King Lear* (1904); incidental mus. for *Le *Martyre de Saint Sébastien* by D'Annunzio (orch. Debussy and Caplet) (1911); *La *Chute de la Maison Usher* (1908–17, unfin. opera after Poe).

ORCH.: *Printemps* (1887); *Prélude à l'*Après-midi d'un faune* (1892–4); 3 *Nocturnes* (1897–9); *La *Mer* (1903–5); 3 *Images* (1905–12); *Fantaisie*, pf., orch. (1889); *Rapsodie*, sax., orch. (1901–8); *Danse sacrée et danse profane*, hp., str. (1904); *Berceuse héroïque* (1914, also for pf.).

CHAMBER MUSIC: str. qt. (1893); *Première rapsodie*, cl., pf. (1901–8); *Syrinx*, fl. (1913); vc. sonata (1915); sonata for fl., va., hp. (1915); vn. sonata (1916–17).

CHORAL: *L'*Enfant prodigue*, cantata, sop., ten., bar., ch., orch. (1884, rev. 1906–8); *La Damoiselle élue* (*The *Blessed Damozel*), cantata, sop., women's ch., orch. (1887–8, re-orch. 1902); 3 *Chansons de Charles d'Orléans*, unacc. SATB (1898–1908).

PIANO: 2 *Arabesques* (1888–91); *Suite bergamasque* (1890, rev. 1906); *Pour le Piano* (1896–1901); *Estampes* (1903); *L'*Isle joyeuse* (1904); *Images* I (1905), *Images* II (1907); *Children's Corner* (1906–8); 12 *Préludes*, Book I (1910), Book II (1912–13); 12 *Études* (Books I and II, 1915).

PIANO DUET: *Petite Suite* (1886–9); *Marche écossaise* (1891) (orch. version by Debussy); 6 *Épigraphes antiques* (1914) (orch. Escher, 1976–7).

2 PIANOS: *Lindaraja* (1901); *En blanc et noir* (1915).

SONGS: *Mandoline* (1880–3); *Cinq poèmes de Baudelaire* (1887–9); *Ariettes oubliées* (1888); *Fêtes galantes* I (1882, rev. 1891–2) and II (1904); *Proses lyriques* (1892–3); *Chansons de Bilitis* (1897–8); *Trois ballades de Villon* (1910) (also with orch. acc.); *Trois ballades de Mallarmé* (1913).

ARRANGEMENTS: Orch. of 2 of Satie's *Gymnopédies* 1896; pf. transcrs. of Wagner, Schumann, Gluck, Raff, Saint-Saëns, and Tchaikovsky.

début (Fr.). Beginning. First public appearance.

decani (Lat.). Of the dean, i.e. that side of the choir of a cath., etc., on which the Dean sits, now normally the south side. In church mus., passages marked *decani* must be taken by the singers on that side. See also *cantoris*.

deceptive cadence. Same as Interrupted cadence, i.e. chord of the dominant followed by that of submediant.

decibel. Logarithmic unit which expresses difference between different intensities of sound-levels or differently-powered electric signals.

décidé (Fr.), **deciso** (It.). Decided. With decision (i.e. firmly, not flabbily). So the It. superlative, *decisissimo*.

decimette. A comp. for 10 performers.

Decker, Franz-Paul (*b* Cologne, 1922). Ger. conductor. Mus. dir. Crefeld 1946–50, Wiesbaden opera 1950–3, municipal mus. dir. Wiesbaden 1953–6, mus. dir. Bochum 1956–64, chief cond. Rotterdam PO 1962–8. Mus. dir. Montreal SO 1967–75, mus. adv. Calgary PO 1975–7, Winnipeg SO 1981–2, mus. dir. Barcelona SO from 1986, chief cond. New Zealand SO 1990 (having been prin. guest cond. 1980–9).

Decoration Day. 2nd movt. of Ives's *New England Holidays* for orch., sometimes played separately. Comp. 1912.

decrescendo; decresciuto (It.). Decreasing, decreased, i.e. getting gradually softer.

Dedler, Rochus (*b* Oberammergau, 1779; *d* Vienna, 1882). Ger. composer of the Passion Play mus. used at Oberammergau.

De Fabritiis, Oliviero (Carlo) (*b* Rome, 1902; *d* Rome, 1982). It. conductor and composer. Début Rome 1920. Worked in Salerno and Rome, then was art. secretary Rome Opera House 1932–43. In 1938 began summer perfs. at Baths of Caracalla. Cond. many opera perfs. in which Gigli sang. Brit. début Edinburgh Fest. 1963 (San Carlo co. in *Adriana Lecouvreur*). CG début 1965. Comp. songs and other vocal mus.

Défauw, Désiré (*b* Ghent, 1885; *d* Gary, Ind., 1960). Amer. (Belg.-born) violinist and conductor. London début 1910. Formed Allied Str. Qt.

(which incl. L. *Tertis) 1914–18. Prof. at Brussels Cons. from 1926. Cond. Défauw concerts and Brussels Cons. orch. (1926–40). Est. Orchestre National de Belgique 1937. Went to USA 1938. Cond., Chicago SO 1943–7. Returned to Belgium 1949 but then went back to USA as cond. Gary SO 1950–8.

De Fesch, William (*b* Alkmaar, 1687; *d* London, ?1757). Flemish composer, organist, cellist, and violinist. Choirmaster, Antwerp Cath., 1725–31. Settled in London 1733. First vn. in Handel's orch. 1746; dir. of orch. at Marylebone Gardens 1748–9. Wrote oratorios, masses, concs., and songs.

De Gaetani, Jan(ice) (*b* Massillon, Ohio, 1933; *d* Rochester, NY, 1989). Amer. mezzo-soprano. NY début 1958. Specialist in contemp. mus. Gave f.ps. of Crumb's *Ancient Voices of Children* (1970) and Maxwell Davies's *Stone Litany* (1973). Teacher at Eastman Sch. from 1973. Noted exponent of solo part in Schoenberg's *Pierrot Lunaire*.

Degeyter, Pierre. See *Internationale*.

degree. A note's classification regarding its position in the scale. When a note is 3 degrees from another, the interval separating them is a 4th. The notes of the major scale are called the 1st, 2nd, etc. degrees of the scale, returning to the first degree. Alternative names for the 7 degrees are tonic, supertonic, mediant, subdominant, dominant, submediant, and leading-note.

De Greef, Arthur. See *Greef, Arthur de*.

degrees and diplomas in music. (1) BRITISH UNIVERSITY DEGREES. The degrees in music given by Brit. and Irish universities are Bachelor (BMus or MusB), Master of Music (MMus), and Doctor (DMus or MusD). Universities which confer a MMus degree are Birmingham, Bristol, Cambridge, Durham, East Anglia, Edinburgh, London, Manchester, Newcastle upon Tyne, and Surrey.

In several universities it is possible to obtain by research in musical subjects the degree of LittM, LittB, LittD, EdM, and PhD (or MLitt, BLitt, DLitt, MEd, and DPhil)—Bachelor and Doctor of Letters, and Doctor of Philosophy. At Reading, music may be studied with physics for BSc.

By an old custom dating from the 13th cent., the Archbishop of Canterbury (by virtue of his former office of Legate of the Pope) has the power to grant degrees, and he sometimes exercises this power by conferring the doctorate of music. These degrees are known as Canterbury Degrees (DMus Cantuar) or (from the Archbishop's London palace, from which they are issued) Lambeth Degrees.

Various universities in the Commonwealth confer music degrees, their requirements being not so much standardized as those of British universities.

At some Brit. universities music can now be taken as one of the subjects for a degree in Arts. Through the Council for National Academic

Awards, some polytechnics and colleges of technology award a BA degree for music.

(2) DIPLOMAS. The diploma-conferring bodies in the list now to be given are recognized as genuine public bodies. Their diplomas are usually graded as follows: (a) Associateship, (b) Licentiateship (not always present), (c) Fellowship. This is not quite invariable, however; for instance, the Royal Academy of Music confers Licentiateship upon external or internal candidates. Fellowship is reserved by some institutions as a purely honorary distinction.

ROYAL ACADEMY OF MUSIC (founded 1822). FRAM (limited to 150 distinguished past students); Hon RAM (honorary members); ARAM; LRAM (open to non-students and with the differentiation, 'teacher' or 'performer'); SPECIAL DIPLOMA of the Teachers' Training Course.

ROYAL COLLEGE OF MUSIC (founded 1883, succeeding the National Training Coll. of Music, founded 1873). FRCM (honorary, limited to 50); Hon RCM (distinguished non-students); Hon ARCM (distinguished past students); ARCM by examination, open to non-students and with the differentiation, 'teacher' or 'performer'); MMus RCM (Master of Music—severe and varied tests; open to non-students); Teachers' Training Course certificate awarded to selected students from certain colleges for a 1-year course.

ASSOCIATED BOARD The RAM and RCM combine, under the title 'Royal Schools of Music, London' with also Royal Northern College and Royal Scottish Academy, to confer in the Commonwealth the diploma, formerly known as LAB (Licentiate of the Associated Board), now entitled LRSM, London. This is the Overseas equivalent of LRAM and ARCM.

ROYAL COLLEGE OF ORGANISTS (founded 1864), ARCO; FRCO, with an additional (optional) diploma entitling the candidate to add the letters ChM (i.e. Choirmaster). In 1936 the Archbishop of Canterbury instituted a Diploma in Church Music to the examination for which he admits only FRCOs holding the ChM diploma, who on passing his examination become ADCMs.

TRINITY COLLEGE OF MUSIC (founded 1872 and a teaching school of music in Univ. of London). ATCL; LTCL; FTCL (these in executive subjects—as Teacher or Performer); AMusTCL; LMusTCL (these in theoretical subjects). GTCL; Hon. FTCL Hon TCL (FTCL awarded also for orig. composition).

GUILDHALL SCHOOL OF MUSIC AND DRAMA (founded 1880). BMus (degree course); AGSM (internal students); LGSM (internal and external students); FGSM (honorary—limited to 100); GGSM (internal students); Hon GSM (honorary—limited to 100).

ROYAL MANCHESTER COLLEGE OF MUSIC (founded 1893). ARMCM (after a 3 years' course and examination) and FRMCM (honorary only) also Hon RMCM. This college was amalgamated in 1972 into Royal Northern College of Music.

ROYAL NORTHERN COLLEGE OF MUSIC, MANCHESTER (founded 1972, being amalgamation of RMCM

and Northern School of Music). GMusRNCM; GRNCM; PPRNCM (Professional Performance Course).

BIRMINGHAM CONSERVATORY (founded 1887). ABSM; ABSM (TTD), Teacher's Training Diploma; LBSM; GBSM (after Graduate Course); FBSM (honorary).

ROYAL SCOTTISH ACADEMY OF MUSIC AND DRAMA (founded 1929). Dip RSAM and (in musical education) Dip Mus Ed RSAM (both after a full course in the Academy and examination).

LONDON COLLEGE OF MUSIC (founded 1887). Diplomas include ALCM, LLCM, FLCM, GLCM, AMusLCM, LMusLCM.

ROYAL MILITARY SCHOOL OF MUSIC (Kneller Hall). Graduation is indicated by the letters psm, meaning 'passed school of music'.

BANDSMAN'S COLLEGE OF MUSIC. This examining body was instituted in 1931 with unpaid officials and described as The National Institutions of the Brass Band Movement. It awards, after examination, 3 diplomas, BBCM (Bandmaster), ABCM, and LBCM.

OVERSEAS SCHOOLS OF MUSIC. Some of the universities in different parts of the Commonwealth, having schools of music attached, grant a diploma. The Royal Canadian College of Organists grants diplomas of ARCCO and FRCCO.

(3) AMERICAN DEGREES. The number of universities, colleges, schools of music, etc., conferring music degrees is well over 700, of which over half are at bachelor level only. The oldest undergraduate degrees are BA and BMus. Many music courses are for 4 years, most of them involving practical work such as conducting. Degrees in theory, musicology, and performance in some universities are Master of Music (MM) and Master of Music Education (MME). There are also DMA (Doctor of Musical Arts) and MMA.

(4) AMERICAN DIPLOMAS. The USA, fortunately, does not possess the bewildering variety of diploma-conferring institutions of Britain, nor are alphabetical distinctions of any kind so much valued. The Amer. Guild of Organists (1896) confers diplomas of Associateship and Fellowship—AAGO and FAGO: when the examination as choirmaster is passed the letters ChM may be added.

Degrigny, Nicolas. See *Grigny, Nicolas de*.

dehors (Fr.). (1) Outside, as in *en dehors*, from the outside.

(2) Prominent. Applied musically to a melody which the composer intends to be particularly prominent.

Deidamia. Opera in 3 acts by Handel (his last), to lib. by Rolli. Comp. 1740, prod. London 1741, Hartford, Conn., 1959. Revived London 1955 and subsequently in Ger.

Deirdre of the Sorrows. (1) Opera by Karl *Rankl, based on Synge's play, which won Fest.

of Britain prize, 1951, but was not prod.

(2) Lyric drama in 1 act by John J. Becker (1945).

De Koven, (Henry Louis) **Reginald** (*b* Middletown, Conn., 1859; *d* Chicago, 1920). Amer. composer and conductor. Family moved to Eng. in 1872. Returned to USA where he became successful composer of light operas, mus. critic, and founder and cond. of Washington PO (1902–5). Wrote 2 operas, *The Canterbury Pilgrims* (NY Met 1917) and *Rip Van Winkle* (Chicago and NY 1920). Operettas incl. *Don Quixote* (1889) and *Robin Hood* (1890). Comp. over 400 songs, pf. sonata, and ballets.

Delacôte, Jacques (*b* Remiremont, Vosges, 1942). Fr. conductor. Won Mitropoulos Comp., NY, 1971. Début with NYPO 1972. Since then has cond. at all major opera houses and with many leading orchs.

Delage, (Charles) **Maurice** (*b* Paris, 1879; *d* Paris, 1961). Fr. composer, pupil of Ravel. Student of Indian mus. and wrote *Quatre poèmes hindous* for v. and orch. (1921). Orch. version of *Debussy's *Chansons de Bilitis* 1926.

Delalande, Michel Richard. See *Lalande, Michel-Richard de*.

de Lara, Isidore. See *Lara, Isidore de*.

Delibes, (Clément Philibert) **Léo** (*b* St Germain-du-Val, nr. Le Mans, 1836; *d* Paris, 1891). Fr. composer and organist. Org., St Pierre de Chaillot, 1853–62. Became acc. at Théâtre Lyrique, 1853. First operetta, *Deux Sous de Charbon*, 1855, led to series of popular short works in this genre. 2nd chorusmaster at Opéra 1865. Wrote ballets *Coppélia* (1870) and *Sylvia* (1876), and 3 works for the Opéra-Comique, *Le Roi l'a dit* (1873), *Jean de Nivelle* (1880), and *Lakmé* (1883). A 4-act opera, *Kassya*, was left unfinished, completed by Massenet, and staged 1893. Wrote incidental mus. for *Le Roi s'amuse* (1882) and 15 songs, best-known being *Les Filles de Cadiz*. Org., St Jean-St François, 1862–71. Prof. of comp., Paris Cons. 1881. Name frequently misspelt 'Délibes'.

delicato (It.). Delicate. So *delicatamente*, delicately; *delicatissimo*, as delicately as possible; *delicatezza*, delicacy.

délié (Fr.). Untied. (1) The notes separated from each other, i.e. staccato.

(2) Unconstrained in style.

(3) Supple (fingers).

delirio (It.). Frenzy. So *delirante*, frenzied.

Delius, Fritz later **Frederick** (Theodor Albert) (*b* Bradford, Yorks., 1862; *d* Grez-sur-Loing, Fr., 1934). Eng. composer. Fourth of 14 children of a Ger. couple who had settled in Eng. to engage in the wool trade. The father, Julius Delius, was a mus. lover, helping to organize Hallé concerts and entertaining musicians like Joachim and Piatti in his home, but implacably opposed to mus. as a career for his son, despite Fritz's talent and aptitude. The youth tried to accede to his father's wishes by entering business, but he had no gift for textile commerce and in 1884 went to Florida to manage an orange-plantation at Solana Grove. The oranges were neglected while Delius studied mus. with Thomas F. Ward, a Jacksonville organist. A year later he himself set up as a vn. teacher first in Jacksonville, then at Danville, Virginia, eventually taking an organist's post in NY. The Negro melodies he heard in Florida deeply influenced him, as can be heard in *Appalachia*. By now his father was prepared to allow him to enter the Leipzig Cons. (1886). Academic tuition held no attractions, however, and Delius went to live in the Paris of the 90s where his circle incl. Gauguin, Ravel, Munch, and Strindberg. Already, on a holiday in Norway in 1887, he had become a close friend of *Grieg and deeply attached to Scandinavian life and literature.

His *Florida* suite was perf. privately in Leipzig, 1888. While in Paris he comp. his first opera, *Irmelin* (1890–1, f.p. Oxford 1953). This was followed by *The Magic Fountain* (1894–5, f.p. BBC studio broadcast 1977), songs, the first Vn. Sonata, the tone-poem *Over the Hills and Far Away* (begun *c*.1893), and another opera, *Koanga* (1896–7). In 1899 a concert of his works was given in London which encouraged him to complete his orch. nocturne *Paris: the Song of a Great City*. This was perf. at Elberfeld, 1901, cond. by Hans *Haym and a year later in Berlin under Busoni. Haym also cond. f.p. of the Pf. Conc., in Elberfeld 1904, with Julius Buths as soloist. Haym, together with Fritz *Cassirer, was Delius's earliest champion, being followed some years later in England by Wood and, in particular, *Beecham. Until about 1904 Delius pubd. his works under the name Fritz Delius.

From 1897, Delius lived at Grez-sur-Loing, near Fontainebleau, with the artist Jelka Rosen, whom he married in 1903. From 1899 to 1902 he worked on 2 operas, *A Village Romeo and Juliet*, and *Margot-la-Rouge*, and revised *Appalachia* (begun *c*.1896). His reputation in Ger. was greater at this time than in his native land but the balance was corrected from 1907 with f.ps. in England of a series of works: 1907: pf. conc. (London, soloist Szanto, cond. Wood); 1908: *Paris* (Liverpool, cond. Beecham), *Life's Dance* (first version) (London, cond. Arbós), *Brigg Fair* (Liverpool, cond. Bantock), *Sea Drift* (Sheffield, cond. Wood); 1909: *A Mass of Life* (London, cond. Beecham), *In a Summer Garden* (first version) (London, cond. Delius), *Dance Rhapsody No.1* (Hereford, cond. Delius).

In 1908–10 he comp. his last opera *Fennimore and Gerda*, prod. Frankfurt 1919. During the 1914–18 war he left Grez for Eng. for a time, composing *Dance Rhapsody No.2*, vn. sonata, vc. sonata, conc. for vn. and vc., str. qt., vn. conc., *Eventyr*, and a *Requiem* (text by H. Simon) 'dedicated to the memory of all young artists fallen in the war'. This last work was perf. in 1922 and was so savagely criticized for its 'atheism' that it remained unperf. again for over 40 years. Shortly after the war he wrote a vc. conc. and the incidental mus. to Flecker's play *Hassan* (1923). In 1922 Delius developed the first signs of progressive paralysis, said to have resulted from syphilis contracted in Paris in 1890s, or even perhaps in Florida. Four years later he became blind and helpless. From 1928 he was enabled to continue composing through the assistance of a young Yorkshire musician, Eric *Fenby, who offered his services as amanuensis. Among the works comp. in this period were *A Song of Summer*, the 3rd vn. sonata, *Songs of Farewell*, *Fantastic Dance*, and an *Idyll* based on material from *Margot-la-Rouge*. In 1929 Delius was made a CH and went to London to attend a fest. of 6 concerts of his mus. organized by Beecham. He died 5 years later, being buried at Grez, but in May 1935 was reinterred at Limpsfield, Surrey.

Delius's mus. is chromatic in harmony and belongs in form and spirit to the post-Wagnerian world of Chausson, Debussy, Strauss, and Mahler. He is *par excellence* the composer-poet of regret for time past, of the transience of human love, but there is also a vigorous ecstatic elation in sections of *A Mass of Life* and the *Song of the High Hills*. Though he despised the classical procedures, his sonatas and concs. succeed because of the way in which he adapted his rhapsodic manner to suit his own version of sonata form. The exquisite orch. scoring of such short works as *On hearing the first cuckoo in spring* and the intermezzo, *Walk to the Paradise Garden*, from *A Village Romeo and Juliet*, have ensured him a regular place in the Eng. repertory, and his songs and unacc. choral works are also very fine. Prin. works:

OPERAS: *Irmelin* (1890–2); *The *Magic Fountain* (1894–5, rev. 1898); *Koanga* (1896–7, rev. 1898); *A *Village Romeo and Juliet* (1899–1901); *Margot-la-Rouge* (1901–2); *Fennimore and Gerda* (1908–10).

MELODRAMA: *Paa Vidderne*, speaker, orch. (poem by Ibsen, 1859–60, set to Ger. trans., *Auf dem Hochgebirge*, by L. Passarge). Comp. 1888.

INCIDENTAL MUSIC: *Folkeraadet* (Parliament), play by G. Heiberg (1897); *Hassan*, play by James Elroy Flecker (1920–3).

ORCH.: *Florida Suite* (1886–7, rev. 1889); *Sleigh Ride*; *Marche Caprice* (1888; *Sleigh Ride* orch. 1889, *Marche Caprice* rev. 1890); *Summer Evening* (1890); *Paa Vidderne* (On the Mountains), sym.-poem (1890–1, rev. 1892); *Over the Hills and Far Away* (?1893–??); *La *Calinda* (from *Koanga*, 1896–7, arr. Fenby 1938); *Life's Dance* (1899, rev. 1901 and 1912); *Paris: the Song of a Great City* (1899); *Appalachia, American Rhapsody* (1st vers. 1896. See VOICE(S) & ORCH.); *Intermezzo: *Walk to the Paradise Garden* (1906, addition to *A Village Romeo and Juliet*); *Brigg Fair: an English Rhapsody* (1907); *In a Summer Garden* (1908, rev. 1913); *Dance Rhapsody* No.1 (1908), No.2 (1916); *2 Mood Pictures for small orch.*: *On hearing the first cuckoo in spring* (1911–13), *Summer Night on the River* (1911); *North Country Sketches* (1913–14); *Air and Dance*, str. (1915); *Eventyr* (1917); *2 *Aquarelles* (arr. for str.

by Fenby, 1938, from 2 unacc. ch. 1917); *A Song before Sunrise* (1918); *A Song of Summer* (1930); *Fantastic Dance* (1931); *Irmelin Prelude* (1931).

CONCERTOS: pf. (1st version in 3 movts. 1897, rev. 1898; rev. in 1 movt. 1906–7); vn. and vc. (1915, f.p. 1920, arr. for vn. and va. by Tertis 1934–5); vn. (1916, f.p. 1919 Sammons, Boult); vc. (1921, f.p. 1923 Frankfurt); *Caprice and Elegy*, vc., chamber orch. (1930, also for vc. and pf. or va. and pf. 1931); *Suite* (incl. *Pastorale*), vn., orch. (1888); *Légende*, vn., orch. (1895).

VOICE(S) & ORCH.: *Maud* (Tennyson), song cycle, v., orch. (1891); *Zarathustra's Night Song*, bar., male ch., orch. (1898); *Appalachia, ch., bar., orch. (1902–3); *Sea Drift*, bar., ch., orch. (1903–4); *A *Mass of Life*, SATB soloists, double ch., orch. (1904–5); *Cynara*, bar., orch. (1907, rev. 1928–9); *Songs of Sunset*, mez., bar., ch., orch. (1906–8); *Song of the High Hills*, ch., orch. (1911); *Arabesk*, bar., ch., orch. (1911); *Requiem*, sop., bar., ch., orch. (1913–16); *A Late Lark* (Henley), v., orch. (1921–5); *Songs of Farewell*, double ch., orch. (1930); *Idyll: Once I passed through a populous city*, sop., bar., orch. (1930–2).

VOICE(S) & PIANO: 5 *Songs from the Norwegian* (1888); 7 *Songs from the Norwegian* (1889–90, No. 3 with Eng. words, 1930, known as *Twilight Fancies*); 3 *English Songs* (Shelley) (1891); 2 *Songs* (Verlaine) (1895); 7 *Danish Songs* (1897); 5 *Songs* (4 to poems by Nietzsche) (1898); 2 *Songs* (1900); *Summer Landscape* (1902); *The nightingale has a lyre of gold* (Henley) (1910); *I-Brasil* (1913); *On Craig Dhu* (1907); *Midsummer Song* (1908); *Wanderer's Song* (1908); *To be sung of a summer night on the water* (unacc.) (1917, arr. for str. by Fenby as 2 *Aquarelles*, 1938); *The Splendour Falls* (unacc.) (1923).

CHAMBER MUSIC: str. qt. (1916, scherzo added 1919, incorp. themes from abandoned 1888 str. qt. 3rd movt., *Late Swallows*, arr. for str. by Fenby 1963, other 3 movts. 1977 with title *Sonata for Strings*); vn. sonata (1892, unpubd.), No.1 (1905–14, f.p. 1915), No.2 (f.p. 1924, arr. for va. by Tertis), No.3 (1930, arr. for va. by Tertis); vc. sonata (1916).

PIANO: *Zum Carnival* (1886); 3 *Preludes* (1923); 5 *Pieces* (1923).

Della Casa, Lisa (*b* Burgdorf, nr. Berne, 1919). Swiss soprano. Début Solothurn-Biel 1941 as Butterfly. Member of City Th., Zurich, 1943–50, singing Pamina, Gilda, Serena in *Porgy and Bess*, and creating role of the Young Woman in Burkhard's *Die schwarze Spinne*, 1949. Sang at Vienna State Opera 1947–74; Salzburg Fest. début 1947 (Zdenka in *Arabella*). Sang a variety of Strauss roles at Salzburg—Countess in *Capriccio*, Chrysothemis, Marschallin, and Ariadne—also Mozart's Countess, Donna Elvira, and Pamina. Created three roles in *Der *Prozess*, Salzburg 1953. Glyndebourne début 1951. First sang Arabella Zurich 1950. CG début 1953; Bayreuth Fest. 1952; NY Met 1953–68. Retired 1974. One of most lustrous of Strauss singers. Made first commercial recording of *Vier letzte Lieder* (1953, cond. Böhm).

Deller, Alfred (George) (*b* Margate, 1912; *d* Bologna, 1979). Eng. countertenor. Lay clerk

Canterbury Cath. 1940–7. Was heard in 1943 by Tippett, who invited him to sing at a Morley Coll. concert. Sang Purcell's *Come, ye Sons of art, away* on opening night of BBC Third Programme, Sept. 1946. Full-time career from 1947. Formed Deller Consort 1950 for authentic perf. of baroque mus. (début Salzburg Fest. 1972). Deller's artistry almost solely responsible for revival of counterten. v. and its use in Purcell, Handel, Monteverdi, etc. Created role of Oberon in *A Midsummer Night's Dream*, 1960. OBE 1970. Son Mark Deller (*b* St. Leonards, 1938) is also counterten.

Dello Joio, Norman (*b* NY, 1913). Amer. composer, pianist, and organist. Son of NY organist and choirmaster, was influenced from childhood by Gregorian chant and It. opera. Studied with Hindemith at Tanglewood 1941 and at Yale Univ. 1941–3. Org., St Ann's Church, NY, 1934–40. Mus. dir. Loring Dance Players 1941–3. Prof. of comp., Mannes Coll. 1956–72, prof. of mus., Boston Univ. 1972–9. His mus. is noted for melodic content rather than for adventurous technique, and he displays a natural gift for opera and ballet (several works for Martha Graham). Prin. works incl.:

OPERAS: *The Triumph of St Joan* (1950); *The Ruby* (1953); *The Trial at Rouen* (1955–6); *The Triumph of St Joan* (1958–9, a new version); *Blood Moon* (1961); *Nativity: A Canticle for the Child* (opera-oratorio) (1987).

BALLETS: *Diversion of Angels* (1948); *Seraphic Dialogue* (1951, material from *The Triumph of St Joan*); *Time of Snow* (1968).

ORCH.: *Sinfonietta* (1940); *To a Lone Sentry* (1943); *On Stage* (1945); *Concert Music* (1945); *Serenade* (1948); *New York Profiles* (1949); *The Triumph of St Joan Symphony* (1951); *Air Power* (1957); *Five Images* (1967); *Homage to Haydn* (1969); *Satiric Dances*, band (1975); *Colonial Variations* (1976); *Ballabili* (1981); *Variants on a Bach Chorale* (1985).

CONCERTOS: fl., str. (1939), 2 pf. (1941), harmonica (1944), hp. (1945); *Ricercari*, pf., orch. (1946); concertato, cl. (1949); *Fantasy and Variations*, pf. (1961); *Lyric Fantasies*, va., str. (1973); *Notes from Tom Paine*, pf., band (1975).

CHORAL: *The Mystic Trumpeter* (1943); *Psalm of David* (1950); *Song of Affirmation* (1952); *Prayers of Cardinal Newman* (1960); *Songs of Walt Whitman* (1966); Mass (1968); *Evocations* (1970); Mass (1976); *As of a Dream*, solo vv., ch., narr., dancers, orch. (1978); *Love Songs at Parting*, ch., pf. (1981); *I Dreamed of an Invincible City*, ch., pf./org. (1984).

CHAMBER MUSIC: vc. sonata (1937); vn. sonata (1938); 3 pf. sonatas (1943, 1944, 1948); trio (1944); str. qt. (1974); tpt. sonata (1979); *Concert Variations*, pf. (1980); *Reflections on a Christmas Tune*, ww. quintet (1981); *Song at Springtide*, pf. 4 hands (1984); *Short Intervallic Studies*, pf. (1988). Also songs and incidental mus. for TV.

Del Mar, Norman (René) (*b* Hampstead, 1919; *d* Bushey, Herts, 1994). Eng. conductor, horn-player, and author. Hn.-player in Beecham's RPO, becoming ass. cond. 1947–8. Founded Chelsea SO 1944, giving perfs. of works then little known in

Eng., e.g. Busoni's pf. conc. and Mahler's 2nd Sym. Prin. cond. EOG 1948–56. Cond. Yorkshire SO 1954–5. Cond. BBC Scottish SO 1960–5, Göteborg SO 1969–73. Art. dir. Århus SO 1985–8. Prof. GSMD 1952–60. Guest cond. of leading orchs. Cond. f.p. of Britten's *Let's Make an Opera*, 1949. Cond. f. London p. (concert) of Strauss's *Daphne*, 1990. Author of 3-vol. survey of mus. of R. Strauss (1962–72), monograph on Mahler's 6th Sym. (1980), *Anatomy of the Orchestra* (1981), *Orchestral Variations* (1981), *A Companion to the Orchestra* (1987), and *Conducting Beethoven* (1992). CBE 1975. His son Jonathan (*b* London, 1951) is also a cond.

Del Monaco, Mario (*b* Florence, 1915; *d* Mestre, Venice, 1982). It. tenor. Sang in opera at Mondalfo, nr. Pesaro, at age of 13. Début Pesaro 1939 (Turiddù in *Cavalleria Rusticana*); Milan 1941; CG 1946 (with San Carlo co.); Amer. début S. Francisco 1950; NY Met 1950–8. Verdi's Otello among his prin. roles—he sang it 427 times during his career. Retired 1973.

Delogu, Gaetano (*b* Messina, 1934). It. conductor. Winner of Florence young cond. comp. 1964, Mitropoulos comp., NY, 1968. Cond. Teatro Massimo, Palermo, 1975–8. Mus. dir. Denver SO 1979–86.

De Los Angeles, Victoria. See *Los Angeles, Victoria de*.

Delsarte, François Alexandre Nicolas Chéri (*b* Solesmes, 1811; *d* Paris, 1871). Fr. tenor and singing teacher. Created system known as 'Delsarte method' by which singers were taught to match the emotion of the text with their facial expression (a method prone to unfortunate distortion).

Del Tredici, David (Walter) (*b* Cloverdale, Calif., 1937). Amer. composer and pianist. Turned to comp. 1958, encouraged by Milhaud. Ass. prof. of mus., Harvard Univ. 1966–72; on mus. faculty Boston Univ. 1973–84. Teacher at City Coll. of City Univ., NY, from 1984. Pulitzer Prize in Mus., 1980. Works incl.:

Night Conjure-Verse, 2 Joyce poems, sop., mez. or counterten., wind, str. qt. (1965); *Syzgy*, 2 Joyce poems, sop., hn., chamber orch. (1966); *The Last Gospel*, amplified sop., rock group, ch., orch. (1967); *Pot-Pourri*, amplified sop., rock group, ch., orch. (1968); *The Lobster Quadrille*, extract from *In Wonderland*, folk group, orch. (1969, rev. 1974); *Vintage Alice*, text from L. Carroll, amplified sop., folk group, chamber orch. (1972); *Adventures Underground* (Carroll), amplified sop., folk group, orch. (1973); *In Wonderland* (Carroll) *Part I, A Scene with Lobsters*, amplified sop., folk group, orch. (1969–74), *Part II*, amplified sop., orch. (1975); *Final Alice* (Carroll), amplified sop., folk group, orch. (1976); *Annotated Alice*, amplified sop., folk group, orch. (1976); *Child Alice*, orch., in 4 parts: *In memory of a summer day, Happy Voices, All in the golden afternoon*, and *Quaint Events* (1977–81, f.p. Aspen 1984); *March to Tonality*, orch. (1983–5); *Haddock's Eyes*, sop., chamber ens. (1985–6); *Steps*, orch. (1990); *Brass Sym.*, brass quintet (1992); *Heavy Metal Alice*, brass quintet (1995); *Chana's Story*, sop., pf. (1996); *Song of Solomon*, song-cycle., v., pf. (1996–2000); *My Favourite Penis Poems*, sop., bar., pf. (1998–2002); pf. trio (2002); *4 Heartfelt Anthems*, children's ch. (2003); *In Wartime*, wind band (2003); *Paul Revere's Ride*, sop., ch., orch. (2005).

De Luca, Giuseppe (*b* Rome, 1876; *d* NY, 1950). It. baritone. Début Piacenza 1897 (Valentine in *Faust*); La Scala 1903–10, creating role of Sharpless in *Madama Butterfly*, 1904; CG début 1907; NY Met 1915–35 and 1939–40 (last role Rigoletto). Created Gianni Schicchi, NY 1918. Became teacher at Juilliard Sch. and gave last NY recital in Nov. 1947.

De Lucia, Fernando (*b* Naples, 1860; *d* Naples, 1925). It. tenor. Opera début Naples 1885 in *Faust*. Became exponent of *verismo* heroes (Turiddù, Canio, etc.). Sang in f.p. of *L'amico Fritz* (Rome, 1891). London début 1887 (Drury Lane); CG 1892. Retired 1917, but sang at Caruso's funeral, 1921. Made over 400 recordings.

DeMain, John (Lee) (*b* Youngstown, Ohio, 1944). Amer. conductor. Apprentice, NY City Opera 1972. Ass. cond. St Paul Chamber Orch. 1972–4. Mus. dir. Texas Opera Th. 1974–6, Houston Grand Opera 1979–93, Chautauqua Opera 1982–7, Opera Omaha 1983–91. At Houston cond. f.ps. of Bernstein's *A Quiet Place* (1983), Adams's *Nixon in China* (1987), and Tippett's *New Year* (1989).

démancher (Fr., from *manche*, neck). (1) To move the left hand along the neck of a str. instr.

(2) To move the left hand closer to the bridge of a str. instr.

Demessieux, Jeanne Marie-Madeleine (*b* Montpellier, 1921; *d* Paris, 1968). Fr. organist and composer. Org., Saint-Esprit, Paris, from age 12. First recital Paris 1946, London 1947, Edinburgh 1948, Salzburg Fest. 1949; Amer. début 1953. Won praise for remarkable powers of improvisation. Prof., Liège Cons., 1952. Org., Madeleine, from 1962. First woman invited to play in Westminster Cath. and Westminster Abbey. Played at inaugural ceremony Liverpool Metropolitan Cath., 1967.

Demetrio e Polibio. Opera in 2 acts by Rossini to lib. by Vincenza Mombelli. His first opera, written in 1806 when he was 14. Orch. for str. only. Prod. Bologna 1812, Manchester (RMCM) 1969.

demi-cadence. Same as imperfect cadence (half close), i.e. chord of the tonic or other chord followed by that of dominant.

demi-jeu (Fr.). Half-play, i.e. at half power (in org. and harmonium mus., etc.).

demi-pause (Fr.). Half-rest, minim rest.

demisemiquaver (♬) the thirty-second note, i.e. $\frac{1}{32}$ the time-value of the whole-note or semibreve. See *note values*.

demi-ton (Fr.). Semitone.

demi-voix (Fr.). Half voice, i.e. half the vocal power (It. *mezza voce*).

Dempsey, Gregory (*b* Melbourne, 1931). Australian tenor. Studied as bar., but made début as ten. at National Opera of Victoria, 1954 (Don Ottavio in *Don Giovanni*). Moved to London 1962, joining SW Opera (later ENO), where his roles incl. Peter Grimes, Mime, David, Tom Rakewell, and Don José. Created Boconnion in Bennett's *The Mines of Sulphur*, 1965. Sang title-role in f. London p. of *The Excursions of Mr Brouček* (ENO 1978). Amer. début S. Francisco 1966. Sang Dionysus in f. Brit. stage p. of *The Bassarids*, 1974. CG début 1972. Member of Australian Opera.

Demus, Jörg (Wolfgang) (*b* St Pölten, 1928). Austrian pianist. Début Vienna 1943, London 1950. Foreign tours after 1951. Salzburg Fest. début 1960. Won Busoni Prize, Bolzano, 1956, and Harriet Cohen Bach Medal 1977. Acc. to *Schwarzkopf and *Fischer-Dieskau. Has collection of historical kbd. instrs. Author, with P. *Badura-Skoda, of *Beethoven's Piano Sonatas* (1970).

Dench, Chris (*b* London, 1953). Eng. composer. Awarded Kranichsteiner prize at Darmstadt fest. of new mus. 1984. Lived in Italy 1987–8 and in Berlin from 1988. His mus. has been taken up by leading contemp. mus. ens., e.g. Arditti Quartet and Ensemble Intercontemporain, and played at Venice Biennale, Almeida Fest., etc. Some of his mus. explores dense microtonal polyphony.

Denève, Stéphane (*b* Tourcoing, 1972). Fr. conductor. Studied Paris Cons., graduating 1995. Ass. to Solti 1995 with Orch. de Paris and for *Don Giovanni* at Opéra 1996. Cond. *Die Zauberflöte* Dusseldorf 1997. CG 2004 (*Così fan tutte*). Mus. dir. RSNO from 2005. Frequent guest cond. of Amer. orchs.

Denhof Opera Company. Short-lived but significant body formed in 1910 by Ernst Denhof (*d* 1936), Ger.-born resident of Edinburgh, to give provincial perfs. of Wagner's *Ring* in English. *Balling cond. f.ps. in Edinburgh, 1910, followed in 1911 by tours to Leeds, Manchester, and Glasgow, and to these cities again in 1912 plus Hull and Liverpool. Repertory by now incl. *Elektra* (in Eng.) and *Die Meistersinger*, with *Pelléas* and *Der Rosenkavalier* added in 1913, in which year co. ran into financial trouble in Manchester, being rescued and absorbed by Beecham's co. (Scotland did not hear a complete *Ring* cycle again until 1971.)

Denison, John (Law) (*b* Reigate, Surrey, 1911). Eng. horn-player and concert administrator. Hn.-player in BBCSO, LPO, and CBSO 1934–9; ass. mus. dir., Brit. Council 1946–8; mus. dir., Arts

Council from 1948; gen. man. Royal Festival Hall, 1965–70; dir., South Bank Concert Halls 1971–6. CBE 1960.

Denisov, Edison (*b* Tomsk, 1929; *d* Paris, 1996). Russ. composer. Trained as mathematician, but taught himself gui. and cl. before studying pf. Persuaded by Shostakovich to study comp. with *Shebalin at Moscow Cons. 1951–6. Taught at Moscow Cons. from 1960. Worked at Experimental EMS, Moscow, 1968–70. Student of Russ. folkmus. Comps. incl.:

OPERAS: *Soldier Ivan* (1959); *L'Écume des Jours* (1977–80).

BALLET: *Confession* (1984).

ORCH.: sym. in C (1955); *Sinfonietta on Tadzhik Themes* (1957); *Crescendo e Diminuendo*, hpd., 12 str. (1966); *Peinture* (1970); vc. conc. (1973); *Aquarelle*, 24 str. (1975); fl. conc. (1975); vn. conc. (1978); pf. conc. (1978); *Partita*, vn., orch. (1980); conc., bn., vc. (1982); *Tod ist ein langer Schlaf*, vars. on theme by Haydn, vc., orch. (1981–2); *Chamber Sym.* (1982–3); *Epitaphe*, chamber orch. (1983); *Colin et Chloé* (1983, suite from opera *L'Écume des Jours*); conc., 2 va., hpd., str. (1984); *Happy End*, str. (1985); *Pictures of Paul Klee*, ens. (1986); va. conc. (1986); ob. conc. (1986); *Variations on Bach Chorale Es ist genug* (1986); sax. conc. (1993, re-working of va. conc.).

VOCAL: *Canti di Catulli*, bass, 3 tb. (1962); *Soleil des Incas*, sop., ens. (1964); *Chansons italiennes*, sop., ens. (1966); *Pleurs*, sop., pf., perc. (1966); *5 Geschichten vom Herrn Keuner*, ten., 7 instr. (1968); *Automne* (1969); *Chants d'automne*, sop., orch. (1971); *La vie en rouge*, v., ens. (1973); *Requiem*, sop., ten., ch., orch. (1980); *Lumière et ombres*, bar., pf. (1982); *Ton image charmante*, v., orch. (1982); *Venue du printemps*, unacc. ch. (1984); *Eternal Light*, ch. (1988).

CHAMBER MUSIC: sonata, 2 vn. (1958); str. qt. (1961); vn. sonata (1963); *Ode in memory of Che Guevara*, cl., pf., perc. (1967); *Musique romantique*, ob., hp., str. trio (1969); *3 Pieces*, vc., pf. (1969); str. trio (1969); *D-S-C-H* (1969); wind. quintet (1969); sonata, alto sax., pf. (1970); pf. trio (1971); vc. sonata (1971); *Canon in memory of Igor Stravinsky*, fl., cl., hp. (1971); solo cl. sonata (1972); sonata, fl., gui. (1977); solo vn. sonata (1978); conc. for gui. solo (1981); trio, ob., vc., hpd. (1981); solo bn. sonata (1982); sonata, vn., org. (1982); *5 Études*, bn. (1983); sonata, fl., hp. (1983); *Diane dans le vent l'automne*, va., vib., pf., db. (1984); quintet, cl., str. (1988).

Denner, Johann Christoph (*b* Leipzig, 1655; *d* Nuremberg, 1707). Ger. instrument-maker. In attempting to improve the Fr. *chalumeau he is credited by some historians with inventing the *clarinet *c.*1690. Subject of opera by Weigmann *Der Klarinettenmacher* (1913).

Dent, Edward (*Joseph*) (*b* Ribston, Yorks., 1876; *d* London, 1957). Eng. scholar, teacher, and author. Taught mus. at Cambridge Univ. 1902–18, and was involved in prod. of *Die Zauberflöte* in his trans. in 1911, when this opera was virtually

unknown in Brit. Prof. of mus., Cambridge Univ. 1926–41. Active in many Eng. operatic ventures and esp. as translator of libs. His trans. of 4 Mozart operas contributed largely to their re-evaluation in Eng. In 1919 he helped found Brit. Mus. Soc. (disbanded 1933) and in 1922 organized a fest. of contemp. chamber mus. in Salzburg from which developed the *ISCM. Dent became first pres., 1923–37. Pres., Int. Musicological Soc. 1931–49, RMA 1928–35. Ed. *The Beggar's Opera*, 1944. Contrib. to many encyclopaedias and dictionaries, critic, and author of books *Alessandro Scarlatti* (1905), *Mozart's Operas* (1913, rev. 1947 and 1955), *Ferruccio Busoni* (1933), and *Handel* (1934).

Denza, Luigi (*b* Castellammare di Stabia, Naples, 1846; *d* London, 1922). It. composer. Wrote opera and 600 popular songs, best-known being *Funiculì, Funiculà*, 1880, comp. for opening of Naples funicular railway. Settled in London 1879. Prof. of singing, RAM, 1898–1922.

déploration (Fr.). A poem of mourning, and therefore its musical setting. Term generally confined to Renaissance comps. written in memory of a composer, e.g. Andrieu's for Machaut, Ockeghem's for Binchois, and Josquin Desprès's for Ockeghem.

De profundis (Out of the depths). Psalm 129 in the Vulgate (following the Septuagint) and 130 in the Eng. Authorized and Revised versions (following the Hebrew). It is one of the 7 Penitential Psalms (see *psalm*) and, attached to its traditional plainsong, has a place in the Office of the Dead of the RC Church. It has been set by composers many times.

der (Ger.). (1) The (masc. sing.). (2) Of the (fem. sing.).

De Reszke, Édouard [Mieczyslaw, Edward] (*b* Warsaw, 1853; *d* Garnek, 1917). Polish bass, brother of Jean *de Reszke. Début at Théâtre des Italiens, Paris, as the King in first Paris *Aida* cond. Verdi, 1876. London CG 1880; Chicago 1891. Stalwart of NY Met 1891–1903. Notable in Wagner, first in It. then in Ger. (King Marke, Sachs, Hagen), but his most famous role was Mephistopheles in *Faust*. Retired 1903.

De Reszke, Jean [Mieczyslaw, Jan] (*b* Warsaw, 1850; *d* Nice, 1925). Polish tenor, brother of Édouard *de Reszke. Début (as bar. and as Giovanni di Reschi), Turin and London 1874 (singing Alfonso in *La Favorite*). His brother persuaded him he was really a ten. and after further study from 1876 he sang *Robert le Diable* in Madrid 1879. After 5 fallow years he had a great success in Massenet's *Hérodiade* (Paris, 1884) and *Le Cid* (1885). Sang Faust at 500th Paris perf. in 1887 (with Édouard as Mephistopheles). London début as ten. 1887; CG 1888, returning nearly every year until 1900. Amer. début Chicago 1891; NY Met 1891–1901. Late in career sang Wagner roles of Walther, Tristan, and Siegfried. Retired 1902, and taught in Paris and Nice. Regarded as one of greatest operatic tens.

De Reszke, Joséphine (*b* Warsaw, 1855; *d* Warsaw, 1891). Polish soprano, sister of above. Début Venice 1874. Paris Opéra 1875–84 (début as Ophélia in Thomas's *Hamlet*). Début CG 1881 as Aida. Retired 1885 on marriage.

D'Erlanger, Baron Frédéric [Regnal, Frédéric] (*b* Paris, 1868; *d* London, 1943). Eng. composer (of Ger. and Amer. parents) (Eng. cit.). Wrote several operas, incl. *Inez Mendo* (CG 1897) and *Tess* (based on Hardy's novel, Naples 1906, CG 1909 with Destinn), *Requiem* (1931), vn. conc., and chamber mus. Banker by profession and financial supporter of CG between the wars.

Dermota, Anton (*b* Kropa, 1910; *d* Vienna, 1989). Austrian tenor. Début Vienna 1936 (First Armed Man in *Die Zauberflöte*), appearing mainly there and at Salzburg for the rest of his career, notably in Mozart roles. CG début 1947. Sang Florestan in *Fidelio* at reopening of Vienna State Opera, 1955. Retired 1966 and taught at Vienna Acad. of Mus.

Dernesch, Helga (*b* Vienna, 1939). Austrian soprano, later mezzo-soprano. Berne Opera 1961–3 (début as Marina in *Boris Godunov*); Wiesbaden 1963–6; Cologne 1966–9; Bayreuth Fest. 1965–9; Salzburg Easter Fest. 1969–73; Salzburg Fest. 1982. Brit. début with Scottish Opera 1968; CG 1970; Chicago 1971; Vienna 1972. Created Goneril in Reimann's *Lear*, Munich 1978, and Hecuba in his *Troades* (1986). Outstanding in Strauss and Wagner. Mez. roles from 1979. NY Met début 1985.

des (Ger. singular; Fr. plural). Of the. Also (Ger.), the note D♭.

De Sabata, Victor [Vittorio] (*b* Trieste, 1892; *d* S. Margherita, 1967). It. conductor and composer. Cond. Monte Carlo Opera 1918 (*La traviata*), becoming cond. there 1919–29, where he cond. f.p. of *L'Enfant et les Sortilèges* (1925). Cond. La Scala, Milan, 1930–57 (début with *La fanciulla del West*), art. dir. 1953–7. Cond. Bayreuth (*Tristan*) 1939. Took Scala Co. to CG 1950. Salzburg Fest. début 1952. Frequent guest cond. of concerts and opera throughout world. Wrote 2 operas (one unfinished, the other prod. La Scala 1917), 3 sym.-poems, and other works. Retired 1957.

De Saram, Rohan (*b* Sheffield, 1939). Sri Lankan cellist. After Eur. recitals made Amer. début in NY, 1960. Settled in Eng. 1972, joining teaching staff of TCL. Wide repertory from Haydn to Xenakis, specializing in contemp. works. Cellist of *Arditti String Quartet.

descant. Like *'faburden' a puzzling term because at different periods used with different significances, chief of which are as follows: (1) A term, usually spelt *discant*, for a form of the 12th cent. part-writing known as *organum. (2)

A part extemporized by a singer to a non-extemporized part sung by another singer. (3) The art of composing or singing part-music. (4) The soprano part in choral music. (5) In modern hymn singing, a freely written or improvised soprano part added to a hymn tune while the tune itself is sung by the rest of the choir or by the congregation.

descant viol. The treble viol. See *viol*.

Desderi, Claudio (*b* Alessandria, 1943). It. bass-baritone and conductor. After concerts, made opera début Edinburgh Fest. 1969 with Maggio Musicale as Gaudenzio in Rossini's *Il Signor Bruschino*. CG début 1976 with La Scala co. in Rossini roles. Salzburg Fest. 1977; Glyndebourne 1981; Royal Opera début 1987. Cond. *Così fan tutte* and *Le nozze di Figaro*, Turin 1989. Cond. *Così fan tutte* for GTO, 1991.

Deses (Ger.). The note D♭♭.

desiderio (It.). Desire. Hence *con desiderio*, longingly.

Desmond, Astra (*b* Torquay, 1893; *d* Faversham, 1973). Eng. mezzo-soprano. First London recital 1915. Sang title-role in Boughton's *Alkestis* 1922. Became notable exponent of Eng. mus., esp. Elgar and Vaughan Williams (one of orig. 16 singers in *Serenade to Music*), but also sang in 12 languages and wrote books on songs of Grieg, Dvořák, Sibelius, and Schumann. Prof. of singing, RAM 1947–63. CBE 1949.

Désormière, Roger (*b* Vichy, 1898; *d* Paris, 1963). Fr. conductor and composer. Played fl. in Paris orchs. Cond. début Concerts Pleyel 1921. Cond. Diaghilev Ballet 1925–30. Opéra-Comique 1937, becoming mus. dir. 1944–6. Cond. *Pelléas* at CG 1949. Cond. early perfs. of works by Messiaen and Boulez. Retired 1950.

Desprès, Josquin. See *Josquin Desprès*.

Dessau, Paul (*b* Hamburg, 1894; *d* E. Berlin, 1979). Ger. composer and conductor. Opera coach, Hamburg, 1913–14. Cond. Cologne Opera 1918–23, Berlin State Opera 1926. Lived in Paris 1933–9, USA 1939–45, then returned to Ger. Close assoc. of Brecht, having written incidental mus. to several of his plays. Other works incl. 5 str. qts.; *Deutsches miserere*, choral work to text by Brecht; operas *Die Verurteilung des Lukullus* (The Trial of Lucullus, lib. by Brecht, 1949), *Puntila* (lib. after Brecht, 1957–9), *Lanzelot* (1969), *Einstein* (1971–3); *In memoriam Bertolt Brecht*, orch. (1957); *Requiem für Lumumba*, sop., bar., spkr., ch., ens. (1963); 2 syms. (1926, 1934, rev. 1962); 3 *Orchestermusik* (1955, 1967, 1973); and many songs.

Dessay, Natalie (*b* Lyon, 1965). Fr. soprano. Studied at Bordeaux Cons. and at Paris Opéra's Ecole d'Art Lyrique, where she sang Elisa in Mozart's *Il re pastore*. Won int. Mozart comp. in Vienna and was engaged for coloratura roles such as Blondchen, Adèle, and Zerbinetta. Joined Vienna State Opera 1993. Aix Fest. 1994 (Queen of Night). NY Met 1994 (Fiakermilli). Milan 1995 (Olympia). Salzburg Fest. 1997 (Queen of Night). CG début 2003 (Ophélie in *Hamlet*), Santa Fe 2002 (concert, her Amer. début), opera 2004 (*La sonnambula*).

Destinn, Emmy [Kittl, Ema] (*b* Prague, 1878; *d* České Budějovice, 1930). Cz. soprano. Trained as violinist but her vocal prowess was noticed and she studied with Marie Loewe-Destinn, whose name she adopted. Début Berlin Kroll Opera 1898 (Santuzza in *Cavalleria rusticana*) repeating role 2 months later at Court Opera where she remained until 1908. Sang at CG 1904–14 and 1919, and NY Met 1908–16 and 1919–21. Senta in first Bayreuth *Fliegende Holländer*, 1901; Diemut in *Feuersnot* 1901 and first Berlin Salome 1906. First Butterfly at CG 1905 (with Caruso) and Tatyana in *Eugene Onegin* 1906. Created role of Minnie in *La fanciulla del West* 1910. In 1914–18 war adopted name Ema Destinnová; was interned on her Bohem. estate for duration because of her sympathy with Cz. national movt. Returned to Met and CG 1919 as Aida. Retired from stage 1926 but sang in London at concert cond. by Wood in 1928.

Destouches, André-Cardinal (*b* Paris, 1672; *d* Paris, 1749). Fr. composer. Superintendent, Paris Opéra, 1713, dir. 1728–30. Best-known work is 3-act opera *Issé*, heroic pastorale prod. Fontainebleau 1697. It was one of his operas, *Omphale* (1701), that sparked off the 'Querelle des *Bouffons*'.

détaché (Fr.). Detached, i.e. staccato. (1) *grand détaché*, staccato with a full bow for each note. (2) *petit détaché*, staccato with the point of the bow for each note. (3) *détaché sec*, same as *martelé* (hammered).

detached console. Placed at a distance from the org. so that the player can hear the full effect as his listeners hear it. In electric orgs. such a console may be movable.

Detroit Symphony Orchestra. Founded 1914 with Weston Gales as cond. 1914–18, followed by Ossip *Gabrilowitsch 1918–35. Victor Kolar and guest conds. succeeded the latter, but after difficult times the orch. disbanded 1949. Reorganized 1952. First European tour 1979. Plays in Orchestra Hall, built 1919, restored 1989 seating *c*.2,200 and with reputation for outstandingly fine acoustic. Conds.: Paul *Paray 1952–63; Sixten Ehrling 1963–73; Aldo Ceccato 1973–6; Antal Dorati 1977–81; Gary Bertini 1981–3; Günther Herbig 1984–90; Neeme Järvi 1990–2005.

Dettingen Te Deum and Anthem. Comp. by Handel, to celebrate Brit. defeat of Fr. at Dettingen, nr. Frankfurt, 1743. First sung at Chapel Royal, St James's, Nov. 1743. Anthem's text begins 'The King shall rejoice'.

Deuteromelia (Gr.). 'Second honey.' 2nd coll. of Eng. rounds and catches pubd. 1609 by T. *Ravenscroft. See *Pammelia*.

Deutsch, Otto Erich (*b* Vienna, 1883; *d* Vienna, 1967). Austro-Eng. music scholar and art critic. Wrote book on Schubert 1905 and biog. 1913–14. Worked at Vienna Univ. art-history library 1909–12. Mus. lib. to A. van *Hoboken 1926–35. Went to Eng. 1939, settling in Cambridge. Naturalized 1947, returned to Vienna 1952. Ed., Brit. Union Catalogue of Early Mus. 1946–50. Author of books on Handel (1955), Haydn, Schumann, and Beethoven, but his masterpieces are his books on Schubert. These incl. an edn. of all documents, pictures, and relevant material (1914, Eng. edn. 1946) and a thematic catalogue (1951, rev. by others 1978) which gave all Schubert's works D nos. Also wrote documentary biography of Mozart (1961, Eng. edn. 1963, suppl. 1978).

Deutsche Motette (German Motet). Motet by R. Strauss, Op.62, for sop., alto, ten., and bass soloists and 16-part unacc. mixed ch., to words by Rückert, comp. 1913, rev. 1943.

deutscher Tanz, deutsche Tänze (Ger.). German dance(s). Peasant dance from Ger. and Switzerland, like slow waltz. Adopted particularly by Mozart and Schubert.

Deutsches Requiem, Ein (A German Requiem). Choral work, Op.45, by Brahms for sop. and bar. soloists, ch., and orch. Comp. 1861–8, though what is now 2nd movt. was comp. in 1857. So called because text is not that of the RC Liturgy but consists of passages selected by Brahms from Luther's trans. of the Bible. 7 movts. First 3 movts. perf. Vienna, Dec. 1867. 2nd perf. Bremen Cath. 10 Apr. 1868, with 3 movts. added. A month later he inserted new 5th movt., *Ihr habt nun Traurigkeit*, for sop., in memory of his mother, *d* Feb. 1865. First complete perf. Leipzig 18 Feb. 1869, cond. Reinecke.

Deutschland über Alles. (Ger. 'Germany beyond everything' or 'Germany before everything'), known also as the *Deutschlandlied* ('Germany Song'). A poem of aspiration for the unity of the Ger. peoples written in the period which preceded the 1848 revolutionary disturbances, by August Heinrich Hoffmann (generally called Hoffmann von Fallersleben, 1798–1874). Sung to the tune Haydn wrote (or adapted, for there is a similar tune in Telemann) as Austrian national anthem, the *Emperor's Hymn*. Nat. anthem of German Fed. Republic from 1922 until 1945. Reinstated 1950 with 3rd verse ('Einigkeit und Recht und Freiheit', 'Unity and Right and Freedom') replacing the first with its controversial reference to 'über Alles'.

deux (Fr.). Two. *a deux*, for 2 vv. or instr., or (sometimes) short for 'a *deux temps*'. In orch. mus., however, this expression has 2 opposite meanings: (*a*) 2 separate instr. parts are now merged in 1 line of mus.; (*b*) 1 instr. part is now divided, the players becoming 2 bodies.

Deux Journées, Les (The Two Days). Opera in 3 acts by Cherubini to lib. by J.-N. Bouilly.

Generally known in Britain as *The Water Carrier*, and in Ger. as *Der Wasserträger*. Prod. Paris 1800, London 1801, New Orleans 1811.

Deux Pigeons, Les (The Two Pigeons). Ballet in 3 acts by Messager, lib. by H. Régnier and Mérante, choreog. Mérante. Prod. Paris 1886. New version choreog. Ashton, London 1961.

deux temps (Fr.). Two beats (1) In 2/2 time.

(2) *valse à deux temps* has the following varied meanings; (*a*) In normal Waltz (3/4) time with 2 dance steps to a measure, on the first and 3rd beats; (*b*) In 6/4 or 6/8 time, with steps on the 1st and 4th 'beats'; (*c*) Having 2 values of beat, as in Gounod's *Faust* where 2 waltzes are combined, one of them in 3/4 time and the other in 3/2, 2 measures of the 3/4 being heard against 1 measure of the 3/2 and thus rhythmically conflicting.

development (also called *free fantasia*, or *working-out*. Fr. *développement*; Ger. *Durchführung*, i.e. 'through-leading'; It. *svolgimento*, i.e. 'unfolding'). The treatment of the detailed phrases and motifs of a previously heard theme ('subject') in such a way as to make new passages, often of a modulatory nature. The second section of sonata form, coming between exposition and recapitulation, is the development. With the expansion of the symphony, the development section became increasingly complex and important. Beethoven departs from convention in his 3rd sym. by introducing new thematic material in this section. There is also a development in **fugue*.

Devienne, François (*b* Joinville, 1759; *d* Charenton, 1803). Fr. woodwind player (fl., ob., and bn.) and composer. Played bn. in Paris Opéra orch. 1779, later in Loge Olympique. Soloist (fl. and bn.) at Concert Spirituel 18 times, 1782–5. Prof. at newly-founded Paris Cons. 1795. Comp. many works for fl. and wrote a method for it (1794). Also comp. 11 operas and much chamber mus.

Devil and Daniel Webster, The (1) Opera in 1 act by Douglas *Moore to lib. by Stephen Vincent Benet based on his own story. Comp. 1938. Prod. NY 1939.

(2) Film score by *Herrmann from which he prod. 5-movt. suite. Comp. 1941. F.p. Philadelphia, 1942.

Devil and Kate, The (Dvořák). See *Kate and the Devil*.

devil in music. See *tritone*.

Devils of Loudun, The (*Diably z Loudun*). Opera in 3 acts by *Penderecki to his own lib. based on John Whiting's play (1961) from A. Huxley's novel (1952), in Eng. trans. by Erich Fried. Comp. 1968–9. Prod. Hamburg 1969, Santa Fe 1969, London (SW) 1973.

'Devil's Trill' Sonata (*Trillo del Diavolo* or *Sonata del Diavolo*). Nickname of vn. sonata in G minor by *Tartini, comp. *c*.1714, which has a long trill in the last of its 4 movts. The legend is that Tartini dreamed he had made a deal with the Devil to whom he gave his vn. The Devil played a

solo so beautiful that Tartini awoke and tried to play what he had heard. He failed but comp. the 'Devil's Trill'. The sonata was found by *Baillot (1771–1842) and first pub. in *L'Art du violon* (1798, 1801) by Cartier. Legend is subject of ballet *Le Violon du diable* with mus. by Pugni, Paris 1849.

Devil Take Her, The. Comic opera in prol. and 1 act by A. Benjamin to lib. by A. Collard and J. B. Gordon. Prod. London 1931, cond. Beecham.

Devin du village, Le (The Village Soothsayer). Opera (*intermède*) in 1 act by *Rousseau to his own lib. Prod. Fontainebleau 1752, Paris 1753, London 1766, NY 1790. Lib. of Mozart's *Bastien und Bastienne is based on a parody.

De Vito, Gioconda (*b* Martina Franca, Lecce, 1907; *d* Rome, 1994). Eng. violinist of It. birth. Won international comp. Vienna 1932. Prof. of vn., Accademia di S. Cecilia, Rome. Visited London 1947 to make records. Public début 1948 (LPO). Specialist in standard repertory, notably Brahms concerto. Taught at Bari Cons. Retired 1961.

Dexter, John (*b* Derby, 1925; *d* London, 1990). Eng. stage director. Worked for Eng. Stage Co. at Royal Court, London, 1957–72. Assoc. dir., Nat. Th. 1963. First opera prod. Berlioz's *Benvenuto Cellini*, CG 1966. Prod. operas in Hamburg 1969–72 and Paris 1973. Dir. of prod., NY Met 1974–81, when he introduced many 20th cent. works new to the Met audience, e.g. by Weill, Britten, and Poulenc. Staged f. Brit. p. of Penderecki's *Devils of Loudun* (SW 1973).

D'Hardelot, Guy. See *Hardelot, Guy d'*.

Diabelli, Antonio (*b* Mattsee, Salzburg, 1781; *d* Vienna, 1858). Austrian composer and publisher. Choirboy at Salzburg Cath. Encouraged to comp. by Michael Haydn. Went to Vienna in 1803 as teacher of pf. and guitar and as proof-reader. Entered publishing 1818, founded Diabelli and Co.,1824, publishing works by Beethoven, Schubert, and Czerny. Wrote operetta, masses, pf. pieces, and songs. See *Diabelli Variations*.

Diabelli Variations. Beethoven's Thirty-Three Variations on a Waltz by Diabelli, Op.120, for pf., comp. 1819–23. The publisher *Diabelli commissioned 50 composers to write a variation apiece on his theme and was delighted to receive 33 from Beethoven, instantly recognizing the work as a major masterpiece. Among the other composers who responded to Diabelli's request were Liszt (aged 11), Schubert, Drechsler, Schenk, Czerny, Kalkbrenner, Pixis, Moscheles, Stadler, Sechter, Hoffmann, and Archduke Rudolph.

diabolus in musica (Lat.). The devil in mus., i.e. the *tritone. Term is derived from various prohibitions on using this awkward interval.

Diaghilev, Serge [Dyagilev, Sergey] (Pavlovich) (*b* Selistchev, Novgorod, 1872; *d* Venice, 1929). Russ. impresario. Art. adviser to Mariinsky Theatre 1899–1901. In 1908 organized Paris concerts of Russ. mus. and prod. *Boris Godunov* with *Chaliapin. In 1909 he was invited to present a season of Russ. opera and ballet in Paris, scoring a major triumph with the ballet, for which he engaged the dancer Nijinsky, choreog. Fokine, and the painters Bakst and Benois. From this season the sensational Ballets Russes developed, transforming the ballet world. Diaghilev directed the co. until his death, surviving financial crises and personal quarrels which threatened to tear it apart. Over the years he called on an astonishing range of talents, not only among dancers (Nijinsky, Karsavina, Massine, Sokolova, Dolin, etc.) but choreographers (Fokine, Nijinsky, Massine, Nijinskaya, Balanchine), designers (Bakst, Benois, Matisse, Picasso, Utrillo, Derain) and composers (scores commissioned from Ravel, Stravinsky, Falla, Debussy, Prokofiev, Milhaud, Satie, Strauss, Poulenc, Auric, Lambert, and Berners). See *Ballet*.

dialogue. (1) Vocal work, mainly from medieval times to 17th cent., in which echo, alternation, or contrast suggested spoken dialogue.

(2) Spoken dialogue is used in some types of opera, e.g. Fr. *opéra-comique*, Ger. *Singspiel*, Sp. *zarzuela*, and Eng. ballad opera (and the operas of Gilbert and Sullivan). In Beethoven's *Fidelio* there is spoken dialogue and *melodrama. In some cases spoken dialogue has been replaced by accompanied recitative comp. by someone else (e.g. Guiraud for Bizet's *Carmen*). There are examples of a brief spoken passage used in opera to great dramatic effect, e.g. in Britten's *Peter Grimes*.

dialogues des Carmélites, Les. (The Carmelites' dialogues). Opera in 3 acts by Poulenc to his own lib. after Georges Bernanos's play adapted from novel *Die letzte am Schafott* (The Last on the Scaffold) by G. von le Fort (1931) and film scenario by Bruckenberger and Agostini. Comp. 1953–6. Prod Milan, Paris, and San Francisco 1957, CG 1958. Known in Eng. as *The Carmelites*.

Diamand, Peter (*b* Charlottenburg, 1913; *d* Amsterdam, 1998). Dutch administrator, born an Austrian. Secretary to *Schnabel 1934–9. Ass. to dir. Netherlands Opera 1946–8, dir. Holland Fest. 1947–65. Dir. Edinburgh Fest. 1966–78. Gen. man. RPO 1978–81. Dir., Mozart Fest., Paris, 1980–7. Hon. CBE 1972.

Diamond, David (Leo) (*b* Rochester, NY, 1915; *d* Rochester, NY, 2005). Amer. composer. Sym. in one movement perf. at Eastman Sch. 1931. Juilliard Award 1937, Guggenheim Fellowship 1938, 1941, Amer. Acad. in Rome Award 1942. Lived in Florence 1953–65. Head of comp. dept., Manhattan Sch. of Mus., NY, 1965–7. His mus. owes something to his admiration for Ravel and Stravinsky and is strongly contrapuntal. He adopted serialism in the 1950s. Works incl. 11 syms. (1940–92); *Psalm* for orch. (1936); *Elegy in Memory of Ravel* (1938); *Rounds* for str. (1944); *Timon of Athens* (1949); *The World of Paul Klee* (1957); 2-pf. conc.; pf. conc.; 3 vn. concs. (1936–67); vc. conc.;

11 str. qts.; pf. qt.; pf. quintet; vn. sonata; *L'Ame de Debussy* (song-cycle); vc. sonata; *Choral Symphony: To Music* for male soloists, ch., and orch. (1967); *The Noblest Game*, opera (1971); fl. conc. (1984–5); *Kaddish*, vc., orch. (1987–9); *Sinfonietta* for orch. (1989–90); trio, vn., cl., pf. (1993–4); *Night Thoughts* for small orch. (1995–6); 52 preludes and fugues for pf.; songs, etc.

diapason (Gr.). Through all. (1) Greek name for the octave.

(2) The name of certain org. stops which are the foundation tone of the instr. and are either 'open' or 'stopped' according to whether the ends of the pipes are clear or plugged (plugged stops are lower in pitch by an octave). *open diapason, 8'*, is the chief manual stop. There are also *stopped diapason*, *horn diapason*, and *diapason phonon* in which the lips of the pipes are leathered to refine the tone.

(3) In Fr., *diapason normal* is a standard indication of pitch: A = 440 vibrations per sec.

diapente (Gr.). The interval of the perfect 5th.

diaphone. Org. stop (open diapason) invented by Robert Hope-Jones (1859–1914) which was actuated by vibratory apparatus to increase loudness.

diaphony. Gr. term for dissonance, applied to form of *organum. Some define it as a freer form, admitting other intervals than the perfect ones, others consider it to be a later form, admitting of contrary motion, part-crossing, etc.

Diary of One who Disappeared (*Zápisník zmizelého*). Song-cycle by Janáček, comp. 1917–19, for ten., cont. (or mez.), 3 women's vv., and pf. Setting of 22 anonymous poems, No.13 being represented by a pf. solo (*intermezzo erotico*). All the vv. are heard only in No.9, women's vv. only in No.10, ten. and cont. in No.11, the remainder being for ten. F.p. Brno 1921, f.p. in England, London 1922. Eng. trans. by Bernard Keeffe.

diatonic. The *diatonic scales* (see *scale*) are those of the major and minor keys, and diatonic passages, intervals, chords, and harmonies are those made up of the notes of the key prevailing at the moment. The *modes must also be considered diatonic. See also *chromatic*.

Díaz, Justino (*b* San Juan, Puerto Rico, 1940). Puerto Rican bass-baritone. Début Puerto Rico 1957 as Ben in *The Telephone*. Sang with New England Opera Th., Boston, 1961. NY Met début 1963; Salzburg Fest. 1966. Created role of Antony in Barber's *Antony and Cleopatra*, NY Met 1966, and of Francesco in Ginastera's *Beatrix Cenci*, Kennedy Center Opera House, Washington DC, 1971. CG début 1976; S. Francisco 1982. Sang Iago in Zeffirelli film of *Otello* (1986).

Dibdin, Charles (*b* Southampton, 1745; *d* London, 1814). Eng. composer, impresario, and singer. Choirboy, Winchester Cath. 1756–9. From 1764 in London wrote words and mus. of many popular 'musicals'. In 1789 began 'table entertainments' at which he sang his own songs. Th. manager 1796–1805. Best-known songs are 'The Bells of Aberdovey' from *Liberty Hall* (Drury Lane 1785) and the beautiful 'Tom Bowling' from table entertainment *The Oddities* (Lyceum 1789).

Dichterliebe (Poet's Love). Cycle of 16 songs for v. and pf. by Schumann, Op.48 (1840), being settings of Heine.

Dichtung (Ger.). Poem. Hence *symphonische Dichtung*, sym.-poem. R. Strauss used the term *Tondichtung*, tone-poem.

Dickie, Brian (James) (*b* Newark, 1941). Eng. opera dir. Art. dir., Wexford Fest. 1967–74. On Glyndebourne staff from 1962, gen. admin. 1982–8. Dir. Canadian Opera Co., Toronto, 1989–93.

Dickie, Murray (*b* Bishopton, nr. Glasgow, 1924; *d* Cape Town, 1995). Scottish tenor and producer. Début London 1947 (Almaviva in *Il barbiere di Siviglia* at Cambridge Th.); CG 1948–52 (sang in f.p. of Bliss's *Olympians*, 1949); Glyndebourne 1950; Vienna State Opera 1951; Salzburg Fest. 1954; NY Met 1962. Prod. J. Strauss's *Ein Nacht in Venedig*, ENO 1976.

Dickinson, Meriel (*b* Lytham St Annes, 1940). Eng. mezzo-soprano. Member BBC Ch. 1963–4, solo recitalist and oratorio.

Dickinson, Peter (*b* Lytham St Annes, 1934). Eng. composer and pianist. Extra-mural staff tutor in mus. Birmingham Univ., 1966–70. Prof. of mus., Keele Univ., 1974–84, Goldsmiths Coll., London, from 1991. Authority on Amer. mus. Works incl.:

THEATRE: *Vitalitas*, ballet (1959; orch. of *Variations* for pf. 1957); *The Judas Tree*, 5 speaking parts, 2 tens., ch., and orch. (1965).

ORCH.: *Monologue*, strs. (1959); *Transformations, Homage to Satie* (1970); concs.: org. (1971), str., perc., elec. org. (1971), pf. (1978–84), vn. (1986); *The Unicorns*, brass band (1982); *Merseyside Echoes* (1988); *Jigsaws*, ens., hp., perc. (1988).

VOCAL: 4 *Auden Songs*, sop. or ten., pf. (1956); 4 *Poems of Alan Porter*, counterten., hpd. (1968); *e. e. cummings Song Cycle*, mez., pf. (1965 rev. 1970); *Winter Afternoons* (Emily Dickinson), cantata, 6 solo vv., db. (1971); *Lust*, 6 vv. (1974); *Schubert in Blue*, mez., pf. (1977); *The Unicorns*, sop., brass band (1982); *Stevie's Tunes*, mez., sop. (1984); *A Mass of the Apocalypse*, ch., 2 perc., pf. (1984); *Tiananmen 1989*, double ch., tubular bells (1990); *Summoned by Mother*, mez., hp. (1990).

CHAMBER MUSIC: vn. sonata (1961); *Fanfares and Elegies*, 3 tpts., 3 tbs., org. (1967); *Hymns, Blues, and Improvisations*, str. qt., pf., tape (1973); str. qt. No.1 (1958, rev. 1974), No.2, with tape or pf. (1975); *Hymns, Rags and Blues*, vns., cl., pf. (1985); *London Rags*, 2 tpt., hn., tb., tuba (1986); *Auden*

Studies, ob., pf. (1988); *Cellars Clough Duo*, 2 gui. (1988); 5 *Explorations*, gui. (1989); *Swansongs*, vc., pf. (1992).

KEYBOARD: 5 *Forgeries*, pf. duet (1963); *Paraphrase II*, pf. (1967); 3 *Satie Transformations*, pf. (1970); *Rags, Blues and Parodies*, pf. (1970–86); *Piano Blues*, pf. (1973); *Blue Rose*, pf. (1979); *Hymn-Tune Rag*, pf. (1985); *Blue Rose Variations*, org. (1985); *Patriotic Rag*, pf. (1986); *Sanctus and Benedictus*, org. (1998); *A Millennium Fanfare*, org. (1999).
Also choral works, church music, and pieces for org.

diction. Properly, verbal phrasing, or skill in the choice of words, but used in context of singing to denote clear and correct enunciation.

didjeridu. Australian aborigines' wind instr., straight (over 3′ in length), end-blown, and capable of producing a variety of sounds, such as trills, croaks, gurgles, and imitations of birds and animals. The player can breathe through the nose without interrupting the sound he is making.

Dido and Aeneas. Opera in prol. and 3 acts by Purcell to lib. by Nahum Tate, after his play *Brutus of Alba* (1678) and Book 4 of Virgil's *Aeneid*. Presumed f.p. Josias Priest's sch. for young gentlewomen, Chelsea, in 1689 or 1690, but recent scholarship by Bruce Wood and Andrew Pinnock suggests comp. and perf. dates of 1683–4. Staged in London *c*.1700 and *c*.1704 and not again until RCM 1895 (Lyceum Th.). F.p. in NY 1923 (at Hotel Plaza). Several versions survive, the score held by St Michael's College, Tenbury, being accepted as standard. Another important version was found at Tatton Hall, Cheshire. *Dido's Lament*, *When I am laid in earth*, occurs in Act 3.

DiDonato, Joyce (*b* Prairie Village, Kansas, 1969). Amer. mezzo-soprano. Studied at Acad. of Vocal Arts, Philadelphia (1993–6). 2nd prize Domingo Operalia 1998. Won Richard Tucker Award 2002. Santa Fe Opera apprentice singer. Santa Fe début 2000 (Cherubino); CG 2003 (Fox in *Cunning Little Vixen*); Paris Opéra 2002 (Rosina); La Scala, Milan, 2001 (Angelina in *La Cenerentola*); NY Met 2005 (Cherubino).

Dido's Lament. Aria for Dido at end of Act 3 of Purcell's *Dido and Aeneas*, beginning with words 'When I am laid in earth'. Orch. arr. is played annually at Remembrance Day service at Cenotaph, London.

die (Ger.). The.

Diepenbrock, Alphons (*b* Amsterdam, 1862; *d* Amsterdam, 1921). Dutch composer. Influential teacher. Wrote chiefly church mus. (2 settings of *Te Deum*, a *Stabat mater*, and the *Missa in die festo* of 1891), the *Hymnen an die Nacht* (1899) for v. and orch., and incidental mus. to plays. Befriended and admired by *Mahler.

Dieren, Bernard van (*b* Rotterdam, 1887; *d* London, 1936). Dutch composer, long resident in Eng. Trained as scientist, but began to write mus. criticism and in 1909 settled in London as correspondent for several European periodicals. His works became the subject of a cult among leading Brit. intellectuals of the 1920s, e.g. Sitwells, Gerald Cooper, Heseltine, Gray, and others. Successive efforts to persuade his contemporary public and later generations of his genius have made little ground, the mus. being less novel than is suggested. Works incl. *The Tailor* (comic opera) (1917); *Symphony on Chinese Themes* (with vv.) (1914); *Serenade*; 6 str. qts.; solo vn. sonata; songs. Wrote book on Epstein (1920) and vol. of criticism, *Down Among the Dead Men* (1935).

dièse (Fr.). Sharp (♯).

Dies Irae (Day of Wrath). A section of the Requiem Mass. The poem is probably by Thomas of Celano (*d* *c*.1250). The plainsong tune has frequently been introduced into instr. mus., as in Berlioz's *Symphonie fantastique*, Saint-Saëns's *Danse macabre*, Rachmaninov's *Paganini Rhapsody*, etc. Settings of the Requiem by Verdi, Berlioz, and others contain vivid depictions of the *Dies Irae*.

diesis (It.). (1) Sharp (♯).
(2) In acoustical theory the minute interval between the sum of 3 major 3rds (in perfect tuning) and an octave.

Dies Natalis (Lat. 'Birthday'). Cantata, Op.8, by *Finzi, for sop. or ten. and str., composed between 1926 and 1939, f.p. 1940. It is in 5 movts., the 1st instrumental, the 2nd a setting of a prose passage from *Centuries of Meditations* by T. Traherne (1638–74), and the last 3 being settings of Traherne poems.

differential tone (or resultant tone). In acoustics: (1) When two loud notes are played, another, lower, note may sometimes be heard which corresponds to the difference in vibration between the original 2 notes.
(2) When a note higher than the original 2 may be heard which corresponds to the sum of their vibrations.

digital. Any one of the keys comprising the kbd. of a pf. or similar instr. For digital recording, see *gramophone recordings*.

digitorium. A small portable apparatus for the use of kbd. players wishing to strengthen their fingers. It usually had no more than 5 keys and these had strong springs so that considerable force was required to depress them. Invented by Myer Marks about the middle of the 19th cent.

Dillon, James (*b* Glasgow, 1950). Scottish composer. As a boy, played in pipe band. Studied medieval, Renaissance, and non-Western mus. Awarded Kranichsteiner prize, Darmstadt 1982. His mus. was featured at Bath and La Rochelle fests., 1984. Works incl.: *Babble*, 40 vv. (1974–6); *Dillug Kefitsah*, pf. (1976); *Cumha*, 12 str. (1976–8); *Incaain*, 16 vv. (1977); *Ariadne's Thread*, va. (1978); *Crossing Over*, cl. (1978); *Ti-re-Ti-ke-Dha*, solo drum (1979); . . . *Once Upon a Time*, 10 instr. (1980); *Spleen*, pf. (1980); *Who do you Love*, v., 8 instr.

(1980–1); *Evening Rain*, solo v. (1981); *Parjanya-Vata*, vc. (1981); *Come Live with Me*, mez., 4 instr. (1981); *A Roaring Flame*, v., contrabass (1981–2); *Time Lag Zero*, v., va. (1982); *East 11th St. NY 10003*, perc. (6 players) (1982); str. qt. No.1 (1983), No.2 (1991), No.3 (1998); *Zone* (. . . . *de azul*), 8 instr. (1983); *Le Rivage*, wind quintet (1984); *Sgothan*, fl. (1984); *helle Nacht*, orch. (1986–7); str. trio (1991); *Blitzschlag*, fl., orch. (1995); *Eos*, vc. (1999); *Vapor Musik*, 4 vv., str. qt. (1999); *Via sacra*, orch. (2000); vn. conc. (2000); *Book of Elements I–V*, pf. (1997–2002); *Philomela*, opera, 3 vv., small orch., elec. (2003–4).

diluendo (It.). Dissolving, i.e. dying away.

dilungando (It.). Lengthening.

diminished intervals. Perfect or minor intervals which are reduced chromatically by a semitone are diminished intervals. For practical purposes this term is useful only when applied to the diminished 5th (semitone less than perfect 5th) and diminished 7th (semitone less than minor 7th).

diminished triad. A *triad of which the 5th is diminished.

diminuendo (It.). Diminishing, i.e. gradually getting quieter (>).

diminution. Shortening of the time-values of the notes of melodic parts. Opposite of *augmentation. In *canon by diminution* the imitating vv. are in shorter notes than the one they are imitating.

Dimitrij. Opera in 4 acts by Dvořák to lib. by Marie Červinková-Riegrová based on writings by Mikovec and on Schiller's *Demetrius*. Comp. 1881–2, prod. Prague 1882. Rev. 1883, prod. Prague 1883; further rev. 1885, prod. Prague 1892. Revised again 1894–5 with much recomposition, and prod. that year in Prague. For a prod. in 1904, Dvořák reverted to a combination of the earlier and latest versions. Brit. f.p. Nottingham 1979. US f.p. NY (concert) 1984.

Dimitrova, Ghena (*b* Beglej, Bulgaria, 1941; *d* Milan, 2005). Bulg. soprano. Joined Bulg. Nat. Opera, début in Skopje 1965 as Abigaille in *Nabucco*. Sang in It. from 1970 and in Vienna 1978. Amer. début Dallas 1981; London début 1983; La Scala 1983; CG 1984; Salzburg Fest. 1984; NY Met 1988. Sang Lady Macbeth with Royal Opera in Greece 1986 and Aida at Luxor 1987.

di molto (It.). Of much, i.e. very. Augments the word to which it is applied, e.g. *allegro di molto*, very fast.

D'India, Sigismondo (*b* Palermo, *c*1582; *d* ?Modena, before 1629). It. composer and singer. Said to be of noble birth and spent 1600–10 travelling in It., visiting several courts. Probably met Monteverdi in Mantua 1606. Dir. of chamber mus. to the Duke of Savoy in Turin, 1611–23, during which period most of his mus. was written. Moved to Modena 1623–4, then to Rome where in 1625 his sacred opera *Sant' Eustachio* was perf. in Cardinal Maurizio's palace. Returned to Modena 1626. Regarded as most important composer of secular vocal mus. in early 17th-cent. It. after Monteverdi. Collections of his works were pubd. in Milan and Venice from 1609 to 1623. Blended styles of Marenzio, Wert, Gesualdo, and Monteverdi into a rich polyphonic style of his own, with daring harmonies and treatment of dissonance.

D'Indy, (Paul Marie Théodore) **Vincent** (*b* Paris, 1851; *d* Paris, 1931). Fr. composer and teacher. In 1872 he sent a pf. qt. to *Franck, who agreed to teach him. As a member of Franck's class at the Paris Cons. he imbibed not only Franck's teaching, but also his lofty and idealistic attitude to art. To supplement his studies, d'Indy in 1872 became 2nd perc. player in the Colonne Orch., and from 1875 to 1879 was ch.-master of the Concerts Colonne. Public début as composer 1874. In 1876 he attended the first Bayreuth Fest., having been introduced to Wagner's mus. by Duparc in 1869, and became fervent enthusiast of *The Ring*. Keenly interested in education, d'Indy in 1894 accepted invitation from *Bordes to join him and Guilmant in founding the Schola Cantorum for the study of church mus. In 1900 this became a general mus. sch. at which d'Indy taught comp. until his death, becoming sole dir. in 1911. His teaching methods are described in his 3-vol. *Cours de Composition*, written in assoc. with A. Sérieyx. His pupils incl. Satie, Auric, Roussel, Turina, and Roland-Manuel. D'Indy was also active in assisting Lamoureux to introduce Wagner's works to Paris, was a champion of Debussy, and revived the mus. of Monteverdi, Rameau, Gluck, and Bach. He wrote several books (incl. biography of Franck), toured as cond. abroad, ed. old mus. (incl. several Monteverdi operas), and pubd. colls. of folk-songs. His comps. are characterized by rich orchestration, a vein of folk-like melody, and often employ Franck's 'cyclic method'. Chief among them are:

OPERAS: *Le Chant de la cloche* (1879–83); *Fervaal* (1889–95); *L'Étranger* (1898–1901); *La Légende de Saint-Christophe* (1908–15); *Le Rêve de Cynias* (1922–3).

ORCH.: *La Forêt enchantée* (1878); *Wallenstein*, trilogy (1874–82); *Symphonie sur un chant montagnard français (Symphonie Cévenole)* (1886); *Istar* (1896); 2nd Sym. (1902–3); *Jour d'été à la montagne* (1905); *Le Poème des rivages* (1920–1).

CHORAL: *Sainte Marie-Magdaleine*, cantata (1885); *Sur la Mer* (1888); *Deus Israël* (1896).

CHAMBER MUSIC: 3 str. qts.; vc. sonata; vn. sonata; pf. quintet; str. sextet.

PIANO: *Promenades, Schumanniana, Menuet sur le nom de Haydn, Conte de fées*.

Dinner Engagement, A. 1-act comic opera by Lennox Berkeley to lib. by Paul Dehn (1912–76). Prod. Aldeburgh 1954.

Dinorah, ou le pardon de Ploërmel. 3-act opera by Meyerbeer to lib. by Barbier and Carré. Prod. Paris and London 1859, New Orleans 1861. Contains the coloratura sop. 'Shadow Song'.

Dioclesian (*The Prophetess, or The History of Dioclesian*). Semi-opera in 5 acts by Purcell (1690). Dialogue by T. Betterton, adapted from Fletcher and Massinger. Prod. London, May 1690. For revival in London, 1724, Pepusch wrote new mus.

diplomas. See *degrees and diplomas*.

Dippel, (Johann) **Andreas** (*b* Kassel, 1866; *d* Hollywood, Calif., 1932). Ger. tenor and impresario. Member of opera cos. in Bremen 1887–92 and Vienna 1893–8. Débuts: NY Met 1890; CG 1897; Bayreuth 1889. At NY Met 1890–1908, becoming joint man. with *Gatti-Casazza 1908–10. Man., Chicago Opera, 1910–13. Sang over 150 roles, notably those by Wagner, and was famous for ability to replace indisposed colleague at very short notice.

direct. The sign at the end of a page or line (in older mus.) to give warning of the next note.

dirge (Lat. *naenia*). Burial or memorial song, often with character of funeral march. Shakespeare's *Dirge for Fidele* (*Cymbeline*) has been set by several composers incl. Vaughan Williams (1922) and Finzi (1942). The 15th cent. Lyke-wake Dirge was set by Stravinsky (*Cantata* 1952), Britten (*Serenade* 1943), and Whittaker (1924).

Dirge for Two Veterans. (1) Setting of text from Whitman's *Drum Taps* (1865) by Holst for male vv., brass, and perc. Comp. 1914.

(2) Setting of same text for ch. and orch. by Vaughan Williams, comp. 1911 and incorporated into his cantata *Dona nobis pacem* (1936) as 4th movt.

Dirigent, dirigieren (Ger.). 'Conductor', 'to conduct'.

Dis (Ger.). The note D♯.

disc (Amer. *disk*). Gramophone record.

discant. Same as *descant.

discography. A list of gramophone recordings, either of those of the mus. of a particular composer, or those made by an individual artist, orch., or instr. combination. When an artist has recorded for several cos. and in several countries, these can require considerable and valuable research. A discography is becoming a standard feature of many books on music.

discord. A chord which is restless, jarring to the ear, requiring to be resolved in a particular way if its presence is to be justified by the ear (or the note or interval responsible for producing this effect).

disjunct motion. A note which moves to another note or an adjacent note by a leap. See *motion*.

dissonance. See *discord*.

Dissonanzen Quartett (Les Dissonances). Ger. and Fr. nicknames for Mozart's Str. Qt. No.19 in C major, K465, comp. 1785. The introduction contains remarkable use of dissonance.

Di Stefano, Giuseppe (b Motta Santa Anastasia, nr. Catania, 1921). It. tenor. Début 1946 Reggio Emilia as Des Grieux in *Manon*. La Scala début 1947; NY Met 1948–65; S. Francisco 1950; Brit. début Edinburgh Fest. 1957; CG 1961. Sang often with *Callas, making recordings with her, and partnering her on her 1973–4 concert tour.

Distratto, Il (The Distraught Man). Nickname for Haydn's sym. in C major, No.60 in Breitkopf edn. of syms. 6 movts. are derived from Haydn's incidental mus. (1774) for J. F. Regnard's play *Le Distrait* (Ger. *Der Zerstreute*), revived at Eszterháza that year.

dital harp. Obsolete instr. invented in 1798 by Edward Light, a teacher of guitar: it was at first called *harp guitar*. By 'dital' is meant a finger-key (actually played by the thumb): each dital raised the pitch of a string by a semitone. Another name was *harp lute*, the appearance of the instr. suggesting the body of a lute continued upwards by that of a small harp.

dithyramb (from Gr. *dithyrambos*). In ancient Greece an intoxicated song in honour of the god Dionysus; in modern usage applied to a comp. of wild, passionate character.

Dittersdorf, Karl Ditters von [Ditters, Karl] (b Vienna, 1739; d Neuhof, 1799). Austrian composer and violinist. From 1751 to 1761 in private orch. of nobleman who paid for his vn. and comp. lessons. Kapellmeister to various princes, esp. to Prince-Bishop of Breslau 1770–95. Ennobled 1773. Wrote 11 *Singspiele* for court ht. at Oels after 1793. Prolific composer, works incl. 40 operas (incl. *Doktor und Apotheker* (1786), *The Marriage of Figaro* (c.1789, lost), and *The Merry Wives of Windsor* (1796)); c.120 syms. (incl. 12 syms. after Ovid's *Metamorphoses*); 35 concs.; 5 str. qts.; 12 str. quintets; 14 str. trios; 17 vn. sonatas; 30 pf. sonatas; and quantities of church mus.

div. Abbreviation for *divisi*.

diversions. Occasional synonym for variations.

Divertimenti by Mozart. Mozart's comps. to which he gave the title Divertimento are: E♭ (K113, 1771, wind, str.), D major (K131, 1772, wind., str.), D major (K136, 1772, str. qt.), B♭ (K137, 1772, str. qt.), F major (K138, 1772, str. qt.), E♭ (K166, 1773, wind), B♭ (K186, 1773, wind), C major (K187, 1773, wind), C major (K188, 1773, wind., timp.), D major (K205, 1775, wind, str.), F major (K213, 1775, wind), B♭ (K240, 1776, wind), F major (K247, 1776, hns., str.), D major (K251, 1776, wind., str.), E♭ (K252, 1776, wind), F major (K253, 1776, wind), B♭ (K254, 1776, pf. trio), B♭ (K270, 1777, wind), B♭ (K287, 1777, 2 hn., str.), F major (K288, 1777 (fragment) wind., str.), E♭

(K289, 1777, wind), D major (K334, 1779–80, 2 hn., str.), E♭ (K563, 1788, str. trio), E♭ (K Anh.226, wind), B♭ (K Anh.227, wind).

divertimento (It.). Amusement. (1) An 18th-cent. suite of movts. of light, recreational mus., sometimes for open-air perf., for a small no. of players. Mozart wrote 25, calling them Divertimenti or sometimes serenades or cassations. In the 20th cent. composers use the term to denote a not-too-serious work.
(2) Fantasia on airs from operas, etc.

divertissement (Fr.). Amusement. The same as *divertimento, with the additional meaning of an entertainment of dances and songs inserted in an 18th-cent. stage spectacle or sometimes in a ballet or opera (as in Gounod's *Faust* or Delibes's *Coppélia*). The term is also applied to a suite of dances unconnected by a story. Ibert's *Divertissement* is an orch. work derived from mus. for the film *The Italian Straw Hat*.

Dives and Lazarus, 5 Variants of. Work by Vaughan Williams for str. and harp(s) comp. 1939 for NY World Fair. F.p. NY 1939. *Dives and Lazarus* is Eng. folk-song.

Divina Commedia, Symphony to (Liszt). See *Dante Symphony*.

Divine Office. The Canonical Hours of the RC Church (*Matins, Lauds, Prime, Terce, Sext, None, Vespers*, and *Compline*: these are daily said by all the clergy and in cath. and monastic churches are daily said or sung). Also *Matins* and *Evensong* in the Church of England.

Divine Poem, The (*Bozhestvennaya poema*). Title of Scriabin's Sym. No.3 in C minor, Op.43, comp. 1902–4, f.p. Paris 1905, NY 1907, London 1913. Illustrates his theosophical ideas; the 3 movts. are entitled *Struggles, Delights*, and *Divine Play*.

divisi (It.). Divided, often abbreviated to 'div.'. Term used, for instance, where orch. str. parts are written in double (or more) notes, and the players, instead of individually attempting to play all the notes of each chord, are to divide themselves into 2 (or more) groups to perform them.

divisions. (1) (17th and 18th cents.) The splitting up of the notes of a tune into shorter notes, i.e. a form of variation; this was especially common in viol playing and was extemporized.
(2) Long vocal runs, as in Bach, Handel, and other 18th-cent. composers. Obsolete term.

division viol. Small bass viol for the playing of popular sets of (often extemporized) variations.

Dixieland. Style of instr. jazz-playing from c.1912, also called 'New Orleans' or 'classic' style. Had elements of ragtime and blues with own distinctive improvisation. Dixieland bands were divided into 2 sections, one providing rhythm and harmony, the other melody and extemporization. The melody section consisted of tpt. or cornet, cl., and tb. (and, later, sax.); the rhythm section of pf. and/or banjo, trap drums, and sousaphone, tuba, or plucked db. Outstanding Dixieland performers were Louis Armstrong, Kid Ory, King Oliver, Sidney Bechet, Jelly Roll Morton, and Earl Hines.

Dixon, (Charles) **Dean** (b NY, 1915; d Zug, Switz., 1976). Amer. conductor, one of the first blacks to achieve fame as a symphonic cond. Début NY Town Hall 1938, NYPO 1941, and then other leading orchs. Founded Amer. Youth Orch. 1944. In 1949 cond. in Scandinavia. Cond. Israel PO 1950–1. Mus. dir. Gothenburg SO 1953–60, Hesse Radio SO 1961–74, Sydney SO 1963–7. British début 1963 with BBCSO. Series of concerts with leading Amer. orchs. after 1970.

Djamileh. 1-act opera by Bizet to lib. by L. Gallet based on Alfred de Musset's poem *Namouna* (1832). Prod. Paris 1872, Manchester 1892, London 1893.

do. The name for *ut or C in the Romance languages, introduced by G. M. *Bononcini, 1673. See *doh*.

Dobbs, Mattiwilda (b Atlanta, 1925). Amer. coloratura soprano. Won Geneva Fest. first prize 1951 and appeared in concerts in Scandinavia, Fr., etc. Opera début as Stravinsky's Nightingale, Holland Fest. 1952. First black singer to appear at La Scala 1953. Outstanding Zerbinetta in *Ariadne auf Naxos*, Glyndebourne 1953. CG début 1954. Member of NY Met co. from 1956. In the 1970s was visiting prof. at several Amer. univs.

Dobrowen, Issay (Alexandrovich) [Barabeichik, Ishok Israelevich] (b Nizhny Novgorod, 1891; d Oslo, 1953). Russ.-born conductor, pianist, and composer. Début as cond. Moscow 1919 (Bolshoy 1921). Worked at Dresden with Fritz Busch, cond. first Ger. perf. of *Boris Godunov* (Dresden, 1922). Worked in Vienna, Sofia, and Budapest, frequent visitor to USA (Amer. début S. Francisco SO 1931). Cond. Göteborg SO 1939, Stockholm Royal Opera from 1941. Cond. and prod. Russ. operas at Scala from 1948. Comps. incl. concs. for pf. and vn. Became Norweg. cit. in 1930s.

Dobrowolski, Andrzej (b Lemberg, now Lwów, 1921). Polish composer and teacher. Worked for Polish radio experimental studio. From 1954 teacher at Warsaw Acad. Works incl. sym. vars. (1949); sym. (1955); bn. conc. (1953); wind trio (1955); *Music for Orch. I* (1969), *II* (1971), *III* (1972–3), *IV (A-La)* (1974), *V (Passacaglia)* (1979), *VI* (1981–2); *Music*, chamber orch. (1982–3); *Music*, orch., ob. (1984–5); *Flütchen*, chamber ens., reciter (1986); *Musik für Grazer Bläserkreis*, 8 tpt., 8 tb., 8 hn., perc. (1984); *Music for Magnetic Tape No.1* (1963) (reproduced on p. 230); *Music*, tape, ob. (1965); *Music*, magnetic tape, db. (1977); *Music*, magnetic tape, cl. (1980); songs; and *musique concrète*.

Docteur Miracle, Le (Doctor Miracle). Operetta in 1 act by Bizet to lib. by Battu and Halévy. Prod. Paris 1857, London 1957, also 1-act operetta by

Lecocq, prod. Paris 1857, the day before Bizet's, both works being entries in competition sponsored by Offenbach and being adjudged joint winners. F. Eng. stage p. of Lecocq, London 1984.

Doctor of Music. Highest mus. degree in Brit., Commonwealth, and USA. According to individual univ. style, abbreviated to D.Mus., Mus.D., or Mus. Doc.

dodecaphonic (Gr.). 12 sounds. Adjective describing the system of comp. with 12 notes (dodecaphony). In the dodecaphonic scale the 12 notes are considered to be of equal status and are so treated. See *atonal* and *note-row*.

Dodge, Charles (b Ames, Iowa, 1942). Amer. composer. Specialist in elec. and computer-programmed mus. Teacher at Columbia Univ. 1967–9, 1970–7; assoc. prof. of mus., Brooklyn Coll. of City Univ. of NY, 1977–80, prof. from 1980. Works incl. *Changes*, computer-synthesized sounds on tape (1970); *Earth's Magnetic Field*, elec. on tape (1970); *Extensions*, tpt., computer synthesis (1973); *Palinode*, orch., computer synthesis (1976); *Mingo's Song*, computer-synthesized v. (1983); *The Waves*, sop., computer synthesis (1984); *Song Without Words*, computer synthesis (1986); *Wedding Music*, vn., computer synthesis (1988); *The Voice of Binky*, computer synthesis (1989).

Dodgson, Stephen (b London, 1924). Eng. composer. Works incl. opera *Margaret Catchpole* (1979); 2 gui. concs. (1959, 1972); 3 pf. sonatas (1959, 1975, 1983); pf. quintet (1966); 2 pf. trios (1967, 1973); *Magnificat* (1975); *Epigrams from a Garden*, cont., cls. (1977); bn. conc. (1969); *Sir John*, cantata, ch., hn. trio (1980); cl. conc. (1983); tb. conc. (1986); str. qt. (1986); and songs.

doglia (It.). Sorrow. So *doglioso*, sorrowful; *dogliosamente*, sorrowfully.

doh. In Tonic sol-fa the spoken name for the tonic (first degree) of the scale. *Doh* sharpened becomes *de*.

Dohnányi, Christoph von (b Berlin, 1929). Ger. conductor. Grandson of Ernö *Dohnányi. Ass. cond. to Solti, Frankfurt Opera 1952. Gen. mus. dir. Lübeck 1957–63, Kassel 1963–6, Frankfurt 1968–77, Hamburg 1977–84. Chief cond. W. Ger. Radio SO 1964–70, Cleveland Orch. 1984–2002, Philharmonia Orch. 1997–2008. Salzburg Fest. début 1962; Brit. début 1965 (LPO); CG 1974; Amer. opera début Chicago 1969; NY Met 1972. Cond. f.p. of Henze's *Der junge Lord* (Berlin 1965). Cond. *Der Ring*, Vienna 1992–3.

Dohnányi, Ernö [Ernst von] (b Pozsony, now Bratislava, 1877; d NY, 1960). Hung. composer, pianist, and conductor. Pianist of int. repute 1897–1908 (début Berlin 1897). London début 1898 (Beethoven G major conc. at Richter concert). Prof of pf., Berlin Hochschule, 1908–15. Dir. Budapest Cons. 1919. Dir. Hungarian radio 1931, Hochschule 1934. Cond. Budapest PO 1919–44. Salzburg Fest. début 1929. Settled in

USA 1949 at Florida State Univ., Tallahassee, as prof. of pf. and comp. His mus. has nationalist flavour but much less than that of Bartók and Kodály. Prin. works:

OPERAS: *Tante Simona* (Dresden 1913); *The Tower of Voivod* (Budapest 1922); *The Tenor* (Budapest 1929).

ORCH.: sym. in D minor (1900–1), in E (1943–4, rev. 1953–6); pf. conc. No.1 (1897–8), No.2 (1946–7); vn. conc. No.1 (1914–15), No.2 (1949–50); *Suite* in F♯ minor (1908–9); *Variations on a Nursery Song*, pf., orch. (1913).

CHAMBER MUSIC: 3 str. qts. (1899, 1906, 1926); 2 pf. quintets (1895, 1914); vc. sonata (1899); vn. sonata (1912); sextet (1935); *Passacaglia*, fl. (1959).

PIANO: 4 *Klavierstücke*; 4 *Rhapsodies, Variations, Passacaglia*, and *Ruralia Hungarica* (1923, orch. 1924).

Doktor, Paul (Karl) (*b* Vienna, 1919; *d* NY, 1989). Austrian-born violist. Prin. violist Lucerne SO 1940–7. Won Geneva Int. Fest. 1942. Went to USA 1947. Salzburg Fest. début 1955. Lect., violist in resident qt., Univ. of Michigan 1948–51; prof. of va., Mannes College of Mus., 1953–70. Summer faculty Colorado College from 1957. On staff Juilliard Sch. from 1971. Soloist with leading orchs., ed. of va. mus.

Doktor Faust. Opera in 2 prols., interlude, and 3 scenes by Busoni to his own lib., comp. 1916–24, the final scene being completed by *Jarnach. Prod. Dresden (Busch) 1925, London (concert) 1937, (stage, ENO) 1986, NY (concert) 1964, Reno (stage) 1974. A new completion by Antony Beaumont (1984), based on hitherto unknown sketches for the missing scenes acquired from Jarnach in 1974, was prod. Bologna 1985 and also used in ENO prod. (1986).

dolcan (org. stop). Same as *dolce.

dolce (It.). Sweet (with the implication of 'soft' also) or gentle. Hence *dolcissimo*, very sweet; *dolcemente*, sweetly; *dolcezza*, sweetness.

dolce or **dolcan** (org. stop). Soft open metal *diapason; pipes are of inverted conical shape; 8′ length and pitch.

dolente (It.). Doleful, sorrowful. So the adverb *dolentemente* and the superlative *dolentissimo*.

Dollarprinzessin, Die (The Dollar Princess). Operetta in 3 acts by *Fall, to lib. by A. M. Willner and F. Grünbaum based on comedy by Gatti-Trotha. Prod. Vienna 1907, Manchester 1908, London and NY 1909 (with additional numbers by Jerome Kern).

Dolly. Pf. suite by Fauré, Op.56, comp. 1893–6, for 4 hands. 6 movts. are: *Berceuse, Mi-a-ou, Le Jardin de Dolly, Kitty-valse, Tendresse*, and *Le Pas espagnol*. Orch. version by *Rabaud, 1906.

Dolmetsch, Arnold (*b* Le Mans, 1858; *d* Haslemere, 1940). Swiss musician and maker of old instr. Taught vn. Dulwich Coll. 1885–9. Restored old instrs., made his first lute 1893, clavichord 1894, hpd. 1896. Worked on early kbd. instr. at Chickering's pf. factory, Boston, Mass., 1902–9; in charge Gaveau's hpd. dept., Paris, 1911–14. Settled in Eng. at Haslemere, Surrey, 1917, establishing workshop for manufacture and repair of clavichords, hpds., viols, lutes, recorders, etc., and founding (1925) annual fest. at which old mus. was perf. by himself and his family on authentic instr. His book *The Interpretation of the Music of the 17th and 18th Centuries* (1915) was the first comprehensive survey of its field.

Dolmetsch, Carl (Frederick) (*b* Fontenay-s-Bois, 1911; *d* Haslemere, 1997). Eng. recorder-player, son of Arnold *Dolmetsch. Was a virtuoso, touring the world. Also maker of recorders and player of vn. and lute. Ed. of recorder mus. Dir., Haslemere Fest. from 1940. CBE 1954.

dolore (It.). Sorrow, dolour, pain. Hence *doloroso*, dolorous, painful, and the adverb, *dolorosamente*.

Dolzflöte (Ger.). Same as It. *flauto dolce*, i.e. a soft-toned org. stop of fl. tone.

Domestic Symphony (Strauss). See *Symphonia domestica*.

Domgraf-Fassbänder, Willi (*b* Aachen, 1897; *d* Nuremberg, 1978). Ger. baritone, father of Brigitte *Fassbaender. Operatic début Aachen 1922 as the Count in *Le nozze di Figaro*. Prin. lyric bar., Berlin State Opera 1928–45. Sang Figaro in *Le nozze di Figaro* at opening night of Glyndebourne Opera, 1934. Salzburg Fest. 1937. Chief producer, Nuremberg Opera, 1953–62. On retirement became dir. of opera studies, Nuremberg Cons.

dominant. (1) 5th degree of major or minor scale, thus if the key is B (major or minor) the dominant is F♯. Chords built on this note are *dominant chords*, the most important being the *dominant seventh* which is a chord consisting of the common chord of the dominant with the minor 7th from its root added, e.g. in key C it is G–B–D–F. Like all intervals of a 7th, the dominant 7th is a discord. It normally resolves on the tonic or submediant chord, the note constituting the 7th falling a semitone, allowing the 3rd (i.e. the leading note of the scale) to rise to the tonic. More rarely the 7th can remain as a note common to the following chord, usually the 1st or 2nd inversion of the subdominant. The three inversions of the dominant seventh chord are, of course, in common use.

(2) See *modes*.

dominant cadence. Same as imperfect cadence, or half close.

Domingo, Plácido (*b* Madrid, 1941). Sp. tenor and conductor. Début as bar. 1957 in zarzuela. Opera début as ten. in Monterrey, Mexico, 1961 (Alfredo in *La traviata*). Member of Israeli Nat. Opera 1962–5. Amer. début 1961 (Dallas); NY début 1965 with City Opera; NY Met début 1968; La Scala 1969; Brit. début London, 1969; CG 1971. Sang his first Otello Hamburg 1975. Salzburg Fest. début 1975 (title-role in *Don*

Carlos). Outstanding exponent of lyrical and heroic roles of It. opera, but also a fine Lohengrin and Walther in *Die Meistersinger*. Sang Parsifal at La Scala and NY Met 1991 and at Bayreuth 1993; sang Siegmund in *Die Walküre*, Vienna 1992. Has also cond. opera, incl. *Die Fledermaus* (CG 1983) and *La bohème* (NY Met 1985). Autobiography *My First Forty Years* (NY 1983). Hon. KBE 2002. One of Three Tenors with *Carreras and *Pavarotti.

Dominguez, Oralia (*b* S. Luis Potosi, Mexico, 1928). Mexican mezzo-soprano. Operatic début, Nat. Opera of Mexico, 1950. Sang from 1953 at world's leading opera houses, also concerts and recitals. Début La Scala 1953 in *Adriana Lecouvreur*. CG début 1955; with Glyndebourne co. at Edinburgh 1955; Glyndebourne 1957.

Dominicus Mass, or **Pater Dominicus Mass**. Mozart's Mass in C, K66 (1769). Written for the first celebration of mass at St Peter's, Salzburg, by a young priest (Cajetan Hagenauer) who had taken that name. Revived in Vienna, 1773.

domp(e). See *dump*.

domra. Russ. instr., like *balalaika, played by plucking. Has convex back like *mandolin.

Dona nobis pacem (Give us peace). (1) Part of the *Mass.
(2) Cantata by Vaughan Williams to text selected from the Bible, Whitman, and a parliamentary speech by John Bright. Comp. 1936, except for movt. *Dirge for Two Veterans* (1911). F.p. Huddersfield 1936, London 1936 (broadcast), 1938 (public).

Donath, Helen [Erwin, Helen] (*b* Corpus Christi, Texas, 1940). Amer. soprano. Sang Inez in *Il trovatore*, Cologne 1960. Member of Cologne Opera 1962–3; Hanover 1963–7; Salzburg Fest. 1967; Amer. début (S. Francisco) 1971; CG 1979. Roles incl. Ilia, Zerlina, Mimi, Martinů's Julietta, and the Governess in *The Turn of the Screw*. Frequent recitalist in *Lieder* and concert-hall choral works. Husband is Klaus Donath, former mus. dir. Darmstadt Opera.

Donaueschingen. Town in Germany with a mus. tradition going back to 17th cent. but notable especially for foundation in 1921 of first fest. devoted exclusively to contemp. mus. Fest. programmes 1921–6 planned mainly by Hindemith and Joseph Haas and incl. works by Krenek and Hába. In 1926 fest. was moved to Baden-Baden, with emphasis on chamber opera, and in 1930 to Berlin, where competition from New Mus. fest. proved too great. In 1950 fest. was revived in collab. with SW Ger. Radio, Baden-Baden, using radio orch. under Rosbaud and, from 1964, Ernest Bour. Among composers brought to the fore at post-1950 fests. are Boulez, Stockhausen, Xenakis, Nono, Ligeti, Berio, Fortner, Penderecki, and Henze. F.ps. there incl. Hindemith's *Kammermusik No.1* (1922), Webern's *6 Songs*, Op.14 (1924),

Schoenberg's *Serenade*, Op.24 (1924), Boulez's *Poésie pour pouvoir* (1958), Messiaen's *Chronochromie* (1960), and Stockhausen's *Mantra* (1970).

Don Carlos. 5-act opera by Verdi, to French lib. by Méry and du Locle after Schiller's play, comp. 1866–7, prod. Paris 1867, London CG 1867, NY 1877. This orig. version was heavily cut in Paris; the f.p. of the uncut score was in a BBC studio production in 1973, cond. by John Matheson. There was a stage perf., omitting only the ballet *La Pérégrina*, in Boston, Mass., 1975. In 1882–3 Verdi reduced it to 4 acts by omitting Act I (the 'Fontainebleau scene'), prod. Milan 1884, and in 1886 he restored orig. Act I to the 4-act rev. It. version is properly known as *Don Carlo*. In recent years both 5- and 4-act versions have been perf.

Dönch, Karl (*b* Hagen, 1915; *d* Vienna, 1994). Ger. bass-baritone. Operatic début Görlitz 1936. Sang in Reichenberg and Bonn. Salzburg Fest. début 1946. Vienna Opera from 1947. Roles there incl. Beckmesser, Doctor in *Wozzeck*. NY Met 1959–60, 1966–7. Bregenz Fest. 1955–84. Dir., Vienna Volksoper 1973–86.

Don Giovanni (*Il dissoluto punito, ossia Il Don Giovanni*; The Rake punished, or Don Giovanni). *Dramma giocoso* in 2 acts by Mozart (K527) to lib. by da Ponte based on the Don Juan legend as told in Bertati's play (1775). Comp. 1787. Prod. Prague 1787, Vienna 1788 (with extra material), London 1817 (or earlier), NY 1826. See also *Don Juan*.

Donington, Robert (*b* Leeds, 1907; *d* Firle, Sussex, 1990). Eng. author, composer, musicologist, and authority on old instruments. Expert player of viola da gamba; worked with Dolmetsch at Haslemere. Played in Eng. Consort of Viols 1935–9, London Consort 1950–60, Donington Consort 1956–61. Prof. of mus. at several Amer. univs. 1961–71. Comp. 12-note works. Several books on early mus. but most famous books are his *Wagner's 'Ring' and its Symbols* (1963), a detailed exposition of the psychological basis of *Der Ring des Nibelungen*; and two major books on performance practice in early mus., *The Interpretation of Early Music* (London, 1963) and *Performer's Guide to Baroque Music* (London, 1973). He also wrote *The Rise of Opera* (London, 1981). OBE 1979.

Donizetti, Gaetano (*b* Bergamo, 1797; *d* Bergamo, 1848). It. composer, principally of operas. Pupil of *Mayr at Bergamo and of Padre Mattei at Bologna. His *Enrico di Borgogna* was prod. Venice, 1818, and *Zoraida di Granata* was a success in Rome in 1822. In the next 8 years he wrote nearly 30 operas which were perf. throughout It. His first int. success was with *Anna Bolena* (1830), and this was followed by the comedy *L'Elisir d'Amore* (1832), and by his masterpiece *Lucia di Lammermoor* (1835). For Paris, 1840, he comp. the light-hearted *La Fille du Régiment* and the large-scale *La Favorite*. His last success was also in Paris, with *Don Pasquale* in 1843. Donizetti was prof. of counterpoint at Naples

Cons. 1835–7, becoming dir. in 1837. He became paralysed and mentally unbalanced as a result of syphilis in 1844.

Donizetti's ability to write at great speed has prejudiced attitudes to the quality of his work. He wrote specifically for a generation of great singers such as Grisi, Mario, Lablache, and Tamburini. However, although he catered for their ability and agility, the tendency to underrate the melodic and dramatic content of his operas has only recently been corrected by a more discriminating willingness to recognize Donizetti's brilliance as a rival in comic opera to Rossini; and to acknowledge the debt, in the form of recognizable borrowings, owed to him by Verdi, who clearly appreciated his dramatic mastery. Recently several of Donizetti's lesser-known operas have been revived and found to have unsuspected merit. He also wrote church mus., 18 str. qts., and some orch. works. A list of his operas follows:

Il pigmalione (1816); *L'ira d'Achille* (1817); *Enrico di Borgogna*; *Una follia* (both 1818); *Il falegname di Livonia*; *Le nozze in villa* (both 1819); *Zoraide di Granata*; *La zingara*; *La lettera anonima*; *Chiara e Serafina* (all 1822); *Il fortunato inganno*; *Alfredo il Grande* (both 1823); *L'ajo nell'imbarazzo*; *Emilia di Liverpool* (both 1824); *Alahor in Granata*; *Gabriella di Vergy* (2nd version 1838); *Elvida* (all 1826); *Olivo e Pasquale*; *Il borgomastro di Saardam*; *Le convenienze teatrali* (2nd version, *Le convenienze ed inconvenienze teatrali*, 1831), *Otto mesi in due ore* (all 1827); *Alina, regina di Golconda*; *Gianni di Calais*; *L'esule di Roma* (all 1828); *Il Giovedì Grasso*; *Il Paria*; *Elisabetta al castello di Kenilworth* (all 1829); *Il diluvio universale*; *I pazzi per progetto*; *Imelda de' Lambertazzi*; *Anna Bolena* (all 1830); *Gianni di Parigi*; *La Romanziera e l'uomo nero*; *Francesca di Foix* (all 1831); *Fausta*; *Ugo, conte di Parigi*; *L'elisir d'amore*; *Sancia di Castiglia* (all 1832); *Il furioso all'isola di San Domingo*; *Parisina*; *Torquato Tasso*; *Lucrezia Borgia* (all 1833); *Rosmonda d'Inghilterra*; *Gemma di Vergy* (both 1834); *Marino Faliero*; *Lucia di Lammermoor*; *Maria Stuarda* (all 1835); *Belisario*; *Il campanello di notte*; *L'assedio di Calais*; *Betly* (all 1836); *Roberto Devereux*; *Pia de' Tolomei* (both 1837); *Poliuto* (2nd version, *Les martyrs*, 1840); *Maria di Rudenz*; *Elisabetta di Siberia* (all 1838); *Le *Duc d'Albe* (incomplete, 1839); *La *Fille du régiment*; *La *Favorite* (rev. and expansion of *L'ange de Nisida* of 1839) (both 1840); *Adelia, o La Figlia dell'arciere*; *Rita, ou le mari battu*; *Maria Padilla* (all 1841); *Linda di Chamounix*; *Caterina Cornaro* (both 1842); *Don Pasquale*; *Maria di Rohan*; *Dom Sébastien, roi de Portugal* (all 1843).

Don Juan. (1) The legend of the libertine Don Juan has been the basis of many plays since that of Tirso di Molina in 1630, and of many operas, Mozart's *Don Giovanni* being the best-known. Other composers who have treated the subject incl. Melani, Gazzaniga, Fabrizi, Federici, Dibdin, Pacini, Dargomyzhsky, Delibes, Alfano, and Goossens.

(2) Tone-poem, Op.20, by Richard Strauss, based on poem by Lenau, comp. 1888, f.p. Weimar 1889.

(3) Ballet-pantomime in 3 acts, music by Gluck, lib. by Calzabigi, based on Molière. Prod. Vienna 1761.

Donna Diana. Opera in 3 acts by *Rezníček to lib. by composer based on Moreto's comedy *El Lindo Don Diego* (1654). Prod. Prague 1894. Rev. 1908 and 1933.

Donohoe, Peter (*b* Manchester, 1953). Eng. pianist and conductor. Recital début, Manchester. Joint silver medal, Moscow Tchaikovsky Comp. 1982. Cond. Northern Chamber Orch. 1984–7, Orch. of the Mill, CBSO etc. Champion of contemp. mus. and noted for his playing of Liszt and Messiaen.

Don Pasquale. 3-act *opera buffa* by Donizetti to lib. by Ruffini and composer based on Anelli's lib. for Pavesi's *Ser Marc' Antonio* (1810) and ultimately derived from Ben Jonson's *Epicene*. Prod. Paris and London 1843, New Orleans 1845.

Don Quichotte (Don Quixote). Opera in 5 acts by Massenet to lib. by Henri Cain after J. Le Lorrain's play *Le chevalier de la longue figure* (1906) based on Cervantes's novel (1605, 1615). Comp. 1908–9. Prod. Monte Carlo 1910, London 1912, New Orleans 1912, NY Met 1926. Title-role comp. for *Chaliapin.

Don Quichotte à Dulcinée. 3 songs for v. and pf. by Ravel to poems by Paul Morand. Comp. 1932–3 (his last work). Also version for v. and orch. Written for a film starring Chaliapin but not used, Ibert's 4 songs being used instead.

Don Quixote. (1) Cervantes's novel, pubd. in 2 parts (1605, 1615), has been the inspiration of many mus. works. Operas on the subject have been comp. by Förtsch, Conti, Boismortier, Paisiello, Piccinni, Salieri, Hubaček, Garcìa, Mendelssohn, Mercadante, Donizetti, Macfarren, Clay, Jaques-Dalcroze, Heuberger, and Falla. Incidental mus. to a play by D'Urfey was written by Purcell and Eccles, 1694–5.

(2) Tone-poem, Op.35, by R. Strauss, comp. 1896–7, f.p. Cologne 1898. Introduction, theme and 10 variations, and finale, with solo parts for vc. and va. Sub-titled *Fantastische Variationen über ein Thema ritterlichen Charakters* (Fantastic Variations on a theme of knightly character).

(3) Ballets on the subject are also numerous, including Petipa's of 1869 with mus. by Minkus. More recent ballet mus. has been composed by Petrassi (1947), Ibert (1950), and *Gerhard (1940–1, 1947–9, SW, choreog. N. de Valois 1950).

dopo (It.). After.

Doppel (Ger.). Double.

Doppel B or **Doppel-be** (Ger.). Double flat.

Doppelchor (Ger.). Double chorus.

Doppelfagott (Ger.). Double bassoon.

Doppelflöte (Ger.). Double flute. Wooden org. stop; sometimes end-plugged pipes: generally 8' pitch (name comes from pipes having 2 mouths, one on each side, producing a loud and pure fl. tone).

Doppelfuge (Ger.). Double fugue.

Doppelkreuz (Ger.). Double sharp.

Doppelschlag (Ger.). Double stroke, i.e. the *gruppetto.

Doppeltaktnote (Ger.). Double-measure-note, or two-bar note. The Breve, or Double Whole-note.

doppelt so schnell (Ger.). Twice as fast.

doppio (It.). Double. So *doppio diesis, doppio bemolle*, double sharp, double flat; *doppio movimento*, double speed (i.e. twice the preceding speed).

doppione. Rare medieval double-bore reed-cap wind instr., though experts have discovered that it was later blown directly. Had parallel conical bores, each with a basic set of 7 finger-holes.

Doppler, (Albert) **Franz** (Ferenc) (*b* Lemberg, 1821; *d* Baden, nr. Vienna, 1883). Austrian flautist, conductor, and composer. First fl., Pest Opera orch. 1847–58, Vienna Opera orch. from 1858. Prof. of fl., Vienna Cons. from 1865. Cond. ballet at Vienna Opera. Comp. 7 operas, ballets, fl. concs., etc.

Dorabella. The 10th (Intermezzo) of Elgar's *Enigma Variations*. Mus. portrait of Dora Penny (Mrs Richard Powell), nickname being reference to *Così fan tutte*. Mrs Powell's book *Edward Elgar: Memories of a Variation* (London 1937) gives interesting domestic glimpses of the composer.

Doráti, Antal (*b* Budapest, 1906; *d* Gerzensee, nr. Berne, 1988). Hung.-born conductor and composer (Amer. cit. 1947). Early career as opera cond. in Budapest (1924–8), Dresden (1928–9), and Munster (1929–32), then 2nd cond. Ballet Russe de Monte Carlo 1935–7, cond. orig. Ballet Russe 1938–41, and Ballet Th. 1941–5. Settled in USA 1940. Salzburg Fest. début (concert) 1946 (Mozarteum Orch.), (opera) 1959 (première of H. Erbse's *Julietta*). Prin. cond. Dallas SO 1945–9, Minneapolis SO 1949–60, BBCSO 1962–6, Stockholm PO 1966–70, National Sym. of Washington DC 1970–6, RPO 1975–8, Detroit SO 1977–81. Comp. sym., vc. conc., cantata, ballet, and str. qt. Arr. ballet mus. Cond. recording with Philharmonia Hungarica of complete Haydn syms. and several Haydn operas. Hon. KBE 1983.

Dorfmann, Ania (*b* Odessa, 1899; *d* NY, 1984). Russ. pianist. As a child played duo recitals with Heifetz. Eur. tours 1920–6; later career mainly in USA. NY début 1936. Teacher at Juilliard Sch. from 1966.

Dorfmusikanten Sextett (Mozart). See *Musical Offering*.

Dorian mode. The Mode represented by the white keys of the pf. beginning at D. See *modes*.

Dorian (Doric) Toccata and Fugue. Name given to a Toccata and Fugue in D minor by Bach because orig. copy omitted key-signature and thus suggested Dorian Mode.

Dorow, Dorothy (*b* London, 1930). Eng. soprano. Exponent of 20th-cent. mus., singing in London from 1958. Sang in Brit. première of Schoenberg's *Herzgewächse* (1960) and of works by Birtwistle, Nono, Maderna, Dallapiccola, Ligeti, Boulez, Goehr, and Bennett. Sang Hilda Mack in f. Brit. p. of Henze's *Elegy for Young Lovers*, Glyndebourne 1961. Lived in Sweden 1963–77, Holland from 1977. CG début 1983. Has taught at cons. in Holland.

dot, dotted note. Mark in notation. (1) Placed above a note indicates *staccato. (2) Placed after a note lengthens it by half. But in music up to and including Bach and Handel the addition intended was merely *approximately* half, something being left to the decision of the performer, e.g. a dotted quaver and a semiquaver in one part, played against a triplet of quavers in another part, might accommodate itself to that latter rhythm,

being rendered thus

Also in a very slow movt. ♩. ♪ might be rendered ♩.. ♪. It was, indeed, to meet this latter case that the DOUBLE DOT (the 2nd dot adding half the value of the 1st one) was introduced in 1769 by Mozart's father, Leopold Mozart.

doublé (Fr.). The *gruppetto (ornament).

double. (1) (Fr.). A variation, especially one with elaborate ornamentation. Similar to Eng. 'division'.
(2) Indicates a lower octave, e.g. double bassoon plays an octave below bassoon.
(3) Singers who perform two roles in one work and instrumentalists who play more than one instr. in a comp. e.g. fl. doubles piccolo.

double action. The mechanism of a *harp invented by *Érard, so called to distinguish it from earlier models on which pitches could be raised only by a semitone.

double appoggiatura. See *acciaccatura*.

double bar. The double perpendicular line marking the end of a comp. or of some section thereof. (It may or may not coincide with a single bar line and if it does not do so has no rhythmic function.) Usually reinforced when they mark the end of the work. With dots on either side of the lines they indicate that the previous or subsequent section is to be repeated.

double bass (or contrabass). Largest and lowest-pitched of bowed string instruments, derived from the *violone. Formerly had 3 strings but now generally has 4, usually tuned at the interval of a 4th. Compass from E just over an octave below bass stave upwards for nearly 3 octaves. Some instruments have 5 strings, extra string sounding B below bottom E. Generally an orchestral instrument, but occasionally used in chamber music and very occasionally as solo concerto instrument. Used in jazz and dance bands, mostly pizzicato.

double-bass clarinet. Also known as pedal cl., or contrabass cl., in B♭. Mainly used by military bands. Part written 9th higher than sounds.

double bassoon (contrabassoon; Fr. 'contrebasson'; Ger. 'Kontrafagott'). Wind instr. octave deeper than *bassoon and notated octave higher than it sounds, though Wagner and Debussy sometimes wrote for it at pitch. Some baroque examples were made but standard modern design is Heckel's (1876). Conical bore tube is 18' long, with 5 parallel sections connected by 4 U-bends. Crook fits into metal tube. Brahms scored for it in his 1st Sym. In Strauss's *Salome* there is a long solo for the instr. when Jokanaan descends into his cell.

double-bass saxhorn. In B♭ or C. Almost identical with B♭ bass tuba, but with range complete at bottom. Sometimes treated as *transposing instr.

double-bass (contrabass) **trombone**. Pitched an octave below ten. tb.

double-bass (contrabass) **tuba**. One of the tuba family, pitched an octave below ten. tuba. Has wide conical bore and cup-shaped mouthpiece. Wagner used one to strengthen the bass of his 8-part harmony by doubling it an octave lower.

double-bass viol. Also known as violone or consort viol. Sounded an octave below bass viol. See *viol*.

double-bémol (Fr.). Double flat.

double C. Sometimes used to indicate the note C, 2 lines below the bass stave.

double choir (or chorus). Ch. arranged in 2 equal and complete bodies with a view not merely to singing in 8 parts but also to responsive effects, etc. Much used by Venetian composers of 16th and 17th cents.

double concerto. A conc. with 2 prin. instr., either of the same kind, as in double pf. conc., or different, as in Brahms's conc. for vn. and vc. Also used to denote use of 2 orchs. (generally str.), e.g. Tippett's Conc. for double str. orch.

double counterpoint. Invertible *counterpoint concerning 2 vv. (permitting vv. to change places, the higher becoming lower and vice versa).

double-croche (Fr.). Double-hook, i.e. semiquaver or 16th-note.

double-curtal. 16th-cent. instr., being a larger or different size of the *curtal or dulcian, ancestor of the bn. In Eng. it meant the bass curtal.

double-dièse (Fr.). Double sharp.

double dot. See *dot*.

Double English horn. Org. stop of *Hope-Jones invention: 16' *chorus reed

double flat. The sign when placed before a note, indicates that its pitch is lowered a whole-step or tone. The resultant note has a simpler enharmonic name, e.g. on the pf., A♭♭ is G natural. See *inflection of notes*.

double fugue. A *fugue with 2 subjects. There are 2 types: (1) in which the subjects appear from the start, and (2) in which the first subject is treated for a time, the other then appearing and being similarly treated, after which the 2 are combined.

double-handed. Term applied to band of players that is convertible from wind to str. or to full orch; or to an instrumentalist who can play 2 different instr.

double harp. Early form of harp which had only 2 rows of str., diatonically tuned. Intermediate semitones could be obtained only by shortening the length of a str. with the thumb while plucking it with a finger. Not the same as *double action* harp.

double horn. Valve *horn pitched in both F and B♭ alto.

double octaves. In pf.-playing, octaves played simultaneously in both hands.

double open diapason. *Diapason org. stop of 16' pitch.

double organ. (1) (obsolete). Either one with a full kbd., descending to 8' C or 12' G, or one with 2 manuals.
(2) (modern, sometimes used in USA). Org. with separate 'sanctuary' division.

double pedal. Harmonic *pedal in which 2 notes are held, generally tonic and dominant.

double reed. Wind instr. such as ob., cor anglais, Heckelphone, bn., and double bn., whose mouthpiece consists of 2 pieces of cane between which air is blown so that the 2 reeds vibrate against each other.

double-sharp. The sign x which, placed before a note, raises it by a whole-step or tone. As with *double-flat, the resultant note can be more simply named, e.g. Fx is G on the pf. See *inflection of notes*.

double stopping. Term used of str. instr., to indicate stopping and playing on 2 str. simultaneously to produce a 2-part effect. Also used, loosely, when one or both of the str. are 'open'.

double suspension. Harmonic term, when 2 notes of a chord are held over as a momentary discordant part of the following combination. Resolved by moving to notes which form real part of 2nd chord.

double tonguing. Fast method of articulation while playing wind instr. such as fl. and piccolo. Obtained by alternation of the sounds T and K or D and G when the mouth is applied to the embouchure. See *tonguing*.

double virginals. A virginals of which the kbd. descended to C below bass stave.

double whole-note. Amer. term for the *breve.

doubling. Term meaning (1) duplication of a melody by several performers, e.g. 'the solo soprano's part is doubled by the oboe'.
(2) duplication of instr. by one player, the commonest orch. example being the doubling of piccolo by one of the flautists, i.e. the 2nd flautist plays piccolo instead of fl. when required.

douçaine. Medieval reed instr. about which information is very scanty, but it is thought to have been of ten. pitch and soft in tone.

Douglas, Barry (*b* Belfast, 1960). Brit. pianist. London début 1981. Silver medal, Rubinstein Comp., Israel, 1983, bronze medal Van Cliburn Comp., Fort Worth, Texas, 1985, gold medal Tchaikovsky Comp., Moscow, 1986. NY début 1988 (Carnegie Hall).

Douglas (Leigh Pemberton), **Nigel** (*b* Lenham, Kent, 1929). Eng. tenor. Début Vienna 1959 (Rodolfo in *La bohème*). Prin. ten. Zurich Opera House from 1964; Vienna Volksoper 1964–8, Scottish Opera 1968–71, WNO 1971. Repertoire of over 80 roles, incl. Loge, Herod, Peter Grimes, Vere, and Aschenbach. Sang Kent in f. Brit. p. of Reimann's *Lear* (ENO 1989). Expert on Viennese operetta. Frequent broadcaster of mus. talks and author of *Legendary Voices* (1992) and *More Legendary Voices* (1994).

Douglas, (Richard) **Roy** (*b* Tunbridge Wells, 1907). Eng. composer, arranger, and music editor. Orch. of Chopin for ballet *Les Sylphides* used by many cos. Worked closely with Vaughan Williams 1944–58, and wrote book about their assoc. *Working with RVW* (1972). Comp. and arr. of mus. for brass band.

doux, douce (Fr.). Sweet, gentle. *doucement*, sweetly, gently.

Dow, Dorothy (*b* Houston, Texas, 1920; *d* Galveston, Tex., 2005). Amer. soprano. Sang and dir. NY choirs 1938–44. Début Buffalo 1944 (Santuzza in concert perf. of *Cavalleria rusticana*). Created Susan B. Anthony in f.p. of V. Thomson's *The Mother of Us All*, Columbia Univ., NY, 1947. Member of Zurich Opera 1948–50; La Scala from 1950. Sang the Woman in f. Amer. p. of Schoenberg's *Erwartung* (NYPO 1951)). Glyndebourne début 1952. Sang Renata in f. stage p. of Prokofiev's *The Fiery Angel* (Venice, 1955).

Dowd, (Eric) **Ronald** (*b* Sydney, NSW, 1914; *d* Sydney, NSW, 1990). Australian tenor. Début 1948, Perth (Hoffman). Toured Australia singing Florestan, Alfredo, Cavaradossi, Lohengrin, etc. Joined SW Opera in London 1956. Sang Mahony in f. Brit. p of Weill's *Rise and Fall of the City of Mahagonny* (SW 1963). Created Mosbie in Goehr's *Arden Must Die* (Hamburg, 1969). CG début 1960. Joined Australian Opera and sang Pierre in Prokofiev's *War and Peace* at opening of Sydney Opera House, 1973. Was also noted for his singing of Elgar's Gerontius, often with Barbirolli.

Dowland, John (*b* London, ?1563; *d* London, 1626). Eng. composer, singer, and lutenist. Mus.B. Oxon 1588. From 1580 to 1584 was in service of Brit. Ambassador to Paris where he became RC. Lutenist at courts at Brunswick, Hesse, Venice, Florence, and Nuremberg, 1595. Lutenist to King of Denmark 1598–1606. Returned to London 1606; lutenist to Lord Howard de Walden 1606–12; musician to James I 1612. Though noted in his day as a virtuoso lutenist and singer, he is now recognized as a great composer, whose songs melodically and harmonically advanced the 'art song'. His printed songs numbered 87 of which 84 appeared in 4 vols.: 3 *Books of Songs or Ayres*, 1597, 1600, 1603, and *A Pilgrims Solace*, 1612), and 3 in his son Robert's *Musical Banquet*, 1614. Among his finest songs are *Awake, Sweet Love; Come again Sweet Love; Fine Knacks for Ladies; Flow my Tears; Flow not so fast, ye Fountains; In Darkness let me Dwell; Sweet, stay awhile; Weep ye no more, sad Fountains; Welcome black night*. Among his other comps. are the *Lachrimae of 1604, which contains 21 instr. items incl. the celebrated *Semper Dowland semper dolens*, and many pieces for solo lute, incl. *Walsingham, Loth to Depart, My Lady Hunsdons Puffe, Queen Elizabeths Galliard*, and *Dowlands Adew*.

down-beat. Downward movement of a cond.'s. stick or hand, in particular when indicating first beat of the bar. See also *up-beat*.

Down by the Greenwood Side. Dramatic pastoral by *Birtwistle to lib. by Michael Nyman for sop., mime and speech, and chamber ens. Comp. 1968–9.

Downes, (Sir) **Edward** (Thomas) (*b* Birmingham, 1924). Eng. conductor and horn-player. Cond. first opera, *Le nozze di Figaro*, while a teacher at Aberdeen Univ. Ass. cond. Carl Rosa Opera 1950–1; staff cond. CG 1951–69. First Eng. cond. after

1945 to conduct full *Ring* cycle (CG 1967); mus. dir. and chief cond. Australian Opera 1972–6. In 1970s cond. BBC studio perfs., the f. complete ps. in Brit., of *Die Feen*, *Das Liebesverbot*, and *Rienzi*, the first two being their f. complete ps. Prin. cond., BBC Philharmonic 1980–91; prin. cond. CG from 1991. Cond. f.p. of Maxwell Davies's *Taverner*, 1972, and first opera perf. in Sydney Opera House (*War and Peace*, 28 Sept. 1973). Completed Prokofiev's *Maddalena*, conducting f.p. in a BBC broadcast, March 1979. Cond. f. Brit. professional ps. of Verdi's *Stiffelio*, in his own edn., CG 1993. Trans. Russ. libs., e.g. *Khovanshchina and **Katerina Izmaylova*. CBE 1986. Knighted 1991.

Downes, Ralph (William) (*b* Derby, 1904; *d* London, 1993). Eng. organist. Ass. org., Southwark Cath. 1923–5. Lect. Princeton Univ., NJ, 1928–35; org., London Oratory 1936–77; designed many important orgs. incl. RFH. Prof. of org., RCM, 1954–75. CBE 1969.

doxologia, doxology (from the Gr. *doxa*, glory, and *logos*, discourse). Any liturgical formula of praise, as the *Gloria patri* (Glory be to the Father, etc., i.e. the lesser doxology, or doxologia parva, used at the end of the Psalms), or the *Gloria in excelsis Deo* (Glory to God in the highest—the greater doxology, or doxologia magna).

The 'greater doxology' is a part of the Roman Mass (sung to differing plainsong according to the feast); properly it should be left to the priest until the words 'Et in terra pax', when the choir should enter, but composers such as Bach, Mozart, and Beethoven have ignored this. In its Eng. wording the greater doxology is a part of the Anglican Communion Service.

D'Oyly Carte, Richard (*b* London, 1844; *d* London, 1901). English impresario and producer of light operas, who brought together the librettist Gilbert and the composer Sullivan for *Trial by Jury*, 1875. Partnership so successful he built theatre, the Savoy, which opened 1881 with *Patience*. His attempt to launch English grand opera with Sullivan's *Ivanhoe*, 1891, failed. His widow Helen (*d* 1913) continued management of 'Savoy operas', followed by son Rupert (1876–1948) and granddaughter Bridget. The Gilbert and Sullivan operas were generally presented in Britain professionally by the D'Oyly Carte Opera Co. until 1982 (they were known more widely as 'D'Oyly Carte operas' than as 'Savoy operas') but the D'Oyly Carte's exclusive ownership of them ended with expiry of Sullivan's copyright in 1950 and other opera companies have produced them, e.g. ENO, with prods. by Jonathan Miller and Ken Russell.

Dragonetti, Domenico (*b* Venice, 1763; *d* London, 1846). It. virtuoso on double-bass. In orch. of St Mark's Venice, at age 18. Went to London 1794, playing in opera orch. and giving nationwide recitals with cellist *Lindley. Twice visited Vienna, where he knew Haydn and Beethoven.

Played db. in f.p. of Beethoven's 9th Sym. Comp. solos for db. At 82 in 1845 led db. section in Bonn Beethoven Fest.

dramatic. (1) Applied to sop., ten., etc., a powerful singer with a style suitable for forceful operatic roles.

(2) Applied strictly to mus., this adjective signifies mus. written for the stage, but the much more general meaning is mus. of strongly theatrical spirit and effect, e.g. Tchaikovsky's 4th Sym., Berlioz's *Symphonie Fantastique*, Strauss's *Don Juan*, Beethoven's *Appassionata Sonata*, etc.

dramaturg. Official at opera houses who keeps up to date with scholarly research, adapts libs., edits programmes, works as press officer, and sometimes produces. Orig. a Ger. post, there are now 'dramaturges' at CG and ENO.

drame lyrique (Fr.). Lyric drama, i.e. serious opera. Debussy thus described his *Pelléas et Mélisande*.

dramma giocoso (It.). Comic drama. 18th-cent. It. term for comic operas containing tragic features. Used by Mozart to describe *Don Giovanni* and by Haydn for several of his operas.

dramma per musica (It.). Drama through music. 17th- and 18th-cent. It. term for serious opera.

drängend (Ger.). Urging forward, hurrying.

drawstop. The part of an *organ which operates a row of pipes. See *stop*.

Dream of Gerontius, The. Setting by Elgar, Op.38, for mez., ten., bass, ch., semi-ch., and orch. of Cardinal J. H. Newman's poem (1866). Comp. 1899–1900 (some sketches 1896). F.p. Birmingham 1900, cond. Richter. F. London p. 1903. Although frequently described and classified as an oratorio, this is not a term Elgar approved in this connection and does not appear on the score.

Dreigroschenoper, Die (The Threepenny Opera). Play with mus. in prol. and 8 scenes by *Weill, text being a modern interpretation of Gay's *The Beggar's Opera* based on a trans. by Elisabeth Hauptmann with lyrics (some from Kipling and Villon) by Bertolt Brecht. Prod. Berlin 1928, NY 1933, London 1956. Eng. trans. and adaptation by *Blitzstein prod. Brandeis, Mass., 1952, and NY 1954.

Drei Pintos, Die (The Three Pintos). Comic opera in 3 acts left unfinished by Weber and completed by Mahler. Weber began work in 1820 on lib. by Theodor Hell (Karl Winkler) based on story *Der Brautkampf* by C. Seidel. Work on mus. for *Preciosa* and the commissioned operas *Euryanthe* and *Oberon* prevented Weber composing for *Die drei Pintos* beyond 1821. On his death in 1826, he left sketches for 7 out of 17 numbers, a total of 1,700 bars of which only 18 were scored. In 1826 these were taken to Meyerbeer, who kept them until 1852 but did nothing with them. In 1887 Weber's grandson invited Mahler, then 2nd cond. at Leipzig Opera, to complete the work, which he undertook by using Weber's sketches and extending the opera to 21 numbers in length by inserting other pieces by Weber and sections comp. by himself based on Weber's themes. The result is a remarkable example of posthumous collaboration. Prod. Leipzig 1888, cond. Mahler; London 1962; St Louis 1979; Wexford 2003.

Dresden. City in Germany (Saxony) with long mus. tradition. Its archives mention an organist in 1370 and from about 1420 three wind players were instructed to play on 29 major church fests. At the court mus. first achieved prominence *c*.1540. In the 18th cent. artistic life at court was on a grand scale and among the court composers and Kapellmeisters of that era were Zelenka, Lotti, Hasse, and J. S. Bach (who held the title 1736–50 but was active only in Leipzig at this period). By the end of the cent. Dresden's reputation for It. opera was high. A German Opera was founded in 1817 with Weber as cond. Weber's ideals were continued 17 years after his death by Wagner, whose own *Rienzi* was produced in Dresden in 1842, followed by *Der fliegende Holländer* 1843 and *Tannhäuser* 1845. The Royal Saxon Opera House, designed by Gottfried Semper, was opened 1841. This was burned down 1869 and his second building was opened 1878. Dresden's most illustrious operatic period dates from the appointment as cond. in 1882 of Ernst von Schuch. He championed Wagner's later operas and those of Richard Strauss whose *Feuersnot* (1901), *Salome* (1905), *Elektra* (1909), and *Der Rosenkavalier* (1911) had their f.ps. under Schuch. After Schuch the opera was cond. by Fritz Reiner (1914–21), but it was Fritz Busch (1922–33) who revived its glories and continued the Strauss assoc. with f.ps. of *Intermezzo* (1924) and *Die ägyptische Helena* (1928). He also cond. new operas by Hindemith (*Cardillac*, 1926) and Busoni (*Doktor Faust*, 1925). Driven out by the Nazis, Busch was succeeded by Karl Böhm, although Clemens Krauss cond. the f.p. of Strauss's *Arabella* in 1933. Under Böhm (1934–42), Strauss's *Die schweigsame Frau* (1935) and *Daphne* (1938) were first performed, also Sutermeister's *Romeo und Julia* (1940). Böhm was succeeded by Karl Elmendorff (1943–4). The opera house was bombed in 1945 and the co. moved into a rebuilt theatre in 1948. In 1977, rebuilding began of the Semper Opera House to a design faithful to the original, and it opened in February 1985 with *Der Freischütz*. Cond. of Staatskapelle from 1945 to 1950 was Joseph Keilberth. His successors were Rudolf Kempe (1950–3), Franz Konwitschny (1953–5), Lovro von Matačić (1956–8), Otmar Suitner (1960–4), Kurt Sanderling (1964–7), Martin Turnovsky (1967–8), Siegfried Kurz (1971–5), Herbert Blomstedt (1975–85), Hans Vonk (1985–91), Giuseppe Sinopoli (1991–2001), Bernard Haitink (2002–4), and Fabio Luisi (from 2007). Operas given f.ps. in Dresden since 1945 incl. Blacher's *Die Flut* (1947), and U. Zimmermann's *Levins Mühle* (1973). The opera dir. from 1973 to 1981 was Harry Kupfer, and Joachim Herz 1985–91.

Orch. mus. in Dresden has been provided by two orchs., the venerable Staatskapelle (which plays for the opera) and the Philharmonic. The Staatskapelle dates its origins to the 16th cent. and has had various guises. One of them, from 1923, was as the Saxon State Orch. cond. by Busch and later by Böhm. The Philharmonic was founded in 1871, though under another name. Its conds. incl. Strauss, Bülow, Nikisch, Mottl, and Edwin Lindner. Its greatest period, which incl. fests. of modern mus., was under Paul van Kempen (1934–42). After 1945 conds. incl. Heinz Bongartz (1947–64), H. Förster (1964–7), Kurt Masur (1967–72), Günther Herbig (1972–7), Herbert Kegel (1977–85), Hans Vonk (1985–91), Jörg Peter Weigle (1991–2001), Marek Janowski (2001–3), and Rafael Frühbeck de Burgos (from 2004).

Other composers beside Wagner to have lived in Dresden were Schumann (1844–50), who cond. the *Liedertafel* and founded a choir, and Rachmaninov (1906–9).

Dresden Amen. Setting of *Amen* comp. by J. G. *Naumann (1741–1801) in Threefold Amen of Royal Chapel of Dresden. Quoted by Mendelssohn in his *Reformation Sym.* (1830–2) and by Wagner in *Parsifal* (1878–82).

Drew, David (*b* London, 1930). Eng. mus. critic and publisher. Mus. critic *New Statesman*, 1959–67, ed. *Tempo* from 1971. Specialist in Messiaen, Weill, Stravinsky, Gerhard, and other 20th-cent. figures. On staff Boosey and Hawkes from 1975.

droit, droite (Fr.). Right, e.g. *main droite*, right hand. But *droit* as a noun means right in another sense, e.g. *Droits d'exécution*, Performing Rights.

drone. Pipe or pipes sounding continuous note of fixed pitch as a permanent bass, e.g. of bagpipes. Hence *drone bass* applied to orch. mus.

Drottningholm. Swedish opera house on Lake Mälaren in royal palace. First th. built there 1754. Burnt down 1762 and replaced in 1766 (with additions 1791). Commissioned by Gustavus III and not used after his assassination in 1792. In 1920 orig. wooden machinery, controlled by wheel system, was found to be still working. Th. reopened 1922 for occasional perfs. Annual fest. begun 1953, based mainly on 18th-cent. repertory. Orch. wears period costume and plays period instrs. Mus. dirs. have included Charles Farncombe 1970–9, Arnold Östman 1980–91, Elisabeth Söderström 1992–5.

Druckman, Jacob (*b* Philadelphia, 1928; *d* Milford, Conn., 1996). Amer. composer. Taught at Juilliard Sch. 1957–72. Dir. Yale Univ. Sch. of Mus. EMS 1971–2. Pulitzer Prize 1972 for *Windows*, f.p. Chicago SO cond. Maderna. Comp.-in-residence NYPO 1982–6. Works incl. conc. for str. (1951); ballet mus.; 3 str. qts. (1948, 1966, 1981); *Valentine*, db. solo (1969); *The Sound of Time* for sop. and orch. (1965); *Animus* I, II, III, and IV (1966, 1968, 1969, 1977), for instr. and tape; *Lamia*, sop. and orch. (1974); *Chiaroscuro*, orch. (1976); *Other Voices*, brass quintet (1976); va. conc. (1978); *Aureole*, orch. (1979); *Prism*, 3 pieces for orch. after

Charpentier, Cavalli, and Cherubini (1980); *Tromba marina, 4 db.* (1981); *Athanor,* in mem. Vincent Persichetti, winds, brass, perc. (1987).

drum. Percussion instrument of several kinds consisting of hollow wood or metal cylinder over which a skin is stretched (the drumhead). Sound is obtained by striking the skin with a stick. Among the leading types of drum are:

(1) KETTLEDRUM (It. *timpano*; plur. *timpani*. The spelling '*tympani*' is incorrect). Tuned to a definite pitch. A bowl of metal with, stretched over its open end, a membrane of which the tension can be increased or decreased by turning screws (in machine drums) or by some mechanical method. The playing is by means of 2 drumsticks, with heads of material which varies according to the tone-quality desired. Up to and including Beethoven the orch. player had 2 kettledrums normally tuned to the tonic and dominant (doh and soh) of the key in use; nowadays he has usually 3, and sometimes more. Both repeated notes and rolls are played. Forms of 'muffling' (= muting, see *mute*) are possible, such as placing a cloth over the drumhead. Most composers up to and including Mozart notated for the kettledrums as one of the *transposing instruments, the part being written in key C (i.e. the notes shown being C and G) and the actual pitch of the 2 notes being indicated at the outset by some such indication as timpani in D, A (according to the key of the piece). The current method is to show the actual notes to be played with all sharps and flats indicated. The use of pedals for mechanical tuning is widespread and enables *glissando* effects. In mounted military bands the kettledrum is used, one being slung on each side of the horse. Introduction of the kettledrum into the orch. is generally attributed to Lully in his opera *Thésée* (1675).

(2) SIDE-DRUM or SNARE-DRUM. Of indefinite pitch. A small cylindrical drum with parchment at each end, one end having strings (*snares*) across it, to add a rattling effect and so increase the brilliance of the tone, the other end being left clear for the use of 2 drumsticks. It can be muted by placing a handkerchief or a wooden wedge between the snares and the parchment.

(3) TENOR DRUM. Larger than the *side-drum and without snares. It is rarely used in the sym. orch.

(4) BASS DRUM. Indefinite and low pitch. Large and shallow, used in the sym. orch., military band, and dance band (in which the drumstick is often worked by a pedal). Played with skinheads perpendicular.

(5) TRAP DRUM. Drum equipment used in dance bands and theatre pit, comprising *bass drum with *cymbal attached, both being played with foot pedal. Drummer thus has both hands free to play snare drum.

Drum Mass (Haydn). See *Paukenmesse.*

Drummond, (Sir) **John** (Richard Gray) (*b* London, 1934; *d* Brighton, 2006). Eng. administrator and producer. Worked as writer, produ-

cer, and ed. for BBC radio and TV, 1958–78. Dir., Edinburgh Fest. 1978–83. Controller, BBC Music from 1985, Radio 3 1987–91. Art. dir. European Arts Fest. 1991–3. Dir., Henry Wood Prom. Concerts 1992–5. CBE 1993. Knighted 1995.

Drum Roll Symphony (Haydn). See *Paukenwirbel.*

D.S. Abbreviation for **dal segno.*

DSCH. Personal motto, derived from letters of his name, by Dmitri Shostakovich, notated as D–E♭–C–B. Occurs in several of his works, incl. 8th str. qt., 10th and 15th syms., and 1st vn. conc.

dub. Old Eng. for *tabor.

Dubensky, Arkady (*b* Vyatka, Russia, 1890; *d* Tenafly, NJ, 1966). Russ.-born violinist and composer. Leader, Moscow Imperial Opera Orch. for 9 years. Went to NY 1921, joining NYSO until merger with NYPO of which he became member until 1953. Comp. for unusual combinations, e.g. *Fugue,* 18 vn.; *Fugue,* 4 bn.; *Suite,* 9 fl.; Ov., 18 toy tpt.; *Fantasy on Negro Themes,* tuba, orch.; tb. conc.; concerto grosso, 3 tb., tuba, orch. Also wrote operas, str. qts., and works for conventional orch. forces.

Dubois, (François Clément) **Théodore** (*b* Rosnay, 1837; *d* Paris, 1924). Fr. composer, organist, and teacher. Choirmaster, Ste Clotilde 1862–9, Madeleine 1869–77; succeeded Saint-Saëns as org. of Madeleine 1877–1906. Prof. of harmony, Paris Cons. 1871–90, dir. 1896–1905. Resigned after protests over exclusion by jury, incl. Dubois, of Ravel from entering for *Prix de Rome* for 4th time. Wrote 7 operas, ballet, oratorios, cantatas, orch. works, incl. 3 syms., 2 pf. concs., and vn. conc.

Ducasse, Jean J. A. Roger. See *Roger-Ducasse, Jean J. A.*

Duc d'Albe, Le (The Duke of Alba). (1) 4-act opera by Donizetti, to lib. by Scribe, written for Paris 1839 but not prod. Score recovered at Bergamo 1875, completed by Salvi, and prod. as *Il duca d'Alba,* Rome 1882. Scribe altered lib. and re-sold it to Verdi in 1853 as *Les *Vêpres siciliennes,* Verdi only discovering 30 years later that it had been used by Donizetti.

(2) Opera, *Il Duca d'Alba,* by Pacini to lib. by Piave, 1842.

Dudamel, Gustavo (*b* Barquisimeto, 1981). Venezuelan conductor. Studied vn. from age 8. Cond. youth orch. aged 13, programme incl. his own tb. conc. Studied cond. in Caracas with Rodolfo Saglimbeni from 1996 and J.-A. Abreu from 1999. Mus. dir. Simón Bolívar Nat. Youth Orch. of Venezuela from 1999. Won first Gustav Mahler/Bamberg SO cond. comp. 2004. Prof. début 2004 (Philharmonia Orch. in Bonn). Débuts: Israel PO 2004; Gothenburg SO (BBC Proms) 2005; Los Angeles PO 2005; CBSO, RLPO, Boston SO, Dresden Staatskapelle, all 2006. Opera début

Staatsoper, Berlin, 2006 (*L'elisir d'amore*); La Scala début 2006 (*Don Giovanni*). Prin. cond. Gothenburg SO from 2007.

Dudelkastensack, or **Dudelsack** (Ger.). Bagpipe.

due (It.). Two. (1) *a due*, either (*a*) div. between 2 instr. or vv., or (*b*) 2 instr. or vv. to join in playing the same line.

(2) *due corde*. Two strings, i.e. in vn. mus., etc., divide the passage over 2 str.

Due Foscari, I (The Two Foscari). 3-act opera by Verdi to lib. by Piave, based on Byron's drama (1821). Comp. 1844, rev. 1845–6. Prod. Rome 1844, London and Boston, Mass., 1847.

Duenna, The, or The Double Elopement. (1) 3-act opera comp. and compiled by Thomas Linley senior and junior to text by Sheridan (who was Linley senior's son-in-law). Prod. London 1775, NY 1786.

(2) 4-act opera by Prokofiev, to his own lib. based on Sheridan with verses by Mira Mendelson, and sometimes known as *Betrothal in a Monastery*. Comp. 1940–1, prod. Prague 1946, London 1980, Glyndebourne 2006.

(3) 3-act opera by *Gerhard to his own lib. after Sheridan. Comp. 1945–7, rev. 1950. BBC broadcast 1949. Prod. (concert) Frankfurt 1951. F. stage p. Madrid, 1992; f. Brit. stage p. Leeds 1992 (Opera North).

duet (Fr. *duo*; Ger. *Duett*; It. *duo* or *duetto*). Any combination of 2 performers (with or without acc.), or a comp. for such, as in pf. duet.

Du Fay, Guillaume (*b* Bersele, nr. Brussels, 1397; *d* Cambrai, 1474). Fr. composer. Illegitimate son of a priest, took his mother's name of Du Fayt. Known in his early years as Willem Du Fayt, later as Guillaume Du Fay. Choirboy at Cambrai Cath. Went to It. in his twenties and fled from Bologna to Rome in 1428, staying until 1433. Sang in the papal chapel. Met *Binchois in 1434. Returned to Cambrai 1439. His connection with the Burgundian court is now thought to have been unlikely. Was most acclaimed comp. of 15th cent. Nearly 200 of his works have survived incl. 8 complete Masses and 84 songs. Use of a secular *cantus firmus* such as 'L'homme armé' in a Mass possibly originated with him. Was basically a conservative comp., but his warm harmonies and expressive tunes anticipate the Renaissance. Undoubtedly his melodic clarity stemmed from his It. years. Composed the earliest Requiem Mass, now lost.

Dukas, Paul (*b* Paris, 1865; *d* Paris, 1935). Fr. composer. Awarded 2nd *Prix de Rome* 1888. Early works influenced by Wagner. Scored major success in 1897 with orch. scherzo *L'Apprenti Sorcier*. Perhaps his finest work is his opera *Ariane et Barbe-Bleu* (Paris, 1907) based like Debussy's *Pelléas* on a Maeterlinck play and finding, like Debussy, symbolic and emotional depths in the text which are luminously translated into mus. Also wrote ballet *La Péri* (1912), and pf. sonata (1901)

said to be the first by a major Fr. composer. Prof. of orch., Paris Cons. 1910–13, of comp., 1928–35. Wrote much criticism. Pubd. very little mus. after 1920 and destroyed his unpubl. works before he died. Aided Saint-Saëns in completion of Guiraud's opera *Frédégonde*, orchestrating first 3 acts. Ed. several Rameau operas. Prin. works:

OPERA: *Ariane et Barbe-Bleu (1899–1906).

BALLET: La *Péri (1911–12).

ORCH.: ov. *Polyeucte* (1892); sym. in C (1896);
   *L'*Apprenti Sorcier* (1897); *La Péri*, suite.

CHAMBER MUSIC: *Villanelle* (hn. and pf.).

PIANO: sonata in E♭ minor (1899–1901); *Variations, Interlude et Final (sur un thème de Rameau)* (1903); *Prélude élégiaque* (1908); *La Plainte au loin du faune* (1920).

SONG: *Sonnet de Ronsard* (1924).

Duke Bluebeard's Castle (*A Kékszakállú herceg vára*). Opera in 1 act, Op.11, by Bartók, comp. 1911, to lib. by Béla Balázs (after fairy-tale by Perrault), for sop. and bar. Rev. 1912 and 1918. First perf. Budapest 1918, Dallas (concert) 1946, NY 1952, London 1957.

Duke, Vernon. See *Dukelsky, Vladimir*.

Dukelsky, Vladimir (*b* Parfianovka, 1903; *d* Santa Monica, Calif., 1969). Russ.-born composer (Amer. cit. 1936). Settled in NY 1922. Ballet *Zéphyr et Flore* prod. Diaghilev, 1925. Wrote several other ballets; operas; 4 syms.; oratorio; pf. conc.; vn. conc.; vc. conc.; pf. sonata; hpd. sonata. Changed name (at Gershwin's suggestion), and as Vernon Duke wrote mus. for musical comedies (notably *Cabin in the Sky*, 1940), films, etc. Best-known song is *April in Paris*.

dulcet. Org. stop: a *dulciana of 4′ length and pitch.

dulcian. Alternative name for the *curtal.

dulciana. Soft org. stop usually in Brit. of *diapason class, and in USA of str.-toned class.

dulciana mixture. Org. *Mixture stop of soft tone, generally on swell or echo manual.

dulcimer. Old instr. A shallow closed box over which are stretched wires to be struck with 2 wooden hammers held in the player's hands. Still in use in E. Europe for traditional mus. (known in Hung. as *cimbalom*). In USA is wrongly applied to plucked zither-like folk-instr.

dulcitone. Kbd. instr. similar to *celesta, but with steel tuning forks instead of steel plates. In Fr. known as *typophone*. Used by *d'Indy in *Chant de la Cloche*.

Dumbarton Oaks Concerto. Name given to Stravinsky's Conc. in E♭ for chamber orch. (15 instr.) (comp. 1937–8) because it received its f.p. in May 1938 (cond. by N. Boulanger) at Dumbarton Oaks, the estate in Washington DC of Mr & Mrs R. W. Bliss who commissioned this 'little concerto in the style of the Brandenburg Concertos'.

dumka (plural *dumky*). A type of Slavonic folk-ballad, Ukrainian in orig., in which elegiac and fast tempi alternate. Term was used by *Dvořák for movts. in his str. sextet and pf. quintet. His *Dumky* trio is the nickname for his pf. trio, Op.90, comprising 6 *dumka* movts. His pf. sonata, Op.35 (1876) is also known as the *Dumka*.

dump, dumpe. Title given to some Eng. kbd. pieces of the 16th and early 17th cents., often in variation form and possibly elegiac in intention ('down in the dumps', for example, means 'in a depressed mood'). *My Ladye Careys Dompe* is a typical (though anonymous) example.

Dunhill, Thomas (Frederick) (*b* London, 1877; *d* Scunthorpe, 1946). Eng. composer and writer. Ass. mus. master, Eton College, 1899–1908, also teaching harmony and counterpoint at RCM. Comps. incl. sym.; operetta *Tantivy Towers* (lib. by A. P. Herbert, prod. London 1931); *Elegiac Variations* for orch.; vn. sonata; wind quintet; pf. quintet; 2 pf. trios; str. qt.; many songs incl. *The Cloth of Heaven* (Yeats). Wrote several books, subjects incl. Mozart's str. qts., Elgar, and chamber mus.

Dunstable [Dunstaple], **John** (*b* c.1390; *d* London, 1453). Eng. composer, astrologer, and mathematician. Leading Eng. composer of first half of 15th cent. Enjoyed Eur. reputation, attested by discovery of his works in early It. and Fr. colls. Was member of households of John, Duke of Bedford and Humphrey, Duke of Gloucester, the latter a noted patron of the arts. Travelled to Europe and was given land holdings in Normandy. Influenced *Du Fay and *Binchois. Probably first to write instr. acc. for church mus. Wrote masses, isorhythmic motets, etc. Buried in St Stephen's, Walbrook, London (destroyed in Great Fire of 1666). Some works attrib. to him are now known to be by Lionel Power, Binchois, Binet, and others.

duo (It.). Two. (1) duet, usually but not exclusively for instrs.
  (2) 2 performers, or a work written for them. In USA a *duo*-pianist is member of a 2-pf. duo.

duodrama. A work for 2 actors to speak to orch. acc. Mozart admired the form.

Duparc, Elisabeth ['Francesina'] (*d* ?1778). Fr. soprano trained in It. Opera engagement London 1736. Sang in Handel's *Faramondo* and *Serse* in 1738 and thenceforward was almost exclusively a Handel singer, being his leading sop. from 1738 to 1745. Sang in *Messiah*, April 1745.

Duparc, (Marie Eugène) **Henri** (Fouques-) (*b* Paris, 1848; *d* Mont-de-Marsan, 1933). Fr. composer. Extremely self-critical, destroying most of his early works. His 16 songs, orig. in idiom and fore-telling impressionism, are models of sensitivity to the poetic text combined with melodic inspiration and a harmonic style based on Wagner. They were comp. between 1868 and 1884. After 1885 he wrote nothing owing to an incurable nervous disease. His output is as follows:

SONGS: (with pf. acc., but † = orch. version provided

by Duparc): †*Chanson triste* (1868 or 9); *Soupir* (1869); *Romance de Mignon* (1869); *Sérénade* (1869); *Le galop* (1869); †*Au pays où se fait la guerre* (?1869–70, orig. title *Absence*); †*L'Invitation au voyage* (1870); †*La vague et la cloche* (1871, comp. for orch., with pf. acc. supplied later first by d'Indy then by Duparc); *Elégie* (1874); *Extase* (1874, ?rev. 1884); †*Le Manoir de Rosemonde* (1879 or 82); *Sérénade Florentine* (?1880–1); †*Phidylé* (1882); *Lamento* (1883 or 5); †*Testament* (1883 or 5); †*La Vie antérieure* (1884).

VOCAL: *La fruite*, sop., ten., pf. (1871); *Benedicat vobis Dominus*, motet, STB (1882).

ORCH.: *Poème Nocturne* (1874, orig. in 3 movts., but only No.1, *Aux étoiles*, survives); *Lénore*, sym.-poem (1875).

PIANO: *5 Feuilles volantes* (?1867–9).

duplet. Pair of notes of equal time-value, written where number of beats cannot be divided by 2. See *irregular rhythmic groupings*.

duple time. Where the primary division is into 2 e.g. 2/4 as distinct from triple time (primary division into 3) or quadruple (division into 4). See *time signature*.

Duplex-Coupler Piano. Pf. invented 1921 by *Moór. Has 2 manuals, the upper tuned an octave higher. These are placed so that the hand can easily move from one to the other or play on both together. Thus, scales in 10ths are played as scales in 3rds as on a normal pf. The manuals can be instantly coupled, so that scales in octaves can be played as scales in single notes.

duplex instruments (Brass). These exist in 2 types: (a) those planned to produce 2 qualities of tone by the provision of 2 bells of different bore, and (b) those planned to play in either of 2 different keys (i.e. from either of 2 different *fundamental notes) without change of quality of tone (e.g. the double hn. in F and B♭) by the provision of double lengths of valve tubing.

duplex scaling. System by which those portions of pf. str. which are normally dumb, lying beyond each end of the vibrating portion, are left free and tuned so as to correspond with some of the harmonics of the main note of the str. See *aliquot scaling*.

Duport, Jean Louis (*b* Paris, 1749; *d* Paris, 1819). Fr. cellist and composer. Court cellist in Berlin 1792–1806, court musician to ex-King of Spain at Marseilles, 1807–12. Prof. of vc., Paris Cons. 1813–16. Wrote 6 vc. concs. and many solo pieces, also still-important method, *Essai sur le doigter du violoncelle et la conduite de l'Archet*.

Duport, Jean Pierre (*b* Paris, 1741; *d* Berlin, 1818). Fr. cellist. Début Concert Spirituel, Paris, 1761. Member of Frederick the Great's court orch., Berlin, 1773–1811, dir. of court concerts 1787–1806. Beethoven's 2 vc. sonatas Op.5 may have been written for him and f.p. in Berlin by Beethoven and Duport, 1796. Mozart wrote variations for pf. on a minuet by Duport (K573), 1789.

Dupré, Desmond (John) (b London, 1916; d nr. Tonbridge, 1974). Eng. lutenist, guitarist, and viol player. Lute-song duo with Alfred *Deller from 1950, touring widely. Many solo recitals. Recorded J. S. Bach's sonatas for va. da gamba and hpd. with Thurston *Dart. Member of Morley Consort, Jaye Consort of Viols, Musica Reservata, etc.

Du Pré, Jacqueline (b Oxford, 1945; d London, 1987). Eng. cellist. Suggia award, Queen's Prize. Public début at age 7. Début recital Wigmore Hall 1961. RFH début 1962 in Elgar's conc., with which she became closely identified, playing it also on first NY appearance, 1965 (cond. Dorati), and recording it with Barbirolli and with her husband, Daniel *Barenboim, whom she married 1967. Salzburg Fest. 1968. Perf. in chamber mus. trio with Barenboim and P. *Zukerman. Career halted 1973 by illness. OBE 1976.

Dupré, Marcel (b Rouen, 1886; d Meudon, nr. Paris, 1971). Fr. organist and composer. *Prix de Rome* 1914. Org., St Vivien, Rouen, at age 12. Ass. org. to Widor at St Sulpice, Paris, from 1906; succeeded him 1934. Played all J. S. Bach's org. works at Paris Cons. 1920, first time such a perf. had been given. London début 1920, NY 1921. Noteworthy improviser. Prof. of org., Paris Cons. 1926–54. Ed. org. works of Bach, Handel, Schumann, Liszt, Franck, etc. Comp. sym., vn. sonata, cantatas, and many org. works incl. 2 org. syms., org. conc., *Poèmes symphoniques*, and *Poèmes héroïques* (1937), org., brass, perc.

Duprez, Gilbert(-Louis) (b Paris, 1806; d Paris, 1896). Fr. tenor, composer, and teacher. Opera début Paris 1825 (Almaviva in *Il barbiere di Siviglia*). Wrote opera *La cabane du pêcheur*, a failure at Versailles 1826. Had first success as dramatic ten. in Turin 1831 in *Il *Pirata*. Sang Arnold in It. première of *Guillaume Tell* (Lucca 1831). Created several Donizetti roles, incl. Edgardo in *Lucia di Lammermoor* (Naples 1835). On return to Paris 1837, had immense success with Paris audiences. Created title-role in *Benvenuto Cellini* (1838) and roles in works by Auber, Halévy, and Verdi. Sang in London 1844–5 (Edgardo). Taught at Paris Cons. 1842–50. Founded vocal sch., 1853. First great *tenore di forza*.

dur (Ger.). Major (key), e.g. *dur Ton, dur Tonart*, major key; *A dur*, A major.

duramente (It.). With hardness, harshness, sternness.

Durand. Fr. mus. publishers (Durand, Schoenewerk, & Cie) founded 1869 in Paris by mus. critic Auguste Durand (1830–1909). Became Durand et Fils 1891. Complete editions of Rameau begun 1894 (ed. Saint-Saëns). Pubd. editions of Chopin by Debussy and of Schumann by Fauré. Composers in firm's list incl. Debussy, Ravel, Saint-Saëns, Milhaud, Poulenc, d'Indy, Messiaen, Ibert, and others.

durch (Ger. through). **durchaus** (throughout). **durchkomponiert** or **durchcomponiert** (through-

composed). Applied to songs of which the music is different for each stanza of the poem, i.e. the opposite of *strophic; but use of the term has been widened to mean a composition which has been 'fully worked out', 'thoroughly composed', as opposed to something that seems episodic or patchy. **durchdringen** (through-forcing) penetrating, shrill. **durchführung** (through-leading) *development. **durchweg** (1) throughout, altogether. (2) generally, nearly always.

Durey, Louis (b Paris, 1888; d St Tropez, 1979). Fr. composer. In 1917 joined Milhaud, Honegger, and others under leadership of Satie as 'les nouveaux jeunes', becoming *Les *Six* in 1920. Abandoned them in 1921. Joined Fr. Communist party 1936. After 1945 became Progressist, one of group of Fr. composers who wrote mus. of deliberate 'mass appeal' in accordance with Communist doctrines on art. Works incl. *Judith*, monodrama (1918); *L'Occasion*, lyric drama (1928); *Fantaisie Concertante*, vc., orch. (1947); pf. concertino (1956); *Mouvement symphonique* (1964); *Sinfonietta* (1966); *Obsession*, wind inst. (1970); 3 str. qts.; 3 sonatines, fl., pf.; and songs.

Durkó, Zsolt (b Szeged, 1934; d Budapest, 1997). Hung. composer. Broke away from influence of Kodály, all his work being atonal. Prof. of comp. Budapest Acad., 1970–80. Works incl. *Organismi*, vn., orch. (1964); *Fioriture* (1965–6); Str. qt. No.1 (1966), No.2 (1969, rev. 1970); *Altamira*, ch., orch. (1967–8); *Burial Prayer*, oratorio, ten., bar., ch., orch. (1967–72); *Cantilène*, pf., orch. (1968); *Moses*, opera (1972, prod. Budapest 1977); *Chamber Music*, 2 pf., 11 str. (1973); *Dwarfs and Giants*, pf. (1974); *Turner Illustrations*, orch. (1976); *Refrains*, vn., orch. (1978); pf. conc. (1980); *Movements*, tuba, pf. (1980); *Széchenyi Oratorio* (1981–2); *Impromptus in F*, fl. and ens. (1984); *Wind Octet* (1988); *Ilmarinen*, ch. (1989).

Dürr, Alfred (b Charlottenburg, 1918). Ger. musicologist and writer. Member, Johann-Sebastian-Bach-Inst., Göttingen, 1951–83 (ass. dir. 1962–81). Ed. Bach-Jahrbuch 1953–74. Ed. of works for Bach neue Ausgabe sämtlicher Werke. Books incl. Bach's Christmas Oratorios (1967), *The Cantatas of J. S. Bach* (1971, rev. 1985), and Bach's St John Passion (1988).

Duruflé, Maurice (b Louviers, 1902; d Paris, 1986). Fr. composer and organist. Org., St Étienne-du-Mont, Paris, from 1930. Ass. to M. *Dupré at Paris Cons. from 1942, prof. of harmony 1943–69. Works incl. *Requiem*, Op.9 (1947, rev. 1961), 3 *Dances for Orch.* (1932), *Messe-cum jubilo* (1966), motets, and org. works.

Dušek, František (b Chotěborky, 1731; d Prague, 1799). Bohem. pianist and composer. Prominent teacher in Prague. Close friend of Mozart. Comp. syms., chamber mus.

Dušek [Dussek], **Jan Ladislav** (b Čáslav, 1760; d St Germain-en-Laye, 1812). Bohem. pianist and composer. Began career as virtuoso pianist in Malines, 1779, then had comp. lessons from

C. P. E. Bach in Hamburg 1782. Visited Ger., Russia, Fr., and It. as pianist; settled in London 1789–99, appearing with Haydn. Served various royal patrons after 1803, the last being Talleyrand (Prince of Benevento). Prolific composer, works incl. 34 pf. sonatas; 15 pf. concs.; conc. for 2 pf.; pf. trios; ballad-opera; mass; 38 vn. sonatas; 16 fl. sonatas; etc. (much of it worth exploring).

Dušek (*née* Hambacher), **Josefa** (*b* Prague, 1754; *d* Prague, 1824). Bohem. soprano, composer, and pianist, wife of František *Dušek. Friend of Mozart who wrote concert aria *Bella mia fiamma, addio* (K528, 1787), for her. First singer of Beethoven's *Ah, perfido!* Op.65, 1796, also probably written for her.

Dushkin, Samuel (*b* Suwalki, Poland, 1891; *d* NY, 1976). Amer. violinist of Polish birth, pupil of Auer and Kreisler. Eur. début 1918. Gave f.p. 1924 of orch. version of Ravel's *Tzigane*. Stravinsky wrote vn. conc. for him, 1931, f.p. Berlin that year, also *Duo Concertant*, of which he and Stravinsky gave f.p. Berlin 1932.

Dutilleux, Henri (*b* Angers, 1916). Fr. composer. Won *Prix de Rome* 1938. Joined French Radio 1943, becoming dir. of mus. productions 1945–63. Prof. of comp., École Normale de Musique 1961 (pres. from 1969), Paris Cons. 1970–1. Regarded as natural successor to Ravel and Roussel. Works incl.:

BALLETS: *Le Loup* (1953); *Summer's End* (1981).

ORCH.: syms.: No.1 (1951), No.2 (*Le double*) (1959); *Métaboles* (1964); *Tout un monde lontain*, vc., orch. (1970); *Timbres, espace, mouvement ou La nuit étoilée* (1977, rev. 1991); *L'arbre des songes*, vn., orch. (1985); *Mystère de l'instant*, 24 str., cimbalon, perc. (1989).

CHAMBER MUSIC: *Sarabande et Cortège*, bn., pf. (1942); Sonatine, fl., pf. (1943); ob. sonata (1947); *Choral, Cadence et Fugato*, tb., pf. (1950); *3 Strophes sur le nom de SACHER*, vc. (1976); *Ainsi la nuit*, str. qt. (1976–7); *Diptyque, Les Citations*, ob., hpd., db., perc. (1988, 1991).

PIANO: *Au gré des ondes*, 6 short pieces (1946); sonata (1948); *Tous les chemins* (1961); *Bergerie* (1963); *Résonances* (1964); *Figures de Résonances*, 2 pf. (1970); *Le jeu des contraires* (1988).

Dutoit, Charles (Edouard) (*b* Lausanne, 1936). Swiss violist and conductor. Began career as violist in Lausanne Chamber Orch. but also guest cond. of Suisse Romande Orch. Art. dir. Zurich Radio Orch. 1964–71, chief cond. Berne SO 1967–77, cond. Montreal SO 1977–90, chief cond. Orchestre National de Paris 1990–2001. Eng. début 1966, especially assoc. with RPO. Visits to N. and S. America and Japan. NY Met début 1987.

Duval, Denise (*b* Paris, 1921). Fr. soprano. Début Bordeaux 1943 (Lola in *Cavalleria Rusticana*), then member of Folies Bergères. Début Opéra-Comique, Paris, 1947 as Butterfly. Created Thérèse in *Les *mamelles de Tirésias* (1947), and sang Blanche in Paris première of *Les *Dialogues des Carmélites* (1957). Created Elle in *La *Voix humaine* (Paris

1959) and sang role at Edinburgh Fest. 1960. Sang Mélisande, Glyndebourne 1962. Retired 1965 and taught at École Française de Mus., Paris.

dux. The v. in a canon which first enters with the melody to be imitated. Also called antecedent. See also *canon*.

Dux, Claire (*b* Witkowicz, 1885; *d* Chicago, 1967). Polish soprano. Opera début Cologne 1906 as Pamina in *Die Zauberflöte*. Berlin Opera 1909–18. CG début 1913; Chicago Opera 1921–3. Retired after her third marriage.

Dvořák, Antonín (Leopold) (*b* Nelahozeves, Bohemia, 1841; *d* Prague, 1904). Cz. (Bohem.) composer. Son of a village butcher, Dvořák as a child helped in the shop and also showed talent as a violinist. At 14 he was sent to relatives in Zlonice to learn Ger.; while there he was taught va., org., pf., and counterpoint by A. Liehmann. From 1857 to 1859 he attended the Org. Sch., Prague, leaving to become va. player in a band and later in the orch. of Prague Nat. Th., 1866–73, playing under Smetana. At this time he comp. several works which he later destroyed or withdrew, the most significant being a song-cycle *Cypress Trees* from which he drew themes in later years (for the Vc. Conc., for example). The cycle was a tale of disappointed love, the result of Dvořák's disappointment that a girl he adored married someone else. (He later married her sister.) Like most young composers of the time, his natural tendencies were complicated by the inescapable influence of Wagner. His first opera, *Alfred* (1870) was Wagnerian in tone. Three years later he had his first major success with a cantata, *Hymnus (The Heirs of the White Mountain)*, which enabled him to give up his orch. playing. In 1874 his sym. in E♭ won him an Austrian nat. prize, Brahms being on the jury. Two years later the Moravian duets won him the same prize, and Brahms recommended them to the publisher Simrock. The nationalist element in such works as the *Slavonic Rhapsodies*—the results of Smetana's beneficial influence—earned Dvořák increasing recognition and requests for new works e.g. from Joachim for a vn. conc. and from Hans *Richter for a sym. Both Richter and *Bülow championed his mus. in their concerts. In 1884 he paid the first of 9 visits to England and cond. his *Stabat Mater* which had scored a tremendous success the previous year under *Barnby. His popularity in Britain was immediate and sustained both as comp. and cond., and he was financially successful enough to be able to buy an estate in S. Bohemia. Several of his works were written for or first perf. in Eng., e.g. the sym. in D minor (No.7), comp. for the Phil. Soc. (1885), the cantata *The Spectre's Bride* (Birmingham, 1885), the oratorio *St Ludmila* (Leeds, 1886), the sym. in G major (No.8) (Phil. Soc. 1888), and the *Requiem* (Birmingham, 1891). Cambridge made him Hon. D.Mus. in 1891 and in the same year he was appointed prof. of comp. at Prague Cons. The Cons. granted him leave to accept the invitation of Mrs Jeanette Thurber, founder in 1885 of the Nat. Cons. of Mus., NY, to become dir. of the cons. He remained in Amer. for 3 years, a fruitful period in which he wrote some of his finest works, incl. the 'New World' Sym., the vc. conc., the Biblical Songs, the str. qt. Op.96, and the str. quintet Op.97. His art seems to have been intensified by a combination of the influence of Negro melodies and of a deep home-sickness. He returned to his teaching post in Prague in 1895, becoming dir. of Prague Cons. in 1901. His pupils incl. his son-in-law *Suk, and *Novák. In his last years he devoted his creative energies to symphonic poems and to operas.

Dvořák's mus. is a particularly happy result of the major influences on his art: Wagner, Brahms, and folk mus. His innate gift for melody was Schubertian and his felicitous orchestration, often reflecting natural and pastoral elements, is of an art that conceals art. But a tendency to regard him as blithely naïve would be both un-just and misleading, for his mastery of form and his contrapuntal and harmonic skill are the manifestations of a powerful mus. intellect. The nationalist feeling in his mus. is beautifully in-tegrated into classical structures and his use of Cz. dances and songs, such as the furiant, polka, skočná (reel), dumka, and sousedská (slow waltz), is in no way bizarre. His syms., the vc. conc., and perhaps above all his chamber mus. show the best side of his work; the operas, apart from Rusalka, are only just beginning to travel outside Czechoslovakia; and the choral works which won him such a following in late Victorian Eng. are due for rehabilitation. For many years it was customary to credit him only with the 5 syms. pubd. in his lifetime, but the 4 early examples have now been accepted into the canon and the whole series is numbered chronologically. Prin. works:

OPERAS: Alfred (unpubd.) (1870); King and Charcoal Burner (Král a uhlíř) (1871, totally re-composed 1874, rev. 1887), Op.14; The Stubborn Lovers (Tvrdé palice) (1874), Op.17; Vanda (1875, rev. 1879, 1883) Op.25; The Peasant a Rogue (Šelma sedlák) (1877), Op.35; *Dimitrij (1881–2, revs. 1883, 1885, 1894–5), Op.64; The *Jacobin (1887–8, rev. 1897), Op.84; *Kate and the Devil (Čert a Káča) (1898–9), Op.112; *Rusalka (1900), Op.114; Armida (1902–3), Op.115.

SYMPHONIES: No.1 in C minor (The *Bells of Zlonice) (1865) (no Op. no., recovered 1923, pubd. 1961); No.2 in B♭ (1865) (no Op. no.); No.3 in E♭ (1873), (no Op. no. but orig. Op.10); No.4 in D minor (1874) (no Op. no. but orig. Op.13, pubd. 1912); No.5 in F major (1875, rev. 1887), Op.76 (orig. Op.24 and formerly No.3); No.6 in D major (1880), Op.60 (formerly No.1); No.7 in D minor (1884–5), Op.70 (formerly No.2); No.8 in G major (1889), Op.88 (formerly No.4); No.9 in E minor (From the *New World) (1893), Op.95 (formerly No.5).

ORCH.: sym.-poems: The Water sprite (Vodník), Op.107 (1896); The *Noonday Witch (Polednice), Op.108 (1896); The Golden Spinning Wheel (Zlatý Kolovrat), Op.109 (1896); The *Wood Dove (Holoubek), Op.110 (1896); Heroic Song, Op.111 (1897); Ovs.: My Home,

Op.62a (1882); Hussite (Husitská), Op.67 (1883); Cycle, *Nature, Life and Love comprising *Amid Nature, Op.91, *Carneval, Op.92, and *Othello, Op.93 (1891–2); Serenade in E major, str., Op.22 (1875); Suite in D (Czech), Op.39 (1879); Serenade in D minor, wind, vc., bass, Op.44 (1878); 3 *Slavonic Rhapsodies in D, G minor, and A♭, Op.45 (1878); 8 *Slavonic Dances, 1st series, Op.46 (1878), 8 (2nd series) Op.72 (1886); Legends, Op.59 (1881); Scherzo capriccioso, Op.66 (1883); Symphonic variations, Op.78 (1877, orig. Op.40).

SOLOIST & ORCH.: vc. conc. in A major (1865, with pf. acc. only. Orch. Raphael 1928, Burghauser 1975, vc. part ed. Sádló); Romance for vn., Op.11 (1873–7, arr. of andante con moto of str. qt. in F minor, Op.9, of 1873); pf. conc. in G minor, Op.33 (1876); Mazurka for vn., Op.49 (1879); vn. conc. in A minor, Op.53 (1879–80); Rondo for vc., Op.94 (1893); Forest Calm, for vc. (1891); vc. conc. in B minor, Op.104 (1894–5).

CHAMBER MUSIC: string quartets: F minor, Op.9 (1873), A minor, Op.12 (1873), A minor, Op.16 (1874), D minor, Op.34 (1877), E♭, Op.51 (1878–79), C major, Op.61 (1881), E major, Op.80 (1876, orig. Op.27), F major (the *'American'), Op.96 (1893), A♭, Op.105 (1895), G major, Op.106 (1895). Also several without Opus no. incl. Cypresses (Cypřiše) (1887); string quintets: G major, Op.77, with db. (1875, orig. Op.18), E♭, Op.97 (1893); string sextet: A major, Op.48 (1878); pf. trios: B♭, Op.21 (1875), G minor, Op.26 (1876), F minor, Op.65 (1883), E minor (Dumka) Op.90 (1890–1); pf. qts.: D major, Op.23 (1875), E♭, Op.87 (1889); pf. quintet: A major, Op.81 (1887); *Bagatelles (Maličkosti), 2 vn., vc., harmonium (or pf.), Op.47 (1878); Terzetto, 2 vn., va., Op.74 (1887); vn. sonata: F major, Op.57 (1880); vn. sonatina in G, Op.100 (1893).

CHORAL: Stabat Mater, Op.58 (1876–7, orig. Op.28); The *Spectre's Bride, Op.69 (1884); *St Ludmila, Op.71 (1885–6); Mass in D, Op.86 (1887, rev. 1892); Requiem, Op.89 (1890); The American Flag, Op.102 (1892); Te Deum, Op.103 (1892); Hymn of the Czech Peasants (Hymna ceského rolnictva), Op.28 (1885); with 4-hand acc., Hymnus, Op.30 (1872, orig. Op.4); *Amid Nature (Vpřírodě), 5 ch., Op.63 (1882).

SONGS: cycle, Cypress Trees, 18 songs to words by Pflager (1865), unpubd. in orig. form but pubd. as 4 Songs, Op.2, 8 Love Songs, Op.83 (1888) and Cypress Trees for str. qt; 5 Evening Songs, Op.31 (1876); 3 Modern Greek Songs, Op.50 (1878); 7 *Gipsy Songs, Op.55 (1880; No.4 is *Songs my Mother taught me); 4 Songs, Op.82 (1887–8); 10 *Biblical Songs, Op.99 (1894, Nos. 1 and 5 are orch.).

PIANO: Silhouettes, Op.8 (1879); Dumka and Furiant, Op.12 (1884); *Dumka, Op.35 (1876); Theme and Variations, Op.36 (1876); Scottish Dances, Op.41 (1877); 4 Pieces, Op.52 (1880); 8 Waltzes, Op.54 (1879–80; Nos. 1 and 4 arr. for str. qt.); 6 Mazurkas, Op.56 (1880); Poetic Tone Pictures (Poetické nálady), Op.85 (1889); Suite in A, Op.98 (1894, arr. for orch.); 8 *Humoresques, Op.101 (1894; No.7 is the famous one); Éclogues (1880); Album Leaves (1881).

PIANO DUETS: 16 *Slavonic Dances*, Opp. 46 and 72 (2 sets of 8; also for orch.); *Legends*, Op.59 (1881, also for orch.); *From the Bohemian Forest (Ze Šumavy)*, Op.68 (1884).

Dvořákova, Ludmila (*b* Kolín, 1923). Cz. soprano. Opera début Ostrava 1949 (as Káťa Kabanová). Bratislava Opera 1952–4; Prague 1954–60; Berlin State Opera from 1960. First sang Brünnhilde (*Ring*) in Berlin 1962, Isolde in Karlsruhe 1964. Vienna début 1965; Bayreuth 1965; NY Met 1966. Sang Brünnhilde in *Ring* cycles CG 1966–71. Deutsche Oper am Rhein, Dusseldorf, 1973–4. Mez. roles from late 1970s. Visited Japan with Berlin and Hamburg State operas 1982 and 1984.

Dvorsky, Peter (*b* Partizánske, nr. Topol'čany, 1951). Slovak tenor. Début Bratislava 1972 (Lensky in *Eugene Onegin*). Won Geneva int. comp. 1975. Débuts: Vienna 1977; NY Met 1977; Milan 1978; CG 1978; Salzburg Fest. 1989.

Dwarf, The (Zemlinsky). See *Zwerg, Der*.

Dykes, John Bacchus (*b* Hull, 1823; *d* Ticehurst, Sussex, 1876). Eng. church composer. Org., St John's, Hull, while schoolboy. Precentor of Durham Cath. 1849–62, and vicar of St Oswald's, Durham, from 1862. Submitted 7 hymn-tunes to mus. ed. of *Hymns Ancient and Modern*, all being accepted. Eventually contrib. 60 tunes to first edn. (1861), the most popular being *Nearer My God to Thee*, *Eternal Father, Strong to Save, Our blest Redeemer, Holy, holy, holy, The King of Love my Shepherd is, Jesu, Lover of my Soul*, and *Lead, Kindly Light*.

Dykes Bower, John. See *Bower, John Dykes*.

Dylan, Bob [Zimmerman, Robert Allen] (*b* Duluth, Minn., 1941). Amer. singer and songwriter. Self-taught in pf., gui., and harmonica. Formed rock and roll band 1955. When at Univ. of Minnesota, 1959–60, played in coffee houses. His 'talking blues', in nasal speech-song style, attracted attention and he was among leaders of 1960s folk-song revival. His songs and lyrics were popular with Amer. youth as part of protest and rights movements in 1960s, most famous being *Blowin' in the wind* (1962) and *The times they are a-changin'* (1964). Appeared in London 1965 with Joan Baez. Started folk-rock style with elec. gui. and rock-band accompaniment at Newport Fest., 1965. Other songs incl. *Mr Tambourine Man* (1965) and *Lay, Lady, Lay* (1969).

dynamics. The gradations of vol. in mus., e.g. *forte, piano, crescendo*, etc.

Dyson, (Sir) **George** (*b* Halifax, Yorks., 1883; *d* Winchester, 1964). Eng. composer, teacher, and organist. Spent 1904–8 in It. and Ger. on Mendelssohn Scholarship. From 1908–37 was mus. master at a succession of Eng. schs. incl. Rugby, Wellington, and Winchester (1924–37). Taught at RCM becoming dir. 1937–52. Comps. incl. *In Honour of the City*, ch., orch. (1928); *The *Canterbury Pilgrims*, sop., ten., bar., ch., orch. (1929–31); *St Paul's Voyage to Melita* (1933); *The Blacksmiths*, ch., orch. (1934); Sym. in G (1937); *Quo Vadis* (1939); vn. conc. (1942); *Sweet Thames Run Softly* (1954); *Benedicite*, bar., ch., org. (1955). Knighted 1941, KCVO 1953.

Dzerzhinsky, Ivan (*b* Tambov, 1909; *d* Leningrad, 1978). Russ. composer. His operas were upheld as models when Shostakovich was in disgrace with Soviet authorities for his *Lady Macbeth of the Mtsensk District*. Works incl. the operas *Quiet Flows the Don* (1935); *Virgin Soil Upturned* (1937); *Blood of the People* (1941); *Nadezhda Svetlova* (1943); and *A Man's Destiny* (1961). Also 3 pf. concs. (1932, 1934, 1945), sym.-poem, songs, etc.

E. Note of the scale: 3rd degree of natural scale of C. Thus, E♭, E♭♭, E♮, E♯, E♯♯. Keys of E major and E minor, E♭ major and E♭ minor. E♭ is also indication of *transposing instr. (e.g. the E♭ cl.) on which written note C sounds as E♭.

e (It.). And. See *ed*.

Eadie, Noël (*b* Paisley, 1901; *d* London, 1950). Scottish soprano. Début London, CG 1926 (Woglinde in *Das Rheingold*), BNOC 1928; Chicago Opera 1931–2; Glyndebourne 1935–6; SW, and other cos. Sang Sandrina in f. Eng. p. of *La finta giardiniera*, London 1930.

Eaglen, Jane (*b* Lincoln, 1960). Eng. soprano. Studied at RNCM. Début 1984, ENO, as Lady Ella in *Patience*. CG début 1986; Scottish Opera 1988; Vienna State Opera 1991–2. Sang Brünnhilde in Scottish Opera's *Die Walküre*, Glasgow 1991, and title-role in *Norma* 1993. Proms début 1989; Seattle 1994.

Eames, Emma (Hayden) (*b* Shanghai, 1865; *d* NY, 1952). Amer. soprano. Paris Opéra 1889–91, making début as Juliette in *Roméo et Juliette*. Débuts: CG 1891; Amer. (Chicago) 1891; NY Met 1891. Member of Met co. until 1909, incl. Mrs. Ford in Amer. première of *Falstaff*, 1895. Last stage appearances Boston 1911, thereafter recitals. Autobiography *Some Memories and Reflections* (NY 1927, 1977).

ear, playing by. The ability to play an instr. intuitively, without instruction, or to improvise without a score.

early music. Term by which is generally understood mus. comp. from earliest times up to and incl. mus. of Baroque era. With growth of interest in mus. of this period and especially the use of authentic instrs. in perf., various 'early mus.' consorts and ens. were formed. The periodical *Early Music* was founded in 1973 by John Thomson and has been pubd. since then by Oxford University Press. Later eds. have been Nicholas Kenyon and Tess Knighton.

Early Music Consort. Group of musicians founded by David *Munrow in 1967 to perform Renaissance and other early mus. on orig. instrs. such as rebec, sackbut, shawm, curtall, etc. Many recordings.

Easdale, Brian (*b* Manchester, 1909; *d* London, 1995). Eng. composer. Comps. incl. operas *Rapunzel* (1927), *The Corn King* (1935), and *The Sleeping Children* (1951); also pf. conc. (1938), song-cycles, and film and th. mus.

East [Easte, Est, Este], **Michael** (*b c.*1580; *d* Lichfield, 1648). Eng. composer and organist. Choirmaster, Lichfield Cath. Wrote madrigals, anthems, and mus. for viols. His 5-part madrigal

Hence Stars is in *The *Triumphs of Oriana*. Also wrote madrigal called *O metaphysical tobacco* (1606).

East [Easte, Est, Este], **Thomas** (*b c.*1550; *d* London, 1608). London mus. publisher. Issued Byrd's psalms, sonnets, and songs (1588), works by other madrigalists (Morley, Mundy, and Wilbye), and 4-part settings of psalms (1592). Printed Dowland's *Second Book of Songs or Airs* (1600) and John Danyel's *Songs for the Lute Viol and Voice* (1606).

Eastman, George (*b* Waterville, NY, 1854; *d* Rochester, NY, 1932). Amer. industrialist. In 1880 developed process for making dry plates for photocopy and in 1884 founded Eastman Dry Plate and Film Co. In 1892 this became Eastman Kodak Co. Gave more than 75 million dollars to scientific and cultural organizations, founding Eastman Sch. of Mus. of Univ. of Rochester, NY, in 1919.

Eastman School of Music. Dept. of Univ. of Rochester, NY. Founded 1919 through munificence of George *Eastman, inventor of Kodak photographic process, and opened in 1921. Dir. 1924–64 was Howard *Hanson.

Easton, Florence (Gertrude) (*b* South Bank, Yorks, 1882; *d* NY, 1955). Eng. soprano. Opera début as Shepherd in *Tannhäuser* with Moody-Manners Co., Newcastle upon Tyne, 1903. Joined Savage Co., Baltimore, 1904–5, 1906–7. Member Berlin Royal Opera 1907–13; Hamburg Opera 1912–16; Chicago 1915–17; NY Met 1917–29 and 1935–6; CG 1927 and 1932; SW 1934. Created Lauretta in *Gianni Schicchi* (NY Met 1918). Repertory of 150 very varied roles in 4 languages and could learn a new score in 12 hours. Resplendent Brünnhilde with Melchior in *Siegfried*, CG 1932. Retired 1936.

Eastwood, Thomas (Hugh) (*b* Hawley, Hants, 1922; *d* 1999). Eng. composer. Worked for Brit. Council in Ankara 1948–51, and Berlin 1951–4. On council of SPNM 1959–70. Art. dir. Andover Fest. 1985–6. Mus. dir. Latin-Amer. Arts Assoc. 1986. Works incl. 3 operas (one of them *Christopher Sly*, 1950); cantatas; chamber mus.; songs; and incidental mus. for plays incl. John Osborne's *Look Back in Anger* (1956). Made new realization of *Love in a Village* for BBC (1964).

Eben, Petr (*b* Žamberk, Cz., 1929). Cz. composer and pianist. Assoc. prof., Prague Univ. from 1955. Taught at RNCM 1977–8. Comps. incl. pf. conc. (1961); oratorio *Apologia Sokratus* (1964); *Laudes*, org. (1964); *Ubi caritas et amor*, ch. (1965); wind quintet (1965); brass quintet (1969); *Okna*, tpt., org. (1976); *Mutationes*, 2 org. (1980); *Faust*, org. (1980); str. qt. (1981); *Curses and Blessings*, ballet

(1983); org. conc. (1983); *Landscapes of Patmos*, org., perc. (1984); *Desire of Ancient Things*, unacc. ch. (1985); pf. trio (1986); *Festive Voluntary, Variations on Good King Wenceslas*, org. (1986); *Hommage à Dietrich Buxtehude*, org. (1987); *Job*, org. (1987); *3 Jubilations*, org., brass (1987); *2 Invocations*, tb., org. (1988).

Ebert, (Anton) **Carl** (*b* Berlin, 1887; *d* Santa Monica, Calif., 1980). Ger.-born operatic producer and impresario. Trainee actor in Berlin under tutelage of Max Reinhardt. Actor in Frankfurt and Berlin 1915–27. Dir., Darmstadt State Th. 1927–31 (staging *Le nozze di Figaro* and *Otello* in 1929), Berlin State Opera 1931–3. Left Ger. for Buenos Aires, working at Teatro Colón with Fritz *Busch. Prod. *Die Entführung*, Salzburg 1932 (cond. Busch). Producer, Glyndebourne Fest. from first season in 1934 to 1939, and 1947–59. Organized Turkish Nat. Opera 1937–47, dir., opera dept. Univ. of S. Calif. 1948–54. Prod. f.p. of *The Rake's Progress*, Venice 1951. Returned to Berlin State Opera 1954–61; NY Met 1959–62. Set new standards of ens. and detailed rehearsal in Verdi and Mozart. CBE 1960.

Ebert, Peter (*b* Frankfurt, 1918). Ger. opera producer, son of Carl *Ebert. Has worked at Glyndebourne, Rome, Venice, Wexford, Los Angeles, and Copenhagen. Chief producer Hanover State Opera and Deutsche Oper am Rhein 1954–64; dir. of prods. Scottish Opera 1965–75; gen. administrator Scottish Opera 1977–80.

Ebony Concerto. For cl. and orch. by *Stravinsky. Comp. 1945 for jazz musician Woody Herman who was soloist with his band at f.p. in NY 1946. Jazz slang for cl. is 'ebony stick'.

Eccles, John (*b* London, *c.*1668; *d* Hampton Wick, 1735). Eng. composer. Prolific writer of th. mus., incl. Congreve's *The Way of the World* and masque *The Judgement of Paris*. Collab. with Purcell on *Don Quixote* (1694–5). Comp. opera *Semele* (*c.*1706) to same lib. as Handel. Master of King's Band 1700. Pubd. 100 songs in 1710.

Eccles [Eagles], **Solomon** (*b* London, 1618; *d* London, 1682). Eng. composer and performer on virginals and viol. On becoming Quaker *c.*1660, publicly burned his mus. and instrs. on Tower Hill, later accompanying George Fox to W. Indies.

Ecclesiastical modes. See *modes*.

échappé. See *changing note*.

échelle (Fr.). Ladder, i.e. scale (*gamme* is the more usual word for the mus. scale). **échelette** (Fr.). Little ladder, i.e. *xylophone.

echo cornet. Organ stop of gentle tone (see *cornet stop*).

echo gamba. A soft type of organ stop.

Echoklavier (Ger.). Echo-keyboard. *Choir organ (not echo organ).

echo organ. An org. manual with very soft stops to give an echo effect.

Eckhardt-Gramatté, Sophie-Carmen (Sonia) (*b* Moscow, 1899; *d* Stuttgart, 1974). Russ.-born Canadian composer, violinist, and pianist. Toured as duo with Edwin *Fischer in Ger. 1925. Career as solo violinist and pianist from age 11, but later concentrated on comp. Works incl. 3 pf. concs.; 2 vn. concs.; conc. for orch.; triple conc. (tpt., cl., bn.); bn. conc.; 2 syms.; 3 str. qts.; 6 pf. sonatas; 2 vn. sonatas; and other chamber works. Settled in Canada 1953 (cit. 1958).

Éclat (Fragment). Work for chamber orch. (15 instr.) by Boulez, comp. 1965. F.p. Los Angeles 1965, London 1966. Expanded and rev. 1970 as *Éclat/Multiples*, f.p. London 1970, but regarded as 'work in progress'.

eclecticism. Term frequently used to describe a composer's conscious use of styles alien to his nature, or from a bygone era. Also used pejoratively when applied to mus. in which the composer, thought to be lacking originality, has freely drawn on other models.

eclogue. Short pastoral poem (sometimes used as title of a piece of mus.).

écossaise. A type of contredanse (see *country dance*) in duple time. The orig. of the name is a mystery, since there appears to be nothing Scottish about the character of the mus. It is not the same as the *Schottische.

ed (It.). 'And' (version of *e* as used before a vowel). Thus the title of Bellini's opera may be given as *I Capuleti e (ed) i Montecchi*.

Eda-Pierre, Christiane (*b* Fort-de-France, Martinique, 1932). Fr. soprano. Début Nice 1958 (Leila in Bizet's *Les pêcheurs de perles*). Aix-en-Provence 1959; Paris Opéra-Comique 1961; Paris Opéra 1962; CG 1966; Wexford 1966; NY Met 1976 with Paris Opéra, then returning from 1980; Salzburg Fest. 1980. Created Angel in Messiaen's *St François d'Assise* (Paris 1983). Prof., Paris Cons. from 1977.

Edelmann, Otto (Karl) (*b* Brunn am Gebirge, 1917; *d* Vienna, 2003). Austrian bass. Début Gera 1937 (as Mozart's Figaro). Sang at Nuremberg 1938–40. Prisoner-of-war in Russ. for 2 years. Joined Vienna Opera 1947; Salzburg Fest. 1948 and sang Ochs in *Der Rosenkavalier* in f.p. in new Grossesfestspielhaus, 26 July 1960; Bayreuth 1951; Brit. 1952 (Edinburgh Fest.). Regular visitor to NY Met (début 1954) and S. Francisco.

Eden and Tamir. Israeli piano duo formed 1952 by Bracha Eden (*b* Jerusalem, 1928) and Alexander Tamir (*b* Vilnius, 1931). Both studied at Rubin Acad., Jerusalem until 1952 and at Aspen in 1955 with Vronsky and Babin. Début Israel 1954, NY 1955, London 1957. Have revived many two-piano works by Clementi, Dussek, and Hummel. Gave f. Amer. p. of Lutosławski's *Paganini Variations* and f. public. p. of pf. duet version of Stravinsky's *Rite of Spring*.

Eder, Helmut (*b* Linz, 1916; *d* Salzburg, 2005). Austrian composer. Taught at Linz Cons. from 1950, organizing its EMS 1959. Taught at Salzburg Mozarteum from 1967. Cond. Mozarteum Orch. at Salzburg Fest. 1972. Works incl.

OPERAS: *Oedipus* (1958); *Der Kardinal* (1962); *Die weise Frau* (1968); *Konjugationen 3* (for TV, 1969); *Der Aufstand* (1975); *Georges Dandin oder Der betrogene Ehemann* (1978–9); *Mozart in New York* (1991).

BALLETS: *Moderner Traum* (1957); *Anamorphose* (1963); *Die Irrfahrten des Odysseus* (1964–5).

ORCH.: 5 syms. (1950–80, No.4, *Choral*, 1973–5, No.5 for org., 1979–80); ob. conc. (1962); 3 vn. concs. (1963, 1964, 1981–2); bn. conc. (1968); *Pastorale*, str. (1974); conc. for vc., db., orch. (1977–8); vc. conc. (1981); *Haffner Concerto*, fl., orch. (1984); *Concertino* for classical orch. (1984).

CHAMBER MUSIC: str. qt. (1948); pf. trio (1971); *Szene*, 6 hn. (1977); cl. quintet 1982); qt. for fl. and str. trio (1983).

Edgar. 4-act opera by Puccini to lib. by F. Fontana after A. de Musset's verse-drama *La Coupe et ses lèvres* (1832). Comp. 1884–8. Prod. Milan 1889; NY 1956. Rev. 3-act version f.p. Ferrara 1892. Further rev. 1901, 1905 (Buenos Aires, 1905).

Edinburgh Festival. 3-week annual int. fest. of the arts held in Scottish capital Aug.–Sept., with strong emphasis on opera, concerts, and recitals. Founded 1947 with Rudolf Bing as dir.; he was succeeded by Ian Hunter 1949–55, Robert Ponsonby 1955–60, Earl of Harewood 1961–5, Peter Diamand 1966–78, John Drummond 1979–83, Frank Dunlop 1984–91, Brian McMaster 1992–2006, Jonathan Mills from 2007. Many distinguished visiting cos. have supplied opera, incl. Glyndebourne, Stuttgart, Stockholm, Hamburg, Prague, Belgrade, La Scala, Florence, Deutsche Oper, Bavarian State, and Scottish. Visiting orchs. and soloists incl. virtually all the most celebrated. Several works have had f. Brit. ps. at fest., incl. the following operas: *Mathis der Maler* (1952); *The Rake's Progress* (1953); *La vide breve* (1958); *La voix humaine* (1960); *Love for Three Oranges* and *The Gambler* (both 1962); *From the *House of the Dead* (1964); *Intermezzo* (1965); *The *Excursions of Mr Brouček* (1970); *Die Soldaten* (1972); *Mary, Queen of Scots* (1977); *The Lighthouse* (1980); *Juha* (1987); *Nixon in China* and *Greek* (both 1988).

A feature is the very lively 'fringe', events outside the official programme, some of which have 'stolen the show'.

E dur (Ger.). The key of E major.

Edwards, Richard (*b* Somerset, 1524; *d* London, 1566). Eng. composer, poet, and scholar. Member of Chapel Royal by 1557 and Master of the Children of the Chapel Royal from 1561. Best known for his madrigal *In going to my naked bed*. His *Damon and Pythias* (1564) has been described as early 'mus. drama'.

Edwards, Ross (*b* Sydney, NSW, 1943). Australian composer. Went to London 1969. Returned to Australia 1972. Taught in mus. dept., Univ. of Sydney. Lect., NSW Cons. from 1976. Comps. incl.:

STAGE: *Christina's World*, 2 mez., ten., bar., tape, ens. (1983).

ORCH.: *Mountain Village in a Clearing Mist* (1973); pf. conc. (1982); *Maninyas*, vn., orch. (1988); *Varrageh*, solo perc., orch. (1989); *Aria and Transcendental Dance*, hn., str. (1990).

INSTR.: *Shadow D-Zone*, fl., cl./bcl., perc., pf., vn., vc. (1977); *Laikan*, fl., cl., perc., pf., vn., vc. (1979); *Reflections*, pf., 3 perc. (1985).

CHORAL: *5 Carols From Quem Quaeritis*, unacc. women's ch. (1967); *Antifon*, ch., brass sextet, org., 2 perc. (1973); *Ab estasis foribus, 5 Mediaeval Latin Lyrics*, unacc. ch. (1980); *Flower Songs*, ch., perc. (1986–7).

VOICE(S) & INSTR.: *The Hermit of Green light*, v., pf. (1979); *Maninya I*, v., vc. (1981); *Maninya V*, v., pf. (1986).

CHAMBER MUSIC: *Monos I*, vc. (1970); *The Tower of Remoteness*, cl., pf. (1978); *Maninya II*, str. qt. (1982); *10 Little Duets*, 2 high instr. (1982); *Marimba Dances*, marimba (1982); *Maninya III*, wind quintet (1985); *Maninya IV*, cl. (or bcl.), tb., marimba (1985–6).

PIANO: *Monos II* (1970); *5 Little Piano Pieces* (1976); *Kumari* (1980–1); *Etymalong* (1984).

Edwards, Sian (*b* West Chiltington, Sussex, 1959). Eng. conductor. Won first Leeds cond. comp. 1984. Guest cond. of major Brit. and Amer. orchs. Opera début, Scottish Opera, Glasgow 1986 (Weill's *Rise and Fall of the City of Mahagonny*). Glyndebourne début 1987; GTO 1988; CG début 1988, first woman to cond. opera there. Cond. f.p. of Turnage's *Greek*, Munich 1988. ENO début 1990, mus. dir. 1993–5.

Edwards, Terry (*b* London, 1939). Eng. chorusmaster. Prof. début as bass in Prom. concert chorus, 1966. Bass, then manager, John Alldis Choir and Schütz Choir, 1970–86. Founder and dir. London Voices from 1973; founder and art. dir. Electric Phoenix from 1978; art. dir. London Sinfonietta Voices and Chorus from 1980. Chorusmaster for Solti in Verdi perfs. in Chicago 1987–9. Chorus dir. Royal Opera, CG, 1992–2004.

EFDSS. *English Folk Dance and Song Society.

Egdon Heath. Orch. work, Op.47, by Holst, comp. 1927 and inspired by the Dorset landscape described as 'Egdon Heath' in Thomas Hardy's *The Return of the Native* (1878). Sub-titled 'Homage to Thomas Hardy'. Commissioned by NY SO which gave f.p. 1928. F.p. in England, Cheltenham 1928, cond. Holst, and London 10 days later (all these perfs. were in Feb.).

Egk, (Mayer) **Werner** (*b* Auchsesheim, Bavaria, 1901; *d* Inning, Bavaria, 1983). Ger. composer and conductor. Cond. for Bavarian radio 1930–3 and at Berlin State Opera 1937–41. Dir., Berlin Hochschule für Musik 1950–3. Very active on behalf of performing rights, etc. Controversial figure, his opera *Peer Gynt* being banned by Nazis because of its satire on régime, but he wrote mus. for Berlin Olympic Games 1936 and was head of the Ger. Union of Composers 1941–5. Colouristic and rhythmical features of his work derive from admiration for Stravinsky. Works incl.:

OPERAS: *Columbus* (1933 radio, 1942 stage); *Die Zaubergeige* (1935, rev. 1954); *Peer Gynt (1938); *Circe* (1945, rev. 1966 as *17 Tage und 4 Minuten*); *Irische Legende (after Yeats, 1955, rev. 1970); *Der Revisor* (after Gogol's The *Government Inspector, 1957); *Die Verlobung in San Domingo* (1963).

BALLETS: *Joan von Zarissa* (1940); *Abraxas* (1947–8); *Ein Sommertag* (1950); *Die chinesische Nachtigall* (1953); *Casanova in London* (1969).

ORCH.: *Geigenmusik*, vn. and orch. (1936); *Olympische Festmusik* (1936); *Französische Suite* (after Rameau, 1949); *Variations on a Caribbean Theme* (1959); *Orchestra Sonata No.2* (1969); *Spiegelzeit* (1979).

VOICE & ORCH.: *Variations on an Old Viennese Song*, coloratura sop. (for singing-lesson scene in *Il barbiere di Siviglia*) (1938); *La Tentation de Saint Antoine*, mez., str. qt. (1947, rev. for mez., str. qt., str. 1952); *Chanson et Romance*, coloratura sop. (1953).

CHORAL: *Furchtlosigkeit und Wohlwollen*, oratorio (1931, rev. 1959); *Mein Vaterland* (1937).

Egmont. Ov. and 9 items of incidental mus., Op.84, by Beethoven to Goethe's historical drama about the Flemish aristocrat Egmont who defied Philip of Spain and was beheaded in 1567. Comp. 1809–10.

Egorov, Yuri (b Kazan, 1954; d Amsterdam, 1988). Russ. pianist. Won prize at Long–Thibaud comp., Paris, 1971, 3rd prize Moscow Tchaikovsky comp. 1974. Amer. début 1978. Settled in Holland. Some recordings.

eguale (It.). Equal. So *egualità*, *egualezza*, equality; *egualmente*, equally. *voci eguali*, *equal voices.

Egyptian Helen, The (Strauss). See *Ägyptische Helena, Die*.

Ehrling, Sixten (b Malmö, 1918; d NY, 2005). Swed. conductor and pianist. Opera début as cond., Stockholm Royal Opera 1940, concert début Göteborg 1942. Prin. cond. Stockholm Royal Opera 1953–70. CG début 1960. Cond. Detroit SO 1963–73. NY Met 1973–7 (first Met. Ring for 78 years). Mus. adv. Denver SO 1978–85, art. adv. San Antonio SO 1985–8.

Eighteen-Twelve (1812). Concert-ov., Op.49, by Tchaikovsky, comp. 1880, commemorating Napoleon's retreat from Moscow in 1812 and incorporating *La Marseillaise* and the Tsarist nat. anthem. Orig. idea was for perf. in a Moscow square with large orch., military band, cath. bells, and cannon fire. Sometimes still perf. with cannon (esp. at Royal Albert Hall popular Tchaikovsky evenings).

eight-foot. Term in org. mus. for sound of normal pitch, the lowest pipe of normal pitch being theoretically 8′ in length.

eighth note. The quaver in Amer. terminology.

Eight Songs for a Mad King (Maxwell Davies). See *Songs for a Mad King, Eight*.

Eimert, Herbert (b Bad Kreuznach, 1897; d Cologne, 1972). Ger. composer and theorist. Worked for Cologne Radio 1927–33 and 1945–65. Mus. critic *Kölnische Zeitung* 1936–45. Founder-dir., EMS, Cologne, 1951–62. Co-ed. *Die Reihe* 1955–62. Prof. and dir. EMS, Cologne Hochschule für Musik 1965–71. Assoc. with Stockhausen and Ger. *avant-garde* in propounding theories of elecs. Works incl. 2 str. qts. (1925, 1944); *Tanzmusik*, sax., fl., mechanical instr. (1926); *Glockenspiel*, tape (1953); and other works on tape. Author of textbooks on atonality, 12-note technique, and elec. music.

Eine kleine Nachtmusik (Mozart). See *Kleine Nachtmusik, Eine*.

Einem, Gottfried von (b Berne, 1918, d Oberndürnbach, 1996). Austrian composer. Chorus coach Berlin State Opera and at Bayreuth 1938–43; resident comp. and mus. adv. Dresden State opera 1944. One of Salzburg Fest. administrators 1948–66; lect., Vienna Konzerthaus Gesellschaft 1946–66; prof. of comp., Vienna Hochschule für Musik 1965–72. Essentially a tonal composer, Einem had considerable success in the opera house where his melodic gifts and command of colour were well deployed. Works incl.:

OPERAS: *Dantons Tod (1944–6); *Der* *Prozess (1950–2); *Der Zerrissene* (1961–4); *Der Besuch der alten Dame* (The *Visit of the Old Lady, 1970); *Kabale und Liebe* (1970–5); *Jesu Hochzeit* (1978–9); *Prinz Chocolat* (1982–3); *Tulifant* (1990).

BALLETS: *Prinzessin Turandot* (1942–3); *Rondo vom goldenen Kalb* (1950); *Glück, Tod und Traum* (1953); *Medusa* (1957).

ORCH.: *Capriccio* (1943); *Concerto for Orch.* (1943); *Meditations* (1954); pf. conc. (1955); *Symphonische Szenen* (1956); *Ballade* (1957); *Dance-Rondo* (1959); *Philadelphia Symphony* (1960); *Nachtstück* (1960); vn. conc. (1966–7); *Hexameron* (1969); *Bruckner Dialog* (1971); *Wiener-Symphonie* (1976); *Ludi Leopoldini* (1980).

CHORAL: *Hymnus an Goethe*, cont., ch., orch. (1949); *Von der Liebe*, high v., orch. (1961); *Kammergesänge* (1965); *Rosa mystica*, bar., orch. (1972); and songs.

CHAMBER MUSIC: vn. sonata (1949); 2 pf. sonatinas (1947); 3 str. qts. (1975, 1977, 1980); solo vn. sonata (1975); wind quintet (1976).

Ein' feste Burg (A Safe Stronghold). Luther's setting of Ps.46 in his own trans.; tune adapted by him from a plainsong melody. Quoted by several composers, e.g. in Meyerbeer's *Les Huguenots*, Mendelssohn's *Reformation Sym.*, and Wagner's *Kaisermarsch*.

Einstein, Alfred (b Munich, 1880; d El Cerrito, Calif., 1952). Ger. scholar and writer (Amer. cit. 1945). Ed. *Zeitschrift für Musikwissenschaft* 1918–33; mus. critic *Münchner Post* 1919–27, *Berliner Tageblatt* 1927–33. Ed. 9th–11th edns. Riemann's *Musiklexikon* (1919, 1922, 1929). Lived in London and It. 1933–9; settled in USA 1939. Prof. of mus., Smith Coll., Northampton, Mass., 1939, later teaching at other Amer. univs. Rev. Köchel's Mozart catalogue 1937. Books incl. *History of Music* (1917, and many later edns.), *Gluck* (1936), *Mozart, his character, his work* (1945), *The Italian Madrigal* (1949), *Schubert* (1951). No relation to the physicist Albert Einstein.

Einstein on the Beach. Opera in 4 acts and 5 'knee plays' (intermezzos) by Philip *Glass and Robert Wilson to a lib. ('spoken texts') by C. Knowles, L. Childs, and S. M. Johnson. Comp. 1974–5. Prod. Avignon 1976, NY Met 1976, Stuttgart 1989.

einstimmig (Ger.). One-voiced, i.e. for one part.

Eis (Ger.). The note E♯.

Eisenberg, Maurice (*b* Königsberg, 1902; *d* NY, 1972). Ger.-Amer. cellist and teacher. Baltimore. Début with Philadelphia Orch. 1916, later becoming its prin. cellist until 1919, when he joined NYSO. Went to Eur. 1927. Member of Menuhin Trio. Founder and art. dir. London Int. Violoncello Centre. Prof. of vc., École Normale, Paris, 1929–39, Juilliard Sch. from 1964.

Eisis (Ger.). The (theoretical) note E♯♯.

Eisler, Hanns (*b* Leipzig, 1898; *d* Berlin, 1962). Ger. composer. His Marxist beliefs led him from 1927 to a more 'popular' style, and he wrote political marching-songs, chs., and th. mus. in collab. with Brecht. Exiled in 1933, he worked in Paris, London, Copenhagen, and USA, settling in Hollywood 1938 where he taught at the Univ. of S. Calif. and worked on films with Chaplin. He wrote (in Eng.) the book *Composing for the Films* (1947). McCarthy drive against Communists in 1947 led to a deportation order. He returned to Vienna and in 1949 settled in (East) Berlin, organizing workers' choirs and writing popular songs (incl. the DDR anthem). Nevertheless many of his comps. were in advanced 12-note technique. Works incl. 600 songs, mus. for 40 plays and over 40 films. The following have words by Brecht: *Die Massnahme* (1930); *Deutsche Sinfonie* (1935–9); *Lenin-Requiem* (1937); *Die Teppichweber von Kujan-Bulak* (1957); *Solidaritätslied* (1930); *Kinderlieder* (1951); *Die Mutter* (Gorky and Brecht, 1931); *Die Rundköpfe und die Spitzköpfe* (1934–6); *Galileo Galilei* (1946); *Die Gesichte der Simone Machard* (1946); *Schweyk im zweiten Weltkrieg* (1957).

Also *Kleine Sinfonie* (1932); 5 *Orchestral Pieces* (1938); *Chamber Symphony* (1940); Str. Qt. (1937); *Nonet* (1939); *Theme and Variations* for pf. (1940); septet (variations on Amer. nursery songs) (1941); pf. quintet (1944); septet No.2 (1947); pf. sonatas (1924 and 1943); *Ernste Gesänge* (bar. and orch.) (1962).

Eisteddfod (Welsh, 'Session', from *eistedd*, 'to sit'. Plural *Eisteddfodau*). The nat. Welsh gathering of bards and celebration of Welsh language and culture, dating in its present form from 1817, though it is said to date back, in one form or another, as far as the 7th cent., with a suspen-

sion throughout the entire 18th cent. and a few years before and after it. It now takes place annually (in Aug.) alternately in towns in N. and S. Wales. Degrees conferred on musicians by Gorsedd Beirdd Ynys Prydain (Throne of Bards of the Isle of Britain) are *Cerdd Ofydd* (Music Ovate), *Cerddor* (Musician), and *Pencerdd* (Chief Musician). Many local *Eisteddfodau* exist in the form of competitive fests. An int. *Eisteddfod*, at which choirs and dancers from all over the world compete, has been held annually in Llangollen since 1947.

Eitner, Robert (*b* Breslau, 1832; *d* Templin, Berlin, 1905). Ger. musicologist and composer. Settled in Berlin 1853 as teacher, and gave concerts of his own comps. 1857–9. Began research into 16th- and 17th-cent. works. Prin. achievement, begun 1882, was his *Biographisch-bibliographisches Quellen-Lexikon der Musiker und Musikgelehrten* (10 vols., 1900–4). Wrote opera *Judith* and a pf. fantasia on themes from *Tristan und Isolde*.

Ek, Gunnar (*b* Åsarum, 1900; *d* Lund, 1981). Swed. composer, organist, and cellist. Cellist in Stockholm film industry orch. 1928–37. Composer of syms., *Swedish Fantasy* for orch., pf. conc., and *Doomsday Cantata*.

Elder, Mark (Philip) (*b* Hexham, 1947). Eng. conductor and bassoonist. Chorister, Canterbury Cath. Mus. staff, Wexford fest. 1969–70. Ass. to R. *Leppard at Glyndebourne 1970 and chorusmaster 1970–2. Début with RLPO, 1971. Australian Opera 1972–4; ENO 1974, becoming ass. cond.; mus. dir. 1979–93; CG 1976; Glyndebourne 1995. Cond. f. Brit. stage p. of Busoni's *Doctor Faustus* (ENO 1986). Bayreuth, 1981. Mus. dir. Rochester PO 1989–94; prin. guest cond. CBSO 1992–2000. Prin. cond. Hallé Orch. from 2000. CBE 1989.

electric action. Means of permitting air to enter an org. pipe by electrical device, after key has been depressed.

electric guitar. *Guitar, used in pop groups or jazz bands, connected by wire to electrical apparatus which amplifies or modifies the sound. Used in Tippett's *The Knot Garden*, Stockhausen's *Gruppen*, and Boulez's *Domaines*.

electric musical instruments. Instrs. in which the use of elec. devices such as valves and photocells determines or affects the actual sound of the note prod. Before the full-scale development of *electronic music several electric instr. were pioneered. Chief among these were the *sphaerophon, the *theremin, the *trautonium, the *ondes Martenot, the *hellertion, the *electronde, and the *rhythmicon.

electric organ. Organs of various makes (most notably by the Hammond Instr. Co. of Chicago) which work on an electro-magnetic principle. Their tone is prod. not from pipes but by means of rotating discs with electro-magnetic pick-ups. They are popular as domestic instr.

Electrification of the Soviet Union, The. Opera in 2 acts by Nigel Osborne to lib. by Craig Raine based on B. Pasternak's novel *The Last Summer* and his poem *Spectorsky*. Comp. 1986–7. Prod. Glyndebourne 1987.

electrochord. Trade name of elec. instr. resembling a pf., in which the str. are set vibrating by hammers. There is no soundboard, vibrations being picked up electrically and amplified through a loudspeaker. Variations of tone-quality and vol. can be controlled.

electrofonic violin. Semi-elec. instr. developed in 1938 by Marshall Moss, leader of the Nat. SO, Washington, and William Bartley, an engineer. The vn., which has no sound-board, is played in the usual way, the mechanically-prod. vibrations being picked up by electro-magnets or a microphone and amplified through a loudspeaker. Similar instr., and a vc., was developed by Vierling, and there is a 5-string electric vc. by Karapetov.

electronde. Elec. instr. developed by Martin Taubman in 1933. On similar lines to *theremin, but by pressing a switch at the same time as moving his hand over the antenna, the player can obtain a staccato effect. It also enables playing of rapid passages.

electronic music. Mus. prod. by elec. means, the resulting sounds being recorded on tape. At first the term applied strictly to sounds synthesized electronically, to differentiate from *musique concrète*, which was assembled from normal mus. and everyday sounds. But by now it covers both groups. Attempts to produce elec. sounds began in the USA and Canada in the 1890s. Early in the 20th cent., experiments were made in Ger. by Fischinger; and in USSR in the 1930s elec. mus. was prod. by the use of photo-electric techniques rather than by oscillator. In fact, the development of elec. mus. has proceeded step by step with the invention of equipment: telephone, loudspeaker, microphone, tape, film sound-track, oscillator, gramophone recording, etc. For composers, an important milestone was reached with experiments at Bonn Univ. in 1949–50 followed by a public perf. at Darmstadt in 1951. The first elec. mus. studio was est. 1951 by W. Ger. Radio, Cologne, dir. by Herbert *Eimert. Other studios were set up in Milan, Tokyo, London, Warsaw, Brussels, Munich, Eindhoven, Paris, and at Columbia Univ., NY.

In the 1950s the comp. of elec. works was a slow and laborious business, chiefly because of the comparatively primitive equipment in the early studios. A comp. consisting of hundreds of predetermined and separately recorded sounds which would last a few minutes could take weeks to assemble on the final tape. The equipment in the early studios generally comprised: (a) *sine-tone generators*. Sine-tones are pure sounds which have no harmonics and are on a single frequency of even dynamic level. To build a complex tone at least 8 generators were needed.

(b) *white sound generator*. White sound comprises all audible frequencies sounding together. (c) *square wave generator*. Square waves are richly harmonic and produce contrasts to sine-tones. (d) *filters*. Devices which, as their name implies, can 'filter' sound, or extract a single sine-tone from the white sound. Filters are classified according to their frequency-response characteristics, i.e. low-pass, high-pass, band-pass, and band-stop. For example, the band-pass filter passes only the sound-waves within a specified band of frequencies grouped round a centre frequency. (e) *ring modulator*. Used to combine several sound signals so that the sound output comprises the sums and differences of all the input-frequency components. (f) *variable speed tape recorders*. Varying speeds of playing the tape are used to speed up or slow down specific effects. (g) *dynamic suppressor*. A device which allows signals to be cut out below a selected level of dynamics, thus introducing a 'chance' element.

Among the most celebrated elec. pieces composed in the 1950s were Eimert's *Fünf Stücke*, Stockhausen's *Gesang der Jünglinge* (which incl. a boy's v., fragmented and superimposed upon itself, thereby creating a bridge with *musique concrète*), Krenek's *Spiritus Intelligentiae Sanctus*, Berio's *Mutazioni*, and Maderna's *Notturno*. But it should be remembered that in 1939–42 John *Cage's first 3 *Imaginary Landscapes* incl. the use of records played at different speeds, audio oscillators, and an amplified wire coil. The first public concert of elec. mus. was given by *Ussachevsky and *Luening in Museum of Modern Art, NY, on 28 Oct. 1953.

Elec. mus. was revolutionized in the 1960s by the invention of voltage-controlled sound *synthesizers*, especially the model developed in 1964–5 by the American Robert A. *Moog. This instr. dispensed with the drudgery of tape-splicing and cutting. It not only presented composers with a complete spectrum of new sounds, but could be made to play itself in a remarkable variety of sounds which could be recurrent or otherwise, as required. By the fitting of a control device known as a *sequencer*, the synthesizer can be used by a composer to memorize a long and complicated mus. compilation and play it 'live' without recording or tape-editing. Because of the synthesizer's astonishing imitative qualities, its use has been commercialized and vulgarized, but its potentiality as a serious instr. is still being explored and awaits a Wagner to exploit it to the full. Its main working principle, greatly oversimplified, is that the oscillators used as sound sources are also used to 'control' each other. Some synthesizers have a kbd., often with its own tuned oscillator, or set to act as a voltage control.

The sequencer is a small variety of the other revolutionary device also introduced in the 1960s, *digital computer synthesis*. Control by digital computer means that the equipment the composer uses is supplied with a 'memory'. For example, a work comp., or 'programmed', for voltage-controlled equipment by means of punched paper tape has an intrinsic major problem in that the system has no way of storing information until it is needed; everything must be supplied in detail each time it is required. The computer memorizes all this information. The disadvantages of a computer are those inherent in 'programming', and it remains to be seen whether a supreme work of art will evolve by this system. The advantages of elec. mus. for th., radio, and film incidental mus. are obvious, and so far it is in these fields that the best results have been achieved.

Notation of elec. mus. obviously bears no relation to conventional mus. notation, and since the principal feature of an elec. work is that it is predetermined and mechanically produced, notation as a guide to performers is unnecessary. But 'live' elec. mus. is a developing art-form, and graphic directions in pitch (frequency) etc. are provided in 'realization' scores which provide all

Dobrowolski: *Music for Magnetic Tape No. 1*

MUZYKA NA TASME MAGNETOFONOWA Nr 1

ANDRZEJ DOBROWOLSKI (1963)

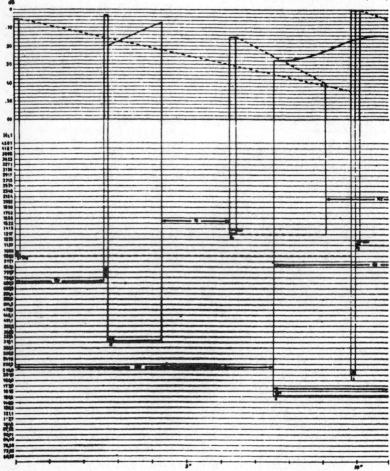

the technical data necessary to reproduce the piece. 'Representational' scores, for the score reader, are slightly less fearsome. An illustration of a typical elec. score or graph will give the reader a better idea of what is involved (see p. 224).

Among composers who have prod. elec. works are: Cage, Berio, Stockhausen, Wuorinen, Blacher, Boulez, Babbitt, Pousseur, Badings, Varèse, Davidovsky, Ligeti, Takemitsu, Penderecki, and Xenakis.

Interested readers who wish for fuller and more technical information than can be provided here are referred to Reginald Smith Brindle's *The New Music* (London, 1975), to which this entry acknowledges its indebtedness, and to Tristram Carey's *Illustrated Compendium of Musical Technology* (London, 1992). See also *computers in music*.

electrophone. Term for mus. instr. which produce sound by electronic means, either by oscillation or by electromagnetic or electrostatic methods. Does not cover instr. in which tone is conventionally produced and then electronically modified (e.g. electric guitar, piano, double bass). Classification added to four devised by C. Sachs and E. M. von Hornbostel and pubd. in *Zeitschrift für Ethnologie*, 1914, i.e. *aerophones, *chordophones, *idiophones, and *membranophones.

elegia, elegiaco (It.). *Elegy, elegiac.

elegy, élégie (Fr.). A song of lament for the dead or for some melancholy event, or an instr. comp. with that suggestion, such as Elgar's *Elegy for Strings* and Fauré's *Élégie*.

Elegy for Young Lovers. Opera in 3 acts by Henze to lib. (in Eng.) by Auden and Kallman (Ger. trans. by Ludwig Landgraf). Comp. 1959–61. Prod. Schwetzingen 1961, Glyndebourne 1961 (Act III, Sc.7 and 8 omitted), NY (Juilliard Sch.) 1965.

Elektra. Opera in 1 act by R. Strauss to lib. by Hofmannsthal based on Sophocles' *Electra*. Comp. 1906–8. Prod. Dresden 1909, NY and London 1910.

elevatio (Lat.), **elevation** (Eng.). Mus. (choral or organ) perf. during the Elevation of the Host in the RC Church.

Elgar, (Sir) **Edward** (William) (*b* Broadheath, Worcester, 1857; *d* Worcester, 1934). Eng. composer and cond. He was the son of a mus.-shop proprietor in Worcester who was also an organist, pf.-tuner, and teacher. He showed an early aptitude for mus., learning the org., vn., and other instr. He hoped, on leaving school at 15, to go to Leipzig Cons. but his father could not afford to send him, so after a brief spell in a solicitor's office, he helped his father in the shop and became his ass. organist at St George's RC Church, Worcester. Soon he was playing the vn. in several local orchs. or chamber groups and became cond. of several. With his brothers and friends he formed a wind quintet, for which he comp. several works. His first comps. had been written during childhood, incl. mus. for a play written and prod. by the Elgar children, *The Wand of Youth*, which he adapted as 2 orch. suites in 1907–8. In 1877 he went to London for vn. lessons from Pollitzer but abandoned them when he realized he would not become a virtuoso. He played in the 2nd vns. in the 3 Choirs Fest. orch. at Worcester in 1878. The following year he became bandmaster at the county lunatic asylum at Powick where members of the staff played weekly for dances. Elgar made several arrs. of operatic arias for concerts there and also comp. a series of quadrilles. In 1882 he joined the 1st vns. in a Birmingham orch. cond. by W. Stockley who incl. Elgar's *Sérénade mauresque* in a concert in 1883. For the next 6 years, until his marriage in 1889, Elgar was in demand locally in many mus. capacities but he was unknown outside the Midlands apart from a perf. of his *Sevillana* at a Crystal Palace concert in May 1884. After his marriage to a general's daughter in 1889, Elgar gave up his work in Malvern and Worcester and went to London, but met with no success there. He returned to Malvern a year later to resume his teaching and other activities. In the meantime, however, the 1890 3 Choirs Fest. at Worcester had commissioned a work from him, the concert-ov. *Froissart*. In 1893 he comp. a secular cantata, *The Black Knight*, which was the first of a series of choral works taken up by the great Midlands choral socs. Its successors were *King Olaf* (1896), *The Light of Life* (1896), and *Scenes from the Bavarian Highlands* (1896). For Queen Victoria's Diamond Jubilee in 1897 Elgar comp. an *Imperial March* which *Manns cond. at the Crystal Palace and which the Queen requested should be incl. in the State Concert marking the Jubilee. Its success led to a commission from the Leeds Fest., the result being the large-scale cantata *Caractacus* (1898). At this time, Elgar was still earning his living as a vn. teacher; his first large-scale London success came in 1899 when *Richter cond. the f.p. of the *Variations on an Original Theme (Enigma)*, one of Elgar's greatest and best-known works. A few months later Clara Butt sang the *Sea Pictures* at the Norwich Fest. Commissioned to write a big choral work for the 1900 Birmingham Fest., Elgar, a Catholic, chose to set Newman's poem *The Dream of Gerontius*. The f.p. was a failure, but the worth of the mus. was recognized and two Düsseldorf perfs. followed, after the 2nd of which Richard Strauss hailed Elgar as the foremost Eng. composer of the day. From that day there developed an Elgar vogue on the Continent, and several conds. such as Weingartner, Strauss, Steinbach, and Busoni incl. his works in their programmes. The neglect of the previous 25 years in Eng. was forgotten (though not by Elgar) overnight as he became the most talked-about composer of the day. From 1901 until 1914 were the years of greatest acclaim for Elgar in his lifetime, and he responded with a succession of splendid works incl. the *Cockaigne* ov., the oratorios *The Apostles* and *The Kingdom*, 2 syms., a vn. conc. (for *Kreisler), the *Introduction and Allegro* for str., the choral ode *The*

Music Makers, and the symphonic study *Falstaff*. The 1st Sym. (1908) in particular had an astonishing initial success, being perf. 100 times in just over a year in cities as far apart as Manchester, Vienna, St Petersburg, Rome, and Budapest. However, the work which had made him a household name was No.1 of a set of *Pomp and Circumstance* Marches, f.p. 1901. The splendid tune of the trio section caught the ear of King Edward VII who suggested that it should be set to words. When in 1902 it emerged in the *Coronation Ode* as *Land of Hope and Glory* it soon became clear that Elgar had comp. an alternative nat. anthem. Elgar was knighted in 1904 at age 47, and in 1911 became a member of the OM. He visited the USA to cond. his own works and spent several periods in It. From 1905 to 1908 he was Peyton Prof. of Mus., Birmingham Univ. He was appointed cond. of the LSO for 1911–12 and in 1912 moved from Hereford to a large house in Hampstead.

During the 1914–18 war Elgar wrote several patriotic works, including the recitation with orch. *Carillon*, the symphonic prelude *Polonia*, and the Binyon settings *The Spirit of England*. He also wrote incidental mus. for a children's play, *The Starlight Express*, and a ballet *The Sanguine Fan*. In 1918–19 he wrote 3 chamber works, a vn. sonata, str. qt., and pf. quintet, and a vc. conc. These were to be his last major works. In 1920 his wife died and for the last 14 years of his life he wrote hardly anything that was not concocted from earlier sketches. In this last period he prod. incidental mus. for 2 plays, *Arthur* and *Beau Brummel*, a 5th *Pomp and Circumstance* march, the *Nursery Suite*, and the *Severn Suite*. He was at work on a Ben Jonson opera, *The Spanish Lady*, and a 3rd sym. at the time of his death. In 1923 he returned to live in Worcestershire and often appeared throughout the country as cond. of his own works. He became Master of the King's Musick in 1924 and was created a baronet in 1931. He was the first great composer to realize the possibilities of the gramophone and from 1914 to 1933 made many recordings of his own mus. which are important historical documents, the most celebrated being that of the vn. conc. made in 1932 with the 16-year-old *Menuhin. KCVO 1928. GCVO 1933.

Elgar's greatness as a composer lies in his ability to combine nobility and spirituality of utterance with a popular style. Side by side with his large-scale works are dozens of lighter pieces distinguished by melodic charm and fine craftsmanship. Learning entirely by the practical experiences of his youth, he became one of the supreme masters of the orch., but his command of choral effects in his masterpiece *The Dream of Gerontius* is no less wonderful. His harmonic language derives from Schumann and Brahms coloured by the Wagnerian chromaticism endemic to his generation, the whole being lightened by a gracefulness akin to Bizet and Saint-Saëns. Like his personality, his mus. veers from extrovert warmth and geniality to a deep introspective melancholy. His prin. works are:

THEATRE (incl. recitations): Incidental mus., funeral march, and song for *Grania and Diarmid* (Yeats and Moore), Op.42 (1901); *The *Crown of India*, masque, Op.66 (1902–12); *Carillon*, Op.75, reciter, orch. (1914); incidental mus. for *The *Starlight Express* (Blackwood and Pearn), Op.78 (1915); *Une voix dans le désert*, Op.77, reciter, sop., orch. (1915); *The *Sanguine Fan*, ballet, Op.81 (1917); *Le drapeau belge*, Op.79, reciter, orch. (1917); incidental mus. to *Arthur* (Binyon) (1923); incidental mus. to *Beau Brummel* (Matthews) (1928).

ORCH.: *Froissart*, Op.19 (1890); *Serenade* for str. in E minor, Op.20 (1892); *Sursum Corda*, Op.11 (1894); *Imperial March*, Op.32 (1897); *Enigma Variations*, Op.36 (1898–9); *Pomp and Circumstance Marches*, Op.39, No.1 in D major, No.2 in A minor (1901), No.3 in C minor (1904), No.4 in G major (1907), No.5 in C major (1930); *Cockaigne*, Op.40 (1900–1); *In the South (Alassio)*, Op.50 (1904); *Introduction and Allegro* for str., Op.47 (1905); *The *Wand of Youth Suites* Nos. 1 and 2, Opp. 1a and 1b (1907 and 1908 respectively); sym. No.1 in A♭ major, Op.55 (1907–8); *Elegy* for str., Op.58 (1909); vn. conc. in B minor, Op.61 (1909–10); *Romance* for bn., Op.62 (1910); sym. No.2 in E♭ major, Op.63 (1903–11); *Coronation March*, Op.65 (1911); *Suite, Crown of India*, Op.66 (1912); *Falstaff*, Op.68 (1902–13); *Sospiri* for str., hp., org., Op.70 (1914); *Polonia*, Op.76 (1915); vc. conc. in E minor, Op.85 (1918–19); *Empire March* (1924); *Severn Suite*, Op.87, brass band (1930), for orch. (1932); *Nursery Suite* (1931).

VOICES & ORCH.: *The *Black Knight*, cantata, Op.25 (1889–93); *Scenes from the *Bavarian Highlands*, Op.27 (1896); *The *Light of Life (Lux Christi)*, oratorio, Op.29 (1895–6, rev. 1899); *Scenes from the Saga of *King Olaf*, cantata, Op.30 (1894–6); *The *Banner of St George*, ballad, Op.33 (1896–7); *Caractacus*, cantata, Op.35 (1898); *The *Dream of Gerontius*, Op.38 (1899–1900); *Sea Pictures*, songcycle, mez., orch., Op.37 (1897–9); *Coronation Ode*, Op.44 (1902); *The *Apostles*, oratorio, Op.49 (1901–3); *The *Kingdom*, oratorio, Op.51 (1901–6); 3 Songs with orch., Op.59 (1909–10); *The *Music Makers*, choral ode, Op.69 (1902–12); *The *Spirit of England*, Op.80 (1915–17).

PART-SONGS & CHURCH MUSIC: *Ave, verum corpus*, Op.2, No.1 (1887); *Ecce sacerdos magnus*, ch., org. (1888); *My love dwelt in a northern land* (1889); *Spanish Serenade*, Op.23 (1891, with orch. 1892); *Te Deum and Benedictus*, Op.34 (1897); *The Sword Song*, from *Caractacus* (1898); *To her beneath whose steadfast star* (1899); *Weary Wind of the West* (1902); 5 *Part-Songs from the Greek Anthology*, Op.45 (1902); *Evening Scene* (1905); 4 *Part-Songs*, Op.53 (1907); *The Reveille*, Op.54 (1907); *Angelus*, Op.56 (1909); *Go, Song of Mine*, Op.57 (1909); *O hearken thou*, offertory, Op.64 (Coronation 1911); *Great is the Lord* (Psalm 48), Op.67 (1912); *Give Unto the Lord* (Psalm 29), Op.74 (1914); 2 *Choral Songs*, Op.71 (1914); *Death on the Hills*, Op.72 (1914); 2 *Choral Songs*, Op.73 (1914); *The Wanderer* and *Zut, zut, zut* (1923).

CHAMBER MUSIC: *Promenades* for wind quintet (1878); *Harmony Music*, wind quintet (1879);

Allegretto on GEDGE, vn., pf. (1885); **Salut d'Amour*, Op.12, for pf. solo, for vn. and pf., for orch., and in many other arrs. (1888–9); *Liebesahnung*, vn., pf. (1889); *La Capricieuse*, Op.17, vn., pf. (1891); *Very Easy Melodious Exercises in the 1st Position*, Op.22, for vn. (1892); *Études caractéristiques*, Op.24, vn. (1882–92); *Chanson de Nuit, Chanson de Matin*, Op.15, Nos. 1 and 2, vn., pf. (later orch.) (No.1 pubd. 1897, No.2 pubd. 1899); vn. sonata in E minor, Op.82 (1918); str. qt. in E minor, Op.83 (1918); pf. quintet, Op.84 (1918–19).

SHORT PIECES FOR SMALL ORCH.: *Cantique*, Op.3 (1912 orch. of 1897 organ solo *Adagio solenne*); *Rosemary* (1914 orch. of 1882 pf. solo); **Sevillana*, Op.7 (1884); *Salut d'Amour*, Op.12 (1888); 3 *Bavarian Dances*, Op.27 (Nos. 1, 3, and 6 of *From the Bavarian Highlands*) (orch. 1897); *Minuet*, Op.21 (1899 orch. of 1897 pf. solo); *Chanson de Nuit*; *Chanson de Matin*, Op.15, Nos. 1 and 2 (1901 orch.); *Sérénade lyrique* (1899); *Dream Children*, Op.43 (1902); *Carissima* (1913); *Minuet (Beau Brummel)* (1928); *Mina* (sketched for pf. 1932, orch. 1933).

SOLO SONGS: *Through the long days* (1885); *The Wind at Dawn* (1888); *Queen Mary's Song* (1889); *Like to the Damask Rose* (1893); *Shepherd's Song* (1893); *Rondel* (1894); *After* (1895); *Love Alone Will Stay* (incorporated into *Sea Pictures* as *In Haven*) (1897); *Pipes of Pan* (1900); *In the Dawn*; *Speak, Music* (1902); *Land of Hope and Glory* (1902); *Pleading* (1908); *The Torch*; *The River* (1909–10); *The Fringes of the Fleet* (1917); and many more.

PIANO: *Rosemary (Douce Pensée)* (1882, orch. 1914); *May Song* (1901, orch. 1928); *Concert Allegro*, Op.46 (1901); *Dream Children*, Op.43 (1902); *Skizze* (1903); *In Smyrna* (1905); *Echo's Dance* (from *Sanguine Fan*) (1917); *Sonatina* (1889, rev. 1930); *Adieu* (1932); *Serenade* (1932).

ORGAN: *11 Vesper Voluntaries*, Op.14 (1889–90); Sonata in G major, Op.28 (1895); Sonata No.2, Op.87a (arr. by Atkins of *Severn Suite*) (1932–3).

TRANSCRIPTIONS FOR ORCH.: *J. S. Bach: Fugue in C minor* (Elgar Op.86) f.p. London 1921; *Fantasy in C minor*, f.p. Gloucester 1922; *Handel: Overture in D minor*, f.p. Worcester 1923; *Chopin: Funeral March from Pf. Sonata in B♭ minor*, 1933.

UNCOMPLETED: Sym. No.3, Op.88 (begun c.1932), perf. edn. by A. Payne, f.p. 1998; *The *Spanish Lady*, opera, Op.89 (begun c.1932), perf. vers. by P. M. Young, 1995; pf. conc., Op.90 (sketches date from 1909), perf. edn. by R. Walker, f.p. 1997; *Pomp and Circumstance March No.6*, perf. vers. by A. Payne, f.p. 2006.

Elias, Brian (David) (*b* Bombay, India, 1948). Eng. composer. Works incl. *La Chevelure*, sop., chamber ens. (1967); *ELM*, sop., ten., pf. (1969); 5 *Pieces for Right Hand*, pf. (1969); *Piece*, vc. (1970); *Peroration*, solo sop. (1973); *Proverbs of Hell*, unacc. ch. (1975); *Tzigane*, vn. (1978); *Somnia*, ten., orch. (1979); *At the Edge of Time*, ten., pf. (1982); vn. conc. (1984); *L'Eylah* (1984); *Geranos*, chamber ens. (1985); 5 *Songs to Poems by Irina Ratushinskaya*, mez., orch. (1989); *Hymns to Sts Cosmo and Damian*, counterten., 2 ten., bar., hurdy-gurdy (1991); *Fanfare*, orch. (1993); *Laments*, 6 female vv. (1998); *The*

House that Jack Built, orch. (2001); 3 *Songs* (Christina Rossetti), alto, hp. (2003); *A Talisman*, orch. (2004); *Infida's Song*, mez., pf. (2004).

Elijah (*Elias*). Oratorio, Op.70, by Mendelssohn to text selected from the Bible by Julius Schrubring. For sop., cont., ten., bass, and treble soloists, boys' ch., ch., and orch. Comp. 1846, f.p. Birmingham 1846, Hamburg 1847, NY 1851.

Elisabetta, Regina d'Inghilterra (Elizabeth, Queen of England). Opera in 2 acts by Rossini to lib. by Giovanni Schmidt, after C. Federici's play (1814) based on Sophia Lee's novel *The Recess* (1783–5). Prod. Naples 1815; London 1818. First opera in which Rossini provided orch. acc. for all the recitatives. Ov. is same as for *Aureliano in Palmira* and *Il barbiere di Siviglia*. Comp. for Isabella *Colbran, whom Rossini later married.

Elisir d'amore, L' (The Elixir of Love). Comic opera in 2 acts by Donizetti to lib. by Romani after Scribe's lib. *Le Philtre* for Auber (1831). Prod. Milan 1832, London 1836, NY 1838.

Elizalde, Federico (*b* Manila, 1907; *d* Manila, 1979). Sp. composer, conductor, and pianist. Won first prize as pianist at 14 at Madrid Cons. From 1926 to 1929 was in Eng. where he influenced development of jazz, particularly by his arrangements for a band at the Savoy Hotel 1927–9. Cond., Manila SO, 1930. President, Manila Broadcasting Co., 1948. Comps. incl. vn. conc. (1943); pf. conc. (1947); opera *Paul Gauguin* (1948); *Music for 15 soloists*, etc.

Ella, John (*b* Leicester, 1802; *d* London, 1888). Eng. writer, violinist, and impresario. Dir. of mus. society at London home of Lord Saltoun, 1826–46. Founded and dir. chamber mus. concerts known as the *Musical Union* 1845–80, writing series of analytical notes. Critic of *Morning Post* 1828–42, *Athenaeum* 1831–4, and other journals.

Eller, Heino (*b* Yur'yev (now Tartu), 1887; *d* Tallinn, 1970). Estonian composer. Taught theory and comp. at Tartu mus. sch. 1920–40, prof. of comp. Tallinn Univ. 1940–70. *Tubin was his pupil. Works incl. 3 syms. (1936, 1947, 1962); sym.-poems *Twilight* (1917), *Dawn* (1918), *Nocturnal Sounds* (1920), *Apparitions* (1924), *The Eagle's Flight* (1949), *The Singing Fields* (1951); vn. conc. (1933, rev. 1965); *Sinfonietta*, str. (1965); 4 pf. sonatas (1920, 1938, 1944, 1958); 2 vn. sonatas (1922, 1946); 5 str. qts. (1925, 1930, 1945, 1954, 1959); and nearly 200 short pf. pieces.

Ellington, Duke (Edward Kennedy) (*b* Washington, DC, 1899; *d* NY, 1974). Amer. composer, pianist, and jazz-band leader. One of the most influential figures in the history of jazz. From 1927 to 1932 his band established its fame at the Cotton Club, NY. Later it toured Europe (1933 and 1939), attracting and influencing several composers; though re-formed several times, some of its members remained with Ellington for over 30 years. Among his most celebrated players were Johnny Hodges (sax.), Barney Bigard (cl.), Cootie Williams (tpt.), Lawrence Brown (tb.), and Harry Carney (bar. sax.). Wrote about 6,000 comps., among best known being *Mood Indigo, Solitude, Caravan, Sophisticated Lady, Black and Tan Fantasy, Creole Love Call*, and *Black, Brown, and Beige*.

Ellis, David (*b* Liverpool, 1933). Eng. composer and administrator. Comps. awarded Royal Philharmonic prize, RCM patrons' award, and Morley College opera prize. Joined staff of BBC, Manchester, 1964 with responsibility for BBC Northern SO (now BBC Philharmonic) programmes. Head of Mus., BBC North, 1978–86. Art. dir., Northern Chamber Orch. 1986–94. Works incl.:

OPERA: *Crito*, Op.21 (1963).

ORCH.: sym. No.1, Op.38 (1973), No.2, Op.52 (1995), No.3 (*Images from beyond Infinity*), Op.59 (1998); *Sinfonietta*, Op.13 (1953); vn. conc., Op.22 (1958); pf. conc., Op.27 (1962); *Dance Rhapsody*, Op.28 (1963); *Fanfares and Cadenzas*, Op.31 (1968); *L*, Op.41 (1977); *Contraprovisations (on a Theme by John McCabe)*, Op.51 (1994); *Fantasia (quasi una sonata)*, Op.53 (1996); *Attleborough Tuckets*, Op.65 (2001); *Desinent*, Op.79 (2005).

CHAMBER ORCH.: *Diversions*, Op.39 (1974); *In Nomine* (1963); *Sequentia III (Tenebrae)*, Op.32 (1970); *Circles* (1979); *Capriccio 'The Bear'* (1981); vc. conc., Op.43 (1978, rev. 2004); *Divertimento elegiaco*, Op.54a (2003).

STRING ORCH.: *Diversions on a Theme of Purcell*, Op.16 (1956); *Solus*, Op.37 (1973); *Suite franglaise* (1987); *Sinfonia con variazioni*, Op.49a, bass tuba, str. (1992); *2 Fantasias*, Op.50 (1993); bn. conc., Op.71 (2002).

CHORAL: *Magnificat* and *Nunc Dimittis*, ch., org. (1964); *Psalm 115*, ch., brass, org., Op.33 (1970); *Carols for an Island Christmas*, Op.34, ch., ens. (1971); *Sequentia IV (Visions)*, Op.36, ten., bar., ch., org., perc. (1972); *Sequentia V (Genesis)*, Op.40, ch., orch. (or org.) (1975); *Jubilate (Festival Introit)*, ch., org., bells (1978); *A Distant Horizon*, Op.58, ch., org./pf., brass quintet, bells (1997).

CHAMBER MUSIC: str. trio, Op.9 (1954); wind quintet, Op.17 (1956); sonata for db., Op.42 (1977); str. qt. No.1, Op.45 (1980), No.2, Op.56 (1996), No.3, Op.70 (2002); *Aubade*, hn., pf. (1981); *Two for Six*, sax. qt., Op.55 (1996); *Epiphany Nocturne*, Op.62, tpt., bn., pf. (1999); *Elegiac Variations*, Op.66, recs., va., vc. (2001); *Low Priority*, Op.74, db./vc., pf. (2002); *For One who Listens in Secret*, Op.75, jazz ens., vc., bcl. (2003); *Music in a Bottle*, Op.77, No.1, pf. (2004), No.2, v., 1 instr. (2006).

PIANO: sonatina, Op.2 (1953); sonata, Op.12 (1956); *3-Note Variables*, Op.60 (1998); *Old Willows*, Op.64 (2000).

Ellis [Elsas], **Mary** (*b* NY, 1900; *d* London, 2003). Amer.-born Eng. soprano. Début NY Met 1918. Created Novice in *Suor Angelica* and sang Lauretta in *Gianni Schicchi*. Also sang with Caruso and Chaliapin. Had Broadway success in title-role of Friml's *Rose Marie*, 1924. Settled in Eng., singing in Kern's *Music in the Air* (1933) and Novello's *Glamorous Night* (1935), *The Dancing Years* (1939), and

Arc de Triomphe, based on life of Mary *Garden (1943). Also acted in plays by Coward, Rattigan, and O'Neill. Appeared in TV play at age of 92.

Ellis, Osian (Gwynn) (*b* Ffynnongroew, 1928). Welsh harpist and singer. Member of Melos Ens. Former prin. harpist LSO. Recitals, tours, and recordings. Britten wrote Harp Suite in C, Op.83, for him. Prof. of hp., RAM, 1959–89. CBE 1971.

Ellsworth, Warren (*b* Worcester, Mass., 1950; *d* Houston, 1993). Amer. tenor. Début Houston Opera as bar. (Malatesta in *Don Pasquale*), as ten. Houston 1979 (Prince Paul in *Grande Duchesse de Gérolstein*). Brit. début WNO 1981 and in 1983 sang Parsifal, cond. Goodall; Bayreuth Fest. 1984; CG 1986 (with WNO); ENO (Parsifal). CG (with Royal Opera) 1988. Joined Deutsche Oper, Berlin, 1989, where his roles incl. Don José, Samson, Siegmund, Lohengrin, and Parsifal. Last sang in London 1991.

Elman, Mischa (*b* Talnoye, Russia, 1891; *d* NY, 1967). Russ.-Amer. violinist (Amer. cit. 1923). Child prodigy. Professional début St Petersburg and Berlin 1904, London 1905 (Glazunov conc.). First played in NY 1908, thereafter maintaining brilliant int. reputation. Gave f.p. in Boston, Mass., 1943, of Martinů's 2nd vn. conc., written for him.

Elmendorff, Karl (*b* Düsseldorf, 1891; *d* Hofheim am Taunus, 1962). Ger. cond. Held cond. posts in Munich, Düsseldorf, and Berlin. Bayreuth Fest. 1927–42. Cond. Dresden State Opera, 1942–5, Wiesbaden 1948–56. Cond. f. Dresden p. of Strauss's *Capriccio*, 1944.

Elming, Poul (*b* Ålborg, 1949). Danish tenor. Recital début 1978. Sang bar. roles with Jutland Opera, Århus, 1979–84 and at Royal Opera, Copenhagen, 1984–9. After further studies, made début as ten. Copenhagen 1989 (Parsifal); Bayreuth 1990; CG 1990.

Eloy, Jean-Claude (*b* Mont-Saint-Aignan, nr. Rouen, 1938). Fr. composer. Visited USA 1964 and 1967–9. Worked at EMS, Cologne, 1972. Works incl. *Stèle pour Omar Khayyám*, sop., hp., pf., perc. (1960); *Étude III* (Sym. No.1) (1962); *Equivalences*, 18 instr. (1963); *Poly-chronies* I and II for wind and perc. (1964); *Macles* I/II, 6 groups of instr. (1967); *Faisceaux-Diffractions*, 28 instr. (1970); *Kamakala*, 3 ens., 3 ch. (1971); *Shanti*, 6 solo vv., instrs., elec. (1972–3, rev. as *Vers l'étendue*, orch. 1974); *Kshara-akshara*, sop., ch., 3 orch. groups (1974); *Fluctuante-Immuable*, orch. (1977); *Yo-In* (Reverberations), 4 tapes, perc. (1980).

El Salón México. Orch. work by *Copland based on popular Mexican themes. Comp. 1933–6, f.p. Mexico SO 1937. Also arr. by composer for solo pf.

Elsner, Joseph Xaver (*b* Grottkau, 1769; *d* Warsaw, 1854). Silesian composer. While at Breslau Jesuit Gymnasium 1781–8, played vn. in opera orch. Gave up medicine for mus. 1789. Kapellmeister, Lemberg, 1792–9. Cond. in Warsaw from 1799, in charge of opera until 1824 and becoming dir. of Cons. 1821–30. Taught Chopin. Comp. 20 operas, 8 syms., ballet, concs., etc.

Elwell, Herbert (*b* Minneapolis, 1898; *d* Cleveland, 1974). Amer. composer and critic. Mus. critic, *Cleveland Plain Dealer* 1932–65. Head of comp., Cleveland Inst. 1928–45. Teacher of comp. Oberlin Cons. from 1945. Works incl. ballet *The Happy Hypocrite* (1925), 2 str. qts., *Lincoln: Requiem aeternam* (1947), *Introduction and Allegro* for orch. (1942), etc.

Elwes, Gervase (Cary) (*b* Northampton, 1866; *d* Boston, Mass., 1921). Eng. tenor. Did not become professional musician until 1903, having begun diplomatic career. Soon in demand for *Lieder* recitals and as notable exponent of Evangelist in Bach's *St Matthew Passion* and of Gerontius in Elgar's choral masterpiece which he first sang under Weingartner in 1904. Gave recitals in Ger., partnered by the pianist Fanny Davies. First singer of Vaughan Williams's *On Wenlock Edge* (1909). Sang in f.p. in England of Mahler's *Das Lied von der Erde* (1914). Fund est. in his memory is now the *Musicians' Benevolent Fund.

embellishments. See *ornaments*.

embouchure. (1) In brass and some woodwind playing, the mode of application of the lips, or their relation to the mouthpiece.
(2) (Fr.). The *mouthpiece of a brass instr.

Emerald Isle, The. Posthumous comic opera in 2 acts by Sullivan, begun 1900 and completed by Edward German. Lib. by Basil Hood. Prod. Savoy Th. 1901.

Emmanuel, (Marie François) **Maurice** (*b* Bar-sur-Aube, 1862; *d* Paris, 1938). Fr. composer and scholar. Prof. of mus. history Paris Cons. 1909–36. Authority on Gr. mus., about which he wrote extensively. Comp. 2 operas, 2 syms., str. qt., and suite on popular Gr. airs for vn. and pf.

E moll (Ger.). The key of E minor.

'Emperor' Concerto. Nickname by which Beethoven's pf. conc. No.5 in E♭ major, Op.73, is known in Eng. and USA. Not known when or by whom this title was conferred, but it is not inapt.

'Emperor' Quartet (*Kaiserquartett*). Nickname for Haydn's str. qt. in C major, Op.76 No.3, because the slow movt. is a set of variations on the tune he wrote for the *Emperor's Hymn.

Emperor's Hymn (*Gott erhalte Franz den Kaiser*, i.e. God preserve the Emperor Francis). Tune found in many hymn-books under the name *Austria*. The nat. hymn of Austria from the time of comp. of the tune by Haydn in 1797 to the creation of the Republic in 1918. Thereafter the tune was officially retained, but other words adopted, *Sei gesegnet ohne Ende* (Thine be never-ending blessings) by Ottokar Kernstock.

The orig. words were by Lorenz Leopold Haschka (1749–1827). Haydn, whose instructions were to compose something approaching in merit the Eng. nat. anthem, took a folk melody of his childhood, which probably suggested itself to him as fitting metrically and rhythmically the opening lines, and altered and extended its later part. For the tune in Ger. see *Deutschland über Alles*.

Emperor Waltz (Strauss). See *Kaiser-Walzer*.

Empfindung (Ger.). Feeling, sentiment; hence *empfindungsvoll*, feelingly.

enchaînez (Fr.). Chain together, join up (i.e. next movt. to be played without break).

Enchanted Lake, The (*Volshebnoye ozero*). Symphonic poem by *Lyadov, comp. 1909.

Encina [Enzina], **Juan del** (*b* Salamanca, 1468; *d* Léon, *c*.1530). Sp. composer and poet. Chorister, Salamanca Cath. Served 2nd Duke of Alba, 1492–8, then worked in Rome. Archdeacon of Málaga 1510–12, in Rome 1512–19, then prior of Léon from 1519. Wrote several eclogues (pastoral plays) and a large number of songs for 3 or 4 vv. His *Cancionero*, 1495, was an anthology of plays and poems.

encore (Fr.). Again. In Eng. has been adopted as the word of demand for the repetition of a perf. (properly, perhaps, of the same piece, but often used of a return to the platform to give additional perf., either of the same or another piece). Also used as verb (to encore).

Although a Fr. word, *encore* entered the Eng. language as a corruption of It. *ancora* (with the same meaning), which, from the early 18th cent. onwards, was used by audiences at the It. Opera in London (together with the words *altra volta*, another time). The Fr. use *bis* (Lat., twice; verb *bisser*).

Endless Parade. Work for solo tpt., vib., and str. by *Birtwistle. Comp. 1986–7 and f.p. Zurich May 1987 by Håkan *Hardenberger (tpt.) and the Collegium Musicum, cond. Paul Sacher, who commissioned it. F. London p. 1987.

end-plugged. Term for org. flue pipes with a stopper at the top which lowers their pitch by an octave.

energia (It.). Energy. *energico*, energetic.

Enescu, George [Enesco, Georges] (*b* Liveni-Virnav, Romania, 1881; *d* Paris, 1955). Romanian composer, violinist, and conductor. First public recital as violinist at age 7 in Băile Slănic, now Slănic Moldova. Concert of his works in Paris 1897. Frequent appearances as cond. until 1951—début Bucharest 1898—and as sonata recitalist with Cortot. Amer. début NY 1923. His vn. pupils incl. Menuhin, Grumiaux, and Gitlis. His comps. use Romanian folk-idioms and are also influenced by late romanticism. They incl.: *Œdipe (4-act opera, 1921–32); Sym. No.1 (1905),

No.2 (1912–14), No.3, with ch. and pf. solo (1916–21), No.4 (1934), No.5, ten., ch., orch. (1941); *Symphonie concertante*, vc., orch. (1901); 2 *Romanian Rhapsodies* (1901); 3 vn. sonatas (1897, 1899, 1926); 2 vc. sonatas (1898, 1935); str. octet (1900); 2 pf. sonatas (1924, 1933–5); 2 pf. quintets (1895, 1940); 2 str. qts. (1916–20, 1950–3); 2 pf. qts. (1909, 1943–4); *Chamber symphony*, 12 instr. (1954); and songs.

Enfance du Christ, L' (The Childhood of Christ). Oratorio, Op.25, by Berlioz for soloists, ch., and orch., to text by composer. Comp. 1850–4. F.p. Paris 1854, Manchester 1880.

Enfant et les sortilèges, L' (The Child and the Spells). *Fantaisie lyrique* in 2 parts by Ravel, to lib. by Colette. Comp. 1920–5. Prod. Monte Carlo 1925, San Francisco 1930, Oxford 1958, London, SW 1965, CG 1983, NY Met 1981.

Enfant prodigue, L' (The Prodigal Son). (1) Cantata by Debussy, comp. 1884, for sop., ten., and bar. soloists, ch., and orch. It won Debussy the *Prix de Rome*. F.p. Paris 1884 with acc. for 2 pf. Orch. rev. 1906 and 1908.

(2) Opera by Auber, 1850.

See *Prodigal Son* for Prokofiev ballet and Britten church parable.

En-Gedi (In the wilderness). F. X. Huber's lib. for Beethoven's oratorio *Christus am Ölberge* (1803) was replaced in Eng. by new text by H. Hudson, changing story to that of 'David in the Wilderness' in view of 'objectionable nature' of orig. words.

Engel, Karl (*b* Theiedewiese, 1818; *d* Kensington, 1882). Ger. pianist and writer. Settled London, *c*.1845, where he formed valuable library and coll. of ancient instr. Among his writings are *Introduction to the Study of National Music* (1866) and *Researches into the Early History of the Violin Family* (1883).

Engelstimme (Ger.). Angel-voice. The *vox angelica* stop on the organ.

englisches Horn (Ger.). English horn, i.e. *cor anglais*.

English Bach Festival. Annual series of concerts and operas founded 1963 by Lina *Lalandi, Greek-born harpsichordist and singer. Orig. based at Oxford, but transferred mainly to London 1968. Joint art. dirs. Lalandi and J. A. Westrup 1963–70, Lalandi from 1971. Programmes are based on Bach but widened to incl. operas by Rameau, Handel, Vivaldi, and Rossini. Some of the opera perfs. have been at CG. Stravinsky cond. his own works in 1964. Much contemp. mus. perf., incl. f. Brit. ps. of works by Skalkottas, Xenakis, Stockhausen, Ligeti, Messiaen, Smalley, and Lutyens.

English Baroque Soloists. Ensemble performing with period instruments founded by John Eliot *Gardiner in 1978 and often appearing in company with the Monteverdi Choir. Has made many highly-praised recordings, incl. Bach's B minor Mass and *St Matthew Passion*, Beethoven's *Missa solemnis*, Mozart pf. concs., syms., and *Requiem*, Monteverdi *Vespers*, and Purcell semi-operas. Salzburg Fest. début 1990 (Monteverdi's *Orfeo*).

English Cat, The. Story for singers and instrs. in 2 acts by *Henze to lib. by Edward Bond after Balzac's tale *Peines de cœurs d'une chatte anglaise* (1840). Comp. 1980–3, rev. 1990. Prod. Schwetzingen (in Ger. trans.) 1983, cond. Dennis Russell Davies; Paris 1984, Santa Fe 1985 (first perf. with orig. Eng. text). Rev. vers. prod. Montepulciano 1990, London (GSMD) 1991.

English Chamber Orchestra. Orig. name was Goldsbrough Orch., founded 1948 by Arnold Goldsbrough and Lawrence Leonard to perf. *baroque mus. Present name adopted 1960 when repertory was expanded to cover mus. of all periods written for 'Mozart-sized' ens. Assoc. with *Aldeburgh Fest. from 1961, playing in premières of Britten's *A Midsummer Night's Dream*, *Owen Wingrave*, church parables, and Cello Sym. Has also given f.ps. of works by Maw, Birtwistle, Tavener, Richard Rodney Bennett, etc. No prin. cond. before 1985, but worked closely with Britten, Leppard, Barenboim, Davis, Zukerman, and others. Jeffrey Tate appointed first prin. cond. 1985. Salzburg Fest. début 1987 (cond. Tate). Many recordings. Worldwide tours, incl. Japan, the Americas, Europe, Israel, etc.

English fingering. The (obsolete) 'Eng.' system of marking printed pf. mus. with the composer's or ed.'s suggested *fingering, whereby a cross represented the thumb and the figures 1 to 4 the fingers (as opposed to 'continental' system using 1 for thumb and 2 to 5 for fingers which is in general use today).

English Folk Dance and Song Society. Amalgamation in 1932 of Folk Song Society (founded 1898) and Eng. Folk Dance Soc. (1911), with general aim of preserving songs and dances of Brit. people. H.Q. in Cecil Sharp House, London, where library and archives are housed.

English horn. See *cor anglais*.

English Hymnal, The. Coll. of Eng. hymns and tunes pubd. 1906 (rev. 1933) ed. by Percy Dearmer with *Vaughan Williams as mus. ed. Incl. several hymn tunes by Vaughan Williams and others by his Eng. contemporaries, several being adaptations of folk-songs.

English Lyrics. Title given to 12 sets of songs (74 in all) for v. and pf. by *Parry, all settings of Eng. poetry. 1st set (4 songs) 1881–5, 2nd (5) 1874–85, 3rd (6) 1895, 4th (6) 1885–96, 5th (7) 1876–1901, 6th (6) 1903, 7th (6) 1888–1906, 8th (6) *c*.1904–6, 9th (7) 1908, 10th (6) 1909, 11th (8) 1910–18, 12th (7) various dates, some very early, posth. pubd. 1920. The last 2 sets were selected and ed. by Dr Emily Daymond.

English Madrigal School. First complete edn. of Eng. madrigals, 1588–1624, transcr., scored, and ed. by Dr E. H. *Fellowes and pubd. in 36 vols., 1913–24.

English Music Theatre. Title from 1976 of former English Opera Group, founded by Benjamin Britten, Eric Crozier, and John Piper in 1946 to perf. chamber operas old and new. Closely connected with Britten's operas, but also gave f.ps. of Walton's *The Bear* and Birtwistle's *Punch and Judy*. Has toured abroad widely, incl. USSR (1964). From 1961 administered and financed by CG. Re-formed 1976 under joint dir. of Colin Graham and Steuart Bedford with aim of longer season and to embrace opera, operetta, musicals, and less conventional works, all generalized as 'music theatre'. Ceased to exist 1980.

English National Opera. English opera company with policy of usually performing operas in English. It assumed this name in 1974, six years after having moved into the London Coliseum in St Martin's Lane from its previous headquarters at Sadler's Wells, a th. in N. London (Rosebery Avenue). Sadler's Wells was so named because in 1683 a Mr Sadler discovered a well in his garden with supposedly medicinal properties and enlarged his buildings and grounds to accommodate customers, for whom he also provided entertainment. In 1765 a th. was built on the site. Various entertainments were given there before it fell into disuse. In 1925 a public appeal raised £70,000 in 5 years to restore the th. as a home for opera and drama like the Old Vic. It opened, with a capacity of 1,650, in Jan. 1931 under management of Lilian *Baylis. Opera and ballet alternated with Shakespeare prods., between SW and Old Vic, but from 1934–5 the opera was based at SW. In next 5 years, several operas had their f.ps. and f.ps. in England (incl. Rimsky-Korsakov's *Snow Maiden* and the orig. *Boris Godunov*), and many famous Eng. singers and conds. worked there. During war, co. concentrated on touring but was built up again under directorship of Joan Cross. For return to its London home in June 1945 the co. produced a new opera by Benjamin Britten, *Peter Grimes*. In 1947, Norman Tucker became co-dir. (dir. 1954–66) and post-war mus. dirs. incl. James Robertson 1946–54, Alexander Gibson 1957–9, Colin Davis 1959–65, Charles Mackerras 1970–8, Charles Groves 1978–9, Mark Elder 1979–93, Sian Edwards 1993–5, Paul Daniel 1997–2005, and Edward Gardner from 2006. Since 1950 new operas by Berkeley, Gardner, Richard Rodney Bennett, Malcolm Williamson, Gordon Crosse, David Blake, Stephen Oliver, John Buller, Jonathan Harvey, and Judith Weir, have been prod. Janáček perfs. by SW and ENO est. the composer in the Brit. public's favour, and there were famous prods. at SW of *Così fan tutte, Rusalka, Simon Boccanegra* (its f. Brit. p., 1948), and many other operas. Stephen Arlen was dir. 1966–72, succeeded by the Earl of Harewood, whose tenure ended in 1985 when he was succeeded by Peter Jonas. On Jonas's departure to Munich in 1993, Dennis Marks became gen. dir. Arlen pioneered the co.'s move from the Rosebery Avenue th. to the London Co-

liseum in 1968. A feature of Arlen's management was the engagement of Reginald Goodall to conduct Wag-ner's *Mastersingers* and later the complete *Ring* in a new Eng. trans. by Andrew Porter, and with Rita Hunter as Brünnhilde. SW/ENO gave the f. Brit. p. of *The *Devils of Loudun* (1973) and f. Brit. stage p. of *The *Bassarids* (1974). Under the triumvirate of Jonas, Elder, and the prod. David Pountney, after 1985 the ENO won a reputation for innovative, radical, and often controversial prods. Among f. Brit. ps. in this period were *Le *Grand Macabre* (1982), **Akhnaten* (1985), and Reimann's *Lear* (1989), and the première was given of *The *Mask of Orpheus* (1986). Marks was succeeded in 1998 by Nicholas Payne, who resigned in 2002. His successor, Séan Doran, left in 2006 and was followed by John Berry and Loretta Tomasi. A separate opera co., ENO North, based in Leeds, was founded Nov. 1978, with David Lloyd-Jones as mus. dir. Its name was changed to *Opera North in 1981. For SW Ballet, see *Royal Ballet*.

English Opera Group. See *English Music Theatre*.

English Singers, The. Title of group of 6 singers specializing in Eng. madrigals and folk-song arrs. who gave 1st concert in 1920. Visited Prague 1922 and later toured in Berlin, Vienna, Holland, and the USA. Orig. members were Flora Mann, Winifred Whelen, Lillian Berger, Steuart Wilson, Clive Carey, and Cuthbert Kelly. In 1924 Nellie Carson, Norman Stone, and Norman Notley replaced Whelen, Wilson, and Carey, and there were further changes before final disbandment.

English Suite, An. Suite in G in 7 movts. for str. orch. by Parry. The 5th (*Pastoral*) movt. dates from 1890, some from 1914 and other parts from 1916. Left unfinished and put in final form by Dr Emily Daymond. Pubd. 1921, f.p., in public 1922.

English Suites. Set of 6 kbd. suites by Bach, pubd. posthumously. Title seems to have arisen from the existence of MS copy (in the possession of Bach's youngest son, Johann Christian) describing the work as *fait pour les Anglais* ('made for the English'). See also *French Suites*; *German Suites*.

Englund, (Sven) **Einar** (*b* Ljugarn, Gotland, Sweden, 1916; *d* Ljugarn, 1999). Finn. composer, conductor, pianist, and writer. Cond., pianist, and reviewer for Finn. radio and TV from 1950; mus. critic, Helsinki *Hufvudstadsbladet* from 1957. Taught comp. at Sibelius Acad. from 1958. Works incl. 7 syms. (1946, 1948, 1969–71, 1976, 1977, 1984, 1988); vc. conc. (1954); 2 pf. concs. (1955, 1974); pf. sonata (1978); vn. sonata (1979); conc. for 12 vcs. (1980–1); vn. conc. (1981); vc. sonata (1982); pf. trio (1982); fl. conc. (1985); str. qt. (1985); *Intermezzo*, ob. (1987); and mus. for films, th., and radio.

enharmonic intervals. Those *intervals which differ from each other in name but not in any other way (so far as modern kbd. instr. are concerned). For example: C to G♯ (augmented 5th) and C to A♭ (minor 6th). Hence *enharmonic change*, the change of a note in a part, e.g. from D♯ to E♭.

Enigma Variations (*Variations on an Original Theme (Enigma)*). Elgar's Op.36 for full orch., comp. 1898–9. F.p. London, 19 June 1899; finale rev. for 3rd perf. Sept. 1899. The 'Enigma' is the theme itself, probably representing Elgar, but he said 'through and over the whole set another and larger theme "goes", but is not played'. Identity of this 2nd theme, if it exists, has never been established despite many ingenious guesses. The work is ded. 'to my friends pictured within', each variation being a mus. sketch. Initials or pseudonyms disguise the individuals but their identities are: 1. CAE (Lady Elgar); 2. HDS-P (Hew Steuart-Powell); 3. RBT (R. B. Townshend); 4. WMB (W. Meath Baker); 5. RPA (Richard P. Arnold); 6. Ysobel (Isabel Fitton); 7. Troyte (A. Troyte Griffith); 8. WN (Winifred Norbury); 9. Nimrod (A. J. Jaeger); 10. Dorabella (Dora Penny); 11. GRS (G. R. Sinclair, but more accurately his bulldog Dan); 12. BGN (Basil G. Nevinson); 13. *** (Lady Mary Lygon); 14. EDU (Elgar). Also 1-act ballet by *Ashton, f.p. CG 1968 (uses orig. ending to finale). Arr. for brass band by Eric *Ball, 1984.

enlevez (Fr.). Take up, i.e. remove (e.g. pedal or mute).

En Saga (A Saga). Symphonic poem by Sibelius, Op.9, 1892, rev. 1901.

ensalada (Sp.). Salad. Comical Sp. 16th-cent. choral pieces, using combination of texts in various languages.

ensemble (Fr.). Together. (1) Any combination of performers, but especially a small group playing individual parts.

(2) The quality in perf. implying the greater or lesser exhibition of the co-operative spirit, e.g. unanimity of attack, balance of tone, etc., thus giving rise to such expressions as 'good ens.', 'poor ens.', etc. A *morceau d'ensemble* (e.g. in an operatic context) is a piece in which several performers combine.

Entführung aus dem Serail, Die. (The Abduction from the Seraglio). Opera (*Singspiel*) in 3 acts by Mozart (K384) for Ger. lib. by Gottlob Stephanie adapted and enlarged from C. F. Bretzner's lib. for André's *Belmont und Constanze* (1781). Comp. 1781–2. Prod. Vienna 1782, London 1827, NY 1860. In 19th cent. was sung in It. in Eng., hence spurious title *Il seraglio*.

entr'acte (Fr.). Between the acts. Strictly the interval between the acts of a play or opera, but in mus. parlance refers to the piece of orch. mus. played at such times, e.g. Schubert's entr'actes for *Rosamunde*.

entrada (Sp.). Same as *entrée*.

entrée (Fr.). Entrance. (1) A 17th- and 18th-cent. term for an instr. piece before a ballet.

(2) An act in an *opéra-ballet* of which every act is self-contained (corruption of *entremets*, 'side-dish', old title for a kind of masque).

(3) The opening moment of any part of a work.

Entremont, Philippe (b Rheims, 1934). Fr. pianist and conductor. Winner Belgian State Comp., Brussels, 1951. Amer. début NY 1953. Specialist in Fr. mus. but wide repertory. Mus. dir. Vienna Chamber Orch. 1976–80; cond. New Orleans PO 1980–5; mus. dir. Denver SO 1987–9; mus. dir. Colonne Orch., Paris, from 1988. Salzburg Fest. début 1985.

envelope. Term in elec. mus. for those characteristics of amplitude which determine the growth and decay of a signal.

Éolides, Les (The Breezes). César Franck's symphonic poem, comp. 1876, based on poem by Leconte de Lisle describing flight of the breezes, daughters of Aeolus, over the southern lands. F.p. Paris 1877.

Eötvös, Peter (b Székelyudvarhely, 1944). Hung. conductor and composer. Played in Stockhausen's elec. ens. in Cologne from 1968. Worked in Cologne's West Ger. radio EMS 1971–9. Cond., Ensemble Intercontemporain, Paris, 1979–91. Cond. f.p. of Stockhausen's *Donnerstag aus Licht*, Milan 1981. Also cond. f.ps. of Donatoni's *Duo pour Bruno*, 1975; Stockhausen's *Michaels Reise um die Erde* (Act II of *Donnerstag aus Licht*, 1978); Reich's *Desert Music*, 1984; Birtwistle's *Earth Dances*, 1986; and Amy's *Missa cum jubilo*, 1988. Comps. incl. *Hochzeitmadrigal*, 6 soloists (1963, rev. 1976); *Intervalles-Intérieures*, var. instr. (1981); *Pierre-Idyll*, chamber orch. (1984); *Chinese Opera*, chamber orch. (1986); *The Metal Space*, 7 brass, 2 perc. (1990); *Korrespondenz*, str. qt. (1992); *Atlantis*, vv., large ens., synth. (1995); *Three Sisters*, opera (1996–7); *2 Monologues*, bar., orch. (1998); *Replica*, va., orch. (1998); *As I Crossed a Bridge of Dreams*, mus. th. (1998–9); *Le Balcon*, opera (2001–2); *Jet Stream*, tpt., orch. (2002); CAP-KO, conc. for acoustic pf., kbd., orch. (2005).

epicedium. Dirge or lament, e.g. Purcell's *The Queen's Epicedium*, 1695.

epilogue. A concluding piece: in opera, for example, sometimes addressed directly to the audience, as in Stravinsky's *The Rake's Progress*. Term has been used as description of movts. in their syms. by Vaughan Williams and Bax.

episode. In comps. designed on one of the regular patterns, a section containing thematic material of secondary importance is sometimes called an episode. It can also contain new material. In *rondo form, the contrasting sections between returns of the main material are sometimes called episodes. In *fugue form, an episode follows the exposition and is a passage of connective material, usually a development of a theme from the exposition, leading to another entry or series of entries of the subject. One function of the fugal episode is to effect modulation to various related keys so that later entries may take advantage of this variety.

Epitaffio per García Lorca (Epitaph for García Lorca). Work by *Nono, comp. 1951–3, in 3 parts: 1. *Espana en la corazón*, sop., bar., small ch., and instr. 2. *Y su sangre ya viene cantando*, fl. and small orch. 3. *Memento*, female speaker, speaking choir, ch., and orch.

epithalamium (Lat., Eng. epithalamion). A marriage song or wedding hymn. Vaughan Williams's cantata *Epithalamion* (1957) has words selected from Spenser's poem of that name.

éponge, baguette d' (Fr.). Sponge-headed drumstick.

Epstein, Julius (*b* Agram, 1832; *d* Vienna, 1926). Croatian pianist, prof. at Vienna Cons. 1867–1901. Taught Mahler and recognized his genius even as a boy. His son Richard (*b* Vienna, 1869; *d* NY, 1919) was his pupil. He lived in London 1909–14, then in NY. Was accomp. to Destinn, Sembrich, Gerhardt, and chamber-mus. partner of Kreisler and Elman, also playing with Rosé and Bohemian Qt.

Epstein, Matthew (*b* NY, 1947). Amer. opera administrator. Joined Columbia Artists Management 1973. Art. adv., Chicago Lyric Opera 1980 and consultant to Kennedy Center, Santa Fe Opera, Netherlands Opera, and S. Francisco Opera (from 1992). Supervised concert perfs. of opera at Carnegie Hall, NY, 1982–6. Art. dir. of opera, Brooklyn Acad. of Mus. 1987–90. Gen. dir. WNO 1992–4.

equale, equali (Old It.). (1) Equal. (2) 18th-cent. term for a funeral qt. of instr. of the same kind, usually tbs.; or mus. for such, e.g. Beethoven's 3 *Equali* (1812) in D minor, D major, and B major, 2 of which, with vocal parts added by Seyfried, were perf. at Beethoven's funeral.

equal temperament. See *temperament*.

equal voices (It. *voci eguali*; Lat. *voces aequales*; Ger. *gleiche Stimmen*). A choral comp. is said to be for 'equal vv.' when it is for vv. of the same kind, generally for 2 sop. or 3 sop. (sch. mus. and mus. for women's choirs). In such mus., in fairness to the vv. of the performers, the parts are usually so arr. that sometimes one v. and sometimes another is at the top. Occasionally the term is less correctly used as implying 'for children's vv.' (unmixed with adults) or 'for women's vv.' (unmixed with men's), or vice versa.

Érard [Erhard], **Sébastien** (*b* Strasbourg, 1752; *d* La Muette, nr. Paris, 1831). Fr. founder of firm of pf. and hp. manufacturers. Went to Paris 1768, built first Fr. pf. 1777. Est. firm with his brother in Paris 1779. Opened London branch 1786 working there until 1796, in which year, in Paris, he made his first grand pf. Patented improvements to pf. (repetition action) and hp. (double-action mechanism). Succeeded by nephew Pierre Érard (1796–1855). London branch closed 1890. Amalgamated with Gaveau, 1960.

Erb, Donald James (*b* Youngstown, Ohio, 1927). Amer. composer. Played tpt. in dance bands. Teacher at Cleveland Inst. 1953–61, comp.-in-res. 1966–81, prof. of mus. Indiana Univ. Sch. of Mus.

1984–7, prof. of comp., Cleveland Inst. from 1987. Comp.-in-res. St Louis SO 1988–90. Comps. incl. several works involving tape and synthesizers, but many works employ more conventional means. The latter incl. vc. conc. (1975); tb. conc. (1976); tpt. conc. (1980); contrabn. conc. (1984); cl. conc. (1984); *Concerto for Orch.* (1985); conc. for brass and orch. (1986); *Woody*, cl. (1988); *Solstice*, chamber orch. (1988); Sym. for Winds (1989); *Bulgarian Bop*, tb., jazz ens. (1990); vn. conc. (1993); vn. sonata (1994); hp. sonata (1997); str. qt. No.3 (1995); *Dance You Monster*, tpt. (1998); *3 Pieces for Db. Alone* (1999).

Erb, Karl (*b* Ravensburg, 1877; *d* Ravensburg, 1958). Ger. tenor. Début with Stuttgart Opera 1907 (Kienzl's *Der Evangelimann*); Lübeck Opera 1908–10; Munich opera 1913–25, where he created title-role in *Pfitzner's Palestrina* 1917. Salzburg Fest. 1925; CG 1927. Retired from stage 1930 (last role was Florestan in *Fidelio*). Noted exponent of Evangelist in Bach's *St Matthew Passion*. His wife was the sop. Maria *Ivogün.

Erede, Alberto (*b* Genoa, 1908; *d* Monte Carlo, 2001). It. conductor. Début Rome 1930. Mus. dir. Salzburg Opera Guild 1935–8. Ass. to Busch at Glyndebourne 1934–9, cond. *Le nozze di Figaro* and *Don Giovanni* 1938–9. Amer. début NBC orch., NY 1937. Cond. Turin Radio SO 1945–6; New London Opera Co. 1946–8; NY Met 1950–5 and 1974–5; Deutsche Oper am Rhein, Dusseldorf, 1956–62. Cond. Bayreuth 1968. Guest cond. CG 1958; Scottish Opera 1975. Returned to Rome Opera 1988.

Erickson, Robert (*b* Marquette, Mich., 1917; *d* San Diego, 1997). Amer. composer. Teacher at S. Francisco Cons. 1957–66 and at Univ. of Calif., San Diego, from 1967. Began as 12-note composer but changed course in 1957 with his str. qt. No.2 where he showed new interest in qualities of sound which led him to introduce improvisation into his *Chamber Concerto* (1960) and pf. conc. (1963). He began to use tape in 1964, employing *musique concrète* processes. Works comp. in this idiom incl. *Ricercar*, 3 db. (1967); *Pacific Sirens*, 10–14 instr. on tape (1968); *High Flyer*, amplified fl. (1969). Later works incl. *Rainbow Rising* (1974); *Garden*, vn., orch. (1977); *East of the Beach*, small orch. (1980); *Auroras*, orch. (1982); *Sierra*, ten. or bar., chamber orch. (1984); *Solstice*, str. qt. (1984–5); *Dunbar's Delight*, timp. (1985); Trio, cl., vc., hp. (1986); *Fives*, va., vc., ca., bcl., pf. (1988); *Music for Tpt., Str., Timp.* (1990).

Erkel, Ferenc (*b* Gyula, 1810; *d* Budapest, 1893). Hung. composer. Cond. Budapest Nat. Th. 1838–74. Founder and cond. Budapest Phil. 1853–71. Prof. of pf., Hung. Nat. Acad. of Mus., dir. 1875–88. One of first Hung. 'nationalists', striving to est. nat. opera. His first opera, *Bátori Mária* (1840), was followed by *Hunyádi László* (1844, rev. 1885) and by *Bánk Bán* (1844–52, prod. 1861) which is traditionally perf. on nat. holiday. Other operas are *Dózsa György* (1866), *Brankovics György* (1874), and *King István* (1874–84).

Erlanger, Camille (*b* Paris, 1863; *d* Paris, 1919). Fr. composer. Works incl. *Requiem* for double ch. and several operas (*Le Juif polonais*, 1900; *Le Fils de l'étoile*, 1904; *Bacchus triomphant*, 1909; *Le Barbier de Deauville*, 1917).

Erlebach, Philipp Heinrich (*b* Esens, Friesland, 1657; *d* Rudolstadt, 1714). Ger. composer who was for 33 years Kapellmeister in Rudolstadt, 1681–1714. Among surviving works are 6 sonatas for vn., bass viol, and continuo (1694), 2 vols. of songs (1697, 1710), and sacred mus.

Erleichterung (Ger.). An 'easing', i.e. a simplified version.

Erlkönig (The Erl-King). Ballad by Goethe, the Erl-King being a King of all the spirits who appears to a child and entices him to death. Poem comes from Goethe's ballad-opera *Die Fischerin* (1782) and first mus. setting was an 8-bar melody written by Corona Schröter, actress who played the fisherwoman at the f.p. It was then set by Reichardt, Klein, and Zelter, but the best-known settings (for v. and pf.) are those by Schubert (D328), 1815, and Loewe, 1818. Sketches of an abandoned Beethoven setting exist. Special importance of Schubert's setting is the difficult and vivid acc., which revolutionized the art of acc. for composers and pianists.

Ermler, Mark (*b* Leningrad, 1932; *d* Seoul, 2002). Russ. conductor. Concert début, Leningrad PO 1952. Opera début Leningrad 1953 (*Die Entführung*). Joined Bolshoy Opera, Moscow, 1956, ballet début 1964. Brit. début 1974 (with Bolshoy Ballet, London). Toured with Bolshoy Opera to Canada, Fr., Japan, It., USA (1975), and W. Ger. CG ballet début 1985, opera 1986. Cond. *War and Peace*, Seattle 1990.

Ernani. 4-act opera by Verdi to lib. by Piave based on Hugo's *Hernani* (1830). Comp. 1843–4. Prod. Venice 1844, London 1845, NY 1847.

erniedrigen (Ger.). To lower (pitch).

Ernst, Heinrich Wilhelm (*b* Brünn (Brno), 1814; *d* Nice, 1865). Moravian violinist and composer. Modelled his style on that of *Paganini. Lived in Paris 1831–8, toured Europe 1838–44. Frequent visitor to London after 1843, settling there in 1855, and playing in qt. with Joachim, Wieniawski, and Piatti. Viola soloist in Berlioz's *Harold en Italie*, with comp. conducting, on several occasions. Comp. vn. concs., *Élégie* (1840), *Le Carnaval de Venice* (1844), and 6 *Polyphonic Studies* for solo vn.

Ernste Gesänge, Vier (Four Serious Songs) (Brahms). See *Vier ernste Gesänge*.

Eroica Symphony (*Sinfonia Eroica*). Sym. No.3 in E♭ major, Op.55, by Beethoven, comp. 1803–4, f.p. 1804, f.pub.p. 1805. Orig. called *Bonaparte*, this title being erased by Beethoven on hearing that Napoleon had proclaimed himself emperor. On publication it bore the title *Sinfonia Eroica*, composta per festeggiare il Sovvenire di un grand Uomo (Heroic Symphony, composed to celebrate the memory of a great man). Finale is set of variations on theme taken from Beethoven's ballet *Die Geschöpfe des *Prometheus* (1801).

'Eroica' Variations. Title given (not by Beethoven) to his pf. variations in E♭ major, Op.35, comp. 1802, based on theme from his ballet *Die Geschöpfe des *Prometheus*, 1801, also used in *Eroica Sym. Sometimes known as *Prometheus Variations*. Theme is used again for No.7 of 12 *Kontretänze* for orch., WoO 14, pubd. 1803.

Erös, Peter (*b* Budapest, 1932). Hung. conductor. Left Hung. 1956, assisting Fricsay at Holland Fest. 1958–61. Ass. cond. Concertgebouw Orch., 1960–5. Cond., Malmö SO 1966–8. Mus. dir. San Diego SO 1972–80. Cond. Australian Broadcasting Commission 1975–9. Mus. dir. Peabody SO, Baltimore, 1982, and chief cond. Ålborg SO from 1983.

erotikon (Ger.). Love-song.

erst, erste (Ger.). First.

ersterbend (Ger.). Dying away.

Erste Walpurgisnacht, Die (The First Walpurgis Night). Mus. by Mendelssohn, Op.60 (comp. 1831, rev. 1842) to Goethe's ballad, for soloists, ch., and orch. Walpurgis Night is spring fest. when witches ride to the Brocken in Harz Mountains.

Erwartung (Expectation, Suspense). Monodrama in 1 act by Schoenberg, Op.17, to lib. by Marie Pappenheim, for sop. and orch. Comp. 1909. Prod. Prague 1924 (cond. Zemlinsky), London, NY 1951 (concert), and Washington D.C. 1960 (but Schoenberg cond. a BBC concert perf. in London 1931).

erweitert (Ger.). Widened, broadened (i.e. slower and with steadiness).

Erzähler (Ger., 'narrator'). (1) The Evangelist in settings of the Passion.
  (2) Soft organ-stop of 8′ length and pitch, invented by Skinner of Boston, Mass., giving octave above the fundamental.

Es (Ger.). The note E♭.

Escales (Ports of call). Orch. suite by Ibert, comp. 1922. The 3 ports are said to be Palermo, Tunis, and Valencia.

Eschenbach [Ringmann], **Christoph** (*b* Breslau, 1940). Ger. pianist and conductor. Won Steinway pf. comp. 1952; first prize in first Clara Haskil comp., Montreux, 1965. London début 1966; Salzburg Fest. 1967; Amer. 1969 (Cleveland Orch.). Gave f.p. of Henze's 2nd pf. conc. (Bielefeld, 1968). Début as cond. 1972. Opera début, Darmstadt 1978 (*La traviata*); CG 1984. Cond. Tonhalle Orch., Zurich, 1982–5. Mus. dir. Houston SO 1988–99, Orch. de Paris from 2000, Philadelphia Orch. from 2003.

Escher, Rudolf George (*b* Amsterdam, 1912; *d* DeKoos, 1980). Dutch composer. In 1960–1 worked in Delft EMS and similar studio at Utrecht State Univ. Writer on Ravel and Debussy. Taught at Inst. for Mus. Science, Utrecht, 1964–75. Comps. incl. *Le Tombeau de Ravel*, fl., ob., hpd., vn., va., vc. (1952); Owen's *Strange Meeting*, bar., pf. (1952); 2 syms. (1953–4, 1958); *Summer Rites at Noon*, 2 orchs. facing each other (1962–9); *The Persians*, narr., male vv., orch. (1963); wind quintet (1966–7); *Univers de Rimbaud*, ten., orch. (1970); solo cl. sonata (1973); *3 Poems by Auden*, ch. (1975); fl. sonata (1975–7); *Sinfonia*, 10 instr. (1976); *Trio*, cl., va., pf. (1978). Orch. Debussy's *Six épigraphes antiques* (1976–7).

Esclarmonde. Opera (*opéra romanesque*) in 4 acts and prol. by Massenet to lib. by Alfred Blau and Louis de Gramont based on medieval romance *Partenopoeus de Bloix* (before 1188). Comp. 1888 for Amer. sop. Sibyl Sanderson, who first sang title-role. Prod. Paris 1889; New Orleans 1893, NY Met 1976; CG 1983.

Eses (Ger.). The note E♭♭.

Es moll (Ger.). The key of E♭ minor.

espagne (Fr.). Spain. **espagnol, espagnole** (Fr.), **espagn(u)olo, espagn(u)ola** (It.). Spanish. Used in titles of works such as *Rapsodie espagnole* (Ravel), *Symphonie espagnole* (Lalo).

España (Spain). Orch. rhapsody by *Chabrier, f.p. 1883, in which Sp. tunes and rhythms are quoted. He visited Sp. 1882–3. Pf piece and song based on it by other hands.

Espansiva, Sinfonia (Expansive Symphony). Title of *Nielsen's 3rd sym., Op.27, comp. 1910–11, f.p. Copenhagen 1912. F. Brit. p., London 1962.

Espert, Nuria (*b* Barcelona, 1935). Sp. stage director. Was actress in Barcelona th. co., 1947–52. First prod. was Lorca's *The House of Bernarda Alba*, Hammersmith 1986. First opera prods., *Madama Butterfly* (Scottish Opera, Glasgow, 1987; CG 1988). Prod. *Elektra* (Brussels 1988; Barcelona 1990), *Rigoletto* (CG 1988), *La traviata* (Glasgow 1989), and *Carmen* (CG 1991).

Esposito, Michele (*b* Castellammare, Naples, 1855; *d* Florence, 1929). It. composer and pianist. Lived in Paris 1878–82. In 1882 became prof. of pf., Royal Irish Acad. of Mus., Dublin. Founded and cond. Dublin Orch. Soc. 1899. Hon DMus, Dublin, 1917. Works incl. operetta *The Postbag* (1902); cantata *Deirdre* (1897); *Irish Symphony* (1902); str. qt.; vc. sonata; etc. Mentor of Hamilton *Harty.

espressione (It.).Expression. **espressivo**. Expressively.

esquisse (Fr.). *Sketch.

Esquivel Barahona, Juan de (*b* Ciudad Rodrigo, c.1563; *d* Ciudad Rodrigo, after 1613). Sp.

composer and church musician. Choirmaster, Ciudad Rodrigo Cath. 1608–13. Ranked by some as equal of Victoria. Wrote over 60 motets.

esraj. Indian mus. instr. played with a bow and having 4 melodic str. and 10 to 15 sympathetic understr. Tone like a vn. but with more resonance. Fingerboard has 20 movable frets.

essential note. An actual note of a chord, as distinct from a passing note, suspension, appoggiatura, etc. These latter are 'unessential notes'.

Esswood, Paul (Lawrence Vincent) (*b* West Bridgford, 1942). Eng. countertenor. Lay vicar, Westminster Abbey choir 1964–71. Début 1965 (*Messiah*). Opera début 1968 (Berkeley, Calif.) in f. Amer. p. of Cavalli's *Erismena*. Salzburg Fest. début 1971. Founder of Pro Cantione Antiqua singers. Prof., RCM 1973–85 and from 1985. Sang in Monteverdi operas at Milan 1978. Sang in f.p. of Penderecki's *Paradise Lost* (Chicago 1978), and Glass's *Akhnaten* (Stuttgart 1984).

Estampes (Engravings). 3 pieces for pf. by Debussy comp. 1903. Movements are *Pagodes* (Pagodas), *Soirée dans Grenade* (Evening in Granada), and *Jardins sous la pluie* (Gardens in the rain). F.p. as complete set Paris 1904. No.1 orch. Caplet, No.2 orch. Büsser.

estampie (Fr.), **estampida** (Provençal). Type of troubadour tune for dancing, sometimes with words, in form of a *rondeau.

Estes, Simon (Lamont) (*b* Centerville, Iowa, 1938). Amer. bass-baritone. Began career in Ger., 1965, singing Ramfis in *Aida* at Deutsche Oper, Berlin. Silver medal, Moscow Tchaikovsky comp., 1966, and was invited to sing with S. Francisco opera and Chicago Lyric. Glyndebourne début 1972. Sang with NY Met co. on its visit to Vienna 1976. Milan 1977; Hamburg 1978; Bayreuth 1978; Salzburg Fest. 1983; CG 1986. Amer. recital début, Carnegie Hall, NY, 1980, and sang Wotan in Met concert perf. of *Die Walküre*, Act III, 1981. NY Met stage début 1982. Sang Gershwin's Porgy there in first Met perf. of opera, 1985.

Esther. Oratorio by Handel to text by S. Humphreys after Racine. F.p. as masque *Haman and Mordecai*, 1720, at Cannons but expanded into concert oratorio 1732. First Eng. oratorio.

estinguendo (It.). Extinguishing, i.e. dying away.

estinto (It.). Extinct. As soft as possible.

Estrada, Carlos (*b* Montevideo, 1909; *d* Montevideo, 1970). Uruguayan composer and conductor. Founded Montevideo SO 1959. Taught harmony Montevideo Univ. 1950–6. Works incl. oratorio *Daniel* (1942); 2 syms. (1951, 1967); mus. drama *L'Annonce faite à Marie* (1943); and many shorter pieces.

estribillo (Sp.). A choral movement at the beginning or end of a *villancico.

Estro armonico, L' (Harmonious Inspiration). Title of Vivaldi's Op.3, 12 concs. for various instrs., pubd. Amsterdam 1711, 6 of which were transcr. by J. S. Bach. Comprised conc. in D for 4 vn. (RV549), in G minor for 2 vn. and vc. (RV578), in G for vn. (Bach BWV978, RV310), in E minor for 4 vn. (RV550), in A for 2 vn. (RV519), in A minor for vn. (RV356), in F for 4 vn. and vc. (RV567), in A minor for 2 vn. (Bach BWV593, RV522), in D for vn. (Bach BWV972, RV230), in B minor for 4 vn. and vc. (Bach BWV1065, RV580), in D minor for 2 vn. and vc. (Bach BWV596, RV565), in E for vn. (Bach BWV976, RV265).

Eszterháza. A castle on the S. side of the Neusiedlersee in Hungary which was opened in 1766 as a seat of the Esterházy family. It stood in marshy country and was very isolated, but it contained an opera house and a marionette th. Scene of f.ps. of many works by Joseph Haydn, who was engaged in 1761 by Prince Paul Anton Esterházy (1711–62) and became Kapellmeister in 1766 under his successor Prince Nicolaus (1714–90). From 1776 to 1790 over 100 different operas were perf. there, of which only 6 were by Haydn. Others were by Cimarosa, Paisiello, Bianchi, Salieri, Traetta, Gluck, Grétry, etc. Haydn as Kapellmeister was responsible for 1,200 of these perfs. In 1779 opera house burnt down and was rebuilt within a year.

Eternal Father, Strong to Save. Hymn, words by William Whiting (1825–78), written in 1860 and pubd. in *Anglican Hymn Book* (1868) in orig. version beginning 'O thou who bidd'st the ocean deep'. Revs. appeared in *Hymns Ancient and Modern* 1861 and appendix to *Psalms and Hymns* 1869. Known as 'the Navy's hymn'. Tune by J. B. *Dykes.

Et Exspecto Resurrectionem Mortuorum (And I look forward to the resurrection of the dead). Orch. work by *Messiaen for woodwind, brass, metal perc. Comp. 1964. Commissioned by French Govt. and ded. to memory of dead of two World Wars. F.p. Sainte-Chapelle, Paris, 1965, cond. Baudo, later in Chartres Cath. in presence of Gen. de Gaulle.

ethnomusicology. Study of music, instruments, and dance, usually of oral tradition, in countries not linked with European art music, e.g. tribal mus. and dances in Africa, Asia, India, China, Japan, etc. Term is attrib. to Jacop Kunst in subtitle of book, Amsterdam 1950.

Et incarnatus est. See *Mass*.

Et in Spiritum Sanctum. See *Mass*.

Et in unum Dominum. See *Mass*.

Etler, Alvin (*b* Battle Creek, Iowa, 1913; *d* Northampton, Mass., 1973). Amer. composer and oboist. Oboist, Indianapolis SO 1938–40. On faculty of Yale Univ. Sch. of Mus. 1942–6, Cornell Univ. 1946–7, Univ. of Illinois 1947–9, and Smith Coll.

1949–73. From 1968 chairman, Hampshire Coll. elec. workshop. Works incl. sym., 2 str. qts.; 2 wind quintets; conc. for orch.; conc. for vn. and wind quintet; conc. for wind quintet and orch.; brass quintet; conc. for str. qt. and orch.; etc.

Étoile, L' (The Star). Comic opera in 3 acts by Chabrier to lib. by E. Leterrier and A. Vanloo. Comp. 1877. Prod. Paris 1877, Edinburgh 1984 (Opéra de Lyon), Leeds 1991 (Opera North).

Étoile du Nord, L' (The North Star). 3-act comic opera by Meyerbeer to lib. by Scribe. Prod. Paris 1854, London 1855, New Orleans 1855. Incorporated 6 items from Meyerbeer's opera *Ein Feldlager in Schlesien* (1844, rev. as *Vielka*, 1847).

Eton College Manuscript (Eton Choir Book). A book of choral mus. at Eton College, dating from between 1490 and 1504.

étouffer (Fr., imperative *étouffez*; past participle *étouffé*). To stifle, i.e. to damp, e.g. with vn. mute, pf. pedal, etc. *étouffoir*, damper (pf. pedal).

Et resurrexit. See *Mass*.

étude (Fr.). Study. Comp. intended as a basis for the improvement of the performer's technique. In pf. mus. the term is especially applied to a short piece restricted to the exploitation of one kind of passage. Masterpieces of this kind suitable for public perf. as well as private practice were written by Chopin and Debussy.

Études d'exécution transcendante (Fr., 'Transcendental Studies'). 12 pieces for solo pf. by Liszt, comp. 1851 and based on his *24 Grandes Études* of 1837 and *Mazeppa* of 1840. The titles are 1. *Preludio*, 2. in A minor, 3. *Paysage*, 4. *Mazeppa*, 5. *Feux follets*, 6. *Vision*, 7. *Eroica*, 8. *Wilde Jagd*, 9. *Ricordanza*, 10. in F minor, 11. *Harmonies du soir*, 12. *Chasse-neige*.

Études d'exécution transcendante d'après Paganini (Transcendental Studies after Paganini). Transcr. for pf. by Liszt, 1838, of 6 of *Paganini's vn. caprices, incl. *La *Campanella*. Rev. and re-issued 1851 as *Grandes Études de Paganini*.

Études symphoniques (Symphonic Studies). Schumann's Op.13 for pf. solo with orig. title *Etuden im Orchester-Charakter von Florestan und Eusebius*, comp. 1834–7, rev. 1852, first pubd. 1837, ded. to Sterndale *Bennett. The first version contained 12 studies; in 1852, Schumann omitted Nos. 2 and 9 and rewrote finale. Wieck's 1862 edn. restored Nos. 2 and 9. Five further variations, orig. suppressed, have since been discovered and are included in some perfs.

etwas (Ger.). Some, something, somewhat.

Eugene Onegin (Evgeny Onyegin). 3-act opera by Tchaikovsky to lib. by composer and K. S. Shilovsky based on Pushkin's poem (1831). Comp. 1877–8. Prod. Moscow 1879, London 1892, NY Met 1920 (but concert perf. NY 1908).

Eulenburg, Ernst (*b* Berlin, 1847; *d* Leipzig, 1926). Ger. music publisher. Founded firm in Leipzig 1874, taking over in 1892 the series of miniature scores, *Kleine Partitur-Ausgabe*, pubd. by Albert Payne, and later Donajowski's edn.

Eulenburg, Kurt (*b* Berlin, 1879; *d* London, 1982). Son of E. *Eulenburg. Succeeded as head of firm 1926, enlarging no. of miniature scores and publishing scholarly edns. by *Blume, *Einstein, and others. Went to Switzerland 1939. Opened new London co. 1939, with branch in Zurich. Settled in London 1945. Edn. acquired by *Schott 1957, but retained identity. On Eulenburg's retirement in 1969, Roger Fiske was ed. 1969–76, succeeded by Philip Cranmer.

Eulenspiegel, Till (Strauss). See *Till Eulenspiegel*.

euphonium. (1) Member of the tuba family of brass instrs., being a tenor tuba in B♭. Mainly used in brass and military bands, many solos for euphonium having been written.

(2) Instr. invented by Chladni in 1790, made of glass plates and rods and with a pleasant but soft tone.

eurhythmics. Method invented by *Jaques-Dalcroze for expressing rhythmical aspect of mus. through gymnastic exercises.

Euryanthe. 3-act opera by Weber to lib. by Helmina von Chézy after 13th-cent. Fr. romance. Comp. 1822–3. Prod. Vienna 1823, London 1833, NY Met 1887. Because of weaknesses of lib. various attempts have been made to renovate *Euryanthe*, but it is best perf. as Weber left it, flaws and all.

Evans, (Dame) **Anne** (*b* London, 1941). Eng. soprano of Welsh parentage. Sang minor roles in Geneva. Prin. sop. ENO 1968–78 (début as Mimi). WNO début Cardiff 1974 and has since sung with them many roles incl. Brünnhilde in *Ring* cycle (1984–5 and with WNO at CG 1986) and Isolde (1993). Bayreuth début 1983; sang Brünnhilde in *Ring* cycle at Bayreuth 1989–92, and has sung role in Berlin, Nice, Paris, Turin, and Zurich. Returned to ENO 1990 as Ariadne. NY Met début 1992. DBE 2000.

Evans, Edwin (*b* London, 1874; *d* London, 1945). Eng. critic. His father was a writer on mus. and trans. Wagner's *Opera and Drama*. Took up financial journalism, but turned to mus. 1901 and became expert on Russ. composers. Champion of Debussy and young Eng. composers. Critic, *Pall Mall Gazette* 1912–23. Then worked with Ballets Russes. Critic, *Daily Mail* from 1933. Wrote biography of Tchaikovsky, many essays, trans. *Louise* and *Pelléas et Mélisande*. Succeeded *Dent as president of ISCM, 1938.

Evans, (Sir) **Geraint** (Llewellyn) (*b* Cilfynydd, Pontypridd, 1922; *d* Aberystwyth, 1992). Welsh baritone and opera producer. Début CG 1948 (Nightwatchman in *Die Meistersinger*), becoming one of leading int. bars., his best roles incl. Falstaff, Figaro, Papageno, Wozzeck, Beckmesser, and Leporello. Débuts: Glyndebourne 1950–61; S. Francisco 1959; La Scala 1960; Vienna 1961; Salzburg Fest. 1962; NY Met 1964; Paris 1975. Created roles of Mr Flint (*Billy Budd*, CG 1951), Mountjoy (*Gloriana*, CG 1953), and Antenor (*Troilus and Cressida*, CG 1954). Retired 1984 (last opera perf. CG 4 June 1984) but appeared at Glyndebourne gala concert as speaker, July 1992. Autobiography *A Knight at the Opera* (1984). CBE 1959. Knighted 1971.

Evans, Nancy (*b* Liverpool, 1915; *d* Aldeburgh, 2000). Eng. mezzo-soprano. Opera début London 1938 in Sullivan's *The Rose of Persia*, followed by small roles at CG 1939. Alternated with Kathleen Ferrier as Lucretia in f.p. of *The Rape of Lucretia*, Glyndebourne 1946. Created role of Nancy in *Albert Herring*, Glyndebourne 1947. Sang Polly in Britten's version of *The Beggar's Opera* with EOG 1948. Also notable concert career. Britten wrote *A Charm of Lullabies* for her, f.p. 1948. After retirement, taught at Britten-Pears Sch. at Snape Maltings. OBE 1991.

Evans, Peter (Angus) (*b* West Hartlepool, 1929). Eng. teacher and musicologist. Mus. master, Bishop Wordsworth's Sch., Salisbury, 1951–2; lecturer, Durham Univ. 1953–61; prof. of mus., Southampton Univ., 1961–92. Cond., Southampton Phil. Soc. Author of *The Music of Benjamin Britten* (1979, rev. 1989).

Evans, Rebecca (Ann) (*b* Pontrhydyfen, Wales, 1963). Welsh soprano. Career as nurse before studying at GSMD. Young Welsh Singer of the Year 1991. Début WNO 1990 (Gretel). Sang title-role in *Cendrillon* (WNO) 1993. S. Francisco début 1995; débuts: Munich 1995 (Ilia in *Idomeneo*); Santa Fe 1995 (Susanna); CG 1998 (Susanna); NY Met 1999 (Sophie in *Werther*); ENO 2002 (Romilda in *Xerxes*). Has sung with major internat. orchs. and conds., and given many recitals, incl. Wigmore Hall, London.

Evening Hymn. Song by Purcell to words by Fuller, 1688, beginning 'Now that the sun hath veiled his light'. Arr. for v. and str. by Vaughan Williams 1912.

Evenings in the Orchestra (*Les Soirées de l'orchestre*). Entertaining and instructive coll. of criticisms and essays by Berlioz, pubd. in Paris in 1853 and Eng. trans. by Jacques *Barzun, 1956.

Éventail de Jeanne, L' (Jeanne's Fan). Ballet in 10 nos. choreog. Y. Franck and A. Bourgat, commissioned in 1927 for her Paris ballet school by Jeanne Dubost, who gave the 10 leaves of her fan to 10 composers, asking each to compose a no. Those participating were Ravel, Ferroud, Ibert, Roland-Manuel, Delannoy, Roussel, Milhaud, Poulenc, Schmitt, and Auric. Ravel's 1-minute *Fanfare* is marked *Wagneramente*.

Eventyr (Once Upon a Time). Ballad for orch. by Delius after Asbjörnsen's fairy tales. Comp. 1917, f.p. 1919 cond. Wood.

Everding, August (*b* Boltrop, 1928; *d* Munich, 1999). Ger. stage director and administrator. Manager, Munich Chamber Players 1963–73. First opera prod. Munich 1965 (*La traviata*). Resident dir., Hamburg State Opera 1973–7. Gen. Intendant, Bavarian State Opera, Munich, 1977–93; Bayreuth 1969 (*Der fliegende Holländer*); Salzburg Fest. 1973; NY Met 1971; CG 1979; Chicago 1992 (*Ring* cycle).

Everyman. (1) Oratorio by Walford *Davies based on medieval mystery play, Leeds 1904.

(2) Incid. mus. for small orch. by Sibelius, 1916, for prod. of Hofmannsthal's version of *Everyman* (*Jedermann*).

(3) 6 monologues for bar. or cont. and pf. or orch. from Hofmannsthal's *Jedermann* by Frank *Martin, 1943.

evirato (It.). Unmanned. 18th-cent. type of male singer whose boy-sop. v. had been preserved by castration. Same as **castrato*.

evovae or **euouae**. This 'word' consists of the vowels of 'seculorum, Amen', being the last words of the Gloria Patri (see *doxologia*), and is used as a name for the cadential endings of the Gregorian Psalm tones. These letters are often placed under the notes of the plainsong as an abbreviation of the words they represent.

Ewing, Maria (Louise) (*b* Detroit, 1950). Amer. mezzo-soprano. Prof. début 1973, Ravinia Fest. with Chicago SO. Débuts: NY Met 1976 (Cherubino in *Le nozze di Figaro*), La Scala 1976; Salzburg Fest. 1976; Glyndebourne 1978; CG 1988. Sang Carmen in new prod. CG 1991. In concert-hall excels in Fr. mus.

Excursions of Mr Brouček, The (*Výlety páně Broučkovy*). Opera in 2 parts by Janáček. Lib. of Part 1, *Mr Brouček's Excursion to the Moon*, adapted from satirical novel (1887) by S. Čech (1846–1908) by V. Dyk, K. Mašek, Z. Janke, F. Gellner, J. Mahen, and F. S. Procházka; Part 2, *Mr Brouček's Excursion to the XVth Century*, adapted from S. Čech's satirical novel (1888) by Procházka. Comp. 1908–17. Janáček himself wrote most of lib. of Part 1. F.p. Prague 1920; f. Brit. p. Mar. 1970 (BBC studio, cond. Mackerras), f. Brit. stage p. Edinburgh, Sept. 1970; London (ENO) 1978. F. Amer. p. S. Francisco (concert) 1981, Bloomington (stage) 1981.

Execution of Stepan Razin, The (*Kazn' Stepana Razina*). Cantata by Shostakovich, Op.119, to text by Yevtushenko, for bass, ch., and orch. Comp. 1964, f.p. Moscow 1964.

exercise. (1) An instr. passage purely for technical practice and with little or no artistic interest.

(2) In the 18th cent., a kbd. suite such as D. Scarlatti's early sonatas, pubd. as *Esercizii*.

(3) Comp. submitted by candidates for certain univ. mus. degrees.

Expert, Henri (*b* Bordeaux, 1863; *d* Tourettes-sur-Loup, 1952). Fr. musicologist. Joint founder, 1903, *Société d'Études Musicales*. Specialist in mus. of Fr. Renaissance period, publishing 23 vols. and 5 subsidiary sections.

exposition. (1) In sonata form, the first section of a comp. in which the prin. themes are ex-

pounded before they are developed.

(2) In fugue the first statement of the subject by all the 'voices' in turn.

expression. That part of a composer's mus. such as subtle nuances of dynamics which he has no full means of committing to paper and must leave to the artistic perception and insight of the executant. All he can do is to indicate speed and the kind of mood to be expressed by means of conventional mus. terms written on the score. A large part of the cond.'s art is the imparting of expressive qualities to the perf.

expressionism. Term borrowed from painting, generally assoc. with work of the early 20th-cent. Ger. artists of the Munich 'Blaue Reiter' group led by Kandinsky. Prin. characteristics were avoidance of representational forms and interest in psychological impulses. These were musically reflected in works of Schoenberg, Webern, and Berg. But, like *impressionism, the term is vague.

expression stop. A stop in a harmonium or other reed org. When drawn, the passage of the air is made to short-circuit the reservoir through which it otherwise passes, and this gives the feet great control over degrees of force and accent.

Exsultate, jubilate (Rejoice, be glad). Motet by Mozart (K165) for sop., orch., and org., comp. 1773. 3rd movt. is famous setting of 'Alleluia'. Orig. comp. for castrato Venanzio *Rauzzini.

extemporization. See *improvisation*.

extension organ. Same as unit org., i.e. built on the principle of saving space and money by making a comparatively small no. of pipes produce something of the effect of a larger number by 'borrowing'. The pipes of an 8' stop may, for example, be made to do duty also for a 4' by a connection which draws on them an octave higher throughout (as in cinema orgs.).

extravaganza (from It. 'stravaganza'). A mus. work which intentionally caricatures conventional procedures, such as Mozart's *Ein musikalische Spass* (*A *Musical Joke*), and especially a 19th-cent. Eng. form of stage entertainment with mus.

Eybler, Joseph Leopold Edler von (*b* Schwechat, 1765; *d* Schönbrunn, Vienna, 1846). Austrian composer. Befriended by Haydn. Chorusmaster Schottenkloster, Vienna, 1794–1824. Vice-Kapellmeister, Viennese Imperial court, from 1804 until he succeeded Salieri in 1824 as court composer. Comp. opera, oratorio, masses, requiem, syms., pf. solos, and other works. Friend of Mozart, whom he nursed in last illness. Asked by Mozart's widow to complete the *Requiem* but did not finish the task.

ezcudantza. Basque fest. dance for 2 performers with acc. of pipe and tabor, and sometimes of v.

F

F. Note of the scale, 4th degree of natural scale of C. Thus F♭, F♭♭, F♮, F♯, F𝄪. Keys of F major and F minor, F♯ major, F♯ minor. 'In F' is also an indication of *transposing instr. on which written note C sounds as F (e.g. hns., F tpt.). The F clef is the bass clef.

F. Prefix given to numbers in the catalogue of Vivaldi's works by Antonio Fanna. Superseded by that of *Ryom.

f. Abbreviation of *forte* (It., 'loud', 'strong'), hence degrees of increasing loudness, *ff* (fortissimo), *fff* (triple forte), and sometimes more.

fa. The 4th degree of the major scale, according to the system of vocal syllables derived from Guido d'Arezzo, and so used (spelt *fah*) in *Tonic Sol-fa (also in that system the 6th degree of the minor scale; see *tonic sol-fa*). In many countries, however, the name has become attached to the note F, in whatever key this may occur.

Faber, Heinrich (*b* Lichtenfels, before 1500; *d* Ölsnitz, 1552). Ger. music theorist. Prof. of mus., Wittenberg Univ. Author of Lat. compendium of mus. (1548) later trans. into Ger. by *Vulpius (Halle, 1608).

Faber Music. Mus. publishing branch of book publishers Faber & Faber; est. 1964, becoming separate co. 1966. Catalogue incl. mus. by Britten, Holst, Arnold, G. Benjamin, R. Smalley, Harvey, Muldowney, Howard Blake, C. and D. Matthews, Knussen, and Vaughan Williams, in addition to works by Mahler and Schoenberg and by It. Baroque composers.

faburden (Eng.), **fauxbourdon** (Fr.), **falsobordone** (It.). Literally, false bass, or drone. This term has had a surprisingly large number of different applications at different periods.

(1) In very early use, the acc. in parallel 3rds and 6ths of a plainsong melody.

(2) In 15th cent., any added part to such a plainsong melody, both parts moving at the same rate. Apparently used especially of such passages interpolated among unison singing of the plainsong, e.g. in the psalms.

(3) About the same period, also used of the same kind of liturgical singing as that mentioned under (2), but without plainsong in any of the vv. (This is sometimes spoken of as 'free' faburden as distinct from the previous type, spoken of as 'strict'.)

(4) A sort of chanting in which the whole of a phrase was declaimed on one chord, except that the cadence was harmonized as such. (The same mus. was used for every verse of a psalm, etc., as is done today with the Anglican Chant.)

(5) Sometimes applied to a sort of monotoning.

(6) A drone bass, such as that of a bagpipe.

(7) In 16th- and 17th-cent. Eng. usage, sometimes applied to the ten. part of a metrical psalm tune, etc., which part then usually carried the melody.

(8) A refrain to the verses of a song.

(9) Nowadays (as with descant) the word is used in Brit. for a freely-written sop. part added to a hymn tune while the tune itself is sung by the ten. vv. of the ch. or by the congregation, or (more commonly in recent years) for a 4-part harmonization with the tune in the ten.—this last a revival of the old English practice.

When this word is used in old mus. treatises or in the modern mus. historical works any of the above senses may be intended. See also *fauxbourdon*.

Façade. 'Entertainment' by *Walton, being acc. for small chamber ens. (9 players) to poems by Edith Sitwell declaimed in notated rhythm by a speaker or speakers. Comp. 1921, f.p. (private) 1922, (public) 1923. This version has been several times rev. with many substitutions of items. Final pubd. version (1951) contains 21 items. 8 unpubd. nos. perf. under title *Façade Revived*, London 1977, 3 of these were rejected before publication and 3 others (Nos. 4, 6, 7) substituted by composer; rev. and re-worked version perf. 1979 as *Façade II*. Prin. revs. of *Façade I* 1926, 1928, 1942. Also arr. by composer for larger orch. (without poems) as 2 Suites (No.1, of 5 items, f.p. London 1926; No.2, of 6 items, f.p. NY and London 1938). Also arr. as ballet, with choreog. by Gunter Hess, f.p. Hagen, Westphalia, 1929; with choreog. by Frederick *Ashton f.p. London 1931 (7 items), extra item 1935, 2 further addns. 1940; Ashton ballet of work with reciter and chamber ens. f.p. Snape, Suffolk, and London 1972. Many arrs. by others of items from *Façade* for a variety of combinations.

Faccio, Franco (Francesco Antonio) (*b* Verona, 1840; *d* Monza, 1891). It. conductor and composer. Served in Garibaldi's army 1866. Prof. of harmony, Milan Cons. 1868. Chief cond. La Scala from 1871. Cond. f. It. p. of *Aida* (1872) and f.p. of *Otello* (1887). Cond. first Wagner opera in It. (*Lohengrin*, 1873) and first London *Otello* (1889). Also cond. f.ps. of operas by Ponchielli (*La Gioconda*), Catalani, and Puccini (*Le villi* and *Edgar*). Comp. operas *I profughi Fiamminghi* (Milan 1863), *Amleto* (lib. by *Boito, Genoa 1865), cantata *Le Sorelle d'Italia* (text by Boito, 1861), 3 syms., str. qt., and songs.

Fach (Ger.: 'Compartment', division). *zweifach*, twofold, *dreifach*, threefold, etc. Most commonly used to indicate a division of, e.g., the first vns. of an orch., but there is an org. application indicating the no. of ranks in a mixture stop. In an operatic context it denotes the classification of parts—the 'voice-category'—for all opera roles in Ger. opera houses. Whereas Cherubino is regarded as sop. role in *Fach* system, it is mez. in Italy and elsewhere.

Fachiri (*née* d'Arányi), **Adila** (*b* Budapest, 1886; *d* Florence, 1962). Hung.-born violinist, sister of Jelly d'*Arányi. *Joachim was her great-uncle. Vienna début 1906 (Beethoven conc.). Foreign tours with her sister. Eng. début Haslemere 1909. Settled and married in Eng., continuing to appear as orch. soloist and in chamber mus. Holst's double concerto (1930) was comp. for her and her sister.

facile (Fr.). Easy. **facilement** (Fr.), **facilmente** (It.). Easily, i.e. fluently and without an effect of striving.

facilità (It. 'facility'). (1) Ease, fluency.
(2) Simplification, as of a virtuoso solo passage brought within the range of less skilled performers.

Fackeltanz (Ger.). 'Torch dance', more often a torchlight procession to mus. Spontini, Meyerbeer, and others have comp. these dances, which were usually part of a wedding or similar celebration.

fado. A type of popular Portuguese song and dance with gui. acc., apparently dating from *c*.1850.

fa fictum. A term used in connection with the *hexachords—the note B flattened (in the soft hexachord).

Fagan, Gideon (*b* Somerset West, Cape Province, 1904; *d* Cape Town, 1980). S. African conductor and composer. Cond. BBC Northern Orch. 1939–42, Johannesburg Orch. 1949–52. Mus. dir. S. African Broadcasting Corp. 1963–6, lect. Univ. of Cape Town 1967–73. Cond. several London musicals. Comps. incl. *Afrikaans Folktune Suite*.

FAGO. Fellow of the American Guild of Organists.

Fagott (Ger.), **fagotto** (It.), **fagote** (Sp.). (1) The *bassoon. The name derives from *fagotto* (It., 'bundle of sticks'), possibly applied jokingly to the *phagotum*, a kind of bagpipe invented by Canon Afranio of Ferrara in 1521. In the 16th cent. the word *fagotto* covered a range of instr., such as the *curtal or *dulcian which are forerunners of the modern bn.
(2) Organ stop, same as bn.

fah. See *fa*.

Fair at Sorochintsī, The (Mussorgsky). See *Sorochintsy Fair*.

Fairfax, Bryan (Lancelot Beresford) (*b* Sydney, 1930). Australian conductor and violinist. Violinist Hallé Orch. 1954–6. Founded Polyphonia Orch. 1961 for perf. of new or rarely heard mus. Cond. f.p. of Brian's *Gothic Symphony*, 1961, con-

cert perf. of Britten's *Gloriana*, London 1963 (on night of composer's 50th birthday), and f. Brit. pub. p. of Nielsen's *Sinfonia espansiva* (1962). Also cond. f. Brit. p. of Shostakovich's 3rd sym. (1962) and Grainger's *The Warriors* (1970).

Fair Maid of Perth, The (Bizet). See *Jolie Fille de Perth, La*.

Fairy Queen, The. Semi-opera, but really a succession of masques, by Purcell in prol. and 5 acts, to lib. (by E. Settle?) based on Shakespeare's *A Midsummer Night's Dream* (which is not quoted). Prod. London 1692, London 1911 (Morley Coll., cond. Holst), Cambridge (stage) 1920, S. Francisco 1932. Score was lost by 1700 but a partly autograph full score was found in library of RAM, 1901. First work staged at CG after World War II.

Fairy's Kiss, The (Stravinsky). See *Baiser de la fée, Le*.

Falkner, (Sir) (Donald) **Keith** (*b* Sawston, Cambs., 1900; *d* Bungay, 1994). Eng. baritone and administrator. Sang in opera (BNOC) but best known as oratorio soloist. On retirement became teacher. Brit. Council mus. officer for It. 1946–50; teacher at Cornell Univ. 1950–60; dir., RCM, 1960–74. Knighted 1967.

Fall, Leo(pold) (*b* Olomouc, 1873; *d* Vienna, 1925). Austrian composer. Th. cond., Berlin, Hamburg, and Cologne. Comp. 2 operas, but greatest success with operettas, e.g. *Der Rebell* (1905); *Der Fidele Bauer* (1907); *Die *Dollarprinzessin* (1907); *Brüderlein fein* (1909); *The Eternal Waltz* (London 1911); *Die Rose von Stamboul* (1916); and *Madame Pompadour* (1922).

Falla, Manuel de [Falla y Matheu, Manuel Maria de] (*b* Cádiz, 1876; *d* Alta Gracia de Córdoba, Argentina, 1946). Sp. composer and pianist. He was taught the pf. by his mother and harmony by 2 local musicians, but his ambition was to be a composer and he wrote 2 *zarzuelas, the first of which was prod. in 1902. Falla then studied comp. in Madrid for 3 years with *Pedrell, who imparted the doctrine that a nation's mus. should be based on folk-song. However, it was to the spirit rather than to the letter of Sp. folk-mus. which Falla turned. In 1905 he won the Madrid Acad. of Fine Arts prize for the best lyrical drama by a Sp. composer with his 2-act opera *La Vida Breve* (but it was not perf.). In the same year he won the Ortiz y Cusso prize for Sp. pianists. For 2 years he taught the pf. in Madrid and in 1907 went to Paris, where he became the friend of and was greatly influenced by Dukas, Ravel, and Debussy. Ricardo *Viñes played the *4 Spanish Pieces* for pf. in Paris in 1908, and Falla himself introduced them to London at his début there in 1911. *La Vida breve* was produced in Nice and Paris in 1913 and in Madrid in 1914. The ballet-pantomine *El amor brujo* followed in 1915. In 1916 he completed his most ambitious and successful concert work (begun in Paris 1909), the *Noches en los jardines de España* (Nights in the Gardens of Spain) for pf. and orch. Falla's fame was est., however, in 1919 by Diaghilev's prod. in London of the ballet *El sombrero de tres picos* (Tricorne, or The *Three-Cornered Hat). In 1919 Falla also completed his major work for solo pf., *Fantasía Bética*, dedicated to Arthur *Rubinstein. Bética was the Roman name (Baetica) for Andalusia. After World War I, Falla's style was less colourfully but no less inherently Sp.—it is truer to say that the popular Andalusian folk element was succeeded by a re-creation of the severer style of the early Sp. polyphonic masters. From this period come the chamber opera (based on an incident in *Don Quixote*) *El Retablo de Maese Pedro* (*Master Peter's Puppet Show), f.p. 1923, and the hpd. conc. (1926) ded. to Wanda *Landowska. In 1926 he began work on an enormous 'scenic cantata' *Atlántida* which was left unfinished and was completed by E. *Halffter. In 1939, after cond. 4 concerts in Buenos Aires, he settled in Argentina. Prin. comps.:

OPERAS: La *Vida breve* (1904–5); *Fuego Fatuo* (based on Chopin) (1918–19); *El Retablo de Maese Pedro* (1919–22).

BALLETS: El *Amor Brujo* (1915); *El sombrero de tres picos* (1918–19, being rev. version of *El corregidor y la molinera*, 1916–17).

ORCH.: *Noches en los jardines de España* (1909–15), pf., orch.; Suites Nos. 1 and 2 from *El sombrero de tres picos* (1919).

CHAMBER MUSIC: *Psyche* for mez., fl., harp, vn., va., vc. (1924); conc. for hpd. (or pf.), fl., ob., cl., vn., vc. (1923–6).

CHORAL AND VOCAL: *Atlántida*, scenic cantata, unfinished (completed by Halffter); 3 *Melódies*, v., pf. (1909); *Siete Canciones Populares Españolas* (7 Spanish Popular Songs), v., pf. (1914–15); *Soneto a Córdoba*, v., hp. (1927); *Balada de Mallorca* (after Chopin), mixed ch. (1933).

PIANO: *Nocturno* (1899); *Serenata andaluza* (1899); *Vals-capricho* (1900); *Serenata* (1901); *Cuatro Piezas Españolas* (4 Spanish Pieces), (1907–8); *Fantasía Bética* (1919); *Homenajes* (Homages) 1. *Fanfare on the name of *Arbós, 1933, orch. 1938; 2. A Claude Debussy (elegia de la guitarra), also for guitar as Homenaje a Debussy, 1920, orch. 1939; 3. Rapel de la Fanfare, 1941; 4. A Paul Dukas (Spes Vitae), 1935, orch. 1939; 5. Pedrelliana, 1938. *Ritual Fire Dance, Dance of Fear, Pantomime, Récit du Pêcheur, arr. by Falla from ballet El Amor Brujo; suite from 7 Spanish Popular Songs, arr. by Falla; Dance of Miller's Wife and Miller's Dance, from El Sombrero de tres picos, arr. Falla.

ARRS. BY OTHERS: La Vida breve: 2 Spanish Dances, pf. solo and pf. duet, arr. Samazeuilh; 1st Spanish Dance, vn., pf., arr. Kreisler; 2 Spanish Dances, orch. Chapelier; 7 Spanish Popular Songs, orch. by Halffter; Suite for vn. and pf. arr. P. Kochanski; for vc. and pf., arr. M. Maréchal.

Fallows, David (Nicholas) (*b* Buxton, 1945). Eng. musicologist. Has held academic posts at Studio der frühen Musik, Munich, 1968–70, Univ. of Wisconsin-Madison 1973–4, and Manchester Univ. from 1976. Wrote on many medieval subjects and on tempo and expression marks in *The New Grove Dictionary of Music & Musicians* (1980). Many articles on his special subjects. Writes mus. criticism. Author of *Dufay* (1982).

false accent. When the accent is removed from 1st beat of a bar to 2nd or 4th.

false close. See *cadence*.

false relation. In harmony, the appearance of a note with the same letter-name in different parts (or 'voices') of contiguous or the same chords, in one case inflected (♯ or ♭) and in the other uninflected (e.g. F♮ and F♯). Amer. term is 'cross-relation'.

falsetto (It.). Singing method used by males, particularly tens., to achieve a note or notes higher than comes within the normal range of their v. Often used for comic effect, e.g. Falstaff imitating the Merry Wives in Verdi's opera.

falsobordone (It.). Same as Eng. *faburden*.

Falstaff. (1) Comic opera in 3 acts by Verdi (his last) to lib. by Boito after Shakespeare's *The Merry Wives of Windsor* and *King Henry IV*, Parts 1 and 2. Comp. 1889–92, rev. 1893 and 1894. Prod. Milan 1893, CG 1894, NY Met 1895. Operas on same subject incl. those by *Dittersdorf (1796), *Salieri (1798), *Balfe (1838), *Nicolai (*Die lustigen Weiber von Windsor*, 1849), Holst (*At the Boar's Head*), and Vaughan Williams (*Sir John in Love*, 1924–8).

(2) Symphonic study in C minor, with 2 interludes, Op.68, for orch. by Elgar. Comp. 1902–13. F.p. Leeds Oct. 1913, f. London p. Nov. 1913.

Fanciulla del West, La (The Girl of the Golden West, literally 'The Girl of the West'). 3-act opera by Puccini to lib. by Civinini and Zangarini based on Belasco's play *The Girl of the Golden West* (1905). Comp. 1908–10. F.p. NY Met 1910; CG and Rome 1911.

fancy. Eng. 16th- and 17th-cent. equivalent of *fantasia.

fandango. A lively Sp. dance believed to be of S. Amer. origin. It is in simple triple or compound duple time, and of ever-increasing speed, with sudden stops during which the performers (a single couple) remain motionless, and with intervals during which they sing. Acc. is normally by guitar or castanets. There is a fandango in Mozart's *Figaro*.

fanfare. (1) (Eng.). Flourish of tpts., or other instrs. in imitation of them, as a means of proclamation, such as a military signal.

(2) (Fr.). Brass band (as distinct from *Harmonie*, a band of mixed brass and woodwind).

Fanfare for the Common Man. Orch. work by *Copland, comp. 1942 as one of series of wartime fanfares commissioned by Eugene Goossens, who cond. f.p. with Cincinnati SO, March 1943. Incorporated into 3rd sym. (1944–6).

Fanny Robin. Opera in 1 act by Harper to his own lib. derived from Hardy's *Wessex Poems* (1898) and *Far From the Madding Crowd* (1874). Comp. 1974, prod. Edinburgh (Scottish Opera) 1975.

Fanshawe, David (*b* Devon, 1942). Eng. composer. Has devoted much time to research into African folk mus. and into that of Iraq and Tonga. Works incl. *Escapade I* and *II* for pf.; *Fantasy on Dover Castle*, orch.; *Requiem for the Children of Aberfan*, orch.; *African Sanctus* (orig. version 1972, rev. 1977); *Salaams*, tone-poem (1978); *The Awakening*, vc./va., pf. (1992); *Celtic Lullaby*, vv. (1998); *Millennium Fanfare and Millennium March*, orch./band (1999).

Fantaisies Symphoniques. Sub-title of 6th Sym. by Martinů, Comp. 1951–3, f.p. Boston 1955.

fantasia (It.), **fantaisie** (Fr.), **Fantasie** (Ger.). Fantasy or fancy. Generally a comp. in which form is of secondary importance, although the 16th-cent. It. fantasia was an instr. comp. in strict imitation of a vocal motet. In Eng. in the 16th and 17th cents. the term 'fancy' was used for comps. for both kbd. and str. instr., notably consorts of viols. Such comps. were usually contrapuntal and in several sections often with a common theme, thus being an early form of variations. In the 20th cent. the chamber mus. patron *Cobbett revived the form, preferring the spelling phantasy. Sweelinck and Bach used the term fantasia for their organ comps. in which the character of the mus. suggested an improvisational character or the play of free fancy. In the 19th cent. the term was applied by Schumann, Chopin, and others to short mood pieces, e.g. Schumann's *Fantasiestücke*. Other meanings of the word are:
   (1) a comp. comprising a string of tunes, e.g. from an opera, as in Liszt's pf. fantasies on operatic arias.
   (2) Development section in sonata-form, i.e. free fantasia.
   (3) Title of film first shown in 1940, made by Walt Disney, in which cartoons (some merely abstract patterns) were set to famous pieces of music played by the Philadelphia Orch. conducted by Stokowski. The items were: J. S. Bach's *Toccata and Fugue in D minor* (transcr. Stokowski); Tchaikovsky's *Nutcracker Suite*; Ponchielli's *Dance of the Hours*; Beethoven's *Pastoral Symphony*; Dukas's *L'Apprenti sorcier*; Stravinsky's *The Rite of Spring*; Mussorgsky's *Night on the Bare Mountain*; and Schubert's *Ave Maria*. See *film music*.

Fantasia Bética. Work for pf. by Falla, completed 1919 and ded. to Arthur Rubinstein who commissioned it and gave f.p. in NY 1920. Baetica was Roman name for Andalusia.

Fantasia Concertante on a Theme of Corelli. Work for str. by *Tippett, comp. 1953 for Edinburgh Fest. on tercentenary of Corelli's birth. Str. div. into concertino (2 solo vn. and vc.), conc. grosso (half remaining body), conc. terzo (other half). Theme taken from Corelli's Conc. Grosso Op.6 No.2, and work quotes Bach's *Fugue on themes of Corelli*.

Fantasia Contrappuntistica. Work for solo pf. comp. by Busoni in 3 versions between 1910 and 1912. Sub-titled *Preludio al Corale 'Gloria al Signori nei Cieli' e fuga a quattro soggetti obbligati sopra un frammento di Bach*. Arr. for 2 pfs., 1921. Adapted for org. by work's dedicatee Wilhelm Middelschulte. Based on Bach's Contrapunctus XVIII from *The Art of Fugue*, in desire to complete Bach's unfinished fugue. Busoni created 4th subject (Bach having comp. only 3), and added 5th.

Fantasia on a Theme by Thomas Tallis. Comp. by Vaughan Williams for double str. orch. and str. qt., f.p. Gloucester 1910, London 1913 (rev.). Further rev. 1919. Tallis's theme is No.3 ('Why fumeth in fight') of 9 psalm tunes comp. 1567 for Archbishop Parker's Psalter.

Fantasia on a Theme of Handel. Comp. for pf. and orch. by *Tippett, comp. 1939–41, f.p. London 1942 by Phyllis Sellick, cond. Walter Goehr.

Fantasia on British Sea Songs. Compilation of trad. and other songs made by Henry J. *Wood for concert on 21 Oct. 1905 to celebrate centenary of Nelson's victory at Trafalgar and which became (and remains) traditional finale to Last Night of London Promenade Concerts, with the audience joining in (singing, clapping, and footstamping). In 9 sections: 1, *Naval Bugle calls*. 2, *The anchor's weighed* (solo tpt., solo tb.). 3, *The saucy Arethusa* (solo euphonium). 4, *Tom Bowling* (Dibdin) (solo vc.). 5, *Hornpipe, Jack's the lad* (solo vn., solo fl., solo piccolo). 6, *Farewell and adieu, ye Spanish ladies* (4 tbs.). 7, *Home, sweet home* (Bishop) (solo cl., solo ob.). 8, *See, the conquering hero comes* (Handel) (solo hns.). 9, *Rule, Britannia!* (Arne) (org. and full orch.). For some years the Fantasia was cut, but the practice recently has been to give it in full. Bringing a solo cont. into *Rule, Britannia!* was Sargent's departure from Wood's score.

Fantasia on Christmas Carols. Comp. by *Vaughan Williams for bar., ch., and orch. Founded on traditional carols: 1. The truth sent from above. 2. Come all you worthy gentlemen. 3. On Christmas night. 4. There is a fountain; with fragments of others. F.p. Hereford 1912, London 1913.

Fantasia on 'Greensleeves'. Arr. by Ralph Greaves (1934) for strs. and harp (or pf.) with optional fl.(s) of interlude from Vaughan Williams's opera *Sir John in Love*, middle section being based on folk-song *Lovely Joan*. Several other arrs., none by Vaughan Williams, exist.

Fantasias on an In Nomine by John Taverner. 2 works for orch. by *Maxwell Davies, comp. as studies for his opera *Taverner*. 1st, comp. 1962; 2nd, comp. 1964 (f.p. London 1965, cond. John Pritchard).

Fantasiestücke (Fantasy Pieces). 8 pieces for solo pf., Op.12, by Schumann, 1837–8, with descriptive titles. 3 further *Fantasiestücke* described only by key-signatures were pubd. as Op.111 (1851). Schumann also wrote *Fantasiestücke*, Op.73, for cl. and pf.

farandole (Fr.). Lively Provençal dance in 6/8 time in which, to the acc. of *galoubet* and *tambourin*, the participants danced through the streets holding each other by the hands or by a handkerchief. The *farandole* in Bizet's incidental mus. to *L'*Arlésienne* is based on an authentic Provençal dance-tune but is not in 6/8.

Farewell, Manchester. Jacobite song played while the Young Pretender's army left Manchester in 1745, tune being a hpd. piece, *Felton's Gavotte*, comp. *c.*1740 by Rev. William *Felton, of Hereford.

Farewell Symphony (Haydn). See *Abschiedsymphonie*.

Farinelli [Broschi, Carlo] (*b* Andria, 1705; *d* Bologna, 1782). It. castrato singer. Début Naples, 1720. In 1723 sang title-role in Porpora's *Adelaide*. In 1727 was defeated in public exhibition of vocal skill by Bernacchi, who then taught him. Sang in Vienna and in London, where he joined Porpora's opera co. which was in competition with Handel's. Sang in Madrid, 1737, where Philip V offered him 50,000 francs a year to stay, which he did for 25 years, singing each night to the king. Was instrumental in est. It. opera in Madrid. Left Spain on Charles III's accession in 1759, living in Bologna in some splendour, collecting pictures and playing hpd. and va. d'amore.

Farkas, Ferenc (*b* Nagykanizsa, 1905; *d* Budapest, 2000). Hung. composer. Worked as composer and cond., film studios in Vienna and Copenhagen 1933–6. Prof. of comp., Kolozsvár Cons., 1941–3, dir. 1943–4. Dir. Székesfehérvár Cons., 1946–8. Prof. of comp., Budapest Acad. 1949–75. Comps. incl. 3 operas; 2 ballets; choral works; concs.; chamber mus.; and songs.

Farkas, Ödön (*b* Jászmonostor, 1852; *d* Kolozsvár, 1912). Hung. composer. Wrote 7 operas, sym., 5 str. qts., songs, and choral mus., all of strong Hung. character.

Farmer, John (*b c.*1570; *fl.* 1591–1601). Eng. madrigal composer. Org., Christ Church, Dublin, 1595–9. Lived in London from 1599. Contrib. to *The *Triumphs of Oriana*.

Farnaby, Giles (*b* Truro, 1563; *d* London, 1640). Eng. composer of madrigals, music for virginals, canzonets, psalm-tunes, etc. Over 50 of his virginals pieces are included in *Fitzwilliam Virginal Book*; among the best known are *His dreame*, *A Toye*, and *Loth to depart*. In 1592 contributed to *East's book of psalms; his canzonets for 4 vv. were pubd. 1598.

Farncombe, Charles (Frederick) (*b* London, 1919; *d* London, 2006). Eng. conductor. Founder, Handel Opera Soc., 1955, and dir. to 1985, during which period he cond. several first modern revivals incl. *Deidamia, Riccardo Primo, Alcina,* and *Rinaldo*. Chief cond. Royal Court Th., Drottningholm, 1970–9. Chief guest cond., Badisches Staatstheater, Karlsruhe, from 1979. Mus. dir. London Chamber Opera from 1983. CBE 1977.

Farnes, Richard (*b* Cuckfield, Sussex, 1964). Eng. conductor. Studied at Eton Coll. (1977–82), King's Coll., Cambridge (1983–6), RAM and GSMD (1987–90), Nat. Opera Studio (1993). Kbd. player in Eur. Youth Orch. (1998). On mus. staff at Glyndebourne and Bath Fests. (1992–8). ETO (1992–5). Founded chamber group Equinox 1992. New Israeli Opera, Tel Aviv, 1994 (*Nabucco*). Opera North début 1994 (*Gloriana*). Cond. world première of David Horne's *Friend of the People*, Scottish Opera 1999; Glyndebourne 1997 (*Makropoulos Case*); CG 2002 (*Simon Boccanegra*); mus. dir. Opera North and prin. cond. of the Orchestra of Opera North from 2004.

Farrant, Richard (*b c.*1530; *d* London, 1580). Eng. composer. Choirmaster, St George's Chapel, Windsor 1564–80. Master of Chapel Royal choristers 1569–80. Composer of anthems and songs.

Farrar, Ernest (Bristow) (*b* Lewisham, 1885; *d* in action nr. Le Cateau, Cambrai, 1918). Eng. composer and organist. Friend of Frank *Bridge. Org., Eng. church, Dresden, 1909, then St Hilda's, South Shields, 1910–12 and Christ Church, Harrogate, 1912–16. While at Harrogate gave lessons from 1914 to *Finzi. Enlisted in army 1915; commissioned in Devonshire Regiment 1918. Killed at Battle of Epéhy Ronssoy, Somme Valley, 18 Sept. 1918. Comp. prize in his memory founded at RCM (later twice won by *Britten), but now amalgamated with Sullivan Prize. Bridge's pf. sonata (1921–4) is dedicated to his memory. Works (dates given are either of publication or f.p.) incl.:

ORCH.: Rhapsody No.1 *The Open Road*, after Whitman (1909), No.2 *Lavengro*, after Borrow (1913); sym.-poem *The Forsaken Merman*, after Arnold (1914); *Variations on an Old British Sea Song*, pf., orch. (1915); *English Pastoral Impressions*, suite (1915); *3 Spiritual Studies*, str. (1925); *Heroic Elegy* 'For Soldiers', orch. (1918).

CHORAL: 3 partsongs, mixed ch. (1907); 2 partsongs, male vv. (1909); *The Blessed Damozel*, low v., ch., orch. (1907); *Margaritae Sorori*, unacc. ch. (1916); *Out of Doors*, Whitman suite, ch., orch. (*c.*1911); *A Song of St Francis*, unison, pf. (1919); *Summer* (C. Rossetti), women's vv., pf. or sop., orch. (1918).

CHAMBER MUSIC: vn. sonata (lost); *Celtic Suite*, vn., pf. (1910); *Celtic Impressions*, str. qt. (?).

PIANO: *Valse caprice* (1913); *Miniature Suite* (1913); *Shadow Dance* (1922); *3 Pieces* (1915–27, pubd.); *3 Pieces* (1916); *2 North Country Sketches* (1920).

ORGAN: *Fantasy Prelude* (1908); *3 Chorale Preludes* (1920); *A Wedding Piece* (1925); *Elegy* (1925); *6 Pieces* (1926).

SONGS: 3 songs (1906); *Vagabond Songs*, bar., orch. (1911); *Brittany* (1914); *O Mistress Mine* (1921); *2 Elizabethan Love Songs* (1921).

Farrar, Geraldine (*b* Melrose, Mass., 1882; *d* Ridgefield, Conn., 1967). Amer. soprano. Début, Berlin Court Opera, 1901 (Marguérite in *Faust*). Monte Carlo 1904–6. Sang Mimì and Gilda (*Rigoletto*) to Caruso's Rodolfo and Duke on several occasions. NY Met début 1906; sang Butterfly at its first Met perf. 1907. Member of Met co. until 1922, singing nearly 500 times. Created *Suor Angelica* (NY 1918). Last appearance 1922. Also appeared in many films. Wrote biography *Such Sweet Compulsion* (NY 1938, 1970).

Farrell, Eileen (*b* Willimantic, Conn., 1920; *d* Park Ridge, NJ, 2002). Amer. soprano. Début Columbia Broadcasting Co. 1941, after which she had her own prog. for 6 years. Sang Marie in concert perf. of *Wozzeck*, NY 1951. Stage début 1956 in Tampa, Fla. S. Francisco 1956; NY Met 1960. Sang Brünnhilde and Isolde in concert perfs. with L. Bernstein. Also gifted singer of blues, Gershwin, etc. Prof. of mus., Indiana Univ. Sch. of Mus., Bloomington, 1971–80, Univ. of Me. in Orono from 1984.

farruca. An Andalusian dance of gipsy origin. *Falla, in his ballet *The Three-Cornered Hat*, uses the *farruca* for the Miller's Dance.

Fasano, Renato (*b* Naples, 1902; *d* Rome, 1979). It. conductor, pianist, and composer. Dir., Cagliari Cons. 1931–9. Art. dir., St Cecilia Acad., Rome, 1944–7. Founder and cond., 1947, of Collegium Musicum Italicum which in 1952 became I Virtuosi di Roma, chamber ens. specializing in early mus. Salzburg Fest. début with them 1956. Dir., Venice Cons. 1952–60. Dir., Rome Cons. 1960–72. Pres., St Cecilia Acad., Rome, 1972–6.

Faschingsschwank aus Wien (Viennese Carnival Pranks). Pf. comp. (*Fantasiebilder*) by Schumann, Op.26, comp. 1839. In 5 movts.

Fassbaender, Brigitte (*b* Berlin, 1939). Ger. mezzo-soprano and producer, daughter of Willi *Domgraf-Fassbänder. Début Munich 1961 (Nicklausse in *Les Contes d'Hoffmann*); CG 1971; S. Francisco 1970; Salzburg Fest. 1972; NY Met 1974; Vienna 1976. Member of Bavarian State Opera from 1961. Glyndebourne début 1990 (Clairon in *Capriccio*). Specialist in *travesti* roles. Prod. *Der Rosenkavalier*, Munich 1989. Brit. début as prod., Leeds (Opera North) 1992 (Schreker's *Der ferne Klang*). Outstanding *Lieder* singer.

Fassung (Ger.). Drafting. *neue Fassung*, new version.

Fate (Janáček). See *Osud*.

Fauré, Gabriel (Urbain) (*b* Pamiers, 1845; *d* Paris, 1924). Fr. composer and organist. Org., St Sauveur, Rennes, 1866–70, ass. org. St Sulpice, Paris, 1871–4; choirmaster from 1877 at the Madeleine, org. 1896–1905. Prof. of comp., Paris Cons. 1896, dir. 1905–20. Pupils incl. Ravel, N. Boulanger, Enescu, Schmitt, Koechlin, and Roger-Ducasse. Mus. critic, *Le Figaro*, 1903–21. Fauré's music was slow to gain recognition outside Fr., but he is now acknowledged as one of the greatest of Fr. composers, a master of the

song-cycle, a poet of the kbd., and a profound composer of chamber mus. His delicate and elegant but by no means harmonically unadventurous style has an unsuspected strength and emotional appeal. His opera *Pénélope* is regarded by many as a masterpiece. His best-known work is the *Requiem*, comp. and rev. between 1877 and 1899, but it did not achieve general popularity until after World War II despite the earlier advocacy of Nadia *Boulanger. Prin. works:

OPERAS: *Prométhée*, Op.82 (1900); *Pénélope* (1907–12); *Masques et Bergamasques* (divertissement) (1919).

INCIDENTAL MUSIC: *Caligula* (Dumas), Op.52 (5 movts.) (1888); *Shylock* (Haraucourt after Shakespeare), Op.57 (6 movts.) (1889); *Pelléas et Mélisande* (Maeterlinck), Op.80 (1898); *Le Voile du bonheur* (Clémenceau), Op.88 (1901).

ORCH.: vn. conc., Op.14 (1878–9, unfinished); *Ballade*, pf. and orch., Op.19 (1881); *Pavane* (with optional ch.), Op.50 (1887); suite, *Shylock*, Op.57 (1889); suite, *Pelléas et Mélisande*, Op.80 (4 items) (1901); *Fantaisie* in G major, pf., orch., Op.111 (1919); suite, *Masques et Bergamasques*, Op.112 (4 items) (1919); suite *Dolly*, Op.56 (orch. Rabaud, 1906).

CHAMBER MUSIC: sonata for pf. and vn.: No.1 in A, Op.13 (1875–6), No.2 in E minor, Op.108 (1916–17); pf. qt.: No.1 in C minor, Op.15 (1876–9), No.2 in G minor, Op.45 (1885); pf. quintet: No.1 in D minor, Op.89 (1890–4, 1903–5); No.2 in C minor, Op.115 (1919–21); sonata: No.1 in D minor for pf. and vc., Op.109 (1917), No.2 in G minor, Op.117 (1921); pf. trio in D minor, Op.120 (1922–3); str. qt. in E minor, Op.121 (1923–4); *Berceuse*, pf., vn., Op.16 (1878–9) (also for vn. or vc. and orch.); *Élégie*, pf., vc., Op.24 (1880) (also with orch. 1895); *Romance*, vn., pf., Op.28 (1877); *Romance* in A, vc., pf., Op.69 (1894); *Andante*, pf., vn., Op.75 (1897); *Papillon*, vc., pf., Op.77 (1884) (also for str. quintet or vn. and pf.); *Sicilienne*, vc., pf., Op.78 (1898); *Fantaisie*, fl., pf., Op.79 (1898) (orch. Aubert 1957); *Sérénade*, vc., pf., Op.98 (1908).

CHORAL: *Cantique de Jean Racine*, Op.11 (1865); *La Naissance de Vénus*, Op.29 (1882); *O Salutaris: Maria, Mater Gratiae*, Op.47, Nos. 1 and 2 (1887); *Requiem*, Op.48, sop., bar. soloists, ch., org., orch. (1877, 1887–90, orch. 1899); *Ecce fidelis servus*, Op.54, motet (1890); *Tantum ergo*, Op.55 (1890); *Salve Regina*; *Ave Maria*, Op.67, Nos. 1 and 2 (1894–5).

SONGS & SONG-CYCLES (v. and pf.): *Sylvie*, *Après un rêve*, *Hymne*, *Barcarolle*, Op.7, Nos.1–4 (No.2 orch. Busser 1925) (1870–8); *Nell*, *Le Voyageur*, *Automne*, Op.18, Nos.1–3 (No.3 orch. Busser 1925) (1878); *Les Berceaux*, *Notre Amour*, *Le Secret*, Op.23, Nos.1–3 (No.2 orch. Busser 1925) (1879); 2 *Mélodies*, Op.27 (1882); *Aurore*, *Fleur jetée*, *Les pays des rêves*, *Les Roses d'Ispahan*, Op.39, Nos.1–4 (1884); *Les Présents*, *Clair de Lune*, Op.46, Nos.1–2 (1887); *Larmes*, *Au cimitière*, *Spleen*, *La Rose*, Op.51, Nos.1–4 (1888); 5 *Mélodies* (Verlaine), Op.58 (1891) (sometimes known as 5 *Chansons de Venise*) (*Mandoline*, *En sourdine*, *Green*, *À Clymène*, *C'est l'extase*); *La *Bonne Chanson* (Verlaine cycle), Op.61, Nos.1–9 (1892–4); *Prison*, *Soir*, Op.83, Nos.1–2 (1894); *Le Parfum impérissable*, *Arpège*, Op.76, Nos.1–2 (No.1 orch. Busser 1924) (1897); 3 *Mélodies*, Op.85 (1902); *Le

Plus Doux Chemin, Le Ramier, Op.87, Nos.1–2 (1904); *Le Don silencieux*, Op.92 (1906); *Chanson*, Op.94 (1906); *Vocalise* (1906); *La Chanson d'Ève* (Lerberghe cycle), Op.95, Nos.1–10 (1906–10); *Le *Jardin clos* (Lerberghe cycle), Op.106, Nos.1–8 (1914); *Mirages* (Brimont cycle), Op.113, Nos.1–4 (1919); *C'est la Paix!* Op.114 (1919); *L'*Horizon chimérique* (Mirmont cycle), Op.118, Nos.1–4 (1921).

PIANO: 3 *Romances sans paroles*, Op.17 (1863); *Ballade*, Op.19 (1879); *Impromptus*: No.1 in E♭, Op.25 (1881), No.2 in F minor, Op.31 (1883), No.3 in A♭, Op.34 (1883), No.4 in D♭, Op.91 (1905), No.5 in F♯ minor, Op.102 (1909), No.6, Op.86 bis (see *Harp*); *Nocturnes*: 3 *Nocturnes*, Op.33, No.1 in E♭ minor (1875), No.2 in B major (1881), No.3 in A♭ (1883); No.4 in E♭, Op.36 (1884), No.5 in B♭, Op.37 (1884), No.6 in D♭, Op.63 (1894), No.7 in C♯ minor, Op.74 (1898), No.8 in D♭ (8th of *Pièces brèves*, Op.84 (1898–1902)), No.9 in B minor, Op.97 (1908), No.10 in E minor, Op.99 (1908), No.11 in F♯ minor, Op.104, No.1 (1913), No.12 in E minor, Op.107 (1915), No.13 in B minor, Op.119 (1921); *Barcarolles*: No.1 in A minor, Op.26 (1881), No.2 in G major, Op.41 (1885), No.3 in G♭, Op.42 (1885), No.4 in A♭, Op.44 (1886), No.5 in F♯ minor, Op.66 (1894), No.6 in E♭, Op.70 (1895), No.7 in D minor, Op.90 (1905), No.8 in D♭, Op.96 (1906), No.9 in A minor, Op.101 (1908–9), No.10 in A minor, Op.104, No.2 (1913), No.11 in G minor and No.12 in E♭, Op.105, Nos. 1 and 2 (1913–15), No.13 in C major, Op.116 (1921); *Valses-Caprices*: No.1 in A, Op.30 (1882), No.2 in D♭, Op.38 (1884), No.3 in G♭, Op.59 (1887–93), No.4 in A♭, Op.62 (1893–4); *Mazurka* in B♭, Op.32 (1875); *Thème et variations*, Op.73 (1895) (orch. Inghelbrecht 1955); 8 *Pièces brèves*, Op.84 (1869–1902); 9 *Préludes*, Op.103 (1909–10).

PIANO DUET (4 hands): *Dolly*, Op.56 (1893–6) (orch. Rabaud 1906); *Souvenirs de Bayreuth* (with *Messager) (c.1888; pubd. 1930).

HARP: *Impromptu*, Op.86 (1904) (rearr. for pf. as *Impromptu* No.6, Op.86 bis (1913)); *Une Châtelaine en sa tour*, Op.110 (1918) (arr. Durand for pf.).

Fauré's Requiem. Choral work for sop., bar., ch., orch., and org. by *Fauré, in 7 movts.: 1. *Introit and Kyrie*, 2. *Offertory*, 3. *Sanctus*, 4. *Pie Jesu*, 5. *Agnus Dei*, 6. *Libera me*, 7. *In Paradisum*. Comp. history deserves detailed mention. 1st vers. comp. 1887–8, f.p. at an architect's funeral at the Madeleine, Paris, 16 Jan. 1888, comprising 5 movts: Nos. 1, 3 (comp. 9 Jan. 1888), 4, 5 (comp. 6 Jan. 1888), and 7. Scored for treble v., solo vn., 5 vas., 2 vcs., 3 dbs., 2 hps., timp., org. For f. public p., Madeleine 4 May 1888, with Louis Aubert as treble soloist, 2 tpts. and 2 hns. were added to *Agnus Dei* No.2, with bar. solo, sketched (*Hostias* only) 1887, completed 1889; No.6, also with bar. solo, existed for bar. and org. in 1877 and its final vers. for bar., ch., orch. (with 3 tbs.) was probably f.p. Madeleine 1891, soloist Louis Ballard. Pubd.: V.S. 1900; F.S. 1901 in vers. with large orch. and org. This final vers., of which the MS is lost, was completed 1898–9 but is probably

not all Fauré's work. Scholars believe he was aided by *Roger-Ducasse, who had arr. the work for ch. and pf. 1897–9.

Faust. (1) Opera in 5 acts by Gounod to lib. by Barbier and Carré based on Carré's *Faust et Marguérite* and Goethe's *Faust*, Part I, 1808, 1832 (in Nerval's Fr. trans.). Prod. Paris 1859, London 1863, Philadelphia 1863, NY Met 1883 (inaugural opera).
   (2) Singspiel in 2 acts by Spohr to lib. by J. K. Bernard not based on Goethe, comp. 1813, prod. Prague 1816; rev. 1852 as 3-act opera, prod. London 1852 and 1984.

Faust, Doktor (Busoni). See *Doktor Faust*.

Faust, La Damnation de (Berlioz). See *Damnation de Faust, La*.

Faust, Scenes from Goethe's. Ov. and 6 other movts. for soloists, ch., and orch. by Schumann, comp. 1844–53.

Faust, 2 Episodes from Lenau's. 2 orch. works by Liszt, comp. before 1861, inspired by poem about Faust by Lenau. Titles are *The Night Ride* and *Dance in the Village Inn*, the latter being the *Mephisto Waltz No.1, later transcr. for pf. solo and pf. duet.

Faust Overture, A (*Eine Faust Ouvertüre*). Concert ov. by Wagner, orig. intended as 1st movt. of a Faust Sym., comp. 1839–40, f.p. Dresden 1844. Rev. 1843–4, 1855.

Faust Symphony, A (*Eine Faust-Symphonie*). Sym. by Liszt in 3 character studies (*in drei Charakterbildern*) based on Goethe's poem, with *ad lib* male-v. choral ending. Comp. 1854–7, f.p. 1857, rev. 1880. 3 movts. entitled *Faust, Gretchen*, and *Mephistopheles*.

fauxbourdon (Fr.). Literally 'false bass'. Way of singing improvised polyphony in 15th-cent. mus., particularly that by Burgundian composers. Plainsong melody in treble is acc. by two lower parts, one in parallel sixths, the other a fourth below melody. Similar to but not identical with Eng. *faburden and derivation one from another is disputed.

Favart, Charles-Simon (*b* Paris, 1710; *d* Belleville, 1792). Fr. librettist, composer, and impresario. Stage-manager at Opéra-Comique (which was called Salle Favart after him) 1743–55, writing and adapting works for it. Dir., Comédie-Italienne 1758 to 1762, when it merged with Opéra-Comique. Wrote over 150 opera libs. for composers incl. Grétry, Gluck, and Philidor.

Favola d'Orfeo, La (The Legend [Fable] of Orpheus). (1) *Favola in musica* in prol. and 5 acts by Monteverdi to lib. by Striggio. Prod. Mantua 1607. Rev. in concert version arr. *d'Indy, Paris 1904, London 1924; staged Paris 1911, Oxford 1925; NY Met 1912 (concert), Northampton, Mass., 1929 (stage). Also ed. by *Malipiero, Orff, Westrup, Hindemith, Stevens, Leppard, Whenham, Bartlett, and others.

(2) 1-act opera by Casella, to lib. by C. Pavolini after A. Poliziano's verse-drama (1480). Prod. Venice, 1932.

favola in (or **per**) **musica** (It., 'fable for music'). 17th-cent. term for opera lib. of mythological or legendary character.

Favorite, La (The Favourite). 4-act opera by Donizetti to lib. by Royer, Vaëz, and Scribe. Prod. Paris 1840, New Orleans and London 1843, NY Met 1895 (It. vers.). Also perf. in Italian under titles *Leonora di Guzman* (Padua, 1842) and *Elda* (Milan, 1843), and in Ger. as *Richard und Mathilda* (Cassel, 1841), as well as *La Favorita* (It.). It is a rev. of *L'Ange de Nisida*, in 3 acts by same librettists, comp. 1839 and unperformed.

Fayrfax, Robert (*b* Deeping Gate, Lincs., 1464; *d* St Albans, 1521). Eng. composer and organist. Member of Chapel Royal 1496. Cambridge MusD 1504. Attended Field of the Cloth of Gold, 1520. Comp. 6 masses, motets, other church mus., secular songs, and instr. pieces. First to receive DMus from Oxford Univ. (1511).

FBSM. Fellow of the Birmingham Sch. of Mus.

Fedeltà premiata, La (Fidelity Rewarded). Comic opera in 3 acts by Joseph Haydn to lib. by G. Lorenzi. Comp. 1780. Prod. Eszterháza (inauguration of new th.) 1781, shortened vers. 1782, Vienna 1784, London (Collegiate Th.) 1971, Glyndebourne 1979.

Fedora. 3-act opera by Giordano to lib. by Colautti after Sardou's play (1882). Prod. Milan 1898, London and NY Met 1906.

Fedoseyev, Vladimir (Ivanovich) (*b* Leningrad, 1932). Russ. conductor. Prin. cond., Acad. Orch. of Russ. folk instrs., 1959–74, Moscow Radio and TV SO from 1974. Guest cond. with Eur. orchs. Salzburg Fest. début (concert) 1990 (Moscow Radio SO). Specialist in operas of Rimsky-Korsakov.

Feen, Die (The Fairies). 3-act opera by Wagner (his first) to his own lib. after Gozzi's comedy *La donna serpente* (1762). Comp. 1833–4. Prod. Munich 1888; Birmingham 1969; NY City Opera (concert) 1982.

feierlich (Ger. 'solemn', 'festive'). Expression mark used by Bruckner in his syms. and by Wagner for Siegfried's funeral march in *Götterdämmerung*. Term is assoc. with public celebrations, 'solemn' for religious occasions, 'festive' for secular.

Felciano, Richard (James) (*b* Santa Rosa, Calif., 1930). Amer. composer. Chairman, mus. dept., Lone Mountain Coll., San Francisco, 1959–67. Comp.-in-res., Nat. Centre for experiments in TV, S. Francisco, 1967–71. Teacher at Univ. of Calif., Berkeley, from 1967. Comps. incl. *Sir Gawain and the Green Knight*, opera (1964); *The Captives*, ch., orch. (1965); *Mutations*, orch. (1966); *Glossolalia*,

org., bar., perc., tape (1967); *Soundspace for Mozart*, fl., elec., tape (1970); *Galactic Rounds*, orch. (1972); *In Celebration of Golden Rain*, Indonesian gamelan and pipe org. (1977); *Lumen*, sop., org. (1980); *Orchestra*, orch. (1980); *Crystal*, str. qt. (1981); *Salvadore Allende*, str. qt., cl., perc. (1983); org. conc. (1986); *Shadows*, fl., cl., vn., vc., pf., perc. (1987); *Palladio*, vn., pf., perc. (1989); *Primal Balance*, fl., db. (1991); sym., str. (1993); *Overture concertante*, cl., orch. (1995); str. qt. (1995); *Prelude*, pf. (1997).

Feldman, Morton (*b* NY, 1926; *d* Buffalo, 1987). Amer. composer. Later influenced by the theories and ideas of *Cage, Earle *Brown, Christian Wolff, and David Tudor. Used indeterminacy and graphic notation in his mus. from *Projections* (1950–1). Another major influence was the painting of Jackson Pollock and W. de Kooning, and Feldman said that he tried, in sound, to emulate the world of their art. Low dynamic levels and occasional use of oscillators are also features of his work. Comps. incl.:

OPERA: *Neither* (S. Beckett) (1977).

ORCH.: *Marginal Intersection* (1951); *Atlantis* (1958); *Structures* (1960–2); *In Search of an Orchestration* (1969); *The Viola in My Life IV* (1971); *String Quartet and Orchestra* (1973); *Oboe and Orchestra* (1976); *The Turfan Fragments* (1980); vn. conc. (1984).

INSTR. ENS.: *Projections II* (1951), *V* (1951); *Durations V* (1961); *2 Pieces for 6 Instruments* (1964); *Between Categories* (1969); *The Viola in My Life I and II* (1972); *Routine Investigations* (1976).

CHAMBER MUSIC: *Projection I–V* (1950–1); *3 Pieces*, str. qt. (1956); *Durations I–IV* (1960–2); *Vertical Thoughts I–IV* (1963); *The Viola in My Life III* (1970); *3 Clarinets, Cello and Piano* (1971); *Voice, Violin and Piano* (1976); *String Quartet* (1979), *No.2* (1983); *For John Cage* (1982).

Also vocal and choral works, solo works for vc., perc., and org., and many works for pf. (solo or for 2, 3, 4, or 5 pfs.).

Feldpartita, Feldpartia, or **Feldparthie** (Ger., 'field suite'). Suite for perf. in the open air by a military band. Haydn wrote 6 *Feldpartien*.

Feldpfeife (Ger., 'field pipe'). Renaissance version of the fife, or military fl., used in the Swiss infantry's fife-and-drum corps. Shrill sound due to narrow bore. Also an org. stop.

Fellowes, E(dmund) **H**(orace) (*b* London, 1870; *d* Windsor, 1951). Eng. musicologist and editor. Ordained 1894. Minor canon of St George's Chapel, Windsor, from 1900, and choirmaster 1924–7. Ed. complete works in 36 vols. of the *English Madrigal School* (pubd. 1913–24, rev. 1956 by Dart as *The English Madrigalists*), the *English School of Lutenist Song-Writers* (32 vols., 1920–32, partly rev. 1959–66 by Dart as *The English Lute-Songs*), and the complete works of *Byrd (20 vols., 1937–50, rev. 1962 by Dart, Brett, and Elliott). Also wrote books on the Eng. madrigalists, Byrd and Gibbons. CH 1944.

Felsenstein, Walter (*b* Vienna, 1901; *d* East Berlin, 1975). Austrian opera producer and actor.

Début as actor, Lübeck 1923. Chief opera and drama dir. Basle Stadtth. 1927–9. Opera producer at Cologne (1932–4), Frankfurt (1934–6), Zurich (1938–40), and Schiller Th., Berlin (1940–4). Prod. *Le nozze di Figaro*, Salzburg Fest. 1942. Producer and Intendant, Berlin Komische Oper from 1947, setting new standards in imaginative and totally integrated prod. techniques, particularly in *Die Fledermaus* (1947), *Carmen* (1949), *The Cunning Little Vixen* (1956), *Don Giovanni* (1966), *Fiddler on the Roof* (1971), and *Háry János* (1973). Prod. film version of *Fidelio*. Among producers who worked and studied with him were Joachim *Herz, Harry *Kupfer, Götz *Friedrich, and Ruth *Berghaus.

Felton, William (*b* Drayton, 1715; *d* Hereford, 1769). Eng. composer, organist, harpsichordist, and Anglican clergyman (vicar-choral, Hereford Cath.). His popular hpd. gavotte was adapted for the song *'Farewell Manchester'. Comp. 32 concs. for org. or hpd.

feminine. Term used in such phrases as *feminine cadence* and *feminine ending* to denote relative weakness, e.g. the final chord is reached on a 'weak' beat of the bar. Second subjects in sonata-form are sometimes described as 'feminine', meaning gentler than the first subject. This is a hangover from the age when women were regarded as the weaker sex.

Fenby, Eric (William) (*b* Scarborough, 1906; *d* Scarborough, 1997). Eng. organist, composer, and teacher. His unique claim to fame was that, at the age of 22 and totally unknown, he volunteered to go to Grez-sur-Loing to act as amanuensis to the blind and paralysed *Delius. Several of Delius's late works, incl. *A Song of Summer*, the 3rd vn. sonata, *Songs of Farewell*, *Fantastic Dance*, *Irmelin Prelude* and the *Idyll*, were dictated to Fenby, a laborious and sometimes acrimonious process recorded in Fenby's book *Delius as I knew him* (1936, rev. 1981). Also arr. some of Delius's mus., and after the composer's death in 1934 was active in writing about it, and in working for the Delius Trust. Comps. incl. a sym. and the ov. *Rossini on Ilkla Moor*, and mus. for the film *Jamaica Inn*. Mus. dir. North Riding Training Coll. 1948–62. Prof. of harmony, RAM 1964–77. Art. dir. Delius centenary fest. 1962. OBE 1962.

Fenice, Teatro La. Prin. and extremely beautiful Venetian opera house. Opened 1792, destroyed by fire 1836, rebuilt 1837, restored 1854 and 1938. Again destroyed 1996, reopened 2003. Among operas f.p. there are *L'Italiana in Algeri*, *Semiramide*, *I Capuleti e i Montecchi*, *Ernani*, *Rigoletto*, *La traviata*, *Simon Boccanegra*, *The Rake's Progress*, *The Turn of the Screw*, and *The Fiery Angel*.

Fennell, Frederick (*b* Cleveland, Ohio, 1914; *d* Siesta Key, Flor., 2004). Amer. conductor. Cond. nat. mus. camp, Interlochen, Michigan, 1931–3. On faculty of Eastman Sch. as cond. Little Sym. and Symphonic Band, 1939–65. Founded East-

man Wind. Ens. 1952. Cond.-in-res., Univ. of Miami Sch. of Mus., Coral Gables, Fla., 1965–80. Cond. Kosei wind orch., Tokyo, from 1984.

Fennimore and Gerda. Opera by Delius (his 6th and last) to his own lib., being '2 episodes in the life of *Niels Lyhne* in 11 pictures after the novel by J. P. Jacobsen'. Comp. 1908–10. Prod. Frankfurt 1919; London 1968, St Louis 1981. Intermezzo often perf. as concert item is derived from material in last scene.

Ferdinand III, Emperor of Austria (*b* Graz, 1608; *d* Vienna, 1657). Reigned from 1637. Est. It. opera in Vienna. Comp. *Drama musicum* (1649), Mass, motets, and other church mus. Monteverdi's 8th Book of Madrigals (1638) is dedicated to him.

Ferencsik, János (*b* Budapest, 1907; *d* Budapest, 1984). Hung. conductor. Coach at Hung. State Opera 1927, cond. 1930. Mus. ass. at Bayreuth Fest. 1930–1. Cond. Vienna State Opera 1948–50; chief cond. Hung. Radio and TV SO, 1945–52; Hung. State SO 1952–84; and Budapest PO 1953–76. London début 1957 (LPO), Amer. 1962.

Ferguson, Howard (*b* Belfast, 1908; *d* Cambridge, 1999). N. Irish composer, pianist, and teacher. Prof. at RAM 1948–63. In 1959, after completing his choral work *The Dream of the Rood*, he decided he had said all he wished to say and wrote no more music, concentrating instead on editing of kbd. music. Ed. of complete pf. works of Schubert and of pf. works by Schumann, Brahms, Haydn, Mozart, Beethoven, Mendelssohn, and Tchaikovsky, and of early kbd. works by Eng., Fr., Ger., and It. composers. Works incl.:

ORCH.: *Partita*, Op.5a (1935–6, arr. for 2 pf.,1937); *4 Diversions on Ulster Airs*, Op.7 (1939–42); conc. for pf. and str., Op.12 (1950–1); *Overture for an Occasion*, Op.16 (1952–3).

VOICE(S) ORCH.: *2 Ballads (The Two Corbies, A Lyke-Wake Dirge)*, Op.1, bar., orch. (or pf.) (1928–32); *Amore Langueo*, Op.18, ten., semi-ch., ch., orch. (1955–6); *The Dream of the Rood*, Op.19, sop. or ten., ch., orch. (1958–9).

CHAMBER MUSIC: *5 Irish Folk Tunes*, vc. (or va.), pf. (1927); vn. sonata No.1, Op.2 (1931), No.2, Op.10 (1946); octet, Op.4, 2 vn., va., vc., db., cl., bn., hn. (1933); *5 Pipe Pieces*, treble, alt., and ten. pipes (1934–5); *4 Short Pieces*, Op.6, cl. (or va.), pf. (1932–6); *3 Sketches*, Op.14, fl. (or rec. or ob.), pf. (1932–52); *2 Fanfares*, Op.15, 4 tpt., 3 tb. (1952).

PIANO: *Partita*, Op.5b (1935–6, also for orch.); sonata, Op.8 (1938–40); *5 Bagatelles*, Op.9 (1944).

SONGS: *3 Mediaeval Carols*, Op.3 (1932–3); *Discovery* (5 songs by Denton Welch), Op.13, v., pf. (1951); *5 Irish Folk Songs*, Op.17, v., pf. (1954).

ferial. The word comes from the Lat. *feria*, 'feast day', but has by etymological perversity come to mean an ordinary day, as distinguished from a feast. Hence the application of 'ferial use' to liturgy and mus.

fermata (It.), **Fermate** (Ger.). A pause ⌢. Sometimes the use is a special one—the pause mark in a conc. which indicates the point at which the *cadenza begins.

fermer (Fr., 'to close'; past participle *fermé*). Used in org. mus. as indication to (1) close the swell box, or (2) put a particular stop out of action.

fermo (It.). 'Fixed', in style of perf., as in *canto fermo*.

Ferne Klang, Der (The Distant Sound). 3-act opera by *Schreker to his own lib. Comp. 1903–09. Prod. Frankfurt 1912, BBC studio 1957, Leeds (Opera North) 1992.

Ferneyhough, Brian (*b* Coventry, 1943). Eng. composer. Played in and comp. for brass bands. Emigrated to Switzerland 1969. Lect., Freiberg Hochschule für Musik, 1973–86. Taught comp. at Royal Cons., The Hague, 1986–7; prof. of mus., Univ. of Calif., San Diego, from 1987. Mus. of extreme complexity; elec. devices employed in some works. Works incl.: sonatina, 3 cl. and bn. or bcl. (1963); *4 Miniatures*, fl., pf. (1965); *Prometheus*, wind sextet (1965, rev. 1967); Sonata, 2 pf. (1966); 3 *Pieces*, pf.; *Sonatas*, str. qt. (1967); *Epicycle*, 20 str. (1968); *Missa brevis*, 12 vv. (1969); *Cassandra's Dream Song*, solo fl. (1971); *Sieben Sterne*, org. (1969–70); *Firecycle Beta*, orch. (1969–71); *Transit*, 6 vv., chamber orch. (1972–4, rev. 1975); *Time and Motion Study III*, 16 vv., perc., elecs. (1974); *Time and Motion Study II*, vc., tape, elecs. (1973–6); *Unity Capsules*, fl. (1975–6); *Time and Motion Study I*, bcl. (1971–7); *Funérailles*, str. sextet, db., hp. (1969–77); *La Terre est un homme*, orch. (1977–8); 2nd str. qt. (1979–80); *Lemma-Icon-Epigram*, pf. (1981); *Superscriptio*, piccolo (1981); *Carceri d'Invenzione I*, chamber orch. (1982), *II*, fl., chamber orch. (1983–4), *III*, ww., brass, perc. (1985–6); *Adagissimo*, str. qt. (1983); *Etudes transcendentales*, sop., qt. (1982–5); *Intermedio alla ciaccona*, vn. (1986); *Mnemosyne*, bfl., tape (1986); 3rd str. qt. (1987); 4th str. qt. (1990); *Kurze Schatten*, gui. (1983–9); *Trittico/per G.S.*, db. (1989); *Terrain*, vn., ens. (1992); str. trio (1995); *Algebrah*, ob., str. (1996); *Flurries*, picc., cl., hn., pf., vn., vc. (1997); *Maisons noires*, 22 instrs. (1998); *Doctrine of Similarity*, ch., 3 cl., vn., pf., perc. (2000); *In nomine a 3*, picc., ob., cl. (2001).

Fernflöte (Ger., 'distant flute'). Soft metal org. stop of 8′ length and pitch.

Fernwerk (Ger. 'distant work'). Echo manual of org.

Ferrabosco, Alfonso (*b* Bologna, 1543; *d* Bologna, 1588). It. composer (son of Domenico Ferrabosco who was choirmaster at St Petronio, Bologna, from 1548). Settled in Eng. *c*.1560, entering service of Elizabeth I. In It. 1569–71. Left Eng. 1578 after protesting innocence of charge of robbery and murder. Entered service of Duke of Savoy 1581. Comp. madrigals, motets, and lute pieces. In contest with *Byrd, each set plainsong *Miserere* in 40 different ways.

Ferrabosco, Alfonso (*b* Greenwich, *c*.1575; *d* Greenwich, 1628). Son of above. Violinist in service of James I. Comp. mus. for several of Jonson's masques. Was made 'Composer of King's Music' to Charles I in 1626. Skilled player of lyra viol, for which he wrote fantasies. His 3 sons, Alfonso, Henry, and John, were also musicians in royal service, John becoming org. of Ely Cath.

Ferrara, Franco (*b* Palermo, 1911; *d* Florence, 1985). It. conductor. Début Florence 1938. Went to Holland 1959 to give courses in cond. Famed as a teacher.

Ferras, Christian (*b* Le Touquet, 1933; *d* Paris, 1982). Fr. violinist. Paris début as conc. soloist 1946. Appeared as conc. soloist and recitalist in all leading mus. centres. Gave f. Eng. p. of Fricker's *Rapsodia Concertante*, Cheltenham 1954.

Ferretti, Giovanni (*b* *c*.1540; *d* after 1609). It. composer. Choirmaster Ancona Cath., 1575–9, at Gemona 1586–8, and at Santa Casa, Loreto, 1580–2 and 1596–1603. His 'canzoni alla napolitana' for 5 vv., of which he pubd. 5 books and 2 for 6 vv., were popular throughout Eur. Thomas *Morley acknowledged his influence.

Ferrier, Kathleen (Mary) (*b* Higher Walton, Lancs., 1912; *d* London, 1953). Eng. contralto. Began mus. career as pianist and acc. in N. of Eng. competitive fests. Worked as telephone switchboard operator. Entered singing competition, Carlisle 1937, winning Rose Bowl. London début in *Messiah*, Westminster Abbey 1943, after which she rose rapidly to a leading position among Brit. singers in Elgar's *The Dream of Gerontius*, Bach's *St Matthew Passion*, and other works. Opera début Glyndebourne 1946, CG 1947 (both as Lucretia in *The Rape of Lucretia*). Noted exponent of Mahler's *Das Lied von der Erde* under batons of Walter (with whom she sang the work at Salzburg 1949) and Barbirolli, and frequently appeared in recitals with Britten and Pears. Soloist in f. Brit. p. of Mahler's 3rd sym., 1947. The beauty of her v., combined with a warm and humorous personality, endeared her to audiences, and her early death from cancer was profoundly and widely mourned. Last appearance was at CG 1953 in *Orfeo*, cond. Barbirolli. Royal Phil. Soc. Gold Medal, 1953. CBE 1953.

Fes (Ger.). The note F♭. **Feses**, F♭♭.

Festa, Costanzo (*b* *c*.1490; *d* Rome, 1545). It. composer. Choirmaster at Vatican. Comp. masses, motets, and other church mus., his *Te Deum* still being sung at election of new Pope. Also wrote madrigals, one known in Eng. as *Down in a Flowery Vale*.

festal. Applied in the distinction of ecclesiastical feast days from ordinary, or *ferial days.

Feste Romane (Roman Festivals). Orch. work by Respighi comp. 1928 and f.p. NY 1929 cond. Toscanini. In 4 sections entitled *Circus Maximus*, *The Jubilee*, *The October Festival*, and *Epiphany*.

Festgesang (Festive Hymn). Work for 2 male ch. and brass by Mendelssohn to words by Prof.

Prölss of Freiberg, comp. for fest. at Leipzig 1840 in honour of invention of printing by Gutenberg and f.p. in open market-place. (*Lobgesang* was comp. for same occasion.) 2nd no. of *Festgesang* was adapted by W. H. Cummings to words of hymn *'Hark, the Herald Angels Sing'.

Festin de l'araignée, Le (The Spider's Banquet). Ballet-pantomime with mus. by *Roussel to scenario by G. de Voisins and choreog. by Staats. Prod. Paris 1913. Orch. suite (1912).

festivals (from Lat. *festivalis*, 'festival'). The Eng. derivative 'festival' has come to be applied to gatherings in which one or several of the arts is celebrated. Its first mus. use was possibly the Fest. of the Sons of the Clergy which, from 1698, used an orch. as part of what was really only an elaborate church service. The oldest Eng. fest. in the truer sense is the 3 Choirs Fest., alternating annually between the cath. cities of Gloucester, Hereford, and Worcester. In the 19th cent. the emphasis was on choral mus., and the Handel Fest., the Birmingham, Leeds, Sheffield, and Norwich Fests. flourished. Abroad, the Haydn Fests. in Austria and the 1845 Beethoven Fest. in Bonn were outstanding events. Other famous continental fests. are those at Bayreuth (devoted exclusively to Wagner) and Salzburg (based on Mozart, but with wider scope). Since the end of the 1939–45 war, fests. have developed alongside the growth of tourism. Almost any attractive town (and several unattractive ones) has considered establishing a fest. as a means of attracting visitors. Among the best and longest est. are those at Edinburgh, Cheltenham, Bath, Harrogate, Aldeburgh, York, Haslemere, Holland, Aix-en-Provence, Bregenz, Florence, Savonlinna, Munich, Spoleto, Berkshire (Boston, Mass.), Hollywood Bowl, Ravinia Park (Chicago), Santa Fe, St Louis, Glimmerglass, etc. Some fests. have a theme (one particular composer or one type of mus.); others are just a random coll. of artistic events.

Festivo (Festive). No.3 of Sibelius's 1st set of *Scènes historiques* for orch., Op.25, comp. 1899, rev. 1911.

Festspiel (Ger., 'Festival-play'). A term applied to certain mus. stage works, or works in which mus. has some part. Wagner extended the term in the title to his *Ring* tetralogy, which he called a *Bühnenfestspiel* (Stage-festival-play) and still further in the title of *Parsifal*, described as a *Bühnenweihfestspiel* (stage-consecration festival-play).

Fêtes galantes. Two sets of songs for v. and pf. by Debussy to poems by Verlaine. The first version, comp. 1882, comprised *Pantomime, En sourdine, Mandoline, Clair de Lune*, and *Fantoches*, but three of the songs were revised in 1891–2 and were pubd. in 1903 as Set I (*En sourdine, Fantoches*, and *Clair de Lune*). Set II, comp. 1904, comprises *Les ingénus, Le faune*, and *Colloque sentimental*. No.2 of Set II orch. Roland-Manuel 1923, No.3 orch. Beydts 1929. *Mandoline* and *Pantomime* were issued separately.

Fétis, François (Joseph) (*b* Mons, 1784; *d* Brussels, 1871). Belgian critic, historian, composer, and organist. Org., Douai 1813–18. Prof. of comp., Paris Cons., 1821, librarian 1826–30. Founded and ed. *Revue musicale* 1827–33. Dir., Brussels Cons. 1833–71. Reputation est. by *Biographie universelle des musiciens* (8 vols., 1835–44, 2nd edn. 1860–5; suppl. by Pougin, 2 vols., 1878–80). Also author of vols. of history, theoretical works, and biographies of Paganini and Stradivari. Comp. 8 operas; 2 syms.; 3 pf. quintets; 3 str. qts.; sonatas; church mus.; etc.

Feuermann, Emanuel (*b* Kolomyja, Lwów, 1902; *d* NY, 1942). Austrian-born Amer. cellist (Amer. citizen). Public début at age 11. Teacher of vc. at Cologne Cons. 1917–23, at Berlin Hochschule 1929–33. Amer. début 1934 with Chicago SO. Settled in USA 1938. Frequent soloist with leading orchs. and performer of chamber mus. with Schnabel, Huberman, Rubinstein, and Heifetz.

Feuersnot (Trial by Fire or Fire Famine). 1-act opera by R. Strauss to lib. (*Singgedicht*) by E. von Wolzogen based on Flemish legend. Comp. 1900–1. Prod. Dresden 1901, London 1910, Philadelphia 1927.

Feux d'artifice (Fireworks). Title of pf. prelude by Debussy, last of the 2nd book of 12 (1912–13).

Février, Henry (*b* Paris, 1875; *d* Paris, 1957). Fr. composer. Comp. several operas incl. *Monna Vanna* (1909) and *Gismonda* (1918). Also wrote vn. sonata (1903). Wrote book about Messager.

ff. Abbreviation for *fortissimo*, very loud. Composers occasionally use *fff* and even more.

Ffrangçon-Davies, David (Thomas) (*b* Bethesda, 1855; *d* London, 1918). Welsh baritone. Originally a clergyman, he took up singing and made stage début in opera in London, 1890. Toured USA and Canada 1896–8. High reputation in oratorio. Teacher, RAM 1903–7. Illness cut short career 1907. His daughter Gwen (*b* 1891; *d* 1992) began her career as a sop., singing in *Boughton's *Immortal Hour*, and later became a leading actress, DBE 1991.

Fg. Abbreviation for *Fagott* (Ger.), bassoon.

FGSM. Fellow of Guildhall Sch. of Mus. and Drama.

Fiala, George (*b* Kiev, 1922). Russ.-born Canadian composer. Settled in Canada 1949 (Can. cit. 1955). Comps. incl. pf. conc. (1946), wind quintet (1948); sym. (1950); str. qt. (1956); *Shadows of our Forgotten Ancestors*, orch. (1962); *Canadian Credo*, ch., orch. (1966); *Montréal*, sym. suite (1968); *Serenada concertante*, vc., str. (1968); vc. sonata (1969); vn. conc. (1973); sym. No.4 (*Ukrainian*) (1973); pf. quintet (1982); sax. qt. (1983); *Millennium Liturgy*, cl. (1985); 8 pf. sonatas, two 2-pf sonatas, and *Piano Music No.2* (1987).

Fiala, Joseph (*b* Lochovice, 1754; *d* Donaueschingen, 1816). Cz. composer, oboist, and cellist. Oboist in court band at Oettingen-Wallerstein, 1774–7, during which time he pubd. 6 str. qts. Went to Munich 1777, meeting Mozart, of whom he became close friend. Played in Archbishop of Salzburg's orch. 1778–85, and in Vienna 1785–90. Kapellmeister at Donaueschingen from 1792. Works incl. 12 str. qts.; syms.; concs. for ob., ca., and hn.; pieces for wind band; duos; and sonatas.

Fialkowska, Janina (b Montreal, 1951). Canadian pianist. From 1974 had int. career as soloist with major orchs. Gave f.p. of newly discovered pf. conc. of Liszt, Chicago, May 1990.

fiato (It., 'breath'). Wind instr. are *stromenti a fiato*.

Fibich, Zdeněk (Antonin Václav) (b Všebořice, 1850; d Prague, 1900). Cz. composer. Taught pf. in Paris 1868–9. Returning to Prague, worked as th. cond., but lived mainly from comps. Was first Romantic Cz. composer, in this respect standing apart from Dvořák, Smetana, and Janáček. Among his most remarkable achievements are his concert and stage melodramas, the most ambitious ever written, especially the trilogy *Hippodamia* (1888–91), and his 376 *Moods, Impressions and Reminiscences* for solo piano (1892–9), a 'diary' of his love for his piano pupil, the writer Anežka Schulzová (1868–1905). His operas include *Bukovin* (1870–1); *Blaník* (1874–7); *Nevěsta mesinská* (The Bride of Messina) (1882–3); *Bouře* (The Tempest, after Shakespeare) (1893–4); *Hedy* (1894–5); *Šárka* (1896–7); and *Pád Arkuna* (The Fall of Arkona) (1898–9). Wrote much incidental music; 3 syms.; several sym.-poems; chamber mus.; and over 200 songs. His sym.-poem *At Twilight* (V podvečer) (1893) contains the celebrated *Poem*.

Fibonacci series. See *number systems*.

Ficher, Jacobo (b Odessa, 1896; d Buenos Aires, 1978). Russ. composer and violinist. In 1923 settled in Argentina, founding contemp. mus. group, conducting, and after 1956 teaching comp. at Nat. Cons., Buenos Aires. Comp. incl. 2 Chekhov chamber operas, The **Bear* (1952) and *Proposal of Marriage* (1956); 3 pf. concs. (1945, 1954, 1960); 8 syms. (1932–65); sax. qt.; fl. conc.; 7 pf. sonatas; wind quintet; 4 str. qts. (1927–52); etc.

fiddle. Colloquial term for any kind of bowed instr., especially the vn., or in reference to its use as a 'folk' instr. (as in Mahler's 4th Sym. where a solo vn., specially tuned, is instructed to play *wie ein Fiedel* ('like a fiddle', in folk style). Also name for the medieval ancestor of the vn.

Fiddle Fugue. Nickname for org. fugue in D minor by Bach (because it was arr. from an earlier version for solo vn., 1720).

Fidelio, oder Der Triumph der ehelichen Liebe (Fidelio, or The Triumph of Married Love). Opera in 2 acts by Beethoven, Op.72, to lib. by Josef von Sonnleithner based on Bouilly's *Léonore, ou L'Amour conjugal*. F.p. in orig. 3-act version,

Vienna 1805. Reduced to 2 acts by Stefan von Breuning 1806, prod. Vienna 1806. Further rev., and lib. rev. by G. F. Treitschke, 1814, prod. Vienna 1814, London 1832, NY 1839. Orig. 1805 version, under title **Leonore*, reconstructed in edn. by E. Prieger, 1905. Of the 4 ovs., *Fidelio* (comp. for 1814 revival but not ready for f.p.) is now used in the th. *Leonora* No.2 is thought to have been comp. 1804–5, No.3 in 1806, and No.1 in 1807 for a projected Prague perf. No.3 is sometimes perf. as an entr'acte before final scene. Bouilly's lib. was also the basis of *Gaveaux's *Léonore* (Paris 1798), *Paër's *Leonora* (Dresden 1804), and *Mayr's *L'Amor coniugale* (Padua 1805).

Fiedler, Arthur (b Boston, Mass., 1894; d Brookline, Mass., 1979). Amer. conductor. Joined Boston SO as violinist 1915, later violist. Formed Boston Sinfonietta, conducting it in Boston and on tour. In 1930 became cond. of Boston 'Pops' concerts, spreading their fame through recordings.

Fiedler, (August) Max (b Zittau, 1859; d Stockholm, 1939). Ger. conductor. Taught at Hamburg Cons. from 1882, becoming dir. 1903–8. Cond., Hamburg Phil. 1904–8; Boston SO 1908–12; mus. dir. in Essen 1916–34. Comp. sym., ov., and pf. quintet.

Field, Helen (b Awyn, N. Wales, 1951). Welsh soprano. Début 1976 with WNO as Offenbach's Euridice. Sang many roles with WNO 1976–86, incl. Tatyana, Desdemona, the Vixen, Poppea, Jenůfa, Marzelline, Mimì, Mařenka, Micaela, and Katerina in Martinů's The Greek Passion. CG début 1982; sang with ENO 1983–90; NY Met début 1984. Sang title-role in f. Brit. p. of *Daphne* (Leeds, Opera North, 1987). Created JoAnn in *New Year* (Houston 1989 and in f. Brit. p. at Glyndebourne (her début) 1990. Also many concert appearances.

Field, John (b Dublin, 1782; d Moscow, 1837). Irish pianist and composer. Début in Dublin aged 9. In London became pupil of *Clementi, whose pfs. he exhibited. Played a conc. by Dussek at *Pinto's benefit concert 1798 and his own 1st conc. at King's Th., 1799. In 1802 Clementi took him to Fr., Ger., and Russia, where he settled in St Petersburg in 1803, becoming teacher and touring Europe as virtuoso pianist. Last played in Eng. 1831–2. His importance as a composer for the pf. has only latterly been recognized. He invented the style and name *Nocturne* for short pieces, composing 19. Wrote 7 pf. concs., 4 sonatas, and other works. Schumann and Liszt admired his work, and Chopin developed the nocturne form.

Field-Hyde, Margaret (b Cambridge, 1905; d Goring-on-Thames, 1995). Eng. soprano and violinist. Début 1928 in Cambridge revival of Purcell's *King Arthur*. Specialist in Purcell and Bach, but also in works by Lutyens and other contemps. Founded Golden Age Singers 1950.

Fierrabras. Opera in 3 acts by Schubert (D796) to lib. by J. Kupelwieser after story by J. G. G. Büsching and F. H. von der Hagen in *Buch der*

Liebe (1809) and Friedrich de la Motte Fouqué's *Eginhard und Emma* (1811). Comp. 1823. Prod. Vienna (concert, 3 numbers) 1835, Vienna (Th. an der Wien, cond. Abbado) 1988; Karlsruhe 1897 (with mus. rev. by *Mottl); London (concert extracts) 1938, BBC studio 1971, QEH 1988 (f. prof. p., semi-staged, cond. Tate); Oxford 1986; Philadelphia 1980; Buxton 2000.

Fiery Angel, The (*Ognennyï Angel*; sometimes known as *The Flaming Angel*). Opera in 5 acts, Op.37, by Prokofiev to his lib. based on novel by V. Bryusov (1907). Comp. 1919–23, rev. 1926–7. F.p. Paris (concert) 1954, staged Venice 1955, London and NY 1965. Prokofiev's 3rd Sym. uses themes from the opera.

fife. Ancient side-blown instr. like a high-pitched fl., frequently used in military bands. Modern drum and fife bands incl. low-pitched fls.

fifteenth. A high-pitched *diapason org. stop sounding 2 octaves above the note played; 2′ length and pitch on manuals, 4′ on pedals.

fifth. Interval consisting of 3 whole-tones and a semitone, so-called because no. of notes from one extreme of the interval to the other in the diatonic scale is 5. A perfect 5th is the distance from, for example, C to G. From C up to G♭ is a diminished fifth, and from C up to G♯ is an augmented fifth. See under *consecutive*.

'Fifths' Quartet (Quintenquartett). Name for Haydn's Str. Qt. in D minor, Op.76, No.2 (1797–8) because it begins with melodic leaps of a 5th.

figural, figured (Eng.); **figuré** ('Fr.); **figurato** (It.); **figural, figuriert** (Ger.). Florid. (1) A 'figured chorale', is one in which the melody is acc. by quicker notes in the other parts.

(2) In solo vocal mus. the word implies *coloratura*.

Figuralmusik. See *musica figurata*.

figurato, figurata (It.). See *figural*.

figure. (1) In mus. structure, this word usually carries the same meaning as *Motif*. A 'figure of accompaniment' refers to the mus. cell from which a certain type of song acc. may be evolved.

(2) In dancing the word implies a set of movts. by the dancers as a body, forming a distinct division of the whole. This element is prominent in a *figure dance*, as opposed to a *step dance*, in which it is largely absent.

figured bass. See *basso continuo*.

filare la voce, filar il tuono (It.), **filer la voix (le son)** (Fr.). To draw out the voice (tone). The *messa di voce*; or sometimes understood to mean the holding of a long note without any dynamic fluctuation.

Fille aux cheveux de lin, La (The girl with the flaxen hair). Pf. piece by Debussy, No.8 of his *Préludes*, Book I. Comp. Jan. 1910, f.p. London 1910. Inspired by poem by Leconte de Lisle.

Fille de Madame Angot, La (Mme Angot's Daughter). 3-act operetta by Lecocq to lib. by Clairville, Siraudin, and Koning, after Maillot's vaudeville *Madame Angot* (1796). Prod. Brussels 1872, London 1873, NY 1873.

Fille du Régiment, La (The Daughter of the Regiment). 2-act opera by Donizetti to lib. by V. de Saint-Georges and Bayard. Prod. Paris 1840, London 1843, New Orleans 1843.

Fille mal gardée, La (The Unchaperoned Girl). 2-act ballet to lib. by Dauberval orig. to medley of Fr. songs and airs. Prod. Bordeaux 1789. For 1828 revival in Paris, Hérold provided new score, using some of orig. tunes, extracts from Rossini and Donizetti operas, and his own mus. Mus. for 1864 Berlin version comp. by Hertel. For 1960 London revival to Ashton choreog., John Lanchbery prepared new score based mainly on Hérold but with Hertel's 'Clog Dance'.

film music. Mus. written to acc. action in documentary and feature films. In the days of silent films a pianist or small orch. in the cinema pit provided a mus. commentary on the action, usually by a selection of appropriate popular operatic and orch. items. But the first piece of 'original' film mus. was written by Saint-Saëns (Op.128) for H. Lavedan's film *L'Assassinat du Duc de Guise*, 1908.

An ambitious development for its day was the silent film made in 1924–5 of Strauss's *Der Rosenkavalier*. For this, mus. from the opera was adapted for th. orch., with some additional items for extra scenes. With the advent of the 'talkie' and the development of the sound-track, the opportunities for the use of illustrative mus. were gradually seized and exploited by composers. In Hollywood, the capital of the cinema industry, mus. for many films was written by Max Steiner and Erich *Korngold and later by Miklós *Rózsa, Dmitri Tiomkin, Alfred Newman, and André Previn. Distinguished film music was written by Bernard *Herrmann for Welles's *Citizen Kane* and for a series of Hitchcock films, notably *Psycho*. Fr. composers such as *Auric wrote for films, and in Britain practically all the leading composers—Britten, Walton, Berners, Vaughan Williams, Rawsthorne, Bax, Ireland, Alwyn, Arnold, Richard Rodney Bennett, and many others—have written film mus. Some of the greatest film mus. was written by Prokofiev for Eisenstein's *Alexander Nevsky*, and Shostakovich, Khachaturian, Milhaud, Honegger, and Copland also wrote effective film scores. Walton's *Henry V* and Vaughan Williams's *Scott of the Antarctic* are highly regarded. Mention should also be made of the scores by Michel Legrand, Maurice Jarre, John Barry, Henry Mancini, John Williams, and Burt Bacharach, while Addinsell's clever pastiche of a romantic pf. conc., the 'Warsaw' Conc. from *Dangerous Moonlight*, perhaps made a wider audience aware of the potency of film music. There have been examples of brilliant use in a film of mus. which was not written specially for it, e.g. Rachmaninov's C minor pf. conc. in *Brief*

Encounter; Mozart's C major pf. conc. No.21, K467 (2nd movt.) in *Elvira Madigan*, the 'Sunrise' opening of Strauss's *Also sprach Zarathustra* in *2001—a Space Odyssey*, and the *Adagietto* from Mahler's 5th sym. in *Death in Venice*. In a special category was **Fantasia* (1940), in which Walt Disney cartoons were used to illustrate mus. by Bach, Beethoven, Dukas, Ponchielli, Mussorgsky, Tchaikovsky, Schubert, and Stravinsky, played by the Philadelphia Orch., cond. Stokowski. And there is Schoenberg's *Accompaniment to a Film Scene*, Op.34 (1930), comp. for no particular film or scene.

filter. Elec. device permitting selective transmission of specified frequencies of the input signal by attenuating, or filtering out, unwanted frequencies.

fin (Fr.). End.

fin (It.). Same as **fino*.

final. (1) (Eng.). The note on which the modal scale ends (see *modes*), as on the keynote of the major or minor scale.
(2) (Fr.). **finale*.

finale (It.). End. The last movt. of a work in several movts., i.e. sym., conc., suite, sonata, etc. Also the ens. ending an act of an opera.

Finck [van de Vinck], **Herman** (*b* London, 1872; *d* London, 1939). Eng. composer and conductor. At 16 was pianist and violinist at Palace Th., London, becoming cond. there 1900. Mus. dir. Drury Lane 1922–31. Comp. comic operas, such as *Katinka*, and th. mus. Best known for his short piece *In the Shadows* (1910).

Finck, Hermann (*b* Pirna, 1527; *d* Wittenberg, 1558). Ger. organist and composer of motets, etc. Wrote treatise *Practica Musica* (1556), which deals with plainsong, canons, the modes, and performing practice.

Fine, Irving (*b* Boston, Mass., 1914; *d* Natick, Mass., 1962). Amer. composer and critic. Ass. prof. of mus., Harvard, 1939–50. Chairman, sch. of creative arts, Brandeis Univ., from 1950. Mus. tended towards neo-classicism; in his last years he was attracted by 12-note technique. Works incl. Sym. (1962); *Music for Modern Dance* (1941); *3 Choruses from Alice in Wonderland* (1949), 2nd series (1953); *Mutability*, 6 songs for mez. and pf. (1952); *The Hour Glass*, ch., orch. (1949); *Serious Song*, orch. (1955); *Blue Towers*, orch. (1959); *Diversions*, orch. (1960); vn. sonata; str. qt.; etc.

Fine, Vivian (*b* Chicago, 1913; *d* Bennington, VT, 2000). Amer. composer. Has held several teaching posts, notably at Bennington Coll., Vermont, 1964–87, and from 1931 championed modern pf. mus. Her works incl. pf. conc.; str. qt.; vn. sonata; *Alcestis* (ballet for Martha Graham, 1960); and *A Guide to the Life Expectancy of a Rose* for sop., ten., and chamber ens.

Fingal's Cave (The Hebrides) (*Die Hebriden (Fingals Höhle)*). Ov. in B minor, Op.26, by Mendels-

sohn, who is said to have invented the prin. theme while on a visit to the Hebrides and the island of Staffa in 1829. (In fact he jotted down the theme in a letter written before he went to Staffa. The orig. version was called *The Lonely Island*.) Comp. 1830, rev. 1832. After rev. the work was f.p., as *The Isles of Fingal*, London, CG 1832. It is in effect a descriptive tone-poem.

finger board. In a str. instr., the long strip of hard wood over which the str. are stretched.

Fingerhut, Margaret (*b* London, 1955). Eng. pianist. Greater London Arts Assoc. Young Musician of the Year 1981. Soloist with leading orchs. Specialist in mus. of **Bax.

fingering (of kbd. instr.). Since the end of the 18th cent., this has been standardized on something like modern principles. Before this period there was a good deal of passing of the 3 middle fingers over one another and comparatively little use of the thumb and little finger; this was partly due to the fall of the keys being much shallower than with modern instr. The pf. killed finger-crossing, since it demanded an actual blow (properly a blow by pressure—one sufficient to *throw* the hammer at the strings, yet so exactly controlled as to throw it with either the greater force required by a fortissimo or the lesser required by a pianissimo).

Clementi firmly est. the modern principles of fingering: his use of the thumb was the same as ours, except that he did not use it on the black keys, as is sometimes done today. These modern principles incl. the division of a scale into 2 groups of 3 and 4 notes respectively, with the thumb as the pivot between them, the playing of arpeggio passages on the basis of the octave, some adaptation of fingering to the hand of the individual player, the planning of the fingering of a passage by working backwards from the point at which it is ultimately to arrive, and the division of such a passage into 'physical groups' as units, each of these being considered as a chord.

Organ fingering follows much the same principles as pf. fingering but, as the nature of the instr. generally calls for a perfect legato, more substitution of finger is required, a key often being depressed by one finger and then held by another, so freeing the first for use on another key.

See also *English fingering*.

finite canon. A **canon which is not repeated, the converse of 'perpetual' or 'infinite' canon.

Fink, Bernarda (*b* Buenos Aires, 1955). Argentinian mezzo-soprano of Slovenian parentage. Studied at Inst. of Art, Teatro Colón. Moved to Eur. 1985, singing with all major orchs., giving recitals, and making recordings of Wolf, Schubert, and Dvořák. Opera in Geneva, Prague, Salzburg, Barcelona, etc.

Finlandia. Short work for orch., Op.26, by Sibelius. Comp. 1899 as final tableau (Finland

Awakes!) of nationalist pageant to raise money for a press pension fund in Helsinki (and to support press in its struggle to stay free from Tsarist pressure). Rev. 1900, when it was given title *Finlandia*, and f.p. Helsinki, July 1900. Its patriotic fervour, though no folk-song material was used, led to its adoption as a symbol of Finnish nat. aspirations. F.p. in Eng. 1905 (Liverpool, cond. Bantock).

Finley, Gerald (*b* Montreal, 1960). Canadian baritone. Chorister in Ottawa. Studied at Ottawa Univ. then at RCM, King's Coll., Cambridge, and Nat. Opera Studio. Glyndebourne chorus 1986. NY Met début 1998 (Papageno). Salzburg début 2004 (Guglielmo). Created Harry in Turnage's *The Silver Tassie* (ENO 2000), Jaufré Rudel in Saariaho's *L'amour de loin* (Salzburg 2000), and Oppenheimer in Adams's *Dr Atomic* (San Francisco 2005). Roles incl. Don Giovanni, Onegin, Figaro, Pilgrim, and Owen Wingrave. Recitals feature songs by Ives, Barber, Schubert, and Duparc.

Finney, Ross Lee (*b* Wells, Minn., 1906; *d* Cornel, CA, 1997). Amer. composer and teacher. Taught at Smith Coll., 1929–47. Prof. of mus., Univ. of Michigan 1949–74, where he est. EMS. Since 1950 he has combined in his mus. tonalism with 12-note and serial techniques. Works incl. opera *Weep Torn Land* (1984); 4 syms.; 8 str. qts.; vn. sonatas; vc. sonatas; pf. qt.; pf. quintets; str. quintets; 2 pf. concs.; 2 vn. concs.; alto sax. conc.; and choral pieces.

Finnie, Linda (*b* Scotland, 1952). Scottish mezzo-soprano. Won Ferrier Prize 1974 and won 's-Hertogenbosch comp. 1977. Prof. début 1975 with Scottish Opera (in Robin Orr's *Hermiston*). CG début 1978; ENO 1978 (roles incl. Brangäne, Eboli, Amneris, and Ulrica); WNO 1980; Frankfurt Opera and Nice Opera 1987; Bayreuth Fest. 1988. Many concert-hall perfs. of Mahler and Elgar.

Finnilä, Birgit (*b* Falkenberg, Swed., 1931). Swed. contralto. Exponent of Wagner, Mahler, Brahms, etc. Prof. début Göteborg 1963. Opera début Göteborg 1967 as Gluck's Orpheus. Sang Erda in *Ring* at Salzburg Easter Fests. 1973 and 1974. Paris début 1976; Amer. début, NY 1979; NY Met 1981.

Finnissy, Michael (Peter) (*b* Tulse Hill, London, 1946). Eng. composer and pianist. Formed mus. dept. at London Sch. of Contemporary Dance, teaching there 1969–74. Virtuoso pianist who has commissioned works from Lutyens, Weir, Knussen, Osborne, and Skempton. Taught at Univ. of Sussex 1989–90. Works incl.:

OPERAS: *The Undivine Comedy* (1987–8, rev. 1992, prod. Paris 1988); *Thérèse Raquin* (1992–3, rev. 2005); *Shameful Vice* (1994).

MUSIC THEATRE: *Mysteries*: 1. *The Parting of Darkness from Light*, 2 ten., 2 bar., bass. 2. *The Earthly Paradise*, mez., ten., bass, 2 actors, ens. 3. *The Great Flood*, ten., 4 actors, 4 actresses, 2 instr., 3 perc. 4. *The Prophecy of Daniel*, sop., bar., actor, ch.,

hp., perc. 5. *The Parliament of Heaven*, 3 sop., mez., ten., 2 actors, 3 ch., children's ch., ens. 6. *The Annunciation*. 7. *The Betrayal and Crucifixion of Jesus of Nazareth*. 8. *The Deliverance of Souls*, 2 sop., mez., 2 ten., 2 bar., bass, 4 ch., children's ch., orch. (1972–9); *Bouffe*, for a person alone on stage (1975); *Vaudeville*, mez., bar., 2 mimes, 6 instr., perc. (1983).

ORCH.: *Song II* and *IV* (1963–9); *Song X* (1968–75); *Offshore* (1975–6); *Pathways of Sun and Stars* (1976); *Sea and Sky* (1979–80); *Red Earth* (1988); *Eph-phatha* (1988–9); *Plain Harmony* (1993); *Glad Day* (1994); *Speak its Name!* (1996).

INSTR. ENS.: *Piece to honour Igor Stravinsky*, fl., va., hp. (1971); pf. conc. No.1 (1975), No.2 (1975–6), No.3 (1978), No.7 (1981); *Nobody's Jig*, str. qt. (1980–1); *Australian Sea Shanties II*, recorder consort (1983); str. qt. (1984); str. trio (1986); *Obrecht Motetten I*, 9 instr. (1989), *II*, mand., gui., hp. (1989), *III*, 13 instr. (1990), *IV*, brass quintet (1990), *V*, 11 wind, db., pf. (1992); *Cambridge Codex*, fl., vn., vc., 2 bells (1991); *Mars + Venus*, instr. ens. (1993); *Independence Quadrilles*, pf. trio (1995); *Bright Future Ignoring Dark Past*, pf. trio (2000); *Molly-House*, instr. ens. (2004).

Also choral works; many comps. for vv. and instr. incl. *Sir Tristran*, sop., cl., pf., vn., va., vc. (1978) and *Lay de la Fonteinne*, mez., fl., picc., ob., vib. or pf. (1990); comps. for solo instr. incl. *Ru Tchou*, perc. (1975), *Terekemme*, cembalo (1981), and *Enek*, vn. (1990); and pf. pieces.

fino (It.). As far as, e.g. *fino al segno*, as far as the sign (⌣).

Finta giardiniera, La (The Feigned Garden-Girl). *Opera buffa* in 3 acts (K196) by Mozart to lib. dubiously attrib. Petrosellini, written for *Anfossi (1774), and altered by Coltellini. Comp. 1774. Prod. Munich 1775, NY 1927, London 1930. Anfossi's 3-act opera was prod. Rome 1774, London 1775 (as *La marchesa giardiniera*), and Frankfurt 1782.

Finta semplice, La (The Feigned Simpleton). *Opera buffa* in 3 acts (K51) by Mozart to lib. by Coltellini, after lib. by Goldoni first set by Perillo (1764). Prod. Salzburg 1769, London (Paumgartner ed.) 1956, Boston, Mass., 1961.

Finzi, Gerald (Raphael) (*b* London, 1901; *d* Oxford, 1956). Eng. composer. Taught comp. at RAM 1930–3. After marriage in 1933, he retired to isolated life in countryside, building his own house at Ashmansworth, nr. Newbury. Formed Newbury String Players, 1939. Worked in Ministry of War Transport, 1941–5. For the Newbury players he revived and ed. many 18th-cent. works by Eng. composers such as Boyce, Stanley, and Mudge. Also worked to obtain publication of mus. by Ivor *Gurney, whom he never met. Was collector of rare books and grower of rare apples.

His works, some of them spread over many years and constantly revised, can be broadly linked to the Eng. tradition of Elgar and Vaughan Williams, but the influence on him of these composers can be overstressed. His settings of Eng. poetry, particularly of Thomas Hardy, have a distinctive individuality, with musical imagery to match the verbal. Nor would it be just to describe him as a miniaturist, for such works as *For St Cecilia*, the *Intimations of Immortality*, and the vc. conc. show an ability to handle larger forms. Through Parry, he reached back to J. S. Bach in the vocal style of his masterpiece, the cantata *Dies Natalis*; and the same fluent imaginative vision gives an unfading emotional power to his Shakespeare song-cycle *Let us Garlands Bring* and to his touching Christmas work *In terra pax*. Prin. works:

ORCH.: *A Severn Rhapsody* (1923); *Introit*, vn., orch. (1925, rev. 1935, 1942); *New Year Music* (1926, rev. c.1946); *Eclogue*, pf., str. (1920s, rev. 1940s); *Romance*, str. (1928); *The Fall of the Leaf* (1929, rev. 1939–41, orch. completed by H. Ferguson); cl. conc., str. (1948–9); *Grand Fantasia and Toccata*, pf. orch. (*Fantasia* 1928, rev. 1953, *Toccata* 1953); vc. conc. (1951–5).

CHORAL: *Lo, the full final sacrifice*, with org. (1946, orch. 1947); *Intimations of Immortality*, ten., ch., orch. (1936–8, 1949–50); *For St Cecilia*, ten., ch., orch. (1947); *Magnificat*, with org. (1952, orch. 1956); *In terra pax*, sop., bar., ch., str., hp., cymbals (1954, full orch. 1956).

SOLO VOICE & ORCH. or ENS.: *By Footpath and Stile*, bar., str. qt. (1921–2); **Dies Natalis*, sop. (or ten.), str. (1926, 1938–9); *Farewell to Arms*, ten., str. or small orch. (1925–44); *2 Milton Sonnets*, ten. (or sop.), small orch. (c.1928).

UNACC. VOICES: *3 Short Elegies*, SATB (1926); *7 Part-songs*, SATB (1934–7); *White-flowering days* (in *A Garland for the Queen*), SATB (1953).

VOICE(S) & PIANO: *A Young Man's Exhortation*, 10 songs (Hardy), ten., pf. (1926–33); *Earth and Air and Rain*, 10 songs (Hardy), bar., pf. (1928–36); *Before and After Summer*, 10 songs (Hardy), bar., pf. (1938–49); **Let Us Garlands Bring*, 5 songs (Shakespeare), bar., pf. (also with orch.) (1929–42); *Let us now praise famous men*, male vv., pf. (1952); *Till Earth Outwears*, 7 songs (Hardy), sop. or ten., pf. (1927–55); *I said to Love*, 6 songs (Hardy), bar., pf. (1928–56).

fioritura (It.). Flowering (pl. *fioriture*). In 17th and 18th cents., the vocal decoration of the melody of an operatic aria, etc., usually extemporized during perf. by the singer. Also a common practice in vn. and kbd. playing.

fipple. The block of wood which canalizes the air (i.e. plugs the mouthpiece) in woodwind instr. of the *recorder family, known therefore as 'fipple flutes'.

Firebird, The (*Zhar-Ptitsa*, Fr. *L'Oiseau de Feu*). Ballet (*conte dansé*) in 1 act and 3 scenes by Stravinsky, comp. 1909–10 and orig. choreog. by Fokine, with later versions by Bolm, Balanchine, Lifar, Cranko, and Béjart. Prod. Paris 1910 (Diaghilev Ballets Russes). Based on Russ. fairy-tales. Mus. had 19 sections. Suite, 1911, with orch. as

for ballet, had 5 movts.; rev. and re-orch. (also 5 movts.), 1919; further rev. with orch. as 1919 but with 10 movts., 1945.

Fires of London, The. Instr. ens. founded 1970 by Peter Maxwell Davies after reorganization of *Pierrot Players. Gave many f.ps. of major works by *Maxwell Davies. Disbanded 1987.

Fireworks. Fantasy, Op.4, for large orch. by Stravinsky. Comp. 1908, f.p. St Petersburg 1909.

Fireworks Music (Music for the Royal Fireworks). Suite of 8 movts. by Handel for wind band, comp. for and played at fireworks display in Green Park, London, to mark Peace of Aix-la-Chapelle, 1749. Later Handel added str. parts. Arr. for modern orch. by *Harty and by *Mackerras.

Firkušný, Rudolf (*b* Napajedlá, Moravia, 1912; *d* Staatsburg, NY, 1994). Amer. pianist of Cz. birth. Début Prague 1920, London 1933, NY 1938. Worldwide tours. Settled in USA 1940 and became Amer. cit. Gave f.ps. of 3rd and 4th concs. of Martinů (1949, 1956) and of concs. by Menotti (1945) and Hanson (1948). Salzburg Fest. début 1957. Taught at Berkshire Mus. Center, Juilliard Sch. of Mus. Comp. pf. conc., str. qt., pf. pieces, and songs.

Firsova, Elena (*b* Leningrad, 1950). Russ. composer. Strongly influenced by Edison *Denisov. Her mus. is melodic and introspective, concentrating on vocal settings and chamber ensembles. She has made several settings of the poet Osip Mandelstam. Settled in Eng. 1991. Taught at Dartington 1992. Prof. and comp.-in-res. Keele Univ. from 1993. Works incl.:

OPERAS: *Feast in Plague Time* (Pushkin), Op.7 (1972); *The Nightingale and the Rose* (Wilde and C. Rossetti) (1991).

ORCH.: *5 Pieces*, Op.6 (1971); *Chamber Music*, Op.9 (1973); *Stanzas*, Op.13 (1975); *Autumn Music*, chamber orch., Op.39 (1988); *Nostalgia* (1989); *Pimpinella* (arr. of Tchaikovsky's song, Op.38 No.6) (1989); *Cassandra* (1992); *Mnemosyne*, chamber orch. (1995); Chamber Conc. No.6/Pf. Conc. No.2 (1996); *The Sound of Time Past* (1997); *Leaving*, str. (1998).

SOLO INSTR. & ORCH.: vc. conc. No.1, Op.110 (1973); vn. conc. No.1, Op.14 (1976), No.2, Op.29 (1983); *Postlude*, Op.18, hp., orch. (1977); chamber concs., No.1, Op.19, fl., str. (1978), No.2 (vc. conc. No.2), Op.26 (1982), No.3, Op.33, pf., orch. (1985), No.4, Op.37, hn., ens. (1988); conc. for vn., 13 str. (1993).

VOICE(S) & ORCH.: *Tristia*, Op.22, v., chamber orch. (1979); *The Stone*, Op.28 (1983); *Augury*, Op.38, ch., orch. (1988); *Secret Way*, Op.52, v., orch. (1992); *The Former Things are Passed Away*, sop., bass, ch., chamber orch. (1999).

ENSEMBLE: *Scherzo*, Op.1, fl., ob., cl., bn., pf. (1967); pf. trio, Op.8 (1972); *Capriccio*, Op.15, fl., sax. qt. (1976); *Mysteria*, Op.30, org., perc. (1984); *Music for 12*, Op.34 (1986); *Odyssey*, fl., hn., perc., hp., vn., va., vc. (1990); *The Singing Forest*, 4 rec., str. (1999); *Euphonisms*, euph., pf. (2003).

VOICE & ENS.: *Petrarca's Sonnets*, Op.17 (1976); *Night*, Op.20, v., sax. qt. (1978); *Earthly Life*, Op.31, cantata, sop., ens. (1984); *Forest Walks*, Op.36, sop., ens. (1987); *Stygian Song*, sop., ens. (1989); *The Shell*, Op.49, sop., ens. (1991); *Whirlpool*, Op.50, mez., fl., perc. (1991); *Silentium*, Op.51, mez., str. qt. (1991); *Distance*, Op.53, v., cl., str. qt. (1992); *Before the Thunderstorm*, ens. (1994–5); *Winter Elegy*, counterten., str. trio. (1999).

CHAMBER MUSIC: str. qts.: No.1, 5 *Pieces*, Op.4 (1970), No.2, Op.11 (1974), No.3, *Misterioso*, in mem. Stravinsky, Op.24 (1980), No.4, *Amoroso*, Op.40 (1989), No.5 (1993–4), No.6 (1994), No.7, *Compassione* (1995), No.8, *The Stone Guest* (1995), No.9, *The Door is Closed* (1996), No.10, *La Malinconia* (1998); *Legend*, hn., pf. (1967); *Suite for Viola Solo*, Op.2 (1967); 2 *Pieces*, vn., pf. (1968); vc. sonata, Op.5 (1971); solo cl. sonata, Op.16 (1976); 2 *Inventions*, fl. (1977); 3 *Pieces*, xyl. (1978); 3 *Pieces*, hn., pf. (1980); *Sphinx*, hp. (1982); *Spring Sonata*, Op.27, fl., pf. (1982); *Fantasie*, Op.32, vn. (1985); *Monologue*, bn. (1989); *Verdehr-Terzett*, pf., cl., vn. (1990); *Far Away*, Op.48, sax. qt. (1991); *The Night Demons*, vc., pf. (1993); *Frozen Time*, pf. qt. (1999); *Perpetual Turn*, fl., ob., hp., str. trio (2000); *Epitaph*, str. trio (2003).

UNACC. CHORAL: 3 *Poems by Osip Mandelstam*, Op.3, mixed ch. (1970); *The Bell* (with D. Smirnov), mixed ch. (1976); *Equinox* (1998); *Tears* (2001); *Beauty Will Save the World* (2002).

VOICE & INSTR.: 3 *Romances on Poems by Boris Pasternak*, v., pf. (1966–7); *Creation*, high v., pf. (1967); 2 *Romances on poems by Vladimir Mayakovsky*, v., pf. (1969); *Autumn Songs*, Op.12, v., pf. (1980); 3 *Poems by Osip Mandelstam*, Op.23, v., pf. (1980); *Shakespeare's Sonnets*, Op.25, v., org. (1981); *The Dream*, mez., pf. (1988); 7 *Haiku*, Op.47, sop., sop. lyre (1991); 2 *Sonnets of Shakespeare*, v., org. (1991); *Distance*, v., cl., str. qt. (1992).

PIANO: 2 *Polyphonic Piece* (1966); *Invention à two* (1966); *Elegy*, Op.21 (1979); sonata, Op.35 (1986); *Hymn to Spring* (1993); *Evening Music* (1996); *For Alissa* (Variations) (2002).

first. In orch. parlance this term implies leadership of a section (e.g. 1st cl., or prin. cl.) in addition to, often, a part higher in pitch. The 1st vn. is leader of the orch., but the 1st vns. are a section div. from the 2nd vns. In choral terms a higher-pitched part.

first inversion. That in which the 3rd of a chord becomes the bass, e.g. common chord C–E–G becomes E–G–C or E–C–G.

First Post. Brit. Army bugle-call sounded at 9.30 p.m. which calls all men back to barracks. See also *Last Post*.

first subject. (1) The first melody, motif, or theme in a *sonata-form movt., in the tonic key. (2) First of the 2 themes of a double fugue.

First Walpurgis Night (Mendelssohn). See *Erste Walpurgisnacht*.

Fis (Ger.). The note F♯. **Fisis**, F♯♯.

Fischer, Adam (*b* Budapest, 1949). Hung. conductor. Brother of Ivan *Fischer. Winner of Cantelli cond. comp., Milan, 1973. Cond. Finn. Nat. Opera 1974–7, Karlsruhe Opera 1977–8, Freiburg 1981–3, and Kassel from 1987. Mus. dir. Haydn Fest., Eisenstadt. Débuts: Salzburg Fest. 1980 (concert); Paris Opéra 1984; Amer. 1986 (Boston SO); CG 1989.

Fischer, Annie (*b* Budapest, 1914; *d* Budapest, 1995). Hung. pianist. Début Budapest 1922 in Beethoven's C major conc. Winner, Int. Liszt Competition, Budapest, 1933. Salzburg Fest. 1964. Worldwide tours as conc. pianist and recitalist.

Fischer, Edwin (*b* Basle, 1886; *d* Zurich, 1960). Swiss pianist and conductor. Teacher at Stern Cons., Berlin, 1905–14. Cond. posts in Lübeck 1926–8 and Munich 1928–32. Succeeded Schnabel on staff of Berlin High Sch. for Mus. from 1931. In 1932 formed chamber orch., directing it from the kbd. in concs. (one of first to revive this 18th cent. practice). Salzburg Fest. début 1938. Specialist in, and writer about, mus. of Bach. whose kbd. works he ed. Comp. of pf. works. Also wrote book on Beethoven's sonatas (1956, Eng. trans. 1959).

Fischer, György (*b* Budapest, 1935). Hung. pianist and conductor. Ass. to Karajan at Vienna Opera. Cond. opera in Cologne, Munich, and S. America, specializing in Mozart. Brit. début Cardiff, WNO, 1973 (*Die Zauberflöte*). London début 1979, Camden Fest. (f. Brit. p. of *Mitridate, Rè di Ponto*) Wexford Opera 1984; Australian Opera 1987. Acc. many leading singers, incl. Lucia Popp.

Fischer, Ivan (*b* Budapest, 1951). Hung. conductor. Had cond. engagements in Milan, Florence, Budapest, Vienna before winning Rupert Foundation comp. in Eng. 1976. Joint mus. dir. Northern Sinfonia 1979–82. Opera début Zurich 1977 (*Don Giovanni*). Brit. opera début, Kent Opera 1982; Royal Opera 1983 (Manchester). Mus. dir. Kent Opera from 1984, art. dir. from 1989 until company went into liquidation in 1990. ENO 1987; Vienna 1988. Founder, Budapest Fest. Orch. 1983. Brother of Adam *Fischer.

Fischer, Julia (*b* Munich, 1983). Ger. violinist. Studied vn. from age of 4 with Helge Thelen and pf. with mother, Viera Fischer. Attended Leopold Mozart Cons., Augsburg, with Lydia Dubrowskaya then from 1992 Munich Acad. of Mus. Won Int. Menuhin Comp. 1995 and Eurovision Comp. 1996. Amer. début 1997. Repertory of over 40 concs. and 60 chamber works.

Fischer, Johann (Christian) (*b* Freiburg in Breisgau, 1733; *d* London, 1800). Ger. oboist and composer. Played in court orch. at Dresden from 1764. Went to London, 1768, becoming member of Queen's band and playing at Bach-Abel concerts. Married Gainsborough's daughter 1780. Returned to Continent on disappointment at not being made Master of King's Band 1786.

Returned to London 1790. Died from stroke while performing before royal family. Mozart wrote variations on his Minuet (1773).

Fischer-Dieskau, Dietrich (b Berlin, 1925). Ger. baritone and conductor. Stage début Berlin State Opera 1948 (Posa in *Don Carlos*). Rapidly became one of world's leading singers, outstanding in *Lieder* and in wide range of operatic roles from the Count in *Le nozze di Figaro* to Falstaff, Wozzeck, Don Giovanni, Sachs, Mittenhofer in f.p. of Henze's *Elegy for Young Lovers*, and Lear in f.p. of Reimann's *Lear*. Salzburg Fest. début 1951; Eng. début 1951 (concert); CG 1965; Bayreuth 1954; NY 1955 (recital); Vienna State Opera from 1957. First singer of bar. role in Britten's *War Requiem*, Coventry 1962, and Tippett's *The Vision of St Augustine*, London 1966. Took up cond. 1973. Author of books on Schubert, Schumann, and relationship between Nietzsche and Wagner. His memoirs were pubd. in Stuttgart 1987 and in Eng. trans. (*Echoes of a Lifetime*) 1989. Retired 1992. Gave last perf. 31 Dec. 1992 at Nat. Th., Munich.

Fišer, Luboš (b Prague, 1935; d Prague, 1999). Cz. composer. Emigrated to USA 1971. Comps. incl. operas *Lancelot* (1959–60)), *The Good Soldier Schweik* (1962); 2 syms. (1956, 1960); *15 Prints after Dürer's Apocalypse*, orch. (1964–5); *Caprichos*, singers, ch. (1966); *Requiem*, sop., bar., ch., orch. (1968); *Lament over the Destruction of the City of Ur*, sop., bar., 3 narr., ch., 7 timp., 7 bells. (1969); *Labyrinth*, orch. (1977); *Albert Einstein*, org., orch. (1979); pf. conc. (1980); *Centaurs*, orch. (1983); Sonata, solo va., str. qt. (1991); *Sonata for Leonardo*, gui., str. (1994); *Pastorale for Giuseppe Tartini*, gui., str. (1995); also str. qt. (1955); vc. sonata (1975); pf. trio (1978); and 6 pf. sonatas (1955–78).

Fisher, Sylvia (Gwendoline Victoria) (b Melbourne, 1910; d Melbourne, 1996). Australian soprano. Début Melbourne 1932. CG début 1948, becoming co.'s leading sop. until 1958 in roles such as Isolde, Kostelnička (f. Brit. p. 1956), Brünnhilde, Sieglinde, and the Marschallin. Chicago Opera 1959. Sang with EOG 1963–71 in Britten operas and with SW Co. (later ENO), notably with latter as Elizabeth I in *Gloriana* (1966). Created Miss Wingrave in *Owen Wingrave* (TV 1971, CG 1973).

Fistoulari, Anatole (b Kiev, 1907; d London, 1995). Russ.-born conductor, Brit. cit. from 1940s. Cond. Tchaikovsky's 6th Sym. in Kiev at age of 7. Cond. ballet in Paris 1933 and toured with Ballets Russes de Monte Carlo. Settled in Eng. 1940; prin. cond. LPO 1943–4. Toured USSR with LPO 1956. Guest cond. of world's leading orchs.

Fitelberg, Grzegorz (b Dynaburg, Latvia, 1879; d Katowice, 1953). Polish conductor, violinist, and composer. With *Szymanowski and others, founded 'Young Poland' group of composers in Berlin 1905. Cond. Warsaw PO 1907 (having been its leader); Vienna Opera 1911–14; Petrograd and Moscow 1914–20. Returned to Warsaw PO 1923–

34. Founder and cond. Polish Radio SO 1934–9 and from 1947. Comp. 2 syms. (1903, 1906), vn. conc. (1901), sym.-poem, vn. sonata, etc.

Fitzgerald, Ella (b Newport News, Va., 1918; d Beverly Hills, Calif., 1996). Amer. singer. Sang in Harlem clubs in early 1930s until discovered by Chick Webb with whose band she sang from 1934. On his death in 1939 she led the band until 1942 when she became a free-lance. Toured Eur., Canada, Japan, and USA with Norman Granz's 'Jazz at the Philharmonic' from 1946. In scat-singing, improvised melody and harmony to compete with instrumentalists. Sang at Carnegie Hall, NY, with *Ellington, 1958. Made films and many recordings.

Fitzwilliam Virginal Book. Remarkable MS coll. of early 17th-cent. Eng. mus. for kbd. by (mostly) Eng. composers, comprising 297 pieces. Coll. orig. made by Francis Tregian in 17th cent. Bears present title because it became property of the mus. antiquarian Richard, Viscount Fitzwilliam (1745–1816) who bequeathed it, together with the annual interest on £100,000, to Cambridge Univ. where it is preserved in Fitzwilliam Library. Pubd. 1894–9 in edn. by *Fuller Maitland and Barclay *Squire.

Five, The. Name given to group of 5 Russ. composers, Balakirev, Borodin, Cui, Mussorgsky, and Rimsky-Korsakov, who est. a 'national' sch. of comp. in 19th cent. In Russia they were known as *moguchaya kuchka*, 'the mighty handful', a term invented by the critic Stasov in 1867.

Five Tudor Portraits. Choral suite in 5 movements by Vaughan Williams for mez., bar., ch., and orch. Comp. 1935. Texts are from the poetry of John Skelton (1460–1529) incl. 'The Tunning of Elinor Rumming' and the 'Lament for Philip Sparrow'. F.p. Norwich 1936, London 1937.

fixed-doh. System of sight-singing in which the note C, in every key in which it occurs, is called *doh*, D called *ray*, etc. See *movable-doh*.

Fjeldstad, Øivin (b Christiania, 1903; d Oslo, 1983). Norweg. conductor, composer, and violin teacher. Début as violinist 1921, as cond. 1931. Cond. Norwegian State Broadcasting Orch. 1946–62. Chief cond. Norwegian State Opera 1958–60, Oslo PO 1962–9. Had close assoc. with Nat. Youth. Orch. of GB, taking it on tour to Ger., Russ., and Scandinavia, 1961. Cond. first complete recording of *Götterdämmerung*, with Flagstad and Svanholm, 1956.

flageolet. (1) Late 16th-cent. instr. of end-blown fl. type, with 4 finger-holes and 2 thumb-holes, 'invented' by Sieur de Juvigny of Paris, c.1581. The name has also been applied to earlier instr. of the end-blown fipple type of pipe. Handel wrote for the true flageolet in *Rinaldo*.

(2) Soft organ stop of 2′ length and pitch.

(3) *flageolet notes* is a term applied to harmonics on a str. instr., produced by light stopping of the

str. at natural points of vibration, and so called because the resultant high thin sound is said to resemble that of the flageolet.

Flagstad, Kirsten (Malfrid) (*b* Hamar, Norway, 1895; *d* Oslo, 1962). Norweg. soprano. One of the greatest of Wagnerian singers. Début Christiania (Oslo) Nat. Th. as Nuri in d'Albert's *Tiefland*. Sang wide range of roles in opera and operetta in Scandinavia up to 1932 but was virtually unknown elsewhere until glowing reports of her first Isolde in Oslo in June 1932 led to her engagement in small roles at 1933 Bayreuth Fest. Sang Gutrune and Sieglinde at Bayreuth 1934. NY Met début as Sieglinde 1935, singing Isolde 4 days later and Brünnhilde a month after that. CG début as Isolde 1936. Her int. standing as leading exponent of Wagner's great female roles was thereafter unchallenged until her retirement from the stage in 1953. Though a famous Brünnhilde at La Scala, she never sang Brünnhilde or Isolde at Bayreuth. Sang her main Wagner roles at CG 1948–51 and her last Isolde in Liverpool 1951. Salzburg Fest. début 1949 (Leonore in *Fidelio*). Gave f.p. of Strauss's *Vier letzte Lieder*, London 1950. Dir., Norweg. State Opera 1958–60. Fine exponent of Grieg songs. Her return to Nazi-occupied Norway in 1941 to be with her husband led to a post-war investigation on charges of collaboration (she was cleared) and to hostility to her return to the Met.

flam. Rhythmic 2-note figure in side-drum playing, 'open' or 'closed' according to whether the 1st or 2nd note is on the accented beat.

flamenco. Very rhythmical Sp. dance style, particularly Andalusian. See *cante flamenco*. The 'flamenco' style of gui.-playing, rhythmical and improvisatory, is the opposite of the 'classical'.

Flanagan, William (*b* Detroit, 1923; *d* NY, 1969). Amer. composer and critic. Promoted recitals of Amer. song with Ned *Rorem. Wrote incidental mus. for 4 plays by Albee. Wrote th. and mus. criticism for NY *Herald Tribune*, etc. Works incl. opera *Bartleby* (prod. NY 1961); *Notations* for orch.; song-cycles incl. *The Weeping Pleiades* (Housman); and choral mus.

flat (♭). The sign which, placed before a note, lowers its pitch by a semitone. In Britain, the verb 'to flatten' (past participle 'flattened') is in use; in USA, 'to flat' ('flatted').
    (2) 'Flat' singing or playing is that which departs from correct intonation on the downward side.

flat twenty-first. Rank in an organ mixture stop, sounding 2 octaves and a minor 7th above normal (i.e. interval of minor 21st or compound minor 7th).

flautando, flautato (It., 'fluting', 'fluted'). The prod. of fl.-like notes from the vn., etc., either by bowing near the finger-board with the point of the bow, or by the use of *harmonics.

flautina. A *gemshorn org. stop of 2' length and pitch.

flautist. A fl.-player. Flutist is an older term; 'flautist' is derived from the It. *flauto* and, in Britain, has been retained as a hangover from the 18th-cent. domination of It. mus. and musicians.

flauto (It., 'flute', plural *flauti*). In printed scores since Haydn's time *flauto* implies the side-blown fl. (*flauto traverso*). The small version of this is the *flauto piccolo*, usually called *piccolo. In earlier periods *flauto* sometimes meant the *recorder. J. S. Bach wrote *flauto piccolo* to indicate a small recorder; if he wanted the side-blown flute he wrote *flauto traverso*. For history of fl., see under *flute*.

flauto dolce. Org. stop; much the same as *dolce but more fl.-like.

flauto traverso (It., 'transverse flute'). (1) The side-blown fl., as opposed to the end-blown variety.
    (2) Org. stop of 4' length and pitch.

Flea, Song of the. See *Song of the Flea*.

flebile; flebilmente (It.). Mournful; mournfully. Also faint, feeble.

Fledermaus, Die (The Bat). Operetta in 3 acts by J. Strauss II to lib. by Haffner and *Genée after *Le Réveillon* (1872) by Meilhac and Halévy, this being based on *Das Gefängnis* (The Prison, 1851) by R. Benedix. Comp. 1873–4. Prod. Vienna and NY 1874, London 1876. Eng. versions under titles *The Gay Rosalinda* and *The Merry Countess*. Filmed (1955) as *Oh, Rosalinda! Die Fledermaus* was admitted into the opera repertory by Mahler in Hamburg in 1894 and at the Vienna Hofoper, cond. by composer, in same year. Richard Strauss cond. it in Vienna, 1920, Bruno Walter at CG in 1930, and Karajan in Vienna, 1960.

Fleisher, Leon (*b* San Francisco, 1928). Amer. pianist and conductor. Début at age 7. Appeared in S. Francisco 1942; NY 1944 (cond. *Monteux). First prize Brussels Queen Elisabeth competition 1952. Career as pianist halted by illness 1964 which affected his right hand, but quickly took up repertory for left hand. Début as cond., NY 1970. Assoc. cond. Baltimore SO 1973–7, cond. 1977–8; art. dir. Tanglewood Mus. Center 1985.

Fleming, Amaryllis (*b* London, 1920; *d* London, 1999). Eng. cellist, daughter of artist Augustus John (1878–1961). Won int. comp. Munich. Début as soloist, Newbury 1944 (Elgar conc.). Formed Loveday pf. trio 1949 (with Alan Loveday, vn., and Peggy Gray, pf.) and played in Fidelio Ens. from 1951. Won Queen's Prize 1952. London recital début 1953, Proms début 1953. Gave f.ps. of Arnold Cooke's sonata (Paris 1956), Fricker's sonata (BBC 1956), and Seiber's *Tre pezzi* (Cheltenham 1958, cond. Barbirolli). From 1963 played on Amati 5-string cello and specialized in baroque mus. Formed Fleming String Trio 1968–75 and Parikian-Fleming-Roberts pf. trio 1983–8. Prof. of vc., RCM. Retired 1988.

Fleming, Renée (b Indiana, Pa., 1959). Amer. soprano. Studied singing with Patricia Misslin at State Univ. of NY then with Beverly Johnson at Amer. Opera Center of Juilliard Sch. 1983–7. Prof. début NY 1986 (Constanze). Débuts: NY City Opera 1989 (Mimì); London 1989 (Glauce in *Médée*); NY Met 1991 (*Figaro* Countess). Created roles of Rosina in Corigliano's *The Ghosts of Versailles* (NY Met 1991), Mme de Tourvel in Susa's *The Dangerous Liaisons* (San Francisco 1994), and Blanche DuBois in Previn's *A Streetcar Named Desire* (San Francisco 1998). Roles incl. Strauss's Marschallin and *Capriccio* Countess.

Flesch, Carl (b Moson, Hung., 1873; d Lucerne, 1944). Hung. violinist. Début Vienna 1895. Prof. of vn., Bucharest Cons. 1897–1902, Amsterdam Cons. 1903–8. Taught in Berlin from 1908. NY début 1913. Chief vn. prof. Curtis Institute 1924–8. Returned to Berlin to teach at High Sch. for Mus. 1928–34. Went to London 1934–9, Holland 1939–40. Settled in Lucerne 1943. Ed. of vn. mus. Author of famous method and of several books on vn.-playing. Prize awarded in his memory since 1945.

flessibile, flessibilità (It.). Flexible, flexibility.

Fleury, Louis François (b Lyons, 1878; d Paris, 1926). Fr. flautist, for whom several composers wrote works, including Debussy (*Syrinx*). Played in orchs., and in 1902 joined Société Moderne des Instruments à Vent, becoming dir. 1905–26. Frequent visitor to Eng. and champion of Eng. composers in Eur. Ed. works for fl. by Stanley, Purcell, Blavet, and others.

flexatone. Novelty instr., patented 1922, producing a weird tremolo. A flexible metal sheet is suspended in wire frame with handle. On each side of the metal sheet is a wooden knob on a spring of steel. Performer shakes the instr. so that knobs hit sides of metal. Pitch may be altered by varying pressure on metal sheet. Used by Schoenberg in his *Variations*, Op.31, *Von Heute auf Morgen*, and *Moses und Aron*, by Khachaturian (pf. conc.), and by Henze and Penderecki, among others.

flicorno. It. variety of *saxhorn and *flügelhorn used in military bands. There are 3 sizes: *flicorno basso* (*bassflicorno*), *flicorno basso grave*, and *flicorno contrabasso*.

fliegende Holländer, Der (The Flying Dutchman). Opera in 3 acts by Wagner to his own lib. based on the legend as retold by Heine. Comp. 1840–1, rev. 1842, 1846, and 1852, end of opera and coda of ov. remodelled 1860. Prod. Dresden 1843, London 1870 (in It.; in Ger. 1882), Philadelphia 1876. Orig. intended to be in 1 act, it is now often so perf. (e.g. by Bayreuth 1901 and by CG, ENO, and Opera North).

fliessend (Ger.). Flowing. So **fliessender**, more flowing.

Flight of the Bumble Bee, The. Orch. interlude in opera *The *Legend of Tsar Saltan* (1900) by Rimsky-Korsakov in which a prince becomes a bee and stings his villainous relatives. Many arrs. (some highly spurious) for variety of solo instr.

Flimm, Jürgen (b Giessen, 1941). Ger. theatre and opera director. Studied drama and literature Cologne Univ. Ass. dir. Munich Kammerspiele 1968. Dir. Thalia Th., Hamburg, 1973–4 and 1985–2000. Opera début Frankfurt 1978 (Nono's *Al gran sole cantico d'amore*). Opera prods. incl. *Les Contes d'Hoffmann* (Hamburg 1981), *Così fan tutte* (Amsterdam 1990), *L'incoronazione di Poppea* (Salzburg Fest. 1993), *Der Ring des Nibelungen* (Bayreuth 2000). Has worked in most major opera houses. Drama dir. Salzburg Fest. 2002–4, dir. Ruhr Triennale 2005–7, art. dir. Salzburg Fest. from 2007.

Flonzaley Quartet. Str. qt. founded by patron E. J. de Coppet of NY, in 1902, and named after his residence near Lausanne. Orig. membership A. Betti, A. Pochon, U. Ara and I. d'Archambeau. Toured Europe 1904. 1st NY concert 1905. L. Bailly replaced Ara, 1917, and was replaced by F. d'Archambeau, 1924. I. d'Archambeau replaced by N. Moldavan 1924. Disbanded 1928 (London) after giving 3,000 concerts, mostly in USA.

Flood, The. Mus. play for 3 speakers, ten., and 2 basses, ch., and orch. by *Stravinsky to lib. chosen and arr. by Robert Craft from *Genesis*, and York and Chester cycles of mystery plays. Comp. 1961–2. F.p. on TV (CBS) 1962; f. stage p. Hamburg 1963; London (concert) 1963. See also Britten's *Noye's Fludde*.

Flood, (William Henry) **Grattan** (b Lismore, Ireland, 1859; d Enniscorthy, 1928). Irish organist and writer. Org., Enniscorthy Cath., 1895–1928. Noted collector of Irish folk-tunes; ed. *Moore's Irish Melodies* and wrote memoir of John *Field (Dublin, 1920). Also wrote histories of Irish mus. and monographs on musicians who visited Ireland.

Flor, Claus Peter (b Leipzig, 1953). Ger. conductor. Won cond. comps. in Poland and Denmark. Prin. cond. Suhler PO 1981–4 and guest cond. in Leipzig and Dresden. Prin. cond. Berlin SO 1984, mus. dir. from 1985. Amer. début with Los Angeles PO, Hollywood Bowl, 1985.

Florence. It. city, capital of Tuscany, of great beauty and cultural significance. Sacred mus. flourished there from 14th cent. and reached a high-point in 16th cent. under patronage of Medici family. At the same periods a tradition of secular mus. in the form of madrigals and *Ballate* developed. Florence is also regarded as the birthplace of opera, which emerged as an offshoot of the court th. fests. held at the celebration of Medici weddings together with the interest of Florentine intellectuals, musicians, and poets in ancient Greek musical and dramatic theories. In particular, the informed meetings held at the homes of Giovanni de' Bardi and Jacopo Corsi resulted in the composition of musical dramas by Peri, Caccini, and Cavalieri. First opera is generally believed to have been Peri's *Dafne* (1594–8), perf. in several versions before 1604, followed by his *Euridice* (1600). Pastorals by Monteverdi and Gagliano were perf. in Florence soon after their premières in Mantua.

A rich period occurred at the end of the 17th cent. under Prince Ferdinando de' Medici (1663–1713). It was in his court that Cristofori built the first piano. The prince himself directed operas in the Villa di Pratolino, held nightly chamber concerts, and patronized church mus. During the 18th cent., Neapolitan and Venetian composers tended to dominate the Florentine musical scene. Its internationalization can be attrib. to the extinction of the Medicis in 1737 and their succession by the aristocratic families Habsburg and Lorraine. During the 19th cent., Florence was a centre of symphonic and chamber mus. rather than opera. A pf. factory with Viennese craftsmen was opened in 1828 and a Philharmonic Soc., the first in It., was founded in 1830. Beethoven's symphonies were better known in Florence than in the rest of It. Even so, opera—chiefly at the Teatro della Pergola—was not neglected. First perfs. were given of Donizetti's *Parisina* (1833) and Verdi's *Macbeth* (1847) and f. It. ps. of Weber's *Der Freischütz* (1843) and Meyerbeer's *Dinorah* (1867). The city's mus. life declined after 1870 until its revival in *c.*1913 by Bastianelli and Pizzetti, who were based in Florence as both critics and musicians. They concentrated on contemporary mus. On the occasion in 1923 when Casella cond. Schoenberg's *Pierrot Lunaire*, Puccini met Schoenberg. In 1928 Vittorio *Gui founded and cond. one of It.'s first permanent orchs., the Orchestrale Fiorentina, and in 1933 Guido M. Gatti instituted the Maggio Musicale Fiorentino, a fest. held annually in May and June. It soon became internationally renowned for adventurous opera prods. and excellent concerts. Gui's orch. was renamed Orchestra del Maggio and has been cond. by Walter, Furtwängler, de Sabata, Mitropoulos, and Bruno Bartoletti. Directors of the fest. incl. Mario Labroca (1937–44), Francesco Siciliani (1950–6), and Riccardo Muti (1969–81). Stravinsky's *Oedipus Rex* had its It. première at the Maggio Musicale in 1937. Operatic f.ps. incl. Dallapiccola's *Volo di notte* (1940), Prokofiev's *War and Peace* (1953), Pezzati's *Il sognatore* (1982), and Bussotti's *L'ispirazione* (1988).

Florez, Juan Diego (*b* Lima, 1973). Peruvian tenor. Studied at Lima Cons. 1990–3, Curtis Inst., Pa., 1993–6. Private tuition from Ernesto Palacio. Prof. début Pesaro 1996 (Corradino in *Matilde di Shabran*). Milan 1996 (*Armide*), CG 1998 (Donizetti's *Elisabetta*), Vienna 1999 (Almaviva in *Barbiere*), NY Met 2002 (Almaviva).

florid. Descriptive term for melody embellished by ornaments and trills, either improvised or comp.

florid counterpoint. The 5th species of strict counterpoint in which the added v. employs mixture of the processes of the other 4 species and also introduces shorter notes (eighth-notes).

Floros, Constantin (*b* Thessalonika, 1930). Ger. musicologist of Greek descent. Prof. of musicology, Hamburg Univ., from 1972. Authority on Byzantine neumes (3 vols., 1961) and has written much on Mahler, Beethoven, Brahms, and Bruckner.

Flos Campi (Flower of the Field). Suite by Vaughan Williams for solo va., mixed ch. (wordless), and small orch. F.p. London 1925 (soloist Lionel *Tertis). Each of the 6 movts. is prefaced by a Latin quotation from *The Song of Solomon*.

Floss der Medusa, Das (The Raft of the Medusa). 'Popular and military oratorio' (or cantata) by Henze, to lib. by Ernst Schnabel, for narrator, sop., bar., ch., boys' ch., and orch. Based on historical (1816) event, the subject of Géricault's painting, when the Fr. frigate *Medusa* ran aground, its officers escaping in the boats and leaving the crew to their fate on an improvised raft. Henze's avowedly political and class-conscious work was cause of a famous fracas involving students and police in Hamburg, 1968, which caused cancellation of première. F.p. Vienna 1971, London 1977.

Flothuis, Marius (Hendrikus) (*b* Amsterdam, 1914; *d* Amsterdam, 2001). Dutch composer, musicologist, and critic. Ass. man., Concertgebouw Orch., 1937–42 and 1953–5, art. dir. 1955–74. Mus. critic Amsterdam *Het Vrije Volk* 1945–53. Prof. of musicology, Utrecht Univ. from 1974. Author of books on Monteverdi, Mozart, Eng. composers, etc. Composer of concs. for fl., vn., hn., pf., and cl., vn. sonata, *Hymnus* for sop. and orch., cantatas, song cycles, str. qt., etc.

Flotow, Friedrich von (*b* Teutendorf, 1812; *d* Darmstadt, 1883). Ger. composer. Lived mostly in Paris and Vienna. Intendant, ducal court th. at Schwerin 1855–63. Wrote ballets, chamber mus., and 30 operas of which only *Martha* (1847) and *Alessandro Stradella* (1844) seem to have outlived him.

flotter (Fr., 'to float', present participle *flottant*, 'floating'). An undulating movt. of the bow in str. playing.

flourish. (1) A tpt. call of the fanfare type.
(2) In a more general sense any florid instr. passage.

Flower, (Sir) (Walter) **Newman** (*b* Fontmell Magna, Dorset, 1879; *d* Blandford, 1964). Eng. writer and publisher. Author of books on Handel, Sullivan, and Schubert. Collected mus. autographs and portraits. Chairman, Cassell & Co. (publishers). Knighted 1938.

Flowers o' the Forest. Scottish lament, orig. words of which are lost, but many lines were incorporated into an 18th-cent. version by Jane

Elliott. A new set of words was written c.1765 by Mrs Cockburn to a different tune but is now generally sung to old tune. The flowers are young men, the Forest a district of Selkirk and Peebles; the poem commemorates their death in battle. The tune, played by pipers, is a regular and moving feature of the Remembrance Day ceremony at the Cenotaph in Whitehall, London.

Floyd, Carlisle (b Latta, S. Carolina, 1926). Amer. composer. Taught at Florida State Univ., 1947–76; prof. of mus., Univ. of Houston, from 1976. Works incl. several operas, notably *Susannah* (1955); **Wuthering Heights* (1958); *The Passion of Jonathan Wade* (1962, rev. 1991); *Markheim* (1966); *Of Mice and Men* (1969); *Bilby's Doll* (1976); *Willie Stark* (1981); and *Cold Sassy Tree* (1999).

flue-pipe. Org. pipe into which the air enters directly, i.e. not striking a reed. See *organ*.

Flügel (Ger., 'wing'). The grand pf., formerly the hpd.

Flügelhorn (Ger.). Brass wind instr. with cup-shaped mouthpiece and wide conical bore. Bell held forward. Types are (1) sop. in E♭ (rare). (2) alto in B♭, same compass as cornet in B♭ but mellower in tone. (3) ten. in E♭ (sometimes called *Altflügelhorn* or *Althorn*) or sometimes in F. (2) is the type used in Brit. brass bands and sometimes in orch. comp., e.g. by Vaughan Williams in his 9th Sym. (1956–8). The posthorn solo in 3rd movt. of Mahler's 3rd Sym. is often played by a flügelhorn.

flute (It. *flauto*, Fr. *flûte*, Ger. *Flöte*). Wind instr. of ancient origin formerly made of wood but now of silver and other metals. From medieval times 2 methods of producing sound were used: (a) blowing across a round mouth-hole as on the panpipes or transverse (side-blown) fl.; (b) blowing into a whistle mouthpiece (end-blown) as on the **recorder or **flageolet. The word fl. was used indiscriminately to denote both types during medieval times, but in the baroque period fl. or **flauto specifically meant the end-blown recorder. The modern fl. is descended from the Ger. (transverse) fl. Whereas today it is cylindrical in bore, stopped at one end, until the early 19th cent. it was conical. The player's breath sets in vibration the column of air inside the tube. Acoustically the tube acts as an open one; the mouth-hole serves to prevent its acting as stopped and thus sounding an octave lower. The body orig. had one thumb-hole and from 4 to 8 finger-holes. The 1st key was added in 1677, the 2nd in 1726 by **Quantz, fl. teacher of Frederick the Great. The great fl. virtuoso of the Bavarian Court Orch., Theobald **Boehm, used an 8-key fl., but revolutionized the instr. in 1832 with his 'ring key' system. In 1847 he produced a 15-hole metal instr. with 23 keys and levers. See *alto flute*, *bass flute*.

flûte-à-bec (Fr., 'beaked flute'). **Recorder or **flageolet.

flûte à cheminée (Fr., 'Chimney flute'). Same as **Rohrflöte*.

flute amabile. Org. stop, same as **flûte d'amour*.

flûte à pavillon (Fr., 'tented flute'). Org. stop of 8′ or 4′ length and pitch; each pipe ends in a sort of bell-tent structure.

flûte d'amour (Fr., 'love flute'). (1) Flute pitched a third lower than regular fl.
  (2) Soft org. stop, in Britain, of 8′ or 4′ length and pitch, and in USA of 2′ length and 4′ pitch (being end-plugged).

flûte harmonique (Fr.). (1) **Mouth org.
  (2) An org. stop.

flute stop (on org.). See *Doppelflöte, Fernflöte, flauto traverso, flûte d'amour, Grosseflöte, harmonic flute, Hohlflöte, Rohrflöte, Spitzflöte, Waldflöte, Zauberflöte*.

flutist. Player of the flute (Amer. usage). See *flautist*.

flutter-tonguing (Ger. *flatterzunge*). **Tonguing in the playing of wind instr. is the interruption of the flow of air by a motion of the tongue to produce certain effects. Flutter-tonguing—chiefly on the fl. but possible on the cl. and some brass—consists of a trilling of the letter R while playing a chromatic scale. It was introduced by R. Strauss and Mahler (e.g. in the latter's *Das Lied von der Erde*).

Flying Dutchman, The (Wagner). See *Fliegende Holländer, Der*.

Foerster, Josef Bohuslav. See *Förster, Josef*.

Fogg, (Charles William) **Eric** (b Manchester, 1903; d London, 1939). Eng. composer. Son of C. H. Fogg, who had been Hallé's organist. Chorister at Manchester Cath. Comp. ballet *Hansel and Gretel* and *Scenes from Grimm* for orch. when he was 15. His *Dance Fantasy* (1919) won a **Cobbett Prize. Joined BBC in Manchester 1924 as accomp. and became ass. mus. dir. Also affectionately remembered as 'Uncle Eric' of *Children's Hour*. Other comps. incl. a str. qt. (1922–3) and a bn. conc. played by Archie Camden.

Fokine, Mikhail (Mikhaylovich) [Michel] (b St Petersburg, 1880; d NY, 1942). Russ. dancer and choreographer. Member of Mariinsky Th. Started to teach 1902. Choreog. *The Dying Swan* for Pavlova 1907. Engaged as chief choreog. 1909 by **Diaghilev who recognized his genius as a reformer of ballet methods. Among his greatest ballets were *Les Sylphides, Sheherazade, Firebird, Petrushka, Daphnis et Chloé*, and *Josephslegende*. After break with Diaghilev, worked as freelance, settling in NY 1923.

Foldes, Andor (b Budapest, 1913; d Herrliberg, 1992). Hung.-born Amer. pianist and composer. In 1922, aged 8, was soloist with Budapest PO in Mozart's B♭ major conc. (K450). Won Int. Liszt Prize, Budapest, 1933. Authoritative exponent of mus. of Bartók with whom he worked. Toured Eur. until 1939 when he settled in USA, becoming Amer. cit. 1948. Returned to live in Ger. and Switz. after 1950. Author of books on pf. technique. Some pf. comps.

Foli, Signor [Foley, Allan James] (*b* Cahir, Tipperary, 1835; *d* Southport, 1899). Irish-Amer. bass. Début Catania 1862 as Elmiro in Rossini's *Otello*, and in London 1865 as Saint-Bris in Meyerbeer's *Les Huguenots*. Sang in over 60 operas in London until 1887. Appeared in USA, Russia, and Austria. Sang Daland in f. London p. of *Der fliegende Holländer* (Drury Lane, 1870).

folía, la (Sp., 'the folly'; It. *la follia*). A type of wild Portuguese dance. One particular melody used for the dance attained wide popular currency in the 16th, 17th, and 18th cents., being first mentioned by Salinas in 1577, and subsequently used by numerous composers as an ostinato basis for variations. The best-known set is by *Corelli in his 12th sonata for vn. and hpd., 1700. Other composers to use the melody incl. Vivaldi, Frescobaldi, Lully, Pergolesi, Geminiani, Bach, Grétry, Cherubini, Liszt, Nielsen, Rachmaninov, and Henze.

folk music. Term covering folk-songs and folk dances. Folk-songs are songs of unknown authorship passed orally from generation to generation, sung without acc., and often found in variants (of words and tune) in different parts of a country (or in different countries). Folk-songs were generally found among the country-dwellers, but with the increase of urbanization and industrialization they spread to the towns and factories. In the 19th and early 20th cents. the fear that with the advance of modern life the old customs were dying out led to a major campaign of song coll., in Eng. by Cecil *Sharp, Vaughan Williams, Maud Karpeles, Mrs Leather, Anne Gilchrist, Frank Kidson, and many others; in Hungary by Kodály and Bartók, and similarly in other countries. Many composers have made use of folk-songs in their comps., from Renaissance times to Haydn, Grieg, Dvořák, Tchaikovsky, Bartók, Vaughan Williams, and others. Although folk-songs enshrine the nat. characteristics of their country of origin, they have int. similarities. Most of them are modal. Like every generic term, folk-song is susceptible to many conflicting interpretations, and readers are referred to several important books on the subject. It is also impossible to predict how folk-song may develop in future centuries. It may well be that the popular songs of the 20th cent. by named composers may become (indeed already have become) the folk-songs of a new age. Folk dance is a type of dance which has developed by itself without aid from choreogs., is connected with traditional life, and is passed from one generation to the next.

Folquet de Marseille (*b* ?Marseilles, *c*.1155; *d* Toulouse, 1231). Fr. troubadour, thought also to be rich merchant. Career as troubadour extended from court at Aragon in 1180 to 1195, when he entered Cistercian order. Est. Univ. of Toulouse 1229. In Dante's *Paradiso* (canto ix), Folquet tells of his early 'sinful life' and his conversion. His troubadour songs were ed. by S. Stronski in Kraków, 1910.

fonds d'orgue. 'Foundation tone' and also 'foundation stops' of an org. *Jeux de fonds* means the foundation stops (i.e. all the stops except the mutation and mixture stops).

Fontana, Giovanni Battista (*b* Brescia, ?; *d* Padua, *c*.1630). It. violinist and composer of vn. sonatas. Regarded as a leading figure in the development of the solo sonata.

Fontane di Roma (It., 'Fountains of Rome'). Symphonic poem for orch. by Respighi, comp. 1914–16, in 4 sections, each depicting the sensations of the composer in contemplating 4 of the city's most famous fountains, Vale Giulia at dawn, Tritone in mid-morning, Trevi at noon, and Villa Medici at sunset. F.p. Rome 1917, NY 1919, London 1921.

foot. Unit of length for measuring vibrating air-column, and therefore a measure of pitch. An air-column of 8′ vibrates at twice the speed of a 16′ column, and thus emits a note an octave higher. Org. stops are classified by the sound which will be emitted if the note representing 8′ C is struck. An 8′ stop sounds the note itself, 16′ the note an octave below, 32′ the note two octaves below. A 4′ stop sounds the note an octave above, 2′ two octaves above, 1′ three octaves above.

Foote, Arthur (William) (*b* Salem, Mass., 1853; *d* Boston, 1937). Amer. composer and organist. Recipient of first MA conferred at Harvard for work in mus. Later studied comp. in Paris with Stephen Heller. Org., First Unitarian Church, Boston, 1878–1910. A founder of Amer. Guild of Organists, president 1909–12. Comps. incl. orch. suites; vc. conc.; cantata *The Farewell of Hiawatha*; chamber mus.; vocal works; songs; pf. pieces; and org. mus. Author of books on harmony and fugue.

Forbes, Sebastian (*b* Amersham, 1941). Eng. composer and organist. Producer for BBC 1964–7. Cond. Aeolian Singers 1965–9. Org., Trinity Coll., Cambridge, 1968. Lect. in mus., Bangor, 1968–72, Univ. of Surrey from 1972 (prof. from 1981). Works incl. 3 syms.; 3 str. qts.; trio; pf. quintet; opera; songs; choral mus.; org. sonata; sonata for 8 instr. (pf., fl., ob., cl., hn., vn., va., vc., 1978). Son of W. *Forbes.

Forbes, Watson (*b* St Andrews, 1909; *d* Great Wolford, 1997). Scottish viola player. Violist in LPO, 1932–6, LSO 1936–46. Prof. of chamber mus. RAM 1956–64, of va. 1958–64. Member Aeolian Qt. 1944–64. Head of BBC Mus., Scotland, 1964–72. Made many arrs. and transcrs. for va.

Ford, Andrew (*b* Liverpool, 1957). Eng. composer. Fellow in mus., Bradford Univ., 1978–82, lect. Sch. of Creative Arts, Univ. of Wollongong, NSW, from 1983. Introduced many contemp.

works, e.g. by Stockhausen, to Australia. Comps. incl. opera *Poe* (1981–3); children's opera *The Piper's Promise* (1986–7); 2 chamber concs.; str. qt.; *Imaginings*, pf., orch. (1991); *The Great Memory*, vc., orch. (1994); *Manhattan Epiphanies*, 17 solo str. (1994–9); *The Furry Dance*, orch. (1999); *Sad Jigs*, str. (2005); *An die Musik*, unacc. ch. (2005); *Scenes from Bruegel*, large. ens., tape (2006); and works for solo vn., pf., etc.

Ford, Bruce (*b* Lubbock, Texas, 1956). Amer. tenor. Début while student in *Adriana Lecouvreur*. Sang in f.p. of Floyd's *Willie Stark* (Houston, 1981). Joined Wuppertal Opera 1983–5. Sang with Minnesota Opera 1984 and at Mannheim 1985–7. Débuts: Wexford 1986; CG 1991. Also Salzburg Fest. and La Scala. Specialist in Rossini roles.

Ford, Thomas (*b c*.1580; *d* Westminster, 1648). Eng. composer and lutenist. Musician to Prince Henry, 1611; later one of lutes and voices in service of Prince Charles (later King Charles I), with whom he remained until 1642. His 19 anthems were pubd. 1614 and his *Musicke of Sundrie Kindes* (for voices and bass viols) in 1607.

Forelle, Die (Schubert). See *Trout, The*.

Forgotten Rite, The. Orch. 'prelude' by John Ireland, 1913. The unspecified rite is assoc. with the Channel Islands.

Forkel, Johann Nicolaus (*b* Meeder, 1749; *d* Göttingen, 1818). Ger. organist and writer. Dir. of mus., Göttingen Univ. from 1778, cond. *Akademie* concerts 1779–1815. Wrote several theoretical books, but his *chef d'œuvre* was 1st biography of J. S. Bach (Leipzig 1802). Composer of cantatas, oratorios, and instr. works.

form. The structure and design of a composition. Whereas in the 16th and 17th cents. instr. comps. were usually very brief (e.g. a movt. in a kbd. suite of Byrd or Purcell), by the 19th cent. they were frequently long (e.g. a sonata or sym. movt. of the later Beethoven, Bruckner, and Mahler). This implies an enormous growth in the understanding of the principles of form and in mastery of the application of those principles. In general, however, despite continuous experimentation the mus. forms so far devised can be classified into no more than 6 categories, all of them exploiting the idea of contrast plus variety both in the domain of content (thematic material) and in that of key (combinations of these are, of course, possible, e.g. in simple ternary form each section can be in binary form, and so on).

(1) SIMPLE BINARY FORM (e.g. in the movts. of Bach's kbd. suites) has no strong contrast of material. The 1st section opens in the tonic key and then modulates as it ends, into the key of the dominant (or in the case of a minor key, sometimes the relative major). The 2nd section then opens in that 2nd key and, before it ends, modulates back to the 1st. There are, then, 2 distinct main cadences, or points of rest, the 1st in the dominant (or relative major), and the 2nd in the tonic. This form, although it sometimes

attained fairly considerable dimensions in the 18th cent., is unsuitable for very long pieces, since the variety offered to the listener is almost entirely confined to details of treatment and the element of key, the thematic material employed throughout being the same. This form has been little used since *c*.1750.

(2) TERNARY FORM. This is one of the most commonly used forms for short comps. It consists of a first section (more or less complete and self-contained), a 2nd section, contrasting as to mus. material and key (normally in the dominant or the tonic minor or relative major), and then the first section repeated. See *ABA*.

(3) COMPOUND BINARY FORM (also known as SONATA FORM, because often employed in the first or some other movt. or movts. of a sonata; and as FIRST MOVEMENT FORM for the same reason). This derives historically from simple binary form but has developed into something more resembling ternary form. Like simple binary it falls into 2 sections, of which the 1st modulates to the dominant and the 2nd takes us back to the tonic. But the sections have become elaborated as follows:

1st section. Strain I (*first subject*) in tonic key; followed by Strain II (*2nd Subject*) in dominant key. Those 2 strains (or subjects) are generally contrasted in character. This section is called the *exposition*.

2nd section. Some *development* (also called 'working-out' or 'free fantasia') of the material in the previous section, followed by a repetition (*recapitulation*) of that section, but this time with both subjects in the tonic key so that the piece may end in the key with which it opened.

Further details may incl. (a) a *bridge passage*, leading (in both sections) from the first subject to the second; (b) a closing passage (coda), at the end of each section.

A tendency towards the evolution of simple binary form into compound binary form may be observed in some of Bach's movts., but its first real exploitation is connected with the name and fame of his son, C. P. E. Bach, and the further exploitation and elaboration with the names of Haydn, Mozart, Beethoven, and their contemporaries. This form is still in frequent use, but 20th cent. composers have modified it in detail.

(4) RONDO FORM This may be considered an extension of ternary form. If the 3 sections of that form are indicated by the formula ABA, then the rondo form must be indicated by ABACADA, or some variant of this. (The sections B, C, D, etc. are often spoken of as *episodes*).

SONATA-RONDO FORM, as its name implies, offers a combination of compound binary and rondo forms. The general plan is as follows: *1st section*. Subject I, subject II in another key, subject I repeated. *2nd section*. Development of the previous subject-material. *3rd section*. Subject I and subject II again, but the latter this time in the same key as subject I.

Sometimes the development above mentioned is replaced by new material. And there are other variants.

(5) AIR WITH VARIATIONS. This form, which from the 16th cent. to the present day has been popular with composers of every class from the most trivial to the most serious, consists, as the name implies, of one theme (or 'subject'), first played in its simplicity and then many times repeated with elaborations, each variation thus taking on its own individuality.

There are very many types of comp. to which distinctive names are given, each representing not a 'form' but rather a style in which one of the above forms is presented; such as the nocturne, the gavotte, the barcarolle, the Konzertstück, and others.

With the development of elec. mus. and the use of *aleatory techniques in 20th-cent. comps., the use of form is stretched to meet whatever the composer may wish to do. Infinite flexibility would seem to be the guiding principle in works of this kind.

(6) See *fugue*.

formalism. Alleged fault in comp. by Soviet Union composers for which Prokofiev, Shostakovich, and others were officially criticized, esp. in 1948. The criticism is of too much intellectual emphasis on form as opposed to content, with the suggestion also that the mus. is too 'modern' and discordant.

Forqueray, Antoine (*b* Paris, *c*.1672; *d* Mantes, 1745). Fr. player of viola da gamba, and composer. At age 5, played to Louis XIV, and entered king's service as chamber musician 1689. Retired to Mantes 1728. One of greatest viol virtuosi of his day, rival to *Marais. Comp. *c*.30 viol pieces, pubd. in 5 suites. His son, Jean-Baptiste Antoine (*b* Paris, 1699; *d* Paris, 1782) was also a viol player of some renown, in service of king and Prince de Conti.

Forrester, Maureen (Katherine Stewart) (*b* Montreal, 1930). Canadian contralto. Début Montreal 1953. Recital tour of Europe 1955. Amer. début NY Town Hall 1956. Sang in Mahler's 2nd Sym. at Bruno Walter's invitation, NY 1957. London début, Proms 1957 (Verdi's *Requiem*). Noted as Mahler interpreter, also as Angel in Elgar's *Dream of Gerontius*. Salzburg Fest. 1968 (concert). Opera début Toronto 1961 as Gluck's Orpheus. NY City Opera 1966; S. Francisco 1967; NY Met 1975; CG 1971; Paris 1981. Head of vocal dept., Philadelphia Mus. Acad., 1966–71.

Förster, Josef (Bohuslav) (*b* Dětenice, 1859; *d* Novy Vesteč, 1951). Cz. composer, organist, and critic. Org. St Vojtěch, Prague, 1882–8. Prof. of pf., Hamburg Cons. from 1901 and critic for several Hamburg papers 1893–1903, during which period he was perceptive champion and friend of *Mahler. Prof. of comp. at New Vienna Cons. 1903–18 and critic of *Die Zeit* 1910–18. Prof. of comp., Prague Cons. 1918–22, dir. 1922–31. Works incl. 6 operas, 5 syms., 6 suites, 2 vn. concs., vc. conc., 4 sym.-poems, chamber mus., and songs. His wife was the sop. Berta Foerstrová-Lauterová (*b* Prague, 1869; *d* Prague,

1936), who sang at the Nat. Th., Prague, 1887; Hamburg Opera 1893–1901; Vienna 1901–13, retiring 1914.

Forsyth, Cecil (*b* Greenwich, 1870; *d* NY, 1941). Eng. violist, conductor, composer, and musicologist. Violist in London orchs. Settled in NY 1914. Comps. incl. operas, va. conc., setting of Keats's *Ode to a Nightingale* for bar. and orch., masses, part-songs, chamber mus., and songs. Author of several books incl. *History of Music* (1916, with Stanford) and valuable treatise on orchestration (1914).

Forsyth, Malcolm (Denis) (*b* Pietermaritzburg, 1936). S. African-born Canadian composer, trombonist, conductor, and teacher. Co-principal trombonist Cape Town Municipal Orch. 1961–7. Settled in Canada (Can. cit. 1974). Prin. trombonist Edmonton SO 1973–80. Joined teaching staff of Univ. of Alberta, Edmonton, in 1968, prof. of mus. 1977, art. dir. of mus. dept. 1987–9, and McCall Professor 1990–1. Works incl. 3 syms. (1968–72, 1976, 1980–7); pf. conc. (1973–5); tpt. conc. (1987); *Valley of a Thousand Hills*, orch. (1989); *Kora Dances*, 2 hp. (1990); *Tre vie*, sax., orch. (1992); *Electra Rising*, vc., chamber orch. (1995); *Siyajabula! We Rejoice!*, orch. (1996); *Glasnost*, ch., tape (2000); acc. conc. (2001).

forte (It.). 'Strong', i.e. loud (abbreviation *f*); *fortemente*, 'strongly'.

fortepiano (It.). Same as *pianoforte*, but the term has come to be used to denote the late 18th-cent./early 19th-cent. instr. known to Haydn, Hummel, Beethoven, and Schubert.

For the Fallen. 3rd movt. of Elgar's choral work *Spirit of England*, but perf. 1916 before work as a whole was completed and still often perf. separately. Words by Laurence Binyon.

fortissimo (It.). Very loud (abbreviation *ff*).

Fortner, Wolfgang (*b* Leipzig, 1907; *d* Heidelberg, 1987). Ger. composer, conductor, and teacher. Taught theory and comp. at Church Mus. Inst., Heidelberg, 1931–54; prof. of comp. NW Ger. Mus. Acad., Detmold, 1954–7, and at State Mus. Sch., Freiburg im Breisgau 1957–72. Founded Heidelberg Chamber Orch. 1935. Dir. of *Musica Viva* series in Heidelberg, Freiburg, and Munich. Early music influenced by Hindemith and Stravinsky; he adopted 12-note method in mid-1940s. Comps. incl. 5 operas (among them *Bluthochzeit* (Blood Wedding), after Lorca) (1957), *In seinem Garten liebt Don Perlimplin Belisa*, chamber opera after Lorca (1962), and *Elisabeth Tudor* (1972)); sym. (1947); 4 str. qts.; org. conc.; concs. for pf. (1943), vn. (1947), vc. (1951); *Fantasy on the Name BACH*, 2 pf., orch. (1950); *Movements*, pf., orch. (1953); oratorio *Isaaks Opferung* (1952); ballet *Die Weisse Rose* (1950; after Wilde's *Birthday of the Infanta*); *Variations*, solo vc. (1975); pf. trio (1978); 4th str. qt. (1979); *Immagini*, sop., str. (1979); *Variations*, for chamber orch. (1980); *Petrarca-Sonette*, unacc. ch. (1980); *Madrigal* for 12 vcs. (1980).

'Forty-eight, The' (Bach). See *Wohltemperierte Klavier, Das*.

Forza del Destino, La (The Force of Destiny). 4-act opera by Verdi to lib. by Piave based on Spanish drama *Don Alvaro* (1835) by the Duke of Rivas with scene interpolated from Schiller's *Wallensteins Lager* (1799) trans. by A. Maffei. Comp. 1861–2 for Imperial Th., St Petersburg, where f.p. was given in 1862. Prod. Rome (as *Don Alvaro*) 1863, NY 1865, London 1867. In 1868–9 Verdi made extensive revs. for 1869 Milan prod. and added ov. Lib. rev. by Ghislanzoni.

Foss, Hubert (James) (*b* Croydon, 1899; *d* London, 1953). Eng. pianist and editor. Joined staff of OUP 1921 becoming head of mus. dept. on its foundation in 1924. Pubd. mus. of several Eng. composers, notably Walton and Vaughan Williams. Wrote book about Vaughan Williams (1950).

Foss [Fuchs], **Lukas** (*b* Berlin, 1922). Ger.-born Amer. composer, pianist, and conductor. Settled in USA 1937. Pianist, Boston SO 1944–50. Worked in Rome 1950–2. Prof. of comp., UCLA, 1953–62. Cond. Buffalo PO 1963–70; Brooklyn PO 1971–90; Jerusalem SO 1972–5; mus. dir. Milwaukee SO 1981–6. Foss's mus. is both traditional and experimental, the latter employing indeterminacy though scores are wholly notated. In his *Baroque Variations*, on themes by Bach, Handel, and Scarlatti, the method of 'composition by deletion' is used in an effective and sophisticated manner. Works incl.:

OPERAS: *The Jumping Frog of Calaveras County* (after Mark Twain) (1950); *Griffelkin* (TV, 1955); *Introductions and Goodbyes* (1959).

BALLET: *Gift of the Magi* (1945).

ORCH.: sym. (1945); pf. conc. No.1 (1944, orig. cl. conc. 1941–2), No.2 (1949, rev. 1953); ob. conc. (1950); *Time Cycle*, sop., orch. (1960); vc. concert (vc., orch., tape) (1967); *Baroque Variations* (1967); *Paradigm* perc., gui., 3 other optional instr. (1968); *Orpheus*, vn., va. or vc., orch. (1972), rev. as *Orpheus and Euridice*, 2 vn., orch. (1984); *Solomon Rossi Suite* (1975); *Night Music for John Lennon*, brass quintet, orch. (1981); *Exeunt* (1982); *Renaissance Concerto*, fl., orch. (1986); sym. No.3 (*Symphony of Sorrows*) (1988); cl. conc. No.2 (1989); *American Landscapes*, gui. conc. (1989); pf. conc., left hand (1993); sym. No.4 (*Window to the Past*) (1995); *Capriccio*, vc., small orch. (1999); *Celebration*, 5 brass, orch. (1999); *Solo Transformed*, pf., small orch. (2000); *For Aaron*, small orch. (2002).

VOCAL & CHORAL: *The Prairie* (1944); *A Parable of Death* (1952); *Psalms* (1956); *Time Cycle*, sop., ens. (1960); *American Cantata*, ten., ch., orch. (1976); *13 Ways of Looking at a Blackbird*, sop. or mez., fl., pf., perc. (1978); *Round a Common Centre*, v. and ens. (1979); *De Profundis* (1983); *With Music Strong*, mixed ch., ens. (1988); *Sanctus*, ch., orch. (1994).

CHAMBER MUSIC: str. qts.: No.1 (1947), No.2 (1973), No.3 (1975), No.4 (1998), No.5 (2000); *Composer's Holiday*, vn., pf. (1944); *Capriccio*, vc., pf. (1946); *Echoi*, for cl., vc., perc., pf. (1961–3); *Elytres*, for fl.,

vns., pf., hp., perc. (1964); *Cave of the Winds*, ww. quintet with multiphones (1972); brass quintet (1978); *Curriculum Vitae with Time Bomb*, accordeon, perc. (1980); perc. qt. (1983); hn. trio (1984); *Embros*, various ens. (1985); *Tashi*, 6 instr. (1986); *Central Park Reel*, vn., pf. (1989); *For Toru*, fl., db., str. qt. (1996).

PIANO: *Solo* (1981); *Solo Observed* (1982); *Elegy for Anne Frank* (1989).

Foster, Lawrence (*b* Los Angeles, 1941). Amer. conductor of Romanian origin. Début Los Angeles 1960 with Young Musicians' Foundation Début Orch., which he cond. for 4 years. Cond. S. Francisco Ballet 1962–5. Assoc. cond. Los Angeles PO 1965–8. Won Koussevitzky Memorial cond. prize, Tanglewood, 1966. Eng. début 1967 with ECO, since then being frequent visitor. CG début 1976 (*Troilus and Cressida* in Walton's rev. vers.). Cond. Houston SO 1971–8. Chief cond. Monte Carlo PO and Opera from 1979. Gen. mus. dir. Duisburg 1982–8. Mus. dir. Lausanne Chamber Orch. 1985–90. Cond. Jerusalem SO from 1988. Cond. f.p. of Birtwistle's *The Triumph of Time* (1972).

Foster, Muriel (*b* Sunderland, 1877; *d* London, 1937). Eng. mezzo-soprano. Concert début, Bradford 1896. Became closely assoc. with mus. of Elgar, singing Angel in *Dream of Gerontius* in Düsseldorf and Worcester 1902, at f. London p. 1903, and many other times. Sang in f.ps. of *The Apostles* (1903) and *The Kingdom* (1906), gave f.p. of uncompleted song-cycle Op.59 (1910), and of *The Music Makers* (1912). Also notable Bach singer. Illness compelled premature retirement.

Foster, Stephen (Collins) (*b* Lawrenceville, Pa., 1826; *d* NY, 1864). Amer. composer. Wrote over 200 songs, several of which have come to be regarded almost as Amer. folk-songs. Though a Northerner, several of his songs capture the Southern plantation spirit in an authentic and eloquent manner. Among the best-known are: *Oh! Susanna* (1848); *Old Folks at Home* (1851); *Massa's in de Cold, Cold Ground* (1852); *My Old Kentucky Home* (1853); *Camptown Races* (1854); *Jeanie with the light brown hair* (1854); *Come where my love lies dreaming* (1855); *Old Black Joe* (1860); and *Beautiful Dreamer* (1864, posth.).

Foulds, John (Herbert) (*b* Manchester, 1880; *d* Calcutta, 1939). Eng. composer and cellist. Son of a professional bassoonist. Studied pf. at 4 and started to compose at 7. Became orch. cellist at 14 and until 20 played in th. bands in Manchester region. Joined Hallé Orch. under Richter in 1900. In 1906 was Eng. composer-delegate to Essen Mus. Fest., where he met Mahler and Strauss, and in 1910 went to Munich for f.p. of Mahler's 8th Sym. Comp. incid. mus. for plays prod. by Lewis Casson. Moved in 1912 to London, where he met and eventually married the actress, musician, and writer Maud MacCarthy (1882–1967). Mus. dir., YMCA National Council 1918–23. From 1919 to 1921 he worked on his *World Requiem*, for soloists, ch., and orch. This ambitious work was perf. in Royal Albert Hall at

Armistice Night commemoration ('Festival of Remembrance') in 1923 and for 3 subsequent years. In 1924 wrote incid. mus. for Shaw's *Saint Joan*. In 1927 Foulds went abroad, returning in 1930. Unable to obtain more than a few perfs., he went to India in 1935 to study folk music. In 1937 he was appointed dir. of mus. for All-India radio in Delhi. Formed radio orch. and Indo-European orch. of traditional Ind. instr. In 1939 was transferred to Calcutta to organize mus. at newly established radio station, but died from cholera after only a few days in new post.

Foulds's mus. was perhaps too eclectic to survive but a body of opinion exists which makes high claims for it. Like *Ives he was a tireless experimenter and was ahead of his time in Eng. mus. in working in microtonalities. The modal pf. mus., the str. qt. *Quartetto Intimo*, the Vc. Sonata, the pf. conc. *Dynamic Triptych*, and several songs are splendid mus. and deserve to emerge from oblivion.

foundation. In organ parlance this word is used in 2 different senses. (1) *foundation tone* is that of all the more dignified stops (diapason, the more solid of the fl. stops etc.).

(2) *foundation stops* are all the stops except the mutation and mixture stops.

Fountain, Ian (*b* Welwyn Garden City, 1969). Eng. pianist. Won Viotti-Valsesia int. comp. 1986, joint winner Arthur Rubinstein int. comp., Tel Aviv, 1989. Recital débuts Frankfurt and Munich 1989–90. Conc. début with RLPO 1990. London recital début 1991.

Fountain of Arethusa, The. No.1 of *Myths* (*Mity*), *3 Poems* for vn. and pf. by Szymanowski, Op.30 (1915).

Fourestier, Louis (*b* Montpellier, 1892; *d* Boulogne-Billancourt, 1976). Fr. conductor and composer. Won *Prix de Rome* 1925. Cond. in Marseilles and Bordeaux, then Opéra-Comique, Paris, 1927–32 and Paris Opéra 1938–45. NY Met 1946–8; Salzburg Fest. 1953. Prof. of cond., Paris Cons. 1945–63. Comp. cantatas, symphonic poem, str. qt., etc.

Four Last Songs. (1) See *Vier letzte Lieder* (Strauss).

(2) For v. and pf. by Vaughan Williams, comp. between 1954 and 1958 to words by Ursula Vaughan Williams. Title given by publisher, songs being intended by composer as part of 2 cycles. Individual titles: *Procris, Tired, Hands, Eyes, and Heart*, and *Menelaus*. F.p. as cycle 1960.

Fournet, Jean (*b* Rouen, 1913). Fr. conductor and flautist. Held cond. posts in Rouen 1938, and Marseilles 1940. Worked for Fr. Radio and was mus. dir., Opéra-Comique, Paris, 1944–57. Cond. Netherlands Radio Orch. 1961–8, Rotterdam PO 1968–73. Prof. of cond., École Normale de Paris, 1944–62. Cond. f.p. in Japan of *Pelléas et Mélisande*, Tokyo 1958. Amer. début, Chicago Opera 1965; NY Met 1987. Noted interpreter of *Les *Dialogues des Carmélites*.

Fournier, Pierre (*b* Paris, 1906; *d* Geneva, 1986). Fr. cellist. Début 1925, the year in which he played in f. private p. of Fauré's str. qt. Worldwide tours as recitalist and conc. soloist. Chamber mus. partner of Szigeti, Primrose, Thibaud, Cortot, and Schnabel. Master-class teacher, Paris Cons. 1941–9. Salzburg Fest. début 1958. Frank Martin's vc. conc. and Poulenc's vc. sonata were written for him.

Four Rustics, The (Wolf-Ferrari). See *Quatro rusteghi, I*.

Four Saints in Three Acts. Opera in prologue and 4 acts by Virgil *Thomson to lib. by Gertrude Stein with scenario by M. Grosser. Comp. 1927–8, orch. 1933. Prod. Ann Arbor (concert) 1933; Hartford, Conn., 1934; NY (Broadway) 1934, Met 1973; Paris 1952; London (semi-staged) 1983.

Four Seasons, The (*Le quattro stagioni*). 4 vn. concs. by Vivaldi, No.1 in E (Spring), RV269, No.2 in G minor (Summer), RV315, No.3 in F (Autumn), RV293, No.4 in F minor (Winter), RV297. They are first 4 of 12 vn. concs. of Op.8, *Il cimento dell' armonia e dell' inventione* (The contest between harmony and invention), pubd. Amsterdam 1725. Nos. 9 and 12 also exist as ob. concs. Fl. transcr. of whole work by James Galway.

Four Serious Songs (Brahms). See *Vier ernste Gesänge*.

Four Temperaments, The (1) Sub-title of *Nielsen's Sym. No.2 in C minor, Op.16 (*De Fire Temperamenter*), 1901–2, inspired by a painting of that name, each movt. being descriptive of one of the medieval 'temperaments' of human character: choleric, phlegmatic, melancholic, sanguine.

(2) Sub-title of Hindemith's *Theme and Variations* for str. and pf., 1940, each of the 4 variations denoting a temperament, in the order melancholic, sanguine, phlegmatic, choleric. F.p. Boston 1944. Also ballet, f.p. NY 1946.

fourth. Interval in melody or harmony in which there are 4 steps in the major or minor scale from one extreme to the other (incl. the bottom and top notes). Perfect 4th is the distance from C up to F or from G to C; a semitone more gives the augmented 4th (e.g. C up to F♯).

Fou Ts'ong (*b* Shanghai, 1934). Chinese pianist. Début Shanghai 1951. Won 3rd prize in Bucharest pf. comp. 1953 and Warsaw Chopin comp. 1955. Gave 500 concerts in Eastern Eur. while studying in Poland. Brit. début 1959. Settled in Eng., but int. tours.

Fowke, Philip (Francis) (*b* Gerrards Cross, 1950). Eng. pianist. Début London 1974, Amer. début 1982. Prof. of pf., RAM.

Fowler, Jennifer (*b* Bunbury, W. Australia, 1939). Australian composer. Worked at Univ. of

Utrecht EMS 1968-9. Settled in London 1969. Won 1st prize in int. comp. for women composers, Mannheim 1975.

Fox Strangways, Arthur Henry (*b* Norwich, 1859; *d* Dinton, Salisbury, 1948). Eng. critic and author. Mus. master Wellington Coll., 1893-1901. Mus. critic, *Times* 1911-25, *Observer* 1925-39. Founder and first ed. *Music and Letters* 1920-37. Authority on Indian mus. Joint biographer. (with M. *Karpeles) of Cecil Sharp. Trans. (with S. *Wilson) of *Lieder* of Schubert, Brahms, and Wolf.

fox-trot. Amer. ballroom dance (and the mus. for it) of a kind of march-like ragtime, slow or quick. From *c*.1913 it spread to ballrooms all over the world. The *Charleston* and *Black Bottom* are varieties of it. In several of his works, Peter *Maxwell Davies has made use of the fox-trot for nostalgic and ironic effect.

FRAD. Fellow of the Royal Academy of Dancing (founded 1927; chartered 1936).

Fra Diavolo (Brother Devil). *Opéra-comique* in 3 acts by Auber to lib. by Scribe. Prod. Paris 1830, London and Philadelphia 1831, NY Met 1910.

Frager, Malcolm (*b* St Louis, 1935; *d* Pittsfield, Mass., 1991). Amer. pianist. Début 1941. NY début 1952. Winner of several int. comps. incl. Queen Elisabeth, Brussels, 1960. Tours of Eur. and Russ.

FRAM. Fellow of the Royal Academy of Music.

Française. Old round dance in triple or compound duple time. Very popular in the 1830s.

Françaix, Jean (*b* Le Mans, 1912; *d* Paris, 1997). Fr. composer and pianist. Comp. pupil of N. Boulanger. Frequent soloist in his own works, which are marked by wit and elegance. Wrote mus. for Sacha Guitry films. Comps. incl.:

OPERAS: *Le diable boiteux* (1938); *L'apostrophe* (1940); *Le main de gloire* (1944); *Paris à nous deux* (1954); *La princesse de Clèves*.(1965).

BALLETS: *Sculo de ballo* (1933); *Les malheurs de Sophie* (1935); *Le roi nu* (1935); *Le jeu sentimental* (1936); *La lutherie enchantée* (1936); *Le jugement d'un fou* (1938); *Verreries de Venise* (1938); *Les demoiselles de la nuit* (1948); *Les zigues de mars* (1950); *La dame dans la lune* (1957); *Pierrot ou les secrets de la nuits* (1980).

ORCH.: sym. No.1 (1932), No.2 (1953); pf. concertino (1932); *Suite*, vn., orch. (1934); *Sérénade comique*, vc., small orch. (1934); *Divertissement*, vn., va., vc., orch. (1935); concs.: fl., ob., cl., bn., orch. (1935); pf. (1936), hpd. (1959), 2 pf. (1965), fl. (1966), cl. (1967), vn. No.1 (1968, rev. 1970), No.2 (1979), db. (1974), 2 hp. and 11 str. (1978), bn., str. (1979), gui., str. (1982-3), tb., wind (1984), fl., cl. (1991); *Au musée Grevin*, suite (1936); *Rhapsodie*, va., orch. (1946); *Symphonie d'archets*, str. (1948); *Variations de Concert*, vc., str. (1950); *L'horloge de flore*, ob., orch. (1959); *Le dialogue des Carmélites*, sym. suite (1960); *Sei preludi*, str. (1963); *Jeu poétique*, hp., orch. (1969); *La ville mystérieuse*, fantasy (1973-4);

Thème et variations (1974); *Le gay Paris*, tpt., ww. (1974); *Cassazione*, 3 orchs. (1975); *Chaconne*, hp., 11 str. (1976); *Ouverture anacréontique* (1978); *Tema con variazioni*, cl., str. (1978); *Mozart new-look*, db., 10 wind (1981); *Impromptu*, fl., str. (1983); *Pavane pour un génie vivant à la mémoire de Maurice Ravel*, chamber orch. (1987); Conc. for 15 soloists and orch. (1988).

CHAMBER MUSIC: str. trio (1933); wind qt. (1933); vn. sonata (1934); str. qt. (1934); fl. quintet No.1 (1934), No.2 (1989); *Divertissement*, bn., str. quintet (1942); *Divertissement*, ob., cl., bn. (1947); *L'heure du berger*, fl., ob., cl., bn., hn., pf. (1947); wind quintet No.1 (1948), No.2 (1987); *Divertimento*, hn., pf. (1959); qt., ca., vn., va., vc. (1970); trio, fl., hp., vc. (1971); octet, cl., hn., bn., 2 vn., va., vc., db. (1972); *Aubade*, 12 vc. (1975); cl. quintet (1977); *Danses exotiques*, 12 players (1981); pf. trio (1986); *Dixtour*, wind, str. quintet (1986); *Notturno*, 4 hn. (1987); *Le colloque des deux perruches*, fl., alto fl. (1989); *Élégie*, 10 wind instr. (1990); trio, cl., va., pf. (1990); *Suite*, 4 sax. (1990); *Pour remercier l'auditoire*, fl., cl., hn., vn., vc., pf. (1994).

VOCAL: *3 Épigrammes*, ch., str. quintet or str. orch. (1938); *L'apocalypse selon St Jean*, oratorio, 4 soloists, ch., 2 orchs. (1939); *La cantate de Méphisto*, bass, str. (1952); *Déploration de Tonton, chien fidèle*, mez., str. (1956); *Les inestimables chroniques du bon géant Gargantue*, spkr., str. (1971); *3 poèmes de Paul Valéry*, ch. (1984).

PIANO: *Scherzo* (1932); *5 Portraits de jeunes filles* (1936); *Éloge de la danse* (1947); *8 Danses exotique*, 2 pf. (1957); sonata (1960); *8 Variations on the Name of Gutenberg* (1982); *La promenade d'un musicologue éclectique* (1987).

ORGAN: *Suite carmélite* (1960); *Suite profane* (1984); *Messe de mariage* (1986).

Francesca da Rimini. The story of the adulterous lovers Paolo and Francesca in canto V of Dante's *Inferno* has been the basis of several comps.:

(1) Symphonic fantasy by Tchaikovsky, Op.32, 1876, based on picture by Doré.

(2) Opera in 4 acts by Zandonai to lib. by T. Ricordi after play by d'Annunzio (1902), after Dante's *Inferno*, canto V. Comp. 1912-13. Prod. Turin and London 1914, NY Met 1916.

(3) Opera in prol., 2 scenes, and epilogue by Rachmaninov to lib. by M. Tchaikovsky after Dante's *Inferno*, canto V. Prod. Moscow 1906. F. Brit. p. Chester 1973.

(4) Sym.-poem by H. Hadley f.p. Boston 1905. Also operas on the subject by Goetz, Pierné, Thomas, *Nápravník, and several other composers.

Francescatti, (René) **Zino** (*b* Marseilles, 1902; *d* La Ciotat, 1991). Fr. violinist (It.-born father). Début at 5, played Beethoven conc. at 10. Toured Brit. 1926 with Ravel. Taught at École Normale de Musique, Paris, from 1927. Salzburg Fest. début 1936. Amer. début 1939 (NYPO). Settled in USA. Soloist with world's leading orchs.

Francesch, Homero (*b* Montevideo, 1947). Uruguayan pianist. Début 1963. Henze wrote *Tristan* for him. London début 1974. Salzburg Fest. début 1986.

Francesina. See *Duparc, Elisabeth*.

Franchetti, (Baron) **Alberto** (*b* Turin, 1860; *d* Viareggio, 1942). It. composer. Dir., Florence Cons., 1926–8. His considerable wealth enabled him to stage his 9 operas which incl. *Asrael* (1887), *Cristoforo Colombo* (1892), *Germania* (1902, CG 1907), *La figlia di Jorio* (1906), and *Notte de Legenda* (1915). Wrote sym. and chamber mus. Verdi recommended that he should comp. *Cristoforo Colombo* to mark 400th anniversary of discovery of America. Was offered Illica's lib. of *Tosca* by Ricordi before Puccini, but withdrew after some persuasion (and because he acknowledged that Puccini would write the better opera).

Francis, Alun (*b* Kidderminster, 1954). Eng. conductor and horn-player. Played hn. in Hallé and Bournemouth SO. Took up cond. 1965. Cond., Ulster Orch. 1966–7, N. Ireland Opera Trust 1974–84; dir., Northwest Chamber Orch., Seattle, 1980–5, Overijssels PO, Holland, 1985–7; chief cond. NW Ger. PO and Berlin SO from 1989. In 1978 cond. revival of Donizetti's *Gabriella di Vergy* in Belfast.

Franck, César (Auguste-Jean-Guillaume-Hubert) (*b* Liège, 1822; *d* Paris, 1890). Belg.-born composer and organist (Fr. cit. 1870). He toured Belgium as a pianist at the age of 13. In 1835 he went to Paris, studying harmony with Reicha and was at the Paris Cons. from 1837 to 1842. On leaving the Cons. he concentrated on comp. and settled in Paris in 1843. In 1853 he became choirmaster, and in 1858 organist, of the church of Sainte-Clotilde, Paris, where his outstanding ability as an improviser drew listeners from far and wide, incl. Liszt who in 1866 likened his skill to that of Bach. He was prof. of org. at the Cons. from 1872. Throughout these years as teacher and organist, his comps. were ignored by the general public. His pupils, led by *d'Indy, organized a concert of his works in Jan. 1887, which, although poorly perf., pleased the uncomplaining composer, who subsequently wrote three of his finest works. The Sym. was received with incomprehension in 1889, but there was an enthusiastic response to the str. qt. He became Chevalier de la Légion d'Honneur in 1885.

In his early works Franck was influenced by the *opéra-comique* composers such as Grétry. His middle years were dominated by works of religious character, his oratorio *Les Béatitudes* occupying him for 10 years. In his later works he developed 'cyclic form' whereby a theme, modified or varied, recurs in each section of the work. His symphonic poems date from the late 1870s and the *Variations Symphoniques* for pf. and orch. from 1885. Franck's harmonic idiom, no doubt influenced by Wagner and by the org.-loft, has a pungent individuality which exerted a powerful sway not only over his pupils but over a much later generation, e.g. *Messiaen. His work also played a large part in restoring French taste for 'pure music', thereby opening the way for Debussy, Ravel, and others. Prin. comps.:

OPERAS: *Le Valet de Ferme, opéra-comique* (1851–2); *Hulda* (1882–5); *Ghisèle* (1889–90, orch. by Chausson, d'Indy, and others).

ORCH.: *Les *Éolides* (1876); *Le *Chasseur maudit* (1881–2); *Les Djinns* (1884, pf. and orch.); *Variations Symphoniques* (1885, pf. and orch.); *Psyché* (1887–8, with ch.); sym. in D minor (1886–8).

CHORAL: *Ruth*, biblical eclogue, soloists, ch., orch. (1843–6); *La Tour de Babel*, oratorio (1865); *Les *Béatitudes*, oratorio (1869–79); *Rédemption*, sop., ch., orch. (1871–2, orch. item and male ch. added 1874); *Rebecca* (1881); *Messe solennelle*, bass, org. (1858); *Mass*, 3 vv. (STB), org., hp., vc., db. (1860); 3 *Offertories*, soloist, ch., org., db.; *Panis angelicus*, ten., org., hp., vc., db. (1872).

CHAMBER MUSIC: pf. trio (1834); *Trois Trios Concertants*, pf., vn., vc. (1841–2); 4th *Trio Concertant* (1842); pf. quintet (1878–9); sonata, pf., vn. (1886, also arr. for pf. and vc. and for pf. and fl.); str. qt. in D major (1889).

PIANO: *Souvenirs d'Aix-la-Chapelle* (1843); *Fantasia on 2 Polish Airs* (1845); *Prélude, Choral, et Fugue* (1884); *Prélude, Aria et Final* (1886–7).

ORGAN: 6 *Pièces pour Grand Orgue* (1862); 44 *Petites Pièces* (1863); 3 *Pièces pour Grand Orgue* (incl. *Pièce heroique*) (1878); *Andantino* (1889); 3 *Chorals* (1890). Also songs and works for harmonium incl. *L'Organiste*, 59 pieces for harmonium (1889–90).

Francœur, François (*b* Paris, 1698; *d* Paris, 1787). Fr. composer and violinist. Twice manager of Paris Opéra (1757–67, 1772–5). Court musician (one of the 24 violones du roi), and superintendent of the King's Music, 1744–76. Wrote vn. sonatas, operas, and ballets. Collab. with F. *Rebel.

François, Samson (*b* Frankfurt, 1924; *d* Paris, 1970). Fr. pianist. Public début at age 6. Winner of several int. prizes. World tours. Amer. début 1947. Fine exponent of Mozart and Debussy.

Francs Juges, Les (The judges of the secret court). Ov., Op.3 by Berlioz, comp. 1826 to opera in 3 acts (libretto by H. Ferrand). 1st version of opera composed 1826, expanded in 1829, and recast in 1833 as 1-act intermezzo, *Le cri de guerre de Brisgaw*. Ov. and 6 numbers survive.

Frank, Alan (Clifford) (*b* London, 1910; *d* London, 1994). Eng. publisher, editor, writer, and clarinettist. Joined OUP staff 1927, music ed. 1948, head of mus. dept. 1954–75. His wife was the composer Phyllis *Tate.

Frankel, Benjamin (*b* London, 1906; *d* London, 1973). Eng. composer and conductor. Watchmaker's apprentice. Studied mus. in Ger., returning to London (GSMD) 1923. Worked as café musician and as jazz-band violinist, leader, and orchestrator (orch. of Coward's *Operette* and many C. B. Cochran revues). On staff GSMD 1946. Many of his more serious comps. are in 12-note system. Wrote 8 syms., vn. conc., va. conc., 5 str. qts., and mus. for over 100 films.

Frankenstein, Alfred (Victor) (*b* Chicago, 1906; *d* S. Francisco, 1981). Amer. critic of music and art. Educated Chicago Univ., where he was on staff 1932–4. Clarinettist in Chicago Civic Orch. before becoming writer. Mus. critic *San Francisco Chronicle* 1934–75. Found and pubd. (1939) sketches by V. Hartmann which inspired Mussorgsky's *Pictures at an Exhibition* and ed. illustrated edn. of score (1951).

Frankfurt Group. Group of Eng. composers (Norman O'Neill, Roger Quilter, Cyril Scott, and Balfour Gardiner) who were pupils of Iwan *Knorr at Frankfurt Hoch Cons. in late 1890s.

Frankl, Peter (*b* Budapest, 1935). Hung.-born pianist (Brit. cit. 1967). First prize in pf. comps. in Paris 1957, Munich 1957, Rio de Janeiro 1959. Frequent conc. soloist. Member of chamber mus. trio with György Pauk (vn.) and Ralph Kirshbaum (vc.).

Franklin, David (*b* London, 1908; *d* Evesham, 1973). Eng. bass. Discovered as amateur by John Christie 1934. Début Glyndebourne 1936. Sang Banquo in f. Brit. p. of 1865 vers. of *Macbeth*, Glyndebourne 1938. Leading bass CG 1947–50. Notable Ochs in *Der Rosenkavalier*. Also concert work (*Gerontius*, etc.). Throat ailment caused retirement 1951. Thereafter worked as effective broadcaster, lect., and writer. Librettist of *Tate's *The Lodger*. Autobiography *Basso Cantante* (1969).

Franquin, Merri (*b* Lanøn, 1848; *d* Paris, 1934). Fr. trumpeter. Prof. of tpt., Paris Cons. Invented 5-piston tpt. Author of tpt. method.

Frantz, Justus (*b* Hohensalza, 1944). Ger. pianist. Launched career in 1967 and played series of Mozart concs. with Berlin PO, cond. Karajan. Amer. début 1975. Toured USA, Japan, and Eur. 1983 in duo with Christoph *Eschenbach. Prof. of pf., Hamburg Hochschule für Mus. from 1985. Founded Schleswig-Holstein Fest. 1986. Played complete cycle of Mozart concs. in several Eur. cities 1987–8.

Franz [Knauth], **Robert** (*b* Halle, 1815; *d* Halle, 1892). Ger. composer. A set of his songs was highly praised by Schumann in 1843 and won the attention of Mendelssohn, Liszt, and others. Appointed org. at Halle, becoming mus. dir. of Halle Univ. 1851. Retired 1868 because of illness; thereafter ed. works of Bach and Handel, supplying additional accs., and comp. some choral mus. His reputation rests on his 300 *Lieder*, which some enthusiasts rank alongside those of Schubert and Schumann.

Frauenliebe und -Leben (Woman's Love and Life). Song-cycle for sop. or mez. and pf., Op.42, by Schumann, being settings of 8 poems by Adalbert von Chamisso. Comp. 1840.

Frau ohne Schatten, Die (The Woman without a Shadow). Opera in 3 acts by R. Strauss to lib. by Hofmannsthal. Comp. 1914–17. Prod. Vienna 1919, San Francisco 1959, London 1967.

FRCCO. Fellow of the Royal Canadian College of Organists.

FRCM. Fellow of the Royal College of Music.

FRCO. Fellow of the Royal College of Organists.

Freccia, Massimo (*b* Florence, 1906; *d* Ladispoli, Rome, 2004). It. conductor and composer. Cond., Budapest SO 1933–5. Amer. début 1938. Cond. Havana PO 1939–43; New Orleans SO 1944–51; Baltimore SO 1952–9; chief cond. Radio-televisione Italiana (RAI) Orch., Rome, 1959–63. Guest cond. of many other orchs.

Frederick the Great (Friedrich II, King of Prussia) (*b* Berlin, 1712; *d* Potsdam, 1786). Ger. sovereign (reigned 1740–86) who was also composer, flautist, and patron of music. Pupil of Hayne and *Quantz. Est. court orch. Berlin 1740, and opera house 1742. Employed C. P. E. Bach as harpsichordist from 1740, and J. S. Bach visited the court at Potsdam, 1747, the *Musical Offering* being the result (based on theme supplied by Frederick). Other notable musicians in Frederick's service incl. the Graun brothers and Quantz. Comp. syms., opera, marches, arias, etc. Wrote libs. for K. H. *Graun.

Fredigundis. Opera in 3 acts by F. *Schmidt to lib. by B. Warden and I. M. Welleminsky after Felix Dahn. Comp. 1916–21. Prod. Berlin 1922.

Fredman, Myer (*b* Plymouth, 1932). Eng. conductor. On staff Glyndebourne Opera 1959–74 (chorus master 1962–7); prin. cond. GTO 1968–74 (mus. dir. from 1971). Mus. dir. Adelaide Opera from 1975. Head of opera, NSW Cons. (now State Cons.), Sydney, 1981–92.

free canon. Form of *canon in which the intervals of the imitating v. remain the same numerically, but not necessarily as to quality (e.g. a major 3rd may become a minor 3rd).

free counterpoint. See *counterpoint*.

Freed, Isadore (*b* Brest-Litovsk, 1900; *d* Rockville Center, NY, 1960). Russ.-born conductor and pianist. Emigrated to USA as child. Pf. pupil, 1924, of Josef *Hofmann. Studied comp. with *Bloch and *d'Indy. Cond. Concert Spirituel, Paris, 1930–3. Head of mus. dept., Hartt Coll. of Mus., Hartford, Conn., 1944–60. Comps. incl. opera; ballet; 2 syms.; vn. conc.; vc. conc.; va. rhapsody; 3 str. qts.; choral works; and pf. pieces.

Freedman, Harry (*b* Łódź, 1922; *d* Toronto, 2005). Polish-born Canadian composer. Taken to Canada at age of 3 (Can. cit. 1931). Studied to become painter at Winnipeg Sch. of Art 1936–40, but influence of jazz turned his interest to mus. Played ca. in Toronto SO 1946–70. Founder and pres., 1975–8, Canadian League of Composers. Comps. incl. opera *Abracadabra* (1979); ballet *Oiseaux exotiques* (1984–5); 3 syms. (1954–60, 1966, 1983, rev. 1985); *Concerto for Orchestra* (1982); *The Sax Chronicles*, sax., orch. (1984); *A Dance on the Earth*, orch. (1988); wind quintet (1962); *Blue*, str.

qt. (1980); *Fragments of Alice*, sop., alt., bar., chamber orch. (1976); *Rhymes from the Nursery*, children's ch. (1986); *A Dance on Earth*, orch. (1988); *Touchings*, perc. ens., orch. (1989); *Another Monday Gig*, jazz ens. (1991); *Indigo*, 22 solo str. (1994); *Saxtet*, sax. qt. (1995); *Higher*, bcl., vc. (1996); *Graphic 8*, str. qt. (2000); *Romp and Reverie*, fl. (2002); *Phoenix*, str. qt. (2003).

free fantasia. Same as 'development' in compound binary form, etc. See also *form* (3).

Freeman, David (*b* Sydney, NSW, 1952). Australian director. Founded Opera Factory in Sydney 1973, Opera Factory Zurich 1976, and Opera Factory London 1981. In London he prod. world première of Nigel Osborne's *Hell's Angels* (1986, lib. by Freeman) and Birtwistle's *Yan Tan Tethera* (1986). Also prod. Mozart's da Ponte operas, with *Così fan tutte* set on a bathing beach. Prods. for ENO incl. f. Brit. p. of Glass's *Akhnaten* (1985) and world première of Birtwistle's *The Mask of Orpheus* (1986). CG début 1992 (*The Fiery Angel*). Has worked with Opera North, and in Fr., Ger., and USA. Prods. are notable for emphasis on acting, black humour, and concentration on sexual nuances. Married to sop. Marie Angel.

Frei aber Froh (Ger., 'Free but happy'). Brahms's personal motto, the initial letters of which (F–A–F) he used as the basic thematic structure of his 3rd sym. (1883).

Freischütz, Der (The Freeshooter). 3-act opera by Weber to lib. by Friedrich Kind after a story by Apel and Laun in *Gespensterbuch* (1811). Comp. 1817–21. Prod. Berlin 1821, London 1824, NY 1825.

Freitas Branco, Luìs de (*b* Lisbon, 1890; *d* Lisbon, 1955). Portuguese composer. Taught at Lisbon Cons. and held govt. posts from which he was removed between 1939 and 1947 because of his protests over persecution of artists in Ger. and It. Comp. 5 syms. (1924–52); concs. for vn., pf., and vc.; chamber mus.; choral works. Wrote educational books.

Freitas Branco, Pedro de (*b* Lisbon, 1896; *d* Lisbon, 1963). Portuguese conductor and composer, brother of Luìs de *Freitas Branco. Founded Portuguese Opera Co. 1926. Cond. state sym. orch. from 1934. Cond. Venice Biennale 1943. Guest cond. in Fr., Ger., Sp., Eng. (Hallé Orch. etc.).

Frémaux, Louis (Joseph Felix) (*b* Aire-sur-Lys, 1921). Fr. conductor. Cond. Nat. Orch. Monte Carlo 1956–66, Rhône-Alpes PO 1968–71, prin. cond. and mus. dir. CBSO 1969–78; prin. cond. Sydney SO 1979–81.

Fremstad, Olive [Rundquist, Olivia] (*b* Stockholm, 1871; *d* Irvington, NY, 1951). Swed. soprano (Amer. cit.). Her adoptive parents emigrated to Minnesota when she was in her early teens, when she expected to become pianist, having made recital début at age 12. Opera

début Boston 1890 (Lady Saphir in *Patience*). Went to NY 1890, becoming cont. soloist at St Patrick's Cath. Lilli Lehmann convinced her she was sop. or mez. Soloist 1895 at Cologne Fest., leading to engagement with Cologne Opera, début 1895 (Azucena in *Il trovatore*). Bayreuth 1896; London 1902; Munich Opera 1900–3; NY Met 1903;. Increasingly specialized in Wagner roles e.g. Kundry, Isolde, and especially Brünnhilde, of which she was one of greatest interpreters, but sang Carmen opposite Caruso 1906 and Salome in the single perf. at NY Met 1907. Farewell appearance at Met 1914, but sang opera at Boston and Chicago, and gave final recital, NY 1920.

French horn. Coiled brass wind instr. (tube over 11′ in all) of conical ¼″ bore, with funnel-shaped mouth-piece and bell of 11–14″ diameter. The hn. was one of the earliest primitive instrs., being used for military purposes and esp. for hunting. The modern hn. was developed in Fr. (hence the name). It has existed in 2 forms: (a) *natural, but with *crooks*. This is the instr. for which the older classical composers wrote and is said to have been introduced into the orch. by Lully in his comedy-ballet *La Princesse d'Elide*, Paris 1664. A notational convention existed whereby if notes occurred low enough to demand the use of the bass clef, they were written an octave lower than that pitch demanded. All parts were written as if in the key of C, with sharps and flats inserted as accidentals. Certain notes not in tune with the modern tempered scale were modified by the insertion of a hand in the bell ('stopped notes'). (b) *with valves*. The Fr. hn. was equipped with rotary valves in about 1827 and this instr. gradually displaced (a). Schumann was among the first to specify its use, and Wagner abandoned (a) in and after *Lohengrin* (1848). Traditionally the valved hn. is pitched in F, but other pitches exist. Compass is from B′ upwards for about 3½ octaves. The 'double hn.' pitched in both F and B♭ alto, is normally used today. The valves act much as the old crooks did but of course more speedily. Notation is without key signature, written a perfect 5th higher than it is intended to sound. There is a modern tendency to use a key signature, which, from the use of the F pitch, necessarily has a flat less or sharp more than the actual key. The hn.'s place in the sym. orch. has grown in importance since the 19th cent., composers such as Mahler and Strauss sometimes specifying 8 hns. Orch. parts assume that the higher notes will be played by the odd-numbered players, the lower by the even. Many hn. concs. have been written (e.g. by Mozart, Strauss, Hindemith), and it is also employed in chamber works (notably Brahms's hn. trio). The Fr. hn. is also used in military bands, but not in brass bands where the term is colloquially used to denote the ten. saxhorn.

French overture. 17th- and 18th-cent. form of the piece of orch. mus. played before an opera or oratorio (see *overture*). It was orig. developed by Lully, and was in 3 movts., slow, quick, slow.

French sixth. A type of *augmented 6th, containing an augmented 6th, major 3rd, and augmented 4th (taking key C as example: A♭–C–D–F♯).

French Suites. Name (possibly unauthorized) given to a set of 6 kbd. suites by Bach, comp. *c*.1722. See also *English Suites, German Suites*.

Freni [Fregni], **Mirella** (*b* Modena, 1935). It. soprano. Début Modena 1955 (Micaela in *Carmen*). Netherlands Opera 1959–60. Débuts: Glyndebourne 1960; CG 1961; Wexford 1962; La Scala 1962; NY Met 1965; Salzburg 1966. One of outstanding singers of her generation.

Frescobaldi, Girolamo (*b* Ferrara, 1583; *d* Rome, 1643). It. composer and organist. Held post at Antwerp, becoming org. at St Peter's, Rome, 1608–28 (30,000 are said to have attended his f.p. there, an indication of his reputation as a virtuoso). Org. at Florentine court 1628–33, returning to St Peter's thereafter. Comp. motets and madrigals, Masses and Magnificats, but prin. achievements were his toccatas, fugues, ricercari, and capriccios for org. and hpd. His mus. had strong influence on Ger. mus. through his pupil *Froberger. Baroque music for the next century was influenced by Frescobaldi's development of variation-form.

frets. Strips of wood or metal (orig. cords) on the fingerboard of certain str. instrs. e.g. guitar, viol, lute (though not vn. family). They indicate the length of str. required to produce a given note—the player presses his finger against a fret to shorten the vibrating length of str.

fretta (It.). Haste. Hence *frettevole, frettoso, frettoloso, frettolosamente*, 'hurried'.

Fretwell, Elizabeth (*b* Melbourne, 1922; *d* Sydney, 2006). Australian soprano. Début Australian Nat. Opera 1947 (Senta in *Der fliegende Holländer*). Dublin Grand Opera 1954. Prin. sop. SW Opera from 1955 (a famous Violetta in *La traviata*). First Brit. Ariadne in Strauss's opera. Notable exponent of Britten roles. Returned to Australia 1970 and sang at opening of Sydney Opera House 1973. OBE 1977.

Freund, Marya (*b* Breslau, 1876; *d* Paris, 1966). Fr. (Polish-born) soprano and teacher. Début 1909. Became authoritative interpreter of contemp. composers; one of first to sing 12-note works. Created part of Wood Dove in Schoenberg's *Gurrelieder* (1913), was speaker in first Fr. and Eng. perfs. of *Pierrot Lunaire* (but not at f. Berlin p.). Teacher in Paris for over 30 years.

Frey, Paul (*b* Heidelberg, Toronto, 1942). Canadian tenor. Prof. ice-hockey player until injury forced retirement. Opera début Toronto 1978 as Massenet's Werther. Basle Opera from 1979. Débuts: Brit. 1986 (Edinburgh Fest.); Munich 1986; Bayreuth début 1987; NY Met 1987; CG 1988. Cologne Opera 1990–1. Sang the Emperor in Sawallisch's recording of *Die Frau ohne Schatten*.

Frick, Gottlob (*b* Olbronn, 1906; *d* Pforzheim, 1994). Ger. bass. Stuttgart Opera chorus 1927–31. Solo début 1934 at Coburg (Daland in *Der fliegende Holländer*). Sang at Freiberg and Königsberg 1934–9. Member of Dresden State Opera 1940–50; Berlin State Opera 1950–3; Munich and Vienna from 1953. Débuts: CG 1951; Salzburg 1955; NY Met 1961. Noted for Wagner roles of Hagen, Hunding, and Gurnemanz. Bayreuth 1957–64. Retired 1970 but sang Gurnemanz (*Parsifal*) at CG 1971, and made other occasional appearances.

Fricker, Peter Racine (*b* London, 1920; *d* Santa Barbara, 1990). Eng. composer. Served RAF 1941–6. Won Clements Prize 1947 with wind quintet, and Koussevitzky award with his sym. No.1 (f.p. cond. Barbirolli, Cheltenham 1950). Won Arts Council Fest. of Britain award for young composers, 1951, with vn. conc. Prof. of comp., RCM 1955–64, dir. of mus., Morley Coll., 1952–64, visiting prof. of mus., Univ. of Calif. (S. Barbara) 1964, prof. from 1965, chairman of mus. dept. 1970–4. One of first post-1945 Eng. composers to develop individual style derived from influences of Bartók, Stravinsky, and Schoenberg. Prin. comps.:

ORCH.: sym. No.1 (1949), No.2 (1950–1), No.3 (1960), No.4 (1966), No.5 (1975–6); *Prelude, Elegy, and Finale*, str. (1949); *Dance Scene* (1954); *Litany*, double str. orch. (1955); *3 Scenes* (1966); *7 Counterpoints* (1967); *Sinfonia in memoriam Benjamin *Britten*, 17 wind instr. (1976–7); *Concerto for Orchestra* (1986); *Walk by Quiet Waters* (1989).

CONCERTOS: vn. (1949–50); cor anglais and str. (or pf.) (1950); 3 pf., str., timp. (1951); va. (1952); pf. (1952–4); vn. No.2 (*Rapsodia Concertante*) (1952–4); *Toccata*, pf. (1958–9); *Laudi Concertati*, org., orch. (1979); *Rondeaux*, hn., orch. (1982).

VOICE & INSTR(S).: *Night Landscape*, sop., str. trio (1947); *3 Sonnets by Cecco Angiolieri*, ten., 7 instr. (1947); *Tomb of St Eulalia*, elegy, counter-tenor, va. da gamba, hpd. (1955); *Cantata*, ten., chamber orch. (1962); *O Longs désirs*, 5 songs, sop., orch. (1963); *The Day and the Spirits*, sop., hp. (1966–7); *Some Superior Nonsense*, ten., chamber ens. (1968); *The Roofs*, coloratura sop., perc. (1970); *Come, sleep*, cont., alto fl., bcl. (1972); *2 Songs*, bar., pf. (1977).

CHORAL: *Madrigals* (a cappella) (1947); *Musick's Empire*, ch., small orch. (1955); *The *Vision of Judgement*, oratorio, sop., ten., ch., orch. (1957–8); *Ave Maris Stella* (1967); *Magnificat* (1968); *Whispers at these Curtains*; bar., ch., boys' ch., orch. (1984).

CHAMBER MUSIC: wind quintet (1947); str. qt. No.1 (1947), No.2 (1952–3), No.3 (1975), No.4 (1976); vn. sonata No.1 (1950), No.2 (1988); hn. sonata (1955); vc. sonata (1956); octet (1957–8); *Serenade No.1*, 6 instr. (1959), No.2, fl., ob., pf. (1959), No.3, sax. qt. (1969); *4 Dialogues*, ob., pf. (1965); *Fantasy*, va., pf. (1966); *Refrains*, ob. (1968); *3 Arguments*, bn., vc. (1969); *Paseo*, gui. (1969); *The Groves of Dodona*, 6 fl. (1973); *Spirit Puck*, cl., perc. (1974); *Aspects of Evening*, vc., pf. (1985).

KEYBOARD: *Suite*, hpd. (1957); *Variations*, pf. (1957–8); *14 Aubades*, pf. (1958); *12 Studies*, pf. (1961); *Episodes I*, pf. (1967–8), *II*, pf. (1969); sonata, 2 pf. (1977); *Anniversary*, pf. (1978).

ORGAN: *Sonata* (1947); *Choral* (1956); *Pastorale* (1959); *Ricercare* (1965); *6 Pieces* (1968); *Toccata* (1968); *Praeludium* (1970); *Intrada* (1971); *Trio Sonata* (1974); *Invention and Little Toccata* (1976).

Fricsay, Ferenc (*b* Budapest, 1914; *d* Ermatingen, Switz., 1963). Hung. conductor. Cond. at Szeged 1933–9. Prin. cond. Budapest Opera 1939–45. Cond. f.ps. of *Einem's Dantons Tod (Salzburg Fest. 1947, his début there), and Orff's Antigonae (Salzburg 1949). Cond. Berlin Städtische Opera 1948–52, Munich Opera 1956–8, Deutsche Oper, Berlin, from 1961, inaugurating rebuilt th. with *Don Giovanni*. Prin. cond. RIAS Orch., Berlin, 1948–54. Mus. dir. Bavarian State Opera 1956–8. Brit. début, Edinburgh Fest. 1950; Amer. début 1953. Cond. Houston SO 1954.

Fried(-Biss), Miriam (*b* Satu-Mare, Romania, 1946). Israeli violinist of Romanian birth. Won Paganini comp., Genoa, 1968 and Queen Elisabeth comp., Brussels, 1971. NY début 1969. Brit. début, Windsor Fest. 1971 with Menuhin Fest. Orch.

Fried, Oskar (*b* Berlin, 1871; *d* Moscow, 1941). Ger.-born conductor, horn-player, and composer (Russ. cit. 1940). Hn.-player in Frankfurt Opera orch. 1889. Guest cond. of most leading Eur. orchs., specially active in Berlin: cond. Stern Choral Soc. from 1904, Gesellschaft der Musikfreunde 1907–10, Berlin SO 1925–6. Left Berlin in 1934 for Russ. Cond. ballet at Salzburg Fest. 1925. Cond. opera at Tbilisi and was chief cond. Moscow All-Union Radio Orch. Champion of Delius, Mahler, and others among his contemporaries. His comps. incl. opera *Die vernarrte Prinzess; Verklärte Nacht*, mez., ten., orch. (1901); and *Das trunkene Lied*, sop., cont., bass, ch., orch. (1904).

Friedenstag (Day of Peace). 1-act opera by R. Strauss to lib. by J. Gregor (from an idea and with emendations by S. Zweig) based on Calderón's play *La Rendición de Breda* (1625). Comp. 1935–6. Prod. Munich 1938. F. Amer. p. Los Angeles (Univ. of S. Calif., in English), 1957; NY (concert) 1989. F. Eng. p. BBC broadcast (concert perf.) 1971; public concert perf. London 1985.

Friedheim, Arthur (*b* St Petersburg, 1859; *d* NY, 1932). Ger pianist, composer, and teacher. Was pupil of Liszt and acted as his secretary. Lived and worked in USA 1891–5. Prof. of pf., RMCM 1903–4. Cond. in Munich, 1908–10, returning to USA. Settled in NY 1914 but became prof. of pf., Canadian Acad., Toronto, 1921. Ed. complete works of Chopin, transcr. Liszt works, and comp. operas and pf. concs.

Friedman, Ignaz (*b* Podgórze, nr. Kraków, 1882; *d* Sydney, NSW, 1948). Polish pianist and composer. Début Vienna. Toured in Eur. and USA, living in Berlin until 1914, then in Copenhagen and, from 1940, in Australia. Frequently partnered *Huberman in vn. sonatas. Ed. Chopin's works. Comp. chamber mus. and songs.

Friedrich, Götz (*b* Naumburg, 1930; *d* Berlin, 2000). Ger. opera producer. Studied in Weimar and joined *Felsenstein at the Komische Oper,

Berlin, 1953. First prod. *Così fan tutte* 1958, dir. of prods. 1968. Chief prod. Hamburg 1973–81. First Bayreuth prod. 1972 (*Tannhäuser*). Prin. prod. CG 1976–81 and among his prods. there staged *The Ring* (1974–6 and 1989–91). Prod. f.p. Berio's *Un Re in Ascolto* (his Salzburg Fest. début, 1984), Rihm's *Oedipus*, Berlin 1987. USA début prod. *Wozzeck* (Houston 1982). An avowed Marxist, his political leanings were reflected in his prods. Intendant, Deutsche Oper, Berlin, from 1980. Married to soprano Karan Armstrong (*b* 1941).

Friend, Lionel (*b* London, 1945). Eng. conductor. Début WNO, Swansea, 1969 (*La traviata*). Cond. at WNO 1968–72; Cassel Opera 1972–5. Staff cond. ENO 1976–89; mus. dir. Nexus Opera from 1981, New Sussex Opera from 1989.

Friml, Rudolf (*b* Prague, 1879; *d* Hollywood, 1972). Cz. composer who settled in USA 1906. First visited USA 1901 as pianist with Jan *Kubelik. Played his pf. conc. with NYSO and comp. pf. works and chamber mus. Fame rests on series of popular operettas: *The Firefly* (1912); *Katinka* (1915); *Rose Marie* (1924); and *The Vagabond King* (1925). His popular 'Donkey Serenade' was added to *The Firefly* when it was filmed in 1937.

Friskin, James (*b* Glasgow, 1886; *d* NY, 1967). Scottish pianist and composer. Taught at Royal Normal Coll. for Blind, 1909–14. Settled in USA 1914, devoting most of time to teaching and to recitals of Bach's mus., in which he specialized. Taught at Inst. of Mus. Art, NY, and Juilliard Sch. for a total of 50 years. Wrote str. qt., pf. trio, pf. qt., pf. quintet, vn. sonata. His wife was the composer Rebecca *Clarke.

Frith, Benjamin (*b* Sheffield, 1957). Eng. pianist. Début London 1981. Joint winner, Busoni int. pf. comp. 1986, joint winner Arthur Rubinstein int. pf. masters comp., Tel Aviv, 1989.

FRMCM. Fellow of the Royal Manchester College of Music.

FRNCM. Fellow of the Royal Northern College of Music, Manchester.

Froberger, Johann Jacob (*b* Stuttgart, 1616; *d* Héricourt, 1667). Ger. composer and organist. Org. at court of Vienna 1637, but spent next 4 years in Italy as pupil of *Frescobaldi. Visited Belgium, Germany, Holland, France, and England before returning to Vienna as court org. 1653–8. Comp. much for org. and hpd. (toccatas, capriccios, ricercari, etc.).

frog. Device in str. instr. which secures hair of the bow and holds it away from the stick at the lower end. Sometimes called 'heel' or 'nut'.

'Frog' Quartet. (Ger. *Froschquartett*). Nickname of Haydn's Str. Qt. in D major, Op.50, No.6 (1787) because of the 'croaking' theme in the finale.

Froissart. Concert-ov., Op.19, by Elgar comp. for and f.p. at Worcester Fest. 1890. Title refers to passage in Scott's *Old Mortality* in which

Claverhouse speaks of his enthusiasm for the historical romances and *Chronicles* of the Fr. writer Jean Froissart (1337–1410). Score is headed by Keats quotation 'When chivalry lifted up her lance on high'.

From Bohemia's Meadows and Forests (*Z Českych Luhu a Haju*). The 4th symphonic poem of Smetana's *Má Vlást*, often played separately.

From My Life (*Z mého života*; Ger. *Aus meinem Leben*). Title of Smetana's 2 str. qts. (E minor, 1876, and D minor, 1882–3) although it has become customary to apply it only to No.1. Autobiographical character of this qt. culminates in sustained high E in finale depicting whistling in composer's ear which in 1874 heralded his deafness.

From Stone to Thorn. Work by *Maxwell Davies for mez. and instr. ens. to poem by George Mackay Brown. F.p. Oxford 1971, with Mary Thomas (mez.) cond. composer.

From the Bavarian Highlands (Elgar). See *Bavarian Highlands, Scenes from the*.

From the Diary of Virginia Woolf. Song-cycle of 8 songs for medium v. and pf. by *Argento with text from V. Woolf: 1. *The Diary*, 2. *Anxiety*, 3. *Fancy*, 4. *Hardy's Funeral*, 5. *Rome*, 6. *War*, 7. *Parents*, 8. *Last Entry*. Comp. 1974. F.p. Minneapolis, 1975 (Janet Baker and Martin Isepp).

From the House of the Dead. See *House of the Dead, From the*.

Frosch (Ger., 'frog'). The nut of the vn. bow. *am Frosch*, 'at the nut'. See *frog*.

frottola (It., plural *frottole*). A late 15th- and early 16th-cent. popular unacc. It. choral form, a type of simple *madrigal similar to the Eng. ayre. The same mus. was sung to each verse and the tune was invariably in the highest part.

FRSAMD. Fellow of the Royal Scottish Academy of Music and Drama.

FRSCM. Fellow of the Royal School of Church Music.

Frühbeck de Burgos, Rafael (*b* Burgos, 1933). Sp. conductor. Prin. cond. Bilbao orch. 1958–62; Madrid Nat. Orch. 1962–79; Düsseldorf SO 1966–70; Montreal SO 1974–6; Vienna SO from 1991. Guest cond., prin. Eur. and Amer. orchs., incl. Nat. SO of Washington from 1980. Salzburg Fest. début 1988.

Fry, William (Henry) (*b* Philadelphia, 1813; *d* Santa Cruz, 1864). Amer. composer, music critic, and author. In 1845 wrote *Leonora*, regarded as first significant Amer. opera. From 1846 spent 6 years in London and Paris as correspondent of NY *Tribune*, meeting Berlioz and others. On return to NY as mus. critic of *Tribune*, championed Amer. composers. Wrote another 3 operas, syms., church mus., etc.

FTCL. Fellow of Trinity College of Music, London.

FTSC. Fellow of the Tonic Sol-fa College of Music.

Fuchs, Carl (*b* Offenbach, 1865; *d* Manchester, 1951). Ger. cellist. Prin. cellist Hallé Orch., Manchester, 1887–1914. Prof. of vc. RMCM 1893–1914 and 1921–42. Member of Brodsky Qt. 1895–1926. Pubd. a vc. method (3 vols.) 1906.

Fuchs, Johann (Nepomuk) (*b* Frauenthal, 1832; *d* Vöslau, 1899). Austrian conductor and composer. Cond. opera at Pressburg (1864) and at Cassel, Cologne, Hamburg, and Leipzig. Mus. dir., Vienna Opera from 1880. Dir., Vienna Cons. from 1893. Wrote opera *Zingara* (1872).

Fuchs, Marta (*b* Stuttgart, 1898; *d* Stuttgart, 1974). Ger. soprano. Début as mez., Aachen 1928–30. Salzburg Fest. 1929. Dresden Opera from 1930 until retirement in 1945. Also member of Berlin Staatsoper. Sang sop. roles from 1933. Bayreuth début 1933. Sang Isolde at Bayreuth 1938 and Brünnhilde 1938–42. CG début 1936 (with Dresden co.).

Fuchsova, Liza (*b* Brno, 1913; *d* London, 1977). Cz. pianist. Début with Czech PO. Settled in London 1939. Member of Dumka Trio. Excelled in chamber mus. Teacher in later years.

fuga (Lat., It. 'flight'). Since mid-17th cent. this term has meant It. equivalent of *fugue. From Middle Ages to early 17th cent. denoted strict imitation or an individual point of imitation.

Fuga alla giga (Fugue in Jig-style). A fugue in G by J. S. Bach for org., so called from its rhythmic nature.

fugara. Org. stop; a rather rougher toned variety of *gamba*.

fugato. A passage in fugal style. See *fugue*.

Fugère, Lucien (*b* Paris, 1848; *d* Paris, 1935). Fr. baritone. Began career in cabaret, making début 1870 in *café-concert*. Sang over 100 roles at Opéra-Comique 1877–1910. CG début 1897; Paris Opéra 1910–13, singing Sancho Panza in f. Paris p. of *Don Quichotte. Sang Dr Bartolo in *Le nozze di Figaro*, in Paris at age of 85 (1933).

fughetta. A short *fugue.

fugue (Fr. 'fugue', Ger. 'Fuge', It. 'fuga'). Type of contrapuntal comp. for particular no. of parts or 'voices' (described thus whether vocal or instr., e.g. fugue in 4 parts, fugue in 3 vv.). The point of fugue is that the vv. enter successively in imitation of each other, the 1st v. entering with a short melody or phrase known as the *subject* (different from sonata-form 'subject' in that it is merely melodic and short). When all the vv. have entered, the *exposition* is over. Then (normally) there comes an episode or passage of connective tissue (usually a development of something that has appeared in the exposition) leading to another entry or series of entries of the subject, and so on until the end of the piece, entries and episodes alternating.

Contrasts of key constitute an important element in fugal construction. In the exposition the subject first appears, naturally, in the tonic key; the 2nd v. to enter with it does so a 5th higher (or 4th lower), i.e. in the dominant key, the name *answer* now being attached to it; the 3rd is a repetition of the subject (in a higher or lower octave) and so on, subject and answer, tonic and dominant keys, thus appearing alternately, according to the no. of 'voices' engaged. One function of the *episodes* is to effect modulation to various related keys, so that the later entries may have the advantage of this variety, but once the exposition is over it is not considered necessary that further series of entries shall always alternate as to keys in the subject-answer manner.

In addition to the subject there is often a *counter-subject* appearing in the exposition and probably later to the fugue. It is of the nature of a melodic acc. to the answer and subject (generally in double *counterpoint). The v. which has just given out the subject or answer then goes on to the countersubject whilst the next v. is giving out the answer or subject and so on.

Sometimes in later entries there is overlapping of the subject, each v., as it gives out, not waiting for the previous v. to finish it but breaking in, as it were, prematurely. This device, which is called *stretto*, tends to increase the emotional tension of the entry in which it occurs.

Occasionally, after the exposition (and possibly before the 1st episode) there is a *counter-exposition*, much like the 1st exposition in that the same 2 keys are employed. Appearances of the subject (in the exposition or elsewhere) are sometimes separated by something of the nature of the episode, but shorter, called a *codetta*.

The exist 2 types of fugue with 2 subjects (or *double fugue*), one in which the 2 subjects appear together from the outset, and another in which the 1st subject is treated for a certain time, the other then appearing and being likewise treated, after which both are combined. In choral fugues (e.g. in an oratorio movement) there is sometimes a free instr. part, an *accompanied fugue*. The device of *pedal is often employed in fugue, especially near its close.

There are cases in which, instead of the answer being an exact replica of the subject (*real answer*), it is slightly changed in 1 or 2 of its intervals (*tonal answer*), resulting respectively in a *real fugue* and a *tonal fugue* (an absurdity since the tonal treatment may not extend beyond the exposition).

A shortened type of fugue is sometimes called a *fughetta*. A passage in fugal style, not in itself an actual fugue, is called *fugato*.

The above descriptions are of the academic fugue form, but the great composers have, naturally, varied it, e.g. Bach in *Die Kunst der Fuge*. Superb fugues occur in many works, e.g. Beethoven's *Grosse fuge* for str. qt., Op.133, in Elgar's *Introduction and Allegro* for str., and in many choral comps. Fugue-form is also used effectively in opera, e.g. the finale of Act 2 of *Die Meistersinger von Nürnberg* and the finale of *Falstaff*.

fuguing tune. An 18th-cent. type of hymn-tune in which one or more vv. fell silent and then came in with an imitation of some preceding v. Popular in USA, particularly those by *Billings.

Fujikawa, Mayumi (*b* Asahigawa, Japan, 1946). Japanese violinist. Won Vieuxtemps grand prix, Verviers 1970, and 2nd prize in Tchaikovsky comp., Moscow, 1970. London début 1975 (with LSO, cond. Previn). Plays in pf. trio with Michael Roll (pf.) and Richard Markson (vc.).

Fuleihan, Anis (*b* Cyprus, 1900; *d* Stanford, Calif., 1970). Cyprian-born Amer. composer, conductor, pianist, and teacher. Settled in USA 1915, début as pianist NY 1919. Comp. ballets for Bolm and Denishaw cos. in 1920s. Prof. of mus., Indiana Univ. 1947–52, dir., Nat. Cons., Beirut, 1953–60. Cond. Tunis orch. 1963–5. Returned to USA as teacher at Illinois Univ. Comps. incl. opera; 2 syms.; 3 vn. concs.; 3 pf. concs.; concs. for vc., bn., *Theremin, fl., va.; 5 str. qts.; 41 pf. sonatas; songs.

full anthem. Anglican church anthem sung by full choir throughout, as opposed to *verse anthem*.

full close. Perfect *cadence, i.e. chord of the dominant followed by that of the tonic.

Fuller Maitland, J(ohn) **A**(lexander) (*b* London, 1856; *d* Carnforth, 1936). Eng. critic, editor, and harpsichordist. Started career as mus. critic, *Pall Mall Gazette*, 1882–4, *Manchester Guardian* 1884–9, chief critic of *The Times* 1889–1911. One of founders of Folk Song Soc. 1898, having collaborated with L. *Broadwood in *English County Songs*, 1893. Ed. 2nd edn. *Grove's Dictionary of Music and Musicians* (1904–10). Ed. (with W. Barclay *Squire) *Fitzwilliam Virginal Book* (1894–9). Also wrote books on Schumann, Brahms, Joachim, J. S. Bach, and 19th-cent. Eng. mus.

Füllflöte (Ger.). A 'full-toned' (i.e. loud) fl. stop on the org.

Fülligstimmen (Ger., 'full-toned voices'). Org. stops of loud tone.

full mixture. Org. *mixture stop of which pipes are of diapason scale.

full orchestra. The orch. of the normal 4 main sections (str., woodwind, brass, perc.) at concert-hall strength.

full organ. As an indication in org. music, directs the player to use great coupled to swell, with all the louder stops on both manuals.

Füllstimme (Ger., 'filling-voice'). (1) A middle strand (*ripieno*) in the texture of a choral or instr. comp. which may be considered purely accessory.
(2) An additional orch. part (see *ripieno*).
(3) The mixture stop of an org.

full to mixtures. Org. composers' term meaning use all loud stops except reeds.

functional analysis. Form of analysis of a comp., without words, simply by musical extracts showing its structural features and thematic developments, invented for radio by Hans *Keller because he believed that writing or talking about music distorts the music (though he valuably did a lot of both).

fundamental. A chord in which the lowest note is that from which the chord is derived. *Fundamental bass* is the imaginary bass of a passage, consisting not of its actual bass notes but of the roots of its chords, i.e. the bass of its chords when in root position.

fundamental discord. A discordant chord of which the discordant note forms a real part of the chord, i.e. not a mere suspension, anticipation, or retardation. Or the discordant note itself (e.g. dominant 7th, etc.).

fundamental note. The primary note of the harmonic series.

funèbre (Fr.), **funebre** (It.). Funeral. *marche funèbre* or *marcia funebre*, funeral march.

funeral marches. Among the best known of these (all of them in some public use on occasions of mourning) are the following: (1) Handel's *Dead March in Saul* (from the oratorio of that name); (2) The 2nd movt. of Beethoven's 3rd Sym. (*Eroica*); (3) The 3rd movt. of Chopin's 2nd pf. sonata (in B♭ minor, Op.35); (4) Chopin's *Marche funèbre* in C minor, Op.72b.

There are also (5) Beethoven's march 'sulla morte d'un eroe' (on the death of a hero), which is a movt. in his pf. sonata in A♭, Op.26; (6) Mendelssohn's *Song without Words* No.28, in E minor (the title *Funeral March* not, however, authentic); (7) Siegfried's Funeral March from Wagner's *Götterdämmerung*; (8) Grieg's Funeral March for Nordraak (military band, but scored also by Halvorsen for orch.); (9) Berlioz's *Funeral March for the Last Scene of 'Hamlet'* (Op.18, No.3, 1848). Several symphonic movts. (e.g. Elgar's 2nd Sym. *larghetto* and various examples in the works of Mahler) have the character if not the title of funeral marches.

Funeral March of a Marionette (*Convoi funèbre d'une marionette*). Light-hearted piece by Gounod comp. as pf. solo 1872 and orch. 1879.

fünf (Ger.). Five. *Fünfstimmig*, '5-voiced', i.e. in 5 parts.

Funiculì, funiculà. Song comp. by *Denza, 1880, in honour of the opening of the Naples funicular railway. Quoted by R. Strauss, who was apparently under the impression that it was a genuine folk-song, in *finale* of *Aus Italien*, 1886.

fuoco (It.). Fire, e.g. *con fuoco*, with a combination of force and speed. (But *focoso*, fiery.)

Für Elise (For Elise). Bagatelle in A minor for pf. by Beethoven, comp. *c*.1810. Autograph score is inscribed 'Für Elise am 27 April zur Erinnerung von L. v. Bthvn'. Theory put forward by Max Unger that 'Elise' may have been copyist's mis-reading of Therese (von Brunswick) with whom Beethoven was in love and among whose papers the score was discovered. Pubd. 1867.

furia (It.). Fury. So *furioso, furibondo*, furious; *furiosamente*, furiously.

furiant. A rapid Bohemian dance of decided yet frequently-changing rhythm. Dvořák used the title for several movements, but in some of his examples the rhythm remained unchanged.

Furlanetto, Ferruccio (*b* Pordenone, Sicily, 1949). It. bass. Début 1974 Lonigo, Vicenza, as Sparafucile in *Rigoletto*. Sang in Turin, Venice, Parma, and Milan (La Scala début as Banquo in *Macbeth*). Amer. début New Orleans 1978; S. Francisco 1979; Glyndebourne 1980; Salzburg Fest. 1986; CG 1988; NY Met 1990.

furniture, fourniture (in org. terminology). A powerful *mixture stop.

furore (It.). (1) Fury.
(2) Enthusiasm.

Fürst, Janos (*b* Budapest, 1935). Hung. conductor. Formed Irish Chamber Orch. 1963. London début 1972 with RPO. Chief cond. Malmö Orch. 1974–8, mus. dir. Aalborg SO 1980–3. Mus. dir. opera and sym. concerts in Marseilles. Cond RTE Orch., Dublin, 1983–9 (Mahler cycle 1988–9). Mus. dir. Winterthur Municipal Orch., from 1990. Has cond. opera for ENO, Scottish Opera, and in Scandinavia. Amer. début 1990 (Indianapolis SO).

Fürstner. Ger. firm of music publishers. Founded Berlin 1868 by Adolph Fürstner (*b* Berlin, 1833; *d* Bad Nauheim, 1908), who was head clerk of *Bote & Bock before launching his own firm. In 1872 bought Dresden firm of Meser, thereby acquiring Wagner's *Rienzi, Der fliegende Holländer*, and *Tannhäuser* and some works by Liszt. Later acquired Massenet operas and Leoncavallo's *Pagliacci*. In 1900 put Richard Strauss under contract and thereby became publisher of *Salome*. Succeeded by son Otto (*b* Berlin, 1886; *d* London, 1958) who pubd. Strauss operas from *Elektra* to *Arabella*, Pfitzner's *Palestrina*, and light salon mus. Left Ger. 1933 and settled in Eng. where he formed Fürstner Ltd. Leased Ger. publishing rights to Oertel. Succeeded by his widow Ursula, who in 1970 acquired the rights of Fürstner Ltd. Firm now known as Fürstner London.

Furtwängler, (Gustav Heinrich Ernst Martin) **Wilhelm** (*b* Berlin, 1886; *d* Ebersteinburg, 1954). Ger. conductor and composer. Répétiteur, Breslau Stadttheater 1905–6, Zurich 1906–7, Munich court opera with Mottl 1907–9. 3rd cond. under Pfitzner at Strasbourg 1910–11. Dir., Lübeck Opera and cond. of Lübeck SO 1911–15. Cond. Mannheim Opera 1915–20. Tonkünstler Orch., Vienna, 1919–24. Leipzig Gewandhaus Orch. 1922–8, Berlin PO 1922 (for most of the rest of his life), Vienna PO 1924 (prin. cond. 1927–8, 1933–54). Bayreuth Fest. 1931 (*Tristan*),

1936, 1937, 1943, 1944, 1951 (Beethoven's 9th Sym. only). London début 1924, NY 1925, CG début 1935. Regularly cond. Salzburg Fest. (début 1937) and perfs. of *Ring* at La Scala. In concert-hall gave memorable perfs. of the classics, Bruckner, Tchaikovsky, Strauss, etc., and championed music of Stravinsky and other 20th-cent. composers. Cond. f.ps. of Bartók's 1st pf. conc. (Frankfurt 1927), Schoenberg's *Variations*, Op.31 (Berlin 1928), Hindemith's sym. *Mathis der Maler* (Berlin 1934), and Strauss's *Vier letzte Lieder* (London 1950). Controversy over his position during Nazi régime led to withdrawal of his appointment as cond. NYP-SO, 1936 and as cond. of Chicago SO 1949. Fled to Switz. to avoid arrest, 1945. Cleared of pro-Nazi activities 1946 and resumed his int. career, visiting London several times. One of the great masters of the art of cond. Comp. 3 syms., pf. conc., and chamber mus.

Fussell, Charles (Clement) (*b* Winston-Salem, N. Car., 1938). Amer. composer and conductor. Taught theory and comp. at Univ. of Mass., 1966–76, founding Group for New Music, 1974. Teacher of comp., N. Car. Sch. of the Arts, Winston-Salem, 1976–7, Boston Univ. from 1981. Works incl opera *Caligula* (1962); 3 syms. (1963, 1964–7, 1978–81); *Northern Lights* (2 portraits for chamber orch. of Janáček and Munch) (1977–9); *Virgil Thomson Sleeping*, chamber orch. (1981);

Greenwood Sketches, str. qt. (1976); several vocal works incl. *Wilde*, 2 monologues for bar. and orch. (1989–90).

futurism. Artistic movt. which began in 1909 when *Marinetti published his futurist manifesto in a Paris newspaper. Aim was to emphasize dynamic force and motion in industrial soc. Musically this meant all kinds of noise, and special instr. were invented, such as exploders, thunderers, and whistlers. Prominent in the movt. were Francesco Pratella (1880–1955), who composed for a standard orch., and Luigi Russolo (1885–1947), a painter, who wanted every kind of sound to be mus. material. Two of his works, perf. London 1914, were *The Awakening of a Great City* and *A Meeting of Motorcars and Aeroplanes*. Movement petered out *c*.1918, but left its mark.

Fux, Johann Joseph (*b* Hirtenfeld, nr. Graz, 1660; *d* Vienna, 1741). Austrian composer, organist, and theorist. Org., in Vienna 1696, court composer 1698–1705, choirmaster St Stephen's Cath. 1705, vice-Kapellmeister 1713, Kapellmeister and imperial choirmaster 1715. Opera *Constanza e Fortezza* perf. Prague 1723 during coronation festivities. His *Gradus ad Parnassum* (Vienna 1725) formulated rules for counterpoint. Wrote over 400 works, incl. 20 operas, 14 oratorios, *c*.80 masses, instr. partitas, etc.

G

G. Note of the scale: 5th degree of natural scale of C. Thus G♭, G♭♭, G♮, G♯, G♯♯. Keys of G major and G minor. 'In G' signifies either in key of G major or *transposing instr. on which written note C sounds as G (e.g. alto flute in G).

G. In Fr. org. mus., *grand orgue*, i.e. 'Great Org'.

G. Letter prefix to lists of works by Beethoven and Liszt compiled for *New Grove Dictionary of Music and Musicians* (1980).

G. Abbreviated prefix to nos. in the catalogue of Boccherini's works compiled by Yves Gérard (*b* 1932) and pubd. 1969.

Gabrieli, Andrea (*b* Venice, *c*.1510; *d* Venice, 1586). It. organist and composer. Singer at St Mark's, Venice, 1536. Met Lassus when in Ger. 1562, forming lasting friendship. Org. St Mark's 1566–86. Pupils incl. *Hassler, *Sweelinck, and his nephew Giovanni *Gabrieli. Wrote 7 masses and a large quantity of sacred motets and secular madrigals, psalm-settings, and org. works.

Gabrieli [Gabrielli], **Domenico** (*b* Bologna, 1651; *d* Bologna, 1690). It. cellist and composer of a dozen operas, oratorios, and instr. pieces.

Gabrieli, Giovanni (*b* Venice, *c*.1554; *d* Venice, 1612). It. composer and organist, nephew of A. *Gabrieli whose pupil he was. Second org., St Mark's, Venice, from 1585. One of the great Venetian composers of motets with instr. accs. His mus. made use of the special antiphonal effects of vv. and brass obtainable in St Mark's. Comps. incl. *Canzone* for various combinations; 2 sets of *Sacrae symphoniae* (1597 and 1615), the first set containing the celebrated *Sonata pian' e forte alla quarta bassa*; concertos; and many motets incl. *Angelus ad pastores, O magnum mysterium, Exaudi Deus, Hodie Christus natus est, Jubilate Deo, Regina coeli, Sancta et immaculata virginitas*, etc. Also wrote many secular madrigals. Pupils incl. *Schütz and Praetorius.

Gabrieli Quartet. Brit. qt. formed in 1966. Members are Kenneth Sillito (*b* Newcastle upon Tyne, 1939) and Brendan O'Reilly (*b* Dublin, 1934) (who in 1969 replaced Claire Simpson) vns., Ian Jewel (*b* London, 1944), va., and Keith Harvey (*b* Liverpool, 1938), vc. Début London 1967. Wide repertory, incl. many 20th-cent. works.

Gabrilowitsch, Ossip (Salomonovich) (*b* St Petersburg, 1878; *d* Detroit, 1936). Russ.-born pianist, composer, and conductor (Amer. cit.). Début Berlin 1896, followed by Eur. tours and Amer. début 1900. Took up cond. *c*.1905 in Vienna and Paris. Friend of Mahler. Cond. Konzertverein Orch., Munich, 1910–14. Settled NY, 1914, début there as cond. in 1917. Cond., Detroit SO, 1918–35. From 1928 also cond. Philadelphia Orch. Continued annual recital tours

of USA as pianist. Comp. pf. pieces, songs, etc. His wife, Clara Clemens, a contralto, was Mark Twain's daughter.

Gade, Niels (Vilhelm) (*b* Copenhagen, 1817; *d* Copenhagen, 1890). Danish composer, organist, and violinist. Joined royal orch. as violinist 1834. Royal stipend enabled him to travel to It. and Ger. Mendelssohn cond. Gade's 1st Sym., rejected by Copenhagen, at Leipzig 1843 with much success. This led to friendship when Gade went to Leipzig and became ass. cond. of Gewandhaus concerts 1844–6, cond. 1847–8. Returned to Copenhagen, and re-organized Mus. Soc., establishing permanent orch. and choir and cond. f. Danish p. of Bach's *St Matthew Passion* and his own syms. Nos. 4 to 8. Court Kapellmeister 1861, but resigned after a few months. Co-dir. of newly founded Copenhagen Acad. of Mus. 1866. Visited Eng. 1876 to conduct his cantata *The Crusader* at Birmingham Fest. His comps., influenced by Mendelssohn and Schumann, are of persuasive charm and skill. They incl. 8 syms.; ovs.; suites; vn. conc.; opera-ballet *The Fairy Spell*; str. qt.; pf. trio; str. quintet; str. octet; str. sextet; pf. pieces; cantatas; and songs.

Gadski, Johanna (*b* Anklam, Prussia, 1872; *d* in car accident, Berlin, 1932). Ger. soprano. Début Kroll Oper, Berlin, 1889 in Lortzing's *Undine*, remaining for 5 years. Amer. début 1895 with Damrosch Opera Co. at NY Met. Sang Wagner roles with this co. for three seasons. CG début 1898; sang Eva at Bayreuth 1899; NY Met début as member of the co. 1900, singing there until 1917, her roles incl. Brünnhilde and Isolde, and Verdi's Aida, Amelia, and Leonora. From 1929 sang in Wagnerian co. which toured USA.

Gage, Irwin (*b* Cleveland, Ohio, 1939). Amer. pianist. Career devoted to acc. leading singers, incl. Fischer-Dieskau, Hermann Prey, Christa Ludwig, Gundula Janowitz, Elly Ameling, Lucia Popp, Brigitte Fassbaender, Arleen Augér, Edita Gruberova, Cheryl Studer, Thomas Hampson, and Francisco Araiza. Salzburg Fest. début 1970 (recital with Tom Krause).

Gagliano. 18th-cent. Neapolitan family of vn. makers. Chief members were Alessandro, active up to *c*.1730, his sons Gennaro and Niccoló and grandsons Ferdinando and Giuseppe.

Gagliano, Marco da (*b* Florence, 1582; *d* Florence, 1643). It. composer, one of the founders of opera. Educated as priest. Choirmaster, Florence Cath. 1608. His opera *Dafne* (1607, prod. Mantua 1608) was rated highly by *Peri; its preface anticipated Gluck in advocating the importance of dramatic reality. Collab. with Peri on *Il medoro* (1616, lost). *Dafne* and last opera, *La flora* (1628), survive. Also comp. madrigals, motets, etc.

Gaîté parisienne (Parisian gaiety). Ballet in 1 act to Rosenthal's arr. of mus. by Offenbach, lib. Comte Etienne de Beaumont, choreog. Massine. Prod. Monte Carlo 1938. Some characters taken from Offenbach's La *Vie parisienne*.

Gál, Hans (b Brunn am Gebirge, Vienna, 1890; d Edinburgh, 1987). Austrian-born composer, pianist, and writer. Début as pianist 1910. Lect., Vienna Univ. 1919–28. Dir., Mainz municipal coll. of mus. 1929–33. Cond., Vienna Concert Orch. and Bach Soc. 1933–8. Settled in Edinburgh 1938, lect. Edinburgh Univ. 1945–65. Author of books on Brahms, Wagner, Schubert, Verdi, and Vienna. Comps. incl. 5 operas; 4 syms.; *Lilliburlero: Improvisations on a Martial Melody*, orch. (1946); vn. conc.; vc. conc.; concertinos for pf., str. and vn., str.; 2 str. qts.; pf. qt.; pf. trio; str. trio; choral mus.; pf. pieces. OBE 1964.

Galamian, Ivan (Alexander) (b Tabriz, Iran, 1903; d NY, 1981). Amer. violinist and teacher (of Armenian parentage). Paris début 1924. Taught at Russ. Cons., Paris, 1925–39 and at École Normale de Musique 1936–9. Settled in NY 1939. Joined faculty of Curtis Inst. 1944, and Juilliard Sch. of Mus. 1946. Outstanding teacher whose pupils incl. Itzhak Perlman, Michael Rabin, Kyung-Wha Chung, Miriam Fried, Pinchas Zukerman, and Jaime Laredo. Wrote 2 books on vn. playing and technique.

galant (Fr., Ger.). Courtly. 18th-cent. term to describe elegant style (Fr. *style galant*; Ger. *galanter Stil*) favoured by, for example, J. C. Bach, the Stamitzes, and early Mozart.

galanterien (Ger.), **galanteries** (Fr.). In the classical *suite 3 movts. which were not looked upon as essential to the scheme but rather as interpolations of light relief. They usually comprised any of the following: minuet, gavotte, bourrée, passepied, loure, polonaise, air.

Galilei, Vincenzo (b S. Maria a Monte, c.1520; d Florence, 1591). It. composer and lutenist. Associate of members of Bardi's *Camerata from which first opera perfs. developed. Pubd. 2 books of madrigals and one of lute pieces. Also mus. theorist: author of *Dialogo della musica entica e della moderna* (1581). His *Il fronimo* (1568, rev. 1584) is a valuable treatise on lute-playing. His son Galileo Galilei was the great astronomer.

Galin-Paris-Chevé. Fr. sight-singing system, devised by Pierre Galin (1786–1821), Aimé Paris (1798–1866), Nanine Paris (d 1868), and Émile J. M. Chevé (1804–64), on movable-doh lines and with a practical device for acquiring the sense of time-values of notes. See also *Tonic Sol-fa*.

galliard (It. *gagliarda*; Fr. *gaillard*). Lively dance, from 15th cent. or earlier, in simple triple time. Featured a group of 5 steps, and was therefore sometimes called *cinque passi* (It.), *cinque pas* (Fr.), and *cinque pace* or *sink-a-pace* (Eng.). Often paired and contrasted with the slower *pavan, this assoc. being the origin of the *suite. Vaughan Williams's *Job* contains a modern galliard.

Galli-Curci, Amelita (b Milan, 1882; d La Jolla, Calif., 1963). It. soprano. Début as Gilda in *Rigoletto* at Trani, 1906, then sang in It., Egypt, Spain, Russ., and C. and S. Amer. Amer. début Chicago 1916, then Chicago Opera 1916–24; NY Met 1921–30. Brilliant agility in coloratura roles such as Gilda, Violetta, and Elvira in I *Puritani*. Retired 1937. Never sang in opera in Brit., but gave recitals.

Galliera, Alceo (b Milan, 1910; d Brescia, 1996). It. conductor and composer. Teacher of org. comp., Milan Cons., 1932. Cond. début, Rome 1941. Guest cond. of many orchs. and of opera at La Scala. Salzburg Fest. 1948 (Vienna PO). Mus. dir. Victoria SO, Melbourne, 1950–1. Resident cond., Carlo Felice opera house, Genoa, 1957–60, subsequently art. dir. and resident cond. Orch. Municipale de Strasbourg 1964–71. Comps. incl. ballet, orch. mus., chamber works, and songs.

Gallo, Domenico (fl. mid-18th cent.). It. composer and violinist. May have been born in Venice c.1730. Pubd. 6 sonatas for 2 vn. and continuo in Venice and another set of 6 sonatas for 2 fl. and continuo in London. Thirty-six of his trio sonatas are in the coll. at Burghley House, Stamford, Lincs., and Naples and Bologna Cons. have some of his church mus. A set of 12 of his trio sonatas was pubd. in 1780 as by Pergolesi. Some were used by Stravinsky in *Pulcinella* on the wrong assumption that they were by Pergolesi.

Gallus. See *Händl, Jacob*.

galop or **galopade**. 19th-cent. ballroom round dance in simple duple time, with a change of step, or hop, at the end of every mus. phrase. Koenig's *Posthorn Galop* f.p. in Eng., 1844. Galops have been included in 20th-cent. Soviet ballets.

Galpin, Francis William (b Dorchester, 1858; d Richmond, Surrey, 1945). Eng. clergyman and authority on ancient musical instruments. Books incl. catalogue of Eur. instrs. in Metropolitan Museum, NY (1902), study of instrs. of American Indians, history of sackbut, etc. In 1946 the Galpin Soc. was formed in London to continue his work.

Galuppi, Baldassare (b Island of Burano, nr. Venice, 1706; d Venice, 1785). It. composer. From 1728 comp. several operas for It. ths. Visited London 1741–3, with considerable operatic success at King's Th., Haymarket. Ass. choirmaster of St Mark's, Venice, 1748, choirmaster 1762. Visited St Petersburg 1766–8. His 112 operas incl. *Adriano in Siria* (1740); *Didone abbandonata* (1741); *Scipione in Cartagine* (1742); *Il filosofo di campagna* (1752); *Il re pastore* (1762); and *Ifigenia in Tauride* (1768). Also wrote oratorios, church mus., hpd. sonatas. Browning's poem *A Toccata of Galuppi's* refers to an imaginary comp.

Galway, (Sir) **James** (*b* Belfast, 1939). Irish flautist. Flautist, SW Orch. 1960–5, CG 1965. Prin. flautist, LSO 1966–7; RPO 1967–9; Berlin PO 1969–75. After 1975 soloist with orchs. and chamber groups. Salzburg Fest. début 1990. OBE 1977. Knighted 2001.

gamba (It.). Leg. (1) Abbreviation of **viola da gamba*.

(2) Str.-toned org. stop of 8′ (sometimes 4′ or 16′) length and pitch. Metal pipes often taper towards top and sometimes widen again into an inverted bell (*bell gamba*). The *bearded gamba* is a variety with a small roller before the mouth of each pipe.

Gamba, Piero (Pierino) (*b* Rome, 1937). It. conductor and pianist. Child prodigy, son of professional violinist, who cond. an orch. in Rome Opera House in Beethoven's 1st sym. at age of 8. Toured Eur. and N. and S. Amer. London début 1948, cond. Beethoven and Dvořák in Harringay Arena. Moved to Madrid 1952 and resumed career in late 1950s. Visited London 1959–63 and recorded Beethoven's 5 pf. concs. with Julius Katchen. Mus. dir., Winnipeg SO 1970–81; Adelaide SO 1980–8.

Gambler, The (*Igrok*). Opera in 4 acts, Op.24, by **Prokofiev to his own lib. based on Dostoyevsky's short story (1866). Comp. 1915–17, 2nd version 1927–8. Prod. Brussels 1929, NY 1957, Edinburgh 1962, London (ENO) 1983. Orch. suite, *4 Portraits and the Dénouement*, Op.49, f.p. Paris 1932.

Gamblers, The. Unfinished opera by Shostakovich, planned as Op.63, to his own lib. based on comedy *The Gamblers* by Nikolai Gogol (1832) for six male solo vv. and large orch. Begun 1941, abandoned 1942 when not quite 8 of 25 scenes were completed. F.p. (concert) Leningrad 1978, cond. Rozhdestvensky. Completed by Krzysztof Meyer, 1981. Scherzo of va. sonata (1975) uses mus. from *The Gamblers*.

gamelan. Type of orch. found in S. E. Asia, particularly Indonesia (e.g. Java). Incl. str. and woodwind instrs., but is notable for range of perc. such as gongs, drums, chimes, marimbas, etc. The visit of a Javanese gamelan to the Paris Exposition of 1889 had a marked influence on **Debussy.

Game of Cards (Stravinsky). See *Jeu de cartes*.

gamme (Fr.). Scale.

gamut. (1) Properly, the note G at the pitch now indicated by the lowest line of the bass staff. Greek G or 'gamma' was used for its designation, and as the note just mentioned was the 'ut' ('doh') of the lowest **hexachord, this portmanteau word was adopted as a name for it.

(2) By extension, the word came to be used as a comprehensive name for the whole series of hexachords as displayed in writing.

(3) By a further extension it came to mean 'scale' in general (Fr. *gamme*).

(4) Also came to mean the whole range of mus. sounds from the lowest to the highest; and to be

applied in a metaphorical way to a singer's or actor's range, e.g. 'He covered the whole gamut of tragic expression'.

ganz (Ger.). Quite, whole, e.g. *ganzer Bogen*, whole bow; *gänzlich*, completely.

ganze, ganze Note (Ger.). Same as **Ganzetaktnote*.

ganze Pause (Ger.). Whole-note (semibreve) rest.

Ganzetaktnote (Ger.). Whole-measure note, or whole-bar note, i.e. the whole-note, or semibreve.

Gänzl, Kurt (Friedrich) [Gallas, Brian Roy] (*b* Wellington, NZ, 1946). NZ writer. After studying classics in NZ, went to London Opera Centre for a year but took up writing on operetta and mus. th. Wrote *The British Musical Theatre* (1986, 2 vols.), *Encyclopaedia of World's Musicals* (1994) and, with Andrew Lamb, *Gänzl's Book of the Musical Theatre* (1988).

gapped. Term applied to a scale, indicating inclusion of intervals of more than a tone's distance, e.g. the **pentatonic scale.

García, Manuel del Populo Vicente (*b* Seville, 1775; *d* Paris, 1832). Sp. tenor, composer, and singing teacher. Choirboy, Seville Cath., at age 6. Sang in Paris 1808 and 1819–23, Naples 1811–16, creating Almaviva in *Il barbiere di Siviglia*, and London 1817–19. Sang Almaviva in première of *Il barbiere* in Paris, London, and NY. Returned to London 1823, founding singing sch. Est. It. opera co. in NY 1825–6, giving US première of *Don Giovanni* with da Ponte in audience. Took co. to Mexico 1827–8 where bandits robbed him of all his earnings (some £6,000). Returned to Paris first as a singer, then teacher. Comp. 97 operas. Pupils incl. his daughters Maria **Malibran and Pauline **Viardot.

García, Manuel Patricio Rodriguez (*b* Zafra, Madrid, 1805; *d* London, 1906). Sp. bass and singing teacher, son of above. Trained in singing by his father, going to USA in 1825 where he sang Figaro in *Il barbiere di Siviglia* in NY. From 1829 devoted himself to teaching. Prof. of singing, Paris Cons. 1847–50. First to make scientific study of v. production. Invented laryngoscope, 1855. Pubd. *Mémoire sur la voix humaine* (1840) and *Traité complet de l'art du chant* (1840, trans. into It., Ger., and Eng.). Settled in London 1848, becoming prof. at RAM until 1895. Pupils incl. Jenny Lind, Julius Stockhausen, Santley, and Mathilde Marchesi.

García, Maria Felicitá. See *Malibran, Maria Felicitá*.

García, Pauline. See *Viardot-García, Pauline*.

Gardelli, Lamberto (*b* Venice, 1915; *d* Munich, 1998). Swed. conductor and composer of It. birth. Répétiteur, Rome Opera, with **Serafin. Opera début as cond. Rome 1944 (*La traviata*). Cond., Stockholm Opera 1946–55; Danish Radio SO 1955–61 and 1986–9; Budapest Opera 1961–5 and from 1990. Prin. cond. Munich Radio SO

1983–8. Glyndebourne début 1964; Amer. début NY (Carnegie Hall) 1964; NY Met 1966–8; CG 1969. Comp. 5 operas.

Garden, Mary (*b* Aberdeen, 1874; *d* Inverurie, 1967). Amer. soprano of Scot. birth. Taken to USA as a child. Befriended by Amer. sop. Sibyl *Sanderson who sent her to Carré, dir. of Opéra-Comique. Studied title-role of Charpentier's *Louise* and took over from the indisposed Marthe Rioton midway through a perf. in April 1900. Created role of Mélisande in Debussy's opera, 1902, at composer's request. Further successes followed in operas by Massenet, Saint-Saëns, Leroux, and Erlanger. CG 1902–3 (Juliette). After hearing her as Manon, Massenet wrote *Chérubin* (1905) for her. Joined Manhattan Opera, NY, 1907–10 (début in Amer. première of *Thaïs*) and later sang in f. Amer. p. of *Pelléas et Mélisande*, Feb. 1908. Chicago Opera from 1910, becoming dir. 1921–2 and remaining until 1931. Last operatic appearance, Opéra-Comique, Paris, 1934 in Alfano's *Risurezzione*. Taught at Chicago Mus. Coll. 1935 and acted as adviser on opera scenes in Hollywood films. Returned to Scotland 1939. With Louis Biancolli, wrote *Mary Garden's Story* (NY 1951).

Garden of Fand, The. Symphonic poem by *Bax, comp. 1913–16, f.p. Chicago 1920. Fand is a heroine in Irish legend and her garden was the sea. Used for ballet *Picnic at Tintagel* by Ashton, NY 1952.

Gardiner, (Henry) **Balfour** (*b* London, 1877; *d* Salisbury, 1950). Eng. composer. Mus. master, Winchester Coll. 1907. Promoted concerts of contemp. Eng. mus. 1910–20, and was especial champion of *Holst, for whom he arr. a private f.p. of *The Planets* in Queen's Hall, London, cond. by Boult in 1918. He also enabled Delius to continue to live in Fr. by buying his house at Grez-sur-Loing. Comp. sym., *Shepherd Fennel's Dance*, orch. (after Hardy), *News from Whydah*, ch., orch., chamber mus., and songs.

Gardiner, (Sir) **John Eliot** (*b* Fontmell Magna, Dorset, 1943). Eng. conductor, great-nephew of Balfour *Gardiner. Founded Monteverdi Choir 1964, Monteverdi Orch. 1968, English Baroque Soloists (period instr.) 1978, and Orchestre révolutionnaire et romantique 1990. Prof. début 1966. Has made new edns. of Monteverdi's *Vespers* (1967), and Rameau's *Dardanus*, *Les Fêtes d'Hébé*, and *Les Boréades*. Cond. f. staged p. of *Les Boréades*, Aix 1982 and f. modern revival of Berlioz's *Mass*, Paris 1993. SW début 1969; CG 1973. Youngest cond. to appear at Henry Wood Proms. (1968). Prin. cond. CBC Vancouver Orch. 1980–3, art. dir. Göttingen Handel Fest. 1981–90, mus. dir. Lyons Opera 1982–8. Salzburg début 1990. Prin. cond. N Ger. Radio Orch., Hamburg, 1991–4. At Lyons cond. operas by Charpentier, Handel, and Leclair, revived Chabrier's *L'Etoile* and cond. *Pelléas et Mélisande* in a score which was scrupulously close to Debussy's autograph. CBE 1990. Knighted 1998.

Gardner, Edward (*b* Gloucester, 1974). Eng. conductor. Studied King's Coll., Cambridge, and RAM. Assoc. cond. Hallé Orch. 2001–4. Mus. dir.

GTO 2004–6. Paris Opéra 2005 (*Seven Deadly Sins*), ENO 2005 (*Così fan tutte*). Cond. f. Brit. p. of Adams's *Death of Klinghoffer*, Edinburgh 2005. Mus. dir. ENO from 2006.

Gardner, John (Linton) (*b* Manchester, 1917). Eng. composer and pianist. Dir. of mus. Repton School 1939–40. Mus. staff, CG 1946–52; tutor, Morley Coll. 1952–76, dir. of mus. 1965–9; dir. of mus. St Paul's Girls' School 1962–75; prof. of comp., RAM 1956–75. Comps. incl. operas *The Moon and Sixpence* and *Tobermory* (1-act, 1977); orch.: 3 syms. (1946–7, 1985, 1989); *Variations on a Waltz by Nielsen* (1952); pf. conc. (1957); *An English Ballad* (1969); chamber mus.: str. qt. (1939); ob. sonata (1953); *Sonata da chiesa*, 2 tpt., org. (1976, rev. 1977); choral: *Jubilate Deo* (1947); *Ballad of the White Horse*, bar., ch., orch. (1959); *A Latter Day Athenian Speaks* (1962); *Cantiones sacrae* (1952); Mass in C (1965); *Cantata for Christmas* (1966); *Proverbs of Hell* (1967); *Cantata for Easter* (1970); *The Entertainment of the Senses*, 5 singers, 6 players (words by Auden and Kallman) (1974); *English Dance Suite* (1977); *Mass in D* (1983); ob. conc. (1990); *Stabat Mater* (1993). Also th. and film scores. CBE 1976.

Garland for the Queen, A. Collection of songs for unacc. mixed ch. by 10 Brit. composers to texts by 10 contemporary Brit. poets written to celebrate coronation of Elizabeth II in 1953 (in emulation of *The *Triumphs of Oriana* in Elizabeth I's reign). Works and composers (with poets' names in parentheses) were: *Aubade for Coronation Morning*, Bliss (Henry Reed); *What is it Like to be Young and Fair?*, Bax (C. Bax); *Dance, Clarion Air*, Tippett (Fry); *Silence and Music*, Vaughan Williams (Ursula Wood); *Spring at this Hour*, Berkeley (P. Dehn); *The Hills*, Ireland (J. Kirkup); *Inheritance*, Howells (De La Mare); *White Flowering Days*, Finzi (Blunden); *Canzonet*, Rawsthorne (MacNeice); and *Salutation*, Rubbra (Hassall). F.p. London, 1 June 1953.

Garrett, Lesley (*b* Thorne, Doncaster, 1955). Eng. soprano. Joint winner, Ferrier memorial comp. 1979. Opera début London, as Alice in *Le Comte Ory*, ENO 1980; Wexford Fest. 1980 and 1981; Buxton Fest. 1981; WNO début 1981. Sang with ENO from 1984 incl. Susanna, Despina, Yum-Yum, Adele, and Janáček's Vixen. Glyndebourne début 1984. CBE 2002.

Garsington Opera. Annual summer fest. of (usually) 3 operas staged in gardens of Garsington Manor near Oxford. Founded 1989 by Leonard Ingrams (1941–2005). Has made speciality of works by Strauss (f. Eng. stage p. of *Die ägyptische Helena* 1997), Haydn, and Rossini. Gen. dir. Anthony Whitworth-Jones from 2006.

Gaspard de la nuit. Set of 3 pf. pieces by *Ravel, comp. 1908: 1. *Ondine*, 2. *Le Gibet*, 3. *Scarbo*. Composite title taken from prose-ballads by A. Bertrand, sub-titled *Fantaisies à la manière de Rembrandt et de Callot* (1842).

Gasparini, Francesco (*b* Camaiore, 1668; *d* Rome, 1727). It. composer. Choirmaster at Venice

1701–13, engaging Vivaldi as vn. teacher; choirmaster St Lorenzo in Lucina, Rome, 1717–25; choirmaster St John Lateran, Rome, from 1725 but did not assume post because of illness. Wrote oratorios, cantatas, church mus., and many operas, incl. *Amleto* (1705) which is not based on Shakespeare's play. Wrote treatise (1708) on hpd. acc.

Gasteen, Lisa (*b* Brisbane, 1957). Australian soprano. Worked in family business, then entered Queensland Cons. 1980 to study with Margaret Nickson. Nat. Opera Studio 1985–6. Prof. début 1985 Lyric Opera, Queensland (Diana in *Orpheus in the Underworld*). Won Cardiff Singer of the World Comp. 1991. Débuts: Brit. 1992 (Scottish Opera in Glasgow, Leonore in *Trovatore*); USA 1994 (Washington, DC); NY Met 1997 (Aida); CG 2002 (Isolde); Paris 2005 (Isolde). Has sung Brünnhilde in complete *Ring* cycles in Meiningen, Adelaide (2004), Vienna (2005), and London (CG 2005–6). Active concert and recital career.

Gatti, Daniele (*b* Milan, 1962). It. conductor. Opera début Milan 1982 (*Giovanna d'Arco*). Débuts: La Scala 1988; Amer. (Chicago) 1991; CG 1992; NYPO 1995. London concert début 1993 (LSO). Mus. dir. Accademia di S. Cecilia, Rome, from 1992; mus. dir. RPO from 1996.

Gatti, Guido (Maggiorino) (*b* Chieti, 1892; *d* Grottaferrata, nr. Rome, 1973). It. critic and scholar. At 20, appointed ed. of weekly *Reforma musicale*. Leading mus. figure in Turin until *c*.1940. Founded and ed. review *Il pianoforte* 1920 (re-titled *La rassegna musicale* 1928) until its demise 1962. Dir.-gen. Teatro di Torino 1925–31. Sec.-gen. Florence Maggio Musicale from 1933. Instrumental in persuading leading It. composers to write film mus. Ed. of several periodicals, contributor to many dictionaries.

Gatti-Casazza, Giulio (*b* Udine, 1868; *d* Ferrara, 1940). It. impresario. Gave up career as naval engineer to succeed father as dir. of municipal th., Ferrara, 1893; dir. of La Scala 1898–1908, working with *Toscanini and helping to popularize Wagner in It. trans. Dir. NY Met 1908–35, when he staged over 5,000 perfs. of 177 works. Took Toscanini to NY with him, thus inaugurating the cond.'s Amer. career. Encouraged Amer. composers to write operas and secured for the Met the f.ps. of *Königskinder* (1910) and *La fanciulla del West* (1910).

Gauntlett, Henry John (*b* Wellington, Salop, 1805; *d* London, 1876). Eng. organist and composer. Practised for 15 years as lawyer. Org., St Olave's, Southwark 1827. Lect., London Inst. 1837–43. Chosen by Mendelssohn to play org. in f.p. of *Elijah* at Birmingham, 1846. Expert in Gregorian chant. Designed orgs., initiating several reforms. Said to have comp. several thousand hymn tunes, among them *Once in Royal David's City* (1849), with words by Mrs Cecil Frances Alexander.

Gavazzeni, Gianandrea (*b* Bergamo, 1909; *d* Bergamo, 1996). It. conductor, composer, and critic. In 1930s wrote opera, ballet, oratorio, vc. conc., and vn. conc., then devoted more time to writing and cond., eventually giving up composing and discouraging perfs. of his works. Cond. début 1940. Cond., La Scala from 1948 (art. dir. 1965–8). Débuts: Brit. (Edinburgh Fest.) 1957; Amer. (Chicago) 1957; Salzburg Fest. 1961; Glyndebourne 1965; NY Met 1976.

Gaveaux, Pierre (*b* Béziers, 1760; *d* Paris, 1825). Fr. composer and tenor. From 1792 about 30 of his operas were prod. at Opéra-Comique, incl. *Léonore* (1798, in which he sang Florestan) to a lib. which was prin. source of lib. for Beethoven's *Fidelio*. Wrote revolutionary hymn *Le Réveil du peuple* (1795).

gavotte. Old Fr. dance in common time beginning on 3rd beat of the bar. Originated in Pays de Gap where the inhabitants were known as 'gavots'. Popularized at court of Louis XIV, where Lully comp. several examples. Became optional movement of baroque suite. Some examples by 20th-cent. composers, e.g. Prokofiev in his *Classical Symphony* and Schoenberg in his Suite for String Orch.

Gavrilov, Andrei (*b* Moscow, 1955). Russ. pianist. Won Tchaikovsky Comp., Moscow, 1974. Salzburg Fest. début 1974. Brit. début, London 1976 and then with all major London orchs. Amer. début NY 1985. Has appeared in Eur., at many fests., and plays regularly in USA.

Gawain. Opera in 2 acts by *Birtwistle to lib. by David Harsent after *Sir Gawain and the Green Knight* (anon., 14th cent.). Comp. 1987–90, rev. 1994. Prod. London (CG) 1991.

Gawriloff, Saschko (*b* Leipzig, 1929). Ger. violinist. Leader, Dresden PO 1947–8, Berlin PO 1948–9, Berlin Radio SO 1949–53, Frankfurt Museum Orch. 1953–7, Hamburg Radio SO 1961–6. Salzburg Fest. début 1985. Taught at Nuremberg Cons. 1957–61, NW Ger. Mus. Acad. 1966–9. Head of master classes, Cologne Hochschule für Mus. As soloist has played with world's leading orchs. and given f.ps. of works by Maderna, Schnittke, and Ligeti (vn. conc.).

Gay, John (*b* Barnstaple, 1685; *d* London, 1732). Eng. poet, playwright, and theatre manager. Wrote lib. for Handel's *Acis and Galatea*, and for The *Beggar's Opera* (1728) and its sequel *Polly* (1729). Built first CG th., 1732.

Gayane (*Gayeneh*). Ballet in 4 acts, mus. by *Khachaturian, lib. Derzhavin, choreog. Anisimova. Comp. 1940–2, rev. 1952 and (with new plot) 1957. Prod. Leningrad 1942. Earlier version, *Happiness*, prod. Erevan 1939. Contains famous 'Sabre Dance'. Also 3 orch. suites.

Gazza ladra, La (The Thieving Magpie). Opera in 2 acts by Rossini to lib. by Gherardini after comedy *La Pie voleuse*, 1815, by d'Aubigny and Caigniez. Prod. Milan 1817, London 1821, New Orleans 1928. Though the opera was not revived until 1965 in Florence, the ov., in Rossini's most brilliant style, remained popular. Wexford Fest. 1959; Leeds (Opera North) 1992.

Gazzaniga, Giuseppe (b Verona, 1743; d Crema, 1818). It. composer. Comp. 47 operas, of which most successful was *Don Giovanni Tenorio ossia Il Convitato di pietra*, Venice 1787 and in Paris and Lisbon 1792 and London 1794. Choirmaster, Crema Cath. 1791.

Gazzelloni, Severino (b Roccasecca, 1919; d Cassino, 1992). It. flautist. Son of tailor and began career in village band. Début Rome 1945. Prin. fl., It. Radio SO 1946–77. Renowned for playing *avant-garde* works. Also specialized in baroque mus. as well as playing pieces by Beatles and other pop musicians. Played on soundtrack of films. Lifelong Communist.

GBSM. Graduate of Birmingham School of Music.

G Clef. See *great staff*.

Gebrauchsmusik (Ger.). Utility music. Term applied in 1920s to works (by Hindemith, Weill, Krenek, and others) influenced to some social or educational purpose instead of being 'art for art's sake'. Later disowned by Hindemith.

gebunden (Ger.). Bound. Used musically in the sense of 'tied' or 'slurred'.

gedackt, gedeckt (Ger.). Covered. Soft organ stop approaching fl. quality. The name comes from end-plugged pipes of 8′, 16′, 4′ (occasionally 2′) pitch.

gedämpft (Ger.). Damped. When applied to str. and brass instr., it means 'muted'; to drums, 'muffled'; and to pf., 'soft-pedalled'.

Gedda [Ustinov], **Nicolai** (b Stockholm, 1925). Swed. tenor of Russ. descent. Début Stockholm 1951 in Sutermeister's *Der rote Stiefel*, leading to appearances at La Scala 1953; Paris 1954; London (CG) 1954; Vienna 1957. Amer. début (Pittsburgh) 1957; Salzburg Fest. 1957; NY Met 1957–79 (created Anatol in Barber's *Vanessa*, 1958). Also specialized in operetta by Lehár, etc. Frequent singer of *Lieder* and oratorio (has recorded Elgar's *Dream of Gerontius*).

gedeckt. See *gedackt*.

gehend (Ger.). Going. Same as *andante*.

Geige (Ger., plural *Geigen*). Fiddle. Originally any bowed instr., now the vn.

Geigen (Principal). Organ stop; a slightly str.-toned diapason of 8′ (sometimes 4′) length and pitch.

Geigenwerk. Obsolete kbd. instr. invented in Nuremberg 1575 by Hans Haiden. A type of

hurdy-gurdy with brass and steel str. activated by 5 or 6 parchment-covered wheels set in motion by treadle.

Geiringer, Karl (Johannes) (b Vienna, 1899; d Santa Barbara, Calif., 1989). Amer. musicologist and writer of Austrian birth. Curator of collections of Vienna Gesellschaft der Musikfreunde 1930–8. Ed. rare works by Haydn, Brahms, Schubert, Schumann, etc. Went to London 1938, worked for BBC and taught at RCM 1939–40. From 1940 resident of USA. Prof. of mus. history and theory, Boston Univ., 1941–62. Prof. of mus. Univ. of California, Santa Barbara, 1962–72. Books incl. biographies of Haydn (1946, rev. 1961, 1982), and Brahms (1934), *The Bach Family* (1954), *Structure of Beethoven's Diabelli Variations* (1964), and *Johann Sebastian Bach* (1966).

Geister Trio (Ghost Trio). Name for Beethoven's pf. trio in D major, Op.70 No.1, comp. 1808. Mysterious atmosphere of slow movt., which has a theme intended for a projected *Macbeth* opera, gave rise to nickname.

gekkin. Japanese str. instr. with circular body like banjo. Has 9 frets and 4 strs., tuned in pairs.

Geliot, Michael (b London, 1933). Eng. opera and theatre producer. Staged f. Brit. p. of Liebermann's *School for Wives*, Cambridge 1958. Worked at SW 1960–3 and Glyndebourne 1960–1. For New Opera Co., prod. Weill's *Mahagonny* (1963). Dir. at London Traverse Th. 1966–8. Resident prod. WNO 1966–9, dir. of prod. 1969–74, art. dir. 1974–8, prin. prod. 1978–83. Prod. *Lulu* (2-act version) WNO, 1971. Staged f.p. *Taverner*, CG 1972. Also dir. of f. Brit. p. of *Boulevard Solitude* (SW 1962), *Cardillac* (New Opera Co. at SW, 1970), and Martinů's *The Greek Passion* (WNO 1981). Prod. at Wexford, Glasgow, Zurich, Amsterdam, and Munich. Trans. several operas.

Gellenflöte. (Ger.). *clarinet.

Gellhorn, Peter (b Breslau, 1912; d Kingston-upon-Thames, 2004). Ger.-born conductor, pianist, and composer. Settled in Eng. Mus. dir. Toynbee Hall, London, 1935–9; ass. cond. SW Opera 1941–3; cond. Royal Carl Rosa Opera 1945–6; on cond. and mus. staff CG 1947–53; cond. and ch. master Glyndebourne, 1954–61 and from 1974; dir., BBC Chorus 1961–72. Co-founder and mus. dir., Opera Barga, Italy, 1967–9. Prof., GSMD. Visiting coach and occasional cond., RCM Opera Sch., 1981–8.

Geminiani, Francesco (b Lucca, 1687; d Dublin, 1762). It. violinist and composer. In Naples opera orch. 1711–14. Lived in London from 1714, with intervals in Dublin 1733–40 and 1759–62, and Paris 1749–55. When playing for George I in 1716 was accomp. at the hpd. by Handel. Wrote *The Art of Playing on the Violin* (London 1751). Also wrote *Art of Accompaniment* (1754) and *Art of Playing the Guitar or Citra* (1760). Comp. 42 concerti grossi; over 40 vn. sonatas; 6 vc. sonatas; ballet *La foresta incantata* (Paris 1754); etc.

Gemshorn (Ger.). chamois horn. (1) Obsolete medieval type of fl. with sharply-tapering conical bore, made from animal horn (cow, ox, or goat, rather than chamois). Disappeared from use in mid-16th cent.

(2) Light-toned organ stop with conical pipes, usually 4′ length and pitch.

Gendron, Maurice (b Nice, 1920; d Grez-sur-Loing, 1990). Fr. cellist and conductor. Début London 1945 (f. Eur. p. of Prokofiev's vc. conc., Op.58). Played at Aldeburgh Fests. World-wide tours as conc. soloist and recitalist. Master classes in Fr. and Ger. Ass. cond. Bournemouth Sinfonietta 1971–2.

Genée, (Franz Friedrich) **Richard** (b Danzig, 1823; d Baden, 1895). Ger. composer and conductor. Th. cond. in various cities 1847–67; cond. at Theater an der Wien, Vienna, 1868–78. Comp. over a dozen operettas, librettist of others incl. Die *Fledermaus. Collab. with F. Zell (Camillo Walzel) on operettas for Suppé and Millöcker.

Generalbass (Ger.). See *basso continuo*.

general pause. Rest or pause for all executants.

General William Booth Enters into Heaven. (1) Song by *Ives to words by Vachel Lindsay, for v. and pf., 1914, also for bass soloist, ch., and chamber orch. Pubd. in collection *19 Songs*.

(2) For ten., male vv., and chamber orch., 1932, by Philip *James.

Genoveva. (1) Opera in 4 acts, Op.81, by R. Schumann to his own lib. based on 2nd draft of R. Reinick's adaptation of plays by Tieck (1799) and Hebbel (1843). Comp. 1847–9. Prod. Leipzig 1850, London 1893.

(2) Opera in 4 scenes and an interlude by Detlev Müller-Siemens, to lib. by Julie Schrader. Comp. 1977. Prod. TV 1977.

Gentlemen's Concerts. Series of concerts in Manchester begun as gathering of amateur flautists c.1770. Concert hall built 1777. Gave enterprising programmes but declined in 1840s. Revived by appointment of Charles *Hallé as cond. 1849, but subsequently overshadowed by foundation of Hallé's own concerts and orch. 1858. Survived until 1920.

Gentle Shepherd, The. Scot. ballad opera in 5 acts to lib. by Allan Ramsay who selected traditional airs as mus. (1728) for what was orig. (1725) a comedy without songs. Prod. Edinburgh 1729, London 1730.

Genzmer, Harald (b Blumental, Bremen, 1909). Ger. composer. Chorus répétiteur, Breslau Opera, 1934–7. Prof. of comp. Hochschule für Musik, Freiburg, 1946–56, Akademie der Tonkunst, Munich, 1957–74. Made special study of elec. instr. the *Trautonium for which he wrote 2 concs. (1939, 1952). Other works incl. Bremer Symphony (1942); sym. No.1 (1957), No.2 (1958), No.3 (1986); Musik for strings (1942); concs.: 3 for pf. (1948–74), vc. (1950), fl. (1954), vn. No.1 (1959), No.2 (1969), va.

(1967), org. (1971), vc., db., str. (1985); choral works; str. qt.; hp. septet; 2 fl. sonatas; 2 vn. sonatas; recorder sonata; suite for trautonium and pf. His Mass in E (1953) is highly regarded.

Georgian, Karine (b Moscow, 1944). Russ. cellist. Soloist with Russ. orchs. Amer. début 1969 (NY with Chicago SO). Prof. of vc. at Staatliche Hochschule für Mus., Detmold, from 1984.

Gergiev, Valery (Abissalovich) (b Moscow, 1953). Russ. conductor. Ass. cond. to Temirkanov at Kirov Th., Leningrad (now Mariinsky Th., St Petersburg) 1977. Won 2nd prize at Karajan cond. comp., Berlin 1977. Chief cond., Armenian State Orch. 1981–5. London début 1988 with LSO, followed by CBSO and RLPO. Succeeded Temirkanov as chief cond. and art. dir. Kirov Opera and Ballet Th., 1988. Prin. cond. Rotterdam PO from 1995. Prin. cond. LSO from 2006. NY Met début 1994 (Otello). At his instigation, co-operation in prods. begun with Royal Opera, CG (Tarkovsky and Boris Godunov, Moshinsky and Otello, Freeman and The Fiery Angel).

Gerhard, Roberto (b Valls, Tarragona, 1896; d Cambridge, 1970). Composer and pianist with Swiss-Ger. father and Alsatian mother, who identified himself with Sp. mus. and eventually became Eng. cit. Added Hispanic 'o' to his forename in 1940. Returned to Barcelona to teach 1929 but moved first to Paris then to Eng. after Republican defeat in Sp. Civil War, having been adviser to Ministry of Fine Arts in Catalan Govt. 1937–8. Visited Ger. for first time for 20 years in 1951 to hear concert perf. of The Duenna in Frankfurt. Taught at Dartington 1956 and Tanglewood 1961. Last visit to Spain 1967. Left 5th sym. incomplete. CBE 1967.

Influenced at first by Debussy and Ravel, Gerhard became a Schoenberg pupil on the strength of his 7 Hai-Ku for sop., wind, and pf. (1922). His wind quintet (1928) was basically serial but not 12-note and, despite the influence of Schoenberg, his mus. of this date remained tonal in essence and had a distinctive Sp. melodic and rhythmic flavour. On settling in Cambridge in 1939 he seemed to expand as a composer. His idiosyncratic 12-note serial method was first used in 3 Impromptus for pf., 1950, comp. for Marion Stein (then Countess of Harewood). This period of his development culminated in the 3-act Sheridan opera The Duenna (1945–7, rev. 1950) where a Sp. idiom is combined with tonal, bitonal, and serial harmonic styles. For 3 years Gerhard reassessed his attitude to Schoenbergian methods and studied the serial opinions of *Hauer and A. Hába. His pf. conc. (1951) is consistently 12-note but was not 'strict' and drew on early Sp. kbd. styles. In a series of splendidly individual works from 1952 onwards, Gerhard adopted Hába's 'athematicism'. Sometimes, as in his 3rd sym. ('Collages'), he combined orch. sound with elec. tape. All his mus. has imaginative genius and colour, its fundamentally lyrical and original nature never being sacrificed to doctrinaire procedures. Prin. works:

OPERAS: *The *Duenna* (after Sheridan) (1945–7, rev. 1950) (BBC broadcast 1949, concert perf. Frankfurt 1951, f. stage p. Madrid 1992); *El Barberillo di Lavapies*, zarzuela (1954).

BALLETS: *Ariel* (1934); *Soirées de Barcelone* (1936–8); *Alegrías* (1942); *Pandora* (1943–4); **Don Quixote* (1940–1, 1947–9).

ORCH.: *Albada, Interludi i Danza* (1936); *Hommaje a Pedrell*, sym. (1941), its final movt. pubd. separately as *Pedrelliana* (1941); vn. conc. (1942–3); pf. conc., with str. (1951); sym. No.1 (1952–3), No.2 (1957–9, recomp. as *Metamorphoses* 1967–8), No.3 ('Collages') (1960), No.4 ('New York') (1967); hpd. conc. with str. and perc. (1955–6); *Concerto for Orchestra* (1965); *Epithalamion*, orch. (reworking of film score *This Sporting Life*, 1963) (1966); *Hymnody*, 11 players (1963); *Leo*, chamber sym., 10 players (1969).

VOICE(S) & INSTR(S).: *L'alta Naixença del Rei en Jaume*, cantata, sop., bar., ch., orch. (1932); *L'Infantament meravellos de Shahrazada*, sop., pf. (1917); *7 Hai-Ku*, v., 5 instr. (1922); *The Akond of Swat*, v., perc. (1954); *The Plague*, spkr., ch., orch. (after Camus) (1963–4).

CHAMBER MUSIC: pf. trio (1918); va. sonata (1950); str. qt. No.1 (1950–5), No.2 (1960–2); Nonet, 8 wind instr., accordion (1956); *Libra*, fl., cl., vn., gui., pf., perc. (1968); vc. sonata (1956).

PIANO: *Alegrías*, 2 pf. (1942); *Dances from Don Quixote* (1947); *3 Impromptus* (1950).

INCIDENTAL MUSIC: *Cristóbal Colón* (Madariaga, BBC 1943); *Don Quixote* (Linklater, BBC 1940); *Conquistador* (MacLeish, BBC 1953); *L'Etranger* (Camus, BBC 1954); and for several Shakespeare prods. at Stratford-upon-Avon, beginning with *Romeo and Juliet* (1949). Wrote mus. for films, incl. *Secret People* (1952) and *This Sporting Life* (1963, much of it unused).

Gerhardt, Elena (*b* Leipzig, 1883; *d* London, 1961). Ger.-born mezzo-soprano (orig. sop.) (Brit. cit.). Studied Leipzig Cons. 1900–4 and with A. Nikisch, who later often acted as her acc., as at her début, 1903, on her 20th birthday. After a few appearances at Leipzig, rejected opera in favour of the recital platform, becoming outstanding exponent of Ger. *Lieder*, esp. Wolf, Brahms, Schubert, R. Strauss. Eng. début 1906, Amer. 1912. Settled in London 1934. Sang during war at Nat. Gallery concerts and for a time afterwards, then became teacher.

Gericke, Wilhelm (*b* Schwanberg, 1845; *d* Vienna, 1925). Austrian conductor and composer (under pseudonym Wenzel Ecker). Th. cond., Linz, from 1865; 2nd cond. Vienna Opera from 1874. Succeeded Brahms as cond. of Gesellschaft Konzerte, Vienna, 1880. Cond. Boston SO 1884–9, returning to Vienna and the Gesellschaft 1890–5. Resumed Boston post 1898–1906, when he retired. Comp. operetta, requiem, orch. mus., songs, etc.

German, (Sir) **Edward** [Jones, German Edward] (*b* Whitchurch, Salop, 1862; *d* London, 1936). Eng. composer. Played in th. orchs., soon becoming cond. Mus. dir., Globe Th. from 1888, writing incidental mus. for Shakespeare's plays (incl. some of Irving's prods.) which made him famous. Greatest success was patriotic operetta *Merrie England* (1902). Among his popular songs are *Rolling Down to Rio* (1903) and *Glorious Devon* (1905). Also wrote attractive mus. for pf. Knighted 1928. Prin. works:

LIGHT OPERAS: *The *Emerald Isle* (1901, completion of *Sullivan's last work); **Merrie England* (1902); *A Princess of Kensington* (1902); **Tom Jones* (1907); *Fallen Fairies* (1909).

THEATRE MUSIC: *Richard III* (1889); *Henry VIII* (1892); *Romeo and Juliet* (1895); *As You Like It* (1896); *Much Ado About Nothing* (1898); *Nell Gwyn* (1900).

ORCH.: Syms. No.1 (1887, rev. 1890) and No.2 ('Norwich', 1893); *Hamlet*, sym.-poem (1897); *Welsh Rhapsody* (1904); *Coronation March* (based on *Henry VIII*) (1911); *Theme and 6 Diversions* (1919).

German dance. See *deutscher Tanz*.

Germani, Fernando (*b* Rome, 1906; *d* Rome, 1998). It. organist, composer, and scholar. Head of org. studies, Curtis Inst. 1936–8. London début 1936. First org., St Peter's, Rome, 1948–59. Worldwide recital tours. Ed. of **Frescobaldi's org. works (1936) and author of an org. method (1942–52).

German Requiem, A (Brahms). See *Deutsches Requiem, Ein*.

German sixth. Type of **augmented 6th chord.

German Suites. Unauthorized title for the set of 6 kbd. partitas by J. S. Bach. See also *French Suites*; *English Suites*; *Klavierübung*.

Gershwin, George [Gershwin, Jacob] (*b* Brooklyn, NY, 1898; *d* Hollywood, Calif., 1937). Amer. composer and pianist. Son of Russ. Jewish migrants who went to USA *c.*1893 (family name Gershovitz). Pf. lessons 1913 from Charles Hambitzer; later studied theory and harmony with Rubin Goldmark and Edward Kilenyi for whom he wrote a str. qt. (1919). In 1914 left school to work as pianist and 'song plugger' for Remick, a publisher of popular mus. Wrote his first song in 1916 and his first Broadway musical, *La La Lucille*, in 1919. For the next 14 years a Gershwin musical was a feature of NY theatrical life. His first outstanding 'hit' was the song *Swanee* (1919), which became assoc. with Al Jolson. In 1924 he enjoyed success in a new genre, that of applying jazz idioms to concert works, when his *Rhapsody in Blue* for pf. and orch. had its f.p. From then until the end of his life he produced larger-scale works alongside the songs (many with words by his elder brother Ira (Israel)) he wrote for musicals and, after 1931, films. The Pf. Conc. of 1925 was followed by *An American in Paris*, a second *Rhapsody*, the *Cuban Overture*, and in 1935 by the opera *Porgy and Bess* which is still the only opera by an Amer. composer to become est. in the repertory.

Gershwin's melodic gift was phenomenal. His songs contain the essence of NY in the 1920s and have deservedly become classics of their kind, part of the 20th-cent. folk-song tradition in the sense that they are popular mus. which has been spread by oral tradition (for many must have sung a Gershwin song without having any idea who wrote it). His larger-scale works, melodically remarkable as might be expected, suffer from his haphazard mus. education and lack of grounding in counterpoint, theory, etc. (*Rhapsody in Blue* was orchestrated by Ferde *Grofé, but Gershwin himself scored the later works.) He went for lessons to Henry Cowell and Joseph Schillinger, and there can be little doubt that had he lived longer he would have progressed to considerable symphonic achievement. As it is, his mixture of the primitive and the sophisticated gives his mus. individuality and an appeal which shows no sign of diminishing. Prin. works:

OPERAS: *Blue Monday* (1-act; item in *George White's Scandals* 1922 but withdrawn after 1 perf.; retitled *135th Street* and revived Miami 1970); *Porgy and Bess* (1934–5).

ORCH.: *Rhapsody in Blue* (pf. and orch.) (1924); pf. conc. in F major (1925); *An *American in Paris* (1928); *Second Rhapsody* (pf. and orch.) (1931); *Cuban Overture* (1932); *'I Got Rhythm' Variations* (pf. and orch.) (1934).

MUSICALS: *The Passing Show of 1916*; *La La Lucille* (1919); *George White's Scandals* (1920–4); *A Dangerous Maid* (1921); *Sweet Little Devil* (1924); *Primrose* (1924); *Lady, Be Good!* (1924); *Song of the Flame* (1925); *Tell Me More* (1925); *Tip Toes* (1925); *Oh, Kay!* (1926, lyrics by P. G. Wodehouse); *Strike up the Band* (1927, 2nd vers. 1930); *Funny Face* (1927); *Rosalie* (1928); *Treasure Girl* (1928); *Show Girl* (1929); *Girl Crazy* (1930); *Of Thee I Sing* (1931, lyrics by George F. Kaufman); *Pardon my English* (1933); *Let 'em eat Cake* (1933).

FILMS: *Delicious* (1931); *Shall We Dance?*; *A Damsel in Distress* (1937); *The Goldwyn Follies* (1938); *The Shocking Miss Pilgrim* (1946); *Kiss Me, Stupid* (1964).

PIANO: 3 Preludes (1926) (transcr. for vn. and pf. by Heifetz).

SONGS: Among the best of hundreds of songs are *Swanee*; *The Man I Love*; *Embraceable You*; *I Got Rhythm*; *Fascinating Rhythm*; *'S Wonderful*; *Lady Be Good*; and *Love Walked In*. The popular *Summertime* is from *Porgy and Bess*.

Gertler, André (*b* Budapest, 1907; *d* Brussels, 1998). Hung. violinist. Frequently gave recitals with Bartók as pianist. Settled in Brussels where he founded Gertler Qt., 1931–51. On staff Brussels Cons. 1940–54. Conc. soloist with leading orchs. Salzburg Fest. 1955. Prof., Cologne Hochschule für Mus. 1954–9, Hanover Acad. 1964–78.

Ges (Ger.). G♭, Geses, G♭♭.

Gesamtkunstwerk (Ger.). Unified work of art. Wagner's term for a dramatic work in which drama, music, poetry, song, and paintings should be united into a new and complete artform. This theory is expounded in his *Das Kunstwerk der Zukunft* (The Art-work of the Future, 1849).

Gesang der Jünglinge (Song of the Young Boys). Elec. comp. (on tape) by *Stockhausen, 1955–6, comprising spoken and sung boy's v. so altered and multiplied by various devices that it sounds to be many vv., with elec. sounds added.

Gesang der Parzen (Song of the Fates). Ballad, Op.89, by Brahms for 6-part ch. and orch., comp. 1882. Text by Goethe.

Geschöpfe des Prometheus, Die (Beethoven). See *Prometheus, Die Geschöpfe des*.

Gesellschaft der Musikfreunde, Wien (Society of Friends of Music, Vienna). Founded 1813, through efforts of Joseph von Sonnleithner, with Beethoven's friend and pupil, Archduke Rudolph, as patron, to perf. oratorios in the Riding School, but later had own home. Also founded cons., library, and museum. A choral soc., Singverein, of over 300 members, was founded 1858, and an Orchesterverein in 1860. Gesellschaft concerts were cond. by members until 1851 when Hellmesberger was appointed. Successors incl. Brahms, *Gericke, Richter, Franz Schalk, and Furtwängler. The soc. archives contain priceless manuscripts by Beethoven (*Sinfonia Eroica*), Haydn, Mozart, Schubert, Schumann, Brahms, Wagner, and Johann Strauss II. Also possesses Beethoven's ear-trumpet.

Gessendorf, Mechthild (*b* Munich, 1937). Ger. soprano. Member of Vienna Chamber Opera from 1961, then sang in Bremen and Bonn opera cos. Joined Bavarian State Opera, Munich, singing Strauss roles such as the Empress and Marschallin, also Aida, Elisabeth (*Don Carlos*), and in *The Turn of the Screw*. Salzburg Fest. début 1982; Bregenz 1983; Amer. (Tulsa) 1983; Met 1986; CG 1987. London concert début 1989. Sang Wagner and Strauss roles in most Eur. opera houses and fests.

gestopft (Ger.). Stopped. (1) 'Stopped' hn. notes are those prod. with the bell of the instr. more or less closed by the hand.

(2) An equivalent for *gedämpft.

Gesualdo, Don Carlo, Prince of Venosa (*b* Naples, *c*.1560; *d* Gesualdo, Avellino, 1613). It. composer and lutenist. Pubd. 4 books of madrigals from 1594 to 1596 when at court of the Estensi at Ferrara. Returned to Naples 1597. Two further books of madrigals pubd. 1611; these contain harmonic complexity and modernity far in advance of his contemps. in the 20th cent., for example, these madrigals inspired and fascinated Stravinsky. Also wrote motets and religious songs. In 1590 his first wife and her lover were murdered on Gesualdo's orders, an event which is explored in a book on Gesualdo by Cecil *Gray and Philip Heseltine (1926).

Geszty [Witkowsky], **Sylvia** (*b* Budapest, 1934). Hung. soprano. Début Budapest Opera 1959. Member of Berlin State Opera 1961–70 (début as Amor in Gluck's *Orfeo*); Berlin Komische Oper

1963–70; Hamburg State Opera 1966–73; Stuttgart Opera from 1971. CG début 1966; Salzburg 1967; Glyndebourne 1971; Amer. (Los Angeles) 1973. Recorded Zerbinetta, her outstanding role, with Kempe.

geteilt, getheilt (Ger.). Divided, e.g. of vns., corresponding to *divisi*. Sometimes abbreviated as *get*.

Gewandhaus (Ger.). Cloth hall. Leipzig's concert hall. Concerts began in Bach's time, being held in a private house, then in an inn. In 1781 they moved to the Gewandhaus, where they were given until 1885, when a new hall was built.

gewöhnlich (Ger.). Usual. Used in scores to countermand previous indication that the instr. concerned was to play in some unusual way, e.g. the vn. after it has been playing *am Griffbrett* (near the fingerboard).

gezogen (Ger.). Drawn. (1) Drawn out, sustained. (2) Same as *portamento.

GGSMD. Graduate of Guildhall School of Music and Drama.

Ghazarian, Sona (*b* Beirut, 1945). Lebanese soprano. Member of Vienna State Opera from 1972, her roles incl. Oscar in *Un ballo in maschera* and Violetta in *La traviata*. Salzburg Fest. début 1973. Met début 1989.

Ghedini, Giorgio (Federico) (*b* Cuneo, 1892; *d* Nervi, 1965). It. composer. Ass. cond. Teatro Regio, Turin. Prof. of harmony and comp. Turin Cons. 1918–37, Parma Cons. 1938–41, Milan Cons. 1941–51, dir. 1951–62. Ed. works by Monteverdi, A. and G. Gabrieli, Frescobaldi, Schütz, etc. 8 operas incl. *Re Hassan* (1938), *Billy Budd* (1949), and *L'ipocrita felice* ('The Happy Hypocrite', Max Beerbohm, 1956). Also wrote sym.; *Concerto dell' albatro*; *Canzoni* for orch.; pf. conc.; double vc. conc.; 2 vn. concs.; va. conc.; chamber mus.; choral works; and songs.

Gheorghiu, Angela (*b* Adjud, Romania, 1965). Romanian soprano. Début with Bucharest Opera 1990. CG début 1992; Vienna opera début 1992; NY Met 1993. Roles incl. Mimì and Violetta.

Ghiaurov, Nicolai (*b* Velingrad, Bulgaria, 1929; *d* Modena, 2004). Bulgarian bass. Played vn., cl., tb., and pf. by age of 14. Opera début Sofia 1955 (Don Basilio in *Il barbiere di Siviglia*). Vienna début 1957; member of Bolshoy Opera from 1958. Frequent guest singer at La Scala (début 1960). Débuts: CG 1962; Salzburg Fest. 1962; Amer. (Chicago) 1963; NY Met 1965. Notable roles were Boris and King Philip in *Don Carlos*. Sang title-role in Massenet's *Don Quichotte*, Paris 1974.

Ghislanzoni, Antonio (*b* Lecco, 1824; *d* Caprino-Bergamasco, 1893). It. writer. Career as bar. in Fr. and It. 1846–55, his roles incl. Carlo in Verdi's *Ernani*. Ed. *Gazzetta musicale*, Milan. Author of at least 80 opera libs., incl. that for Verdi's *Aida* (1871). Helped Verdi with rev. of *La forza del destino* (1869) and *Don Carlos* (1872).

Ghiuselev [Gyuselev], **Nicola** (*b* Pavlikeni, 1936). Bulg. bass. Début Sofia 1961 with Bulg. Nat. Opera as Timur in *Turandot*. NY Met début 1965; Holland Fest. 1966; CG 1976. Returned to CG 1990 as Galitzky in *Prince Igor*.

Ghosts of Versailles, The. Grand *opera buffa* in 2 acts by *Corigliano to lib. by William M. Hoffman based on Beaumarchais's play *La mère coupable* (1792), comp. 1980–91. Prod. NY Met 1991.

Ghost Trio (Beethoven). See *Geister Trio*.

Giacomini, Giuseppe (*b* Veggiano, Padua, 1940). It. tenor. Début Vercelli 1966 (Pinkerton in *Madama Butterfly*). Sang in Berlin and Vienna from 1972; Hamburg 1973; La Scala 1974; Paris 1975; Amer. (Conn. Opera) 1975; NY Met 1976; CG 1980. Sang Otello in San Diego 1986 and elsewhere.

Gianni Schicchi. 1-act opera by Puccini to lib. by Forzano based on incident in Dante's *Inferno*, canto 30. Comp. 1917–18. Prod. NY Met 1918, Rome 1919, London 1920. The 3rd of Puccini's *Trittico*, the others being Il *tabarro and *Suor Angelica*.

Gianoncelli, Bernardo (*d* before 1650). It. composer and lutenist in first half of 17th cent. One of last It. composers for lute. Little known biographically. In 1650 his widow pubd. *Il liuto di Bernardo Gianoncelli* in his memory (only surviving copy in Biblioteca Nazionale Marciana, Venice). Contains several suites, arr. according to key. Best-known piece was *Bergamasca*, of which a lute arr. by Chilesotti was pubd. 1891. Also orch. version by *Respighi.

'Giant' Fugue. Nickname for Bach's organ fugue in D minor in Part III of the *Klavierübung*. So called because of giant-like strides of a pedal figure:

Giardini, Felice de (*b* Turin, 1716; *d* Moscow, 1796). It. violinist and composer. Chorister, Milan Cath. Played in opera orchs. in Rome and Naples. Toured Ger. and Eng. 1750, settling in latter as leader of orch. at It. Opera, which he managed 1756–65. Leader of orch. at 3 Choirs Fest. 1770–6. Left Eng. 1784, returning 1790 to start comic opera co. in London. It failed and he took it to Moscow. Wrote operas, oratorio *Ruth*, 54 vn. sonatas, 12 vn. concs., 18 str. qts., etc.

Gibbons, Orlando (*b* Oxford, 1583; *d* Canterbury, 1625). Eng. composer, organist, and virginalist. Entered choir of King's Coll., Cambridge, 1596. Org., Chapel Royal from 1604. MusB

Cambridge Univ. 1606, DMus Oxford 1622. Chamber musician to King, 1619, org. Westminster Abbey from 1623. Composer of noble church mus., incl. many anthems (e.g. *This is the Record of John*), motets and madrigals (e.g. *The Silver Swan*), 40 kbd. pieces, incl. contribution to *Parthenia*, 30 fantasies for viols, several pavans and galliards, and 3 *In nomines*. One of the greatest of the early Eng. composers. His father, William, brothers Edward, Ellis, and Ferdinando, and son Christopher Gibbons were musicians.

Gibbs, (Cecil) **Armstrong** (*b* Great Baddow, 1889; *d* Chelmsford, 1960). Eng. composer. On staff RCM 1921–39. Comp. 5 operas, 3 syms., ob. conc., incidental mus., choral works, cantatas, church mus., but best known for waltz *Dusk* and for his many songs, several being settings of Walter De La Mare (such as the popular *Five Eyes*). Festival adjudicator 1923–52.

Gibet, Le (The Gallows). Second of 3 pf. pieces by Ravel under title *Gaspard de la Nuit*, 1908.

Gibson, (Sir) **Alexander** (Drummond) (*b* Motherwell, Scotland, 1926; *d* London, 1995). Scot. conductor. Répétiteur and ass. cond., SW Opera 1951–2, ass. cond. BBC Scottish SO 1952–4, staff cond. SW Opera 1954–7, mus. dir. 1957–9. Prin. cond. Scot. Nat. Orch. 1959–84. Founded Scottish Opera 1962, mus. dir. 1962–87. CG début 1957 (*Tosca*). Amer. début 1970. During his 25 years with Scottish Opera, cond. f. complete p. of Berlioz's *Les Troyens* (1969), first *Ring* cycle perf. outside London for over 38 years (1971, sung in Ger.); and f.ps. of Orr's *Full Circle* (Glasgow 1968) and Hamilton's *The Catiline Conspiracy* (Stirling 1974). CBE 1967. Knighted 1977.

Gielen, Michael (Andreas) (*b* Dresden, 1927). Austrian conductor, composer, and pianist. Family emigrated to Argentine 1939. Studied Buenos Aires, where he perf. all Schoenberg's pf. works, 1942–9. Mus. staff, Teatro Colón, Buenos Aires, 1947–50. Joined staff of Vienna State Opera 1950, becoming resident cond. 1954–60. Chief cond. Royal Swed. Opera, Stockholm, 1960–5. Cond. W. Ger. Radio Orch., Cologne, 1965–9. Mus. dir., Nat. Orch. of Belg. 1969–72; mus. dir. Netherlands Opera 1973–4. NY début 1971. Salzburg Fest. début 1972. Mus. dir., Frankfurt Opera, 1977–87. Chief guest cond., BBCSO 1979–82. Mus. dir., Cincinnati SO 1980–6. Cond. Baden-Baden Radio SO 1986–99. Prof. of cond., Salzburg Mozarteum 1987–95. Particularly noted for championship of contemp. music. Comps. incl. chamber cantatas, choral works, and chamber mus.

Gieseking, Walter (Wilhelm) (*b* Lyons, 1895; *d* London, 1956). Ger. pianist. Début 1912 followed by int. tours. London début 1923. NY 1926, Paris 1928. Salzburg Fest. 1939. Renowned for playing of Debussy and Ravel, but also for Beethoven and Brahms. Comp. pf. pieces and songs.

giga. See *gigue*.

Gigault, Nicolas (*b* ?Paris, *c*.1627; *d* Paris, 1707). Fr. organist and composer. Org. at four Paris churches (St Honoré 1646–52, St Nicolas-des-Champs 1652–1707, St Martin-des-Champs from 1673, Hôpital du St Esprit from 1685) and owned large collection of instr., both kbd. and stringed. Regarded as equal of Couperin as executant. His *Livre de musique* (1683) contains 20 noëls with variations, the earliest known example of this genre.

gigg, gigge. Old Eng. spellings of *jig* or *gigue*.

Gigli, Beniamino (*b* Recanati, 1890; *d* Rome, 1957). It. tenor. First prize int. contest, Parma, 1914. Début Rovigo 1914 (Enzo in *La Gioconda*), followed by appearances in Bologna, Naples, Berlin, Dresden, Turin, Rome, Madrid, and Monte Carlo. La Scala début 1918 with Toscanini (Faust in Boito's *Mefistofele*). NY Met 1920–32 and 1938–9; CG 1930–1, 1938–9, 1946; Salzburg Fest. 1936 (concert). Still sang superbly on tour of USA 1955. Excelled as Rodolfo (*La bohème*), Duke of Mantua (*Rigoletto*), and Cavaradossi (*Tosca*). Sang Ruggero in *La rondine* at its NY Met première, 1928.

Gigout, Eugène (*b* Nancy, 1844; *d* Paris, 1925). Fr. organist, composer, and teacher. Prof. of org. École Niedermeyer, Paris, 1863–85 and 1900–5. Org., St Augustin, Paris, 1863–1925, touring widely and becoming known for brilliant improvisations. Founded own (state-assisted) org. sch. 1885. Prof. of org., Paris Cons., from 1911. Worked as mus. critic and comp. many works for org.

gigue, giga (Fr., It.). Jig. (1) A lively rustic Eng., Scot., and Irish dance type (see jig), usually in compound duple or triple time, with the characteristic rhythm etc. Eng. virginalists were first to use the *gigue*, which was introduced to the Continent by *Froberger, 1657, though the term had appeared in 1648 in a lute piece by Ebner. Pieces in gigue style were absorbed into the suite as the customary closing movts.: in Bach's gigues the 2 halves of binary form often opened in something like fugal style, the subject of the first half being often inverted as that of the 2nd half. (Occasionally Bach applied the term 'gigue' loosely to a piece in simple duple or quadruple time.)

(2) Medieval name for str. instr.

Gigues (Debussy). See *Images*.

Gilbert, Anthony (*b* London, 1934). Eng. composer. Lect. in comp. Goldsmiths' Coll., London Univ., 1969–73. Ed. of contemp. mus. Schott's, London, from 1965. Head of comp. RNCM 1973–99. Head of comp. dept., NSW Cons., Sydney, 1978–9. Prin. works incl.:

OPERAS: *The Scene Machine* (1970); *The Chakravaka-Bird*, radio opera (1977).

ORCH.: *Sinfonia*, chamber orch. (1965); *Peal II*, big band (1968); symphony (1973, rev. 1985; *Regions*, rev. and incorporated as middle movt.); *Crow-Cry*, chamber orch. (1976); *Towards Asavari*, pf., orch.

(1978); *Koonapippi*, youth orch. (1981); *Dream Carousels*, wind band (1988); *Mozart Sampler With Ground* (1991); *Igorochki*, concertini recs., chamber orch. (1992); vn. conc. (*On Beholding a Rainbow*) (1998); *Another Dream Carousel*, str. (2000); *Sheer*, str. (2003).

INSTR. ENS.: *Serenade* 6 instr. (1963); *Brighton Piece*, perc., ens. (1967); *O'Grady Music*, cl., vc., toy instr. (1971); *Canticle I (Rock-song)*, fls., obs., cls., hns., hp., pf. (1973), 2nd vers. fls., cls., hp. (1979); *Calls Around Chungmori*, ens., workshop ens., audience (1980); *Little Dance of Barrenjoey*, chamber ens. (1981); *Upstream River Rewa*, narr., Indo-Eur. ens. (1991); *Ziggurat*, bcl., mar. (1994); *Stars*, rec., pf. (1995); *Midwales Lightwhistle Automatic*, rec., pf. (1996); *Réflexions, Rose Nord*, bcl., vib. (1996); *Sinfin 2*, 4 vib. (2000); str. qt. No.4 (2002); *Dark Singing, Dancing Light*, bn., str. quintet/ens. (2005).

BRASS: *Fanfarings Nos. 1 & 2* (1983), *Nos. 3 & 4* (1986–7), *No.5* (1988), *No.6* (1992).

CHORAL: *Missa brevis*, unacc. (1965); *Canticle II (Anger)*, male vv. (1974); *Chant of Cockeye Bob*, children's vv., instr. (1981); *Beastly Jingles*, sop., ens. (1981); *Handles to the Invisible (Day)*, ch. (1995, rev. 2003).

VOICE(s) & INSTR(s).: *Love Poems*, sop., cl., vc., accordeon (1970), vers. for sop., cl., bcl., chamber org. or harmonium (1972); *Long White Moonlight*, sop., elec. db. (1980); *Beastly Jingles*, sop., ens. (1984); *Certain Lights Reflecting*, sop., orch. (1988–9); *Vers de lune*, sop., fl., vc., perc. (1999); *Tinos*, sop., cl., vib. (2004); *Encantos*, sop./mez., cl., vib., gui. (2004).

Also many chamber works and kbd. pieces.

Gilbert, Henry F(ranklin Belknap) (*b* Somerville, Mass., 1868; *d* Cambridge, Mass., 1928). Amer. composer. Great interest in folk music and Negro melodies. Works incl. *Comedy-Overture on Negro Themes* (1905); *3 American Dances* (1911); *Negro Rhapsody* (1913); symphonic prol. *Riders to the Sea* (1915); ballet *Dance in Place Congo* (1918).

Gilbert, Kenneth (*b* Montreal, 1931). Canadian harpsichordist and organist. Church org. in Montreal 1952–67. London début 1968. Taught at Montreal Cons. 1957–74, McGill Univ. 1964–72, and Laval Univ., Quebec, 1969–76. Prof. of hpd. at Stuttgart Hochschule für Musik and Salzburg Mozarteum and at Paris Cons. from 1988. Ed. of F. Couperin's *Pièces de clavecin* (4 vols., 1969–72) and of complete sonatas of D. Scarlatti (11 vols., 1971–85).

Gilbert, (Sir) **W**(illiam) **S**(chwenck) (*b* London, 1836; *d* Harrow Weald, 1911). Eng. poet and playwright, librettist of 14 operettas (the 'Savoy Operas') with *Sullivan from 1871 to 1896. Knighted 1907. The libretti for Sullivan were: *Thespis* (1871); *Trial by Jury* (1875); *The Sorcerer* (1877, rev. 1884); *HMS Pinafore* (1878); *The Pirates of Penzance* (1879); *Patience* (1881); *Iolanthe* (1882); *Princess Ida* (1884); *The Mikado* (1885); *Ruddigore* (1887); *The Yeomen of the Guard* (1888); *The Gondoliers* (1889); *Utopia (Limited)* (1893); *The Grand Duke* (1896).

Gilels, Emil (*b* Odessa, 1916; *d* Moscow, 1985). Soviet pianist. At age of 5 entered Odessa Cons.,

début there 1929. Pupil of Heinrich Neuhaus at Moscow Cons. 1935–8. First prize Brussels pf. competition 1938. Début in Paris and London 1954, Philadelphia 1955. Salzburg Fest. début 1969. Brilliant interpreter of Prokofiev sonatas, and also of classics.

Gillis, Don (*b* Cameron, Missouri, 1912; *d* Columbia, S. Carolina, 1978). Amer. composer. Played tb. in jazz bands. Worked as composer, arranger, and trombonist, Fort Worth Radio, Texas, 1932–5. Programme dir. and producer NCB, NY, 1944–54, working with Toscanini. His comps. are in a popular and traditional style, influenced by jazz, hymns, dances, and Sibelius, Strauss, etc. Composer of 10 short operas; 12 syms. and sym. No.5½ ('for fun'); 2 pf. concs.; *The Crucifixion* (oratorio); str. qts.

Gilson, Paul (*b* Brussels, 1865; *d* Brussels, 1942). Belg. composer and critic. Mus. critic *Le Soir* 1906–14. Prof. of harmony, Brussels Cons. 1899–1909, Antwerp Cons. 1904–9. Founded *La Revue musicale belge* 1924. Strong influence on younger school of Belg. composers 1920–40. Inspector gen. of Belg. sch. mus. 1909–30. Comp. operas, cantatas, orch. works, and chamber mus.

gimel. See *gymel*.

Ginastera, Alberto (*b* Buenos Aires, 1916; *d* Geneva, 1983). Argentinian composer. Ballet suite *Panambí* performed in Buenos Aires 1937. Guggenheim fellowship 1942. Lived in NY 1945–7. Returned to Argentina 1948 to teach and compose (though falling foul of Peron régime). Founded various mus. schs., incl. Centre for Advanced Mus. Studies, Buenos Aires, of which he became dir. 1962–9. Settled in Geneva 1971. His mus. was in a nationalistic idiom up to about 1958 when he adopted more advanced procedures incl. serialism (first apparent in the 1952 pf. sonata), microtones, and aleatory rhythms. His operas have attracted wide attention. Works incl.:

OPERAS: *Don Rodrigo*, 3 acts (prod. Buenos Aires, 1964); *Bomarzo*, 2 acts (prod. Washington 1967, London 1976); *Beatrix Cenci*, 2 acts (prod. Washington 1971).

BALLETS: *Panambí* (1934–6); *Estancia* (1941).

ORCH.: suite, *Panambí* (1937); *Ollantay* (1947); *Variaciones concertantes* (1953); *Pampeana No.3* (1954); *Concerto per corde* (1965); *Estudios sinfónicos* (1967); *Glosses sobre temes de Pau Casals* (1976–8); *Iubilum* (1980).

CONCERTOS: pf. No.1 (1961), No.2 (1972); vn. (1963); hp. (1956); vc. No.1 (1968), No.2 (1980).

CHORUS & ORCH.: Ps. 150 (1938); *Turbae ad Passionem Gregorianam*, 3 singers, boy's ch., ch., and orch. (1974).

VOICE & ORCH.: *Cantáta para América mágica*, sop., perc. (1960); *Sinfonia, 'Don Rodrigo'*, sop., orch. (1964); cantata *Bomarzo*, narr., bar., orch. (1964, distinct from opera of same name); *Milena*, sop., orch. (1971); *Serenata*, vc., bar., chamber orch. (1973).

CHAMBER MUSIC: Duo, fl., ob. (1945); str. qts., No.1 (1948), No.2 (1958), No.3 (1973, with sop.); pf.

sonatas, No.1 (1952), No.2 (1981), No.3 (1982); pf. quintet (1963); *Puneia No.2 'Hommage à Paul Sacher'*, vc. (1976); gui. sonata (1976); vc. sonata (1979); *Variations and Toccata sopra 'Aurora Lucis Rutilat'*, org. (1980).

Gioconda, La (The Joyful Girl). Opera in 4 acts by *Ponchielli, to lib. by 'Tobia Gorrio' (Arrigo Boito), based on Hugo's play *Angelo, Tyran de Padoue* (1835). Prod. Milan 1876, CG and NY Met 1883. Contains in Act 3 Sc.2 the ballet 'Dance of the Hours'.

giocoso (It.). Jocose, merry, playful. So the adverb *giocosamente*.

gioia, gioja (It.). Joy. So *gioiante, gioioso*; *gioiosamente*, joyful.

Gioielli della Madonna, I (The Jewels of the Madonna). Opera in 3 acts by *Wolf-Ferrari, lib. Golisciani and Zangarini (text rev. 1933). Prod. Berlin 1911 in vers. by H. Liebstöckl, Chicago and CG 1912, Genoa 1913, Wexford 1981.

Giordano, Umberto (*b* Foggia, 1867; *d* Milan, 1948). It. composer. First success 1892 in Rome with opera *Mala vita*, an example of the *verismo* sch. which he continued to exploit. Later successes were *Andrea Chénier* (Milan 1896), *Fedora* (Milan 1898), and *Madame Sans-Gêne* (NY 1915, cond. Toscanini).

Giorno di regno, Un (King for a Day). Comic opera in 2 acts by Verdi to lib. by Romani orig. written (as *Il finto Stanislao*) for Gyrowetz in 1818. Comp. 1840. Prod. Milan 1840, NY 1960 (Amato Opera Co., concert perf.), London 1961, Wexford 1981.

Giovanna d'Arco (Joan of Arc). Opera in prologue and 3 acts by Verdi, lib. by Solera, based on Schiller's *Die Jungfrau von Orleans* (1801). Comp. 1844–5, rev. 1845. Prod. Milan 1845, NY (concert) and London 1966.

Gipps, Ruth (*b* Bexhill-on-Sea, 1921; *d* Eastbourne, 1999). Eng. composer, conductor, oboist, and pianist. Oboist in professional orchs. and concert pianist until 1952, ch.-master City of Birmingham Choir, 1948–50; cond. London Repertoire Orch. 1955–86; founder and cond. Chanticleer Orch. from 1961. Taught at TCL 1959–66. Prof. at RCM 1967–77. Comps. incl. 5 syms (1942–82); concs. for pf., vn., vn. and va., ob., cl., hn., and double bn; cantata *Goblin Market*; tonepoem for wind instrs.; *Magnificat*; and *The Cat for 2 soloists, ch., orch. MBE 1981.

Gipsy Baron, The (Strauss). See *Zigeunerbaron, Der*.

Gipsy Princess, The (Kálmán). See *Csárdásfürstin, Die*.

Gipsy Songs, Seven. For ten. and pf. by Dvořák, Op.55, to words by Heyduk, comp 1880. 1. *My Song Resounds*. 2. *My Triangle is Singing*. 3. *Silent the Woods*. 4. *Songs my Mother Taught me*. 5. *Sound the Fiddle*. 6. *Clean Cotton Clothes*. 7. *To the Heights of Tatra*.

Girl I left behind me, The. The words can be traced back to the end of the 18th cent.; so can the tune, sometimes known as *Brighton Camp*. It is played in the Brit. Army on occasions of departure.

Girl of the Golden West, The (Puccini). See *Fanciulla del West, La*.

Gis (Ger.). G♯. **Gisis**, G♯♯.

Giselle, ou Les Wilis (Giselle, or the Wilis). 'Fantastic ballet' in 2 acts, mus. *Adam, choreog. Coralli and Perrot, f.p. Paris 1841. Lib. based on legend recounted by Heine. Carlotta Grisi danced first Giselle. F.p. London, Vienna, St Petersburg 1842. Modern prods. are based on Petipa's last St Petersburg prod. of 1884. The Wilis are the ghosts of girls who die before their intended marriages.

gitano, gitana (Sp.). Gipsy.

Gitlis, Ivry (*b* Haifa, 1922). Israeli violinist. Gave first public concert at age of 8. Début with Brit. orchs. after Second World War. Won Thibaud Prize 1951. Début with Israel PO 1952. Settled in Paris. Noted for playing of contemp. mus.

gittern. Medieval forerunner of guitar, heyday being 14th cent.

giù (It.). Down, e.g. *arcata in giù*, 'down-bowed'.

Giuditta. Opera in 3 acts by *Lehár, lib. Knepler and Löhner. Prod. Vienna 1934, with *Tauber and Novotná. Lehár's only opera.

Giuliani, Mauro (*b* Bisceglie, 1781; *d* Naples, 1829). It. guitar virtuoso and cellist. Lived in Vienna 1806–19, during which time he knew Beethoven (and played in vc. section at f.p. of 7th Sym., 1813). Toured Russ. and Eng. before settling in Naples. Comp. over 200 works for gui.

Giulietta e Romeo. See *Romeo and Juliet*.

Giulini, Carlo Maria (*b* Barletta, 1914; *d* Brescia, 2005). It. conductor. Début Rome 1944.. Mus. dir. It. Radio 1946–51. Cond. first opera in broadcast perf. of *La traviata*. Stage opera début Bergamo 1950 (*La traviata*). La Scala 1951–6 (prin. cond. from 1953). Brit. début 1955 at Edinburgh Fest. when he cond. the Glyndebourne Co. in *Falstaff*. Later cond. many London concerts with Philharmonia Orch. (memorable perfs. of Verdi *Requiem*); guest cond. Hallé Orch. 1968. Amer. début 1955; CG 1958–67 and 1982; Salzburg Fest. début 1970. Joint cond. Chicago SO (with *Solti) 1969–72. Prin. cond. Vienna SO 1973–6. Chief cond. Los Angeles PO 1978–84.

Giulio Cesare in Egitto (Julius Caesar in Egypt). (1) Opera in 3 acts by Handel, lib. by N. F. Haym adapted from G. F. Bussani's *Giulio Cesare in Egitto* (1677). Prod. London 1724, Northampton, Mass., 1927, Glyndebourne 2005.
  (2) Opera in 3 acts by *Malipiero, to own lib.

based on Shakespeare's play. Prod. Genoa 1936. (3) Other operas on this subject by Cavalli, Sartorio, Freschi, Keiser, Graun, and others.

giustamente (It.). With exactitude i.e. unvarying speed and rhythm.

giustiniana. Type of love song popular in 15th and 16th cents. named after poet Leonardo Giustiniani (*c*.1385–1446). After about 1560 name was applied to type of *villanella* in which text is about three men who still desire sexual encounters but are too old to find them except with prostitutes. Coll. pubd. by Scotto 1570 incl. examples by A. Gabrieli and Merulo.

giusto (It.). Just, strict. *allegro giusto* means either a strict allegro or a moderate allegro (neither too fast nor too slow). *tempo giusto* means either 'strict' time or 'suitable' time.

Glagolitic Mass (*Glagolská mše*). Mass for sop., cont., ten., bass, ch., and orch. by Janáček, comp. 1926, f.p. Brno 1927, Norwich 1930. Text adapted from Ordinary of the Mass by Miloš Weingant. Movts. entitled: Kyrie (*Gospodi pomiluj*); Gloria (*Slava*); Credo (*Věruju*); Sanctus (*Svet*); Agnus Dei (*Agneče Božij*). Vernacular version of Ordinary was taken by Janáček from church magazine. He mistakenly called Old Slavonic language of time of St Cyril and St Methodius (9th cent.) 'glagolitic', which properly refers only to Old Slavonic script and alphabet. Mus. contains important org. part. Because of inadequacies among singers and instrumentalists at the f.p., Janáček made cuts and alterations which found their way into the pubd. score after his death. It is probable that he did not intend them to be other than emergency measures. The orig. vers. had its f.p. in Manchester 1993 (Manchester Univ.) and has been recorded.

Glanville-Hicks, Peggy (*b* Melbourne, Victoria, 1912; *d* Sydney, NSW, 1990). Australian-born composer (Amer. cit. 1948). Lived in NY 1942–59, organizing concerts of modern mus. and working as critic of *NY Herald Tribune* 1948–58. Went to live in Greece 1959. Her mus. combines serialism with the use of oriental and ancient modes.

Glasenapp, Carl (Friedrich) (*b* Riga, 1847; *d* Riga, 1915). Ger.-Russ. teacher and writer. Authority on Wagner. Wrote 2-vol. life and works of Wagner 1876–7, rewritten in 6 vols. (1894–1911, Eng. trans. by Ashton Ellis); also ed. Bayreuth letters and archives for publication.

glass armonica (Ger. Glasharmonika). Obsolete mus. instr., also known as 'musical glasses', comprising either (a) drinking glasses filled with water to different heights in order to leave a larger or smaller area of glass free to vibrate, and so to produce different notes; or (b) glass basins, graduated in size, fixed to a spindle revolved by pedal mechanism, the bottoms of the basins running in a trough of water, so as to be kept permanently damp. Sound is produced by rubbing the rims of the glasses with a wet finger. Gluck performed in London on the first type, Mozart on the second, for which he and Beethoven wrote mus. Donizetti wrote a part for glass (h)armonica in Lucia's Mad Scene in *Lucia di Lammermoor*, the alternative being fl.; and R. Strauss used it in his opera *Die Frau ohne Schatten*. George *Crumb revived the instr. in last movt. of his *Black Angels* for elec. str. qt. Bruno Hoffmann is the 20th cent. virtuoso of the instr. Benjamin Franklin invented an improved vers. *c*.1761.

glass dulcimer. Strips of glass struck with hammers. Occasionally provided with mechanism and kbd.

Glass, Louis (Christian August) (*b* Copenhagen, 1864; *d* Copenhagen, 1936). Danish composer. Worked as pianist and cellist. Works incl. syms.: No.1 (1893), No.2 (1898–9), No.3 (*Wood Symphony*) (1901), No.4 (1900–1), No.5 (*Sinfonia svastica*) (1919), No.6 (*Bird of the Scyldings*) (1926); ovs. *Der Volksfeind* and *Dänemark*; dance-poem *Artemis* (1917); 4 str. qts.; pf. trio; 2 vn. sonatas; pf. pieces.

Glass, Philip (*b* Baltimore, 1937). Amer. composer. Studied fl. at Peabody Cons. at age of 8. Working on a film in Paris with Ravi Shankar awakened interest in non-Western mus. Under this influence, devised a style whereby within a strong diatonic framework, his work was based on 5 or 6 notes with no harmonic change but powerful rhythmical steadiness. This produced a mus. similar to that of Steve Reich and Terry Riley although he did not then know their work. The result has been called *'minimalist' music, because there was maximum repetition of a minimum amount of material. In 1968 founded Philip Glass Ensemble, comprising keyboards (incl. elec. org.) and wind instr. Prin. comps.:

OPERAS: **Einstein on the Beach*, in collab. with Robert Wilson (1974–5); *Madrigal Opera* (Amsterdam, 1980); *Satyagraha* (Rotterdam, 1980); *The Photographer* (Amsterdam, 1982); *The CIVIL WarS* (1982–4); **Akhnaten* (1980–3); *The Juniper Tree*, in collab. with Robert Moran (Cambridge, Mass., 1985); *A Descent into the Maelstrom* (1986); *The Fall of the House of Usher* (Cambridge, Mass., 1988; Llantwit Major, Wales, 1989); *The Making of the Representative for Planet 8* (Houston, 1988; London (ENO) 1988); *1000 Airplanes on the Roof* (Vienna Airport, 1988); *Hydrogen Jukebox* (Philadelphia (concert); Charleston, S. Car., 1990); *The Voyage* (NY Met, 12 Oct. 1992) [Columbus Day]); *The White Raven* (1993); *Orphée* (1993); *Monsters of Grace* (1997); *Galileo Galilei* (2001); *The Sound of a Voice* (2003); *Waiting for the Barbarians* (2005).

ORCH.: *Music in Similar Motion* (1969); *Façades*, chamber orch. (1981); *Glassworks*, chamber orch. (1981); *Company*, str. (1983); *Dance from Akhnaten* (1984); *Music from the Civil Wars* (Cologne section), opt. ch. (1984); *The Light* (1987); vn. conc. (1987); *The Canyon* (1988); Sym. No.1 (*Low*) (1992), Sym. No.2 (1994), Sym. No.3, str. (1995), Sym. No.4 (*Heroes*) (1996), Sym. No.5 (*Choral*) (1999), Sym. No.6 (*Plutonian Ode*) (2002), Sym. No.7 (*A Toltec*

Symphony) (2005), Sym. No.8 (2005); *The Transformer*, orch., synth. (1995); conc., sax. qt., orch. (1995); *Days and Nights in Rocinha* (1997); *Tirol Conc.*, pf., orch. (2000); *Dancissimo* (2001); vc. conc. (2001); pf. conc. No.2 (2004).

CHORUS & ORCH.: *Music from the Civil Wars* (Rome section), sop., alto, ten., bar., bass, ch. (1984); *Itaipu* (1989); *Psalm 126*, ch., spkr., orch. (1998); *Passion of Ramakrishna* (2006).

CHORUS: *Wind Song*, unacc. (1968); *Another Look at Harmony* (Part 4), ch., org. (1974); *Fourth Series*, Part I, ch., org. (1978); *Vessels* (from *Koyaanisqatsi*), 2 sop., mez., ten., bar., bass, kbd. (1981); *3 Songs*, unacc. (1986).

CHAMBER MUSIC: Str. Qts. No.1 (1966), No.2 (*Company*) (1983), No.3 (*Mishima*) (1985), No.4 (*Boczak*) (1989), No.5 (1993); *Arabesque in memoriam*, fl.; *Strung Out*, amp. vn. (1969); *Modern Love Waltz*, fl., cl., 2 kbd., opt. hp., vib. (1979); *Floe*, fl., sop. sax., ten. sax., 2 hn., pf. (1983); *Prelude to Endgame*, db., 4 timp. (1986); *In the Summer House*, vn., vc., v., synth. (1993); *Songs of Milarepa*, bar., str. orch. (1997); *Dracula*, str. qt., pf., perc. (1998); *The Hours*, pf., hp., cel., str., perc. (2002).

VOICE (& INSTR.): *A Madrigal Opera*, 2 sop., ten., bar., bass, vn. doubling va. (1979); *Habeve Song*, sop., cl., bn. (1983); *Hymn to the Sun* (from *Akhnaten*), counterten. (1984); *Changing Opinion* (with Paul Simon), v., fl., pf. (1986); *Forgetting* (with L. Anderson), v., str. qt. (1986); *Freezing* (with Suzanne Vega), v., str. qt. (1986); *Lightning* (with David Byrne), v., fl., sop. sax., ten. sax. (1986); *Fifty-Fifty Chance*, v., vns., va., vc., gui. (1990); *Planctus*, v., pf. (1997).

KEYBOARD: *Modern Love Play*, pf. (1977); *Fourth Knee Play*, pf. (1977); *Dance No.2*. org. (*Fourth Series*, Pt.2) (1979), No.4 (Pt.4) (1979); *Mad Rush*, pf. (*Fourth Series*, Pt.3) (1979); *Metamorphoses*, pf. (1989); *Tesra*, pf. (1993); *Now, So Long After that Time*, pf. (1994); *Trilogy Sonata*, pf. (2000); *A Musical Portrait of Chuck Close*, pf. (2005).

FILM MUSIC: *Koyaanisqatsi* (1983); *Mishima* (1985); *Hamburger Hill* (1987); *Powaqqatsi* (1987); *The Thin Blue Line* (1988); *The Secret Agent* (1996); *Truman Sleeps* (1998); *The Music of Undertow* (2004); *Taking Lives* (2004).

Glazunov, Alexander (Konstantinovich) (*b* St Petersburg, 1865; *d* Neuilly-sur-Seine, 1936). Russ. composer. Pupil of Rimsky-Korsakov 1880–1. Balakirev cond. his first sym. in 1882, the work being hailed as a precocious masterpiece. Glazunov later met Liszt at Weimar and was influenced by his and Wagner's mus. Cond. in Paris 1889 and London 1896–7. Became dir. of St Petersburg Cons. 1905 after which his comps. became fewer. Left Russia 1928, visited USA 1929, then lived in Paris. Cosmopolitan rather than nationalist in mus. style. Works incl.:

BALLETS: *Raymonda* (1896–7); *The *Seasons* (1899).

ORCH.: syms. No.1 (1881, rev. 1885, 1929), No.2 (1886), No.3 (1890), No.4 (1893), No.5 (1895), No.6 (1896), No.7 (1902), No.8 (1906), No.9 (unfinished 1909, perf. Moscow 1948); *Suite caractéristique*

(1887); *Stenka Razin* (1885); *The Sea* (1889); *Carneval* ov. (1892); *Chopiniana* (1893); *Scènes de ballet* (1895); vn. conc. (1904); pf. conc. No.1 (1910), No.2 (1917); sax. conc. (1931).

CHAMBER MUSIC: 7 str. qts. (1882–1930); str. quintet (1895); sax. qt. (1932).

PIANO: sonatas Nos. 1 and 2 (1901); *Nocturne* (1889); *Grand Concert Waltz* (1893); *Suite* for 2 pf. (1920). Also songs.

glee. A choral comp. in a number of short self-contained sections, each expressing the mood of some particular passage of the poem set, the mus. predominantly harmonic (i.e. in blocks of chords), rather than contrapuntal. Properly it is for solo male vv. (unacc.). It flourished *c*.1750–*c*.1830, during which time a remarkable series of able composers, such as Samuel Webbe, made lavish contributions to the repertory, but subsequently gave way gradually to the *part-song. It is a purely Eng. form, and was much fostered by the popularity of glee clubs. (In USA this name has been applied to univ. mus. clubs with more general aims.)

Glennie, Evelyn (*b* Aberdeen, 1965). Scottish percussionist. During childhood became profoundly deaf. Played in Nat. Youth Orch. of Scot. London début 1986. Has played with all leading orchs. and given solo recitals. Many composers have written works for her. Gave f.p. of John McLeod's *The Song of Dionysus*, Proms 1989, and James MacMillan's *Veni, Veni, Emmanuel*, Proms 1992. Recipient of many awards. OBE 1992.

gli, glie (It.). 'The' (a form of plural).

Glière [Glier], **Reinhold** (Moritsovich) (*b* Kiev, 1875; *d* Moscow, 1956). Russ. composer and conductor. Dir. and prof. of comp., Kiev Cons. 1913–20, then taught at Moscow Cons. His ballet *The Red Poppy* was one of first 'social realism' works of Soviet régime. The conservative-nationalist nature of his idiom was much to liking of official party arbiters of taste. Works included 3 syms.; 4 str. qts.; *March of the Red Army*, wind instrs. (1924); operas *Shakh Senem* (1923–5) and *Rachel* (1943); ballets *The Red Poppy* (1926–7, rev. 1949) and *The Bronze Horseman* (1948–9); hp. conc. (1938); vc. conc. (1945–6); 123 songs; 175 pf. pieces; and much chamber mus.

Glimmerglass Opera. Opera fest. founded in 1975 near Cooperstown, NY. Name derives from that given by James Fenimore Cooper in his *Leather-Stocking Tales* to Lake Otsega, on the shores of which the fest. takes place. 8-week summer season of 45 perfs. of 4 operas, all in new prods., perf. in 900-seat Alice Busch Opera Th. (opened 1987). All operas sung in Eng. until 1992, now some original-language perfs. with surtitles. Many new or rare works given in co-operation with NY City Opera, such as William Schuman's *A Question of Taste* (1989) and the f. Amer. p. of Mozart's *Il re pastore* (1991). Visitors picnic in the grounds near the lake. Several Britten operas have been staged. Art. dir. Paul Kellogg 1979–2006 (and of NY City Opera 1996–2007); mus. dir. and prin. cond. Stewart Robertson 1988–2006. Gen. and art. dir. Michael McLeod from 2006.

Glinka, Mikhail (Ivanovich) (*b* Novospasskoye, Smolensk, 1804; *d* Berlin, 1857). Russ. composer, regarded as founder of nat. sch. and the first Russ. composer to be accepted outside Russia. Son of wealthy landowner. Interest in mus. aroused *c*.1815 when he heard a Crusell cl. qt. During general education in St Petersburg from 1817 had 3 pf. lessons from John *Field. Also studied vn. and harmony. Worked in Ministry of Communications 1824–8 but gave recitals as amateur singer. In 1828 began serious study of comp. with Zamboni. Went to Milan 1830 where homesickness led him to contemplate writing a truly nat. opera, then to Vienna and Berlin 1833, studying comp. with Siegfried Dehn. Returned to St Petersburg to compose opera *A Life for the Tsar*, successfully prod. 1836. Appointed Kapellmeister, Imperial Chapel 1837. His second opera *Ruslan and Lyudmila* was prod. 1842. In 1844 visited Paris, meeting Berlioz, travelling on to Sp. where the folk-dance rhythms fascinated him. Returned to Russ. 1847, but made several more foreign journeys. Works incl.:

OPERAS: *A *Life for the Tsar (Ivan Susanin)* (1834–6); *Ruslan and Lyudmila* (1837–42).

ORCH.: sym. in B♭ (*c*.1824); *Valse fantaisie* (1839–56); *Capriccio brillante* (1845); *Kamarinskaya* (1848); *Night in Madrid* (1848).

CHAMBER MUSIC: str. qt. No.1 (1824), No.2 (1830); sextet for pf. and strs. (1832); *Trio pathétique*, pf., cl., bn. (1832). Also pf. and vocal works.

glissando (bastard It. from Fr. *glisser*, to slide). (1) (pf., harp, xylophone, vibraphone, etc.) The drawing of a finger down or up a series of adjacent notes.

(2) (bowed instrs.) Passing all or part of the way from one note to another on the same str., in much the same way as above and with much the same effect—with the difference that the pitches passed through, instead of representing the fixed tones and semitones of a scale, are infinite in number. Tb. can also perform a satisfactory glissando.

Globokar, Vinko (*b* Anderny, Fr., 1934). Fr.-born Yugoslav trombonist and composer. Visited USA 1965–6. Prof. of tb. at Cologne Musikhochschule from 1968. Active at IRCAM, Paris, from 1975. By remarkable virtuosity extended range of tb. into *avant-garde* mus., making the instr., as has been said, not only talk but sing, scream, weep, and laugh. Works written for him by Kagel, Berio, and Stockhausen.

Glock, (Sir) **William** (Frederick) (*b* London, 1908; *d* 2000). Eng. critic, administrator, and pianist. Mus. critic *Daily Telegraph* 1934, *Observer* 1934–45, *New Statesman* 1958–9. Dir., summer sch. of mus., Bryanston, 1948–52, Dartington Hall 1953–79. Founder and ed. *The Score* 1949–61. Controller of mus. BBC 1959–72, achieving catholic expansion of repertory, bringing Boulez to conduct BBCSO, and extending scope and range of Henry Wood Promenade Concerts. Chairman, British section ISCM 1954–8. Art. dir., Bath Fest. 1976–84. Autobiography 1992. CBE 1964. Knighted 1970.

Glocke(n) (Ger.). Bell(s). In orch. scores means tubular bells.

Glockenspiel (Ger.). Play of bells. Perc. instr. of tuned metal bars, with compass of 2 to 3 chromatic octaves, emitting brittle bell-like sound when played with kbd. or (more commonly) by small hand-held hammers. Orch. glockenspiel is played in horizontal position; in military bands it is carried vertically, bars being mounted in lyre-shaped frame (hence alternative name bell-lyra). First used 1739 by Handel in *Saul* (where he called it a carillon) and later by Mozart in *Die Zauberflöte* (1791). K. Salomon wrote glockenspiel conc., 1948.

Gloria in Excelsis Deo (Lat.). 'Glory to God in the highest'. The 'doxologia magna' (see *doxologia*), an amplification of the song of the angels announcing the birth of Christ. It occurs in the Roman Mass and in the Communion Service of the Anglican Church.

Gloriana. Opera in 3 acts, Op.53, by Britten, comp. 1952–3, lib. W. Plomer after L. Strachey's *Elizabeth and Essex*. Commissioned by CG for coronation of Elizabeth II, who attended f.p. at CG on 8 June 1953, 6 days after her coronation. Cincinnati (concert) 1956, f. Amer. stage p. San Antonio 1984 (ENO tour).

Glossop, Peter (*b* Sheffield, 1928). Eng. baritone. Opera début in Sheffield 1949 (Coppélius/Dr Miracle in *Les contes d'Hoffmann*). Joined SW ch. 1952. Member SW Opera, 1952–62, CG 1962–5, thereafter guest singer at leading opera houses. Won int. comp. for young singers, Sofia, 1961; Verdi gold medal, Parma, 1964. Débuts: La Scala 1965; NY 1967; Met 1971; Vienna 1968; Salzburg Fest. 1970.

glottal stop. See *coup de glotte*.

Glover, Jane (Alison) (*b* Helmsley, Yorks., 1949). Eng. conductor and musicologist. Début Oxford Univ. Opera Gp. 1971 (*Le nozze di Figaro*). Prof. cond. début Wexford 1975. Has ed. and cond. operas by Cavalli and Monteverdi. Art. dir., London Mozart Players from 1984. Chorus dir., Glyndebourne, 1980–4, prin. cond. Huddersfield Choral Soc. 1988–97. Cond. GTO 1981 (art. dir. 1982–5); Glyndebourne 1982; CG début 1988; ENO 1989. Art. dir. Buxton Fest. 1993, but resigned before taking office. Lect. in mus. St Hugh's Coll., Oxford, 1976–84, St Anne's Coll. 1976–80, Pembroke Coll. 1979–84. Wrote *Mozart's Women* (2005). CBE 2003.

Gluck, Alma [Fiersohn, Reba] (*b* Bucharest, 1884; *d* NY, 1938). Amer. soprano of Romanian birth. Opera début with Met company in 1909 (Sophie in *Werther*). Member of Met company 1909–12. From 1913 appeared mainly as concert singer.

Noted for purity of vocal tone. Her second husband was the violinist Efrem Zimbalist (married 1914). Daughter by first husband was Marcia Davenport (Abigail Gluck), the novelist and writer on music.

Gluck, Christoph Willibald von (*b* Erasbach, 1714; *d* Vienna, 1787). Ger. composer. Went to Prague Univ. in 1732 to study mus. and philosophy, also learning vc. In 1735 travelled to Vienna under protection of Prince Lobkowitz. Joined private orch. of Prince Melzi, who engaged him for his orch. in Milan 1737. There he probably studied with *Sammartini. Wrote his first opera *Artaserse*, 1741, 7 more following up to 1744. Travelled with Prince Lobkowitz to London 1745, composing 2 operas prod. 1746, meeting Handel, and giving 2 concerts as performer on *glass armonica. After 1746 travelled in Austria and Denmark and again visited Prague and Naples. In 1754 Empress Maria Theresa appointed him opera Kapellmeister to court th. in Vienna, a post which required him to compose in the more lively and flexible style of the fashionable Fr. *opéras-comiques*. During 1755–61 he was closely assoc. with Durazzo (court th. Intendant), Quaglio (scene-painter), Angiolini (dancer), and the poet Calzabigi, with whom he evolved his operatic 'reforms' in which the singers' claims were subjugated to those of the drama, with *recitativo accompagnato* ousting the more formal *secco* recit. His ballet *Don Juan* (1761) and opera *Orfeo* (1762) embodied these principles which reached full expression in *Alceste* (1767), an anticipation of Wagner's music-drama. Gluck set forth his operatic creed in the preface to *Alceste*.

He resigned his Vienna court post in 1770 and in 1773 went to Paris, having been contracted to compose *Iphigénie en Aulide* for the Opéra. Its prod. in 1774 was followed by a slightly rev. Fr. version of *Orfeo* and 2 years later of *Alceste*. Jealousy of Gluck's success in Paris led to an engineered quarrel with the It. composer *Piccinni, who was asked to set the same lib. on which Gluck was known to be working. Gluck destroyed his sketches but composed *Armide* (1777), followed by *Iphigénie en Tauride* (1778). In 1779 he returned to Vienna and retired, living in a grand manner and dying after defying his doctor by drinking a post-prandial liqueur. The simplicity and sublimity of Gluck's melodies, supported by a vivid dramatic sense, have ensured the survival of a large proportion of his mus. Works incl.:

OPERAS: *Artaserse* (Milan 1741); *La caduta dei giganti* and *Artemene* (London 1746); *La Semiramide riconosciuta* (Vienna 1748); *La contesa dei Numi* (Copenhagen 1749); *La clemenza di Tito* (Naples 1752); *Le *Cinesi* (1754); *La danza* (Vienna 1755); *Il rè pastore* (Vienna 1756); *Orfeo ed Euridice* (Vienna 1762); *Telemaco* (Vienna 1765); *Paride ed Elena* (Vienna 1770); *Iphigénie en Aulide* (Paris 1774); *Orphée* (Paris 1774); *Alceste* (Vienna 1767, Paris 1776); *Armide* (Paris 1777); *Iphigénie en Tauride* (Paris 1778); *Echo et Narcisse* (Paris 1779).

OPÉRAS-COMIQUES: *L'Île de Merlin* and *La Fausse Esclave* (Vienna 1758); *La Cythère assiégée* (Schwetzingen 1759); *L'Arbre enchanté* (Vienna 1759); *La Rencontre imprévue* (often known as *The Pilgrimage to Mecca*) (Vienna 1764).

BALLETS: *Don Juan* (Vienna 1761); *Semiramide* (Vienna 1765).

MISC.: *De Profundis*, ch.; 6 sonatas a tre (London 1746); 9 syms. (Vienna 1753).

Glückliche Hand, Die (lit. The Blessed Hand; The Knack). Drama with mus. in 1 act by Schoenberg, Op.18, lib. composer. Comp. 1910–13. Prod. Vienna 1924, Philadelphia and NY Met 1930, London 1962 (concert perf.). Contains mimed parts for man and woman. Use of coloured lights also has fundamental importance.

Glyndebourne. House and estate near Lewes, Sussex, in grounds of which the owner, John *Christie, built opera house with (as it was thought) eccentric idea of staging ideal perfs. of opera in beautiful setting. Inspiration for enterprise was Christie's wife, the soprano Audrey *Mildmay. First Glyndebourne Fest. began on 28 May 1934 with Mozart's *Le nozze di Figaro*, followed the next evening by *Così fan tutte*. Fritz Busch was the cond. with Carl *Ebert as producer and, later, Rudolf *Bing as administrator, a team which set new standards for Brit. opera. In 1939 the th. was enlarged to seat 539 instead of 300; in 1951 there was room for 592 and by 1977 for 830. The original th. was demolished at the end of the 1992 season and a new one built, with a capacity of around 1,200. This opened on 28 May 1994, the 60th anniversary of the first Glyndebourne perf., with *Le nozze di Figaro*, cond. by Haitink. While mus. considerations have always been paramount, Glyndebourne has also always had a special significance because of the beauty of the gardens. The tradition of a long dinner interval, during which visitors can picnic in the grounds (marquee when wet) or dine in the restaurant, is a big social attraction, so that what began as a risky venture lasting a few days is now a fully booked-up annual season extending from late May to late August.

After the war Glyndebourne re-opened in 1946 with Britten's *Rape of Lucretia*. There were no perfs. in 1948 and 1949 but Glyndebourne presented operas at the *Edinburgh Fest. from 1947 to 1951. On Busch's death in 1951, Vittorio *Gui became chief cond. He was succeeded in 1960 by John *Pritchard who first joined the mus. staff in 1947 and retired in 1977. Bernard *Haitink was mus. dir. 1977–87, Andrew *Davis 1989–2000, Vladimir Jurowski from 2001. When Ebert retired in 1959, Gunther Rennert became chief producer. He was succeeded by John *Cox 1971–83, Sir Peter *Hall 1984–90, and Graham *Vick 1994–2002. Although Glyndebourne's basic diet is the operas of Mozart, it has also staged *Don Pasquale* and several Rossini operas (under Gui) including successful revivals of *Le Comte Ory*, *La Cenerentola*, and *L'italiana in Algeri*. The f. Eng. p. of Verdi's 1865 rev. of *Macbeth* was at Glyndebourne

1938. A speciality has been made of Richard Strauss's operas, with *Der Rosenkavalier* (in a reduced orchestration exclusively made by Strauss for Glyndebourne), *Ariadne auf Naxos, Capriccio, Intermezzo, Die schweigsame Frau*, and *Arabella*. The prod. of *Idomeneo* restored Mozart's *opera seria* to general circulation. Among adventurous prods. have been Stravinsky's *The Rake's Progress*; Busoni's *Arlecchino*; Gluck's *Alceste* and *Orfeo*; Einem's *The Visit of the Old Lady*; Henze's *Elegy for Young Lovers*; Donizetti's *Anna Bolena*; Cavalli's *Ormindo* and *Calisto*; Monteverdi's *L'incoronazione di Poppea* and *Il ritorno d'Ulisse in patria*; Maw's *Rising of the Moon*, Britten's *A Midsummer Night's Dream, Albert Herring, Death in Venice* and *Peter Grimes*; Prokofiev's *Love for 3 Oranges*; Janáček's *The Cunning Little Vixen, Jenůfa* and *Káťa Kabanová*; Knussen's *Where the Wild Things Are*; Gershwin's *Porgy and Bess*; Osborne's *Electrification of the Soviet Union*; and Tippett's *New Year* (which was a joint commission with Houston Grand Opera and the BBC). Many of the world's great operatic artists have sung at Glyndebourne, which has a penchant for discovering a rising star some years before everyone else. Scrupulous attention is paid to sets and lighting, with the engagement of such artists as Oliver Messel, Osbert Lancaster, Erté, John Piper, John Gunter, John Bury, and David Hockney. In recent years it has become the custom to perf. one of the season's operas in a semi-staged version at the Prom. concerts in the RAH, London. Many of the Glyndebourne prods. have been filmed for TV and some are available on video. For the prods. of *Le nozze di Figaro* in 1989 and *Così fan tutte* in 1991, period instrs. of the Orch. of the Age of Enlightenment were used. In 1968 the Glyndebourne Touring Co. (GTO) was formed to make an autumn tour (usually to Oxford, Bristol, Norwich, Southampton, and Stoke-on-Trent) with some of the Sussex prods. sung by casts specially recruited to give opportunities to the best of young Brit. singers, but with a stiffening of est. artists. It gave its first London season at SW in 1992. Just as the RPO or LPO (since 1964) is engaged for Glyndebourne itself, the GTO has used the Northern Sinfonia, Bournemouth Sinfonietta, and London Sinfonietta, but in 1989 it formed its own orch. Art. dirs. of GTO have been Myer Fredman (1968–74), Kenneth Montgomery (1975–6), Nicholas Braithwaite (1977–80), Jane Glover (1982–5), Graeme Jenkins (1986–91), Ivor Bolton (1992–7), Louis Langrée (1998–2002), and Edward Gardner (2004–6).

GMusRNCM. Graduate, with honours, of the *Royal Northern College of Music, Manchester.

GO. In Fr. org. mus., *grand orgue*, i.e. 'great org.'.

Gobbi, Tito (*b* Bassano del Grappa, nr. Venice, 1913; *d* Rome, 1984). It. baritone and opera producer. Début Gubbio 1935 as Rodolfo in *La Sonnambula*. Sang Germont *père* in *La traviata* in Rome 1937 and title-role in *Wozzeck* at f. It. p. 1942. La Scala 1942; S. Francisco 1948; Salzburg 1950; CG 1951; NY Met 1956. Sang regularly at CG. Sang with Chicago Lyric Opera 1954–73. Outstanding

actor as well as singer: notable for interpretations of Scarpia, Rigoletto, Macbeth, Iago, Falstaff, and Boccanegra. Début as producer, Chicago and CG 1965. Repertory of 100 operas.

Godard, Benjamin (Louis Paul) (*b* Paris, 1849; *d* Cannes, 1895). Fr. composer and violinist. Cond. Concerts Modernes, Paris 1885–6. Prof. of instr. ens., Paris Cons., from 1887. Wrote 2 vn. concs., pf. conc., syms., and 8 operas (from which only the *Berceuse* for ten. from *Jocelyn* (1888) seems to have survived). Some of the instr. works are still played.

God bless the Prince of Wales. Song with words written in Welsh by Ceiriog Hughes and mus. by Henry Brinley Richards (1817–85). They were pubd. together in 1862. F.p. London 14 Feb. 1863 by Sims Reeves, preparatory to wedding of Prince of Wales on 10 March.

Goddard, Arabella (*b* St Servan, 1836; *d* Boulogne, 1922). Fr.-born pianist of Eng. origin. Pupil of Thalberg, Kalkbrenner, and J. W. Davison (mus. critic of *The Times*) whom she married 1859. London début 1850. Among first to play Beethoven's last sonatas in London. Retired 1880.

Godfrey, (Sir) **Daniel** [Dan] (Eyers) (*b* London, 1868; *d* Bournemouth, 1939). Eng. conductor (son, grandson, and nephew of military bandmasters). Cond. military bands 1890, opera in S. Africa 1891–2. Engaged at Bournemouth in 1893 to form municipal orch. to give sym. concerts in the Winter Gardens. These he cond. until 1934, introducing many new works to Brit. audiences and making the concerts a particular forum for the f.ps. of works by Brit. composers. Knighted 1922. See *Bournemouth Symphony Orch.*

Godowsky, Leopold (*b* Soshly, nr. Vilna, 1870; *d* NY, 1938). Polish-born pianist and composer (Amer. cit. 1891). Toured USA 1884–6 (début Boston 1884) and again in 1890, after which he became a pf. teacher in Philadelphia and, in 1894, dir. of pf. sch. at Chicago Cons. 1895–1900. Returned to Berlin 1900–9, teaching and touring as recitalist. Dir., Master sch. of pf.-playing, Vienna Acad., 1909–14. Returned to USA 1912, settling there 1914. Career ended by illness 1930. Comps. incl. *53 Studies on Chopin Études, Triakontameron* (30 pf. pieces each comp. on a different day), the *Java Suite* (12 pieces), 4 symphonic metamorphoses for pf., and numerous pf. transcrs.

God Save the Queen (King). The tune of the Brit. 'National Anthem' must long have been the best-known tune in the world, having at one time or another been borrowed by about 20 countries as that of their official nat. song. The popularity of the words and tune in Brit. seems to date from the time of the landing of the Young Pretender, 1745, when they were introduced in London th. and widely taken up, being sung on several successive nights at Drury Lane and Covent Garden theatres in Sept. of that year. The authorship of both words and tune is obscure, but it existed in some form before 18th cent.

The tune is in rhythm and style a galliard. There is a Geneva tune of this type with some phrases resembling those in God Save the Queen; it was introduced in 1603 at a banquet celebrating the first anniversary of the unsuccessful attempt of the Duke of Savoy to seize the city (the 'Escalade'). An Eng. Christmas carol printed in 1611, *Remember, O thou Man*, shows similar resemblances. Much stronger resemblances are seen in a kbd. piece by John *Bull (though in the minor), and his name is sometimes attached to the tune. The earliest known source is in a vol. of songs, *Harmonia anglica*, issued by John Simpson in London in 1744.

In the Amer. colonies and the USA the tune has at different times been sung to many different sets of words, e.g. *God Save America*, *God Save George Washington*, *God Save the Thirteen States*, etc. The present words *My country, 'tis of Thee*, date from 1831 and are the work of the Rev. Samuel Francis Smith. The name usually given to the tune is *America*.

Many composers, incl. Beethoven, Weber, Marschner, Paganini, Brahms, Donizetti, and Verdi have introduced the tune into their comps. or based works on it.

Gods go a-begging, The. Ballet in 1 act to mus. by Handel arr. *Beecham, choreog. Balanchine, prod. Diaghilev's Ballet Russe, London, 1928. Later choreog. by N. de Valois 1936, Lichine 1937. Also orch. suite.

Godunov, Boris (Mussorgsky). See *Boris Godunov*.

Goehr, (Peter) **Alexander** (*b* Berlin, 1932). Eng. composer of Ger. birth, son of Walter *Goehr. Contemp. at RMCM of Maxwell Davies, Birtwistle, and Ogdon. On mus. staff BBC 1960–8; comp.-in-res. New England Cons. 1968–9; assoc. prof. of mus. Yale Univ. 1969–70; prof. of mus. Leeds Univ., 1971–6; prof. of mus. Cambridge Univ. 1976–99. Dir., Leeds Fest., 1975. Goehr's mus. employs serialism but rejects elec. devices. He is among leaders of group of Eng. composers influenced by 2nd Viennese Sch. and his mus. can be described as essentially radical-conservative in idiom. Works incl.:

OPERAS: *Arden muss sterben (Arden must die) (1966); Behold the Sun, or Die Wiedertäufer (The Anabaptists) (1981–4); Arianna (1993–5).

BALLET: *La belle dame sans merci* (1958).

MUSIC THEATRE: *Triptych*, 3-part th. piece for actor, 2 mimes, 5 singers, instr. group, 1. *Naboth's Vineyard* (1968), 2. *Shadowplay* (1970), 3. *Sonata about Jerusalem* (1970); *Kantan and Damask Drum* (1997–8).

ORCH.: *Fantasia* (1954, rev. 1959); *Hecuba's Lament* (1959–61); vn. conc. (1961–2); *Little Symphony* (1963); *Little Music for Strings* (1963); *Pastorals* (1965); *3 Pieces from Arden Must Die* (1967); *Romanza*, vc., orch. (1968); *Konzertstück*, pf., orch. (1969); *Symphony in 1 Movement* (1969, rev. 1981); Conc. for 11 instrs. (1970); pf. conc. (1972); *Chaconne*, 19 wind instrs. (1974); *Metamorphosis/Dance* (1973–4); *Fugue on Psalm IV*, str. (1976); *Romanza on Psalm IV*, str. (1977); *Sinfonia* (1979);

Deux Études (1980–1); *Symphony with Chaconne* (1985–6); *Still Lands*, 3 pieces, small orch. (1988–90); *Variations on Bach's Sarabande from English Suite in E minor*, wind instr., timp. (1990); *Colossos or Panic*, symphonic fragment after Goya (1991–2); *Cambridge Hocket*, 4 hns., orch. (1993); *Uninterrupted Movement*, solo vc., 4 vcs., vc. ens. (1996); *Schlussgesang*, va., orch. (1997); *. . . kein Gedanke, nur ruhige Schlaf*, in memoriam Olivier Messiaen, chamber orch. (1998); *. . . second musical offering (GFH 2001)* (2001); *Marching to Carcassonne*, sop., 12 instr. (2002).

CHORAL & VOCAL: *The Deluge*, cantata after da Vinci, sop., alto, fl., hn., tpt., hp., and strs. (1957–8); *Sutter's Gold*, cantata, bass, ch., orch. (1959–60); *2 Choruses* (Milton and Shakespeare) (1962); *5 Poems and an Epigram of William Blake*, ch., tpt. (1964); *Orpheus Songs*, sop. (1971); *Psalm IV*, sop., alto, women's ch., va., org. (1976); *Babylon the Great is fallen*, ch., orch. (1979); *Das Gesetz der Quadrille*, bar., pf. (1979); *Behold the Sun*, concert aria, sop., vib., ens. (1981); *2 Imitations of Baudelaire*, unacc. ch. (1985); *Eve Dreams in Paradise*, mez., ten., orch. (1988); *Carol for St Steven* (1989); *Sing, Ariel*, mez., 2 sop., 5 instr. (1989–90); *The Mouse Metamorphosed into a Maid*, unacc. v. (1991); *The *Death of Moses*, sop., cont. or male alto, ten., bar., bass, ch., mixed children's ch. (or semi-ch. of women's vv.), 13 instr. (1991–2); *Psalm 39*, chamber ch., wind ens. (1992–3); *Lamento of 'Arianna'*, sop., ens. (1994–5); *3 Sonnets and 2 Fantasias*, counterten., viol consort (2000).

CHAMBER MUSIC: pf. sonata (1951–2); *Suite*, fl., cl., hn., hp., vn., va., vc. (1961); *3 Pieces*, pf. (1964); pf. trio (1966), str. qt. No.1 (1956–7, rev. 1988), No.2 (1967), No.3 (1975–6), No.4 (1990); *Nonomiya*, pf. (1969); *Paraphrase*, cl. (1969); *Lyric Pieces*, wind septet, db. (1974); *Prelude and Fugue*, 3 cl. (1978); *Lento e Sostenuto*, str. qt. (1956–7, rev. 1983, orig. slow movt. of str. qt. No.1); vc. sonata (1988); *5 Objects Darkly*, bcl., hn., vn., va., pf. (1997); *Duos*, vn., 2 vas. (1998); pf. quintet (2000); *. . . around Stravinsky*, vn., wind quintet (2002); *2 notes only for Ollie*, 11 players (2002).

Goehr, Walter (*b* Berlin, 1903; *d* Sheffield, 1960). Eng. conductor and composer of Ger. birth. Cond. Berlin radio 1925–31, composing for it opera *Malpopita*. Settled in Eng. 1933 and known professionally as George Walter until 1948. Mus. dir., Columbia Graphophone Co. 1933–9. Cond. BBC Th. Orch. 1945–8. Cond. Morley Coll. concerts 1943–60. Ed. Monteverdi's *Vespers* (York 1954) and *L'incoronazione di Poppea*. Wrote scores for radio, films, and th. Orch. Mussorgsky's *Pictures from an Exhibition*. Cond. f.ps. of Britten's *Serenade* (1943), Tippett's *A Child of Our Time* (1944), Seiber's *Ulysses* (1949), and A. Goehr's *The Deluge* (1959); and f. Brit. p. of Mahler's 6th Sym. (BBC 1950).

Goerne, Matthias (*b* Weimar, 1967). Ger. bass-baritone. Studied with H. J. Beyer in Leipzig, then with Elisabeth Schwarzkopf and Dietrich Fischer-Dieskau. Won many prizes, incl 1st prize in Hugo Wolf Comp. 1990. Prof. début Leipzig

1990 (*St Matthew Passion*, cond. Masur). Opera début Cologne 1990 (title-role in *Der Prinz von Hamburg*). Brit. début London 1995 (Wigmore Hall recital), CG 2000 (Wozzeck). Salzburg Fest. début 1997 (Papageno). Has sung at many leading opera houses, incl. NY Met. Teacher at Robert Schumann Mus. Sch., Düsseldorf, from 2004.

Goetz, Hermann (*b* Königsberg, 1840; *d* Hottingen, Zurich, 1876). Ger. composer. Org. at Winterthur 1863–7, moving to Zurich where he comp. his successful opera *The Taming of the Shrew* (prod. 1874). His sym. was also much admired and is convincing evidence of a rare talent prematurely cut short. Works incl.:

OPERAS: *Die heiligen drei Königen* (with pf. acc.) (1865); *Der widerspenstigen Zähmung* (*The *Taming of the Shrew*) (1868–72); *Francesca da Rimini* (1875–6, completed by Ernst Frank).

ORCH.: *Frühlingsouvertüre* (1864); pf. conc. (1867); vn. conc. (1868); Sym. in F (1873).

CHAMBER MUSIC: pf. trio (1863); str. qt. (1865); pf. qt. (1867); pf. quintet (1874).

Also songs and pf. pieces.

Goff, Thomas (Robert Charles) (*b* London, 1898; *d* London, 1975). Eng. builder of clavichords, harpsichords, and lutes. Gift of a clavichord in 1932 impelled him to build one. Began business in partnership with J. C. Cobby 1933, later opening his own London headquarters. His particular achievement has been to adapt tone and dynamics to modern concert hall requirements. Adopted clavichord design of Herbert Lambert of Bath.

Golani, Rivka (*b* Tel Aviv, 1946). Israeli violist. Moved to Canada 1974. Début with Israel PO. Champion of contemp. mus. and fine interpreter of Bartók's va. conc. Made first recording of Tertis's transcr. of Elgar vc. conc.

Gold and Silver (Ger. *Gold und Silber*). Waltz by Lehár comp. for gold and silver ball given by Prince Metternich, Jan. 1902.

Goldberg, Johann (Gottlieb Theophilus) (*b* Danzig, 1727; *d* Dresden, 1756). Ger. organist, composer, and klavier player. Chamber musician to Count Brühl 1751–6. Wrote 2 kbd. concs., 6 fl. trios, etc. Bach gave him a copy of his 30 vars. for hpd.—the *Goldberg Variations*, pubd. *c*.1741 in *Klavier-Übung*, iv—but the story that they were commissioned for him to play is doubtful.

Goldberg, Reiner (*b* Crostau, 1939). Ger. tenor. Opera début as Luigi in Puccini's *Il tabarro*, Dresden 1966. Dresden State Opera 1973–7, Berlin State Opera from 1977. Débuts: CG 1982; Paris 1982; Salzburg Fest. 1982; NY 1983; La Scala 1984; Bayreuth 1988; NY Met 1992. Sang Parsifal on sound-track of Syerberg's film. Mainly assoc. with Wagner leading roles.

Goldberg, Szymon (*b* Włocławek, Pol., 1909; *d* Toyama, Japan, 1993). Pol.-born violinist and conductor (Amer. cit. 1953). Début Warsaw 1921.

Leader, Dresden PO 1925–9, Berlin PO 1929–34. Member of trio with *Hindemith and *Feuermann 1930–4. Settled in London and USA. Duo with Lili Kraus 1935–40. Member of fest. pf. qt., Aspen, Colorado, 1951–65. Solo concert violinist from 1955. Cond. Netherlands Chamber Orch. 1955–78. Cond. Manchester Camerata 1977–9. Teacher at Juilliard Sch. of Mus. 1978–80, Curtis Inst. 1980–1, Manhattan Sch. of Mus., NY, from 1981.

'Goldberg' Variations. 30 variations on an orig. theme for 2-manual hpd., by Bach. Nickname arose from story, now thought to be untrue, that they were commissioned by the Russ. ambassador to Saxony, Count Keyserlingk, for J. G. T. *Goldberg to play. Bach gave Goldberg a copy of the work.

Golden Age, The (*Zolotoy vek*). Ballet in 3 acts with mus. by Shostakovich, choreog. Kaplan and Vaynonen. Prod. Leningrad 1930. Also orch. suite, Op.22a.

Golden Cockerel, The (*Zolotoy petushok*). Opera (his 14th and last) in 3 acts by Rimsky-Korsakov, lib. Belsky after Pushkin's poem (1834) which is based on two tales from *The Alhambra* by Washington Irving (1783–1859). Prod. Moscow 1909, London 1914, NY Met 1918. Comp. 1906–7, but perf. was banned in the composer's lifetime because of the opera's satire on autocracy. The indefensible habit of referring to it by the Fr. title *Le Coq d'or* arose from the prod. by Diaghilev in Paris, 1914, when all the roles were enacted by dancers while singers sat at the sides of the stage.

Golden Legend, The. Cantata by Sullivan for soloists, ch., and orch. to text based on Longfellow's poem. Comp. for Leeds Fest. 1886.

'Golden' Sonata. Nickname, but not the composer's, for Purcell's Sonata in F for 2 vns., va. da gamba, and org. or hpd., No.9 of 10 sonatas posthumously pubd. 1697.

Goldmark, Károly (*b* Keszthély, Hung., 1830; *d* Vienna, 1915). Hung. composer and violinist, son of a cantor. After playing in th. orchs., settled in Vienna 1850 as composer, teacher, and critic. His tuneful, colourful mus. is remembered today chiefly through his sym.-poem *Rustic Wedding* (1875). Comp. 6 operas incl. *Die *Königin von Saba* (The Queen of Sheba) (1875) and *Ein Wintermärchen* (*A Winter's Tale*, after Shakespeare) (1908); sym. in C minor; sym. in E♭; ov. *Sakuntala*; 2 vn. concs.; str. qt.; vc. sonata; etc.

Goldmark, Rubin (*b* NY, 1872; *d* NY, 1936). Amer. composer, nephew of K. *Goldmark. Dir., Colorado Coll. Cons. 1895–1901. Teacher of pf. and theory in NY 1902–24; dir. of comp. dept., Juilliard Sch. 1924–36. Wrote *Requiem* for orch. (1919), *Hiawatha* (1900), *Negro Rhapsody*, and several chamber works.

Goldsborough, Arnold (Wainwright) (*b* Gomersal, 1892; *d* Tenbury Wells, 1964). Eng.

keyboard-player, conductor, and teacher. After being sub-org. at Manchester Cath., became org., St Anne's, Soho, 1920–3, ass. org. Westminster Abbey 1920–7, teacher at RCM from 1923, dir. of mus. Morley Coll. 1924–9, org., St Martin-in-the-Fields 1924–35. Founded Goldsborough Orch. 1948 for perf. of mus. by Purcell, Handel, Bach, etc., and himself played hpd. and continuo. In 1960 it was renamed ECO.

Goldschmidt, Berthold (*b* Hamburg, 1903; *d* London, 1996). Ger.-born composer and conductor (Brit. cit. 1947). Ass. cond. Berlin State Opera 1926–7. Cond. Darmstadt Opera 1927–9. Guest cond. Leningrad PO 1931. Artistic adviser Berlin State Opera 1931–3. His opera *Der gewaltige Hahnrei* (The Mighty Cuckold) was successfully prod. in Mannheim 1932, but plans for further prods. were forbidden by the Nazis. (It was perf.—and recorded—in Berlin in Dec. 1992.) Settled in Eng. 1935. Cond. Glyndebourne co. in Verdi's *Macbeth* at first Edinburgh Fest. 1947. Aided and adv. Deryck *Cooke in preparing perf. version of Mahler's 10th sym., and cond. f. complete p. London 1964. His second opera, *Beatrice Cenci* (1949–50), won a Fest. of Britain prize but was not perf. until a concert perf. in London in 1988. Visited USA 1983, returning there 1985 when his cl. qt. had its f.p. at Univ. of Pasadena. Simon *Rattle cond. his *Ciaconna Sinfonica* (1936) at 1987 Berlin Fest. (its f.p. was Vienna 1960). Both operas, as well as other works, were perf. in Germany in 1994. Works incl.:

OPERAS: *Der gewaltige Hahnrei* (1930–1); *Beatrice Cenci* (1949–50).

BALLET: *Chronica* (1938).

ORCH.: ov., *The Comedy of Errors* (1925); *Passacaglia* (1925); *Marche militaire* (1932); vc. concertino (1933); vn. conc. (1933, rev. 1955); *Ciaconna Sinfonica* (1936); *Sinfonietta* (1945); hp. conc. (1949); vc. conc. (1953); cl. conc. (1954); *Intrada*, wind. orch. (1985).

CHAMBER MUSIC: str. qts.: No.1 (1925), No.2 (1936), No.3 (1988–9), No.4 (1992); pf. sonata (1926); cl. qt. (1983); pf. trio (1985); *Berceuse*, vn., vc. (1990), str. trio (*Retrospectrum*) (1991); *Fantasy*, hp., ob., vc. (1991); *Capriccio*, vn. (1992); *Rondeau*, vn., pf. (1994).

SONGS: *Mediterranean Songs* (1958); *Les petits adieux*, bar., orch. (1994).

Goldschmidt, Otto (*b* Hamburg, 1829; *d* London, 1907). Ger.-born pianist, composer, and conductor. Moved to London 1848. In 1851 visited USA as acc. for Jenny *Lind, whom he married 1852 in Boston. They lived in Dresden 1852–5, but returned to London 1858, Prof. of pf. RAM from 1863, vice-prin. 1866. Mus. organizer Rugby Sch. 1864–9. Founded and cond. London Bach Choir 1875. Cond. f. complete p. in Eng. of Bach's Mass in B minor, April 1876. Comp. oratorio *Ruth*, pf. conc., songs, part-songs, etc.

Goldstone, Anthony (*b* Liverpool, 1944). Eng. pianist. Début Manchester 1965, RMCM orch. cond. Barbirolli. Won int. prizes in Munich and

Vienna. London début 1968. Was member of pf. trio with Ralph Holmes (vn.) and Moray Welsh (vc.).

Golem. Opera in 2 parts (Prelude and Legend) by Casken, to lib. by composer and Pierre Audi, comp. 1988–9. F.p. London, 1989; f. Amer. p. Omaha, 1990. Won first Britten Award for Composition, 1990. Also an opera by Larry Sitsky, f.p. Sydney, NSW, 1993.

Golliwogg's Cakewalk. 6th item of Debussy's *Children's Corner* suite for pf. (1906–8).

Golovin, Andrei (*b* Moscow, 1950). Russ. composer. Comps. incl. Syms. No.1 (1976), No.2 (1981), No.3 (1986), No.4 (1992); Concert Sym. for va., vc., orch. (1980); ob. sonata (1980); pf. sonata (1981); va. sonata (1982); str. qt. (1982); pf. sonatina (1986); Concert Sym. for va., pf., orch. (1988); sym. (1990); *Plain Songs*, cantata, mez., bass, pf., chamber orch. (1991); *2 Songs without Words*, ens. (1993); *The Twilight*, mez., pf. (1995); *First Love*, opera (1996); *Canto d'atessa*, vn., orch. (1999).

Golschmann, Vladimir (*b* Paris, 1893; *d* NY, 1972). Fr.-born conductor of Russ. parentage (Amer. cit. 1947). Founded Golschmann concerts, Paris, 1919, for perf. of contemp. mus., in particular mus. of *Les *Six*. Also cond. f.ps. of chamber operas by Schmitt, Milhaud, and Ibert. Cond. for Diaghilev ballets. NY début 1924. Cond. Scottish Orch. 1928–30. Prin. cond. St Louis SO 1931–56; Tulsa SO 1958–61; Denver SO 1964–70.

Goltz, Christel (*b* Dortmund, 1912). Ger. soprano. Début 1935 at Fürth (Agathe in *Der Freischütz*). Joined opera co. at Plauen and became member Dresden State Opera 1940–50. Débuts: CG 1951; Salzburg Fest. 1951; NY Met 1954. Vienna State Opera 1951–70, esp. in Strauss roles. Created title-role in Liebermann's *Penelope* (Salzburg 1954). Repertory of over 120 parts. Noted for her Salome, Elektra, Marie, Isolde, and Tosca.

Gomez, Jill (*b* New Amsterdam, Brit. Guiana, 1942). W. Indian-born soprano. Opera début Cambridge 1967. GTO 1968 (Adina in *L'elisir d'amore*); Glyndebourne 1969. Created Flora in *The *Knot Garden*, CG 1970. Débuts: Wexford 1974; ENO 1984. Has sung with EOG, Scottish Opera, WNO, Kent Opera; also concert career, esp. in certain contemp. works, e.g. McCabe's *Notturni ed alba* and David Matthews's *Cantiga*, f.p. 1988. Created Duchess in Adès's *Powder her Face*, 1995.

gondola song. (1) A *barcarolle type of comp., supposed to recall the singing of Venetian gondoliers at their work. It is generally in 6/8 or other compound time.

(2) Name given by Mendelssohn to 3 of his *Songs without words* (No.6 in G minor, No.12 in F♯ minor, and No.29 in A minor), and also to another pf. piece, *Auf einer Gondel* (On a Gondola) in A major, 1837.

Gondoliers, The, or The King of Barataria. Operetta in 2 acts by Sullivan, lib. Gilbert. Prod. London 1889, NY and Capetown 1890.

gong. Perc. instr., also called tam-tam, of Chinese origin, being a large round sheet of metal turned up at the edge to form a kind of dish. Struck with felt mallet. Of indefinite pitch, but Puccini in *Turandot* and Vaughan Williams in his 8th Sym. require tuned gongs.

Goodall, (Sir) **Reginald** (*b* Lincoln, 1901; *d* Bridge, nr. Canterbury, 1990). Eng. conductor. Lincoln Cath. choir sch. 1910–14. Lived in Toronto and attended univ. there, studying with Healey Willan. Returned to Eng. to study RCM 1925–8. Org., St Alban's, Holborn, 1929–36, where he cond. f. Brit. ps. of Bruckner sacred works and early works by Britten. Opera début cond. *Carmen* in semi-amateur perf., London 1936. Became ass. to Albert Coates at CG 1936. Ass. cond. Royal Choral Soc. 1936–9. Cond., Wessex PO, Bournemouth, 1940–3. Cond. at SW Opera from 1944. Cond. f.p. of *Peter Grimes*, June 1945. Cond. SW Opera-Ballet 1945–6. Glyndebourne début 1946 (*The Rape of Lucretia*). On mus. staff of CG from 1946, but went abroad to assist Furtwängler, Krauss, and Knappertsbusch. Cond. *Tannhäuser*, SW 1960. Overdue recognition as a Wagner cond. came in 1968 when he cond. SW *Mastersingers*. This was followed by hugely successful cycles, in English, of *The Ring* from 1973. Cond. *Parsifal* at CG 1971, *Tristan und Isolde* with WNO (recorded) 1979, *Tristan* (ENO 1981), *The Valkyrie* (WNO 1984), *Parsifal* (ENO 1986). CBE 1975. Knighted 1985.

Goode, Richard (Stephen) (*b* NY, 1943). Amer. pianist. Début NY 1962 (NY Young Concert Artists). Eur. début Spoleto Fest. 1964. Member of Boston Symphony Chamber Players 1967–9 and of Chamber Mus. Soc. of Lincoln Center, NY, 1969–79 and 1983–9. Won 1st prize Clara Haskil comp. 1973. Wide repertory and has recorded complete cycle of Beethoven sonatas.

Good Friday Music (*Karfreitagzauber*). The mus. in Wagner's *Parsifal* Act 3, Sc.1 as Parsifal is anointed in preparation for his entry into the castle of the Grail. Sometimes perf. as separate concert piece.

Good-Humoured Ladies, The (*Les femmes de bonne humeur*). Choreog. comedy in 1 act to mus. by D. Scarlatti arr. by V. *Tommasini, choreog. Massine. Prod. Rome 1917.

Goodman, Benny [Benjamin] (David) (*b* Chicago, 1909; *d* NY, 1986). Amer. clarinettist and jazz musician. Trained in mus. at synagogue. Prof. début 1921 at Central Park Th., Chicago. Joined Ben Pollack's band as a soloist 1925. Went to NY with Pollack and after 1929 worked as freelance. In 1934 formed his own 12-piece band, inaugurating the 'swing era'. In 1935 formed a trio with Teddy Wilson (pf.) and Gene Krupa (drums), expanding it in 1936 to a quartet with Lionel Hampton (vib.). In 1938 recorded Mozart cl. quintet with Budapest Qt. and commissioned

Contrasts from Bartók, giving f.p. in NY 1939 with Szigeti and Bartók. Soloist with NYPO (cond. Barbirolli) in Mozart conc. Commissioned concs. from Copland and Hindemith 1947, and appeared as soloist with Amer. orchs. in works by Bernstein, Brahms, Debussy, Weber, Nielsen, Prokofiev, Poulenc, and Stravinsky. Re-formed own band 1940 and again 1948. Toured Russ. 1962. Played at Aldeburgh Fest. 1985.

Goodman, Roy (*b* Guildford, Surrey, 1951). Eng. conductor and violinist. From 1971 worked as mus. teacher in comprehensive schs. Specialist in perf. on original instrs. Dir. of Early Mus., RAM. Founded Brandenburg Consort (Reading) 1975. Co-dir., Parley of Instrs. 1979–86. Prin. cond. Hanover Band from 1986, with which he has recorded period perfs. of Haydn, Mozart, Beethoven, Schubert, Mendelssohn, and Weber, and toured USA three times between 1988 and 1990.

Goodwin, (Trevor) **Noël** (*b* Fowey, 1927). Eng. critic and author. Ass. mus. critic, *News Chronicle* 1952–4, *Manchester Guardian* 1954–5. Mus. and dance critic *Daily Express* 1956–78. Exec. ed. *Music and Musicians* 1963–71. Overseas news ed., *Opera*, from 1985. Books incl. *London Symphony* (1954) and *A Knight at the Opera* (1984, with Sir Geraint *Evans).

Goodwin, Ron(ald) (Alfred) (*b* Plymouth, 1925; *d* London, 2003). Eng. composer and conductor. Has comp. mus. for many films, best-known being *Those Magnificent Men in Their Flying Machines* (1965); *Where Eagles Dare* (1969); *The Battle of Britain* (1969); *The Little Mermaid* (1973); *The Happy Prince* (1974); *One of Our Dinosaurs is Missing* (1975); *Force 10 from Navarone* (1978); *Valhalla* (1986).

Goose of Cairo, The (Mozart). See *Oca del Cairo, L'*.

Goossens, Eugene (*b* Bruges, 1845; *d* Liverpool, 1906). Belg. conductor. Cond. of opera in Belgium, Fr., and It., then in Eng. from 1873. Cond. Carl Rosa Opera 1883–93 (prin. cond. from 1889). Org., St Anne's RC Church, Liverpool.

Goossens, Eugene (*b* Bordeaux, 1867; *d* London, 1958). Fr.-born conductor, son of above. Studied Brussels Cons. 1883–6. Lived in Eng. from 1873. Worked with father for Carl Rosa, then prin. cond. of various other cos. Prin. cond. Carl Rosa 1899–1915. Cond. for Beecham co. from 1917, and BNOC from 1926.

Goossens, (Sir) (Aynsley) **Eugene** (*b* London, 1893; *d* Hillingdon, 1962). Eng. conductor, violinist, and composer, son of above. Violinist in Queen's Hall Orch. 1911–15. Ass. cond. to Beecham 1916–20. Cond. f. Eng. concert p. of Stravinsky's *The Rite of Spring*, London 1921. Cond. opera and ballet CG 1921–3. Went to USA, becoming cond. Rochester PO 1923–31 and Cincinnati SO 1931–47. Cond. Sydney SO, NSW, and dir. NSW Cons. 1947–56. Knighted 1955. Comps. incl.:

OPERAS: **Judith* (1 act, lib. Arnold Bennett, CG 1929); *Don Juan de Manara* (4 acts, lib. by Bennett, CG 1937).

ORCH.: *Sinfonietta* (1922); ob. conc. (1927); sym. No.1 (1940), No.2 (1942–4).

CHORAL: *Silence* (1922); *Apocalypse*, oratorio (1950–4).

CHAMBER MUSIC: *Phantasy* for str. qt. (1915); str. qts. No.1 (1915), No.2 (1942); *2 Sketches (By the Tarn* and *Jack o'Lantern*); str. qt. (1916); pf. quintet (1919); concertino for str. octet (1930).

Goossens, Leon (*b* Liverpool, 1897; *d* Tunbridge Wells, 1988). Eng. oboist, brother of above. Prin. oboist Queen's Hall Orch. 1914, later at CG. Prin. ob. LPO from its formation, 1932–9. Then free-lance as soloist and chamber mus. player. Prof. of oboe RAM 1924–35, RCM 1924–39. Brilliant virtuoso for whom several composers—e.g. Elgar, Vaughan Williams, Britten, Gordon Jacob, and Eugene Goossens—wrote works. Teeth and lips injured in car accident 1962 but he developed a new technique and resumed his career 1966, play-ing with almost undiminished skill. CBE 1950.

Goossens, Marie (Henriette) (*b* London, 1894; *d* Dorking, 1991). Eng. harpist, sister of above. Dé-but Liverpool 1910. Prin. harpist CG, Diaghilev Ballet seasons, Queen's Hall Orch. 1920–30, LPO 1932–9, LSO 1940–59, London Mozart Players from 1972. Prof. of hp., RCM 1954–67. OBE 1984.

Goossens, Sidonie (*b* Liscard, Cheshire, 1899; *d* Betchworth, Surrey, 2004). Eng. harpist, sister of above. Début with orch. 1921. Prin. harpist BBC SO 1930–80, being especially adept at mastering *avant-garde* scores, e.g. those by Boulez. Prof. of hp., GSMD from 1960. MBE 1974. OBE 1981.

gopak (hopak). A lively Russ. folk dance in duple time.

Gorchakova, Galina (*b* Nonokuznetsk, 1962). Siberian soprano. Début Sverdlovsk Opera 1988 (Tatyana in *Eugene Onegin*). Brit. début 1991 (Proms.); CG début 1992; NY Met 1992. Member of Kirov Opera for several years.

Górecki, Henryk (Mikołaj) (*b* Czernica, Rybnik, 1933). Polish composer. On leaving school in 1951, became primary school teacher. Began for-mal music studies in Rybnik, 1952. Rector of Ka-towice Cons. 1975–9. Won first prize at several composers' competitions. His *Beatus Vir* was first perf. at Kraków in 1979 on occasion of Pope John Paul II's visit to Poland. Górecki was among Polish composers who took advantage of relative 'thaw' in 1950s in relations with West and came to know mus. of Xenakis, Stockhausen, Nono, Messiaen, and others. But his own mus., initially influenced by Webernian serialism and later by clusters, has never made use of elec. instr. and has developed a highly individual style, going back for inspiration to 14th-cent. Polish chants, to Palestrina's poly-phony, and to the richness of the Wagnerian orch. His 3rd Sym. (1977) achieved worldwide popular-ity, perhaps because its reliance on modal and

triadic structures and its preoccupation with slow tempos are in strong contrast to the dissonance of many contemp. works.

Gorr, Rita [Geirnaert, Marguérite] (*b* Zelzaete, Belg., 1926). Belg. mezzo-soprano. Début Ant-werp 1949 as Fricka in *Die Walküre*. Strasbourg Opera 1949–52. Won Lausanne int. comp. 1952, then joined Paris Opéra. Débuts: Bayreuth 1958; CG 1959; La Scala 1960; NY Met 1962. Sang Mme de Croissy in *Les dialogues des Carmélites* at Lyons and Seattle 1990, and Herodias in *Salome* at Lyons 1990.

Gossec, François (Joseph) (*b* Vergnies, 1734; *d* Passy, 1829). Belg. composer. Boy chorister Ant-werp Cath. Went to Paris 1751 where he was helped by *Rameau for whose patron's private band he comp. first Fr. syms. from 1754. Also comp. str. qts. for Prince de Condé, whose service he entered 1762–9. Dir., Concert Spirituel 1773–7. 2nd cond. at Opéra 1780–2. Organized and dir. École Royale de Chant 1784–95, when it became the Nat. Cons. Prof. of comp. at Paris Cons. 1795–1815. Comp. about 30 syms., 20 operas, church and choral mus. (incl. many pieces in favour of the Revolution), and ballets. His *Te Deum* (1790) anticipated Berlioz in requiring 1,200 singers and 300 wind instrs. A bold innovator in orches-tration.

Gossett, Philip (*b* NY, 1941). Amer. musicolo-gist. Joined faculty of mus., Princeton Univ. 1964–5. At Univ. of Chicago was ass. prof. 1968–73, assoc. prof. 1973–7, prof. 1977–84, chairman, dept. of mus. 1978–84, Dean, Division of the Humanities, from 1990. Int. authority on mus. of Rossini, being gen. ed. of complete edn. from 1979. Adv. to several opera houses on vocal ornamentation. Co-ordinating ed. of works of Verdi from 1983. Co-ed. with Charles Rosen of facsimile series *Early Romantic Operas* (NY, 1978–83, in 44 vols.), and author of *The Tragic Finale of Tancredi* (Pesaro, 1977) and *Anna Bolena and the Artistic Maturity of Gaetano Donizetti* (Oxford 1984).

Gothic Symphony. Havergal *Brian's 1st Sym., comp. 1919–27, in 4 movts., the last of which is setting of *Te Deum* for 4 vv., ch., children's ch., 4 brass groups, and very large orch. F.p. London 1961; f.p. with complete forces required, Hanley 1978.

Götterdämmerung (Twilight of the Gods). Mus. drama in prol. and 3 acts by Wagner to his own lib. The final opera in his tetralogy *Der *Ring des Nibelungen*. Comp. 1869–74. Prod. Bayreuth 1876, London 1882, NY Met 1888.

Gottschalk, Louis Moreau (*b* New Orleans, 1829; *d* Tijuca, nr. Rio de Janeiro, Brazil, 1869). Amer. pianist, conductor, and composer. His pf. début in 1844 was praised by Chopin. On return to USA toured widely, playing and conducting his own sentimental and naive mus. for unso-phisticated audiences who enjoyed his virtuoso panache and his arrs. of nat. airs. Collapsed on stage in Rio after playing a piece called *Morte!* and died a month later. Wrote 2 operas; 2 syms.; *Grande Tarantelle*, *The Union*, and *Marcha triunfal y final de opera*, all for pf. and orch.; and pf. pieces such as *The Dying Poet* (1863–4).

Gould, Glenn (Herbert) (*b* Toronto, 1932; *d* Toronto, 1982). Canadian pianist, composer, and writer. Début Toronto at age of 14 in Beethoven's 4th pf. conc; Washington DC and NY 1955, Eur. tour 1957, London 1958. Salzburg Fest. début 1958. Toured USSR. Exceptionally wide repertory, from 16th-cent. kbd. works to jazz. Highly idiosyncratic performer with mannerisms to match. In 1964 gave up public perf. in favour of recordings. Recorded complete cycle of Schoenberg. Brilliant and controversial writer whose essays were publ. in *The Glenn Gould Reader* (1985).

Gould, Morton (*b* Richmond Hill, NY, 1913; *d* Orlando, Fla., 1996). Amer. composer, conductor, and pianist. Member of Radio City Mus. Hall staff 1931–46. Worked for NBC and CBS broadcasting systems. His mus. contains popular Amer. mus., jazz, and more formal structures. Brilliant orchestrator. Works incl.:

BALLETS: *Interplay* (1943); *Fall River Legend* (1947); *Fiesta* (1953).

ORCH.: *Little Symphony* (1939); syms. No.1 (1942), No.2 (*Marching Tunes*) (1944), No.3 (1947, rev. 1948); pf. conc. (1937); vn. conc. (1938); *American Symphonette* No.1 (*Swing*) (1935), No.2 (1936), No.3 (1937), No.4 (*Latin American*) (1940); *Lincoln Legend* (1941); va. conc. (1943); va. concertette (1943); *Concerto for Orchestra* (1944); *Minstrel Show* (1946); Conc. for tap dancer and orch. (1952); *Jekyll and Hyde Variations* (1957); *St Lawrence Suite* (1958); *Prisms* (1962); *Venice*, audiograph for 2 orch. (1966); *Columbia* (1966); *Vivaldi Gallery*, for str. qt., div. orch. (1967); *Troubadour Music*, 4 guitars, orch. (1968); *Symphony of Spirituals* (1976); *Burchfield Gallery* (1981); fl. conc. (1984); *Chorales and Rags* (1988); *Concerto Grosso* (1988).

Also chamber works, and much mus. for films and TV.

Gounod, Charles (François) (*b* Paris, 1818; *d* St-Cloud, 1893). Fr. composer, conductor, and organist. Won *Grand Prix de Rome* 1839; impressed by Rome and made special study of Palestrina. Became org. at Paris church and studied for priesthood but eventually decided to devote himself to comp. Wrote several operas from 1851 but had no real success until *Faust* in 1859, which became and remained one of the most popular of all operas. Later operas were less successful, though *Roméo et Juliette* survives and the delightful *La Colombe* has been rediscovered. Also wrote many choral works and lived in Eng. 1870–5, becoming first cond. of what is now Royal Choral Soc. His oratorios *La Rédemption* and *Mors et vita* were comp. for the Birmingham and Norwich Fests. of 1882 and 1885. Gounod's mus. has considerable melodic charm and felicity, with admirable orchestration. He was not really a master of the large and imposing forms, in this way perhaps being a Fr. parallel to Sullivan. Works incl.:

OPERAS: *Sapho* (1851); *La Nonne sanglante* (1854); *Le Médecin malgré lui* (1858); *Faust (1859); *La Colombe* (1860); *Philémon et Baucis* (1860); *La Reine de Saba* (1862); *Mireille (1864); **Roméo et Juliette* (1867); *Cinq Mars* (1877); *Polyeucte* (1878); *Le Tribut de Zamora* (1881).

ORCH.: sym. No.1 in D (1855), No.2 in E♭ (*c.*1854); *Petite Symphonie* in B♭, for 9 wind instrs. (1885).

ORATORIOS: *La Rédemption* (1868–81); *Mors et Vita* (1885).

CANTATAS: *Marie Stuart* (1837); *Gallia* (1871).

CHURCH MUSIC: *Messe a tre* (1841); *Messe solennelle* (1849); *Messe solennelle de Ste Cécile* (1855); *Messe à Jeanne d'Arc* (1887); three Requiems; Stabat Mater, Te Deum, Magnificat, etc.

MISC.: *Funeral March of a Marionette* (for pf., 1872, orch. 1879); *Méditation sur le premier prélude de S. Bach*, pf., vn. or vc., org. or vc. *ad lib* (1853, being 1st prelude of Bach's '48' with counterpoint melody by Gounod. In 1859 this was arr. as a solo song, *Ave Maria*, mélodie religieuse adaptée au premier prélude de J. S. Bach); many songs.

Government Inspector, The (*Der Revisor*). Opera in 5 acts by *Egk to his own lib. based on play by Gogol (1836). Prod. Schwetzingen 1957; London (SW, New Opera Co.) 1958; NY City Opera 1980.

Goyescas (*Los majos enamorados*) (Sp. 'Goya-like works', or 'Youth in Love'). (1) 2 sets of pf. pieces, 7 in all, by *Granados, inspired by paintings of Goya, comp. 1911, f.p. 1914. Titles are 1. *Los requiebros* (Loving words), 2. *Coloquio en la reja* (A conversation through the grating), 3. *El fandango del candil* (Kitchen fandango), 4. *Quejas o la maja y el ruisenor* (Lament, or The Maja and the Nightingale), 5. *El amor y la muerte* (Love and death), 6. *Epilogo: la serenada del espectro* (Epilogue: The ghost's serenade), 7. *El pelele* (The worthless man).

(2) Opera in 3 scenes by Granados, amplified and scored (at the suggestion of the Amer. pianist Ernest Schelling) from the above pf. pieces, with Sp. lib. by F. Periquet. Prod. NY Met 1916, London 1951. See also *Maja y el ruisenor*.

GP. (1) *General pause, of 1 or 2 bars for all performers.

(2) (Fr.). *grand et positif*, i.e. great and choir organs to be coupled.

GPR. (Fr.). *grand-positif-récit*, i.e. great, choir, and swell organs to be coupled.

GR. (Fr.). *grand récit*, i.e. great and swell organs to be coupled.

grace notes. *Ornaments in vocal and instr. mus., indicated in very small notation.

Gradual. (1) The Respond sung in the service of the Mass between the Epistle and Gospel.

(2) The book containing the concentus of the traditional plainsong of the Mass, i.e. it is the

choir's (or congregation's) mus. companion to the Missal—in which last the only mus. is the *accentus or priest's parts.

Gradualia. Motets by William Byrd. Book I (1605) contains 32 for 5 vv., 20 for 4, and 11 for 3; Book II (1607) contains 9 for 6 vv., 17 for 5, and 19 for 4.

Gradus ad Parnassum (Steps to Parnassus (the abode of the muses)). (1) Title of treatise on *counterpoint by J. J. *Fux, 1725.

(2) Series of 100 studies by *Clementi, pub. 1817 (50 ed. *Bülow; complete series ed. Vogrich, 1898).

(3) 1st piece in Debussy's *Children's Corner* is called *Dr Gradus ad Parnassum* (a parody of a Clementi study).

Graf, Hans (*b* Linz, 1949). Austrian conductor. Cond., Iraqi Nat. SO 1975. Début Vienna Opera 1977. 1st prize Karl Böhm cond. comp., Salzburg 1979. Salzburg Fest. début 1983. Mus. dir. Salzburg Mozarteum Orch. 1984–92. Paris Opéra 1984 (*Die Entführung*). Has cond. opera in Munich, Venice, Berlin, Bregenz, Helsinki, and concerts in Russ., It., and Eng.

Graffman, Gary (*b* NY, 1928). Amer. pianist. Recital début NY 1938, conc. début with Philadelphia Orch. 1947; Eur. 1956, followed by world-wide tours. Leventritt Award 1949. In 1979 lost use of right hand through carpal-tunnel syndrome. Joined faculty of Curtis Inst. 1980, becoming art. dir. 1986.

Graf von Luxemburg, Der (Lehár). See *Count of Luxemburg, The*.

Graham, Colin (*b* Hove, 1931). Eng. stage director, designer, and opera producer. Studied RADA 1951–2 and worked for several years as stage man. Début as prod. Aldeburgh 1958 (*Noye's Fludde*). Art. dir. EMT 1976–9; dir. of prods., EOG 1961–75; assoc. dir. of prod. SW/ENO 1967–75 (début 1961, *The Cunning Little Vixen*, dir. 1976–82, art. dir., Aldeburgh Fest. from 1968. Close assoc. with operas of Britten, notably the premières of the 3 church parables 1964–8, *Owen Wingrave* (stage première, CG, 1973), and *Death in Venice* (Snape 1976). Opera prods. for Glyndebourne (début 1970, *The *Rising of the Moon*, CG (début 1961, Gluck's *Orpheus*), Scottish Opera (1968 at Edinburgh Fest., *Peter Grimes*), NY Met (1974, *Death in Venice*). Prod. f.ps. of Josephs's *Rebecca* (Leeds [Opera North] 1983) and Corigliano's The *Ghosts of Versailles* (NY Met 1991). Art. dir., Opera Theater of St Louis from 1978. OBE 2002.

Graham, Martha (*b* Allegheny, 1894; *d* NY, 1991). Amer. dancer, choreographer, teacher, and ballet company director. Began studying at Denishawn 1916, member of Denishawn Dancers till 1923. Founded own co. 1929. Developed own technique and became leading exponent of modern dance in USA, exerting enormous influence and producing many famous pupils. Comps. who wrote ballets for her co. incl. Hindemith, Hunter Johnson, Copland,

Chávez, Barber, Menotti, Schuman, Dello Joio, Hovhaness, and Seter. Cond. ballet at Salzburg Fest. 1989.

Graham, Susan (*b* Roswell, New Mexico, 1960). Amer. mezzo-soprano. Studied with Marlena Malas at Manhattan Sch., NY. Prof. début 1988, St Louis (Erika in *Vanessa*). Débuts: NY Met 1991 (2nd Lady in *Zauberflöte*); Salzburg Fest. 1992 (Cecilio in *Lucio Silla*); CG 1993 (Massenet's Cherubin); La Scala 1995 (*Damnation of Faust*); Paris 1996 (Dorabella). Created title-role in Goehr/Monteverdi *Arianna* (CG 1995), Jordan Baker in Harbison's *The Great Gatsby* (NY Met 1999), Sister Helen Prejean in Heggie's *Dead Man Walking* (San Francisco 2000), and Sandra Finchley in Picker's *An American Tragedy* (NY Met 2005). Outstanding as Strauss's Octavian and Composer and in songs of Ives, Rorem, Barber, Hahn, Berlioz, and Chausson.

Grainger, Percy (Aldridge) (*b* Brighton, Victoria, 1882; *d* White Plains, NY, 1961). Australian-born composer and pianist (Amer. cit. 1918). Recital début in London, June 1901; conc. début Bath 1902 (Tchaikovsky B♭ minor). In 1903 toured Australia, NZ, and S. Africa. In London in 1906 he was befriended by *Grieg, who greatly admired his playing and invited him to Norway to make a special study of the pf. conc. in A minor, a work of which he remained a notable interpreter. Collected and ed. Eng. folksongs, incl. *Brigg Fair*, collected at N. Lincs. mus. competition fest. at Brigg, 1905. His arr. of it was admired by *Delius, whose orch. rhapsody was based on this tune. Delius and Grainger remained close friends. Grainger's NY début was in 1914, after which the USA became his home. Although best-known as a composer for his lighter works such as *Shepherd's Hey*, usually based on traditional tunes, his folksong arrs. for ch., e.g. *Shallow Brown*, are original and impressive and won the admiration of Britten. He was a lifelong experimenter and something of an eccentric, a very lively and stimulating figure. He rejected It. as the language in which to indicate tempo etc. in scores and used colloquial Eng., e.g. 'Linger very slightly. Quicker lots bit by bit'. As early as 1937 he comp. what he called 'free mus.' for primitive elec. instrs. Prin. works:

ORIGINAL: KEYBOARD: *Over the Hills and Far Away*, 2 pf. (1916–18); *Colonial Song*, pf. (1914); *Handel in the Strand*, pf. (1930), 2 pf. (1947); *Hill Song No.1*, 2 pf. (1921), *No.2*, 2 pf. (1907); *Mock Morris*, pf. (1910), 2 pf. (1910); Suite, *In a Nutshell*, 2 pf. (1916); *The Warriors*, 2 pf., 6 hands (1922); *Walking Tune*, pf. (c.1905).

ORCH.: *Colonial Song* (1905–12, rev. c.1928); *Handel in the Strand*, str. (1932); *Mock Morris*, str. (1910), orch. (1914); Suite, *In a Nutshell* (1905–16); *The Warriors*, 3 pf., orch. (1912–16).

LARGE WIND ENS.: *Colonial Song*, band (1918); *Over the Hills and Far Away*, band, pf. (1916–19); *Hill Song*

No.2, band (1901, rev. 1911, 1940–6); *Marching Song of Democracy*, band (1948).

CHORAL & VOCAL: *Colonial Song*, sop., ten., hp., orch. (1905–12, rev. 1914), sop., ten., pf. trio (1912); *Danny Deever*, male vv., orch./bar., male vv., pf. (1903, 1922–4); *Marching Song of Democracy*, ch., org., orch. (1901–17); *Recessional*, ch. (1905, 1929).

CHAMBER MUSIC: *Colonial Song*, pf. trio (1912); *Handel in the Strand*, pf. trio (1911–12); *Hill Song No.1*, 22 instr. (1921, rev. 1923), *No.2*, 22 wind/cymbal (1907, rev. 1911, 1940–6); *Mock Morris*, str. sextet (1910), vn., pf. (1910); *Walking Tune*, wind quintet (1900–5).

FOLK-SONG SETTINGS: KEYBOARD: *Country Gardens, pf. (1908–18), 2 pf. (1918) orch. by L. Artok; *Green Bushes*, 2 pf., 6 hands (1919); *Irish Tune from Co. Derry* (*Londonderry Air*), pf. (1911); *Lincolnshire Posy*, 2 pf. (1937–8); *Molly on the Shore*, pf. (1918), 2 pf. (1947); *My Robin is to the Greenwood Gone*, pf. (1912); *Shepherd's Hey*, pf. (1911), 2 pf. (1947); *Spoon River*, pf. (1919–22), 2 pf. (1932, rev. 1946).

ORCH.: *Irish Tune from Co. Derry*, str. (1913); *Molly on the Shore*, str. (1907, rev. c.1911), orch. (1914); *Shepherd's Hey*, orch. (1912–13); *Ye Banks and Braes*, orch. (1932).

LARGE WIND ENS.: *Irish Tune from Co. Derry*, band (1917); *Lincolnshire Posy*, band (1906–37); *Molly on the Shore*, band (1920); *Shepherd's Hey*, band (1918); *Spoon River*, band (1933); *Ye Banks and Braes*, band (1949).

CHORAL & VOCAL: *Bold William Taylor* (1908); *Brigg Fair* (1906, rev. 1911); *Died for Love* (1906–7); *Early One Morning* (1901, 1939–40); *I'm Seventeen Come Sunday* (1905–12); *Irish Tune from Co. Derry* (1902, 1920); *Shallow Brown* (1910, rev. 1923–5); *Six Dukes Went A-Fishin'* (1905, 1910–12); *Sir Eglamore* (1904, rev. 1912–13); *Pretty Maid Milking Her Cow* (1920); *Lost Lady Found* (1905–10); *Men of Harlech* (1904); *Three Ravens* (1902, rev. 1943–9); *Willow, Willow* (1898–1911); *Ye Banks and Braes* (1901).

CHAMBER & INSTR.: *Early One Morning* (1901, 1939–40); *Green Bushes* (1905–6, rev. 1921); *Irish Tune from Co. Derry*, str. and hn. (1913); *Molly on the Shore*, str. qt. (1907, rev. c.1911), vn., pf. (1914); *My Robin is to the Greenwood Gone*, 2 wind, 6 str. (1904, 1912), pf. trio (1912); *Shepherd's Hey*, 11 or 12 instr. (1908–9); *Spoon River*, 2 pf., harmonium (1929).

Gramophone. Monthly magazine specializing in reviews and news of recordings and technical equipment. Founded by Compton Mackenzie (1883–1972) in April 1923.

gramophone (phonograph) recordings. The idea of recording sound by attaching a needle to a membrane vibrating in sympathy, and by allowing its point to mark a plate travelling at a fixed speed, dates from as early as the beginning of the 19th cent., the object being to add to acoustical knowledge about the differences in the vibrations evoked by sounds of various pitches and timbres. The Amer. Edison, in 1877 constructed such an apparatus, with the intention that it should be used in a 'dictating machine': this he called *The Phonograph—the Ideal Amanuensis*, and the records, on wax cylinders, he called phonograms. The vv. of many celebrities of the day were crudely preserved in this way (e.g. Gladstone, Irving, Tennyson) and in 1878 Lily Moulton, an amateur singer, sang into Edison's device. Other musicians, incl. Brahms, made recordings in the 1880s.

Emile Berliner, a Ger.-born citizen of the USA, had by 1888 obtained patents for important improvements—a circular plate of a shellac mixture instead of a waxed cylinder, and a horizontal motion of the needle instead of a perpendicular one (i.e. a motion making lateral impressions on the sides of a spiral track instead of the previous 'hill and dale' impressions), and his principles were in time developed and universally adopted. The patented title for the instr. which played Berliner's discs was 'grammophone', but the less accurate 'gramophone' was adopted.

The flat disc record led to a boom among commercial cos. for preserving the vv. of celebrated singers. The first singer to record commercially and to make a reputation thereby was the Russian sop. Maria Mikhailova. Soon Calvé, Van Rooy, Plançon, Kirkby-Lunn, Albani, Maurel, and Ben Davies were recorded, but it was the ten. *Caruso who 'made' the gramophone record. Instrumentalists, too, were recorded, among them Grieg, Sarasate, Joachim, and Pugno. The historical importance of these discs is obvious, and many of them have been transferred on to modern records and tapes.

So far the processes used had been purely 'acoustic', the result of the direct action of sound vibrations. The human v. could be fairly satisfactorily and faithfully recorded by this means, but attempts to record orch. mus. were crude and primitive. In 1925 appeared the earliest electrically made records, in which the vibrations had been received by means of a microphone and converted into electrical vibrations, causing, in turn, mechanical vibrations in a steel or fibre needle travelling over the recording disc. It was found that by the use of electric-made records operating at the standard speed of 78 revolutions per minute, very much more faithful reproductions could be secured, and the acoustic-made record in time disappeared from the market. The motive power of the Edison and early Berliner instrs. had been supplied by a handle turned by the operator. This was superseded by a clock-spring device, which in the more expensive instrs. was, in turn, superseded by electric power obtained by plugging to the domestic electric circuit: such instrs. also reproduced the sounds by electric means, reversing the above process of electrical recording. The new apparatus was very commonly combined with one for the reception of radio broadcasting, and called a radiogram. During the 1920s and 1930s recordings of most of the world's great orchs. and chamber groups were made, the perf. of great artists such as Rachmaninov, Kreisler, and Heifetz were preserved, and the composers Elgar and Strauss cond. their own mus. for the gramophone. Whole operas were issued, and the significance of the gramophone as an educative force and as a means of widening the public's repertory became apparent.

A great disadvantage of the 78 rpm record was that comps. were dissected into sides lasting less than 5 minutes. An opera could run to 40 or more sides. It was in 1948 that (in the USA) all the problems inherent in trying to combine a narrower groove and slower speed without loss of 'high fidelity' throughout the greater part of the range of audible frequencies were satisfactorily solved.

This was when the Columbia co. announced the long-playing (LP) disc. Attempts to introduce LPs had been made in 1904 and 1931, but the 1948 version offered an average of 23 mins. per side at 33 rpm, with the advantages of records made from non-breakable material, with greatly improved recording techniques, and with light-weight pick-ups and sapphire and diamond needles. At first there was some resistance and a 'battle' between 33 and 45 rpm (for short items). In Brit., Decca was the first firm to market LPs (1950), the EMI group not following until 1952. However, the artistic advantage of being able to record a whole opera on 6 or 8 sides, a Mozart sym. on one side, and to offer complete recitals by singers and instrumentalists on one record revolutionized the industry and listening habits. The standards of recording improved constantly with the advent of the record 'producer' who, like an opera producer, governed the whole recording process. It could be argued that the remarkable growth of the public appetite for the mus. of Mahler is partly due to the fact that LPs enabled his vast syms. to be recorded easily. The rise of the LP was paralleled by the growth of high-fidelity—'Hi-fi'—reproductive equipment —the coupling of amplifier, speakers, pick-up, and needle-cartridge instead of the mass-produced radiogram.

The other great single factor in LP recording was the use of magnetic tape instead of wax or acetate for the orig. recording process. Experiments with tape were made, esp. in Ger., in the late 1930s and early 1940s. Tape enables long stretches of mus. to be recorded without a break; it also enables flaws and errors to be corrected by the re-recording of the offending bar or two, so that a final recording may be, and often is, a compilation of the best of several 'takes', skilfully ed. The next 'recording revolution' was in 1958 with the introduction of stereophonic (as opposed to monophonic) sound, whereby the sound of instrs. or singers was as realistically 'placed' as in the hall or opera house. Eventually 'stereo' replaced 'mono' entirely; and demands for still more realistic and spectacular sound led in the 1970s to 'quadraphonic' recordings (which means that the engineers have fed four independent signal channels into the master tape).

In 1979 recordings made by the even more accurate *digital* tape process appeared on the market from Decca. This system of recording on tape differs from the conventional magnetic system in measuring the shape of the changes in air pressure (sounds) so that the sounds received through the microphone are stored in a computer as a series of numbers (digits). No matter how often the numbers are re-converted into sounds they cannot become distorted. Thus the tape recording is more accurate, has less background noise and no speed variations, and can be re-recorded without loss in quality. In some digital systems the shapes are measured 40,000 times a second.

In 1983 the *compact disc* was introduced, bringing exceptional clarity and dynamic range into recording. It is the first sound reproduction system to dispense with contact between disc and stylus or between cassette and tape-recorder heads. Thus any hiss or hum is eliminated, also any damage to the grooves. The compact disc has a coating of acrylic plastic to protect it from scratches or other damage. The rotating disc is played by a small low-powered laser which directs a beam of infra-red light on to it, translates a reflected message as a digital code and converts it into sound. The laser's collection and transference of the recorded message is achieved by a technology derived from computers. During recording, a machine makes a series of sound 'samples' at the rate of 44,000 per second. These are converted into a binary code (noughts and ones). This code is inscribed in the form of billions of microscopic pits on the surface of the disc in a spiral 2½ miles long (the disc has a diameter of 4.7"). The laser reads the code by focusing on the line of dots as the disc rotates. When the laser fixes on one of the pits, its beams scatter. When it hits the reflecting surface between the pits, it shines back to produce a pattern which re-creates the original binary code. The code is converted into electrical impulses and passed through amplifiers to the speakers in the normal way. The process was pioneered independently by Philips and the Sony Corporation of Japan, who joined in 1980 to produce the first players for the Eur. market.

Of less commercial success at first was the issue of recordings as tapes instead of discs (mono from 1951, stereo from 1956 in the USA). These did not appeal to the public until the introduction of the automatic cassette in 1965. Soon the sales of cassettes threatened to rival those of discs. The development of digital audio tape was yet another step forward.

Alongside the enormous expansion of recording has developed the 'literary' side of the gramophone, not only expert reviewing, but the specialized compilation of lists of recordings made by individual artists, these being known as *discographies.

Granados (y Campina), **Enrique** (*b* Lérida, 1867; *d* at sea, 1916). Sp. composer and pianist. Début recital Barcelona 1890. Founded Soc. of Classical Concerts, Barcelona, 1900, and his own pf. sch., Academia Granados, 1901. Famous as brilliant pianist especially of his own comps. These pf. pieces are elegant and poetic; so are his songs, many of them in the style of 18th-cent. tonadillas. Best known of his orch. comps. is the Intermezzo from his opera *Goyescas*, based on the pf. suite of the same name which created a sensation in Paris in 1914. He and his wife were drowned when the liner *Sussex* was torpedoed by a Ger. U-boat in the Eng. Channel. Prin. works:

ZARZUELAS & OPERAS: *Maria del Carmen* (1898); *Petrarca, Picarol* (1901); *Follet* (1903); *Gaziel* (1906); *Liliana* (1911); **Goyescas* (1914–15).

ORCH.: suites: *Elisenda* (*c.*1910); *Navidad; Suite Arabe; Suite Gallega; La Nit del mor*; sym.-poem; *Serenata; Tres danzas españolas* (orch. de Grignon).

VOICE & PIANO: *Colección de canciones amatorias; Colección de tonadillas, escritas en estilo antiguo,* etc.

PIANO: *10 Sp. Dances* (1892–1900); *6 Pieces on Sp. Popular Songs; Rapsodia Aragonesa; Escénas Romanticas; 7 valses poéticos; Bocetos; 6 Studies in Expression; *Goyescas* (1911).

gran cassa (It.). Big box, i.e. bass drum.

gran coro (It.). Full organ.

grand chœur (Fr.), sometimes abbreviated to *Gd. chœur* or *Gd. Ch.* 'Large choir', or 'full organ'.

Grand Duke, The, or The Statutory Duel. Comic opera by Sullivan, lib. Gilbert, their last and unsuccessful collaboration. Comp. 1895–6. Prod. London and Berlin 1896, NY 1937.

Grand Duo. Sub-title given by publisher in 1838 to Schubert's Sonata in C major for pf., 4 hands (1824, D813) comp. at Zseliz. Once thought to be piano version of a 'lost' symphony, but this theory is totally discredited by recent scholarship. Orch. versions by Joachim and Anthony Collins.

Grande Duchesse de Gérolstein, La. *Opéra bouffe* in 3 acts by Offenbach, lib. Meilhac and Halévy. Prod. Paris, NY, and London 1867.

Grande sonate pathétique. Fr. title given by Beethoven to his pf. sonata in C minor, Op.13, comp. 1798–9.

grandezza (It.). Grandeur, dignity. **grandioso** (It.). With dignity.

Grandi, Alessandro (*b* ?1575; *d* Bergamo, 1630). It. composer of motets, madrigals, and church music. Choirmaster of Bergamo churches and of Ferrara Cath., 1615. In 1617 he became ass. choirmaster to Monteverdi at St Mark's, Venice; and from 1627 until his death was choirmaster of S. Maria Maggiore, Bergamo.

grand jeu (Fr.). Full organ (or harmonium, of which a combination stop is so named).

Grand Macabre, Le (The Grand Macabre). Opera in 2 acts by *Ligeti, lib. M. Meschke and comp., freely adapted from M. de Ghelderode's play *La balade du Grand Macabre*. Comp. 1972–6. Prod. Stockholm 1978, cond. Elgar Howarth who also cond. f. Eng. p. ENO 1982 (trans. by G. Skelton).

Grand' Messe des Morts (High Mass for the Dead). Fr. title of *Berlioz's Requiem Mass, Op.5, for ten., boys' ch., ch., and orch., commissioned 1836 and f.p. Paris, Dec. 1837.

grand opera. Imprecise term, generally taken to mean either (a) opera in which every note of the lib. is sung, i.e. no spoken dialogue, or (b) 'serious' opera as distinct from operetta. *grand*

opéra (Fr.) means an epic or historical work in 4 or 5 acts, using large orch., the ch. and incl. a ballet.

grand orchestre (Fr.). (1) Full orchestra.
 (2) Large orchestra.

grand orgue (Fr.). (1) Full organ or great organ (see *organ*). (2) Pipe organ—as distinct from reed organ, i.e. from American organ or cabinet organ.

Grand Prix de Rome. 1st prize in the **Prix de Rome* contest of the Fr. Acad. of Fine Arts.

grand staff, or **grand stave**. See *great staff.*

Grange, Philip (*b* London, 1956). Eng. composer. Northern Arts Fellow in comp., Durham Univ. 1988–9. Lect. in comp., Exeter Univ. from 1989. Works incl. *3 Piano Pieces* (1976); pf. sonata (1978); *Cimmerian Nocturne*, chamber ens. (1979); sextet, wind quintet and pf. (1980); *3 Pieces*, cl., orch. (1981); *The Kingdom of Bones*, mus. th. (1982–3); *Nocturnal Image*, vc., pf. (1984); *La ville entière*, cl., pf. (1984); *Variations* (1986); *Out in the Dark* (1986); *In memoriam HK*, tb. (1986); *The Dark Labyrinth* (1987); *Concerto for Orchestra* (1988); *In a Dark Time* (1989); *Changing Landscapes* (1990); *Focus and Fade*, orch. (1992); *Lowry Dreamscape*, brass band (1993); *Bacchus Bagatelles*, wind quintet (1993); *Homage to Chagall*, pf. trio (1995); *A Puzzle of Shadows*, ens. (1997); cl. conc. (2000); *Lament of the Bow*, chamber orch. (2000).

Grania and Diarmid. Play by W. B. Yeats and George Moore (staged as *Diarmuid and Grania*) for which Elgar wrote incidental mus. Op.42, Dublin Gaiety Th., 21 Oct. 1901. Most frequently played item is the *Funeral March*, f. London p. 1902.

graphic scores. Scores by 20th-cent. *avant-garde* composers which employ drawn visual analogues in order to convey the composer's intentions with regard to the required sounds and textures. Earliest example is thought to have been *Feldman's *Projections* 1950–1. Some graphic scores indicate distinct mus. parameters, as in Feldman, Stockhausen, and Ligeti. Others deliberately omit any notational sign or mus. indication, seeking only to stimulate the performer's creativity. Examples by Bussotti and Earle Brown are often pictorially delightful if musically enigmatic. (See example from Logothetis's *Agglomeration* on page 310.)

Grappelli, Stephane (*b* Paris, 1908; *d* Paris, 1997). Fr. jazz violinist. Had classical training and turned to jazz in late 1920s. Formed Quintet of the Hot Club of France 1934 with the guitarist Django Reinhardt. Lived in Eng. 1940–8. Amer. début, Newport, RI, 1969; NY début 1974 (Carnegie Hall). In 1973 formed popular partnership with *Menuhin, resulting in recordings, later with Nigel *Kennedy.

Graubart, Michael (*b* Vienna, 1930). Austrian-born comp., conductor, teacher, and flautist. Freelance flautist 1953–7. Cond. amateur orchs.

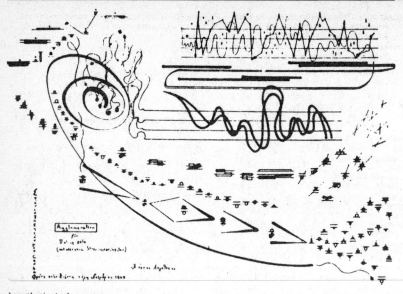

Logothetis: *Agglomeration*

and choirs from 1953—Ars Nova Chamber Orch. 1960, Hampstead Chamber Orch. 1962–6. Mus. dir. Focus Opera Group 1967–71. Teacher and cond. at Morley Coll. from 1966, dir. of music 1969–91. Ed. of works by Monteverdi, Du Fay, and Pergolesi. Comps. incl. va. concertino, *Aria* for orch., and works incorporating elec. tape.

Graun, Karl (Heinrich) (*b* Wahrenbrück, Saxony, 1704; *d* Berlin, 1759). Ger. tenor and composer. Sang as ten. at Brunswick Opera 1725, but became 2nd Kapellmeister there 1726 and wrote several operas. Entered service of Crown Prince Frederick at Rheinsberg 1735. When Frederick (the Great) became King, Graun was made cond. of Berlin Royal Opera, 1740, for which he wrote 26 It. operas, incl. *Rodelinda* (1741), *Cesare e Cleopatra* (1742, revived Berlin 1992), and *Ezio* (1755), and dramatic cantatas. Also wrote Passion-cantata *Der *Tod Jesu* (1755). Instr. works incl. hn. conc.

grave (It., Fr.). (1) (as a term of expression), slow and solemn.

(2) (as a term of pitch), low.

(3) (in Fr. org. mus.) *octaves graves* means sub-octave coupler.

grave mixture. Org. *mixture stop* of 2 ranks (12th and 15th).

Graves, Alfred (Perceval) (*b* Dublin, 1846; *d* Harlech, 1931). Irish poet, folksong collector, and school inspector. Collab. with Stanford in publication of Irish folksongs, many of which he collected, incl. the Co. Kerry tune for which he wrote the words *Father O'Flynn*. Provided first two sets of words for tune *Londonderry Air. Father of poet Robert Graves.

gravicembalo (It., probably corruption of *clavicembalo*). The hpd.

Gray, Cecil (*b* Edinburgh, 1895; *d* Worthing, 1951). Scot. composer and critic. Settled in London 1915. Joint ed. with Philip Heseltine of periodical *The Sackbut*. Mus. critic *Nation and Athenaeum* 1925–30, *Daily Telegraph* 1928–32, *Manchester Guardian* 1932. Wrote 3 operas to his own libs.: *Deirdre, Temptation of St Anthony*, and *The Trojan Women*. Wrote lib. on Gesualdo for opera by Walton, but no mus. was comp. His reputation rests on his books, which incl. *A Survey of Contemporary Music* (1924), *Carlo Gesualdo, Musician and Murderer* (with P. Heseltine) (1926), *History of Music* (1928), *Sibelius* (1931), *Peter Warlock* (1934), *Predicaments* (1936), and *Contingencies* (1947).

Gray, Linda Esther (*b* Greenock, 1948). Scottish soprano. Kathleen Ferrier memorial prize 1972; John Christie award 1973. Opera début as Mařenka in *The Bartered Bride* and Poppea at SW 1970 while a student. Sang Mimì with GTO, 1972. Glyndebourne début 1973; Paris 1976; Scottish Opera 1974–9; ENO début 1978. Sang Isolde in Ger. with WNO 1979 and in Eng. for ENO, both cond. Goodall. CG début 1980; Amer. début Dallas 1981.

grazia; grazioso; graziosamente (It.). Grace; graceful; gracefully.

great organ (great). Chief division (manual and its controlled equipment) of an org. Full org. is always played from the great kbd. coupled to other divisions.

great staff or **great stave** (or grand staff or stave). Notational device introduced by mus. pedagogues for the purpose of explaining the clefs—

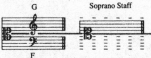

The two staves in common use are brought near together. It suffices then to place between them one extra line for Middle C ('middle' in a double sense: in the middle of this diagram, as it is in the middle of the piano kbd.). The C clef is placed on this line. The treble (or G) clef now comes 2 lines above and the bass (or F) clef 2 lines below. The treble staff, bass staff, soprano staff (in some choral use in Ger. still), the *alto staff* (in use in older choral mus., in mus. for the viola, etc.) and the *tenor staff* (in use in the older choral mus., for the tb., etc.) are seen as sections of the 'great staff', with Middle C as the pivot.

G	Soprano Staff	Alto Staff	Tenor Staff

F

Greef, Arthur de (*b* Louvain, 1862; *d* Brussels, 1940). Belg. pianist and composer. Prof. at Brussels Cons. 1885–1930. Toured widely. Especial champion of mus. of his friend Grieg. Comp. sym., 2 pf. concs., 2 vn. sonatas, and songs.

Greek. Opera in 2 acts by Mark-Anthony Turnage to lib. by composer and Jonathan Moore from S. Berkoff's play *Greek*. Comp. 1986–8. Prod. Munich 1988, Edinburgh Fest. 1988, London (ENO) 1990.

Greek Passion, The (*Řecké pašije*). Opera in 4 acts by *Martinů to lib. by composer and N. Kazantzakis after latter's novel *Christ Recrucified* (1948) trans. into Eng. by J. Griffin. Comp. 1956–7, rev. 1958 and 1959. Prod. Zurich 1961, Cardiff (WNO) 1981.

Green. Poem by Verlaine set for v. and pf. by Debussy, 1887–8, as No.5 of *Ariettes oubliées*, and by Fauré, 1891, as No.3 of 5 *Mélodies*, Op.58. Also set as *Offrande* by R. Hahn, 1895.

Greenbaum, Hyam (*b* Brighton, 1901; *d* Bedford, 1942). Eng. conductor and violinist. Member of Queen's Hall Orch. and of Brosa Qt. 1924–5. Mus. dir. to impresario C. B. Cochran for his revues, 1930–4. Cond. BBC TV Orch. 1936–9, BBC Revue Orch. 1939–42. Confidant of Lambert, Rawsthorne, and Walton (some of whose film mus. he orchestrated).

Greenberg, Noah (*b* NY, 1919; *d* NY, 1966). Amer. conductor and music editor, specializing

in medieval and Renaissance mus. Served in US Merchant Marines 1944–9. Founded NY Pro Musica 1952 to perf. early mus. in authentic fashion. In 1958 revived medieval drama *The Play of Daniel*, touring Europe with it in 1960.

Greene, Harry Plunket (*b* Old Connaught House, Co. Wicklow, 1865; *d* London, 1936). Irish bass-baritone. Sang in London concerts from 1888 (début in *Messiah* at Stepney), opera from 1890, but later confined himself to songs and oratorio. First interpreter of songs, some written for him, by Parry, Stanford, and Vaughan Williams. First singer of bass parts in Elgar's *Dream of Gerontius*, 1900. Later became teacher. Wrote biography of Stanford and *Interpretation in Song* (1924). Married Parry's daughter Gwendolen, 1899.

Greene, Maurice (*b* London, 1696; *d* London, 1755). Eng. composer and organist. Org., St Paul's 1718, and Chapel Royal, 1727. Master of the King's Musick, 1735. Prof. of mus., Cambridge Univ. from 1730. Began great collection of Eng. cath. mus. which he bequeathed to *Boyce, who completed and pubd. it. Comp. an-

thems (best-known *Lord let me know mine end*), oratorios, org. pieces, opera, and songs.

Greenfield, Edward (Harry) (*b* Westcliff-on-Sea, 1928). Eng. music critic and broadcaster. Joined *Manchester Guardian* 1953, working as lobby correspondent in House of Commons. Record critic from 1955, mus. critic from 1964, chief mus. critic 1977–93. Contrib. to *Gramophone* from 1960. Co-ed. of *Stereo Record Guide* from 1960. Regular broadcaster. Author of monographs on Puccini (1958), Joan Sutherland (1972) and André Previn (1973). OBE 1994.

Greenhouse, Bernard (*b* Newark, NJ, 1916). Amer. cellist and teacher. Prin. cellist CBS SO 1938–42; member Dorian Str. Qt. 1939–42, Navy Str. Qt. 1942–5. Recital début NY 1946, annual recitals to 1957. Taught at Juilliard Sch. 1951–61. Member, Harpsichord Qt. 1947–51, Bach Aria Group 1948–76. Founder member Beaux Arts Trio 1955–87. Prof. of vc., Manhattan Sch. of Mus., NY, 1950–82; Juilliard Sch. 1951–61; Hartt Cons., Hartford, 1956–65; Indiana Univ. Sch. of Mus., Bloomington, summers 1956–65; State Univ. of NY 1960–85; New Eng. Cons., Boston, from 1986; State Univ. of NJ from 1987.

Greensleeves. Old Eng. tune twice mentioned by Shakespeare in *The Merry Wives of Windsor* and by other writers of this and later periods. It is first referred to in the Stationers' Co. Register in 1580, when it is called 'a new Northern Dittye', but there is evidence that it is of earlier date. There seem to be many ballads to the tune, also some examples of its conversion to sacred use, as, for instance (again in 1580), 'Green Sleeves moralized to the Scripture'. During the Civil War of the 17th cent. 'Greensleeves' was a party tune, the Cavaliers setting many political ballads to it. From this period the tune is sometimes known as The Blacksmith, under which name Pepys alludes to it (23 Apr. 1660). The tune is sung by Mistress Ford in Act 3 of Vaughan Williams's opera Sir John in Love to the words printed in A Handefull of Pleasant Delites, 1584. An orch. fantasia from the opera is frequently played. The tune is also used by *Holst in his St Paul's Suite for strs. and in his Suite No.2 for military band, and by Busoni in *Turandot.

Gregor, Bohumil (b Prague, 1926). Cz. conductor. Début Prague 1947. Ass. cond. Brno Opera, 1949–51, mus. dir. Ostrava Opera 1958–62, cond. Prague Nat. Th. 1962–6, Stockholm Opera 1966–9, Hamburg Opera 1969–72. Specialist in operas of Janáček. Brit. début Edinburgh Fest. 1964 (f. Brit. p. of From the *House of the Dead) and 1970 (f. Brit. p. of The *Excursions of Mr Brouček); Amer. début, S. Francisco 1969 (Jenůfa), returning to cond. Salome and Otello.

Gregor, Joseph (b Czernowitz, now Cernăuti, 1888; d nr. Vienna, 1961). Austrian writer and librettist. Assisted Max Reinhardt in Berlin prod. of Goethe's Faust, Part 2, 1910. On staff Vienna Nat. Library from 1918, founding theatrical archive 1922 and motion-picture archive 1929. Wrote 3 opera libs. for Richard Strauss between 1935 and 1940: *Friedenstag, *Daphne, and Die *Liebe der Danae. Wrote books on Viennese th. history, also on Strauss and Clemens Krauss. Correspondence with Strauss pubd. 1955.

Gregorian Chant. Solo and unison plainsong choral chants assoc. with Pope Gregory I which became the fundamental mus. of the RC Church. See Plainsong.

Gregorian Tones. The 8 plainsong melodies prescribed for the psalms in the RC Church, one in each of the 8 modes. They have alternative endings (or 'inflexions') so as to connect properly with the various following *antiphons. The *Tonus Peregrinus is additional to the 8.

Gregson, Edward (b Sunderland, 1945). Eng. composer and conductor. Prof. in mus. at Goldsmiths' Coll., Univ. of London and prof. of comp. RAM. Principal, RNCM, from 1996. Has cond. f.ps. of works by Brit. composers and was a cond. at the Berio Fest. in London, 1989. Wrote mus. for York Mystery Plays, 1976, and for Royal Shakespeare Co.'s Plantagenets trilogy 1988. Wrote title-mus. for BBC TV's Young Musician of the Year comp. (1988). Comps. incl.:

ORCH.: Music for Chamber Orch. (1968); tuba conc. (1976, arr. for orch. 1978); tb. conc. (1979); Metamorphoses, with elec. (1979); tpt. conc. (1983, rev. 2001); Contrasts (1983); Flourish (1978, rev.

1986); The Plantagenets Trilogy, th. band (1988); Blazon (1992); cl. conc. (1994); pf. conc., wind orch. (1995, rev. 1997); Stepping Out (1996); Three Matisse Impressions (1997); vn. conc. (2000); sax. conc. (2006).

WIND & BRASS: Quintet, 2 tpt., hns., tb., tuba (1967); March Prelude, brass band (1968); tuba conc. (band vers. 1976, wind band 1984); Equale Dances, 2 tpt., hns., tb., tuba (1983); Dances and Arias, brass band (1984); Sonata, 4 tb. (1984); Festivo, wind band (1985); Occasion, brass band (1986); Processional, brass quintet (1992); The Kings Go Forth, wind band (1996); Partita, wind band (1999); The Trumpets of the Angels, brass band (2000); An Age of Kings, brass band (2004).

VOCAL & CHORAL: In the Beginning, mixed ch., pf. (1966, rev. 1981); Missa brevis pacem, bar., boys' ch., wind (or mixed children's vv. or women's vv.), wind ens. (1987); Make a Joyful Noise, mixed ch., org., brass, perc. (1988); A Welcome Ode (1997); . . . and the seven trumpets (1998); The Dance, Forever the Dance (1999).

PIANO: Six Little Pieces (1982); sonata (1983, rev. 1986).

Greindl, Josef (b Munich, 1912; d Vienna, 1993). Ger. bass. Début Krefeld 1936 as Hunding in Die Walküre. Dusseldorf Opera 1938–42; Berlin Staatsoper 1942–8, Städtische Oper from 1948; Vienna Staatsoper from 1956. Bayreuth début 1943 (Pogner in Die Meistersinger), leading bass there from 1951. Salzburg 1949; NY Met 1952. Moses in first Ger. prod. of Moses und Aron, Berlin 1959. Guest appearances (esp. in Wagner) in London, USA, It. Prof. of singing, Vienna Hochschule from 1973.

grelots (Fr.). Little bells (e.g. sleigh bells, sometimes used in the orch.).

Grenadiere, Die beiden (The Two Grenadiers). Song for v. and pf. by R. Schumann, to poem by H. Heine (1797–1856), being No.1 of Romanzen und Balladen, Vol. II, Op.49 (1840). Also set by Wagner for v. and pf., 1840.

Gresham Professorship. In the will of Sir Thomas Gresham (c.1519–79), founder of London Royal Exchange, provision was made for 7 professorships in various subjects and for a lecture on mus. John *Bull was first mus. prof. (1596–1607). Later incumbents have incl. Sir Frederick Bridge, Sir Walford Davies, and Peter Latham.

Gretchen am Spinnrade (Gretchen at the Spinning-wheel). Song for v. and pf. by *Schubert to text from Goethe's Faust, comp. 19 Oct. 1814 (D118).

Grétry, André Ernest Modeste (b Liège, 1741; d Montmorency, Paris, 1813). Belg. (later Fr.) composer. Comp. mass for 4 vv. 1759, thereby winning patronage enabling study in Rome 1761–5. His intermezzo La Vendemmiatrice was successfully prod. 1765. Visited Geneva, where he met Voltaire, and returned to Paris 1767. In Paris his opéras-comiques, from Le Tableau parlant, 1769, quickly found favour. During the next 35 years he wrote some 50 operas, of which the best were *Zémire et Azor* (1771), *L'Amant jaloux* (1778), *L'Épreuve villageoise* (1784), *La Caravane du Caire* (1783) and *Panurge dans l'île des lanternes* (1785). His finest work is said to be his most serious opera, *Richard Cœur de Lion* (1784). Also comp. requiem, motets, str. qts., 6 pf. sonatas, fl. conc., and songs. His melodic gift was immense, but his lack of mastery of harmony and counterpoint was a permanent defect. Wrote several treatises. Standard edn. of his works in 42 vols. financed by Belg. Govt. from 1883.

Grieg, Edvard (Hagerup) (*b* Bergen, 1843; *d* Bergen, 1907). Norweg. composer, conductor, and pianist. (Great-grandfather was Scotsman named Greig.) Early tuition from mother, who was gifted pianist. On advice of violinist Ole *Bull, went to study at Leipzig Cons., working so hard that his health was permanently impaired. Settled in Copenhagen, being encouraged (but not taught) by *Gade. In 1865–6 visited Rome where he comp. his concert ov. *In Autumn* which later won Stockholm Acad. of Mus. prize. Married his cousin, the sop. Nina Hagerup, in 1867, she being the inspiration and interpreter of many of his songs. Settling in Christiania (Oslo), became teacher and cond. His comps. earned admiration of Liszt, whom he met in Rome 1870 where Liszt played Grieg's pf. conc. from MS at sight. In 1874 Grieg received life annuity from Norweg. Govt. and was asked by Ibsen to write incidental mus. to *Peer Gynt*. This had its f.p. in 1876 and made Grieg a nat. figure. He was a great favourite in Eng., where he and his wife gave recitals. He received Hon. D Mus. Cambridge 1894 and Oxford 1906. Befriended Delius and Percy Grainger. Grieg's mus. eschews the larger forms of opera and sym. (he wrote a sym. in 1864 but forbade perfs. after a few had been given, though this edict has been posthumously ignored) but within his chosen scale it is deeply poetic, superbly fashioned, and, in the songs especially, emotionally passionate. His nationalist idiom transcends local boundaries by reason of the strong individuality of his work. Comps. incl.:

INCIDENTAL MUSIC: *Sigurd Jorsalfar* (Bjørnson), Op.22 (1872); *Peer Gynt* (Ibsen), Op.23 (1874–5, rev. 1885, 1891–2).

ORCH.: *In Autumn*, concert ov., Op.11 (1866); *Peer Gynt*, suite No.1 from incid. mus., Op.46 (1874–5, rev. 1885, 1891–2), suite No.2, Op.55 (1874–5, rev. 1891 and 1892); 3 pieces from incid. mus. for *Sigurd Jorsalfar*, Op.56 (1872, rev. 1892); *Lyric Suite* (orch. of 4 items from Op.54 for pf.) (1904); pf. conc., Op.16 (1868, rev. 1906–7); 2 *Elegiac Melodies* (*Heart's Wounds* and *Last Spring*), Op.34 (version for str. of 2 songs from Op.33); *Holberg Suite*, str., Op.40 (1884) (also for pf.); 2 *Melodies*, str., Op.53 (1891); 2 *Norwegian Melodies*, str., (1869), orch. (1895), Op.63; 4 *Symphonic Dances*, Op.64 (orch. of work for pf., 4 hands) (1896–7); Sym. (1863–4, withdrawn by composer but perf. Oslo 1980 and recorded).

CHORUS AND ORCH.: *Before the Cloister Gate*, soloists, women's ch., Op.20 (1871); *Olaf Trygvason*, soloists, ch., Op.50 (1873, rev. 1889).

VOICE AND ORCH.: *Bergliot*, reciter, orch., Op.42 (1871, orch. 1885); *The Mountain Thrall*, bar., 2 hn., str., Op.32 (1877–8); 6 *Songs*, v., orch. (incl. 'Solvejg's Song' from *Peer Gynt*) (1870–80, rev. 1891–4).

CHAMBER MUSIC: Vn. Sonata, No.1 in F, Op.8 (1865); No.2 in G, Op.13 (1867), No.3 in C minor, Op.45 (1886–7); Str. Qt. in G minor, Op.27 (1877–8); vc. sonata in A minor, Op.36 (1883).

PIANO: 4 *Pieces*, Op.1 (1861); 4 *Humoresques*, Op.6 (1865); sonata in E minor, Op.7 (1865); *Lyric Pieces*: Book 1 (8 items), Op.12 (1867), Book 2 (8 items), Op.38 (1883), Book 3 (6 items), Op.43 (1884), Book 4 (7 items), Op.47 (1885–8), Book 5 (6 items), Op.54 (1891) (those orch. as *Lyric Suite* are No.1, *Shepherd's Boy*, 2, *Norwegian Rustic March*, 3, *Nocturne*, and 5, *March of the Dwarfs*), Book 6 (7 items), Op.57 (1893), Book 7 (6 items), Op.62 (1895), Book 8 (6 items), Op.65 (1897) (No.6 *Wedding Day at Troldhaugen*, also for orch.), Book 9 (6 items), Op.68 (1898), Book 10 (6 items), Op.71 (1901); *Sketches of Norwegian Life*, Op.19 (1870–1); *Ballade* in G minor, Op.24 (1875–6); 4 *Albumblätter*, Op.28 (1878); *Holberg Suite*, Op.40 (1884); 6 *Songs* transcr. for pf., Op.52 (incl. 'Solvejg's Song' as No.4); 19 *Norwegian Folk Tunes*, Op.66 (1896); *Norwegian Peasant Dances*, Op.72 (1902–3); *Moods*, Op.73 (1903–5).

PIANO (4 HANDS): 2 *Symphonic Pieces*, Op.14 (1863–4); 4 *Norwegian Dances*, Op.35 (also orch.) (1881); 2 *Waltz Caprices*, Op.37 (1883); *Symphonic Dances*, Op.64 (also orch.) (1897).

SONGS: Grieg's songs, numbering over 120, were pubd. as follows: 4 *Songs*, Op.2; 6 *Songs*, Op.4; 4 *Songs*, Op.5; 4 *Songs and Ballads*, Op.9; 4 *Songs*, Op.10; 4 *Songs*, Op.15; 8 *Songs*, Op.18; 4 *Songs*, Op.21; 3 *Songs from Peer Gynt* (1. *Solvejg's Song*, 2. *Solvejg's Cradle Song*, 3. *Peer Gynt's Serenade*), Op.23; 5 *Songs*, Op.25; 4 *Songs*, Op.26; 12 *Songs*, Op.33; 5 *Songs*, Op.39; 4 *Songs*, *From Fjeld and Fjord*, Op.44; 6 *Songs* (Ger. words), Op.48; 6 *Songs*, Op.49; 5 *Songs*, Op.58; 6 *Songs*, Op.59; 5 *Songs*, Op.60; 7 *Children's Songs*, Op.61; *Haugtussa* (The Mountain Maid), cycle of 8 songs, Op.67 (1895); 5 *Songs*, Op.69; 7 *Songs*, Op.70. The best-known individual titles with opus numbers are: *Hope* (or *Ambition*), Op.26, No.3; *'Neath the Roses*, Op.39, No.3; *Autumn Song*, Op.18, No.3; *A Dream*, Op.48, No.6; *Eros*, Op.70, No.2; *The First Meeting*, Op.21, No.4; *From Monte Pincio*, Op.39, No.5; *The Hut*, Op.18, No.4; *I love thee*, Op.5, No.3 (1864); *Spring*, Op.33, No.2; *The Swan*, Op.25, No.1; *With a Water Lily*, Op.25, No.3.

Griffes, Charles (Tomlinson) (*b* Elmira, NY, 1884; *d* NY, 1920). Amer. composer. Taught at boys' school in Tarrytown, NY, from 1908 until his death. His mus. was beginning to be recognized as important just before he died. Much influenced by Fr. mus. impressionists, he also used Japanese and Amer.-Indian themes and oriental scales. In his later works, polymetric and polytonal features occur. Prin. works:

DRAMATIC: *The Kairn of Koridwen*, dance-drama, 5 ww., cel., hp., pf. (1916); *Shojo*, Japanese dance-pantomime, 4 ww., strs., hp., perc. (1917).

ORCH.: *Nocturne* (1919); *The *White Peacock* (orch. in 1919 of No.1 of *4 Roman Sketches* for pf. of 1915–16); *Poem*, fl., orch. (1918); *The *Pleasure Dome of Kubla Khan* (sym.-poem after Coleridge arr. from pf. piece of 1912) (1917).

VOICE & PIANO: *Tone Images*, mez. (Wilde and Henley) (1912); *3 Songs* (1916); *3 Poems of Fiona MacLeod*, sop. (also with orch.) (1918).

CHAMBER MUSIC: *2 Sketches Based on Indian Themes*, str. qt. (c.1918).

PIANO: *3 Tone Pictures* (1911–12); *The Pleasure Dome of Kubla Khan* (1912, orch. 1917); *Fantasy Pieces* (1912–14); *4 Roman Sketches* (1915–16); Sonata (1917–18).

Griffiths, Paul (*b* Bridgend, Glam., 1947). Eng. music critic. Freelance critic from 1971. Chief mus. critic *The Times* 1982–92; *New Yorker* 1992–6, *New York Times* 1996–2005. Contributor (especially on late 20th cent. subjects) to *New Grove Dictionary of Music and Musicians* (1980) and *New Oxford Companion to Music* (1983). Author of monographs on Boulez, Cage, Maxwell Davies, and Ligeti, and *A Concise History of Modern Music* (1978), *The String Quartet* (1983), *Bartók* (1984), *An Encyclopaedia of 20th Century Music* (1986), *Stravinsky* (1992), and *Penguin Companion to Classical Music* (2004). Compiled Mozart *pasticcio*, *The Jewel Box*, for Opera North (f.p. Nottingham 1991). Trans. *Die Zauberflöte* (1993). Librettist for Carter's *What Next?* (1998).

Grigny, Nicolas de (*b* Rheims, 1672; *d* Rheims, 1703). Fr. organist. Org. Rheims Cath. from 1695. Comp. of *Pièces d'Orgue*, admired by Bach.

Griller, Sidney (Aaron) (*b* London, 1911; *d* London, 1993). Eng. violinist. Founded Griller Str. Qt. 1928 (disbanded 1961), resident qt. at Univ. of Calif. Head of str. dept., Royal Irish Acad. of Mus., Dublin, 1963–73. Head of chamber mus., RAM, 1964–82. CBE 1951.

Grinke, Frederick (*b* Winnipeg, 1911; *d* Ipswich, 1987). Brit. violinist of Canadian birth. Member of Kutcher Qt. for 6 years, leader of Boyd Neel Orch. 1937–46, later becoming soloist and teacher. Champion of Eng. mus., notably that of Vaughan Williams, Rubbra, Berkeley. CBE 1979.

Grisélidis. Opera (*conte lyrique*) in prol. and 3 acts by Massenet to lib. by A. Silvestre and E. Morand after their play *Grisélidis* (1891) based on story in Boccaccio's *Decameron* (1349–51). Comp. 1894, rev. 1898. Prod. Paris 1901, NY (Manhattan Opera Co.) 1910, Wexford 1982, London (GSMD) 1993.

Grisi, Carlotta (*b* Visinada, 1819; *d* St Jean, Switz., 1899). It. dancer. Contract at Paris Opéra 1841, creating divertissement in *La favorite* with

Petipa and title-role in *Giselle*. London début 1836. Most admired ballerina of her time. Cousin of the sisters *Grisi.

Grisi, Giuditta (*b* Milan, 1805; *d* Robecco d'Oglio, nr. Cremona, 1840). It. mezzo-soprano. Début Vienna 1826 in Rossini's *Bianca e Falliero*. Sang several seasons in Venice. Bellini wrote role of Romeo for her in *I Capuleti e i Montecchi*. Sang Norma at Bologna 1833. Retired 1838.

Grisi, Giulia (*b* Milan, 1811; *d* Berlin, 1869). It. soprano, sister of Giuditta, who taught her. Début in Bologna 1828 as Emma in Rossini's *Zelmira*. Milan 1831. Created Juliet opposite her sister in *I Capuleti e i Montecchi* and Adalgisa in *Norma*. Sang regularly in Paris 1832–49, making her début in the title-role of *Semiramide* and creating roles of Elvira in *I Puritani* and Norina in *Don Pasquale*. London début 1834, singing there every season except 1842, until 1861. US début 1854. One of great singers of her day. Partnered often by the ten. Mario, her lifelong companion, with whom she visited Russ., USA, and Spain. Retired 1861.

Grist, Reri (*b* NY, 1932). Amer. soprano. Began career in Broadway musicals (*Carmen Jones* and *West Side Story*). Début with NY City Opera, 1959, and Santa Fe Opera. Cologne 1960 (Queen of Night in *Die Zauberflöte*); Salzburg 1964. Sang at Milan, Chicago, Munich, Vienna, Glyndebourne. CG 1962, NY Met 1966.

Gritton, Susan (*b* Reigate, 1965). Eng. soprano. Read botany at Oxford and London Univs. before taking up singing. Won Ferrier Prize 1994. London recital début 1994. Extensive international concert career. Glyndebourne début 1994 (Barbarina). Roles incl. Governess (*Turn of the Screw*), Handel's Fulvia and Cleopatra, and Marzelline (*Fidelio*). ENO principal from 2000. CG début 1997 (*The Pilgrim's Progress*).

GRNCM. Graduate of the *Royal Northern College of Music, Manchester.

Grobe, Donald (*b* Ottawa, Ill., 1929; *d* Berlin, 1986). Amer. tenor. Opera début in *Rigoletto*, Chicago 1952. Salzburg Fest. début 1962. Member of Deutsche Oper, Berlin, from 1960, where he created Wilhelm in *Der *junge Lord* (1965) and sang Aschenbach in Ger. première of *Death in Venice* (1974). Débuts: Brit. 1965 (Edinburgh Fest. with Bavarian Nat. Opera); NY Met 1968; CG 1972 (with Bavarian Nat. Opera).

Grofé, Ferde [Grofe, Ferdinand Rudolf von] (*b* NY, 1892; *d* Santa Monica, Calif., 1972). Amer. composer, conductor, and arranger. Violist in Los Angeles SO for 10 years, also played pf. and vn. in th. bands. Work as arranger admired by the band-leader Paul Whiteman, who engaged him to arr. the symphonic jazz which was attracting attention. Thus he orchestrated *Gershwin's *Rhapsody in Blue* (1924). Wrote several works in popular symphonic idiom e.g.

Mississippi Suite, Hollywood Suite, and, most popular of all, *Grand Canyon Suite* (1931), cond. Paul Whiteman; also 1-movt. pf. conc. (1932–59).

gros, grosse (Fr.). Great, large. In the case of an org. stop this means of low pitch, e.g. 16′ instead of 8′.

gross, grosse (Ger.). Great, large. *grösser*, greater.

grosse caisse (Fr.). big box, i.e. *bass drum (It. *gran cassa*).

Grosseflöte (Ger.). Large flute. (1) The normal fl. (2) Metal org. stop of 8′ length and pitch.

Grosse Fuge (Great Fugue). Fugue in B♭ major for str. qt. by Beethoven. Intended as finale of his Str. Qt. No.13 in B♭ major, Op.130, comp. 1825–6. After f.p. in March 1826, the publisher Artaria persuaded Beethoven to substitute a less onerous finale, so the fugue was detached and pubd. as separate work, Op.133, in 1827. Beethoven made arr. for pf., 4 hands, Op.134. In recent times, some qts. have restored it as finale of Op.130. Although it is customary to refer to it by its Ger. title, Beethoven wrote the title in Fr., *Grande Fugue tantôt libre tantôt recherché*.

Grosse Orgelmesse (Great Mass with Organ). Popular name for Haydn's Mass No.2 in E♭, 1766, in which the org. has an important part. See also *Kleine Orgelmesse*.

grosses Orchester (Ger.). Full orch.

grosse Trommel (Ger.). Great drum, i.e. *bass drum.

gros tambour (Fr.). Great drum. Same as *grosse caisse, i.e. *bass drum.

ground bass (It. *basso ostinato*, 'obstinate bass'). Short thematic motif in bass which is constantly repeated with changing harmonies while upper parts proceed and vary. Originated in *cantus firmus* of choral mus. and became popular in 17th cent., particularly in Eng., as a ground for variations in str. mus. Hence the no. of 'divisions on a ground'. Examples exist by Byrd, Purcell, Frescobaldi, Carissimi, and Cavalli. See *chaconne*.

Groupe de Recherches Musicales (Group for musical research). EMS (the first), est. at Fr. Radio in 1951 by Pierre *Schaeffer, which has exerted wide influence on composers invited to work there, e.g. Messiaen, Boulez, Stockhausen, Berio, and Xenakis.

Grout, Donald Jay (*b* Rock Rapids, Iowa, 1902; *d* Skaneateles, NY, 1987). Amer. musicologist and teacher. Taught at Harvard 1936–42; assoc. prof. of mus., Univ. of Texas 1943–5; prof. of mus. Cornell Univ. 1945–70. Books incl. *A Short History of Opera* (1947, rev. 1965), *History of Western Music* (1960, rev. 1973). Editor of operas of A. Scarlatti.

Grove, (Sir) **George** (*b* Clapham, 1820; *d* Sydenham, 1900). Eng. writer on music and teacher. Trained as civil engineer, constructing several railway stations and also taking part in building of Crystal Palace, of which he was secretary 1852–73. From 1856 became increasingly involved in mus., writing programme notes for Crystal Palace concerts for 40 years. Went with Sullivan to Vienna in 1867 on successful quest for missing items of Schubert's *Rosamunde* mus. and at the same time propounding the now disproved theory of a 'lost' *Gastein* sym. by Schubert. In 1873 began work on compilation of vast *Grove's Dictionary of Music and Musicians*, pubd. in 4 vols. at intervals from 1879 to 1889. First dir. of RCM 1882–94. Also wrote *Beethoven and his Nine Symphonies* (1884). Among his other activities were building lighthouses in W Indies, founding Palestine Exploration fund, ed. biblical dictionary, primer of geography, and *Macmillan's Magazine* (1868–83). Knighted 1883.

Groves, (Sir) **Charles** (Barnard) (*b* London, 1915; *d* London, 1992). Eng. conductor. Ch. master at BBC 1938–42. Assoc. cond. BBC Th. Orch. 1942–4. Cond. BBC Northern Orch., Manchester, 1944–51, Bournemouth SO 1951–61, WNO 1961–3, Royal Liverpool PO 1963–77, ENO 1978–9. During his time in Liverpool, cond. cycle of Mahler syms. and many works by Eng. composers from Elgar to Maxwell Davies. OBE 1958, CBE 1968. Knighted 1973.

Grove's Dictionary of Music and Musicians. Largest and most far-ranging mus. dictionary pubd. in Eng. First compiled and ed. by George *Grove (1879–89, 4 vols.); 2nd edn. ed. J. A. *Fuller Maitland (1904–10, 5 vols.); 3rd edn. ed. H. C. Colles (1927, 5 vols.); 4th edn. ed. H. C. Colles (1940, 5 vols. + suppl.); 5th edn. ed. Eric Blom (1954, 9 vols. + suppl.); 6th edn. ed. Stanley Sadie (1980, 20 vols., title changed to *The New Grove Dictionary of Music and Musicians*, 2nd edn. 2001, 29 vols.). The *New Grove* has had 'satellite' pubs., incl. *Dictionary of Musical Instruments* (1984), *Dictionary of American Music* (4 vols., 1986), *Concise Dictionary of Music* (1988), *Dictionary of Opera* (4 vols., 1992), and *Dictionary of Women Composers* (1994).

Growing Castle, The. Chamber opera in 2 acts by *Williamson, for 4 singers and chamber ens., to his own lib. based on Strindberg's *Dream Play*. Comp. 1968. Prod. Dynevor Fest. 1968.

GRSM. Graduate of the *Royal Schools of Music.

Gr. Tr. Abbreviation for *grosse Trommel* (Ger.), bass drum.

Gruber, Franz Xaver (*b* Unterweizburg, 1787; *d* Hallein, nr. Salzburg, 1863). Austrian composer, great-great-grandfather of H. K. *Gruber. Although a manual labourer, studied org. and, at 28, became org. at Oberndorf. On Christmas Eve 1818, the curate brought him a poem to be set to mus. The result was the carol *Stille Nacht, heilige Nacht* (Silent Night, Holy Night).

Gruber, H(einz) **K**(arl) (*b* Vienna, 1943). Austrian composer, double-bass player, and baritone. In Vienna Boys' Choir, 1953–7. Db. player in Die Reihe ens. from 1961. Prin. db., Tonkünstler Orch.

1963–9. Co-founder of 'MOB Art and Tone ART' ens., 1968–71. Joined Austrian Radio SO 1969. Soloist in *Frankenstein!!*, Liverpool 1978. Success of this work led to other commissions and to international fame. His mus. borrows from all sources to become unpredictably original and outrageous, but always intrinsically Viennese. Works incl.:

STAGE: *Die Vertreibung aus dem Paradies* (The Expulsion from Paradise), melodrama (1966, rev. 1979); *Gomorra* (1990–1); *Gloria von Jaxtberg* (1992–3); *der herr nordwind* (2003–5).

ORCH.: *Manhattan Broadcasts*, light orch. (1962–4); *Frankenstein!!*, pan-demonium, bar. *chansonnier*, orch. (1976–7); *Phantom-Bilder*, small orch. (1977); vn. conc. No.1 ('. . . *aus schatten duft gewebt*') (1977–8, rev. 1992), No.2 (*Nebelsteinmusik*), vn., str. (1988); *Charivari* (1981, rev. 1984/1999); *Rough Music*, conc., perc., orch. (1982–3); vc. conc. (1989); tpt. conc. (*Ariel*) (1999); *Dancing in the Dark* (2002).

ENS.: *3 MOB Pieces*, 7 instr., perc. (1968, rev. 1977); *Frankenstein!!*, ens. version, bar., 12 players (1979); *Anagramm*, 6 vcs. (1987); *Overture: Gloria von Jaxtberg* (1992); *Zeirfluren*, mixed ens./chamber orch. (2001).

BRASS BAND: *Demilitarized Zones* (1979).

CHORAL: *5 Kinderlieder*, unacc. female vv. (1965, rev. 1980).

CHAMBER MUSIC: *4 Pieces*, solo vn. (1963); *6 Episodes from a Discontinued Chronicle*, pf. (1967); *Castles in the Air*, pf. (1981); *Exposed Throat*, tpt. (2000).

TV FILM: *Bring me the head of Amadeus* (1991).

Gruberova, Edita (*b* Bratislava, 1946). Slovak soprano. Opera début Bratislava 1968 as Rosina in *Il barbiere di Siviglia*. Vienna State Opera début 1970. Joined Vienna co. 1972, singing coloratura roles. Débuts: Glyndebourne 1973; Salzburg Fest. 1974; NY Met 1977; CG 1984. Major success as Zerbinetta (*Ariadne auf Naxos*).

Gruenberg, Erich (*b* Vienna, 1924). Austrian-born violinist and conductor (Brit. cit. 1950). Leader, Palestine Broadcasting Orch. 1938–45. Settled in London 1946. Leader Stockholm PO 1956–8, LSO 1962–5, RPO 1972–6. Frequent chamber-music player in str. qts. and pf. trios. Champion of contemp. vn. concs. Prof. at RAM. OBE 1994.

Gruenberg, Louis (*b* nr. Brest-Litovsk, now Brest, 1884; *d* Los Angeles, 1964). Russ.-born Amer. composer and pianist. Début as pianist with Berlin PO, 1912. Gave up concert touring for comp. on return to USA. Head of comp. dept., Chicago Mus. Coll., 1930–3. Comps. strongly influenced by jazz. Success with opera *The Emperor Jones* (based on O'Neill play), NY Met 1933. His vn. conc. was written for Heifetz. Also wrote film scores. Comps. incl.: *The Emperor Jones* (1933); *Green Mansions* (for radio) (1937); *Volpone* (1945); operas; 5 syms. (1919–48); *The Hill of Dreams*, orch. (1921); *Jazz Suite* (1929); 2 pf. concs.; vn. conc. (1944); 2 vn. sonatas; str. qt.; pf. quintet; pf. pieces incl. *Jazzberries*, *6 Jazz Epigrams*, etc.

Grumiaux, Arthur (*b* Villers-Perwin, Belg., 1921; *d* Brussels, 1986). Belg. violinist. Début Brussels 1940, career then interrupted by war. Début in London 1945, then worldwide career as leading soloist. Prof. of vn., Brussels Cons., from 1949. Salzburg Fest. début 1949. Became a baron 1973.

Grümmer, Elisabeth (*b* Niederjeutz, Alsace-Lorraine, 1911; *d* Berlin, 1986). Ger. soprano. Began career as actress in Aachen. Singing début there 1940 (at *Karajan's suggestion) as First Flower Maiden in *Parsifal* and then Oktavian in *Der Rosenkavalier*. Sang opera in Duisburg and Prague. Berlin Städtische (later Deutsche Oper) 1946–72. Sang Ellen Orford in f. Berlin p. of *Peter Grimes*. Débuts: CG 1951; Salzburg 1953; Bayreuth 1957; NY Met 1967. Notable in Wagner, Mozart, and Strauss.

Grundstimmen (Ger.). Ground voices: foundation-stops of an org.

Grundheber, Franz (*b* Trier, 1937). Ger. baritone. Member of Hamburg Opera from 1966. Vienna début 1983 as Mandryka in *Arabella*. Salzburg Fest. début 1984; CG 1992.

Gruppen (Groups). Comp. for 3 orchs. by *Stockhausen, 1955–7, each placed in a different part of the hall and each playing different mus. F. Brit. p. 1967.

gruppetto (It.). Grouplet. The turn, a type of ornament in vocal and instr. mus. *gruppetto* implies a 4-note figure, the note above, the note itself, the note below, and the note itself. This figure is perf. *after* the note itself or *instead of* it, according to whether the turn sign is placed *after* the note itself or *over* it.

The inflection of the upper or lower note of the turn (in either form) is shown by the placing of a sharp, flat, natural, etc., sign above or below.

When the *gruppetto* occurs after the note the taste of the performer governs the division of the time available. The general principle seems to be that the *gruppetto* is to be perf. fairly rapidly. To bring this about, the first example just given (if occurring in a slow tempo) might be treated thus:

whilst in a very quick tempo it might be treated as follows (indeed there might be no time to treat it in any other way):

The number of different examples given in different textbooks is very large, and no two textbooks quite agree, but the above statement gives the chief general principles accepted by all. They also apply, of course, to the inverted turn, which begins with the *lower* auxiliary note, instead of the upper one.

GSMD. *Guildhall School of Music and Drama.

G string (vn.). The lowest str., possessing a rich tone. Composers sometimes direct that a passage should be played entirely on that str. Bach's so-called 'Air on the G string' is really the 2nd movt. from his 3rd orch. suite in D, rearr. by *Wilhelmj in 1871 as a vn. solo in the key of C, the melody transposed down a 9th, and with pf. acc.

Guadagni, Gaetano (*b* Lodi, *c.*1725; *d* Padua, 1792). It. castrato contralto, later soprano. Début Parma 1746. Joined *buffa* co. which visited Eng. 1748, remaining there and in Dublin until 1755. Handel engaged him to sing in *Messiah* 1750, and *Samson*. After studying with Conti in Lisbon, created role of Orpheus in Gluck's *Orfeo ed Euridice*, Vienna 1762, and *Telemaco*, 1765. Several arias in *Messiah*, incl. 'But who may abide', were transposed or rewritten for him by Handel.

guajira. Sp. dance, with rhythm constantly alternating between 6/8 and 3/4. Also found in varied form in Cuba where it is a narrative folk-song.

guaracha, guarracha. Sp. and Mexican folk dance in 2 sections respectively in triple and duple time. Dancer usually accompanies himself on gui.

Guarneri [Guarnerius]. It. family, makers of vns., vcs., etc. in 17th and 18th cents. Founder was Andrea (*b* Cremona, *c.*1626; *d* Cremona, 1698),

fellow-pupil with *Stradivari of Nicola *Amati. His sons were Pietro Giovanni (*b* Cremona, 1655; *d* Mantua, 1720) who settled as vn.-maker in Mantua, and Giuseppe Giovanni Battista (*b* Cremona, 1666; *d* Cremona *c.*1739) who developed an individual style. But most celebrated of family was Bartolomeo Giuseppe (*b* Cremona, 1698; *d* Cremona, 1744), nephew of Andrea, and known as 'del Gesù', from the letters I.H.S. on his labels. Regarded as 2nd only to Stradivari. Revived early Brescian sch. traditions, making instrs. with rich, powerful tone. One was owned by *Paganini, who bequeathed it to city of Genoa.

Guarneri Quartet. Amer. str. qt. formed 1964 in Vermont at suggestion of Alexander Schneider. Members were Arnold Steinhardt (*b* Los Angeles, 1937) and John Dally (*b* Madison, Wisc., 1936) vns., Michael Tree (*b* Newark, NJ, 1935) va., and David Soyer (*b* Philadelphia, 1925) vc. Visited London 1970 to perf. all Beethoven's quartets, which it has also recorded.

Guarnieri, (Mozart) **Camargo** (*b* Tiété, São Paulo, 1907; *d* São Paulo, 1993). Brazilian composer and conductor. Went to Paris 1938, studying comp. and orch. with *Koechlin. Returned to São Paulo, becoming cond. of Phil. Soc. and prof. at Cons. Colourful mus. using Brazilian folk mus. at times. Comps. incl. 2 operas; 4 syms. (1944–63); *Dansa Brasileira* for orch.; *Brasiliana*, suite for orch.; 5 pf. concs. (1936–70); 2 vn. concs. (1940, 1953); 3 str. qts. (1932–62); 5 vn. sonatas (1930–62); pf. pieces; songs.

Gubaidulina, Sofia (*b* Chistopol, Tatar, 1931). Russ. composer. In 1975, with Artyomow and Suslin, founded Astreya, a group which improvised on rare Russ., Caucasian, and Central Asian folk instr. Her *Stufen* for orch. won first prize at Rome int. comp. competition 1975. Regarded, with *Schnittke and *Denisov, as one of leaders of Soviet mus. since death of Shostakovich. Has wide literary interests and her music is influenced by religious faith. Comps. incl.: *Fatseliya*, sop., orch. (1956); pf. quintet (1957); *Chaconne*, pf. (1962); *Allegro rustico*, fl., pf. (1963); sonata, pf. (1965); *Night in Memphis*, mez., male vv., orch. (1968); *Musical Toys*, pf. (1969); *Fairytale Poem*, orch. (1971); str. qts.: No.1 (1971), No.2 (1987), No.3 (1987), No.4 (1990); *Roses*, sop., pf. (1972); conc., bn., low str. (1975); conc. for sym. orch. and jazz band, with 3 sop. (1976); *Light and Darkness*, org. (1976); *Hour of the Soul*, perc., mez., orch. (1976–88); *Misterioso*, 7 perc. (1977); *Sounds of the Forest*, fl., pf. (1978); *De profundis*, bayan (1978); *In croce*, vc., org. (1979); *Offertorium*, vn. conc. (1980, rev. 1982, 1986); sonata (*Rejoice!*), vn., vc. (1981); *7 Words*, vc., bayan, str. (1982); *Quasi hoquetus*, va., bn., pf. (1984); *Stimmen . . . Verstummen . . .*, sym. in 12 movts., orch. (1986); *Hommage à T. S. Eliot*, sop., octet (1987); *Answer without Question*, 3 orchs. (1988); *Jauchzt vor Gott*, ch., org. (1989); *Oration for the Age of Aquarius*, opera-ballet-oratorio (1991); *Jetzt immer Schnee*, cantata, vv., instr. (1993); *Zeitgestalten* (*Figures of Time*), orch. (1993–4); va. conc. (1996); *Two Paths: A Dedication to Mary* *and Martha*, 2 va., orch. (1998); *Johannes-Passion*, soli, ch., orch. (2000); *The Light of the End*, orch. (2003); *Verwandlung*, tb., sax. qt., vc., db., tam-tam (2004); *The Deceitful Face of Hope and Despair*, fl., orch. (2005); *Feast during a Plague*, orch. (2006).

Gueden, Hilde (*b* Vienna, 1917; *d* Klosterneu-berg, 1988). Austrian soprano. Worked in oper-etta at 16. Opera début as Cherubino, Zurich 1939. Went to Munich Staatsoper 1942 on recom-mendation of Strauss and Clemens Krauss. Also sang in Rome and Florence 1942–5. Salzburg Fest. début 1946. Vienna Staatsoper 1947–73. CG début 1947 (visit of Vienna co.). Kammersän-gerin, Vienna Opera, 1950. NY Met début 1951, singing there for 9 seasons. Sang Anne in Amer. première of *The Rake's Progress* 1953. Specialized in Strauss roles (Daphne, Sophie, etc.), Mozart, Verdi, but equally at home in Weill and Lehár.

Guerre des bouffons. See *Bouffons, Querelle des*.

Guest, Douglas (Albert) (*b* Mortomley, Yorks., 1916; *d* Minchinhampton, 1996). Eng. organist and composer. Dir. of mus., Uppingham Sch. 1945–50, org., Salisbury Cath. 1950–7, org. Wor-cester Cath. 1957–63, dir. of mus. Westminster Abbey 1963–81, prof. RCM 1963–81. CVO 1975.

Guest, George (Hywel) (*b* Bangor, N. Wales, 1924; *d* Cardiff, 2003). Welsh organist and conductor. Org. and choirmaster St John's Coll., Cambridge, 1951–91, making it one of the finest choirs in the world, with a continental rather than Eng. style. Ass. lect. in mus., Cambridge Univ. 1953–6. lect. 1956–82. Prof. of harmony and counterpoint, RAM, 1960–1. Org., Cambridge Univ. 1974–91. Art. dir. Llandaff Fest. 1985. CBE 1987.

Guglielmi, Petro Alessandro (*b* Massa, 1728; *d* Rome, 1804). It. composer. First of many operas perf. in Naples 1757; wrote 25 in next decade, several of them (e.g. *La sposa fedele*) being popular throughout Eur. Lived in London 1767–72, writ-ing several operas incl. *Ezio* (King's Th., 1770). On return to Naples, his output showed no sign of slackening and he also wrote oratorios. Choir-master of St Peter's, Rome, 1793.

Gui, Vittorio (*b* Rome, 1885; *d* Florence, 1975). It. conductor and composer. Début Rome, 1907 (*La Gioconda*). Ass. to Toscanini, Milan, 1923–5 (début with *Salome*) and 1932–4. Cond. Florence Orch. 1928–40, helped to found (1933) Maggio Musicale Fiorentino, where he cond. rarities such as *Luisa Miller*, *Armide*, and *Médée*. First It. invited to cond. at Salzburg Fest., preceding Tos-canini by 3 weeks in 1933. Took over from Tos-canini as cond. of *Falstaff* for 1938 fest. CG début 1938. Cond., Glyndebourne Opera 1952–60, after which 'artistic counsellor'. Last cond. at Glynde-bourne in 1964. Noted for revivals of neglected and rare Rossini operas, e.g. *L'italiana in Algeri* (Turin 1925, with *Supervia*) and *Le Comte Ory* (Glyndebourne, 1955). Comp. operas, sym.-poems, and critical essays.

Guidarini, Marco (*b* Genoa, 1960). It. conductor. Début as cellist then turned to cond. Cond. *Fal-*

staff, Lyons 1986. Wexford Fest. 1988; London début 1989 (QEH); Opera North 1989; WNO 1990; ENO 1990; Scottish Opera 1991; GTO 1992.

Guido d'Arezzo [Aretinus] (*b* Paris, c.995; *d* Avel-lano, after 1033). It. theorist, teacher, and monk who reformed mus. notation. Educated in Bene-dictine Abbey and Pomposa, nr. Ferrara, where his innovations trained singers to learn new chants quickly. Lived in Arezzo from c.1025, training singers for the cathedrals. Pubd. his theories in *Micrologus* (1025). Called to Rome by the Pope, 1028, to explain his innovations. In-ventor of *solmization, whereby names 'ut', 're', 'mi' etc. were used as indications of relative posi-tions of notes of the scale; and of the 'Guidonian Hand', an aid to memory in which tips and joints of the fingers are given names of various notes. See *hexachords*.

Guilbert, Yvette (*b* Paris, 1865; *d* Aix-en-Prov-ence, 1944). Fr. *diseuse*, folk-singer, and actress. Protégée of Charles Zidler, impresario of Paris Hippodrome. Début as actress 1877. In 1890 be-gan to sing her own or individual arr. of others' songs at café-concerts and had immense success at Moulin Rouge, Montmartre. Eng. début 1893, Amer. début 1896. From 1901 sang a new reper-tory from medieval period to 19th cent., acc. by instr. quintet. Her artistry was admired by Verdi and Gounod, among many others.

Guildhall School of Music and Drama. Mus. acad. est. 1880 by Corporation of City of London in warehouse at Aldermanbury. Moved in 1887 to Blackfriars, when number of students had risen in 7 years from 62 to 2,700. Buildings extended in 1898 and 1970. In 1977 moved to present building in *Barbican Arts Centre. Name changed to add 'and Drama' in 1935. Full-time courses. First prin. Weist-Hill 1880–92, followed by Sir Joseph Barnby 1892–6, W. H. Cummings 1896–1910, Sir Landon Ronald 1910–38, Edric Cundell 1938–59, Gordon Thorne 1959–65, Allen Percival 1965–78, John Hosier 1978–88, Ian Hors-brugh 1989–2002, Genista McIntosh 2002–3, Barry Ife from 2003.

Guillaume Tell (William Tell). Opera in 4 acts by Rossini (his last) to lib. by de Jouy and Bis after Schiller's play (1804) based on the legend. Prod. Paris 1829, London 1830 (in version adapted by Planché and Bishop) and 1839 (orig. version), NY 1831. Operas on same subject by Grétry (1791) and B. A. Weber (1795).

Guiraud, Ernest (*b* New Orleans, 1837; *d* Paris, 1892). Fr. composer and teacher. Won *Grand Prix de Rome*, 1859 (as his father had done in 1827). First opera, *Le Roi David*, prod. New Orleans 1852. On staff Paris Cons. from 1876, prof. of comp. from 1880. Wrote treatise on instrumentation. Comp. several operas, the last, *Frédégonde*, being completed by Saint-Saëns (1895), ballet *Gretna Green*, and other works, but remembered today because he comp. the recits. for *Carmen* and com-pleted orchestration of *Les contes d'Hoffmann*. Compiled Suite No.2 from Bizet's *L'Arlésienne*.

guitar (Fr. *guitare*, Sp. *guitarra*). Stringed instr., plucked and fretted, of ancient origin, its 16th-cent. ancestor being the Sp. *vihuela de mano*. Not unlike a lute but with flat or slightly rounded back. Now has 6 courses, tuned E–A–d–g–b–e′. Became very popular in 19th cent: first great virtuoso of int. fame was Fernando Sor, 1778–1839; while such composers as Boccherini, Berlioz, and Paganini played and comp. for the instr. Present-day revival initiated by Spaniard Francisco Tárrega (1852–1909), and popularity has continued in 20th cent. with emergence of virtuosi such as Segovia, John Williams, and Julian Bream. Concs. have been written for guitar by Villa-Lobos, Ponce, Castelnuovo-Tedesco, Stephen Dodgson, Arnold, and Richard Rodney Bennett. Also used in popular mus. (skiffle, pop, folk, etc.) and in jazz (especially elec. gui. (connected to amplifier) and bass guitar). See *Hawaiian guitar*.

Gulda, Friedrich (*b* Vienna, 1930; *d* Weissenbach am Altersee, 2000). Austrian pianist and composer. Début 1944. 1st prize Geneva int. contest 1946. Worldwide reputation as recitalist. NY début 1950. Salzburg Fest. début 1951. Also jazz player, having comp. several jazz pieces. Comp. 2 pf. concs. and cadenzas for several repertory concs.

Gung'l, Joseph (*b* Zsàmbèk, Hung., 1810; *d* Weimar, 1889). Hung. composer and bandmaster. Formed own 36-man band in Berlin 1843, touring Eur. and visiting USA 1849. Kapellmeister to Emperor of Austria from 1876. Comp. over 300 dances and marches.

Guntram. Opera in 3 acts by R. Strauss (his 1st) to his own lib. Comp. 1887–93. Prod. Weimar 1894. Rev. 1934–9. Revived at Weimar 1940. F. Eng. p. BBC broadcast 1981; NY (concert) 1983.

Gurlitt, Manfred (*b* Berlin, 1890; *d* Tokyo, 1973). Ger. composer and conductor. Cond. at Essen 1911–12, Augsburg 1912–14, and Bremen 1914–27. His comps. were banned by the Nazis. Went to Japan 1939, forming Gurlitt Opera Co. Works incl. 9 operas (incl. **Wozzeck*, 1920–5, prod. Bremen 1925) *Goya Symphony* (1938), *Shakespeare Symphony* (choral) (1954), pf. quintet, chamber conc., and songs.

Gurney, Ivor (*b* Gloucester, 1890; *d* Dartford, 1937). Eng. composer, organist, and poet. Ass. org. Gloucester Cath. 1906–11. Joined army 1915, gassed at Passchendaele 1917. Wrote poetry, setting several of his own poems to mus. as well as poetry by Housman, etc. Song-cycles, of touching beauty and promise, incl. *Ludlow and Teme*, for ten., str. qt., and pf., and *The Western Playland* for bar., str. qt., and pf. Other songs incl. *Desire in Spring*, *Sleep*, *In Flanders*, and *Severn Meadows*. Returned to RCM 1919 but declared insane 1922. In last years of his life various friends, incl. Marion Scott, Howells, Finzi, and Ferguson, prepared the best of his work for pub., but over 200 songs remain in MS, also 6 vn. sonatas, 5 str. qts., and *A Gloucestershire Rhapsody* for orch.

Gurrelieder (Songs of Gurre). Work by Schoen-berg, comp. 1900–3 and 1910–11 and given no Op. no., being setting for 5 soloists, speaker, 3 male chs., mixed ch., and orch. of a Ger. trans. from the Danish of poems by J. P. Jacobsen. (Gurra is castle where the 14th-cent. heroine Tove lives.) Mus. is in Schoenberg's Wagnerian style but foreshadows his maturity. Requires huge orch. incl. 10 hn., 8 fl., 4 Wagner tubas, 6 timp., and iron chains. F.p. Vienna 1913, cond. F. Schreker; London (broadcast) 1928; Philadelphia 1932, cond. Stokowski. The *Song of the Wood Dove* (*Lied der Waldtaube*) was arr. by Schoenberg for v. and chamber orch. 1922.

gusla (gusle, guzla). Ancient 1-str. bowed instr. still popular in some Slavonic regions (not to be confused with **gusli*).

guslar. A player on the **gusli*.

gusli (guslee). Ancient Russ. instr. of the zither family (not to be confused with **gusla*). Imitated by Rimsky-Korsakov in his opera *Sadko*.

Gustafson, Nancy (*b* Evanston, Ill., 1956). Amer. soprano. Début S. Francisco Opera 1983 (Woglinde in *Die Walküre*). Sang Donna Elvira (*Don Giovanni*) with Glyndebourne in Hong Kong 1986. Glyndebourne début 1988; CG 1988; Scottish Opera 1989; NY Met 1989; La Scala 1990.

Gutheil-Schoder, Marie (*b* Weimar, 1874; *d* Bad Ilmenau, 1935). Ger. soprano. Début Weimar 1891 and sang Carmen 1895. Engaged for Vienna Opera by Mahler, 1900, remaining until 1926. Sang Susanna in *Le nozze di Figaro*, cond. Mahler, Salzburg 1906. Sang Oktavian in *Der Rosenkavalier* at its Vienna première, 1911, and at CG 1913 (her only London appearance). Outstanding actress, hence success in *Elektra*, *Carmen*, etc. Sang in f.p. of Schoenberg's 2nd str. qt. (Vienna 1908, with Rosé Qt.) and created The Woman in *Erwartung* (Prague, 1924). After retiring, taught and directed in Vienna and Salzburg. Prod. Salzburg Fest. 1926 (*Don Giovanni*) and 1930 (*Iphigénie en Aulide*).

Guthrie, (Sir) **Tyrone** (*b* Tunbridge Wells, 1900; *d* Newbliss, Ireland, 1971). Eng. producer. Started career as actor, then became dir. of Old Vic, London, 1933–4, 1937, and 1953–7. Founder, Shakespeare Fest. at Stratford, Ontario, dir. 1953–7. Founded Guthrie Th., Minneapolis, 1963. Prod. first CG *Peter Grimes* 1947 and Britten's vers. of *The Beggar's Opera*, Cambridge 1948. Knighted 1961.

Gutiérrez, Horacio (*b* Havana, 1948). Cuban-born pianist (Amer. cit. 1967). Début with Havana SO 1959. Soloist in concs. with leading US and Eur. orchs. 2nd prize Tchaikovsky comp. 1970.

Gutman, Natalia (*b* Moscow, 1942). Russ. cellist. Began studies aged 5. Won comps. in Moscow, Prague, Munich and Vienna. Has played with leading orchs. in Russia, Eur., and Amer. Plays in chamber concerts with Svyatoslav Richter.

Salzburg Fest. début 1985. Perfs. works by contemp. Russ. composers (Denisov, Gubaidulina, and Schnittke). Has recorded both Shostakovich vc. concs.

Guy, Barry (*b* London, 1947). Eng. composer and double-bass player. Prin. db. player in several chamber orchs., incl. Academy of Ancient Mus., City of London Sinfonia, and Orch. of St John's, Smith Square. Founder and artistic dir., London Jazz Composers' Orch. Works incl. *Incontri*, vc., orch. (1969–70); 3 str. qts. (1969, 1970, 1973); *'D'*, 15 solo str. (1972); *Anna*, amplified db., orch. (1974); *Songs from Tomorrow*, orch. (1975); *Play*, chamber ens. (1976); *Eos*, db., orch., (1977); *Pf, ff*, vc., perc., pf. (1979); *Bitz*, septet (1979, rev. 1981); *Voyages of the Moon*, db., orch. (1983); *Flagwalk*, 14 solo str. (1983); *rondOH!*, pf., vn., db. (1985); *Video Life*, db., elec. (1986); *'UM 1788'* (1989); *Look up* (1990); *Theoria* (1991); *Buzz*, ens. (1995).

Gwendoline. Opera in 3 acts by Chabrier to lib. by C. Mendès. Comp. 1885. Prod. Brussels 1886; San Diego, Calif., 1982; London, 1983.

gymel, gimel (from Lat. *gemellus*, twin). The word has been used in mus. in 3 senses, all with the idea of twinship. (1) Style of singing alleged to have been common in parts of Britain as early as the 10th or 11th cents. Whilst one body of singers took the tune of a song another body would extemporize a part in 3rds beneath it.

(2) Type of comp. found in the 14th and early 15th cents. in which, whilst the main tune, or *cantus firmus, was sung in a lower v., 2 upper vv. sang an acc. in which they moved independently of the other v. but in 3rds with one another.

(3) In 16th-cent. choral mus. the word *gymel* on a vocal part means that the singers of that part are here divided (same as *divisi*). The restoration of the status quo is then indicated by the word *semel*.

Gymnopédies. 3 pf. pieces by *Satie, comp. 1888. Nos. 1 and 3 orch. by Debussy 1896, No.2 by Roland-Manuel and also by Herbert Murrill. Title refers to Ancient Greek annual fest. in Sparta in honour of Apollo, the Gymnopaidiai being choral dances perf. by naked men and boys divided by age into 3 choruses.

Gyrowetz, Adalbert [Jirovec, Vojtěch] (*b* Budějovice, 1763; *d* Vienna, 1850). Bohemian composer and conductor. His work was admired by Mozart in Vienna in 1785. Was of much assistance to Haydn, whom he idolized, during his two visits to Eng. Kapellmeister and Intendant of Vienna court ths. 1804–31. Pallbearer at Beethoven's funeral, 1827. Comp. 30 operas (incl. *Hans Sachs*, 1833), 25 ballets, 40 syms., 45 str. qts., pf. sonatas, etc.

Gyuselev, Nicola. See *Ghiuselev, Nicola*.

H

H (Ger.). B♮, *H dur* being key of B major and *H moll* key of B minor.

H. Abbreviated prefix to nos. in Imogen *Holst's thematic catalogue of her father Gustav *Holst's works, e.g. *Brook Green Suite* (H190).

Haas, Joseph (*b* Maihingen, 1879; *d* Munich, 1960). Ger. composer. Taught comp. at Stuttgart Cons. 1911–21, Munich 1921–50. One of founders of *Donaueschingen Fest., 1921. Wrote biography of Reger (1949). Works incl. operas *Tobias Wunderlich* (1937) and *Die Hochzeit des Jobs* (1944); oratorios *Das Lebensbuch Gottes* (1934), *Lied von der Mutter* (1939), *Das Jahr im Lied* (1952), and *Die Seligen* (1956); 2 str. qts. (1908, 1919); vn. sonata; and other choral mus. and song-cycles.

Haas, Karl (Wilhelm Jacob) (*b* Karlsruhe, 1900; *d* London, 1970). Ger.-born conductor and musicologist. Mus. adv. Karlsruhe and Stuttgart radio. Settled in Eng. 1939. Founded London Baroque Ens. 1941 to perform then unfamiliar mus. from baroque period. Public début, Nat. Gallery, 1943, last concert 1966. Ed. works of Cherubini, Boccherini, Haydn, etc.

Haas, Monique (*b* Paris, 1906; *d* Paris, 1987). Fr. pianist. Began concert career 1927. Worldwide tours. Salzburg Fest. 1951. Specialist in Ravel and other contemp. works. Taught at Paris Cons. Recorded complete pf. works of Debussy.

Haas, Pavel (*b* Brno, 1899; *d* Auschwitz, 1944). Cz. composer. Studied Brno Cons. 1919–21 and in Janáček's master class 1920–2, then worked as private comp. teacher. Sent to Terezin concentration camp 1941, where he continued to compose. Was moved to Auschwitz 1944 and gassed. Works incl. opera *The Charlatan* (1934–7, prod. Brno 1938); sym. (1941); 3 str. qts. (1920, 1925, 1938); wind quintet (1929); *Suite*, ob., pf. (1939); *4 Songs on Chinese Poetry*, bass, pf. (1944), and choral works.

Haas, Robert (Maria) (*b* Prague, 1886; *d* Vienna, 1960). Ger.-Cz. conductor and musicologist. Ass. to G. *Adler in Vienna 1909, cond. th. orchs. 1910–13. Mus. librarian Vienna State Library, 1920–45. Prof. Vienna Univ. 1930. Ed. works by Monteverdi etc., but best known for his editorship of complete edn. of Bruckner's works from 1932 to 1949 when he was succeeded by *Nowak. Haas restored the syms. nearer to the form in which Bruckner intended they should be heard. Author of books on Vienna Opera (1926), Mozart (1933), and Bruckner (1934).

Hába, Alois (*b* Vizovice, 1893; *d* Prague, 1973). Cz. composer. Worked in Vienna as proofreader for Universal Edition, thereby learning Schoenberg's works. Studied oriental mus. and also Moravian folk-mus. Became prin. propagator of *microtonal mus., founding and directing dept. of ¼-tone and ⅙-tone mus. at Prague Cons. 1924–51. Wrote comps. in ¼-tones, ⅙-tones, and some in ⅕-tones. Developed harmonic theory in ¼-tone, ⅙-tone, and 12-tone systems. ¼-tone and ⅙-tone instrs. (3 types of pf., harmonium, cls., and tpts.) were made for him. Folk music also influenced his works, and his 12-note works, while never abandoning tonality, are on Schoenbergian principles. Works incl.: Operas *Matka* (The *Mother) in ¼ tones (1927–9, rev. 1964), *Přůd Královtsvi Tvé* (*Nezaměstnani*) (Thy Kingdom Come (The Unemployed)) in ⅙ tones (1932–42), and *Nová Země* (The New Land) (1935–6); 16 str. qts., some in ¼, ⅙ and ⅘ tones; fantasias for vc. and for pf. in ¼ tones; vn. conc. (1954); va. conc. (1956); symphonic fantasia *Cesta Života* (The Way of Life) (1934); and *Fantasia* for nonet (1932, 12-tone) and ⅐ tone, 1932.

Hába, Karel (*b* Vizovice, 1898; *d* Prague, 1972). Cz. composer and violist, brother of Alois *Hába. Ed., Cz. nat. radio journal 1929–50. Violist Cz. PO 1929–36. Like his brother's, his works employ microtones. They incl. 4 operas: *Jánošík* (1929–32), *Stará historie* (Old History) (1934–7), *Smoliček* (1950), *Kalibův zlocïn* (1957–61); vn. conc. (1927); vc. conc. (1935); 2 syms. (1947–8, 1953–4); str. qts.; choral works; and chamber mus.

habanera (Fr. *havanaise*). Slow Cuban (orig. African) song and dance (Habana = Havana), which became very popular in Sp. It is in simple duple time and dotted rhythm. Famous examples are the habanera in Bizet's opera *Carmen* ('L'Amour est un oiseau rebelle') which is an adaptation of a popular song by *Yradier, and the *Habanera* for 2 pfs. by Ravel, later incorporated in his *Rapsodie espagnole* for orch.

Habeneck, François (Antoine) (*b* Mézières, 1781; *d* Paris, 1849). Fr. conductor, composer, and violinist. First vn. in Paris Opéra orch. 1815, dir. 1821–4, and cond. 1824–47 (chief cond. from 1831). Cond. f.ps. of *Guillaume Tell* (1829), *La Juive* (1835), and *Les Huguenots* (1836). Ass. prof. of vn., Paris Cons. 1808–16, teaching special class 1825–48. Founded Société des Concerts du Conservatoire 1828, conducting it until 1848 and introducing Beethoven's syms. to Fr. Cond. f.ps. of some works by Berlioz incl. the *Requiem* (1837) and the opera *Benvenuto Cellini* (1838).

Hackbrett (Ger.). Chopping board, i.e. *dulcimer.

Hacker, Alan (Ray) (*b* Dorking, 1938). Eng. clarinettist and conductor. Member of LPO 1958–66. Founder-member, *Pierrot Players 1967. Founded Matrix 1971, Music Party (for period perf.) 1972, Classical Orch. 1977. Member, Fires of London, 1970–6. Prof. of cl., RAM, 1960–76; lect., Leeds

Univ. 1972–3, York Univ. from 1976. Dir., York Early Music Fest. 1975–85. Revived basset cl. and restored orig. text of Mozart's conc. and quintet 1967; revived baroque cl. 1975. Gave f.ps. of works by Boulez, Goehr, Birtwistle, Maxwell Davies, D. Blake, Feldman, and Stockhausen. Took up cond. in 1970s. Cond. f. prod. of complete *La finta giardiniera* of Mozart, Swedish Nat. Opera 1986–7. Cond. Keiser's *Claudius* (1703) at Vadstena Acad., Sweden 1989. Cond. f.p. of Weir's *The Vanishing Bridegroom*, Glasgow 1990 (Scottish Opera). Has also cond. opera in Stuttgart. OBE 1998.

Hadley, Jerry (*b* Princeton, Ind., 1952). Amer. tenor. Début Saratoga 1978 as Lyonel in *Martha*. Joined NY City Opera 1979 (début as Arturo in *Lucia di Lammermoor*), later singing Werther, Tom Rakewell, Rodolfo, and Pinkerton. Eur. début Vienna 1982. Débuts: Glyndebourne 1984; CG 1984; NY Met 1987. Sang title-role in concert perf. of Bernstein's *Candide*, cond. by composer, London 1989.

Hadley, Patrick (Arthur Sheldon) (*b* Cambridge, 1899; *d* King's Lynn, 1973). Eng. composer. Taught at RCM 1925–62. Prof. of mus., Cambridge Univ., 1946–62. Comps. influenced by folk mus., Eng. poetry, Vaughan Williams, and Delius, mainly for vv. and orch. They incl.: *Ephemera*, sop. or ten., chamber orch. (1929); *Scene from Hardy's The Woodlanders*, sop., orch. (1926); *The Trees so high*, bar., ch., orch. (1931); *La Belle Dame sans merci*, ten., ch., orch. (1935); *The Hills*, sop., ten., ch., orch. (1944); *Scene from Shelley's The Cenci*, sop., orch. (1951); and *Fen and Flood*, ten., bass, ch., orch. (1954). Also many songs.

Hadow (Sir) **W**(illiam) **H**(enry) (Sir Henry) (*b* Ebrington, Glos., 1859; *d* London, 1937). Eng. educator, writer, and composer. Lect. on mus. Oxford Univ. 1890–9; prin., Armstrong Coll., Newcastle upon Tyne, 1909–19; vice-chancellor, Sheffield Univ. 1919–30. Comp. chamber mus. and songs. Books incl. *Studies in Modern Music* (1892, 1894, new edn. 1926), *English Music* (1931). Gen. ed. *Oxford History of Music* from 1896 and wrote Vol. V (*The Viennese Period*), 1904, 2nd edn. 1931. Knighted 1918.

Haebler, Ingrid (*b* Vienna, 1926). Austrian pianist. Début Salzburg 1937. Salzburg Fest. début 1954. Won Munich and Geneva int. comps. 1954. Specialist in Mozart concs. and Schubert sonatas. Teacher, Salzburg Mozarteum from 1969. Mozart Medal, Vienna, 1971.

Haefliger, Ernst (*b* Davos, 1919). Swiss tenor. Début Geneva 1942 (Evangelist in Bach's *St John Passion*). Salzburg Fest. début 1949. Glyndebourne début 1956. Noted *Lieder* singer. Prof. of singing, Munich Hochschule für Musik from 1971. Wrote *Die Singstimme* (Berne 1983). Retired 1995.

Haenchen, Hartmut (*b* Dresden, 1943). Ger. conductor. Cond., Halle SO 1966–72. Mus. dir. Zwickau Opera 1972–3. Guest cond. Dresden State Opera 1974–6. Cond. Mecklenburg Staatskapelle 1976–9. Prof. of cond. Dresden Hochschule 1980–6. Mus. dir. Netherlands Opera, Amsterdam, from 1985. CG début 1991 (Gluck's *Orfeo ed Euridice*).

Haendel, Ida (*b* Chelm, Poland, 1923). Polishborn British violinist. Début London 1937 in Brahms conc., cond. Wood. Settled in Eng. and became Brit. cit., but toured worldwide. In 1952 left Eng. to live in Canada. Toured Russ. 1966. Sibelius Medal 1982. CBE 1991.

Haffner Serenade. Nickname of Mozart's Suite in D major, K250, comp. 1776 for a marriage in the Salzburg family of Haffner.

Haffner Symphony. Nickname of Mozart's Sym. No.35 in D major, K385, arr. from a serenade (but not the D major, K250) written for the Haffner family in 1782.

Hagegård, Håkan (*b* Karlstad, 1945). Swed. baritone. Début Stockholm (Papageno in *Die Zauberflöte*). Débuts: Glyndebourne 1973; NY Met 1978; CG 1987; Chicago 1988. Sang Papageno in Bergman film of *Die Zauberflöte*, 1975. Created Beaumarchais in Corigliano's *The Ghosts of Versailles*, NY Met 1991.

Hager, Leopold (*b* Salzburg, 1935). Austrian conductor and organist. Opera début Mainz 1958 (*L'italiana in Algeri*). Ass. cond. Mainz Opera 1958–62; prin. cond. Linz Landesth. 1962–4, Cologne 1964–5, Freiburg 1965–9. Prin. cond. Salzburg Mozarteum Orch. 1969–81. Salzburg Fest. début 1954 (as org.). Cond. f. modern p. of *Mitridate, Rè di Ponto*, Salzburg Fest. 1971. Vienna début 1973; NY Met 1976; CG 1978; Buenos Aires 1977. Has recorded many of Mozart's early operas.

Hagley, Alison (*b* London, 1961). Eng. soprano. Sang title-role in *Rodelinda* at Aldeburgh Fest. 1985 and in *La finta giardiniera*, Camden Fest. 1986. Débuts: Glyndebourne 1988; CG 1989; ENO 1991. Sang Mélisande in *Pelléas et Mélisande*, cond. Boulez, WNO 1992.

Hahn, Hilary (*b* Lexington, Va., 1979). Amer. violinist. Entered Suzuki class, Peabody Cons., Baltimore, 1983. Studied with Klara Berkovich 1984–9. 1st recital 1988. Studied at Curtis Inst., Pa., 1990–9 with Jascha Brodsky. Soloist with Baltimore SO cond. Zinman 1991, followed by débuts in Philadelphia, Pittsburgh, Cleveland, and NY. Ger. début Munich 1995 in Beethoven conc. with Bavarian Radio SO, cond. Maazel. Continued studies with Jaime Laredo. Gave f.p. of Edgar Meyer's conc., St Paul 1999.

Hahn, Reynaldo (*b* Carácas, 1874; *d* Paris, 1947). Fr. composer and conductor. Mus. critic *Le Figaro* 1934. Mus. dir. Paris Opéra 1945–6. His operas incl. 2 special successes, *Ciboulette* (1923) and *Le marchand de Venise* (1935). The mus. comedy *Mozart* (1925) (with lib. by Sacha Guitry) was also popular, not least for having Yvonne *Printemps in the title-role. Though he wrote ballets, operetta, a cantata, pf. conc., vn. conc., vc. conc., str.

qt., and incid. mus., he is best remembered by his elegant and charming songs (which he sang, acc. himself). They incl. *Si mes vers avaient des ailes*. Was intimate friend of Marcel Proust.

Hail to the Chief. March played at formal Amer. events to announce arrival of the President. Comp. *c.*1812 by James Sanderson (1769–?1841), an Englishman. Words (never now sung) from Sir Walter Scott's *The Lady of the Lake* (1810). First used at a pres. inauguration 1837 (Martin Van Buren).

Haïm, Emmanuelle (*b* Paris, 1962). French conductor and kbd. player. Studied pf. with Yvonne Lefébure, org. with André Isoir, and hpd. with Kenneth Gilbert and Christophe Rousset. Became vocal coach at baroque mus. centre of Studio Versailles-Opéra and then at CNSM Paris. Continuo player and ass. in various opera houses. In 2000 founded baroque ens. *Le Concert d'Astrée*, which toured to London and int. fests. Cond. Handel's *Rodelinda* for GTO 2001. Salzburg Easter Fest. 2004 (OAE in Charpentier's *David et Jonathas*). Netherlands Opera 2007 (Monteverdi's *Orfeo*).

hairpins. Nickname for the signs < and > which represent **crescendo* and **diminuendo* respectively.

Haitink, Bernard (*b* Amsterdam, 1929). Dutch conductor. Violinist in Netherlands Radio PO, becoming prin. cond. 1956. Guest cond. Concertgebouw Orch. 1958–60, becoming joint prin. cond. with *Jochum) 1961, prin. cond. 1964–87. Amer. début 1958 (Los Angeles), Brit. début 1959 (visit with Concertgebouw Orch.). Prin. cond. LPO 1967–79 (art. dir. from 1970). Brit. opera début, Glyndebourne 1972 (*Die Entführung*), CG 1977. Mus. dir. Glyndebourne Opera 1977–87. NY Met début 1982. Mus. dir. CG 1987–2002, where he cond. *Ring* cycles 1989–91 and again 1994–6. Mus. dir. Staatskapelle Dresden 2002–4. Specialist in syms. of Mahler and Bruckner. Hon. KBE 1977. Hon. CH 2002.

Hajdu, André (*b* Budapest, 1932). Hung.-born Israeli composer and musicologist. Taught at Tunis Cons. 1959–61. Emigrated to Israel 1966, becoming teacher at Tel Aviv Acad. 1967. Works incl. pf. conc. (1968); *Ludus Paschalis*, 8 soloists, children's ch., 9 instr. (1970); *Terouath Melech*, cl., str. (1973); *Stories about Mischievous Boys*, orch. (1976); *5 Sketches in a Sentimental Mood*, pf. qt. (1976); *Concerto for 10 Little Pianists and Grand Orchestra* (1978); *Plasmas*, 10 players (1982); *Overture in the Form of a Kite*, orch. (1985); pf. conc. No.2, with chamber orch. (1990), orch. (1991); *Dreams of Spain*, cantata (1991); *Job and his Comforters*, oratorio (1992); *Symphonie Concertante*, fl., ob., cl., hn., vn., vc., str. (1993); *Book of Challenges I & II*, kbd. (1991–9); *Mishna Variations*, str. qt. (1991); *Shadows and Echoes*, db., chamber ens. (2004); *A Late Sonata*, pf. (2005).

Halb, Halbe (Ger.). Half. *Halbe, Halbenote, halbe Taktnote*, half-note (minim); *Halbe-pause*, half-rest (minim rest).

Halbprinzipal (Ger.). Half diapason, i.e. 4′. Principal (org. stop).

Halbsopran (Ger.). Mezzo-soprano.

Halbtenor (Ger.). Baritone.

Hale (Halle), Adam de la. See *Adam de la Halle*.

Hale, Robert (*b* Kerryville, San Antonio, Tex., 1943). Amer. bass-baritone. Début Denver 1965 (Figaro in *Le nozze di Figaro*). Joined NY City Opera 1967. Eur. début, Cologne Opera 1983; CG 1988; La Scala 1989; NY Met 1990; Salzburg Fest. 1990.

Halek, Vačlav (*b* Prague, 1937). Cz. composer. Comps. incl. 2 pf. concs., 2 str. quintets, sym., tb. conc., vn. and pf. conc., *Battle for Peace* for org. and strs., choral works.

Halévy [Lévi], **Jacques** (François Fromental Elie) (*b* Paris, 1799; *d* Nice, 1862). Fr. composer. *Grand Prix de Rome* 1819 with cantata *Herminie*. Achieved fame with opera *La *Juive*. Taught at Paris Cons. from 1827. *Chef du chant* Paris Opéra 1829–45. Comp. over 30 operas, several ballets, cantatas, and songs.

half cadence. See *cadence*.

half close. See *cadence*.

Halffter, Cristóbal (*b* Madrid, 1930). Sp. composer and conductor. Nephew of Ernesto and Rodolfo *Halffter. Worked for Sp. radio. Teacher of comp. and theory, Madrid Cons. 1961–6 (dir. 1964–6), lect. at Univ. of Navarra 1970–8. Art. dir. EMS, Freiburg, 1979. Works incl.:

OPERA: *Don Quichotte* (1970).

ORCH.: 5 *Microforms* (1960); sym. for 3 groups of instrs. (1963); *Sequences* (1965); *Anillos* (1967–8); *Fibonaciana*, fl., str. (1969); *Requiem por la Libertad Imaginada* (1971); vc. conc. (1974); *Elegies for death of 3 Spanish poets* (1974–5); *Pourquoi*, 12 str. (1974–5); vn. conc. (1979); vc. conc. No.1 (1979), No.2 (1985); *Tiento* (1980); *Fantasia on a Theme of Handel*, str. (1981); *Sinfonia ricercata*, org., orch. (1982); fl. conc. (1982); *Versus* (1983); conc., vn., va., orch. (1984); *Paraphrase on Handel Theme* (1984); *Tiento del primer tono y batalla imperial* (1986); *Dortmund Variations* (1986–7); pf. conc. (1987–8); *Prelude to Nemesis* (1988–9); *Conc. for Four*, sax. qt., orch. (1989–90); vn. conc., str. (1990–1); *Daliniana*, chamber orch. (1993–4); *Odradek – Homage to Kafka* (1996); *Divertimento: Haldbéniz* (2000).

CHORAL: *Yes Speak Out Yes*, UNO cantata, sop., bar., ch., orch. (1968); *In expectatione resurrectionis Domini*, bar., male ch., orch. (1965); *Symposion*, bar., ch., orch. (1968); *In memoriam Anaick*, reciter, ch., orch. (1967); *Jarchas de dolor de Ausencia*, 12 vv. (1979); *Dona nobis pacem*, mixed ch., ens. (1984); *Prelude for Madrid '92*, ch., orch. (1991); *Veni creator spiritus*, ch., ens. (1992); *De verborum et speculorum ludis*, ch., perc., elec. pf., org. (1999–2000).

CHAMBER MUSIC: *Codex*, gui (1963); str. qt. No.1 (1955), No.2 (1970), No.3 (1978); *Variations on the Theme 'Sacher'*, vc. (1975); *Fandango*, 8 vc. (1988–9); *Fractal*, sax. qt. (1991); *Le Sommeil*, chamber orch. (1994); *Tinguely Fanfare*, brass ens. (1996); *Solo*, vc. (2000).

Halffter [Escriche], **Ernesto** (*b* Madrid, 1905; *d* Madrid, 1989). Sp. composer and cond. Lived in Portugal until he founded chamber orch. in Seville. Works incl. gui. conc. (1968), *The Death of Carmen* (1977), orch. pieces, pf. mus., etc. Completed Falla's *Atlántida*, f.p. Milan 1962.

Halffter [Escriche], **Rodolfo** (*b* Madrid, 1900; *d* Mexico City, 1987). Sp.-born composer (Mexican cit. 1939), brother of Ernesto *Halffter. Influenced by Schoenberg. Settled in Mexico 1939. Founded Mexican contemp. ballet co. 1940 and publishing house 1946. Ed., *New Music*, 1946–52. Composed orch. works and chamber mus.

half-note (♩). Half the time-value of the whole-note or semibreve. In Eng. usage 'minim' (from Lat. *minima*). See also *rests*; *names of notes*.

Halíř, Karel [Karel] (*b* Hohenelbe, 1859; *d* Berlin, 1909). Bohemian violinist. Leader of several Ger. orchs. incl. Berlin Court Opera orch. 1893–1907. 2nd violinist in Joachim Qt. 1897–1907. Formed Halíř Quartet 1898.

Halka (Helen). Opera in 4 (orig. 2) acts by Moniuszko to lib. by Wolski after Wójcicki's story *Góralka*. F. (concert) p. Wilno (Vilnius) 1848; (rev. vers.) Warsaw 1858; NY 1903; London 1961.

Hall, Marie (Paulina) (*b* Newcastle upon Tyne, 1884; *d* Cheltenham, 1956). Eng. violinist. Début Prague 1902, London 1903, NY 1905. Made first recording (severely abridged) of Elgar's vn. conc., cond. by composer, 1916. Gave f.p. of Vaughan Williams's *The Lark Ascending* 1920.

Hall, (Sir) **Peter** (Reginald Frederick) (*b* Bury St Edmunds, 1930). Eng. theatrical producer. Dir., Oxford Playhouse 1954–5; man. dir. Royal Shakespeare Co. 1960–8; dir., Nat. Th. 1973–88. Appointed joint dir. CG 1971, but resigned before taking office. Art. dir. Glyndebourne 1984–90. First opera prod., Gardner's *The Moon and Sixpence*, SW 1957. Produced Wagner's *Ring* at Bayreuth 1983. His other prin. opera prods. have been: CG: *Moses und Aron* (1965), *Die Zauberflöte* (1966), *The Knot Garden* (1970, its f.p.), *Eugene Onegin* (1971), *Tristan und Isolde* (1971), *Salome* (1988, orig. from Los Angeles, 1986); Glyndebourne: Cavalli's *Calisto* (1970), Monteverdi's *Il Ritorno d'Ulisse in Patria* (1972), *Le nozze di Figaro* (1973 and 1989), *Don Giovanni* (1977), *Così fan tutte* (1978), *Fidelio* (1979), *A Midsummer Night's Dream* (1981), Gluck's *Orfeo* (1982), *L'incoronazione di Poppea* (1984), *Carmen* (1985), *Albert Herring* (1985), *Simon Boccanegra* (1986), *La traviata* (1987), *Falstaff* (1988), *Otello* (2001), *La Cenerentola* (2005); NY Met: *Macbeth* (1982), *Carmen* (1986). Prod. world première of Tippett's *New Year* (Houston, 1989, Glyndebourne 1990). CBE 1963. Knighted 1977.

Hall, Richard (*b* York, 1903; *d* Horsham, 1982). Eng. composer, teacher, and poet. Played vc. and org. Org., Dorchester Abbey, Oxon, 1923. Org. scholar Peterhouse, Cambridge Univ., 1923–4. Ordained in C of E. Precentor, Leeds Parish Church 1926–36. Left church 1936, chiefly because of growing interest in Eastern religion and philosophy. Mus. adv., Lancs. Community Council 1936–40. Prof. of harmony and comp., RMCM, 1938–56. Influential teacher, pupils incl. Maxwell Davies, A. Goehr, Birtwistle, D. Wilde, and A. Butterworth. Dir. of mus. Dartington Hall 1956–65, founding Dartington Str. Qt. Ordained as Liberal Catholic priest 1959. Minister, Unitarian Church, Moretonhampstead 1965–7, Horsham 1967–76, Billingshurst 1968–76. Pubd. 7 books of poetry 1970–5. Comps., influenced by Delius, Scriabin, Schoenberg, and Berg, incl. 5 syms.; pf. conc.; 2 str. qts.; 19 pf. sonatas (1934–5); vc. conc.; *Lyric Pieces*, orch. (1946); sym.-poem *Lemura*; *Creator Spiritus*, vv., orch.; *Rhapsody*, org., str. (1929); orch. fantasy *The Sheep Under the Snow*; songs; etc.

Hallé, (Sir) **Charles** [Halle, Karl] (*b* Hagen, Ger., 1819; *d* Manchester, 1895). Ger.-born pianist and cond. Child prodigy pianist. Went to Paris 1836 to improve pf. technique, becoming friend of Chopin, Liszt, and Berlioz. Début in Paris in pf. trio with Alard and Franchomme, 1840. Concert tour of Ger. 1842, London 1843. Instituted first Paris series of chamber concerts 1847. Settled in Eng. 1848. First pianist to play complete series of Beethoven pf. sonatas in London (also in Manchester and Paris). Invited to settle in Manchester, 1848, where he lived for the rest of his life. Founded chamber concerts in Manchester 1848–9, choral soc. 1850, became cond. of *Gentlemen's Concerts orch. 1849, cond. his first concert 1850. Founded his own series of orch. concerts Jan. 1858, thereby inaugurating what are still known as the *Hallé Orch. and Hallé Concerts. Regularly appeared as soloist in concs. and as recitalist. Annual visits to London, Edinburgh, etc. Champion of new works, esp. those of Berlioz. Cond. f.p. in Eng. of *Symphonie Fantastique* (1879), *L'Enfance du Christ* (1880), and *La Damnation de Faust* (1880) and of Tchaikovsky's 5th sym. (1893). Cond. opera seasons in Manchester 1854–5, London 1860–1. Cond. Bristol Festival 1873–93. Toured Australia 1890 and 1891 and S. Africa 1895 with 2nd wife, the violinist Wilhelmina Norman-*Neruda. First Prin., RMCM 1893–5. Knighted 1888.

Hallelujah Chorus. Usually taken to mean one particular ch. out of many which exist, i.e. that which closes Part II of Handel's *Messiah*. At one of the 3 London perfs. in CG Th. in 1743, the whole assembly, led by George II, rose to its feet as the ch. opened, and remained standing to the end, thus establishing a tradition which is sometimes still maintained by Brit. audiences.

Hallé Orchestra. Manchester's prin. sym. orch., founded 1858 by Charles *Hallé, after success of series of orch. concerts at 1857 Art Treasures Exhibition. Hallé remained cond. (and proprietor and prin. pf. soloist) until death in 1895. In inter-regnum Frederic *Cowen was cond. until 1899 when Hans *Richter took up post offered to him in 1895. Concerts managed from 1898 by non-profit-making Hallé Concerts Soc. (today with con-siderable financial support from Arts Council, private patronage, and local govt.). Richter left in 1911 and was succeeded in 1912 by Michael *Bal-ling who remained until 1914. Then Hamilton *Harty, 1920–33. Beecham was a frequent visitor 1933–40. Sargent was prin. cond. 1939–42. Orch. reconstituted 1943 on annual basis giving many more concerts and John *Barbirolli was ap-pointed cond., retaining post until his death in 1970. Succeeded by James *Loughran 1971–83; Stanislaw *Skrowaczewski 1984–92; Kent *Na-gano 1992–2000; Mark Elder from 2000. Among works f.p. by Hallé are Elgar's *In the South* (1904) and 1st Sym. (1908) and Vaughan Williams's 7th and 8th syms. (1953 and 1956). Orch. gives regular series in Sheffield and Bradford, tours throughout Britain, and has made many overseas tours.

halling. Popular solo Norweg. dance, probably from the Hallingdal. The mus. is in simple duple time, and the steps are remarkably vigorous. Acc. played on 'Hardanger fiddle', vn. strung with 4 stopped and 4 sympathetic str.

Halm, Hans (*b* Munich, 1898; *d* Munich, 1965). Ger. musicologist. Dir., mus. section, Munich State Library from 1938. After death of *Kinsky, completed and pubd. his thematic catalogue of Beethoven's works (1955).

Halsey, Louis (Arthur Owen) (*b* London, 1926). Eng. conductor. Founded and cond. Elizabethan Singers 1953–66, Louis Halsey Singers from 1967, Thames Chamber Choir from 1964. Mus. prod., BBC, from 1963.

Halsey, Simon (*b* Kingston-upon-Thames, 1958). Eng. conductor. Cond., Scottish Opera-Go-Round 1980–1. Dir. of mus., Warwick Univ. 1980–8. Chorusmaster CBSO from 1982. Ass. dir., Philhar-monia Ch. from 1986. Mus. dir., CBTO from 1987. Dir., ch. of Academy of Ancient Mus. from 1988. Ch. dir., Flanders Opera, Antwerp, from 1991.

Hambourg, Mark (*b* Bogutchar, 1879; *d* Cam-bridge, 1960). Russ.-born pianist (Brit. cit. 1896). Début with Moscow PO 1888. London début 1889. Pupil of *Leschetizky in Vienna 1891–5. Many world tours.

Hamburg. N. German city and port with long mus. tradition. Famous figures in its church mus. history who held office of Musikdirektor der Hauptkirchen incl. Sartorius (1604–37), Selle (1638–63), Telemann (1721–67), C. P. E. Bach (1767–88), and C. F. G. Schwencke (1788–1822). In 17th cent. Hamburg was leading centre of N German org. mus. Schnitger (1648–1719) was important org. builder and among distinguished orgs. were the Praetorius brothers, Reincken, and Lübeck. Became opera centre in 1678. Keiser, who moved to Hamburg in 1695, wrote over 50 operas for the company he directed from 1703 to 1706, with Handel as apprentice. Telemann wrote several operas for Hamburg. In 19th cent., Bernhard Pollini (Pohl) from 1874 established a Wagnerian reputation and engaged Mahler as cond. (1891–7). Later conds. incl. Klemperer (1910–12), Pollak (1917–31), and Böhm (1931–4). Opera house bombed 1943, rebuilt 1955. Conds. after 1945 incl. Arthur Gruber (1946–50), Leo-pold Ludwig (1951–71), Horst Stein (1972–7), Christoph von Dohnányi (1977–84), Gerd Albrecht 1988–2005, and Simone Young from 2006. Producers such as Günther Rennert and inten-dants such as Tietjen (1954–9), R. Liebermann (1959–73), August Everding (1973–7), and Peter Ruzicka (1988–97), lifted Hamburg to a leading place in European opera. Orch. concerts devel-oped *c*.1660. C. P. E. Bach arr. concerts from 1768 for the next 20 years. Hamburg Philharmonic Orch. gave first concert in Jan. 1829 but was eclipsed from 1886 by concerts given by the opera orch. under Hans von Bülow. But Muck from 1922 transformed the playing until, when he retired in 1933, the orch. was merged with the opera orch. under joint cond. of Jochum and Schmidt-Isserstedt. After 1945 conds. incl. Keil-berth and Sawallisch. In 1945 Schmidt-Isserstedt became chief cond. of Hamburg radio orch. which later toured Eng., Russ., and USA. Known as North German Radio SO from 1951. Gave f.p. (concert) of Schoenberg's *Moses und Aron*, 1954. Atzmon was chief cond. 1972–9, Tennstedt 1979–82, Wand 1982–91, John Eliot Gardiner 1991–4, Herbert Blomstedt 1996–8, Christoph Eschenbach 1998–2004, Christoph von Dohná-nyi from 2004.

Hamburger, Paul (*b* Vienna, 1920; *d* Yeovil, 2004). Austrian-born pianist and critic. Settled in Eng. Worked with EOG 1953–6, Glyndebourne 1956–62. Staff acc. BBC 1962–75. BBC producer 1976–81. Frequent acc. and chamber mus. player. Has contributed to pubd. symposiums on Britten, Mozart, and Chopin. Translator of Bruno Walter's *Music and Music-Making* (1961) and of Hans Hollander's *Janáček* (1963). Professor of piano and singing at GSMD from 1982.

Hamilton, Iain (Ellis) (*b* Glasgow, 1922; *d* London, 2000). Scot. composer and pianist. Cl. quintet perf. 1949; 2nd sym. (1951) won Kousse-vitzky award. Lect., Morley Coll. 1952–9, London Univ. 1955–60. Prof. of mus., Duke Univ., N Car., 1961–78, becoming chairman, mus. dept. 1966–7. Returned to Eng. 1981. Early works showed influences of Bartók and Hindemith, and in the *Sinfonia* he used serial procedures. Growing inter-est in vocal and operatic mus. has eased ten-dency to austerity in his mus. Works incl.:

OPERAS: *Rondo*, 1-act opera buffa; *Agamemnon*, 2-act (1967–9); *Royal Hunt of the Sun*, 2-act (1967–9); *Pharsalia* 1-act (1968); *The *Catiline Conspiracy* (1972–3); *Tamburlaine* (1976); *Anna Karenina* (1978); *Dick Whittington* (1980–1); *Lancelot* (1982–3); *The Tragedy of Macbeth* (1990).

BALLET: *Clerk Saunders* (1951).

ORCH.: *Variations* for str. (1948); syms.: No.1 (1950), No.2 (1951), No.3 (*Spring*) (1981), No.4 in B (1981);

concs.: cl. (1950); pf. No.1 (1949), No.2 (1960 rev. 1967); vn. No.1 (1952), No.2 (*Amphion*) (1971); jazz tpt. (1958); org. (1964); *Sinfonia Concertante*, vn., va., orch. (1950); *Sinfonia*, 2 orch. (1958–9); *Circus*, 2 tpt., orch. (1969); *Voyage*, hn., orch. (1970); *Commedia: Concerto for Orch.* (1972–3); *The Alexandrian Sequence*, chamber orch. (1976).

VOCAL & CHORAL: *The Bermudas* for bar., ch., and orch. (1956); *Nocturnal*, 11 solo vv. (1959); *Dialogues*, coloratura sop., small orch. (1965); *Epitaph For This World and Time*, 3 ch., 3 org. (1970); *Te Deum; The Descent of the Celestial City*, vv., org. (1972); *The Golden Sequence*, ch., org. (1973); *To Columbus*, ch., brass, perc. (1975); *Cleopatra*, dramatic scene, sop., orch. (1978); *Requiem*, unacc. ch. (1979); Mass in A, unacc. ch. (1980); *Vespers*, ch., 2 pf., hp., perc. (1980); *The Morning Watch*, ch., 10 winds (1981); *St Mark Passion*, SATB soloists, ch., orch. (1982).

CHAMBER MUSIC: str. qt. (1949), 2nd str. qt. (1965); cl. quintet No.1 (1948), No.2 (*Sea Music*) (1974); sonatas: va. (1951), cl. (1954), vc. No.1 (1958), No.2 (1974), fl. (1966), 3 winds (1966); octet for str. (1954); *Hyperion*, pf., cl., hn., vn., vc. (1977); *Spirits of the Air*, bass tb. (1977); octet (1983–4).

PIANO: sonata No.1 (1951 rev. 1971), No.2 (1973), No.3 (1978); *3 Pieces* (1955); *Nocturnes with cadenzas* (1963); *Palinodes* (1972).

Hamlet. Shakespeare's play (1600–1) has inspired operas and orch. mus. e.g.

(1) Opera in 5 acts by Ambroise Thomas to lib. by Barbier and Carré, prod. Paris 1868, London 1869, NY 1872.

(2) Opera (*Amleto*) by *Faccio to lib. by Boito, prod. Genoa 1865.

(3) Sym.-poem by Liszt, comp. 1858 as prelude to play.

(4) Fantasy-ov. Op.67a by Tchaikovsky, 1888, and incid. mus. (16 items) Op.67b, 1891.

(5) Opera in 3 acts by *Searle to his own lib., prod. Hamburg 1968, London 1969.

(6) Ballets on the subject have used mus. by Tchaikovsky, Clerico, Gallenberg, Blacher, and Shostakovich.

(7) Other operas on the subject by Gasparini, D. Scarlatti, Mercadante, Grandi, and Szokolay among others.

(8) Film music by Shostakovich and Walton.

Hammerklavier Sonata. Title generally applied solely to Beethoven's pf. sonata No.29 in B♭ major, Op.106, comp. 1817–18, but in a letter written in Jan. 1817 Beethoven said he had decided to use the word 'Hammerklavier' (Ger., 'pianoforte') on all his pf. mus. with Ger. titles, adding 'this is to be clearly understood once and for all'.

Hammerstein, Oscar (I) (*b* Stettin, 1846; *d* NY, 1919). Ger.-Amer. impresario and businessman. Settled in NY 1863, making fortune from inventions such as cigar-making machine. From 1890 built and managed various ths. In 1906 built Manhattan Opera House, NY, engaging superb singers and producing adventurous repertory,

incl. first NY perfs. of *Louise, Pelléas et Mélisande*, and *Elektra*. In 1908 built Philadelphia Opera House, run in assoc. with his NY co. The Met in 1910 bought his interests and stipulated he should not produce opera in NY, Boston, Philadelphia, or Chicago for 10 years. So in London he built London Opera House (Stoll, Kingsway), opening in 1911 but failing after 2 seasons. Built Lexington Opera House, NY, in 1913, but the Met legally restrained him from producing opera there.

Hammerstein, Oscar (II) (*b* NY, 1895; *d* Doylestown, Penn., 1960). Amer. librettist and producer, grandson of above. Wrote mus. comedy *Always You* in 1920. Then with Otto Harbach worked on a number of shows. In 1927 collab. with Kern on *Show Boat*, later with Romberg, Friml, Gershwin, and most notably with Richard Rodgers in *Oklahoma!* (1943), *Carousel* (1945), *Allegro* (1947), *South Pacific* (1949), *The King and I* (1951), *Flower Drum Song* (1958), and *The Sound of Music* (1959). Wrote lib. for *Carmen Jones* (1943), the brilliant adaptation of *Carmen* as an Amer. musical.

Hammond, (Dame) **Joan** (Hood) (*b* Christchurch, NZ, 1912; *d* Bowral, NSW, 1996). Australian soprano of New Zealand birth. Played vn. in Sydney SO for 3 years. Début as singer Sydney 1928 (Giovanna in *Rigoletto*). London début 1938 (*Messiah*) and in opera in Vienna 1938. Later career in opera houses in London, Vienna, Moscow, and Netherlands, repertory incl. Aida, Fidelio, and some Wagner. Member Carl Rosa Co. 1942–5. CG début 1948; Amer. début (NY City Opera) 1949. Sang title-role in f.p. in Eng. trans. of *Rusalka*, SW 1959. Worked as journalist in Australia, also excellent golfer. Retired 1965. Autobiography *A Voice, A Life* (1970). OBE 1953, CBE 1963, CMG 1972, DBE 1974.

Hammond Organ. Type of elec. org. invented and manufactured by Hammond Organ Co., Chicago (first introduced 1933). Usually has 2 manuals and pedal kbd. Sound is prod. and controlled by electricity in simulation of pipeorg. Inventor, Laurens Hammond, also produced the solovox, the chord organ, and the novachord.

Hammond-Stroud, Derek (*b* London, 1926). Eng. baritone. Début London (St Pancras Fest.) 1955 (Pluto in concert perf. of Haydn's *Orfeo*). Stage début London (St Pancras Fest.) 1957 (Publius in *La Clemenza di Tito*). Prin. bar. SW Opera 1961–71. Débuts: CG 1971; Glyndebourne 1973; Amer. (Houston) 1975; NY Met 1977. Noted for Beckmesser in *Die Meistersinger* and for Alberich in *Ring* cycle, both with SW/ENO, cond. by Goodall. OBE 1987.

Hampe, Michael (Hermann) (*b* Heidelberg, 1935). Ger. director. Studied vc., musicology, and philosophy. Worked as prod. at municipal theatres in Berne 1961–4 and Zurich 1965–70. Dir., Nat. Th., Mannheim, 1972–5. Intendant, Cologne Opera from 1975. Prod. opera at Salzburg (début 1982, *Così fan tutte*), Vienna, Paris, Milan, Edinburgh Fest., and London. CG début 1984 (*Andrea Chénier*).

Hampel, Anton Joseph (*b* Prague, *c*.1710; *d* Dresden, 1771). Bohemian-born horn-player. In Dresden court orch. from, probably, 1731 where he was first to develop method of playing chromatic scale by hand-stopping. In about 1753 devised way of inserting crooks into body of horn rather than at the mouthpiece. Wrote hn. concs.

Hampson, Thomas (*b* Elkhart. Ind., 1955). Amer. baritone. Won Lotte Lehmann award 1978, 2nd prize at 's-Hertogenbosch int. comp. 1980, and first place in NY Met auditions 1981. Member Deutsche Oper am Rhein, Dusseldorf, 1981–4. Title-role in Henze's *Der Prinz von Homburg*, Darmstadt 1982, and Guglielmo in *Così fan tutte*, St Louis 1982. Santa Fe début 1983. Recital débuts: London 1983, NY 1985. Opera débuts: NY Met 1986; Salzburg 1988; CG 1993. Fine singer of Schubert and Brahms *Lieder* and of Mahler cycles. Co-ed., critical edn. of Mahler songs.

Hanacca, Hanakisch (Ger.; Fr. *hanaise*). A Moravian dance in simple triple time; a sort of quick polonaise.

handbells. Small bells attached to the hands by leather straps and played by striking them together. Used for practice by change ringers.

Handel, George Frideric [Händel, Georg Friedrich] (*b* Halle, 1685; *d* London, 1759). Ger.-born composer and organist (Eng. cit. 1726). Son of a barber-surgeon who opposed mus. as his son's career though he permitted lessons from *Zachau, composer and org. of Liebfrauenkirche, Halle. Handel studied law at Halle Univ., turning to full-time mus. when his father died. He went to Hamburg in 1703 where he joined the opera house under the composer Reinhard *Keiser, playing 2nd vn. in the orch. His first opera *Almira*, written because Keiser lost interest in the lib., which Handel took over, was prod. there in 1705, being followed by 3 others. In 1706 Handel went to Italy in a prince's retinue, meeting Corelli, the Scarlattis, and other leading figures, and rapidly attaining mastery of It. style in opera, chamber mus., and vocal mus. He was acclaimed as a genius, the rival of his It. contemporaries. His opera *Rodrigo* was perf. in Florence in 1707 and *Agrippina* in Venice in 1709. The following year he was appointed court cond. in Hanover and was also invited to write an opera (*Rinaldo*) for London, where he quickly realized the possibilities for his own success and, after settling his affairs in Hanover, settled there permanently.

For the next 35 years Handel was immersed in the ups and downs of operatic activity in London where the It. *opera seria* was the dominant force. In 1712 he received a pension of £200 a year for life from Queen Anne, this being increased to £600 by King George I, his former ruler in Hanover, for whom in 1717 he comp. the famous *Water Music* suite. From 1717 to 1720 Handel was resident comp. to the Earl of Carnarvon (Duke of Chandos from April 1719) at his palace of Cannons in Edgware. The 11 *Chandos Anthems* were the chief fruit of this appointment. In 1719 Handel, in assoc. with G. *Bononcini and *Ariosti, was a mus. dir. of the so-called Royal Acad. of Mus. (not a coll. but a business venture to produce It. opera). Handel travelled abroad to engage singers and in the 8 years until the acad. closed because of lack of support he comp. 14 operas, among them *Radamisto, Rodelinda, Admeto*, and *Tolomeo*. In 1727, for the coronation of George II, Handel wrote 4 anthems, incl. *Zadok the Priest*, which has been sung at every Brit. coronation since then.

The success of Gay's *The Beggar's Opera* and imitative works was the prin. cause of the falling-away of support for Handel's co. He went to It. to hear operas by composers such as Porpora and Pergolesi and to engage the leading It. singers. Back in London in partnership with Heidegger at the King's Theatre, Handel wrote *Lotario* (1729), *Partenope* (1730), and *Orlando* (1733). In 1734 he moved to the new CG Th., for which he wrote two of his greatest operas, *Ariodante* (prod. Jan. 1735) and *Alcina* (prod. Ap. 1735), but he recognized that the popularity of It. opera was declining and began, somewhat unwillingly, to develop the genre of dramatic oratorios which is perhaps his most orig. contribution to the art of mus. *Esther* (1732 in rev. form) and *Acis and Galatea* are typical examples. Ironically, released from the conventions of *opera seria*, Handel's dramatic gifts found wider and more expressive outlets in the oratorio form. Scores contain stage directions and the use of ch. and orch. became more dramatic and rich. He cond. several oratorio perf. in London, 1735, playing his own org. concs. as entr'actes. Nevertheless he continued to write operas and between 1737 and 1740 comp. *Berenice, Serse, Imeneo*, and *Deidamia*.

In 1737 Handel's health cracked under the strain of his operatic labours and he had a stroke. Following his recovery, he wrote a series of oratorios, incl. *Messiah*, prod. Dublin, 1742. By this work his name is known throughout the world, yet it is something of an oddity in Handel's work since he was not a religious composer in the accepted sense. But its power, lyricism, sincerity, and profundity make it one of the supreme mus. creations as well as an outstanding example of devotional art. It was followed by *Samson, Judas Maccabaeus*, and *Solomon*. The success of these works made Handel the idol of the Eng., and that popularity dominated Eng. mus. for nearly 150 years after his death. Not until Handel's operas were revived in Ger. in the 1920s was the perspective corrected and the importance of that branch of his art restored. Superb as are Handel's instr. comps. such as the *concerti grossi*, sonatas, and suites, it is in the operas and oratorios that the nobility, expressiveness, invention, and captivation of his art are found at their highest degree of development. He did not revolutionize operatic form but he brought the novelty of his genius to the genre as he found it. The scene-painting and illustrative qualities of his orchestration are remarkable even at a period when naive and realistic effects were common currency.

For the last 7 years of his life Handel was blind, but he continued to conduct oratorio perfs. and to revise his scores with assistance from his devoted friend John Christopher Smith. His works were pubd. by the Ger. *Handel Gesellschaft* in a complete edn. (1859–94) of 100 vols., ed. *Chrysander, and a new edn., the *Hallische Handel-Ausgabe*, is in progress. Prin. comps.:

OPERAS: Hamburg: *Almira, Nero* (lost) (both 1705); *Florindo e Dafne* (lost) (1707); Florence: *Rodrigo* (1707); Venice: *Agrippina* (1709); London: *Rinaldo* (1711, rev. 1731), *Il pastor fido* (1712; 2nd version with ballet *Terpsicore*, 1734); *Teseo* (1712); *Silla* (1714); *Amadigi di Gaula* (1715); *Radamisto* (1720, rev. 1720, 1721, 1728); *Muzio Scevola, Floridante* (both 1721); *Ottone* (1722); *Flavio* (1723); *Giulio Cesare in Egitto* (1723–4); *Tamerlano* (1724, rev. 1731); *Rodelinda, regina de'Longobardi* (1725); *Scipione, Alessandro* (both 1726); *Admeto, Riccardo I* (both 1727); *Siroe, Tolomeo* (both 1728); *Lotario* (1729); *Partenope* (1729–30, rev. 1730, 1736); *Poro* (1731); *Ezio, Sosarme* (both 1732); *Orlando* (1733); *Arianna* (1734); *Ariodante, *Alcina* (both 1735); *Atalanta* (1736); *Arminio, Giustino, *Berenice* (all 1737); *Faramondo, *Serse* (both 1738); *Imeneo* (1738–40); *Deidamia* (1740).

ORCH.: *Water Music* (c.1717); *Music for Royal Fireworks* (1749).

DRAMATIC ORATORIOS: Rome: *La Resurrezione, Trionfo del Tempo* (1708); Naples: *Aci, Galatea e Polifemo* (1709); Hamburg: *Der für die Sünde der Welt gemartete und sterbende Jesus* (Brockes Passion) (?1716); London: *Haman and Mordecai* (masque 1720, later rev. as *Esther* in 1732); *Acis and Galatea* (1718; rev. 1732 incorporating part of 1708 cantata on same subject, and 1743); *Deborah* (1733); *Athalia* (1733); *Alexander's Feast* (1736); *Israel in Egypt* (1738); *Saul, Ode for St Cecilia's Day* (1739); *L'Allegro, il Pensieroso ed il Moderato* (1740); *Messiah* (1741); *Samson* (1741–2); *Joseph and his Brethren, *Semele* (1743); *Belshazzar, Hercules* (1744); *Occasional Oratorio, *Judas Maccabaeus* (1746); *Alexander Balus, *Joshua* (1747); *Solomon, Susanna* (1748); *Theodora, Alceste* (1749); *Choice of Hercules* (1750); *Jephtha* (1751); *Triumph of Time and Truth* (1757).

CANTATAS AND CHAMBER DUETS: Handel comp. 100 of the former and 20 of the latter. Among the best known are *Silete Venti*, sop., instr. (1729); *La terra è liberata* (*Apollo e Dafne*), sop., bass, instr. (c.1708); and *O numi eterni* (*La Lucrezia*), sop., continuo (1709).

CHURCH MUSIC: *Gloria Patri* (1707); *Utrecht Te Deum and Jubilate* (1712–13); *Dettingen Te Deum* (1743); 11 *Chandos Anthems* (1717–18); 4 *Coronation Anthems* (1727: *The King Shall Rejoice; Let thy hand be strengthened; My heart is inditing; *Zadok the Priest*); *The Ways of Zion do Mourn*, funeral anthem for Queen Caroline (1737).

VOCAL: *Birthday Ode for Queen Anne* (1713); 9 *German Arias* (1729).

INSTRUMENTAL AND CHAMBER MUSIC: 6 *Concerti Grossi*, str., ww., continuo, Op.3 (1734); 12 *Concerti Grossi*, str., optional wind, Op.6 (1739); 5 *Concerti*, orch. (1741); 6 *organ concerti*, Op.4 (1738); 6 *organ concerti*, Op.7 (1760); 6 *organ concerti* (1740); 15 *chamber sonatas* (fls., recorders), Op.1 (1724); 3 *concerti a due cori*; 2 ob. sonatas; 12 fl. sonatas; 6 trio sonatas; 9 trio sonatas, Op.2 (1722–33); 7 trio sonatas, Op.5 (1739); va. da gamba sonata; 8 *suites de pièces*, hpd. (1720); 8 *suites de pièces* (1733, these incl. the well-known *Chaconne* in G); 6 Fugues (1736). See also *Harmonious Blacksmith*.

Handel Opera. Founded 1955 as Handel Opera Society by Charles *Farncombe, at suggestion of E. J. *Dent, to revive interest in Handel's operas. First prod. was *Deidamia*, 1955, at St Pancras Town Hall. Moved in 1959 to Sadler's Wells Th. Revived over 20 Handel works, many for the first time since Handel's lifetime. Name changed to Handel Opera 1980. Singers who appeared with the company incl. Richard Lewis, Geraint Evans, James Bowman, Janet Baker, Joan Sutherland, and Anna Reynolds. Ceased 1985.

Handford, Maurice (*b* Salisbury, 1929; *d* Warminster, 1986). Eng. conductor and horn-player. Prin. hn. Hallé Orch. 1949–61. Assoc. cond. Hallé Orch. 1966–71. Staff cond. CBSO 1970–4; prin. cond. Calgary PO 1971–5.

hand horn. The 'natural' *French horn, i.e. without valves, which can produce only the notes of the harmonic series, together with some obtained by placing the hand in the bell of the instr.

Händl, Jacob (*b* Ribniča, 1550; *d* Prague, 1591). Slovenian composer. Was singer in imperial chapel, Vienna, by 1574. Choirmaster to Bishop of Olmütz, 1579–85, later cantor in Prague. Wrote 16 masses, many motets, and other church mus. Handel's *Funeral Anthem* is based on a Händl motet. Also known as Gallus.

Handley, Vernon (George) (*b* Enfield, 1930). Eng. conductor. Cond. Tonbridge Phil. Soc. 1958–61, Proteus Choir 1962–81. Cond. Guildford PO and Ch. 1962–83. Cond. LPO and Bournemouth SO in 1961. Prof., RCM 1966–72. Cond. Ulster Orch. 1985–9 and Malmö SO 1985–91. Specialist in Eng. mus. CBE 2004.

hand organ. *Barrel organ. The word 'hand' distinguishes it from the 'finger organ' (played from a kbd.).

Handy, W(illiam) **C**(hristopher) (*b* Florence, Alabama, 1873; *d* NY, 1958). Amer. composer whose parents had been slaves. Left home at 18 to become vagrant musician, playing tpt. in brass bands. Toured South with own orch. 1903–21. Became co-proprietor of mus. publishing business in Memphis. Among works he published were his own *Memphis Blues* (1912) and *St Louis Blues* (1914). Known as 'father of the blues'.

Hann, Georg (*b* Vienna, 1897; *d* Munich, 1950). Austrian bass-baritone. Served in Austrian Army in First World War. Bavarian State Opera, Munich, 1927–50 (created La Roche in *Capriccio*, 1942). Salzburg Fest. début 1931, singing there until 1949. Sang at Paris, Berlin, La Scala, CG (with Vienna co. 1947). Sang both buffo and dramatic roles, incl. Falstaff, Leporello, Ochs, Rigoletto, Sarastro, and Amfortas.

Hanover Square Rooms. Formerly London's prin. venue for concerts, built by Gallini, J. C. *Bach, and K. F. *Abel and opened in 1775 with a Bach–Abel subscription concert. *Salomon est. concerts there in 1786 at which, in 1791–2 and 1794–5, Haydn's 12 Salomon syms. were introduced. The Phil. Soc.'s concerts were given there 1833–69. Closed 1874.

Hänsel und Gretel. Opera in 3 acts by *Humperdinck to lib. by Adelheid Wette (his sister) based on story by brothers Grimm in *Kinder und Hausmärchen* (1812–14). F.p. Weimar 1893 (R. Strauss cond.); London 1894; NY 1895.

Hansen. Danish publishers of mus., founded 1853 by Jens Wilhelm Hansen. At first published educational mus., but later issued works by Gade and other Danish composers. Branch opened in Leipzig 1887 (closed during Second World War) and a Swedish branch, Nordiska Musikforlag, in 1915. New Ger. branch established 1951 in Frankfurt and in 1957 assoc. began with London firm of J. & W. Chester. Composers in Hansen list incl. Nielsen, Holmboe, Backer-Grøndhal, Svendsen, Sinding, Alfvén, Rosenberg, Bäck, Sibelius, and Kilpinen. Recently some Lutosławski has been published by them.

Hans Heiling. Opera in prol. and 3 acts by *Marschner to lib. by Devrient. Comp. 1831–2. F.p. Berlin 1833, Oxford 1953, Wexford 1983.

Hanslick, Eduard (*b* Prague, 1825; *d* Baden, nr. Vienna, 1904). Austrian critic and writer of Cz. descent. Deeply impressed by Wagner's *Tannhäuser* in Dresden, 1845, about which he wrote long critical article. Settled in Vienna 1846, contrib. articles on mus. and in 1848 becoming mus. ed. of *Wiener Zeitung*, while working as civil servant. Mus. critic *Die Presse* 1855–64, *Die Neue Freie Presse* 1864–95. His book *Vom Musikalisch-Schönen* (*Beauty in Music*) was pubd. 1854. Lect. in history and aesthetics of mus., Vienna Univ., 1856–95 (prof. from 1861). His *Beauty in Music* aligned him with the purist Leipzig school, represented by Mendelssohn, Schumann, and Brahms, against the Weimar school of Liszt and Wagner whose 'music of the future' had to comprise elements other than mus. His early admiration of Wagner changed to critical hostility with his review of *Lohengrin* in Vienna in 1858. Wagner's reaction was such that in the orig. poem of *Die Meistersinger* the character of Beckmesser was called Veit Hanslich. But those who regard Hanslick merely as the bigoted opponent of Wagner,

Strauss, Bruckner, etc. should read his criticism, which is among the best and most penetrating ever written.

Hanson, Howard (Harold) (*b* Wahoo, Nebraska, 1896; *d* Rochester, NY, 1981). Amer. composer and educator, of Swed. descent. First Amer. to win *Prix de Rome*, 1921, spending 3 years at Amer. Acad. in Rome. In 1924 became dir. of Eastman Sch. of Mus., holding this post for 40 years. Est. Amer. fests. at Rochester in 1925 at which hundreds of works by Amer. composers have received f.ps. Dir. of Inst. of Amer. Mus., Rochester Univ., from 1964. Known as 'the American Sibelius', his mus. reflects a similar romantic outlook firmly rooted in tonality, His book *Harmonic Materials of Modern Music* (NY 1960) shows his grasp of contemporary technical devices. His opera *Merry Mount* was cond. by Serafin at NY Met in 1934. Prin. works:

OPERAS: *Californian Forest Play* (1919); *Merry Mount* (1933); *Nymph and Satyr* (1978).

ORCH.: syms., No.1 (*Nordic*) (1921), No.2 (*Romantic*) (1930), No.3 (1938), No.4 (*Requiem*) (1943), No.5 (*Sinfonia Sacra*) (1955), No.6 (1968), No.7 (*Sea*), with ch. (1977); *Lux aeterna*, sym.-poem with va. obbl. (1923); org. conc. (1926); *Pan and the Priest*, sym.-poem with pf. obbl. (1926); *Merry Mount Suite* (1937); pf. conc. (1948); *Mosaics* (1958); *Summer Seascape* (1958); *Summer Seascape II* (1966); *Bold Island Suite* (1961); *Dies Natalis I* (1967); *Young Composer's Guide to the 6-Tone Scale* (1971–2).

CHORAL: *Lament for Beowulf*, ch., orch. (1923–5); *Heroic Elegy*, ch., orch. (1927); 3 *Songs from Drum Taps*, vv., orch. (1935); *Song of Democracy*, soloists, ch., orch. (1956); *Song of Human Rights*, cantata (1963); *Streams in the Desert*, ch., orch. (1969); *New Land, New Covenant*, oratorio (1976); *Prayer for the Middle Ages*, unacc. ch. (1976).

CHAMBER MUSIC: pf. quintet (1916); str. qt. (1923). Also works for pf. and songs.

Happy Birthday to You. Song comp. by Mildred Hill (1859–1916) of Louisville, Kentucky, and published by Clayton F. Summy, head of Chicago mus. pub. firm (est. 1888) as 'Good morning to all' in *Song Stories for the Kindergarten*, 1893, and later as march 'Happy birthday', 1934. Pubd. as song 'Happy birthday to you' with words by Patty Smith Hill (1868–1916) in *Union School Chorus Music*, 1935. Popular as choral greeting on birthdays. Used—not knowing it was Summy's copyright—by Stravinsky as basis for his short *Greetings Prelude*, comp. for Monteux's 80th birthday, 1955.

Happy End. Comedy with mus. in 3 acts by Weill to lib. by D. Lane (Elisabeth Hauptmann) and lyrics by Brecht. Comp. 1928–9. Prod. Berlin 1929. Contains songs 'Bilbao Song' and 'Surabaya Johnny'.

Happy Prince, The. Opera in 1 act by *Williamson for children's and women's vv., pf. duet, perc., and optional str. quintet, to his own lib. based on Oscar Wilde's fairy-tale. Comp. 1964–5. Prod. Farnham Fest., 1965.

Harawi, Chant d'Amour et de Mort. Song-cycle by Messiaen for sop. and pf. (1945), one of 3 of his works inspired by Tristan and Isolde legend (the others being 5 *Rechants and *Turan-galîla). F.p. Brussels 1946.

Hardelot, Guy d' [Mrs. W. I. Rhodes, *née* Helen Guy] (*b* Hardelot, Boulogne, 1858; *d* London, 1936). Fr. composer. Toured USA with Calvé, 1896. After marriage, settled in London. Wrote many songs (incl. *Because*, 1902) which went into repertory of Melba, Calvé, Plançon, Maurel, and others.

Hardenberger, Håkan (*b* Malmö, 1961). Swed. trumpeter. Won prizes at comps. in Paris, Munich, and Geneva. Brit. début Crystal Palace 1984 in Howarth's tpt. conc. Proms 1986 in Crosse's *Array*. Gave f.p. of Birtwistle's *Endless Parade*, Zurich, 1987.

Harding, Daniel (*b* Oxford, 1975). Eng. conductor. Ass. to Rattle at CBSO, début as cond. 1994; ass. to Abbado at Berlin PO, début 1996. Prin. cond. Trondheim SO 1997–2000. Mus. dir. Ger. Chamber PO, Bremen, 1997–2003; Mahler CO from 2003; Swedish Radio SO from 2007. Salzburg Fest. début 2003 (Staatskapelle Dresden), Vienna PO début 2004. Has cond. opera at Aix Fest. CG 2002 (*The Turn of the Screw*), Milan 2005 (*Idomeneo*).

Harewood, George (Henry Hubert Lascelles), **7th Earl of** (*b* London, 1923). Eng. opera administrator, writer, and editor. Enthusiasm for opera intensified when prisoner of war. Assoc. with EOG from its inception. Founded magazine *Opera* 1950 (ed. 1950–3). Board of dir. CG 1951–3 and 1969–72, controller of opera planning 1953–60. Dir., Leeds Fest. 1958–74; dir., Edinburgh Fest. 1961–5. Man. dir. SW Opera (ENO) 1972–85, chairman 1986–95. Art. dir. Adelaide Fest. 1988. Ed., 8th, 9th, 10th, and 11th edns. of *Kobbé's Complete Opera Book*, 1954, 1976, 1987, and 1997; *Kobbé's Illustrated Opera Book* (1989); autobiography *The Tongs and the Bones* (1982). KBE 1986.

Harfe (Ger.). Harp.

Hark, the Herald Angels Sing. Hymn orig. written by Charles Wesley (1743) beginning 'Hark, how all the welkin rings'. G. Whitefield incl. it in his *Collection* of 1753, substituting the familiar first line. It was further altered in other hymn publications in 1760, 1774, and 1775. In 1782 it was added to the suppl. of Tate and Brady. Dr. W. H. Cummings, org. of Waltham Abbey, fitted the tune of the 2nd no. of Mendelssohn's *Festgesang to the words for his choir and pubd. the adaptation in 1856. It soon became very popular. Mendelssohn thought the tune would 'never do to sacred words'.

harmonica. Name given at different times to various mus. instrs. Today its prin. meaning is the mouth-organ, a small wind instr. invented in 1830s with metal reeds, one to each note, which is held against the lips and moved from side to side according to the note desired. The term also meant mus. glasses (see *glass armonica*).

harmonic bass. Org. stop; same as *acoustic bass.

harmonic flute. Org. stop usually of 8' length but 4' pitch, pipes being pierced at half-length: silvery tone.

harmonic piccolo. Org. stop of 4' length and 2' pitch—on principle of *harmonic flute.

harmonics. Any note prod. by an instr. is accompanied by a number of other notes at fixed intervals above it. These are heard as the constituents of the single note, but can be prod. separately. On str. instrs. this is done by touching the string lightly at various points ('nodes') so splitting up the vibrations and producing notes of a flute-like purity (in Ger. and Fr. harmonics are indeed called *flageolet*). The lowest tone of the harmonic series (the 'fundamental') is the 1st harmonic, the next lowest the 2nd harmonic, and so on. Other tones are the 'upper partials' or 'overtones', at fixed intervals above the fundamental, an octave, then a perfect 5th, etc. On an open str. the result is a 'natural' harmonic; on a 'stopped' str. (a finger used to stop and another lightly placed) it is an 'artificial' harmonic. In brass instrs. harmonics are produced by varying the method of blowing. Every note of normal mus. instr. is a combination of the fundamental and certain upper partials. The only exception is the tuning-fork.

harmonic trumpet. Org. stop (see *trumpet*) embodying (in upper pipes, at any rate) constructional principle of *harmonic flute; 8' pitch.

harmonie (Fr., Ger., 'harmony'). *harmonie, musique d'harmonie, Harmoniemusik*, etc. means (1) a band of woodwind, brass, and perc. instr., as distinct from *fanfare*, a band of brass and perc.; or (2) the wind instr. of an orch.

harmonie, basse d' (Fr.). *Ophicleide.

harmonie, cor d' (Fr.). Valveless Fr. hn. See *hand horn*.

harmonie, trompette d' (Fr.). The ordinary modern *trumpet.

Harmonie der Welt, Die (The Harmony of the World). Opera in 5 acts by Hindemith to his own lib. based on life of 17th-cent. astronomer Johannes Kepler (author of *De harmonia mundi*). Comp. 1956–7 (earlier sketches). Prod. Munich 1957. Preceded by orch. sym. in 3 movts. comp. 1951, F.p. Basle 1952, f. Brit. p. Edinburgh 1953 cond. Furtwängler.

Harmonielehre (Ger.). Study, teaching, and theory of *harmony.

Harmoniemesse (Wind-band Mass). Popular name for Haydn's Mass No. 12 in B♭, of 1802, which makes a fuller, but not exclusive, use of wind instr. than is common in Haydn's Masses.

Harmoniemusik (Ger.). Mus. for wind instr.

Harmonious Blacksmith, The. Nickname for air and variations in Handel's 5th hpd. suite in E in the 1st set of 8 suites (1720). The name was bestowed after Handel's death and has no connection with the circumstances of the work's comp.

harmonium. Small portable example of the reed org. family dating from early 19th cent. Perfected by Debain of Paris *c*.1842, but the instr. made by Alexandre achieved wider popularity. It is blown by 2 pedals operated by left and right foot working in alternate strokes to drive air through bellows. Used as substitute for org. to acc. hymns etc., but has been used by Dvořák in his *Bagatelles* (with 2 vn. and vc.) and by R. Strauss in *Ariadne auf Naxos*.

harmony. The simultaneous sounding (i.e. combination) of notes, giving what is known as vertical mus., contrasted with horizontal mus. (*counterpoint). Composers, in much the greater proportion of their mus., maintain in their minds some melody which ranks as the principal one, and which they intend the listener to recognize as such, whilst other melodies which are combined with it, or chords with which it is acc., rank as subsidiary. The word *chord may be defined as any combination of notes simultaneously perf., and even when the main process in the composer's mind is a weaving together of melodic strands he has to keep before him this combinational element, both as regards the notes thus sounded together and the suitability of one combination to follow and precede the adjacent combination.

At different periods composers have given more attention to one or the other of the two aspects of their work: (a) the weaving together of melodic strands and (b) the chords thus brought into existence from point to point.

The former aspect of the result is the *contrapuntal* element (see *counterpoint) and the latter the *harmonic* element. In less elaborate mus. (as, for instance, a simple song with pf. acc.) the contrapuntal element may be unimportant or even non-existent. Counterpoint necessarily implies also harmony, but harmony does not necessarily imply counterpoint.

Over a long period the resources of harmony may be said to have widened: new combinations introduced by composers of pioneering spirit have been condemned by unaccustomed ears as ugly, have then gradually come to be accepted as commonplace, and have been succeeded in their turn by other experimental combinations. The following definitions concern traditional and basic harmonic procedures:

(*a*) DIATONIC HARMONY: harmony which confines itself to the major or minor key in force at the moment. CHROMATIC HARMONY: harmony which employs notes extraneous to the major or minor key in force at the moment.

(*b*) OPEN HARMONY: harmony in which the notes of the chords are more or less widely spread. CLOSE HARMONY: harmony in which the notes of the chords lie near together.

(*c*) PROGRESSION: the motion of one note to another note or one chord to another chord.

(*d*) TRIAD: a note with its 3rd and 5th (e.g. C–E–G). COMMON CHORD: a triad of which the 5th is perfect. MAJOR COMMON CHORD: a common chord of which the 3rd is major. MINOR COMMON CHORD: a common chord of which the 3rd is minor. AUGMENTED TRIAD: a triad of which the 5th is augmented. DIMINISHED TRIAD: a triad of which the 5th is diminished.

(*e*) ROOT of a chord: that note from which it originates (e.g., in the common chord C–E–G we have C as the root, to which are added the 3rd and 5th). INVERSION of a chord: the removal of the root from the bass to an upper part. FIRST INVERSION: that in which the 3rd becomes the bass (e.g. E–G–C or E–C–G). SECOND INVERSION: that in which the 5th becomes the bass (e.g. G–E–C or G–C–E). THIRD INVERSION: in a 4-note chord that inversion in which the fourth note becomes the bass (e.g., in the chord G–B–D–F the form of it that consists of F–G–B–D or F–B–G–D, etc.). FUNDAMENTAL BASS: an imaginary bass of a passage, consisting not of its actual bass notes but of the roots of its chords, i.e. the bass of its chords when uninverted.

(*f*) CONCORD: a chord satisfactory in itself (or an interval that can be so described; or a note which forms a part of such an interval or chord). CONSONANCE: the same as *concord*. DISCORD: a chord which is restless, requiring to be followed in a particular way if its presence is to be justified by the ear (or the note or interval responsible for producing this effect). See, for instance, the examples given under *dominant (seventh)* and *diminished (seventh)*. DISSONANCE: the same as *discord*. RESOLUTION: the satisfactory following of a discordant chord (or the satisfactory following of the discordant note in such a chord). SUSPENSION: a form of discord arising from the holding over of a note in one chord as a momentary (discordant) part of the combination which follows, it being then resolved by falling a degree to a note which forms a real part of the second chord. DOUBLE SUSPENSION: the same as the last with 2 notes held over.

(*g*) ANTICIPATION: the sounding of a note of a chord before the rest of the chord is sounded. RETARDATION: the same as a suspension but resolved by *rising* a degree.

PREPARATION: the sounding in one chord of a concordant note which is to remain (in the same 'part') in the next chord as a discordant note. (This applies both to fundamental discords and suspensions.)

UNPREPARED SUSPENSION: a contradiction in terms meaning an effect similar to that of suspension but without 'preparation'.

FUNDAMENTAL DISCORD: a discordant chord of which the discordant note forms a real part of the chord, i.e. not a mere suspension, anticipation, or retardation. Or the said discordant note itself (e.g. *dominant seventh, diminished seventh*, etc.).

PASSING NOTE: a connecting note in one of the melodic parts (not forming a part of the chord which it follows or precedes).

(*h*) FALSE RELATION: the appearance of a note with the same letter-name in different parts (or 'voices') of contiguous chords, in one case inflected (sharp or flat) and in the other uninflected.

(*i*) PEDAL (or 'point d'orgue'): the device of holding on a bass note (usually tonic or dominant) through a passage including some chords of which it does not form a part. INVERTED PEDAL: the same as the above but with the held note in an upper part. DOUBLE PEDAL: a pedal in which two notes are held (generally tonic and dominant).

From Wagner onwards the resources of harmony have been enormously extended, and those used by composers of the present day often submit to no rules whatever, being purely empirical, or justified by rules of the particular composer's own devising. Among contemp. practices are:

Bitonality—in which two contrapuntal strands or 'parts' proceed in different keys.

Polytonality—in which the different contrapuntal strands, or 'parts', proceed in more than one key.

Atonality—in which no principle of key is observed.

Microtonality—in which scales are used having smaller intervals than the semitone.

In the 20th cent. greater freedom in the treatment of the above procedures has developed, together with a much wider application of dissonance. Chords of 7th, 9th, 11th, and 13th are treated as primary chords, and there has been a return to the use of pentatonic scales, medieval modes, and the whole-tone scale. A prin. revolution *c*.1910 was the abandonment of the triad as the prin. and fundamental consonance. Composers such as Bartók, Stravinsky, Schoenberg, and Webern widened the mus. spectrum of tone-colour by showing that any combination of notes could be used as a basic unresolved chord. The tritone has been used as the cause of harmonic tensions in place of tonic-dominant relationships. Another 20th-cent. harmonic feature is the 'layering' of sound, each layer following different principles of organization. Milhaud produces bitonal passages from two layers in different tonalities.

Since 1950 much mus. has been comp. in which harmony has hardly any place, for example in some of the serial works of Boulez and Stockhausen. Where non-pitched sounds are used, harmony no longer exists and its place is taken by overtones, densities, and other concomitants of 'clusters', etc.

In amplification of this entry see *added sixth*, *augmented*, *consecutive*, *counterpoint*, and *chromatic intervals*.

Harnoncourt, Nikolaus (*b* Berlin, 1929). Austrian conductor, cellist, and musicologist. Founder-member Concentus Musicus of Vienna 1954, reviving early mus. on orig. instr. Amer. and Brit. débuts 1966. Prof. of mus. Mozarteum and Inst. of Musicology, Salzburg Univ., from 1972. Ed. of perf. edns. of Monteverdi's *Il ritorno d'Ulisse in Patria* and *L'incoronazione di Poppea* and of Bach choral works. Has cond. Mozart operas and other works with modern orchs. Salzburg Fest. début 1992.

Harold en Italie (Harold in Italy). Sym. (No.2) for orch., with solo va., by Berlioz, Op.16, inspired by Byron's *Childe Harold*. After a Paris concert of Berlioz's mus. in Dec. 1833, Paganini asked Berlioz for a va. work in which he could display his Stradivarius instr. Berlioz sent him the 1st movt. which Paganini rejected because it gave him too little to play. The work was completed in 4 movts. and f.p. Paris 1834, solo va. C. *Urhan.

harp. This instr., of very ancient lineage, can be simply defined as an open frame over which is stretched a graduated series of str., set in vibration by plucking with the fingers. In the modern orch. hp. the series is not normally chromatic, as it is in the pf., having merely 7 different notes with the octave, these being in the major scale of B (treated for convenience as that of C♭). There are 7 pedals, each affecting one note of this foundational scale; each pedal works to 2 notches, and by depressing it to its first or 2nd notch, respectively, the vibrating lengths of all the relevant strings are simultaneously shortened by fractions representing a semitone and a tone: thus all keys become possible, and by depressing all the pedals together the pitch of the complete instr. can be raised from C♭ (the normal key) to C♮ or C♯. The usual compass is 5½ octaves from C. Chords are normally played in more or less rapid succession of their notes, in the form understood by the word *arpeggio* (It. *arpa*, hp.). The typical 'sweeping' (*glissando*) action of the hand may be used in many kinds of scale (but evidently not in the chromatic scale, nor in any other scale passage employing more than 8 notes to the octave). In addition, of course, single str. may be plucked individually or in small groups. The instr. described above is the *double-action* hp., introduced by Érard (*c*.1810), the word 'double' marking its differences from its predecessors on which the pitches could be raised only a semitone.

One earlier form of the hp. is the *Welsh harp* or *telyn*, with 3 rows of str., the 2 outer rows (tuned in unison or octaves) giving the diatonic scale and the inner row the intermediate semitones: a simple modulation was effected by touching one of the inner str.

The hp. has been much used as a solo instr. in Wales from time immemorial and in Eng. domestically during the Victorian period. It was a frequent member of the early 17th-cent. orch. but in later times was rarely found again in orch. use until the 19th cent. when the great Romantic orchestrators—Berlioz, Wagner, Strauss, Mahler, Elgar, etc.—made effective use of it. In the 20th cent. it has been used in chamber mus. (e.g. by Debussy and Ravel). There are several hp. concs.

See also *chromatic harp, double harp, clàrsach, dital harp, aeolian harp.*

Harper, Edward (James) (*b* Taunton, 1941). Eng. composer, pianist, and conductor. Lect., Faculty of Mus., Edinburgh Univ. from 1964 (Reader from 1989), dir., New Music Group of Scotland 1975. Comps. incl.:

OPERAS: **Fanny Robin* (1974); *Hedda Gabler* (1984–5); *The Mellstock Quire* (1986–7); *Lochinvar, a Children's Opera* (2000).

ORCH.: pf. conc. (1969); *Bartók Games* (1972); sonata for chamber orch. (1972); *Fantasias I* (1975) and *V* (1985), chamber orch.; *Fern Hill*, chamber orch. (1976); sym. (1978–9); *Fantasia IV*, vn., pf., small orch. (1980); cl. conc. (1981–2); *Intrada after Monteverdi* (1983, orch. of 1982 chamber ens.); *Double Variations*, ob., bn., wind ens. (1989); *Etude for Orchestra* (1999).

CHAMBER ENS.: quintet for fl., cl., vn., vc., pf. (1973–4); *Ricercari in memoriam Luigi Dallapiccola* (1975); *Fantasia II*, 11 solo str. (1976); *Fantasia III*, brass quintet (1977); *Intrada after Monteverdi* (1982); str. qt. (1986); *In Memoriam*, vc., pf. (1989–90); trio, cl., vc., pf. (1997); *Souvenir*, 2 pf., vib., mar. (1998); *The Ash Grove*, str. qt. (2003).

CHORAL: *Chester Mass*, ch., orch. (1979); *Mass: Qui creavit coelum*, unacc. ch. (1986–7); *The Lamb*, sop., ch., orch. (1990); *The Voice of a City*, ch., chamber orch., org. (2000).

VOCAL: *7 poems by e. e. cummings*, sop., orch. (1977); *Caterwaul*, sop., db. (1986); *Homage to Thomas Hardy*, bar., chamber orch. (1990).

Harper, Heather (Mary) (*b* Belfast, 1930). Irish soprano. Sang in BBC Chorus. Opera début Oxford 1954 as Lady Macbeth. Sang The Woman in f. Brit. stage p. of Schoenberg's *Erwartung*, 1960. Glyndebourne début 1957; CG 1962; Bayreuth 1967; NY Met 1977. Outstanding roles incl. Elsa, Arabella in Strauss's opera, Ellen Orford, and the Governess in *The Turn of the Screw*. Sang in f.p. of Britten's *War Requiem*, 1962 and Tippett's 3rd Sym. 1972. Created Mrs Coyle in *Owen Wingrave*, TV 1971. Retired from stage 1984, but sang Nadia in *The Ice Break* at Proms 1990. Prof. of singing RCM from 1985, teacher of singing, Britten-Pears Sch., Snape, 1985–2002 (dir. of singing 1986–7). Sang at Proms 1994. CBE 1965.

Harp Quartet. Name for Beethoven's str. qt. No.10 in E♭ major, Op.74, comp. 1809, because of hp.-like pizzicato arpeggios in 1st movt.

harpsichord family (virginals, spinet, harpsichord). The *harpsichord* is a wing-shaped kbd. instr. in which the str. are plucked mechanically. It was developed during the 15th cent., the earliest surviving example (in the Victoria and Albert Museum, London) having been made in Bologna in 1521, but there are illustrated representations of the instr. dating from nearly a century earlier, and a reference in a Ger. poem of 1404 to the *clavicimbalum*, the earliest recorded use of the name from which the It. word *clavicembalo* is derived. The hpd. is fundamentally a mechanized *psaltery. Each key operates a mechanical device known as the 'jack', equipped with a small leather or quill plectrum attached

to a pivoted tongue. When the key is released the jack descends and, by positioning of a spring, the tongue pivots back, allowing the plectrum to pass the str. silently on its return. When the jack is back in its orig. position, a felt damper silences the vibration of the str. Very few contrasts of tone or dynamics are possible, variation in finger touch having little effect.

Italy was the home of the first important sch. of hpd. makers; at the end of the 16th cent., however, Antwerp became the centre of activity, particularly for the family of Ruckers. Their aim was to give the players some tonal contrast, a typical Ruckers single-manual instr. having a compass of four octaves from C and two sets of strings, one 8′ and one 4′. Hand stops in the right-hand side of the case brought one or both sets of jacks into contact with the strings. Ruckers also prod. a 2-manual hpd., the lower manual a 4th below the upper. From the 17th cent. to the end of the 18th, the hpd. was the indispensable supporting basis for continuo in almost every instr. combination, as well as being a popular domestic instr. With the development of the pf., the hpd. fell into semi-oblivion during the 19th cent., but in the 20th it has been revived both by modern composers, several of whom—e.g. Falla and McCabe—have written concs. for it, and in the authentic perf. of baroque mus. The **Dolmetsch* family played a major part in the revival, and there are several distinguished modern hpd. manufacturers. 20th-cent. virtuosi have incl. Wanda *Landowska and Ralph *Kirkpatrick.

virginal or *virginals*. This plucked kbd. instr. was first mentioned *c.*1460. The origin of the name is not, as is generally supposed, Eng. nor has it anything to do with Elizabeth I, but it is widely accepted that the name derives from the fact that young ladies were regularly depicted playing the instr. The main differences from the hpd. are in the oblong shape of the soundbox, the placing of the str. parallel to the kbd. instead of at right-angles, and the existence of 2 bridges. Sometimes one sees references to 'double virginals' or 'a pair of virginals'. The origins of these terms are obscure, since a double-manual virginal was extremely rare; a likely explanation is that they referred to the instr.'s compass. Eng. virginal mus. of the 17th cent. is of major importance; colls. of it incl. the **Fitzwilliam Virginal Book*, **Mye Ladye Nevells Booke*, and **Benjamin Cosyns Virginal Book*. The earliest pubd. coll. was **Parthenia* (1611).

spinet. This resembles the virginals in having one str. to a note, but differs from it in being not rectangular but wing-shaped in an uneven 6 sides with the longest containing the kbd. It has a 4-octave compass. The str. either run roughly parallel to the kbd. as with the virginals, or diagonally in front of the player. (In the *clavicytherium*, however, a rarer form than that described above, the str. ran perpendicularly like those of an upright pf.) The spinet was in use from the later 15th cent. to the end of the 18th.

Harrell, Lynn (*b* NY, 1944). Amer. cellist. Début recital, NY 1960. Prin. cellist Cleveland Orch.,

1965–71. Soloist since 1971, appearing with major Amer., Brit., and European orchs. Brit. début 1975, with LSO. Salzburg Fest. début 1979. Taught at Univ. of Cincinnati Coll.-Cons. of Mus. 1971–6, Juilliard Sch. 1976–86, Univ. of S. Calif., Los Angeles, 1986–92; int. chair of vc. studies, RAM 1986–93. Prin., RAM, 1993–4.

Harrhy, Eiddwen (Mair) (*b* Trowbridge, Wilts., 1949). Welsh soprano. Won Imperial League of Opera prize. Opera début as Ilia in *Idomeneo*, Oxford 1974, and made strong impression in Handel operas in 1974. CG début 1974; ENO 1977. Amer. début (Los Angeles) 1986.

Harries, Kathryn (*b* Hampton Court, 1951). Eng. soprano. Concert début London 1977. Presented BBC TV programme *Music Time*. Opera début Cardiff (WNO) 1983 (Flower Maiden in *Parsifal*). Débuts: Buxton Fest. 1983; ENO 1983; Scottish Opera 1985 (created Hedda Gabler in Harper's opera); NY Met 1986; CG 1989. Sang Dido in f. complete p. in France of *Les Troyens*, Lyons 1987 (also for Scottish Opera 1990).

Harris, (Sir) **Augustus** (*b* Paris, 1852; *d* Folkestone, 1896). Eng. impresario. Son of CG stage-manager. Ass. manager to Mapleson. Manager, Drury Lane, 1879–94, managing Carl Rosa opera seasons there 1883–7. Formed opera co. 1887, engaging de Reszke, Maurel, Melba, etc. Manager, CG from 1888, achieving brilliant success, paying careful attention to production details. Introduced opera in its orig. language to CG and was sturdy champion of Wagner's operas, presenting *Ring* cycles at CG 1892, cond. Mahler. Knighted 1891.

Harris, Renatus (*b* France, *c*.1652; *d* Salisbury, 1724). Eng. organ-builder (of 39 instr.). His grandfather (Renatus), father (Thomas), and sons (Renatus and John) were also org.-builders.

Harris, Roy (Ellsworth) (*b* Lincoln County, Nebraska, 1898; *d* Santa Monica, Calif., 1979). Amer. composer. His 1st sym., cond. Koussevitzsky in Boston, 1934, earned him the reputation as America's leading symphonist, confirmed by 3rd sym. in 1939. Taught at many colls., incl. Juilliard Sch. (1932–40), Cornell Univ. (1940–2), and Univ. of Calif., Los Angeles, 1961–73. His music is basically diatonic and consonant, its rugged rhythmic qualities and falling intervals, combined with a melodic flavour of hymn-tunes and folk-tunes, making him an Amer. counterpart of Janáček, without the Czech's genius. Prin. works:

ORCH.: syms.: No.1 (*Symphony 1933*) (1934), No.2 (1936), No.3 (1939), No.4 (*Folksong*, with ch.) (1940), No.5 (1943), No.6 (*Gettysburg Address*) (1944), No.7 (1952), No.8 (1962), No.9 (*Polytonality*) (1963), No.10 (*Abraham Lincoln*), ch., brass, 2 amp. pf., perc. (1965), No.11 (1968); No.12 (*Père Marquette*), ten. or spkr., orch. (1968–9, final vers. 1969); No.13 (but premièred as No.14!) (*Bicentennial*), ch., orch. (1976); *American Portraits* (1929); *When Johnny Comes Marching Home* (1935); *Prelude and Fugue* for str. (1936); *Farewell to Pioneers*

(1936); *Time Suite* (1937); *Ode to Friendship* (1944); conc. for 2 pf. (1946); accordion conc. (1946); *Kentucky Spring* (1949); vn. conc. (1949–51); pf. conc. (1953); *Ode to Consonance* (1957); *Elegy* (1958); *Epilogue to Profiles in Courage: J.F.K.* (1963–4); *Horn of Plenty* (1964); conc., amp. pf., wind, perc. (1968).

CHORAL: *Songs for Occupations* (unacc.) (1934); *Symphony for Voices* (unacc.) (1936); *Challenge 1940*, bar., ch., orch. (1940); *Cantata*, ch., org., brass (1943); *Mass*, male ch., org. (1943); *Psalm 150* (1955); *Give me the splendid silent sun*, bar., orch. (1959); *Canticle to the Sun*, coloratura sop., chamber orch. (1961); *Jubilation*, ch., brass, pf. (1964).

CHAMBER MUSIC: *Songs for a Rainy Day* for str. qt. (1925); str. qts. No.1 (1930), No.2 (1933), No.3 (1939); str. sextet (1932); pf. trio (1934); pf. quintet (1936); str. quintet (1940).

PIANO: sonata (1929); *Little Suite* (1938); *American Ballads* (1942).

Harris, (Sir) **William** (Henry) (*b* London, 1883; *d* London, 1973). Eng. organist and composer. Org., New Coll., Oxford, 1919–28, Ch. Ch., Oxford, 1928–33, St George's Chapel, Windsor, 1933–61. Cond., Oxford Bach Choir 1926–33. Prof. of org. and harmony RCM, 1923–53. Dir. of mus. studies, Royal Sch. of Church Mus., 1956–61. Comp. *The Hound of Heaven* for bar., ch., and orch., church mus., and org. works. KCVO 1954.

Harrison, Beatrice (*b* Roorkee, India, 1892; *d* Smallfield, Sussex, 1965). Eng. cellist. Début with Queen's Hall Orch. 1907. Frequently played in recitals with her violinist sister May (1891–1959). Delius's double conc. was written for them. Notable exponent of Elgar conc., which she recorded twice with the composer. Gave f.p. of Delius's vc. sonata, 1918, and f. Eng. p. of his vc. concerto, 1923, also f. Eng. p. of Ravel's sonata for vn. and vc., and Kodály's unacc. sonata. In early BBC broadcasts played vc. in Surrey wood to acc. of nightingale. Her sister (May) studied at RCM and with Auer in St Petersburg. London début in Mendelssohn conc.

Harrison, Jonty (*b* Scunthorpe, 1952). Eng. composer. Member of Nat. Youth Orch. of GB. Studied comp. with Bernard Rands. Worked at Nat. Th., London. Dir., Electro-Acoustic mus. studio, Birmingham Univ., from 1980. Worked at IRCAM 1982 and Groupe de Recherches Musicales, Paris, 1986. Many elec. comps.

Harrison, Julius (Allan Greenway) (*b* Stourport, 1885; *d* Harpenden, 1963). Eng. composer, conductor, and writer. Cond. opera CG 1913. In Paris 1914 to help Nikisch and Weingartner prepare Wagner perfs. Conducted for Beecham Co. and BNOC (1922–7). Cond. Scottish Orch. 1920–3. Cond., Hastings Municipal Orch. 1930–40 (doing splendid work for Brit. mus.). Prof of comp. RAM. Works, influenced by Elgar, incl. Mass in C and *Requiem*; cantata *Cleopatra*; suite *Worcestershire*

Pieces; *Cornish Sketches* for str., *Bredon Hill* for vn. and orch., str. qt., songs, etc. Contributor to various books on mus.; specialist on Brahms.

Harrison, Lou (*b* Portland, Oregon, 1917; *d* Lafayette, IN, 2003). Amer. composer and teacher. Organized concerts with John *Cage. Taught at Mills Coll., 1936–9. Went to NY 1943, writing mus. criticism for *Herald-Tribune* 1945–8 and working as copyist and ballet composer. Ed. some of *Ives's mus., incl. 3rd sym. of which he cond. f.p. 1947. Later taught in N Carolina and took many jobs not connected with mus. Also invented new methods of clavichord construction and built a Phrygian *aulos. His works reflect his busy and restless outlook: they combine Schoenbergian and aleatory procedures, use quartertones, call for extraordinary devices for producing unusual sounds, and emulate medieval polyphony and gamelan rhythms. Taught at San José State Univ. 1967–82, Mills Coll. 1980–5. Comps., in many genres, incl. operas *Rapunzel* (1954) and *Young Caesar* (1971); 14 ballets; ww. sextet *Schoenbergiana*; pf conc. (1985); *A Cornish Lancaran*, sax., gamelan (1986); *Grand Duo*, vn., pf. (1988); pf. trio (1990); *Suite for Percussion* (1992); *Tandy's Tango*, pf. (1992); *Vestiunt silve*, mez., fl., 2 va., hp. (1994); *A Parade for MTT*, orch. (1995); *Music for Remy*, ob., perc. (1998); hp. sonata (1999); 4 syms.; chamber mus.; choral works; songs; and gamelan pieces.

Hart, Fritz (*b* London, 1874; *d* Honolulu, 1949). Eng. conductor and composer. Friend of Holst, Vaughan Williams, and Hurlstone. Became th. cond. and went in 1908 to Australia. Dir., Melbourne Cons. 1915–35. Cond. Melbourne SO 1928. Prof. of mus., Univ. of Hawaii 1936–42. Cond. Honolulu SO 1932–49. Wrote 20 operas, 514 songs, sym. (1934), 3 vn. sonatas, 2 str. qts., and choral works. Style influenced by Eng. folksong.

Hartmann, Karl Amadeus (*b* Munich, 1905; *d* Munich, 1963). Ger. composer. Works perf. in 1930s but he withdrew from public life because of opposition to Nazi régime. After 1945 organized Musica Viva concerts of new works in Munich. His mus. is very much of its time, with marked polyphonic tendencies and showing traces of such varied influences as Bruckner, Berg, Stravinsky, and Blacher. Comp. 8 syms. (No.1 for cont. and orch. to text by Whitman) between 1936 and 1962; also 2 str. qts. (1933 and 1945–6); chamber opera *Des Simplicius Simplicissimus Jugend* (comp. 1934–5, prod. Cologne 1949); vn. conc.; pf. conc.; va. conc.

Hartmann, Rudolf (*b* Ingolstadt, 1900; *d* Munich, 1988). Ger. opera producer and impresario. Chief resident producer Altenberg 1924, Nuremberg 1928–34 and 1946–52; Berlin State Opera 1934–8. Many prods. at Salzburg Fest. 1931–69 (début with *Die Entführung*). Specially assoc. with cond. Clemens Krauss and operas of R. Strauss at Munich as chief prod. 1938–44 and intendant 1953–67. Prod. *Die Meistersinger* at Bayreuth 1951. At CG prod. *Elektra* (1953), *Ring* cycle

(1954), *Arabella* (1965), and *Die Frau ohne Schatten* (1967). Author of *Richard Strauss, the Staging of his Operas and Ballets* (Fribourg 1980, Eng. trans. 1981).

Harty, (Sir) (Herbert) **Hamilton** (*b* Hillsborough, Co. Down, 1879; *d* Brighton, 1941). Irish composer, conductor, organist, and pianist. Church org. at age 12, later holding posts in Belfast and Dublin. Settled in London 1900 where he quickly won attention as composer and as brilliant pf. accompanist. Gradually his conducting took priority. Cond. opera at CG and LSO concerts. Appointed permanent cond. Hallé Orch. 1920, holding post until 1933 and re-establishing orch. as one of finest in Eur. Cond. f. Eng. p. of Mahler's 9th Sym., Manchester 1930, and of Shostakovich's 1st Sym., Manchester 1932, also f. public p. of Lambert's *Rio Grande*, Manchester 1929. Cond. f.p. of Walton's 1st sym. (London 1934 without *finale*, London 1935 complete). Cond. LSO and other orchs. from 1933. Comps. incl. pf. quintet; *Irish Symphony*; vn. conc.; pf. conc.; *Ode to a Nightingale* for sop. and orch.; sym.-poems *With the Wild Geese* and *The Children of Lir*; cantata *The Mystic Trumpeter*, ch., orch.; also modern orchestrations of Handel's *Water Music* and *Fireworks Music*. Knighted 1925.

Harvey, Jonathan (Dean) (*b* Sutton Coldfield, 1939). Eng. composer and teacher. Cellist in Nat. Youth Orch. On staff, mus. dept., Southampton Univ. 1964–77, Sussex Univ. 1977–93 (prof. from 1980); Stanford Univ. 1993–2000. Comps., some of which use tape, incl.:

OPERA: *Inquest of Love* (1991–2).

CHURCH OPERA: *Passion and Resurrection* (1981).

ORCH.: sym. (1966); *Benedictus* (1970); *Persephone Dream* (1972); *Inner Light III* (1975); *Smiling Immortal* (ballet), chamber orch., pre-prepared tape (1977); *Bhakti*, 15 instr., quad. tape (1982); *Madonna of Winter and Spring*, orch., synth., elec.) (1986); *Lightness and Weight*, tuba, orch. (1986); *Timepieces* (1987); vc. conc. (1990); *Fanfare for Utopia*, chamber orch. (1995); perc. conc. (1997); *Calling across Time*, chamber orch. (1998); *Tranquil Abiding*, chamber orch. (1998).

INSTR. AND CHAMBER: *Dialogue*, vc., pf. (1965); *4 Images after Yeats* (1969); *Inner Light I*, instr., tape (1973); pf. trio (1971); str. qts. No.1 (1977), No.2 (1988), No.3 (1995), No.4 (with live elec.) (2003); *Concelebration*, fl., cl., vc., pf., perc. (1979, rev. 1980); *Modernsky Music*, 2 ob., bn., hpd. (1981); *Curve with Plateaux*, vc. (1982); *Valley of Aosta*, 13 players (1988); *Serenade in homage to Mozart*, 10 wind (1991); *Chant*, va. (1992); *Lotuses*, fl. qt. (1992); *Sufi Dance*, gui. (1997); *Death of Light, Light of Death*, ob./ca., hp./tam-tam, vn., va., vc. (1998); *Bird Concerto with Pianosong*, pf., chamber orch., live elec. (2001); *Moving Trees*, chamber ens. (2002); *Jubilus*, va., chamber ens. (2003); trio, cl., vn., pf. (2004); *Run before Lightning*, fl., pf. (2004).

VOCAL AND ORCH.: *Cantata I* (1965), *Cantata IV—Ludus Amoris*, sop., ten., spkr., ch., orch. (1969); *Cantata VI*, ch., str. (1970); *Cantata VII—On Vision*, sop., ten., spkr., chamber group, tape (1971); *Inner*

Light II, vv., ens., tape (1977); *Hymn*, ch., orch. (1979); *The Path of Devotion*, ch., orch. (1983); *The Angels*, unacc. ch. (1994); *Ashes Dance Back*, ch., elec. (1997); *White as Jasmin*, sop., orch. (1999); *Mothers Shall Not Cry*, sop., ten., female ch., orch., elec. (2000); *Remember, O Lord*, unacc. ch. (2003).

VOICE AND INSTR(S).: *Angel Eros*, v., str. qt. (1973); *Cantata II–3 Lovescapes*, sop., pf. (1967); *Cantata III*, sop., chamber ens. (1969); *Cantata V—Black Sonnet*, 4 singers, wind quintet (1970); *The Dove Descending*, ch., org. (1975); *Cantata X—Spirit Music*, sop., 3 cl., pf. (1975); *Magnificat and Nunc Dimittis*, ch., org. (1978, rev. 2002); *Nachtlied*, sop., pf., tape (1984); *Song Offerings*, sop., 8 players (1985); *From Silence*, sop., vn., va., perc., 3 synth., tape (1988); *You*, sop., cl., va., vc., db. (1992); *Sweet/Winterhart*, ch., vn. (2001); *Chu*, sop., cl., vc. (2002); *Buddhist Song*, mez., pf., *No.1* (2003), *No.2* (2004).

TAPE: *Time-Points*, magnetic tape (1970); *Veils and Melodies*, 3 prepared tapes (1978); *Mortuos plango, Vivos voco*, computer-manipulated concrete sounds (1980); *Ritual Melodies* (1989); *Mythic Figures*, tape (2001).

Harvey, Trevor (Barry) (*b* Freshwater, I.o.W., 1911; *d* London, 1989). Eng. conductor, critic, and broadcaster. Worked for BBC (ass. ch. master) 1935–42. Free-lance cond. from 1946. Cond. Sir Robert Mayer children's concerts 1951–73, Brit. Youth Orch. 1960–72.

Harwood, Basil (*b* Woodhouse, Glos., 1859; *d* London, 1949). Eng. composer and organist. Org., Ely Cath., 1887–92, Ch. Ch., Oxford, 1892–1909. Comp. of org. sonatas and many church anthems, etc.

Harwood, Elizabeth (Jean) (*b* Barton Seagrave, 1938; *d* Ingatestone, Essex, 1990). Eng. soprano. Won Ferrier Prize 1960. Opera début Glyndebourne 1960 (Second Boy in *Die Zauberflöte*). SW 1961–5; CG début 1967; Salzburg Fest. 1970; NY Met 1976. Particularly fine Strauss singer. Recorded title-role in *Die lustige Witwe* with Karajan and Tytania in *A Midsummer Night's Dream*, cond. Britten. Also outstanding exponent of oratorio (Handel, Elgar), and of English song.

Háry János (John Háry). Opera in prol., 4 parts, and epilogue by Kodály to lib. by Paulini and Harsányi after poem *The Veteran* by Garay. Comp. 1925–6. Prod. Budapest 1926, NY 1960, London 1967. Orch. suite of 6 movts. drawn from opera f.p. NY 1927, cond. Mengelberg.

Haskil, Clara (*b* Bucharest, 1895; *d* Brussels, 1960). Romanian pianist, later Swiss citizen. Début Bucharest 1904. Concert career began in 1910. Exponent of classical and early romantic composers.

Hasler, Hans. See *Hassler, Hans*.

Hassan, or The Golden Journey to Samarkand. Play by James Elroy Flecker (1884–1915) for the first prod. of which in Darmstadt 1923 Delius comp. (1920–3) incid. mus. incl. songs,

dances, and choral episodes. Prod. London later in 1923. The *Intermezzo* and *Serenade* exist in several arrs. and there is a *Suite* arr. Fenby 1933.

Hasse, Johann (Adolph) (*b* Bergedorf, 1699; *d* Venice, 1783). Ger. composer. Sang at Hamburg Opera as ten. 1718–19, then at Brunswick where his opera *Antioco* was prod. 1721. Went to Naples 1724, writing several popular operas. Married singer Faustina *Bordoni in 1730. Dir., Dresden court opera 1731–63, also visiting London and It. Most of his MSS destroyed in siege of Dresden. Moved to Vienna 1763, comp. operas to Metastasio librettos in opposition to Gluck and eventually setting almost all Metastasio's opera texts. Lived in Venice from 1775. Despite nationality, It. by style and inclination. Wrote over 100 operas, also masses, oratorios, sinfonias, etc. Hearing Mozart's *Ascanio in Alba* in 1771 said: 'This boy will cause us all to be forgotten'.

Hassid, Josef [Chasyd, Joseph] (*b* Suwalki, Poland, 1923; *d* Epsom, 1950). Pol. violinist. At age of 10 entered Wieniawski comp., 1934 (1st and 2nd prizewinners were Ginette *Neveu and David *Oistrakh). First London recital 1938. Début with orch. 1938 (Tchaikovsky conc. with LPO). Last concert London 1941. Career terminated by mental illness.

Hassler [Hasler], **Hans Leo** (*b* Nuremberg, 1562; *d* Frankfurt-am-Main, 1612). Ger. composer and organist. Org. at Augsburg 1586–1600, Nuremberg 1601–8, Dresden from 1608. Wrote It. *canzonette, cantiones sacrae*, madrigals, masses, and motets.

Haubenstock-Ramati, Roman (*b* Kraków, 1919; *d* Vienna, 1994). Austrian composer (Polish-born). Mus. dir., Radio Kraków 1947–50. Dir., state mus. library and prof. of mus., Tel Aviv Acad. 1950–7. Worked at Fr. Radio *musique concrète* studio, 1957. Settled in Vienna 1957–68, working for Universal Edition. Composer of several elec. works. Much concerned with new methods of notation. Organized first exhibition of graphic scores, Donaueschingen 1959.

Hauer, Josef Matthias (*b* Wiener Neustadt, 1883; *d* Vienna, 1959). Austrian composer. Met Schoenberg 1919. In 1919, independently of Schoenberg, developed 12-note system and wrote his first 12-note piece, *Nomos*. Method based on 44 combinations (tropes) of 12 notes of the octave, each subdivided into 6-note groups. Did not get on well with Schoenberg because of his insistence that he first 'discovered' 12-note composition, even to proclaiming it on his stationery. Works incl. operas *Die schwarze Spinne* (1932, f.p. Vienna 1966) and *Salambo* (1930, f.p. Vienna 1983); oratorio *Wandlungen*; pf. conc.; vn. conc.; Hölderlin songs; 3 str. qts. From 1939 all his works bore the title *Zwölftonspiel* (12-note piece).

Haugland, Aage (*b* Copenhagen, 1944; *d* Copenhagen, 2000). Danish bass-baritone. Début Oslo 1968 in Martinů's *Comedy on the Bridge*. Member of Danish Royal Opera from 1973. CG début 1975. Sang Hagen in *The Twilight of the Gods*, ENO 1975. Amer. début (St Louis) 1979; NY Met 1979; Milan 1981; Salzburg 1982; Bayreuth 1983. Roles incl. Hunding, Hagen, King Mark, Fafner, Klingsor, Boris, Ochs, Wozzeck.

Haugtussa (Norweg. The Mountain Maid). Song-cycle for sop. and pf., Op.67, by Grieg, comp. 1895, being settings of 8 poems by Arne Garborg written in archaic Norweg. and pubd. 1895. The songs are 1. *Det syng* (The Singing), 2. *Veslemy* (Little Maid), 3. *Blaaberri* (Bilberry slopes), 4. *Mote* (Meeting), 5. *Elsk* (Love), 6. *Killingsdans* (Kidlings' dance), 7. *Vond dag* (Evil Day), 8. *Ved gjaetlebekken* (By the brook).

Hauk, Minnie [Hauck, Amalia Mignon] (*b* NY, 1851; *d* Tribschen, Lucerne, 1929). Amer. soprano. Début Brooklyn 1866 (Amina in *La sonnambula*). CG 1868. First Amer. and London Carmen, but also famous as Norma, Amina, and other *bel canto* roles. Sang title-role in *Manon* at its Amer. première 1885. NY Met 1891. Formed own opera co., but after one year retired to live with husband in Wagner's villa Tribschen. After war became blind and poor; supported by funds from Amer. opera enthusiasts.

Haunted Ballroom, The. Ballet in 1 act, mus. and lib. by Geoffrey Toye, choreog. by de Valois. Prod. London 1934.

Hauptstimme (Ger.). Prin. v. or part.

Hauptthema (Ger.). Prin. subject of a comp.

Hauptwerk (Ger., 'chief work'). great organ.

Hausegger, Siegmund von (*b* Graz, 1872; *d* Munich, 1948). Austrian composer and conductor. Cond. Frankfurt Museum concerts 1903–6, Hamburg PO 1910–20, Konzertverein, Munich (Munich PO from 1928) 1920–38. Dir., Munich Acad. of Mus. 1920–34. Wrote 2 operas, symphonic poems, songs, etc.

Hausmann, Robert (*b* Rottleberode, 1852; *d* Vienna, 1909). Ger. cellist. Member of Count Hochberg's qt., Dresden, 1872–6; of Joachim Qt. 1879–1907. Prof. of vc. Berlin Hochschule from 1876. Gave f.p. of Brahms's 2nd vc. sonata, Op.99, in 1886 and, with Joachim, of Brahms's double conc. (Cologne 1887).

hautboy. Obsolete Eng. name for *oboe, derived from Fr. *hautbois* ('loud wood') from which the It. *oboe* was derived.

Hautcousteaux, Artus. See *Auxcousteaux, Artus*.

haute danse (Fr., 'high dance'). An old general term covering any dance in which the feet were lifted, as distinguished from the *basse danse*, in which they were kept close to the floor.

havanaise (Fr.). Same as *habanera*.

Hawaiian guitar. Type of guitar introduced by Portuguese which has distinctive str. tunings.

The str. are 'stopped' with a small moveable metal bar which goes across all str., in order to obtain the characteristic portamento effect.

Hawes, William (*b* London, 1785; *d* London, 1846). Eng. composer, conductor, and violinist. Violinist, CG orch. 1802–5. Gentleman, Chapel Royal, 1805, master of choristers 1817. From 1812, master of choristers, St Paul's Cath. Dir. of Eng. opera at Lyceum Th., 1824–36. Had pub. business in the Strand and was org. of Lutheran Chapel of the Savoy. Adapted many operas for Eng. stage, incl. *Così fan tutte* and *Don Giovanni*. Introduced *Der Freischütz* to Eng., 1824, adding some airs of his own. Wrote glees and madrigals.

Haydn, Franz Joseph (*b* Rohrau, 1732; *d* Vienna, 1809). Austrian-born composer of pure Ger. stock. The son of a farmer-wheelwright, Haydn showed immediate mus. precocity and at the age of 5 was given into the care of a Hainburg schoolmaster called Franck, who taught him the rudiments of mus. At 8 went to Vienna as choirboy at St Stephen's. When his v. broke at 17, he lived in poverty as a teacher and became accompanist and servant to the It. composer and teacher *Porpora. He worked for two aristocratic patrons in 1750s, and in 1761 was engaged as vice-Kapellmeister at Eisenstadt, Hungary, by Prince Paul Esterházy. Haydn remained with the Esterházy household for 30 years, for both Prince Paul and his successor Prince Nikolaus, who reigned from 1762 to 1790, were passionate mus.-lovers. In 1766 Nikolaus built the palace of Eszterháza (modelled on Versailles) on the south side of the Neusiedlersee, spending the greater part of each year in this isolated home. Haydn's art benefited from this seclusion. 'There was no one near to confuse me, so I was forced to become original', he said. His duties were numerous; besides administrative work and caring for the court musicians, he cond. the orchestra, arr. and dir. operatic perfs., played in chamber mus., and produced a stream of works in many genres, incl. incidental mus. for plays, to please his patron. Haydn's fame spread from Eszterháza throughout Austria, Ger., and It. as his syms. were pubd. Fr. edns. of his works began to appear in the 1760s and later in London. In 1785 he was commissioned by Cadiz to compose an oratorio without words on the Saviour's 7 Last Words, and by the Parisian soc. Concert de la Loge Olympique to compose 6 syms. By this time he had become friends with Mozart, for whom he had the highest admiration. Their works from this date (1781) betray mutual influence. Haydn's life at Eszterháza ended in 1790 when Prince Nikolaus died and his successor dismissed the musicians, though leaving Haydn his salary and title. Haydn left the castle for Vienna where he accepted an invitation from the impresario J. P. *Salomon to visit London. He stayed in England from 1 Jan. 1791 to the middle of 1792, being fêted, lionized, and entertained by royalty. He comp. syms. 93–98 on this visit, when he was deeply impressed by the 1791 Handel Fest. in Westminster Abbey. In

July 1791 the hon. degree of D.Mus. was conferred on him by Oxford Univ. On his return to Vienna he bought a house there and accepted Beethoven as a pupil, an uneasy relationship for both great men. In 1794 he visited Eng. again, having been commissioned by Salomon to write 6 new syms. This 2nd visit lasted from Feb. 1794 to Aug. 1795 and was even more successful artistically and, especially, financially than the first. The Esterházy family had now reconstituted their mus. est., but Haydn comp. only for special occasions and was allowed to concentrate on his work as a composer. Between 1796 and 1802 he wrote 6 magnificent settings of the Mass. In 1797 he comp. his *Gott erhalte Franz den Kaiser*, which was adopted as Austria's nat. anthem. But his chief pre-occupation at this time was his oratorio *Die Schöpfung* (The Creation), f.p. privately in Vienna, 1798. This was followed by *Die Jahreszeiten* (The Seasons), f.p. 1801. From then on, Haydn's health began to fail and, though he made several more public appearances, he died during the Fr. occupation of Vienna.

If Haydn's life was comparatively uneventful, his vast output of mus. is notable for the number of delights and surprises contained in almost every work. Yet though the number and magnitude of Haydn masterpieces are constantly amazing, his mus. for long failed to exert as powerful a sway over the public as that of Mozart and Beethoven. He is regarded as the 'father' of the sym. (which he was not) and of the str. qt., but some treasurable Haydn lies in his vocal mus., in his oratorios, masses, and in his operas (which are still in process of re-discovery). In all his mus. his inventive flair seems inexhaustible. He delighted in exploiting the capabilities of solo instr. and virtuoso performers, and every genre in which he worked he enlarged, extended, and re-shaped. The syms. are a remarkable example of his development of a particular form, hallmarked by deep feeling, drama, elegance, wit, and, in the final 12, a Mozartian perfection of all these qualities combined. But much the same can be said of the qts. and masses; nor should the kbd. sonatas be overlooked.

The cataloguing of Haydn's works has been the object of considerable scholarship. It was begun in 1766 by Haydn himself, aided by the Esterházy court copyist Joseph Elssler, whose son Johann (1769–1843) later became Haydn's copyist and faithful servant. Haydn worked on this list until about 1805. Pohl prepared a MS catalogue, and for the Breitkopf und Härtel complete edn. Mandyczewski assembled his list of 104 syms. (omitting 3 now acknowledged as such). Modern scholarship, led by H. C. Robbins *Landon, has amended this list, and a thematic catalogue has been ed. by *Hoboken in which works are given Hob. nos. in the manner of Köchel's Mozart catalogue.

Haydn's works are too numerous to be listed in full detail. The following is a concise list of the prin. comps.:

OPERAS: 20 were comp., some of the first being lost. The extant 15 incl. *La Canterina* (1766); *Lo Speziale*

(1768); *Le Pescatrici* (1769); *L'*infedeltà delusa* (1773); *L'incontro improvviso* (1775); *Il *mondo della luna* (1777); *La *vera costanza* (1777–8, rev. 1785); *L'*isola disabitata* (1779, rev. 1802); *La *fedeltà premiata* (1780, rev. 1782); *Orlando Paladino* (1782); *Armida* (1783); *Orfeo ed Euridice* (1791); also 5 puppet operas incl. *Philemon und Baucis* (1773) and *Dido* (1776).

MASSES: No.1 in F (*Missa brevis*) (1750); No.2 in E♭ (*Grosse Orgelmesse*) (1766); No.3 in C (*St Cecilia*) (1776); No.4 in G (1772); No.5 in B♭ (*Kleine Orgelmesse*) (c.1775); No.6 in C (*Mariazellermesse*) (1782); No.7 in C (*In tempore belli—*Paukenmesse*) (1796); No.8 in B♭ (*Heiligmesse*) (1796); No.9 in D minor (*Nelson*) (1798); No.10 in B♭ (*Theresienmesse*) (1799); No.11 in B♭ (*Schöpfungsmesse*) (1801); No.12 in B♭ (*Harmoniemesse*) (1802). Also Mass in G (c.1750).

CANTATAS & ORATORIOS: *Stabat Mater* (1767); *Applausus* (1768); *Il Ritorno di Tobia* (1774–5); *Die sieben letzten Worte unseres Erlösers am Kreuz* (The *Seven Last Words of Our Saviour on the Cross, 1st version (str. qt.) 1785, choral version 1795–6); *Die Schöpfung* (The *Creation) (1796–8); *Die Jahreszeiten* (The *Seasons) (1799–1801).

SYMPHONIES: Nos. 1–5 (1757); No.6 in D (*Le *Matin*), No.7 in C (*Le Midi*), No.8 in G (*Le Soir*) (c.1761); No.9 in C (c.1762); No.10 in D (c.1761); No.11 in E♭ (c.1760); No.12 in E, No.13 in D (1763); No.14 in A, No.15 in D (1764); No.16 in B♭, No.17 in F, No.18 in G, No.19 in D, No.20 in C (all before 1766, prob. 1761–2); No.21 in A, No.22 in E♭ (*The *Philosopher*), No. 23 in G, No.24 in D (1764); No.25 in C (c.1761–3); No.26 in D minor (*Lamentatione*) (c.1770); No.27 in G (c.1760); No.28 in A, No.29 in E, No.30 in C (*Alleluia*), No.31 in D (*Horn Signal*) (1765); No.32 in C, No.33 in C (c.1760); No.34 in D minor (c.1766); No.35 in B♭ (1767); No.36 in E♭ (c.1761–5); No.37 in C (c.1757); No.38 in C (*Echo*) (c.1766–8); No.39 in G minor (c.1768); No.40 in F (1763); No.41 in C (c.1769); No.42 in D (1771); No.43 in E♭ (*Merkur*), No.44 in E minor (*Trauer*) (c.1771); No.45 in F♯ minor (*Abschied*), No.46 in B, No.47 in G (1772); No.48 in C (*Maria Theresia*) (c.1768–9); No.49 in F minor (*La *Passione*) (1768); No.50 in C (1773); No.51 in B♭, No.52 in C minor (c. 1771–3); No.53 in D (*L'*Impériale*) (c.1780); No. 54 in G, No.55 in E♭ (*Der *Schulmeister*), No.56 in C (1774); No.57 in D (1774); No.58 in F, No.59 in A (*Feuersymphonie*) (c.1776–8); No.60 in C (*Il *Distratto*) (1774); No.61 in D (1776); No.62 in D, No.63 in C (*La *Roxolane*) (c.1780); No.64 in A (c.1775); No.65 in A (c.1771–3); No.66 in B♭, No.67 in F, No.68 in B♭, No.69 in C (*Laudon*) (c.1778); No.70 in D (1779); No.71 in B♭ (c.1779–80); No.72 in D (c.1763–5); No.73 in D (*La *Chasse*) (1780–1); No.74 in E♭ (1780); No.75 in D (1779); No.76 in E♭, No.77 in B♭, No.78 in C minor (1782); No.79 in F, No.80 in D minor, No.81 in G (1783–4); No. 82 in C (*Bear*) (1786); No.83 in G minor (*La *Poule*) (1785); No.84 in E♭ (1786); No.85 in B♭ (*La *Reine*) (1785); No.86 in D (1786); No.87 in A (1785); No.88 in G, No.89 in F (c.1787); No.90 in C, No.91 in E♭ (1788); No.92 in G (*Oxford*) (1789); No.93 in D, No.94 in G

(*Surprise*), No.95 in C minor, No.96 in D (*Miracle*) (1791, London); No.97 in C (1792, London); No.98 in B♭ (c.1792, London); No.99 in E♭ (1793, Austria); No.100 in G (*Military*), No.101 in D (*Clock*), No.102 in B♭ (1794, London); No.103 in E♭ (*Paukenwirbel*, Drum Roll), No.104 in D (*London*) (1795, London).

CONCERTOS: vc. in C (c.1765), in D (1783); Klavier in D (c.1784), Klavier and str. in G; hn. No.1 in D (1762), No.2 in D (c.1764); 2 hn. and str. in E♭; for *lira organizzata* No.1 in C, No.2 in G, No.3 in G, No.4 in F, No.5 in F (c.1786); org. conc. (1756); for tpt. in E♭ (1796); for vn. No.1 in A, No.2 in C, No.3 in G (c.1765); for vn., pf., and str. in F (1766); *Sinfonia Concertante* in B♭ for ob., bn., vn., vc. (1792).

STRING QUARTETS: Op.1 (6 qts., 1760); Op.2, Nos. 7–12 (Nos. 9 and 11, with 2 hn. added) (1755–60); Op.9 (6 qts., 1771); Op.17, Nos. 25–30 (1771); Op.20, Nos. 31–6 (1772); Op.33, Nos. 37–42 (1781); Op.42, No.43 (1758); Op.50, Nos. 44–9 (c.1787); Op.51, Nos. 50–6 (1785, *Seven Last Words from the Cross*); Op.54, Nos. 57–9 (c.1788); Op.55, Nos. 60–2 (c.1788); Op.64, Nos. 63–8 (c.1790); Op.71, Nos. 69–71 (1793); Op.74, Nos. 72–4 (1793); Op.76, Nos. 75–80 (c.1797); Op.77, Nos. 81–2 (c.1799); Op. 103, No.83 (1802–3).

KEYBOARD: 62 sonatas (c. 1761–94), *Variations* in F minor (1793).

CHAMBER MUSIC: 32 pf. trios; 6 sonatas for klavier and vn.; fl. qts; lute qt.; divertimentos for str. trio; str. trios; 126 *baryton trios; 32 pieces for mechanical clocks; and *Notturnos* for lira organizzata.

SOLO CANTATAS: *Arianna a Naxos* for sop./mez. (1790); *Berenice che fai* (1795).

VOCAL: qts. and trios (1796 and 1799); *Alfred—Chorus of the Danes* (1796); 12 canzonettas to Eng. words for solo v. and pf. (1794–5) incl. *My mother bids me bind my hair*, *Spirit's Song*, *Piercing Eyes*, *She never told her love*; 450 arrs. of Brit. folk-songs (1791–1805).

Haydn, (Johann) **Michael** (*b* Rohrau, 1737; *d* Salzburg, 1806). Austrian-born composer, brother of Franz Joseph *Haydn. Chorister, St Stephen's, Vienna, 1745–55, also deputy org. Court mus. and Konzertmeister to Archbishops of Salzburg 1763 to end of his life. Wrote 40 syms., vn. concs., hn. concs., tpt. conc., hpd.-and-va. conc., fl. concs., 12 str. quartets, operas, masses, and vast amount of other church mus. *Weber and *Diabelli were among his pupils. His *Requiem* in C minor was perf. at his brother's funeral.

'Haydn' Quartets. Name customarily given to set of 6 str. qts. by Mozart (No.14 in G, K387 (1782), No.15 in D minor, K421 (1783), No.16 in E♭, K428 (1783), No.17 in B♭, *Hunt*, K458 (1784), No.18 in A, K464 (1785), No.19 in C, *Dissonanzen*, K465 (1785)), because he ded. them to Haydn, who played 1st vn. in perfs. at Mozart's house (Mozart played the va.).

Hayes, William (*b* Gloucester, 1707; *d* Oxford, 1777). Eng. composer and organist. Org., Worcester Cath., 1731–4, Magdalen Coll., Oxford, 1734–

42, prof. of mus., Oxford Univ., 1742–77. Champion of Handel's mus. Comp. cantatas, catches, glees, church mus.

Haym, Hans (*b* Halle, 1860; *d* Elberfeld, 1921). Ger. conductor and composer. Mus. dir. Elberfelder Gesangverein, 1890–1920. Friend and champion of Delius. In Elberfeld cond. f.p. of *Over the Hills and Far Away* (1897), *Paris* (1901), unpubd. 1st version (1897) of pf. conc. (1904), *Appalachia* (1904), and f. complete p. in Ger. of *A Mass of Life*, 1909.

Haym, Nicola (Francesco) (*b* Rome, 1678; *d* London, 1729). It. cellist, composer, and librettist, of Ger. parentage, who took leading role in establishing It. opera in London. Played violone in private orch. in Rome under Corelli 1694–1700. From 1701 to 1711 was in London as chamber musician to Duke of Bedford. Played vc. in orch. when Clayton's *Arsinoe* was first all-sung opera in It. style to be given at Drury Lane. Wrote lib. for Handel's *Teseo* (1713) and between 1723 and 1728 wrote 7 more libs. for him, *Ottone*, *Flavio* (1723), *Giulio Cesare*, *Tamerlano* (1724), *Rodelinda* (1725), *Siroe*, *Tolomeo* (1728). From 1718 was string bass player in service of Duke of Chandos at Cannons, playing in Handel oratorios. Comp. oratorios, anthems, etc.

Haymon, Cynthia (*b* Jacksonville, Fla., 1958). Amer. soprano. Début Sante Fe 1984 in f. Amer. p. of *We Come to the River*. Sang Xanthe at Sante Fe 1985 in Amer. première of *Die Liebe der Danae*. Created title-role in Musgrave's *Harriet, the Woman Called Moses*, Norfolk, Va., 1985. Eur. début 1986 at Glyndebourne as Bess in *Porgy and Bess*. Sang Liù (*Turandot*) with Royal Opera, CG, on tour of Far East, and Mimì at CG.

Haywood, Lorna (Marie) (*b* Birmingham, 1939). Eng. soprano. Début Juilliard 1964 (title role in *Kát'a Kabanová*). CG début 1966; SW 1970. Specialized in Janáček roles, notably Jenůfa, Kát'a, and Málinka in *The Excursions of Mr Brouček* (ENO 1978).

Head, Michael (Dewar) (*b* Eastbourne, 1900; *d* Cape Town, 1976). Eng. composer, singer, and pianist. Prof. of pf. RAM, from 1927. Comps. incl. cantata, light operas, works for ob., and many songs (in which he acc. himself).

Headington, Christopher (John Magenis) (*b* London, 1930; *d* Les Houches, Switz., 1996). Eng. composer, pianist, and writer. Joined BBC mus. staff 1964. Comps. incl. pf. preludes; 3 pf. sonatas; vn. conc. (1959); pf. qt. (1978); *The Healing Fountain (in memoriam Benjamin Britten)* (1979); pf. conc. (1982); *Sinfonietta* (1985); bn. conc. (1990); pf. conc. (1991); *In Commendation of Music*, unacc. ch. (1992); *Elgar Variations*, vn., hn., pf. (1993); sym. (1996); 3 str. qts.; song-cycles; etc. Author of *The Orchestra and its Instruments* (1965), *Britten* (1981), and *Peter Pears: a Biography* (1992).

head voice. Method of vocal tone prod. in high register, so called because singer experiences sensation of v. vibrating in the head. See also *chest voice*.

Healey, Derek (*b* Wargrave, 1936). Eng. composer. Taught at Univ. of Victoria, BC, 1969–71, Toronto Univ. 1971–2, Univ. of Guelph Coll. of Arts 1972–8. Prof. of theory and comp., Univ. of Oregon from 1979. Works incl. opera *Seabird Island* (1977); 2 ballets; *Arctic Images*, orch. (1971), 3 syms.; str. qt. (1961); vc. sonata (1971); *Solana Grove*, wind quintet (1982); and other chamber works and pf. pieces.

Hear my Prayer (*Hör mein Bitten*). Hymn by Mendelssohn for sop. solo, choir, and org. (also orch.) comp. 1844 for Bartholomew's concerts in Crosby Hall, London, where f.p. 1845. Contains section 'O for the wings of a dove', sometimes perf. separately.

Heart of Oak (*not* 'Hearts of Oak'). This bold patriotic song comes from a pantomime, *Harlequin's Invasion*, written by Garrick in 1759, the mus. being supplied by *Boyce. It is a topical song, alluding to 'this wonderful year' (the victories of Minden, Quiberon Bay, and Quebec).

Heart's Assurance, The. Song-cycle for high v. and pf. by *Tippett on poems by Sidney Keyes and Alun Lewis. Commissioned by Peter Pears. Comp. 1950–1. F.p. London 1951 (Pears and Britten).

Heath, Dave (*b* Manchester, 1956). Eng. composer and flautist. Had a jazz band in London while studying fl. Won Wavendon Allmusic Comp. of the Year Award, 1990, for composers who wrote mus. which crosses barriers between classical, jazz, rock, and other types. Several of his works perf. by Nigel *Kennedy. Many of his rhythms are rock based, with tonal harmonies. Works incl.:

ORCH.: *Rise from the Dark* (1984); *The Frontier*, str. (1989); *Out of the Cool*, vn., orch. (orch. version of chamber work, 1989); *Cry from the Wild: Flute Concerto No.1*, fl., orch. (1991); *The Connemara: Flute Concerto No.2*, fl., str. (1992); *Alone at the Frontier*, improvised solo instr., ch., orch. (1992); *The Four Elements*, perc., str. (1993); vn. conc. (*The Celtic*), vn., str., sax. (1994); perc. conc. (*African Sunrise/Manhattan Rave*) (1995); *Moroccan Fantasy*, sax., orch. (1997); fl. conc. (fl., perc., str.) (2000); *Sirocco*, conc. for ob., vn., chamber orch. (2002).

CHAMBER MUSIC: *Rumania*, fl., vn. or sax., pf. (1979); *Coltrane*, solo wind instr. (1979); *Beyond the Dark*, fl., hp. (1985); *On Fire*, vc. or vn., pf. (1986); *Forest*, fl., cl. or hp., str. qt. (1988); *Gorbachev*, pf. trio (1993); *Rain, Fire and Passion*, bfl., str. (1995); *Lochalsh*, vn. (or vn., str.) (1995); *Darkness to Light*, pf., perc. (1997); *Dawn of a New Age*, perc., sax. (1999); *Gottlieb*, org. (2001); *The Beloved*, sop., treble, ch., ob., org. (2001); *Golden Sunset*, solo fl., 7 fls. (2003).

PIANO: *Fight the Lion* (1982).

Heather, William. See *Heyther, William*.

Hebden, John (*fl.* 1740–50). Eng. cellist, bassoonist, and composer. Prin. cellist in London th. orchs. Comp. 6 concerti grossi for str. which

were ed. R. Wood in 1980 and revived, after 200 years of neglect, by the Scottish ens. Cantilena. Also wrote 6 solos for fl. and continuo.

Hebrides, The (Mendelssohn). See *Fingal's Cave*.

Heckel, Johann Adam (*b* Adorf, 1812; *d* Biebrich, 1877). Ger. instrument-maker. Founded own firm at Biebrich, 1831. Worked on improvements to bn. and cl. Son Wilhelm (1856–1909) invented *heckelphone 1904.

Heckelclarina. Rare type of cl. invented by Ger. firm of Heckel expressly for shepherd's pipe part in Act 3 of Wagner's *Tristan und Isolde* (cor anglais is usually preferred).

Heckelphone. Bass ob. (octave lower than ob.) made by Ger. firm of Heckel in 1904. Used by R. Strauss in *Salome* and *Elektra* and by Delius, as 'bass oboe' in *Dance Rhapsody No.1, Fennimore and Gerda, Songs of Sunset, Arabesk*, and *Requiem*.

Hedley, Arthur (*b* Newcastle upon Tyne, 1905; *d* Birmingham, 1969). Eng. scholar and writer. Specialist in mus. of Chopin, about whom he wrote book and many articles.

heel. That end of the bow of a str. instr. at which it is held, to be distinguished from the other end, which is called 'point'.

Heger, Robert (*b* Strasbourg, 1886; *d* Munich, 1978). Ger. composer and conductor. Cond. début Strasbourg 1907; opera cond. Nuremberg 1913–21, Vienna 1925–33, Berlin 1933–50, Munich from 1950. Salzburg Fest. début 1927 (*Le nozze di Figaro*). Cond. many times at CG 1925–35, esp. operas of Strauss, and cond. f. Brit. p. of *Capriccio* 1953. Cond. celebrated abridged recording of *Der Rosenkavalier*, 1933, with Lehmann, Schumann, Olczewska, and Mayr. Comp. 5 operas, incl. *Lady Hamilton* (1951); 3 syms.; vn. conc.; vc. conc.; cantatas; and songs.

Heggie, Jake (*b* West Palm Beach, 1961). Amer. pianist and composer. Studied in Orinda, Calif., with Ernst Bacon, 1977–9, in Paris for 2 years, then at UCLA (piano with Johana Harris, comp. with Roland Bourland, Paul DesMarais, and David Raksin). Regular accomp. to many singers (Frederica von Stade, Thomas Hampson, Jennifer Larmore, etc.). Comp.-in-res. San Francisco Opera from 1998. Received Guggenheim Fellowship 2005. Works incl. *Dead Man Walking*, opera (1998–2000); *The End of the Affair*, opera (2003, rev. 2004–5); *At the Statue of Venus*, scena (2005); str. qt. (*Lugalla*) (1984); *Glengariff Trio*, vn., vc., pf. (1985); *Divertimento*, 2 pf. (1990); *Homage à Poulenc*, pf. (1992); *From Emily's Garden*, song-cycle, sop., fl., vn., vc., pf. (1999); *Cut Time*, var. for pf., chamber orch. (2001); vc. conc. (*Holy the Firm*) (2002); and over 200 songs and song-cycles, highly thought of by many Amer. singers.

Heifetz, Jascha (*b* Vilna, Lithuania, 1899; *d* Los Angeles, 1987). Russ.-born violinist (Amer. cit. 1925). Lessons at 3 from father, public début in Vilna at 5. Entered St Petersburg Cons. at 8. Gave first public concert in St Petersburg, 1911. While still student, aged 11, played Tchaikovsky conc. with Berlin PO under Nikisch, 1912, in Vienna under Safonov, and in Leipzig. Family went to USA 1917, where Heifetz made début in Carnegie Hall that year. Thereafter worldwide reputation as among very greatest violinists. London début 1920. Commissioned Walton conc., 1939, also concs. by Castelnuovo-Tedesco, Korngold, and Louis Gruenberg. After 1974 played principally in chamber mus. Taught at Univ. of Calif, Los Angeles, 1962–72. Made many arrs. for vn. of mus. by Bach, Vivaldi, and others. Most celebrated transcr. is *Hora staccato* by Grigoras Dinicu.

Heiligmesse (Holy Mass). Popular name, derived from the special treatment of the words 'Holy, holy' in the Sanctus, for Haydn's 8th Mass in B♭, 1796.

Heinze, (Sir) **Bernard** (Thomas) (*b* Shepparton, Victoria, 1894; *d* Sydney, NSW, 1982). Australian conductor and teacher. Dir. of mus. Australian Broadcasting Co. 1929–32. Prof. of mus., Melbourne Univ., 1925–57, dir. State Cons., NSW 1957–66. Cond. Melbourne SO 1933–49. Knighted 1949.

Heldenbariton (Ger., 'heroic baritone'). Baritone with exceptional power for such roles as Telramund in *Lohengrin*.

Heldenleben, Ein (A Hero's Life). Orch. tone-poem, Op.40, by R. Strauss. Comp. 1897–8, f.p. 1899 in Frankfurt (though ded. to Mengelberg and Concertgebouw Orch. of Amsterdam). In the 5th of the 6 sections, the 'Hero's Works of Peace', Strauss quotes from several of his own comps.

Heldentenor (Ger., 'heroic tenor'). Ten. with powerful v. of wide range capable of such parts as Huon in Weber's *Oberon*, Bacchus in Strauss's *Ariadne auf Naxos*, and most of the Wagner ten. parts.

Helffer, Claude (*b* Paris, 1922; *d* Paris, 2004). Fr. pianist. After war studied harmony and comp. with Leibowitz. Début Paris 1948. Specialist in 20th-cent. pf. mus., having given f.ps. of works by Amy. Salzburg Fest. 1989. Has recorded complete solo pf. music of Schoenberg, also works by Boulez and Barraqué.

helicon. Form of bass tuba made so that it may be wrapped round the player's body and rest on the shoulder (useful when played on the march). So called because of helical (spiral) shape. Largely displaced by modified version, *sousaphone.

Heliogabalus Imperator. Tone-poem ('allegory for music') by Henze (1971–2) after Enzensberger. F.p. Chicago (cond. Solti) 1972.

Hellertion. Elec. instr. developed in Frankfurt in 1936 by Bruno Helberger and Peter Lertes. Similar to *theremin, but with a guide kbd. and pedals to regulate vol. and tone-quality. Range of nearly 6 octaves, capable of 4-part harmony,

and able to simulate human v. and some instrs. Played by pressure on 4 leather bands stretched across front, which sets up a current.

Hellflöte (Ger.). Clear flute (an org. stop).

Hellmesberger, Joseph (*b* Vienna, 1828; *d* Vienna, 1893). Austrian violinist, conductor, and teacher. Father and brother were also violinists. Pupil of father. Cond., Vienna Gesellschaft concerts 1851–9, prof. of vn., Vienna Cons. 1851–77, dir. 1851–93. Leader, Vienna PO 1855–77 and of opera orch. 1860–77. Founder and leader, Hellmesberger Qt., 1849–91.

Hellmesberger, Joseph (*b* Vienna, 1855; *d* Vienna, 1907). Austrian violinist and composer, son of above. 2nd vn. in Hellmesberger Qt. from 1875, succeeding as leader 1891. Leader Vienna PO 1870–84. Prof. of vn., Vienna Cons. from 1878. 2nd cond., Vienna Opera 1899. Cond. Vienna PO 1901–3. Court cond. Stuttgart 1904–5. Comp. 10 operettas.

Helm, Everett (*b* Minneapolis, 1913; *d* Berlin, 1999). Amer. composer and writer. In 1941 worked with Milhaud at Mills Coll. Holder of various teaching posts. Active as mus. critic from 1948. Works incl. opera, sym. for str., 2 pf. concs., 2 str. qts., 2 pf. sonatas, db. conc., etc. Author of books on Bartók, Liszt, and the *chansons* of Arcadelt.

Heltay, László (István) (*b* Budapest, 1930). Brit. conductor of Hung. birth (Brit. cit. 1962). On staff Budapest Radio 1952–6. Left for Eng. 1956. Founded Schola Cantorum, Oxford, 1960. Dir. of mus., Merton Coll., Oxford, 1962–4. Ass. cond. NZBC SO 1964–6. Dir. of mus., Gardner Centre, Sussex Univ., from 1968. Cond., Collegium Musicum of London from 1970. Founded Brighton Fest. Chorus.

Hely-Hutchinson, (Christian) **Victor** (*b* Cape Town, 1901; *d* London, 1947). S. African-born Eng. composer, conductor, pianist, and administrator. After teaching mus. in S. Africa, joined BBC staff 1926, becoming head of mus., Midlands Region (Birmingham), 1933–4. Prof. of mus., Birmingham Univ. 1934–44. Dir. of mus., BBC, 1944–7. Works incl. *A Carol Symphony*, pf. quintet, va. sonata, and settings of Edward Lear's *Nonsense Songs*.

hemidemisemiquaver (♬). The 64th note (i.e. 1/64th of a semibreve in value).

Heming, Percy (*b* Bristol, 1883; *d* London, 1956). Eng. baritone. Opera début with Beecham co., London, 1915 as Mercutio in *Roméo et Juliette*. Prin. bar. BNOC from 1922, SW 1933–5. Ass. art. dir. (to Beecham), CG 1937, art. dir. CG Eng. Co. 1937–9. Art. adv., CG 1946–8. Notable Amfortas, Scarpia, and Ford. Toured USA 1920 as Macheath in *The Beggar's Opera*.

hemiola or **hemiolia**. This rhythmic device consists of superimposing 2 notes in the time of 3, or 3 in the time of 2, e.g.:

A rhythmic device much used in cadential progressions by composers up to and including the baroque period.

Hemmings, Peter (William) (*b* Enfield, 1934; *d* Piddlehinton, Dorset, 2002). Eng. administrator and singer. Repertory and planning man., SW Opera 1959–65, gen. man. New Opera Co. 1957–65; gen. administrator Scottish Opera 1962–77; dir. Australian Opera 1977–80. Man. dir. LSO 1981–4. Dir. Los Angeles Music Center Opera (which he helped to create) from 1984. OBE 1998.

Hempel, Frieda (*b* Leipzig, 1885; *d* Berlin, 1955). Ger. soprano. Début Breslau, then Berlin 1905 (Mrs Ford in *Die lustigen Weiber von Windsor*) and Schwerin 1905–7. Berlin Opera 1907–12. London début CG 1907; NY Met 1912–19. First Berlin (1911) and NY (1913) Marschallin in *Der Rosenkavalier*. Retired from opera 1921 (Chicago), continuing to give concerts.

Hemsley, Thomas (Jeffrey) (*b* Coalville, 1927). Eng. baritone. Stage début London 1951 as Aeneas to Flagstad's Dido. Prin. bar., Aachen Opera 1953–6, Deutsche Oper-am-Rhein 1957–63, Zurich Opera 1963–7; Glyndebourne 1953–61; Bayreuth 1968–70; CG début 1970. Guest singer Scottish Opera, ENO, WNO (1977–85), and Kent Opera. Notable Beckmesser. Created Demetrius in *A Midsummer Night's Dream*. Also noted singer in oratorio, cantatas, and of *Lieder*. Professor of singing at GSMD from 1987. CBE 2000.

Hen, The (Haydn). See *Poule, La*.

Henderson, Roy (Galbraith) (*b* Edinburgh, 1899; *d* Bromley, 2000). Scottish baritone. Début Queen's Hall, London, 1925 as Zarathustra in Delius's *A Mass of Life*. Opera début CG 1929 as Donner in *Das Rheingold*. Member Glyndebourne co. 1934–9 (Papageno, Guglielmo, and sang Count in *Le nozze di Figaro* on opening night, 1934). Noted in concert and recital work. One of orig. 16 soloists in *Serenade to Music* (1938). Retired 1952. Prof. of singing RAM 1940–74. Private pupils incl. Kathleen *Ferrier. Cond. of several choirs, incl. Nottingham Oriana Choir 1936–52. CBE 1970.

Hendricks, Barbara (*b* Stephens, Ark., 1948). Won Geneva int. comp. 1971. Opera début NY 1973 in V. Thomson's *Four Saints in Three Acts*, followed by concert tour of Eur. Débuts: S. Francisco 1974; Glyndebourne 1974; Carnegie Hall 1975; CG 1982; NY Met 1986; Salzburg Fest. 1977. Sang Mimì in film of *La bohème* 1988. Concert appearances with most leading conds., and recitalist.

Henry, Pierre (*b* Paris, 1927). Fr. composer. Dir., Groupe de Recherches de Musique Concrète, Fr. Radio, 1950–8, working with Pierre *Schaeffer. Founded first private EMS in Fr. at Apsome, 1958. Works incl. *Le Voile d'Orphée* (1953), *La Reine verte* (1963), *Messe de Liverpool* (1967), *Gymkhana* (1970), *Dieu* (1976), *Paradis perdu* (1982), *Une maison de sons* (1989), *Schubertnotizen I–II* (1994), *Les Sept Péchés capitaux* (1998), all with elecs.

Henry VIII (*b* Greenwich, 1491; *d* Windsor, 1547). Eng. king (from 1509). Talented musician and composer. Attrib. to him are 17 songs and several pieces for viols. The anthem *O Lord, the Maker of All Things*, however, is not by Henry, as was long supposed, but by W. Mundy. Only surviving sacred work is 3-part motet *Quam pulchra es*.

Henry VIII. (1) (*Henri VIII*) Opera in 4 acts by Saint-Saëns to lib. by Détroyat and Silvestre, comp. 1883. Prod. Paris 1883, CG 1889, NY 1983. Rev. to 3 acts 1889, restored to 4 in 1909.

(2) Incidental mus. to Shakespeare's play by Sullivan, 1878, and by *German, 1892.

Henry Watson Music Library. Prin. mus. library in Manchester, part of the corporation's Central Reference Library. Basis was coll. of 5,000 books and many more scores handed over in 1899 by Henry Watson (*b* Burnley, 1846; *d* Salford, 1911), organist, cond., and teacher at RMCM, to Manchester Corporation and since greatly expanded.

Henschel, (Sir) **George** [Isidor Georg] (*b* Breslau, 1850; *d* Aviemore, Scotland, 1934). Eng. baritone, pianist, conductor, and composer of Ger. birth (Brit. cit. 1890). Public début as pianist, Berlin 1862. Leipzig Cons. 1867–70; Berlin Royal Cons. 1870–4. Sang Hans Sachs in concert perf. of *Die Meistersinger*, Munich 1868. In 1875 sang in Bach's *St Matthew Passion*, cond. by Brahms, of whom he became close friend. London début 1877. First cond. Boston SO 1881–4. Prof. of singing, RCM 1886–8 and Inst. of Mus. Art, NY, 1905–8. Cond., London Symphony Concerts 1886–96. Cond. Scottish Orch. 1891–5. Acc. himself as singer. Continued to broadcast and record until past 70. Comp. 3 operas, str. qt., choral works, songs, etc. Knighted 1914.

Henschel, Jane (*b* California, 1960). Amer. mezzo-soprano. Sang in Gilbert and Sullivan operettas in Los Angeles. Aspen Mus. Fest. 1977 (Ottavia in *L'incoronazione di Poppea*). Aachen Opera 1977–80, Wuppertal from 1980, and Dortmund. Sang Brangäne, Amneris, Eboli, and baroque roles (Vivaldi's *Juditha triumphans*). Netherlands Opera 1992; CG début 1992; Glyndebourne début 1994.

Henselt, Adolf von (*b* Schwabach, Bavaria, 1814; *d* Warmbrunn, Silesia, 1889). Ger. pianist and composer. Went to St Petersburg 1838, becoming court pianist and teacher of Royal family. No tours after 1838 yet acclaimed as one of greatest pianists. Comp. pf. conc., 2 sets of 12 Studies, pf. pieces, etc.

Hen Wlad fy Nhadau. See *Land of my Fathers*.

Henze, Hans Werner (*b* Gütersloh, Westphalia, 1926). Ger. composer and cond. Studied at

Brunswick State Mus. Sch. 1942–4, Heidelberg 1946. Studied Schoenberg's 12-note system with *Leibowitz at Darmstadt 1948. Mus. dir. Hessian State Opera's ballet, Wiesbaden, 1950. Settled in Italy 1953. Politically Henze moved in the 1960s to the extreme Left and many of his works after that date reflected revolutionary ideals and dogmas. Henze's mus. style is bewilderingly diverse, reflecting his fertile imaginative gifts and his refusal to be 'tied down' by formulae. As much a Fr. or It. composer as Ger., he can adopt at will Schoenbergian, Stravinskyan, or aleatory styles. Sensuous lyricism, rich and delicate tone-colours, and easy mastery of choral writing are among the prin. features of his work. Wrote *Music and Politics* (Ithaca, NY, and London, 1982). Prin. works:

OPERAS AND MUSIC THEATRE: *Das Wundertheater* (1-act, after Cervantes, for actors and orch., 1948; new version for singers 1964); *Boulevard Solitude* (1951); *König Hirsch* (1953–5; reduced version as *Il Re Cervo*, 1962); *Der *Prinz von Homburg* (after Kleist) (1957–8, rev. 1991); *Elegy for Young Lovers* (1959–61); *Der *junge Lord* (1964); *Das ende eine Welt* (1964, stage version of radio opera, 1953); *Ein Landarzt* (1964, stage version of radio opera, 1951); *The *Bassarids* (1965); *Moralities* (3 scenic cantatas to Auden text, 1967); *Der langwierige Weg in die Wohnung der Natascha Ungeheuer* (The Tedious Way to the Place of Natasha Ungeheuer) (1971); *La Cubana* (vaudeville, 1973); *We Come to the River* (lib. by E. Bond) (1974–6); *Don Chisciotte della Mancia* (version of Paisiello, 1976); *Pollicino* (children's opera, 1979); *Il Ritorno di Ulisse in Patria* (realization of Monteverdi, 1980–2); *The *English Cat* (lib. by E. Bond) (1980–3, rev. 1990); *Das *verratene Meer* (1986–9); *Venus and Adonis* (1993–5); *L'Upupa und der Triumph der Sohnesliebe* (2003).

RADIO OPERAS: *Ein Landarzt* (Kafka) (1951); *Das Ende einer Welt* (1953).

BALLETS: *Ballett-Variationen* (1949, *Suite* 1949); *Rosa Silber* (1950, *Suite* 1950); *Maratona* (1956, *Suite* 1956); *Undine* (1956–71, 2 *Suites* 1958); *Tancredi* (1964 rev. of *Pas d'action* 1952, *Suite* 1952); *Orpheus* (1978).

CHAMBER BALLETS: *Jack Pudding* (1949, *Suite* 1949); *Die schlafende Prinzessin* (arr. of Tchaikovsky for small orch. 1951); *Labyrinth* (1951, choreog. fantasy for orch. 1950); *Der Idiot* (1952); *Des Kaisers Nachtigall* (after Andersen, 1959, *Suite* 1959).

INCIDENTAL MUSIC: *Der tolle Tag* (Beaumarchais) (1951); *Les Caprices de Marianne* (Musset/Ponnelle) (1962); *Der Frieden* (Aristophanes/Hacks) (1964).

ORCH.: syms.: No.1 (for chamber orch. 1947, rev. 1963), No.2 (1949), No.3 (1949–50), No.4 (1955), No.5 (1962), No.6, for 2 chamber orch. (1969), No.7 (1982–4), No.8 (1992–3), No.9 (1995–7), No.10 (1997–2000); *Symphonic Interludes from Boulevard Solitude* (1953); *Quattro Poemi* (1955); *Antifone* (1960); *Los Caprichos* (1963); *Symphonic Interludes from Der junge Lord* (1964); 3 *Symphonic Studies* (1955–64); *The Hunt of the Maenads* (from *The Bassarids*) (1965); *Telemanniana* (1967); *Heliogabalus Imperator* (1971–2); *Tristan,

preludes for pf., orch., tape (1973); *Ragtimes and Habaneras*, brass band (1975); *Suite from Pollicino* (1979); 2 *Dramatic Scenes from Orpheus* (1979); *Barcarola* (1983); *Allegro brillante* (1989); *Introduction, Theme and Variations*, vc., hp., str. (1992); 7 *Boleros* (from *Venus and Adonis*) (1996); *Fraternité* (1999); *A Tempest* (2000); *Scorribanda sinfonica* (2001); *Sebastian im Traum* (2003–4).

CHAMBER ORCH.: *Sinfonie* (1947, rev. for full orch. as sym. No.1, 1963); *Symphonic Variations* (1950); *Sonata for Strings* (1957–8); 3 *Dithyrambs* (1958); 4 *Fantasies* (3 movts. from *Chamber Music 1958* with new *Adagio*), 8 instr. (1963); *In memoriam: Die weisse Rose* (1965); *Fantasia für Streicher* (1966, from film mus. for *Der junge Törless*); *Fragments from a Show* (from *Natasche Ungeheuer*), hn., 2 tpt., tb., tuba (1971); *Suite* from film mus. *Katharina Blum* (1975); *Amicizia*, cl., tb., vc., pf., perc. (1976); *Aria de la folia española*, orch., also chamber orch. (1977); *Apollo trionfante*, wind, perc., db. (1979); *Arien des Orpheus*, guitar, hp., hpd., str. (1979); *Canzona*, ob., 3 vas., vc., pf., hp. (1982); *I Sentimenti di Carl P. E. Bach* (transcr. of *Fantasia* for pf. and vn., 1787), fl., hp., str. (1982); *Cinque piccoli concerti* (interludes from *The English Cat*), 8 instr. (1983); *Sonata for 6* (1984); 12 *kleine Elegien*, Renaissance instr. (1986); *Requiem* (9 *Spiritual Concertos*), pf., tpt., large chamber orch. (1990–2); *Toccata for 19 instrs.* (1996).

CONCERTOS: chamber conc., pf., fl., str. (1946); vn. conc. No.1 (1947), No.2, vn., bass-bar., 33 instr., tape (1971), No.3 (1996); concertino, pf., wind, perc. (1947); pf. conc. No.1 (1950), No.2 (1967); *Jeux des Tritons* (from *Undine*), pf., orch. (1956–7/ 1967); *Ode to the West Wind*, vc., orch. (1953); *Concerto per il Marigny*, pf., 7 instr. (1956); double conc., hp., ob., str. (1966); db. conc. (1966); *Compases para preguntas ensimismadas*, va., 22 players (1969–70); *Il Vitalino raddoppiato*, vn., chamber orch. (1977); *Musik*, vc., chamber orch. (1977); *Le Miracle de la Rose*, cl., 13 instr. (1981); gui. conc. (1986); 7 *Liebeslieder*, vc., orch. (1984–5).

VOICE AND INSTR.: *Ein Landarzt*, monodrama, bar., orch. (1951–64, see also RADIO OPERA); *Whispers from Heavenly Death* (Whitman), high v., 8 instr. (or pf.) (1948); *The Reproach* (*Der Vorwurf*) (Werfel), aria for bar., tpt., tb., str. (1948); *Apollo and Hyacinth*, alto, 9 instr. (1949); 5 *Neapolitan Songs*, mez. or bar., chamber orch. (1956); *Nocturnes and Arias*, sop., orch. (1957); *Chamber Music 1958* (Hölderlin), ten., guitar, 8 instr. (1958); 3 *Hölderlin Fragments*, v., guitar (1958); *Ariosi* (Tasso), sop., vn., and orch. (or pf. 4 hands) (1963); *Being Beauteous* (Rimbaud), coloratura sop., hp., 4 vc. (1963); *Essay on Pigs*, bar., chamber orch. (1968); *El Cimarrón*, bar., fl., guitar, perc. (1969–70); *Voices* (22 songs), mez., ten., 15 instr. (1973); *The King of Harlem*, mez., instr. ens. (1979); 3 *Auden Poems*, v., pf. (1982–3); *Drei Lieder über den Schnee*, sop., bar., cl., bn., hn., 2 vn., va., vc., db. (1989); *Heilige Nacht*, med. v., rec./fl./ob./vn. (1993); *Sechs Gesänge aus dem Arabischen*, ten., pf. (1997–8).

CHORAL: 5 *Madrigals*, ch., 11 instr. (1947); *Lullaby of the Blessed Virgin*, boys' ch., 9 instr. (1948); *Chorus of the Captured Trojans* (from Goethe's *Faust II*), ch., orch. (1948, rev. 1964); *Novae de Infinito Laudes, cantata, 4 solo vv., ch., small orch. (1962); *Cantata della Fiaba Estrema*, sop., small ch., 13 instr. (1963); *Choral Fantasia* (Bachmann), chamber ch., tb., 2 vc., db., org., perc., timp. (1964); *Muses of Sicily* (Virgil), conc. for ch., 2 pf., wind, timp. (1966); *Das *Floss der Medusa*, oratorio for sop., bar., speaker, ch., 9 boys' vv., orch. (1968); **Jephte* (realization of Carissimi's oratorio, 1650), 3 sop., alto, ten., 2 bass, 6 vv., instr. (wind, hp., perc., guitar, banjo, mandolin) (1976); *Canzoni für Orpheus*, unacc. ch. (1980); *Hirtenlieder* (from *Venus and Adonis*), 6 vv. or unacc. chamber ch. (1993–5).

CHAMBER MUSIC: str. qts.: No.1 (1947), No.2 (1952), No.3 (1975–6), No.4 (1976), No.5 (1976); vn. sonata (1946); sonatina, fl., cl. (1947); *Chamber Sonata*, pf., vn., vc. (1948, rev. 1963); *Serenade*, vc. (1949); *Quintet*, fl., ob., cl., hn., bn. (1952); *3 Tentos* (from *Chamber Music 1958*), guitar (1958); *Der junge Törless*, fantasia (after work for str. orch.), str. sextet (1966, trans. of *Fantasia für Streicher*); *Memorias de El Cimarrón*, guitar (1970); *Carillon, Récitatif, Masque*, mandolin, guitar, hp. (1974); *Royal Winter Music* (2 sonatas on Shakespearean characters), guitar (1975–6 and 1979); *L'Autunno*, wind quintet, fl., cl., ob., hn., bn., with interchangeable instr. (1977); sonata, solo vn. (1977); va. sonata (1979); *Capriccio, vc.* (1983); *Selbst- und Zwiegespräche*, va., gui., small org. (1984–5); *Serenade*, vn. (1986); *Für Manfred*, vn. (1989); *Five Night Pieces*, vn., pf. (1990); *Adagio, adagio*, vn., vc., pf. (1993); *Notturno*, fl., db., pf. (1995); *Monotaurus Blues*,

6 perc. (1996); trio, vn., va., vc. (1998).

KEYBOARD: *Variations*, pf. (1949); pf. sonata (1959); *Lucy Escott Variations*, pf. or hpd. (1963); *6 Absences*, hpd. (1961); *Divertimenti*, 2 pf. (1964); *Toccata senza Fuga* from *Orpheus*, org. (1979); *Euridice*, hpd. (1981); *La mano sinestre*, pf. (left hand) (1988); *Toccata mistica*, pf. (1994); *Olly on the Shore*, pf. (2001); *Scorribanda pianistica*, pf. (2003).

Heppner, Ben (b Murrayville, B.C., 1956). Canadian tenor. In mid-1980s sang Mozart, Rossini, and Donizetti roles in Toronto, then emerged as dramatic ten. Début 1987, Victoria State Opera, Melbourne (Bacchus in *Ariadne auf Naxos*). In 1988 sang Zinovy in *Lady Macbeth of the Mtsensk District* in Toronto. Débuts: Chicago 1988; S. Francisco and Stockholm 1989; Milan and CG 1990; Amsterdam 1991; NY Met 1996 (Hermann).

heptatonic. Scale or mode based on seven pitches to the octave.

Herabstrich (Ger.). Down-bow, in vn. and va. playing. **Heraufstrich** is up-bow.

Herbage, Julian (Livingston) (b Woking, 1904; d London, 1976). Eng. musicologist and writer. Career in th. before joining BBC 1927–46 (ass. dir. of mus. 1940–6). Helped to plan and produce Promenade concerts until 1961. Ed. and cond. works by Locke, Purcell, Bach, Arne, and Handel. Wrote books and essays on Handel's *Messiah*,

Sibelius, Bax, and Tchaikovsky. With wife Anna Instone (b Cardiff, 1912; d London, 1978), presented BBC's weekly *Music Magazine* on radio 1944–73.

Herbert, Victor (b Dublin, 1859; d NY, 1924). Irish-born composer, conductor, and cellist (Amer. cit.). Prin. cellist Stuttgart court orch. 1883–6. Went to USA 1886, becoming prin. cellist NY Met orch., and in other orchs. Also appeared as soloist and cond. military bands. First operetta, *Prince Ananias* (NY 1894) was success and was followed by over 30 others, incl. *Naughty Marietta* (1910) and *Sweethearts* (1913). Wrote 2 operas, *Natoma* (1911) and *Madeleine* (1914). Cond., Pittsburgh SO 1898–1904. Also comp. symphonic poem *Hero and Leander*, 2 vc. concs. (1885, 1894), *Irish Rhapsody*, etc.

Herbig, Günther (b Ústì nad Labem, Cz., 1931). Cz.-born Ger. conductor. Cond. Dresden PO 1972–7, Berlin SO 1977–83. Eng. début 1973, London. Chief guest cond., BBC Northern SO (now BBC Philharmonic) 1980–4. Cond. Detroit SO 1984–9, Toronto SO 1989–94.

Herincx, Raimund [Raymond] (b London, 1927). Eng. bass-baritone. Sang in concerts in Belg. and Fr. 1950. Opera début Cardiff (WNO) 1957, as Boito's Mefistofele, later singing Scarpia, Nabucco, and Pizarro. SW Opera 1957–67 (incl. Segura in f.p. of *Our Man in Havana*, 1963). NY concert début 1966; CG début 1968. Created Faber in *The Knot Garden* (CG 1970), the White Abbot in *Taverner* (CG 1972 and at Amer. première, Boston 1986), and the Governor in *We Come to the River* (CG 1976). Sang Wotan and Hagen in ENO *Ring* cycle 1970–4 and in Seattle 1977–81. Salzburg Easter Fest. début 1973; NY Met début 1977.

Herman, Woody [Woodrow] (Charles) (b Milwaukee, 1913; d Los Angeles, 1987). Amer. jazz saxophonist, clarinettist, and composer. Formed own band 1936, reformed 1946, 1947 and 1950. Worldwide tours. Comps. incl. *Blues in the Night* and *At the Woodchoppers' Ball*. Stravinsky wrote his *Ebony Concerto* for him, 1945, f.p. NY 1946.

Hérodiade (Herodias). Opera in 4 acts (orig. 3 acts) by Massenet to lib. by P. Milliet and 'H. Grémont' (G. Hartmann) after story by Flaubert (1877). Comp. 1878–81, rev 1883. Prod. Brussels (3-act vers.) 1881, Paris 1884, New Orleans 1892, London (under title *Salome*) 1904 (all in 4-act vers.).

Hérold, (Louis Joseph) **Ferdinand** (b Paris, 1791; d Les Ternes, Paris, 1833). Fr. composer. *Grand Prix de Rome* 1812. First opera prod. Naples 1815. Returned to Paris 1815, composing 12 operas and several ballets in 14 years. Gained biggest success with **Zampa* (1831) followed by *Le Pré aux Clercs* (1832). Among his ballets were *La *Fille Mal Gardée* (1828) and *La Belle au Bois dormant* (1829). Also comp. 2 syms., 3 str. qts., 4 pf. concs., and pf. pieces.

Herreweghe, Philippe (b Ghent, 1947). Belgian conductor and chorusmaster. Founded Collegium

Vocale of Ghent, 1969. Perf. early mus. with Ton Koopman and Gustav Leonhardt. With Philippe Beaussant, founded Ens. Vocal La Chapelle Royal, 1977. Participated in *Towards Bach* series, London 1989. Cond., Eur. Vocal Ens. from 1989. Cond., Mahler/Schoenberg concerts with Ens. Musique Oblique, 1991.

Herrmann, Bernard (*b* NY, 1911; *d* Hollywood, 1975). Amer. composer and conductor. Founder-cond. New Chamber Orch. 1931–4. Mus. dir. CBS 1934–40, cond.-in-chief CBS SO 1942–59. Champion of Ives's mus. and also of Eng. composers—not only Elgar and Vaughan Williams, but Rubbra, Brian, Bax, Cecil Gray, and Cyril Scott. Also an enthusiast for Raff. Lived in London for several months each year. Wrote 49 film scores, several of them for Orson Welles (*Citizen Kane*, 1941; *The Magnificent Ambersons*, 1942) and Hitchcock (*North by Northwest*, 1959; *Psycho*, 1960). Among his other film scores were *Jane Eyre* (1943); *Anna and the King of Siam* (1946); *The Ghost and Mrs Muir* (1947); *The Snows of Kilimanjaro* (1952); *The Man Who Knew Too Much* (1956); *Journey to the Centre of the Earth* (1959); *Fahrenheit 451* (1966); *Sisters* (1972); and *Taxi Driver* (1976). He used electric vn. and electric bass in *The Day the Earth Stood Still* (1951), one of the first examples of elec. mus. in films. His opera *Wuthering Heights* and other comps. have an expressive and lyrical warmth which compensate for some lack of originality. Comps. incl.:

OPERAS: *Wuthering Heights (1943–51); A Christmas Carol, TV (1954); A Child is Born, TV (1955).

ORCH.: sym. No.1 (1939–41); vn. conc. (unfinished, 1937); For the Fallen (1943); Suite, The *Devil and Daniel Webster (1941); *Welles Raises Kane (1942); Sinfonietta, str. (1935).

CHORAL: *Moby Dick, cantata for 2 ten., 2 basses, male ch., and orch. (1937–8); Johnny Appleseed (1940).

CHAMBER MUSIC: str. qt. (1932); Echoes for str. qt. (1965); Aubade, 14 instr. (retitled Silent Noon) (1933); Souvenirs de Voyage, cl. quintet (1967).

Herstrich (Ger.). A bow movt. towards the player, i.e. the down stroke in vc. and db. playing. See also *Hinstrich*.

Hertel, Johann Wilhelm (*b* Eisenach, 1727; *d* Schwerin, 1789). Ger. violinist and composer. Kapellmeister at Schwerin from 1754. Wrote 36 sym., several conc., pf. sonatas, etc.

Hertz, Alfred (*b* Frankfurt, 1872; *d* San Francisco, 1942). Ger.-born Amer. conductor. Début Halle 1891. Held various cond. posts in Ger.; in 1902 went to USA (becoming Amer. cit.). Cond. of Ger. operas at NY Met 1902–15, during which time he cond. f. stage p. of *Parsifal outside Bayreuth in 1903, thereby infringing Bayreuth copyright and ensuring that no Ger. opera house again employed him. Cond. first Amer. perfs. of *Salome* (1907) and *Der Rosenkavalier* (1913) and f.p. of several Amer. operas. Cond. CG 1910. Cond. S. Francisco SO 1915–29. Founded summer concerts at Hollywood Bowl in 1922 and cond. over 100 concerts there.

herunterstimmen (Ger.). 'To tune down' a str. to (*nach*) a specified note.

Herunterstrich (Ger.). Down-bow in vn. and va. playing.

Hervé [Ronger, Florimond] (*b* Houdain, 1825; *d* Paris, 1892). Fr. composer, conductor, actor, singer, and organist. Org., St Eustache, Paris, 1845–53. Cond. several th. orchs. in Paris and appeared as singer and actor, sometimes in his own works. Wrote over 100 operettas, incl. *Don Quixote et Sancho Pança* (1848), and *Le Petit Faust* (1869). Cond. at Empire Th., London, from 1886. Also wrote 'heroic symphony' *The Ashanti War* (London 1874).

Herz, Joachim (*b* Dresden, 1924). Ger. producer. Worked with Dresden Touring Opera 1951–3, was *Felsenstein's ass. at Berlin Komische Oper 1953–6. Cologne Opera 1956–7; dir. Leipzig Opera 1957–76. Intendant Berlin Komische Oper 1976–81; prin. dir. of prod., Dresden Opera 1981–90. Among his famous prods. were *Albert Herring* (Dresden 1955), *Der fliegende Holländer* (Bolshoy, Moscow, 1963), and *Guillaume Tell* (Buenos Aires 1966). His *Ring* cycle at Leipzig 1973–6 stressed what Herz saw as capitalist oppression and class distinctions. Brit. début ENO 1975; WNO 1978 (*Madama Butterfly*, restoring some of orig. mus. and much anti-Amer. sentiment).

Herzogenberg, Heinrich von (Baron von Herzogenberg-Peccaduc) (*b* Graz, 1843; *d* Wiesbaden, 1900). Austrian pianist and composer. Dir., Bach-Verein, Leipzig, 1875–85. Prof. of comp. Berlin Hochschule für Musik 1885. Dir., Meisterschule für Komposition, Berlin, 1888–92 and 1897–1900. Wrote 3 syms., 3 oratorios, mass, requiem, chamber mus., etc.

Hes (Ger.). The note B♭. (Usually, however, the Germans call this note B; see *H*, above.)

Heseltine, Philip. See *Warlock, Peter*.

Hess, (Dame) **Myra** (*b* London, 1890; *d* London, 1965). Eng. pianist. Début 1907, London (Beethoven 4th conc., cond. Beecham). Thereafter one of England's leading pianists, especially in mus. of Schumann, Beethoven, Mozart, and Bach. Amer. début 1922. Her transcr. of chorale from Bach's church cantata No.147 under title 'Jesu, joy of man's desiring' was immensely popular. During World War II, founded and dir. series of lunchtime recitals at *Nat. Gallery, London, which played important role in sustaining morale. CBE 1936, DBE 1941.

Hess, Willy (*b* Mannheim, 1859; *d* Berlin, 1939). Ger. violinist. Lived in USA 1865–72, making début with Theodore *Thomas Orch. Leader, opera orch., Frankfurt, 1878–86. Prof. of vn., Rotterdam Cons. 1886–8. Leader, Hallé Orch. 1888–95; prof. of vn. RMCM 1893–5, Cologne Cons. 1895–1903 (also leader of Cologne Gürzenich Concerts and Qt.), RAM 1903–4. Leader, Boston SO 1904–10. Prof. of vn. Berlin Hochschule 1910–28 and leader of Haliř Qt., Darmstadt 1931–3.

heterophony (Gr., 'other voice'). Vague term, coined by Plato, used to describe simultaneous variation of one melody. Also applied to vocal mus. of Near and Far East, when an instr. embellishes the vocal part.

Heuberger, Richard (Franz Joseph) (*b* Graz, 1850; *d* Vienna, 1914). Austrian composer, conductor, and critic. Cond. Vienna Singakademie 1878–81, Männergesangverein 1902–9. Mus. critic in Munich and Vienna 1881–1901. Prof., Vienna Cons. from 1902; ed. of various periodicals. Comp. 3 operas, sym., cantata, partsongs, and 6 operettas incl. *Der *Opernball* (The Opera Ball, 1898),

Heure espagnole, L' (The Spanish Hour). Opera (*comédie musicale*) in 1 act by *Ravel to lib. based on his own comedy by Franc-Nohain. Comp. 1907–9. Prod. Paris 1911, London 1919, Chicago 1920.

Heward, Leslie (Hays) (*b* Littletown, Liversedge, 1897; *d* Birmingham, 1943). Eng. conductor and composer. Chorister, Manchester Cath., 1910, ass. org. 1914. Mus. dir., Westminster Sch. 1920. Cond. opera for BNOC. Mus. dir. S. African Broadcasting Corporation and cond. Cape Town Orch., 1924–7. Cond. CBSO 1930–43. Cond. f.p. of Moeran's Sym. in G minor, London 1938.

hexachord. A group of 6 consecutive notes regarded as a unit for purposes of singing at sight—somewhat as the octave is in 'movable-doh' systems. It was introduced (or perfected) by *Guido d'Arezzo in the 11th cent. and was still widely current up to the 17th.

There were 3 different hexachords, the *hard* one beginning on G, the *natural* one beginning on C, and the *soft* one beginning on F. It will be realized that these overlapped in their range, and that a singer reading a piece of mus. might have to pass from one to another if its compass extended beyond one of those sets of 6 notes.

The names of the notes were taken from the opening syllables of 6 lines of a Lat. hymn, which syllables happened to ascend a degree with each succeeding line. These names were *ut, re, mi, fa, sol*, and *la*. Letter names were also then in use for the notes, but these were *absolute* names, as they are still, whereas the hexachordal names were *relative* to the group in use at the moment, as their successors the modern tonic sol-fa names are relative to the *key in use at the moment: the sol-fa system (on its pitch side) may, indeed, be looked upon as a modernization of the hexachordal system, which served well in the period of simple modal mus. (see *modes*) but was incapable of application to the increasing complexities of a key system.

To the hexachords Guido added the device of The Guidonian Hand.

In the 20th cent. the term is applied to a coll. of 6 pitch classes considered either simultaneously or as a succession, esp. in reference to segments of 12-note rows. Unconnected with medieval term.

Hexaméron (Six Parts). 6 variations for pf. on march from Bellini's *I Puritani*, each written by a different composer-pianist—Liszt, Thalberg, Pixis, Herz, Czerny, and Chopin—with introduction, connecting links, and finale by Liszt. F.p. Paris charity concert 1837, the composers sitting at a pf. apiece and each playing his own variation. Liszt later added orch. acc. and played whole series at recitals.

hexatonic. Mode or scale based on system of six different pitches to the octave, as in *whole-tone scale.

Heyther [Heather], **William** (*b* Harmondsworth, *c*.1584; *d* Westminster, 1627). Eng. musician. Sang in Westminster Abbey choir 1586–1615. Gentleman of Chapel Royal from 1615. Founded mus. lect. at Oxford Univ. 1626–7. Oxford chair of mus. is named after him.

Heyworth, Peter (Lawrence Frederick) (*b* NY, 1921; *d* Athens, 1991). Amer.-born Eng. music critic. Mus. critic of the London *Observer* 1955–91. Biographer of *Klemperer and champion of 20th-cent. mus.

Hiawatha. Cantata in 3 parts by *Coleridge-Taylor, text from Longfellow's poem of this title. Part 1, *Hiawatha's Wedding Feast*, f.p. London 1898, Part 2, *The Death of Minnehaha*, f.p. Hanley 1899, Part 3, *Hiawatha's Departure*, f.p. London 1900 (as part of f. complete p. of trilogy). Frequently perf. in pageant form.

Hickox, Richard (Sidney) (*b* Stokenchurch, Bucks., 1948). Eng. conductor. Début as prof. cond. London (St John's, Smith Square) 1971. Cond. and mus. dir. City of London Sinfonia from 1971. Founder Richard Hickox Singers 1971. Org. and master of mus., St Margaret's, Westminster, 1972–82. Mus. dir., London Symphony Chorus 1976–91, prin. cond. from 1991; assoc. cond. LSO from 1985. Art. dir. Northern Sinfonia 1982–90. Ass. cond. San Diego SO 1983–4. Cond., BBC Nat. Orch. of Wales 2000–6. Mus. dir. Opera Australia from 2005. Co-founder Collegium Musicum, for baroque perfs. and recordings, 1990. Opera débuts: RNCM 1974; ENO 1979; Los Angeles Opera 1986; CG 1985. Cond. of many recordings of Brit. mus. CBE 2002.

Hidalgo, Elvira de (*b* Aragón, 1892; *d* Milan, 1980). Sp. soprano. Début Naples 1908 as Rosina in *Il barbiere di Siviglia*. NY Met début 1910; BNOC at CG 1924. Became teacher at Athens (pupils incl. *Callas), and Ankara.

hidden fifths (or octaves). The progression in similar motion of 2 parts to perfect 5th (or octave) from such an interval in the same 2 parts in the previous chord, so that a pedant might find a 5th (or octave) in intermediate hiding (e.g. C–G in ten. and sop. proceeding to A–E in next chord).

Higglety Pigglety Pop! Fantasy opera in 1 act (9 scenes) by Knussen to lib. by Maurice Sendak and composer, based on a children's book by Sendak. Comp. 1984–90. Prelim. vers. prod. Glyndebourne 1985. Final vers. London 1991.

Hildegard of Bingen (*b* Bemersheim, 1098; *d* Rupertsberg, 1179). Ger. abbess, mystic, and writer. Took veil at 15. Became superior at Benedictine monastery of Disibodenberg 1136. *c*.1147 founded monastery on the Rupertsberg, near Bingen, Rhine Valley. Wrote lyrical poetry from 1140, setting it to her own mus., much of it of strong individuality and complexity. She collected it together in 1150s under title *Symphonia armonie celestium revelationum*. Her morality play, *Ordo Virtutum*, a kind of pre-opera, representing the struggle for the soul between 16 virtues and the devil, contains 82 melodies. Edn. of her mus., ed. by J. Gmelch, pubd. Düsseldorf 1913.

Hill, Alfred (Francis) (*b* Melbourne, 1870; *d* Sydney, NSW, 1960). Australian conductor, composer, violinist, and teacher. Settled in NZ where he collected Maori mus., using it in his comps. Prof. of harmony and comp., NSW Cons. 1915–35. Works incl. 9 operas; 10 syms.; cantata *Hinemoa*; *Maori Rhapsody*; 17 str. qts.; songs, etc. OBE 1953, CMG 1960.

Hill, Edward Burlingame (*b* Cambridge, Mass., 1872; *d* Francestown, NH, 1960). Amer. composer. Taught at Harvard Univ. 1908–40 (prof. from 1928). Influenced by Fr. mus. and wrote book *Modern French Music* (Boston, 1924). Comps. incl. 3 syms. (1928, 1931, 1937); vn. conc. (1938); sym.-poem *The Fall of the House of Usher* (1920); str. qt. (1935); pf. qt. (1937).

Hill, Martyn (*b* Rochester, 1944). Eng. tenor. Concert-hall and recital career in Bach, Stravinsky, and much Eng. mus., notably Britten. Gave f.p. of Elliott Carter's *In Sleep, In Thunder*, London 1982. GTO début (at Glyndebourne) 1985 (Idomeneo), Glyndebourne 1988; Scottish Opera 1986; Amer. (NH) 1988.

Hill & Son, W. Firm of London organ-builders, later W. Hill & Son & Norman & Beard. Founded 1755 by John Snetzler. William Hill became partner in 1825, firm changing name to his in 1838. Built orgs. in York Minster, Ely, Worcester, and Manchester Caths., Birmingham Town Hall, etc.

Hill & Sons, W. E. London firm of violin makers and dealers founded by Joseph Hill (1715–84).

Hillbilly Songs. The traditional songs (largely of European origin) of the primitive peoples of the mountain regions (e.g. Appalachians) of the SE parts of the USA. Term 'hillbilly mus.' was used to describe country mus. as a whole.

Hiller, Ferdinand (von) (*b* Frankfurt, 1811; *d* Cologne, 1885). Ger. pianist, conductor, and composer. With Hummel, visited Beethoven on his deathbed, 1827. Lived in Paris 1828–35; first to play Beethoven's 5th pf. conc. in Paris. Cond., Leipzig Gewandhaus Orch. 1843–4 and held cond. posts in Frankfurt, Düsseldorf, and Col-

ogne. Founded Cologne Cons., 1850, becoming dir. until 1884. Cond. of It. opera in Paris 1852–3. Wrote 6 operas; 2 oratorios; 3 syms.; 3 pf. concs.; vn. conc.; cantatas; chamber mus.; and pf. pieces.

Hiller [Hüller], **Johann Adam** (*b* Wendisch-Ossig, 1728; *d* Leipzig, 1804). Ger. composer. Settled in Leipzig 1758, becoming cond. of several organizations. Regarded as founder of the *Singspiel, which he based on the Ger. Lied. First of these was *Die verwandelten Weiber oder Der Teufel ist los*, 1766, followed by 13 others. Also wrote church mus. and secular songs. Ed. of *Wöchentliche Nachrichten*, first specialist periodical on mus.

Hiller, Lejaren (*b* NY, 1924; *d* Buffalo, 1994). Amer. composer. Worked as research chemist; experimented in composition with computers, collaborating with Leonard Isaacson with whom in 1957 he produced *Illiac Suite* (named after the computer). This was first computer-composition. Dir., experimental mus. studio, Illinois Univ. 1958–68; prof of comp., State Univ. of NY, Buffalo, from 1968 (prof. of mus. from 1980). Works incl. pf. conc. (1949); 2 syms. (1953, 1960); *Computer Cantata* (1963); *7 Electronic Studies* (1963); *Rage over the Lost Beethoven* (1972); 7 str. qts.; 6 pf. sonatas; and many works for stage, films, and TV.

Hilton, Janet (Lesley) (*b* Liverpool, 1945). Eng. clarinettist. Prin. cl., WNO orch. 1970–3, SCO 1973–80. Taught at RSAMD 1974–80, RNCM 1982–6. Head of ww. Birmingham Cons. 1993–8, RCM from 1998.

Hilton, John (*b c.*1560; *d* Cambridge, 1608). Eng. composer and organist. Counterten., Lincoln Cath. 1584. Org., Trinity Coll., Cambridge, from 1594. Wrote anthems and madrigals, latter incl. *Fair Oriana, Beauty's Queen* in *The *Triumphs of Oriana*.

Hindemith, Paul (*b* Hanau, 1895; *d* Frankfurt, 1963). Ger.-born Amer. composer, conductor, violist, and teacher (Amer. cit. 1945). Became first violinist in Frankfurt Opera orch. 1915 and Rebner Qt. Served in Ger. Army 1917–19, but continued to compose and to play in str. qt. Returned to opera orch. Left Rebner Qt. 1921. Two 1-act operas, *Mörder, Hoffnung der Frauen* and *Das Nusch-Nuschi*, cond. by Fritz Busch, Stuttgart 1921 and by Ludwig Rottenberg (whose daughter, Gertrud, Hindemith married in 1924) in Frankfurt 1922 (with a 3rd opera *Sancta Susanna*). These works, disowned as prentice pieces, had a *succès de scandale*. His 2nd str. qt. was perf. Donaueschingen 1921, by qt., with Hindemith as violist, led by Licco Amar. This led to the permanent est. of the Amar Qt., which played only modern works. Hindemith left the Frankfurt Opera orch. in 1923, concentrating on his work with the Amar Qt. and as a member of the selection committee for Donaueschingen fests.

In 1927 Hindemith became teacher of comp. at Berlin Hochschule für Musik. Among his pupils were Franz *Reizenstein, Walter *Leigh, and

Arnold *Cooke. Also working in Berlin were 2 conds. who had championed Hindemith's mus., *Furtwängler at the Phil. and *Klemperer at the *Kroll Opera. In 1929, because of pressure of work, Hindemith disbanded the Amar Qt. His satirical opera Neues vom Tage (News of the Day) was prod. in Berlin under Klemperer in summer 1929 (the first opera to incl. a sop. singing in her bath, which shocked Hitler); and his cantata Lehrstück, to a text by Brecht, created a scandal at the 1929 Baden-Baden Festival. In Oct. 1929 Hindemith made his first visit to London, where he was soloist in the f.p. of *Walton's va. conc., having met Walton at Salzburg in 1923.

In 1933, the year Hitler came to power, Hindemith began work on an opera on the subject of the painter Matthias Grünewald, a medieval artist with a social conscience. He arr. 3 interludes as a suite, which he called the Mathis der Maler (Matthias the Painter) Sym. These were performed by the Berlin PO under Furtwängler in Mar. 1934 and were an immediate success. But official criticism of his mus. now began to be voiced publicly. Furtwängler wrote an article in Nov. 1934 defending Hindemith and opposing his 'political denunciation'. As a result of the ensuing controversy, the Nazis forbade prod. of the Mathis opera. In 1935 Hindemith accepted an invitation from Turkey to est. a mus. sch. On his return from Ankara, he found the régime friendlier towards him and a Frankfurt première for Mathis seemed possible. But in 1936, after 'demonstrative' applause for *Kulenkampff's playing of the new vn. sonata, Goebbels banned all further perfs. of Hindemith's mus. After a further spell in Turkey in 1937, Hindemith resigned from the Berlin Hochschule and visited NY to give lectures. He then settled in Switzerland, and in May 1938 Mathis der Maler was staged in Zurich, but mention of the event was forbidden in Ger. newspapers. In Feb. 1940 he sailed for the fourth time to the USA, this time to stay indefinitely. He was appointed visiting prof. of the theory of mus. at Yale Univ., and also was head of advanced comp. at the Berkshire summer fest. at Tanglewood, where his pupils in 1940 incl. Lukas *Foss and Leonard *Bernstein. He returned to Europe in 1947, visiting Italy, Holland, Belgium, Eng., Ger., Austria, and Switzerland where he renewed friendship with Furtwängler. In 1949-50 he spent a year at Harvard Univ. as Norton Prof., giving the Charles Eliot Norton lectures, later pubd. as A Composer's World. In 1951 he accepted a teaching post at Zurich Univ., dividing his time with his duties at Yale, but in 1953 resigned from Yale and returned to Europe. Cond. Vienna PO at Salzburg Fest. (1952) and Beethoven's 9th Sym. at Bayreuth (1953).

Hindemith is invariably associated with the term *Gebrauchsmusik (utility mus.) but this is a misleading and drab name for his attitude to his art, which was that audiences should participate as well as listen. In his Berlin teaching days, therefore, he comp. works which could be used for teaching and would also provide material for amateurs. His title for this type of work was Sing- und Spielmusik (Music to Sing and Play). Examples are his children's opera Wir bauen eine Stadt (Let's Build a Town—echoed years later by Britten in Let's Make an Opera)—and Plöner Musiktag (A Day of Music in Plön), which is a series of instr. and choral pieces written for schoolchildren in Schleswig-Holstein.

Like his friend Walton, Hindemith began as an enfant terrible and ended by being regarded by the avant-garde as an ultra-conservative. He rejected the extremist methods of the avant-garde (but this did not prevent him from writing for an early elec. instr., the *trautonium). His early works show the influences of Strauss and Reger, succeeded by Stravinsky and Bartók. As his style developed, his rhythmic drive and partiality for contrapuntal textures grew more evident, coupled with a reticent lyricism. This lyricism grew more evident at the time of Mathis der Maler, while his harmonic idiom was based on well-controlled dissonant tensions. Tonality was the firm basis of all his comps. The severe reaction against his mus., which eventually slackened, was as unjust as it was unthinking. The best of his mus. occupies an important place in the history of 20th-cent. comp. Prin. works:

OPERAS: Mörder, Hoffnung der Frauen (Murderer, the Hope of Women), 1-act, text by Kokoschka, Op.12 (1919); Das *Nusch-Nuschi, 1-act, text by Blei, Op.20 (1920); Sancta Susanna, 1-act, text by Stramm, Op.21 (1921); *Cardillac, Op.39 (1926, new version 1952); *Hin und Zurück, Op.45a (1927); *Neues vom Tage (1928-9, new version 1953); *Mathis der Maler (1933-5); Die *Harmonie der Welt (The Harmony of the World) (1956-7); The *Long Christmas Dinner (Das lange Weihnachtsmahl) (1960). Also realization of Monteverdi's Orfeo (1943).

THEATRE PIECES: Tuttifäntchen, mus. for children's Christmas play (1922); Lehrstück (Lesson on Consent), cantata to text by Brecht (1929); Wir bauen eine Stadt, children's opera (1930).

BALLETS: Der Dämon, Op.28 (1922); *Nobilissima Visione (1938); Hérodiade (1944).

ORCH.: Lustige Sinfonietta, Op.4 (1916); Dance Suite, Das Nusch-Nuschi, Op.20 (1921); Concerto for Orchestra, Op.38 (1925); Concert Music, pf., brass, hps., Op.49 (1930); Concert music, str., brass, Op.50 (1930); Philharmonic Concerto (1932); sym., *Mathis der Maler (1934); Symphonic Dances (1937); suite *Nobilissima Visione (1938); The *Four Temperaments, theme and vars., str., solo pf. (1940, perf. as ballet 1946); Sym. in E♭ (1940); *Symphonic Metamorphosis of Themes by Carl Maria von Weber (1940-3); Symphonia Serena (1946); Sinfonietta in E (1949-50); sym. in B♭, concert band (1951); Sym. Die *Harmonie der Welt (1951); Pittsburgh Symphony (1958); March (1960).

*KAMMERMUSIK SERIES: No.1 (small orch.) Op.24 (1922); Kleine Kammermusik (wind quintet) Op.24 No.2 (1922); No.2 (pf. conc. with 12 instr.) Op.36 No.1 (1924), No.3 (vc. conc. with 10 instr.) Op.36 No.2 (1925), No.4 (vn. conc.) Op.36 No.3 (1925),

No.5 (va. conc.) Op.36 No.4 (1927), No.6 (va. d'amore conc.) Op.46 No.1 (1927), No.7 (org. conc.) Op.46 No.2 (1927).

CONCERTOS (besides those above): *Concert Music*, va., large chamber orch., Op.48 (1930); *Concert Piece*, trautonium, str. (unpubd.) (1931); *Der* *Schwanendreher, va., small orch., based on folk-songs (1935); *Trauermusik, va., str. (1936); vn. conc. (1939); vc. conc. (1940); pf. conc. (1945); cl. conc. (1947); hn. conc. (1949); conc. for ww., hp., orch. (1949); conc., tpt., bn., str. (1949); org. conc. (1962).

CHORUS & ORCH.: *Das Unaufhörliche* (The Perpetual), oratorio, sop., ten., bar., and bass, ch., orch., text by G. Benn (1931); Requiem **When Lilacs Last in the Dooryard Bloom'd* (text by Whitman), mez., bar., ch., orch. (1946); *Ite, angeli veloces* (Go, flights of angels), cantata to text by Claudel in 3 parts: I, *Triumphgesang Davids*, alto, ten., ch., orch., wind band, spectators (1955), II, *Custos quid de nocte*, ten., ch., orch. (1955), III, *Cantique de l'espérance*, mez., ch., orch., wind band, spectators (1953); *Mainzer Umzug*, sop., ten., bar., ch., orch. (1962).

VOICE & ORCH.: *Die* *junge Magd, 6 Trakl songs, cont., fl., cl., str. qt., Op.23 No.2 (1922); *Das* *Marienleben, 15 Rilke songs, sop., pf., Op.27 (1922–3; rev. version 1948, begun 1936; version with orch. Nos.1–4 1938, Nos.5–6 1959); *Die Serenaden*, cantata, sop., ob., va., vc., Op.35 (1924).

CHAMBER MUSIC: 3 *Pieces*, vc., pf., Op.8 (1917); str. qt. No.1, Op.10 (1918), No.2 Op.16 (1920), No.3, Op.22 (1921), No.4, Op.32 (1923), No.5 (1943), No.6 (1945); vn. sonata in E♭, Op.11 No.1, in D, Op.11 No.2 (1918); va. sonata in F, Op.11 No.4, solo va., Op.11 No.5, vc. sonata, Op.11 No.6 (1919); solo va. sonata, Op.25 No.1, va. d'amore sonata, Op.25 No.2, solo vc. sonata, Op.25 No.3, va. sonata (unpubd.), Op.25 No.4 (1922); cl. quintet, Op.30; solo va. sonata (unpubd.), Op.31 No.4, *Canonic sonata*, 2 fl., Op.31 No.3 (1923); sonatas for solo vn., Op.31 Nos. 1 and 2 (1924); str. trio, Op.34 (1924); 3 *Pieces* for cl., tpt., vn., db., pf. (1925); trio for pf., va., heckelphone (or tenor sax.), Op.47 (1929); 14 *Easy Duets*, 2 vn. (1931); str. trio (1933); *Scherzo*, va., vc. (1934); vn. sonata in E (1935); fl. sonata (1936); bn. sonata; 3 *Easy Pieces*, vc., pf.; qt., cl., vn., vc., pf.; ob. sonata (1938); va. sonata in C; vn. sonata in C; cl. sonata; hp. sonata; tpt. sonata (all 1939); ca. sonata; tb. sonata; *A Frog he went a-courting*, vars., vc., pf. (all 1941); sax. sonata (1943); vc. sonata; septet for wind instr. (both 1948); db. sonata (1949); sonata for 4 hn. (1952); tuba sonata (1955); octet (1957–8).

PIANO: *Tanzstücke*, Op.19 (1920); *Suite 1922* (1922); *Klaviermusik*, Op.37 (Part I 1925, Part II 1926); mus. for film *Vormittagsspuk*, player-pf. (unpubd.) (1928); pf. sonata No.1 in A, No.2 in G, No.3 in B♭ (1936); sonata (4 hands) (1938); sonata for 2 pf. (1942); *Ludus Tonalis (1942).

ORGAN: org. sonatas Nos. 1 and 2 (1937), No.3 (1940).

VOCAL: 8 *Lieder*, sop., pf., Op.18 (1920); *Das Marienleben*, sop., pf., Op.27 (1922–3, rev. 1936–48); 6 *Songs on Old Texts*, unacc. ch., Op.33 (1923); 4 3-part choruses for boys (1930); 2 *Hölderlin Songs* (1933); 4 *Hölderlin Songs* (1935); 5 *Songs on Old Texts*, unacc. ch. (rev. version to Eng. texts of 6 Songs, 1923, Nos. 1, 2, 3, and 6, with new song *Wahre Liebe*, 1937); 3 *Choruses*, male vv., 6 *Chansons*, ch., *Variations on an Old Dance Song*, male vv. (all 1939); *La Belle Dame Sans Merci*, v., pf.; 7 *Songs to Eng. texts* (both 1942); *Sing on There in the Swamp*, v., pf. (1943); *To music* (1944); *Apparebit repentina dies*, ch., brass (1947); 2 Songs to words by Oscar Cox, v., pf. (1955); 12 *Madrigals*, ch. (1958); Mass, unacc. ch. (1963). 13 *Motets*, sop. or ten., pf. (comp. in following order: No.8 (1940–1), No.13 (1943), Nos. 2 and 11 (1944), Nos. 5 and 7 (1958), Nos. 3, 4, 6, 9, 10 (1959), Nos. 1 and 12 (1960).

COMMUNAL & EDUCATIONAL MUSIC: *Spielmusik*, str., fls., obs., Op.43 No.1; *Lieder für Singkreise* (Songs for Group Singing), unacc. ch., Op.43 No.2 (1926); *Schulwerk für Instrumental-Zusammenspiel* (Educational Music for Instrumental Ensembles), str., Op.44 (1927); *Sing- und Spielmusik für Liebhaber und Musikfreunde* (Music to Sing and Play, for Amateurs and Music-lovers), Op.45; *Frau Musica*, 2 solo vv., ch., str., Op.45 No.1 (1928, as *In Praise of Music* 1943); *Plöner Musiktag* (1932).

BOOKS: *The Craft of Musical Composition* (*Unterweisung im Tonsatz*) Vol. I, *Theoretical* (1935–7), Vol. II, *Exercises in 2-part writing* (1938–9), Vol. III, *3-part Writing* (posth.); *A Concentrated Course in Traditional Harmony* (1942–3); *Elementary Training for Musicians* (1945–6); *A Composer's World: Horizons and Limitations* (Norton Lectures, Harvard 1949–50; pubd. in Eng. 1950, in Ger. as *Komponist in seiner Welt*, 1953); *Johann Sebastian Bach, Heritage and Obligation* (Frankfurt Lecture, 1950).

Hindemith, Variations on a Theme of. Orch. work by *Walton comp. 1962–3 to commission by Royal Phil. Soc. for its 150th anniversary concert. Theme is from 2nd movt. of Hindemith's vc. conc. (1940) and 7th var. quotes 4 bars from *Mathis der Maler*. F.p. London 1963, cond. composer.

Hines [Heinz], **Jerome** (Albert Link) (*b* Los Angeles, 1921; *d* NY, 2003). Amer. bass and composer. Début S. Francisco 1941 (Monterone in *Rigoletto*). Won Caruso Award and NY Met début 1946. Eur. début (Edinburgh Fest.) 1953; Bayreuth 1958. Sang Boris in Russian at Bolshoy, 1962, and later in Leningrad, and in orig. vers. at Met 1975. Wrote opera *I am the Way*, on life of Christ, Philadelphia 1969. Autobiography *This is my Story, This is my Song* (NJ 1968) and wrote *Great Singers on Great Singing* (London 1982).

Hinrichsen, Max (*b* Leipzig, 1901; *d* London, 1965). Ger.-born publisher. Joint man. dir. Peters Edition, Leipzig, 1931–7. Went to London 1937, founding Peters Edition, London, and Hinrichsen Edition. Contrib. valuably to revival of early Eng. organ and choral mus. Authority on J. S. Bach.

Hinstrich (Ger., 'away-stroke'). The up-bow on vc. and db. (see also *Herstrich*).

Hin und Zurück (There and Back). Opera (*Sketch mit Musik*) in 1 act by *Hindemith to lib. by M. Schiffer based on Eng. revue sketch. Prod. Baden-Baden 1927; Philadelphia 1928; London 1958. The plot and, in part, the mus. go into reverse at the half-way point.

Hippolyte et Aricie. Opera in prologue and 5 acts by Rameau to lib. by S.-J. Pellegrin. prod. Paris 1733, rev. vers. 1742. Modern revival Paris (concert) 1902, Geneva (stage) 1903; Birmingham (in English) 1965; NY (concert) 1954, Boston (stage) 1966.

Hirokami, Jun'ichi (*b* Tokyo, 1958). Japanese conductor. Ass. cond. Nagoya PO 1983. Guest cond. of Orchestre National de France 1986, Israel PO 1988. London début 1989 (LSO). Opera début 1989, Australian Opera (*Un ballo in maschera*). Prin. cond. of Norrkoeping SO from 1991.

Hirt (Ger.). 'Herd', 'Herdsman'. *Hirtenlied*, 'Herdsman's Song', etc.

Hirt auf dem Felsen, Der (Schubert). See *Shepherd on the Rock, The*.

His (Ger.). The note B♯. *Hisis*, the (probably theoretical) note B♯♯.

Hislop, Joseph (*b* Edinburgh, 1884; *d* Lundin Links, 1977). Scot. tenor and teacher. Début at Swed. Royal Opera 1914. CG début 1920. Distinguished operatic career. Taught at GSMD and at Royal Academy, Stockholm, 1936–49.

Histoire du Soldat, L' (The Soldier's Tale). Work in 2 parts by Stravinsky 'to be read, played, and danced'. Comp. 1918 to Fr. text by C. F. Ramuz based on Russ. tale. Orch. of 12 instrs., 2 speaking parts, 2 danced parts (no singers). Prod. Lausanne 1918, NY 1928, London (concert 1920). Also suite of 8 movts. with orig. orch. or of 5 movts. for vn., cl., and pf. (Lausanne 1919).

Histoires naturelles (Natural histories). Song-cycle for v. and pf. by Ravel to poems by Jules Renard, comp. 1906, f.p. Paris 1907. 1. *Le Paon* (The Peacock), 2. *Le Grillon* (The Cricket), 3. *Le Cygne* (The Swan), 4. *Le Martin-pêcheur* (The king-fisher), 5. *La Pintade* (The guinea-fowl). Orch. version by M. Rosenthal.

hitschiriki. Japanese instr. like a bamboo fl., with 7 finger-holes and 2 thumb-holes. Shrill tone.

hityokin. Japanese vertical fl. made of bamboo.

HMS Pinafore, or The Lass that loved a Sailor. Comic opera by Sullivan to lib. by Gilbert. Comp. 1878. Prod. London (Opéra Comique), Boston, and S. Francisco 1878; NY and Philadelphia 1879.

Hob. Abbreviated prefix to nos. in the *Hoboken catalogue of Haydn's works.

hoboe (Hoboy). Name sometimes given to the *oboe.

Hoboken, Anthony van (*b* Rotterdam, 1887; *d* Zurich, 1983). Dutch musicologist. In 1927 founded Vienna nat. archive of photographs of mus. MSS. Compiler of definitive catalogue of Haydn's works in 2 vols., 1957 and 1971. Works are given 'Hob.' nos., followed by Roman numeral and Arabic figure, e.g. Hob. IV:6.

Hobrecht, Jacob. See *Obrecht, Jacob*.

Hochschule, Berlin. In full the Staatliche Akademische Hochschule für Musik, formerly the Royal High School for Mus. Founded 1869, with Joachim as dir.

Hochzeit des Camacho, Die (The Wedding of the Camacho). Comic opera in 2 acts by Mendelssohn, Op.10, to lib., probably by F. Voight, based on an episode in *Don Quixote*. Comp. 1825. Prod. Berlin 1827, Chicago (concert) 1875, Oxford 1987.

Hochzeitsmarsch (Ger.). Wedding march.

hocket ('hiccough'; Lat. *hoquetus*, Fr. *hoquet*, It. *ochetto*). Device in medieval vocal mus. whereby rests were inserted into vocal parts, even in the middle of words, to intensify expressive effect.

Hoddinott, Alun (*b* Bargoed, 1929). Welsh composer. Lect., Cardiff Coll. of Mus. and Drama 1951. Lect., Univ. Coll., S. Wales, 1959–65, Reader 1965–7, Prof. of Mus. 1967–87. Art. dir. Cardiff Fest. of 20th cent. Mus. 1966–89. Comps. are strongly structured, romantic in feeling, and deeply serious. Serialist technique used without strict formal adherence. Arnold Bax Medal 1957. CBE 1983. Prin. works:

OPERAS: *The Beach of Falesá* (3 acts, lib. by Glyn Jones based on story by R. L. Stevenson, prod. Cardiff 1974); *The Magician* (1 act, lib. by John Morgan, prod. Cardiff 1976—previously as *Murder the Magician* on TV 1976); *What the Old Man Does is Always Right* (1 act, lib. by Myfanwy Piper, prod. Fishguard 1977); *The *Rajah's Diamond* (1978–9) (1 act, lib. by Myfanwy Piper, prod. TV 1979); *The Trumpet Major* (3 acts, lib. by Myfanwy Piper based on T. Hardy, prod. Manchester (RNCM) 1981); *The Tower* (1998–9) (3 acts, lib. by J. Owen, prod. Swansea 1999).

ORCH.: syms., No.1 (1955), No.2 (1962), No.3 (1968), No.4 (1969), No.5 (1973), No.6 (1984), No.7, org., orch. (1989), No.8, brass, perc. (1992), No.9 (*A Vision of Eternity*), sop., orch. (1992); No.10 (1999); *Fugal Overture* (1951); *Nocturne* (1952); *Serenade for Strings* (1957); *Welsh Dances*, 1st Suite (1958), 2nd (1969), 3rd (1985), 4th (1989); *Folk-Song Suite* (1962); *Sinfonia*, str. (1964); ovs., *Jack Straw* (1964), *Pantomime* (1966); *Variants* (1966); *Night Music* (1966); *Sinfoniettas*, No.1 (1968), No.2 (1969), No.3 (1970), No.4 (1971); *Concerto Grosso* No.1 (1965), No.2 (1966); *Fioriture* (1968); *Divertimento* (1969); *Investiture Dances* (1969); *The Sun, the Great Luminary of the Universe* (1970); *Aubade* (1971); *The Hawk is set free* (1972); *The Floore of Heav'n* (1973);

Welsh Airs and Dances, sym. wind band (1975); *Landscapes* (1975); *French Suite* (1977); *Nightpiece* (1977); *Passaggio* (1977); *Lanterne des Morts* (1981); *5 Studies* (1982); *Quodlibet on Welsh Nursery Tunes* (1982); *Hommage à Chopin* (1984); *Scena*, str. (1985); *Concerto for Orchestra* (1986); *Star Children* (1989); *Rhapsody on Welsh Tunes* (1989); *Prelude, Nocturne and Dance*, hp., str. (1990); *Dragon Fire*, timp., perc., orch. (1998); *Celebration Dances* (1998).

CONCERTOS: cl., No.1 (1949), No.2 (1987); ob. (1955); hp. (1958); va. (1958); pf., No.1 with wind and perc. (1960), No.2 (1960), No.3 1966); vn. (1961); org. (1967); hn. (1969); *Prelude, Nocturne and Dance*, hp., str. (1959–90); *Aubade and Scherzo*, hn., str. (1965); *Nocturnes and Cadenzas*, vc., orch. (1969); *The Heaventree of Stars*, vn., orch. (1980); *Doubles*, ob., hpd., str. (1982); *Scenes and Interludes*, tpt., hpd., str. (1984); *Divisions*, hn., hpd., str. (1986); *Triple Conc.*, vn., vc., pf. (1986); *Noctis Equi*, vc., orch. (1989); vn. conc. No.2 (*Mistral*) (1995); tpt. conc. (*Shining Pyramid*) (1995).

CHORAL: *Job*, bass, ch., orch. (1962); *Cantata Dives and Lazarus*, sop., bar., ch., orch. (1965); *Black Bart*, ballad, ch., orch. (1969); *Eryri*, ch., orch. (1969); 4 *Welsh Songs*, male vv., orch. or pf. (1971); *The Tree of Life*, sop., ten., ch., org., orch. (1971); *The Silver Swimmer*, ch., pf. duet (1973); cantata *Sinfonia Fidei*, sop., ten., ch., orch. (1977); *Dulcia Iuventutis*, ch., pf. duet (1978); *Hymnus ante Somnum*, male ch., org. (1979); *Voyagers*, bar., male ch., orch. (1981); *The Charge of the Light Brigade*, male ch., pf. (1982); *In Parasceve Domini: III Nocturno*, women's vv., pf. (1982); *Ingravescentem Aetatem*, ch., pf. duet (1983); *The Bells of Paradise*, bar., ch., orch. (1984); *Lady and Unicorn*, ch., pf. (1985); *The Legend of St Julian*, narr., ch., orch. (1987); *Emynau Pantycelyn*, bar., ch., orch. (1989); *Lines from Marlowe's Dr Faustus*, ch., brass (1989); *May Song*, children's ch., orch. (1992); *Missa Sancti David*, ch., org., pf. duet, perc. (1994); *Mass of the Pilgrims*, bar., ch., pf. duet, org. (1996); *Magnificat and Nunc dimittis (St David's Service)*, ch., org. (1996).

CHAMBER MUSIC: str. qts. No.1 (1966), No.2 (1984), No.3 (1988), No. 4 (1996); pf. septet (1957/73); sextet, ww., str. (1960); *Divertimento*, ob., cl., hn., bn. (1963); hp. sonata (1964); suite for hp. (1967); cl. sonata (1967); *Divertimenti*, fl., cl., bn., hn., str. qt. (1968); *Nocturnes and Cadenzas*, cl., vn., vc. (1968), vc. (1979), fl. (1979); *Sonata-Notturno*, hp. (1969/90); vn. sonatas, No.1 (1969), No.2 (1970), No.3 (1972), No.4 (1976), No.5 (1991), No. 6 (1997); vc. sonata No.1 (1970), No.2 (1977), No. 3 (1996); pf. trio, No.1 (1970), No.2 (1984), No. 3 (1996); hp. fantasy (1970); hn. sonata (1971); pf. quintet (1972); *Ritornelli*, No.1, tb., wind, perc. (1974), No.2, brass quintet (1979), No.3, 4 db. (1981); *Italian Suite*, rec. (fl.), gui. (1977); gui. sonatina (1978); *Scena*, str. qt. (1979); *Quodlibet on Welsh Nursery Tunes*, brass quintet (1983); *Masks*, ob., bn., pf. (1983); *Bagatelles*, ob., hp. (1984); *Chorales, Variants, and Fanfares*, org., brass quintet (1992); quintet (fl., ob., cl., hn., bn. (1992); 6 *Bagatelles*, vn., 2 va., vc. (1994); sonata, ob., hp. (1995); *Tempi*, hp. (1997); 5 *Bagatelles*, wind quintet (1999).

SONGS: *A Contemplation Upon Flowers*, 3 songs, sop., orch. (1976); *Landscapes*, ten., pf. (1975); *Roman Dream*, scena, sop., ens. (1968); *Ancestor Worship*, bar., pf. (1977); 6 *Welsh Folk Songs*, sop., pf. or hp. (1982); *The Silver Hound*, scena, pf. (1985); *Songs of Exile*, ten., orch. (1989); *Paradwys Mai*, sop., pf., str. quintet (1992); *'one must always have love'*, sop., pf. (1994); *Tymhorau*, bar., pf. (1995); *Grongar Hill*, bar., str. qt., pf. (1998); *To the Poet*, bass-bar., pf. (1999).

PIANO: sonatas, No.1 (1959), No.2 (1962), No.3 (1965), No.4 (1966), No.5 (1968), No.6 (1972), No.7 (1984), No.8 (1986), No.9 (1989), No.10 (1989), No.11 (1993), No.12 (1994); *Dark March* (1995).

ORGAN: *Toccata alla giga* (1964); *Intrada* (1967); *Sarum Fanfare* (1970); sonata (1978); *Passacaglia and Fugue* (1985).

Hodgson, Alfreda (*b* Morecambe, 1940; *d* Prestwich, Manchester, 1992). Eng. mezzo-soprano. Début Liverpool 1961, London 1963. Several appearances in opera, but mainly heard in oratorio, Mahler, Elgar, etc. ENO début 1974 (Ulrica in *A Masked Ball*); CG 1983 (*L'Enfant et les Sortilèges*).

Hodie (Lat. 'On this day'). Christmas cantata for mez., ten., bar., boys' vv., ch., and orch. by Vaughan Williams, comp. 1953–4, f.p. Worcester 1954, cond. composer. Orig. title *This Day (Hodie)*, the composer preferring *Hodie*, which has been generally adopted. Text, selected by composer, incl. settings of words from Bible, Milton, Herbert, Hardy, Drummond, Coverdale, Ballet, and Ursula Vaughan Williams.

Hoelscher, Ulf (*b* Kitzingen, 1942). Ger. violinist. Salzburg Fest. début 1977. Gave f.ps. of concs. by Kirchner (1984) and Franz Hummel (1987), and of Reimann's for vn. and vc. (Montreux, 1989). Plays chamber mus. with Michel Béroff and in trio with Heinrich Schiff and Christian Zacharias. Prof., Berlin Hochschule der Kunste from 1987.

Hoffman, Grace (*b* Cleveland, Ohio, 1925). Amer. mezzo-soprano. Début 1951 with US Touring Co. (Lola in *Cavelleria Rusticana*). Member of Zurich Opera 1953–5. Débuts: Bayreuth 1957; NY Met 1958; CG 1959. Prof. of singing, Stuttgart Hochschule für Mus., from 1978.

Hoffmann, Bruno (*b* Stuttgart, 1913; *d* 1991). Ger. player of and composer for *glass armonica. Début London 1938 when he revived Mozart's quintet (K617). His name for the instr. is 'glass harp'.

Hoffmann, E(rnst) T(heodor) A(madeus) (orig. Wilhelm, but adopted name Amadeus in homage to Mozart) (*b* Königsberg, 1776; *d* Berlin, 1822). Ger. writer, music critic, composer, and conductor. Was th. cond. from 1808 at Bamberg, Leipzig, and Dresden. Comp. 10 operas, incl. *Undine* (Berlin 1816), ballet, sym., mass, pf. sonatas, etc. Best known for his essays and tales, which have remarkable bizarre humour. His character, the Kapellmeister Kreisler, inspired Schumann's *Kreisleriana*. He himself is the hero of Offenbach's *Les contes d'Hoffmann*.

Hoffmann, Karl (*b* Smichov, 1872; *d* Prague, 1936). Cz. violinist. Founded Bohemian Str. Qt. 1892. Prof. of vn., Prague Cons., from 1922.

Hoffmeister, Franz Anton (*b* Rothenburg, 1754; *d* Vienna, 1812). Ger. composer and music publisher. Mus.-dealer in Vienna 1784–98; founded Bureau de Musique, Leipzig, 1800, with Kühnel. Returned to Vienna 1805, becoming active as composer. Wrote many works for fl., cl., and str.; over 65 syms.; 9 operas; 12 pf. sonatas; songs; church mus., etc.

Hoffnung, Gerard (*b* Berlin, 1925; *d* Hampstead, 1959). Ger.-born artist, humorist, and tubaplayer. Settled in Brit. as child. Contrib. as freelance artist to various publications from 1940. Made series of illustrations, 1949, to Ravel's *L'Enfant et les sortilèges*. Founded Hoffnung Mus. Fests. at which various witty mus. parodies were perf. Drew series of amusing drawings of mus. subjects. Soloist in London, 1958, in Vaughan Williams's tuba conc.

Hofmann, Josef [Kazimierz, Józef] (*b* Podgorze, Kraków, 1876; *d* Los Angeles, 1957). Polish-born pianist and composer (Amer. cit. 1926). Son of a pianist-cond. and opera singer, showed prodigious talent and made début as pianist at 6, appearing as soloist with Berlin PO at 9. Toured Eur., made NY début at 11 (1887). Amer. tour halted midway by action of soc. for prevention of cruelty to children, enforcing unwilling retirement until he was 18. Returned to Eur. to study (unsuccessfully) with Moszkowski and then as only private pupil of Anton Rubinstein. Returned to platform 1894, followed by regular world tours. Settled principally in USA from 1898. Dir. of Curtis Inst. 1926–38. Final recital, NY 1946. One of greatest players of Chopin, Liszt, and romantics. Comp. sym., 5 pf. concs., pf. sonatas, and many pf. pieces. Sometimes used pseudonym 'Michel Dvorsky'.

Hofmann, Peter (*b* Marienbad, 1944). Ger. tenor. Début Lübeck 1972 (Tamino), member Stuttgart Opera from 1973. Sang Siegmund in the 1976 centenary prod. of *The Ring* at Bayreuth and at CG. Vienna 1976; S. Francisco 1977. Sang Parsifal at CG 1979 and Salzburg Easter Fest. 1980. Recorded Tristan with Bernstein, 1983. Also a rock singer.

Hofmannsthal, Hugo von (*b* Vienna, 1874; *d* Rodaun, nr. Vienna, 1929). Austrian author, poet, and playwright. With Max Reinhardt and others, founded Salzburg Fest. in 1920. Librettist for several works of Richard Strauss: the operas *Elektra* (1906–8), *Der Rosenkavalier* (1909–10), *Ariadne auf Naxos* (1912, 2nd version 1916), *Die Frau ohne Schatten* (1914–18), *Die ägyptische Helena* (1924–7), and *Arabella* (1928–32), the ballet *Josephslegende* (1913–14); *Der Burger als Edelmann* (*Le Bourgeois Gentil-*

homme) (1912 and 1917); ed. with Strauss of Beethoven's ballet *Die Geschöpfe des Prometheus*; cantata *Tüchtigen stellt das schnelle Glück* (1914). Also librettist for Wellesz's *Alkestis* (1922–3). Plays incl. *Alkestis* (1893), *Elektra* (1903), and *Jedermann* (1912).

Hofoper (Ger., 'Court opera'). Title given up to 1918 to the Court or Royal opera houses in many Ger. and Austrian cities, e.g. Vienna Hofoper, which became *Staatsoper (State Opera) in 1919.

Hogwood, Christopher (Jarvis Haley) (*b* Nottingham, 1941). Eng. harpsichordist and conductor. Founder-member with David *Munrow of Early Music Consort, 1967–76. Frequent broadcaster. Founder and dir., Academy of Ancient Music, 1973–2006. Cond. with St. Paul's Chamber Orch., Minn., from 1987, prin. guest cond. from 1991. Author of book on the trio sonata, 1979, and on Handel, 1984. Recorded complete Mozart syms. with period instrs. CBE 1989.

Hohlflöte (Ger., 'hollow flute', i.e. hollow-sounding fl.). Metal or wooden org. stop of 8′ length and pitch.

Holberg Suite (*Holbergiana*; Ger. *Aus Holbergs Zeit*, From Holberg's Time). Pf. suite in 5 movts. by Grieg comp. 1884 and orch. for str. in same year, both versions Op.40. Written to celebrate bicentenary of birth of Norweg. dramatist Ludvig Holberg (1684–1754).

Holborne, Anthony (*d* ?London, 1602). Eng. composer. Pubd. *The Cittharn Schoole* (1597, modern edn. by Kanazawa 1973) containing 58 pieces for cittern and bass viol; and 5-part *Pavans, Galliards, Almans, and other Short Aires* (1599), containing 65 pieces.

Holbrooke, Joseph [Josef] (Charles) (*b* Croydon, 1878; *d* London, 1958). Eng. composer and pianist. Mus.-hall pianist at age of 12. Pianist-cond. for travelling pantomime 1899. After perf. of his tone-poem *The Raven* (1900) his works were much in demand at Eng. fests., but did not hold their place and are rarely heard. Comp. trilogy of Celtic operas 1911–15. Controversial writer (e.g. *Contemporary British Composers* 1925) and frequent polemicist against Establishment. Prin. works:

OPERAS: *Pierrot and Pierrette* (1909); trilogy, *The Cauldron of Anwen* comprising *Dylan* (1909), *The Children of Don* (1911), *Bronwen* (1920).

ORCH.: 4 syms.; sym.-poems, *The Raven* (1900), *Ulalume* (1904), *Queen Mab*, ch., orch (1902), *Byron*, with ch. (1906), *Apollo and the Seaman*, with ch. (1907); *Variations on Three Blind Mice* (1900); vn. conc. (1917); vc. conc. (1936).

Also much chamber mus., pf. pieces, songs, etc.

Hold, Trevor (James) (*b* Northampton, 1939; *d* Wadenhoe, Northants, 2004). Eng. composer and poet. Lect. on mus. Aberystwyth and Liverpool Univs., later on staff of Leicester Univ. Works incl.: *Gunpowder Plot Music*, orch.; ov. *My Uncle Silas*; *Rondo*, str. orch.; *Requiescat*, spkr., ch., brass sextet; *The*

Falcon, church drama; *The Pied Piper*, entertainment for children; *Early One Morning*, high v., gui.; *Cinquefoils*, pf. quintet.

Holden, Amanda (*b* London, 1948). Eng. writer, translator, and pianist. Worked as pianist, accomp., and teacher GSMD 1973–86. Gen. ed. *The Viking Opera Guide*, 1993; *The New Penguin Opera Guide*, 2001. Trans. incl. *L'Italiana in Londra, Falstaff, Ariodante, Lohengrin, Le nozze di Figaro, Idomeneo* and *La Clemenza di Tito*. Contrib. to *The Mozart Compendium*, 1990. Surtitles for several CG prods.

Hölderlin-Fragmente, Sechs (Six Hölderlin Fragments). Setting by Britten, Op.61, for v. and pf. of 6 poems by German poet Hölderlin. Comp. 1958.

Holidays Symphony (Ives). See *New England Holidays*.

Holl, Robert (*b* Rotterdam, 1947). Dutch bass. Won 's-Hertogenbosch int. comp. 1971, Munich int. comp. 1972. Sang with Bavarian State Opera, Munich, from 1973, and concentrated on concert career from 1975. Bayreuth 1996 (Sachs.).

Höller, Karl (*b* Bamberg, 1907; *d* Hausham, 1987). Ger. composer. Teacher at Hoch Cons., Frankfurt, 1937–46, Munich Hochschule für Mus. 1949–72. Comp. 2 syms.; *Variations on a Theme of Sweelinck*, orch.; 2 vn. concs.; 2 vc. concs.; org. conc.; 6 str. qts.; 8 vn. sonatas; film mus.

Höller, York (Georg) (*b* Leverkusen, 1944). Ger. composer. Répétiteur, Bonn municipal th., 1968–9. Worked with Stockhausen at Cologne EMS and with Boulez at IRCAM 1978. Prof. of analysis and mus. theory, Cologne Musikhochschule 1975–89; dir., EMS, Cologne radio from 1990. Comps. incl.:

OPERAS: *Der Meister und Margarita* (1984–8); *Caligula* (1992).

ORCH.: *Topic* (1967); 2 pf. concs. (1970, 1983–4); *Chroma* (1972–4); *Arcus* (1978); *Umbra* (1979–80); *Mythos* (1979–80); *Résonance*, with tape (1981–2); *Schwarze Halbinseln*, with tape (1982); *Traumspiel*, sop., orch., tape (1983); *Magische Klanggestalt* (1984); cl. conc. (1984); *Improvisation sur le nom de Pierre Boulez*, 17 instr. (1985); *Fanal*, tpt., orch. (1990); *Pensées*, pf., orch., elec. (1991); *Margaritas Traum* (suite from *Der Meister und Margarita*), sop., orch., tape. (1991); *Aura* (1992–3); *Gegenklänge*, 18 instr. (1996); *Widerspiel*, 2 pf., orch. (1996–9); *Aufbruch* (1999).

CHAMBER MUSIC: vc. sonata (1969); *Epitaph*, vn., pf. (1969); *Antiphon*, str. qt. (1977); *Moments musicaux*, fl., pf. (1979); *Pas de deux*, vc., pf. (1993); *Tagträuma*, 7 tone-poems, vn., vc., pf. (1994–5); str. qt. No.2 (1997).

ELECTRONIC: *Horizont* (1972); *Tangens* (1973); *Klanggitter* (1976).

PIANO: *5 Pieces* (1964); *Diaphonie*, 2 pf. (1965); *Sonate informelle* (1968); sonata No.2 *Hommage à Franz Liszt* (1987); *Hommage à Bernd Alois Zimmermann* (1996); *Partita*, 2 pf. (1996).

Holliger, Heinz (*b* Langenthal, Switz., 1939). Swiss oboist and composer, husband of Ursula *Holliger. Won comps. at Geneva (1959) and Munich (1961). Prin. ob., Basle Orch. 1959–64. Salzburg Fest. début 1961. Prof. of ob., Freiburg Musikhochschule, from 1966. Works written for him by Berio, Huber, Krenek, Henze, Penderecki, Lutosławski, Ligeti, Stockhausen, Carter, Ferneyhough, Takemitsu, etc. His own comps. incl. *Erde und Himmel*, cantata, ten., 5 instr.; *Elis*, 3 nocturnes, pf. (1961); 3 *Liebeslieder*, alto, orch.; *Schwarzgewebene Trauer*, sop., 3 instr.; 4 *Bagatelles*, sop., pf. (1963); *Glühende Rätsel*, alto, instr. (1964); *Der magische Tänzer*, 2 singers, 2 dancers, 2 actors, ch., orch., tape (1965); *Trio*, ob., va., hp. (1966); *Siebengesang*, ob., orch., vv., amplifiers (1967); *h*, wind quintet (1968); *Dona nobis pacem*, 12 unacc. vv. (1968–9); *Pneuma*, 34 winds, org., perc., radios (1970); *Cardiophonie*, 1 wind player (1971); Str. Qt. (1974–5); *Atembogen*, orch. (1975); *Chaconne*, vc. (1976); *Come and Go*, chamber opera (1976–7); *NOT 1*, monodrama, sop., elec. (1980); *Ad marginem*, chamber orch., elec. (1983); *Engführung*, chamber orch. (1983–4); *Der ferne Klang*, chamber orch., elec. (1983–4); *Schaufelrad*, chamber orch., opt. women's vv. (1983–4); *Turm-Musik*, fl., orch., elec. (1984); *Tonscherben*, orch. (1985); *What Where*, chamber opera (1988); *Scardanelli-Zyklus* (1975–91): 1. *Die Jahreszeiten*, unacc. ch. (1975–9), 2. *(t)air(e)*, fl. (1980–3), 3. *Übungen zu Scardanelli*, small orch., tape (1978–85), 4. *Ostinato funebre*, small orch. (1991); *(S)iratό*, orch. (1992–3); *Hommage à Soutter*, vn., orch. (1993–5); *Mileva-Lieder*, sop., pf. (1994); *Schneewittchen*, opera (1997–8); *Partita*, pf. (1999); *ConcErto?* ... *cErtO!*, soloists, chamber orch. (2001).

Holliger, Ursula (*b* Basle, 1937). Swiss harpist. Soloist with leading orchs. Works have been comp. for her and her husband, Heinz *Holliger, by Henze, Lutosławski, Denisov, Krenek, and Ligeti. Salzburg Fest. début 1974. Prof. of hp., Basle Mus. Acad.

Holloway, Robin (Greville) (*b* Leamington Spa, 1943). Eng. composer. Lect. in mus., Cambridge Univ. from 1975. One of most gifted and interesting of post–1960 school of Eng. composers, with a richly romantic style owing something to Strauss but not merely backwards-looking. Works incl.:

OPERA: *Clarissa (1968–76); *Boys and Girls Come Out to Play* (1991–5).

ORCH.: Concertino No.1 (1964, new finale 1968–9), No.2 (1967, menuetto added 1974), No.3 (*Homage to Weill*), 11 players (1975), No.4 (*Showpiece*), 14 players (1982–3); *Concerto for Orchestra* (1966–9); *Second Concerto for Orchestra* (1979); *Third Concerto for Orchestra* (1981–94); *Fourth Concerto for Orchestra* (2006–7); *Divertimento No.1* (amateur orch.) (1968); *Scenes from Schumann*, 7 paraphrases (1969–70); *Domination of Black*, sym.-poem (1973–4); *Romanza*, vn., small orch. (1976); *Idyll*, small orch., No.1 (1979–80), No.2 (1982–3), No.3 (*Frost at Midnight*) (1993); *Aria (Dark Air)*, chamber orch. (1979–80); hn. conc. (divided into *Sonata* and *Adagio and*

Rondo) (1979–80); *Serenata Notturna*, 4 hn., small orch. (1982); *Seascape and Harvest* (1983–4); va. conc. (1983–4); *Romanza*, ob., str. (1984); *Ballad*, hp., small orch. (1984–5); bn. conc. (1984–5); *Inquietus* (1986); conc. for cl., sax. (1988); *Panorama* (1988); vn. conc. (1988–9); *Wagner Nights* (1989); *Serenade for Strings* (1990); cl. conc. (1996); db. conc. (1996); *Scenes from Antwerp* (1997); sym. (1998–9); *Est blanc et noir* (2002); *Praeludium* (2002).

ENS.: *Garden Music*, 8 players (1962, rev. 1967); conc., org., wind (1965–6); *Fantasy-Pieces*, on Heine *Liederkreis* of R. Schumann, 13 players (1971); *Evening with Angels*, 16 players (1972); *Divertimento No.2*, wind nonet (1972); *The Rivers of Hell*, 7 players (1977); *Serenade* in C, octet (1979); *Ode*, 4 winds, str. (1980); *Serenade* in G, str. sextet, db. (1986); *Summer Music*, ob., cl., str. qt. (1991); *Winter Music*, ob., cl., tpt., vn., vc., pf. (1992); pf. trio (1994); *5 Haydn Miniatures*, ens. (1999).

VOICE(S) & ORCH.: *The Wind Shifts*, 8 poems of W. Stevens, high v., str. (1970); *Cantata on the Death of God*, sop., ten., bass, spkr., ch., org., orch. (1972–3); *Sea-Surface Full of Clouds*, cantata, sop., cont., counterten., ten. soloists, small ch., chamber orch. (1974–5); *Clarissa Symphony*, sop., ten., orch. (1976, 1981); *Brand*, ballad, solo vv., ch., org., orch. (1981); *Peer Gynt*, solo vv., ch., actors, mimes, dance, and film (1984); *The Spacious Firmament*, ch., orch. (1990).

VOICE(S) & ENS.: *3 Poems of William Empson*, mez. and ens. (1964–5); *Music for Eliot's 'Sweeney Agonistes'*, 3 or 4 speakers and 5 players (1965); *In Chymick Art*, cantata, sop., bar., 3 players (1965–6); *Melodrama*, 3 poems of S. Plath, speaker, male ch., ens. (1967); *Divertimento No.3* (*Nursery Rhymes*), sop., wind quintet (1977); *Conundrums* (*Divertimento No.4*), sop., wind quintet (1977, 1979); *Moments of Vision*, speaker, vn., vc., pf., perc. (1984); *Love Will Find a Way*, v., ens. (1992); *A Song of Defiance*, sop., ens. (1996); *A Page from a Humument*, sop., ens. (2006).

UNACC. CHORUS: *The Consolation of Music* (1967–71–77); *5 Madrigals* (1973); *Hymn for Voices* (1977); *He-She-Together* (1978); *Anthem* (1982); *Hymn to the Senses* (1990); *Lord, What is Man?*, motet (1990–1).

SONG-CYCLES & SONGS: *4 Housman Fragments*, sop., pf. (1965–6); *4 Poems of Stevie Smith*, unacc. sop. (1968–9); *Banal Sojourn*, 7 Stevens poems, high v., pf. (1971); *Georgian Songs*, 10 songs, bar., pf. (1972); *5 Little Songs about Death* (S. Smith), unacc. sop. (1972–3); **Lights Out*, 4 songs, bar., pf. (1974); *In the Thirtieth Year*, 5 songs, ten., pf. (1974); *Author of Light*, 4 songs, cont., pf. (1974); *The Leaves Cry*, 2 songs, sop., pf. (1974); *This is Just to Say*, ten., pf. (1977); *The Blue Doom of Summer*, v., hp. (1977); *Willow Cycle*, ten., hp. (1977); *From High Windows*, 6 poems by P. Larkin, bar., pf. (1977); *Killing Time*, unacc. sop. (1978); *The Noon's Repose*, 3 songs, ten., hp. (1978–9); *Wherever We May Be*, 5 songs by R. Graves, sop., pf. (1980–1); *The Lovers' Well*, bass-bar., pf. (1981); *Women in War*, revue, 4 female vv., pf. (1982); *The Food of Love*, ten., unacc. ch. (1996).

CHAMBER MUSIC: *3 Slithy Toves*, 2 cl. (1978); sonata for vn. solo (1981); *Suite for Saxophone* (1982);

Serenade in E♭, wind quintet, str. quintet (1983); *First Partita*, hn. (1985); *Second Partita*, hn. (1985); pf. trio (1994); sonata, db. (1999); sonata, vc. (2000); *Canzona and Toccata*, tpt., org. (2002).

BRASS BAND: *From Hills and Valleys* (1983); *Men Marching* (1983).

KEYBOARD: *Fantasy*, org. (1986); *Wedding Suite*, org. (1999; 2003–4); *Ballade*, pf. (2000).

Hollreiser, Heinrich (*b* Munich, 1913). Ger. conductor. Began career with opera posts in Wiesbaden, Darmstadt, and Mannheim. Munich Staatsoper 1942. Mus. dir. Düsseldorf Opera 1945–52, Vienna 1952–61, Deutsche Oper, Berlin, 1961–4. Bayreuth 1973–5 (début in *Tannhäuser*). Cond. *Ring* in Vienna 1976. Cond. f. Ger. p. of *Peter Grimes* (Hamburg, 1947). Amer. début 1978 (Cleveland Orch.).

Hollweg, Werner (Friedrich) (*b* Solingen, 1936). Ger. tenor. Début Vienna 1962. Sang opera in Bonn 1963–7. Gelsenkirchen 1967–8. Salzburg Fest. début 1969; CG 1976; Paris Opéra 1986. Created Matthew Levi in **Höller's Die Meister und Margarita* (Paris 1989).

Hollywood Bowl. Natural open-air amphitheatre (65 acres) near Los Angeles, Calif., purchased in 1919 and in which since 1922 concerts of the Los Angeles PO are given annually for 9 weeks from July to Sept. Seats 25,000.

Holmboe, Vagn (*b* Horsens, Jutland, 1909; *d* Ramløse, Denmark, 1996). Danish composer. In 1930s collected Romanian and Danish folk music. Teacher Royal Danish Institute for Blind 1940–9, mus. critic *Politiken* 1947–55. Teacher at Royal Danish Cons. 1950–65. Comps. incl. 12 syms. (1935–88); 3 operas; *Requiem for Nietzsche* (1963–4); 3 chamber syms.; 20 str. qts. (1948–75); 13 chamber concs. (1939–56); 14 motets.

Holmès [Holmes], **Augusta** (Mary Anne) (*b* Paris, 1847; *d* Paris, 1903). Fr. composer of Irish parentage. Pseudonym Hermann Zenta. Pupil of César Franck. Declined offer of marriage from Saint-Saëns and had three daughters by Catulle Mendès. Wrote syms., sym.-poems, 4 operas, and choral works.

Holmes, Ralph (*b* Penge, 1937; *d* Beckenham, 1984). Eng. violinist. London début 1951 with RPO. Amer. début 1966. Prof. of vn., RAM, from 1964. Had all major 20th-cent. vn. concs. in his repertoire. Also played in chamber mus.

Holoman, D(allas) **Kern** (*b* Raleigh, NC, 1947). Amer. musicologist, bassoonist, and conductor. Prin. bn., Triangle SO, NC, 1965–9. Founding dir., Early Music Ensemble 1973–7, 1979. Chairman, mus. dept., Univ. of Calif. at Davis, 1980–8. Authority on Berlioz. Publications incl. *Catalogue of the Works of Hector Berlioz* (1987), *Berlioz* (biography, 1989).

Holst, Gustav (Theodore) (*b* Cheltenham, 1874; *d* London, 1934). Eng. composer of Swed. descent. Trained as a pianist, his father being a pf.

teacher. In 1892 he became organist and choirmaster at Wyck Rissington, Glos. His operetta *Lansdowne Castle* was prod. in Cheltenham in 1893, after which his father sent him to the RCM to study comp. under Stanford and the org. under Hoyte. At the same time he learned the tb., his pf.-playing being handicapped by chronic neuritis in the arm. In coll. holidays he played the tb. on seaside piers in the White Viennese Band. He left the RCM in 1898, having formed there a lifelong friendship with Vaughan Williams which extended to frank and detailed criticism of each other's comps. He worked as a trombonist in the Carl Rosa Opera 1898–1900 and Scottish Orch. 1900–3 and learned a smattering of Sanskrit in order to be able to trans. hymns from the *Rig Veda* which he wished to set to mus. His *Cotswolds Symphony* (unpubd.) was perf. in Bournemouth 1902 by Dan *Godfrey and in 1905 his *Mystic Trumpeter* was perf. at the Queen's Hall. In 1903 he became mus. teacher at a Dulwich girls' sch., holding this post until 1920, and in 1905 he became dir. of mus. at St Paul's Girls' Sch., Hammersmith, retaining this appointment until his death. At this time, too, like Vaughan Williams, he became deeply interested in Eng. folksong, and in 1907 became mus. dir. at Morley Coll., holding this post until 1924. At all the schs. where he taught he raised both standards and taste. In 1908 he went on holiday to Algeria (bicycling in the desert), the direct mus. result of which was an orch. suite *Beni Mora*. On return he comp. his chamber opera *Savitri*. In 1911 he cond. at Morley College the f. modern p. of Purcell's *The Fairy Queen*, and in 1913 began work on a large-scale orch. suite *The Planets*, sketching *Mars* just before World War I began in 1914. In that year he set Whitman's *Dirge for 2 Veterans* for male vv., brass, and drums. At this time he went to live in Thaxted, Essex, where in 1916 he organized a Whitsuntide Fest., singing and performing mus. by Bach, Byrd, Purcell, and Palestrina. Later that year *Savitri* was prod. in London and in 1917 Holst began his choral work *The Hymn of Jesus*. He was unfit for war service, but in 1918 was offered the post of YMCA mus. organizer among the troops in the Near East. As a parting present a wealthy friend, Balfour Gardiner, arranged a private perf. of *The Planets* in Queen's Hall, cond. Adrian Boult. The f. public p. was in 1919 and was Holst's first major public success. On return to Eng. later in 1919 he was appointed prof. of mus. at University Coll., Reading, and joined the teaching staff of the RCM. His comic opera *The Perfect Fool* was perf. at CG in 1923 while Holst was conducting at a fest. at the Univ. of Michigan at Ann Arbor. In 1924 he comp. his *Choral Symphony* on poems by Keats which was f.p. at the 1925 Leeds Fest., the same year that his 1-act Falstaff opera *At the Boar's Head* was staged by the BNOC. The ill-health from which he had always suffered in some degree plagued him more after he fell from a platform while rehearsing at Reading in 1923 and comp. became an arduous burden. But in 1927 he wrote his tone-poem *Egdon Heath* (the title given

by Thomas Hardy to a stretch of countryside in Dorset), to a commission from the NYSO. This was followed in 1929 and 1930 by *12 Songs by Humbert Wolfe*, the Double Conc., an opera *The Wandering Scholar*, the *Choral Fantasia* (perf. 1931 at the Gloucester 3 Choirs Fest.), and the prelude and scherzo, *Hammersmith*, for orch. These works gave promise of a new, richer, and more lyrical phase, as did the *Brook Green Suite* and *Lyric Movement* of 1933. But in 1934, after an operation, Holst died in the plenitude of his powers. His mus., while owing something to folk-song influence and to the madrigalian tradition of Byrd and Weelkes, is intensely orig. and has a visionary quality similar to that found in Vaughan Williams but expressed with more austerity and greater natural technical facility. His *Planets* suite is markedly eclectic, but its finest movts., *Mars*, *Venus*, *Saturn*, and *Neptune*, show varied aspects of Holst's style. His genius as a teacher and his feeling for the community spirit engendered by mus. also contributed to the outstanding part he played in Eng. mus.-making in the first two decades of the 20th cent. Prin. works:

OPERAS: *Savitri, Op.25 (1908); The *Perfect Fool, Op.39 (1918–22); *At the Boar's Head, Op.42 (1924); The *Wandering Scholar, Op.50 (1929–30).

BALLET: *The Lure* (1921, ed. for orch. by I. Holst and C. Matthews, 1981).

ORCH.: *Suite de Ballet* in E♭, Op.10 (1899); *A Somerset Rhapsody*, Op.21b (1906–7); *2 Songs Without Words*, Op.22 (1906); *Beni Mora, Oriental Suite in E minor, Op.29 No.1 (1909–10, rev. 1912); *Suite No.1* in E♭, Op.28a, military band (1909), *Suite No.2* in F, Op.28b (1911); *Invocation*, vc., orch. (1911); *St. Paul's Suite*, Op.29 No.2, str. (1912–13); *Japanese Suite*, Op.33 (1915); Suite, The *Planets, Op.32 (1914–16); Ballet mus. from *The Perfect Fool*, Op.39 (1918); *A Fugal Overture*, Op.40 No.1 (1922); *Fugal Concerto*, Op.40 No.2, fl., ob. (or 2 vn.), str. (1923); *Egdon Heath, Op.47 (1927); *A Moorside Suite*, brass band (1928); conc., 2 vn., orch., Op.49 (1929); *Hammersmith*, Op.52, prelude and scherzo for military band and for orch. (1930–1); *Capriccio*, jazz-band piece (1932, ed. Imogen Holst 1967); *Brook Green Suite, str., optional ww. (1933); *Lyric Movement*, va., orch. (1933); *Scherzo* (from unfinished sym.) (1933–4).

CHORAL: 5 *Part-Songs* Op.9a (1899–1900); *Ave Maria*, Op.9b, female vv. (1900); 5 *Part-Songs*, Op.12 (1902–3); *King Estmere*, Op.17, Old English ballad, ch., orch. (1903); The *Mystic Trumpeter, Op.18, scena, sop., orch. (1904, rev. 1912); *Songs from 'The Princess'*, Op.20a, female vv. (1905); 3 *Choral *Hymns from the Rig Veda, Op.26 No.1, ch., orch. (1908–10), Op.26 No.2 (3 Hymns), female vv., orch. (1909), Op.26 No.3 (4 Hymns), female vv., hp. (1909–10), Op.26 No.4 (4 Hymns), male vv., str., brass (1912); *Hecuba's Lament*, Op.31 No.1, cont., female ch., orch. (1911); The *Cloud Messenger*, Op.30, ode, ch., orch. (1910, rev. 1912); 2 *Psalms*, ch., str., org. (1912); *Hymn to Dionysus*, Op.31 No.2, female ch., orch. (1913); *Dirge for 2 Veterans, male vv., brass, perc. (1914); *This have I done for my true love*, Op.34, unacc. ch. (1916); 6

Choral Folksongs, Op.36, unacc. ch. (1916); 3 *Festival Choruses*, with orch. (1916); *The *Hymn of Jesus*, Op.37, 2 ch., women's semi-ch., orch. (1917); **Ode to Death*, Op.38, ch., orch. (1919); *I vow to thee, my country*, unison song with orch. (to central melody from *Jupiter*, No.4 of *The Planets*) (1921); *First Choral Symphony*, Op.41, sop., ch., orch. (1923–4); 2 *Motets*, Op.43, unacc. ch. (1924–5); 7 *Part-Songs*, Op.44 (to poems by Bridges), female vv., str. (1925–6)—No.7 is **Assemble, all ye maidens*; *The Golden Goose*, Op.45 No.1, choral ballet with orch. (1926); *The Morning of the Year*, Op.45 No.2, choral ballet with orch. (1926–7); **Choral Fantasia*, Op.51, sop., ch., org., brass, perc., str. (1930); 12 *Welsh Folksongs*, unacc. ch. (1930–1); 6 *Choruses*, Op.53 (to words trans. from Lat. by Helen Waddell), male vv., str. (or org., or pf.) (1931–2); 6 *Canons* (to words trans. from Lat. by H. Waddell), equal unacc. vv. (1932).

CHAMBER MUSIC: pf. trio in E (1894); 6 *Instrumental pieces* (variously for 2 vn., vn. (or vc.), and pf.) (1902–3); wind quintet (1903); *Terzetto*, fl., ob., va. (1925).

PIANO: 2 *Pieces* (1901); *Toccata* (1924); *Chrissemas Day in the Morning*, Op.46 No.1 (1926); 2 *Folksong Fragments*, Op.46 No.2 (1927); *Nocturne* (1930); *Jig* (1932).

SOLO SONGS: 4 *Songs*, Op.4, v., pf. (1896–8); 6 *songs*, Op.15, bar., pf. (1902–3); 6 *Songs*, Op.16, sop., pf. (1903–4); 9 **Hymns from the Rig Veda*, Op.24, v., pf. (1907–8); 4 *Songs*, Op.35, v., vn. (1916–17); 12 *Songs by Humbert Wolfe*, Op.48, v., pf. (1929); 2 *Canons* (to words trans. from Lat. by H. Waddell), 2 equal vv., pf. (1932).

Holst, Henry (*b* Copenhagen, 1899; *d* Copenhagen, 1991). Danish violinist. Début Copenhagen 1919. Leader, Berlin PO 1923–31. Prof. of vn. RMCM 1931–46, 1950–3, RCM 1946–54, Royal Danish Cons. from 1953; guest prof. Tokyo 1961–3. Frequent conc. soloist. Gave f. Eng. p. of Walton conc. 1941.

Holst, Imogen (Clare) (*b* Richmond, Surrey, 1907; *d* Aldeburgh, 1984). Eng. conductor, composer, editor, and writer. Daughter of Gustav *Holst. Ed. several of her father's works and cond. them for recordings. Mus. dir., arts centre, Dartington Hall, 1943–51. Dir. of Aldeburgh Fest. and mus. ass. to *Britten, 1952–64. Comps. incl. str. quintet (1981). Author of biography and other books about Gustav Holst, also on Britten and Byrd. CBE 1975.

Holt, Simon (*b* Bolton, 1958). Eng. composer. Featured comp., Bath Fest. 1985. Has written several works to commissions from London Sinfonietta and Nash Ensemble. Works incl.:

OPERA/MUS. THEATRE: *The Nightingale's to Blame*, opera (1998); *Who Put Bella in the Wych Elm?* sop., bar., pf., vn., orch. ens., elec. (2002).

ORCH.: *Syrensong* (1987); *walking with the river's roar*, va., orch. 1990–1); *Minotaur Games* (1993); *witness to a snow miracle*, vn., orch. (2005).

INSTR. ENS.: *Palace at 4 am*, fl., ob., cl., vc. (1980); *Mirrormaze*, 3 fl., 2 ob., 2 cl., 2 hn., perc., db. (1981); *Kites*, fl., ob., cl., bn., hn., str. quintet

(1983); *Shadow Realm*, cl., vc., hp. (1983); . . . *era madrugada*, picc., cl., hn., pf., va., vc., db. (1984); *Burlesca oscura*, cl. quintet (1985); *Capriccio spettrale*, fl., cl., hn., tpt., 2 vn., 2 va., vc., db. (1988); *Danger of the Disappearance of Things*, str. qt. (1989); *Sparrow Night*, fl., ob., cl., hn., hp., pf., vn., va., vc., db. (1989); *Lilith*, fl., cl., hn., hp., vn., va., vc., db. (1990); *Icarus Lamentations*, 2 cl., cimbalon, hp., str. (1992); *Daedalus Remembers*, vc., ens. (1995); *eco-pavan*, pf., ens. (1998); *The Coroner's Report*, ens. (2004).

INSTR. ENS. & VOICE(S): *Wyrdchanging*, mez., 2 fl., ob., cl., bcl., hn., perc., 3 vn., va., 2 vc., db. (1980); *Canciones*, mez., fl., ob., hn., hp., str. quintet (1986); *Ballad of the Black Sorrow*, 2 sop., mez., ten., bar., bass, fl., ob., 2 cl., bn., hn., 2 tpt., tb., hp., 4 vn., 2 va., 2 vc., 2 db. (1988); *A Song of Crocuses and Lightning*, sop., hn., hp., va., db. (1989); *Tanagra*, sop., fl., ob., bcl., hn., perc., hp., vn., vc., db. (1991); *A Knot of Time*, sop., cl., va., db. (1992); *Sunrise/ Yellow Noise*, sop., instr. ens. (1999); *Boots of Lead*, alto, instr. (2002).

CHAMBER MUSIC: *Lunas Zauberschein*, mez., bfl. (1979); *Maïastra*, fl. (1981); *Banshee*, ob., perc. (1994); *Sphinx*, ca., perc. (2000); *Odradek*, picc., bfl., tpt., glock. (2002); *feet of clay*, vc. (2003); *the other side of silence*, fl., va., hp. (2004); *brief candles*, cl. (2004).

PIANO: *Piano Piece* (1984); *Tauromaquia* (1985); *Duendecitos* (1988); *Nigredo* (1994); *The night of the blood red moon* (2000); *ashes, ashes* (2004); *Klop's last bite* (2005).

Holý, Alfred (*b* Oporto, 1866; *d* Vienna, 1948). Portuguese harpist of Cz. origin. Prin. hp. Ger. Opera in Prague 1885–96, Berlin Royal Opera 1896–1903, Vienna Opera 1903–13, Boston SO 1913–28. Taught at New Eng. Cons., Boston. Comp. works for hp. Strauss commissioned from him two books of studies for his own orch. hp. parts.

Holy Boy, The. No.3 of 4 *Preludes* for pf. by *Ireland, comp. 1913–15. Orch. for str. 1941, for str. qt. 1941; arr. for org. (by Alec Rowley) 1919, for brass ens. (by R. E. Stepp) 1950, for v. and pf. (poem by Herbert S. Brown) 1938, for unacc. ch. 1941, for str. qt. 1941.

Holy Sonnets of John Donne. Setting of 9 Donne sonnets for high v. and pf. Op.35, by Britten. Comp. 1945 after visit to Ger. concentration camps.

Holzblasinstrumente (Ger., 'wood-blown instruments'). The woodwind.

Holzflöte (Ger.). 'Wooden flute' (org. stop).

Holztrompete (Ger.). (1) Wooden tpt., or Alphorn; Swiss folk instr. for playing simple tunes. (2) Wooden instr. with bell of cor anglais, one valve, and cup mouthpiece invented to play shepherd's tune in Act 3 of Wagner's *Tristan und Isolde* (nevertheless, a cor anglais is usually employed for this passage).

Homage March. See *Huldigungsmarsch*.

Homage to the Queen. Ballet in 1 act, mus. by Malcolm Arnold, choreog. Ashton, prod. London 1953 on night of Queen Elizabeth II's Coronation.

Homer, Sidney (*b* Boston, Mass., 1864; *d* Winter Park, Fla., 1953). Amer. composer. Taught harmony and counterpoint, New Eng. Cons., Boston, 1893–1900. Married cont. Louise Beatty, 1895. Wrote about 100 songs, among them *Bandanna Ballads* (which incl. *The Banjo Song*) and *The Song of the Shirt*. Wrote org. sonata (1922), pf. quintet (1932), and str. qt. (1937).

Home, Sweet Home. Melody by Henry *Bishop, comp. 1821 for album of nat. airs, described as 'Sicilian'. In 1823, with words by J. H. Payne (1791–1852), incorporated in Bishop's opera *Clari*. Tune occurs, altered, in Donizetti's *Anna Bolena*, leading to action by Bishop for 'piracy and breach of copyright'.

Homme Armé, L' (The Armed Man). Old Fr. folk-song used by Du Fay, Palestrina, and more than 20 other composers in 15th, 16th, and 17th cents. as a *cantus firmus in their Masses, which then became known by this title. *Maxwell Davies, in the 20th cent., wrote *Missa super 'L'Homme Armé'* for speaker and ens. (1968).

homophone. 2 harp str. tuned to produce the same note.

homophony (Gk., 'Same-sounding'). Term applied to mus. in which the parts or vv. move 'in step' with one another, instead of exhibiting individual rhythmic independence and interest, as in *polyphony. Many modern hymn-tunes are homophonic, whereas Bach's settings of Ger. chorales and many Handelian choruses are polyphonic.

Honegger, Arthur (*b* Le Havre, 1892; *d* Paris, 1955). Swiss composer. Member of group of Fr. composers known as Les *Six from 1920. His *Le Roi David* won him wider fame in 1921, but this was eclipsed in 1924 by f.p. of his representation of a locomotive in *Pacific 231*. From these works he moved nearer to a neo-romantic style with overtones of baroque influence from his admiration for Bach. His mus. remained tonal and often has strong emotional impact, as in his dramatic oratorio, based on a Claudel 'mystery play', *Jeanne d'Arc au bûcher*. His syms. were championed by the cond. Charles *Munch. He visited the USA several times and despite ill-health taught in his last years at the École Normale in Paris. Prin. works:

THEATRE: *Le *Roi David*, dramatic psalm (1921); *Judith*, biblical opera (1925); *Antigone* (1927); *Amphion*, ballet-melodrama, speaker, bar., 4 female vv., ch., orch. (1929); *Jeanne d'Arc au bûcher*, stage oratorio (1934–5); *L'*Aiglon, 5-act opera with *Ibert (1935); *Charles le téméraire* (1943–4).

BALLETS: Les *Mariés de la Tour Eiffel* (with Les Six) (1921); *L'appel de la montagne* (1945).

ORCH.: *Pastorale d'été* (1920); *Chant de Joie* (1923); *Pacific 231* (1923); concertino, pf., orch. (1924); *Rugby* (1928); vc. conc. (1929); syms., No.1 (1929–30), No.2, str., tpt. (1941), No.3 (*Liturgique*) (1945–6), No.4 (*Deliciae basiliensis*) (1946), No.5 (*Di tre re*) (1951); *Mouvement symphonique No.3* (1932–3); *Nocturne* (1936); *La Construction d'une cité* (with Milhaud) (1937); concerto da camera, fl., ca., str. (1948); *Monopartita* (1951).

VOICE AND ORCH.: Chanson de Ronsard, with fl. and str. (1924); 3 Chansons populaires (1926).

CHORAL: Cantique des Cantiques (1926); Les Cris du Monde (1930–1); La Danse des Morts (Claudel), solo vv., ch., orch. (1938); Chant de libération (1944); Une Cantate de Noël (1941/1953).

CHAMBER MUSIC: str. qts., No.1 (1916–17), No.2 (1936), No.3 (1936–7); sonatas for pf. and vn., No.1 (1916–18), No.2 (1919); va. sonata (1920); vc. sonata (1920); vn. sonatina (1932); vn. sonata (1940).

Also incid. mus. for plays, mus. for films (incl. *Les Misérables* (1934), *Mayerling* (1935), and *Pygmalion* (1938)), radio mus., many songs, and pf. pieces.

Höngen, Elisabeth (*b* Gevelsberg, 1906; *d* Vienna 1997). Ger. mezzo-soprano. Opera début Wuppertal 1933 (Verdi's Lady Macbeth). Düsseldorf opera 1935–40; Dresden 1940–3; Vienna State Opera from 1943. Débuts: Salzburg Fest. 1948; CG 1947; Bayreuth 1951; NY Met 1952. Teacher at Vienna Acad. 1957–60. Specialist in dramatic roles (Ortrud, Dyer's Wife, Carmen, and Amneris). Retired 1971.

Hook, James (*b* Norwich, 1746; *d* Boulogne, 1827). Eng. composer and organist. Org. and composer Marylebone Gardens 1769–73, Vauxhall Gardens 1774–1820. Wrote oratorio, org. conc., pf. sonatas, cantatas, and over 2,000 songs, best-known being *Sweet Lass of Richmond Hill*.

hopak. See *gopak*.

Hope, Daniel (*b* London, 1974). Eng. violinist. Studied with Zakhar Bron and at RAM. In 1985 chosen by Menuhin to perform Bartók duos for Ger. TV. Gave over 60 recitals with Menuhin 1985–99. Soloist with leading orchs. Advocate of Schnittke, Takemitsu, and Kurtág. Gave f.p. of revised Berg conc., Vienna 1996. Member of Beaux Arts Trio from 2002.

Hopkins [Reynolds], **Antony** (*b* London, 1921). Eng. composer, pianist, and educator. Mus. dir. Intimate Opera Co., 1952, writing several chamber operas for it. Composer of mus. for films, radio, and th. His series 'Talking About Music' was regular and valuable contribution to educational radio, 1954–92. Works incl. operas *Lady Rohesia* (1948), *Three's Company* (1954), ballet *Café des Sports*, and pf. mus. CBE 1976.

Hopkins, Bill (George William) (*b* Prestbury, Ches., 1943; *d* Chopwell, nr. Newcastle upon Tyne, 1981). Eng. composer. Lect., Newcastle upon Tyne Univ. from 1979. Works influenced by Boulez and Barraqué, about both of whom he wrote major articles. His *Sensation* (1965) for sop., ten. sax., tpt., hp., and va. is a setting of Rimbaud and Samuel Beckett.

Hopkins, John (Raymond) (*b* Preston, nr. Hull, Yorks, 1927). Eng. conductor and administrator. Apprentice cond. Yorkshire SO 1948–9, ass. cond. BBC Scottish Orch. 1949–52, cond. BBC Northern Orch. 1952–7. Went to NZ as cond. Nat. Orch. 1957–63. Dir. of mus. Australian Broadcasting Commission 1963–73. Dean of Sch. of Mus., Victoria Coll. of Arts, Melbourne, 1973–86. Dir., NSW Cons. of Mus., Sydney, from 1986. OBE 1970.

Hopkinson, Francis (*b* Philadelphia, 1737; *d* Philadelphia, 1791). Amer. composer, harpsichordist, poet, lawyer, and politician (one of signatories of Declaration of Independence, 1776). Wrote first surviving piece of mus. by an American, *Ode to Music* (1754).

hoquet. Same as **hocket*.

Horenstein, Jascha (*b* Kiev, 1898; *d* London, 1973). Russ.-born conductor (Austrian cit., then Amer. cit.). Became ass. cond. to Furtwängler in Berlin 1921–3. Cond. Vienna SO 1923, then worked in Berlin and at Düsseldorf Opera from 1929. After 1933 worked in Fr., Russ., Poland, and Belg. Amer. début 1940. Cond. f. Paris p. of *Wozzeck* (1950) and of *From the *House of the Dead* (1951). Cond. f. Amer. p. (concert) of **Doktor Faust*, NY 1964. Frequent guest cond. of Brit. orchs. CG début 1961 (*Fidelio*). Fine interpreter of Mahler and Bruckner.

Horigome, Yuzuko (*b* Tokyo, 1957). Japanese violinist. Won first prize Queen Elisabeth of the Belgians int. comp., Brussels 1980. London début March 1983, Vienna début 1983.

Horizon Chimérique, L' (The Fanciful Horizon). Song-cycle of 4 songs by Fauré, Op.118, to poems by J. de la Ville de Mirmont, comp. 1921, f.p. 1922.

horn. (1) See *horn family*.
(2) Org. stop like **trumpet* but fuller and smoother in tone.

Horn, Charles Edward (*b* London, 1786; *d* Boston, Mass., 1849). Eng. composer and singer. Son of Karl F. Horn. Settled in USA 1833, returned to Eng. 1843, but settled finally in Boston from 1847. Comp. oratorios, operettas, and songs incl. **Cherry Ripe* and *On the Banks of Allen Water*.

horn diapason. 8′ org. stop of str.-like tone ('Horn' being a misnomer).

Horne, David (*b* Stirling, 1970). Scottish pianist and composer. Won Musicians' Union prize for outstanding promise at Huddersfield Fest. 1986, Nat. Mozart Comp. 1987, pf. section of BBC Young Musician of the Year 1988, and Yorkshire Arts Assoc. young composer's prize at Huddersfield 1988. BBC Proms début 1990 (Prokofiev's 3rd conc.). Works incl. str. qt. (1988); *Splintered Unisons*, cl., vn., vc., pf. (1988); *towards dharma...*,

6 players (1989); *light, emerging*, orch. (1989); *Out of the Air*, ens. (1990); *Contraries and Progressions*, fl., cl., pf., vn. (or va.), vc. (1991); *Nocturnes and Nightmares*, pf. (1991); *The Burning Babe*, children's ch., ens. (or pf.) (1992); *Northscape*, ens. (1992); *3 Dirges*, fl., hp. (1992); *The Lie*, cantata, sop., ten., ch., ens. (1992–3); pf. conc. (1992–3); *Jason Field*, chamber opera (1993); *Magnificat and Nunc Dimittis* (1993); *Travellers*, opera (1994); *Undulations*, str. qt. (1995); *Aureole*, bn., tape (1996); *Beyond the Blue Horizon*, mus. th. (1996–7); *Filters*, va., pf. (1998); *Friend of the People*, opera (1998–9); *Pan's Song*, sop., vn., vc., cl., pf. (1999); *Blunt Instruments*, large ens. (2000); *Elegy*, tpt., pf. (2000); *The Year's Midnight*, ten., ch., orch. (2002); double vn. conc. (2 vns., str.) (2003); Conc. for Orch. (2003); *Flight from the Labyrinth*, str. qt. (2004); *Gossamer*, sax. qt. (2004); *Splintered Instruments*, orch. (2004); double conc., pf. quintet (2005).

Horne, Marilyn (Bernice) (*b* Bradford, Penn., 1934). Amer. mezzo-soprano. Dubbed singing v. (for Dorothy Dandridge) in film of *Carmen Jones*, 1954. Opera début as Hata in *The Bartered Bride*, Los Angeles 1954. Member of Gelsenkirchen opera co. 1956–60. Débuts: Salzburg Fest. 1957; S. Francisco 1960; NY 1961; CG 1965; La Scala 1969; NY Met 1970. Appeared in series of 19th cent. *bel canto* operas in partnership with Joan **Sutherland, beginning in NY in *Beatrice di Tenda* (1961) and incl. *Semiramide* and *Les Huguenots*. Last Rossini role CG 1993 (Isabella in *L'italiana in Algeri*). Repertory from Handel to Wagner.

horn family. Brass instr. The modern hn. is an intricately coiled tube of over 11′; it is of ½″ bore at one end but widens gradually until it terminates in a large bell of 11″–14″ diameter: the mouth-piece is funnel-shaped. All these details differentiate it from the **trumpet*. The principle on which the notes are obtained is that of all brass instr.

There are 2 main forms of the hn.: the *natural horn* and the *valve horn*. The natural horn is restricted, at any given moment, to one pitch of the harmonic series; the valve horn can at will be switched from the harmonic series at one pitch to that of another, so making any note of the chromatic scale instantaneously available. Its technique is more difficult to acquire than that of any other instr. in the orch.

The **basset-horn* and **cor anglais* are not horns but reed instruments.

See *French horn*.

hornpipe. The word has 2 meanings: (1) An obsolete instr., consisting of a wooden pipe with a reed mouthpiece (a single 'beating' reed), and, at the other end, a hn. as 'bell'. Common in the Celtic parts of Brit.

(2) A dance once popular in the Brit. Isles only, to which that instr. was orig. the usual acc. Properly a solo dance; earlier examples of the mus. are in simple triple time, but by the end of the 18th cent. this had changed to simple duple. This dance was later chiefly kept up by sailors. Purcell, Handel, and others wrote hornpipes.

Horn Signal. Nickname for Haydn's sym. in D major, 1765, No.31 in Breitkopf edn. (Hob. I: 31). So called because of calls written for 4 horns in slow movt.

Horoscope. Ballet in 1 act, lib. and mus. by Constant Lambert, choreog. Ashton. Comp. 1937. Prod. London 1938. Orch. suite.

Horowitz, Joseph (b Vienna, 1926). Austrian-born Eng. composer, conductor, and teacher. Settled in Eng. in 1938. Ass. dir. Intimate Opera Co. 1952–63, ass. cond. Glyndebourne 1956, prof. of comp., RCM 1961. Composer of two 1-act operas, 16 ballets, vn. conc., tpt. conc., chamber mus. Arr. of witty parodies for Gerard *Hoffnung's mus. fests. in London.

Horowitz, Vladimir (b Kiev, 1903; d NY, 1989). Russ.-born pianist (Amer. cit. 1944). Début Kiev 1920. Toured Eur., making Berlin début 1926. Amer. début 1928; London début 1928. Settled in US, marrying Toscanini's daughter. Career as int. virtuoso of highest rank interrupted by illness 1936–9. From 1953 played only for recordings. Returned to concert-platform, NY 1965. Acc. to Fischer-Dieskau and played chamber mus. with Rostropovich and Stern. Played at the White House for President Carter 1978. Gave his first Eur. recital for 31 years in London, May 1982. Returned to Russ. for series of recitals 1986. Made last recording on 1 Nov. 1989, four days before his death.

Horst, Louis (b Kansas City, 1884; d NY, 1964). Amer. pianist, conductor, composer, and teacher. Closely assoc. with modern US dance. Cond. for Denishawn Co. 1915–26, mus. dir. for Martha Graham 1926–48. Teacher of dance comp. in NY 1928–64. Scores for Graham incl. *Frontier* and *Celebration*.

Horszowski, Mieczyslaw (b Lwów, 1892; d Philadelphia, 1993). Polish-born pianist (Amer. cit. 1948). Début Warsaw 1902 (Beethoven's 1st conc.). Toured Eur., frequently partnering *Casals. Solo recitals Milan. Settled USA 1942. On staff Curtis Inst. from 1941. Played at Aldeburgh Fest. in 1980s and gave recital in Los Angeles in Jan. 1990.

Hosokawa, Toshio (b Hiroshima, 1955). Japanese composer and pianist. Won several comp. prizes, incl. Valentino Bucchi, Rome, 1980, and Berlin Philharmonic centenary 1982. Comp.-in-residence at fests. in Davos, Warsaw, Darmstadt, Geneva, London, and Seattle. Works incl.:

OPERAS: *Vision of Lear* (1997–8); *Hanjo* (2004).

ORCH.: *Ferne-Landschaft I* (1987); fl. conc. *'Per-Sonare'* (1988); *Hiroshima Requiem* (1988–92): in 3 movts., each of which can be perf. separately: 1. *Preludio—Night*, orch. (1989), 2. *Death and Resurrection*, spkrs., solo vv., mixed ch., children's ch., tape, orch. (1989), 3. *Dawn*, orch. (1992); *Landscape III*, vn., orch. (1993); *To the Sea*, pf., orch. (1998–9); *Ceremonial Dance*, str. (2000); *RH-Turning*, hp., orch. (2001).

CHORUS: *Ave Maria* (1991); *Ave Maria Stella* (1991); *Seascapes – Night*, ch., hp., 2 vn., va., vc., 2 perc. (1997); *Weihnachtskantate*, sop., alt., ch., orch. (2002).

ENSEMBLE: *Manifestation*, vn., pf. (1981); *Dan-so*, vn., vc., pf. (1984); *Sen II*, vc. (1986), *IV*, org. (1990), *V*, accordeon (1991); *In Tal der Zeit . . .*, str. qt., pf. (1986); *Renka I*, sop., gui. (or hp.) (1986), *II*, sop., chamber ens. (1987), *III*, sop. or mez., vn., va. da gamba, hp. (1990); *Fragmente II*, alto fl., str. qt. (1989), *III*, wind quintet (1989); *Birds Fragments I*, mez., alto fl., hp. (1990); *Intermezzo*, lute (1991); *Landscape*, str. qt. (1992); *Vertical Time Study I*, cl., vc., pf. (1992); *Landscape II*, hp., str. qt. (1993); *Interim*, hp., chamber ens. (1994); *Voyage III*, tb., ens. (1997); *Metamorphosis*, cl., perc., str. (2000); *A Song from Far Away*, 6 players (2005–6).

Also several comps. for Japanese instr.

Hotter, Hans (b Offenbach-am-Main, 1909; d Munich, 2003). Austrian bass-baritone. Began as org. and choirmaster; turned to singing and made début in Passau 1929 (*Messiah*). Prof. début Munich 1930 (bar. soloist in Hindemith's oratorio *Lehrstück*, cond. Scherchen). Opera début Troppau 1930 (Wolfram in *Tannhäuser*). Sang in Prague 1932–4 and Hamburg 1934–45. Member of Bavarian State Opera, Munich, 1937–72, Vienna Opera 1939–70. Débuts: London (BBC recital) 1947; CG 1947; NY Met 1950; Bayreuth Fest. 1952; Salzburg Fest. 1942. Created Commandant in *Friedenstag* (1938) and Olivier in *Capriccio* (1942). Sang Jupiter in unofficial Salzburg f.p. of *Die *Liebe der Danae*, 1944. Prod. *Ring* at CG 1962–4. Outstanding Wotan in *Ring*; his last Wotan in Paris, 1972. Vienna farewell 1978. Sang Schigolch in *Lulu* in S. Francisco 1989 and Paris 1991. Has appeared often as speaker in Schoenberg's *Gurrelieder*. One of greatest singers of his generation.

Hotteterre, Jacques(-Martin) ('le Romain') (b Paris, 1674; d Paris, 1763). Fr. flautist, bassoonist, and instrument maker, best known of Fr. family of ww. instr. makers, composers, and performers active in 17th and 18th cents. Called himself 'le Romain' probably because of visit to It. in his youth. By 1708 was bassoonist in Grands Hautbois and flautist in 'chamber of the king'. Much sought-after as teacher. The flutes he made are magnificent instrs. Wrote *Principes de la flûte traversière* (1707, Eng. trans. 1968), *L'art de préluder sur la flûte traversière* (1719), and *Méthode pour la musette* (1737). Pubd. 2 books of suites for fl. and bass (1708, 1715).

Hough, Stephen (b Heswall, Ches., 1961). Eng. pianist. Won Naumburg int. pf. comp. London Proms début 1985. Perf. at Ravinia Fest., Chicago, 1984–5. Soloist with leading Brit. and Amer. orchs.

Housatonic at Stockbridge, The. 3rd movt. of Ives's *Three Places in New England* for orch., sometimes played separately.

House of the Dead, From The (Z Mrtvého Domu). Opera in 3 acts by Janáček to his own lib. based on Dostoyevsky's novel (1862) about his experiences in prison. Comp. 1927–8. Prod. Brno 1930, Edinburgh 1964, London 1965, NY 1990. Part of orch. prelude was taken by Janáček from unfinished vn. conc. (1927–8) to be called *Pilgrimage of the Soul* (*Putováné dušičky*). Problem arises over final 17 bars of this opera inserted by O. Zítek, B. Bakala, and O. Chlubna at the f.p. (1930) which is choral and optimistic; Janáček's orig. ending was more realistic, with an orch. epilogue of 27 bars, and this has been restored in perfs. cond. by Mackerras, Armstrong, and others.

Houston Grand Opera. Opera company in Texas, USA, founded 1955 by Walter Herbert, who was succeeded as gen. man. by David Gockley (1972–2005) and Anthony Freud from 2005. Since 1987 has perf. in Wortham Th. Center, comprising two auditoriums, Cullen Th. (seating 1,100) and Brown Th. (2,300). Under mus. dir. John *DeMain (1979–93), co. est. a high reputation. Patrick Summers mus. dir. from 1998. At its Spring Opera Fest. in 1975, it staged Joplin's *Treemonisha*, followed in 1976 by Gershwin's *Porgy and Bess*. Every season since 1973 has incl. a world première or a prod. of a 20th-cent. masterpiece, e.g. *Lulu* and *Peter Grimes*. Among operas f.p. in Houston are Pasatieri's *The Seagull* (1974); Floyd's *Bilby's Doll* (1976), *Willie Stark* (1981), and *Passion of Jonathan Wade* (1991, rev. of 1962 vers. which had première in NY); Bernstein's *A Quiet Place* (1983); Glass's *Akhnaten* (1984) and *The Making of the Representative for Planet 8* (1988); Adams's *Nixon in China* (1987); Tippett's *New Year* (1989); Stewart Wallace's *Harvey Milk* (1995); Floyd's *Cold Sassy Tree* (2000); and Jake Heggie's *The End of the Affair* (2004).

Houston Symphony Orchestra. Founded in Houston, Texas, 1913 with Julian Paul Blitz as cond., succeeded 1916 by Paul Berge until 1917. Reorganized 1930, with Frank St Leger as cond. 1931–5, Ernst Hoffmann 1936–47. Hoffmann increased size and standards of orch. Conds. after him included Efrem Kurtz 1948–54; Beecham 1954–5; Stokowski 1955–60; Barbirolli 1961–7; Previn 1967–9; Foster 1971–8; Comissiona art. adv. 1980, cond. 1984–8; Eschenbach 1988–99; Hans Graf from 2002.

Hovhaness, Alan (*b* Somerville, Mass., 1911; *d* Seattle, 2000). Amer. composer, conductor, and organist of Armenian and Scot. descent. Worked in Boston 1940–7, taught at Boston Cons. 1948–52, then settled in NY. Prolific composer, deeply interested in Eastern mus. style, which embraces aleatory procedures as in *Lousadzak* (Coming of Light) 1944, combines Western elements with modal harmony, Eastern rhythms, and the exotica of Chinese and Balinese instrs. Works incl. 67 syms. (1936–92); 10 operas; *Mysterious Mountain*, orch.; *Fantasy on Japanese Woodprints*, xyl., orch. (1965); *And God Created Great Whales* (1970) for humpbacked whale solo (on tape) and orch.; choral works; chamber mus.

Howard, Ann (*b* Norwood, 1936). Eng. mezzo-soprano. Début with WNO 1964 (Azucena in *Il trovatore*), then joined SW. A noted Carmen for ENO from 1970. Amer. début New Orleans 1971; CG 1973. Created Leda in Bennett's *The Mines of Sulphur* (SW 1965), Mrs Danvers in Josephs's *Rebecca* (Opera North, 1983) and Elsie Worthing in Blake's *The Plumber's Gift* (ENO 1989). Sang Mescalina in f. Brit. p. of Ligeti's *Le grand macabre* (ENO 1982).

Howard, Brian (*b* Sydney, NSW, 1951). Australian composer and conductor. Worked as répétiteur with Australian Opera. Head of mus. dept., W Australian Acad. of Performing Arts Cons. of Mus. Works incl. chamber operas *Inner Voices* (1979, rev. 1980) and *Metamorphosis* (1983); *Il Tramonto della Luna*, orch. (1971); *The temple of the Golden Pavilion*, orch. (1978); *Chanson de la plus haute tour*, ens. (1980); *The Rainbow Serpent*, ens. (1982); *A Fringe of Leaves*, ch., str. (1982); *Fly Away Peter*, wind quintet (1984); *Sun and Steel*, str. ens. (1985); *Whitsunday*, chamber opera (1988); *Wildbird Dreaming*, orch. (1988); *The Wide Sargasso Sea*, chamber opera (1997).

Howard, Jason (*b* Merthyr Tydfil, 1960). Welsh baritone. Sang Ballad Singer in RCM perf. of *Gloriana*, 1988. After early experience in roles such as Alfio (*Pagliacci*) and Sharpless (*Madama Butterfly*), sang Mozart roles with Scottish Opera. Opera North 1992; Amer. début (Seattle) 1993. Many concert-hall appearances in oratorio, etc.

Howard, Leslie (John) (*b* Melbourne, Victoria, 1948). Australian pianist and composer. Début Melbourne 1967, London 1975. On teaching staff Monash Univ. 1970–3. Notable Liszt exponent. Composer of opera, hn. sonata, etc.

Howarth, Elgar (*b* Cannock, Staffs., 1935). Eng. conductor, composer, and trumpeter. Trumpeter in orch. of ROH, CG, 1958–63. Prin. tpt., RPO 1963–9. Member of London Sinfonietta 1968–71, Philip Jones Brass Ens. 1965–76. Guest cond. London Sinfonietta from 1969, dir. from 1973. Cond. f.p. of Ligeti's *Le grand macabre*, Stockholm 1978, and London première, ENO 1982. CG début 1985 (Tippett's *King Priam*). Cond. Brit. première of Nielsen's *Maskarade* (Opera North 1990), f.p. Birtwistle's *The Mask of Orpheus* (ENO 1986), *Gawain* (CG 1991), and *The Second Mrs. Kong* (GTO, at Glyndebourne, 1994). For Garsington Opera has cond. Strauss's *Arabella*, *Capriccio*, *Die schweigsame Frau*, *Die Ägyptische Helena*, *Die Liebe der Danae*, and *Daphne* and Janáček's *Šárka* and *Osud*. Has often cond. and comp. for brass band.

Howarth, Judith (*b* Ipswich, 1960). Eng. soprano. Début 1984 in Mozart arias with ECO. Opera début in Mozart roles at RSAMD. Won Decca-Ferrier prize 1985. CG début 1985 (First Maid in Zemlinsky's *Der Zwerg*). Has sung Susanna in *Le nozze di Figaro* (Opera North) and Zerlina in *Don Giovanni* (Scottish Opera). Amer. début Seattle 1989; Proms début 1991; Salzburg Fest. 1991. Recorded Walton's *Cressida* 1995.

Howell, Dorothy (*b* Handsworth, 1898; *d* Worcester, 1982). Eng. composer and pianist.

Prof. of harmony and comp. RAM 1924–70. Comp. incl. sym.-poem *Lamia* (1919); *Koong Shee*, orch. (1921); pf. conc. (1923); ov. *The Rock* (1928); chamber mus.; masses; and songs.

Howell, Gwynne (Richard) (*b* Gorseinon, 1938). Welsh bass. Sang Hunding, Fasolt, and Pogner while student at RMCM. Joined SW Opera 1968 (début as Monterone in *Rigoletto*). Débuts: Glyndebourne 1969; CG 1970; NY Met 1985. Created Richard Taverner in *Taverner*, CG 1972. Sang Sachs in *Die Meistersinger* with ENO (also Gurnemanz, Philip II, and Bluebeard). Also fine singer in oratorio and concert repertoire. CBE 1998.

Howells, Anne (Elizabeth) (*b* Southport, 1941). Eng. mezzo-soprano. Sang Eros in f. Eng. p. of Gluck's *Paride ed Elena* while student at RMCM. Glyndebourne ch. 1964–7. Débuts: WNO 1966 (Flora in *La traviata*); CG 1967; Glyndebourne 1967; Amer. (Chicago) 1972; NY Met 1975; Salzburg 1976. Created Lena in Bennett's *Victory*, London 1967, Cathleen in Maw's *The Rising of the Moon*, Glyndebourne 1970, and Régine in Liebermann's *La Forêt*, Geneva 1987.

Howells, Herbert (Norman) (*b* Lydney, Glos., 1892; *d* London, 1983). Eng. composer, organist, and teacher. *Mass in Dorian Mode* perf. Westminster Cath. 1912. Sub-org., Salisbury Cath., 1917. Several comp. perf. at 3 Choirs Fests. in 1920s. Succeeded Holst as dir. of mus., St Paul's Girls' Sch., 1936–62, prof. of mus., London Univ., 1954–64. On staff RCM from 1920 (never retired and was teaching until late 1970s). Frequent adjudication at mus. fests. Org., St John's Coll., Cambridge, 1941–5. His work, influenced by Elgar and Vaughan Williams, has strong individuality, at its finest in the *Missa Sabrinensis* and at its most eloquent in the *Hymnus Paradisi*, where some affinity with the choral writing of Delius may be detected. One of few 20th cent. composers to write for clavichord. The pieces in his two major works for it are musical portraits of friends, incl. Herbert Lambert, Thomas Goff, Vaughan Williams, Finzi, etc. CBE 1954, CH 1972. Prin. works:

ORCH.: *Merry-Eye* and *Puck's Minuet* (1917–20); *Procession* (1922); *Pastoral Rhapsody* (1923); pf. conc. No.1 (1913), No.2 (1925); *Pageantry Suite*, brass band (1934); *Elegy for Strings* (1937); *Fantasia*, vc., orch. (1937); *Concerto for Strings* (1938); *Music for a Prince* (1948); *Three Figures*, brass band (1960).

CHORAL: *Mass in the Dorian Mode (Missa sine nomine)*, unacc. ch. (1912); *Sir Patrick Spens*, bar., ch., orch. (1917); *3 Carol-Anthems*, ch. (1918–20; No.2 is *A Spotless Rose*); *Requiem*, unacc. ch. (1932); *A Kent Yeoman's Wooing Song*, 2 soloists, ch., orch. (1933); *Hymnus Paradisi*, sop., ten., ch., orch. (1938, f.p. 1950); *Missa Sabrinensis*, sop., cont., ten., bar., double ch., orch. (1953); *Inheritance* (1953, in *Garland for the Queen*); *St. Paul's Service* (1954); *An English Mass*, ch., str., org. (1955); *Stabat Mater*, ten., ch., orch. (1963); *Take him, earth, for cherishing* (motet on the death of Pres. Kennedy) (1964); *The Coventry Mass*, ch., org. (1964).

VOICE AND ACC.: 4 *French Chansons*, v., pf. (1918); *In Green Ways*, v., pf. (1915, rev. with orch. 1928); *King David*, v., pf. (1921); *Sine Nomine*, soloists, org., orch. (1922).

CHAMBER MUSIC: pf. qt. in A minor (1916); *Phantasy Quartet* (1916–17); *In Gloucestershire*, str. qt. (1916–30); *Rhapsodic Quintet*, cl., str. (1919); vn. sonata (1923); cl. sonata (1946).

ORGAN: 2 sonatas (1911, 1932); 3 *Rhapsodies* (1915–18), 4th *Rhapsody* (1958); *Fugue, Chorale, and Epilogue* (1939); *Sarabande for the Morning of Easter* (1940); *Master Tallis's Testament* (1940); *De Profundis* (1958).

CLAVICHORD: *Lambert's Clavichord*, 12 pieces (1926–7); *Howells's Clavichord*, 20 pieces (1941–61).

Also about 65 songs incl. several settings of De La Mare, of which *King David* (1921) is a favourite, and many sacred works.

Howes, Frank (Stewart) (*b* Oxford, 1891; *d* Oxford, 1974). Eng. music critic. Staff mus. critic for *The Times* 1925–60 (chief critic from 1943). Chairman, Eng. Folk Dance and Song Soc. 1938–45 and ed. of its journal 1927–46. Author of books on Vaughan Williams, Walton, Eng. mus. renaissance, and aesthetics. Lecturer at RCM. CBE 1954.

Hoyland, Vic(tor) (*b* Wombwell, Yorks., 1945). Eng. composer. Haywood Fellow in mus., Birmingham Univ. 1980–3, lect. at Barber Inst., Birmingham Univ., from 1985. Works incl.:

MUSIC THEATRE: *Xingu*, orch., 3 groups of children (1979); *Michelagnolio*, bar., 6 male vv., 23 instr. (1981); *Crazy Rosa, La madre*, mez., ens. (1988).

ENSEMBLE (& with voice(s)): *ES*, ch., 3 spkr., ens. (1971); *Jeux-Thème*, mez., chamber ens. (1972); *Ariel*, v., fl., ens. (1974–5); *Esem*, db., ens. (1975); *Serenade*, 14 players (1979); *Reel*, double-reed instr. (1980); *Andacht zum Kleinen*, 9 players (1980); *Fox*, chamber ens. (1983); *Seneca/Medea*, vv., ens. (1985); *In transit*, orch. (1987); *Hoquetus David*, ens. (1987); *Of Fantasy, Of Dreams and Ceremonies*, 13 solo str. (1989); *November 2nd*, mez., va., vc., db., 2 bcl. (1992); *Vixen*, orch. (1996).

CHAMBER MUSIC: *Quartet Movement*, str. qt. (1982); *Quintet of Brass* (1985); str. qt. (1985); *Work-out*, tb. (1987); *Work-out for marimba* (1988); pf. trio (1989); pf. quintet (1990); *The Other Side of the Air*, pf. (1992); Chamber Conc., pf., ww., brass., perc. (1993); *Bagatelles* (str. qt. No.3) (1995).

hrotta. Another name for the *crwth.

Hubay, Jenö (*b* Budapest, 1858; *d* Budapest, 1937). Hung. violinist, composer, and conductor. Public début at 11. Paris début 1878. Prof. of vn., Brussels Cons. 1882–6, Pest Cons. 1886–1919, dir. Budapest Acad. 1919–34. Led str. qt. Pupils incl. Szigeti, Telmányi, and Jelly d'Arányi. Comp. 8 operas, incl. *Der Geigenmacher von Cremona* (1893) and *Anna Karenina* (1915); 4 syms., incl. *Dante Symphony* (ch.); 4 vn. concs.; chamber mus., etc. Ed. posth. works of his friend Vieuxtemps.

Huber, Hans [Johann Alexander] (*b* Eppenburg, 1852; *d* Locarno, 1921). Swiss composer. Taught Basle Mus. Sch. 1889–1918 (dir. from 1896).

Comps incl. syms. (incl. No.1, *William Tell* and No.2, *Böcklin*); 4 pf. concs.; vn. conc.; 2 pf. qts.; 5 pf. trios; 10 vn. sonatas; 5 vc. sonatas; 5 operas; oratorio; cantatas.

Huber, Klaus (*b* Berne, 1924). Swiss composer and violinist. Taught vn. Zurich Cons. 1950–60, Lucerne Cons. 1960–3, Basle Mus. Acad. from 1961. Comps. incl.: *Invention and Chorale*, orch. (1956); *Noctes intelligibilis lucis*, ob., hpd. (1961); *Moteti cantiones*, str. qt. (1963); *Tenebrae*, orch. (1966–7); *James Joyce Music*, hp., hn., orch. (1966–7); *Psalm of Christ*, bar., ens. (1967); *Tempora*, vn. conc. (1969–70); *Jot oder Wann kommt der Herr Zurück*, opera (1973); *Turnus*, orch., tape (1974); *Im Paradies* (1974–5); *Litania instrumentalis*, orch. (1975); *Ohne Grenze und Rand*, va., orch. (1976–7); *Von Zeit zu Zeit*, str. qt. (1984–5); *Protuberanzen*, orch. (1985–6); *Spes contra spem*, v., narr., orch. (1986–8); *Winter Seeds*, acc. (1993); *Intarsi*, chamber conc., pf., 17 instrs. (1993–4); *Metanoia*, org. (1995); *Ecce homines*, str. quintet (1997–8); *Bicinium, an Old Man*, bass-bar., vn. (2005).

Huberman, Bronislaw (*b* Czestochowa, 1882; *d* Cosier-sur-Vévey, 1947). Polish violinist. Début aged 7 in Spohr's 2nd conc.; London début 1894; played Brahms conc. in composer's presence 1896. Int. career, based on Vienna until 1936. First tour of USA 1896–7. Founded Palestine SO (now Israel PO) 1936 in assoc. with the cond. William Steinberg.

Hucbald (*b* nr. Tournai, *c*.840; *d* Saint-Amand, Tournai, 930). Fr. monk, remembered for his treatise *De harmonica institutione* (? *c*.880) which describes the gamut and the modes.

Huddersfield Choral Society. Amateur choir founded in Huddersfield, Yorkshire, in 1836. Regular concerts given since 1881. During 1930s had 400 members, but has since been reduced to 230. Has sung at most Brit. fests. and made many recordings. Its *Messiah* perf. is renowned. First overseas tour to Netherlands, 1928. Vienna Mus. Fest. 1958, Boston, Mass. 1965. Has also visited Berlin, Brussels, and Lisbon. At one time had its own orch. but now sings with independent orchs. Sir Henry Coward and Sir Malcolm Sargent were conds. for over 30 years each. Other conds. have incl. John Pritchard (1973–80); Owain Arwel Hughes (1980–6); Jane Glover (1988–97); and Martyn Brabbins 1997–2006. Chorus-masters have incl. Herbert Bardgett, Eric Chadwick, and Douglas Robinson. For centenary (1936) Vaughan Williams wrote *Dona Nobis Pacem*.

Hueber, Kurt Anton (*b* Salzburg, 1928). Austrian composer. Taught musical acoustics, Vienna Hochschule für Musik from 1980. Works incl.: opera *The Canterville Ghost* (1990–1); TV opera *Schwarz und Weiss* (1968); *Symchromie I*, orch. (1970), *II* (1972); *Formant spectrale*, str. (1974); *Requiem* (1977); va. sonata (1964); tpt. sonata (1967); *Intrada*, tpt., org. (1980); *Capriccio*, vc. (1981); *Shakespeariana*, fl. (1989); *Passages into the Wind*,

mez./alto, pf. (1992); *Scene and Song*, 1854, bass, chamber ens. (1994); *Kamaloka*, chamber ens. (1996).

Huggett, Monica (*b* London, 1953). Eng. violinist. Co-founder with T. Koopman of Amsterdam Baroque Orch. 1980 (leader until 1987). Has given many perfs. on gut-str. vn. with Hanover Band, Academy of Ancient Mus., etc.

Hughes, Arwel (*b* Rhosllanerchrugog, 1909; *d* Cardiff, 1988). Welsh composer and conductor. On staff BBC in Wales from 1935 (head of music, BBC Wales 1965–71). Cond. BBC Welsh Orch. 1950. Comp. opera *Menna* (1950–1); sym. (1971); suite for orch.; 3 str. qts.; oratorio, etc. OBE 1969.

Hughes, Herbert (*b* Belfast, 1882; *d* Brighton, 1937). Irish composer and critic. Collected and arr. many Irish folk-songs. Mus. critic, *Daily Telegraph*, 1911–32.

Hughes, Owain Arwel (*b* Cardiff, 1942). Welsh conductor, son of Arwel *Hughes. Professional career began 1968. Guest cond., WNO and ENO. Mus. dir., Royal Nat. Eisteddfod of Wales, 1977, Huddersfield Choral Soc. 1980–6. OBE 2004.

Hughes, Spike (Patrick Cairns) (*b* London, 1908; *d* Brighton, 1987). Eng. writer, composer, and broadcaster, son of Herbert *Hughes. Wrote incid. mus. for Cambridge Univ. prods. and for plays by Congreve and Yeats. For a time led jazz band, making many recordings 1930–3. Mus. critic *Daily Herald* 1933–6. Jazz critic of *The Times* 1957–67. Comps. incl. light music, film scores, etc. His *Cinderella* (1938) was first opera specially comp. for TV. Brilliant broadcaster. Author of books on operas of Mozart, Puccini, and Verdi, history of Glyndebourne Opera (1965, rev. 1981), and 2 vols. of entertaining autobiography.

Hugh the Drover, or Love in the Stocks. Opera in 2 acts by Vaughan Williams to lib. by Harold Child. Comp. 1910–14, rev. 1924 and 1956. Prod. London 1924, Washington 1928.

Huguenots, Les. Opera in 5 acts by *Meyerbeer to lib. by Scribe and Deschamps. Prod. Paris 1836, New Orleans 1839, London 1842.

Huldigungsmarsch (Ger., 'Homage March'). (1) By Wagner, 1864, in honour of his patron, King Ludwig II of Bavaria. Orig. for military band. Orch. version 1865, partly scored by Raff 1871, f.p. at laying of foundation stone at Bayreuth, 1872.

(2) By Liszt, in honour of Grand Duke of Saxe-Weimar. For pf., 1853, scored by Raff 1853; rev. and re-scored by Liszt 1857.

(3) By Grieg, Op.56, No.3, in the *Sigurd Jorsalfar* mus., also known as 'Triumphal March'.

Hullah, John (Pyke) (*b* Worcester, 1812; *d* London, 1884). Eng. composer, organist, and educator. Propagator from 1840 of Wilhem's fixed-doh method of sight-singing. Prof. of vocal mus., King's Coll., London, 1844–74, and taught at Queen's Coll., Bedford Coll., and six London teacher-training colls. Inspector of Training Schools UK from 1872. Comp. operas (one to lib. by Dickens), church mus., part-songs, and songs.

Humble, (Leslie) **Keith** (*b* Geelong, Vict., 1927; *d* Geelong, 1995). Australian composer and pianist. Mus. dir. Centre of Amer. Studies in Paris 1960–6. Lect. in comp. Melbourne Univ. 1966–70, establishing EMS. Prof. of mus., Univ. of Calif., San Diego, 1971–4. Foundation prof. at La Trobe Univ., Vict., from 1974. Mus. dir. Australian contemp. ens. 1975–8. Order of Australia 1982. Works incl. str. trio (1953); series of 9 works called *Nunique* (1968–84), and of 5 called *Arcade* (1969); *Après la légende*, pf., orch. (1969); *La légende*, cantata, v., ch., instr., elec. (1970); trio, vn., cl., pf. (1982); trio, fl., perc., pf. (1985); *Etchings*, perc. qt. (1988); *Four All Seasons*, str. qt. (1989); sonata, fl., pf. (1990–1); *In pace*, ch., perc., hp. (1991); sonata, tb., pf. (1992); *Sym. of Sorrows*, orch. (1993).

Hume, Tobias (*b* ?*c*.1569; *d* London, 1645). Eng. composer and army officer. His *First Part of Ayres* for lyra-viol was pub. 1605, with fanciful titles such as 'Tickle me quickly' and the instruction, thought to be the first recorded use of *col legno*, to 'drum this with the back of the bow'. In 1607 his *Captaine Humes Poeticall Musicke* constituted the largest pubd. repertory of solo lyra-viol music to that date.

Humfrey [Humphrey], **Pelham** (*b* London, 1647; *d* Windsor, 1674). Eng. composer. Chorister of Chapel Royal 1660–4. Visited Fr. 1664–7. Gentleman of Chapel Royal 1667, Master of the Children 1672. Taught Purcell. Comp. incidental mus. to Shadwell vers. of Shakespeare's *The Tempest*, sacred and secular songs, anthems, and other church mus. Contrib. to *Club Anthem*.

Hummel, Johann Nepomuk (*b* Pozsony, 1778; *d* Weimar, 1837). Austrian pianist and composer. Lived and studied pf. with Mozart 1785–7. Début Vienna 1787 at Mozart concert. Kapellmeister to Prince Esterházy 1804–11. Kapellmeister at Stuttgart 1816–18, then at Weimar 1819–37. Toured extensively, conducting the Ger. Opera in London, 1833. Pubd. pf. sch. 1828. Comp. numerous works incl. pf. concs. and sonatas, tpt. conc., bn. conc., mandolin conc., operas, oratorios, and much chamber mus. incl. *Septet militaire* and pf. quintet. Mus. has melodic grace and abundant craftsmanship. Pf. writing influenced Chopin. His relationship with Beethoven fluctuated but they were reconciled at Beethoven's death-bed. Was pall-bearer at Beethoven's funeral and played at his memorial concert. Schubert dedicated his last 3 pf. sonatas to him (but publisher altered the dedications after Schubert's death).

humoresque (Fr.), **Humoreske** (Ger.). Title given by some composers to a lively and capricious (sometimes a little sad) instr. comp. Famous examples are by Dvořák (particularly No.7 of his 8 *Humoresques* for pf., Op.101, 1894), and Schu-

mann, for pf., Op.20, 1839. Mahler orig. conceived his 4th Sym. as a 'symphonic Humoresque'.

Humperdinck, Engelbert (*b* Siegburg, 1854; *d* Neustrelitz, 1921). Ger. composer. Met Wagner in It. 1879 and was invited to assist in preparation for prod. of *Parsifal* at Bayreuth. Taught theory, Barcelona Cons., 1885–6, Cologne Cons. 1887–8. Teacher of harmony, Hoch Cons., Frankfurt, 1890–7 (prof. from 1896), also acting as mus. critic for *Frankfurter Zeitung*. His opera *Hänsel und Gretel*, which effectively uses a Wagnerian idiom for a fairytale, was a success at Weimar, 1893 (where R. Strauss cond. f.p.), and subsequently elsewhere ever since. His other operas failed to emulate its success, although *Königskinder* (f.p. NY Met 1910) has had several modern revivals. Dir., Berlin Akademische Meisterschule for comp. 1900–20. Prin. works:

OPERAS: *Hänsel und Gretel (1893); Dornröschen (1902); Die Heirat wider Willen (1905); *Königskinder (1908–10); Die Marketenderin (1914); Gaudeamus (1919).

ORCH.: Humoreske (1879); Ov., Der Zug des Dionysos (1880); Die maurische Rhapsodie (1898).

CHAMBER MUSIC: str. qts.: No.1 in E minor (1873), No.2 (1876), No.3 (1920); Notturno, vn., pf.

INCID. MUSIC: Königskinder (1895–7, later rev. as opera, 1908–10); The Merchant of Venice (1905); The Winter's Tale (1906); The Tempest (1906); Romeo and Juliet (1907); As You Like it (1907); Lysistrata (1908); The Miracle (1911); The Blue Bird (1912).

Also many songs.

Humphrey, Pelham. See *Humfrey, Pelham*.

Hungarian Dances (*Ungarische Tänze*). 21 pf. duets by Brahms pubd. in 4 vols. between 1852 and 1869. 3 were orch. by him, and he arr. some for pf. solo (Nos. 1–10).

Hungarian Rhapsodies. 19 comps. for pf. by Liszt, comp. 1846–85. Of these 6 were orch. in collab. with Franz Döppler, others by various composers. The *Hungarian Fantasia* for pf. and orch. is based on No.14. There are discrepancies between the numbering of pf. and orch. versions.

Hungarian String Quartet. Founded in Budapest 1935, disbanded 1970. Orig. members were Sandor Végh, Péter Szervánsky (vns.), Dénes Koromzay (va.), and Vilmos Palotai (vc.). Shortly Zoltán *Székely became leader, with Végh as 2nd vn. Végh was succeeded in 1940 by Alexandre Moskowsky, who was succeeded in 1959 by Michael Kuttner. In 1956 Palotai was replaced by Gabriel Magyar. After being resident in Holland, the qt. moved to USA 1950. Salzburg Fest. début 1958. Many famous recordings, notably of Beethoven and Bartók. At time of disbandment membership was Székely, Kuttner (vns.), Koromzay (va.), and Magyar (vc.).

Hunnenschlacht (Battle of the Huns). 11th of Liszt's 13 symphonic poems. Comp. 1856–7, f.p. Weimar 1858. Inspired by Kaulbach's mural of legend of battle in the air between ghosts of slain Huns and Romans after Battle of Chalons in 451.

Hunt, Donald (Frederick) (*b* Gloucester, 1930). Eng. conductor, organist, and composer. Ass. org. Gloucester Cath. 1948–54, dir. of mus. Leeds Parish Church 1957–74, org. Worcester Cath. 1974–96. Cond. Halifax Choral Soc. 1957–88. Composer of church mus., org. sonata, carols, etc. OBE 1993.

Hunt, The (Haydn). See *Chasse, La*.

Hunt, Thomas (*fl.* early 17th cent.). Eng. composer of church music, etc. Contributed madrigal *Hark, did you ever hear so sweet a singing*? to *The *Triumphs of Oriana* (1601).

Hunter, Rita (Nellie) (*b* Wallasey, 1933; *d* Sydney, NSW, 2001). Eng. soprano. Joined SW ch. 1954. Toured with Carl Rosa Opera 1956 (début as Inez in *Il trovatore*). SW début 1960; CG 1963. Prin. sop. SW (later ENO) from 1965, the Brünnhilde of their Eng. *Ring* cycle, 1970. NY Met début 1972. Australian Opera from 1981. Autobiography *Wait till the Sun Shines, Nellie* (London, 1986). CBE 1980.

Hunt Lieberson, Lorraine (*b* San Francisco, 1954; *d* Santa Fe, 2006). Amer. mezzo-soprano. Studied at S. José State and Boston Cons. Violist in Berkeley Free Orch. and in Boston. Took up singing at age of 26. Sang at Pepsico Summerfare Fest., Purchase, NY, in Peter Sellars's prod. of Handel's *Giulio Cesare*. This led to many recordings of Handel operas and oratorios cond. by Nicholas McGegan. Paris Opéra 1993 (title-role in Charpentier's *Médée*). Boston Lyric Opera 1994 (Carmen). Glyndebourne 1996 (Irene in Sellars's prod. of Handel's *Theodora*). NY Met 1999 (created Myrtle Wilson in Harbison's *The Great Gatsby*). Created Triraksha in Peter Lieberson's *Ashoka's Dream* (Santa Fe 1997). Sang in f.p. of Adams's *El Niño*, Paris 2000. Large concert and recital repertory.

Hunt Quartet. Nickname for Mozart's Str. Qt. No.17 in B♭ (K458, 1784), ded. to Haydn, and so called because of the 1st subject of 1st movement.

hüpfend (Ger., 'hopping'). In str. playing, 'with springing bow', i.e. *spiccato*.

Hurd, Michael (John) (*b* Gloucester, 1928; *d* Portsmouth, 2006). Eng. composer, conductor, author, and teacher. Prof. of theory, Royal Marines Sch. of Mus. 1953–9. Comps. incl. operas, cantatas, church mus., chamber mus., songs. Books on Britten, Boughton, Elgar, Vaughan Williams, Gurney, Tippett, opera, sea shanties, soldiers' songs; author of *The Oxford Junior Companion to Music* (1979), *The Orchestra* (1981), *An Outline History of European Music* (1968, rev. 1988), and *Letters of Gerald Finzi and Howard Ferguson* (co-ed., 2001).

hurdy-gurdy (*organistrum, symphonia, chifonie, organica lyra, vielle à roue* 'wheel fiddle'). A portable medieval str. instr., shaped like a viol, dating (in Eur.) from early 12th cent. First str. instr. to which kbd. principle was applied. The instr. is hung round the player's neck or strapped to the body at an angle which lets the keys fall back under their own weight. Bowing action replaced by wheel cranked by a handle. Outer rim of wheel, coated with resin, makes all str. resonate at once, providing a continuous drone like a bagpipe. Fingering is also mechanized, the same str. being stopped at different points to produce required scale. Orig. required 2 players, but during 13th cent. improvements enabled solo perf., thus transforming its use from a cumbersome instr. to one capable of providing dance mus. By 14th cent. there were 6 str. and a kbd. compass of 2 chromatic octaves. Application of the term to any instr. worked by turn of a handle, e.g. barrel-org., street pf., is incorrect. See *lira organizzata*.

Hurford, Peter (John) (*b* Minehead, 1930). Eng. organist and composer. Début, London (RFH) 1957. Master of the Mus., St Albans, 1958–78. Visiting artist-in-res., Sydney Opera House 1979–82. Specialist in baroque period. Comps. incl. church mus. and org. suites. OBE 1984.

Hurlstone, William (Yeates) (*b* London, 1876; *d* London, 1906). Eng. composer and pianist. Soloist in own pf. conc., London, 1896. Wrote 12 chamber works, incl. str. qt. (1906), ballad *Alfred the Great*, and *Fantasie-Variations on a Swedish Air* (1903) for orch. Prof. of counterpoint RCM, from 1905.

Hurst, George (*b* Edinburgh, 1926). Eng. conductor of Romanian and Russ. parentage. Cond., York SO Penn., 1950–5, London début 1953 (with LPO); ass. cond., LPO 1955–7; prin. cond., BBC Northern SO 1958–68; Bournemouth SO 1969–71; art. adviser and cond. Bournemouth Sinfonietta to 1978; cond. Nat. SO of Ireland 1990–3.

hurtig (Ger.). *allegro*, i.e. nimble, quick.

Husa, Karel (*b* Prague, 1921). Amer. composer and conductor of Cz. birth. Cond. of various orchs. in Prague and Paris. Ass. prof. Cornell Univ. Mus. Dept. 1954–61, prof. 1961–92. Taught at Ithaca Coll. 1967–86. Comps. incl.:

BALLET: *The Trojan Women* (1980).

ORCH.: 3 *Frescoes* (1947); pf. concertino (1949); sym. No.1 (1953), No.2 (*Reflections*) (1983); *Portrait*, str. (1953); 4 *Easy Pieces*, ob., tpt., perc., str. (1955); *Fantasies* (1956); *Poem*, va., orch. (1959); *Mosaïques* (1961); *Elegy and Rondo*, alto sax., orch. (1961); *Serenade*, wind quintet, str. (1963); conc., brass quintet and str. (1965); *Music for percussion* (1966); conc., alto sax. and band (1967); *Music for Prague* (1968); 2 *Sonnets from Michelangelo* (1971–2); *The Steadfast Tin Soldier*, speaker, orch. (1974); *Pastoral*, str. (1980); *Symphonic Suite* (1984); *Concerto for Orchestra* (1986); org. conc. (1987); tpt. conc. (1987); vc. conc. (1988); *Ov. Mladi* (*Youth*) (1991); vn. conc. (1992); *Celebración* (1996).

CHORAL: *An American Te Deum*, bar., ch., wind ens.

(1976), bar., ch., orch. (1978); *Cantata*, male ch., brass quintet (1983); *Song (Good Night)*, unacc. ch. (2000).

CHAMBER MUSIC: str. qts. No.1 (1948), No.2 (1953), No.3 (1968), No.4 (1989); vn. sonatina (1945); *Evocations of Slovakia* for cl., va., and vn. (1951); wind trio (1966); pf. sonata (1949); vn. sonata (1972–3); *Landscapes*, brass quintet (1977); *Sonata a tre*, vn., cl., pf. (1981); *Recollections*, wind quintet, pf. (1982); *Variations*, pf. qt. (1984); *Memories*, ens. (1992); *5 Poems*, wind quintet (1994); *Midwest Celebration (Fanfare)*, chamber ens. (1996); *Postcard from Home*, sax., pf. (1997); *Les Couleurs fauves*, chamber ens. (1997).

Hüsch, Gerhard (*b* Hanover, 1901; *d* Munich, 1984). Ger. baritone. Début Osnabrück 1923 in Lortzing's *Der Waffenschmied*. Sang in opera in Bremen 1924–7, Cologne 1927–30, and Berlin 1930–42. CG début 1930; Bayreuth 1930 and 1931. Particularly noted for *Lieder* singing.

Hüttenbrenner, Anselm (*b* Graz, 1794; *d* Ober-Andritz, 1868). Austrian composer and pianist. Knew Beethoven well and was at his deathbed. Comp. 6 operas; 8 syms.; 10 masses; 4 Requiems; 2 str. qts.; and 200 songs (among them *Erlkönig*). Many Schubert MSS, incl. that of 'Unfinished' Sym., were in his possession after the composer's death until 1865.

Hvorostovsky, Dmitri (*b* Krasnoyarsk, Siberia, 1962). Siberian baritone. Sang with Krasnoyarsk Opera from 1986. Won Glinka prize 1987, Toulouse singing comp. 1988, Cardiff Singer of the World comp. 1989. London recital début 1989, NY 1990. Western opera début, Nice 1989 (Yeletsky in *Queen of Spades*); CG 1992; Amer. opera début (Chicago) 1993.

hydraulis. Ancient instr., also known as water org., said to have been invented by Gr. Ktesibios *c*.250 BC. Resembled small modern org. Kbd. operated by series of levers, each with a return mechanism, pressed down by fingers to obtain required notes. Water was used to stabilize wind pressure. In 4th cent. AD hydraulic mechanism was replaced by bellows, enabling much louder tone. See also *organ*.

hymn. Song of praise to the deity or a saint. Particularly assoc. with Anglican church where words and melodies of hymns are especially popular for congregational singing. Books of hymns and hymn-tunes of special significance are *Hymns Ancient and Modern* (1861 and many subsequent edns.), *The Yattendon Hymnal* (Bridges, 1899), *The English Hymnal* (1906, rev. 1933, mus. ed. Vaughan Williams, in which some folk tunes were adapted as hymn-tunes), and *Songs of Praise* (1925, rev. 1931, mus. ed. Vaughan Williams and Martin Shaw) in Eng. hymn-books, tunes are given an identifying title such as a Latin translation, or the name of a town or village, e.g. Down Ampney (Vaughan Williams's birthplace) is title of his *Come down, O love divine*.

Hymnen (Anthems). Comp. by *Stockhausen which exists in 3 versions, incl. one for elec. instr. and *musique concrète*, and one with added soloists (both 1966–7). A shorter version with orch. was made in 1969. The anthems are nat. anthems.

Hymn of Jesus, The. Work for 2 ch., women's semi-ch., and orch., Op.37, by Holst to words trans. by Holst from the apocryphal Acts of St John. Comp. 1917. F.p. London 1920, cond. Holst.

Hymns from the Rig Veda. 23 settings by Holst of his trans. of words from the Sanskrit. There are 5 sets: *9 Hymns*, solo v., pf., Op.24 (1907–8); *3 Choral Hymns*, Group I, ch., orch., Op.26 (1908–10); *3 Choral Hymns*, Group II, women's vv., orch., Op.26 (1909); *4 Choral Hymns*, Group III, women's vv., hp., Op.26 (1909–10); *4 Choral Hymns*, Group IV, men's vv., str., brass, Op.26 (1912).

Hymn to St Cecilia. Setting of text by W. H. Auden for unacc. 5-part ch. by Britten, Op.27. Comp. 1942. F.p. London 1942.

Hymn to St Magnus. Work by *Maxwell Davies for sop. and chamber ens. F.p. London 1972, cond. composer.

Hymnus Amoris (Hymn of Love). Cantata, Op.12, by Nielsen, comp. 1896 to Danish text by A. Olrik, Latin text by J. L. Heiberg, for sop., ten., bar., and bass soloists, children's ch., mixed ch., male ch., and orch. F.p. Copenhagen 1897, cond. Nielsen; f. Eng. p. Birmingham 1959.

Hymnus Paradisi (Hymn of Paradise). Requiem by *Howells for sop., ten., ch., orch., to texts selected by him from Latin Mass for the Dead, Psalm 23, Psalm 121, the Burial Service, and the Salisbury Diurnal (trans. G. H. Palmer). Comp. 1938 in memory of his son, but not released for perf. until 1950 (Gloucester Fest.). Some of the themes in *Hymnus Paradisi* were first employed in Howells's *Requiem* for unacc. ch., comp. in 1936. The *Requiem* was reassembled from MS and perf. in 1980.

Hynninen, Jorma (*b* Leppävirta, Finland, 1941). Finn. baritone. Won Lappeenranta singing comp. 1969. Concert début Helsinki 1970, opera début with Finn. Nat. Opera, Helsinki, 1970 (Silvio in *Pagliacci*). Débuts at Vienna, Hamburg, and Milan 1977; Munich 1979; Paris 1980. Created Topi in Sallinen's *The Red Line*, Helsinki 1978. Sang this role with Finn. Nat. Opera at CG 1979 and NY Met 1983. Created the King in Sallinen's *The King Goes Forth to France*, Savonlinna Fest. 1984 and his *Kullervo* (Los Angeles 1992). Sang Rigoletto and title-role in Merikanto's *Juha*, Edinburgh 1987. Art. dir., Finn. Nat. Opera 1984–90.

Hytner, Nicholas (*b* Manchester, 1956). Eng. theatre and opera director. Prod. Weill's *The Threepenny Opera* while at Cambridge. First prof. opera prod. was *The Turn of the Screw* for Kent Opera, 1979, also directing *Le nozze di Figaro* (1981) and *King Priam* (1983) for this co. For ENO prod. *Rienzi* (1983), *Xerxes* (1985), *The Magic Flute* (1988), and *The Force of Destiny* (1992). CG début 1987 with Sallinen's *The King Goes Forth to France*, followed by Tippett's *The Knot Garden* (1988). Glyndebourne 1991 (*La clemenza di Tito*), 2006 (*Così fan tutte*). Prods. abroad incl. Paris 1987, Geneva 1989. In the th., his prods. incl. *The Scarlet Pimpernel*, *Miss Saigon*, *Edward II*, *Carousel* (Nat. Th. 1992), *The Madness of George III*, and *The Importance of Being Earnest*. Dir. Nat. Th. from 2003.

i (It.). The (masc. plural).

Ibéria. No.2 of Debussy's **Images* for orch. Comp. 1905–8, f.p. 1910, Paris. In 3 sections: 1. *Par les Rues et par les chemins* (By highways and byways); 2. *Les Parfums de la nuit* (Night Scents); 3. *Le Matin d'un jour de fête* (Morning of festival day). This evocation of Sp. was written by a composer who went to Sp. for one day in his life—to see a bullfight.

Iberia. 4 books (1906–9) containing 12 pf. pieces by **Albéniz, several being orch. by **Arbós.

Ibert, Jacques (François Antoine) (*b* Paris, 1890; *d* Paris, 1962). Fr. composer. Dir., Fr. Acad., Rome, 1937–60 (excl. 1939–45), ass. dir. Paris Opéra and Opéra-Comique 1955–6. Works, light and witty in style, incl.:

OPERAS: *Persée et Andromède* (1921); *Angélique* (1926); *Le Roi d'Yvetot* (1928); *Gonzague* (1930); *L'*Aiglon* (with Honegger, 1936); *Les petites Cardinal* (with Honegger, 1937); *Barbe-bleue* (radio, 1943).

BALLETS: *L'*Éventail de Jeanne* (with 9 other composers, 1927); *Le Chevalier errant* (1935); *Les amours de Jupiter* (1945); *Circus* (1952).

ORCH.: *Ballade de la geôle de Reading* (1920); **Escales* (1922); vc. conc. (1926); *Divertissement* (1928, adaptation from mus. for Lebiche's play *Un Chapeau de paille d'Italie* (The Italian Straw Hat)); fl. conc. (1933); *Diane de Poitiers*, 2 suites (1934); concertino da camera, alto sax. (1935); *Ouverture de fête* (1940); *Symphonie Concertante*, ob., str. (1949); *Louisville Concerto* (1953); sym. No.2 ('Bostoniana') (1955); *Hommage à Mozart* (1956); *Bacchanale* (1956).

CHAMBER MUSIC: *Capriccio*, 10 instr. (1938); str. qt. (1937–42); trio, vn., vc., hp. (1942); *2 Interludes*, fl., vn., hpd. (or hp.) (1946).

VOICE & PIANO (or ORCH.): *2 Mélodies*, medium v., pf. (1910); *3 Chansons de Charles Vildrac*, medium v., pf. (1928); *La verdure dorée*, medium v., pf. (1924); *4 Chants*, medium v., pf. (1927); *4 Chansons de Don Quichotte*, low v., pf. (or orch.) (1932); *Chanson de rien*, medium v., pf. (1934); *Le Petit Âne blanc* (The Little White Donkey) (1940, from *Histoire No.2* for pf., 1921); *Complainte de Florinde*, mez., pf. (or hp.) (1951).

Ice Break, The. Opera in 3 acts by **Tippett to his own lib., comp. 1973–6. Prod. CG 1977, Kiel 1978 (as *Wenn das Eis bricht*), Boston, Mass., 1979.

idée fixe (Fr.). Fixed idea. Term used by **Berlioz, in his *Symphonie fantastique* and elsewhere, for what is in essence a **leitmotiv* or **motto theme. Berlioz borrowed the term from medicine, where it means 'a delusion that impels towards some abnormal action'.

idiophone. Term for mus. instr. which produce sound from their own substance, e.g. castanets,

cymbals, bells, etc. Can be struck, plucked, blown, or vibrated by friction. One of 4 classifications of instr. devised by C. Sachs and E. M. von Hornbostel and pubd. in *Zeitschrift für Ethnologie*, 1914. Other categories are **aerophones, **chordophones, and **membranophones, with **electrophones added later.

Idomeneo, Rè di Creta, ossia Ilia ed Idamante (Idomeneus, King of Crete, or Ilia and Idamantes). Opera seria in 3 acts by Mozart (K366) (comp. 1780–1) to It. lib. by G.B. Varesco, after Danchet's lib. for **Campra's *Idoménée* (1712) and the ancient legend. For Vienna private perf. in 1786 Mozart made additions to the score incl. new sop. aria *Non temer, amato bene* (K490), now sung in many modern perfs. Prod. Munich 1781, Karlsruhe 1917, Dresden 1925, Glasgow 1934, Tanglewood 1947, Glyndebourne 1951; NY 1951, Met 1982; London 1962, CG 1978. For revival at Vienna, 1931, R. Strauss ed. (liberally) the score and added mus. of his own, with text rewritten by L. Wallerstein, and Wolf-Ferrari ed. the work for Munich, 1931. Many textual and other special musicological problems attend this opera. For details, see W. Mann's *The Operas of Mozart* (1977).

idyll. In literature a description (prose or verse) of happy rural life, and so sometimes applied to a mus. comp. of peaceful pastoral character (e.g. Wagner's **Siegfried Idyll*).

Idyll: Once I Passed through a Populous City. For sop., bar., and orch. by Delius to text by Whitman. Comp. 1930–2, containing re-working of parts of early opera, **Margot-la-rouge* (1901–2).

Igloi, Thomas (George) (*b* Budapest, 1947; *d* London, 1976). Hung.-born cellist. Début London 1969. Winner, BBC vc. comp. 1969, Casals int. vc. comp., Florence, 1971; soloist with leading orchs.

il (It.). The (masc. sing.).

Illica, Luigi (*b* Piacenza, 1857; *d* Piacenza, 1919). It. playwright and librettist. Wrote, or helped to write, 35 opera libs., among them those for Puccini's *Manon Lescaut* (1893) and, with Giacosa, *La bohème* (1898), *Tosca* (1900), and *Madama Butterfly* (1904); also for Catalani's *La Wally* (1892), Giordano's *Andrea Chénier* (1896), and Mascagni's *Iris* (1898).

Illuminations, Les (The Illuminations). (1) Song-cycle for high v. and str. orch., Op.18, by Britten, comp. 1938–9, text being 9 prose-poems by Fr. poet Arthur Rimbaud written 1872–3 (*Les Illuminations* and *Poèmes en prose*). The movements are: 1. *Fanfare*, 2. *Villes*, 3 (a) *Phrase*, (b) *Antique*, 4. *Royauté*, 5. *Marine*, 6. *Interlude*, 7. *Being beauteous*, 8. *Parade*, 9.

Départ. F.p. London, 1940 (Nos. 5 and 7 perf. separately in Birmingham and London 1939).
(2) Song-cycle for sop. and chamber ens. by *Furrer, comp. 1985.

Images (Pictures). Title given by Debussy to 2 works: (1) *Images* for orch. (*Gigues*, 1909–12, orch. *Caplet; *Ibéria*, 1905–8, and *Rondes de Printemps*, 1905–9). F.p. as triptych, Paris 1913 cond. Pierné. (2) 2 sets for solo pf., set 1 (1905) containing *Reflets dans l'eau, Hommage à Rameau, Mouvement*; set 2 (1907) containing *Cloches à travers les feuilles, Et la lune descend sur le temple qui fut*, and *Poissons d'or.*

Imaginary Landscape. Title of 5 perc. works by *Cage in which he also developed his interest in unusual and elec. sounds. No.1 (1939), 2 variable speed gramophone turntables, frequency recordings, muted pf., cymbal; No.2 (*March*), perc. quintet (1942); No.3 (1942), perc. sextet; No.4 (*March No.2*), 12 radios, 24 players, cond. (1951); No.5 (1952) is a score for making a recording on tape using any 42 gramophone records.

Imai, Nobuko (*b* Tokyo, 1943). Japanese violist. Won Munich and Geneva int. va. comps. She was violist in Vermeer Qt. 1974–9. Settled in Eng. and became solo violist with leading orchs. One of orig. soloists in f.p. of Tippett's Triple Conc., 1980. Salzburg Fest. début 1990.

Imbrie, Andrew (Welsh) (*b* NY, 1921). Amer. composer and pianist. Taught at Univ. of Calif. from 1948 (prof. from 1960). *Prix de Rome* 1947, working in Rome 1947–51, 1953–4. Works incl. operas *Christmas in Peebles Town* (1962–3) and *Angle of Repose* (1975–6); 4 syms.; vn. conc.; vc. conc.; 3 pf. concs.; fl. conc.; *Legend*, orch.; chamber sym.; vc. sonata; 5 str. qts. (1942–87); pf. sonata; *Psalm 42*, male ch., org.; *On the Beach at Night* (1948); *Drum Taps*, ch., orch. (1961); *Requiem*, sop., ch., orch. (1984); *Earplay Fantasy*, vn., vc., fl., cl., pf., perc. (1995); *Spring Fever*, 2 vn., va., vc., db., fl., ob., cl., pf., perc. (1996); *Chicago Bells*, vn., pf. (1997); pf. qt. (1998); *Songs of Then and Now*, sop., alto, vn., vc., fl., cl., pf., perc. (1998); *From Time to Time*, 2 vn., va., 2 vc., fl., ob., cl., bn., perc. (2000).

Imeneo (Lat., 'Hymen'). Opera in 3 acts by Handel to lib. anonymously adapted from Stampiglia's *Imeneo* (1723). Comp. 1738–40 (incl. mus. from pasticcio *Giove in Argo* and Op.6 concs.). Prod. London 1740, Dublin (concert) 1742. Revived in rev. by A. Lewis, Birmingham 1961, in Handel's vers. SW Th., London 1984.

imitation. Compositional device in part-writing involving repetition by one v. of more or less the phrase previously stated by another v. In *canon and *fugue, imitation is according to a strict regulated pattern.

imitazione, aria d'. See *aria*.

Immortal Hour, The. Mus. drama in 2 acts by *Boughton to own lib. based on works of 'Fiona Macleod' (William Sharp). Prod. Glastonbury 1914, London 1922, NY 1926.

imperfect cadence. See *cadence*.

'imperfect' time. See *common time*.

Impériale, L' (The Imperial). Nickname for Haydn's Sym. in D major, No.53 in Breitkopf edn., comp. *c*.1780. Name first used in 19th-cent. Paris catalogue of Haydn syms. for unknown reason.

Imperial Mass. Another name for Haydn's *Nelson Mass*.

Importance of Being Earnest, The. Opera in 3 acts by Castelnuovo-Tedesco to his own lib. based on Wilde's play (1895). Comp. 1961–2. Prod. NY 1975, Florence 1984.

Impresario, The (*Der Schauspieldirektor*). Comedy with mus. in 1 act (K486) by Mozart to lib. by G. Stephanie. Comp. 1785–6. Prod. Vienna 1786, London 1857, NY 1870.

impressionism. Term used in graphic art from 1874 to describe the work of Monet, Degas, Whistler, Renoir, etc., whose paintings avoid sharp contours but convey an 'impression' of the scene painted by means of blurred outlines and minute small detail. It was applied by musicians to the mus. of Debussy and his imitators because they interpret their subjects (e.g. *La Mer*) in a similar impressionistic manner, conveying the moods and emotions aroused by the subject rather than a detailed tone-picture. To describe Debussy's harmony and orchestration as impressionist in the sense of vague or ill-defined is to do them a severe injustice. Some of the technical features of musical impressionism included new chord combinations, often ambiguous as to tonality, chords of the 9th, 11th, and 13th being used instead of triads and chords of the 7th; *appoggiaturas used as part of the chord, with full chord included; parallel movement in a group of chords of triads, 7ths, and 9ths, etc.; whole-tone chords; exotic scales; use of the modes; and extreme chromaticism.

impromptu (Fr.). Literally 'improvised' or 'on the spur of the moment', but in 19th cent., name given to short piece of instr. mus., often in song-like form, e.g. those by Schubert, Chopin, and Schumann. In 20th cent., term has been used by Britten for rev. 3rd movt. of his pf. conc.

improvisation (or extemporization). A perf. according to the inventive whim of the moment, i.e. without a written or printed score, and not from memory. It has been an important element in mus. through the centuries, viz. (1) from the 12th to the 17th cents., in vocal descant when a part was improvised by one singer to a notated part sung by another. (2) In 17th and 18th cents. in the *'divisions' of viol players, i.e. the improvised decoration of the notes of a tune by shorter notes. Also the kbd. player's improvisation of the figured bass. (3) In the 18th cent. the filling-in of the preludes to kbd. suites which Handel and others often indicated merely as a series of chords from which the perf. was to develop his material. (4) From 18th cent., the *cadenza in concs. (sometimes written out, but often left to the virtuoso to invent). (5) In 18th and early 19th cents., the kbd. perfs. by which Bach, Mozart, Beethoven, Hummel, Clementi, and others enthralled their audiences by brilliant displays of improvisation. (6) The same as (5) by organists such as Bruckner and Widor, this practice still being fairly common among organists. (7) In jazz, improvisation by solo instrumentalists is part of the idiom's attraction. (8) *Aleatory or indeterminate features of 20th-cent. works are of an improvisatory nature. (9) The term is sometimes used as the title of a notated work which is intended to convey an impression of improvisation.

in alt (It.). Notes are *in alt* which are in the octave immediately above the top line of the treble stave; the next octave is *in altissimo*.

In a Summer Garden. Rhapsody for large orch. by Delius, comp. 1908. F.p. London 1909, rev. version Edinburgh 1913. The garden was Delius's own at Grez.

Inbal, Eliahu (*b* Jerusalem, 1936). Israeli cond. Won Cantelli int. competition for conds., Novara, 1963. Salzburg Fest. début 1969 (Vienna PO). Mus. dir. Frankfurt Radio SO 1974–90. Opera début Bologna 1969 (*Elektra*). Art. dir., La Fenice, Venice, 1983–6. Cond. Berlin SO 2001–6. In 1986 in Venice cond. perfs. on same day of Verdi's *Stiffelio* and its rev. vers. *Aroldo*. Recorded all Mahler syms.

incalcando (It.). Warming-up, i.e. getting faster and louder.

incidental music. Mus. written for atmospheric effect or to accompany the action in a play. It was provided 'incidentally' as far back as Gr. drama. Purcell wrote much incidental mus. for the th. of his day, and there are dozens of superb examples since the early 19th cent., e.g. Beethoven's for Goethe's *Egmont*, Mendelssohn's for Shakespeare's *A Midsummer Night's Dream*, Grieg's for Ibsen's *Peer Gynt*, Bizet's for Daudet's *L'Arlésienne*, Fauré's and Sibelius's for Maeterlinck's *Pelléas et Mélisande*, Walton's for Shakespeare's *Macbeth*, etc. Music for films and TV is also in a sense 'incidental music'.

Incoronazione di Poppea, L' (The Coronation of Poppaea). Opera in prol. and 3 acts by Monteverdi (his last) to a lib. by Busenello after Tacitus and others. Comp. 1642. Prod. Venice 1643, Naples 1651, Paris, concert version ed. d'Indy, 1905, stage 1913, Northampton, Mass., 1926, Oxford 1927, London (RAM) 1969. First opera on an historical, other than biblical or mythical, subject. In the 20th cent. there have been several edns., incl. those by Krenek, d'Indy, Benvenuti, Malipiero, Ghedini, W. Goehr, Redlich, Harnoncourt, Curtis, and R. Leppard (first vers. f.p. Glyndebourne 1962, London 1971; second vers. f.p. Glyndebourne 1984). New edn. by Roger Nor-

rington for Kent Opera 1974. In some respects this was the first 'modern' opera by virtue of its treatment of human emotions and personalities and its anticipation of a *leitmotiv* technique of comp. Scholars agree that some sections of the score were written by Sacreti, Benedetto Ferrari, and Cavalli. Final duet, text and mus., are probably by Ferrari.

Incorporated Society of Musicians. Assoc. of professional musicians founded in 1882. Meetings are held regularly in regional branches, and an annual conference is held in one of the large cities of the UK. Examinations conducted by the soc. were dropped in 1928.

Incredible Flutist, The. Ballet with mus. by Walter *Piston. Prod. 1938. Concert suite from the ballet f.p. 1940.

Indes galantes, Les (The courtly Indies). Opéra-ballet in prol. and 4 *entrées* by *Rameau to lib. by Louis Fuzelier. Prod. Paris 1735, with 4th *entrée* 1736. First modern revivals, Paris 1952, NY 1961, London 1974. Each *entrée* tells a love-story from a different part of the world: 1. *Le Turc généreux* (The generous Turk). 2. *Les Incas de Pérou* (The Incas of Peru). 3. *Les Fleurs, feste Persane* (The Flowers, Persian festival). 4. *Les Sauvages* (The Savages).

indeterminacy. Much the same as *aleatory, but specially the principle by which a decision of the performer of a comp. replaces a decision of the composer.

India, Sigismondo d'. See *D'India, Sigismondo*.

Indianische Fantasie (Indian Fantasy). Busoni's Op.44 for pf. and orch. Comp. 1913. Based on Amer. Indian themes.

Indianisches Tagebuch (Indian Diary). Work by Busoni, Book I being for pf. solo and Book II for orch. Comp. 1915.

Indian Queen, The. Semi-opera in prol. and 5 acts by Purcell. Comp. 1695, with text by Dryden and R. Howard about rivalry between Mexicans and Peruvians. His last major work, left unfinished. Prod. London 1695, the final masque in Act V being by his brother, Daniel Purcell.

In dulci Jubilo (In sweet joy). 14th-cent. Ger. macaronic carol; Eng. version *c*.1540. Popular setting for solo vocal octet and 5-pt. chorus by Robert L. Pearson dates from 1834.

Indy, Vincent d'. See *D'Indy, Vincent*.

Inextinguishable, The (*Det uudslukkelige*). Title of Sym. No.4 by Carl *Nielsen, comp. 1915–16. F.p. Copenhagen 1 Feb. 1916; f.p. in England, London, 22 June 1923, cond. Nielsen.

Infedeltà delusa, L' (It., 'Deceit Outwitted'). Opera in 2 acts by Joseph Haydn to lib. by Coltellini, rev. by C. Friberth. Comp. 1773. Prod.

Eszterháza 1773. F. modern p. of orig. score, Hungarian Radio 1952, stage Budapest 1955; London (concert) 1960, (stage, Camden Fest.) 1964.

infinite canon (perpetual canon). Canon in which each v., having reached the end, begins again, and so indefinitely.

inflection. In plainsong, the general name given to such parts as are not in monotone, i.e. incl. the intonation, mediation, and ending, and excl. the recitation.

inflection of notes.

Sharp ♯	Double Sharp ×
Raising the note a half-step or semitone	Raising the note a full-step or tone
Flat ♭	Double Flate ♭♭
lowering the note a half-step or semitone	lowering the note a full-step or tone

After a sharp or flat the natural sign ♮ restores the note to its normal pitch.

After a double sharp or double flat the sign ♯ or ♭ (or ♮♯ or ♮♭) changes the pitch of the note to that of a single sharp or flat.

After a double sharp or double flat the sign ♮ (rarely given ♮♮) restores the note to its normal pitch.

Any of these various signs is understood to affect not only the note before which it immediately occurs, but also, unless contradicted, any other notes on that same line or space of the staff throughout the measure (bar), and if the last note of the measure is thus inflected and is tied to the same note at the opening of the next measure, that latter also is understood to be included in the inflection.

Additions are made to the names of the notes as shown below.

Because of several irregularities in the Ger. names it has been thought best to set these out in full. Notice particularly the names marked *.

Inghelbrecht, Désiré (Émile) (b Paris, 1880; d Paris, 1965). Fr. conductor and composer. Cond. Swedish Ballet in Paris and London 1919–23. Ass. cond. Opéra-Comique 1924–5, cond. 1932. Ass. cond. Pasdeloup concerts 1928–32. Cond., Paris Opéra 1945–50. Founded Fr. Nat. Radio Orch. 1934, cond. 1934–44, 1951–8. Author of several books. Comp. opera, 4 ballets, choral, orch., chamber mus., and songs. *La Nursery* (1905–11) is 5 suites of pf. pieces for 4 hands for children, later orch. Wrote Kipling-based work, *Mowgli*, v., orch. (1946).

In Honour of the City. Cantata by *Dyson, setting of poem by William Dunbar (1465–1520), f.p. Lincoln 1928.

In Honour of the City of London. Cantata for ch. and orch. by *Walton, setting of poem by William Dunbar, f.p. Leeds 1937; f. London p. Dec. 1937, cond. Walton.

in modo di (It.). In the manner of.

innig (Ger.). Inmost, heartfelt. So the noun *Innigkeit*. Word frequently used by Eng. mus. critics to describe mystical or spiritual passages in the mus. of, for instance, Beethoven and Bruckner.

In nomine (In the name). A type of contrapuntal instr. comp. by 16th-cent. Eng. comps., usually for consort of viols but sometimes for lute or kbd. based on a version of a piece of plainchant. First used by *Taverner, when he comp. an instr. piece based on the theme to which he set the words 'In nomine Domini' in his *Gloria Tibi Trinitas* Mass. This set a fashion, and the name 'In nomine' was adopted for this type of piece. Several 20th-cent. composers have quoted *In Nomines* in their works, e.g. Maxwell Davies and R. Smalley.

Inoue, Michiyoshi (b Tokyo, 1946). Japanese conductor. Began career as ass. cond., Tokyo Metropolitan SO. Mus. dir. Japan PO from 1983, Kyoto SO from 1990. La Scala début 1971. Guest cond. of Eur. and Amer. orchs.

	♯	×	♭	♭♭	♮
English	sharp	double sharp	flat	double flat	natural
German	Cis	Cisis	Ces	Ceses	The sign is
	Dis	Disis	Des	Deses	called Quadrat
	Eis	Eisis	Es	Eses	or
	Fis	Fisis	Fes	Feses	*Auflösungszeich-*
	Gis	Gisis	Ges	Geses	*en* (release-sign)
	Ais	Aisis	As	Ases	
	*His	*Hisis	*B	*Bes	
	(The sign is called *Kreuz*)	(The sign is called *Doppelkreuz*)	(The sign is called *Be*)	(The sign is called *Doppel-Be*)	
French	dièse	double-dièse	bémol	double-bémol	bécarre
Italian	diesis	doppio diesis	bemolle	doppio bemolle	bequadro

Institut de recherche et de co-ordination acoustique-musique. Laboratories and elec. studios, part of the Georges Pompidou Centre, Paris, inaugurated 1977 under directorship of *Boulez, for experiment and research into modern compositional techniques. Known as IRCAM.

instrumentation. Writing of mus. for particular instrs., especially referring to composer's knowledge of what is practicable on various instrs. Also used in sense of *orchestration.

instruments, musical. Objects or devices for producing mus. sound by mechanical energy or electrical impulses. They can be classified as: (1) Str. (plucked or bowed). (2) Wind (played by blowing direct into the mouthpiece or through a reed). (3) Perc. (of determinate or indeterminate pitch). (4) Elec. Note that the pf., though it has str., is percussive in its mechanism, so is not easily classified. For the classifications of instr. by C. Sachs and E. M. von Hornbostel pubd. in 1914, see *aerophones, chordophones, idiophones,* and *membranophones,* with *electrophones* as additional category. For the Sachs–Hornbostel introduction to their classifications, see *New Grove*, Vol. 9, pp. 241–5.

intavolatura (It.). Entablature. Term denoting 'scoring' used in Elizabethan period. Referred to arr. of madrigals for kbd. perf.

Intégrales. Work for small orch. and perc. by *Varèse, comp. 1924–5, f.p. NY 1925.

Intendant (Ger.). Superintendent. Administrative dir. (not necessarily artistic or mus. dir.) of a Ger. opera house or th.

interlude. Piece of mus. played between other pieces, such as an org. passage played between verses of a hymn, or between the acts of a play, or between scenes in an opera (e.g. the *Sea Interludes* in Britten's *Peter Grimes*). Also used as a title of a mus. work without above connotations.

intermezzo (intermedio) (It.; Fr. *intermède*). In the middle. This word has undergone several changes in application, viz., (1) Originally, in 16th-cent. It., a mus. entertainment interpolated between sections of more serious fare, such as songs or madrigals, or between the acts of a play. Earliest recorded was at Florence 1539. In France, the *intermèdes* were sometimes on a sumptuous scale and sometimes comprised ballet only. Those by Lully for Molière's plays preceded or followed the comedy in addition to separating its acts and in some cases had nothing to do with the plot, e.g. the *Ballet des Nations* which concluded *Le bourgeois gentilhomme* (1670).

(2) With the development of *opera seria*, based invariably on mythological legends, the *intermezzo* became popular because of its contrasted, more realistic, and topical, often comic, characters. At the beginning of the 18th cent., comic characters were admitted into *opera seria* in scenes near the end of an act, thus forming a separate plot, an *intermezzo*. Most popular of these *intermezzi* was Pergolesi's *La serva padrona*

(The maid as mistress) (1733). From this form developed *opera buffa.

(3) By the 19th cent. the word had come to be applied in the same sense as *interlude; and for a short orch. piece inserted into an opera to denote a lapse of time, as in Mascagni's *Cavalleria Rusticana*, or summarizing events as in the 'Walk to the Paradise Garden' in Delius's *A Village Romeo and Juliet*.

(4) A short movt. in a sym., conc., or sonata, e.g. the slow movement of Schumann's pf. conc.

(5) Short independent pf. pieces by Brahms, Schumann, etc.

Intermezzo. 'Bourgeois comedy with symphonic interludes' in 2 acts by R. Strauss, comp. 1917–23 to his own lib. (based on a marital incident in his life, the two main characters being portraits of himself and his wife Pauline). Prod. Dresden 1924, Vienna 1927, NY (concert) 1963, Curtis Inst., Philadelphia (stage) 1977, Edinburgh 1965, Glyndebourne 1974.

Internationale. Socialist song composed by P. Degeyter (1848–1932) to words by Eugène Pottier, a Lisle woodworker. Was official anthem of Communist Russia until 1 Jan. 1944. Not the same as *The Red Flag*.

International Folk Music Council. Organization formed in London in 1947 at conference representing 28 countries. First pres. Vaughan Williams, succeeded 1958 by Maud *Karpeles. Devoted to int. research into folk mus., arranges fests., etc.

International Musical Society. Soc. devoted to musicological research, having about 20 nat. sections which combined for purposes of publication and conferences. Founded 1899 in Leipzig, terminated 1914 by World War I. Work carried on by *International Musicological Society.

International Musicological Society (International Society for Musical Research). Founded 1927 to resume and continue the work of the *International Musical Society. Headquarters at Basle. Publishes journal, *Acta Musicologica*.

International Society for Contemporary Music. Soc. founded after fest. by young Viennese composers in Salzburg in 1922, under first presidency of E. J. *Dent. Many nat. sections. Annual fest. held each year at a different place, at which the works of contemporary composers of all nationalities are given a hearing. Works to be played are chosen by int. jury. Known as ISCM.

interpretation in mus. is merely the act of perf., with the implication that in it the performer's judgement and personality have a share. Just as there is no means by which a dramatist can so write his play as to indicate to the actors precisely how they should speak his lines, so there is no means by which a composer can indicate to a performer the precise way in which his mus. is to be sung or played—so that no two performers will adopt the same slackenings and

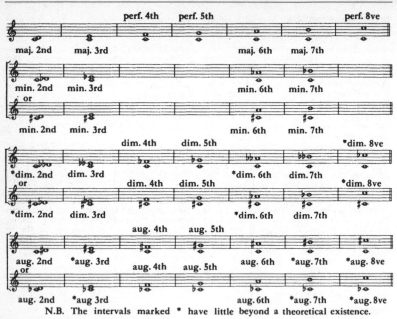

maj. 2nd   maj. 3rd   perf. 4th   perf. 5th   maj. 6th   maj. 7th   perf. 8ve

min. 2nd   min. 3rd   min. 6th   min. 7th
or
min. 2nd   min. 3rd   min. 6th   min. 7th

dim. 4th   dim. 5th   *dim. 8ve
*dim. 2nd   dim. 3rd   *dim. 6th   dim. 7th
or   dim. 4th   dim. 5th   *dim. 8ve
*dim. 2nd   dim. 3rd   *dim. 6th   dim. 7th

aug. 4th   aug. 5th
aug. 2nd   *aug. 3rd   aug. 6th   *aug. 7th   *aug. 8ve
or   aug. 4th   aug. 5th
aug. 2nd   *aug 3rd   aug. 6th   *aug. 7th   *aug. 8ve

N.B. The intervals marked * have little beyond a theoretical existence.

hastenings of speed (incl. *rubato*), the same degree of emphasis on an accented note, and so forth. The matter is further complicated by composers' latitude in use of metronome markings as applied to a term such as *allegro* or *moderato* (e.g. varying in one work from ♩ = 160 to ♩ = 100 for *allegro*). Thus there is no 'right' or 'wrong' interpretation in the strict sense, but in matters of style and taste, a performer's 'interpretation' may be felt by listeners to be out of sympathy with, or a distortion of, the composer's intentions.

interrupted cadence. Chord of the dominant followed by that of sub-mediant.

interval. (See examples above.) The 'distance' between 2 notes is called an 'interval', i.e. the difference in pitch between any 2 notes. The 'size' of any interval is expressed numerically, e.g. C to G is a 5th, because if we proceed up the scale of C the 5th note in it is G. The somewhat hollow-sounding 4th, 5th, and octave of the scale are all called *perfect*. They possess what we may perhaps call a 'purity' distinguishing them from other intervals. The other intervals, in the ascending major scale, are all called *major* ('major 2nd', 'major 3rd', 'major 6th', 'major 7th').

If any major interval be chromatically reduced by a semitone it becomes *minor*; if any perfect or minor interval be so reduced it becomes *diminished*; if any perfect or major interval be increased by a semitone it becomes *augmented*.

Enharmonic intervals are those which differ from each other in name but not in any other way (so far as modern kbd. instruments are concerned). As an example take C to G♯ (an augmented 5th) and C to A♭ (a minor 6th).

Compound intervals are those greater than an octave, e.g. C to the D an octave and a note higher, which may be spoken of either as a major 9th or as a compound major 2nd.

Inversion of intervals is the reversing of the relative position of the 2 notes defining them. It will be found that a 5th when inverted becomes a 4th, a 3rd becomes a 6th, and so on. It will also be found that perfect intervals remain perfect (C up to G a perfect 5th; G up to C a perfect 4th, etc.), while major ones become minor, minor become major, augmented become diminished, and diminished become augmented.

Every interval is either *concordant* or *discordant*. The concordant comprise all perfect intervals and all major and minor 3rds and 6ths; the discordant comprise all augmented and diminished intervals and all 2nds and 7ths. It therefore follows that all concordant intervals when inverted remain concordant and all discordant intervals remain discordant.

In the Faery Hills (*An Sluagh Sidhe*). Sym.-poem by Bax, comp. 1909, f.p. London 1910. The Faery Hills are in Co. Kerry, Ireland. One of 3 tone-poems comp. under the composite title *Eire*.

In the South (Alassio). Concert-ov. (tone-poem) by Elgar, Op.50, Comp. and f.p. London 1904. Sketched at Alassio, the work being an impression of It., its landscape and its imperial past.

In the Steppes of Central Asia (*V sredney Azii*, In Central Asia). 'Orchestral picture' by *Borodin, comp. 1880 to acc. *tableau vivant* at exhibition marking Alexander II's silver jubilee. Represents approach and passing of a caravan.

Intimate Letters (*Listy důvěrné*). Sub-title of Janáček's Str. Qt. No.2, comp. in 22 days 1928; so called because it is autobiographical in content, the letters concerned being those he wrote to Kamila Stoesslová between 1917 and 1928 (he wanted to call it 'Love Letters'). F.p. Brno 1928; f.p. in England 1936 (broadcast).

Intolleranza 1960 (Intolerance 1960). Opera in 2 parts for 5 singers, mime, ch., and orch. by *Nono to his own lib. based on an idea by A. M. Ripellino. The lib. is assembled from the writings of eight authors, incl. Brecht, Eluard, and Sartre. Comp. 1960–1. Prod. Venice 1961; Boston 1965.

intonation. (1) The opening phrase of a *plainsong melody, perhaps so called because it was often sung by the precentor alone, giving the pitch and (in the Psalms) the 'tone' of what was to follow.
(2) The act of singing or playing in tune. Thus we speak of a singer or instrumentalist's 'intonation' as being good or bad.

intoning. The singing upon one tone or note, as is done by the clergy in parts of the Roman, Anglican, and other liturgies.

intrada. The It. equivalent of the Fr. *entrée*. Used as name for a movt. by 18th-cent. composers and also in 20th cent. (e.g. in Vaughan Williams's *Concerto Grosso* and Janáček's *Glagolitic Mass*).

introduction. The beginning of a piece of mus., sometimes but not necessarily thematically linked to what follows (as in Elgar's *Introduction and Allegro for Strings*). Many syms., especially among those by Haydn, Mozart, and Beethoven, have extensive slow introductions to the first movt.

Introduction and Allegro. (1) Elgar's Op.47, for str. qt. and str. orch., comp. 1905 (theme sketch 1901) and f.p. London 1905. Contains melody inspired by hearing Welsh singers on a distant hillside.
(2) Schumann's *Introduction and Allegro* for pf., Op.143, also known as *Concert Allegro*, was comp. in 1853. His *Introduction and Allegro Appassionato* for pf. and orch., Op.92, was comp. in Dresden in 1849.
(3) *Bliss wrote an *Introduction and Allegro* for full orch. (1926).
(4) Ravel's Septet (1905) is entitled *Introduction and Allegro* for hp., fl., cl., str. qt.

Introit. Part of the Proper of the Mass. Initial chant, usually comprising antiphon with one verse and the Gloria patri. Also org. piece which replaces all or part of the sung Introit.

Invention. Name given by J. S. Bach to 15 of his shorter kbd. comps. in 2 parts or 'voices', in his *Klavierbüchlein*, 1720. They are highly contrapuntal, being largely in the nature of imitation. Each works out some short melodic motif. Bach also left another 15 comps. in the same style, now known as his '3-part Inventions', to which he gave the title 'Symphonies'. The term was used before Bach's day for short vocal or instrumental pieces by Dowland, Janequin, and Negri, among others. It has occasionally been revived in the 20th cent., e.g. by Blacher and Berg.

Inventionshorn, Inventionstrompete (Ger.). Invention horn, invention trumpet. The prefix 'inventions' has been used to characterize several novelties. The *Inventionshorn* was the work of Charles Clagget (1740–*c*.1795) who united 2 instr., one in D and the other in E♭, in such a way that the player had both at command and could thus gain the advantage of the full chromatic scale. Clagget's work, patented 1788, was made possible by the invention, by the hn. player Hampel of Dresden, of curved sliding crooks called 'inventions', hence the name. The term *Inventionstrompete* seems to have been applied not only to the tpt. equivalent of the *Inventionshorn* but also to 2 earlier novelties, a short horn in F with crooks for every key down to B♭, and the 'Italian trumpet' (coiled into horn shape).

inversion. Literally, the turning upside down of a chord, interval, counterpoint, theme, or pedal point. A chord is said to be inverted when not in its 'root position'. For inversion of intervals, see *interval*.

inversion, canon by. See *canon*.

inverted cadence. See *cadence*.

inverted mordent. See *mordent*.

inverted pedal. See *harmony*.

inverted turn. See *gruppetto*.

invertible counterpoint. See *counterpoint*.

Invisible City of Kitezh, The Legend of the (*Skazaniye o nevidimom grade Kitezhe i deve Fevronii*; The legend of the invisible city of Kitezh and of the Maiden Fevronia). Opera in 4 acts by Rimsky-Korsakov to lib. by V. Belsky. Comp. 1903–5. Prod. St Petersburg 1907; London (concert) 1926; Ann Arbor (concert) 1932, Philadelphia (stage) 1936; Edinburgh (stage) 1995.

Invitation to the Dance (*Aufforderung zum Tanz*). Title of Rondo Brillant in D♭, Op.65, for pf. by Weber (1819), representing a ballroom scene. Arr. for small orch. by *Lanner, *c*.1828. Often heard in arr. for orch. by Berlioz (1841), and sometimes, much altered, in one by Weingartner. Adopted by Diaghilev's Russian Ballet as mus. for *Le Spectre de la rose*.

In Windsor Forest. Cantata for ch. and orch. by Vaughan Williams containing 5 items adapted from his opera *Sir John in Love*. F.p. London 1931.

Iolanta (Tchaikovsky). See *Yolanta*.

Iolanthe, or The Peer and the Peri. Operetta in 2 acts by Sullivan to lib. by Gilbert. Prod. London and NY 1882.

Ionian mode. See *modes*.

Ionisation. Work for perc. instr. by *Varèse comp. 1929–31, f.p. NY, 1933.

Iphigénie en Aulide (Iphigenia in Aulis). Opera in 3 acts by Gluck to lib. by Du Roullet after Racine's play based on Euripides. Prod. Paris 1774; Oxford 1933; Philadelphia 1935. Gluck used three numbers from *Don Juan* in this score. Operas on same subject by Caldara (1718), Porpora (1735), Jommelli (1751), Sarti (1777), Soler (1779), Zingarelli (1787), and Cherubini (1788).

Iphigénie en Tauride (Iphigenia in Tauris). Opera in 4 acts by Gluck to lib. by Guillard after G. de la Touche's play based on Euripides. Prod. Paris 1778, London 1796, NY Met 1916 (in version by R. Strauss, 1889–90). Ger. version 1781. Also opera by Desmarets (1704), and Jommelli (1771), among others.

Ippolitov-Ivanov, Mikhail (Mikhaylovich) (*b* Gatchina, 1859; *d* Moscow, 1935). Russ. composer and conductor. Reputation est. with *Caucasian Sketches* for orch. 1894. Prof. of comp. and harmony, Moscow Cons. 1893–1935 (dir. 1905–22). Cond., Mamontov Opera, Moscow, 1898–1906, Bolshoy Opera from 1925. Wrote patriotic songs and marches such as *Song of Stalin*. Comp. 6 operas, the best of which (*The Last Barricade*, 1933–4) dealt with a Revolutionary subject. In 1925 orch. newly discovered St Basil scene in Mussorgsky's *Boris Godunov*; added 3 acts to Mussorgsky's unfinished opera *The Marriage* in 1931. Comp. sym., symphonic poem, 2 str. qts., vn. sonata, cantatas, songs, etc.

Iradier, Sebastián de. See *Yradier, Sebastián de*.

IRCAM. See *Institut de recherche et de co-ordination acoustique-musique*.

Ireland, John (Nicholson) (*b* Bowdon, Ches., 1879; *d* Washington, Sussex, 1962). Eng. composer and pianist. Org., St Luke's, Chelsea, 1904–26. Prof. of comp. RCM 1923–39, pupils incl. Britten, Bush, Moeran, Searle, and Arnell. He made his reputation with chamber mus. and with pieces for pf. solo in which his understanding of the instr. is paramount. His songs are in the best Eng. tradition and are typical of Ireland's style, which nevertheless owes more to French influences than to English and has an individual restraint and austerity which is highly attractive. He did not compose syms. or large-scale choral works, but his orch. tone-poems and ovs. are colourfully scored and his pf. conc., with its racy jazz interludes, is among the best in the genre by an Eng. composer. Prin. works:

ORCH.: *Tritons*, symphonic prelude (1899); *Orchestral Poem in A minor* (1904); *The *Forgotten Rite*, prelude (1913); *Bagatelle* (orig. for vn., pf. 1911, arr. orch. 1916); *Mai-Dun*, symphonic rhapsody (1920–1); pf. conc. in E♭ (1930); *Downland Suite*, str. (1932); *Legend*, pf., orch. (1933); *A London Overture* (reworking of *Comedy Overture*, brass, 1936); arr. brass, unpubd., no date); *Concertino Pastorale*, str. (1939); *The Holy Boy*, orig. pf. prelude (1913), str. (1941); *Epic March* (1941–2); *Satyricon*, ov. (1944–6); *The Overlanders*, suite (1965, arr. Mackerrras from film mus. 1946–7).

CHORUS & ORCH.: *Vexilla Regis* (1898); *Greater Love Hath No Man*, motet (1911, orch. 1922); *These Things Shall Be*, cantata, bar. (or ten.), ch., orch. (1936–7); *Man in his labour rejoiceth*, ch., brass band (1947).

BRASS BAND: *A Downland Suite* (1932); *Comedy Overture* (1934, re-worked as *A London Overture* 1936, arr. for wind band 1986); *Maritime Overture* (1944); *The Holy Boy* (orig. pf. prelude 1913), arr. by Robert E. Stepp (1950).

VOICES: *Te Deum* in F, ch., org. (1907); *Greater Love Hath No Man* (sometimes called *Many Waters cannot quench Love*), motet, treble, bar., ch., org. (1911, with orch. 1922); *Jubilate* in F, ch., org. (1914); *An Island Hymn*, male vv. (1915, rev. as *Island Praise*, 1955); *They Told Me, Heraclitus*, unacc. male vv. (1924); *New Prince, New Pomp*, carol, unacc. male vv. (1927); *The *Holy Boy*, unacc. carol (orig. pf. prelude 1913–15), arr. vv. (1941); *Adam Lay Ybounden*, unacc. carol (1956); *Island Praise*, unacc. male vv. (1955, rev. of *An Island Hymn*, 1915).

CHAMBER MUSIC: sextet, cl., hn., str. qt. (1898); str. qts.; No.1 in D minor (1897), No.2 in C minor (1897); *Cavatina*, vn., pf. (1904); *Phantasy Trio* in A minor (1908); vn. sonata No.1 in D minor (1908–9, rev. 1917), No.2 in A minor (1915–17); Bagatelle, vn., pf. (1911, arr. orch. by L. Bridgewater, 1916); pf. trio in E (1917); vc. sonata in G minor (1923, arr. for va. by *Tertis, 1941); pf. trio in E minor (1938, based on unpubd. trio of 1912–13); *Fantasy Sonata*, cl., pf. (1943); *The Holy Boy* (orig. pf. prelude, 1913), arr. vc., pf. (1919), va. (by L. Tertis, 1925), str. qt. (1941), fl., pf. (by J. Galway, 1987).

SONGS & SONG-CYCLES: 5 *Songs of a Wayfarer* (c.1905–11); *Marigold* (1913); *Sea Fever* (1913); *I Have Twelve Oxen* (1918); *If there were Dreams to sell* (1918); *The *Land of Lost Content* (6 Housman poems) (1920–1); *The Vagabond* (1922); *When I am dead, my dearest* (1924, arr. v., str. qt. 1924); 3 *Hardy Songs*, v., pf. (1925); 5 *Poems by Thomas Hardy*, bar., pf. (1926); *We'll To The Woods No More* (3 Housman poems), v., pf. (1926–7); 6 *Songs Sacred and Profane*, v., pf. (1929–31); *The Holy Boy* (orig. pf. piece, 1913, arr. as song to poem by Herbert S. Brown 1938); *Five 16th Century Poems*, v., pf. (1938).

PIANO: *Decorations* (3 pieces incl. *The Island Spell*) (1912–13); 3 *Dances* (1913); 4 *Preludes* (No.3 is *The Holy Boy*) (1913–15); *Rhapsody* (1915); 3 *London*

Pieces (No.1 is *Chelsea Reach*) (1917–20); *Merry Andrew* (1918); *The Towing-Path* (1918); Sonata in E minor-major (1918–20, rev. 1951); *Summer Evening* (1919); *The Darkened Valley* (1920); 2 *Pieces* (*For Remembrance* and **Amberley Wild Brooks*) (1921); *On a Birthday Morning* (1922); *Equinox* (1922); *Prelude* in E♭ (1924); 2 *Pieces* (1925); sonatina (1926–7); *Ballade of London Nights* (c.1929, pubd. 1968); *Indian Summer* (1932); *Green Ways* (3 *Lyric Pieces*) (1937); **Sarnia: An Island Sequence* (3 pieces) (1940–1); 3 *Pastels* (1941); *Columbine* (1949).

ORGAN: *Intrada* (1904); *Villanella* (1904, arr. for orch. by L. Bridgewater 1941 and by R. Binge 1949); *Menuetto-Impromptu* (1904); *Marcia popolare* (1904); *Alla marcia* (1911); *Capriccio* (1911); *Sursum corda* (1911); *The Holy Boy*, orig. pf. prelude 1913 (1919).

Iris. Opera in 3 acts by Mascagni, to lib. by Illica. Prod. Rome 1898; rev. version Milan 1899, Philadelphia 1902, London 1919, Wexford 1995.

Irische Legende (Irish Legend). Opera in 5 scenes by **Egk to his own lib. based on Yeats's *The Countess Cathleen* (1892). Prod. Salzburg 1955. (Rev. 1970).

Irish Symphony. (1) Sub-title of Stanford's Sym. No.3 in F minor, Op.28, comp. 1887.

(2) Title of sym. by **Harty, based on Irish folksongs; popular scherzo 'The Fair Day' often played separately. Comp. 1904, rev. 1915 and 1923.

(3) Title of sym. in E minor by Sullivan, 1864–6.

Irmelin. Opera in 3 acts by Delius to his own lib. Comp. 1890–2, prod. Oxford 1953. The *Irmelin*

Prelude (1931) is an independent orch. comp. based on themes from the preludes to Acts 1 and 3 of the opera.

irregular cadence. See *cadence*.

irregular rhythmic groupings. Various combinations are possible other than those shown below, and it is hardly possible to list them or to lay down rules. When an irregular combination occurs the performer should observe the other notes of the measure, and he will quickly realize into what fraction of the measure the irregular grouping is to be fitted.

Irving, (Kelville) **Ernest** (*b* Godalming, 1878; *d* Ealing, 1953). Eng. conductor, particularly of theatre and film music. Cond. at nearly all London th. between 1900 and 1940. Mus. dir., Ealing film studios 1935–53, engaging several leading Brit. composers to write film mus. Expert on chess.

Irving, Robert (Augustine) (*b* Winchester, 1913; *d* Winchester, 1991). Eng. conductor. Répétiteur at CG 1936 and mus. master of Winchester Coll. Ass. cond. BBC Scottish Orch. 1945–8, mus. dir. SW (later Royal) Ballet 1949–58, NY City Ballet from 1958 (cond. them at Salzburg Fest. 1965).

Isaac [Isaak], **Heinrich** (*b* Brabant, c.1450; *d* Florence, 1517). Flemish composer. From 1485 to 1493 in service of Lorenzo de' Medici at Florence as org., choirmaster, and teacher of his children. Court composer at Innsbruck 1500–1. Returned to Florence 1502 and also served at Ferrara. Comp. much church mus. (36 masses), and many secular songs. Motets pubd. in 3 vols. as *Choralis*

Duplet or Couplet	Two in the time of three:
Triplet (see also under 'Sextolet' below)	Three in the time of two:
Quadruplet	Four in the time of three:
Quintuplet	Five in the time of four —or of three:
Sextolet or Sextuplet (and Double Triplet)	Six in the time of four: (really a triplet) If a grouping of 3+3 is desired it should be written as below: (really a double triplet)
Septolet, or Septuplet, or Septimole	Seven in the time of four —or of six:

Constantinus (1550). Modern complete edn. of his works, ed. F. Lerner, begun in 1974. Regarded as one of major figures of the *Desprès era.

Isaacs, (Sir) **Jeremy** (*b* Glasgow, 1932). Eng. opera administrator and television director. Granada TV prod. 1958–65, with BBC 1965–8. Controller of features, Thames TV 1968–74, dir. of progs. 1974–8. Chief Exec., Channel 4, 1981–7. Gen. dir. ROH, CG, 1988–97. Knighted 1996.

ISCM. *International Society for Contemporary Music.

Isepp, Martin (Johannes Sebastian) (*b* Vienna, 1930). Austrian-born Eng. pianist and harpsichordist, son of singing-teacher Hélène Isepp. Worked with EOG in 1950s. On staff Glyndebourne Opera 1957–93 (chief coach 1973–8, head of mus. staff 1978–93). Head of opera training, Juilliard Sch. 1973–7; head of mus. studies, Nat. Opera Studio from 1978. Assoc. with opera training schools in Banff, Alberta, and Ischia. Acc. to several leading singers. Has cond. Mozart operas at NY Met, Glyndebourne, and with GTO.

Ishikawa, Shizuka (*b* Tokyo, 1954). Japanese violinist. She won 2nd prize in Wieniawski int. comp. 1972 and silver medal, Queen Elisabeth comp., Brussels, 1976. Soloist at many fests. and with leading orchs.

Islamey. Oriental fantasy for pf. by *Balakirev, 1st version, comp, 1869, 2nd version, comp. 1902. Orch. by Casella 1907.

Isle joyeuse, L' (The Island of Joy). Pf. piece by Debussy comp. 1904 and inspired by one of Watteau's 2 pictures, *L'Embarquement pour Cythère*, which delicately depicted early 18th-cent. scene of party about to embark for the island sacred to Venus.

Isle of the Dead, The (*Ostrov myortvykh*). Symphonic poem Op.29 by Rachmaninov, comp. 1909 and inspired by Böcklin's painting of that name (*Insel der Toten*). F.p. Moscow 1909.

ISM. *Incorporated Society of Musicians (Brit).

Isokoski, Soile (*b* Posio, Finland, 1957). Finnish soprano. Studied at Sibelius Acad., Helsinki. Solo début 1986. 2nd prize in Cardiff Singer of the World 1987. Won Elly Ameling comp. 1988, Tokyo int. comp. 1990. Noted interpreter of Sibelius and Strauss songs. Opera roles incl. Mozart Countess and Fiordiligi, Strauss Countess and Marschallin, Marguerite, Desdemona, Eva, Donna Anna.

Isola disabitata, L' (The Deserted Island). (1) Opera (*azione teatrale*) in 2 parts by Haydn to lib. by Metastasio. Comp. 1779, rev. 1802. Prod. Eszterháza 1779, Washington DC 1936, Wexford 1982.
(2) Opera in 3 acts by G. Scarlatti to lib. by Goldoni. Prod. Venice 1757.

isometric (from Gr. *isos*, equal). Having the same rhythm in every v. or part (i.e. proceeding in chords rather than in freely moving counterpoint).

isorhythm (from Gr. *isos*, equal). Term coined in 1904 by F. Ludwig to describe the principle found in medieval mus., *c*.1300–1450, whereby the same rhythmic pattern recurs in successive repetitions of the melody. It was usually applied to the ten. part of a motet which would consist of a short repeated rhythmic pattern; the melody in the ten. part was also often repeated but not in synchronization with the rhythmic repetition. Rhythmic repetition was known as *talea*, melodic as *color*. In the mus. of Machaut and de Vitry, the rhythmic pattern was not repeated in the same note values but in proportional diminution, e.g. original values were halved or reduced by a third. Eng. composers at the end of the 14th cent. developed isorhythm in all vv., so that it took two appearances of the *talea* to accommodate one of the *color*.

Isouard, Nicoló (*b* Valletta, Malta, 1775; *d* Paris, 1818). Maltese composer of Fr. origin, known sometimes as Nicoló or Nicolo de Malta. First opera prod. Florence 1794. Returned to Paris 1799, becoming popular opera composer in rivalry to Boieldieu. Of over 35 operas prod. in 16 years, the best was *Cendrillon* (1810), but also set *Il barbiere di Siviglia* (*c*.1796) and *Joconde* (1814). Comp. sacred works, airs, and romances.

Israel in Egypt. Oratorio by Handel, to Biblical text probably compiled by him. Comp. 1738, f.p. London 1739. Famous for its superb double choruses. The ch. *Egypt was glad* was borrowed, unacknowledged, from a canzona by *Kerll—indeed, up to a third of the music was taken from other composers.

Israel Philharmonic Orchestra. Formerly known as Palestine SO, founded in 1936 by *Huberman. Toscanini cond. first concert, December 1936. Since 1951 has made frequent tours. Chief conds. have incl. Jean Martinon, Paul Kletzki and, since 1968, Zubin Mehta, but many guest conds., notably Bernstein. Salzburg Fest. début 1971 (cond. Mehta). Based in Tel Aviv.

Israel Symphony. For 2 sop., 2 cont., bass, and orch. by Bloch. Comp. 1912–16; f.p. NY 1916.

Isserlis, Steven (*b* London, 1958). Eng. cellist. Début London 1977. Quickly est. as one of leading cellists, with acclaimed recordings of Elgar conc., Britten Cello Sym., Tchaikovsky *Rococo Variations* (orig. vers.), and Bloch *Schelomo*. Gave f.p. of Tavener's *The Protecting Veil*, 1989. CBE 1998.

Istel, Edgar (*b* Mainz, 1880; *d* Miami, 1948). Ger. composer and musicologist. Writer and teacher in Munich 1900–13; lect. in Berlin 1913–19; worked in Sp. 1920–36, leaving there for Eng. and then (1938) USA. Comp. 5 operas and choral works; author of several books on Wagner, also on Cornelius, Paganini, comic opera, etc.

istesso (It.). Same. Used in such connections as *l'istesso tempo*, 'The same speed'—usually meaning that, though the nominal value of the beat has changed, its actual time duration is to remain the same: for instance, the former beat may have been (say in 4 time) and the new one (say in 6 time) and these are to have the same time value.

Istomin, Eugene (George) (*b* NY, 1925; *d* Washington, DC, 2003). Amer. pianist of Russ. parentage. Won Leventritt Award 1943. Début with Philadelphia Orch., 1943. Prades Fest. with Casals 1950. Founded pf. trio with Isaac Stern and Leonard Rose, 1961.

istrumento d'acciaio (It.). Instrument of steel. Mozart's name for his *glockenspiel in Die Zauberflöte.

Italiana in Algeri, L' (The Italian girl in Algiers). Comic opera in 2 acts by Rossini to lib. derived from Anelli's lib. for Mosca's opera of same name (1808). Prod. Venice 1813, London 1819, NY 1832.

Italian Caprice. Orch. work by Tchaikovsky, Op.45, comp. 1880, often known by mixed It.-Fr. title *Capriccio italien*.

Italian Concerto. Instr. comp. by Bach for solo hpd. with 2 manuals, pubd. in 2nd section of *Klavierübung, 1735. He seems to have used the term to draw attention to the facts that there are (a) passages of alternation and contrast, and (b) 3 movts., so resembling the It. *concerto grosso*.

Italian Girl in Algiers, The (Rossini). See *Italiana in Algeri, L'*.

Italian Serenade (*Italienische Serenade*). Work for str. qt. by Wolf, 1887. Later arr. for orch. (1892) and ed. Reger.

Italian sixth. See *augmented intervals*.

Italian Song-book (Wolf). See *Italienisches Liederbuch*.

Italian Symphony. Title given by Mendelssohn to his Sym. No.4 in A major, Op.90. Begun in It. 1830-1 and completed 1833 but not pubd. until 1847 (it was his 3rd sym. in order of comp.). F.p. London 1833.

Italienisches Liederbuch (Italian Songbook). 46 songs for v. and pf. by *Wolf, all being settings of poems trans. from the It. by Paul von Heyse (1830-1914) and pubd. in 1860 under title *Italienisches Liederbuch*. Wolf's songs were comp. in 2 parts, Book I of 22 songs 1890-1, Book 2 of 24 songs in 1896. Some were later orch. by Wolf, others by Reger.

Iturbi, José (*b* Valencia, 1895; *d* Los Angeles, 1980). Sp. pianist and conductor. Head of pf. dept., Geneva Cons. 1919-23. London début 1923, Philadelphia 1928. Began active cond. career 1933 in Mexico City and NY. Mus. dir. Rochester PO 1935-44. Appeared in several films.

Ivan IV. Correct name of opera in 4 (orig. 5) acts by Bizet to lib. by F. H. Leroy and H. Trianon orig. written for Gounod. Comp. ?1862-3, rev. 1864-5. Efforts to have it prod. having failed, Bizet withdrew it. Incomplete MS of score passed to Paris

Cons. in 1929. Private stage perf. of this version was given at Mühringen Castle, Württemberg, 1946 under title *Ivan le Terrible*. Completed and rev. (reduced to 4 acts) by Henri Busser, perf. Bordeaux 12 Oct. 1951, Cologne 1952, Liverpool 1955. Bizet used portions of score in other works. Perf. of orig. version broadcast by BBC 1975.

Ivanhoe. (1) Opera in 3 acts by Sullivan (his only 'grand opera') to lib. by J. Sturgis after Scott's novel (1819). Comp. 1890. Prod. London 1891 (run of 160 perfs.); Berlin 1895; Boston 1991.
(2) *Pasticcio* by Rossini, Paris 1826, CG 1829, NY 1832, rev. Mont Pellier 1990.

Ivan Susanin. Orig. title of Glinka's opera *A *Life for the Tsar* by which it became known in Communist and some other countries.

Ivan the Terrible (Rimsky-Korsakov). See *Maid of Pskov, The*.

Ives, Charles (Edward) (*b* Danbury, Conn., 1874; *d* NY, 1954). Amer. composer, one of the most extraordinary and individual figures in the history of Western music. In his works, many of the innovatory and radical procedures adopted by younger *avant-garde* composers are anticipated or foreshadowed in some degree. His father was a town bandmaster who experimented with tone clusters, polytonality, quartertones, and acoustics, inspiring similar interests in his son. What fascinated George Ives, and later his son, was the clash of rhythm and tone resulting from two bands playing different tunes at a parade, or from his wife whistling at her housework and a boy elsewhere practising the pf. He would make Charles sing in a key different from the acc. 'to stretch our ears'.

At 14 Charles became organist at Danbury Baptist Church, composing in 1891 his *Variations on 'America'*. He entered Yale Univ. in 1894, studying org. with Dudley Buck and comp. with Horatio Parker (with whose conventional outlook Ives soon grew weary). Ives wrote his first sym. while at Yale, played the org. at Centre Church on the Green, and tried out some of his comps. on the local th. orch. In 1898 he graduated and moved to NY as a clerk in an insurance co., taking up several organist posts. In 1907 he and a friend formed their own insurance agency, which became very successful. Ives divided his time between business and mus., working long hours and damaging his health. He worked on a 2nd Sym. from 1900 to 1902 and a 3rd from 1904-11. Mahler was interested in this latter work but died before he could conduct it. From 1910 to 1918 Ives was at his most prolific, working on several comps. simultaneously. In 1918 he was seriously ill, sustaining cardiac damage; he gradually reduced his business activities, retiring in 1930, and he comp. little new after 1917, devoting the rest of his life to revising his comps. and thereby contributing to the chaotic state of his MSS, which led to untold difficulties in perf. He planned a *Universe Symphony* in which several different orchs., with huge choirs, were to be stationed in valleys, and on top of mountains.

In 1919 Ives decided to publish some of his mus., without copyright or performing rights. The vast *Concord Sonata* and 114 songs were issued in this way. The first perf. in NY of orch. mus. by Ives was in Jan. 1927 when Eugene Goossens cond. the 2nd movt. of the 4th Sym. It was a failure. However, Ives's mus. was beginning to attract champions, among them the lecturer Henry Bellamann, the French pianist Robert Schmitz, and the composers and conds. Henry *Cowell, Wallingford *Riegger, Carl *Ruggles, Nicolas *Slonimsky and, later, Bernard *Herrmann and Lou *Harrison. Slonimsky bravely cond. perfs. of *Three Places in New England* in Boston, NY, and Los Angeles between 1930 and 1932 and later cond. Ives works in Europe. Slonimsky also made the first Ives recording (1934) and Herrmann cond. the first Ives broadcast (1933). The pianist John Kirkpatrick devoted nearly 10 years to mastering the complexities of the *Concord Sonata* in consultation with Ives and played it in NY and elsewhere in 1939, arousing considerable enthusiasm. (It was f.p. in New Orleans in 1920.) In 1947 the 3rd Sym., perf. in NY that year, won the Pulitzer Prize, to Ives's dismay (he gave the prize money away). The 4th Sym. was not heard in its entirety until 11 years after Ives's death, when Stokowski cond. it in NY on 26 Apr. 1965.

Ives's mus. is sometimes called primitive but is in fact highly sophisticated. It is, like it or not, entirely honest mus., the outpouring of its stubborn and unusual creator, who delighted in pointing out that he had written most of his works before those by Stravinsky and Hindemith which some critics claimed had influenced him. The juxtaposition of incongruous elements, derived from the Danbury bands, occurs even in his earliest works. His *Psalm 67* of 1893 is in 2 keys throughout. Even in the Dvořákian 1st Sym. the use of tonality is remarkably free and unconventional. Jazz is drawn upon in his first pf. sonata; in the psalm settings for choir of 1896–1900 occur whole-tone scales, a 12-note row, tone clusters, polytonality, and polyrhythms. Aleatory procedures are anticipated in *The Unanswered Question* where the cond. is told to cue in various parts at will. In several of the orch. works the memory of the 2 bands playing different marches in different keys and tempi is vividly re-created. He 'borrowed' consistently from popular sources such as songs and hymns, or from other composers—over 170 such sources have been positively identified by scholars. Prin. works:

ORCH.: sym., No.1 in D minor (1895–8), No.2 (1900–2, some sketches earlier), No.3 (*The Camp Meeting*) (1904–11), No.4 (1910–16, with ch. in finale); *Variations on 'America'* (orch. arr. by W. Schuman) (dates of comp. of the syms. are approximate, since Ives himself said he was not sure when he wrote them); *New England Holidays (sometimes called Holidays Symphony)*: 1. *Washington's Birthday*. 2. *Decoration Day*. 3. *Fourth of July*. 4. *Thanksgiving and/or Forefathers' Day* (with ch.) (1904–13); *The *Unanswered Question* (1906, rev. c.1932); *Over the Pavements* (1906); *Central Park in the Dark in the

Good Old Summertime (1906); *Set* for th. or chamber orch. (1906–11); *Robert Browning Overture* (1908–12); *Orchestral Set No.1 (*Three Places in New England*) (1908–14); *Orchestral Set No.2 (1909–15); *The Gong on the Hook and Ladder (or Firemen's Parade on Main Street)* (1911); *Tone Roads No.1 (1911), No.3 (1915); *Universe Symphony* (incomplete, 1911–16); *Rainbow* (1914, as song 1921); *Hymn* (arr. for orch. 1921); *Orchestral Set. No.3* (1919–27); *Largo Cantabile* (1921).

CHORAL: *Easter Carol*, ch., orch. (1892); *The Circus Band*, bass, ch., orch. (1894); *Psalm 54* (c.1896), *Psalm 150*, unacc. ch., orch., and org. or orch. (1896), *Psalm 90*, sop., ten., ch., orch. (1896–1901, 1923–4); *Psalm 14* (c.1897), *Psalm 25* (c.1897), *Psalm 67* (1898), *Psalm 100* (c.1898), *Psalm 135* (c.1899), 3 *Harvest Home Chorales*, ch., orch. or ch., brass, org. (c.1898–1912); *The Celestial Country*, cantata (1899); *On The Antipodes* (1904), ch., orch. 1915, v., pf. 1923; *Serenity*, ch., orch. (1909), v., pf. (1919); *The New River*, ch., orch. (1911, rev. 1913 and ?1921); *Duty*, ch., orch. (c.1912); *Lincoln The Great Commoner*, ch., orch. (1912), v., pf. (1914); *Vita*, ch., orch. or org. (1912), v., pf. (1921); *December*, ch., orch. (1912–13); *Walt Whitman*, ch., orch. (1913), v., pf. (1921); *General William Booth Enters Into Heaven*, bass, ch., orch. (also v., pf.) (1914); *Majority*, ch., orch. (1914–15), v., pf. (1921); *An Election, or Nov.2, 1920*, male vv. or unison ch., orch. (1920), v., pf. (1921).

CHAMBER MUSIC (incl. v. and chamber ens.): *Song for Harvest Season*, mez., brass quintet (c.1893); str. qt. No.1 (*A Revival Service*) (1896), No.2 (1907–13); *The Children's Hour*, mez., ch., orch. (1901); *From the Steeples and the Mountains*, brass quintet (1901); *Largo*, vn., cl., pf. (1901); vn. sonata No.1 (1903–8), No.2 (1903–10), No.3 (1902–14), No.4 (1892–1906, 1914–15); pf. trio (1904–11); *Chromatimelodtune*, brass qt., pf. (1909, 1913, 1919); *The Indians*, mez., chamber orch. (1912), v., pf. (1921).

PIANO: over 20 *Studies* for pf., incl. Nos. 2, 5, 6, 7, 8, and 9 (*The Anti-Abolitionist Riots*), Nos. 15, 18, 20, 21 (*Some South-Paw Pitching*), No.22 (*Twenty-Two*), and No.23 (*Baseball Take-off*) (1907–9); 5 *Take-Offs* (*Seen and Unseen, Rough and Ready, Song without (good) Words, Scene Episode, Bad Resolutions and Good*) (1906–7); sonata No.1 (1901–9), No.2 (*Concord, Mass. 1840–1860*) with solos for va. and fl. (1911–15); *3-Page Sonata* (1905); 6 *Protests* (*Varied Air and Variations*) (1916); 3 *Quarter-Tone Piano Pieces* for 2 pf. (1923–4); *Celestial Railroad*, arr. from 2nd movt. of 4th Sym. (c.1924).

ORGAN: *Variations on a National Hymn, 'America'* (c.1891, also arr. for orch. by W. Schuman); *Prelude, Adeste Fideles* (1897).

SONGS: pubd. in the following colls.: 3 *Songs*; 4 *Songs*; 7 *Songs*; 9 *Songs*; 10 *Songs*; 11 *Songs and 2 Harmonizations*; 12 *Songs*; 13 *Songs*; 14 *Songs*; 19 *Songs*; 34 *Songs*; *Sacred Songs*.

Ivogün, Maria [Kempner, Ilse] (*b* Budapest, 1891; *d* Beatenberg, Switz., 1987). Hung. soprano. Début Munich 1913 (Mimì in *La bohème*). Member of Munich Opera 1913–25. Created Ighino in Pfitzner's

Palestrina, Munich 1917 (her husband, Karl *Erb, created the title-role). CG début 1924 (Zerbinetta in *Ariadne auf Naxos*, a role in which Strauss described her as 'without rival'), Berlin Municipal Opera 1925–34. Salzburg Fest. début 1925. Devoted herself to teaching after retirement.

Iwaki, Hiroyuki (*b* Tokyo, 1932; *d* Tokyo, 2006). Japanese conductor. Ass. cond. NKH (Japanese radio) SO 1954–65. Mus. dir. Fujiwara Opera Co. 1965–7. Guest cond. Hamburg, Vienna, and Berlin 1966–9. Mus. dir. NKH SO from 1969. Cond., Melbourne SO 1974–89, Kanazawa SO from 1988.

J

jabo (or **jaleo**) (Sp., in old Sp. *xabo*, or *xaleo*). A solo dance in a slow triple rhythm.

jack. See *harpsichord*.

Jackson, Francis (Alan) (*b* Malton, 1917). Eng. organist, composer, and conductor. Org., Malton church 1933–40; org. and master of the mus., York Minster 1946–82. Frequent recitalist. Comps. incl. monodramas (spkr., ch., and orch.); org. sonatas; *Variations on a Theme by Vaughan Williams*; sym. in D minor (orch.); and numerous org. pieces, anthems, canticles, etc. OBE 1978.

Jackson, Richard (*b* Cornwall, 1960). Eng. baritone. Founder-member of *Songmakers' Almanac. Concert repertoire incl. Bach, Handel, Monteverdi, and Elgar. Has sung with GTO, Kent Opera, and Handel Opera Soc.

Jacob, Gordon (Percival Septimus) (*b* London, 1895; *d* Saffron Walden, 1984). Eng. composer, teacher, and conductor. On staff RCM as prof. of theory, comp., and orchestration 1926–66. Author of textbooks on orchestration and its technique. Transcr. for full orch. and brass band Vaughan Williams's *English Folk-Song Suite*, orig. for military band, and for full orch. his *Variations* for brass band. Comps. incl. 2 syms. (1929, 1944), sinfonietta (1942), 2 va. concs. (1925, 1979), 2 pf. concs. (1927, 1957), bn. conc. (1947), hn. conc. (1951), vn. conc. (1953), 2 ob. concs. (1933, 1956), cl. conc. (1980), ballets, and numerous arrs. CBE 1968.

Jacobi, Frederick (*b* San Francisco, 1891; *d* NY, 1952). Amer. composer, conductor, and pianist. Ass. cond. NY Met 1913–17. Studied mus. of Pueblo Indians, living among them in New Mexico and Arizona. Indian themes and Jewish liturgical mus. are the main influences on his works. Taught at Juilliard Sch. 1936–50. Comp. opera *The Prodigal Son* (1943–4), 2 syms., *Indian Dances* for orch., *Sabbath Evening Service*, *Ode to Zion*, vc. conc., pf. conc., vn. conc., 3 str. qts., pf. pieces, songs.

Jacobin, The (*Jakobín*). Opera in 3 acts by Dvořák to lib. by M. Červinková-Riegrová. Comp. 1887–8, rev. 1897. Prod. Prague 1889 (rev. vers. Prague 1898); London 1947, Manchester and Cardiff 1980 (f. prof. Brit. ps., jointly RNCM and WNO); Washington 1979.

Jacobs, Arthur (David) (*b* Manchester, 1922; *d* Oxford, 1996). Eng. music critic, editor, and translator. Mus. critic *Daily Express* 1947–52, then freelance critic for var. newspapers. Deputy ed. *Opera* magazine 1962–71; ed. *British Music Yearbook* 1971–80; ed. *A New Dictionary of Music* (1958, rev. 1967, 1973, and as *New Penguin Dictionary of Music*, 1978); *Choral Music* symposium 1963; *Pan Book of Opera* (with S. Sadie, 1966, rev. 1984); *Penguin Dictionary of Musical Performers*, 1990. Wrote *A Short History of Western Music* (1972), *Arthur Sullivan, a Victorian Musician* (1984, 2nd edn. 1992), biography of Sir Henry Wood (1994), and contrib. to many other books and publications. Librettist of *Maw's *One-Man Show* (1964) and trans. over 20 opera libs. Lect. in mus. history, etc., at RAM 1964–79. Head of mus. dept., Huddersfield Polytechnic, 1979–85 (prof. from 1984). Visiting lect. to several Amer. univs.

Jacobs, Paul (*b* NY, 1930; *d* NY, 1983). Amer. pianist and harpsichordist. Specialized in Baroque mus. on hpd. and *avant-garde* works on pf. Worked in Eur. 1951–60. Gave recital of all Schoenberg's pf. works in Paris. Pianist and harpsichordist to NY Philharmonic Soc., 1962–74. Taught at Brooklyn Coll. and Manhattan Sch. of Mus., NY.

Jacobs, René (*b* Ghent, 1946). Belg. countertenor, conductor, and editor. Sang with early mus. ens. such as Leonhardt Consort and La Petite Bande. Formed own ens., Collegium Vocale. Cond. Cavalli's *Giasone* in own edn., Innsbruck Fest. 1988. Salzburg Fest. début 1993, cond. Monteverdi's *L'Orfeo* in his own edn.

Jacques, Reginald (*b* Ashby-de-la-Zouch, 1894; *d* Stowmarket, 1969). Eng. conductor and composer. Org., Queen's Coll., Oxford. Cond. Oxford Harmonic Soc. 1923–30, Oxford Orch. Soc. 1930–6, London Bach Choir 1932–60. First mus. dir. of CEMA (later Arts Council) 1940–5. Founded Jacques Orch. 1936, remaining cond. Author of books on school mus. and v. training. CBE 1954.

Jadlowker, Hermann (*b* Riga, 1877; *d* Tel Aviv, 1953). Latvian tenor. Début Cologne 1897 (Gomez in Kreutzer's *Das Nachtlager in Granada*). After singing in Stettin and Riga, sang with Karlsruhe Opera 1906–10 and at Kroll Opera from 1907. Berlin Court Opera 1909. NY Met 1910–12. Created Bacchus in *Ariadne auf Naxos* (Stuttgart 1912). Berlin State Opera 1922–3. Returned to Riga as chief cantor of synagogue 1929–38 and taught at Riga Cons. 1936–8. Emigrated to Palestine 1938 and taught in Tel Aviv.

Jaeger, August (Johannes) (*b* Düsseldorf, 1860; *d* London, 1909). Ger. musician who settled in Eng. in 1878, working for printer of maps in the Strand, London. Joined staff of mus. publishers, Novello, in 1890, becoming head of publishing office. Was responsible for seeing works by Novello composers into print, especially those by Elgar, whose greatness he recognized. Became intimate friend of Elgar, their correspondence having since been pubd. Immortalized in Elgar's *Enigma Variations* as 'Nimrod' (Nimrod in the

Bible was a hunter; *Jäger* = hunter in Ger.). To say, as is sometimes committed to print, that he was 'Elgar's publisher' is inaccurate.

Jahn, Otto (*b* Kiel, 1813; *d* Göttingen, 1869). Ger. archaeologist, philologist, and writer on music. Held professorial posts in archaeology and philology in Greifswald, Leipzig, and Bonn. Author of *Life of Mozart* (1st edn., 4 vols. Leipzig 1856–9, 2nd edn., 2 vols. 1867; 3rd edn. 1889–91, and 4th edn. 1905–7, both prepared by Herman Deiters; 5th edn. 1919–21, rev. by Herman Abert; 6th edn. 1955, rev. by Anna Amalie Abert; Eng. trans. by Pauline Townsend 1882). Collected material for biographies of Haydn and Beethoven which was passed, respectively, to Pohl and Thayer. One of founders in 1850 of *Bach Gesellschaft.

Jahreszeiten, Die (Haydn). See *Seasons, The*.

Jakobsleiter, Die (Jacob's Ladder). Unfinished oratorio by Schoenberg, comp. 1917–22, for sop., 3 tens., 2 basses, speaking ch., ch., and orch., to his own text. Scoring completed by Winfried Zillig. F.p. (1st part) Hamburg 1958; (completed version) Vienna 1961; f.p. in England, London 1965; f. Amer. p. Santa Fe 1968.

Jalas [Blomstedt], **Jussi** (*b* Jyväskylä, 1908; *d* 1985). Finn. conductor. Cond. at Finn. Nat. Th. 1930–45, cond. Helsinki Nat. Opera 1945–73. Guest cond. in Eng., USA, and Europe. Son-in-law of Sibelius.

jaleadas (Sp.). The 'seguidillas jaleadas' dance (see *seguidilla*) is a vigorous form, showing the influence of the *cachucha.

Jalousieschweller (Ger.). Venetian-blind swell. The org. swell pedal.

Jamaican Rumba. Short piece for 2 pf. by Arthur Benjamin, pubd. in 1938 as No.1 of 2 *Jamaican Pieces*. Arr. for many other combinations, particularly small orch.

James, Philip (*b* Jersey City, NJ, 1890; *d* Southampton, NY, 1975). Amer. composer and conductor. Cond. operettas of Victor Herbert 1919–22. Faculty of Mus. NY Univ. 1923 (head of dept. 1933–55). Founder-cond. New Jersey SO 1922–9, Bamberger Little Sym. 1929–36. Won NBC prize 1932 for satirical suite *Station WGZBX*. Works incl. ballet *Judith* (1927); ov. *Bret Harte*; 2 syms.; sym.-poems; choral works (incl. *General William Booth Enters Into Heaven*); chamber mus.

jam session. Informal perf. by jazz musicians improvising collectively.

Janáček, Leoš (*b* Hukvaldy, E. Moravia, 1854; *d* Moravská, Ostrava, 1928). Cz. composer, conductor, organist, and teacher. Although he was 47 when the 20th cent. began, he is essentially a 20th-cent. composer. His father was a choirmaster. At 11, Janáček entered the Augustinian monastery, Brno, as a choirboy, studying mus. with Pavel Křižkovský. In 1872 he became a junior master at Brno teachers' training coll., and was at the Prague Organ Sch., 1874–6. He went to Leipzig and Vienna in search of fame and fortune but returned disappointed to Brno as mus. master at the training coll. His early comps. met with little success, but he became deeply involved with Moravian folk music, working with Bartoš on editing, harmonizing, and performing folk-songs. He also founded Brno Organ Sch. in 1881, becoming dir. and remaining as organizer until 1919. In 1894 he began work on his 3rd opera, *Jenůfa*, which was perf. in Brno with considerable success in January 1904, the year of his 50th birthday. He had every right to expect it would then be staged in Prague, but some years earlier he had severely criticized a comp. by Karel Kovařovic who was now head of the Prague Opera. He refused to hear *Jenůfa* and it took Janáček's friends until 1916 to have the work accepted for Prague—even then, Kovařovic insisted on 'editing' it himself, for which he received a royalty. Nevertheless the opera was a triumph, as it was in Max Brod's Ger. version in Vienna and Cologne in 1918. This success at the age of 62, coupled with the formation of the Cz. republic, was a tremendous creative spur to Janáček and in the last 10 years of his life he produced a series of works full of originality, vitality, and power. The opera *The Excursions of Mr Brouček* (1917) and the orchestral rhapsody *Taras Bulba* (1918) were followed by the song-cycle *The Diary of One Who Disappeared*, the operas *Káťa Kabanová* and *The Cunning Little Vixen*, the concertino for pf. and chamber orch., the *Sinfonietta*, 2 str. qts., the wind sextet *Mládí*, the *Glagolitic Mass*, and 2 more operas, *The Makropulos Affair* and *From the House of the Dead*. Mus. history can offer few, if any, parallels with this upsurge of sustained inspiration—an inspiration partly derived from his love for a young married woman, Kamila Stösslová, whom he met in 1917 and to whom he wrote over 600 letters. He visited London for a concert of his works in 1926.

Janáček's early works belong to the 19th-cent. world of Dvořák and Smetana. But in his maturity, from *Jenůfa* onwards, his individual style developed. His works are based on short bursts of melody, strongly rhythmical, like vocal exclamations, these deriving from his fascination by speech-rhythms. He noted in sketch-books phrases he overheard in town and countryside, particularizing the moods in which they were spoken. The melodic fragments undergo sudden changes of tonality and mood, being built by simple but unusual means to strong emotional climaxes. His harmonic language, however, was in no way innovatory. His staple fare in this respect comprised common chords, 7ths, 9ths, and the whole-tone scale, but what is unusual is his spacing and juxtaposition of chords. His orchestration is equally striking and unusual, often seeming harsh and raw but invariably being apt and effective. He liked to use instr. at the extremes of their range.

Janáček's operas have held their place in the repertory since they were first perf. in Europe but only since the 1950s has the Eng. public been awakened to their originality and beauty, largely through the efforts of the cond. Charles *Macker-ras, who has also purged the scores of corruptions and accretions by other hands. The emotional range of the operas is wide: jealousy, hatred, love, and guilt are explored in *Jenůfa* and *Káťa Kabanová*, nature and the eternal round of the seasons in the fantasy *The Cunning Little Vixen*, satire in *The Excursions of Mr Brouček*, and harsh reality in *The Makropulos Affair* and the extraordinary *From the House of the Dead*—yet in all these disparate works the principal element is a compelling faith in humankind and its grip on life. Prin. works:

OPERAS: *Šárka* (text by Zeyer) (1887–8, rev. 1918 and 1924); *The Beginning of a Romance (Počátek Románu)* (1891, prod. 1894); *Her Foster-Daughter (Její Pastorkyňa,* known as **Jenůfa)* (1894–1903, 1st rev. 1906); *Fate (*Osud)* (1903–5, rev. 1906–7); *The *Excursions of Mr Brouček (Výlet páně Broučkovy)* (1908–17); **Káťa Kabanová (Katya Kabanova)* (1919–21); *The *Cunning Little Vixen (Příhody lišky Bystroušky)* (1921–3); *The *Makropulos Affair (Věc Makropulos)* (1923–5); *From the *House of the Dead (Z Mrtvého Domu)* (1927–8).

ORCH.: *Suite for Strings* (1877); *Idyll for strings* (1877); *Suite* (c.1891); *Lachian Dances (Lašske tance)* (1889–90); ov. *Jealousy (Žárlivost)* (1894); ballad *The Fiddler's Child (Šumařovo Dítě)* (1912); rhapsody **Taras Bulba* (1915–18); sym.-poem *The Ballad of Blaník (Balada blanická)* (1920); *Sinfonietta* (1926); sym.-poem *Danube (Dunaj)* (1923–8, completed by O. Chlubna); vn. conc. *(Pilgrimage of the Soul)* (c.1926–8, sketches completed by M. Stědroň and L. Faltus, 1988. See *From the *House of the Dead*).

CHORUS & ORCH.: *Lord, have mercy on us (Hospodine pomiluj ny),* double ch., solo qt., wind orch., org., hp. (1897); *Amarus,* sop, ten., bar., ch., orch. (c.1897, rev. 1901, 1906); *At the Inn of Solan (Na Solani Čarták),* ten., male ch., orch. (1911); *The Eternal Gospel (Věčné Evangelium),* sop., ten., ch., orch. (1914–15); **Glagolitic Mass (Glagolská mše),* sop., alto, ten., bass, ch., org., orch. (1926); *Nursery Rhymes (Říkadla),* 9 vv., pfs., 11 instr. (1925, rev. 1927).

CHORUS: *Ploughing (Oriani),* male ch. (1876); *The Wild Duck (Kačena Divoka)* (c.1885); *4 Choruses,* male vv. (1886); *The Wreath (Vinek),* 4 male ch. (1904); *4 Moravian Choruses,* male vv. (1904); *Songs of the Hradčany (Hradčanské Piškičky),* 3 male vv. (1916); **Diary of One Who Disappeared (Zápisník Zmizelého),* song-cycle, ten., cont., 3 women's vv., pf. (1917–19); *Wolf Tracks (Vlčí stopa),* sop., women's ch., pf. (1916); *Kaspar Rucky,* women's ch. (1916); *Teacher Halfar (Kantor Halfar),* male vv. (1906, rev. 1917); *The Czech Legions (České Legie),* male ch. (1918); *The Wandering Madman (Potulny šilenec),* sop., male ch. (1922).

CHAMBER MUSIC: *Dumka,* vn., pf. (c.1880); *Fairy Tale (Pohádka),* vc., pf. (1910, 2nd version 1923); vn. sonata (1914, rev. 1921); str. qt. No.1 (**Kreutzer Sonata)* (1923–4), No.2 (**Intimate Letters)* (*Listy důvěrné)* (1928); *Youth (*Mládí),* wind sextet (1924); concertino for pf., chamber orch. (c.1925); *Capriccio,* pf. (left hand), chamber orch. (c.1926).

PIANO: *Vallachian Dances* (1888); *National Dances of Moravia,* for pf. (4 hands), Books 1 and 2 (1891),

Book 3 (1893); *On an Overgrown Path (Po zarostlém Chodníčku),* 15 short pieces (7 orig. for harmonium) (1901–8); *Sonata 1:x:1905* (A street scene; *Z ulice)* (the day a worker was killed by a soldier for demonstrating for a Cz. univ. in Brno); *In the Mists (V mlhách)* (1912); *Moravian Dances,* 2 books (1912); *In the Threshing House* (1913).

SOLO VOICE: *Song of Spring,* v., pf. (1897); *Folk Poetry of Hukwald,* 13 songs for v., pf. (1899); *A Garland of Moravian Folk Songs,* 53 songs coll. by Bartoš and Janáček, with pf. acc. by Janáček, Book 1 (1892), 2 (1901).

Janáček Quartet. Cz. str. qt. formed 1947 by students of Brno Cons. First public concert, Brno, Oct. 1947. Adopted name Janáček Qt. after Prague début 1949. First visit to Brit. 1958. Made close study of Janáček's two qts., also those by Bartók, Shostakovich, Britten, and Novák. Always performs from memory.

Janequin [Jannequin]. **Clément** (*b* Châtellerault, nr. Poitiers, *c.*1485; *d* Paris, 1558). Fr. composer. Choirmaster, Angers Cath. 1534–7. Comp. over 250 *chansons,* some of which were pubd. by Attaignant. Settled in Paris 1549, becoming *compositeur du roi.* Entered Paris Univ. as a student when over 70. Wrote two Masses based on two of his *chansons.* Introduced bird-song and other programmatic effects. His *Le bataille de Marignan* (1515) imitates sword-clashes, warriors' cries, and other sounds.

Janiewicz [Yaniewicz], **Feliks** (*b* Wilno, 1762; *d* Edinburgh, 1848). Polish violinist and composer. Violinist in royal chapel of King of Poland 1777–84. Visited Vienna 1785, meeting Haydn and Mozart; then 3 years in It.; Paris 1787–90. Visited Eng. 1792, playing in London, Bath, Liverpool, and Manchester. Took part in Haydn's London concerts 1794. Settled in Liverpool 1800, founding publishing firm 1803. One of founders of Phil. Soc., London. Lived in Edinburgh from 1815, retiring in 1829. Comp. vn. concs., chamber mus., etc.

Janigro, Antonio (*b* Milan, 1918; *d* Milan, 1989). It. cellist and conductor. Début 1934. Worldwide reputation as solo cellist. Head of advanced vc. class, Zagreb Univ. 1939–53; cond. Zagreb radio-TV orch. 1954–64; founder of chamber ens., *I solisti di Zagreb* (12 musicians) 1954, cond. until 1967 (Salzburg Fest. 1956); cond. Angelicum Orch., Milan, 1965–7; cond. Saar chamber orch. from 1968; head of advanced vc. class Schumann Cons., Düsseldorf, 1965–74. Cond. f.ps. of works by Ligeti and Penderecki.

Janis [Yanks], **Byron** (*b* McKeesport, Penn., 1928). Amer. pianist. Début Pittsburgh 1937. Recital début, NY 1948. Eur. début, Amsterdam 1952; toured USSR 1960 and 1962. In 1960s continued career despite arthritis in both hands. In 1967 in Fr., discovered autograph MSS of two Chopin waltzes, Op.70, No.1 and Op.18.

Janissary music (Ger. *Janitscharenmusik*). Term once used for the imitation-Turkish mus. produced by triangle, cymbals, and bass drum as in Mozart's *Die Entführung aus dem Serail*. The Janissaries were the Sultan's bodyguard, disbanded 1826, who had a band.

Janowitz, Gundula (*b* Berlin, 1937). Ger. soprano. Début Vienna State Opera 1959 as Barbarina in *Le nozze di Figaro*, singing with this co. for 30 years, especially in Mozart and Strauss roles. Bayreuth Fest. 1960–2; Salzburg début 1963, singing many roles there until 1981; NY Met début 1967. Sang Countess in *Figaro* at re-opening of Paris Opéra 1973. CG début 1976; Glyndebourne 1964. Dir., Graz Opera 1990–1. Noted *Lieder* singer.

Janowski, Marek (*b* Warsaw, 1939). Polish-born conductor (Ger. cit.). Ass. cond. in Aachen, Cologne, and Düsseldorf opera houses. Mus. dir. Freiburg Opera 1973–5, Dortmund 1975–9. Cond. New PO of Radio France from 1984, Gürzenich Orch., Cologne, 1986–91. Cond. Berlin Radio SO from 2001, Orch. de la Suisse Romande from 2005. London début 1969 (Brit. première of *Der *junge Lord* with Cologne Opera). Amer. opera début Chicago 1980; NY Met 1984. Art. adv. RLPO 1983–6.

Janssen, Herbert (*b* Cologne, 1892; *d* NY, 1965). Ger.-born baritone (Amer. cit. 1946). Début Berlin 1922 (Herod in Schreker's *Der Schätzgraber*). Member of Berlin State Opera 1922–38. CG 1926–39. Bayreuth 1930–7. Member of NY Met 1939–52. Singer of Wagnerian roles such as Gunther, Kothner, Amfortas, and Kurwenal, later in career Wotan and Sachs.

Janssen, Werner (*b* NY, 1899; *d* NY, 1990). Amer. composer and conductor. Cond. début Rome 1931. Amer. début with NYPO 1934. Cond. Baltimore SO 1937–9; Janssen SO of Los Angeles 1940–52; Utah SO 1946–7; Portland SO 1947–9; San Diego PO 1952–4. Comps. incl. *Louisiana Suite* (1929–30), *Dixie Fugue* (1932), 2 str. qts., film mus.

Jansons, Mariss (*b* Riga, 1943). Latvian conductor, son of Arvid *Yansons. 2nd prize, Karajan cond. comp. 1971. Ass. cond. Leningrad PO. Prin. cond. Oslo PO 1979–2000; Pittsburgh SO 1997–2002; Bavarian Radio SO from 2003; Royal Concertgebouw from 2004. Amer. début (with Oslo PO) 1987. Salzburg Fest. début 1990.

Japanese fiddle. A 1-str. instr. sometimes seen in the hands of Eng. street perfs., etc.

Jaques-Dalcroze, Émile (*b* Vienna, 1865; *d* Geneva, 1950). Swiss composer and teacher. On staff Geneva Cons. 1892, developing his *gymnastique rythmique*, known as *Eurhythmics, exercises for expressing rhythmical aspects of mus. by physical movements. Influence on ballet. Taught method 1910–14 at Hellerau, Dresden. Founded Institut Jaques-Dalcroze in Geneva 1915. Wrote several books on subject. Comp. 5 operas (incl. *Sancho Panza*, 1896), operetta, 2 vn. concs., 3 str. qts., pf. pieces, etc.

Jardin clos, Le (The Enclosed Garden). Song-cycle of 8 songs for high or medium v. and pf. by Fauré, Op.106, to poems by Charles van Lerberghe, comp. 1914, f.p. 1915.

Jarnach, Philipp (*b* Noisy, 1892; *d* Börnson, 1982). Ger. composer of Sp. birth. Taught at Zurich Cons. 1915–21. Mus. critic, *Börsen-Kurier*, Berlin, 1922–7. Disciple (not pupil) of *Busoni, whose opera *Doktor Faust* he completed. Prof. of comp., Cologne Cons. 1927–49; dir., Hamburg Cons. 1949–70. Taught Weill and formed friendship with Schoenberg. Comp. orch. and choral works, str. qt., unacc. vn. sonatas, 2 pf. sonatas, etc.

Järnefelt, Armas (*b* Viborg (now Viipuri), 1869; *d* Stockholm, 1958). Finnish-born composer and conductor (Swed. cit. 1910). Cond. Viipuri orch. 1898–1903, Helsinki opera 1903–7, Royal Opera, Stockholm, 1907–32, Finn. Nat. Opera 1932–6, Helsinki PO 1942–3. Brother-in-law of *Sibelius. Said to have introduced Wagner's mus. to Finland. Comps. incl. *Praeludium* for orch. (1907), *Berceuse*, pf. pieces, etc.

Jarre, Maurice (*b* Lyons, 1924). Fr. composer. Comp. *Passacaille* in memory of Honegger (1956), *Mobiles*, vn., orch. (1961), incid. mus. for Molière's *Don Juan* (perf. at Salzburg Fest. 1955), and many film scores incl. *Dr Zhivago* (1965).

Jarred, Mary (*b* Brotton, Yorks., 1899; *d* Farnborough, 1993). Eng. contralto. Hamburg Opera 1929–32 (Nurse in *Die Frau ohne Schatten*), London (SW) début 1933; CG, and Margret in BBC concert perf. of *Wozzeck*, cond. Boult 1934 (its f. Brit. p.); Glyndebourne co. 1953 (at Edinburgh Fest.) and at Glyndebourne 1954 and 1955. Notable also for singing in oratorio and as the Angel in Elgar's *The Dream of Gerontius*. One of the original 16 singers in Vaughan Williams's *Serenade to Music*, 1938. Retired 1955. Prof. of singing, RAM, 1965–73, and also taught privately.

Jarrett, Keith (*b* Allentown, Pa., 1945). Amer. jazz pianist and composer of Scottish-Irish and Hungarian descent. Child-prodigy pianist. In early teens toured with Fred Waring and his Pennsylvanians. Was offered schol. to study with N. Boulanger in Paris but went instead to NY where he formed his own jazz group and occasionally played with a Miles Davis band. His solo piano improvisations embrace classical and jazz history, rarely with direct quotations, and he has been classified with the 'back to romanticism' movement of Rochberg and Del Tredici. Has been soloist in pf. concs. by Lou Harrison, Hovhaness and McPhee. Comps. incl. *Ritual* for pf. and *The Celestial Hawk*, a pf. conc.

Järvi, Neeme (*b* Tallinn, Estonia, 1937). Estonian-born conductor (Amer. cit. 1983). Won St Cecilia Acad., Rome, cond. comp. 1971. Début at Kirov Th. (*Carmen*). Mus. dir. Estonian State SO. Dir., Estonian Opera 1964–77. NY Met début 1979 (*Eugene Onegin*). Emigrated to USA 1980. Cond., Göteborg SO 1982–2004. Prin. guest cond. CBSO 1981–4, prin. cond. SNO 1984–8. Mus. dir. Detroit SO 1990–2005. Mus. dir. New Jersey SO and Hague Residentie Orch. from 2005.

Järvi, Paavo (*b* Tallinn, Estonia, 1962). Estonian conductor, son of Neeme *Järvi. Studied perc. and cond. at Tallinn Mus. Sch. until moving in 1980 to USA, where he studied at Curtis Inst. and at Los Angeles Phil. Inst. with *Bernstein. Guest cond. of many Eur. and Amer. orchs., incl. CBSO. Salzburg Fest. début 2004. LSO début 2006. Art. adv. to Estonian Nat. SO. Mus. dir. Cincinnati SO from 2001. Mus. dir. Frankfurt Radio SO from 2006.

jazz (etymology obscure). A term, which came into general use *c.*1913–15, for a type of mus. which developed in the Southern States of USA in the late 19th cent. and came into prominence at the turn of the century in New Orleans, chiefly (but not exclusively) among black musicians. Elements which contributed to jazz were the rhythms of W. Africa, European harmony, and Amer. 'gospel' singing. Before the term *jazz* was used, ragtime was the popular name for this genre. Ragtime lasted from *c.*1890 to *c.*1917. It was an instr. style, highly syncopated, with the pf. predominant (though a few rags had words and were sung). Among the leading exponents of the pf. rag were Scott *Joplin, Jelly Roll Morton, and J. P. Johnson, with the cornettists Buddy Bolden and King Oliver. Some rags were notated (e.g. Joplin's *Maple Leaf Rag*) but the majority were improvised. About 1900 also, the 'blues' craze began. 'Blues' implies a largely vocal form and a depressed frame of mind on the part of the perf. The form originated from Negro spirituals, and made use of a blend of major and minor harmony, and non-tempered scale intervals. In instr. blues the prominent instrs. were tpt., cornet, cl., sax., or tb. A leading figure of the blues era was the black composer W. C. *Handy whose *Memphis Blues* (1909) and *St Louis Blues* (1914) are jazz classics. Outstanding blues singers have been Bessie Smith and, later, Billie Holiday.

The subsequent history of jazz has embraced a diversity of styles, e.g. *Dixieland*, from *c.*1912, which borrowed elements from both ragtime and blues and made a feature of group improvisation led by the trumpeter. The principal Dixieland musicians included the trumpeters King Oliver and Louis *Armstrong, the trombonists Kid Ory and Jack Teagarden, the saxophonist Sidney Bechet, the pianists Jelly Roll Morton and Earl Hines. In the 1920s, jazz became more sophisticated as it spread to New York, Paris, and London and became a social 'rage'. The jazz arranger emerged and with him the bigger band: harmony became more conventional, melodies were played by a full instr. section with the solos as central display-pieces, like cadenzas. These 'big bands' had marked individual styles. Paul Whiteman popularized 'symphonic jazz' using vns. and elaborate arrs. At the other extreme was the Negro style of Duke *Ellington, the first great jazz composer. A 'Chicago' style revived smaller bands and more improvisation (its star was the trumpeter Bix Beiderbecke).

The 1930s coincided with the style known as 'swing'. The swing bands—led by such virtuoso instrumentalists as Benny *Goodman (cl.), Jimmy Dorsey (alto sax.), Gene Krupa (drums), Glenn *Miller (tb.), Tommy Dorsey (tb.), Artie Shaw (cl.)—concentrated on precision, arr., and good ens. work. Though Ellington's band was influenced by swing, its members were such superb players and such strong individualists that improvisation still played a large part in his comps. Swing yielded in the 1940s to 'be-bop', allied to scat singing (vocalizing to nonsense syllables). Tempi were fast and great virtuosity was needed. The dominant player was the alto saxophonist Charlie *Parker (1920–55). Also important were Dizzy Gillespie (trumpeter), Stan Getz (tenor saxophonist), and Kenny Clarke and Max Roach (drummers). 'Be-bop' was later rechristened 'modern jazz'. Among its derivatives were 'cool' jazz, led by Getz and Miles Davis, and by Shorty Rogers (tpt.) and Lennie Tristano (pf.). In the 1960s 'free jazz' was pioneered but the jazz scene was overshadowed by the emergence of 'pop' and the pop groups, e.g. the *Beatles, the *Rolling Stones, and many others, these comprising usually a vocalist, guitarist(s), and perc. 'Hard rock' was a development from this period, and elec. instrs. were commandeered, as in other branches of mus.

The influence of jazz on so-called 'serious music' has been widespread and beneficial. Ives composed ragtime pieces for th. orch. as early as 1902; Debussy in 1908 wrote the *Golliwogg's Cakewalk*; Ravel used the blues in his vn. sonata, and both his pf. concs. are jazz-influenced; Stravinsky wrote ragtime pieces and composed the *Ebony Concerto* (1945) for Woody Herman; Hindemith, Poulenc, Weill, Krenek, Lambert, Copland, and Tippett all used jazz features, as did Berg in *Lulu*. Duke Ellington and Bill Russo are among the leading composers of jazz, while those who have written works throwing a bridge between jazz and symphonic forms incl. Gershwin, Rolf Liebermann, Leonard Bernstein, Gunther Schuller, Richard Rodney Bennett, and John Dankworth.

Jazz Calendar. Ballet in 7 parts, mus. by Richard Rodney *Bennett, choreog. Ashton, comp. 1963–4, prod. CG 1968. Based on rhyme 'Monday's Child is Fair of Face' . . . etc.

Jeanne d'Arc au bûcher (Joan of Arc at the Stake). (1) Dramatic oratorio for 4 speakers, 3 sops., cont., ten., bass, ondes Martenot, ch., and orch. by Honegger to text by Claudel. Comp. 1934–5. F.p. Basle 1938; f.p. in England, London, BBC 1947, staged 1954; S. Francisco 1954.

(2) Scena for mez. and pf. by Liszt, 1845 (arr. for v. and orch. 1858, rev. 1874).

Jeffreys, George (*b c.*1610; *d* Weldon, Northants, 1685). Eng. composer. Org. to Charles I at Oxford during Civil War. In 1646 became steward to Sir Christopher (later Lord) Hatton at Kirby, Northants, remaining until death. Worked as amateur composer, only one work being published in lifetime. Wrote mainly church mus., influenced by

It. Baroque, particularly Monteverdi and Gesualdo. Collected works ed. Peter *Aston, from 1970. Works incl. 35 Eng. anthems, over 70 Latin settings, secular songs, str. fantasias (1629), and mus. for plays (1631).

Její Pastorkyňa (Janáček). See *Jenůfa.*

'Jena' Symphony. Name given to orch. work found by F. *Stein in 1909 at Jena, Ger., and long attrib. to Beethoven. H. C. Robbins Landon in 1957 est. it was comp. by Friedrich *Witt.

Jenkins, John (*b* Maidstone, 1592; *d* Kimberley, Norfolk, 1678). Eng. composer. Musician in service of Charles I and Charles II but mainly in private service in Norfolk. Wrote over 800 instr. works, incl. Fancies for viols or org., 12 sonatas for 2 vns., str. bass, and continuo (org. or theorbo) (1660), light pieces called rants, and songs, catches, etc.

Jenkins, Newell (Owen) (*b* New Haven, Conn., 1915; *d* Hillsdale, NY, 1996). Amer. conductor and scholar. Début as cond., Freiburg 1935 (*Dido and Aeneas*). Founded Yale Opera Group, New Haven, 1940. Cond., Bologna Chamber Orch. 1948–53. Founder and dir., Piccola Accademia Musicale, Florence, 1952. Founder, Clarion Concerts, NY, 1956. Taught at NY Univ. 1964–74 and Univ. of Calif. at Irvine 1971–9. Expert on music of Sammartini, J. M. Kraus, and Cherubini.

Jenůfa. Opera (Moravian music drama) in 3 acts by Janáček. This is title by which it is known outside Czechoslovakia, where it retains its orig. title of *Her Foster-daughter* (*Její Pastorkyňa*). Lib. by composer based on story by G. Preissová. Comp. 1894–1903, rev. 1906, 1911, 1916. Prod. Brno 1904, Prague 1916, Vienna 1918, NY Met 1924, London 1956. Orig. version of ov., comp. 1894, was pubd. in 1906 as independent orch. piece *Jealousy* (*Žárlivost*). Since 1916 opera has usually been performed in edn. with re-orch. by Prague cond. Karel Kovařovic, but Mackerras and others have restored orig. scoring.

Jephte. (1) Oratorio by *Carissimi to Lat. text based on biblical words. For 6 vv. and continuo; comp. 1650. Version by Henze for 7 solo vv., 6 vv. ch., 4 fl., perc., hp., guitar, mandolin, banjo, 1976.

(2) Oratorio (*Jephtha*) by Handel to text by Morell based on Bible. Comp. 1751. F.p. London 1752.

Jeremiah. Sym. No.1 by Leonard Bernstein for orch. with mez. soloist in last movement to words from *Book of Jeremiah*. F.p. Pittsburgh, Jan. 1944, cond. Bernstein, with Jennie Tourel.

Jerger, Alfred (*b* Brünn, Vienna, 1889; *d* Vienna, 1976). Austrian bass-baritone. Began career as operetta cond., Zurich 1913; singing début Zurich 1917 (Lothario in Thomas's *Mignon*). Munich Opera 1919–21 at Strauss's invitation; Vienna 1921, remaining as leading bar. until 1953, singing 150 roles. Salzburg Fest. début 1922 (title-role in *Don Giovanni*, cond. Strauss), singing there frequently until 1959. Created The Man in

Schoenberg's *Die glückliche Hand*, Vienna 1924, and Mandryka in *Arabella*, Dresden 1933 and CG 1934. Temporary dir., Vienna State opera 1945. After retirement was prod. at Vienna Volksoper and teacher at Acad.

Jeritza, Maria [Jedlitzka, Mizzi] (*b* Brno, 1887; *d* Orange, NJ, 1982). Moravian-born Amer. soprano (Amer. cit. 1943). Opera début as Elsa in *Lohengrin* at Olmütz, 1910. Engaged 1912 for Vienna Volksoper. Created role of Ariadne in both versions of *Ariadne auf Naxos*, Stuttgart 1912 and Vienna 1916. After Emperor Franz Josef heard her sing in Bad Ischl in 1912, became member of Vienna Court (State) Opera 1913–32, 1949–52, creating role of the Empress in *Die Frau ohne Schatten* (1919) and singing first Vienna Jenůfa (1918) and first Vienna Marietta in *Die *tote Stadt* (1920). NY Met 1921–32, where she was first Amer. Jenůfa, Turandot, and Helen (*Die ägyptische Helena*). CG 1925–6. Last Met appearance as Roselinda in *Die Fledermaus* 1951. Of striking personal beauty and acting ability.

Jerusalem. (1) Setting for unison ch. by C. H. *Parry of Blake's poem *Milton*. Comp. and f.p. 1916. Orch. by Elgar for Leeds Fest. 1922.

(2) Oratorio by H. H. Pierson, Norwich Fest. 1852.

Jérusalem. Opera in 4 acts by Verdi to lib. by Royer and Vaëz being Fr. version (1847) of Verdi's opera *I *Lombardi alla prima crociata* (1842). Little of Solera's orig. plot was kept, ballet was added, and much of the mus. material was re-ordered, cut, and revised, with a considerable amount of new mus. (It. vers. is *Gerusalemma*.) Prod. Paris 1847, New Orleans 1850, La Scala 1850, Leeds (Opera North) 1990.

Jerusalem, Siegfried (*b* Oberhausen, 1940). Ger. tenor. Began career as bassoonist in various Ger. orchs. (Stuttgart Radio SO 1972–7). Opera début Stuttgart 1975 (First Prisoner in *Fidelio*). Sang Lohengrin, Darmstadt and Aachen 1976, Hamburg 1977. Bayreuth début 1977; Salzburg Fest. début 1979. Deutsche Oper, Berlin, 1977–80. NY Met début 1980; ENO 1986; CG 1986. Many Wagner roles.

Jessonda. Opera in 3 acts by Spohr to lib. by E. Gehe after A. M. Lemièrre's play *La veuve de Malabar*. Comp. 1822–3. Prod. Kassel 1823, London 1840, Philadelphia 1864.

Jesu, Joy of Man's Desiring. Eng. name for chorale *Jesu, bleibet meine Freude* in J. S. Bach's church cantata No. 147, *Herz und Mund und Tat und Leben*, orig. orch. for tpt., ob., str., and org. but best known in pf. transcr. by Myra *Hess of choral arr. by Hugh P. Allen with poem by Robert Bridges. Chorale melody is *Werde Munter* by Johann Schop, 1641.

jeu (Fr.; plural *jeux*). (1) Game, play, etc.

(2) Stop (org.), e.g. *jeux d'anche*, reed stops; *jeux de fonds*, foundation stops (see *fonds d'orgue*); *grand jeu* or *plein jeu*, full org.

Jeu de cartes (Card Game). Ballet 'in 3 deals' with lib. and mus. by Stravinsky, comp. 1936, choreog. Balanchine, prod. NY Met 1937. Also orch. suite.

jeu de clochettes (Fr.). Play of little bells, i.e. *glockenspiel.

Jeune, Claude le (*b* Valenciennes, *c*.1530; *d* Paris 1600). Fr. composer of psalm-settings and many secular *chansons* and instr. pieces. Known to have worked in Paris from 1564. Promoted new style of comp. in which mus. was made to follow metrical rhythm of text (*Vers mesurez*). Mastercomposer to Henri IV, 1596.

Jeune France, La (Fr.). Young France. Group of Fr. composers formed in Paris in 1936 to re-establish then unfashionable idea of 'a personal message' in comp. Members were *Baudrier, *Jolivet, *Daniel-Lesur, and *Messiaen.

Jeunesse d'Hercule, La (The Youth of Hercules). Symphonic poem by Saint-Saëns, Op.50, 1877.

Jeunesses Musicales (Fr.). Musical Youth. Int. organization initiated by Marcel Cuvelier in Belg., 1940. In 1945 *La Fédération internationale des jeunesses musicales* was founded, later with 35 member-nations. Aim to spread love of mus. among youth of all lands. Arr. congresses and exchange-visits. Int. founder-members incl. Alicia de Larrocha, Sir Robert Mayer, Joan Miró, Henryk Szeryng, and Nicanor Zabaleta.

Jeux (Games). Ballet (*poème dansée*) by Debussy comp. in 1912–13 and f.p. Paris 1913 by Diaghilev's co. with choreog. by Nijinsky. The scenario, also by Nijinsky, involves a game of tennis.

Jeux d'eau (Fountains). Work for solo pf. by Ravel, comp. 1901, f.p. Paris 1902.

Jeux d'enfants (Children's Games). Suite of 12 pieces for pf. duet comp. by Bizet in 1871. Nos. 2, 3, 6, 11, and 12 were orch. by Bizet as *Petite Suite d'Orchestre* and perf. Paris 1873. Five were orch. also by Karg-Elert (Nos. 6, 3, 4, 11, and 12 in order of perf.) and Nos. 6, 3, 2, 11, and 12 were arr. by H. Finck.

Jewels of the Madonna, The (Wolf-Ferrari). See *Gioielli della Madonna, I.*

Jewess, The (Halévy). See *Juive, La.*

Jewish music. It is apparent from the Old Testament and from archaeological discoveries that instr. and vocal mus. has always played a part in Jewish life, both on sacred and secular occasions. After the destruction of the Second Temple, instr. mus. was banned as a token of mourning, but the *shofar was retained as the ritual horn and decorative bells were attached to the curtain covering the Ark. Instr. mus. was later permitted at weddings and festive events. The oldest element of synagogue mus. is still the cantillation of biblical texts, from which synagogue prayer chants derived. These chants were orally transmitted from generation to generation by cantorcomposers. In the middle of the 19th cent. cantorial schools were founded as moves towards a printed repertory began. 19th-cent. Jewish liturgical composers incl. Solomon Sulzer (1804–90), Samuel Naumburg (1815–80), Hirsch Weintraub (1811–81), and Boruch Schorr (1823–1904). In the 20th cent., liturgical services have been comp. by Paul Ben-Haim, *Bloch, *Milhaud, and *Castelnuovo-Tedesco.

Jew's harp (Fr. *rebube*, *guimbarde*; Ger. *Trumpel*; It. *scacciapensieri*). One of the simplest and most widely distributed instr., being found throughout Europe and Asia. It consists of a tiny iron frame, open at one end, in which end a single strip of metal vibrates. The frame is held between the teeth, and the strip then twanged by the finger. The strip, in itself, is obviously capable of producing only one note, but the harmonics of this note become available by resonance, through various shapings of the cavity of the mouth. Thus tunes can be played.

The origin of the name is unknown and seems to be unconnected with Jewry. The name 'Jew's trump' was recorded in 1545.

jig. (1) A dance once popular in Eng., Scot., and Ireland, in the last of which its popularity was of longest duration. For its general character and music see *gigue*.

(2) In the late 16th and 17th cents., the term was applied to a lively song and dance item, of comic character, used to terminate theatrical perfs.

(3) Title of last movement of an 18th-cent. orch. suite. See *gigue*.

Jílek, František (*b* Brno, 1913; *d* Brno, 1993). Cz. conductor, pianist, and composer. Cond. Brno Opera, 1936–9. Ass. cond. Ostrava Opera 1939–48, cond. Brno Opera 1948–52, art. dir. 1952–78. Chief cond. Brno State PO 1978–83. Also cond. in Helsinki, Florence, Leipzig. Prof. of cond., Janáček Acad. of Mus. Arts. Authority on Janáček., cond. all his operas in Brno 1958, and on Smetana and Martinů.

Jingling Johnny (Fr. *pavillon chinois* or *chapeau chinois*). Perc. instr., now obsolete, also known as 'Turkish Crescent' or 'Turkish Jingle'. Used in military bands. It comprised a long stick surmounted by a tent-shaped construction, with an inverted crescent lower down the stick, small bells and the like being suspended from both of these. Used by Berlioz in his *Symphonie funèbre et triomphale.*

Jo, Sumi (*b* Seoul, 1962). Korean soprano. Début Trieste 1986 (Gilda in *Rigoletto*). Débuts: Salzburg Fest. 1988; La Scala; NY Met 1989; CG 1991.

Joachim, Joseph (*b* Kitsee, 1831; *d* Berlin, 1907). Hung. violinist and composer. Gave first concert at age of 7. Studied in Vienna 1839–43 under Hellmesberger and Boehm. Went to Leipzig Cons. 1843, where he was welcomed by the dir.,

Mendelssohn, playing at *Gewandhaus concerts and, in 1844, in London (Beethoven conc.). In 1849 became leader of Weimar court orch., under Liszt, and leader and soloist to the King of Hanover 1853–66. Met and became friend of Brahms. In 1868 went to Berlin as dir. and prof. of vn. at the new *Hochschule für ausübende Tonkunst*, forming *Joachim Quartet following year. Frequent visitor to England (hon. Mus.D., Cambridge, 1887). Superb interpreter of classical conc., especially that by Beethoven (for which he wrote cadenzas). Dedicatee and first player of Brahms's conc., and dedicatee of Dvořák's conc., which he refused to play. Rift in friendship with Brahms when marriage broke up and Brahms sided with Frau Joachim (the singer Amalie Weiss) in the divorce suit. This rift was healed by Brahms's Double Conc., 1887. One of conds., Berlin PO 1882–7. Comp. 3 vn. concs. (incl. *Hungarian Concerto*), 5 ovs., songs, etc. Orchestrated Schubert's *Grand Duo* (1855).

Joachim Quartet. Str. qt. founded in Berlin in 1869 by Joseph *Joachim, who was 1st vn. 1869–1907. Annual series of concerts in Berlin from 1869. Visits to Vienna, Budapest, Rome, Paris, and London (1900). K. Halíř led the qt. during Joachim's illness in 1907, and formed his own qt. after Joachim's death.

Job. (1) Masque for dancing in 9 scenes and epilogue by Vaughan Williams, founded on Blake's *Illustrations of the Book of Job*. Comp. 1927–30. F.p. (concert) Norwich 1930, (ballet) London 1931.
(2) Oratorio by Parry, f.p. Gloucester 1892.
(3) Opera (*sacra rappresentazione*) in 1 act by Dallapiccola, text by composer from *Book of Job*, comp. 1950, f.p. Rome 1950.

Jochum, Eugen (*b* Babenhausen, 1902; *d* Munich, 1987). Ger. conductor. Opera coach at Munich 1924–5, Kiel 1926–7. Cond. Kiel Opera 1927–9. Chief cond., Duisburg 1930. Cond. for Berlin radio and State Opera 1932–4. Mus. dir. Hamburg State Opera 1934–49, Hamburg PO 1934–49. Chief cond. Bavarian Radio SO 1949–61. Salzburg Fest. début 1945 (Mozarteum Orch.); Bayreuth Fest. 1953 (*Tristan und Isolde*). Amer. début 1958. Joint chief cond. Concertgebouw Orch., Amsterdam, 1961–4; chief cond. Bamberg SO 1969–78. Regular visitor to Eng. as cond. of LPO. Cond. laureate LSO 1975.

jodelling (yodelling; from Ger. *Jodel*). A type of vocal expression common in Switzerland and the Tyrol, which employs an alternation of normal v. production with falsetto in simple rhythmic tunes.

Johannesburg Festival Overture. Ov. by *Walton written for 70th anniv. of city of Johannesburg, 1956. F.p. Johannesburg, cond. Sargent, 1956, f. Eng. p. Liverpool, cond. Kurtz, 1956.

Johannesen, Grant (*b* Salt Lake City, 1921; *d* Munich, 2005). Amer. pianist. Début 1944 with

NYPO. Several tours of Europe and USSR. Taught at Aspen Mus. Sch. 1960–6. Mus. dir., Cleveland Inst. of Mus. 1974–7, pres. 1977–85.

John [João] **IV, King of Portugal** (*b* Villa-Viøsa, 1603; *d* Lisbon, 1656). Patron of music and composer of church music such as well-known *Crux fidelis*. Wrote defence of 'modern music' 1649. His magnificent library of church mus. was destroyed in Lisbon earthquake 1755.

Johnny strikes up (Krenek). See *Jonny spielt auf*.

John of Fornsete (*b* Forncett, Norfolk; *d* 1238 or 9). Eng. monk at Reading Abbey where he kept the records and hence is credited as being composer of *Sumer is icumen in*, although scholars insist that all theories about him are without foundation.

Johnson, Edward (*fl.* 1570–1602). Eng. composer of madrigals, virginals pieces (3 in *Fitzwilliam Virginal Book*) and psalm-tunes. Contrib. 6-part madrigal *Come, blessed byrd*, to *The *Triumphs of Oriana*. Employed as musician by Kitson family at Hengrave Hall, Suffolk, in 1570s. Cambridge MusB 1594.

Johnson, Edward (*b* Guelph, Ontario, 1878; *d* Guelph, 1959). Can.-born tenor and opera administrator (Amer. cit. 1922). Début NY 1907 in O. Straus's *Waltz Dream*. It. début Padua 1912 (under name Edoardo di Giovanni). Sang first It. Parsifal at La Scala under Toscanini 1914. Prin. ten. roles in Milan, Rome, Buenos Aires, Rio, and Madrid 1914–19; Chicago Opera 1919–21; NY Met 1922–34. Gen. man. NY Met 1935–50. Hon. CBE 1935.

Johnson, Graham (*b* Bulawayo, 1950). Rhodesian-born Eng. pianist. Début, London 1972. Art. dir. *Songmakers' Almanac from 1976. Accomp. to Schwarzkopf, de los Angeles, Baker, etc. Recorded all Schubert's songs with various singers. OBE 1994.

Johnson, Hunter (*b* Benson, N. Car., 1906; *d* Smithfield, N. Car., 1998). Amer. composer. Head of comp. dept., Michigan Univ. 1929–33. Won Amer. *Prix de Rome* 1933, going to Eur. for 2 years' study. Teacher at Manitoba Univ. 1944–7, Cornell Univ. 1948–53. Illinois Univ. 1959–65, Texas Univ. 1966–71. Comps. incl. sym. (1931); pf. conc. (1935); *Concerto for Orchestra* (1944); 4 ballets incl. *Letter to the World* (1940) and *The Scarlet Letter* (1975); chamber mus., etc.

Johnson, John (*b* c.1540; *d* c.1595). Eng. composer and lutenist at court of Elizabeth I from 1579. Developed lute duet. Earliest of major lutenists of period.

Johnson, Robert (*b* London, c.1583; *d* London, 1633). Eng. composer and lutenist. Appointed as one of King's Musicians 1604. Composed instr. pieces, catches, and songs. His settings of *Full Fathom Five* and *Where the Bee Sucks* from Shakespeare's *The Tempest* are thought to have been comp. for the orig. prod. Also wrote mus. for plays by Ben Jonson and for Webster's *The Duchess of Malfi* ('Oh, let us howl', *c*.1613).

Johnson, Robert Sherlaw (*b* Sunderland, 1932; *d* Appleton, Oxon., 2000). Eng. composer and pianist. Lect., Leeds Univ., 1961–5, York Univ., 1965–70, Oxford Univ. from 1970. Specialist in mus. of *Messiaen and author of book on him. Works incl. opera *The *Lambton Worm* (1977); *Songs of Love and Springtime*, sop., pf.; 3 pf. sonatas (1963, 1967, 1976); *The Resurrection of Fêng-Huang*, sop., unacc. ch. (1968); *7 Short Piano Pieces* (1968); *The Praises of Heaven and Earth*, sop., pf., tape (1969); *Green Whispers of Gold*, sop., pf., tape (1971); *Carmina Vernalia*, sop., chamber orch. (1972); *Triptych*, fl., cl., va., vc., pf., perc. (1973); *Asterogenesis*, pf. (1973); *Festival Mass of the Resurrection*, ch., orch. (1974); *Where the Wild Things Are*, sop., tape; 2 str. qts. (1974); cl. quintet (1974); sonata, fl., vc. (1975); *Anglorum Feriae*, sop., ten., ch., orch. (1977); *Veritas veritatis*, 6 vv. (1980); pf. conc. (1983); *Encounters*, cl., str. qt., pf. (1988); *Sinfonietta Concertante* (1989); *Hymn to the Seasons*, sop., cl., pf. (1990); *Fanfares and Chorales*, 4 hn., 4 tpt., 4 tb. (1992).

Jolas, Betsy [Illous, Elizabeth] (*b* Paris, 1926). Fr.-born Amer. composer. Her Amer. parents took her to USA 1940. Won prize in Besançon int. cond. comp. 1953 and many subsequent awards. Replaced Messiaen at his Paris Cons. course 1971–4, joining faculty 1975. Teacher at many Amer. univs. and colls.

Jolie Fille de Perth, La (The Fair Maid of Perth). Opera in 4 acts by Bizet to lib. by St Georges and Adenis, based on Scott's novel (1823). Comp. 1866. Prod. Paris 1867, Manchester and London 1917.

Jolivet, André (*b* Paris, 1905; *d* Paris, 1974). Fr. composer. One of founders of *Jeune France* group 1936. Cond. and later mus. dir. Comédie-Française 1943–59, prof. of comp., Paris Cons. 1965–70. Interested in and influenced by oriental mus. and unusual instr. sonorities. Prin. works:

STAGE: *Dolorès, ou le miracle de la femme laide*, opera (1942); *L'inconnue*, ballet (1950); *Ariadne*, ballet (1964–5).

ORCH.: syms., No.1 (1953), No.2 (1959), No.3 (1964); *5 Danses rituelles* (1939); *Symphonie des danses* (1940); *Guignol et Pandore* (1943); concertino for tpt., str., pf. (1948); concs.: ondes Martenot (1947), fl. (1949), pf. (1950), hp. (1952), bn. (1954), tpt. No.2 (1954), perc. (1958), vc. No.1 (1962), No.2 (1966), vn. (1972); *Suite transocéane* (1955); *3 Interludes de la vérité de Jeanne* (1956); *Suite française* (1957); *Les amants magnifiques*, variations on Lully (1960); sym. for str. (1961); *Heptade* for tpt. and perc. (1971); *Yin-Yang*, 11 solo str. (1974).

VOICE AND ORCH.: *3 Chants des hommes*, bar. (1937); *Les Trois Complaintes du soldat* (1940); *La vérité de Jeanne*, oratorio (1956); *Songe à nouveau rêve*, sop. (1970).

CHORUS: *Kyrie* (1938); *La Tentation dernière de Jeanne d'Arc* (1941); Mass, *Uxor tua* (1962); *Le Coeur de la matière* (1965).

CHAMBER MUSIC: str. qt. (1934); *Pastorales de Noël*, fl., bn., hp. (1943); *Poèmes intimes*, v., pf. or chamber orch. (1944); *Chant de Linos*, fl., pf., or fl., vn., va., vc., hp. (1944); *Sérénade*, wind quintet (1945); *Suite rapsodique*, vn. (1965); *Cérémonial en hommage à Varèse* for 6 percussionists (1968); *Controversia*, ob., hp. (1968); *Arioso barocco*, tpt., org. (1969); *Heptade*, tpt., perc. (1971–2).

PIANO: *Mana* (1935); sonata No.1 (1945), No.2 (1957); *Hopi Snake Dance*, 2 pf. (1948); *Patchinko*, 2 pf. (1970).

Also incidental mus., songs, etc.

Joll, Phillip (*b* Merthyr Tydfil, 1954). Welsh baritone. Sang Wotan in *Das Rheingold* at RNCM 1978. Prof. début ENO 1978 (the Bonze in *Madam Butterfly*). Joined WNO 1979, singing several prin. roles, incl. Wotan in *Ring* cycle 1983–5 (perf. also at CG 1986). CG début 1982; NY Met début 1987.

Jommelli, Niccolò (*b* Aversa, Naples, 1714; *d* Naples, 1774). It. composer. Comp. first opera 1737. Worked in Rome and Bologne 1740–1 and in Venice 1741–7. Visited Vienna 1749, forming friendship with *Metastasio, most of whose texts he subsequently used, several of them more than once. Kapellmeister to Duke of Württemberg, Stuttgart, 1753–69, composing 17 operas. Returned to Naples 1769, but his work no longer found favour. Comp. over 80 operas and much church mus. Anticipated Gluck in use of dramatic recit. and in abandonment of *da capo* arias unless they had dramatic point. Among his many operas were: *L'errore amoroso* (1737); *Merope* (1741); *Achille in Sciro* (1749); *Ifigenia in Aulide* (1751); *La clemenza di Tito* (2 versions, 1753 and 1765); *Fetonte* (1753, 2nd vers. 1768); *Armida abbandonata* (1770); *Ifigenia in Tauride* (1771).

Jonas, (Sir) Peter (*b* London, 1946). Eng. administrator. Worked as extra and stagehand at Glyndebourne while student at Sussex Univ. Ass. to mus. dir. Chicago SO 1974–6, art. administrator 1976–85. Gen. dir., ENO, 1985–93. Intendant, Bavarian State Opera, Munich, 1993–2006. Noted for encouragement of contemp. composers and innovative prods. CBE 1992. Knighted 2000.

Jones, Daniel (Jenkyn) (*b* Pembroke, 1912; *d* Swansea, 1993). Welsh composer and conductor. Works incl. 12 syms;, vn. conc.; operas *The Knife* and *Orestes*; oratorio *St Peter*; cantata *The Country Beyond the Stars*; incidental mus. for *Under Milk Wood* (Dylan Thomas); 8 str. qts.; str. trio; sonata for 3 kettledrums. Friend since schooldays of Dylan Thomas, whose complete poems he ed. 1971. OBE 1968.

Jones, Della (*b* Neath, 1946). Welsh mezzo-soprano. Won Ferrier memorial schol. 1969. Début Geneva 1970 (Fyodor in *Boris Godunov*). SW début 1973, member of ENO 1977–82; WNO début 1977. Created Dolly in Hamilton's *Anna Karenina* 1981 (ENO). CG début 1983. Has sung with Scottish Opera and Opera North. Amer. début Los Angeles 1986.

Jones, Geraint (Iwan) (*b* Porth, 1917; *d* 1998). Welsh organist, conductor, and harpsichordist.

Org. at Nat. Gallery Concerts 1940–4. Founder, Geraint Jones Singers and Orch. 1951. Mus. dir. Lake District Fest. 1960–78. Art. dir. Salisbury Fest. 1972–7. Prof. RAM.

Jones, (Dame) **Gwyneth** (*b* Pontnewynydd, 1936). Welsh soprano. Début Zurich 1962 (Gluck's Orpheus). Sang Lady Macbeth (1963) and Leonore in *Fidelio* (1964) for WNO. Member of Royal Opera, CG, from 1963. Frequent guest appearances at Vienna Opera from 1966, Rome, Munich, Milan, S. Francisco, Chicago. NY début 1966, NY Met 1972; Bayreuth début 1966 and sang Brünnhilde in *Der Ring des Nibelungen* at centenary Bayreuth Fest. 1976, and at S. Francisco 1990, CG 1991, and NY Met 1993. Salzburg Fest. 1979. CBE 1976. DBE 1986. Shakespeare Prize 1987.

Jones, Philip (*b* Bath, 1928; *d* London, 2000). Eng. trumpet-player. Prin. tpt. in most leading Brit. orchs. incl. CG, RPO (1956–60), Philharmonia (1960–4), LPO (1964–5), New Philharmonia (1965–7) and BBC SO (1968–71). Founder and dir. Philip Jones Brass Ens. 1951–86. Head of Wind and Perc., RNCM, 1975–7, GSMD 1983–8. Principal TCL 1989–94. OBE 1977. CBE 1986.

Jones, Robert (*b* c.1485; *d* c.1535). Eng. composer and singer. Member of Chapel Royal under Henry VII and Henry VIII. Was at Field of the Cloth of Gold 1520. Only 3 comps. survive: *Missa* 'Spes nostra' in 5 parts, *Magnificat* in 5 parts, and 3-part song 'Who shall have my fayr ladye?'

Jones, Robert (*b* c.1570; *d* c.1615). Eng. composer and lutenist. Wrote 5 sets of 'songs and ayres' and set of madrigals. Contributed *Fair Oriana* to *The *Triumphs of Oriana* (1601).

Jones, Sidney (*b* London, 1861; *d* London, 1946). Eng. composer of operettas, notably *The Geisha*, prod. London and NY 1896. Son of bandmaster. Became cond. Prince of Wales Th., London, for which he wrote *A Gaiety Girl* (1893) and other musical comedies. Cond. Empire Th. from 1905 to retirement in 1916.

jongleur (Fr., 'juggler'). Medieval Fr. mus. entertainer or wandering minstrel who sang, played an instr., and was juggler and acrobat. See *Meistersinger, ménestrel*, and *Minnesinger*.

Jongleur de Notre-Dame, Le (Our Lady's Juggler). (1) Opera (*miracle*) in 3 acts by Massenet to lib. by M. Léna from Anatole France's story *L'étui de Nacre* (1892), itself based on *Le tombleur de Notre-Dame* (1870s). Comp. 1900. Prod. Monte Carlo 1902, CG 1906, NY (Manhattan Op. Co.) 1908.

(2) Masque by *Maxwell Davies for mime, bar., chamber ens., and children's band, f.p. St Magnus Fest., Orkney, 1978.

Jonny spielt auf (Johnny strikes up). Opera in 2 parts (11 scenes) by *Krenek, Op.45, to his own lib. Comp. 1925–6. Prod. Leipzig 1927, NY Met 1929, Leeds (Opera North) 1984. First opera to use jazz, Johnny being a Negro jazz player.

Joplin, Scott (*b* nr. Marshall, Texas, ?1868; *d* NY, 1917). Black Amer. composer and ragtime pianist. Played pf. in brothels of St Louis and Chicago. Formed Scott Joplin Ragtime Opera Co. 1903 to perf. his ragtime opera *A Guest of Honour*. Settled in NY, 1907. Pf. rags incl. *Maple Leaf Rag*, *The Entertainer*, and *Wall Street Rag*. Wrote 3-act opera, *Treemonisha* (1908–11, orchestrated 1915). It received a single perf. without scenery in 1915 and its failure contributed largely to the composer's death. Revival of popular enthusiasm for Joplin's mus. in mid-1970s due mainly to efforts of Amer. pianist and musicologist Joshua Rifkin. *Treemonisha* was first staged Atlanta 1972 (orig. orch. is lost). Posthumous Pulitzer Prize 1976.

Jordá, Enrique (*b* San Sebastian, 1911; *d* Brussels, 1996). Amer. conductor of Sp. birth. Début Paris 1938. Cond. Madrid SO 1940–5, Cape Town SO 1948–54, San Francisco SO 1954–63, Antwerp PO 1970–5, Euskadi SO 1982–4. Cond. f.p. of Roy Harris's 8th Sym., S. Francisco 1962.

Jordan, Armin (Georg) (*b* Lucerne, 1932; *d* Basle, 2006). Swiss conductor. Début Bienne Opera 1957. Chief cond., Bienne Opera 1961–6, Zurich Opera 1963–8, St Gallen 1968–71, Basle Opera 1968–9. Mus. dir. Lausanne Chamber Orch. 1973–85, Orchestre de la Suisse Romande 1985–97.

Joseph. (1) Oratorio by Handel (*Joseph and His Brethren*) perf. London 1744, New Orleans 1812.

(2) 3-act opera by *Méhul, to lib. by Duval. Prod. Paris 1807, Philadelphia 1828, London (concert) 1841, CG (rev. Weingartner) 1914.

(3) Oratorio by Macfarren, 1877 Leeds Fest.

Josephs, Wilfred (*b* Newcastle upon Tyne, 1927; *d* London, 1997). Eng. composer. Won 1st Milan int. comp. competition in 1963 with *Requiem*. Prolific composer of mus. for TV and films. Works incl.:

OPERAS: *Pathelio* (1963); *The Appointment* (TV, 1968); *Through the Looking Glass and What Alice Found There*, children's opera (1977–8); *Rebecca* (1982–3); *Alice in Wonderland*, children's opera (1985–8).

BALLETS: *The Magic Being* (1961); *La Répétition de Phèdre* (1964–5); *Equus* (1978); *Cyrano de Bergerac* (1985).

ORCH.: syms.: No.1 (1955, rev. 1957–8, 1974–5), No.2 (1963–4), No.3 (*Philadelphia*), chamber orch. (1967), No.4, alto, bar., orch. (1967–70), No.5 (*Pastoral*) (1970–1), No.6, sop., bar., ch., orch. (1972–4), No.7 (*Winter*), chamber orch. (1976), No.8 (*The Four Elements*), sym. band (1975–7), No.9, *Sinfonia Concertante*, chamber orch. (1979–80), No.10 (*Circadian Rhythms*) (1985), No.11 (*Fireworks*), sym. band (1992), No.12 (*Sinfonia Quixotica*) (1995); *Elegy*, str. (1957); *Concerto da camera*, vn., pf., chamber orch. (1959); *A Tyneside Overture* (1960); *Monkchester Dances* (1961); *Cantus Natalis*, vc. conc. (1961–2); pf. conc. No.1 (1965), No.2

(1971), No.3 (1993–4); *Canzonas on a Theme of Rameau*, str. (1965); *Polemic*, str. (1967); *Rail* (1967); ob conc. (1967–8); *Serenade* (1968) *Variations on a Theme of Beethoven* (1969); double vn. conc. (1969); *Saratoga Concerto*, gui., hp., hpd., chamber orch. (1972); Ov., *The 4 Horsemen of the Apocalypse* (1973–4); Concerto for Brass Band (1974); cl. conc. (1975); *Eve (d'après Rodin)*, sym.-poem (1977–8); *Concerto d'amore*, 2 vn., orch. (1979); db. conc. (1980); Ov., *The Brontës* (1981); perc. conc. (1982); va. conc. (1983); *Caen Wood* (1985); *Fanfare Prelude* (1986); *Battle of Britain Suite*, wind band (1989–90); vn. conc. (1992); *Celebration* (1994).

CHORAL AND VOCAL: *12 Letters*, after Belloc, narr., cl., str. trio., pf. (1957); *Requiem* (1962–3); *Mortales*, oratorio (1967–9); *Nightmusic*, mez. (or cont., or ten., or bar.), orch. (1970); *Songs of Innocence*, ch., children's ch., orch. (1972); *Aeroplanes and Angels*, solo vv., pf. duo (1977–8); *Spring Songs*, SATB (1981); *Fish Heaven*, mez., fl. (1991).

CHAMBER MUSIC: str. qts.: No.1 (1954), No.2 (1958), No.3 (1971), No.4 (1981); sonata, solo vn. (1957); *Requiescant pro defunctis judaeis*, str. quintet (1961); octet (1964); vn. sonata No.1 (1965), No.2 (1975); trio, fl., vn., vc. (1966); str. trio (1966); sonata, solo vc. (1970); hn. trio (1971); sonata, brass quintet (1974, rev. 1981); pf. quintet (1974–6); *Waltz and Song*, fl., cl., hn., hp., str. (1975); fl. sonata (1976–7); wind quintet (1977); conc. for 4 pf., 6 perc. (1978); ob. qt. (1979); db. sonata (1980); *8 Aphorisms*, 8 tb. (1981); cl. quintet (1985); *Northumbrian Dances*, sop. sax., pf. (1986); *Serenade to the Moon*, 4 cl. or 4 sax., or fl., ob., cl., bn., or str. qt. (1987); ob. sonata (1988); *Papageno Variations*, ww. sextet (1989); pf. trio No.2 (1996).

PIANO: *29 Preludes* (1969); *Doubles*, 2 pf. (1970–3); *Sonata Duo*, 2 pf. (1976); *Byrdsong*, pf. and org. (1981).

ORGAN: *Fantasia on 3 Notes* (1978); *Tombeau* (1980); *Testimony*, in memoriam DSCH (1981); sonata (1992).

Josephslegende (The Legend of Joseph). Ballet in 1 act with mus. by R. Strauss to lib. by H. Kessler and H. von Hofmannsthal, choreog. Fokine. Comp. 1913–14. Prod. Paris (Diaghilev) and London, 1914, with Massine as Joseph. Also symphonic fragment for orch., 1947, f.p. Cincinnati 1949.

Joshua. Oratorio by Handel. Text by Rev. T. Morell. F.p. London 1748.

Josquin Desprès [Desprez, des Pres, and several other spellings], (*b* ?Picardy, *c.*1440; *d* Condé-sur-l'Escaut, Hainaut, 1521). Fr.-Flemish composer. Possibly a pupil of *Ockeghem. From *c.*1459 to 1504 was in It., first as singer in Milan Cath. and employee of Sforza family. Went to Rome in 1484 in service of Cardinal Ascanio Sforza and as member of papal chapel. Became choirmaster at Ferrara, 1503. Returned to Low Countries 1504, after outbreak of plague, where he became provost of church at Condé. Regarded as most gifted and influential composer of his time. Was no radical innovator but successfully developed existing and unexplored techniques. Was

particularly successful in giving dramatic emphasis to the texts he set by means of word-rhythms and imitation. Although his early masses used a *cantus firmus*, later ones employed parody techniques and were sometimes based on a motto theme or a series of canons. Similarly in motets he abandoned a plainchant *cantus firmus* in favour of imitative devices. Some of his *chansons* were on erotic and frivolous texts and he was one of the first to appropriate tunes from court and theatre for his serious works. His work was so popular that many forgeries were published. He wrote 18 masses (the best-known being *Ave Maris Stella*, *L'homme armé*, and *Pange lingua*), nearly 100 motets, and over 70 secular works.

jota, la. A lively dance in triple time from N. Spain. It is perf. by one or more couples, acc. by a gui. player who also sings, and castanets.

Joubert, John (Pierre Herman) (*b* Cape Town, 1927). S. African composer. Settled in Brit. 1946. Lect. in mus. at Hull Univ. 1950–62 and Birmingham Univ. 1962–86. Works incl.:

OPERAS: *Antigone*, radio (1954); *Silas Marner* (1961); *The Quarry* (1964); *The Prisoner* (1973); *The Wayfarers* (1983); *Jane Eyre* (1987–9).

ORCH.: *Symphonic Prelude* (1953); vn. conc. (1954); syms.: No.1 (1955), No.2 (1970); pf. conc. (1958); *Sinfonietta* (1962); bn. conc. (1974); *Threnos*, hpd., 12 solo str. (1974); *Déploration* (1978); *Temps perdu*, str. (1984); *A Song for Stephen* (2003); *Nativity Prelude* (2004).

CHORAL: *The Burghers of Calais*, sop., counterten., 2 ten., bar., bass, ch., chamber orch. (1953); *Urbs Beata*, ten., bar., ch., orch. (1963); *The Martyrdom of St Alban*, spkr., ten., bass, ch., chamber orch. (1968); *The Raising of Lazarus*, mez., ten., ch., orch. (1970); *Herefordshire Canticles*, sop., bar., ch., boys' ch., orch. (1979); *Gong-Tormented Sea*, bar., ch., orch. (1981); *The Instant Moment*, bar., str. (1986); *Missa brevis*, ch., chamber orch. (1988); *Rochester Triptych*, ch., orch. (1997); *Vertue*, sop., ten., mixed vv. (1999).

UNACC. VOICES: *There Is No Rose* (1954); *Welcome Yule* (1958); *The Beatitudes* (1964); *4 Stations on the Road to Freedom* (1972); *2 Antiphons*, male vv. (1974); *3 Portraits* (1983); *3 Carols* (1984); *Rotate Coeli* (1985).

VOICE(S) & INSTR(S).: *Great Lord of Lords*, ch., org. (1954); *Missa beata Ioannis*, ch., org. (1961); *Te Deum*, sop., ch., org. (1964); *Lord, Thou hast been our refuge*, ch., org. (1967);; *Magnificat* and *Nunc dimittis*, ch., org. (1968); *I will lift up mine eyes*, women's vv., pf. (1969); *3 Hymns to St Oswald*, ch., org. (1972, rev. 1974); *Music for a Pied Piper*, ch., rec., 2 vn., bass viol, violine, 2 lutes (1985); *Autumn Rain*, ch., pf. (1985); *Vision and Prayer*, ch., pf. (4 hands) (1986); *Missa brevis*, ch., org. (1988); *For the Beauty of the Earth*, ch., pf. (2001).

SONGS & SONG-CYCLES: *2 Invocations* (Blake), ten., pf. (1958); *6 Poems of Emily Brontë*, high v., pf. (1969); *African Sketchbook*, 4 vv., wind quintet (1970);

Crabbed Age and Youth, counterten., rec., viola da gamba, hpd. (1974); *The Turning Wheel*, sop., pf. (1979); *The Hour Hand*, sop., rec. (1984).
CHAMBER MUSIC: str. qts.: No.1 (1950), No.2 (1977), No.3 (1986), No.4 (1987); va. sonata (1951); str. trio (1958); *Octet* (1961); *Kontakion*, vc., pf. (1971); *Chamber Music for Brass Quintet* (1985); pf. trio (1986); *Improvisations*, rec., pf. (1988); *Landscapes*, sop., vn., vc., pf. (1992); *Six Miniatures after Kilvert*, vn., va. (1997).
PIANO: Sonatas: No.1 (1957), No.2 (1972); *Divertimento*, pf. duet (1950); *Dance Suite* (1956); *Lyric Fantasy* (2000).

Journet, Marcel (*b* Grasse, 1867; *d* Vittel, 1993). Fr. bass. Début Bézier, 1891 (Balthasar in *La favorite*). Sang in Brussels 1894–1900. CG début 1897. Sang in London until 1907, returning 1927–8. NY Met 1900–8; Paris Opéra 1908–32; Chicago 1915–18; La Scala 1917–28. Noted interpreter of Méphistophélès, Colline, and Escamillo.

Joyce, Eileen (Alannah) (*b* Zeehan, Tasmania, 1912; *d* Limpsfield, Surrey, 1991). Australian pianist and harpsichordist. London début Prom. concert cond. Wood (1930). Soloist with all leading orchs. Gave early Brit. perfs. of concs. by Shostakovich and Khachaturian. CMG 1981.

Jubilate. Psalm 100 in Authorized Version of Bible (Ps. 99 in Latin Psalter). Used in Anglican service as alternative to Benedictus. Has been set to mus. by many composers, incl. G. Gabrieli, Purcell, and Britten.

Judas Maccabaeus. Oratorio by Handel to text by Rev. T. Morell based on biblical incidents. Comp. in summer of 1746 on commission from Frederick, Prince of Wales, to celebrate Eng. victory over Young Pretender at Culloden and return of victorious general, Duke of Cumberland, to London. (Part 3 contains ch. *See the Conquering Hero Comes*.) Prod. London 1747.

Judd, James (*b* Hertford, 1949). Eng. conductor. After working at London Opera Centre, was ass. cond. Cleveland Orch. 1973–5. Assoc. cond. Eur. Community Youth Orch. 1978. Co-founder and cond. Chamber Orch. of Eur. 1981. Mus. dir. Florida PO, Fort Lauderdale, 1987–2001, Eur. Community Youth Orch. 1990. Art. dir. Florida Grand Opera 1993–6; cond. NZ SO from 1999.

Judd, Terence (*b* London, 1957; *d* Beachy Head, 1979). Eng. pianist. Won Nat. Junior pf. comp. 1967. 1st prize Brit. Liszt comp. 1976. 4th place Tchaikovsky comp., Moscow, 1978. Annual prize awarded in his memory.

Judith. (1) Oratorio by Parry, f.p. Birmingham Fest. 1888.
(2) Opera in 3 acts by *Honegger to lib. by R. Morax, comp. 1925, prod. Monte Carlo 1926.
(3) Opera in 1 act by E. Goossens to lib. by Arnold Bennett, prod. London and Philadelphia 1929.
(4) Oratorio by Thomas Arne, words by Bickerstaffe, f.p. London 1761.

Juditha Triumphans (Judith triumphant). Oratorio (RV644) by Vivaldi to lib. by Cassetti, f.p. Venice 1716, f. stage ps. Schwetzingen 1981, London 1984.

Juha. Opera in 3 acts by *Merikanto to lib. by A. Ackté after novel by J. Aho. Comp. 1920–2. F.p. Finn. Radio 1958, (stage) Lahti Mus. Coll., Finland, 1963, Edinburgh Fest. 1987.

Juilliard Quartet. Amer. str. qt. founded in 1946 by William Schuman when pres. of Juilliard Sch. of Mus., NY. Specializes in contemporary mus., but has also recorded and given several cycles of all the Beethoven qts. Membership has altered more than once except for the 1st vn. Robert Mann (*b* Portland, Oregon, 1920).

Juilliard School. Amer. mus. coll. in NY. Named after Augustus D. Juilliard (*b* at sea, 1836; *d* NY, 1919), NY cotton merchant, who left around 20 million dollars for creation of Juilliard Musical Foundation, 1920. School founded as Juilliard Graduate Sch. 1924, entrance only by competitive exam. before entire faculty, each student having to re-qualify in this manner every year of their course. Merged with Inst. of Mus. Art (founded by F. Damrosch and J. Loeb in 1905) in 1946, the Inst. becoming the Undergraduate Sch. of the Juilliard, with Graduate Sch. retaining orig. identity. The composer William Schuman was pres. 1945–62, Peter Mennin 1962–83, Joseph W. Polisi from 1984. In Nov. 1969 the Sch. moved to its own building as a constituent part of the Lincoln Center for the Performing Arts. This building has 4 auditoria, incl. opera th. Name changed from Juilliard School of Mus. to Juilliard Sch. because of est. of dance dept. in 1952 and drama division in 1968.

Juive, La (The Jewess). Opera in 5 acts by Halévy to lib. by Scribe. Prod. Paris 1835, New Orleans 1844, NY 1845, London 1846.

juke boxes. Automatic coin-operated machines for playing gramophone records, orig. installed in Amer. inns, etc., and common in Britain in the last few decades. (Name derived from 'jouke'; local inns in southern states of USA being called 'jouke joints', perhaps from Old Eng. *jowken*, to rest or sleep.)

Julien. Opera in prol. and 4 acts by Charpentier to his own lib. Sequel to *Louise*. Prod. Paris 1913, NY 1914.

Julietta (Cz. *Snář*, The Dream-Book). Opera in 3 acts by Martinů to his own lib. based on the play *Juliette, ou La Clé des songes* (Julietta, or The Key of Dreams) (1930) by Georges Neveux. Comp. 1936–7. Prod. Prague 1938, London (New Opera Co. at the Coliseum) 1978.

Julius Caesar (Handel). See *Giulio Cesare*.

Jullien [Julien], **Louis** (Georges Maurice Adolphe Roch Albert Abel Antonio Alexandre Noé Jean Lucien Daniel Eugène Joseph-le-brun

Joseph-Barème Thomas Thomas Thomas-Thomas Pierre Arbon Pierre-Maurel Barthélemi Artus Alphonse Bertrand Dieudonné Emanuel Josué Vincent Luc Michel Jules-de-la-Plane Jules-Bazin Julio César) (*b* Sisteron, 1812; *d* Paris, 1860). Fr. conductor, composer, and impresario. Sponsored at his baptism by 36 members of local Phil. Soc., each of whom contrib. a name. Early ventures led to insolvency; fled to London where he promoted opera and promenade concerts 1838–59 with his own orch. which he cond. in highly flamboyant style. Engaged Berlioz to cond. four operas at Drury Lane, 1847, resulting in first bankruptcy. Employed what today would be called 'publicity gimmicks'. Comp. an opera *Pietro il Grande* (CG 1852). Toured USA 1853–4. Lost all his mus. in CG fire 1856, investments failed 1857. Returned to Paris 1859, was arrested for debt, released, and then put in asylum where he died. Pioneer in use of the baton. Notwithstanding his indulging in such showmanship as being handed a jewelled baton on a silver salver, he had the best players in London in his orch. and was a serious figure in the popularization of mus.

Jumping Frog of Calaveras County, The. Opera in 1 act by Lukas *Foss to lib. by J. Karsavina after story by Mark Twain. Prod. Bloomington, Ind., 1950.

June, Ava (*b* London, 1931). Eng. soprano. Member of SW chorus 1953, becoming prin. sop. 1957. CG début 1958 (Voice from Heaven in *Don Carlos*). Won Sofia int. comp. 1963. Sang with WNO and in S. Francisco (1974, her Amer. début), but sang mainly with ENO, roles incl. Sieglinde (in *Ring* cycle cond. Goodall).

Jung, Manfred (*b* Oberhausen, 1940). Ger. tenor. Début as Arindal in Wagner's *Die Feen*, Bayreuth Youth Fest. 1967. Bayreuth ch. 1970–3, début as soloist Dortmund 1974. Member Düsseldorf Opera from 1977. Bayreuth Fest. 1977–86. Sang Siegfried in TV version of Chéreau's prod. of *The Ring*. Salzburg Easter Fest. 1980. In addition to Wagner roles, sings Strauss's Herod and Aegisthus.

Junge Lord, Der (The Young Lord). Comic opera in 2 acts by Henze to lib. by I. Bachmann after fable *Der Scheik von Alexandria und seine Sklaven* (1827) by W. Hauff. Comp. 1964. Prod. Berlin 1965; San Diego 1967; London 1969 (visit by Cologne Opera).

Junge Magd, Die (The Young Servant). 6 songs by Hindemith to poems by Trakl, set for alto v., fl., cl., and str. qt. His Op.23 No.2. Comp. 1922, f.p. Donaueschingen 1922.

Jungwirth, Manfred (*b* St Pölten, 1919; *d* 1999). Austrian bass. Début Bucharest 1942 (Mephistopheles in *Faust*). Salzburg Fest. début 1946 (concert), opera 1985 (La Roche in *Capriccio*). Won int. singing comp. Geneva 1948. Sang in Innsbruck, Zurich, Berlin, Düsseldorf, Frankfurt (1960–7), and Vienna from 1967. Débuts: Brit. (Glyndebourne) 1965; Vienna (1967), S. Francisco (1971), NY Met (1974); CG 1981.

'Jupiter' Symphony. Nickname for Mozart's Sym. No.41 in C major, K551 (1788). Not known why or when name originated, but possibly first used in programme of Phil. Soc. of London concert cond. *Bishop on 26 March, 1821. Mozart's son F. X. Mozart said that the nickname was coined by the impresario *Salomon.

Jürgens, Jürgen (*b* Frankfurt am Main, 1925; *d* Hamburg, 1994). Ger. conductor. Dir. of Hamburg Monteverdi Choir 1955. Joined staff of Hamburg Univ. as lect. 1960, becoming mus. dir. 1966 and prof. 1977. Ed. of works by Monteverdi and A. Scarlatti. His choir's repertory ranged from Ockeghem and Monteverdi to Henze.

Jurinac, Sena [Srebrenka] (*b* Travnik, Yugoslavia, 1921). Austro-Croatian soprano of Bosnian birth. Début Zagreb 1942 as Mimì in *La bohème*. Member, Vienna State Opera 1944–83. London début 1947 with Vienna State Opera. Salzburg Fest. 1947–80; La Scala 1948; Glyndebourne 1949–56; Memorable in Mozart roles and as Composer in *Ariadne auf Naxos* and Oktavian in *Der Rosenkavalier*). S. Francisco 1959; Chicago 1963. In latter part of her career sang Kostelnička in *Jenůfa*.

Jurowski, Vladimir (*b* Moscow, 1972). Russ. cond. Studied Moscow Cons. Moved to Ger. 1990, studying at Mus. High Schs. of Dresden and Berlin (cond. with Rolf Reuter). Int. opera début Wexford Fest. 1995 (*May Night*), CG 1995 (*Nabucco*). Chief cond. Komische Oper, Berlin, 1996–2000. NY Met 1999 (*Rigoletto*). WNO 2000 (*Queen of Spades*). Mus. dir. Glyndebourne from 2001. Prin. cond. LPO from 2007.

just intonation. System of instr. tuning whereby a single scale, usually C, was determined according to ratio of its notes. Those far removed from C would be severely out of tune, hence the introduction of equal temperament as substitute for this 'natural' non-tempered scale.

K

K. Abbreviated prefix given to nos. in (1) *Köchel catalogue of Mozart's works; the letter is followed by a numeral, e.g. K491 (C minor pf. conc.).
(2) *Kirkpatrick catalogue of Domenico Scarlatti's works.

Kabaivanska, Raina (Yakimova) (*b* Burgas, 1934). Bulg. soprano. Début Sofia Nat. Opera 1957 (Tatyana in *Eugene Onegin*). It. début La Scala 1961; CG 1962; NY Met 1962; Paris 1975 Salzburg 1981. Renowned Tosca and Butterfly in leading It. opera-houses.

Kabalevsky, Dmitry (Borisovich) (*b* St Petersburg, 1904; *d* Moscow, 1987). Russ. composer and pianist. Worked as pf. teacher and silent-cinema pianist 1922–5. His pf. conc. 1929 won him fame in Soviet Union. In 1932, when Union of Soviet Composers was formed, he helped to organize Moscow branch, thereafter holding various administrative posts and writing many articles on Soviet mus. and composers. His output in the next 5 years was prolific, incl. 3 syms., the 3rd of which was a requiem for Lenin. Ass. prof. of comp., Moscow Cons. from 1932, prof. from 1939. During World War II he wrote numerous patriotic works, having joined Communist party in 1940. His post-war efforts reflected the official policy of 'Socialist realism'. His works comp. specially for young musicians are regarded as of particular significance. The West knows his instr. works better than his operas and operettas which are perf. in Russia. Prin. works:

OPERAS: *The Craftsman of Clamecy* (known in West as *Colas Breugnon*) (1936–8, rev. 1953, 1969); *Into the Fire (Before Moscow)* (1942); *The Taras Family* (incorporating much of *Into the Fire*) (1947, 2nd version 1950, 3rd version 1967); *Nikita Vershinin* (1954–5); *Spring Sings* (1957); *In the Magic Forest* (1958); *The Sisters* (1967).

ORCH. AND CHORAL: syms.: No.1 in C♯ minor (1932), No.2 in C minor (1934), No.3 in B♭ minor (*Requiem* with ch.) (1933), No.4 in C minor (1954); *The Comedians*, suite (1940); *Suite for Jazz Orch.* (1940); *Parade of Youth* with ch. (1941); *The Mighty Homeland*, 2 soloists and ch. (1941–2); *The People's Avengers*, suite for ch. and orch. (1942); *Suite, Romeo and Juliet* (1956); *Song of Morning, Spring, and Peace*, children's ch. (1957–8); *Leninists*, 3 ch. and orch. (1958–9); *Spring*, sym.-poem (1960); *Requiem*, mez., bar., double ch., and orch. (1962); *Of the Homeland*, children's ch. and orch. (1965); *Letter to the 30th Century*, oratorio (1972).

CONCERTOS: pf., No.1 in A minor (1928), No.2 in G minor (1935), No.3 in D major (1952), *Rhapsody* for pf. and orch. (1963); vn. conc. in C major (1948); vc. conc. No.1 in G minor (1948–9), No.2 in C major (1964).

CHAMBER MUSIC: str. qts. No.1 in A minor (1928), No.2 in G minor (1945); vc. sonata (1962).
PIANO: sonata No.1 in F major (1927), No.2 in E♭ major (1945), No.3 in F major (1946); *4 Preludes* (1927–8); *30 Children's Pieces* (1938–9); *24 Preludes* (1943–4).
SONGS: *3 Poems of A. Blok* (1927–8); *8 Songs for children's ch.* (1932); *7 Merry Songs* (English nursery-rhymes) (1944–5); *10 Shakespeare Sonnets* (1953–5); *5 Romances* (1963–4).
Also ch. and film mus.

Kaddish. Doxology, one version of which became Jewish mourners' prayer. Set by *Josephs in his *Requiem* and by *Bernstein as 3rd Sym. Ravel borrowed one of the liturgical versions (chanted as the prayer for dew on Passover) for the second of his *Deux mélodies Hébraïques* (1914).

Kadosa, Pál (*b* Léva, Hungary (now Czechoslovakia), 1903; *d* Budapest, 1983). Hung. composer and pianist. Taught pf. at Fodor Cons. 1927–43. Prof. and dean of pf. faculty, Budapest Acad. from 1945. Works incl. 2 operas; 8 syms.; 5 cantatas (incl. *Stalin's Oath*, 1949); 4 pf. sonatas; 4 pf. concs.; va. conc.; conc. for str. qt. and orch.; 3 str. qts., etc.

Kaffeecantate (J. S. Bach). See *Coffee Cantata*.

Kagel, Mauricio (*b* Buenos Aires, 1931). Argentinian-born composer, conductor, and teacher. Choral coach and cond. at Teatro Colón, 1955–6. Moved to Cologne 1957, working at EMS. Has worked in th. as composer and dir. of his own works since 1963. His mus. uses tape and elec. procedures; also he has demanded 'screams and yells' from singers and the sound of balls thrown on a kettle-drum. In his later works, visual and theatrical elements ('mixed media') have predominated. Many of the scores involve *indeterminacy. Works incl.: Str. Sextet (1953); *Tower Music*, pre-recorded *concrète* instr. sounds for 24 groups of loudspeakers, with light projections (1953); *Anagrama*, 4 soloists, ch., chamber ens. (1957–8); *Heterophonie* (1959–60); *Antithèse*, actor, elec., audience sounds (1962); *Diaphonie*, 2 projectors, ch., orch. (1962–4); *Tremens*, scenic montage (1963–5); *Kommentar und Extempore*, soliloquies with gestures (1965–7); *Music for Renaissance Instruments* (1965–7); Str. Qt. (1966–8); *Ludwig Van* (1969); *Variations without Fugue*, orch. (1971); *Programm, Gespräche mit Kammermusik*, vv., ens. (1971–2); *Zwei-Mann-Orchester* (1973); *1898*, children's ch., instr. (1973); *Kantrimusik, Pastorale für Stimmen und Instrumente* (1973–5); *Die Erschöpfung der Welt (The Exhaustion of the World)*, mus. th., 6 solo vv., 6 actors, 2 chs., orch. (1974–8); *Mare Nostrum* (1975); *Bestiarium* (1975); *Die Umkehrung Amerikas*, radio play (1976); *Variété*, concert spectacle (1977); *Dressage*, 3 perc. instr. (1977); th. piece *Ex-Position*, with gymnasts (1978); *Rhythm-machines*, gymnasts or dancers, 2 perc., rhythm-generators (1978); *Chorbuch* (1978) (arr. of 53 Bach chorales for amp. mixed ch. and pf.); *Aus Deutschland*, *lieder*-opera (1981); *Lekture von Orwell*, stage work (1984); *La trahison orale*, orch. (1984); *2 Ballads of Guillaume de Machaut* (1984); *Nach einer Sankt-Bach-Passion* (1985); pf. trio (1985); *A Letter*, mez., orch. (1986); *Dance School*, ballet (1988); *Quodlibet*, women's vv., orch. (1988); 3rd str. qt. (1988); *Osten*, salon orch. (1989); *Fragende Ode*, ch., wind., perc. (1989); *Liturgian* (1990); *Opus 1990* (1991); *'den 24. XII. 1931'* (1991).

Kahane, Jeffrey (Alan) (*b* Los Angeles, 1956). Amer. pianist and conductor. Début S. Francisco 1978. Second in Clara Haskil comp. 1977, 4th in Van Cliburn comp. 1981, and winner of Arthur Rubinstein comp. 1983. NY début 1983, London 1985. Cond. début Oregon 1988. Mus. dir. Santa Rosa SO 1995–2005, Los Angeles CO from 1996, Colorado SO from 2005.

Kahnt, Christian Frederik (*b* Leipzig, 1823; *d* Leipzig, 1897). Ger. music publisher. Founded his firm at Leipzig 1851. Pubd. works by Liszt and Mahler. Firm moved to Bonn 1950 and then to Wasserburg.

Kaim, Franz (*b* Kirchheim, 1856; *d* Munich, 1935). Ger. patron of music who built concert-hall and founded Kaim concerts in Munich 1891, starting orch. (Kaim Orch.) 1893. Works by Mahler and Strauss were perf. at Kaim concerts which, in 1908, were absorbed by new Konzertverein. The orch. in 1924 became the Munich PO.

Kaipaiinen, Jouni (Ilari) (*b* Helsinki, 1956). Finn. composer. Comps. incl. TV opera *The Miracle of Konstanz* (1985–7); 3 str. qts. (1973, 1974, 1984); *5 Poems of René Char*, sop., orch. (1978–80); *Ladders to Fire*, conc. for 2 pf. (1979); sym. (1980–5); cl. trio (1983); trio, fl., bn., pf. (1986); pf. trio (1986–7); *Carpe Diem!*, cl. conc. (1990); ob. conc. (1994); va. conc. (1997); bn. conc. (2005).

Kaisermarsch (Emperor March). Orch. work by Wagner, comp. 1871 to celebrate Ger. victory in Franco-Prussian War of 1870 and election of Wilhelm I as Ger. emperor. F.p. Berlin 1871.

Kaiserquartett (Haydn). See *'Emperor' Quartet*.

Kaiser von Atlantis, oder Die Tod-Verweigerung, Der (The Emperor of Atlantis, or The Refusal to Die). Legend in 4 scenes, Op.49, by *Ullmann to lib. by Peter Kien. Comp. 1943 in concentration camp of Theresienstadt (Terezin), where rehearsals were held in 1944. Prod. Amsterdam 1975, S. Francisco 1977, London 1985.

Kaiser-Walzer (Emperor Waltz). Waltz, Op.437, by Johann Strauss II, comp. 1888 in honour of Emperor Franz Josef to mark 40th anniversary of his accession. Arr. for chamber ens. 1925 by *Schoenberg.

Kajanus, Robert (*b* Helsinki, 1856; *d* Helsinki, 1933). Finn. conductor and composer. Founded Helsinki Phil. Soc., 1882, cond. Helsinki PO until 1932. Taught mus. at Helsinki Univ. 1897–1926

(prof. from 1908). Friend and interpreter of Sibelius, several of whose syms. he cond. for early recordings. Comp. syms., cantatas, hymns, etc.

Kakadu Variations. Variations on 'Ich bin der Schneider Kakadu' for pf. trio, Op.121a, by Beethoven, probably comp. in 1798 but not pubd. until 1824. Song is by Wenzel Müller from mus. play *Die Schwestern von Prag* (The Sisters from Prague) (1794). Kakadu is Ger. for cockatoo, but in this case refers to a character in the play.

Kalbeck, Max (*b* Breslau, 1850; *d* Vienna, 1921). Ger. author, critic, and librettist. Mus. critic *Schlesische Zeitung* 1875, later for *Breslauer Zeitung*. Moved to Vienna 1880. Wrote for *Wiener allgemeine Zeitung*, then for *Neue freie Presse* 1883–6, *Neues Wiener Tageblatt* 1886–90, and *Wiener Montags-Revue* from 1890. Partisan of Brahms, whose biog. he wrote (Berlin 1904–14, pubd. in 8 half-vols.). Ed. some vols. of Brahms's letters (Vols.I–II, Berlin 1907, VIII, Berlin 1915, IX–XII, Berlin 1917–19). Also wrote 3 books on Wagner's operas, new libretti for Mozart's *Bastien und Bastienne* and *La finta giardiniera*, and libs. for Johann Strauss II (*Jakuba*, 1894) and Georg Henschel (*Nubia*, 1899).

Kalevala (from *Kaleva*, Finland). Finn. nat. epic, transmitted orally over several centuries, on which Sibelius based several works. In 1835 Elias Lönnrot published an edn. of 12,000 verses and in 1849 a 2nd edn. of 23,000 verses in trochaic verse, unrhymed, divided into 50 cantos or runes. This has been trans. into Swed., Ger., Eng., and Fr. Sibelius works which draw on it incl. *Kullervo, *Pohjola's Daughter*, and the *Lemminkäinen* works.

Kalichstein, Joseph (*b* Tel Aviv, 1946). Israeli pianist. Début NY, 1967. 1st prize Leventritt comp. 1969. Eur. début London 1970 (LSO, cond. Previn). Thereafter int. concert career. Salzburg Fest. début 1977.

Kalinnikov, Vasily (Sergeyevich) (*b* Govt. of Orel, 1866; *d* Yalta, 1901 (old calendar 1900)). Russ. composer and conductor. Bassoonist in th. orchs. Ass. cond. Moscow It. Opera 1893–4. Ill-health compelled resignation. Comp. 2 syms., cantata, str. qt., etc.

Kalisch, Alfred (*b* London, 1863; *d* London, 1933). Eng. music critic and librettist. Began writing on mus. 1894, working for various papers (*The World* 1899–1915). Strong champion of R. Strauss in Eng.; trans. libs. of *Salome, Elektra, Der Rosenkavalier* (much bowdlerized), and *Ariadne auf Naxos*. Also trans. lib. of Mascagni's *Iris*.

Kalkbrenner, Friedrich (Wilhelm) (*b* nr. Kassel, 1785; *d* Enghien-les-Bains, 1849). Fr. pianist, teacher, and composer. Of Ger. extraction. Lived in London 1814–23. Joined pf.-making firm of *Pleyel in Paris, 1824, establishing himself as renowned teacher. Chopin was his friend and dedicated his E minor pf. conc. to him. Wrote pf. method. Comp. 4 pf. concs., 13 pf. sonatas, and much chamber mus.

Kalliwoda [Kalivoda], **Johann Wenzel** [Jan Václav] (b Prague, 1801; d Karlsruhe, 1866). Bohemian composer and violinist. Played in Prague th. orch. 1816–21. For over 30 years Kapellmeister at court of Donaueschingen. Comp. 2 operas, 7 syms. (1826–41), str. qts., ob. conc., song-cycle *Das deutsche Lied*.

Kallman, Chester (b Brooklyn, NY, 1921; d Athens, 1975). Amer. poet and librettist. Joint librettist with Auden for Stravinsky's *The Rake's Progress* and Henze's *The Bassarids* and *Elegy for Young Lovers*. Also joint translator, with Auden, of *Die Zauberflöte*. Trans. libs. of Monteverdi's *L'incoronazione di Poppea*, Verdi's *Falstaff*, Donizetti's *Anna Bolena*, Mozart's *Die Entführung aus dem Serail*, and Bartók's *Bluebeard's Castle*.

Kálmán, Emmerich [Imre] (b Siófok, 1882; d Paris, 1953). Hung.-born composer. Settled in Vienna until 1938. In Paris 1938–40, USA 1940–6 (Amer. cit. 1942). Lived in Paris from 1949. Wrote successful operettas, e.g. *Tatárjárás* (The Gay Hussars) (1908); *Fräulein Susi* (1915); *Die Csárdásfürstin* (The Gipsy Princess) (1915); *Gräfin Mariza* (Countess Maritza) (1924); *Die Zirkusprinzessin* (The Circus Princess) (1926).

Kalmus, Alfred (August Uhlrich) (b Vienna, 1889; d London, 1972). Eng. music publisher of Austrian birth. Joined mus. publishers Universal Edition in Vienna, 1909. Went to London 1936 and opened branch of Universal Ed. Unceasing champion of 20th-cent. composers, incl. Schoenberg, Berg, Webern, Bartók, Janáček, Berio, Boulez, Stockhausen, Birtwistle, David Bedford, and Hugh Wood.

Kamarinskaya (Wedding Song). Orch. fantasia on 2 Russ. folk-songs by Glinka, comp. 1848 in Warsaw. Title refers to Russ. dance. Version generally played contains revs. by Glazunov and Rimsky-Korsakov.

Kaminski, Joseph (b Odessa, 1903; d Gedera, Israel, 1972). Russ.-born violinist and composer. Went to Tel Aviv 1935, becoming leader Palestine SO (later Israel PO) 1937–69. Wrote vn. conc., tpt. concertino, str. qts., etc.

Kammer (Ger.). Chamber. So *Kammercantate*, chamber cantata (see *cantata*); *Kammerduett*, *Kammertrio*, chamber duet, chamber trio (i.e. for a room rather than a concert hall); *Kammerconcert*, *Kammerkonzert*, either chamber concert, or chamber conc.; *Kammermusik*, chamber mus.; *Kammersymphonie*, chamber sym.

Kammermusik (Chamber Music). Title given by *Hindemith to 7 instr. works comp. between 1922 and 1927: No.1 for small orch.; No.2, pf. conc.; No.3, vc. conc.; No.4, vn. conc.; No.5, va. conc.; No.6, viola d'amore conc.; No.7, org. conc.

Kammersänger(in) (Ger.). Chamber Singer. Esteemed honorary title bestowed by Ger. and Austrian govts. on distinguished singers.

Kamu, Okko (Tapani) (b Helsinki, 1946). Finn. conductor, composer, and violinist. Début as violinist early 1950s, in str. qt. 1965, as cond. 1968–9. Violinist in Helsinki PO 1965–6, leader Finn. Nat. Opera Orch. 1966–9, 3rd cond. at Nat. Opera 1968–9. Won first Karajan cond. comp. 1969. Guest cond. Royal Swedish Opera 1969–70. Cond. Finn. Radio SO 1970–7. Chief cond. and mus. dir. Oslo PO 1975–9. Chief cond. Helsinki PO 1979–90. Prin. cond. Dutch Radio SO 1983–6, Sjaelland (Denmark) SO from 1988. Chief cond. Finnish Nat. Opera 1996–9. Guest cond. of Brit. orchs. (London début 1970, New Philharmonia). Cond. f.ps. of Sallinen's *The Red Line* (1978) and *The King Goes Forth to France* (1984). NY Met 1983; CG 1987 (Brit. première of *The King Goes Forth to France*). Composer of film mus., songs for children, etc.

Kanawa, Kiri te. See *Te Kanawa*, (*Dame*) *Kiri*.

Kancheli, Giya (Alexandrovich) (b Tbilisi, 1935). Georgian composer. On staff Tbilisi Cons. from 1970. Influenced by jazz and by Copland and Crumb. Prin. works: syms.: No.1 (1967), No.2 (1970), No.3, with ten. (1973), No.4 (1974), No.5 (1977), No.6 (1980), No.7 (1983); *Concerto for Orchestra* (1962); *Largo and Allegro*, str., pf., timp. (1963); *The Pranks of Hanum*, mus. comedy (1973); *Music for the Living*, multi-media opera (1984); *Sweet Sadness*, boys' ch., orch. (1985); va. conc. (*Mourned by the Wind*) (1989), version for vc., orch. (1996); *Night Prayers*, str. qt., tape (1992); *Psalm 23*, sop., chamber orch. (1993); *Magnum ignotum*, wind, db., tape (1994); vc. conc. (1995); *Valse Boston*, pf., str. (1996); *Time . . . and Again*, vn., va., vc. (1998); *And Farewell Goes Out Sighing . . .* , counterten., vn., orch. (1999); *Ergo*, orch. (2000); much music for theatre and films (incl. *The Gladiator*, 1983).

K. Anh. Köchel Anhang, the appendix to Köchel's catalogue of Mozart's works, some of which have the suffix K. Anh. followed by a number. In the main, works of dubious attribution are confined to the appendix.

kantele. Finnish variety of *gusli, plucked with the fingers.

Kapell, William (b NY, 1922; d nr. S. Francisco, in air crash, 1953). Amer. pianist of Russ. and Polish parentage. Brilliant virtuoso with deep musical sensibility.

Kapelle (Ger.). Chapel. A term at one period applied to the whole staff of clergy, musicians, etc., attached to a royal chapel or the like. In time it came to be used for any organized body of musicians employed at court, etc., and from this it ultimately became a designation for any orch. body, from sym. orch. to dance band.

Kapellmeister (Capellmeister) (Ger.). The dir. or cond. of a *Kapelle*. *Kapellmeistermusik* became, sometimes unfairly, a derogatory term applied to mus. 'composed to order'.

Kaplan, Mark (b Cambridge, Mass., 1953). Amer. violinist. Won comp. at age of 8 and went to Juilliard Sch. as pupil of Dorothy DeLay. Prof. début

1973. Eur. début 1980. Gave f. Eur. p. of *Neikrug's vn. conc., Manchester 1986 (Hallé Orch. cond. L. *Foster).

Kapr, Jan (*b* Prague, 1914; *d* Prague, 1988). Cz. composer, pianist, and teacher. Mus. dir. Prague Radio 1939–46, prof. of comp. Janáček Acad., Brno, 1961–70. Works incl. opera; 10 syms. (1943–85); 7 str. qts. (No.6 with bar. solo) (1937–76); 3 pf. sonatas; vn. conc.; cl. concertino.

Karajan, Herbert von (*b* Salzburg, 1908; *d* Anif, Salzburg, 1989). Austrian conductor. Début Salzburg Landestheater 1927 in *Fidelio*. Cond. Ulm Opera 1929–34; Aachen 1934–42; Berlin State Opera 1938–45; art. dir. Vienna State Opera 1957–64. Cond. at Bayreuth 1951–2 (début in *Die Meistersinger*); Salzburg Fest. début 1933 (cond. incid. mus. Goethe's *Faust*), opera 1948 (Gluck's *Orfeo*). Art. dir. Salzburg Fest. 1956–60, thereafter presiding genius until his death (dir. and art. dir. 1964–88). Founded Salzburg Easter Fest. 1967. Cond. Berlin PO 1954–89. Assoc. also with Philharmonia Orch. 1948–54, Vienna SO 1948–58, Orchestre de Paris 1969–71, and La Scala from 1948. NY début 1955; NY Met 1967. Visited NY with Vienna PO 1989. One of outstanding conds. of post-war era, his career having been halted from 1945 to 1947 because of his Nazi affiliations. Also opera producer on stage and film.

karaoke (Japanese, 'empty orchestra'). A style of singing which became popular in Japan in the 1970s, whereby songs were recorded with full accompanimental backing but without vocal line, which could then be added by anyone wishing to do so.

Karel, Rudolf (*b* Pilsen, 1880; *d* Theresienstadt (Terezin), 1945). Cz. composer. Prof. of comp. and orch., Prague Cons., 1923–41. Wrote 2 operas; sym.; sym.-poems (incl. *The Demon* 1920); oratorio *Resurrection*; cantatas; chamber mus.; etc. Died in Ger. concentration camp, after arrest in 1943 for membership of Cz. resistance. While there comp. children's opera *3 Hairs of the Wise Old Man*.

Karelia. Ov. and suite for orch., Opp. 10 and 11 by Sibelius, comp. 1893. Karelia is province in southern Finland.

Karfreitagzauber (Wagner). See *Good Friday Music*.

Karg-Elert [Karg], **Sigfrid** (*b* Oberndorf-am-Neckar, 1877; *d* Leipzig, 1933). Ger. composer, pianist, and organist. Prof. at Leipzig Cons. from 1919, succeeding Reger. Best known for strikingly orig. org. comps. Works incl. pf. conc.; 5 pf. sonatas; 28 pf. preludes; vc. sonata; vn. sonata; str. qt.; chamber sym.; org. sonata; *66 Chorale Improvisations* for org. (1908–10); *Fantasia and Fugue in D* for organ; *20 Chorale Preludes and Postludes* for org. (1912); 2 sonatas for harmonium; *Scènes pittoresques* for harmonium; choral works. Arr. Elgar's syms. for pf. solo.

Karłowicz, Mieczysław (*b* Wiszniewe, 1876; *d* Zakopane, Tatra Mountains, 1909). Polish composer. Gave up career as violinist because of bad health,

concentrated on comp. Dir., Warsaw Mus. Soc. 1904–6. In 1907 settled at Zakopane, at foot of Tatra Mountains. Died in avalanche. Works incl. sym. ('Revival', *Odrodzenie*) (1902); vn. conc. (1902); and several sym.-poems, incl. *Stanisław i Anna Oświecimowie*. Strongly supported 'Young Poland' group of Szymanowski, Fitelberg, and Szeluto. His sym.-poems, in an individual style derived from Wagner and Strauss, reflect Schopenhauerian obsessions with love, death, and pantheism.

Karnéus, Katarina (*b* Stockholm, 1965). Swed. mezzo-soprano. Studied at TCL (1988–92), and Nat. Opera Studio (1993–4). Won Cardiff Singer of the World Comp. 1995. Recital débuts: Wigmore Hall (1995), Salzburg Fest. (1996), Edinburgh Fest. (1998), Lincoln Center, NY (2001). Opera débuts: Brussels 1998 (Cherubino); Glyndebourne Fest. 1998 (Dorabella); NY Met 1999 (Varvara in *Káťa Kabanová*); Munich 1999 (Annio in *La clemenza di Tito*); WNO, Cardiff, 2000 (Oktavian); CG 2002 (Annio).

Karpath, Ludwig (*b* Budapest, 1816; *d* Vienna, 1936). Austrian music critic and singer. Sang small bass roles with Nat. Opera Co., USA, 1886–8. Engaged by Mahler for bass roles at Budapest Opera 1889 but dismissed a few days later. On return to Vienna, became mus. critic of *Neues Wiener Tageblatt* 1894–1921. Wrote book on Wagner.

Karpeles, Maud (*b* London, 1885; *d* London, 1976). English folk-song collector, editor, and scholar. With sister Helen, was one of folk dancing team who illustrated Cecil *Sharp's lectures. Assoc. with Sharp's folk-song collecting from 1903, she went with him 1916–18 to Appalachian Mts., collecting over 500 songs which had travelled to N. Amer. with early immigrants. Also went alone to Newfoundland 1929 and 1930 to collect 191 songs there, pubd. in 2 vols. 1934. Held many administrative folk-song posts, incl. hon. secretaryship *English Folk Dance and Song Society. In 1947 she founded International Folk Music Council, attending its conferences in many countries, first as secretary and later pres. Wrote biography of Cecil Sharp in collab. with A. H. Fox Strangways 1933 (rev. edn. under her name alone, 1967). Ed. many cols. of folk-songs. OBE 1961.

Karr, Gary (Michael) (*b* Los Angeles, 1941). Amer. double-bass player. Début recital NY 1962, also soloist with NYPO European tour 1964. Has commissioned concertos from Henze, Arnold, and Schuller. Plays on 1611 Amati db. once owned by Koussevitzky.

Kars, Jean-Rodolphe (*b* Calcutta, 1947). Austrian pianist. London début 1967. Winner of 1968 Messiaen Comp., Royan.

Kasprzyk, Jacek (*b* Biala, 1952). Polish conductor. Début Warsaw Opera 1975. Prin. cond. Polish Nat. Radio SO 1976–82. Settled in Eng. 1982, making début with Philharmonia Orch. Cond. at Stockholm Royal Opera, Scottish Opera, and Opera North. Prin. cond. North Netherlands Orch. 1991–5. Prin. cond. and mus. adv. Polish Nat. Opera 1998–2005 (also gen. dir. 2002–5).

Káťa Kabanová (Katya Kabanova). Opera in 3 acts by Janáček to his own lib. based on the play *The Storm* (*Groza*) (1859) by A. N. Ostrovsky (1823–86) in Cz. trans. by V. Červinka. Comp. 1919–21. Prod. Brno 1921, London (SW) 1951, Cleveland, Ohio, 1957. (This was first Janáček opera to be staged in London, but a Brno perf. had been broadcast in 1948.)

Katchen, Julius (*b* Long Branch, NJ, 1926; *d* Paris, 1969). Amer. pianist. Début 1937 with Philadelphia Orch. Settled in Paris and had int. career as virtuoso with wide repertory.

Kate and the Devil (*Čert a Káča*). Opera in 3 acts by Dvořák to lib. by A. Wenig. Comp. 1898–9. Prod. Prague 1899; Oxford 1932, Wexford 1988; Berkeley, Calif., 1988.

Katerina Izmaylova. Title given to rev. version (1955–63) of Shostakovich's 4-act opera *Lady Macbeth of the Mtsensk District* (*Ledi Makbet Mtsenskovo uyezda*), comp. 1930–2 as Op.29. Lib. by A. Preys and composer, after story (1865) by N. Leskov. Prod. Moscow 1934, Cleveland, Ohio, 1935, London (concert) 1936. Rev. version, Op.114, Moscow 1963, London CG, 1963, San Francisco 1964. Orig. version was unperf. in USSR after Jan. 1936 when Soviet newspaper *Pravda* attacked it as 'leftist' and discordant, but there were prods. in Venice 1947 and Düsseldorf 1959. See also *Lady Macbeth of the Mtsensk District*.

Katin, Peter (Roy) (*b* London, 1930). Eng.-born pianist (Canadian cit.). Début London 1948. Noted as interpreter of Chopin, Rachmaninov, and Tchaikovsky. Prof. of pf., RAM, 1956–69 and at Univ. of W. Ontario, 1978–84.

Katz, Mindru (*b* Bucharest, 1925; *d* Istanbul, 1978). Romanian-born Israeli pianist. Début with Bucharest PO 1947. Début in West (Paris) 1957, London début 1958. Settled in Israel 1959. On staff Rubin Acad. of Mus., Tel Aviv Univ., 1962 (prof. from 1972). Died during recital.

Kaufman, Louis (*b* Portland, Oregon, 1905; *d* Los Angeles, 1994). Amer. violinist. Won Loeb Prize 1927. Noted champion of contemp. mus., giving f.p. of vn. conc. by Dag *Wirén (Stockholm 1953), f. Eng. p. of Piston's vn. conc. (London 1956), and of works by Milhaud and Martinů. Ed. vn. sonatas of Telemann.

Kaufmann, Julie (*b* Iowa, 1950). Amer. soprano. Début at Hagen, then Frankfurt. Munich début 1983 (Despina in *Così fan tutte*); CG début 1984; Salzburg Fest. début 1987. Member of Bavarian State Opera, Munich, from 1984.

Kay, Ulysses Simpson (*b* Tucson, Arizona, 1917; *d* Englewood, NJ, 1995). Amer. composer. Won *Prix de Rome* and worked in It. 1949–52. Worked for Broadcast Music Inc., NY, 1953–68. Prof. of mus., Lehman Coll. of City Univ., NY, 1968–88. Works incl. 5 operas; sym.; ob. conc.; *Concerto for Orchestra*; *Suite* for orch.; ballet *Dance Calinda*; cantata *Song of Jeremiah*; 3 str. qts.; pf. sonata; fl. quintet, etc.

kazoo (Fr. *mirliton*). Children's mus. instr., consisting of a short tube with membrane at each end, played by humming or singing into a side-hole to produce effect of comb-and- paper.

Kb. (Ger.). Abbreviation for *Kontrabass*, i.e. the db.

Keal, Minna [Nerenstein, Mina] (*b* London, 1909; *d* Bucks., 1999). English composer. After some chamber works had been perf., gave up composing 1929 to help in family business. Resumed comp. studies in 1974. Comps. incl. str. qt. (1978); wind quintet (1980); sym. (1980–4); *Cantillation*, vn., orch. (1986–8); vc. conc. (1988–93).

Keeffe, Bernard (*b* London, 1925). Eng. conductor. Prof. of cond. TCL from 1966. Noted broadcaster and introducer of televised mus. Made Eng. trans. of Janáček's *Diary of One who Disappeared*. Prod. and cond. 1955–60, head of BBC radio opera 1959, controller of opera planning, CG 1960–2. Cond., BBC Scottish SO 1962–4.

Keel Row (Keel = boat). Song of unknown orig. which first appeared in print in *A Collection of Favourite Scots Tunes* (Edinburgh, *c*.1770) but is principally assoc. with Newcastle and Tyneside district. Quoted by Debussy in the 3rd movt. (*Gigues*) of his **Images* for orch.

keen (Irish *caoine*). Irish funeral song acc. by wailing (keening). Reproduced in Vaughan Williams's opera **Riders to the Sea*.

Keene, Christopher (*b* Berkeley, Calif., 1946; *d* NY, 1995). Amer. conductor. Founded own opera co. while at Univ. of Calif., staging two of Britten's operas. Worked as ass. to Kurt Adler at San Francisco Opera 1966. San Diego Opera 1967. Ass. to Menotti, Spoleto Fest. 1968, when he cond. *The Saint of Bleecker Street*. Mus. dir. Amer. Spoleto Fest. at Charleston 1977–80, Syracuse SO 1975–84, ArtPark, Lewiston, NY, 1974–89. Cond. f.p. of Villa-Lobos's *Yerma*, Santa Fe, 1971. NY Met début 1971; NY City Opera 1970 (mus. dir. 1983–6, gen. dir. from 1989); CG début 1973. Advocate of operas of Philip *Glass. Cond. f. NY stage p. of *Moses und Aron*, 1990.

Keenlyside, Simon (*b* London, 1959). English baritone. Zoology degree at Cambridge, then studied with John Cameron at RNCM. Tauber Prize 1986. Prof. début Hamburg 1987. Member of Scottish Opera 1988–93. CG début 1989 (Silvio in *Pagliacci*); ENO 1990 (Guglielmo in *Così fan tutte*); American début 1993 (San Francisco, Olivier in *Capriccio*); La Scala 1995 (Papageno in *Zauberflöte*); NY Met 1996 (Belcore in *L'elisir d'amore*). Created Prospero in Adès's *The Tempest* (CG 2004) and Winston Smith in Maazel's *1984* (CG 2005). Excellent as Billy Budd, Don Giovanni, Papageno, Pelléas. Also outstanding recitalist, especially in Schubert's *Winterreise*. CBE 2003.

Keilberth, Joseph (*b* Karlsruhe, 1908; *d* Munich, 1968). Ger. conductor. Joined Karlsruhe's opera co. as répétiteur 1925, becoming cond. Mus. dir. 1935–40. Cond., Ger. PO, Prague, 1940–5. Mus. dir. Dresden State Opera 1945–50; cond. Bavarian State Opera, Munich, 1951–68 (mus. dir. from 1959); art. dir. Hamburg PO 1950–9, cond. Bamberg SO 1949–68. Bayreuth Fest. 1952–6; Salzburg Fest. 1957–62. Notable Strauss interpreter. Died while cond. *Tristan und Isolde* at Nationalth., Munich.

Keiser, Reinhard (*b* Teuchern, 1674; *d* Hamburg, 1739). Ger. composer. At court of Brunswick 1694 where he succeeded Kusser. Moved to Hamburg 1695, achieving success with opera *Mahumet II*. In next 40 years comp. over 100 operas for Hamburg, becoming cond. of the opera 1696–1702 and dir. 1703–7. Regarded at one time as greatest orig. genius Ger. had prod. His operas contain magnificent florid arias and instrumentation which was emulated by *Handel, who was violinist and harpsichordist for Keiser at Hamburg. Keiser's operas incl. *Der hochmütige, gestürtzte und wieder erhabene Croesus* (1710, rev. 1730, modern edn. 1912, rev. 1958); *Die Römische Unruhe* (1705); *Die verdammte Staat-Sucht* (1705); *Fredegunda* (1715); and *Der Lächerliche Prinz Jodelet* (1726). Keiser also wrote dramatic and striking oratorios, and settings of the Passions.

Kelemen, Zoltán (*b* Budapest, 1926; *d* Zurich, 1979). Hung. bass-baritone. Début Augsburg 1959 (Kecal in *The Bartered Bride*). Member of Cologne Opera from 1961 to death. Bayreuth Fest. 1964 (Alberich). Sang in f.p. of *Die *Soldaten*, Cologne 1965. London début SW 1969 (with Cologne Opera); Salzburg 1965;, NY Met 1968; CG 1970.

Kell, Reginald (Clifford) (*b* York, 1906; *d* Frankfort, Kentucky, 1981). Eng. clarinettist. Prin. cl. Beecham's LPO 1932–6 and CG orch. 1932–6, LSO 1936–9, Liverpool PO 1942–5, and Philharmonia 1945–8. Went to USA 1948. Prof. at Aspen Mus. Fest., Colorado, 1951–7. Returned to Eng. 1971, but died in USA. Prof. cl., RAM, 1935–9 and 1958–9. Noted for artistic use of vibrato. Published Kell method, NY 1968.

Keller, Hans (Heinrich) (*b* Vienna, 1919; *d* Hampstead, 1987). Austrian-born violinist, violist, music critic, and author (Eng. cit. 1948). Member of BBC mus. division 1959–79. Joint ed. of book on Britten. Contrib. to many periodicals. Authority on assoc. football. See *functional analysis*.

Kelley, Edgar (Stillman) (*b* Sparta, Wisconsin, 1857; *d* NY, 1944). Amer. composer, organist, and author. Org. in S. Francisco and Oakland, mus. critic, *S. Francisco Examiner* 1893–5. Worked in S. Francisco 1880–6 and 1892–6, coming into contact with Chinese and their mus. Acting prof. and orch. cond., Yale Univ. Sch. of Music 1901–2. Taught in Berlin 1902–10, returning to USA to teach comp. at Cincinnati Cons. Works incl. incidental mus. to *Macbeth* and *Ben Hur*; 2 syms. (No.1

Gulliver—His Voyage to Lilliput, Op.15; No.2 *New England*); pantomime suite *Alice in Wonderland*; *Pilgrim's Progress*; pf. quintet; str. qt., etc.

Kelly, Bryan (*b* Oxford, 1934). Eng. composer, pianist, and conductor. Taught at RSAMD. Prof. of comp. RCM 1962–84. Moved to It. 1984. Has written several works for children. Prin. comps.:

ORCH.: syms.: No.1 (1983), No.2 (1986); *Latin Quarter Overture* (1955); *Music for Ballet* (1957); *The Tempest Suite*, str. (1964); *Cookham Concertino* (1969); ob. conc. (1972); gui. conc. (1978); for brass band: *Divertimento* (1969); *Edinburgh Dances* (1973); *Andalucia* (1976); *Concertante Music* (1979); sym. (1988).

CHAMBER MUSIC: *3 Pieces*, vn., pf. (1959); *Aubade, Toccata, and Nocturne*, gui. (1964); *2 Concert Pieces*, cl., pf. (1964); *Zodiac*, cl., pf. (1978); *Suite parisienne*, brass quintet (1979); *Brass Bagatelles*, hn. or bar. or euph., pf. (2003); *Globe Theatre Suite*, rec./picc., pf. (2005).

CHORUS & ORCH.: *Tenebrae Nocturnes*, ten., ch., orch. (1965); *The Shell of Achilles*, ten., orch. (1966); *Stabat Mater*, sop., bass, ch., orch. (1970); *At the round earth's imagined corners*, ten., ch., str. (1972); *Let there be light*, sop., narr., ch., orch. (1972–3); *Latin Magnificat*, ch., ww. (1979); *Missa brevis* (1991); *Dover Beach* (1995); *Canterbury Responses*, unacc. ch. (2003); *Kentucky Canticles*, ch., org. (2005).

VOCAL: *Magnificat and Nunc Dimittis* ('Latin American'), ch., org. (1965); *Sleep Little Baby*, carol, SATB (1968); *O Be Joyful* (Caribbean Jubilate), ch., org. (1970); *Abingdon Carols*, unacc. ch. (1973); *Te Deum and Jubilate*, ch., org. (1979).

KEYBOARD: pf. sonata (1971); *Prelude and Fugue*, org. (1960); *Pastorale and Paean*, org. (1973).

CHILDREN: *Herod, do your worst*, nativity opera (1968); *On Christmas Eve*, suite of carols, vv., pf. (1968); *The Spider Monkey Uncle King*, opera pantomime (1971); *Half a Fortnight*, unison vv., pf., perc. (1973).

Kelly, Michael (*b* Dublin, 1762; *d* Margate, 1826). Irish tenor and composer. Début Dublin 1779 in Piccinni opera. Sang at Vienna Court Opera, 1783–7, becoming friend of Mozart and creating roles of Basilio and Curzio in *Le nozze di Figaro*, 1786. Sang in London 1787; actor-man. King's Th., London, 1793. Comp. mus. for plays and songs. Retired 1811. Wrote amusing and informative *Reminiscences* (1826; ed. R. Fiske, 1975).

Kelterborn, Rudolf (*b* Basle, 1931). Swiss composer and conductor. Taught and cond. at Basle (1956–60) and at Detmold (1960–8). Prof. of comp. Zurich Musikhochschule 1968–75 and 1980–3. Head of mus., Swiss Radio, 1975–80. Dir., Basle Music Acad. from 1983. Works incl. 7 operas, incl. *Ein Engel kommt nach Babylon* (An Angel comes from Babylon) (1977) and *Julia* (1990–1); oratorio *Die Flut*; 4 syms. (1967–86, incl. No.3, *Espansioni*, for orch., bar., and tape); 6 str. qts.; 2 chamber syms.; octet, etc.

Kemble, Adelaide (*b* London, 1814; *d* Warsash, Hants., 1879). Eng. soprano. Concert début London 1835. Went to It. to study with *Pasta. Opera début as Norma, Venice 1839. Sang same role in Eng. at CG, 1841. Retired 1843 on marriage to E. J. Sartoris.

Kemp [Mikley-Kemp], **Barbara** (b Kochem an der Mosel, 1881; d Berlin, 1959). Ger. soprano. Début Strasbourg 1903 (Priestess in *Aida*). Sang in Rostock 1906–8, Breslau 1908–13. Leading sop. Berlin Opera 1913–31. NY Met 1922–4. Bayreuth Fest. 1914 and 1924–7. Gave f.p. of Strauss's *3 Hymns*, Op.71, Berlin 1921. Wife of Max von *Schillings. NY Met début 1923 (created title-role in Schillings's *Mona Lisa*). Became stage dir. in Berlin in 1930s.

Kemp, Ian (b Edinburgh, 1931). Scottish musicologist and teacher. Worked for Schott's 1954–64. Lect. in mus. Aberdeen Univ. 1964–71, Cambridge Univ. 1972–6. Prof. of mus. Leeds Univ. 1977–81, Manchester Univ. 1981–91. Author of books on Tippett and Hindemith, ed. Vol.13 *New Berlioz Edition*.

Kempe, Rudolf (b Niederpoyritz, Dresden, 1910; d Zurich, 1976). Ger. conductor. Began career as oboist in Dortmund, becoming prin. oboist Leipzig Gewandhaus Orch. 1929–36. Début as cond. Leipzig 1935 (*Der *Wildschütz*), after which he became répétiteur and junior cond. Leipzig Opera 1936–42. Cond. Chemnitz Opera 1945–8, Weimar 1948–9, Dresden 1950–3, Munich 1952–4. Débuts: CG 1953 with Munich company (*Arabella*); NY Met 1955; Salzburg 1955; Bayreuth 1960 (new prod. of *Der Ring des Nibelungen*). Cond. *Ring* cycles at CG 1955–9. Succeeded Beecham as chief cond. RPO 1961–3, art. dir. from 1964, prin. cond. for life from 1970. Cond. Delius centenary fest. 1962. Art. dir. Tonhalle Orch., Zurich, 1965–72, Munich PO 1967. Prin. cond. BBC SO 1975–6. Recorded complete orch. works of R. Strauss.

Kempen, Paul van (b Zoeterwoude, Leyden, 1893; d Hilversum, 1955). Dutch conductor and violinist. Leader, Concertgebouw Orch. under *Mengelberg. Leader of several Ger. orchs. before becoming cond. in Oberhausen, 1932. Cond. Dresden PO 1934–42. Cond. Berlin State Opera 1940, Aachen Opera 1942–3. Chief cond. Hilversum Radio from 1949, and in Bremen from 1953.

Kempf, Freddy (b London, 1977). Eng. pianist of Ger. father and Japanese mother. Played Mozart conc. (K414) with RPO aged 8. Won BBC Young Mus. of the Year 1992; 3rd prize in Tchaikovsky Int. Comp., Moscow, 1998. Has played throughout Eur., the Americas, Asia, and Australia. Also plays chamber mus.

Kempff, Wilhelm (Walter Friedrich) (b Jüterbog, 1895; d Positano, It., 1991). Ger. pianist and composer. Reputation grew from 1916 as virtuoso pianist, especially in assoc. with Berlin PO. Dir., Stuttgart Hochschule für Musik, 1924–9. London début 1951, Amer. début NY 1964. Gave annual courses at Positano from 1957. Salzburg Fest.

1958. Noted for playing of Beethoven and classics. Comp. opera *King Midas*, 2 syms., vn. conc., pf. conc., chamber mus., and choral works.

Kennedy, Nigel (b Brighton, 1956). Eng. violinist. Début London 1977. Toured Hong Kong and Australia as soloist with Hallé Orch., 1981. Amer. tour 1985. Regular jazz/improvisation concerts with S. *Grappelli. In 1993 stated he had retired from classical mus. platform.

Kennedy Center for Performing Arts. Arts centre in Washington, DC, opened in 1971 and named in honour of late President J. F. Kennedy (assassinated 1963). Contains concert hall seating 2,700, opera house (2,300), and drama th. First event was *Bernstein's *Mass* (Sept. 1971).

Kennedy-Fraser, Marjory (b Perth, 1857; d Edinburgh, 1930). Scots singer and collector of folk-songs. As child, toured as acc. to father, the singer David Kennedy (1825–86). When widowed, taught singing and in 1905 visited Outer Hebrides, where she began coll. of folk-songs which she arr. and pubd. for v. and pf.

Kenny, Yvonne (b Sydney, NSW, 1950). Australian soprano. Début London 1975 (concert perf. of Donizetti's *Rosamunde d'Inghilterra*). Débuts: CG 1976; ENO 1977; Salzburg Fest. 1984; Glyndebourne 1985. Victoria State Opera from 1978. Order of Australia 1989.

Kent bugle. Obsolete (since 1815) bugle with keys similar to saxophone. Invented 1810 by Irish bandmaster Halliday and named after Duke of Kent, who took interest in it.

Kentner, Louis [Lajos] (Philip) (b Karvinna, Hungary (now Czechoslovakia), 1905; d London, 1987). Hung.-born pianist (Brit. cit. 1946). Recital début 1920, soon making int. reputation. Settled Eng. 1935. Salzburg Fest. début 1954. NY début 1956. Gave f. Hung. p. of Bartók's 2nd pf. conc., Budapest 1933, f.p. (with Ilona Kabos) of conc. for 2 pf. and perc., London 1942, and f.p. in Europe of 3rd pf. conc., London 1946. Noted player of Liszt. CBE 1978.

Kenton, Stan(ley Newcomb) (b Wichita, Kansas, 1912; d Hollywood, 1979). Amer. band leader, pianist, and composer. Protagonist of 'progressive jazz'. Established reputation at ballroom in Balboa, Calif., where his *Peanut Vendor* became a hit. Wrote ballet *Homage to the Princess*, 1956, for wedding of Prince Rainier of Monaco to Amer. actress Grace Kelly. Elaborate arrs. a feature of his later style.

Kent Opera. Eng. opera company founded 1969 by Norman Platt and Roger Norrington. Regularly played in Canterbury and Tunbridge Wells, toured widely in the southern counties and visited Manchester and various fests. Casts were mixture of experienced and new singers, and repertory extended from well-known Verdi, Mozart, and Britten to rare works by Handel (f.p. of *Atalanta* since 1736 in 1970), Telemann, and others. Staged Tippett's *King Priam* in 1984–5 season. Gave world première of Judith Weir's *A Night at the Chinese Opera* (Cheltenham, 1987). Norrington's edns. of 3 Monteverdi operas (*The Coronation of Poppea*, *Orfeo*, and *The Return of Ulysses*) were given in 1974, 1976, and 1978. Ivan Fischer succeeded Norrington as mus. dir. in 1984 and remained with the company until it went into liquidation in 1990 after Arts Council withdrew funding. Revived 1994. From 2002, art. dir. Roger Butlin, mus. dir. Gary Cooper.

Kenyon, Nicholas (Roger) (*b* Altrincham, 1951). Eng. music critic, broadcaster, and administrator. Worked for BBC mus. division and as freelance critic 1975–9. Mus. critic, the *New Yorker* 1979–82, *The Times* 1982–5, *The Listener* 1982–7, *The Observer* 1985–92. Ed., *Early Music* to 1992. Controller Radio 3, BBC, 1992–8; dir., Henry Wood Proms from 1996. Author of *The BBC Symphony Orchestra 1930–80* (1981), *Simon Rattle: the Making of a Conductor* (1987, rev. 2001); *The Faber Pocket Guide to Mozart* (2005). CBE 2001.

keraulophon (Gr.). Horn-pipe voice. Rarely-found metal labial org. stop of 8′ pitch, resembling Fr. hn. in tone quality and invented in 1843 for org. of St Paul's, Knightsbridge. Before that it was a variety of basset-hn. stop.

Kerman, Joseph (Wilfred) (*b* London, 1924). Amer. scholar and critic. Prof. of mus., Univ. of Calif. 1974–88, having previously been on staff 1951–71. Prof. of mus. Oxford Univ. 1971–4. Books incl. *Opera as Drama* (1956, 2nd edn. 1989, in which *Tosca* is described as 'a shabby little shocker'), *The Beethoven Quartets* (1967), *Contemplating Music* (Eng. title *Musicology*) (1985), and *The Art of Fugue: Bach's Fugues for Keyboard, 1715–1750* (2006).

Kern, Adele (*b* Munich, 1901; *d* Munich, 1980). Ger. soprano. Début Munich 1924 (Olympia in *Les contes d'Hoffmann*). Frankfurt Opera 1924–9. Vienna State Opera 1929–30, Munich Opera 1937–46. CG début 1931. Salzburg Fest. 1927–35. One of singers in famous Clemens *Krauss perfs. of Strauss and Mozart in Frankfurt, Munich, and Vienna. Retired 1947.

Kern, Jerome (David) (*b* NY, 1885; *d* NY, 1945). Amer. composer. Wrote his first successful song in 1905. Comp. several popular musicals incl. *Oh, Boy!* (1917); *Sally* (1920); *Sunny* (1925); *Show Boat* (1927); *Music in the Air* (1932); and *Roberta* (1933). *Show Boat* (first musical to enter an opera co.'s repertory, NY City Opera 1954) contained the songs 'Ol' Man River', first sung by Paul *Robeson, and 'Can't help Lovin' dat Man of Mine'. Also comp. 'Smoke Gets in your Eyes' (in *Roberta*), 'All the things you are', and other popular melodies, several being featured in films. Words for several of his songs (most famous being 'Bill') were written by P. G. Wodehouse.

Kerr, Harrison (*b* Cleveland, Ohio, 1897; *d* Norman, Oklahoma, 1978). Amer. composer. Dean of Coll. of Fine Arts, Oklahoma Univ., 1949–60, comp.-in-res. 1960–8. Works incl. opera *The Tower*

of Kel (1958–60); 3 syms.; vn. conc.; 2 pf. sonatas; str. qt.; pf. trio; vn. sonata; *Sinfonietta* for chamber orch.

Kertész, István (*b* Budapest, 1929; *d* drowned while swimming, Kfar Saba, Israel, 1973). Hung.-born conductor (Ger. cit.). On staff Budapest Acad. 1952–7, then cond. at Györ, Hung., 1953–5, Budapest State Opera 1955–7, Augsburg 1958–63. Mus. dir. Cologne Opera 1964–73, where he cond. Ger. première of Verdi's *Stiffelio*. Prin. cond. LSO, 1965–8 and guest cond. of most leading orchs. Brit. début 1960 (Liverpool); Amer. début 1961; Salzburg Fest. 1961; CG 1965.

Kes, Willem (*b* Dordrecht, 1856; *d* Munich, 1934). Dutch conductor and violinist. Leader of several Dutch orchs., first cond. Concertgebouw Orch. of Amsterdam 1888–95, Scottish Orch. 1895–8. Cond. Moscow Phil. Soc. 1898, dir. Moscow mus. sch. 1901–5. Dir., Koblenz orch. and mus. sch. 1905–26. Comp. sym., vn. conc., vc. conc., and songs.

Ketèlbey, Albert (William) [Vodorinski, Anton] (*b* Birmingham, 1875; *d* Cowes, IoW, 1959). Eng. composer and conductor. Cond. London th. orchs. Comp. comic opera, *Concertstück* for pf. and orch., wind quintet, but best known for orch. works such as *In a Monastery Garden* (1915), *In a Persian Market* (1920), *Bells Across the Meadows* (1921), and *Sanctuary of the Heart* (1924).

kettledrum. See *drum*.

Kettledrum Mass (Haydn). See *Paukenmesse*.

Keuris, Tristan (*b* Amersfoort, Holland, 1946; *d* Amsterdam, 1996). Dutch composer. Won Matthijs Vermeulen Prize with his *Sinfonia*, 1975. Head of comp., Utrecht Cons. Comps. incl.:

ORCH.: *Quintet* (1966–7); *Soundings* (1970); Conc. for alto sax. (1971); *Sinfonia* (1975); *Serenade* (1976); pf. conc. (1980); *Movements* (1982); *7 Pieces*, bcl., orch. (1983); vn. conc. (1984); conc. for sax. qt. (1986); *Aria*, fl., orch. (1987); *Symphonic Transformations* (1987); *Catena: Refrains and Variations*, 31 wind instr., perc., cel. (1988); *Intermezzi*, 9 winds (1989); *3 Sonnets*, alto sax., orch. (1989); org. conc. (1993).

VOCAL: *Choral Music I* (1969); *To Brooklyn Bridge*, 24 vv., 4 cl., 4 sax., 2 pf., 2 hp., 3 db. (1988).

CHAMBER MUSIC: str. qts.: No.1 (1982), No.2 (1985); *Quartet*, 4 sax. (1970); pf. sonata (1970); *Concertante Music*, cl., ob., bn., pf., 5 str. (1972–3); *Music*, vn., cl., pf. (1973); *Fantasia*, fl. (1976); *Concertino*, bcl., str. qt. (1977); vn. sonata (1977); *Quartet*, 3 cl., bcl. (1983); *Music for Saxophones*, 4 sax. (1986); *5 Pieces*, brass quintet (1988).

key. (1) As a principle in mus. comp., implies adherence, in any passage, to the note-material of one of the major or minor scales (see *scale*)—not necessarily a rigid adherence (since other notes may incidentally appear), but a general adherence, with a recognition of the *tonic (or

*key-note) of the scale in question as a principal and governing factor in its effect. For instance we speak of a passage as being 'in the key of' C major, or F minor, and also use the same terms to describe a comp. (or movement) as a whole—in this latter case implying merely that the key mentioned is that in which the piece begins and sometimes but not always (e.g. Mahler) ends and is its governing one (see *modulation*). If a piece in several movements is so spoken of it does not necessarily mean more than that the first movement (usually also the last one) is in that key.

The element of key crept into European mus. in the early 17th cent., as the *modes gradually fell out of use: it remained of supreme importance to the end of the 19th cent. but in the 20th cent., many composers, led by *Schoenberg, have abandoned tonality. See *atonal*.

(2) A lever on an instr. which is depressed by finger or foot to produce a note, e.g. on a pf. by finger, on an org. by foot, on woodwind by finger (the levers covering the airholes).

keyboard. (1) A frame, or set, of *keys presented in a continuous arr. The purpose of kbds. is to enable the 2 hands (e.g. on pf. or harmonium) or the 2 hands and 2 feet (org.) readily to control the sounds from a much larger number of str., reeds, or pipes than could otherwise be controlled. One standardized apparatus of this sort, which has been gradually developed over a long period, has come to be universally adopted: it is by no means the most convenient imaginable, but the conservatism of musicians will probably prevent its supersession unless some drastic change in the scales used in mus. (e.g. by the general adoption of *microtones) makes such a change imperative. The unchanging span of the octave is determined by the average span of the human hand.

The earliest kbd. was, apparently, that of the org., used for perf. of sacred melodic plainsong. In those days, mus. was still modal and the longer finger-keys, as we still have them, were all that were needed. With the coming into use of the practice of *musica ficta a B♭ was found to be desirable and space for it was made by placing a short finger-key between the A and B♮ (it appears that a few kbds. like this still existed as late as the beginning of the 17th cent.). Other finger-keys were similarly added, and our present-day kbd. of 7 different long and broad keys and 5 short and narrow ones so came into existence. This still leaves out many notes (e.g. B♯, if required, has to be played as C, F♭ as E, etc.). The restricted no. of keys which the individual

can manipulate, and the necessity of avoiding the high cost of providing a large number of extra organ pipes, str., etc., precluded the provision of further finger-keys, and the difficulty was overcome by methods of tuning, at first, partially, with mean-tone tuning and then, fully, with equal temperament tuning (see *temperament*). There have been a good many attempts at the invention of a kbd. which would be free (or largely free) from this principle of compromise, but whilst some of them have been scientifically interesting none has proved of practical value in mus. making. Various ingenious inventions, such as the Janko kbd., have also proved ephemeral.

(2) The term is also used generally, as in 'keyboard works', to indicate that the works may be played on more than one kind of kbd. instr.

keyboard of light. See *Prometheus, the Poem of Fire*.

key (keyed) bugle. Treble brass instr. of the *ophicleide type, introduced about 1810 but fading from the scene when the modern *cornet appeared. See also *Kent bugle*.

keyed (bass) horn. Not a hn., but an improved form of *serpent, without that instr.'s twisting shape.

key-note. The prin. (and lowest) note of the scale out of which a passage is constructed. Same as *tonic.

Keys, Ivor (Christopher Banfield) (*b* Littlehampton, 1919; *d* Birmingham, 1995). Eng. teacher, composer, and organist. Ass. org. Ch. Ch., Oxford, 1938–40, 1946–7. Dir. of mus., Queen's Coll., Belfast, prof. 1951. Prof. of mus. Nottingham Univ. 1954–68, Birmingham Univ. 1968–86. Comps. incl. cl. conc., vc. sonata, choral works. Frequent broadcaster. Author of books on Brahms and Mozart. CBE 1976.

key-signature. The sign, or no. of signs, written at the beginning of each staff, to indicate the *key of the comp. Use of a key-signature dispenses with the need to write *accidentals (sharps or flats) for the notes affected throughout the comp. The keys of C major and A minor require no accidentals. The 'natural' form of the minor scale determines key-signature. Major and minor key-signatures are indicated thus:
The white note in each case represents the major key, the black note the minor key with the same signature (called 'relative minor').

Starting from C, the keynotes of the sharp

keys rise 5 notes (a perfect 5th) each remove, and the keynotes of the flat keys fall 5 notes (a perfect 5th) each remove. In the sharp major keys the keynote is immediately above the last sharp.

In the flat major keys the keynote is 4 notes below the last flat (i.e. is at the pitch of the last flat but one in the signature).

Three notes down any major scale is the keynote of its relative minor or, conversely, 3 notes up any minor scale is the keynote of its relative major.

Keys with 6 sharps (F♯ major and D♯ minor) are (on kbd. instr.) the equivalents of the keys with 6 flats (G♭ major and E♭ minor), and keys with 7 sharps (C♯ major and A♯ minor) are the equivalents of the keys with 5 flats (D♭ major and B♭ minor). Composers use either one or the other of these signatures, but it is much easier to write in D♭ with 5 flats than in C♯ with 7 sharps.

The order of the sharps in the signatures is by rising 5ths, and the order of the flats by falling 5ths.

Sharps—F C G D A E B—*Flats*

Thus, one order is the other reversed.

Khachaturian, Aram (Ilyich) (*b* Tbilisi (Tiflis), 1903; *d* Moscow, 1978). Armenian composer. Planned to be biologist, but at 19 became vc. student, later joining comp. class. His trio (1932) attracted the attention of Prokofiev, who arranged perf. in Paris. His 1st sym. (1934) was a success at its f.p. in April 1935, but even greater was that of his pf. conc. (1936). Held various state posts. His 2nd sym. and vc. conc. incurred official disapproval in 1948 and he switched to comp. of film mus. In 1950 he began to teach at Gnesin Inst. and Moscow Cons. and developed as cond. of his own works, travelling to It., Eng., Latin America, and elsewhere. In 1956 his ballet *Spartacus* was acclaimed by Moscow critics as a masterpiece. His mus. is colourful and has continued the nationalist tradition of the St Petersburg sch. Prin. works:

BALLETS: *Happiness* (1939); **Gayane* (incorporating mus. from *Happiness*) (1940–2, rev. 1952; 2nd version with new plot 1957); **Spartacus* (1954, rev. 1968).

ORCH. AND CHORUS: syms.: No.1 in E minor (1934), No.2 in A minor (1943), No.3 (1947); *Dance Suite* (1932–3); *Poem about Stalin*, with ch. (1938); 3 *Suites* from *Gayane* (1943); *Ode in memory of Lenin* (1948); 4 *Suites* from *Spartacus* (Nos. 1–3, 1955–7, No.4, 1967); *Ode of Joy*, mez. and ch. (1956); *Lermontov Suite* (1959).

CONCERTOS: pf. in D♭ major (1936); vn. in D minor (1940); vc. in E major (1946); conc.-rhapsody for pf. (1955, rev. 1961); conc.-rhapsody for vn. (1961); conc.-rhapsody for vc. (1962).

CHAMBER MUSIC: vn. sonata in D (1932); trio for pf., cl., and vn. (1932).

PIANO: *Poem* (1927); 7 *Recitatives and Fugues* (1928–66); *Suite* (1932); 3 *Marches* (1929–34); sonatina in C (1958); sonata (1961).

INCIDENTAL MUSIC: *Macbeth* (1934, 1955); *King Lear* (1958).

FILMS: *Lenin* (1948–9); *Battle of Stalingrad* (1949); *Othello* (1955).

Khamma. Ballet-pantomime in 3 scenes (*légende dansée*) by Debussy, scenario by W. L. Courtney and Maud Allan. Comp. and pubd. 1911–12 with pf. acc. Prelude orch. Debussy, rest by Koechlin under composer's supervision, 1912–13, f.p. Paris 1924. First stage perf. Paris 1947.

Kharitonov, Dimitri (*b* Leningrad, 1958). Russ. baritone. Won several singing comps. Prin. bar. Odessa Opera 1984, Bolshoy Opera, Moscow, 1985–8. Settled in Eng. 1989. Amer. début Chicago 1990 (Sonora in *La fanciulla del West*). ENO début 1990; Glyndebourne 1992.

Khovanshchina (The Khovansky Affair). Unfinished opera in 5 acts by Mussorgsky to lib. by composer and V. Stasov. Comp. 1873. Completion and orch. by Rimsky-Korsakov, prod. St Petersburg 1886 and 1911; Paris and London 1913 in version altered by Stravinsky and Ravel; Philadelphia 1928. Later completed by Shostakovich (1959), prod. Leningrad 1960.

Khrennikov, Tikhon (Nikolayevich) (*b* Elets, 1913). Russ. composer. Held various official Soviet posts; as sec.-gen. of Union of Soviet Composers, denounced Prokofiev and Shostakovich for *formalism in 1948, and a generation later Schnittke and Gubaidulina. Leader of Soviet Composers' Union, for over 25 years. Teacher of comp., Moscow Cons. from 1963. Works incl. 5 operas; 3 syms.; vc. conc.; vn. conc.; 2 pf. concs.; songs; and film scores.

Kienzl, Wilhelm (*b* Waizenkirchen, 1857; *d* Vienna, 1941). Austrian composer. Cond. opera in Crefeld and Graz; 1st cond. Hamburg Opera 1890–2, court cond. Munich 1892–4. Adopted Wagnerian principles for his 10 operas and mus. plays, most successful being *Der Evangelimann* (The Evangelist) (1894). In 1918 wrote new nat. anthem for Austria which replaced Haydn's from 1920 to 1929, when Haydn's was reinstated.

Kiepura, Jan (*b* Sosnowiec, 1902; *d* Rye, NY, 1966). Polish tenor. Début Lwów 1924 as Faust. Sang leading operatic roles in Vienna (1926–37), Berlin, Milan, Budapest, and Buenos Aires (1926–39). Created Stranger in Korngold's *Das Wunder der Heliane* (1927). Amer. début Chicago 1931; NY Met début 1938. Made career in films. Sang with wife, Hung. sop. Marta Eggerth (*b* 1912).

Kilpinen, Yrýo (Henrik) (*b* Helsinki, 1892; *d* Helsinki, 1959). Finn. composer and critic. Mus. critic in Helsinki 1919–31. Taught at Helsinki Cons. State pension enabled him to compose. Wrote over 800 songs, also pf. sonatas, etc.

Kim, Young-Uck (*b* Seoul, 1947). S. Korean violinist. Début 1968 with Philadelphia Orch., cond. Ormandy. Eur. tour as soloist with Berlin PO, Vienna PO., Concertgebouw Orch., and LSO. Formed trio with Emanuel Ax (pf.) and Yo-Yo Ma (vc.).

Kimm, Fiona (*b* Ipswich, 1952). Eng. mezzo-soprano. Member of CG chorus 1975–7. Glynde-bourne début (with GTO) 1978 (First Lady in *Die Zauberflöte*). Joined ENO 1979; CG début 1983. Has sung major roles with Opera North and Scottish Opera. Salzburg Fest. début 1990.

Kindermann, Johann Erasmus (*b* Nuremberg, 1616; *d* Nuremberg, 1655). Ger. composer and organist. By 15 was singing and playing vn. in concerts in Frauenkirche, Nuremberg. Went to It. 1635, possibly becoming pupil of Monteverdi and Cavalli. In 1640 became org. of Egidien-kirche, Nuremberg, being also in demand as teacher. His *Harmonia organica* (1645) contains 25 contrapuntal pieces. Comp. over 100 pieces for wind or strings and many for str. and hpd. Perhaps the first Ger. composer to employ *scordatura.

Kinderscenen (Scenes from childhood). Suite of 13 pieces for pf. by *Schumann, Op.15, comp. 1838. No.7 is *Träumerei.

Kindertotenlieder (Songs of the death of children). Song-cycle of 5 songs for bar. (or cont.) and orch. or pf. by *Mahler, to poems by Rückert. Comp. 1901–4, pubd. 1905, f.p. Vienna 1905.

Kindler, Hans (*b* Rotterdam, 1892; *d* Watch Hill, R.I., 1949). Dutch-born (later Amer. cit.) cellist and conductor. Taught in Berlin from 1911 and was prin. vc. at Deutsches Opernhaus. Went to USA 1914, prin. cellist Philadelphia Orch. 1914–21. Took up cond. 1927 in Philadelphia. Founded Nat. SO, Washington, DC, 1931, remaining cond. until 1948.

King, Alec [Alexander] **Hyatt** (*b* Beckenham, 1911; *d* Southwold, 1995). Eng. librarian, bibliographer, and critic. Joined staff Brit. Museum 1934. Supt., mus. room at BM, 1944–73, mus. librarian, reference division, Brit. Library, 1973–6. Authority on Mozart, Handel, and mus. printing.

King, James (*b* Dodge City, 1925; *d* Naples, Flor., 2005). Amer. tenor. Began career as bar. Prof. opera début Florence 1961 (Cavaradossi in *Tosca*). Amer. début S. Francisco 1961. Made career mainly in Eur., singing Bacchus (*Ariadne auf Naxos*) at Vienna début 1963. Débuts: Salzburg Fest. 1962; Bayreuth 1965; NY Met 1966; CG 1967.

King, Robert (*fl.* London 1676–1728). Eng. composer of songs and th. mus. Member of Charles II's band from 1680 remaining in royal band until 1728. Promoted public concerts in London from 1689.

King, Robert (John Stephen) (*b* Wombourne, 1960). Eng. conductor and harpsichordist. Dir., The King's Consort from 1979. Mus. dir. European Baroque Orch. 1986, Nat. Youth Mus. Th. from 1987.

King, (Dame) Thea (*b* Hitchin, 1925). Eng. clarinettist. Played in SW orch. 1950–2, Portia Wind Ens. 1955–68. Prin. cl. London Mozart Players 1956–64, ECO from 1964. Member of Melos Ens.

from 1974. On staff RCM 1961–87, GSMD from 1987. Specialist in 20th-cent. Brit. mus., but has also revived 18th- and 19th-cent. works for cl., e.g. those by Crusell. OBE 1985. DBE 2001.

King Arthur, or The British Worthy. Semi-opera in prol., 5 acts, and epilogue by Purcell to lib. by Dryden, but really a play with extensive mus. Prod. London 1691, NY 1800.

King Christian II. Play by Adolf Paul for which in 1897–8 *Sibelius wrote incidental mus., suite from it (7 movts.) being his Op.27.

Kingdom, The. Oratorio, Op.51, by Elgar for sop., cont., ten., and bar. soloists, ch., and orch. to words mostly selected from the Bible. Comp. 1901–6. Sequel to *The *Apostles*. F.p. Birmingham 1906.

King Goes Forth to France, The (*Kuningas lähtee Ranskaan*). Opera in 3 acts, Op.53, by *Sallinen to lib. by P. Haavikko. Comp. 1983. Prod. Savonlinna 1984, Kiel (in German) 1986, Santa Fe (in English) 1986, London (CG) 1987.

King Lear. Mus. works inspired by Shakespeare's play (1606) incl.

(1) ov. by Berlioz, Op.4, comp. 1831;
(2) ov. and incid. mus. by Balakirev, 1859–61;
(3) 2 movements of incid. mus. by Debussy 1904;
(4) opera by Reimann, 1978;
(5) opera by Sallinen, 1998–9;
(6) mus. by Shostakovich, comp. 1970, for Russ. film of Shakespeare's play in B. Pasternak's trans.

Various opera composers, incl. Verdi and Britten, have contemplated but abandoned *King Lear* projects.

King of Prussia Quartets. Title given to the last 3 str. qts. written by Mozart—No.21 in D, K575 (1789), No.22 in B♭, K589 (1790) and No.23 in F, K590 (1790)—commissioned by King Friedrich Wilhelm II of Prussia, a cellist (hence the prominent vc. parts). 6 were requested, but only 3 written.

King Olaf, Scenes from the Saga of. Cantata, Op.30, by Elgar for sop., ten., and bass soloists, ch., and orch. on text by Longfellow with additions by Acworth. Comp. 1894–6, f.p. Hanley, Staffs, 1896, London (Crystal Palace) 1897.

King Priam. Opera in 3 acts by *Tippett to his own lib. based on Homer's *Iliad*. Comp. 1958–61. Prod. Coventry 1962, Karlsruhe 1963, London (concert) 1980, Canterbury (and tour) by Kent Opera 1985 (cond. E. Howarth), S. Francisco 1994.

King Roger (*Król Roger*). Opera in 3 acts by *Szymanowski to lib. by J. Iwaszkiewicz and composer. Comp. 1918–24. Prod. Warsaw 1926; Palermo 1949; London 1975; Long Beach, Calif., 1988.

King's Singers, The. Male-v. ens. of 6 singers (2 counterten., ten., 2 bar., bass) formed in 1968 and so called because orig. members, with one Oxonian exception, were choral scholars at King's College, Cambridge. Specialize in part-songs and in arrs. of various genres, incl. humorous songs. Range from Monteverdi to Noël Coward, with several works written specially for them.

King Stag (Henze). See *König Hirsch*.

Kinsky, Georg (Ludwig) (*b* Marienwerder, 1882; *d* Berlin, 1951). Ger. musicologist. Self-taught in mus. Curator, Heyer Music History Museum., Cologne, 1908–27. Lect. in musicology, Cologne Univ. 1921–32. Prepared catalogue of Beethoven's works, completed after his death by Hans Halm, pubd. 1955.

Kipnis, Alexander (*b* Zhitomir, Ukraine, 1891; *d* Westport, Conn., 1978). Russ.-born bass (Amer. cit. 1931). Sang in operetta, Berlin 1913. Hamburg Opera 1915–17, Wiesbaden 1917–22, Berlin State Opera 1919–35. Left Ger. 1935. Vienna Opera 1935–8. Débuts: US (Baltimore 1923); Chicago Opera 1923–32; NY Met 1940; CG 1927; Bayreuth Fest. 1927; Glyndebourne 1936; Salzburg Fest. 1937. Also notable *Lieder* singer. Taught at Juilliard Sch. until he was past 80.

Kipnis, Igor (*b* Berlin, 1930; *d* Redding, Conn., 2002). Amer. harpsichordist and critic, son of Alexander *Kipnis. Début NY 1959 (hpd.), Indianapolis 1981 (as fortepianist). Eur. tour 1967. Assoc. prof. of fine arts, Fairfield Univ., Conn., 1971–5, artist-in-residence 1975–7. Has taught at summer courses in Tanglewood and Indianapolis. Works written for him by Rochberg, Rorem, Kolb, R. R. Bennett, and McCabe.

Kirchner, Leon (*b* Brooklyn, NY, 1919). Amer. composer, pianist, and conductor. Taught at Univ. of S. Calif., Los Angeles 1951–4, Mills Coll., Oakland, 1954–61, and Harvard Univ. 1961–89 (prof. of mus. from 1966). Comp., in idiom of Berg and Schoenberg but not 12-note, incl.: opera *Lily* (1973–6); *Sinfonia*; 2 pf. concs.; 3 str. qts.; conc. for vn. vc., 10 winds, perc.; pf. sonata; choral mus.; etc.

Kirchner, Volker David (*b* Mainz, 1942). Ger. composer and violinist. Played cl. and pf. in jazz bands. Prin. violist Rhenish Chamber Orch. 1962–4. Violinist in Frankfurt Radio SO 1966–88. Comp. incid. mus. for over 20 plays. Works incl.: operas *Die Trauung* (1974), *Die fünf Minuten des Isaak Babel* (1977–9), and *Belshazar* (1984–5); *Orphischer Gesang*, str. sextet, str. orch. (1975–6); pf. trio (1979); *Totentanz*, orch. (1980); *Nachtstück*, va., small orch. (1980–1); *Der blaue Harlekin (Hommage à Picasso)*, 8 winds (1981); vn. conc. (1981–2); *Bildnisse* I, orch. (1981–2), II, orch. (1983–4); str. qt. (1982–3); pf. sonata (1985–6); *Lamemnto e danza d'Orfeo*, hn., pf. (1986–7); *Orfeo*, bar., hn. pf. (1986–7); *Und Salome sprach . . .*, vc. (1987); *Schibboleth*, va., orch. (1989); *Hortus magicus*, orch. (1994); *Labyrinthos*, actor, v., small orch. (1994–5); *Dybuk*, mar. (1995); *Gilgamesh*,

opera, 3 acts (1996–8); ob. conc. (1997–80); *Ahasver*, oratorio (1998–2000); trio, vn., va., vc. (1999); *Con mortuis in lingua mortua*, org. (2000).

Kirchschlager, Angelika (*b* Salzburg, 1965). Austrian mezzo-soprano. Studied pf. at Salzburg Mozarteum and singing at Vienna Acad. of Mus. with Walter Berry. Engaged by Vienna Kammeroper 1990 (Pamina). Prizewinner Vienna Belvedere comp. 1991. Strauss and Mozart roles in Vienna etc. Amer. début Seattle 1997 (Octavian). NY Met 1997 (Annio in *La clemenza di Tito*). Created role of Sophie in Maw's *Sophie's Choice* (CG 2002). Glyndebourne 2005 (Sesto in Handel's *Giulio Cesare*).

Kirckman, Jacob (*b* Bischweiler, nr. Strasbourg, 1710; *d* Greenwich, 1792). Ger. organist and composer. Settled in Eng. *c.*1730 to work for Tabel, hpd.-maker, and became first of line of distinguished hpd.-makers. Wrote several org. pieces. Succeeded by nephew, Abraham, who extended business to pf. manufacture and made last hpd. in 1809. Business merged with Collard, 1898.

Kirkby, (Carolyn) **Emma** (*b* Camberley, 1949). Eng. soprano. Taught before London début in 1974. Specialist in early mus. and has sung with Academy of Ancient Music, London Baroque, and Consort of Musicke. Amer. début 1978 and three tours of Middle East 1980–3, with lutenist Anthony Rooley. Repertory ranges from the Italian quattrocento to arias by Handel, Mozart, and Haydn. Opera début Bruges 1983 (Mother Nature in *Cupid and Death* by C. Gibbons and M. Locke). Amer. opera début 1989. OBE 2000.

Kirkby-Lunn, Louise (*b* Manchester, 1873; *d* London, 1930). Eng. mezzo-soprano. Début Drury Lane, London, 1893 in Schumann's *Genoveva*. Début CG 1896. Carl Rosa Opera 1897–9, CG 1901–14, 1919–22, NY Met 1902–3, 1906–8, 1912–14. Notable in Wagner roles. Sang with BNOC 1919–22. Sang Elgar's *Sea Pictures* in NY, cond. Mahler, 1910.

Kirkpatrick, John (*b* NY, 1905; *d* Ithaca, NY, 1991). Amer. pianist. Member of mus. faculty, Cornell Univ. 1946–68 and Yale Univ. 1968–73. Gave f.p. of Ives's *Concord Sonata*, NY, Jan. 1939, playing from memory.

Kirkpatrick, Ralph (*b* Leominster, Mass., 1911; *d* Guilford, Conn., 1984). Amer. harpsichordist. Début, Cambridge, Mass., 1930. Prof. of mus., Univ. of Calif. 1964, Yale Univ. 1940–76 (prof. from 1965). Biography of Domenico Scarlatti (1953) incorporated catalogue of his works which has been accepted as definitive, works being given *'K'* nos. Ed. of over 60 Scarlatti sonatas, J. S. Bach's *'Goldberg' Variations*, etc.

Kirshbaum, Ralph (Henry) (*b* Denton, Texas, 1946). Amer. cellist and conductor. Début with orch. Dallas 1959. Won Cassadó comp., Florence, 1969, and Tchaikovsky comp., Moscow, 1970. Settled in London 1971. NY début 1975. Plays in pf. trio with *Pauk (vn.) and *Frankl (pf.). Soloist, with Pauk and *Imai, in f.p. of Tippett's triple conc. (1980). Gave f. Amer. p. of Maxwell Davies's vc. conc., Cleveland 1989. Senior vc. tutor, RNCM.

Kirsten, Dorothy (*b* Montclair, NJ, 1910; *d* Los Angeles, 1992). Amer. soprano. Opera début Chicago 1940 (Poussette in *Manon*). In Chicago sang Musetta to Grace Moore's Mimì in *La bohème*. NY début 1942; NY City Opera 1944; NY Met 1945; S. Francisco 1947. Sang Cressida in f. Amer. p. of *Troilus and Cressida* (S. Francisco 1955). First American sop. to appear at Moscow Bolshoy, 1962. Sang in several films, incl. *The Great Caruso* with Mario Lanza (1950). Autobiography *A Time to Sing* (1982).

Kiss, The (*Hubička*). Opera in 2 acts by Smetana, comp. 1875–6 to lib. by E. Krásnohorská, after story by K. Světlá (1871). Prod. Prague 1876; Chicago 1921; Liverpool 1938.

Kissentanz (Ger.). *Cushion dance.

Kissin, Evgeny (*b* Moscow, 1971). Russ. pianist. Played Beethoven sonatas and a Mozart conc. at 7. Prof. début with orch. 1983 (both Chopin concs. with Moscow PO). Played Tchaikovsky 1st conc. with Berlin PO, cond. Karajan, 1987. Brit. début 1987; London début 1988; Amer. début (NY) 1990, followed by Carnegie Hall recital.

kit. Pocket fiddle, about 16" in length, used by dancing masters in the 18th and early 19th cents.

kitchen department. Humorous term referring to orch.'s perc. section.

Kitezh, The Legend of the Invisible City of (Rimsky-Korsakov). See *Invisible City of Kitezh, The Legend of the*.

kithara. Ancient Gr. str. instr. shaped like lyre but plucked by fingers.

Kittl, Johann Friedrich [Jan Bedřich] (*b* Orlik nad Vltavou, 1806; *d* Lissa, 1868). Ger.-Bohemian composer. Mendelssohn cond. his 2nd sym. in Leipzig, 1840. Dir., Prague Cons. 1843–65. Friend of Wagner, who gave him his lib. *Die Franzosen vor Nizza* which he comp. as *Bianca und Giuseppe* (1848). Also wrote 3 other operas, 4 syms., chamber mus., pf. pieces, and songs.

Kjerulf, Halfdan (Charles) (*b* Christiania, 1815; *d* Grefsen, 1868). Norweg. composer, nationalist in feeling. Wrote over 100 songs, many being settings of Bjørnson, choral and pf. comps. His songs combined influence of Ger. *Lieder* with Norweg. folk mus., paving the way for Grieg.

Kl. Abbreviation for *Klarinette* (Ger.), i.e. *clarinet.

Klafsky, Katharina (*b* Sz. János, Hungary, 1855; *d* Hamburg, 1896). Hung. soprano. In ch. of Vienna Komische Oper 1874. Sang opera at Leipzig 1876–86. London début 1882 in *Die Walküre*.

Hamburg Opera 1886–95. Sang in London 1892, under Mahler. Married cond. Otto Lohse 1895. Prin. sop., Damrosch Ger. Opera, NY, 1895–6.

Klagende Lied, Das (The Song of Sorrow). Cantata by *Mahler, to his own text, for sop., cont., ten., bass, ch., and orch. Orig. version in 3 parts 1880: 1. *Waldmärchen* (Forest Legend), 2. *Der Spielmann* (The Minstrel), 3. *Hochzeitsstück* (Wedding Piece). Rev. 1888 into 2 parts, *Waldmärchen* being omitted. Further rev. 1893–1902. F.p. Vienna 1901. F.p. of complete orig. version: Vienna (radio) 1935. F. Eng. p. of rev. version, Oxford 1914, cond. Boult, London 1956, cond. W. Goehr, of orig. version, London 1970, cond. Boulez. F.p. of orig. orch. of all 3 parts, Manchester 1997, cond. K. Nagano.

Klangfarbenmelodie (Ger.). Melody of tone colours. Term introduced by Schoenberg in his *Harmonielehre* (1911) to describe the contrasts in timbre which he introduced in the 3rd of his 5 *Orchestral Pieces* (1909) and which now constitute a structural element in modern comp. comparable in importance with pitch, duration, etc. Further explorations into the possibilities of melodic construction with points of tone colour were carried out by Webern.

Klappenhorn (from Ger., *Klappen*, keys). *key bugle.

Klarinette(n) (Ger.). *clarinet(s).

Klaviatur (Ger.). *keyboard.

Klavier (Clavier) (Ger.). Keyboard. Term for pf., hpd., clavichord, or any other domestic kbd. instr. In Eng. the word is chiefly used as synonym for organ manual.

Klavierauszug (Ger.). Pf. arr.

Klavierbüchlein (Little keyboard-book). Title given by J. S. Bach to 3 colls. of his kbd. mus.:
(1) Pieces for the instruction of his eldest son, Wilhelm Friedemann *Bach, 1720.
(2) Similar but small coll. for his 2nd wife, Anna Magdalena, 1722.
(3) Larger coll. for his wife, 1725, incl. some vocal pieces.

Klavierstück (Ger.). Pf. piece.

Klavierstücke I–XI (Piano Pieces I–XI). 11 pf. pieces by *Stockhausen comp. between 1952 and 1956, with IX and X rev. 1961. Many new techniques of pf.-playing are introduced for perf. of these pieces. The XIth is one of the first works in *open form. It has 19 sections printed on one large sheet of paper; the player has to play any piece at random, selecting his own tempo etc. Other permutations follow. F. complete p. Darmstadt 1966 (Aloys Kontarsky).

Klavierübung (Klavier Exercise). J. S. Bach's title, borrowed from *Kuhnau, for hpd. and org. works issued in 4 sections: (a) 6 partitas or *German Suites, 1731; (b) 2 pieces for double-manual hpd., the *Italian Concerto* and Partita in B minor (or French Overture) 1735; (c) org. works incl. 'St Anne' Fugue 1739; (d) *'Goldberg' Variations*, 1742.

Klebe, Giselher (Wolfgang) (*b* Mannheim, 1925). Ger. composer. Worked for Berlin Radio 1946–9. Prof. of comp. and theory, NW Ger. Mus. Acad., Detmold, from 1957. Uses serialism in several comps. Works incl. 13 operas (incl. *Figaro lässt sich scheiden* (Figaro seeks a divorce) (1962–3) and *Ein wahrer Held* (based on Synge's *Playboy of the Western World*) (1972–3); 4 ballets; 7 syms.; 15 solo concs.; 3 str. qts.; vocal mus.

Klecki, Pawel. See *Kletzki, Paul*.

Klee, Bernhard (*b* Schleiz, 1936). Ger. conductor and pianist. Ass. to Ackermann and Sawallisch at Cologne Opera. Cond. début Cologne 1960 (*Die Zauberflöte*). Worked in opera houses in Salzburg 1962–3, Oberhausen 1963–5, Hanover 1965–6. Mus. dir. Lübeck Opera 1966–73. Brit. début Edinburgh Fest. 1969 (with Hamburg Opera); CG 1972; Salzburg Fest. 1973; Amer. début 1974 (NYPO). Chief cond. Hanover Radio SO 1976–9 and from 1991. Mus. dir. Düsseldorf SO 1977–87, chief guest cond. BBC Philharmonic 1985–9. Acc. in recitals with sop. Edith *Mathis.

Kleiber, Carlos (*b* Berlin, 1930; *d* Ljubljana, 2004). Ger.-born conductor (Austrian cit. 1980). Son of Erich *Kleiber. Répétiteur, Gärtnerplatz, Munich, 1953. Cond. Potsdam Opera, 1954–6 (début in Millöcker's *Gasparone*), Vienna Volkstheater 1956–8. Cond. Düsseldorf Opera 1956–64, Zurich Opera 1964–6, Stuttgart from 1966, Munich from 1968. Cond. *Wozzeck* at Edinburgh Fest., 1966. Débuts: Bayreuth Fest. 1974; CG and La Scala 1974; Amer. (S. Francisco) 1977; NY Met 1988.

Kleiber, Erich (*b* Vienna, 1890; *d* Zurich, 1956). Austrian-born (Argentinian cit. 1938) conductor. Cond., Darmstadt court th. 1912–18, Wuppertal 1919–21, Düsseldorf 1921, Mannheim 1922–3. Berlin début 1923 (*Fidelio*). Gen. mus. dir. Berlin State Opera 1923–34, one of its most brilliant periods, incl. Janáček's *Jenůfa*, 1924, and f.p. of *Wozzeck*, 1925 (after, it is said, 137 rehearsals). Amer. début 1930 with NYP-SO. Resigned post 1934 over *Hindemith controversy with Nazis and their ban on *Lulu*. Left Ger. 1934 for S. Amer. Salzburg Fest. 1935. Cond. Buenos Aires 1936–49, Amsterdam 1933–8. British concert début 1935. Début CG 1938, working there regularly 1950–3, cond. f. Eng. stage p. of *Wozzeck* (1952). It. operatic début, Florence 1951. Vienna début 1951. Returned to post at Berlin State Opera 1955, but resigned because of political interference before taking it up.

klein, kleine (Ger.). (1) Little, as in *kleine Flöte* (little fl., i.e. piccolo), *Eine kleine Nachtmusik* (A Little Night Music).

(2) Minor (of intervals).

Kleine Nachtmusik, Eine (A Little Night Music, or Serenade). Comp. in 4 movements (K525) by

Mozart (for which occasion is not known) dating from 10 Aug. 1787. It is the Serenade No.13 in G major, scored for 2 vn., va., and bass, or small str. orch. Orig. MS recovered in 1955, indicates that a 5th movement, a 1st minuet, was torn out.

Kleine Orgelmesse (Little Organ Mass). Nickname for Haydn's Mass No.5 in B♭ (see also *Grosse Orgelmesse*).

kleine Trommel (Ger.). Small drum. The *sidedrum; otherwise snare-drum.

Klemperer, Otto (*b* Breslau, 1885; *d* Zurich, 1973). Ger.-born conductor and composer (Israeli cit. 1970). Cond. Reinhardt's prod. of Offenbach's *Orpheus in the Underworld*, Berlin 1906. Later encouraged by Mahler, whom he assisted with rehearsals of 8th Sym., Munich 1910. Cond. of opera Ger. Nat. Th., Prague, 1907–10, Hamburg 1910–12, Bremen 1913, Strasbourg 1914–17, Cologne 1917–24, Wiesbaden 1924–7, Berlin 1927–33 (first at Kroll Opera [until 1931], then State Opera). Cond. Bruckner's 8th sym. at his Salzburg Fest. début 1933, opera 1947 (*Le nozze di Figaro*). Cond. Los Angeles PO 1933–9. Seriously ill 1939, remaining partially paralysed. Budapest Opera 1947–50; Montreal SO 1950–3. Began assoc. with Philharmonia Orch., London, 1947, becoming prin. cond. 1959 and cond. for life in 1964. Cond. series of famous Beethoven concerts. Cond. and prod. *Fidelio* at CG 1961, *Die Zauberflöte* 1962, and *Lohengrin* 1963. Retired 1972. Comp. 6 syms., opera *Das Ziel* (1915, rev. 1970), 9 str. qts., and 100 songs.

Klenau, Paul (August) **von** (*b* Copenhagen, 1883; *d* Copenhagen, 1946). Danish composer and conductor. Cond. Freiburg Opera 1907 and 1912–17. Stuttgart 1909–12. Cond. Danish Phil. Soc. 1920–6. Champion of Delius's mus. Comp. 7 operas, incl. *Kjarten und Gudrun* (1924), *Rembrandt van Rijn* (1937), and *Elisabeth von England* (1938, rev. as *Die Königin*, 1940); 7 syms. (1908–41); str. qt.; pf. pieces; and orch. work *Bank Holiday, Souvenir of Hampstead Heath* (1922).

Klenovsky, Nikolay (Semyonovich) (*b* Odessa, 1857; *d* Petrograd, 1915). Russ. composer and conductor. Ass. cond. Moscow Imperial Opera (1883–93). Dir. Tiflis Mus. Sch. from 1893. Wrote ballets, cantatas, th. mus.

Klenovsky, Paul. Pseudonym under which Sir Henry *Wood made orch. transcription (1929) of Bach's Toccata and Fugue in D minor (in order to confuse the critics). *Klen* is the Russian word for a maple tree.

Kletzki [Klecki], **Paul** [Pawel] (*b* Łódź, 1900; *d* Liverpool, 1973). Polish-born (later Swiss) conductor and violinist. Violinist, Łódź PO 1914–19. Studied and cond. in Berlin 1921–33. Taught comp., Milan, 1933–8. Settled in Switz., 1939. Guest cond. of leading Eng. orchs. after 1947 (début with Philharmonia). Salzburg Fest. 1962.

Cond., Dallas SO 1958–61, Orchestre de la Suisse Romande 1968–70. Frequent cond. Israel PO. Comp. 4 syms., pf. conc., vn. conc., 4 str. qts.

Kl. Fl. Abbreviation for *kleine Flöte* (Ger.), i.e. *piccolo.

Klien, Walter (*b* Graz, 1928; *d* Vienna, 1991). Austrian pianist. Prizes at int. contests at Bolzano 1952, Paris and Vienna 1953. Int. tours. Recorded complete solo pf. works of Brahms, Mozart, and Schubert. Salzburg Fest. début 1963. Duo partner of Wolfgang *Schneiderhan from 1963.

Klindworth, Karl (*b* Hanover, 1830; *d* Stolpe, 1916). Ger. pianist, conductor, and composer. Worked in London as cond., pianist, teacher, and impresario 1854–68. Prof. of pf., Moscow Cons. 1868–81, settling in Berlin 1882, where he cond. Berlin PO and founded pf. cons. (1884), which merged in 1895 with Scharwenka's cons. Arr. Wagner's *Ring* for pf. Critical edn. of Chopin. Wrote many pf. pieces.

Klosé, Hyacinth (Eléonore) (*b* Corfu, 1808; *d* Paris, 1880). Fr. clarinettist. Prof. of cl., Paris Cons.,1839–68. Improved method of fingering 1843. Wrote methods of cl. and sax., pieces for cl. and military band.

Kluge, Die (The Clever Girl, or The Wise Woman). Opera in 12 scenes by *Orff to his own lib. which is synthesis of different versions of folktale. Comp. 1941–2. Prod. Frankfurt 1943, Cleveland, Ohio, 1949, London 1959.

Kmentt, Waldemar (*b* Vienna, 1929). Austrian tenor. Toured Holland and Belgium with opera co. as student. Vienna début 1950 (Beethoven's 9th Sym.), opera début Volksoper 1951 (Prince in *Love for Three Oranges*). Vienna State Opera from 1952. Sang Jaquino (*Fidelio*), 1955, at re-opening of Vienna State Opera House. Salzburg début 1955; Bayreuth 1968.

Knaben Wunderhorn, Des (Youth's Magic Horn). Anthology of Ger. folk poetry pubd. 1805–8, ed. by Arnim and Brentano, songs from which have been set by several composers incl. Strauss and, particularly, *Mahler, who comp. over 20 *Wunderhorn* songs for v. and pf. or orch. and incorporated *Wunderhorn* songs into his 2nd, 3rd, and 4th syms. F. Eng. p. of Mahler's *Des Knaben Wunderhorn* (10 songs for sop. and bar.) in orch. version, London, Nov. 1961, cond. B. Fairfax.

Knapp, Peter (*b* St Albans, 1947). Eng. baritone. Début 1973 (Count in *Figaro* with GTO). Joined Kent Opera. Sang title-role in *King Roger* with New Opera Co. 1975. ENO début 1977. Formed Singers' Company (later Travelling Opera) 1978. Created Maxim in Josephs's *Rebecca* (Leeds, Opera North, 1983).

Knappertsbusch, Hans (*b* Elberfeld, 1888; *d* Munich, 1965). Ger. conductor. Début Mulheim 1910. Ass. to S. Wagner and Richter at Bayreuth 1910–12. Opera posts at Bochum, Elberfeld

(1913–18), Leipzig (1918–19), Dessau (1919–22). Cond. Bavarian State Opera, Munich, 1922–36. Salzburg Fest. début 1929 (concert), opera début 1937 (*Der Rosenkavalier* and *Elektra*). Cond., Vienna State Opera 1937–44. Regular cond. Bayreuth Fest. from 1951. Returned to Munich 1945. Only London appearance, *Salome*, CG 1937. Superb interpreter of Wagner and Strauss.

kneifend (Ger.). Plucking (same as *pizzicato).

Kneller Hall. Headquarters of *Royal Military School of Music (founded 1857) at Whitton, Twickenham, Middlesex. Former home of painter Sir Godfrey Kneller (1646–1723).

Knight, Gillian (*b* Redditch, 1939). Eng. mezzo-soprano. Sang with D'Oyly Carte Co. 1959–64. SW début 1968 (Ragonde in *Le Comte Ory*). CG début 1970. Created Rose Parrowe in *Taverner*, CG 1972. Amer. début 1979 (Tanglewood); Wexford Fest. 1990.

Kniplová (*née* Pokorná), **Naděžda** (*b* Ostrava, 1932). Cz. soprano. Sang with Janáček Opera, Brno, 1959–64, then became prin. at Prague Nat. Th. Salzburg Easter Fest. 1967 (Brünnhilde), summer Fest. 1971 (Janáček's *Glagolitic Mass*). Outstanding in strongly dramatic roles, e.g. Smetana's Libuše, Janáček's Emilia Marty and Kostelnička, Isolde, Tosca, Ortrud, and Renata in *The Fiery Angel*.

Knipper, Lev (Konstantinovich) (*b* Tiflis, 1898; *d* Moscow, 1974). Russ. composer. Works incl. 14 syms. (1929–54), several with choral finales; 5 operas; sym.-poem; vn. conc.; film mus.; chs.; songs, etc.

Knorr, Iwan (*b* Mewe, W. Prussia, 1853; *d* Frankfurt-am-Main, 1916). Ger. composer and teacher. From 1886, prin. teacher of comp., Hoch Cons., Frankfurt, where he had several distinguished pupils, incl. Pfitzner and Ernst Toch, and Eng. composers who became known as 'Frankfurt group', i.e. N. O'Neill, Cyril Scott, Roger Quilter, and Balfour Gardiner. Dir. of Cons. 1908–16. Wrote operas, orch. mus., and songs.

Knot Garden, The. Opera in 3 acts by *Tippett to his own lib. Comp. 1966–70. Prod. CG 1970, Evanston Univ., Ill., 1974, Paris 1994. Orch. reduced for chamber ens. of 22 players by M. Bowen, 1982–3. See also *Songs for Dov*.

Knoxville: Summer of 1915. Samuel *Barber's Op.24, scena for sop. and orch., to a prose text by James Agee, comp. 1947 and f.p. Boston 1948 (sop. Eleanor Steber, cond. Koussevitzky). Arr. for sop. and chamber orch. 1950, f.p. Dumbarton Oaks, Washington DC, 1950 (sop. Eileen Farrell, cond. Wm. Strickland).

Knüpfer, Paul (*b* Halle, 1866; *d* Berlin, 1920). Ger. bass. Début Sondershausen 1885. Leipzig 1887–98; Berlin 1898–1920; Bayreuth Fest. début 1901; CG début 1909. First singer in England of Baron Ochs in *Der Rosenkavalier* (1913), and Gurnemanz (*Parsifal*).

Knussen, (Stuart) **Oliver** (*b* Glasgow, 1952). Eng. composer and conductor. Began to compose at age of 6. In 1968, aged 16, cond. LSO in f.p. of his 1st sym. Awarded fellowship at Tanglewood 1970. Taught comp. RCM junior dept. 1977–82. Co-ordinator of contemp. mus., Tanglewood, 1986–98. Co-art. dir., Aldeburgh Fest. 1983–98. Prin. cond. London Sinfonietta 1998–2002. CBE 1994. Prin. works:

OPERAS: *Where the Wild Things Are*, Op.20 (1979–83); *Higglety Pigglety Pop!* (1984–90).

ORCH.: syms.: No.1, Op.1 (1966–7), No.2, Op.7, sop. and small orch. (1970–1), No.3, Op.18 (1973–9); *Symphony in One Movement*, Op.5 (1969/2000); *Choral*, Op.8, wind, perc., dbs. (1970–2); *Music for a Puppet Court*, Op.11 (1972/1983); *Ophelia Dances*, Book I, Op.13, for 9 instr. (1975); *Coursing*, Op.17, chamber orch. (1979, rev. 1981); *The Wild Rumpus*, Op.20b (from *Where the Wild Things Are*) (1983); *Fanfares for Tanglewood*, 13 brass, perc. (1986); *Flourish with Fireworks*, Op.22 (1988); *The Way to Castle Yonder*, Op.21a (from *Higglety Pigglety Pop!*) (1988–90); hn. conc., Op.28 (1994); vn. conc., Op.30 (2002).

VOICE & ENS.: *Hums and Songs of Winnie-the-Pooh*, Op.6, sop., ens. (1970–83); sym. No.2, Op.7, sop., small orch. (texts by Trakl and Plath) (1970–1); *Rosary Songs*, Op.9, sop., cl., va., pf. (1972); *Océan de Terre*, Op.10, sop., ens. (1972–3, rev. 1976); *Trumpets*, Op.12, sop., 3 cl. (1975); *Songs and a Sea Interlude*, Op.20a, sop., orch. (from *Where the Wild Things Are*) (1979–81); *4 Late Poems and an Epigram of Rainer Marie Rilke*, Op.23, unacc. sop. (1988); *Whitman Settings*, Op.25a, sop., orch. (or pf.) (1991–2).

CHAMBER MUSIC: *Processionals*, Op.2, wind quintet and str. qt. (1968–78); *Masks*, Op.3, fl. (1969); *Fire*, Op.4, fl., str. trio (1969); *3 Little Fantasies*, Op.6a, wind quintet (1970, rev. 1976); *Autumnal (Triptych, Pt. I)*, Op.14, vn., pf. (1976–7); *Cantata (Triptych, Pt. III)*, Op.15 (1977); *Elegiac Arabesques*, Op.26a (1991); *Songs Without Voices*, Op.26, 8 instr. (1991–2).

PIANO: *Sonya's Lullaby (Triptych, Pt. II)*, Op.16 (1977–8); *Variations*, Op.24 (1989); *Prayer Bell Sketch* (1997).

Koanga. Opera in prol., 3 acts, and epilogue by Delius to lib. by C. F. Keary after G. W. Cable's novel *The Grandissimes* (1880). Comp. 1896–7, rev. 1898. Extracts perf. in concert version London 1899. F.p. Elberfeld 1904, cond. *Cassirer; f. Eng. p. CG 1935 cond. Beecham (with lib. rev. by Beecham and E. Agate); f. Amer. p. Washington 1970. Concerns slaves on Mississippi plantation. See also *Calinda, La*.

Kobbé, Gustav (*b* NY, 1857; *d* Long Island, 1918). Amer. music critic and writer. From 1880 mus. critic for several NY papers, incl. the *Herald* for 18 years. Attended first *Parsifal* at Bayreuth 1882. Wrote 2-vol. life of Wagner (1890), and several other books. His *chef d'oeuvre* was *The Complete Opera Book*, a coll. of synopses and analyses of a large number of operas which was on the point of completion when he was killed by a seaplane striking his sailing-boat. 1st edn. pubd. 1922, with additions by Katherine Wright. Extensive rev. 1954 ed. by Earl of Harewood, who has continued revs. up to 11th edn., 1997 with Anthony Peattie.

Kochánski, Pawel [Paul] (*b* Odessa, 1887; *d* NY,

1934). Polish violinist. Leader of Warsaw PO at 14 in 1901. Prof. of vn., Warsaw Cons. 1907–13, St Petersburg Cons. 1913–17, Kiev Cons. 1919–20. Amer. début NY 1921. Taught at Juilliard Sch. from 1924. Friend of *Szymanowski who wrote *Myths* (1915) and 1st vn. conc. (1916) for him.

Köchel, Ludwig von (*b* Stein, nr. Krems-on-the-Danube, 1800; *d* Vienna, 1877). Austrian botanist and mineralogist with immense admiration for music of Mozart. Compiled chronological thematic catalogue—*Chronologisch-thematisches Verzeichnis*—of Mozart's works, giving each a 'Köchel number' (e.g. K488) by which they are now universally identified. First pubd. Leipzig 1862. Various revs. have been pubd., one being by A. Einstein, 1937. 6th edn. 1964.

Kocsis, Zoltán (*b* Budapest, 1952). Hung. pianist and composer. Won Hung. Radio Beethoven Comp. 1970. Toured USA 1971, London and Salzburg débuts 1972. Liszt Prize 1973. Comps. incl. *Memento (Chernobyl '86)* for orch.

Koczwara, Franz. See *Kotzwara, Franz*.

Kodály, Zoltán (*b* Kecskemét, 1882; *d* Budapest, 1967). Hung. composer and teacher. He was born and had his early education in Galánta. His father, a state railways employee, played the vn., his mother the pf., and he grew up in a mus. atmosphere. He attended the Nagyszombat Gymnasium 1892–1900, during which period his first orch. work was played by the school orch. In 1900 he entered Budapest Univ. and the Franz Liszt Acad. of Mus., where his teacher was Hans (János) Koessler, who also taught *Bartók and *Dohnányi. He met Bartók after his graduation, in 1905, and embarked on his first foray as a folk-song collector in Galánta. In 1906 his symphonic poem, *Summer Evening*, had its f.p. Kodály continued his folk-song collecting between 1907 and 1914. Although he was insistent on folk mus. as a basis of nat. culture, he had a wider view of the mus. scene and travelled to Bayreuth, Salzburg, Berlin, and Paris. He taught theory at the Liszt Acad. in 1907, and took over the comp. classes from Koessler in 1908 (prof. from 1911). From that time, too, he was closely involved with the mus. curriculum in Hung. schs., and with Bartók he formed an organization for the perf. of contemporary mus. Alongside these activities he produced a steady flow of comps.

In 1923, for the 50th anniversary of the unification of Buda and Pest as the capital, he comp. *Psalmus Hungaricus*, which was soon perf. throughout Europe and America under leading conds. such as Toscanini, Mengelberg, and Furtwängler. In 1926 he completed his opera *Háry János*, firmly rooted in folklore. Another opera, *The Spinning Room*, followed in 1932, and the orch. *Dances of Galánta* in 1933. In the same year Kodály and Bartók were requested by the Hung. Acad. of Sciences to prepare for publication all available folk mus. material. After Bartók went to the USA, Kodály took over sole editorial control. The first vol. appeared in 1951. Two important commissions were for the Amsterdam Concertgebouw

Orch.'s 50th anniv., 1939 (*Variations on a Hungarian Folk Song, The Peacock*) and the 50th anniv. of the Chicago SO, 1941 (*Concerto for Orchestra*). These were in contrast to the dozens of works for children's vv. which occupied him for the last 30 years of his life. He retired from the Liszt Acad. in 1942. After World War II he travelled to Fr., Eng., the USA, and USSR to cond. his own works. A 3rd opera, *Czinka Panna*, was prod. in 1948. His sym., in memory of Toscanini, was prod. at Lucerne in 1961. He visited the USA again in 1965 and 1966.

Kodály's mus. is not as advanced in its harmonic idiom as Bartók's and is less cosmopolitan. But it has the merits of complete conviction, finished craftsmanship, and melodic inspiration. Prin. works are:

OPERAS: *Háry János* (1925–6); *The Spinning Room* (1924–32); *Czinka Panna* (1946–8).

ORCH.: *Summer Evening* (1906, rev. 1929–30); Suite, *Háry János* (1927); *Dances of Marosszék* (1930, arr. of work for pf. 1927); *Dances of Galánta* (1933); *Variations on a Hungarian Folk Song, The *Peacock* (1938–9); *Concerto for Orchestra* (1939–40); sym. (1930s–61).

CHORUS & ORCH.: *Psalmus Hungaricus*, ten., ch., and orch. (1923); *Te Deum of Budavár* (1936); *Missa brevis* (1944); *At the Grave of the Martyr* (1945); *The *Music Makers*, vv., orch. (1964).

CHORUS AND ORGAN, PIANO, etc: *Pange lingua* (1929); *Hymn to King St Stephen* (1938); *Laudes Organi* (1966).

UNACC. CHORAL: *Evening* (1904); *Birthday Greeting* (1931); *Jesus and the Traders* (1934); *Ode to Ferenc Liszt* (1936); *Molnár Anna* (1936); *The Peacock* (1937); *Forgotten Song of Bálint Balassi* (1942); *Lament* (1947); *Hymn of Zrínyi* (1954); *Mohács* (1965).

CHAMBER MUSIC: str. qts., No.1 (1908–09), No.2 (1916–18); sonata for vc. and pf. (1909–10); *Duo*, vn., vc. (1914); Solo vc. sonata (1915); *Capriccio*, solo vc. (1915); Serenade, 2 vn. and va. (1919–20). Also many folk-song arrs., children's chs., singing exercises, and transcrs. (Bach, etc.).

Koechlin, Charles (*b* Paris, 1867; *d* le Canadel, Var, 1950). Fr. composer. Wrote large amount of mus., much of it still rarely heard. Followed no 'school' or fashion, his music being influenced both by medieval procedures and by Satie, Stravinsky, etc. Bitonality and near-atonality feature in his works, some of which are marked by complex polyphony. Wrote several symphonic poems based on Kipling. One of founders, 1909, of Société Musicale Indépendante. Author of treatises, and of books on Debussy and Fauré. Prin. works:

THEATRE: *Jacob chez Laban* (1-act 'biblical pastorale') (1896–1908); *La Forêt païenne* (ballet) (1911–25).

ORCH.: *7 Stars Symphony* (on characters of film stars) (1933); *Symphony of Hymns* (1936); sym. No.2 (1943–4); *3 Poèmes*, after Kipling (1899–1910); *La Course de printemps*, after Kipling (1925–7); *La Loi de la jungle*, after Kipling (1939); *Les Bandar-Log*, after Kipling (1939–40); *Le Buisson ardent* (1938, 1945); *La Forêt* (1897–1907); *Partita* for chamber orch. (1945).

CHAMBER MUSIC: 3 str. qts. (1911–13, 1915–16, 1921); fl. sonata (1913); va. sonata (1906–15); ob.

sonata (1911–16); vn. sonata (1916); vc. sonata (1917); bn. sonata (1919); hn. sonata (1918–25); 2 cl. sonatas (1923); wind trio (1924); *Primavera* for fl., vn., va., vc., hp. (1936); septet for wind quintet, ca, alto sax. (1937); *Epitaphe de Jean Harlow*, fl., alto sax., pf. (1937).

PIANO: *Paysages et marines* (*c*.1916); *L'Ancienne Maison de campagne* (1932–3).

Koellreutter, Hans-Joachim (*b* Freiburg, 1915; *d* São Paolo, 2005). Ger. composer and flautist. Taught at Brazilian Cons., Rio de Janeiro, 1937–52. Founder and dir., Free Acad. of Mus., São Paulo 1952–5, and mus. dept., Bahia Univ. 1952–62. Head of programmes, Goethe Institute, Munich, 1963–5; dir., Ger. cultural institute, New Delhi, 1965–9. Prin., New Delhi Sch. of Mus. 1966–9. Dir. of Goethe Inst., Tokyo, 1970–5. Prof. at São Paulo Cons. from 1984. Works incl. chamber sym.; 4 *Pieces* for orch.; 2 fl. sonatas; vn. sonata; *Mùsica* for orch.; *Concretion* for orch.; *India Report* for sop., spkr., speaking ch., and orch.; *Composition 70* for sitar and chamber orch.

Kogan, Leonid (*b* Dnepropetrovsk, 1924; *d* Mytishcha, nr. Moscow, 1982). Ukrainian-born violinist. Début Moscow 1941. London début 1955; Amer. début 1958; Salzburg Fest. début 1966. On staff Moscow Cons. from 1952 (prof. 1963, head of vn. dept. 1969). First Soviet violinist to play and record Berg conc. In trio with *Gilels (pf.) and *Rostropovich (vc.).

Koizumi, Kazuhiro (*b* Kyoto, 1949). Japanese conductor. Worked for 2 years with Seiji Ozawa. Ass. cond. Japan Philharmonic 1970–2. Won Karajan comp., Berlin, 1972. Salzburg Fest. début 1976. Mus. dir. New Japan PO 1975–80, Winnipeg SO 1983–9. Chief cond. Tokyo Metropolitan Orch. 1984–7.

Kokkonen, Joonas (*b* Iisalmi, Finland, 1921; *d* Järvenpää, 1996). Finn. composer and pianist. Teacher, Sibelius Acad. 1950–9 (prof. of comp. 1959–63). Wrote mus. criticism 1947–63. Works incl. 5 syms.; vc. conc.; 3 str. qts.; pf. trio; pf. qt.; vc. sonata; *Missa a cappella*; *Symphonic Sketches*; opera *The *Last Temptations* (1975); *Requiem* (1981).

Kolb, Barbara (*b* Hartford, Conn., 1939). Amer. composer. Worked as mus. copyist in NY 1965. Won Amer. *Prix de Rome* 1970. Asso. prof. of mus. theory Brooklyn Coll. 1973–5. Residency at IRCAM, Paris, 1983–4. Prin. works:

ORCH.: *Soundings* (2 conds.) (1971–2, rev. 1975, 1978); *Grisaille* (1978–9); *Yet That Things Go Round*, chamber orch. (1986–7, rev. 1988); *The Enchanted Loom* (1988–9, rev. 1992); *Voyants*, pf., chamber orch. (1991); *All in Good Time* (1993).

ENS.: *Crosswinds*, wind. ens., perc. (1969); *Trober Clus* (1970); *Chromatic Fantasy*, narr., 6 instr. (1979); *The Point that Divides the Wind*, org., perc., 3 male vv. (1981–2); *Millefoglie*, computer tape, ens. (1984–5, rev. 1987); *Cloudspin*, org., brass (1991); *Introduction and Allegro*, wind band (2001).

CHAMBER MUSIC: *Rebuttal*, 2 cl. (1965); *Chansons bas*, sop., hp., 2 perc. (1966); *Figments*, fl., pf. (1967, rev. 1969); *Looking for Claudio*, gui., tape (1975);

Homage to Keith Jarrett and Gary Burton, fl., vib. (1976, rev. 1977); *Songs Before an Adieu*, sop., fl./alto fl., gui. (1976–9); *3 Lullabies*, gui. (1980); *Related Characters*, tpt. (or cl., alto sax., va.), pf. (1980); *Cavatina*, vn. (or va.) (1983, rev. 1985); *Time . . . and Again*, ob., str. qt., tape (1985); *Umbrian Colours*, vn., gui. (1986); *Introduction and Allegro*, gui. (1988); *Broken Slurs*, gui. (1988, rev. 1992, 2001); *Extremes*, fl., vc. (1989); *Sidebars*, bn., pf. (1995–6).

KEYBOARD: *Solitaire*, pf., tape. (1971); *Toccata*, hpd., tape. (1971); *Spring River Flowers Moon Night*, 2 pf., tape (1974–5); *Appello*, pf. (1976); *Cloudspin*, org., tape (1991); *Antoine's Tango*, pf. (2001).

Kolisch, Rudolf (b Klamm am Semmering, 1896; d Watertown, Mass., 1978). Amer. violinist of Austrian birth. After childhood injury, used bow in left hand. Formed Kolisch Qt. 1922, which toured Europe, Africa, and USA where its members settled in 1935. Played standard repertory from memory and championed works by Schoenberg (Kolisch's brother-in-law after 1924), Berg, and Webern. Gave f.ps. of Schoenberg's 3rd and 4th str. qts. (1927 and 1937), Berg's *Lyric Suite* (1927), Webern's str. trio (1928) and str. qt. (1938), Bartók's 5th str. qt. (1935) and 6th str. qt. (1941). Quartet disbanded 1941. Kolisch led Pro Arte Qt. from 1942 and taught at Univ. of Wisconsin 1944–67.

Kollo [Kollodziejski], **René** (b Berlin, 1937). Ger. tenor. Début Brunswick 1965 (in *Oedipus Rex*). Düsseldorf Opera 1967–71. Débuts: Bayreuth 1969; Salzburg 1972; CG 1976; NY Met 1976. Leading Wagnerian roles at Salzburg Easter Fest. 1974 (Lohengrin), Vienna, Munich, Berlin, etc.

Kol Nidrei [Kol Nidre] (All vows). (1) For vc. and orch., Op.47, by Bruch, comp. 1881. Arr. for vc. and pf.
(2) Setting for rabbi, ch., and orch., Op.39, by *Schoenberg (1938), f.p. Los Angeles 1938 cond. Schoenberg.
The *Kol Nidrei* is the opening prayer of the Jewish service on the eve of the Day of Atonement (*Yom Kippur*). It probably originated among the Ashkenazi Jews of mediaeval Ger. Tune (traditional) is not used by Sephardim. *Ketèlbey (non-Jewish composer), inserted whole motif into his *Sanctuary of the Heart* (1924).

Kolodin, Irving (b NY, 1908; d NY, 1988). Amer. music critic. Ass. mus. critic to W. J. Henderson, NY *Sun* 1932, eventually becoming chief critic until 1950. Mus. critic *Saturday Review*, 1947–82. Also critic of recordings in several publications. Author of history of NY Met, and other books. Taught at Juilliard Sch. from 1968.

kolomyika. A quick Polish dance in duple time, usually with slow introduction (*dumka). Popular among the mountain peasants of Poland.

Kondrashin, Kyril (Petrovich) (b Moscow, 1914; d Amsterdam, 1981). Russ. conductor. Cond., Maly Opera, Leningrad, 1936–43, Bolshoy Opera, Moscow, 1943–56. Brit. and Amer. débuts 1958.

Prin. cond. Moscow PO 1960–75. Ass. prin. cond. Concertgebouw Orch., Amsterdam, 1975–81. Cond. f.ps. of Shostakovich's 13th Sym. (1962), *The Execution of Stepan Razin* (1964), and 2nd vn. conc. (1967). Recorded all Shostakovich syms. Emigrated to West 1978.

Konetzni(-Wiedmann), [Konerczny], **Anny** (b Ungarisch-Weisskirchen, 1902; d Vienna, 1968). Austrian soprano, sister of Hilde *Konetzni. Sang in Vienna Volksoper ch. Stage début Chemnitz 1927 as cont. Sang in the *Ring* in Paris 1929. Joined Berlin Staatsoper 1931; Vienna Opera from 1933. Débuts: NY Met 1934; Salzburg Fest. 1934; CG 1935 (Brünnhilde), returning in same role 1951.

Konetzni [Konerczny], **Hilde** (b Vienna, 1905; d Vienna, 1980). Austrian soprano, sister of Anny *Konetzni. Début Chemnitz 1929 (Sieglinde in *Die Walküre*, with Anny as Brünnhilde). Joined Ger. Th., Prague, 1929; Vienna Opera 1936. Salzburg Fest. début 1936; CG début 1938.

König Hirsch (King Stag). Opera in 3 acts by *Henze to lib. by H. von Cramer after Gozzi. Comp. 1953–5. Prod. (heavily cut) Berlin 1956; rev. 1962 as *Il Re Cervo*, f.p. Kassel 1963, Santa Fe 1965, BBC 1973. F.p. of complete score of orig. vers., Stuttgart (staged) 1985.

Königin von Saba, Die (The Queen of Sheba). Opera in 4 acts by K. Goldmark to lib. by S. H. Mosenthal. Prod. Vienna 1875, NY 1885, Manchester 1910.

Königskinder (The King's Children). 3-act opera by Humperdinck to lib. by 'Ernst Rosmer' (Elsa Bernstein-Porges) after her play of same name. Humperdinck wrote incidental mus. for the play in 1894 and adapted it as a melodrama employing rhythmically notated *Sprechgesang* (1895–7). Perf. in this vers. Munich and London 1897, NY 1898. In 1908–10 he expanded and rev. this as an opera, prod. NY Met 1910, London 1911.

König Stephan (King Stephen). Ov. and incidental mus. by Beethoven, Op.117, comp. 1811 for prol. by Kotzebue written for opening night of Ger. th. in Budapest, 1812 (see also *Ruinen von Athen, Die*).

Kontakte (Contacts). Comp. by *Stockhausen for pf., perc., and elec. sounds on 4-track tape. Comp. 1959–60.

Kontarsky, Alfons (b Iserlohn, 1932). Ger. pianist, brother of Aloys *Kontarsky. Held seminars at Darmstadt summer schools 1962–9. Has appeared as pf. duo with brother since 1955, giving f.ps. of works by Berio, Bussotti, Kagel, Pousseur, Stockhausen, and Zimmermann.

Kontarsky, Aloys (b Iserlohn, 1931). Ger. pianist, brother of Alfons *Kontarsky. Formed pf. duo with brother 1955. Gave f. complete p. of Stockhausen's *Klavierstücke I–XI*, Darmstadt 1966. Formed duo with cellist Siegfried *Palm.

Kontrabass (Ger.). Db., generally the str. instr.

Kontrabassposaune (Ger.). *Double-bass trombone.

Kontrafagott (Ger.). *Double bassoon.

Kontra-Punkte (Counter-points). Work by *Stockhausen, 1952–3, for 10 instr. (fl., cl., bcl., bn., tpt., tb., pf., hp., vn., vc.). It is a rev. of a work for orch. *Punkte* (1952), itself rev. in 1962.

Konwitschny, Franz (*b* Fulnek, N. Moravia, 1901; *d* Belgrade, 1962). Ger. conductor. Played vn. and va. in various orchs. Cond. début 1927, working in opera 1927–49). Cond., Leipzig Gewandhaus Orch. 1949–62, Dresden State Opera 1953–5, Berlin State Opera 1955–62. Cond. *The Ring* at CG, 1959. Salzburg Fest. 1961.

Konzert (Ger.). (1) concert.
(2) concerto.

Konzertstück (Ger.). Concert piece, generally with the implication of 'concerted' piece, i.e. for solo instr. and orch. Term often applied to short or 1-movement concs., e.g. Weber's *Konzertstück* for pf. and orch.

Koopman, Ton (*b* Zwolle, Holland, 1944). Dutch harpsichordist, organist, and conductor. Leader of Musica da Camera and Musica Antiqua. Formed Amsterdam Baroque Orch. 1977. Specialist in early mus. performances.

Koppel (Ger.). Coupler (organ).

Korchinska, Maria (Countess Benckendorff) (*b* Moscow, 1895; *d* London, 1979). Russ.-born harpist. Prin. harpist Bolshoy Th., 1918–24, prof. of hp., Moscow Cons., 1918–24. Settled in Eng. 1924. Gave f.p. of Bax's *Fantasy Sonata* for hp. and va., dedicated to her, 1927.

Kord, Kazimierz (*b* Pogórze, 1930). Polish conductor. Warsaw Opera 1960–2. Art. dir. Kraków Opera 1962–8. Mus. dir. Polish Nat. Orch. 1968–73. NY Met début 1972; CG début 1976. Art. dir. Warsaw PO from 1977. Cond. Cincinnati SO 1980–2. Chief cond. SW German Radio SO 1980–6.

Korean Temple Block. An oriental addition to the 20th-cent. dance-band drummer's equipment. A skull-shaped hollow block of wood, in several sizes giving different pitches, struck with a drum-stick. Used in some symphonic works. Similar to the *Chinese temple block*.

Korn, Peter (Jona) (*b* Berlin, 1922; *d* Munich, 1998). Ger.-Amer. composer and conductor. Founder and cond. Los Angeles New Orch. 1948–56. Teacher of comp., Trapp Cons., Munich, 1960–1, dir., Strauss Cons., Munich, from 1967. Works incl. opera *Heidi in Frankfurt* (1961–3); 3 syms. (1941–69); *Tom Paine* ov.; vc. conc.; concertino for hn.; sax. conc.; vc. sonata; ob. sonata; hn. sonata; str. qt.; pf. sonata, etc.

Kornett (Ger.). The modern *cornet or the ancient *cornett.

Korngold, Erich (Wolfgang) (*b* Brünn, 1897; *d* Hollywood, Calif., 1957). Austrian-born composer and conductor (Amer. cit. 1943). Son of mus. critic Julius *Korngold. Child prodigy as pianist and composer. His *Der Schneemann* was a sensation at the Vienna Court Opera 1910 and Schnabel played a pf. sonata he wrote at 13. His one-act operas *Violanta* and *Der Ring des Polykrates* were premièred in Munich in 1916 cond. by Bruno Walter. In 1920 his opera *Die tote Stadt* (The Dead City) had simultaneous premières in Hamburg and Cologne. Cond., Hamburg Opera 1921. Prof., Vienna State Acad., 1931. Settled in USA 1934, writing mus. for many successful films until 1947. Prin. works:

STAGE: *Der Schneemann* (pantomime, orch. Zemlinsky) (1910); *Der Ring des Polykrates* (1916); *Violanta* (1916); *Die *tote Stadt* (1919–20); *Das Wunder der Heliane* (Hamburg, 1927); *Die Kathrin* (1937, f.p. Stockholm 1939); *Die stumme Serenade* (1946).

ORCH.: sym. in F♯ major (1951–2); *Schauspiel-Ouvertüre* (1911); *Sinfonietta* (1912); *Symphonic Serenade* for str. (1947); pf. conc. for left hand (1923); vn. conc. (1945); vc. conc. (1946).

PIANO: *Fairy-Tale Pictures* (1910); pf. sonatas: No.1 (1908), No.2 (1910), No.3 (1931).

CHAMBER MUSIC: str. qts., No.1 in A (1924), No.2 in E♭ (1935), No.3 in D (1945); pf. trio (1910); vn. sonata; pf. quintet; str. sextet.

FILM MUSIC: *Give Us This Night, Captain Blood, The Prince and the Pauper, The Adventures of Robin Hood, The Sea Hawk, The Private Lives of Elizabeth and Essex, Between 2 Worlds, Devotion*, etc.

In the 1920s Korngold re-orchestrated, re-arr., and practically re-comp. (for Theater an der Wien) operettas by Strauss (incl. *Eine Nacht in Venedig*), Offenbach, and Fall.

Korngold, Julius (*b* Brünn, 1860; *d* Hollywood, Calif., 1945). Austrian music critic, father of Erich *Korngold. Mus. critic *Neue Freie Presse*, Vienna, 1902–34. Collab. with son on lib. of Erich's opera *Die *tote Stadt* under joint pseudonym 'Paul Schott'.

kosakisch, kosatcheck, or **kosachok**. A Cossack dance, the mus. of which is in quick duple time and of ever-increasing speed, and is often in the minor.

Kosler, Zdeněk (*b* Prague, 1928; *d* Prague, 1995). Cz. conductor. Début, Prague Nat. Th., 1951 (*Il barbiere di Siviglia*). Won int. cond. comp. Besançon 1956 and Mitropoulos comp. NY 1963, after which he was ass. cond. to Bernstein with NYPO 1963–4. Opera dir., Olomouc 1958–62, Ostrava Opera 1962–6; cond. Prague SO 1966–7; mus. dir. Berlin Komische Oper 1966–8; cond. Czech PO 1971–80; chief cond. of opera at Slovak Nat. Th., Bratislava, 1971–6; chief cond. Prague Nat. Th. 1980–5 and 1989–91. Brit. début 1975.

Kossuth. Symphonic-poem in 10 tableaux by *Bartók, based on life of Lajos Kossuth (1802–94), leader of unsuccessful Hungarian uprising against Austria, 1848–9. Comp. 1903. F.p. Budapest 1904; f. Eng. p. Manchester 1904 (cond. Richter). Contains distorted version of Austrian national hymn.

Kostelanetz, André (*b* St Petersburg, 1901; *d* Port-au-Prince, Haiti, 1980). Russ.-born conductor (Amer. cit. 1928). Settled in USA 1922 and worked as rehearsal accomp. at NY Met. Cond. for CBS 1930. Guest cond. of NYPO. Widely known for luscious arrs. of light mus. in which he cond. his own orch. Cond. f.p. of Walton's *Capriccio burlesco* (dedicated to him) NY 1968.

Kotelettenwalzer (Ger.). See *Chopsticks.*

koto. 13-stringed Japanese psaltery, strs. being of waxed silk, tuned by movable bridges. 6′ in length, 3″ high and 9″ wide. Rests on floor, the right end being raised by 2 small legs. Player sits on his heels, plucking the strs. with right hand and using plectra on thumb and first 2 fingers, modifying pitch with left hand. Used in ritualistic mus. and regarded since 17th cent. as Japanese nat. instr.

Kotzwara, Franz [Koczwara, František] (*b* Prague, 1750; *d* London, 1791). Bohemian-born violinist, double-bass player, and composer. Settled in London 1775 and spent some time in Ireland in late 1780s. Was db. player at King's Th., London, in 1791. Won popularity with fantasia *The *Battle of Prague* (*c.*1788), for pf. and optional extra instrs. Died during perverted sexual practice with prostitute who was acquitted of his murder.

Koussevitzky [Kussevitzky], **Serge** [Sergey] (Alexandrovich) (*b* Vishny Volochek, 1874; *d* Boston, Mass., 1951). Russ.-born conductor and double-bass player (Amer. cit. 1941). Joined Bolshoy Th. orch., becoming prin. db. 1901–5. Recognized as db. virtuoso, making public début Moscow 1901. Début outside Russ., Berlin 1903. Début as cond., Berlin PO 1908. Db. soloist début, London, 1907, cond. 1908. With first wife, Natalie, founded pub. firm 1909, profits going to Russ. composers. Founded and cond. Koussevitzky SO 1910–18, and championed mus. of Scriabin. Dir., State SO, Petrograd, 1917–20, dir., Grand Opera of Moscow 1918. Left Russia for Paris, founding orch. and conducting Concerts Koussevitzky 1921–8. Cond., Boston SO 1924–49, giving many f.ps. of mus. by Amer. composers. Especial champion of Sibelius. Est. Berkshire Music Center at Tanglewood, Mass., in 1940 with Copland as ass. dir. Koussevitzky taught cond. there. Through Koussevitzky Mus. Foundation, founded 1943 in memory of wife, commissioned many works, incl. Bartók's *Concerto for Orchestra* and Britten's *Peter Grimes.* Second wife Olga (1901–78), whom he married in 1947, was very active on behalf of foundation. Koussevitzky composed conc. for db. and other pieces for the instr.

Kout, Jiří (*b* Novedvory, 1937). Cz. conductor. Cond. Pilsener Opera and SO. Won cond. comps. in Besançon 1965 and Brussels 1969. Prin. cond. Deutsche Oper am Rhein, Düsseldorf 1978–84, prin. res. cond. Deutsche Oper, Berlin, from 1990. Amer. début Los Angeles 1988; NY Met début 1991; CG début 1993.

Kovacevich [Bishop-Kovacevich], **Stephen** (*b* Los Angeles, 1940). Amer. pianist and conductor of Yugoslav parentage, living in Eng. Début 1951 (San Francisco). Brit. début Wigmore Hall, 1961. Dedicatee and first player of Richard Rodney Bennett's conc. (1968) and gave f.p of Tavener's (1979). Prof. of pf., RAM, from 1986. Took up cond. and frequently appears with Northern Sinfonia.

Kovacić, Ernst (*b* Kapfenberg, Styria, 1943). Austrian violinist. Outstanding champion of contemp. composers, notably Schwertsik, Gruber, Eder, and many Brit. composers of whose concs. he gave f.p. Salzburg Fest. début 1979. Gave f. Brit. p. of Janáček vn. conc. (Liverpool 1989).

Kovařovic, Karel (*b* Prague, 1862; *d* Prague, 1920). Cz. conductor and composer. Harpist at Prague Nat. Th. 1879–85. Cond. some of first concerts of Czech PO 1896–8. Dir. of opera Prague Nat. Th. from 1900. Cond. f.p. of Dvořák's *Rusalka,* 1901, and operas by Ostrčil, Foerster, and Novák. Cond. f. Prague p. of Janáček's *Jenůfa,* 1916, having for 12 years rejected it because of a personal grudge, and rev. and reorch. parts of it. Comp. 5 operas between 1883 and 1901, 3 ballets, pf. conc., and 3 str. qts. (1878–94).

Kowalski, Jochen (*b* Wachow, 1954). Ger. countertenor. Sang David in *Die Meistersinger* at Komische Oper while a student. Prof. début Handel Fest., Halle, 1982, in *Muzio Scevola.* Member of Berlin Komische Oper from 1983. Paris début 1987; Vienna 1987; CG 1989 (with Komische Oper), CG Royal Opera début 1990.

Koželuh [Kozeluch], **Jan** [Johann Anton] (*b* Velvary, 1738; *d* Prague, 1814). Cz. composer and organist. Taught in Prague. Kapellmeister, Prague Cath. from 1784. Wrote operas, church mus., bn. conc., pf. conc., etc. Known as 'the masterly contrapuntist'. Cousin of Leopold *Koželuh.

Koželuh [Kozeluch], **Leopold** [Jan Antonín] (*b* Velvary, 1747; *d* Vienna, 1818). Cz. composer and teacher. Instructor to Viennese aristocracy. Refused to succeed Mozart at Salzburg 1781, but succeeded him as court composer in Prague 1792. Wrote operas, ballets, oratorio, 28 syms., 22 pf. concs., about 80 pf. trios, and 50 pf. sonatas. Arr. Scottish, Irish, and Welsh folk songs for George Thomson of Edinburgh.

Kožená, Magdalena (*b* Brno, 1973). Cz. mezzo-soprano. Studied singing at Brno Cons. 1987–91 with Neva Megová, then at Coll. of Perf. Arts, Bratislava, 1991–5 with Eva Blahová. Won 6th int. Mozart comp. Salzburg 1995. Opera début Brno 1995 (Dorabella). Vienna Volksoper début

1996 (Annius), Drottningholm 1998 (Paris in Gluck's *Paride ed Elena*), Aix Fest. 1999 (*L'incoronazione di Poppea*), Salzburg Fest. 2002 (Zerlina), London 2003 (Gluck's Paris, concert), Glyndebourne 2003 (Idamante), NY Met 2006 (Dorabella).

Kraft, Anton (*b* Rokitzan, Pilsen, 1749; *d* Vienna, 1820). Cz. cellist and composer. Father of Nicolaus *Kraft. Haydn persuaded him to join Eszterháza orch. 1778–90. Played in court orch., Bratislava, 1790–6, then in Prince Joseph Lobkowitz's orch. in Vienna. Taught in Vienna 1820. Haydn's vc. conc. in D was once attrib. to him. His fine playing inspired vc. part of Beethoven's triple conc.

Kraft, Nicolaus (*b* Eszterháza, 1778; *d* Cheb, Cz., 1853). Cz. cellist and composer, son and pupil of Anton *Kraft. Member of Prince Joseph Lobkowitz's orch. from 1796 and of Schuppanzigh's str. qt. which gave f.ps. of several Beethoven qts. Wrote 4 vc. concs. and many salon pieces.

Kraft, William (*b* Chicago, 1923). Amer. composer and timpanist. Prin. timpanist Los Angeles PO 1955–81. Comp.-in-residence, Los Angeles PO 1981–5. Visiting Prof., Univ. of S. Calif., Los Angeles, 1988–90. Jazz-influenced comps. incl.:

OPERA: *The Red Azalea* (1997–2002).

ORCH.: sym., str., perc. (1961); *Concerto grosso*, vn., vc., fl., bn., orch. (1961); conc. for 4 perc., orch. (1966); *Configurations*, conc. for 4 perc., jazz orch. (1966); *Contextures: Riot-Decade '60* (1967); pf. conc. (1973); *Tintinnabulations: Collage No.3* (1974); *Andirivieni*, tuba, orch. (1978, rev. as tuba conc. 1979); *Double Play*, vn., pf., chamber orch. (1982); timp. conc. (1983); *Contextures II: The Final Beast*, sop., ten., chamber orch. (1984; for sop., ten., boys' ch., orch., 1986); *Interplay* (1984); *A Kennedy Portrait*, narr., orch. (1988); *Veils and Variations*, hn., orch. (1988); *Vintage 1990–91* (1990); conc. for 4 perc. and wind ens. (1995).

CHAMBER MUSIC: *Nonet*, brass, perc. (1958); *Triangles*, perc., 10 instr. (1965–8); *In Memoriam Igor Stravinsky*, vn., pf. (1972–4); *In the Morning of the Winter Sea*, vc., perc. (1975); *Weavings*, str. qt., perc. (1984); *Mélange*, fl., cl., vn., vc., pf., perc. (1985); *Quartet for the Love of Time*, cl., vn., vc., pf. (1987); *Quartet for Percussion* (1988); *Cadeau*, fl., pf. (1992); *Brazen*, brass, timp., org. (1996).

PERCUSSION: *Theme and Variations*, perc. qt. (1956); *Suite*, 4 perc. (1958); *Encounters I*, perc., tape (1975); *Variations for King George*, timp. (1980).

Krakoviak, Krakowiak. (1) Polish dance from Kraków district, in lively 2/4 time, with distinctive syncopation.
(2) Title of Chopin's concert rondo for pf. and orch., Op.14, comp. 1828.

Krämerspiegel (Shopkeeper's Mirror). Cycle of 12 songs, Op.66, for v. and pf. by R. Strauss to poems by Alfred Kerr (1867–1948), comp. 1918. Poems contain satirical and punning references to most of leading Ger. mus. publishers with whom Strauss was in dispute over copyright.

One of the work's melodies (in songs Nos. 8 and 12) was used again by Strauss over 20 years later as the 'Moonlight Music' and elsewhere in his last opera *Capriccio*.

Krasner, Louis (*b* Cherkassy, Russ., 1903; *d* Boston, Mass., 1995). Russ.-born Amer. violinist. Taken to USA as child. Début Vienna. Commissioned and gave f.p. of Berg's conc., Barcelona 1936. Gave f.p. of Schoenberg's conc., Philadelphia 1940. Leader, Minneapolis SO 1944–9. Prof. of vn., Syracuse Univ. 1949–72. Taught at New Eng. Cons. from 1974.

Kraus [Trujillo], **Alfredo** (*b* Las Palmas, Canary Is., 1927; *d* Madrid, 1999). Sp. tenor of Austrian descent. Won Geneva int. comp. 1956. Opera début Cairo 1956 (Duke in *Rigoletto*). Eur. début Venice 1956; London début Stoll Th. 1957; CG 1959; La Scala 1960; Amer. début Chicago 1962; NY Met 1966; Salzburg Fest. 1968. Outstandingly elegant lyric tenor.

Kraus, Lili (*b* Budapest, 1903; *d* Asheville, N. Car., 1986). Hung.-born pianist (Brit. cit. 1948). World tours and soloist with leading orchs. Salzburg Fest. 1934. Specialist in Mozart. First to record all Mozart pf. sonatas and first to perf. all his concs. in NY, 1966–7. Duo with Szymon *Goldberg 1935–40. Interned in Java 1942–5.

Kraus, Otakar (*b* Prague, 1909; *d* London, 1980). Cz.-born baritone (Brit. cit.). Début Brno 1935 (Amonasro in *Aida*). Prin. bar., Bratislava Opera 1936–9, then settled in Eng. 1940, singing with Carl Rosa Opera 1943–6. Joined EOG 1946, creating Tarquinius in Britten's *Rape of Lucretia*. Netherlands Opera 1950–1. Member of CG Opera Co. 1951–73. Created Nick Shadow in *The Rake's Progress* (Venice, 1951), Diomede in *Troilus and Cressida* (CG 1954), and King Fisher in *The Midsummer Marriage* (CG 1955). Sang Alberich at Bayreuth Fest. 1960–2. OBE 1973.

Krause, Tom (*b* Helsinki, 1934). Finn. baritone. Début Helsinki 1957 (concert); opera début Berlin 1959 (Escamillo in *Carmen*). Member of Hamburg Opera from 1962. Created title-role in Searle's *Hamlet*, Hamburg 1968. Bayreuth début 1962; Brit. début Glyndebourne 1963; NY Met 1967; Salzburg Fest. 1968.

Krauss, Clemens (Heinrich) (*b* Vienna, 1893; *d* Mexico City, 1954). Austrian conductor. Opera début Brno 1913 (*Zar und Zimmermann*). Cond., Ger. th., Riga, 1913–14, Nuremberg 1915–16. Worked in Stettin 1916–21 and Graz 1921–2. Ass. cond. Vienna State Opera 1922–4, earning admiration of R. Strauss of whom he became close friend and great interpreter. Dir., Frankfurt Opera 1924–9; Vienna 1929–34; Berlin 1934–7; Munich 1937–43; Vienna 1947–54. His Munich period was notable for superb standard of prods. Salzburg Fest. début 1926 (*Ariadne auf Naxos*). London début CG 1934; Amer. début 1929 NYP-SO; Bayreuth 1953. Frequent cond. of Vienna PO, Frankfurt Museum concerts. Cond. f.p. of

Arabella (Dresden 1933), *Friedenstag* (Munich 1938), *Capriccio*, for which he wrote part of lib. (Munich 1942), and *Die *Liebe der Danae* (Salzburg 1944 dress reh. and Salzburg 1952). Married sop. Viorica *Ursuleac.

Krebs, Johann (Ludwig) (b Buttelstedt, 1713; d Altenburg, 1780). Ger. organist and composer. Held org. posts at Zwickau, Zeitz, and Altenburg. Wrote religious choral works, fl. sonatas, fl. trios, and much org. mus., some of which is heard today.

Krehbiel, Henry (Edward) (b Ann Arbor, Mich., 1854; d NY, 1923). Amer. music critic, author, and editor. Mus. critic *Cincinnati Gazette* 1874–80, NY *Tribune* 1880–1923. Champion of Brahms, Dvořák, and Wagner. Bitterly attacked Strauss's *Salome* and was severely critical of Mahler as composer and cond. Wrote several books. Pubd. Eng. version of *Parsifal*. Rev. and completed Eng. text of Thayer's *Life of Beethoven* (3 vols. 1921).

Kreisler, Fritz (Friedrich) (b Vienna, 1875; d NY, 1962). Austrian-born violinist and composer (Amer. cit. 1943). Entered Vienna Cons. at age 7. Amer. début 1888 in Boston, followed by tour with pianist Moriz *Rosenthal. Returned to Europe and abandoned mus. career, studying medicine in Vienna and art in Rome and Paris. Resumed career as violinist Jan. 1898 in Vienna. Returned to USA 1900–1. London début, Philharmonic Soc., May 1902. His brilliant technique and unmistakably personal tone put him in the forefront of int. violinists. In 1910 gave the f.p. of Elgar's conc., which is ded. to him. Lived in NY 1915–24 but later returned to Eur. and in 1938 became Fr. citizen. Made many recordings. Returned to NY 1940, thereafter living chiefly in USA. Comp. str. qt. and many pieces for vn., of which the best-known are *Caprice Viennois, Liebesfreud, Liebesleid, Schön Rosmarin* and *Tambourin Chinois*. Also transcr. works by Dvořák, Paganini, and Tartini. Wrote cadenzas for Beethoven and Brahms concs.

Kreisleriana. Set of 8 fantasy pf. pieces by Schumann, Op.16, comp. 1838 and ded. to Chopin (rev. 1850). Title refers to the character Kreisler in E. T. A. Hoffmann's stories.

Kreizberg, Yakov (b Leningrad, 1959). Russ.-born conductor. Brother of Semyon *Bychkov. Emigrated to USA 1976. Became ass. to Tilson Thomas with Los Angeles PO. Won Stokowski cond. comp., NY, 1986. Mus. dir. Mannes Coll. Orch., 1985–8. Gen. mus. dir. Krefeld Opera from 1988. Mus. dir. and chief cond., Komische Oper, Berlin, from 1994. Prin. cond. Bournemouth SO 1995–2000. Toronto début 1990; Glyndebourne début 1992; London (ENO) 1994.

Kremer, Gidon (b Riga, 1947). Latvian violinist. 1st prize at Paganini comp., Genoa, 1968, and Tchaikovsky comp., Moscow, 1970. Amer. début

NY 1977. Duo recitalist with Martha *Argerich. Performs many contemp. works, notably by Schnittke, Gubaidulina, and Pärt.

Krenek [Křenek], **Ernst** (b Vienna, 1900; d Palm Springs, Calif., 1991). Austrian-born composer (Amer. cit. 1945). His chamber mus., neo-classical in style, was played at Donaueschingen and Nuremberg, and his *Die Zwingburg*, to a text by Franz Werfel, was prod. in Berlin, 1924, under Kleibecategr. In 1925–7 he was ass. to Paul Bekker as gen. man. of opera at Kassel and Wiesbaden. In 1926 he completed his opera *Jonny spielt auf* (Johnny strikes up), using jazz idiom. After rejection by several Ger. opera houses, it was staged in Leipzig in 1927 and was a sensational success, being perf. in over 100 cities and trans. into 20 languages. It made Krenek's name and fortune. He returned to Vienna in 1928 and made extensive study of 12-note technique, later writing for *Frankfurter Zeitung* 1930–3. During this time he wrote an elaborate opera, *Karl V*, using the 12-note method. (Its scheduled prod. in Vienna was cancelled when the Nazis occupied Austria and he was categorized as a composer of 'degenerate music'. It was perf. in Prague, 1938.) In some later works he employed a free atonal technique and also applied a 'principle of rotation', in which serial variants are formed through the systematic exchange of the pitches of a given series with their adjacent pitches. He also used elec. procedures and later returned to a more lyrical style. He emigrated to USA in 1938, becoming prof. of mus. at Vassar Coll. 1939–42 and at Hamline Univ., St Paul, 1942–7. In 1948 he settled near Los Angeles, devoting his time to comp., lecture-tours, etc. After 1945 he preferred his name to be spelt simply as Krenek. Prin. works:

OPERAS: *Die Zwingburg*, Op.14 (lib. by Werfel) (1922); *Der Sprung über den Schatten*, Op.17 (1923); *Orpheus und Eurydíke*, Op.21 (lib. by Kokoschka) (1923); *Bluff*, Op.36 (1924–5); *Jonny spielt auf*, Op.45 (1925–6); *Der Diktator*, Op.49 (1926); *Das geheime Königreich*, Op.50 (1926–7); *Schwergewicht* (1926–7); *Leben des Orest*, Op.60 (1928–9); *Kehraus um St Stephan*, Op.66 (1930); *Karl V*, Op.73 (1930–3); *Cefalo e Procri*, Op.77 (1933–4); *Tarquin*, Op.90 (1940); *What Price Confidence?*, Op.111 (1945–6); *Dark Waters* (1950); *Pallas Athene weint* (1952–5); *The Bell Tower* (1955–6); *Ausgerechnet und verspielt* (1961); *Der goldene Bock*, Op.186 (1963); *Der Zauberspiegel* (1966); *Sardakai* (1967–9).

BALLETS: *Der vertauschte Cupido*, after Rameau (1925); *8-Column Line*, Op.85 (1939); *Jest of Cards* (1957).

ORCH.: syms.: No.1, Op.7 (1921), No.2, Op.12 (1922), No.3, Op.16 (1922), No.4, Op.34, wind, perc. (1925), No.5 (1949), sym. (unnumbered, 1947), *Little Symphony*, Op.58 (1928), Sym. *Pallas Athene* (1954), Symphonic mus., 9 instr., Op.11 (1922); pf. concs.: No.1, Op.18 (1923), No.2, Op.75 (1937), No.3 (1946), No.4 (1950); 2-pf. conc. (1951); *Concerto grosso* No.1, Op.10, (1921), No.2, Op.25 (1924); vn. concs.: No.1, Op.29 (1924), No.2 (1954); *7 Pieces*, Op.31 (1924); *Potpourri*, Op.54 (1927); *Symphonic Piece*, str., Op.86 (1939); *Little Concerto*, pf., org., chamber orch., Op.88 (1940);

I Wonder as I Wander, variations on N. Car. folk-song, Op.94 (1942); *Symphonic Elegy*, str. (on death of Webern) (1946); *Brazilian Sinfonietta*, str. (1952); *Kette, Kreis und Spiegel* (1956–7); *Quaestio temporis* (1958–9); *Marginal Sounds* (1960); conc., vn., pf., small orch. (1950); vc. conc. No.1 (1953), No.2 (1982); *Capriccio*, vc., small orch. (1955); hp. conc. (1951); *Horizon Circled* (1968); *Dream Sequence*, concert band (1975); conc., org., str. (1979); *Im Tal der Zeit*, sym. sketch (1979); org. conc. (1982).

CHAMBER MUSIC: str. qts.: No.1, Op.6 (1921), No.2, Op.8 (1921), No.3, Op.20 (1923), No.4, Op.24 (1923–4), No.5, Op.65 (1930), No.6, Op.78 (1937), No.7, Op.96 (1943–4), No.8 (1952); vn. sonata (1919); *Suite*, Op.28, cl., pf. (1924); Suite, solo vc., Op.84 (1939); org. sonata, Op.92, No.1 (1941); fl. and va. sonatina, Op.92, No.2 (1942); sonata, solo va., Op.92, No.3 (1944); *Pentagram*, wind quintet (1957); str. trio No.1 (1948), No.2 (1987); wind quintet (1951); solo vn. sonata (1948); va. sonata (1948); ob. sonatina; guitar suite; fl. piece in 9 phases (1959).

CHORAL: *The Seasons* (Hölderlin), Op.35 (1925); *Symeon der Stylit* (1935–87); *Lamentatio Jeremiae Prophetae*, Op.93 (1941); *The Santa Fe Time Table* (1945); *In Paradisum* (1945); 6 *Motets* (Kafka) (1959); *Canon 'Igori'* (for Stravinsky's 80th birthday, 1962); *German Proper of the Mass for Trinity Sunday* (1966–7); *Opus sine nomine*, oratorio (1989).

SONGS: 9 *Songs* (1921–3); *Reisebuch aus den österreichischen Alpen* (Diary from the Austrian Alps), Op.62, 20 songs to own words (1929); *Die Nachtigall*, Op.68 (1931); 5 *Songs* (Kafka) Op.82 (1938); *Ballad of the Railroads* (1944); *Sestina*, sop., 10 players (1957); *Wechselrahmen* (Change of Frames), 6 *songs*, sop., pf. (1968).

PIANO: sonatas: No.1, Op.2 (1919), No.2, Op.59 (1928), No.3, Op.92 No.4 (1943), No.4 (1948), No.5 (1950), No.6 (1951); 2 Suites, Op.26 (1924); 5 Pieces, Op.39 (1928); completion of Schubert's C major sonata (1921); *Echoes from Austria* (1958); 8 Pieces (1946); *George Washington Variations* (1950); 6 *Vermessene* (1958).

ELECTRONIC: *Spiritus intelligentiae Sanctus*, oratorio, vv. and sounds (1956); *San Fernando Sequence* (1963); *Quintina*, sop., tape, chamber ens. (1965).

MISCELLANEOUS: Edn. and orch. of Monteverdi's *L'incoronazione di Poppea* (Vienna 1937); perf. version of 1st and 3rd movts. of Mahler's 10th sym. (with Berg and F. Schalk) (Vienna 1924).

Krenn, Werner (*b* Vienna, 1943). Austrian tenor. Member of Vienna Boys' Choir. Bassoonist in Vienna SO 1962–6, then turned to singing. Stage début Berlin 1966 (in Purcell's *Fairy Queen*). Salzburg Fest. début 1967; Brit. début Scottish Opera 1970. Also successful *Lieder* singer.

Krenz, Jan (*b* Włocławek, 1926). Polish conductor and composer. Cond. Lódź PO 1945, Poznań PO 1948–9. Worked with G. Fitelberg. Chief cond. and art. dir. Polish Radio SO, Katowice, 1953–67. Cond., Danish Radio SO 1966–8. Eng. début with BBC SO 1961. First cond. at Warsaw Opera 1967–73, later perm. guest cond. Mus. dir.

Bonn Orch. 1979–82. Orch. works by Polish composers. Comps. incl. sym., 2 str. qts., pf. concertino.

Kreutzer, Conradin (*b* Messkirch, Baden, 1780; *d* Riga, 1849). Ger. composer and conductor. Held several Kapellmeister posts: to King of Württemberg, at Donaueschingen (1818–22), Vienna (1822–7, 1829–32, 1833–40), and Cologne (1840–2). Wrote operas, incl. *Das Nachtlager von Granada* (1834), oratorios, 3 pf. concs., incid. mus., chamber works, and songs.

Kreutzer, Rodolphe (*b* Versailles, 1766; *d* Geneva, 1831). Fr. violinist and composer. Début Paris, Concert Spirituel 1780 (in Stamitz conc.). 1st vn. in *Chapelle du Roi* 1785, and soloist at Paris Théâtre des Italiens 1790. Two operas prod. there. Prof. of vn., Paris Cons. 1795–1826, compiling (with Baillot) the establishment's vn. method. In 1798 visited Vienna where he met Beethoven, who ded. to him his A major sonata, Op.47, completed 1803, and known as *Kreutzer Sonata*. 1st vn., Paris Opéra, from 1801, cond. there 1816–24, dir. 1824–6. Retired 1826. Comp. over 40 operas and ballets; 19 vn. concs.; 17 str. qts.; 15 trios; 3 double concs.; sonatas; and many vn. pieces incl. 20 *Études ou Caprices*.

Kreutzer Sonata. (1) Nickname of Beethoven's vn. sonata in A major, Op.47 (1803) ded. to the Fr. violinist Rodolphe *Kreutzer, who is believed never to have played it. F.p. by George *Bridgetower (vn.) and Beethoven (pf.), Vienna 1803.

(2) Sub-title often given to Janáček's Str. Qt. No.1, comp. 1923–4 and incorporating part of scrapped pf. trio of 1908–9. On the score Janáček wrote: 'Inspired by L. N. Tolstoy's *Kreutzer-sonata*' (novel pubd. 1890). F.p. Prague 1924 (Bohemian Qt.); London 1926.

Kreuz (Ger.). Cross. Ger. for the *sharp sign (♯).

Křička, Jaroslav (*b* Kelč, Moravia, 1882; *d* Prague, 1969). Cz. composer and conductor. Prof. at Prague Cons., from 1918, later becoming dir. Comp. 2 syms., 13 operas, several str. qts., mus. for Maeterlinck's *The Blue Bird*, song-cycles, and works for children.

Krieger, Johann (*b* Nuremberg, 1651; *d* Zittau, 1735). Ger. composer and organist. Court organist, Bayreuth, 1672–7. Town mus. dir., Zittau 1681–1735. Comp. preludes and fugues for organ much admired by Handel. Also wrote songs and church mus.

Krips, Henry (Joseph) (*b* Vienna, 1912; *d* Adelaide, 1987). Austrian-born conductor (Australian cit. 1944), brother of Josef *Krips. Cond. début Vienna Burgtheater 1932. Cond. Innsbruck 1933–4; Salzburg 1934–5; Vienna 1935–8. Emigrated to Australia 1938 and formed Krips-de Vries Opera Co. Prin. cond. W. Australia SO 1948–72 and S. Australia SO 1949–72. Worked for Australian Broadcasting Commission. Lived in London from 1972. Cond. at SW from 1967, mainly operetta.

Krips, Josef (*b* Vienna, 1902; *d* Geneva, 1974). Austrian conductor. Cond. at Vienna Volksoper 1921–4; Dortmund 1925–6; Karlsruhe 1926–33; Vienna State Opera 1933–8; Belgrade Opera 1938–9. Salzburg Fest. début 1935. Banned by Nazis from conducting, 1939–45. Cond. first opera perf. in Vienna after war in 1945, playing major part in restoring Vienna Opera's reputation 1945–50. Re-opened Salzburg Fest. 1946 (*Don Giovanni*). Guest cond. Eng. orchs. (Hallé, etc.) from 1947. Débuts: CG 1947 (with Vienna co.), CG Royal Opera 1963; NY Met 1966. Cond.-in-chief LSO 1950–4; Buffalo PO 1954–63; S. Francisco SO 1963–70.

Kroll Oper. Ger. opera house in Berlin, extant 1924–31. Was planned by Wilhelm II in 1896, the Theater am Königplatz (orig. built by Joseph Kroll in 1844) being purchased. Delays postponed opening until 1924, as home of Berlin's Grosse Volksoper. Under *Klemperer 1927–31, the Kroll was among most adventurous opera houses of world, performing many contemp. works, e.g. by Stravinsky, Janáček, Hindemith, and Schoenberg. Nazis took over th. as home of Reichstag, 1933.

Krombholc, Jaroslav (*b* Prague, 1918; *d* Prague, 1983). Cz. conductor. Guest cond. Prague Nat. Th. and Czech PO 1940. Cond., Ostrava Opera 1944–5. On staff Prague Nat. Th. from 1945, 1st cond. 1963–8; head, Prague Nat. Th. Opera 1968–70; chief cond. Nat. Th. Opera 1970–5. Chief cond. Cz. Radio SO 1973–8. Cond. opera in Vienna, Budapest, Warsaw, Naples, Russia, and London (CG début 1959; ENO début 1978. Notable for perfs. of Janáček, Smetana, Martinů, Novák, and Shostakovich.

Krommer, Franz (*b* Kamenitz, Moravia, 1759; *d* Vienna, 1831). Moravian composer and violinist. Served in various court mus. posts, until succeeding Koželuh as Vienna court Kapellmeister 1818, last to hold this post. Prolific composer of mus. for wind instrs., syms., masses, cl. conc., etc.

Kronos Quartet. String quartet founded in Seattle 1973 by David Harrington and re-formed in 1978 in San Francisco. Plays almost exclusively contemp. mus. incl. rock transcrs. Has given over 400 f.ps. of works by Carter, Feldman, Reich, Rihm, Gubaidulina, and others.

Krueger, Karl (*b* Atchison, Kansas, 1894; *d* Elgin, Ill., 1979). Ger.-Amer. conductor. New Eng. Cons. 1914–15. Org., St Ann's, NY, 1916–20. Went to Eur. 1920. Ass. cond. Vienna State Opera 1919–24; Cond., Seattle SO 1925–32; Kansas City PO 1933–43; Detroit SO 1943–9. Cond. several opera premières with NY Music Guild.

Krumhorn, Krummhorn (Ger.). *Crumhorn.

Krummbogen, Krummbügel (Ger.). Bent-arch. or **Stimmbogen**, Tuning-arch. Crook (of a brass instr.).

Krumpholtz, Johann (Baptist) (*b* Budenuce, nr.

Zlonice, 1742; *d* Paris, 1790). Bohemian harpist and composer. Originated several improvements in the hp., incl. invention of hp. with two pedals, loud and soft. Comp. several works for hp. Drowned himself in Seine because of wife's infidelity with J. L. *Dušek.

Krumpholtz, Wenzel (*b* Budenice, nr. Zlonice, 1750; *d* Vienna, 1817). Bohemian violinist, mandolin-player, and composer, brother of Johann Baptist *Krumpholtz. Violinist in Court opera orch., Vienna, from 1796. Friend and champion of Beethoven, who composed a mandolin sonata for him and the vocal trio *Gesang der Mönche* in his memory.

Kubelik, Jan (*b* Michle, nr. Prague, 1880; *d* Prague, 1940). Cz.-born violinist and composer (Hung. cit. 1903). Father of Rafael *Kubelik. Concert début Prague, Vienna, 1898. London début 1900. Notable virtuoso. Last concert 1940 (Prague). Comp. 6 vn. concs. and *American Symphony* (1937).

Kubelik, (Jeroným) **Rafael** (*b* Býchory, 1914; *d* Lucerne, 1996). Cz.-born conductor and composer (Swiss cit. 1966), son of Jan *Kubelik. Début with Czech PO 1934; accompanist to father 1935–6; cond. Czech PO 1936–9, Brno Opera 1939–41, chief cond. Czech PO 1941–8. Left Cz. 1948, vowing never to return under Communism. Amer. début Chicago 1949. Salzburg Fest. début 1950 (Vienna PO). Cond. Chicago SO 1950–3; SW début 1954; mus. dir. CG 1955–8 (incl. f. stage ps. in Eng. of *Jenůfa* and *Les *Troyens*); cond. Bavarian Radio SO 1961–79. Mus. dir. NY Met 1973–4. Retired 1985 but returned to Cz. 1990 in triumph (after its liberation from Communism) to cond. 2 perfs. of *Má Vlast*. Works incl. 2 syms.; 5 operas; 4 str. qts.; vn. conc.; vc. conc.; songs; chamber mus.

Kubik, Gail (Thompson) (*b* S. Coffeyville, Oklahoma, 1914; *d* Covina, Calif., 1984). Amer. composer and violinist. Confidant of N. Boulanger from 1937. Taught at several Amer. mus. colls. 1934–40. Comp. mus. for films, radio, and TV. Works incl. 3 syms.; 2 vn. concs.; folk-opera *A Mirror for the Sky*; pf. sonata; *In Praise of Johnny Appleseed*, bass, ch., orch.; *Gerald McBoing Boing* (film cartoon score and concert version).

Kubla Khan, Pleasure Dome of (Griffes). See *Pleasure Dome of Kubla Khan*.

Kuhlmann, Kathleen (*b* San Francisco, 1950). Amer. mezzo-soprano. Début Chicago 1979 (Maddalena in *Rigoletto*). Eur. début Cologne 1980; La Scala 1980; CG 1982; Glyndebourne 1983; Salzburg 1985.

Kuhn, Gustav (*b* Turrach, nr. Spittal, 1947). Austrian conductor. Cond. Turkish State Opera, Istanbul, 1970–3 (début *Fidelio*), art. dir. Netherlands Opera Forum 1974–5, cond. Dortmund Opera 1975–7. Res. cond. Vienna Opera 1977–80. Mus. dir. Berne Opera 1979–83, Bonn

Opera 1982–5. Art. dir. Rome Opera from 1986. Salzburg Fest. début 1978; Glyndebourne début 1980; Amer. début Chicago 1981; CG 1981.

Kuhnau [Kuhn], **Johann** (*b* Geising, Bohemia, 1660; *d* Leipzig, 1722). Bohemian composer and lawyer. Org., St Thomas's, Leipzig, from 1684, cantor 1701. Bach's immediate predecessor at Leipzig. Wrote ably for clavichord and hpd., composing exercises which he called *Klavierübung*, a term later used by Bach. Among first to compose sonatas (as distinct from suites).

Kuijken, Sigiswald (*b* Dilbeck, nr. Brussels, 1944). Belgian violinist, viol-player, and conductor. Self-taught on baroque vn., which he played from 1970, having begun to learn old technique of vn.-playing in 1969. Member of *avant-garde* Musique Nouvelle to 1974 and Alarius Ens. 1964–72. Taught baroque vn., Hague Cons., from 1971. Founded baroque orch. La Petite Bande 1972. London début 1986. Founded Kuijken Str. Qt. 1986. Recorded Bach sonatas with *Leonhardt.

kujawiak. A quick Polish dance in triple time, slower form of *mazurka. Distinctive for misplaced accents.

Kulenkampff, Georg (*b* Bremen, 1898; *d* Schaffhausen, 1948). Ger. violinist and teacher. Prof. of vn., Berlin Hochschule für Musik, 1923–6. Leading soloist in Ger. between World Wars I and II, also member of pf. trio with Edwin Fischer (pf.) and Enrico Mainardi (vc.) and partnered by Georg *Solti in several sonata recitals. Succeeded Flesch at Lucerne Cons. 1943. Salzburg Fest. 1948. Career cut short by paralysis. Several memorable recordings, particularly of Beethoven conc.

Kullervo. (1) Symphonic poem, Op.7, by Sibelius for sop., bar., male ch., and orch., 1892, based on Finnish legends in the *Kalevala. F.p. 1892, then withdrawn and not perf. again until 1958.

(2) Sym. by R. *Kajanus.

(3) Opera in 2 acts by *Sallinen to his own lib. based on play *Kullervo* by A. Kivi (1864). Comp. 1987–8. Prod. Los Angeles 1992.

Kullman, Charles (*b* New Haven, Conn., 1903; *d* New Haven, Conn., 1983). Amer. tenor of Ger. parents. Concert début NY 1924. Opera début (Pinkerton in *Madama Butterfly*) with Amer. Opera Co. 1929, then went to Berlin, making début at *Kroll Oper, 1931. Berlin State Opera 1932–4. CG début 1934–5; NY Met 1935; Salzburg Fest. début 1934. Sang ten. songs in Walter's first (1936) recording of Mahler's *Das Lied von der Erde*. Taught at Bloomington, Ind., 1956–71.

Kunad, Rainer (*b* Chemnitz, 1936; *d* Reutlingen, 1995). Ger. composer. Dir. of stage mus. at Dresden State Th. 1960–74. Prof. of comp., Dresden Hochschule für Mus. 1978–84. Settled in what was then W. Ger., 1984.

Kunst der Fuge, Die (The Art of Fugue). Posthumous and unfinished work by J. S. Bach, comp. 1748–9, pubd. posthumously 1750, and designed

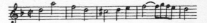

to establish the possibilities of a simple subject in the various types of fugal and canonic writing.

It is not clear what medium was intended to be employed, or, indeed, whether actual perf. was in view. Modern edns. for pf., org., and versions for str. instr. and for orch. have appeared. Completions of the final fugue have been made by Donald *Tovey and by *Busoni in his *Fantasia contrappuntistica*.

Kunstlied (Ger.). Art-song (as distinct from *Volkslied*, folk-song).

Kunz, Erich (*b* Vienna, 1909; *d* Vienna, 1995). Austrian bass-baritone. Opera début Troppau 1933 (Osmin in *Die Entführung*). Joined Glyndebourne ch. 1935. Member Vienna State Opera from 1940. Débuts: Salzburg Fest. 1942; Bayreuth Fest. 1943; NY Met 1952; CG 1947 (with Vienna co.); Glyndebourne 1948. Notable Papageno and Beckmesser. Also superb singer of operetta.

Kuolema (Death). Play by A. Järnefelt for Helsinki prod. of which in 1903 *Sibelius wrote incidental mus. incl. *Valse triste* and *Scene with cranes*.

Kupfer, Harry (*b* Berlin, 1935). Ger. producer. Ass. at Landesth., Halle (début 1958, *Rusalka*). Worked in Stralsund 1958–62 and Chemnitz 1962–6. Opera dir., Weimar Nat. Th. 1966–72 and taught at Liszt Musikhochschule 1967–72. Début Berlin (then E. Berlin) State Opera 1971 (*Die Frau ohne Schatten*). Opera dir. and chief prod. Dresden State Opera 1971–81. Bayreuth Fest. 1978; Brit. début Cardiff 1978; ENO 1981; Salzburg Fest. 1986; CG 1993. Prod. *Der Ring des Nibelungen* at Bayreuth 1988. His prods. are much concerned with social realities and psychological motivation.

Kupferman, Meyer (*b* NY, 1926; *d* NY, 2003). Amer. composer and clarinettist. Début NY 1946. Teacher of comp. and chamber mus. at Sarah Lawrence Coll., NY, from 1951. Mus., some of it highly experimental, influenced by jazz and 12-note system. Works incl. 6 operas (incl. *Dr Faustus Lights the Lights*, 1953, lib. by Gertrude Stein); 5 ballets; 11 syms.; *Concerto for Orchestra*; 3 pf. concs.; 2 vc. concs.; vn. conc.; tuba conc.; cl. conc.; *Lyric Symphony*; 7 str. qts.; *Cycle of Infinities*, over 25 works of various kinds all based on same 12-note row and, principally, same theme; choral works; pf. pieces; and songs.

Kupper, Annelies (Gabriele) (*b* Glatz, 1906; *d* Munich, 1987). Ger. soprano. Taught mus. in Breslau 1929–35. Her singing was heard by mus. dir. of Breslau Opera who engaged her. Début 1935 as Second Boy in *Die Zauberflöte*. After 1937 she was at Schwerin and Weimar; Hamburg State Opera 1940–6; Bavarian State Opera, Munich,

1946–66. Bayreuth début 1944; Salzburg Fest. début 1950. Sang Danae in official f.p. of *Die *Liebe der Danae*, Salzburg 1952. CG début 1953.

Kurtág, György (*b* Lugoj, Romania, 1926). Romanian-born composer (Hung. cit. 1948). Worked as tutor at Bartók mus. sch., Budapest, 1958–63 and as coach of Nat. Philharmonia 1960–8. Prof. of pf., later of chamber mus., Budapest Acad. 1967–86. Beginning as a disciple of Bartók and Kodály, he later was influenced by Webernian serialism. Works incl.:

ORCH. (& VOICE): va. conc. (1954); *4 Capriccios*, Op.9, sop., chamber ens. (1971); *Messages of the late Miss R. V. Troussova*, Op.17, sop., chamber ens. (1976–80); *. . . quasi una fantasia . . .*, Op.27, No.1, pf., instr. (1987–8); *Grabstein für Stefan*, Op.15c, gui., instr. (1989); double conc., Op.27, No.2, pf., vc., 2 chamber ens. (1989–90); *Samuel Beckett: What is the Word*, Op.30b, alto (recit.), vv., chamber ens. (1991); *Stele* (1994); *. . . concertante . . .*, vn., va., orch. (2003).

CHAMBER MUSIC: str. qt., Op.1 (1959); wind quintet, Op.2 (1959); *8 Duos*, Op.4, vn., cimbalon (1961); *The Sayings of Péter Bornemisza*, Op.7, sop., pf. (1963–8); *In memory of a Winter Sunset*, Op.8, sop., vn., cimbalon (1969); *4 Songs to Poems by János Pilinszky*, Op.11, bass or bass-bar., chamber ens. (1975); *S.K. Remembrance Noise*, Op.12, sop., vn. (1975); *In memoriam György Zilcz*, 2 tpt., 2 tb., tuba (1975); *Hommage à András Mihály*, Op.13, str. qt. (1977); *Microludes*, str. qt. (1977); *Herdecker Eurythmie* (Op.14a, fl., tenor lyre, Op.14b, vn., tenor lyre, Op.14c, spkr., tenor lyre) (1979); *Bagatelles*, Op.14d, fl., pf., db. (1981); *The Little Predicament*, Op.15b, picc., tb., gui. (1978); *Scenes from a Novel*, Op.19, sop., vn., db., cimbalon (1981–2); *Attila-József Fragments*, Op.20, sop. (1981); *7 Songs*, Op.22, sop., cimbalon (or pf.) (1981); *13 Pieces for Cimbalon*, 2 cimbalons (1982); *Kafka-Fragmente*, Op.24, sop., vn. (1985–6); *3 Old Inscriptions*, Op.25, sop., pf. (1986); *Requiem for the beloved*, Op.26, sop., pf. (1986–7); *Officium Breve in memoriam Andreae Szervánszky*, Op.28, str. qt. (1988–9); *Hölderlin: An . . .*, Op.29, ten., pf. (1988–9); *Samuel Beckett: What is the Word*, Op.30, vn., pf. (1990, see Orch. above); *Ligatura—Message to Frances Marie (the Answered Unanswered Question)*, Op.31b, vc. with 2 bows, 2 vn., cel. or 2 vc., 2 vn., cel. or 2 org., cel. (or upright pf.) (1989); *Hommage à R. Sch.*, Op.15d, cl., va., pf. (1990); *Trio Movement*, pf. trio (2005).

INSTR. SOLOS: *Suite*, pf. duet (1950–1); *8 Piano Pieces*, Op.3 (1960); *Signs*, Op.5, va. (1961); *Splinters*, Op.6b, cimbalon (1973), Op.6c, pf. (1973); *Pre-Games*, pf. (1973); *Games*, pfs., in 4 books (1973–6); *János Pilinszky: Gérard de Nerval*, vc. (1986); *Message to Frances-Marie*, Op.31a, vc. with 2 bows (1989); *3 in memoriam*, pf. (1–2–3 hands) (1988–90); *Ligature e Versetti*, org. (1990).

CHORAL: *Beads* (1950–1); *Omaggio a Luigi Nono*, Op.16 (1979); *8 Choruses*, Op.23 (1981/2–84); *Songs of Despair and Sorrow*, ch., orch. (1994).

TAPE: *Mémoire de Laïka*, synthesizers and real sounds (joint work of Kurtág and G. Kurtág jnr.) (1990).

Kurtz, Efrem (*b* St Petersburg, 1900; *d* London, 1995). Russ.-born conductor (Amer. cit. 1944). Early cond. engagements with Berlin PO, 1921–4. Mus. dir. Stuttgart PO 1924–33, during which time he cond. much ballet in Eur. and toured with Anna Pavlova 1928–31. Cond. ballet at Salzburg Fest. 1931 and 1932. Cond. Ballet Russe de Monte Carlo 1933–42. Chief cond. Kansas City PO 1943–8, Houston SO 1948–54. Joint cond. Liverpool PO 1955–7. Returned to Leningrad and Moscow as guest cond. 1966. Second wife was Amer. flautist Elaine Shaffer.

Kurz, Selma (*b* Biala, Silesia, 1874; *d* Vienna, 1933). Austrian soprano. Opera début Hamburg 1895 (*Mignon*). Frankfurt Opera 1896–99. Engaged by Mahler for Vienna Opera 1899, singing there until 1927, first in lyric roles, then as coloratura. First Zerbinetta in rev. vers. of *Ariadne auf Naxos*, Vienna 1916. CG 1904–7 and again in 1924. Salzburg Fest. 1922.

Kusche, Benno (*b* Freiburg, 1916). Ger. bass-baritone. Début Coblenz 1938. Sang at Augsburg 1939–45. Member of Bavarian State Opera, Munich, from 1946 for over 30 years. Débuts: Salzburg Fest. 1949; CG 1952; Glyndebourne 1954; NY Met 1971. Düsseldorf Opera from 1958.

Kussevitzky, Serge. See *Koussevitzky, Serge*.

Kutcher Quartet. Eng. str. qt. noted for perf. of contemporary works. Founded by Samuel Kutcher (*b* London, 1899; *d* London, 1984) in 1924. Other members were Peter Tas (2nd vn.), Raymond Jeremy (va.), and Douglas Cameron (vc.) (succeeded by John Barbirolli).

K.V. Ger. usage for the *Köchel abbreviation, from *Köchel-Verzeichnis* (Köchel Index).

Kvapil, Jaroslav (*b* Fryšták, Moravia, 1892; *d* Brno, 1959). Cz. composer, conductor, and teacher. Pupil of Janáček at Brno org. sch. 1906–9 and of Reger, Leipzig Cons. 1911–13. Prof., Brno Cons. from 1919; Choirmaster and cond. Brno Beseda 1919–47; taught at Janáček Acad., Brno, 1947–57. Works incl. 4 syms.; 2 vn. concs.; ob. conc.; pf. conc.; *Burlesque*, fl., orch.; opera *Romance in May* (Prague 1950); cantata *The Lion's Heart* (Brno 1931); 6 str. qts. (1914–51); pf. quintet; 3 pf. sonatas. Cond. first Cz. perf. of Bach's *St Matthew Passion* (1923).

Kynaston, Nicolas (*b* Morebath, Devon, 1941). Eng. organist. Début RFH 1966. Org. of Westminster Cath. 1961–71. Toured USA 1974. Specialist in Fr. works, notably Messiaen and Franck.

Kyrie (Gr.). Lord. The section of the Ordinary of the *Mass which follows the Introit. Has 3 parts, *Kyrie eleison, Christe eleison, Kyrie eleison*, thrice repeated ('Lord have mercy, Christ have mercy, Lord have mercy'). In medieval times, the *Kyrie* was set as an independent movt., but after *Du Fay it was incorporated as the 1st movt. of a series.

Kyung-Wha Chung. See *Chung, Kyung-Wha*.

L

L. Abbreviated prefix given to nos. in the *Longo catalogue of Domenico Scarlatti's kbd. works. A later catalogue was prepared by R. *Kirkpatrick.

la. The 6th degree of the major scale, according to the system of vocal syllables derived from *Guido d'Arezzo (see *hexachord), and so used (spelt *lah*) in *tonic sol-fa, in which it is also the 1st degree of the minor scale. In many countries, however, the name has become attached (on 'fixed-doh' principles) to the note A, in whatever key this may occur.

Labbette, Dora (*b* Purley, 1898; *d* Purley, 1984). Eng. soprano. Début 1917. Sang often in oratorios and concert works with Beecham, making speciality of Delius. Opera début Oxford, 1934. CG début (under name Lisa Perli), CG 1935 (Mimì in *La bohème*). Fine actress, which made memorable her perfs. of Desdemona, Mélisande, and Vreli in *A Village Romeo and Juliet*.

Labèque, Katia and Marielle (*b* Hendaye, 1950 and 1952 respectively). Fr. piano duo. Début Bayonne 1961. Soon established themselves as specialists in works of Messiaen, Boulez, and Berio. Also play jazz, collaborating with John McLaughlin, guitar.

Labialstimme (Ger., plural *Labialstimmen*). Flue stop (on the org.).

Lablache, Luigi (*b* Naples, 1794; *d* Naples, 1858). It. bass of Fr. and Irish parentage. Début Naples 1812 in Fioravanti's *La molinara*. La Scala début 1817. Stayed for six seasons. Int. career followed (in Vienna he sang in Mozart's *Requiem* at Beethoven's funeral, 1827). London début 1830. Became great favourite in Paris and London 1830–56. Created Sir George Walton in *I Puritani* (Paris 1835), title-role in *Don Pasquale* (Paris 1843), and Massimiliano in *I *Masnadieri* (London 1847). St Petersburg 1852. Famous Bartolo and Leporello. V. had compass of 3 octaves. Taught Queen Victoria singing. Retired 1856.

Laburda, Jiří (*b* Soběslav, 1931). Cz. composer. His cantata *Glagolitica* won Esplá Prize at Alicante 1966 and *Metamorphoses* the Spreckelsen Prize in Hanover 1968. Works incl.: ballet *Les petits riens* (1967); pf. conc. (1969); sym. (1975); accordeon conc., str. (1978); *Pastorale*, fl., str. (1981); *Festive Overture* (1983); *Divertimento*, str. (1983); chamber conc., vc., orch. (1986); *Glagolitica*, soloists, ch., org., brass, perc. (1964); *Metamorphoses*, soloists, narr., ch., orch. (1966); *Wedding*, women's vv., soloists, pf. (1980); *Memento*, male ch., pf. (1985); tpt. sonatina (1971); *Partita*, vn. (1976); sonata, 2 pf., perc. (1976); 8 pf. sonatas (1978–99); tb. sonata (1979); str. qt. (1982); pf. quintet (1983); cl. sonata (1984); *Prague Bridges*, suite, brass quintet, pf. (1984); tuba sonata (1987); trio, ob., cl., bn. (1989); *Romantic Valses for Piano*, pf. (1988, 1992); 4 sonatas, org. (1992–9); bn. conc., str. (1997); vc. conc., str. (1998); ov., sym. wind orch., perc. (2000); sym., sym. wind orch. (2002); *Moravian Songs*, ch., vc. or unacc. (2002).

Lachner, Franz (*b* Rain am Lech, 1803; *d* Munich, 1890). Ger. conductor and composer. Most eminent of remarkable mus. family. Taught and played org. in Munich 1822. Went to Vienna 1823, becoming friend of Schubert. Cond. at Kärntnerthor Th., 1827–34. Opera cond., Mannheim, 1834–6. Cond. Munich Court Opera 1836–65 (dir. from 1852). Resigned over differences with Wagner. Responsible for eminence of Munich Opera. Comp. operas, masses, oratorios, 8 syms., chamber mus., etc. Cherubini's *Médée* is usually perf. in his edn. which omits the spoken dialogue.

Lachrimae. 21 pieces for 5 viols and lute by *Dowland pubd. 1604, of which 7 pavans are entitled *Lachrimae*. The other 14 are dances such as galliards. Each of the Pavans ('sevean teares figured in sevean passionate pavans') begins with the theme of Dowland's song *Flow my tears* followed by variations.

Lachrymae. 'Reflections on a song of John Dowland' for va. and pf. by Britten, Op.48, comp. 1950. Arr. for va. and orch. 1976, f.p. Recklinghausen 1977.

Lacrimosa. See *Requiem*.

lacrimoso, lagrimoso (It.). Lachrymose, tearful.

Lady in the Dark. Mus. play in 2 acts by *Weill to book by Moss Hart and lyrics by Ira Gershwin. Comp. 1939–40. Prod. Boston 1940, NY 1941 (with Gertrude Lawrence and Danny Kaye, cond. Abravanel). Extended score based on autograph full score and rehearsal material ed. by D. Loud and J. Mauceri 1986. Prod. Edinburgh Fest. (concert perf.) by Scottish Opera) 1988, cond. Mauceri.

Lady Macbeth of the Mtsensk District, The (*Ledi Makbet Mtsenskovo uyezda*). Opera in 4 acts by Shostakovich to lib. by composer and A. Preys after short story by N. Leskov (1846). Comp. 1930–2. Prod. Leningrad 1934, Moscow 1934 (2 days later under title *Katerina Izmaylova*), Cleveland 1935, London (concert) 1936. Opera had nearly 200 perfs. in two years in Moscow and Leningrad. In Jan. 1936 Stalin and Soviet officials attended Moscow perf. at Bolshoy Th. and two days later an article, inspired and perhaps even written by Stalin and headed 'Muddle instead of music', violently attacked the opera as 'screaming' and obscene. There were no more perfs. After Stalin's death in 1953, opera was revised (1956–62) but not prod. until 1963 (Moscow) as *Katerina Izmaylova*, Op.114. Orig. vers. revived

Düsseldorf 1959 and outside Russ. has now replaced rev. vers. Prod. London (ENO) 1987, S. Francisco 1964, CG 2004.

Lady of Shalott, The. Cantata by Phyllis Tate, setting of Tennyson's poem, for ten., va., perc., 2 pf., and celesta. Comp. 1956 for 10th anniv. of BBC 3rd Programme. Also cantata by Maurice Jacobson.

Lady Radnor's Suite. Suite in 6 movts. for str. orch. by *Parry comp. 1894 for orch. cond. by amateur musician, Lady Radnor.

Lage (Ger.). Position, e.g. in str. instr., or inversion of chord.

lah. See *la*.

lai, lay (Fr.). A 13th- and 14th-cent. Fr. songform, consisting usually of 12 unequal stanzas sung to different tunes. Later examples are in several vv. Also a purely instr. piece.

Lajtha, László (*b* Budapest, 1892; *d* Budapest, 1963). Hung. composer, writer, and folk music expert. 1910 joined Bartók and Kodály in expeditions to collect folk songs, later acting independently. After war service, joined staff of Nat. Cons., Budapest, where he was prof. 1919–49. Comp. 9 syms. (1936–61); vc. conc.; 2 masses; 10 str. qts. (1923–53); opera; and 3 ballets. Kossuth Prize 1951.

Lakes, Gary (*b* Dallas, 1950). Amer. tenor. Début Seattle Opera 1981 (Froh in *Das Rheingold*). Débuts: Mexico City 1983; NY Met 1986; London Proms 1991. Sings *Heldentenor* roles of Siegmund, Emperor (*Die Frau ohne Schatten*), and Bacchus (*Ariadne auf Naxos*).

Lakmé. Opera in 3 acts by Delibes to lib. by Gondinet and Gille after P. Loti's novel *Rarahu ou Le Mariage de Loti* (1879). Prod. Paris and Chicago 1883, London 1885.

Lalande, Michel-Richard de (*b* Paris, 1657; *d* Versailles, 1726). Fr. composer and organist, contemporary of *Lully. Org. of 4 Paris churches in 1670s. Taught daughters of Louis XIV, becoming Master of King's chamber mus., 1685. Dir. of royal chapel 1714–23, having been *sous-maître* since 1683, and eventually holding seven court posts. Comp. lavish court ballets and church mus.

Lalandi, Lina (Madeleine) (*b* Athens, 1920). Gr.-born harpsichordist and clavichordist (Brit. cit.). London début 1954. Founder and art. dir., Eng. Bach Fest. Trust 1963. OBE 1975.

Lalo, Édouard-Victor-Antoine (*b* Lille, 1823; *d* Paris, 1892). Fr. composer of Sp. descent. Pubd. songs 1848–9. Played in Armingaud Qt. from 1855. Vn. conc. played by Sarasate 1874, who a year later gave f.p. of *Symphonie espagnole*. Of his operas, only *Le Roi d'Ys* had any success. His son, Pierre Lalo (*b* Puteaux, 1866; *d* Paris, 1948) was a mus. critic and wrote a book on Wagner (1933). Works incl.:

OPERAS: *Fiesque* (1866–8); *Le *Roi d'Ys* (1875–87); *La Jacquerie* (1891–2, completed by Coquard 1894).
BALLET: *Namouna* (1882).
ORCH.: *Allegro symphonique* (1875); *Rapsodie norvégienne* (1881); sym. in G minor (1886); concs.: vn. (1873), *Symphonie espagnole*, vn., orch. (1874), *Fantaisie norvégienne*, vn., orch. (1880), *Concerto russe*, vn., orch. (1883), vc. (1877), pf. (1888–9).
CHAMBER MUSIC: 3 pf. trios (1850, 1852, 1889); vn. sonata (1853); vc. sonata (1856); str. qt. (1859, rev. 1880).

Lambert, (Leonard) Constant (*b* Fulham, London, 1905; *d* London, 1951). Eng. composer, conductor, and critic. Ballet *Romeo and Juliet* commissioned by Diaghilev and prod. Monte Carlo 1926. Series of brilliant works est. him with Walton among leading younger Eng. composers. Influenced by jazz, esp. Duke Ellington. His biggest success was with *The Rio Grande*, a setting of Sacheverell Sitwell (1927). Took leading part in est. of British ballet, and made th. orch. version of Vaughan Williams's *Job*, 1931. Cond. Camargo Society ballet 1930 and ballet and opera at SW, being mus. dir. Vic-Wells ballet from its foundation in 1931 until 1947, then mus. adviser SW Ballet from 1948. Cond. Purcell's *The Fairy Queen*, in a vers. by him and E. J. Dent, at CG 1946, the first post-war perf. there. Brilliant writer, his book *Music, Ho!* (1934) being an important and idiosyncratic commentary on contemporary mus. at that date. Witty conversationalist. Notable narrator in Walton's *Façade* with Edith Sitwell. Champion of mus. of *Boyce, several of whose works he arr. Also advocate for Liszt when it was unfashionable in Eng. to admire him. Prin. works:

BALLETS: *Romeo and Juliet* (1924–5); *Pomona* (1926); *Apparitions* (orch. of Liszt) (1936); *Horoscope* (1937); *Tiresias* (1950–1).
INCID. MUSIC: *Jew Süss* (1929); *Salome* (1931); *Hamlet* (1944).
ORCH.: *Champêtre* (1926); *Elegiac Blues* (1927, orch. of pf. piece); *Music for Orch.* (1927); pf. conc. (1931); *Aubade héroïque* (1942); incidental mus. for *Hamlet*.
CHORAL: *The *Rio Grande*, pf., ch., orch. (1927); *Summer's Last Will and Testament*, bar., ch., orch. (1932–5); *Dirge* (from *Cymbeline*), ten., bar., male ch., str. (or pf.) (1940).
VOCAL: 8 *Poems of Li-Po*, v., pf. or 8 instr. (1926–9).
PIANO: *Pastorale* (1926); *Elegiac Blues* (1927, also orch.); sonata (1928–9); *2 pièces nègres pour les touches blanches*, 4 hands (1949).

Lambton Worm, The. Opera in 2 acts by R. Sherlaw *Johnson to lib. by Anne Ridler based on medieval legend. Comp. 1977. Prod. Oxford 1978.

lament. Piece of elegiac mus. expressing grief, specifically mus. for bagpipes at Scottish clan funerals.

Lamentations. Lamentations of the prophet Jeremiah sung to plainchant melodies (or other settings such as the great ones by Tallis) in RC churches in the week before Easter. Gr. word *Threni* sometimes used.

Lamentation Symphony. Nickname for Haydn's Sym. No.26 in D minor, 1770, because certain themes resemble the plainsong melodies sung in RC churches in the week before Easter. Also sometimes known, for unknown reason, as 'Christmas' Sym. (*Weihnachtssymphonie*).

lamento (It.). Lament. In 17th-cent. opera, a tragic aria usually placed before the climax of the plot. A famous example is Monteverdi's **Lamento d'Arianna*.

Lamento d'Arianna (Ariadne's Lament). Only surviving section of Monteverdi's opera **Arianna*, 1608. Arr. by Monteverdi as 5-part madrigal *Lasciatemi morire* (Leave me to die), Book VI, 1614; this book also incl. *O Teseo mio*, reduced from 20 bars of *Lasciatemi morire*. Also arr. by Monteverdi as one of his *Selva Morale e Spirituale* (1640), *Pianto della Madonna* on the *Lamento d'Arianna: Jam moriar fili mi*, for solo v.

Lamond, Frederic(k) (Archibald) (*b* Glasgow, 1868; *d* Stirling, 1948). Scot. pianist and composer. Church organist at age 12. Début Berlin 1885, followed by int. tours. Visited Russia 1896. Specially noted as Beethoven player. Prof. of pf., The Hague Cons., from 1917. Lived in Berlin 1904–39. Toured USA 4 times between 1922 and 1929 and taught at Eastman Sch. Later prof. of pf., RSAMD. Comp. sym., pf. trio, vc. sonata, pf. pieces.

Lamoureux, Charles (*b* Bordeaux, 1834; *d* Paris, 1899). Fr. conductor and violinist. Played in orch. at Opéra. Ass. cond. *Société des Concerts du Conservatoire* 1872–7. Cond. Opéra-Comique 1876–7, Opéra 1877–9. In 1881 founded *Nouveaux Concerts*, later known as *Concerts Lamoureux*. Among first to champion Wagner in France (cond. f. Paris p. of *Lohengrin*, 1887) and young Fr. composers such as Lalo, Dukas, and Chabrier. Visited London 1881, and took orch. there 1896–9. Succeeded by son-in-law **Chevillard. Mus. dir. Paris Opéra 1891–2. Lamoureux Orch., under various distinguished conds., has remained among leading European orchs.

Lamperti, Francesco (*b* Savona, 1813; *d* Cernobbio, nr. Como, 1892). It. teacher of singing. Dir. with Masini of Teatro Filodrammatico at Lodi which attracted students from all over Europe. Prof. of singing, Milan Cons., 1850–75, pupils incl. Albani, Sembrich, Stolz, Waldmann, and Campanini. His son Giovanni Battista (*b* Milan, 1839; *d* Berlin, 1910) was his pupil and also a singing-teacher. Author of *The Technique of Bel Canto* (1905).

Lancashire Sol-fa. System of sight-singing more properly called 'Old English Sol-fa', since it was universally used in Eng. from at least the early 17th cent. and its latest textbook appeared in 1879. It is a method of solmization applied to the normal staff notation; the first 3 notes of every major scale are called *fa-sol-la*, and so are the second 3 notes, the remaining note being called *mi*; the minor scale is read as if its notes were those of the relative major. In Amer. often called *Fasola*.

lancers. Type of **quadrille dance popular in 19th-cent. Eng.

Lanchbery, John (*b* London, 1923; *d* Melbourne, 2003). Eng. conductor and composer. Mus. dir. London Metropolitan Ballet 1947–9. Cond. SW Th. Ballet 1951–60. Prin. cond. Royal Ballet 1960–72. Mus. dir. Australian Ballet 1972–7, Amer. Ballet 1978–80. Arr. mus. for *House of Birds*, *La Fille mal gardée*, *A Month in the Country*, *Mayerling*, *The Dream*, *Tales of Beatrix Potter*, *The Merry Widow*.

Lancie, John (Sherwood) **de** (*b* Berkeley, Calif., 1921; *d* Walnut Creek, Calif., 2002). Amer. oboist and teacher. Oboist, Pittsburgh SO 1940–2. Served in US Army and in 1945 was at Garmisch where he met Richard Strauss and inquired if he had ever thought of writing an ob. conc. Strauss said 'No', but a conc. soon followed (which de Lancie recorded). Oboist, Philadelphia Orch. 1946–74 (prin. from 1954). Teacher at Curtis Inst. 1954–74, dir. 1977–85. Commissioned and gave f.p. of Françaix's *L'horloge de Flore* (Philadelphia 1961) and Benjamin Lees's ob. conc. (1963).

Landi, Stefano (*b* Rome, *c.*1586; *d* Rome, 1639). It. composer and teacher. Singer in Rome churches up to 1618 when he became choirmaster to Bishop of Padua, where he wrote his first opera, *La Morte d'Orfeo*. Returned to Rome 1620, serving Borghese and Barberini families. Sacred opera *Il Sant' Alessio* (1632), perf. at Barberini palace, had elaborate stage effects, and was first opera to have ovs. in the form of sinfonias. One of musicians chosen by Pope Urban VIII in 1634 to prepare new hymn-book pubd. in Antwerp in 1643 (now lost). His *Arie*, of which he pubd. six books, are conventional.

Landini [Landino], **Francesco** (*b* Florence, 1325; *d* Florence, 1397). It. composer, who lost his sight as child but played org., lute, fl., and other instrs. Comp. madrigals and over 140 *ballate* (type of *virelai*). Org., monastery of S. Trinità, Florence, 1361; *capellanus*, church of S. Lorenzo, 1365–97.

Landini Cadence. Cadence named after Francesco **Landini, in which the 6th degree is inserted between leading-note and the octave. Found in works of **Machaut, Desprès, Palestrina, Victoria, and Monteverdi.

Ländler (Ger.). Type of slow waltz originating in the Landel (part of Austria north of Ems river). Examples were comp. by Mozart, Haydn, Beethoven, and Schubert, and the rhythm is employed by Mahler in his syms. and by Berg in his vn. conc.

Land of Hope and Glory. Title of finale for cont., ch., and orch. of Elgar's **Coronation Ode*

(1902), words by A. C. Benson. Tune is adaptation of melody of trio section of *Pomp and Circumstance March* No.1 in D. Also pubd. as separate song for cont. and orch., this being the version now generally and communally sung (with words different from those in *Coronation Ode*).

Land of Lost Content, The. Song-cycle by *Ireland, comp. 1920–1, of 6 poems from A. E. Housman's *A Shropshire Lad*. Orig. for high v. and pf. Titles are: 1. *The Lent Lily*, 2. *Ladslove*, 3. *Goal and wicket*, 4. *The vain desire*, 5. *The Encounter*, 6. *Epilogue*. Written for Gervase *Elwes, who died before he could sing it. Ireland set 3 more Housman poems under title *We'll To The Woods No More* (1926–7), No.3 being for pf. alone.

Land of my Fathers (*Hen Wlad fy Nhadau*). Nat. anthem of Wales always sung to orig. Welsh words. Comp. 1856, words by Evan James (1809–78) of Pontypridd, music by his son James James (1832–1902). Orig. name was *Glan Rhondda*. F.p. 1856 by Elizabeth John, aged 16, in Methodist chapel in Maesteg. First appeared in print 1860 in John Owen's *Gems of Welsh Melody*. Was sung as finale to each day's proceedings of Nat. *Eisteddfod held in Ruthin, 1868, and thereafter gradually came to be adopted as Welsh nat. anthem.

Land of Smiles, The (*Das Land des Lächelns*). Operetta in 3 acts by Lehár to lib. by L. Herzer and F. Löhner based on earlier (1923) operetta *Die gelbe Jacke* (The Yellow Jacket), prod. Vienna 1923. F.p. Berlin 1929 (with Tauber); London 1931; Vienna (State Opera), 1938.

Land of the Mountain and the Flood. Ov. by Hamish MacCunn, comp. 1887 when he was 19.

Landon, Christa (*b* Berlin 1921; *d* Funchal, Madeira, 1977). Ger. musicologist, first wife of H. C. Robbins *Landon. Assisted in search for rare Haydn MSS. Ed., works of J. S. Bach, Mozart, and Haydn. Edn. of Haydn's pf. sonatas pubd. in 3 vols., Vienna 1963–6.

Landon, H(oward) **C**(handler) **Robbins** (*b* Boston, Mass., 1926). Amer. musicologist. Settled in Vienna 1948, undertaking meticulous research into life and mus. of Joseph Haydn. Author of book on Haydn syms. (1955) and of *Haydn: Chronicle and Works* (5 vols., 1976–80), *Haydn: a Documentary Study* (1981) and *Haydn: His Life and Music* (1988, with D. Jones), also of edn. of syms. Discovered correct attrib. of *'Jena' Symphony*. Joint ed. with D. Mitchell of *The Mozart Companion* (1956, rev. 1965); and author of *Beethoven: a Documentary Study* (1970), *Mozart's Last Year* (1988), *Mozart: the Golden Years* (1989), *Mozart and Vienna* (1991). Gen. ed. *The Mozart Compendium* (1990), *Vivaldi, Voice of the Baroque* (1993).

Landowska, Wanda (Alexandra) (*b* Warsaw, 1877; *d* Lakeville, Conn., 1959). Polish-born harpsichordist and pianist. Settled in Paris 1900, touring Europe and USA in recitals of baroque mus. on pf. and hpd. Head of hpd. class, Berlin Hochschule, 1913 (interned during 1914–18

war). First in 20th cent. to play continuo of *St Matthew Passion* on hpd. (Basle, 1919). Returned to Fr. 1919–38 as teacher and to give concerts of early mus. Falla (1926) and Poulenc (1929) comp. hpd. concs. for her. Author of *Musique Ancienne* (1909).

Lang, Aidan (*b* Kingston-on-Thames, 1957). Eng. opera director. Studied Eng. and drama at Birmingham Univ. (1977–80). Began as staff prod. for Opera 80, Glyndebourne, and WNO in the 1980s. Prin. assoc. dir. of Glyndebourne Fest. and dir. of prods. GTO 1990–9 (incl. the Brit. première (1993) of Siegfried Matthus's *Cornet Rilke's Songs of Love and Death*). Art. dir. Opera Zuid, Netherlands, 1990–8 and of Buxton Festival 2000–6; gen. dir. NZ Opera from 2006. Has prod. operas for all the major Brit. companies and throughout Eur. Dir. Brit. première of Delius's *The Magic Fountain*, Scottish Opera 1999. Salzburg début 2005 (*The Turn of the Screw*). In Brazil, prod. the country's first Wagner *Ring*, at Teatro Amazonas, Manaus, 2005.

Láng, Paul Henry (*b* Budapest, 1901; *d* Lakeville, Conn., 1991). Hung.-born musicologist and critic (Amer. cit. 1934). Chamber-mus. pianist and orch. bassoonist in Budapest. Went to USA 1928. Ass. prof. of mus. Vassar Coll., 1930–1, assoc. prof. of mus. Wells Coll., 1931–3, assoc. prof. of musicology, Columbia Univ. 1933–9, prof. 1939–69. Mus. critic, *NY Herald Tribune* 1954–63. Ed., *Musical Quarterly* 1945–73. Author of several books incl. *Music in Western Civilisation* (NY, 1941), *George Frideric Handel* (NY 1966), *Critic at the Opera* (NY 1971), and the anthologies *The Concerto 1800–1900* (NY 1969) and *The Symphony 1800–1900* (NY 1969).

Langdon, Michael [Birtles, Frank] (*b* Wolverhampton, 1920; *d* Hove, 1991). Eng. bass-baritone. Joined CG ch. 1948. Début CG 1950 (Nightwatchman in *The *Olympians*, in Manchester). Prin. bass at ROH 1957–77. NY Met 1964. Created roles of Lieut. Ratcliffe in *Billy Budd* (1951), Recorder of Norwich in *Gloriana* (1953), He-Ancient in *The Midsummer Marriage* (1955), the Doctor in *We Come to the River* (1976). Sang Ochs over 100 times worldwide. Final appearances CG 1985 (Frank in *Die Fledermaus*). Dir., Nat. Opera Studio, 1978–86. CBE 1973.

Lange (*née* Weber), **Aloysia** (*b* ?Mannheim, *c*.1761; *d* Salzburg, 1839). Ger. soprano, sister of Mozart's wife Constanze. Munich début 1779 (Schweitzer's *Alceste*). Vienna début 1779. Married actor and painter Joseph Lange, 1780. Mozart comp. 2 substitute arias (K418 and 419) for her for Anfossi's *Il curioso indiscreto* in 1783. From 1785 sang mainly at Kärntnertortheater. Sang Donna Anna in Vienna première of *Don Giovanni*, Burgth. 1788.

Langford, Samuel (*b* Manchester, 1863; *d* Manchester, 1927). Eng. music critic. Mus. critic,

Manchester Guardian, 1905–27. His widow Lesley was a singing teacher in Manchester and London for 50 years after his death.

Langgaard, Rued (Immanuel) (*b* Copenhagen, 1893; *d* Ribe, 1952). Danish composer and organist. Début as org. 1904. His 1st sym. (1908–11) was perf. in Berlin, 1913. Influenced at first by Liszt and Bruckner, entered experimental phase 1916–24. Later became disciple of Nielsen and eventually Hindemith. In 1920s, after an Ivesian period, abandoned experimentation for a romantic style. Increasingly isolated, he became org. of Ribe Cath. in 1940. Works incl. opera *Antikrist* (1921–39); 16 syms. (1908–51); vn. conc. (1943–4); 8 str. qts. (1914–31); 5 vn. sonatas (1915–49); vocal and choral works; 6 pf. sonatas; 100 org. preludes; 150 songs.

Langlais, Jean (*b* La Fontenelle, 1907; *d* Paris, 1991). Fr. organist and composer, blind from infancy. Teacher of org., comp., and choral singing, Institut National des Jeunes Aveugles, from 1931, prof. from 1971. Teacher of org., Schola Cantorum, Paris, 1961–76. Org., St Clotilde, Paris, 1945–88. Works incl. 3 *Poèmes évangéliques* (1932); *Suite française* (1948); *American Suite* (1959); *Suite baroque* (1974); *Progression, 5 Pièces* (1979); and 2 org. syms. (1942, 1977).

Langridge, Philip (Gordon) (*b* Hawkhurst, Kent, 1939). Eng. tenor. Began singing 1962. Début Glyndebourne 1964 (Footman in *Capriccio*). Specialist in Britten roles for CG and ENO. CG début 1983. Co-created title-role in Birtwistle's *The Mask of Orpheus*, ENO 1986, and Kong in *The Second Mrs. Kong*, Glyndebourne (GTO) 1994. NY Met début 1985; Salzburg Fest. 1987. Also exponent of Janáček roles and a notable Bénédict in Berlioz's opera. Pelegrin in f. Brit. p. of *New Year*, Glyndebourne 1990. CBE 1994.

langsam (Ger.). Slow. *langsamer*, slower.

Lanier [Laniere], **Nicholas** (*b* London, 1588; *d* London, 1666). Eng. composer. Protégé of Cecil family 1605–13. Wrote mus. for 4 masques by Ben Jonson. Appointed master of mus. to Prince Charles in 1618, so when the prince became Charles I in 1625 Lanier became first Master of the King's Mus. Held same office under Charles II from 1660. Comp. cantatas and songs. Skilled painter who bought pictures in It. for Charles I between 1625 and 1628, purchasing Duke of Mantua's coll. for over £25,000.

Lankester, Michael (*b* London, 1944). Eng. conductor and composer. Cond. début ECO, London 1967. Cond. of opera at RCM 1969–80 (head of opera dept. 1975). Mus. dir. Nat. Th., 1969–75, Surrey PO 1974–9. Founder, Contrapuncti. At Britten's request in 1976, made orch. suite of ballet *The Prince of the Pagodas*, f.p. London 1979 (Proms.). Ass. cond. 1980–2, assoc. cond. 1982–4, and cond.-in-res. 1984–8 of Pittsburgh SO. Mus. dir., Hartford (Conn.) PO 1986–2001.

Lanner, Joseph (Franz Karl) (*b* Vienna, 1801; *d* Oberdöbling, 1843). Austrian conductor and composer. Began career by arranging potpourris of popular melodies for his ens. to play. In demand at court balls and other entertainments. Formed qt. in which Johann *Strauss I was violinist 1819–25. Appointed Kapellmeister, 2nd Bürger Regiment. In rivalry with Strauss, comps. incl. 112 waltzes, also 10 quadrilles, 3 polkas, 28 galops, 6 marches, and 25 *Ländler*. Arr. Weber's *Invitation to the Dance* (1819) for small orch., *c*.1828.

Lanza, Mario [Coccozza, Alfred Arnold] (*b* Philadelphia, 1921; *d* Rome, 1959). Amer. tenor and actor. Worked in family grocery business. Had audition with *Koussevitzky in 1942 and was awarded schol. to Tanglewood. After wartime military service, signed film contract and was chosen in 1951 for the title-role in *The Great Caruso*. Made best-selling record, *Be My Love*. His voice was heard also in *The Student Prince* (1954).

Lara, Isidore de (Cohen) (*b* London, 1858; *d* Paris, 1935). Eng. composer and pianist. Comp. several operas perf. at CG, Monte Carlo, Paris, and NY Met, incl. *The Light of Asia* (1892), *Amy Robsart* (1893), *Messaline* (1899), *Naïl* (1910), *The Three Musketeers* (1920). Wrote many songs and organized concerts of new chamber works.

Laredo (y Unzueta), **Jaime** (Eduardo) (*b* Cochabamba, Bolivia, 1941). Amer. violinist of Bolivian birth. Début S. Francisco 1952. Won Queen Elisabeth of Belgians competition, 1959. NY début 1960, London 1961. World tours. Specialist in Bach and Handel.

largamente (It.). Broadly. Slowish and dignified (see also *largo*), more usually applied to style of perf. than to specific tempo.

Large, Brian (*b* London, 1937). Eng. musicologist, pianist, writer, and TV producer. Worked at Prague Nat. Th. in 1960s. Specialist in Cz. mus.; author of books on Smetana, Martinů, and Cz. opera. Joined BBC, becoming chief opera prod. 1974. Videotaped *Ring* cycles at Bayreuth 1980 and 1991 and at NY Met 1990.

larghetto (It.). The diminutive of *largo*. Slow and dignified, but less so than *largo*; *larghezza*, breadth.

largo (It.). Broad. Slow, dignified in style; *largo di molto*, very slow and dignified, etc.

Largo (Handel). Title universally applied to the many spurious, if pleasing, instr. arrs. of the aria *Ombra mai fù* (which in fact is marked *larghetto*), from *Handel's opera *Serse*.

larigot (old name for flageolet). Org. stop; same as *nineteenth*.

Lark Ascending, The. Romance for vn. and orch. or chamber orch. by Vaughan Williams inspired by poem of that name by G. Meredith (1828–1909). Comp. 1914, rev. 1920, f.p. in arr. for vn. and pf. 1920, in orch. version 1921.

Lark Quartet (Haydn). See *Lerchenquartett*.

Larmore, Jennifer (*b* Atlanta, 1958). Amer. mezzo-soprano. Studied Westminster Choir Coll. of Princeton, NJ, with John Bullock and Regina Resnik. Début S. Barbara 1982 (Rosina in *Il barbiere di Siviglia*). Prof. début Nice 1986 (Sesto in *La clemenza di Tito*). Won Richard Tucker prize 1994. Débuts: Vienna 1998 (Isabella in *L'Italiana in Algeri*); La Scala, Milan, 1992 (Isolier in *Le Comte Ory*); CG 1992, NY Met 1995 (both as Rosina); Salzburg Fest. 1993 (Dorabella). Sang Olympic Hymn at closing of Olympic Games, Atlanta 1996. Created Elizabeth Griffiths in Picker's *An American Tragedy*, NY Met 2005. Also recitalist and concert singer in USA and Eur. Carnegie Hall concert 2006.

Larner, Gerald (*b* Leeds, 1936). Eng. music critic. Joined *Guardian* staff in Manchester as ass. mus. critic 1962; chief Northern mus. critic 1965–93. Art. dir. Bowdon Fest. 1980–4. Trans. lib. of Wolf's *Der Corregidor* into Eng. Wrote lib. for McCabe's *The Lion, the Witch, and the Wardrobe* 1971. Wrote *Ravel* (1996). Critic for *The Times* 1993–2001.

Larrocha, Alicia de (*b* Barcelona, 1923). Sp. pianist. First public appearance at age of 5. Concert début Madrid 1935. In late 1940s made int. reputation. London début, 1953; NY début 1955; Salzburg Fest. début 1986. Notable interpreter of Albéniz and Granados.

Larsén-Todsen, Nanny (*b* Hagby, 1884; *d* Stockholm, 1982). Swed. soprano. Début Stockholm Royal Opera 1906 (Agathe in *Der Freischütz*), singing there until 1923 in roles ranging from Mozart to Strauss and Wagner. Sang Isolde cond. Toscanini, La Scala 1924. NY Met 1925–7; CG début 1927; Bayreuth 1927–31.

Larsson, Lars-Erik (*b* Akarp, 1908; *d* Helsingborg, 1987). Swed. composer, conductor, and critic. Ch. master Stockholm Opera 1931. Worked as critic. Cond. for Swed. radio 1937–54, prof. of comp., Stockholm Cons., 1947–59, dir. of mus. at Uppsala Univ. 1961–5. Works incl. 3 syms. (1928, 1936, 1945); 3 concert ovs.; sinfonietta for str.; serenade for str.; sax. conc.; vn. conc.; vc. conc.; 12 concertinos; opera; cantata; 3 str. qts.

La Rue, Pierre de (*b* ?Tournai, *c*.1460; *d* Courtrai, 1518). Flemish composer. Singer at Siena Cath. 1483–5. Returned to Netherlands *c*.1490 and was ten. at 's Hertogenbosch Cath. 1489–92 and in Burgundian court chapel. Moved to Mechelen 1508. Became abbot at Courtrai 1516. Exemplar of medieval Netherlands style of comp. Wrote 31 Masses, mostly on plainchant *cantus firmus* but some on secular tunes, e.g. 'L'Homme armé'. About 30 motets survive, also 30 secular *chansons*.

La Scala, Milan (Teatro alla Scala). It. opera house built in 1778 and named after Regina della Scala, wife of a Duke of Milan, who had founded a church on the site in 14th cent.

Opened on 3 Aug. 1778, with opera by *Salieri. All the great 19th-cent. It. composers wrote works for La Scala. Among f.ps. were *La Gazza Ladra* (Rossini), *Lucrezia Borgia* (Donizetti), *Norma* (Bellini), *Otello* and *Falstaff* (Verdi), *Madama Butterfly* and *Turandot* (Puccini). *Toscanini was chief cond. 1898–1902, 1906–8 and 1921–9, periods during which the greatest opera singers of the world worked in the co. Victor *de Sabata took over dir. in 1930, continuing until 1957. In more recent times Claudio *Abbado and Riccardo *Muti have been the outstanding La Scala cond. Bombs almost destroyed the Scala in Aug. 1943 but by 1946 it had been rebuilt as before in time for opening concert on 11 May cond. Toscanini. Seats 3,600. Maria *Callas was in the co. 1950–8 and Renata *Tebaldi 1949–54. Chamber th. for 600, *La Piccola Scala*, was opened in Dec. 1955 and closed in 1983.

Lassen, Eduard (*b* Copenhagen, 1830; *d* Weimar, 1904). Danish conductor, composer, and opera director. Prix de Rome 1851. Succeeded Liszt as opera dir. at Weimar 1858–95. His opera *Landgrave Ludwigs Brautfahrt* (or *Le roi Edgard*) was prod. Weimar 1857 under Liszt's sponsorship. Comp. mus. for Goethe's *Faust*, 2 syms., and vn. conc.

Lasso, Orlando di. See *Lassus, Orlande de*.

Lass of Richmond Hill, The. Song with mus. by James *Hook and words by L. McNally. (N.B. The song refers to Richmond, Yorks., not Surrey.)

lassù. Slow section of *csárdás*.

Lassus, Orlande de (Roland) [It. Orlando di Lasso] (*b* Mons, 1532; *d* Munich, 1594). Flemish composer. In boyhood and youth travelled in Sicily and Italy in service of various aristocrats. Choirmaster, St John Lateran, Rome, 1553–4. Returned to Flanders, settling in Antwerp. Pubd. first vol. of madrigals, motets, and *chansons*, 1556. Entered service of Duke of Bavaria at court in Munich, 1556, becoming Kapellmeister 1563, the year he began his 7 *Penitential Psalms* (1563–70). Wrote nearly 2,000 works, mainly motets, madrigals, masses, canzonas, *chansons*, and psalms. Ranked with Palestrina and Victoria as among supreme masters of 16th-cent. polyphonic art. Complete catalogue of works pubd. Berlin 1956 (ed. W. Boettcher).

Last Post. British Army bugle call. The *First Post* at 9.30 p.m. calls all men back to barracks and the *Last Post* at 10 p.m. ends the day. By a natural and poetical association of ideas it has become the custom to sound the same call at military funerals.

Last Rose of Summer, 'Tis the. Old Irish air, orig. *Castle Hyde*, which became *The Groves of Blarney c*.1790 by R. A. Millikin, and was incl. by Thomas Moore, to his own new words, in his *Irish Melodies* (1813). Beethoven set the air, Mendelssohn wrote a pf. fantasia on it (Op.15, 1827), and it is sung by a sop. in Act 2 of Flotow's *Martha*.

Last Sleep of the Virgin, The (*Le Dernier Sommeil de la Vierge*). Orch. interlude from Massenet's oratorio *La Vierge* (1880), much favoured as an encore by *Beecham and the RPO.

Last Temptations, The (*Viimeiset kiusaukset*). Opera in 2 acts by *Kokkonen to lib. by L. Kokkonen, based on life of Finn. evangelist Paavo Ruotsalainen (1777–1852). Comp. 1973–5. Prod. Helsinki 1975, London (Finn. Nat. Opera) 1979.

László, Magda (*b* Marosvásárhely, 1919; *d* Viterbo, Italy, 2002). Hung. soprano. Budapest Opera 1943–6 (début as Elisabeth in *Tannhäuser*), then settled in Italy. Created the Mother in *Il *prigioniero* (radio 1949, Florence 1950). Glyndebourne 1953 and 1962. Created Cressida in *Troilus and Cressida*, CG 1954.

Late Swallows. Title of 3rd movt. of Delius's 2nd str. qt. (1916). Arr. for str. orch. by Fenby 1963 (f.p. Houston SO, Barbirolli, 1963).

Latham-Koenig, Jan (*b* London, 1953). Eng. conductor and pianist. Founded Koenig Ens. 1976. Concert pianist until 1981. Member of Cantiere Internazionale d'Arte, Montepulciano, 1981–6, when he cond. operas and cycle of Mahler syms. ENO début 1987; Wexford Fest. 1987; Vienna début 1988, CG 1995. Conducts many rare and contemp. works.

laùd. Sp. form of lute.

Lauda Sion (Praise, O Zion). One of the *Sequences allowed to remain in the liturgy of the RC Church when the Council of Trent (1545–63) abolished the rest. It has its traditional plainsong, but has also been set by composers. The words were written by St Thomas Aquinas (*c*.1264) for the feast of Corpus Christi (on which they are still sung).

Laudi Spirituali (Spiritual songs. More correctly *Laude spirituali*). Popular devotional songs sung by the *Laudesi*, a Florentine confraternity instituted in 1233. Music was at first in unison but later in parts. 1st pubd. coll. 1485. Regarded as forerunner of oratorio.

Laudon Symphony. Haydn's own sub-title for his sym. in C major, No.69 in Breitkopf edn., which he ded. to the Austrian field-marshal Ernst Gideon Freiherr von Loudon (to give him his correct spelling) (1716–90).

Lauds. The 2nd of the Canonical Hours of the RC Church, formerly sung at sunrise.

Lauri-Volpi, Giacomo (*b* Lanuvio, Rome, 1892; *d* Valencia, Spain, 1979). It. tenor. Opera début under name Giacomo Rubini at Viterbo 1919 (Arturo in *I Puritani*), under own name Rome 1920 (Des Grieux in *Manon*). Engaged by Toscanini for La Scala 1922 and sang there regularly in 1930s and 1940s. NY Met 1923–33. Sang Calaf in f. Amer. p. of *Turandot*, 1926. CG début 1925. Wrote 5 books of memoirs and history of vocal music.

Laute (Ger.). The *lute.

Lautenmacher (Ger., Fr. *luthier*). Maker of str. instrs.

Lavallée, Calixa (*b* Verchères, Quebec, 1842; *d* Boston, Mass., 1891). Fr.-Canadian composer and pianist. Travelling th. musician and teacher from 1857. On return to Canada, tried and failed to found state-supported cons. and opera co. Taught at Petersilea Acad., Boston, from 1881 and was mus. dir. RC cath. Wrote operas, sym., oratorio, 2 str. qts., vn. sonata, etc., also Canadian nat. song. **O Canada!* (1880) to words by Adolphe B. Routhier (Eng. vers. 1908 by R. Stanley Weir).

Lawes, Henry (*b* Dinton, Wilts., 1596; *d* London, 1662). Eng. composer and singer. Gent. of Charles I's Chapel Royal from 1626 and appointed as one of King's musicians 1631. Wrote mus. for Milton's masque *Comus* at Ludlow, 1634, taking part of Attendant Spirit. Reinstated in court posts 1660. Comp. anthem *Zadok the Priest* for Charles II's coronation, songs, and madrigals.

Lawes, William (*b* Dinton or Salisbury, 1602; *d* Chester, 1645). Eng. composer, brother of Henry *Lawes. One of private musicians attached to Charles I before and after he became King (1625). Comp. songs, madrigals, mus. for viols, and a large amount of mus. for the stage. Regarded as one of the greatest and most influential of Eng. composers. Joined royal army in Civil War in 1642 and was killed in siege of Chester.

Lawrence, Marjorie (Florence) (*b* Dean's Marsh, Australia, 1909; *d* Little Rock, Arkansas, 1979). Australian soprano. Opera début Monte Carlo 1932 (Elisabeth in *Tannhäuser*). Paris Opéra 1933–6; NY Met 1935–41. Stricken with poliomyelitis during *Die Walküre* at Mexico City 1941. Despite inability to walk unaided, continued opera career, incl. Wagnerian roles in which she excelled, and gave recitals. After retirement in 1952, prof. of v. Tulane Univ., 1956–60, prof. of v. and dir. of opera workshop, S. Illinois Univ. from 1960. CBE 1977.

Lawton, Jeffrey (*b* Oldham, 1939). Eng. tenor. Began amateur career with Manchester Opera Co. Sang Otello with the co. in 1975. Prof. début 1981 with WNO (Florestan in *Fidelio*). Sang Siegfried in WNO *Ring* cycle 1985 (CG 1986) and Tristan 1993 (also CG). Paris and Brussels 1987. Opera North début 1988. Cologne 1988 and 1989.

lay. See *lai*.

Layton, Robert (*b* London, 1930). Eng. critic and administrator. On mus. staff BBC since 1959. Author of books on Berwald and Sibelius. Trans. Erik Tawaststjerna's 3-vol. biography of Sibelius. Sole authority on Danish composer Esrum-Hellerup.

Lazarev, Alexander (*b* Russia, 1945). Russian conductor. Won Karajan cond. comp., Berlin

1972. Cond. Bolshoy Th., Moscow, from 1973 (chief cond. and art. dir. 1987–95). Founded Bolshoy Ens. of Soloists 1978 to perf. contemp. mus. Brit. début 1987 (RLPO). Prin. Cond. RSNO 1997–2005.

Lazarof, Henri (b Sofia, 1932). Bulg.-born composer and teacher (Amer. cit. 1959). Emigrated to Palestine 1946. Taught French at UCLA 1959–62. On mus. faculty 1962–87 (retiring as prof. emeritus). Artist-in-res. Univ. of W. Berlin 1971–2. Comps. incl. 3 ballets; concs. for pf. (1957), va. (1961), vc. (1968), vn. (1985), cl. (1989); Chamber Sym. (1977); 3 str. qts. (1956, 1962, 1980); vn. sonata (1958); wind trio (1981); octet, fl., ob., cl., vn., vc., db., pf., perc. (1988).

Lazarus, oder Die Feier der Auferstehung (Lazarus, or The Feast of the Resurrection). Unfinished oratorio ('Easter Cantata') by Schubert (D689), to text by A. H. Niemayer (1754–1828) comp. 1820. What remains contains marvellous mus.

LBCM. Licentiate of the Bandsman's College of Music.

LBSM. Licentiate of the Birmingham School of Music.

leader. (1) (Amer. concertmaster; Ger. *Konzertmeister*). Prin. 1st vn. of sym. orch.

(2) Often used in USA for cond., e.g., 'Ormandy leads the Philadelphia Orch. in . . .'.

(3) 1st vn. of str. qt. or other chamber group.

leading note. 7th degree of the scale, semitone below the tonic. So called because of tendency to rise, or 'lead', to the tonic. In minor keys is sometimes flattened in descent.

leading seventh. Chord of minor 7th on *leading note of major scale (e.g. in C Major, B–D–F–A).

Lead, Kindly Light. Hymn, words by John Henry Newman (1801–90), written after an illness in Sicily. Tune, *Lux benigna*, by Rev. John Bacchus Dykes, organist, first pubd. 1867, under name *St Oswald* in *Psalms and Hymns for the Church, School and Home*, ed. D. T. Barry, 1867, and a year later in appendix to *Hymns Ancient and Modern*. Another tune, *Alberta*, by W. H. Harris in *Songs of Praise*, enlarged edn., 1931.

Lear. Opera in 2 parts by *Reimann to lib. by Claus Henneberg based on Shakespeare's play *King Lear* (1606). Comp. 1976–8. Prod. Munich 1978 (Fischer-Dieskau as Lear). S. Francisco 1981, Paris 1982, London (ENO) 1989. See also *King Lear*.

Lear (*née* Shulman), **Evelyn** (b Brooklyn, NY, 1926). Amer. soprano. Sang in musicals, then went for voice tuition at Juilliard Sch. Won Fulbright schol. to Ger. 1955. Brit. début 1957 (Strauss's *Vier letzte Lieder* with LSO). Opera début Berlin 1958 (Composer in *Ariadne auf Naxos*). Salzburg Fest. début 1962. Sang title-role in *Lulu*, Vienna 1962 and London 1966, and Marie in

Wozzeck in Vienna, Berlin, Munich, S. Francisco, NY Met, and Milan (1971). CG début 1965; NY Met début 1967. Notable Marschallin in *Der Rosenkavalier*, singing role at farewell Met appearance 1985, but sang Countess Geschwitz in *Lulu* in Chicago 1987.

Lebègue, Nicolas-Antoine (b Laon, c.1631; d Paris, 1702). Fr. organist and composer. Org., church of St Merry, Paris, 1664–1702, and court org. to Louis XIV, 1678. Comp. 2 vols. of hpd. works (1677, 1687) and 3 vols. of org. pieces (1676 and after 1678).

Lebewohl, Das (The Farewell). Beethoven's (therefore the correct) title for his pf. sonata No.26 in E♭ major Op.81a, usually known as 'Les Adieux'. Comp. 1809–10.

lebhaft (Ger.). Lively. So *lebhafter*, livelier; *lebhaftigkeit*, liveliness.

Lebrun, Ludwig August (b Mannheim, 1752; d Berlin, 1790). Ger. oboist and composer. Member of Mannheim court orch. 1764–90. Comp. 7 ob. concs., 12 ob. trios, fl. conc., etc. Married sop. Franziska Danzi (1756–91), with whom he toured It., Fr., Ger., Austria, and Eng.

Lechner, Leonhard (b Adige valley, S. Tyrol, c.1553; d Stuttgart, 1606). Austrian composer. Chorister at Munich court, 1564–8, under Lassus, an edn. of whose motets he pubd. 1579. Taught in Nuremberg 1575–84. Kapellmeister at Württemberg from 1587. Comp. masses, motets, and psalms. First composer to set a complete cycle of Ger. poems to mus. (*Deutsche Sprüche von Leben und Tod*).

Leclair, Jean-Marie (b Lyons, 1697; d Paris, 1764). Fr. composer and violinist, known as 'the elder' to distinguish him from his brother. Began career as dancer at Lyons Opera. Went to Turin as ballet-master 1722 and took up vn. Settled in Paris 1723 and played at Concert Spirituel 1728 and in opera orch. 1729–35, during which time he studied comp. Court mus. in Paris 1733–7. Wrote opera *Scylla et Glaucus* (Paris 1746, revived in concert perf., London 1979) and ballets, and many vn. works incl. concs., sonatas, trios. Murdered by his nephew outside his house. His brother, also Jean-Marie (b Lyons, 1703; d Lyons, 1777), was a violinist and composed vn. sonatas and choral works.

Lecocq, (Alexandre) **Charles** (b Paris, 1832; d Paris, 1918). Fr. composer. His setting of *Le *Docteur Miracle* (with *Bizet's) won prize offered by Offenbach, 1856. From 1868 to 1911 produced a series of popular operettas of which most successful were *Fleur-de-Thé* (1868), *La Fille de Madame Angot* (1872) and *Giroflé-Girofla* (1874). Comp. ballet *Le cygne* (1899).

Lecuona, Ernesto (b Guanabacoa, 1896; d S. Cruz de Tenerife, 1963). Cuban composer and pianist. Leader of dance band, Lecuona's Cuban Boys. Lived for a time in NY, writing for musicals, films, and radio. Wrote 2 zarzuelas, *Rapsodia negra* for pf. and orch. (1943), and many songs, incl. *Andalucía*.

Ledger, (Sir) **Philip** (Stevens) (*b* Bexhill-on-Sea, 1937). Eng. organist, conductor, pianist, and harpsichordist. Master of Mus., Chelmsford Cath. 1962–5; dir. of mus., Univ. of E. Anglia 1965–73; dir. of mus. and organist King's Coll., Cambridge, 1974–82. One of art. dirs. of Aldeburgh Fest. 1968–89. Prin., RSAMD 1982–2002. CBE 1985. Knighted 1999.

ledger lines (leger lines). Short lines added below or above the stave to accommodate notes too high or too low for the stave itself.

Leech, Richard (*b* Binghamton, Calif., 1956). Amer. tenor. First sang as bar., then sang Offenbach's Hoffmann while student. Sang in concerts and operas in Amer. from 1980. Eur. début Berlin 1987 (Raoul in *Les Huguenots*). NY City Opera 1988; NY Met début 1990; La Scala début 1990.

Leeds Festival. Mus festival, principally choral, held in Yorkshire city of Leeds since 1858 when it marked opening of town hall. Second festival, cond. by Costa, was in 1874, third in 1880 (Sullivan), after which it was held triennially until 1970. Under Sullivan festival acquired international status, with choral works commissioned from Dvořák, Massenet, Sullivan, Parry, and Stanford. When Sullivan retired, Stanford took over until 1910. Among works first perf. at Leeds festivals were Elgar's *Caractacus* (1898) and *Falstaff* (1913), Vaughan Williams's *A Sea Symphony* (1910), Holst's *Choral Symphony* (1925), Walton's *Belshazzar's Feast* (1931), Britten's *Nocturne* (1958), and Blake's *Lumina* (1970). Directors in recent years have included Earl of Harewood and John Warrack.

Leeds Piano Competition. International competition for pianists est. 1963 by Fanny Waterman and Marion Thorpe (then Lady Harewood). Held triennially. Winners have been Michael Roll (1963), Rafael Orozco (1966), Radu Lupu (1969), Murray Perahia (1972), Dmitri Alexeev (1975), Michel Dalberto (1978), Ian Hobson (1981), Jon Kimura Parker (1984), Vladimir Ovchinnikov (1987), Artur Pizarro (1990), Ricardo Castro (1993), Ilya Itin (1996), Alessio Bax (2000), Antti Siirala (2003), Sunwook Kim (2006). Many pianists who have come second in the Leeds comp. have had international careers, including Viktoria Postnikova (1966), Craig Sheppard (1972), and Mitsuko Uchida (1975, when Andras Schiff was joint 3rd and Myung-Whun Chung joint 4th!). In 1981 Peter Donohoe was placed 6th.

leer (Ger.). Empty; applied to open str. of vn., etc.

Lees [Lysniansky], **Benjamin** (*b* Harbin, Manchuria, 1924). Amer. composer of Russ. parentage. Went to Europe 1954, returning to USA 1962. Teacher at several Amer. colleges. Awarded Arnold Bax Medal 1958. Prin. works:

OPERAS: *The Oracle* (1955); *The Gilded Cage* (1963); *Medea in Corinth* (1970).

BALLET: *Scarlatti Portfolio* (1979).

ORCH.: syms.: No.1 (1953), No.2 (1958), No.3 (1969), No.4 (*Memorial Candles*), mez., vn., orch. (1985), No.5 (*Kalmar Nyckel*) (1986); pf. conc. No.1 (1955), No.2 (1966); vn. conc. (1958); *Profile* (1952); *Interlude*, str. (1957); *Concertante breve*, ob., 2 hn., str. (1959); *Concerto for Orchestra* (1959); *Prologue, Capriccio, and Epilogue* (1959); ob. conc. (1963); conc., str. qt., orch. (1964); *Spectrum* (1964); Conc., chamber orch. (1966); *Silhouettes* (1967); *The trumpet of the Swan*, narr., orch. (1972); *Études*, pf., orch. (1974); *Passacaglia* (1975); *Labyrinths*, sym. wind band (1975); *Variations*, pf., orch. (1976); conc., ww. quintet, orch. (1976); *Mobiles* (1980); double conc., pf., vc., orch. (1982); conc., brass, orch. (1983); *Portrait of Rodin* (1984); hn. conc. (1992); *Borealis* (1993); *Celebration* (1996); perc. conc. (1999).

VOICE(S) & ORCH.: *Songs of the Night*, sop., 13 instr. (1955); *Visions of Poets* (Whitman), sop., ten., ch. (1961); *Echoes of Normandy*, ten., tape, org., orch. (1994); *The Nervous Family*, ch., bn., orch. (2004).

SONGS & SONG-CYCLES: *Songs of the Night*, sop., pf. (1952, with instr. 1955); *3 Songs*, cont., pf. (1959); *Cyprian Songs*, bar., pf. (1960); *Staves*, sop., pf. (1977); *Paumanok*, mez., pf. (1980).

CHAMBER MUSIC: str. qts., No.1 (1952), No.2 (1955), No.3 (1982), No.4 (1989), No.5 (2002), No.6 (2005); hn. sonata (1952); vn. sonata No.1 (1953), No.2 (1972), No.3 (1991); *3 Variables*, ob., cl., bn., hn., pf. (1955); *Invenzione*, vn. (1965); *Study No.1*, vc. (1970); *Collage*, wind quintet, perc., str. qt. (1973); *Soliloquy Music from King Lear*, fl. (1975); *Dialogue*, vc., pf. (1977); sextet (wind quintet and pf.) (1977); vc. sonata (1981); pf. trios, No.1 (1983), No.2 (*Silent Voices*) (1998); *Contours*, pf., vn., vc., cl., hn. (1994); *Night Spectres*, vc. (2000); *Tapestry*, fl., cl., vc., pf. (2003); *Landscape (after Yves Tanguy)*, vn. (2004).

PIANO: sonatas: No.1 (1949), No.2 (1950), No.3 (1956), No.4 (1963); sonata, 2 pf. (1951); *Fantasia* (1954); *Sonata breve* (1956); *6 Ornamental Études* (1957); *Kaleidoscopes* (1958); *3 Preludes* (1962); *Odyssey*, pf. (1970); *Fantasy Variations* (1983); *Mirrors* (1992–2003); *Tableau*, 2 pf. (2003).

Leeuw, Ton de (*b* Rotterdam, 1926; *d* Paris, 1996). Dutch composer. Dir. of sound, Dutch Radio Union 1954–60. Teacher at Amsterdam Univ. from 1963 (dir. 1971–3). Works influenced by Schoenberg, *musique concrète*, Pijper's 'germ-cell' melodic principle, and Asian mus. Has used proportional rhythmic notation to represent unlimited scale of note-values. Works incl.: radio oratorio *Job* (1956); opera *The Dream* (1962–3); TV opera *Alceste* (1963); ballet *The Bees* (1965); orch.: 2 vn. concs. (1953, 1961); *Ombres* (1961); *Symphonies for Winds*, 29 wind instr. (1963); *Spatial Music I-IV, Litany of our Time* (1965–8); *Syntaxis* (1968); *Gending*, Javanese gamelan (1975); *Résonances* (1985); conc., gui., str. (1989); chamber mus.: str. qts. No.1 (1958), No.2, with tape (1964); str. trio (1948); vn. sonata (1951); *The Four Seasons*, hp. (1964); *Music*, ob. (1969); *Reversed Night*, fl. (1971); *Midare*, marimba (1972); *Canzone*, brass (1974); *Modal Music* (accordeon) (1978–9); *Apparences I*, vc.

(1986–7); choral: *Car nos vignes sont en fleur*, 12 vv. (1981); *And They Shall Reign Forever*, mez., cl., hn., pf., perc. (1981); *Les chants de Kabir*, solo vv. (1985); *Transparence*, ch., brass (1986); keyboard: pf. sonatina (1949); sonata, 2 pf. (1950); *5 Études* (1951); *3 African Studies* (1954); *Sweelinck Variations*, org. (1972–3); tape: *Electronic Suite* (1958); *Clair-Obscur* (1982).

LeFanu, Nicola (Frances) (*b* Wickham Bishops, Essex, 1947). Eng. composer and teacher, daughter of Elizabeth *Maconchy. Cobbett chamber mus. prize 1968, 1st prize BBC young composers' comp. 1971. Taught at Francis Holland Sch., London, 1969–72, St Paul's Girls' Sch. 1975–7. Lect., Morley Coll. 1976, lect. in mus., King's Coll., London Univ. from 1977, comp.-in-res. NSW Cons. 1979. Prof. of mus., York Univ., from 1994. Works incl.:

OPERAS: *Anti-World*, mus. th., dancer, sop., bar., alt. fl., cl., perc. (1972); *Dawnpath*, chamber opera (1977); *The Old Woman of Beare*, monodrama (1981); *The Story of Mary O'Neill*, radiophonic opera, sop., 16 vv. (1986); *The Green Children*, children's opera (1990); *Blood Wedding* (1991, prod. London 1992); *The Wildman* (1994).

BALLET: *The Last Laugh* (1972).

ORCH.: *Preludio I*, str. (1967); *Preludio II*, str. (1976, rev. of I); *The Hidden Landscape* (1973); *Columbia Falls* (1975); *Farne* (1980); *Variations*, pf., orch. (1982); conc., alto sax., str. (1989); conc., cl., str. (1997).

CHORAL & VOCAL: *Il Cantico del Cantici II* (1968); *But Stars Remaining*, sop. (1970); *Christ Calls Man Home*, unacc. SATB (1971); *Rondeaux*, ten., hn. (1972); *Paysage*, bar. (1973); *The Valleys Shall Sing*, ch., wind (1973); *The Same Day Dawns*, sop., 5 players (1974); *The Little Valleys*, 4 unacc. sop. (1975); *For We Are the Stars*, 16 vv. (1978); *Like a Wave of the Sea*, ch., ens. of early instrs. (1981); *A Penny for a Song*, sop., pf. (1981); *Rory's Rounds* (1983); *Trio II: Song for Peter*, sop., cl., pf. (1983); *Stranded on my Heart*, ten., ch., str. (1984); *I am Bread*, sop., pf. (1987); *The Silver Strand*, unacc. SATB (1989); *Cancion de la Luna*, counterten., str. qt. (1994–5); *At the Blue Hour*, ch., vc. (1995); *On the Wind*, unacc. ch. (1997).

CHAMBER & INSTR.: *Soliloquy*, ob. (1966); Variations, ob. qt. (1968); *Chiaroscuro*, pf. (1969); *Abstracts and a Frame*, vn., pf. (1971); *Songs and Sketches*, vcs. (1971); *Omega*, org. (1972, rev. 1984); *Collana*, 6 instr. (1976); *Deva*, vc., 7 instr. (1979); *Trio I*, fl., vc., perc. (1980); *Moon Over Western Ridge Mootwingee*, sax. qt. (1985); *Invisible Places*, cl. quintet (1986); *Lament*, ob., cl., va., vc. (1988); str. qt. (1988); *Lullaby*, cl., pf. (1988); *Nocturne*, vc., pf. (1988); str. qt. No.1 (1988), No.2 (1997).

Lefébure, Yvonne (*b* Ermont, Seine-et-Oise, 1898; *d* Paris, 1986). Fr. pianist. Prof., École Normale de Musique, Paris, from 1924, Paris Cons. 1952–67. Salzburg Fest. 1937. Int. career as recitalist and soloist. Also writer and lecturer.

legato (It.). Bound together. Perf. of mus. so that there is no perceptible pause between notes, i.e.

in a smooth manner, the opposite of *staccato. Indicated by slur or *curved line. On str. instrs., legato passages are played with one stroke of the bow; in vocal mus., the legato passage is sung in one breath. *Legato touch* in pf. playing requires holding down one key until the finger is on another. Superlative is *legatissimo*.

Legend (Ger. *Legende*). Title given to short comps. of lyrical or epic character. Well-known examples are *Dvořák's *Legends*, Op.59 (orch. from pf. duet) and Sibelius's 4 *Lemminkäinen Legends* for orch., Op.22.

Legende von der Heiligen Elisabeth, Die (The Legend of St Elizabeth). Oratorio by Liszt comp. 1857–62, f.p. Budapest 1865. Staged as opera-oratorio Weimar 1881 and NY Met 1918.

Legend of Joseph (Strauss). See *Josephslegende*.

Legend of the Invisible City of Kitezh (Rimsky-Korsakov). See *Invisible City of Kitezh, The Legend of the*.

Legend of Tsar Saltan, The. Opera in prol. and 4 acts by *Rimsky-Korsakov to lib. by Belsky after Pushkin's poem (1832). Comp. 1899–1900. Prod. Moscow 1900, London 1933, NY 1937. One of orch. interludes is *Flight of the Bumble Bee.

leger lines. See *ledger lines*.

Legge, Walter (*b* London, 1906, *d* S. Jean, Cap Ferrat, 1979). Eng. impresario, critic, and author. Joined Gramophone Co. (HMV) 1927, becoming recording manager and holding similar post with Columbia from 1938. Ass. to Beecham at CG 1938–9. Instrumental in putting many famous artists under recording contract. Organized Wolf and Beethoven Sonata socs. for recordings. Contributed criticisms to *Manchester Guardian* 1934–8. Dir. of mus. ENSA 1942–5. Founded *Philharmonia Orch. 1945. Prod. or supervised many famous recordings, incl. Furtwängler's of *Tristan und Isolde*, Karajan's of *Falstaff* and *Der Rosenkavalier*, many by Callas, Lipatti's pf. recordings, Klemperer's legacy, and Neveu's Sibelius vn. conc. Married sop. Elisabeth *Schwarzkopf 1953.

legg(i)ero, legg(i)ere (It.). Light. So *legg(i)eramente* or *legg(i)ermente*, lightly, *legg(i)erezza, legg(i)eranza*, lightness; *leggerissimo*, as light as possible.

leggiadro, leggiadretto (It.). Graceful. So *leggiadramente*, gracefully.

leggio (It., from *leggere*, to read). Music desk.

legno (It.). Wood. *col legno*, 'with the wood', i.e. in str. playing, tapping the str. with the stick of the bow instead of using the hair, thus producing a rather bizarre sound as in finale of Berlioz's *Symphonie Fantastique*. *Bacchetta di legno*, wooden-headed drumstick, *strumenti* (*stromenti*) *di legno*, woodwind instrs.

Legrand, Michel (*b* Paris, 1932). Fr. composer and conductor. Soon became known as brilliant orchestrator of light mus. and jazz. Cond. for Maurice Chevalier in Paris and NY 1954–5. Gained reputation with music for *Les Parapluies de Cherbourg* (1964). Comp. many film scores, among them *Un Homme et Une Femme* (1961), *The Thomas Crown Affair* (1968), *Summer of '42* (1971), *The Go-Between* (1971), *The Three Musketeers* (1974), *The Hunter* (1980), *Yentl* (1983), *Never Say Never Again* (1983), *Dingo* (1991), *Ready to Wear* (1994), and *Aaron's Magic Village* (1997).

Legrenzi, Giovanni (*b* Clusone, nr. Bergamo, 1626; *d* Venice, 1690). It. composer and choirmaster. Organist in Bergamo 1645–55, Ferrara 1656–65 (while there he wrote his first operas). At Conservatorio dei Mendicanti, Venice, 1671–81, when he became deputy choirmaster at St Mark's succeeding to the chief post in 1685. Comp. 19 operas, much instr. mus., 7 oratorios, masses, psalms, motets, church sonatas.

Lehár, Ferencz [Franz] (*b* Komáron, 1870; *d* Bad Ischl, 1948). Austro-Hung. composer. Advised by Dvořák to concentrate on comp. Joined Elberfeld opera orch. as violinist, then became ass. leader of his father's band. Cond. of various army bands 1890–1902. Cond., Theater an der Wien, Vienna, 1902. His *Wiener Frauen* was produced there Nov. 1902 and after its success he stayed in Vienna and devoted his time to comp. His operetta, *Die lustige Witwe* (The *Merry Widow*) was a colossal success not only at its Vienna première in 1905 but all over the world ever since. He was the bridge between the Strausses and Zeller and the later Oskar Straus, Fall, and Kálmán. In the 1920s the v. of Richard Tauber became indelibly associated with Lehár roles and one above all—in *Das Land des Lächelns* (The *Land of Smiles*)—a rev. of *Die gelbe Jacke* (1923)—in 1929. He wrote a full-scale opera, *Giuditta* (Vienna State Opera, 1934) and several other operettas: *Der Graf von Luxemburg* (The *Count of Luxemburg*) (1909), *Zigeunerliebe* (1910), *Frasquita* (1922), *Paganini* (1925), *Der *Zarewitsch* (1926), and *Friederike* (1928). Also wrote sonatas, sym.-poems, vn. conc., marches, and dances (incl. the concert-waltz *Gold and Silver*, 1902). His villa in Bad Ischl is now a museum and an annual Lehár Fest. is held in the spa. Cond. Vienna PO in prog. of his mus., Salzburg Fest. 1940.

Lehel, György (*b* Budapest, 1926; *d* Budapest, 1989). Hung. conductor. Début 1946. Prin. cond. Budapest Radio SO from 1962. Brit. début, Cheltenham 1968. Kossuth Prize 1973.

Lehmann, Lilli (*b* Würzburg, 1848; *d* Berlin, 1929). Ger. soprano. Childhood in Prague: studied pf. at 6 and at 12 was acc. to her mother, a sop., who also taught her singing. Début Prague 1865 as 1st Boy in *Die Zauberflöte*. Member, Berlin Opera 1869–85 (début as Marguerite de Valois in *Les Huguenots*), singing lyric and coloratura roles. At first Bayreuth Fest. 1876 sang Woglinde, Helmwige, and Waldvogel (Wood Bird) in *The Ring*. London début 1880. Sang Isolde at CG 1884 cond. Richter. Début NY Met 1885. Was first Amer. Isolde (1886) and Brünnhilde in *Siegfried* (1887) and

Götterdämmerung (1888). On return to Ger. in 1889 was banned from all opera by Kaiser because she had overstayed her leave. Ban lifted 1891. Excelled as Mozart singer and sang at Salzburg Fest. 1905, later becoming art. dir. Returned to Met 1891–2 and 1898–9. Sang Isolde in Vienna 1909 and continued recitals until 1920. Was superb actress and her vocal and dramatic range covered Wagner to Bellini, Mozart, and Beethoven; also Suppé and Offenbach—in all, 170 roles in 119 operas. Taught for nearly 40 years, pupils incl. *Farrar and *Fremstad. Author and translator of several books. Autobiography *My Path Through Life* (NY and London 1914, 1977).

Lehmann, Liza [Elizabeth] (Nina Mary Frederika) (*b* London, 1862; *d* Pinner, 1918). Eng. composer and soprano. Successful career as concert singer (début London 1885) ended in 1894, then devoted herself to comp. Best-known work is song-cycle *In a Persian Garden*, setting for SATB of 30 quatrains from FitzGerald's *Rubaiyát of Omar Khayyám* (f.p. London 1896).

Lehmann, Lotte (*b* Perleberg, 1888; *d* Santa Barbara, Calif., 1976). Ger.-born soprano (Amer. cit. 1945). Début Hamburg 1909 as 3rd Boy in *Die Zauberflöte*. Vienna début 1914. Joined Vienna Opera 1916, remaining until 1938, singing leading roles in Wagner, Strauss, Mozart, Puccini, and Beethoven. First to sing successively all 3 sop. roles in *Der Rosenkavalier* (Sophie, Oktavian, and Marschallin), eventually becoming outstanding Marschallin of her time. Created the Composer in *Ariadne auf Naxos* (1916), Dyer's Wife in *Die Frau ohne Schatten* (1919), and Christine in *Intermezzo* (Dresden 1924). First Vienna Arabella (1933). London début 1914 as Sophie; CG début 1924 as Marschallin (her first assumption of this role) and sang there yearly until 1935 and again in 1938. Salzburg Fest. début 1926; Amer. début (Chicago) 1930; NY Met 1934–45. Settled in USA at Santa Barbara 1938, est. sch. of singing there. Sang last Marschallin at San Francisco 1946. Farewell recital, Santa Barbara, Aug. 1951. Pupils incl. Grace *Bumbry and Jeannine *Altmeyer. Gave master-classes in London 1957 and 1959. Directed prod. of *Der Rosenkavalier* at NY Met 1962. Wrote books, novel, and poems. Autobiography *My Many Lives* (NY 1948).

Lehnhoff, Nikolaus (*b* Hanover, 1939). Ger. director. Ass. to Wieland Wagner and Karl Böhm at Bayreuth in 1960s. Opera début Paris 1972 (*Die Frau ohne Schatten*). Prod. *The Ring* S. Francisco 1983–5 and Munich 1987. Prod. *Elektra*, Chicago 1975 and *Salome* NY Met 1989. At Glyndebourne prod. *Káťa Kabanová* (1988), *Jenůfa* (1989), *The Makropulos Affair* (1995), *The Bartered Bride* (1999), *Tristan und Isolde* (2003). Salzburg Fest. début 1990 (*Idomeneo*); La Scala 1990 (*Meistersinger*); ENO 1996 (*The Prince of Homburg*); CG 1997 (*Palestrina*).

Leibowitz, René (*b* Warsaw, 1913; *d* Paris, 1972). Polish-born Fr. composer, conductor, and musicologist. Settled in Paris 1926. Powerful advocate of Schoenberg's 12-note system, influencing

Boulez and Henze. Cond. and teacher at Darmstadt Fest. from 1949. Author of several books on dodecaphonic mus. Prolific composer of operas, syms., concs., chamber mus.

Leichtentritt, Hugo (*b* Pleschen, 1874; *d* Cambridge, Mass., 1951). Ger. composer, teacher, and scholar. Went to USA 1889. Taught comp. and aesthetics at Klindworth-Scharwenka Cons., Berlin, 1901–24 and worked as critic in Berlin 1901–17. Returned to USA 1933 as lect. at Harvard until retirement in 1940. Author of many books incl. biographies of Chopin, Busoni, and Handel, ed. of old mus., and prolific composer in all forms.

Leider, Frida (*b* Berlin, 1888; *d* Berlin, 1975). Ger. soprano. Début Halle 1915 (Venus in *Tannhäuser*). Opera at Rostock 1917–18, Königsberg 1918–19, Hamburg 1919–23, then Berlin State Opera 1923–40, esp. in Wagner roles (a great Isolde and Brünnhilde). CG début 1924 (Isolde), returning annually until 1938; La Scala 1927; Chicago Opera 1928–32; NY Met 1933–4; Bayreuth 1928–38. Gave many *Lieder* recitals (Berlin début 1927). Producer and teacher after 1945. Autobiography *Das war mein Teil* (1959, in Eng. as *Playing My Part*, 1966).

Leiferkus, Sergei (Petrovich) (*b* Leningrad, 1946). Russ. baritone. Sang at Maly Th., Leningrad, 1972–8. Joined Kirov (now Mariinsky) Opera, Leningrad, 1978, having sung Andrei in *War and Peace* there, 1977. Wexford Fest. début 1982 (Marquis in Massenet's *Grisélidis*). Scottish Opera début 1985; ENO 1987; CG 1989 (but 1987 with Kirov. co.); Opera North 1988; Amer. début Boston 1987; Glyndebourne 1989. London recital début 1989. Sang Ruprecht in *The *Fiery Angel*, BBC Proms 1991 (and CG 1992).

Leigh, Adèle (*b* London, 1928; *d* London, 2004). Eng. soprano. Member of CG co. 1948–56 (début as Xenia in *Boris Godunov*). Created 2 roles in *The Pilgrim's Progress* (CG 1951) and Bella in *The Midsummer Marriage* (CG 1955). Amer. début Boston 1959; NY 1960; Zurich Opera from 1961. Prin. sop. Vienna Volksoper 1963–72. Came out of retirement to sing Gabrielle in *La *vie parisienne*, Brighton Fest. 1984, and Heidi in Sondheim's *Follies*, London 1987. Teacher at RNCM from 1992.

Leigh, Walter (*b* London, 1905; *d* in action nr. Tobruk, 1942). Eng. composer. Wrote two light operas, *The Pride of the Regiment* (1932) and *Jolly Roger* (1933), incid. mus. (incl. *A Midsummer Night's Dream*), concertino for hpd. and str. (1936), songs, chamber mus.

Leighton, Kenneth (*b* Wakefield, 1929; *d* Edinburgh, 1988). Eng. composer and pianist. Comp. fellowship Leeds Univ. 1953–5; lect. then reader in mus., Edinburgh Univ. 1956–68; lect. in mus., Oxford Univ. 1968–70. Prof. of mus., Edinburgh Univ. 1970–88. Works incl.:

OPERA: *Columba*, Op.77 (1980).

ORCH.: concs.: vn., Op.12 (1952); va., hp., Op.15 (1952); vc., Op.31 (1956); pf.: No.1, Op.11 (1951,

rev. 1959), No.2, Op.37 (1960), No.3, Op.57 (1969); org., Op.58 (1970); hpd., rec., str. (1982); syms.: No.1, Op.42 (1964), No.2 (*Sinfonia Mistica*), Op.69, sop., ch., orch. (1974), No.3 (*Laudes musicae*), Op.90, ten., orch. (1983); *Dance Suite* No.1, Op.53 (1968), No.2, Op.59 (1970), No.3 (*Scottish Dances*) (1983).

VOICE(S) & INSTR(S).: *A Christmas Carol*, Op.21, bar., ch., str., pf. (1953); *The Light Invisible, sinfonia sacra*, Op.16, ten., ch., orch. (1958); *Laudes Montium*, Op.71, bar., ch., orch. (1975); *Animal Heaven*, Op.83, sop., recorder, vc., hpd. (1980); *Earth, Sweet Earth*, Op.94, ten., pf. (1986).

VOICE(S) & ORGAN: *Magnificat and Nunc Dimittis*, ch., org. (1959); *Alleluia Amen*, bar., ch., org. (1961); *Te Deum*, sop., bar., ch., org. (1964); *Let All the World in Every Corner Sing*, ch., org. (1965); *Adventate Deo*, ch., org. (1970); *Awake My Glory*, Op.79, sop., ch., org. (1979); *These are Thy Wonders*, Op.84, ten. or sop., org. (1981); *The World's Desire*, Op.91, ch., org. (1984); *The Beauty of Holiness*, mez., ch., org. (1988).

UNACC. VOICES: *3 Carols*, Op.25, sop., ch. (1948–56); *Hymn of the Nativity*, sop., ch. (1960); *Mass*, Op.64, SATB soli, double ch., org. (1964); *Lift Up Your Heads*, ch. (1966); *Missa brevis*, Op.50, ch. (1967); *6 Elizabethan Lyrics*, Op.65, women's vv. (1972); *Evening Hymn*, sop., ch. (1979); *What Love is this of Thine?*, sop., bar., ch. (1985).

CHAMBER MUSIC: *Fantasia on the Name BACH*, Op.29, va., pf. (1955); pf. quintet, Op.34 (1959); *7 Variations*, Op.43, str. qt. (1964); pf. trio, Op.46 (1965); vc. sonata, Op.52 (1967); *Contrasts and Variants*, Op.63, pf. qt. (1972); *Fantasy on a Chorale*, Op.80, vn., org. (1980); *Fantasy-Octet 'Homage to Percy Grainger'*, Op.87, str. (1982).

PIANO: *Fantasia Contrappuntistica, 'Homage to Bach'*, Op.24 (1956); *Pieces for Angela*, Op.47 (1966); sonata, Op.64 (1972); *Household Pets*, Op.86 (1981); *Sonata for Four Hands*, Op.92, pf. duet (1985); *Prelude, Hymn, and Toccata*, Op.96, 2 pf. (1987).

ORGAN: *Prelude, Scherzo and Passacaglia*, Op.41 (1963); *Et Resurrexit*, Op.49 (1966); *Martyrs*, Op.73, org. duet (1976); *Veni Redemptor*, Op.93 (1985); *Veni Creator Spiritus* (1987).

Leinsdorf [Landauer], **Erich** (*b* Vienna, 1912; *d* Zurich, 1993). Austrian-born conductor (Amer. cit. 1942). Rehearsal pianist for Weber's choir 1932–4. Ass. cond. to Bruno Walter and Toscanini at Salzburg Fest. 1934–7. Opera cond. Bologna 1936; ass. cond. NY Met from 1937 (début 1938 in *Die Walküre*), succeeded *Bodanzky as chief cond. of Ger. repertory 1939–43. Cond. Cleveland Orch. 1943–4; Rochester PO 1947–55. Mus. dir., NY City Opera 1956–7. Cond. NY Met 1957–62; Boston SO 1962–9; prin. cond. W. Berlin Radio SO 1978–80.

Leipzig. Ger. city in Saxony with long tradition of sacred and secular music. St Thomas's Church became town church 1755. Several distinguished musicians were Kantor there, one of the finest being Johann *Kuhnau, org. from 1684 and Kantor 1701–22. He was succeeded in 1723 by J. S. Bach who stayed until his death in 1750. Like Kuhnau, he became dissatisfied with standards of perf., but many of his church cantatas were written for the choir. His successors incl. J. A. Hiller (1789–1804) and Karl Straube (1918–40). The first opera written for Leipzig was N. A. Strungk's *Alceste* (1694). Telemann comp. at least 20 operas for Leipzig. The Schauspielhaus was built 1766 after which opera was regularly perf. It became the Stadttheater 1817. The Neues Stadttheater opened 1867. Lortzing was cond. of opera in Leipzig 1844–5; among his successors were Julius Rietz (1847–54), Anton Seidl (1878–80), Arthur Nikisch (1879–89), Gustav Mahler (1886–8), Otto Lohse (1912–23), Gustav Brecher (1923–33), Paul Schmitz (1933–51). Krenek's *Jonny spielt auf* (1927) and Weill's *Aufstieg und Fall der Stadt Mahagonny* (1930) were f.p. in Leipzig. Opera house was destroyed by bombs 1943. After 1945 Leipzig was in East German (Communist) zone. Joachim Herz was dir. 1959–76. After Ger. reunification (1989), Udo Zimmermann became Intendant 1990 and mus. dir. was Lothar Zagrosek.

Leipzig's concert tradition began in 17th cent. In 1781 a new Gewandhaus (Cloth Hall) was built, enabling the Gewandhaus concerts to become the most important in the city, the first being given on 25 Nov. 1781, cond. by Hiller. Mozart gave a concert of his own works there 1789. Mendelssohn was cond. 1835–47. During his régime Bach's *St Matthew Passion* was revived and f.ps. were given of Schumann's 1st, 2nd, and 4th syms., Schubert's 'Great' C major sym., and Mendelssohn's 3rd sym. and vn. conc. Rietz was cond. 1854–60, Carl Reinecke 1860–95. Brahms cond. all his syms. in Leipzig and his vn. conc. had its première there 1879. New Gewandhaus opened 1884. Conds. were Arthur Nikisch (1895–1922), Furtwängler (1922–9), Bruno Walter (1929–33), Hermann Abendroth (1934–46). Gewandhaus was bombed 1943 and rebuilt 1978. Since 1946 conds. have incl. Franz Konwitschny (1949–62), Vaclav Neumann (1964–8), Kurt Masur (1970–98), Herbert Blomstedt (1998–2005), Riccardo Chailly from 2005.

Leipzig also has a radio orch., founded 1924. The Cons. was founded in 1843 through Mendelssohn's efforts and has remained one of the leading institutions of its kind. Leipzig is also the home of org.-builders, several mus. publishers, e.g. Breitkopf & Härtel, Hoffmeister & Kühnel, and C. F. Peters, and of mus. journals such as the *Allgemeine musikalische Zeitung* (1798) and *Neue Zeitschrift für Musik*.

leise (Ger.). Soft, gentle, as in *Leise, leise*, Agathe's aria in Act 2 of *Der Freischütz*. *leiser*, softer.

Leitmotiv (leading motive). A term (often misspelt *leitmotif*) first used *c*.1865 by A. W. Ambros in article about Wagner operas and Liszt sym.-poems. 'Representative theme' is a good Eng. alternative. Composers throughout history have used the device in one form or another, e.g. Gluck and Mozart, Weber in *Der Freischütz*, Mendelssohn, Berlioz (the *idée fixe* in the *Symphonie Fantastique*), but it was raised to its highest and most complex form by Wagner, especially in *Der Ring des Nibelungen*, where the subtle combinations of *leitmotiv* create symphonic textures.

Leitner, Ferdinand (*b* Berlin, 1912; *d* Forch, nr Zurich, 1996). Ger. conductor. Ass. to *Busch at Glyndebourne 1935. Opera cond. Berlin 1943, Hamburg 1945–6, Munich 1946–7. Mus. dir. Stuttgart Opera 1947–69 (gen. mus. dir. from 1950), conducting 13 prods. by Wieland Wagner and f.ps. of Orff's *Oedipus der Tyrann* (1959) and *Prometheus* (1968). Cond. Zurich Opera 1969–84. Prin. cond. Hague PO 1976–80, RAI Orch., Turin, 1986–90. Amer. début Chicago 1969; Salzburg Fest. 1985.

Lejeune, Claude. See *Jeune, Claude le*.

Lekeu, Guillaume (*b* Heusy, Belg., 1870; *d* Angers, 1894). Belg. composer. Died of typhoid, leaving small body of works of exceptional promise and beauty, all comp. between 1887 and 1892.

Lélio, ou Le Retour à la vie (Lélio, or The return to life). Monodrama by Berlioz, his Op.14 *bis*, comp. 1831–2 as a sequel to *Symphonie Fantastique*. For speaker, 2 ten., bar., ch., orch. F.p. Paris, Nov. 1832.

Lemare, Edwin (Henry) (*b* Ventnor, IoW., 1865; *d* Los Angeles, 1934). Eng. organist and composer. Held various org. posts, incl. St Margaret's, Westminster, 1897–1902, and gave many recitals. Visited USA 1900 and settled there holding org. posts in Pittsburgh, S. Francisco, Portland (Maine), and Chattanooga. Composed 2 org. syms. and other works. The song *Moonlight and Roses*, his best-known comp., was adapted from an *Andantino* for org.

Lemmens-Sherrington, Hellen (*b* Preston, 1834; *d* Brussels, 1906). Eng. soprano. London début in concerts, then with Eng. Opera 1860–5 and at CG 1866. Long career in opera and oratorio, being regarded as leading Eng. sop. of her day. First prof. of singing, RMCM 1893–7. Retired 1894 and taught at Brussels Cons. Married Nicolas Jacques Lemmens (1823–81), Belg. organist, composer, and teacher at Brussels Cons.

Lemminkäinen Legends (*Lemminkäis-sarja*). Suite for orch. Op.22 by Sibelius containing 4 movts.: 1. *Lemminkäinen and the Maidens of the Island* (*Lemminkäinen ja saaren neidot*) comp. 1895, rev. 1897, 1939. 2. *Lemminkäinen in Tuonela* (*Lemminkäinen Tuonelassa*) comp. 1895, rev. 1897, 1939. 3. *The Swan of Tuonela* (*Tuonelan joutsen*) comp. 1893, rev. 1897, 1900. 4. *Lemminkäinen's Return* (*Lemminkäisen paluu*) comp. 1895, rev. 1897, 1900. No.3 was conceived as prelude to abandoned opera *The Burning of the Boat* (*Veenen luominen*) and No.2 also had operatic origins. F.p. 1895 version, Helsinki 1896, cond. Sibelius; f.p. 1897 revision, Helsinki 1897, cond. Sibelius; f. Eng. p. of complete 1897 version, BBC 1950, cond. Cameron; f.p. of Nos. 1 and 2 outside Finland, Bournemouth 1937, cond. Wood; f. Eng. p. No.3, London 1905, cond. Wood; f. Eng. p. No.4, BBC Newcastle station broadcast 1925, cond. E. Clark.

Lemnitz, Tiana (Luise) (*b* Metz, 1897; *d* Berlin 1994). Ger. soprano. Opera début Heilbronn 1921 (Lortzing's *Undine*). Aachen Opera 1922–8; Hanover 1928–33; Dresden State Opera 1933–4; Berlin State Opera 1934–57. Buenos Aires 1936 and 1950; CG début 1936; Salzburg 1939. Wide repertory from Pamina to Jenůfa. A fine Oktavian. Last appearance, Berlin *Lieder* recital 1957.

Léner Quartet. Hung. str. qt. formed in 1918 by 4 members of Budapest Opera Orch.—Jenö Léner (*b* Szabadka, 1894; *d* NY, 1948), Joseph Smilovits, Sandor Roth, and Irme Hartman. Début Budapest 1919, Vienna and Paris 1920, NY 1929. Became one of leading qts. of inter-war period, making first recording of all the Beethoven qts. Disbanded 1942. Reorganized, with partly new membership, 1945, but finally disbanded on Léner's death, 1948.

Lengnick & Co. English music publishing firm founded 1892 by Alfred Lengnick (*d* 1904). Acquired by Schott and became limited co., 1924. Specialists in educational mus. Eng. representatives of Ger. firm Simrock. Among Brit. comps. in its list are Alwyn, Arnold, Maconchy, Rubbra, Simpson, and Wordsworth. In 1991 Complete Music Ltd. bought Lengnick as its classical division. In recent years composers pubd. by them incl. David Ellis, Adam Gorb, and John Veale.

Leningrad Philharmonic Orchestra. See *St Petersburg Philharmonic Orchestra*.

Leningrad Symphony. Sub-title of *Shostakovich's sym. No.7 in C major, Op.60, comp. 1941 during Ger. siege of Leningrad. F.p. Kuibyshev 1942; f. Eng. p. London 1942 cond. Wood. Ballet made from 1st movt., 1961, Kirov Ballet (choreog. Igor Belsky).

lent (Fr.), **lento** (It.). Slow. So *lentando*; *lentato* (It.). slowing, slowed (same as *rallentando*); *lentement* (Fr.), *lentamente* (It.), slowly; *lenteur* (Fr.), *lentezza* (It.), slowness; *lentissimo*, very slow.

Lenya, Lotte [Blamauer, Karoline] (*b* Vienna, 1898; *d* NY, 1981). Austrian-born singer of mezzo-soprano quality (Amer. cit.). Went to Zurich 1914. Member of *corps de ballet*, Zurich Stadttheater and made stage acting début at Schauspielhaus. Moved to Berlin 1920, where she met the playwright Bertolt *Brecht and the composer Kurt *Weill, whose wife she became in 1926. Singing début Baden-Baden 1927 (*Mahagonny*). Created Jenny in *Die Dreigroschenoper*, Berlin 1928. Her distinctive singing style and accomplished acting made a major contribution to the success of the Brecht–Weill collaborations, especially in such songs as 'Pirate Jenny', 'Surabaya Johnny' and 'Alabama Song'. With Weill, went to USA in 1933 and made new career in plays and films, incl. *From Russia with Love*.

Leonard, Lawrence (*b* London, 1925; *d* Hanpstead, London, 2001). Eng. conductor. Ass. cond. BBC Northern SO. Assoc. cond. Hallé 1964–6; cond. and mus. dir. Edmonton SO, Canada, 1969–74. Cond. f.p. in Eng. of *West Side Story*, 1958.

Leoncavallo, Ruggiero (*b* Naples, 1857; *d* Montecatini, 1919). It. composer. Completed first opera, *Chatterton*, in 1876 and planned trilogy on Renaissance Italy of which only 1st part *I Medici* (1893) was written. Was café pianist for many years, travelling through Eur. and settling in Paris. Fame rests on successful *Pagliacci* (Milan 1892, cond. Toscanini). His *La *bohème* (1897) suffered from comparison with Puccini's, prod. 15 months earlier. Wrote series of operettas, but failed to win an audience. Last opera was *Edipo Re* (Chicago 1920). His *Zazà* (Milan 1900) has been revived, notably at Wexford 1990 (as was his *La bohème* in 1994).

Leonhardt, Gustav (*b* 's Graveland, Holland, 1928). Dutch harpsichordist, organist, and conductor. Début Vienna 1950. Prof. of hpd., Vienna Acad. 1952–5, Amsterdam Cons. from 1954. Ed. of Bach's *Die Kunst der Fuge*, and works of Sweelinck. Founded Leonhardt Consort 1955. Has cond. opera in addition to many concerts.

Leoni, Franco (*b* Milan, 1864; *d* Hampstead, 1949). It. composer. Settled in London 1891–1914 and in later years. Comp. 3 oratorios, all perf. in London, and several operas, best-known being *L'*Oracolo* (London 1905).

Leoni, Leone (*b* Verona, *c*.1560; *d* Vicenza, 1627). It. composer. Choirmaster, Vicenza Cath., from 1588. Wrote 180 motets and 120 madrigals for double ch. Some motets had instr. acc.

Leonore. Beethoven's intended title for his opera *Fidelio* (but not used at 1805 f.p. as is sometimes supposed) and the name of its heroine. The 3 ovs. are known in Eng. as *Leonora* (see *Fidelio*).

Léonore, ou L'Amour conjugal (Leonora, or Married Love). Opera in 2 acts by *Gaveaux to text by J. N. Bouilly. Prod. Paris 1798. First setting of story used by Paër (1804), Mayr (1805), and Beethoven (*Fidelio*, 1805).

Leopold I (*b* Vienna, 1640; *d* Vienna, 1705). Emperor of Austria who reigned 1658–1705. Patron of mus., esp. opera. Comp. instr. sonatas, etc.

Leopold II (*b* Vienna, 1747; *d* Vienna, 1792). Emperor of Austria who reigned 1790–2. Grand Duke of Tuscany 1765–90, influencing mus. life there and in Vienna. Paid for perfs. of several innovatory operas by *Traetta. On succeeding his brother Joseph II, he began a major reform of Viennese court opera, introducing singers from Florence.

Leppard, Raymond (John) (*b* London, 1927). Eng.-born conductor, composer, harpsichordist, and musicologist (Amer. cit.). Début London 1952 and often cond. Goldsbrough Orch. (later ECO). CG début 1959 (Handel's *Solomon*), Glyndebourne 1962; SW 1965. Prin. cond. BBC Northern SO 1973–80. Amer. (concert) début NY 1969, opera début Santa Fe 1974; NY Met 1978. Settled in USA 1976. Prin. guest cond. St Louis SO 1984–90, mus. dir. Indianapolis SO 1987–2001. Editorial realizations of Monteverdi's *Ballo delle Ingrate*

(1958), *L'incoronazione di Poppea* (1962), *Orfeo* (1965), and *Il ritorno d'Ulisse* (1972), and of Cavalli's *Messa Concertata* (1966), *Ormindo* (1967), *Calisto* (1969), *Egisto* (1974), *Orione* (1980), also *Magnificat* (1970). These have been criticized on the grounds that they are harmonically too rich, musicologically too imprecise, contain too many transpositions, and too much music comp. by Leppard, but there is no doubt that they popularized baroque opera and paved the way for other, more austere, editions. Also effective cond. of standard orch. repertoire. CBE 1983. Wrote *The Real Authenticity* (London 1988) and *Raymond Leppard on Music: an Anthology of Critical and Personal Writings* (1993).

Lerchenquartett (Lark Quartet). Nickname of Haydn's str. qt. in D, No.11 of the *Tostquartette*; it is sometimes described as Op.64, *No.5. Its nickname is derived from the opening. The rhythm of the last movement has given rise to another, less frequently used, nickname, the 'Hornpipe' Qt.

Le Roux, François (*b* Rennes, 1955). Fr. baritone. Sang with Opéra de Lyon 1980–5. Paris Opéra début 1985, as Debussy's Pelléas, the role in which he first appeared at La Scala (1986), Vienna (1988), Helsinki (1989), and Cologne (1992). Glyndebourne début 1987; CG 1988. Created title-role in Birtwistle's *Gawain* (CG 1991).

Leroux, Xavier (Henry Napoléon) (*b* Velletri, It., 1863; *d* Paris, 1919). Fr. composer. *Prix de Rome* 1885. Prof. of harmony, Paris Cons., 1896–1919. Wrote series of operas incl. *Evangéline* (1895), *La Reine Fiammette* (1903), *William Ratcliff* (1905), *Le Chemineau* (1906), and *Le fille de Figaro* (1913–14). Ed. periodical *Musica*.

Les Adieux (Beethoven). See *Lebewohl, Das*.

Leschetizky, Theodor [Leszetycki, Teodor] (*b* Lancut, Poland, 1830; *d* Dresden, 1915). Polish pianist, teacher, and composer. Public début at age of 10. Dir. of pf. studies, St Petersburg Cons. 1862–78, then settled in Vienna, where est. own sch. Retired from concert-giving 1886. Developed a teaching 'method' and attracted pupils from the world over. Among them were *Paderewski, *Schnabel, *Moiseiwitsch, and *Gabrilowitsch. Wrote 2 operas and pf. pieces.

lesson. Term used in 17th and 18th cents. for short kbd. piece or exercise, and often synonymous with sonata.

lesto (It.). Quick. So *lestamente*, quickly; *lestissimo*, very quickly.

Le Sueur, Jean François (*b* Drucat-Plessiel, nr. Abbéville, 1760; *d* Paris, 1837). Fr. composer. Held church posts, becoming choirmaster of Nôtre Dame, Paris, 1786, and engaging large orch. to dramatize perfs. of masses and motets. Dismissed 1788 because of opposition aroused. From 1792 wrote *grands opéras*. Inspector, Paris Cons. 1795–1802. Succeeded Paisiello as Choirmaster to Napoleon, 1804–30. Prof. of comp., Paris Cons., from 1818. Pupils incl. Berlioz.

Lesur, Daniel. See *Daniel-Lesur, Yves*.

Let's Make an Opera. 'Entertainment for young people', Op.45 by Britten, lib. by Eric Crozier. In 2 parts, first being preparations by children and adults to put on an opera, second being the opera itself, *The Little Sweep* (acc. for str. qt., pf. 4 hands, and perc.). Audience participates in 4 songs. Comp. and f.p. Aldeburgh 1949; St Louis 1950.

Let us Garlands Bring. Song-cycle of 5 songs by *Finzi for bar. and pf. (or orch.) to words by Shakespeare. Comp. 1929–42. F.p. London, 12 Oct. 1942, on 70th birthday of Vaughan Williams, to whom it is dedicated. 1. *Come away, death* (1938); 2. *Who is Sylvia?* (1929); 3. *Fear no more the heat o' the sun* (1929); 4. *O mistress mine* (1942); 5. *It was a lover and his lass* (1940).

letzt (Ger.). Last, e.g. *Vier letzte Lieder*, Four Last Songs (Strauss).

Leutgeb, Ignaz (Joseph) (*b* ?Salzburg, *c*.1745; *d* Vienna, 1811). Austrian hornplayer for whom Mozart wrote his 4 hn. concs. 1st hn. in archbishop's orch. at Salzburg from 1770, but was given leave to play in Paris, Vienna, and Milan. Settled in Vienna 1777 when he inherited a cheese-shop.

Levant, Oscar (*b* Pittsburgh, 1906; *d* Beverly Hills, Calif., 1972). Amer. pianist and composer. Settled in Hollywood in 1920s, becoming close friend and interpreter of *Gershwin. Career as wit on radio and TV and as film actor. Author of entertaining books. Wrote 2 pf. concs., str. qt., etc.

levare (It.). To lift, or take off (past participle *levato*, plural *levati*; imperative *levate*). *Si levano i sordini*, the mutes are taken off.

Leventritt Competition. Int. competition, alternately for violinists and pianists, est. 1939 by Leventritt Foundation, NY, in memory of Edgar M. Leventritt, lawyer and patron of mus. Prin. award is series of engagements with major orchs., an honorarium, and offer of recording contract.

Levi, Hermann (*b* Giessen, 1839; *d* Munich, 1900). Ger. conductor. Held cond. posts at Saarbrücken, Rotterdam, and Karlsruhe (1864–72) before becoming chief cond. Munich Opera 1872–96. Fine interpreter of Wagner; cond. f.p. of *Parsifal*, Bayreuth 1882, and mus. at Wagner's funeral. Rev. libs. of Mozart operas and trans. text of Berlioz's *Les Troyens*. Comp. pf. conc.

Levine, James (*b* Cincinnati, 1943). Amer. conductor and pianist. Solo pianist with Cincinnatti SO at age of 10. Ass. cond. to *Szell, Cleveland Orch., 1964–70. NY Met début 1971 (*Tosca*), becoming prin. cond. 1973, mus. dir. 1975, and art. dir. 1986. Cond. Munich PO 1999–2004. Mus. dir. Boston SO from 2004. Cond. Met premières of *I Vespri Siciliani* (1974), *Lulu* (1977), *Idomeneo* (1982), and *Porgy and Bess* (1985). Brit. début Llandudno

(WNO) 1970; Salzburg Fest. début 1975 (concert), opera 1976; Bayreuth début 1982. Cond. *Ring* at NY Met 1989 and Bayreuth 1994.

Levy, Marvin (David) (*b* Newark, NJ, 1932). Amer. composer and critic. Worked as mus. critic 1952–8. Commissioned by NY Met in 1961 to compose opera based on O'Neill's *Mourning Becomes Electra* (f.p. 1967). Composer of 5 operas, choral works, sym., pf. conc., chamber mus.

Lewenthal, Raymond (*b* S. Antonio, Texas, 1926; *d* Hudson, NY, 1988). Amer. pianist, writer, musicologist, and editor. Specialist in Liszt and neglected 19th-cent. composers. Ed. pf. mus. of *Alkan.

Lewis, (Sir) **Anthony** (Carey) (*b* Bermuda, 1915; *d* Haslemere, 1983). Eng. conductor, composer, editor, and teacher. On BBC mus. staff 1935–46. Prof. of Mus., Birmingham Univ. 1947–68. Prin., RAM 1968–82. Composer of hn. and tpt. concs. Founder and ed. *Musica Britannica.* Cond. of many Handel opera revivals. Ed. of Handel operas, Purcell's *Fairy Queen*, etc. CBE 1967. Knighted 1972.

Lewis, Henry (*b* Los Angeles, 1932; *d* NY, 1996). Amer. conductor, clarinettist, and double-bass player. Db. in Los Angeles PO. Member and later cond. US 7th Army SO 1955–7. Founder and dir. String Soc. of Los Angeles (later Los Angeles Chamber Orch.). Ass. cond. Los Angeles PO 1961–5, mus. dir. Los Angeles Opera Co. 1965–8. Prin. cond. NJ SO 1968–76. NY Met début 1972 (*La bohème*), first black cond. to work there. Chief cond. Dutch Radio SO, Hilversum, from 1989.

Lewis, Jeffrey (*b* Port Talbot, 1942). Welsh composer, organist, pianist, and teacher. Pianist, Paris Chamber Ens. 1967–8. Lect. in 20th-cent. comp. City of Leeds Coll. of Mus. 1969–72. Lect., Mus. Dept., Univ. Coll. of N. Wales, Bangor, 1973–87, senior lect. 1987–92. Comps. incl. *Aurora, Fanfares with Variations, Mutations* I (orch.), II (organ); *Sonante*, cl., pf. (1985); *Lux Perpetua* (1992); *Antiphon*, tpts., org. (1994).

Lewis, Keith (*b* Methven, NZ, 1950). NZ tenor. Won Ferrier memorial schol. 1976, John Christie Award 1979. From 1976 sang with Chelsea Opera Group and Eng. Bach Fest. GTO début 1977 (Don Ottavio in *Don Giovanni*). Glyndebourne 1978; CG 1978; ENO 1982; S. Francisco 1984; Salzburg Fest. début 1989. Also concert career.

Lewis, Paul (*b* Liverpool, 1973). Eng. pianist. Studied at Chetham's Sch. of Mus., Manchester, and GSMD. Pupil of Brendel from 1993. Specialist in Beethoven, Mozart, and Schubert.

Lewis, Richard [Thomas, Thomas] (*b* Manchester, 1914; *d* Eastbourne, 1990). Eng. tenor and conductor. Opera début with Carl Rosa co. 1939 (Almaviva in *Il barbiere di Siviglia*). Began concert career in Denmark 1946. Eng. concert début Brighton 1947. Glyndebourne début 1947. Sang Peter Grimes at CG 1947 and Albert Herring with EOG 1948. Created role of Troilus in *Troilus*

and Cressida CG 1954 and at S. Francisco 1955, and roles of Mark (*The Midsummer Marriage*, 1955) and Achilles (*King Priam*, 1962). Sang in f.p. of Stravinsky's *Canticum Sacrum*, Venice 1956. Sang Aron in *Moses und Aron* at CG 1965, in Boston (stage) 1966, and in Paris 1973. Successful concert career in oratorio, esp. Gerontius which he recorded with both Barbirolli and Sargent. Took up cond. 1975. CBE 1963.

Leygraf, Hans (*b* Stockholm, 1920). Swed. pianist, composer, and conductor. Début 1929 with Stockholm SO. Specialist in Mozart; on teaching staff Salzburg Mozarteum from 1956. Composer of pf., orch., and chamber works.

lezginka. A dance of the Mohammedan tribe the Lezghins (on the Persian border).

LGSMD. Licentiate of the Guildhall School of Music and Drama.

LH. Abbreviation for Left Hand.

Lhévinne, Josef (*b* Orel, 1874; *d* NY, 1944). Russ. pianist and teacher. Début, Moscow 1889 (Beethoven 5th conc.). Prof. of pf., Moscow Cons. 1902–6. NY début 1906 with Russ. SO. Many world tours. Lived in Ger. 1907–19, settled in USA 1920. Salzburg Fest. 1932. On teaching staff Juilliard Sch. from 1922.

Lhévinne, (*née* Bessie), **Rosina** (*b* Kiev, 1880; *d* Glendale, Calif., 1976). Russ. pianist and teacher. Wife of Josef *Lhévinne, whom she married in 1898 on leaving Moscow Cons. Toured widely, gave many recitals with husband. Still gave recitals in mid-1960s. On staff Juilliard Sch. from 1922. Pupils incl. Van Cliburn, James Levine, Garrick Ohlsson, and John Browning.

Liadov, Anatol. See *Lyadov, Anatol.*

liberamente (It.). Freely (i.e. with regard to tempo, rhythm, etc.).

libretto (It.). Little book. The text of a vocal work, particularly opera. Author is 'librettist'. First known was for Peri's *Dafne* (1594–8). Among famous librettists have been *Metastasio, *da Ponte, Scribe, Romani, Piave, *Illica, *Gilbert, *Boito, *Hofmannsthal, Auden and Kallman, and Myfanwy Piper. Some composers have written own libs., e.g. Wagner, Leoncavallo, Delius, and Tippett.

licenza (It.). Licence, freedom (in such expressions as *con alcuna licenza*, with some licence, i.e. freedom as to tempo and rhythm or to form of a work).

Licette, Miriam (*b* Chester, 1892; *d* Twyford, 1969). Eng. soprano. Début Rome 1911 (Butterfly). Member of Beecham co. 1916–20, BNOC 1922–8. Sang in CG int. seasons 1919–29.

Lichnowsky, (Prince) **Karl** (*b* Vienna, 1761; *d* Vienna, 1814). Austrian aristocrat of Polish descent. Patron of mus., maintaining str. qt. and sponsoring orch. concerts at his entertainments.

Pupil and patron of Mozart, who accomp. him to Prague, Leipzig, Dresden, and Berlin 1789. Beethoven's Opp. 1, 13, 26, and 36 are ded. to him. Employed str. qt. led by Schuppanzigh which gave f.ps. of qts. by Haydn and Beethoven.

Lichnowsky, (Count) **Moritz** (b Vienna, 1771; d Vienna, 1837). Austrian aristocrat, brother of Prince Karl. Intimate friend of Beethoven, whose Opp. 35, 51, and 90 are ded. to him and his wife. Was also patron of Chopin.

Licht: Die sieben Tage der Woche (Light: The Seven Days of the Week). Cycle of seven operas by *Stockhausen, one for each day of the week, composed 1977–2003, for various combinations of solo voices and instrs., solo dancers, choruses, orchestras, ballet, mime, and elec. Many of the acts can be performed separately:

Montag aus Licht (*Monday from Light*), in greeting, 3 acts, and farewell, comp. 1984–8, f.p. Milan 1988.

Dienstag aus Licht (*Tuesday from Light*), in greeting, 2 acts, and farewell, comp. 1977, 1987–91, f.p. Leipzig 1993.

Mittwoch aus Licht (*Wednesday from Light*), in greeting, 4 scenes, and farewell, comp. 1995–7.

Donnerstag aus Licht (*Thursday from Light*), in greeting, 3 acts, and farewell, comp. 1978–80, f.p. Milan (La Scala) 1981. Act 2, *Michaels Reise um der Erde* (*Michael's Journey around the Earth*) has been perf. as a tpt. conc.

Freitag aus Licht (*Friday from Light*), in greeting, 2 acts, and farewell, comp. 1991–4, f.p. Leipzig 1996.

Samstag aus Licht (*Saturday from Light*), in greeting and 4 scenes, comp. 1981–3, f.p. Milan 1984.

Sontag aus Licht (*Sunday from Light*), in 6 scenes and a farewell, comp. 1998–2003.

lié (Fr.). Bound, i.e. (1) Slurred; (2) Tied.

Liebe der Danae, Die (The Love of Danae). Opera in 3 acts by R. Strauss, comp. 1938–40 to lib. by J. Gregor using a draft by Hofmannsthal. Prod. Salzburg 1952, London 1953, Los Angeles 1964 (in Eng.). But dress reh. was given at Salzburg 1944 in Strauss's presence, before ths. were closed by Nazi edict.

Liebermann, Lowell (b NY, 1961). Amer. composer, conductor, and pianist. Début as pianist NY (Carnegie Hall) 1978. Youngest comp. to receive Ives Schol. 1980. Grand prize, Delius comp. competition 1987. Ives Fellowship, Amer. Acad. and Inst. of Arts and Letters, 1990. Comps. incl. opera (*The Picture of Dorian Grey*, 1995); 2 syms. (1982, 1999); 3 pf. concs. (1983, 1992, 2006); conc. for vn., pf., str. qt. (1989); vn. conc. (2001); conc. for orch. (2002); 2 str. qts. (1979, 1998); 3 pf. sonatas (1977, 1983, 2002); 3 vc. sonatas (1978, 1998, 2005); pf. quintet (1990); *Missa brevis*, ten., bar., ch., org. (1985); song-cycles; kbd. solos.

Liebermann, Rolf (b Zurich, 1910; d Paris, 1999). Swiss composer, pupil of *Vogel. Head of orch.

div., Swiss Radio 1950–7, head of mus. N. Ger. Radio, Hamburg, 1957–9, dir. Hamburg Opera 1959–73 and 1985–8, Paris Opéra 1973–80. Champion of modern works, his Hamburg years seeing many splendid prods. of new operas by Einem, Searle, Menotti, Henze, Penderecki, Kagel, and others. Used 12-note system in his own works which incl.: operas: *Leonore 40/45* (Basle 1952), *Penelope* (Salzburg 1954), *The School for Wives* (Louisville 1955, rev. as *Die Schule der Frauen*, Salzburg 1957), *La forêt* (1987), *Acquittal for Medea* (1995, rev. as *Medea*, 1998); orchestral: *Furioso* (1947), Sym. No.1 (1949), conc. for jazz band and sym. orch. (1954); also pf. quintet (1987); and songs.

Lieberson, Lorraine Hunt. See *Hunt Lieberson, Lorraine.*

Lieberson, Peter (b NY, 1946). Amer. composer. Son of ballerina Vera Zorina. Studied at Columbia Univ. 1972–6 with Babbitt, Wuorinen, and Martino, later at Boulder, Colorado, with Chogyam Trungpa. Works incl. pf. conc. (1980); va. conc. (1982); *Drala*, orch. (1986); *The Gesar Legend*, orch. (1988); *The World's Turning*, orch. (1991); *King Gesar*, opera (1992); *The Five Great Elements*, orch. (1995); *Processional*, orch. (1995); *Ashoka's Dream*, opera (1996–7); *6 Realms*, vc. conc. (2000); *Rilke Songs*, mez., orch. (2001); *Ah*, orch. (2002); pf. conc. No.3 (2003); *Neruda Songs*, mez., orch. (2005).

Liebesgeige (Ger.) . Love-fiddle. *Viola d'amore.

Liebesliederwalzer (Love-song waltzes). Brahms's Op.52 (containing 18 waltzes) for pf. duet with 4 vv. (SATB) *ad lib.* 1868–9. Op.52a (1874) is minus the vocal parts. Followed in 1874 and 1877 by the *Neue Liebesliederwalzer*, also with v. parts *ad lib.*

Liebesmahl der Apostel, Das (The Love-Feast of the Apostles). 'Biblical scene' for male ch. and orch. (which enters late in the work) by Wagner, who also wrote the text. Comp. 1843. F.p. Dresden 1843.

Liebesoboe (Ger.). Love-oboe, i.e. oboe d'amore. (See *oboe family.*)

Liebestod (Ger.). Love-death. Title generally applied to Isolde's aria at end of Act III of Wagner's *Tristan und Isolde* (or to orch. arr. of it, often played as concert-piece with the Prelude to Act 1). But Wagner applied the term to the love duet in Act II.

Liebesträume (Love-dreams). 3 nocturnes for pf. (c.1850) by *Liszt, the 3rd in A♭ being the best-known. They are transcrs. of his songs *Hohe Liebe* (c.1849), *Gestorben war ich* (c.1849), and *O Liebe, so lang du lieben kannst.* (c.1845).

Liebesverbot, Das (The Ban on Love). Opera in 2 acts by Wagner to his own lib. based on Shakespeare's *Measure for Measure* (1604–5). Comp. 1835–6. Prod. Magdeburg 1836, Munich 1923, London 1965 (abridged), Wexford 1994 (abridged).

Lieblich Gedackt (from Ger. *Lieblich*, 'lovely'). Org. stop, same as *Gedackt.*

Lied, Lieder (Ger.). Song, songs. *Lieder* have existed since before 1400, but they are principally associated in the public mind with a distinctive type of Ger. solo vocal comp. which came into being as an outcome of the Romantic movt. of the late 18th and early 19th cents. In this type the quality of the verse selected is very important. The treatment of the poem may be either 'verse-repeating' (strophic) or 'through-composed' (*durchkomponiert*) (i.e. either the same for every stanza or different for each), according to the lyrical or dramatic demands of the poem. The pf. part (simple or highly elaborate) is more than a mere acc. and, as much as the vocal part, demands artistic interpretation. Some great names in the history of *Lieder* are *Schubert, J. *Loewe, *Schumann, *Franz, *Brahms, *Wolf, *Mahler, and *Strauss. Certain poets recur frequently in these composers' *Lieder*, e.g. Goethe, Dehmel, Eichendorff, Heine, Hesse, Liliencron, Mayrhofer, Mörike, Rilke, Rückert, Schack, Schiller, Trakl, Tieck. A *Lieder* recital should correctly contain only Ger. songs. A succinct appreciation of singing *Lieder* has been made by Peter *Stadlen: 'The elusive art of suggesting the dramatic content of a text by other than operatic means.'

Lieder eines fahrenden Gesellen (Songs of a Wayfarer). Song-cycle of 4 songs by Mahler to his own poems (based on, or imitative of, *Des *Knaben Wunderhorn*) for bar. or mez. and pf. or orch. The movements are: 1, *Wenn mein Schatz Hochzeit macht* (When my sweetheart has her wedding); 2. *Ging heut' Morgen übers Feld* (I walked this morning through the fields); 3. *Ich hab' ein glühend Messer* (I have a gleaming knife); 4. *Die zwei blauen Augen* (Her two blue eyes). Comp. 1884, orch. and rev. 1892–3, further rev. 1896. F.p. Berlin 1896. Thematically linked to First Sym.

Liederkranz (Ger.). Song-wreath, i.e. *song-cycle.

Liederkreis (Ger.). General term for song-cycle; used specifically by Schumann for 2 sets of songs, his 9 Heine settings, Op.24, and his 12 Eichendorff settings, Op.39, both 1840. Term first used by Beethoven to describe *An die ferne Geliebte*.

Liedertafel (plural *Liedertafeln*) (Ger.). Song table. Name given to Ger. male-v. singing socs. which flourished in the nationalistic climate of the early 19th cent. Originally convivial occasions at which the members sat round a table with refreshments, but the aims later became more artistic. Particularly assoc. with expatriates.

Liederzyklus (Ger.). *Song-cycle.

Lied ohne Worte (Ger.; Fr. *Chanson sans paroles*). Song without words. Term introduced by Mendelssohn to describe pf. solo in which song-like melody progresses against acc. Pubd. in 8 books each containing 6 pieces: *Book 1*, Op.19, 1829–30; *Book 2*, Op.30, 1835; *Book 3*, Op.38, 1837; *Book 4*, Op.53, 1841; *Book 5*, Op.62; *Book 6*, Op.67, 1843–5; *Book 7*, Op.85, 1842; *Book 8*, Op.102, 1842–5. Most of the titles given to these pieces were not Mendelssohn's, but the 3 *Venetian Gondola Songs* were. He also wrote a *Lied ohne Worte* for vc. and pf., Op.109.

Lied von der Erde, Das (The Song of the Earth). Sym. for cont. (or bar.), ten., and orch. by Mahler, being settings of 6 Ger. versions by Hans Bethge (with additions by Mahler) of Chinese poems (some wrongly attrib. by Bethge). The movts. are: 1. *Das Trinklied vom Jammer der Erde* (Drinking-Song of Earth's Sorrow); 2. *Der Einsame im Herbst* (The Lonely One in Autumn); 3. *Von der Jugend* (Of Youth); 4. *Von der Schönheit* (Of Beauty); 5. *Der Trunkene im Frühling* (The Drunkard in Spring); 6. *Der Abschied* (The Farewell). Comp. 1907–9. F.p. Munich 1911, London 1914, Philadelphia 1916.

Lie Strewn the White Flocks. 'Pastoral' by Bliss for mez., ch., and orch. f.p. London 1929. Settings of poems by Jonson, Fletcher, Poliziano, Theocritus, and Robert Nichols.

Lieutenant Kijé. 5-movt. symphonic suite for orch., Op.60, by Prokofiev, derived from mus. he wrote for film of same name. Comp. 1934; suite f.p. Paris 1937.

Life for the Tsar, A (*Zhizn' za tsarya*). Opera in 4 acts and epilogue by *Glinka to lib. by Baron Yegor Rosen and others on subject suggested by poet Zhukovsky. Comp. 1834–6. Prod. St Petersburg 1836; London 1887; S. Francisco 1936. Prague prod. of 1866 was first perf. of Russ. opera abroad. Orig. title was *Ivan Susanin*, the peasant who, by misleading Polish troops in 1613, saved life of Tsar Mikhail, founder of Romanov dynasty, at sacrifice of his own. During rehearsals Tsar Nicholas I visited Bolshoy Th., with result that the opera was ded. to him and he suggested new title. After 1917 revolution, subject was embarrassing to régime and various attempts to adapt mus. to new subjects were made. In 1938 S. M. Gorodetsky re-wrote lib., re-focusing interest on leaders of uprising against Poles and restoring orig. title. Prod. Moscow 1939.

Life's Dance. Tone-poem for orch. by Delius, after Hilge Rode's play *Dansen Gaar*. 1st version 1899 as *La Ronde se déroule* (The Dance goes on), rev. 1901 as *Life's Dance*, final rev. for publication 1912. F.p. of orig., London 1899; 1st rev. Düsseldorf 1904 cond. *Buths, final version Berlin 1912 cond. *Fried.

ligature. (1) The sign which in early notation (13th–16th cent.) combines several notes into one symbol:

(2) The slur which in modern notation of vocal mus. shows that the 2 or more notes it affects are to be fitted to the same syllable, or, in instr. mus., that the notes are to be phrased together. (3) The *tie or bind—a use of the word better avoided as unnecessary and confusing.

(4) The adjustable metal band which in instr. of the cl. family secures the reed to the mouthpiece. Some clarinettists use string ligature.

See *curved line, various uses of*.

Ligendza, Caterina [Beyron, Kattarina] (*b* Stockholm, 1937). Swed. soprano. Opera début Linz 1965 (Countess in *Le nozze di Figaro*). Saarbrucken Opera 1966–9; Deutsche Oper, Berlin, 1970–88. Became notable for Wagner roles. Salzburg Easter Fest. 1969; La Scala 1970; Bayreuth Fest. 1971–7; NY Met 1971; CG début 1972; Vienna 1973. Retired from stage 1988.

Ligeti, András (*b* Hungary, 1953). Hung. conductor. Leader, Hung. State Opera orch. 1976–80. Assoc. cond. Budapest SO from 1985. Brit. début 1989 (BBCSO).

Ligeti, György (Sándor) (*b* Dicsöszentmáron, 1923; *d* Vienna, 2006). Hung.-born composer (Austrian cit. 1967). Lect., Budapest Acad., 1950–6. Left Hungary 1956, going to work first at Cologne EMS 1957–8, then settling in Austria. Lect. at Darmstadt mus. courses 1959–72. Prof. of comp., Hamburg Mus. Acad. 1973–89. Though elec. stimulated his urge to compose, from 1958 he wrote only for 'live' performers. His orch. writing uses precisely calculated textures and dense (but not thick) scoring, deriving ultimately from Webern (Ligeti's term is 'micropolyphony'). Prin. works:

OPERA: Le **Grand Macabre* (1972–6, rev. 1995, in 2 acts, f.p. Stockholm 1978).

ORCH.: *Apparitions* (1958–9); **Atmosphères* (1961); **Lontano* (1967); **Melodien* (1971); **San Francisco Polyphony* (1973–4).

SOLOIST & ORCH.: vc. conc. (1966); double conc., fl., ob. (1972); pf. conc. (1985–8); vn. conc. (1990, 1992); hn. conc. (1998–9, rev. 2003).

CHORAL: *Requiem*, sop., mez., 2 ch., orch. (1963–5); *Lux aeterna*, 16-part ch. (1966); *Clocks and Clouds*, 12-voice women's ch., orch. (1972–3); *Scenes and Interludes from Le Grand Macabre*, sop., mez., ten., bar., opt. ch., orch. (1978); *Nonsense Madrigals*, 6 vv. (1988).

SMALL ORCH.: *Ballad and Dance on Romanian Folk Songs* (1949–50); *6 Miniatures*, 10 wind instr. (1953, scored 1975 by F. Wanek); *Fragment*, 11 instr. (1961); *Adventures*, 3 singers, 7 instr. (1962); *Nouvelles Aventures*, 3 singers, 7 instr. (1962–5); **Ramifications*, str., or 12 solo str. (1968–9); Chamber Conc., 13 instr. (1969–70).

CHAMBER MUSIC: vc. sonata (1948–53); 10 *Pieces*, wind quintet (1968); str. qts. No.1 (*Métamorphoses nocturnes*) (1953–4), No.2 (1968); *6 Bagatelles*, wind quintet (1953); hn. trio (*Hommage à Brahms*) (1982); sonata, vn. (1991–4).

KEYBOARD: *Musica Ricercata*, 11 pieces, pf. (1951–3); *Continuum*, hpd. (1968); 3 *Pieces* (*Monument, Selbstporträt, Bewegung*), 2 pf. (1976); *Passacaglia ungherrese*, hpd. (1978); *Hungarian Rock*, hpd. (1978); *Etudes*, Bk.1 (1985), Bk.2 (1988–94), Bk.3 (1995).

ORGAN: *Volumina* (1961–2, rev. 1966); 2 *Studies* (1967, 1969).

MISCELLANEOUS: *Artikulation*, tape (1958); *Poème symphonique*, 100 metronomes (1962); *Horizont*, recorder (1971).

light. Adjective applied somewhat patronizingly and vaguely to mus. which is supposed to need less concentration than 'serious music' (another objectionable term). Thus there are also 'light' orchs. and 'light' opera. 'Light' mus. can refer to Elgar's shorter pieces or to works by composers such as Ronald **Binge. 'Light opera' probably means **Merrie England* rather than *The Merry Widow*, but such classification is imprecise.

Light Cavalry (*Leichte Cavallerie*). Operetta by Suppé, in 2 acts, lib. by C. Costa; prod. Vienna 1866. Ov. exceedingly popular.

Lighthouse, The. Chamber-opera in 1 act with prologue by **Maxwell Davies to his own lib. Comp. 1979. Based on actual event in 1900 when the 3 keepers of the Flannan lighthouse in the Outer Hebrides unaccountably disappeared. F.p. Edinburgh 1980. London 1981, Boston 1983.

Light of Life, The (*Lux Christi*). Oratorio, Op.29, for SATB soloists, ch., and orch. by Elgar to text by E. Capel-Cure. Comp. 1895–6, rev. 1899. F.p. Worcester 1896.

Lights Out. (1) Song-cycle of 6 songs, settings of poems by Edward Thomas (1878–1917) by Ivor **Gurney, comp. 1918–25, for v. and pf.

(2) 4 poems of Edward Thomas for bar. and pf. by R. **Holloway, Op.24, 1974.

Lilac Time (Berté). See *Blossom Time*.

Lilburn, Douglas (Gordon) (*b* Wanganui, NZ, 1915; *d* Wellington, NZ, 2001). NZ composer. Cobbett Prize 1939. Lect. in mus., Victoria Univ. Coll., Wellington, NZ, 1947–79 (prof. from 1970) and dir. of its EMS 1970–9. Comps. incl. 3 syms. (1949, 1951, rev. 1974, 1961) and other orch. works; str. qts.; vn. sonatas; str. trio; pf. sonata; cl. sonata; song-cycles.

Lill, John (Richard) (*b* London, 1944). Eng. pianist. Début London 1963. First prize Moscow Tchaikovsky comp. 1970. Outstanding Beethoven player. OBE 1978.

Lilliburlero. Tune of unknown origin, first appeared in print in 1686 in a book of 'lessons' for the recorder or fl., where it is styled 'Quickstep'. In the following year it achieved popularity set to satirical verses (with the mock Irish word 'Lilliburlero' as a refrain) referring to the appointment to the Lord-Lieutenancy of Ireland of General Talbot, newly-created Earl of Tyrconnel, whose name is mentioned several times. It has remained a song of the Orange party to the present day, set to different words as 'Protestant Boys'. In Purcell's *Musick's Handmaid*, it appears under the title 'A New Irish Tune' as a hpd. piece: Purcell also used it as a **ground bass in mus. for the play *The Gordian Knot unty'd* (1691).

Lima, Luis (*b* Cordoba, Arg., 1948). Arg. tenor. Début Lisbon 1974 (Turiddù in *Cavalleria rusticana*), then sang in Ger. opera houses 1974–6.

LIN

Amer. début NY 1976 (concert); La Scala 1977; NY Met 1978; Salzburg Fest. 1984; CG 1985; S. Francisco 1992.

Lin, Cho-Liang (*b* Taiwan, 1960). Chinese-born violinist (Amer. cit. 1988). First public appearance at age of 7. Won Taiwan nat. youth comp., 1970. First prize in Queen Sofía int. comp., Madrid, 1977. Amer. début 1976 (Philadelphia), London 1976.

Lincoln Center for the Performing Arts. Arts centre in NY with following constituents: Metropolitan Opera House, Avery Fisher (formerly Philharmonic) Hall, Juilliard Sch., State Th. (headquarters of NY City Opera and City Ballet), Repertory Th., Film Soc., and Chamber Mus. Soc. First building to open was Philharmonic Hall, home of NYPO in place of Carnegie Hall, 1962. State Th. opened 1964, new Met 1966, and Juilliard Sch. 1969.

Lincoln Portrait, A. Work for speaker and orch. by Copland, comp. 1942. F.p. Cincinnati, May 1942. Spoken words are taken from speeches and letters of Abraham Lincoln. Proposed perf. at Pres. Eisenhower's inauguration, 1953, was banned because of Copland's alleged Communist sympathies. Among those who have appeared as the spkr. are Eleanor Roosevelt, Adlai Stevenson, Henry Fonda, John Gielgud, Katharine Hepburn, Margaret Thatcher, and Gen. Norman Schwarzkopf.

Lincoln, the Great Commoner. Song by Ives to words by Edwin Markham, ch. and orch. 1912, v. and pf. 1914.

Lind, Jenny (Johanna) (*b* Stockholm, 1820; *d* Malvern Wells, Worcs., 1887). Swed. soprano. Made first stage appearance in Stockholm at age of 10. Début Stockholm Opera 1838 (Agathe in *Der Freischütz*). Dissatisfied with her v., went to Paris 1841 to study with M. P. R. *García. Meyerbeer commended her to Berlin, where she sang Norma, 1844, and sang leading role in Meyerbeer's *Ein Feldlager in Schlesien* (later rev. as *L'*Étoile du Nord*). After singing in Hamburg, Stockholm, Frankfurt, Vienna (1846), and elsewhere, causing a sensation wherever she appeared, she made her London début at Her Majesty's, 1847, as Alice in *Robert le Diable*. In same year created role of Amalia in *I Masnadieri*. Excelled in brilliant coloratura roles (*Sonnambula*, etc.). Retired from opera (last perf. London, May 1849), thereafter singing only in oratorio and concerts. Visited US 1850–2 under auspices of Barnum and acc. by Julius Benedict, the conductor, and Giovanni Belletti, the bar. who had advised her to consult García in 1841. In Boston, Mass., married the cond. Otto *Goldschmidt, returning with him to Dresden 1852–5 and then to London, where she helped him to found the *Bach Choir. Retired 1870. Prof. of singing RCM from 1883. Her voice was remarkable for its purity and agility in cadenzas and ornamentation. Known as 'The Swedish Nightingale'.

Linda di Chamounix. Opera in 3 acts by Donizetti to lib. by Rossi based on *vaudeville La Grâce de Dieu* by d'Ennery and Lemoine (1841). Comp. 1842. Prod. Vienna 1842, London 1843, NY 1847, Wexford 1983.

Lindberg, Magnus (*b* Helsinki, 1958). Finnish composer and pianist. Studied elec. mus. with Osmo Linderman at Sibelius Acad. and at EMS studio in Stockholm. Works incl. *Arabesques*, wind quintet (1978); *Linea d'Ombre*, fl., sax., gui., perc. (1981); *Action-situation-signification*, hn., perc., vc., pf., live elec. (1982); *Zona*, vc., 7 instr. (1983); *Kraft*, orch. and soloist ens. (1983–5); *Metal Work*, accordeon, perc. (1984); *UR*, vn., vc., db., cl., pf., synthesizers, micro-computers (1986); *Faust*, tape (1985); *Twine*, pf. (1988); *Schlagwerk*, 2 pf., 2 perc., live elec. (1988–9); *Kinetics* (1989); *Marea* (1990); *Jeux d'anches* (1990); *Joy* (1990); *Moto* (1990); *Steamboat Bill Jr.* (1990); pf. conc. (1991); *Corrente* (1991–2), II (1994); *Duo concertante* (1992); *Aura*, vc. (1994); *Symphonic Triptych*, pf., str. (*Feria* [1997], *Cantigas* [1997–9], *Parade* [2001]); vc. conc. (1997–9); cl. conc. (2000–1); *Partia*, vc. (2001); *Bright Cecilia*, orch. (2002); Conc. for Orch. (2002–3); *Mano a mano*, gui. (2004); *Sculpture*, orch. (2005); vn. conc. (2006).

Linde, Hans-Martin (*b* Werne, 1930). Ger.-born Swiss recorder-player, flautist, and composer. Solo flautist W. Ger. Radio Cappella Coloniensis 1951–6. On staff of Schola Cantorum, Basle, from 1957, teaching baroque fl. and recorder. Member of Schola Cantorum Basiliensis, cond. of vocal ens. from 1965 and chamber orch. from 1970. Specialist in early mus. Duo with Frans *Brueggen. Formed Linde Consort.

Lindholm [Jonsson], **Berit** (Maria) (*b* Stockholm, 1934). Swedish soprano. Début Stockholm 1963 as Countess in *Le nozze di Figaro*. CG début 1966; Bayreuth 1967–74; Scottish Opera 1971; Amer. début (S. Francisco) 1972; NY Met 1975.

Lindley, Robert (*b* Rotherham, 1776; *d* London, 1855). Eng. cellist, pupil of Cervetto. Prin. cellist of opera orch. in London 1794–1851. Recital partner with *Dragonetti. First prof. of vc. RAM 1822. Comp. vc. pieces.

linear counterpoint. Term used specifically to describe type of 20th-cent. counterpoint with emphasis on the individual strands of the fabric rather than on their harmonic implications—but all counterpoint is by nature linear.

Linke Hand (*Links*) (Ger.). Left hand.

Linley, Thomas (*b* Badminton, 1733; *d* London, 1795). Eng. composer. Taught and gave concerts in Bath. Later joint manager of oratorios at Drury Lane Th., London, which he partly owned from 1776. Wrote mus. for many plays, incl. R. B. Sheridan's *The Duenna* (1775), also songs, cantatas, madrigals, and elegies. Daughter Elizabeth (1754–92), sop., married Sheridan.

Linley, Thomas (*b* Bath, 1756; *d* Grimsthorpe, Lincs., 1778). Eng. composer and violinist, son of

Thomas *Linley. Friend of Mozart. Wrote opera *The Cady of Baghdad* (1778), oratorio, incidental mus. (incl. *The Duenna* with his father), 6 vn. sonatas, at least 20 vn. concs. (only one survives), and songs. Twice painted by Gainsborough. Drowned in boating accident.

Linz Symphony. Mozart's Sym. No.36 in C major (K425), comp. Linz 1783 and first played there.

Lipatti, Dinu (Constantin) (*b* Bucharest, 1917; *d* Geneva, 1950). Romanian pianist and composer. 2nd prize, Vienna int. contest 1934. On staff Geneva Cons. 1943–6. Superb artist, whose career was ended by leukaemia. Visited Eng. 4 times 1946–8. Comp. concertino for pf. and chamber orch. (1936), *Romanian Dances* for orch., and pf. sonata for left hand (1941).

Lipkin, Malcolm (Leyland) (*b* Liverpool, 1932). Eng. pianist and composer. Début as pianist, Holland 1951, London 1952. Extramural lect., Oxford Univ. 1965–75, Kent Univ. from 1975. Prin. works:

ORCH.: syms.: No.1 (*Sinfonia di Roma*) (1958–65), No.2 (*The Pursuit*) (1975–9), No.3 (*Sun*) (1979–86); pf. conc. (1957); vn. conc. No.1 (1951–2), No. 2 (1960–2); fl. conc. (1974); *Pastorale*, hn. and str. (1963, rev. 1979); *Mosaics* (1966, rev. 1969); ob. conc. (1989); *From Across La Manche*, str. (1998); *Festivo*, str. (2004).

CHORAL & VOCAL: *Psalm 96*, ch., orch. (1969); *The White Crane*, young vv., orch. (1972); *Five Songs*, sop., pf. (1978); *The Knight of the Grail*, alto, female vv., pf. (1993).

CHAMBER MUSIC: str. qt. (1951); vn. sonata No.1 (1957), No.2 (1997); *Suite*, fl., vc. (1961); str. trio (1963–4); *Interplay*, treble recorder, va. da gamba, hpd., perc. (1975); *Clifford's Tower*, fl., ob., cl., bn., hn., vn., va., vc. (1977); *Pastorale*, hn. (or ob.), pf. (1979); *Naboth's Vineyard*, recorders, vc., hpd. (1981–2); wind quintet (1985); pf. trio (1988); *Variations on a Theme of Bartók*, str. qt. (1989–90); *Dance Fantasy*, vn. (1991); *5 Bagatelles*, ob., pf. (1993); *Pierrot Dances*, va., pf. (1998); *Little Suite*, fl., pf. (2000); *3 Pieces for Children*, instr. ens. (2001–3).

PIANO: sonata No.3 (1951, rev. 1979), No.4 (1955, rev. 1987), No.5 (1986), No.6 (2002); *Nocturne* No.1 (1987), No.2 (1995), No.3 (1999), No.4 (2000), No.5 (2001), No.6 (2002).

Lipovšek, Marjana (*b* Ljubljana, 1946). Slovene mezzo-soprano. Joined Vienna Opera 1979. Member of Bavarian State Opera, Munich, from 1983. Salzburg Fest. début 1981 (Emilie in f.p. of Cerha's *Baal*). Created Rosa Sacchi in Penderecki's *Die schwarze Maske*, Salzburg 1986. London début 1988; CG début 1990; NY Met 1990.

Lipp, Wilma (*b* Vienna, 1925). Austrian soprano. Début Vienna 1943 (Rosina in *Il barbiere di Siviglia*). Vienna State Opera from 1945. Salzburg Fest. début 1948; CG 1951; Bayreuth 1951; Glyndebourne 1957; S. Francisco 1962.

Lipton, Martha (*b* NY, 1916). Amer. mezzo-soprano. Début as recitalist. Opera début NY 1941 (Pauline in *Queen of Spades*). NY City Opera début 1944; NY Met 1944. Made nearly 300 appearances at Met 1941–61. Sang in Amer. première of Wolf's *Der Corregidor*, NY 1952 (concert). Guest singer in Vienna and Paris. Prof. of singing, Indiana Univ. Sch. of Mus. from 1960.

lira (It.). (1) The *lyre.

(2) One of names indiscriminately applied in medieval times to various bowed str. instrs., e.g. *rebec* and *vielle*.

(3) Part of compound name of such old instr. as *lira da braccio*, offshoot of the fiddle which evolved in 2nd half of 15th cent. and in size approximated to modern va. It had 7 str., incl. 2 drones, and was used by recitalists who improvised polyphonic accs. It was played against the shoulder, like a vn. Leonardo da Vinci played it. From it developed the *lirone* or *lira da gamba*, a combination of bass viol and lira da braccio, held between knees like a vc. It had drone strs., and from 9 to 14 stopped str., tuned in 4ths, 5ths, and octaves. Used in court entertainments *c*.1550–1650, and in *intermedii*.

lira organizzata (It.). Organ lyre. Obsolete str. instr. like hurdy-gurdy, in which wooden wheel replaced bow and small org. attachment was built into body to enrich tone-colour effects. Haydn wrote 6 concs. (of which 5 survive) *c*.1786 and 9 *Notturnos* (of which 8 survive) for 2 *lire organizzate* in 1788–90 for King Ferdinand IV of Naples who enjoyed playing duets with his teacher. The 2nd and 4th movts. of his Sym. No.89 in F are revs. of material used in the 5th of these concs., and the 2nd movt. of his Sym. No.100 ('Military') originated in 3rd conc.

Lisle, Claude Joseph. See *Rouget de Lisle, Claude Joseph*.

Lisley, John (*fl*. 17th cent.). Eng. composer. Madrigal *Fair Cytherea* incl. in *The *Triumphs of Oriana*.

List, Eugene (*b* Philadelphia, 1918; *d* NY, 1985). Amer. pianist. Début with Los Angeles PO 1930. Gave f. Amer. p. of Shostakovich's 1st conc., Philadelphia 1934. Played at Potsdam Conference, July 1945, in presence of Churchill, Truman, and Stalin. Champion of *Gottschalk. Prof. of pf., Eastman Sch. of Mus. 1964–75, then at NY Univ.

l'istesso (It.). See *istesso*.

Liszt, Ferencz [Franz] (baptized as Franciscus) (*b* Raiding, Hung., 1811; *d* Bayreuth, 1886). Hung. composer and pianist. A child prodigy, he gave his first pf. recital at age 9. Went to Vienna in 1821, having lessons from Salieri and Czerny. Played in Paris 1823 and London 1824 (where he was received by George IV). Returned to Eng. in 1825 and 1826; operetta *Don Sanche* was prod. in Paris, 1825, where he lived 1823–35, becoming friend of Berlioz and Chopin and of leading literary figures and painters. His fame as a virtuoso pianist, flamboyant in style and taste, was at its height. From 1833 he lived with Countess Marie d'Agoult; of their 3 children, Cosima (b 1837) became the wife of *Bülow and then of *Wagner. He returned to Vienna in 1838 and to London in 1840 and 1841. Until 1847 he toured widely, incl. Russia, his mistress by now being Princess Carolyn Sayn-Wittgenstein.

In 1848 he became Kapellmeister at the Weimar court, staying until 1859. In this decade he made Weimar a pre-eminent mus. centre, conducting a vast number of works, notably by Berlioz and by his friend Wagner whom he had met in 1842. In 1850 he conducted the f.p. of *Lohengrin. These were also rich years for Liszt's own work; he wrote his Faust and Dante syms., 12 symphonic poems, and much else. From 1860 Liszt lived in Rome in the Villa d'Este, and in 1865 took minor orders, becoming the Abbé Liszt. He comp. much religious mus. at this period, incl. The Legend of St. Elizabeth and Christus. From 1869 he divided his time between Rome, Weimar, and Budapest, and his amorous adventures were still the talk of Europe. In the last 5 years of his life he concentrated on teaching, his pupils incl. *Ziloti, *Lamond, *Rosenthal, and *Weingartner, and entered a new and important compositional phase in which his harmonic innovations, always a significant feature, anticipated the 'impressionism' of Debussy, e.g. in Nuages gris and the Csárdás macabre. In 1886 he made a 'jubilee tour' to mark his 75th birthday, revisiting Paris and London.

As a pianist, Liszt was, from all reliable accounts, among the greatest, if not the greatest, there has ever been. His comps. have taken longer to win a rightful place, but they are now recognized as occupying a high place for their own virtues as well as for their undoubted influence on Wagner, R. Strauss, and subsequent composers. The pf. works are in a category of their own, the symphonic poems developed a new art-form, the syms. are compelling and imaginative, the religious works are moving and visionary, and the songs hold their own in high company. He remains a romantic enigma of mus., a genius with a touch of the charlatan, a virtuoso with the flair of an actor-manager, a man generous to colleagues and to the young. His championship of Wagner in the Weimar years, with its subsequent effect on Brahms and Schumann, thereby causing the great schism in 19th-cent. mus., had incalculable results on the art. Prin. works:

OPERA: Don Sanche (1824–5, collab. Paer).

SYMPHONIES: A *Faust Symphony, for ten., male ch., orch. (1854–7, rev. 1880); *Dante Symphony (1855–6, with choral Magnificat as last movt.).

SYMPHONIC-POEMS: Ce qu'on entend sur la montagne ('Bergsymphonie') (What one hears on the mountain) (1848–9, orch. Raff, rev. 1850, 1854); Tasso: lamento e trionfo (1849, orch. Conradi, rev. 1850–1, orch. Raff, rev. 1854); Les *Préludes (1848, rev. before 1854); *Orpheus (1853–4); *Prometheus (1850, orch. Raff, rev. 1855); *Mazeppa (1851, orch. with Raff, rev. before 1854; based on 1840 pf. study); Festklänge (1853); Héroïde funèbre

(1849–50, orch. Raff, rev. c.1854); Hungaria (1854); *Hamlet (1858); *Hunnenschlacht (1856–7); Die Ideale (1857); Von der Wiege bis zum Grabe (From the Cradle to the Grave) (1881–2).

MISC. ORCH.: 2 Episodes from Lenau's *Faust: 1. Der nächtliche Zug (The Night Ride), 2. Der Tanz in der Dorfschenke (Dance in the Village Inn, also *Mephisto Waltz No.1) (before 1861); *Mephisto Waltz No.2 (1880–1); Huldigungsmarsch (1853, rev. 1857, orig. for pf.); 3 Odes funèbres (Les Morts; La Notte; Le triomphe funèbre du Tasse (1860–6); *Rákóczy March (1865); 6 *Hungarian Rhapsodies (orch., in collab. with F. Doppler, from pf. solos. Orch. No.1 is pf. No.14, No.2 (No.12), No.3 (No.6), No.4 (No.2), No.5 (No.5), No.6 (No.9, 2nd version) (date unknown).

PIANO & ORCH.: conc. No.1 in E♭ (1849, collab. Raff; rev. 1853, 1856), No.2 in A major (1839, rev. 1849–61); Malédiction, pf., str. (c.1840); Fantasia on Themes from Beethoven's Ruins of Athens (?1852); Fantasia on Hungarian Folk Melodies (Hungarian Fantasia, based on Hungarian Rhapsody No.14 in F minor for solo pf.) (?1852); *Totentanz (1849, rev. 1853, 1859); *Rapsodie espagnole (c.1863 solo pf., orch. Busoni).

SACRED CHORAL: Die *Legende von der heiligen Elisabeth, oratorio, sop., cont., ten., 3 bar., bass, ch., org., orch. (1857–62); *Christus, oratorio, sop., cont., ten., bar., bass, ch., org., orch. (1862–7); Cantico del Sol di S. Francesco d'Assisi, bar., male ch., org., orch. (1862, rev. 1880–1); Mass, 4 male vv., org. (1848, rev. 1859; 2nd version, 1869); Missa solemnis, sop., cont., ten., bass, ch., orch. (1855, rev. 1857–8); Missa Choralis, ch., org. (1865); Hungarian Coronation Mass, sop., cont., ten., bass, orch. (1867); Requiem, 2 ten., 2 bass, male vv., org., opt. brass (1867–8); Psalm 13, ten., ch., orch. (1855, rev. 1859); Psalm 116, male vv., pf. (1869); Ave verum corpus, ch., opt. org. (1871); St Christopher, bar., women's ch., pf., harmonium (after 1874); Via Crucis (1878–9); Rosario (1879); Psalm 129, bar., male vv., org. (1881); Qui seminant in lacrimis, mixed ch., org. (1884); Salve Regina, unacc. ch. (1885).

SECULAR CHORAL: Second Beethoven Cantata, sop., cont., ten., bass, double ch., orch. (1869–70); An die Künstler, 2 ten., 2 bass, male ch., orch. (1853, orch. Raff, rev. 1853, 1856); Choruses from Herder's Entfesseltem Prometheus, sop., cont., 2 ten., 2 bass, double ch., orch. (1850, orch. Raff, rev. 1855); Hungaria 1848, cantata, sop., ten., bass, male vv., orch. (1848, orch. Conradi); Für Männergesang, 12 songs, some with acc. (1842–59).

CHAMBER MUSIC: Romance oubliée, pf. qt. (1880); La lugubre gondola, pf. trio (1882, also pf. solo); At Richard Wagner's Grave, str. qt., harp (1883).

PIANO: Étude en 12 Exercises (1826); 24 Grandes Études (1837); *Mazeppa (1840, orch. 1851); 6 *Études d'exécution transcendante d'après Paganini (1838, rev. 1851 as Grandes Études de Paganini); 12 *Études d'exécution transcendante (Transcendental Studies) (1851); Apparitions (1834); Album d'un voyageur (3 books, 1835–6); 3 *Sonetti del Petrarca (?1839–46); Venezia e Napoli (c.1840, rev. 1859); *Années de pèlerinage, Book 1 'Switzerland', 9 pieces (1848–54, all but 2 pieces based on Album d'un voyageur),

Book 2 'Italy', 7 pieces (1837–49), Book 3, 7 pieces (1867–77); *Harmonies poétiques et réligieuses*, 10 pieces (1845–52); 6 **Consolations* (1849–50); *Grosses Konzertsolo* (?1849, arr. 2 pf. *c*.1855 as *Concerto pathétique*, and for pf. and orch. as *Grand Solo de Concert* ?1850); **Liebesträume—3 Notturnos* (*c*.1850, transcr. of songs); *Scherzo und Marsch* (1851); Sonata in B minor (1852–3); *Huldigungsmarsch* (1853, arr. for orch. 1853, rev. 1857); *Berceuse* (1854, rev. 1862); 2 *Concert Studies* (*Waldesrauschen, Gnomenreigen*) (?1862–3); 2 *Légendes* (St Francis of Assisi preaching to the birds, St Francis of Paule walking on the waves) (1863); *'Weinen, Klagen, Sorgen, Zagen'* prelude (1859); *Rapsodie espagnole* (*c*.1863); *Weihnachtsbaum*, 12 pieces (1874–6); *Nuages gris* (1881); *La lugubre gondola* (1882); *R.W.-Venezia* (1883); **Mephisto Waltz No.3* (1883); *4 Valses oubliées* (1881–?1885); *Csárdás macabre* (1881–2); *Mephisto Waltz No.4* (1885); *Csárdás obstiné* (1886); 19 **Hungarian Rhapsodies* (1846–85, see also ORCH.) (No.1 in C♯, 1846; No.2 in C♯, 1847; No.3 in B♭; No.4 in E♭; No. 5 *Heroïde-élégiaque* in E minor; No.6 in D♭; No.7 in D minor; No.8 in F♯; No.9 in E♭, 1st version pubd. 1848, 2nd version pubd. 1853; No.10 in E; No.11 in A minor; No.12 in C♯; No.13 in A minor; No.14 in F minor; No.15 *Rákóczy March*, 1st version pubd. 1851, 2nd version pubd. 1871; No.16 in A minor, 1882; No.17 in D minor; No.18 in C♯, 1885; No.19 in D minor, 1885).

PIANO TRANSCRIPTIONS: Liszt's transcr. of his own works are too numerous for listing here. A selective list follows of his transcr. of works by other composers (operatic transcr. are listed separately): J. S. BACH: *Fantasia and Fugue in G minor* (BWV 542) (1863); BEETHOVEN: Syms. Nos. 5, 6, and 7 (1837), remaining 6 (1863–4), *Septet*, Op.20 (1841); BERLIOZ: *Symphonie fantastique* (1833, finale rev. 1864–5), *Harold en Italie* (*c*.1836, rev. 1862), *Danse des Sylphes* (*c*.1860); CHOPIN: 6 *Chants Polonais* (1847–60); MENDELSSOHN: 7 *Lieder* (1840); PAGANINI: *Grand Fantasia de bravoure sur La Clochette* (on *La Campanella* from Violin Conc. in B minor, Op.7) (1831–2, rev. as No.3 of *Études d'exécution transcendante d'après Paganini*, 1838); ROSSINI: 12 *Soirées Musicales* (1837), *Ov., William Tell* (1838); SAINT-SAËNS: *Danse macabre* (1876); SCHUBERT: 12 *Lieder* (1837–8), *Schwanengesang* (1838–9), *Winterreise* (1839); SCHUMANN: *Widmung* (1848).

PIANO TRANSCRIPTIONS FROM OPERAS: BELLINI: *Réminiscences des Puritains* (1836), *Hexaméron* (vars. on march from *I Puritani*, collab. with Thalberg, Pixis, Herz, Czerny, Chopin) (1837), *Fantaisie sur les motifs favoris de l'opéra La Sonnambula* (1839, rev. 1840–1), *Réminiscences de Norma* (1841); DONIZETTI: *Réminiscences de Lucia di Lammermoor* (1835–6), *Réminiscences de Lucrezia Borgia* (1840); HALÉVY: *Réminiscences de La Juive* (1835); MEYERBEER: *Grande Fantaisie sur des thèmes de l'opéra Les Huguenots* (1836), *Réminiscences de Robert le Diable* (1841); MOZART: *Réminiscences de Don Juan* (1841); TCHAIKOVSKY: *Eugene Onegin: Polonaise* (1880); VERDI: *Concert Paraphrase on Themes from Ernani* (1847), *Miserere du Trovatore* (1859), *Rigoletto:*

paraphrase de concert (1859), *Don Carlos: Coro di festa e marcia funebre* (1867–8), *Réminiscences de Simon Boccanegra* (1882); WAGNER: *Phantasiestück on themes from Rienzi* (1859), Ov. *Tannhäuser* (1848), *2 Pieces from Lohengrin* (1854), *Isoldes Liebestod* (1867), *Am stillen Herd* from *Die Meistersinger* (1871), *Feierlicher Marsch zum heiligen Gral, Parsifal* (1882); WEBER: *Fantasia on Themes from Der Freischütz* (1840), Ov. *Oberon* (1843), Ov. *Der Freischütz* (1846).

ORGAN: *Prelude and Fugue on the Name of Bach* (1885, rev. 1870); *Requiem* (1879); *At Richard Wagner's Grave* (1883).

SONGS (selected list): *Tre *Sonetti di Petrarca* (1838–9); *Die Loreley* (Heine) (1841); *Mignons Lied* (Goethe) (1842); *Es war ein König in Thule* (Goethe) (1842); *Oh! quand je dors* (Hugo) (1842); *Du bist wie eine Blume* (Heine) (*c*.1843); **Jeanne d'Arc au bûcher* (Dumas) (1845, arr. v. and orch. 1858, rev. 1874); *En ces lieux* (Monnier) (1854); *Die drei Zigeuner* (Lenau) (1860); *Go not, happy day* (Tennyson) (1879); *Verlassen* (Michell) (1880).

litany. Christian prayer for supplication—'Deliver us, O Lord', etc.—often set to mus. Sometimes the title of instr. works, e.g. **Fricker's Litany* for double str. orch.

Litolff, Henry Charles (*b* London, 1818; *d* Paris, 1891). Fr. composer and pianist of Anglo-Alsatian parentage. Début London 1832. Settled in Paris 1835. Cond. at Warsaw 1841–4. In Dresden 1844 taught Hans von Bülow. On visit to Eng. 1845, in abortive attempt to divorce first wife, he was sent to jail but escaped to Holland with help of jailer's daughter. Became mus. publisher, Brunswick, 1851, on marriage to widow of publisher G. M. Meyer (firm's name changed to Henry Litolff Verlag). Pioneered popular cheap edns. 1861. Court cond. Saxe-Coburg-Gotha 1855. Settled in Paris 1869 to cond. and compose. Wrote 6 operas, operettas, oratorio, *Scenes from Goethe's Faust*, pf. solos, chamber mus., and 5 *Concerts-symphoniques* for pf. and orch. (No.4, *c*.1852, contains often-played *Scherzo*). The Litolff pub. firm was modernized by his adopted son Theodor (1839–1912). It was taken over by Peters of Leipzig, 1940.

Little, Tasmin (*b* London, 1965). Eng. violinist. Studied at Menuhin Sch. and GSMD. Rapidly became one of leading Brit. violinists of her generation. Fine interpreter of Delius and Elgar concs. Gave f.p. of Robert **Saxton's vn. conc., Leeds 1989.

Little Clavier-book (Bach). See *Klavierbüchlein*.

Little Night Music, A. Eng. trans. of Mozart's title *Eine *kleine Nachtmusik*. Also title of Amer. musical (1973) by Stephen **Sondheim.

Little Organ-book (J. S. Bach). See *Orgelbüchlein*.

Little Organ Mass (Haydn). See *Kleine Orgelmesse*.

'Little Russian' Symphony. Nickname for **Tchaikovsky's Sym. No.2 in C minor (1872), so-called because of use of folk-songs from Ukraine ('Little Russia'). 2nd vers. 1879–80.

Little Sweep, The (Britten). See *Let's Make an Opera*.

Litton, Andrew (*b* NY, 1959). Amer. conductor. Won BBC Rupert Foundation int. cond. comp. 1982. London début 1982 Proms (BBCSO). Ass. cond. Nat. SO, Washington, 1982–6. Prin. cond. Bournemouth SO 1988–94. Mus. dir. Dallas SO 1994–2006. NY Met début 1989 (*Eugene Onegin*).

liturgy. This, properly, means the service of the Christian Eucharist, but in ordinary usage is now applied to any written and officially authorized form of service. The evolution of liturgies has had a great influence on the development of mus., especially because, for many centuries, almost the only literate and trained musicians were those of the Church and the only fully organized mus. that of its services.

lituus. Ancient Roman cavalry tpt., made of bronze. Bell was curved and upturned to give shape of letter J. In Cantata No.118, Bach scored for 2 *litui* (ten. tpts.).

liuto (It.). The *lute.

Liverpool Philharmonic Orchestra. See *Royal Liverpool Philharmonic Orchestra*.

Lloyd, Edward (*b* London, 1845; *d* Worthing, 1927). Eng. tenor. Gentleman of Chapel Royal 1869–71. Had great success at Gloucester Fest. 1871 in Bach's *St Matthew Passion*, leading to outstanding career in oratorios and cantatas. Amer. début 1888. Sang ten. part in f.ps. of Elgar's *King Olaf*, 1896, and *The Light of Life*, 1896, and was first Gerontius in 1900, the year of his retirement. Returned to sing at King George V's Coronation, 1911, and at a benefit concert in 1915.

Lloyd, George (*b* St Ives, Cornwall, 1913; *d* London, 1998). Eng. composer. Composer of operas to libs. by his father, William Lloyd (*Iernin*, 1933–4; *The Serf*, 1936–8; and *John Socman*, 1951); 12 syms., 4 pf. concs., 2 vn. concs., pf. and vn. pieces, *A Symphonic Mass*, ch., orch. (1992), etc. OBE 1970.

Lloyd, Jonathan (*b* London, 1948). Eng. composer. Lived in Paris 1969–70. Attended Ligeti's classes at Tanglewood, 1973. Was busker and street musician 1974–7. Works incl.:

MUSIC THEATRE: *Scattered Ruins*, sop., ens. (1973); *Musices Genus*, sop., ens. (1974); *The Adjudicator*, community opera (1986).

FILM: *Blackmail* (mus. for 1929 Hitchcock silent thriller) (1992–3).

ORCH.: syms.: No.1 (1983), No.2 (1983–4), No.3, 18 instr. (1987), No.4 (1988), No.5 (1989); va. conc. (1979–80); *Rhapsody*, vc., orch. (1982); *There*, gui., str. (1991); *Tolerance* (1993); vn. conc. (1995).

ENSEMBLE: *Waiting for Gozo* (1981); *Don't Mention the War*, 8 players (1982); *Time Between Trains* (1984); *The New Ear* (1985); *Almeida Dances* (1986); *Dancing in the Ruins* (1990).

CHAMBER MUSIC: str. qt. No.1 (*Of Time and Motion*) (1984); str. quintets No.1 (1982), No.2, mandolin, lute, guitar, hp., db. (1982); wind quintet (1982);

brass quintet (1982); ob. sonata (1985); *One Step More*, fl., ob. d'amore, vc., hpd. (1986); *He will make it*, vc. (1988); *Restless Night*, wind quintet (1991); *Ballad for the Evening of a Man*, fl., vn., va., vc. (1992); *Blessed days of blue*, fl., str. (1995).

VOICE(S) & INSTR(S).: *Everything Returns*, sop. (wordless), orch. (1977–8); *If I Could Turn You On*, sop., chamber orch. (1981); *Marching to a Different Song*, sop., chamber orch. (1991); *People your Dreams*, mez., ens. (1994).

VOCAL: *Mass*, 6 solo vv. (1983); *Missa brevis*, unacc. double ch. (1984); *Revelation*, 8 vv. (1990); *And Beyond*, ch., chamber orch. (1996).

Lloyd, Richard (*b* Stockport, 1933). Eng. organist and composer. Sub-organist, Salisbury Cath. 1957–66, organist, Hereford Cath. and cond. 3 Choirs Fest. 1966–74, Durham Cath. 1974–85. Composer of anthems etc., mus. for children.

Lloyd, Robert (Andrew) (*b* Southend-on-Sea, 1940). Eng. bass-baritone. Début London (Univ. Coll.) 1969 (Don Fernando in Beethoven's *Leonore*). SW 1969–72. Glyndebourne début 1972; CG from 1972; La Scala 1976; S. Francisco 1975; NY Met début 1988. Munich Critics' Prize 1979. Sang Gurnemanz in Syberberg film of *Parsifal*, 1981. First Briton to sing Boris at Kirov Opera, 1990. Fine interpreter of *Winterreise*. Recorded Elgar's *The Dream of Gerontius* with Boult. CBE 1991.

Lloyd-Jones, David (Mathias) (*b* London, 1934). Eng. conductor. Guest cond. with many opera cos., incl. CG début 1971 (*Boris Godunov*); Wexford 1967; Scottish Opera début 1967; WNO début 1967; and BBC TV opera. Prin. cond. Opera North (Leeds) 1978–90. Cond. f. Eng. ps. of Fauré's *Pénélope* (1970) and Haydn's *La fedeltà premiata* (1971) and f. Eng. stage p. of Prokofiev's *War and Peace* (SW début, 1972). With Opera North, cond. f.p. of Josephs's *Rebecca* (Leeds, 1983), and f. Brit. ps. of Krenek's *Jonny spielt auf* (Leeds, 1984) and Strauss's *Daphne* (Leeds, 1987). Prepared critical edns. of *Boris Godunov* (1975), *Prince Igor* (1982), and *The Gondoliers* (1984). Translator of several Russ. operas.

Lloyd Webber, Andrew (Lord Lloyd Webber of Sydmonton) (*b* London, 1948). Eng. composer. With Tim Rice (*b* 1944) as librettist, comp. highly successful musicals, *Joseph and the Amazing Technicolor Dreamcoat* (1968), *Jesus Christ Superstar* (1970), and *Evita* (1976). Wrote *Jeeves* (1975) on text by Alan Ayckbourn, *Variations* (1978) for vc. and jazz ens. (for brother Julian *Lloyd Webber), musical *Cats* based on poems by T. S. Eliot (1981), *Song and Dance* (1983), *Starlight Express* (1984), *Phantom of the Opera* (1986), *Aspects of Love* (1989), *Sunset Boulevard* (1993), *Whistle Down the Wind* (1996, rev. 1998), *The Beautiful Game* (2000), *The Woman in White* (2004), and *Requiem*, sop., ten., treble, ch., orch. (1984). Also film music, incl. *The Odessa File* (1974). Knighted 1992. Life peer 1997.

Lloyd Webber, Julian (*b* London, 1951). Eng. cellist. Début London 1972. Gave f. London p. of

Bliss conc. at composer's request, 1972. Amer. début 1980. Rodrigo wrote conc. for him, 1981. Soloist with leading Brit. orchs. Brother, Andrew *Lloyd Webber, wrote *Variations* for vc. and jazz ens. for him.

Lloyd Webber, William (*b* London, 1914; *d* London, 1982). Eng. organist, composer, and teacher. Father of Andrew and Julian *Lloyd Webber. Studied at RCM 1931–5. Dir., London Coll. of Mus. 1964–82. Prof. of comp., RCM, 1946–82. Mus. dir. Central Hall, Westminster, 1946–82. Works incl. sonatina, fl., pf. (1941); tone-poem *Aurora* (1951); sonatina, va., pf. (1952); *Missa Sanctae Mariae Magdalenae*, ch., org. (1979); songs; choral pieces; and org. works.

Lobgesang (Hymn of Praise). Symphony-cantata in B♭ (Sym. No.2) by Mendelssohn for ch. and orch., Op.52, in 4 movements of which only last is choral. F.p. Leipzig 1840, Birmingham 1840.

Lobkowitz, (Prince) **Joseph Franz Maximilian** (*b* Roudnice nad Labem, 1772; *d* Třeboň, 1816). Member of Bohemian aristocratic family who had a tradition of patronage of music. Sang bass in Handel's *Alexander's Feast* in Vienna in 1812. Also violinist and cellist. On board of administrators of Vienna court theatres, 1807–14, being sole dir. of opera. Founder-member of Gesellschaft der Musikfreunde. Commissioned Haydn's Op.77 str. qts. F.p. of Beethoven's 'Eroica' Sym. given in his home 1804. Beethoven dedicated his Op.18 str. qts., the 3rd, 5th, and 6th Syms., the Triple Conc., the str. qt. Op.74, and the song-cycle *An die ferne Geliebte*, to him.

Locatelli, Pietro (Antonio) (*b* Bergamo, 1695; *d* Amsterdam, 1764). It. violinist and composer. Settled in Amsterdam 1729, where he est. concert series. A great virtuoso, he introduced new effects and techniques. Comp. 12 concerti grossi, *L'Arte del Violino*, containing 12 concs. and 24 caprices for str. qt. and continuo, 6 vn. concs., 6 str. trios, 12 solo vn. sonatas, etc.

Locke [Lock], **Matthew** (*b* Exeter, *c*.1622; *d* London, 1677). Eng. composer, especially of theatre music. Convert to Catholicism *c*.1650. Composer-in-ordinary to Charles II, 1661. Wrote incidental mus. for Shadwell's and Davenant's versions of Shakespeare plays (e.g. *Macbeth* and *The Tempest*), many anthems, 6 suites (some for recorder), *Music for his Majesty's Sackbuts and Cornetts, Melothesia* (studies for continuo, 1673). Also wrote pamphlets defending his style.

Lockhart, James (Lawrence) (*b* Edinburgh, 1930). Scottish conductor, organist, and pianist. Ass. organist and chorusmaster, St Giles Cath., Edinburgh, 1946–51; org. and choirmaster, St John the Divine, Kennington, 1951–3, All Souls, Langham Place, 1953–4. Apprentice cond. Yorkshire SO 1954–5. Ass. cond. Munster Opera 1955–6, Bavarian State Opera, Munich, 1956–7, Glyndebourne 1957–9, répétiteur Glyndebourne 1962–8. Prof. of cond. RCM 1962–72. Mus. dir.

WNO 1968–73; cond. Kassel Opera 1972–80. NY Met début 1984 (with ENO). Dir. of opera, RCM 1986–93, of London Royal Schools' vocal faculty, from 1993. Frequent accompanist to sop. Margaret Price.

loco (It.). Place. Term used after a sign indicating perf. an octave higher or lower than written (*8va sopra*, or *8va bassa*) to remind the performer that the effect of that sign is now cancelled. The expression *al loco* (at the place) is often used.

Lodger, The. Opera in 2 acts by Phyllis Tate to lib. by David Franklin based on novel by Mrs Belloc-Lowndes. Comp. 1959–60. Prod. RAM London 1960, Manchester RMCM 1970. The lodger of the title is Jack the Ripper.

Lodoïska. Opera in 3 acts by Cherubini to lib. by Fillette-Loraux, based on episode in Louvet de Couvrai's novel *Les amours du chevalier du Faublas*. Prod. Paris 1791; NY 1826; London 1962. Also subject of operas by *Kreutzer (1791), *Storace (1794), and *Mayr (1796).

Loeffler, Charles (Martin Tornow) (*b* Mulhouse, Alsace, 1861; *d* Medfield, Mass., 1935). Alsatian-Amer. composer and violinist. Son of writer whose pseudonym was Tornow. Played in private orch. In 1881 went to USA, becoming deputy leader Boston SO, 1882, staying until 1903, after which he concentrated on comp. Works, which reflect Fr. impressionist techniques, incl. 3 operas, sym.-poems, choral settings (incl. Whitman's *Beat! Beat! Drums!*), chamber mus., and songs. Many unpub. pieces.

Loeillet, Jacques (*b* Ghent, 1685; *d* Ghent, 1748). Belg. composer, brother of Jean Baptiste *Loeillet. Also flautist, oboist, and violinist. Oboist at Munich. Court oboist to Louis XV, 1727–46. Wrote fl. sonatas, vn. pieces, etc.

Loeillet, Jean Baptiste (*b* Ghent, 1680; *d* London, 1730). Belg. composer, flautist, and harpsichordist. Brother of Jacques *Loeillet. Settled in London 1705, playing in th. orch. and teaching hpd. Introduced transverse fl. to London. Comp. many works for his instrs.

Loesser, Frank (*b* NY, 1910; *d* NY, 1969). Amer. composer. Settled in Hollywood 1931. Wrote several successful Broadway musicals (*Guys and Dolls*, 1950, *The Most Happy Fella*, 1956, and *How to succeed in Business Without Really Trying*, 1961) and many songs incl. 'Praise the Lord and pass the ammunition' (1942).

Loewe, Frederick (*b* Vienna, 1901; *d* Palm Springs, Calif., 1988). Austrian-born (later Amer.) composer. Settled in USA 1924. Wrote mus. for *Brigadoon* (1947), *Paint Your Wagon* (1951), *My Fair Lady* (1956, mus. version of Shaw's *Pygmalion*), *Camelot* (1960, mus. version of White's *The Once and Future King*), and *Gigi* (film). All these were in collab. with librettist Alan Jay Lerner (*b* NY, 1918; *d* NY, 1986).

Loewe, (Johann) **Karl** (Gottfried) (*b* Löbejün, nr. Halle, 1796; *d* Kiel, 1869). Ger. composer, organist, conductor, and singer. Mus. dir. at Stettin 1821–66. Cond. at Düsseldorf and Mainz fests., 1837. Visited Eng. 1847. Developed ballad for v. and pf. as art-form, setting *Erlkönig*, *Edward*, *Tom der Reimer*, etc. His ballads, legends, *Lieder*, and *Gesänge*, over 500 in all, were publd. in 17 vols. 1899–1903. Also wrote 6 operas; 18 oratorios; cantatas; 2 syms.; 2 pf. concs.; 4 str. qts.; pf. trio; 4 pf. sonatas, etc. Entered 6-week trance, 1864, a similar event causing his death.

Loewenberg, Alfred (*b* Berlin, 1902; *d* London, 1949). Ger.-born musicologist who settled in Eng., 1934. Compiled *Annals of Opera 1597–1940* (Cambridge 1943, rev. ed. Zurich 1954 and 1978, by H. D. Rosenthal) which lists details of 4,000 opera perfs. in chronological detail.

Logier, Johann Bernhard (*b* Kassel, 1777; *d* Dublin, 1846). Ger.-born flautist, bandmaster, organist, and piano-teacher. Went to Eng. in 1791 and settled in Dublin 1809, opening music-shop and conducting at th. In 1814 invented and patented the *Chiroplast*, evolving system of teaching based on its use in training the hands for pf.-playing. Went to Berlin for 3 years. Returned to Dublin 1829, managing a music-shop. His *Thoroughbass* (1818) was first textbook studied by Wagner. Wrote pf. conc., sonatas, etc.

Logothetis, Anestis (*b* Pyrgos, Bulgaria, 1921; *d* Vienna, 1994). Bulg.-born Gr. composer. Used graphic and other notation from 1959. (See illustration p. 310). Works incl. *Agglomeration*, vn., str. (1960); *Labyrinthos* (1965); ballet *Odysseus* (1963); *Styx*, orch. of plucked str. instr. (1969); *Anastasis*, vv., tape, film, TV, instr. (1969); *Emantionen*, cl., tape (1973); *Daidalia*, mus. th. (1976–8); *Rondo*, orch. (1979); *Wellenformen 1981*, computer (1981–2); *Symphonietten*, chamber ens. (1981–7); *Meridiane I und Bretiengrade*, soloists, orch. (1981–8).

Lohengrin. Opera in 3 acts by Wagner to his own lib. Comp. 1846–8. Prod. Weimar (cond. Liszt) 1850, NY 1871, London 1875. The Bridal Chorus (wedding march), adapted by innumerable organists for church weddings, occurs early in Act 3, Scene 1. Lohengrin, Knight of the Holy Grail, is the son of *Parsifal*.

Löhr, Hermann (Frederic) (*b* Plymouth, 1872; *d* Tunbridge Wells, 1943). Eng. composer. Wrote popular ballads, e.g. *Where my caravan has rested* (1909) and *Little grey home in the West* (1911).

L'Oiseau Lyre (Lyrebird Press). Fr. firm of mus. publishers, founded in Paris 1932 by Louise Dyer, an Australian, who built up a catalogue of limited edns., incl. Byzantine liturgical mus., medieval polyphonic mus., motets by Attaignant, kbd. works by Byrd, complete edn. of Couperin, etc. Dyer worked in Oxford 1940–5, returning to Paris after the war. She died 1962, when her husband, Jeffrey Hanson, ran firm until 1971. His widow Margarita Hanson then added further vols. Head-

quarters moved to Les Remparts, Monaco. Recordings issued since *c*.1938, label now being part of Decca (Polygram) group.

Lolli, Antonio (*b* Bergamo, *c*.1725; *d* Palermo, 1802). It. violinist and composer. Solo violinist at Württemberg court in Stuttgart 1758–72 and in Moscow with Catherine the Great 1774–83. Visited London 1785 and 1791. Inveterate gambler, died in poverty. Regarded as greatest violinist of his time, forerunner of Paganini. Wrote 17 vn. concs., 30 vn. sonatas.

Lombard, Alain (*b* Paris, 1940). Fr. conductor. Cond. début 1951 with Pasdeloup Orch. Gold medal, Mitropoulos Comp. 1966. Ass. cond., Lyons Opera 1961–5. Amer. début (concert) NY 1963; Met 1966. Mus. dir. Miami PO 1966–74. Salzburg Fest. début 1971. Mus. dir. Strasbourg PO 1972–83, Opéra du Rhin 1974–80, Paris Opéra 1981–3, Opéra-Comique 1983–6. Art. dir. Orch. National Bordeaux Aquitaine from 1988.

Lombardi alla Prima Crociata, I (The Lombards at the First Crusade). Opera in 4 acts by Verdi to lib. by Solera after Grossi's poem of same name. Comp. 1842–3, rev. 1843. Prod. Milan 1843, London 1846, NY 1847 (first Verdi opera in USA). Fr. version under title *Jérusalem*.

London. Eng. city, capital of Great Britain. One of main musical centres of the world, with rich and varied activities in all branches of the art. From 18th cent. has enjoyed visits from leading performers and composers. Among the latter, Handel, J. C. Bach, Mozart, Haydn, Chopin, Weber, Mendelssohn, Liszt, Berlioz, Wagner, Bruckner, Mahler, Strauss, Hindemith, Ligeti, Berio, and Stockhausen are prominent. This summary of London music will be divided into sections, for ease of reference.

OPERA. The first real operatic perf. in London was at Rutland House, 1656, when Davenant's *The Siege of Rhodes* (mus. by 5 composers) was given. Purcell's *Dido and Aeneas* was perf. at a Chelsea school in 1689. Drury Lane Th. was used for opera in the 1690s. Handel's first operatic perfs. in London after 1711 were mainly at the King's Th., Haymarket. Rival perfs. were given at Lincoln's Inn Fields and *Covent Garden. From the 1830s the Lyceum and Drury Lane staged important opera seasons. The King's (re-named Her Majesty's in 1837) was the home of It. opera, but the first London *Ring* cycle was given there in 1882. After being rebuilt smaller in 1897, Her Majesty's was used less frequently for opera, although *Beecham cond. Strauss's *Feuersnot* there in 1910 and the first version of *Ariadne auf Naxos* in 1913. The BNOC gave seasons there after 1924. The first th. on the Covent Garden site opened in 1732. Several Handel operas and oratorios were perf. there. The th. was rebuilt in 1782 and enlarged in 1792. It burned down in 1808 and was re-opened in 1809, *Bishop being dir. 1810–24. Weber's *Oberon* had its f.p. there in 1826. Fire destroyed this building in 1856, the present th. opening in 1858. Mainly It. operas were perf., but the first

Ring cycle, cond. by Mahler, was given in 1892. From 1896 to 1924, CG was run by a syndicate. In 1908 and 1909, Richter cond. the *Ring* in English. Between 1910 and 1914 Beecham introduced *Elektra*, *Salome*, and *Der Rosenkavalier* to London and held the lease of the th. 1919–20. Many famous singers and conductors appeared there up to 1939. During the Second World War, CG was a dance hall, but re-opened in 1946 with Purcell's *The Fairy Queen* and David *Webster as admin. of the CG Opera Company. This became the Royal Opera in 1969. From 1931 London's second opera house was *Sadler's Wells in Rosebery Avenue which housed the Vic-Wells Opera (SW Opera from 1934) until 1939 and from 1945 to 1968 (it re-opened on 7 June 1945 with f.p. of *Peter Grimes*). The company moved to the Coliseum in 1968 and changed its name in 1974 to *English National Opera. Smaller companies and visiting companies continue to use Sadler's Wells. The forerunner of Sadler's Wells was the Old Vic where Lilian Baylis had first staged opera in 1900. Until 1935 Vic-Wells Opera and Vic-Wells Ballet used both the Old Vic and Sadler's Wells.

ORCHESTRAS. Public concerts in London date from 1672. Thomas Britton's weekly gathering at Clerkenwell lasted from 1678 to 1714. Subscription concerts were held at Hickford's Rooms, James Street, from 1729 to *c*.1752. Geminiani ran rival concerts from 1731 to 1738. The J. C. Bach–C. F. Abel concerts began in 1765 at Carlisle House, Soho Square, and moved to Hanover Square Rooms in 1775. They ceased in 1782. Concerts organized by Cramer, Clementi, and *Salomon ran from 1783 to 1793, but Salomon left to launch his own series in 1783 (it was to this series that Haydn came). In the 19th cent. concerts were given first in the Argyll Rooms, at the corner of Oxford and Argyll Streets, and it was there that the *Philharmonic Society gave its first concert on 8 March 1813. The building was demolished in 1818 and the New Argyll Rooms opened in 1820 (they burned down in 1830). The Philharmonic moved to the King's Th. in 1830, to Hanover Square Rooms 1833–68, St James's Hall 1869–93, Queen's Hall 1894–1941, Royal Albert Hall 1941–51, Festival Hall from 1951. Important orch. concerts were given at the Crystal Palace, Sydenham, cond. by August Manns 1855–1901, where the members of the orch. played continually together and were London's first permanent orch. The opening of the *Royal Albert Hall in 1871 added a hall with a capacity of 6,500 to London's musical life. It was used mainly for large-scale events until 1941 when the destruction of Queen's Hall meant that nearly all symphony concerts were given there. It has remained the home since 1941 of the Promenade Concerts, founded in 1895 by Robert Newman and Henry J. *Wood. The Queen's Hall, Langham Place, had opened in 1893 and was renowned for its acoustics. It replaced the St James's Hall, Piccadilly, built in 1858. The Richter concerts were given there from 1877 and, even though the Queen's Hall by then existed, Elgar's *Enigma*

Variations had their f.p. at a Richter concert in St James's Hall in 1899. It was demolished in 1905. London's principal concert hall since 1951 has been the *Royal Festival Hall on the South Bank, with the Queen Elizabeth Hall and Purcell Room as smaller adjuncts since 1967 but not entirely replacing for recitals the usefulness since 1901 of the *Wigmore Hall (Bechstein Hall until 1917) in Wigmore Street. The latest additions are the *Barbican Concert Hall and the Cadogan Hall.

No other city in the world supports as many orchestras as London. The *BBC SO (founded 1930) and the orchestras of the Royal Opera House and ENO are independent bodies and do not, as they once would have done, share players with others. The four principal symphony orchs. are *London Symphony (founded 1904), *London Philharmonic (founded 1932), *Philharmonia (founded 1945), and *Royal Philharmonic (founded 1946). In addition there are the *English Chamber Orchestra (founded 1948, renamed 1960), *Academy of St Martin-in-the-Fields (founded 1958), *London Mozart Players (founded 1949), *London Sinfonietta (founded 1968), and Orchestra of *St John's, Smith Square (founded 1973). Among the choirs are the *Bach Choir (founded 1876), *Royal Choral Society (founded 1871), John *Alldis Choir (founded 1962), London Choral Society (founded 1903), Monteverdi Choir (founded 1964), London Philharmonic Choir (founded 1947), London Symphony Chorus (founded 1966), and Philharmonia Chorus (founded 1957).

COLLEGES. The *Royal Academy of Music was founded in 1822, the *Royal College of Music in 1882, *Trinity College of Music in 1872, the *Guildhall School of Music and Drama in 1880, and the *London College of Music in 1887. In addition the Univ. of London has a thriving musical wing.

MISCELLANEOUS. In festivals, libraries, publishing firms, and not least the churches, from Westminster Abbey, Westminster Cathedral, St Paul's Cathedral, the Temple Church, and much besides, London's music is blessed by abundance. The capital is fortunate in having and holding so much; the only cavil is that some Londoners sometimes assume that nowhere else (in Britain) has anything.

London [Burnstein], **George** (*b* Montreal, 1919; *d* Armonk, NY, 1985). Amer. baritone of Russo-Jewish parentage. Début in concert perf. of A. *Coates's *Gainsborough's Duchess*, Hollywood Bowl 1941, under name Geo. Burnson. S. Francisco Opera 1943 (Monterone in *Rigoletto*). Member of Bel Canto Trio (with Frances Yeend, sop., and Mario *Lanza, ten.), touring USA from 1947. Vienna Opera from 1949; NY Met 1951–66; Bayreuth début 1951; Glyndebourne 1950; La Scala 1952; Salzburg Fest. 1952. First Amer. to sing Boris Godunov at Bolshoy, Moscow, 1960. Sang Wotan in complete *Ring*, prod. Wieland Wagner, Cologne 1962–4. Mandryka in NY Met's first *Arabella*, 1955. Gave up opera through ill-health in 1966. Art. admin., Kennedy Center, Washington, 1968–71. Gen. dir. Music Center

Opera Assoc., Los Angeles, 1971–7, Opera Soc. of Washington, DC, 1975–7. Début as stage director, Seattle 1973.

London College of Music. Mus. sch. founded (privately) 1887. Incorporated 1939. Recognized as examining body. Awards diplomas GLCM, GLCM (Hons.), FLCM, L(Mus.)LCM, ALCM, and LLCM. Dirs. have included W. *Lloyd Webber (1964–82) and J. *McCabe (1983–90).

London Consort of Viols. Ens. formed in 1948.

Londonderry Air. Irish folk-tune first pubd. in 1855 in *Petrie coll. Several sets of words have been fitted to it: 'Would I were Erin's apple blossom' by A. P. Graves, 'Emer's Farewell', also by Graves, and 'Danny Boy' by F. E. Weatherly. Arr. for various combinations by *Grainger (as *Irish Tune from County Derry*).

London Mozart Players. Chamber orch. specializing in mus. of Mozart and Haydn founded in 1949 by Harry *Blech. First concert, Wigmore Hall, London, 11 Feb. 1949. Developed from London Wind Players, formed by Blech in 1942. Tours to It., Switzerland, Holland, Sweden, and Ger. Many fest. appearances. Blech art. dir. until 1984; Jane *Glover 1984–91; Matthias Bamert mus. dir. 1993–2000; Andrew Parrott from 2000.

London Opera House. Th. built in Kingsway, London, in 1911 by Oscar *Hammerstein I as home for resident opera co. After 2 seasons it closed, becoming variety th. under name Stoll. Vladimir Rosing staged an opera season in 1915 (giving f.p. in England of *Queen of Spades*). It. opera seasons 1949 and 1952–7, Zagreb Opera visit 1955, *Porgy and Bess* 1953. Now demolished.

London Overture, A. Orch. work by *Ireland, 1936, a re-working of material from *Comedy Overture*, written for brass band 1934. One of prin. themes said to be inspired by bus cond.'s call of 'Piccadilly!' Arr. for brass band by Ireland (date unknown).

London Philharmonic Orchestra. Founded by Sir Thomas Beecham in 1932 as his answer to BBC SO, with several superb players, e.g. Paul Beard (vn.), George Stratton (vn.), Anthony Pini (vc.), Gerald Jackson (fl.), Leon *Goossens (ob.), Reginald Kell (cl.), Gwydion Holbrooke (bn.), Marie Goossens (hp.). No connection with Phil. Soc. First concert, Queen's Hall, London, 7 Oct. 1932. Toured Ger. 1936. Toured Far East 1969 (cond. Pritchard), China 1973 (cond. Pritchard). Self-governing from 1939. Prin. conds.: Sir Adrian *Boult (1951–7); William *Steinberg (1958–62); John *Pritchard (1962–7); Bernard *Haitink (1967–79); Sir Georg *Solti (1979–83); Klaus *Tennstedt (1983–7); Franz Welser-Möst 1990–6; Kurt Masur 2000–7; Vladimir Jurowski from 2007. CG opera 1933–9. *Glyndebourne Opera from 1964.

London Sinfonietta. Eng. chamber orch. founded by David Atherton and Nicholas Snowman

in 1968, with Atherton as first mus. dir. Specializes in 20th-cent. mus. and has given well over 200 f.ps. and f.ps. in Eng. Elgar Howarth regular cond. from 1973 and Simon Rattle works often with it. Paul Crossley joint art. dir. 1988–94. Markus Stenz prin. cond. 1994–8; Oliver Knussen 1998–2002.

London String Quartet. Founded 1908 by Warwick Evans, cellist, with Albert *Sammons and Thomas Petre, vns., and H. Waldo Warner, va. First public concert Bechstein Hall, London, 26 Jan. 1910. Sammons succeeded by James Levey 1917–27, in turn succeeded by John Pennington, 1927–35. Petre absent 1914–19. Warner succeeded 1929 by Philip Sainton, in turn succeeded by William Primrose 1930–5. Toured USA and Canada annually 1920–35. Set high standards. Disbanded Jan. 1935. Gave f.ps. of several British works and in 1914 perf. 3 movts. of Schoenberg's 2nd str. qt. Name acquired 1958 by qt. comprising Erich Gruenberg and Lionel Bentley (vns.), Keith Cummings (va.), and Douglas Cameron (vc.). They had been New London Quartet 1950–6. Disbanded 1961.

London Symphonies. Collective name given to Joseph Haydn's last 12 syms., Nos. 93–104 in Breitkopf ed., all written for the London impresario J. P. *Salomon and first played in London during Haydn's visits, 1791–2 and 1794–5. The last, No.104, is usually known as the 'London', for no special or good reason. The list which follows gives the syms. in chronological order of comp., with Breitkopf numbering, according to the Haydn scholar H. C. Robbins *Landon:

No.	Date on score	F.p.
96 ('Miracle')	London 1791	1791
95	London 1791	1791
93	London 1791	Feb. 1792
94 ('Surprise')	London 1791	Mar. 1792
98	London 1792(?)	Mar. 1792
97	London 1792	May 1792
99	(Austria 1793)	Feb. 1794
100 ('Military')	London 1794	Mar. 1794
101 ('Clock')	London 1794	Mar. 1794
102	London 1794	Feb. 1795
103 ('Drum Roll')	London 1795	Mar. 1795
104 ('London')	London 1795	Mar. 1795

London Symphony, A. Sym. by *Vaughan Williams (his 2nd, first wholly orch.) comp. 1911–13, f.p. 1914, rev. 1918, 1920, 1933. Though not programmatic, contains picturesque features such as Westminster chimes, lavender-seller's cry, jingle of hansom-cabs, and street musicians.

London Symphony Orchestra. Founded 1904, self-governing from start, by players who seceded from Henry Wood's Queen's Hall Orch. because he banned the system of deputies (by which a player could unilaterally send a deputy to a concert while he took a more lucrative engagement). First concert Queen's Hall, London, 9 June 1904, cond. *Richter, who remained prin. cond. until 1911. Toured USA 1912 cond.

Nikisch. Also assoc. with Elgar as cond. (he was prin. cond. 1911–12). For many years was regular orch. at 3 Choirs Fests. Conductors have incl. Albert *Coates and *Harty. Those appointed prin. cond. since 2nd World War have been Josef *Krips (1950–4), Pierre *Monteux (1961–4), Istvan *Kertész (1965–8), André *Previn (1968–79), Claudio *Abbado (1979–88), Michael Tilson *Thomas (1988–95), Colin *Davis (1995–2006), Valery *Gergiev from 2006. Salzburg Fest. début 1973 (cond. Previn).

Long, Kathleen (b Brentwood, 1896; d Cambridge, 1968). Eng. pianist. Début 1915. On staff of RCM 1920–64. Specialized in Mozart and Fr. composers, e.g. Fauré *Ballade*. Player in chamber mus. with Casals, Sammons, and others. Sonata partnership with Antonio Brosa 1948–66. CBE 1957.

Long, Marguerite (Marie Charlotte) (b Nîmes, 1874; d Paris, 1966). Fr. pianist and teacher. On staff 1906–40 (prof. of pf. from 1920). Founded own sch. 1920, being joined 1940 by *Thibaud. Career of over 70 years. Noted interpreter of contemp. composers and early champion of Debussy (whose pupil she was) and Ravel. Ravel's pf. conc. in G major is ded. to her; she gave f.p. Paris, Jan. 1932 and f.p. in England, London, Feb. 1932, both cond. by composer. Also gave f.p. of Ravel's *Le Tombeau de Couperin*, April 1919. Author of book *At the piano with Debussy* (1960).

longa (Lat.). Long. Time-value of a note in medieval notation system; was intermediate of *maxima* and *brevis*. A double long was equal to 4 breves.

Long Christmas Dinner, The. Opera in 1 act by Hindemith to lib. by Thornton Wilder after his play. Comp. 1960. Prod. Mannheim (as *Das lange Weihnachtsmahl* in Ger. trans. by Hindemith) 1961, Rome 1962. F.p. of orig. Eng. text NY 1963 (Juilliard. Sch.), London 1967.

long drum. Ten. drum—but sometimes the name is applied to the bass drum.

Longo, Alessandro (b Amantea, 1864; d Naples, 1945). It. pianist and composer. Prof. of pf., Naples Cons., 1897–1934. Ed. complete hpd. works of D. *Scarlatti in 11 vols., giving each work a Longo (*L.) no. This numbering system has been superseded by that of *Kirkpatrick.

lontano (It.). (1) Distant, e.g. *come da lontano*, as if from a distance, i.e. faintly; *lontananza*, distance.
(2) Chamber ens. founded and dir. by Odaline de la *Martinez.
(3) Orch. work by Ligeti. See below.

Lontano (In the distance). Work for orch. by *Ligeti, comp. 1967, f.p. Donaueschingen 1967; f. Eng. public p., Manchester 1972 (cond. Loughran).

López-Cobos, Jesús (b Toro, 1940). Sp. conductor. Won Besançon int. cond. comp. 1969. Concert début 1969, Prague Spring fest.; opera

début Venice 1969 (*Die Zauberflöte*); Deutsches Oper, Berlin, 1970; Amer. début (S. Francisco) 1972; CG 1975; NY Met 1978. Gen. mus. dir. Deutsche Oper 1981–90 (cond. co. in first *Ring* cycle staged in Japan, 1987). Cond., Sp. Nat. Orch. 1984–9, mus. dir. Cincinnati SO 1986–2000, mus. dir. Lausanne Chamber Orch. 1990–2000.

Loppert, Max (Jeremy) (b Johannesburg, 1946). S. African music critic, settled in Eng. Mus. critic of *Financial Times* 1982–96. Assoc. ed. of *Opera* 1986–90. Contrib. to periodicals.

Lord, David (Malcolm) (b Oxford, 1944). Eng. composer, conductor, and lecturer. Works incl. *Incantare*, orch.; hpd. conc.; several song-cycles, incl. *The Wife of Winter* (comp. for Janet *Baker).

Lorelei [Loreley]. **Die**. (1) Unfinished opera, Op.98, by Mendelssohn (1847) to lib. by E. von Giebel based on Ger. legend of beautiful woman who sings on a mountain by the Rhine, luring sailors to death on the rocks below. Some fragments, incl. an *Ave Maria*, sometimes perf. in concert-hall. Operas on subject also by Ignaz Lachner (1846), Wallace (1847), Bruch (1863), Catalani (1890, rev. of *Elda*, 1880), and others.
(2) Song by Liszt for v. and pf. to Heine's poem (1841), also with orch. and transcr. for pf. solo.
(3) Song by Friedrich Silcher (1789–1860) for v. and pf. to Heine's poem.

Lorengar, Pilar (b Zaragoza, 1928; d Berlin, 1996). Sp. soprano. Début in zarzuelas 1949. Concert début 1952. NY début 1955 (Rosario in concert perf. of *Goyescas). CG début 1955; Glyndebourne 1956; Salzburg Fest. 1961; S. Francisco 1964; NY Met 1966. Member Deutsche Oper, Berlin, 1958–91.

Lorentzen, Bent (b Stenvad, 1935). Danish composer. Taught at Århus Cons. 1962–71. After Darmstadt in 1965, turned to elec. mus. Worked in Stockholm EMS 1967–8. Settled in Copenhagen 1971. His opera *Euridice* (1965) won 1970 Italia Prize. Also much chamber and choral mus. in addition to works on tape.

Lorenz, Max (b Düsseldorf, 1901; d Salzburg, 1975). Ger. tenor, specializing in Wagner and as Verdi's Otello. Début Dresden 1927 (Walther in *Tannhäuser*). Berlin State Opera 1929–44, Vienna State Opera 1929–33, 1936–44, 1954. NY Met 1931–4 and 1947–50; CG 1934 and 1937; Bayreuth Fest. 1933–41 and 1952. Created Josef K. in Einem's *Der Prozess* (his Salzburg Fest. début, 1953), Der Podestà in Liebermann's *Penelope* (1954), 1st Kaufmann in Egk's *Irische Legende* (1955), and Der alte Torbern in Wagner-Régeny's *Das Bergwerk zu Falun* (1961), all at Salzburg Fest.

Loriod, Yvonne (b Houilles, Seine-et-Oise, 1924). Fr. pianist. Married *Messiaen in 1961. Expert in Messiaen's mus., most of which she has recorded. Prof. of pf. Paris Cons. Gave f. Paris ps. of concs. by Mozart, Bartók, and Schoenberg, and of works by Jolivet, Barraqué, Boulez, and Messiaen. Amer. début 1949.

Lortzing, (Gustav) **Albert** (*b* Berlin, 1801; *d* Berlin, 1851). Ger. composer, actor, tenor, and librettist. Played pf., vn., and vc., and comp. from early youth. Married actress in 1823 and worked as actor. First opera *Ali Pascha von Janina* prod. in Münster, 1824. Leading ten. at Leipzig State Th. 1833–43. While there, his operas *Die beiden Schützen* (1837) and *Zar und Zimmermann* (1837) were successfully perf. His *Hans Sachs* (1840) and *Casanova* (1841) failed, but *Der *Wildschütz* (1842) was a triumph. In *Undine* (1845), he made use of *leitmotiv*. In 1846 he went to Vienna, returning to Leipzig 1849 for his *Rolands Knappen*. Financial troubles led him to accept Berlin post in 1850 conducting farces and vaudevilles, and largely caused his death. His last work was operetta *Die Opernprobe* (The Opera Rehearsal), 1851, prod. in Frankfurt day before he died.

Los Angeles, Victoria de [García, Victoria López] (*b* Barcelona, 1923; *d* Barcelona, 2005). Sp. soprano. Début while student in Monteverdi's *Orfeo*. Professional début as Mimì, Barcelona 1941. Won Geneva int. fest. 1947. Eng. début, BBC 1949; CG 1950; Amer. début NY 1950; Met 1951; Bayreuth Fest. début 1961. Notable interpreter of Mimì, Butterfly, Carmen, Dido, etc., also of Mozart and Wagner roles. Retired from stage 1969, but continued to give recitals.

Los Angeles Philharmonic Orchestra. Founded 1919 with W. H. Rothwell as cond. 1919–27. Since Dec. 1964 has played in Dorothy Chandler Pavilion of Los Angeles Mus. Center. Gives summer concerts in Hollywood Bowl. Prin. cond.: Georg *Schnéevoigt (1927–9), Artur *Rodzinski (1929–33), Otto *Klemperer (1933–9), Alfred *Wallenstein (1943–56), Eduard *van Beinum (1956–9), Zubin *Mehta (1962–77), Carlo Maria *Giulini (1978–84), André Previn (1986–9), Esa-Pekka Salonen from 1992. Toured Eur., Iran, and India under Mehta 1967.

Lost Chord, The. Song by *Sullivan, comp. 1877 in sorrow at his brother's death. Poem by Adelaide Anne Procter. Regarded as the archetypal Victorian drawing-room ballad.

Lothar, Mark (*b* Berlin, 1902; *d* Munich 1985). Ger. composer. Worked as accomp. to singers in 1920s. Mus. dir. in Berlin and Munich 1933–56. Wrote operas *Tyll* (1928), *Lord Spleen* (based on Jonson's *Epicoene*, as was Strauss's *Die schweigsame Frau*) (1930), *Münchhausen* (1933), *Rappelkopf* (1958). Also choral works, chamber mus., pf. pieces, and many songs.

Lott, (Dame) **Felicity** (Ann) (*b* Cheltenham, 1947). Eng. soprano. Opera début, Unicorn Opera, Abingdon, 1973 (Seleuce in Handel's *Tolomeo*). ENO début 1975; CG 1976 (created Lady 3/Girl 3 in *We Come to the River*); GTO 1976; Glyndebourne 1977; Amer. début (concert) 1984; Munich 1988 (Christine); NY Met 1990; Vienna State Opera 1991; Salzburg Fest. 1992. Member of *Song-

makers' Almanac. Outstanding in leading Strauss roles (Marschallin, Octavian, Arabella, Christine, Countess). CBE 1990. DBE 1996.

Lotti, Antonio (*b* Venice, *c*.1667; *d* Venice, 1740). It. composer and organist. In St Mark's choir 1687, chief org. 1704 and choirmaster 1736. Wrote 24 operas between 1693 and 1717. Stayed in Dresden 1717–19, writing 3 operas there, and *Constantino* for Vienna. Comp. only church mus. (of high quality) after 1719. Book of madrigals (1705).

Loughran, James (*b* Glasgow, 1931). Scottish conductor. Won first prize Philharmonia Orch. cond. comp., 1961. London début with Philharmonia 1961; assoc. cond. Bournemouth SO 1962–5; prin. cond. BBC Scottish SO 1965–71; prin. cond. Hallé Orch. 1971–83, Bamberg SO 1978–83. Amer. début 1972 (NYPO). Opera début London (SW) 1963 (f.p. of Williamson's *Our Man in Havana*). CG début 1964. Chief cond. Åarhus SO 1996–2003.

Louise. Opera (*roman musical*) in 4 acts by G. *Charpentier to his own lib. Completed 1896. Prod. Paris 1900, NY 1908, London 1909. Sequel *Julien* (1913).

Louis Ferdinand, Prince (Prince Friedrich Christian Ludwig of Prussia) (*b* Friedrichsfelde, 1772; *d* in battle Saalfeld, 1806). Ger. composer and pianist, nephew of Frederick the Great. Virtuoso pianist. Wrote large amount of chamber mus. Admirer of Beethoven, who dedicated 3rd pf. conc. to him.

loure (Fr.). Type of Fr. bagpipe; also dance, like a slow jig, acc. by this instr.

louré. Term applied in string-playing to a type of slurred staccato and formerly called *portato*. An on-string stroke is executed at moderate speed.

Lourié, Arthur (Vincent) (*b* St Petersburg, 1892; *d* Princeton, NJ, 1966). Russ.-born composer (Amer. cit. 1947). Settled in Paris 1923–40, then he moved to USA 1941. Friend of Stravinsky. Experimented with atonality and quarter-tones, but later adopted modal style. Works incl. 2 operas, 2 syms., several large-scale religious works, 3 str. qts. Wrote biography of *Koussevitzky (Eng. edn. 1931).

Louvier, Alain (*b* Paris, 1945). Fr. composer and teacher. Last recipient of *Grand Prix de Rome*, 1968. Dir., Nat. Mus. Sch., Boulogne-Billancourt 1972–85. Dir., Paris Cons. from 1986. Works incl. *Hommage à Gauss*, vn., orch. (1968); *4 Poèmes de Mallarmé*, sop., narr., orch. (1968); *Suite*, chamber orch. (1977); *Concerto for Orchestra*, with elec. (1982); *Clamavi*, vc., perc. (1995); *Missa de angelis*, ch., 2 hn., perc. (1999); str. qt. (2000); *Heptagone*, fl., cl., hp., pf., vn., va., vc. (2004); *Solstices*, treble vv., pf. (2005); and many chamber works. Uses ondes Martenot and elec. in several of his comps.

Love for Three Oranges (*Lyubov k tryom apelsinam*). Opera in prologue and 4 acts by Prokofiev, Op.33, to Fr. lib. by composer based on Gozzi's play *Fiabe dell' amore delle tre melarance* (1761). Comp. 1919. Prod. Chicago 1921, London 1963. Orch. suite 1923.

Love in a Village. Ballad opera (*pasticcio*) in 3 acts with mus. collected and arr. by T. Arne and comp. by him and 16 other composers. Prod. London 1762, Charleston 1766. New edn. by Arthur *Oldham, Aldeburgh Fest. 1952.

Loveland, Kenneth (*b* Sheerness, 1915; *d* Cwmbran, 1998). Eng. music critic. Mus. critic *S. Wales Daily Argus* (of which he was also for a time ed.). Lect. on mus. Contributor to *The Times* and periodicals.

Love of the Three Kings (Montemezzi). See *Amore dei tre re, L'*.

Love-potion, The (Donizetti). See *Elisir d'amore, L'*.

Lover and the Nightingale, The (Granados). See *Maja y el ruisenor, La*.

Love-song Waltzes (Brahms). See *Liebesliederwalzer*.

Love, the Magician (Falla). See *Amor brujo, El*.

Love went a-Riding. Song for v. and pf. (or orch.) by Frank Bridge. Comp. 1914. Poem by Mary Coleridge (1861–1907).

Löwe, Ferdinand (*b* Vienna, 1865; *d* Vienna, 1925). Austrian conductor. Taught pf. and choral singing at Vienna Cons. 1883–96. Cond. Kaim Orch., Munich, 1897. Ass. cond. Vienna Opera 1898–1900. Cond. Vienna Konzertverein Orch. (now Vienna SO) 1904–24. Dir. Vienna Music Acad. 1918–22. Disciple and interpreter of Bruckner; one of those, who from friendliest if misguided motives, persuaded him to rev. and cut his syms. Ed. of spurious first pubd. edn. of 9th Sym. (1903), heavily cut and rev.

lower mordent. See *mordent*.

LRAM. Licentiate of the Royal Academy of Music.

LRSM. Licentiate of the Royal Schools of Music.

LTCL. Licentiate of Trinity College of Music, London.

LTSC. Licentiate of the Tonic Sol-fa College.

Lubbock, John (*b* Much Hadham, 1945). Eng. conductor and chorusmaster. Founded his own orch. 1967 while a student. Sang in LSO Ch., John Alldis Ch., and Swingle Singers. In 1972 his orch. was appointed res. orch. of St John's, Smith Square, Westminster. Début with LPO 1987. Dir. sch. children's orch., Snape Maltings, from 1982. Wexford Fest. 1992 (*The Dream of Gerontius*).

Lubin, Germaine (Léontine Angélique) (*b* Paris, 1890; *d* Paris, 1979). Fr. soprano. Début Paris Op-

éra-Comique 1912 (Antonia in *Les contes d'Hoffmann*). Sang Strauss's Ariadne at f. Paris p. Paris Opéra 1916–44. Created Charlotte in Milhaud's *Maximilien* (1932). CG début 1937; Bayreuth Fest. 1938, first Fr. singer to appear there. Imprisoned 3 years, 1944, for collab. with Ger. occupation. Gave recitals 1952 and 1954 and taught singing.

Lubotsky, Mark (*b* Leningrad, 1931). Russ. violinist. Début Moscow 1950 (Tchaikovsky conc.). Teacher at Gnesin Inst., Moscow, 1967–76. London début 1970 in Britten's conc., which he recorded with the composer. Prof. of vn., Sweelinck Cons., Amsterdam, from 1976, Hamburg Hochschule für Musik from 1986.

Lucas, Leighton (*b* London, 1903; *d* London, 1982). Eng. conductor and composer. Began career as dancer in Diaghilev Ballet 1918–21, acquiring mus. knowledge by own initiative. Became ballet cond. at 19; composer of religious works and film mus. (incl. *Target for Tonight*, 1941).

Luchetti, Veriano (*b* Viterbo, 1939). It. tenor. Sang at Wexford Fest. 1965 (Alfredo in *La traviata*). CG début 1973; La Scala début 1975; Salzburg Fest. 1985.

Lucia di Lammermoor. Opera in 3 acts by Donizetti to lib. by Cammarano based on Scott's novel *The Bride of Lammermoor* (1819). Prod. Naples 1835, London 1838, New Orleans 1841. The famous 'Mad Scene', one of the finest vehicles for a brilliant but sensitive coloratura sop., is usually perf. as Act 3, Sc. 1 (the original Sc. 1 is usually omitted, although it has been recorded). In the orig. score Lucia is acc. in this scene by glass hp., but a fl. is generally substituted.

Lucier, Alvin (*b* Nashua, New Hampshire, 1931). Amer. composer. Choral dir., Brandeis Univ. 1962–70. Founded Sonci Arts Union 1966, elec. mus. performing group. Prof. at Wesleyan Univ. 1970–84 (head of dept. from 1979). Has worked mainly with elec. apparatus. In his *Music for a Solo Performer* (1965), 3 electrodes are attached to the performer's scalp picking up 10-cycle alpha brain waves. This signal is amplified and filtered, and directed to loudspeakers which activate sympathetic responses in perc. instrs. Various other unconventional sources of sound are used in his works.

Lucio Silla. *Dramma per musica* in 3 acts (K135) by Mozart to lib. by G. da Gamerra, altered by Metastasio. Prod. Milan 1772, Prague 1929, Dresden 1955, London 1967, Baltimore 1968. Also operas by Anfossi (1774) and J. C. Bach (1775).

Lucky Hand, The (Schoenberg). See *Glückliche Hand, Die*.

Lucrezia Borgia. Opera in prol. and 2 acts by Donizetti to lib. by Romani based on Hugo's tragedy (1833). Prod. Milan 1833, London 1839, New Orleans 1843. At Paris prod. 1840, Hugo raised objections. The opera was withdrawn and the lib. re-written as *La Rinegata*, the action being re-located in Turkey.

Ludus Tonalis (The Play of Notes). Pf. studies in counterpoint, tonal organization, and pf. playing by Hindemith, comp. 1942, f.p. Chicago 1943. Comprises prelude, 12 fugues with 11 interludes, and postlude (inverted version of prelude).

Ludwig II, King of Bavaria (*b* Nymphenburg, 1845; *d* Lake Starnberg, 1886). Succeeded his father, Maximilian II, in 1864. Was passionate admirer of Wagner's mus., becoming his generous patron, buying him houses, and planning to build th. in Munich to stage *Der Ring des Nibelungen*. Prime mover in Munich premières of *Tristan und Isolde* (1865), *Die Meistersinger von Nürnberg* (1868), *Das Rheingold* (1869), and *Die Walküre* (1870). Because of scandal of Wagner's affair with Cosima von Bülow, Wagner had to leave Munich, but despite breach in their friendship Ludwig continued to provide support, and helped Wagner financially in building of Bayreuth Festspielhaus and Villa Wahnfried. A fascinating historical figure, his alleged 'madness' is at the least questionable.

Ludwig, Christa (*b* Berlin, 1924). Ger. soprano and mezzo-soprano. Début Frankfurt 1946 (Orlofsky in *Die Fledermaus*), remaining until 1952. Sang in opera in Darmstadt, Hanover, and Hamburg. Salzburg Fest. début 1955, appearing there regularly until 1993. Vienna Opera 1955–93. Amer début Chicago 1959; NY Met début 1959; CG début 1968. Outstanding Marschallin and Oktavian, Eboli and Leonore (*Fidelio*). Also noted interpreter of *Lieder*, Mahler's orch. song-cycles, Verdi *Requiem*, etc. Retired 1994.

Ludwig, Leopold (*b* Witkowitz, 1908; *d* Lüneburg, 1979). Austrian conductor. Began career at Opava, 1931. Mus. dir. Oldenburg 1936, Vienna Opera 1939–43, Berlin State Opera 1943–51. Mus. dir. Hamburg Opera 1951–70, conducting many contemporary works and taking company to Edinburgh (1952), London 1962 (f. Brit. p. of Berg's *Lulu*), and NY (1967). Glyndebourne 1959; NY Met 1970.

Luening, Otto (*b* Milwaukee, Wisconsin, 1900; *d* NY, 1996). Amer. composer, conductor, teacher, and flautist. Worked as flautist and accompanist, 1915. Cond. opera in Munich and Zurich 1917–20. One of founders of Amer. Grand Opera Co., Chicago, 1920. Dir., opera dept., Eastman Sch. of Mus. 1925–8. Taught in Cologne 1928–32, Univ. of Arizona 1932–4, Bennington Coll., Vermont, 1934–44. Prof. of mus. Barnard Coll., NY, 1944–7. On philosophy faculty, Columbia Univ., 1949–68. Co-dir. Columbia-Princeton Elec. Mus. Center 1959–80. Taught comp. Juilliard Sch. 1971–3. Large body of comps. incl. opera *Evangeline* (Longfellow); *A Wisconsin Symphony*; fl. concertino; *Kentucky Concerto* for orch.; song settings of Whitman and Blake; chamber mus. incl. 3 str. qts.; various sonatas; *Sonority Canon* for 2 to 37 fl.; and pf.

pieces. Comp. several elec. works, e.g. *Fantasy in Space*, fl. on tape, and *Synthesis* for orch. Also elec. works in collab. with V. *Ussachevsky, incl. *A Poem in Cycles and Bells*, tape recorder and orch.; and mus. for prods. of Shaw's *Back to Methuselah* and Shakespeare's *King Lear*.

luftig (Ger.). Airy.

Luisa Miller. Opera in 3 acts by Verdi to lib. by Cammarano after Schiller's play *Kabale und Liebe* (1784). Comp. 1849. Prod. Naples 1849, NY 1854, London 1858.

Luisi, Fabio (*b* Genoa, 1959). It. conductor. Began to study piano aged 4 and graduated from Paganini Cons. 1978. Studied with Ciccolini in Paris. Attended Graz Univ. of Mus. to study with Milan Horvat. First post at Graz Opera as acc. and cond. 1983. Concert début Martina Franca, Italy (Cimarosa's *Requiem*), and Graz Opera (Donizetti's *Viva la Mama*), both 1984. Founder and art. dir. Graz SO 1990–5. Art. dir. and chief cond. Tonkünstlerorch., Vienna, 1995–2000. Mus. dir. and art. dir. Orch. de la Suisse Romande 1997–2002. NYPO début 2000, NY Met 2005 (*Don Carlos*). Salzburg Fest. début 2002 (*Die Liebe der Danae*). Chief cond. Vienna SO from 2005. Gen. mus. dir. Semperoper, Dresden, and chief cond. Staatskapelle Orch. from 2007.

Lukomska, Halina (*b* Suchedniów, 1929). Polish soprano. Won 's Hertogenbosch Comp. 1956. Specialist in works of Webern, Boulez, Lutosławski, and Serocki. Recorded Boulez's *Pli selon pli* with composer.

lullaby (Fr. berceuse; Ger. Wiegenlied). Cradle-song, usually in triple rhythm. Vocal lullabies occur in mus. of all periods. There are also instrumental lullabies, such as Chopin's *Berceuse*, Op.57 (1843–4).

Lully, Jean-Baptiste [Lulli, Giovanni Battista] (*b* Florence, 1632; *d* Paris, 1687). It.-born composer (Fr. nationality from 1661). At 14 went to Fr. and worked as page to cousin of Louix XIV until prowess as dancer and mime was noted. Entered service of Louis XIV 1653, composing instr. mus. for the court ballets. Some time before 1656 he became leader of 'les petits violons du Roi', a band of 21 players (an offshoot of the '24 violons du roi'). 'Instrumental composer to the King' 1653–61, 'Superintendent of Mus. and chamber mus. composer' 1661–2; 'music master to Royal Family' from 1662. From 1664 collab. with Molière in series of comedy-ballets which were forerunners of Fr. opera, the last and most famous being *Le Bourgeois Gentilhomme*, in which Lully danced role of the Mufti. Having assimilated both It. and Fr. styles and tastes, from 1673 he turned to opera comp. and obtained from the King exclusive rights to arrange operatic perfs. in Paris. For the next 14 years, working with the poet Quinault, he not only wrote about 20 operas and ballets, but prod. and cond. them and trained the singers with firm discipline. He developed the formal 'French Ov.' and replaced It. *recitativo secco* with acc. recit., placing special emphasis on a style of declamation suited to Fr. language. He introduced professional female dancers into the ballet. A supreme courtier and intriguer, he nevertheless made Fr. opera a popular art. His death was caused by a gangrenous abscess which formed in his foot after he struck it with the long staff he used for beating time on the floor while conducting a *Te Deum* to celebrate Louis XIV's recovery from illness. Prin. works:

OPERAS (*tragédies en musique*): *Les Fêtes de l'Amour et de Bacchus* (1672); *Cadmus et Hermione* (1673); *Alceste* (1674); *Thésée* (1675); *Atys* (1676); *Isis* (1677); *Psyché* (1678); *Bellérophon* (1679); *Proserpine* (1680); *Persée* (1682); *Phaëton* (1683); *Amadis de Gaule* (1684); *Roland* (1685); *Armide* (1686); *Acis et Galathée* (1686); *Achille et Polixène* (with Colasse, 1687, prod. posthumously).

COMEDY-BALLETS with MOLIÈRE: *Le mariage forcé* (1664); *L'amour médecin* (1665); *La Princesse d'Elide* (1664); *Le Sicilien* (1667); *Georges Dandin* (1668); *Monsieur de Pourceaugnac* (1669); *Les amants magnifiques* (1670); *Le *Bourgeois Gentilhomme* (1670).

CHORAL: Motets for 2 choirs (1684); *Miserere* (1664); *Te Deum* (1677); *De Profundis* (1683); 5 *Grands Motets* (1685).

Lulu. Opera in 3 acts by Berg to his own lib. based on Frank Wedekind's *Erdgeist* (1895) and *Die Büchse der Pandora* (1901). Comp. 1929–35, but full score of Act III uncompleted. Prod. Zurich 1937. Vienna 1962, London 1962 (SW, visit of Hamburg Co.), Cardiff (WNO) 1971. Lulu, a *femme fatale*, sinks to prostitution and ends as a victim of Jack the Ripper. Mus. is founded on a single note-row, from which are derived *leitmotiv* assoc. with certain characters, differing from *Wozzeck* where each scene has a formal designation. After death of Berg's widow in 1977, short score of Act III was orch. by Friedrich *Cerha and opera was given complete for first time at Paris Opéra 1979, cond. Boulez. Also Santa Fe, 1979 (in English), CG 1981. A 5-movt. suite for orch. (*Lulu-Symphonie*) was f.p. in Berlin, cond. E. Kleiber, 1934.

Lumbye, Hans Christian (*b* Copenhagen, 1810; *d* Copenhagen, 1874). Danish conductor and composer of galops, marches, and polkas. Known as 'the Northern Strauss'. Dir. of Tivoli Gardens, Copenhagen, 1843–72.

Lumsdaine, David (*b* Sydney, NSW, 1931). Australian composer. Lect. in mus., Durham Univ., where he inaugurated EMS. Prin. works:

ORCH.: *Variations* (1957); *Episodes* (1968–9); *Hagoromo* (1975–7); *Shoalhaven* (1982); *Mandala V* (1988); *A Garden of Earthly Delights*, vc., orch. (1992).

CHAMBER ORCH.: *Mandala II* (1969); *Looking Glass Music* (1970); *Salvation Creek with Eagle* (1974); *Sunflower* (1975); *Mandala III*, pf. and ens. (1978); *Empty Sky, Mootwingee*, fl., tb. or hn., vc., perc., 2 pf. (1986); *A Dance and a Hymn for Alexander*

Maconchy, ens. (1988); *Round Dance*, sitar, tabla, fl., vc., pf. (1989); *Rain Drums*, 4 perc. (1993); *Kali Dances*, chamber ens. (1994).

BRASS BAND: *Evensong* (1975).

VOICE(S) & CHAMBER ENS.: *Annotations of Auschwitz*, sop. and ens. (1964, rev. 1970); *Easter Frescoes*, sop., ens. (1966, rev. 1971); *Aria For Edward John Eyre*, sop., ens. (1972); *Tides*, narrator, 12 vv., perc. (1979); *The Ballad of Perse O'Reilly*, ten., male ch., 2 pf. (1953–81); *What Shall I Sing?* sop., 2 cl. (1982).

CHAMBER MUSIC: *Mandala I*, wind quintet (1967); *Caliban Impromptu* (1972); *Mandala IV*, str. qt. (1983).

PIANO: *Kelly Ground* (1966); *Flights*, 2 pf. (1967); *Kangaroo Hunt*, pf., perc. (1971); *Ruhe Sanfte, Sanfte Ruh'* (1974); *Cambewarra* (1980).

SOLO VOICE: *My Sister's Song*, sop. (1974).

TAPE: *Babel* (1968); *Big Meeting*, elec. fantasy (1978); *Wild Ride to Heaven* (with N. *LeFanu), 'radiophonic adventure playground' (1980).

Lumsden, (Sir) **David** (James) (*b* Newcastle upon Tyne, 1928). Eng. organist, harpsichordist, chorusmaster, and administrator. Org., Nottingham Univ., 1954–6; dir. mus., Keele Univ., 1956–9; org., New Coll., Oxford, 1959–78; Prin., RSAMD 1978–82; Prin., RAM 1982–93. Authority on Eng. lute mus. Knighted 1985.

lungo, lunga (It.). Long; *lunga pausa* (1) long pause; (2) long rest.

luogo (It.). Same as *loco*.

Luonnotar. Tone-poem for sop. and orch., Op.70, by Sibelius, to words from Finnish epic *Kalevala* telling of creation of the world. Comp. 1910–13.

Lupu, Radu (*b* Galati, 1945). Romanian pianist. First prize Van Cliburn comp. 1966, Enescu int. comp. 1967, and Leeds int. comp. 1969. First London recital, Nov. 1969. USA tour 1972 (début with Cleveland Orch.). Settled in Eng. Salzburg Fest. début 1979.

lur. (1) A prehistoric bronze tpt.

(2) A wooden tpt.-like instr. used by herdsmen in Scandinavia as the *Alphorn, which it somewhat resembles, is in Switzerland.

lusigando. A term that appears sometimes in Debussy's mus. Apparently a mistake for *lusingando*.

lusingando (It.). Flattering, i.e. play in a coaxing, intimate manner. So, too, *lusinghevole, lusinghevolmente, lusinghiero, lusingante*.

Lustigen Weiber von Windsor, Die (The Merry Wives of Windsor). Opera in 3 acts by *Nicolai to lib. by S. H. Mosenthal based on Shakespeare's comedy (1600–1). Comp. 1846–7. Prod. Berlin 1849, Philadelphia 1863, London 1864 (in It.), 1878 (in Eng.), 1907 (in Ger. at CG).

Lustige Witwe, Die (Lehár). See *Merry Widow, The*.

lute. Fretted str. instr. of great antiquity played by plucking with the fingers (occasionally with a plectrum in earlier types). The 'long lute', with neck longer than the body, dates back at least to 2000 BC. The short lute, with neck slightly shorter than the body, dates from c.800 BC. It was transformed into the European lute, with distinct neck and central soundhole, probably in Spain in 14th cent. Has a round body, like halved pear, flat neck with 7 or more frets, and separate pegbox usually bent back from neck at angle. In 16th cent. had 11 str. in 6 courses, tuned to convenient pitch. Up to 6 bass courses were added in 17th cent., unalterable in pitch. In mid–17th cent., new system of tuning (called *nouveau ton*) was introduced by Denis Gaultier. Lutes were much used for solos, acc., and in ens. Their mus. was played not from notation but from *tabla-ture which in the 16th and 17th cents. took the form of a staff with a space for each str. and small letters placed within the space to indicate the fret to be used. Small marks above the staff gave the duration of the sounds.

Many varieties of lute were used in the 16th and 17th cents., when it was the chief domestic inst. They incl. *mandola*, *mandolin*, *angelica*, and larger, deeper lutes called *archlutes*, of which the 'long' was the *chittarone and the 'short' the *theorbo. All have the characteristic round back, differentiating them from the flat-back *guitar family. In the 17th cent., lute music was chiefly cultivated in Fr., Ger., and Eng. (*Dowland was probably the greatest lute composer) while Sp. and It. turned to the guitar. The literature of lute mus. stretches from 1507 to c.1770, among the latest composers to compose for it being Handel, J. S. Bach, Reusner, and Weiss. It came to be used in orch. mus., and there is a part for lute in Bach's *St John Passion* (1723). With the 20th-cent. revival of interest in early mus. the lute has regained considerable popularity, especially through the agency of virtuosi such as Julian *Bream and Nigel North.

The term is also used generically for a large group of str. instr., e.g. fiddles, viols, vielle, etc.

lute harpsichord (Ger. *Lautenclavicymbel*). Hpd. with gut instead of metal strs., so-called because of lute-like sound. In 1740 J. S. Bach had one made for his use.

lutenist (lutanist). Player of the *lute.

luth (Fr.). The *lute.

Luther, Martin (b Eisleben, 1483; d Eisleben, 1546). Ger. Protestant church reformer. Player of lute and fl. Est. congregational singing. Wrote treatise on mus. (1538) and words of many hymns and chorales (possibly the mus., too), best-known being *Ein' feste Burg ist unser Gott* (A safe stronghold our God is still).

luthier (Fr., from *luth*, lute; Ger. *Lautenmacher*). A maker of str. instr., nowadays usually those of the vn. family.

Lutosławski, Witold (b Warsaw, 1913; d Warsaw, 1994). Polish composer, pianist, and conductor. Prisoner-of-war of Germans 1939 but escaped and worked as pianist in Warsaw cafés 1940–5. His earlier works were comp. under the restraints imposed by official insistence on a style based on folk-song, but the *Concerto for Orchestra* (1950–4) is a successful example from this period. Secretly he developed his own method of 12-note chords, entirely different from Schoenberg's which he disliked. This method was used in his *Funeral Music* for str. and his 2nd sym. In *Gry weneckie* (*Venetian Games*) of 1960–1, he employed *aleatory procedures within strictly defined limits. His later works combine this technique with more traditional forms such as *ostinato* and harmonic patterns. The mus. texture is all-important.

When conditions in Poland were relaxed after 1956, he travelled to the USA and Britain to teach and give seminars and soon acquired a high reputation in the West. Many prizes and honours came his way and he was acclaimed for a succession of works such as *Paroles tissées*, commissioned by Peter *Pears, *Livre pour Orchestre*, *Mi-Parti*, the str. qt., and the vc. conc. written for *Rostropovich. In his later works, such as the superb 3rd and 4th Syms., the pf. conc., and the song-cycle *Chantefables et Chantefleurs*, it became even more apparent that his music derived from Debussy and early Stravinsky through Bartók to Messiaen. The craftsmanship of his mus. is impeccable and he was an outstanding cond. of it, as his many recordings testify. Prin. comps.:

ORCH.: *Symphonic Variations* (1938); syms: No.1 (1941–7), No.2 (1965–7), No.3 (1972–83), No.4 (1991–2); *Overture*, str. (1949); *Little Suite*, chamber orch. (1950, rev. 1951 for full orch.); 5 *Folk-Songs*, str. (1952, from *Folk Melodies* for pf.); *Concerto for Orchestra* (1950–4); *Muzyka żalobna* (Funeral Music), str. (1958); 3 *Postludes* (1958–63); *Gry weneckie* (*Venetian Games*) (1960–1); *Livre pour orchestre* (1968); *Cello Concerto* (1969–70); *Preludes and Fugue*, 13 solo strings (1972); *Mi-Parti* (1976); *Variations on a Theme of Paganini*, version for pf. and orch. (1978, see 2 PIANOS); *Novelette* (1978–9); Conc. for ob., hp., chamber orch. (1979–80); *Chain I*, chamber orch. (1983), *Chain II*, dialogue, vn., orch. (1985), *Chain III* (1986); pf. conc. (1988); *Partita*, vn., orch. (vers. of chamber work, 1984) (1988); *Slides*, 11 soloists (1988); *Interludium*, chamber orch. (1989).

VOICE(S) & ORCH.: 2 *Fragments from a Requiem*, v., ch., orch. (1937); *Silesian Triptych*, sop., orch. (1951); 3 *Poems of Henri Michaux*, ch., wind, 2 pf., hp., perc. (1963); *Paroles tissées*, ten., 20 solo instr. (1965); *Les espaces du sommeil* (The spaces of sleep), bar., orch. (1975); *Chantefables et Chantefleurs*, sop., orch. (1990).

CHAMBER MUSIC: 30 small pieces for woodwind (1943–4); wind trio (1954); *Dance Preludes*, cl., pf. (1954, rev. 1955 for cl., small orch., 1959 for nonet); str. qt. (1964); *Epitaph*, ob., pf. (1979); *Grave*, vc., pf. (1981); *Partita*, vn., pf. (1984), vn., orch. (1988).

2 PIANOS: *Variations on a Theme of Paganini* (1941); vers. for pf., orch. (1978).

PIANO: sonata (1934); *Folk Melodies* (1945, Nos. 9–12 rev. 1954 for 4 vn. as 4 *Silesian Folk-Songs*; 5 of them arr. for str. as 5 *Folk-Songs*, 1952); *Invention* (1983).

VOICE(s) & PIANO: 20 *Polish Carols* (1946); 5 *Songs* (1957, rev. 1958, mez., 30 instr.); *Tarantella*, bar., pf. (1990).

BRASS: *Mini Overture* (1981).

lutto (It.). Mourning. So *luttoso* or *luttuoso*, mournful; *luttosamente*, mournfully.

Lutyens, (Agnes) **Elisabeth** (*b* London, 1906; *d* London, 1983). Eng. composer. One of first Eng. composers to use 12-note system. Comp. nearly 200 scores for films and radio, also incidental mus. for plays. Helped to found Macnaghten-Lemare concerts, London, 1931, and founded Composers' Concourse 1954. Author of books (autobiography *A Goldfish Bowl*, 1972), and articles. CBE 1969. Prin. works:

OPERAS: *Infidelio* (1954); *The Numbered* (1965–7); *Isis and Osiris* (1969–70); *Time off? Not a Ghost of a Chance!* (charade in 4 scenes with 3 interruptions) (1967–8); *The Goldfish Bowl* (1975); *Like a Window* (1976).

ORCH.: *3 Pieces* (1939); 5 chamber concs. (1939–46); *3 Symphonic Preludes* (1942); va. conc. (1947); *Quincunx* (with sop. and bar.) (1959–60); *Music for Orchestra* I (1955), II (1962), III (1963), IV (1981); *Chorale* (1956); *Symphonies*, pf., wind, hps., perc. (1961); *Music for Piano and Orchestra* (1964); *Novenaria* (1967); *The Winter of the World* (1974); *Eos* (1975); *Rondel* (1976); *Concert Aria*, female v., orch. (1976); *6 Bagatelles* (1976); *Nox*, pf., 2 chamber orchs. (1977); *Tides* (1978); *Echoi*, with mez. (1979); *Rapprochement* (1980); *Six* (1980); *Wild Decembers* (1980).

VOICE(s) & INSTRS.: *O Saisons, O châteaux* (Rimbaud), sop., str. (1946); *Nativity*, sop., str. (1951); *De Amore* (Chaucer), sop., ten., ch., orch. (1957); *Catena*, sop., ten., 21 instr. (1961); *The Valley of Hatsu-se*, sop., fl., cl., vc., pf. (1965); *Akapotik Rose*, sop., ens. (1966); *And Suddenly It's Evening*, ten., 11 instr. (1967); *Essence of Our Happinesses*, ten., ch., orch. (1968); *A Phoenix*, sop., vn., cl., pf. (1968); *Anerca*, speaker, 10 guitars, perc. (1970); *Vision of Youth*, sop., 3 cl., pf., perc. (1970); *Islands*, sop., ten., speaker, ens. (1971); *Requiescat* (in mem. Stravinsky), sop., str. trio or mez., 2 cl., bcl. (1971); *Dirge for the Proud World*, sop., counterten., hpd., vc. (1971); *The Tears of Night*, counterten., 6 sop., 3 instr. ens. (1971); *Chimes and Cantos*, bar., ens. (1972); *Laudi*, sop., 3 cl., pf. (1973); *Fleur du Silence*, ten., ens. (1980); *Mine Eyes, My Bread, My Spade*, ten., str. qt. (1980). *Chorale Prelude and Paraphrase*, ten., str. quintet, pf., perc. (1977); *Elegy of the Flowers*, ten., 3 instr. groups (1978); *Cantata*, sop., instr. ens. (1979); *Cantata* (Beaudelaire), sop., cont., bar., ens. (1979); *Echoes*, cont., fl., cor ang., str. qt. (1979); *Concert Aria* ('Dialogo'), sop., ens. (1980);

CHORAL: *Encomion*, brass, perc. (1963); *Voice of Quiet Waters*, orch. (1972); *Counting Your Steps*, 4 fl., 4 perc. (1972); *The Roots of the World*, vc. obbl. (1979).

UNACC. CHORAL: *Excerpta Tractata—Logico Philosophici* (Wittgenstein), motet (1952); *The Country of the Stars* (1963); *The Hymn of Man*, male vv. (1965), rev. for mixed vv. (1970); *Magnificat and Nunc Dimittis* (1965); *The Tyme doth Flete* (1968); *Verses of Love* (1970); *Roads*, 2 sop., counterten., ten., bar., bass (1973); *Sloth—One of the Seven Deadly Sins*, 2 counterten., ten., 2 bar., bass (1974); *It is the Hour* (1976).

STRING QUARTETS: No.2 (1938), No.3 (1949), No.6 (1952), No.12 (1981); Op.139 (1979); Op.158 (1982); *Plenum III* (1973); *Mare et Minutiae* (1976); *Doubles* (1978); 'Diurnal', Op.146 (1980).

CHAMBER ENS.: str. trio (1939); *Concertante*, fl., cl., vn., vc., pf. (1950); *Nocturnes*, vn., vc., gui. (1955); *Capricii*, 2 hp., perc. (1955); *6 Tempi*, 10 instr. (1957); wind quintet (1960); str. quintet (1963); wind trio (1963); *Fantasie-Trio*, fl., cl., pf. (1963); str. trio (1964); *Scena*, vn., vc., perc. (1964); *Music for Wind* (1964); *The Fall of the Leafe*, ob., str. qt. (1966); *Music for Three*, fl., ob., pf. (1966); *Horai*, vn., hn., pf. (1968); *Driving Out the Death*, ob., str. trio (1971); *Rape of the Moone*, wind octet (1973); *Plenum II*, ob., 13 instr. (1973); *Kareniana*, va., 10 instr. (1974); *Go, Said the Bird*, elec. gui., str. qt. (1975); *Fantasia*, alto sax., 3 instr. groups (1977); *O Absalom . . .*, vn., ob., va., vc. (1977); *Trio*, cl., vc., pf. (1979); *Branches of the Night and of the Day*, hn., str. qt. (1981).

CHAMBER MUSIC (1 or 2 instr., classified instrumentally): *Duo No.3*, vn., pf. (1957); *Scroll for Li-Ho*, vn., pf. (1967); *Prelude*, solo vn. (1979); *Madrigal*, ob., vn. (1977); *Morning Sea*, ob., pf. (1979); *Déroulement*, ob., gui. (1980); *Sonata*, solo va. (1938); *Aptote*, solo va. (1948); *Echo of the Wind*, solo va. (1981); *9 Bagatelles*, vc., pf. (1942); *Duo No.2*, vc., pf. (1956–7); *Constants*, vc., pf. (1976); *The Tides of Time*, db., pf. (1969); *Variations*, fl. (1957); *Footfalls*, fl., pf. (1978); *Presages*, ob. (1963); *5 Little Pieces*, cl., pf. (1945); *Valediction*, cl., pf. (1954); *Tre*, cl. (1973); *Soli*, cl., db. (1980); *This Green Tide*, basset hn., pf. (1975); *Duo No.1*, hn., pf. (1956–7); *The Dying of the Sun*, gui. (1969); *Romanza*, gui. (1977); *The Living Night*, perc. solo (1981).

SONGS (with pf. unless otherwise stated): *2 Songs by W. H. Auden* (1942); *9 Songs* (Stevie Smith) (1948); *3 Songs* (Dylan Thomas), sop., instr. (1953); *In the Temple of a Bird's Wing*, bar. (1956 and 1965); *The Egocentric*, ten. or bar. (1968); *Lament of Isis on the Death of Osiris*, solo sop. (1969); *The Supplicant*, bass (1970); *In the Direction of the Beginning*, bass (1970); *Oda a la Tormenta*, mez. (1970); *Dialogo*, ten., lute (1972); *2 Songs* (D. H. Lawrence), unacc. v. (1974); *The Hidden Power*, 2 unacc. vv. (1974); *Of the Snow*, 3 unacc. vv. (1974); *Nocturnes and Interludes*, sop. (1976); *Variations: Winter Series—Spring Sowing*, sop. (1977); *By All These . . .*, sop., gui. (1977); *She Tells Her Love While Half Asleep* (R. Graves), solo sop. (1979); *That Sun*, cont. (1979); *The Singing Birds*, speaker, va. (1980).

PIANO: *5 Intermezzi* (1941); *3 Improvisations* (1948); *Piano e Forte* (1958); *5 Bagatelles* (1962); *Helix* (1967); *Plenum I* (1972); *The Ring of Bone*, with opt. speaking v. or vv. (1975); *5 Impromptus* (1977); *7 Preludes* (1978); *The Great Seas* (1979); *3 Books of Bagatelles* (1979); *La Natura dell'Acqua* (1981).

HPD.: *Pietà* (1975).

ORGAN: *Sinfonia* (1955); *Epithalamium*, with opt. sop. (1968); *3 Short Pieces* (1969); *Plenum IV* (1974).

Also many film, radio, and theatre scores.

Luxon, Benjamin (Matthew) (*b* Redruth, 1937). Eng. baritone. Sang with EOG 1963–70. Numerous recitals and concerts. Opera at Aldeburgh. Débuts: Glyndebourne 1972; CG 1972 (created Jester, *Death, and Joking Jesus* in *Taverner*); ENO 1974; Scottish Opera 1983; NY Met 1980; Los Angeles 1988. Created role of Owen Wingrave in Britten's opera (BBC TV 1971 and CG 1973). Noted as Don Giovanni. CBE 1986.

Lvov, Alexey (Fyodorovich) (*b* Reval, 1798; *d* nr. Kovno, 1870). Russ. composer, conductor, and violinist. In 1837 succeeded father as dir. of St Petersburg court choir, remaining there until 1861. Played his own vn. conc. at Leipzig, 1840. Led str. qt. Wrote 3 operas, vn. conc., 24 caprices, church mus., and Imperial nat. anthem, *God Save the Tsar* (1833), quoted by Tchaikovsky in *1812 Overture*.

Lyadov, Anatoly (Konstantinovich) (*b* St Petersburg, 1855; *d* Novgorod, 1914). Russ. composer. Prof. of comp. St Petersburg Cons. Researched Russ. folk mus. with *Balakirev and *Lyapunov. His tone poems for orch. incl. *The Enchanted Lake* (*Volshebnoye ozero*) (1909), *Baba Yaga* (1904), and *Kikimora* (1910). Collab. in Borodin's *Paraphrases* (*Chopsticks version). Orig. choice to comp. mus. for ballet *The Firebird*, but because he did not begin work on it, it was passed to *Stravinsky.

Lyapunov, Sergey (Mikhaylovich) (*b* Yaroslavl, 1859; *d* Paris, 1924). Russ. composer. Ass. dir. Imperial choir, St Petersburg, 1884–1902. Worked with *Lyadov and *Balakirev on folk-song research. Prof., St Petersburg Cons. 1910–18. Ed. correspondence between Balakirev and Tchaikovsky. Works incl. 2 syms., 2 pf. concs., *Variations on Ukrainian Themes*, pf., orch., vn. conc., many songs, and pf. pieces.

Lydian mode. See *modes*.

Lyke-Wake Dirge. 15th-cent. anonymous Eng. poem set by *Britten in his *Serenade* for ten., hn., and str. (1943), by *Stravinsky in his *Cantata* (1951–2), and by Whittaker for ch. and orch. (1924).

Lympany, (Dame) **Moura** [Johnstone, Mary] (*b* Saltash, 1916; *d* Menton, Fr., 2005). Eng. pianist. Public début 1929, Harrogate. Int. career. Gave f. London p. of Khachaturian's pf. conc. CBE 1979. DBE 1992.

Lynn, (Dame) **Vera** [Lewis (*née* Welch), Vera Margaret] (*b* London, 1917). Eng. singer. Début 1924. Sang with Joe Loss Band 1935–7, Ambrose 1937–40. Known during Second World War as 'Forces' Sweetheart' as result of her many broadcasts and visits to the Services abroad, incl. Burma from 1944. Best-known songs incl. *We'll meet again, Yours*, and *The White Cliffs of Dover*. OBE 1968. DBE 1975.

lyra (Lira). (1) The *lyre.

(2) Early Ger. name for *hurdy-gurdy; see *lira*.

lyra organizzata. See *lira organizzata*.

lyra viol. Small bass *viol.

lyre. Ancient Gr. instr., like small harp, in which strings were fixed to a cross-bar between 2 arms and plucked by fingers or plectrum.

Lyre-Bird Press. See *L'Oiseau Lyre*.

lyric. (1) Strictly, vocal perf. with *lyre; hence *lyric drama* = opera of all kinds (Fr. *drame lyrique*), *lyric stage* = operatic stage.

(2) Short poem, not epic or narrative; composers such as Grieg adapted this meaning to mus., e.g. *Lyric Piece, Lyric Suite*.

(3) Vocal description, e.g. *lyric tenor, lyric soprano*, somewhere between 'light' and 'heavy' vocal weight, capable of sustaining long flowing lines.

(4) The words of a song in a 'musical' or of a popular 20th-cent. song.

Lyric Suite. (1) Orch. by Grieg (1904) of 4 of his 6 *Lyric Pieces* (Book 5), Op.54 (1891) (*Shepherd's Boy, Norwegian March, Nocturne*, and *March of the Dwarfs*).

(2) Work for str. qt. in 6 movts. by *Berg, comp. 1925–6, f.p. Vienna 1927. 2nd, 3rd and 4th movts. arr. for str. orch. 1928, f.p. Berlin 1929. Research has disclosed that the *Lyric Suite* was a manifestation of Berg's love for Hanna Fuchs-Robettin, wife of a Cz. paper manufacturer and sister of the novelist Franz Werfel. He met her in 1925. In addition to quotations from Wagner's *Tristan*, Zemlinsky's *Lyric Symphony*, and his own *Wozzeck*, Berg used the notes representing Hanna's and his initials (H (B nat.), F, A, and B) in the note-row which is the basis of the work. The 6th movt., *Largo desolato*, exists also in version with mez. voice as setting of S. George's trans. of Baudelaire's 'De profundis clamavi'. F.p. of suite with vocal *finale*, NY 1979, f. Eng. p., BBC broadcast 1979.

Lyrische Symphonie (Lyric Symphony). Zemlinsky's Op.18, being seven songs after poems by Rabindranath Tagore (*b* Calcutta, 1861; *d* Calcutta, 1941) in Ger. trans. by the composer, for sop., bar., and orch. Comp. 1922–3. 7 poems are: 1. *Ich bin friedlos* (I am restless), 2. *Mutter, der junge Prinz muss an unsere Türe vorbeikommen* (Mother, the young Prince is to pass our door), 3. *Du bist die Abendwolke* (You are the evening cloud), 4. *Sprich zu mir Geliebter!* (Speak to me, my love), 5. *Befrei mich von den Banden deiner süsse Lieb!* (Free me from the bonds of your sweetness, my love!), 6. *Vollende denn das letzte Lied und lass uns auseinandergehn* (Then finish the last song and let us leave), 7. *Friede, mein Herz* (Peace, my heart). In the *Lyric Suite*, which is dedicated to Zemlinsky, Berg in the 4th movt. quotes the principal theme from No.3 of the *Lyrische Symphonie*, which occurs at the words 'Du bist mein Eigen' ('You are my own'). F.p. Prague 1924, cond. Zemlinsky; f. Eng. p. 1977, BBC broadcast, cond. Süsskind.

Lysy, Alberto (Ivan) (*b* Buenos Aires, 1935). Ukrainian-Argentine violinist and conductor. First prize, Queen Elisabeth comp., Brussels, 1955. Later studied with Menuhin. Founded chamber orch. in Buenos Aires, 1965. Dir., Camerata Lysy, Gstaad, and Int. Menuhin Sch., Gstaad.

Lysy, Antonio (*b* Rome, 1963). Argentinian cellist, son of Alberto *Lysy. Soloist with many chamber ens., incl. Camerata of Salzburg, with Sandór Vegh.

Lyttelton, Humphrey (Richard Adeane) (*b* Eton, 1921). Eng. jazz trumpeter, band-leader, and cartoonist. Prof. career began 1947. Formed own band 1948. Also writer and broadcaster.

M

M. Surnames beginning M', Mc, or Mac, are all treated, in accordance with most British reference books (though not with Amer. dictionaries), as though spelt Mac.

ma (It.). 'But', as in *ma non troppo*, 'but not too much'.

Ma, Yo-Yo (*b* Paris, 1955). Fr.-born Amer. cellist of Chinese parents. Gave first recital at age of 6. In 1970s achieved international eminence as soloist with world's leading orchs. Salzburg Fest. début 1978. Gave f.p. of H. K. Gruber's conc., Tanglewood 1989.

Maag, Peter (*b* St Gall, Switz., 1919; *d* Verona, 2001). Swiss conductor and pianist. Cond. Düsseldorf Opera 1952–5, Bonn Opera 1956–9. Chief cond. Vienna Volksoper 1964–7; mus. dir. Parma Opera from 1971, Turin Opera 1974–6. Brit. débuts 1959 (CG and Glyndebourne); Amer. 1959 (Minneapolis SO), NY. Met 1972; Salzburg Fest. début 1962. Conducted many unfamiliar operas and championed 20th-cent. works.

Maayani, Ami (Hay) (*b* Ramat-Gan, Israel, 1936). Israeli composer and conductor. Cond. of Israel Youth Orch. Comps. incl. 4 syms.; 2 hp. concs.; vn. conc.; vc. conc.; va. conc.; gui. conc.; 2-pf. conc.; *Qumran*, 'symphonic metaphor' for orch.; *Mismorim*, high v., orch., etc.

Maazel, Lorin (Varencove) (*b* Neuilly, 1930). Amer. conductor, composer, and violinist. Cond. at NY World Fair and Hollywood Bowl 1939 when a child, leading Amer. orchs., incl. NYPO, NBC SO, Chicago, and Cleveland, from 1941. Violinist in Pittsburgh SO from 1948. Cond. in It. from 1953. Mus. dir. Deutsche Oper 1965–71; Berlin Radio SO 1965–75. Débuts: Bayreuth Fest. 1960; NY Met 1962; Salzburg Fest. 1963; CG 1978. Ass. prin. cond. New Philharmonia 1970–2; cond. and mus. dir. Cleveland Orch. 1972–82; chief cond. Orch. Nat. de France 1977–82, mus. dir. 1988–91; prin. cond. Pittsburgh SO 1988–96; Bavarian Radio SO 1992–2002, NYPO from 2002. Dir., Vienna Opera 1982–6 (first Amer. to hold post) but left amid controversy in 1984. Comp. opera *1984* (CG, 2005).

Macal, Zdeněk (*b* Brno, 1936). Cz.-born conductor (Amer. cit. 1992). Cond. Moravian PO (Olomouc) 1963–7. Won Besançon int. cond. competition 1965. Début with Czech PO 1966. Settled in Switzerland 1969. Brit. début Bournemouth SO 1969. Cond. Cologne Radio SO 1970–4. Amer. début Chicago SO 1972. Chief cond. Hanover Radio SO 1980–3. Mus. dir. Milwaukee SO from 1986; cond. Sydney SO 1986; prin. cond. San Antonio SO 1988–92; art. adviser 1992–3, then art. dir. New Jersey SO from 1993. Prin. cond. Czech PO from 2003.

McAllister, Rita (Margaret Notman) (*b* Mossend, Lanarks., 1946). Scottish writer and composer. Lect. in mus., Edinburgh Univ. Composer of str. qt., song-cycles, cantata, etc. Authority on Prokofiev and other 20th-cent. Russ. composers.

Macbeth. (1) Opera in 4 acts by Verdi, his 10th, to lib. by Piave (with additions by A. Maffei) based on Shakespeare's tragedy. Comp. 1846–7. Prod. Florence 1847, NY 1858, Manchester 1860. Rev. 1864–5 for Paris 1865 (in Fr. trans.), this version (in It.) now being generally used. Glyndebourne 1938 (cond. Fritz Busch). NY (44th St. Th.) 1941.
(2) Sym.-poem Op.23 by R. Strauss, comp. 1887–8, rev. 1889–90, f.p. Weimar 1890 cond. Strauss.
(3) Opera in prol. and 3 acts by Bloch to Fr. lib. by Edmond Fleg, after Shakespeare. Comp. 1903–9, prod. Paris 1910, Naples 1938, Cleveland 1957, Milan 1960, London (RFH) 1973.
(4) Opera by L. Collingwood, lib. selected from Shakespeare. Prod. London 1934.

McCabe, John (*b* Huyton, 1939). Eng. composer, pianist, and critic. As pianist specializes in 20th-cent. Eng. mus. and Haydn. Pianist-in-residence Univ. Coll., Cardiff, 1965–8. Dir., London Coll. of Mus. 1983–90. CBE 1985. Prin. comps.:

OPERAS: *The Lion, The Witch, and The Wardrobe* (1968); *The Play of Mother Courage* (1974).
BALLETS: *The Teachings of Don Juan* (1973); *Mary, Queen of Scots* (1975); *Edward II* (1994–5).
ORCH.: syms.; No.1 (*Elegy*) (1965), No.2 (1970–1), No.3 (*Hommages*) (1978), No.4 (*Of Time and the River*) (1994–5); Concerto for Chamber Orch. (1962, rev. 1968); *Variations on a Theme of Hartmann* (1964); *Concertante Variations on a Theme of Nicholas Maw* (1970); *The *Chagall Windows (1974); *Sonata on a Motet*, str. (1976); 2 *Suites* from ballet 'Mary, Queen of Scots' (1976); *Jubilee Suite* (1977); *The Shadow of Light* (1979); *Concerto for Orchestra* (1982); *Rainforest*, 10 players (1984); *Tuning* (1985); *Fire at Durilgai* (1988); *Red Leaves* (1991); *Pilgrim*, str. (1998); sym. '*Edward II*' (1998); *Arthur Pendragon* (2000); *Les Martinets noirs*, 2 vns., str. (2003).
CONCERTOS: pf., No.1 (1966), No.2 (1970), No.3 (*Dialogues*) (1976, rev. 1977); vn., No.1 (1959), No.2 (1980); cl. (1971); *Concerto funèbre*, va., chamber orch. (1962); *Chamber Conc.*, va., vc., orch. (1965); *Concertante*, hpd., chamber ens. (1965); *Concertino*, pf. duet, orch. (1968); *Metamorphosen*, hpd., orch. (1968); ob. d'amore (1972); cl. (1977); *Rainforest II*, hpd., str. (1987); *Double Concerto*, ob., cl. (1987–8); fl. (1990); ob. (1995).
VOICE & ORCH.: *Notturni ed Alba*, sop., orch. (1970); *Voyage*, 5 soloists, boys' ch., ch., orch. (1972); *Time Remembered*, sop., ens. (1973); *Stabat Mater*, sop., ch., orch. (1976); *Reflections on a Summer Night*, ch., orch. (1976); *Music's Empire*, 16 solo vv., or SATB

soli and ch., or ch. only, orch. (1981); *Wind, Sand and Stars*, sop., ens. (1992); *Songs of the Garden*, ch., brass quintet, org. (2004).

CHAMBER MUSIC: *Partita* for str. qt. (1960); 3 *Pieces*, cl., pf. (1964); str. trio (1965); *Fantasy*, brass qt. (1965); *Movements*, cl., vn., vc. (1964, rev. 1966); *Partita*, vc. (1966); *Nocturnal*, pf., str. qt. (1966); *Rounds*, brass quintet (1967); *Canto*, gui. (1968); ob. qt. (1968); conc., pf., wind quintet (1969); *Canzona*, wind, perc. (1970); str. qts. No.2 (1972), No.3 (1979), No.4 (1982), No.5 (1989); *The Goddess Trilogy*, hn., pf. (1973–5); *Dances*, tpt., pf. (1980); *Desert I: Lizard*, fl., ob., cl., bn., perc. (1981), *II: Horizon*, 10 brass (1981), *III: Landscape*, pf. trio (1982), *IV: Vista*, rec. (1983); *January Sonatina*, cl. (1990); *Harbour with Ships (Five Impressions)*, brass quintet (1991); *Postcards*, wind quintet (1991); sonata, vc., pf. (1999); *Domestic Life*, rec., pf. (2000); *The Woman by the Sea*, pf., str. qt. (2001); *Les Oiseaux*, fl., hp. (2004); *Spielend*, 2 vns. (2004); *Hawk in Winter Light*, brass quintet (2005).

BRASS BAND: *Images* (1978); *Cloudcatcher fells* (1985); *Desert II (Horizon)* (arr. 1987); Ov., *Northern Lights* (1992); *Salamander* (1994); *The Maunsell Forts* (2001–2).

WIND BAND: Sym. for 10 wind instr. (1964); *Images* (1978, arr. from brass); *Canyons* (1991).

VOCAL: *Great Lord of Lords* (1966); *Hymn to God the Father* (1966); *Canticles for Salisbury* (1966); *Aspects of Whiteness* (1967, rev. 1969); *The Morning Watch* (1968); *Norwich Canticles* (1970); *Behold a Silly Tender Babe* (1975); *Motet* (1979); *Siberia* (1980); *Visions* (1983); *Scenes in America Deserta* (1986); *Proud Songsters* (1989); *Amen/Alleluia* (1991); *From 'Cartography'* (2002); *The Evening Watch*, unacc. ch. (2003).

PIANO: *Variations* (1963); 5 *Bagatelles* (1964); *Fantasy on a Theme of Liszt* (1967); *Intermezzi* (1968); *Capriccio* (1969); *Sostenuto* (1969); *Gaudi* (1970); *Aubade* (1970); *Basse Danse*, 2 pf. (1970); *Couples* (1975); *Mosaic Study* (1980); *Afternoons and Afterwards* (1981); *Lamentation Rag* (1982); *Haydn Variations* (1983); *I have a bonnet trimmed with blue*, pf. duet (1992); *Tenebrae* (1992–3).

ORGAN: *Sinfonia* (1961); *Dies Resurrectionis* (1963); *Prelude* (1964); *Johannis-Partita* (1964); *Elegy* (1965); *Miniconcerto*, organ, perc., and audience (485 penny whistles) (1966).

McCartney, (Sir) **Paul** (*b* Liverpool, 1942). Eng. songwriter, guitarist, pianist, and organist. Wrote first song 1956. Member of the *Beatles pop group 1960–70; formed new group Wings 1971. Comp. *Liverpool Oratorio* (with Carl Davis), 1991, and many songs (some with John Lennon) incl. *Eleanor Rigby*, *Yesterday*, etc. Mus. for several films. Over 200,000,000 recordings of his comps. sold. MBE 1965. Knighted 1997.

McCormack, **John** (*b* Athlone, 1884; *d* Dublin, 1945). Irish-born tenor (Amer. cit. 1919). Without previous instruction, won gold medal at Nat. Irish Fest. 1903. Opera début (as Giovanni Foli) Savona 1906 (Fritz in *L'*Amico Fritz*). London début in concert 1907, later that year at CG; NY début, Manhattan Opera 1909; NY Met 1910. Member Boston Opera 1910–11, Chicago 1912–14. Last

sang in opera Monte Carlo 1923 and devoted himself to concerts and recitals. Famous also for singing of Irish and sentimental ballads. Made papal Count, 1928. Last London concert 1938, but sang for charity and on radio during the Second World War and made recordings to 1942.

McCracken, **James** (*b* Gary, Indiana, 1926; *d* NY, 1988). Amer. tenor. Opera début in Colorado 1952 (Rodolfo in *La bohème*). NY Met 1953. Sang opera in Zurich and elsewhere until return to Met 1963 as Otello, a role with which he became closely identified throughout world. Salzburg Fest. 1963; CG début 1964.

MacCunn, **Hamish** (*b* Greenock, 1868; *d* London, 1916). Scottish composer and conductor. Prof. of harmony RAM 1888–94 and at GSMD from 1912. Cond. Carl Rosa Opera after 1898 and later for Beecham co. Wrote several operas, incl. *Jeanie Deans* (1894) and *Diarmid* (1897), cantatas, incl. *The Wreck of the Hesperus* (1905), concert-ovs., *Land of the Mountain and the Flood* (1887) and *The Ship o' the Fiend* (1888), part-songs, songs, pf. pieces.

Macdonald, **Hugh** (John) (*b* Newbury, 1940). Eng. lecturer and musicologist. On mus. staff Cambridge Univ. 1966–71, Oxford Univ. 1971–80. Specialist in Berlioz, becoming gen. ed. New Berlioz edn., 1965. Cond. Cambridge Phil. Soc. 1969–71. Prof., Glasgow Univ., 1980–7. Prof. of mus., Washington Univ., St Louis, from 1987.

MacDonald, **Malcolm** (Calum) (*b* Nairn, 1948). Scottish critic and composer. Composer of songs and pf. pieces. Author of many articles and of books on Havergal Brian, J. H. Foulds, and Schoenberg.

MacDowell, **Edward** (Alexander) (*b* NY, 1860; *d* NY, 1908). Amer. composer and pianist. Teacher of pf., Darmstadt Cons. 1881. In 1882 visited Liszt at Weimar; on Liszt's recommendation, *First Modern Suite* for pf. and 1st pf. conc. were publd. From 1885 to 1888 lived at Wiesbaden. Returned to USA 1888, settling in Boston. Soloist in f.p. of 2nd pf. conc., NY 1889. First head of mus. dept., Columbia Univ., NY, 1896–1904. His mus. is romantic in style and charmingly melodic. The MacDowell Colony in Peterboro, New Hampshire, where composers and other artists can work peacefully, was founded in his memory. Prin. works:

ORCH.: sym.-poems *Hamlet* and *Ophelia* (1885), *Lancelot and Elaine* (1886), *Lamia* (1887–8), Suite No.1 (1888–93), No.2 (*Indian*) (1891–5).

CONCERTOS: pf., No.1 in A minor (1882), No.2 in D minor (1884–6); *Romance*, vc., orch. (1888).

PIANO: *1st Modern Suite* (1880–1), *2nd Modern Suite* (1882–3); *Forest Idyls* (1884); *Idyls* (1887, rev. as 6 *Idyls After Goethe*, 1901); *12 Studies* (1890); Sonatas: *Tragica* (1893), *Eroica* (1895), *Norse* (1900), *Keltic* (1900); *12 Virtuoso Studies* (1894); *10 Woodland Sketches* (1896, No.1 is *To a Wild Rose*); *8 Sea Pieces* (1898); *6 Fireside Tales* (1902); *10 New England Idyls* (1902).

Also many songs, part-songs, arrangements, and works pubd. under pseudonym Edgar Thorn.

McEwen, (Sir) **John** (Blackwood) (*b* Hawick, 1868; *d* London, 1948). Scottish composer and teacher. Prof. of harmony and comp., RAM, 1898–1924, prin. 1924–36. Benefactor of chamber concerts. Knighted 1931. Works incl. *Solway Symphony* (1911); va. conc.; ov. *Grey Galloway*; 17 str. qts. (incl. *Biscay*); choral mus.; str. quintet; pf. pieces; songs, etc.

Macfarren, (Sir) **George** (Alexander) (*b* London, 1813; *d* London, 1887). Eng. composer and teacher. Prof., RAM 1837–87. Cond. at CG from 1845. Prof. of mus., Cambridge Univ., 1875. Prin., RAM 1875–87. Knighted 1883. Blind by 1860, dictating to amanuensis. Works incl. 12 operas (*Don Quixote*, 1846, *Robin Hood*, 1860, *She Stoops to Conquer*, 1864), 9 syms., oratorios, cantatas, ov. *Chevy Chase* (1836), pf. conc., vn. conc., sonatas, str. qts., and much church mus. Also wrote textbooks on harmony and articles for *Grove's Dictionary*, etc. Ed. works by Purcell and Handel, and colls. of Eng., Scottish, and Irish songs.

McGegan, Nicholas (*b* Sawbridgeworth, Herts, 1950). Eng. conductor, keyboard-player, and flautist. Joined staff of RCM as prof. of baroque fl. 1973–9, mus. history 1975–9, and dir., early mus. 1976–80. Artist-in-residence Washington Univ., St Louis, 1979–84. Mus. dir. Philharmonia Baroque Orch., S. Francisco, from 1985, and Göttingen Handel Fest. 1991. Cond. of Handel operas throughout world. Scottish Opera 1991; ENO 1993.

MacGregor, Joanna (*b* London, 1959). Eng. pianist and composer. London début 1985. Gave f.p. of Wood's pf. conc., London (Proms) 1991, and of Birtwistle's *Antiphonies* (cond. Boulez) London, 1993. Also performer of Berio, Xenakis, Murail, and Takemitsu. Has comp. mus. for plays and TV.

McGuire, Edward (*b* Glasgow, 1948). Scottish composer and flautist. Won Nat. Young Composers' comp. 1969. Flautist with folk group The Whistlebinkies from 1973. Prin. works:

OPERAS: *The Loving of Etain* (1990); *Cullercoats Tommy* (1993); *Cake Talk*, children's opera (1996).

BALLETS: *Peter Pan* (1989); *The Spirit of Flight* (1991); *Defying Fate* (2005).

ORCH.: *Calgacus* (1977); *Source* (1979); gui. conc. (1988); *A Glasgow Symphony* (1990); *Scottish Dances* (1990); tb. conc. (1991); *Symphonies of Scots Song* (1992); acc. conc., acc., str. (1999); *Ceòl Mor, Ceòl Beag*, chamber orch. incl. bagpipes (2000); db. conc. (2000); *Chinese Air and Dances*, str. (2004).

ENS.: *Rebirth* (1967–74); *Interregnum* (1974); *Liberation* (1975); *Euphoria* (1980); *Riverside*, folk group, orch. (1991); *Symphonies of Trains* (1992); *Sidesteps* (1992); *Zephyr* (1993); *Earthrise*, brass band (2003).

VOICE & INSTR(S).: *Quest*, sop., ens. (1978); *Moonsongs*, sop., db. (1979); *Prelude 8*, ten., tape delay (1981); *5 Songs*, female v., va., pf. (1982); *Citysongs*, bar., pf. (1983); *Life-Songs*, 12 solo vv., 2 vn., va., vc., db. (1983); *Songs of New Beginnings*, mez., fl., ob., cl., bn., hn. (1984); *Loonscapes*, sop., 2 vn., va., vc., db.

(1986); *The Web*, sop., pf., fl., va., gui., perc. (1989); *Cameron's Lament*, ch., fl., pf. (1997); *The De'il's Awa' wi' th' Excise Man*, ch., cl., 2 vn., va., vc., hp. (2003).

CHAMBER MUSIC: *7 Modal Duets*, va., vc. (1966–75); *3 Dialogues*, fl., ob. (1966–78); *3 Dialogues*, vc., pf. (1966–82); *Trio*, fl., ob., bn. (1967–71, rev. 1977–81); *Chamber Music*, 3 cl., hp., pf. (1968); *Prelude 1*, vc. (1975), *2*, bcl. (1975), *3*, fl. (1976–82), *5*, gui. (1981), *6*, va. (1981), *9*, cl., tape delay (1972–82); *Rant*, vn. (1977); *Divertimento*, 20 vas. (1979); *Movement*, fl., va., hp. (1979); wind octet (1980); quintet No.1, pf., cl., vn., va., vc. (1981), No.2, fl., cl., vn., vc., pf. (1986); *Fast Peace II*, vc., org. (1982); str. qt. (1982); *Fantasy Qt.*, pf., vn., va., vc. (1984); str. trio (1986); *3 Dialogues*, va., db. (1987); *Elegy*, pf. trio (1991); *Eastern Echoes*, fl., gui. (1991); *Fountain of Tears*, fl., gui. (1992); *Remembrance*, ob. trio (1993); *Air and Dances*, vn., pf. (1995); *Caprice*, fl., pf. (1999); *Chinese Knotwork*, 4 cl. (2001); *Aria*, fl., pf. (2004).

KEYBOARD: *12 White-Note Pieces*, pf. (1971); *12 Studies in C major*, pf. (1971); *Reflections*, 2 pf. (1979); *Prelude 4*, org. (1980); *Fast Peace I*, pf. (1980); *Prelude 7*, pf. (1981–2).

Machaut [Machault], **Guillaume de** (*b* Reims, *c*.1300; *d* Reims, 1377). Fr. composer, cleric, poet, and diplomat. Secretary to John, Duke of Luxembourg from *c*.1323 to 1346. Later in service of King of Navarre, King of Cyprus, Duke of Berry, and others. Canon of churches at Reims, Verdun, and S. Quentin. Comp. motet for election of Archbishop of Reims, 1324. Outstanding practitioner of **ars nova* and among first to comp. polyphonic setting of poetry in fixed forms (*ballade, rondeau*, and *virelai*), to write in 4 parts, and to compose integrated setting of entire Ordinary of the Mass. Also among last to compose in the medieval forms of **lai* and *dit*. His most important works are probably the *Messe de Notre Dame* for 4 vv. and the *Voir Dit* (Tale of Truth), a collection of letters, lyrics, and song-settings (*ballades* and *rondeaux*) written in praise of a woman (Péronne d'Armentières). Machaut's works, which incl. 23 motets, have appeared in 3 complete edns., by Ludwig (1926, 1954), Schrade (1956), and Sylvette Leguy (Paris, from 1977).

machicotage. (1) Extemporary ornamentation of plainsong by the priest. Machicots were members of the lower clergy who were singers (Lat. *macicoti*; It. *maceconchi*).

(2) Addition of an improvised 2nd part to a plainsong.

(3) Singing of inferior quality.

mächtig (Ger.). Mighty, powerful.

McIntire, Dennis (Keith) (*b* Indianapolis, 1944). Amer. historian and lexicographer. Ass. and research ed., *Lincoln Library of Essential Information* (1967). Dismayed by errors in reference books, supplied corrections and additions to several mus. dictionaries. Ass. to N. *Slonimsky on 7th and 8th edns. of *Baker's Biographical Dictionary of Musicians* (1984 and 1991). Adv. to *Encyclopaedia Britannica* from 1991.

McIntyre, (Sir), **Donald** (Conroy) (*b* Auckland, NZ, 1934). Eng. bass-baritone of NZ birth. Opera début, Cardiff (WNO) 1959 (Zaccaria in *Nabucco*). Member SW Opera 1960–7. CG début 1967; Bayreuth début 1967. In 1973 became first British singer to sing Wotan in Bayreuth *Ring* cycle and sang role in 1976 centenary cycle. Wotan in CG *Ring* cycle 1974. NY Met début 1975. Sang Prospero in f. Eng. p. of Berio's *Un re in ascolto* (CG 1989). OBE 1977. CBE 1985. Knighted 1992.

Mackenzie, (Sir) **Alexander** (Campbell) (*b* Edinburgh, 1847; *d* London, 1935). Scottish composer, violinist, conductor, and teacher. In Edinburgh 1865–79 as violinist, cond., etc. Lived in Florence 1879–88. Prin., RAM 1888–1924. Cond., Philharmonic Soc. 1892–9, giving f. Eng. p. of Tchaikovsky's 6th sym. (1894). Knighted 1895, KCVO 1922. Works incl. 5 operas (incl. *The Cricket on the Hearth*, 1900); oratorios (incl. *The Rose of Sharon*, 1884, rev. 1910); cantatas (incl. *The Dream of Jubal*, 1889); 3 *Scottish Rhapsodies*; vn. conc. (1885); *Pibroch*, vn., orch. (1889); *Scottish Concerto*, pf., orch. (1897); chamber mus.; and songs.

Mackerras, (Sir) (Alan) **Charles** (MacLaurin) (*b* Schenectady, NY, 1925). Australian conductor and oboist. Prin. ob. Sydney SO 1943–6. Went to Eng. 1946. Cond. début, SW Opera 1948 (*Die Fledermaus*), staff cond. 1949–54. Prin. cond. BBC Concert Orch. 1954–6. CG début 1963. First cond., Hamburg State Opera 1966–70. Mus. dir. SW Opera (ENO from 1974) 1970–8; prin. cond. Sydney SO 1982–5. Mus. dir. WNO 1987–91. Cond. f.p. in England of a Janáček opera, *Káťa Kabanová*, SW 1951, following with several other Janáček operas, some of which he has ed. Awarded Janáček Medal, 1978. Arr. mus. by Sullivan for ballet *Pineapple Poll* and reconstructed his lost vc. conc. Also arr. mus. by Verdi for *The Lady and the Fool*. Has cond. and ed. operas by Handel, J. C. Bach, and Gluck. His *Marriage of Figaro* at SW 1965 was remarkable for addition of ornamentation and for 18th cent. appoggiaturas. NY Met début 1972; Glyndebourne début 1990. CBE 1974. Knighted 1979. CH 2003. First recipient of Queen's Medal for Music, 2005.

Mackey, **Steven** (*b* Frankfurt, 1956). Ger.-born Amer. composer and guitarist. Assoc. prof. of mus., Princeton Univ. Works commissioned by Kronos Qt., Dawn Upshaw, and Concord Qt. They incl. *Among the Vanishing*, sop., str. qt. (1989); *On the Verge/Troubadour Songs*, elec. gui., str. qt. (1990); *On all fours*, str. qt. (1990); *TILT*, orch. (1992); *Physical Property*, elec. gui., str. qt. (1992); *Eating Greens*, orch. (1993); *Fusion Time*, gui. (1994); *Great Crossing*, *Great Divide*, str. qt. (1996); *Busted*, solo perc. (2001); *The Attic which is Desire*, ch., ww. quintet, hp. (2002); *'Lude*, str. qt. (2003); *Dreamhouse*, bar., orch. (2003); *Animal, Vegetable, Mineral*, sax. qt. (2004), for sax. qt., orch. (2005).

McKie, (Sir) **William** (Neil) (*b* Melbourne, Victoria, 1901; *d* Ottawa, 1984). Australian organist and conductor. Dir. of mus., Clifton College, 1926–30, Melbourne city organist 1931–8, Magdalen College, Oxford, 1938–41, organist and master of choristers, Westminster Abbey 1941–63, Dir. of mus. for coronation of Queen Elizabeth II, 1953. Knighted 1953.

McLaughlin, **Marie** (*b* Motherwell, 1954). Scot. soprano. Won schol. to London Opera Centre, 1977. Sang Tatyana in *Eugene Onegin*, cond. Rostropovich, at Snape, 1978. Débuts: London (ENO) 1978; CG 1980; Glyndebourne 1985; NY Met 1986; Salzburg Fest. 1987; La Scala 1988. Other operatic roles incl. Zdenka, Gilda, and Jenny in Weill's *Mahagonny*. Sings frequently at Salzburg, Vienna, Geneva, Chicago, and NY.

McLeod, **John** (*b* Aberdeen, 1934). Scottish composer and conductor. Has occupied various cond. and teaching appointments. Visiting lect. RSAMD from 1985. Prin. works:

ORCH. (incl. v. and orch.): 2 syms.; *The Shostakovich Connection* (1974); *Lieder der Jugend*, ten., orch. (1978); *The Seasons of Dr. Zhivago*, bar., orch. (1982); *The Gokstad Ship* (1982); *Hebridean Dances* (1982); *The Whispered Name*, sop., hp., str. (1986); perc. conc. (1987); pf. conc. (1988); *A Dramatic Landscape*, cl., wind band (1990); vc. conc. (1996); *Sun Dances* (2000); cl. conc. (2005).

CHORAL: *Hebridean Prayers*, ch., clarsach, org. (1979); *Canciones de los Angeles*, mez., ens. (1980); *Stabat Mater*, sop., bar., ch., orch. (1985); *Songs from the Small Zone*, sop., ch., pf. (1989); *The Chronicle of Saint Machar*, bar., ch., children's ch., pf., org., perc., str. (1998).

CHAMBER MUSIC: str. trio (1970); cl. quintet (1973); str. qt. (1986); vn. sonata (1986); *Fêtes galantes*, 2 vn., vc., hpd. (1991); *Small Pleasures*, ob., cl., bn. (1992); *A Moment in Time*, vn., vc., cl., pf. (2002); *Chinese Whispers*, brass quintet (2005).

Also much keyboard and vocal music.

MacMillan, (Sir) **Ernest** (Campbell) (*b* Mimico, Ontario, 1893; *d* Toronto, 1973). Canadian conductor, organist, and composer. Concert organist from age 10. ARCO at age of 13, FRCO at 17. Studied Edinburgh with Niecks and Hollins, then Paris. At Bayreuth 1914 and interned throughout war, gaining his Oxford D.Mus. while prisoner. Org., Timothy Eaton memorial church, Toronto, 1919–25. Prin., Toronto Cons. of Mus. 1926–42, dean of mus. Toronto Univ. 1927–52. Cond., Toronto SO 1931–56, Toronto Mendelssohn Ch. 1942–57. Comp. choral works and arr. Canadian folk-songs. Knighted 1935 (first Canadian 'for services to mus.').

MacMillan, **James** (*b* Kilwinning, Ayrshire, 1959). Scot. composer. Lect. in mus., Manchester Univ. 1986–8. Collab. with SCO in educational projects. Comp.-in-res., St Magnus Fest. 1989. Teacher at RSAMD from 1990. His mus. broke away from *avant-garde* and academic preoccupations in 1982 in favour of a more direct style reflecting his interest in Scot. nationalism and his Roman Catholicism. CBE 2004. Prin. works:

OPERAS: *Tourist Variations*, chamber opera (1991); *Inés de Castro* (1992–3).

MUSIC THEATRE: *Búsqueda*, narr., 8 actors, 3 sop., ens. (1988); *Visitatio Sepulchri*, 7 singers, chamber orch. (1993); *Parthenogenesis* (2000).

ORCH.: *Into the Ferment*, ens., orch. (1988); *Tryst* (1989); *The Exorcism of Rio Sumpúl*, chamber orch. or mixed ens. (1989); *The Confessions of Isobel Gowdie* (1990); *The Berserking*, pf. conc. (1990); *Sinfonietta* (1991); *Veni, Veni, Emmanuel*, perc. conc. (1992); *Epiclesis*, tpt. conc. (1993); *VS* (1993); *Britannia*, ov. (1994); *The World's Ransoming*, ca. conc. (1996); vc. conc. (1996); *Ninian*, cl. conc. (1996); *Vigil*, sym. (1997); *The Birds of Rhiannon* (opt. ch.) (2001); *A Deep but Dazzling Darkness*, vn., small orch., tape (2001–2); Sym. No.2, chamber orch. (1999), No.3 (*Silence*) (2002); *A Scottish Bestiary*, org., orch. (2003–4).

BAND: *Festival Fanfares*, brass (1986); *Sowetan Spring*, wind (1990).

ENS. & CHAMBER MUSIC: *Study on 2 Planes*, vc., pf. (1981); *3 Dawn Rituals* (1983); *The Road to Ardtalla*, sextet (1983); *2 Visions of Hoy*, ob., ens. (1986); *Litanies of Iron and Stone*, cl., sop. sax., tb., tape (1987); *Untold*, wind quintet (1987, rev. 1991); *Variations on 'Johnny Faa'*, sop., fl., vc., hp. (1988); *After the Tryst*, vn., pf. (1988); *Visions of a November Spring*, str. qt. (1988, rev. 1991); *. . . as others see us . . .*, mixed ens. (1990); *Tuireadh (Requiem)*, cl., str. qt. (1991); *Intercession*, 3 ob. (1991); *Scots Song*, sop., chamber quintet (1991); *Kiss on Wood*, vn., pf. (1993); *Cumnock Fair*, pf. sextet or pf., str. (1999); *Memento*, str. qt. (1994); *Adam's Rib*, brass quintet (1995); vc. sonata No.1 (1999), No.2 (2000); *From Galloway*, cl. (2000); *Invocation*, v., cl., drumkit, pf., db (2003); *HB to MB*, vc. (2004).

CHORAL & VOCAL: *Beatus Vir*, ch., org. (1983); *Cantos Sagrados*, ch., org. (1989); *Catherine's Lullabies*, ch., brass, perc. (1990); *Divo Aloysio Sacrum*, ch., org. (opt.) (1991); *Scots Song*, v., pf. (1991); *7 Last Words from the Cross*, ch., str. (1993); *The Children*, mez./ bar., pf. (1994); *Raising Sparks*, mez., ens. (1997); *The Company of Heaven*, children's ch., org. (1999); *Nunc dimittis*, ch., org. (2000).

PIANO: sonata (1985); *A Cecilian Variation for JFK* (2nd movt. of *Kennedy Variations*, others being by Victory, Mathias, and M. Berkeley) (1991); *Angel* (1993); *Lumen Christi* (1997); *For Ian* (2000); *25th May 1967* (2002).

MacMillan, (Sir) **Kenneth** (*b* Dunfermline, 1929; *d* London, 1992). Scottish dancer, choreographer, and director. Joined SW Th. Ballet 1946. Choreog., Royal Ballet, 1965. Ballet dir., Deutsche Oper, Berlin, 1966–9. Dir., Royal Ballet 1970–7, prin. choreog. from 1977. Choreog. incl.: *Somnambulism* (*Kenton, 1953); *Rite of Spring* (Stravinsky, 1962); *Romeo and Juliet* (Prokofiev, 1965); *Song of the Earth* (Mahler, 1965); *Checkpoint* (Gerhard, 1970); *7 Deadly Sins* (Weill, 1973); *Manon* (Massenet, 1974); *Elite Syncopations* (Joplin, 1974); *The Four Seasons* (Verdi, 1975); *Rituals* (Bartók, 1975); *Requiem* (Fauré, 1976); *Mayerling* (Liszt, 1978); *My Brother, My Sisters* (Schoenberg and Webern, 1978); *La fin du jour* (Ravel, 1979); *Gloria* (Poulenc, 1980); *Isadora* (R. R. *Bennett, 1981); *Orpheus* (Stravinsky, 1982); *The Prince of the Pagodas*

(Britten, 1985); *Winter Dreams* (Tchaikovsky, 1991); and *The Judas Tree* (Elias, 1992). Knighted 1983.

Macnaghten, Anne (Catherine) (*b* Whitwick, Leics., 1908; *d* Hitchin, Herts, 2000). Eng. violinist. Founder and leader Macnaghten Str. Qt. 1932–40 and co-founder in 1931 with Iris Lemare and E. Lutyens of Macnaghten concerts at which works by young Brit. composers, eg. Britten, were introduced. Quartet reorganized 1947. CBE 1997.

McNair, Sylvia (*b* Mansfield, Ohio, 1956). Amer. soprano. Début in *Messiah*, Indianapolis 1980. Opera début NY 1982 (Sandrina in Haydn's *L'infedeltà delusa*). European début, Schwetzingen 1984 (created title-role in Kelterborn's *Ophelia*). Débuts: Glyndebourne 1989; Salzburg Fest. and CG 1990; NY Met 1991. Has sung with many leading Eur. and Amer. orchs. and with ens. cond. by *Harnoncourt and *Gardiner. Marian Anderson Award 1990.

Maconchy, (Dame) **Elizabeth** (*b* Broxbourne, 1907; *d* Norwich, 1994). Eng. composer of Irish parentage. While she was studying in Prague, her pf. concertino was perf. by Prague PO, 1930. In the same year her suite *The Land* was played at the London Proms. Her ob. quintet won *Daily Telegraph* chamber mus. prize, 1933. She concentrated on chamber mus., inspired by Bartók's example. Her mus. is contrapuntal and tends to have short concise thematic material, but a freer, more passionate style developed in later works. Cobbett Medal for chamber mus. 1960, CBE 1977. DBE 1987. Nicola *LeFanu is her daughter. Prin. works:

OPERAS: 3 1-act operas, *The Sofa* (1956–7), *The Departure* (1960–1), *The Three Strangers* (Hardy) (1958–67) (1st perf. as trilogy, Middlesbrough 1977); *The Birds* (1967–8); *The Jesse Tree*, masque (1970); *The King of the Golden River* (1975).

ORCH.: Suite, *The Land* (1930); ov. *Proud Thames* (1953); *Concertino*, pf., orch. (1930); *Dialogue*, pf., orch. (1940); *Concertino*, cl., str. (1945); *Serenata Concertante*, vn., orch. (1963); *Concertino*, bn., str. (1959); *Variazioni Concertante* (1965); *Music*, brass, ww. (1965); *3 Cloudscapes* (1968); *3 Poems by Gerard Manley Hopkins*, high v., chamber orch. (1964–70); *Ariadne* (C. Day Lewis), sop., orch. (1970); *Epyllion*, vc., 15 str. (1975); *Sinfonietta* (1975–6); *Romanza*, va., small orch. (1979); *Little Symphony* (1980); *Tribute*, vn., ens. (1982–3); *My Dark Heart*, sop., ens. (1982); *Music for Strings* (1983); *Concertino*, cl., small orch. (1985); *Life Story*, str. (1985).

CHORAL: cantata, *Samson and the Gates of Gaza* (1964); *And Death Shall Have No Dominion*, ch., brass (1969); *Prayer Before Birth*, women's vv. (1972); *Sirens' Song*, unacc. (1974); *2 Epitaphs*, unacc. women's ch. (1975); *4 Miniatures*, unacc. (1978); *The Leaden Echo and the Golden Echo*, ch., alto fl., va., hp. (1978); *Héloise and Abélard*, dramatic cantata, sop., ten., bar., ch., orch. (1978); *Creatures*, ch. (1979); *There is no rose*, ch. (1984); *O Time, turn back*, 16 vv., ens. (1984); *Still Falls the Rain*, double ch. (1985); *The Bellman's Carol*, unacc. ch. (1985).

SONGS & SONG-CYCLE: *The Garland*, sop., pf. (1938); *3 Donne Songs*, ten., pf. (1966); *Sun, Moon, and Stars*, sop., pf. (1978); *My Dark Heart*, sop., ens. (1982); *L'Horloge*, sop., cl., pf. (1983); *In memory of W. B. Yeats*, sop., pf. (1985); *Butterflies*, mez., hp. (1986).

CHAMBER MUSIC: Str. Qts. No.1 (1933), No.2 (1937), No.3 (1938), No.4 (1939–43), No.5 (1948), No.6 (1950), No.7 (1955–6), No.8 (1966), No.9 (1968–9), No.10 (1971–2), No.11 (1976), No.12 (1979), No.13 (1984); ob. quintet (1933); *Reflections*, ob., cl., va., hp. (1961); *Notebook*, hpd. (1965–6); *3 Bagatelles*, ob., hpd. (1972); *3 Songs*, ten., hp. (1974); *3 Pieces*, hp. (1976); *Contemplation*, vc., pf. (1978); *Colloquy*, fl., pf. (1978–9); *Fantasia*, cl., pf. (1979); *Piccola Musica*, str. trio (1980); wind quintet (1980); *Trittico*, 2 ob., bn., hpd. (1981); *Tribute*, vn. and 8 wind (1982); *5 Sketches*, va. (1984); *Excursion*, bn. (1984); *Narration*, vc. (1985).

McPhee, Colin (*b* Montreal, 1900; *d* Los Angeles, 1964). Canadian-born Amer. composer and pianist. Lived in NY 1926–34, then in Bali 1934–6, studying native mus. and using its procedures in his *Tabuh-Tabuhan*, for 2 pf., and orch. (1936). Taught at Univ. of Calif. 1960–4. Other works incl. pf. conc. (1923); *Balinese Ceremonial Music*; 3 syms.; and conc. for wind orch. Arr. Britten's *Variations on a Theme of Frank Bridge* for 2 pf., 1942, and interested Britten in *gamelan.

McQueen, Ian (*b* Glasgow, 1954). Scot. composer. Wrote 1-act opera *Judit och Holofernes*, prod. at Vadstena Castle, Sweden, 1987, and 3-act *Fortunato*, prod. by Norrlandsoperan at Umea, Sweden, 1993.

McVicar, David (*b* Glasgow, 1967). Scottish opera and theatre director. Studied acting, design, and directing at RSAMD. Opera début Leeds 1993 (Opera North, *Il re pastore*); Scottish Opera 1996 (*Idomeneo*); ENO 1998 (*Manon*); CG 2001 (*Macbeth*, with which he also made his débuts at the NY Met and the Mariinsky); Glyndebourne Fest. 2002 (*Carmen*); Salzburg Fest. 2003 (*Les Contes d'Hoffmann*). Dir. his first Wagner, Strasbourg 2007 (*Der Ring*).

Madama Butterfly. Opera orig. in 2 acts by Puccini, comp. 1901–3, to lib. by Giacosa and Illica based on Belasco's play (1900) which was taken from a story by J. L. Long (based on a real event). Prod. Milan 1904. New version, with Act 2 divided into 2 parts, separated by interval, prod. Brescia 1904 (3 months later), London 1905, Washington (in Eng.) 1906, NY Met 1907. Version usually perf. today dates from prod. in Paris, 1906, for which Puccini made further cuts and revs. WNO prod. 1978 restored over 400 measures of 1904 score. Orig. vers. given complete, Venice 1982 and Leeds (Opera North) 1991.

Madame Chrysanthème. Ballet in 1 act to mus. by Rawsthorne, lib. and choreog. by Ashton. Prod. London 1955.

Madame Sans-Gêne ('Madame Carefree'). Opera in 3 acts by Giordano to lib. by Simoni after play by Sardou and Moreau. Comp. 1913–14. Prod. NY Met and Turin 1915.

Maddalena. Opera in 1 act, Op.13, by Prokofiev to his own lib. based on play by M. G. Liven-Orlova (1905). Comp. 1911, partly orch. 1912, rev. 1913. Orch. completed 1977–8 by Edward Downes. Prod. Manchester (concert) 1978, cond. Downes, Graz (stage) 1981, cond. Downes.

Maddalena, James (*b* Lynn, Mass., 1954). American baritone. Début 1974 with Boston Pops Orch. Began assoc. with the producer Peter Sellars 1981, singing in Mozart, Haydn, and Handel operas. Created Nixon in Adams's *Nixon in China*, Houston 1987, the Captain in Adams's *The Death of Klinghoffer*, Brussels 1991, and Merlin in Tippett's *New Year*, Houston 1989. Glyndebourne début 1990.

Madeira [Browning], **Jean** (*b* Centralia, Ill., 1918; *d* Providence, RI, 1972). Amer. mezzo-soprano. Solo pianist with St Louis SO 1930, then had singing lessons. Opera début 1943, Chautauqua (Nancy in *Martha*). Appeared at San Carlo and on European tour in title-role of *The *Medium*. NY Met début 1948, becoming member of co. 1956–71. Member of Vienna Opera 1955. CG début 1955. Débuts: Bayreuth 1956; Salzburg 1954. Created Circe in Dallapiccola's *Ulisse*, Berlin 1968. A memorable Klytemnästra.

Maderna, Bruno (*b* Venice, 1920; *d* Darmstadt, 1973). It. composer and conductor, among leaders (with *Berio) of the It. *avant-garde*. After service in World War II, was encouraged by Virgil Thomson and met *Boulez. Taught at Venice Cons. 1947–50 and at Darmstadt summer courses (from 1951). With Berio, founded EMS of It. Radio at Milan, 1955, later becoming mus. dir. Milan Radio. Brilliant cond. of 20th-cent. mus. Cond. many modern operas in Europe. Visited USA 1965 to conduct *Nono's *Intolleranza* at Boston and sym. concerts in Chicago and NY. Salzburg Fest. 1973. His early works were influenced by Bartók and Stravinsky. He adopted serialism in 1951 and Webernian features entered his work. He also used elec. media, usually in combination with live perf. However complex his mus., his native It. lyricism was always present. Prin. works:

THEATRE PIECE: *Hyperion* (Venice 1964), composite work i.e. *Dimensioni III* + *Aria da Hyperion* + 2-track tape; *Hyperion II* (*Dimensioni III* + cadenza for fl. + *Aria da Hyperion*); *Hyperion III* (*Hyperion* + *Stele per Diotima*); *Dimensioni IV* (*Dimensioni III* + *Stele per Diotima*); *Satyricon* (1973).

ORCH.: *Serenata* for 11 instr. (1946, rev. 1954); *Introduzione e Passacaglia* (1947); *Quadrivium* (1948); Conc. for 2 pf. and chamber orch. (1948); *Studi per 'Il Processo' di Kafka*, for reciter, sop., and small orch. (1949); fl. conc. (1954); *Composizione in 3 tempi* (1954); *Serenata II* for 11 instr. (1957); pf. conc. (1959); vn. conc. (1969); conc. for ob., chamber ens., tape *ad lib* (1962, rev. 1965); *Dimensioni III* for sop., fl., and orch. (1963); *Aria da Hyperion* for sop., fl., and orch. (1964); *Stele per Diotima* (1965); ob. conc. (1967); *Music of Gaiety* (based on virginals pieces by Byrd, Farnaby,

Dowland, and Philips) (1969); *Juilliard Serenade (Free Time I)* (1970); *Venetian Journal* for ten. and chamber orch. (1971); *Giardino Religioso* (1972); *Aura* (1972); *Biogramma* (1972).

TAPE: *Musica su 2 dimensioni*, fl. and 2-track tape (1952, rev. 1958); *Notturno* (1956); *Syntaxis* (2-track) (1957); *Continuo* (1958); *Dimensioni II* (2-track) (1960); *Tempo libero I* (1971); *Ages* (1972).

CHAMBER MUSIC: str. qt. (1955); *Aulodia per Lothar*, ob. d'amore, guitar ad lib (1965); *Widmung* for vn. (1967); *Solo* (1971); *Dialodia*, 2 fl., recorder, ob. (1972); *Y después*, guitar (1972).

madrigal (It. *madrigale*; orig. *matricale*—pastoral in the mother-tongue). Vocal comp., of It. origin, for several vv., usually unacc. but sometimes with instr. acc. Texts usually secular (amorous, satirical, or allegorical), but there are *madrigali spirituali*. Madrigals were first sung in It. towards the end of the 13th cent. and early examples survive by Giovanni da Cascia and Jacopo da Bologna. The form was revived in a different style in the 16th cent. by It. composers and by the Flemish Arcadelt, Verdelot, and Willaert. It became more complex and experimental in the hands of *Lassus, *Palestrina, and A. *Gabrieli and achieved its finest flowering in the works of Donati, Marenzio, Gesualdo, and, especially, Monteverdi. In the 17th cent. it was superseded by the cantata.

The singing of It. madrigals was imported to Eng. by It. composers such as *Ferrabosco the elder who worked at Elizabeth I's court. Nicholas Yonge, of St Paul's Cath., formed a madrigal choir and in 1588 pubd. *Musica Transalpina, a coll. of It. madrigals to Eng. words. Eng. composers such as *Byrd, *Morley, and later *Weelkes and *Wilbye, wrote superb madrigals, though they did not always call them by that name. In the 19th cent., mock-madrigals were composed by *Sullivan and *German.

See also *Fellowes, E. H.*

madrigal comedy. Short drama set to mus. as series of secular vocal pieces (madrigals or some other vocal form). First known example was Vecchi's *L'Amfiparnaso* (1594), followed by Banchieri's *La pazzia senile* (1598).

madrigale. See *madrigal*.

Madrigali guerrieri e amorosi (Madrigals of love and war). Monteverdi's 8th book of madrigals, 1638, which contains 58 items, some purely instr., some for 8 vv. with 2 vn. and basso continuo. Contains whole of *Il ballo delle ingrate*, also separate extracts from it, and whole of *Il *combattimento di Tancredi e Clorinda*, with separate extracts from it.

Maelzel [Mälzel], **Johann Nepomuk** (*b* Regensburg, 1772; *d* aboard ship, La Guiara, Venezuela, 1838). Ger. inventor of mechanical musical devices. Settled in Vienna 1792. Constructed *panharmonicon, a mechanical orch. (exhibited in Vienna 1908) for which his friend Beethoven wrote his *Battle Symphony* (1813). Made mus.

chronometer based on Stöckel's invention and, in 1814, a metronome, based on an idea from Winkel of Amsterdam. The 2nd movt. of Beethoven's 8th sym. begins with a theme said to derive from a canon extemporized by Beethoven at a supper in honour of Maelzel, the tickings of the chronometer being represented by staccato 16th-notes, i.e. 'Ta-ta-ta-ta . . . lieber Maelzel'.

maestoso (It.). Majestic, dignified, hence *allegro maestoso*.

maestro (It.). Master. Title given in Italy to celebrated composers, conds., and teachers, e.g. *Maestro Verdi, Maestro Toscanini, Maestro Martini*. The tendency has grown in USA (and has spread) to use it as a synonym only for conds., e.g. 'the maestro'. *Maestro di cappella* was the mus. dir. of a chapel or of an aristocratic mus. est.; *maestro al cembalo* was the musician who, in 17th and 18th cents., directed perfs. from the hpd. or other continuo instr.

Maestro di Cappella, Il (The Chorus Master). Intermezzo by Cimarosa, comp. *c*.1786–93, for bar. and orch. Ov. is that of Cimarosa's opera *L'Impresario in angustie*, prod. 1786.

Maestro di Musica, Il (The Music Master). Comic opera in 1 act, being altered version of *Orazio*, opera by P. Auletta to lib. by A. Palombo. Prod. Naples *c*.1737. Often wrongly attrib. *Pergolesi.

Magaloff, Nikita (*b* St Petersburg, 1912; *d* Vevey, Switz., 1992). Russ. pianist and composer (Swiss cit. 1956). Began career in duo with *Szigeti (vn.), then soloist with orchs. and recitalist in Europe and USA. Prof. of pf. Geneva Cons. 1949–59, then gave summer courses at Taormina and Siena. Salzburg Fest. début 1961 (Beethoven conc. No.5, Dresden Staatskapelle cond. Szell). Comp. vn. sonatina, songs, and pf. pieces.

Magelone, Die schöne (The fair Magelone). 15 songs or romances for solo v. and pf. by Brahms, Op.33, settings of extracts from the novel *Die schöne Magelone* by Ludwig Tieck (1773–1853). Comp. 1861–8.

Maggini, Giovanni (Paolo) (*b* Botticino-Marino, 1580; *d* Brescia, *c*.1630). It. maker of violins, violas, cellos, and double-basses. Valued nearly as highly as instrs. by *Stradivari and *Guarneri. Introduced many improvements, particularly in way the wood was cut.

maggiolata (It.). May song, or spring song—either traditional or comp.

maggiore (It.). Major.

maggot. Old Eng. word meaning 'fanciful idea', used by 16th- and 17th-cent. composers in titles of instr. pieces, often country dances, e.g. 'My Lady Winwoods Maggot'. Revived in 20th-cent. by Peter *Maxwell Davies in his *Miss Donnithorne's Maggot*.

Magic Flute, The (Mozart). See *Zauberflöte, Die*.

Magic Fountain, The ('Watawa'). Opera in 3 acts by Delius to lib. by comp. and Jutta Bell (?1857–1934). Comp. 1894–5, rev. 1898 (makes use of some of *Florida* suite for orch. 1888). F. (concert) p. BBC broadcast recorded in London, July 1977 and relayed on 20 Nov. 1977. Recording of broadcast issued 1980. Brit. stage première Glasgow 1999, Scottish Opera, cond. Richard Armstrong, dir. Aidan Lang.

Magnard, Albéric (*b* Paris, 1865; *d* Baron, 1914). Fr. composer. Comps. are of strong structure, somewhat austere in effect. Wrote 3 operas (*Yolande* 1888–91, *Guercœur* 1897–1900, *Bérénice* 1905–9); 4 syms. (1889–90, 1892–3, rev. 1896, 1895–6, 1911–13); *Chant funèbre*, orch.; str. qt.; songs; pf. pieces. Died when his house was set on fire when he refused to surrender after shooting dead 2 German soldiers who had entered his property. Almost all his MSS were burned with him.

Magnificat (Lat.). Canticle of the Virgin Mary ('My soul doth magnify the Lord') as it appears in St Luke's Gospel. The Lat. name is first word of Vulgate trans. (Magnificat anima mea Dominum). Part of RC Vespers and of Anglican Evensong (where mus. setting is followed by *Nunc Dimittis). Sung to plainchant in RC service and to Anglican chant in latter, but there are many comp. settings for church and concert perf., e.g. by Dunstable, Du Fay, Lassus, Palestrina, Monteverdi, Bach, Schütz, and Vaughan Williams.

Mahler, Gustav (*b* Kalíšt, Bohemia, 1860; *d* Vienna, 1911). Austrian composer, conductor, and pianist. Began to learn pf. at age 6, giving public recital in 1870. Entered Vienna Cons. 1875. Became friendly disciple, but not pupil, of *Bruckner, helping to make pf. duet arr. of 3rd Sym. (1878). While at Cons. comp. and played in perfs. of his own pf. quintet and vn. sonata. On leaving Cons. in 1878 comp. cantata *Das klagende Lied*, entering it in 1881 for Beethoven Prize but it was rejected. Began career as cond. 1880 at Hall, Upper Austria, followed by posts at Laibach (Ljubljana), Olmütz (1883), and Kassel 1883–5. While in the Kassel post he had an unhappy love-affair recorded in his song-cycle *Lieder eines fahrenden Gesellen*. Moved to Prague, 1885, and the next year to Leipzig as 2nd cond. to *Nikisch. While there he was invited by Weber's descendants to construct an opera from the fragments of *Die drei Pintos*. This, when prod. in 1888, was very successful. That year he went to Budapest Opera as chief cond. There his genius as cond. and administrator had full rein for the 1st time. In 1889 he conducted the f.p. of his 1st Sym., then simply described as 'symphonic poem'.

In 1891 Mahler became chief cond. of Hamburg Opera, where he built up a co. of remarkable singers (whom he coached also to be singer-actors), and introduced many new works. He took the co. to London in 1892, his only visit, for perfs. of Wagner's *Ring* and *Tristan*, and Beethoven's *Fidelio*. His 2nd Sym. (*Resurrection*) was completed 1894 and perf. in Berlin 1895. For the rest of his life Mahler divided his time between comp. in the summer and cond. in the winter. His mus. met at first with hostility, but its quality was recognized by his contemporary Richard Strauss. In 1897, having converted from Judaism to Roman Catholicism, he became dir. of the Vienna Court Opera, inaugurating a glorious decade during which he set standards still scarcely surpassed and, with Alfred Roller and others, revolutionized the production, design, and lighting of operas. Built remarkable ens. of singers incl. Mildenburg, Gutheil-Schoder, Slezak, and Mayr. In 1902 he married Alma Schindler, also a musician, by whom he had 2 daughters (the elder died in 1907, aged 4). Between 1896 and 1907, when he resigned his post after controversy, he comp. his Syms. 3 to 8, the song-cycle *Kindertotenlieder*, and other songs with orch. Each of the syms. was on a huge scale, but perfs. were becoming more frequent throughout Europe, especially through the championship of *Mengelberg.

Mahler made his Amer. début on 1 Jan. 1908 conducting *Tristan* at the NY Met. In 1909 he was appointed cond. of the reorganized NYPO. In 1910 in Munich he cond. the first 2 perfs. of his 8th Sym. (*Symphony of a Thousand*), returning to NY 2 months later. From 1907 he lived under the shadow of death from a heart ailment. This led in 1911 to a severe blood infection which caused his premature death on 18 May. He left 3 large posthumous works, the song-sym. *Das Lied von der Erde* and Syms. 9 and 10. *Das Lied* and the 9th were f.p. in 1911 and 1912 respectively cond. by Bruno *Walter in Munich and Vienna. The 10th was long thought to be unfinished and only 2 movts. were pubd. and played until the Eng. scholar Deryck *Cooke discovered in 1960 that the work was complete in short score and made a performing version.

Mahler's greatness as a cond. was never contested. But his comps. for many years were regarded with fanatical admiration by a handful of disciples and admirers and equally fanatical scorn by a larger section of musicians. However, the championship of certain conds. and critics led gradually in the late 1950s to a fervent revival of interest. His works were frequently recorded and entered the repertories of the world's leading orchs. to public acclaim. His mus. appealed both to those elements who cherished its romantic eloquence and to the *avantgarde* who recognized that it bridged the divide between the old and the new. Deeply personal in expression, the extreme chromaticism of works such as the 9th Sym. anticipates the innovations of Schoenberg. The unconventional form of the syms., their juxtaposition of popular elements with mystic passages, the *concertante* use of solo instrs., the complex and subtle instr. polyphony, the contrasts of irony, pathos, childlike simplicity, and psychological insight, all appealed to later 20th-cent. composers; and audiences found in his mus. a cogent and comprehensive expression of the anxieties and complexities of modern life. He championed the younger generation in his lifetime and became their idol after his death. Prin. works:

OPERA: Completion of Weber's *Die *drei Pintos*. F.p. Leipzig 1888, f.p. in England 1962.

SYMPHONIES: No.1 in D major (1884–8, rev. 1893, 1896 reduced from 5 to 4 movts., and 1897–8; excluded movt., *Blumine*, restored in some 20th-cent. perf.). F.p. Budapest 1889, f.p. in England 1903. No.2 in C minor (*Resurrection*; 1888–94, rev. 1910), for sop., cont., ch., and orch. F.p. Berlin 1895, f.p. in England 1931. No.3 in D minor (1895–6), for cont., women's and boys' chs., and orch. F.p. Krefeld 1902, f.p. in England 1947. No.4 in G major (1899–1900, rev. 1910), sop. solo in finale. F.p. Munich 1901, f.p. in England 1905. No.5 in C♯ minor (1901–2, rev. 1904–10). F.p. Cologne 1904, f.p. in England 1945 (*Adagietto* only 1909). No.6 in A minor (1903–5, rev. 1908), f.p. Essen 1906, f.p. in England 1950 (broadcast relay 1947). No.7 in B minor (1904–5, rev. 1909), f.p. Prague 1908, f.p. in England 1913. No.8 in E♭ major (1906–7), for 8 soloists, ch., boys' ch., and orch. F.p. Munich 1910, f.p. in England 1930. No.9 in D major (1909–10). F.p. Vienna 1912, f.p. in England 1930. No.10 in F♯ major (1910). F.p. of *Adagio and Purgatorio* Vienna 1924, f.p. in England *Adagio* 1948, *Adagio* and *Purgatorio* 1955. F.ps. of Cooke version: London 1960 (scherzos incomplete), London 1964 (full perf. vers.), London 1972 (final rev.). Note that Mahler himself cond. the f.ps. of the first 8 syms. (Strauss did not conduct f.p. of No.2, as often stated).

SONG-SYMPHONY: *Das *Lied von der Erde* (The Song of the Earth) for cont. (or bar.), ten., and orch. (1907–9). F.p. Munich 1911; f.p. in Eng. 1914; f.p. in Amer., Philadelphia 1916.

CANTATA: *Das *klagende Lied* (The Song of Sorrow) for sop., cont., ten., bass, ch., and orch. (1878–80). Orig. in 3 parts. Rev. 1888 to 2 parts. Further rev. 1893–1902. F.p. Vienna 1901, f.p. in England 1956 (vers. with pf. acc. cond. Boult at Oxford, 1914). F.p. of complete 1880 version Vienna 1935, f.p. in England 1970. F.p. of orig. orch. of all 3 parts, Manchester 1997.

SONG-CYCLES: *Lieder eines fahrenden Gesellen* (Songs of a Wayfarer) for v. and pf./orch. (1884, rev. c.1892, 1896). F.p. Berlin 1896, f.p. in England 1927. *Kindertotenlieder* (Songs of the Death of Children) for bar. (or cont.) and orch./pf. (1901–4). F.p. Vienna 1905, f.p. in England 1913 (pf.), 1924 (orch.).

SONGS: 3 *Songs* for ten. and pf. (1880); 5 *Songs* for v. and pf. (1880–3), later (1892) pubd. as Book I of *Lieder und Gesänge aus der Jugendzeit* (Songs of Youth). Books II and III (comp. 1888–91) are 9 settings from *Des *Knaben Wunderhorn*; *Lieder aus Des Knaben Wunderhorn*, 12 settings for v. and orch./pf. (1888–99); 3 songs from *Des Knaben Wunderhorn*: *Wir geniessen die himmlischen Freuden* (1892; incorporated into finale of 4th Sym. 1899), *Revelge* (1899), *Der Tamboursg'sell* (1901); 5 *Lieder nach Rückert* for v. and orch./pf.: 1. *Ich atmet'*

einen linden Duft (1901), 2. *Liebst du um Schönheit* (1902), 3. *Blicke mir nicht in die Lieder* (1901), 4. *Ich bin der Welt abhanden gekommen* (1901), 5. *Um Mitternacht* (1901). F.p. Vienna 1905 (excluding No.2).

CHAMBER MUSIC: vn. sonata (1876); pf. quintet in A minor (1876); pf. qt. in A minor (1876).

ARRANGEMENTS: J. S. Bach's Suite for Orch. in 4 movts. (1st and 2nd from Suite No.2, 3rd and 4th from Suite No.3). F.p. NY 1909; Schubert's Str. Qt. in D minor (*Death and the Maiden*), for str. orch., c.1894; Beethoven's Str. Qt. in F minor, Op.95, for str. orch. (f.p. Vienna, Jan. 1899) and Str. Qt. in C♯ minor, Op.131, for str. orch.; Bruckner's 3rd Sym. for pf. 4 hands (1878). Also re-orch. Schumann's 4 syms.

Maid as Mistress, The (Pergolesi). See *Serva padrona, La*.

Maid of Orleans, The. Opera in 4 acts by Tchaikovsky, comp. 1878–9 to his own lib. based on Schiller's play about Joan of Arc., rev. 1882. Prod. St Petersburg 1881; Reno, Nev., 1976; London (Collegiate Th.) 1978.

Maid of Pskov, The (*Pskovityanka*). Opera in prologue and 3 acts by *Rimsky-Korsakov to his own lib. after play by Mey (1860). Comp. 1868–72. Prod. St Petersburg 1873; Moscow 1898, rev. version 1876–7, 3rd version 1891–2, prod. St Petersburg and Moscow 1896, London 1913. Also known under title *Ivan the Terrible*, bestowed by Diaghilev, Paris 1909.

Maid of the Mill, The (Schubert). See *Schöne Müllerin, Die*.

Mai-Dun. Symphonic rhapsody for orch. by *Ireland comp. 1920–1. Title refers to prehistoric Dorset fortification, Maiden Castle.

Mainardi, Enrico (*b* Milan, 1897; *d* Munich, 1976). It. cellist and composer. Gave master classes from 1933 at S. Cecilia Acad., Rome, Salzburg Mozarteum, and Lucerne Cons. Salzburg Fest. début 1948. Wrote 3 vc. concs., conc. for 2 vcs., solo vc. sonatas, etc. Recorded *Don Quixote* with Strauss conducting (1933).

Mainzer, Joseph (*b* Trier, 1801; *d* Salford, 1851). Ger. singing teacher, also mining engineer, priest, composer, and critic. Became priest 1826, later abbé. Taught singing at Trêves, later Brussels. In Paris from 1834 where he pubd. several mus. textbooks. Went to London 1841, then Edinburgh, settling in Manchester 1847. There he est. singing courses based on *Wilhem system. His *Singing for the Million* (1841) had large sale. Founded *Musical Times and Singing-Class Circular* 1842, taken over by Novello 1844 as *Musical Times*. His methods were challenged by those of *Hullah. Comp. 2 operas.

Maisky, Mischa (*b* Riga, 1948). Russ.-born Israeli cellist. Début with Leningrad PO 1965. Emigrated to Israel 1973 and became Israel cit. Studied with Piatigorsky in Calif. Winner, Cassado comp., Florence 1973. Amer. début NY 1973 (Pittsburgh SO). London début 1976 (RPO), recital début 1977. Salzburg Fest. début 1990.

maître de chapelle (Fr.). Equivalent of Ger. **Kapellmeister*.

maîtrise. A Fr. choir sch.

Maja y el ruisenor, La (The Maja and the Nightingale). No.4 of the *Goyescas* by Granados orig. for pf., later incorporated as song into Scene 2 of opera *Goyescas* and frequently heard as separate concert aria with orch.

major bass. Organ stop of 16' pitch, generally an *open diapason*.

major common chord. A common chord incl. the major 3rd.

major flute. Loud org. stop of 8' or 16' length and pitch.

major scale. See *scale*.

Makrokosmos. 12 fantasy-pieces after the Zodiac for amplified pf. by **Crumb*, comp. 1972. They are studies in *avant-garde* pf. technique, each being assoc. with a sign of the Zodiac and with a friend of the composer's who was born under that sign.

Makropulos Affair, The (*Věc Makropulos*; literally 'The Makropulos Thing', hence variations in trans. title, e.g. 'The Makropulos Case', 'The Makropulos Secret'). Opera in 3 acts by Janáček to his own lib. based on play (1922) of same name by Karel Čapek (1890–1938). Comp. 1923–5. F.p. Brno 1926, London 1964, S. Francisco 1966.

Maksymiuk, Jerzy (*b* Grodno, 1936). Polish conductor, composer, and pianist. Cond., Teatr Wielki, Warsaw, 1970–2. Founder-cond. Polish Chamber Orch. Prin. cond. Polish Nat. Radio orch. 1975–7. Brit. début 1977 (with Polish CO). Cond. BBC Scottish SO 1983–93. Salzburg Fest. début 1985. ENO début 1991 (*Don Giovanni*). Comp. ballet, *Capriccio* for pf. and orch. (1969), str. trio, and pf. pieces for children.

Mal (Ger.). Time, in such contexts as *Erste Mal*, 1st time; *2 Mal* (*Zweimal*), twice, etc.

malagueña (Sp.). (1) Sp. dance of fandango variety from Málala and Murcia, exported to Mexico by Sp. settlers.

(2) Sp. gipsy song involving improvisation and cadenzas and sung by amorous youths with guitar accompaniment. Instr. malagueñas occur in Chabrier's *España* (1883), Ravel's *Rapsodie espagnole* (1907), and Albéniz's *Iberia* (1906–9).

Malbrouck s'en va-t-en guerre (Malbrouck goes off to the war). 18th-cent. Fr. nursery song. In Britain the tune is sung to either 'For he's a jolly good fellow', or 'We won't go home until morning'. Sung to various different sets of words, it has enjoyed great European popularity.

It is usually stated that 'Malbrouck' refers to the 1st Duke of Marlborough, but the name is found in medieval literature.

Malcolm, George (John) (*b* London, 1917; *d* London, 1997). Eng. harpsichordist, pianist, conductor, and composer. Master of the Music, Westminster Cath. 1947–59. On staff RAM. Art. dir. Philomusica of London 1962–6. Frequent recitalist. Assoc. with Britten's mus. CBE 1965.

Malcuzyński, Witold (*b* Koziczyn, nr. Vilnius, 1914; *d* Palma, Majorca, 1977). Polish pianist. Settled Paris 1939, début there 1940. NY début 1942. Worldwide tours. Specialized in Chopin, Liszt, etc.

male voice choir (or **chorus**). One (usually) of men only but it may be of boys and men.

male voice quartet. 4 male vv., either alto, 1st and 2nd ten., and bass ('with alto lead'), or 1st and 2nd ten. and 1st and 2nd bass ('with tenor lead').

Malfitano, Catherine (*b* NY, 1948). Amer. soprano. Prof. operatic début Denver 1972 (Nannetta in *Falstaff*). Minnesota Opera 1972–3, NY City Opera 1974–9. Eur. début 1974, Netherlands Opera. Salzburg Fest. début 1976; NY Met 1979; Vienna 1982; Munich 1985; CG 1988. Sang Cleopatra in revival of Barber's *Antony and Cleopatra*, Chicago 1991. A notable Salome.

Malgoire, Jean-Claude (*b* Avignon, 1940). Fr. conductor and oboist. In 1966 founded La Grande Écurie et la Chambre du Roy which specializes in baroque mus., mixing modern instr. with restored models. Has cond. revivals of Rameau's *Hippolyte et Aricie* (Eng. Bach Fest.) and Campra's *Tancrède* (Copenhagen and Aix).

Malibran (*née* García), **Maria** (Felicità) (*b* Paris, 1808; *d* Manchester, 1836). Sp. mezzo-soprano. Studied with her father, Manuel **García*. Sang in Paër's *Agnese* in Naples at age 5. First public perf. Paris 1824. Opera début London (King's Th.) 1825 as Rosina in *Il barbiere di Siviglia*. Went to NY 1825 singing leading roles in her father's It. opera co. While there married François Eugène Malibran, but the union was short-lived. Début Paris Opéra 1828. Triumphs followed in London (CG début 1833), Naples, Rome, Bologna, Venice, Lucca, and Milan (La Scala début 1834). In 1836 married Belg. violinist Charles de **Bériot* with whom she had lived since 1830. Fell from horse in London, Apr. 1836 (while pregnant), her injuries leading to her death in Sept. when she collapsed after singing a duet at a Manchester fest. Her v. was notable for its colour and range, and was described as 'like the costliest gold, but it had to be mined, forged, and stamped like metal under the hammer to make it malleable'. Her roles ranged from Angelina in *La Cenerentola* to Norma, Maria Stuarda, and Leonore. Her lively temperament, intensity as an actress, and exciting life made her a legend. She was a fine pianist and also comp. songs and nocturnes. Her younger sister was Pauline *Viardot.

malimba. See *marimba*.

malinconia, malinconico (It.). Melancholy. So *malinconoso, malinconioso, malinconicamente*, in melancholy fashion. Walton marked the slow movt. of his 1st Sym. 'con malincolia' (sic).

Malipiero, Gian Francesco (b Venice, 1882; d Treviso, 1973). It. composer. Settled in Venice 1904–15, but spent some months in Berlin in 1908–10 attending lectures by Bruch. In this period, in the Marciana Library, Venice, he discovered and transcr. the almost forgotten works of Monteverdi, Galuppi, Tartini, Stradella, etc. This determined him to rebel against the 'operatic tyranny' of It. mus. life. In 1913 he met *Casella, who became his colleague in the struggle. Became prof. of comp., Parma, 1921–3. Then settled at Asolo. Taught comp. at Liceo B. Marcello, Venice, from 1932, becoming dir. 1939–52. Pubd. complete edn. in 16 vols. of Monteverdi 1926–42 which stimulated present revival of interest. Also ed. many vols. of Vivaldi's complete works. Author of books on Vivaldi, Monteverdi, and Stravinsky. He destroyed most of his mus. written before 1914, but thereafter he was a prolific composer and wrote many operas. His mus., naturally influenced by the early It. composers, also shows traces of Debussy's impressionism and, in the 1920s, the angularity of a Janáček. The later works border on atonality, but he rejected serialism. Prin. works:

OPERAS: *L'Orfeide* (triptych: *La Morte delle maschera*, 1921–2, *Sette canzoni* (1918–19), *Orfeo*, 1919–20); *S. Francesco d'Assisi* (1920–1); *Tre Commedie Goldoniane* (triptych: *La bottega da caffè*, 1922, *Sior Todero Brontolon*, 1922, *Le baruffe chiozzote*, 1920); *Filomela e L'infatuato* (1925); *Merlino mastro d'organi* (1926–7); *Il Mistero di Venezia* (triptych: *Le Aquile di Aquileia*, 1928, *Il finto Arlecchino*, 1925, *I Corvi di S. Marco*, 1928); *Torneo Notturno* (1929); *I Trionfi d'amore* (triptych: *Castel smeraldo, Mascherate, Giochi olimpici*, comp. 1930–1. No.2 perf. 1937 as *Il festino*); *La Favola del figlio cambiato* (1932–3); *Giulio Cesare* (1934–5); *Antonio e Cleopatra* (1936–7); *Ecuba* (1940); *La Vita sogno* (1940–1); *I Capricci di Callot* (1941–2); *L'Allegra brigata* (1943); *Vergilii Aeneis* (1943–4); *Mondi celesti e infernali* (1948–9); *Il Figliuol prodigo* (1952); *Donna Urraca* (1953–4); *Il Capitan Spavento* (1954–5); *Venere prigioniera* (1955); *Rappresentazione e festa di Carnasciale e della Quaresima* (1961); *Don Giovanni* (1962); *Le Metamorfosi di Bonaventura* (1963–5); *Don Tartufo Bacchettone* (1966); *Il Marescalco* (1960–8); *Gli eroi di Bonaventura* (1968); *Uno dei dieci* (1970); *L'Iscariota* (1970).

BALLETS, etc.: *Pantea* (1917–19); *Stradivario* (1947–8); *Il Mondo Novo* (1950–1).

ORCH.: syms.: No.1 ('in 4 movements like the 4 seasons', 1933), No.2 (*Elegiaca*, 1936), No.3 (*delle Campane*, 1944–5), No.4 (*In Memoriam*, 1946), No.5 (*Concertante, in Eco*, 1947), No.6, for str. (1947),

No.7 (*delle Canzoni*, 1948), No.8 (*Sinfonia brevis*, 1964), No.9 (*dell' ahimè*, 1966), No.10 (*Atropo*, 1967), No.11 (*delle cornamuse*, 1970); *Sinfonia in un tempo* (1950); *Sinfonia dello Zodiaco* (1951); *Impressioni dal Vero* I (1910–11), II (1915), III (1921–2); *Pause del Silenzio* I (1917), II (1925–6); *Concerti* (1931); *4 Invenzioni* (1933), *Vivaldiana* (1952).

INSTR. & ORCH.: *Variazioni senza Tema*, pf., orch. (1923); vn. conc. No.1 (1932), No.2 (1963); pf. conc. No.1 (1934), No.2 (1937), No.3 (1948), No.4 (1950), No.5 (1958), No.6 (1964); vc. conc. (1937); Triple Conc. (1938); *Dialogo*, 2 pf. (1956); fl. conc. (1968).

VOICES & ORCH.: *La Principessa Ulalia*, cantata (1924); *La Cena*, soloists., ch., orch. (1927); *La Passione*, soloists., ch., orch. (1935); *Missa pro mortuis*, bar., ch., orch. (1938); *Vergilii Aeneis*, heroic sym., 7 soloists., ch., orch. (1943–4); *La festa della Sensa*, bar., ch., orch. (1948); *Magister Josephus*, 4 vv., small orch. (1957).

VOICES & CHAMBER ENS.: *De profundis*, v., va., bass drum, pf. (1937); *Universa Universis*, male ch., chamber orch. (1942); *Mondi celesti*, v., 10 instrs. (1948); *Ave Phoebe dum queror*, ch., 20 instrs. (1964).

CHAMBER MUSIC: str. qt. No.1 (1920), No.2 (1923), No.3 (1931), No.4 (1934), No.5 (1950), No.6 (1947), No.7 (1950), No.8 (1963–4) No.5 based on material from opera *I Capricci di Callot*, 1941–2); Sonata, vn., vc., pf. (1927); vc. sonatina (1942); wind quintet (1956).

Also songs and pf. pieces.

Malipiero, Riccardo (b Milan, 1914; d Milan, 2003). It. composer. Adopted 12-note system 1945 and helped to organize first Int. Congress of 12-note mus., Milan, 1949. Works incl. 3 operas (incl. *La donna e mobile*, 1954); vn. conc.; wind quintet; *6 Poems of Dylan Thomas*, sop., 10 instr.; *Requiem*; 3 syms.; 2 vc. concs.; vn. conc.; picc. conc.; 2 pf. concs.; 3 str. qts.; pf. quintet; ob. sonata; conc. for ballerina and orch.

malizia (It.). Malice. The scherzo of Walton's 1st sym. is marked *presto, con malizia*.

Malko, Nikolay (Andreyevich) (b Brailov, 1883; d Sydney, NSW, 1961). Russ.-born conductor (Amer. cit. 1946). Cond. opera and ballet, St Petersburg 1908–18. Prof. Leningrad Cons. 1918–26, cond. Leningrad PO 1926–9. Cond. f.p. of Shostakovich's 1st and 2nd Syms., Leningrad 1926 and 1927. Prof. Moscow Cons. 1927–33. Went to Eng. Amer. début 1938. Settled in Chicago 1940. Cond. Yorkshire SO 1954–5, Sydney SO 1957–61.

Mallinger [Lichtenegger], **Mathilde** (b Agram, 1847; d Berlin, 1920). Croatian soprano. Début Munich 1866 (as Norma). Created role of Eva in *Die Meistersinger von Nürnberg*, Munich 1868. Berlin Opera 1869–82, prof. of singing Prague Cons. 1890–5, Berlin Eichelberg Cons. from 1895. Taught Lotte *Lehmann.

mamelles de Tirésias, Les (The Breasts of Tirésias). *Opéra-bouffe* in prologue and 2 acts by Poulenc to lib. based on play by Apollinaire. Comp.

1944. Prod. Paris 1947, Brandeis Univ. 1953, Aldeburgh 1958 (vers. with 2 pfs.), Leeds 1978, London (SW) 1978.

Ma mère l'Oye (Mother Goose). Suite in 5 movts. by Ravel based on fairy-tales by Péricault. Orig. for 4 hands (1 pf.) (1908–10), orch. 1911 and prod. as ballet (to scenario by Ravel), Paris 1912. There are differences between the 2 versions. The 5 movts. of piano suite are (1) *Pavane de la Belle au Bois dormant* (Sleeping Beauty's Pavan), (2) *Petit Poucet* (Tom Thumb), (3) *Laideronette Impératrice des Pagodes* (Empress of the Pagodas), (4) *Les Entretiens de la Belle et la Bête* (Conversations of Beauty and the Beast), (5) *Le Jardin féerique* (The Fairy Garden). For the ballet Ravel added a *Prélude*, the *Danse du Rouet* and 4 extensive interludes.

Man. (1, It.) Short for *mano*, hand.
(2, Ger.) Short for *Manuale*, manual (of organ); Man. I = Great; II, Swell; III, Choir; IV, Solo (but occasionally another numeration is used, based on position, i.e. I, Choir; II, Great; III, Swell; IV, Solo).

manchega. An especially lively type of *seguidilla* danced in the La Mancha province of Spain.

Manchester Camerata. Chamber orchestra founded in Manchester in 1972 under auspices of BBC Radio Manchester. Maximum strength 38 players. Became autonomous organization in 1979. Main series in Manchester but plays throughout North West of England and has visited France, Norway, and Hong Kong. Prin. conds.: Frank Cliff 1972–7; Szymon Goldberg 1977–80; Manoug Parikian 1980–4; Nicholas Braithwaite 1984–91; Nicholas Kraemer 1992–5; Sachio Fujioka 1995–2000; Douglas Boyd from 2000. London début 1983, cond. Braithwaite (Croydon 1976, cond. Goldberg). Played for opera at Buxton Fest.

Manchester School. Title given to group of composers—*Maxwell Davies, *Birtwistle, *Goehr, and *Ogdon—who studied in Manchester (RMCM and Univ.) under Richard *Hall in late 1950s and gave concerts there.

Mancinelli, Luigi (*b* Orvieto, 1848; *d* Rome, 1921). It. conductor, composer, and cellist. Th. orch. cond. Rome 1874. Dir. Liceo Musicale, Bologna, 1881–6. Cond. opera Drury Lane, London, 1887, CG 1888–1905; cond. f.ps. in England of *Falstaff* and *Tosca*. Mus. dir. Madrid Th. Royal 1887–93. Chief cond. It. opera at NY Met 1893–1903. Cond. Teatro Colón, Buenos Aires, 1908–13. Comp. operas *Ero e Leandro, Paolo e Francesca*, and *A Midsummer Night's Dream*, also choral works and church mus.

Mancini, Henry (Nicole) (*b* Cleveland, Ohio, 1924; *d* Beverley Hills, 1994). Amer. composer, conductor, and arranger. Pianist and arranger, Tex Beneke orch. 1945–7. On mus. staff Universal Internat. Pictures, 1952–8. Guest cond. leading sym. orchs. Comp. over 70 film scores, incl. *Breakfast at Tiffany's*, with its hit-song *Moon River* (1961); *The Days of Wine and Roses* (1962); *The Pink Panther* (1964); and the TV serial *The Thorn Birds* (1983).

Mandeal, Cristian (*b* Rupea, 1946). Romanian conductor. Studied piano, comp., and cond. at Brasov Mus. High Sch. and Mus. Acad., Bucharest (1965–75), then with *Karajan (1980) and *Celibidache (1990). Became répétiteur at Bucharest Romanian Opera. Gen. dir. and prin. cond. George Enescu PO, Bucharest, from 1987; art. dir. Haifa SO 1999–2002. First prin. guest cond. of Hallé Orch., from 2005. Cond. Brit. première of Enescu's *Oedipe* (Edinburgh Fest. 2002).

mandola, mandora, mandore (from Gr. *pandoura*). Ancient instr. (possibly as early as 9th cent.), a small ancestor of the *lute. Popular in Sp. and It., reaching Eng. at end of 14th cent. Had 9 frets and up to 6 str. Played with plectrum and used for popular mus.-making. Ancestor of *mandolin.

mandolin(e). Plucked str. instr. of lute family, of It. orig., usually with 8 str. tuned in pairs and played with plectrum, generally in a sustained tremolo. Used in informal mus.-making, but occurs in several famous scores, e.g. *Alexander Balus* (Handel, 1747), *L'Amant jaloux* (Grétry, 1778), *Don Giovanni* (Mozart, 1787), *Otello* (Verdi, 1887), 7th Sym. and *Das Lied von der Erde* (Mahler), *Serenade* (Schoenberg), *5 Pieces* (Webern), *Agon* (Stravinsky), etc. Beethoven wrote some pieces for mandolin and pf., and Vivaldi several concs.

Mandoline. Poem by Verlaine set for v. and pf. by Debussy, 1882, as No.3 of *Fêtes galantes* (orig. version), and by Fauré, 1891, as No.1 of 5 *Mélodies*, Op.58. Also set as *Fêtes galantes* by R. Hahn, 1895.

mandora. See *mandola*.

Manduell, (Sir) **John** (*b* Johannesburg, 1928). S. African-born Eng. administrator and composer. On staff of BBC 1956–68 (chief planner, Mus. Prog. 1964–8). Dir. of Mus., Lancaster Univ. 1968–71. Prin., RNCM 1972–96. Dir., Cheltenham Fest. 1969–94, having been programme adv. 1961–7. Works inc. ov. *Sunderland Point*, double conc., str. qt. CBE 1982. Knighted 1989.

Mandyczewski, Eusebius (*b* Czernowitz, 1857; *d* Vienna, 1929). Austrian musicologist and conductor. Cond. Vienna Singakademie 1880, and archivist *Gesellschaft der Musikfreunde*. On staff Vienna Cons. from 1897. Ed. the *Lieder* in complete Schubert ed. 1897, 3 vols. of Haydn syms., works by Beethoven and Brahms. Wrote songs and pf. pieces.

Manfred. Verse-drama by Byron (1817) on which are based (1) Ov. and 15 items of incidental mus. by Schumann, Op.115 (1848–9); (2) Sym. (unnumbered) by Tchaikovsky, Op.58 (1885).

Mangeot, André (Louis) (*b* Paris, 1883; *d* London, 1970). Eng. violinist and impresario of

Fr. birth. Settled in London, becoming Brit. cit. Played in Queen's Hall Orch. under Wood and CG orch. under Richter (1908). Founded International Str. Qt. 1919, specializing in Brit. works and contemporary mus. Gave f. Eng. p. of Fauré's str. qt. 1925. Ed. 17th-cent. Eng. works for str. (with Peter Warlock). Formed André Mangeot Qt. 1948.

Manhattan School of Music. Mus. coll. in NY City, founded 1917, permanent charter 1925. Pres. John *Brownlee 1958–69; George Schick 1969–76; John Crosby 1976–86; Gideon Waldrop 1986–9; Peter C. Simon 1989–92; Marta Casals-Istomin 1992–2005; Robert Sirota from 2005. Moved into buildings vacated by *Juilliard School 1962.

mani (It., plural of *mano*). Hands.

manica (It.). Shift (on vn., etc.; see *position*).

manichord. See *monochord*.

manico (It.). Fingerboard (vn., etc.).

Manieren (Ger.). *Ornaments, or graces.

Mann, William (Somervell) (*b* Madras, 1924; *d* Bath, 1989). Eng. music critic. Ass. mus. critic *The Times* 1948–60, chief mus. critic 1960–82. Author of books on operas of R. Strauss (1964) and Mozart (1977). Many trans. of libs., incl. *Der Ring des Nibelungen* (1964), and *Tristan und Isolde* (1968), and song-texts.

Männergesangverein (Ger.). Male singing society, i.e. male v. ch. Developed from *Liedertafel*.

Manners, Charles [Mansergh, Southcote] (*b* London, 1857; *d* Dublin, 1935). Irish bass and impresario. Joined D'Oyly Carte Opera 1881, created Private Willis in *Iolanthe* 1882. Carl Rosa co., then CG from 1890. Amer. début 1893. Married sop. Florence Moody 1890 and with her est. *Moody-Manners Opera Co., 1898–1916.

Mannes, Leopold (Damrosch) (*b* NY, 1889; *d* Vineyard Haven, Mass., 1964). Amer. pianist, composer, teacher, and inventor. Son of David Mannes and nephew of Walter *Damrosch. Teacher of comp. at *Mannes Sch. 1927–31, dir. 1940–8, president 1950–64. Founded pf. trio 1948–55. Gave up mus. for period in 1920s while with Leopold Godowsky jr. he invented Kodachrome photographic colour process at Eastman Kodak Co., Rochester, NY. Wrote orch. and chamber mus.

Mannes College of Music. Mus. coll. in NY City founded 1916 as Mannes Mus. Sch. by violinist and cond. David Mannes (*b* NY, 1866; *d* NY, 1959) and his wife Clara (1869–1948). Charter 1960. Charles Kaufmann dean 1979–95, Joel Lester from 1996.

Mannheim School. Name given by modern musicologists to group of 18th-cent. Ger. composers based on Mannheim and assoc. with the court of

the Elector of Pfalzbayern (1724–99). Their importance, shared to some extent with similar progressives in Vienna, Italy, and Bohemia, was in laying foundation of the sym. as it was to be developed by Haydn and Mozart. They were headed by Johann W. *Stamitz (1717–57), followed by Ignaz Holzbauer (1711–83, in Mannheim from 1753), F. X. *Richter (1709–89, in Mannheim from 1747), *Cannabich (1731–98), and Stamitz's sons Karl (1745–1801) and Anton (1754–1809). The elder Stamitz joined the Mannheim orch. in 1745, soon becoming cond. He founded a new style of perf. suited to his works. Features of this style incl. melodic prominence of vns., extended crescendi and precise dynamics, tremolando, and replacement of improvised continuo by written-out parts.

Manning, Jane (Marian) (*b* Norwich, 1938). Eng. soprano, expert in contemporary music. Début London 1964 (Park Lane Group) in songs by Webern, Messiaen, and Dallapiccola. Has given f.ps. of numerous works by Eng. composers. Wexford Fest. 1976. Formed Jane's Minstrels 1988. Sang in première of Cage's *Europeras 3 and 4*, London 1990. OBE 1990.

Manns, (Sir) **August** (Friedrich) (*b* Stolzenberg, 1825; *d* Norwood, 1907). Ger.-born conductor (Brit. cit.). After studies, was prin. clarinettist in Danzig military band. In 1848 became first violinist in *Gung'l's orch., Berlin. Bandmaster, Königsberg and Cologne 1851–4. Went to London 1854 as ass. cond. of Crystal Palace band. In 1855 became cond. and augmented band to sym. orch. From 1855 to 1901, when orch. was disbanded, Manns's Crystal Palace concerts were most enterprising concerts in Eng., where many works received their f.ps. in England. Manns cond. first London perf. of mus. by Elgar. Instituted Saturday popular concerts 1856. Cond. Handel Fest. 1883–1900. Knighted 1903.

Manon. Opera in 5 acts by *Massenet to lib. by Meilhac and Gille, after Prévost's novel *Histoire du Chevalier Des Grieux et de Manon Lescaut* (1731). Comp. 1882–3, rev. 1884. Prod. Paris 1884, Liverpool and NY 1885, CG 1891, NY Met 1895. Massenet wrote 1-act sequel *Le Portrait de Manon* (1894). Operas on same subject by *Auber (see below), *Puccini (see below), Balfe (*The Maid of Artois*, 1836), and Henze (*Boulevard Solitude*, 1951).

Manon Lescaut. (1) Opera in 4 acts by Puccini to lib. by Giacosa, Illica, G. Ricordi, Praga, and Oliva, after Prévost's novel. Comp. 1890–2. Prod. Turin 1893, Milan 1894 (rev. vers.), CG and Philadelphia 1894, NY 1898 (Met 1907).

(2) *Opéra-comique* in 3 acts by Auber to lib. by Scribe, after Prévost's novel. Comp. 1855. Prod. Paris 1856.

Manowarda, Josef von (*b* Kraków, 1890; *d* Berlin, 1942). Austrian bass. Sang in Graz 1911–15. Vienna Volksoper 1915–18, member Vienna Opera 1919–42 (created Spirit Messenger in *Die Frau ohne Schatten* on his début there). Berlin State

Opera 1934–42. Salzburg Fest. from 1922; Bayreuth début 1931. Outstanding King Mark and Gurnemanz. Taught at Vienna Acad. of Mus. 1932–5.

Mantovani, (Annunzio Paolo) (*b* Venice, 1905; *d* Tunbridge Wells, 1980). It.-born Eng. conductor and violinist (Brit. cit. 1933). Formed hotel orch., Birmingham, 1923. Recitalist in London. Broadcasting orch. from 1927. Mus. dir. for many musicals, esp. those by Noël Coward. Famous for 'singing strings' sound, heard chiefly in arrs. by Ronald *Binge.

Mantra. Work for 2 amplified, ring-modulated pf. by *Stockhausen, comp. 1969–70. F.p. 1970, London 1971. Fully notated. Pianists also play perc. instr. (wood-block and little bells). Title refers to Indian word for a mystical repetition, a 'sound which makes one see'.

manual. Any of the org. kbds. provided for the hands (as opposed to pedal-kbd.). Hpds. have 1st and 2nd manuals (kbds.).

Manuale (Ger.). Manual (of organ). See *Man*.

Manualkoppel (Ger.). Manual coupler, i.e. (usually) Swell to Great.

Manuel [Lévy], **Roland** (Alexis) [sometimes Roland-Manuel or Manuel-Lévy] (*b* Paris, 1891; *d* Paris, 1966). Fr. composer and critic. Comp. operettas, ballets, pf. conc., etc. Wrote 3 books on Ravel. On staff Paris Cons. from 1947.

Manzoni Requiem. Title sometimes given to Verdi's *Requiem*, which was comp. in memory of It. novelist and poet Alessandro Manzoni (1785–1873). F.p. Milan 1874, London 1875.

maraca (plural *maracas*). Lat.-Amer. perc. instr. made from a pair of dried Cuban gourds, with beans or beads inside. Shaken by handle to produce a rattling effect. (Sometimes made of other materials with lead shot inside, to give a stronger effect.) Usually played as a pair. Used by dance-bands, also in concert works by 20th-cent. composers such as Varèse, Prokofiev, Bernstein, Arnold, McCabe, etc.

Marazzoli, Marco (*b* Parma, *c*.1602 or *c*.1608; *d* Rome, 1662). It. composer, singer, and harpist. Singer in papal chapel 1637–62. With V. *Mazzocchi, wrote what is believed to be first comic opera, *Chi soffre, speri* (Rome 1639, rev. of *Il falcone*, 1637), also other operas, oratorios, cantatas, etc. Connected with Fr. court in Rome from 1643 and dedicated his opera *La vita humana* (1656) to Queen Christina of Sweden.

marcando; marcato (It.). Marking; marked, i.e. each note emphasized; *marcatissimo* is the superlative.

Marcello, Alessandro (*b* Venice, 1669; *d* Venice, 1747). It. violinist, composer, and mathematician, brother of Benedetto *Marcello. Comp. cantatas, concs. for fls. and vns., and for ob. and fl.

His ob. conc. in D minor was transcr. by J. S. Bach (BWV974) (erroneously attrib. to Vivaldi and later to B. Marcello).

Marcello, Benedetto (*b* Venice, 1686; *d* Brescia, 1739). It. composer. Wrote oratorios, cantatas, instr. concs., and settings of 50 psalms for vv. with instr. acc. Pupils incl. the singer Faustina *Bordoni and the composer *Galuppi.

march (Fr. *marche*, Ger. *Marsch*, It. *marcia*). Form of mus. to accompany the orderly progress of large group of people, especially soldiers; one of earliest known mus. forms. Military marches are of 4 kinds: funeral (4/4 time), slow (usually 4/4), quick (2/4 or 6/8), and double-quick. The march entered art mus. in 17th cent. in the works of *Couperin and *Lully, but there are marches in virginals pieces by Byrd. Marches occur in the operas of Mozart (e.g. *Die Entführung*, *Figaro*, *Così fan tutte*, and *Zauberflöte*); Schubert wrote *Marches militaires* and Beethoven incorporated a *funeral march into his *Eroica* sym., as did Chopin into a pf. sonata. Famous operatic marches were written by Meyerbeer, Wagner, and Verdi. It was further developed in the sym. by Berlioz, Mahler, Tchaikovsky, and Elgar. Military marches for concert perf. by sym. orch. were written by Elgar (*Pomp and Circumstance*) and R. Strauss. Some of the best military marches were written in the 19th cent. by *Sousa, Johann Strauss I, and *Lanner.

Marchand, Louis (*b* Lyons, 1669; *d* Paris, 1732). Fr. organist and composer. Org., Nevers Cath. at age of 14. Org., royal chapel 1708–14. High reputation in Fr. as kbd. virtuoso. On tour of Ger. in 1717, he was involved in projected org. competition with Bach in Dresden, but withdrew at the last minute, afraid of failure. Returned to Fr. as teacher. Works incl. kbd. pieces, opera, cantata, airs, and 3 *Cantiques spirituels* (texts by Racine). Teacher of *Daquin.

Marchesi, Blanche (*b* Paris, 1863; *d* London, 1940). Fr. soprano, daughter of Mathilde *Marchesi. Concert début Berlin 1895, operatic début Prague 1900 (Brünnhilde in *Die Walküre*). Joined *Moody-Manners co. Sang Wagner roles at CG from 1902, toured USA (twice), Russ., and Eur. Settled in London to teach.

Marchesi de Castrone [Graumann], **Mathilde** (*b* Frankfurt, 1821; *d* London, 1913). Ger. mezzo-soprano and teacher. Concert début, Frankfurt 1844. Sang in London, 1849. Made only one appearance in opera, in Bremen 1852 (Rosina in *Il barbiere di Siviglia*). Married It. bar. and teacher Salvatore Marchesi (1822–1908) in 1852. Prof. of singing Vienna Cons. 1854–61 and 1869–78, Cologne Cons. 1865–8. Taught at own sch. in Paris 1861–5 and from 1881. Wrote vocal method and 24 books of exercises. Pupils incl. Calvé, Eames, Melba, Klafsky, and Kurz.

Marcovici, Silvia (*b* Bacau, Romania, 1952). Romanian-born violinist. Soloist with Hague

Residentie Orch. in 1967. In 1969 won Thibaud-Long comp. in Paris, Enescu comp., Bucharest 1970. London début 1970 (LSO). Chosen by Stokowski as soloist at his 90th birthday concert in 1971. Emigrated to Israel in 1976, settling later in Ger.

Margot-la-Rouge ('A Night in Paris'). Unpubd. opera in 1 act by Delius to libretto by 'Rosenval' (Berthe Gaston-Danville), comp. 1901–2. Vocal score by Ravel 1902 (pubd. Paris c.1905). See *Idyll*. F.p. (in orch. by Fenby) BBC studio broadcast 1982; f. stage p. (in orig. Delius orch.) St. Louis 1983; f. London stage p. 1984.

Maria di Rohan. Opera in 3 acts by Donizetti to lib. by Cammarano based on a play, *Un duel sous le Cardinal de Richelieu*, by Lockroy and Badon. Prod. Vienna 1843, London 1847, NY 1849.

Maria Golovin. Opera in 3 acts by *Menotti to his own lib. Prod. Brussels and NY 1958, London 1976.

Mariani, Angelo (*b* Ravenna, 1821; *d* Genoa, 1873). It. conductor and composer. Early comps. admired by Rossini. Début as opera cond. Messina 1844. Cond. *I *due Foscari* in Milan, 1846. Court cond., Copenhagen 1847–8. Cond., Genoa 1852–73. Cond. It. premières of *Lohengrin* and *Tannhäuser*, and many important Verdi perfs. Outstanding interpreter of Verdi. Comp. requiem, cantatas, songs.

Maria Stuarda. Opera in 2 or 3 acts by Donizetti to lib. by G. Bardari based on Schiller's play. Act I, sc.iii, is often called Act II. When perf. was forbidden at Naples in 1834, mus. was used for opera with different plot, *Buondelmonte*. F.p. of *Maria Stuarda*, Milan 1835, NY (concert) 1964, NY City Opera 1972, London 1966 (St Pancras Fest.), 1973 (SW at Coliseum). Discovery of missing autograph score led to more authentic 2-act vers., prod. Bergamo 1989.

Marienleben, Das (The Life of Mary). Settings by Hindemith, Op.27, for sop. and pf. of 15 poems by R. M. Rilke, comp. 1922–3, f.p. Frankfurt 1923. New and rev. version, worked on 1936–48, f.p. Hanover 1948. 4 songs orch. by Hindemith 1938, 2 more 1959.

Mariés de la Tour Eiffel, Les (The newly-weds of the Eiffel Tower). Ballet in 1 act with mus. by 5 of *Les *Six* (excl. Durey). Lib. by Cocteau, choreog. by Börlin. Prod. Paris 1921.

marimba. Lat.-Amer. perc. instr. of African origin. It consists of strips of wood of different length with (tuned) resonators underneath, the whole fixed in a frame and struck with drumsticks—in fact, a super-xylophone large enough for perf. by 4 players (or *marimberos*), standing or sitting side by side. Now made with bars of rosewood and tubular metal resonators which are struck with soft-headed hammers held by the player(s). Grainger scored for the marimba in the suite *In a Nutshell* before 1916. *Milhaud wrote a

conc. for marimba and vibraphone (1947) and *Creston a conc. for marimba (1940). It now frequently occurs in orch. works.

The S. African original, known to Afrikaans-speaking Europeans as the *kaffir piano*, is called the *malimba* by natives.

Mario, Giovanni (Matteo) (Cavaliere de Candia) (*b* Cagliari, 1810; *d* Rome, 1883). It. tenor. Army career took him to Paris, 1836, where he was persuaded to become opera singer because of exceptional beauty of v. Début Paris Opéra 1838, title-role in *Robert le Diable*. It. Opera in Paris, 1840. London début, Her Majesty's, 1839, singing there until 1846. CG 1847–71. With Giulia *Grisi, his lifelong companion after 1839, *Tamburini, and *Lablache sang in f.p. of *Don Pasquale*, Paris 1843, creating Ernesto. Sang Duke in f. London p. of *Rigoletto*, 1853. Handsome in appearance and fine actor. Retired 1871.

Maritana. Opera in 3 acts by W. V. *Wallace to lib. by E. Fitzball (with interpolated lyrics by Alfred Bunn) after play *Don César de Bazan* by D'Ennery and Dumanoir. Prod. London 1845, Philadelphia 1846, NY 1848.

Mark, Peter (*b* NY City, 1940). Amer. violist and conductor. Prin. violist, Juilliard Orch. 1960–3, Chicago Lyric Opera 1964–6, ass. prin. violist Los Angeles PO 1968–9. CG début 1982. Solo violist in f.p. of conc. by his wife Thea *Musgrave (Hallé Orch., cond. Loughran, 1975). Art. dir. and cond. Virginia Opera Assoc. from 1975.

Markevitch, Igor (*b* Kiev, 1912; *d* Antibes, 1983). It. conductor, composer, and writer of Russ. birth. London début 1929 as soloist in his pf. conc. Début as cond. 1930 (Amsterdam). Mus. dir. Stockholm SO 1952–5, Montreal SO 1957–61. Salzburg Fest. début 1952. Amer. début Boston SO 1955. Cond., Lamoureux Orch. 1957–61, Spanish Radio-TV orch. 1965–8; dir., Monte Carlo Opera 1968. Fine interpreter of Stravinsky. Prin. works: ORCH.: *Sinfonietta in F* (1928–9); pf. conc. (1929) *Concerto grosso* (1930); *Partita*, pf., small orch. (1931) *Rébus* (1931); *L'envoi d'Icare* (1932, also for 2 pf. and perc.), re-comp. as *Icare* (1943); *Hymnes* (1932–3); *Petite Suite d'après Schumann* (1933); *Hymne à la morte*, small orch., opt. cont. (1936); *Cantique d'amour* (1936); *Le nouvel âge* (1937, also for 2 pf.); *Le bleu Danube* (on themes of J. Strauss) (1944); *Bach's Musical Offering*, arr. fl., ob., ca., bn., vn., va., vc., hpd., soloists, str. (1949–50).

CHORAL & VOCAL: *Cantate* (Cocteau), sop., male ch., orch. (1930); *Psalm*, sop., orch. (opt. ch. of 6 sop.) (1933); *Paradise Lost*, oratorio, sop., mez., ten., ch., orch. (1934–5); *3 Poems*, high v., pf. (1935); *La taille de l'homme*, sop., 12 instr. (1938–9); *Lorenzo il magnifico*, sop., orch. (1940).

CHAMBER MUSIC: *Sérénade*, vn., cl., bn. (1931); *Galop*, fl. (opt.), ob., cl., bn., hn., pf., vn., vc., perc. (1932).

PIANO: *Stefan le poète* (1939–40); *Variations, Fugue and Envoi on a Theme of Handel* (1941).

markiert (Ger.). Marked, i.e. clearly accented, or brought out. Used in connection with, for instance, the emphasis given to a melody above its acc.

markig (Ger. 'vigorous'). Directive frequently found in Bruckner scores, e.g. *sehr markig* in finale of 8th Sym.

Marriage, The (*Zhenitba*). (1) Unfinished opera by Mussorgsky to his own lib. based on Gogol's comedy (1842). 1 act completed 1868. Concert perf. at Rimsky-Korsakov's house 1906, stage (with pf. acc.) St Petersburg 1908, first full prod. in Rimsky's rev., Petrograd 1917. Others who have orch. the score are Gauk (1917), d'Harcourt (1930), Duhamel (1954), and Rozhdestvensky (1982).
(2) Opera in 1 act by Martinů to his own lib. after Gogol. Amer. TV (NBC) 1953; stage prod. Hamburg 1954.

Marriage of Figaro, The (Mozart). See *Nozze di Figaro, Le*.

Marriner, (Sir) **Neville** (*b* Lincoln, 1924). Eng. conductor and violinist. Taught at Eton Coll. 1948. Member of Martin Str. Qt. 1949. Prof. of vn. RCM 1949–59. Violinist in Philharmonia Orch. 1952–6, prin. 2nd vn. LSO 1956–8. Founder, *Academy of St Martin-in-the-Fields, 1958; dir. 1958–78. Cond. Los Angeles Chamber Orch. 1969–79. Début as opera cond. RNCM 1977 (*La bohème*). Prin. cond. Minnesota Orch. 1979–86, cond. Stuttgart Radio SO 1983–9. Salzburg Fest. début 1982 (Academy of St Martin-in-the-Fields). CBE 1979. Knighted 1985.

Marschalk, Max (*b* Berlin, 1863; *d* Poberowad-Ostsee, 1940). Ger. music critic and composer. Friend of R. Strauss and Mahler. Critic for Berlin *Vossische Zeitung* 1894–1933. Wrote incidental mus. to plays (incl. some by his brother-in-law Gerhardt Hauptmann), orch. works, and songs.

Marschner, Heinrich (August) (*b* Zittau, 1795; *d* Hanover, 1861). Ger. composer and conductor. Went to Vienna 1817 and met Beethoven. Success of his opera *Heinrich IV und d'Aubigné*, prod. by Weber at Dresden 1820, led to his appointment there as co-cond. with Weber. Appointed mus. dir. 1824, resigning on Weber's death 1826. Kapellmeister, Leipzig, 1827–30, where his *Der *Vampyr* (1828) was successful. In Dec. 1829 *Der Templer und die Jüdin*, based on Scott's *Ivanhoe*, was prod. Court Kapellmeister, Hanover, 1831–59. Most famous opera, *Hans Heiling*, prod. Berlin 1833. 8 other operas followed, none successful. Wrote incidental mus. to Kleist's *Prinz von Homburg*, also 7 pf. sonatas, pf. trios, songs, etc. Occupies place between Weber and Wagner in history of Romantic opera.

Marschner, Wolfgang (*b* Dresden, 1926). Ger. violinist. Taught at Essen, Cologne, and at Freiburg from 1963. Gave f. London p. of Schoenberg's vn. conc.

Marseillaise, La. Fr. nat. anthem (first line 'Allons, enfants de la patrie'). Words and mus., by Claude Joseph *Rouget de Lisle, written on 24 Apr., 1792, under title *Chant de guerre pour l'armée du Rhin* (War song for the Rhine army). Received present title when sung by battalion of Marseilles troops as they entered Paris. Quoted by Schumann in *Faschingsschwank aus Wien* and *Die beiden Grenadier*, by Elgar in *The Music Makers*, and by Tchaikovsky in his *1812* ov. Elaborately arr. for soloists, ch., and orch. by Berlioz.

Marsh, Roger (*b* Bournemouth, 1949). Eng. composer. Lect., Keele Univ. 1978–88 (head of mus. dept. from 1985). Lect., York Univ. from 1988. Comps. incl. several for mus. th.; chamber mus. (some incl. vocalist); and works using elecs. or amp. of vv. or standard instrs.

Marshall, Lois (Catherine) (*b* Toronto, 1924; *d* Toronto, 1997). Canadian soprano, later mezzosoprano. Début Toronto 1947 (Bach's *St Matthew Passion*). Opera début Toronto 1952 (Queen of Night in *Die Zauberflöte*). NY recital 1952. London début 1956 (RPO, cond. Beecham). Mezzo roles from mid-1970s. Teacher at Toronto Univ. from 1976. Companion of Order of Canada, 1968.

Marshall, Margaret (*b* Stirling, 1949). Scottish soprano. First prize Munich comp. 1974. London début 1975, Edinburgh Fest. 1978. Opera début Florence 1978 (Euridice in Gluck's *Orfeo*); CG 1980; La Scala and Salzburg 1982; Amer. 1980. OBE 1999.

Marteau sans maître, Le (The hammer without a master). Work by *Boulez for cont., alto fl., va., guitar, vibraphone, xylorimba, and perc. Comp. to text by René Char 1952–4, rev. 1957. F.p. Baden-Baden June 1955, cond. Rosbaud, Paris 1956, cond. Boulez, London 1960, cond. Boulez.

martelé (Fr.). Hammered—referring to the manner of playing bowed instr. by a series of short, sharp blows with the bow upon the str. The point of the bow is to be used for this process unless the heel is indicated by the expression *martelé du talon* (see also *détaché*).

martellando; martellato (It.). Same as *martelé*, though the words are sometimes applied to pf. playing and even singing.

Martenot, Maurice (*b* Paris, 1898; *d* Paris, 1980). Fr. musician and inventor of the *ondes Martenot. Prof. at École Normale de Musique, Paris, and dir. of École d'Art Martenot, Neuilly. Gave demonstration of his elec. mus. instr. the ondes musicales, as it was first called, at the Paris Opéra, 20 April 1928. First work written for it was Dimitri Levidis's *Poème symphonique*.

Martha, or Richmond Fair (*Martha, oder der Markt von Richmond*). 4-act opera by Flotow to lib. by W. Friedrich after V. de Saint-Georges's ballet-pantomime *Lady Henriette* for which Flotow had comp. some mus. Makes use of 'The Last Rose of Summer', as 'Letzte Rose'. Prod. Vienna 1847, London 1849, NY 1852.

Martin, Frank (*b* Geneva, 1890; *d* Naarden, Holland, 1974). Swiss composer, pianist, and harpsichordist. Settled in Paris 1923–6, returning to

Geneva to teach at Inst. Jaques-Dalcroze 1927–38. Founder and dir. Technicum moderne de musique, Geneva, 1933–9. Taught Cologne Hochschule für Musik 1950–7. Works of high quality, notable for delicate colouring, contrapuntal skill, and expressive nature. Used 12-note system very freely in late works. Prin. comps.:

OPERAS: *Der Sturm* (The *Tempest*) (1952–5); *Monsieur de Pourceaugnac* (1960–2).

BALLETS: *Die blaue Blume* (1936); *Fairy-Tale of Cinderella* (1941); *Ein Totentanz zu Basel in Jahre 1943* (1943).

ORCH.: *Symphonie burlesque sur des thèmes savoyards* (1915); *Esquisses* (1920); *Rythmes* (1926); *Guitare* (1933); 5 *Ballades*: alto sax., str., pf. (1938); fl., str. (1939); pf. (1939); tb. (1940); vc., small orch. (1949); **Petite Symphonie Concertante*, hp., hpd., pf., str. (1944–5, for full orch. 1946); Concerto, 7 winds, timp., str. (1949); *Passacaille*, str. (1952, orig. for org. 1944), for orch. (1963); *Études*, str. (1956); *Les 4 Éléments* (1963).

CONCERTOS: pf. conc. No.1 (1934), No.2 (1968–9); vn. conc. (1951); hpd. conc. (1952); vc. conc. (1966); *Triptych*, vn., orch. (1973–4).

VOICE & ORCH.: *Der Cornet* or *Die Weise von Liebe und Tod des Cornets Christoph Rilke*, cont., small orch. (1942–3); *Sechs Monologe aus Jedermann* (Hofmannsthal), bar. or cont. (1943, orch. 1949).

CHORAL: *Mass* (1922–6); *Le vin herbé*, secular oratorio on Tristan legend (1938–41); *In terra pax*, oratorio (1944); *Golgotha*, oratorio (1945–8); *Le mystère de la Nativité* (1957–9); *Pilate* (1964); *Requiem* (1971–2); *Et la vie l'emporta*, chamber cantata (1974, orch. B. Reichel).

CHAMBER MUSIC: pf. quintet (1919); str. trio (1936); str. qt. No.1 (1936), No.2 (1967); vn. sonata No.1 (1913), No.2 (1931–2).

Martineau, Malcolm (b Edinburgh, 1960). Scottish pianist/accompanist. Studied at St Catherine's Coll., Cambridge (1978–81), and RCM (1981–4). Teachers incl. Joyce Rathbone, Geoffrey Parsons, and Kendall Taylor. Gave own series at St John's, Smith Square, of complete songs of Debussy and Poulenc (1990–1), Britten cycle at Wigmore Hall (1995–6), and Hugo Wolf cycle at Edinburgh Fest. (1998). Débuts: Wigmore Hall (1984), Aix-en-Provence Fest. (1991), Edinburgh Fest. (1992), Salzburg Fest. (1994). Amer. début 1991 (Philadelphia). NY (Carnegie Hall) 1996 (with Bryn Terfel). Accomp. to many leading singers and instrumentalists: Bryn Terfel, Thomas Allen, Barbara Bonney, Felicity Lott, Emma Johnson, etc. Has appeared throughout Eur., N. Amer., and Australia.

Martinelli, Giovanni (b Montagnana, 1885; d NY, 1969). It. tenor. Played in regimental band, where his v. was noticed by bandmaster. Début Milan 1910 in Rossini's *Stabat Mater*. Opera début Milan 1910 (as Ernani) after which he was engaged by Puccini to sing Dick Johnson in Eur. première of *La Fanciulla del West* (Rome, 1911). London début CG 1912; Amer. début Philadelphia 1913; NY Met 1913. Member of NY Met

1913–43, singing in 36 operas. Met farewell 1946 (gala concert), then taught in NY. Last appearance Seattle 1967.

Martinez, Odaline de la (b Matanzas, Cuba, 1949). Cuban-born conductor and composer (Amer. cit. 1971). Emigrated to USA 1961. Founded chamber ens. Lontano 1976 for perf. of contemp. works which she cond. Cond. f.p. of Goldschmidt's *Beatrice Cenci*, London 1988. Works incl. *Phasing*, chamber orch. (1975); *Lamento*, amp. vocal qt., tape. (1978); opera *Sister Aimée* (1978–83); str. qt. (1985).

Martini, Giovanni (Battista) [Giambattista; known as 'Padre Martini'] (b Bologna, 1706; d Bologna, 1784). It. composer and theorist. Studied mus. and mathematics. Entered monastery 1721, but abandoned monastic life and returned to Bologna 1722. Choirmaster, S. Francesco, Bologna, 1725. Took minor orders 1725, ordained priest 1729 and devoted much time to scientific aspects of mus., amassing library of 17,000 books. Pupils incl. J. C. Bach, Grétry, Mozart, and Jommelli. Wrote church mus., instr. sonatas, and theoretical books.

Martini, Giovanni (Paolo) (Martini il Tedesco, 'Martini the German'; [Schwarzendorf, Johann Paul Aegidius]) (b Freistadt, 1741; d Paris, 1816). Ger. organist and composer. After service with King Stanislaus, settled in France 1764, changing name to Martini. Held various court posts, was th. cond., and taught comp. at Paris Cons. 1800–2. Chief cond. royal court orch. 1814. Wrote operas, church mus., military mus., and songs, of which best-known is *Plaisir d'amour*.

Martino, Donald (James) (b Plainfield, NJ, 1931; d on cruise, off coast of Antigua, 2005). Amer. composer. Assoc. prof. of mus., Yale Univ. 1958–69. Prof. of comp., New England Cons., Boston, 1970–80. Prof. of mus., Harvard Univ. from 1983. Some of mus. uses 12-note technique and dense polyphonic textures. Works incl. Sym.; *Quodlibets*, fl.; *Contemplations*, orch.; pf. fantasy; cl. trio; pf. conc.; vc. conc.; triple conc., cl., bcl., contrabcl.; 5 str. qts.; *The White Island*, ch., chamber orch.; sax. conc. (1987); vn. conc. (1996); cl. conc. (2003); Conc. for Orch. (2004).

Martinon, Jean (b Lyons, 1910; d Paris, 1976). Fr. conductor, violinist, and composer. Prisoner-of-war for 2 years during which he comp. several works. Cond. f.p. of one of these in Paris, which led to post at Bordeaux 1943–5. Ass. to Munch with LPO 1947–9. Cond. Radio Eireann Orch. 1948–50. Mus. dir. Lamoureux Orch., 1951–8, Israel PO 1958–60, Düsseldorf SO 1960–6, Chicago SO 1963–9 (Amer. début Boston 1957), French Radio Orch. 1968–75, Hague Residentie 1975–6. First Frenchman to win Mahler Medal. Wrote 4 syms.; opera; oratorio; 2 vn. concs.; vc. conc.; 2 str. qts., etc.

Martinů, Bohuslav (Jan) (b Polička, 1890; d Liestal, Switz., 1959). Cz. composer and violinist. Vn.

lessons at 6; began composing at 10. Violinist, Czech PO 1918–23, whose cond. *Talich performed Martinů work in Prague 1923. Went to Paris 1923 to study with Roussel. Stayed until 1940, when he escaped to Portugal and in 1941 settled in USA where he composed 5 syms. Returned to Europe 1953, living in Fr. and Switz. Prolific composer in all mus. forms. Remained essentially Cz. despite long exile. His works are uneven and flawed, but the best, such as the opera *Julietta* and the syms., are progressive and full of rhythmical energy and imagination. Basically diatonic, but with wide, sometimes dissonant, harmonic range. Prin. works:

OPERAS: *The Soldier and the Dancer* (1926–7); *The Knife's Tears* (1928); *The Three Wishes* (opera-film, 1929); *The Miracles of Mary* (1933–4); *The Voice of the Forest* (1935); *Comedy on the Bridge* (comp. 1935, radio 1937, rev. 1950, stage 1965); *Theatre Behind the Gate* (1935–6); *Julietta* (1936–7); *Alexandre Bis* (1937); *What Men Live By* (1951–2); *The *Marriage* (TV, 1952); *Mirandolina* (1953–4); *The Greek Passion* (1956–9); *Ariadne* (1958).

BALLETS: *Ištar* (1918–22); *Who is the Most Powerful in the World?* (1922); *Revolt* (1925); *The Butterfly that Stamped* (1926); *Kitchen Revue* (1927); *Špaliček* (The Chap Book, singing ballet) (1931–2); *The Strangler* (1948).

ORCH.: syms.: No.1 (1942), No.2 (1943), No.3 (1944), No.4 (1945), No.5 (1946), No.6 (*Fantaisies symphoniques*) (1951–3); *The Angel of Death*, sym.-poem (1910); *Half-Time* (1924); *Le Bagarre* (Tumult) (1926); *Le jazz* (1928); *Serenade* (1930); Sinfonia Concertante, 2 orch. (1932); *Inventions* (1934); *Concerto Grosso* (1937); *Double Concerto*, 2 str. orch., pf., timp. (1938); *Memorial to Lidiče* (1943); *Intermezzo* (1950); *The Rock* (1957); *3 Estampes* (1958).

CONCERTOS: pf., No.1 (1925), No.2 (1934), No.3 (1947–8), No.4 (*Incantations*) (1955–6), No.5 (*Fantasia Concertante*) (1957), Concertino (*Divertimento*), left hand (1926), Concertino (1938), 2 pfs. (1943); vn., No.1 (1932–3), No.2 (1943), 2 vns. (1950); vc., No.1 (1930, rev. 1955), No.2 (1944–5), Concertino (1924); Misc., str. qt. and orch. (1931), 2 concertinos, pf. trio, str. (1933), hpd. (1935), fl., vn. (1936), *Concerto da camera*, vn., pf., perc., str. (1941), *Sinfonia Concertante*, ob., bn., vn., vc. (1949), *Rhapsody-Concerto*, va. (1952), vn., pf. (1953), ob. (1955).

CHORAL: *Czech Rhapsody*, bar., ch., org., orch. (1918); *Hymn to St James*, sop., alt., bass, narr., ch., ens. (1954); *The Mount of Three Lights*, ten., bar., male ch., orch. (1954); *The Epic of Gilgamesh*, sop., ten., bar., bass, ch., orch. (1954–5); *The Opening of the Wells*, sop., cont., bar., women's ch., ens. (1955); *Mikeš of the Mountains*, sop., ten., ch., ens. (1959); *The Prophecy of Isaiah*, sop., cont., bar., male vv., va., tpt., pf., timp. (1959).

CHAMBER MUSIC: str. qts., No.1 (1918), No.2 (1925), No.3 (1929), No.4 (1937), No.5 (1938), No.6 (1946), No.7 (*Conc. da camera*) (1947); nonet, wind quintet, pf. qt. (1924–5), nonet, wind quintet, str. trio, db. (1959); pf. quintet (1911); str. quintet (1927); wind quintet (1930); pf. quintet No.1 (1933), No.2 (1944); pf. qt. (1942); ob. qt.

(1947); str. trios, No.1 (1923), No.2 (1934); pf. trios, No.1 (1930), No.2 (1950), No.3 (1951); vn. sonatas, No.1 (1927), No.2 (1931), No.3 (1944); vc. sonatas, No.1 (1939), No.2 (1941), No.3 (1952); va. sonata (1955); fl. sonata (1945); cl. sonatina (1956); tpt. sonatina (1956).

Many kbd. pieces and songs.

Martín y Soler, Vicente (b Valencia, 1754; d St Petersburg, 1806). Sp. composer. Went to Italy 1780, Vienna 1785, and St Petersburg 1788 as dir. of It. opera. Wrote 20 operas, several to libs. by da Ponte, incl. *Una cosa rara* (1786, from which Mozart quoted in the supper scene of *Don Giovanni*), *Il burbero di buon core* (1786), and *L'arbore di Diana* (1787), and two to libs. by Catherine II of Russia. In London 1794–6, returning to Russia as teacher.

Martland, Steve (b Liverpool, 1958). Eng. composer. Formed Steve Martland Band. His works, anti-romantic and rejecting traditional classical ens., aim (in his words) 'to return music to the streets'. They incl. *Remembering Lennon*, 7 players (1981, rev. 1985); *Babi Yar*, orch. (1983); *Drill*, 2 pf. (1987); *Albion*, tape, film (1987–8); *Skywalk*, 5 vv. or mixed ch. (1989); *Crossing the Border*, str. (1990–1); *Wolf-gang*, 6 Mozart arias arr. for wind octet (1991); *Patrol*, str. qt. (1992); *Beat the Retreat*, 11 players (1995); *Shepherd's Song*, unacc. ch. (1997); *Dividing the Lines*, brass band (1999); *Hard Times*, solo str., ens. (2000).

Marton (née Heinrich), **Eva** (b Budapest, 1943). Hung. soprano. Opera début Budapest 1963 (Queen in *The Golden Cockerel*). Member of Hung. State Opera 1963–71; Frankfurt Opera 1971–7; Hamburg State Opera from 1977. Amer. début NY 1975 in f.p. of Hovhaness's oratorio *The Way of Jesus*. Débuts: NY Met 1976; Bayreuth 1977; Salzburg Fest. 1982; S. Francisco 1985; CG 1987. Admired exponent of Strauss roles—Elektra, Empress, Dyer's Wife—and of Verdi and Wagner heroines.

Marttinen, Tauno (b Helsinki, 1912). Finnish composer. Dir., Hämeenlinna Inst. of Mus. 1950–75. Works incl. 9 syms. (1958–87); 15 operas (incl. *The Cloak*, after Gogol); 3 Kalevala cantatas; ballets; 2 pf. concs.; vn.conc.; vc. conc.; cl. conc.; fl. conc.; 2 str. qts.; pf. sonata (*Notre Dame*), etc.

Martucci, Giuseppe (b Capua, 1856; d Naples, 1909). It. conductor, pianist, and composer. Prof. of pf. Naples Cons. 1880–7. Toured Europe 1875. Dir., Liceo Musicale, Bologna, 1886–1902, Naples Cons. 1902–9. Est. orch. concerts at which he introduced many modern works to It. audiences. Cond. f.p. in Italy of *Tristan und Isolde*, Bologna 1888. Comp. 2 syms.; 2 pf. concs.; pf. quintet; 2 pf. trios; vc. sonata; many pf. pieces. Made many transcrs. of classical works.

Martyrdom of St Magnus, The. Chamber opera (mus. th.) in 1 act by *Maxwell Davies to his own lib. adapted from 'Magnus' by George Mackay Brown. For ten., 2 bar., bass, sop., and chamber ens. Comp. 1976–7. Prod. St Magnus Cath., Kirkwall (Orkney) 1977, London 1977, Liverpool 1978.

Martyre de Saint-Sébastien, Le (The Martyrdom of St Sebastian). Mus. by Debussy comp. in 1911 for 5-act mystery-play (*mystère*) by D'Annunzio perf. Paris in that year. For sop., 2 cont., ch., and orch. Symphonic fragments (4 movts.) f.p. in Eng. 1915, cond. Wood.

Marusin, Yury (*b* Perm', 1947). Russ. tenor. Début at Maly Th. 1972. Joined Kirov Opera, making Brit. début with them at CG 1987 (Lensky in *Eugene Onegin*). Glyndebourne début 1992.

Marx, Joseph (*b* Graz, 1882; *d* Graz, 1964). Austrian composer. Prof. of theory, Vienna Acad. of Mus. 1914–22, dir. 1922–4. Rector, Vienna Hochschule für Musik, 1924–7. Mus. critic, *Neues Wiener Journal* 1931–8. Taught at Graz. Univ. 1947–57. Noted for his 120 songs, but also wrote *Romantic* pf. conc., *Autumn Symphony*, pf. qt., vc. sonata, choral works, etc.

Mary, Queen of Scots. (1) Opera in 3 acts by Thea *Musgrave to her own lib. based on Amalia Elguera's play *Moray*. Comp. 1976–7. Prod. Edinburgh 1977, Stuttgart and Norfolk, Virginia, 1978, Bielefeld 1984.

(2) Ballet with mus. by John *McCabe, prod. Glasgow 1975.

(3) See *Maria Stuarda*.

marziale (It.). Martial.

Masaniello. Name usually given in Britain to Auber's opera in 5 acts *La Muette de Portici* (The Dumb Girl of Portici) to lib. by Scribe and Delavigne. Prod. Paris 1828, London 1829, NY 1831. Perf. in Brussels in 1830 led to Belgian revolt (plot being based on Neapolitan uprising against Spanish oppressors, 1647).

Mascagni, Pietro (*b* Leghorn, 1863; *d* Rome, 1945). It. composer and conductor. Joined touring opera co. as cond. Settled as pf. teacher at Cerignola. In 1889 won first prize in competition sponsored by publisher Sonzogno with 1-act opera *Cavalleria rusticana*. The abundant success of this work overshadowed his remaining operas, and the assertion that he is a one-opera composer (*verismo* at that) has only recently been challenged. In his later years he associated himself with Mussolini's Fascist régime. Prin. comps.:

OPERAS: *Pinotta* (1882–3); *Guglielmo Ratcliff* (1882–8, rev. 1894); *Cavalleria rusticana* (1889); *L'*Amico Fritz* (1890–1); *I rantzau* (1892); *Silvano* (1895); *Zanetto* (1896); *Iris* (1897–8); *Le maschere* (1899–1900, rev. 1905, 1931); *Amica* (1905); *Isabeau* (1908–10); *Parisina* (1912–13); *Lodoletta* (1916–17); *Sì*, operetta (1919); *Il piccolo Marat* (1919); *Nerone* (1934).

CHORAL: *Poema leopardiano*, cantata for Leopardi centenary (1898); *Requiem* in memoriam Re Umberto (1900); *Inno del Lavro* (1928); *Inno del Avanguardisti* (1929).

mascarade (Fr.). In earlier use this means *masque* and in later use masquerade, i.e. masked ball.

Maschinenpauken (Ger.). Mechanically-tuned kettledrums. See *drum*.

mask, maske. Old spellings of *masque*. Sometimes found attached to, for instance, a virginals piece, where it probably implies a dance of a suitable character for use in a masque.

Maskarade (Masquerade). Opera in 3 acts by *Nielsen to lib. by V. Andersen based on play (1724) by Holberg. Comp. 1904–6. Prod. Copenhagen 1906; St Paul, Minn., 1972; London (Morley Coll.) 1986; Leeds (Opera North) 1990; CG 2005.

Masked Ball, A (Verdi). See *Ballo in maschera, Un*.

Mask of Orpheus, The. Opera in 3 acts by *Birtwistle to lib by Peter Zinovieff. Comp. 1973–5, 1981–4. F.p. London (ENO) 1986.

Mask of Time, The. Work for sop., mez., ten., bar., ch., and instr., in two parts, by *Tippett. Comp. 1980–2. F.p. Boston, Mass., April 1984, cond. Sir Colin Davis. F. European p. London, July 1984, cond. Andrew Davis.

Masnadieri, I (The Robbers). Opera in 4 acts by Verdi to lib. by Maffei from Schiller's play *Die Räuber* (1781). Comp. 1846–7. Prod. London 1847 (with Jenny Lind; only Verdi opera written for London); NY 1860. Revived It. Radio 1951, London (Camden Fest.) 1962, and WNO 1977 (Cardiff and elsewhere).

Mason, Benedict (*b* Budleigh Salterton, 1955). Eng. composer. Won several prizes incl. Britten composers' comp. (1988), Clements memorial (1987), and Guido d'Arezzo int. comp. (1988). Also Fulbright Fellowship 1990, Siemens Stiftung Preis 1992. Several works commissioned and f.p. by Ensemble Modern, London Sinfonietta, Asko Ens., and Ens. Intercontemporain. Works incl.: *Playing Away*, opera (1993–4); *Ohne Missbrauch der Aufmerksamkeit*, theatre piece (1993); Double Conc., hn., tb., ens. (1989); *!*, 14 players (1992); *Quantized Quantz*, fl., live elec., computer, and tape, with readings (1992); *ChaplinOperas*, mez., bass-bar., 22 players, with silent film (1988); 2 str. qts. (1987, 1993); *6 Études*, pf. (1988); *Self-Referential Songs and Realistic Virelais*, sop., ens. (1990); conc. for va. section (1990); cl. conc. (1995); sackbut conc. (1997); tpt. conc. (1997); *felt|ebb|thus|brink|here|array|telling*, chamber orch. (2001); Double Conc., db., tuba (2005). Wrote *Outside Site Unseen and Opened* (1998).

Mason, Colin (*b* Northampton, 1924; *d* London, 1971). Eng. music critic. Authority on Bartók. Mus. critic *Manchester Guardian* 1950–64, *Daily Telegraph* from 1964. Ed. suppl. *Cobbett's Cyclopedia of Chamber Music* 1963. Ed. *Tempo* 1964–71. Active in promotion of contemporary works.

Mason, Daniel Gregory (*b* Brookline, Mass., 1873; *d* Greenwich, Conn., 1953). Amer.

composer, writer, and teacher. Joined mus. faculty Columbia Univ. 1905, becoming prof. 1929. Retired 1942. Wrote several books. Comps. incl. 3 syms. (No.3 *A Lincoln Symphony*), qt. on Negro themes, *Elegy* for pf., pf. qt., etc.

masque (or **mask** or **maske**). An aristocratic ceremonial entertainment in the 17th cent., consisting of a combination of poetry, vocal and instr. mus., dancing, acting, costume, pageantry, and scenic decoration, applied to the representation of allegorical and mythological subjects. It was much cultivated in It., from which country Eng. seems to have learnt it, then carrying it to a very high pitch of artistic elaboration. It developed from the *intermedii* and from mystery plays. In Elizabethan times, among the authors employed was Ben Jonson, a supreme master of the Eng. masque; he sometimes enjoyed the collab. of Inigo Jones as designer of the decorations and machinery. Among composers of masque mus. were *Campion, *Coprario, *Lanier, and the younger *Ferrabosco. From a literary point of view the most famous masque is Milton's *Comus* (1634); for this the mus. was supplied by Henry *Lawes, but the finest masques of this period had music by his brother William. Masques continued under the Puritan régime of the Commonwealth and Protectorate, some being arr., by authority, for entertainment of distinguished foreign visitors. After the Restoration, masque episodes were popular in plays, and music for them was composed by John Blow, Pelham Humfrey, Louis Grabu, and Henry Purcell. A late example is Arne's *Alfred* (1740), written for perf. in the Prince of Wales's garden: from it comes the song *Rule, Britannia!*

In the 20th cent. Vaughan Williams described his ballet *Job* as a 'masque for dancing', to indicate that 19th-cent. type of choreog. would not be appropriate. Lambert's *Summer's Last Will and Testament* is described as a masque.

Masques et Bergamasques (Masks and Bergomasks). Divertissement by Fauré to scenario by R. Fauchois, comp. 1919, prod. Monte Carlo 1919. Suite for orch., Op.112, 4 movts., f.p. Paris 1919, London 1920.

Mass. Owing to the importance the RC Mass holds in the minds of worshippers and the opportunities it offers for mus. participation it has exercised a large influence upon the development of mus. High Mass is sung, Low Mass is spoken. The Proper of the Mass (i.e. the parts which vary from season to season and day to day) has naturally usually been left to its traditional plainsong treatment. The 5 passages that are frequently set for ch., or for ch. and soloists, are: (a) *Kyrie* (Lord have mercy), (b) *Gloria in excelsis Deo* (Glory be to God on high), (c) *Credo* (I believe), (d) *Sanctus*, with *Benedictus* properly a part of it, but in practice often separated (Holy, Holy . . . Blessed . . .), (e) *Agnus Dei* (O Lamb of God). These are, properly, the congregational element in the Ordinary, or Common of the Mass, i.e. the invariable part. Innumerable mus. settings have been

provided by hundreds of composers of all European nations. The earliest polyphonic setting was probably that by *Machaut in 14th cent. In the 15th cent. *Du Fay and others introduced secular tunes as a *cantus firmus*, e.g. the folk song *L'Homme armé*. A high point was reached at the end of the 16th cent., when the unacc. choral contrapuntal style of comp. reached its apogee (Palestrina in It., Byrd in Eng., Victoria in Sp., etc.). In the 17th and 18th cents. the development of solo singing and increased understanding of the principles of effective orch. acc. led to great changes in the style of mus. treatment of the Mass, and the settings of the late 18th-cent. and early 19th-cent. composers (Haydn, Mozart, Weber, Schubert, etc.), however musically effective, have not the devotional quality of the settings of the late 16th and early 17th cents. The practice had grown up of treating the 5 passages above mentioned as the opportunity for providing an extended work in oratorio style, two outstanding examples of this being the Mass in B minor of J. S. Bach (1724–49) and the Mass in D of Beethoven (1819–22). Many impressive settings have been comp. since Beethoven, e.g. by Bruckner, and in the 20th cent. by Stravinsky, Vaughan Williams, Rubbra, and many others.

In large-scale settings the above-mentioned 5 passages tended to become subdivided. The great setting by Bach is as follows: (a) *Kyrie eleison* (Lord, have mercy), *Christe eleison* (Christ, have mercy), *Kyrie eleison* (Lord, have mercy); (b) *Gloria in excelsis Deo* (Glory be to God on high), *Laudamus te* (We praise Thee), *Gratias agimus tibi* (We give Thee thanks), *Domine Deus* (Lord God), *Qui tollis peccata mundi* (Who takest away the sins of the world), *Qui sedes ad dexteram Patris* (Who sittest at the right hand of the Father), *Quoniam tu solus sanctus* (For Thou only art holy), *Cum Sancto Spiritu* (With the Holy Spirit); (c) *Credo in unum Deum* (I believe in one God), *Patrem omnipotentem* (Father almighty), *Et in unum Dominum* (And in one Lord), *Et incarnatus est* (And was incarnate), *Crucifixus* (Crucified), *Et resurrexit* (And rose again), *Et in Spiritum Sanctum* (And (I believe) in the Holy Spirit), *Confiteor unum baptisma* (I confess one baptism); (d) *Sanctus* (Holy), *Hosanna in excelsis* (Hosanna in the highest), *Benedictus qui venit* (Blessed is he that cometh); (e) *Agnus Dei* (O Lamb of God), *Dona nobis pacem* (Give us peace). See also *Missa* and *Requiem*.

Massenet, Jules (Émile Frédéric) (*b* Montaud, St Étienne, 1842; *d* Paris, 1912). Fr. composer. Won *Grand Prix de Rome* and spent 3 years in Rome; returned to Paris 1866, his first (1-act) opera being prod. at Opéra-Comique 1867. His oratorios est. his name until the opera *Hérodiade* (a version of the Salome story) in 1881, but his greatest success came in 1884 with *Manon*. He was prof. of advanced comp. at Paris Cons. 1878–96. Among his later successes was *Don Quichotte*, prod. Monte Carlo 1910, with Chaliapin in the title-role. Massenet used Wagner's *leitmotiv* device, but translated it into his melodious and agreeable style, a style considered by some to be saccharine but which has won admiration in the later 20th cent. for its stylishness, craftsmanship, sense of th., and understanding of the human v. Prin. works:

OPERAS: *La Grand' Tante* (1867); *Don César de Bazan* (1872); *Le *Roi de Lahore* (1875–6); **Hérodiade* (1878–81, rev. 1883); **Manon* (1882–3, rev. 1884); *Le *Cid* (1884–5); **Werther* (1885–7); **Esclarmonde* (1888); *Le Mage* (1889–90); *Amadis* (1889–90, 1910–11); **Thaïs* (1892–3, rev. 1897); *Le Portrait de Manon* (1893); *La *Navarraise* (1893); **Grisélidis* (1894, rev. 1898); **Cendrillon* (1895); *Sapho* (1896, rev. 1909); *Le *Jongleur de Notre-Dame* (1900); *Roma* (1902, 1909); **Chérubin* (1902–3); *Ariane* (1904–5); *Thérèse* (1905–6); *Bacchus* (1907–8); **Don Quichotte* (1908–9); *Panurge* (1911); *Cléopâtre* (1911–12).

BALLETS: *Le Carillon* (1892); *Cigale* (1904); *Espada* (1908).

ORATORIOS & CANTATAS: *David Rizzio* (1863); *Marie-Magdeleine* (1873, rev. as opera 1906); *Eve* (1875); *Narcisse* (1877); *La Vierge* (1880); *Biblis* (1886); *La Terre Promise* (1900).

ORCH.: *Scènes hongroises* (1871); **Scènes pittoresques* (1874); *Scènes napolitaines* (1876); *Scènes alsaciennes* (1881); *Marche solennelle* (1897); *Fantaisie*, vc. and orch. (1897); pf. conc. (1903).

Also about 200 songs, some with orch.

mässig (Ger.). (1) Moderate, moderately, *mässiger*, more moderate and *mässigen*, to moderate.

(2) In the style of (e.g. *marschmässig*, in march style).

Mass in D (*Missa Solemnis*). For sop., cont., ten., and bass soloists, ch., org., and orch. by Beethoven, Op.123, comp. 1819–22. F.p. complete, St Petersburg, April 1824; f.p. (incomplete) to Ger. words, Vienna May 1824 in first part of concert which incl. f.p. of 9th Sym.; complete but private perf. London 1832; public, but probably incomplete, London 1839; first complete public perf. in London 1846.

Mass of Life, A (*Eine Messe des Lebens*). Choral work by Delius for SATB soloists, double ch., and orch. to Ger. text selected by F. *Cassirer from Nietzsche's *Also sprach Zarathustra*. Comp. 1904–5. F.p. of Part 2 only, Munich 1908; f. complete p. London 1909 (in Eng.) cond. Beecham. In 1898 Delius wrote unpubd. setting of the 'Midnight Song' from *Zarathustra* for bar., male ch., and orch. (perf. London 1899). This, revised, was incorporated into the Mass.

Mass of Pope Marcellus (Palestrina). See *Missa Papae Marcelli*.

Masson, Diego (*b* Tossa, Sp., 1935). Fr. conductor. Worked as perc. player in Paris in 1960s, particularly at Domaine Musical, and founded his ens. Musique Vivante in 1966. Took part in several Stockhausen f.ps. and recorded Boulez's *Domaines*. Mus. dir. Marseilles Opéra. London début 1971 (SW, *The *Nightingale* with visiting co.). ENO début 1980 (*La Damnation de Faust*). Cond. f.ps. of Harper's *Hedda Gabler* (Scottish Opera 1985), and Saxton's *Caritas* (Wakefield, Opera North, 1991).

Master Class. Form of teaching in which celebrated performer instructs a group of pupils in front of other pupils or a paying audience. Master classes have become a popular feature at festivals and on television, but there is sometimes doubt as to whether the pupils benefit from what can, in effect, become a solo perf. by the teacher.

Master of Music. Degree awarded at some Brit. and Amer. univ., according status between Bachelor and Doctor of Mus.

Master of the King's (Queen's) Music. Title of the only surviving music post in the British royal household; carries honorarium and no fixed duties. The post originated in reign of Charles I (office being held by Nicholas Lanier) and meant the head of the sovereign's private band which accompanied him or her wherever he or she went. In 1660 Charles II est. a band of 24 players of str. instr. Since 1893 the post has been given to some eminent musician, usually a composer, who will write a fanfare, march, or larger work for some royal or state occasion, and is an influential figure in the mus. world generally (mus. equivalent of the Poet Laureate). Holders of the post since 1660 (some dates conjectural) are: Nicholas Lanier, 1660; Louis Grabu, 1666; Nicholas Staggins, 1674; John Eccles, 1700; Maurice Greene, 1735?; William Boyce, 1755; John Stanley, 1779; William Parsons, 1786; William Shield, 1817–29; Christian Kramer, 1834; George Frederick Anderson, 1848–70; William George Cusins, 1870–93; Walter Parratt, 1893–1924; Edward Elgar 1924–34; Walford Davies, 1934–41; Arnold Bax, 1942–53; Arthur Bliss, 1953–75; Malcolm Williamson 1975–2003; Peter *Maxwell Davies from 2004.

Master Peter's Puppet Show (*El Retablo de Maese Pedro*). 1-act opera by *Falla to lib. by composer based on incident in Cervantes's *Don Quixote* (Part 2, Ch. 26). For singers, puppets, and chamber orch. Comp. 1919–22. F.p. (concert) Seville, Mar. 1923; stage (private) Paris, June 1923; Paris, Nov. 1923; Bristol 1924; NY 1925.

Mastersingers of Nuremberg, The (Wagner). See *Meistersinger von Nürnberg, Die*.

Masterson, Valerie (*b* Birkenhead, 1937). Eng. soprano. Début Salzburg Landesth. 1963 (Frasquita in *Carmen*). D'Oyly Carte Opera Co. 1966–70. SW début at Coliseum 1971 and became member of SW (later ENO) from 1972. CG début 1974; Paris 1978; Amer. début S. Francisco 1980. Combines brilliant coloratura with rich dramatic qualities, hence her particular success as Violetta. Also admired as Handel singer. CBE 1988.

Masur, Kurt (*b* Brieg, Silesia, 1927). Ger. conductor. Cond., Erfurt 1951–3, Leipzig City Th. 1953–5, Dresden PO 1955–8, Schwerin 1958–60. Chosen by Felsenstein as mus. dir., Berlin Komische Oper 1960, staying until 1964. Returned to Dresden PO 1964–7; cond., Leipzig

Gewandhaus Orch. 1970–98. Eng. début 1973. Prin. cond. NYPO 1991–2002, LPO 2000–7, mus. dir. French Nat. Orch. from 2001.

Masurok, Yury. See *Mazurok, Yury*.

Mata, Eduardo (*b* Mexico City, 1942; *d* in air crash, Cuernavaca, Mex., 1995). Mexican conductor and composer. Cond. and mus. dir. Mexican Ballet Co. 1963–4, Guadalajara SO 1965–6, Orch. Phil. UNAM, Mexico City 1966–76; prin. cond. Phoenix SO, Ariz., 1972–8, Dallas SO 1977–93. Guest cond. of European orchs. Comps. incl. 3 syms.; ballet suite *Debora*; str. qt.; pf. sonata; *Trio to Vaughan Williams*, etc.

Matačić, Lovro von (*b* Sušak, 1899; *d* Zagreb, 1985). Croatian conductor. Début Cologne Opera 1919; cond. opera Ljubljana 1924–6, Belgrade 1926–31, Zagreb 1932–8, returning to Belgrade as dir., 1938–42. Cond. Vienna Volksoper 1942–5. Chief cond. Dresden Opera 1956–8 and at Berlin jointly with Konwitschny. Guest cond. Vienna and Milan 1958, Chicago 1959. Chief cond. Frankfurt Opera 1961–5; cond. Zagreb PO 1970–80, Monte Carlo Opera 1974–8.

Matassins, Mattachins. The dance also known as **Bouffons*.

matelotte (from Fr. *matelot*, sailor). Dutch sailors' dance like a hornpipe, perf. in wooden shoes, the dancers' arms being interlaced behind their backs.

Materna, Amalie (*b* St Georgen, 1844; *d* Vienna, 1918). Austrian soprano. Début Graz 1864 as soubrette, then sang in operetta in Vienna. Member, Vienna Court Opera 1869–97 (début as Sélika in *L'Africaine*). Created title-role in Goldmark's *Die Königen von Saba*. Chosen by Wagner as Brünnhilde for first Bayreuth *Ring* 1876 and as Kundry in *Parsifal* 1882. Sang at Wagner's London concerts, 1877, and NY Met 1885. Joined W. Damrosch's Ger. opera co., NY 1894. Taught after retirement, but last sang in public in 1913 at Wagner centenary concert in Vienna.

Mathias, William (*b* Whitland, Dyfed, 1934; *d* Menai Bridge, 1992). Welsh composer and pianist. Bax Soc. prize 1968. Lect. in mus., Univ. Coll. of N. Wales, Bangor, 1959–68, senior lect. in comp. Edinburgh Univ. 1968–70, prof. of mus. and head of mus. dept., Univ. Coll. of N. Wales 1970–88. Art. dir. N. Wales Mus. Fest. from 1972. CBE 1985. Prin. works:

OPERA: *The Servants* (1980).

ORCH.: syms.: No.1 (1966), No.2 (*Summer Music*) (1982–3), No.3 (1991); *Divertimento*, str. (1958); *Music for Strings* (1961); *Serenade, Invocation and Dance* (1962); *Dance Overture* (1962); *Concerto for Orchestra* (1966); *Litanies* (1966); *Sinfonietta* (1967); *Holiday Overture* (1971); *Celtic Dances* (1972); *Laudi* (1973); *Vistas* (1975); *Dance Variations* (1977); *Melos* (1977); *Helios* (1977); *Requiescat* (1978); *Carnival of Wales* (1987); *Threnos*, str. (1990); *In Arcadia* (1991–2).

CONCERTOS: pf. No.1 (1955), No.2 (1961), No.3

(1968); hp. (1970); hpd., str., perc. (1971); cl. (1975); hn. (1984); org. (1984); ob. (1990); vn. (1991); fl. (1992).

VOICE(S) & ORCH. or PIANO: *Ave Rex*, mixed ch., orch. (1969); *Elegy for a Prince*, bar., orch. (1972); *A Vision of Time and Eternity*, cont., pf. (1972); *This Worldes Joie*, soloists, ch., orch. (1974); *The Fields of Praise*, ten., pf. (1977); *A May Magnificat*, double ch. (1977–8); *Shakespeare Songs*, ch., pf. (1978); *Songs of William Blake*, mez., hp., pf., cel., str. (1979); *Lux Aeterna*, sop., mez., cont., ch., boys' ch., org., orch. (1981–2); *Psalm 67* (*Let the People Praise Thee, O God*), ch., org. or orch. (1981); *Angelus*, women's vv. (1983); *Let Us Now Praise Famous Men*, ch., orch. (1984); *Jonah: a Musical Morality*, bar., ten., ch., orch. (1988); *World's Fire*, sop., bar., ch., orch. (1989).

CHURCH: *Festival Te Deum* (1965); *Magnificat and Nunc Dimittis* (1970); *Missa brevis*, No.1 (1973), No.2 (1984); *Te Deum*, sop., mez., ten., ch., orch. (1981); *Tantum Ergo*, ch., org. (1983); *Come, Holy Ghost* (1992); *Ad majorem Dei gloriam* (1992).

CHAMBER MUSIC: str. qt. No.1 (1968), No.2 (1982), No.3 (1980); *Sonatina*, cl., pf. (1957); vn. sonata, No.1 (1962), No.2 (1984); wind quintet (1963); pf. sonata, No.1 (1964), No.2 (1979); *Soundings*, brass quintet (1988); *Summer Dances*, brass quintet (1990).

ORGAN: *Partita* (1962); *Variations on a Hymn-Tune* ('*Braint*') (1962); *Invocations* (1967); *Fantasy* (1978); conc. (1984); *Fenestra* (1989).

Mathieson, Muir (*b* Stirling, 1911; *d* Oxford, 1975). Scottish conductor and composer. Occasional opera cond. at SW but prominent as cond. of film mus. Worked for Sir Alexander Korda, film producer, 1931–9. Mus. dir. Govt. film units 1940–5, then for J. Arthur Rank films. Responsible for persuading Bliss, Vaughan Williams, Walton, Britten, Benjamin, and Bennett to compose for films. OBE 1957.

Mathis, Edith (*b* Lucerne, 1938). Swiss soprano. Début Lucerne 1956 (Second Boy in *Die Zauberflöte*). Cologne Opera 1959–62; Salzburg Fest. 1960; Deutsche Oper, Berlin, 1963; Hamburg State Opera 1960–72; Glyndebourne début 1962; CG 1970; NY Met 1970. Specialist in Mozart roles and songs.

Mathis der Maler (Matthias the Painter). Opera in 7 scenes by *Hindemith to his own lib. based on life of Matthias Grünewald (*c*.1460–1530) and his altar-piece at Isenheim. Comp. 1933–5. Prod. Zurich 1938, London (concert) 1939, (stage) CG 1995, Edinburgh 1952. Boston Univ. 1956. Nazis banned Ger. première in 1935. Also Sym. for orch. in 3 movts.: (1) *Engelkonzert* (Angels' Concert), (2) *Grablegung* (Burial), (3) *Versuchung des heiligen Antonius* (Temptation of St. Anthony). F.p. Berlin 1934, cond. Furtwängler.

Matilde di Shabran. *Opera buffa* in 2 acts by Rossini to lib. by Ferretti, who rewrote an earlier lib. 3 nos. comp. by Pacini. F.p. cond. by Paganini. Prod. Rome 1821; London 1823; NY 1834; Paris 1857.

Matin, Le; Midi, Le; Soir, Le (Morning, After-noon, Evening). Nickname for 3 Haydn syms., Nos. 6–8 in Breitkopf edn., Hob. I:6–8. (respec-tively in D, C, and G), comp. *c.*1761. The last is also known as *Le Soir et la tempête* (Evening and Storm).

Matrimonio segreto, Il (The Secret Marriage). Opera buffa in 2 acts by Cimarosa to lib. by G. Bertati after the comedy *The Clandestine Marriage* (1766) by Colman and Garrick. Prod. Vienna 1792, London 1794, NY 1834.

Mattachins. See *Bouffons*.

Matthay, Tobias (Augustus) (*b* London, 1858; *d* High Marley, Haslemere, 1945). Eng. pianist, composer, and teacher. Joined staff RAM 1876, becoming prof. of pf. 1880–1925. Gave up career as concert pianist to teach. Opened pf. sch. in London 1900. Pupils incl. Myra Hess, Irene Schar-rer, Harriet Cohen, and York Bowen. Evolved own method of teaching, based on close observa-tion of physical and psychological aspects of pf.-playing. Comp. much mus. and wrote several books on the pf.

Mattheson, Johann (*b* Hamburg, 1681; *d* Ham-burg, 1764). Ger. composer, singer, harpsichord-ist, and theorist. Entered opera ch. 1690, singing tenor roles 1697–1705 during which time he wrote 5 operas and met Handel, with whom he fought a duel after an argument during a perf. of Mattheson's opera *Cleopatra* in 1704. Mus. dir. Hamburg Cath. 1715–28. Comp. church cantatas. Wrote 8 operas, 24 oratorios and cantatas, 12 fl. sonatas, and much else. Also wrote important books, full of advanced views and much histor-ical material. One of his operas was *Boris Goude-now* (Hamburg, 1710).

Matthews, Colin (*b* London, 1946). English com-poser. Awards for comp. incl. BBC chamber mus. prize 1970, and Ian Whyte award 1975. Taught at Sussex Univ. 1972–3 and 1976–7. Author of study of Mahler and authority on Berg. Collab. with D. *Cooke on perf. version of Mahler's 10th Sym. (1964–74). Worked for Britten in composer's last years, 1971–6 and subsequently ed. several of Brit-ten's early and unpubd. scores. Prin. works:

ORCH.: *Fourth Sonata* (1974–5); *Night Music* (1976–7); *Little Suite* No.1 (1979), No.2 (1979); *Sonata No.5 (Landscape)* (1977–81); vc. conc. No.1 (1983–4), No.2 (1996); *Night's Mask*, chamber orch. (1984); *Cortège* (1988); *Chiaroscuro* (1990); *Machines and Dreams (Toy Symphony)* (1991); *Broken Symmetry* (1991–2); *Hidden Variables* (orch. vers.) (1992); *Memorial* (1992–3); *Threnody* (1995–6); *Elegeia*, small orch. (1998); *Unfolded Order* (1999); *Pluto the Renewer* (for Holst's *Planets*) (2000); hn. conc. (2001); *Bright Cecilia* (2002); *Vivo* (2002); *Reflected Images* (2002–3).

INSTRS.: *Ceres*, 3 fl., gui., perc., 2 vc., db. (1972) *Specula*, fl., keyed perc., hp., va. (1976–7); *Rainbow Studies*, fl., ob., cl., bn., pf. (1977–8); *Suns Dance*, picc., ob., bcl., dbn., hn., str. quintet (1984–5); *Hidden Variables*, 15 players (1988–9); *Quatrain*, wind,

brass, perc. (1989); *Contraflow*, 14 players (1992); *Three Interludes*, cl., va., pf. (1994); *Capriccioletto*, vn., pf. (1998); *Bassoonova*, bn. (2003).

VOICE & INSTR(S).: *Un colloque sentimental*, v., pf. (1971–8); *5 Sonnets: to Orpheus*, ten., hp. (1975–6); *Shadows in the Water*, ten., pf. (1978–9); *Cantata on the Death of Antony*, sop., chamber ens. (1988–9); *Strugnells Haiku*, v., pf. or chamber ens. (1989); *Aubade*, v., pf. (1990); *Continuum*, mez., small orch. (1999–2000); *A voice to wake*, sop., chamber ens. (2004–5).

CHORAL: *Second-hand Flames*, 5 vv. (1982); *A Rose at Christmas*, double mixed ch. (1990); *Metamorphosis*, ch., orch. (1995–6); *Aftertones*, sop., ch., orch. (1999–2000); *Estrangement*, unacc. ch. (2002).

CHAMBER MUSIC: str. qt. No.1 (1979), No.2 (1985), No.3 (1993–4); *Partita*, vn. (1975); ; *Little Suite*, hp. (1979); ob. qt. No.1 (1981), No.2 (1988–9); *Divertimento*, double str. qt. (1982); *Triptych*, pf. quintet (1984); *5 Duos*, vc., pf. (1987); *5 Untitled Flute Pieces*, fl. (1987–9); *3-Part Chaconne*, str. trio, pf. (left hand) (1989); *Duologue*, ob., pf. (1991); *To Compose without the least Knowledge of Music . . .*, wind sextet (1991); *Palinode*, vc. (1992); *A Quick Start*, hn., 2 tpts., tb., tuba (2001); *Little Berceuse*, cl., str. qt. (2004).

PIANO: *5 Studies* (1974–6); *Suite* (1977–9); *11 Studies in Velocity* (1987); *3 Preludes* (2003).

Matthews, David (*b* London, 1943). Eng. compo-ser and writer, brother of Colin *Matthews. Worked with Britten and helped D. *Cooke on perf. version of Mahler's 10th Sym. Author of book on mus. of *Tippett (1980). Prin. works:

ORCH.: syms.: No.1 (1975, rev. 1978), No.2 (1976–9), No.3 (1983–5), No.4, chamber orch. (1989–90), No.5 (1998–9); *September Music* (1979); vn. conc. No.1 (1980–2), No.2 (1997–8); *White Nights*, fantasy, vn., small orch. (1980); *Introit*, 2 tpt., str. (1981); *In the Dark Time* (1984–5); *Variations*, str. (1986); *Chaconne* (1986–7); *The Music of Dawn* (1989–90); *Romanza*, vc., chamber orch. (1990); *Scherzo capriccioso* (1990); *Capriccio*, 2 hn., str (1991); ob. conc. (1991–2); *From Sea to Sky*, ov. (1992); *A Vision and a Journey* (1993); *2 Pieces*, str. (1996–2000); *Winter Remembered*, va., str. (2001); vc. conc. (2001–2); *Scherzo* (2003–4).

VOICE(S) & INSTR(S).: *3 Songs*, sop., orch. (1968–71); *Stars*, ch., orch. (1970); *The Golden Kingdom*, high v., pf. (1979–83); *Cantiga*, sop., chamber orch. (1987–8); *Marina*, bar., basset hn., vc., pf. (1988); *From Coastal Stations*, medium v., pf. (1990–1); *The Sleeping Lord*, sop., fl., cl., hp., str. qt. (1992); *Spell of Sleep*, 2 cl., va., vc., db. (1992); *2 Housman Songs*, sop., str. qt. (1996); *Winter Passions*, bar., cl., vn., va., vc., pf. (1999); *L'Invitation au voyage*, sop., cl., vn., va., vc., pf. (2003); *Movement of Autumn*, sop., small orch. (2004–5).

UNACC. CHORUS: *The Company of Lovers* (1980); *The Ship of Death* (1988–9); *Fanfare for the Queen Mother* (1990); *The Doorway of the Dawn* (1999); *Aequam memento* (2004).

CHAMBER MUSIC: str. qts., No.1 (1970, rev. 1980), No.2 (1974–6), No.3 (1977–8), No.4 (1981), No.5 (1984), No.6 (1991), No.7 (1993), No.8 (1998), No.9 (2000), No.10 (2000–1); *Duet Variations*, fl., pf.

(1982); *Winter Journey*, vn. (1982–3); pf. trio (1983); cl. qt. (1984); *3 Studies*, vn. (1985); *Aria*, vn., pf. (1986); , No. 8 (1998), No. 9 (2000) No. 10 (2000–1); *Concertino*, ob., str. qt. (1986–7); str. trio No.1 (1989), No.2 (2003); pf. sonata (1989); *Long Lion Days*, vc., pf. (1991); *Three to Tango*, pf. trio (1991), No.2 (1993–4); pf. quintet (2004); *Little Serenade*, str. qt. (2004); *Journeying Songs*, vc. (2004).

Matthews, Denis (*b* Coventry, 1919; *d* Moseley, Birmingham, 1988). Eng. pianist. Début, London (Prom) 1939. Soloist with all leading orchs. Noted Mozartian and brilliant lecturer. Gave f.p. of Rubbra's pf. conc. 1956. Prof. of mus., Newcastle upon Tyne Univ. 1972–84. CBE 1975.

Matthus, Siegfried (*b* Mallenuppen, 1934). Ger. composer. Comp.-in-residence Komische Oper, Berlin, from 1964. Works incl.:

OPERAS: *Lazerillo vom Tormes* (1960–3); *Der letzte Schuss* (1966–7); *Noch ein Löffel Gift, Liebling?* (1971–2); *Omphale* (1972–3); *Judith* (1982–4); *Die Weise von Liebe und Tod des Cornets Christoph Rilke* (1983–4); *Graf Mirabeau* (1987–8); *Desdemona und ihre Schwestern* (1992).

ORCH.: syms.: No.1 (*Dresden*) (1969), No.2 (1976), No.3 (*Gewandhaus*) (1992–3); *Concerto for Orchestra* (1963); *Inventions* (1964); *Tua res agitur*, 15 instr., perc. (1965); vn. conc. (1968); pf. conc. (1970); *Serenade* (1974); vc. conc. (1975); *Responso* (1977); *Visions*, str. (1978); fl. conc. (1978); Chamber Concerto, fl., hpd., str. (1980–1); *Der Wald*, kettledrum conc. (1985); ob. conc. (1985); *Die Windsbraut* (1985); triangle conc. (1985); *Nächtliche Szenen im Park* (1987); conc., *Ornamenlose Freude*, 3 tpts., str. (1989).

VOCAL: 5 *Love Songs*, sop., orch. (1961–2); *Das Manifest*, cantata (1965); *Chamber Music*, cont., 3 female vv., 10 instr. (1965); *Galileo*, v., 5 instr., tape (1966); *Voical Symphony*, sop., bar., 2 ch., orch. (1967); *Kantate von den Beiden*, narr., bar., sop., orch. (1968); *Vocalises*, sop., fl., db., perc. (1969); *Laudate pacem*, oratorio (1974); *Unter dem Holunderstrauch*, sop., ten., orch. (1976); *Holofernes Portrait*, sop., orch. (1981); *Nachtlieder*, bar., str. qt., hp. (1987); *Wem ich zu gefallen suche*, ten., bar., pf. (1987).

CHAMBER MUSIC: *Music*, 4 obs., pf. (1968); sonatina, pf., perc. (1970); octet (1970); str. qt. (1972); trio, fl., va., hp. (1971); octet (1989).

PIANO: *Variations* (1958); *Konzertstück* (1958).

Mattila, Karita (Marjatta) (*b* Somero, 1960). Finn. soprano. Sang Donna Anna in *Don Giovanni* at Savonlinna 1981 while student. Début with Finn. Nat. Opera 1982 (Countess in *Le nozze di Figaro*). Won the first Cardiff Singer of the World comp. 1983. Débuts: Amer. (Washington DC) 1983); CG 1986; Salzburg Fest. 1987; NY Met 1990.

mattinata (It.). A morning song, or a piece with that assoc., i.e. the same as *aubade* (Fr.), *alborada* (Sp.), and *Morgenlied* (Ger.).

Matton, Roger (*b* Granby, Quebec, 1929; *d* Quebec City, 2004). Canadian composer. Researcher

and ethnomusicologist, Laval Univ., Quebec, 1956–76. Works incl. sax. conc.; conc. for 2 pf. and perc. and for 2 pf. and orch.; *Te deum*, bar., ch., orch., elec.; *Tu es Petrus*, orch.

Mauceri, John (Francis) (*b* NY, 1945). Amer. conductor. Cond. Yale Univ. SO 1968–74. Opera début Wolf Trap Fest. 1973 (**Saint of Bleecker Street*). Cond. f. Eur. p. of Bernstein's *Mass*, Vienna 1973. Eur. opera début Spoleto 1974 (Menotti's *Tamu-Tamu*). Brit. opera début 1974; NY Met début 1976; ENO 1983; Royal Opera 1983 (Manchester). Brit. concert début 1976 (SNO). Cond. at NY City Opera 1977–82. Mus. dir. Washington Opera 1980–2, American SO 1984–7, Scottish Opera 1987–93. Co-operated with Bernstein on final rev. vers. of *Candide* (Scottish Opera, 1988). Cond. f. Brit. p. of Weill's *Street Scene*, Glasgow (Scottish Opera) 1989. Cond. f. Eur. p. of rev. vers. of Blitzstein's *Regina*, Glasgow (Scottish Opera) 1991.

Maultrommel (Ger.). *Jew's harp.

Maurel, Victor (*b* Marseilles, 1848; *d* NY, 1923). Fr. baritone. Début Marseilles 1867 (*Guillaume Tell*), Paris Opéra 1868. Sang in St Petersburg, Cairo, and Venice before appearing at La Scala 1870. London début CG 1873, singing there until 1904, particularly in Wagner. NY début 1873. Returned to Paris Opéra 1879. Went into operatic management 1883. Sang in f.p. of *Hérodiade* 1881, and title-role in rev. vers. of *Simon Boccanegra*, 1881. Created Iago in *Otello*, Milan 1887, Tonio in *Pagliacci*, Milan 1892, and title-role in *Falstaff*, Milan 1893. NY Met début 1894. Appeared as actor for short time, then settled NY as teacher 1909. Designed sets for Gounod's *Mireille*, NY Met 1919. Wrote 4 books on singing.

Maurerische Trauermusik (Masonic Funeral Music). Work in C minor by Mozart (K477) scored for 2 ob., cl., 3 basset hn., double bn., 2 hn., and str. Comp. in July 1785 for installation of a master (a ritual which includes funerary imagery) and perf. again in Nov. 1785 at memorial service for two of Mozart's lodge brothers.

mauresco (Sp.), **mauresque** (Fr.). Moorish (see also *moresca*). Elgar wrote a *Sérénade mauresque*.

Má Vlast (My Country). Cycle of 6 symphonic poems by Smetana, comp. 1872–9. They are: 1. *Vyšehrad* (The High Citadel), 2. *Vltava* (River Moldau), 3. *Šárka* (leader of Bohem. Amazons), 4. *Z Českych Luhů a Hájů* (From Bohemia's Meadows and Forests), 5. *Tabor* (stronghold of the Hussites), 6. *Blánîk* (Valhalla of the Hussite heroes: a mountain in S. Bohemia).

Mavra. Opera in 1 act by Stravinsky to lib. by Kochno after Pushkin's poem *The Little House at Kolomna* (1830). Comp. 1921–2. Prod. Paris 1922, London (broadcast) and Philadelphia 1934, Edinburgh 1956, London (stage, Collegiate Th.) 1979.

Maw, (John) Nicholas (*b* Grantham, 1935). Eng. composer. Fellow Commoner in Creative Arts, Trinity Coll., Cambridge, 1966–70. Prof. of comp.

Peabody Inst., Baltimore. One of the generation of 'modern romantics' whose mus., while contemp. in some of its procedures, remains attached to traditional forms and outlook. Prin. works:

OPERAS: *One-Man Show* (2 acts, 1964, rev. 1966, 1970); *The *Rising of the Moon* (1967–70, rev. 1970–1); *Sophie's Choice* (2000–2).

ORCH.: *Sinfonia* (1966); *Sonata*, str., 2 hn. (1967); *Concert Music* (derived from *Rising of the Moon*, 1972); **Odyssey* (1972–87); *Serenade* (1973, rev. 1977); *Life Studies I–VIII*, 15 solo str. (1972, 1976); *Summer Dances* (1981); *Toccata* (1982); *Morning Music* (1982); *Spring Music* (1982–3); *Sonata Notturna*, vc., str. (1985); *The World in the Evening* (1988); *Little Concert*, ob., str., 2 hn. (1988); *American Games*, wind band (1991); *Shahnama* (1992); vn. conc. (1993); *Dance Scenes* (1995); *Variations in Old Style* (1995); ca. conc. (2005).

VOICE(S) & ORCH. OR INSTR(S).: *Nocturne*, mez., chamber orch. (1958); *Scenes and Arias*, sop., mez., cont., orch. (1961–2, rev. 1966); *La Vita Nuova* (The New Life), sop., chamber ens. (1979); *Roman Canticle*, mez., fl., va., hp. (1989).

VOICE(S) & PIANO etc: *The Voice of Love*, mez. (1966); *6 Interiors*, ten., gui. (1966); *5 American Folksongs*, sop. (1990); *The Head of Orpheus*, sop., 2 cl. (1992).

VOCAL: *5 Epigrams* (1960); *Our Lady's Song* (1962); *Corpus Christi Carol* and *Balulalow* (1964); *5 Irish Songs* (1972); *Te Deum* (1975); *Nonsense Songs* (1976); *The Ruin*, with hn. obbl. (1980); *3 Hymns* (1989); *One Foot in Eden, Here I Stand* (1990); *Sweté Jesu* (1992).

CHAMBER MUSIC: fl. sonatina (1957); *Chamber Music*, ob., cl., hn., bn., pf. (1962); str. qt. No.1 (1965), No.2 (1982), No.3 (1994–5), No.4 (2005); *Epitaph, Canon in mem.* Stravinsky, fl., cl., hp. (1971); fl. qt. (1981); *Night Thoughts*, fl. (1982); *Ghost Dances*, 5 players (1988); *Music of Memory*, gui. (1989); pf. trio (1990–1); vn. sonata (1996–7).

Maxwell, Donald (b Perth, 1948). Scot. baritone.

Début with Scottish Opera 1977 (Morton in *Mary, Queen of Scots*) and many roles with Scottish Opera. WNO début 1982. Buxton Fest. début 1979; Wexford Fest.; CG début 1987. Sang Iago, Falstaff, and Golaud for WNO in prods. by Peter *Stein. Dir., Nat. Opera Studio, from 2002.

Maxwell Davies, (Sir) Peter (b Salford, 1934).

Eng. composer, conductor, and teacher. With Birtwistle, Goehr, and Ogdon, known as *Manchester School. In 1957 won It. Govt. scholarship and studied in Rome with *Petrassi. His *Prolation* won Olivetti Prize 1958 and was f.p. ISCM fest., Rome 1959. Mus. dir. Cirencester Grammar Sch. 1959–62. Resident composer Adelaide Univ. 1966. In 1967 was founder and co-dir. of chamber ens., Pierrot Players, formed to perf. contemp. works; this was reorganized 1971 as The *Fires of London (disbanded 1987), for which many of Maxwell Davies's works have been written. Since 1970 he has lived intermittently in Orkney, where the landscape and solitude have had an undoubted effect on his music, notably in the chamber opera *The Martyrdom of St Magnus* and the syms. He founded the St Magnus Fest. in 1977 and was art. dir. 1977–86. In 1986 received

commission from Strathclyde local authority for 10 concs. for soloists from SCO. Mus. dir., Dartington Hall summer sch. 1979–84. Master of the Queen's Music from 2004.

Maxwell Davies soon became one of the most important of the Eng. so-called *avant-garde*. Like Britten, he has enjoyed writing for specific performers and his wide-ranging imagination has devised striking sounds, freakish perhaps but always springing from a genuine mus. impulse. Rhythms are sometimes complex, vocal lines angular. He developed *music theatre*, staged pieces for a single performer, as in the remarkable *Eight Songs for a Mad King*. His music is marked also by a strong dramatic impulse which found full outlet in the operas *Taverner* and *The Lighthouse*. He has been inspired by the ability to combine and contrast the music of medieval times with his own idiom, and has also made much use of the 1920s fox-trot rhythm for nostalgic purposes. CBE 1981. Knighted 1987. Prin. works:

OPERAS: *Taverner* (1962–70, rev. 1983); *The *Martyrdom of St Magnus* (1976–7); *The Two Fiddlers* (children's opera) (1978); *The *Lighthouse* (1979); *Resurrection* (1987); *Redemption* (1988); *The Doctor of Myddfai* (1993–6).

THEATRE PIECES: *Notre Dame des Fleurs*, sop., mez., counterten., ens. (1966); *Vesalii Icones* (*Images from Vesalius*), dancer, vc., ens. (1969); *Eight *Songs for a Mad King*, male v., ens. (1969); *Blind Man's Buff*, sop., mez., mime, stage band (1972); *Miss Donnithorne's Maggot*, mez., ens. (1974); *Le *Jongleur de Notre Dame*, mime, bar., ens., children's band (1978); *Cinderella* (for children) (1980); *The Medium*, mez. (1981); *The Rainbow* (for children) (1981); *The No.11 Bus*, mez., ten., bar., 2 dancers, mime, ens. (1983–4); *The Great Bank Robbery* (for children) (1989); *Jupiter Landing* (for children) (1989); *Dinosaur At Large* (for children) (1989); *Dangerous Errand* (for children) (1990); *The Spiders' Revenge* (for very young children) (1991); *A Selkie Tale* (for children) (1992).

BALLETS: *Salome* (1978); *Caroline Mathilde* (1990).

ORCH.: syms: No.1 (1973–6), No.2 (1980), No.3 (1984), No.4 (1989), No.5 (1993–4), No.6 (1995–6), No.7 (1998–9), No.8 (*Antarctic*) (2000–1); *Prolation* (1958); *5 Klee Pictures* (1959, rev. 1976); *Fantasia on an In Nomine of John Taverner: 1st* (1962), *2nd* (1964); *St Thomas Wake* (1969); *Worldes Blis* (1969); *A Mirror of Whitening Light* (1977); *Dances from 'Salome'* (1979); *An Orkney Wedding with Sunrise* (1985); vn. conc. (1985); *Jimmack the Postie* (1986); tpt. conc. (1988); *Ojai Festival Overture* (1991); *Caroline Mathilde*, suite (1991); *Sir Charles: his Pavan* (1992); *A Spell for Green Corn: the MacDonald Dances* (1993); *Chat Moss* (1993); *Cross Lane Fair* (1994); *The Beltane Fire*, choreographic poem (1994–5); pf. conc. (1997); picc. conc. (1997); hn. conc. (1999); *A Dance on the Hill* (2002).

STRATHCLYDE CONCERTOS: No.1, ob. (1987), No.2, vc. (1988), No.3, hn., tpt. (1989), No.4, cl. (1990), No.5, vn., va. (1991), No.6, fl. (1991), No.7, db. (1992), No.8, bn. (1993), No.9, chamber (1994), No.10, orch. (1995).

VOICE(S) & ORCH. OR CHAMBER ENS.: 5 Motets, SCTB soloists, double ch., instr. (1959); *O magnum mysterium, cycle of carols, ch., instr., org. (1960); Te Lucis ante Terminum, ch., chamber orch. (1961); Frammenti di Leopardi, cantata, sop., cont., instr. (1962); Veni Sancte Spiritus, sop., cont., bass, ch., orch. (1963); Ecce Manus Tradentis, ch., instr. (1965); *Revelation and Fall, sop., 16 instr. (1965); The Shepherd's Calendar, young vv., instr. (1965); *Missa super 'L'Homme Armé', speaker, ens. (1967–8, rev. 1971); *From Stone to Thorn, mez., chamber ens. (1971); *Hymn to St Magnus, sop., chamber ens. (1972); Fool's Fanfare, sop., ens. (1972); Tenebrae super Gesualdo, mez., gui., chamber ens. (1972); *Stone Litany, mez., orch. (1973); Fiddlers at the Wedding, mez., chamber ens. (1973–4); My Lady Lothian's Lilt, mez., ens. (1975); Anakreontika, Gr. songs, mez., instr. (1976); The Blind Fiddler, sop., instr. (1976); Kirkwall Shopping Songs, children's vv., instr., pf. (1979); Black Pentecost, mez., bar., instr. (1979); Solstice of Light, ten., ch., org. (1979); Into the Labyrinth, ten., orch. (1983); Agnus Dei, 2 sop., va., vc. (1984); First Ferry to Hoy, children's ch., ens. (1985); Excuse me, v., ens. (1986); Winterfold, mez., ens. (1986); 6 Songs for St Andrews, children's ch., orch. of classroom instrs. (1988); The Turn of the Tide, children's ch., ens. (1992); The Three Kings, sop., mez., ten., bar., ch., orch. (1995); Job, sop., alt., ten., bass, ch., orch. (1997); The Jacobite Rising, sop., mez., ten., bar., ch., orch. (1997); Sea Elegy, sop., mez., ten., bar., ch., orch. (1998); Canticum canticorum, sop., alt., ten., bass, ch., orch. (2001).

CHAMBER ENS.: Alma Redemptoris Mater, 6 wind instr. (1957); St Michael, sonata, 17 wind instr. (1957); Ricercar and Doubles, 8 instr. (1959); Sinfonia, chamber orch. (1962); 7 In Nomine (1963–5); Shakespeare Music (1964); *Antechrist (1967); Stedman Caters (1968); Eram quasi agnus, motet, instr. (1969); Points and Dances from 'Taverner' (1970); Canon in Memory of Igor Stravinsky (1972); Renaissance Scottish Dances (1973); Psalm 124 (1974); Ave Maris Stella (1975); Runes from a Holy Island (1977); Our Father Whiche in Heaven Art (1977); Dances from 'The Two Fiddlers' (1978); A Welcome to Orkney (1980); The Bairns of Brugh (1981); Image, Reflection, Shadow (1982); Sinfonia Concertante (1982); Sinfonietta Accademica (1983); Unbroken Circle (1984); Mishkenot (1988).

SOLO VOICE(S) & ONE INSTR.: Shall I Die for Mannis Sake?, sop., alto, pf. (1965); Dark Angels, sop., guitar (1974); The Yellow Cake Revue, 6 cabaret songs, v., pf. (1980); The Medium, mez. (1981); Tractus, v., gui. (1990).

VOICES ONLY (SATB unless specified): 4 Carols (1962); The Lord's Prayer (1962); Ave, Plena Gracia, with opt. org. (1964); 5 Carols, women's vv. (1966); Ave Rex Angelorum, with opt. org. (1976); Westerlings (1977); Songs of Hoy (1981); Seven Songs Home (1981); Lullabye for Lucy (1981); One Star at Last (1984); Hallelujah! the Lord God Almightie, with org. (1989); Apple-Basket, Apple-Blossom (1990); Hymn to the Word of God, tenor soloists, SATB ch. (1990); Corpus Christi, with Cat and Mouse (1993); A Hoy Calendar (1993); Il rozzo martello (1997); A Dream of Snow (2000); 2 Motets (2003); Michael Archangelus (2004); O verbum patris (2005); St Bartholomew's Prayer (2005).

CHAMBER MUSIC: Sonata, tpt., pf. (1955); cl. sonata (1956–7); Sextet (1958); str. qt. (1961); Solita, fl. with mus. box (1966); Hymnos, cl., pf. (1967); Stedman Doubles, cl., perc. (1968); Bell Tower (Turris Campanarum Sonantium), perc. (1971); Ara Coeli: Lullaby for Ilian Rainbow, gui. (1972); The Door of the Sun, va. (1975); The Kestrel paced round the Sun, fl. (1975); The Seven Brightnesses, cl. in B♭ (1975); 3 Studies for Percussion (1975); Nocturne, alto fl. (1979); Little Quartets, str., No.1 (1980), No.2 (1981); sonatina, tpt. (1981); Hill Runes, gui. (1981); 2 Gesualdo Motets, brass quintet (1982); The Pole Star, brass quintet (1982); 4 Tallis Voluntaries, brass quintet (1982); Sea Eagle, hn. (1982); Birthday Music for John, fl., va., vc. (1983); sonatine, vn., cimbalom (1984); gui. sonata (1984); For Grace of Light, ob. (1991); Naxos Str. Qts.: No.1 (2002), No.2 (2003), No.3 (2003), No.4 (2004), No.5 (2004), No.6 (2005), No.7 (2005); pf. trio (2003).

PIANO: 5 Pieces (1956); 5 Little Pieces (1967); Sub tuam protectionem (1970); Ut Re Mi (1971); Stevie's Ferry to Hoy (1976); 4 Lessons for 2 Keyboards (1978); Sonata (1980–1).

ORGAN: 3 Preludes (1976); sonata (1982).

BRASS BAND: March: The Pole Star (1982); 4 Tallis Voluntaries (1982); 2 Gesualdo Motets (1982).

REALIZATIONS: Purcell: Fantasia on a Ground and 2 Pavans, chamber ens. (1968), Fantasia on One Note, instr. (1973); Gabrieli: Canzona, wind and str. (1969); Buxtehude: Cantata: Also hat Gott die Welt geliebet, sop., fl., vn., vc., hpd. (1971); J. S. Bach: Prelude and Fugue in C♯ minor, instr. (1972), Prelude and Fugue in C♯ major, instr. (1974); Dunstable: Veni Sancte Spiritus, instr. (1972); Kinloch: Kinloch His Fantassie, instr. (1976); Anon.: Scottish 16th cent.: 4 Instrumental Motets, instr. (1973–7), Renaissance Scottish Dances, instr. (1973).

MISC.: The Devils, mus. for K. Russell film (1971); The Boy Friend, mus for K. Russell film and arrs. of Wilson's songs from musical (1971).

Maybrick, Michael (b Liverpool, 1844; d Buxton, 1913). Eng. baritone and composer. Under pseudonym 'Stephen Adams' wrote popular ballads, e.g. Star of Bethlehem and The Holy City.

Mayer, (Sir) Robert (b Mannheim, 1879; d London, 1985). Ger.-born businessman and patron of music. Met Brahms. Settled in London 1896 (Eng. cit. 1902). Founder (1923), Robert Mayer children's concerts, founder and chairman, Youth and Music. Knighted 1939, CH 1973, created KCVO on his 100th birthday, 5 June 1979. His first wife Dorothy (née Moulton Piper) (b Crouch End, London, 1886; d Henham, Essex, 1974) was one of the first sopranos to sing mus. by Schoenberg and Stravinsky in Britain before 1914. She also wrote biographies of Marie-Antoinette, the artist Angelika Kauffman, and of Spohr (London 1959).

Mayerl, Billy (William Joseph) (b London, 1902; d Beaconsfield, 1959). Eng. pianist and composer. Played Grieg conc. at Queen's Hall 1914. Gave f.

London p. of *Rhapsody in Blue*. In 1921 joined Savoy Havana Band. Wrote many syncopated comps. for pf., incl. *Marigold* (1927) and *Jasmine* (1929). Regular and popular radio performer.

Mayer-Lismann, Else (Mitia) (*b* Frankfurt, 1914; *d* London, 1990). Ger. musician and lecturer. Settled in Eng. Art dir. Mayer-Lismann Opera Workshop. MBE 1984.

May Night (*Mayskaya Noch*). Opera in 3 acts by Rimsky-Korsakov to his own lib. based on story by Gogol in *Evenings on a Farm near Dikanka* (1831–2). Comp. 1878–9. Prod. St Petersburg 1880, London (Drury Lane) 1914.

Mayr, Richard (*b* Henndorf, nr. Salzburg, 1877; *d* Vienna, 1935). Austrian bass-baritone. Début Bayreuth 1902 (Hagen). Vienna Opera 1902–35, début under Mahler (Don Gomez in *Ernani*). Most famous role was Ochs in *Der Rosenkavalier*, written with him in mind though he did not create it. Salzburg Fest. début 1921; CG début 1924; NY Met 1927. Created role of Barak in *Die Frau ohne Schatten*, Vienna 1919. Also concert career, singing in f.p. of Mahler's 8th Sym. (Munich 1910, cond. Mahler).

Mayr, (Johannes) **Simon** (*b* Mendorf, Bavaria, 1763; *d* Bergamo, 1845). Ger.-born composer. First opera *Saffo* (1794) was successful and was followed by 67 others until 1824, his popularity in Italy being immense until eclipsed by Rossini's. Choirmaster, S. Maria Maggiore, Bergamo, 1802; prof. of counterpoint at inst. 1805–26. Taught Donizetti. Also comp. instr. works, e.g. 2 pf. concs., and songs.

Mayuzumi, Toshiro (*b* Yokohama, 1929; *d* Kawasaki, 1997). Japanese composer. Organizer of modern mus. group *Ars Nova Japonica*, and has worked in Tokyo Radio EMS. Works combine Japanese sources with *avant-garde* Western methods. Wrote mus. for film *The Bible* (1965). Other orch. comps. are *Essay*, str.; *Bacchanale*; *Mandala*, sym.; *Microcosmos*; *Fireworks*; *Samsara*; *Texture*; *Tonepleromas 55*; *Phonologie symphonique*; *Sphénogrammes*; *The Birth of Music*; xyl. concertino; perc. conc.; opera: *The Temple of the Golden Pavilion (Kinkakuji)*; ballets: *Bugaku*; *Olympics*; *The Kabuti*; cantatas: *Nirvana sym.*; *Pratidesana*; elec. tape: *Aoi-no-ue* (Princess Hollyhock); *Campanology*; *Olympic Campanology*; *3 Hymns*; *Variations sur 7*.

Mazeppa. (1) Pf. pieces by *Liszt, 1st (1840), 2nd No.4 of *Études d'exécution transcendante* (1851); and sym.-poem for orch. (1851) based on Hugo's story (also for 2 pf. 1855, and pf. 4 hands 1874).

(2) Opera in 3 acts by Tchaikovsky to lib. by composer and Burenin after Pushkin. Comp. 1881–3. Prod. Moscow 1884, Liverpool 1888, Boston 1922, London (ENO) 1984. Mazeppa (1644–1709) was Russ. historical character.

mazurka. A traditional Polish country dance (orig. sung as well as danced). Originated in Mazovia, near Warsaw, inhabitants being Mazurs. It spread in the early 18th cent. to Ger. and then to Paris, and early in the 19th to Brit. and the USA. It is in triple time with a certain accentuation of the 2nd beat of each measure and an ending of the phrases on that beat; dotted notes are a feature. It is not a fast dance, and a certain aristocratic pride of bearing, sometimes combined with a touch of abandon, helps to differentiate it from the waltz. Its place in concert mus. was est. by *Chopin, who wrote *c*.60 for pf. These are in a greatly refined style and the tempo and rhythm are sometimes changed from those that are traditional.

The *polka-mazurka* differs from the Polka in being in triple time and from the Mazurka in having an accent on the 3rd beat of the measure.

Mazurok, Yury (*b* Krasnik, Poland, 1931). Polish-born Russ. baritone. Joined Bolshoy Th., 1963 (début as Onegin). Prizewinner in comps. at Prague (1960), Bucharest (1961), and Montreal (1967). CG début 1975; Amer. début S. Francisco 1977; NY Met 1978; Vienna 1979.

Mazzocchi, Domenico (*b* Città Castellana, 1592; *d* Rome, 1665). It. composer and lawyer. Wrote opera (1626), oratorio *Querimonia di S. Maria Maddalena* (Plaint of St Mary Magdalene, 1631), and pubd. book of madrigals (1640) in which signs < and > for crescendo and diminuendo, *f* for *forte*, *p* for *piano*, and *tr* for trill first appear.

Mazzocchi, Virgilio (*b* Veja, 1597; *d* Città Castellana, 1646). It. composer, brother of Domenico *Mazzocchi. Choirmaster, St John Lateran, Rome, 1628–9, when he moved to similar post at St Peter's. With *Marazzoli, wrote what is said to be first comic opera, *Chi soffre, speri* (Rome 1639, rev. of *Il falcone*, 1637). Also wrote vocal mus.

M.D. = *main droite* (Fr.) or *mano destra* (It.), i.e. right hand. Sometimes, also, used as abbreviation of Musical Director.

me (mi). The 3rd degree of the major scale, according to the system of vocal syllables derived from Guido d'Arezzo (see *hexachord), and so used (spelt *me*) in *tonic sol-fa, in which it is also the 5th degree of the minor scale. In many countries, however, the name has become attached (on 'fixed-doh' principles) to the note E, in whatever key it may occur.

Meale, Richard (Graham) (*b* Sydney, NSW, 1932). Australian composer. From 1955 gave recitals of contemp. pf. mus. Cond. f. Australian p. of *Pierrot Lunaire*, 1959. In 1961 visited Spain, developing interest in work of the poet Lorca. Up to this point his comps. had been of the Bartók-Hindemith genre; thereafter he followed Messiaen and Boulez, with a further influence from Indonesian mus. Programme planner for ABC 1961–8. Lect., Elder Cons. of Mus., Adelaide Univ. 1969–88. MBE 1971. Order of Australia 1985. Prin. works:

OPERAS: *Voss* (1979–86); *Mer de Glace* (1986–91).

ORCH.: fl. conc. (1959); *Homage to Garcia Lorca*, 2 str. orch. (1964); *Images (Nagauta)* (1966); *Nocturnes*, vib., hp., cel., orch. (1967); *Very High Kings*, 2 pf., org., orch. (1968); *Clouds Now and Then* (1969); *Soon It Will Die* (1969); *Variations* (1970); *Evocations*, ob., chamber orch., vn. obbl. (1973); *Viridian*, str. (1979); sym. (1993–4); *3 Miro Pieces* (2002).

INSTR.: *Divertimento*, vn., pf., vc. (1959); fl. sonata (1960); *Las Alborados*, fl., hn., vn., pf. (1963); *Intersections*, fl., va., vib., pf. (1965); *Cyphers*, fl., va., vib., pf. (1965); wind quintet (1970); *Interiors/ Exteriors*, 2 pf., 3 perc. (1970); *Incredible Floridas*, fl., cl., vn., vc., pf., perc. (1971); *Plateau*, wind quintet (1971); *Fanfare*, brass (1978); str. qt. No.1 (1974), No.2 (1980), No.3 (1995); *Mélisande*, fl. (1996); *Palimpsest*, ens. (1999).

PIANO: *Sonatina patetica* (1957); *Orenda* (1959); *Coruscations* (1971).

measure. (1) Old Eng. term, now adopted in USA and reintroduced into Britain in 19th cent. by John *Curwen, indicating time-content of notational space between one bar-line and the next, e.g. '2 beats in the bar'.

(2) The bar-line itself. Note that the Eng. 'bar' is the same as Amer. 'measure'; Amer. 'bar' means Eng. 'bar-line'.

(3) A stately Eng. dance of 15th and 16th cents. ('trod a measure' is a frequent phrase in Elizabethan drama).

Meck, Nadezhda von (*b* Znamenskoye, nr. Smolensk, 1831; *d* Wiesbaden, 1894). Russ. patroness of Tchaikovsky, whom she never met. Gave him annual grant of 6,000 roubles to devote himself to comp. This was abruptly terminated, possibly because of family pressure on her, in 1890. Their correspondence was pubd. in USSR 1934–6. 4th Sym. ded. to her. In 1880 and 1881 Debussy worked for her as a pianist.

Médée (*Medea*). Opera in 3 acts by Cherubini to lib. in Fr. by F. B. Hoffman based on Euripides. Prod. Paris 1797, Berlin 1800, London 1865. Spoken dialogue of orig. set to mus. by F. Lachner 1854 and by Arditi for London prod. 1865. F.p. in England of orig. score Durham 1967, Univ. of Hartford, Conn., 1970. Operas on same subject by several composers, incl. Kusser (1692), M. A. Charpentier (1693), Mysliveček (1764), J. A. Benda (1775), Mayr (1813), and Milhaud (1938). Also ballet by S. Barber (1946).

medesimo (It.). Same, e.g. *medesimo movimento*, the same speed.

medial cadence. One in which leading chord is inverted instead of being in root position.

mediant. The 3rd degree of the major or minor scale. So called because it is midway between the tonic and the dominant.

mediation. Inflection in *plainchant occurring at the end of first section of a psalm-tune.

Medicean Edition. See *plainsong*.

Medium, The. Opera in 2 acts by *Menotti to his own lib. Comp. 1945. Prod. Columbia Univ. 1946; rev. vers. NY 1947, London 1948.

medley. Similar to *pot-pourri: a collection of parts or passages of well-known songs or pieces arranged so that the end of one merges into the start of the next.

Medtner, Nicolai [Nikolay] (Karlovich) (*b* Moscow, 1880; *d* London, 1951). Russ. composer and pianist. Prof. at Moscow Cons. 1902–3, 1909–10 and 1914–21. Left Russ. 1921, living in Ger. and France and touring as virtuoso pianist. Amer. début 1924 with Philadelphia Orch. Wrote much pf. mus.; was influenced by Ger. romanticism. Wrote book, 1935, opposing modern innovations and affirming faith in tonality. Wrote 3 pf. concs. (1914–18, 1920–7, 1940–3); 9 pf. sonatas (1896–1935); many genre pieces for pf., e.g. series called 34 *Fairy-Tales* (1905–29); and many songs. Settled in Eng. 1935. Patronized by Maharajah of Mysore.

Meet My Folks! 'Theme and relations', Op.10, by *Crosse, comp. 1964, being settings of poems by Ted Hughes for speaker, children's ch., perc. band, ob., cl., bn., hn., tpt., vc., pf., and percussionists. F.p. Aldeburgh Fest. 1964.

Mefistofele (Mephistopheles). Opera in prol., 5 acts, and epilogue by *Boito to his own lib., based on both parts of Goethe's *Faust*. Comp. 1866–7. Prod. Milan 1868. Rev. vers. in 4 acts prod. Bologna 1875, second rev. vers. Venice 1876, London 1880, Boston (in English) and NY 1880.

megaphone. A large speaking tpt. Also a device introduced by Edison for listening at a distance of some miles without the use of wires or electricity—practically an improved ear-tpt. on a large scale.

Mehta, Zubin (*b* Bombay, 1936). Indian conductor, violinist, and pianist. Son of Mehli Mehta (*b* Bombay, 1908; *d* S. Monica, Calif., 2002, founder of Bombay SO and at one time violinist in Hallé Orch. before settling in USA). Won first prize, Liverpool int. cond. comp. 1958, this leading to guest engagements throughout world. Amer. début 1960 (Philadelphia Orch.). Mus. dir.: Montreal SO 1961–7; Los Angeles PO 1962–77; NYPO 1978–91; Israel PO from 1977 for life; prin. dir. Maggio Musicale, Florence, from 1985; mus. dir. Bavarian State Opera 1998–2006. Opera début Montreal 1964. Salzburg Fest. 1962; NY Met 1965; CG 1977.

Méhul, Étienne-Nicolas (*b* Givet, nr. Mezières, 1763; *d* Paris, 1817). Fr. composer. Organist at convent at age 10. Taken to Paris 1778 by rich amateur who recognized his talent, studying under Edelmann. Befriended by *Gluck who advised him to compose for the stage. His *Euphrosine et Coradin* (1790) won him fame and imparted new dramatic force to *opéra-comique*. 30 other stage-works followed in next 17 years, most famous being *Joseph* (1807) in which his strong dramatic sense and lyrical vein are found at their best. Taught at Paris Cons. 1793–1815.

Fortunes declined after fall of his patron Napoleon. Also wrote ballets, cantatas, songs, a Mass, and syms. His operas incl.: *Euphrosine et Coradin* (1790), *Stratonice* (1792), *Le Jeune Sage et le vieux fou* (1793), *Le Jeune Henri* (1797), *Ariodant* (1799), *Les Deux Aveugles de Tolède* (1806), *Uthal* (1806), *Joseph* (1807), *Le Prince troubadour* (1813), *L'Oriflamme* (1814).

Meier, Johanna (*b* Chicago, 1938). Amer. soprano. Début NY City Opera 1969 (Countess in *Capriccio*), singing many roles for the co. NY Met début 1976; Bayreuth Fest. 1981.

Meier, Waltraud (*b* Würzburg, 1956). Ger. mezzo-soprano. Sang in chorus of Würzburg Opera, making solo début 1976 (Cherubino in *Le nozze di Figaro*). Joined Mannheim Nat. Th. 1978. Dortmund Opera 1980–3. Bayreuth Fest. début 1983; CG début 1985; NY Met début 1987.

Meistersinger (Mastersingers). Middle-class Ger. literary and mus. movement of 15th and 16th cents. cultivated by craftsmen's guilds and representing continuation of aristocratic *Minnesinger of preceding 2 centuries. Movement declined in 17th cent., the Ulm school being disbanded in 1839 and its last survivor dying in 1876. The conduct of a mastersingers' guild was very much as depicted by Wagner in his opera *Die *Meistersinger von Nürnberg*. Rigid and pedantic rules governed the weekly meetings (after church on Sunday); competitions were held and prizes awarded; members were promoted into various classes: *Schüler* (apprentice), *Schulfreund* (friend), *Sänger* (singer), *Dichter* (poet), *Meister* (master). Title *Dichter* was awarded for new poem (*Lied, Gesang*), *Meister* for new melody (*Ton, Weise*). Several of the characters in Wagner's opera were historical personages, e.g. Konrad Nachtigall and especially Hans Sachs (1494–1576). Some attractive songs by Sachs survive, but generally Meistersinger melodies are dull and suffer from a surfeit of coloratura.

Meistersinger von Nürnberg, Die (The Mastersingers of Nuremberg). Opera in 3 acts by Wagner to his own lib. based on Wagenseil and other sources. Gives accurate and heartwarming picture of medieval guild of *Meistersinger, several of whom, notably Hans Sachs, actually lived. Comp. 1862–7. Prod. Munich 1868, London (Drury Lane) 1882, NY Met 1886, Bayreuth 1888.

Melba, (Dame) **Nellie** [Mrs Helen Porter Armstrong (*née* Mitchell)] (*b* Richmond, Melbourne, 1861; *d* Sydney, NSW, 1931). Australian soprano. Début in opera in Brussels 1887 as Gilda in *Rigoletto*, CG 1888, Paris 1889. Her London triumphs date from her Juliette (Gounod) in 1889 and she appeared regularly at CG until 1914 (except 1909) and then in 1919, 1922–4 (BNOC), and 1926. Débuts La Scala and NY Met both 1893. In 1897–8 toured USA with own co. and was member of Manhattan Opera Co. for several seasons from 1907. Also sang with Chicago Opera. Final operatic appearance CG 1926 as Mimì (in *La*

bohème, recording exists). V. notable for purity, freshness, and brilliance of ornamentation in coloratura roles. Her stage name was adopted in tribute to Melbourne. The ice-cream sweet *pêche Melba* and Melba toast are named after her. DBE 1918, GBE 1929.

Melchior, Lauritz [Hommel, Lebrecht] (*b* Copenhagen, 1890; *d* Santa Monica, Calif., 1973). Danish-born tenor (Amer. cit. 1947). Début Copenhagen as bar. 1913 (Silvio in *Pagliacci*). Début as ten. 1918 (title-role in *Tannhäuser*), at suggestion of Mme. Charles *Cahier. Financed by novelist Hugh Walpole. London début CG 1924. Studied Wagner roles at Bayreuth, singing there 1924–31. Amer. début NY Met 1926. One of most famous Wagnerian *Heldentenors*, singing Tristan over 200 times.

melisma (Gr. 'song'; plural *melismata*). A group of notes sung to a single syllable, as opposed to coloratura. Used in plainsong and in other song. *Melismata* is title of vocal pieces (madrigals, etc.) pubd. 1611 by Thomas *Ravenscroft.

Mellers, Wilfrid (Howard) (*b* Leamington, 1914). Eng. composer, critic, and teacher. Lect. at Cambridge 1945–8, Birmingham Univ. 1948–60, Pittsburgh Univ. 1960–3. Prof. of mus., York Univ., 1964–81; visiting prof. of mus., City Univ. from 1984. Interested in bridging gap between symphonic mus., jazz, pop, and folk mus. Has written ten books on Couperin, Bach, Beethoven, Vaughan Williams, and Amer. mus. Works incl. cantatas, song-cycles, chamber mus., and songs. OBE 1982.

mellophone. Brass instr. of semi-conical bore, coiled in circular shape and played with a cup mouthpiece. Has 3 piston valves. Sometimes used as substitute for French hn., being easier to play but not so rich in tone.

melodia. Org. stop of *Hohlflöte type popular in USA, of 8′ length and pitch.

melodic minor scale. See *scale*.

mélodie (melody). Term applied to Fr. solo song with acc., counterpart of the Ger. *Lied.

Melodien (Melodies). Work for orch. by *Ligeti, comp. 1971, f.p. Nuremberg 1971.

melodrama. Dramatic comp., or part of play or opera, in which words are recited to a mus. commentary. Popularized late in 18th cent. Where one or two actors are involved, 'monodrama' or 'duodrama' is term used. J. A. *Benda's *Ariadne auf Naxos* (1774) and *Medea* (1775) are early examples. Mozart used melodramatic monologues in *Zaide* (1780). *Fibich wrote a trilogy *Hippodamia* (1888–91). Famous operatic examples occur in the dungeon scene of *Fidelio*, the Wolf's Glen in *Der Freischütz*, Gertrude's aria in Marschner's *Hans Heiling*, the Empress in Act III of *Die Frau ohne Schatten*, and in *Peter Grimes*. Other examples are R. Strauss's *Enoch Arden* (1898), Honegger's *Jeanne d'Arc au bûcher* (1935), Bliss's *Morning Heroes*

(1930), and Vaughan Williams's *An Oxford Elegy*
(1949). The word has also come to mean an
over-dramatic play, hence the adjective 'melodramatic', but in a musical connotation the orig.
meaning is conveyed.

melodramma (It.). 17th-cent. term for opera.
Nothing to do with **melodrama.*

melody (from Gr. 'Melos'). A succession of notes,
varying in pitch, which have an organized and
recognizable shape. Melody is 'horizontal', i.e.
the notes are heard consecutively, whereas in
*harmony notes are sounded simultaneously
('vertical'). The mus. of many primitive races still
remains purely melodic, as does European folk-
song and also plainsong. Many apparently
simple folk melodies will be found, on examination, however, to be highly organized,
e.g. as regards the use at different pitch levels of
some simple, brief *motif, the adroit use of a
high note as a point of climax, etc.; many such
melodies will be found to be cast in some definite form, such as simple ternary form.

*Rhythm is an important element in melody,
whether it be the prose rhythm of primitive
mus., plainsong, and the comps. of some modern
composers, or the metrical rhythm of most
other mus. Indeed this element is so much a governing factor in the effect of a melody that if,
while the notes of a popular melody are left intact, the rhythm is drastically altered, it becomes
difficult to recognize the melody. The rhythm of
many melodies is extraordinarily subtle and
repays close study.

Once harmony had become an element in
mus. it began to influence melody in this way—
that melodic passages are often found to be
based on the notes of a chord (with or without
added decorative or intermediate notes).

It is difficult to define 'originality' in melody.
Apparently it lies mainly in mere detail, since,
on critical examination, what we accept as an
orig. melody is often found closely to resemble
some previous and quite well-known melody. It
is often difficult to see what has led to the popularity of a particular melody, or what it is that
gives some melodies durability while others
prove to be merely ephemeral: however, it will
generally be found that the long-lived melodies
possess the valuable quality of logical organization.

Racial and nat. feeling expresses itself strongly
in melody, particular scales, intervals, and
rhythms being typical of the mus. of particular
races or nations.

The word is also sometimes used as the title
for a small, simple piece, e.g. Rubinstein's *Melody*
in F.

melophone. Wind instr. with free-beating reeds,
air being supplied by bellows operated by right
hand and concealed in body of guitar or vc. Invented 1837 by Leclerc of Paris.

Melos Ensemble. Eng. instr. ensemble formed
1950 by Cecil *Aronowitz (va.), Gervase de Peyer

(cl.), Richard Adeney (fl.), and Terence Weil (vc.)
as a group of up to 12 players (str. quintet, wind
quintet, hp., and pf.). Took part in f.p. of Britten's
War Requiem (1962). Amer. début 1966.

Melos Quartet of Stuttgart. Ger. string qt.
founded in 1965. Won Geneva int. comp. 1966.
Recorded all Beethoven qts. 1968–70. Salzburg
Fest. début 1980. Personnel unchanged in first
20 years of existence.

Melusina, The Fair (*Märchen von die schönen
Melusine*). Ov. in C major by Mendelssohn, Op.32,
comp. 1833 and prompted by Conradin Kreutzer's opera *Melusine*.

membranophone. Term for mus. instr. which
produce sound from tightly stretched membranes, either struck (as in drums) or 'singing'
(as the kazoo). One of four classifications of instr.
devised by C. Sachs and E. M. von Hornbostel and
pubd. in *Zeitschrift für Ethnologie*, 1914. Other categories are *aerophones, *chordophones, and
*idiophones, to which *electrophones were later
added.

Memento Vitae (Memory of Life). Conc. for
orch. in homage to Beethoven by *Musgrave,
comp. 1969–70, f.p. Glasgow 1970, cond. Loughran.

Memorial to Lidiče. Work for orch. by Martinů
f.p. NY 1943; comp. in memory of Cz. village
annihilated in Nazis' reprisal.

Mendelssohn [Mendelssohn Bartholdy], **Fanny
Cäcilie** (*b* Hamburg, 1805; *d* Berlin, 1847). Ger.
amateur pianist and composer, sister of Felix
*Mendelssohn. Published 6 of her songs with her
brother's, and (in her own name) 2 books of *Lieder ohne Worte* for pf., also oratorio, pf. qt., songs,
and part-songs. Married painter Wilhelm Hensel
in 1829.

Mendelssohn [Mendelssohn Bartholdy], (Jakob
Ludwig) **Felix** (*b* Hamburg, 1809; *d* Leipzig,
1847). Ger. composer, pianist, organist, and conductor. Grandson of Moses Mendelssohn, philosopher, and son of banker Abraham who added
Bartholdy to his surname when he became Protestant Christian. Felix was 2nd of 4 children,
eldest being Fanny *Mendelssohn, almost as
good a pianist as her brother. His first pf. lessons
were from his mother and in Berlin he was
taught harmony by Karl Zelter. Boy prodigy as
pianist, making public début at 9. In 1819 his
setting of Ps. 19 was sung by Berlin *Singakademie*.
In 1821 Zelter took him to Weimar to visit
Goethe, a warm friendship developing between
the 72-year-old poet and the boy of 12, who was
already a prolific composer. His comic opera, *Die
Hochzeit des Camacho* was completed 1825 and
produced 1827. In 1826, at age 17, he comp. the
ov. to *A Midsummer Night's Dream*, adding the
remainder of the incidental mus. 16 years later.
Attended Berlin Univ. 1826–9, and finally determined upon mus. as a profession. In Mar. 1829,
he cond. Bach's *St Matthew Passion* at the *Singakademie* (its f.p. since Bach's death in 1750), one of

his many services to the Bach revival. Visited Eng. 1829, giving one of f.ps. there of Beethoven's 'Emperor' conc. From the outset he received adulation from Eng. public. Before leaving, toured Scotland and was inspired by scenery to write *Hebrides* ov. Toured Ger., Austria, and It. in next 2 years, composing 2 syms. and publishing first book of *Lieder ohne Worte*. Further visits to London 1832 and 1833 (when he cond. f.p. of his *Italian* Sym.).

Appointed cond., Lower Rhine Mus. Fest., Düsseldorf 1833–6 and cond. of Leipzig Gewandhaus Orch. 1835–46. Married 1837 and in next few years wrote several of his finest works, incl. *Lobgesang*, the *Variations Sérieuses*, and vn. conc. Organized new cons. of mus. at Leipzig, becoming dir. when it opened in 1843 as well as teaching pf. and comp., with Schumann as associate. Made 8th visit to Britain 1844, and returned in 1846 to cond. f.p. of oratorio *Elijah* at Birmingham Fest. Last (10th) visit was in 1847, when he conducted *Elijah* in London, Manchester, and Birmingham, and played for Queen Victoria and Prince Albert. Severe overwork, combined with the shock of his sister Fanny's sudden death in May 1847, led to his own death in Nov. of that year.

Mendelssohn's gifts were phenomenal. He was a good painter, had wide literary knowledge, and wrote brilliantly. He was a superb pianist, a good violist, an exceptional organist, and an inspiring cond. He had an amazing mus. memory. He was generous to other musicians, and keen to raise standards of popular taste. His genius as a composer led Bülow to describe him as the most complete master of form after Mozart. In him, a classical upbringing was combined with romantic inclination, imparting to his work a poetic elegance which has caused it to be regarded as superficial because of its lack of impassioned features. The popularity of his work in the 19th cent. was followed by a severe reaction, partly caused by a puritanical feeling that his life had been too comfortably easy, but the pendulum has swung again and the best qualities of his music, its craftsmanship, restraint, poetry, inventive orchestration, and melodic freshness are now highly valued. Prin. works:

THEATRE: *Die *Hochzeit des Camacho*, Op.10, comic opera (1825); incidental mus. to A *Midsummer Night's Dream*, Op.61 (1842); *Son and Stranger (Die Heimkehr aus der Fremde)*, operetta, Op.89 (1829); *Lorelei*, unfinished opera (1847).

ORCH.: 13 early syms. for str.; syms.: No.1 in C minor, Op.11 (1824), No.2 (*Lobgesang* in B♭, Op.52 (1840), No.3 in A minor, Op.56 (*Scotch* (1830–42), No.4 in A, Op.90 (*Italian*) (1830–1, 1833), No.5 in D minor, Op.107 (*Reformation* (1830–2); ov. *Ruy Blas*, Op.95 (1839), ov. A *Midsummer Night's Dream*, Op.21 (1826), ov. *Hebrides* (*Fingal's Cave (Fingals Höhle)*), Op.26 (1830, rev. 1832); *Meeresstille und Glückliche Fahrt* (*Calm Sea and Prosperous Voyage*), Op.27 (1832); *Die schöne Melusine* (Fair *Melusina*), Op.32 (1833).

CONCERTOS, etc: pf.: No.1 in G minor, Op.25 (1832), No.2 in D minor, Op.40 (1837); *Capriccio brillant* in B minor, Op.22 (1832), *Rondo brillant* in E♭,

Op.29 (1834), *Serenade and Allegro giocoso* in B minor, Op.43 (1838); vn., in E minor, Op.64 (1844); conc. in A minor, pf., str. (op. posth.) (1822); conc. in D minor, vn., str. (op. posth.) (1822); conc. in E, 2 pf., orch. (op. posth.) (1823); conc. in A♭, 2 pf., orch. (1824).

CHORAL: *Die *erste Walpurgisnacht* (The First Walpurgis Night), Op.60 (1831, rev. 1842); oratorios: *St Paul*, Op.36 (1834–6); *Elijah*, Op.70 (1846, rev. 1846–7); *Christus*, Op.97, unfinished (1847); *Lobgesang* (Hymn of Praise, sym. No.2 in B♭), Op.52 (1840); *Lauda Sion*, Op.73 (1846); *Hear My Prayer* (1844); 9 settings of Psalms.

CHAMBER MUSIC: str. qts.: No.1 in E♭, Op.12 (1829), No.2 in A minor, Op.13 (1827), No.3 in D, No.4 in E minor, No.5 in E♭, Op.44 Nos. 1, 2 and 3 (1837–8), No.6 in F minor, Op.80 (1847); str. qt. in E♭ (1823); *4 Pieces*, str. qt., Op.81: *Andante* in E major (1847), *Scherzo* in A minor (1847), *Capriccio* in E minor (1843), *Fugue* in E♭ (1827); pf. qts.: No.1 in C minor, Op.1 (1822), No.2 in F minor, Op.2 (1823), No.3 in B minor, Op.3 (1824–5); va. sonata in C minor (1824); cl. sonata in E♭ (1824); vn. sonata in F minor, Op.4 (1825); *Variations concertantes*, pf., vc., Op.17 (1829); str. quintets: No.1 in A, Op.18 (1831), No.2 in E♭, Op.87 (1845); *Octet* in E♭, str., Op.20 (1825); scherzo from Octet arr. for orch.; vc. sonatas: No.1 in B♭, Op.45 (1838), No.2 in D, Op.58 (1843); pf. trios: No.1 in D minor, Op.49 (1839), No.2 in C minor, Op.66 (1845); *Lied ohne Worte* in D, vc., pf., Op.109 (1845); sextet in D, Op.110 (1824); *Concertstück*, No.1 in F minor, cl., corno di bassetto, pf., Op.113 (1833), No.2 in D minor, Op.114 (1833).

PIANO: *Capriccio* in F♯ minor, Op.5 (1825); sonatas: E major, Op.6 (1826), G minor, Op.105 (1821), B♭, Op.106 (1827); 7 *Characteristic Pieces*, Op.7 (1827); *Rondo capriccioso*, Op.14; *Lieder ohne Worte*, Book 1, Op.19 (1829–30), II, Op.30 (1835), III, Op.38 (1837), IV, Op.53 (1841), V, Op.62, VI, Op.67 (1843–5), VII, Op.85 (1842), VIII, Op.102 (1842–5); *Fantasy*, Op.28 (1833); 3 *Capriccios*, Op.33 (1833–5); *Variations sérieuses* in D minor, Op.54 (1841); *Variations*, Op.82 (1841), Op.83 (1841); *Allegro brillant*, pf. duet, Op.92 (1841); 3 *Preludes and Studies*, Op.104 (1836–8); *Capriccio* in E, Op.118 (1837).

VOICE & PIANO: 12 *Songs*, Op.8 (1830); 12 *Songs*, Op.9 (1829); 6 *Songs*, Op.19a (1830); 6 *Songs*, Op.34 (1834–7); 6 *Songs*, Op.47 (1839); 6 *Songs*, Op.57 (1839–42); 6 *Songs*, Op.71 (1845–7); 3 *Songs*, Op.84 (1831–9); 6 *Songs*, Op.86 (1826–47); 6 *Songs*, Op.99 (1841–5); 2 *Sacred Songs*, Op.112 (1835).

PART-SONGS: 6 for SATB, Op.41 (1834); 6 SATB, Op.48 (1839); 6 TB, Op.50 (1837–40); 6 SATB, Op.59 (1837–43); 6 2-part songs, Op.63 (1836–44); 4 TB, Op.75 (1837–44); 4 TB, Op.76 (1840–7); 3 2-part songs, Op.77 (1836–47); 6 SATB, Op.88 (1839–47); 4 TB, Op.100 (1839–44); 4 TB, Op.120 (1837–47); these are settings mainly of Heine, Goethe, Eichendorff, Fallersleben, Uhland, and Scott; *Festgesang*, male vv. and brass (1840).

ORGAN: 3 Preludes and Fugues, Op.37 (1833–7); 6 Sonatas, Op.65 (1839–44); *Andante and Variations* in D (1844).

ménestrel (Fr.). Minstrel. Type of Fr. public mus. entertainer in 14th cent., orig. called *ménestrier*, the profession being known as *ménestrandie*. Spreading over the channel to Eng., the term became 'minstrel'. The minstrels (in effect professional musicians) formed a guild *c*.1350. See also *jongleurs*, *Meistersinger*, and *Minnesinger*.

Mengelberg, (Josef) **Willem** (*b* Utrecht, 1871; *d* Zuort, Switz., 1951). Dutch conductor. Mus. dir., Lucerne 1891. Appointed permanent cond. of *Concertgebouw Orch. of Amsterdam 1895, remaining until 1945 and making it one of the great orchs. of the world. He particularly championed works of *Mahler and *Strauss in early years of 20th cent., winning friendship and admiration of both composers, who went to Amsterdam to conduct the orch. in their own works. Strauss ded. *Ein Heldenleben* to Mengelberg and the orch. In 1920 Mengelberg held a fest. in Amsterdam at which all Mahler's syms. and other major works were perf., the first such proclamation of faith in the composer. Amer. début NYPO 1905, London 1911. Cond. NYPO, 1921–9. Prof. of mus., Utrecht Univ. from 1933. Salzburg Fest. début 1934 (Vienna PO). Frequent guest cond. of Eng. orchs. In 1945, because of alleged collaboration with the Nazi conquerors of Holland, was forbidden by Dutch govt. to 'exercise his profession in public in any matter whatever for a period of 6 years 1945–51'. He died in exile in the 6th year of this 'sentence', the justice of which is now questioned.

Mennin [Mennini], **Peter** (*b* Erie, Penn., 1923; *d* NY, 1983). Amer. composer. First recipient of Gershwin Memorial Award. Taught comp., Juilliard Sch., 1947–58. Dir., Peabody Cons., Baltimore, 1958–62. President, Juilliard Sch. 1962–83. Comps., somewhat severe in style, won many awards. They incl. 9 syms. (1942–81; No.4 (*The Cycle*) employs ch.); pf. conc.; vn. conc.; vc. conc.; *Sinfonia* for chamber orch.; *Concertato*; *Moby Dick* (1952); *Sinfonia* for large orch.; cantata *The Pied Piper of Hamelin*; 2 str. qts.; org. sonata; pf. sonata; songs, etc.

meno (It.). Less, as in *meno mosso*, less moved, i.e. slower.

Menotti, Gian Carlo (*b* Cadegliano, It., 1911). It.-born composer, librettist, and conductor, mainly resident in USA and Scotland. Taught at Curtis Inst. 1948–55. Formed lifelong friendship with the composer Samuel *Barber. His tendency as composer was always towards opera and his first adult essay, *Amelia Goes to the Ball*, was cond. by *Reiner in 1937 and later at NY Met. As with all his operas, he wrote his own lib. First outstanding success was in 1946 with *The Medium*, but this was eclipsed in 1950 by *The Consul*, dealing with the plight of refugees at the mercy of heartless bureaucracy. *Amahl and the Night Visitors* was the first opera to be written for TV in America. His works have achieved considerable popularity and his intention to bring opera nearer to the Broadway theatregoer has been achieved if at some cost in originality of expression. But of his

dramatic effectiveness and melodic gift there can be no doubt. Founded Fest. of Two Worlds at Spoleto, It. and Charleston, USA, 1958. Wrote lib. for Barber's operas *Vanessa* (1957) and *A Hand of Bridge* (1958). Prod. *Vanessa* (Salzburg 1958). Works incl.:

OPERAS: *Amelia Goes to the Ball (Amelia al Ballo) (1934–7); The Old Maid and the Thief (1939); The Island God (1942, withdrawn); The *Medium (1945); The *Telephone (1946); The *Consul (1949); *Amahl and the Night Visitors (1951, TV); The *Saint of Bleecker Street (1954); *Maria Golovin (1958); The Last Savage (1963); The Labyrinth (TV, 1963); Martin's Lie (1964); Help! Help! the Globolinks (1968, children); The Most Important Man (1971); Tamu-Tamu (1973); The Hero (1976); The Egg (1976); The Trial of the Gipsy (1978); Chip and his Dog (1978); La Loca (1979); A Bride from Pluto (1981–2); The Boy Who Grew Too Fast (1982); Goya (1986); The Wedding (1988); The Singing Child (1993).*

BALLETS: *Sebastian (1944); Errand into the Maze (1947); The Unicorn, the Gorgon, and the Manticore (1956).*

ORCH.: pf. conc. No.1 (1945), No.2 (1982); *Apocalypse*, sym.-poem (1951); vn. conc. (1952); triple conc. a tre (1970); *Halcyon Symphony* (1976); db. conc. (1983); *Goya Suite* (1987).

VOCAL: *The Death of the Bishop of Brindisi (1963); Landscapes and Remembrances (1976); Nocturne, sop., str. qt., hp. (1982); For the Death of Orpheus, ten., ch., orch. (1990); Oh llama de amor viva, bar., ch., orch. (1991); Gloria, ten., ch., orch. (1995); Jacob's Prayer, ch., orch. (1997).*

mensural music. In the 13th to 16th cents. the contrast to *musica plana* (plainsong). It is polyphonic mus. in which every note has a strictly determined value, distinct from the free rhythm of Gregorian chant.

mensural notation. System of mus. notation est. *c*.1250 by Franco of Cologne and used until 1600. All shapes of notes and pauses had definite time values, in contrast with system of preceding epoch (modal notation) in which pattern of series of ligatures was key to required values. Basis of modern system.

Mentzer, Susanne (*b* Philadelphia, 1957). Amer. mezzo-soprano. Début Houston 1981 (Albina in Rossini's *La donna del lago*). From 1982 sang with Dallas, Washington, Chicago, Philadelphia, and NY City Operas. Débuts: Eur. (Cologne) 1983; CG 1985; Salzburg Fest. 1987; NY Met 1989.

menuet (Fr.), **Menuett** (Ger.). See *minuet*. The spelling *menuetto*, used by Beethoven, is incorrect.

Menuhin, Hephzibah (*b* S. Francisco, 1920; *d* London, 1981). Amer. pianist, sister of Yehudi *Menuhin. Début, S. Francisco 1928. Soloist in concs. and frequent recitalist with her brother. Settled in Australia 1938, but continued to tour.

Menuhin, Yehudi (Lord Menuhin of Stoke d'Abernon) (*b* NY, 1916; *d* Berlin, 1999). Amer.-born violinist and conductor (Brit. cit. 1985).

Child prodigy. First public recital S. Francisco 1924. Début with orch. S. Francisco 1926, NY 1927. In 1929 played concs. by Bach, Beethoven, and Brahms in one programme with Berlin PO cond. *Walter, in Berlin, Dresden, and Paris. London début 1929, LSO cond. F. Busch. In 1932 recorded Elgar's conc., cond. by composer, and played work under his baton in Paris 1933. First recitals with sister Hephzibah in NY, London, and Paris 1934, followed by world tour of 73 cities. His career and talent continued beyond the 'prodigy' years. Bartók wrote the solo vn. sonata for him (1944). Gave many concerts for troops during World War II. After war continued his career as most famous of modern vn. virtuosi, but settled in Eng. and also began to conduct in 1957 (fest. at Gstaad). Salzburg Fest. début 1946 (Bach vn. conc. No.2, Mozarteum Orch. cond. Dorati), as cond. 1986 (Chamber Orch. of Europe). Art. dir. Bath Fest. 1959–69, conducting many concerts with own chamber orch. US début as cond. 1966. Founded Menuhin Sch. of Mus., now at Stoke d'Abernon, Surrey, 1963. Did much to encourage Western interest in Indian mus. Autobiography *Unfinished Journey* (1977). Hon. KBE 1965. OM 1987. Life peer 1993.

Mephisto Waltzes (*Mephistowalzer*). Mephisto is abbreviation for Mephistopheles. 4 works by Liszt. No.1, orig. for orch. as No.2 (*Der Tanz in der Dorfschenke*) of *2 Episodes from Lenau's* *Faust* (before 1861), was transcr. for pf. solo and pf. duet (1881); No.2, orig. for orch., transcr. pf. solo and duet (1881); No.3 for pf. (1883) orch. Riesenauer; No.4 for pf. (1885, pubd. 1952).

Mer, La (The Sea). 3 symphonic sketches for orch. by Debussy comp. 1903–5, f.p. Paris 1905; London 1908 (cond. Debussy). Movts. are named *De l'Aube à midi sur la mer* (From dawn to noon on the sea), *Jeux de vagues* (Play of the waves), and *Dialogue du vent et de la mer* (Dialogue of the wind and the sea).

Merbecke [Merbeck, Marbeck, Marbecke], **John** (b Windsor, c.1510; d Windsor, c.1585). Eng. composer and organist. Condemned to death as heretic 1543, but pardoned. In 1550 wrote first setting of prayer-book liturgy as authorized by 1549 Act of Uniformity. Compiled first biblical concordance in Eng. and wrote theological pamphlets and studies of Calvinism.

Mercadante, (Giuseppe) **Saverio** (Raffaele) (b Altamura, 1795; d Naples, 1870). It. composer. Early works were instr. and choral, but turned to opera in 1819 and wrote nearly 60 up to 1856. With *Il giuramento* (1837), he threw off the Rossinian idiom of his earlier works and developed greater dramatic power in the orch. in the style of Meyerbeer, but his works have failed to hold the stage except for occasional perfs. in Italy and in concert versions in Vienna. Choirmaster, Novara Cath., 1833. Dir., Naples Cons., 1840–70. Wrote 17 masses, orch. fantasies, songs, etc. Operas incl. *Maria Stuarda* (1821); *Elisa e Claudio* (1821); *Amleto* (1822); *Don Chisciotte*

(1829); *Francesca da Rimini* (1830–1); *I briganti* (1836); *Il bravo* (1839); *La Vestale* (1840); *Violetta* (1853). Blind from 1862.

Mercurio, Steven (b Bardonia, NY, 1956). Amer. composer and conductor. Ass. cond. Brooklyn PO 1984–7, NY Met 1987–90. Prin. cond. Opera Co. of Philadelphia from 1990. Mus. dir. Festival of Two Worlds (Spoleto and Charleston) from 1992. Devised new ending to Puccini's *Turandot* from Alfano sketches. Works incl. *For Lost Loved Ones*, orch. (1980–4); *A Moon for the Misbegotten*, vn., pf. (1987); *Serenade*, ten., orch. (1990).

Merikanto, Aarre (b Helsinki, 1893; d Helsinki, 1958). Finn. composer. Taught at Sibelius Acad., Helsinki, 1936–58 (prof. of comp. from 1951). Many of his works were not perf. until after his death, incl. the opera *Juha*, regarded by some as comparable with Janáček. Prin. works.

OPERA: *Juha* (1920–2).

ORCH.: syms.: No.1 (1916), No.2 (1918), No.3 (1953); pf. conc. No.1 (1913), No.2 (1937), No.3 (1955); vn. conc. No.1 (1916), No.2 (1925), No.3 (1931), No.4 (1954); vc. conc. No.1 (1919), No.2 (1941–4); *Lemminkäinen*, sym. suite (1916); conc. for vn., cl., hn., str. sextet (1925); *Notturno*, sym.-poem (1929).

CHAMBER MUSIC: str. qt. No.1 (1913), No.2 (1939); str. trio (1912); pf. trio (1917); nonet (1926); str. sextet (1932).

Merrick, Frank (b Clifton, Glos., 1886; d London, 1981). Eng. pianist and composer. First public appearance, Clifton 1895; London début 1903. Diploma of Honour, Rubinstein Competition, St Petersburg, 1910. Prof. of pf., RMCM 1911–29. On staff RCM 1929–56, TCL 1956–75. Comps. incl. 2 pf. concs. and 'completion' of Schubert's 'Unfinished' Sym., also settings of Esperanto poems. Espoused cause of many unfashionable composers and of Brit. composers, e.g. Ireland, Bax, Rawsthorne, etc. CBE 1978.

Merrie England. Light opera in 2 acts by *German to lib. by Basil Hood, introducing Queen Elizabeth I, Raleigh, and other Elizabethan characters. Comp. 1902. Prod. London (Savoy Theatre) 1902.

Merrill, Robert [Miller, Merrill] (b Brooklyn, NY, 1917; d NY, 2004). Amer. baritone. Début Trenton 1944 (Amonasro in *Aida*). Won Met Auditions of Air, 1945, making début there in Dec. 1945. Sang in Toscanini opera recordings. Long career at Met in roles such as Figaro, Rigoletto, Iago, and Scarpia. CG début 1967. Wrote autobiography *Once More from the Beginning* (NY 1965).

Merritt, Chris (Allan) (b Oklahoma City, 1952). Amer. tenor. Apprentice at Santa Fe Opera. Début Salzburg Landesth. 1978 (Lindoro in *L'Italiana in Algeri*). Augsburg Opera 1981–4. Débuts: NY City Opera 1981; Paris Opera 1983; CG 1985. Specialist in Rossini roles, singing at Pesaro.

Merry Widow, The (*Die lustige Witwe*). Operetta in 3 acts by Lehár to lib. by V. Léon and L. Stein after Meilhac's comedy *L'Attaché d'ambassade.* Comp. 1905. Prod. Vienna 1905 (first Widow was Mizzi Günther), London (Lily Elsie) and NY 1907. Merry Widow's name is Hanna Glawari.

Merry Wives of Windsor, The (Nicolai). See *Lustigen Weiber von Windsor, Die.*

messa di voce (It.). Placing of the voice. Practice in *bel canto* of singing a crescendo then a diminuendo on a held note. Not to be confused with *mezza voce.*

Messager, André (Charles Prosper) (*b* Montluçon, 1853; *d* Paris, 1929). Fr. composer, organist, and conductor. Org., St Sulpice, 1874. Cond., Paris Opéra-Comique 1898–1903, 1919–20. Cond. f.p. of Debussy's *Pelléas et Mélisande* (1902), which is ded. to him. Art. dir. CG 1901–6, dir. and chief cond. Paris Opéra 1907–15. Cond. Société des Concerts du Cons., 1908–19 (touring Argentina 1916, USA 1918). Wrote several successful light operas. Works incl.:

OPERAS: *La Béarnaise* (1885); *La Basoche* (1890); *Madame Chrysanthème* (1893); *Les p'tites Michu* (1897); **Véronique* (1898); *Fortunio* (1907); *Béatrice* (1914); **Monsieur Beaucaire* (1919).
BALLETS: *Les *deux pigeons* (1886); *Le Chevalier aux fleurs* (1897).
Also wrote sym. and pf. pieces.

Messa per i defunti (Mass for the Dead). See *Requiem.*

Messe des Morts (Mass of the Dead). See *Requiem.* For that by Berlioz, see *Grand' Messe des Morts.*

Messiaen, Olivier (Eugène Prosper Charles) (*b* Avignon, 1908; *d* Clichy, Hauts-de-Seine, 1992). Fr. composer, organist, and teacher. In his youth he studied Indian and Greek mus. rhythms, plainchant, and folk mus. He also notated the songs of all French birds, classifying them by region. Several of his works quote and make great use of birdsong. In 1931 he became organist of L'Église de la Trinité, Paris, holding the post for over 40 years. In 1936 he became a teacher at the École Normale de Musique and Schola Cantorum, and founded *Jeune France*, a group of young musicians, with Jolivet, Daniel Lesur, and Baudrier. He was imprisoned by the Germans for 2 years during the war, but on release, 1942, he was appointed a teacher at Paris Cons. (harmony, then analysis from 1947 and comp. from 1966). His pupils incl. Boulez, Stockhausen, Barraqué, Xenakis, Amy, Sherlaw Johnson, and Goehr. His 2nd wife, the pianist Yvonne Loriod, exercised great influence on his work.

Messiaen's mus., which is among the most influential and idiosyncratic of the century, was compounded from his deep Catholic faith, his celebration of human love, and his love of nature. He gave a new dimension of colour and intensity to org. mus., making special use of acoustic reverberations and contrasts of timbres. His harmony, rich and chromatic, derived from

Debussy's use of 7ths and 9ths and modal progressions of chords. In his orch. works he made use of the *ondes Martenot* in the vast *Turangalîla-symphonie* and of exotic perc. instrs., giving an oriental effect. Birdsong was also a major feature. His treatment of rhythm was novel, involving irregular metres, some of them originating in ancient Gr. procedures. Messiaen also acknowledged the supremacy of melody. Prin. works:

OPERA: **Saint François d'Assise* (lib. by comp., f.p. Paris 1983) (1975–83).
ORCH.: *Le Banquet eucharistique* (1928); *Les *Offrandes oubliées* (1930); *Le tombeau resplendissant* (1931); *Hymne au Saint Sacrement* (1932); *L'*Ascension* (1933); **Turangalîla-symphonie* (1946–8); *Réveil des oiseaux* (1953); **Oiseaux exotiques* (1955–6); **Chronochromie* (1960); *7 Haï-Kaï* (1962); *Couleurs de la cité céleste* (1963); **Et exspecto resurrectionem mortuorum* (1964); **Des canyons aux Étoiles* (1970–4); *Un vitrail et des oiseaux* (1986); *La ville d'en haut* (1987); *Éclairs sur l'au-delà* (1988–92); *Un sourire* (1989).
VOCAL & CHORAL: *2 Ballades de Villon*, v., pf. (1921); *3 Mélodies*, sop., pf. (1929); *La mort du nombre* (1929); *Mass*, 8 sop., 4 vn. (1933); *Vocalise*, sop., pf. (1935); **Poèmes pour Mi*, sop., pf. (1936), orch. (1937); *O sacrum convivium* (1937); *Chants de terre et de ciel* (1938); *3 Petites Liturgies de la présence divine*, women's ch., pf., ondes Martenot, orch. (1944); *Chants des Déportés*, sop., ten., ch., orch. (1945); **Harawi, chant d'amour et de mort*, sop., pf. (1945); *5 *Rechants*, 12 unacc. vv. (1948); *La *Transfiguration de Notre Seigneur Jésus-Christ*, ten., bar., ch., pf., orch. (1965–9).
PIANO: *8 Préludes* (1929); *Fantaisie burlesque* (1931); *Pièce pour le tombeau de Paul Dukas* (1936); **Visions de l'Amen*, 2 pf. (1943); *Rondeau* (1943); *20 *Regards sur l'Enfant Jésus* (1944); *Cantéyodjayâ* (1948); *4 Études de rythme* (1949–50); **Catalogue d'oiseaux* (1956–8); *La Fauvette des jardins* (1970); *Petites esquisses d'oiseaux* (1985).
ORGAN: *Variations Écossaises* (1928); *Le Banquet céleste* (1928); *Diptyque* (1929); *Apparition de l'Église éternelle* (1931); *L'*Ascension* (1934); *La *Nativité du Seigneur* (1935); *Les *Corps glorieux* (1939); *Messe de la Pentecôte* (1950); *Livre d'orgue* (1951); *Verset pour la fête de la dédicace* (1960); *Méditations sur le mystère de la Sainte Trinité* (1969); *Livre du Saint Sacrement* (1984).
MISC. INSTRS.: *Thème et Variations*, vn., pf. (1932); *Fêtes des belles eaux*, 6 ondes Martenot (1937); *2 Monodies en quart de ton*, ondes Martenot (1938); **Quatuor pour la fin du temps*, vn., cl., vc., pf. (1940); *Le Merle noir*, fl., pf. (1951); *Timbres-durées, musique concrète* (1952); *Le Tombeau de Jean-Pierre Guézec*, hn. (1971).

Messiah. Oratorio by Handel to lib. selected from scriptures by Charles Jennens. Comp. between 22 Aug. and 14 Sept. 1741, though parts are adaptations from other works by Handel. F.p. Dublin, 13 April 1742; London, 23 March 1743; Boston, Mass., 25 Dec. 1818 (extracts in NY 1770). There is no single definitive version, Handel having altered, rewritten, and added numbers for various perfs. It became the custom in the 19th cent. to perf. *Messiah* with grossly inflated forces, but in the mid-20th cent. various performing edns. restored the work nearer to its original proportions and reverted to the correct tempo and rhythm for many nos. Mozart composed additional accs. for *Messiah* for an occasion when no org. was available to provide the figured bass, and these are still frequently used.

Messing (Ger.). Brass. So *Messinginstrumente*, brass instr.

mesto (It.). Mournful, sad. So *mestizia*, sadness.

mesure (Fr.). (1) measure, bar.
(2) time; e.g. *à la mesure = a tempo*.

metallophone. Percussion instr. comprising series of tuned metal bars arr. in a single or double row. *Orff scored for it in some of his comps. Far Eastern versions influenced development of *glockenspiel and *vibraphone.

Metamorphosen. Study in C minor for 23 solo str. by R. Strauss, comp. 1944–5 during the destruction of the Ger. cultural world in which he had lived. Quotes from funeral march of Beethoven's *Eroica* Sym. F.p. Zurich 1946 cond. Paul Sacher; f. Eng. p. London, Dec. 1946 (Boyd Neel Orch.).

Metamorphoses after Ovid, Six. Work for solo ob., Op.49, by Britten, comp. 1951. Movts. are entitled *Pan, Phaeton, Niobe, Bacchus, Narcissus*, and *Arethusa*. F.p. Thorpeness 1951 (Joy Boughton).

metamorphosis. Term used to describe manner in which composer may change tempo, rhythm, and notes of a theme yet preserve its essential and recognizable characteristics. Employed by Liszt in his symphonic poems and by Elgar and Franck in syms. Hindemith's *Symphonic Metamorphosis of Themes by Weber* and Britten's 6 *Metamorphoses after Ovid* are modern examples of the device. Strauss's use of the term in his *Metamorphosen* refers to Goethe, not to mus. form.

Metamorphosis of Themes by Weber, Symphonic (Hindemith). See *Symphonic Metamorphosis of Themes by Weber*.

Metastasio [Trapassi], **Pietro Antonio Domenico Bonaventura** (*b* Rome, 1698; *d* Vienna, 1782). It. poet and librettist. Pubd. first work at 14 and later enjoyed protection of the singer Marianna Benti-Bulgarelli. Lived in Vienna as court poet from 1730 and devoted himself to providing composers with opera libs., mainly on classical subjects. They were set over 800 times by different composers. Some texts from his vast output were used up to 70 times. *Artaserse* was set by 40 composers. Among those who set his libs. were Galuppi, Gluck, Handel, Hasse (who set nearly all), Jommelli, Koželuh, Mercadante, Meyerbeer, Mozart, Paisiello, Piccinni, Spontini, etc. Gluck's opera reforms were directed against the highly formal, artificial, and conventional nature of Metastasio's works, with the development of the plot being halted continually for dis-

plays of vocal agility. Among Metastasio's libs. were *Didone abbandonata, La Clemenza di Tito*, and *Il Rè Pastore*.

Metcalf, John (*b* Swansea, 1946). Welsh composer. Assoc. art. dir. (from 1986) and comp.-in-residence (from 1991), Banff Centre, School of Fine Arts, Alberta. Works incl. operas *The Journey* (1981), *Tornrak* (1986–90), *Chair in Love* (2005); mus. th. *The Crossing* (1981); *The Boundaries of Time*, cantata (1985); hn. conc. (1972), cl. conc. (1982), *Music of Changes*, orch. (1981), *Orchestral Variations* (1990); pf. trio (1988); *Museum of the Air*, mez., orch. (1997); *Paradise Haunts*, vn., orch. (1998); *Passus*, orch. (2000); *Mapping Wales*, hp., str. (2001); *Plain Chants*, sop./mez., unacc. ch. (2001); *Cello Sym.*, vc., orch. (2004); *Line Dance*, str. (2005); and songs.

metre. Term used of regular succession of rhythmical impulses, or beats, in poetry and mus., e.g. 3/4 and 6/8 being described as different kinds of metres. Rhythm is no longer accepted as a sufficiently precise definition, *metre* being considered as the basic pulse and rhythm as the actual time-patterns of the notes within a measure. E.g., in 3/4 the 3 beats—strong, weak, weak—are metrical, while the time-values of the notes actually heard are the rhythm.

metrical psalm. A psalm versified in a regular syllabic metre which thus can be sung to a hymn-tune. Brought to Britain by Calvinists fleeing to Eng. and Scotland from Geneva. Famous treasury of Eng. sacred tunes is Sternhold and Hopkins's metrical psalter (London 1562). It was followed by other such psalters (Este's 1592, Ravenscroft's 1621, Playford's 1677, Tate and Brady's 1696).

metric modulation. Term and technique introduced by Amer. composer Elliott *Carter for changing the rhythm (not necessarily the metre) from one section to another.

metronome. Apparatus for sounding an adjustable number of beats per minute and therefore for fixing the tempo of a comp. An early form, called *chronomètre*, was available at end of 17th cent. and further experiments followed. The idea of the clockwork model patented by *Maelzel seems to have been appropriated from the Dutch inventor D. N. Winkel. Maelzel est. a metronome factory in Paris, 1816. The one most commonly used is a pyramidal wooden instrument at the front of which a perpendicular steel strip, about 7½″ long by ⅛″ wide, is pivoted. The principle is that of a double pendulum (an oscillating rod weighted at both ends). The upper weight is movable along the steel strip, and according to its position on the rod the number of oscillations per minute can be made to vary between 40 and 208. The rod beats (or 'ticks') as it swings back and forth and a bell may be incorporated which can be set to ring every 2, 3, or 4 beats. Maelzel's graduated scale, fixed to the case, gives speed of oscillation. A composer who wants 78 quarternote (crotchet) beats in a minute will write

'M.M. (Maelzel metronome) ♩ = 78'. A spiral spring, which is wound up like a clock, keeps the instrument beating for a considerable period. Battery and electronically operated metronomes have been marketed. A pocket metronome shaped like a wrist-watch was designed in Switzerland about 1945 and others have been invented which can be synchronized to cope with the complex rhythms found in many modern scores.

It should be mentioned that some composers' metronome markings are suspect. Editors of early works have in many cases added metronome marks which they think are feasible. The ticking of Maelzel's metronome is supposed to have inspired the theme of the 2nd movt. of Beethoven's 8th sym. Several 20th-cent. composers have incorporated the ticking of actual metronomes into their scores, e.g. *Ligeti's sym.-poem for 100 metronomes and Gordon *Crosse's *Play Ground*.

Metropolitan Opera House. Chief Amer. opera house, now a constituent of NY's *Lincoln Center for the Performing Arts. Opened Sept., 1966, with Barber's *Antony and Cleopatra*. Seating capacity 3,800. Orig. 'Met' opened 1883, with *Faust*. After first season, Leopold Damrosch was appointed art. dir., but died before his first season was over and was succeeded by Anton Seidl and by Walter Damrosch, son of Leopold, who remained until 1890–1, giving all operas in Ger. Singers at the Met in the period up to 1903 incl. Nilsson, Materna, Sembrich, Nordica, Eames, the de Reszkes, Calvé, Melba, Plançon, Maurel, and Scotti. In 1903 Heinrich Conried became manager, engaging Caruso, Fremstad, Farrar, and Chaliapin. In 1907 he brought Mahler as cond., but resigned in 1908 and was followed by the joint direction of Andreas Dippel and Giulio Gatti-Casazza who engaged Toscanini as cond. Dippel resigned in 1910 and Gatti-Casazza remained until 1935. An outstanding occasion was the f.p. in 1910 of *La Fanciulla del West*, with Caruso, Destinn, and Toscanini. Toscanini resigned in 1914–15 and was followed by a group of conductors among whom Bodanzky, Serafin, and Wolff were outstanding. During Gatti-Casazza's régime operas by Strauss, Janáček, Respighi, and others had their first Amer. performances. Gigli, Ponselle, Pinza, Flagstad, Leider, Melchior, Muzio, Jeritza, and Tibbett were among the principal singers. Gatti-Casazza's successor was Herbert Witherspoon, who died almost immediately and the management passed to Edward Johnson, a member of the company since 1922. In his 15 years he encouraged Amer. singers, e.g. Warren, Peerce, Tucker, Traubel, Thebom, and strengthened the conducting by engaging Stiedry, Walter, Busch, Szell, Reiner, and others. From 1950 to 1972, Rudolf Bing was manager. In his régime stage techniques were modernized and theatrical producers engaged. He extended the season from 30 to 45 weeks. Great singers in his era incl. Callas, Tebaldi, Price, Merrill, de los Angeles, Bergonzi, and Siepi. Bing was succeeded by Goeran Gentele, who was killed before taking office, though not before he had appointed the Met's first mus. dir. Rafael Kubelik. The manager from 1972 was Schuyler Chapin. He appointed James Levine mus. dir. in 1975 and artistic control has increasingly passed to the cond. Chapin left in 1975 and was succeeded by Anthony Bliss 1975–85, Bruce Crawford 1986–9, Hugh Southern 1989–90, Joseph Volpe 1990–2006, and Peter Gelb from 2006. First broadcasts from Met 12 Jan. 1910 (Act II of *Tosca*), 13 Jan. (*Cav.* and *Pag.*). NBC relays began Christmas Day 1931 (*Hänsel und Gretel*) and since 1932 the Saturday matinées have been relayed nationally. Corigliano's *The *Ghosts of Versailles* (1991) was first opera commissioned by Met since 1966.

Mewton-Wood, Noel (*b* Melbourne, 1922; *d* London, 1953). Australian pianist. London début 1940 (Beethoven's C major conc., cond. Beecham). Regarded as one of greatest pianists of his day. Brilliant exponent of Bliss's conc., Tippett's 1st sonata, and of works by Busoni and Britten. Acc. Pears in song-cycles by Tippett. Gave f.p. of rev. version of Britten's pf. conc. 1946.

Meyer, Ernest (Hermann) (*b* Berlin, 1905; *d* Berlin, 1988). Ger. musicologist and composer. After meeting *Eisler in 1929, joined Ger. Communist party and cond. workers' choruses. With advent of Nazis, fled to London where he was helped by Alan *Bush and cond. Labour Choral Union. In 1948 went to E. Berlin as prof. and dir. of musicological inst. of Humboldt Univ. until 1970. Wrote book on Eng. chamber mus. from Middle Ages to Purcell (1946, rev. 1982). Comps. incl. opera *Reiter der Nacht* (1969–72); sym. for pf. and orch.; vn. conc.; hp. conc.; va. conc.; sym.; 6 str. qts.; pf. trio; choral works; and over 200 mass songs.

Meyer, Kerstin (Margareta) (*b* Stockholm, 1928). Swedish mezzo-soprano. Début Stockholm 1952 (Azucena in *Il trovatore*). Guest singer in opera Vienna, Venice, Hamburg, Berlin, from 1956. Sang in Eng. from 1960. Débuts: Salzburg Fest. 1957; CG 1960; NY Met 1960; Glyndebourne 1961; Bayreuth 1962. Striking singing-actress, notably in modern operas. Dir., Stockholm opera sch. from 1984. Hon. CBE 1985.

Meyerbeer, Giacomo [Beer, Jakob Liebmann] (*b* Berlin, 1791; *d* Paris, 1864). Ger. composer who worked mainly in Paris. After receiving legacy from relative named Meyer converted his name into Meyerbeer, 1810. Child prodigy pianist, playing Mozart conc. in Berlin at age 11. His comic opera was a failure in Vienna, where he was urged by Salieri to study vocal methods in It. He fell under Rossini's spell in 1815 and wrote 6 It. operas between 1817 and 1824, all successful, especially *Il Crociato in Egitto*. Weber advised him to turn to Ger. opera, but after the Paris première of *Il Crociato* in 1826 he concentrated on Fr. opera, spending the next few years assimilating Fr. history and character. He collaborated with the librettist Scribe and their first opera, *Robert le*

Diable, in 5 acts and on a grand scale, was an unprecedented success. This was followed by *Les Huguenots* and *Le Prophète*. He was *Generalmusíkdirektor* in Berlin 1842–9, during which time he wrote *Ein Feldlager in Schlesien* for Jenny *Lind, later incorporating some of its nos. into *L'Étoíle du Nord*. The success of Meyerbeer's pageant-like operas irked Wagner (who nevertheless learned from them in early works like *Rienzi*) and Meyerbeer, born of Jewish parentage, was bitterly attacked in Wagner's pamphlet *Das Judentum in der Musik* in spite of the fact that Meyerbeer had assisted him early in his career. He returned to Paris in 1863 to supervise rehearsals of his longest opera, *L'Africaine*, on which he had been working for nearly 25 years but he became ill and died. It had been customary to deride Meyerbeer for an eclecticism which lacked sufficient inner conviction to give his operas life beyond their day and away from the spectacular dramatic productions they received in Paris. Revivals of his operas, however, have revealed virtues which were his alone, and, as with so many other figures in mus. history, it would be rash to write him off as forgotten. Prin. works:

OPERAS: *Jephtas Gelübde* (1812); *Wirth und Gast* (1813, rev. 1820 as *Alimelek*); *Romilda e Costanza* (1817); *Semiramide Riconosciuta* (1819); *Emma di Resburgo* (1819); *Margherita d'Anjou* (1820); *L'esule di Granata* (1822); *Il Crociato in Egitto* (1824); *Robert le Diable* (1831); *Les Huguenots* (1836); *Le *Prophète* (1836–40); *Ein Feldlager in Schlesien* (1844, rev. 1847 as *Vielka*); *L'*Étoíle du Nord* (1854); *Le Pardon de Ploërmel* or *Dinorah* (1859); *L'*Africaine* (1837–64). Also called oratorio, songs, and church mus.

Meyerowitz, Jan [Hans-Hermann] (*b* Breslau [now Wroclaw, Poland], 1913; *d* Colmar, nr Labaroche, 1998). Ger.-born composer (Amer. cit. 1951). Settled in USA 1946, teaching at Tanglewood 1948–51, Brooklyn 1954–61, and in NY from 1962. Works incl. 9 operas, e.g. *Esther* (1957); choral works incl. *The Glory Around His Head* (1955), *Stabat Mater, e. e. cummings Cantata* (1949–56), *Emily Dickinson Cantata* (1948), *Robert Herrick Cantata* (1948–54); Sym. *Midrash Esther* (1957); fl. conc., vc. sonata, songs, etc.

mezzo, mezza (It.). Half. *mezza voce*, half-voice, i.e. half the vocal (or instr.) power possible. (Not to be confused with *messa di voce*.) *mezzo-forte*, half-loud, i.e. neither loud nor soft.

mezzo-soprano (It.). Half-soprano. Female (or artificial male) v. midway between sop. and cont. Vocal range from B below middle C upwards for 2 octaves. Several operatic roles written for sops. are traditionally sung by and better suited to mezzos, e.g. Dorabella in *Così fan tutte*, Carmen, Oktavian in *Der Rosenkavalier*, the Composer in *Ariadne auf Naxos*. Occasionally a singer will describe herself as 'mezzo-contralto', meaning a little lower in range than mezzo-soprano.

mf. = *mezzo forte*, half-loud.

M.G. = *main gauche* (Fr.). Left hand.

mi. See *me*.

Mi. *Messiaen's intimate name for his first wife, the violinist Claire Delbos, for whom he wrote his *Poèmes pour Mi* (1936).

Miaskovsky, Nikolai. See *Myaskovsky, Nikolay*.

Michaels-Moore, Anthony (*b* Grays, Essex, 1957). Brit. baritone. Opera début (Opera North) 1985 (Messenger in *Oedipus Rex*). Won Pavarotti Comp. 1988. On staff of CG from 1987. Débuts: ENO 1987; Amer. (Philadelphia Opera) 1989; La Scala début 1993; NY Met 1996. Sang Don Ferdinand in f. stage p. of Gerhard's *The Duenna*, Madrid 1992.

Micheau, Janine (*b* Toulouse, 1914; *d* Paris, 1976). Fr. soprano. Début Paris (Opéra-Comique) 1933 (Newspaper Girl in *Louise*). Paris Opéra from 1940, creating Manuela in Milhaud's *Bolívar* (1950). CG 1937; S. Francisco 1938; Chicago 1956. Prof. of singing, Paris Cons. from 1960. Notable Mélisande and Micaela.

Michelangeli, Arturo Benedetto (*b* Brescia, 1920; *d* Lugano, 1995). It. pianist. 1st prize Geneva Int. Mus. Comp. 1939. Prof. of pf., Bologna Cons. 1939–41. Eng. début 1946. Amer. début 1948. Toured Russ. 1964. Art. dir., int. pianists' acad., Brescia 1964–9. Remarkable artist, but appearances infrequent.

Michelangelo Buonarroti, Suite on Verses of. 11 settings by Shostakovich, Op.145, for bass and pf., comp. 1974, f.p. Leningrad 1975. Orch. version, Op.145a, 1974, f.p. Moscow 1975.

Michelangelo Sonnets (Britten). See *Seven Sonnets of Michelangelo*.

mi contra fa. The *tritone (interval of 3 whole tones), from F up or down to B, difficult to sing, thus giving rise to the saying 'Mi contra fa diabolus est in musica' ('Mi against fa [the Hexachord system names for these notes] is the devil in music').

microtone. All intervals which lie between the semi-tones of the 12-note, equal-tempered tuning system. Several 20th-cent. composers have experimented in microtones and quarter-tones. Joseph Yasser proposed a scale of 19 notes per octave and Adriaan Fokker 31 per octave, but little mus. has been written using these temperaments because instrs. are not designed to play them. Elec. instrs., however, enable division of intervals other than the octave in equal intervals, as in *Stockhausen's *Gesang der Jünglinge*. Among the earliest composers to employ microtones were *Ives, *Bartók, and *Bloch but as incidental features. More systematic use was devised by A. *Hába, J. *Carrillo, and H. Partch.

middle C. The note C found at approx. middle of pf. kbd., commonly tuned to 256 Hz. The pitch represented by note on 1st ledger line below treble stave, or 1st above bass stave.

Midi, Le (Haydn). See *Matin, Le.*

Midori [Goto, Mi Dori] (*b* Osaka, 1971). Japanese violinist. Début NY 1982 (NYPO cond. Mehta). Toured Asia with NYPO. Subsequently soloist with leading Amer., Brit., and Eur. orchs. Played at White House 1983. NY recital début (Carnegie Hall) 1990.

Midsummer Marriage, The. Opera in 3 acts by *Tippett to his own lib. Comp. 1946–52. Prod. London 1955, S. Francisco 1983, NY 1993. *Ritual Dances* from Act II are often perf. as concert piece and were f.p. before opera was prod. (Basle 1953, Liverpool 1954).

Midsummer Night's Dream, A. Play (1593–4) by Shakespeare which has attracted several composers. (1) *The Fairy Queen*, 1691, adaptation (by E. Settle?) of Shakespeare for which *Purcell wrote incidental mus. Shakespeare's text is not quoted.

(2) *Mendelssohn composed an Ov. in E major, Op.26, in 1826 when he was 17, adding additional items of incidental mus., Op.61, for a prod. of the play at Potsdam in Oct. 1843, these being: 1. *Scherzo* (entr'acte after Act 1). 2. *Melodrama*. 2a. *Fairy March* (Act 2). 3. *You spotted snakes* (2 sop. and ch.) (Act 2). 4. *Melodrama* (Act 2). 5. *Intermezzo* (entr'acte after Act 2). 6. *Melodrama* (Act 3). 7. *Nocturne* (entr'acte after Act 3). 8. *Melodrama* (Act 4). 9. *Wedding March* (after end of Act 4). 10. *Melodrama*. 10a. *Funeral March* (Act 5). 11. *Bergomask Dance* (Act 5). 12. *Melodrama*. 12a. *Finale* (Act 5).

(3) Incidental mus. by *Orff commissioned by Nazis when Mendelssohn's mus. was banned. 1st version 1939 (f.p. Frankfurt 1939; withdrawn), 2nd version 1944 (withdrawn), 3rd version 1952 (f.p. Darmstadt 1952), 4th version 1964 (f.p. Stuttgart 1964).

(4) Opera in 3 acts by *Britten to lib. (Shakespeare's text) abbreviated by composer and Peter Pears. Comp. 1959–60. Prod. Aldeburgh 1960, S. Francisco and CG 1961, NY 1963, Glyndebourne 1981.

Migenes, Julia (*b* NY, 1945). Amer. soprano. As child, appeared at NY Met as Butterfly's son. Sang on Broadway in *West Side Story* and *Fiddler on the Roof*. NY City Opera début 1965 (Annina in *The Saint of Bleecker Street*). Vienna Volksoper 1973–8 in Mozart roles. S. Francisco 1978; NY Met début 1979; Geneva 1983; Vienna State Opera 1983; CG 1987. Sang Carmen in Rosi's film, 1984.

Mighty Handful (Russ., *Moguchaya kuchka*). Term coined by critic V. Stasov and applied to the 5 Russ. composers Balakirev, Borodin, Cui, Mussorgsky, and Rimsky-Korsakov who were consciously nationalist in their approach to mus. Sometimes known as 'the *Five' or the 'Mighty Five'.

Mignon. Opera in 3 acts by Ambroise Thomas to lib. by Barbier and Carré based on Goethe's novel *Wilhelm Meisters Lehrjahre* (1795–6). Prod. Paris 1866, London 1870, New Orleans 1871, NY 1883.

Mihály, András (*b* Budapest, 1917; *d* Budapest, 1993). Hung. composer. Teacher of chamber mus. Budapest Acad. from 1950. Founder and cond. Budapest Chamber Ens. 1968. Dir., Hung. State opera 1978–87. Works incl. 3 syms.; vc. conc.; pf. conc.; vn. conc.; opera *Together and Alone* (1965); 3 str. qts.; choral works, etc.

Mikado, The, or The Town of Titipu. Operetta in 2 acts, comp. 1884–5 by Sullivan to lib. by Gilbert. Prod. London, NY, Chicago, and Sydney, NSW, 1885.

Mikrokosmos. 153 'progressive pieces for pianoforte' by Bartók comp. between 1926 and 1939 and pubd. in 6 vols. 7 pieces (Nos. 69, 113, 123, 127, 135, 145, 146) transcr. by Bartók for 2 pf. 7 pieces (Nos. 102, 117, 137, 139, 142, 151, 153) transcr. by Tibór Sérly for orch. 5 pieces (Nos. 102, 108, 116, 139, 142) transcr. by Sérly for str. qt.

Milan. See *La Scala*.

Milanov [Kunc], **Zinka** (*b* Zagreb, 1906; *d* Manhattan, 1989). Croatian soprano. Début Ljubljana 1927 (Leonora in *Il trovatore*). Prin. sop., Zagreb Opera 1928–35, singing 350 perfs. all in Croatian. Débuts: Salzburg Fest. 1937; NY Met 1937, appearing there regularly until 1966, excluding 1941–2 and 1947–50; Chicago 1940; S. Francisco 1943; La Scala 1950; CG 1956.

Milanova, Stoika (*b* Plovdiv, Bulgaria, 1945). Bulgarian violinist. 1st prize City of London int. competition 1970, also Flesch prize. London début 1970. Hongkong Fest. with Hallé Orch. 1976. Recitals with Radu Lupu.

Mildenburg, Anna von (*b* Vienna, 1872; *d* Vienna, 1947). Austrian soprano. Début Hamburg 1895 (Brünnhilde) under *Mahler, whose mistress she was for a time and about whom she wrote a valuable book of memoirs. Became eminent in Wagner: Bayreuth 1897 (Kundry in *Parsifal*), CG 1906 (Isolde, and Elisabeth in *Tannhäuser*). Sang at Vienna Opera in Mahler's directorship and was regular member of co. 1908–16. Outstanding Klytemnästra in *Elektra* (first London Klytemnästra, 1910). Prof. of singing, Munich Acad. of Mus. from 1921 and stage dir. Nat. Th., Munich, 1921–6. Salzburg Fest. début 1922 as actress, recital 1927. Last appearance, Augsburg 1930 (Klytemnästra). Taught in Berlin 1938. Married the writer Hermann Bahr, 1909, with whom she wrote *Bayreuth und das Wagnertheater* (Leipzig, 1910).

Mildmay, Audrey (*b* Herstmonceux, 1900; *d* London, 1953). Eng. soprano. Toured N. Amer. 1927–8 as Polly in *The Beggar's Opera*. Sang with Carl Rosa and SW. Married John *Christie of *Glyndebourne, 1931, who built opera house for her and launched famous summer opera fest. 1934. Sang Susanna (*Le nozze di Figaro*), Zerlina (*Don Giovanni*), and Norina (*Don Pasquale*) at Glyndebourne. Retired 1943. Edinburgh Fest. was her idea.

Milhaud, Darius (*b* Aix-en-Provence, 1892; *d* Geneva, 1974). Fr. composer and pianist. Entered Paris Cons. 1909, studying with Gédalge, Widor, and d'Indy. Attaché at Fr. legation, Rio de Janeiro, 1917–19, meeting Claudel, poet-diplomat, who was to write libs. for several of his works. Returned Paris 1919, becoming known as one of *Les* *Six who owed allegiance to Satie and Cocteau. Visited USA 1922 as pianist in his own works. Left Fr. 1940, settling in USA, teaching at Mills Coll., Oakland, Calif., 1940–71 and in summers at Aspen, Colorado. Also taught at Paris Cons. 1947–71. Extremely prolific composer, despite handicap of precarious health from late 1920s when rheumatic condition necessitated use of wheelchair. Dominating feature of his mus. is use of *polytonality. Experimented with many instr. combinations and also with tape. Prin. works:

OPERAS: *Esther de Carpentras* (1910–14); *La brebis égarée* (1910–15); *Les Malheurs d'Orphée* (1925); *Le Pauvre Matelot* (1926); trilogy: *L'enlèvement d'Europe* (1927), *L'abandon d'Ariane* (1928), *La déliverance de Thésée* (1928); **Christophe Colomb* (1928); *Maximilien* (1930); *Médée* (1938); *Bolívar* (1943); *David (1952); *Fiesta* (1958); *La Mère Coupable* (based on 3rd play of Beaumarchais's Figaro trilogy) (1964–5); *St Louis* (1970).

BALLETS: *L'Homme et son désir* (1918); *Le* *Bœuf sur le toit (1919); *Les* **Mariés de la Tour Eiffel* (1921); *La* **Création du monde* (1923); *Le Train bleu* (1924); *La Bien-Aimée* (after Schubert and Liszt) (1928); *La Mort d'un tyran* (1933); *Mme Miroir* (1948); *Jeux de printemps* (Imagined Wing) (1944); *The Bells* (1946); *Les Rêves de Jacob* (1949); *Vendange* (1952); *Le rose des vents* (1958); *La branche des oiseaux* (1965).

THEATRE: *Agamemnon*, incidental mus. to Claudel adaptation of Aeschylus (1913–14); *Protée*, incidental mus. to drama by Claudel (1913–19); *Les Choëphores*, Claudel, after Aeschylus (1915); *Les Euménides*, Claudel, after Aeschylus (1917–22); *L'Annonce faite à Marie*, incidental mus. to Claudel drama (1932); *Le Jeu de Robin et Marion*, mystery play after *Adam de la Halle (1951); *L'Opéra des gueux*, arr. of *The Beggar's Opera* (1937).

ORCH.: Syms. Nos. 1–12 (1940–62, No.3 *Hymnus ambrosianus* with ch.); 3 syms. for small orch. (*Le Printemps* (1917), *Pastorale* (1918), *Sérénade* (1921)); *Dixtur à cordes* (1921); *Dixtur d'instruments à vents* (1922), 10 str. instr., 10 wind instr., 4 vv., ob., vc.) (1917–22); *Saudades do Brazil* (1920–1, orig. for pf.); *Suite provençale* (1937); *Suite française* (1945); va. conc. (1927); 2 vc. concs. (1935, 1946); cl. conc. (1941); hp. conc. (1954).

PIANO & ORCH.: 5 concs.; 5 *Études* (1920); *Le Carnaval d'Aix* (1926); Conc. for 2 pf. (1942).

VIOLIN & ORCH.: *Concertino de printemps* (1934); 3 concs. (1927–58) (No.3 *Concerto Royal*).

MISC.: Conc., perc., small orch. (1930); Suite for harmonica (or vn.), orch. (1942); *L'Apothéose de Molière*, hpd., str. (1948); conc. for *marimba, vib., orch. (1947); *Concertino d'hiver*, tb., str. (1953).

CHAMBER MUSIC: 18 str. qts. (1912–51; Nos. 14 and 15 can be played separately or together as an octet, 1949); 2 vn. sonatas (1911, 1917); *La*

**Cheminée du roi René*, suite (1939); str. trio (1947); str. septet (1964); sonatinas for vn. and va., fl. and pf., cl. and pf.; sonatas for va., and for vn. and hpd.; *Élégie* for vc. and pf. (1945).

PIANO: Sonata No.1 (1916), No.2 (1949); *Saudades do Brazil* (1920–1, also orch.); *L'Album de Madame Bovary* (1934); *Le Candélabre à sept branches* (1951); *Scaramouche for 2 pf. (1939); *Paris*, suite of 6 pieces for 4 pf. (1948); *6 Danses en 3 mouvements*, 2 pf. (1970).

VOCAL & CHORAL: *Machines agricoles*, v., 7 instr. (1919); *Catalogue des fleurs*, v., chamber orch. (1920); Sym. for vocal qt., ob., vc. (1923); *Cantate de la paix* (1937); *Les quatre éléments*, sop., ten., orch. (1938); *Cantate de la guerre*, unacc. ch. (1940); *Kaddisch*, v., ch., org. (1945); *Sabbath Morning Service*, bar., ch., org. (1947); *Cantate de l'initiation*, ch., orch. (1960); *Pacem in terris*, ch., orch. (1963).

Also many songs and music for about 30 films, 1929–59, incl. *Madame Bovary* (dir. J. Renoir, 1933) and *Péron et Evita* (1958).

Militärtrommel (Ger.). *side-drum.

Military, The. Nickname of Haydn's Sym. in G, No.100 in Breitkopf edn., comp. 1794 in London. So called because of 'military' instrs. and solo tpt.-call in 2nd movt.

military band. This term is used in Britain to describe either an actual army (or naval or airforce) band or for one on the same model, i.e. comprising both brass and woodwind instr. The composition of such bands varies widely in different countries, and even in different regimental or other units of the same country. One common Brit. combination is as follows: (a) 1 picc. (or fl., or both); 1 ob.; 1 small cl., 12–14 ordinary cl., 2 bass cl.; 1 alto and 1 ten. sax; 2 bn. (b) 4 hn., 2 bars., 2 euphoniums, 4 basses (bombardons). (c) 4 cornets; 2 tpt.; 3 tb. (d) 2 drummers with a variety of perc. instr. Sometimes, when conditions of perf. allow, 1 or 2 str. db. may appear, as an alternative to the same number of bass wind instr. Bands in USA vary from the above scheme merely in detail.

The score and parts of the military band, unlike those of the brass band, employ the ordinary orch. system of notation. The term 'wind band' is used in USA.

Milkina, Nina (*b* Moscow, 1919). Russ.-born pianist. Début Paris 1930, with Lamoureux Orch. Specialist in Mozart and 18th-cent. chamber mus. Settled in Eng.

Miller, (Alton) **Glenn** (*b* Clarinda, Iowa, 1904; *d* between London and Paris, 1944). Amer. trombonist, band-leader, composer, and arranger. Played in various bands from 1921 until joining Dorsey brothers' orch. 1934. Devised reed section of cl. and 4 sax. while with Ray Noble 1935. Formed own band 1937, dissolved 1938; second band, formed 1938, became one of best-known and most popular in the world because of its characteristic sound, exemplified in recordings such as *Moonlight Serenade, Chattanooga Choo-Choo, In the Mood, American Patrol,* etc. Disbanded 1942 when Miller joined US Army. In 1944 assembled service band and went to Eng. same year. Disappeared on flight to Paris, Dec. 1944, aircraft never being found. Band continued under other leaders, notably Ray McKinley (1956–65).

Miller, (Sir) **Jonathan** (*b* London, 1934). Eng. stage director. Qualified in medicine, Cambridge Univ., where he was one of four co-authors and performers in revue *Beyond the fringe,* 1961. High reputation as prod. of Shakespeare and other classics. Opera début 1974, prod. Brit. première of Goehr's *Arden must die,* New Opera Co.; Glyndebourne 1975 (*The *Cunning Little Vixen*). Worked regularly with Kent Opera and ENO. NY Met début 1991; CG 1995. CBE 1983. Knighted 2002.

Millo, Aprile (*b* NY, 1958). Amer. soprano. Sang High Priestess in *Aida* while at San Diego Opera Center 1977–80. Début Salt Lake City 1980 (Aida). La Scala début 1982; WNO 1984; NY Met 1984.

Millöcker, Carl (*b* Vienna, 1842; *d* Baden, 1899). Austrian composer and conductor. Cond. posts at Graz and Vienna, where he was cond. and composer at Theater an der Wien 1869–83. Prolific composer of operettas, best-known of which are *Der tote Gast* (1865), *Der *Bettelstudent* (1882), *Gasparone* (1884), *Der arme Jonathan* (1890).

Mills, Charles (*b* Asheville, N. Carolina, 1914; *d* NY, 1982). Amer. composer. Played in jazz bands from age 17. Winner of several prizes. Commissioned by *Mitropoulos to compose work for NYPO, 1951. Prin. works incl. 6 syms.; pf. conc.; fl. conc.; *Theme and Variations* for orch.; ob. concertino; and many chamber works, some involving jazz groups.

Milner, Anthony (Francis Dominic) (*b* Bristol, 1925; *d* Alfaz del Pi, Alicante, 2002). Eng. composer. Taught at Morley Coll. 1946–62. Dir. and harpsichordist, London Cantata Ens., 1954–65. Lect. at RCM 1961–89 and at King's Coll., London, 1966–71. Lect. in mus., Goldsmith's Coll., London Univ. 1974–80. Visited USA as lecturer 1965–7. Also writer on mus. Works mainly choral, with strong religious (RC) basis, incl.:

ORCH.: sym. No.1 (1972), No.2, ten., ch., orch. (1978), No.3 (1986); *Variations* (1958); *Divertimento* for str. (1961); Chamber Sym. (1968); conc. for symphonic wind band (1979); conc. for str. (1982); ob. conc. (1994).

CHORUS & ORCH.: *Salutatio angelica* (1948); *The City of Desolation* (1955); *St Francis* (1956); *The Water and the Fire* (1960–1); *Break to be Built, O Stone* (1962); *Festival Te Deum* (1967); *Roman Spring* (1969); *Motet for Peace* (1973); *Emmanuel,* counterten., ch., org., str. (1975); *Festival Chant,* ch., org. (1980); *The Gates of Spring* (1988); *The Gates of Summer,* sop., ten., ch., str. (1990).

UNACC. CHORUS: *Mass* (1951); *Benedic anima mea Dominum* (1954); *The Harrowing of Hell* (1956); *Cast*

Wide the Folding Doorways of the East (1963); *Ashmansworth* (1963); *The Leaden Echo and the Golden Echo* (1974).

VOICE & INSTR.: *The Song of Akhenaten,* sop., chamber orch. (1957); *Our Lady's Hours,* sop., pf. (1957); *Midway,* mez., chamber orch. (1974).

CHAMBER MUSIC: ob. qt. (1953); wind quintet (1964); str. qt. (1975); pf. sonata (1989).

Milnes [Blumer], **Rodney** (*b* Stafford, 1936). Eng. critic and author, specialist in opera. Worked in journalism before specializing in mus. Opera critic, *Spectator,* 1970–90, *Evening Standard* 1990–2, *The Times* 1992–2002. Assoc. ed. *Opera* from 1976, deputy ed. from 1984, ed. 1986–99. Translator of several operas, incl. *Rusalka,* *Osud,* and *Tannhäuser.* OBE 2002.

Milnes, Sherrill (*b* Downers Grove, Ill., 1935). Amer. baritone. Opera début Boston Opera Co., 1960 (Masetto in *Don Giovanni*). Member Goldovsky Opera Co. 1960–5; NY City Opera 1964–7; NY Met 1965; London début 1969; CG début 1971. Has cond. opera recordings. Created Adam in *Mourning Becomes Electra* (NY Met 1967).

Milstein, Nathan (Mironovich) (*b* Odessa, 1903; *d* London, 1992). Russ.-born violinist (Amer. cit. 1942). Début Odessa 1920. Toured Russia 1921 in duo with *Horowitz. In Brussels 1925 met and was encouraged by Ysaÿe. Amer. début 1929 with Philadelphia Orch., thereafter settling there. Taught in NY and Zurich. Salzburg Fest. début 1954. Authority on Romantic composers. Ed. of vn. mus. Autobiography *From Russia to the West* (1990).

Milton, John (*b* Stanton St John, nr. Oxford, *c.*1563; *d* London, 1647). Eng. composer of madrigals, viol music, and psalms. Chorister, Ch. Ch., Oxford, 1572–7. Contributed 'Fair Orian' to *The *Triumphs of Oriana.* Father of poet John Milton.

mime. Acting in dumb-show (or the actor in such) sometimes acc. by mus.

Mime. The Nibelung dwarf, brother of Alberich, who rears Siegfried in Wagner's *Der Ring des Nibelungen.*

mimodrama. Play or drama in which action is carried on in dumb-show, often to mus. Differs from ballet because movts. are not formalized.

minaccevole; minaccevolmente (It.). Menacing; menacingly. So also *minacciando, minaccioso, minacciosamente.*

Mines of Sulphur, The. Opera in 3 acts by Richard Rodney Bennett to lib. by Beverley Cross. Comp 1963. Prod. London (SW) 1965 cond. C. Davis, Milan 1966, Glimmerglass 2004.

minim. See *half-note.*

minimalism. Term applied to style of mus. which began in 1960s involving repetition of short musical motifs in a simple harmonic idiom. The minimum of material is repeated to maximum hypnotic effect, much like some oriental mus. Its practitioners are called minimalists, prominent among whom are Philip *Glass, Terry *Riley, and Steve *Reich. The case of John *Adams is more complex.

Minkowski, Marc (*b* Paris, 1962). Fr. bassoonist and conductor. Played in orchs. and in ens. such as Les Arts Florissants. Studied cond. at Pierre Monteux Cond. Sch. in Hancock, Maine. Formed Les Musiciens du Louvre 1982. Cond. Lully's *Phaéton* for reopening of Lyon Opéra 1993. Cond. Paris Opéra 1996 (*Idomeneo*). Salzburg Fest. début 1997 (*Entführung aus dem Serail*). Mus. dir. Flanders Opera from 1998. Aix-en-Provence Fest. 1999. Débuts: Los Angeles PO (2000); OAE, Berlin PO, CBSO (all 2003). Has cond. most major Eur. opera companies and orchs. and perf. with Les Musiciens du Louvre at major Eur. opera fests.

Minkus, Léon [Aloisius Ludwig] (*b* Vienna, 1826; *d* Vienna, 1917). Austrian composer of ballet music. Collab. with Delibes on *La Source*, Paris 1866. Settled in Russia and wrote mus. for many Petipa ballets in St Petersburg, incl. *Don Quixote* (1869) and *La Bayadère* (1877). Court comp. of ballet mus. for imperial theatres in St Petersburg 1872–85. Retired 1891 and returned to Vienna. From mus. point of view, had misfortune to be contemporary of Tchaikovsky.

Minneapolis Symphony Orchestra. See *Minnesota Orchestra*.

Minnelied (Ger.). Love song.

Minnesinger (Ger.). 'Singer(s) of love'. Ger. equivalent of troubadours, flourishing in 12th- and 13th-cent. guilds. Mainly of aristocratic orig. in contrast to *Meistersinger* who were of merchant class. Among the most celebrated *Minnesinger* were Walther von der Vogelweide (*d* 1230), Neidhardt von Reuenthal (*c*.1180–1240), Heinrich von Meissen (Frauenlob, *d* 1318), Hermann, the Monk of Salzburg (*c*.1350–1410), and Oswald von Wolkenstein (*c*.1377–1445). Wagner's *Tannhäuser* and Strauss's *Guntram* are operas dealing with the *Minnesinger* class.

Minnesota Orchestra. Name since 1968 of Minneapolis SO, USA, giving regular series of subscription concerts in Minneapolis and St Paul. Founded 1903 by Emil *Oberhoffer who was cond. until 1922, followed by Bruno *Walter 1922–3, Henry Verbrugghen 1923–31, Eugene *Ormandy 1931–6, Dimitri *Mitropoulos 1937–49, Antal *Dorati 1949–60, Stanislaw *Skrowaczewski 1960–79, Neville *Marriner 1979–86, Edo de *Waart 1986–95, Eiji Oue 1995–2002, Osmo Vänskä from 2003.

minor (It. *minore*; Fr. *mineur*). Opposite of major, applied to *scale, key, chord, and intervals.

minor common chord. Common chord of which the 3rd is minor.

minor intervals. See *interval*.

minor scale. See *scale*.

minstrels. (1) See *menéstrel*.
(2) Black-faced entertainers, 'nigger minstrels', popular in USA (though not with genuine blacks) from about 1830s whose songs and humour were based on those of Negroes. Debussy's *Minstrels* in his *Préludes* (Book 1, No.12), refers to these mus.-hall troupes.

Minton, Yvonne (Fay) (*b* Sydney, NSW, 1938). Australian mezzo-soprano. Won international vocalist comp. at 's Hertogenbosch 1961. Opera début London 1964 (Lucretia in Britten's opera). CG début 1965. Created Thea in *The Knot Garden* (CG 1970). Cologne Opera from 1969. Chicago 1970; NY Met 1973; Bayreuth 1974; Salzburg Fest. 1978. Australian Opera 1972–3. Sang Countess Geschwitz in first 3-act *Lulu*, Paris 1979. Many concert appearances. After brief retirement, returned at Florence 1990 and at Adelaide 1991. Glyndebourne début 1994. CBE 1980.

Mintz, Shlomo (*b* Moscow, 1957). Russ.-born Israeli violinist and conductor. First recital 1966. Soloist in Mendelssohn conc. with Israel PO, cond. Mehta, 1968. Studied at Juilliard Sch. 1973. Amer. début 1973 in NY. Brit. début Brighton Fest. 1976, Salzburg Fest. début 1980. Mus. adv. Israel CO 1989–93.

minuet (Eng.), **menuet** (Fr.), **Menuett** (Ger.), **minuetto** (It.). Dance in triple time, orig. as Fr. rustic dance and adapted by the court in the 17th cent. So called because of small, dainty step (*menu* = small) which is characteristic. Soon taken up by composers of art mus. from *Lully onwards and became one of optional movts. of the *suite. It also occurred in ovs. by Bach and Handel. In 18th cent. it was used in syms. (and other forms) by Wagenseil, Haydn, Mozart, and others, becoming the standard 3rd movt. until supplanted from Beethoven onwards by the *scherzo. Normally in ABA form, the B section being a contrasting minuet called 'trio' because some Fr. composers wrote it in 3-part harmony or reduced the performers to 3. Note that, although Beethoven and other composers used it in their scores, the word *menuetto* does not exist in any language.

Minute Waltz. Nickname for Chopin's Waltz in D♭, Op.64, No.1, comp. 1847, on the assumption that it can be played in 1 minute—but only if played too fast.

Miracle. Nickname of Haydn's Sym. in D major, No.96 in Breitkopf edn., comp. London 1791. So called in error because it used to be said that at its f.p. in London on 11 Mar. 1791 the audience rushed forward at the end to congratulate the composer, thereby escaping injury when a chandelier collapsed on to their vacated seats. Research has est. that this incident occurred during Haydn's 2nd visit to London, at a concert on 2 Feb. 1795 and that the sym. which had been played, and which therefore really deserves the nickname, was Haydn's No.102 in B♭.

Miracle in the Gorbals. Ballet in 1 act, mus. by Bliss, lib. by M. Benthall, choreog. R. Helpmann. Prod. London 1944. The Gorbals was a notorious slum district of Glasgow.

miracle plays, mysteries, and moralities. The custom of teaching Bible stories by means of sacred dramas (often in church) is venerable. These dramas were known as *miracle plays* (or, simply, *miracles*), another name, given by writers on the subject (apparently first in the 18th cent.), being *mystery*. Of similar character were the plays which, personifying virtues and vices, taught moral lessons, e.g. *moralities*. Plays of such types as these are recorded as early as the 4th cent. In Eng., there are records of them from the 11th to the 16th cents., some of the finest being perf. in York and Chester. Even today there are traces of them in the rural perfs. of mummers in the N. of Eng. (e.g. the play of St George and the Dragon).

Corpus Christi (June) was in some cities a great occasion for plays in the streets (at Chester 24 such played in a single day, moving to different locations, with all 24 given at each). Some of the plays involved a good deal of singing, and contained the seeds of the future masque, oratorio, and opera. In the 20th cent. several composers have based works on the old mystery plays, notably Stravinsky and Britten (whose *Noye's Fludde* is a fine example). Vaughan Williams described his opera based on Bunyan's *The *Pilgrim's Progress* as a morality.

Miraculous Mandarin, The (*A csodálatos mandarin*). Pantomime in 1 act, Op.19, by Bartók to scenario by Menyhért Lengyel, f.p. in Cologne 27 Nov. 1926. Orch. suite f.p. Budapest 1928. Comp. 1918–19, rev. 1924 and 1926–31. Censorship dogged the early history of this work, which was not perf. in Budapest until 1946, the year after Bartók's death.

Mireille. Opera in 3 (orig. 5) acts by *Gounod to lib. by Carré based on Mistral's poem *Mirèio* (1859). Prod. Paris and London 1864 in 5-act vers. Paris, Dec. 1864 in 3-act revision, Chicago 1880. Modern practice is to perf. reconstruction of orig. 5-act score.

Miricioiu, Nelly (*b* Adjud, 1952). Romanian soprano. Début Iasi 1974 (Queen of Night in *Die Zauberflöte*). Brasov Opera 1975–8. Brit. début 1981 (Glasgow); CG 1982. Has sung in S. Francisco and San Diego. Salzburg Fest. début 1992.

mirliton. Generic term applied to acoustical devices, many of folk origin, which modify tonal characteristics of other instruments by means of vibration of their membrane, as in comb and paper.

Miroirs (Mirrors). Set of 5 epoch-making pf. pieces by Ravel, comp. 1905, entitled *Noctuelles, Oiseaux tristes, Une Barque sur l'océan, *Alborado del Gracioso, La Vallée des cloches*. In 1908 Ravel scored *Une Barque sur l'océan* for orch., followed in 1912 by *Alborado*.

Mirror Canon, Mirror Fugue. Canon or fugue in which the parts (or vv.) and intervals appear in the score simultaneously both the right way up and upside down, as if a mirror lay between them.

Mirror on which to Dwell, A. Cycle of 6 songs for sop., picc., 2 fl., ob., cor anglais, E♭ cl., bass cl., perc., pf., vn., va., vc., db. by *Carter to poems by Elizabeth Bishop, comp. 1975, f.p. NY Feb. 1976, London Nov. 1976. Titles are: 1. *Anaphora*, 2. *Argument*, 3. *Sandpiper*, 4. *Insomnia*, 5. *View of the Capitol from the Library of Congress*, 6. *O Breath*.

Miserere. Ps. 51 (50 in RC numeration). In the RC Church it is sung in the service of *Lauds. It has frequently been set by composers. A famous operatic setting occurs in Act 4 of *Il trovatore*, for sop., ten., ch., and orch.

Miserly Knight, The (*Skupoy rytsar*). Opera in 3 scenes, Op.24, by *Rachmaninov, a setting of Pushkin's poem (1830). Comp. 1903–5, prod. Moscow 1906, Boston 1910, Glyndebourne 2004.

missa (Lat.). *Mass. Thus one finds *missa brevis*, short mass; *missa cantata*, sung mass; *missa ad fugam* or *missa ad canones*, mass in fugal or canonic style; *missa sine nomine*, mass without a name, i.e. comp. (in 15th and 16th cents.) with orig. material and not, as was customary, on an existing plainsong or secular melody.

Missa in tempore belli (Mass in time of war) (Haydn). See *Paukenmesse*.

Missa Papae Marcelli (Mass of Pope Marcellus). Mass for 6 vv. by Palestrina comp. *c*.1561. The Pope Marcellus II, who resigned after only a few weeks, showed a desire to promote a reform in church mus. and this Mass is traditionally assoc. with the circumstance. But the romantic legend that has grown around the occurrence has no historical basis.

Missa pro defunctis (Mass for the dead). See *Requiem*.

missa solemnis (Lat., 'Solemn Mass'). (1) Mass in which all sections—apart from the readings of the Epistle and the Gospel—are sung either in polyphony or plainchant. Term is also applied to elaborate ceremonial setting.

(2) See *Mass in D* (Beethoven).

Missa super L'homme armé. Work for speaker or (male or female) singer and chamber ens. by *Maxwell Davies, comp. 1967–8, rev. 1971. F.p. London 1968, rev. Perugia 1971. See *Homme armé, L'*.

Miss Donnithorne's Maggot. Th. piece by *Maxwell Davies for mez. and chamber ens. (incl. 4 metronomes, football rattle, bosun's whistle, chamois leather rubbed on glass). Text by Randolph Stow. F.p. Adelaide, S. Australia, 1974, with Mary Thomas (mez.), cond. composer.

Miss Julie. (1) Opera in 2 acts by Ned *Rorem to lib. by Kenward Elmslie after the play by Strindberg (1889), comp. 1965, prod. NY 1965. Rev. to last act 1978, prod. NY 1979.

(2) Ballet in 2 acts, based on Strindberg. Choreog. MacMillan, mus. by *Panufnik. Prod. Stuttgart 1970.

(3) Opera in 2 acts by W. *Alwyn to his own lib. based on Strindberg. Comp. 1961–76. F.p. (broadcast) 1976.

(4) Opera by Bibalo, to lib. based on Strindberg, comp. 1973, orch. rev. 1983–4.

mistero, misterio (It.). Mystery. *misterioso*, mysteriously; *misteriosamente*, in a mysterious manner.

misura (It.). Measure. (1) in the Eng. sense of 'bar'.

(2) In the general sense of regularity. So *alla misura*, in strict time; *senza misura*, without strict time. And so, too, *misurato*, measured, i.e. strictly in time.

Mitchell, Donald (Charles Peter) (*b* London, 1925). Eng. publisher, critic, and author. Man. dir., Faber Music 1965–71, chairman 1977–86. Chairman, Performing Right Soc. 1989–93. Visiting Fellow, Sussex Univ. 1970, prof. of mus. 1971–6. Founder and co-ed., *Music Survey* 1947–52; mus. critic for *Musical Times* 1953–7, *Daily Telegraph* 1959–64; ed. *Tempo* 1958–62. Joint ed. *Benjamin Britten* (1952), *The Mozart Companion* (with H. C. Robbins Landon, 1956). Ed. *Gustav Mahler* by Alma Mahler (Eng. edn.). Author of *Gustav Mahler: Vol. I, The Early Years* (1958 rev. ed. 1979), *Vol. II, The Wunderhorn Years* (1975), and *Vol. III, Songs and Symphonies of Life and Death* (1985); *The Language of Modern Music* (1963); *Benjamin Britten, 1913–76: Pictures from a Life* (with J. Evans, 1978); *Britten and Auden in the Thirties* (1981); *Letters from a Life: Selected Letters and Diaries of Benjamin Britten* (with P. Reed, Vol. I 1923–39 and Vol. II 1939–45 (1991)); *Cradles of the New, Writings on Music 1951–1991*, ed. M. Cooke (1995). CBE 2000.

Mitchell, Howard (*b* Lyons, Nebraska, 1911; *d* Ormond Beach, Fla., 1988). Amer. conductor and cellist. Prin. cellist, Nat. SO, Washington, 1933–44, then ass. cond. 1944–9, cond. and mus. dir. 1949–69. Mus. dir. Nat. Orch. of Uruguay from 1970.

Mitchinson, John (*b* Blackrod, Lancs., 1932). Eng. tenor. Founder-member of BBC Northern Singers, 1953. Sang in concert perf. *Don Giovanni*, *Chelsea Opera Group*, 1955. Operatic stage début 1959 (Jupiter in Handel's *Semele* for Handel Opera Soc.). Successful career in concert hall and opera house. Sang with ENO 1972–8 and WNO 1978–82. Notable interpreter of Mahler's *Das Lied von der Erde*, Stravinsky's *Oedipus Rex*.

Mitridate, Rè di Ponto (Mithridates, King of Pontus). Opera seria (K87) in 3 acts by Mozart to lib. by V. A. Cigna-Santi, after Racine. Prod. Milan, 1770, Salzburg 1971, London (concert) 1979, NY 1985, Wexford 1989 (and in London), CG 1992.

Mitropoulos, Dimitri (*b* Athens, 1896; *d* Milan, 1960). Gr.-born conductor, pianist, and composer (Amer. cit. 1946). Répétiteur, Berlin State Opera 1921–5. Cond. Odeon Cons. Orch., Athens, 1924–9. Cond., Paris SO 1932–6. US début with Boston SO 1936. Cond. Minneapolis SO (now *Minnesota Orch.) 1937–49, NYPO 1949–58. NY Met début

1954. Salzburg Fest. début 1954. Cond. f.p. of Barber's *Vanessa* NY Met 1958 and at Salzburg Fest. 1958. Fine exponent of 20th-cent. mus. Wrote opera, *Soeur Béatrice* (1918), and orch. works. Int. competition for young cond. named in his memory. Died after heart attack while rehearsing Mahler's 3rd Sym.

Mitte (Ger.). Middle, e.g. *Auf der Mitte des Bogen*, In the middle of the bow.

mixed chorus, mixed voices. Body containing male and female vv.

mixed media. Term for theatrical works, events, or 'happenings' in which several forms of art are merged, e.g. mus., dance, film, elec. devices, etc. *Avant-garde* composers such as Cage, Berio, Xenakis, Stockhausen, and Reich have created mixed media works.

mixer. Elec. device which combines several signals and routes them to one or more channels corresponding to tracks on a magnetic tape, or to a loudspeaker.

Mixolydian mode. See *modes*.

mixture stop. Org. stop in which each fingerkey (or pedal-key) played operates on a group of pipes corresponding to the fundamental and some of the higher harmonics of the note of that key. The group may be of from 2 to 10 pipes and the stop is then spoken of as having that number of *ranks* (indicated in order specifications in Roman figures). It cannot be used alone, but adds brightness and richness when combined with stops of normal pitch in 'Full Organ', etc. See also *sesquialtera*.

M.K. Abbreviation for *Manualkoppel* (Ger.), i.e. manual coupler (in org. mus.—followed by an indication of the particular manuals to be coupled).

Mlada. Opera in 4 acts by Rimsky-Korsakov to his own lib. based on lib. for earlier scheme for opera-ballet to be written in collab. with Borodin, Cui, and Mussorgsky, with ballet mus. by *Minkus. Comp. 1889–90. Prod. St Petersburg 1892, London (semi-staged) 1989, Glasgow (Bolshoy Co.) 1990.

Mládí (Youth). Suite in 4 movts. for wind sextet by Janáček, comp. 1924. For fl./picc., ob., cl., hn., bn., and bcl. F.p. Brno 1924, f.p. in England, London 1926.

Mlynarski, Emil (Simon) (*b* Kibarty, Lithuania, 1870; *d* Warsaw, 1935). Polish composer, violinist, and conductor. Int. career as violinist. Ass. cond. Warsaw Opera 1897–1903, cond., Warsaw PO 1901–5, dir. Warsaw Cons. 1904–7 and 1919–22. Cond. Scottish Orch., 1910–16. Cond., Bolshoy Th. Orch., Moscow, 1914–17. Dir., Warsaw Opera 1919–28. Teacher of cond., Curtis Inst. 1929–31. Wrote opera, sym., and 2 vn. concs.

M.M. (1) See *metronome*.

(2) Abbreviation for Master of Music (sometimes M.Mus.).

M.Mus. See *Master of Music*.

Moby Dick. (1) Cantata for 2 ten., 2 basses, male ch., and orch. by *Herrmann to text selected by W. Clark Harrington from Herman Melville's novel (1851). Comp. 1937–8, f.p. NY 1940.

(2) Sym.-poem by Douglas *Moore (1927).

(3) 'Concertato' for orch. by *Mennin (1952).

modal. Pertaining to the *modes; style of comp. in which the modes are used.

moderato (It., 'restrained', 'moderate'). Direction used either alone, as in Elgar's Vc. Conc., or as qualification of another direction, e.g. *allegro moderato* (a bit slower than *allegro*). Fr. *modéré*.

modes. (1) Names for each of the ways of ordering a scale, i.e. *major mode* and *minor mode*.

(2) The scales which dominated European mus. for 1,100 years (approx. AD 400 to AD 1500) and strongly influenced composers for another hundred years (up to *c*.1600). They have since reappeared from time to time in the work of some composers, especially in the 20th cent. Throughout that total period of 1,500 years the plainsong of the Church, which is entirely 'modal', has continued to accustom the ears of fresh generations to the melodic effect of the modes. But the description 'church modes' or 'ecclesiastical modes' is wrong, since their use was general.

The available mus. material at the time when the modes became accepted was that which may be nowadays conveniently represented by the white keys of the pf. or org., the notes of which constitute (with slight differences of tuning) the scale worked out scientifically in the 4th cent. BC by Pythagoras and the Gr. thinkers of his time. In the 2nd cent. AD the Greeks were using this scale in 7 different ways: Gr. influence was strong in the early Christian Church and changes in the modal system developed among singers as a practical measure. In the 5th cent. 4 modes were adopted (authentic modes) and at the time of Pope Gregory (*c*.540–604) 4 more were added (plagal) and later 4 more, making 12. In the Authentic modes, the 5th note (the dominant), was much used as a reciting-note in plainsong, and the first (the final), as a cadence-note, to close a passage. The authentic modes may be re-created by playing on the pf. octave scales of white notes beginning respectively on D, E, F, and G. A melody played in one of the modes and then in another will alter in some of its intervals and hence in its general effect, as opposed to a melody played in our 12 major or minor scales, which are all alike as to intervals.

The *plagal modes* were merely new forms of the others, being the same 4 taken in a compass lying not between final and final of the corresponding authentic modes but between their dominant and dominant, the final, on which the cadences fell, thus coming in the middle. In order to avoid having the reciting note at the very top or bottom of the series of notes a new one was chosen, lying 3 notes below the original, and this was now regarded as the dominant. The whole series was now as follows (A = authentic and P = plagal):

Mode	Range	Dominant
I (A)	D–D	A
II (P)	A–A	F
III (A)	E–E	C[†]
IV (P)	B–B	A
V (A)	F–F	C
VI (P)	C–C	A
VII (A)	G–G	D
VIII (P)	D–D	C[†]

[†] The dominants of the two modes so marked (one of them authentic and the other plagal) would normally be B, but this being found an unsuitable note C was adopted instead.

(It will be noted that the odd-numbered modes are the authentic ones and the even-numbered the plagal.)

Nearly a thousand years after Gregory a Swiss monk, Henry of Glarus, or Henricus Glareanus, brought forth, in a book called *Dodecachordon* (1547), a theory that there should, historically, be 12 modes instead of 8. He added modes on A and C (none on the unsuitable B), with their plagal forms, so that the table above was complemented as follows:

Mode	Range	Dominant
IX (A)	A–A	E
X (P)	E–E	C
XI (A)	C–C	G
XII (P)	G–G	E

Glareanus gave his 12 modes what he thought to be their orig. Gr. names and these (though incorrect) have become accepted:

I. Dorian
II. HypoDorian
III. Phrygian
IV. HypoPhrygian
V. Lydian
VI. HypoLydian
VII. Mixolydian
VIII. HypoMixolydian
IX. Æolian
X. HypoÆolian
XI. Ionian
XII. HypoIonian

It should be clearly understood that the difference between the various modes is not one of pitch but of the order in which fall the tones and semitones. Any mode could be taken at another than its original pitch (i.e. transposed), but in that case its intervals remained as before. Thus the whole series could be set out as beginning on C, when the Dorian and Lydian (to take two examples) would appear as follows:

The authentic modes shown uniformly with C as final (with the semitones marked)

With the development of harmonized music the modal system in time tended to disintegrate: the

I. Dorian.

V. Lydian

two authentic modes added by Glareanus (the Ionian and Aeolian) were felt to be the most suited to harmony and have remained as our 'major' and 'minor' scales. The other modes, however, are in use in plainsong, some folk-song, and occasionally in the work of certain composers such as Vaughan Williams, Bartók, and Kodály.

modinha. Type of song (not folk song) popular in Portugal and Brazil in the 18th and 19th cents.

Mödl, Martha (*b* Nuremberg, 1912; *d* Stuttgart, 2001). Ger. soprano, originally mezzo-soprano. Opera début Remscheid 1942 (Hänsel). Düsseldorf Opera 1945–9 as mez., Hamburg Opera 1949–55, also Vienna State Opera. CG 1949–50 and 1953; NY Met début 1957 Sang as dramatic sop. from 1950; Bayreuth 1951 (Kundry in *Parsifal*), singing other roles incl. Brünnhilde and Isolde until 1967. Salzburg Fest. début 1964. Sang in premières of Reimann's *Melusine* (Schwetzingen 1971) and *Die Gespenstersonate* (Berlin 1984), Fortner's *Elisabeth Tudor* (Berlin 1972), Einem's *Kabale und Liebe* (Vienna 1976), and Cerha's *Baal* (Salzburg 1981). Sang the Countess in *Queen of Spades* in Vienna at the age of 80.

modo (It.). (1) Manner, e.g. *in modo di*, in the manner of.
(2) Mode (see *modes*).

modulation. The changing from one key to another in the course of a section of a comp. by evolutionary mus. means (not just by stopping and starting anew in another key) and as a part of the work's formal organization. The simplest and most natural modulations are to the related keys (or attendant keys) i.e. to the relative minor or major, to the *dominant and its relative major or minor and to the *subdominant and its relative minor or major. The *tonic major and minor are also related keys, modulation from one to the other being simple, but they are not usually so described. *Chromatic modulation*, found frequently in Wagner, Franck, and Strauss, in general means altering a chord by means of a chromatic change. It can also be achieved by moving basses up or down major or minor 3rds. *Enharmonic modulation* covers the use of chords altered by *enharmonic means, e.g. turning a dominant 7th chord to a Ger. 6th. Modulation becomes less of a feature in atonal mus. because of the enlargement of the

scale. First composers to use modulation may have been Obrecht and Desprès. Chromatic modulation occurs in madrigals of *Gesualdo and *Monteverdi. John Bull's organ fantasia *Ut, re, mi, fa, sol, la* modulates a whole tone upward successively into different keys. With J. S. Bach, modulation became integral part of *fugue.

modulator. (1) Elec. device by which frequency or amplitude of a waveform can be changed.
(2) Diagram used in teaching of *tonic sol-fa on which note-names are ranged in order perpendicularly.

Modus Lascivus. The Ionian mode, the same as the major scale of C.

Moeran, E(rnest) **J**(ohn) (*b* Heston, Middx., 1894; *d* Kenmare, Co. Kerry, 1950). Eng. composer of Irish descent. Collected folksongs in Norfolk, where he lived for several years. Mus. first heard in London 1923. Comps., which are predominantly lyrical, incl.:

ORCH.: *In the Mountain Country* (1921); *Rhapsodies* Nos. 1 and 2 (1924); *Whythorne's Shadow* (1931); *Lonely Waters* (1932); Sym. in G minor (1934–7); *Overture for a masque* (1944); *Sinfonietta* (1944); *Serenade in G* (1948).

CONCERTOS: vn. (1942); *Rhapsody*, pf., orch. (1943); vc. (1945).

CHAMBER MUSIC: str. qt.; vn sonata; sonata, 2 unacc. vns. (1935); ob. qt. (1946); vc. sonata (1947); *Prelude*, vc., pf. (1948).

PIANO: 3 *Pieces* (1919); *Theme and Variations* (1920); *On a May Morning, Stalham River, Toccata* (1921); 3 *Fancies* (1922); 2 *Legends* (1923); *Bank Holiday, Summer Valley* (1925); *Irish Love Song* (1926); *White Mountain* (1927); *Prelude and Berceuse* (1933).

SONG-CYCLE: *Ludlow Town*, 4 Housman songs, bar., pf. (1920).

Moevs, Robert Walter (*b* La Crosse, Wisconsin, 1920). Amer. composer and pianist. Taught at Harvard Univ. 1955–63. On mus. staff Rutgers Univ., NJ, from 1964 (prof. from 1968, chairman, mus. dept. 1974–81). Influenced by Boulez and describes his method of comp. as 'systematic chromaticism', a modified serial technique. Works incl. ballet *Endymion*; *3 Symphonic Pieces*; concerto grosso for pf., perc., orch. (1960, rev. 1968); *Cantata sacra*; other choral works incl. *A Brief Mass*, ch., org., vib., gui., db. (1968); 3 str. qts. (1957, 1989, 1995); sonata for solo vn.; pf. sonata, etc.

Moffo, Anna (*b* Wayne, Penn., 1932; *d* Manhattan, NY, 2006). Amer. soprano. Opera début, Spoleto 1955 (Norina in *Don Pasquale*). Amer. début Chicago Lyric Opera 1957; Salzburg Fest. 1957; NY Met 1959; CG 1964.

Moise (Rossini). See *Mosè in Egitto*.

Moiseiwitsch [Moiseivich], **Benno** (*b* Odessa, 1890; *d* London, 1963). Russ.-born pianist (Brit.

cit. 1937). First appeared in Eng. at Reading, 1908, London 1909. Continental tours, then settled in Eng. 1914. Expert in classical repertory but noted above all for his playing of mus. of Rachmaninov, regarded as surpassed in its day only by composer himself. CBE 1946.

Moldau. Ger. title for *Vltava* in Smetana's *Má Vlast*.

Moldenhauer, Hans (*b* Mainz, 1906; *d* Spokane, Wash., 1987). Amer. musical scholar of Ger. birth. Emigrated to USA 1938. Founded Spokane Cons. 1942 (pres. from 1946). Lect., Univ. of Washington. Creator and dir. of Moldenhauer Archive, large coll. of MSS, letters, documents, etc., relating especially to Webern about whom he wrote the authoritative study *Anton von Webern: Chronicle of his Life and Work* (NY and London 1978, Ger. trans. 1979).

Molinari, Bernardino (*b* Rome, 1880; *d* Rome, 1952). It. conductor. Cond. Augusteo, Rome, 1912–43. Frequent guest cond. Europe and USA (Amer. début 1928, NYPO). Expert in 20th-cent. mus., esp. *Respighi and *Malipiero.

Molinari-Pradelli, Francesco (*b* Bologna, 1911; *d* Bologna 1996). It. conductor. Began career 1938. Cond. *L'Elisir d'amore*, Bologna 1939. Mainly cond. of opera, esp. at La Scala from 1946. CG 1955; S. Francisco 1957; Vienna 1959; NY Met 1966–73.

Molinaro, Simone (*b* Genoa, *c*.1565; *d* Genoa, 1615). It. composer. Choirmaster, Genoa Cath., from *c*.1602. Wrote motets, masses, madrigals, canzonets, church mus., but principally works for lute. Ed. *Gesualdo's six books of 5-vv. madrigals, 1613.

Molique, Wilhelm Bernhard (*b* Nuremberg, 1802; *d* Cannstadt, Stuttgart, 1869). Ger. violinist and composer. Member of orch. at Theater an der Wien, then leader of Munich court orch. 1820–6. Cond. royal orch., Stuttgart, 1826–49. London début 1840 in his 5th conc. Settled in Eng. 1849–66 as soloist and teacher. Prof. of comp., RAM 1861–6. Wrote 6 vn. concs.; 8 str. qts.; sym.; oratorio; vc. conc.; vn. solos; etc.

moll (Ger.). Minor, in the sense of key, e.g. *A moll*, A minor; *moll Ton*, or *moll Tonart*, minor key.

Moll, Kurt (*b* Buir, Cologne, 1938). Ger. bass. Sang minor roles at Cologne Opera 1958–61. Début as Lodovico in *Otello* at Aachen 1961. Aachen Opera 1961–3, Mainz 1963–6, Wuppertal 1966–9. Joined Hamburg Opera 1970. Débuts: Salzburg Fest. 1970; Bayreuth Fest. 1972; Amer. (S. Francisco) 1974; La Scala 1974; CG 1977; NY Met 1978; Chicago 1983; NY recital début 1984.

molto (It.). Much, very, e.g. *allegro molto*, very quickly.

Momente (Moments). Comp. by *Stockhausen for sop. solo, 4 ch. groups, and 13 instrumentalists. The first 'Donaueschingen' version dates from 1961–4, the 2nd 'Europa' from 1972.

moment-form. Type of work devised by *Stockhausen, the 'moment' being a short part of a comp. having its own mus. characteristic. What occurs within this moment may be regarded as more important than the succession between moments, which may be indeterminate as in Stockhausen's *Momente* (1961–4).

moment musical (Fr.). Musical moment. Title popular in 19th cent. for short pf. pieces, e.g. Schubert's 6 *Moments musicaux* (D780), completed 1828.

Mompou, Federico (*b* Barcelona, 1893; *d* Barcelona, 1987). Sp. (Catalan) pianist and composer. Wrote most of his works in Barcelona 1914–21, mainly pf. pieces in what he called *primitivista* style (no bar-divisions, key-signatures, or cadences). Lived in Paris 1921–41, when he again returned to Barcelona and composed further pf. works and songs, religious settings for ch. and orch., and mus. for guitar.

Monckton, Lionel (*b* London, 1861; *d* London, 1924). Eng. composer. Began career as barrister but became mus. critic, *Daily Telegraph*, for brief period. Composer of popular light operas, e.g. *A Country Girl* (1902), *Our Miss Gibbs* (1909), *The Arcadians* (1909), *The Quaker Girl* (1910), etc.

Mond, Der (The Moon). Opera in 1 act by *Orff to his own lib. after Grimm. Comp. 1937–8, rev. 1945. Prod. Munich 1939, NY 1956.

Mondo della luna, Il (The World on the Moon). Opera in 3 acts by Haydn to lib. by Goldoni (set previously by Galuppi and also by Paisiello, Piccinni, and others). Comp. 1777. Prod. Eszterháza 1777; NY 1949; London (incomplete) 1951, (complete) 1960. Restored by Robbins Landon and prod. Holland Fest. 1959, Buxton Fest. 1997, Garsington 2000.

Moniuszko, Stanisław (*b* Ubiel, Lithuania, 1819; *d* Warsaw, 1872). Polish composer. Lived in Warsaw from 1858. Cond. Warsaw Opera and prof. at Cons. Regarded as foremost Polish 19th-cent. composer after *Chopin. His opera *Halka* is regarded as first Polish nat. opera (2-act version 1846–7, rev. in 4 acts 1857 and prod. Warsaw 1858). Wrote other operas, none as successful, incl. *Straszny Dwór* (The Haunted Manor) 1861–4. Composed sym.-poem *Bajka* (Fairy Tale), 7 masses, a *Requiem* (1890), and over 300 songs.

Monk, William (Henry) (*b* London, 1823; *d* London, 1889). Eng. composer and organist. Choirmaster King's College, London, 1847, organist 1849, prof. of vocal mus. 1874. Ed., 1861, of *Hymns Ancient and Modern*. Wrote mus. of hymn *Abide with me* ('Eventide').

Monn, Georg (Matthias) (*b* Vienna, 1717; *d* Vienna, 1750). Austrian organist and composer. Org., Karlskirche, Vienna, from *c*.1738. Wrote 21 syms., 7 hpd. concs., and a vc. conc. of which *Schoenberg made an edition in 1911–12.

mono. Abbreviation for *monophonic with special meaning in gramophone recording when long-playing records first appeared. Mono records were recorded on one channel requiring only one loudspeaker as opposed to stereophonic 2-channel recording. Gradually stereo ousted mono, but certain transfers from the pre-LP recording era can only be made in mono.

monochord (Gr.). One string. (1) Scientific instr. consisting of soundbox over which is stretched a single string which can be divided at any point by a movable bridge, the position of which can be exactly determined by scale of measurements on the surface across which it moves. By altering the ratios in which the str. is vibrating, different notes of the *harmonic series may be prod. Used in Ancient Egypt and Ancient Gr. and is still used by modern acousticians.

(2) In later medieval times, monochords were made with 2 or 3 str., capable of emitting intervals and chords. These were ancestors of *clavichord, sometimes called in It. *monocordo*.

monocordo (It.). One string. Term used in str. playing to indicate when certain passage or whole piece is to be perf. entirely on one str. Orig. with *Paganini in his 'Napoleon' Sonata for G str.

monodrama (Gr.). Single play. Stage work involving only one character, e.g. Schoenberg's *Erwartung*, and Poulenc's *La *Voix humaine*.

monody, monodic. Term sometimes used as synonym of *monophonic mus. or for acc. solo song, but properly it is a particular kind of acc. solo song which developed *c.*1600 as a reaction against 16th-cent. polyphonic style. It is distinguished by recit.-like, sometimes florid, v.-part and figured-bass acc. The members of *Bardi's Camerata in Florence wrote in monodic style, Caccini publishing a coll. of monodies, *Le nuove musiche*, in 1602. By 1613 it was adopted for instr. mus. e.g. in trio sonatas of Rossi and Marini.

monophony, monophonic (Gr.). One sound. Mus. which has a single melodic line of notes without harmonies or melody in counterpoint, as opposed to *polyphony and *homophony. Oldest type of mus., being only type perf. in Ancient Gr., early church mus. (Gregorian etc.), and mus. of *Minnesinger, *Meistersinger, etc. All this mus. was in monophonic notation, which is a term covering several systems. For special 20th-cent. application, see *mono*.

monothematic (Gr.). Having only one theme, and therefore applied to comp. or movts. based on one subject, e.g. a figure. Finales of several Haydn syms. are examples of monothematic construction.

monotone (Gr.). Recitation of liturgical text on unaltered pitch as in prayers, psalms, etc.

Monsieur Beaucaire. Operetta in prol. and 3 acts by Messager to lib. by A. Rivoire and P. Veber based on novel by Booth Tarkington. Eng. vers.

by Frederick Lonsdale with lyrics by Adrian Ross, prod. Birmingham, London, and NY 1919. Fr. vers. prod. Paris 1925.

Montagnana, Domenico (*b* Lendinara, *c.*1687; *d* Venice, 1750). It. violin-maker. Lived in Cremona and Venice. His instr. are scarce and very valuable. The vcs. are especially fine. Believed to have made only one va., which once belonged to Lionel *Tertis.

Montague, Diana (*b* Winchester, 1954). Eng. mezzo-soprano. Opera début GTO 1977 (Zerlina in *Don Giovanni*). CG 1978–83; Bayreuth 1983; Salzburg Fest. 1986; NY Met 1987; Glyndebourne 1989. Concert career in Mozart, Bach, Rossini, Berlioz.

Montague, Stephen (*b* Syracuse, NY, 1943). Amer. composer and pianist. In Warsaw on Fulbright schol. 1972–4. Settled in London 1974. Career as virtuoso pianist. Formed pf. duo 1985 with Philip Mead, touring Eur., N. Amer., and Scandinavia. Co-founder of Electro-Acoustic Music Assoc. of Great Britain. Was Florida junior college tennis champion. Works incl.:

BALLETS: *Into the Sun*, 4-channel tape, perc., prepared pf. (1977); *Median* (comprising *Prologue* and *From the White Edge of Phrygia*) (1984); *The Montague Stomp* (1984).

ORCH.: *Voussoirs*, with elec. (1970–2); *Sound Round*, with elec. (1973); *At the White Edge of Phrygia*, chamber orch. (1983), for full orch. (1984); *Prologue* (1984); pf. conc. (1988); *Snakebite*, chamber orch. (1995); *How Slow the Wind*, v., chamber orch. (1995); pf. conc. (1997); *The Creatures Indoors*, narr., orch. (1997); *Snowscape: St Pölten*, str. (2001); fl. & hp. conc., chamber orch. (2002).

KEYBOARD (some with tape): *Strummin'*, pf., str., lighting, tape (1974–81); *Tongues of Fire*, pf., elec., tape (1983–90); *Haiku*, pf., digital delay, tape (1987); *Behold a Pale Horse*, org. (1990); *After Ives . . .*, pf., tape, live elec. (1991–3); *Phrygian Tucket*, hpd., tape (1994); *Tsunami*, pf. (1997); *5 Easy Pieces*, pf. (1998–2002); *Dark Train Comin'*, hpd., tape (2001); *Toccare Incandescent*, org. (2003).

Also vocal and choral works; and many comps. for various chamber ens. (incl. 4 str. qts., 1989–2004), many of which use live elec. and tape.

Montarsolo, Paolo (*b* Portici, 1925; *d* Rome, 2006). It. bass. Début Bologna 1950 (Lunardo in *I *quattro rusteghi*). Débuts: Glyndebourne 1957; Amer. 1957; Salzburg Fest. 1968; NY Met 1975; CG 1976 (with La Scala co.), with Royal Opera 1988. Specialized in *buffo* roles. Directed over 30 operas.

Montemezzi, Italo (*b* Vigasio, 1875; *d* Vigasio, 1952). It. composer. Intended for engineering career, but in Milan decided to become musician and at 3rd attempt was admitted to Milan Cons. His diploma work, *Cantico dei cantici* (1900) was cond. by Toscanini. His first opera was prod. Turin 1905, but he achieved fame in 1913 with

L'*amore dei tre re, a work in **verismo* style but influenced by Debussy also. Lived in USA 1939–49. Prin. works:

OPERAS: *Giovanni Gallurese* (Turin 1905); *Hellera* (Turin 1909); *L'*amore dei tre re* (Milan 1913); *La nave* (Milan 1918); *La notte di Zoraima* (Milan 1931); *L'incantesimo* (NY radio 1943, Verona 1952).

ORCH.: sym.-poems: *Paolo e Virginia* (1929); *Italia mia!* (1944).

Monteux, Pierre (*b* Paris, 1875; *d* Hancock, Maine, 1964). Fr.-born conductor (Amer. cit. 1942). Played va. in orch. of Paris Opéra-Comique (was prin. va. at f.p. of *Pelléas et Mélisande*, 1902). Early years as cond. with Diaghilev's Ballets Russes in Paris, when he cond. f.ps. of **Petrushka* (1911), **Rite of Spring* (1913), **Jeux* (1913) and **Daphnis et Chloé* (1912). Cond. Paris Opéra 1913–14, incl. f.p. of The **Nightingale*. Salzburg Fest. 1916 (Vienna PO). Cond. NY Met 1917–19 and 1953–6, and cond. f. Amer. p. of The **Golden Cockerel*, 1918. Boston SO 1919–24 (introducing much modern mus.). Cond. Orchestre Symphonique de Paris 1929–38. Cond. S. Francisco SO 1935–52. Prin. cond. LSO 1961–4. Outstanding interpreter of Fr. and Russ. mus., but of much else besides.

Monteverdi, Claudio (Giovanni Antonio) (*b* Cremona, 1567; *d* Venice, 1643). It. composer. Chorister, Cremona Cath. At 16, when he was already a fine organist and viol player, he pubd. some sacred madrigals. Entered service of Duke of Mantua as viol player and singer of madrigals. Went with Duke on military expeditions to Danube and Flanders, 1595 and 1599. Heard and was influenced by Florentine operas of the **Camerata*, notably Peri's *Euridice*, 1600. His own first opera, *La favola d'Orfeo* was prod. in 1607, notable in history of mus. because for the first time the acc. was for a full (by the standards of the time) orch. The following year his *Arianna* was perf. at a ducal wedding celebration in Mantua; only the *Lamento*, which was immediately popular, survives. He left Cremona after the death of the Duke in 1612 and in 1613 became Master of Mus. of the Venetian Republic. For St Mark's, Venice, he composed a superb stream of sacred works which spread his fame throughout Europe. He received a visit from **Schütz* and his works were studied by M. **Praetorius* in Ger., **Mersenne* in Fr., and **Tomkins* in Eng. 12 of the operas he had written in Mantua were destroyed there in 1630 when it was sacked by Austrian troops. In the same year the plague ravaged Venice; the combination of these catastrophes probably accounts for Monteverdi's admission to holy orders in 1632. When the first opera house, San Cassiano, was opened in Venice in 1637, Monteverdi's interest in opera was re-kindled and for the remaining 6 years of his life he comp. a series of works of which only 2 survive.

Monteverdi's place in the history of Renaissance mus. can be justly compared to Shakespeare's in literature. Working from traditional beginnings, he transformed every genre in

which he worked by imaginative use of available styles rather than by revolutionary means. His madrigals cover a period of 40 years, from publication of the 1st book in 1589 to the 8th in 1638 (the 9th was pubd. posthumously in 1651). He soon introduced instr. accs., and chromatic modulations, and the dramatic nature of the mus. foreshadows the solo cantata and operatic recit., culminating in *Il combattimento di Tancredi e Clorinda* (1624) which is a miniature opera in style, acc. by str. and employing descriptive effects.

His sacred mus. veered between elaborate traditional polyphony and an advanced concerted style in which elements from his secular madrigals and operas lend colour and drama to the text, as in the famous *Vespers* comp. for Mantua in 1610. The operas take the Florentine **melodramatic* and monodic form and embellish it with all that he learned from It. madrigalists and Fr. composers. They are, in effect, the first mus. dramas, making use of what came to be known as **leitmotiv* and deploying many startling dramatic devices. They are also the first operas in which the characters are recognizably human rather than symbolic figures. Above all, the melodic genius and fertility of his mus. and its harmonic adventurousness are what make it so attractive and 'contemporary' in the 20th cent. Naturally, the scores present many musicological problems; their solution by various eds. has caused considerable disagreement among students of the period. Prin. works:

OPERAS & BALLETS: *La *favola d'Orfeo* (1607); **Arianna* (1608, lost); *Il ballo delle Ingrate* (1608); *Tirsi e Clori* (1616); *Favola di Peleo e di Theti* (1617, lost); *Il matrimonio d'Alceste con Admeto* (1618, lost); *Andromeda* (1619, lost); *Commento d'Apollo* (1620, lost); *La finta Pazza Licori* (1627, lost); *Mercurio e Marte* (1628, lost); *Adone* (1639, lost); *Le nozze d'Enea con Lavinia* (1641, lost); *Il *Ritorno d'Ulisse in patria* (1640); *L'*incoronazione di Poppea* (1642).

SACRED: *Madrigali spirituali*, 4 vv. (1583); **Vespro della Beata Vergine* (1610); *Mass, In illo tempore*, 6 vv. (1610); *Masses*, 4 vv., and psalms (1650); *Selva morale e spirituale* (1641) for varying numbers of vv. with varied instr. acc. in most cases; and a large number of motets, etc.

SECULAR VOCAL: *Canzonette* for 3 vv. (1584); *Madrigali*: Book I for 5 vv. (1587), II for 5 vv. (1590), III for 5 vv. (1592), IV for 5 vv. (1603), V for 5 vv., some with instr. acc. (1605), VI for 5 vv., some with instr. acc.; includes **Lamento d'Arianna* of 1608 (1614), VII for vv. from 1 to 6, with instr. acc., incl. *Lettera amorosa* (1619), VIII **Madrigali guerrieri e amorosi* (Madrigals of Love and War) for vv. from 1 to 8 with instr. acc., incl. *Il *Combattimento di Tancredi e Clorinda* of 1624 (1638), IX *Madrigali e Canzonette* for 2 to 3 vv., 4 with basso continuo (1651); 10 **Scherzi musicali* for 1 or 2 vv., all with basso continuo (1632); 15 *Scherzi musicali* for 3 vv., unacc. (1607).

Montgomery, Kenneth (Mervyn) (*b* Belfast, 1943). Irish conductor. Début Glyndebourne 1967 (*L'elisir d'amore*). Staff cond. SW 1967–70.

Ass. cond. Bournemouth SO and Sinfonietta from 1970; dir. Bournemouth Sinfonietta 1973–5. Mus. dir. GTO 1975–6. Cond. at Wexford, 1972; Netherlands Opera 1972 and 1975. Prin. cond. Netherlands Radio Orch. from 1976. CG début 1975. Art. and mus. dir. Opera Northern Ireland from 1985. Dir. opera studies Royal Cons., The Hague, from 1991.

Mont Juic. Orch. suite of Catalan dances in 4 movts. by *Britten (Op.12) and L. Berkeley (Op.9). Comp. 1937. Berkeley wrote 1st and 2nd movts., Britten 3rd and 4th. 3rd movt. is a Lament sub-titled *Barcelona, July 1936*. F.p. BBC concert 8 Jan. 1938.

Montoya, Carlos (*b* Madrid, 1903; *d* Wainscott, Long Is., NY, 1993). Sp. guitarist whose skill in *flamenco style achieved its recognition on a par with classical style. Played in cafés at age 14. In 1928 toured Europe with dancer La Argentina. First solo recitals 1948. Comp. and arr. mus. for flamenco guitar but could not read mus.

Montreal Symphony Orchestra. Canadian orch., the successor of several previous organizations. From 1897 to 1907 an orch. with this name was cond. by Joseph Goulet, a Belg. violinist who lived in Montreal from 1890. Douglas Clarke, dean of faculty of mus., McGill Univ., in 1930 formed sym. orch. which survived until 1941 and introduced many important works and soloists to Canada. A rival orch., sharing some of the players, was formed in 1935 as Les Concerts Symphoniques, sometimes cond. by Wilfrid *Pelletier and after 1941 by the Belg. Désiré *Défauw. In 1954 orch. was re-named Orchestre Symphonique de Montréal—Montreal SO. Conds. after Défauw: O. Klemperer 1950–3; I. Markevich 1955–60; Z. Mehta 1961–7; F.-P. Decker 1968–75; R. Frühbeck de Burgos 1975–6; Charles Dutoit 1978–2002; Kent Nagano from 2006.

Montsalvatge, Xavier (*b* Gerona, 1912; *d* Barcelona, 2002). Sp. composer. Wrote opera *El gato con botas* (Puss in Boots) (1947); *Mediterranean Symphony*, orch. (1949); 3 *Divertimenti*, pf. (1941); *Concerto breve*, pf., orch.; *Poema concertante*, vn., orch. (1952); and 5 *Canciones negras*, sop., pf. (1945).

Moody, Fanny (*b* Redruth, 1866; *d* Dundrum, Co. Dublin, 1945). Eng. soprano. Début London 1885; stage début with Carl Rosa Opera, Liverpool, 1887 (Arline in *The Bohemian Girl*). Married Charles *Manners 1890, with whom she formed *Moody-Manners Opera Company. Sang at CG and was first Eng. Tatiana in *Eugene Onegin* (1892).

Moody-Manners Opera Company. Touring opera co. formed 1898 by Charles *Manners and his wife Fanny *Moody and disbanded 1916. At its peak was split into 2 cos., one of 175 members, the other of 95.

Moog, Robert (Arthur) (*b* Flushing, NY, 1934; *d* Asherville, N. Car., 2005). Amer. audio-engineer and inventor. Pres., Moog Mus. Inc., Williamsville, NY. Invented and patented Moog *synthe-sizer (1965), manufactured by his co., which greatly increased options open to composers of elec. mus.

Moonlight and Roses. See *Lemare, E. H.*

Moonlight Sonata. Popular nickname of Beethoven's Pf. Sonata No.14 in C♯ minor, Op.27 No.2, comp. 1800–1. The nickname originated in review by poet Heinrich Rellstab (1799–1860) in which he wrote that the first movement reminded him of moonlight on Lake Lucerne—a misleading approach to a movement with almost the character of a funeral march.

Moór, Emanuel (*b* Kecskemét, Hung., 1863; *d* Mont Pèlerin, Montreux, 1931). Hung. composer, pianist, and conductor. Toured Europe and USA 1885–7 as pianist and cond. Wrote 4 operas (incl *La Pompadour*, 1901); 8 syms.; 3 pf. concs.; 2 vc. concs.; 4 vn. concs.; triple conc.; hp. conc.; va. conc.; much chamber mus.; and over 500 songs. Invented *Duplex-Coupler pf., 1921, with 2 kbds. tuned octave apart.

Moore, Douglas (Stuart) (*b* Cutchogue, NY, 1893; *d* Greenport, NY, 1969). Amer. composer, organist, and teacher. Ass. prof. of mus. Columbia Univ., NY, 1926, becoming head of mus. dept. 1940 and MacDowell Prof. of Mus. 1943–62. Works steeped in Amer. legends and history. Wrote 2 books. Prin. comps.:

OPERAS: *The *Devil and Daniel Webster* (1938); *The Emperor's New Clothes* (1948); *The Ballad of Baby Doe* (1956); *Carrie Nation* (1966).

ORCH.: *Symphony of Autumn* (1930), Sym. No.2 (1945); *Pageant of P. T. Barnum* (1924); *Moby Dick* (1927); *Village Music* (1941); *Symphony in A* (1945); *Farm Journal* (1947).

CHAMBER MUSIC: vn. sonata (1929); str. qt. (1933); cl. quintet (1946); pf. trio (1953).

CHORAL: *Simon Legree* (1938); *Prayer for the United Nations* (1943).

Moore, Gerald (*b* Watford, 1899; *d* Penn, Bucks, 1987). Eng. pianist, known as one of the finest of accompanists. Spent boyhood in Canada. First recorded for HMV 1921. Accomp. to tenor John *Coates from 1925. From early 1930s emerged as sensitive accompanist to leading singers. After 1945 closely assoc. with Kathleen *Ferrier, Elisabeth *Schwarzkopf (with whom he made his Salzburg Fest. début, 1954), Victoria de *los Angeles, Janet *Baker, Dietrich *Fischer-Dieskau, and others. Made many records. Wrote several books, incl. *The Unashamed Accompanist* (1943, rev. 1957) and *Am I Too Loud?* (1962). Frequent broadcaster. Retired from concerts 1967 but continued to record and lecture. CBE 1954.

Moore, Grace (*b* Nough, Tenn., 1898; *d* Kastrup Airport, Copenhagen, in air crash, 1947). Amer. soprano. After singing in cafés, night-clubs, and revues went in 1926 to Fr. to study for 2 years. Début Paris and Nice 1927 with Amer.-Ger. Opera Co. NY Met 1928–32 (début as Mimì in *La bohème*), and 1935–46; CG 1935; Paris Opéra-Comique 1928, 1938, 1946; Salzburg Fest. 1946.

Sang *Louise* in Paris after study with *Charpentier. Appeared in several films, incl. *One Night of Love*, *New Moon*, and *Love Me Forever*. Autobiography *You're Only Human Once* (1944).

Moore, Jerrold Northrop (*b* Paterson, NJ, 1934). Amer. musicologist. Taught at Rochester Univ. 1958–61. Curator of historical sound recordings, Yale Univ. 1961–70. Settled in Eng. 1970, becoming a leading authority on Elgar and the history of gramophone recording. Joint ed. of Elgar Complete Edition. Ed. *Music and Friends: Seven Decades of Letters to Adrian Boult* (1979). Author of *An Elgar Discography* (1963), *Elgar: a Life in Photographs* (1972), *Elgar on Record* (1974), *A Voice in Time: the Gramophone of Fred Gaisberg* (1976), *Spirit of England: Edward Elgar in his World* (1984), and *Edward Elgar: a Creative Life* (1984). Ed., *Elgar and his Publishers: Letters of a Creative Life*, Vols. I and II (1987), *Edward Elgar: the Windflower Letters* (1989), *Edward Elgar: Letters of a Lifetime* (1990), and *Elgar: Child of Dreams* (2004). Compiled and wrote *Vaughan Williams: a Life in Photographs* (1992).

Moore, Thomas (*b* Dublin, 1779; *d* Devizes, 1852). Irish poet and musician. Self-taught musically. In 1802 began to write words and mus. of songs pubd. 1807–8 as *Irish Melodies*. By 1834, 10 sets of these melodies and folk-song arrs. had been pubd., the last 2 being harmonized by *Bishop. Among the most enduring of his songs were *The Last Rose of Summer* (incorporated into Flotow's *Martha*), *The Harp that Once in Tara's Halls*, and *The Minstrel Boy*, the words of which he set to traditional tunes. His *Lalla Rookh* (1817) with its 4 interpolated poems (e.g. *Paradise and the Peri*), became the basis of several mus. comps. (by Spontini, Berlioz, Rubinstein, Stanford, Schumann, and Bantock).

Morales, Cristóbal de (*b* Seville, *c*.1500; *d* ?Marchéna, 1553). Sp. composer. Chapelmaster, Àvila Cath., 1526–8, Plasencia Cath. 1528–31. Member of Papal Choir, Rome, 1535–45. While in It. comp. most of his church mus. which ranks him with Victoria and Palestrina as a master of polyphony. Returned to Toledo 1545–7, chapelmaster at Málaga Cath. 1551–3.

moralities. See *miracle plays*.

Moralt, Rudolf (*b* Munich, 1902; *d* Vienna, 1958). Ger. conductor. Ch. trainer Munich Opera 1919–23, then opera cond. at Kaiserslautern 1923–8, 1932–4, Brno 1932–4, Brunswick 1934–6, and Graz 1937–40. Salzburg Fest. début 1939. Regular cond. Vienna Opera 1940–58. Relative of Richard Strauss.

Moran, Robert (Leonard) (*b* Denver, 1937). Amer. composer. Dir., West Coast Mus. Ens., S. Francisco. Comp.-in-res. Portland State Univ. 1972–4 and Northwestern Univ. 1977–8. Moved to NY 1978 and Philadelphia 1985. Among his works, using aleatory techniques, are *L'après-midi du Dracoula*, for any group of instrs. (1966); *Smell Piece for Mills College*, for frying pans and foods (1967, 'orig. intended to produce a conflagration

sufficiently thermal to burn down the college'). Operas incl. *The Juniper Tree* (1985, in collab. with *Glass). His *Hitler: Geschichten aus der Zukunft* (1981) was banned in Ger. Later operas incl. *Desert of Roses* (1989–90, f.p. Houston 1992); *From the Towers of the Moon* (1990); *The Dracula Diary* (1994); *Remember Me to Him* (1996).

morasco. See *moresca*.

morbido; morbidezza (It.). Soft, gentle; softness, gentleness. (Not morbid, or morbidity.)

morceau (Fr.). Piece. So *morceau symphonique*, symphonic piece. (For *morceau d'ensemble* see *ensemble*.)

Morceaux en forme de poire, Trois (3 Pear-shaped pieces). Work for pf., 4 hands, by *Satie, 1903, containing, title notwithstanding, 7 items. Orch. version by R. Désormière.

mordent (from It. *mordere*, to bite). Mus. *ornament shown by a sign over the note. There are upper and lower mordents.

In Ger. *Mordent* means only the lower mordent. Examples are:

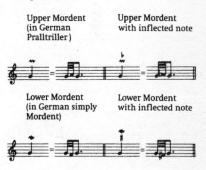

In the case of the upper mordent these 'crushed in' notes are the main note itself and the note above; if the latter is to be inflected in any way the necessary sign ($\sharp \natural \times \flat \flat$) appears *above* the mordent sign.

In the case of the lower mordent the 'crushed in' notes consist of the note itself and the note below; if this latter is to be inflected in any way the necessary sign appears *below* the lower mordent sign (the interval is generally that of a semitone).

There is a confusion of terminology. The terms 'mordent' and 'inverted mordent' are very commonly used for the two forms, but some call the first one shown above the 'mordent' and the second one the 'inverted mordent', and others reverse these titles. The one way of avoiding all misunderstanding is always to use the words 'upper' and 'lower'. In addition to these 2 forms, others were used by earlier composers but in modern edns. those are set out in full. See also *acciaccatura*.

Mordkovitch, Lydia (b Saratov, 1950). Russ.-born violinist. Emigrated to Israel 1974, then settled in Eng. Brit. début with Hallé Orch. 1979. Proms début 1985. Advocate of 20th cent. concs., notably those of Moeran, Prokofiev, Shostakovich, and Szymanowski.

morendo (It. 'dying'). Instruction for the mus. to die away gradually, often used by Verdi (also by Beethoven, at end of slow movt. of str. qt. Op.74).

moresca (moresco), **morisca** (morisco). A Moorish dance. Apparently the name (which was common from the 15th to 17th cents.) did not carry any fixed implications as to rhythm or style. Often it was applied to any rough-and-ready grotesque dance employing animal costumes, etc. In *Arbeau's Orchésographie (1588–9)*, it is said that some performers blacked their faces to resemble Moors and wore bells on their legs; this has led to speculation that the Eng. *Morris dance is a derivation.

Moreschi, Alessandro (b Montecompatri, nr. Rome, 1858; d Rome, 1922). It. castrato, the last. Sang in Sistine Chapel 1883–1913. Known as 'L'angelo di Roma' because of vocal purity. A recording exists.

moresque (Fr.). Same as *moresca.

Morgenblätter (Morning leaves, or morning newspapers). Title of waltz, Op.279, by Johann Strauss II comp. for Vienna Press Ball (1864).

Morhange, Charles Henri. Real name of *Alkan.

Mörike-Lieder (Songs of Mörike). 53 songs by Hugo *Wolf for solo v. and pf. to poems by the Ger. poet Eduard Friedrich Mörike (1804–75), comp. 1888, incl. *Elfenlied, Gesang Weylas, Der Feuerreiter*, and *An die Geliebte*. 11 of them were later orchestrated.

Morison, Elsie (Jean) (b Ballarat, 1924). Australian soprano. Début Melbourne 1944 (in *Messiah*). London début 1948 (in *Acis and Galatea*). In SW Opera Co. 1948–54 and at CG 1953–62, also many concert appearances in oratorio, etc. Sang Blanche in Eng. première of *Les *dialogues des Carmélites*, CG 1958, and Anne Trulove in f. Brit. p. of *The Rake's Progress* by Glyndebourne at Edinburgh Fest. 1953 and at Glyndebourne 1954. Wife of Rafael *Kubelik, whom she married in 1963.

Mørk, Truls (b Bergen, 1961). Norwegian cellist. Finalist and prizewinner Tchaikovsky comp., Moscow 1982. NY recital début 1986, London 1988. Proms début 1989 with Oslo PO. Founder and art. dir. Stavanger int. chamber mus. fest.

Morlacchi, Francesco (b Perugia, 1784; d Innsbruck, 1841). It. composer. Wrote cantata for Napoleon's coronation as King of It. in Milan 1805. Comp. 8 *opera buffa* 1807–10, then went to Dresden as cond. of It. opera there, remaining until his death. Wrote many operas, incl. *Il nuovo barbiere di Siviglia* (Dresden, 1816), and much

church mus. Morlacchi's absences in It. caused Weber, appointed Kapellmeister at Dresden, 1817, to overwork.

Morley, Thomas (b ?Norwich, 1557; d London, 1602). Eng. composer. Pupil of *Byrd. Mus.B., Oxford Univ., 1588. Organist, St Paul's Cath. c.1589–92. Almost certainly worked as a government spy. Gentleman of Chapel Royal 1592. In 1598, granted by Elizabeth I exclusive licence for 21 years to print song-books of all kinds and mus. paper. Thus he pubd. not only his own mus. but that of his contemporaries. Pubd. and ed. *The Triumphs of Oriana* (1601), to which he contributed *Arise, awake* for 5 vv. and *Hard by a crystal fountain* for 6 vv. Was one of great masters of Eng. madrigal. Probably friend of Shakespeare: setting of *It was a lover and his lass* for *As You Like It* may have been for orig. prod., 1599. Specialized in balletts. Also wrote church mus., incl. Burial Service; lute songs, and *A Plaine and Easie Introduction to Practicall Musicke* (1597). Among his works and publications were: *Canzonets* for 3 vv. (1593), *Madrigals* for 4 vv. (1594), *1st Book of Balletts*, 5 vv. (1595), *1st Book of Canzonets*, 2 vv. (1595), *Canzonets*, 4 vv. (selected from 'best It. authors' but incl. 2 by Morley) (1597), *Madrigals*, 5 vv. (selected from 'best It. authors') (1598), *1st Book of Consort Lessons*, 6 instr. (1599), *1st Book of Ayres*, lute and bass viol (1600), *The *Triumphs of Oriana*, 5 and 6 vv. 'by divers several authors' (1601).

Morley College. Non-vocational adult education centre in London, founded 1889. Has flourishing and adventurous mus. dept., dirs. of which have incl. Holst (1907–24), Goldsbrough (1924–8), Arnold Foster (1928–40), Tippett (1940–51), Fricker (1952–64), Gardner (1965–9), Graubart (1969–91), Hanson from 1991.

Morning Heroes. Sym. for orator, ch., and orch. by Bliss, f.p. Norwich Festival 1930. Comp. in memory of his brother, killed in 1914–18 war in which Bliss also served. Texts used are Iliad, Whitman, Li-Tai-Po, Wilfred Owen, and Robert Nichols.

Mornington, Garret Colley Wesley, 1st Earl of (b Dangan, Co. Meath, 1735; d Kensington, 1781). Irish composer and landowner, father of Arthur Wellesley, first Duke of Wellington (surname changed to Wellesley after Mornington's death). Self-taught in mus. Founded Dublin Acad. of Mus. Prof. of mus., Dublin Univ. 1764–74. Excelled in composing glees. Wrote church mus., incl. fine setting of the Burial Service, and an unpublished cantata, *Caractacus*.

Moross, Jerome (b Brooklyn, NY, 1913; d Miami, 1983). Amer. composer. Belonged to 'young composers' group', NY 1934–6. Went to Hollywood 1938 to write and arrange film mus. In 1940 collab. with Copland on mus. for *Our Town*. Works incl.: *Paul Bunyan* (ballet, 1934); *Frankie and Johnnie* (ballet, 1938); *Susanna and the Elders* (ballet-opera, 1940); *The Eccentricities of Davy Crockett* (ballet-opera, 1945); *Gentlemen, Be Seated!* (opera, 1955–6); sym. (1941–2); *Suite* for chamber orch. (1934); sonata for db. and pf.

Morris, Gareth (Charles Walter) (*b* Clevedon, 1920). Eng. flautist. Début as soloist, London 1939. Played with Boyd Neel Orch. and in Dennis Brain Wind Quintet. Prof. of fl., RAM, 1945–85. Prin. fl., Philharmonia Orch. 1948–72. Always played wooden fl.

Morris, James (Peppler) (*b* Baltimore, 1947). Amer. bass-baritone. Début Baltimore 1967 (Crespel in *Les contes d'Hoffmann*). Débuts: NY Met 1971; Glyndebourne 1972; Salzburg Fest. 1982. Sang Wotan in *Die Walküre* at Baltimore 1984 and, after coaching by Hans *Hotter, sang role in S. Francisco and Vienna 1985, at Munich 1987, Berlin 1987, NY Met 1989, and CG 1988–91. Sings Wotan on recordings of *Ring* cond. by Haitink and by Levine.

Morris, Morrice. A type of Eng. folk dance for men, assoc. with Whitsuntide and perf. to the acc. of pipe, tabor, fiddle, concertina, and accordeon. The dancers wear bells on their shins: sometimes they are dressed to represent characters (the Queen of the May, the Fool, etc.). The mus. is usually in duple or quadruple time. Some Eng. villages possess Morris troupes whose origin goes back to an unknown antiquity. Conjecture that the dance derives from the *moresca* is unsubstantiated.

Morris, R(eginald) **O**(wen) (*b* York, 1886; *d* London, 1948). Eng. teacher and composer. On staff RCM 1920–6. Dir. of theory and comp. Curtis Inst. 1926–8; rejoined RCM 1928–48. Author of several textbooks incl. *Contrapuntal Technique in the 16th Century* (1922). Had many distinguished pupils. Comp. sym. (1935), vn. conc., vc. suite, str. qts., songs, and folk-song arrs. Brother-in-law of *Vaughan Williams. Compiled crosswords for *The Times*.

Morris, Wyn (*b* Trelech, 1929). Welsh conductor. Founder-cond., Welsh SO 1957–60. Cond., Royal Choral Soc. 1968–70, Huddersfield Choral Soc. 1969–74. Specialist in mus. of Mahler. Cond. f.p. final rev. of Cooke perf. version of Mahler's 10th Sym., 1972.

Morrison, (Stuart) **Angus** (*b* Maidenhead, 1902; *d* London, 1989). Eng. pianist. Teacher at RCM 1926–72. Début, London 1923. Also played in trio with Jean Pougnet (vn.) and Anthony Pini (vc.). Champion of Fr. and Eng. composers, friend of Walton, Lambert, etc. Played solo pf. part in f.p. (broadcast) of Lambert's *Rio Grande*, 1928. CBE 1979.

Mort de Cléopâtre, La (The Death of Cleopatra). Lyric scene for sop. or mez. and orch. by Berlioz, comp. 1829 as entry for *Prix de Rome* but no prize was awarded. Part of a larger cantata, *Cléopâtre*, the rest being destroyed.

Mortier, Gerard (*b* Ghent, 1943). Belg. administrator. Ass. admin., Flanders Fest. 1968–72.

Worked at Deutsche Oper am Rhein, Düsseldorf, 1973. Ass. admin. Frankfurt Opera 1973–7. Dir., artistic prod., Hamburg Opera 1977–9. Programme consultant, Paris Opéra 1979–81. Gen. dir., Théâtre de la Monnaie, Brussels, 1981–92, a decade of expansion and enterprise in choice of works, producers, and designers. Art. dir. Salzburg Fest. 1992–2001; dir. Paris Opéra from 2004.

Mortimer, Harry (Henry) (*b* Hebden Bridge, Yorks., 1902; *d* London, 1992). Eng. brass-band conductor and trumpeter. Member of celebrated brass-band family. Cornet-player at 7. Trumpeter in Hallé Orch. (under Harty) 1926–30, Liverpool PO 1930–4, BBC Northern Orch. 1935–42. Cond. several championship brass bands, incl. Foden's, Fairey Aviation, Munn and Felton's, Morris Motors, and Black Dyke Mills. Brass and military bands supervisor, BBC 1942–64. CBE 1984.

Moscheles, Ignaz (*b* Prague, 1794; *d* Leipzig, 1870). Ger.-Bohemian pianist, composer, and teacher. Made pf. score of *Fidelio*, 1814, under Beethoven's supervision. After success of his *Variations*, Op.32, in 1815 he toured Europe for 10 years, visiting London 1821 and 1823. Gave pf. lessons to *Mendelssohn 1824. Settled in London 1826. Cond. f. (private) London p. of Beethoven's *Missa Solemnis*, 1832; and 9th Sym. 1837 and 1838 at Philharmonic Soc. Founded series of chamber concerts and played Bach and Scarlatti on hpd. Prof. of pf. at new Leipzig Cons. 1846–70. Comp. 8 pf. concs. (1819–38) and numerous other works. Trans. Schindler's biography of Beethoven into Eng., 1841.

Mosè in Egitto (Moses in Egypt). Opera (*azione tragica-sacra*) in 4 acts (orig. 3) by Rossini to lib. by A. L. Tottola. Prod. Naples 1818 (the well-known 'Prayer' being added for 1819 revival), Vienna 1821 (in Ger.), London 1822 (in It. as *Pietro l'Eremita* (Peter the Hermit)), CG 1833 (in Eng. as *The Israelites in Egypt* with additions from Handel's *Israel in Egypt*), NY 1835. 4-act version with Fr. lib. by Balocchi and de Jouy and mus. substantially rev., prod. Paris 1827 under title *Moïse et Pharaon*. This version prod. CG (under title *Zora*) 1850, NY 1860.

Moser, Edda (Elisabeth) (*b* Berlin, 1938). Ger. soprano, daughter of Hans Joachim *Moser. Début Berlin Städtische Oper 1962 (Kate Pinkerton in *Madama Butterfly*). Sang at Hagen and Bielefeld from 1964. Sang in f.p. of Henze's *Das Floss der Medusa*, Vienna 1971. Salzburg Easter Fest. début 1968; NY Met 1968; Salzburg Fest. 1970. Sang title-role in Matthus's *Omphale*, Cologne 1979.

Moser, Hans Joachim (*b* Berlin, 1889; *d* Berlin, 1967). Ger. musicologist, singer, teacher, and historian. Son of Andreas Moser, violinist. Prof. of musicology, Halle Univ. from 1922, Heidelberg from 1925. Salzburg Fest. début 1925 (in Hofmannsthal's *Das Salzburger grosse Welttheater*). Dir. State Acad. for Sch. and Church Mus., Berlin, 1927–33. Prof. of musicology, Jena Univ. 1947; dir., Berlin Cons. 1950–60. Arr. Weber's *Euryanthe* with new text, Berlin 1915; ed. Handel's *Orlando* (1922); ed. works of Weber with A. Sandberg. Author of many books of mus. history and biography, incl. *Musiklexikon* (1932–5, 1955, suppl. 1963); *Geschichte der deutschen Musik* (3 vols., 1920–4); *J. S. Bach* (1935); *Heinrich Schütz* (1936, rev. 1954); *Gluck* (1940); *Handel* (1941); *Weber* (1941); *Goethe and Music* (1949); *Buxtehude* (1957). Also composer.

Moser, Thomas (*b* Richmond, Va., 1945). Amer. tenor. Opera début Graz 1975. Munich Opera 1976 (Belmonte in *Die Entführing*); Vienna Opera from 1977 in Mozart roles. NY City Opera 1979; Salzburg Fest. 1976. Created Tenor in *Un *re in ascolto* (Salzburg 1984).

Moses und Aron (Moses and Aaron). Opera in 3 acts (3rd act lib. only) by Schoenberg to his own lib. Comp. 1930–2. Prod. (concert) Hamburg 1954, stage Zurich 1957, Berlin 1959, London CG 1965, Boston 1966, Paris 1975, Salzburg 1987. Schoenberg in 1951 said that the 3rd act could be spoken, but Scherchen in Berlin had it spoken to mus. taken from Act 1. Most perfs. keep to 2 completed acts. Act 2 contains *Dance Before the Golden Calf*, f.p. Darmstadt 1951.

Moshinsky, Elijah (*b* Shanghai, 1946). Australian director. In 1970s and 1980s prod. Shakespeare and the classics for Nat. Th., London, and BBC TV. Operatic career began at CG 1975 with *Peter Grimes*, followed there by many productions. For ENO prods. incl. Brit. première of Ligeti's *Le Grand Macabre* (1984). NY Met début 1980. WNO début 1994.

mosso (It.). Moved, e.g. *più mosso*, more moved, i.e. quicker.

Mossolov, Alexander (Vasilyevich) (*b* Kiev, 1900; *d* Moscow, 1973). Russ. composer. Early songs had newspaper advertisements as texts. Was among first proponents of 'Soviet realism' under name 'constructivist music', e.g. ballet *The Factory* (1927), which employed metal sheet, shaken in the orch., for realistic effects (perf. also as concert piece under names 'Music of the Machines' or 'Iron foundry'). This was criticized in Russia as 'decadent'. Mossolov was back in favour during 1941–5 war with patriotic works. Wrote 4 operas; 6 syms. (1928–50); 2 pf. concs. (1927, 1932); vc. conc.; vn. conc.; chamber mus.; and songs.

Moszkowski, Moritz (*b* Breslau, 1854; *d* Paris, 1925). Polish-Ger. pianist and composer. Début Berlin 1873, London 1886. Settled in Paris 1897. Wrote opera, ballet, vn. conc., pf. conc., and many songs, but chiefly known for his lighter pf. pieces, esp. his *Spanish Dances* for pf. duet. Pupils incl. Josef Hofmann, Wanda Landowska, Joaquin Nin, and Joaquin Turina.

motet. A form of short unaccompanied choral comp. which eventually superseded *conductus, although both were in use from 13th to early 16th cents. In 13th, 14th, and 15th cents. the motet was exclusively sacred and was based on a pre-existing melody and set of words to which other melodies and words were added in counterpoint. *Machaut, *Desprès, *Ockeghem, and others were masters of the motet. *Du Fay introduced secular melodies as the *cantus firmus* of the motet. By the 16th cent., the motet reached its apogee as a sacred comp., with the madrigal as its secular counterpart. Palestrina wrote about 180 motets. Victoria, Morales, Tallis, Byrd, Bull, and Taverner were great composers of motets, sometimes called *Cantiones Sacrae*. J. S. Bach wrote motets (incl. *Singet dem Herren*), 4 of them for 8 vv. Soon the term came to be loosely applied by composers, sometimes to works with acc. and even to works for solo v. and acc. In some cases, e.g. Parry's *Songs of Farewell*, the words are not ecclesiastical. Generally today the term signifies a church choral comp. with Lat. words not fixed in the Liturgy. In 1951–2 Bernard Naylor wrote 9 motets to Eng. texts as a cycle for the 9 major church festivals.

Mother, The (*Matka*). Opera in 10 scenes by A. *Hába to his own lib. Prod. Munich 1931, rev. version Florence 1964. First opera to employ quarter-tones.

Mother Goose (Ravel). See *Ma mère l'Oye*.

motif (Fr.; Eng. *motive*; Ger. *motiv*). The shortest intelligible and self-existent melodic or rhythmic figure (e.g. the first 4 notes of Beethoven's 5th Sym.). Every 'theme' or 'subject' perhaps has several *motifs*, and almost every mus. passage will be found to be a development of some *motif*. But the word has, in mus. analysis, been used as a synonym for 'theme'; and Wagner's extension of it to *leitmotiv* has further complicated the issue. The adjective 'motivic' is an invention of analytical writers, functional but ugly and better avoided.

motion. (1) Term which denotes the course upwards or downwards of a melody or melodies. In the combination of any 2 'voices' or 'parts' of a comp., if they proceed in the same direction (notationally considered), they are said to be in *similar motion*, if in opposite directions, in *contrary motion*. If one part holds (or repeats) a note and the other part moves up or down from it, that is *oblique motion*. Similar Motion in which the parts proceed by the same intervals (numerically considered) is *parallel motion*.

(2) In the shaping of a single part progress of one note to an adjacent note by step is called *conjunct motion* and progress to some other note by leap *disjunct motion*.

moto (It.). Motion. *con moto*, with motion, i.e. quickly. *moto perpetuo* (It.). Perpetual motion. See *perpetuum mobile*.

motor rhythm. 20th-cent. term for the type of rhythm which is as though mechanized, i.e. like the sound of an engine. The ugly adjective 'motoric' has, alas, been coined as descriptive of this kind of comp. or passage of comp.

Mottl, Felix (Josef) (b Unter-Sankt-Veit, nr. Vienna, 1856; d Munich, 1911). Austrian conductor and composer. Appointed as one of Wagner's assistants at first Bayreuth Fest., 1876, becoming one of group of young admirers in Wagner's circle. Cond. Karlsruhe Opera 1881–1903, setting high standards. Cond. first complete perf. of Les Troyens (on 2 consecutive evenings), Karlsruhe 1890. Cond. Bayreuth Fest. 1886–92. Cond. CG 1898–1900, NY Met 1903. Cond. Munich Opera 1903–11, Vienna PO 1904–7. Comp. 4 operas, str. qt., songs, etc. Ed. vocal scores of all Wagner's works, made reduced orch. score for some of the operas. Orchestrated Wagner's 5 Wesendonck-Lieder. Also ed. Berlioz works. Collapsed while conducting Tristan and died a few days later.

motto theme. A theme which recurs, sometimes transformed, throughout the course of a comp., e.g. in Beethoven's 5th, Tchaikovsky's 4th and 5th, and Elgar's 1st Syms. It is akin to Wagner's leitmotiv, Berlioz's idée fixe, and Liszt's metamorphosis of themes.

Mount of Olives (Beethoven). See Christus am Ölberge.

Moussorgsky, Modest. See Mussorgsky, Modest.

mouth organ. See harmonica.

mouthpiece (Fr. bec (woodwind); embouchure (brass)). Part of a woodwind or brass instr. which is inserted in the player's mouth or to which he applies his lips in order to produce a sound.

Mouton, Jean (b Holluigue, c.1459; d St Quentin, 1522). Fr. composer. Served at courts of Louis XII and François I. Wrote at least 15 masses, over 100 motets, and chansons. Teacher of *Willaert. His music has great technical polish, excellent contrapuntal mastery, and flowing polyphony, but perhaps lacks brilliance of Desprès.

mouvement (Fr., abbreviated to mouvt.). Movt., either in the sense of motion, or a section of a large comp., such as a sym. (see movement). Sometimes (as in Debussy), the word is used to indicate a return to the orig. speed after some tempo deviation. Mouvement perpétuel is the Fr. equivalent of *perpetuum mobile.

movable-doh. A term applied to that system of sight-singing in which doh is the name applied to the keynote of every major scale, ray to the 2nd note, me to the 3rd, and so on—as distinct from the *fixed-doh system in which C is, in every key in which it occurs, called doh, D called ray, and so on. (See sight-reading, tonic sol-fa.)

movement. The primary, self-contained sections of a large comp. (sym., conc., sonata, suite, etc.), so called because each movt. of a work usually has a separate tempo indication. Some comps. are in 1 movt., e.g. Sibelius's 7th Sym., and in many composer marks movts. to follow on from each other without a break. The word sometimes occurs in the title of a work, e.g. Stravinsky's Symphony in 3 Movements and his *Movements for pf. and orch.

Movements. Work in 5 short sections for pf. and orch. by Stravinsky, comp. 1958–9. F.p. NY 1960. Used as mus. for ballet to choreog. by Balanchine, prod. NY, 1963.

movimento (It.). Motion, as distinct from movt. in the structural sense. Doppio movimento means 'at double the preceding speed'.

Moyse, Marcel (Joseph) (b Saint-Amour, Jura, 1889; d Brattleboro, Vermont, 1984). Fr. flautist and teacher. Prin. fl. in several Paris orchs. Prof. of fl., Paris Cons. 1932–49. Went to USA 1949 and with Rudolf *Serkin and others organized Marlboro Fest. at Brattleboro. Gave master classes in Switz. and Japan. Cond. Mozart and Dvořák in NY at age of 92. Wrote studies for fl. and compiled a manual.

Mozart, (Johann Georg) **Leopold** (b Augsburg, 1719; d Salzburg, 1787). Ger. composer and violinist. Educated in Augsburg 1727–35. Went to Salzburg Benedictine Univ. 1737. Played in orch. of Prince-Archbishop of Salzburg from 1743, becoming court composer and Vice-Kapellmeister 1762. Father of 2 prodigiously talented children, Wolfgang and Anna, to whose training and exploitation he devoted much time. Comp. many types of mus., incl. famous *Toy Symphony (simplified and reduced version of a Cassation in G) and author of influential vn. method, 1756.

Mozart, Wolfgang Amadeus [baptized Johannes Chrysostomus Wolfgangus Theophilus] (b Salzburg, 1756; d Vienna, 1791). Austrian composer, keyboard-player, violinist, violist, and conductor. Son of Leopold *Mozart, Vice-Kapellmeister to Prince-Archbishop of Salzburg, Mozart showed exceptional musical precocity, playing the klavier at 3 and composing at 5. His elder sister Maria Anna (1751–1829) was also a brilliant kbd. player and in 1762 Leopold decided to present his children's talents at various European courts. They first visited Munich and Vienna in 1762. Wolfgang was now able to play the vn. without having had formal teaching. In 1763 a longer journey began, from Munich, Augsburg, Frankfurt, and other cities to Cologne, Brussels, and Paris. They spent a fortnight at Louis XV's court at Versailles. In Apr. 1764 they arrived in London and were received by George III. While in London, Wolfgang studied with *Abel, comp. with J. C. *Bach, and singing with the castrato Manzuoli. He wrote his first 3 syms. in London. After visits to Holland and Switzerland, the Mozart family returned to Salzburg in Nov. 1766. Further visits to Vienna were made in 1767 and 1768 and Mozart comp. 2 operas, La finta semplice and Bastien und Bastienne. In Dec. 1769, Leopold took Mozart to It. where the boy's genius was everywhere acclaimed. He was taught by *Martini and met Nardini, *Jommelli, and Burney. In Rome he heard Allegri's *Miserere* and wrote it out from memory. His opera *Mitridate, Rè di Ponto* was successfully prod. in Milan in Dec. 1770. Two further visits to It. speedily followed, but the new prince-archbishop of Salzburg was less well-disposed towards the Mozarts and in 1777 Mozart left on a tour with his mother, Leopold not being well enough to go. They visited Munich, Augsburg, Mannheim (where he heard the famous orch.) and arrived in Paris in 1778. Mozart's mother died there in July of that year. No longer a *Wunderkind*, Mozart had less appeal for the Parisians, who were engrossed in the Gluck-Piccinni controversy. Unable to obtain a court post, Mozart returned to Salzburg where he spent the next 2 years as court and cath. org. amid growing hostility to the archbishop. In 1780 the Elector of Bavaria commissioned an opera from Mozart (*Idomeneo*), prod. in Munich, Jan. 1781. On Mozart's return to Salzburg he had a final confrontation with the archbishop and resigned. He went to Vienna, where he married Constanze Weber in Aug. 1782, a few days after the first perf. of his opera *Die Entführung aus dem Serail*. The last 9 years of his life were a juxtaposition of financial troubles with an astonishing outpouring of masterpieces in almost every genre. In 1785 he frequently played the va. in str. qts. with Dittersdorf and Haydn. To the latter, who regarded Mozart as the greatest composer he knew, Mozart dedicated 6 str. qts. in the autumn of 1785, when he also began work on *Le nozze di Figaro*. He frequently appeared as soloist in his own kbd. concs. Although *Figaro* was rapturously received in Vienna in 1786, it was taken off after 9 perfs., but was the rage of Prague when prod. there in 1787. During his visit to the Bohemian capital, Mozart's Sym. in D (K504, No.38) received its f.p., thereafter being known as the 'Prague Sym'. He was subsequently commissioned to write an opera for Prague for the following autumn. The result was *Don Giovanni*, written in a few months while the 2 str. quintets in C major and G minor and *Eine kleine Nachtmusik* were also composed. In the same year Leopold Mozart died at Salzburg. The new opera was a success in Prague, but initially failed in Vienna, where it was prod. with some extra numbers in May 1788. A month later Mozart began to compose the first of his 3 last syms., completing them between 26 June and 10 Aug. In 1789, under severe financial pressure, he played a conc. in Dresden on the way to Berlin. He visited Leipzig, playing Bach's org. at St Thomas's. In Berlin King Friedrich Wilhelm II, a cellist, commissioned 6 str. qts. of which only 3 were written. In the autumn Emperor Joseph II of Austria commissioned a new comic opera, *Così fan tutte*, which was prod. early in 1790. Joseph died shortly afterwards, but Mozart's hope of being appointed by Leopold II Kapellmeister in place of Salieri was not fulfilled. In 1791 he was approached by the actor-manager Schikaneder with a view to composing a fairy-tale opera on a lib. concocted by Schikaneder. *Die Zauberflöte*

was almost completed by July, the month in which Mozart received a commission to compose a *Requiem* for an anonymous patron (Count F. von Walsegg who wished to pass it off as his own). Mozart deferred work on it to compose an adaptation of Metastasio's *La clemenza di Tito* for Leopold II's coronation as King of Bohemia in Prague in Sept. This prod. was supervised by Mozart, who returned to Vienna, wrote the cl. conc., cond. the f.p. of *Die Zauberflöte*, and then resumed work on the *Requiem*. But his health, which had been deteriorating for some time, now became critical and he died on 5 Dec., leaving the *Requiem* to be completed by his pupil Süssmayr. He was buried in accordance with the Emperor Joseph II's regulations, with others who had died at the same time, and the location of his grave remains unknown. The circumstances of Mozart's death have given rise to many sensational theories, none proved, and there is much medical speculation on the cause of death.

The extent and range of Mozart's genius are so vast and so bewildering that any concise summing-up of his achievement must risk being trite. He took the mus. small-change of his day, learned from childhood in the courts of Europe, and transformed it into a mint of gold. His sense of form and symmetry seems to have been innate and was allied to an infallible craftsmanship which was partly learnt and partly instinctive. In his operas he not only displayed hitherto unequalled dramatic feeling, but widened the boundaries of the singer's art through contact with some of the greatest vv. of his day and, with his amazing insight into human nature, at once perceptive and detached, he created characters on the stage who may be claimed in their context as the equal of Shakespeare's. His music was supranational, combining It., Fr., Austrian, and Ger. elements. Not by revolutionary deliberation but by the natural superiority of the mus. he wrote, he changed the course of the sym., the pf. conc., the str. qt., the sonata, and much more besides. Perhaps the only element missing from his mus. is the worship of Nature which Beethoven and later 19th-cent. composers were to supply. There are brilliance and gaiety on the surface of Mozart's mus., but underneath a dark vein of melancholy which gives his works (*Così fan tutte* in particular) an ambivalence which is continually fascinating and provocative. 'Mozart *is* music', a critic said, and most composers since 1791 have agreed. A selective list of prin. works follows. Some of the dates, which are *Köchel's, are conjectural:

OPERAS: *Apollo et Hyacinthus*, intermezzo (K38, 1767); **Bastien und Bastienne* (K50, 1768); *La *finta semplice* (K51, 1769); **Mitridate, Rè di Ponto* (K87, 1770); *Ascanio in Alba* (K111, 1771); *Il sogno di Scipione* (K126, 1771); **Lucio Silla* (K135, 1772); *La *finta giardiniera* (K196, 1774); *Il **Rè Pastore* (K208, 1775); **Zaide* (K344, 1779–80); **Thamos, König in Ägypten* (K345, 1773, rev. 1776 and 1779–80, incid. music); **Idomeneo, Rè di Creta* (K366, 1780–1); *Die **Entführung aus dem Serail* (K384, 1781–2); *L'**Oca del Cairo* (K422, 1783); *Lo sposo deluso* (K430,

1783); *Der Schauspieldirektor* (The *Impresario) (K486, 1785–6); *Le *nozze di Figaro* (K492, 1785–6); *Don Giovanni* (K527, 1787); *Cosi fan tutte* (K588, 1789); *Die *Zauberflöte* (The Magic Flute) (K620, 1790–1); *La *clemenza di Tito* (K621, 1791).

BALLET MUSIC: *Les *Petits Riens* (K Anh. 10, 1778); for *Idomeneo* (K367, 1780).

SYMPHONIES (numbered according to Breitkopf and Härtel edn.): No.1 in E♭ (K16, 1764); No.4 in D (K19, 1764); No.5 in B♭ (K22, 1765); No.6 in F (K43, 1767); No.7 in D (K45, 1768); No.8 in D (K48, 1768); No.9 in C (K73, 1771); No.10 in G (K74, 1770); No.11 in D (K84, 1770); No.12 in G (K110, 1771); No.13 in F (K112, 1771); No.14 in A (K114, 1771); No.15 in G (K 124, 1772); No.16 in C (K128, 1772); No.17 in G (K129, 1772); No.18 in F (K130, 1772); No.19 in E♭ (K132, 1772); No.20 in D (K133, 1772); No.21 in A (K134, 1772); No.22 in C (K162, 1773); No.23 in D (K181, 1773); No.24 in B♭ (K182, 1773); No.25 in G minor (K183, 1773); No.26 in E♭, ov. for *Thamos* (K184, 1773); No.27 in G (K199, 1773); No.28 in C (K200, 1773); No.29 in A (K201, 1774); No.30 in D (K202, 1774); No.31 in D (*Paris, K297, 1778); No.32 in G, probably ov. to *Zaide* (K318, 1779); No.33 in B♭ (K319, 1779); No.34 in C (K338, 1780); No.35 in D (*Haffner, K385, 1782); No.36 in C (*Linz, K425, 1783); No.37 in G (only introduction, rest by M. Haydn) (K444, 1783); No.38 in D (*Prague, K504, 1786); No.39 in E♭ (K543, 1788); No.40 in G minor (K550, 1788); No.41 in C (*Jupiter, K551, 1788); also various others, some only fragmentary, and some probably of doubtful authenticity.

MISC. ORCH.: *Cassations*: B♭ (K99, 1769); *Kontretänze* (Country Dances): B♭ (K123, 1770), Set of 6 (K462, 1784), *Das Donnerwetter* (K534, 1788), *La Bataille* (K535, 1788), Set of 2 (K565, 1788), *Der Sieg vom Helden Koburg* (K587, 1789), Set of 2 (K603, 1791), E♭ (K607, 1791), Set of 5 (K609, 1791), G major (K610, 1791); *German Dances*: Set of 6 (K509, 1787), Set of 6 (K536, 1788), Set of 6 (K567, 1788), Set of 6 (K571, 1789), Set of 12 (K586, 1789), Set of 6 (K600, 1791), Set of 4 (K602, 1791), Set of 3 (K605, 1791), C major (K611, 1791); *Divertimenti*: No.1 in E♭ (K113, 1771), No.2 in D (K131, 1772), D (K136, 1772), B♭ (K137, 1772), F (K138, 1772), No.3 in G (K166, 1773), No.4 in B♭ (K186, 1773), No.5 in C (K187, ?1773), No.6 in C (K188, 1776), No.7 in D (K205, 1773), No.8 in F (K213, 1775), E♭ (K226, 1775), B♭ (K227, 1775), No.9 in B♭ (K240, 1776), No.10 in F (K247, 1776), No.11 in D (K251, 1776), No.12 in E♭ (K252, 1776), No.13 in F (K253, 1776), No.14 in B♭ (K270, 1777), No.15 in B♭ (K287, 1777), F (K288, 1777), No.16 in E♭ (K289, 1777), No.17 in D (K334), 1779); *Serenades*: G (K63, 1769), No.1 in D (K100, 1769), No.2 in F (*Kontretanz*) (K101, ?1776), No.3 in D (K195, 1773), No.4 in D (K203, 1774), No.5 in D (K204, 1775), *Serenata notturna*, No.6 in D for 2 orch. (K239, 1776), No.7 in D (*Haffner, K250, 1776), No.8 in D (*Notturno* for 4 orch., K286, 1776–7), No.9 in D (*Posthorn*, K320, 1779), No.10 in B♭ for 13 wind instr. (K361, 1784), No.11 in E♭ for wind (K375, 1781), No.12 in C minor for wind (K388, 1782),

No.13 in G for str., *Eine *kleine Nachtmusik* (K525, 1787); *Maurerische Trauermusik* (Masonic Funeral Music) (K477, 1785); *Ein musikalischer Spass* (A *musical joke) (K522, 1787); *Sinfonia Concertante* in E♭ for ob., cl., bn., hn. (K297b, 1778, considered doubtful attribution by some scholars; also Marches, Minuets, Gavottes.

CONCERTOS: PIANO: No.1 in F (arr. of sonata-movts. by Raupach and Honauer, K37, 1767), No.2 in B♭ (arr. of sonata-movts. by Raupach and Schobert, K39, 1767), No.3 in D (arr. of sonata-movts. by Honauer, Eckart, and ?C. P. E. Bach, K40, 1767), No.4 in G (arr. of sonata-movts. by Honauer and Raupach, K41, 1767), No.5 in D (K175, 1773), No.6 in B♭ (K238, 1776), No.7 in F (K242, 1776), No.8 in C (K246, 1776), No.9 in E♭ (K271, 1777, No.10 in E♭ (K365, ?1779), No.11 in F (K413, 1782–3), No.12 in A (K414, 1782), No.13 in C (K415, 1782–3), No.14 in E♭ (K449, 1784), No.15 in B♭ (K450, 1784), No.16 in D (K451, 1784), No.17 in G (K453, 1784), No.18 in B♭ (K456, 1784), No.19 in F (K459, 1784), No.20 in D minor (K466, 1785), No.21 in C (K467, 1785), No.22 in E♭ (K482, 1785), No.23 in A (K488, 1784–6), No.24 in C minor (K491, 1786), No.25 in C (K503, 1786), No.26 in D, *Coronation (K537, 1787–8), No.27 in B♭ (K595, 1788–90); 2 PIANOS: E♭ (K365, 1779); 3 PIANOS: F major (K242, 1776); Concert Rondo in D (K382, 1782), in A (K386, 1782).

VIOLIN: No.1 in B♭ (K207, 1773), No.2 in D (K211, 1775), No.3 in G (K216, 1775), No.4 in D (K218, 1775), No.5 in A (K219, 1775, with alternative Adagio in E, K261, 1776), *Rondo* in C (K373, 1781); 2 VIOLINS: Concertone in C (K190, 1773); VIOLIN & VIOLA: Sinfonia Concertante in E♭ (K364, 1779); BASSOON: B♭ (K191, 1774); CLARINET: A major (K622, 1791); FLUTE: No.1 in G (K313, 1778), No.2 in D transcr. from ob. conc. in C (K314, 1778); *Andante* in C (K315, 1778); FLUTE & HARP: C major (K299, 1778); HORN & STRINGS: No.1 in D (K412, 1791), No.2 in E♭ (K417, 1783), No.3 in E♭ (K447, 1787), No.4 in E♭ (K495, 1786), No.5 in E♭, fragment (K494a, 1786); Concert Rondo for hn. and orch. in E♭ (K371, 1791); OBOE: C major (K271k, 1777, transcr. for fl. as conc. No.2 in D).

CHURCH MUSIC: *Kyrie* in F (K33, 1766), *Missa brevis* in G (K49, 1768), in D minor (K65, 1769), in C (K115, 1773), in F (K116, 1771), in F (Mass No.6) (K192, 1774), in D (K194, 1774), in C (Mass No.10) (K220, 1775), in C (K258, 1776), in C (Mass No.13) (K259, 1775 or 1776), in B♭ (K275, 1777); Mass in C, *Dominicus (K66, 1769), No.4 in C minor, *Waisenhausmesse* (K139, 1768), No.7 in C, *Missa in honorem Sanctissimae Trinitatis* (K167, 1773), in C (K257, 1776), in C, *Missa longa* (K262, 1775), No.16 in C, *Coronation (K317, 1779), in C major, *Missa solemnis* (K337, 1780), No.18 in C minor, unfinished (K427, 1782–3); *Regina Coeli* (K127, 1772); Motet, *Exsultate, jubilate for sop., orch., and organ (K165, 1773); *Dixit Dominus* (K193, 1774); *Litaniae Lauretanae* (K195, 1774); *Litaniae de venerabili altaris Sacramento* (K243, 1776); *Vesperae de Dominica* (K321, 1779); *Kyrie* in D minor (K341, 1780–1); *Vesperae Solennes de Confessore* (K339,

1780); Motet, *Ave verum corpus* (K618, 1791); *Requiem Mass* in D minor (unfinished) (K626, 1791).

CHORUS & ORCH.: *Die Schuldigkeit des ersten Gebotes*, pt. I of sacred drama (K35, 1767); *Grabmusik*, Passion cantata (K42, 1767); *La Betulia liberata*, oratorio (K118, 1771); **Davidde Penitente*, oratorio, mainly based on Mass in C minor, K427 (K469, 1785); *Die Maurerfreude*, cantata (K471, 1785); *Eine kleine Freimaurer-Kantate* (K623, 1791).

UNACC. VOICES: *God is our Refuge*, sacred madrigal (K20, 1765); *5 Riddle Canons* (K89a, 1770); numerous *Canons* comp. between 1782 and 1788, also various secular trios, qts., and chs.

SOLO VOICE & ORCH. (mainly concert arias): *Per pietà, bell' idol mio*, sop. (K78, *c*.1766); Scena and aria, *Misera, dove son? Ah, non son'io che parlo*, sop. (K369, 1781); Scena and rondo (extra number for *Idomeneo*) *Non più, tutto ascoltai. Non temer, amato bene*, sop. (K490, 1786); Scena and rondo, *Ch'io mi scordi di te. Non temer amato bene*, sop. with pf. obbl. (K505, 1786); Scena and aria, *Bella mia fiamma. Resta, oh caro*, sop. (K528, 1787); aria, *Un bacio di mano*, for Anfossi's *Le gelosie fortunate*, for bass (K541, 1788); rondo, extra aria for Susanna in *Figaro*, *Al desio di chi t'adora*, sop. (K577, 1789); *Un moto di gioia*, sop., extra number for Susanna in *Figaro* (K579, 1789); *Schon lacht der holde Frühling*, sop. for **Paisiello's Il Barbiere di Siviglia* (K580, 1789); *Vado, ma dove?*, sop., for Martin's *Il burbero di buon core* (K583, 1789); *Rivolgete a lui lo sguardo*, bass, orig. for *Così fan tutte* (K584, 1789); *Per questa bella mano*, bass (K612, 1791).

STRING QUARTETS: No.1 in G (K80, 1773–5), No.2 in D (K155, 1772), No.3 in G (K156, 1772), No.4 in C (K157, 1772–3), No.5 in F (K158, 1772–3), No.6 in B♭ (K159, 1773), No.7 in E♭ (K160, 1773), No.8 in F (K168, 1773), No.9 in A (K169, 1773), No.10 in C (K170, 1773), No.11 in E♭ (K171, 1773), No.12 in B♭ (K172, 1773), No.13 in D minor (K173, 1773), Nos. 14–19 'Haydn Quartets': No.14 in G (K387, 1782), No.15 in D minor (K421, 1783), No.16 in E♭ (K428, 1783), No.17 in B♭ (*Hunt, K458, 1784), No.18 in A (K464, 1785), No.19 in C (*Dissonanzen, K465, 1785), No.20 in D (*Hoffmeister*, K499, 1786), Nos. 21–23 (*King of Prussia Quartets'): No.21 in D (K575, 1789), No.22 in B♭ (K589, 1790), No.23 in F (K590, 1790); *Adagio and Fugue* in C minor, fugue identical with K426 for 2 pf. of 1783 (K546, 1788).

STRING QUINTETS: No.1 in B♭ (K174, 1773), No.2 in C minor, arr. of *Serenade No.12* for wind, K388 (K406, 1786), No.3 in C (K515, 1787), No.4 in G minor (K516, 1787), No.5 in D (K593, 1790), No.6 in E♭ (K614, 1791).

CLARINET QUINTET: A major (K581, 1789); CLARINET TRIO, E♭ for cl., va., pf. (K498, 1786).

FLUTE QUARTETS: No.1 in D (K285, 1777), No.2 in A (K285a, 1777), No.3 in C (K285b, 1777), No.4 in A (K298, 1778); FLUTE (or vn.) SONATAS, with hpd.: No.1 in B♭ (K10, 1764), No.2 in G (K11, 1764), No.3 in A (K12, 1764), No.4 in F (K13, 1764), No.5 in C (K14, 1764), No.6 in B♭ (K15, 1764).

HORN QUINTET: E♭ (K407, 1782).

OBOE QUARTET: F major (K370, 1781).

PIANO QUARTETS: No.1 in G minor (K478, 1785), No.2 in E♭ (K493, 1786).

PIANO & WIND QUINTET (pf., ob., cl., hn., bn.): E♭ (K452, 1784).

PIANO TRIOS: No.1 in B♭ (K254, 1776), No.2 in G (K496, 1786), No.3 in B♭ (K502, 1786), No.4 in E (K542, 1788), No.5 in C (K548, 1788), No.6 in G (K564, 1788); in D minor/major, completed by Stadler (K442, 1783).

MISC. CHAMBER WORKS: *Adagio and Rondo* in C minor for glass armonica, fl., ob., va., vc. (K617, 1791); *Adagio* for cor anglais and str. (K580a, 1789); *Adagio in Canon* in F for 2 basset hn. and bn. (K410, 1783); *Adagio* in F for 2 cl. and 3 basset hns. (K411, 1783); *12 Duets* for 2 basset hns. (K487, 1786); *Duo* for vn. and va., No.1 in G (K423, 1783), No.2 in B♭ (K424, 1783); *5 Divertimenti* for 2 cl. and bn. (K229, 1783); *Minuet* in D, 2 vn., 2 hn., bass (K64, 1769); *7 Minuets with Trio*, 2 vn. and bass (K65a, 1769); *Adagio* in C for glass armonica (K356, 1791).

SONATAS: BASSOON & CELLO: B♭ (K292, 1775); PIANO: No.1 in C, No.2 in F, No.3 in B♭, No.4 in E♭, No.5 in G, No.6 in D (K279–284, 1774, No.6, 1775), No.7 in C (K309, 1777), No.8 in A minor (K310, 1778), No.9 in D (K311, 1778), No.10 in C, No.11 in A, No.12 in F, No.13 in B♭ (K330–333, 1778), No.14 in C minor (K457, 1784), No.15 in C (K545, 1788), No.16 in B♭ (K570, 1789), No.17 in D (K576, 1789); VIOLIN & PIANOFORTE: No.1 in C (K6, 1762–4), No.2 in D (K7, 1763–4), No.3 in B♭ (K8, 1763–4), No.4 in G (K9, 1764), Nos. 5–10, K10–15 (see under *flute*), No.11 in E♭, No.12 in G, No.13 in C, No.14 in D, No.15 in F, No.16 in B♭ (K26–31, 1766), No.17 in C (K296, 1778), No.18 in G, No.19 in E♭, No.20 in C, No.21 in E minor, No.22 in A, No.23 in D (K301–306, 1778), No.24 in F (K376, 1781), No.25 in F (K377, 1781), No.26 in B♭ (K378, 1779), No.27 in G major/minor (K379, 1781), No.28 in E♭ (K380, 1781), No.29 in A (K402, 1782, completed by Stadler), No.30 in C (K403, 1782, unfinished), No.31 in C (K404, 1782, unfinished), No.32 in B♭ (K454, 1784), No.33 in E♭ (K481, 1785), No.34 in A (K526, 1787), No.35 in F (K547, 1788). Also sonata movt. in C minor (K396, 1782, completed by Stadler).

STRING TRIOS: B♭, 2 vn. and bass, (K266, 1777), *Divertimento* in E♭, vn., va., vc. (K563, 1788). Also 6 *Fugue* arrs. from J. S. and W. F. Bach, with orig. introductions (K404A, 1782).

PIANO (4 HANDS): Sonatas: in B♭ (K358, 1774), D (K381, 1772), F (K497, 1786), C (K521, 1787); *Fugue* in G minor (K401, 1782); *Andante and Variations* (K501, 1786).

2 PIANOS: *Fugue* in C minor (K426, 1783, arr. for str., with short *Adagio* as preface, 1788), Sonata in D (K448, 1781).

SOLO PIANO (except Sonatas): *Minuet and Trio* in G, *Minuet* in F, *Allegro* in B♭, *Minuet* in F, *Minuet* in F (K1–5, 1761–2), 8 *Variations on 'Laat ons juichen'* (air by C. E. Graaff) in G (K24, 1766), 7 *Variations on 'Wilhelmus van Nassouwe'* (K25, 1766), 12 *Variations on a Minuet by Fischer* (K179, 1774), *Andantino* in E♭ (K236, 1790), 9 *Variations on 'Lison dormait'* from Dezède's *Julie* (K264, 1778), 12 *Variations on 'Ah, vous dirai-je, maman'* (K265, 1778),

8 *Variations on a March in Grétry's 'Mariages Samnites'* (K352, 1781), 12 *Variations on 'La Belle Françoise'* (K353, 1778), 12 *Variations on 'Je suis Lindor' in Beaumarchais's 'Le Barbier de Séville'* (K354, 1778), *Minuet in D* (K355, c.1786), *Fantasia and Fugue in C* (K394, 1782), *Capriccio in C* (K395, 1778), *Fantasia in D minor* (K397, 1782), 6 *Variations on Paisiello's 'Salve tu, Domine'* (K398, 1783), *Suite in C* (K399, 1782), 1st movt. of Sonata in B♭ (K400, 1782), *Kleiner Trauermarsch in C minor* (K453a, 1784), 10 *Variations on Unser dummer Pöbel meint* from Gluck's *La rencontre imprévue* (K455, 1784), *Fantasia in C minor* (K475, 1785), *Rondo in D* (K485, 1786), *Rondo in F* (K.494, 1786), 12 *Variations on an Allegretto in B♭* (K500, 1786), *Rondo in A minor* (K511, 1787), *Allegro and Andante* (K533, 1788, often used with *Rondo*, K494, as finale to make 'Sonata No.18'), *Adagio in B minor* (K540, 1788), 9 *Variations on a Minuet by Duport* (K573, 1789), *Gigue in G* (K574, 1789), 8 *Variations on Schack's 'Ein Weib ist das herrlichste Ding'* (K613, 1791).

ORGAN: Sonatas with orch.: C major (K263, 1776), C major (K278, 1777), C major (K329, 1779); 14 Sonatas for org. and str., comp. between 1767 and 1780.

MECHANICAL ORGAN: *Adagio and Allegro in F minor* (K594, 1790), *Fantasia in F minor* (K608, 1791), *Andante in F* (K616, 1791).

SONGS (v. and pf.): Mozart wrote about 40 solo songs and *Lieder*, of which the best known are: *Die Zufriedenheit* (K349, 1780), *Ah, spiegarti, O Dio* (K178, 1772), *Oiseaux, si tous les ans* (K307, 1777), *Komm, liebe Zither* (with mandolin) (K351, 1780), *An die Hoffnung* (K390, 1782), *Gesellenreise* (K468, 1785), *Der Zauberer* (K472, 1785), *Die betrogene Welt* (K474, 1785), *Das Veilchen* (K476, 1785), *Lied der Freiheit* (K506, 1786), *Die Alte* (K517, 1787), *Die Verschweigung* (K518, 1787), *Das Lied der Trennung* (K519, 1787), *Als Luise* (K520, 1787), *Abendempfindung* (K523, 1787), *An Chloe* (K524, 1787), *Des kleinen Freidrichs Geburtstag* (K529, 1787), *Das Traumbild* (K530, 1787), *Die kleine Spinnerin* (K531, 1787), *Sehnsucht nach dem Frühlinge* (K596, 1791), *Das Kinderspiel* (K598, 1791), *Eine kleine deutsche Kantate, 'Die ihr des unermesslichen Weltalls'* (K619, 1791).

ADDITIONAL ACCOMPANIMENTS TO WORKS BY HANDEL: *Acis and Galatea* (K566, 1788), *Messiah* (K572, 1789), *Alexander's Feast* (K591, 1790), *Ode for St Cecilia's Day* (K592, 1791).

Mozart and Salieri (*Motsart i Sal'yeri*). Opera in 1 act and 2 scenes by Rimsky-Korsakov to his own lib. based on Pushkin's poem (1830). Comp. 1897. Prod. Moscow 1898, London (concert) 1927, Forest Park, Penn., 1933.

Mozartiana. Sub-title of Tchaikovsky's Suite No.4 for Orch. comp. 1887, the 4 movts. consisting of arrs. of Mozart's (1) *Gigue* for pf. (K574), (2) *Minuet* for pf. (K355), (3) *Ave verum corpus* (K618) in orch. arr. by Liszt, (4) *Variations* for pf. on *Unser dummer Pöbel meint* from Gluck's *La rencontre imprévue* (K455).

mp. *mezzo piano*, half-soft.

Mravinsky, Evgeny (Alexandrovich) (*b* St Petersburg, 1906; *d* Leningrad, 1988). Russ. conductor. Cond., Leningrad Th. of Opera and Ballet 1932–8. Prin. cond., Leningrad PO from 1938 to his death. Prof., Leningrad Cons. Cond. f.ps. of Shostakovich's 5th, 6th, 8th, 9th, and 10th Syms. and other works.

M.S. *mano sinistra* (It.), left hand.

Muck, Karl (*b* Darmstadt, 1859; *d* Stuttgart, 1940). Ger. conductor and pianist. Chorus master Zurich, then posts as opera cond. at Salzburg, Brno, and Graz. Cond., Deutsches Landestheater, Prague, 1886. Cond. first Moscow and St Petersburg perfs. of *The Ring*, 1889. Cond. Berlin Opera 1892–1912 (chief cond. from 1908). CG London 1899. Bayreuth 1901–30. Joint cond. Vienna PO 1903–6. Cond. Boston SO 1906–8, becoming chief cond. 1912–18. Outcry against him when USA entered war led to his internment. Cond. Hamburg PO 1922–33. Salzburg Fest. 1925.

Mudd, John (*b* London, 1555; *d* Peterborough, 1631). Eng. composer. Matriculated, Cambridge Univ. 1573. Org., Peterborough Cath. 1583–1631. Wrote church mus., anthems, etc.

Mudge, Richard (*b* Bideford, 1718; *d* ?Bedworth, Warwicks., 1763). Eng. composer and clergyman. Known principally for 6 concerti grossi, pub. 1749, tpt. conc., etc. Modern edns. of concerti arr. by G. *Finzi.

Muette de Portici, La (Auber). See *Masaniello*.

Muffat, Georg (*b* Mégève, Alsace, 1653; *d* Passau, 1704). Ger. composer and organist. Org. of Strasbourg Cath. until 1675, to Bishop of Salzburg c.1687. Org. and later Kapellmeister to Bishop of Passau from 1690. Wrote many org. works, concerti grossi, etc.

Muffling (of drums). A way of muting kettledrums (e.g. at a funeral) by placing a cloth over the surface. Nowadays it is usual to use sponge-headed drumsticks instead.

Mugnone, Leopoldo (*b* Naples, 1858; *d* Capodichino, Naples, 1941). It. conductor and composer. Cond. at Teatro alla Fenice, Naples, 1874. Cond. f.p. of *Cavalleria rusticana*, Rome 1890, and *Tosca*, Rome 1900. Cond. La Scala from 1891. London CG 1905–6, 1919 (Brit. première of *Iris*), and 1925. Début USA 1920. Comp. operas.

Mühlfeld, Richard (*b* Salzungen, 1856; *d* Meiningen, 1907). Ger. clarinettist. Joined Grand Duke's orch. at Meiningen as violinist. Self-taught clarinettist, becoming prin. cl., Meiningen Orch., 1876, and at Bayreuth 1884–96. Brahms's cl. works (trio, Op.114, quintet, Op.115, and 2 sonatas, Op.120) were written for him.

Muldowney, Dominic (John) (*b* Southampton, 1952). Eng. composer and conductor. Mus. dir. Nat. Th. 1981–97. Prin. works:

THEATRE: *An Heavyweight Dirge* (1971); *Klavier-Hammer* (1973); *Da Capo al Fine*, tape for ballet

(1975); *Earl of Essex's Galliard* for 3 actors, dancer, and instr. (1976); ballet *Macbeth* (1979); realization *The Beggar's Opera* (1982); *The Brontës*, ballet (1995); *The Voluptuous Tango*, radio opera (1996).

ORCH.: *Driftwood to the Flow*, str. (1972); *Music at Chartres*, chamber orch. (1974); *Perspectives*, full orch. (1975); Conc., 4 vn. and str. (1980); pf. conc. No.1 (1983), No.2 (2002); saxophone conc. (1984); vn. conc. (1989); *3 Pieces for Orch.* (1990–1); perc. conc. (1991); ob. conc. (1991–2); vn. conc., vn., orch., tape, 2 conds. (1992); tpt. conc. (1992–3); tb. conc. (1995–6); *Conc. Grosso* (1996–7); cl. conc. (1997); *The Brontës Suite* (1998).

CHAMBER ENSEMBLE: *Love Music for Bathsheba Everdene and Gabriel Oak* (1974); *Solo/Ensemble* (1974); *3-part Motet* for 11 instr. (1976); *12 Shorter Chorale Preludes of Bach* arr. for 8 woodwind instr. (1976); *10 Longer Chorale Preludes of Bach* arr. for 8 woodwind instr. (1976); *Variations after Sweelinck* (1977); *Double Helix* (1977); *Entr'acte* (1977); *Six Chorale Preludes* (1986); *Sinfonietta* (1986); *Ars subtilior*, ens., tape (1987); *Un carnaval Cubiste*, 10 brass players and metronome (1989).

CHAMBER MUSIC: *In a Hall of Mirrors*, alto sax., pf. (1979); Pf. Trio (1980); Str. Qt. No.1 (1973), No.2 (1980); *Golden Moments*, vc., db. (1992); *The Anatomy Lesson*, vn., pf. (1993); sonata, 4 vns., str. (1994).

CHORAL AND VOCAL: *Bitter Lemons* for women's vv. (1970); *Cantata* for soloists, speakers, 2 vc. and perc. (1975); *Procurans Odium*, sop. and 8 instr. (1977); *Five Psalms*, sop., ten., ch., wind, tape (1979); *5 Theatre Poems* (Brecht), mez. and ens. (1980–1); *From Little Gidding* (Eliot), bar., treble, pf. (1980); *In Dark Times* (Brecht), sop., alto, ten., bass, ens. (1981); *Sports et Divertissements*, narr., ens. (1981); *The Duration of Exile*, mez., ens. (1983); *A Second Show*, cont., hp., vn., alto sax., tape (1983); *Maxims*, bar., ens. (1986); *Lonely Hearts*, mez., ens. (1988); *On Suicide*, v., ens. (1989); *Out of the East*, 2 vv., ens. or pf. (1990); *Never let me see you suffer*, v., pf. (1993); *The Fall of Jerusalem*, sop., ten., bar., ch., children's ch., orch. (1998–9).

PIANO: *A Little Piano Book*, 24 pieces (1979); *Paraphrase on Machaut's Hoquetus David* (1987); *The Ginger Tree* (1989).

Müller, Maria (*b* Theresienstadt (now Terezin), nr. Litoměřice, 1898; *d* Bayreuth, 1958). Cz. soprano. Début Linz 1919 (Elsa in *Lohengrin*). NY Met début 1925, singing each season until 1934–5. Sang in Berlin and regularly at Bayreuth 1930–44. Salzburg Fest. début 1931; CG début 1934. One of most radiant singers of Eva.

Müller-Hartmann, Robert (*b* Hamburg, 1884; *d* Dorking, 1950). Ger.-born composer, teacher, and critic (Brit. cit. 1948). Worked as mus. critic on several papers. Taught at Bernuth Cons., Hamburg; lect., Hamburg Univ. 1923–33; mus. adv., N. German Radio, 1931–3. Settled in Eng., 1933, becoming friend of Vaughan Williams, whose *The *Pilgrim's Progress* he partially trans. into Ger. Works incl. Sym. (1927), ov., *Leonce and Lena* (1922), *Variations on a Pastoral Theme* (1925), Sinfonietta (1943), *Craigelly Suite* (1944), chamber mus., pf. pieces, and songs.

Müller-Siemens, Detlev (*b* Hamburg, 1957). Ger. composer and conductor. Settled in Basle 1989. Prof. of comp., Basle Mus. Acad. from 1991. Works incl.:

OPERAS: *Genoveva* (1977); *Die Menschen* (1989–90); *Bing* (1999–2001).

ORCH.: *Concerto*, 19 players (1975); *Scherzo und Adagio patetico* (1976); *2 Pieces*, chamber orch. (1977); *Passacaglia* (1978); Sym. No.1 (1978–80); pf. conc. (1980–1); *Under Neonlight I*, chamber orch. (1981); va. conc. (1983–4); *4 Passages* (1988); hn. conc. (1988–9); conc. for vn., va., orch. (1992–3); *Phoenix*, 13 instr. (1993); *Tom-a-Bedlam*, instr. vers. (1990–1, 1993); *Refuge*, small orch. (1997–8); *Light Blue, almost White* (in memoriam Olivier Messiaen), small orch. (1998).

VOCAL: *Songs and Pavanes*, ten., orch. (1984–5); *Arioso*, sop., ten., hn., ch., orch. (1986); *2 Holderlin Songs*, sop., pf. (1999–2000).

CHAMBER MUSIC: *Nocturne*, vn., pf. (1975); *Variations on a Schubert Ländler*, wind quintet, str. quintet (1977–8); *Les sanglots longs des violons de l'automne*, fl., ob., cl., bn., pf., str. qt. (1984–5); Octet, cl., hn., bn., 2 vn., va., vc., db. (1988–9); Sextet (1993); *Cuts*, sax., ens. (1996); str. trio, vn., va., vc. (2002); *Bedlam Dances*, fl., perc. (2003).

PIANO: *Under Neonlight II*, 2 pf. (1980–3), *III*, pf. (1987).

Müller von Asow, Erich (*b* Dresden, 1892; *d* Berlin, 1964). Ger. musicologist. Dir., contemporary mus. fest., Dresden, 1917. Ed. of 5-vol. edn. of Mozart family's correspondence, 1942. Author of books on Schütz, Handel, and Reger. Ed., thematic catalogue of R. Strauss's works (1959–74, continued by A. Ott and F. Trenner). Ed. of mus. dictionaries.

Mulliner Book. MS coll. of Eng. mus. containing 131 comps., mainly for kbd. but also for cittern, made by Thomas Mulliner *c*.1560. Pubd. in modern notation 1951, ed. Denis Stevens, rev. 1962.

Mullings, Frank (Coningsby) (*b* Walsall, 1881; *d* Manchester, 1953). Eng. tenor. Début Coventry 1907 as Faust. Denhof Co. 1913, Beecham Co. 1916–21, BNOC 1922–9. First to sing Parsifal in Eng. (CG 1919). Noted singer of Otello and Tristan. Later taught at Birmingham Sch. of Mus. 1927–46 and RMCM 1944–9.

Mullova, Viktoria (*b* Moscow, 1959). Russ. violinist. Public début 1971 (Vieuxtemps 5th conc.). Won Sibelius comp., Helsinki 1981 and gold medal in Tchaikovsky comp., Moscow 1982. Left Russ. to pursue int. career.

Mumma, Gordon (*b* Framingham, Mass., 1935). Amer. composer. Co-founder, Co-operative Studio for Elec. Mus., Ann Arbor, 1958–66. Composer with Merce Cunningham Dance Co. 1966–74. Teacher at Univ. of Calif., Santa Cruz, 1973–5 (prof. from 1975). Prof. at Mills Coll., Oakland, from 1981. Among first to use live elec. mus.

processes, devising a computerized system which he called cybersonics. Comps. incl. *Swarm*, for vn., concertina, bowed crosscut saw, and cybersonic modification.

Munch, Charles (*b* Strasbourg, 1891; *d* Richmond, Va., 1968). Alsatian-born conductor and violinist (Fr. cit. 1920). Prof. of vn., Strasbourg Cons., 1919–25 and leader of Strasbourg orch.; prof. Leipzig Cons. 1925–32 and leader of Gewandhaus Orch. Début as cond. Paris 1932. Founder and cond., Orchestre de la Société Philharmonique 1935–8. London début 1938. Cond., Société des Concerts du Conservatoire 1938–46 and prof. of cond. Paris Cons. Salzburg Fest. début 1946; US début Boston 1946. Cond. Boston SO 1949–62; dir., Berkshire Mus. Center 1951–62. Toured Europe, Far East, and Australia with Boston SO. Organized Orchestre de Paris 1967.

Münchinger, Karl (*b* Stuttgart, 1915; *d* Stuttgart, 1990). Ger. conductor. Cond. Hanover SO 1941–3. Founder-cond. *Stuttgart CO, 1945, with which he made many int. tours. London début 1949. Salzburg Fest. début 1952. Recorded Bach's Brandenburg Concertos three times—in mono, stereo, and quadraphonic sound. Retired 1988.

Mundharmonika (Ger.). Mouth harmonica, i.e. mouth organ.

Mundy, John (*b* c.1555; *d* Windsor, 1630). Eng. composer and organist, son of William Mundy. Org., St George's Chapel, Windsor, for over 40 years. Wrote pieces for viols and madrigals, incl. *Lightly she tripped* for 5 vv. in *The *Triumphs of Oriana*. His kbd. fantasia *Faire Wether* has descriptions of lightning and thunder.

Munich Philharmonic Orchestra. Orch. in Munich, Bavaria, founded 1924 on basis of former *Kaim Orch. (1893–1923). Cond. have incl. Siegmund von Hausegger (1920–38), Oswald Kabasta (1938–45), Hans Rosbaud (1945–8), Fritz Rieger (1949–66), Rudolf Kempe (1967–76), Sergiu Celibidache (1979–96), James Levine (1999–2004), and Christian Thielemann (from 2005).

Munrow, David (John) (*b* Birmingham, 1942; *d* Chesham Bois, 1976). Eng. player of recorder, crumhorn, etc., and specialist in early music and its instruments. Founder-dir. of Early Music Consort, 1967; lect. in history of early mus., Leicester Univ. from 1967. Prof. of recorder, RAM, from 1969. Frequent broadcaster. Comp. and arr. mus. for films and TV. Author of *Instruments of the Middle Ages and Renaissance*, 1976.

Murail, Tristan (*b* Le Havre, 1947). Fr. composer. Won *Prix de Rome* 1971. In 1973 joined with others to found Groupe de l'Itinéraire, comprising composers and performers interested in new links between elec. and traditional instrs. Teacher at courses in computer mus. organized by IRCAM and Paris Cons.

Murder in the Cathedral (Pizzetti). See *Assassinio nella cattedrale*.

Murdoch, William (David) (*b* Bendigo, Australia, 1888; *d* Holmbury St Mary, Surrey, 1942). Australian pianist. Settled in Eng. 1905 and made reputation as chamber mus. player, especially in assoc. with Albert *Sammons (vn.). Prof. of pf. at RAM 1930–6. Wrote books on Brahms and Chopin, and arr. Bach's works for pf. Was pianist in f.p. of Elgar's Pf. Quintet (1919).

Muris, Johannes de [Murs, Jehan des] (*b* Lisieux diocese, *c*.1300; *d* *c*.1350). Fr. music theorist. Wrote treatise *Musica speculativa* at Sorbonne, Paris, 1323, and 4 other treatises, incl. one on counterpoint. Opposed the innovations of the *ars nova*.

Murphy, Suzanne (*b* Limerick, 1941). Irish soprano. Début Dublin (Irish Nat. Opera) in *La Cenerentola*. Prin. sop. with WNO 1976–85 with very wide repertory. Vienna début 1987.

Murray, Ann (*b* Dublin, 1949). Irish-born mezzo-soprano. Opera début with Scottish Opera as Alceste (Snape Maltings, 1974). Débuts: CG 1976; NY City Opera 1979; Salzburg Fest. 1981; NY Met 1984. Notable Béatrice in Berlioz's opera, Buxton Festival 1980 and ENO 1990. Specialist in *travesti* roles (Composer, Octavian, Xerxes, etc.). Song recitalist and oratorio singer. Hon. DBE 2002.

Mus. Abbreviation for 'Music', as in B.Mus. (Bachelor of Music), D.Mus. (Doctor of Music), etc.

musette. (1) Type of Fr. bagpipe popular in court circles in 17th and 18th cents. Was bellows-blown and had 4 or 5 drones enclosed in cylinder. Used in orch. by Lully.
(2) Variety of gavotte in which persistent drone bass suggests the above instr. Vaughan Williams's ob. conc. (1944) has a *musette* in 2nd movt.

Musgrave, Thea (*b* Barnton, Midlothian, 1928). Scottish composer and conductor. Lect. in mus., London Univ. 1959–65. Taught at Univ. of California 1970. Her mus. developed from early diatonicism to a more chromatic idiom and to use of serialism; from various elements she has forged a mature style capable of rich expressiveness as in her opera *Mary, Queen of Scots*. In her orch. works, solo instr. are often given virtuoso opportunities; and in her cl. conc. the soloist moves about the orch. to play with different sections in the manner of a jazz improvisation. CBE 2002. Prin. comps.:

OPERAS: *The Abbot of Drimock*, 1-act (1955); *The Decision*, 3 acts (1964–5); *The *Voice of Ariadne* (1972–3); *Mary, Queen of Scots*, 3 acts (1976–7); *A Christmas Carol* (1978–9); *An Occurrence at Owl Creek Bridge*, radio opera (1981); *Harriet, the Woman Called Moses* (1984, rev. 1985); *Simón Bolívar* (1993–4); *The Mocking Bird*, chamber opera (2000); *Pontalba* (2003).

BALLETS: *A Tale for Thieves* (1953); *Beauty and the Beast* (1968–9); *Orfeo*, with dancer (see Chamber Music below).

ORCH.: *Obliques* (1958); *Themes and Interludes* (1962); *Sinfonia* (1963); *Festival Overture* (1965); **Nocturnes and Arias* (1966); *Concerto for Orchestra* (1967); cl. conc. (1967); *Night Music* (1969); **Memento Vitae* (homage to Beethoven) (1969-70); hn. conc. (1971); va. conc. (1973); *Space Play*, conc. for 9 instr. (1974); *Peripateia* (1981); *Moving into Aquarius* (1984, with R. R. Bennett); *The Seasons* (1988); *Rainbow* (1990); *Autumn Sonata*, bcl., orch. (1993); ob. conc. (*Helios*) (1994); *Phoenix Rising* (1997); *Echoes of Past Time*, ca., tpt., str. (1997); *Aurora*, str. (2000); *Turbulent Landscapes*, orch. (2003); *Wood, Metal and Skin*, perc., orch. (2004).

CHORAL AND VOCAL: *5 Love Songs*, ten., gui. (1955); *Song for Christmas*, v., pf. (1958); *Triptych*, ten., small orch. (1959); *The Phoenix and the Turtle*, ch., orch. (1962); *The Five Ages of Man*, ch., orch. (1963); *Memento creatoris*, ch. (1967); *Rorate coeli*, unacc. (1974, rev. 1976); *The Last Twilight*, ch., brass, perc. (1980); *The Lord's Prayer*, ch., org. (1983); *Black Tambourine*, women's vv., pf., perc. (1985); *Monologues of Mary, Queen of Scots*, sop., orch. (1977/ 1986); *For the Time Being: Advent*, narr., ch. (1986); *Midnight*, unacc. ch. (1992); *On the Underground Set I* (1994), *II* (1994), *III* (1995); *A la esperanza (Hope)*, sop., org. (1998); *Celebration Day*, ch., orch. (1999); *Journey into Light*, sop., orch. (2005).

CHAMBER MUSIC: Str. qt. (1958); *Colloquy*, vn., pf. (1960); Trio, fl., ob., pf. (1960); *Serenade* (1961); Chamber Conc. No.1 (1962), No.2 (1966), No.3 (1966); *Soliloquy*, gui., prerecorded tape (1966); Impromptu No.1, fl., ob. (1967), No.2, fl., ob., cl. (1970); *Elegy*, va., vc. (1970); *From One to Another I*, va., tape (1970, orch. vers. va., 15 str. *From One to Another II*, 1980); *Orfeo I*, fl., tape (1975, orch. vers. fl., 15 str., *Orfeo II*, 1975); *Fanfare*, brass quintet (1982); *Pierrot*, cl., vn., pf. (1985); *The Golden Echo I*, hn., tape (1986); *The Golden Echo II*, hn., 16 accomp. hns. (1986); *Narcissus*, fl. with digital delay (1987); *Wild Winter*, ens. (1993); *Three Women*, sop., narr., orch. (1997); *Lamenting with Ariadne*, ens. (1999); *Canta, Canta*, cl., pf., vc. (1997); *Ring out Wild Bells*, cl./vn., vc./pf. (2000); *Going North*, ch., 2 cl. (2004).

Musica Antiqua (Lat.). Old music. Coll. of 190 pieces of mus. compiled and ed. by John Stafford Smith and pubd. 1812. Ranges from ancient chants by Merbecke to Norman *chansons*, and masques from time of James I of Eng.

musica ficta (Lat.). Feigned music. **musica falsa** (It.). False music. In early mus., the sharpening or flattening of certain notes, conventionally prescribed or permitted in modal mus. (see *modes*) to avoid certain awkward intervals, etc. Its prevalence in mus. up to and incl. that of the 16th cent. requires considerable knowledge of performing practice of the period on the part of modern eds. In most modern edns. the necessary alterations are written in.

musica figurata (It.), **Figuralmusik** (Ger.). The term has 2 meanings: (1) Contrapuntal mus. in which the various melodic strands move more or less independently, shorter notes in one v. against longer in others—as distinct from mere 'note against note' counterpoint; (2) Decorated melody in plainsong, etc., as distinct from the more sober type (such decorated plainsong is also known as *musica colorata*, coloured music).

Musical America. American monthly mus. magazine founded as a weekly in 1898. Among eds. have been J. C. Freund, Deems Taylor, Oscar Thompson, and Everett Helm. Absorbed by *High Fidelity*, 1965.

musical box. Toy in which pins on a rotating barrel pluck the teeth of a comb. These teeth are graduated in length, thus providing a scale of notes from which tunes can be produced. (Multiple sets of pins produce several tunes.) Mechanism usually activated by lifting of lid.

musical comedy (musicals). Type of musical entertainment, 20th-cent. development of operetta, which relies for its popular success on a succession of catchy and easily memorable tunes, either as songs, duets, or choruses. Some early Eng. examples date from end of 19th cent., e.g. Lionel Monckton's *The Runaway Girl* (1898), but perhaps the first of the kind were Osmond Carr's *In Town* (1892) and Sidney Jones's *A Gaiety Girl* (1893), both staged by George Edwardes at the Prince of Wales Th., London. These were followed by Leslie Stuart's *Florodora* (1899), *The Arcadians* (Monckton, 1909), and *The Maid of the Mountains* (Fraser-Simson, 1916). The outstanding success of the First World War was Norton's *Chu Chin Chow* (1916). After 1918 American shows began to visit London and the names became familiar of Youmans (*No, No, Nanette*, 1924), Jerome Kern (*The Cabaret Girl*, 1922, *Sunny*, 1925, *Show Boat*, 1927), Gershwin (*Oh Boy*, 1917, *Lady, Be Good*, 1924, *Funny Face*, 1927, *Girl Crazy*, 1930, *Strike up the Band*, 1930), Rodgers and Hart (*The Girl Friend*, 1926, *Evergreen*, 1930, *On Your Toes*, 1936, *Pal Joey*, 1940), Cole Porter (*Gay Divorce*, 1932, *Nymph Errant*, 1933, *Anything Goes*, 1934). Emigré European composers such as Victor Herbert, Rudolf Friml (*Rose Marie*, 1924, *The Vagabond King*, 1925), and Sigmund Romberg also contributed to the transatlantic successes. Romberg's shows incl. *The Student Prince* (1924), *The Desert Song* (1926), and *New Moon* (1928).

In England two native composers dominated the musicals of the 1930s, Noël Coward with *Bitter-Sweet* (1929) and *Operette* (1938), and Ivor Novello with *Glamorous Night* (1935), *Careless Rapture* (1936), and *The Dancing Years* (1939). Scarcely less popular were Vivian Ellis's *Mr Cinders* (1929), *Jill Darling* (1934), and *Under Your Hat* (1938), while Noel Gay's *Me and My Girl* (1937) made 'The Lambeth Walk' almost a national song for a time. After the Second World War, the 1930s type of musical comedy lingered on with Ellis's *Bless the Bride* (1947), Novello's *King's Rhapsody* (1949), Wilson's *The Boy Friend* (1953), and Julian Slade's *Salad Days* (1954). But the death-knell of this genteel kind of affair was sounded by the record-breaking *Oklahoma!* (1943) of Rodgers and Hammerstein, first of an amazing series of shows from this duo: *Carousel* (1945), *South Pacific* (1949), *The King and I* (1951), *Flower Drum Song* (1958), and *The Sound of Music* (1959). The stronger construction of these musicals attracted into the popular th. such choreographers as Agnes de Mille, Jerome Robbins, and George Balanchine. Comparable with them were Irving Berlin's *Annie Get Your Gun* (1946) and *Call Me Madam* (1950), Porter's *Kiss Me Kate* (1948, based on *The Taming of the Shrew*), and *Can-Can* (1953), and (a new team) Frederick Loewe's and Alan Jay Lerner's *Brigadoon* (1947), *Paint Your Wagon* (1951), **My Fair Lady* (1956, based on Shaw's *Pygmalion*), and *Camelot* (1960).

A tougher vein was exploited by Leonard *Bernstein with *On the Town* (1944), *Wonderful Town* (1953), and *West Side Story* (1957). The lyrics of the last-named were written by Stephen Sondheim, who later comp. some of the best musicals of the 1970s in *Company* (1970), *A Little Night Music* (1973), and *Pacific Overtures* (1976). The Brit. challenge to the Amer. dominance after 1946 was best represented by Lionel Bart's *Fings ain't wot they used t'be* (1959) and *Oliver!* (1960, based on *Oliver Twist*), Bricusse's and Newley's *Stop the World—I Want to Get Off* (1961), *Charlie Girl* (1965, Taylor and Heneker), but it was left to Andrew *Lloyd Webber to chart a new course with *Joseph and the Amazing Technicolor Dreamcoat* (1968), *Jesus Christ Superstar* (1970), *Evita* (1976, a life of Eva Peron) (all with Tim Rice), *Cats* (1981, based on T. S. Eliot poems), *Phantom of the Opera* (1987), *Aspects of Love* (1989), *Sunset Boulevard* (1993), *Whistle Down the Wind* (1996, rev. 1998), *The Beautiful Game* (2000), and *The Woman in White* (2004). Other significant musicals of the second half of the 20th cent. have been Frank Loesser's *Guys and Dolls* (1950), *The Most Happy Fella* (1956), and *How to Succeed in Business Without Really Trying* (1961), Adler's and Ross's *The Pajama Game* (1954) and *Damn Yankees* (1955), Jule Styne's *Funny Girl* (1964), Herman's *Hello Dolly!* (1964), Bock's *Fiddler on the Roof* (1964), Leigh's *Man of La Mancha* (1965, based on *Don Quixote*), Kander's *Cabaret* (1966, based on Isherwood's *Goodbye to Berlin*), MacDermot's *Hair* (1967, a 'rock' musical which incorporated elec. sounds), Marvin Hamlisch's *Chorus Line* (1975), and C.-M. Schönberg's *Les Misérables* (1980) and *Miss Saigon* (1989).

musical glasses. See *glass armonica*.

Musical Joke, A (*Ein musikalischer Spass*). Divertimento in F for 2 hn. and str. qt. by Mozart (K522) comp. Vienna, 1787, as satire on composers and perfs. of popular mus.

Musical Offering, The (*Das musikalische Opfer*). Coll. of 13 comps. by Bach (BWV 1079) in various contrapuntal forms, all using a theme given to Bach for extemporization by King Frederick the Great of Prussia in Potsdam in 1747. Some are for kbd., 2 for fl., and others for no particular medium. Nos.1–8 constitute the actual offering, the remainder having been added later. Modern performing edns. exist and various composers have orchestrated certain items, e.g. Webern *Ri-*

cercare. The pieces are: 1. *Ricercare a 3*, 2. *Canon perpetuus*, 3. *Canon a 2 violini in unisono*, 4. *Canon a 2 per motum contrarium*, 5. *Canon a 2 per augmentationem*, 6. *Canon a 2 per tonos*, 7. *Canon a 2*, 8. *Canon a 2 quaerendo invenietis*, 9. *Canon perpetuus*, 10. *Canon a 4*, 11. *Fuga canonica*, 12. *Trio sonata*, 13. *Ricercare a 6*.

musical switch. A medley constructed out of snatches of popular tunes dovetailed into each other so that one tune is 'switched', after a few measures, to another.

Musical Times. Eng. monthly mus. magazine founded 1844. Eds. have incl. W. McNaught (father and son), Martin Cooper, Harold Rutland, Andrew Porter, Stanley Sadie, Andrew Clements, Basil Ramsey, and Antony Bye.

musica mensurata (Lat.). Measured music. Medieval system of notation, necessitated by invention of figured mus. to denote relative duration and pitch of each note of plainchant to be sung.

Music and Letters. Eng. mus. quarterly founded 1920 by A. H. Fox Strangways, who was ed. until 1937. Succeeded by Eric Blom 1937–50, Richard Capell 1950–4, Blom 1954–9, J. A. Westrup 1959–76, Denis Arnold and Edward Olleson 1976–80, Edward Olleson and Nigel Fortune 1981–6, Nigel Fortune and John Whenham 1986–92, Nigel Fortune and Tim Carter 1992–9, Nigel Fortune and Daniel Chua (from 2005), and Nigel Fortune and Daniel Grimley (from 2006).

musica reservata (Lat.). Reserved music. (1) Term coined in early 16th cent., possibly for expressive style of composers such as Desprès and for its method of perf., but exact meaning is unknown. One view applies it to mus. employing exceptional reserve in use of ornamentation and another theory is that it meant mus. reserved for what would now be called 'highbrows'.

(2) Name of London ens. formed 1960 to perform early mus. in authentic manner.

Musica Transalpina. First printed coll. of It. (i.e. transalpine) madrigals with Eng. words, compiled and pubd. in London by Nicholas Yonge in 2 vols., 1588 and 1597 (both It. and Eng. words were given). Had great influence on Eng. composers. Vol.I contained 57 pieces, incl. examples by Marenzio, Palestrina, Byrd, de Lassus, and others; 2nd vol. of 24 pieces incl. Ferrabosco, Marenzio, Venturi, etc.

music centre. Really a place, e.g. a hall, on which mus. activity is centred, but the term has been appropriated by commerce for piece of equipment in which stereo record-player, cassette-player, recording equipment, and sometimes radio are all assembled into single item of domestic furniture.

music drama. Term used by Wagner after *Lohengrin* to describe his operas in order to emphasize that the mus., dramatic, and scenic elements were on equal terms—a fusion of the arts as Gluck had proposed. Yet the old It. description of opera was *dramma per musica*.

Music for a While. Song by *Purcell, part of his incidental mus. to Dryden's play *Oedipus*, 1692.

music hall. Strictly, the place where a particular type of variety entertainment was held, often attached to a public house or containing a bar where customers could drink while they listened and watched; but the term also means the entertainment itself. It flourished in Brit. from c.1850 to 1914. Among the most famous London music-halls were the Surrey (Southwark), the Bedford (Camden Town), the Metropolitan (Edgware Road), and Collins's (Islington). By 1870 there were said to be 200 in London and 300 elsewhere. Many 'acts' were performed; musically the halls' importance lay in the association of a popular song with a particular performer, e.g. Charles Coborn and *Two Lovely Black Eyes*, Eugene Stratton and *Lily of Laguna*, Albert Chevalier and *My Old Dutch*, Harry Champion and *Any Old Iron*, Harry Lauder and *Roamin' in the gloamin'*, Vesta Victoria and *Waiting at the Church*, Florrie Forde and *Down at the ol' Bull and Bush*, Will Fyffe and *I Belong to Glasgow*, and Ella Shields and *Burlington Bertie from Bow*. After 1914 consumption of food and drink in the auditorium was forbidden and the music-hall gave way to the variety theatre and its stars like Gracie Fields and Hetty King. Something of the music-hall spirit survives in North of England working-men's clubs. It is an irony that while the songs and their singers have acquired a kind of immortality in Eng. theatrical folklore, the names of the composers are scarcely remembered, with the exception of Leslie Stuart, who wrote for Eugene Stratton. Thousands of music-hall songs, for example, were comp. by Joseph Tabrar, yet for one whose melodies reached more lips than Mozart's and Beethoven's, the reward has been almost total obscurity.

Musicians' Benevolent Fund. British mus. charity founded in 1921 orig. as fund in memory of the ten. Gervase *Elwes. Maintains a residential home for elderly and retired musicians, and helps many other musicians in various ways.

Musicians' Company. See *Worshipful Company of Musicians*.

Musicians' Union. Brit. trade union formed in 1921 by amalgamation of Nat. Orch. Assoc. of Professional Musicians (1891) and Amalgamated Musicians' Union (1893). Objective is to improve pay and conditions of professional musicians.

Music Makers, The. Ode, Op.69, for cont. or mez., ch., and orch. by Elgar, to poem by A. O'Shaughnessy (1844–81), in which several self-quotations occur (e.g. from *Enigma Variations*, 1st sym., vn. conc., etc.). Comp. 1911–12, with earlier sketches. F.p. Birmingham 1912. Also set for vv. and orch. by Kodály, 1964.

musicology (Ger. *Musikwissenschaft*). Mus. scholarship. A 20th-cent. word taken into the Eng. language (from the Fr. *musicologie*), but the Ger. term *Musikwissenschaft* was coined by J. B. Logier in 1827. It may be said to cover all study of mus. other than that directed to proficiency in perf. or comp. Thus, a musicologist is one who is a specialist in some mus. study.

Among the divisions of musicology are acoustics; the physiology of v., ear, and hand; the psychology of aesthetics and, more directly, of mus. appreciation and education; ethnology so far as it bears on mus. (incl. folksongs, folk dances, etc.); rhythm and metrics; modes and scales; the principles and development of instrs.; orchestration; form; theories of harmony; the history of mus.; the bibliography of mus.; terminology—and so forth.

The International Mus. Soc. (IMS, 1900–14) had as its purpose the promotion of musicological study, and its post-war successor made its purpose clear in its name—'Société Internationale de Musicologie' (SIM, founded 1928, publishes journal *Acta Musicologica*). There are also nat. musicological socs. in many countries. A Brit. musicological soc. (The Royal Mus. Assoc.) has existed since 1874, and the Amer. Musicological Soc. was founded in 1934: both socs. publish journals.

music theatre. A type of comp., sometimes quasi-operatic but more usually a concert piece, for which a semi-staged presentation is necessary. It developed after about 1950, esp. in USA and Ger. An Eng. example is *Maxwell Davies's *Eight *Songs for a Mad King*. In some examples of the genre, the visual and dramatic elements dominate the musical factors.

Musikalische Opfer, Das (Bach). See *Musical Offering, The*.

Musin, Ilya (*b* Kostzomo, 1902; *d* London, 1999). Russ. conductor and teacher. Son of Jewish watchmaker. Studied Petrograd (later Leningrad, now St Petersburg) Cons. from 1919 (entering on the same day as Shostakovich). Gifted pianist. Studied cond. from 1924 with Nikolay Malko. Taught at Leningrad Cons. from 1929. Cond. Minsk PO from 1937. After the war, refused to join the Creative Union of Musicians and Composers, and thus unable to obtain top cond. posts. Strict but beloved teacher, governed by 19th-cent. Russ. mus. principles. Most major conds. of the 20th and 21st cents. studied with Musin, incl. Gergiev, Bychkov, Sian Edwards, Caetani, Temirkanov, and Kreizberg. First travelled outside Russ. in 1991. Cond. RPO in London 1996.

musique concrète (Fr.). Concrete music. Mus. prepared from recorded sounds, either natural (e.g. birdsong) or man-made (traffic, instr. etc.). Term originated by Pierre *Schaeffer in 1948 to differentiate between mus. assembled from concrete sound objects and mus. based on the abstract medium of notation. Strictly, *musique* *concrète* should not be modified electronically but the distinction between it and electronically synthesized sound has been increasingly blurred until the term elec. mus. covers the whole process.

Mussorgsky, Modest (Petrovich) (*b* Karevo, Pskov, 1839; *d* St Petersburg, 1881). Russ. composer. Showed mus. talent as a child but was destined for an army career. In 1857 he met Balakirev in St Petersburg and studied with him, resigning his commission the next year. His early songs and pf. pieces show little sign of his later achievement, but by 1864 he was writing fine songs. He started and abandoned 2 operas, but began work in 1868 on *Boris Godunov*, which he rev. when it was rejected by the Imperial Th. On its prod. in 1874 it pleased audiences but not musicians, who resented its unconventional methods and unusual style in which speech-inflexion governed the vocal lines. Over the next few years Mussorgsky worked on 2 operas, but his heavy drinking, a habit acquired at cadet school, sapped his capacity for concentrated work. He was one of the group of 5 Russ. composers of nationalist tendencies known as the *'Mighty handful'. After his death his works were completed and 'improved' by Rimsky-Korsakov and others, but in the 20th cent. his realistic and progressive qualities have been recognized and his orig. scores have been restored where possible. Prin. comps.:

OPERAS: *Salammbô* (unfinished, 1863–6); *The *Marriage* (1 act only finished) (1868); *Boris Godunov* (1868–9, rev. 1871–2, rev. 1873); *Mlada* (projected 4-act opera-ballet of which Cui, Rimsky-Korsakov, and Borodin were to compose the other 3 acts, 1872); *Khovanshchina* (1873, 5th act unfinished); *Sorochintsy Fair* (1876–81, unfinished).

ORCH.: *Night on the Bare Mountain* (1867, rev. 1872, 1874).

PIANO: *Souvenir d'Enfance* (1857); *Intermezzo* (1861, orch. and expanded 1867); *Memories of Childhood* (1865); *Pictures at an Exhibition* (1874).

SONGS: Many solo songs and 3 song-cycles: *The Nursery* (7 songs) (1868–72); *Sunless* (6 songs) (1874); *Songs and Dances of Death* (4 songs) (1875–7). (The famous *Song of the Flea* dates from 1879.)

Mustel organ. Kbd. 'cabinet organ' invented by V. Mustel (*b* Le Havre, 1815; *d* Paris, 1890), whose son Auguste (1842–1919) patented the celesta in 1886.

muta (It., plural *mutano*). Change, e.g. of kettledrum tuning. *muta D in C* means change tuning from D to C (no connection with the word 'mute'). Also used in connection with change of crook in brass instr.

mutation stop. Org. stop sounding not at normal or octave pitch, but at pitch of one of the non-octave harmonics. See *Quint, Twelfth, Seventeenth, Nineteenth, Flat Twenty-first*.

mute. A mechanical device used to reduce the tonal vol. of an instr. and usually indicated by

the term *con sordini*. (1) In bowed instr. a small clamp to be placed on the bridge. (2) In brass instr. a pear-shaped stopper to be pushed into the bell or, in the case of the hn., putting the hand in the bell. It is impossible to mute woodwind instr. (3) With the kettledrums muting was formerly effected by placing a cloth over the parchment heads but it is usual now to employ sponge-headed drumsticks instead. (4) In the pf. the sound is muted by the left (soft) pedal. The mute should not be confused with the damper.

Muti, Riccardo (*b* Naples, 1941). It. conductor. Cantelli Prize 1967. Opera début Florence 1966 in work by Paisiello. Salzburg Fest., 1971; Amer. début Philadelphia Orch. 1972; Vienna 1973; CG 1977. Chief cond., (New) Philharmonia Orch. 1973–82 (mus. dir. from 1979). Art. dir., Florence Fest. (Maggio Musicale) 1977–81. Prin. guest cond., Philadelphia Orch. from 1977, prin. cond. 1981–92. Mus. dir. La Scala 1986–2005.

Mutter, Anne-Sophie (*b* Rheinfeldin, 1963). Ger. violinist. Won 1st prize at young musicians' nat. comp. at age of six. After hearing her at 1976 Lucerne Fest., *Karajan invited her to appear with Berlin PO at Salzburg Easter Fest. 1977. Salzburg Fest. début 1977. Eng. début 1977. Moscow début 1985. Amer. début Washington, NY recital début 1988. Gave f.p. of Lutosławski's *Chain II*, 1986. First holder of chair of vn. studies, RAM, 1986.

Muzio, Claudia (*b* Pavia, 1889; *d* Rome, 1936). It. soprano. Daughter of ass. stage manager at CG and NY Met. Début Arezzo 1910 (Massenet's Manon). La Scala début 1913; CG 1914; NY Met 1916–22 and 1933–4; Chicago 1922–31. Created role of Giorgetta in Puccini's *Il tabarro*, NY 1918. Notable interpreter of Violetta, Desdemona, and Tosca.

Myaskovsky, Nikolay (Yakovlevich) (*b* Novogeorgyevsk, 1881; *d* Moscow, 1950). Russ. composer. Prof. of comp. Moscow Cons., 1921–50, pupils incl. Kabalevsky, Khachaturian, and Shebalin. One of composers denounced by Soviet officials in 1948 for *formalism. Wrote 27 syms., the first in 1908, the last being perf. posthumously. No.19 is for military band. Also comp. sym.-poems *Nevermore* (after Poe's *The Raven*) and *Alastor* (after Shelley); sinfonietta; vn. conc. (1938); vc. conc. (1944–5); 13 str. qts. (No.1 1929–30, No.13 1949); 9 pf. sonatas; and many songs.

My Country (Smetana). See *Má Vlast*.

Myers, Rollo (Hugh) (*b* Chislehurst, 1892; *d* Chichester, 1985). Eng. writer on music. Mus. critic for *Times* then *Daily Telegraph* 1920–34. On BBC staff 1935–44. British Council officer in Paris 1944–5. Ed. *The Chesterian* 1947. Author of books on 20th-cent. mus. generally and on Satie and Debussy in particular. Trans. Strauss-Rolland correspondence (London, 1968).

My Fair Lady. Musical version of G. B. Shaw's play *Pygmalion* (1912) with music by Frederick

*Loewe and words by Alan Jay Lerner (b NY, 1918; d NY, 1986). F.p. NY 1956, London 1958, and has been in performance somewhere in the world almost ever since. Roles of Eliza Doolittle and Prof. Higgins created by Julie Andrews and Rex Harrison, the latter successfully employing a type of *Sprechstimme* for his songs. Film version 1964.

My Ladye Nevells Booke (My Lady Nevill's Book). Coll. of 42 virginals pieces by Byrd transcr. in 1591 by John Baldwin of Windsor for the use of Lady Nevell, or Nevill, believed by Dr. E. H. *Fellowes to have been Rachel, wife of Sir Edward Nevill. Modern ed. by Hilda Andrews, 1926.

Mysliveček, Josef (b Ober-Sárka, nr. Prague, 1737; d Rome, 1781). Bohemian composer. His first opera *Medea* was a big success in Parma, 1764, followed by *Il Bellerofonte*, Naples 1767. Went to Vienna and Munich 1772. In 1773 he composed *La Clemenza di Tito* for Venice. Mozart admired his pf. sonatas and praised his oratorio *Abramo ed Isacco*, Munich 1777. Comp. 27 operas, 6 oratorios, and instr. works of all kinds.

mysteries. See *miracle plays*.

Mystic Trumpeter, The. (1) Scena, Op.18, by Holst for solo v. (usually sop.) and orch. to words by Whitman, comp. 1904, rev. 1912, f.p. 1905 (rev. version f.p. 1913).

(2) Setting of same text for vv. and orch. by Harty, 1913.

(3) Symphonic fantasy after Whitman for orch. by F. S. Converse, 1904.

N

Nabokov, Nicolai (Nicolas) (*b* Lubcha, nr. Minsk, 1903; *d* NY, 1978). Russ.-born composer (Amer. cit. 1939). Lived in Paris and Ger. 1926–33. Ballet-oratorio *Ode* prod. by Diaghilev's ballet co., 1928. Settled in USA 1933, teaching at various colls. and univs. Worked for US Government in Berlin 1945–7; sec.-gen., Congress for Cultural Freedom 1951–66. Art. dir., Berlin Fest. of the Arts 1963–6. Comps. incl. operas (incl. *Love's Labour's Lost* (lib. by Auden and Kallman, 1970)); ballets; 3 *Symphonies lyriques*, orch.; pf. conc.; vc. conc.; and choral works.

Nabucco (Nabucodonosor, Nebuchadnezzar). Opera in 4 acts by Verdi to lib. by T. Solera written for and rejected by Nicolai. Comp. 1841, rev. 1842. Prod. Milan 1842, London 1846, NY 1848.

nach (Ger.). After, in the manner of, according to, towards, to. Hence *nach und nach*, bit by bit; *nach Es*, now tune to E♭; etc.

Nachschlag (Ger., 'after stroke'). (1) The 2 notes that end the turn closing a shake. See *trill*.

(2) Any ornamental note or notes added after another note; such notes decorate the following note, but take their time-value from the preceding note, and are therefore classified as an 'after-stroke'.

Nachspiel (Ger.). Afterplay. The equivalent of *postlude.

Nachtanz (Ger.). After-dance. Term applied to the 2nd of the two dance tunes which were commonly paired from the 15th to the 17th cents., i.e. pavan and galliard, passamezzo and saltarello, sarabande and gigue, etc. (The Saltarello, especially, is known by this name.)

Nachthorn (Ger.). Org. stop, same as *cor de nuit.

Nacht in Venedig, Eine (A Night in Venice). Operetta in 3 acts by Johann Strauss II to lib. by 'F. Zell' (Camillo Walzel) and Genée. Prod. Berlin 1883, NY 1889, London 1944.

Nachtmusik (Ger.). Night-music. A serenade, e.g. Mozart's Serenade in G, *Eine *kleine Nachtmusik*.

Nachtstück (Ger.). Night-piece. (1) The Ger. equivalent of *nocturne.

(2) A piece which conveys the impressions or feelings of night, such as the central (3rd) movt. of Bartók's *Concerto for Orchestra*.

Nacht und Träume (Night and Dreams). Song for v. and pf. by Schubert (D827) to poem by Matthäus von Collin (1779–1824), comp. 1825.

Nagano, Kent (George) (*b* Morro Bay, Calif., 1951). Amer. conductor of Japanese descent. Worked with Opera Co. of Boston 1977–9. Mus. dir. Berkeley SO from 1978 (cond. f. Amer. p. (concert) of *Palestrina*, 1982). Cond., Opéra de Lyon 1988–98. Mus. dir. Hallé Orch. 1991–2000; chief cond. Berlin Radio SO 2000–6; mus. dir. Los Angeles Opera 2001–6; cond. Bavarian State Opera from 2006; cond. Montreal SO from 2006. Cond. f. London p. of Messiaen's *St François d'Assise* (concert perf.) 1988. Cond. and recorded Strauss's Fr. vers. of *Salome*, Lyon 1990. Cond. f.p. of Adams's *The Death of Klinghoffer*, Brussels 1991. NY Met début 1994.

nail fiddle (nail violin, nail harmonica). 18th-cent. instr. consisting of a semicircular board with nails, graduated in size, fastened around the curve: it was held in the left hand and the nails bowed with the right.

Naldi, Romolo (*b* ?Bologna, *c*.1550; *d* Rome, 1612). It. priest who lived in Rome and Bologna. Comp. book of madrigals (1589), book of motets (1600), and other pieces.

Namensfeier (Name Day). Concert ov. in C major by Beethoven, Op.115, comp. 1814 for name-day festivities of Emperor Francis II of Austria. F.p. 1815, pubd. 1825.

names of the notes and rest values. The Eng. names of the longer notes are based upon the old Lat. names of the early Middle Ages. The earlier It. names are similar. The Fr. names stand alone as being purely descriptive of the appearances. The Ger. names are arithmetical, and the Amer. practically a trans. of them. The Amer. and Ger. names require no remembering, being logically descriptive of time-values. They are undoubtedly the best, and the Amer. names are now largely adopted in the Commonwealth. See table on p. 522.

Nancarrow, Conlon (*b* Texarkana, Ark., 1912; *d* Mexico City, 1997). Amer.-born composer (Mexican cit. 1956). Was jazz trumpeter. Lived in Mexico 1939–79, having been refused Amer. passport because he fought for Republicans in Sp. Civil War. His mus. can be notated only by perforating player-piano rolls to mark notes and rhythms and perf. only by activating the rolls. Comps. incl. *Sarabande and Scherzo*, ob., bn., pf. (1930); *Blues*, pf. (1935); *Prelude*, pf. (1935); *Toccata*, vn., pf. (1935); *Septet* (1940); *Sonatina*, pf. (1940); *Trio*, cl., bn., pf. (1942); *Suite for Orch.* (1943); 3 str. qts. (No.1, 1945, No.2 unfinished, No.3, 1987); and more than 50 *Studies* for player piano (1951–93).

Nänie (Ger., from Lat. *Naenia*, 'dirges'). Ode by Brahms, Op.82, for ch. and orch., comp. 1880–1, to text by Schiller.

Nanino, Giovanni Maria (*b* Tivoli, *c*.1545; *d* Rome, 1607). It. composer. Ten. at S. Maria Maggiore, Rome, becoming choirmaster in 1567.

Names of the Notes and Rest Values
English, Italian, French, German, and American

	English	Italian	French	German	American
▮ ✕	breve	breve	carrée (square) or brève	Doppeltakt-note (double measure note)	double whole-note
○ ▾	semibreve	semibreve	ronde (round)	Ganze Takt-note (whole measure note)	whole-note
♩ ▬	minim	minima or bianca (white)	blanche (white)	Halbe (half) or Halbenote or Halbe Taknote	half-note
♩ 𝄽	crotchet	semiminima or nera (black)	noire (black)	Viertel (quarter)	quarter-note
♪ ♪	quaver	croma	croche (hook)	Achtel (eighth)	eighth-note
♫ ♫	semi-quaver	semi-croma	double-croche (double-hook)	Sechzehntel (sixteenth)	sixteenth-note
♬ ♬	demisemi-quaver	biscroma	triple-croche (triple-hook)	Zweiund-dreissigstel (thirty-second)	thirty-second note
♬ ♬	hemidemi-semiquaver	semi-biscroma	quadruple-croche (quadruple-hook)	Vierund-sechzigstel (sixty-fourth)	sixty-fourth note

(The word 'Rest' is in It. *Pausa*; Fr. *Silence*, or *Pause*; Ger. *Pause*).

Choirmaster S. Luigi de' Francesi, Rome 1575–7. Ten. in Sistine Chapel ch. from 1577, becoming choirmaster 1586. Est. Rome's first public sch. of mus. to be run by an Italian, being helped by his brother G. B. Nanino and Palestrina. Wrote madrigals, motets, canzonets, etc. Regarded as one of greatest contrapuntists of his time.

Napoleon, Ode to (Schoenberg). See *Ode to Napoleon Buonaparte*.

napolitana (It.), **napolitaine** (Fr.). A light and simple type of madrigal, presumably of Neapolitan origin, and much like the **villanella*. During the 20th cent. a certain type of mus.-hall song also took the name 'Napolitana': it usually had verses in the minor and chs. in the major.

Nápravník, Eduard (Francevič) (*b* Býšt, Bohemia, 1839; *d* Petrograd, 1916). Bohemian composer and conductor. Went to St Petersburg 1861 to conduct prince's orch., succeeding Lyadov as cond. of Imperial Russ. Opera 1869–1916. Raised standards and cond. over 4,000 opera perfs., incl. f.ps. of Mussorgsky's *Boris Godunov*, Rimsky-Korsakov's *The Maid of Pskov*, and of 3 operas by Tchaikovsky. Cond. sym. concerts 1870–82. Wrote 4 operas, incl. *Francesca da Rimini* (1902), 4 syms., pf. conc., 3 str. qts., songs, etc.

Nardini, Pietro (*b* Leghorn, 1722; *d* Florence, 1793). It. violinist and composer. Solo violinist at court of Stuttgart, 1762–5; dir. of mus. to Duke of Tuscany 1770. Wrote 16 vn. concs., vn. sonatas, str. qts., etc.

narrator (It. *testo*, 'witness'). Singer or speaker in oratorios, cantatas, and sometimes operas who tells the basic story of the work, normally in recit. Among the first works to use a narrator was **Monteverdi's dramatic madrigal *Il combattimento di Tancredi e Clorinda* (1624). In the Passion settings of the 17th and 18th cents. the narrator is often called the Evangelist, e.g, in Bach's *St Matthew Passion*. Narr. are used in many 20th-cent. works, e.g. Stravinsky's *The Soldier's Tale*, Vaughan Williams's *An Oxford Elegy*, and Honegger's *Le Roi David*. The Male and Female Ch. in *The *Rape of Lucretia* (1946) act as narrators.

Narváez, Luis de (*b* 1500; *d* c.1555). Sp. player of **vihuela* for which he wrote many pieces. Said to have introduced variation-form into Sp. mus.

Nash, Heddle (*b* London, 1894; *d* London, 1961). Eng. tenor. Chorister, Westminster Abbey. Début Milan 1924 (Almaviva in *Il barbiere di Siviglia*). Sang opera in London at Old Vic and SW from 1925. Sang with BNOC 1926–9; CG 1929–39, 1947–8; Glyndebourne 1934–8. Outstanding in Mozart and Rossini tenor roles, and a famous David in *Die Meistersinger*. Also had successful career in oratorio, e.g. *Messiah*, and was one of finest interpreters of Elgar's Gerontius, which he recorded 1944.

Nash, Peter Paul (*b* Leighton Buzzard, 1950). Eng. composer. Comp. Fellow, Leeds Univ. 1976–8. BBC Radio 3 producer, 1985–7. Works incl. str. trio (1982); *Études*, orch. (1983–4); *Figures,* hp. (1985); str. qt. (1987); Sextet, pf., wind quintet (1987); sym. No.1 (1991), No.2 (1997); *Apollinaire Choruses* (1995).

naso, nasetto (It.). Nose, little nose. The point of the vn. bow.

National Anthems. Songs or hymns adopted by certain nations to be perf. on official occasions and to represent them at int. events, e.g. when a competitor is awarded a medal in the Olympic Games. They are the mus. equivalent of the flag. Among the best-known (with author and composer, where both are known) are: Australia (since 1974): *Advance Australia Fair* (P. D. McCormick). Austria (since 1947): *Land der Berge, Land am Strome* (Preradovi; mus. doubtfully attrib. Mozart); (before 1919): *Gott erhalte unsern Kaiser* (Haschka; J. Haydn, 1797. In 1919 a new anthem, *Deutsch-Österreich, du herrliches Land* (Renner; Kienzl, 1919) was chosen, but abandoned in 1929 when Haydn's tune was reinstated until 1947). Belgium: *Après des Siècles d'esclavage*, known as *La *Brabançonne* (Dechet, whose text was replaced 1860 by another by Rogier; F. van Campenhout, 1830). Chile: *Dulce patria, recibe los votos* (Pintado, rev. 1847 by Lillo; Carnicer, 1828). China: *March on, brave people of our nation* (collective text; Nie Erh, 1932). Czechoslovakia: 1 (Czech): *Kde domov mūj?* 'Where is my home?' (Tyl; Skroup); 2 (Slovak): *Nad Tatrousa blýska* 'On Tatra mountains lightning strikes' (Matúška; trad.). Denmark: *Kong Kristian* (Ewald; ?Rogert, 1779). Finland: *Oi maamme, Suomi synnyinmaa!* 'O our native land' (Runeberg; Pacius, 1848). France: *Allons, enfants de la patrie*, known as *La *Marseillaise* (R. de Lisle 1792, words and mus.). Germany (before 1945): *Deutschland, Deutschland über Alles* (Fallersleben; J. Haydn); since 1950, *Einigkeit und Recht und Freiheit* (to Haydn's tune). Great Britain: *God Save the King (Queen)*. Greece: *Segnorizo apo tin Kopsi* (Solomós; Mantzaros, 1828). Ireland: *Sinne Fianna Fail at' fé gheall ag Eirinn* 'Soldiers are we whose lives are pledges to Ireland' (Heaney; Kearney). Israel: *Kol od balevav* (known as *Hatíkvah* (N. H. Imber, 1878; mus. trad., arr. S. Cohen). Italy: *Fratelli d'Italia* (Mameli; Novaro, 1847). Netherlands: *Wilhelmus von Nassouwe* (Marnix, *c*.1570; mus. in A. Valerius, *Gedenck-Clanck*, 1626). Norway: *Ja, vi elsker dette landet* (Bjørnson, 1864; *Nordraak). Poland: *Jeszcze Polska nie zgineta* (Wybicki; trad.). Russia: *Patriotic Song* (Glinka, arr. A. Petrov). USA: *The Star-spangled Banner* (F. Scott Key, 1814; mus. by John Stafford Smith comp. for *To Anacreon in Heaven*).

National Broadcasting Company of America. See *NBC Symphony Orchestra* and *NBC Television Opera*.

National Conservatory of Music of America. Mus. coll. founded in NY and Washington in 1885 by Mrs Jeannette M. Thurber with charters from NY State and the US Congress. *Dvořák was dir., 1892–5. Tuition free until 1915.

National Federation of Music Societies. Brit. organization founded 1935 by Sir George *Dyson with general aim of improving and advancing education by promoting 'art and the practice and the public performance' of mus. About 1,100 mus. socs. belong to the Federation, which aids them financially.

National Gallery Concerts. Famous series of weekday lunchtime concerts given in Nat. Gallery, London, during World War II from 10 Oct. 1939 to 10 Apr. 1946 (a total of 1,698 concerts). Est. by Dame Myra *Hess, who herself played many times. Several works f.p. at these concerts. Proceeds (nearly £16,000) went to Musicians' Benevolent Fund.

Nationalism in Music. A mus. movt. which began during the 19th cent. and was marked by emphasis on nat. elements in mus. such as folksongs, folk dances, folk rhythms or on subjects for operas and symphonic poems which reflected nat. life or history. It burgeoned alongside political movements for independence, such as those which occurred in 1848, and as a reaction to the dominance of Ger. mus. Haydn was an early 'nationalist' in his use of folk-song in many works. Chopin, by his use of Polish dance rhythms and forms, e.g. the mazurka and the *Krakowiak, was a nationalist and wrote a *Fantasia on Polish Airs* in 1828. In Russ., Glinka's *A Life for the Tsar* (1836) began the nationalist movement, which was sustained by Cui, Mussorgsky, Balakirev, Rimsky-Korsakov, etc. Liszt expressed the Hungarian spirit in his works, and this spirit was later intensified by Bartók and Kodály. Smetana, Dvořák, and Janáček were leading nationalists in Bohemia; in Norway, Grieg; Finland, Sibelius; Spain, Falla, Albéniz, and Granados; England, Holst and Vaughan Williams; USA, Copland, Gershwin, Ives, and Bernstein; Brazil, Villa-Lobos.

National Opera Studio. Training sch. for opera singers, providing one-year courses for advanced post-graduate trainees. Dir., Michael *Langdon 1978–86, Richard Van Allan 1986–2001, Donald Maxwell from 2001. Established in 1978 as replacement for London Opera Centre (founded 1963), whose first dir. was H. *Procter-Gregg, succeeded by James *Robertson 1964–78. The Centre took over the work of the National Sch. of Opera, directed from 1948 by Joan *Cross and Anne Wood.

National Sound Archive. Organization founded 1948 by Patrick Saul and incorporated 1951 in London for preservation of recordings of all kinds, which are then made available for study. Originally known as British Institute of Recorded Sound.

National Symphony Orchestra. Amer. orch. founded in Washington DC, 1931 by Hans Kindler, who was cond. until 1948, when Howard Mitchell succeeded him. Mitchell was succeeded by Antal Dorati, 1970–6, *Rostropovich 1977–94, Leonard Slatkin from 1996. From 1971 concerts given in Kennedy Center for the Performing Arts. Orch. toured Russ. with Rostropovich 1990.

National Training School of Music. Mus. coll. founded in Kensington, London, 1873 (although the idea originated with Prince Albert, who died in 1861). Opened 1876, with Sullivan as prin., until succeeded by Stainer in 1881. Absorbed in 1882 by *Royal College of Music, which opened 1883.

National Youth Orchestra of Great Britain. Sym. orch. for children aged between 13 and 19 founded in 1947 by Ruth Railton (later Dame Ruth King). Assembled in Bath 1947 under conductorship of Reginald Jacques. Players selected by audition, the orch. assembling in school holidays for rehearsal and study under guest cond. Very high standard achieved and many players have 'graduated' into leading sym. orchs.

Nativité du Seigneur, La (The Birth of the Lord). 9 meditations in 4 books for organ by *Messiaen, comp. 1935.

natural. (1) A note that is neither raised ('sharpened') nor lowered ('flattened').
(2) The sign ♮, which, after a note has been raised by a sharp or double-sharp, or lowered by a flat or double-flat, restores it to its orig. pitch. After a double-sharp or double-flat the change to a single one is sometimes indicated ♮♯ or ♮♭ (at other times by the single accidental).
(3) Type of *harmonic in str.-playing.

naturale (It.). Natural. Direction to perf. to return to a natural style after performing in some unusual way, e.g. falsetto, or muted.

natural harmonics. *Harmonics produced from an open str., as distinct from artificial harmonics produced from a stopped str.

natural keys. Keys with no sharp or flat in the signature, i.e. C major and A minor.

natural trumpet (Ger. *Naturtrompete*). A tpt. without *crooks which can produce only notes of the harmonic series of its fundamental note. From 17th cent. to late in the 19th, crooks were used, i.e. additional lengths of tubing which lowered the pitch of the fundamental note and thus of the whole harmonic series. However, crooks could not be very quickly changed, removed, or inserted. In his *Pastoral Symphony* (1921), *Vaughan Williams requires use of the natural tpt.

Nature, Life, and Love. Cycle of ovs. by Dvořák, comprising *Amid Nature* (*V přírodě*), *Carneval* (*Karneval*), and *Othello*, comp. 1891–2.

Natürlich (Ger.). Natural (in same sense as given under *Naturale*).

Naumann, Johann Gottlieb (*b* Blasewitz, Dresden, 1741; *d* Dresden, 1801). Ger. composer. Court composer of sacred mus., Dresden, 1764. In It. 1765–8 when he wrote several operas incl. *La Clemenza di Tito* (1769) and *Armida* (1773). Kapellmeister, Dresden from 1776. Went to Stockholm 1777 to reform Court orch. and to conduct opera. Was guest opera cond. and comp., Copen-

hagen, 1785–6, returning to Dresden as Oberkapellmeister. Comp. 24 operas, 13 oratorios, 21 masses, 18 syms., chamber mus., etc. Comp. so-called 'Dresden Amen', from his Threefold Amen.

Navarra, André (*b* Biarritz, 1911; *d* Siena, 1988). Fr. cellist. Played in Krettly Str. Qt. 1929–35. Début as soloist Paris, 1931. Eng. début 1950 (Cheltenham in Elgar conc., cond. Barbirolli). World tours as soloist with orch. Salzburg Fest. 1960. Gave f.p. of Jolivet's conc. 1962. Prof. of vc., Paris Cons., from 1949. Taught in Siena 1954–88.

Navarraise, La (The Girl from Navarre). Opera (lyric episode) in 2 acts by Massenet to lib. by Jules Claretie and Henri Cain after Claretie's story *La Cigarette* (1890). Comp. 1893. Prod. CG 1894, Bordeaux 1895, NY Met 1895.

Navarro, Garcia (*b* Chiva, 1941; *d* Madrid, 2001). Sp. conductor. Won 1st prize Besançon cond. comp. 1967. Mus. dir. Valencia SO 1970–4, ass. cond. Noordhollands PO, Haarlem, 1974–8. Mus. dir. Portuguese Radio SO 1976–8, Lisbon Nat. Opera 1980–2. Gen. mus. dir. Stuttgart State Th. from 1987. CG début 1979; Salzburg Fest. début 1983.

NBC Symphony Orchestra. Orch. created in NY in 1937 by the NBC specially for Toscanini, who had just left the NYPO. Made many recordings. When Toscanini retired in 1954, orch. was disbanded by the NBC but continued for another decade as co-operative enterprise under name 'Symphony of the Air'.

NBC Television Opera. Opera co. formed by NBC in NY in 1949 with Peter Herman Adler as mus. dir. Gave first Amer. perfs. of *Billy Budd* and *War and Peace*. Commissioned Menotti's *Amahl and the Night Visitors* and gave f.p. of Martinů's *The Marriage*. Company has toured in over 50 Amer. cities.

Neaman, Yfrah (*b* Sidon, Lebanon, 1923; *d* London, 2003). Lebanese-born violinist. Début Paris 1939. London début 1944. Settled in Eng. as base for int. career. Head of Str., GSMD. OBE 1983.

Neapolitan School. Term applied, with little real justification, to 18th-cent. school of comp. said to have originated in Naples or been cultivated by composers who studied there. Among these were A. Scarlatti, Porpora, Pergolesi, Jommelli, Anfossi, Piccinni, Paisiello, and Cimarosa, most of whom were active outside Naples and Italy.

Neapolitan Sixth. A chromatic chord. It is a major common chord on the flattened supertonic in its 1st inversion, e.g. in key C it comprises F–A♭–D♭. Reason for its name is unknown, since it occurs in 17th-cent. mus. before the so-called Neapolitan sch. existed, e.g. in mus. by Carissimi, Corelli, and Purcell (in *King Arthur*).

Nearer, My God, to Thee. Hymn existing in 2 vers., Eng. and Amer., both set to verses (1841) by

Eng. poet Sarah Flower Adams (1805–48). Eng. vers. comp. by John *Dykes. Was sung by passengers as liner *Titanic* sank in 1912. Amer. hymn is sung to tune *Bethany* (1859) by Lowell Mason (1792–1872).

Neary, Martin (Gerard James) (*b* London, 1940). Eng. organist, harpsichordist, and conductor. Org., St Margaret's, Westminster, 1965–71, Winchester Cath. 1972–87, Westminster Abbey 1988–98. Prof. of org. TCL 1963–72. Dir., Southern Cathedrals Fest. 1972–87. Ed. of org. works. Cond. f.p. of Tavener's *Ultimos Ritos* 1979, and Jonathan Harvey's *Passion and Resurrection* 1981. CBE 1998.

Neate, Charles (*b* London, 1784; *d* Brighton, 1877). Eng. pianist, cellist, and composer. Début as pianist CG 1800. Founder-member of Phil. Soc., London, 1813. Visited Beethoven in Vienna, 1815, and acted as his agent in Eng. First to play Beethoven's 5th ('Emperor') pf. conc. in London, at Philharmonic Soc. concert, 8 May 1820. Wrote pf. sonatas.

Neblett, Carol (*b* Modesto, Calif., 1946). Amer. soprano. Toured as soloist with Roger Wagner Chorale. Début 1969, NY City Opera (Musetta in *La bohème*). Débuts: Chicago 1975; Vienna 1976; CG 1977; Salzburg Fest. 1976; NY Met 1979. Sang Didon in *Les Troyens*, S. Francisco 1991.

Nebuchadnezzar (Verdi). See *Nabucco*.

neck. The projecting portion of a str. instr. such as a vn. or lute, which carries the fingerboard and terminates in the peg-box.

Neefe, Christian Gottlob (*b* Chemnitz, 1748; *d* Dessau, 1798). Ger. musician who taught *Beethoven at Bonn. Court org., Bonn, 1782, becoming Kapellmeister 1783. Cond. opera at Dessau 1796. Wrote 8 operas, concs., church mus., etc.

Neel, (Louis) **Boyd** (*b* Blackheath, 1905; *d* Toronto, 1981). Eng.-born conductor (Canadian cit. 1961). Qualified as naval officer and doctor of medicine, but turned to mus., founding Boyd Neel Str. Orch. 1933 which rapidly achieved an int. reputation for its perfs. of Eng. and other mus., notably of the baroque era, which was at that time rarely played with chamber forces. Played at Salzburg Fest. 1937, giving f. public p. of Britten's specially commissioned *Variations on a Theme of Frank Bridge*. Cond. Robert Mayer Children's Concerts 1946–52. Dean of Toronto Royal Cons., 1953–70. Cond., Mississauga SO 1971–8. Boyd Neel Orch. renamed Philomusica of London 1957. CBE 1953.

Negro Spiritual. See *Spiritual*.

Neidlinger, Gustav (*b* Mainz, 1912; *d* Bad Ems, 1991). Ger. bass-baritone. Opera début Mainz 1931. Hamburg Opera 1936–50, Stuttgart Opera from 1950. Bayreuth Fest. 1952–75; Salzburg Fest. 1942; London (RFH) 1955; CG 1963; NY Met 1972. Renowned for singing of Alberich, Pizarro, and Klingsor (*Parsifal*).

Neikrug, Marc (Edward) (*b* NY, 1946). Amer. pianist and composer. Comp.-in-res. Marlboro Fest. 1972. Formed duo with Pinchas *Zukerman. Salzburg Fest. début 1978 (recital with Zukerman). Works incl. opera *Los Alamos* (1988); concs.: pf. (1966); cl. (1970); va. (1974); vn. (1985); fl. (1989); 2 str. qts. (1969, 1972); *Rituals*, fl., hp. (1976); Concertino, ens. (1977); *Continuum*, vc., pf. (1978); *Cycle of 7*, pf. (1978); *Kaleidoscope*, fl., pf. (1979); *Eternity's Sunrise*, orch. (1979–80); *Through Roses*, mus. th. (1980); *Duo*, vn., pf. (1983); *Chetro Ketl*, orch. (1986); sym. No.1 (1992); pf. conc. (1995); *Suite from Los Alamos*, orch. (1998); vn. conc. No.2 (*Departures and Remembrance*) (1999).

Nell. Poem by Leconte de Lisle set for v. and pf. by Fauré (Op.18 No.1, 1880).

Nelson. Opera in 3 acts by Lennox *Berkeley to lib. by Alan Pryce-Jones. Comp. 1953. F.p. London (concert perf.) 1953, stage (SW) 1954.

Nelson, John (*b* San José, Costa Rica, 1941). Amer. conductor. Cond. NY concert perf. of *Les Troyens* 1972. Opera stage début NY City Opera 1972 (*Carmen*). NY Met début 1973. Cond. Amer. première of *Owen Wingrave*, Santa Fe 1973. Mus. dir. Indianapolis SO 1977–88, Opera Th. of St Louis 1985–92.

Nelson, Judith (*b* Chicago, 1939). Amer. soprano. Opera début Berkeley 1976 (Roberto in A. Scarlatti's *Griselda*). Eur. début Brussels 1979. Specialist in early mus. but also sings contemp. works.

Nelson Mass (*Nelsonmesse*). Nickname for Haydn's Mass No.9 in D minor (*Missa in angustiis*) (Mass in time of peril), comp. 1798. A legend says that the work celebrates Nelson's victory at Aboukir Bay in 1798, another that Nelson heard it perf. at Eisenstadt in 1800.

Nelsova [Katznelson], **Zara** (*b* Winnipeg, 1918; *d* NY, 2002). Canadian-born cellist (Amer. cit. 1953). Début London 1931 (Lalo conc. with LSO, cond. Sargent). Prin. cellist Toronto SO 1940–3. Amer. début, NY 1942. Worldwide tours. On staff Juilliard Sch. from 1962. Gave f.p. of Hugh Wood's vc. conc., London 1969.

Nelsson, Woldemar (*b* Kiev, 1938). Russ. conductor. Attended master classes at Moscow and Leningrad Cons. Won 1st prize Moscow cond. comp. 1971, becoming ass. to Kondrashin with Moscow PO. Emigrated to W. Ger. 1977. Cond. f.p. of Henze's ballet *Orpheus*, Stuttgart 1979 (also at NY Met). Bayreuth Fest. 1980–5. Gen. mus. dir. Cassel State Th. 1980–7. Cond. f.p. of Penderecki's *Die schwarze Maske*, Salzburg Fest. 1986.

nenia (It. 'Dirge'). In Ancient Rome, a funeral song in praise of the dead. Schiller's *Nänie* were set by Goetz (1874), Brahms (1880–1), and Orff (1956). Term has also been used by Birtwistle in his *Nenia on the death of Orpheus* (1970).

Nenna, Pomponio (*b* Bari, *c*.1550; *d* Rome, 1613). It. composer influenced by *Gesualdo, in whose service he was employed *c*.1594–9. Pubd. seven books of madrigals, six for 5 vv. 1582–1608 and 1618 (posth.), for 4 vv. 1613. Active mainly in Naples and Rome.

Neo-Bechstein Piano. Semi-elec. pf. dating from 1931, based on research by W. Nernst of Berlin. Str. are set in vibration by hammers, but blow required is very light ($\frac{1}{20}$ that given on ordinary pf). No sound-board, the vibrations being amplified through a loudspeaker. Vol. or tone controlled by pedal acting on the amplifier.

Neo-classicism. Term applied to 20th-cent. mus. trend which developed in the 1920s, when several composers wrote works in 17th- and 18th-cent. forms and styles as a reaction against the excessive orchestration of the late 19th-cent. romantics. Prokofiev's *Classical Symphony* (1916–17) and R. Strauss's *Ariadne auf Naxos* (1912) can be claimed as neo-classical, but the movt. began in earnest with Stravinsky (*Capriccio* for pf. and wind, pf. conc., *Pulcinella*, vn. conc., *Oedipus Rex*, etc.) and Hindemith. In Eng. Vaughan Williams's vn. conc. (orig. *Concerto Accademico*) of 1925 was neo-classical in style, though, because for most composers the model was Bach, neo-baroque might be a more accurate description. (Prokofiev's *Classical Symphony*, being a pastiche of Haydn, is truly named.)

nera (It.). Black. Crotchet or quarter-note.

Neri, Massimiliano (*b* ?Brescia, ?1615; *d* Bonn, 1666). It. composer. Org. at St Mark's, Venice 1644–64. Court org., Cologne, 1664. Wrote motets, *Sonate e canzone* (1644), and instr. sonatas (1651).

Nerone (Nero). (1) Opera in 4 acts by *Boito to his own lib. Begun in 1877 and still incomplete when Boito died in 1918. Completed by Toscanini, Tommasini, and Smareglia and prod. Milan 1924, Rome 1928.

(2) Opera in 3 acts by Mascagni to lib. by Targioni-Tozzetti after comedy by P. Cossa (1872). Comp. 1934. Prod. Milan 1935.

Neruda, Wilma [Wilhelmina] (*b* Brno, 1839; *d* Berlin, 1911). Bohem. violinist. Début Vienna 1846. Toured Ger. as prodigy; London début 1849. Many tours of Europe and Russia. Married the Swed. composer *Norman 1864, playing under name Norman-Neruda. Regular visitor to Eng. after 1869. In 1888 married Sir Charles *Hallé with whom she gave many recitals, touring S. Africa and Australia. Retired 1895 when Hallé died, but resumed playing 1898, touring USA 1899. Lived in Berlin from 1900.

Nesterenko, Yevgeny (*b* Moscow, 1938). Russ. bass. Début Maly 1963 (Gremin in *Eugene Onegin*).

Among finest Russ. basses, a notable Boris, and also excellent in It. repertory. Joined Bolshoy Opera 1971. Sang Boris with Bolshoy co. at La Scala 1973 (début with Scala co. 1978); Vienna 1974; NY Met 1975; CG 1978. Noted interpreter of Shostakovich's 14th Sym.

Netrebko, Anna (*b* Krasnodar, 1972). Russ. soprano. Studied at St Petersburg Cons. and later with Renata Scotto. Won Nat. Glinka Comp., Moscow, 1993. Début in concert at Bolshoy Opera 1993. Kirov (Mariinsky) Opera début, St Petersburg, 1994 (Susanna). Amer. opera début San Francisco 1995 (Glinka's Lyudmila). Brit. début Kirov, Drury Lane 1997 (Xenia in *Boris Godunov*), CG 2000 (Natasha in *War and Peace*). Salzburg Fest. 2002 (Natasha), NY Met 2002 (Natasha). Amer. recital début San Francisco 2005, NY (Carnegie Hall) 2006.

Neues vom Tage (News of the Day). Comic opera in 3 parts by Hindemith to lib. by Marcellus Schiffer. Comp. 1928–9. Prod. Berlin 1929. Rev. (mus. and text) by Hindemith 1953, prod. Naples 1954, Cologne 1956, Santa Fe (in Eng.) 1961.

Neumann, Angelo (*b* Vienna, 1838; *d* Prague, 1910). Austrian tenor and impresario. Début 1859. Sang at Vienna Court Opera 1862–76. Man. of Leipzig Opera 1876–82, Bremen Opera 1882–5, Prague Landestheater 1885–1910 (among conds. he engaged there was Mahler). Formed touring co. based on Leipzig to give Wagner's operas, especially *Der Ring des Nibelungen*, in London, Paris, Rome, St Petersburg, etc.

Neumann, František (*b* Přerov, 1874; *d* Brno, 1929). Cz. conductor and composer. Worked in various Ger. and Cz. opera houses 1903–19. On *Janáček's recommendation, appointed cond. Brno Nat. Th. 1919–29. Collab. closely with Janáček and cond. f.ps. of *Káťa Kabanová* (1921), *The Cunning Little Vixen* (1924), *Šárka* (1925), and *The Makropulos Affair* (1926), also f.ps. of operas by Novák and Ostrčil. His 8 operas incl. *Die Brautwerbung* (Linz, 1901), *Liebelei* (Frankfurt, 1910), *Herbststurm* (Berlin, 1919), and *Beatrice Caracci* (Brno, 1922).

Neumann, Václav (*b* Prague, 1920; *d* Vienna, 1995). Cz. conductor and violist. Violist in Smetana Qt. and prin. violist in Czech PO, both from 1945. Deputy cond. Czech PO 1948. Cond. Prague SO 1956–63, Prague PO 1963–4, Komische Oper, Berlin, 1956–64, Leipzig Gewandhaus Orch. and Leipzig Opera 1964–7; chief cond. Czech PO 1968–89. Mus. dir. Stuttgart Opera 1969–72. Salzburg Fest. début 1971. NY Met début 1985. Cond. Felsenstein's famous Berlin production of *The *Cunning Little Vixen*, 1956.

neum(e)s (from Gr. *neuma*, 'gesture' or 'sigh'). System of mus. notation from 7th to 14th cents. Orig. generating forms were grave and acute accents with a horizontal line, but developed into elaborate system for plainsong manuals of the church. Gave precise indication of pitch, but at first were merely approximate indications to singer of shape of the melody.

Neuwirth, Olga (b Graz, 1968). Austrian composer. Started to play trumpet aged 7. Studied at San Francisco Cons. with Elinor Armer 1986–7, Vienna Cons. with Erich Urbanner 1987–93, and IRCAM with Tristan Murail 1993–4. Winner of several prizes, mainly for electro-acoustic works. Works incl. *Bählemms Fest*, opera (1999); *Clinamen/Nodus*, orch. (2000); *Lost Highway*, mus. th. (2003); *. . . ce qui arrive*, mus./video (2004); *locus . . . doublure . . . solus*, pf., ens. (2005–6).

Nevada, Mignon (Mathilde Maria) (b Paris, 1886; d Long Melford, 1971). Eng. soprano, daughter of Amer. sop. Emma Nevada (1859–1940) with whom she studied. Opera début Rome 1907 (Rosina in *Il barbiere di Siviglia*), CG 1910. Also sang in Milan, Paris, and other opera houses. Beecham considered her to be the best Desdemona in *Otello*.

Neveu, Ginette (b Paris, 1919; d San Miguel, Azores, in air crash, 1949). Fr. violinist. Début with Paris Colonne Orch. 1926. Won Wieniawski Prize, Warsaw int. competition, 1935. Amer. début 1937, Eng. 1945. Brilliant interpreter of Sibelius conc.

Nevin, Ethelbert Woodbridge (b Edgeworth, Penn., 1862; d New Haven, Conn., 1901). Amer. composer and pianist. Appeared as soloist in concs. in Pittsburgh and wrote popular songs and pf. pieces despite intermittent ill-health. *The Rosary* (1898) and *Mighty Lak' a Rose* (1901) were his most popular songs, the former achieving a sale of 6 million copies in 30 years. His pf. piece *Narcissus* (1891) was also a best-seller.

New England Conservatory of Music. Mus. sch. in Boston, Mass., founded in Feb. 1867 by Eben Tourjée (b Warwick, R.I., 1834; d Boston, Mass., 1891) in assoc. with Robert Goldbeck. Within 10 years it was largest mus. sch. in the USA with over 14,000 graduates. After Tourjée, dirs. were Carl Faelton (1891–7), George W. Chadwick (1897–1931), Wallace Goodrich (1931–42), Harrison Keller (1942–66), Gunther Schuller (1966–77), J. S. Ballinger (1977–82), Lawrence Lesser (1983–96), Robert Freeman (1997–9), and Daniel Steiner (2000–6). Cons. has Afro-Amer. dept. and courses in jazz and ragtime. Members of Boston SO are among teaching staff.

New England Holidays. Sym. (unnumbered) by *Ives for orch., comp. 1904–13. Movts. entitled 1. *Washington's Birthday*. 2. *Decoration Day*. 3. *Fourth of July*. 4. *Thanksgiving and/or Forefathers' Day* (with ch.).

Newlin, Dika (b Portland, Oregon, 1923). Amer. musicologist and composer. Est. mus. dept. at Drew Univ., Madison, NJ, 1952, teaching there until 1965. Prof. of mus., North Texas State Univ. 1965–73 and Virginia Commonwealth Univ.

from 1978. Has written on Mahler, Bruckner, and Schoenberg. Trans. Schoenberg's *Style and Idea* (1950). Composer, in 12-note method, of 3 operas; pf. conc.; sym. for ch. and orch.; pf. trio; *Chamber Symphony*, etc.

Newman, Ernest [Roberts, William] (b Everton, Lancs., 1868; d Tadworth, 1959). Eng. music critic and author. Began career as bank employee 1889–1904, writing on economics and mus. Wrote first book, *Gluck and the Opera*, in 1895 and *A Study of Wagner* in 1899. On staff Birmingham Midland Institute of Mus. 1903–5. Mus. critic *Manchester Guardian* 1905–6, *Birmingham Post* 1906–19, *Observer* 1919–20, *Sunday Times* 1920–58. Authority on Wagner, of whom he wrote 4-vol. biography (1928–47) in addition to *Wagner as Man and Artist* (1914, rev. 1924), *Fact and Fiction about Wagner* (1931), and *Wagner Nights* (1949). Also wrote studies of Elgar (1906), Wolf (1907), and Strauss (1908), *The Unconscious Beethoven* (1927), *The Man Liszt* (1934), *Opera Nights* (1943), *More Opera Nights* (1954), and other books. Trans. most of Wagner's libs., incl. perf. versions of *Tannhäuser* and *Die Meistersinger*.

Newman, Robert (b 1859; d London, 1926). Eng. bass and impresario. After singing career, became man. of Queen's Hall, London, 1893 and started Promenade concerts in assoc. with Henry J. *Wood in 1895.

Newmarch (née Jeaffreson), **Rosa** (Harriet) (b Leamington, 1857; d Worthing, 1940). Eng. writer on music. Went to Russia in 1897, working under Stasov at Imperial Public Library and meeting leading Russ. composers. On return to Eng. did much to spread the fame of these composers and from 1908 to 1927 wrote programme notes for the Promenade concerts. Wrote several books and translated libs. of Russ. operas. Also early advocate of Sibelius and Janáček (whose *Sinfonietta*, 1926, is ded. to her). Organized Janáček's visit to London 1926.

new music (Ger. *Neue Musik*). Term which periodically recurs in the history of mus., e.g.

(1) *ars nova* of 14th cent.

(2) *nuove musiche* of 17th cent. when new monodic style transformed the art. In 1602 G. Caccini pubd. *Le nuove musiche* (The New Musics) containing arias and madrigals with monodic recitative.

(3) The mus. of Liszt, Wagner, and their followers from c.1850, compared with the 'traditional' Brahms.

(4) In 20th cent., atonal and elec. mus.

New Opera Company. Formed in Cambridge in late 1950s by Leon Lovett, Peter Hemmings, and Brian Trowell as part-amateur, part-professional co. It began to give short London seasons at SW in 1957, making a speciality of rare, modern, or Eng. operas. Among works staged were Stravinsky's *The Rake's Progress* (f. London p., 1957); Benjamin's *A Tale of Two Cities* (1957); Vaughan Williams's *Sir John in Love* (1958); and British premières of: Egk's *Der Revisor* (1958); Dallapiccola's *Il prigioniero* (1959); Schoenberg's *Erwartung*

(1960); Henze's *Boulevard Solitude* (1962); Proko-fiev's *The Fiery Angel* (1965); Shostakovich's *The Nose* (1973); Goehr's *Arden Must Die* (1974); Szyma-nowski's *King Roger* (1975); Ginastera's *Bomarzo* (1976); Martinů's *Julietta* (1978); Brian Howard's *Inner Voices* (1983). Withdrawal of grant killed company in 1984.

New Philharmonia Orchestra. See *Philharmonia Orchestra*.

News of the Day (Hindemith). See *Neues vom Tage*.

Newsome, Roy (*b* Elland, Yorks., 1930). Eng. con-ductor, composer, teacher, and adjudicator. Major figure in brass band world. Cond., Black Dyke Mills Band 1966–77, Besses o' th' Barn 1978–85, Williams Fairey 1986–9, Sun Life Band from 1990. Head of Band Studies, Salford Coll. of Technology 1976–89. Mus. dir. Nat. Youth Brass Band of Gt. Britain from 1984. Has comp. conc. for pf. and brass band and other pieces.

Newstone, Harry (*b* Winnipeg, 1921; *d* Victoria, BC, 2006). Eng. conductor. Formed Haydn Orch. 1949. Mus. dir. Sacramento SO 1965–78. Dir. of mus., Kent Univ. (UK) 1979–86. Specialist in clas-sical period, but also fine interpreter of Scandi-navian and Brit. music.

Newton, Ivor (*b* London, 1892; *d* Bromley, 1981). Eng. pianist, principally accompanist. Worked with many celebrated artists, e.g. Melba, Ger-hardt, Gigli, McCormack, Flagstad, Chaliapin, Casals, Ysaÿe, Menuhin, etc. Salzburg Fest. 1946 (recital with Grace *Moore). Autobiography *At the Piano—Ivor Newton* (1966). CBE 1973.

New World, From the (*Z nového světa*). Sub-title given by Dvořák to his 9th (5th in the old num-bering) sym. in E minor, Op.95, comp. 1893 and f.p. NY Dec. 1893 cond. Anton Seidl. Some themes are regarded as in the spirit of Amer. Negro folk tunes but none is directly quoted, though the resemblance of one to 'Swing low, sweet chariot' is often noticed. On the other hand, the Bohemian element is equally strong. The main theme of the *largo* has been made into a Negro spiritual to the words 'Goin' Home'. Dvořák himself hoped to write an opera based on Longfellow's *Hiawatha* and he said that the *largo* was a study for it.

New Year. Opera in 3 acts by *Tippett to his own lib. Comp. 1986–8. F.p. Houston 1989, Glynde-bourne 1990, BBC TV 1991. Orch. suite, f.p. Chel-tenham 1990.

New York City Opera. Opera co.—originally City Center Opera Co.—founded 1943 as part of NY City Center of Music and Drama. First prod. (*Tosca*) in Feb. 1944, Laszlo Halász being mus. dir. until 1951, succeeded by Joseph Rosenstock 1952–5, Erich Leinsdorf 1956–7, Julius Rudel 1957–79, Christopher Keene 1983–6. Beverly *Sills was dir. 1979–88; Keene 1989–95; Paul Kellogg 1996–2006. Moved to NY State Theatre

in Lincoln Center 1966. Follows adventurous pol-icy, presenting unusual and modern operas. Has nurtured many fine singers, best known of whom are the sops. Beverly Sills, Ashley Putnam, and Carol Vaness, the ten. Plácido Domingo, and the bar. Samuel Ramey.

New York Philharmonic Orchestra. America's oldest sym. orch., founded 1842 as Phil. Soc. of NY. Up to 1892 the conds. incl. Leopold Dam-rosch and Theodore Thomas. Since then the usual rule has been for there to be a 'permanent' or prin. cond. with some guest conds., the post being one of the most highly prized in the mus. world: Anton Seidl (1891–8); Emil Paur (1898–1902); Walter Damrosch (1902–3); guest cond. (1903–6) incl. Wood, Weingartner, R. Strauss, and F. Steinbach; Vasily Safonov (1906–9); Gustav Mahler (1909–11); Josef Stransky (1911–21); Willem Mengelberg (1921–9); Arturo Toscanini (1928–36) (jointly with Mengelberg 1928–9); John Barbirolli (1936–42); Artur Rodzinski (1943–7); Bruno Walter (1947–9); Leopold Stokowski and Dimitri Mitropoulos (1949–50); Dimitri Mitropoulos (1950–8); Leonard Bernstein (1958–69, with whom the orch. made its Salzburg Fest. début 1959); Pierre Boulez (1971–7); Zubin Mehta (1978–91): Kurt Masur (1991–2002); Lorin Maazel from 2002. Bernstein in 1969 became cond. laureate for life. The orch. merged in 1928 with the *New York Symphony Orchestra, becoming the Philharmonic-Symph-ony Orchestra of New York, but is now simply the NYPO.

New York Symphony Orchestra. Founded by Leopold Damrosch, 1878, who was cond. until his death in 1885. Succeeded by his son Walter until merger with *New York Philharmonic Or-chestra in 1928.

NHKSO (Nippon Hōsō Kyōkai Symphony Orches-tra). First Japanese prof. orch., formed 1926 as New Orchestra, which later became Japan SO. In 1951 changed to present name when the broad-casting network NKO took over responsibility for the orch. Mus. dirs. have incl. Joseph Rosenstock (1937–41); Charles Dutoit (from 1998); and Vla-dimir Ashkenazy (from 2004).

Nicholls, Agnes (*b* Cheltenham, 1877; *d* London, 1959). Eng. soprano. Opera début London 1895 as Purcell's Dido. CG 1901–24. Sang with Denhof, Beecham, and BNOC cos. Amer. début Cincinnati Fest. 1904. Sang Sieglinde in *Die Walküre* and Brünnhilde in *Siegfried* in first Eng. *Ring* at CG in 1908 cond. Richter. Successful career in oratorio, singing in f.p. of Elgar works. Wife of cond. Sir Hamilton *Harty. Works were written for her by Parry and Harty. CBE 1923.

Nicholson, George (*b* Durham, 1949). Eng. com-poser and pianist. Several comps. commissioned by BBC and by various contemp. mus. groups. Member of chamber group Nomos. Works incl.:

THEATRE: *The Arrival of the Poet in the City*, melodrama for actor and 7 instr. (1982–3).

ORCH.: *Recycle*, 11 instr. (1975–6); *1132* (1976); *The Convergence of the Twain*, chamber orch. (1978); *Chamber Concerto*, 13 instrs. (1979–80); *Sea-Change*, 14 str. (1988); vc. conc. (1990); fl. conc. (1993); *Fenestrae*, 15 instr. (1998); Conc. for Orch. (2004–5).

VOCAL: *Colloque sentimental*, sop., hp. (1976); *Rondeau*, sop. (1977); *Settings*, sop., pf. (1977); *Hallel*, sop., org. (1979); *Alla Luna*, sop., cl., pf. (1981); *Aubade*, sop., 5 players (1981); *Vignette*, sop., pf. (1983); *Peripheral Visions*, sop., pf. (1983); *A World of Imagination*, unacc. ch. (1984); *Blisworth Tunnel Blues*, sop., chamber orch. (1984–6); *Letters to the World*, sop., rec., vc., hpd. (1997–9); *Idyll*, sop., 5 instr. (2003); *Embers*, sop., ob., cl., hn., vn., va., vc., vib. (2004).

CHAMBER MUSIC: *Overtune*, 7 wind instr. (1976); str. qt. No.1 (1976–7), No.2 (1984–5), No.3 (1995); brass quintet (1977); *The Seventh Seal*, va. (1977); *Nodus*, cl., pf. (1978); *Winter Music*, cl., hp., perc. (1978); *N'est-ce pas . . . ?*, vn. (1979); *Slide Show*, tb. (1981); *So Low*, db. (1981); *Ancient Lights*, fl., cl., bass cl., vn., va., vc., pf. (1982); *Movements*, 6 instr. (1982–3); *Sound Progressions Newly Minted*, brass quintet (1983); *Stilleven*, 5 instr. (1985); *3 Nocturnes*, cl., vn., vc., pf. (1986); *Romanza*, vn., pf. (1987); *Spring Songs*, rec. (1991); *Muybridge Frames*, tb., pf. (1992); *Ave atque vale*, fl., pf. (1994); *(termiJné*, 2 bcl., pf. (1995); *Fills*, cl. (2000); *Shailing and Wambling*, va., vc. (2001); *Mr Biberian his Dompe*, gui. (2002); *Hic Harold Rex interfectus est*, sax., hn., tpt., hp., gui., str. qt., perc. (2004).

PIANO: Sonata (1983); *Cascate* (1985); *Impromptu* (1988); *All Systems Go* (1989); *For Miles* (1991–2); *In Accord* (1997).

Nicholson [Nicolson], **Richard** (*b* c.1570; *d* Oxford, 1639). Eng. composer and organist. Org. and choirmaster Magdalen Coll., Oxford, from 1595. First prof. of mus., Oxford Univ., 1626–39. Wrote madrigals, motets, and *Joan, quoth John, when will this be?* a madrigal cycle for 3 vv. which has been called the first song-cycle. Contrib. 5-part madrigal *Sing shepherds all* to The **Triumphs of Oriana*.

Nicholson, (Sir) **Sydney** (Hugo) (*b* London, 1875; *d* Ashford, Kent, 1947). Eng. organist and composer. Org., Carlisle Cath. 1904–8, Manchester Cath. 1908–18, Westminster Abbey 1918–27. Founder-dir. Sch. of Eng. Church Mus., 1927, which became *Royal School of Church Music 1945. Wrote church mus. and org. pieces. Ed. 1916 supplement to *Hymns Ancient and Modern*. Knighted 1938.

Nicolai, (Karl) **Otto** (Ehrenfried) (*b* Königsberg, 1810; *d* Berlin, 1849). Ger. composer and conductor. Taught mus. in Berlin 1830–3, singing in Singakademie. Public concert in Berlin 1833, appearing as composer, singer, and pianist. Went to Rome 1833–6 as org. of Prussian embassy chapel. Kapellmeister and singing master of Kärntnerthor Th., Vienna, 1837, returning to Rome 1838, where he comp. several operas in It. style. Kapellmeister, Vienna Court Opera 1841–7, founding Phil. concerts 28 March 1842. Credited with being first to insert Beethoven's *Leonora No.3*

ov. into *Fidelio* as entr'acte (1841). Dir., Berlin Opera 1847, where his most successful opera, *Die *Lustigen Weiber von Windsor*, was prod. 2 months before his death. Also wrote 2 syms., pf. conc., str. qt., etc.

Nicolet, Aurèle (*b* Neuchâtel, 1926). Swiss flautist and teacher. Won fl. prize Geneva int. comp. 1948. Prin. fl. Winterthur Orch. 1948–50, Berlin PO 1950–9. Salzburg Fest. début 1958. Prof., Berlin Hochschule für Musik 1953–65, then taught in Freyburg and Basle. Noted player of classics and of contemp. works written for him by Huber, Kelterborn, Takemitsu, and Denisov.

Nicolini [Grimaldi, Nicolino] (*b* Naples, 1673; *d* Naples, 1732). It. castrato contralto. Sang in It. 1694–1708, being closely assoc. with operas of A. Scarlatti. Went to London where he achieved enormous success 1708–11 and 1714–18. Sang in many of Handel's operas and created roles of Rinaldo (1711) and Amadigi (1715). Returned to It. to sing in opera in Rome, Venice, and Naples.

Niedermeyer, (Abraham) **Louis** (*b* Nyon, Switz., 1802; *d* Paris, 1861). Swiss composer. Wrote unsuccessful operas for Paris. Took over sch. of church mus. now known as École Niedermeyer. Wrote mass and other religious works.

Niederschlag (Ger.). (1) down-beat (up-beat being *Aufschlag).

(2) In str. playing, down-stroke of the bow (also called *Niederstrich*).

Nielsen, Carl (August) (*b* Nørre-Lyndelse, 1865; *d* Copenhagen, 1931). Danish composer, violinist, and conductor. Showed mus. talent as child and became military trumpeter at 14 at Odense 1879–83. Formed str. qt. in 1882. Joined th. orch. as violinist, 1886, and was violinist in Royal Chapel orch. 1889–1905. Studied at Royal Cons., Copenhagen, 1884. Made some appearances as cond., and became a cond. at Royal Th., Copenhagen, 1908–14. Cond. Copenhagen Mus. Soc. 1915–27. On staff of Royal Danish Cons. from 1915, becoming dir. 1931. Visited Berlin 1921, London 1923, and Paris 1926 to conduct his own works. For many years his mus. was little known outside Denmark, but after World War II the power and originality of his syms. spread to other countries. The 5th Sym. contains an early aleatory feature, when the side-drummer is instructed to improvise so as to drown the rest of the orch. His First Sym. of 1891–2 is one of earliest examples of 'progressive tonality', i.e. it begins in one key and ends in another. Prin. comps.:

OPERAS: *Snefrid*, melodrama (1893); **Saul and David* (1898–1901); **Maskarade* (1904–6).

INCIDENTAL MUSIC: *Hr. Oluf han rider* (Master Oluf Rides) (1906); *Tove* (1906–8); *Willemoes* (1907–8); *Foraeldre* (1908); *Hagbarth og Signe* (1910); *St Hansaftenspil* (1913); *Faedreland* (1915); *Løgneren* (1918); *Aladdin* (1918–19); *Cosmus* (1921–2); *Ebbe Skammelsen* (1925); *Amor og Digteren* (Love and the Poet) (1931); *Paaske-aften* (1931).

ORCH.: syms.: No.1 in G minor (1891–2), No.2 (*The *Four Temperaments*) (1901–2), No.3 (**Sinfonia* *espansiva*) with sop. and bar. (1910–11), No.4 (*Det uudslukkelige*, The *Inextinguishable*) (1915–16); No.5 (1921–2), No.6 (**Sinfonia semplice*) (1924–5); *Little Suite*, str. (1888); *Helios*, ov. (1903); *The Dream of Gunnar* (*Saga-Drøm*) (1908); vn. conc. (1911); *Franz Neruda in memoriam*, speaker, orch. (1918); *Pan and Syrinx*, pastorale (1917); *7 Pieces from 'Aladdin'* (1918–19); fl. conc. (1926); *En Fantasirejse til Faerøerne* (An Imaginary Trip to the Faroe Islands), rhapsody (1927); cl. conc. (1928).

CHORAL: **Hymnus Amoris*, sop., ten., bar., bass, children's ch., male ch., mixed ch., orch. (1896); *Søvnen* (Sleep), ch., orch. (1904); *Fynsk Foraar* (Springtime on Fyn), sop., ten., bass-bar., ch., orch. (1921); *Hyldest til Holberg* (Homage to Holberg), solo vv., ch., orch. (1922); *Hymne til Kunsten* (Hymn to Art), sop., ten., ch., wind instr. (1929); *3 Motets*, unacc. ch. (1929); various occasional cantatas, incl. one for the 50th anniv. of Danish Cremation Union (1931).

CHAMBER MUSIC: str. qts.: in D minor (1882–3), in F (1887), No.1 in G minor (1888), No.2 in F minor (1890), No.3 in E♭ (1898), No.4 in F (1906/19); str. quintet in G (1888), wind quintet (1922); vn. sonatas: in G (1881–2), No.1 in A (1895), No.2 (1912); *Ved en ung Kunstners Baare* (At the bier of a young artist), str. qt., db. (1910); *Prelude and Theme with Variations*, solo vn. (1923); *Serenata in vano*, cl., bn., hn., vc., db. (1914).

PIANO: *2 Characteristic Pieces* (c.1882–3); *5 Pieces* (1890); *Symphonic Suite* (1894); *6 Humoresque-Bagatelles* (1894–7); *Festive Prelude to the New Century* (1899); *Chaconne* (1916); *Theme with Variations* (1916); *Suite* (1919); *Tre Klaverstykker* (3 Pieces) (1928); *Piano Music for Young and Old*, 24 5-finger pieces (1930).

VOICE & PIANO: *5 Poems by J. P. Jacobsen* (1891); *6 Songs and Verses by J. P. Jacobsen* (1891); *6 Songs* (Holstein) (1894); *7 Strophic Songs* (1905–7); *Tove*, 3 songs for Holstein's play (1906–8); *Willemoes*, 5 songs for L. C. Nielsen's play (1907–8); *Hymn to Denmark* (1917); *3 Songs from 'Aladdin'* (1918); *20 Popular Melodies* (1917–21); *Balladen om Bjørnen* (Ballad of the Bear) (1923); *10 Little Danish Songs* (1923–4).

ORGAN: *29 Short Preludes* (or for harmonium) (1929); *2 Preludes* (1930); *Commotio* (1931).

Nielsen, Riccardo (*b* Bologna, 1908; *d* Ferrara, 1982). It. composer. Earlier works in neo-classical idiom, later in 12-note; incl. radio opera *La via di Colombo* (NY 1953), which won 1953 Italia Prize; *L'incubo*, monodrama (Venice 1948); 2 syms.; conc. for orch.; vn. conc.; pf. concs.; chamber mus.

niente (It.). Nothing. Term used (especially by Vaughan Williams) to indicate that the sound is gradually to fade out of earshot.

Nietzsche, Friedrich Wilhelm (*b* Röcken, 1844; *d* Weimar, 1900). Ger. philosopher, poet, and amateur composer. Prof. of classical philology, Basle Univ. 1869–79. Distinguished between 'Romantic' and 'Dionysian' in music. Friend and ardent disciple of Wagner from 1868 but turned

against him and denounced his influence in 3 pamphlets, the last and most effective of them being *Der Fall Wagner* (1888). Instead, championed Bizet. Wrote songs, pf. pieces, and choral mus. His epic prose-poem *Also sprach Zarathustra* (1883–5) inspired mus. from R. Strauss, Mahler, and Delius.

Nigg, Serge (*b* Paris, 1924). Fr. composer. In 1945–8 studied 12-note technique with R. Leibowitz. Later reacted against atonality and turned to more accessible idiom. Prof. of orch., Paris Cons. Works incl. symphonic poems *Timour* (1944), *Pour un poète captif* (1950); 2 pf. concs.; vn. conc.; fl. conc.; vn. sonata; 3 pf. sonatas; *Jérôme Bosch Symphony* (1960); *Mirrors for William Blake*, pf., orch. (1978); str. qt. (1982); *Du clair au sombre*, song-cycle, sop., chamber orch. (1986); *Poème pour orchestre* (1989); *Deux images de nuit*, pf. (1999); vn. conc. No.2 (2001).

Night at the Chinese Opera, A. Opera in 3 acts by Judith *Weir to her own libretto based partly on Chi Chun-Hsiang's *The Chao Family Orphan* (13th cent.). Comp. 1986–7. Prod. Cheltenham 1987, London 1987, Santa Fe 1989.

nightingale. Imitative toy instr. used in an oratorio by A. Scarlatti, in Leopold Mozart's *Toy Symphony*, and in Crosse's *Play Ground*.

Nightingale, The (Russ. *Solovey*; Fr. *Le Rossignol*). Opera in 3 acts by Stravinsky to lib. by composer and S. Mitusov, based on Hans Andersen. Comp. 1908–9, 1913–14. Prod. Paris and London 1914, NY Met 1926. Also *Song of the Nightingale* (*Le Chant du Rossignol*) sym.-poem in 3 parts based on mus. from the opera, 1917. F.p. Geneva 1919; f.p. in England, London 1920; *Songs of the Nightingale and Chinese March* for vn. and pf., transcr. Stravinsky and S. Dushkin, 1932.

Night on the Bare Mountain (*Ivanova noch na lisoy gore*, St John's Night on the Bare Mountain). Orch. work by Mussorgsky inspired by witches' sabbath in Gogol's story *St John's Eve*. Comp. 1867 for orch., rev. as choral piece for inclusion in opera *Mlada*, 1872, again rev. as choral introduction to Act 3 of **Sorochintsy Fair*, 1874. This final version was freely rev. and orch. by Rimsky-Korsakov, 1908, and it is this version which is well-known, though it is scarcely accurate to describe it as by Mussorgsky.

Night Ride and Sunrise. Tone poem for orch., Op.55, by *Sibelius, comp. 1907, f.p. St Petersburg 1909 (cond. Ziloti), f.p. in England Hastings 1930.

Nights in the Gardens of Spain (Falla). See *Noches en los jardines de España*.

Nijinskaya [Nijinska], **Bronislava** (*b* Minsk, 1891; *d* Los Angeles, 1972). Dancer and choreographer. Sister of Vaclav *Nijinsky. Created roles in Diaghilev ballets (*Carnaval*, 1910 and *Petrushka*, 1911). Returned to Russ. 1914 but left 1921 to rejoin Diaghilev co. as dancer, prod., and choreographer. Created *Renard* (1922), *Les Noces* (1923), *Les Biches*, and *Le train bleu* (1924). Worked as choreog. for Paris Opéra, Teatro Colón in Buenos Aires, and with Ida Rubinstein co. (*Le Baiser de la Fée*, *Boléro*, 1928, *La Valse*, 1929). Later worked for Max Reinhardt in Berlin and opened ballet sch. in Los Angeles 1938. Guest choreog. for various cos. in 1940s. Prod. *Les Biches* (1964) and *Les Noces* (1966) for Royal Ballet at CG.

Nijinsky [Nizhinsky], **Vaclav** (*b* Kiev, 1889; *d* London, 1950). Russ. dancer. Entered St Petersburg ballet sch. 1898, graduated 1907. Joined Mariinsky Th. Danced with Pavlova in Fokine's *Pavillon d'Armide* (1907). Met *Diaghilev and became prin. attraction in Paris seasons of Ballet Russe. Noted for his dancing in *Les Sylphides* (1909), *Shéhérazade* (1910), *Spectre de la Rose* and *Petrushka* (1911), *Daphnis and Chloë* (1912). Resigned from Mariinsky co. 1911 because his costume in *Giselle* was considered indecent. Choreographer for Diaghilev prods. of *L'Après-midi d'un Faune* (1912), *Jeux* (1913), and *Le Sacre du Printemps* (1913). His marriage led to break with Diaghilev. Estab. own co. 1914 but it failed. Rejoined Diaghilev 1916, choreographing *Till Eulenspiegel*. Last solo perf. St Moritz 1919. Spent last years in mental hospitals. One of the greatest artists in history of ballet.

Nikisch, Arthur (*b* Lébényi Szent-Miklós, 1855; *d* Leipzig, 1922). Hung. conductor and violinist. Child prodigy pianist. Played vn. in orch. at laying of Bayreuth foundation stone, May 1872. Violinist, Vienna Court Opera Orch. 1874–7. Engaged by A. *Neumann as ch. master, Leipzig Opera, 1877, 2nd cond. there 1878, 1st cond. 1879–89 (with Mahler as 2nd cond. 1886–8). Cond. Boston SO 1889–93. Dir. Budapest Opera 1893–5. Cond. Leipzig Gewandhaus Orch. and Berlin PO from 1895. Frequent guest cond. in Eng. and USA. Took LSO on first Amer. tour 1912. Cond. opera at CG 1907, 1912 (Holbrooke's *Children of Don*), and 1913–14 (*The Ring*). Cond. much Eng. mus. incl. Elgar's 1st Sym. and f.p. of Butterworth's *Shropshire Lad* Rhapsody (Leeds 1913). Was excellent pf. accomp., notably with his pupil Elena *Gerhardt. Comp. chamber mus. and cantata.

Nikolayeva, Tatyana (Petrovna). (*b* Bezhiza, 1924; *d* S. Francisco, 1993). Russ. pianist, teacher, and composer. Won 1st prize 1950 at Leipzig Bach bicentennial fest. Teacher at Moscow Cons. 1959–65, prof. from 1965. Shostakovich wrote his *24 Preludes and Fugues* (1950–1) for her: she gave f.p. 1952. Brit. début Leeds 1984 (on jury Leeds pf. comp. and gave recital there). London début 1986. Salzburg Fest. début 1987. NY début 1993 (aged almost 70!). Comps. incl. syms., 2 pf concs., pf. quintet, 24 studies for pf., and songs.

Nilsson [Svennsson], (Märta) **Birgit** (*b* Bjärlov, Västra Karup, 1918; *d* Bjärlov, 2005). Swed. soprano. Opera début Stockholm 1946 (Agathe in *Der Freischütz*). Sang variety of roles in Stock-

holm, esp. Wagner, Verdi, Puccini, and Strauss. Glyndebourne 1951. Sang Brünnhilde in *Der Ring des Nibelungen*, Munich 1955. Bayreuth début 1954 and sang Brünnhilde there in 1960s, being acknowledged as Flagstad's successor as leading Wagnerian sop. Outstanding Turandot at La Scala 1958. CG début 1957; Amer. début (S. Francisco) 1956; NY Met 1959. Retired 1984.

Nilsson, Bo (*b* Skelleftehamn, Sweden, 1937). Swed. composer, largely self-taught. Serialist and has used elec. and *avant-garde* techniques. Works incl. *Frequenzen*, chamber ens. (1956); *20 Clusters* for picc., ob., and cl. (1958–9); cantata *And the hands of his eyes were slowly turning back* (1959); *Entrée*, orch., tape (1962–3); *Szene* I, II, and III, chamber ens. (1960–2); *Versuchungen*, orch. in 3 groups (1963); *La Bran*, sax., ch., orch. (1963–76); *Revue*, orch. (1967); *Attraktionen*, str. qt. (1968); *Design*, vn., cl., pf. (1968); *Rendezvous*, pf. (1968); *Caprice*, orch. (1970); *Nazm*, reciter, solo vn., ch., jazz group, orch. all amp. (1973); *Taqsim-Caprice-Maqam*, ens. (1974); *Szene IV*, jazz sax., ch. (1975); *Déjà connu, déjà entendu*, wind quintet (1976); *Madonna*, mez., ens. (1977); pf. quintet (1979); *Wendepunkt*, brass, live elec. (1981); *Carte Postale a Sten Frykberg*, brass quintet (1985).

Nilsson, Christine [Törnerhjelm, Kristina] (*b* Sjöabol, 1843; *d* Stockholm, 1921). Swed. soprano. Début Paris 1864 (Violetta in *La traviata*); London 1864 and sang opera regularly in London, incl. CG, until 1881 and gave farewell concert there in 1891. Created Ophelia in Thomas's *Hamlet*, Paris Opéra 1868. Amer. début (NY Acad. of Mus.) 1871; NY 1871–4 and 1883–4. Sang Marguerite in *Faust* on opening night of NY Met 1883.

Nimphes des Bois (Fr. 'Wood Nymphs'). Title of poem by Jehan Molinet which is combined with the Latin Requiem as text for the six-part motet-chanson *La Déploration de la mort de Johannes* (*Jehan*) *Ockeghem* by Josquin *Desprès. Written and composed 1497 (Ockeghem died on 6 Feb., 1497). Text refers to several contemporary composers, incl. Josquin himself. Requiem chant is used as *cantus firmus* to principal setting.

Nimrod. 9th (*adagio*) of Elgar's *Enigma Variations*. So called because it is a portrait of Elgar's friend A. J. Jaeger (Jäger is Ger. for hunter: Nimrod was 'mighty hunter' in Old Testament). Enshrines a day when the two men discussed Beethoven slow movts. and is often used as a commemorative separate item.

Nimsgern, Siegmund (*b* St Wendel, 1940). Ger. bass. Between 1967 and 1971 won singing comps. at 's Hertogenbosch, Cologne, Munich, and Berlin. Début Saarbrücken 1967 (Lionel in *Maid of Orleans*). Salzburg Fest. début 1970. Member of Saarbrücken Staatstheater 1971–4, then Deutsche Oper-am-Rhein. Brit. début 1972; CG 1973; Amer. début (S. Francisco) 1974; NY Met 1978. Sang Wotan at Bayreuth 1983–5.

Nin (y Castellanos), **Joaquín** (*b* Havana, 1879; *d* Havana, 1949). Cuban pianist, composer, and musicologist. Prof. of pf., Schola Cantorum, 1905–8. Worked in Berlin 1908–10. Specialized as pianist in old and modern Sp. mus. Ed. several vols. of early Sp. mus. Wrote pf. works, songs, guitar pieces, etc.

nineteenth. Org. mutation stop. Length and pitch 1⅓′, pitch being thus a 19th (2 octaves and a 5th) above normal.

ninth. *Interval of 9 steps, if bottom and top notes are counted. Chord of the 9th is common chord plus the 7th and 9th.

Ninth Symphony. Although several composers published 9 syms., e.g. Mahler, Bruckner, Dvořák, and Vaughan Williams, this term to the general mus.-lover means one work, Beethoven's Sym. No.9 in D minor, the 'Choral'.

Nixon in China. Opera in 2 acts by John *Adams to lib. by Alice Goodman. Comp. 1984–7. Prod. Houston 1987, Edinburgh 1988. Plot is based on visit of US President Nixon to China in 1972 and characters also include Pat Nixon, Henry Kissinger, Mao Tse-tung and Mme Mao, and Chou en Lai.

nobile (It.). Noble.

Nobilissima Visione (Most noble vision). Choreographic legend in 1 act and 5 scenes, lib. and mus. by Hindemith based on life of St Francis of Assisi. Choreog. Massine, who danced in f.p. London (Drury Lane) 1938. Danced in USA under title *Saint Francis*. Also orch. suite in 3 movts.

nobilmente (It.). Nobly, in a noble style. Directive closely, almost exclusively, assoc. with mus. of Elgar, who first used it in a pubd. score in the pf. transcription of 'Nimrod' in the *Enigma Variations* (1899), but not in full score. First used in pubd. orch. score in *Cockaigne* concert-ov., 1901. Though widely regarded as symbol of Elgar's 'ceremonial' manner, it should be noted that he did not apply it to the *Pomp and Circumstance* marches, nor to the *Coronation Ode*, but used it for themes of a particular emotional intensity, as in the vn. and vc. concs., and the syms. Vaughan Williams also used the term in his *Coastal Command* film mus., 1942.

Noble, Dennis (William) (*b* Bristol, 1899; *d* Jávea, Spain, 1966). Eng. baritone. Heard by Percy *Pitt singing in cinema and offered CG audition. Début there 1924. Sang there regularly until 1938 and also in 1947. Also with BNOC and Carl Rosa. Sang bar. part in f.p. of Walton's *Belshazzar's Feast*, Leeds 1931.

Noble, Ray (mond Stanley) (*b* Brighton, 1903; *d* London, 1978). Eng. bandleader, composer, and arranger. Nephew of T. Tertius *Noble. Worked as arranger for publisher and at BBC with Jack Payne. From 1929 his New Mayfair Orch., with Al Bowlly as singer, made many broadcasts and

recordings. Went to USA 1934 where Glenn *Miller helped him to assemble band which made début at Rainbow Room, NY, 1935. Moved to Los Angeles 1929. Comps. incl. *Goodnight, Sweetheart* (1931); *Love is the sweetest thing* (1932); *The very thought of you* (1934); *The touch of your lips* (1936); and *Cherokee* (1938).

Noble, T(homas) **Tertius** (*b* Bath, 1867; *d* Rockport, Mass., 1953). Eng. organist and composer. Studied at RCM with Parratt, Frederick Bridge, and Stanford. Ass. org., Trinity Coll., Cambridge, 1890–2. Org., Ely Cath. 1892–8, York Minster 1898–1912, St Thomas's Church, NY, 1912–47. Comps. incl. anthems, hymns, cantata, and org. pieces.

Noces, Les (Russ. *Svadebka*; Eng. 'The Wedding'). 'Choreographic scenes with song and music' by Stravinsky (words adapted by composer from popular sources) for mixed ch., 4 soloists, 4 pf., and 17 perc. instr., in 4 scenes: *The Blessing of the Bride, The Blessing of the Bridegroom, The Bride's Departure from her Parents' Home*, and *The Wedding Feast*. 1st version 1917 unfinished (scored for full wind, str. octet, with cimbalom, hps., perc., and harmonium. Completed 1971 by R. Craft and C. Matthews). 2nd version 1919, for perc., harmonium, cimbalom, and pianola. Prod. Paris 1923, choreog. *Nijinskaya, cond. Ansermet. Later choreog. Béjart.

Noches en los jardines de España (Nights in the Gardens of Spain). Symphonic impressions for pf. and orch. by Falla, comp. 1909–15, f.p. Madrid 1916, f.p. in England, London 1921 (soloist Falla); f.p. in Amer., Boston, Mass., 1924. Movts. are: 1. *En el Generalife*. 2. *Danza lejana* (Dance in the distance). 3. *En los jardines de la Sierra de Córdoba*.

nocturne (Fr., 'pertaining to night'). A comp. which suggests a nocturnal atmosphere, e.g. Haydn's *Notturnos* for *lira organizzata*, Mozart's *Serenata Notturna*, but more specifically a short pf. piece of romantic character. First to use the title for this genre was John *Field, followed by *Chopin. An expressive melody in the right hand is accompanied in the left by broken chords.

Nocturne. Song-cycle for ten., 7 obbl. instr., and str. orch., Op.60, by Britten, comp. 1958. Settings of 8 poems about night by Shelley, Tennyson, Coleridge, Middleton, Wordsworth, Owen, Keats, and Shakespeare. The opening poem is acc. by str. only, each succeeding setting is dominated by an obbl. instr. (bn., harp, hn., timp., cor anglais, and fl. and cl.), and the finale is for the full complement. Ded. to Mahler's widow. F.p. Leeds 1958.

Nocturnes. Symphonic triptych for orch., and in the last movt. women's ch., by Debussy, comp. 1897–9. The 3 movts. are *Nuages* (Clouds); *Fêtes* (Festivals); and *Sirènes* (Sirens). F.p. (Nos. 1 and 2), Paris 1900; f. complete p. Paris 1901. F.p. in England, London 1909, cond. Debussy. Arr. for 2 pf., 4 hands, by Ravel 1909.

Nocturnes and Arias. (1) Orch. work by *Musgrave comp. 1966, f.p. Zurich, cond. N. Del Mar.
(2) Settings by *Henze of poems by I. Bachmann for sop. and orch. Comp. 1957. F.p. Donaueschingen (Gloria Davy, H. Rosbaud).

node (of a vibrating string). Point of rest between two vibrating portions.

Noël (Fr.); **Nowell** (Eng.). A popular Christmas song or carol. In Eng. several 15th-cent. carols begin with the word 'Nowell' and *Busnois (c.1430–92) wrote a work for 4 vv. with the word 'Noël' as the sole text. In the 17th cent. the name 'noël' was given to organ pieces to be played during the Christmas services and based on Christmas melodies.

noire (Fr.). The crotchet or Amer. quarter-note.

None. The 6th of the Canonical Hours of the RC Church. Properly it takes place at 3 p.m. (i.e. the '9th hour').

nonet (Eng.); **nonette** (Fr.); **Nonett** (Ger.); **nonetto** (It.). Comp. for 9 solo instr. or 9 vv. Famous examples are by Spohr, Rheinberger, Stanford, Ravel (3 *Poèmes de Mallarmé* for v. and 9 instr.), and Webern (*Concerto*, Op.24).

non-harmonic note. Term in harmonic analysis meaning a note not part of the chord with which it sounds and therefore requiring explanation, e.g. *passing-note or *appoggiatura.

Nonnengeige (Ger.). Nun's fiddle. The *tromba marina.

Non Nobis Domine (Not unto us, O Lord). Vocal canon, said to be by *Byrd, sung at the end of banquets or other festive occasions as a kind of 'grace after meat'.

Nono, Luigi (b Venice, 1924; d Venice, 1990). It. composer. Entered Venice Cons. 1941, studying comp. with *Malipiero (1943–5) and later with *Maderna and H. *Scherchen. Also studied law at Padua Univ., graduating 1946. Early works showed Webern's influence, later works became dominated by his commitment to Communist political and social causes and themes. What may be called the 'protest' element in his mus., expressed by heavy use of perc. and by use of pre-recorded tape, has not entirely obscured a characteristically Italian lyricism, such as may be found in his early works and in *Liebeslied*. Prin. comps.:

OPERAS: *Intolleranza 1960 (1960–1); *Al gran sole carico d'amore* (1974–5; rev. 1977).

ORCH.: *Variazioni canoniche* (1950); *Composizione I* (1951); *Due espressioni* (1953); *Composizione II* (1959); *Per Bastiana Tai-Yang Cheng*, orch., tape (1967); pf. conc. No.1 (1972), No.2 (1975); *A. C. Scarpa architetto, ai suoi infiniti possibili* (1984); *No hay caminos, hay que caminar . . . A. Tarkovsky* (1987).

INSTRUMENTAL: *Polifonica–Monodia–Ritmica*, 7 players (1951); *Canti per tredici* (1955); *Incontri*, 24 instr. (1955); *Varianti*, vn., str., woodwinds (1957); *Con Luigi Dallapiccola*, 6 perc., elec. (1979); *Fragmente-Stille an Diotima*, str. qt. (1979–80); *Omaggio a György Kurtag*, tb., elec. (1983).

CHORUS & ORCH.: *Epitaffio per García Lorca* (1951–3); *Il mantello rosso*; ballet for sop., bar., ch., orch. (1953); *La victoire de Guernica* (1954); *Liebeslied* (1954); *Il canto sospeso* (1956); *La terra e la compagna*, sop., ten., ch., instr. (1958); *Coro di Didone* (1958); *Canciones a Guiomar I*, sop., 6-part women's ch., instr. (1962); *II*, 12-part women's ch., instr. (1963); *Ricorda cosa ti hanno fatto in Auschwitz*, solo vv., tape (1966); *Non consumiamo Marx*, vv., tape (1969); *Un volto e del mare*, vv., tape (1969); *Voci destroying Muros*, women's ch., orch. (1970); *Y entonces comprendio*, 6 women's vv., ch., tape (1970); *Ein Gespenst geht um in der Welt*, sop., ch., orch. (1971).

UNACC. VOICES: *'Ha venido'*, sop. solo and 6-part sop. ch. (1960); *Sarà dolce tacere*, 8 vv. (1960); *Siamo la gioventù del Vietnam* (1973).

VOICE(S) & ORCH.: *Canti di vita e d'amore (Sul ponte di Hiroshima)*, sop., ten., orch. (1962); *La fabbrica illuminata*, mez., tape (1964); *Como una ola de Fuerza y Luz*, sop., pf., orch., tape (1972); *Das atmende Klarsein*, bfl., ch., elec. (1980–1); *Quando stanno morendo . . .*, 4 women's vv., bfl., vc., elec. (1982); *Guai ai gelidi mostri*, 2 alts., fl., cl., tuba., va., vc., db., elec. (1984); *A Pierre: Dell'azzuro silenzio inquietum*, ch., fl., cl., elec. (1985); *Risonanze erranti a M. Cacciari*, alt., fl., tuba., perc., elec. (1986); *Découvrir la subversion: Omaggio a E. Jabès*, mez., narr., tuba., hn., elec. (1987).

TAPE: *Omaggio a Vedova* (1960); *Music for Die Ermittlung (Weiss)* (1965); *Contrappunto dialettico alla mente* (1968); *Musiche per Manzu* (1969); *Für Paul Dessau* (1974); *Notturni-albe* (1974); *Sofferte onde serene* (1976).

Noonday Witch, The (The Mid-day Witch, Cz. *Polednice*). Sym.-poem for orch., Op.108, by Dvořák, comp. 1896.

Noras, Arto (Erkki) (b Turku, 1942). Finn. cellist. 2nd prize Tchaikovsky Competition, Moscow, 1966. Soloist with leading orchs. Exponent of Walton and Bliss concs. Gave f.p. of conc. by *Sallinen, 1976.

Norberg Schulz, Elizabeth (b Norway, 1959). Norweg. soprano. Gave *Lieder* recitals and sang *Les *Illuminations*, Snape 1981. Won Spoleto Fest. singing comp. 1985, and sang various operatic roles in Italy. Visited Japan with La Scala co. 1988 (Musetta in *La bohème*). Rome Opera 1989; Maggio Musicale, Florence, 1989; Salzburg Fest. début 1992.

Nordgren, Pehr Henrik (b Saltvik, 1944). Finn. composer. Works incl. chamber opera *The Black Monk* (1981); orch.: *Euphonie I* and *II* (1967), *III* (1975), *IV* (1981); vn. conc. No.1 (1969), No.2 (1977), No.3 (1981), No.4 (1994); va. conc. No.1 (1970), No.2 (1979), No.3 (1986); cl. conc. (1970); *Autumnal Concerto*, Japanese trad. instr. (1974); sym. No.1 (1974), No.2 (1989), No.3 (1993), No.4 (1997), No.5 (1998), No.6 (1999–2000), No.7 (2003); pf. conc. No.1 (1975), No.2 (2001), pf. left hand

(2004); vc. conc. No.1 (1980), No.2 (1983), No.3 (1992), No.4 (1994), No.5 (2005); Concerto for Str. (1982); *HATE-LOVE*, vc., str. (1987); chamber mus.: str. qt. No.1 (1967), No.2 (1968), No.3 (1976), No.4 (1983), No.5 (1986), No.6 (1989), No.7 (1992), No.8 (1999), No.9 (2004); wind quintet No.1 (1970), No.2 (1975); Qt. No.1 for trad. Japanese instr. (1974), No.2 (1978); pf. quintet (1978), pf. trio (1980); vocal: *Agnus Dei*, sop., bar., ch., orch. (1970); *Alex*, TV opera (1982–3); *Going On*, db., perc. (1991); *Equilibrium*, str. (1995); *Zest*, sax., vc., pf. (1999); gui. conc. (2003–5); acc. conc. (2006).

Nordheim, Arne (*b* Larvik, Norway, 1931). Norweg. composer. Worked as mus. critic 1960–8. From 1968 concentrated on elec. mus. not only in the concert-hall but by providing 'accompaniment' for an Oslo sculpture. Works incl.:

ORCH.: *Canzona* (1960); *Floating* (1970); *Katharsis*, suite (1962); *Epitaffio*, orch., magnetic tape (1963); *Greening* (1973); *Zimbel* (1974); *Spur*, accordeon, orch. (1974); *Doria*, ten., orch. (1974–5); *Be Not Afeared*, sop., bar., ens., tape (1978); *Tempora noctis*, sop., mez., orch., tape (1979); *Tenebrae*, vc., orch. (1981–2); *Varder*, tpt., orch. (1986); *Rendezvous*, str. (1987); *Monolith* (1990); *Acantus firmus Olympiadis*, Hardanger fiddle, tpts., str., tape (1992); *Music for the Winter Olympics 1994*, orch. (1994); vn. conc. (1996).

ELECTRONIC: *Favola*, musical play for TV, sop., ten., ch., orch., elec. sound (1965); *Evolution*, elec. and concrete sound on tape (1966); *Colorazione*, Hammond org., perc., 2 tape-recorders, amplifiers, loudspeakers (1968); *Solitaire*, elec. and concrete sound on tape (1968); *Partita II*, electric gui. (1969); *Lux et tenebrae* (1970); *Pace* (1970); *Osaka-Music* (1970); *Dinosauros*, accordion, elec. sounds (1970); *Return of the Snark*, tb., tape (2000).

Also ballets, chamber mus., and choral works.

Nordica [Norton], **Lillian** (*b* Farmington, Maine, 1857; *d* Batavia, Java, 1914). Amer. soprano. Concert débuts NY 1876, London 1878, under name Lilly Norton. Milan 1879 (as 'Nordica') as Elvira (*Don Giovanni*). Paris début 1882; NY (Acad. of Mus.) 1883; CG 1887; NY Met 1891. First Amer. to sing at Bayreuth, 1894 (Elsa in *Lohengrin*). Became noted singer of Isolde, Brünnhilde, and Kundry in USA and Europe from 1895 to her death.

Nordraak, Rikard (*b* Christiania, 1842; *d* Berlin, 1866). Norweg. composer. Advocate of Norweg. nationalism and influenced Grieg. Wrote Norweg. nat. anthem *Ja, vi elsker dette landet* ('Yes, we love this land') (1863–4).

Norfolk Rhapsody. Orch. work in E minor by Vaughan Williams comp. 1906 and rev. in early 1920s. Based on 3 folk-songs collected in Norfolk in 1905 by composer. F.p. London 1906. 2 other *Norfolk Rhapsodies*, in D minor and G minor, were written and f.p. in Cardiff 1907, the orig. plan being a 'Norfolk Symphony', but they were withdrawn in 1914. No.2 recorded 2002.

Nørgård, Per (*b* Gentofte, 1932). Danish composer. Worked as mus. critic in Copenhagen 1958–62. Taught at Odense Cons. 1958–60, Copenhagen Cons. 1960–5, and Århus Cons. from 1965 (prof. of comp. from 1987). Works make use of complex contrapuntal techniques and of some aspects of serialism. In 1959 developed 'the infinite row', a 12-note series which expands, it is said, to infinity, and has combined this with rhythms expressed in graphic notation. Works incl.:

OPERAS: *The Labyrinth* (1963); *Gilgamesh* (1971–2); *Siddharta* (1973–9); *The Divine Circus* (1982); *Nuit des hommes* (1996).

BALLETS: *Le Jeune Homme à marier* (Scenario by Ionesco) (1964); *Tango Chicane* (1976); *Trio* (1972).

ORCH.: syms. No.1 (1953–5), No.2 (1970), No.3, ch., orch. (1972–5), No.4 (1981), No.5 (1990), No.6 (1997–9); *Constellations*, conc. for 12 solo str. or 12 str. groups (1958); *Lyse Danse* (1959); *Fragment VI*, 6 orch. groups (1959–61); *Iris* (1966–7); *Luna* (1967); *Voyage into the Golden Screen*, chamber orch. (1968–9); *Doing*, wind orch. (1969); *Lilá*, 11 instr. (1972); *Dream Play*, chamber orch. (1975); *Jousting*, small orch. (1975); *Twilight*, orch., conga player, dancer (opt.) (1977); *For a Change*, perc. conc. (1982); *Burn* (1984); *Illumination* (1984); *Between*, vc., orch. (1985); *Prelude to Breaking* (1986); *Remembering Child*, va., chamber orch. (1986); *Helle Nacht*, vn. conc. (1987); *Pastorale*, str. (1988); *King, Queen, and Ace*, hp., chamber ens. (1989); *Spaces of Time*, pf., ens. (1991); *Night-Symphonies, Day Breaks* (1991); *Scintillation*, 7 instr. (1993); *Voyage into the Broken Screen* (1995); *Bach to the Future* (1996–7); *Terrains vagues* (1999–2000).

CHORAL & VOCAL: *Babel*, oratorio (1964); *Libra*, ten., gui., 2 mixed ch., 2 vibs. or 2 pf. (1973); *Singe die Gärten*, 8 vv., 8 instr. (1974); *Frostsalmer*, 16 vv. (1976); *Sea-Drift*, sop., ens. (1978); *Entwicklungen*, alt., ens. (1986); *L'enfant et l'aube*, sop., ten., ens. (1988); *November-Prelude*, sop., ens. (1993); *Inner and Outer Landscape*, male ch. (1995); *Something about the Lark and the Lark itself*, ten., cl., vn., vc., pf. (1998); *Morning Myth*, ch. (2000).

CHAMBER MUSIC: str. qts.: No.1 (1952), No.2 (1952–8), No.3 (*3 Miniatures*) (1959), No.4 (*Dreamscape*) (1969), No.5 (*Inscape*) (1969), No.6 (*Tintinnabulary*) (1986), No.7 (1993), No.8 (*Night Descending*) (1996–7); Quintet, fl., vn., va., vc., pf. (1951–2); solo vc. sonata (1952, rev. 1953); *Diptychon*, vn., pf. (1953); wind quintet (1970); *Spell*, cl., vc., pf. (1973); *Nova genitura*, sextet (1975); sextet, perc. ens. (1981); *I Ching*, perc. (1982); *Solo Intimo*, vc., pf. (1983); *Ode to Plutonium*, sop., vc. (1984); *9 Friends*, pf. or harmonica (1985); *Lin*, cl., vc., pf. (1986); *Hut ab*, 2 cl. (1988); *Syn*, brass quintet (1988); *Swan descending*, hp. (1989); *Re-Percussion*, perc. duo (1991); *Variations in search of a theme*, vc., gui. (1991); *Tjampuan*, vn., vc. (1992); *Roads to Ixtlan*, sax. qt. (1992–3); *Letters of Grass*, cl., pf. (1992–3); *Dancers around Jupiter*, sax. qt. (1994–5); *Wintermusic*, fl., cl., vc., perc., gui., org. (1998); *Lamentation or Dance*, vn., gui. (1998); *A Nervous Fanfare*, sax., 2 tpt., 2 tb., perc. (1999).

KEYBOARD: pf. sonatas: No.1 (1953, rev. 1956), No.2 (1957); *Partita concertante*, org. (1958); *Sketches*, pf.

(1959); *9 Studies*, pf. (1959); *4 Fragments*, pf. (1959–61); *Grooving*, pf. (1967–8); *Canon*, org. (1971); *Turn*, pf. or hpd. (1973); *Maya*, pf. (1983); *Achilles and the Tortoise*, pf. (1983); *2 Small Pieces* (from *Babette's Feast*), pf. (1987); *Trepartita*, org. (1988); *Remembering*, pf. (1989); *Light of a Night*, pf. (1989); *Gemini Rising*, hpd. (1990); *The Blessed*, org. (1995); *Star Barcarole*, pf. (1995); *Esmeralda*, acc. (1997); *Make your Choice, Mr Schneider*, pf. (1998).

Norma. Opera in 2 acts by Bellini to lib. by Romani after play by Soumet. Comp. 1831. Prod. Milan 1831, London 1833, Paris 1835, New Orleans 1836, NY 1841 (in English). The heroine, Norma, is a Druid priestess. Wagner cond. *Norma* in Riga 1837 and when in Paris in 1839 wrote an aria, 'Norma il predisse', for Lablache to sing as Oroveso, but it was not performed.

Norman, Jessye (*b* Augusta, Georgia, 1945). Amer. soprano. Won Munich int. mus. comp. 1968. Opera début, Deutsche Oper, Berlin, 1969 (Elisabeth in *Tannhäuser*). Débuts: Florence 1971; La Scala 1972; CG 1972; Amer. (Hollywood Bowl) 1972; Salzburg Fest. 1977; NY Met 1983. Noted *Lieder* singer and interpreter of such works as Berlioz's *Les nuits d'été*. Settled in Eng.

Norman, (Frederick Vilhelm) Ludwig (*b* Stockholm, 1831; *d* Stockholm, 1885). Swed. composer and conductor. Cond. Royal Orch., Stockholm, 1859–79. Prof. of comp., Royal Swed. Acad. 1858–61. Married violinist Wilma *Neruda, 1864. Wrote 4 syms., pf. conc., 6 str. qts., pf. quintet, vc. sonata, vn. sonata.

Norrington, (Sir) Roger (Arthur Carver) (*b* Oxford, 1934). Eng. conductor and advocate of period-style performance. Cond. début 1962 with Schütz Chorale. Mus. dir. *Kent Opera 1966–84, Schütz Choir of London, London Str. Players, and London Baroque Ens. SW début 1973; CG 1986; Amer. (Oakland) 1974. Prin. cond. Bournemouth Sinfonietta 1985–9. NY début 1989. Salzburg Fest. début 1989. Mus. dir., Orch. of St Luke's, NY, 1990–4; prin. cond. Stuttgart Radio SO from 1998. Cond. Brit. stage première of Rameau's *Les Boréades*, RAM 1985. OBE 1980. CBE 1990. Knighted 1997. Ed. of *L'incoronazione di Poppea*, *Orfeo*, and *Il ritorno d'Ulisse in patria* (Kent Opera, 1974, 1976, 1978).

Norris, David Owen (*b* London, 1953). Eng. pianist. Int. career as soloist and as acc. to major singers and instr. soloists. In early career was répétiteur CG, dir. of fests. in Cardiff and Petworth. Prof. of pf. RAM, 1978–92. Prof. of vocal accompaniment RCM from 1998. Lect. at Southampton Univ. Often plays on early pfs. Frequent broadcaster.

Norris, Geoffrey (*b* London, 1947). Eng. musicologist and author. Lect., RNCM 1975–6. Specialist in Russ. composers. Author of books on Rachmaninov and Rimsky-Korsakov. Mus. critic for *Times*, then for *Daily Telegraph* (chief critic from 1995). Deputy ed., *New Oxford Companion to Music* 1977–83.

North, Alex (*b* Chester, Pa., 1910; *d* Pacific Palisade, Calif., 1991). Amer. composer and conductor. Cond. for dance troupe in Mexico 1939. During war service comp. scores of over 25 documentary films. After 1946 concentrated on film mus. Was nominated 15 times for Academy Award and finally was awarded Oscar in 1986. Among his film scores were: *A Streetcar Named Desire* (1951); *Death of a Salesman* (1951); *The Rose Tattoo* (1955); *The Sound and the Fury* (1959); *Spartacus* (1960); *The Children's Hour* (1961); *The Misfits* (1961); *The Agony and the Ecstasy* (1965); *Who's Afraid of Virginia Woolf?* (1966); *Bite the Bullet* (1975); *Under the Volcano* (1984); *The Penitent* (1986); *Good Morning, Vietnam* (1988). Other works incl. ballets *American Lyric* (1937), *Golden Fleece* (1941), and *Daddy Long Legs Dream* (1955, for Astaire-Caron film); *Revue*, cl., orch. (1946); Syms. No.1 (1947), No.2 (1968), No.3 (1971). His commissioned score for Kubrick film *2001: A Space Odyssey* was not used and became basis of 3rd Sym.

North, Roger (*b* ?Tostock, Suffolk, *c*. 1651; *d* Rougham, Norfolk, 1734). Eng. author, lawyer, and musician. M.P. and Attorney-Gen. under James II but in 1688 retired to country life at Rougham. Wrote many essays on mus. His reminiscences span from the time of consorts of viols heard in his boyhood to Purcell and the It. 'invasion' of early 18th cent. They are specially valuable for their detailed discussion of performing practice in his lifetime.

Northcott, Bayan (Peter) (*b* Harrow-on-the-Hill, 1940). Eng. music critic and composer. Mus. critic *New Statesman* 1973–5, *Sunday Telegraph* 1975–87, *Independent* from 1987. Author of book on A. Goehr Works incl. *Sonata*, ob. (1978); *6 Japanese Lyrics*, sop., cl., vn. (1979); *Fantasia*, gui., str. (1981–2); *Hymn to Cybele*, cont., ten., bar., ch., perc., db. (1983); *Sextet*, fl./picc., cl./bcl., pf., perc., vn., vc. (1985); conc. for hn. and ens. (1990–8), *3 English Lyrics*, sop., cl., va., db. (1988); *Ave Regina Celorum/Alleluia*, mez., ten. (1997); *Memento*, sop., fl. (1999); *Alma Redemptoris Mater*, 3 ten. (or 2 ten., 1 bar.) (2000).

North Country Sketches. Orch. work by *Delius, comp. 1913–14, in 4 movts.: 1. *Autumn* (The wind soughs in the trees). 2. *Winter landscape*. 3. *Dance*. 4. *The march of Spring* (Woodlands, meadows, and silent moors). F.p. London 1915, cond. Beecham.

Northern Sinfonia. Chamber orch. based at Newcastle upon Tyne serving north-eastern area of Eng., though it regularly plays in London. Founded as freelance orch. in 1958 by Michael Hall; became first permanent chamber orch. in Brit. 1961. Has made several overseas tours, played for opera, and made several recordings. Conductors: Hall 1958–64, Rudolf Schwarz 1964–73 (with Boris Brott 1964–7); Christopher Seaman 1973–9; Tamás Vasáry and Ivan Fischer 1979–82; Richard Hickox 1982–90; Heinrich Schiff from 1990–6; Jean-Bernard Pommier 1996–2002; Thomas Zehetmair from 2002. N. Marriner was ass. cond. 1971–3. Title changed to Northern Sinfonia of England in 1982.

Northumbrian Bagpipes. See *bagpipe*.

Nose, The (*Nos*). Opera in 3 acts by Shostakovich, Op.15, to lib. by E. Zamyatin, G. Yunin, A. Preys, and composer, after Gogol. Comp. 1927–8. Prod. Leningrad 1930; London, SW, New Opera Co. 1973. Suite, Op.15A, comprising 7 sections from opera, f.p. Moscow 1928, cond. Malko.

Noseda, Gianandrea (*b* Milan, 1964). It. conductor. Studied pf. and comp. in Milan and cond. with Myung-Whun Chung and Valery Gergiev. Won Douai int. comp. 1994. Cond. début Milan 1994 with Giuseppe Verdi Orch. First foreign prin. guest cond. of Mariinsky (Kirov) Opera and Ballet 1997. Guest cond. of world's leading orchs. Los Angeles Opera 2001 (*Queen of Spades*), CG 2002, NY Met 2002 (both *War and Peace*). NYPO 2005. Prin. cond. BBCPO from 2002.

nota cambiata (It.). Exchanged note. See *changing note*.

notation and nomenclature. The methods of writing down mus. so that it can be performed. These are devices for which the human being long felt no need, and although every race has its mus. they are still unknown to the larger part of the world's population. They are apparently purely European in origin and even in Europe thousands of tunes existed which were transmitted by one generation to another without achieving the dignity of being recorded on paper until the folksong collectors came on to the scene.

The naming of notes by letters of the alphabet goes back as far as the Ancient Greeks; the Romans also possessed an alphabetical system. In both cases, however, this nomenclature served rather the purposes of scientific discussion than those of performance.

An early (7th-cent.) system of notation was that of *neum(e)s*. Our conventional signs for the turn and the trill are derived from details of neum notation. The present exactitude in pitch indication has been effected by adding to the one line of the early neum notation. Plainsong now uses a *staff of 4 lines, and other mus. one of 5 lines. The *clef derives from neum notation: attached to the Staff it fixes the pitch of one of its lines as middle C or some other note, from which all the others may be deduced.

Proportional notation of an exact character (i.e. as to the time values) began in the 10th cent. when the primitive developments of polyphony brought about its necessity. Definite notes, of different shapes according to their intended proportionate length, were devised, from which our present series of semibreve (whole-note), minim (half-note), etc. is derived. *Bar lines became common only during the 16th and 17th cents. (the earliest use dates from 1448): they were at first casually drawn as aids to the eye—the idea of making them of equal time-value coming later. They first arose in choral scoring to demonstrate the coincidence of the different vv., and were originally not present in the independent vocal parts for the use of singers.

Adjustments to and changes in traditional staff notation have increased in the 20th cent., particularly since *c.*1950 when total serialism, aleatory procedures, etc. have required a parallel development of notational signs, resulting in some confusion where individual composers have devised their own methods which may use terms employed by another composer for a different effect. Some mus. cannot be written at all in conventional notation. The subject is too large for more than an outline to be given here, but some of the changes can be mentioned briefly.

With the arrival of atonal and 12-note mus., conventional pitch notation, with its selection of accidentals, tended to become unworkable, but no new system has been generally adopted, and makeshift adaptation of conventional methods has been favoured by performers. Systems of microtonal notation devised by A. *Hába and J. Carillo have not lasted.

Traditional notation is little use in pulseless mus. and in mus. in which different and often complicated rhythms progress simultaneously at different speeds. To cope with notating these durations, *proportionate notation has been employed, whereby durational proportions are transmuted into the graphic equivalent of notes spaced out horizontally along the staff according to their durations.

For graphic notation, see the separate entry under *graphic scores*. Mention may be made here of 2 explicit new notational systems which have not yet found acceptance. *Equiton* uses only 2 staff lines per octave. The 12 chromatic notes are notated with alternating black and white note-heads and without accidentals. Note-heads appear below, on, and above each staff line; and those between the staff-lines occur close to lower or upper line and centred between the lines. Those close to the lines have ledger lines drawn through them. Notation of durations is proportionate. *Klavarscribo* uses a staff in which lines and spaces run vertically, being grouped according to the black and white keys of the keyboard. No accidentals are needed. Black-and-white note-heads are used for easy identification with corresponding keys. The mus. is read from top to bottom. Notation of durations is proportionate and bar-lines are horizontal.

Below is a selection of some of the generally accepted new notational symbols:

note. (1) A single sound of a given mus. pitch and duration; in Amer. called a *tone*.

(2) A written sign representing (1).

(3) A finger-key of the pf., organ, accordion, etc. to produce a sound of particular pitch.

note-row (Amer. 'tone-row'). In 12-note mus., the order in which the composer decides to arrange the 12 notes within the octave, this order acting as the basis for the comp. (almost like a motto-theme). Strictly no note should be repeated before the row comes to an end, but the rhythm in which they are presented may be.

Also, any note in the row may appear an octave higher or lower than it did originally and the whole row can be used at any higher or lower level. But successive composers have broken the rules.

notes inégales (Fr. 'unequal notes'). Rhythmic convention whereby certain divisions of the beat move in alternately long and short values (or vice versa) even when written as equal to avoid monotony of rhythm. Inequality was normal feature of musical teaching in 17th and 18th cents. in France and Germany, the degree being left to the judgement of the performer. Its use in baroque performance in modern times is subject of much controversy.

note values.

1 whole-note (semibreve)

equals

2 half-notes (minims)

or

4 quarter-notes (crotchets)

or

8 eighth-notes (quavers)

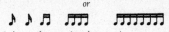

or

16 sixteenth-notes (semiquavers)

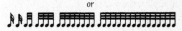

or

32 thirty-second notes (demisemiquavers).

After this follow 64th notes (hemidemisemiquavers) and, occasionally, notes of 128 to the whole-note.

A dot after a note increases its value by half; thus (but see exception mentioned under *dot, dotted note*). A double dot after a note increases its value by a half plus a quarter; thus . A third dot has very occasionally been used; thus

Notre Dame (Our Lady). Romantic opera in 2 acts by F. *Schmidt to lib. by composer and Leopold Wilk after Hugo. Comp. 1902–4, 1904–6. Prod. Vienna 1914. The Intermezzo is a popular concert-piece.

Nottebohm, (Martin) **Gustav** (*b* Lüdenscheid, Westphalia, 1817; *d* Graz, 1882). Ger. composer and musicologist. Settled in Vienna 1846, became friend of Brahms, and wrote some minor works, but is known for his valuable research into Beethoven's sketchbooks embodied in three books, pubd. 1872 and 1887 (posth.). Also pubd. thematic catalogues of works of Beethoven (1868) and Schubert (1874). One of first authorities in textual criticism.

Notturni ed Alba (Nocturnes and Dawn). Song cycle for sop. and orch. in 5 movts., to words from medieval Lat. texts, by *McCabe. F.p. Hereford Fest. 1970. Perf. as ballet, Westfalen, 1976.

notturnino (It.). A miniature *nocturne.

notturno. See *nocturne*.

novachord. Patented elec. kbd. instr. invented by Laurens Hammond. It has 6-octave kbd. like that of a pf. Chords and not just single notes can be played. Tone is varied by manual controls and vol. is controlled by pedals, which also sustain notes.

Novák, Jan (*b* Nová Říša na Moravě, 1921; *d* Ulm, 1984). Cz. composer. Settled Brno 1948, but emigrated to Denmark 1968–70, thereafter to It. The neo-classical style of his early works gave way in 1958 to employment of jazz elements and 12-note techniques. Works incl.: *Passion Play* (1965); ob. conc. (1952); 2-pf. conc. (1955); *Philharmonic Dances*, orch. (1955–6); *Variations on a Theme of Martinů*, orch. (1959, pf. version 1949); *Concentus*

Eurydicae, guitar, str. (1971); *Dido*, speaker, mez., male vv., orch. (1967); *Orpheus et Eurydice*, sop., va. d'amore, pf. (1971); *Voces latinae*, ch., drum, pf., db. (1975); *Ludi concertantes*, 18 instr. (1981); *Symphonia bipartita* (1983); and pf. pieces.

Novák, Vítězslav (*b* Kamenice, Cz., 1870; *d* Skuteč, 1949). Cz. composer. Prof. of comp. Prague Cons. 1909–39, influencing and teaching many Cz. composers. His early works were Brahmsian in style but he became more nationalist under the influence of Janáček. Works incl.:

OPERAS: *Zvíkovský rarášek* (The Imp of Zvíkov) (1913–14); *Karlštejn* (1916, rev. 1925, 1930); *Lucerna* (The Lantern) (1919–22, rev. 1930); *Děduvů odkaz* (Grandfather's Legacy) (1926, rev. 1942).

ORCH.: *Serenade* in F (1894); pf. conc. (1895); *3 Bohemian Dances* (1897); *V Tatrách* (In the Tatras), sym.-poem (1902); *Slovak Suite* (1903); *South Bohemian Suite* (1936–7); *De Profundis* (1941); *St Wenceslas Triptych* (1941).

CHORAL: *6 Men's Choruses* (1906); *Bouře* (The Storm), sea fantasy, soloists, ch., orch. (1908–10); *Svatební Košile* (The Spectre's Bride), soloists, ch., orch. (1912–13); *Podzimní symfonie* (Autumn Sym.), ch., orch. (1931–4); *Májová symfonie* (May Sym.), soloists, ch., orch. (1943); *Hvězdy* (Stars), female vv., orch. (1949).

CHAMBER MUSIC: pf. trios: G minor (1892), D minor (1902); pf. qt. (1894, rev. 1899); pf. quintet (1896, rev. 1897); str. qts.: in G (1899), in D (1905), in G (1938); vc. sonata (1941).

PIANO: *Variations on a Theme of Schumann* (1893); *Sonata eroica* (1900); *Exotikon* (1911); *6 Sonatinas* (1919–20).

Novelette (Eng.), **Novellette** (Ger.). A term introduced by Schumann as a compliment to the Eng. soprano Clara *Novello as the title for his 8 pf. pieces Op.21, 1838. They have no individual titles but each, says the composer, is to be taken as the mus. equivalent of a romantic story. A few other composers have adopted the term: it has no special connotation as to form.

Novello, Clara (Anastasia) (*b* London, 1818; *d* Rome, 1908). Eng. soprano, daughter of Vincent *Novello. Concert début Windsor, 1832. Sang solo sop. part in f. Eng. p of Beethoven's Mass in D, 1832. Sang at Worcester Fest. 1833 and in Mendelssohn's *St Paul*, Birmingham 1837. Mendelssohn engaged her for Leipzig Gewandhaus concerts, leading to triumphs in Ger. Opera début Bologna, 1841, in *Semiramide*. Gave up career on marriage in 1843, but resumed it in 1849. On return to Eng. in 1851, became leading oratorio singer in choral fests. Retired 1861.

Novello, Ivor [Davies, David Ivor] (*b* Cardiff, 1893; *d* London, 1951). Welsh composer, actor, playwright, and impresario, son of choral conductor Clara Novello-Davies (1861–1943). Composer of *Keep the Home Fires Burning* (1914), one of the most popular songs during 1914–18 war. Wrote, comp., and acted in successful mus. comedies, e.g. *Glamorous Night* (1935); *Careless Rapture* (1936); *Crest of the Wave* (1937); *The Dancing Years* (1939); *Arc de Triomphe* (1943); *Perchance to Dream* (1945); and *King's Rhapsody* (1949). Most had lyrics by Christopher Hassall (1912–63). Acted in Shakespeare.

Novello, Vincent (*b* London, 1781; *d* Nice, 1861). Eng. organist, publisher, and composer of It. origin. Org., Portuguese Embassy chapel, London, 1797–1822. Founded publishing house *Novello and Co. 1811. Founder-member of Phil. Soc. Comp. sacred mus. and ed. classics. Pubd. 5 vols. of 17th-cent. It. church mus. under title *The Fitzwilliam Music*, 1825, and 5 vols. of Purcell's sacred mus., 1826–9. In 1829 organized fund to assist Mozart's widow, going to Salzburg to give her the money. Diaries of this journey pubd. 1955 as *A Mozart Pilgrimage*. Also helped to prepare way for Bach revival in Eng.

Novello and Co. Eng. music publishers, founded in London 1811 by Vincent *Novello. His son Alfred, from 1829 to 1857, followed by Henry Littleton (1823–88), made the business extremely successful by issuing standard edns. of the classics, particularly choral works. Most Eng. Victorian oratorios and cantatas were pubd. by Novello, incl. those by *Elgar. Its house magazine, *The *Musical Times*, remains one of the most respected publications, but has been pubd. by Orpheus Publications from 1988.

Novotná, Jarmila (*b* Prague, 1907; *d* NY, 1994). Cz. soprano. Début Prague 1925 as Mařenka in *The Bartered Bride*. Sang Gilda (*Rigoletto*) in Verona Arena 1928, then in Berlin at Kroll Oper and Staatsoper. Vienna Opera 1933–8, where she was a distinguished Oktavian in *Der Rosenkavalier* and created title-role in Lehár's *Giuditta*, with *Tauber, 1934. Débuts: Salzburg Fest. 1935; La Scala 1937; Amer. (S. Francisco) 1939; NY Met 1940–56.

Nowak, Leopold (*b* Vienna, 1904; *d* Vienna, 1991). Austrian musicologist. Prof. at Vienna Univ. 1932–73. Dir., mus. division, Vienna Nat. Library 1946–69. Author of books on Liszt (1936), Haydn (1951), and Bruckner (1947, 1973). Ed., following R. *Haas in 1945, of complete works of Bruckner.

Now Thank We All Our God (*Nun danket alle Gott*). Ger. hymn. Words by Lutheran prelate Martin Rinckart (1586–1649), mus. by Johannes Crüger (1598–1662). J. S. Bach used melody as basis of his choral prelude of same name (BWV657).

Noye's Fludde. Setting by Britten, Op.59, of Chester miracle play for adults' and children's vv., children's ch., chamber ens., and children's orch. Comp. 1958. F.p. Aldeburgh Fest. (Orford Church) 1958.

Nozze di Figaro, Le (The Marriage of Figaro). *Commedia per musica* in 4 acts (K492, 1785–6) by Mozart to lib. by da Ponte after Beaumarchais's comedy *La Folle Journée, ou Le Mariage de Figaro* (1778). Comp. 1786. Prod. Vienna 1786, London 1812, NY 1824, Met 1894.

nuance (Fr.). Shade, distinction, gradation. A word frequently used by writers on mus. to imply those delicate differences of intensity and speed which largely constitute the character of a perf.

Nuits d'été, Les (Summer Nights). 6 songs, Op.7, by Berlioz to poems by Théophile Gautier. Comp. 1840–1, rev. 1843 and 1856. Orig. for mez. or ten. with pf. acc. Berlioz orchestrated *Absence* in 1843, and the rest in 1856. The songs are: 1. *Villanelle*. 2. *Le Spectre de la rose*. 3. *Sur les lagunes*. 4. *Absence*. 5. *Au Cimetière*. 6. *L'Île inconnue*. It is a rare v. which can encompass all these songs. The pubd. version for v. and pf. is marked 'for mez. or ten.', but in orchestrating the songs Berlioz specified the v. for each song as follows: 1. mez. or ten. 2. cont. 3. bar., cont., or mez. 4. mez. or ten. 5. ten. 6. mez. or ten.

numbers. Term used for self-contained item in a musical or opera (because each piece of this kind is separately numbered in the score). A 'number opera' is an opera in which these divisions occur, as opposed to Wagner's later operas, for example, where each act is written continuously without internal divisions or pauses.

number systems. J.-J. *Rousseau introduced a system of numerical notation in which the first 8 numerals are substituted for the 8 notes in the scale. Nos. are popular among 20th-cent. composers, because of the concept of 'parameters', in which mus. sounds are regarded as the sum of several components (pitch, duration, intensity, timbre, and position in space). What is called the *Fibonacci series (each no. the sum of the previous 2) has been used to control these components by such composers as Krenek, Stockhausen, Maxwell Davies, and Nono.

Nunc Dimittis. The Song of Simeon in St Luke's Gospel (Lord, now lettest thou thy servant depart in peace). It is a part of the service of Compline in the RC Church and of that of Evensong in the Anglican Church. It has its traditional plainsong in the former, and is often sung to an Anglican chant in the latter. It has also been set innumerable times by church composers, usually as an adjunct to a *Magnificat.

Nun danket alle Gott. See *Now Thank We All Our God*.

Nun's Fiddle. The *tromba marina.

nuove musiche. See *new music*.

Nurock, Kirk (b Camden, NJ, 1948). Amer. composer. In 1971 developed vocal technique called 'natural sound' in which audience participation is welcomed. Animal noises are used in several works. Comps. incl. *Audience Oratorio* (1975); *Mowgli*, mus. th. (1978–84); *Bronx Zoo Events* (1980); *Sonata for Piano and Dog* (1982); *Expedition*, jazz trio, Siberian husky (1984); *Haunted Messages*, pf., bark-ing audience (1984); *The Incurable Dorothy Parker*, song-cycle, sop., pf. (1986); *Gorilla, Gorilla*, pf. (1988); *3 Screams*, 2 amp. pf. (1990).

Nursery Suite. 7-movt. orch. suite by Elgar, f.p. London 1931, and ded. to the then Duchess of York (later Queen Elizabeth the Queen Mother) and her daughters Princess Elizabeth (later Queen Elizabeth II) and Princess Margaret Rose. Ballet with choreog. by N. de Valois, London 1932.

Nusch-Nuschi, Das. 1-act opera by Hindemith, Op.20, 'for Burmese marionettes' to lib. by Franz Blei. Comp. 1920. Prod. Stuttgart 1921.

Nussbaum, Der (The Nut tree). Song for v. and pf. by R. Schumann, to poem by Julius Mosen (1803–67), being No.3 of cycle *Myrthen*, Op.25 (1840).

nut. (1) On a str. instr., the slight ridge over which the str. pass on leaving the pegs. On a *ukelele and similar instr. a moveable nut is placed on the fingerboard which can shorten all str. equally and thus raise the pitch.
(2) Device at the heel of the bow of a vn., etc., which adjusts the tension of the bow-hairs.

Nutcracker (Russ. *Shchelkunchik*, Fr. *Casse-Noisette*). Ballet in 2 acts and 3 scenes with mus. by *Tchaikovsky, Op.71, comp. 1891–2, choreog. by Ivanov, and lib. by Petipa based on Hoffmann's *Der Nüssknacker und der Mäusekönig* (The Nutcracker and the King of the Mice). Prod. St Petersburg 1892 as double bill with opera *Yolanta*, London (complete) 1934. Has been choreog. also by Balanchine, Cranko, Nureyev, etc. Orch. suite of 8 numbers, Op.71a, arr. Tchaikovsky, 1892.

Nyman, Michael (b London, 1944). English composer and writer. Visited Romania to collect folksongs. Wrote on mus., 1964–76, in *The Listener*, *New Statesman*, and *Spectator*. Claims to have introduced word 'minimalism' as a description of mus. (in review of Cornelius *Cardew's *The Great Learning*). In 1974 wrote *Experimental Music—Cage and Beyond*, in which he celebrated Cage's influence in freeing composers from restraints of academic serialism. In 1976 was invited by Birtwistle to arr. 18th-cent. Venetian popular mus. for Nat. Th. prod. of Goldoni's *Il Campiello*. Formed band to perf. it and after run of play ended, began to write mus. for band (all instr. amp.) to play. Collaboration with the film maker Peter Greenaway from 1977 established him as a leading film composer. Several of his works, e.g. *I'll Stake my Cremona to a Jew's Trump* (1983), metamorphose material taken from Mozart, symbolic of a distinctive style devised by creative synthesis of many strands from many periods. Works incl.:

OPERAS: *The Man Who Mistook His Wife For a Hat* (1987); *Letters, Riddles and Writs* (1991); *Noises, Sounds and Sweet Airs* (1994); *Facing Goya* (2000); *Man and Boy: Dada* (2003); *Love Counts* (2004).

BALLET & DANCE: *Basic Black* (1984); *A Broken Set of Rules* (1984); *Portraits in Reflection* (1985); *And Do

They Do (1986); *Touch the Earth* (1987); *Miniatures* (Str. Qt. No.2) (1988); *Configurations* (Str. Qt. No.2) (1989); *The Fall of Icarus* (1989); *Garden Party* (1990); *La Princesse de Milan* (1991).

FILM SCORES: *A Walk Through H* (1977); *Tom Philips* (1977); *1–100* (1977); *Vertical Features Remake* (1978); *The Falls* (1980); *Brimstone and Treacle* (1982); *The Draughtsman's Contract* (1982); *Frozen Music* (1983); *Nelly's Version* (1983); *The Cold Room* (1984); *A Zed and Two Noughts* (1985); *L'ange frénetique* (1985); *The Disputation* (1986); *Ballet Méchanique* (1986); *Photographic Exhibits* (1987); *Drowning by Numbers* (1988); *La traversée de Paris* (1989); *The Cook, the Thief, His Wife and Her Lover* (1989); *Prospero's Books* (1990); *Les enfants volants* (1991); *The Piano* (1992); *The Diary of Anne Frank* (1995); *The End of the Affair* (1999).

ORCH.: *A Handsom, Smooth, Sweet Smart Clever Stroke: Or Else Play Not At All* (1983); *Taking a Line for a Second Walk* (1986); *Where the Bee Dances* (1991); *The Upsidedown Violin* (1992); *MGV* (1993); pf. conc. (1993); conc., hpd., str. (1995); Double Conc., vc., sax. (1997); *a dance he little thinks of* (2001); *The Claim for Orchestra* (2003); vn. conc. (2003); marimba conc. (2006).

CHAMBER & ENS. (for Nyman band unless otherwise indicated): str. qts. No.1 (1985), No.2 (1988), No.3 (1990), No.4 (1995); *Bell Set No.1*, multiple perc. (1974); *In Re Don Giovanni* (1977); *Waltz in F* (1978); *M Work* (1981); *Think Slow, Act Fast* (1981); *Five Orchestral Pieces Opus Tree* (1981); *The Disposition of the Linen* (1982); *Four Saxes*, 3 sop. sax., 1 tenor sax. (1982); *Queen of the Night* (1982); *Time's Up*, gamelan (1983); *I'll Stake My Cremona to a Jew's Trump*, elec. modified vn. and va, and vv. (1984); *Bird Work* (1984); *Swan Rot*; *Angelfish Decay*, 2 vns., hpd. or pf.; *Bisocosis Populi*; *Car Crash*; *Zoo Caprices*, vn.; *Child's Play*, 2 vns., hpd. or pf.; *Delft Waltz*; *Venus de Milo*; *Vermeer's Wife*; *Lady in the Red Hat* (all 1985); *Taking a Line for a Second Walk*, 2 pf. (1986); *Dead Man's Catch*; *Drowning by Number 2*; *Drowning by Number 3*; *Endgame*; *Knowing the Ropes*; *Bees in Trees*; *Sheep and Tides*; *Wedding Tango* (all 1988); *Book Depository* (1989); *Miserere Paraphrase*, vn., pf. (1989), also for str. qt. and pf. (1991), 5 pf. (1991),

sop. and band (1991); *Cornfield*; *History of Sycorax*, *Miranda*, *Prospero's Curse*, *Prospero's Magic*, *Shaping the Curve*, sop., sax., pf. (all 1990); *Masque Arias*, brass quintet (1991); *Goodbye Frankie, Goodbye Benny*, vn., vc., pf. (1992); *The Convertibility of Lute Strings*, hpd. (1992); *For John Cage*, 10-piece brass ens. (1991); *Suite: The Draughtsman's Contract* (1993); *Songs for Tony*, sax. qt. (1993); *The Commissar Vanishes* (1999); *Yellow Beach*, pf./vn., vc. (2002); *Compiling the Colours (Samhitha)*, mand., band (2003); *For John Peel*, pf. trio (2004); *24 Hour Sax Quartet*, sax. qt. (2004); *Exit, No Exit*, 2 bcl./ 2 vn., va., vc. (2005).

CHORAL & VOCAL: *Bird List Song*, sop., band (1979); *A Neat Slice of Time*, ch., amp. pf. (1980); *The Abbess of Andouillets*, solo SATB (1984); *Memorial*, sop., band; *Miserere*, sop., ch., band; *L'Orgie Parisienne*, sop. or mez., band; *Out of the Ruins*, ch., opt. org.; *Ah!, ça ira*, sop., ch., band (all 1989); *6 Celan Songs*, mez., band; *The Masque*, 3 sop., band; *5 Ariel Songs*, sop. or mez., band (all 1990); *Letters, Riddles and Writs*, mez. or counterten., bass, and band; *Miranda*, 5 sop., band; *Miraculous Possession*, 3 sop., band; *Polish Love Song*, sop. and 6 instr. (all 1991); *Anne de Lucy Songs*, sop., pf.; *Miserere Paraphrase*, sop., band; *Mozart on Mortality*, sop., 6 instr.; *Self-Laudatory Hymn of Inanna and her Omnipotence*, counterten. and viols (all 1992); *Balancing the Books*, unacc. ch. (1999); *The Waltz Song*, ch., pf. (1995); *Mosè*, ch., str. (2001); *A Child's View of Colour*, children's vv., str. quintet (2003); *Acts of Beauty*, sop., instrs. (2004).

Nymphs and Shepherds. Song by *Purcell, part of his incidental music for Shadwell's play *The Libertine*, 1692. Often sung by sop., but made famous in choral version recorded by Manchester schoolchildren's choirs cond. *Harty in 1929.

NZ. Neue Zeitschrift für Musik. Ger. bi-monthly periodical, orig. *Neue Leipziger Zeitschrift für Musik*, founded in Leipzig by Schumann in 1834. Ed. Schumann until 1844. Present title adopted 1979.

O

o, od (It.). Or.

obbligato (It.; Fr. *obligé*; Ger. *obligat*). Indispensable. Adjective attached to the name of an instr., e.g. 'vc. obbligato', where the instr.'s part is obligatory, and special or unusual in effect. To use the term in the opposite sense of optional or *ad libitum* is wrong, as is the frequently-encountered spelling *obligato* (favoured by Britten).

Oberhoffer, Emil (*b* Munich, 1867; *d* San Diego, Calif., 1933). Ger.-born pianist and conductor (Amer. cit. 1893). Went to USA in 1885. Settled in St Paul, Minn., 1897 as cond. of local mus. soc. His efforts led in 1903 to formation of Minneapolis SO, which he cond. until 1922. See *Minnesota Orch.*

Oberlin, Russell (*b* Akron, Ohio, 1928). Amer. countertenor. Soloist with NY Pro Musica Antiqua 1953–9. Début CG 1961 as Oberon in *A Midsummer Night's Dream*. Taught at Hunter Coll., NY., from 1966.

Oberlin Conservatory of Music (Oberlin, Ohio). Founded 1865 within Oberlin College (founded 1833). Renowned internationally as mus. school of highest calibre. Deans of the Cons. have been: George Whipple Steele (1867–71); Fenlon B. Rice (1871–1901); Charles Walthall Morrison (1902–24); Frank Holcolm Shaw (1924–49); David Ritchie Robertson (1949–60); James Stanley Ballinger (1961–3); Norman Lloyd (1963–5); Robert Pratt Fountain (1965–70); Emil Charles Danenberg (1970–5); David S. Boe (1975–90); Thomas F. Kelly (1990–1); Karen L. Wolff (1991–9); Kathryn Stuart (1996–7); Robert K. Dodson (1999–2004); and David H. Stull (from 2004).

Oberon, or The Elf-King's Oath. Opera in 3 acts by Weber to Eng. lib. by J. R. Planché, after W. Sotheby's trans. (1798) of Wieland's poem *Oberon* (1780), which is based on the 13th-cent. Fr. *chanson de geste*, *Huon de Bordeaux*. Comp. 1825–6. Prod. London, CG 1826, cond. Weber; Leipzig 1826; NY 1828. Other operas on subject by Kunzen (*Holger Danske*, 1789) and P. Wranitzky (*Oberon, König der Elfen*, 1789).

obertas(s). A nat. Polish round dance of rather wild character, in quick triple time.

Oberto, Conte di San Bonifacio (Oberto, Count of Bonifacio). Opera in 2 acts by Verdi to lib. by A. Piazza, rev. with additions by T. Solera. Comp. 1835–9 as *Rocester*, rev. 1840–1, being Verdi's first opera to be prod. (Milan 1839). Chicago 1903 (concert version), London (concert) 1965, (stage, Collegiate Th.) 1982, NY 1978, Leeds 1994.

Oberwerk (Ger.). Upper-work, i.e. swell org. (Abbreviated to 'Obw' or 'O.W.')

oblique motion. See *motion*.

oboe. Org. reed stop of 8' pitch, imitative of instr. whose name it bears.

oboe family. The ob. is a woodwind instr. blown through a double reed and with a compass from the B♭ below middle C upwards for over 2½ octaves. Standard orch. instr., also in chamber mus. and military bands. It is the note A sounded on the oboe to which the rest of the orchestra tune their instr. Many concs. have been written for its solo use, e.g. by Vivaldi, Albinoni, R. Strauss, Vaughan Williams, Martinů, etc. Derives from the *shawm and the *curtal. Known in Fr. and Eng. in the 17th cent. as *hautbois* and *hautboy*. There also exist: (1) *oboe d'amore* (ob. of love): pitched a minor 3rd below normal oboe. Has pear-shaped bell, which gives it its mellow and individual tone-colour, and is midway in size between ob. and cor anglais. Was favoured by Bach, but subsequently neglected. In 20th cent, has been used by R. Strauss in *Symphonia Domestica*, Holst in *Somerset Rhapsody*, Ravel in *Boléro*, Janáček in several works, incl. operas, and John McCabe has written a conc. for it (1972). (2) *oboe da caccia* (hunting ob.): obsolete predecessor of cor anglais. See also *cor anglais, bassoon, Heckelphone, shawm*.

Oborin, Lev (Nikolayevich) (*b* Moscow, 1907; *d* Moscow, 1974). Russ. pianist. Taught at Moscow Cons. from 1928, becoming prof. 1935. Début 1924. Won first Warsaw int. Chopin comp. 1927. Gave f.p. of Khachaturian's pf. conc., Leningrad 1937. Many successful pupils, incl. *Ashkenazy.

Obraztsova, Elena (Vasilyevna) (*b* Leningrad, 1937). Russ. mezzo-soprano. Opera début Moscow 1963 (Marina in *Boris Godunov*). Won 1st prize, Tchaikovsky comp., Moscow, 1970. Has sung in Milan, Hamburg, Vienna, etc. NY Met (with Bolshoy Co.) 1975, début with Met co. 1976; S. Francisco 1975; La Scala 1976; Salzburg Fest. 1978; CG 1985. Début as prod., Bolshoy, Moscow, 1986–7 (*Werther*).

Obrecht [Obertus], **Jacob** (*b* Bergen-op-Zoom, *c*.1451; *d* Ferrara, 1505). Flemish composer. Kapellmeister, Utrecht, *c*.1476–8; worked in Cambrai 1484–5. Was in Ferrara 1487–8. Choirmaster, Bruges 1490–1. Wrote much church mus., incl. masses, motets, etc., and secular songs. Forerunner of Josquin *Desprès. Used secular *cantus firmus* in his masses, e.g. *Missa super Maria Zart*. Used number symbolism in his works, cabalistic significance having been discovered in many of his structures, e.g. the number of *tactus* in his *Missa 'Sub tuum praesidium'* is 888, the symbol of Christ. Some of his works are deliberately imitative of other composers. The 'boundless exuberance', as one scholar has put it, of his music ranks it with the greatest of its time.

Obw. Abbreviation for *Oberwerk* (i.e. swell org. in Ger. org. mus.).

O.C. Abbreviation for *organo corale* (It.), choir org.

Oca del Cairo, L' (The Goose of Cairo). Unfinished *opera buffa* in 2 acts (K422) by Mozart 1783 to lib. by Varesco; prod. Frankfurt 1860 (concert), Paris 1867, London 1870, Salzburg 1936. Several modern edns., incl. one by *Redlich, prod. London (SW) 1940, NY 1953.

O Canada! Canadian nat. song, especially popular among Fr.-Canadians. The mus., by Calixa *Lavallée, comp. 1880, was orig. a hymn in honour of St John the Baptist.

ocarina (It. 'little goose'). Small keyless wind instr., shaped rather like an egg with holes for fingers and invented *c*.1860. Made of earthenware or metal. Mainly used as a toy and sometimes nicknamed 'sweet potato' (as in once-popular song *Sweet Potato Piper*).

Oceanides, The (*Aallottaret*). Symphonic poem for orch. by Sibelius, Op.73, comp. 1914. F.p. Norfolk, Conn., 1914, cond. Sibelius.

Ockeghem [Okeghem], **Johannes** (Jean) (*b* *c*.1410; *d* ?Tours, 1497). Fr.-Flemish composer. In 1443 was singer in Notre Dame, Antwerp, and was member of chapel of Duke of Bourbon at Moulins, nr. Dijon, 1446–8. About 7 years later was at Fr. court, where he stayed for the rest of his life, serving three successive kings. Travelled on court missions to It. and Sp. Leading composer of period between Du Fay and Josquin Desprès, but only 14 Masses, fewer than a dozen motets, and about 20 *chansons* survive, enough to show his stature. Style noted for contrapuntal richness. His *Missa 'Fors seulement'* was one of first parody Masses, based on one of his own *chansons*. His *Missa pro Defunctis* is earliest surviving requiem, Du Fay's having been lost. His *chansons* were the 'popular songs' of his day. After he died, Molinet's commemorative poem *Nimphes des Bois* was set to mus. by Desprès.

O Come, all ye Faithful. See *Adeste Fideles*.

Octandre (Plant with 8 stamens). Work for small orch. (woodwind, brass, db.) by Varèse, comp. 1923, f.p. NY 1924.

octave. Interval of 8 notes, counting bottom and top notes. Notes an octave apart have same letter-names. Interval from, say, D to next D above is *perfect octave*; from D up to D♭ and from D up to D♯ are *diminished* and *augmented* octaves respectively. So *double octave*, 2 octaves; *at the octave*, to be perf. octave higher than written; *in octaves*, to be perf. with each note doubled one or more octaves above or below.

octave coupler. Device on org. or hpd. with which note struck is doubled an octave higher.

octave flute (It. *ottavino*). *piccolo.

octave quint. Organ stop same as *twelfth.

octaves graves, octaves aiguës. In Fr. org. mus. mean, respectively, the sub- and super-octave couplers.

octave signs

8va or *8* ottava, i.e. perform an octave higher than written.	*8va bassa* or *8va sotto* perform an octave lower than written (*sotto* = under).
loco place, i.e. (after playing octave higher or lower) resume the playing as written.	*con 8* play the passage not in single notes, as marked, but in octaves (the added line of octaves will be above if the passage occurs in the treble of a pf. piece, and below if in the bass)

octavin (Fr.). The 'fifteenth' stop of the org. So *octavin harmonique*, harmonic piccolo.

octet (Fr. *octuor, octette*; It. *ottetto*; Ger. *Oktett*). Any combination of 8 performers or any piece of mus. comp. for such. The normal str. octet is for 4 vn., 2 va., 2 vc., as in Mendelssohn's. Schubert's Octet is for 2 vn., va., vc., db., cl., bn., and hn. That by Stravinsky is for wind instr.

octo-bass. A str. db. 10' high invented by the great Paris *luthier* J. B. Vuillaume in 1849 and recommended by Berlioz. The stopping was controlled by levers operated by the left hand and the feet; the instr. was bowed in the normal way. It had a range of 2 octaves and a 5th. Failed to catch on but a conc. was written for it in 1984.

octuor. See *octet*.

od (It.). Or.

ode. In literature, a lyrical poem. In Ancient Greece an ode was recited to mus. acc. In its mus. sense, the term often means a ceremonial work, e.g. Purcell's *Ode for St Cecilia's Day* and Elgar's *Coronation Ode*, but sometimes the term is used for works with particular significance to the composer, e.g. Elgar's *The Music Makers* and Stravinsky's *Ode: Elegiacal Chant*.

Ode for St Cecilia's Day. (1) Title of 4 choral works by *Purcell, 2 comp. in 1683, another probably of that date, a 4th in 1692. All except one (Lat.) have Eng. texts.

(2) Choral work by Handel, 1739, being setting of Dryden's poem (1698).

(3) Cantata by Hubert *Parry, 1889.

There are many other works with this title.

Ode to Death. Setting for ch. and orch., Op.38, by Holst of text by Whitman. Comp. 1919. F.p. Leeds Fest. 1922, London 1923.

Ode to Napoleon Buonaparte. Setting by Schoenberg, Op.41, of Byron's poem (1814) for str. qt., pf., and reciter (whose part is rhythmically notated at approx. pitch). Comp. 1942. Version (Op.41b) for str. orch., pf., and reciter f.p. NY 1944.

Odyssey. Orch. work lasting 90 mins. by Nicholas *Maw, comp. between 1972 and 1987. F.p. (incomplete) London 1987 (BBC Prom., cond. Elder), f. complete p. London 1989, BBCSO cond. Bernas. Rev. with opt. cuts, perf. Birmingham 1990 (CBSO, cond. Rattle).

O.E. Abbreviation for *organo espressivo* (It. swell organ).

Œdipe (Oedipus). Opera in 4 acts by *Enescu to lib. by E. Fleg based on Sophocles. First sketches 1910, comp. 1921/2–1932. Orch. extracts perf. 1924 and 1925. Prod. Paris 1936, Brussels 1956, Bucharest 1958.

Oedipus Rex (King Oedipus). Opera-oratorio in 2 acts by Stravinsky to lib. by J. Cocteau trans. into Lat. by J. Daniélou and based on Sophocles. Comp. 1926–7. Prod. Paris 1927 (as oratorio), London 1928 (broadcast), 1936 (concert). F. stage p. Vienna 1928; Boston (concert) 1928, Philadelphia (stage) 1931, NY Met 1981; Edinburgh (stage) 1956.

Oestvig, Karl (Aagaard) (*b* Christiania, 1889; *d* Oslo, 1968). Norweg. tenor. Opera début Stuttgart 1914. Vienna State Opera 1919–27. Created Emperor in *Die Frau ohne Schatten*, 1919. Berlin State Opera 1927–30. Fine Wagnerian singer. Retired 1932. Became teacher and dir., Oslo Opera 1941.

Offenbach, Jacques [Jacob] (*b* Deutz, nr. Cologne, 1819; *d* Paris, 1880). Ger.-Fr. composer, conductor, and cellist. Orig. surname Eberst, Wiener, or Levy: took name Offenbach because family came from Offenbach-am-Main. Son of cantor of Cologne synagogue. Studied Paris Cons. 1833–7, also playing vc. in Opéra-Comique orch. Cond. at Théâtre Français, 1849–55. From 1853 began to compose operettas, writing no fewer than 90 in the next quarter-cent. Man. of Théâtre Comte, renaming it Bouffes-Parisiens. The best of his lighter works, *La Belle Hélène, Orphée aux Enfers*, etc., symbolize the Fr. 2nd Empire, but his fame rests equally securely on his sole grand opera *Les contes d'Hoffmann*, on which he worked for many years. It was prod. after his death in a version rev. and largely orchestrated by *Guiraud. Among his chief works are:

OPERAS: *Die Rheinnixen* (Vienna 1864); *Les contes d'Hoffmann* (The *Tales of Hoffmann*) (1877–80).
BALLET-PANTOMIME: *Le Papillon* (1860).
OPERETTAS: *Barbe-bleue* (1866); *La *Belle Hélène* (1864); *Les Bergers de Watteau* (1865); *Daphnis et Chloé* (1860); *Les Deux Aveugles* (1855); *Dragonette* (1857); *La Fille du tambour-major* (1879); *Geneviève de*

Brabant (1859, rev. 1875); *La *Grande Duchesse de Gérolstein* (1867); *Madame Favart* (1878); *Le Mariage aux lanternes* (1857); *Monsieur Choufleuri* (1861); *Orphée aux enfers* (*Orpheus in the Underworld*) (1858, rev. 1874); *La *Périchole* (1868, rev. 1874); *Princesse de Trébizonde* (1869); *Robinson Crusoé* (1867); *La *Vie parisienne* (1866, rev. 1873; see also *Gaîté parisienne*); *Pomme d'api* (1873); *Whittington and his Cat* (1874).

offertory (Fr. offertoire; Lat. offertorium). The Offertory of the Mass consists of an *Antiphon, a part of the Proper of the Mass, sung just after the Credo, while the priest is preparing the bread and wine and offering them upon the altar. The plainsong setting is generally insufficient to occupy the time, so a motet or org. voluntary may be interpolated.

Offrandes oubliées, Les (The Forgotten Offerings). Work for orch. by *Messiaen, comp. 1930, f.p. Paris 1931. In 3 parts, *The Cross, The Sin, The Eucharist*.

Ogdon, John (Andrew Howard) (*b* Mansfield, 1937; *d* London, 1989). Eng. pianist and composer. As a student gave f.ps. of his own works and those by fellow-students Goehr and Maxwell Davies. Played Brahms's 1st conc. with Barbirolli, 1956, when still a student; début with Hallé Orch. 1957. Joint first prize (with *Ashkenazy), Moscow Tchaikovsky comp. 1962. Brilliant exponent of Liszt, Busoni, Alkan, in addition to wide repertory of concs. NY début 1963. Taught at Indiana Univ. Sch. of Mus., Bloomington, 1976–80. Composer of pf. conc., etc.

O God, our Help in Ages Past. Hymn, words (based on Psalm 90) by Isaac Watts (1674–1748), first pubd. in his *Psalms of David* (1719) with first words 'Our God, our help' which were altered to 'O God' by John Wesley in *Collection of Psalms and Hymns* (1737). Tune (attrib. William *Croft) first appeared anonymously, set to Psalm 42, in 1708 *Supplement* to Tate and Brady Psalms. Known as *St Anne*, Croft being organist of St Anne's, Soho, in 1708. First line of tune is stock 18th-cent. phrase and is found in J. S. Bach's org. fugue in E♭ which is therefore known in Eng. as 'St Anne Fugue'. Has claim to be most popular of all hymns, and is especially assoc. with Remembrance Day services.

Ohana, Maurice (*b* Casablanca, 1914; *d* Paris, 1992). Fr. composer and pianist of Spanish descent. Career as pianist until outbreak of war in 1939. On return to Paris, 1946, formed Groupe Zodiaque 'to defend freedom of expression against dictatorial aesthetic attitudes'. Wrote much of importance for pf. His comps. shun serialism but are complex in other ways. Works incl. operas *Autodafé* (1971–2) and *La Célestine* (1982–6); *3 Graphiques*, gui. conc. (1950–7); *Anneau de Tamarit*, vc., orch. (1976); pf. conc. (1980–1); 2 str. qts. (1963, 1979–80); many choral works; much chamber mus.; *24 Preludes*, pf. (1972–3) and other kbd. pieces; and incid. mus. for plays, films, and radio.

Ohlsson, Garrick (*b* Bronxville, 1948). Amer. pianist. Winner of Busoni comp., It., 1966, Montreal comp. 1968, Warsaw int. Chopin comp. 1970. Int. career as soloist and recitalist.

Oiseaux exotiques (Exotic birds). Orch. work by *Messiaen for pf., 2 cl., xylophone, glockenspiel, perc., small wind orch., comp. 1955–6. F.p. Paris 1956, Loriod (pf.), R. Albert (cond.).

Oistrakh, David (*b* Odessa, 1908; *d* Amsterdam, 1974). Russ. violinist and conductor. Played Glazunov conc. with composer conducting, Kiev 1926. Moscow début 1928, joining staff of Cons. 1934. 1st prize Brussels Ysaÿe Int. Comp., 1937. Début Paris and London 1953, USA 1955. Salzburg Fest. début 1972 (soloist and cond.). Dedicatee and first performer of both Shostakovich vn. concs., No.1 (1955); No.2 (1967). One of greatest violinists of his day.

Oistrakh, Igor (*b* Odessa, 1931). Russ. violinist, son of David *Oistrakh. Début 1948. Frequently appeared as joint recitalist with his father, also in Bach's double vn. conc. and in Mozart's Sinfonia Concertante, with father as violist. Won Wieniawski comp., Poznań, 1952. On staff Moscow Cons. from 1958. Salzburg Fest. début 1980.

Okeghem, Johannes. See *Ockeghem, Johannes*.

Oklahoma! Amer. musical with mus. by Richard Rodgers and lyrics by Oscar Hammerstein II based on *Green Grow the Lilacs* by Lynn Riggs. Generally held to have pioneered new type of musical show. Prod. NY 1943, London 1947, Paris 1955. Film 1955. Contains songs *O, What a Beautiful Morning* and *The Surrey with the Fringe on Top*, among others equally good.

Oktave (Ger.). Octave. So *Oktavflöte*, octave flute, i.e. *piccolo; *Oktavkoppel*, octave coupler.

Olczewska, Maria [Berchtenbreitner, Marie] (*b* Ludwigsschwaige, nr. Donauwörth, 1892; *d* Klagenfurt, 1969). Ger. mezzo-soprano. Began career in operetta. Opera début Crefeld 1917 (Page in *Tannhäuser*). Heard by *Nikisch, who engaged her for Leipzig Opera 1917–20. Hamburg Opera 1920–3 (creating Brigitte in *Die *tote Stadt*, 1920), Vienna 1921–3, Munich 1923–5. Member of Vienna State Opera 1925–30, being a notable Oktavian in *Der Rosenkavalier*. Sang at CG 1924–32, Chicago Opera 1928–32, NY Met 1933–5. Prof., Vienna Acad. 1947–9. Fine Wagnerian singer.

Old Hall Manuscript. Early 15th-cent. coll. of church mus. found in the library of St Edmund's Coll., Old Hall, Herts., first described in 1903 and pubd. 1933–8. Sold privately to Brit. Library 1973. It offers a valuable opportunity of studying the choral style of a period *c*.1415. Comprises 140 folios of church mus. by composers of the Chapel Royal.

Oldham, Arthur (William) (*b* London, 1926; *d* Villejuif, Fr., 2003). Eng. composer, chorusmaster, and pianist. Mus. dir. Ballet Rambert. Adapted Arne's *Love in a Village* for Aldeburgh

Fest., 1952. Works incl. ballets *Mr Punch* (1946) and *Bonne-1952* (Bouche); choral works; *Divertimento* for str. etc. Ch.-master of Scottish Opera 1966–74, LSO Chorus 1969–76. Founded ch. of Orchestre de Paris 1975 and of Concertgebouw Orch. 1979. OBE 1990.

Old Hundredth (Amer. Old Hundred). Metrical psalm tune of uncertain origin. Its name indicates that it was set to the 100th psalm in the 'old' version of the metrical psalms, i.e. Sternhold and Hopkins as distinct from Tate and Brady. The edn. of this version in which it first appeared was Daye's of 1560–1, where it was set to the words 'All people that on earth do dwell' by W. Kethe. But the history of the tune goes back to Marot and Béza's Genevan Psalter of 1551, in which it is attached to the 134th psalm. An even earlier form of the tune appears in the Antwerp collection *Souter Liederkens* (1540). A ceremonial arr. of the tune for ch., congregation, orch., organ, and 'all available trumpets' was made by Vaughan Williams for the coronation of Elizabeth II, 1953. (It was also perf. at his funeral in Westminster Abbey, 1958).

Old King Cole. Ballet for orch. and ch. (ad lib.) by Vaughan Williams to lib. by Mrs E. Vulliamy, prod. Cambridge 1923. Based on Eng. folk dances; score incorporates some folk-songs.

Old Vic. Familiar name for S. London th. properly the Royal Victoria Hall, Waterloo Road. Built 1818 as Royal Coburg Hall, being renamed 1833 and becoming mus.-hall. Bought in 1880 by Emma Cons, a social reformer, who renamed it Royal Victoria Coffee Hall and staged operatic excerpts. In 1898 her niece Lilian *Baylis took over and, with courageous single-mindedness, developed the th. as a home for cheap-seat Shakespeare and opera, the latter being given twice a week and on alternate Saturday matinées. In 1931 the opera was transferred to new SW Th. and eventually to Coliseum as English National Opera.

ole (Sp.). A gipsy type of *seguidilla also known as *polo* or *romalis*.

Oleg, Raphael (*b* Paris, 1959). Fr. violinist. Won 1st prize, Moscow Tchaikovsky comp. 1986. Brit. début 1987 (Brahms conc., with LSO cond. Tate). Tokyo début 1989.

oliphant (from Fr. *cor d'olifant*, elephant's horn). Holeless type of cow-horn made of ivory, introduced into the W. from Byzantium in medieval times. Became symbol of royalty, owing to rich carving and decoration.

Oliver, Stephen (*b* Liverpool, 1950; *d* London, 1992). Eng. composer. Taught for 2 years at Huddersfield Sch. of Mus. Prolific composer of operas and mus. th. *Perseverance* calls for rock group, dance band, and skiffle group. Works incl.:
THEATRICAL (incl. OPERA): *Slippery Soules*, Christmas drama (1969, rev. 1976, 1988); 3 *Instant Operas* (*Paid Off*, *Time Flies*, *Old Haunts*) (1973); *Sufficient*

Beauty (1973); *A Fur-Coat for Summer* (1973); *Perseverance* (1973–4); *Past Tense* (1974); *Cadenus Observ'd* (solo bar., 1974); **Tom Jones* (1974–5); *Bad Times* (1975); *The Great McPorridge Disaster* (1976); *The Waiter's Revenge* (1976); *The Garden* (1977); *The Girl and the Unicorn*, children's opera (1978); *The Duchess of Malfi* (1971, rev. 1978); *The Dreaming of the Bones* (1979); *Jacko's Play* (1979); *Nicholas Nickleby* (1980); *Euridice* (1981, arr. of Peri's opera); *Sasha* (1982); *Peter Pan* (1982); *Blondel* (1983); *Britannia Preserv'd* (1984); *The Ring* (1984); *Beauty and the Beast* (1984); *Mario and the Magician* (1988); *Timon of Athens* (1990–1).

ORCH.: *The Boy and the Dolphin* (1974); *Luv* (1975); sym. (1976, rev. 1983); conc., rec., str. (1988).

CHAMBER & INSTR.: *Music for the Wreck of the Deutschland*, pf. quintet (1972); *Ricercare I*, cl., vn., vc., pf. (1973); *Bad Times*, bar., str. qt. (1975); *The Elixir*, bar., cl., ch. (1976); *The Dong with a Luminous Nose*, narr., str. (1976); gui. sonata (1978); *The Key to the Zoo*, spkr., 2 ob., bn., hpd. (1980); *Ricercare II*, 2 ob., 22 cl., 3 bn., 2 hn. (1981); *Ricercare III*, gui., va., vc. (1983); *Ricercare V*, brass quintet (1986).

VOCAL: *Sirens*, bar., pf. (1972); *Magnificat and Nunc Dimittis* (1976); *Exchange*, counterten., ten., bar., pf. (1978); *The Child from the Sea*, treble, ch., orch. (1980); *A Man of Feeling*, sop., bar., pf. (1980); *A String of Beads*, ch., orch. (1980); *Trinity Mass*, unacc. (1981); *Beauty and the Beast*, solo vv., orch. (1984); *Seven Words*, ch., str. (1985); *Ricercare IV*, counterten., 2 ten., bar. (1986); *2 Songs and a Scene from Cymbeline*, bar., pf. (1986); *Exposition of a Picture*, ten., bar., str. qt. (1986).

Olivero, Magda (*b* Saluzzo, 1910). It. soprano. Opera début Turin 1933 (Lauretta in *Gianni Schicchi*). Was Cilea's favourite interpreter of Adriana Lecouvreur. Retired 1941 on marriage, but returned 1951 in Brescia (Adriana Lecouvreur, at composer's request). London 1952. Sang in USA 1966–77, début in Dallas 1966; NY 1970; Met début 1975. Notable singing-actress.

Oliveros, Pauline (*b* Houston, 1932). Amer. composer. Worked at S. Francisco Tape Centre 1961–6. Worked with David Tudor, pianist, and Elizabeth Harris, dancer-choreog., 1963–6. Dir., tape mus. centre, Mills Coll., 1961–7; teacher of elec. mus., Univ. of California, San Diego, from 1967 (prof. 1970–81). After 1963 her works used mixed media and she prefers live elec. perf. to prepared tape. Has written a trio for fl., pf., and page-turner (1961) and a work for orch., ch., elecs., and lights called *To Valerie Solonis and Marilyn Monroe in recognition of their desperation* (1970). Among her other works are *The Chicken who Learned How to Fly*, vv., narr., synth. (1985); *The New Sound Meditation*, vv. (1989); *All Fours of the Drum Bum*, drum kit (1990); *Cicada Song*, acc. (1996); and *Timeless Pulse*, perc., elec. (2002).

Olympians, The. Opera in 3 acts by **Bliss to lib. by J. B. Priestley. Prod. London 1949.

O magnum mysterium (O great mystery). Cycle of 4 carols for mixed ch. with instr. sonatas and fantasia for org. by **Maxwell Davies. Written for Cirencester Grammar Sch., 1960. Numerous other settings of this text incl. a masterpiece by *Victoria.

O'Mara, Joseph (*b* Limerick, 1861; *d* Dublin, 1927). Irish tenor and impresario. Début London 1891 in title-role of **Ivanhoe. Sang Wagner roles at CG, then became prin. ten. of **Moody-Manners co., 1902–10. Joined Beecham's co. at CG 1910–12. Formed O'Mara Co. 1912, appearing with it until 1924. Retired 1926.

Omar Khayyám. Work for cont., ten., bass soloists, ch., and orch. by Bantock to text drawn from Edward FitzGerald's *Rubaiyát of Omar Khayyám* (1859). In 3 parts (Birmingham 1906, Cardiff 1907, Birmingham 1909, then perf. complete in London and Vienna 1912).

Omphale's Spinning-wheel (Saint-Saëns). See *Rouet d'Omphale, Le*.

Oncina, Juan (*b* Barcelona, 1925). Sp. tenor. Début Barcelona 1946 (Des Grieux in *Manon*). It. début Bologna 1946, singing in It. until 1962 and specializing in Rossini and Donizetti roles. Glyndebourne 1952–65. Retired 1974.

ondeggiando, ondeggiante, ondeggiamento (It.). Undulating, i.e. **tremolo or **vibrato, or (also) any swaying effect.

ondes Martenot. Elec. instr. (originally named *ondes musicales*) developed by Maurice **Martenot, a Fr. musician, who patented it in 1922 and produced it in 1928. Looks like a **spinet, with a kbd. of 5 octaves but can produce only one note at a time. Uses oscillating valves like **theremin, but is operated by a wire across the kbd., the player producing the desired pitch by manipulating the wire which moves a variable condenser, the kbd. serving as a guide. The signal is amplified through a loudspeaker. Tone-colour and timbre are obtained by pressing a button, and vol. is controlled by a key. First demonstrated in Paris 20 Apr. 1928; first comp. to use it was *Poème symphonique* by Dimitri Levidis, 23 Dec. 1928. The instr. is used in **Messiaen's **Turangalîla Symphony* and in **Honegger's **Jeanne d'Arc au bûcher*.

Ondine. (1) See *Undine*. (2) (Ravel). See *Gaspard de la nuit*.

Ondříček, František (*b* Prague, 1857; *d* Milan, 1922). Cz. violinist and composer. Début Paris 1882, followed by tours. Gave f.p. of Dvořák's vn. conc., Prague 1883. Settled in Vienna 1907, forming qt. Prof. of vn. Vienna Cons. 1911–19, Prague Cons. 1919–22. With Mittelmann, wrote vn. method (1908). Composed vn. conc. and other vn. pieces.

O'Neill, Dennis (*b* Pontardulais, 1948). Welsh tenor. Wexford Fest. 1973 (Messenger in *Ivan Susanin*) and in Glyndebourne chorus 1974. S. Australian Opera 1974–6. Sang with Scottish Opera and WNO 1979; CG début 1979; Glyndebourne 1980; Amer. début (Dallas) 1983; Vienna 1983; NY Met début 1986 (on tour), in NY 1987. CBE 2000.

O'Neill, Norman (*b* London, 1875; *d* London, 1934). Eng. composer and conductor. Treasurer, Royal Phil. Soc. 1918–34. Teacher of harmony and comp., RAM 1924–34. Mus. dir. Haymarket Th. 1908–19, 1920–34, composing incidental mus. for Maeterlinck's *The Blue Bird* (1909) and Barrie's *Mary Rose* (1920). Also wrote orch. works and chamber mus. (See also *Frankfurt Group*.)

one-step. Amer. dance in simple duple time and rather more vigorous than the *fox-trot. Became popular *c*.1910.

ongarese (It.). Hungarian.

On Hearing the first Cuckoo in Spring (Delius). No.1 of *2 Mood Pictures* for small orch. comp. 1911–13, f.p. Leipzig 23 Oct. 1913, cond. Nikisch, f.p. in England 1914 (cond. Mengelberg). Main theme based on No.14 ('In Ola Valley') of Grieg's *Norwegian Folk Tunes*, Op.66.

Onslow, Georges (Louis) (*b* Clermont-Ferrand, 1784; *d* Clermont-Ferrand, 1853). Fr. pianist and composer (Brit. father, Fr. mother). Settled in Fr., giving pf. recitals and lessons. Wrote 3 comic operas, 4 syms., 35 str. qts., 34 str. quintets, and other chamber works.

On this Island. 5 songs for high v. and pf. by Britten, Op.11, to poems by W. H. Auden. Comp. 1937. F.p. BBC broadcast 1937.

Onward, Christian Soldiers. Hymn with words by the Rev. S. Baring-Gould, first pubd. 1868 in appendix to *Hymns Ancient and Modern*, with tune by J. B. *Dykes adapted from slow movt. of Haydn's Sym. No.53. Became popular when set by *Sullivan in 1871 as 'St Gertrude', pubd. in *The Hymnary* (ed. Barnby), but first pubd. in *Musical Times*. Holst set same words in 1924.

On Wenlock Edge. Song-cycle by Vaughan Williams to 6 poems from A. E. Housman's *A Shropshire Lad* (1896) for ten., str. qt., and pf. Comp. 1908–9. F.p. 1909. Also arr. by composer for ten. and orch. (f.p. 1924). First item of cycle is the poem *On Wenlock Edge*.

op. (plural opp.). Abbreviation for *opus.

open. (1) Applied to bowed or plucked instr., a str. which is allowed to vibrate throughout its full length, i.e. not 'stopped' by a finger pressed on it.
  (2) Of a hn., not 'stopped' by the placing of the hand inside the bell.

open diapason. The chief manual stop of the org., 8′ in length, contrasted with the 'stopped diapason'.

open form. A structural procedure whereby the sequence and/or construction of parts of a notated work are variable. First employed by *Ives, *Cowell, and *Grainger, but developed as

indeterminacy by *Cage and Earle *Brown. In Boulez's 3rd pf. sonata, for example, the 5 movts. may be played in any order except the 3rd which must stay central.

open harmony. Harmony in which the notes of the chords are widely spread.

opening cuts. Phrase used in operatic parlance, meaning that passages of an opera which are usually omitted are being performed.

Oper (Ger.). Opera. Also refers to an opera co., e.g. Vienna Staatsoper (Vienna State Opera co. implied).

Opera. Monthly magazine covering news and reports of all operatic matters founded 1950 by Earl of Harewood, who was ed. until 1953, when he was succeeded by Harold *Rosenthal. Rodney Milnes ed. 1986–99, John Allison from 2000.

opera (It., work, but actually plural of Lat. *opus*, a work; Fr. *opéra*; Ger. *Oper*). The term is an abbreviation of *opera in musica*. Opera is a drama set to mus. to be sung with instr. acc. by singers usually in costume. Recit. or spoken dialogue may separate the *numbers, but the essence of opera is that the mus. is integral and is not incidental, as in a 'musical' or play with mus.
  Although literary dramas and *sacre rappresentazione* were its precursors in some respects, opera is generally said to have originated in Florence towards the close of the 16th cent. (see *Camerata*) with the earliest examples by *Peri and *Caccini. Recit. was the dominant feature, but with *Monteverdi, whose operatic career extended from 1607 to 1642, opera developed rapidly, borrowing elements from the madrigal and from the ornate Venetian church mus. The aria became an important element, and in *L'incoronazione di Poppea*, the insight shown into the humanity of the characters anticipated 19th-cent. developments. *Cavalli followed Monteverdi's lead, but a more formal approach was reintroduced by A. *Scarlatti, who comp. 115 operas between 1679 and 1725. He introduced instr. acc. for recit. in 1686. During the 17th cent. opera was pioneered in Fr. by *Lully and *Rameau and in Ger. by *Schütz and *Keiser. But the next great figure in operatic history was *Handel, whose operas were mostly comp. for London (between 1711 and 1741) in the It. *opera seria* style. His glorious solo arias were written for the brilliant techniques and skills of the great *castrato* singers of his day and for equally fine sops.; in addition, he imparted a lengthened degree of dramatic tension to the form both in arias and recits. It was left to J. C. *Bach in his London operas of the 1760s to restore the ch. to a place in opera, as was done also by *Gluck, whose operas were written between 1741 and 1779. Gluck's *Orfeo*, written for Vienna in 1762, is a revolutionary opera because it exploits to the full the mus. and dramatic possibilities of the lib. Gluck scrapped the *da capo* aria, which was a primary cause of holding up the dramatic development of the plot, and in his preface to *Alceste* (1767) he wrote of reducing

mus. to its true function 'which is that of seconding poetry in the expression of sentiments and dramatic situations of a story'. Although *opera seria* was to reach its culmination with Mozart's *Idomeneo* (1781), Gluck's reforms effectively killed it off, even if fashion still prevented him from carrying out his theories fully.

*Haydn's operas, mostly written for Eszterháza, are rich in mus. content but were eclipsed by the works of genius with which *Mozart ended the 18th cent., operas which brought the orch. into the forefront of the art, giving it a whole new dimension. Moreover they were works which defied classification under the old headings of *opera seria* and *opera buffa*. After *Don Giovanni* almost anything was possible.

The beginning of the 19th cent. was given a post-Mozartian sparkle by the brilliance, wit, and zest of *Rossini's comic operas, and a generation of remarkable singers was served by Rossini, *Bellini, and *Donizetti. In Ger. the romantic movt., with its interest in folklore and fantasy, found an operatic spokesman in *Weber, whose *Der Freischütz*, *Oberon*, and *Euryanthe* opened the way for the colossal transformation wrought by *Wagner, who in his maturity dispensed with the established *number opera and converted recit. and aria into a seamless, continuous, and symphonic web of mus., with the orch. almost an extra character on the stage. He preferred the term 'music drama' to 'opera', wrote his own libs., and viewed opera as an amalgam of all the arts. In one sense his operas were a reaction against the spectacular 'singers' operas' of *Meyerbeer which he had seen in his Parisian youth. Meyerbeer was Ger., but it is with Paris that he is assoc., enjoying success while the much more talented *Berlioz had little operatic success in his lifetime, though his *Les Troyens* is now recognized as a major masterpiece. The operas of Massenet, Gounod, Bizet, and Saint-Saëns dominated Fr. mus. in the latter half of the 19th cent. But next to Wagner the outstanding figure was *Verdi, also born in 1813, who learned much from Donizetti and refined and developed his art, keeping to a number-opera format, from *Oberto* of 1837–8 to the magical *Falstaff* of 1889–92.

Nationalist opera was principally an E. European development, beginning with *Glinka's *A Life for the Tsar* in 1836 and continuing with *Mussorgsky's *Boris Godunov* and Borodin's *Prince Igor*. Tchaikovsky's operas, of which *Eugene Onegin* is the best known, were not overtly nationalist, however. *Smetana in Bohemia with *Dalibor* and *The Bartered Bride* est. a Cz. operatic tradition which reached its apogee in the first quarter of the 20th cent. with the powerful, realistic, and orig. operas of *Janáček.

In Ger. the greatest post-Wagnerian figure in opera was Richard *Strauss, whose first opera, *Guntram*, was prod. 1894 and his last, *Capriccio*, in 1942. He was continually trying to find new ways of reconciling words and mus., several of his works having the advantage of fine libs. by the Austrian poet Hofmannsthal. Other major

operas from Ger. and Austria in the 20th cent. were written by *Berg (*Wozzeck* and *Lulu*), Schoenberg, Pfitzner, Schreker, Korngold, Einem, Orff, and Henze.

After Verdi in It. came the *verismo* (reality) movt., in which operas, often but not necessarily in contemporary settings, strove to present the harsh realities of the situations with which they dealt. In many cases these derived from the realistic novels of Fr. literature in the late 19th cent., e.g. Zola, but like all such categorizations, *verismo* is hard to define and it could easily be said that Verdi's *La traviata* is *verismo*. However, the term is generally applied to the works of *Mascagni, *Leoncavallo, *Montemezzi, *Leoni, and, though he is a special case, to *Puccini, whose operas achieved and have retained a wide popularity because of their mus. and dramatic colour and immediate appeal. *La bohème* in particular is among the most frequently perf. of all operas, with *Madama Butterfly* running it close.

Opera in Eng. was for many years mainly an imported commodity. Only *Purcell's short *Dido and Aeneas* (1683–4) and the ballad-opera *The *Beggar's Opera* (1728) were of any quality among native products, although Balfe's *The Bohemian Girl* (1843) achieved popularity. *Sullivan wrote a grand opera (*Ivanhoe*) but won immortality through the light operas written in collab. with Gilbert in which his flair for parody and pastiche could be exploited to the full. *Vaughan Williams comp. 5 operas which have excellent mus. qualities but are still held to be dramatically weak. *Britten, with *Peter Grimes* in 1945, showed that Eng. had at last produced a natural operatic composer, as was shown by the eagerness with which these works were also staged abroad. He wrote several operas which needed only a chamber orch. and also developed a genre which he called 'church parables'. These are midway between opera and medieval morality play. The example of Britten was followed by Tippett, Bennett, Walton, Maxwell Davies, Birtwistle, Oliver, Tavener, Weir, Adès, and many others.

In the USA, native opera took even longer than in Brit. to find its feet. *Gershwin's *Porgy and Bess* has a claim to be the first successful Amer. opera. Operas by the It.-born *Menotti and by *Barber and *Argento followed the European tradition, and qualities of exuberance, raciness, and wit which the Americans bring to mus. have been channelled most effectively into the genre of 'musical' such as *Oklahoma!* and *Kiss Me Kate*. This genre was sophisticated by Sondheim's *A Little Night Music*. The 'minimalist' composers Philip *Glass and John *Adams have written successful operas, notably the former's *Akhnaten* and the latter's *Nixon in China*. A NY Met commission which scored a success was Corigliano's *The Ghosts of Versailles*.

Some great composers have written only one opera, the supreme examples being *Beethoven, whose *Fidelio* is regarded by many as the greatest of all operas, and *Debussy (*Pelléas et Mélisande*), while others have written none, e.g. Brahms, Bruckner, Elgar, Mahler, Ives, and Rubbra. Yet opera remains for most composers the greatest and most attractive challenge. With the development of mechanical and elec. techniques and the advance of the stage producer to an importance comparable with that of the cond., the staging of operas has grown more exciting and controversial, and has been exploited in the works of Henze, Maxwell Davies, *Ginastera, and others. It has also become more expensive. Finance was a contributory cause of Britten's development of chamber operas, and has also led to the emergence of *music theatre, a genre in which works of quasi-operatic character, sometimes involving only one singer or reciter, can be perf. either with a minimum of stage trappings (costumes, etc.) or with none at all but purely as a concert performance. A remarkable example of mus. theatre at its best is Maxwell Davies's Eight *Songs for a Mad King. Yet even here it can be argued that 20th-cent. mus. theatre is merely a reversion to Monteverdi's Il combattimento di Tancredi e Clorinda.

The term opera not only covers the form of mus. composition but the whole business of performing opera. Thus it embraces the famous opera houses and cos. of It. in Milan, Rome, Naples, and Venice, of other parts of Europe in Vienna, Salzburg, Berlin, Dresden, Frankfurt, Munich, Bayreuth, and Paris, of Russia in Moscow and Leningrad, in the USA in NY and Chicago, and in Eng. in London. Two prin. cos. work in London, the Royal Opera at CG, and ENO at the Coliseum. Outside London there is the summer fest. at *Glyndebourne, Sussex, but opera is provided on almost an all-the-year-round basis by the regional cos., Scottish Opera (based in Glasgow), WNO (Cardiff) and Opera North (Leeds). These cos. also tour. There are also many other cos., e.g. GTO and ETO, which provide excellent perfs. and reflect the immense development of operatic life in Britain since 1945. All these activities, except Glyndebourne, are heavily subsidized. Commercial sponsorship of opera has become a valuable and necessary contribution to its continuance.

Opéra, Paris. See Paris Opéra.

opéra-ballet. Stage work, especially assoc. with Campra and Rameau in Fr. in the late 17th and early 18th cents., in which equal or nearly equal importance is given to singing and dancing.

opera buffa (It.; Fr. opéra-bouffe). Comic opera, the opposite of *opera seria. Began as use of a comic subject involving characters drawn from everyday life. Examples are Mozart's Le nozze di Figaro, Rossini's Il barbiere di Siviglia, and Donizetti's Don Pasquale.

opéra-comique (Fr.). Comic opera. By no means the Fr. equivalent of opera buffa, and it has changed its meaning several times. It now means opera in which there is spoken dialogue, but the subject-matter ought to be light-hearted and treated thus. Beethoven's Fidelio and Bizet's Carmen are technically opéras-comiques but cannot be classified as such.

Opéra-Comique, Paris. See Paris, Opéra-Comique.

Opera North. Opera company based in Grand Th., Leeds, Yorkshire, formed in 1978 as northern arm of English National Opera at the London Coliseum. F.p. November 1978, Grand Th., Leeds, Saint-Saëns's Samson et Dalila. As financial independence grew, co. altered name from English National Opera North to Opera North in 1981. Gives regular seasons in Manchester, Nottingham, Sheffield, Hull, etc. Commissioned Wilfred Josephs's Rebecca (1983) and Benedict Mason's Playing Away (1994). Gave f. Eng. ps. of *Jonny spielt auf (1984), *Daphne (1987), *Jérusalem (1990), and Der *ferne Klang (1992), and f. Brit. stage p. of Verdi's first opera, Oberto (1994). First visit to London 1994 (Gloriana at CG). Mus. dir. David Lloyd-Jones from formation until 1990; Paul Daniel 1990–7; Steven Sloane 1999–2003; Richard Farnes from 2004.

opera-oratorio. Term used by Stravinsky to describe his *Oedipus Rex, which is designed to be presented on the stage but in the static manner of a concert perf. of an oratorio.

opera seria (It.). Serious opera. In the 17th and 18th cents., opera seria was the chief operatic genre, becoming very formal and complex, with elaborate display arias. Mythological subjects were the norm, and most of these were written for various composers by the librettist *Metastasio. The last and greatest examples of the form were Mozart's Idomeneo (1781) and La clemenza di Tito (1791).

Opera Theatre of St Louis. Annual summer opera fest. held in St Louis, Miss., founded 1976 by Richard Gaddes and in first 25 seasons presented 15 world premières and 19 Amer. premières. Colin Graham art. dir. from 1986, Stephen Lord mus. dir. from 1986. Operas perf. in Eng. in 987-seat Loretto-Hilton Center on campus of Webster Univ. Audiences dine in garden setting. Singers whose careers blossomed at this fest. incl. Christine Brewer, Susan Graham, Dwayne Croft, and Sylvia McNair.

operetta (It.; Fr. opérette). Little opera. Strictly a play with ov., songs, entr'actes, and dances, but the term has become synonymous with 'light opera', e.g. Offenbach's La Belle Hélène and Strauss's Die Fledermaus, and 'musical comedy', e.g. Coward's Bitter-Sweet.

Opernball, Der (The Opera Ball). Operetta in 3 acts by *Heuberger to lib. by Léon and Waldberg after the farce Les Dominos roses by Delacour and Henniquin. Prod. Vienna 1898, NY 1909. Contains the sop. aria Geh'n wir in's Chambre séparée.

Oper und Drama (Ger.). Opera and Drama. Long essay by *Wagner, written in Zurich 1850–1, in which he expounded his theories on mus. drama, speech-origins, etc.

ophicleide. (1) Obsolete keyed brass instr. of conical bore and played with cup mouthpiece. Was a development of the *serpent and existed in alto, bass, and double-bass sizes, but only the bass was much used. Was used in military bands and is also incl. in early scores of Mendelssohn, Berlioz, Verdi, and Wagner. Superseded by the bass tuba.

(2) org. stop like *tuba*.

Opie, Alan (*b* Redruth, 1945). Eng. baritone. Opera début SW 1969 (Papageno in *Die Zauberflöte*). CG début 1971. Created Oblonsky in Hamilton's *Anna Karenina*, ENO 1981. Title-role in *Háry János*, Buxton Fest. 1982. Bayreuth début 1987 (Beckmesser in *Die Meistersinger*).

Oppens, Ursula (*b* NY, 1944). Amer. pianist. Début NY 1969. Won Busoni int. pf. comp. 1969. Specialist in contemp. mus., works having been comp. for her by Rzewski, Carter, and Wuorinen. Teacher at Brooklyn Coll., NY City Univ.

op. posth. Posthumous work, i.e. work pubd. after composer's death. See *opus*.

opus (Lat.). Work. Word used, followed by a number, e.g. Opus 50, for the numbering of a composer's works. This numbering gives a rough idea of the order in which works were comp., but can be misleading. Sometimes the Opus no. is allotted by the composer, sometimes by the publisher. Some composers, e.g. Mozart, Haydn, did not number their works; some, e.g. Elgar, gave some works opus nos. and not others; some, e.g. R. Strauss, did likewise but also reallotted opus nos. so that much confusion arises in his case. Dvořák allowed early works to be given late opus nos. by his publisher. In many cases an opus no. covers a group of works, in which case the numbering is subdivided, e.g. Op.59, No.3, or in a style often used, Op.59/3. In other cases, 2 versions of the same work exist and the composer uses letters after the number to differentiate them, e.g. Op.49a, Op.49b. Although the Latin plural of opus is opera, it has become customary to write 'opuses', to avoid confusion, just as in Italian 'opera' has become a singular noun with the plural *opere*.

Oracolo, L' (The Oracle). Opera in 1 act by F. *Leoni to lib. by C. Zanoni from a story 'The Cat and the Cherub' by C. B. Fernald. Prod. CG 1905, NY Met 1915.

Oramo, Sakari (*b* Helsinki, 1965). Finn. conductor and violinist. Trained as violinist and played in Avanti! CO, becoming leader of Finn. Radio SO. Studied cond. with Jorma Panula at Sibelius Acad. 1989–92. Cond. début 1993 with Finn. Radio SO, leading to appointment as co-prin. cond. Prin. cond. CBSO 1998–2008 (mus. dir. from 1999). Toured with CBSO in Eur., Japan, and Scandinavia. Chief cond. Finn. Radio SO from 2003. Prin. cond. Kokkola Opera from 2006. Specialist in Finn. mus. and has cond. many Eng. works.

Oration. 'Concerto elegiaco' for vc. and orch. by Frank *Bridge, comp. 1930. F.p. BBC 1936, Florence Hooton (vc.), cond. Bridge.

oratorio. (1) Strictly, a mus. setting of a religious lib. for solo singers, ch., and orch., in dramatic form but usually perf. without scenery or costumes in concert-hall or church. The form originated in plays given in the Oratory of S. Philip Neri, Rome, in the mid-16th cent., the mus. form developing *c*.1600. The first oratorio was Cavalieri's *La rappresentazione di anima e di corpo* (The Representation of Soul and Body), a morality set to music and perf. in costume. Later oratorios, in concert-form, were written by *Carissimi, A. *Scarlatti, *Schütz, *Handel (esp. *Messiah*, the most popular of all oratorios), *Haydn, *Spohr, *Beethoven, and *Mendelssohn (*Elijah*). Elgar wrote 3 oratorios (but *The Dream of Gerontius* is not an oratorio).

(2) The term is also applied to works similar to these cited above but on a non-religious subject, e.g. Handel's *Semele*, *Tippett's *A *Child of our Time*. Stravinsky's *Oedipus Rex* is described as an *opera-oratorio.

Orb and Sceptre. Coronation march by *Walton, comp. 1952–3 for coronation of Elizabeth II, and f. public p. in Westminster Abbey, cond. Boult, 2 June 1953.

Orchésographie. Treatise on dancing by Thoinot *Arbeau, written in Fr. and pubd. 1588–9. Important source of information on ancient dances and their tunes. They are described in a dialogue with his pupil Capriol, hence the title *Capriol Suite* for *Warlock's work based on several of the dance tunes.

orchestra (Fr. *orchestre*, Ger. *Orchester*). A mixed body of instrumentalists for the perf. of symphonic and other works. There are various types of orch., e.g. symphony orchestra, a body of (usually) over 90 players able to play elaborate works; chamber orchestra, small version of above (from, say, 15 to 45 players); string orchestra, strings only; theatre orchestra, medium-size orch. used for musicals, etc., and often incl. saxs.

The orch. has changed and developed over the centuries, the standard version today comprising str., woodwind, brass, and perc. In the 17th cent. the orch. was a haphazard affair, often incl. viols, fls., obs., cornetts, tbs., drums, and hpd. In the 18th cent., with instr. improvements, vns. ousted viols. Accs. were realized by the harpsichordist or org. from a figured bass. From *c*.1800, the orch. became more elaborate and composers more skilled in its use, obtaining tone-colour by subtle combinations and by solo passages. In Beethoven's 1st Sym. (1800) the orch. consisted of: vns., div. into 1st and 2nd sections, vas., vcs., dbs., fls., obs., cls., bns., tpts., hns., timp. Later composers added the harp and Berlioz enlarged the woodwind, brass, and perc. departments, as did Wagner and Liszt. Towards the end of the 19th and in the 20th cents., composers enlarged the orch. enormously, and we have

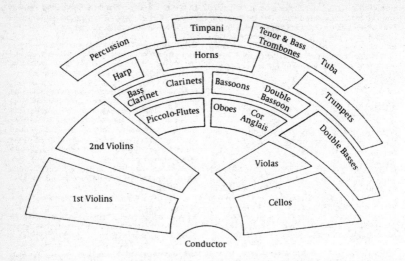

the marvellously rich, exotic, and grandiose orch. works of Strauss, Mahler, Elgar, Havergal Brian, Ravel, Stravinsky, and many more. Huge brass sections are often a feature of their scores, with triple or quadruple woodwind (i.e. 3 or 4 of each instr.). Later in the 20th cent. even more variety in orch. use is encountered, with reversions to small combinations of instr., works scored for solo instr. and wind or brass instr. only, exotic perc. effects, and of course the addition of elec. instr., tape-recorded and synthesized effects.

The lay-out of the standard sym. orch. is normally as shown in the diagram above, but certain works call for special seating arrangements and some conds. have individual preferences.

Orchestral Employers' Association. British advisory and consultative committee of which the members are the managers of the prin. London and provincial sym. and opera orchs. Acts as advisory and consultative body on matters of common interest and represents its members in negotiations with Musicians' Union on pay and conditions, and in representations to the Govt. Works in assoc. with *Arts Council.

orchestral oboe. org. stop.

Orchestral Pieces, Five (*Fünf Orchesterstücke*). Work for large orch. by Schoenberg, Op.16, comp. June–Aug. 1909, rev. 1922 and 1949 (reduced to normal-sized orch.). F.p. Berlin (Nos. 1, 2, and 4), Feb. 1912, arr. Webern for 2 pf., 8 hands; f. complete p. London 1912, cond. Wood (also cond. Schoenberg in London 1914). Arr. for chamber orch. 1925 by Felix Greissle.

Orchestral Set. Name of 2 orch. works by *Ives.

No.1 is usually known as *Three Places in New England*, 1908–14; No.2, comp. 1909–15, has 3 movts.: 1. *An Elegy to our Forefathers*; 2. *The Rockstrewn Hills Join in the People's Outdoor Meeting*; 3. *From Hanover Square North at the end of a Tragic Day (1915), the Voice of the People again Rose.*

Orchestration. (1) The art of scoring mus. for an orch. or band. Many composers show special skill in this, e.g. Haydn, Mozart, and Beethoven, while Berlioz, Wagner, Mahler, Elgar, Strauss, Ravel, Rimsky-Korsakov, and Britten were all masters of the art.

(2) Arr. of a work for orch. which was comp. for another medium, e.g. Ravel's orchestration of his own *Ma mère l'Oye*, written for pf. duet.

Orchestre de la Société des Concerts du Conservatoire. Fr. symphony orch. inaugurated by *Habeneck on 5 Feb. 1828, with Beethoven's *Eroica* Sym., and comprising over 80 past and present students of the Conservatoire. Habeneck was succeeded by Girard (1849), Tilmant (1861), and Hainl (1864). Towards the end of the century Messager was cond. and after 1945 Munch and Cluytens were associated with it. Disbanded 1967 and succeeded by the Orchestre de *Paris.

Orchestre de la Suisse Romande. Orch. based on Geneva founded 1918 by Ernest *Ansermet (as Orchestre Romand), who was cond. until 1966. His successors have been Paul *Kletzki 1967–9, Wolfgang *Sawallisch 1970–80, Horst *Stein 1980–5, Armin *Jordan 1985–97, Fabio Luisi 1997–2002, Pinchas Steinberg 2002–5, Marek Janowski from 2005.

Ord, Boris (Bernhard) (*b* Bristol, 1897; *d* Cambridge, 1961). Eng. organist, choirmaster, and composer. On staff of Cologne Opera 1927. Org. and choirmaster, King's Coll., Cambridge, 1929–57, popularizing through radio the famous Christmas Eve Fest. of Nine Lessons and Carols; lect. in mus., Cambridge Univ. 1936–58; cond. Cambridge Univ. Mus. Soc. 1936–54. Wrote one carol, *Adam lay y-bounden* (1957). CBE 1958.

ordinario (It.). Ordinary, normal, e.g. *tempo ordinario*.

ordre (Fr.). Term synonymous with *suite used by F. *Couperin and his contemporaries.

O'Regan, Tarik (*b* London, 1978). Eng. composer. Studied at Oxford and Cambridge Univs. Comp.-in-res. Corpus Christi Coll., Cambridge. Moved to NY 2004. Fulbright Chester Schirmer Fellowship in comp., Columbia Univ. Research affiliate on visiting faculty, Yale Univ. Inst. of Sacred Mus. Works incl.:

OPERA: *Heart of Darkness*, 4 singers, 13 instr. (2006).
ORCH.: *Clichés* (2000); *Hudson Lullaby* (2004); *The Pure Good of Theory* (2004).
CHORAL: *Agnus Dei*, ch., org. (2001); *Corpus Christi Service*, ch., org. (2001); *Magnificat & Nunc dimittis*, vc./sax., ch. (2001); *Beatus auctor saeculi*, unacc. ch. (2003); *Alleluia, laus & Gloria*, women's vv. (2004); *Bring rest, sweet dreaming child*, ch., hp., org. (2004); *Cantate domino*, ch., org. (2004); *De Sancto Ioanne Baptista*, ch., org. (2004); *Dorchester Canticles*, ten., ch., org., opt. hp. (2004); *Gloria*, ch., org. (2004); *Threnody*, ch., str. (2004); *Lamentation*, male ch. (2005); *We Remember Them*, sop., ch. (2005); *And there was a great calm*, sop., women's ch., str. (2005); *Triptych*, ch., str. (2005).
SOLO VOICE: *The Appointment*, bar., pf. (2004); *3 Andrew Motion Settings*, bar., pf. (2005).
CHAMBER MUS.: *Fragments*, str. qt. (2005).
PIANO: *3 Miniatures* (1999); *Lines of Desire* (2005).

Orel, Alfred (*b* Vienna, 1889; *d* Vienna, 1967). Austrian musicologist. Librarian, music div., Austrian Nat. Library 1918–40 and of Vienna Univ. musicological institute. Worked with R. *Haas from 1934 on collected works of Bruckner. Wrote books on Beethoven, Bruckner, Mozart, Schubert, Wolf, and Brahms, and ed. coll. of Bruckner's letters and other documentary sources.

Orfeo ed Euridice (Orpheus and Eurydice). (1) Opera (*azione teatrale per musica*—theatrical action for mus.) in 3 acts by Gluck to lib. by Calzabigi based on mythological legend. Prod. Vienna 1762, London 1770 (*pasticcio*), 1773 (orig. form); NY 1863, Met 1891. Title-role sung at f.p. in Vienna by alto castrato Gaetano *Guadagni. For Parma prod. 1769, male sop. sang role. Fr. version, *Orphée*, to trans. by Moline with title-role transposed for high ten. prod. Paris 1774. (Some mus. from ballet *Don Juan* recurs, and other new mus. was added.) Orfeo is now generally sung by mez. but sometimes by bar. or counterten. Ed. by Berlioz prod. Paris 1859 (with Viardot as Orpheus).

(2) *L'anima del filosofo, ossia Orfeo ed Euridice*. Opera in 4 acts by Haydn (Hob. XXVIII:13) to lib. by C. F. Badini after Ovid's *Metamorphoses*, Books IX and X. Comp. 1791 for King's Th., London, but not perf. F.p. Florence 1951, cond. E. *Kleiber; London (concert) 1989.

See also *Favola d'Orfeo* (Monteverdi) and *Orpheus*. Many composers have written works on the Orpheus legend, from Peri and Landi to Benda, Cannabich, Malipiero, Krenek, and Birtwistle.

Orff, Carl (*b* Munich, 1895; *d* Munich, 1982). Ger. composer, teacher, and conductor. Studied Munich Acad., leaving to join army 1914. Worked in opera houses and returned to Munich 1920 for further study with Kaminsky. In 1924 founded the Günther School, Munich, where his life-long interest in children's mus. education began. About this time he made edns. of several operas by Monteverdi, incl. *L'incoronazione di Poppea*, comp. cantatas and an *Entrata* for orch. 'after William Byrd'. In 1937, when his *Carmina Burana* was f.p., he disowned all his previous works, though some were later rev. and restored. From then he comp. exclusively for the stage, though not conventionally (*Carmina Burana*, for example, is usually given in a concert version). His mature style is dry and staccato, with much use of perc. and the content of the mus. based on rhythmic patterns and their variations. Harmony is reduced to basic elements, and melody is nearer to rhythmic speech than to the 'expressive' ideal of other composers. Prin. works:

STAGE: *Trionfi—Trittico Teatrale* (Triumphs—theatrical triptych): 1. *Carmina Burana* (Songs of Beuren), *cantiones profanae* (1935–6), 2. *Catulli Carmina* (Songs of Catullus), *ludi scaenici* (1943), 3. *Trionfo di Afrodite* (Triumph of Aphrodite), *concerto scenico* (1950–1). *Der *Mond* (The Moon), *ein kleines Welttheater* (1937–8, rev. 1945); *Antigonae* (1940–9); *Die *Kluge* (The Clever Girl) (1941–2); *Die *Bernauerin* (1944–5); *Astutuli* (1945–6); *Comoedia de Christi Resurrectione*, an Easter play (1955); *Oedipus der Tyrann* (1957–8); *Ludus de Nato Infante Mirificus*, a Christmas play (1960); *Ein Sommernachtstraum* (A *Midsummer Night's Dream*), incidental mus. for Shakespeare (1939, rev. 1944, 1952, 1964); *Prometheus* (1963–7); *De temporum fine comoedia* (1969–71).
CHORUS & ORCH.: *Die Sänger der Vorwelt* (The Singer of Former Times) (1955); *Nänie und Dithyrambe* (1956); *Rota* (1972).
EDUCATIONAL: *Das Schulwerk, Musik für Kinder*, 5 vols. (1930–5, rev. 1950–4).
ARRANGEMENTS: Monteverdi: *L'incoronazione di Poppea* (1925, rev. 1940); *Lamenti* (triple bill, prod. Schwetzingen 1958, of *Lamento d'Arianna*, 1925, rev. 1940, *La Favola d'Orfeo*, 1925, rev. 1931, 1940, *Il ballo delle ingrate*, 1925, rev. 1940).

organ (Ger. *Orgel*; Fr. *orgue*; It. *organo*). Kbd. instr. operated by air blown by a *bellows* through *pipes* to sound the notes. Often known as 'the king of instruments' because of its normal large size, although it is made in various sizes. The phrase was coined by *Machaut, who was probably referring also to the organ's versatility.

The principles of construction, in primary outline, are:

(1) A row of *pipes*, graduated as to size (and hence as to pitch), is placed in a corresponding row of holes in a *windchest*, which is fed by a *bellows*.

Under each hole in the *windchest* is a *pallet*, i.e. a type of hinged cover which can be opened and closed.

The *pallets* are operated, in the older orgs., by a series of rods, called *stickers*, and these are connected with the kbd. of the instr. by levers called *backfalls* and rods called *trackers*: thus on depressing a finger-key a current of air is admitted to its particular pipe, and on releasing it the current of air is then cut off. In many modern organs, instead of the *sticker-backfall-tracker* action there are the tubes of a *pneumatic action* or the wires of an *electric action*.

What has been described is a theoretical org. of only one row of pipes. But in practice the windchest has several such rows, the pipes being some of wood and some of metal, some of normal pitch and some of a pitch an octave below or above that pitch, etc., some being simple ('flue') pipes and others supplied with a vibrating tongue of metal called a *reed*, and so on. The pallets extend, *from front to back*, under each of these rows, so admitting air to, or excluding it from, the pipes related to one finger-key of the organ, whilst *from side to side* of the windchest, under each row of pipes, runs a board with holes in it, called a *slider*; when slid into one position the holes in this board coincide with those under the pipes and so permit the pallets to operate as regards that row; when slid into another position they no longer coincide, and so cut off the operation of the pallets in admitting air. The sliding is accomplished (mechanically, pneumatically, or electrically) by connection with *handles* or other devices; these are the *drawstops*, *stop-keys*, etc., respectively, each of which operates one row of pipes—called a *register* or *stop* (we speak of an organ of '20 stops', of '100 stops', etc.).

A kbd. operated by the hands is called a *manual* and one operated by the feet, a *pedal-board*. All orgs. nowadays possess both types of kbd. When an instr. contains any considerable number of stops, differentiation in their use is made easier by their being distributed over 2, 3, or 4 manuals (occasionally more). These are banked up stepwise before the player. The chief manual is that of the *great organ*, which contains a variety of stops, incl. especially many of robust tone. Above it is that of the *swell organ*, the pipes belonging to which are enclosed in a *swell box*—with Venetian shutters which by means of a swell pedal can be opened or closed, so increasing or diminishing the volume of tone. Below the great organ manual, in a 3-manual organ, is that of the *choir organ* which contains softer stops, intended originally in a church, chiefly for the acc. of the choral body. If there is a 4th manual (above the swell manual) it is that of the *solo organ* (with special stops of the character indicated by that name), and there may also be an *echo organ*, with very soft stops.

(2) The two varieties of stop are respectively called *flue pipes* and *reed pipes*. Both are graduated in size, the larger producing the lowest notes and the smaller the highest. The normal pitch of an organ (the same, properly, as that of a pf.) is the product of any set of open-ended flue pipes of which the largest (representing C two lines below the bass staff) is 8' long, the length of the remaining pipes of the set diminishing by half as each octave is ascended. The tone from the stops with these pipes of normal size can be reinforced by that from others of abnormal size, with their pipe for low C 4' or 2' long (so that the whole stop concerned gives an effect respectively 1 or 2 octaves higher than the normal) or, on the other hand, 16' or even 32' long (so that the stop concerned gives an effect respectively 1 or 2 octaves lower than normal). There are also stops of other lengths which give intermediate pitches reinforcing some of the natural harmonics of the normally pitched stops: these are called *mutation stops* or, if several rows (*ranks*) of them are operated in chorus as though they made one, **mixture stops*. The chief stops on the *pedal organ* are pitched an octave below those of the manuals (i.e. whereas the chief stops of the manuals are 8' stops, those of the pedal are 16' stops).

Besides 'open-ended flue pipes' there are flue pipes which have a stopper at the top ('end-plugged' is a term used in various entries in this dictionary), which lowers their pitch by an octave. The chief manual stop of the organ is the 8' *open diapason: but there is generally also a *stopped diapason*, also, from its pitch, spoken of as an 8' stop although, in actual physical length, 4'. (These stops are also to be found in the pedal department.)

By a system of *couplers* (see *couples*) the pedal organ can have one or more of the manuals connected with it. Some of the organ's stops are imitative of other instrs. such as the flute, the orchestral oboe, clarinet, and trumpet (the last 3 being *reed stops*), and the *gamba* (a *string-toned* stop, supposed to reproduce the tone of the old viola da gamba). Stops presumably intended to be imitative are the *vox humana* (a reed stop) and the *vox angelica* or *voix céleste* (with 2 flue pipes to each note slightly out of tune with each other, so producing a somewhat mysterious effect—or, if only one, by the drawstop simultaneously bringing into action some normally tuned soft stop). The *tremulant* is not a stop, though operated by the player by similar means: it causes a slight fluctuation of the tone.

History: the org. is the oldest kbd. instr. The first was built by Ktesibios, a Gr. engineer living in Alexandria, in the 3rd cent. BC. This was called the *hydraulis, and wind pressure was stabilized by the use of water. During the 4th cent. AD bellows replaced the hydraulic mechanism (creating the pneumatic org.), and thereby increasing the vol. of sound. In the medieval org., pipes were of the 'flute' type (voiced with a lip, like the recorder); instead of the hydraulis kbd.

(levers, each with a return mechanism, which were depressed by fingers to play notes), there was a series of tongues or sliders which were pulled or pushed manually; 2 players were often required, seated at the same manual; pipes sometimes outnumbered sliders by 10 to 1 and each note was prod. by a simultaneous 'mixture' of different pipes, producing a variety of timbre and pitch—there were unisons (basic pitch), octaves (octave higher), and quints (1 or more octaves plus a 5th higher).

During the 13th and 14th cents. the fashion for building very large instrs. was succeeded by a trend to smaller varieties, with the clumsy slider movement being replaced by the more flexible and sensitive kbd. One of the most popular types of org. from the 13th to the 16th cent. was the portative org. (organetto), so called because it could be carried. There were usually 2 rows of pipes giving a range of up to 2 octaves. The player provided his own air supply, using the right hand for the kbd. and the left for the bellows. The portative org. was monophonic, suited to playing a solo dance-tune. The 'great' church org. gained additional kbds. to offer variety of tone, that at Halberstadt, Ger., built in 1361, having 3 manuals and a pedal kbd. It had 20 bellows worked by 10 men. When the wind pressure was strong, the player had to use the full power of his arm to hold down a key. Between the cath. and the portative orgs. in size was the positive, which could be used in church and for chamber mus. It required 2 or 3 sets of bellows and someone else to operate them so that the player could use both hands on the kbd. Though not portable, the positive could be easily moved, smaller versions often standing on a table. In Eng. it became known as the 'chair' org., corrupted into 'choir' org.

At the close of the Middle Ages, several improvements occurred in construction of large church orgs., making them less unwieldy. By the beginning of the 16th cent. the kbd. had been altered to make it as responsive as that of smaller orgs; registration for each kbd. could be controlled by stops which worked in a similar way to the slider mechanism; in addition to open and stopped 'flue' pipes, there were 'reed' pipes employing a single vibrating tongue and a resonator; stops were contrasted, many of them being designed to imitate instr., and couplers were used to join manual to manual or manual to pedals. Further improvements were added over the course of the next century. Pedals were not introduced into Eng. org.-building until nearly the end of the 18th cent. In Paris, 1867, electricity was first used to activate the key action. Since that time every kind of refinement has been introduced to make orgs. capable of a wider and subtler range of tone-colour. The elec. org. was introduced in 1935. See also *regal*.

organistrum. The *hurdy-gurdy.

Organ Solo Mass. Mozart's Mass in C, K259 (1776). So named because there is an important org. solo in the Benedictus.

organum. An early form of melodic harmonization which flourished from c.900 to 1200. In plainchant the melody was harmonized by addition of 1, 2, or 3 parts, usually parallel.

Orgelbüchlein (Little Organ Book). Unfinished coll. of 46 short chorale preludes for org. by Bach (164 were intended), written for instruction and for pedalling practice.

orgue de Barberie. Small mechanical organ played by turning a handle. At one time frequently heard in Eng. streets.

orgue expressif (Fr.). *harmonium.

O'Riada, Seán [Reidy, John] (*b* Cork, 1931; *d* London, 1971). Irish composer. Ass. mus. dir. Radio Éireann 1954–5, mus. dir. Abbey Th., Dublin, 1955–62. Lect., Univ. Coll., Cork, 1963–71. Works incl. 2 ballets; *The Banks of Sullane*, sym. essay (1956); *Nomos No.4*, pf., orch. (1957–8); *Requiem for a Soldier*, sop., ten., bar., ch., org. (1968).

Orlando. (1) Opera in 3 acts by Handel to anon. lib. based on C. S. Capece's *L'Orlando* (1711) after Ariosto's 16th-cent. poem *Orlando furioso* (Mad Orlando). Comp. 1732. Prod. London 1733.
(2) Opera in 3 acts by Vivaldi (*Orlando furioso*) to lib. by Braccioli after Ariosto. Prod. Venice 1727.

Orlando Paladino. Opera in 3 acts by Haydn to lib. by N. Porta based on version by P. Guglielmi (1771) of Ariosto's *Orlando furioso*. Prod. Eszterháza 1782, Prague 1791, Dresden 1792.

Orloff, Vladimir (*b* Odessa, 1928). Russ.-born cellist. Prof., Vienna Acad. 1967, Toronto Univ. 1971–91. Début, Bucharest 1947. First prize Bucharest int. comp. 1947, Warsaw int. comp. 1955.

Ormandy, Eugene [Blau, Jenö] (*b* Budapest, 1899; *d* Philadelphia, 1985). Hung.-born conductor (Amer. cit. 1927). Toured Europe as child prodigy until 1914. Head of master classes, Budapest Cons. 1919. Went to USA 1921, becoming leader and, in 1924, cond. of orch. at Capitol cinema, NY. Cond. Minneapolis SO 1931–6; ass. cond. (with Stokowski) Philadelphia Orch. 1936–8, mus. dir. 1938–80. NY Met début 1950 (*Die Fledermaus*). Salzburg Fest. 1955. Hon. KBE 1976.

ornaments (Fr. *agréments*; It. *fioriture*; Ger. *Verzierungen*, *Manieren*). Embellishments and decorations of a melody as expressed through small notes or special signs. Further detail will be found under *acciaccatura, *appoggiatura, *mordent, *gruppetto, and *trill. In early vocal mus. and opera, embellishments were improvised by the singers, some of whom carried them to great lengths. In the 19th and early 20th cents. this improvised ornamentation became almost unknown (except in jazz), but since the 1950s it has been restored to some perf. of oratorios and operas, incl. (under Charles Mackerras and others) the operas of Mozart.

Ornstein, Leo (*b* Kremenchug, 1892; *d* Green Bay, Wisc., 2002). Russ.-born composer and pianist (Amer. cit.). Settled in USA 1907, studying in NY, where he made début 1911. Became leading soloist in Amer. and Europe. Introduced pf. mus. of Schoenberg to USA. Retired from public perf. in 1935 to devote time to comp. Taught in Philadelphia and founded Ornstein Sch. of Mus. (retiring 1955). His early works (c.1913) were regarded as extremely discordant and innovatory. Prin. comps. incl.: *Lysistrata Suite* for orch. (1930); *Nocturne and Dance of the Fates*, orch. (1936); vn. sonata (1917); pf. conc. (1923); *Hebraic Fantasy*, vn. and pf. (1929); 3 str. qts. (No.1, ?1940; No.2, incomplete, ?1930; No.3, 1976); vc. sonata (1916); and for pf.: *Wild Men's Dance* (1912), *Impressions of Chinatown* (1917), *Poems of 1917* (1919), 20 *Waltzes* (1955–68), *Tarantella* (1958), *Mindy's Piece* (1967), *The Deserted Garden* (1982), and 8 sonatas.

Orozco, Rafael (*b* Córdoba, 1946; *d* Rome, 1996). Sp. pianist. Won Leeds int. pf. comp. 1966. Int. career.

orpharion. Development of the *cittern very popular in Eng. in 16th and 17th cents. Had 15 frets and wire strings. Bridge was fixed and the str. ran over a small metal saddle into the bridge and were fastened to small metal pegs driven into lower side of bridge. Orig. had 6 courses but a 7th was added c.1600. Specified as alternative to lute in several books of lute tablature.

Orphée aux enfers (Offenbach). See *Orpheus in the Underworld*.

Orpheus. (1) Sym.-poem by Liszt, comp. 1853–4 as introduction to his Weimar prod. of Gluck's *Orfeo*.
   (2) Ballet in 3 scenes to mus. by Stravinsky, comp. 1947, choreog. Balanchine, prod. NY 1948, Hamburg 1962. Other versions choreog. Cranko, Georgi, and others.
   (3) Ballet in 2 acts by Henze, scenario by Edward Bond. Comp. 1978. Prod. Stuttgart 1979.

Orpheus Britannicus. The 'British Orpheus', i.e. Purcell. Title given to 2 posthumous vols. of Purcell's vocal mus. pubd. by H. Playford (1698–1702), also to vol. of his songs pubd. by J. Walsh (1735). *Britten and Pears realized and ed. 18 of these solo songs for v. and pf. and 6 duets for high and low vv. and pf. They also made a Suite of Songs for high v. and orch. and arr. 3 songs for high v. and orch.

Orpheus in the Underworld (*Orphée aux Enfers*). *Opéra-fantastique* by Offenbach to lib. by Crémieux and Halévy. Comp. in 2 acts 1858, rev. and prod. in Paris in 4-act version 1874. Prod. Paris (2-act version) 1858; NY 1861; London 1865 (adapted by Planché as *Orpheus in the Haymarket*).

Orr, Buxton (Daeblitz) (*b* Glasgow, 1924; *d* London, 1997). Scottish composer. Wrote film and th. mus. 1955–61. Cond. London Jazz Composers' Orch. 1970–80, Guildhall New Mus. Ens. from 1975. Works incl. opera *The Wager* (1961–2); *A*

Celtic Suite, str., (1968); tb. conc. (brass band) (1971); *Interplay*, jazz orch. (1973); *Ring in the New*, mus. th. (1986).

Orr, Robin [Kemsley, Robert] (*b* Brechin, 1909; *d* Cambridge, 2006.). Scottish composer, organist, and teacher. Ass. lect. in mus., Leeds Univ., 1936–8; org., St John's Coll., Cambridge, 1938–41, 1945–51; lect. in mus., Cambridge Univ. 1947–56; prof. of comp., RCM, 1950–6; prof. of mus., Glasgow Univ., 1956–65; prof. of mus., Cambridge Univ., 1965–76; chairman, Scottish Opera, 1962–76; dir., Cambridge Arts Th. 1970–6; dir., WNO 1977–83. Works incl. operas *Full Circle* (1967), *Hermiston* (1975), and *On the Razzle* (1988); 3 syms. (1965, 1971, 1978); *Sinfonietta Helvetica* (1990); *Rondo des Oiseaux*, rec. (1993); *O Gracious Light*, unacc. ch. (1999); *For Christmas: A Carol*, unacc. ch. (2001); chamber mus.; and songs. CBE 1972.

Orthel, Léon (*b* Roosendaal, 1905; *d* The Hague, 1985). Dutch composer and pianist. Teacher of pf., Royal Cons., The Hague, 1941–71, and of comp., Amsterdam Cons. 1949–71. Works incl. 6 syms. (1931–61); 2 vc. concs.; chamber mus.; and songs.

Ortiz, Cristina (*b* Bathia, Brazil, 1950). Brazilian pianist. Won 1st prize Cliburn comp. 1969. Recital début NY 1971; London début 1973; Salzburg Fest. début 1983. Settled in London 1973. Soloist with leading orchs.

O Salutaris Hostia (O saving victim). RC hymn sung at Benediction and some other services to plainsong melody or one of many comp. settings.

Osanna. It. form of 'Hosanna'.

Osborne, Charles (Thomas) (*b* Brisbane, 1927). Australian critic and writer. Ass. ed. *London Magazine* 1957–66; ass. literary dir., Arts Council 1966–71, literary dir. 1971–86. Author of books on operas of Verdi (1969), Mozart (1978), Puccini (1982), Strauss (1988), Wagner (1990), and *bel canto* composers (1994); ed. of coll. of Verdi's letters (1971), *The Dictionary of Composers* (1977), *Dictionary of Opera* (1983), and *The Opera Lover's Companion* (2004). Contrib. to many periodicals.

Osborne, George (Alexander) (*b* Limerick, 1806; *d* London, 1893). Irish pianist. Self-taught till age 18. Went to Paris 1826, becoming friend of Chopin, Berlioz, Hallé, etc. Settled as teacher in London 1843 and became dir. of Philharmonic Soc. Comp. chamber mus., pf. pieces, and 33 vn. duos in collab. with de Bériot.

Osborne, Nigel (*b* Manchester, 1948). Eng. composer. In Poland worked with live elec. mus. group. Won Swiss Radio prize 1971 with cantata *7 Words*. Lect. in mus., Nottingham Univ. 1978–90, prof. of mus., Edinburgh Univ. from 1990. Among his works are:

OPERAS: *Hell's Angels* (1985); *The *Electrification of the Soviet Union* (1986–7); *Terrible Mouth* (1992); *Sarajevo* (1993–4); *The Piano Tuner* (2004).

ORCH.: vc. conc. (1977); fl. conc. (1980); vn. conc. (1990); *Hommage à Panufnik*, str. (1993); *The Art of Fugue* (1994); ob. conc., chamber orch. (1998).

CHAMBER MUS.: *Remembering Esenin*, vc., pf. (1974); *After Night*, gui. (1977); sonata, pf. (1981); *Mbira*, vn., pf. (1985); *Zone*, ob., cl., str. trio (1989); *Sarajevo*, cl., vc., pf. (1994); str. qt. No.1 (1999); *The Piano Tuner*, pf., vn., vc. (2004).

VOICE & ENS.: *I am Goya*, bass-bar., fl., ob., vn., vc. (1977); *The Cage*, ten., ens., elec. (1981); *Pornography*, mez., ens. (1986).

CHORAL: *7 Words*, 2 ten., bass, ch. (1971); *Heaventree*, unacc. (1973); *Gnostic Passion*, unacc. (1980); *Choralis I, II, and III*, 6 vv. unacc. (1981–2); *Tracks*, 2 ch., orch., wind band (1990).

ELEC.: *Musica da Camera*, vn., tape-delay, audience (1975); *Poem Without a Hero*, sop., mez., ten., bass, elec. (1980); *The Four-Loom Weaver*, mez., tape (1985).

oscillator. That part of electrical generator which produces a repetitive waveform. The term is sometimes used to mean the whole generator.

ossia (It. *o sia*, 'it may be'). (1) Term used in the sense of 'or else' to indicate an alternative version of a mus. passage, e.g. composer's simplified alternative for a difficult section, or ed.'s emendation of composer's text where it is presumed to be wrong.
(2) Used in opera titles in the sense of 'or', e.g. *Il dissoluto punito, ossia Il Don Giovanni*.

Osten, Eva Plaschke von der (*b* Heligoland, 1881; *d* Dresden, 1936). Ger. soprano. Début Dresden 1902 as Urbain in *Les Huguenots*. Prin. sop., Dresden Opera, 1902–27. Created role of Oktavian in *Der Rosenkavalier* 1911. Was first Dresden Ariadne, Dyer's Wife (*Die Frau ohne Schatten*), and Kundry (*Parsifal*). Member Ger. Opera Co., USA, 1923–4. After retirement became prod. at Dresden. Wife of Friedrich Plaschke (1875–1951), bass-bar. at Dresden and later stage dir.

ostinato (It.). Obstinate, persistent. A persistent mus. phrase or rhythm. A basso ostinato is a figure in the bass which is persistently repeated.

Östman, Arnold (*b* Malmö, 1939). Swedish conductor. Art. dir. Vadstena Acad. 1969–79 where he cond. many baroque operas by Monteverdi, Stradella, etc. Mus. dir. Drottningholm 1979–91, staging operas by Mozart, Gluck, and others, with period instr. London début 1983 (*Il matrimonio segreto* at SW). CG début 1984; Wexford Fest. 1986.

Ostrčil, Otakar (*b* Prague, 1879; *d* Prague, 1935). Cz. composer and conductor. Chief cond. Prague Nat. Opera 1920–35. Champion of Cz. operas and of contemp. opera generally. Cond. f.p. of Janáček's *The Excursions of Mr Brouček*, Prague 1920. Comp. 7 operas, sym., sym.-poems.

Osud (Fate). Opera in 3 acts by Janáček to lib. by composer adapted by Fedora Bartošová. Comp. 1903–5, rev. 1906–7. F.p. Brno (broadcast) 1934. F. stage p. Brno (in version by V. Nosek) 1958,

orig. version České Budějovice 1978. F. public p. in Eng. (concert) London 1983. F. Eng. stage p. London (ENO) 1984.

Otaka, Tadaaki (*b* Kamakura, 1947). Japanese conductor. Teacher at Toho-Gakuen Sch. from 1970. Prin. cond. Tokyo PO 1974–81, Sapporo SO 1981–6, BBC Welsh SO (known from 1993 as BBC National Orchestra of Wales) 1987–96.

Otello (Othello). (1) Opera in 4 acts by Verdi to lib. by Boito based on Shakespeare's tragedy *Othello, the Moor of Venice* (1604–5). Comp. 1884–6. Prod. Milan 1887, NY 1888, London 1889, NY Met 1894.
(2) Opera (*Otello, ossia Il Moro di Venezia*) in 3 acts by Rossini to lib. by di Salsa. Prod. Naples 1816, London 1822, NY 1826.

ôter (Fr.). To take off. *ôtez les sourdines*, take off the mutes. In org. mus. *ôter* means to discontinue use of a stop.

Othello. Ov. for orch. Op.93, by Dvořák, comp. 1891–2 as 3rd of cycle of 3 ovs. called *Nature, Life, and Love*, the others being *Amid Nature* and *Carneval*. See also *Otello*.

ottava (It., sometimes abbreviated '8va'). Octave. Indications to play a passage an octave higher are *all'ottava* (at the octave), *ottava alta* (high octave), and *ottava sopra* (octave above). Indications to play an octave below written pitch are *ottava bassa* (low octave), and *ottava sotto* (octave below). An expression meaning 'play in octaves' is *coll' ottava* (with the octave).

ottavino (It.). Modern name for small fl., known in other countries as *piccolo*.

Otter, Anne Sofie von (*b* Stockholm, 1955). Swedish mezzo-soprano. Sang with Basle Opera 1982–5 (début as Alcina in Haydn's *Orlando paladino*). CG début 1985 (Cherubino); Amer. début (Chicago concert) 1985; NY Met 1988 (Cherubino). Salzburg Fest. début 1989. Sang Carmen at Glyndebourne 2002.

Otterloo, (Jan) **Willem van** (*b* Winterswijk, 1907; *d* Melbourne, Australia, 1978). Dutch conductor, cellist, and composer. Cellist, Utrecht SO 1932, ass. cond. 1933, chief cond. 1937–49. Cond., Residentie Orch., The Hague, 1949–73; Melbourne SO 1967–73; Sydney SO 1973–8; Düsseldorf SO 1974–7. Wrote sym., orch. suites, chamber mus., org. pieces.

Ottone. Opera in 3 acts by Handel to lib. by N. Haym adapted from Pallavicino's *Teofane* (1719). Comp. 1722. Prod. London 1723. Rev. 1723, 1726, 1734. Revived (ed. O. Hagen) Göttingen 1921, London (SW) 1971.

ottoni (It.). Brass instrs.

Our Hunting Fathers. Symphonic song-cycle for high v. and orch., Op.8, by Britten to text devised by W. H. Auden. F.p. Norwich Fest. 1936, cond. Britten. F. London p. 1937, cond. Boult.

Our Man in Havana. Opera in 3 acts by Williamson to lib. by Sidney Gilliat based on Graham Greene's novel. Comp. 1962–3. Prod. London 1963.

Ours, L' (Haydn). See *'Bear' Symphony*.

Ouseley, (Sir) **Frederick** (Arthur) **Gore** (*b* London, 1825; *d* Hereford, 1889). Eng. organist, composer, pianist, and clergyman. Child prodigy musician. Succeeded to baronetcy 1844. Ordained as clergyman 1849. Precentor, Hereford Cath., 1855. Prof. of mus., Oxford Univ. 1855–89 (instituted formal exams. for degrees of Mus.B. and Mus.D.). Founded St Michael's Coll., Tenbury, 1854, with special emphasis on church mus. Wrote oratorios, church mus., org. pieces, and an opera (1834) on Metastasio's libretto *L'Isola disabitata*. Ed. sacred works of O. Gibbons.

Ousset, Cécile (*b* Tarbes, 1936). French pianist. Gave first recital aged 5. First prize in pf. on graduation at age 14. Brit. début Edinburgh Fest. 1980. Amer. début 1984.

Ovchinikov, Vladimir (*b* Belebey, 1960). Russ. pianist. 2nd prize Montreal comp. 1980; joint silver medal (with P. *Donohoe), Tchaikovsky comp., Moscow, 1982; winner, Leeds pf. comp. 1987. London début 1987. Teacher at RNCM 1994.

overblow. To blow a woodwind instr. so hard that its notes are stepped up from basic pitch. This is usually an octave but the cl. overblows a 12th.

overstrung. When the str. of a pf. are set at two differing levels and crossing, to give greater length of str.

overtone. Any note of the harmonic series except the fundamental.

overture (from Fr. *ouverture*, opening). (1) Piece of instr. mus. which precedes opera, oratorio, or play. *Lully est. the *French overture* in a 3-movt. style of slow–fast(fugal)–slow (concluding section). The *Italian overture*, introduced by A. *Scarlatti, also had 3 movts., quick–slower–quick (see *symphony*). Gluck was the first to give ovs. a thematic connection with what followed. Weber's ovs. were orchestral synopses of the opera. But in It. opera, ovs. were still used as a way of stopping the audience talking and giving latecomers a chance to reach their seats. Thus one of Rossini's ovs. did duty for 3 of his operas (incl. *Il barbiere di Siviglia*). Wagner preferred the term *Vorspiel* (Prelude). In the 20th cent., operatic ovs. have become rare, composers often bringing up the curtain immediately. Strauss's orch. introduction to *Der Rosenkavalier* is almost an ov., as is the sextet which opens *Capriccio*. For his comic opera *Die schweigsame Frau* he wrote a *potpourri*, a medley of tunes from the opera in the style of the composers of light operas, e.g. Sullivan.
(2) Term sometimes used as equivalent of

suite (by Handel and Bach) or *symphony* (Haydn's London programmes 1791).
(3) See *concert overture*.

Overture, Scherzo, and Finale. Orch. work by Schumann, Op.52, comp. 1841, rev. 1845.

O.W., in Ger. org. mus. = *Oberwerk*, i.e. swell org.

Owen Wingrave. Opera in 2 acts by Britten, Op.85, to lib. by Myfanwy Piper based on Henry James. Comp. for BBC TV (16 May 1971) and later rev. for first stage perf. at CG 10 May 1973. Santa Fe 1973, GTO 1995.

Owl and the Pussy-Cat, The. (1) Setting for speaker, fl., vc., and guitar by *Searle (1951) of poem by Edward Lear (1870).
(2) Setting for v. and pf. by Stravinsky (1966).

Oxford Elegy, An. Work for narrator, small mixed ch., and chamber orch. by Vaughan Williams, with text adapted from Matthew Arnold's poems *The Scholar Gipsy* (1853) and *Thyrsis* (1867), comp. 1949. Some of text is spoken, some sung by ch., also wordless part for ch. F. public p. Oxford 1952.

Oxford Symphony. Nickname for Haydn's Sym. No.92 in G (Hob. I: 92) because it was perf. when Haydn received hon. doctorate at Oxford Univ. in 1791. Comp. 1789 with no thought of Oxford.

Oxford University. Eng. university which has awarded degrees in music since 1499 (B.Mus. and D.Mus.). William Heather (Heyther) founded lectureship in music in 1627, the holder of the post of choragus eventually becoming known as professor. Post of choragus re-established 1848. Professorship was long regarded as sinecure. Profs. of mus. since 1797: William Crotch (1797–1847), H. R. Bishop (1848–55), F. A. Gore Ouseley (1855–89), John Stainer (1889–1900), Hubert Parry (1900–8), Walter Parratt (1908–18), Hugh Allen (1918–46), J. A. Westrup (1947–71), Joseph Kerman (1971–4), Denis Arnold (1975–86), Brian Trowell (1988–96), Reinhard Strohm (from 1996). The Faculty of Music was created in 1944, largely thanks to Allen.

Ox Minuet (Ger. *Ochsenmenuett*). Minuet attrib. J. Haydn but comp. by his pupil I. X. von Seyfried (1776–1841) who introduced it into his opera *Das Ochsenmenuett* (1823), compiled mainly from Haydn's works. Based on legend that Haydn wrote a minuet for a butcher who gave him an ox in return.

Ozawa, Seiji (*b* Fenytien (now Shenyang), China, 1935). Japanese cond. Won int. cond. comp., Besançon, 1959. Début Tokyo, NHK Orch. Ass. cond. to Bernstein, NYPO 1961–2 and 1964–5. Cond. Ravinia Park Fest., Chicago, 1964–8; Toronto SO 1965–9; S. Francisco SO 1970–6; Boston SO 1973–2004; Vienna State Opera from 2004. London début 1965; Salzburg Fest. début 1966 with Vienna PO, opera 1969 (*Così fan tutte*, this being his opera début); CG 1974; NY Met 1992. Cond. f.p. of Messiaen's *St François d'Assise* (Paris, 1983).

P

P. Abbreviated prefix to numbers in the *Pincherle catalogue of Vivaldi's works.

p. Abbreviation of *piano* (It., soft), hence *pp*, *ppp*, and sometimes even quieter (Verdi optimistically uses *pppp* in his *Requiem*, also Elgar in *Enigma Variations*).

P. In Fr. org. mus., this abbreviation sometimes means *Pédales* (pedals) and sometimes *Positif* (choir org.).

Pachelbel, Johann (*b* Nuremberg, 1653; *d* Nuremberg, 1706). Ger. organist and composer. Deputy org., St Stephen's Cath., Vienna, 1673–6. Court org. Eisenach 1677. Org., Protestant Predigerkirche, Erfurt, 1678–90. Court org., Stuttgart, 1690–2. Org., St Sebald, Nuremberg, 1695–1706. His comps. influenced Bach. Works incl. *Hexachordum Apollinis* (1699), 6 sets of airs and variations for hpd.; 78 chorale preludes (1693), incl. *Ein' feste Burg, Nun komm der Heiden Heiland, Vom Himmel hoch*, etc.; *Aria Sebaldina*, variations in F minor for hpd.; *Canon and Gigue* in D for 3 vns. and continuo; *Chaconne and 13 variations* for hpd., etc. His church music, for long disregarded, has been highly revalued, particularly his sacred concertos and his 13 settings of the *Magnificat*.

Pachmann, Vladimir de (*b* Odessa, 1848; *d* Rome, 1933). Russ.-born pianist (It. cit. 1928). Début Odessa 1869, then retired for 8 years' further study; reappeared in public but then retired again for 2 years. From age of 32 became popular and successful recitalist, especially in mus. of Chopin. Début USA 1891. Eccentric platform-manner, often making remarks to the audience in praise of himself or in disparagement of other pianists, and crawling under the pf. after a recital to look for the wrong notes he had played!

Pacific 231. 'Mouvement symphonique' for orch. by Honegger, 1923. F.p. Paris 1924, f.p. in England, Manchester 1924. Pacific 231 is a locomotive.

Pacini, Giovanni (*b* Catania, 1796; *d* Pescia, 1867). It. composer and teacher. His first opera was unperformed, but his second was prod. in Milan in 1813. After writing nearly 50 operas, mostly comic, by 1835, abandoned stage for 5 yrs, discouraged by success of Rossini, Bellini, and Donizetti. Founded mus. sch. at Viareggio 1835; head of ducal chapter at Lucca 1837. Returned to stage with tragedy, *Saffo* (Naples 1840). Its success induced him to write another 40 operas, mostly tragic. *Maria Tudor* (1843) was revived at Camden Fest. 1983. Also wrote quantities of church mus., 6 str. qts., and a *Dante Symphony*. *Saffo* revived Wexford 1995.

Paderewski, Ignacy Jan (*b* Kuryłówka, 1860; *d* NY, 1941). Polish pianist, composer, and states-man. Pf. teacher at Warsaw Cons. 1879–83. Début Paris 1888, London 1890, NY 1891. Became one of the most famous int. pianists. Began composing at age 6. Up to 1899 he wrote mainly pf. solos, incl. the *Tatra Album* (1885), based on songs and dances of the Polish Tatra mountain-dwellers. In the 1890s he comp. a vn. sonata, the *6 Humoresques de Concert* for pf. (No.1 of which is the famous Minuet in G), a pf. conc. in A minor, and the *Polish Fantasy* for pf. and orch. His opera *Manru* (1897–1900) had its f.p. in Dresden 1901 and was given at the NY Met in 1902. In 1903 he wrote a pf. sonata, 12 songs to Fr. poems by Mendès, and a set of Variations for pf. His *Sym.*, avowedly patriotic, was completed in 1907 and f.p. Boston, Mass., 1909. In 1910 he spoke at the unveiling of a monument in Kraków and thereafter symbolized Polish aspirations. During the 1914–18 war he worked ceaselessly for the Polish cause. When Poland was created an independent nation in 1919 he became Prime Minister and Foreign Minister of the first govt. but retired a year later after disagreement with other politicians. In 1922 he resumed his recitals, raising large amounts of money for war victims. He sponsored several competitions and est. scholarships. In 1936 he appeared in a film, *Moonlight Sonata*, and in 1936–8 supervised a complete Chopin edn. pubd. in Warsaw. He died when Poland was again enslaved. Hon. GBE 1925.

padiglione (It.). Pavilion, tent. Hence, the bell of a wind instr. *padiglione cinese*, Turkish Crescent or *Jingling Johnny.

Padmâvatî. Opera-ballet in 2 acts by *Roussel to lib. by L. Laloy. Comp. 1914–18. Prod. Paris 1923, London (concert) 1969.

Padmore, Elaine (*b* Haworth, Yorks, 1945). Eng. administrator and soprano. Joined BBC as mus. prod.; chief opera prod. 1976–82. Art. dir. Wexford Fest. 1982–94, Dublin Grand Opera 1989–90, Royal Danish Opera, Copenhagen, 1993–9. Dir. of opera, CG, from 2000.

padovana (It.). See *pavan*.

paean. Song of triumph or praise (orig. to Apollo).

Paer, Ferdinando (*b* Parma, 1771; *d* Paris, 1839). It. composer. Orig. violinist but gave it up for comp. First opera prod. Parma 1791, then went as cond. to Venice where he wrote several more light operas. Worked in Vienna 1797–1802. Became Kapellmeister at Dresden 1802 and wrote *Leonora* (1804), on same plot as Beethoven was to use in *Fidelio* in 1805. In 1807 went to Paris as cond. of Opéra-Comique and *maître de chapelle* to Napoleon I. Succeeded Spontini 1812 as dir. of Théâtre-Italien. Dismissed 1827, becoming cond. of royal chamber mus. 1832. Wrote 53 operas, also oratorios, masses, cantatas, and numerous instr. works.

Paganini, Niccolò (*b* Genoa, 1782; *d* Nice, 1840). It. violinist and composer. Regarded as greatest of all vn. virtuosos. Made first tour at 13 and comp. difficult pieces for himself to play. During a love affair in 1801–4 he took up the guitar, for which he composed 6 str. qts. with a guitar part, and other works. Returned to platform 1805 with sensational success. Dir. of mus. to Princess of Lucca 1805–9. Milan début 1813, Vienna 1828, Paris and London 1831. In Paris in 1833 commissioned va. conc. from Berlioz, the result being *Harold en Italie*, but he never played it. From 1834 he made few appearances: for some years he had been suffering from cancer of the larynx which killed him in 1840. He left a fortune and was generous to colleagues in need. Owned vns. by Stradivarius, Guarnerius, and Amati, also Stradivarius va. and db. His Mephistophelean appearance led to stories that his virtuosity stemmed from diabolical powers; he was a skilled showman and although his feats as a virtuoso are no longer regarded as unique or unapproachable, he pioneered the use of harmonics, tuned his instr. to obtain special effects, used several styles of bowing, and exploited staccato and pizzicato as never before. His intonation was unfailingly accurate. Works incl.:

VN. CONCS.: No.1 in E♭ (usually played in D) (?1817), No.2 in B minor, with *Rondo à la clochette* (1826), No.3 in E major (1826), No.4 in D minor (1830), No.5 in A minor (1830), and the so-called No.6 in E minor (comp. *c*.1815) (and others lost).

VN. AND ORCH.: *Le Streghe* (Witches' Dance) based on air by Süssmayer; Variations on *God Save the King*; *Moto perpetuo, allegro de concert*; Variations on *Non più mesta* (*La Cenerentola*); Variations on the air *Di tanti palpiti* (*Tancredi*).

VC. AND ORCH.: *Variations on Theme of Rossini* for 2 vc.

SOLO VN.: *24 Caprices* (*c*.1805); Variations on *Le Carnaval de Venise*; *Duo in C*; Recitative and Variations on 3 airs for the 4th string.

CHAMBER MUSIC: 12 sonatas for vn. and guitar; 6 qts. for vn., va., guitar, and vc.; vn. sonata with vn. and vc. acc.; *Terzettos* for vn., vc., guitar; 3 str. qts. (1800–5).

Paganini Transcriptions. There are several transcrs. by other composers of Paganini comps. and several comps. based on the theme of his *Caprice* No.24 in A minor (e.g. Brahms's *Variations on a Theme of Paganini* for pf., 1862–3; Rachmaninov's *Rhapsody on a Theme of Paganini*, for pf. and orch., 1934; Blacher's *Variations on a Theme of Paganini*, for orch., 1947; Lutosławski's *Variations on a Theme of Paganini*, for 2 pf., 1941; Rochberg's *50 Caprice-Variations*, for solo vn. 1970). Schumann wrote *12 Études de Concert* based on Paganini's *Caprices* in 2 sets, Op.3, 1832, Op.10, 1833. Liszt wrote a *Grande Fantaisie de Bravoure sur la clochette* (1831–2), on a theme from vn. conc. No.2 in B minor, Op.7, and 6 *Études d'exécution transcendante d'après Paganini* (1838, rev. 1851 as *Grandes études d'après les caprices de Paganini*, No.3 being *La campanella*).

Pagliacci (Strolling players, or Clowns). Opera in prologue and 2 acts by *Leoncavallo to his own lib. Prod. Milan 1892, CG and NY 1893. Customarily perf. in double bill with *Mascagni's *Cavalleria rusticana*, the result being colloquially known as 'Cav and Pag'.

Paik, Kun Woo (*b* Seoul, 1946). Korean pianist. NY recital début 1971; London 1974.

Paine, John Knowles (*b* Portland, Maine, 1839; *d* Cambridge, Mass., 1906). Amer. composer, organist, and teacher. Became instructor in mus., Harvard Univ. 1862, ass. prof. of mus. 1873, prof. 1875–1906 (the first Amer. prof. of mus.). Pupils incl. D. G. Mason, J. A. Carpenter, and Richard Aldrich. Wrote 2 operas, 2 syms., choral works incl. Mass in D (1866–7), and chamber mus.

Paisiello, Giovanni (*b* Roccaforzata, nr. Taranto, 1740; *d* Naples, 1816). It. composer. In youth wrote mainly church mus., but discovered flair for opera buffa and wrote his first comic operas for Bologna 1764. Settled in Naples as rival of Piccinni, then of Cimarosa. Went to St Petersburg 1776 as court cond. and master of It. opera to Catherine the Great, while there composing his *Il barbiere di Siviglia* (1782) which had such great success in It. that Rossini's later setting (1816) encountered resentment. Returned to Naples 1784 as court cond. to Ferdinand IV. Sided with Napoleon in 1799 and went to Paris 1802 to organize and direct the mus. of his chapel. On return to Naples, remained out of favour with Bourbons and died in relative poverty. Wrote over 100 operas, many of them accomplished and pleasant, 12 syms., kbd. concs., comic cantatas, and other works. Prin. operas were: *Don Chisciotte* (1769); *Achille in Sciro* (1778); *La serva padrona* (1781); *Il *barbiere di Siviglia* (1782); *Il re Teodoro in Venezia* (1784); *La Molinara* (1789); *Nina* (1789); *Didone abbandonata* (1794); *Proserpina* (1803).

Palestrina. Opera (*Musikalische Legende*) in 3 acts by *Pfitzner to his own lib. Comp. 1911–15. Prod. Munich 1917, London (Abbey Opera) 1981, Berkeley (concert) 1982, CG 1997. Based on untrue legend that Palestrina comp. the *Missa Papae Marcelli* to persuade the Council of Trent not to ban polyphonic mus.

Palestrina, Giovanni Pierluigi da (*b* Palestrina, nr. Rome, *c*.1525; *d* Rome, 1594). It. composer who took his name from his birthplace. Chorister at S. Maria Maggiore, Rome, in 1537. Studied in Rome *c*.1540. Organist and choirmaster, Palestrina, 1544. In 1550 the Bishop became Pope Julius III and in 1551 summoned Palestrina to Rome as choirmaster of Cappella Giulia, a nursery for Sistine Choir. The following year Palestrina published his first book of Masses. In 1555 a new Pope, Paul IV, dismissed Palestrina and two others from the Sistine Choir because they were married. Palestrina was appointed choirmaster of St John Lateran in 1555 in succession to *Lassus. For this church he wrote his

Lamentations. He resigned in 1560 over dissatisfaction with the way the choirboys were fed, becoming choirmaster of S. Maria Maggiore in 1561. He pubd. his first book of motets 2 years later. In 1567 he resigned to enter service of Cardinal Ippolito d'Este, having become dissatisfied with the papal reforms of church mus. which rendered 2 of his masses unliturgical because they contained words foreign to the mass. In addition, others of his masses incl. secular songs, such as *L'*Homme armé*. The cardinal kept a mus. establishment at his palace in Tivoli (the Villa d'Este). In 1571 Palestrina became dir. of the Cappella Giulia. Over the next few years he lost both his sons and his wife through epidemics and decided to become a priest. But after a few weeks he changed his mind and married again, his new wife being the rich widow of a fur merchant. Palestrina formed a partnership with one of the men in the business and made a fortune which enabled him in the last 13 years of his life to publish 16 colls. of his mus.

Palestrina's mus. is marked by flowing, smooth lines and a rich beauty of sound in the way vv. are blended. He had neither the range nor the inventiveness of Byrd and Lassus, but the skill with which his sacred works are based on the secular madrigal gives his mus. special characteristics which are greatly admired. His works incl.:

MASSES: 4 for 8 vv.; 22 for 6 vv. (incl. *Missa Papae Marcelli* and *Hexachord Mass*); 39 for 4 vv. (incl. *Missa brevis*, 1570); 29 for 5 vv. (incl. *L'Homme armé*).

MOTETS: 6 for 12 vv. (incl. *Stabat Mater*); 56 for 8 vv.; 2 for 7 vv.; 34 for 6 vv.; 79 for 5 vv.; 67 for 4 vv.; 29 settings for 4 vv. from the *Song of Solomon*.

CANTIONES SACRAE: 2 for 8 vv.; 4 for 4 vv.

MAGNIFICATS: 35 on the 8 tones.

OTHER WORKS: Hymns for 4 vv.; Offertories for 5 vv.; Lamentations for 4 vv.; Psalms for 12 vv.; Litanies; Antiphon; Sacred Madrigals for 5, 4, and 3 vv.; Secular Madrigals.

Palm, Siegfried (*b* Wuppertal, 1927; *d* Frechen-Buschbell, 2005). Ger. cellist. Cellist in Lübeck municipal orch. 1945–7, NW Ger. Radio SO 1947–62, Cologne Radio SO 1962–7. Member, Harmann Qt. 1951–62. Soloist with leading orchs. from 1962. Teacher of vc. class, Cologne Nat. College of Mus. from 1962 (dir. from 1972). Dir., Deutsche Oper, Berlin, 1977–81. Salzburg Fest. début 1985. Developed cello technique to suit *avant-garde* works. Was first to play works by Penderecki, Xenakis, Zillig, Ligeti, Zimmermann, and Blacher. Penderecki wrote *Capriccio per Siegfried Palm* (1968).

Palmer, Felicity (Joan) (*b* Cheltenham, 1944). Eng. soprano, later mezzo-soprano. Sang in professional choirs, notably John Aldiss Ch. Won Kathleen Ferrier Memorial Schol. 1970. London début 1970 (Purcell's *Dioclesian*). Opera début, Kent Opera (Dido) 1971, then with ENO at Coliseum. Débuts: Amer. (Houston Opera) 1973;

Glyndebourne 1985; La Scala 1987; Salzburg Fest. 1988. Specialist in Fr. songs (notably Messiaen and Poulenc) and admired in Gluck's *Armide*. CBE 1993.

Palmer, Robert (*b* Syracuse, NY, 1915). Amer. composer. On faculty Kansas Univ. 1940–3. Teacher of comp. at Cornell Univ. 1943–80. Influenced by Quincy *Porter and Bartók. Works incl.:

ORCH.: *Concerto for Orchestra* (1940); *Symphonic Variations* (1945); sym. No.1 (1953), No.2 (1966); *Centennial Overture* (1966); pf. conc. (1968–70); *Symphonia Concertante*, 9 instr. (1972); *Organon II*, str. (1975); conc., 2 pf., 2 perc., str., brass (1984).

CHORAL: *Abraham Lincoln Walks at Midnight* (1948); *Slow, Slow, Fresh Fount* (1953); *Nabuchodonosor*, oratorio (1960–4); *Portents of Aquarius*, ch., org. (1975).

CHAMBER MUSIC: str. qts. Nos. 1–4 (1939–59); pf. sonatas No.1 (1938, rev. 1946), No.2 (1942, rev. 1948), No.3 (1979); pf. qt. No.1 (1947), No.2 (1974); pf. quintet (1950); va. sonata (1951); wind quintet (1951); cl. quintet (1952); pf. trio (1958); 2 vc. sonatas (1976, 1983).

Palmgren, Selim (*b* Pori, 1878; *d* Helsinki, 1951). Finn. composer, pianist, and conductor. Held cond. posts in Finland 1902–12. Toured USA 1921 as acc. to his wife, who sang his songs. Taught at Eastman Sch. 1923–6. Prof. of harmony, Sibelius Acad., Helsinki, 1936–51. Wrote 2 operas, 5 pf. concs. (1903–41), songs, and many short pf. pieces.

palotache (*palotás*). Hung. type of instr. piece in dance style (2 beats to the measure), derivative of the *verbunkos*.

Pammelia (from Gk., all honey). First coll. of vocal rounds, catches, and canons pubd. in Eng. (by T. Ravenscroft, 1609, 2nd edn. 1618). Part 2 (*Deuteromelia*) pubd. 1609. No composers' names given.

pandiatonicism. Term coined by Amer. musicologist *Slonimsky to describe the free use in chord-formation of the 7 degrees of the *diatonic scale, e.g. the added 6th in jazz.

pandora, pandore. See *cittern*.

pandorina. Small type of wire-strung lute.

Panerai, Rolando (*b* Campi Bisenzio, 1924). It. baritone. Début Florence 1946 (Enrico in *Lucia di Lammermoor*). Naples Opera 1947–8; La Scala début 1952. Created Ruprecht in stage première of *The *Fiery Angel*, Venice 1955. Sang title-role in It. première of *Mathis der Maler*, 1957. Salzburg Fest. début 1957; CG début 1960. Amer. début (S. Francisco) 1958.

panharmonicon. Mechanical orch. invented by *Maelzel in 1805. Beethoven wrote his *Battle Symphony* (1813) for it.

Panizza, Ettore (*b* Buenos Aires, 1875; *d* Milan, 1967). Argentinian conductor of It. descent. Début Rome 1899. Cond. at CG, 1907–14, 1924. Ass.

cond. to Toscanini at La Scala, 1921–9. Cond., La Scala, 1930–2, 1946–8; NY Met 1934–42; Colón, Buenos Aires, 1921–67. Wrote 4 operas, ed. Berlioz's treatise on orchestration (1913). Cond. f.p. of d'Erlanger's *Tess* (CG 1909).

Pannain, Guido (*b* Naples, 1891; *d* Naples, 1977). It. musicologist, author, and composer. Prof. of mus. history, Naples Cons. 1915–61. Wrote 3 operas, 2 vn. concs., va. conc., pf. conc., hp. conc., *Requiem, Stabat Mater,* and other works, but best-known for historical books. Wrote *Modern Composers*, pubd. in Eng. 1932. Mus. critic for various journals 1920–57.

pan-pipes (Pandean Pipes, Syrinx). Instr. of classical antiquity, ancestor of the fl. Series (4 to 12 or more) of short vertical pipes of wood, cane, or pottery fixed side by side and graduated in length to give the pitches of the different notes. The player blows across the open ends. The ancient Greeks credited the god Pan with its invention. Used by Papageno in Mozart's *Die Zauberflöte*.

Pantaleon. (1) Large dulcimer invented by Pantaleon Hebenstreit (1667–1750).
   (2) Term used by Ger. writers in late 18th cent. to describe a small square piano.

pantomime (from Gk., 'all imitating'). (1) Play in which artists use dumb show.
   (2) Mimed episode in larger work, e.g. in Ravel's ballet *Daphnis et Chloé* when story of Pan and Syrinx is mimed.
   (3) Type of Eng. stage show usually presented at the Christmas period, loosely based on a fairy-story, containing songs, and in former times concluding with harlequinade.

pantonality. Term coined by R. *Réti in 1958 to describe extension of tonality in late 19th cent., as developed by Debussy, Wagner, and others, whereby the mus. cannot be said to be 'in' a key but moves in and out of discernible key centres without becoming atonal. Thus it applies to mus. by Bartók, Hindemith, Stravinsky, and others.

pantoum (Fr., from Malay *pantum*). Type of verse quatrain of Malayan origin adapted in Fr. verse by 18th-cent poet Evariste Parny and by Victor Hugo. The term was used by Ravel to describe 2nd movt. (scherzo) of his pf. trio (1914).

Panufnik, (Sir) **Andrzej** (*b* Warsaw, 1914; *d* Twickenham, 1991). Polish-born composer and conductor (Brit. cit. 1961). Cond. Kraków PO 1945–6, Warsaw PO 1946–7. Guest cond. leading orchs. Left Poland in protest against political regimentation 1954, settling in Eng. Cond. CBSO 1957–9, resigning to concentrate on comp. His mus. has extraordinary intensity and power. His works up to 1944 were destroyed during the Warsaw uprising of that year. Some of the 'revisions' of pre–1944 works are reconstructions. Knighted 1991. Prin. comps.:

BALLET: *Miss Julie* (Stuttgart 1970).

ORCH.: syms: *Sinfonia Rustica* (1948, rev. 1955), *Sinfonia Elegiaca* (1957, rev. 1966), *Sinfonia Sacra* (1963), *Sinfonia di Sfere* (1975), *Sinfonia Mistica* (1977), *Sinfonia Votiva* (1981, rev. 1984), sym. No.9 (1986); sym. No.10 (1988, rev. 1990); *Tragic Overture* (1942, rev. 1945, 1955); *Lullaby*, 29 str., 2 hp. (1947, rev. 1955); *Nocturne* (1947, rev. 1955); *Heroic Overture* (1952, rev. 1969); *Rhapsody* (1956); *Polonia* (1959); *Autumn Music*, chamber orch. (1962, rev. 1965); pf. conc. (1962, rev. 1970, recomposed 1972, 1982); *Landscape*, str. (1962, rev. 1965); *2 Lyric Pieces* (1963); *Hommage à Chopin*, fl., str. (orch. 1966); *Katyń Epitaph* (1967, rev. 1969); vn. conc., with str. (1971); *Sinfonia Concertante*, fl., hp., str. (1973); *Metasinfonia*, org., timp., str. (1978); *Concerto Festivo* (1979); Concertino, timp., perc., str. (1979–80); *A Procession for Peace* (1982–3); *Arbor Cosmica*, str. (1983); bn. conc. (1985); *Harmony*, chamber orch. (1989).

VOCAL: *5 Polish Peasant Songs*, sop., fls., cls. (1940, rev. 1945, 1959); *Hommage à Chopin*, sop., pf. (1949, rev. 1955, orch. version 1966); *Song to the Virgin Mary*, unacc. ch. (1964), arr. str. sextet (1987); *Universal Prayer*, sop., cont., ten., bass., ch., 3 hp., org. (1968–9); *Thames Pageant*, cantata (1969); *Invocation for Peace*, trebles, 2 tpt., 2 tb. (1972); *Winter Solstice*, sop., bar., ch., brass, timp. (1972); *Dreamscape*, v., pf. (1977).

CHAMBER MUSIC: pf. trio (1934, rev. 1945, 1977); *Triangles*, 3 fls., 3 vc. (1972); *Prelude and Transformations*, str. qt. No.1 (1976), No.2, *Messages* (1980), No.3 *Wycinanki* (1990); str. sextet, *Trains of Thought* (1987).

PIANO: *12 Miniature Studies* (1947, rev. 1955, 1964); *Reflections* (1968); *Pentasonata* (1984).

Panzéra, Charles (*b* Hyères, 1896; *d* Paris, 1976). Swiss baritone. Opera début Opéra-Comique 1919 as Albert in *Werther*. Later was celebrated Pelléas. Noted recitalist and interpreter of Fr. song. Prof. of singing, Paris Cons., 1949. Also taught at Juilliard Sch. Author of *L'Art de chanter* (1945).

Papaïoannou, Yannis (Andreou) (*b* Cavala, Greece, 1911; *d* Athens, 1989). Gr. composer. Primarily self-taught as comp., but had lessons from Honegger in Paris 1939. Taught comp. Hellenic Cons. 1954. Pioneer in Gr. of *avant-garde* resources. Adopted total-serial methods in his syms. from 1963 and also used other techniques. Influenced by tribal mus. and Byzantine chant. Works incl. 5 syms. (1946–64); pf. conc.; conc. for orch.; *Hellas*, symphonic poem after Shelley; str. qt.; pf. sonata; guitar suite; ob. qt.; and cantatas to texts by C. Cavafy.

Pape, René (*b* Dresden, 1964). Ger. bass. Sang in Dresden Kreuzchor and studied at Carl Maria von Weber High Sch. for Mus. Prof. début (while student) 1988 (Speaker in *Die Zauberflöte*). Berlin Staatsoper from 1988, roles incl. Sarastro, Rocco, Hunding, and King Mark. Débuts: Salzburg Fest. 1990 (Sarastro); La Scala 1991 (Sarastro), NY Met 1992 (in Seville), 1995 (in NY), Bayreuth 1994 (Fasolt), Vienna 1996, CG 1997, San Francisco 2001, Glyndebourne 2003. Sang his first Boris, Berlin 2005.

Papillons (Butterflies). 12 short dance pieces for pf. solo, Op.2, by Schumann, comp. 1829–31, inspired by masked-ball scene at end of Jean-Paul Richter's *Flegeljahre* (Age of Indiscretion). Also title given to hpd. piece by F. Couperin and pf. piece by Grieg (Op.43 No.1, 1884).

Pappano, Antonio (*b* London, 1959). Eng. conductor and pianist. Studied pf., comp., and cond. in USA. Répétiteur in opera houses in NY, Chicago, Barcelona, and at Bayreuth as ass. to Barenboim. Opera début Oslo 1987 (*La bohème*). Mus. dir. Norske Opera, Oslo, 1990–2. CG début 1990 (*La bohème*). Mus. dir. Théâtre de la Monnaie, Brussels, 1992–9. Vienna début 1993 (*Siegfried*), NY Met 1997 (*Eugene Onegin*), Bayreuth 1999 (*Lohengrin*). Mus. dir. Royal Opera, CG (youngest to hold post), from 1999, mus. dir. Accademia Nazionale di S. Cecilia, Rome, from 2005. Guest cond. of many orchs. Pf. accomp. to singers worldwide.

Parade. 'Ballet réaliste' in 1 act with mus. by *Satie to lib. by Cocteau, choreog. Massine, décor Picasso. Prod. Paris 1917 (Diaghilev's Ballet Russe, cast incl. Lopokova and Massine).

Paradis, Maria Theresia von (*b* Vienna, 1759; *d* Vienna, 1824). Austrian pianist, blind from childhood, also org., composer, and singer. Visited most European capitals, incl. London. Mozart's pf. conc. in B♭ major (K456, 1784) was written for her. She comp. in a specially devised notation and founded a mus. sch. for girls.

Paradise and the Peri (*Das Paradies und die Peri*). Part 2 of T. Moore's poem *Lalla Rookh* (1817), the Peri being a benign spirit in Persian mythology seeking re-admission to Paradise. 3 comps. based on it, by (1) Schumann, Op.50, cantata for soloists, ch., and orch., based on free trans., f.p. Leipzig 1843.
  (2) Sterndale Bennett, fantasy-ov., Op.42, comp. 1862.
  (3) J. F. Barnett, cantata for soloists, ch., and orch., 1870.

Paradise Lost. (1) Opera in 2 acts by *Penderecki to lib. by Christopher Fry adapted from Milton's poem (1658–64, pubd. 1667). Comp. 1976–8. Prod. Chicago, 1978, Stuttgart 1979.
  (2) Dramatic cantata by Christopher Steel, Op.34, for sop., ten., and bass soloists, ch., and orch. Comp. 1966. F. public p. Gloucester Fest. 1974.

parameter. Orig. mathematical term, in musical connotation refers to 'dimension' of a sound, its pitch, loudness, duration, rhythm, and (controversially) timbre.

paraphrase. (1) Compositional process in polyphonic works of 15th and 16th cent., involving quotation in one or more vv. of a plainchant melody, usually one that has been altered rhythmically or melodically.
  (2) In 19th cent., term applied to works based on existing melodies or comps., especially as a vehicle for virtuosity. Thus, Liszt's many 'paraphrases' for pf. of arias from It. operas.

  (3) Scottish paraphrases are metrical versions of scriptural passages sung to psalm tunes in the Church of Scotland.

Paraphrases. Collection of pf. duets (24 variations and 14 other pieces) based on *Chopsticks, by Borodin, Rimsky-Korsakov, and others incl. Liszt.

Paray, Paul [Charles, M. A.] (*b* Le Tréport, 1886; *d* Monte Carlo, 1979). Fr. conductor and composer. Won *Prix de Rome*. Ass. cond. Lamoureux Orch. from 1920, prin. cond. from 1923. Cond. Monte Carlo Orch. 1928–32, Orch. of Concerts Colonne, Paris, 1932–40 and 1944–52. Amer. début 1939. Mus. dir. Detroit SO 1952–63. Last appearance as cond., Curtis Inst. 1978. Wrote syms., ballet, *Mass for the 500th Anniversary of the Death of Jeanne d'Arc* (1931), str. qt., etc.

pardessus de viole. Type of *viol, smaller than the treble, with 5 strings.

Parepa-Rosa, Euphrosyne (*b* Edinburgh, 1836; *d* London, 1874). Scottish soprano. Début Malta 1855 as Amina in *La sonnambula*. London début at Lyceum Th. 1857 (Elvira in *I Puritani*). Sang at CG and Her Majesty's 1859–65 and in Handel fests. 1862 and 1865. Toured USA 1865 with Carl Rosa, whom she married 1867, when they formed Parepa-Rosa Grand English Opera Co. Had range of 2 octaves. Prin. sop. Carl Rosa Opera Co. Career in oratorio also.

Parergon (Gr., 'supplementary work'). Term used by R. Strauss in title of his *Parergon zur Symphonia Domestica*, Op.73, for pf. (L.H.) and orch., 1925, comp. for Paul Wittgenstein and using theme from earlier *Symphonia Domestica.

Paride ed Elena (Paris and Helen). Opera in 5 acts by Gluck to lib. by Calzabigi. Prod. Vienna 1770, Manchester (RMCM) 1963 (in Eng. trans. by Arthur Jacobs).

Paris Conservatoire de Musique. Free sch. of mus. est. in Paris 1795 incorporating 2 previous schs. Among dirs. have been Sarrette, Cherubini, Auber, Thomas, Dubois, Fauré, and Rabaud. For its distinguished teachers and pupils, see this dictionary *passim*. Since 1911 has been in rue de Madrid.

Paris Opéra. French opera house, its official title being *Académie de Musique, Paris*. Opened 1671. Controlled by *Lully 1672–87. Destroyed by fire 1763, also the next building 1781. In 1794 moved to rue de Richelieu as Théâtre des Arts, then to rue Favart 1821 and to rue Lepeletier 1822. Great period in its history followed, with operas by Meyerbeer, Auber, and Hérold and commissioned works from Rossini (*Guillaume Tell*), Verdi (*Don Carlos* and *Les Vêpres siciliennes*). New th. opened 1875, commonly known as Salle Garnier (after its architect). Accommodates 2,600 people and has large stage (100' wide and 112' deep). With opening of Opéra Bastille in 1990, the Paris Opéra is now used both for opera and ballet. See also *Paris, Opéra-Comique*.

Paris, Opéra-Comique. Opera house in Paris, orig. housing Fr. mus. works with spoken dialogue. It has had a chequered history: opened 1715, closed 1745, reopened 1752. Moved to the rue Favart 1782 (still sometimes being known as the *Salle Favart. Closed 1801, amalgamated with a rival co. Works by Méhul, Boïeldieu, and Auber were produced there in the first half of the 19th cent. as well as *La Fille du régiment* (1840). Later, *Les contes d'Hoffmann*, *Lakmé*, and several operas by Massenet, incl. *Manon* and *Cendrillon*, had their f.ps. there. The building was burned down in 1887, the co. finding haven elsewhere until 1898 when the present th. opened. *Pelléas et Mélisande* was given its f.p. in the new th. in 1902. In 1959 administration of the Opéra-Comique and the Paris Opéra was merged under A. M. Julien, succeeded 1962 by *Auric, 1969–71 by Nicoly. The th. closed in 1972 and reopened 1973 as *Opéra Studio de Paris* under dir. of Louis Erlo. Opéra Studio moved to Lyons 1976, and Opéra-Comique, dir. by R. Liebermann, 1973–80, opened with old name of Salle Favart.

Paris, Orchestre de. Fr. sym. orch. founded in 1967 when the Orchestra de la Société des Concerts du Conservatoire (founded in 1828) was disbanded. Conds.: Munch (1967–8); Karajan (1969–71); Solti (1972–5); Barenboim (1975–88); Bychkov (1989–98); Dohnányi (1998–2000); Eschenbach (from 2000).

Paris Symphonies (Haydn). Set of 6 syms. by Joseph Haydn, Nos. 82–87 (Hob. I:82–7), comp. 1785–6 and commissioned by Comte d'Ogny, one of backers of a Masonic Parisian concert society, 'Le Concert de la Loge Olympique'. F.ps., Paris 1787. The works are: No.82 in C, *L'Ours* (The *Bear); No.83 in G minor, *La *Poule* (The Hen); No.84 in E♭; No.85 in B♭, *La *Reine* (The Queen); No.86 in D; No.87 in A. Haydn's next 5 syms., Nos. 88–92, were also written for Paris.

Paris Symphony. Nickname of Mozart's sym. No.31 in D (K297), comp. in Paris, 1778, where it was f.p. at the Concert Spirituel on Corpus Christi Day, 18 June 1778.

Paris: The Song of a Great City. Nocturne for orch. by Delius, 1899. F.p. Elberfeld 1901 cond. *Haym, Liverpool and London 1908, cond. Beecham. Used for ballet by F. Ashton, SW 1936 (Fonteyn and Helpmann).

Parker, Charlie [Christopher jr., Charles] (*b* Kansas City, 1920; *d* NY, 1955). Amer. jazz alto and tenor saxophonist and composer, known as Bird or Yardbird. Became full-time professional musician on leaving school in 1935. Worked mainly in Kansas City 1935–9 with blues and jazz groups. First visited NY 1939. Joined Earl Hines's band 1942 and Billy Eckstine band 1944. Led own group 1945, worked with Dizzy Gillespie (trumpeter) and began to make recordings. In 1946 worked in Los Angeles, returning to NY 1947. His greatest period was 1947–51, when he made over half his surviving records and visited

Europe three times. His last years were shadowed by drug addiction and alcoholism. Parker was one of the most influential figures in jazz and a leader in the development of bop in the 1940s. His outstanding achievement was his improvisation.

Parker, Horatio (William) (*b* Auburndale, Mass., 1863; *d* Cedarhurst, NY, 1919). Amer. composer, organist, and teacher. Held org. posts in NY, and taught at Nat. Cons. when Dvořák was dir. Org. and mus. dir. Trinity Church, Boston, 1893–1902. Prof. of mus., Yale Univ., 1894–1919 (dean from 1904). Taught *Ives. His oratorio *Hora Novissima* (1893) was the first work by an Amer. to be perf. at a 3 Choirs Fest. (Worcester 1899). His *Wanderer's Psalm* was perf. Hereford 1900, Part 3 of *Legend of St Christopher* at Worcester 1902, complete work Bristol 1902. Also wrote 2 operas (*Mona*, 1910, won NY Met prize and was prod. there 1912), sym., sym.-poem, org. conc., chamber mus., ch. works, org. pieces, and songs.

parlando, parlante (It.). Speaking (also **parlato**, spoken). (1) In vocal mus., a directive for the tone of the v. to approximate to speech.

(2) In instr. mus., it calls for an expressive freedom greater than is implied by *cantabile*.

Parma, Ildebrando da. See *Pizzetti, Ildebrando*.

parody. The only true use of the term applies to the 18th- and 19th-cent. parodies of the popular or most talked-about operas of the day, e.g. that of Wagner's *Tristan* prod. in Munich 1865 and called *Tristanderl und Süssholde*. Examples of parodies of one composer by another or of a type of composition are to be found in Bartók's *Concerto for Orchestra* (where Shostakovich is the target), Britten's *A Midsummer Night's Dream* (Italian 19th-cent. opera), and Walton's *The Bear* (various).

Parody Mass (Lat. *Missa parodia*). Misleading term for a 15th- and 16th-cent. Mass which incorporated material derived from a motet, *chanson*, or madrigal. There was nothing of 'parody' about this practice, merely the use of already existing material.

Paroles tissées (Woven words). Work for ten. and 20 solo instr. by *Lutosławski, comp. 1965. Text by Jean-François Chabrun. Commissioned and first sung by Peter *Pears.

Parratt, (Sir) **Walter** (*b* Huddersfield, 1841; *d* Windsor, 1924). Eng. organist and composer. Pupil of his father Thomas, who was org. Huddersfield parish ch. 1812–62. Held org. post at age of 11. Org., Great Witley, Worcs., 1864–8, Wigan 1868–72, Magdalen Coll., Oxford, 1872–82, St George's Chapel, Windsor, 1882–1924. Prof. of org. RCM 1883–1923. Prof. of mus., Oxford Univ., 1908–18, dean of mus., London Univ. from 1916. Master of the Queen's (King's) Mus. 1893–1924. Bach specialist. Some comps. Knighted 1892, KCVO 1921.

Parrott, Andrew (*b* Walsall, 1947). Eng. conductor. Began cond. at Oxford; dir. mus. Merton Coll. and research into perf. practice of 16th- and 17th-cent. mus. Founded Taverner Choir 1973 and later Taverner Consort and Players. Prom. début 1977 with Monteverdi Vespers, RFH 1979. Gave f.p. in London of Bach's Mass in B minor with period instr.; also perfs. of *St Matthew Passion* and *Brandenburg* concs. with authentic instr. Has cond. ECO, London Bach Orch., and Concerto Amsterdam. Assoc. with Tippett and recorded his mus. for *The Tempest*, 1983. Salzburg Fest. début 1987. Cond. f.p. Weir's *A Night at the Chinese Opera*, Cheltenham 1987. Art. dir. Kent Opera 1989. CG début 1993. Mus. dir. London Mozart Players from 2000. Wrote *New Oxford Book of Carols* (co-ed., 1992); *The Essential Bach Choir* (2000, trans. Ger. 2003).

Parrott, (Horace) **Ian** (*b* London, 1916). Eng. composer and teacher. Lect., Birmingham Univ. 1947–50; prof. of mus., Univ. Coll., Aberystwyth, 1950–83. Author of books on orchestration, Elgar, and Cyril Scott's pf. music. Comp. operas (incl. *The Black Ram*, 1951–3); 3 syms.; sym.-poem *Alamein*; pf. conc.; cor anglais conc.; ob. qt.; pf. trio; choral works; etc.

Parry, (Sir) (Charles) **Hubert** (Hastings) (*b* Bournemouth, 1848; *d* Rustington, Sussex, 1918). Eng. composer, teacher, and writer. Studied Oxford Univ. (co-founder of Mus. Club) with Sterndale Bennett and Macfarren. Entered business 1871 but 3 years later gave it up for mus. Studied pf. with E. Dannreuther, who introduced his pf. conc., 1880. His choral works, especially *Blest Pair of Sirens* (1887), est. him, with Stanford, in the forefront of Brit. composers at a time when Brahms and Bach were the admired models. He wrote prolifically in several genres (composing an unprod. opera, *Guenever* 1885–6), and exerted a beneficial influence on Eng. mus. through his educational work. He joined staff of RCM 1883, becoming dir. 1894 until death. Prof. of mus., Oxford Univ. 1900–8. His *Songs of Farewell* are masterpieces of *a cappella* writing and his settings of English poetry, in the sets known as the *English Lyrics*, are extremely felicitous. In 1916 he wrote the unison setting of Blake's 'Jerusalem' which has become a nat. song like Elgar's 'Land of Hope and Glory'. The scorn poured on Parry's choral works by Bernard Shaw put them into critical purdah for many years, but the best of them are re-emerging, to be regarded with delighted surprise, notably *The Soul's Ransom* and the *Nativity Ode*. His chamber music, too, amply rewards exploration. Wrote several books, among them *Studies of the Great Composers* (1886), *The Evolution of the Art of Music* (1896), *Style in Musical Art* (1911), *J. S. Bach* (1909). Knighted 1898, baronet 1903. Prin. comps.:

OPERA: *Guenever* (1885–6, rev. 1886).

INCIDENTAL MUSIC: *The Birds* (1883, rev. 1903); *The Frogs* (1891, rev. 1909); *Hypatia* (1893); *Agamemnon* (1900); *The Clouds* (1905); *The Acharnians* (1914).

ORCH.: syms. No.1 in G (1880–2), No.2 in F ('Cambridge') (1882–3, rev. 1887, 1895), No.3 in C ('English') (1887–9, rev. 1895, 1902), No.4 in E

minor (1888–9, 2nd version 1909–10, rev. 1916), No.5 in B minor ('1912', orig. *Symphonic Fantasia*) (1912); *Allegretto scherzando* in E♭ (1867); *Intermezzo religioso* (1868); *Concertstück* in G minor (1877); pf. conc. in F♯ (1878–80, rev. 1895); *Suite Moderne* (1886, rev. 1892); *Suite* for str. in E minor (1892); *Overture to an Unwritten Tragedy* (1893, rev. 1897, 1905); *Lady Radnor's Suite*, str. (1894); *Symphonic Variations* (1897); *Elegy for Brahms* (1897); *From Death to Life*, sym.-poem (1914); *An English Suite*, str. (1890–1918).

ORATORIOS & SACRED: *Magnificat and Nunc Dimittis* in A (1864); *Te Deum* in E♭ (1873); *Judith*, SATB soloists, ch., orch. (1888); *Ode on St Cecilia's Day*, sop., bass, ch., org. (1889); *Job*, sop., ten., 2 basses, ch., orch. (1892); *King Saul*, SATB soloists, ch., orch. (1894); *Te Deum* (1900); *The Love that casteth out fear*, ch., orch. (1904); *The Soul's Ransom*, sinfonia sacra, sop., bass, ch., orch. (1906); *Te Deum* in D (Coronation) (1911); *Ode on the Nativity*, sop., ch., orch. (1912).

MOTETS & ANTHEMS: *De Profundis*, sop., 12 vv., orch. (1891); *Crossing the Bar* (1903); *Voces clamantium*, sop., bass, ch., orch. (1903); *Beyond these voices there is peace*, sop., bass, ch., orch. (1908); *Songs of Farewell* (*My soul, there is a country*, 1916, *I know my soul hath power*, 1916, *Never weatherbeaten sail*, 1916, *There is an old belief*, 1916, *At the round earth's imagin'd corners*, 1917, *Lord, let me know mine end*, 1918); *I Was Glad*, with processional music (1902, Coronation).

SECULAR CHORAL: *Scenes from Shelley's* *Prometheus Unbound*, cont., ten., bass, ch., orch. (1880, rev. 1881, 1885); *The Glories of Our Blood and State*, ch., orch. (1883, rev. 1908, 1914); *Blest Pair of Sirens*, ch., orch. (1887); *L'Allegro ed Il Penseroso*, sop., bass, ch., orch. (1890, rev. 1909); *The Lotos-Eaters*, sop., ch., orch. (1892); *Invocation to Music*, sop., ten., bass, ch., orch. (1895); *Ode to Music*, sop., ten., bass, ch., orch. (1901); *War and Peace*, SATB soloists, ch., orch. (1903); *The Pied Piper of Hamelin*, ten., bass, ch., orch. (1905, rev. 1910); *The Vision of Life*, sop., bass, ch., orch. (1907, rev. 1914); *The Chivalry of the Sea*, ch., orch. (1916); *England*, unison song (1916); *Jerusalem*, choral song, unison vv., orch. (1916).

CHAMBER MUSIC: nonet in B♭ for wind (1877); str. quintet in E♭ (1884, rev. 1896, 1902); pf. qt. in A♭ (1879); str. qts., No.1 in G minor (1867), No.2 in C minor (1868), No.3 in G (1878–80); pf. trios, No.1 in E minor (1877–8), No.2 in B minor (1884), No.3 in G (1884–90); 3 *Movements*, vn., pf. (1863); 2 *Duettinos*, vc., pf. (1868); *Romance in D*, vn. (1866–8); *Allegretto pastorale* in G, vn., pf. (1870); 6 *Freundschaftslieder*, vn., pf. (1872); *Fantasie-sonata* in B minor, vn., pf. (1878); vc. sonata in A (1879); *Partita in D minor*, vn., pf. (1877–86); vn. sonata in D minor (1875); *12 Short Pieces*, vn., pf. (1895); *Suite in D*, vn., pf. (1907); *Suite in F*, vn., pf. (1907).

PIANO: *Andante* in C (1867); *Sonnets and Songs Without Words*, Set I (1868), II (1867–75), III (1870–7); 7 *Charakterbilder* (1872); *Variations on an Air by Bach* (1873–5); sonatas, No.1 in F (1877), No.2 in A (1876–7); *Theme and 19 Variations* in D minor (1878); *10 Shulbrede Tunes* (1914); Suite, *Hands Across the Centuries* (1918).

SONGS: Over 40 part-songs (1864–1918); over 100 songs for v. and pf., 74 of them in 12 sets of *English Lyrics*.

Parry, John (*b* Bryn Cynan, *c.*1710; *d* Ruabon, 1782). Welsh harpist. Although blind, became most distinguished player of his time in Brit. From 1734 to death was in service of Williams Wynn family at Wynnstay, Ruabon. His playing impressed Handel, and the Prince of Wales (later George III) became his patron. After he had played at Cambridge 1757, the poet Thomas Gray was inspired to complete his ode *The Bard*. Composed for the hp. and the gui. In collab. with Evan Williams, another harpist, pubd. first coll. of Welsh melodies (1742), later adding two more coll. under his own name. These contributed to the popularity of the hp. melody in the late 18th cent.

Parry, Joseph (*b* Merthyr Tydfil, 1841; *d* Penarth, 1903). Welsh composer. Prof. of mus., Univ. Coll., Aberystwyth 1873–9, ran private mus. sch. in Swansea 1881–8, and became lect. in mus. at Univ. Coll. of S. Wales and Monmouthshire, Cardiff, 1888–1903. Wrote 7 operas, 3 oratorios, cantatas, and hymn-tunes, incl. the superb *Aberystwyth* (1877), to which are usually sung the words 'Jesu, Lover of my Soul'. Tune appeared in *Ail Lyfr Tonau ac Emynau*, 1879.

Parsifal. Sacred fest. drama (*Bühnenweihfestspiel*) in 3 acts by Wagner to his own lib. His last opera, composed 1877–82, f.p. Bayreuth 1882 cond. Levi, NY Met 1903, CG 1914. (Concert perfs., London 1884, NY 1886.) Wagner wanted *Parsifal* to be perf. nowhere but at Bayreuth, and the Bayreuth Fest. had a copyright on the work until 31 Dec. 1913. Nevertheless this was infringed by the NY Met and in Zurich in 1903 and by perfs. in Boston, Mass., and other Amer. cities 1904–5, in Amsterdam 1905, and in Buenos Aires and Rio 1913.

Parsley, Osbert (*b* 1511; *d* Norwich, 1585). Eng. composer and singer. Singer in Norwich Cath. choir for over 50 years, according to tablet there in his memory. Wrote church mus. for Eng. and Latin rites, incl. two 4-part morning services, *Magnificat* and *Nunc Dimittis*, and anthem. Also wrote for viols.

Parsons, Geoffrey (Penwill) (*b* Sydney, NSW, 1929; *d* London, 1995). Australian pianist and accompanist. Toured Australia with Essie Ackland 1948 and with Peter *Dawson 1949. Went to London 1950 as acc. to Dawson and settled there. World tours as acc. to leading singers, e.g. Janet Baker, Nicolai Gedda, Elisabeth Schwarzkopf, Hans Hotter, Jessye Norman, and Thomas Hampson. Salzburg Fest. début 1977. OBE 1977.

part (Fr. *partie* or *voix*; Ger. *Part* or *Stimme*; It. *parte* or *voce*). (1) The mus. from which a particular perf. or singer in an ens. works, e.g. bass part, ob. part. One speaks of 'score and parts', to denote the full score (containing all the parts) and the individual parts.

(2) Individual line of notes to be perf. by any instr. or v., or group of instrs. or vv., thus, Fugue in 4 parts, etc.

(3) A division of a large comp., e.g. Part I of *The Dream of Gerontius*. See also *colla parte*.

Pärt, Arvo (*b* Paide, 1935). Estonian composer. Worked for Estonian radio 1958–67. Emigrated in 1980, settling in (West) Berlin 1982. Early works influenced by Shostakovich, but later adopted strict serialism and eventually collages and minimalism. Works incl.:

ORCH.: syms.: No.1 (1963), No.2 (1966), No.3 (1971); *Nekrolog* (1960); *Perpetuum mobile* (1963); *Pro et Contra*, vc. conc. (1966); *Credo*, pf., ch., orch. (1968); *If Bach had kept bees (Wenn Bach Bienen gezüchtet hätte)*, 2 versions, hpd., elec. (1978), hpd., 20 str. (1980); *Tabula rasa*, double conc., 2 vn. (or vn. and va.), str., prepared pf. (1977); *Fratres*, str., perc. (1977, rev. 1991), vn., str. (1977, rev. 1991) (see also ENSEMBLE and CHAMBER MUSIC); *Summa*, str. (1980–91) (see also CHORAL and CHAMBER MUSIC); *Cantus in memory of Benjamin Britten*, str., bell (1980); *Festina lente*, str., opt. hp. (1988, rev. 1990); *Silouan's Song (My Soul yearns after the Lord . . .)*, str. (1991); *Trisagion*, str. (1992, rev. 1994); *Mein Weg*, 14 str. (1999); *Orient & Occident*, str. (2000); *Lamentate*, pf., orch. (2002).

CHORAL: *Cantate Domino Canticum Novum* (Ps. 95), vv., instr. (1977–91); *Missa syllabica*, vv., instr. (1977–91); *De profundis*, male ch., perc. (opt.), org. (1980); *Summa*, unacc. ch. or 4 soloists (1980–90) (see also ORCH. and CHAMBER MUS.); *St John Passion*, ten., bass, vocal qt., ch., ob., bn., vn., vc., org. (1982); *By the Waters of Babylon*, ch., instr. (1984), with org. (1991); *Te Deum*, 3 ch., pf., tape, str. (1984–5, rev. 1986); *7 Magnificat Antiphons*, unacc. ch. (1988, rev. 1991); *Magnificat*, unacc. ch. (1989); *Nun eile ich zu euch*, unacc. ch. or soloists (1989); *Miserere*, 5 soloists, ch., ens., org. (1989, rev. 1990); *Mother of God and Virgin*, unacc. ch. (1990); *Beatus Petronius*, 2 ch., 2 org. (1990); *Statuit ei Dominus*, 2 ch., 2 org. (1990); *The Beatitudes*, ch. or soloists, org. (1990, rev. 1991); *Berlin Mass*, ch. or soloists, org. or str. (1990–1, rev. 1997); *An den Wassern zu Babel*, ch., org. (1991); *Litany*, ch., orch. (1994); *I am the true vine*, unacc. ch. (1996); *Canon of Repentance*, unacc. ch. (1997); *Kanon Pokajanen*, unacc. ch. (1997); *Triodion*, unacc. ch. (1998); *My Heart's in the Highlands*, ch., org. (2000); *. . . which was the son of . . .*, unacc. ch. (2000); *Nunc dimittis*, unacc. ch. (2001); *Salve Regina*, ch., org. (2002); *In principio*, ch., orch. (2003).

VOICE(S) & INSTR(S).: *Sarah was 90 years old*, sop., 2 ten., perc., org. (1983–90); *Psalm 121*, ten. or bar., str. qt. (1984); *Es sang vor langen Jahren*, motet, counterten., vn., va. (1984); *Psalm 117 and Psalm 131*, sop., cont., counterten., ten., bass (1984); *Stabat Mater*, sop., cont., ten., vn., va., vc. (1985); *Zwei Wiegenlieder*, 2 female vv., pf. (2002); *L'Abbé Agathon*, sop., 4 va., 4 vc. (2004).

ENSEMBLE: *Collage on BACH*, str., ob., hpd., pf. (1964); *Fratres*, chamber ens. (1977) (see also CHAMBER MUS.); *Arbos*, chamber ens. (1977), 7 fl., 3 triangles (opt.) (1977), 9 brass instr., perc. (1977–86).

CHAMBER MUSIC: wind quintet (1964); *Fratres*, vn., pf. (1977–80), 4, 8, or 12 vc. (1977–83), str. qt. (1977–85), vc., pf. (1977–89), wind octet, perc. (1977–90); *Spiegel im Spiegel*, vn., pf. (1979); *Pari intervallo*, 4 fl. (1980) (see also ORGAN); *Summa*, vn., 2 va., vc. (1980–90), str. qt. (1980–91) (see also ORCH. and CHORAL); *Sarah was 90 years old*, 2 pfs., tpt. or sop. (1983) (see also VOICE(S) & INSTR(S).); *Psalom*, str. qt. (1986–91); *Passacaglia*, vn., pf. (2003).

PIANO: *Diagrams* (1964); *Für Alina* (1976); *Variationen zur gesundung von Arinuschka* (1977).

ORGAN: *Trivium* (1976); *Pari intervallo* (1980) (see also CHAMBER MUSIC); *Annum per annum* (1980); *Mein Weg hat Gipfel und Wellentäler* (1985).

Part Books (Ger. *Stimmbücher*). MS or printed books of 15th and 16th cents. containing mus. for an individual v. in a polyphonic comp.

Partch, Harry (*b* Oakland, Calif., 1901; *d* San Diego, 1974). Amer. self-taught composer and inventor. Comp. several large works before he was 25 but destroyed them. Wandered over USA during depression as hobo. In 1943, while a lumberjack, he received Guggenheim award enabling him to develop 20 instrs. he had invented. He used system of intonation with 43 notes to octave; instrs. incl. the 'marimba eroica', 'chromelodeon', etc. Research assoc., Wisconsin Univ. 1944–7. Works incl. *Windsong*, *Barstow*, *2 Settings from Finnegans Wake*, and *And on the 7th Day Petals Fell in Petaluma*.

Partenope. Opera in 3 acts by Handel to lib. adapted from S. Stampiglia's *Partenope* (1699, rev. 1708). Comp. 1729–30, rev. 1730 and 1736. F.p. London 1730. F. modern ps. Göttingen 1935 (ed. F. Lehmann), Abingdon 1961, Omaha 1988, London 1995.

Parthenia (Gk. 'Maidenhood'). Title of 1st book of kbd. mus. printed in Eng. 1611 containing 21 pieces by Byrd, Bull, and Gibbons–'*Parthenia*, or the Maidenhead of the first music that ever was printed for the virginals.' Reprinted 1613 and several other times in 17th cent. Reprints 1847, in facsimile by O. E. Deutsch, 1943, and edn. by Thurston Dart, 1961. A companion work, *Parthenia inviolata* (pun on 'Inviolated' and 'set for the viol') was pubd. shortly after *Parthenia* containing 20 anon. pieces for virginals and bass viol. Only known copy in NY Public Library.

partials. Constituents of the notes of the *harmonic series, the main (fundamental) note being the first partial and the remainder the upper partials.

Particell (Ger.). Short *score.

partie. See (1) *part*; (2) *suite*.

partimento (It.). Division. Practice in 17th and 18th cents. of improvising melodies above a written bass. In Eng. viol-playing, 'divisions' on a ground were a form of *partimento* technique.

partita (It.). Strict mus. meaning of this term is a variation, the total comp. being the plural *partite*. But the ungrammatical custom of applying *partita* to a composite work such as a suite has developed from the 6 Partitas in Bach's *Klavierübung* (1731). Bach's 3 suites for solo vn. are actually termed on the autograph score *Partia*.

partition (Fr.). *Score.

partito (It.). Divided.

Partitur (Ger.), **partitura** (It.). *Score.

Partos, Ödön (*b* Budapest, 1907; *d* Tel Aviv, 1977). Hung.-Israeli composer and violist. Worked in Berlin 1928–33, Budapest, 1933–6. Settled in Palestine 1938 as prin. violist in Palestine SO (later Israel PO) until 1956. Dir., Tel Aviv Acad. of Mus. (later Rubin Acad. of Tel Aviv Univ.) from 1951, becoming prof. there 1961. Comps. incl. *Yizkor* (*In Memoriam*), va., str. (1946); *Choral Fantasia on Yemenite Jewish Themes* (1946); 3 va. concs. (1949, 1957, 1962); vn. conc. (1958); *Arabesque*, ob. and chamber orch. (1975); *Improvisation*, 12 hps. (1960); *Ballade*, pf. qt. (1977); 2 str. qts., and songs.

Partridge, Ian (*b* Wimbledon, 1938). Eng. tenor. Began career as accompanist, but sang in Westminster Cath. Choir 1958–62. Début Bexhill 1958. *Lieder* recitalist and specialist in Eng. songs. CG début 1969 (Iopas in *Les Troyens*). Salzburg Fest. début 1989. Often acc. at pf. by his sister Jennifer (*b* New Malden, 1942). CBE 1991.

part-song. Strictly any song written for several vocal parts, but in practice, a comp. for male, female, or mixed vv. (usually but not necessarily unacc.) which is not contrapuntal like the *madrigal but has the melody in the highest part with accompanying harmonies in the other vv. Either through-composed (*Durchkomponiert*) or strophic (verse-repeating). Is a particularly Eng. genre, developing in popularity with growth of choral socs. in early 19th cent., so there are many examples by Pearsall, Barnby, Stanford, Elgar, Delius, Warlock, and many others. But examples exist by Schubert, Schumann, Mendelssohn, Brahms, etc.

part-writing (Ger. *Stimmführung*; Amer. voiceleading). The organization of a comp. so that each individual part is blended into a euphonious whole.

pas (Fr.). (1) A step in dancing and ballet, e.g. *pas seul*, solo dance, *pas de deux*, dance for 2, *pas d'action*, dramatic ballet scene.
(2) Not, as in *pas trop vite*, not too fast.

Pas d'acier, Le (Prokofiev). See *Age of Steel, The*.

Pasdeloup, Jules-Étienne (*b* Paris, 1819; *d* Fontainebleau, 1887). Fr. conductor. On staff Paris Cons. 1841–68, becoming cond. of students' orch., 1853. In 1861 founded Concerts Populaires and cond. many works by contemporary

Fr. composers, also much Wagner. After his death concerts continued for a time under name Concerts Pasdeloup.

Pashley, Anne (*b* Skegness, 1937). Eng. soprano. Stage début 1959 with Handel Opera Soc. in *Semele*. Glyndebourne 1963; CG 1965. Also sang with ENO, WNO, Scottish Opera, and at Aldeburgh Fest. and with leading orchs. Olympic runner in 1956 Games at Melbourne.

Paskalis, Kostas (*b* Levadis, 1929). Gr. baritone. Début Athens 1954 (Rigoletto). Athens Opera 1951–8. Vienna Opera 1958–79. Brit. début Glyndebourne 1964; NY Met 1965; Salzburg 1966; CG 1969. Notable exponent of Verdi roles. Dir., Nat. Opera of Greece from 1988.

pasodoble (Sp.). Double step. 20-cent. Sp. dance in quick 2/4 time. The tango-pasodoble in *Walton's *Façade* is a parody (using 'I do like to be beside the seaside').

passacaglia. See *chaconne*.

passage. Section of a comp. which perhaps has no structural significance, e.g. a pizzicato passage, which may last only 2 bars. 'Passage-work' is often applied to brilliant display for the soloist.

passaggio (It. 'passage'). (1) The point at which two of the three vocal registers (high, middle, and low) meet.

(2) Transition section in Baroque composition.

passamezzo, pass'e mezzo (It.). Dance in quicker tempo. It. dance of 16th and 17th cents. similar to *pavan but faster and less serious. Examples by Byrd and Philips are in *Fitzwilliam Virginal Book.

passecaille (Fr.). Passacaglia. See *chaconne*.

passepied (Fr.; Eng. 'paspy'). Pass-foot. Lively dance in 3/8 or 6/8 said to have originated among sailors of Basse-Bretagne and introduced to Paris in late 16th cent. by street dancers, becoming popular at courts of Louis XIV and Louis XV. Examples in Fr. operas of the period, e.g. by *Campra. The term was incorrectly applied by Debussy to a 2-in-a-measure piece.

passing-notes. Harmonic term to describe note which forms a discord with the chord with which it is heard but is melodically placed between two non-discordant notes.

Passion Music. The practice of setting to mus. the Passion of Christ, for perf. during Holy Week, has 2 connected origins—the old mysteries (see *Miracle Plays*) and (a more direct and obvious source) a very ancient Holy Week practice of reading or reciting in church, in a more or less dramatic fashion, the story of the Passion of Christ. It is known to have existed in the 4th cent.; by the 8th its character was determined as follows: a priest recited, in Lat., the story of the Passion from one of the Gospels, in a speaking voice except for the words of Christ, which he

gave out to a traditional plainsong. By the 12th cent. 3 of the clergy took part, a ten. as Narrator, a bass as Christ, and an alto as the Crowd (Turba). By the 15th cent. Passions of more musically elaborate character became common. The Reformation brought a further development. The Ger. (Lutheran) reformers, acting on their principle that the people should be able to follow the words of the service, adapted it to the Ger. language.

In the 16th cent., unacc. polyphonic settings of the complete Lat. text of the Passion were based on a plainchant *cantus firmus*. Among many such settings were those of *Obrecht, Daser, Ruffo, Lassus, Victoria, and Byrd. One of the earliest settings by an Eng. composer was that by Richard *Davy.

Outstanding examples of the Ger. type of Passion are the settings of *Schütz (1585–1672). He adopted a type of recit. derived from the new It. style but which also had considerable affinity with the old plainsong. The 4-part chs. are acc. by str. The various characters are allotted to different vocal soloists and the works can be designated as 'oratorio Passions'. In the 17th cent. the 'Passion oratorio' developed, in which the biblical text was replaced by a metrical paraphrase, as in *Keiser's *Der blutige und sterbende Jesus* (1704). But Bach, in his great *St John* and *St Matthew* Passions, combined both types of setting, making use of biblical text, paraphrases, chorales, arias, and imparting to the mus. a startlingly dramatic quality. In the 19th cent. oratorios on biblical subjects replaced the strict Passion settings, but *Penderecki in the 20th cent. had remarkable success with his *St Luke Passion* (1963–6), leading to Passions by Pärt and others.

Passione, La. Nickname for Haydn's Sym. in F minor, No.49 in Breitkopf edn., comp. 1768. Begins with *adagio* suggestive of Passion mus.

Pasta (*née* Negri), **Giuditta** (*b* Saronno, nr. Milan, 1797; *d* Blevio, nr. Lake Como, 1865). It. soprano. Among greatest of opera singers. Début Milan 1816 in her teacher Scappa's *Le tre Eleonore*. London début 1817 (Telemachus in Cimarosa's *Penelope*; later sang Cherubino and Despina). Caused sensation in Paris, 1821–2. The immense range of her v. and her dramatic gifts were matched by poignancy of expression, though she was an uneven artist. Sang regularly in London, Paris, and St Petersburg 1824–37. Created role of Amina in *La sonnambula*, Milan 1831, and title-roles in *Norma* (Milan 1831, London 1833), *Beatrice di Tenda* (Venice 1833), and *Anna Bolena* (Milan 1830).

pasticcio (It.). Pie, pasty. (1) A dramatic entertainment with songs, ensembles, dances, and other items assembled from the works of several composers, thus giving the audience a medley of their favourite tunes. Popular in 18th cent., e.g. *Thomyris* (1707).

(2) An opera in which each act is by a different composer, e.g. *Muzio Scevola* (1721) by Amadei, Bononcini, and Handel.

(3) Instr. comp. containing different sections or items by different composers, e.g. Diabelli's *Väterlandischer Künstlerverein* (1823–4), containing variations by 50 composers; the **Hexaméron* (1837), and *L'*Éventail de Jeanne* (1927).

pastiche (Fr.). Imitation. Not the same as **pasticcio*, being a work deliberately written in the style of another period or manner, e.g. Prokofiev's *Classical Symphony* and Stravinsky's *Pulcinella*. Although *pastiche* has a meaning as 'medley', it is invariably applied musically in the sense outlined above.

pastoral, pastorale. (1) Type of instr. or vocal comp., generally in 6/8 or 12/8, which suggests rustic or bucolic subject, often by imitation of shepherd's pipe. A 20th-cent. use of the term is **Bliss's Pastoral, *Lie Strewn the White Flocks*.
   (2) Stage piece dealing with legendary or pastoral subject. Began as a play but in Fr. pastorals were set to mus. as an early form of *opéra-ballet* and were at height of popularity in 17th and 18th cents. Handel's *Acis and Galatea* is an example.

pastorale (Fr.). **Pastoral.

Pastorale d'été (Summer Pastoral). Symphonic-poem for small orch. by Honegger, comp. 1920. F.p. Paris 1921.

Pastoral Sonata. Publisher's name for Beethoven's pf. sonata No.15 in D major, Op.28, comp. 1801 (presumably because of rustic rhythm in finale).

Pastoral Symphony. (1) sym. No.6 in F major, Op.68, by Beethoven, comp. 1807–8, f.p. Vienna 1808. A 'programme symphony' in which birdsong and a storm are represented. Each movt. has a title, viz. 'Awakening of happy feelings on arriving in the country', 'By the brook', 'Joyous gathering of country folk—storm', 'Shepherd's song; happy and thankful feelings after the storm'.
   (2) 3rd Sym. by Vaughan Williams comp. 1916–21, rev. 1950–1, f.p. London 1922. Last movt. has wordless solo for sop. (or cl.).
   (3) Short orch. movt. in Handel's *Messiah*, depicting calm of first Christmas Eve.

Pastor Fido, Il (The Faithful Shepherd). Opera in 3 acts by Handel to lib. by Rossi based on Guarini's pastoral play (1585). Prod. London 1712 (2nd vers. 1734, 3rd vers. with prologue *Terpsicore*, 1734), NY 1952. Also opera by **Salieri (1789).

pastourelle (Fr.). Light Fr. song of pastoral type, popular in 18th cent.

Patanè, Giuseppe (b Naples, 1932; d Munich, 1989). It. conductor. Début Naples 1951 (*La traviata*). Ass. cond., Teatro S. Carlo 1951–6. Res. cond. Deutsche Oper, W. Berlin, 1962–8. Débuts: Amer. (S. Francisco) 1967; CG 1973; NY Met 1975, appearing there regularly until 1982. Co-prin. cond. American SO in NY 1982–4. Chief cond.

Mannheim Nat Th. from 1987, Munich Radio Orch. from 1988. Had heart attack while conducting *Il barbiere di Siviglia*.

'Pathetic' Symphony. Subtitle, authorized by composer, of **Tchaikovsky's sym. No.6 in B minor, Op.74. After f.p. in St Petersburg 1893, Modest Tchaikovsky suggested title 'Tragic' but composer demurred, immediately agreeing to *Pathetic*. No reason in Eng. why Fr. title *Symphonie Pathétique* should be used. Note that Russ. word *patetichesky* means 'passionate' or 'emotional' rather than 'pathetic'.

Pathétique Sonata (Pathetic Sonata). Beethoven's pf. sonata No.8 in C minor, Op.13, comp. 1798–9 and entitled by him, in Fr., *Grande sonate pathétique* (meaning 'passionate' or 'emotional' rather than 'pathetic'—see above entry).

Patience, or Bunthorne's Bride. Operetta in 2 acts by **Sullivan to lib. by Gilbert. Comp. 1880–1. Prod. London 1881, St Louis 1881, NY 1882. Satire on 'aesthetic' movt. Ov. arranged by Eugen d'Albert.

Patterson, Paul (Leslie) (b Chesterfield, 1947). Eng. composer. Dir. of contemp. mus. Warwick Univ. 1974–80. Prof. of comp. and dir. elec. studies RAM from 1975, head of comp. 1987–97, prof. from 1997. Works, some using elec. tape and **aleatory methods, incl.:

ORCH.: tpt. conc. (1969); *Partita* (1970); *Symphonic Study II* (1971); hn. conc., str. (1971); *Strange Meeting* (1975); *The Circular Ruins* (1975); cl. conc., str. (1976); *Concerto for Orchestra* (1981); *Sinfonia for Strings* (1982); *Europhony* (1985); *Propositions*, harmonica, str. (1987); *White Shadows on the Dark Horizon* (1989); sym. (1990); vn. conc., str. (1992); *Festivo* (1993); *Ov.: Songs of the West*, orch. (1995); *Four Rustic Sketches* (1997); *The City Within* (2000); *Jubilee Dances* (2003); *Three Little Pigs*, narr., hp., orch. (2003); *Orchestra on Parade*, orch. (2004).

CHAMBER MUSIC: *Rebecca*, spkr., ens. (1966); wind quintet (1967); wind trio (1968); *Conversations*, cl., pf. (1974); *Diversions*, sax. qt. (1976); *Deception Pass*, brass (1980); *At the Still Point of the Turning World*, octet (1980); *Duologue*, ob., pf. (1984); str. qt. (1986); *Memories of Quiberville*, tb. qt. (1986); Suite, vc. (1987); *Tides of Mananan*, va. (1988); *Westerly Winds*, wind quintet (1999); *Deviations*, str. octet (2001); *Tate Modern Mobiles*, large ens. (2003).

CHORAL: *Kyrie*, ch., pf. (2 players) (1972); *The Abode of the Dead/You'll Never be Alone*, vv., ens. (1973); *Requiem*, ch., orch. (1975); *Sing Praises!* ch., orch. (1980); *The Canterbury Psalms*, ch., orch. (1981; ch., brass, org. 1984); *Mass of the Sea*, SATB soloists, ch., orch. (1983; rev. for sop., bass, ch., orch. 1983–4); *Missa brevis*, unacc. ch. (1985); *Stabat Mater*, mez., ch., orch. (1985–6); *Magnificat and Nunc Dimittis*, ch., org. (1986); *Te Deum*, sop., ch., orch. (1988); *Revolting Rhymes*, narr., ens. (1992); *Hell's Angels*, ch., ens. (1998); *Gloria*, ch., orch. (1999); *Millennium Mass*, sop., ch., orch. (1999); *The Fifth Continent*, ch., brass ens. (2005).

PIANO: *Country Search* (1974); *3 Portraits* (1984); *A Tunnel of Time* (1988).

patter-song. Comic song, prevalent in opera, which is a rapid iteration of words, the mus. merely being lightly supportive. Examples exist in Haydn, Mozart, and Rossini operas; there are many in the Sullivan operettas (e.g. 'My name is John Wellington Wells', from *The Sorcerer*). Usually solos, but *Ruddigore* has a patter-trio.

Patti, Adelina [Adela] (Juana Maria) (*b* Madrid, 1843; *d* Craig-y-Nos Castle, nr. Brecon, Wales, 1919). It. soprano. Daughter of singers. Taken to NY as child, touring USA as child prodigy for 3 years, accomp. by her brother-in-law Maurice Strakosch and the violinist Ole *Bull. In 1857 toured with pianist Gottschalk. Studied singing with Strakosch. Opera début 1859 in *Lucia di Lammermoor* at Acad. of Mus., NY. London début CG 1861; Paris 1862; Vienna 1863. Rapidly recognized as leading sop. of day and *Grisi's successor. V. had great range, flexibility, and purity of tone. Essentially a coloratura sop., but sang dramatic roles such as Leonora in *Il trovatore* and Violetta in *La traviata*. First London *Aida* (1876). In 25 consecutive CG seasons sang over 30 roles by Donizetti, Bellini, Rossini, Verdi, Meyerbeer, etc. Zerlina in *Don Giovanni* was her only Mozart role. La Scala début 1877; NY Met 1887. CG farewell 1895; sang last operas in Monte Carlo and Nice 1897. Toured N. and S. Amer. and the world's capitals. Highest-paid singer of her day. Farewell concert, London 1906, followed by provincial tour. Retired to her castle in Wales but gave charity concert in 1914. Buried in Paris.

Patzak, Julius (*b* Vienna, 1898; *d* Rottach-Egern, 1974). Austrian tenor. Intended to be cond. but turned to singing, making début Reichenberg Opera 1926 (Radames in *Aida*). Munich Opera 1928–45; Vienna Opera 1945–60; CG début 1938; Salzburg Fest. début 1938. Outstanding Florestan in *Fidelio* and in title-role of *Palestrina*. Created Desmoulins in *Dantons Tod*, Salzburg 1947. Superb singer of *Lieder*, oratorio, etc.

Pauk, György (*b* Budapest, 1936). Hung. violinist. Won Paganini comp., Genoa 1956, Munich comp. 1957, Long-Thibaud comp., Paris 1959. Eng. début 1961, settling in London. Prof. of vn. RMCM 1964, RAM from 1987. Soloist with leading orchs. and member of trio, often with Peter *Frankl (pf.) and Ralph *Kirshbaum (vc.). Has given f.ps. of several contemp. concs.

Pauke(n) (Ger.). Kettledrum(s). See *drum*.

Paukenmesse (Kettledrum Mass). Popular subtitle for Haydn's Mass No.7 in C major, comp. 1796 and named by composer *Missa in tempore belli* (Mass in time of war).

Paukenwirbel Symphonie (Drum-roll Symphony). Nickname for 11th of Haydn's 'London' Syms., No.103 in E♭ major in Breitkopf edn., because it opens with a roll on the kettledrums.

Paul Bunyan. (1) Choral operetta by Britten in 2 acts and prol. to text by Auden. F.p. Columbia Univ., NY, May 1941. Then withdrawn until rev. in 1974 and publication as Op.17. First complete perf. in England, BBC broadcast, Feb. 1976; f. stage p. Aldeburgh, June 1976; f. professional Amer. p., St Louis 1984.

(2) Ballet for puppets and solo dancer by W. Bergsma, 1937, prod. S. Francisco 1939; also orch. suite 1937, rev. 1945.

Paulus (Mendelssohn). See *St Paul*.

Paulus, Stephen (Harrison) (*b* Summit, NY, 1949). Amer. composer. Founded Minn. composers' forum 1973, acting as managing composer until 1984. Comp.-in-res. Minnesota Orch. 1983–7, Atlanta SO 1987–91. Comps. incl. 9 operas (*The Village Singer*, 1977; *The Postman Always Rings Twice*, 1981, orch. suite 1986; *The Woodlanders*, 1984; *Harmoonia*, 1990; *The Woman of Otawia Crossing*, 1995; *The Three Hermits*, 1997; *Summer*, 1999; *Heloise and Abelard*, 2002; *Hester Prynne at Death*, 2004); *Concerto for Orch.* (1983); *Symphony in 3 Movements* (1985); vn. conc. (1987); *Symphony for Strings* (1989); 2 str. qts.; conc. for vn. and vc. (1994); *Partita Appassionata*, vn., pf. (1996); *Art Suite*, vc., pf. (1999); *Fanfare: UNM 150*, brass quintet (2000); *King David's Dance*, org. (2002); *Erotic Spirits*, sop., orch. (2004); *Above Me, Round Me Lie*, ch., org. (2004); *A Heartland Portrait*, bar., pf. (2005); and choral pieces.

Pauly, Rose [Pollak, Rose] (*b* Eperjes, 1894; *d* Kfar Shmaryan, nr. Tel Aviv, 1975). Hung. soprano. Début Hamburg 1918 in *Martha*. Cologne Opera 1922–7 (where in 1922 she sang title-role in Ger. première of *Káťa Kabanová*). Salzburg début 1922; Kroll Oper, Berlin 1927–31; Vienna 1923–38; NY Met 1938–40; CG début 1938. Notable in Strauss roles of Elektra, Dyer's Wife, and Salome. Retired to Israel.

Paumgartner, Bernhard (*b* Vienna, 1887; *d* Salzburg, 1971). Austrian conductor, composer, and musicologist. Son of Hans Paumgartner and Rosa Papier. Cond. at Vienna Opera 1911–12, but became one of leading organizers of Salzburg Fest., often conducting there. Comp. mus. for Hofmannsthal's *Jedermann*, 1920. Dir. Salzburg Mozarteum 1917–38, 1945–59. Founded Salzburg Mozart Chamber Orch. Visited USA 1965. Comp. operas, ballet, and other works. Wrote books on Mozart (1927), Salzburg (1935), Schubert (1943), and J. S. Bach (1950).

pausa (It.). Rest (*not* pause, which is *fermata*). So *lunga pausa*, a long rest.

pause (Eng.). (1) The sign ⌢ which means that the note or rest so indicated must be held longer than usual (at performer's discretion). Placed over a bar line, it means a short silence. The Fr. term is *point d'orgue*.

(2) In the phrase General Pause (G.P.) it means the whole orch. is briefly silent.

Pause (Ger.). (1) A pause, as in Eng.
(2) Rest.
(3) Interval of a concert.

pause (Fr.). (1) Pause.
(2) Rest, especially a whole-note rest and a measure rest.

pavan (Fr. *pavane*; It. *pavana*; old forms incl. *pavin*, *pavyn*, *paven*, etc.). The pavan was a dance of It. orig., popular in the 16th and 17th cents., and as the name sometimes appears as *padovana* it is assumed that its orig. home was Padua. It was in simple duple time, and of stately character. In Italy the pavan gave way to the passamezzo by the mid-16th cent., but was given a new lease of life by its treatment by Eng. composers, e.g. Byrd, Dowland, Bull, and Philips. It was usually paired with the *galliard* and their assoc. was the orig. of the *suite. Some 19th- and 20th-cent. composers have written works to which they gave the name *Pavan*, e.g. Fauré's *Pavane*, *Ravel's *Pavane pour une infante défunte*, and the *Pavan* in Vaughan Williams's *Job.

Pavane. Work by *Fauré, Op.50, for orch. with optional mixed ch. Comp. 1887, f.p. Paris 1888.

Pavane pour une infante défunte (Pavan for a dead Infanta). Pf. piece by *Ravel comp. 1899 (f.p. 1902), orch. by composer 1910 (f.p. Paris 1910). Recalls Sp. court custom of solemn ceremonial dance at time of royal mourning.

Pavarotti, Luciano (*b* Modena, 1935). It. tenor. Won int. comp. at Reggio Emilia 1961, making opera début there later that year as Rodolfo in *La bohème*. Rapid success. CG début 1963 (Rodolfo); Glyndebourne 1964 (Idamante in *Idomeneo*); La Scala début 1965 (Rodolfo); Amer. début Miami 1965 (Edgardo in *Lucia di Lammermoor*); S. Francisco 1967; NY Met 1968 (both as Rodolfo). Toured Australia 1965 with Joan *Sutherland. Salzburg Fest. début (recital) 1976, (opera) 1978 (Italian Singer in *Der Rosenkavalier*). Sang Otello 1991 in concert perfs. in Chicago and NY, cond. Solti, later recording it. During late 1980s became idol of both operatic and non-operatic public, achieving apogee of fame in 1990 when he sang 'Nessun dorma' from *Turandot* in connection with football World Cup. One of Three Tenors with *Domingo and *Carreras.

pavillon (Fr.). Pavilion. The bell of a brass instr. e.g. tpt., hn., etc. So called because of tent-like shape. The direction to brass-players 'pavillons en l'air' means hold the bells high (in order to increase vol.).

pavillon chinois (Fr.). See *Jingling Johnny*.

Payne, Anthony (Edward) (*b* London 1936). Eng. composer and critic. Illness halted his creative work 1961–5, but his *Phoenix Mass* was start of new phase. Mus. critic *Daily Telegraph* 1965–87, *The Independent* 1987–97, *Country Life* from 1995. Author of books on Schoenberg (1968) and Frank Bridge (1984). Made performing edition (1993–4) of Elgar's 3rd Sym., f.p. 1998. Works incl.:

ORCH. & INSTRUMENTAL: *Contrapuncti*, str. (1958, rev. 1979); *The Spirit's Harvest*, orch. (1972–85); *Conc. for Orch.* (1974); *The World's Winter*, sop., fl., ob., cl., hn., hp., str. trio (1976); *Fire on Whaleness*, brass band, perc. (1976); *The Stones and Lonely Places Sing*, chamber ens. (1979); *The Song of the Clouds*, ob., 2 hn., str., perc. (1979–80); *A Day in the Life of a Mayfly*, fl., cl., pf., vn., vc., perc. (1981); *Spring's Shining Wake*, orch. (1982); *Songs and Seascapes*, str. (1984); *The Song Streams in the Firmament* (1986); *Half Heard in the Stillness*, orch. (1987); *Time's Arrow*, orch. (1990); *River-Race*, brass ens., perc. (1990); *Hidden Music*, orch. (1992); *Orch. Variations: The Seeds Long Hidden'*, orch. (1994); *Visions and Journeys*, orch. (2002).

CHORAL & VOCAL: *Phoenix Mass*, ch., 3 tpt., 3 tb. (1965–9, with add. 1972); *2 Songs Without Words*, male v. quintet (1970); *A Little Passiontide Cantata*, unacc. ch. (1974); *First Sight of Her and After*, 16 solo vv. (1975); *A Little Whitsuntide Cantata*, unacc. ch. (1977); *A Little Ascensiontide Cantata*, unacc. ch. (1977); *The Sea of Glass*, ch., org. (1977); *Evening Land*, sop., pf. (1981); *A Little Christmastide Cantata*, unacc. ch. (1983); *Alleluias and Hockets*, ch., orch. (1987); *Adlestrop*, sop., pf. (1989); *Aspects of Love and Contentment*, sop., fl., cl./hp., 2 vn., va., vc (1991); *Break, Break, Break*, unacc. ch. (1996); *Poems of Edward Thomas*, sop., pf. qt. (2003).

CHAMBER MUSIC: *Paraphrases and Cadenzas*, cl., va., pf. (1969); *Sonatas and Ricercars*, wind quintet (1970); str. qt. (1978); *Footfalls Echo in the Memory*, vn., pf. (1978); *Evening Land*, sop., pf. (1981); *Consort Music*, str. quintet (1987); *Sea-Change*, septet (1988); *The Enchantress Plays*, bn., pf. (1990); *Symphonies of Wind and Rain*, ens. (1993); *Empty Landscape—Heart's Ease*, ens. (1995); *The Woodlanders*, sop., 2 cl., vn., vc (1999); hn. trio, hn., vn., pf. (2006).

KEYBOARD: *Paean*, pf. (1971); *Reflections in the Sea of Glass*, org. (1983).

Payne, Nicholas (*b* Bromley, 1945). Eng. opera administrator. Worked in finance dept., CG, 1968–70. Subsidy Officer, Arts Council, 1970–6. Financial controller, WNO, 1976–82. Gen. admin., Opera North 1982–93. Dir. of opera, CG, 1993–8. Gen. dir. ENO 1998–2002. Dir. Eur. Opera from 2003.

Peabody Conservatory. Sch. of mus. at Baltimore, Maryland, USA, which also houses library and art gallery. Founded 1857 as Peabody Inst., but opening as mus. cons. delayed until 1868. Confers degrees of B.Mus., M.Mus., and Doctor of Musical Arts. Named after Amer. businessman and philanthropist George Peabody (*b* South Denvers, Mass., 1795; *d* London, 1869) who gave $1.5 million for its foundation.

Peacock Variations. *Variations on a Hungarian Folk-Song 'The Peacock'* for orch. by Kodály, comp. 1938–9, commissioned for 50th anniv. of Concertgebouw Orch. of Amsterdam, 1939.

Pearl Fishers, The. See *Pêcheurs de perles, Les*.

Pears, (Sir) **Peter** (Neville Luard) (*b* Farnham, 1910; *d* Aldeburgh, 1986). Eng. tenor and organist.

Org., Hertford Coll., Oxford, 1928–9. Dir. of mus., Grange Sch., Crowborough, 1930–4. Had lessons from E. *Gerhardt. In BBC Singers 1934–7, New Eng. Singers 1936–8. Went to USA with friend Benjamin *Britten 1939, returning 1942. Stage début Strand Th., London, 1942 as Hoffmann in *The Tales of Hoffmann*. SW Opera 1943–6; EOG from 1946. Closely assoc. with mus. of Britten, giving f.ps. of many works (*Serenade, Nocturne, Seven Sonnets of Michelangelo, Holy Sonnets of John Donne*) and creating several of Britten's operatic roles, i.e. title-roles in *Peter Grimes* and *Albert Herring* and Male Chorus in *The Rape of Lucretia*, Captain Vere in *Billy Budd*, Essex in *Gloriana*, Quint in *The Turn of the Screw*, Flute in *A Midsummer Night's Dream* (of which he was co-librettist with Britten), Madwoman in *Curlew River*, Sir Philip Wingrave in *Owen Wingrave*, Aschenbach in *Death in Venice*. Created Pandarus in Walton's *Troilus and Cressida*, CG 1954. Sang ten. part in f.p. of Britten's *War Requiem* 1962. Notable singer of Schubert, Bach (Evangelist), and of Vašek in *The Bartered Bride*. The recitals Pears and Britten gave together from 1937 until Britten's stroke in 1973 were a feature of international musical life throughout the period. Salzburg Fest. 1952 (recital, accomp. Britten). NY Met début 1974 (Aschenbach). Writer on mus. and ed. (with Britten) of Purcell. CBE 1957. Knighted 1978.

Pearsall, Robert (Lucas) (*b* Clifton, 1795; *d* Wartensee, 1856). Eng. composer. Lived mainly abroad. Wrote madrigals in 16th-cent. style. Comp. many part-songs, incl. *O Who will o'er the Downs so Free?* His setting for 8 solo vv. and 5-part chorus of the Ger. macaronic carol *In dulci jubilo* was made in 1834 and pubd. in 1836. Also comp. *Requiem* 1853–6.

Pearson, H. H. See *Pierson, Henry Hugo*.

Peasant Cantata (*Bauernkantate*). Light-hearted cantata by Bach, 1742, to lib. by Picander. It is Cantata No.212, *Mer hahn en neue Oberkeet*, for sop., bass, hns., fl., str., and continuo.

Pêcheurs de perles, Les (The Pearl Fishers). 3-act opera by Bizet to lib. by Cormon and Carré. Comp. 1863. Prod. Paris 1863, London 1887 (under title *Leila*, the heroine's name), Philadelphia 1893. Action set in Ceylon (Sri Lanka).

ped. Abbreviation for *pedal. In pf. mus., means that the sustaining pedal is to be depressed until its release is indicated. In org. mus., means that mus. is to be played on the *pedal-board.

pedal. (1) In *harmony, a note sustained below changing harmonies and called a *pedal-point* or *pedal-bass*. If sustained but not in the bass, it is an *inverted pedal*.

(2) Lowest, i.e. fundamental, note of *harmonic series, esp. in brass instrs.

(3) Lever operated by the foot, as in hp., hpd., kettledrum, org., and pf.

pedal-board. Kbd. played with the feet, as on an org. Also found (rarely) in hpd., clavichord, and pf.

pedal clarinet. Same as db. cl., a very rare form of cl., used mainly in military bands.

pédalier (Fr.). *Pedal-board or *pedal-piano.

Pedalpauken (Ger.). Mechanically-tuned kettle-drums.

pedal-piano. Pf. fitted with pedal kbd. in addition to manual. Used by orgs. for practice at home. Schumann and Alkan comp. for it.

pedal-point. See *pedal (1)*.

Pedrell, Felipe (*b* Tortosa, 1841; *d* Barcelona, 1922). Sp. composer and musicologist. Believed that a nation should base its mus. on its folk-song. Ed. early Sp. church and secular mus., and complete works of *Victoria (Leipzig, 1902–13). Taught at Madrid Cons. 1895–1903, pupils incl. *Albéniz, *Granados, and *Falla. Comp. several operas, orch. works, and church mus.

Peerce, Jan [Perelmuth, Jacob Pincus] (*b* NY, 1904; *d* New Rochelle, NY, 1984). Amer. tenor. Trained as violinist, played and sang in dance-bands. Sang at Radio City Music Hall 1933–9. Opera début Philadelphia 1938 (Duke in *Rigoletto*). NY Met début 1941, becoming regular member of co. until 1966 and singing several times in Toscanini's NBC opera broadcasts. In 1956 was first Amer. to sing at Bolshoy since Second World War. Broadway début 1971 as Tevye in *Fiddler on the Roof*. Made several films. Retired 1982. Brother-in-law of Richard *Tucker.

Peer Gynt. Play by Ibsen for which Grieg comp. 23 items of incidental mus., Op.23, 1874–5, f.p. Christiania, Feb. 1876. Later arr. for pf., 4 hands, then as 2 orch. suites: No.1 (Op.46, 1874–5, rev. 1888): 1. *Morning*, 2. *Death of Aase*, 3. *Anitra's Dance*, 4. *In the Hall of the Mountain King*; No.2 (Op.55, 1874–5, rev. 1891 and 1892): 1. *Abduction of the Bride* and *Ingrid's Lament*, 2. *Arabian Dance*, 3. *Peer Gynt's Homecoming*, 4. *Solvejg's Song*. Additional items sometimes perf. are *Wedding March, Solvejg's Cradle Song, Prelude, Dance of the Mountain King's Daughter*. Incidental mus. also comp. by *Saeverud, 1947 (2 orch. suites pubd.). Also opera by *Egk (Berlin 1938).

Peeters, Flor (*b* Thielen, 1903; *d* Antwerp, 1986). Belg. organist and composer. Organist Mechelen Cath. from 1923. Prof. of org., Lemmens Inst. 1925–52, Royal Cons., Ghent, 1931–8, Tilburg 1935–48, and Royal Flemish Cons., Antwerp, 1948–68 (dir. from 1952). Ed. early Flemish, Dutch, and Eng. org. works and wrote 3-vol. org. method (*Ars Organi*, 1952). World tours as org. recitalist. Noted exponent of mus. of his friend Tournemire. Created Baron Peeters, 1971. Comps. incl.:

ORGAN: *Variations and Finale* (1929); *Toccata, Fugue, and Hymn on Ave Maris Stella* (1931); *Flemish*

Rhapsody (1935); *Passacaglia and Fugue* (1938); *Sinfonia* (1940); conc. (1944); *Lied Symphony* (1948); 3 *Preludes and Fugues* (1950); org. and pf. conc. (1951); *Hymn Preludes for Liturgical Year* (1959–64); 6 *Lyrical Pieces* (1966); 10 *Inventions* (1969); 10 *Preludes on Old Flemish Songs* (1972); *Introduzione, fugato con corale supra 'Pro Civitate'* (1976).

VOICE(S) AND ORGAN: *Mass for St Joseph* (1929); *Speculum vitae*, sop. (1935); *Jubilate Deo* (1936); *Te Deum* (1945); *Missa festiva* (1958); *Entrata festiva* (1959); *Magnificat* (1962); *Canticum gaudii* (1971–2).

peg (Ger. *Wirbel*; Fr. *cheville*; It. *bischero*). Movable wooden pin set in head of instr. of vn. family and used to adjust the tension of the str.

Peinemann, Edith (*b* Mainz, 1937). Ger. violinist. First taught by father, who was leader of Mainz orch. Won Munich int. comp. 1956. NY début 1965 with Cleveland Orch., cond. Szell. Prof., Frankfurt Hochschule für Mus. from 1976. Recital duo with Jörg Demus. Salzburg Fest. début 1977.

Pelléas et Mélisande. (1) Opera (*drame lyrique*) in 5 acts, 12 *tableaux*, by Debussy, comp. 1893–5 and 1901–2, being a nearly complete setting of the text of Maeterlinck's play of this name (1892). Prod. Paris 1902, NY 1908, London 1909.
(2) Sym.-poem (*Pelleas und Melisande*) after Maeterlinck, Op.5, by Schoenberg, comp. 1902–3 and f.p. 1905 (Vienna). F.p. in England 1930.
(3) Incidental mus. to Maeterlinck's play by Sibelius, Op.46, comp. 1905 for prod. in Helsinki. Suite of 9 items for small orch. pubd. 1905.
(4) Incidental mus. to Maeterlinck's play by Fauré, Op.80, comp. 1898 for London prod. (cond. Fauré). Suite of 4 items for orch. pubd. 1900 and f.p. 1901 (also arr. for pf. solo, and pf., 4 hands).

Pelletier, Wilfrid (*b* Montreal, 1896; *d* NY, 1982). Canadian conductor. Ass. cond. Montreal Opera Co., then of NY Met 1921, becoming cond. there 1928–50. Initiated Met Auditions of the Air. Cond. Ravinia Park, Chicago, and S. Francisco Opera. Cond. sym. concerts in Montreal 1935–51. Dir. Montreal Cons. 1943–61. Cond. Quebec SO 1951–66. Companion of Order of Canada, 1968.

Penderecki, Krzysztof (*b* Debica, 1933). Polish composer. Won all 3 prizes at Warsaw autumn fest. 1959. Teacher at Kraków High Sch. for Mus. from 1958, dir. 1972–87. Teacher at Yale Univ. 1973–8. In 1974 appeared at Salzburg Fest., conducting his *Magnificat*. After 1960 abandoned Boulez-influenced style and was one of first *avant-garde* composers to experiment with sounds such as sawing wood, rustling paper, typewriters, knocking, hissing, screeching, etc., and various orig. effects obtained from conventional instr. by unconventional means, in particular microtonal glissandi and dense clusters. In choral mus., the singers are asked to articulate consonants rapidly, to hiss and to whistle. Never-

theless these freakish effects are put to artistic use and his *St Luke Passion* (1966) was an immediate success with a wide public. In the 1970s, with the *Christmas Symphony* and the vn. conc., he moved towards a more conservative and traditional idiom, although his Salzburg opera *Die schwarze Maske* was violently radical. Prin. works:

OPERAS: *The* **Devils of Loudun (Diably z Loudun)* (1968–9); *Paradise Lost (1976–8); *Die* *schwarze Maske (1984–6); *Ubu Rex* (1990–1).
ORCH.: *Emanations*, 2 str. orch. (1958); *Anaklasis*, 42 str., perc. (1959–60); *Threnody for the Victims of Hiroshima (Tren pamieci ofiarom Hiroszimy)* 52 str. (1960); *Fonogrammi*, fl., chamber orch. (1961); *Polymorphia*, 48 str. (1961); *Fluorescences* (1961–2); *Canon*, 52 str., 2 tapes (1962); *Sonata*, vc., orch. (1964); *Capriccio*, ob., str. (1964); *De natura sonoris* (Of the nature of sound) I (1966), II (1971); *Pittsburgh Overture*, wind (1967); *Capriccio*, vn., orch. (1967); *Prélude*, wind, perc., dbs. (1971); vc. conc. No.1 (1966–7, rev. 1971–2), No.2 (1982); *Partita*, hpd., 5 elec. amplified solo instr., orch. (1971); *Actions*, jazz ens. (1971); sym. No.1 (1972–3), No.2 (*Christmas*) (1979–80), No.3 (1988), No.4 (1989), No.5 (1991–2); *Intermezzo*, 24 str. (1973); vn. conc. (1976–7, rev. 1988), No.2 (1992–5); *Als Jabob erwachte (The Dream of Jacob)* (1974); *Adagio* from *Paradise Lost* (1979); *Passacaglia* (1988); *Adagio* (1989); *Sinfonietta*, str. (1991); *Sinfonietta*, cl., str. (1994); *Passacaglia*, str. (1996); pf. conc. (2002).
VOICES & ORCH.: *From the Psalms of David*, ch., chamber ens. (1958); *Strophes* (Strofy), sop., narr., 10 instr. (1959); *Dimensions of Time and Silence (Wymiary czasu i ciszy)*, ch., chamber ens. (1959–60); *Cantata in honorem Almae Matris Universitatis Iagellonicae*, ch., orch. (1964); *St Luke Passion, narr., sop., bar., bass, 3 ch., boys' ch., orch. (1962–5); *Dies Irae*, sop., ten., bass, ch., orch. (1967); *Utrenja: Part I, *The Entombment of Christ*, sop., cont., ten., 2 basses, 2 ch., orch. (1969–70), Part II, *The Resurrection of Christ*, sop., alt., ten., 2 basses, boys' ch., 2 ch., orch. (1970–1); *Kosmogonia*, sop., ten., bass, ch., orch. (1970); *Canticum Canticorum Salomonis* (Song of Songs), ch., chamber orch., opt. dance pair (1970–3); *Magnificat*, bass, boys' vv., 7 male vv., 2 ch., orch. (1973–4); *Prelude, Visions, and Finale (Paradise Lost)*, sop., mez., ten., counterten., 2 bars., ch., orch. (1979); *Te Deum*, sop., mez., ten., bass, 2 ch., orch. (1979–80); *Lacrimosa (Polish Requiem)*, sop., ch., orch. (1980); *Polish Requiem*, SATB soloists, ch., orch. (1980–4); *7 Gates of Jerusalem*, soloists., narr., 3 ch., orch. (1996); *Credo*, sop., 2 mez., ten., bass, children's ch., ch., orch. (1997–8).
UNACC. CHORUS: *Stabat Mater*, 3 mixed ch. (1962); *Miserere (St Luke Passion)*, opt. boys' ch., 3 mixed ch. (1965); *In pulverem mortis (St Luke Passion)*, 3 mixed ch. (1965); *Ecloga VIII* (Virgil), 6 male vv. (1972); *Agnus Dei (Polish Requiem)* (1981); *Song of Cherubim* (1986); *Veni Creator* (1987).
CHAMBER MUSIC: str. qts., No.1 (1960), No.2 (1968); vn. sonata (1953); 3 *Miniatures*, cl., pf. (1956); *Capriccio per Siegfried Palm*, vc. (1968); *Capriccio tuba* (1980); *Cadenza*, va. (1984); *Per Slava*, vc.

(1985–6); *Prelude*, cl. (1987); *Der Unterbrochene Gedanke*, str. qt. (1988); *String Trio* (1990); *Entrata*, brass, timp. (1994).

TAPE: *Psalmus* (1961); *Brigade of Death* (1963).

Pénélope. (1) Opera (*poème lyrique*) in 3 acts by *Fauré to lib. by René Fauchois. Comp. 1907–12. Prod. Monte Carlo and Paris 1913, London, 1970.

(2) Opera semi-seria in 2 parts by Liebermann to text by H. Strobel. Prod. Salzburg 1954. Other operas on Penelope legend are by Monteverdi (*Il *ritorno d'Ulisse in patria*), Cimarosa, Galuppi, Piccinni, and Jommelli.

penillion. Type of Welsh traditional singing in which improvised or set poems are sung in counterpoint to well-known melody played by harpist. Also title of orch. work by Grace *Williams, comp. 1955.

Pennario, Leonard (*b* Buffalo, NY, 1924). Amer. pianist. Public début at 7, played with Dallas SO at 12 (Grieg conc.). Served in World War II but made NY début with NYPO, cond. Rodzinski, 1943; on resumption of career played in trio with Heifetz (vn.) and Piatigorsky (vc.). First toured Eur. 1952. Many tours as conc. soloist.

Penny for a Song, A. Opera in 2 acts by Richard Rodney Bennett to lib. by Colin Graham from play by John Whiting. Prod. London (SW) 1967.

pentatonic scale (from Gr. *pente*, five). Scale of 5 notes widely found in folk mus. (Scottish, Chinese, Negro, etc.) and found as early as 2000 BC. Can be easily prod. by playing 5 black keys only of pf., beginning with F♯. The tune of *Auld Lang Syne* is pentatonic.

Pentland, Barbara (Lally) (*b* Winnipeg, 1912; *d* Vancouver, 2000). Canadian composer. Taught theory and comp. Toronto Cons. 1943–9, Univ. of B.C., Vancouver, 1949–63. Works incl. 4 syms.; 5 str. qts.; pf. conc.; org. conc.; vn. sonata, etc.

Pépin, Clermont (*b* St Georges de Beauce, 1926). Canadian composer. Teacher of comp., Montreal Cons. 1955–64, dir. 1967–72. Works incl. 5 syms.; 2 pf. concs.; 5 str. qts.; sym.-poem *Guernica*; ballets *The Gates of Hell* and *The Phoenix*.

Pepusch, Johann Christoph (*b* Berlin 1667; *d* London, 1752). Ger.-born composer, conductor, and organist. Mainly self-taught; expert in theory and history. Settled in London 1704. Played va. and hpd. in Drury Lane orch. One of founders of *Academy of Ancient Music. Org. and comp. to Duke of Chandos 1715–31. From 1715 comp. mus. for operas and masques at Drury Lane and Lincoln's Inn Th. Probably comp. ov. for Gay's The *Beggar's Opera* (1728), but there is no evidence that he arranged the airs. Wrote treatise on harmony (1730) and other theoretical books.

per (It.). By, through, for, in order to, etc., e.g. *per stromentati*, for instrs.

Perahia, Murray (*b* NY, 1947). Amer. pianist and conductor. Début NY 1968. Winner Leeds

Int. pf. comp. 1972. Soloist with leading orchs. Frequently conducts from kbd. in perfs. of Mozart concs. First London recital 1973. Co-art. dir. Aldeburgh Fest. 1982–9. Salzburg Fest. début 1989. Hon. KBE 2004.

percussion. Name for family of instrs. (perhaps the most ancient in existence) which are usually played by striking a resonating surface with a stick or the hand, or by a pedal. The pf. may be used percussively (as in Orff, Stravinsky, Bartók, etc.) but is not classified as a perc. instr., nor is the celesta. The instr. are divided into those of definite pitch—*kettledrum, *tubular bells, *glockenspiel, *vibraphone, *xylophone, *marimba—and those of indefinite pitch—*triangle, *gong, *castanets, *whip, *rattle, *anvil, *bass drum, ten. *drum, *side-drum, *tabor, *tambourine, *bongo, and *cymbals. Various unusual devices such as iron chains, motor horns, tin sheet, come into the perc. section.

perdendo, perdendosi (It.; Fr. *se perdant*). Losing oneself, i.e. gradually dying away.

perfect cadence. See *cadence*.

Perfect Fool, The. Comic opera in 1 act by Holst, Op.39, to lib. by composer. Comp. 1918–22. Prod. London, CG 1923 cond. E. Goossens; Wichita 1962. Also separate orch. suite of ballet mus., f.p. 1920.

perfect intervals. See *interval*.

perfect pitch. See *absolute pitch*.

perfect time. See *common time*.

performance practice (Ger. *Aufführungspraxis*). The way in which mus. is perf., especially as it relates to the quest for the 'authentic' style of performing the mus. of previous generations and eras. Its study covers notation, ornamentation, instruments, voice production, tuning and pitch, and the size of ensembles and choruses.

Performing Right Society. Brit. assoc. of composers, authors, and mus. publishers founded 1914 for the purpose of collecting royalties for the non-dramatic public perf. and broadcasting of members' works. (Often incorrectly described as the Performing Rights Society.)

Pergolesi, Giovanni Battista (*b* Jesi, nr. Ancona, 1710; *d* Pozzuoli, nr. Naples, 1736). It. composer, violinist, and organist. Principally talented as composer of comic operas, the first of which, *Salustia*, was a failure in Naples in 1732. In 1733 he comp. *Il prigioner superbo*, now forgotten except for its 2-act intermezzo *La *serva padrona*, which has remained popular. Other operas, recently revived, incl. *Lo frate 'nnamorato* (1732), *Adriano in Siria* (1734), and *Il flaminio* (1735). His *Stabat Mater* (1736) for male sop., male alto, and orch. is still perf. After his early death from tuberculosis, many works were and still are falsely ascribed to him, such as the comic opera *Il maestro di musica*, concs., and songs. Stravinsky in *Pulcinella* 'recomposed' material by Pergolesi, but even there some of the attributions are false.

Peri, Jacopo (*b* Rome or Florence, 1561; *d* Florence, 1633). It. composer, pupil of Malvezzi, and singer. Entered service of Medici court 1588 and Mantuan court from early 1600s. Probably one of group of poets and musicians assoc. in Florence with Jacopo Corsi and Count *Bardi in last quarter of 16th cent. (see *Camerata*), and whose interest in reviving elements of Gr. drama led to comp. in monodic style of what is regarded as the first opera or mus.-drama, *Dafne* (1594–8), to which Peri contrib. the recitatives and some other items in collab. with Corsi. This was followed by *Euridice* (1600), parts of which were comp. by Peri's rival Caccini. Peri later wrote other operas, some in collab., ballets, madrigals, etc., only a few of which survive. Org. at Badia, Florence, 1579–1605.

Péri, La (The Peri). Ballet (*poème dansé*) by Dukas, Comp. 1911–12, choreog. Clustine, f.p. Paris 1912. Orch. suite from mus.

Périchole, La. *Opéra-bouffe* by Offenbach to lib. by Meilhac and Halévy after Mérimée's *Le Carrosse du Saint Sacrement*. Orig. in 2 acts (1868), rev. in 3 acts (1874). Prod. Paris 1868, NY 1869, London 1870.

Périgourdine. Old Fr. dance to mus. in compound duple time which was sung by the dancers. Its native home was Périgord.

Perle, George (*b* Bayonne, NJ, 1915). Amer. composer. Prof. of mus., Queens Coll., City Univ. of NY, 1961–84, having held teaching posts at other univs. from 1949. Comp.-in-residence, S. Francisco SO 1989–91. Authority on music and life of Alban Berg. Author of *Serial Composition and Atonality* (1962, 6th edn. 1991), *Twelve-Tone Tonality* (1977), *The Operas of Alban Berg, Wozzeck* (1980), *Lulu* (1985). As a composer evolved his own serialist method. Works incl. *Hebrew Melodies* for vc. (1945); 8 str. qts. (some withdrawn); 4 wind quintets; vc. conc. (1966); *3 Movements*, orch. (1960); *6 Bagatelles*, orch. (1965); *Sonnets to Orpheus*, ch. (1974); *A Short Symphony* (1980); vc. sonata (1985); *Dance Fantasy*, orch. (1986); pf. conc. No.1 (1990), No.2 (1992); *Adagio*, orch. (1992); *Duos*, hn., str. qt. (1995); *Critical Moments*, fl./picc., cl., vn., vc., pf., perc. (1996); *Chansons cachées*, pf. (1997).

Perlemuter, Vlado (*b* Kowno [Kaunas], 1904; *d* Paris, 2002). Fr. pianist of Polish birth. Learned all Ravel's pf. mus. between 1925 and 1927 and played it to the composer. His other specialization was Chopin. Prof. of pf., Paris Cons. 1950–77.

Perlman, Itzhak (*b* Tel Aviv, 1945). Israeli-born violinist (Amer. cit.). Recital on Amer. radio at age 10, Carnegie Hall 1963, with leading orchs. from 1964. London début 1968; Salzburg Fest.

début 1972. Assoc. in chamber mus. with Barenboim, Ashkenazy, Zukerman, etc. Plays seated because of polio.

Pérotin [known as Perotinus Magnus] (*c*.1160–1205 or 1225). Fr. composer whose identity is unknown. Choirmaster of chapel on site of present Notre Dame Cath., Paris, and leader of what became known as Notre Dame Sch. Wrote liturgical mus. in style known as *ars antiqua* and took leading part in revision of Léonin's theoretical treatise *Magnus liber*. Among his finest vocal works is the *Beata viscera*.

perpetual canon. A *canon so arr. that each v., having arrived at the end, can begin again, and so continue indefinitely.

perpetuum mobile (Lat.; It. *moto perpetuo*). Perpetually in motion. Title often given to type of instr. comp. based on rapid, repetitive note-patterns.

Perséphone. Melodrama in 3 scenes by Stravinsky to lib. by André Gide, choreog. Jooss, for narr., ten., ch., children's ch., and orch. Comp. 1933–4. Prod. Paris 1934, London (concert) 1934, London (stage) CG 1961, Santa Fe (stage) 1961. In ballet version, performer of Perséphone must recite and dance, but the role is now often divided between 2 performers, on Stravinsky's suggestion.

Persichetti, Vincent (Ludwig) (*b* Philadelphia, 1915; *d* Philadelphia, 1987). Amer. composer, conductor, and teacher. Teacher of comp. at Philadelphia Cons. 1941–7 and at Juilliard Sch. from 1947 (chairman of comp. dept. from 1963). Publishing executive and lecturer. Prolific and fluent composer in wide range of styles. Works incl. opera *The Sibyl* (1976); 9 syms.; 15 serenades; pf. conc.; 12 pf. sonatas; 6 pf. sonatinas; 9 hpd. sonatas; 4 str. qts.; septet *King Lear*; pf. quintet; *Stabat Mater*; songs; and 25 works (1965–86), mostly for solo instr., under name *Parable*. Wrote *Twentieth-Century Harmony* (NY, 1961).

Pert, Morris (*b* Edinburgh, 1947). Scottish composer. Won Royal Phil. Soc. award for orch. work *Xumbu-Ata* (1970). Worked for 2 years with Japanese percussionist Stomu Yamash'ta, then formed own experimental mus. group 'Suntreader'. Worked for 18 years as session musician in major London recording studios and made arrs. for Classic Rock series by LSO. Works comp. since 1971 incl. 2 ballets; incid. mus.; 4 syms.; vocal and choral mus.; pieces for kbd.; works using tape.

Perti, Giacomo Antonio (*b* Bologna, 1661; *d* Bologna, 1756). It. composer. Choirmaster at St Petronio, Bologna, 1696–1756. Wrote about 30 operas, several in collab., and few of which survive, but later devoted himself to religious works, especially oratorios, cantatas, and masses. Also wrote sonatas for vn. and vc. and other instr. works.

Pertile, Aureliano (*b* Montagnana, 1885; *d* Milan, 1952). It. tenor. Début Vicenza 1911 (Lionel in *Martha*). Sang in Naples, Milan, and Buenos Aires. La Scala début 1916; NY Met 1921–2; CG 1927–31. Leading ten. La Scala 1921–37, where he was greatly admired by Toscanini after his singing as Faust in Boito's *Mefistofele*. Created Boito's Nerone (1924). Later in his career he often sang Otello. Retired 1946. Prof. of singing, Milan Cons., 1945–52.

pes (Lat.). Foot. (1) Name for the ten. in Eng. mus. MSS of 13th and 14th cents., also for 2 lower parts in *Sumer is icumen in* (as ground bass).

(2) Synonym for *podatus*, a melodic figure in the old *neum notation.

pesante (It.). Heavy or heavily as in *allegro pesante*, implying that the whole passage is to be perf. with weight, as opposed to *allegro marcato*, which means that individual notes or groups of notes are to be emphasized.

Pešek, Libor (*b* Prague, 1933). Cz. conductor. Founder-cond. Prague Chamber Harmony 1959 and of Sebastian Orch. 1965. Mus. dir. Cz. State Chamber Orch. 1969–77, Frysk Orkest (Netherlands) 1969–75 and Overijssels PO (Netherlands) 1975–9. Cond., Slovak PO 1981–2. Res. cond. Czech PO from 1982. Prin. cond. RLPO 1987–97. Hon. KBE 1996.

Peter and the Wolf (*Petya i volk*). Symphonic fairy-tale for narrator and orch., Op.67, by Prokofiev to his own lib. Comp. 1936. F.p. Moscow Children's Theatre Centre 1936, f. Eng. p. London 1941. The boy Peter's fooling of a wolf is narrated and brilliantly illustrated by solo orch. instrs.; the work is delightful in itself and a wonderful way of instructing children (and others) how to identify orch. instr.

Peter Grimes. Opera in prol. and 3 acts by *Britten, Op.33, to lib. by Montagu Slater (1902–56) based on poem 'The Borough' (1810) by George Crabbe (1754–1832). Comp. 1944–5. F.p. London, SW, 7 June 1945; Tanglewood, Mass. 1946; CG 1947.

Peters, Carl Friedrich (*b* Leipzig, 1779; *d* Sonnenstein, Bavaria, 1827). Ger. mus. publisher who bought Kühnel and Hoffmeister's business (est. 1800) in 1814 and pubd. first complete edns. of Bach and Haydn. On his death business was continued by others, notably, after 1863, by Max Abraham (1831–1900) who developed the 'Peters Edition' of inexpensive classic scores and est. the Peters Library, opening it to the public in 1894. He enriched the firm's catalogue with works by Brahms, Grieg, Bruch, and Wagner. His nephew, Henri Hinrichsen (*b* Hamburg, 1868; *d* Theresienstadt, 1942), assumed control on Abraham's death, expanded the catalogue with works by Wolf, Mahler, Reger, Pfitzner, and Strauss (7 of his tone-poems), and was joined in partnership by his three sons in 1931 and 1933. One of these, Max (1901–65), settled in London 1937 where he est. Hinrichsen Edition in 1938 (Peters Edn. from 1975). His brother Walter (1907–69) settled in

USA 1936 where he est. C. F. Peters Corp. 1948, publishing many important Amer. composers. The third son, Hans-Joachim (1909–40) died in the Perpignan concentration camp. Leipzig house passed into other hands 1939, but Peters Edition was restored to Hinrichsen family in 1948. Firm of Peters Edition became state-owned company in Leipzig, also the Peters Library. Hinrichsen interest divided into 3 equal partners in London, NY, and Frankfurt. Peters Frankfurt acquired Belyayev Edition in 1971.

Peters [Peterman], **Roberta** (*b* NY, 1930). Amer. soprano. Début NY Met 1950 (Zerlina in *Don Giovanni*). Sang at Met until 1985 in variety of roles. CG début 1951; Salzburg Fest. début 1963. Sang in *The King and I* on Broadway 1973.

Peter Schmoll und seine Nachbarn ('Peter Schmoll and his Neighbours'). Opera (*Singspiel*) in 2 acts by Weber, to lib. by Joseph Türk based on novel by C. G. Cramer (1798–9). Dialogue now lost. Comp. 1801–2. Prod. Augsburg 1803 (and possibly Munich 1807). Revived Lübeck 1927 with new dialogue by K. Eggert. Reconstructed version by H. Hasse prod. Freiburg 1943. Version based on idea of R. Lauckner by W. W. Göttig published 1963.

Peterson, Oscar (Emmanuel) (*b* Montreal, 1925). Canadian jazz pianist. Joined Johnny Holmes Orch. 1944–7. Went to NY 1949, appearing at 'Jazz at the Philharmonic' concert and becoming recognized as one of leading jazz players of his time. Recordings and international tours followed. Appeared with guitarist (drummer after 1959) and bass player. Influenced by pianism of Art Tatum and vocal style of Nat King *Cole. Officer of Order of Canada 1973. Chancellor of York Univ., Toronto, 1991–4.

petite flûte (Fr.). Little flute, i.e. the *piccolo.

Petite Messe solennelle (Little Solemn Mass). Setting of Mass by Rossini for sop., cont., ten., and bar. soloists, ch. of 12 singers, 2 pf., and harmonium, 1863. F.p. Paris 1864. Arr. 1867 for full orch. by composer. The 'petite' does not refer to the work's size but is Rossini's too modest evaluation of its importance.

Petite Suite (Little Suite). Work for pf. 4 hands by Debussy comp. 1886–9 (arr. for pf. solo by Durand 1906). 4 movts. are *En bateau* (In a boat), *Cortège* (Funeral Procession), *Menuet*, and *Ballet*. Orch. version by Busser, 1907 (also version for small orch. by Mouton, 1909).

Petite Symphonie (Little Symphony). Work in 4 movements for 9 wind instr. (2 each of obs., cls., hns., and bns., and 1 fl.) by *Gounod, comp. 1885 for Paul Taffanel, Fr. flautist, and f.p. by *Société de Musique de la Chambre pour Instruments à Vent*, Paris 1885.

Petite Symphonie Concertante (Little concertante symphony). Work by Frank *Martin for harp, hpd., pf., and 2 str. orchs. Comp. 1944–5, arr. for full orch. 1946. F.p. Zurich 1946.

Petits Riens, Les (The Little Nobodies). Ballet mus. by Mozart (K Anh. 10) comp. in Paris, June 1778, for a perf. of a ballet-divertissement *Les Petits Riens* with lib. and choreog. by the Parisian ballet-master Jean Noverre. Mus. lost until 1872, when found in library of Paris Opéra.

Petrarch Sonnets, Three (Liszt). See *Sonetti di Petrarca*.

Petrassi, Goffredo (*b* Zagarolo, 1904; *d* Rome, 2003). It. composer. Worked in Rome mus. store and was given harmony lessons in his free time. Studied S. Cecilia Cons., Rome, 1928–33. Taught at S. Cecilia Acad. 1934–6, 1959–74, and at S. Cecilia Cons. 1939–59. Dir., La Fenice, Venice, 1937–40. Comps. in neoclassical style, using 12-note method in later works. Prin. works:

OPERAS: *Il Cordovano* (1944–8); *La Morte dell' Aria* (1950).

BALLETS: *La Follia di Orlando* (1942–3); *Ritratto di Don Chisciotte* (1945).

ORCH.: *Divertimento* (1930); *Ouverture da concerto* (1931); *Passacaglia* (1931); *Concertos for Orchestra*, No.1 (1933–4), No.2 (1951), No.3 (*Récréation Concertante*) (1952–3), No.4, str. (1954), No.5 (1955), No.6 (*Invenzione concertata*), brass, str., perc. (1956–7), No.7 (1961–2, rev. 1964), No.8 (1970–2); pf. conc. (1936–9); fl. conc. (1960); *Estri*, for 15 instr. (1966–7); *Poems* (1977–80); *Frammento* (1983).

CHAMBER MUSIC: *Sonata da camera* (1948); *Dialogo angelico*, 2 fl. (1948); *Musica a due*, 2 vc. (1952); str. qt. (1956–7); str. trio (1959); *Nunc*, gui. (1971); *Ala*, fl., hpd. (1972); *4 odi*, str. qt. (1973–5); *Sestina d'autunno*, 6 instrs. (1981–2); *Inno*, 12 brass (1984); *Duetto*, vn., va. (1985).

CHORAL: *Salmo 9*, ch. and orch. (1934–6); *Magnificat*, sop., ch., and orch. (1939–40); *Coro di morti*, male ch., 3 pf., brass, perc. (1940–1); *Noche oscura*, cantata (1950–1); *Beatitudines*, bar., 5 instr. (1969); *Orationes Christi*, ch., brass, 8 vn., 8 vc. (1974–5); *Tre cori sacri*, unacc. ch. (1980–3); *Laudes creaturarum*, narr., 6 instr. (1982); *Kyrie*, ch., str. (1986).

Petri, Egon (*b* Hanover, 1881; *d* Berkeley, Calif., 1962). Ger. pianist of Dutch ancestry. Son of H. V. Petri, violinist and composer. Int. reputation from 1920. Prof. of pf. RMCM, 1906–10. Prof. at Berlin Hochschule für Musik 1921–5. Lived in Poland 1925–39. Amer. début, NY 1932. Pianist-in-residence, Cornell Univ. 1940–6; Mills Coll., Oakland, 1947–57; S. Francisco Cons. 1952–62. Returned to Europe to teach in Basle 1957. Last recital 1960. Specialist in Liszt and Busoni. Collab. with Busoni in edn. of Bach.

Petri, Michala (*b* Copenhagen, 1958). Danish recorder player. Began to play at age of 3; début on radio at age of 5. Concert début Copenhagen 1969. Amer. début, NY 1982. Has commissioned several works.

Petrić, Ivo (*b* Ljubljana, 1931). Slovenian composer. Influenced in early works by *Bartók, turned to new types of sound after encountering mus.

of *Lutosławski, *Ligeti, and *Penderecki. Works incl. *Goga* Sym. (No.1) (1954); *Concerto grosso* (1955); fl. conc. (1955); sym. No.2 (1957), No.3 (1960); cl. sonata (1956–7); cl. conc. (1958); *Symphonic Mutations* (1964); *Musique Concertante*, pf., orch. (1971); *Dialogues concertantes*, vc., orch. (1972); *3 Images*, vn., orch. (1973); *Nocturnes et Jeux* (1973); *Gemini Conc.*, vn., vc., orch. (1975); *Thus played Kurent*, va., orch. (1976); *Jeux concertants*, fl., orch. (1978); *Toccata concertante*, 4 perc., orch. (1979); *The Song of Life*, mez., orch. (1981); *The Picture of Dorian Grey* (1984); tpt. conc. (1986); *Dresden Concerto*, 15 str. (1987); *Jeux*, v., hp. (1965); *Jeux II*, vocal and instr. sounds on tape (1966); *Intégrals en couleur*, chamber ens. (1968); str. qt. (1969); *3 Satires after Kriloff*, ch., ens. (1970); *Meditations*, pf. trio (1971); *Capriccio*, vc., 8 instr. (1973); *Summer Music*, fl., pf. (1973); *Autumn Music*, vn., pf. (1974); 3 wind quintets (1953, 1959, 1974); vn. sonata (1976); *Winter Music*, cl., pf. (1977); conc. for 5 perc. (1978); *Leipzig Chamber Music*, 5 players (1983); *Quatuor 1985*, str. qt. (1985); *Fantasies and Nocturnes*, vn., ch., pf. (1986); *Gallus Metamorphoses*, orch. (1992); *The Song of Life*, mez., orch. (1995); *Four Seasons*, orch. (1996); *Diptykhos*, 12 sax. (1996); hn. conc. (1997); *Trio lirico*, cl., va., pf. (1999); *Three Places in Scotland*, orch. (2000); *Metamorphosis on A*, str. (2001); *Macphadraig's Second Scottish Diary*, pf. (2002); *Preludes*, gui. (2003); *Episodes concertantes*, vn., vc. (2004).

Petrushka. (The title *Pétrouchka* is merely the Fr. transliteration of the Russ. and should properly be used only in Fr.) Ballet (burlesque) in 4 tableaux with mus. by Stravinsky, comp. 1910–11 to lib. by Benois, choreog. by Fokine. Prod. Paris (Diaghilev Ballet) 1911, London 1911, NY 1916. Nijinsky created title-role, Karsavina the Ballerina. Orch. suite f.p. Paris (cond. Monteux) 1914; re-orch. 1947 as suite in 4 parts with 15 movts. 3 movts. (*Russian Dance, In Petrushka's Cell*, and *Shrove-tide Fair*) arr. for pf. by Stravinsky, 1921. Version for 2 pf. arr. Babin exists, also Suite of 5 pieces arr. for pf. by Szántó, 1922.

Pettersson, (Gustaf) **Allan** (*b* Västra Ryd, 1911; *d* Stockholm, 1980). Swed. composer and violist. Violist, Stockholm PO 1940–50. Comps. incl. 16 syms. (1950–80); conc. for vn. and str. qt; vn. conc.; 3 concs. for str. orch.; 7 sonatas for 2 vn.; song-cycle *Vox Humana* for soloists, ch., and orch.; songs, etc.

petto, voce di (It.). *Chest v.

Peyer, Gervase (Alan) **de** (*b* London, 1926). Eng. clarinettist and conductor. Début, broadcast of Mozart conc. while at school. Founder member, Melos Ens. 1950. Prin. cl., LSO, 1955–71. Dir. LSO wind ens., appearing at Salzburg Fest. 1973. Ass. cond. Haydn Orch. Prof. of cl., RAM, 1959–68. Played with Chamber Music Soc. of Lincoln Center, NY, 1969–89. Gave f.p. of works by Musgrave, Hoddinott, Sebastian Forbes, and others.

pezzo (It., plural *pezzi*, 'piece'). A comp., the word sometimes being used as part of the title, e.g. *Pezzo concertante, Tre pezzi*.

Pfeife (Ger.). Fife, fl. org. pipe.

Pfitzner, Hans (Erich) (*b* Moscow, 1869; *d* Salzburg, 1949). Ger. composer and conductor. Taught pf. Coblenz Cons. 1892–3. Cond. Mainz mus. th. 1894–6. Taught comp. and cond. Stern Cons., Berlin, 1897–1907. First cond. Theater des Westens, Berlin, 1903–6. Municipal mus. dir. and dir. of Cons., Strasbourg, 1908–18, becoming mus. dir. Strasbourg Opera 1910–16. Taught in Berlin 1920–9. Prof. of comp., Munich Acad. 1929–34. Influenced by Wagner and Schopenhauer. Well-known as writer on mus. and determined critic of modern tendencies. Mahler cond. two of his operas in Vienna, but his chief success was with *Palestrina* (Munich 1917) which has remained in the repertory in Ger. and has won many admirers beyond its frontiers. The Nazis upheld his mus. as in the best Ger. tradition and contrasted it with the 'degeneracy' of Strauss. After the 1939–45 war he was found in penury in a Munich home for the aged by the president of the Vienna PO who took him to Vienna where he was supported by the orch. His mus. is romantic in a Wagner-Strauss idiom; his songs in particular are beautiful. Prin. works:

OPERAS: *Der arme Heinrich* (1891–3); *Die *Rose vom Liebesgarten* (1897–1900); *Das Christelflein* (comp. as incid. mus. 1906, converted into opera 1917); *Palestrina* (1911–15); *Das Herz* (1931).

ORCH.: *Scherzo* (1888); *Kleine Symphonie* (1939); *Fantasie* (1947); pf. conc. (1922); vn. conc. (1923); vc. conc. No.1 (1935), No.2 (1944); sym. in C♯ minor (adapted from 2nd str. qt.) (1932); sym. in C (1940).

INCIDENTAL MUSIC: *Das Fest auf Solhaug* (Ibsen) (1889–90); *Das Käthchen von Heilbronn* (Kleist) (1905); *Das Christelflein* (Stach) (1906, reworked as opera 1917).

CHORAL: *Der Blumen Rache*, ballad for alto, women's ch., and orch. (1888); *Columbus*, 8-part unacc. ch. (1905); *Rundgesang zum Neujahrsfest*, bass, ch., and pf. (1901); *Von deutscher Seele*, cantata for 4 soloists, ch., and orch. (1921, rev. 1937); *Das dunkle Reich* (1929).

CHAMBER MUSIC: str. qt. No.1 (1902–3), No.2 (1925), No.3 (1942); pf. trio (1896); pf. quintet (1908); vc. sonata (1890); pf. sextet (1945).
Over 90 *Lieder* with pf. acc. and songs with orch.

Phaedra. (1) Dramatic cantata by Britten, Op.93, for mez. and small orch., being setting of extracts from Racine's *Phèdre* trans. by Robert Lowell. Comp. 1975. Ded. to Dame Janet Baker, who gave f.p. Aldeburgh 1976.

(2) Monodrama for mez. and orch. by G. *Rochberg, Comp. 1973–4 (text drawn from Lowell by Gene Rochberg). F.p. NY, 1976, by Neva Pilgrim with Syracuse SO, cond. D. Loebel.

Phaëton. Symphonic poem, Op.39, by Saint-Saëns, comp. 1873. Also opera by Lully (Paris, 1683).

phagotum. Instr. invented *c*.1520 by Canon Afranio of Ferrara (*c*.1489–*c*.1565), being a kind

of bellows-blown bagpipe. Nothing to do with bn. (fagott), the only feature in common being use of parallel bores.

Phantasie (Ger.). Fantasy, fancy, hence *Phantasiestück* (more commonly spelt *Fantasiestück*), 'fantasy piece'. See *fantasia*.

phantasy. Same as fantasy, but this spelling was preferred by W. W. *Cobbett when he est. his prize in 1906 for works comp. in this form. Hence the large number of Eng. works with this word in their title, e.g. *Phantasy Quintet* by Vaughan Williams, *Phantasy Quartet* by Britten.

Philadelphia Orchestra. Amer. sym. orch. founded 1900 by Fritz Scheel, who remained cond. until 1907. Succeeded by Karl Pohlig 1907–12. The orch.'s fame and style (rich and virtuoso) were est. under the conductorship 1912–38 of Leopold *Stokowski, who also introduced many new and adventurous works to Amer. audiences (e.g. Mahler's 8th Sym., 1916, and works by Schoenberg). Eugene *Ormandy was co-cond. 1936–8 and succeeded Stokowski, occupying the post for the next 40 years and consolidating the orch.'s position as among the world's greatest. Riccardo *Muti prin. cond. 1981–92, Wolfgang *Sawallisch 1993–2002, Christoph Eschenbach from 2003. Salzburg Fest. début 1987, cond. Muti.

Philharmonia Orchestra. Eng. sym. orch. founded 1945 by Walter *Legge primarily to make recordings for the Gramophone Co. Cond. on records and in the concert-hall incl. Karajan, Klemperer, Toscanini, Furtwängler, Strauss, Giulini, Cantelli, and Dobrowen. Became principally assoc. with Otto Klemperer (prin. cond. 1959–73), who was made 'conductor for life'. In 1964, after Legge had attempted to disband it, orch. became self-governing body named New Philharmonia, the 'New' being dropped in 1977. Salzburg début 1990 (cond. Sinopoli). Lorin Maazel assoc. prin. cond. 1971–3; Riccardo Muti prin. cond. 1973–82; Giuseppe Sinopoli 1984–94; Christoph von Dohnányi 1997–2008.

Philharmonic Society (of London). See *Royal Philharmonic Society*.

Philidor [Danican]. Fr. family of musicians over several generations, *c*.1600–1800. Best-known was François André (*b* Dreux, 1726; *d* London, 1795), famous as composer (pupil of Campra) and as chess-player. Visited London annually to play chess from 1745 and heard Handel's operas. Settled in Paris 1754, composing successful comic operas, e.g. *Tom Jones* and *L'amant déguisé*. His father, André (*b* Versailles, *c*.1647; *d* Dreux, 1730) played ob., crumhorn, and bn. and was composer. Compiled (1684–1730) coll. of Fr. court mus. from reign of Henri III to end of 17th cent., some of which is in Versailles Municipal Library, and a large part, formerly at St Michael's College, Tenbury, is now in the Bibliothèque Nationale, Paris.

Philips, Peter (*b* c.1561; *d* Brussels, 1628). Eng. composer and organist. Choirboy, St Paul's Cath., London, 1574. First comp., a keyboard pavan, 1580. Fled country 1582 because he was RC. Org., Eng. Coll. in Rome 1582–5. In 1585 entered service of Lord Thomas Paget and travelled to Switz., Sp., and France with him. Settled in Antwerp 1590 as court org. Visited Sweelinck in Amsterdam 1593. Was arrested 1593 and accused of conspiracy to assassinate Elizabeth I, but was exonerated and released. 1st book of madrigals pubd. 1596. Entered service of Archduke in Brussels 1597 as one of 3 organists of vice-regal chapel, a post he held until he died. John Bull visited him in 1613. Comp. motets, madrigals, masses, and psalms, all of high quality and interest.

Phillips, Peter (*b* Southampton, 1953). Eng. conductor. Founded choir, Tallis Scholars, 1978, which quickly won high reputation for perfs. of works by Lassus, Gesualdo, Victoria, Josquin, Byrd, Taverner, Palestrina, and others. Toured Australia 1984, Amer. 1988. Proms début 1988 (Victoria *Requiem*). Author of *English Sacred Music 1549–1649* (1991). Occasional writer on cricket.

'Philosopher, The' (*Der Philosoph*). Nickname of Haydn's Sym. No.22 in E♭ (Hob. I:22) comp. 1764. Known by this title in Haydn's lifetime in reference to opening *adagio*. Haydn said he had once written a sym. in which God speaks to an unrepentant sinner: this could be the work. A 2nd version, omitting the *adagio*, was printed in Paris by Venier in 1773.

Phoebus and Pan (Eng. title for *Der Streit zwischen Phoebus und Pan*, 'The Strife between Phoebus and Pan'). Cantata by J. S. Bach (BWV 201), comp. ?1729, to lib. by Picander (based on Ovid) satirizing hostile mus. critic. Sometimes staged as opera.

Phoenix Mass. Choral work by *Payne for mixed ch., 3 tpt., and 3 tb., comp. 1965–9 with 39 bars added to *Agnus Dei* in 1972.

phoneuma. Very soft org. stop of *dulciana* tone and *quintatön* effect.

phonograph. Same as gramophone and used in USA. The term was devised by Edison for his recording machine, the record or wax cylinder being called a *phonogram*.

phrase. Short section of a comp. into which the mus., whether vocal or instr., seems naturally to fall. Sometimes this is 4 measures, but shorter and longer phrases occur. It is an inexact term: sometimes a phrase may be contained within one breath, and sometimes sub-divisions may be marked. In notation, phrase-marks are the slurs placed over or under the notes as a hint of their proper punctuation in perf. (see *curved line, various uses of*). The art of phrasing by a perf. is often instinctive and is one of the features by which a supreme artist may be distinguished from one of lesser inspiration, whether cond., singer, or instrumentalist.

Phrygian Mode. The 3rd of the ecclesiastical *modes, represented by white keys of pf. beginning on E.

piacevole (It.). Agreeable.

Piaf [Gassion], **Edith** (Giovanna) (*b* Paris, 1915; *d* Mougins, 1963). French *chanteuse*. As a child, assisted her father in his circus act. At 15 became street singer and was nicknamed *Piaf* (sparrow) because of her ragged appearance. Radio début 1936 and was helped by Maurice Chevalier to become leading music-hall star. During war entertained Fr. prisoners in Ger. and was accused of collaboration but exonerated. Toured USA 1947. Her most famous songs were *Non, je ne regrette rien* and her own *La vie en rose*, sung in a powerful, strident style which captivated audiences. Wrote 2 books of memoirs, pubd. 1958 and 1964.

piangendo, piangente (It.). Weeping; **piangevole, piangevolmente**. Plaintive; plaintively.

piano (It.). Soft, quiet. (1) Instruction to play softly (abbreviation *p*, or *pp*, *pianissimo*, very softly). Opposite of *forte*, loud.

(2) Eng. term for kbd. instr. whose full name is *pianoforte* (It.), soft-loud. This instr. is, with regard to its str. and hammers, a descendant of the *dulcimer, and, to its kbd., a descendant of the *harpsichord and *clavichord. The modern pf. has an iron frame and is either *grand* (str. horizontal) or *upright* (str. vertical). It normally has 88 keys, with a standard compass of 7⅓ octaves, but some models by Bösendorfer have a compass of 8 octaves.

Although there are other claimants to the invention of the instrument, it is generally accepted that the earliest instr. of this type was made in Florence, c.1698–1700, by Bartolomeo *Cristofori, who prod. what he called a *gravicembalo col piano e forte*, i.e. a 'harpsichord with loudness and softness': for the hpd.'s plucking of the str. he had substituted the blows of a series of hammers, and it was this that gave the players of his instr. their new power of control of degrees of force. The Cristofori pfs. had a range of 4 to 4½ octaves.

Cristofori's idea was taken up in Ger. by the org.-builder Gottfried Silbermann, who in 1726 made 2 pfs. which he submitted to Bach, whose opinion of them was unfavourable and perhaps led to the improvements which apparently were introduced. In 1747 Bach, on a visit to the court of Frederick the Great at Potsdam, played the Silbermann pfs. there. All pfs. up to this point were of the hpd. shape—rather like what we now call the grand pf., with the str. horizontal and in line with the relevant finger-keys. The first pf. in clavichord shape, known as the square pf., was made by Frederici of Gera, but he was closely followed by one of Silbermann's apprentices, Johannes Zumpe, who went to London and introduced there the popular rectangular form of the instr. Further impetus to the pf. was given by J. C. Bach, when he settled in London, and by *Clementi. Developments in the 'action' of the instr. were made by Backers, John Broadwood, and Stodart. Broadwood made changes in the square pf. In Fr., Érard made the square, and later grand pfs., while the Austrian Andreas Stein found a way of giving extra lightness of touch to the grand. The first Amer.-built pfs. were by J. Behrent in Philadelphia, 1775.

The *upright pianoforte*, in which the str. run perpendicularly, was developed by John Isaac Hawkins of Philadelphia (1800) and Robert Wornum, jun., of London (1811, perfected 1829): the existing model is largely founded on that of Wornum. From the middle of the 19th cent. it superseded the square form, but was itself almost ousted in the 20th cent. by the 'baby', i.e. small-sized, grand.

Hawkins also introduced the iron frame. One advantage was the possibility of using str. at higher tension than the wooden frame allowed, so making possible the use of thicker wire, producing a fuller tone. The tension of a single str. today may be 180–200 lb., the varying stress of the different sizes of str. being more or less equally distributed by *overstringing*, i.e. by one group of str. passing more or less diagonally over another: this principle as applied to the pf. dates from *c*.1835, but there had previously been occasional overstrung clavichords.

18th-cent. hpds. had more than 1 str. to each note and Cristofori's pf. had 2 throughout: the modern pf. has 1 string for a few of the very lowest notes, 2 for the middle register, and 3 for the highest (on account of the decrease of resonance with the shorter str.): the lowest str. are wrapped with a copper coil to increase their mass without too greatly decreasing their flexibility.

The *sound-board* of a pf. (lying behind the str. in an upright and below them in a grand) fulfils the same function as the body of a vn.: without it the tone of the instr. would be very faint and thin. The *sustaining pedal*, when depressed, removes the whole series of dampers from the str.: thus any note or chord played can be given some duration, even though the finger or fingers have been removed from the keys, and also the harmonics of the str. sounded are enriched by the sympathetic resonance of those derived from other freely-vibrating str., resulting in a fuller tone. (It is a mistake to call this pedal the 'Loud Pedal' as it is as much used in soft passages as in loud.) This pedal must of course normally be lifted at a change of harmony, as otherwise confusion will result. There is in most instr. manufactured in the USA and Canada a *sostenuto pedal*. It ingeniously enables the player to make (within limits) a selection as to the notes he wishes to be held over. It was introduced by the Steinway firm and perfected in 1874. The *soft pedal* may act in one of several ways: (a) in grands by moving the kbd. and set of hammers sideways, so as to leave unstruck 1 str. of each note (see *corda*); (b) in uprights by moving the whole set of hammers nearer to the str., so that the force of their blows is diminished, or by interposing a piece of felt between hammer and str. (a crude method now little used). Many contemporary pianos are made only in Japan.

Experiments in the construction of the pf. have been frequent; these have included pfs. with double kbd.; pfs. with indefinitely prolonged sounds (by means of a revolving wheel or other imitation of the vn. bow, or of a current of air

tending to keep the str. in vibration, or by some electrical device); pfs. with tuning-forks in place of str. (incapable of getting out of tune); combinations of the pf. principle with that of some other instr. (e.g. fl., organ, hpd., clavichord); quarter-tone pfs. (see *microtone*); various applications of electricity, etc. See *keyboard* for experimental kbds.; see *prepared piano*; see *aliquot* and *duplex* scaling.

The pf. is, of course, principally used as a solo instr., or as the solo instr. in a conc. with orch., or in chamber mus. (pf. trio, pf. qt., etc.). But many composers in the 20th cent. have used it as an orch. instr., e.g. Stravinsky in *Petrushka*, Vaughan Williams in *Sinfonia Antartica*, Bartók in *Music for Strings, Percussion, and Celesta*, and numerous other works. Stravinsky's *Les Noces* is scored for 4 pf. used as perc. instrs. Later composers, from *Cage onwards, have conjured new sounds from the pf. by making adjustments to the str. (see *prepared piano*), having them plucked by hand, or used as resonators.

Since its first appearance, the pf. has called forth executants of varying styles and techniques. C. P. E. Bach was among the first to develop the new methods of playing so different from those required for hpd. and clavichord, followed by *Clementi. Absolute evenness of touch was his ideal, inculcated also in his pupil *Cramer. The Viennese-made pf. was lighter, with less sonorous tone, than the heavier English type. Mozart's playing was attuned to the Viennese action. His most famous pupil was *Hummel. But Beethoven used an Eng. pf., suitable to his energetic and dynamic playing. He was the first fully to profit by the opportunities afforded by the sustaining pedal. His example was followed by Schubert, Schumann, *Chopin, and Mendelssohn, whose works would be unimaginable on a pedalless instr. John *Field developed the 'singing touch' of legato playing and his exploitation of the *nocturne* influenced Chopin whose playing and comps. for the pf. opened up new possibilities of tone-colour. *Liszt was the first of the virtuosi whose technique rivalled Paganini's on the vn., expanding it beyond all previous bounds, and pointing the way to the harmonic experiments of Debussy and Ravel and even to the percussive effects of Stravinsky and Bartók. Other great 19th-cent. executants were Rubinstein, Thalberg, and Bülow, while among the great composer-pianists born in the 19th cent. were Busoni, Rachmaninov, and Bartók. The 20th cent. has been rich in superb virtuosi. One need name only Arthur Rubinstein, Arrau, Horowitz, Michelangeli, and Richter as exemplars.

pianoforte (It.). 'Soft-loud'. The *piano.

pianola. Patented name (by the Aeolian Corp.) for one of the group of pfs. known as 'player-pianos'. These instr. are fitted with a mechanism by which the keys are depressed not by the fingers but by air-pressure supplied through bellows and pedals or by electricity. The air-pressure is applied through perforations on a paper roll which unwinds and which are arranged so that a comp. is played. It is not necessary for the perforations to be restricted to the number of notes which can be played by 2 (or 4) hands. In some cases the rolls reproduce an artist's nuances in performance, such as *crescendos, diminuendos*, and tempo changes, the instr. then reproducing this perf. (hence the name reproducing piano). The first of this kind was the Welte-Mignon, invented by Edwin Welte in Freiburg in 1904. Historic rolls of this kind, first developed in 1904 by Welter and Sons in Ger., preserve, for example, the playing of their own mus. by Mahler, Strauss, Debussy, Rachmaninov, Busoni, and Gershwin. Works were comp. for the player-piano by Stravinsky, Hindemith, Casella, Howells, and others. Some of these perfs. have been transferred to CDs. Further developments made possible by use of encoded magnetic tape cassettes. In 1978 an ordinary piano fitted with computer and tape interface, could re-play a perf. controlled by the tape. In 1986 Bösendorfer manufactured a computer-assisted model.

piano quartet. Group of 4 players—usually pianist, violinist, violist, and cellist—or work written for them to perform.

piano quintet. Group of 5 players—usually pianist, 2 violinists, violist, cellist—or work written for them, but one of the most famous works, Schubert's 'Trout' quintet, is for pf., vn., va., vc., and db.

piano score. Score in which the orch. parts and vocal parts (if any) are reduced to a pf. part.

piano signs for 'spreading' of chords
Instead of attacking the notes of the chord simultaneously

('Arpeggriated', i.e. harp-fashion)

written   played

ultaneously, play them from the bottom upwards, holding each as struck. (Occasionally in early mus. the notes are to be played from the top downwards and the question as to which is intended is sometimes a difficult one.)

Sometimes the wavy line is not continuous between the two staves, and then it is to be understood that the composer intends the arpeggio effect to go on in the two hands simultaneously.

It is to be noted that all spread chords should be so played as not to destroy the rhythm of the passage.

piano trio. Group of 3 players—pianist, violinist, cellist—or work written for them to perform.

Piatigorsky, Gregor (*b* Ekaterinoslav, 1903; *d* Los Angeles, 1976). Russ.-born cellist (Amer. cit. 1942). Joined Lenin Qt. 1919 and in same year became prin. vc. of Moscow Bolshoy Opera orch. Left Russ. 1921, becoming prin. vc. Berlin PO under Furtwängler 1924–8. Played in *Don Quixote* many times cond. by Strauss, who admired him greatly. Formed sonata partnership with *Schnabel. Amer. début in Oberlin, Ohio, 1929, followed by Dvořák conc. in NY. In 1930s played in trio with Horowitz and Milstein. Taught at Curtis Inst. 1942–51 and at Univ. of S. Calif., Los Angeles, 1962–76. Gave f.ps. of concs. by Castelnuovo-Tedesco (1935), Hindemith (1941), and Walton (1957). Comp. works for vc. and wrote autobiography, *Cellist*, 1965.

piatti (It.). *Cymbals.

Piatti, Alfredo (Carlo) (*b* Borgo di Canale, nr. Bergamo, 1822; *d* Crocetta di Mozzo, nr. Bergamo, 1901). It. cellist and composer. Début Milan 1837, Paris and London 1844. Annual visitor to London, being particularly assoc. with the Monday and Saturday Popular Chamber Concerts 1859–98. Lived in London from 1846 and was cellist in Joachim Qt. Piatti prize for cellists at RAM is in his memory. Wrote 2 vc. concs., 6 vc. sonatas, other chamber works, and ed. vc. sonatas by other composers. His 1720 Stradivari vc., now known as 'the Piatti', is lent to the winner of the triennial Piatigorsky Award in NY.

Piave, Francesco Maria (*b* Murano, 1810; *d* Milan, 1876). It. poet and librettist. Son of Murano glass-maker. Became proof reader in Venice and began to write opera libs. Was recommended to Verdi and wrote libs. for 10 Verdi operas—*Ernani* (1844), *I due Foscari* (1844), *Macbeth* (with Mattei, 1847), *Il corsaro* (1848), *Stiffelio* (1850) rev. as *Aroldo* (1857), *Rigoletto* (1851), *La traviata* (1853), *Simon Boccanegra* (1857), and *La forza del destino* (1862). Also wrote libs. for Balfe, Mercadante, and Ricci brothers.

pibroch (Gaelic *piobaireachd*). Type of Scot. Highland bagpipe mus. in the form of variations.

Picardie, tierce de (Fr.). Picardy third. See *tierce de Picardie*.

Piccaver [Peckover], **Alfred** (*b* Long Sutton, Lincs., 1884; *d* Vienna, 1958). Eng. tenor. Début

Prague 1907 as Gounod's Romeo. Leading ten. at Vienna Opera 1910–37; Chicago 1923–5; CG 1924; Salzburg Fest. 1927. Noted for smooth legato and noble phrasing. Returned to London 1937–55, giving some lessons, but went back to Vienna as guest for re-opening of State Opera 1955 and remained to teach.

picchettato, picchiettato, picchiettando (It.). Knocked, knocking. In the playing of bowed instr., detaching the notes (see also *spiccato*).

Piccinni, Niccolò (*b* Bari, 1728; *d* Passy, 1800). It. composer. First opera, *Le donne dispettose* was success in Naples, 1755. His most popular opera buffa, *La cecchina, ossia La buona figliuola*, 1760, based on Richardson's *Pamela*, was perf. throughout Europe. Wrote about 100 operas for It. theatres. Second choirmaster, Naples Cath. and taught singing. Most of his operas were perf. in Rome, but he fell out of favour in 1753 when *Anfossi came to the fore. In 1776 moved to Paris to write Fr. operas. His first was *Roland* (1778). This was perf. in the midst of the celebrated Gluck-Piccinni feud, engineered by the composers' supporters. The dir. of the Paris Opéra arranged for each to compose *Iphigénie en Tauride*. Gluck's version came first, 1779, and eclipsed Piccinni's of 1781. After Gluck left Paris, *Sacchini became a rival. Piccinni became a teacher at the École Royale de Chant 1784, but returned to Naples 1791 after outbreak of the Revolution. There he was suspected of political intrigue and lived for 4 years under virtual house arrest. Returned to Paris 1798 but his star had waned. His operas, no rivals to Gluck's, nevertheless have excellent qualities. They incl. *Il curioso del suo proprio danno* (1756), *La Cecchina* (1760), *L'Olimpiade* (1761), *Alessandro nelle Indie* (1758, rev. 1774), *Didon* (1783), *Pénélope* (1785), *La serva onorata* (1792).

piccolo (from It. *flauto piccolo*, little flute; also known as octave flute, It. *ottavino*). Small fl. pitched octave higher than concert fl., used in orch. and military band. Famous picc. parts occur in Beethoven's *Egmont* ov. and in Sousa's march *The Stars and Stripes Forever*. Also organ stop, metal or wood, of 2′ length and pitch.

Picker, Tobias (*b* Manhattan, NY, 1954). Amer. composer. Started to compose aged 8, encouraged by Menotti. Studied at Manhattan Sch. of Mus. (comp. with C. Wuorinen, orch. with J. Corigliano), Juilliard Sch., and Princeton Univ. (with Babbitt). Won many prizes, incl. Charles Ives Scholarship and Guggenheim Foundation fellowship. Comp.-in-res. Houston SO 1985–90. Comps. incl.:

OPERAS: *Emmeline* (1996); *Fantastic Mr Fox* (1997–8); *Thérèse Raquin* (1999–2000); *An American Tragedy* (2005–6).

ORCH.: sym. No.1 (1982), No.2, sop., orch. (1986), No.3, str. (1988); pf. conc. No.1 (1980), No.2 (1983), No.3 (1986); vn. conc. (1981); *The Encantadas*, narr., orch. (1983); *Old and Lost Rivers* (1986); *Romances and Interludes*, ob., orch. (1989);

Bang! amp. pf., orch. (1992); *And Suddenly it's Evening* (1994); va. conc. (1994); vc. conc. (1999); *Tre sonetos de amour*, bar., orch. (2000).

VOCAL: *Aussöhnung*, medium/high v., pf. (1984); *Half a Year Together*, medium/high v., pf. (1987); *The Rain in the Trees*, fl., v., orch. (1993); *Irrational Exuberance*, medium-high/high v., pf. (2001); *I am in Need of Music*, medium/high v., pf. (2004).

CHAMBER MUSIC: *Rhapsody*, vn., pf. (1978); *Nova*, pf. quintet (1979); *The Blue Hula*, fl., cl., vib., glock., maracas, vn., vc., pf. (1981); *Dedication Anthem*, band (1984); str. qt. No.1 (1987), No.2, with bass (1988); *Invisible Lilacs*, vn., pf. (1991); *Suite*, vc., pf. (1998).

PIANO: *Pianorama*, 2 pf. (1984); *Old and Lost Rivers* (1986); *The Blue Hula* (1990); *4 Etudes for Ursula* (1996).

Pickett, Philip (*b* London, 1950). Eng. recorder-player and conductor. Specialist in early mus. for recorder. Prof. of Early Mus., GSMD, from 1972. Dir., New London Consort, appearing at major Eur. fests.

Pick-Mangiagalli, Riccardo (Strakonice, 1882; *d* Milan, 1949). Bohemian-born composer and pianist of partly It. descent; naturalized It. Began career as pianist in Vienna before turning to composing. Dir., Milan Cons. 1936–49. Wrote operas, sym.-poems, chamber mus., and songs.

Pictures at an Exhibition (*Kartinki s vystavki*). Pf. comp. by Mussorgsky, 1874, being mus. representation of 10 pictures at a memorial exhibition for Russ. artist Victor Hartmann, who died in 1873, with a 'promenade' as linking passage. Orch. versions by Ravel, Henry Wood, Stokowski, Ashkenazy, Elgar Howarth (brass and perc.), and others. The titles of the pieces are: *The Gnome, The Old Castle, Tuileries, Bydlo* (Polish for cattle), *Unhatched chickens, Samuel Goldenberg and Shmuyle, Market-place at Limoges, Catacombs, Baba-yaga* (*The Hut on Fowl's Legs*), *The Great Gate of Kiev*.

pied en l'air (Fr.). Foot in the air. A particular motion in the *galliard.

pieno, piena (It.). Full. *organo pieno*, full organ; *coro pieno*, full choir (contrasted with passages for smaller ens.); *a voce piena*, with full v.

Pierné, (Henri Constant) **Gabriel** (*b* Metz, 1863; *d* Ploujean, Finistère, 1937). Fr. composer, organist, and conductor. Succeeded Franck as org., Ste-Clotilde, 1890–8. Ass. cond., Concerts Colonne 1903, becoming prin. cond. 1910–34. Works incl. ballet *Cydalise et le Chèvre-pied* (Cydalise and the Satyr), 1923, from which comes the 'Entry of the Little Fauns'; oratorios *La Croisade des Enfants* (The Children's Crusade), 1902, and *Les enfants à Bethléem*, 1907; pf. conc., incidental and chamber mus.

Pierrot Lunaire (Moonstruck Pierrot). Melodrama for female v., pf., fl., picc., cl., bass cl., vn., va., and vc., Op.21, by Schoenberg, comp. 1912, f.p. Berlin 1912, London 1923. Cycle of '3 times

7' songs—in *Sprechgesang*—to poems by Albert Giraud trans. from Fr. into Ger. by O. E. Hartleben. The titles are: I, *Mondestrunken, Colombine, Der Dandy, Eine blasse Wäscherin, Valse de Chopin, Madonna, Der kranke Mond*. II, *Die Nacht, Gebet an Pierrot, Raub, Rote Messe, Galgenlied, Enthauptung, Die Kreuze*. III, *Heimweh, Gemeinheit, Parodie, Der Mondfleck, Serenade, Heimfahrt, O alter Duft*.

Pierrot Players. Instr. ens. founded 1967 by *Maxwell Davies and Harrison *Birtwistle for perf. of contemporary mus., particularly their own. Title adopted because of frequent perf. of Schoenberg's *Pierrot Lunaire*. Re-organized 1970 as *Fires of London.

Pierson [Pearson], **Henry Hugo** (*b* Oxford, 1815; *d* Leipzig, 1873). Ger. composer and teacher of Eng. origin. Lived in Ger. 1839–44. In 1846 appointed prof. of mus., Edinburgh Univ., resigning after a few months to settle in Ger. Wrote several operas, prod. Brno (1845) and Hamburg (1848), oratorios, incl. *Jerusalem* (Norwich, 1852), music for Goethe's *Faust, Part II* (Hamburg 1854), sym.-poem *Macbeth* (1859), part-song *Ye Mariners of England*, and other pieces. His songs are regarded as of considerable interest and originality.

piffaro, piffero (It.). In 16th cent., generic term for any kind of pipe. Specifically a rustic wind instr. of the *shawm family. When Handel wrote *pifa* above his 'Pastoral Symphony' in *Messiah* he was referring to the *piffero*.

Pijper, Willem (*b* Zeist, 1894; *d* Leidschendam, 1947). Dutch composer. Mus. critic in Utrecht 1918–23. Prof. of comp. Amsterdam Cons. 1925–30. Dir., Rotterdam Cons. 1930–47. Most prominent Dutch composer of his generation. Works incl. 2 operas; 3 syms. (1918, 1921, 1926); *6 Symphonic Epigrammata*; pf. conc.; vn. conc.; vc. conc.; 5 str. qts.; 2 pf. trios; and other chamber mus.

Pilarczyk, Helga (*b* Schöningen, Brunswick, 1925). Ger. soprano. Début Brunswick 1951 as mez. Brunswick Opera 1951–4; Hamburg Opera 1954–68. Glyndebourne début 1958 (Composer in *Ariadne auf Naxos*) and CG 1959. Amer. début Washington DC 1962; NY Met 1965. Specialist in 20th-cent. roles. Sang in f.p. of Henze's *König Hirsch*, Berlin 1956.

Pilgrim's Progress, The. There have been several mus. settings based on the allegory by John Bunyan (Part I 1674–9, II 1684). The best-known are:
(1) Opera (morality) in 4 acts by *Vaughan Williams to his own adaptation of Bunyan, with Christian's name altered to Pilgrim. Comp. between 1925 and 1951, rev. 1951–2. Prod. CG 1951, Cambridge 1954, Manchester (RNCM) 1992; f. Amer. p. Provo, Utah, 1968. Act IV, Sc. 2 is *The *Shepherds of the Delectable Mountains*, which had been prod. as a separate 'pastoral episode' in London in 1922. Vaughan Williams also comp. incidental mus. (some of it later incorporated into the opera) for BBC prod. of *The Pilgrim's Progress* in 1943. His 5th

Sym. (1938–43) uses themes from the opera, which at that time he did not expect to finish.
(2) Oratorio for soloists, ch., and orch. by *Bantock, 1928.
(3) Oratorio by Robin *Milford, 1932.

Pilkington, Francis (*b* c.1570; *d* Chester, 1638). Eng. composer. Lay clerk, Chester Cath., from 1602, later clergyman, and precentor of the cath. from 1623. Wrote songs with lute or viola da gamba (1605), 2 sets of madrigals (1614 and 1624), and religious part-songs. Contrib. 5-part madrigal *When Oriana Walked to Take the Air* to *The *Triumphs of Oriana*.

Pimlott, Steven (Charles) (*b* Manchester, 1953). Eng. theatre director and oboist. Staff prod. ENO 1976. Prod. for Opera North from 1978, incl. *The Bartered Bride, Nabucco*, and *Prince Igor*. Prod. *Carmen* at Earl's Court 1989. Prod. musicals *Carousel* (Manchester 1985), *Carmen Jones* (Sheffield 1986), *Sunday in the Park with George* (London, Nat. Th., 1990). Has also prod. Molière's *The Miser* (Nat. Th. 1991) and Shakespeare's *Julius Caesar* (RSC 1991).

Pincé (Fr.). Pinched, i.e. *pizzicato. Also formerly a type of *mordent.

Pincherle, Marc (*b* Constantine, Algeria, 1888; *d* Paris, 1974). Fr. musicologist. After 1918 taught history of vn. at École Normale de Musique, Paris. Editor-in-chief *Monde musical* 1925–7, *Musique* 1927–30. Art. dir. Société Pleyel 1927–55. Specialist in Fr. and It. mus. of 17th and 18th cents. His 1948 book on Vivaldi was a pioneering study and was followed by another in 1955 (Eng. trans. 1957). Wrote 2 books on Corelli (1933, 1954), and books on Kreisler and Roussel.

Pineapple Poll. Ballet in 1 act and 3 scenes, lib. and choreog. by John Cranko to mus. by Sullivan arr. by *Mackerras. Prod. SW 1951. Story taken from W. S. Gilbert's Bab Ballad 'The Bumboat Woman's Story'. Also concert suite.

Pines of Rome (*Pini di Roma*). One of 3 symphonic poems by *Respighi about Rome. Comp. 1923–4 (f.p. Rome 1924, London 1925). Score incl. nightingale on a gramophone record. 4 sections are: *Villa Borghese, A Catacomb, Janiculum*, and *Appian Way*.

Pini, Anthony (*b* Buenos Aires, 1902; *d* ?London, 1989). Eng. cellist. Prin. cellist LPO 1932–9, RPO 1947–63, CG 1964. Soloist with leading orchs. Prof. of vc. RCM. Member of several quartets and chamber ensembles.

Pini-Corsi, Antonio (*b* Zara (now Zadar), Dalmatia, 1858; *d* Milan, 1918). It. baritone. Début Cremona 1878 (Dandini in *La Cenerentola*). La Scala début 1893 (Rigoletto), then chosen by Verdi to create role of Ford in *Falstaff*, Milan 1893. Sang at CG 1894–6, 1902–3; NY Met 1899–1914. Created Schaunard in *La bohème* (Turin, 1896), Happy in *La fanciulla del West* (NY, 1910), and Innkeeper in *Königskinder* (NY 1910). Last sang in 1917 in Milan.

Pinkham, Daniel (*b* Lynn, Mass., 1923). Amer. composer, harpsichordist, organist, and conductor. Has held various teaching posts. Works incl. 4 syms.; pf. conc.; 2 vn. concs.; chamber opera *The Garden of Artemis*, arr. (with additions) of *The Beggar's Opera* (1956); *Wedding Cantata; Christmas Cantata; St Mark's Passion* (1965); *Requiem*; org. conc. (1970); *Signs of the Zodiac* (1964), orch.; *Garden Party*, opera (1976); *Before the Dust Returns*, ch., instrs. (1981); *Dallas Anthem Book*, ch., orch. (1984); *The Creations of the World*, narr., ch., instrs. (1994); *Called Home*, mez., pf. (1996); str. trio (1998); *The Covenant Motets*, ch., org. (2001); Sonata, tpt., pf. (2006); *The Garden of the Muses*, org. (2006).

Pinnock, Trevor (David) (*b* Canterbury, 1946). Eng. harpsichordist and conductor. Chorister, Canterbury Cath. Solo début London 1968. Played with Galliard Harpsichord Trio 1966–72. Founder and mus. dir., The English Concert 1972–2003, specializing in perf. of early mus. on period instrs. First tour of N. Amer. 1983. NY Met début 1988; Salzburg Fest. 1988. Founded Classical Band of NY, 1989, cond. 1989–90. Prin. cond. Nat. Arts Centre Orch., Ottawa, 1991–6. CBE 1992.

Pinto, George Frederic (Saunders) (*b* Lambeth, 1785; *d* Camden Town, 1806). Eng. violinist, composer, and pianist. Wrote 5 pf. sonatas and 3 vn. sonatas. The pf. sonatas, written when he was 16, have been ed. by N. *Temperley and revived (1979) by John *McCabe, who has shown them to be works of extraordinary merit, which could easily be mistaken for mature Schubert.

Pinza, Ezio (*b* Rome, 1892; *d* Stamford, Conn., 1957). It. bass. Début Soncino, 1914 (Oroveso in *Norma*). After army service, made Rome début 1920 as King Mark in *Tristan*. Sang at La Scala 1921–4; NY Met 1926–48; CG 1930–9; Salzburg Fest. début 1934. Repertory of nearly 100 roles. A great Don Giovanni. His noble voice and fine looks were matched by dramatic ability. After his operatic career, appeared in musicals and films, notably in *South Pacific* on Broadway (1949).

piobaireachd. See *pibroch*.

pipe. (1) Hollow cone or cylinder in which air vibrates to produce a sound, e.g. in an org. or a blown wind instr.
(2) A simple woodwind instr. without any mechanism such as bamboo pipes, or the 3-holed pipe used in Eng. folk dances together with the tabor.
(3) The *bagpipe.

Piper (*née* Evans), (Mary) **Myfanwy** (*b* London, 1911; *d* Fawley Bottom, Kent, 1997). Eng. librettist. Married John Piper (1903–92), the artist and scenic designer, in 1935. Wrote libs. for three Britten operas: *The Turn of the Screw* (1954, based on Henry James), *Owen Wingrave* (1971, also Henry James), and *Death in Venice* (1973, based on Thomas Mann). For Hoddinott she wrote *What the Old Man Does is Always Right* (1977), *The Rajah's Diamond* (1979), and *The Trumpet Major* (1981, based on Thomas Hardy).

piqué (Fr.). Pricked. A bowed instr. term, same as *spiccato*.

Pique Dame (Queen of Spades). (1) Operetta by Suppé, 1862.
(2) For Tchaikovsky opera, see *Queen of Spades*.

Piquiren (Ger.). To play *spiccato*.

Pirata, Il (The Pirate). Opera in 2 acts by Bellini to lib. by Romani based on I. J. S. Taylor's play *Bertram, ou Le Pirate*. Comp. 1827. Prod. Milan 1827, London 1830, NY 1832.

Pirates of Penzance, The, or The Slave of Duty. Operetta in 2 acts by Sullivan, comp. 1879, to lib. by Gilbert. Prod. Paignton, Devon, and NY 1879, London 1880.

Pires, Maria-João (*b* Lisbon, 1944). Portuguese pianist. Gave her first recital aged 5, soloist in Mozart conc. when 7. Won 1st prize Beethoven comp., Brussels 1970. Salzburg Fest. 1984. London début 1986, N. Amer. début 1986. Toured USA 1988. Has recorded all Mozart sonatas.

pirouette (Fr.). Spinning-top. (1) Funnel-shaped reed shield, made in variety of shapes, used on *shawm and *rackett against which player could press his lips while taking projecting part of reed into his mouth. Helped to avoid lip-fatigue and protected reed.
(2) In dancing, one or more turns of the body on one leg, with the point of the working leg usually touching knee of supporting leg.

Pisk, Paul (Amadeus) (*b* Vienna, 1893; *d* Los Angeles, 1990). Austrian-born composer and musicologist (Amer. cit. 1941). Worked as mus. critic in Vienna 1921–34. Settled in USA 1936, becoming prof. of mus. Redlands Univ., Calif., head of mus. dept. 1948–50; prof. of mus., Univ. of Texas, Austin, 1951–63, Washington Univ., St Louis 1963–72. Wrote *Life and Works of Schütz* (1972). Works incl. *3 Ceremonial Rites* for orch., str. qt., cantata *Die neue Stadt*, etc.

piston. (1) A type of valve in brass instr., bored with passages which, when it is depressed within its casing, deflect the air-stream passing through it into the valve tubing. First valve lowers pitch a tone, 2nd a semitone, 3rd 2 semitones. If a 4th valve is added, it is adjusted to lower pitch 2 tones and a semitone, or a perfect 4th. New harmonic series can be prod. from these valves singly or in combination.
(2) (Fr.). Abbreviation for *cornet-à-pistons*, the *cornet.

Piston, Walter (Hamor) (*b* Rockland, Maine, 1894; *d* Belmont, Mass., 1976). Amer. composer. Began career as architectural draughtsman and after First World War played sax. in dance halls and restaurants. Joined mus. faculty at Harvard 1926, becoming prof. of mus. 1944–60. Boston SO gave f.ps. of 11 of his works between 1927 and 1971. Author of 3 important textbooks, *Harmony* (1941), *Counterpoint* (1947), *Orchestration* (1955). His pupils incl. Bernstein and Carter. Prin. works:

ORCH.: *Concerto for Orchestra* (1933); syms.: No.1 (1937), No.2 (1943), No.3 (1948), No.4 (1951), No.5

(1956), No.6 (1955), No.7 (1960), No.8 (1965); *Sinfonietta* (1941); vn. conc. No.1 (1939), No.2 (1960); pf. concertino (1937); *Symphonic Suite* (1948); va. conc. (1957); double pf. conc. (1959); *3 New England Sketches* (1959); *Variations* for vc. and orch. (1967); cl. conc. (1967); *Ricercare* (1968); *Fantasia*, vn. and orch. (1970); fl. conc. (1971); conc. for str. qt., woodwind, perc. (1976).

BALLET: *The *Incredible Flutist* (1938), also orch. suite (1938).

CHAMBER MUSIC: fl. sonata (1930); ob. suite (1931); str. qts., No.1 (1933), No.2 (1935), No.3 (1947), No.4 (1951), No.5 (1962); pf. trio No.1 (1935), No.2 (1966); vn. sonata (1939); fl. quintet (1942); pf. quintet (1949); wind quintet (1956); str. sextet (1964); pf. qt. (1964); *Duo*, vc., pf. (1976).

pitch. The location of a sound in the tonal scale, depending on the speed of vibrations from the source of the sound, fast ones producing a high pitch and slow ones a low. The rate of vibration per second is the note's 'frequency'. By int. agreement of 1939, renewed and extended in 1960, the present-day standard of 'concert-pitch' to which instr. are tuned is that in which the A directly above middle C has 440 (double) vibrations per second (440 Hz), which makes middle C 261.6 Hz. This replaced the standard of 435 (diapason normal) fixed in Paris in 1859 and confirmed in Vienna in 1885. Before then, a variety of pitches existed. In Eng. in the 16th cent., domestic kbd. pitch was about 3 semitones lower than today's pitch and the church mus. pitch over 2 semitones higher. Between 1700 and 1850, the note A varied between 415 and 429. Pitch can now be measured electronically, but still the most common way is by a tuning-fork. See *A*.

Pitch Names of the Notes

English	C	D	E	F	G	A	B
German	C	D	E	F	G	A	H
French	ut *or* do	ré	mi	fa	sol	la	si
Italian	do	re	mi	fa	sol	la	si

Note that Eng. B♭ = Ger. B; and that Eng. B = Ger. H.

pitchpipe. Small wooden pipe of square section, about 18″ in length, with whistle mouthpiece, used in 18th and 19th cents. Leather-covered wooden stopper can be inserted to shorten pipe and thus raise the pitch. On the stem of the stopper the various notes were marked. Principally used in churches that had neither organ nor band of musicians.

Pitfield, Thomas (Baron) (*b* Bolton, 1903; *d* Bowdon, Cheshire, 1999). Eng. composer and

teacher, also poet, artist, and craftsman. Joined staff RMCM 1947, becoming prof. of comp. and later at RNCM until 1973. Pupils incl. A. Goehr, Maxwell Davies, and McCabe. Comps. incl. pf. conc., cantata *A Sketchbook of Women*, songs, and chamber mus. Autobiography: *No Song, No Supper* (1986) and *A Song After Supper* (1991).

Pitt, Percy (*b* London, 1869; *d* London, 1932). Eng. conductor. Ass. cond. CG 1902, mus. dir. Grand Opera Syndicate (CG) 1907–24. Assoc. with Beecham Opera Co. 1915–18. Art. dir. BNOC 1920–4, mus. adv. to BBC 1922–4, mus. dir. BBC 1924–9. Cond. BBC's first public sym. concert, Central Hall, Westminster, Feb. 1924, and first opera relay from CG (*Hänsel und Gretel*) Jan. 1923. Also composer of sym., sym.-poem, incid. mus., etc.

Pittsburgh Symphony Orchestra. US orch., founded 1895, first concert 27 Feb. 1896, cond. Frederic Asker. Prin. conds., Victor *Herbert, 1898–1904; Emil Paur, 1904–10. Guest conds. incl. R. Strauss in 1903–4 season and Elgar in 1906–7. Disbanded March 1910, re-formed 1926. Cond. Antonio Modarelli 1930–7. Reorganized 1937 by *Klemperer. Prin. conds.: Fritz *Reiner, 1938–48; William *Steinberg, 1952–76; André Previn, 1976–84; Lorin Maazel 1988–96; Mariss Jansons 1997–2002; Andrew Davis from 2005. Toured Europe and Middle East 1963, Japan and Korea 1972 with Steinberg; Europe 1978 with Previn; Salzburg Fest. 1985, cond. Maazel. Moved into new hall, Heinz Hall for Performing Arts, 1971.

Pitz, Wilhelm (*b* Breinig, 1897; *d* Aachen, 1973). Ger. chorus-master, conductor, and violinist. Violinist, Aachen City Orch., 1913–33. Ch.-master Aachen Opera 1933–61, also mus. dir., Aachen Choral Soc. Cond., Aachen Opera from 1946. Ch.-master Bayreuth Fest., 1951–71. First ch.-master, Philharmonia Ch. 1957–71, establishing very high standards. Hon. OBE 1970.

più (It.). More. *più lento*, slower; *più mosso*, more moved, i.e. quicker, etc.

piva (It.). (1) Bagpipe.
(2) 16th-cent. dance step.

Pixis, Johann Peter (*b* Mannheim, 1788; *d* Baden-Baden, 1874). Ger. pianist, teacher, and composer. After concert career became teacher in Munich, Vienna, Paris (from 1823), and Baden-Baden from 1840. Wrote operas, sym., pf. conc., 2 str. qts., and joined Chopin, Liszt, Czerny, Thalberg, and Herz as contributor to the *Hexaméron.

Pizarro, Artur (*b* Lisbon, 1968). Portuguese pianist. Won int. comp. Lisbon 1987, Florida pf. comp. 1988, Leeds int. pf. comp. 1990. London début 1989. Proms début 1991 (Ravel conc.).

Pizzetti, Ildebrando (*b* Parma, 1880; *d* Rome, 1968). It. composer and teacher, sometimes known as 'Ildebrando da Parma'. Taught at Parma Cons. until 1908, moving to Cherubini Inst., Florence (dir. 1917–24). Dir. Milan Cons. 1924–36, prof. of comp. S. Cecilia Acad., Rome,

1936–58. Though associated briefly with It. *avant-garde* of his day (Malipiero, Casella, etc.), he later advocated a return to 'tradition'. His mus. character was divided between a deeply religious vein, which is reflected in his operas (at the other extreme from those of Puccini) and a hedonistic vein which found expression in collab. with d'Annunzio, for whose plays he wrote incidental mus. Toscanini cond. 2 of his operas in Milan. His choral works are especially fine. Prin. comps.:

OPERAS: *Fedra* (1909–12); *Debora e Jaele* (1915–21); *Lo straniero* (1922–5); *Fra Gherardo* (1925–7); *Orséolo* (1931–5); *L'Oro* (1938–42); *Vanna Lupa* (1947–9); *Ifigenia* (1950); **Assassinio nella Cattedrale* (1957); *Il calzare d'argento* (1961); *Clitennestra* (1961–4).

ORCH.: *Per l'Edipo Re di Sofocle* (1903); suite, *La pisanella* (1913); *Sinfonia del fuoco* (1914); *Concerto dell' estate* (1928); *Rondo Veneziano* (1929); pf. conc. (*Canti della Stagione Alta*) (1930); vc. conc. (1933–4); sym. (1940); vn. conc. (1944); *Preludio a un altro Giorno* (Prelude to Another Day) (1952); hp. conc. (1958–60).

CHORUS & ORCH.: *Agamemnon* (1931); *Epithalamium* (1939); *Cantico di Gloria 'Attollite Portas'* for 3 ch., 24 wind instr., 2 pf., perc. (1948); *Vanitas Vanitatum*, cantata (1958).

UNACCOMPANIED VOICES: *2 canzoni corali* (1913); *Canto d'amore* (1914); *Requiem* (1922–3); *De profundis* (1937); *2 composizioni corali* (1961).

Pizzi, Pier Luigi (*b* Milan, 1930). It. director and designer. Designed first opera, *Don Giovanni*, in Genoa 1952. Handel's *Orlando* in Florence 1959 established him as specialist in Baroque opera. This led to series of Rameau prods. at Aix-en-Provence and other Fr. fests. Prod. and designed *I Capuleti e i Montecchi*, CG 1984, *Les Troyens* for opening of Opéra Bastille, Paris 1990, and first modern staging of **Traetta's Buovo d'Antona*, Venice 1993.

pizzicato (It., abbreviated to *pizz.*; Fr. *pincé*). Pinched. Direction that notes on str. instr. are to be prod. by plucking, not bowing, the str. An early use occurs in Monteverdi's *Il combattimento di Tancredi e Clorinda* (1624), but Tobias Hume in *Harke, harke*, one of his 'Musicall Humors' from *The First Part of Ayres* (1605, *Musica Britannica* IX, 116), written for bass viol and lyra viol, instructs the performers to 'play 9 letters (i.e. notes) with your fingers'. In his vn. conc. (1910), Elgar uses the direction *pizzicato tremolando*, meaning that the players should 'thrum' rapidly with the fingers across the str.

P.K. (Ger.). Abbreviation used in org. mus. for *Pedalkoppel* (pedal-coupler), followed by indication of the particular manual to be coupled to the pedal.

Pk (Ger.). Abbreviation found in orch. scores for *Pauken*, kettledrums. See *drum*.

plagal cadence. Cadence with subdominant preceding the tonic, normally both in root position. Known also as 'Amen cadence', because it was used for the Amen of hymns in the 15th and 16th cents. Use revived by Hindemith.

plainchant. Same as **plainsong*.

plainsong. The large body of traditional ritual melody of the Western Christian Church, in its final form called Gregorian chant. Comprises single line of vocal melody, properly (but not always nowadays) unacc. in free rhythm, not divided into bar-lengths. Has own system of notation, employing stave of 4 lines instead of 5. The word is a trans. of *cantus planus*—in contra-distinction to *cantus figuratus* (florid song, implying a counterpoint added to the traditional melody) or *cantus mensuratus* (measured song, implying the regularity of rhythm assoc. with harmonic mus.). The Eastern (or 'Greek') branch of the Christian Church and the Jewish Synagogue have similar bodies of melodic ritual song, but the term *plainsong*, as ordinarily used, does not incl. them.

Plainsong rhythm is the free rhythm of speech; it is a prose rhythm, which of course arises from the unmetrical character of the words to be recited—psalms, prayers, and the like.

In character, plainsong falls into two essentially distinct groups—the responsorial (developed from recitation of psalms round a 'dominant'), and antiphonal (developed as pure melody).

Plainsong developed during the earliest centuries of Christianity, influenced possibly by the mus. of the Jewish synagogue and certainly by the Gr. modal system (see *modes*). A major reform was instituted in the 6th cent. at, it is said, the request of Pope Gregory.

Further reform was attempted at the end of the 16th cent., but the results were disastrous. **Palestrina* was charged with the work of revising the plainsong of the Gradual, Antiphonal, and Psalter, but died almost immediately after accepting the commission. Felice Anerio and Soriano undertook the work, and their edn. was pubd. by the Medicean Press in 2 vols., 1614–15. This *Medicean Edition*, as it is called, with its addition and suppression of melismata, its altered melodies, and its new ones, became the basis for many cheaper performing edns. In the 18th cent. there was a fashion for introducing grace notes and passing notes into the plainsong (called in Fr. **machicotage*). In the 19th cent. there was another cry for reform and the famous Ratisbon (Regensburg) edns. appeared—unfortunately based on the *Medicean Edition*. Years of controversy followed, for the Benedictine monks of Solesmes, in Fr., had long been at work in the most scientific spirit, photographing and collating innumerable manuscripts, in all the libraries of Europe. They pubd. their Gradual in 1883 and their Antiphonal in 1891. The Ratisbon edn. had had papal privileges conferred upon it, but in 1903 these expired and in the same year Pius X was chosen Pope and he at once issued his famous *Motu Proprio* on church mus., laying down, among other things, the importance of plainsong and the necessity of taking it from early and pure sources.

Among the reforms of the Solesmes monks (who, temporarily driven from France by anti-clerical legislation in 1901, carried on their work for some years in Eng.) was the introduction of a lighter and more rhythmic manner of perf.

Planché, James Robinson (*b* London, 1796; *d* London, 1880). Eng. writer for the theatre and authority on costume. Trans. many opera libs. (incl. those of operas by Rossini, Bellini, Offenbach, Mozart, etc.). Made Eng. version of Weber's *Der Freischütz* and was librettist for *Oberon*.

Plançon, Pol [Paul-Henri] (*b* Fumay, 1851; *d* Paris, 1914). Fr. bass. Opera début Lyons 1877 (Saint-Bris in *Les Huguenots*), Paris 1880. Paris Opéra 1883–93; CG 1891–1904; NY Met 1893–1908. V. of great range and flexibility.

Planets, The. Suite for orch. by Holst, his Op.32. Comp. 1914–16. 7 movts. based on astrological assocs.: 1. *Mars, the Bringer of War*; 2. *Venus, the Bringer of Peace*; 3. *Mercury, the Winged Messenger*; 4. *Jupiter, the Bringer of Jollity*; 5. *Saturn, the Bringer of Old Age*; 6. *Uranus, the Magician*; 7. *Neptune, the Mystic* (with wordless female ch.). F.p. (semi-private) 1918; excl. Nos. 2 and 7, 1919; complete 1920, all cond. Boult. In 2000 an 8th movt., *Pluto, the Renewer*, was comp. by Colin Matthews, with an off-stage female ch. F.p. Manchester 2000, Hallé Orch. and Ch., cond. Nagano.

Planquette, (Jean) **Robert** (*b* Paris, 1848; *d* Paris, 1903). Fr. composer. Began career by writing songs for the 'cafés-chantants', then turned to comic opera. Wrote about 20 operettas, most popular being *Les *cloches de Corneville* (1877). Also *Rip Van Winkle* (1882), *Surcouf* (1887, as *Paul Jones* 1889), and *Panurge* (1895).

plaqué (Fr.). Non-arpeggiated. Indication that notes of a chord should be played simultaneously.

Plasson, Michel (*b* Paris, 1933). Fr. conductor. Won 1st prize Besançon int. comp. 1962. Mus. dir. Metz 1966–8. Dir. of orch. and of Théâtre du Capitole, Toulouse, 1968–83. Cond. Orch. Nationale du Capitole de Toulouse from 1983. Mus. dir. Dresden PO 1994–9. CG début 1979 (*Werther*).

playera (Sp.). Sp. *seguidilla* of Andalusian orig. which is sung and danced.

player-piano. See *pianola*.

Playford, John (*b* Norfolk, 1623; *d* London, 1686). Eng. music publisher. Began business in 1647. In 1650 he registered *The English Dancing Master* (pubd. 1651), source-book of folk mus., followed by many other important publications. On his death Purcell wrote an elegy. His son Henry (1657–*c*.1720) pubd. works by Purcell, also **Orpheus Britannicus*, and later founded concerts in London and Oxford.

Play of Daniel, The. Medieval liturgical drama which exists in several versions, only the Beauvais version having survived with mus. complete. Comp. between 1227 and 1234 for perf. at Beauvais Cath. during matins probably on 1 Jan. In 2 parts,

1st dealing with Daniel at Belshazzar's court, 2nd with Daniel's trials at the court of Darius. Several modern edns., incl. one by David Wulstan.

Pleasants, Henry (*b* Wayne, Pa., 1910; *d* London 2000). Amer. music critic and writer. Central Eur. mus. correspondent for *NY Times* 1945–55. London mus. critic of *International Herald-Tribune* from 1967. His books *The Agony of Modern Music* (1955) and *Death of a Music?* (1961) were seriously critical of contemp. trends in composition, and his *Opera in Crisis* (1989) exposed the deficiencies of so-called innovative prods. Ed. and trans. the criticisms of Hanslick in *Vienna's Golden Years of Music 1850–1900* (1950). He wrote *The Musical Journeys of Louis Spohr* (1961), *The Musical World of Robert Schumann* (1965), and *The Music Criticism of Hugo Wolf* (1979). Also wrote *The Great Singers* (1966).

Pleasure Dome of Kubla Khan, The. Symphonic poem by *Griffes based on Coleridge's poem. Orig. pf. piece, comp. 1912; orch. 1917, f.p. Boston SO 1919.

plectrum. Small thin piece of horn, wood, tortoiseshell, metal, ivory, or other material used to pluck the str. of certain str. instrs. such as zither, mandolin, lyre, lute, banjo, etc. On the hpd. it is a part of the mechanism.

Pleeth, William (*b* London, 1916; *d* London, 1999). Eng. cellist. Début Leipzig 1932, London 1933. Soloist with orchs. but principally chamber mus. player. Cellist in Blech Quartet 1936–41, Allegri Quartet 1953–67. Prof. of vc., GSMD, 1948–78. Pupils incl. Jacqueline *du Pré. OBE 1989.

plein jeu (Fr.). Full play. (1) Type of org. mixture stop incl. only unison, octave, and 12th.
(2) Full org. in Fr. mus.

Pletnev, Mikhail (*b* 1957). Russian pianist and conductor. Gold Medal, Tchaikovsky int. pf. comp., Moscow, 1978. Founded Russ. Nat. Orch. 1990 and was its mus. dir. until 1999. International tours as pianist and cond.

Pleyel, Ignaz (Joseph) (*b* Ruppersthal, Vienna, 1757; *d* Paris, 1831). Austrian composer, violinist, pianist, and founder of piano firm. Became choirmaster at Strasbourg Cath. 1789. Cond. concerts in London 1791–2. Set up as mus. dealer in Paris 1795, founding pf. factory 1807. Composed 29 syms., 45 str. qts., 18 fl. qts., 2 vn. concs., 4 vc. concs., 2 pf. concs., 6 pf. sonatas, etc. His son Camille (1788–1855) became his partner in 1821 and they were joined by *Kalkbrenner in 1824. Camille was succeeded by Auguste Wolff. After Wolff's death, his son-in-law Gustave Lyon (1857–1936) assumed control. In 1961 firm was merged with Gaveau-Érard, but still made pianos under name Pleyel. Merged firm bought by Schimmel of Brunswick, 1976.

Pli selon pli (Fold upon fold). 'Portrait of Mallarmé' for sop. and orch. by Boulez. In 5 sections, some involving choice of order by cond. Comp. 1957–62 but liable to continuous rev. First Brit. perf. Edinburgh, Aug. 1965, cond. Boulez.

Plishka, Paul (*b* Old Forge, Pa., 1941). Amer. bass. Début 1961 with Paterson Lyric Opera. Sang with Met Nat. Co. (touring) 1965–7, then joined main NY Met co, making début 1967 as the Monk in *La *Gioconda*. In 25 seasons at Met sang over 50 roles. Also CG, Berlin, Chicago, and S. Francisco.

plötzlich (Ger.). Suddenly.

Plowright, Rosalind (Anne) (*b* Worksop, 1949). Eng. soprano, formerly mezzo-soprano. Opera début RMCM 1968 in f. Brit. p. of J. C. Bach's *Temistocle*. ENO début 1975 (Page in *Salome*). GTO début 1976. Won Sofia int. comp. 1979. CG 1980; Amer. début 1982. Fine singer of Verdi's Desdemona and Strauss's Danae and Ariadne. Sang Aida at CG 1984, Elena in *The Sicilian Vespers*, ENO 1984, and title-role in Cherubini's *Médée*, Buxton Fest. 1984.

Ployer, Barbara von (*fl.* 1770–90). Austrian pianist. Pf. and comp. pupil of Mozart, who in 1784 wrote for her his pf. concs. No.14 in E♭ (K449) and No.17 in G (K453) of which she gave f.ps. in Vienna. Also played the sonata in D for 2 pf. (K448) with Mozart. Daughter of Court Councillor Gottfried Ignaz von Ployer, from 1780 agent of Salzburg Court in Vienna.

pneuma (Gr.). Breath, breathing. Term applied to the florid passages sung to a single vowel at the end of certain pieces of plainsong. Such final vocalises were also known as *jubili*, indicating their intention as expressions of pious joy.

pneumatic action. See *organ*.

pochette (Fr.; It. *sordino*). Little pocket. Small type of vn. formerly used by 17th-cent. dancing-masters, and known in Eng. as a kit. Name may well have come from the leather case in which the instr. was kept.

poco (It.). A little, rather, e.g. *poco lento*, rather slow. *Poco a poco* means little by little, so *poco a poco animando*, becoming livelier by degrees. *Pochetto, pochettino*, very little, very little indeed, *pochissimo*, the least possible.

podatus. See *pes*.

poem. Literary term introduced into music by Liszt with the expression 'symphonic poem' to apply to his narrative orch. works. Famous individual works bearing this title are the *Poem* by *Fibich, a movt. from his orch. serenade *At Twilight* (*V Podvečer*), and the *Poème* for vn. and orch., 1896, by Chausson.

Poème de l'amour et de la mer (Poem of Love and the Sea). Work for v. and orch. (or pf.) in 3 parts by Chausson, to words by Maurice Bouchor. Comp. 1882–90, rev. 1893, f.p. Brussels 1893, f.p. in England, London 1919 (with orch.).

Poèmes pour Mi (Poems for *Mi). Song-cycle by *Messiaen, to his own poems, for sop. and pf. (1936); for sop. and orch. (1937). F.p. Paris 1937.

Poem of Ecstasy (*Poema ekstasa*; Fr. *Le Poème d'extase*). Orch. work by *Scriabin, Op.54, comp. 1905–8 and f.p. NY 1908, London 1910. Inspired by his theosophical ideas on love and art.

Poem of Fire (Scriabin). See *Prometheus, the Poem of Fire*.

Poet and Peasant (*Dichter und Bauer*). Play in 3 acts (1846) by K. Elmar, for which ov. and incidental mus. were comp. by *Suppé.

Poet's Echo, The. Setting by Britten for high v. and pf., Op.76, of 6 poems (in Russ.) by Pushkin, comp. 1965 for *Vishnevskaya and *Rostropovich, who gave f.p. in Moscow Cons. Dec. 1965.

Pogorelich, Ivo (*b* Belgrade, 1958). Serbian pianist, son of db. player. Won Casagrande competition at Terni 1978 and 1st prize in Montreal int. comp. 1980. His failure to reach the final rounds of the 1980 Int. Chopin Comp. in Warsaw led to resignation from the jury of Martha *Argerich and to the launching of his career. NY and London débuts 1981. Salzburg Fest. 1983. Settled in Eng. 1982.

Pohjola's Daughter. Symphonic fantasia for orch., Op.49, by Sibelius comp. 1906 and based on legend from the *Kalevala. F.p. St Petersburg 1906, cond. by composer.

Pohl, Carl Ferdinand (*b* Darmstadt, 1819; *d* Vienna, 1887). Ger. musicologist and organist. Archivist and librarian of Vienna Society of the Friends of Music (*Gesellschaft der Musikfreunde*) 1866–87. Began huge biography of Haydn of which he completed only Vol. I (pubd. in 2 parts 1875, 1882). Wrote book on *Mozart and Haydn in London* (1867), living in London 1863–6 while engaged on research, and treatise on glass armonicas (1862) (he was grandson of first maker of them).

poi (It.). Then, e.g. (after some direction for the repetition of a passage) *poi la coda*, then the coda.

point. (1) The tip of the bow of vn., etc., opposite to that held by the hand.
(2) Same as *pedal.
(3) See *pointing.

point d'orgue (Fr.). Organ-point. (1) *Pedal.
(2) The pause-sign,
(3) A cadenza in a conc., so-called because of pause sign indicating where it begins.

pointillist(e). A term used in painting (meaning the use, by Seurat and other Post-Impressionists, of separate dots of pure colour instead of mixed pigments) and borrowed by writers on mus. to describe passages where the notes seem to be in 'dots' rather than in melodic phrases, e.g. in the mus. of Webern.

pointing. In Anglican chant, the allotting of syllables to the notes on which they are to be sung (as in psalms and canticles). First attempt to present pointing in printed form was by Robert Janes, organist of Ely Cath., in 1837.

Poisoned Kiss, The, or The Empress and the Necromancer. Opera (romantic extravaganza) by Vaughan Williams to lib. by Evelyn Sharp (1869–1955) derived from Richard Garnett's *The Poison Maid* and Nathaniel Hawthorne's *Rapaccini's Daughter*. Comp. 1927–9, rev. 1934–5, 1936–7, 1956–7. Prod. Cambridge and London 1936, NY 1937. Spoken dialogue rev. by Ursula Vaughan Williams in 1957 and subsequently. All characters have botanical names, e.g. Amaryllus and Persicaria.

polacca (It.). *polonaise.

Polacco, Giorgio (*b* Venice, 1875; *d* NY, 1960). It. conductor. Début London 1891 (Gluck's *Orfeo ed Euridice*). Cond. Milan, Genoa, Rome, and in St Petersburg, where he won fame as a Wagnerian. Amer. début S. Francisco 1905. NY Met 1912–17; Chicago Grand Opera 1918–19, 1921, and Chicago Civic Opera 1922–30. CG début 1913.

Polaski, Deborah (*b* Richmond Center, Wisconsin, 1949). Amer. soprano. Career in Ger. opera houses from 1976. Bayreuth 1988 and 1994 (Brünnhilde in *Ring* cycle). Roles incl. Isolde, Sieglinde, Marie (*Wozzeck*), and Elektra.

Poldowski. Pseudonym of Lady (Irene) Dean Paul (*b* Brussels, 1880; *d* London, 1932), daughter of the violinist *Wieniawski. Composed popular ballads, sometimes singing them to her own pf. accompaniment.

poliphant. Eng. instr. of early 17th cent., strung with wire and evidently mixing the qualities of harp, lute, and theorbo. Had 37 str.

'Polish' Symphony. Nickname for Tchaikovsky's Sym. No.3 in D, Op.29, because finale is in *polonaise rhythm. Comp. 1875.

polka. Bohem. dance which originated in the early 19th-cent. and quickly spread throughout Europe. It was a round dance in quick duple time, with steps on the first 3 half-beats of the measure and a sort of rest on the 4th. Introduced to Prague 1837, Vienna and St. Petersburg 1839, Paris 1840, and London 1844. The mus. bears some resemblance to that of the Schottische, and a particular kind was, in fact, called *Schottische bohème* (or *Polka tremblante*). One of the first uses of the Polka in art-mus. was by *Smetana in *The Bartered Bride*.

Pollak, Anna (*b* Manchester, 1912; *d* Hythe, Kent, 1996). Eng. mezzo-soprano of Austrian parentage. Began career as actress. Début London 1945 as Dorabella in *Così fan tutte*. Created Bianca in *The Rape of Lucretia*. Glyndebourne début 1952; CG 1952. Prin. mez. SW 1945–62, guest artist 1962–8. OBE 1962.

Pollak, Egon (*b* Prague, 1879; *d* Prague, 1933). Cz.-born Austrian conductor. Ch. cond. Prague 1901. Cond. Bremen Opera 1905–10, Leipzig 1910–12, Frankfurt 1912–17. Mus. dir. Hamburg Opera 1922–31. Cond. Chicago Opera 1915–16,

1929–32. CG début 1914. Noted cond. of Wagner and Strauss. Cond. Hamburg première (1920) of Korngold's *Die tote Stadt*. Died conducting *Fidelio*.

Pollini, Bernhard [Baruch Pohl] (*b* Cologne, 1838; *d* Hamburg, 1897). Ger. impresario, formerly tenor (début in *I Puritani*, Cologne 1857). Later, bar. with It. Opera Co. of which he became man. Dir. of It. opera St Petersburg and Moscow. Dir., Hamburg Opera 1876–97, engaging Mahler as cond. in 1891.

Pollini, Maurizio (*b* Milan, 1942). It. pianist and conductor. Début at age of 9. Won Warsaw Chopin Comp. 1960. After that appeared in Europe and USA as recitalist and concerto soloist, working often with conductor Claudio *Abbado. Wide repertory, from Bach to *avant-garde* works such as Boulez's 2nd sonata. Played complete pf. mus. of Schoenberg and was soloist in f.p. of Nono's *Como una ola de fuerza y luz*, Milan 1972. Salzburg Fest. début 1973. Like Ashkenazy, Barenboim, Perahia, and others, has often conducted from keyboard. Opera début as cond. Pesaro 1981 in Rossini's *La donna del lago* after which he regularly cond. Rossini operas.

Polly. Ballad opera in 3 acts written 1729 by Gay, with mus. arr. attrib. *Pepusch and extra songs by Samuel Arnold. Sequel to *The *Beggar's Opera*. Prod. London 1777, NY 1925. Rev. version with text by Clifford Bax and mus. arr. Frederic Austin prod. London 1922. Another modern version by John Addison (Aldeburgh 1952).

polo. Andalusian folk-song (and dance) in moderate 3/8 with syncopations and vocal coloraturas on words such as 'Ole' and 'Ay'. Example comp. by M. *García in his opera *El criado fingido* was quoted by Bizet in prelude to Act IV of *Carmen*. No.7 of Falla's *7 Spanish Popular Songs* is a polo.

polonaise (Fr.), **Polonäse** (Ger.), **polacca** (It.). A nat. Polish dance, in simple triple time and of moderate speed; it should, perhaps, more properly be described as a stately ceremonial procession rather than a dance, and probably originated among the aristocracy in 16th cent. Certain rhythms are characteristic, such as the frequent division of the first beat of the measure with accentuation of its 2nd half, the ending of phrases on the 3rd beat of the measure, etc. Many composers, incl. Bach, Handel, Mozart, Beethoven, and Schubert, have written polonaises; Chopin's 13 examples, in which he found an outlet for his patriotic feeling, are outstanding.

Polonia. (1) Concert-ov. by Wagner, comp. 1836. F.p. Palermo 1881, London 1905.
(2) Symphonic prelude for orch., Op.76, by Elgar, f.p. 1915.
(3) Suite for orch. by *Panufnik, comp. and f.p. 1959. Polonia means Poland.

Polovtsian Dances. Sequence of choral and orch. pieces forming ballet scene in Act 2 of

*Borodin's opera *Prince Igor*. The Polovtsy were nomadic invaders of Russia.

polska. Scandinavian dance in simple triple time, so-called because of its Polish origin (it derives from the Mazurka). Dates from the union of Swedish and Polish crowns in 1587.

Polstertanz (Ger.). Pillow dance. Same as *Kissentanz* or *cushion dance.

polyphony (Gr.). Many sounds. Mus. in which several simultaneous v. or instr. parts are combined contrapuntally, as opposed to monophonic mus. (single melody) or homophonic mus. (one melodic line, the other parts acting as acc.). In historical terms, polyphonic era is defined as 13th–16th cents., but polyphony survived beyond 1700.

polyrhythm. Several different rhythms perf. simultaneously, as in many 20th-cent. works. Mozart combined 3 different dance-rhythms simultaneously in *Don Giovanni*.

polytonality. The simultaneous use of more than one key in different contrapuntal strands, an effect found in works by Holst, Milhaud, Bartók, and others. The use of only two keys is *bitonality.

pommer. Type of *shawm, forerunner of the ob. Often taken as meaning a large (lower-pitched) instr., but antiquarian authorities apply the term indiscriminately.

Pommier, Jean-Bernard (*b* Béziers, 1944). Fr. pianist. Won first prize, int. comp. *Jeunesses Musicales* 1960, thereafter soloist with world's leading orchs. Salzburg Fest. début 1971; Amer. début 1973–4. Has acted as conductor/soloist with Northern Sinfonia and other ensembles. Art. dir., Northern Sinfonia 1996–2002.

Pomp and Circumstance. Title given by Elgar (quoting Act 3 of Shakespeare's *Othello*) to set of 5 marches for sym. orch., Op.39: No.1 in D major and No.2 in A minor, comp. and f.p. Liverpool 1901; No.3 in C minor, comp. and f.p. London 1904; No.4 in G major, comp. and f.p. London 1907; No.5 in C major, comp. and f.p. London 1930; No.6 in G minor, perf. vers. by A. Payne, f.p. 2006. Altered trio section of No.1 became finale, with words by A. C. Benson beginning *'Land of Hope and Glory', of *Coronation Ode* 1902.

Ponce, Manuel (Maria) (*b* Fresnillo, 1882; *d* Mexico City, 1948). Mexican composer. Lived in Paris 1925–33. Taught at Nat. Cons., Mexico City, 1909–15, 1917–22, becoming dir. 1934–5. Founded mus. journal, 1936–7, and was first Mexican composer to carry out research on Creole and Meztiso folklore, which, together with Fr. composers such as Dukas, influenced his mus. Wrote many works for guitar, incl. 24 Preludes, 5 sonatas, and *Concierto del sur* (1941), also 2 pf. concs., vn. conc., and over 100 songs and 100 pf. pieces.

Ponchielli, Amilcare (*b* Paderno, 1834; *d* Milan, 1886). It. composer. Org. at Cremona. First opera, *I promessi sposi*, prod. Cremona 1856 and in rev. version at Milan 1872. Comp. ballet and several operas of which only *La *Gioconda* (Milan 1876) has held its place. Choirmaster Bergamo Cath., 1881. Taught comp. Milan Cons. from 1880, pupils incl. Puccini and Mascagni.

Ponnelle, Jean Pierre (*b* Paris, 1932; *d* Munich, 1988). Fr. director and stage designer. First success as designer was in *Boulevard Solitude* (Hanover 1952) and *König Hirsch* (Berlin 1956). First opera prod. was *Tristan und Isolde*, Düsseldorf 1962. Later he prod. and dir. it at Bayreuth (1981). Worked regularly at La Scala, Cologne (Mozart cycle), Zurich (Monteverdi cycle, cond. Harnoncourt), and S. Francisco where he staged over 20 operas. CG début 1962, designs of *L'heure espagnole*, and was prod./designer there of *Don Pasquale* (1973), *Aida* (1984), and *L'Italiana in Algeri* (1988). Glyndebourne 1977, dir. and designed *Falstaff*. Salzburg Fest. début 1968, prod. and designer *Il barbiere di Siviglia*; later stagings there incl. *Le nozze di Figaro*, *Così fan tutte*, *Die Zauberflöte*, *La Clemenza di Tito*, *Don Giovanni*, *Idomeneo*, *Les contes d'Hoffmann*, and *Moses und Aron*. Made films of many of his prods.

Pons, Juan (*b* Ciutadella, Minorca, 1946). Sp. baritone. Began career as ten. in Barcelona. CG début 1979; Paris 1983; NY Met début 1986 (Scarpia in *Tosca*).

Pons, Lily [Alice Joséphine] (*b* Draguignan, nr. Cannes, 1898; *d* Dallas, 1976). Fr.-born soprano (Amer. cit. 1940). Opera début, Mulhouse 1928 as Lakmé. Recommended to *Gatti-Casazza of NY Met where she made début as Lucia di Lammermoor in 1931, singing there for 28 seasons. CG 1935. Made several films.

Ponselle [Ponzillo], **Rosa** (*b* Meriden, Conn., 1897; *d* Green Valley, Baltimore, 1981). Amer. soprano. First sang in cinemas and in vaudeville act with her sister Carmella. At Caruso's suggestion, although she had never sung in opera, was engaged for Leonora in *La forza del destino*, NY Met 1918. Sang at Met 1918–37, CG 1929–31. One of greatest sops. of cent. in such roles as Norma, Violetta, Rachel (*La Juive*), and the *Trovatore* Leonora. Retired at height of powers and taught at Baltimore, becoming art. dir. of civic opera.

Ponsonby, Robert (Noel) (*b* Oxford, 1926). Eng. arts administrator. On Glyndebourne staff 1951–5. Art. dir. Edinburgh Fest 1956–60. Gen. admin. SNO 1964–72. Controller of Mus., BBC, 1972–85. Art. dir. Canterbury Fest. 1986–8. CBE 1985.

ponticello (It.). Little bridge. Bridge of a str. instr. The direction *sul ponticello* means 'play with the bow as close as possible to the bridge' to produce a special 'metallic' tone-quality. In *bel canto* singing it means the join between the chest and head registers.

pop. Abbreviation for 'popular'. Earlier meaning meant concerts appealing to a wide audience. The London Popular Concerts were founded by *Benedict in 1858 and continued until 1898. Since the late 1950s, however, *pop* has had the

589   POSITION

special meaning of non-classical mus., usually in the form of songs, perf. by such artists as the Beatles, the Rolling Stones, Abba, etc. Thus 'pop groups' (performers of pop, usually singer(s), guitars, drums, sometimes sophisticated elec. effects), and 'pop festivals'.

Popp, Lucia (*b* Uhorška Veš, 1939; *d* Munich, 1993). Cz.-born Austrian soprano. Début Bratislava 1963 (Queen of Night in *Die Zauberflöte*). Sang Barbarina (*Le nozze di Figaro*) in Vienna 1963, and was engaged by State Opera, where she then sang regularly. Débuts: Salzburg Fest. 1963; CG 1966; NY Met 1967. She was a notable singer of Strauss roles, and of Mozart and Janáček. Also successful concert and recital career.

Popper, David (*b* Prague, 1843; *d* Baden, Vienna, 1913). Bohem. cellist, pupil of Goltermann at Prague Cons. Played in orch., then from 1863 rose to leading position among world's cellists. Prin. cellist, Vienna Opera 1868–73. Member of Hubay Qt. Taught at Budapest Acad. from 1896. Composed 4 vc. concs.; *Requiem* for 3 vc. and orch. (1892); str. qt.; suites for vc.; and many short vc. pieces incl. the well-known *Dance of the Elves*.

Porgy and Bess. Opera in 3 acts by Gershwin to lib. by DuBose Heyward and I. Gershwin after novel *Porgy* (1925) by DuBose and Dorothy Heyward. Comp. 1934–5. Prod. Boston, Mass., and NY 1935, Copenhagen 1943, London 1952, NY Met 1985, Glyndebourne 1986.

Porpora, Nicola Antonio (*b* Naples, 1686; *d* Naples, 1768). It. composer and singing teacher. Earliest operas prod. in Naples (from 1708). Taught in Naples 1715–21, producing many brilliant graduates. As teacher, held posts in several It. cities, in Ger., and in Austria. Went to London 1733 to est. opera in rivalry to Handel but was no match for him. Returned to Venice and Vienna (where Haydn was for a time his pupil), and eventually to Naples where he comp. his last opera, 1760. Died in poverty. Wrote 48 operas, oratorios, syms., 12 vn. sonatas, etc.

portamento (It.). Carrying. With the v. or a bowed instr., the carrying of the sound from note to note smoothly and without any break, hence very *legato* and momentarily sounding the pitches in between any 2 indicated by the notation. See *curved line, various uses of*.

portando, portato (It.). Carrying, carried. The same as *portamento*.

portative organ. Medieval org. small enough to be carried by the player.

port de voix (Fr.). Carrying of the voice. (1) Vocal *portamento*. (2) An *appoggiatura* from below and above, used especially in Fr. baroque mus.

Porter, Andrew (Brian) (*b* Cape Town, 1928). Eng. music critic. Taught at All Souls, Oxford, 1973–4, and Univ. of Calif., Berkeley, 1980–1.

Mus. critic *Manchester Guardian* 1949, *Financial Times* 1953–74, *New Yorker* 1972–92, *Observer* 1992–7, *Times Literary Supplement* from 1997. Ed., *Musical Times*, 1960–7. Trans. several opera libs. for perf., incl. Wagner's *Der Ring des Nibelungen* (for ENO). Responsible for rediscovery and subsequent performance of first version of Verdi's *Don Carlos*. Published 5 vols. of his collected *New Yorker* criticisms.

Porter, Cole (*b* Peru, Ind., 1891; *d* Santa Monica, Calif., 1964). Amer. composer. First stage prod. in NY was *See America First*, 1916. First big success was *Wake Up and Dream*, London 1929. There followed a long series of Broadway musicals and films, e.g. *Gay Divorce* (1932, filmed as *The Gay Divorcée*, 1934), *Anything Goes* (1934), *DuBarry Was a Lady* (1939), *Panama Hattie* (1940), *Kiss Me, Kate* (1948). His individual songs, marked by witty words, incl. *Begin the Beguine, Let's Do It, Night and Day, Don't Fence Me In, Miss Otis Regrets, You're the Top, I get a kick out of you*, and many others equally good and cherished.

Porter, (William) **Quincy** (*b* New Haven, 1897; *d* Bethany, Conn., 1966). Amer. composer and violist. Taught at Cleveland Inst., 1922–8 and 1931–2. Prof. of mus., Vassar Coll., 1932–8, dean of mus. faculty, New England Cons., 1938–42, dir. 1942–6. Prof. of mus., Yale Univ., 1946–65. Works incl. 2 syms. (1934, 1964); va. conc. (1948); *Concerto concertante* for 2 pf. and orch. (1954); *New England Episodes* (1958); 10 str. qts.; and other chamber mus.

Portsmouth Point. (1) Orch. ov. by *Walton after an etching by Rowlandson (1756–1827). Comp. 1924–5. F.p. Zurich 1926, London 6 days later.
(2) Orch. work by Lord *Berners *c*.1920 of which score is lost; pubd. as pf. solo.

Portunal, Portunalflöte (Ger.). An org. stop of open wooden pipes wider at the top than the bottom. It has a smooth tone.

pos. (1) In Fr. org. mus., *positif* (i.e. choir org.).
(2) In str. mus., *posizione* (It.), *position* (Fr.), *position.

Posaune (Ger.). (1) Tb., but tpt. in biblical sense of 'the last tpt'.
(2) Org. reed stop of 8′ or 16′ pitch.

posément (Fr.). Steadily, sedately.

positif (Fr.). Choir org.

position. (1) In the playing of str. instr., term used for specifying the moving of left hand up or down the finger-board so that the fingers may produce different sets of notes, e.g. first position, 'nearest the pegs', 2nd etc. progressively further from pegs.
(2) How far the slide should be pushed out in tb. playing (first position is least extended).

(3) Lay-out of a chord in harmony to determine which note comes at the bottom, so that one speaks of a chord in 'root position'.

positive organ. Type of small org. which could be placed on floor or table in contrast with *portative organ.

posthorn. Brass instr. without valves or keys which can produce only the notes of one *harmonic series. Made straight, oblong-coiled, or circular-coiled, and once used by postillions for signalling. Mozart's *Serenade* No.9 in D (K320, 1779) is nicknamed *Posthorn*.

Posthorn Galop. Solo (with acc.) for posthorn comp. by cornet-player Koenig, 1844.

postlude. Piece played at the end, i.e. opposite of *prelude.

Postnikova, Viktoria (Valentinovna) (*b* Moscow, 1944). Russ. pianist. Prizewinner, Chopin comp. Warsaw 1965; 2nd prize, Leeds int. comp. 1966. London début 1967. Soloist with world's leading orchs. Salzburg Fest. début 1976. Played in f. Eng. p. of Schnittke's conc. for pf. duet and orch., Huddersfield 1990.

Poston, Elizabeth (*b* Highfield, Herts., 1905; *d* Stevenage, 1987). Eng. composer, pianist, and writer. Lived abroad 1930–9, collecting folksongs. On BBC staff 1940–5, becoming mus. dir. of European Service. Authority on and arranger of folk-songs and carols. Composer of incid. mus. for radio, choral mus., chamber mus., and songs (incl. *Sweet Suffolk Owl*, 1924). Lived in house which was original of E. M. Forster's *Howards End*.

pot-pourri (Fr. 'rotten-pot'). Mus. application of this horticultural term is to a medley of tunes strung together without development. R. Strauss called the ov. to his *Die schweigsame Frau* a 'potpourri'.

Potter, (Philip) **Cipriani** (Hambley) (*b* London, 1792; *d* London, 1871). Eng. composer, pianist, conductor, and teacher. Début as pianist 1816 with Phil. Soc., London. Went to Vienna 1817 to study comp. with A. Förster and was advised by Beethoven. Prof. of pf., RAM from 1822, prin. 1832–59. Introduced 3 Beethoven pf. concs. (Nos. 1, 3, and 4) to Eng. at Phil. concerts. Wagner praised one of his 9 syms. Wrote 3 pf. concs. and much other mus., including *'Enigma' Variations* for pf. (*c*.1825) composed 'in the style of five eminent artists'.

Pouishnoff, Leff (Nicolas) (*b* Odessa, 1891; *d* London, 1959). Russ.-born pianist and composer (Brit. cit. 1935). Début at age 5. London début 1912, USA 1923. Taught in Tbilisi 1913–17. Settled in W., becoming noted interpreter of Romantic mus.

Poule, La (The Hen). Nickname for Haydn's Sym. in G minor, No.83 in Breitkopf edn., comp. 1785. A 19th-cent. accretion, purporting to describe 'clucking' 2nd subject of 1st movt.

Poulenc, Francis (*b* Paris, 1899; *d* Paris, 1963). Fr. composer and pianist. Taught pf. by his mother. At 15 studied with Ricardo Viñes, who encouraged his ambition to compose and introduced him to *Satie, *Casella, *Auric, and others. In 1917 his *Rapsodie nègre* brought his name to notorious prominence in Paris as one of a number of composers—*Les Nouveaux Jeunes*—encouraged by Satie and Cocteau. Even so, his technical knowledge was still scanty and in 1920 he studied harmony for 3 years with *Koechlin, but never studied counterpoint nor orchestration. His knowledge of form was instinctive. In 1920, a mus. critic, Henri Collet, selected 6 of *Les Nouveaux Jeunes* and called them *Les *Six*, Poulenc being among them. They gave concerts together, one of their articles of faith being to draw inspiration from 'Parisian folklore', i.e. street musicians, mus.-halls, circus bands. This milieu is faithfully reflected in Poulenc's settings of Cocteau's *Cocardes*. These caught the ear of Stravinsky who recommended Poulenc to Diaghilev, the result being the ballet *Les Biches* (1923), in which he expressed brittle 1920s sophistication, a faithful understanding of the jazz idiom, and (in the *adagietto*) the romantic lyricism that was increasingly to dominate his work. Perhaps his finest achievements are contained in his many songs for v. and pf., particularly those written after 1935 when he began to acc. the great Fr. bar. Pierre *Bernac. His settings of Apollinaire and of his friend Paul Éluard are particularly good, covering a wide emotional range. He comp. 3 operas, the biggest being *Les dialogues des Carmélites* (1953–6), based on events of the Fr. Revolution, and his religious works have a tuneful ecstatic joy such as one finds elsewhere only in Haydn. He rediscovered his RC faith after the death of a close friend in a car crash, the first musical result being *Litanies à la vierge noire* (1936). Of his instr. works, the org. conc. (1938) is highly original in its treatment of the solo instr. His mus., eclectic yet strongly personal in style, is essentially diatonic and melodious, embroidered with 20th-cent. dissonances. It has wit, elegance, depth of feeling, and a bitter-sweetness which derives from the mixture in his personality of gaiety and manic depression. In 1946 he said: 'I have no system for writing music, thank God! (by system I mean "contrivances")'. Prin. works:

OPERAS: *Le gendarme incompris (comédie-bouffe)* (1921); *Les *mamelles de Tirésias* (1944); *Les *dialogues des Carmélites* (1953–6); *La *voix humaine* (1958).

BALLETS: *Les *Biches* (1923); contribution to *L'*Éventail de Jeanne* (1927); *Les Animaux modèles* (1941).

INCID. MUSIC: *La Reine Margot* (Bourdet), with Auric (1935); *Léocadia* (Anouilh) (1940); *La fille du jardinier* (Exbrayat) (1941); *Le voyageur sans bagages* (Anouilh) (1944); *La nuit de Saint-Jean* (Barrie) (1944); *Le soldat et la sorcière* (Salacrou) (1945); *L'invitation au château* (Anouilh) (1947); *Amphitryon* (Molière) (1947); *Renaud et Armide* (Cocteau) (1962).

FILMS : *La Belle au bois dormant* (1935); *La Duchesse de Langeais* (1942); *Le voyage en Amérique* (1951).

ORCH.: *2 Marches et un intermède*, chamber orch. (1937); *Suite, Les Biches* (1940, rescored); *Suite, Les Animaux modèles* (1942); *Sinfonietta* (1947); *Matelot provençale* (1952); *Bucolique* (1954).

CONCERTOS: *Concert champêtre*, hpd. or pf., orch. (1927–8); *Aubade*, 'concerto choréographique', pf., 18 instr. (1929); 2 pf., orch. (1932); org., str., timp. (1938); pf., orch. (1949).

CHAMBER MUS.: 2-cl. sonata (1918); sonata, cl., bn. (1922); sonata, tpt., tb., hn. (1922); trio, ob., bn., pf. (1926); pf. sextet (1932–9); *Villanelle*, pipe, pf. (1934); vc. sonata (1940–8); vn. sonata (1942–3); str. qt. (1946, destroyed); fl. sonata (1957); *Élégie*, hn., pf. (1957); *Sarabande*, gui. (1960); cl. sonata (1961–2); ob. sonata (1962).

VOICE(S) & INSTR(S).: *Rapsodie nègre*, bar., pf., str. qt., fl., cl. (1917); *Le Bestiaire*, v., fl., cl., bn., str. qt. or v., pf. (1919); *Le Bal masqué*, cantata, bar. (or mez.), chamber ens. (1932); *Colloque*, sop., bar., pf. (1940); *La Dame de Monte Carlo*, sop., orch. (1961).

CHORAL: *Chanson à boire*, unacc. male ch. (1922); *7 Chansons*, unacc. ch. (1936); *Litanies à la Vierge Noire*, women's or children's ch., org. (1936); *Petites Voix*, unacc. ch. (1936); *Mass in G*, unacc. ch. (1937); *Sécheresses*, ch., orch. (1937); *4 Motets pour un temps de pénitence*, unacc. ch. (1938–9); *Exultate*, unacc. ch. (1941); *Salve Regina*, unacc. ch. (1941); *Figure humaine*, cantata, unacc. double ch. (1943); *Un soir de neige*, cantata, 6 unacc. vv. or unacc. ch. (1944); *Chansons françaises*, unacc. ch. (1946); *4 petites prières de St. François d'Assise*, unacc. male ch. (1948); *Stabat Mater*, sop., ch., orch. (1950); *4 Motets pour le temps de Noël*, ch. (1952); *Ave verum corpus*, 3 female vv. (1952); *Laudes de Saint Antoine de Padoue*, unacc. male ch. (1959); *Gloria*, sop., ch., orch. (1959); *7 Répons des ténèbres*, male ch., orch. (1960–2).

PIANO: *3 Pastorales* (1918); *3 mouvements perpétuels* (1918); *Valse* (1919); *5 Impromptus* (1920); *Suite in C* (1920); *10 Promenades* (1921); *Suite, Napoli* (1925); *Pastourelle* (1927); *2 Nouvellettes* (1927–8); *3 Pièces* (1928); *Pièce brève sur le nom d'Albert Roussel* (1929); *8 Nocturnes* (1929–38); *Valse-Improvisation sur le nom Bach* (1932); *15 Improvisations* (1932–59); *Feuillets d'album* (1933); *Villageoises* (1933); *Presto* (1934); *2 Intermezzi* (1934); *Humoresque* (1934); *Badinage* (1934); *Suite française* (1935); *Les Soirées de Nazelles* (1936); *Bourrée, Au Pavillon* (1937); *Mélancolie* (1940); *Intermezzo in A♭* (1943); *Thème varié* (1951); *Novelette* (1959); *Improvisation in D: Hommage à Edith Piaf* (1960).

PIANO & NARRATOR: *L'Histoire de *Babar le petit éléphant* (1940–5).

PIANO (4 HANDS): Sonata (1918).

2 PIANOS: *L'Embarquement pour Cythère* (1951); Sonata (1953); *Elégie* (1959).

SONGS (v., pf. unless otherwise stated): *Toréador* (Cocteau) (1918); *Le Bestiare au cortège d'Orphée* (Apollinaire, 6 songs), v., 7 instr. or pf. (1919); *Cocardes* (Cocteau, 3 songs), v., 5 instr. or pf. (1919); *5 Poèmes de Ronsard* (1924–5); *Chansons gaillardes* (17th-cent. anon., 8 songs) (1926); *Vocalise* (1927); *Airs chantés* (Moréas, 4 songs) (1927–8); *Epitaphe* (Malherbe) (1930); *3 Poèmes de Louise Lalanne* (Apollinaire pseudonym, 3 songs) (1931); *4 Poèmes* (Apollinaire) (1931); *5 Poèmes*

(Jacob) (1931); *8 Chansons Polonaises* (1934); *4 Chansons pour enfants* (Jaboune) (1934–5); *5 Poèmes* (Éluard) (1935); *A sa guitare* (Ronsard) (1935); *Tel jour telle nuit* (Éluard) (1936–7); *3 Poèmes* (Vilmorin) (1937); *2 Poèmes* (Apollinaire) (1938); *Le Portrait* (Colette) (1938); *Miroirs brûlants* (Éluard, 2 songs) (1938); *Priez pour paix* (d'Orléans) (1938); *La Grenouillère* (Apollinaire) (1938); *Ce doux petit visage* (Éluard) (1938); *Bleuet* (Apollinaire) (1938); *Fiançailles pour rire* (Vilmorin, 6 songs) (1939); *Banalités* (Apollinaire, 5 songs) (1940); *Le chemins de l'amour* (from *Léocadia*) (1940); *Chansons villageoises* (Fombeure, 6 songs) (1942, also with chamber orch.); *Métamorphoses* (Vilmorin, 3 songs) (1943); *2 Poèmes* (Aragon) (1943); *Montparnasse*; *Hyde Park* (Apollinaire) (1945); *Le Pont*; *Un Poème* (Apollinaire) (1946); *Paul et Virginie* (Radiguet) (1946); *Le disparu* (Desnos) (1947); *3 Chansons de F. Garcia Lorca* (1947); *Main dominée par le cœur* (Éluard) (1947); '. . . 'mais mourir' (Éluard) (1947); *Calligrammes* (Apollinaire, 7 songs) (1948); *Hymne* (Racine) (1949); *Mazurka* (Vilmorin) (1949); *La Fraîcheur et le feu* (Éluard, 7 songs) (1950); *Parisiana* (Jacob, 2 songs) (1954); *Rosemonde* (Apollinaire) (1954); *Le Travail du peintre* (Éluard, 7 songs) (1956); *2 Mélodies 1956* (Apollinaire and de Baylié) (1956); *Dernier poème* (Desnos) (1956); *Une chanson de porcelaine* (Éluard) (1958); *Fancy* (Shakespeare) (1959); *La Courte Paille* (Carême) (1960).

Poulton, Diana (*b* Storrington, 1903; *d* Heyshott, Sussex, 1995). Eng. lutenist and historian. Co-ed. of lute mus. of *Dowland. Prof. of lute RCM from 1971. Wrote *Life of Dowland* (1972).

Pound, Ezra (Loomis) (*b* Hailey, Idaho, 1885; *d* Venice, 1972). Amer. poet, music critic, and composer. Went to It. 1908, Eng. 1908–20, Paris 1920–4, It. 1924–45. Settled in Rapallo and became champion of Vivaldi. Admiration for Mussolini led him to give many talks on Rome Radio during Second World War. He was arrested in 1944 and sent to a prison camp in Pisa. Sent to USA to be tried for treason, he was declared insane and committed to Amer. mental hospital, 1946–58. Returned to It. 1958. Principally known as poet, but wrote mus. criticism regularly in Eng. from 1908 (a collection, ed. R. M. Shafer, was pubd. 1977). Especially interested in mus. of medieval troubadours. Wrote 1-act opera *Le Testament de François Villon* (1920–1) with help from George Antheil; *Hommage à Froissart* for vn. (1926); *Cavalcanti* (unfinished opera, 1920s).

Pountney, David (Willoughby) (*b* Oxford, 1947). Eng. opera director. Directed first opera 1967 at Cambridge Univ. (Scarlatti's *Trionfo dell' Onore*). Prod. Janáček's *Káťa Kabanová*, Wexford 1972. Dir. of prod., Scottish Opera, 1975–80, where he staged *Die Meistersinger von Nürnberg*, *Eugene Onegin*, *Don Giovanni*, and a notable Janáček cycle in collab. with WNO. Amer. début Houston 1973 (*Macbeth*), ENO 1977 (Blake's *Toussaint*), Australia (Sydney) 1978 (*Die Meistersinger*). Several prods. for Netherlands Opera incl. f.p. of Glass's *Satyagraha* (1980). Dir. of prod. ENO 1982–93, incl. *Lady*

Macbeth of Mtsensk, f. Brit. stage ps. of *Doctor Faust* and *Osud*, and f.p. of Harvey's *Inquest of Love*. Several of his prods. caused controversy. Prod. world première of Floyd's *Bilby's Doll* (Houston 1976), and of Glass's *The Voyage* (NY Met début, 1992). Librettist of Maxwell Davies's opera *The Doctor of Myddfai* (1993–6). CBE 1994.

poussé (Fr.). Pushed. Up-bow (in str. playing), contrasted with *tiré* (pulled), down-bow.

Pousseur, Henri (*b* Malmédy, Belg., 1929). Belg. composer. Taught mus. at Brussels sch. 1950–60. Until 1959 worked in EMS in Cologne and Milan where he was influenced by Webern, Boulez, Stockhausen, and Berio. Comp. his first elec. work in Cologne, 1954. Founder, 1958, and dir. Studio de Musique Electronique, Brussels. Has written many articles on contemp. mus. and trans. Berg's writings into Fr. Taught at Darmstadt summer courses 1957–67. Prof. of mus., State Univ. of NY at Buffalo, 1966–9. Prof. of comp., Liège Cons., 1970–94 (dir. from 1975). Teacher at Liège Univ. 1983–7. Works incl.:

OPERAS: *Votre Faust* (1961–7); *Die Erprobung des Petrus Hebraïcus* (1974); *Leçons d'enfer* (1989–91).

ORCH.: *Symphonies* for 15 instrs. (1955); *Phonèmes Couleurs croisées* (1967); *Les Ephémérides d'Icare II* (1970); *Icare apprenti* (1970); *L'Effacement du Prince Igor* (1971); *Le seconde apothéose de Rameau*, chamber orch. (1981); *Nuits des Nuits* (1985).

CHAMBER MUSIC: *Quintet in mem. Anton Webern* (1955); *Répons* (1960, re-composed 1965); *Ode*, str. qt. (1960–1); *Madrigal II*, fl., vn., viola da gamba, cembalo; *Madrigal III*, cl., vn., vc., 2 perc., pf. (1962); *Echoes I*, vc. (1967); *Echoes II*, mez., fl., vc., pf. (1969); *U oder E-Musik*, str. qt. (1991).

VOICE(S) & INSTR(S).: *Miroir de votre Faust*, pf., sop. ad lib. (1964–5); *Mnemosyne 1*, monody for v. or instr. or ch. (1968); *Echoes II de votre Faust*, mez., fl., vc., pf. (1969); *Chronique berlinoise*, bar., pf. quintet (1976); *Chronique illustrée*, bar., orch. (1976); *Humeurs du futur quotidien*, reciter, orch. (1978); *Tales and Songs from the Bible of Hell*, vv., tape, and live elec. (1979); *Agonie*, elec.vv. (1981); *La Rose des voix*, v., ch., narr., instr. (1982); *La Passion selon guignol*, vocal qt., orch. (1982); *Traverser la Forêt*, narr., 2 vocal soloists, ch., 12 instr. (1987); *Déclaration d'Oranges*, narr., 2 vocal soloists, orch., tape (1989).

ELECTRONIC & TAPE: *Seismogrammes* (1953); *Scambi* (1957); *Rimes pour différentes sources sonores* (1958–9); *3 Visages de Liège* (1961).

PIANO(S): *Mobile*, 2 pf. (1956–8); *Caractères* (1961); *Apostrophes et 6 Réflexions* (1964–6).

Powder her Face. Opera in 2 acts by Adès to lib. by P. Hensher based on life of Margaret, Duchess of Argyll (1912–93). Comp. 1995. F.p. Cheltenham 1995.

Powell, Claire (*b* Tavistock, 1954). Eng. mezzo-soprano. Won Tauber memorial prize 1978. Début GTO (at Glyndebourne) 1978 (2nd Lady in *Die Zauberflöte*). Member of Royal Opera, CG, 1979–85; London recital début 1979. Amer. début (S. Francisco) 1990. Sang Bianca in f. London p. of Zemlinsky's *A Florentine Tragedy* (CG 1985).

Powell, Maud (*b* Peru, Ill., 1868; *d* Uniontown, Pa., 1920). Amer. violinist. Toured Eng. 1883. Eur. début 1885. Amer. début 1885. Promoted works by Amer. composers and gave f. Amer. ps. of concs. by Bruch, Tchaikovsky, Dvořák, and Sibelius. Formed str. qt. 1894–8 and Maud Powell Trio 1908, touring USA 1908–9. Comp. cadenza for Brahms conc.

Powell, Mel (*b* NY, 1923; *d* Los Angeles, 1998). Amer. composer and pianist. Pianist and arr. for Benny Goodman and Glenn Miller bands. Worked in NY 1950–7. On comp. faculty Yale Univ. 1958–69, est. EMS there 1960. Dean of Mus., Calif. Inst. of Arts from 1969 (provost 1972–6, prof. from 1976). His works, even those using elec. means, retain strong traditional features. Works incl. *Filigree Setting*, str. qt. (1959); *Haiku Setting*, v., pf. (1961); *Events*, tape (1963); *Stanzas*, orch. (1965); *Analogs 1–4*, tape (1966); *Immobiles 1–4*, tape and/or orch. (1967); *Immobile 5*, tape, orch. (1969); *Setting*, vn., tape, wind (1972); *Inscape*, ballet (1976); *Variations*, elec. (1976); *Little Companion Pieces*, sop., str. qt. (1979); *Cantilena*, tb., tape (1981); ww. quintet (1984–5); *Invocation*, vc. (1987); *Letter to a Young Composer*, sop. (1987); *3 Madrigals*, fl. (1988); *Computer Prelude*, elec. (1988).

Power, Lionel (*d* Canterbury, 1445). Eng. composer. Supposed colleague of *Dunstable. Wrote 2 treatises on mus. theory and much church mus., incl. *Salve Regina* and *Mater ora filium*. Many works incl. in *Old Hall MS.

Powers, Anthony (*b* London, 1953). Eng. composer. Taught at Dartington Coll. of Arts and Exeter Univ. Prof. of mus. Cardiff Univ. from 2004. Comps. incl.:

OPERA: *The Search for the Simorgh* (1981).

MUSIC THEATRE: *A Sussex Carol*, actors, mimes, sop., ch., orch. (1982).

ORCH.: *Music for Strings* (1984); *Vespers*, 21 solo str. (1986); *Stone, Water, Stars* (1987); vc. conc. (1990); *Architecture and Dreams* (1992); *Terrain* (1992); sym. No.1 (1994–6), No.2 (1999); *. . . further in shadow . . .*, ob., orch. (2001).

ENS.: *Another Part of the Island* (1980); *Nymphéas* (1983); *Chamber Conc.* (1984).

VOICE(S) & INSTR.: *Souvenirs du voyage*, sop., pf. (1979–80); *Rembrandt Dying*, bass, pf. (1984); *The Winter Festival*, mez., 9 instr. (1984–5); *Venexiana I*, 2 ten., 2 vn., vc., hpd. (1985); *II*, 2 high vv., small orch. (1986); *From Station Island*, spkr., bar., ens. (2003).

CHORAL & VOCAL: *Songs for Dark Times*, unacc. ch. (1981); *Memorials of Sleep*, ten., orch. (2000); *Airs and Angels*, sop., bar., ch., orch. (2003).

CHAMBER MUSIC: Sonata, fl., ob., vc., hpd. (1981); *Nocturnes Book I*, tpt., vn., db. (1981), *II*, vc. (1984); quintet, fl., cl., vn., va., vc. (1983); *Sea/Air*, cl. (1985); *Études-Tableau Book I*, pf., vn., vc. (1986), *II*, pf., vn., va., vc., db. (1986); str. qt. No.1 (1987), No.2 (1991), No.3 (1999), No.4 (2005); *Double Sonata*, cl., vn., vc., pf. (1993); *Fast Colours*, fl., cl., vn., vc., pf. (1997); *Capricci*, wind quintet (1994); *Five Philosophical Interludes*, cl. (2001).

PIANO: Sonatas: No.1 (1983), No.2 (1985–6); *The Memory Room* (1991); *Vista* (2003); *Flyer*, 2 pf. (2004).

pp, ppp, etc. Abbreviations for *pianissimo*, very soft.

P.R. In Fr. org. mus., abbreviation for *positif-récit*, i.e. choir-swell (swell to choir coupler).

Practical Cats. Work for speaker and orch. by Rawsthorne, settings of 6 poems from T. S. Eliot's *Old Possum's Book of Practical Cats* (1939). F.p. Edinburgh Fest. 1954.

Praeludium (Lat.). Prelude. Title of popular orch. work by *Järnefelt, first played in Eng. 1909.

Praetorius. Latinized form of Schulz or Schultz adopted by several Ger. musicians in 16th and 17th cents. Among them are: **Hieronymus Praetorius** (*b* Hamburg, 1560; *d* Hamburg, 1629). Comp. church mus., wedding songs, etc., much of it pubd. in 5 vol. *Opus musicum novum et perfectum* (1622–5). **Michael Praetorius** (*b* Kreuzberg, 1571; *d* Wolfenbüttel, 1621). Prolific composer and important mus. historian. Began career as organist, 1604, to Duke of Brunswick. His *Syntagma musicum* (1614–20, 3 vols.) is a wide survey of mus., the 2nd vol. being a prime source of information on mus. instr. of the time.

Prague Symphony. Nickname of Mozart's Sym. No.38 in D (K504) comp. 1786 and f.p. during Mozart's visit to Prague in 1787. In 3 movts.

Pralltriller (Ger.). Upper mordent. See *mordent*.

Prausnitz, Frederik (*b* Cologne, 1920; *d* Lewes, Del., 2004). Ger.-born conductor (Amer. cit.). Début Detroit SO 1944. On staff Juilliard Sch. in various capacities 1947–61. Guest cond. Brit. and Eur. orchs. from 1957. Cond., New Eng. Cons. SO, Boston, 1961–9, Syracuse SO 1971–4, dir. of cond. Peabody Inst., Baltimore, from 1976. Has cond. f. Amer. ps. of works by Dallapiccola, Gerhard, Lutyens, Schoenberg, Stockhausen, Varèse, and Webern. Wrote *Score and Podium* (1983).

Precentor (Lat.). First singer. Ecclesiastical official, in charge of vocal mus. in Anglican caths.

Preciosa. Ger. play about a gipsy by P. A. Wolff for which Weber in 1820 comp. ov., 4 chs., song, 3 melodramas, and dances.

precipitato, precipitoso, etc. (It.). Rushed; impetuously.

pre-classical. Term applied to composers such as C. P. E. Bach who are considered to be later than baroque and leading to the 'classical' style of Haydn, Mozart, etc.

prelude. A piece of mus. which precedes something else, e.g. preceding a fugue; forming 1st movt. of a suite; orch. introduction to opera. Also a self-contained short piece for pf., as those by Chopin, Rachmaninov, Debussy, etc.

Préludes. 2 books of pf. pieces by Debussy. *Book I* (1910): (1) *Danseuses de Delphes* (Dancing Women of Delphi), suggested by a pillar in the Louvre on which are sculptured 3 Bacchantes; (2) *Voiles* (Sails); (3) *Le Vent dans la plaine* (The wind in the plain); (4) *Les Sons et les parfums tournent dans l'air du soir* (Sounds and perfumes in the evening air); (5) *Les Collines d'Anacapri* (The hills of Anacapri); (6) *Des Pas sur la neige* (Footsteps on the snow); (7) *Ce qu'a vu le vent d'Ouest* (What the west wind saw); (8) *La fille aux cheveux de lin* (The girl with the flaxen hair), suggested by a poem of Leconte de Lisle; (9) *La Sérénade interrompue* (The interrupted serenade), Spanish in its idioms; (10) *La Cathédrale engloutie* (The submerged cathedral), based on the legend of the cath. of Ys, with its bell-tolling and chanting under the sea; (11) *La Danse de Puck* (Puck's dance); (12) *Minstrels*—Negro or music-hall type. *Book II* (1912–13): (1) *Brouillards* (Mists); (2) *Feuilles mortes* (Dead leaves); (3) *La Puerta del Vino*—name of famous gate of Alhambra; (4) *Les Fées sont d'exquises danseuses* (Fairies are exquisite dancers); (5) *Bruyères* (Heaths); (6) *General Lavine—eccentric*—Paris mus.-hall performer; (7) *La Terrasse des audiences du clair de lune* (Terrace of Moonlight Audiences); (8) *Ondine*—the water-spirit maiden of the early 19th-cent. story of de la Motte Fouqué; (9) *Hommage à S. Pickwick Esq., P.P.M.P.C.*—with a touch of the Brit. nat. anthem; (10) *Canope* (Canopic vase), ancient Egyptian cinerary urn; (11) *Les Tierces alternées* (Alternating 3rds); (12) *Feux d'artifice* (Fireworks).

Préludes, Les (The Preludes). Symphonic poem by Liszt, comp. 1848, rev. before 1854. Title from one of Lamartine's *Nouvelles Méditations poétiques*, but mus. was orig. comp. as ov. to *Les Quatres Éléments*, 4 male chs. with words by J. Autran and orch. by Conradi. Liszt's preface to rev. score states that life is treated as a series of preludes to the unknown after-life.

preludio (It.). Prelude.

preparation. Device in harmony whereby effect of discord is lessened: the note in a chord which causes the chord to be discordant is sounded in the preceding chord where it is not a cause of discord, i.e. prepared discord. If this course is not followed, the discord is unprepared.

prepared piano. A pf. in which the strs. have been 'doctored' in various ways to produce abnormal tone-qualities. Invented by Henry *Cowell and demonstrated in S. Francisco 1914. Used by *Cage for his *Bacchanale* (1938).

pressando, pressante (It.), **pressant** (Fr.). Pressing on, *accelerando*. Sometimes the Fr. infinitive *presser* is used.

prestant. Org. stop, same as *principal (3) in Brit. and Amer. instr.

presto (It.). Quick. *prestezza*, quickness; *prestamente*, quickly; *prestissimo*, very quick; *prestissimamente*, very quickly.

Preston, Simon (John) (*b* Bournemouth, 1938). Eng. organist, teacher, harpsichordist, and conductor. London début as org. 1962. Sub-org. Westminster Abbey 1962–7. Cond. Oxford Bach Ch. 1967–8. Org., Christ Church, Oxford, 1970–81; lect. in mus. Oxford Univ. 1972–81; org. and master of the choristers, Westminster Abbey, 1981–7.

Prêtre, Georges (*b* Waziers, 1924). Fr. conductor. Dir. of mus., opera houses of Marseilles, Lisle, and Toulouse 1946–55. Mus. dir. Opéra-Comique 1956–9; cond. f. Paris p. of *Capriccio*, 1956. Débuts: London 1961; Amer. (Chicago) 1959; NY Met 1964; Salzburg Fest. 1966. Mus. dir. Paris Opéra 1966–71; prin. cond. Stuttgart Radio SO 1995–8. Cond. at CG 1965 for Callas in *Tosca* and often conducted for her in the theatre and recording studio. Cond. f.ps. of Poulenc's *La Voix humaine* (1959) and *Gloria* (1959).

Previn, André (George) [Andreas Ludwig Priwin] (*b* Berlin, 1929). Ger.-born pianist, conductor, and composer (Amer. cit. 1943). Went to USA 1939. Once a jazz pianist, he later worked as composer and arranger of film mus. in Hollywood. Début as cond., St Louis SO 1962. Cond.-in-chief, LSO, 1968–79; settled in Eng. where he won popular following as presenter of mus. on TV. Champion of Eng. mus., notably Walton and Vaughan Williams (whose 9 syms. he recorded). Cond. Houston SO, 1967–9, Pittsburgh SO 1976–84, mus. dir. RPO 1985–7 and prin. cond. 1987–92, mus. dir. Los Angeles PO 1985–90. Salzburg début 1973. Comps. incl. vc., vn., pf., hn., and gui. concs., chamber mus., and works for solo pf., mus. for 'play for actors and orch', by Tom Stoppard, *Every Good Boy Deserves Favour*, prod. London 1978 (with LSO). Comp. opera, *A Streetcar Named Desire*, 1997, and cond. f.p., San Francisco 1998. Hon. KBE 1996.

Previtali, Fernando (*b* Adria, 1907; *d* Rome, 1985). It. conductor and composer. Ass. to *Gui at Florence Maggio Musicale 1928–36. Cond. It.

Radio Orch. 1936–43, 1945–53, S. Cecilia Orch. 1953–73. Guest cond. European orchs. from 1948. Amer. début, Cleveland Orch. 1955. Noted for radio opera perfs. Author of books on mus. Wrote ballet and other works.

Prey, Hermann (*b* Berlin, 1929; *d* Krailling, nr. Munich, 1998). Ger. baritone. Début Wiesbaden 1952. Hamburg Opera 1953–60. Guest singer Berlin and Vienna Operas from 1956. Salzburg Fest. from 1959. Brit. début 1965 (Storch in *Intermezzo* at Edinburgh Fest. with Bavarian State Opera). Bayreuth début 1965; CG from 1973. Amer. début in *Lieder* 1952, NY Met 1960. Noted for Strauss roles and for Beckmesser in *Die Meistersinger*. Especially fine exponent of *Lieder*. Founder (1976) of annual Schubert fest. at Hohenems.

Pribaoutki (Song games). For v., fl., ob., cor anglais, cl., bn., and str. qt. by *Stravinsky comp. 1914 to Russ. popular texts. F.p. London 1918, cond. Goossens. Items are: 1. *L'Oncle Armand* (*Kornillo*), 2. *Le Four* (*Natashka*), 3. *Le Colonel*, 4. *Le Vieux et le lièvre* (The Old Man and the Hare).

Přibyl, Vilém (*b* Náchod, 1925; *d* Brno, 1990). Cz. tenor. Début as amateur in Hradec Králové 1952 as Lukáš in Smetana's *The Kiss*. Joined Janáček Opera, Brno, 1961 and sang leading Janáček roles, and Radames, Lohengrin, Otello, and Walther. Brit. début Edinburgh Fest. 1964 (title-role in f. Brit. p. of Smetana's *Dalibor* with Prague Nat. Th. Opera). CG 1967; Salzburg Fest. 1971.

Price, Curtis (Alexander) (*b* Springfield, Mo., 1945). Amer. musicologist. Taught at Washington Univ., St Louis, 1974–81, King's Coll., London, 1981–95 (prof. from 1988). Specialist in Eng. dramatic mus. from Purcell to early 19th cent. Author of *Henry Purcell and the London Stage* (1984). Ed. of Purcell's *Dido and Aeneas* (1986). Prin., RAM from 1995. Hon. KBE 2005.

Price, (Mary Violet) **Leontyne** (*b* Laurel, Miss., 1927). Amer. soprano. Sang Mrs Ford in *Falstaff* in student prod. at Juilliard Sch. Chosen by Virgil Thomson to sing in revival of *Four Saints in Three Acts* in NY and Paris, 1952. Sang Bess in *Porgy and Bess* in tour of USA 1952–4 and in Vienna, Berlin, Paris, and London in 1955. Recital début NY 1954, then NBC TV 1955. S. Francisco début 1957; Chicago 1959; Vienna 1958; CG 1958; Salzburg 1959; La Scala 1960; NY Met 1961; Paris 1968. One of finest Verdi sops. of her day and memorable Butterfly and Tosca. Also noted exponent of mus. of Samuel Barber (gave f.p. of his *Prayers of Kierkegaard* with Boston SO cond. Munch, 1954, and created Cleopatra in NY Met première of his *Antony and Cleopatra*, 1966). Last opera appearance was as Aida at NY Met, 3 Jan. 1985.

Price, (Dame) **Margaret** (Berenice) (*b* Blackwood, nr. Tredegar, Wales, 1941). Welsh soprano. Member of Ambrosian Singers 1960–2. Opera début as

Cherubino with WNO 1962 and at CG 1963. Guest singer, especially in Mozart roles, in leading opera houses. Débuts: Glyndebourne 1966; Amer. (S. Francisco) 1969; NY Met 1985; Salzburg Fest. 1975. Has recorded Isolde with C. Kleiber. Noted *Lieder* singer. CBE 1982. DBE 1992.

prick-song. Old Eng. term (prick = mark) for mus. which was written down, i.e. 'pricked' instead of being extemporized or traditional (as plainchant).

Priestman, Brian (*b* Birmingham, 1927). Eng. conductor. Ass. cond. Yorkshire SO 1952–4, mus. dir. Royal Shakespeare Th., Stratford-upon-Avon, 1960–3. Cond. Edmonton SO 1964–8, Baltimore SO 1968–9, Denver SO 1970–8. Prin. cond. NZ Broadcasting Corporation 1973–6, Miami PO 1978–80. Prof. of mus., Univ. of Cape Town Coll. of Mus. 1980–6. Cond. f. Brit. p. of A. Scarlatti's *Griselda* in BBC broadcast 1968.

Prigioniero, Il (The Prisoner). Opera in prol. and 1 act by *Dallapiccola, comp. 1944–8, to lib. by composer after Villiers de L'Isle Adam's *La Torture par l'espérance* (1883) and Charles Coster's *La Légende d'Ulenspiegel et de Lamme Goedzak*. F.p. It. radio 1949. Prod. Florence 1950, NY 1951, London 1959.

prima donna (It.). First lady. Orig. the chief woman singer in an opera cast, but term has been generalized to mean a leading woman singer. Thus, for orig. meaning, one has to use term *prima donna assoluta*, 'the absolute first lady'. The same process has occurred in ballet with *prima ballerina assoluta*.

Prima Donna. Comic opera in 1 act by A. Benjamin to lib. by Cedric Cliffe. Comp. 1933, prod. London 1949, Philadelphia 1955.

Prima la musica e poi le parole (It. 'First the music and then the words'.). Opera in 1 act by Salieri to lib. by Casti. Comp. 1785. Prod. Vienna 1786. Richard Strauss was inspired by it to comp. his last opera, *Capriccio* (1942), on the relative merits of words and mus. in opera.

primo, prima (It.). First. Hence *primo*, top part in pf. duets; *primo uomo*, prin. male singer in opera (orig. the leading castrato); *prima vista*, first sight; *tempo primo*, same tempo as at beginning; *come prima*, as at first; *prima volta*, first time; *sonare a prima vista*, to sight read.

Primrose, William (*b* Glasgow, 1903; *d* Provo, Utah, 1982). Scottish-born violist and violinist (Amer. cit. 1955). Changed from vn. to va. on Ysaÿe's advice and played in London Str. Qt. 1930–5. Settled in USA 1937. Prin. va. NBC SO 1938–42. Many appearances as soloist. Formed str. qt. 1939. Violist in Festival Qt. 1954–62. Commissioned Bartók's va. conc. and gave f.p. with Minneapolis SO, 1949. Taught at Indiana Univ. Sch. of Mus., Bloomington, 1965–72, Brigham Young Univ., Provo, 1979–82. CBE 1953.

Prince Igor. Opera in 4 acts, with prol., by *Borodin to his own lib. after an outline by Vladimir Stasov. Begun in 1869 and left unfinished in 1887. Completed by Rimsky-Korsakov and Glazunov; prod. St Petersburg 1890, London 1914, NY 1915. The Russ. musicologist Lamm has shown that Rimsky and Glazunov deleted nearly 1,800 bars of mus., a fifth of the total. An edn. by Levashov, Fortunatov, and Pokrovsky was perf. in Vilnius 1974 and pubd. in Berlin 1978. There are other performing versions.

Prince of the Pagodas, The. Ballet in 3 acts by Britten, Op.57, choreog. John Cranko, comp. 1956, f.p. CG 1957. 'Pas de six', Op.57a, pubd. separately, for orch. (1957). Inspired by a visit to the Far East. Britten cut the score for CG and for his recording. The complete score has been recorded by Oliver Knussen. Orch. suite, *Prelude and Dances from The Prince of the Pagodas*, arr. N. Del Mar, f.p. 1963; orch. suite (approved by Britten), arr. M. Lankester, f.p. 1979. Another suite has been compiled by A. Previn. New choreog. MacMillan 1985.

Princess Ida, or Castle Adamant. Operetta in 3 acts by Sullivan to lib. by Gilbert. Comp. 1883. Prod. London and Boston, Mass., 1884. Described by Gilbert as 'respectful operatic perversion of Tennyson's *The Princess*.'

principal. (1) Leading player of orch. section, e.g. 'prin. cl.', 'prin. hn.', etc.
(2) Singer who takes main parts in opera—'prin. ten.', meaning ten. who sings prin. roles, not the chief tenor.
(3) Open diapason org. stop of 4' length on manuals or 8' on pedal.

principale (It.). (1) Great org.
(2) Type of 17th- and 18th-cent. tpt. part.

Pringsheim, Klaus (*b* Feldafing, nr. Munich, 1883; *d* Tokyo, 1972). Ger. conductor and composer. Ass. cond. to Mahler at Vienna Opera 1906–9. Cond. Ger. Opera in Prague 1909–14, Bremen Opera 1915–18. Mus. dir. Max Reinhardt ths. in Berlin 1918–25. Cond. all Mahler syms. and songcycles in Berlin 1923–4. Taught at Imperial Acad. of Mus., Tokyo, 1931–7. Mus. adv. Royal Dept. of Fine Arts, Bangkok, 1937–9. Returned to Japan 1939, interned there 1944. Worked in Calif. 1946–51, but returned to Japan where he became dir., Musashino Acad. of Mus., Tokyo. Comps. incl. radio opera, Conc. for Orch., and xyl. conc. His reminiscences of Mahler, pubd. 1973–4, are illuminating.

Printemps (Spring). Symphonic suite for orch. and ch. by Debussy, comp. 1887. Definitive version re-orch. Busser 1913 without ch., f.p. Paris 1913. Not to be confused with *Rondes de printemps* (see *Images*).

Printemps [Wigniolle], **Yvonne** (*b* Ermont, Seine-et-Oise, 1894; *d* Neuilly-sur-Seine, Paris, 1977). Fr. soprano. Début in revue aged 12. In 1916 joined th. co. run by Sacha Guitry (whom she married 1919). They had worldwide success in plays and *opérettes*, incl. Hahn's *Mozart*. After divorce in 1932, she appeared in Noël Coward's *Conversation Piece* (1934) and Oscar Straus's *Les trois valses* (1937). Works were written for her by Poulenc and Hahn.

Prinz von Homburg, Der (The Prince of Homburg). Opera in 3 acts by Henze to lib. by Bachmann after play by Kleist. Comp. 1957–8, rev. 1991. Prod. Hamburg 1960, London 1962. Baritone title-role rewritten for tenor, 1964.

Prise de Troie, La (The Capture of Troy). Part I (Acts 1 and 2) of Berlioz's opera *Les *Troyens*.

Prisoner, The (Dallapiccola). See *Prigioniero, Il*.

Pritchard, (Sir) **John** [Stanley Frederick] (Michael) (*b* London, 1918; *d* Daly City, S. Francisco, 1989). Eng. conductor. Cond., Derby Str. Orch., 1943–52. Répétiteur at Glyndebourne 1947, becoming ch. master and ass. to Fritz Busch 1949 and cond. *Don Giovanni*, *Così fan tutte*, and *Figaro* 1951. Prin. cond. Glyndebourne 1967, mus. dir. 1969–77. Débuts: CG 1952; Salzburg Fest. 1966; Amer. opera début Chicago 1969; NY Met 1971. Cond. f.ps. of *Gloriana* (CG, 1953), *The Midsummer Marriage* (CG, 1955), and *King Priam* (Coventry, 1962), f. Brit. p. of *Elegy for Young Lovers* (Glyndebourne, 1961). Prin. cond. RLPO 1957–63, LPO 1962–7. Cond. Huddersfield Choral Soc. 1973–6, BBC SO 1981–9. Cond. Cologne Opera 1978–89. Joint mus. dir. Opéra National, Brussels, 1981–9; mus. dir. S. Francisco Opera 1986–9. Hamburg Shakespeare Prize 1975. CBE 1962. Knighted 1983.

Prix de Rome. Prizes awarded annually since 1803 by Institut de France to candidates selected by competition from comp. students at Paris Cons. First prize (*Grand Prix de Rome*) entitles winner to live in Rome for 4 years at Villa Medici (Fr. Acad.) while engaging in study and creative work. 2nd prize is a gold medal. Exam. takes place *en loge* (in isolation); candidates must set to mus. a cantata on a given subject. Jury's verdict must be ratified by entire Académie des Beaux-Arts. Among winners have been Berlioz (1830), Gounod (1839), Bizet (1857), Massenet (1863), Debussy (1884), and Charpentier (1887). Ravel's failure to win was subject of famous scandal. Belg. awards prize of same name and does not insist upon residence in Rome. An Amer. *Prix de Rome* was instituted in 1905, the winner to reside at the Amer. Acad. in Rome. No award was made until 1921 (Sowerby). Fr. comp. suppressed 1968; promising young composers etc. now sent to Rome on teachers' recommendations.

Pro Arte Quartet. Belgian str. qt., founded 1912 by graduates from Brussels Cons. Début Brussels 1913, achieving reputation for perfs. of contemporary mus. Eng. début 1925, USA 1926. Perf. annually in Cambridge for a week 1932–8. Title passed to faculty qt. of Univ. of Wisconsin at Madison. Austrian str. qt. of same name founded in Salzburg, 1973.

Pro Cantione Antiqua. Eng. vocal ens. formed in 1968 by Mark Brown, Paul *Esswood, and

James Griffett to perf. mus. of medieval, Renaissance, and baroque eras. Début Westminster Cath., 1968, cond. by Colin Mawby.

Procesión del Rocio, La (The Procession of Rocio). Sym.-poem in 2 parts by Turina, 1913. (The Rocio is a place of pilgrimage near Seville.)

Prodaná Neveštá (Smetana). See *Bartered Bride, The*.

Prodigal Son, The. There are several mus. comps. on this theme, among them:

(1) *L'Enfant Prodigue*, ballet by Prokofiev, Op.46, 1928–9, choreog. Balanchine. prod. Paris 1929.

(2) *The Prodigal Son*, parable for church perf., by Britten, Op.81, to lib. by W. Plomer, prod. Aldeburgh (Orford) 1968, NY 1969.

(3) *L'Enfant Prodigue*, cantata for sop., ten., bar., by Debussy, 1884, with which he won *Prix de Rome*.

(4) *The Prodigal Son*, oratorio by Sullivan, perf. Worcester Fest. 1869.

programme music. Instr. mus. which tells a story, illustrates literary ideas, or evokes pictorial scenes. Though the term originated with Liszt, illustrative mus. has existed for as long as mus. itself. Beethoven's *Pastoral Symphony* is a well-nigh perfect example of mus. which is both illustrative and satisfying purely as mus. In the 19th cent., composers such as Berlioz, Liszt, Tchaikovsky, and R. Strauss lent the full resources of the sym. orch. to this form of mus. art in works such as the *Symphonie fantastique*, *Romeo and Juliet*, and *Don Quixote*. The precept, once widely propagated, that 'absolute mus.' was, *ipso facto*, superior to 'programme mus.' is now, happily, outdated.

progression. The motion of one note to another note or one chord to another chord, in logical progression.

progressive tonality. Beginning a symphonic movt. in one key and ending it in another, as in certain works of *Nielsen and *Mahler.

Prohaska, Felix (*b* Vienna, 1912; *d* Vienna, 1987). Austrian conductor, son of Jaro *Prohaska. Taught at Graz Cons., 1936–9. Cond. of opera in Duisburg 1939–41, Strasbourg 1941–3, Prague 1943–5. Salzburg Fest. début 1945. Cond. and teacher, Vienna, 1946–55; chief cond. Frankfurt Opera 1955–61; Hanover Opera 1965–74. Dir., Hochschule für Musik, Hanover, from 1961.

Prohaska, Jaro(slav) (*b* Vienna, 1891; *d* Munich, 1965). Austrian bass-baritone. Member of Vienna Boys' Choir 1898–1906. Opera début Lübeck 1922. Nuremberg Opera 1925–31, Berlin State Opera 1931–52, Bayreuth Fest. 1933–44. Famous interpreter of Wagnerian roles of Sachs, Wotan, Dutchman, and Amfortas. Salzburg Fest. 1949. Retired 1959. Head of West Berlin Musikhochschule 1947 and dir. of its opera sch. 1952–9. Hermann *Prey was among his pupils.

Prokina, Elena (*b* Odessa, 1964). Russian soprano. Began career as actress. Member of Kirov Opera, Leningrad, 1988–92. Brit. début Edinburgh Fest 1991 (with Kirov Opera in *Khovanschchina*); CG début 1992 (Kirov Opera); London début 1993 (concert); Royal Opera 1994; Glyndebourne 1994; Los Angeles 1994.

Prokofiev, Sergey (Sergeyevich) (*b* Sontsovka, 1891; *d* Moscow, 1953). Russ. composer and pianist. Was taught pf. at age 3 by his mother, who encouraged him to compose (he wrote an opera at age 9). Studied privately with *Glière 1903–4. Entered St Petersburg Cons. 1904, studying harmony and counterpoint with Lyadov, pf. with A. Winkler, and orch. with Rimsky-Korsakov. Later studied pf. with Anna Essipova and cond. with Tcherepnin. Comp. and pubd. several works while student, incl. 2 pf. sonatas and first two pf. concs., all of which were condemned by the critics. Visiting Paris and London in 1914 he met Diaghilev, who commissioned a ballet from him (the war upset this plan and the mus. survives as the *Scythian Suite, Ala and Lolly*). In 1917 he comp. his first sym., the *Classical*, a superb 20th-cent. reincarnation of Haydn. After its f.p. in Petrograd in 1918 he left Russia for USA, appearing in NY as solo pianist in his own works. His opera *Love for Three Oranges* was commissioned by Chicago Opera, perf. 1921. From 1920 he made his home in Paris, writing 3 ballets for Diaghilev, and having several of his works perf. at the orch. concerts cond. *Koussevitzky, another Russ. exile. He completed another opera, *The Fiery Angel*, in 1923, but it was not staged in his lifetime. Never fully at home in the W., Prokofiev re-visited Russia in 1927 and 1929 and returned there to live in 1933, choosing an inopportune moment when the doctrine of 'socialist realism' in the arts had just been propounded. He found an outlet for his particular gifts in film mus.—brilliant scores for *Lieutenant Kijé* and *Alexander Nevsky*—and ballet (*Romeo and Juliet* and, later, *Cinderella*), In 1941 he began work on his most ambitious opera, *War and Peace*, and in 1944 wrote his richest and most heroic sym., the 5th. In spite of its success, he was among those in 1948 condemned for *'formalism' and was compelled to 'confess' his shortcomings in an open letter to the Union of Soviet Composers. He died on the same day as Stalin.

Though regarded as impossibly dissonant and *avant-garde* in his youth, Prokofiev can now be seen as in the direct line of Russ. comps., embodying the bold and colourful strokes of 19th-cent. nationalists into a 20th-cent. style strongly marked by its brittle wit and capacity for pungent dramatic characterization. Like Walton and Poulenc, he was fundamentally a romantic melodist and his style is formed like theirs from a reconciliation of the two strains in his personality, the tough, astringent modernist and the lyrical traditionalist. He was successful in a wide range of works: *War and Peace* is a great opera on the largest scale and *Love for Three Oranges* and *The Fiery Angel* have found their way into the rep-

ertory of several opera houses, the syms. and concs. are fine mus., at least 3 of his ballets are masterpieces, the pf. sonatas are crucial to the 20th-cent. pf. repertory; and in *Peter and the Wolf* he created the most enduring, touching, and instructive of young persons' guides to the orch. Prin. works:

OPERAS: *Maddalena*, Op.13 (1911, rev. 1913, completed in pf. score but only Scene 1 orch. Scenes 2–4 orch. Downes, 1977–8); *The *Gambler* (*Igrok*), Op.24 (1915–17, 2nd version 1927–8); *Love for Three Oranges* (*Lyubov k tryom apelsinam*), Op.33 (1919); *The *Fiery Angel* (*Ognennyï Angel*), Op.37 (1919–23, rev. 1926–7); *Semyon Kotko*, Op.81 (1939); *The *Duenna* (*Betrothal in a monastery*), Op.86 (1940); *War and Peace* (*Voyna i Mir*), Op.91 (1941–3, 1946–7, and rev. up to 1953); *The *Story of a Real Man* (*Povest' o nastoyashchem cheloveke*), Op.117 (1947–8).

BALLETS: *The Buffoon* (*Chout*), Op.21 (1915, rev. 1920); *Age of Steel* (*Le Pas d'acier*), Op.41 (1925–6); *The *Prodigal Son* (*L'Enfant prodigue*), Op.46 (1928–9); *Sur le Borysthène*, Op.51 (1930–1); *Romeo and Juliet*, Op.64 (1935–6); *Cinderella*, Op.87 (1940–4); *The *Stone Flower*, Op.118 (1948–53).

ORCH.: syms.: No.1 (*Classical*), Op.25 (1916–17, f.p. 1918), No.2 in D minor, Op.40 (1924, f.p.p. 1925), No.3 in C minor, Op.44 (1928, f.p. 1929), No.4 in C, Op.47 (1929–30, f.p. 1930, 2nd version, Op.112, 1947), No.5 in B♭, Op.100 (1944, f.p. 1945), No.6 in E♭ minor, Op.111 (1947, f.p. 1947), No.7 in C♯ minor, Op.131 (1951–2, f.p. 1952); *Sinfonietta*, Op.5/48 (1909, 1929); *Esquisse automnale*, Op.8 (1910); *Scythian Suite*, Op.20 (1914–15); *Overture* for 17 instr., Op.42 (1926); *Divertimento*, Op.43 (1929); *Symphonic Song*, Op.57 (1933); suite, *Lieutenant Kijé*, Op.60 (1934); *Egyptian Nights*, Op.61 (1934); *Peter and the Wolf*, narr., orch., Op.67 (1936); *Russian Overture*, Op.72 (1936); *Suite, 1941*, Op.90 (1941).

CONCERTOS: pf.: No.1 in D♭, Op.10 (1911–12), No.2 in G minor, Op.16 (1912–13, rev. 1923), No.3 in C, Op.26 (1917–21), No.4 in B♭, Op.53, left hand (1931), No.5 in G, Op.55 (1932); vn.: No.1 in D, Op.19 (1916–17), No.2 in G minor, Op.63 (1935); vc.: No.1 in E minor, Op.58 (1934, rev. 1938), No.2 in E minor (1950–1) rev. as *Sinfonia Concertante*, Op.125 (1952).

CHAMBER MUSIC: *Overture on Hebrew Themes*, Op.34, cl., pf., str. qt. (1919; orch. version 1934); quintet, wind, str., Op.39 (1924); str. qt. No.1, Op.50 (1930), No.2, Op.92 (1942); sonata for 2 vns., Op.56 (1932); vn. sonata No.1, Op.80 (1938–45), No.2 (from Op.94) (1944); fl. sonata, Op.94 (1943); solo vn. (or unison vns.) sonata, Op.115 (1947); vc. sonata, Op.119 (1949).

CHORAL WORKS: *Seven, They are Seven*, ten., ch., orch., Op.30 (1917–18, rev. 1933); *Mass Songs*, Op.68, ch. (1936); *Cantata on 20th Anniversary of October Revolution*, Op.74, orch., band, perc., 2 ch. (1937); *Songs of Our Days*, Op.77, orch. (1937); *Alexander Nevsky*, Op.78, mez., ch., orch. (1939); *Tale of Boy Who Remained Unknown*, Op.93, ch., orch. (1944); *Winter Bonfire*, reciters, boys' ch., orch. (1949–50); *On Guard For Peace*, oratorio (1950).

PIANO: sonatas: No.1 in F minor, Op.1 (1909), No.2 in D minor, Op.14 (1912), No.3 in A minor, Op.28 (1907–17), No.4 in C minor, Op.29 (1908–17), No.5 in C, Op.38 (1923, rev. as Op.135, 1952–3), No.6 in A minor, Op.82 (1940), No.7 in B♭, Op.83 (1939–42), No.8 in B♭, Op.84 (1939–44), No.9 in C, Op.103 (1947), No.10 (unfinished); *4 Études*, Op.2 (1909); *4 Pieces*, Op.3 (1907–11); *4 Pieces*, Op.4 (1908–13); *10 Pieces*, Op.12 (1908–13); *Sarcasms*, Op.17 (1912–14); **Visions fugitives*, Op.22 (1915–17); *Tales of the Old Grandmother*, Op.13 (1918); *2 Sonatines*, Op.54 (1931); *10 Pieces from Romeo and Juliet*, Op.76 (1937).

SONGS: *The Ugly Duckling*, Op.18 (1914); *5 Poems*, Op.23 (1915); *5 Songs to words of Anna Akhmatova*, Op.27 (1916); *5 Melodies Without Words*, Op.35 (1920); *7 Songs*, Op.79 (1939).

FILM & THEATRE MUSIC: *Lieutenant Kijé* (1934); *Queen of Spades*, Op.70 (1936); *Eugene Onegin*, Op.71 (1936); *Boris Godunov*, Op.74 (1936); **Alexander Nevsky* (1938); *Ivan the Terrible* (1942–5).

prolation. Division in medieval mensural notation of the whole-note (semibreve) into 3 smaller time-units (major prolation) or 2 (minor).

Promenade Concerts. Literally, concerts at which the audience can walk about, but in modern usage concerts at which a section of the audience stands. First Eng. promenade concerts were held in London 1838 under title 'Promenade Concerts à la Musard' (Musard was the leader). Later concerts on similar lines were promoted by *Jullien, *Balfe, Mellon, and others. In 1895 Robert Newman began new series at Queen's Hall, cond. Henry *Wood. These still continue. They have been sponsored by BBC since 1927 (except for 1940 and 1941) and the majority of concerts has been given by BBCSO. After Wood died in 1944, Malcolm Sargent became prin. cond. in 1948, but after his death in 1967 no single cond. dominated. The 'Proms', now held in the Royal Albert Hall and other venues for 8 weeks from mid-July each year, are in effect an enormous mus. fest., embracing semi-staged opera perfs. and chamber mus. Several orchs. take part, each concert is broadcast, and several are televised. The Last Night has become a traditional feature of Brit. life, especially the 2nd half in which the audience enthusiastically joins in the perfs. of Elgar's *Land of Hope and Glory*, Parry's **Jerusalem*, and Wood's **Fantasia on British Sea-Songs*. Various other orchs., e.g. the Hallé, CBSO, RLPO, and RSNO, give their own series of promenade concerts.

Prometheus. (1) Symphonic-poem by Liszt. Orig. comp. (and orch. by Raff) 1850 as prelude to a setting of chs. from Herder's *Prometheus Unbound*. Re-scored by Liszt 1855.

(2) Scenic oratorio in 5 scenes by Wagner-Régeny to lib. by composer after Aeschylus. Comp. and f.p. 1959 (Cassel).

Prometheus, Die Geschöpfe des (The Creatures of Prometheus). Ballet by Beethoven, Op.43, comp. 1800–1 (ov., introduction, and 16 nos.), f.p. Vienna 1801, choreog. Salvatore Viganó. Beethoven used 2 themes from the finale of the ballet in other works, viz. 1. A theme in G major appears as No.11 of the 12 *Kontretänze* for orch., WoO 14. 2. A theme in E♭ major is used as No.7 of the 12 *Kontretänze*, WoO 14; as the theme of the Piano Variations (**Eroica*) Op.35; and as the main theme of the finale of Symphony No.3 (**Eroica*) Op.55.

Prometheus, the Poem of Fire (*Prometei, Poema Ognya*). Sym.-poem in F♯ by Scriabin, Op.60, for orch. with pf., optional ch., and 'kbd. of light' (projecting colours on to screen). Comp. 1908–10, f.p. Moscow 1911, London 1913, NY 1914 (this perf. used 'kbd. of light').

Prometheus Unbound, Scenes from Shelley's. Work by Hubert *Parry for soloists, ch., and orch. to text by Shelley. Comp. 1880, rev. 1881, 1885. F.p. Gloucester 1880, London 1882.

Prophète, Le (The Prophet). Opera in 5 acts by *Meyerbeer to lib. by Scribe. Comp. 1836–40. Prod. Paris and London 1849, New Orleans 1850.

proportion. Conception in medieval mus. theory of relationship between vibration nos. of notes and also between their time-signatures in mensural notation expressed by fractions.

proportionate (proportional) **notation**. In 20th-cent. mus. a graphic method of indicating durations, i.e. instead of traditional notation, the horizontal spacing of symbols represents the intended length of durations.

Proporz, Proportz (Ger.). Same as **Nachtanz*.

prosa, prose. In the Christian church service, the earliest sequences (types of hymn sung to special melodies) were in prose, and this term is sometimes still used instead of sequence.

Proses lyriques (Lyrics in prose). 4 songs for v. and pf. by Debussy to his own texts. Comp. 1892–3. Titles are: *De Rêve* (Of a dream), *De Grève* (About the Shore), *De Fleurs* (About flowers), *De Soir* (About evening).

protest song. Term which gained currency (first in USA) in 1960s for song which voiced feelings of protest about some social or political injustice, real or imagined, or about some int. event which aroused strong emotions, e.g. Amer. part in Vietnam war. A famous example is 'We shall overcome'. Among the prin. singers of the genre were Bob Dylan and Joan Baez.

Prout, Ebenezer (*b* Oundle, 1835; *d* London, 1909). Eng. composer, organist, theorist, and teacher. Largely self-taught. Began career as schoolmaster. Took up mus. 1859. Org. in Islington 1861–73; pf. teacher Crystal Palace Sch. of Art 1861–85. Taught at Nat. Training Sch. for

Mus. 1876–82, RAM from 1879 and GSMD from 1884. Prof. of mus., Trinity Coll., Dublin, 1894–1909. Comp. large number of works in many forms, ed. Handel's *Messiah*, but best known for his mus. textbooks. Wrote 4 syms., 2 org. concs., 2 str. qts., cantatas, and church music.

Prozess, Der (The Trial). Opera in 9 scenes by *Einem, Op.14, to lib. by Blacher and H. von Cramer after novel by Kafka (1925). Comp. 1950–2. Prod. Salzburg 1953.

Prozession (Procession). Comp. by *Stockhausen, 1967, for tam-tam, va., electronium, pf., 2 microphones and controls, 2 filters: 6 players. The players are instructed to play 'events' from other Stockhausen works, i.e. *Mikrophonie I, Gesang der Jünglinge, Kontakte, Momente, Telemusik, Solo*, and *Klavierstücke I–XI*.

Pruslin, Stephen (Lawrence) (b NY, 1940). Amer. pianist and librettist. Settled in London making recital début 1970. Founding member of Fires of London, 1970, and wrote extensively on mus. of Maxwell Davies. Librettist of *Punch and Judy* (1967).

Prussian Quartets (Mozart). See *King of Prussia Quartets*.

Ps. Short for Ger. *Posaunen*, i.e. tbs.

psalm. Hymn acc. by harp or other str. instrs. But by the term is generally understood the Old Testament Book of Psalms. In Christian church services these are sung antiphonally to various chants. Verse paraphrases of the psalms are known as metrical psalms. There are countless settings of individual psalms by composers from Bach to Britten (and by earlier and later composers).

psalmody. Study of the psalms or of the tunes used for metrical psalms.

Psalmus Hungaricus. Work for ten., ch., org., and orch. by Kodály, Op.15, based on text of Psalm 55 in paraphrase of 16th-cent. Hung. poet Mihály Végh. Commissioned for 50th anniv. of union of Buda and Pest. F.p. Budapest 1923, Zurich 1926, Cambridge 1927.

psalter. A collection of Eng. verse paraphrases of the psalms, intended to be sung. Miles Coverdale pubd. a coll. in 1539. The Sternhold and Hopkins coll. appeared in 1549 and was completed by 1564. Other famous psalters were those by John Day, Este, Ravenscroft, Playford, and Tate and Brady.

psaltery. Medieval str. instr., played by plucking with a plectrum or the fingers, trapeze-shaped, and usually strung horizontally over a soundboard. Had sweet, pure tone. Can be played with bow. Tavener scores for 4 bowed psalteries in *Toward the Son* (1982).

psaume (Fr.). *Psalm.

Puccini, Giacomo (b Lucca, 1858; d Brussels, 1924). It. composer. 5th of a line of It. church musicians. Org. at local church. Attended Milan Cons. 1880–3, studying comp. with Bazzini and Ponchielli. Showed bias towards symphonic works, but Ponchielli sensed his pupil's operatic potentiality and persuaded him to enter Sonzogno 1-act opera competition with *Le Villi*. Rejected by the jury, the work was admired by Boito and prod. Milan, 1884. It was heard by Verdi's publisher, Ricordi, who commissioned an opera from Puccini. *Edgar*, when it appeared in 1889, was a failure, but Ricordi's faith was justified in 1893 by *Manon Lescaut*, in which the mature Puccini is already evident in the ardent and profuse melodic mastery which distinguishes the work. Strangely, Puccini's next opera, *La bohème*, prod. Turin 1896, was at first less successful than *Manon*, but it soon became what it remains, probably the most popular and generally beloved opera ever written, a masterpiece of characterization, sentiment, and craftsmanship. With these successes, he was able to build his magnificent house at Torre del Lago. Power of characterization also marked his next opera, *Tosca*, based on a Sardou play. *Madama Butterfly* was his most successful psychological character-study and requires exceptional vocal and histrionic skill from the sop. who sings the heroine. The work was a failure at its Milan première, but Puccini re-cast it in 3 acts for Brescia 3 months later, where it was acclaimed as a triumph and has since almost rivalled *Bohème* in popularity. *Butterfly* was set in Japan and was based on a play by Belasco, who was author of the Amer. melodrama *The Girl of the Golden West* which became Puccini's next opera (*La fanciulla del West*). This was prod. at the NY Met in 1910 but has never attained a popularity equal to its predecessors although on closer acquaintance the mus. is revealed as of very high quality. Similar re-assessment is due to *La rondine* (Monte Carlo 1917). Nothing illustrates Puccini's instinctive theatrical skill more remarkably than the success with which he achieved the difficult feat of combining three contrasting 1-act operas in *Il trittico* (Triptych): a thriller in *Il tabarro*, a sentimental tragedy in *Suor Angelica*, and a comedy in *Gianni Schicchi*. For his next opera Puccini selected a lib. inspired by Gozzi's play *Turandot*. But he died of cancer before he could complete the duet which was planned as the climax of the work. It was completed skilfully by *Alfano and the opera has held its place despite this anti-climax because of the superb mus. earlier in the opera and because the part of the cruel Princess Turandot is a glorious gift to dramatic sops.

Puccini lacks the nobility of Verdi, but few opera composers can rival him in dramatic flair and skill. He is sentimental but it is a sentimentality to which millions are glad to respond. His sense of characterization was highly developed and his genius for orchestration enabled him with a few notes to hold an audience in the palm of his hand. Most of his operas contain a heroine in whom there are elements of the 'little girl', and there is a streak of sadistic cruelty which also marred the personality of the man himself. He continued to develop as an artist and to respond to contemporary influences, from Debussy to Schoenberg. Prin. works:

OPERAS: *Le *Villi* (The Willis) (first, 1-act, version, 1883; 2-act version, 1884); *Edgar* (4-act version, 1884–8; 3-act version 1892, rev. 1901, 1905); *Manon Lescaut* (1890–2); *La *bohème* (1894–5); *Tosca* (1898–9); *Madama Butterfly* (2-act version, 1901–3; 3-act version, 1904; further cuts and rev., 1906); *La *fanciulla del West* (1908–10); *La *rondine* (The Swallow) (1914–16, rev 1918–19); *Il *trittico* (Il *tabarro*, *Suor Angelica*, *Gianni Schicchi*) (1913–18); *Turandot* (1920–6, last scene completed by Alfano).

CHORAL: *Messa di Gloria* in A, for sop., ten., bar., ch., and orch. (1880).

ORCH.: *Preludio sinfonico* (1876); *Capriccio sinfonico* (1883).

CHAMBER MUSIC: *Crisantemi*, str. qt. (1890); *3 Minuets*, str. qt. (1892, Nos. 1 and 3 rev. 1898).

Pugnani, Gaetano (*b* Turin, 1731; *d* Turin, 1798). It. violinist and composer. Travelled widely 1754–70, staying for long spells in Paris (where he was soloist in his own conc. at the Concert Spirituel) and London (where he cond. at the King's Th. and had a success with his opera *Nanetta e Lubino*, 1769). Returned to Turin as orch. leader and teacher. His pupils incl. *Viotti. Comp. operas, cantatas, ballets, vn. conc., 20 vn. sonatas, 6 str. qts., and other works. A *Praeludium and Allegro* said to have been arr. from Pugnani by the violinist *Kreisler was admitted by Kreisler in 1935 to be entirely his own work.

Pugno, (Stéphane) **Raoul** (*b* Montrouge, N. Fr., 1852; *d* Moscow, 1914). Fr.-It. pianist, organist, and composer. Org. St Eugène, Paris, 1872–92. Prof. of harmony, Paris Cons. 1892–6, of pf. 1896–1901. Frequently played in duo with violinist *Ysaÿe. Wrote 4 comic operas, 6 ballets, oratorio, and pf. pieces.

Pulcinella. Ballet, with song, in 1 act by Stravinsky, comp. 1919–20, to lib. and choreog. by Massine. For sop., ten., bass, and small orch. Prod. Paris 1920. The mus., comprising 18 items, is a re-comp. of pieces by *Pergolesi, though at least one is a false attrib., seven from trio sonatas by Domenico Gallo, and one by Count Van Wassenaer. Also suite of 8 movts. for small orch., *c*.1922, rev. 1947. The *Suite italienne* for vc. and pf. (1932) comprises 5 movts. from *Pulcinella*, and the version for vn. and pf. (*c*.1933) has 6.

Pulitzer Prize. Prizes in Amer. journalism, letters, and mus. awarded since 1943 under will of the publisher Joseph Pulitzer (1847–1911). Administered by Columbia Univ., NY. Mus. prize (for comp.) incl. award of $500, and earlier a travelling scholarship of $1,500 was given to a student to enable him or her to study in Europe. Since 1970 mus. critics have been eligible for award for criticism.

Pult (Ger., plural *Pulte*). Orch. mus. stand (shared by 2 performers, such as violinists, playing the same part). *Pultweise*, deskwise, i.e. in order of the players' desks.

Punch and Judy. Opera in 1 act by Birtwistle, lib. by Stephen Pruslin. Comp. 1966–7. F.p. Aldeburgh 1968, Minneapolis 1970, London (concert) 1979, (stage) 1982.

punta (It.). Point. *a punta d'arco*, with the point of the bow.

Punto, Giovanni [Stič, Jan Václav or Stich, Johann Wenzel] (*b* Zehušice, 1746; *d* Prague, 1803). Bohemian horn-player and violinist. Assumed It. name 1766 and in 1768 began European travels, visiting Eng. in 1770 and 1777. At Mainz court 1769–74. Met Mozart in Paris 1778. Worked in Paris 1782–7 and 1789–99. When he visited Vienna in 1800, Beethoven wrote his hn. sonata, Op.17, for him. Acclaimed as virtuoso of highest order. Wrote 11 hn. concs. (pubd. *c*.1787–*c*.1806), 24 hn. qts., 20 hn. trios, 56 hn. duos, other chamber works, and a book of hn. exercises (1795).

punto coronato, punto d'organo (It.). The pause sign.

Purcell, Daniel (*b* London, *c*.1660; *d* London, 1717). Eng. organist and composer, brother of the great Henry *Purcell. Org., Magdalen Coll., Oxford, 1688–95, St Andrew's, Holborn, 1713–17. In 1695 succeeded his brother as composer of incidental mus. for plays and wrote mus. for final masque of Henry Purcell's *The Indian Queen*. Prolific writer of other works.

Purcell, Edward (Cockram) [Edward Purcell Cockram] (*d* 1932). Eng. composer best known for song *Passing by*.

Purcell, Henry (*b* London, 1659; *d* London, 1695). Eng. composer and organist. Son of Thomas Purcell, one of the King's musicians. Boy chorister of Chapel Royal. Studied with *Humfrey and *Blow. In 1674 he was appointed tuner of Westminster Abbey org. and at 18, in 1677, he succeeded Matthew Locke as 'composer to the King's violins' (a str. band of 24 players). He succeeded Blow as organist of Westminster Abbey in 1679. In the following year he pubd. the superb Fantasias for strs., written for his private enjoyment and not for the royal band. From 1680 Purcell began to compose the long series of 'welcome odes' and other official choral pieces, his music by far transcending the doggerel of the words. In that year, too, he comp. the first of the incidental mus. he wrote for the London th., for plays by Dryden, Congreve, Shadwell, Brady, Behn, etc. In 1682 he became one of the 3 organists of the Chapel Royal and in 1683 pubd. his sonatas in 3 parts (2 vn., and bass, with organ or hpd.), in the preface to which he admitted that he had attempted a 'just imitation of the most fam'd Italian masters'. In 1685 his anthem *My Heart is Inditing* was comp. for the coronation of James II and 4 years later he was involved in the coronation of William III and Mary II. In 1689 his only opera, *Dido and Aeneas*, was perf. at Josias Priest's boarding-school for girls at Chelsea, but recent research has convincingly suggested that this may have been a revival and that the opera was comp. at least 5 years earlier, probably 1684. In the last few years of his life, Purcell was increasingly prolific, composing some of his greatest church mus. such as the *Te Deum* and *Jubilate in D*. In 1695, for Queen Mary's funeral, he comp. an anthem (*Thou knowest, Lord, the Secrets of our Hearts*), 4 canzonas for brass, and 2 elegies, which are among his most masterly works and were used for his own funeral later the same year.

Purcell's position as among the greatest of Eng. composers was acknowledged in his lifetime, but it was not until the bicentenary of his death that this judgment came to be accepted by later generations. The work of the Purcell Soc. and of composers such as Holst and Vaughan Williams helped to rehabilitate him, and Benjamin Britten of a later generation paid him the compliment of imitation and also restored many of his works to the concert-hall, aided by the 20th-cent. revival of interest in perf. the mus. of Purcell's time in authentic style. Purcell's brilliance of invention, his sense of drama, and the 'common touch' which endeared him to his contemporaries (both musicians and non-musicians) give his mus. freshness and immediacy. In *Dido and Aeneas*, he comp. the first great Eng. opera and set a new standard of sensitivity to words and word-rhythms in addition to displaying rare depths of emotion. Yet it is in the instrumental works that the real genius of Henry Purcell dwells. Prin. works:

OPERA: *Dido and Aeneas (?1684).

SEMI-OPERAS: The Prophetess, or The History of *Dioclesian (1690); *King Arthur, or The British Worthy (1691); The *Fairy Queen (1692); The *Indian Queen (1695); The Tempest, or The Enchanted Island (?1695. See Weldon, John).

INCIDENTAL MUSIC: Theodosius, or The Force of Love (1680); Amphitryon (1690); Distressed Innocence (1690); The Indian Emperor (1691); The Libertine (?1692); The Double Dealer (1693); Timon of Athens (1694); The Comical History of Don Quixote (1694–5); The Married Beau (1694); Abdelazer (1695); The Mock Marriage (1695); Bonduca, or The British Heroine (1695); The Spanish Friar (1694–5). (See also Songs from Theatre Music, below.)

CHORAL: Behold, I Bring you Good Tidings, Christmas anthem (1687); *Come ye Sons of Art, ode for Queen Mary's birthday (1694); Elegy on the death of Queen Mary (1695); Jehovah, quam multi, motet; Jubilate Deo in D (1694); Let God arise (1679); Magnificat and Nunc Dimittis in G minor; My Beloved Spake (c.1680); My Heart is Inditing, anthem (1685); Now Does the Glorious Day Appear, ode for Queen Mary's birthday (1689); O God, thou art my God, anthem (1682); O God, thou has cast us out, anthem (1682); O Lord God of hosts, anthem (1682); O Sing unto the Lord (1688); *Ode for St Cecilia's Day (1683–92); Rejoice in the Lord Alway, the *Bell anthem (1684–5); Remember not, Lord, our offences,

anthem (1682); Te Deum in D (1694); They that go Down to the Sea in Ships, anthem (1685); Thou knowest, Lord, the Secrets of our Hearts, anthem (*Queen Mary's Funeral Music, 1695); Thy Word is a Lantern, anthem (c.1694).

SONGS FROM THEATRE MUSIC: Cinthia frowns whene'er I woo her (Distressed Innocence, 1690); O Let me Weep; Turn then thine Eyes (The Fairy Queen, 1692); I Sighed and owned my Love (The Fatal Marriage, 1694); I Attempt from Love's Sickness to Fly (The Indian Queen, 1695); Fairest Isle, all Isles Excelling; Shepherd, Leave Decoying (King Arthur, 1691); *Nymphs and Shepherds (The Libertine, ?1692); No, Resistance is but Vain (The Maid's Last Prayer, 1693); Man is for the Woman Made (The Mock Marriage, 1695); *Music for a while (Oedipus, 1692); My Dearest, my Fairest; Sweeter than Roses (Pausania, 1695); Arise ye Subterranean Winds; Halcyon Days; See, see, the Heavens Smile (The Tempest, ?1695).

SONGS: Ah Cruel Nymph; Bess of Bedlam; Fly Swift, ye Hours; The Father brave; I Lov'd fair Celia (1694); I Vowed to Die a Maid; If Music be the food of Love (3 versions 1692, 1693, 1695); Lord, What is Man? (1693); Love Arms himself in Celia's Eyes (1695); Love, thou art Best; Lovely Albina (1695); Morning Hymn; Now that the Sun hath Veiled his Light (*Evening Hymn, 1688); Queen's Epicedium; Sleep, Adam, sleep (1683); Tell me some Pitying Angel (The *Blessed Virgin's Expostulation, 1693); What a Sad Fate is Mine; When Night her Purple Veil.

INSTRUMENTAL: Strings, without continuo: Chacony in G minor, 4 parts; 3 Fantasias, 3 parts (1680); 9 Fantasias, 4 parts (1680); Fantasia upon 1 note, 5 parts; In Nomine, 6 parts; In Nomine, 7 parts; Pavan in G minor, 4 parts. Strings, with continuo: Fantasia on a ground in D, 4 parts; Overtures in G, 4 parts; in D minor, 4 parts; in G minor, 5 parts; 12 Sonatas of 3 parts (1683); 10 Sonatas of 4 parts (pubd. 1697); Sonata in G minor; Suite in G major; Sonata in D for tpt., strs., continuo; Symphoniae sacrae, viol and organ; Trumpet Tune and Air. Brass: March and Canzona for 4 tbs. (*Queen Mary's Funeral Music, 1695).

KEYBOARD: suites for hpd. (pubd. 1696): No.1 in G, No.2 in G minor, No.3 in G, No.4 in A minor, No.5 in C, No.6 in D, No.7 in D minor, No.8 in F; Musick's Handmaid (1689) in 2 parts (No.9 of part 2 is New Irish tune in G, *Lilliburlero); Air in D minor; Fanfare in B♭; Ground in D minor; Hornpipe in E minor; Pavans in A minor and G; Round in D; Toccata in A minor.

ORGAN: Voluntary on the Old 100th; Voluntary in G.

Purgatory. Opera in 1 act by *Crosse, Op.18, to lib. based on play by W. B. Yeats. Comp. 1965. Prod. Cheltenham 1966. For ten., bar., women's ch., and orch. Also opera by *Weisgall.

Puritani di Scozia, I (*I Puritani*; The Puritans of Scotland). Opera in 3 acts by Bellini (his last) to lib. by C. Pepoli after play *Têtes rondes et cavaliers* by F. Ancelot and X. B. Saintine derived from

Scott's *Old Mortality* (1816). Comp. 1834. Prod. Paris and London, 1835, New Orleans 1843, NY 1844.

Pusar, Ana (*b* Celje, 1954). Slovene soprano. Ljubljana Opera 1975–9, singing Rosina, Manon, Tatyana, etc. Won Toti dal Monte comp. and Mario del Monaco comp. 1978. Berlin Komische Oper 1979–85. Sang Marschallin (*Der Rosenkavalier*) at reopening of Dresden Semper Oper 1985. Vienna Opera from 1986 in Mozart and Strauss roles.

Putnam, Ashley (*b* NY, 1952). Amer. soprano. Apprentice with Sante Fe Opera. Début 1976 as Lucia di Lammermoor with Virginia Opera Assoc., Norfolk. 1st prize in Met Auditions 1976. NY City Opera début 1978 (Violetta in *La traviata*). Eur. début Glyndebourne 1978; CG 1986; NY Met 1990.

Putnam's Camp. 2nd movt. of Ives's **Three Places in New England* for orch., sometimes played separately.

Puyana, Rafael (*b* Bogotá, 1931). Colombian harpsichordist. European tour 1955, NY début 1957, London, 1966. Dir., early mus. dept. of summer sch. at Santiago de Compostela, Sp., from 1961. Works written for him, e.g. by Evett, McCabe, Mompou, Orbon.

Pygott, Richard (*fl.* early 16th cent.). Eng. composer. Trained choristers in Wolsey's chapel choir 1517–29. Gentleman of Chapel Royal, 1524–53. Wrote mainly church mus.

Quadrat (Ger.). Natural sign (♮).

quadrille. Type of square dance popular at court of Napoléon I in early 19th cent. In 5 sections (4 of 32 bars each and finale), varying in time-signature from 6/8 to 2/4, the mus. being selected from popular tunes, operatic arias, and sometimes sacred works. Elgar composed a series of quadrilles for use by the band which he cond. for staff dances at a lunatic asylum (1879–84).

quadruple counterpoint. Counterpoint in which 4 vv. are concerned, which are capable of changing places with each other, thus making 24 positions of the v. parts possible.

quadruple-croche (Fr.). Quadruple-hook. Hemidemisemiquaver, or 64th note.

quadruplet. A group of 4 notes, of equal time-value, written to be played in the time of 3. See *irregular rhythmic groupings*.

quadruple time. See *time signature*.

quail. Toy instr. which imitates the cry of the quail; used in 'toy symphonies'. Beethoven imitated the quail in his *Pastoral* Symphony but using normal instrs.

Quantz, Johann Joachim (*b* Oberscheden, Hanover, 1697; *d* Potsdam, 1773). Ger. flautist and composer. Began mus. training 1708. In 1718 was oboist in Polish King's orch. in Dresden and Warsaw, becoming flautist after study with Buffardin. Engaged 1728 as teacher in Dresden of Crown Prince Frederick of Prussia; in 1741, when Frederick became King, entered royal service as court composer, chamber musician, and dir. of royal concerts. Added 2nd key to fl. and invented sliding tuning device. Wrote comprehensive method on fl.-playing (1752 and many subsequent edns.). Comp. 300 fl. concs., 200 fl. sonatas, mostly for the use of his royal patron, 60 trio sonatas, 22 hymns, and some songs.

quartal. Medieval or modern term for harmony in which chords are constructed on basis of superimposed 4ths.

quarter note. The note ♩ as a time-value, called in Eng. the crotchet, although the Amer. usage is gaining wider currency. Quarter-note rests are notated ♩ or ♭.

quarter-tone. An interval of half a semitone (24 quarter-tones to the octave). Introduced into Western mus. in 20th cent. with rise of interest in other cultures, quarter-tones having always been used in Eastern mus. Poses special problems of notation. Some composers who have written in quarter-tones have built special pfs., e.g. Hans Barth and Alois Hába. Boulez, Stockhausen, and other *avant-garde* serial composers have used quarter-tones.

quartet (Fr. *quatuor*; Ger. *Quartett*; It. *quartetto*). A comp. for 4 vv. or instr. or the 4 singers or performers who sing or play such comps. (e.g. Chilingirian Qt.). In the case of perfs., qt. usually implies a str. qt., i.e. 2 vn., va., vc. But there are also pf. qt. (pf. and 3 bowed instr.), ob. qt. (ob. and 3 bowed instr.), etc. In opera, a qt. is for 4 solo vv. (e.g. in the last act of *Rigoletto*). The vocal qt. for unacc. vv. has existed since mid-15th cent.

Quartetto Italiano. It. string quartet formed in 1945, making début at Carpi as Nuovo Quartetto Italiano. Noted for playing its repertory from memory, each piece being most carefully prepared. Outstanding in Debussy, Ravel, and Beethoven. Frequent international tours. Members were Paolo Borciani (*b* Reggo Emilia, 1922), Elisa Pegreffi (*b* Genoa, 1922), Piero Farulli (*b* Florence, 1920; he replaced Lionello Forzanti in 1946), and Franco Rossi (*b* Venice, 1921). Disbanded 1987.

Quartettsatz (Quartet movement). Title given to a movt. in C minor by Schubert (D703, 1820) intended for str. qt. which was never completed.

Quartfagott (Ger.). Medieval bn. pitched a 4th lower than normal.

Quartflöte (Ger.). Small fl. tuned 4th above concert fl.

quasi (It.). As if, almost. Thus, *sonata quasi fantasia*, sonata almost like a fantasia.

Quasthoff, Thomas (*b* Hildesheim, 1959). Ger. baritone. Studied law at Hanover Univ., then from 1972 privately in Hanover with Charlotte Lehmann (singing) and Ernst Huber-Contwig (mus. theory and history). Won various prizes 1988–96. Prof. of vocal studies, Detmold Univ. Mus. Sch. from 1996. USA début Oregon 1995; NY 1998 (*Winterreise*); Carnegie Hall 1999 (Britten's *War Requiem*, Boston SO cond. Ozawa). Opera début Berlin PO (concert) 2002, Salzburg Easter Fest. 2003 (stage) (both as Don Fernando in *Fidelio*, cond. Rattle). Vienna Opera début 2004 (Amfortas in *Parsifal*). Salzburg Fest. début 2004 (recital). Outstanding perf. of *Winterreise* (with Barenboim, pf.).

quatro rusteghi, I (The Four Rustics). Opera in 3 acts by Wolf-Ferrari, lib. by Sugano and Pizzolato based on Goldoni's comedy *I rusteghi* (1760). Comp. *c*.1904–5. Prod. Munich 1906, London (SW) 1946 (as *The School for Fathers*), NY 1951.

quattro (It.). Four. *quattro mani*, four hands; *quattro voci*, four vv.

Quattro pezzi sacri (Four Sacred Songs). Composite title for 4 short works for ch. and orch. by Verdi (1888-97): *Ave Maria, Stabat Mater, Te Deum, Laudi alla Vergine Maria*.

Quatuor pour la fin du temps (Quartet for the end of time). Qt. by *Messiaen for pf., cl., vn., and vc., comp. 1940 while Messiaen was in Silesian prisoner-of-war camp Stalag 8A, where it had its f.p., 15 Jan. 1941.

quaver (Fr. *croche*; Ger. *Achtelnote*; It. *croma*). The 8th-note, notated ♪ (rest notated 𝄾): half value of *quarter-note.

Queen Mary's Funeral Music. Mus. comp. by Purcell for the Westminster Abbey funeral on 5 Mar. 1695 of Queen Mary II wife of William III, who died of smallpox on 28 Dec. 1694. The mus. comprised two of the sentences from the burial service, which he had set at least 12 years earlier; the anthem *Thou knowest, Lord, the Secrets of our Hearts*, specially comp.; 2 canzonas for slide tpts. and tbs.; and a March originally written for a scene in Shadwell's *The Libertine* (?1692), an adaptation of the Don Juan legend. Some of the mus. was perf. in the Abbey in Nov. 1695 for Purcell's funeral.

Queen of Sheba, The (Goldmark). See *Königin von Saba, Die*.

Queen of Spades, The (Russ. *Pikovaya Dama*). Opera in 3 acts by Tchaikovsky to lib. by M. Tchaikovsky and the composer after Pushkin's novel (1833). Comp. 1890. Prod. St Petersburg 1890, NY Met 1910, London 1915.

Queen's Hall. Prin. London concert-hall, in Langham Place, opened 1893 and destroyed by bombing 1941. First home of Henry Wood Promenade Concerts and scene of many illustrious perfs.

Queffélec, Anne (*b* Paris, 1948). Fr. pianist. 1st prize, Munich comp., 1968, finalist Leeds comp., 1969. Soloist with leading orchs. and recitalist.

Queler, Eve (*b* NY, 1936). Amer. conductor and pianist. Cond. début Fairlawn, NJ, 1966 (*Cavalleria rusticana*). Cond. and vocal coach for NY City Opera. Founder, dir., and cond., Opera Orch. of NY from 1967, with which she has cond. concert perfs. of many rarely-heard operas.

Querelle des Bouffons. See *Bouffons, Querelle des*.

Querflöte (Ger.). Transverse fl.

queue (Fr.). Tail. Tail or stem of a note, or tailpiece of vn., vc., etc. *piano à queue* (Fr.). Grand pf.

quick-step. Lively march in 2/4, also known as quick march (*c*.108 steps to the minute). Also a fast version of the foxtrot.

Quiet City. Work by Copland for tpt., ca., and str. Orig. incid. mus. to play by Irwin Shaw. Prod. NY 1939; as orch. work f.p. 1941.

Quiet Flows the Don (*Tikhiy Don*). Opera in 4 acts by Dzerzhinsky to lib. by L. I. Dzerzhinsky on motifs from M. Shokolov's novel. Comp. 1934. F.p. Leningrad 1935.

Quiet Place, A. Opera in 1 act by Bernstein to lib. by S. Wadsworth. Comp. 1983. Houston 1983. Rev. in 3 acts incorporating *Trouble in Tahiti*, Milan 1984.

Quilico, Gino (*b* NY, 1955). Canadian baritone, son of Louis *Quilico. Début 1978 in TV prod. of *The *Medium*. Sang in Canada and USA, then made Eur. début in Paris 1980 (Mercutio in *Roméo et Juliette*). Paris Opéra 1980-3. Débuts: Brit. (Scottish Opera, Edinburgh Fest.) 1982; CG 1983; NY Met 1987; Salzburg Fest. 1988. Created Figaro in Corigliano's *The Ghosts of Versailles*, NY Met 1991.

Quilico, Louis (*b* Montreal, 1929; *d* Toronto, 2000). Canadian baritone. Début with NY City Opera 1953 (Germont *père* in *La traviata*); S. Francisco 1955; CG 1961; NY Met 1972. Sang regularly at Met. Teacher at Univ. of Toronto from 1971.

quilisma (Lat.). Most important of decorative *neums, something like the trill.

Quilter, Roger (*b* Brighton, 1877; *d* London, 1953). Eng. composer. Wrote highly distinguished songs, chiefly settings of Shakespeare, Tennyson (*Now Sleeps the Crimson Petal*), Herrick (cycle, *To Julia*), and others. Wrote opera *Julia* (London 1936), *A Children's Overture*, incidental mus. to children's play *Where the Rainbow Ends*, and some chamber mus.

Quinault, Jean-Baptiste Maurice (*b* Verdun, 1687; *d* Gien, 1745). Fr. composer, actor, and singer. Acted and sang at the Théâtre Français 1912-28, Comédie-Française until 1734. Wrote ballets, *divertissements*, and *intermèdes* for Fr. theatre 1714-32, incl. incid. music for Molière's *Le bourgeois gentilhomme* (1716).

quint. Org. stop sounding a note a 5th higher than key depressed. When on the pedal it is a $10\frac{2}{3}'$ stop designed to be used in conjunction with 16′ stop, producing effect of 32′ stop. *Quintadena* and *quintatön* are types of org. stop which sound not only the note of the key depressed but also the note a 12th higher. Also the 4th partial tone of a bell when it is tuned a 5th above the strike note.

quinte (Fr.). (1) Interval of a 5th.
(2) Obsolete Fr. name for va. (orig. ten. viol with 5 str., pitched 5th lower than vn.).

quintet (Fr. *quintette, quintuor*; Ger. *Quintett*; It. *quintetto*). Comp. for 5 instr. or vv., or the singers or players who perform such comps. In vocal music usually 2 sop., alto, ten., and bass (there are many 5-part madrigals). A str. quintet is usually 2 vns., 2 va., and vc., but sometimes (as in most quintets by Boccherini and in those by Schubert and Vaughan Williams) for 2 vns., va., and 2 vc. A pf. quintet is usually for pf., 2 vns., va., vc., but note that Schubert's 'Trout' Quintet is for pf., vn., va., vc., db. There are also cl. quintets, ob. quintets, etc. The customary wind quintet is for fl., ob., hn., cl., bn., but Elgar's wind quintets are for 2 fl., ob., cl., bn. There are also operatic quintets, the most famous occurring in Act 3 of *Die *Meistersinger von Nürnberg*.

Quintfagott (Ger.). Bn. pitched 5th lower than normal.

quintole (quintuplet). Group of 5 notes, or notes and rests, of equal time-value, written to be played in the time of 4 or 3. See *irregular rhythmic groupings*.

quintuple counterpoint. Counterpoint in which 5 vv. are concerned, which are capable of changing places with each other, so making 120 positions of the v. parts possible.

quintuplet. See *quintole*.

quintuple time. When there are 5 beats to a measure, with prin. accents on 1st, and 3rd or 4th beats according to whether the 5 are a compound of 2/4 and 3/4 or of 3/4 and 2/4. Famous examples are in Chopin's pf. sonata in C minor, Op.4, Wagner's *Tristan und Isolde*, Act III, Sc. 2, and Tchaikovsky's 6th Sym. (2nd movt.).

Quivar, Florence (*b* Philadelphia, 1944). Amer. mezzo-soprano. Member of Juilliard Opera Th., NY. Successful concert-hall career. NY Met début 1977 (Marina in *Boris Godunov*). Salzburg Fest. début 1983.

quodlibet (Lat.). What pleases. Light-hearted comp. comprising several popular tunes or fragments of tunes ingeniously put together, e.g. finale of Bach's *'Goldberg' Variations*, where 2 popular melodies of the day, *Ich bin so lang nicht bei dir g'west* (I've been away from you so long) and *Kraut und Rüben* (Cabbage and turnips), are combined within the harmonic outline of the theme.

R

R. (1) Abbreviation for right, e.g. R.H., right hand, in pf. mus.

(2) Abbreviation for Responsorium in church mus. (Gregorian chant).

(3) Abbreviation for **ripieno* in early orch. mus.

(4) Abbreviation for *clavier de récit*, the swell manual, in Fr. org. mus.

(5) Abbreviation for *ritardando*, found particularly in Elgar's scores.

(6) In catalogues of works of *Vivaldi, abbreviation for Rinaldi or for Ryom (latter usually in form RV).

Raabe, Peter (*b* Frankfurt an der Oder, 1872; *d* Weimar, 1945). Ger. conductor, composer, and scholar. Cond. opera at Königsberg, Elberfeld, Amsterdam 1894–9. Cond., Kaim Orch., Munich and Mannheim, 1903–7. Court cond., Weimar 1907, curator Liszt Museum from 1910. Dir. of mus. Aachen 1920–34. Succeeded R. Strauss as president of Reichsmusikkammer, 1935–45. Chairman, editorial board of Liszt complete edn. Wrote 2-vol. book on Liszt. Comp. songs and pf. pieces.

Raaff, Anton (*b* Gelsdorf, Bonn, 1714; *d* Munich, 1797). Ger. tenor. Sang in It. 1738–42, Ger. 1742–52, Lisbon 1753–5, Madrid 1755–9. In Mannheim from 1770 and Munich from 1779. Went to Paris with Mozart, 1778. Mozart wrote role of Idomeneo for him, 1781.

Rabaud, Henri (Benjamin) (*b* Paris, 1873; *d* Paris, 1949). Fr. composer, conductor, and teacher. Won *Prix de Rome* 1894 with cantata *Daphné*. Cond. Paris Opéra 1908–18 (dir. 1914–18), Boston SO 1918–19. Prof. of harmony, Paris Cons., dir. 1922–41. Wrote 8 operas, incl. *L'Appel de la mer* (*Riders to the Sea) 1924; 2 syms.; sym.-poems; oratorio *Job*; vc. concertino; str. qt.; etc. Wrote vc. method. Orch. Fauré's *Dolly* suite.

Rabin, Michael (*b* NY, 1936; *d* NY, 1972). Amer. violinist, son of violinist in NYPO. Prof. début 1947. Brilliant and sensitive artist whose untimely death ended int. career.

Race, Steve (*b* Lincoln, 1921). Eng. pianist, composer, writer, and broadcaster. Career as jazz pianist followed by success as popular presenter of mus. on radio and TV. Comp. *Variations on a Smoky Theme* for orch., film mus., and *Cyrano de Bergerac* for radio. OBE 1992.

Rachmaninov, Sergei (Vasilyevich) (*b* Semyonovo, Starorussky, 1873; *d* Beverly Hills, Calif., 1943). Russ. composer, pianist, and conductor (Amer. cit. 1943). Entered St Petersburg Cons. 1882; studied pf. with Nikolay Zverev in Moscow, 1885, and began to compose in 1886. Entered Ziloti's pf. class at Moscow Cons. 1888, also studying counterpoint with Taneyev and harmony with Arensky. In 1890 he began to compose his first pf. conc., completing it a year later. In the summer of 1892 he wrote the Prelude in C♯ minor which became his most celebrated comp. His first opera *Aleko* was staged at the Bolshoy, Moscow, in 1893 and praised by Tchaikovsky. It was a success, unlike his first Sym. which received a disastrous perf. under Glazunov in St Petersburg in 1897. Rachmaninov withdrew the work, which was never again played in his lifetime. In 1897–8 he became 2nd cond. of the Moscow Private Russian Opera Co., forming a lifelong friendship with the co.'s then unknown bass *Chaliapin. His first professional visit abroad was to London in 1899, where he played 'the' Prelude and cond. his orch. fantasy *The Rock*. At this time he lost faith in his power of comp., but was helped by hypnosis treatment from Dr Nikolay Dahl, also an amateur musician, who had many talks on mus. with his patient. A few months later Rachmaninov began his 2nd pf. conc., which was a great success at its f.p. and has remained immensely and rightly popular. The conc. was f.p. in Dec. 1900 without the 1st movt.; the f. complete p. was in April 1901. Thenceforward Rachmaninov comp. fluently. He worked simultaneously on 2 operas, *The Miserly Knight* and *Francesca da Rimini*, both of which he cond. at the Bolshoy where he was cond. 1904–6. Worried by political unrest in Russia, he moved to Dresden in 1906, beginning work on a 2nd Sym., the f.p. of which he cond. on a visit to St Petersburg in 1908. His first visit to USA followed in 1909, where he was soloist in the f.p. of his 3rd pf. conc. in NY. He returned to live in Russia, conducting several Moscow Phil. concerts in the 1912–13 season and completing his choral sym. *The Bells*. In 1917 he left Russia for ever and began a new career as int. concert pianist, making America his base. This reduced the time he had for comp. and it was not until 1926 that he completed the 4th pf. conc. he had begun in 1914. The work was played 1927 but was not, and never has been since, a success. After he signed a letter in 1931 attacking the Soviet régime his mus. was banned in Russia until 1933. In 1934 he comp. one of his finest works, the *Rhapsody on a Theme of Paganini*, which was followed in 1936 by the 3rd Sym. In 1938 he was in London to play at Henry Wood's jubilee concert and gave his last London recital in Mar. 1939. He comp. the *Symphonic Dances* for orch. in 1940. Despite failing health he embarked on an arduous Amer. tour in the winter of 1942–3, giving the proceeds to war relief. After playing in Knoxville, Tennessee, on 15 Feb. he became seriously ill and died on 28 Mar.

Rachmaninov was one of the greatest of pianists, as is proved by his recordings not only of his own concs. but of other composers' mus., incl.

sonatas with the violinist Kreisler. The vigour and attention to detail of his cond. are also preserved on records. But it is as a composer that his name will live longest. He was the last of the colourful Russian masters of the late 19th cent., with their characteristic gift for long and broad melodies imbued with a resigned melancholy which is never long absent. His operas have failed to hold the stage, mainly because of defects in their libs., but recordings have enabled their splendid mus. to be appreciated. Three of the 4 pf. concs. are an ineradicable part of the romantic repertory, and the syms., though long overshadowed by the pf. works, have gained esteem and popularity. The songs are at last being recognized as among Russia's best. In his later years his style grew subtler, as can be heard in the *Corelli Variations* for pf., the *Paganini Rhapsody*, the last set of songs, and the *Symphonic Dances*. But his masterpiece is *The Bells*, in which all his powers are fused and unified. Prin. works:

OPERAS: *Aleko (1892); The *Miserly Knight (Skupoy rytsar) Op.24 (1903–5); *Francesca da Rimini, Op.25 (1900, 1904–5); Monna Vanna (1907, one act in pf. score).

ORCH.: Scherzo in D minor (1887); Prince Rostislav (Knyaz Rostislav) (1891); The Rock (Utyos), Op.7 (1893); Caprice bohémien (Kaprichchio na tsiganskiye temi, Capriccio on gipsy themes), Op.12 (1892–4); syms.: No.1 in D minor, Op.13 (1895), No.2 in E minor, Op.27 (1906–8), No.3 in A minor, Op.44 (1935–6, rev. 1938); The *Isle of the Dead (Ostrov myortvikh), Op.29 (1909); *Symphonic Dances, Op.45 (1940).

PIANO & ORCH.: concs.: No.1 in F♯ minor, Op.1 (1890–1, rev. 1917), No.2 in C minor, Op.18 (1900–1), No.3 in D minor, Op.30 (1909), No.4 in G minor, Op.40 (1914–26, rev. 1941); *Rhapsody on a Theme of Paganini, Op.43 (1934).

CHORAL: 6 Choruses, Op.15, women's or children's ch. (1895–6); Spring (Vesna), Op.20, cantata, bar., ch., orch. (1902); Liturgy of St John Chrysostom, Op.31 (1910); The *Bells (Kolokola), Op.35, sym. for sop., ten., bar., ch., orch. (1913); All-Night Vigil (Vsenoshchnoye bdeniye), Op.37, soloists, ch. (1915); 3 Russian Songs, Op.41, ch., orch. (1926).

CHAMBER MUSIC: 2 movts., str. qt. (1889, also arr. for orch. by Rachmaninov, 1891); Trio élégiaque, No.1 in G minor, pf., vn., vc. (1892); 2 Pieces, vc., pf., Op.2 (1892); 2 Pieces, vn., pf., Op.3 (1893); Trio élégiaque, No.2 in D minor, Op.9 (1893); 2 movts., str. qt. (?1896); vc. sonata in G minor, Op.19 (1901).

PIANO: 3 Nocturnes (1887–8); 4 Pieces (?1888); Prelude in F (1891); 5 Morceaux de Fantaisie, Op.3 (No.2 is Prelude in C♯ minor, also arr. for 2 pf., 1938) (1892); 7 Morceaux de Salon, Op.10 (1893–4); 6 Moments Musicaux, Op.16 (1896); Variations on a theme of Chopin, Op.22 (1902–3); 10 Preludes, Op.23 (No.1 in F♯ minor, No.2 in B♭ major, No.3 in D minor, No.4 in D major, No.5 in G minor, No.6 in E♭ major, No.7 in C minor, No.8 in A♭ major, No.9 in E♭ minor, No.10 in G♭ major) (1903, except No.5 in 1901); 13 Preludes, Op.32 (No.1 in C, No.2 in B♭ minor, No.3 in E major, No.4 in E minor, No.5 in G major, No.6 in F minor, No.7 in

F major, No.8 in A minor, No.9 in A major, No.10 in B minor, No.11 in B major, No.12 in G♯ minor, No.13 in D♭ major) (1910); Études tableaux, Op.33 (No.1 in F minor, No.2 in C, No.3 in E♭ minor, No.4 in E♭ major, No.5 in G minor, No.6 in C♯ minor (1911) (3 études of Op.33 were withdrawn by composer before publication: orig. No.4 in A minor (pubd. as Op.39, No.6), orig. No.3 in C minor and orig. No.5 in D minor (both pubd. 1948)); Études tableaux, Op.39 (No.1 in C minor, No.2 in A minor, No.3 in F♯ minor, No.4 in B minor, No.5 in E♭ minor, No.6 in A minor, No.7 in C minor, No.8 in D minor, No.9 in D major (1916–17, except No.6, comp. 1911, rev. 1916); Oriental Sketch (1917); Variations on a Theme of Corelli (La folia) (1931); sonatas: No.1 in D minor (1907), No.2 in B♭ minor (1913, rev. 1931).

PIANO DUET: Romance in G (?1893); 6 Duets, Op.11 (1894).

2 PIANOS: Russian Rhapsody in E minor (1891); Fantaisie-tableaux (Suite No.1), Op.5 (1893), Suite No.2, Op.17 (1900–1).

SONGS: 6 Songs, Op.4 (1890–3); 6 Songs, Op.8 (1893); 12 Songs, Op.14 (1894–6); 12 Songs, Op.21 (1902; No.1 1900); 15 Songs, Op.26 (1906) (No.7 is *To the Children, K detyam); Letter to K. S. Stanislavsky (1908); 14 Songs, Op.34 (1912; No.7 1910; No.14 is *Vocalise, rev. 1915); 6 Songs, Op.38 (1916).

Also several transcr., incl. Scherzo from Mendelssohn's Midsummer Night's Dream and 3 movts. of J. S. Bach's Partita No.3 for solo vn. (all 1933).

racket (Ger. *Rackett*). Renaissance woodwind instr., forerunner of bn., developed in Ger. in late 16th cent., when it was called *Raggett*. Had narrow cylindrical bore of 9 parallel channels drilled in wooden or ivory cylinder and connected alternately top and bottom. Existed in 4 types: ten., bass, quint bass, great bass. Ten. was 4½″ high, great bass just over 12″. During latter part of 17th cent., bass racket was redesigned, with wider expanding conical bore, coiled crook inserted at side, central bulbous bell, and new disposition of finger-holes. This instr., in effect a narrow-bore bn., is known as the baroque racket. Modern versions of both Renaissance and Baroque racket available, former with a plastic reed.

Radamisto. Opera in 3 acts by Handel to anon. lib. adapted from D. Lalli's L'amour tirannico, o Zenobia (Venice, 1710). Comp. 1720, rev. 1720, 1721, 1728. F.p. London 1720; f. modern ps. Göttingen 1927, London 1960. F. Amer. p. Washington DC 1980.

raddoppiare (It.). To double. Hence *raddoppiamento*, doubling.

Radetzky March. March comp. 1848 by Johann Strauss the elder. Radetzky was Austrian field-marshal.

radical bass. Same as fundamental bass; roots of various chords.

radical cadence. Any cadence of which the chords are in root position, i.e. the roots of the chords in the bass.

Raff, (Joseph) **Joachim** (*b* Lachen, Switz., 1822; *d* Frankfurt, 1882). Ger. composer. School-teacher who taught himself pf., vn., and comp. Orchestrated some of Liszt's works at Weimar. Espoused cause of 'music of the future'. Pf. teacher, Wiesbaden, from 1856. Dir., Hoch Cons., Frankfurt, 1877–82. Taught Amer. composer *MacDowell. Prolific and attractive composer whose mus. has enjoyed a modest revival after being almost forgotten except for celebrated *Cavatina* for vn. and pf. Comps. incl. 6 operas; oratorio; 11 syms., incl. No.3 *Im Walde* (In the Forest), No.5 *Lenore*, No.7 *In den Alpen* (In the Alps), No.9 *Im Sommer* (In Summer); pf. conc.; 2 vn. concs.; 2 vc. concs.; 9 str. qts.; 5 vn. sonatas; pf. quintet; octet; sectet; vc. sonata; songs, transcrs., etc.

rāga. Indian melodic type, first mentioned in 5th cent. AD. Various rāga systems have developed over the centuries. A rāga comprises an unchangeable series of notes presented as an ascending and descending scale, some notes being used only in the ascending part, others only in the descending. Rāgas are assoc. with moods, e.g. loneliness, bravery, eroticism, and with particular times of day or year, or with certain ceremonial occasions.

ragtime. Early type of jazz, particularly for solo pf., and comp. rather than improvised. Famous exponent and composer of it was Scott *Joplin. Popular from *c*.1895–1920, when other forms of jazz took over, but it had a revival in 1970s, when Joplin's mus. was used for the film *The Sting*. Stravinsky comp. *Ragtime* for 11 instr. (1918) and *Piano-Rag Music* (1919). A *Rag* is a ragtime comp. To *rag* is to play in ragtime.

Railton, (Dame) **Ruth** (*b* Folkestone, 1915; *d* Dublin, 2001). Eng. pianist and conductor. Début Liverpool 1936. Founder and mus. dir. Nat. Youth Orch. of Great Britain and Nat. Junior Mus. Sch. 1947–65. OBE 1954, DBE 1966.

railway music. Many comps. have reflected interest in railways and railway engines. Perhaps the earliest is Berlioz's *Le chant des chemins de fer*, 1846, which exists in 2 versions: as No.3 of his 6 *Feuillets d'album*, Op.19, for v. and pf., and for v. and orch. The cantata version was written for the opening of the Fr. Northern Railway and was perf. at Lille on 14 June 1846. The text was by Jules Janin. Other works worthy of note are J. Strauss II's *Excursion Train Polka*, Honegger's *Pacific 231*, A. Butterworth's *Trains in the Distance*, Lumbye's *Copenhagen Steam Railway Galop*, Villa-Lobos's *Little Train of the Caipira*, and Krenek's *The Santa Fe Timetable*. Britten's song *Midnight on the Great Western*, from *Winter Words*, Op.52, is also memorable. The first of Webern's *6 Orchestral Pieces*, Op.6, describes a rail journey to visit the graves of his parents. The first piece of *musique concrète* by Schaeffer in 1948 was an assemblage of railway noises called *Étude aux chemins de fer*. There are also Vivian Ellis's light orch. piece *Coronation Scot*, commemorating the L.M.S. 1937 'crack' engine, and the delightful Amer. song *Chattanooga*

Choo-Choo by Gordon and Warren. Possibly the film mus. by Britten for *Night Mail* should also count as railway mus.

Raimondi, Ruggero (*b* Bologna, 1941). It. bass. Opera début Spoleto 1964 (Colline in *La bohème*). Débuts: Glyndebourne 1969; NY Met 1970; Salzburg 1970; CG 1972; member of La Scala Co. from 1970.

'Raindrop' Prelude. Nickname for Chopin's Prelude in D♭, Op.28, No.15 (1839), on unauthenticated supposition that the repeated note A♭ represents raindrops.

Rainier, Priaulx (*b* Howick, Natal, 1903; *d* Besse-en-Chandesse, 1986). S. African composer and violinist. Entered S. African College of Mus. as vn. student 1913. She won vn. scholarship to RAM 1920 and settled in London. Worked as violinist and only concentrated on comp. after grant in 1935. Studied in Paris with Boulanger to 1939. Prof. of comp., RAM, 1943–61. Prin. works:

ORCH.: *Sinfonia da Camera*, str. (1947); *Ballet Suite* (1950); *Phala-Phala*, dance conc. (1960–1); vc. conc. (1964); *Aequora Lunae* (1966–7); *Trios and Triads*, 10 trios, perc. (1969–73); *Ploërmel*, winds, perc. (1973); vn. conc. (*Due canti e finale*) (1977); *Concertante*, ob., cl., orch (1981).

VOCAL: *3 Greek Epigrams*, sop., pf. (1942); *Cycle for Declamation* (Donne), solo sop., ten., or bar. (1954); *Requiem*, ten., unacc. ch. (1955); *Dance of the Rain*, ten., gui. (1961); *The Bee Oracles* (E. Sitwell), ten. or bar., fl., ob., vn., vc., hpd. (1969); *Ubunzima*, ten. or sop., gui. (1973); *Vision and Prayer*, ten., pf. (1973); *Prayers from the Ark*, ten., hp. (1974–5).

CHAMBER MUSIC: str. qt. (1939); *Suite*, cl., pf. (1943); va. sonata (1945); 6 *Pieces*, fl., ob., cl., hn., bn. (1954); *Pastoral Triptych*, ob. solo (1960); *Quanta*, ob., str. trio (1961–2); str. trio (1965–6); *Grand Duo*, vc., pf. (1980–2).

KEYBOARD: *Barbaric Dance Suite*, pf. (1949); *Quinque*, hpd. (1971).

ORGAN: *Gloriana* (1972); *Primordial Canticles* (1974).

Raisa, Rosa [Burchstein, Rosa] (*b* Białystok, Poland, 1893; *d* Pacific Palisades, Calif., 1963). Polish-born soprano. Child singer. Fled from pogrom in Poland to It. Taught by Eva Tetrazzini and by Barbara Marchisio at Naples Cons. Opera début Parma 1913 (Leonora in *Oberto*), then at La Scala 1916 (Aida). Sang Aida at Chicago Opera 1913, becoming member of co. 1917–32, 1933–6. CG début 1914 (Aida). Created role of Asteria in Boito's *Nerone*, Milan, 1924, and was chosen by Puccini to be first Turandot (La Scala 1926). Much admired as Marschallin (*Der Rosenkavalier*), Norma, and Tosca. Retired 1938 and taught in Chicago, where she opened a singing-sch. with her husband, the bar. Giacomo Rimini (1888–1952).

Rajah's Diamond, The. Opera for TV by *Hoddinott to lib. by Myfanwy Piper based on story in R. L. Stevenson's *New Arabian Nights* (1882). Comp. 1978–9. F.p. BBC TV 1979.

Rakastava (The Lover). Comp. by *Sibelius, Op.14, orig. 3 songs for unacc. male ch. with text from Book 1 of *Kanteletar*. 1. *Where is my Beloved?* 2. *My Beloved's Path*. 3. *Good Evening, my Little Bird*. Comp. 1893, f.p. Helsinki 1894. Version for male ch. and str. 1894 (unpubd.). Version for unacc. mixed ch., 1898. Rewritten version for str. orch., triangle, and timp., 1911, in 3 movts.: 1. *The Lover*. 2. *The Path of the Beloved*. 3. *Goodnight—Farewell*.

Rake's Progress, The. (1) Opera in 3 acts and epilogue by *Stravinsky to lib. by W. H. Auden and Chester Kallman based on Hogarth's 8 engravings (1732–3). Comp. 1947–51. Prod. Venice 1951, NY Met and Edinburgh 1953 (by Glyndebourne co.), London (New Opera Co.) 1957.

(2) Ballet in 6 scenes with mus. by Gavin Gordon, choreog. N. de Valois, prod. London 1935.

Rakhmaninov, Sergey. See *Rachmaninov, Sergei*.

Rákóczy March. Hung. march-tune dating from *c*.1809 by unknown composer (possibly János Bihari, gipsy violinist) and named in honour of Prince Francis Rákóczy, leader of the Hung. revolt against Austria, 1703–11. Liszt played it at recitals in Hungary, where its patriotic assocs. brought it into high popularity. Berlioz arr. it as *Marche hongroise*, 1846, and added it to his *Scenes from Faust* when he remodelled it as *La Damnation de Faust*. Also occurs in Johann Strauss's *Zigeunerbaron*.

Ralf, Torsten (Ivar) (*b* Malmö, 1901; *d* Stockholm, 1954). Swed. tenor. Studied Stockholm and Berlin. Opera début Stettin 1930 (Cavaradossi in *Tosca*). Sang opera in Frankfurt 1933–5, Dresden 1935–44. Created Apollo in *Daphne*, 1938. Sang at CG 1935–9 (début as Lohengrin) and 1948, NY Met 1945–8 (début as Lohengrin). Notable Parsifal, Walther (*Die Meistersinger*), and Radames (*Aida*).

Rallentando (It.). Slowing down, gradually. Abbreviated to *rall*. in scores. Virtually the same as *ritardando*.

RAM. *Royal Academy of Music, London.

Rameau, Jean-Philippe (*b* Dijon, 1683; *d* Paris, 1764). Fr. composer, harpsichordist, and organist. Self-taught in harmony and counterpoint. Visited It. 1701. Org., Clermont-Ferrand 1702–5, Paris 1705–8, Dijon 1709–14, Lyons 1714–15, and then Clermont-Ferrand again 1715–22, where he worked on his important *Traité de l'harmonie*, pubd. in Paris 1722, in which he set out the then novel doctrines of inversions of chords and principles of chord-progression. This was followed by other textbooks on harmony between 1726 and 1752, and by his dissertation on methods of acc. for hpd. and org. (1732). Settled in Paris 1722, teaching the hpd. and writing many works for the instr. In 1730 he came under the patronage of Le Riche de la Pouplinière. In 1733, at the age of 50, his first opera, *Hippolyte et Aricie*, met with no success, but he persevered and wrote over 20 operas and opera-ballets, incl. *Castor et Pollux* and *Les Indes galantes*. These works, though controversial because of their novel use of colourful orchestration, bold harmonies, and use of recit., est. Rameau as *Lully's successor in the field of Fr. opera. His champions opposed those of *Pergolesi in the *Querelle des *Bouffons*. In 1745 he was appointed chamber mus. composer to the King. Prin. works:

OPERAS AND OPERA-BALLETS: († = opera-ballet):
Hippolyte et Aricie (1733, rev. 1742); *Les *Indes galantes* (1735–6); *Castor et Pollux* (1737, rev. 1754); †*Les Fêtes d'Hébé* (1739); *Dardanus* (1739, rev. 1744 and 1760); †*Les Fêtes de Polymnie* (1745); *Le Temple de la gloire* (1745, rev. 1746); †*Platée* (1745, rev. 1749); †*La Princesse de Navarre* (1745, rev. 1763); †*Les Fêtes de l'Hymen et de l'Amour* (1747); †*Zaïs* (1748); †*Les Surprises de l'amour* (1748, rev. 1757); †*Pygmalion* (1748); *Nais* (1749); *Zoroastre* (1749, rev. 1756); *Acante et Céphise* (1751); †*La guirlande* (1751); *Daphne et Eglé* (1753); *Les Sybarites* (1753); *Lysis et Delia* (1754); *La Naissance d'Osiris* (1754); *Zéphire* (1757); *Nélée et Mithis* (1757); *Le Retour d'Astrée* (1757); †*Anacréon* (1757); *Les Paladins* (1760); *Les *Boréades (Abaris)* (1763).

CANTATAS & SACRED WORKS: *Thétis* (1718); *Aquilon et Orinthié* (1719); *Les Amants trahis* (1721); *Orphée* (1721); *L'Impatience* (1715–22); *Le Berger fidèle* (1728); *Pour la fête de St-Louis* (1740); *Deus Noster Refugium* (before 1716); *In Convertendo* (1718); *Quam dilecta* (*c*.1720).

CHAMBER MUSIC: *5 Pièces de clavecin en concert* for hpd., va. da gamba, baroque vn. (1741); *5 Concerts* for hpd., vn., fl. (1741).

HARPSICHORD: (pubd. in 3 vols. of suites in Rameau's lifetime): 1. *Prelude*, 2. *Allemande 1*, 3. *Allemande 2*, 4. *Courante*, 5. *Gigue*, 6. *Sarabande 1*, 7. *Sarabande 2*, 8. *La Vénétienne*, 9. *Gavotte*, 10. *Menuet*, 11. *Menuet en rondeau*, 12. *Allemande*, 13. *Courante*, 14. *Gigue en rondeau*, 15. *2nd Gigue en rondeau*, 16. *Le Rappel des oiseaux*, 17. *Rigaudon 1*, 18. *Rigaudon 2*, 19. *Double*, 20. *Musette en rondeau*, 21. *Tambourin*, 22. *La Villageoise* (rondeau), 23. *Les Tendres Plaintes* (rondeau), 24. *Les Niais de Sologne*, 25. *Doubles 1 des Niais*, 26. *Doubles 2 des Niais*, 27. *Les Soupirs*, 28. *La Joyeuse*, 29. *L'Ollette* (rondeau), 30. *L'Entretien des Muses*, 31. *Les Tourbillons* (rondeau), 32. *Les Cyclopes* (rondeau), 33. *Le Lardon* (menuet), 34. *La Boiteuse*, 35. *Allemande*, 36. *Courante*, 37. *Sarabande*, 38. *Les Trois Mains*, 39. *Fanfarinette*, 40. *La Triomphante*, 41. *Gavotte* (with 6 doubles), 42. *Les Tricotets* (rondeau), 43. *L'Indifférente*, 44. *Menuet 1*, 45. *Menuet 2*, 46. *La Poule*, 47. *Les Triolets*, 48. *Les Sauvages*, 49. *L'Enharmonique*, 50. *L'Egyptienne*, 51. *La Dauphine*, 52. *La Laivri* (rondeau), 53. *L'Agaçante*, 54. *La Timide* (rondeau), 55. *La Timide* (rondeau), 56. *L'Indiscrète* (rondeau).

Ramey, Samuel (Edward) (*b* Colby, Kan., 1942). Amer. bass-baritone. Sang with Grass Roots Opera Co., Raleigh, N.C. Début NY City Opera 1973 (Zuniga in *Carmen*), becoming prin. bass. Débuts: Glyndebourne 1976; Chicago and S. Francisco 1979; La Scala and Vienna 1981; CG 1982; NY Met 1984; Salzburg Fest. 1987. Series of Rossini roles at Pesaro 1981–9. Also many Mozart principal roles.

Ramifications. Work for str. orch. or 12 solo str. by *Ligeti, comp. 1968–9, f.p. (str. orch. version) Berlin, April 1969, cond. Gielen; (solo str. version) Saarbrücken, Oct. 1969, cond. Janigro.

Rampal, Jean-Pierre (Louis) (b Marseilles, 1922; d Paris, 2000). Fr. flautist. Solo flautist Vichy Opera 1946–50 and at Paris Opéra 1956–62 and in Orchestre de l'Association des Instruments à Vent. Founded French Wind Quintet 1945 and Paris Baroque Ens. 1953. Toured worldwide after 1945 as soloist in recitals and with orch. Salzburg Fest. début 1957. Prof. of fl. Paris Cons. 1969–82. Gave f.ps. of several contemp. concs. Ed. of much early fl. mus. Author of *Ancient Music for the Flute* (1958), autobiography 1989.

Ranalow, Frederick (Baring) (b Dublin, 1873; d London, 1953). Irish baritone. Successful oratorio singer and prominent member of Beecham Opera Co. as Figaro, etc. Sang part of Macheath in revival of *The Beggar's Opera*, 1920, over 1,600 times.

Ranczak, Hildegard (b Witkowitz in Mähren (now Vitkoviče), 1895; d Vienna, 1987). Bohemian soprano. Début Düsseldorf 1919 (Pamina in *Die Zauberflöte*). Sang opera in Cologne 1923–5 and Stuttgart 1926–8, then joined Bavarian State Opera in Munich, where she sang several Strauss roles incl. Salome, and created Clairon in *Capriccio* 1942. Vienna début 1931; CG 1937. Last role was Carmen in Munich 1950.

Randle, Thomas (Tom) (b Los Angeles, 1958). Amer. tenor. Studied cond. and comp. before having v. training. Sang in concerts in USA and Eur. with leading orchs., specializing in Bach, Handel, and Mozart. Brit. début London (ENO) 1988 (Tamino in *Die Zauberflöte*). Glyndebourne début 1991. Sang Essex in *Gloriana*, Leeds (Opera North) 1993 (and with them at CG 1994). Created Judas in Birtwistle's *The Last Supper* (Berlin, 2000).

Randová, Eva (b Kolin, 1936). Cz. mezzo-soprano. Began career as teacher of mathematics and sport. Début Ostrava 1962 (Eboli in *Don Carlos*). Prague Nat. Opera from 1969 and Stuttgart Opera from 1971. Bayreuth début 1973; Salzburg Fest. 1975; CG 1977; NY Met 1981.

Rands, Bernard (b Sheffield, 1935). Eng.-born composer (Amer. cit. 1983). Lived and studied in It., then spent 2 years in Amer. at Princeton and Univ. of Illinois, Urbana. Member of mus. faculty York Univ. 1968–74. Prof. of mus., Univ. of Calif., San Diego, from 1976. Founder-member of mus.-th. ens., C.L.A.P. Worked in EMS in various cities. His mus., *avant-garde* in style, and sometimes aleatory, is notable for its richly colourful sonorities. Won Pulitzer Prize 1984 with *Canti del Sole* for ten. and orch. Works incl. mus. theatre, orch. works, and vocal mus. Has also written educational mus.

rank. Each separate set of org. pipes, particularly mixture stops.

Ránki, Dezsö (b Budapest, 1951). Hung. pianist. 1st prize Zwickau int. comp. 1969. Liszt Prize 1973. Salzburg Fest. 1984.

Ránki, György (b Budapest, 1907; d Budapest, 1992). Hung. composer. Dir. of mus. Hungarian Radio 1947–8. Awarded Kossuth Prize 1954. Comps. incl. 6 operas, best-known being *King Pomádé's New Clothes*, orig. written for radio in 1951; 5 ballets; 2 syms.; th. and film music.

Rankl, Karl (b Gaaden, 1898; d St Gilgen, 1968). Austrian-born conductor and composer. Cond. Vienna Volksoper 1922–5. Cond. opera at Reichenberg and Königsberg, 1925–8, then ch.-master to Klemperer at Kroll Opera, Berlin, 1928–31. Graz Opera 1932–7, Prague 1937–9. Settled in Eng. 1939. Mus. dir. new CG Opera Co. 1946–51. Prin. cond. Scottish Nat. Orch. 1952–7. Mus. dir. Elizabethan Opera Trust, Sydney, NSW, 1958–60. Wrote 8 syms., oratorio, str. qt., and opera *Deirdre of the Sorrows*.

rant. Old Eng. 17th-cent. dance of the jig variety. It originated in Scotland and N. England. Four examples occur in Playford's *The Dancing Master* (1657 and 1665 revisions).

Ranz des vaches (Kuhreigen, Kuhreihen). Cow-procession. A type of Swiss Alpine melody, sung or played on the *Alphorn to call the cows scattered over the mountain-side. Every district has its own version, some of which (with modifications) have been introduced into comps., e.g. Rossini's *William Tell* ov., Beethoven's *Pastoral* sym., Berlioz's *Symphonie fantastique*, Schumann's *Manfred*, Strauss's *Don Quixote* and *Ein Heldenleben*. Walton's *Façade* contains a parody of a *Ranz des vaches*.

Rape of Lucretia, The. Opera in 2 acts by Britten to lib. by Ronald Duncan after André Obey's *Le viol de Lucrèce*. Comp. 1946, rev. 1947. F.p. Glyndebourne, 1946; London 1946; Chicago 1947; Salzburg 1950. Britten's first chamber opera, comp. for EOG.

rappresentazione (It.). Representation, staged action. Type of staged oratorio, precursor of opera.

Rappresentazione di anima e di corpo, La (The Representation of the soul and the body). Staged oratorio by *Cavalieri to text by Manni. Sometimes described as first opera. Prod. Rome 1600.

Rapsodie espagnole (Spanish Rhapsody). (1) Orch. work in 4 sections by *Ravel, 1907: *Prélude, Malagueña, Habanera, Feria*. The *Habanera* was orig. written for 2 pf., 1895–7 as No.1 of the *Sites auriculaires*.
(2) Work for pf. by Liszt, comp. 1863, arr. for pf. and orch. by Busoni.

raptak (rektah). A whirlwind type of dance which appears in Delibes's opera *Lakmé*.

rasch; rascher (Ger.). Quick; quicker.

Rasiermesserquartett (Razor Quartet). Nickname of Haydn's str. qt. in F minor, Op.55, No.2 (Hob. III:61). The story is that Haydn exclaimed in 1787 when shaving 'I'd give my best quartet for a new razor', and was taken at his word by a visitor, the London mus.-publisher Bland. This qt. was Haydn's side of the bargain.

Rasoumovsky [Razumovsky], **Count** (later Prince) **Andrey** (Kyrilovich) (*b* St Petersburg, 1752; *d* Vienna, 1836). Russ. mus. patron. Admiral in Russ. navy, then ambassador in several capitals, culminating in Vienna 1792–1812. Friend of Beethoven, whose three Op.59 qts. are ded. to him. From 1808 played 2nd vn. in his own qt., trying out Beethoven's chamber mus. for composer.

Rasoumovsky [Razumovsky] **Quartets**. Beethoven's str. qts. Nos. 7, 8, and 9, Op.59, Nos. 1, 2, and 3, in F major, E minor, and C major, comp. 1806 and so called because of ded. to Count *Rasoumovsky, Russ. ambassador in Vienna, who was a keen qt. player. Each qt. contains a Russ. theme; in two cases these are folk-tunes.

rataplan. Onomatopoeic word for sound of a drum. Used as name for solos and ens. in operas by Donizetti, Meyerbeer, and Verdi (*La forza del destino*).

ratchet (Ger. *Ratsche*). Rattle. Percussion instr. of indefinite pitch. A cogwheel is either revolved by means of a handle against one or several tongues of wood or metal, or twirled so that the tongues strike the cogs. Is used by Strauss in *Till Eulenspiegel*, Ravel in his orch. of Mussorgsky's *Pictures at an Exhibition*, and Walton in his *Façade* ballet suite No.1. But of course any instr. producing a rattling noise, such as pebbles shaken in a dried gourd, is a rattle.

Ratsche (Ger.). See *ratchet*.

rattle. See *ratchet*.

Rattle, (Sir) **Simon** (*b* Liverpool, 1955). Eng. conductor. Played perc. in Merseyside Youth Orch. at age of 8 and later in RLPO. Founded and cond. Liverpool Sinfonia 1970–2. First prize John Player int. cond. award 1974, leading to 2-year contract with Bournemouth SO and Sinfonietta. RFH début 1975. Professional opera début 1975, GTO (*The Rake's Progress*). Glyndebourne début 1977. Worked with London Sinfonietta and EMT, 1976. Amer. début 1979, Los Angeles PO. Prin. guest cond. Los Angeles PO from 1981. Prin. cond. CBSO 1980–98. Cond. Berlin PO from 2002. Art. dir. Salzburg Easter Fest. from 2003. Cond. f. Eng. public p. of Janáček's *Osud*, London 1983 (concert). Débuts: ENO 1985; Amer. opera (Los Angeles) 1988; CG 1990; Salzburg Fest. 1993. CBE 1987. Knighted 1994.

Rautavaara, Einojuhani (*b* Helsinki, 1928). Finnish composer. Dir., Käpylä Mus. Sch., Helsinki, 1965–6, lect. in mus. Sibelius Acad. from 1966 (prof. of comp. 1976–90). Comps. incl. 10 operas,

incl. *The Mine* (1957–8, 1960/3), *Apollo contra Marsyas* (1970), *Thomas* (1982–5), *The House of the Sun* (1989–90), *Aleksis Kivi* (1995–6), *Rasputin* (2001–2); *The Temptations*, ballet (1969); 8 syms. (1956–99); 4 pf. concs. (No.0, 1955, No.1, 1969, No.2, 1988–9, No.3, 1998); vc. conc. (1968); fl. conc. (1975); vn. conc. (1977); db. conc. (*Angel at Dusk*) (1980); *Isle of Bliss*, str. (1995); *Adagio celeste*, orch. (2000); *Manhattan Trilogy*, orch. (2002–5); *Book of Visions*, orch. (2004); 4 str. qts. (1952, 1958, 1965, 1975); *Autumn Garden*, chamber orch. (1999); *Requiem in our Time* (1953); *Daughter of the Sea*, sop., ch., orch. (1970); *Nirvana Dharma*, sop., ch., fl. (1979); *4 Songs to Poems of Aleksis Kivi*, unacc. male ch. (1998–2005); *The Trip*, bar./mez., pf. (1977); *In my Beloved's Garden*, song-cycle, v., pf. (1983–7); *Die Liebenden*, song-cycle, v., str. qt. (1958–9, arr. 2001); *Serenades of the Unicorn*, gui. (1977); *Wedding March*, org. (1984); *Passionale*, pf. (2002).

Rautawaara, Aulikki (*b* Vaasa, 1906; *d* Helsinki, 1990). Finnish soprano. Début Helsinki 1932. Sang Countess in *Le nozze di Figaro* in inaugural Glyndebourne season, 1934, returning in this role 1935–8 and as Pamina in *Die Zauberflöte* 1935–8. Salzburg Fest. 1937.

Rauzzini, Venanzio (*b* Camerino, 1746; *d* Bath, 1810). It. composer, male soprano, and teacher. Début Rome 1765. Sang in f.p. of Mozart's *Lucio Silla*, Milan 1772. Mozart wrote *Exsultate, jubilate* for him. Settled in Eng. 1774. Wrote 5 operas for London and 5 for Munich, also chamber mus. and songs. Became singing teacher in London and Bath, pupils incl. Braham, Storace, Kelly, and Elizabeth Billington. Haydn was his guest in 1794.

Ravel, (Joseph) **Maurice** (*b* Ciboure, 1875; *d* Paris, 1937). Fr. composer and pianist. Born in Basque region but spent childhood in Paris. Entered Paris Cons. 1889, studying pf. with Bériot and comp. with Fauré, and remaining for 16 years. By 1895 he had already developed a personal style of comp., but his unconventional harmonies offended academic ears in spite of the classical basis of his work. He competed for the *Prix de Rome* in 1901, 1902, 1903, and 1905. At the last attempt he was eliminated in the preliminary test. The ensuing outcry led to the resignation of Dubois as dir. of the Cons. He had already written several works now acknowledged as masterpieces, incl. the str. qt., *Shéhérazade*, and the *Miroirs* for pf. Though a brilliant orchestrator, several of his works were first written for pf. His outstanding achievement in orch. writing is the ballet *Daphnis et Chloé*, comp. for *Diaghilev and f.p. in 1912. In 1911 his comic 1-act opera *L'Heure espagnole* had not been a success, but was later welcomed for the brilliant piece it is. After service in the 1914–18 war, Ravel captured the savage flavour of the end of an era in his *La Valse*. Fragile health in the last 17 years of his life reduced the number of his comps. but not the quality. To the late years belong his fascinating opera, to a lib. by Colette, *L'Enfant et les sortilèges*, 2 pf. concs., his popular *Boléro* (orginally a ballet score), chamber works, and the *Don Quixote* songs. He occasionally cond. his own works, but held no official posts and had very few pupils, though one of them (for 3 months) was *Vaughan Williams.

Ravel is conveniently classified with Debussy, but their dissimilarities are more striking and significant. He had more respect for classical forms than Debussy and was nearer to the ethos of Saint-Saëns than to that of Massenet. Satie, Chabrier, Strauss, Mussorgsky, the orientalism learned from the 1889 int. Exposition, and jazz were influences on him. Dance rhythms frequently occur in his works. His harmonies, often 'impressionist' in technique, extended the range of tonality by the exploitation of unusual chords and by the use of bitonality. His melodies sometimes have a modal tendency. Repetition, sequences, and variation are preferred to regular development. The charge that he was a miniaturist in his choice of forms can be sustained, but there is nothing small about the invention. That artificiality which led Stravinsky to call him 'a Swiss clock-maker' can also be perceived, but perhaps this is part of the price he paid for the exceptional clarity of his thought and of his scoring. He was one of the great innovators in writing for the pf. Prin. works:

OPERAS: *L'*Heure espagnole* (The Spanish Hour) (1907–9); *L'*Enfant et les sortilèges* (The Child and the Spells) (1920–5).

BALLETS: *Daphnis et Chloé* (1909–12); *Fanfare* for *L'*Éventail de Jeanne* (1927); *Boléro* (1928).

ORCH.: *Shéhérazade*, ov. (1898); *Une barque sur l'océan* (1906, orch. of movt. from *Miroirs*, pf.); *Rapsodie espagnole* (1907); *Pavane pour une infante défunte* (1910, arr. from pf. version); *Ma mère l'Oye* (1911, orch. version of 4-hands pf. work); *Daphnis et Chloé*, Suite No.1 (1911), Suite No.2 (1913); *Valses nobles et sentimentales* (1912, orch. version of pf. work); *Alborada del gracioso* (1918, orch. version of No.4 of *Miroirs* for pf.); *Le *Tombeau de Couperin* (1919, orch. version of pf. work); *La *Valse* (1906–14, 1919–20); *Menuet antique* (1929, orch. version of pf. piece); pf. conc. for left hand (1929–30); pf. conc. in G (1929–31).

CHAMBER MUSIC: str. qt. in F (1902–3); *Introduction and Allegro*, hp., str. qt., fl., cl. (1905); *Pièce en forme d'Habanera*, vn., pf. (version of *Vocalise*, 1907); pf. trio (1914); *Le Tombeau de Claude Debussy*, vn., vc. (1920); sonata, vn., vc. (1920–2); *Berceuse sur le nom de Gabriel Fauré*, vn., pf. (1922); vn. sonata (1923–7); *Tzigane*, vn., pf. (1924, version for vn. and orch. 1924); *Rêves*, v., pf. (1927).

VOICE & ORCH.: *Manteau de fleurs* (1903); *Shéhérazade* (1903); *5 Mélodies populaires grecques* (5 Popular Greek Melodies) (1904–6); *Le Noël des Jouets* (1905, 2nd version 1913); *3 Poèmes de Stéphane Mallarmé*, v., chamber ens. (1913); *2 Mélodies hébraïques* (1919); *Ronsard à son âme* (1924); *Chansons madécasses*, v., fl., vc., pf. (1926); *Don Quichotte à Dulcinée* (1932–3).

VOICE & PIANO: *Un Grand Sommeil noir* (1895); *Sainte* (1896); *2 Épigrammes* (1898); *Manteau de fleurs* (1903); *5 Mélodies populaires grecques* (1904–6); *Le Noël des jouets* (1905); *Les Grands Vents venus d'outre-mer* (1906); *Histoires naturelles* (1906, orch. version by M. Rosenthal); *Sur l'herbe* (1907); *Vocalise en forme d'Habanera* (1907; also version for vn. and pf.); *Tripatos* (1909); *7 Chants populaires* (1910–17; No.4, *Chanson hébraique*, orch. Delage); *2 Mélodies hébraiques* (1914); *3 Chansons* (1916); *Ronsard à son âme* (1924); *Rêves* (1927); *Don Quichotte à Dulcinée* (1932–3).

UNACC VOICES: *3 Chansons* (1915; also v. and pf.).

PIANO: *Menuet antique* (1895); *Pavane pour une infante défunte* (1899); *Jeux d'eau* (1901); *Sonatine* (1905); *Miroirs* (1905); *Gaspard de la Nuit* (1908); *Ma mère l'Oye* (4 hands) (1908–10); *Menuet sur le nom d'Haydn* (1909); *Valses nobles et sentimentales* (1911); *À la manière de (1) Borodin (2) Chabrier* (1913); *Le *Tombeau de Couperin* (1914–17).

2 PIANOS: *Sites auriculaires* (1895–7, unpubd. but No.1, *Habanera*, was incorporated in *Rapsodie espagnole* 1907); *Frontispiece* (1918). (*Ma mère l'Oye* is for 1 pf., 4 hands.)

TRANSCRIPTION, ETC. OF OTHER COMPOSERS: Chabrier: *Menuet pompeux*, orch. (1920); Debussy: *Nocturnes*, 2 pf. (1909), *Prélude à L'après-midi d'un faune*, 2 pf. (1910), *Sarabande*, orch. (1920), *Danse*, orch. (1923); Delius: vocal score of opera *Margot-la-Rouge* (1902); Mussorgsky: *Khovanshchina*, completed and orch. by Ravel and Stravinsky (mostly lost), *Tableaux d'une Exposition* (*Pictures at an Exhibition*), orch. 1922; Satie: *Le Prélude du fils des étoiles*, orch. 1913; Schumann: *Carnaval*, orch. 1914 (unpubd.).

Ravenscroft, Thomas (*b* c.1582; *d* c.1633). Eng. composer and publisher. Ed. of important psalter, *The Whole Booke of Psalmes* (1621), in which he comp. 55 of the 105 settings. Pubd. *Pammelia* (*Musick's Miscellanie*), 1609 (1st coll. of 100 rounds, catches, and canons), and its successor *Deuteromelia*, 1609, coll. of 31 songs and rounds, incl. 'Three blind mice'. Also comp. anthems.

Ravinia. Park in Highland Park, a suburb of Chicago, Ill. Venue for summer season of opera by Ravinia Opera Co., 1911–31. Singers drawn from NY Met and Chicago Opera. Summer fest. organized there since 1936, comprising concerts, recitals, operas in concert form, popular mus., etc. with Chicago SO as mainstay.

ravvivando; ravvivato (It., reviving, brightening up, enlivening). Quickening; quickened.

Rawnsley, John (*b* Colne, 1950). Eng. baritone. Opera début GTO 1975 (Kilian in *Der Freischütz*). Glyndebourne début 1977; WNO 1977; CG 1979; Opera North 1979; ENO 1982; La Scala 1987. Sang Rigoletto in Jonathan Miller's ENO prod. updated to NY in 1950s.

Rawsthorne, Alan (*b* Haslingden, 1905; *d* Cambridge, 1971). Eng. composer and pianist. Taught at Dartington Hall 1932–4, settled in London 1935, concentrating on comp. His mus., overshadowed by that of his contemporary fellow Lancastrian Walton, has style, structural strength, and impeccable craftsmanship. CBE 1961. Prin. works:

BALLET: *Madame Chrysanthème (1955).

ORCH.: syms.: No.1 (1950), No.2 (Pastoral) (1959), No.3 (1964); Symphonic Studies (1939); *Street Corner Overture (1944); *Cortèges, fantasy ov. (1945); Concerto for Strings (1949); Concertante Pastorale (1951); Hallé, ov. (1958); Improvisations on a Theme of Constant Lambert (1961); Concerto for 10 Instruments (1961); Divertimento (1962); Elegiac Rhapsody, str. (1963); Theme, Variations, and Finale (1967); Triptych (1969).

CONCERTOS: pf.: No.1, orig. version (1939) with str. and perc., rev. with full orch. (1942), No.2 (1951); 2 pf. (1968); vn.: No.1 (1948), No.2 (1956); vc. (1966); cl., str. (1936); ob., str. (1947).

VOICE(S) & INSTR(S).: A Canticle of Man, bar., ch., fl., str. (1952); *Practical Cats, spkr, orch. (1954); Medieval Diptych, bar., orch. (1962); Carmen Vitale, sop., ch., orch. (1963); Tankas of the 4 Seasons, ten., chamber ens. (1965); The God in the Cave, ch., orch. (1967).

CHORAL: Canzonet, sop., unacc. ch. (part of A *Garland for the Queen, 1953); 4 Seasonal Songs, unacc. ch. (1956); A Rose for Lidiče, sop., unacc. ch. (1956); Lament for a Sparrow, ch., hp. or pf. (1962).

CHAMBER MUSIC: str. qts.: No.1 (Theme and Variations) (1939), No.2 (1954), No.3 (1965); Concertante, vn., pf. (1934, rev. 1968); va. sonata (1935, rev. 1954); Theme and variations, 2 vn. (1938); Suite, rec., pf. (1939); cl. qt. (1948); vc. sonata (1949); vn. sonata (1959); Concerto, 10 instrs. (1961); pf. trio (1962); quintet (pf., ob., cl., hn., bn.) (1963); pf. quintet (1968); ob. qt. (1970); quintet (pf., cl., hn., vn., vc.) (1970); Elegy (guitar) (1971).

PIANO: 4 Bagatelles (1938); Suite, The Creel, pf. duet (1940); Sonatina (1949); 4 Romantic Pieces (1953); Ballade (1967); Theme and 4 Studies (1971).

Also scores for 22 films.

Raybould, (Robert) **Clarence** (b Birmingham, 1886; d Bideford, 1972). Eng. conductor, pianist, and composer. First to take B.Mus. degree at Birmingham Univ., 1912. Assisted Boughton at early Glastonbury Fests., working later with Beecham Opera Co. and BNOC. Toured Brit. as pianist and accompanist and worked for Columbia Graphophone Co. 1927–31. Joined BBC 1936. Ass. cond. BBCSO 1939–45. Cond. f. Brit. ps. (concert) of *Cardillac 1936 and Mathis der Maler 1939. Founded Nat. Youth Orch. of Wales 1945, cond. until 1966. His opera The Sumida River (anticipating Britten's Curlew River) was perf. in Birmingham 1916.

Razor Quartet (Haydn). See Rasiermesserquartett.

RCM. See Royal College of Music, London.

RCO. See Royal College of Organists.

re. The 2nd degree of the major scale, according to the system of vocal syllables derived from Guido d'Arezzo (see hexachord), and so used (spelt ray) in tonic sol-fa (also in that system the 4th degree of the minor scale; see tonic sol-fa). In many countries the name has become attached (on 'fixed-doh' principles) to the note D, in whatever key this may occur.

real. Term used in certain special senses as opposite to tonal, e.g. in *fugue real answer is when the answer exactly reproduces the subject (except for a 5th displaced), the fugue being a real fugue. In *sequence, if the intervals within a sequence are unaltered, the result is called a real sequence.

realism. Musically this term is applied to (1) operas where the plot or characters are said to be 'true to life' (*verismo) as distinct from remote.

(2) The attitude which was required by the Communist party bureaucracy from Soviet Union composers, meaning that their mus. should be optimistic, easily comprehended, and 'of the people'.

realize. To give full artistic life to mus. left by the composer in a contemp. style, e.g. to fill out the continuo bass line of a 17th- or 18th-cent. comp., to write in ornamentation, to interpret vague directions as to the manner of perf. Thus one speaks of Britten's 'realizations' of Purcell, etc., rather than his 'arrangements', and of Leppard's 'realizations' of Venetian operas compared with 'editions' by Harnoncourt, Glover, etc.

rebec (ribible, rubible). One of the first bowed str. instr., which probably originated in Moslem countries (as rebab or rabab) and was introduced to Europe in 8th cent. AD. It had rounded back carved out of the solid wood, with flat soundboard added. After 15th cent., no. of str. varied from 1 to 5. In Renaissance there were several sizes and pitches of rebec, e.g. sop., ten., and bass. The ten. and bass were probably played gamba-wise, held between knees. Smaller versions were known as ribecchino (It.) or rubechette (Fr.).

Rebel, François (b Paris, 1701; d Paris, 1775). Fr. composer and violinist, son of Jean-Féry *Rebel. Member of Paris Opéra orch. at 13. Music for 18 stage works in collab. with Francœur 1726–60. Joint cond. Paris Opéra 1733–44, later becoming manager. Superintendent of mus. to Louis XV. Wrote cantatas, etc.

Rebel, Jean-Féry (b Paris, 1666; d Paris, 1747). Fr. composer and violinist. One of the '24 violons du Roi', 1705–17. Chamber-composer to king, 1718–27. Violinist and cond., Paris Opéra. Wrote sonatas and pieces for solo vn.

recapitulation. That section of a comp. in sonata form and its variants in which the themes, or some of them, presented in the exposition are repeated, more or less in their orig. form.

Re cervo, Il (Henze). See König Hirsch.

Rechants, Cinq. 5 pieces by Messiaen for 12-v. ch., one of 3 Messiaen works inspired by Tristan and Isolde legend (the others being *Harawi and *Turangalîla). Comp. 1948. F.p. Bordeaux 1950.

récit (Fr.). (1) Short for *recitative.
(2, not abbreviation) Swell org.

recital. Term denoting a mus. perf. by soloists or duettists, e.g. an organ recital, song recital (by 1 or 2 singers), pf. recital, sonata recital. Orig. referred only to singers, but was applied *c*.1840 to Liszt's concert perfs.

recitative (It. *recitativo*). Form of declamatory speech-like singing used especially in opera or oratorio. Serves for dialogue or narrative (as a means of advancing the plot), whereas the subsequent *aria is often static or reflective. In 17th- and 18th-cent. opera, especially *opera seria*, the distinction between recit. and aria was clear, but with Mozart's much more expressive and inventive use of recitative (as in *Don Giovanni*), the convention began to break up. Types of recit. are: *recitativo accompagnato* or *stromentato* (It., acc. or instr. recit.), introduced *c*.1663, in which the v. is acc. by instr.; *recitativo secco* (It., dry recit.), in which the notes and metre of the singing followed the verbal accents, accompanied only by occasional hpd. chords, perhaps with a vc. or other instr. taking the bass line.

recorder (Fr. *flûte à bec*; Ger. *Blockflöte*; It. *flauto diretto*; Sp. *flauta de pico*). Woodwind instr. of ancient lineage, made without reed. Forerunner of the fl., but end-blown through a whistle-mouthpiece. In medieval times, the recorder was known under the Lat. name *fistula*, hence 'fipple-flute'. It had 7 finger-holes in front and a thumbhole behind, and a beak-shaped mouthpiece. The antiquity of the instr. is hard to determine because its playing position is so like that of similar instr. (other whistle types), that contemporary illustrations are of little help. But it has been est. as being in existence in the 12th cent., although the word 'recorder' first appeared in a document in 1388. A recorder tutor was pubd. in Venice, 1535. By the 15th cent. there were several sizes of recorder. Praetorius lists 8, i.e. great bass, quint bass, bass, ten., alto, 2 sop., sopranino. Thus, recorder consorts were a common feature of Renaissance mus. life. The instr. has been widely revived in the 20th cent. both as an easy instr. for children and as part of the revival in performing early mus. on authentic instr. Modern composers have written for it e.g. Britten, Arnold Cooke, and Rubbra. The most common size today is the descant (sop.), but there are also sopranino, treble (alto), ten., and bass.

recte et retro (Lat.). In the right way and backwards. Another name for the *canon cancrizans* in which the theme of a canon is perf. normally in counterpoint with itself perf. backwards.

Redlich, Hans (Ferdinand) (*b* Vienna, 1903; *d* Manchester, 1968). Austrian-born conductor, composer, and scholar (Eng. cit. 1947). Opera cond. Berlin 1924–5, Mainz 1925–9. Settled in Eng. 1939; lect. in mus. Cambridge Univ. 1942–55, Birmingham Univ. 1949–55, Edinburgh Univ. 1955–62. Prof. of mus., Manchester Univ. 1962–8. Ed. of operas and masses by Monteverdi, of Mozart's *L'Oca del Cairo*, and of works by Handel. Comp. vocal works. Author of books on Mahler, Bruckner, Berg, Monteverdi, and Wagner operas.

redowa. Bohemian dance usually in quick 3/4 time. It resembles the Polish dance, the mazurka. See *rejdovačka*.

reed. Sound-producing agent (of thin cane, plastic, or metal) of various mouth-blown wind instr., such as ob. and harmonica, certain org. pipes, etc. A reed which vibrates *against* an air slot is a *beating reed*; one which vibrates *through* such a slot (i.e. from one side to the other) is a *free reed*. Reeds may be either single, as in cl. family, or double (in the latter the two halves of the mouthpiece itself being pieces of reed vibrating against each other, see *oboe*). On an org., the *reed stop* controls pipes which have reeds.

Reed, William (Henry) (*b* Frome, 1876; *d* Dumfries, 1942). Eng. violinist, composer, and author. Violinist in London orchs. Joined LSO on its foundation in 1904 and was its leader 1912–35. Taught at RCM. Close friend of *Elgar, about whom he wrote 2 books and who consulted him on technical points in the Vn. Conc. (1910). Played in f.ps. of Elgar's vn. sonata, str. qt., and pf. quintet. Comp. orch. works, incl. *The Lincoln Imp* (1921), vn. conc., va. rhapsody, 5 str. qts., songs, etc. Long assoc. with 3 Choirs Fest. and is buried in Worcester Cath.

reed-cap instruments. From the late 15th cent. some woodwind instr. were made with a reed-cap which kept the reed from direct contact with the player's lips. The player blew through a slit in the top of the cap to activate the reed. Most reed-cap instr. cannot overblow and have a restricted compass.

reed-organ. Name for kbd. instr. using free-beating reeds and no pipe, as the *harmonium and the *American org. Also for *accordion and *harmonica. See also *regal*.

reel. Dance common in Scotland, parts of England, and Ireland, for 2 or more couples. The mus. is rapid and smoothly flowing and generally in simple quadruple time. The *Highland fling* is a particularly vigorous form of the Scottish reel. Scandinavian countries have similar dances. In N. Amer., the *Virginia reel*, said to be the same as the Eng. dance *Sir Roger de Coverley*, was probably introduced by Eng. settlers.

Reeves, Sims [John] (*b* Shooters Hill, 1818; *d* Worthing, 1900). Eng. tenor. Début as bar., Newcastle upon Tyne 1838 in Bishop's *Guy Mannering*, then studied in Paris and Milan, singing as ten. at La Scala 1846 (Edgardo in *Lucia di Lammermoor*) and London 1846. First sang in oratorio, Norwich Fest. 1848 and thereafter appeared more often on concert-platform than in opera, but sang title-role in f.p. in Eng. of *Faust*. Particularly assoc. with Handel Fests.

Reformation Symphony. Mendelssohn's Sym. No.5 in D minor, Op.107, comp. 1830–2. Written for tercentenary of Augsburg Confession of 1530 but not perf. until 1832 in Berlin. The first and last movts. quote the 'Dresden Amen' and the Lutheran chorale *Ein' feste Burg.

refrain. That part of a song which recurs at the end of each stanza. Refers to both words and mus. Corresponds to poetic 'burden'. In popular 20th-cent. mus., 'chorus' is used as synonym.

regal. Small portable 1-manual org. popular from 15th to 17th cents. Had reed pipes of type known as 'beating reeds' (reeds which vibrate against an air slot). Variety known as Bible Regal folded in two like a book.

Regards sur l'enfant Jésus, Vingt (20 looks at the Child Jesus). 20 pieces for solo pf. by Messiaen, comp. 1944. F.p. Paris 1945 (Loriod).

Reger, (Johann Baptist Joseph) **Max**(imilian) (b Brand, 1873; d Leipzig, 1916). Ger. composer, pianist, organist, and teacher. Wrote most of his org. works by 1900, finding devoted interpreter in Karl *Straube. Lived in Munich from 1901, teaching at Acad. of mus. 1905–6. Dir. of mus. and prof. of comp., Leipzig Univ. 1907–11. Cond. Meiningen Orch. 1911–14. Toured Europe and Russia as organist. Was opponent of 'programme' mus. and comp. only in 'absolute' forms. Master of polyphony and developed complex harmonic procedures. Prolific composer, chief works incl.:

ORCH.: 2 Romances, vn., orch. (1900); Variations and Fugue on a Theme of Beethoven (1915, arr. of 2-pf. work 1904); Sinfonietta in A (1904–5); Serenade in G (1905–6); Variations and Fugue on a Theme of J. A. Hiller (1907); vn. conc. in A (1907–8); Symphonic Prologue for a Tragedy in A minor (1908); pf. conc. in F minor (1910); Comedy Overture (1911); Concerto in Olden Style (1912); Romantic Suite, after Eichendorff (1912); 4 Böcklin Tone-Pictures (1913); Ballet Suite in D (1913); Variations and Fugue on a Theme of Mozart (1914, arr. for 2 pf. 1914).

CHORAL: Hymne an den Gesang, male ch., orch. (1898); 7 Male Choruses (1899); 4 Cantatas (1903–5); 10 Gesänge, male vv. (1904, 1909); Psalm 100, ch., orch., org. (1908–9); Geistliche Gesänge, 5 vv. (1912); Die Weihe der Nacht, male vv., orch. (1911); Römischer Triumphgesang, male vv., orch. (1912).

VOCAL: An die Hoffnung, alto, orch. or pf. (1912); Hymnus der Liebe, bar. or alto, orch. (1914); 12 Sacred Songs, v., pf. or org. or harmonium (1914); also over 250 solo songs, 12 of them with orch. acc.

CHAMBER MUSIC: 6 str. qts. (1888–9, 1900 (2), 1903–4, 1909, 1911); 2 pf. quintets (1897–8, 1901–2); 9 vn. sonatas (1890, 1891, 1892, 1903, 1904, 1905, 1910, 1911, 1915); 3 vc. sonatas (1898, 1904, 1910); 11 sonatas for solo vn. (1900 (4), 1905 (7)); 3 cl. sonatas (1900 (2), 1908–9); 2 pf. qts. (1910, 1914); str. sextet (1910); cl. quintet (1915).

PIANO: 12 Waltz-Caprices, duet (1892); 7 Waltzes (1893); Lose Blätter (1894); 6 Morceaux (1898); 7 Fantasie-Stücke (1898); 7 Charakterstücke (1899); 6 Intermezzi (1900); 7 Silhouettes (1900); 12 Blätter und Blüten (1900–2); 10 Pieces (1901–3); Variations and Fugue on a Theme of J. S. Bach (1904); Aus meinen

Tagebuch (35 little pieces) (1904–12); Variations and Fugue on a Theme of Beethoven, 2 pf. (1904, orch. 1915); 4 Pieces (1901–6); 4 Sonatinas (1905, 1908); Introduction, Passacaglia, and Fugue, 2 pf. (1906); Variations and Fugue on a Theme of Mozart, 2 pf. (1914, arr. of orch. work); Variations and Fugue on a Theme of G. P. Telemann (1914); Träume am Kamin, 12 little pieces (1915).

ORGAN: 3 Pieces (1892); Chorale Fantasia 'Ein' feste Burg' (1898); Fantasia and Fugue in C minor (1898); Sonatas, No.1 in F♯ (1899), No.2 in D minor (1901); Fantasia and Fugue on BACH (1900); 6 Trios (1900); 5 Easy Preludes and Fugues (1904); 12 Pieces (1901); 12 Pieces (1902); 52 Easy Chorale Pieces (1902); 10 Pieces (1903); Variations and Fugue on an Original Theme in F♯ (1903); 13 Chorale Preludes (1901–3); 12 Pieces (1904); 4 Preludes and Fugues (1904); Introduction, Passacaglia, and Fugue in E minor (1913); 9 Pieces (1913); 30 Little Chorale Preludes (1914); Fantasia and Fugue in D minor (1916); 7 Pieces (1915–16).

reggae. Rhythmic mus. indigenous to black culture of Jamaica and originating in mid-1960s; extremely eclectic, being drawn from African religious mus. and cult drum mus., Christian black revival songs, and liturgical mus. of Rastafarian sect. Words usually relate news, social gossip, and political comment. Reggae spread into commercialized jazz field, being known first as 'Rudie Blues', then 'Ska', later 'Blue Beat', and 'Rock Steady'.

Regina. Opera in 3 acts by Blitzstein to his own lib. based on Lillian Hellman's play The Little Foxes. Comp. 1946–9. Prod. NY 1949, Glasgow 1991.

register. (1) Set of org. pipes belonging to a particular stop.
(2) To 'register' a piece of mus. is to select the stops to be employed in its various sections; hence, 'registration', the art of selecting and using stops in playing org. and hpd.
(3) The part of the compass of an instr. having a distinctive tonal quality, e.g. *chalumeau register of cl.
(4) Part of vocal compass, e.g. chest v., high register, etc.

Rehfuss, Heinz (Julius) (b Frankfurt, 1917; d Rochester, NY, 1988). Ger.-Swiss-born bass-baritone and singing teacher (Amer. cit.). Début 1938. Sang in Lucerne 1938–9. Member of Zurich Stadttheater 1940–52. Wide repertory of operatic roles and noted for singing of oratorio. Settled in USA. Sang in f.p. of Intolleranza (Venice 1961). Taught at various schs. of mus.

Reich, Steve [Stephen] (Michael) (b NY, 1936). Amer. composer; one of the *minimalists. Worked with S. Francisco tape mus. centre 1963–5, then est. own EMS in NY and formed own ens., Steve Reich and Musicians, 1966, with which he achieved internat. fame and success. Though influenced to some degree by African and Asian mus., his works deal exclusively with very gradual changes in time. Prin. comps.:

DANCE: *Impact* (1985); *Variations for Vibes, Pianos and Strings*, 3 str. qts., 4 vib., 2 pf., dancers (2005).

MUSIC THEATRE: *The Cave* (1989–93); *3 Tales* (2001).

ORCH.: *Pendulum Music*, 3 or more microphones, amplifiers, loudspeakers, and perf. (1968); *Music for a Large Ensemble* (1978); *Variations*, winds, str., kbd. (1979, rev. 1980); *Eight Lines* (rev. of *Octet*) (1979, rev. 1983); *Three Movements* (1986); *The Four Sections* (1987); *Duet*, 2 vns., str. (1993); *For Strings (with Winds and Brass)*, orch. (1987/2004).

VOICES & ORCH.: *Tehillim*, vv., ens. (1981), vv., chamber orch. (1982); *The Desert Music*, 27 amp. vv., orch. (1982–4), 10 amp. vv., orch. (1985); *Proverb*, vv., ens. (1995); *You Are (Variations)*, vv., chamber orch. (2004); *Daniel Variations*, 6 vv., large ens. (2006).

PERC./KEYBOARD ENS.: *Piano Phase*, 2 pf. or 2 marimbas (1967); *Phase Patterns*, 4 elec. org. (1970); *Four Organs*, 4 elec. org., maracas (1970); *Drumming*, 4 pairs of tuned bongos, 3 marimbas, 3 glockenspiels, 2 female vv., whistling, picc. (1971, in 4 parts each of which may be perf. separately); *Music for Pieces of Wood*, 5 pairs of tuned claves (1973); *Six Pianos* (1973); *Music for Mallet Instruments, Voices, and Organ* (1973); *Music for 18 Musicians*, with 4 wordless female vv. (1976); *Sextet* (1984, rev. 1985); *Six Marimbas* (version of *Six Pianos*) (1986); *City Life*, 17 players (1995).

SOLO INSTR(S). or SMALL ENS.: *Reed Phase*, sop. sax, tape (1966); *Violin Phase* vn., tape or 4 vns. (1967); *Clapping Music*, 2 perf. clapping (1972); *Vermont Counterpoint*, fl. (picc., alto fl.), tape (1982); *New York Counterpoint*, cl., tape (1985), ens. version for 9 cl. (1987); *Electric Counterpoint*, elec. gui., tape (1987), ens. version for 11 elec. gui., 2 elec./bass gui. (1989); *Different Trains*, str. qt., tape (1988); *City Life*, amp. ens. (1995); *Triple Quartet*, str. qt., tape/str. ens./str. orch. (1998); *Dance Patterns*, 2 xyl., 2 vib., 2 pf. (2002); *Cello Counterpoint*, amp. vc., tape (2003).

TAPE: *It's gonna rain* (1965); *Melodica* (1966); *Come Out* (1966).

Reich, Willi (*b* Vienna, 1898; *d* Zurich, 1980). Austrian-born musicologist and critic (Swiss cit. 1961). Ed. journal *23—eine Wiener Musikzeitschrift*, 1932–7, in which he supported Second Viennese School. Settled in Switz. 1938, lecturing in Zurich and writing, from 1948, for *Neue Zürcher Zeitung*. Wrote books on Berg, Mozart, Haydn, Wolf, Wagner, Verdi, Bruckner, Mahler, and Schoenberg.

Reicha, Antonín (*b* Prague, 1770; *d* Paris, 1836). Bohemian, later Fr., composer and flautist. Flautist in Bonn Elector's orch., 1785–94, becoming friend of Beethoven. Lived in Hamburg 1794–9, Paris 1799–1802, Vienna 1802–8, 1808 Paris, becoming prof. of comp. at Paris Cons. from 1818 (pupils incl. Berlioz, Liszt, Franck, and Gounod). Wrote 16 operas; 2 syms.; *Scènes italiennes* for orch.; octet for str. and wind; 24 wind quintets; 20 str. qts.; 24 hn. trios; 12 vn. sonatas; and numerous other chamber works. Remembered almost exclusively for his frequently-played wind quintets, nearly the first of their kind. His *Art du compositeur dramatique* (1833) influenced several 19th cent. opera composers, incl. Meyerbeer.

Reichardt, Johann Friedrich (*b* Königsberg, 1752; *d* Giebichenstein, 1814). Ger. composer, conductor, and writer. Court composer and cond. to Frederick the Great and Frederick II, 1775–94. Instituted many reforms. Visited London and Paris 1785 and again some years later. Dismissed from court post for sympathy with Fr. Revolution. Cond. Kassel Opera 1808. Wrote at least 12 operas, *Singspiele*, setting of Milton's *Morning Hymn*, over 1,500 songs (incl. setting of *Erlkönig*, highly praised by Mendelssohn), and much chamber mus. Author of several books on comp.

Reichmann, Theodor (*b* Rostock, 1849; *d* Marbach, Bodensee, 1903). Ger. baritone. Début Magdeburg 1869. Sang opera in Berlin, Munich, and Hamburg, joining Vienna Opera 1882–9, 1893–1902. Created Amfortas in *Parsifal*, Bayreuth 1882. London début 1882; CG 1884 and 1892 (*Ring* cycles, cond. Mahler); NY Met 1889–91. Last appearance Munich 1902, as Hans Sachs (*Die Meistersinger*).

Reigen, Reihen (Ger.). Round dance, or simply dance. *Elfenreigen*, elf dance, *Gnomenreigen*, gnome dance.

Reilly, Tommy (*b* Guelph, Ontario, 1919; *d* Frensham, Surrey, 2000). Canadian-born mouthorgan player, self-taught. Has transcr. mus. for Bach, Mozart, Smetana, and Chopin for his instr. Works written for him by Spivakovsky and Jacob. Soloist with leading orchs. MBE 1992.

Reimann, Aribert (*b* Berlin, 1936). Ger. composer and pianist. Exceptional accompanist, often with *Fischer-Dieskau (Salzburg Fest. 1971). Comps. influenced by Berg, Webern, and the mus. of India. Abandoned serialism in 1967. Has set texts by Shakespeare and Shelley. Prin. works:

OPERAS: *Ein Traumspiel* (A Dream Play) (1964, after Strindberg); *Melusine* (1970); *Lear* (1976–8, after Shakespeare); *Die Gespensteronate* (1983, after Strindberg); *Troades* (1984–5, after Euripides); *Das Schloss* (1989–91, after Kafka); *Bernarda Albas Haus* (2000).

BALLET: *Stoffreste* (1957), rev. as *Die Vogelscheuchen* (The Scarecrows), lib. by Günter Grass (1970).

ORCH.: *Rondes*, str. (1968); *Loqui* (1969); suite, *Ein Traumspiel* (1965); suite, *Die Vogelscheuchen* (1972); pf. conc. No.1 (1961), No.2 (1972); vn. conc. (1959); *Variations* (1975); *7 Fragmente* (1988); conc., vn., vc., orch. (1989); *9 Pieces* (1993–4); vn. conc. (1995–6); *Spiralat Halom* (2002).

VOCAL: *Ein Totentanz*, bar., chamber orch. (1960); *Hölderlin-Fragmente*, sop., orch. (1963); *Inane*, sop., orch. (1968); *Zyklus*, bar., orch. (1971); *Epitaph*, ten., 7 instr. (1965); *5 Poems of Paul Celan*, bar., pf. (1960); *3 Shakespeare Sonnets*, bar., pf. (1964); *Lines* (Shelley), sop., 14 str. (1973); *Wolkenloses Christfest* (Cloudless Christmas), requiem, bar., vc., orch. (1974); *Verrà la Morte* (Death Shall Come), cantata, sop., ten., bar., 2 ch., orch. (1966); *Lear*, sym., bar., orch. (1980); *Unrevealed*, bar., str. qt. (1980); *Chacun sa Chimère*, ten., orch. (1981); *Requiem*, sop., mez., bar., orch. (1982); *Apocalyptic Fragment*, mez., pf., orch. (1987); *Shine and Dark*, bar., pf. (1990).

CHAMBER MUSIC: pf. sonata (1958); *Canzoni e Ricercare*, fl., va., vc. (1961); *Reflexionen*, 7 instr. (1966); vc. sonata (1963); *Invenzioni* for 12 players (1979); trio, vn., va., vc. (1987); *Solo*, ob. (2001).

Re in ascolto, Un (It. 'A Listening King'). *Azione musicale* in 2 parts by *Berio to his own lib. drawn from Calvino, Auden, Einsiedel, and Gotter. Comp. 1979–83. F.p. Salzburg 1984; London (CG) 1989.

Reine, La (The Queen). Nickname of Haydn's Sym. in B♭, No.85 in Breitkopf edn., comp. 1785, being abbreviation of 'La Reine de France'. No.4 of the *'Paris' syms. and much admired by Marie Antoinette.

Reinecke, Carl (Heinrich Carsten) (*b* Altona, 1824; *d* Leipzig, 1910). Ger. pianist, violinist, composer, conductor, and teacher. Début as violinist 1835. Orch. violinist but then devoted himself to pf., making int. reputation. Court pianist, Copenhagen, 1846–8. After teaching in Cologne, Barmen, and Breslau, settled in Leipzig, becoming cond. of Gewandhaus Orch. 1860–95 and prof. of pf. and comp. at Cons. 1860–97, dir. 1897–1902. Wrote 5 operas; oratorio; cantatas; 3 syms.; 4 pf. concs.; hp. conc.; much chamber mus.; and pf. pieces. Wrote over 40 cadenzas for pf. concs. by other composers.

Reiner, Fritz (*b* Budapest, 1888; *d* NY, 1963). Hung.-born conductor (Amer. cit. 1928). Chorusmaster Budapest Opera 1909. Cond. Budapest Volksoper 1911–14. Chief cond., Dresden Opera 1914–22. Cond. Cincinnati SO 1922–31. Head of orch. and opera depts., Curtis Inst. 1931–41. Cond., Pittsburgh SO 1938–48. CG 1936–7. NY Met 1949–53 and cond. f. Amer. p. of *The Rake's Progress*. Cond., Chicago SO 1953–63. London début with LSO, 1924. CG 1936–7. Salzburg Fest. 1956. Famed interpreter of R. Strauss, Wagner, Bartók.

Reinhardt, Delia (*b* Elberfeld, 1892; *d* Arlesheim, 1974). Ger. soprano. Début Wrocław 1913. Munich Opera 1916–24, Berlin State Opera 1924–32. Sang at CG 1924–9, NY Met 1923–4. A famous Oktavian in *Der Rosenkavalier*, also won acclaim for her Eva, Pamina, and Desdemona.

Reinhardt, Django (Jean Baptiste) (*b* Liberchies, 1910; *d* Fontainebleau, 1953). Belg. jazz guitarist. Burned in fire 1928, mutilation of left hand causing him to devise new fingering method. Worked with the singer Jean Sablon and the violinist Stephane *Grappelli. Founder-member with Grappelli of Quintet du Hot Club de France, 1934. Visited London 1946 and toured USA as soloist with *Ellington's orch. Can be claimed as first really great European jazz musician.

Reinhardt [Goldmann], **Max** (*b* Baden, Austria, 1873; *d* NY, 1943). Austrian theatre director. Began career as actor in Volkstheater, Rudolfsheim, 1892. Worked in Berlin from 1898 and became dir. of Neues Th., creating sensation with his prods. of Maeterlinck's *Pelleas und Melisande*, Wilde's *Salome*, and Hofmannsthal's *Elektra*. First opera prod. was *Orphée aux enfers*, with designs by Ernst Stern, 1906. Prod. (anonymously) f.p. of Strauss's *Der Rosenkavalier* (Dresden, 1911), followed by *La belle Hélène* (Venice, 1911), and *Ariadne auf Naxos* (Stuttgart, 1912). One of founders of Salzburg Fest. 1920, where he prod. Hofmannsthal's *Jedermann* and Goethe's *Faust*. Last major opera prod. was of *Die Fledermaus* (San Remo, 1934), although after emigrating to USA in 1937 he prod. *The Eternal Road*, with mus. by Weill (1937).

Reining, Maria (*b* Vienna, 1903; *d* Deggendorf, 1991). Austrian soprano. Worked in bank before taking up singing. Vienna Opera 1931–3, 1937–55; Darmstadt 1933–5; Bavarian State Opera, Munich, 1935–7. CG début 1938. Toscanini's choice for Eva in Salzburg 1937 *Die Meistersinger*. Chicago 1938, NY City Opera 1949. Prof. of singing, Salzburg Mozarteum 1962. Famous for Strauss roles of Marschallin, Arabella, and Ariadne.

Reissiger, Karl Gottlieb (*b* Belzig, 1789; *d* Dresden, 1859). Ger. composer and conductor. Weber cond. his opera *Didone abbandonata* in Dresden, 1824. Succeeded Weber as dir., Dresden Court Opera, 1826, and was appointed Hofkapellmeister 1828. Made Dresden Opera best in Ger. Cond. f.p. of *Rienzi* 1842, appointing Wagner as 2nd cond. 1843. Wrote 9 operas, incl. *Turandot* (1843).

Reizenstein, Franz (Theodor) (*b* Nuremberg, 1911; *d* London, 1968). Ger.-born composer, pianist, and conductor. Settled in London 1934. Taught pf. at RAM 1958–68, RMCM 1962–8. Works incl. radio opera *Anna Kraus*; oratorio *Genesis*; cantata *Voices of Night* (all to texts by Christopher Hassall); and 2 pf. concs.; 2 vn. concs.; vc. conc.; much chamber mus. incl. 2 pf. sonatas and other kbd. works. Frequently played in various chamber ens. incl. his own pf. trio. Composed 2 of best *Hoffnung concert *pastiches*, *Let's Fake an Opera* and *Concerto popolare* (both 1958).

rejdovačka or **rejdovák**. Bohemian dance in duple time, somewhat like the polka but considered to be a variant of the *redowa.

Rejoice in the Lord Alway. Anthem by H. Purcell known as *Bell Anthem*.

rektah. See *raptak*.

Relâche (theatrical term denoting 'no show' or 'theatre closed'). 'Ballet instantanéiste' in 2 acts and cinematographic entr'acte by René Clair, with music by *Satie to lib. by F. Picabia, choreog. Börlin. Prod. Paris 1924.

related. Term used for one key's harmonic distance from, or closeness to, another. 'Related keys' is an unspecific term, since all keys are related in some way.

relative. Term used to indicate connection between a major and a minor *key having same key signature, e.g. A minor is the *relative minor* of C major, and C major the *relative major* of A minor.

Remedios, Alberto (*b* Liverpool, 1935). Eng. tenor. Opera début London (SW) 1957 (Tinca in *Il tabarro*). CG début 1965. Scored major success as Walther in *The Mastersingers* at SW 1968, under *Goodall. Frankfurt Opera 1968–70. Sang Siegmund and Siegfried in SW *Ring* cycles cond. by Goodall, with Rita *Hunter as Brünnhilde. Amer. début S. Francisco 1973; NY Met début 1976. CBE 1981.

Reményi [Hoffmann], **Ede** [Eduard] (*b* Mistolc, Hung., 1828; *d* San Francisco, 1898). Hung. violinist. Début Pest 1846, London 1848. Was in USA 1848–52. Toured Europe 1852–3 with Brahms as accompanist. Friend of Liszt at Weimar. Visited London 1854, becoming court solo violinist to Queen Victoria 1854–9. Austrian court violinist, 1860. Wrote vn. conc. and other pieces. The 'gipsy' element in some of Brahms's music is probably attributable to his time with Reményi. Died while playing in a concert.

remettre (Fr.). To put back. The imperative *remettez* in Fr. org. mus. means to bring into use some stop that has been temporarily out of action.

Remoortel, Edouard van (*b* Brussels, 1926; *d* Paris, 1977). Belg. conductor. Chief cond., Belg. Nat. Orch. 1951. Cond. St Louis SO 1958–62. Monte Carlo Opera 1965–9.

Renaissance (Fr., 'rebirth'). In mus. parlance, the Renaissance period is that between 'medieval' and 'baroque', i.e. from early 15th to early 17th cents.

Renard (The Fox). 1-act *histoire burlesque chantée et jouée* (burlesque in song and dance) by Stravinsky to his own lib. after A. Afanasyev's Russ. folktales, 1855–64, in Fr. trans. by C. F. Ramuz. Full title: *Bayka pro lisu, petukha, kota da barana* ('Fable of the Vixen, the Cock, the Cat and the Ram'). Comp. 1915–16. Prod. Paris 1922, NY 1923.

Rendall, David (*b* London, 1948). Eng. tenor. Début, GTO 1975 (Ferrando in *Cosi fan tutte*). CG 1975; Glyndebourne 1976; ENO 1976–92; NY City Opera 1978; S. Francisco 1978; NY Met 1980.

Renn, Samuel (*b* Kedleston, Derbyshire, 1786; *d* Manchester, 1845). Eng. organ-builder. Apprenticed *c*.1800 to his uncle James Davis and became his foreman 1808, supervising many installations. On Davis's retirement, Renn took over his Lancashire business and traded as Renn & Boston. Built 100 organs 1822–45. By standardizing dimensions of pipes etc., he reduced costs. Built Chester Cath. organ 1829 and St Philip's, Salford. His nephew James Kirtland took over business

when Renn died, being joined in 1846 by F. W. Jardine. The title Jardine & Co. was adopted 1867 and the firm survived until 1976.

Rennert, Günther (*b* Essen, 1911; *d* Salzburg, 1978). Ger. producer and intendant. Film producer 1933. Worked in opera, at Felsenstein's prompting, at Wuppertal, Frankfurt, and Mainz 1935–9, Königsberg 1939–42, Berlin 1942–4, Munich 1945. Salzburg Fest. début 1947 (*Arabella*), and many prods. until his death. Intendant, Hamburg Opera 1946–56, making it leading Ger. co. of its day and staged such 20th-cent. operas as *Peter Grimes*, *Wozzeck*, *Lulu*, and *The Rake's Progress*. Glyndebourne début 1959 (*Fidelio*), joint art. dir. 1960–7. Guest producer CG, NY Met, and other leading opera houses. Staatsintendant, Bavarian State Opera, Munich, 1967–77.

Rè Pastore, Il, (The Shepherd King). *Dramma per musica* or *Serenata* in 2 acts (K208) by Mozart to lib. by Metastasio. Prod. Salzburg 1775 and 1906, London 1954, Norfolk, Va., 1971. Lib. also used by Hasse, Gluck, and several others.

repeat marks (see p. 619).

répétiteur (Fr.; It. *maestro concertatore*). Rehearser. Member of mus. staff of opera house who coaches singers in their roles and also sometimes acts as chorusmaster, and prompter in perfs. Word is generally used in Eng., otherwise 'coach'. Many distinguished opera conds. have learned their craft as *répétiteurs*. 'Repeat' is orch. players' term for the inside 1st vn. next to the leader.

répétition (Fr.). Repetition, i.e. rehearsal. The *répétition générale* is final dress rehearsal.

repiano. See *ripieno*.

reports, rapports (from Fr. *rapporter*, to carry back). In 17th-cent. mus. parlance, 'report' was equivalent of 'imitation'. It meant the re-introduction, by one v. or part, of a melodic phrase just heard from another. In the Scottish Psalter of 1635 some tunes are headed 'Heere are some Psalmes in Reports'. These are subjected to motet or anthem-like treatment.

reprise (Fr.). Repeat. In comp., a return to the first section after an intervening and contrasting section. In the works of Rameau, Couperin, etc., the term means a short refrain at the end of a movt. and intended to be repeated.

reproducing piano. See *pianola*.

Requiem. The RC Mass for the Dead (Lat. *Missa pro defunctis*) beginning 'Requiem aeternam' (Rest eternal). Text follows that of normal Mass but with Gloria and Credo omitted and Dies Irae added. There are many mus. settings, from the traditional plainsong to elaborate versions more suitable for concert perf. than for liturgical use, e.g. those by Berlioz and Verdi. Other notable settings are by Palestrina, Mozart (incomplete),

repeat marks (for notes)

There is a 'catch' in (c) and (d), the convention not being quite logical. In (c) (3 examples are given) the time-value to be filled is that of *one* of the notes shown (in this case half-note); in (d) the time-value to be filled is that of *both* of the notes shown (in this case eighth notes).

Note. If *tremolo* (or *trem.*) is added to any of the above or similar signs the notes concerned should be repeated very rapidly and without any attention to the exact number of repetitions attained during the time-value available.

repeat marks (for passages)

:‖ means return to :‖ or, if that does not occur, to the beginning of the piece.	D.C. or *Da Capo*, literally 'from the head', i.e. return to the beginning.	D.S or *Dal Segno*, i.e. from the sign, meaning the return to the mark 𝄋.	A.S. (rare) or *Al Segno*, i.e. to the sign. Usually the expression is *D.C. al Segno e poi la Coda*, i.e. 'From the beginning to the 𝄋 and then the Coda'.	*Bis* means perform the passage twice.

To avoid needless writing or engraving (especially in orchestral mus.) the repetition of a short passage is often indicated as:

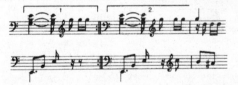   or

Sometimes when a section is marked to be repeated it ends in a way suitable for the return to the beginning, and, having been repeated, ends in a way suitable to proceed to the next section (or to close the whole composition if nothing more follows). The two endings are then shown thus:

Or instead of the '1' there may be used the expression '1ma Volta', or 'Prima Volta', or '1st Time'. Instead of the '2' there may be used the expression '2da Volta', or 'Seconda Volta', or '2nd Time'. When a return to the opening of the piece, or of some section of it, is indicated but only a part is to be repeated and then the piece brought to an end, the word *Fine* (end) shows where to stop.

For instance, a minuet is often followed by another minuet called *trio, after which the first minuet is to be repeated and then an end to be made. In this case the word 'Fine' is placed at the end of the first minuet to indicate that this is the place to conclude when performing the repetition.

Fauré, and Dvořák. A typical disposition of the text in these large settings is: 1. *Requiem aeternam*; *Kyrie eleison*; 2. *Dies Irae* (Day of Wrath) divided into *Tuba mirum* (Hark, the trumpet),

Liber scriptus (A book is written), *Quid sum miser* (How wretched am I), *Rex tremendae* (King of glory), *Recordare* (Remember), *Ingemisco* (Sadly groaning), *Confutatis* (From the accursed),

Lacrimosa (Lamentation); 3. *Domine Jesu Christe* (Lord Jesus Christ); 4. *Sanctus* (Holy); 5. *Agnus Dei* (Lamb of God); 6. *Lux aeterna* (Eternal light); 7. *Libera me* (Deliver me). This is Verdi's scheme: there are several variations of it. Not all Requiem settings follow the Lat. text. Brahms's *Ein *Deutsches Requiem* uses texts from the Ger. Bible. Delius's *Requiem* is a setting of a text by H. Simon and was described as 'pagan'. Hindemith's setting of Whitman's poem 'When Lilacs Last in the Dooryard Bloom'd' is of the character of a Requiem. Britten's *War Requiem* uses the Lat. Mass interspersed with poems by Wilfred Owen. Geoffrey Burgon's *Requiem* also uses several sources. The term is occasionally used in other contexts as in Britten's *Sinfonia da Requiem* for orch.

rescue opera. Type of opera, or *opéra-comique*, popular in Fr. after the Revolution, in which the hero or heroine is saved from some dire fate by human heroism. The most famous rescue opera is Beethoven's *Fidelio* (1805), based on a real-life incident previously used as libretto by *Gaveaux in 1798 (*Léonore, ou l'amour conjugal*).

Resnik, Regina (*b* NY, 1922). Amer. mezzo-soprano. Concert début as sop. Brooklyn Acad. of Mus. 1942, opera début (New Opera Co., NY) 1942 (Lady Macbeth). Débuts: Mexico City 1943; NY City Opera 1944; NY Met 1944–74; S. Francisco 1946; Bayreuth 1953. Changed to mez., 1955. CG début 1957 (Carmen). Salzburg début 1960. Interpreter of Amneris, Carmen, and Klytemnästra. Début as opera dir., Hamburg 1971 (*Carmen*).

resolution. The satisfactory following of a discordant chord (or of the discordant note in such a chord) with a concord or less acute discord.

resoluto, risoluto (It.). Resolute.

resonance. (1) Sympathetic vibration of bodies capable of producing sounds as soon as a pitch similar to that of the body or one of its overtones is heard.
(2) The rebound of vibration-waves from a solid structure such as walls of a hall or church.
(3) Transmission of vibrations from the str. of a str. instr. to a sounding-board.

Respighi, Ottorino (*b* Bologna, 1879; *d* Rome, 1936). It. composer, conductor, string-player, pianist, and teacher. Went to St Petersburg 1900 as first va. in opera orch. and from 1901 studied with *Rimsky-Korsakov, then in Berlin with *Bruch, 1902. From 1903 to 1908 pursued career as violinist and violist and was pianist at Berlin singing-sch. 1908–9. Prof. of comp. at Liceo di S. Cecilia, Rome, 1913; dir. 1924–6. His mus., though based on classical forms, was influenced by the brighter colours of Rimsky-Korsakov and Strauss, and his symphonic poems are notable for their brilliant and luscious scoring. In his operas he reacted against Puccinian 'realism', but they are more impressive orchestrally than vocally. Some of his most tender and exquisite work is to be found in his shorter vocal pieces. Prin. works:

OPERAS: *Re Enzo* (1905); *Semirama* (1910); *Belfagor* (1921–2); *La bella dormente nel bosco* (1916–21); *La campana sommersa* (The Sunken Bell) (1923–7); *Maria Egiziaca* (1929–31); *La Fiamma* (1931–3); *Lucrezia* (1935).

BALLETS: *La *Boutique fantasque* (The Fantastic Toyshop) adapted from mus. by Rossini (1919); *Belkis, Regina di Saba* (1930–1).

ORCH.: *Notturno* (1905); *Sinfonia drammatica* (1913–14); *Fountains of Rome* (*Fontane di Roma*) (1914–16); *Ancient Airs and Dances*, transcr. for orch., 1st series (1917), 2nd series (1924), 3rd series (str.) (1931); *Ballata delle gnomidi* (1918–20); *Pines of Rome* (*Pini di Roma*) (1923–4); *Rossiniana* (from Rossini pf. pieces) (1925); *Vetrate di Chiesa* (Church Windows), 4 symphonic impressions (1925); *Impressione brasiliane*, sym. suite (1927); *Trittico Botticelliano* (1927); *The *Birds* (*Gli uccelli*) (1927); *Feste Romane* (Roman Festivals) (1928); *Metamorphosen modi XII* (1930).

CONCERTOS etc.: pf. conc. (1902); *Concerto in the Old Style*, vn. (1908); *Adagio con variazioni*, vc. (1920); *Concerto Gregoriano*, vn. (1921); *Concerto in modo misolidio*, pf., orch. (1925); *Poema autunnale*, vn., orch. (1920–5); *Toccata*, pf., orch. (1928); conc. for ob., tpt., vn., db., pf., str. (1933).

VOICE(S) & ORCH.: *Aretusa*, mez., orch. (1911); *La primavera*, soloists, ch., orch. (1918–19); *Il Tramonto*, mez., str. qt. (1914); *Deità silvane*, sop., pf. (1917), high v., chamber ens. (1925); *Lauda per la natività del Signore*, sop., cont., ten., ch., orch. (1928–30).

CHAMBER MUSIC: 11 pieces, vn., pf. (1904–7); str. qt. (1907); vn. sonata (1917); Doric str. qt. (1924).

TRANSCRIPTIONS: Monteverdi: *Orfeo* (1935); *Lamento d'Arianna* (1908); Marcello: *Didone*, cantata (1935); Rossini: *Soirées musicales* for ballet *La Boutique fantasque* (1919); J. S. Bach: *Prelude and Fugue* in D, for orch. (1930); *3 Organ Chorals*, for orch. (1931); *Passacaglia* in C minor, for orch. (1934); Vitali: *Chaconne*, for vn., str., org. (1909).

responses. In Anglican church, the replies of the choir (or congregation) to the versicles of the priest. Usually in plainsong. Tallis, Byrd, Gibbons, etc. wrote superb harmonized versions.

responsorio. Type of motet in which a soloist and the choir sing responsively—in Eng. a variety of 'Solo Anthem'.

rest. (1) Musical silence.
(2) Notation of absence of sound in performer's part for a length of time corresponding to a given number of beats or measures, e.g. 4 measures' rest or an 8th-note rest. Notation of rests is as shown:

The $\natural$ rest hangs down; the $\quarternote$ rest remains on the surface. (Imagine the rest of greater value is the heavier.)

The $\quarternote$ rest γ turns to the right (mnemonic: cRotchet–Right; or quaRter Note–Right); the $\eighthnote$ rest γ turns to the left.

In addition to the above there is the double-note rest, occupying the whole space between two lines—$\blacksquare$.

Also, the whole-note rest is used as a whole-measure rest, irrespective of the actual time-value of the measure.

A silence of several measures is often indicated thus (or in some similar way):

Rests can be dotted and doubly dotted, as notes are, and with the same effect: this, however, is less commonly done.

See also *note values*.

restez (Fr.). Remain, i.e. linger on a note rather than hurry off it; in str. mus., remain in the same position for the duration of a passage.

resultant bass. Org. stop; same as *quint*.

resultant tone. When 2 loud notes are heard together they produce a 3rd sound, the resultant tone, corresponding to the difference between the 2 vibration nos.: this (low in pitch) is called a 'difference tone'. They also produce a 4th sound, high and faint, corresponding to the sum of the 2 vibration numbers. This is a 'summation tone'.

Resurrection Symphony. Sub-title of *Mahler's Sym. No.2 in C minor (1888–94, rev. 1910) because finale is setting for sop. and alto soloists, ch., and orch. of the 'Resurrection' (*Aufersteh'n*) chorale by Klopstock (1724–1803).

Retablo de Maese Pedro, El (Falla). See *Master Peter's Puppet Show*.

retardando (It.). Same as *ritardando*.

retardation. In harmony, the same as *suspension*, but with the discord resolved by rising a degree.

retenant; retenu (Fr.). Holding back; held back (immediately, like *ritenuto*, not gradually, like *rallentando*).

Rethberg [Sattler], **Elisabeth** [Lisbeth] (*b* Schwarzenberg, 1894; *d* NY, 1976). Ger.-born soprano (Amer. cit.). Début Dresden 1915 (Arsena in *Zigeunerbaron*). NY Met début 1922, staying with co. until 1942. Salzburg 1922; CG début 1925 and 1934–9. Created title-role in *Die *ägyptische Helena*, Dresden 1928. Many concert appearances. Retired 1942.

Réti, Rudolph (*b* Užice, Serbia, 1885; *d* Montclair, NJ, 1957). Serbian-born musicologist, pianist, and composer. One of founders of ISCM, Salzburg, 1922. Settled in USA 1938. Wrote opera, orch. mus., and other pieces, but best known for books *The Thematic Process in Music* (NY, 1951) and *Tonality, Atonality, Pantonality* (NY, 1958). Gave f.p. of Schoenberg's *3 Piano Pieces*, Op.11, in 1911.

Return of Lemminkäinen (Sibelius). See *Lemminkäinen Legends*.

Reutter, Hermann (*b* Stuttgart, 1900; *d* Heidenheim an der Brenz, 1985). Ger. composer and pianist. Began career as pf. accompanist to Sigrid Onegin and Karl Erb. Taught comp. Stuttgart 1932–6, dir., Berlin Hochschule 1936–45, prof. of comp. Stuttgart Acad. 1952–6, dir. 1956–66, prof. of mus., Munich Acad. from 1966. Prolific composer, especially of *Lieder* (over 200). Friend of Hindemith.

Reveille (from Fr. *réveil*, wakening). The military signal beginning the day (in the Brit. army pronounced 'revelly' or 'revally').

Revelation and Fall. Work for sop. and 16 instr. by *Maxwell Davies to text from Georg Trakl's *Offenbarung und Untergang*. Comp. 1965. F.p. London 1968 (Mary Thomas, mez.) cond. composer.

Revenge, The Choral ballad, setting of Tennyson's poem, by Stanford, Op.24, f.p. Leeds Fest. 1886.

'Revolutionary' Study. Nickname for Chopin's pf. Étude in C minor, Op.10, No.12 (1831), supposedly because it expressed his patriotic fury on hearing that Warsaw had been captured by the Russians; however, the story is unsupported by evidence.

revue. Form of entertainment comprising a series of scenes, without a plot, and sketches, dances, songs, and ballet. Evolved in Fr. in early 19th cent. as purveyor of satire, later becoming more spectacular and including *tableaux vivants*. In 20th cent. became more sophisticated, with personalities like Mistinguett (1873–1956), Maurice Chevalier (1888–1971), and Josephine Baker (1906–75), whose erotic dancing in a 1925 revue caused a scandal. In Brit., revue did not really take root until early in 20th cent. The producer and impresario C. B. Cochran imported Fr. artists, notably Alice Delysia. His revues, with those of André Charlot, dominated the London stage in the 1920s. Noël Coward and Ivor Novello wrote songs for Charlot and Cochran, and Coward later wrote his own revues (e.g. *Tonight at 8.30*). Brit. revue stars incl. Gertrude Lawrence, Beatrice Lillie, Jessie Matthews, Jack Buchanan, and Leslie Henson. Berners comp. his ballet *Luna Park* for Cochran's 1930 revue and Walton his *The First Shoot* for Cochran's *Follow the Sun* (1935–6). 'Intimate' revues by Herbert and Eleanor Farjeon brought fame to Hermione Baddeley and Hermione Gingold. Later developments of revue were the shows which featured Michael Flanders and Donald Swann (*At the Drop of a Hat*, etc.) and the wittily satirical *Beyond the Fringe* (1961). In the USA, revue developed from vaudeville. Its most successful form was in the *Follies* produced by Florenz Ziegfeld annually from 1907 until the mid-1920s.

Reyer, Ernest [Rey, Louis Étienne] (*b* Marseilles, 1823; *d* Le Lavandou, 1909). Fr. composer and critic. Went to Paris 1848. His early operas were praised by Berlioz and his 2-act *Érostrate* was perf. at Baden-Baden at same time as *Béatrice et Bénédict* (1862). Planned opera on Nibelungen legends, but postponed project because of work as critic. Championed Berlioz, Wagner, Bizet, Franck, etc. Eventually the Nibelung opera appeared, **Sigurd* (Brussels and CG 1884, Paris 1885). This was followed by *Salammbô*, based on Flaubert's novel (Brussels 1890, Paris 1892, NY Met 1901). Also wrote choral works and songs.

Reynish, Timothy (John) (*b* Axbridge, 1938). Eng. conductor and horn-player. Prin. hn. with Northern Sinfonia, SW, and CBSO, 1959–71. Guest cond. leading Brit. orchs. 3rd prize Mitropoulos comp., NY, 1971. Head of sch. of wind and percussion, RNCM, 1977–2001.

Reynolds, Anna (*b* Canterbury, 1931). Eng. mezzo-soprano. Opera début at Parma 1960 (Suzuki in *Madama Butterfly*). Débuts: Glyndebourne 1962; CG 1967; NY Met 1968; Salzburg Easter Fest. 1970; Bayreuth 1970. Also sang at La Scala and in Rome and Aix-en-Provence. Notable Angel in Elgar's *The Dream of Gerontius*.

Rezniček, Emil Nikolaus von (*b* Vienna, 1860; *d* Berlin, 1945). Austrian composer and conductor. Cond. of various military bands and th. orchs. House composer, Ger. Opera House, Prague, 1885–8. Military bandmaster, Prague 1888–95. Court cond. Mannheim 1896–9. Settled in Berlin 1902, founding series of orch. concerts and teaching at Klindworth-Scharwenka Cons. from 1906. Mus. dir. Warsaw Phil. and Imperial Opera 1907–9. Returned to Berlin as cond., Komische Oper 1909–11. Taught at Hochschule 1920–6. Visited London 1907 and cond. f.p. of *Harnham Down* by Vaughan Williams. Wrote several operas incl. **Donna Diana* (1894, rev. 1908, 1933) and *Till Eulenspiegel* (1902), requiem, 4 syms., vn. conc., and other orch. works, 3 str. qts., pf. pieces.

rf, rfz. = **rinforzando*.

R.H. Right Hand.

rhapsody. Strictly, from the ancient Gr. usage, the recitation of parts of an epic poem. In mus. the term has come to mean a comp. in one continuous movt., often based on popular, nat., or folk melodies. Thus Liszt's *Hungarian Rhapsodies*, Stanford's *Irish Rhapsodies*, Vaughan Williams's *Norfolk Rhapsody*. Delius's *Brigg Fair*, variations on an Eng. folk-song, is subtitled *An English Rhapsody*, and Rachmaninov's variations on a caprice by Paganini are called **Rhapsody on a Theme of Paganini*. Brahms used the term for works for solo pf. and for his *Alto Rhapsody*, a setting for v., male

ch., and orch. of verses by Goethe. Gershwin used the term for his **Rhapsody in Blue* and Chabrier's *España* is a Sp. rhapsody.

Rhapsody in Blue. Work for pf. and orch. by **Gershwin, among first to combine jazz with symphonic procedures. Comp. Jan. 1924. Orch. by **Grofé. F.p. NY 12 Feb. 1924, Gershwin (pf.) and Paul Whiteman's Orch. Gershwin cut 48 measures after f.p. Grofé re-orch. work in 1926 and 1942, each time for larger orch. The 1942 vers. for sym. orch. is most often used.

Rhapsody on a Theme of Paganini. Work for pf. and orch. by Rachmaninov, Op.43, comp. and f.p. 1934 (Baltimore), f.p. in Eng., Manchester 1935. Contains 24 variations on Paganini's violin Caprice No.24 in A minor.

Rheinberger, Josef (Gabriel) (*b* Vaduz, Liechtenstein, 1839; *d* Munich, 1901). Ger. organist, pianist, conductor, and composer. Org. at Vaduz church at age 7. Taught at Munich Cons. 1859–65 and 1867–1901. Org., St Michael's, Munich, 1860–6, choral cond. in Munich and coach at court opera. Prolific composer of operas, syms., chamber mus., and choral works but remembered almost exclusively through his elaborate and challenging organ comps. which incl. 2 concs., 20 sonatas, 22 trios, 12 *Meditations*, 24 fughettos, and 36 solo pieces.

Rheingold, Das (The Rhine Gold). Prol. in 1 act by Wagner, to his own lib., to his tetralogy *Der *Ring des Nibelungen*. Comp. 1853–4. Prod. separately Munich 1869, London 1882, NY Met 1889; first prod. as part of *The Ring*, Bayreuth 1876.

'Rhenish' Symphony. Name given to **Schumann's Sym. No.3 in E♭ major (No.4 in order of comp.), comp. 1850, f.p. 1851. The 4th of its 5 movts. was inspired by the installation of a cardinal at Cologne on the Rhine.

Rhosymedre (Lovely). Hymn-tune by J. D. Edwards (1805–85), on which Vaughan Williams based the 2nd of his *3 Preludes* for org., founded on Welsh hymn-tunes, 1920.

rhythm (in the full sense of the word) covers everything pertaining to the *time* aspect of mus. as distinct from the aspect of pitch, i.e. it incl. the effects of beats, accents, measures, grouping of notes into beats, grouping of beats into measures, grouping of measures into phrases, etc. When all these factors are judiciously treated by the performer (with due regularity yet with artistic purpose—an effect of forward movt.—and not mere machine-like accuracy) we feel and say that the performer possesses 'a sense of rhythm'. There may be 'free' or 'strict' rhythm.

The human ear seems to demand the perceptible presence of a unit of time (the *beat*); even in the 'free rhythm' of **plainsong this can be felt, though in such mus. the grouping into measures is not present.

Apart from such mus. as that just mentioned it will be found that the beats fall into regular groups of 2s or 3s, or of combinations of these (as a group of 4 made up of 2+2, or a group of 6 made up of 3+3). Such groups or combinations of groups are indicated in our notation by the drawing of bar-lines at regular intervals, so dividing the mus. into *measures* (or 'bars'). The measures, in their turn, can be felt to build up into larger groups, or *phrases* (4 measures to a phrase being a very common but not invariable combination; cf. *phrase*).

It is chiefly *accent* that defines these groupings, e.g. taking the larger groupings, a 4-measure phrase is normally accentuated something like this:

(musical notation example in 2/4)

and if the beats are in any part of the music subdivided into what we may call shorter beat-units sub-accentuations are felt, as

(musical notation example in 2/4)

Where the measures have 3 beats an accented note is followed by 2 unaccented:

(musical notation example in 3/4)

and similarly in a 3-measure phrase the first measure will be more heavily accentuated than the 2 following measures

(musical notation example in 2/4)

It will be seen, then, that what we may call the official beat-unit of a composition is a convention, there being often present smaller units and always present larger units, both of which may be considered beats. Another example of *free rhythm* may be seen in much of the choral mus. of the polyphonic period (madrigals, motets, etc.): these may be said (in literary terms) to be in 'prose rhythm', as opposed to the 'verse rhythm' of most tunes for marching and dancing.

Just as the traditional conception of tonality dissolved at the beginning of the 20th cent., so the organization of rhythm became more elaborate, irregular, and surprising. It can be divided into 2 categories: (1) *metrical*, with irregular groups of short units, (2) *non-metrical*, where there is no perceptible unit of measurement and no 'traditional' tempo. Metrical rhythms predominated at the start of the century, but the different uses possible are illustrated by the contrast between Schoenberg's works *c.*1908–15, where constantly changing tempi and freer use of changing time signatures make the rhythmic structure highly complex, and Stravinsky's of the same period, where there are similar constant changes of time signature but the irregularities are much more clearly defined. *Syncopation* has also invaded all types of mus. Although syncopated rhythm can be found in the earliest music, in the 20th cent. it has stemmed mainly from jazz.

Non-metrical rhythm can be discerned in Wagner and its possibilities were outlined by Busoni, who wrote of the tense silence between movts. being in itself mus. and more 'elastic' than sound. *Messiaen in the late 1930s developed 'ametrical' rhythm and described in a treatise (1944) that the techniques he used were 'augmented or diminished rhythms', 'retrograde' rhythms, and 'polyrhythm'. From 1940 composers such as *Babbitt, *Boulez, and Messiaen himself developed these tendencies, though some find the results 'static' rather than conveying the sense of impetus which is the function of rhythm. Further revolutionary attitudes to rhythm have developed since the 1950s, with the increasing use of *indeterminacy. Composers such as *Cage, *Stockhausen, *Carter, and *Xenakis have written works which leave the choice of duration and tempo to the performer. With the introduction of elec. and scientific techniques into comp., there seems no limit to the expansion and intricacy of rhythmic procedures in mus.

rhythmicon. Kbd. perc. instr. using photo-electric cell and developed by Theremin and the Amer. composer *Cowell in 1931 in order to demonstrate the combination of complex rhythms. Cowell wrote his *Rhythmicana* for it.

ribible or **rubible.** The *rebec*.

Ricci, Federico (*b* Naples, 1809; *d* Conegliano, 1877). It. composer. Choirmaster, imperial theatres of St Petersburg 1853–69. Comp. 19 operas, some in collab. with his brother Luigi *Ricci. One of his solo efforts was *La Prigione di Edimburgo* (1838, based on Scott's *The Heart of Midlothian*, 1818). Also wrote masses and cantatas.

Ricci, Luigi (*b* Naples, 1805; *d* Prague, 1859). It. composer. From 1836 choirmaster of Trieste Cath. Cond. f.p. of Verdi's *Il corsaro*, Trieste 1848. Wrote some 30 operas, some in collab. with his brother Federico *Ricci, incl. *Crispino e la comare* (Venice 1850, Wexford 1979), also masses, songs, etc.

Ricci, Ruggiero (*b* San Francisco, 1918). Amer. violinist. Début S. Francisco at age 10, NY 1929, London 1932. Brilliant int. career. Interpreter of many contemporary concs., such as those by *Ginastera (1963), written for him, Einem, and Schurmann. Special interest in Paganini, whose rediscovered 4th conc. he introduced in 1971. First to record the *24 Caprices* in their orig. form. Salzburg Fest. 1990. Teacher at Juilliard Sch. from 1975.

Ricciarelli, Katia (*b* Rovigo, 1946). It. soprano. Opera début Mantua 1969 (Mimì in *La bohème*). Won Parma comp. 1970. Leading roles in It. opera at world's greatest opera houses. Débuts:

Amer. (Chicago) 1972; CG 1974; NY Met 1975; Salzburg Fest. 1979. Has sung several Rossini roles at Pesaro.

ricercare (ricercar, ricercata) (It., Eng. 'research', Fr. 'recherché'). To seek out. As noun, applied musically in 16th to 18th cents. to (*a*) an elaborate contrapuntal instr. comp. in fugal or canonic style (a famous example being that by Bach in *Das musikalische Opfer*), and (*b*) more loosely to any type of prelude (usually contrapuntal in style).

ricercata (It., past participle of verb *ricercare*, and used as a noun in same sense). See *ricercare*.

Richard III. Play by Shakespeare (1593) for which incidental mus. was composed by Edward *German (1889). Mus. for film of play comp. by *Walton, 1955. Sym.-poem by Smetana, 1858. The nickname 'Richard III' was given to the young Richard Strauss in Ger., indicating that although he was regarded as a successor to Wagner, there could be no Richard II.

Richard Cœur de Lion (Richard the Lionhearted). Opera in 3 acts by *Grétry to lib. by M. J. Sedaine. Prod. Paris 1784, London 1786, Boston 1797. (Rev. in 4 acts Fontainebleau 1785.) Beethoven comp. *8 Vars. on the Romance 'Un fièvre brûlante' from 'Richard Cœur de Lion'*, for pf., *c.*1795 (WoO 72).

Richards, Nansi (*b* Pen-y-bont-fawr, Montgomeryshire, 1888; *d* Pen-y-bont-fawr, 1979). Welsh harpist known as 'The Harpist of Montgomery'. Frequently perf. at *eisteddfodau. Created 'Royal Harpist' at investiture of Prince of Wales, 1911. Toured USA 1924. Annual schol. in her memory awarded to young Welsh harpist.

richettato (It.). Same as *spiccato.

Richter, Hans [Johann] (Baptist Isidor) (*b* Raab (now Györ), Hung., 1843; *d* Bayreuth, 1916). Austro-Hung. conductor. Choirboy in Vienna Court Chapel. Hn.-player, Kärntnerthor Th., Vienna, 1862–6. Worked with Wagner at Tribschen, 1866–7, making fair copy of score of *Die Meistersinger*. Recommended by Wagner to Bülow as chorusmaster, Munich Opera, 1868–9. Cond. Brussels première of *Lohengrin*, 1870. Cond., Budapest Opera 1871–5, 1st Kapellmeister Vienna Opera 1875–1900. Imperial Court Cond. 1893–1900. Cond. Vienna PO 1875–82, 1883–98; and dir., Musikfreunde Gesellschaft 1884–90. Chosen by Wagner to conduct first complete *Ring*, Bayreuth 1876. Went to London as co-cond. with Wagner 1877, thereafter giving annual series of Richter Concerts in London 1879–1902. London opera début, Drury Lane 1882 (f.ps. in England of *Tristan* and *Meistersinger*), CG (Theatre Royal) 1884 and 1903–10 (cond. first *Ring* sung in English, 1908). Permanent cond. Hallé Orch., Manchester, 1899–1911. Prin. cond. LSO, 1904–11. Cond. Birmingham Fest. 1885–1909 (incl. f.p. of Elgar's *The Dream of Gerontius* 1900). Champion of Elgar, also cond. f.ps. of *Enigma Variations* (1899) and 1st

Sym. (1908, ded. to him). Cond. f.p. of Brahms's 2nd and 3rd Syms. and Bruckner's 8th. Retired 1912, last appearance as cond. of *Meistersinger* at Bayreuth. Championed several Eng. composers besides Elgar and during his Hallé years introduced mus. of Bartók and Sibelius. Organized and rehearsed private orch. for f.p. of Wagner's *Siegfried Idyll* on staircase at Tribschen, 1870, playing tpt. (not hn., as often stated).

Richter, Karl (*b* Plauen, 1926; *d* Munich, 1981). Ger. organist, harpsichordist, and conductor. Org., Thomaskirche, Leipzig, 1947–50. Joined staff of Munich Acad., 1951, becoming prof., 1956. Founder-cond. Munich Bach Choir (performed at Salzburg Fest. 1970). Amer. début NY 1965. Specialist in Bach.

Richter, Svyatoslav (Teofilovich) (*b* Zhitomir, 1915; *d* Moscow, 1997). Russ. pianist. Boy prodigy. Répétiteur Odessa Opera 1930, ass. cond. 1933. Début as pianist, Odessa 1934. Of exceptional virtuosity, he soon won int. recognition. Specialist in works of Prokofiev, giving f.ps. of 6th, 7th, and 9th pf. sonatas and conducting f.p. of *Symphony-Concerto* for vc. and orch. (1952, *Rostropovich soloist). London début 1961; Amer. début Chicago and NY 1960–1. Salzburg Fest. début 1964. Equally impressive in concs., solo recitals, and chamber mus. Played at Aldeburgh Fest. in assoc. with *Britten and Rostropovich.

Richter-Haaser, Hans (*b* Dresden, 1912; *d* Brunswick, 1980). Ger. pianist, conductor, and composer. Début Dresden 1928. Cond. Detmold Orch., 1945–7. Prof. of pf., N.W. Ger. Mus. Acad. 1947–62. Amer. début 1959. Salzburg Fest. 1963. Frequent world tours as pianist. Composer of sym., pf. concs., and other works.

Rickenbacher, Karl Anton (*b* Basle, 1940). Swiss conductor. Début RIAS, Berlin. Ass. cond., Zurich Opera, 1966–9. Cond., Freiburg Opera 1969–74. Cond., BBC Scottish SO 1977–80. Guest cond. of leading European orchs.

Ricketts, Frederick Joseph. See *Alford, Kenneth J.*

Ricordi. It. (orig. Sp.) family of music publishers, founded in Milan 1808. Pubd. operas and other works of Bellini, Rossini, and Donizetti. Under Giulio Ricordi (1840–1912), the firm prospered, especially through his championship of and friendship with Verdi, and later Puccini. Succeeded by his son Tito (1865–1933). London branch est. 1824–8, re-est. 1875; Paris 1888; NY 1911 (now closed).

Ridderbusch, Karl (*b* Recklinghausen, 1932; *d* Wels, Austria, 1997). Ger. bass. Opera débuts: Münster 1961; Essen 1962; Düsseldorf 1965; Bayreuth 1967; Vienna 1968; Salzburg Easter Fest. 1968; NY Met 1967; CG 1971. Leading exponent of Wagnerian bass roles, also in choral works by Mozart, Beethoven, etc.

Riddle, Frederick (Craig) (*b* Liverpool, 1912; *d* Newport, IoW, 1995). Eng. violist. On staff RCM.

LSO 1933–8, LPO 1938–52, RPO from 1953. Fine player of Walton conc., of which he made first recording (1937). Prof. of va., RMCM, 1964. OBE 1980.

Riders to the Sea. (1) Opera in 1 act by Vaughan Williams, being an almost verbatim setting of J. M. Synge's play (1904). Comp. 1925–32. Prod. London (RCM) 1937, Cambridge 1938, Cleveland, Ohio, 1950, SW 1953, Naples 1959.
   (2) Opera in 1 act, under title *L'Appel de la mer*, by *Rabaud, based on Synge's play, prod. Paris 1924.

Ridout, Alan (John) (*b* West Wickham, Kent, 1934; *d* Caen, France, 1996). Eng. composer. Lect., Cambridge Univ., 1963–75, prof. RCM 1961–84. Works incl. several operas, 6 syms., *Christmas Oratorio*, chamber mus., song-cycles, etc.

Ridout, Godfrey (*b* Toronto, 1918; *d* Toronto, 1984). Canadian composer. Teacher at Toronto Univ. 1948–82, becoming senior prof., and at Toronto Cons. 1940–82. Works incl. *Esther* (dramatic sym.); *Cantiones mysticae*, No.1 for sop. and orch., No.2 for sop., tpt., str.; chamber mus.; songs.

Riefling, Robert (*b* Oslo, 1911; *d* Oslo, 1988). Norweg. pianist. Début Oslo 1925. Prof., Royal Danish Cons., Copenhagen, 1967–73, Norwegian Mus. H.S., Oslo, from 1973. Many tours of Europe and USA. Specialist in contemporary Scandinavian works by Valen, Saeverud, etc.

Riegel, Kenneth (*b* Womelsdorf, Pa., 1938). Amer. tenor. Début 1965, Santa Fe (Alchemist in *König Hirsch*). NY City Opera 1969–74; NY Met début 1973. Sang Alwa in f.p. of 3-act *Lulu*, Paris 1979, title-role in *Der *Zwerg*, Hamburg 1981, the Leper in f.p. of *Saint François d'Assise*, Paris 1983. CG début 1985; Salzburg Fest. début 1975.

Riegger, Wallingford (Constantin) (*b* Albany, Georgia, 1885; *d* NY, 1961). Amer. composer and conductor. As boy learned vn. and vc. Cond. début with Blüthner Orch., 1910. Returned to USA as cellist in St Paul SO, Minnesota. Returned to Ger., 1913–17, as opera cond. and cond. of sym. concerts. On return to USA he held teaching posts at various univs. until settling in NY, 1923. Wrote several scores for Amer. choreographers, 1930–41. Under several pseudonyms made hundreds of arrs. of various kinds of choral mus. to supplement income. Began composing in a 19th-cent. style; but under influence of the Schoenberg 12-note method became more adventurous. His use of atonality was always individual. Strong rhythmic drive and contrapuntal forms also characterize his mus. Prin. works:

ORCH.: syms.: No.1 (1944, withdrawn), No.2 (1945, withdrawn), No.3 (1946–7), No.4 (1956); *Dichotomy* (1931–2); *Little Black Sambo* (1946); *Music for Orchestra* (1951); *Festival Overture* (1957); *Sinfonietta* (1959); *Duo*, pf., orch. (1960).

DANCE: *Bacchanale* (1930); *Evocation* (1933); *New Dance* (1935); *Candide* (1937); *Case History No . . .* (1937); *Pilgrim's Progress* (1941).

SOLOIST WITH ORCH.: *Variations*, pf., orch. (1952–3); *Variations*, vn., orch. (1959); *Introduction and Fugue*, vc., wind (1960); conc., pf., ww. quintet (1953).

VOCAL: *La Belle Dame sans merci* (1923); *From Some Far Shore* (1946); *The Dying of the Light* (1954); *Who Can Revoke?* (1948).

CHAMBER MUSIC: str. qts.: No.1 (1938–9), No.2 (1948), No.3 (1945–7); *Romanza* for str. qt. (1954); pf. quintet (1951); pf. trio (1930); vn. sonatina (1947); woodwind quintet (1952).

PIANO: *Blue Voyage* (1927); *4 Tone Pictures* (1932); *New and Old* (1944).

Riemann, (Karl Wilhelm Julius) **Hugo** (*b* Gross-Mehlra, 1849; *d* Leipzig, 1919). Ger. musicologist, teacher, and composer. Lect. on mus., Leipzig Univ. 1878. Taught pf., etc., Hamburg Cons. 1881–90, Wiesbaden Cons., 1890–5. Returned to Leipzig 1895, prof. from 1901. Dir., Inst. of Mus. Science 1908. Extremely prolific scholar and ed. of many learned symposiums, etc., trans. many scholarly works. Prin. achievement was his *Musiklexikon* (dictionary of mus.) (1882 and subsequent edns.). Comp. 2 str. qts. and other chamber works.

Rienzi (orig. *Cola Rienzi, der letzte der Tribunen*, Cola Rienzi, the last of the Tribunes). Opera in 5 acts by Wagner to his own lib. based on Bulwer-Lytton's novel (1835) and Mary Russell Mitford's play (1828). Comp. 1838–40. Prod. Dresden 1842, NY 1878, London (in Eng.) 1879.

Ries, Ferdinand (*b* Bonn, 1784; *d* Frankfurt, 1838). Ger. pianist, composer, and conductor, son of Franz Anton *Ries. Pupil of his father and of Beethoven in Vienna 1801–5. Toured Europe and Scandinavia as pianist. Lived in London 1813–24 as pianist and teacher. Worked in Ger., esp. Frankfurt and Aachen, from 1824. Cond. at 8 of Lower Rhine fests. 1825–37. With Wegeler, wrote *Biographical Notices of Beethoven*, 1838. Comp. 3 operas (incl. *Die Räuberbraut*, 1828); 2 oratorios; 18 syms.; 9 pf. concs.; 26 str. qts.; 128 vn. sonatas; 14 pf. sonatas, etc.

Ries, Franz Anton (*b* Bonn, 1755; *d* Godesberg, 1846). Ger. violinist. Leader of Bonn electoral court orch. 1779–94. Friend and teacher of Beethoven. Attended unveiling of Beethoven statue in Bonn, 1845, at age of 89.

Ries, Hubert (*b* Bonn, 1802; *d* Berlin, 1886). Ger. violinist and teacher. Son and pupil of Franz Anton *Ries, also pupil of *Spohr. Settled in Berlin 1824. In court orch. from 1825 (leader 1836). Dir. of Phil. Soc. 1835. Taught at Royal Orch. Sch. 1851–72. Wrote vn. sch., 2 vn. concs., and other works.

Rieti, Vittorio (*b* Alexandria, Egypt, 1898; *d* NY, 1994). It.-born composer (Amer. cit. 1944). Lived in Paris from 1925. Wrote ballets for Diaghilev and mus. for plays and films of Louis Jouvet.

Settled in USA 1940. Taught at various Amer. colleges. Works, often influenced by Stravinsky and Les *Six, incl. 17 ballets; 7 operas; 8 syms.; 3 pf. concs.; 2-pf. conc.; hpd. conc.; 2 vc. concs.; triple conc. (pf., vn., va.); 5 str. qts.; woodwind quintet; pf. pieces; and songs.

Rietz, Julius (*b* Berlin, 1812; *d* Dresden, 1877). Ger. cellist, composer, and conductor. In Berlin th. orch. from 1828; ass. cond. to Mendelssohn at Düsseldorf Opera in 1834, succeeding him 1835. Cond. Leipzig Opera 1847–54, dir. Gewandhaus concerts and teacher of comp., Leipzig Cons., 1848–60. Court cond. Dresden from 1860, also dir., Dresden Cons. from 1870. Wrote 3 operas; operetta; 3 syms.; 4 concs.; *Konzertstück* for ob.; str. qt., etc. Ed. complete works of Mendelssohn.

riff. Jazz term meaning a short, repetitive, but not improvised, instr. passage, e.g. the beginning of *In the Mood*.

Rifkin, Joshua (*b* NY, 1944). Amer. musicologist, composer, and conductor. Worked for Nonesuch Records, NY, 1964–75. Taught at Brandeis Univ. 1970–82. Founder and dir., Bach Ens. from 1978. Researched early perf. practice of Bach and also contrib., both as scholar and performer, to revival of interest in Scott *Joplin.

rigaudon (Fr.), **rigadoon** (Old Eng.). Ancient Provençal type of dance, in simple duple or quadruple time, similar to the *bourrée. Rameau used the rigaudon in nearly all his operas and there are 2 in Fux's *Concentus musicus* (1701). It occurs in suites by Couperin, Lalande, Telemann, Muffat, and others. Also used by Grieg in *Holberg Suite* (1884), Saint-Saëns, MacDowell, and by Ravel in *Le Tombeau de Couperin*.

Rigby, Jean (*b* Fleetwood, 1954). Eng. mezzosoprano. Won ENO young artists. comp. 1981. Member of ENO from 1982 (début as Mercédès in *Carmen*). CG début 1983; Glyndebourne 1985. Created Eurydice in The *Mask of Orpheus*, ENO 1986.

Righini, Vincenzo (*b* Bologna, 1756; *d* Bologna, 1812). It composer, teacher, and conductor. Début as ten. in Parma 1775. Joined opera co. in Prague 1776, composing *Il Convitato di Pietra* (*Don Giovanni*) for it (Haydn later cond. it at Eszterháza.) Dir., It. Opera in Vienna from 1780. In much demand as singing teacher. Kapellmeister, Mainz electoral court 1787–93. Comp. oratorio *Der Tod Jesu* at this time, also highly praised *Missa Solemnis* (1790), the latter perf. at Coronation of Leopold II in Frankfurt. Court cond. and dir. of It. Opera, Berlin, 1793–1806. His operas incl. a setting of Goldoni's *La Vedova Scaltra* (1778), later set by Wolf-Ferrari (1931). Beethoven comp. 24 vars. for pf. on Righini's arietta *Venni amore* in 1790–1 (WoO 65).

Rigoletto. Opera in 3 acts by Verdi to lib. by Piave based on V. Hugo's play *Le Roi s'amuse*

(1832). Orig. title was *La maledizione* (The Curse). Comp. 1850–1. Prod. Venice 1851, London 1853, NY 1855.

Rig Veda (Holst). See *Hymns from the Rig Veda*.

Rihm, Wolfgang (*b* Karlsruhe, 1952). Ger. composer. Studied with Stockhausen 1973 and Huber 1974. Lect. at Karlsruhe Musikhochschule from 1973 (head of its Institute for Modern Music). Works incl.:

STAGE: operas *Faust und Yorick* (1976) and *Jakob Lenz* (1978); music theatre: *Die Hamletmaschine* (1986), *Oedipus* (1986–7), and *Die Eroberung von Mexico* (1987–9); ballet *Tutuguri* (1981–2); *Séraphin* (1993–4).

ORCH.: Syms.: No.1 (1969), No.2 (1975), No.3, sop., bar., ch., orch. (1976–7); pf. conc. (1969); *Lichtzwang*, vn., orch. (1975–6); va. conc. (1979–83); *Abgesangsszene I* (1979), *V* (1979); *Brahmsliebewalzer* (1979–88); *Walzer I*, *Sehnsuchtwalzer* (1979–81), *II, Drängender Walzer* (1986–7); *Klangbeschreibung I*, 2 orch. groups (1982–7), *III* (1984–7); *Dunkles Spiel*, small orch. (1988–90); *Passim* (1989); *Umfassung*, orch. in 2 groups (1990); *La lugubre gondola/Das Eismeer*, 2 orch. groups, pf. (1990–2); *Music for Oboe and Orch.* (1993, rev. 1995); *Form*, 4 ens. (1993–4); *Styx und Lethe*, vc., orch. (1997–8); *Sotto voce*, pf., orch. (1999); *Concerto*, str. qt., orch. (2000); *Verwandlung*, orch. (2002); *2 Other Movements*, orch. (2004).

SOLO VOICE(S) & ORCH. or ENS.: *Sicut cervus desiderat ad fontes aquarum*, sop., ens. (1970); Sym. No.3, sop., bar., ch., orch. (1976–7); *Abgesangsszene II*, bar., orch. (1979–80), *V*, mez., bar., orch. (1979–81); *Andere Schatten*, sop., mez., bar., narr., ch., orch. (1985); *Frau/Stimme*, sop., orch. with sop. (1989); *O meine Seele war ein Wald*, mez., alt., hp., va., vc., db. (1994); *Lied*, middle v., small orch. (1997); *Stilles Stück*, bar., 2 str. qts. (2000); *Bildnis: Anakreon*, ten., cl., hp., vc., pf. (2004).

INSTR. ENS.: *Music-Hall Suite*, cl., 2 sax., tpt., perc., pf., vn., db. (1979); *Chiffre I*, pf., 7 instr. (1982), *III*, 12 players (1983), *IV*, bass cl., dbn., hn., 2 vn., va., vc., db. (1983–4), *VI*, 8 players (1985–6); *Figur*, hp., 4 tb., perc. (1989); *Cantus firmus*, 14 players (1990); *Étude pour Séraphin*, 2 ten. tb., 2 bass tb., 4 bass tubas, 6 perc. players (1991–2).

CHORUS & ORCH. or ENS.: *Hölderlin-Fragmente*, ch., orch. (1977); *Lowry-Lieder*, ch., orch. (1982–7); '*Was aber . . .*', 2 women's vv., orch. (1986); *Départ*, ch., narr., 22 players (1988); *Engel*, 2 male vv., 20 instr. (1989); *Maximum est unum*, 4 sop., alt., 2 ch., org., orch. (1996); *Deus passus (St Luke Passion)*, SMATB soloists, ch., orch. (1999–2000); *Astralis*, small ch., vc., 2 timp. (2001); *Memoria*, boy sop., alt., ch., orch. (1994–2004).

CHAMBER MUSIC: str. qts.: No.1 (1968), No.2 (1970), No.3 (1976), No.4 (1979–81), No.5 (1983), No.6 (1984), No.7 (1985), No.8 (1988), No.9 (1993), No.10 (1997), No.11 (2003–4), No.12 (2000–1); pf. trio (1981); *Fremde Szene I*, vn., vc., pf. (1982), *II* (*Charackterstück*), vn., vc., pf. (1983); *III*, vn., vc., pf. (1983); *Protokoll, ein Traum*, 6 vc. (1987); *Am Horizont*, vn., vc., acc. (1991); *Antlitz*, vn., pf.

(1993); *Über die Linie*, vc. (1999); *Vier Male*, cl. (2000); wind quintet, fl., ob., cl., hn., bn. (2003); *En plein air*, fl., cl., hp., str. qt. (2004).

VOICE & PIANO: *4 Songs of Paul Celan* (1973); *Wölfli-Liederbuch* (1980–1); *Apokryph*, bar., pf. (1997); *Nebendraussen*, v., pf. (1998); *3 Hölderlin Songs*, sop.,/ten., pf., (2004).

KEYBOARD: *2 Fantasies*, org. (1967); *Klavierstück* Nos.4–7 (1974–80); *Ländler*, pf. (1979); *'Bann, Nachtschwärmerei'*, org. (1980); *Maske*, 2 pf. (1985); *Nachstudie*, pf. (1992–4); *Auf einem anderen Blatt*, pf. (2000); *Über-Schrift*, 2 pf. (1992–2003).

Riisager, Knudåge (*b* Port Kunda, Estonia, 1897; *d* Copenhagen, 1974). Danish composer. Worked in Danish Finance Ministry 1925–50. Dir., Royal Danish Cons. 1956–67. Leader of Denmark's progressive composers and noted ballet composer. Wrote 5 syms. (1925–50), 6 str. qts. (1918–43), pf. sonatas, sinfonietta, syms. for str., etc. Best-known of 14 ballets are: *Land of Milk and Honey* (1942), *Qarrtsiluni* (1942), *The Phoenix* (1946), *Étude* (1948), and *The Lady from the Sea* (1960).

Riley, Terry (Mitchell) (*b* Colfax, Calif., 1935). Amer. composer and saxophonist. Frequent tours of Europe as perf. of his own works, which 'take the form of charts of repeated patterns and series, which must assume a form during rehearsal and performance'. Assoc. prof., Mills Coll., Oaklands, Calif., 1971–80. Has comp. many works for *Kronos Qt., incl. 13 str. qts., *The Sands*, conc. for str. qt. (1991), and *The Cusp of Magic*, str. qt., pipa (2004).

Rilling, Helmuth (*b* Stuttgart, 1933). Ger. organist, conductor, and teacher. Founded Gächinger Kantorei 1954 and toured Eur., Asia, N. and S. Amer. London début as org. 1963. Founded Bach-Collegium of Stuttgart 1965 (US tour 1968). Salzburg Fest. cond. début 1987 (choral concert). Prof., Frankfurt Hochschule für Mus. from 1969.

Rimsky-Korsakov, Nikolay (Andreyevich) (*b* Tikhvin, 1844; *d* Lyubensk, 1908). Russ. composer and cond. Born into aristocratic family and had conventional mus. education. Ambition to be sailor; entered Corps of Naval Cadets 1856 in St Petersburg, where he had pf. lessons and attended opera and concerts. Nationalist works of Glinka deeply impressed him and he met and was influenced by Balakirev. Wrote part of a sym., though ignorant of names of chords and of rules of part-writing. Away at sea 1862–5. Completed sym. 1865, first of importance by Russ. composer. In 1865–8 wrote *Sadko* and *Antar*, both later rev. In 1869 was entrusted with completion of Dargomyzhsky's opera *The Stone Guest* and in 1872 completed his own opera *The Maid of Pskov*. In 1871, while still a naval lieutenant and still unlearned in harmony and counterpoint, was appointed prof. of practical comp. and instrumentation, St Petersburg Cons. Taught himself in secret. Inspector of Naval Bands, 1873–84. For several years as part of his self-education

prod. 'academic' comps. incl. str. qt., pf. quintet, pf. fugues, etc. His editing of *100 Russian Folk-Songs*, 1876–7, led him to a new, more attractive phase in his own works, incl. the operas *May Night* and *Snegurochka* (The Snow Maiden). From 1874–81 was dir. of the Free School of Mus. After 1882 much occupied with administration, cond., and rev. and orchestration of *Khovanshchina* and other works by *Mussorgsky. When Borodin died in 1887, completion and orch. of *Prince Igor* was undertaken by Rimsky-Korsakov and his pupil *Glazunov. Rimsky interrupted this to write 2 of his most colourful works, the *Spanish Caprice* and *Sheherazade*. Thereafter, influenced by the first Russ. perfs. in 1888–9 of Wagner's *Ring*, devoted himself to opera. For a time, neurasthenic illness robbed him of the will to work, but he resumed creative work in the 1890s and in 1896 made his version of Mussorgsky's *Boris Godunov* which, though it is now partly discredited, preserved this opera until scholars restored the composer's orig. In 1905, having shown sympathy with revolutionary students, was temporarily removed from his professorship at St Petersburg Cons. and a 2-month ban imposed on perf. of his works. This clash with authority is reflected in his last and satirical opera, *The Golden Cockerel*, which was banned by the govt. and not prod. until after his death. In 1906, rev. *Boris Godunov*, and in 1907 cond. in Paris at Diaghilev's concerts of Russ. mus.

Less talented than his colleagues in the nationalist school, Rimsky-Korsakov excelled them all in the art of clear and colourful orchestration, and to us today his mus. seems to epitomize the brilliance and pageantry of Tsarist Russia. Lately the splendour of his operas has been rediscovered. His influence on his most distinguished pupil, *Stravinsky, can be discerned above all in *The Firebird*. Wrote textbooks on harmony and orchestration, also autobiography. Prin. comps.:

OPERAS: *The *Maid of Pskov (Ivan the Terrible)* (1868–72, rev. 1876–7, rev. 1891–2); *May Night* (1878–9); *Snow Maiden (Snegurochka)* (1880–1, rev. c.1895); *Mlada* (1889–90); *Christmas Eve* (1894–5); *Sadko* (1894–6); *Mozart and Salieri* (1897); *Boyarina Vera Sheloga* (comp. 1876–7 as prol. to *Maid of Pskov*, reconstructed as 1-act opera 1898); *The *Tsar's Bride* (1898); *The *Legend of Tsar Saltan* (1899–1900); *Servilia* (1900–1); *Kashchey the Immortal* (1901–2, rev. 1906); *Pan Voyevoda* (1902–3); *Legend of the *Invisible City of Kitezh and the Maiden Fevronia* (1903–5); *The *Golden Cockerel* (1906–7).

ORCH.: syms.: No.1 in E♭ minor (1861–5, rev. in E minor 1884), No.2 (*Antar*, 1868, rev. 1876 and 1897, symphonic suite 1903), No.3 in C (1866–73, rev. 1885–6); *Overture on 3 Russian Themes* (1866, rev. 1879–80); *Fantasia on Serbian Themes* (1867, reorch. 1886–7); *Sadko*, symphonic picture (1867, rev. 1869, 1891; see also opera); conc., tb., military band (1877); *Sinfonietta on Russian Themes*, str. qt. (1897; rev. and orch. 1880–4); *Skazka* (Legend) (1879–80); pf. conc. (1882–3); *Fantasia on Russian Themes*, vn., orch. (1886);

Spanish Caprice (1887); *Sheherazade* (1888); *Russian Easter Festival Overture* (1888); *Dubinushka* (1905).

CHORAL: *Alexey the Man of God*, ch., orch. (1877); *Svitezyanka*, cantata (1897); *Song of Oleg the Wise*, cantata (1899); *From Homer* (1901).

CHAMBER MUSIC: str. qt. (1875); str. sextet (1876); pf. quintet (pf., wind) (1876); *Allegro* in B♭, str. qt. (1899)

TRANSCRIPTIONS etc.: BORODIN: **Prince Igor*, orch. and completed (with Glazunov), prod. 1890; MUSSORGSKY: **Boris Godunov*, re-orch. 1896, rev. 1906, **Khovanshchina*, rev. and orch. 1882–5; DARGOMYZHSKY: *The *Stone Guest*, orch. and completed 1870–1, rev. 1902.

Also songs, chs., folk-song arrs. and pf. pieces.

Rinaldo. (1) Opera in 3 acts by Handel (his first in Eng.) to lib. by Rossi after sketch by Aaron Hill from Tasso's *Gerusalemme liberata* (1562). Prod. London 1711 (rev. vers. 1731). F. modern ps. London 1933, Halle 1954, Houston 1975, NY Met 1984.

(2) Cantata, Op.50, by Brahms for ten., male ch., and orch. (1863–8).

rinforzando; rinforzato (It.). Reinforcing; reinforced, i.e. stress is applied to individual notes or chords. So *rinforza, rinforzamente*; reinforcement. Abbreviation *rf, rfz*.

Ring des Nibelungen, Der (The Nibelung's Ring). 4 operas (mus. dramas) by Wagner, to his own libs., which he called a 'stage festival for 3 days with a preliminary evening' (*Ein Bühnenfestspiel für drei Tage und einen Vorabend*). The cycle, often referred to as 'the tetralogy', is based on versions of the Scandinavian saga of the Nibelungs involving gods and mortals. Among the characters in the operas are Wotan, Alberich, Siegfried, Mime, Siegmund, Loge, Brünnhilde, Fricka, Hagen, Gutrune, Sieglinde, Freia, Fasolt, Fafner, Donner, and the Valkyries. The 4 operas, with details of their f.ps., are: *Das Rheingold* (The Rhine Gold), prol. in 1 act, comp. 1853–4, prod. Munich 1869, Bayreuth (as part of complete *Ring*) 1876, London 1882, NY 1889; *Die Walküre* (The Valkyrie), 3 acts, comp. 1854–6, prod. Munich 1870, Bayreuth (as part of complete *Ring*) 1876, NY (incomplete) 1877, London 1882; *Siegfried*, 3 acts, comp. 1856–7, 1864–71, prod. Bayreuth (as part of complete *Ring*) 1876, London 1882, NY 1887; *Götterdämmerung* (Twilight of the Gods), 3 acts, comp. 1869–74, prod. Bayreuth (as part of complete *Ring*) 1876, London 1882, NY Met 1888. Writing and comp. of *The Ring* occupied Wagner intermittently from 1848 to 1874.

The 1st complete *Ring* cycle, sung in Ger., at **Bayreuth was cond. Hans Richter on 13, 14, 16, and 17 Aug. 1876. The first cycle to be perf. in London was at Her Majesty's, cond. Anton Seidl, on 5, 6, 7, and 9 May 1882. Seidl also cond. (heavily cut) first cycle at NY Met on 4, 5, 8, and 11 March 1889 (although there had been perfs. of the cycle excluding *Das Rheingold* in 1887–8, also under Seidl). F. uncut Amer. p. 1898–9, cond. Schalk. First CG cycle in June 1892, cond. Mahler, but given out of sequence. First cycle in

Eng. trans. at CG cond. Richter, 1908, and in Brit. provinces by **Denhof Co. in Edinburgh 1910, cond. **Balling (Leeds, Manchester, Glasgow 1911, Hull, Leeds, Liverpool 1912); in Bradford 1933, cond. Robert Ainsworth and A. **Coates. No further perfs. in provinces until Scottish Opera cycle (in Ger.) in Glasgow, Dec. 1971. F.ps. of new Eng. trans. by Andrew Porter for ENO 1970–3, complete cycle, London, July-Aug. 1973.

Rinuccini, Ottavio (*b* Florence, 1563; *d* Florence, 1621). It. poet. Wrote earliest opera libs. for **Peri (*Dafne* and *Euridice*), **Monteverdi (*Arianna*), **Gagliano, and **Caccini.

Rio Grande, The. Work by C. **Lambert for ch., orch., and solo pf., comp. 1927, f.p. BBC broadcast 1928; in public, Manchester 1929. Setting of poem by Sacheverell Sitwell.

ripieno (It., 'filling', or 'stuffing'). Replenished, supplementary. (1) The term is used in older mus. to make a distinction between passages to be played by the full body (*ripieno*) and others to be played by a group of soloists (*concertante* (see *concerto*)). The term is in this sense still used in Eng. brass bands, generally misspelt ripiano or repiano. Also used of boys' vv. in Bach's *St Matthew Passion*.

(2) In It. org. mus., mixture.

Ripley, (Maud) Gladys (*b* Essex, 1908; *d* Chichester, 1955). Eng. contralto, largely self-taught. Leading exponent of oratorio roles and of Angel in Elgar's *Dream of Gerontius*. Also sang in opera.

ripresa (It.; Fr. **reprise*). (1) Repeat, of a section of a comp.

(2) Recapitulation section of a movt. in **sonata form.

(3) Revival, of opera, etc.

Rise and Fall of the City of Mahagonny (*Aufstieg und Fall der Stadt Mahagonny*). Opera in 3 acts by Weill to lib. by Brecht. Comp. 1927–9. Prod. Leipzig 1930, NY 1952, S. Francisco 1972, NY Met 1979, London 1963. Developed from 'Songspiel' *Mahagonny* (1927).

Rising of the Moon, The. Opera in 3 acts by **Maw to lib. by Beverley Cross. Comp. 1967–70, rev. 1970–1. Prod. Glyndebourne 1970, Graz (Ger. trans.) by M. Vogel) 1978, Wexford 1994.

risoluto; risolutamente (It.). Resolute; resolutely. So the superlative *risolutissimo*. **risoluzione**, resolution.

rispetto (It., plural *rispetti*). A type of It. folk-song with 8 lines to the stanza. Title used for mus. by Wolf-Ferrari, Malipiero, and others.

rit. Short for **ritardando*.

ritardando, ritardare, ritardato (It.). Holding back, to hold back, held back (gradually, i.e. same as **rallentando*). Abbreviated to 'rit.' (but see also *ritenuto*). **ritardo** (It.). The act of holding back (i.e. of gradually diminishing the speed).

Ritchie, Margaret [Mabel] (*b* Grimsby, 1903; *d* Ewelme, Oxon., 1969). Eng. soprano. Leading Eng. exponent of Schubert *Lieder*. Sang in opera at SW 1944, Glyndebourne 1946–7, CG, EOG, etc. First to sing wordless sop. role in Vaughan Williams's *Sinfonia Antartica* (1953), also in film mus. (1948). Created Lucia in *The Rape of Lucretia* (1946) and Miss Wordsworth in *Albert Herring* (1947).

ritenuto (It.). Held back, i.e. slower (immediately, not gradually as with *ritardando* and *rallentando*). Sometimes abbreviated to *rit.*, or *riten.* Also *ritenendo*, *ritenente*, holding back.

Rite of Spring, The (*Vesna svyashchennaya* (Spring the sacred), Fr. *Le Sacre du printemps*). Ballet (pictures from pagan Russia) in 2 parts, mus. by Stravinsky, lib. Roerich, choreog. Nijinsky. Comp. 1911–13. Prod. Paris and London 1913, Boston and NY 1924 (concert version). Part I: *The Adoration of the Earth*, Part II: *The Sacrifice*. Arr. for pf. 4 hands by composer, 1913. F.p. (cond. Monteux) on 29 May 1913 at Théâtre des Champs-Elysées was occasion of celebrated riot. F. London concert p. 1921.

ritmo (It.). Rhythm, as in *ritmo di tre battute*, rhythm of 3 measures. **ritmico** (It.). Rhythmic.

ritornel (Fr. *ritournelle*; It. *ritornello*; Ger. *Ritornell*). A return (*ritornello* is a little return). (1) The refrain in 14th- and 15th-cent. madrigal-type comps.

(2) An It. folk-song, each stanza of 3 lines, the last line rhyming with the first.

(3) The repetition of the instr. introduction to a song, and hence also the instr. introduction itself.

(4) In the classical conc., the return of the full orch. after a solo passage, same as *tutti*.

(5) Synonym for *da capo*.

Ritorno d'Ulisse in patria, Il (Ulysses's return to his native land). Opera in prol. and 3 acts by *Monteverdi to lib. by G. Badoaro based on Homer's *Odyssey*. Comp. 1640. Prod. Venice 1640. Revived in fragmentary concert-form Brussels 1925, Paris (d'Indy version) 1925, London (d'Indy version broadcast in Eng.) 1928, Florence (Dallapiccola stage version) 1942, Wuppertal (Krenek edn.) 1959, Vienna (Harnoncourt edn.) 1971, Glyndebourne (Leppard edn.) 1972, Washington 1974, Salzburg 1985 (Henze edn.). F. stage p. in Britain was in London, 1965.

Ritter, Alexander (*b* Narva, Estonia, 1833; *d* Munich, 1896). Ger. violinist, composer, and conductor. Married Wagner's niece Franziska, 1854, and joined Liszt circle at Weimar. Cond., Stettin Opera 1856–8. Worked at theatre in Würzburg 1863–82. Violinist in Meiningen Orch. under Bülow, 1882–6 where he met R. Strauss and influenced him to follow Lisztian precepts. Wrote 2 operas, incl. *Der faule Hans* (1885), 6 sym.-poems, str. qt., etc.

Ritual Dances. 4 dances for ch. and orch. in Tippett's opera *The Midsummer Marriage* which are often played separately as a concert work. Three occur in Act 2: *The Earth in Autumn* (The Hound chases the Hare); *The Waters in Winter* (The Otter pursues the Fish); *The Air in Spring* (The Hawk swoops on the Bird). In Act 3 occurs the 4th dance *Fire in Summer* (celebration of carnal love). Comp. 1947–52. F.p. Basle 1953, Liverpool 1954 (before f.p. of opera).

Ritual Fire Dance. One of dances in Falla's ballet *El *Amor Brujo* popularized in composer's pf. arr. and played with exceptional brilliance by Arthur Rubinstein. Also arr. for other instr., eg. vc.

riverso, al. See *rovescio, al*.

Rizzi, Carlo (*b* Milan, 1958). It. conductor. Début Milan 1982 (Donizetti's *L'Aio nell'imbarrazzo*). Brit. début Buxton Fest. 1988 (Donizetti's *Torquato Tasso*). Australian Opera 1989–90. Brit. concert début London 1989 (RPO). CG début 1990. Mus. dir. WNO 1992–2001 and from 2005. NY Met début 1993.

rk. Rank, with reference to the *mixture stops of an org.

RMCM. *Royal Manchester College of Music.

RNCM. *Royal Northern College of Music, Manchester.

Robbins Landon, H. C. See *Landon, H. C. Robbins*.

Robert le diable (Robert the Devil). Opera in 5 acts by *Meyerbeer to lib. by Scribe and Delavigne. Prod. Paris 1831, London 1832, NY 1834.

Roberto Devereux, ossia Il Conte di Essex. Opera in 3 acts by Donizetti to lib. by Cammarano after Ancelot's play *Elisabeth d'Angleterre*. Comp. 1837. Prod. Naples 1837, London 1841, NY 1849.

Roberton, (Sir) **Hugh** (Stevenson) (*b* Glasgow, 1874; *d* Glasgow, 1952). Scottish chorusmaster. Founder and cond. of Glasgow Orpheus Choir, 1906–51, which made several overseas tours and won innumerable competitions. Choir voluntarily disbanded 1951 when Roberton retired, but was later re-formed by younger members as Glasgow Phoenix Choir, with Sir Hugh as hon. pres. Arr. Scottish folk-songs, etc. Knighted 1931.

Roberts, Bernard (*b* Manchester, 1933). Eng. pianist. Début London 1957. Was member of Parikian-Fleming-Roberts Trio. Prof. of pf. RCM.

Robertson, Alec (*b* Southsea, 1892; *d* Midhurst, 1982). Eng. organist, chorusmaster, critic, and broadcaster. Worked for the Gramophone Co. 1920–30. Head of mus. talks, BBC, 1940–52. Authority on plainchant. Author of monographs and books on Schubert, Dvořák, etc. Ed. of several reference books. Reviewer of records in *Gramophone* for nearly 50 years (its music ed. 1952–72). MBE 1972.

Robertson, James (*b* Liverpool, 1912; *d* Ruabon, N. Wales, 1991). Eng. conductor. Chorusmaster, Carl Rosa Opera 1938–9; on staff Glyndebourne 1937–9; dir. and cond. SW Opera 1946–54; cond. NZ Nat. Broadcasting Orch. 1954–7; Carl Rosa Opera 1958; guest cond. SW Opera 1958–63; mus. dir. NZ Opera 1962–3, 1978–81; dir., London Opera Centre 1964–78. CBE 1969.

Robertson, Leroy (*b* Fountain Green, Utah, 1896; *d* Salt Lake City, 1971). Amer. composer. Taught at Brigham Young Univ. 1925–48, prof. of mus. Utah Univ. 1948–62. Comps. incl. *Punch and Judy Overture* (1945); vn. conc. (1948); pf. conc. (1966); vc. conc. (1966); *The Book of Mormon*, oratorio (1953); str. qt.; pf. quintet, etc.

Robertson, Rae (*b* Ardersier, Inverness, 1893; *d* Los Angeles, 1956). Scottish pianist. Began career as solo pianist but formed famous 2-pf. duo with his wife Ethel *Bartlett and toured world. Britten wrote 3 works for them.

Robeson, Paul (Bustill) (*b* Princeton, NJ, 1898; *d* Philadelphia, 1976). Amer. bass and actor. Studied as lawyer, but in 1922 entered professional th. as actor in O'Neill plays. Won int. renown in Kern's musical *Show Boat* (1927) when he sang 'Ol' Man River'. Famous as singer of Negro spirituals. Appeared in films (*Sanders of the River*, etc.) and was a notable Othello. Career halted in 1950s when he fell into disfavour in USA because of alleged Communist sympathies.

Robinson, Christopher (John) (*b* Peterborough, 1936). Eng. organist and conductor. Ass. org., Ch. Ch. Cath., Oxford, 1955–8, New Coll., Oxford, 1957–8; mus. master Oundle Sch. 1959–62; ass. org. Worcester Cath. 1962–3, org. 1963–74. Cond., Oxford Bach Choir 1977, Leith Hill Mus. Fest. 1977–80. Org. and dir. of mus., St John's Coll., Cambridge,1991–2003. Org. and Master of Choristers, St George's Chapel, Windsor. CBE 2004.

Robinson, Faye (*b* Houston, 1943). Amer. soprano. Won 1st prize in S. Francisco Opera auditions. Début NY City Opera 1972 (Micaela in *Carmen*). Opera appearances throughout Eur. and USA. Paris Opéra début 1982. Soloist in f.p. of *The *Mask of Time*, Boston 1984.

Robinson, Forbes (*b* Macclesfield, 1926; *d* London, 1987). Eng. bass. Opera début CG 1954 (Monterone in *Rigoletto*). Prin. bass, CG. Created title-role in *King Priam*, 1962. Took speaking part of Moses in *Moses und Aron*, 1965. Guest singer with WNO, notably as Claggart in *Billy Budd* and as Boris Godunov.

Robinson, Stanford (*b* Leeds, 1904; *d* Brighton, 1984). Eng. conductor. On BBC staff 1924–66. From 1936 was responsible for many distinguished studio opera perfs. Chorus-master BBC 1924–32, founding BBC Singers, BBC Choral Soc. Ch. Cond., BBC SO 1946–9. Opera dir., assoc. cond. BBC SO 1946–9; cond. BBC Opera Orch. 1949–52; chief cond. Queensland SO 1968–9. CG début 1937. OBE 1972.

Robles, Marisa (*b* Madrid, 1937). Sp.-born harpist. Début 1953 with Nat. Orch. of Sp. Prof. of harp, Madrid Royal Cons., 1958. Settled in Eng. 1959. London début 1963. Prof. of hp. RCM from 1971. Hp. tutor Nat. Youth Orch. of G.B. Soloist with leading orchs.

Robson, Christopher (*b* Falkirk, 1953). Scot. countertenor. Concert début London 1976 (Han-

del's *Samson*), opera début Birmingham 1979 (Argones in Handel's *Sosarme*). Member Monteverdi Choir 1974–84, London Oratory Choir 1974–80, King's Consort 1981–6, New London Consort from 1986. Sang with Kent Opera and Handel Opera Society. CG début 1988. Created title-role in Glass's *Akhnaten*, Houston and NY 1984 and London (ENO) 1985.

Rochberg, George (*b* Paterson, NJ, 1918; *d* Bryn Mawr, Pa., 2005). Amer. composer. Teacher, Curtis Inst., 1948–54; chairman, mus. dept., Pennsylvania Univ. 1961–8, prof. of mus. 1968–83. Influenced by Schoenberg and Mahler, his mus. developed an individual type of serialism but later returned to tonality. Author of many critical articles. Works incl.:

OPERA: *The Confidence Man* (1982).

ORCH.: syms. No.1 (1948–57, in 3 movts.; withdrawn 1977; restored to 5 movts. 1977), No.2 (1955–6), No.3, double ch., chamber ch., soloists, orch. (1966–9), No.4 (1976), No.5 (1984), No.6 (1987); *Night Music* (1948); *Cheltenham Concerto* (1958); *Time-Span I* (1960, withdrawn), *II* (1962); *Zodiac* (1965); *Music for the Magic Theater* (1965–9); *Imago Mundi* (1973); vn. conc. (1974); *Transcendental Variations*, str. (based on 3rd movt. of 3rd str. qt.) (1975); ob. conc. (1983); Suite No.1 (from *The Confidence Man*) (1987–8); cl. conc. (1996).

SOLO VOICE & ORCH.: *David the Psalmist*, ten. (1954); *4 Blake Songs*, sop. and ens. (1961); *Music for 'The Alchemist'*, sop. and 11 players (1965); *Tableaux*, sop., 2 actors' vv., ch., and 12 players (1968); *Sacred Song of Reconciliation*, bass-bar. (1970); *Phaedra*, mez. (1973–4); *7 Early Love Songs*, v., pf. (1991).

CHAMBER MUSIC: str. qts., No.1 (1952), No.2, with sop. (1959–61), No.3 (1972), No.4 (1977), No.5 (1978), No.6 (1978), No.7, with bar. (1979); *Duo Concertante*, vn., vc. (1953); *Dialogues*, cl., pf. (1956); *La Bocca della Verità*, ob., pf. (1958–9, vn., pf. 1962); pf. trio (1963); *Contra Mortem et Tempus*, vn., fl., cl., pf. (1965); *50 Caprice-Variations* (after Paganini), solo vn. (1970); *Electrikaleidoscope*, amp. ens. of fl., cl., vc., pf., elec. pf. (1972); *Ricordanza*, vc., pf. (1972); *Ukiyo-e*, harp (1973); pf. quintet (1975); *Slow Fires of Autumn*, fl., hp. (1978); va. sonata (1979); *Duo*, ob., bn. (orig. version 1946) (1979); *Trio*, cl., hn., pf. (1980); str. quintet (1982); pf. qt. (1983); *To the Dark Wood*, ww. quintet (1985); pf. trio (1985); vn. sonata (1988); *Muse of Fire*, fl., gui. (1989–90); *Summer 1990* (pf. trio No.3) (1990); *Circles of Fire*, 2 pf. (1997).

Also many vocal works and pf. pieces.

Roche, Jerome (Lawrence Alexander) (*b* Cairo, 1942; *d* Durham, 1994). Eng. musicologist. Lect., Durham Univ. 1967. Authority on 17th cent. Italian sacred music. Author of books on Palestrina (1972) and Lassus (1982), ed. *Dictionary of Early Music from the Troubadours to Monteverdi* (with E. Roche, 1981), and *North Italian Church Music in the Age of Monteverdi* (1984).

rock. Species of popular mus. originating in USA (as rock 'n' roll) in early 1950s and spreading throughout world. Perf. by 'groups', e.g. of v(v)., guitars, often electronically amplified, and drums. There are sub-species such as *folk rock*, *jazz rock*, and *punk rock*. Rock was used in stage works such as *Hair*, *Tommy*, and *Jesus Christ Superstar*. Words of songs often refer to social themes.

Rock of Ages, Cleft for Me. Hymn, words by Rev. Augustus Montague Toplady (1740–78), Vicar of Broadhembury, Devon, first pubd. in *Gospel Magazine*, ed. Toplady, in 1776. Tune by Richard Redhead, from *Church Hymn Tunes, Ancient and Modern*, 1853.

rococo (from Fr. *rocaille*, fancy rock-work in architecture). In visual arts term is applied to the delicate, diverting style of Watteau and his contemporaries. Mus. application refers to the decorative style e.g. of F. Couperin, and of certain works by Rameau and J. C. Bach. Musically it is a vague term, almost synonymous with *galant* and the 18th cent. and referring to works which are no longer baroque and not yet classical.

Rode, (Jacques) **Pierre** (Joseph) (*b* Bordeaux, 1774; *d* Château de Bourbon, Damazan, 1830). Fr. composer and violinist, pupil in Paris of Viotti, 1787. Début, Paris 1790. Prof. of vn., Paris Cons., from 1795 and solo violinist at the Opéra 1799. Violinist to Napoleon, 1800. Settled in St Petersburg 1803–8. Beethoven wrote vn. sonata in G, Op.96, for him. Skill declined and he abandoned public concerts. Wrote 13 vn. concs., 12 études, 24 caprices, 12 str. qts., and vn. method.

Rodelinda. Opera in 3 acts by Handel to lib. by Haym adapted from Salvi's *Rodelinda, regina de' longobardi* (1710) after Corneille's *Pertharite, roi des Lombards* (1651). Prod. London 1725; f. modern ps. Göttingen 1920, Northampton, Mass., 1931, London 1939, Glyndebourne 1998.

Rodeo. Ballet in 1 act by Copland, 1942, choreog. and lib. by Agnes de Mille. Sub-titled 'The Courting at Burnt Ranch' and set (like **Billy the Kid*) in America's Wild West. Uses traditional songs. Prod. 1942. Suite of 4 movts. for orch. 1943.

Rodgers, Joan (*b* Whitehaven, 1956). Eng. soprano. Won Ferrier Memorial Scholarship 1981. Sang in RNCM operas. Prof. début Aix-en-Provence 1982 (Pamina in *Die Zauberflöte*). Débuts: ENO 1983; CG 1983; Glyndebourne 1989; Salzburg 1991; NY Met 1995. Large concert repertoire. CBE 2001.

Rodgers, Richard (Charles) (*b* Hammels Station, Long Is., 1902; *d* NY, 1979). Amer. composer. With Lorenz Hart as lyric-writer, wrote successful Broadway musicals *The Girl Friend* (1926), *Connecticut Yankee* (1927), *On Your Toes* (1936, incl. ballet *Slaughter on Tenth Avenue*), *Babes in Arms* (1937), *The Boys from Syracuse* (1938), and *Pal Joey* (1940). With Oscar *Hammerstein II, wrote *Oklahoma!* (1943), *Carousel* (1945), *Allegro* (1947), *South Pacific* (1949), *The King and I* (1951), *Flower Drum Song* (1958), and *The Sound of Music* (1959). With

Stephen Sondheim he wrote *Do I Hear a Waltz?* (1965). Many of these made into films. Wrote mus. for TV documentary *Victory at Sea*. Among the songs he composed are 'There's a Small Hotel', 'My Funny Valentine', 'The Lady is a Tramp', 'Bewitched, bothered, and bewildered', 'Blue Room', 'O What a Beautiful Morning', 'Some Enchanted Evening', 'The Sound of Music'.

Rodrigo, Joaquín (*b* Sagunto, 1901; *d* Madrid, 1999). Sp. composer. Almost totally blind from age 3. Won Sp. nat. prize 1925 for orch. work *Cinco Piezas Infantiles*. Prof. of mus. history, Madrid Univ. from 1947. Works incl. sym.-poem *Per la flor del Liri blau* (1934); **Concierto de Aranjuez*, gui., orch. (1939); *Concierto heroico*, pf., orch. (1943); *Concierto de estío*, vn., orch. (1944); *Concierto en modo galante*, vc., orch. (1949); *Concierto serenata*, hp., orch. (1954); *Fantasía para un gentilhombre*, gui., orch. (1954); *Concierto andaluz*, 4 gui., orch. (1967); *Concierto- madrigal*, 2 gui., orch. (1968); *Concierto pastoral*, fl., orch. (1978); *Concierto como un divertimento*, vc., orch. (1979–81); *Concierto para una fiesta*, gui., orch. (1982); *Tres viejos aires de danza* (1994); songs; and choral works.

Rodzinski, Artur (*b* Spalato (now Split), Dalmatia, 1892; *d* Boston, Mass., 1958). Polish-born cond. (Amer. cit. 1933). Début Lwów 1920 (*Ernani*). Cond. opera and concerts in Warsaw 1921–5. Ass. cond. Philadelphia Orch. 1926–9. Cond. Los Angeles PO 1929–33, Cleveland Orch. 1933–43, NYPO 1943–7, Chicago SO 1947–8. Salzburg Fest. début (concert) 1936 (Vienna PO). Trained and selected players for Toscanini's NBC Orch., 1937. Cond. Amer. première of Shostakovich's *The Lady Macbeth of the Mtsensk District*, Cleveland 1935.

Rogé, Pascal (*b* Paris, 1951). Fr. pianist. Début with orch. in Paris at age of 11. Début Paris 1969, London 1969. First prize Marguérite Long-Jacques Thibaud int. competition 1971. Amer. début 1974. Specialist in works of Ravel, Liszt, and Bartók.

Roger-Ducasse, Jean (Jules Aimable) (*b* Bordeaux, 1873; *d* Taillan-Médoc, 1954). Fr. composer and teacher. Prof. of comp., Paris Cons. 1935–40. Works incl. comic opera *Cantegril* (1931), mime-drama *Orphée* (1913), *Suite française*, orch. (1907), pf. qt., str. qt., motets, and songs. Completed and orch. Debussy's *Rhapsody* for sax. and orch. (1919).

Rogers, Bernard (*b* NY, 1893; *d* Rochester, 1968). Amer. composer. Chief critic, *Musical America*, 1913–24. Taught at Eastman Sch. 1929–67. Works incl. operas *The Warrior* (1944), *The Veil* (1950), *The Nightingale* (1954); 5 syms. (1926–58); *To the Fallen*, orch. (1918); oratorio *The Passion* (1942); *The Musicians of Bremen*, narr., 13 instr. (1958); *Variations on a Song of Mussorgsky*, orch. (1960); vn. sonata (1962); 2 str. qts.; and *Dirge for 2 Veterans*, ch., pf. (1967).

Rogg, Lionel (*b* Geneva, 1936). Swiss organist and harpsichordist. Début as organist, Geneva

1961, thereafter world career as recitalist. Prof. Geneva Cons. from 1960. Recorded all J. S. Bach's organ works.

Rohrflöte (Rohr Flute) (Ger.). Reed flute. Org. stop of 4' length and 8' pitch; metal end-plugged pipes with narrow tube through plug. Reed of cl., ob., etc. is Rohrblatt.

Rohrwerk, Rohrstimmen (Ger.). Reed dept. of the org.

Roi Arthus, Le (Fr. 'King Arthur'). Opera in 3 acts, Op.23, by Chausson to his own lib. Comp. 1885–95. Prod. Brussels 1903.

Roi David, Le (King David). 'Psaume dramatique' (dramatic psalm) in 5 parts (28 nos.), by Honegger for narrator, sop., mez., ten., ch., and orch. Comp. 1921. F.p. Mézières, 1921. Rev. and re-orch. 1923, into 3 parts (27 nos.). F.p. Winterthur 1923 (in Ger.), f.p. in England, London 1927. Also orch. suite of 4 nos.

Roi de Lahore, Le (The King of Lahore). Opera in 5 acts by Massenet to lib. by L. Gallet after Comte de Beauvoir's *Voyage autour du monde*, based on story from the Hindu epic *Mahabharata*. Comp. 1875–6. Prod. Paris 1877, CG 1879, New Orleans 1883, Met 1924, Vancouver 1977.

Roi d'Ys, Le (The King of Ys). Opera in 3 acts by *Lalo to lib. by Blau. Comp. 1875–87. Prod. Paris 1888, New Orleans 1890, London 1901.

Roi malgré lui, Le (King despite himself). Opera in 3 acts by *Chabrier to lib. by de Najac and Burani (rev. by Richepin). Comp. 1887. Prod. Paris 1887. Rev. version by A. Carré, 1929. New lib. by J. Sams (*The Reluctant King*), Opera North, Edinburgh 1994.

Roland-Manuel. See *Manuel, Roland*.

Roldán, Amadeo (*b* Paris, 1900; *d* Havana, 1939). Cuban composer, violinist, and conductor. Settled in Cuba 1921 where he was active as cond. and violinist. Cond. Havana PO from 1932. Prof. of comp., Havana Cons. from 1935. Interested in African influence on Cuban mus. His works make liberal use of Afro-Cuban rhythms and themes.

Rolfe Johnson, Anthony (*b* Tackley, Oxon., 1940). Eng. tenor. Took up singing 1967 after being farmer. Début 1973 with EOG in *Iolanta*. Ch. and small roles, Glyndebourne 1972–6. Won John Christie Award. Débuts: ENO 1978; WNO 1979; CG 1988; Salzburg Fest. 1987. Sang Aschenbach (*Death in Venice*) for Scottish Opera, 1983 and Peter Grimes 1994. Also sings *Lieder, Dream of Gerontius*, Bach Passions, etc. Dir. of Singing Studies, Britten-Pears Sch., Snape, from 1990. CBE 1992.

roll (Ger. *Wirbel*). Rapid succession of notes on a drum, becoming almost a continuous sound.

Roll, Michael (*b* Leeds, 1946). Eng. pianist. Dé-

but London 1958 (Schumann conc.). Won 1st prize at 1st Leeds int. comp. 1963. Amer. début 1974; NY début recital 1992.

Rolland, Romain (*b* Clamecy, 1866; *d* Vézelay, 1944). Fr. writer and musicologist. Prof. of mus. hist., Sorbonne, 1903–13. Lived in Switzerland 1913–39. Author of books on Beethoven and Handel. His huge novel, *Jean-Christophe* (1904–12), concerns the life of a composer and won him the Nobel Prize for literature. Friend of R. Strauss (their interesting correspondence has been pubd.).

Roller, Alfred (*b* Brno, 1864; *d* Vienna, 1935). Austrian stage designer and painter. In 1890s helped to found Vienna Sezession with Schiele, Kokoschka, and Klimt. Prof. at Vienna School of Art 1900, dir. 1909–34. Engaged by Mahler at Vienna Court Opera, 1903, to provide new sets for *Fidelio, Don Giovanni, Tristan und Isolde*, and *Das Rheingold* and *Die Walküre*. These revolutionized stage design. Worked closely with Max Reinhardt at Salzburg Fest. Chief designer Vienna Opera 1903–9, 1918–34, and at Burgtheater 1918–34. Designed orig. prods. of Strauss's *Der Rosenkavalier* (Dresden 1911) and *Die Frau ohne Schatten* (Vienna 1919), also first Vienna *Elektra* (1909).

Rolling Stones. Eng. rock group formed in London 1962. Orig members were Mick (Michael Philip) Jagger (*b* 1944) v., Keith Richard (*b* 1944) v. and guitar, Brian Jones (1944–69) guitar and harmonica, Charlie (Charles Robert) Watts (*b* 1942) drums, and Bill Wyman (*b* 1941) bass guitar. Jones's place was taken in 1969 by Mick Taylor, who was succeeded in 1974 by Ron Wood. By 1964 Jagger and Richard were composing most of their material and the group attracted a large following notwithstanding, perhaps because of, its rebellious mode of dress and behaviour. Their songs included *Satisfaction, Mother's Little Helper*, and *Let's Spend the Night Together*. Jagger increasingly became a cult figure among the *avant-garde* of the pop world.

Rollschweller (Ger.). The 'general crescendo' pedal of an org. which gradually brings out all the stops.

romalis (*ole, polo*) (Sp.). Type of *seguidilla*.

Roman Carnival, The (Berlioz). See *Carnaval Romain, Le*.

romance (It. *romanza*, Ger. *Romanze*). Title with no strict formal application—composers use it as they fancy, vocally or instrumentally. Generally it implies a specially personal or tender quality. Mozart called the slow movt. of his pf. conc. No.20 in D minor (K466) a 'Romance'. Schumann wrote *Drei Romanzen*. Vaughan Williams used the term several times: his *The Lark Ascending* for vn. and orch. is a 'Romance' (1914), he wrote a *Romance* for harmonica, str., and pf. (1951), and the slow movt. of the 5th Sym. (1943) is entitled *Romanza*. Elgar wrote a *Romance* for bn. and the 13th 'Enigma' var. is *Romanza*.

romanesca (It.), **romanesque** (Fr.). (1) Probably a kind of *galliard danced in the Romagna.

(2) A certain melody much used in the 17th cent. as a *ground bass.

(3) A type of song (e.g. by Monteverdi).

Roman Festivals (Respighi). See *Feste Romana*.

Romani, Felice (*b* Genoa, 1788; *d* Moneglia, 1865). It. poet and librettist. Wrote over 100 opera libs. for Mayr, Rossini, Bellini, Donizetti, etc. Among best-known are those of *Il Turco in Italia* (1814), *Norma* (1831), *La sonnambula* (1831), *L'Elisir d'amore* (1832), and *Lucrezia Borgia* (1833).

Romanian Rhapsodies. 2 works for orch., No.1 in A and No.2 in D, by *Enescu, Op.11.

Romantic(ism). Term used to describe literature, written mainly in the 2 decades 1830–50, and applied to mus. written in the period *c*.1830 to *c*.1900. It is a vague term, for there are 'Romantic' elements in all mus. of all ages. However, the composers generally classified as Romantic are of the period of Weber, Schubert, Schumann, Chopin, Liszt, Berlioz, Wagner, etc., in whose mus. emotional and picturesque expression appeared to be more important than formal or structural considerations. Thus Romanticism became the antithesis of classicism. In literature the works of Byron, Scott, Wordsworth, Goethe, Hugo, Gautier, and Balzac were the heart of the Romantic movt. and composers such as Berlioz and Liszt were particularly influenced by Byron and Scott. The supernatural element in Romantic literature is reflected musically in works such as Weber's *Der Freischütz*, and the *Witches' Sabbath* movt. of Berlioz's *Symphonie fantastique*. However, Chopin, an essentially Romantic composer, was not influenced by literary models; and many movts. in works by 'Classical' composers such as Haydn, Mozart, Beethoven, and others, have Romantic leanings. As in so many branches of mus., distinctions between one category and another are blurred, thus nationalism, impressionism, and postromanticism all impinge upon Romanticism.

'Romantic' Symphony. (1) Bruckner's sub-title for his Sym. No.4 in E♭ major (1874, rev. 1878, 1879–80, 1881, 1886).

(2) Sub-title of Sym. No.2 by Howard Hanson (1930).

romanza. See *romance*.

rombando (It.). Humming.

Romberg, Sigmund (*b* Nagykanizsa, Hung., 1887; *d* NY, 1951). Hung.-born composer (Amer. cit.). Went to USA 1909, settling eventually in NY. Wrote succession of popular operettas, incl. *Maytime* (1917), *The Student Prince* (1924), *The Desert Song* (1926), *New Moon* (1928), and *Up in Central Park* (1945). Among songs he comp. are 'Deep in my heart, dear', 'One alone', 'Riff Song', 'Lover,

come back to me', 'Softly, as in a morning sunrise', and the Serenade and Drinking Song from *The Student Prince*.

Romeo and Juliet. Several mus. comps. have been based on this Shakespeare tragedy (1594–5). Among them are: (1) *Roméo et Juliette*, dramatic sym., Op.17, for sop., ten., bass, ch., and orch. by *Berlioz, 1838–9.

(2) *Roméo et Juliette*, opera in 5 acts by *Gounod to lib. by Barbier and Carré. Prod. Paris, London, and NY, 1867.

(3) *Romeo and Juliet* (*Romeo i Dzhulietta*), fantasy-ov. for orch. by *Tchaikovsky, 1869 (f.p. 1870), rev. 1870 and 1880 (f.p. 1886). Also duet for sop., ten., and orch., partly based on fantasy-ov., 1893, completed by Taneyev.

(4) *Romeo and Juliet* (*Romeo i Dzhulietta*), ballet in prol., 3 acts, and epilogue by *Prokofiev, Op.64, to lib. by Lavrovsky, Prokofiev, and Radlov, choreog. Psota. Comp. 1935–6. Prod. Brno 1938. Also Symphonic Suite No.1, Op.64b (7 movts.), 1936, No.2, Op.64c (7 movts.), 1937, No.3, Op.101 (6 movts.), 1944.

(5) *Romeo und Julia*, opera by Sutermeister to his own lib. Prod. Dresden 1940.

There are also operas on this subject by *Zandonai, *Zingarelli, and *Blacher. See also *Bellini's *I *Capuleti e i Montecchi*.

Rome Prize (French, Belgian, American). See *Prix de Rome*.

Ronald, (Sir) **Landon** [Russell, Landon Ronald] (*b* London, 1873; *d* London, 1938). Eng. conductor, composer, pianist, and administrator. Son of Henry *Russell. CG coach under Mancinelli 1891, becoming cond. of Augustus Harris's touring opera co. Toured USA as *Melba's accompanist, 1894. CG début as cond. 1896 (*Faust*). Cond. mus. comedy in London 1898–1902. Guest cond. LSO 1904–7 and later of Berlin PO and other leading orchs. Permanent cond. Royal Albert Hall Orch. 1909–14, Scottish Orch. 1916–20. Prin., GSMD 1910–38. Wrote mus. criticism. Friend and interpreter of Elgar, who ded. *Falstaff* to him. Wrote operetta and orch. mus. but remembered chiefly through his song *Down in the Forest*, one of nearly 200. Knighted 1922.

ronde (Fr.). Round. (1) The *whole-note or *semibreve.

(2) A round dance to vocal acc. by the dancers.

rondeau (Fr.). Mus. form so called because of its circle of recurrence. (1) Type of medieval song (also *rondel*) sung by troubadours in which sections of both words and mus. recurred.

(2) Instr. form in 17th and later cents. in which the first section recurs. See *rondo*.

rondeña. A kind of *fandango of southern Sp. (named after Ronda in Andalusia), with the same harmonic peculiarity as the *malagueña.

Rondes de printemps (Debussy). See *Images*.

Rondine, La (The Swallow). Opera in 3 acts by Puccini to lib. by Adami trans. from Ger. lib. by

Willner and Reichert. Comp. 1914–16, rev. 1918–19. Prod. Monte Carlo 1917, NY (Met) 1928, BBC broadcast 1920, London (Fulham) 1965, Leeds (Opera North) 1994.

rondo (It., properly spelt *rondó*). Round. Form of comp., usually instr., in which one section intermittently recurs. By Mozart's day it was the usual form for the last movt. of a conc. or sonata. Frequent pattern is ABACADA etc., A being the recurring rondo theme and B, C, and D contrasting episodes. Mozart and Beethoven combined this with sonata form into a *sonata-rondo*. Strauss's *Till Eulenspiegel* is designated a rondo. The term is also sometimes used in opera for an aria with a slow section followed by a faster one.

Ronger, Florimond. See *Hervé*.

Röntgen, Julius (*b* Leipzig, 1855; *d* Bilthoven, nr. Utrecht, 1932). Ger.-born Dutch composer, pianist, and conductor. Accompanist to distinguished singers. Teacher at Amsterdam Mus. Sch. 1878. Cond. Maatschappij concerts, Amsterdam, 1886–98. Dir., Amsterdam Cons. 1918–24. Comp. 3 operas, 21 syms., 7 pf. concs., 2 vn. concs., 2 vc. concs., chamber mus., songs, etc.

Roocroft, Amanda (*b* Coppull, 1966). Eng. soprano. Sang Fiordiligi (*Così fan tutte*) and Handel's Alcina whilst student at RNCM. Won Decca Kathleen Ferrier Prize 1988. Prof. début Cardiff (WNO) 1990 (Sophie in *Der Rosenkavalier*). Débuts: GTO 1990; CG 1991; Glyndebourne 1991 (all as Pamina in *Zauberflöte*); Munich 1993 (Fiordiligi in *Così fan tutte*). NY Met 1997 (Elvira in *Don Giovanni*).

Rooley, Anthony (*b* Leeds, 1944). Eng. lutenist and specialist in early music. Teacher of gui. and lute, RAM, 1969–71. Founded (with James Tyler) the Consort of Musicke 1969. Author of several articles on lute and aspects of early mus. Frequently partners the sop. Emma *Kirkby*.

root. The note from which a chord originates, the lowest note when the chord is in its 'basic' position, e.g. in chord of C major (common chord) C–E–G, the root is C.

Rootham, Cyril (Bradley) (*b* Bristol, 1875; *d* Cambridge, 1938). Eng. organist and composer. Org., St John's College, Cambridge, from 1901. Lect. in mus. Cambridge Univ. from 1913. Cond. Cambridge Univ. Mus. Soc. 1912–36. Wrote opera, choral works incl. *For the Fallen* (1915), 2 syms., str. qts., songs, etc.

Rorem, Ned (*b* Richmond, Ind., 1923). Amer. composer and author. Worked in NY as copyist to Virgil Thomson. Lived in Morocco and Paris 1949–58. Studied in Fr. with Honegger, 1951–2. In 1951–5 wrote *The Paris Diary of Ned Rorem*, entertaining journal, pubd. 1966. Recipient of several awards and fellowships. Prof. of mus., Buffalo Univ. 1959–61, prof. of comp. Utah Univ. 1965–7. Taught at Curtis Inst. 1980–6. The influence of Poulenc is discernible in his many songs,

of which he is the foremost Amer. composer. His orch. works are colourful and he sometimes uses a modified serial technique. Has written several other books, incl. *Critical Affairs, A Composer's Journal* (1970), *Setting the Tone* (1983), and *Wings of Friendship* (2005).

Rosa, Karl [Carl] (August Nikolaus) [really Karl Rose] (*b* Hamburg, 1842; *d* Paris, 1889). Ger. conductor, violinist, and impresario. Leader of orch. in Hamburg, 1863–5. London début 1866, in USA 1866–71. In NY 1867 married sop. Euphrosyne Parepa and became manager and dir. of opera co. headed by his wife. After her death in 1874 formed *Carl Rosa Opera Co.*, based in Eng. from 1875.

rosalia. Name sometimes given to harmonic real *sequence (because It. popular song *Rosalia, mia cara* began with this device). An example is Diabelli's theme, set by Beethoven and others.

Rosamunde, Fürstin von Cypern (Rosamund, Princess of Cyprus). Play by Helmina von Chézy (1823) for which *Schubert wrote ov., 3 entr'-actes, 2 ballet pieces, and some vocal nos. (D797). The ov. played at the f.p. was that already comp. for *Alfonso und Estrella* and pubd. under that title as Op.69 (D732). What we know as the *Rosamunde* ov. (D644) was written in 1820 for melodrama by Hoffmann called *Die *Zauberharfe* (The Magic Harp).

Rosbaud, Hans (*b* Graz, 1895; *d* Lugano, 1962). Austrian conductor and pianist. Cond. and dir., mus. sch., Mainz 1923–30; chief cond. Frankfurt radio orch. 1928–37; Münster Opera 1938–41; Strasbourg Opera 1941–4; Munich PO 1945–8; SW Ger. Radio Orch. 1948–62; Zurich Tonhalle Orch. 1950 (mus. dir. from 1957). Chief cond. Aix-en-Provence Fest. 1947–59. Frequently cond. at Donaueschingen, promoting early works of Boulez and Stockhausen. Cond. f.p. (radio and stage) of *Moses und Aron* (Hamburg, 1954 and Zurich, 1957). Renowned interpreter and champion of 20th-cent. mus. Cond. f.p. of Bartók's 2nd pf. conc., with composer as soloist, 1933.

Roscoe, Martin (*b* Halton, Ches., 1952). Eng. pianist. Won Brit. Liszt comp. 1976, Sydney int. comp. 1981. Has toured Australia, Middle East, and N. and S. Amer.

rose. Sound-hole cut to aid resonance in the lute, guitar, mandolin, etc. So-called owing to ornamental flower-like shape.

Rosé, Arnold (Josef) (*b* Iasi, Romania, 1863; *d* London, 1946). Austrian violinist. Début Leipzig Gewandhaus 1879. Leader of Vienna Court Opera Orch. and of Vienna PO for 57 years (1881–1938), also frequently led orch. at Bayreuth Fest. Formed and led Rosé Qt. from 1883 (Amer. début Washington DC, 1928). It gave f.ps. of works by Reger and Schoenberg. Taught at Vienna State Acad. 1893–1924. Brother-in-law of Mahler. Fled to Eng. 1938.

Rose, Barry (Michael) (*b* London, 1934). Eng. organist. Org., St Anne's, Chingford, 1946–56. Org.

and choirmaster, Guildford Cath. 1960–74; sub-org., St Paul's Cath., London, 1974–7, choirmaster 1977–84. Choirmaster, King's Sch., Canterbury, 1984–8. Master of Mus., St Alban's Abbey from 1988. CBE 1998.

Rose, Leonard (Joseph) (b Washington DC, 1918; d White Plains, NY, 1984). Amer. cellist. Member of NBC Orch., under Toscanini. Prin. cellist Cleveland Orch. 1939–43, NYPO 1943–51, then successful solo career. Salzburg Fest. 1977. Member of Istomin-Stern-Rose Trio from 1961. Teacher at Curtis Inst. 1951–62 and at Juilliard Sch. 1947–51 and 1962–84. Pupils incl. Lynn Harrell and Yo-Yo Ma.

Roseingrave, Thomas (b Winchester, 1688; d Dunleary, Ireland, 1766). Irish organist and composer. Son and pupil of Daniel Roseingrave (d 1727, org. of Gloucester, Winchester, and Salisbury caths. and of St Patrick's and Christ Church caths., Dublin). Studied in Italy, where he knew both Scarlattis. Organist, St George's, Hanover Sq., 1725–52. Wrote opera, cantatas, extra numbers for D. Scarlatti's opera *Narciso* in London 1720, hpd. pieces, etc.

Rosen, Albert (b Vienna, 1924; d Dublin, 1997). Austrian-born conductor. Opera début Pilsen. Cond., Smetana Th., Prague, 1964. Chief cond., RTE Sym. Orch., Dublin, from 1969. Cond. at Wexford Fest. 1965–94. Amer. début S. Francisco Opera 1980. Cond. Brit. première of Rimsky-Korsakov's *Christmas Eve*, London (ENO) 1988. Mus. dir. Irish Nat. Opera, Dublin, from 1993.

Rosen, Charles (Welles) (b NY, 1927). Amer. pianist and author. Début NY 1951. Prof. of mus., State Univ. of NY from 1971. Among his books are *The Classical Style* (1971); *Schoenberg* (1975); *Sonata Forms* (1980); *The Romantic Generation* (1995); and *Piano Notes: the World of the Pianist* (2002). Noted for his playing of Bach's *Goldberg Variations*, late Beethoven sonatas, and Debussy. Has given important perfs. of Schoenberg, Webern, Carter, and Boulez.

Rosenberg, Hilding (Constantin) (b Bosjökloster, Sweden, 1892; d Stockholm, 1985). Swedish composer, pianist, and conductor. Taught pf. and theory, Stockholm, 1916–30. In 1926 began to work with th. dir. Per Lindberg and in over 25 years wrote incid. mus. for over 40 plays. Cond., Royal Swedish Opera 1932–4. Comps. reflect Scandinavian nationalist tendencies, also influence of Schoenberg.

Rosenkavalier, Der (The Knight of the Rose). Opera in 3 acts by Richard Strauss, his Op.59, to lib. (comedy for mus.) by Hugo von Hofmannsthal. Comp. 1909–10. Prod. Dresden 1911; London and NY Met 1913. Among the famous characters in this opera are the Marschallin (wife of the field-marshal), Oktavian, Sophie, Baron Ochs, and Faninal. For silent film (first shown 1926) with altered plot, much of the mus. of the opera was arr. by others for chamber orch. (1925)

as accompaniment. Strauss cond. for the film in Dresden and London but did not use this reduced score, which was not perf. until recorded in 1980.

Rosenstock, Joseph (b Craców, 1895; d NY, 1985). Polish-born conductor and pianist (Amer. cit. 1949). Cond., Darmstadt Opera 1920–5, Wiesbaden 1927–9, Mannheim 1930–3; mus. dir. Jewish Kulturbund, Berlin, 1933–6. Début NY Met 1929. Cond. in Tokyo 1937–41. Settled in USA 1946. Cond., NY City Opera 1948–56 (dir. from 1952); mus. dir. Cologne Opera 1958–61. Returned to USA 1961, conducting at NY Met 1961–8, and S. Francisco Opera.

Rosenthal, Harold (David) (b London, 1917; d London, 1987). Eng. critic and author. Archivist, Royal Opera House, CG, 1950–6. Ass. ed. *Opera* 1950–3, ed. 1953–86. Books incl. *Two Centuries of Opera at Covent Garden* (1958). Co-ed., *Concise Oxford Dictionary of Opera* (2nd edn., 1979). Revised Loewenberg *Annals of Opera* 1978. Autobiography *My Mad World of Opera* (1982). OBE 1983.

Rosenthal, Manuel [Emmanuel] (b Paris, 1904; d Paris, 2003). Fr. composer and conductor. Cond. of many Fr. orchs.; co-cond., Fr. Nat. Radio Orch. 1934–9, chief cond. 1944–7. Cond. Seattle SO 1949–51. Salzburg Fest. 1959. Prof. of cond., Paris Cons., from 1962. Cond. Liège SO 1964–7. NY Met début 1981. Cond. *Der Ring* at Seattle 1986. Works incl. oratorio *St Francis of Assisi* (1936–9); orch. suite *Joan of Arc* (1936); sym. (1949); mass (1953); operas; and chamber mus. Arr. of ballet *Gaîté parisienne* (1938) from Offenbach themes. Orch. transcrs. of works by Ravel.

Rosenthal, Moriz (b Lemberg, 1862; d NY, 1946). Ukrainian pianist. Début Vienna 1876. Retired from concert platform to study philosophy, Vienna Univ. 1880–6. Began foreign tours 1887, making int. reputation as one of the great pianists 'in the grand manner'. Toured USA 1888–9, partly with Kreisler. London début 1895. Taught at Curtis Inst. Settled in NY 1939.

Roses from the South (*Rosen aus dem Süden*). Waltz, Op.388, by Johann Strauss II. Occurs in operetta *Das Spitzentuch der Königin* (The Queen's Lace Handkerchief), 1880.

Rose vom Liebesgarten, Die (Ger. 'The Rose from the Garden of Love'). Opera in prologue, 2 acts, and epilogue by Pfitzner to lib. by J. Grun. Comp. 1897–1900. F.p. Elberfeld 1901, Vienna 1905 (cond. Mahler).

Rosing, Vladimir (b St Petersburg, 1890; d Los Angeles, 1963). Russ.-born tenor (Amer. cit.). Début St Petersburg 1912 as Lensky in *Eugene Onegin*. London concert début 1913. Settled in London. Dir. and sang in opera season at London Opera House 1915. Gave notable series of recitals in London and elsewhere 1916–21. Toured USA 1922. Dir., opera dept., Eastman Sch. of Mus. 1923. Dir., Amer. Opera Co., 1927–9. In 1936, with Albert *Coates, organized Brit. Mus.-Drama

Opera Co., which survived for one season at CG. Prod. George Lloyd's *The Serf* for Eng. Opera Soc. at CG 1938. Settled in Los Angeles from 1939, becoming ass. dir. S. Calif. Opera Assoc. Dir., NY City Opera, 1950–8.

Ros Marbá, Antoni (*b* Barcelona, 1937). Sp. conductor. Début Barcelona 1962. Cond. Sp. Radio and TV Orch. 1965–8, City of Barcelona Orch. 1967–78, 1981–6, Sp. Nat. Orch. 1978–81, Netherlands Chamber Orch. 1979–86. Mus. dir. Nat. Opera Th., Madrid, from 1987.

Rosselli, Francesco (*b c.*1510; *d* after 1577). It. composer, but may have been French (François Roussel). Choirmaster St Peter's, Rome, 1548–50. Wrote motets, madrigals, and songs.

Rossellini, Renzo (*b* Rome, 1908; *d* Monte Carlo, 1982). It. composer and critic. Taught comp. at Pesaro Cons. 1940–2. Art. dir. Monte Carlo Opera, 1972–6. Wrote several operas, incl. *Una sguàrdo dal ponte* (based on A. Miller's play *A View from the Bridge*, prod. Rome 1961), ballets, orch. works, chamber mus., and scores for films dir. by his brother Roberto Rossellini, incl. *Rome, Open City* (1945).

Rosseter, Philip (*b* 1567 or 8; *d* London, 1623). Eng. composer and lutenist. Wrote half of *Booke of Ayres* (1601) with *Campion, also works for broken consort, etc. Lutenist at court of James I, 1603. Managed company of boy actors (Children of Whitefriars) 1609–17.

Rossi, Mario (*b* Rome, 1902; *d* Rome, 1992). It. conductor. Deputy cond., Augusteo Orch., Rome, 1926–36. Taught cond. at S. Cecilia Acad., Rome, 1931–6. Cond., Maggio Musicale Fiorentino, 1936–44. Opera début Florence 1937 (*Iris*). Salzburg Fest. 1952. Cond., Turin Radio Orch. 1946–69. Advocate of contemp. music.

Rossignol, Le (Stravinsky). See *Nightingale, The*.

Rossi-Lemeni, Nicola (*b* Istanbul, 1920; *d* Bloomington, Ind., 1991). It. bass of mixed It. and Russ. parentage. Opera début Venice (La Fenice) 1946 (Varlaam in *Boris Godunov*). Regular appearances at La Scala 1947–60. Débuts: CG 1952; S. Francisco 1951; NY Met 1953. Sang Claggart in f. It. p. of *Billy Budd* (Florence 1965) and created Tommaso in *L'Assassinio nella cattedrale* (La Scala 1958). Joined faculty of Indiana Univ. in Bloomington, 1980.

Rossini, Gioachino Antonio (*b* Pesaro, 1792; *d* Paris, 1868). It. composer, son of town trumpeter and a singer. As child, apprenticed to blacksmith, sang in churches, and played hpd. in ths. Entered Bologna Acad. 1806 and while a student wrote opera *Demetrio e Polibio*. In 1810 Venetian impresario commissioned him to write comic opera (*La cambiale di matrimonia*), and in 1812 his *La pietra del paragone* was produced at La Scala. 2 operas prod. in Venice, 1813, est. his reputation outside It.—*Tancredi*, an *opera seria*, and *L'Italiana in Algeri*, an *opera buffa*. In 1814 was engaged as

mus. dir. of both Neapolitan opera houses and for San Carlo wrote *Elisabetta, Regina d'Inghilterra*, in which he replaced *recitativo secco* with recits. acc. by str. Other operas for Naples were *Otello* and *Il barbiere di Siviglia*, a failure at first but soon to be hailed as an outstanding *opera buffa*. These were followed by *La Cenerentola*, *La gazza ladra*, and *Mosè in Egitto*. In 1822 married sop. Isabella *Colbran, who had created several of his sop. roles, incl. in 1823 *Semiramide*, the last opera of his It. cycle.

In 1822 Rossini visited Vienna, where he met Beethoven; this was followed by a trip to London, where he was fêted, in 1823–4. In 1824 settled in Paris as dir. of the Théâtre Italien, and wrote 3 operas for Paris, incl. *Guillaume Tell* (1829). Appointed composer to King Charles X in 1825 and after success of *Tell* was commissioned by Govt. to write 5 operas in 10 years. But the 1830 revolution dethroned Charles, and the new govt. set aside the commissions. Rossini left Paris for Italy in 1836 and for the next 19 years composed only three religious works and some occasional pieces. The likely reason is his prolonged neurasthenic ill-health which followed the intensive work on *Guillaume Tell*. In Bologna became hon. pres. of the Liceo Musicale and reformed its teaching methods, but left the town in 1848. In 1855 he and his 2nd wife settled in Paris where, for the remaining 13 years of his life, Rossini was the centre of artistic and intellectual life. He also began to compose again, the *Petite Messe solennelle* in 1863 and the 150-odd piano pieces, songs, and ensembles which he called *Péchés de vieillesse* (Sins of Old Age) (1857–68). Many of these were first perf. at the Rossinis' 'Samedi Soirs'. He was buried in Paris (at his funeral Beethoven's Funeral March from Op.26 was played by an ens. of instr. invented by Adolphe *Sax and many of the greatest singers of the day were soloists, incl. *Patti and *Nilsson). In 1887 he was reinterred in Florence.

Rossini's comic operas have perpetuated his name. Their wit, speed, and grace, their bubbling fun and entirely appropriate orchestration, are perennially fresh. Several of them were written within the space of a fortnight: although there is nothing slipshod about them, the impression of spontaneity remains. Nevertheless his serious works, *Guillaume Tell*, *Tancredi*, and *Semiramide*, contain superb mus., and although *Otello* has yielded to Verdi's masterpiece, it is still worth hearing. His 2 late religious works are masterpieces, and the sparkling str. sonatas (str. qts.) of his youth testify to his grounding in the classics of Haydn and Mozart. Prin. works:

OPERAS: *Demetrio e Polibio (1806); La cambiale di matrimonio (1810); L'equivoco stravagante (1811); L'inganno felice (1811); Ciro in Babilonia (1812); La *scala di seta (1812); La pietra del paragone (1812); L'occasione fa il ladro (1812); Il *signor Bruschino (1812); *Tancredi (1812); L'*Italiana in Algeri (1813); Aureliano in Palmira (1813); Il *Turco in Italia (1814); Sigismondo (1814); *Elisabetta, Regina d'Inghilterra (1815); Torvaldo e Dorliska (1815); Il *barbiere di Siviglia* (1816); *La gazzetta* (1816); *Otello* (1816); *La *Cenerentola* (1816); *La *gazza ladra* (1817); *Armida* (1817); *Adelaide di Borgogna* (1817); **Mosè in Egitto* (1818, rev. as *Moïse et Pharaon*, 1827); *Adina* (1818); *Ricciardo e Zoraide* (1818); *Ermione* (1819); *Eduardo e Cristina* (1819); *La donna del lago* (1819); *Bianca e Faliero* (1819); *Maometto II* (1820); **Matilde di Shabran* (1821); *Zelmira* (1822); **Semiramide* (1823); *Il *viaggio a Reims* (1825); *Le *Siège de Corinthe* (1826, rev. and amplification of *Maometto II*); *Le *Comte Ory* (1828); **Guillaume Tell* (1829).

CANTATAS: *Il pianto d'armonia* (1808); *La morte di Didone* (1811); *Partenope* (1819); *Il vero omaggio* (1823); *Il pianto delle Musi per la morte di Lord Byron* (1823); *Il serto votivo* (1829).

SACRED MUSIC: *Messa di gloria* (1820); *Stabat Mater* (1842); **Petite Messe solennelle* (1863, 1867).

MISCELLANEOUS: *Inno dell' Indipendenza* (1815); *Soirées musicales*, songs and duets incl. *La Danza* (1835); *La Regata Veneziana*, song-cycle (1857).

INSTRUMENTAL: *Introduction and Variations* for cl. and orch. (1809); *Andante con variazioni* in F, ob. and harp; *Prelude, Theme, and Variations*, hn. and pf.; Str. sonatas (*sonatas a quattro*), 2 vn., vc., db. (1804), No.1 in G, No.2 in A, No.3 in C, No.4 in B♭ major, No.5 in E♭, No.6 in D. In 1808 Rossini transcribed 5 of these sonatas as wind qts. which are given here in relation to the numbers of the str. versions: No.1 in F, No.2 in G, No.4 in B♭, No.5 in F, No.6 in D. The str. No.3 has no wind version. A 6th wind qt. (in F, 2 movts.) has no str. equivalent.

PÉCHÉS DE VIEILLESSE: A large number of works for voices and instrs. (incl. *La regata veneziana*, mez., pf.) comp. between 1857 and 1868 and pubd. in 13 albums.

Rostal, Max (*b* Teschen, 1905; *d* Berne, Switz., 1991). Austrian-born violinist, composer, and teacher (Brit. cit.). Leader Oslo PO 1927. Ass. to Flesch 1927–30. Prof., Berlin State Acad. 1930–3. Settled in Eng. 1934. Prof. GSMD 1944–58. Prof. Cologne State Acad. and Berne Cons. from 1957. He was a noted exponent of contemporary mus. and much sought after as teacher. CBE 1977.

Rostropovich, Mstislav (Leopoldovich) (*b* Baku, 1927). Russ. cellist, pianist, and conductor. Début 1942. Won Prague int. comp. 1950. Western début, Florence 1951. Prof. of vc., Moscow Cons. from 1956 and Leningrad Cons. from 1961. One of great cellists of his day, for whom Prokofiev, Shostakovich, and Britten (all of whom were his friends) wrote works. Also gave f.ps. of works by Bliss, Walton, Lutosławski, Panufnik, Dutilleux, and Saxton. Pf. accompanist to his wife, the sop. Galina *Vishnevskaya. London début 1956. Amer. début as cellist, NY 1956. Début as cond., (concert) Gorky 1962, (opera) Moscow 1968 (*Eugene Onegin*); Salzburg Fest. début (cellist) 1969 (Orch. de Paris., cond. Karajan), pf. accomp. 1975. Cond. début in London 1974 (New Philharmonia). Amer. début concert cond., Washington DC 1975, and in opera at S. Francisco 1975 (*Queen of Spades*). Cond. Nat. SO, Washington, 1977–94. Cond. f.ps. of

works by Bernstein, Walton, Schnittke (opera *Life with an Idiot*, 1992), Penderecki, and Gubaidulina. Art. dir., Aldeburgh Fest. 1977–88. Out of favour with Soviet authorities from 1970 because of public defence of dissident novelist Solzhenitsyn and was denied exit from USSR for foreign engagements for over a year until he cond. opera in Vienna. Left USSR with wife 1974, ostensibly for 2 years, but did not return. In 1978 they were deprived of Soviet citizenship, but this was restored in 1990 and he was invited to take the Nat. SO to Russia. Hon. KBE 1987.

Roswaenge [Rosenving-Hansen], **Helge** (*b* Copenhagen, 1897; *d* Munich, 1972). Danish tenor. Début Neustrelitz 1921 (Don José in *Carmen*). Member Cologne Opera 1927–30, Berlin State Opera 1930–44. Débuts: Vienna Opera 1936; CG 1938; Salzburg 1932. Sang Parsifal at Bayreuth 1934 and 1936. Sang opera in Berlin and Vienna after 1945. Concert tour of USA 1962.

rota (Lat.). Wheel. (1) Term occasionally used for *round, as in Reading Rota, i.e. **Sumer is icumen in*, thought to have been comp. by a monk of Reading Abbey.

(2) Hurdy-gurdy.

Rota, Nino (*b* Milan, 1911; *d* Rome, 1979). It. composer. Wrote oratorio at age of 11 and opera at 14. Taught at Liceo Musicale, Bari, from 1939, becoming dir. 1950–78. Comp. 10 operas, 3 syms., concs. for pf., tb., vc., bn., db., and hn., chamber mus., and many film scores for the directors Fellini, de Filippo, Visconti, and Zeffirelli.

Roth, Daniel (*b* Mulhouse, 1942). Fr. organist and composer. Won Chartres int. comp. 1971. Deputy org. Sacré Cœur, Paris, 1963–72, org. 1973–83; prof. of org., Marseilles Cons. 1973–9. Org., St Sulpice, Paris, from 1983. Prof. of org., Saarbrücken Musikhochschule from 1988. Recitals in USA and Europe. Comps. for org. and choir.

Rothenberger, Anneliese (*b* Mannheim, 1924). Ger. soprano noted for Mozart and Strauss operatic roles and for singing of operetta. Début Koblenz 1943. Member Hamburg State Opera 1946–72. Brit. début 1952 (Edinburgh Fest. with Hamburg co. in f. Brit. stage p. of *Mathis der Maler*). Joined Deutsche Oper 1956. Salzburg Fest. début 1954, creating Telemachos in Liebermann's *Penelope*. Débuts: Vienna 1957; Glyndebourne 1959; NY Met 1960.

Rothmüller, Marko (Aron) (*b* Trnjani, 1908; *d* Bloomington, Ind., 1993). Croatian baritone. Opera début Altona, nr. Hamburg, 1932 (Ottokar in *Der Freischütz*). Zagreb Opera 1933–8, Zurich Opera 1938–47, CG 1939 and 1948–55, Vienna Opera 1945–8, NY City Opera 1948–52, Met 1959–64. First stage Wozzeck in Eng. (CG 1952, cond. Kleiber). Created Truchsess in *Mathis der Maler*, Zurich 1938. Glyndebourne début (Edinburgh Fest.) 1949, at Glyndebourne 1951. Joined faculty of Univ. of Indiana, Bloomington, 1955–79, Rubin Acad. of Mus., Jerusalem 1981–2. Also a fine *Lieder* singer.

Rothwell, Evelyn. See *Barbirolli, Evelyn*.

Rothwell, Walter Henry (*b* London, 1872; *d* Los Angeles, 1927). Eng. conductor, composer, and pianist. Toured Europe as pianist, but abandoned kbd. for cond.'s rostrum when he became ass. to Mahler at Hamburg, 1895. Cond. Savage Opera Co. in USA, incl. perfs. of *Parsifal* in English. Cond. Amer. première of *Madama Butterfly* (in Eng.) 1906. Cond. St Paul SO 1908–14, Los Angeles PO 1919–27. Wrote pf. conc., chamber mus., and songs.

Rott, Hans (Johann Carl Maria) (*b* Vienna, 1858; *d* Vienna, 1884). Austrian composer and organist. Close friend of Mahler, whose methods are anticipated in Rott's Symphony in E (1878–80). Became insane 1880.

rotte (or rote). Name applied in Middle Ages to various instr., such as harp, lyre, crwth, and hurdy-gurdy. (Variant of *chrotta, crot*, etc.)

Rouet d'Omphale, Le (Omphale's Spinning-Wheel). First symphonic poem by Saint-Saëns, his Op.31, comp. 1871–2. Omphale was mythical queen to whom Hercules was slave (wearing woman's dress) for 3 years, spinning wool for her.

Rouget de Lisle, Claude Joseph (*b* Lons-le-Saunier, 1760; *d* Choisy-le-roi, 1836). Fr. army engineer, poet, and composer. While stationed in Strasbourg, wrote on 25 April 1792 words and music of *Chant de guerre pour l'armée du Rhin*. This was perf. so often by Marseilles Volunteer Battalion it eventually became known as *La Marseillaise*. Sanctioned as national song in 1795, fell out of favour, restored to respectability 1830, adopted as Fr. nat. anthem 1879.

roulade (Fr.). One of Fr. vocal ornaments, much like **divisions*.

Rouleau, Joseph (Alfred) (*b* Matane, Quebec, 1929). Fr.-Canadian bass. Début Montreal 1951 (in *Un ballo in maschera*). First major appearance, New Orleans 1955 (Colline in *La bohème*). CG début 1957. Repertoire of 70 roles, incl. King Philip, Basilio, Boris, and Arkel.

round. Short unacc. vocal 'perpetual canon' at the unison or octave in which the vv. enter in turn. Popular in Eng. after 16th cent. Famous examples are *Three Blind Mice* and *London's Burning*.

round dance. (1) A dance in which the performers turn round.
   (2) (a more common use of the term) A dance in which they move round in a circle, i.e. a ring dance.

roundelay (Fr. *rondelet*). Country songs or ballads common in 14th cent. So called because of constant recurrence of first verse.

Rounseville, Robert (*b* Attleboro, Mass., 1914; *d* NY, 1974). Amer. tenor. Sang in night-clubs, on radio, and in musicals under name Robert Field. Joined NY City Opera 1948, début as Pelléas opposite Maggie Teyte. Sang Hoffmann in Beecham film version of opera, 1950. Created Tom Rakewell in *The Rake's Progress*, Venice 1951. Returned to Broadway mus. stage, singing in *Candide* and in *Man of La Mancha*.

Rousseau, Jean-Jacques (*b* Geneva, 1712; *d* Ermenonville, 1778). Swiss philosopher, composer, and writer on music. While working as copyist, devised new system of mus. notation which he published in *Dissertation sur la musique moderne* (Paris, 1743). Wrote *opéra-ballet*, *Les muses galantes* (1747), and very successful pastoral opera *Le Devin du village* (Fontainebleau 1752). Took It. side in *Querelle des *Bouffons* and attacked Fr. mus. in his *Lettre sur la musique française* (1753). Pubd. *Dictionnaire de Musique* (1768). Left unfinished opera *Daphnis et Chloé* and wrote about 100 songs.

Roussel, Albert (Charles Paul Marie) (*b* Tourcoing, 1869; *d* Royan, 1937). Fr. composer. Despite showing mus. tendencies as a child, began career as naval officer, his service in Indo-China leaving profound impression. Resigned commission 1894 to study mus. Worked with Gigout and from 1898 to 1909 at Schola Cantorum under d'Indy. Prof. of counterpoint, Schola Cantorum, 1902–14, pupils incl. Satie and Varèse. Served in Fr. army 1914–18, thereafter devoting himself to comp. and living secluded life because of ill-health. Once free of d'Indy influence, Roussel developed a neo-classical style in which strong Stravinskyan rhythms and daring harmonies were blended with a rich, sometimes orientally exotic, orch. palette and expressive melodies. His 3rd and 4th syms. represent him at his most individual, but his ballet *Bacchus et Ariane* is his best-known work. Prin. comps.:

OPERAS: *La naissance de la lyre* (1923–4); *Le Testament de la tante Caroline* (1932–3).

OPERA-BALLET: **Padmâvatî* (1914–18).

BALLET: *Le *Festin de l'araignée* (1912); **Bacchus et Ariane* (1930); *Aeneas* (1935).

INCIDENTAL MUSIC: *Le Marchand de Sable qui passe* (1908).

ORCH.: syms: No.1 (*Le Poème de la forêt*) (1904–6), No.2 in B♭ (1919–21), No.3 in G minor (1930), No.4 in A (1934); *Prelude to Tolstoy's Resurrection* (1903); *Pour une fête de printemps* (1920); 2 suites from *Bacchus et Ariane* (1930); *Suite in F* (1926); pf. conc. (1927); *Petite Suite* (1929); *Sinfonietta*, str. (1934); *Rapsodie flamande* (1936); vc. concertino (1936).

VOICE(S) & ORCH.: *La Ménace* (1908); *Madrigal aux muses* (1923); *Psalm 80*, ten., ch., orch. (1928).

CHAMBER MUSIC: pf. trio (1902); *Divertissement*, pf., 5 wind (1906); vn. sonata No.1 (1907–8), No.2 (1924); *Serenade*, fl., hp., str. trio (1925); *Joueurs de flûte*, fl., pf. (1924); *Trio*, fl., va., vc. (1929); str. qt. (1932); *Andante and Scherzo*, fl., pf. (1934); str. trio (1937).

PIANO: *Rustiques* (1904–6); *Suite* (1909–10); *Sonatina* (1912); *3 Pieces* (1933).

SONGS: 4 *Poèmes d'Henri de Régnier* (1903); 4 *Poèmes d'Henri de Régnier* (1907); *Flammes* (1908); 2 *Songs from the Chinese* (1907–8); 2 *Songs* (*Light, Farewell*) (1918); 2 *Songs* (*Le Bachalier de Salamanque, Sarabande*) (1919); *Jazz dans la nuit* (1928).

Routh, Francis (John) (*b* Kidderminster, 1927). Eng. composer, organist, pianist, and author. Founder-dir., Redcliffe Concerts of Brit. mus., 1963–4. Works incl. sym.; vc. conc.; pf. conc.; double conc.; org. sonatina; 3 concs. for ens.; ob. conc.; *Poème fantastique*, pf., orch. Author of books on the org., contemp. mus., and Stravinsky.

Roux, Gaspard le (*b* Paris, c.1660; *d* c.1705). Fr. composer. Wrote hpd. suites and pieces, motets, airs, etc.

rovescio, al (It.). In reverse. Term which refers either to a passage that can be played backwards as well as forwards, or to a form of canon in which every descending interval in the leading v. is imitated by an ascending one, and *vice versa*.

row. See *note-row*.

Rowe, Tony (*b* Manchester, 1961). Eng. conductor. Founder and cond. Robinson Orch., Cambridge, 1981, Oxford and Cambridge Chamber Orch. 1982. Cond. *Don Giovanni* for Brit. Youth Opera 1987. Cond., Louisville Orch. 1987–8. Won Liverpool int. cond. comp. 1988, 2nd prize Leeds int. cond. comp. 1991. Cond., Vassar Coll. Orch. & Opera 1989–92. Ass. cond. American SO from 1992. Début with RLPO 1992 (Preston).

Rowicki, Witold (*b* Taganrog, Russia, 1914; *d* Warsaw, 1989). Polish conductor and composer. Début as cond. 1933. Chamber mus. performer 1932–45. Founder and mus. dir. Katowice Radio O 1945–50. Chief cond. Warsaw PO (now Nat. PO) 1950–5, 1958–77. Dir., Teatr Wielki opera centre from 1965. Cond. Bamberg SO 1983–6.

Roxburgh, Edwin (*b* Liverpool, 1937). Eng. composer, cond., and oboist. Prin. oboist, SW Opera Orch. 1964–7. Prof. of comp. and dir. 20th cent. dept., RCM, from 1967. Cond. and dir. 20th-Cent. Ens. of London. Works incl.:

BALLET: *The Tower* (1964).

ORCH.: *Variations* (1963); *Montage* (1977); 7 *Tableaux*, tpt. conc. (1979); *Prelude* (1981); *Saturn* (1982); *Serenata* (1983); *Tamesis*, chamber orch. (1983); *Sinfonia Concertante*, ob., hn., vn., vc., chamber orch. (1990); *Dreamtime*, fl., str. (1994); *Lament (for the Victims of Conflict)*, ob., str. (2003).

VOICE(S) & INSTR(S).: *Recitative after Blake*, cont., str. orch. (or str. quintet) (1961–7); *Night Music*, sop., orch. (1969); *How Pleasant to Know Mr Lear*, narr., chamber orch. (1971); *A Scottish Fantasy*, sop., vn., str. (1973); *A Portrait of e. e. cummings*, male and female narr., vn., orch. (1974).

CHORAL: *The Rock*, oratorio, SATB soloists, ch., children's ch., orch. (1979).

UNACC. VOICES: *Westron Wynde*, ten., bar., ch. (1961); *Christ is risen* (1982); *A Passiontide Carol* (1982); *Et*

vitam venturi saeculi (1983); *Pianto* (1985); *The Beginning of Sorrows*, sop., off-stage vocal qt., ch. (2005).

ENSEMBLE: & *sum & silence*, ten., pf., perc. (1965); *Ecclissi*, ob., vn., va., vc. (1971); *Dithyramb II*, pf., 3 perc. (1972); *Convolutions*, sop., ten., alto fl., ob. d'amore, bn., hpd. (1974); *Hexham Tropes*, ob., ob. d'amore, bn., hpd. (1979); *Elegy*, ob., fl., cl., vn., vc., perc. (1982); *Shadow-play*, 2 ob., ca. (1984); *Heliochrome*, cl. qt. (1989).

CHAMBER MUS.: quartet, fl., cl., vn., vc. (1964); *Images*, ob., pf. (1967); *Partita*, vc. (1970); *Dithyramb I*, cl., perc. (1972); *Constellations*, rec. ob. (1973); *Nebula I*, cl. choir (1974), *II*, wind quintet (1974); *Circling the Circlings . . .*, vc., pf. (1977); *At the Still Point of the Turning World*, amp. ob., elec. (1978); wind quintet No.2 (1983); quartet, fl., str. (1984); *Shadow-play*, 2 ob., ca. (1984); *Flute Music*, fl., pf. (1986); *Antares*, ob., pf. (1988); 4 *Soliloquies*, va. d'amore (1988); *Voyager*, 3 ob., 3 ca., 3 bn. (1989); *Star-drift*, fl. (1992); *In such a night as this*, vc., pf. (2005).

PIANO: *Introduction and Arabesques* (1963); *Labyrinth* (1970); 6 *Études* (1980); Sonata (1993); *Reflets dans la glace*, pf. duet (2003).

Roxolane, La. Nickname of Haydn's Sym. No.63 in C major, (Hob. I:63), comp. c.1780. Uses material from earlier mus., incl. incidental mus. for the play *Soliman II* whose heroine was Roxolane.

Royal Academy of Music. College of mus. in London instituted in Tenterden Street, 1822; Royal charter 1830. Lodging and boarding of students discontinued after 1853, when first board of professors was appointed. Moved to Marylebone Road 1912. Wide range of activities: premises incl. concert-hall (Duke's Hall), lecture hall, opera th. (opened 1977), and library. About 700 students, with teaching staff of 150. Prins.: William Crotch 1822–32, Cipriani Potter 1832–59, Charles Lucas 1859–66, W. Sterndale Bennett 1866–75, G. A. Macfarren 1876–87, A. C. Mackenzie 1888–1924, J. B. McEwen 1924–36, S. Marchant 1936–49, R. S. Thatcher 1949–55, Thomas Armstrong 1955–68, Anthony Lewis 1968–82, David Lumsden 1982–93, Lynn Harrell 1993–4, Curtis Price from 1995. RAM is supported by Govt. grant, subscriptions, donations, and fees. F. Brit. p. of Verdi's *Giovanna d'Arco* was given at RAM 1966, f. London stage p. of *L'incoronazione di Poppea* in 1969. (The name Royal Acad. of Mus. was also given to an operatic venture supported by aristocracy, founded successfully in London 1718–19 under directorship of Handel, Bononcini, and Ariosti but which collapsed in 1728.) See also Royal College of Music.

Royal Albert Hall. Large, all-purpose, oval-shaped hall in London (South Kensington) built in memory of Prince Consort (*d* 1861) and formally opened March 1871. Seating capacity 10,000. Venue for many occasions incl. balls, pageants, fest. of remembrance, Miss World competition, etc., but best known as concert hall and especially, since destruction of Queen's Hall (1941), as home of Henry Wood Promenade

Concerts. Formerly acoustically notorious for echo, but this has been largely eliminated by special installations.

Royal Ballet. Name bestowed by Royal charter in 1956 on former SW Ballet (CG), SW Theatre Ballet (SW), and SW Ballet School. Originated in Acad. of Choreographic Art, formed by Ninette de *Valois in London, 1926. This sch. moved in 1931 to newly-built SW Th. under direction of Lilian *Baylis. Became Vic-Wells Ballet, dir. by Constant *Lambert and with *Ashton and de Valois as leading choreogs. Visited Paris 1937, Holland 1940. Became resident co. at CG from 1946, opening with famous prod. of *The Sleeping Beauty*. Second co. (orig. SW Opera Ballet) formed 1946. Many eminent dancers worked for prin. co., incl. Fonteyn (from 1934), Dolin, Helpmann, Turner, Somes, Grey, Shearer, Massine, Nerina, Beriosova, Blair, Nureyev, Sibley, Park, Collier, and Bussell. Choreogs. have incl. Massine, Balanchine, Cranko, Tudor, and MacMillan. NY début 1949. Art. dirs.: Ninette de Valois (1931–63), Frederick Ashton (1963–70), Kenneth MacMillan (1970–7), Norman Morrice (1977–86), Anthony Dowell (1986–2001), Ross Stretton (2001–2), Monica Mason from 2002.

Royal Choral Society. London choir of about 850 vv. which originated in choir formed and cond. by Gounod for opening of *Royal Albert Hall, 1871. Taken over by Barnby, 1872. Name at first was Royal Albert Hall Choral Soc., present name adopted 1888. Barnby was succeeded in 1896 by J. F. Bridge. Sir Malcolm Sargent had long assoc. as cond. from 1929.

Royal College of Music. London mus. college, successor to *National Training School of Music. Founded by Prince of Wales (later Edward VII) in 1882 and opened 1883, when it received Royal charter. Orig. housed in building occupied by Nat. Training Sch., new building in Prince Consort Road, S. Kensington, was opened 1894. Large concert-hall added 1901 and later an opera th. (Parry Theatre) which was replaced in 1986 by Britten Theatre. Further extensions 1964 and 1973. Has superb mus. library and valuable coll. of historical instr. Governed by pres. and council, with dir., board of professors, graduates, and donors. Dirs.: George Grove 1883–94; Hubert Parry 1894–1918; H. P. Allen 1918–37; G. Dyson 1937–52; E. Bullock 1953–60; K. Falkner 1960–74; D. Willcocks 1974–84; M. Gough Matthews 1984–93; Janet Ritterman 1993–2005; Colin Lawson from 2005.

Royal College of Organists. Formed 1864 in London, among aims being to provide examinations and certificates to safeguard standards among organists and also to encourage comp. and study of sacred mus. Orig. housed in Bloomsbury, since 1894 in Kensington Gore in building vacated by RCM. Royal charter 1893.

Royal Concertgebouw Orchestra of Amsterdam. Dutch sym. orch. which plays in the Concertgebouw (Dutch, 'concert building') built Amsterdam, 1888, though the Concertgebouw Soc. was founded 5 years earlier. The first cond. was Willem *Kes, but the orch. became internationally famous under his successor *Mengelberg, cond. 1895 to 1945. Conds. since then have incl. Eduard van *Beinum 1945–59, Bernard *Haitink and Eugen *Jochum jointly 1961–4, Haitink 1964–88, Riccardo Chailly 1988–2004; Mariss Jansons from 2004. Title changed to Royal Concertgebouw Orchestra 1989.

Royal Festival Hall. Concert-hall built in London (by London County Council) on S. Bank of River Thames as part of Fest. of Brit. 1951. Designed by R. H. Matthew, with org. by Harrison and Harrison, Durham. Seating capacity 3,200. Major refurbishment 2005–7. Queen Elizabeth Hall and Purcell Room are part of S. Bank concert-hall 'complex'.

Royal Hunt of the Sun, The. Opera in 3 acts by *Hamilton to his own lib. based on play by Peter Shaffer. Comp. 1967–9. Prod. London 1977.

Royal Irish Academy of Music. Mus. college founded in Dublin, 1848, reorganized 1856. Governed by 24 governors and secretary until appt. of first dir. in 1980s. Dir. John O'Conor from 1994.

Royal Liverpool Philharmonic Orchestra and Society. Soc. founded 1840 since when it has promoted orch. concerts. Opened Phil. Hall 1849, among finest in Europe; destroyed by fire 1933 and replaced 1939 by present fine building. Title 'Royal' bestowed 1957. First cond. was John Russell, succeeded in 1843 by violinist Zeugheer Herrmann, who stayed until his death in 1865. He was followed by Alfred Mellon 1866–7, Julius Benedict 1867–79, Max Bruch 1880–3, Charles Hallé 1883–95, Frederic Cowen 1895–1913. Guest conds. were engaged until the appointment of Malcolm Sargent 1942–8, succeeded by Hugo Rignold 1948–54, Efrem Kurtz and John Pritchard 1955–7, John Pritchard 1957–63, Charles Groves 1963–77, Walter Weller 1977–80, David Atherton 1980–3, Marek Janowski 1983–6, Libor Pešek 1987–97, Petr Altrichter 1997–2000; Gerard Schwarz 2000–6; Vasily Petrenko from 2006.

Royal Manchester College of Music. Mus. college founded in Manchester 1893, with title Royal from inception. Royal charter 1923. Founded on initiative of Sir Charles *Hallé, Prin. 1893–5. Successors: A. Brodsky 1895–1929, R. J. Forbes 1929–53, F. R. Cox 1953–70, J. Wray 1970–2. From 1957 gave 4 diplomas. Premises were in Ducie Street, Manchester. In 1972 merged with Northern Sch. of Mus. to become *Royal Northern College of Music, Manchester.

Royal Military School of Music. Founded 1857 at Kneller Hall, Twickenham, Middlesex, for training of army instrumentalists and bandmasters.

Royal Musical Association. Organization founded by Stainer and Pole in London in 1874 'for investigation and discussion of subjects connected with the art, science, and history of music'. Incorporated 1904, prefix 'Royal' since 1944. Papers, etc., read to the Assoc. are pubd. in its

Proceedings, known since 1988 as *Journal of the RMA*.

Royal Northern College of Music, Manchester. Coll. of mus. opened in Manchester 1972 by amalgamation of Royal Manchester Coll. of Mus. and Northern Sch. of Mus. Housed in new building on Oxford Road containing concert-hall, opera ho., recital room, tutorial rooms, etc. Governed by board of governors. Prins.: Sir John *Manduell (1972–96); Edward Gregson from 1996.

Royal Opera House. See *Covent Garden*.

Royal Philharmonic Orchestra. Sym. orch. founded 1946 by Sir Thomas Beecham, who remained prin. cond. until his death in 1961. Regular orch. at Glyndebourne Fest. 1947–63. Tour of USA 1950 (first Brit. orch. to visit Amer. since LSO 1912). Rudolf *Kempe became ass. cond. 1960, chief cond. 1961–3, art. dir. from 1964 (cond. for life from 1970). Antal *Dorati was appointed cond.-in-chief 1975–8, Walter Weller 1980–5. André Previn from 1985–7 and prin. cond. 1987–92, Yuri Temirkanov prin. cond. 1992–8. Vladimir Ashkenazy mus. dir. 1987–94, Daniele Gatti from 1996. No connection with *Royal Philharmonic Society.

Royal Philharmonic Society. Founded in London, Jan. 1813 for encouragement of orch. and instr. concerts and immediately promoted annual series of concerts. First concert 8 Mar. 1813. Concerts were given at first in Argyll Rooms, then successively at New Argyll Rooms, King's Th., Hanover Sq. Rooms, St. James's Hall, Queen's Hall, Royal Albert Hall, Royal Fest. Hall. Commissioned Beethoven's 9th Sym. (though f.p. in Vienna) and gave the first Eng. perf. under Smart on 21 Mar. 1825. Sent Beethoven £100 on his death-bed and waived claim to its return when it was found among his effects. Since 1871 a replica of Schaller's bust of Beethoven, presented to the Soc. in that year by Mme. F. Linzbauer, has been placed at the front of the platform at every Phil. concert. To commemorate centenary of Beethoven's birth in 1870 a Gold Medal was struck by the Soc. in 1871 and is presented sporadically, at the recommendation of the dirs., to distinguished musicians (composers and executants), being among the most coveted mus. awards. Most of the world's leading musicians have appeared on the Soc.'s platform. Prefix 'Royal' granted 1912.

Royal School of Church Music. Founded as Sch. of Eng. Church Mus. 1927 by S. H. *Nicholson and members of Church Mus. Soc. Royal charter 1945. Main training centre opened 1929 at College of St Nicolas; successively at Chislehurst, Canterbury, and Croydon (since 1953).

Royal Schools of Music. See *Associated Board of the Royal Schools of Music*.

Royal Scottish Academy of Music and Drama. Mus. college in Glasgow, originating from Glasgow Athenaeum Sch. of Mus., founded 1890. In 1929, a Scottish Nat. Acad. of Mus. was formed to combine with univ. faculty of mus., the Prin. combining office with that of univ. prof. of mus. Prefix 'Royal' 1944. Drama sch. added 1950, present title dating from 1968. Separate Prin. appointed 1953. New building opened 1987. Prins.: W. G. *Whittaker 1929–41; Ernest *Bullock 1941–52; H. Havergal 1953–69; K. Barritt 1969–76; D. Lumsden 1978–82; Philip Ledger 1982–2000; John Wallace from 2000.

Royal Scottish National Orchestra. Prin. prof. sym. orch. of Scotland, based in Glasgow and giving regular series of concerts in Glasgow, Edinburgh, and other Scottish towns. Formed 1891 as Scottish Orch., with George *Henschel as cond. 1891–5. His successors were Willem *Kes (1895–8), Max *Bruch (1898–1900), Frederic *Cowen (1900–10), Emil *Mlynarski (1910–16), Landon *Ronald (1916–20), Julius *Harrison (1920–3). From 1923 to 1933 there was no regular cond. except in 1926 when Václav *Talich was in charge. *Barbirolli was cond. 1933–6, followed by *Szell 1936–9, W. *Braithwaite 1940–6, and Walter *Süsskind 1946–52. Reorganized 1950 as Scottish Nat. Orch., with players on annual contracts and much enlarged schedule. Karl *Rankl became cond. 1952–7, Hans *Swarowsky 1957–9, Alexander *Gibson 1959–84, Neeme *Järvi 1984–8, Bryden *Thomson 1988–90, Walter *Weller 1991–7, Alexander Lazarev 1997–2005, Stéphane Denève from 2005. During Gibson's régime the orch. increased its repertory, gave many f.ps., toured abroad, and played in the pit for *Scottish Opera. Stockhausen's *Gruppen, and several works by Henze received first Brit. perfs. from Gibson and SNO, and Scottish composers received particular encouragement. Schoenberg's vn. conc. had first Brit. public perf. in 1960. New Glasgow concert-hall, Royal International Hall, opened 1990. Title 'Royal' granted 1990.

Royal Society of Musicians of Great Britain. Soc. for relief of infirm and distressed musicians and their dependants, founded 1738. Royal charter 1790.

Royal Welsh College of Music and Drama. Welsh mus. coll. founded 1949 as Cardiff Coll. of Mus. in Cardiff Castle. Changed name to Welsh College of Music and Drama in 1970. Royal charter granted in 2002. Moved in 1975 to new building in castle grounds at Cathays Park. Prin. from 1990, Edmond Fivet.

Rozhdestvensky, Gennady (Nikolayevich) (*b* Moscow, 1931). Russ. conductor. Son of cond. Nikolay Anosov (1900–62); took his mother's surname. Ass. cond. Bolshoy Th., 1951, on cond. staff there 1956–60. Chief cond. USSR Radio and TV Orch. 1960–5 and 1970–4; prin. cond. Bolshoy 1965–70. Cond. Russian première of *A Midsummer Night's Dream* (1965). Toured USA 1973 as cond., Leningrad PO. London début 1956; CG début

1970; Salzburg Fest. 1976. Mus. dir., Stockholm PO 1975–7. Chief cond. BBC SO 1978–81. Cond. Vienna SO 1980–2; cond. Royal Stockholm PO 1991–5.

Rózsa, Miklós (*b* Budapest, 1907; *d* Los Angeles, 1995). Hung.-born composer (Amer. cit.). Settled in Paris 1932, then in London, studying at TCL 1936–40. Mus. dir. and composer for Korda films 1936–42. Emigrated to USA 1940. Comp. for MGM 1948–62. Taught at Univ. of S. Calif., Los Angeles, 1945–65. Influenced by folk mus. His film mus. is rich and the essence of 'Hollywood'; his other works combine dissonance and strong rhythms. Prin. comps. are *Concerto for Strings*, pf. conc., vn. conc., vc. conc., 2 str. qts., *Sinfonia Concertante* for vn., vc., and orch., pf. quintet, str. trio, pf. sonata, motet *The Vanities of Life*, etc. Film scores incl. *Knight Without Armour* (1937), *The Thief of Bagdad* (1940), *The Jungle Book* (1942), *Double Indemnity* (1944), *The Lost Weekend* (1945), *Spellbound* (1945), *Double Life* (1948), *The Asphalt Jungle* (1950), *Ben Hur* (1959), *The Private Life of Sherlock Holmes* (1970), and *Dead Men Don't Wear Plaid* (1982).

Rozsa, Vera (*b* Budapest, 1920). Hung.-born mezzo-soprano and teacher (Brit. cit.). Début Budapest 1945 (Hänsel). Sang with Budapest State Opera, Vienna Opera, and with leading orchs. in Eur. and USA. Retired 1975. Taught singing RMCM 1965–70, Opera Studio, Paris, 1975–80. Consultant prof. of singing GSMD from 1980. OBE 1989.

rubato, or tempo rubato (It.). Robbed time. A feature of perf. in which strict time is for a while disregarded—what is 'robbed' from some note or notes being 'paid back' later. When this is done with genuine artistry and instinctive mus. sensibility, the effect is to impart an admirable sense of freedom and spontaneity. Done badly, rubato merely becomes mechanical. The question of rubato in Chopin is particularly contentious, since its use in his mus. may be dangerously open to abuse. Accounts of his playing (and of Mozart's) suggest that he kept the left-hand in strict time, and added rubato with the right.

Rubbra, (Charles) **Edmund** (*b* Northampton, 1901; *d* Gerrards Cross, 1986). Eng. composer and pianist. Worked at 14 as railway clerk. Private comp. lessons from Cyril *Scott. Studied at Reading Univ. 1920–1, comp. with Holst, pf. with E. Howard-Jones at RCM 1921–5, comp. with Holst and Morris. Taught, wrote mus. criticism, and comp. mus for a travelling th. group. Recognition came with perf. of first Sym. (1935–7). Lecturer in mus., Oxford Univ. 1947–68, prof. of comp., GSMD from 1961. Served in army 1941–5 and was ordered to form pf. trio with which he gave concerts to Servicemen and women throughout Brit. and, later, Ger. Contrib. to several works of reference, reviewer, etc. His prolific output covered all forms except for the th., and he was in the mould of Holst and Vaughan Williams, although folk-song as such plays no part in his work. His use of modal harmony and his

large amount of religious mus. are in a particularly Eng. tradition, and his syms. have a mus. substance and spiritual grandeur which have still not been fully appreciated. CBE 1960. Prin. works:

ORCH.: syms.: No.1, Op.44 (1935–7), No.2, Op.45 (1938, rev. 1951), No.3, Op.49 (1939), No.4, Op.53 (1941), No.5, Op.63 (1947–8), No.6, Op.80 (1954), No.7, Op.88 (1957), No.8 (*Hommage à Teilhard de Chardin*), Op.132 (1966–8), No.9 (*Sinfonia Sacra*, 'the Resurrection') for sop., cont., bar., ch., and orch., Op.140 (1971–2), No.10 (Chamber sym.), Op.145 (1974), No.11, Op.153 (1978–9); *Festival Overture*, Op.62; *Improvisations on Virginal Pieces by Giles Farnaby*, Op.50; *Ov., Resurgam*, Op.149; pf. conc., Op.85 (1956); va. conc., Op.75 (1952); vn. conc., Op.103 (1959); *Improvisation*, vn. and orch., Op.89; *Sinfonia Concertante*, pf., orch., Op.38; *Soliloquy*, vc., small orch., Op.57; orchestrations of Brahms's *Variations on a Theme of Handel* and of Rachmaninov's *Prelude in G minor*.

CHORUS & ORCH.: *The Dark Night of the Soul*, Op.41, No.1 (solo cont.); *Song of the Soul*, Op.78; *The Morning Watch* (Vaughan), Op.55; *Cantata di Camera* (Carey and Spenser), Op.111, solo ten.; *Suite, In Die et Nocte Canticum*, Op.129; *Inscape* (G. M. Hopkins), Op.122; *Advent Cantata*, Op.136, solo bar.; *Veni, Creator Spiritus*, Op.130.

UNACC. CHORUS: 5 *Madrigals* (Campion), Op.51; 5 *Motets*, Op.37 (No.3 is Donne's *Hymn to God the Father*); *Missa Cantuariensis*, Op.59; *Missa in honorem Sancti Dominici*, Op.66; 9 *Tenebrae Motets*, Op.72; 3 *Motets*, Op.76; *Agnus Dei*, Op.143; 3 *Greek Folk Songs*, Op.151; *Prayer for the Queen*, Op.152.

CHAMBER MUSIC: str. qts.: No.1 in F minor, Op.35 (1934, rev. 1956), No.2 in E♭, Op.73 (1952), No.3, Op.112 (1962–3), No.4, Op.150 (1976–7); pf. trio No.1, Op.68, No.2, Op.138; *Lyric Movement*, pf., str. qt., Op.24; 4 *Easy pieces*, vn., pf., Op.29; vn. sonatas: No.1, Op.11, No.2, Op.31, No.3, Op.133; *Phantasy*, 2 vn., pf., Op.16; Suite, *The Buddha*, Op.64, fl., ob., vn., va., vc.; *Variations on a Phrygian Theme*, solo vn., Op.105; *Meditations on a Byzantine Hymn*, solo va., Op.117; *Improvisation*, solo vc., Op.124; *Pezzo Ostinato*, hp., Op.102; vc. sonata, Op.60; ob. sonata, Op.100; *Fantasia on a Theme of Machaut*, Op.86, recorder, str. qt., hpd.; sonatina, Op.128, treble recorder, hpd.

KEYBOARD: 8 *Preludes*, pf., Op.131; *Introduction and Fugue*, pf., Op.19; 9 *Pieces*, pf., Op.74: 1. *Question and Answer*, 2. *Pipe Tune*, 3. *Hurdy Gurdy*, 4. *Slow Dance*, 5. *Catch me if you can*, 6. *Peasant Dance*, 7. *Cradle Song*, 8. *The Donkey*, 9. *The Shining River*; *Prelude and Fugue*, Op.69, pf.; *Introduction, Aria, and Fugue*, hpd. (or pf.), Op.104.

SONGS: *Amoretti* (5 Spenser Sonnets), ten., str. qt., Op.43; 5 *Spenser Sonnets*, ten., str. orch., Op.42; 4 *Medieval Latin Lyrics*, bar., str., Op.32; *The Jade Mountain*, high v., hp., Op.116; 3 *Psalms*, low v., pf., Op.61.

Rubens, Paul (Alfred) (*b* London, 1875; *d* Falmouth, 1917). Eng. composer. Wrote some nos. for *Floradora* (1899) and then devoted himself entirely to comp. of light operas, e.g. *Miss Hook of Holland* (1907), *The Balkan Princess* (1910), *Tonight's the Night* (1915), etc.

rubible. The **rebec*.

Rubini, Giovanni-Battista (*b* Romano, 1794; *d* Romano, 1854). It. tenor. Début Pavia 1814 in Generali's *Le lagrimi di una vedova*. Created Lindoro in L'**Italiana in Algeri*, Venice 1815. Sang in Naples 1815–31 and had sensational success in Paris 1825–6 in Rossini operas. La Scala début 1827. Divided time between Paris and London 1831–43 and created ten. roles in several operas by Bellini and Donizetti. Toured with Liszt 1843. Retired, immensely rich, 1845.

Rubinstein, Anton (Grigorievich) (*b* Vikhvatinets, 1829; *d* Peterhof, 1894). Russ. pianist and composer. Début Moscow 1839, European tour 1840–3. Studied comp., Berlin 1844–6. Returned to Russia 1848, then went to Ger. 1854 with many of his own comps. Settled in St Petersburg 1858 as court pianist and cond. Founded St Petersburg Cons. 1862 (dir. until 1867, then 1887–90). Cond. Vienna PO 1871–2. Toured USA 1872–3, giving 215 concerts. Visited Eng. several times between 1841 and 1886. Farewell recitals 1886–7. One of greatest pianists of his day and a prolific composer. Remembered for his *Melody in F* for pf. Other works incl. 20 operas (incl. *The Demon*, 1871); 6 syms., incl. the 'Ocean'; 5 pf. concs.; vn. conc.; 2 vc. concs.; 10 str. qts.; and much other chamber mus.; also pf. pieces and songs.

Rubinstein, Arthur [Artur] (*b* Lódź, 1887; *d* Geneva, 1982). Polish-born pianist (Amer. cit. 1946). Child prodigy, giving recital in Warsaw at age 5. Studied there with Rozycki, then taken by mother to Berlin to play for Joachim. Studied at Warsaw Cons., then aged 10 again sent to Berlin where Joachim, with 3 others, paid for his mus. training with Heinrich Barth (pf., comp., and theory). Played Mozart A major conc. (K488), cond. Joachim, Berlin 1900. First visited USA 1906. London début 1912. Settled in Paris but was in London 1914 and, speaking 8 languages fluently, became wartime interpreter. Gave recitals for charity with violinist **Ysaÿe. Had great success in Spain 1916, becoming noted exponent of Falla's mus. Played frequently in USA 1919–27 but did not gain full success there until 1937. Settled in Hollywood 1939. Gave first post-war recital in Poland 1958 and visited Russ. 1964, but refused to return to Ger. Among greatest pianists of 20th cent., a master in the classics, in Chopin, and in 20th-cent. repertory. Played with almost undiminished power and skill up to his 90th birthday. Last London recital 30 Apr. 1976. Hon. KBE 1977.

Rubinstein, Nikolay (Grigorevich) (*b* Moscow, 1835; *d* Paris, 1881). Russ. pianist and composer, brother of Anton **Rubinstein. Founded Moscow Cons. 1866, remaining dir. until his death. Not-

able teacher, pupils incl. Taneyev and Ziloti. Gave f.p. of Balakirev's *Islamey*. Tchaikovsky's Pf. Trio in A minor was composed in his memory.

Ruckers. Antwerp firm of hpd. and virginals makers between 1579 and 1667, the founder being Hans Ruckers (*c*.1550–1598). Over 100 Ruckers instr. still exist. The aim of the hpds. made between 1580 and 1650 was to offer the player some contrast of tone or register. The single-manual instr. had a short-octave compass of 4 octaves from C and had 2 sets of str., respectively 8′ and 4′. Ruckers also made 2-manual hpds., probably as transposing device to help accompanists. Hans Ruckers was helped and succeeded by his sons Jan (1578-1643) and Andries (1579–*c*.1645).

Ruddigore, or The Witch's Curse. Operetta in 2 acts by Sullivan to lib. by Gilbert. Comp. 1886–7. Orig. title *Ruddy Gore*. Prod. London and NY 1887.

Rudel, Julius (*b* Vienna, 1921). Austrian-born conductor (Amer. cit. 1944). Settled in USA 1938. Cond. small opera socs. in NY and elsewhere, then became rehearsal pianist NY City Opera 1943, ass. cond. 1944 (début *Der Zigeunerbaron*), art. dir. 1957–79. Mus. dir. Kennedy Center, Washington DC, 1971–5. NY Met début 1978; CG début 1984. Cond. Buffalo PO 1978–85. Champion of contemp. works and of lighter stage works.

Ruders, Poul (*b* Ringsted, 1949). Danish composer and organist. Once described himself as 'a film composer with no film'. In several works, mus. of earlier period provides the impetus, e.g. Monteverdi's *Vespers* in *glOriA*, Vivaldi and Schubert in 1st vn. conc. Comps. incl.:

OPERAS: *Tycho* (1986); *The Handmaid's Tale* (1997–8); *Kafka's Trial* (2001–3).

ORCH.: *Capriccio Pian' e Forte* (1978); vn. conc. No.1 (1981), No.2 (1990–1); *Manhattan Abstraction* (1982); *Thus Saw Saint John* (1984); cl. conc. (1985); *Jubileephony* (1986); *Dramaphonia*, pf., orch. (1987); *Monodrama*, solo perc., orch. (1988); *Polydrama*, vc., orch. (1988); *Psalmodies*, gui., orch. (1989); sym. No. 1 (1989), No. 2 (1995–6); *Tundra* (1990); *The Second Night Shade* (1991); *Trapeze* (1992); *Gong* (1992); *Zenith* (1992–3); *Anima* (vc. conc. No.2) (1993); pf. conc. (1994); va. conc. (1994); ob. conc. (1998); *Paganini Variations*, gui., orch. (1999–2000); *Listening Earth* (2001); *Final Nightingale* (2003).

ENS.: *Wind-Drumming*, wind quintet, 4 perc. (1979); *4 Compositions*, fl., cl., hn., pf., str. qt., db. (1980); *Diferencias*, fl., cl., vib., gui., pf., vn., vc. (1980); *Greeting Concertino*, hn., cornet, tb., perc., pf., vn., vc., db. (1982); *4 Dances in One Movement*, small ens. (1983); *Break-Dance*, pf., 2 tpt., 3 tb. (1984); *Corpus cum Figuris* (1985); *Nightshade*, fl., ob., bcl., hn., tb., perc., pf., vn., db. (1987); *Second Set of Variations*, ens. (1994–5); *Sophisticated Caravan Solitude*, ens. (1999); *Abysm*, ens. (2000).

CHORUS: *glOriA*, ch., brass (1981); *3 Motets* (1981–8); *The Death of Queen Dagmar*, unacc. ch. (1990).

SOLO VOICES & INSTR.: *Pestilence Songs*, sop., gui., pf. (1975); *The City in the Sea*, cont., orch. (1990); *The Bells*, sop., chamber ens. (1993); *Andersen Songs* bar., ens. (2003–4); *Sonnet*, mez., ens. (2004).

CHAMBER MUSIC: str. qts. No.2 (1979), No.3 (*Motet*) (1979); *Vox in Rama*, cl., elec. vn., pf. (1983); *Regime*, 3 perc. (1984); *Tattoo for Three*, cl., vc., pf. (1984); *Cembal d'amore*, hpd., pf. (1986); *Throne*, cl., pf. (1988); Trio, vn., hn., pf. (1998); *Serenade on the Shores of the Cosmic Ocean*, acc., str. qt. (2004).

SOLO INSTR.: *Bravour-Studien*, vc. (1976); *Cha Cha Cha*, perc. (1981); *Alarm*, perc. (1983); *Tattoo for One*, cl. (1984); *Variations*, vn. (1989); *Towards the Precipice*, perc. (1990); *Psalmodies Suite*, gui. (1990); *Air with Changes*, hp. (1993); *Chaconne*, gui. (1996); *Reveille – retraite*, tpt. (2003); *Bel canto*, vn. (2004).

KEYBOARD: *Requiem*, org. (1968); pf. Sonatas: No.1 (*Dante Sonata*) (1970), No.2 (1982); *7 Recitatives*, pf. (1977); *13 Postludes*, pf. (1988); *Star-Prelude and Love Fugue*, pf. (1990); *De profundis*, 2 pf., perc. (1990); *Event Horizon*, pf. (2001); *Swinging Bells*, pf. (2002).

Rudolf, Max (*b* Frankfurt, 1902; *d* Philadelphia, 1995). Ger.-born conductor (Amer. cit. 1946). Ass. cond. Freiburg Opera 1922–3, cond. Hesse State Opera 1923–9, Ger. Opera, Prague, 1929–35. Cond. in Sweden 1935–9. Emigrated to USA 1940. Member of mus. staff NY Met 1945–58 (ass. admin. 1950–8), cond. début 1946 (*Der Rosenkavalier*). Mus. dir. Cincinnati SO 1958–70. Head of opera class, Curtis Inst. 1970–3 and from 1981. Cond. Dallas SO 1973–4, New Jersey SO 1976–7, Detroit SO 1983.

Rudy, Mikhail (*b* Tashkent, 1963). Russ. pianist. Won Bach comp. Leipzig 1971 and Marguérite Long comp. Paris 1975. Eur. début Paris 1977. Amer. début 1981. Salzburg Fest. début 1987. London début 1988 (LSO cond. Tilson Thomas).

Rudziński, Witold (*b* Siebiez, Lithuania, 1913; *d* Warsaw, 2004). Polish composer. Taught at Vilna Cons. 1939–42 and Łódź Cons. 1945–7. Cond. Warsaw Opera and PO 1948–9. Prof., Warsaw Acad. of Mus. from 1957. Author of books on Bartók (1964) and ed. of letters of Moniuszko (1954–70). Works incl. operas, oratorios, 2 syms., pf. concs., chamber mus.

Rudziński, Zbigniew (*b* Czechowice, 1935). Polish composer. Mus. dir. Warsaw documentary film studio 1960–7. Prof. of comp., Warsaw Acad. of Mus. from 1973, head of faculty 1980–1, pro-rector 1981–4. Works incl. *Manekiny*, opera (1981); *Antygone*, chamber opera (1979–82); *Moments Musiceaux I, II*, and *III*, orch. (1965–8); Sym., male ch., orch. (1969); *Night Music*, orch. (1970); *Requiem for the Victims of Wars*, ch., orch. (1971); pf. sonata (1975); str. trio (1964); *Es sind keine Traume*, sop., pf. (1987); *3 Romantic Portraits*, 12 sax. (1992).

rueda. Sp. round dance in quintuple time, popular in Castile.

Ruffo, Titta [Ruffo, Cafiero Titta] (*b* Pisa, 1877; *d* Florence, 1953). It. baritone. Opera début as Herald in *Lohengrin*, Rome 1898. Buenos Aires début 1902 (sang regularly there 1908–31). CG 1903; La Scala 1904; Amer. (Philadelphia) 1912; NY Met 1922–9. Superb singer of Verdi bar. roles. Retired 1931.

Rugby. 'Mouvement symphonique' No.2 for orch. by Honegger, 1928. F.p. Paris 1928, f.p. in England, London 1929.

Ruggles, Carl [Charles Sprague] (*b* East Marion, Mass., 1876; *d* Bennington, Vermont, 1971). Amer. composer. Earned living as youth as violinist in Boston th. orchs. Cond. Winona, Minn., SO 1908–12. Moved to NY 1917 and thereafter concentrated on comp. His works were perf. at Varèse's int. composers' guild concerts. Became friend of Ives. Taught comp. at Univ. of Miami 1938–43. His mus. is uncompromisingly dissonant and employed atonal principles long before their general acceptance. Wrote few works, being slow and conscientious worker, discarding many attempts. Prin. comps.:

ORCH.: *Men and Angels* (1920: *Men* destroyed; *Angels* for 6 tpt., rev. 4 tpt., 3 tb., 1938); *Suntreader* (1926–31), rev. as *Men of Men and Mountains*; *Men and Mountains*, small orch. (1924), rev. large orch. 1936, rev. 1941 (comprises *Men*; *Lilacs* for str.; *Marching Mountains*); *Portals* for 13 str. (1925), rev. str. orch. 1929, further rev. 1941 and 1952–3; *Organum* (1944–7).

VOICE & ORCH.: *Vox clamans in deserto*, sop., small orch. (1923, comprises *Parting at Morning* (Browning), *Son of Mine* (Meltzer), *A Clear Midnight* (Whitman)).

SONG: *Toys*, v., pf. (1919).

CHAMBER MUSIC: *Mood*, vn., pf. (*c*.1918).

PIANO: *Evocations*, 4 chants (1935–43, rev. 1954), No.2 orch. 1942, others later.

Ruhe (Ger.). Peace, rest. *ruhig*, peaceful; *ruhelos*, peace-less, restless.

Ruhepunkt; Ruhezeichen (Ger.). Rest-point; rest-sign, i.e. the sign ⌒.

Rührtrommel (Ger.). Tenor drum.

Ruinen von Athen, Die (The Ruins of Athens). Ov. and incidental mus. by Beethoven, Op.113, comp. 1811 for an epilogue by Kotzebue written for first night of Ger. th. in Budapest, 1812. (See also *König Stephan*.) In 1922–4, Strauss and Hofmannsthal ed. and arr. *Die Ruinen von Athen* and included parts of *Die Geschöpfe des* *Prometheus.

Rule, Britannia! Song by *Arne to words by James Thomson, f.p. in masque *Alfred* at Maidenhead, 1 Aug. 1740. Handel quoted it 6 years later in his *Occasional Oratorio*. Beethoven introduced it into his **Battle Sym.* (*Wellington's Victory*) and wrote 5 pf. variations in D on it (pubd. 1804). Wagner wrote an ov. based on it (1837). It has been suggested that it is the 'hidden theme' behind Elgar's *Enigma Variations* (Elgar quoted it in *The Music Makers*).

rule of the octave (It. *regola dell' ottava*). Formula for harmonization of the ascending and descending scale in the bass.

Ruler of the Spirits, The (*Der Beherrscher der Geister*). Concert-ov., Op.27, by Weber, 1811, being rev. of ov. to incomplete opera *Rübezahl*.

rullante, tamburo (It.). Rolling drum, i.e. tenor drum.

rumba. Cuban dance in 8/8 time which extended into world of jazz *c*.1930. Orig. perf. by instr. ens. with singer uttering meaningless phrases and syllables. Arthur Benjamin wrote a **Jamaican Rumba* and rumba rhythm has been used by other composers, e.g. Tippett and McCabe.

Rumford, (Robert) **Kennerley** (*b* Hampstead, 1870; *d* North Stoke, Oxford, 1957). Eng. baritone. Début under Henschel 1893. Gave many popular recitals with his first wife, Clara *Butt.

Runnicles, Donald (*b* Edinburgh, 1954). Scottish conductor. Répétiteur, Nat. Th., Mannheim, 1978, making début as cond. 1980 (*Les contes d' Hoffmann*), chief cond. 1984–7. Ass. cond. at Bayreuth 1982. Prin. cond. Hanover Opera 1987–9. NY Met début 1988; cond. *Der Ring des Nibelungen*, S. Francisco 1990; Vienna début 1990; Glyndebourne début 1991. Mus. dir., Freiburg Opera from 1989, S. Francisco Opera from 1992. Bayreuth début 1993. OBE 2004.

Running Set. Eng. folk dance still in use in Appalachian mountains of USA. Also title of orch. work by Vaughan Williams (1933) based on traditional tunes assoc. with this dance.

Runswick, Daryl (*b* Leicester, 1946). Eng. composer. Jazz player 1968–82 (bass guitar for Frank Sinatra and pianist for Cleo Laine). Db. player in London Sinfonietta 1970–82. Also produced King's Singers recordings and sang in Electric Phoenix. Works incl. *Taking the Air*, rock opera (1989); *I Sing the Body Electric*, vv., tape (1984); *Lady Lazarus*, amp. female v. (1985); *Patents Pending*, 6 solo vv. (1988); *Needs Must When the Devil Drives*, vv., elec. (1990); *Main-Lineing*, cl. qt. (1991). Reorchestrated *Aida* for ens. of 24 players for WNO's *The Drama of Aida* (Mold, 1983)

Rusalka. (1) Opera in 3 acts by Dvořák to lib. by J. Kvapil. Comp. 1900. Prod. Prague 1901, Chicago 1935, London 1950, London (SW) 1959 (first prof. prod. in English), NY Met 1993. Rusalka is a watersprite.
(2) Opera in 4 acts by *Dargomyzhsky to his own lib. after Pushkin (1832). Prod. St Petersburg 1856, Seattle 1921, London 1931.

Rushton, Julian (Gordon) (*b* Cambridge, 1941). Eng. musicologist. Lect., Univ. of East Anglia, 1968–74, Cambridge Univ. 1974–81. Prof. of mus., Leeds Univ. 1982–2002. Specialist in Mozart and Berlioz. His books incl. *The Musical Language of Berlioz* (1983); *W. A. Mozart: Don Giovanni*

(1981); *W. A. Mozart: Idomeneo* (1993); *Elgar, Enigma Variations* (1999); *Mozart: an Extraordinary Life* (2005); *Mozart* (2006).

Ruslan and Lyudmila. Opera in 5 acts by Glinka to lib. by V. F. Shirkov and V. A. Bakhturin based on poem by Pushkin (1820). Comp. 1837–42. Prod. St Petersburg 1842, London 1931, NY 1942 (concert).

Russell, Henry (*b* Sheerness, 1812; *d* London, 1900). Eng. composer, singer, and organist. Org. at Rochester, NY, for several years between *c*.1835 and 1840. Returned to Eng. 1841 and gave popular entertainments at which he sang his own songs, among them 'Cheer, Boys, Cheer' and 'A Life on the Ocean Wave', accompanying himself at the piano. Wrote singing treatise. Had 2 sons, one being Landon *Ronald, the other Henry Russell (*b* London, 1871; *d* London, 1937), impresario and singing teacher who presented opera at CG in 1904 and was dir. of Boston, Mass., Opera Co. 1909–14.

Russian bassoon. Old form of *serpent with bn. shape. Made of wood in 3 or 4 detachable sections, ending in brass bell. 6 finger-holes and 3 or 4 keys.

Russian Quartets (*Die Russischen Quartette*). Name given to Haydn's 6 str. qts., Op.33 (Hob. III:33), 1781, ded. to Grand Duke Paul of Russia. Also known as *Gli Scherzi*, from the character of their minuets, and as *Jungfernquartette* (Maiden qts.).

Russo, William (*b* Chicago, 1928; *d* Chicago, 2003). Amer. composer. Trombonist and composer-arranger for Stan Kenton orch., 1950–4. Dir., Russo Orch., NY, 1958–61 and London Jazz Orch. 1962–5. Teacher and dir. Rock Theater, Peabody Inst., 1969–71, and at Columbia Coll., Chicago, from 1979. Comps. incl. 2 syms.; ballets *Les Deux Errants* (1955) and *The Golden Bird* (1983); operas *John Hooton* (1961) and *A Cabaret Opera* (1985); vc. conc. (1962); *The Civil War*, rock cantata (1968); *David*, rock cantata (1968); *Liberation*, rock cantata (1969); *Street Music*, blues conc., harmonica, pf., orch. (1976); *Urban Trilogy*, orch. (1981); *Memphis*, sax., ens. (1991); many jazz works and film scores.

Russolo, Luigi (*b* Portogruaro, 1885; *d* Cerro di Laveno, 1947). It. composer and painter. Theorist of *futurism movement, for which he also comp. In *L'arte dei rumori* (1913), advocated use of variety of sounds and noises as materials for comp. and invented instrs. for which he developed graphic notation (1926). These were stored in Paris and destroyed during Second World War.

Rustic Wedding (*Ländliche Hochzeit*). Title of sym.-poem in 5 movts. by K. Goldmark, 1876.

Rustle of Spring (*Frühlingsrauschen*). Title of pf. piece (No.3 of 6, Op.32, pubd. 1909) by Sinding, extremely popular and exists in many arrs. Comp. 1896.

Rute, Ruthe (Ger.). Rod. Type of birch brush used to beat the bass drum to obtain special effect. Called for by R. Strauss, Mahler in 7th sym., etc.

Ruth. Opera in 1 act by L. Berkeley to lib. by E. Crozier based on *Book of Ruth*. Prod. London 1956. Also title of various 19th-cent. oratorios.

Rutter, John (*b* London, 1945). Eng. composer. Dir. of mus., Clare Coll., Cambridge, 1975–9. Founded Cambridge Singers 1981 (NY début 1990). Special interest in composing for young people and for amateurs. Works incl.: *Bang!* (opera, 1975); *Partita*, orch. (1975–6); *The Falcon*, ch., semi-ch., boy's ch., and orch. (1969); *Fancies*, ch., orch. (1971); *Gloria*, ch., brass, perc., org. (1974); *5 Childhood Lyrics*, unacc. ch. (1973); *Requiem* (1985); *Te Deum* (1988); *Magnificat*, sop., ch., ens. (1990); *Psalm 150* (2002); anthems, carols, and church mus.

Ruy Blas. Ov. by Mendelssohn, Op.95, comp. 1839 for a Ger. perf. of Victor Hugo's play of that name (1838).

Rydl, Kurt (*b* Vienna, 1947). Austrian bass. Opera début Stuttgart 1973 (Daland in *Der fliegende Holländer*). Débuts: Bayreuth 1975; Vienna 1976; Salzburg 1976; CG 1993. Has recorded Ochs (*Der Rosenkavalier*) with Haitink.

Ryom, Peter (*b* Copenhagen, 1937). Danish musicologist. Catalogued works of Vivaldi (*Verzeichnis der Werke Antonio Vivaldis*, Leipzig 1974, 2nd edn. 1979), superseding earlier catalogues by Fanna, Pincherle, and Rinaldi.

Rysanek, Leonie (*b* Vienna, 1926; *d* Vienna, 1998). Austrian soprano. Opera début Innsbruck 1949 (Agathe in *Der Freischütz*). Munich State Opera from 1952, Vienna State Opera from 1954. Débuts: CG 1953 (with Munich co.); S. Francisco 1956; Salzburg Fest. 1958; NY Met 1959; Bayreuth Fest. 1951. Notable singer of Strauss and Wagner roles. Late in her career sang Janáček roles of Kostelnička and Kabanicha.

Rzewski, Frederic (Anthony) (*b* Westfield, Mass., 1938). Amer. composer and pianist. Professional pianist from 1960. Taught at Cologne courses for new mus., 1963, 1964, 1970. Co-founder, Musica Elettronica Viva studio, Rome, 1966. Returned to NY 1971. Prof. of comp., Liège Cons. from 1977. Disciple of Cage and Stockhausen. Has written works involving dancers, film, tape, etc.

S

S. (1) Abbreviation for **segno, *sinistra, *subito.*

(2) Abbreviation for *schola* (choir) in liturgical books.

(3) Abbreviation for **Schmieder* in catalogue of works of J. S. Bach.

Saariaho, Kaija (*b* Helsinki, 1952). Finnish composer. Studied Sibelius Acad. (1976–81) and Freiburg Musikhochschule (1981–2) with **Ferneyhough and *Huber. From 1982 worked in Paris at IRCAM. Taught at Sibelius Acad. 1997–8. Works often use live elec. and tape. Has written th. mus. and mus. for multimedia. Comps. incl.:

OPERAS: *L'amour de loin* (2003); *Adriana Mater* (2004–5).

ORCH.: *Verblendungen*, orch., tape (1982–4); *Du cristal* (1989–90); . . . *à la fumée*, fl., vc., orch., elec. (1990); *Graal théâtre*, vn., orch. (1994, rev. vn., chamber orch. 1997); fl. conc. (*Aile du songe*) (2001); *Orion*, pf., str. (2002); *Asteroid 4179: Toutatis*, orch. (2005).

CHAMBER MUSIC: *Canvas*, fl. (1978); *Im Traume*, vc., pf. (1980); *Lichtbogen*, fl., 2 vn., va., vc., db., hp., pf., perc., elec. (1985–6); *Petals*, vc. (1988); *For the Moon*, bcl., vc. (1990); *Nocturnes*, vn. (1994); *Neiges*, 8 vc. (1998); *Sept papillons*, vc. (2000); *Terrestre*, fl., perc./hp./vn., vc. (2002).

CHORAL & VOCAL: *The Bride*, sop., 2 fl., perc. (1977); *Study for Life*, female v., dancer, tape, light (1980); *From the Grammar of Dreams*, 2 sop. (1988); *Nuits, adieux*, 4 vv., elec. (1991); *Die Aussicht*, sop., fl., gui., vn., vc. (1996); *Miranda's Lament*, sop., cl., vn., db., hp. (1997); *Message pour Gérard*, mez., fl., hp., 2 perc., vn., va., vc., db. (2000); *Tag des Jahrs*, ch., elec. (2001); *Prospero's Vision*, bar., vn., cl., hp., db. (2002); *Another Heart Beats*, alto, vc., pf. (2003); *La Passion de Simone*, oratorio (2005–6).

Sabbatini, Galeazzo (*b* ?Pesaro, 1597; *d* Pesaro, 1662). It. composer. Canon of Pesaro Cath., 1626–30 and from 1641. Mus. dir. to Duke of Mirandola 1630–9. Comp. madrigals and motets. Wrote treatise on figured bass.

Sacchini, Antonio (Maria Gasparo) (*b* Florence, 1730; *d* Paris, 1786). It. composer, influenced by Gluck's reforms. Active in Venice, Rome, and Naples, 1762–9. Worked in London 1772–81, writing 17 operas which won him popularity. Settled in Paris 1782 where he enjoyed even greater vogue. Piccinni's most formidable rival in It. Wrote over 40 operas, incl. *Semiramide*, *Armido e Rinaldo*, and *Œdipe à Colonne*; 2 syms.; 6 str. qts.

Sacher, Paul (*b* Basle, 1906; *d* Basle, 1999). Swiss cond. Founded Basle Chamber Orch. 1926, Schola Cantorum Basiliensis 1933. Cond. Zurich Collegium Musicum (chamber orch.) from 1941. Dir., Basle Acad. of Mus. 1954–69. Cond. at Glyndebourne 1954–63 (début in The *Rake's Progress*). NY début 1955. Among works commissioned for his Basle and Zurich chamber orchs. are Bartók's *Divertimento* and *Music for Strings, Percussion and Celesta*, Strauss's *Metamorphosen*, and works by many contemp. composers.

Sachs, Curt (*b* Berlin, 1881; *d* NY, 1959). Ger.-born musicologist. Prof. of musicology, Berlin Univ. and curator of state coll. of mus. instrs. Left Ger. 1934, settling first in Paris, then USA. Prof. of Mus., NY Univ. 1937–53. Author of books on instrs., rhythm and tempo, history of dance, etc.

Sachs, Hans (*b* Nuremberg, 1494; *d* Nuremberg, 1576). Ger. shoemaker and poet, foremost of Nuremberg Mastersingers. Wrote over 4,000 master-sch. poems and nearly 2,000 narrative and dramatic poems. His master-songs were pubd. in *Das Singebuch des Adam Puschmann* ed. Münzer (1906). Immortalized by Wagner in *Die Meistersinger von Nürnberg* (1862–7).

sackbut. (1) Early Eng. name for tb. Origin of name unknown (sometimes occurs as *shagbolt*). Used from last years of 15th cent. Most common size was tenor in B♭ which could cope with alto, ten., or bass parts. Adaptable to different pitches. Little different from modern tb. except that modern instr. has bell with greater flare. Matthew **Locke's *Music for His Majesty's Sackbuts and Cornetts* dates from 1661.

(2) Name of mus. periodical founded by Philip Heseltine (Peter **Warlock), 1920.

Sackman, Nicholas (*b* London, 1950). Eng. composer. Taught in London, then lect. in comp., Nottingham Univ., from 1990. Works incl. str. qts. No.1 (1978–9), No.2 (1990–1); *Ensembles and Cadenzas*, vc., 5 players (1972); *From this moment a change*, chamber ens. (1973); *A Pair of Wings*, 3 sops., ens. (1970–3); *Ellipsis*, pf., ens. (1976); *Doubles*, 2 instr. groups (1977–8); *And the World— a Wonder Waking*, mez., 8 instr. (1981); *Holism*, va., vc. (1982); *Time-Piece*, brass quintet (1982–3, rev. 1986); pf. sonata (1983–4); *Corranach*, 7 players (1985); sonata, tb., pf. (1986); *Paraphrase*, wind (1987, rev. 1990); fl. conc. (1988–9); *Hawthorn*, orch. (1991–2); *Scorpio*, perc., pf. (1995); *Caccia*, pf., orch. (1997–8); *Koi*, fl. qt. (1998–9); *Mosaic*, orch. (2002); *Cross Hands*, pf. (2002); *Puppets*, perc. qt. (2003); *Vivace*, chamber orch. (2004).

sacra rappresentazione (It.). 'Sacred representation'. Type of staged oratorio, precursor of opera, popular in Italy up to mid-16th cent.

Sacred and Profane. 8 settings of medieval lyrics for unacc. vv. by Britten, Op.91, comp. 1974–5: 1. *St. Godric's hymn*. 2. *I mon waxe wod*. 3. *Lenten is come*. 4. *The long night*. 5. *Yif ic of luve can*. 6. *Carol*. 7. *Ye that pasen by*. 8. *A death*. F.p. Snape 1975.

Sacred Service (*Avodath Hakodesh*). Setting by Bloch of Jewish Sabbath morning service for bar., ch., and orch. Hebrew text follows 5 traditional chief liturgical sections with additions chosen by Bloch. Comp. 1930–3 after request in 1930 for setting for use in Reform Synagogue, NY. F.p., Turin 1934.

Sacre du printemps, Le. Fr. title for Stravinsky's The *Rite of Spring*.

Sadaï, Yizhak (*b* Sofia, 1935). Bulgarian-born Israeli composer. Teacher in Jerusalem from 1960 and at Tel Aviv Univ. from 1966 (later prof. of mus.). Works incl. *Prélude à Jerusalem*, for 3 reciters, ch., and orch. (1968). Since being influenced by Pierre Schaeffer in 1966, many of his works have used tape.

Sadie, Stanley (John) (*b* Wembley, 1930; *d* Cossington, Somerset, 2005). Eng. critic, writer, and editor. Prof., TCL 1957–65. On mus. staff of The Times 1964–81. Ed., *Musical Times* 1967–87. Ed., *New Grove Dictionary of Music* (6th edn. of Grove's *Dictionary of Music and Musicians*) 1970 (pubd. 1980, 2nd edn. 2001), *New Grove Dictionary of Musical Instruments* (1984), *New Grove Dictionary of American Music* (1986), *New Grove Dictionary of Opera* (1992), *Grove Concise Dictionary of Music* (1988, 2nd edn. 1994), *Cambridge Music Guide* (with A. Latham) (1985), and *Calling on the Composer* (with J. A. Sadie) (2005). Author of books on Handel, Mozart, and Beethoven. CBE 1982. His wife **Julie Anne Sadie** (*née* McCormack) (*b* Eugene, Oregon, 1948) trained as a cellist, taught at Eastman Sch. 1974–6, ed. *Everyman Companion to Baroque Music* (1991), and joint. ed. *New Grove Dictionary of Women Composers* (1994).

Sadko. Opera (*opera-bylina*) in 7 scenes by Rimsky-Korsakov to lib. by composer, V. Stasov, V. Belsky and others. Comp. 1894–6. Prod. Moscow 1898, NY Met 1930, London 1931. Developed from 'symphonic picture' for orch., *Sadko*, comp. 1867, rev. 1869 and 1891.

Sadler's Wells. See *English National Opera*.

Sádlo [Zátvrzský], **Miloš** (*b* Prague, 1912; *d* Prague, 2003). Cz. cellist. Adopted name of his teacher K. P. Sádlo. Début as soloist 1929, London 1937. Studied at Prague Cons. 1938–40 and with Casals in 1955. Member of Prague Qt. (1931–3) and other chamber groups incl. Prague Trio (1966–73). Taught at Prague Acad. from 1950. Gave modern première of Dvořák's A major conc., which he edited.

saeta. Andalusian folk-song sung during Lent or Feast of the Nativity to acc. street processions.

Saeverud, Harald (Sigurd Johan) (*b* Bergen, 1897; *d* Siljustol, Norway, 1992). Norweg. composer. Mus. critic in Bergen 1929–40. Works incl. 9 syms. (1916–66); *Overtura appassionata* (1920); *50 Variazioni piccole*, chamber orch. (1931); ob. conc. (1938); incid. mus. to *Peer Gynt* (1947, 2 orch. suites 1947); pf. conc. (1948–50); vn. conc. (1956); bn. conc. (1963); 3 str. qts. (1969, 1975,

1978); *Fanfare and Hymn*, orch. (1970); wind quintet, fl., ob., cl., hn., bn. (1983); *Åsnes Vals*, pf. (1988); *Scènes macabres*, pf. (1989); Sonatina, va., pf. (1989).

Safonov [Safonoff], **Vasily** (Ilyich) (*b* Itsyursk, Caucasus, 1852; *d* Kislovodsk, 1918). Russ. pianist and conductor. Début St Petersburg 1880. Taught at St Petersburg Cons. 1881–5 and at Moscow Cons. 1885–1905 (dir. 1889–1905). Began career as cond. 1889. NY début 1904, cond. NYPO 1906–9. Dir., Nat. Cons., NY, 1906–9. London début with LSO 1906. Returned to Russia 1911. Notable advocate of Tchaikovsky's mus. First modern cond. to dispense with baton.

Saga, En (Sibelius). See *En Saga*.

sainete (Sp. 'farce', 'titbit'). Sp. form of late 18th-cent. comic opera, usually employing scenes of low life. Among notable composers of *sainetes* was *Soler.

St Anne. Eng. hymn-tune of disputed orig. but probably comp. by William *Croft, who pubd. it in 1708. Usually sung to words 'O God, our help in ages past'. J. S. Bach's Fugue in E♭ for org. (last item of *Klavierübung*, Book 3, 1739) begins with same notes and is known in Eng. as *St Anne Fugue*.

'St Anthony' Variations (Brahms). See *Variations on a Theme by Haydn*.

St Florian. Monastery near Linz, Austria, founded *c*.1070. Has long and strong mus. tradition. Building was reconstructed in Baroque style from 1686 to 1750 with new org. built by F. X. Chrismann, later enlarged to 4 manuals, 103 registers, and 7,343 pipes. *Bruckner was born near St Florian, was a choirboy there and was taught mus. by the monks. Org. there 1848–56. Often revisited St Florian and is buried there. Org. known as 'Bruckner Organ'.

Saint-Foix, Marie Olivier Georges du Parc Poulain, Comte de (*b* Paris, 1874; *d* Aix-en-Provence, 1954). Fr. musicologist. Author, with T. de Wyzewa, of life of Mozart in 5 vols., 1912–46 (last 3 vols. by Saint-Foix alone). Wrote book on Mozart's syms. (1932, Eng. edn. 1947).

Saint François d'Assise (St Francis of Assisi). Opera (*scènes franciscains*) in 3 acts and 8 tableaux by Messiaen to his own lib. Comp. 1975–83. F.p. Paris, Dec. 1983, cond. Ozawa; Boston 1986 (3 scenes); London (concert perf. cond. Nagano) 1988; Salzburg 1993.

St James's Hall. Chief concert-hall in London 1858–1905, in Regent St. Capacity 2,127. Home of chamber concerts known as 'Monday Pops' 1859–98 and 'Saturday Pops' 1865–98, Phil. Soc. concerts, Richter concerts, etc. Superseded by Queen's Hall and subsequently demolished.

St John Passion (*Johannespassion*; properly in Eng. The Passion According to St John). Setting by Bach (BWV245) for solo vv., ch., and orch. of the Passion of Christ narrated in St John's Gospel, with interpolations. F.p. Leipzig, Good Friday 1723, f.p. in England 1872. There are also *St John Passion* settings by Selle (1623), *Schütz (1666), *Telemann (1741), and Pärt (1981-2).

St John's Night on the Bare Mountain (Mussorgsky). See *Night on the Bare Mountain.*

St John's, Smith Square. London church built between 1713 and 1728. Converted into concert-hall 1969 and used often for broadcasts of chamber mus. and chamber ensembles. Orch. of St John's, Smith Square, founded by John Lubbock, 1973.

St Louis Opera. See *Opera Theatre of St Louis.*

St Louis Symphony Orchestra. Second oldest sym. orch. in USA, founded in St Louis, Missouri, March 1881. Complement of about 100 musicians. Since 1968 has played in Powell Symphony Hall. Prin. conds. have incl. Joseph Otten, Alfred Ernst, Max Zach, Rudolph Ganz, Vladimir Golschmann (1931-58), Edouard van Remoortel (1958-62), Eleazar Carvalho (1963-8), Walter Süsskind (1968-75), Jerzy Semkow (1976-9), Leonard Slatkin (1979-95), Hans Vonk (1996-2002), David Robertson from 2002. St Louis also has thriving operatic life.

St Ludmila. Oratorio, Op.71, by Dvořák, comp. 1885-6 and f.p. Leeds Fest. 1886. Text by Vrchlický. For sop., cont., 2 ten., bass, ch., orch.

St Luke Passion. Oratorio by *Penderecki for narrator, sop., bar., bass, boys' ch., 3 mixed ch., and orch. Comp. 1962-5. Commissioned by W. Ger. Radio (Cologne). F.p. Münster Cath. 1966.

St Matthew Passion (*Matthäuspassion;* properly in Eng. *The Passion According to St Matthew*). Setting by Bach (BWV244) for solo vv., ch., and orch. of the Passion of Christ from St Matthew's Gospel with interpolations by Picander. F.p. Leipzig, Good Friday 1727; revived by Mendelssohn, Berlin 1829 (see *Bach Revival*), f.p. London 1854 (incomplete), 1870 (complete, cond. Barnby). There are other settings of the *St Matthew Passion*, incl. those by R. *Davy, *Sebastiani (c.1663), and *Schütz (1665).

St Nicolas. Cantata, Op.42, by Britten, text by Eric Crozier, for solo ten., ch., women's semi-ch., 4 boy singers, str., pf. duet, perc., and org. Comp. 1947-8. F.p. Aldeburgh 1948.

Saint of Bleecker Street, The. Opera in 3 acts by *Menotti to his own lib. Comp. 1953-4. Prod. NY 1954, Milan 1955, London (TV) 1956.

Sainton, Prosper (Philippe Cathérine) (*b* Toulouse, 1813; *d* London, 1890). Fr. violinist. Prof., Toulouse Cons. 1840-5. Settled in London 1845, becoming prof. at RAM, leader of Phil. Soc. orch. 1846-54, CG orch. 1847-71. Wrote 2 vn. concs. and several vn. pieces. Retired 1883.

Sainton-Dolby, Charlotte (Helen) (*b* London, 1821; *d* London, 1885). Eng. contralto. Début as

soloist London 1842. Sang at Leipzig Gewandhaus concerts 1845-6. Mendelssohn wrote cont. part in *Elijah* for her. Married violinist Prosper *Sainton 1860. Opened singing sch. in London 1872. Comp. 4 cantatas.

St Paul (*Paulus*). Oratorio by Mendelssohn, Op.36, for SATB soloists, ch., and orch., comp. 1834-6, f.p. Düsseldorf 1836 cond. composer.

St Paul's Suite. Suite for str. orch., Op.29 No.2, by Holst, comp. 1912-13. Written for sch. orch. of St Paul's Girls' Sch., Hammersmith, where Holst was dir. of mus. from 1905. 4 movts. are *Jig, Ostinato, Intermezzo,* and *Finale: the *Dargason* (in which the tune *Greensleeves* is used as a counterpoint).

St Petersburg Philharmonic Orchestra. Orch. based in St Petersburg. Founded 1921 (as Leningrad PO) from pre-Revolutionary court orch. Prin. conds. Emil Cooper (1921-2), Nikolay Malko (1926-9), Alexander Gauk (1930-3), Fritz Stiedry (1934-7), Evgeny Mravinsky (1938-88, jointly with Kurt Sanderling 1941-60), Yury Temirkanov from 1988. Also closely ass. with it have been Arvid *Yansons and his son Mariss *Jansons. Gave f.ps. of Shostakovich syms. Nos. 1, 2, 3, 5, 6, 9, 10, and 14. Name changed to St Petersburg PO 1991.

Saint-Saëns, (Charles) **Camille** (*b* Paris, 1835; *d* Algiers, 1921). Fr. composer, pianist, and organist. Showed mus. aptitude as child almost comparable with Mozart's. Gave pf. recital in Paris 1846. Entered Paris Cons. 1848, studying org. with Benoist and comp. with Halévy. Organist, Eglise Ste-Merry, Paris, 1853-7, Madeleine 1857-77. In 1852 met and became friends with Liszt, by whom he was much influenced. Wrote his first syms. c.1848 and 1850 (unpubd.) and became pf. prof. at École Niedermeyer 1861-5 (his pupils incl. Fauré and Messager). Wrote first opera 1864-5 and began work on *Samson and Dalila* in 1868. In 1871 was co-founder of Société Nationale de Musique, formed to encourage development of Fr. instr. sch. To this end wrote a series of excellent symphonic poems. By this time was in demand as solo pianist and organist, and was soloist at the f.p. of his 5 pf. concs. between 1865 and 1896. First visit to Eng., 1871, to play Albert Hall org. Liszt prod. *Samson et Dalila* at Weimar 1877, Parisian impresarios regarding the biblical subject as too serious (not prod. at the Opéra until 1892). His best sym., No.3 in C minor (the 'Organ') was ded. to Liszt's memory and f.p. in London, 1886. In later life Saint-Saëns travelled widely and stayed often in Algeria, some of his later works reflecting local colour. Visited USA in 1915. Last visited Eng. 1913 to conduct *The Promised Land* at Gloucester Fest. Wrote coronation march for Edward VII in 1902. Saint-Saëns's output was prolific and extended for most of his 86 years. Elegance of form and line, beautiful harmonies and chords were more important to him than emotional feeling or technical adventure, and his mus. has therefore been condemned for its superficiality and facility. Nevertheless these very qualities, to which may be added graceful melodic invention, have ensured the survival of a large amount of his work. It is significant that he was admired by Ravel, another emotionally undemonstrative composer. His best features are to be found in *Samson et Dalila*, the 3rd Sym., and the pf. concs. Hon. CVO 1902. Prin. comps.:

OPERAS: *Le Timbre d'argent* (1864–5); **Samson et Dalila* (1867–8, 1873–7); *La Princesse jaune* (1872); *Etienne Marcel* (1877–8); *Henri VIII* (1881–2); *Proserpine* (1886, rev. 1889); *Ascanio* (1887–8); *Phryné* (1892); *Frédégonde* (completion of opera by Giraud, 1894–5); *Les Barbares* (1900–1); *Hélène* (1903); *L'ancêtre* (1905); *Déjanire* (1919–20).

ORCH.: syms: No.1 in E♭ (1853), No.2 in A minor (1859), No.3 in C minor, with org. (1886) (2 other syms., 2nd and 3rd in order of comp., 1852 and 1859, were withdrawn by the composer); sym.-poems: *Le *Rouet d'Omphale* (1871–2); **Phaëton* (1873), **Danse macabre* (1874), *La *Jeunesse d'Hercule* (1877); *Marche héroïque* (1871); *Suite Algérienne* (1880); *Une Nuit à Lisbonne* (1880); *Jota Aragonesa* (1880); *Ouverture de fête* (1910).

INSTR(S). & ORCH.: pf. concs.: No.1 in D (1858), No.2 in G minor (1868), No.3 in E♭ (1869), No.4 in C minor (1875), No.5 in F (1896); vn. concs.: No.1 in A major (1859), No.2 in C (1858, pubd. 1879), No.3 in B minor (1880); vc. concs.: No.1 in A minor (1872), No.2 (1902); Miscellaneous: *Introduction and Rondo Capriccioso*, vn. (1863, pubd. 1870), *Romance*, vn. (1874), *Morceau de Concert*, vn. (1880), *Caprice Andalou*, vn. (1904); *Allegro appassionato*, pf. (1884); *Rapsodie d'Auvergne*, pf. (1884); *Africa*, fantasy, pf. (1891); *Tarantelle*, fl., cl. (1857); *Romance*, fl. or vn. (1871); *Odelette*, fl. (1920); *Romance*, hn. or vc. (1874); **Carnaval des Animaux*, 2 pf. and orch. (1886).

CHORUS & ORCH.: *Mass* (1856); *Oratorio de Noël* (1858); *Les Noces de Prométhée* (1867); *Psalm 18* (1865); *Le Déluge* (1875); *Requiem* (1878); *La Lyre et l'harpe* (1879); *Hymne à Victor Hugo* (1881); *Le Feu céleste* (1900); *Psalm 150* (1907); *The Promised Land* (1913); *Hail, California* (1915); *Hymne à la Paix* (1919).

CHAMBER MUSIC: str. qts. No.1 (1899), No.2 (1918); pf. quintet (1865); pf. trio No.1 in F (1863), No.2 in E minor (1892); pf. qt. (1875); *Septet*, pf., str., tpt. (1881); vn. sonata.No.1 in D minor (1885), No.2 in E♭ (1896); *Wedding-Cake*, caprice-valse, pf., str. (1886); *Havanaise*, vn., pf. (or orch.) (1887); vc. sonata No.1 (1872), No.2 (1905); *Cavatina*, ten. tb., pf. (1915); *Elegy* No.1, vn., pf. (1915), No.2 (1920); ob. sonata, cl. sonata, bn. sonata (1921).

PIANO: *6 Bagatelles* (1855); *6 Études* (1877); *6 Études* (1899); *6 Fugues* (1920).

2 PIANOS: *Variations on a Theme of Beethoven* (1874); *Polonaise* (1886); *Caprice Arabe* (1884); *Caprice héroïque* (1898).

ORGAN: *Bénédiction nuptiale* (1859); *3 Preludes and Fugues* (1894); *Marche réligieuse* (1897); *3 Fantaisies* (1857, 1895, 1919).

St Thomas Wake. Foxtrot for orch by *Maxwell Davies on a Pavan by John Bull. Scored for large orch., with many exotic instr., contrasting Bull's tune with 20th-cent. dance-band foxtrot, and in-

spired by composer's memories of air raid on Manchester 1940. Comp. 1969. F.p. Dortmund 1969, cond. composer.

Saite (Ger., plural *Saiten*). String, thus *Saiten-instrumente*, str. instr.

salicional. Org. stop of soft tone, 8′ length and pitch (sometimes 16′). *salicet* is of 4′ length and pitch.

Salieri, Antonio (*b* Legnano, 1750; *d* Vienna, 1825). It. composer and conductor. Taken to Vienna 1766 as protégé of Gassmann. Début as cond. Vienna Court Opera 1770 and in next 4 years had 9 operas prod. Comp. and mus. dir. It. opera in Vienna from 1774. Back in It. 1778–80, writing comic operas for Milan, Venice, and Rome. Succeeded Gluck at Paris Opéra 1784–8. Court cond. Vienna 1788–1824 (of choral concerts only after 1790). Was hostile to Mozart, but there is no truth in legend that he poisoned him (as is depicted in Rimsky-Korsakov's *Mozart and Salieri*). Taught Beethoven, Schubert, and Liszt. Wrote over 40 operas, incl. *Prima la musica, poi le parole* (1786), *Tarare* (1787), *Axur* (1788, reworking of *Tarare*), *Palmira* (1795), and *Falstaff* (1798); 4 oratorios, much church mus., and many vocal and instr. pieces.

Salle Favart. Colloquial name for Paris Opéra-Comique th., which is in the Rue Favart and was for a time known as Théâtre de la rue Favart.

Sallinen, Aulis (Heikki) (*b* Salmi, Finland, 1935). Finn. composer. Manager, Finnish Radio SO 1960–70. Teacher, Sibelius Acad. 1965–81. Became Finn. Government's first Prof. of Arts for Life, 1981. Comps. incl.:

OPERAS: *The Horseman* (*Ratsumies*) (1973–4); *The Red Line* (*Punainen viiva*) (1976–8); *The *King Goes Forth to France* (*Kuningas lähtee Ranskaan*) (1983); **Kullervo* (1987–8); *The Palace* (1994–5); *King Lear* (1998–9).

BALLETS: *Midsommernatten* (from sym. No.3) (1983); *Secret of Heavens* (*Himlens hemlighet*) (from syms. Nos. 1, 3, and 4) (1986); *The Hobbit*, vc., fl. (2000).

ORCH.: syms: No.1 (1971), No.2 (*Symphonic Dialogue*), perc., orch. (1972), No.3 (1974–5), No.4 (1979), No.5 (*Washington Mosaics*) (1985), No.6 (*From a New Zealand Diary*) (1989–90), No.7 (*The Dreams of Gandalf*) (1996), No.8 (*Autumnal Fragments*) (2001); *Concerto for Chamber Orch.* (1960); *Funeral Music* (1962); *Variations* (1963); *Chamber Music I*, str. (1975), *II*, fl., str. (1976), *III* (*The Nocturnal Dances of Don Juanquixote*), vc., str. (1986), *IV* (*Version of Metamorphosen*) (1964/2000), *V* (*Barabbas Variations*) (2000); vn. conc. (1968); vc. conc (1976); *Shadows* (1982); *Fanfare*, ww., brass (1986); *Sunrise Serenade*, 2 tpt., pf., str. (1989); fl. conc. (1994–5); *Introduction and Tango Ov.*, pf., str. (1997); hn. conc. (2002); *Chamber Conc.*, vn., pf., chamber orch. (2004–5); *Chamber Music VI*, str. qt., str. (2006).

CHORAL & VOCAL: *Suita grammaticale*, children's ch., chamber orch. (1971); *4 Dream Songs*, sop., orch. (1972); *Songs from the Sea*, unacc. children's ch.

(1974); *Dies Irae*, sop., bass, male ch., orch. (1978); *Song Around a Song*, unacc. children's ch. (1980); suite, *The Iron Age*, sop., children's ch., ch., orch. (1983); *The Beaufort Scale*, unacc. ch. (1984); *Anthem for Ants*, unacc. children's ch. (1988); *Songs of Life and Death*, bar./mez., ch., orch. (1995); *The Birth of Ale ('Oluen Synty')*, unacc. ch. (1999); *The Barabbas Dialogues*, narr., sop., mez., ten., bass, bass-bar., instr. ens. (2003).

CHAMBER MUSIC: str. qts.: No.1 (1958), No.2 (*Canzona*) (1960), No.3 (*Some Aspects of Peltomiemi Hintrik's Funeral March*) (1969; also for str. orch.), No.4 (*Quiet Songs*) (1971), No.5 (*Pieces of Mosaic*) (1983); *Elegy for Sebastian Knight*, vc. (1964); *Quattro per Quattro*, ob. (or fl. or cl.), vn., vc., hpd. (1965); *Cadenze*, vn. (1965); *4 Études*, vn., pf. (1970); *Chorali*, 2 perc., hp., cel. (1970); solo vc. sonata (1971); *Metamorfora*, vc., pf. (1974); *Canto and Ritornello*, vn. (1975); *Echoes from a Play*, ob., str. qt. (1990); *From a Swan Song*, vc., pf. (1991); *Introduction and Tango Ov.*, pf., str. quintet/str. qt (1997); pf. quintet (2004); sonata, vc., pf. (2004).

SONGS: *Simple Simon and his Dog*, bar., pf. (1978); *Man, is-nothing, is-no-one*, bar., pf. (1978).

KEYBOARD: *Notturno*, pf. (1966); *Chaconne*, org. (1970); *King Lear's Distant War*, pf. (2000).

Salmenhaara, Erkki (*b* Helsinki, 1941; *d* Helsinki, 2002). Finn. composer. Mus. critic in Helsinki 1963–73, lect. Helsinki Univ. from 1963. Works incl. opera *The Woman of Portugal* (1970–2); 5 syms. (1962–89); hn. conc. (1973); vc. conc. (1983–7); *Requiem profanum* (1968–9); *Information Explosion* (elec.); 2 vc. sonatas (1960, 1982); str. qt. (1977); 4 pf. sonatas (1965–80); Suite for Winds (1995).

Salminen, Matti (*b* Turku, 1945). Finnish bass. Sang small parts at Finn. Nat. Opera from 1966; début in major role 1969 (Philip II in *Don Carlos*). Prin. bass Cologne Opera 1972–9. Wexford 1973 (title-role in *Ivan Susanin*). Débuts: CG 1974; Bayreuth 1976; NY Met 1981. Notable singer of Boris Godunov and of major Wagner bass roles.

Salmond, Felix (*b* London, 1888; *d* NY, 1952). Eng. cellist. Début London 1909. Cellist in London Str. Qt. and other chamber mus. ens. Soloist in f.p. of Elgar's Vc. Conc., 1919. Début NY 1922, settling in USA. Formed Trio of NY 1937. Head of vc. dept., Curtis Inst. 1925–42 and taught at Juilliard Sch. 1924–52. Pupils included Leonard *Rose.

Salome. (1) Opera in 1 act by Richard Strauss, being setting of Hedwig Lachmann's Ger. trans. of Wilde's Fr. play *Salomé*. Comp. 1903–5. Prod. Dresden 1905, NY Met 1907, London 1910. Fr. vers. by Strauss to Wilde's text, involving changes to vocal line and scoring, 1905, pubd. 1906. F.p. Paris 1907, concert perf. Montpellier 1989, stage Lyons 1990 (and recorded).

(2) Opera, based on Wilde's play, by Mariotte. Prod. Lyons 1908, Paris 1910.

(3) Drama without words, *La tragédie de Salomé*, by F. Schmitt. Prod. Paris 1907, rev. 1910.

(4) Ballet choreog. Flemming Flindt, mus. by *Maxwell Davies, prod. Stockholm 1978.

Salomon, Johann Peter (*b* Bonn, 1745; *d* London, 1815). Ger.-born violinist and impresario. Played in Bonn court orch. 1758–65. Violinist and composer in royal orch. at Rheinsberg 1764–80. Settled in London 1781, winning special fame as qt. player. Began to organize concerts and introduced Haydn and Mozart syms. at series in 1786. Brought Haydn to Eng. 1790–1 and 1794–5 (hence name 'Salomon symphonies' for Haydn's last 12). Suggested *The Creation* to Haydn. Friend of Beethoven. Co-founder Phil. Soc. of London 1813, leading orch. at first concert. Comp. operas, oratorio, vn. concs. Buried in Westminster Abbey.

Salomon [Salmon], **Karel** (*b* Heidelberg, 1897; *d* Beit Zayit, nr. Jerusalem, 1974). Ger.-Israeli composer, baritone, and conductor. Cond. in Hamburg 1920–6. Settled in Palestine 1933. Mus. dir., Jerusalem Univ., then of Palestine Radio 1936. Mus. dir. Israel radio 1948–57. Works incl. opera *David and Goliath*, 2 syms., pf. conc., vc. conc., glockenspiel conc., chamber mus., etc.

Salomon Symphonies (Haydn). See *London Symphonies*.

Salonen, Esa-Pekka (*b* Helsinki, 1958). Finn. composer and conductor. Began career as hornplayer. London début 1983 (Philharmonia Orch.). Chief cond. Swedish Radio SO 1985–95. Cond. f.p. of Saxton's *The Circles of Light*, 1986. Cond. Messiaen's *Saint François d'Assise*, Salzburg Fest. 1992. CG début 1995. Prin. cond. Los Angeles PO from 1992 and of Philharmonia Orchestra from 2008. Comps. incl.: *Goodbye*, vn., gui. (1979); sax. conc. (1980–1); *Baalal*, tape (1982); *Floof*, sop., small ens. (1990); *Second Meeting*, ob., pf. (1992); *LA Variations*, orch. (1997); *5 Images after Sappho*, sop., 14 instr. (1999); *2 Songs from Kalender Röd*, unacc. ch. (2000); *Dichotomie*, pf. (2000); vc. conc. (*Mania*) (2000); *Foreign Bodies*, orch. (2001); *Insomnia*, orch. (2002); *Wing on Wing*, 2 sop., orch. (2004); *Stockholm Diary*, str. (2004); *Helix*, orch. (2005).

salon music. Term applied, often pejoratively, to mus. of light character which aims to please rather than to be profound, suitable for perf. in a salon. Elgar's lighter works are sometimes called 'salon music' by those who wish to disparage them.

saltando; saltato (It.). Leaping, leapt. Term used in str. playing, meaning with a springing bow, i.e. same as *spiccato.

saltarello (modern It. *salterello*). Lively dance of Sp. and It. provenance in varying metres (6/8, 3/4, 3/8, 6/4), incorporating jumps. In 16th cent. was the after-dance (*Nachtanz*) to a *pavan or *passamezzo, the mus. often being indistinguishable from a galliard. Mendelssohn called the finale of his 'Italian' Sym. a *saltarello*.

saltbox. Traditional handy instr. used when joyous mus. was to be extemporized, domestically or publicly. The lid was flapped up and down and the side battered with a rolling-pin.

Salter, Lionel (Paul) (b London, 1914; d London, 2000). Eng. pianist, harpsichordist, composer, critic, and conductor. Ass. cond. BBC Th. Orch. 1945–6. Mus. supervisor, BBC European service 1948. Head of Mus., BBC TV 1956. Head of TV Opera 1963, Ass. Controller of Mus. 1967–74. Translator of opera libs., ed. of early mus. Authority on jazz.

Salut d'amour (Liebesgruss) (Love's greeting). Short piece by Elgar, Op.12, orig. written as pf. solo 1888, orch. 1889, also arr. for vn. and pf. and for many other combinations.

Salve Regina (Hail, Queen). One of 4 Antiphons to Virgin Mary, probably written in 11th cent. Polyphonic settings became numerous in 15th and 16th cents.

Salzburg Festival. Fest. held annually in Austrian town where Mozart was born. Mus. coll. known as Mozarteum est. there 1880. In 1877, first of 8 Mozart fests. up to 1910 was held there with Richter, Mottl, Mahler, Strauss, Muck, and Schalk among conds. In 1917, Hofmannsthal, Strauss, Max Reinhardt, and Schalk became dirs. of planned new fest. which opened in 1920 with a perf. of Hofmannsthal's Jedermann. The 1921 fest. was devoted to orchestral and chamber works and the Requiem. Four operas were perf. in 1922. In 1927 Festspielhaus was opened as opera house (re-designed 1963), and old riding school (Felsenreitschule) was converted into th. (re-designed 1968–70). Singers engaged were the best from Vienna and Munich, conds. incl. Krauss, Strauss, and Walter. Repertory mainly Mozart and Strauss, with Beethoven's Fidelio, Verdi's Falstaff, and Wagner's Die Meistersinger. Toscanini cond. there 1934–7; followed by Furtwängler, Böhm, etc. After war, fest. resumed 1946. Strauss's Die *Liebe der Danae, which reached dress-rehearsal stage in 1944, had f.p. there 1952. New operas by Einem, Orff, Henze, Nono, Blacher, Liebermann, Egk, Penderecki, etc. prod. there. Fest. also incl. sym. concerts, chamber mus., recitals, plays. Karajan art. dir. 1957–60 and 1964–89. New Festspielhaus opened 1960, seating 2,160. Has largest stage in world, 135′ wide, 70′ deep, and 120′ high. After 2004, small Festspielhaus rebuilt as 'House for Mozart' in time for 2006 festival. When Karajan died, he was succeeded as art. dir. by a triumvirate headed by Gerard Mortier which widened the scope of the fest. Mortier resigned in 2001. Dir. since then: Peter Ruzicka (2002–6), Jürgen Flimm from 2007. In 1967 Karajan est. an Easter Fest. at which the operas prod. incl. Wagner. After Karajan's death, Solti was art. dir. Easter Fest. 1992–3, Abbado 1994–2002, Rattle from 2003.

Salzédo, Carlos (b Arcachon, Fr., 1885; d Waterville, Maine, 1961). Fr.-born harpist and composer (Amer. cit. 1923). Solo harpist Monte Carlo 1905–9, NY Met 1909–13. Founded Salzédo Harp Ens. 1917. Taught at Curtis Inst. and Juilliard Sch. Est. harpists' colony at Camden, Maine, 1931. Wrote hp. sonata, hp. concs., and other works for hp. Devised new effects on instr.

Salzedo, Leonard (Lopès) (b London, 1921; d Leighton Buzzard, 2000). Eng. composer, violinist, and conductor. Violinist in LPO, RPO, etc., 1947–66. Mus. dir., Ballet Rambert 1966–72. Prin. cond. Scottish Th. Ballet 1972–4. Comp. 8 ballets, 7 str. qts., perc. conc., tpt. conc., brass sextet, part-songs, etc.

Salzman, Eric (b NY, 1933). Amer. composer, critic, and impresario. Mus. critic in NY 1958–66. Mus. dir. NY radio station 1962–3, 1968–71. Organized concerts of new mus. in NY and multimedia mus. th. ens., Quog, 1970. Many of his works involve elecs.

Samazeuilh, Gustave (b Bordeaux, 1877; d Paris, 1967). Fr. composer and critic. Wrote criticism for several papers, incl. La Revue musicale. Trans. lib. of Wagner's Tristan und Isolde and Strauss's Capriccio into Fr. Wrote book on Dukas, and autobiography. Comp. sym.-poems, chamber mus., and songs.

samba. Brazilian dance in two forms: rural samba, African-influenced, and urban samba known as the 'samba-carioca', developed from the maxixe, a type of tango. Also a song-form. Modern dance-form, closer to maxixe, has simple 2/4 rhythm. Popularized in Brit. in 1940 by Edmundo Ros.

samisen. Japanese 3-str. guitar, without frets, with strs. of waxed silk played by plectrum called 'batsi'. Wrongly applied to perc. instr. in Puccini's Madama Butterfly and Massenet's Iris.

Sammartini, Giovanni-Battista (b c.1700; d Milan, 1775). It. composer and organist. Leading Milan composer of his day; choirmaster of eight churches. Pioneer of sonata form and teacher of Gluck, 1737–41. Said to have comp. 2,000 works in all genres, incl. operas, over 70 syms., many concs., and str. qts., str. quintets, etc.

Sammons, Albert (Edward) (b London, 1886; d Southdean, 1957). Eng. violinist, mainly self-taught. Solo début 1906. Heard in 1908 by *Beecham while playing in Waldorf Hotel, London, restaurant orch. and became leader of Beecham Orch. Also led orch. of RPS from 1913 and of Diaghilev's Ballets Russes 1911–13. First vn. of London Str. Qt. 1907–16. Became concert soloist, memorable as interpreter of Elgar conc. Gave f.p. of Delius conc. (ded. to him) 1919. Prof. at RCM. Author of book on technique. In 25-year partnership with the pianist William *Murdoch gave f.ps. of many British sonatas, notably Ireland's No.2 (1917). Comp. Phantasy Str. Qt. (winner of *Cobbett Prize). CBE 1944.

Samosud, Samuil (Abramovich) (b Tiflis, 1884; d Moscow, 1964). Russ. conductor, cellist, and teacher. Cellist in various orchs. Cond., Mariinsky Th., Petrograd, 1917–19 and art. dir. Maly Th. 1918–36. Art. dir Bolshoy Th. 1936–43. Taught cond. at Leningrad Cons. 1929–36. Cond. f.ps. of Shostakovich's The Nose and Prokofiev's 7th Sym.

Sams, Eric (b London, 1926; d London, 2004). Eng. writer on music. Civil servant 1950–78.

Authority on codes and ciphers and author of monographs on Schumann's ciphers, Elgar's enigma, and Brahms's 'musical love-letters'. Has also written books about the songs of Wolf (1961, rev. 1983), Schumann (1969, rev. 1975), and Brahms (1972).

Samson. Oratorio by Handel to text from Milton's works, comp. 1741–2, f.p. London 1743.

Samson et Dalila (Samson and Delilah). Opera in 3 acts by Saint-Saëns to Fr. lib. by Lemaire based on Bible. Comp. 1867–8, 1873–7. Prod. Weimar 1877 (in Ger.), NY 1892 (concert), New Orleans 1893 (stage), CG 1893 (concert), 1909 (stage). F.p. in Fr., Rouen 1890, Paris 1892.

Samuel, Harold (*b* London, 1879; *d* Hampstead, 1937). Eng. pianist. As a child played in public houses. Début, London 1894. Became specialist in kbd. mus. of Bach, playing it practically complete in a series of recitals spread over a week (first in London 1921, then in NY 1924, and several times elsewhere). Toured USA almost every year after 1924. Wrote mus. comedy, incid. mus., songs, etc. Prof. of pf. RCM for many years.

San Carlo, Naples, Teatro di. It. opera house ranking next to La Scala. Opened Nov. 1737, destroyed by fire 1816 and replaced in 6 months by present building, seating 3,500. Extensive alterations 1844, modernized stage 1929. Rossini wrote several operas for San Carlo, incl. *Otello*. Donizetti's *Lucia di Lammermoor* and Verdi's *Luisa Miller* had premières there. Co. visited CG 1946.

Sancta Civitas (Holy City). Oratorio by Vaughan Williams, comp. 1923–5, f.p. Oxford 1926. Text from *Revelation*, with additions from Taverner's Bible (1539) and other sources. For bar., ten., ch., boys' ch., and orch.

Sanctus (Holy). One of 5 main parts of the Mass. Settings by innumerable composers.

Sanderling, Kurt (*b* Arys, E. Prussia, 1912). Ger. conductor. Répétiteur at Berlin State Opera, 1931. Left Ger. 1936, becoming cond. Moscow Radio SO 1936–41. Cond., Leningrad PO 1941–60 (jointly with Mravinsky), East Berlin SO 1960–77, Dresden Staatskapelle 1964–7 (Salzburg Fest. début 1965). Eng. début 1970 (with Leipzig Gewandhaus Orch.). Notable interpreter of classics and of Mahler and Shostakovich.

Sanders, John (Derek) (*b* Wanstead, 1933; *d* Hereford, 2003). Eng. organist and conductor. Ass. org., Gloucester Cath. 1958–63. Org., Chester Cath. 1963–7, Gloucester Cath. from 1967. Cond. 3 Choirs Fest. Comp. a *Te Deum*, and other choral works. OBE 1994.

Sanderson, Sibyl (*b* Sacramento, 1864; *d* Paris, 1903). Amer. soprano. Début (as Ada Palmer) The Hague 1888 in title-role of *Manon*. Massenet wrote *Esclarmonde* (1889) and *Thaïs* (1894) for her to exploit the extraordinary range of her v. (g–g″). Saint-Saëns wrote *Phryné* (1893) for her. CG

début 1891, NY Met 1895, but was never as successful as in Paris. Fine actress and very beautiful.

Sándor, György (*b* Budapest, 1912; *d* NY, 2005). Hung.-born pianist (Amer. cit. 1943). Toured Europe 1930–8, settled in USA 1939. London début 1937. Soloist in f.p. of Bartók's 3rd conc., Philadelphia 1946. Recorded all Bartók's and Kodály's pf. mus. and all Prokofiev's solo pf. works. Made pf. transcr. of Dukas's *L'apprenti sorcier*. Taught at Southern Methodist Univ., Dallas, 1956–61, dir. of pf. studies, Univ. of Mich. at Ann Arbor 1961–81, Juilliard Sch. from 1982.

Sandström, Sven-David (*b* Motala, Swed., 1942). Swed. composer. Joined faculty of Stockholm State Coll. of Mus. 1980. Comps. incl. church opera *Strong Like Death* (1978); opera *Slottet det vita* (1981–2); 2 ballets; *Pictures*, perc., orch. (1969); *In the Meantime*, chamber orch. (1970); fl. conc. (1980); vn. conc. (1985); *Invention*, 16 vv. (1969); *Birgitta-Music I* (1973); *Silence*, ten., narr., str. (1979); *Requiem* for child victims of war and racism, 4 soloists, ch., children's ch., orch., tape (1979); *Agnus Dei* (1980); *24 Romantic Studies*, ch. (1988); str. qt. (1969); *Utmost*, wind quintet, brass, perc. (1975); *Sax Music* (1985); *Dance III*, 3 vcs. (1988); *Songs of Love*, sop., orch. (1990); *Laudamus te*, ch. (1993); conc., rec., hpd., str. (1995); *The City*, opera (1996); *Spring Music*, perc. (1997); *Crysaetos*, unacc. ch. (1998); *Credo*, ch. (2000).

San Francisco Opera Co. Founded 1923 by Gaetano Merola, who was dir. until 1953, then succeeded by Kurt Herbert Adler (1953–82); Terence A. McEwen (1982–8); Lotfi Mansouri (1988–2001); Pamela Rosenberg (2001–5); David Gockley from 2006. Ranks with Chicago in importance after NY Met. War Memorial Opera House, seating 3,252, opened Oct. 1932 with *Tosca*. Among modern works staged for the first time in USA at S. Francisco are *Die *Frau ohne Schatten*, The *Makropulos Affair*, Les *Dialogues des Carmélites*, *Troilus and Cressida*, A *Midsummer Night's Dream*, The *Midsummer Marriage*, *King Priam*, A *Streetcar Named Desire*, *Dead Man Walking*, and *Doctor Atomic*. First mus. dir. John Pritchard (1986–89), Donald *Runnicles from 1992.

San Francisco Polyphony. Work for orch. by *Ligeti, comp. 1973–4; f.p. S. Francisco 1975 cond. Ozawa.

San Francisco Symphony Orchestra. Founded 1911 under sponsorship of Mus. Assoc. of San Francisco. Conds.: Henry Hadley 1911–15; Alfred Hertz 1915–29; Basil Cameron and Issay Dobrowen 1930–2; Dobrowen 1932–4; Pierre Monteux 1935–52; Enrique Jorda 1954–63; Josef Krips 1963–70; Seiji Ozawa 1970–6; Edo de Waart 1977–85; Herbert Blomstedt 1985–95 (Salzburg Fest. 1990); Michael Tilson Thomas from 1995. Since 1980 has played in Louise M. Davies Symphony Hall.

Sanguine Fan, The. Ballet by Elgar, Op.81, comp. 1917 to scenario by Ina Lowther based on a fan design drawn in sanguine (blood-red crayon) by Charles Conder showing Pan and Echo with 18th-cent. figures in background. Ballet was f.p. Chelsea 1917 at a matinée to raise money for war charities. After 2 perfs. and a recording of excerpts in 1920, the mus. was unperf. until a recording in 1973. Revived as ballet, choreog. Ronald Hynd, London 1976.

Sankey and Moody. Joint Amer. compilers of hymn-tune collections popular in late Victorian years. Ira David Sankey (1840–1908) was an evangelistic singer from 1871 when he joined forces with D. L. Moody and toured with him in USA and Brit. until 1899. *Sacred Songs and Solos* was pubd. 1873. Moody did not write the words of any hymns. Sankey wrote many tunes and collected as many others.

Santa Fe Opera. Opera co. in Santa Fe, New Mexico, founded 1957 by John *Crosby. Orig. theatre destroyed by fire 1967, rebuilt 1968 (capacity 1,889), again rebuilt 1998 (capacity 2,128). 2-month annual summer fest., theatre being partially in open-air. Adventurous policy, operas receiving f.ps. there incl. Floyd's *Wuthering Heights* (1958), Berio's *Opera* (1970), and Villa-Lobos's *Yerma* (1971). F.p. since 17th cent. of Cavalli's *Egisto*. F. Amer. ps. of Berg's *Lulu* (both incomplete and complete versions), Henze's *Boulevard Solitude* and *The Bassarids*, Strauss's *Daphne*, Shostakovich's *The Nose*, Britten's *Owen Wingrave*, Stephen Oliver's *Duchess of Malfi*, Judith Weir's *Blond Eckbert*, and Thomas Adès's *The Tempest*.

Santa María, Tomás de (*b* Madrid, *c*.1516–20; *d* Ribadavia, 1570). Sp. organist and monk. Wrote works for *vihuela* and other instr.; and a treatise (1565) on playing kbd. or *vihuela* fantasias.

Santi, Nello (*b* Adria, Rovigo, 1931). It. conductor. Début Padua 1951 (*Rigoletto*). Cond. Zurich Opera 1958–69. CG début 1960; Salzburg Fest. 1960; NY Met 1962. Cond. London's first 'arena' opera (*Aida*) at Earl's Court, 1988.

Santini, Gabriele (*b* Perugia, 1886; *d* Rome, 1964). It. conductor. Began career in Rome. Cond. at Teatro Colón, Buenos Aires, for 8 seasons and at Rio de Janeiro. Ass. to Toscanini at La Scala 1925–9. Cond. Rome Opera 1929–33, art. dir. 1944–7. Cond. *La traviata* recording with *Callas.

Santley, (Sir) **Charles** (*b* Liverpool, 1834; *d* London, 1922). Eng. baritone and composer. Opera début Pavia 1857 (as Doctor in *La traviata*), London (concert) 1857, CG 1859. Sang with various Eng. opera cos. Sang Valentin in Eng. première of *Faust*, 1863 (for 1864 revival Gounod added 'Avant de quitter ces lieux' specially for him). Sang at La Scala 1865–6. Sang title-role in Italian in *Der fliegende Holländer*, first London prod. of any Wagner opera (1870). Carl Rosa Co., 1875–6. Notable singer of oratorios etc. (especially *Elijah*), appearing at Leeds Fests., 3 Choirs (1863–1906), Birmingham Fest., Handel Fest. CG fare-

well 1911 but sang in 1915 at concert for Belgian relief. Wrote books on singing, and autobiography. Comp. mass and other church mus. Knighted 1907, year of his golden jubilee.

Santoro, Cláudio (*b* Manáos, Brazil, 1919; *d* Brasilia, 1989). Brazil. composer and violinist. Co-founder Brazilian SO, playing vn. in it 1941–7. Teacher at various Brazil. institutions, mus. dir. Brasilia cultural foundation 1962–7. Mus. dir., Teatro Novo, Rio, 1968–9. Prof. of comp., Heidelberg-Mannheim Hochschule für Musik, 1970–8. Comp. 8 ballets and many scores for radio, TV, and films. Other works incl. 11 syms. (1940–84); 3 pf. concs.; 2 vn. concs.; vc. conc.; 5 vn. sonatas (1940–51); 4 vc. sonatas (1943–63); 7 str. qts. (1943–65); *Ode to Stalingrad* (1947); oratorio *Berlin, 13th August* (1961–2); and songs. 4th sym. is subtitled *Brasília*. Ballet *Zuimaaluti* is based on 5th sym. and was cond. by Santoro at CG 1960. Began as atonalist, later wrote in nationalist style. Was for a time admirer of Communist Russia.

Sanzogno, Nino (*b* Venice, 1911; *d* Milan, 1983). It. conductor, composer, and violinist. Cond. La Fenice Orch., Venice, from 1937. Cond. at La Scala from 1939, being esp. assoc. with 20th-cent. works and cond. f.ps. in Italy of *Lulu* (Venice, 1949), *Troilus and Cressida* (1956), *A *Midsummer Night's Dream* (1961), *Lady Macbeth of Mtsensk*, and world (stage) première of *The *Fiery Angel* (Venice 1955). Inaugurated Piccola Scala 1955. Mus. dir. La Scala, 1962–72. Composer of va. and vc. concs., and chamber mus.

Sapellnikov [Sapelnikoff], **Vasily** (*b* Odessa, 1867; *d* San Remo, It., 1941). Russ. pianist and composer. Début Hamburg 1888 (Tchaikovsky 1st conc.), London 1889. Teacher Moscow Cons. 1897–9. Left Russia 1923, settling in Ger. and It. Wrote opera and pf. mus.

Sapieyevski, Jerzy (*b* Łódž, 1945). Polish-born composer and conductor. Formed own experimental ens. 1966. Settled in USA 1967. Teacher at several Amer. univs. Works incl. double pf. conc., conc. for va. and winds, *Summer Overture*, etc.

sarabande (Sp. Zarabanda). Dance form in 17th and 18th cents. Originated in Lat. America, appearing in Sp. in early 16th cent. Was banned by Philip II in 1583 because it was regarded as loose and ugly, 'exciting bad emotions'. Introduced to Fr. and Eng. in early 17th cent., where a stately version, in slow triple time, was preferred to the lively Sp. original. Sarabandes became a standard movt. of the *suite in instr. works by Purcell, J. S. Bach, and Handel. In 20th cent. it has been revived by Debussy, Satie, Vaughan Williams (in *Job*), and Britten (in *Simple Symphony*).

sarangi. Indian 3-str. viol with 4-cornered, wooden, skin-covered soundbox, wide fingerboard, and 10 or more sympathetic understr. Tone like va. Used to acc. dancing. 4th str.

sometimes added, tuned in unison with highest of other 3 at middle C. Name sometimes applied to other Indian bowed instr.

Sarasate y Navascuéz, Pablo Martín Melitón de (*b* Pamplona, 1844; *d* Biarritz, 1908). Sp. violinist and composer, known as Pablo de Sarasate. Public début aged 8. London début 1861. Had sweet tone and pure style. Lalo comp. *Symphonie espagnole* for him, Bruch his 2nd conc. and *Scottish Fantasy*, and Saint-Saëns his 1st and 3rd concs. and *Introduction and Rondo Capriccioso*. Comp. several vn. pieces, incl. *Zigeunerweisen* and *Jota Aragonesa, Carmen Fantasy* (with orch.), and transcr. Sp. folk mus.

Saraste, Jukka-Pekka (*b* Heinola, 1956). Finn. conductor. Début 1980 with Helsinki PO. Won Nordic cond. comp. 1981. Toured USA with Helsinki PO 1983 as co-cond. with Okko Kamu. London début 1984 (LSO at Proms). Prin. cond. Finnish Radio SO 1987–2001, Scottish Chamber Orch. 1987–94, Toronto SO 1994–2001. Mus. dir. Oslo PO from 2006.

Sarbu, Eugene (*b* Bucharest, 1950). Romanian violinist. Solo début aged 6; won Nat. Fest. of Mus. award, Bucharest, 1958. London début, Proms 1982.

sardana. Nat. Catalonian dance, perf. to acc. of the *fluvial*, Sp. equivalent of pipe and tabor. It is in sections, partly in compound duple and partly in simple duple time. Participants link hands in a large ring, as in the **farandole*.

Sargent, (Sir) (Harold) **Malcolm** (Watts) (*b* Ashford, Kent, 1895; *d* London, 1967). Eng. cond., organist, pianist, and composer. Organist, Melton Mowbray church 1914–24. Mus.D., Durham, 1919. Cond. his own *Impression on a Windy Day* at London Promenade concert 1921. On staff RCM as teacher of cond. from 1923. Cond. opera for BNOC. Mus. dir. Courtauld-Sargent Concerts 1929–40. Cond. of many choral socs., incl. Royal Choral Soc. (from 1928), Huddersfield Choral Soc. (from 1932), Liverpool Welsh Choral Union (from 1941), Leeds Phil. Soc. (from 1947). Prin. cond. Hallé Orch. 1939–42, Liverpool PO 1942–8, BBCSO 1950–7, chief cond., Henry Wood Promenade Concerts 1948–67. Cond. many f.ps. of Brit. works, incl. Walton's *Belshazzar's Feast* (Leeds 1931) and *Troilus and Cressida* (CG 1954). Frequently cond. D'Oyly Carte Opera Co. Guest cond. of int. orchs. and ambassador for Eng. mus. Arr. carols and authentic tune of *Rule, Britannia!* Orchestrated Brahms's *Vier ernste Gesänge* and *Nocturne* from Borodin str. qt. No.2. Knighted 1947.

Šárka. (1) Opera in 3 acts, Op.51, by Fibich to lib. by A. Schulzová. Comp. 1896–7. Prod. Prague 1897, Wexford 1996.

(2) Opera in 3 acts by Janáček to lib. by J. Zeyer. 1st vers. comp. 1887, 2nd vers. 1888 (only 2 acts orchestrated), 3rd vers. 1919 (Act III orch. Chlubna 1918–19). Final rev. 1925. Prod. Brno 1925, Edinburgh (concert) 1993.

(3) 3rd of Smetana's cycle of six sym.-poems **Má Vlast*, comp. 1874–9.

Sarnia. 'An Island Sequence' of 3 pieces for pf. solo by Ireland, comp. 1940–1 and descriptive of the Channel Island. Pieces entitled 1. *Le Catioroc*, 2. *In a May Morning*, 3. *Song of the Springtides*. F.p. 1942 by Clifford Curzon.

sarod. Indian str. instr., bowed or plucked, usually with 6 strs. and 12 to 15 sympathetic str.

sarrusophone. Double-reed woodwind instr., although made of brass, invented 1856 by Fr. bandmaster named Sarrus. Made in 9 sizes (in keys E♭, B♭, and C) from sop. to db. Saint-Saëns and Delius (e.g. in *Songs of Sunset, Dance Rhapsody No.1, Fennimore and Gerda, Arabesk, Song of the High Hills, Requiem, Eventyr*) have scored for db. sarrusophone (usually played by double bn.).

Sarti, Giuseppe (*b* Faenza, 1729; *d* Berlin, 1802). It. composer, conductor, and organist. Org., Faenza Cath. 1748–52; cond. of It. opera and court cond. in Copenhagen 1753–65 and 1768–75. Wrote 20 It. and Danish operas in Denmark. Dir., Ospedaletto Cons., Venice, 1775–9; choirmaster Milan Cath. 1779–84 (teacher of Cherubini); court cond. to Catherine II of Russia 1784–7, dir., Ukraine mus. sch. 1787–91, dir. St Petersburg Cons. from 1793. Made scientific study of acoustics. Wrote over 70 operas, incl. one based on a lib. by Empress Catherine. At Don Giovanni's supper-party in last scene of his opera, Mozart quotes the air *Come un agnello* (Like a lamb) from Sarti's *Fra i due litiganti* (Between Two Litigants).

Sass, Sylvia (*b* Budapest, 1951). Hung. sop. Opera début 1971 (Frasquita in *Carmen*). Salzburg Fest. 1974; Brit. début Scottish Opera, Glasgow, 1975; CG 1976; NY Met 1977. Had lessons from **Callas, whose dramatic gifts she emulates. Fine singer of Judith in *Duke Bluebeard's Castle*.

SATB. Soprano, Alto, Tenor, Bass; meaning either a mixed ch. or 4 soloists.

Satie, Erik [Eric] (Alfred Leslie) (*b* Honfleur, 1866; *d* Paris, 1925). Fr. composer and pianist, son of Fr. father and Scottish mother. Moved to Paris 1878. Worked as pianist in 1888 at Montmartre cabaret. In same year wrote his *Gymnopédies* for pf. Met Debussy in 1890. In 1891 joined Catholic Rosicrucian sect and comp. several works for it. Shortly afterwards seemed almost to have retired from comp., writing fewer than 10 works in 12 years. In 1905 entered Schola Cantorum as pupil of d'Indy and Roussel, leaving in 1908. From about 1910 became something of a cult among young composers attracted by the eccentric, humorous titles of some of his works, e.g. *Trois Morceaux en forme de poire* (Three Pear-shaped Pieces). Strongly influenced group of young composers known as *Les *Six*. Meeting with Cocteau in 1915 led to Diaghilev ballet *Parade* (1917), in which jazz rhythms are used and the instrumentation incl. typewriter, steamship whistle, and siren. Later, was assoc. with Surrealists and Dadaists. Satie's importance lay in directing a new generation of Fr. composers away from Wagner-influenced impressionism towards a leaner, more epigrammatic style. His harmony is often characterized by unresolved chords, which may have influenced Debussy (or he may have learned the device from Debussy—nobody knows). Melody is simple, sometimes slightly archaic, and scoring economical, with few *tutti* passages. *Socrate* is the most ambitious of his works, most of which are comparatively short, the majority being for solo pf. He anticipated many later *avant-garde* trends; e.g. in *Gnossiennes* (1890) there are no bar-lines and the score contains verbal instructions bearing little relation to the mus. But beware—behind the clown's mask is a serious composer. Prin. comps.:

STAGE: *Le Fils des Étoiles*, incidental mus. (1891, prelude re-orch. Ravel 1913); *Geneviève de Brabant*, marionette opera (1899); *Le Piège de Méduse*, lyric comedy (1913); *Parade*, ballet (1917); *Mercure*, ballet (1924); *Relâche*, ballet (1924).

ORCH.: *En Habit de cheval* (1911); *Cinq Grimaces* (1914); *Trois petites pièces montées* (1919, also for pf. 4 hands, 1920); *La belle excentrique* (1920); *Jack-in-the Box* (1900, unperf. pantomime, orch. Milhaud 1926).

CHORAL: *Messe des Pauvres*, with organ or pf. (1895, orch. version by D. Diamond 1960); *Socrate*, 4 sop., small orch. (1918).

VOICE & PIANO: *3 Mélodies de 1886*; *3 Poèmes d'Amour* (1914); *3 Mélodies* (1916); *Ludions* (5 songs) (1923).

VIOLIN & PIANO: *Choses vues à droit et à gauche (sans lunettes)* (1914).

PIANO: *3 Sarabandes* (1887–8, orch. Caby); *3 *Gymnopédies* (1888, Nos. 1 and 3 orch. Debussy 1896, No.2 orch. H. Murrill and by Roland-Manuel); *3 Gnossiennes* (1890, orch. Lanchbery; No.3 orch. Poulenc 1939); *Trois Préludes* from *Le Fils des Étoiles* (1891, orch. Roland-Manuel); *Valse, Je te veux* (c.1900, arr. for v. and orch., also arr. for orch. by C. Lambert); *9 Danses gothiques* (1893); *4 Préludes* (1893, Nos. 1 and 3 orch. Poulenc, 1939); *Prélude de la porte héroïque du Ciel* (1894, orch. Roland-Manuel 1912); *2 Pièces froides* (1897); *3 Nouvelles pièces froides* (pre–1910); *Le Poisson rêveur* (1901; version for pf. and orch. by Caby); *Morceaux en forme de poire*, for 4 hands (1903; orch. Désormière); *12 Petits Chorals* (c.1906); *Passacaille* (1906); *Prélude en tapisserie* (1906); *Aperçus désagréables*, 4 hands (1908–12); *2 Rêveries nocturnes* (1910–11); *En Habit de cheval*, vers. for 4 hands (1911); *3 Véritables Préludes flasques (pour un chien)* (1912); *3 Descriptions automatiques* (1913); *3 Embryons desséchés* (1913); *3 Croquis et agaceries d'un gros bonhomme en bois* (1913); *3 Chapitres tournés en tous sens* (1913); *3 Vieux Séquins et vieilles cuirasses* (1913); *Enfantines* (9 pieces) (1913); *6 Pièces de la période 1906–13*; *21 Sports et divertissements* (1914); *Heures séculaires et instantanées* (1914); *3 Valses du précieux dégoûté* (1914; orch. Greenbaum); *Avant-dernières pensées* (1915); *Parade*, suite for 4

hands from ballet (1917); *Sonatine bureaucratique* (1917); *5 Nocturnes* (1919); *Premier Menuet* (1920).

Satyricon. (1) Comedy ov. by *Ireland, comp. 1944–6, headed by quotation from the *Satyricon* of Petronius.

(2) Opera by Maderna to lib. by composer and I. Strasfogel after Petronius. Comp. 1973. F.p. Scheveningen 1973, Tanglewood 1973, London 1990.

Satz (Ger.). 'Setting'. Term used in several different ways, e.g.: (1) Movt., as in Schubert's qt. movt. (*Quartettsatz*).
(2) Setting or comp. (*Tonsatz*).
(3) Theme or subject, i.e. *Hauptsatz*, first subject or main theme.
(4) Texture.
(5) Style.

saudades (Portuguese). Term expressive of the haunting sense of sadness and regret for days gone by. It has been used (e.g. by Milhaud and Warlock) as a title for pieces of instr. or vocal mus.

Sauer, Emil von (*b* Hamburg, 1862; *d* Vienna, 1942). Ger. pianist and composer. Eng. début 1894. Dir. of pf. master-classes Vienna Cons. 1901–7 and after 1915. Salzburg Fest. 1940. Comp. pf. concs., pf. sonatas, 33 studies, etc. Ed. Brahms's pf. works.

Sauguet, Henri [Jean Pierre Poupard] (*b* Bordeaux, 1901; *d* Paris, 1989). Fr. composer. Became disciple of *Satie and formed group called École d'Arcueil. Best known for his ballets and has also comp. *musique concrète*. Most considerable work is his Stendhal opera *La Chartreuse de Parme* (1927–36, rev. 1968; prod. Paris 1939). Wrote 7 other operas; 25 ballets, incl. *La Dame aux Camélias* (1957, rev. 1960); 3 pf. concs. (1934–63); 4 syms. (1945–71); vn. conc. (1953); harmonica conc. (1970); 3 str. qts. (1926–79); *Requiem* (1954); *Ecce homo* (1965); *Reflets sur feuilles*, orch. (1979); *Messe jubilatoire*, bar., ten., str. qt. (1983); *Sonata d'église*, org. (1984); *Valse anachronique*, pf. (1985); *90 Notes*, fl. (1986); and song-cycles to texts by Eluard, Schiller, Shakespeare, and Mallarmé.

Saul and David (*Saul og David*). Opera in 4 acts by *Nielsen to lib. by Einar Christiansen. Comp. 1898–1901. Prod. Copenhagen 1902, Glasgow (BBC concert perf.) 1959, London (stage) 1977.

Sauret, Emile (*b* Dun-le-Roi, 1852; *d* London, 1920). Fr. violinist and composer. Began European tours at age of 8. London début 1866. Amer. début 1872. Played sonatas with Liszt. Taught in Berlin 1880–9. Prof. of vn., RAM 1890–1903, Chicago Mus. Coll. 1903–6, TCL from 1908. Wrote vn. conc., over 100 vn. pieces, and *Gradus ad Parnassum* for vn. (1894).

sausage bassoon. Name for the *racket (Ger. *Wurstfagott*).

sautillé (Fr.). Springing. Type of bowing on vn., va., vc., and db. like *spiccato*, the bow lightly rebounding off the str.

Savile, Jeremy (*fl.* 1651–65). Eng. composer of songs and part-songs. Remembered for *Here's a health unto his Majesty*.

Savitri. (1) Chamber opera in 1 act, Op.25, by Holst to his own lib. taken from the Sanskrit *Mahabharata*. 3 characters, Savitri (sop.), Satyavan (ten.), Death (bar.), with acc. of 2 fl., cor anglais, and str. Comp. 1908. Prod. London (students) 1916, (professional) 1921, Chicago 1934.
(2) 'Legend' for stage by Molnár (1912).

Savoy Operas. Name by which the operettas of Gilbert and Sullivan are known because from *Iolanthe* (1882) onwards they were prod. at the Savoy Th., London, built specially for them in 1881. The performers were known as 'Savoyards'.

saw, musical. Hand-saw played for novel entertainment by holding it between the knees and playing with a vn. bow, the left hand altering the pitch of the note by bending the saw.

Sawallisch, Wolfgang (*b* Munich, 1923). Ger. conductor and pianist. Début (*Hänsel und Gretel*) as cond. at Augsburg Stadttheater 1947–53, beginning as répétiteur, leaving as first Kapellmeister. Gen. mus. dir., Aachen 1953–7, Wiesbaden 1957–9, Cologne 1959–63. Cond. Vienna SO 1960–70. Gen. mus. dir. Hamburg PO 1961–73. Cond. Orch. de la Suisse Romande 1970–80. Gen. mus. dir., Bavarian State Opera, Munich, 1971–93 (Intendant from 1982). Chief cond. Philadelphia Orch. 1993–2003. Bayreuth Fest. 1957–62; Salzburg Fest. début 1957; Amer. début 1964 (with Vienna SO); CG début 1972 (with Bavarian State Opera in Strauss operas). Fine accompanist to leading singers and instrumentalists.

Sawer, David (*b* Stockport, 1961). Eng. composer. Early works perf. by London Sinfonietta, Music/Rejects London, and Almeida Fest. Works incl. chamber opera *The Panic* (1991); ensemble pieces *Cat's Eye* (1986), *Take Off* (1987), *Good Night* (1989), *Rhetoric* (1989); *Études*, 2 to 6 actors/musicians, ten. sax., 2 tpts., perc. (1984); *Food of Love*, actress, pf. (1988); *Mute*, tb. (1990); *Songs of Love and War*, 24 vv., 2 hp., perc. (1990); *Solo Piano*, pf. (1983); *The Melancholy of Departure*, pf. (1990); *The Memory of Water*, 2 vn., str. (1993); *Byrnam Wood*, orch. (1995); *Tiroirs*, chamber ens. (1996); *Musica ficta*, chamber orch. (1997–8); *Between*, hp. (1998); *From Morning to Midnight*, opera (2001); pf. conc. (2001–2); *Parthenope*, va. (2003); *Rebus*, 15 players (2004).

Sax, Adolphe (Antoine Joseph) (*b* Dinant, 1814; *d* Paris, 1894). Belg. instrument-maker. Exhibited fl. and ivory cl. at Brussels Exhibition 1830, cl. with 24 keys in 1834. Moved to Paris 1842, where he was helped by Berlioz, Rossini, and others. In 1840s invented new brass instr., *saxophone, which he registered in 1846. Also invented the *saxhorn family of instr. (*c.*1845).

saxhorn. Type of brass wind instr. of wide semiconical bore, using cup mouthpiece and played with valves, invented by A. *Sax *c.*1845. There are 7 varieties (deep bass to high treble), i.e. 2 sop., alto, ten., B♭ bass, E♭ bass, and BB♭ bass (BB signifies wider bore). They are transposing instrs.: those used in Brit. brass bands are the E♭ ten. (ten. hn.) and B♭ bar. (bar. hn.), both closely related to the *Flügelhorn. Nomenclature for the group is somewhat confused, e.g. in the 4 higher instrs.:
(a) sopranino saxhorn in E♭ (or F), also called sop. saxhorn or (mistakenly) sop. Flügelhorn, or Flügelhorn piccolo. Little different from E♭ cornet.
(b) sop. saxhorn in B♭ (or C), also called alto saxhorn or (mistakenly) alto Flügelhorn. Little different from B♭ cornet.
(c) alto saxhorn in E♭ (or F), also called saxhorn, or ten. saxhorn, or ten. hn., or alto, or althorn in E♭ (or F).
(d) ten. in B♭ (or C), also called bar., or bar. saxhorn, or althorn in B♭.
The 3 lower saxhorns are whole-tube instrs., the 4 higher are half-tube instrs. The 3 lower instrs. are classified with tubas, e.g.
(e) bass saxhorn in B♭ (or C), almost identical with *euphonium.
(f) bass saxhorn in E♭ (or F), almost identical with E♭ bass tuba, otherwise E♭ bombardon.
(g) double-bass saxhorn in B♭ (or C), almost identical with B♭ bass tuba but with complete range at bottom.
These are not always used as transposing instr.: sometimes the bass clef is used, sometimes the treble clef showing the notes an octave higher than if the bass clef had been used. In each case, middle C represents the octave of the fundamental note.

saxophone. Family of wind instrs. invented by A. *Sax *c.*1840–5 (patented 1846), having metal body. Played with a single beating reed, like cl., but conical in bore, like ob. Complete family is of 8 sizes, alternately in E♭ and B♭, i.e. sopranino in E♭, sop. in B♭, alto in E♭, ten. in B♭, bar. in E♭, bass in B♭, contrabass in E♭, subcontrabass in B♭. All are transposing instr., written in the treble clef, the most commonly used being the alto and ten. The sax.'s tone is extremely flexible and variable, blending well with either woodwind or brass, capable of a fl.-like softness, str.-like richness, and metallic stridency. It is a standard feature of jazz big bands, where a section of saxs. takes the place of a sym. orch.'s str. section (e.g. in Glenn Miller's and Tommy Dorsey's bands). But it has also been effectively used in symphonic mus. Berlioz, Meyerbeer, Bizet, Massenet, Saint-Saëns, and others all scored for the sax. Strauss used 4 saxs. in *Symphonia Domestica* (though he intended saxhorns), and he would have been preceded by Elgar, whose desire for 4 in *Caractacus* was thwarted only by economic considerations. Debussy, Ibert, Milhaud, Villa-Lobos, and Eric Coates have written conc.-like works for sax. and orch. Vaughan Williams uses it effectively in *Job*, and in his 6th and 9th Syms., and innumerable other 20th-cent. composers have called upon it. The idea that it is mainly a jazz instr. and so not quite decent in symphonic mus. is therefore as inaccurate as it is snobbish.

sax(o)tromba. *Sax's modification of the *saxhorn *c*.1850 with a more cylindrical bore between tb. and saxhorn. Seldom used.

Saxton, Robert (Louis Alfred) (*b* London, 1953). Eng. composer. Had help and advice from Britten in his childhood. Head of comp., GSMD, 1990–7, RAM 1997–9, mus. lect. Oxford Univ. from 1999. Works incl.:

OPERA: *Caritas* (1990–1).

ORCH: *Choruses to Apollo* (1980); *Traumstadt* (1980); *Ring of Eternity* (1982–3); *Concerto for Orchestra* (1984); *The Circles of Light*, chamber sym. (1985–6); va. conc. (1986); *Variation on 'Sumer is icumen in'* (1987); *In the Beginning* (1987); *Elijah's Violin* (1988); *Music to Celebrate the Resurrection of Christ* (1988); vn. conc. (1989); *Psalm: a Song of Ascents*, tpt., orch. (1992); vc. conc. (1992–3); sym., sop., bar., orch. (1993–5).

ENSEMBLE: *Reflections of Narziss and Goldmund*, 2 chamber groups, hp., pf. or celesta (1975); *Canzona*, fl., ob., cl., hn., hp., str. trio (1978); *Processions and Dances*, 11 instr. (1981); *Piccola Musica per Luigi Dallapiccola*, fl., ob., va., vc., pf. or celesta (1981).

VOICE(S) & INSTRS.: *La Promenade d'Automne*, sop., fl., cl., perc., pf., str. trio (1972); *Where Are You Going To, My Pretty Maid?*, arr. for sop., fl., cl., hp., guitar, vn., vc. (1973); *What does the song hope for?*, sop., fl., ob., cl., pf., str. trio, tape (1974); *Brise Marine*, sop., pf., tape (1976); *Cantata on Poems of Hölderlin*, ten., counterten., pf. (1979); *Cantata No.2*, ten., ob., pf. (1980); *Cantata No.3*, 2 sop. and tape delay (1981); *Eloge*, sop., fl., ob., cl., hn., pf., str. qt. (1980); *Prayer to a Child*, sop., 2 cl. (1992); *Prayer before Sleep*, sop., vc./pf. (1997).

CHORAL: *Child of Light*, sops., org. (1984); *Rex gloriae (Psalm 24)*, women's vv., org. (1988); *O sing unto the Lord a new song*, ch., org. (1993); *Canticum Luminis*, sop., ch., orch. (1994–5).

UNACC. CHORUS: *Chaconne*, double ch. (1981); *I will awake the dawn*, double ch. (1986–7); *At the Round Earth's Imagined Corners* (1992); *Alternative Canticles* (2002); *5 Motets* (2003).

CHAMBER MUSIC: *Krystallen*, fl., pf. (1973); *Echoes of the Glass Bead Game*, wind quintet (1975); *Poems for Mélisande*, fl., pf. (1977); *Arias*, ob., pf. (1977); *Study for a Sonata*, fl., ob., vc., hpd. (1977); *Toccata*, vc. (1978); *Chiaroscuro*, perc. (1981); *Fantasiestück*, accordion (1982); *The Sentinel of the Rainbow*, sextet (1984); *Night Dance*, gui. (1986–7); *Invocation, Dance and Meditation*, va., pf. (1991); *Paraphrase on Mozart's Idomeneo*, wind octet (1991); *Fantasia*, str. qt. (1994); *A Yardstick to the Stars*, pf. quintet (1994–5); *Sonata on a Theme of Walton*, vc. (2000).

PIANO: *Ritornelli and Intermezzi* (1972); *2 Pieces* (1976); *Sonatas for 2 Pianos* (1977); *Sonata (in memory of Belá Bartók)* (1981); *Chacony*, left-hand (1988).

Sayão, Bidú [Balduina] (de Oliveira) (*b* Rio de Janeiro, 1902; *d* Lincolnville, Maine, 1999). Brazi-

lian soprano. Début Rio 1926 (Rosina in *Il barbiere di Siviglia*). La Scala début 1930. Sang Gounod's Juliette at Paris Opéra and Opéra-Comique 1931. NY début 1935; NY Met 1937–52; Chicago Civic Opera 1941–5, Lyric Opera 1954; S. Francisco 1946–52. Retired 1957.

Saygun, Ahmed Adnan (*b* Izmir, 1907; *d* Istanbul, 1991). Turkish composer. In Paris, 1928–31. Returned to Turkey 1931 to hold various teaching posts: Istanbul Cons. 1936–9, Ankara State Cons. from 1964, Istanbul State Cons. from 1972. Works incl. 4 operas, 4 syms., pf. conc., vn. conc., 3 str. qts., wind quintet, vn. sonata, vc. sonata, etc. Accompanied Bartók in 1936 on folksong collecting journey in Anatolia; in 1976 his *Bartók's Folk Music* was pubd. in Budapest. His oratorio *Yunus Emre* (1946) was cond. by Stokowski in NY 1958.

scacciapensieri (It. 'chase away thoughts'). *Jew's harp.

Scala, La. See *La Scala*.

Scala di seta, La (The Silken Ladder). Opera in 1 act by Rossini to lib. by G. M. Foppa after Planard's lib. for Gaveaux's *L'échelle de soie* (1808). Prod. Venice 1812, London 1954, S. Francisco 1966.

scala enigmatica (Lat.). Enigmatic scale. Term applied to arbitrary scale used by Verdi in his *Ave Maria* (1897), the first of his *Quattro pezzi sacri*. Scale, which sounds like whole-tone scale, is C–D♭–E–F♯–G♯–A♯–B–C.

scale (from It. *scala*, 'staircase', 'ladder'; Ger. *Tonleiter*; Fr. *gamme*). A series of single notes progressing up or down stepwise. Thus, a series of notes within an octave used as the basis of comp. Scales are arbitrary, and the no. in use throughout the world is incalculable.

For the older European scales, used in the Church's plainsong and in folk song, see *modes*. Two of these ancient modes remained in use by composers, when the other 10 were almost abandoned, and these are our major and minor scales—the latter, however, subject to some variations in its 6th and 7th notes. Taking C as the keynote these scales (which have provided the chief material of music from about AD 1600 to 1900) run as follows:

Major scale (semitones 3–4 and 7–8—the two halves thus being alike).

Minor scale—'harmonic' form (semitones 2–3, 5–6, 7–8; there is the interval of the augmented second, 6–7).

Minor scale—'melodic' form (semitones 2–3, 7–8 ascending; 6–5, 3–2 descending; this avoids the interval of the augmented 2nd while allowing the leading note to retain its function of 'leading' to the tonic).

The major and minor scales are spoken of as DIATONIC SCALES, as distinct from a scale using nothing but semitones, which is the CHROMATIC SCALE, for which 2 different notations are employed:

Chromatic scale (in 'melodic' notation—sharps upwards, flats downwards; this notation economizes accidentals).

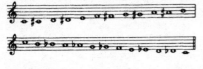

Chromatic scale (in 'harmonic' notation).

This scale when begun on other notes is 'harmonically' notated according to the same principles; for instance, beginning on D it reads:

The scheme is: the notes of the major scale, plus those of the harmonic minor scale, plus the minor 2nd and augmented 4th.

A scale comprising the same notes as the chromatic scale is the *DODECAPHONIC SCALE, in which the 12 notes are considered to be all of equal status and are so treated, whereas the chromatic scale beginning on any particular note is considered to comprise the diatonic scale of that note 'coloured' (this is the literal meaning of 'chromatic') by the addition of the extra semitones.

Scales with smaller intervals than the semitone have been introduced. See *microtone*.

The WHOLE-TONE SCALE is free of semitones and thus allows of only 2 different series, each with 6 notes:

Whole-tone scale.

An extremely widespread scale is the 5-note or PENTATONIC SCALE (common in Scottish, Chinese, and other music):

Pentatonic scale (commonest order of the intervals).

The Scottish Highland Bagpipe is tuned to a scale that cannot be represented in orthodox notation. It is roughly that of the white notes of the piano with the C and F about a quarter of a tone sharp.

Scalero, Rosario (*b* Moncalieri, Turin, 1870; *d* Settimo Vittone, Turin, 1954). It. violinist, composer, and teacher of violin and of composition. Taught in Fr. and It. before going to USA in 1919. Chairman, theory and comp. dept., Mannes Sch. 1919–28; taught at Curtis Inst. 1924–33, 1935–46. Pupils incl. *Barber, *Menotti, and L. *Foss. Wrote vn. conc., chamber mus., songs, etc.

Scapino. Comedy ov. by Walton, comp. 1940 to commission from Chicago SO who gave f.p. in Apr. 1941, cond. Frederick Stock. F. Eng. p. London, Nov. 1941. Rev. 1950. Score is subtitled 'after an etching from Jacques Callot's *Balli di Sfessania*, 1622'. Scapino was comic valet in *commedia dell' arte* and the hero of Molière's *Les Fourberies de Scapin*.

Scaramouche. (1) Suite for 2 pf., 1939, by *Milhaud. Based on incid. mus. for play *The Flying Doctor*, 1937, prod. in Paris at Théâtre Scaramouche, hence title.
(2) Ballet in 3 scenes, mus. by Sibelius (1913), lib. by P. Knudsen, choreog. E. Walbom. Prod. Copenhagen 1922.

Scarbo (Ravel). See *Gaspard de la nuit*.

Scarlatti, (Petro) **Alessandro** (Gaspare) (*b* Palermo, 1660; *d* Naples, 1725). It. composer, specially important in development of opera and considered founder of so-called Neapolitan school. Taken to Rome 1672, said to have studied with *Carissimi, and wrote first opera there 1679. Engaged by Queen Christina of Sweden, then living in Rome, as choirmaster and cond., 1680–4, for her private th. Court cond. to Viceroy of Naples, 1684–1702 and from 1708. Alternated between Rome and Naples for rest of life, in various court and church appointments. Contribution to opera was liberation of dramatic expression. Est. the *da capo* aria, first in *Teodora* (1692), the opera in which orch. ritornello is supposedly used for the first time. The so-called 'It. ov.' was introduced in 1696 in a revival of *Dal male il bene*. In 1685, in *L'Olimpia vendicata*, occurs the first recorded instance of acc. recit. His greatest opera is reckoned to be *Mitridate Eupatore* (1707), comp. for Prince Ferdinando de' Medici, but a failure on its f.p. in Venice. In his late Rome years, the general enthusiasm for opera, stimulated by Scarlatti, overcame all ecclesiastical objections. His 115 operas incl. only one comic opera, *Il trionfo dell'onore* (Naples 1718). Sixty-four survive, wholly or in part, of which revivals show superb craftsmanship and lofty invention, perhaps the best known being the last, *La Griselda* (1721). He also wrote some 20 oratorios, 10 masses, several settings of *Stabat Mater*, etc., over 40 motets, over 600 solo cantatas with basso continuo and 60 with other instr., some 30 chamber cantatas for 2 vv., 28 serenatas, several madrigals, 12 chamber concs., various sonatas, and hpd. pieces, incl. variations on *La Folia*. Father of Domenico *Scarlatti.

Scarlatti, (Giuseppe) **Domenico** (*b* Naples, 1685; *d* Madrid, 1757). It. composer and harpsichordist, son of A. *Scarlatti. Thought to have been pupil of his father and after 1708 of Pasquini and Gasparini in Venice, where he met Handel. In 1709, according to one biographer, Handel's patron, Cardinal Ottoboni, arranged a friendly kbd. contest between Handel and Scarlatti which was a tie, Handel being adjudged the better organist and Scarlatti the better harpsichordist. Worked in Rome 1708–19. Choirmaster to Queen of Poland, composing operas for her private th. in Rome. Choirmaster, Cappella Giulia at St Peter's 1714–19. Court harpsichordist to King of Portugal and teacher of Princess Maria Barbara in Lisbon 1719–28; returned to Italy on leave 1725–9; accompanied Maria Barbara to Spain on her marriage to the Sp. Crown Prince in 1729. Stayed in Madrid for rest of his life, becoming Maria Barbara's *maestro de cámera* when she became queen. Domenico did for kbd.-playing what his father did for opera, by imparting to it a hitherto unsuspected freedom of style. Introduced many new technical devices (rapid repetitions, crossed hands, double-note passages, etc.) and the 550 single-movt. sonatas he wrote in Sp. are exercises (*esercizi*) as well as innovatory comps. foreshadowing sonata form. Also comp. 14 operas, masses, *Stabat Mater* for 10 vv., *Salve Regina*, cantatas, at least 12 concerti grossi, 17 sinfonias, and org. fugues. His works have been catalogued by R. *Kirkpatrick, superseding the *Longo catalogue begun in 1906.

Scarlatti, Giuseppe (*b* Naples, *c*.1718; *d* Vienna, 1777). It. composer, thought to be nephew of D. *Scarlatti. Comp. 31 operas for Turin, Venice, Lucca, Naples, Florence, and Rome, then moved to Vienna where his subsequent operas incl. *La clemenza di Tito* (1760).

scat singing. Jazz term meaning the interpolation of nonsense words and syllables and other vocal effects, introduced in 1920s by Cab Calloway and Louis Armstrong.

Scelsi, Giacinto [Conte Giacinto Scelsi di Valva] (*b* La Spezia, 1905; *d* Rome, 1988). It. composer. Disciple of Schoenbergian serialism, then became interested in Eastern mus. and developed a variety of pre-minimalism, writing works based on one note. Works incl. str. qts., a sinfonietta, 11 pf. suites, and choral pieces. Became a cult figure after his death.

scemando (It.). Diminishing, in vol. of tone. Same as *diminuendo*.

scena (It.). Scene. Prin. meaning of this term is an elaborate concert aria for v. and orch. in several sections, like the cantatas of Haydn, A. Scarlatti, etc. Examples are Beethoven's *Ah! perfido*, Bliss's *The Enchantress*, Barber's *Andromache's Farewell*, and Britten's *Phaedra*. Other meanings are (1) a scene, subdivision of an act in opera; (2) solo operatic movt., less formal than an aria e.g. Leonore's *Abscheulicher!* in Beethoven's *Fidelio*.

Scenes and Arias. Setting of medieval love-letters for sop., mez., cont., and orch. by *Maw, comp. 1961–2, rev. 1966. F.p. London, 1962, cond. N. Del Mar.

Scenes from Childhood (Schumann). See *Kinderscenen*.

Scenes from Comus. Work for sop. and ten. soloists and orch. by Hugh *Wood, comp. 1962–5, commissioned by BBC and f.p. Promenade Concert, London, 1965, cond. Norman Del Mar. Text from Milton's masque *Comus* (1634).

Scenes from Goethe's Faust (Schumann). See *Faust, Scenes from Goethe's*.

Scenes from the Bavarian Highlands (Elgar). See *Bavarian Highlands, Scenes from the*.

Scenes from the Saga of King Olaf (Elgar). See *King Olaf, Scenes from the Saga of*.

Scènes historiques (Historical Scenes). Fr. title given by Sibelius to 2 suites of orch. pieces. No.1 (Op.25) dates from 1899 and comprises *All' Overtura*, *Scène*, and *Festivo* (rev. 1911). No.2 (Op.66) dates from 1912 and comprises *The Chase*, *Love-Song*, and *At the Drawbridge*.

Scènes pittoresques (Picturesque Scenes). Orch. work by Massenet, comp. 1874.

Schaaf, Johannes (*b* Bad Cannstadt, 1933). Ger. producer. Studied medicine, then joined Stuttgart Schauspielhaus, producing Shakespeare, Beaumarchais, Büchner, etc. From 1967 made series of TV films about musicians. Opera prods. at Vienna Volksoper (*Les contes d'Hoffmann*) and State Opera (*Idomeneo*). Salzburg Fest. début, play 1975, opera 1985. CG début 1987.

Schack [Žák], **Benedikt** (*b* Mirotice, 1758; *d* Munich, 1826). Bohem. tenor, composer, flautist, and conductor. Court cond., then joined *Schikaneder's co. 1786 as ten., singing with it in Salzburg, Vienna, Graz, and Munich until 1805. Created Tamino in *Die Zauberflöte*, 1791, playing the fl. himself. Said to be one of group who sang parts of Mozart's *Requiem* to composer on his death-bed. Wrote several operas and church mus. Mozart in 1791 wrote a set of 8 variations for pf. (K613) on the aria *Ein Weib ist das herrlichste Ding*, said to be by Schack.

Schaeffer, Boguslaw (Julian) (*b* Lwów, 1929). Polish composer, mainly self-taught, and pianist. First comp. 1946 in neo-classical style but with atonal leanings. Wrote atonal chamber mus. 1946–8. First composer in E. Europe to use 12-note system for orch. work (*Nocturne*, 1953). In 1955 discovered noteless composing of mus., e.g. in *Study in Diagram* for pf. (1955–6) only intervals, directions of linear motion, and articulations are used. In 1958 wrote *Tertium datur* with geometrical constructions written in graphical notation. Since 1959 his orch. scores have all been for unusual combinations of instr. Has written several jazz comps. since 1962 and elec. pieces since 1964. Many of his works inspired by paintings and literature. Uses 'synectic' method of comp., i.e. performers themselves decide what they understand by special signs and graphics. Has written books on new mus. (1958, 1969), *Sounds and Signs* (1969), and *Introduction to Composition* (1976, Eng. trans.), and is also a successful playwright. Comps. incl. works for stage; 10 syms. (1960–79); 3 pf. concs.; 2 hpd. concs.; 2 vn. concs.; concs. for various other instrs.; 6 str. qts. (1954–73); 2 str. trios; pf. trio; sax. qt.; vocal works; comps. for jazz ens.; many kbd. pieces.; works for elec., some with tape.

Schaeffer, Pierre (Henri Marie) (*b* Nancy, 1910; *d*. Aix-en-Provence, 1995). Fr. composer. Trained as radio technician and worked mostly for RTF, Paris. In 1942 founded acoustical experiments studio. Began experiments in 1948 with comps. based on assemblage of recorded sounds. For these he coined the term *musique concrète*, his first being *Étude aux chemins de fer*, made from the sounds of railway trains. This and 4 other works were broadcast from Paris on 5 Oct. 1948. In 1949 he began to collaborate with the composer Pierre Henry. In 1951 RTF est. a studio under Schaeffer's dir., the first to be devoted to elec. mus. Dir. of research, RTF 1959–75. Prof., Paris Cons. 1968–76. Prin. comps. incl. *Symphonie pour un homme seul* (collab. Pierre Henry, 1949–50, rev. 1966); *Orphée 53* (with Henry, for vn., hpd., 2 singers, and tape, 1951–3); *Sahara d'aujourd'hui* (collab. Henry, 1957); *Études aux objets* (1959, rev. 1966–7); *Les antennas de Jéricho* (1978); *Excusez-moi je meurs* (1981); *Prélude, Chorale et Fugue* (1983).

Schafe können sicher weiden (Sheep may safely graze). Recit. and air by Bach, with obbl. for 2 recorders, in secular cantata *Was mir behagt ist nur die munter Jagd!* (What I enjoy is only the merry chase!) (BWV208, ?1713). Several arrs. of it have been made, among them one by Walton as 7th no. of his ballet *The Wise Virgins* (No.5 in orch. suite), 1940, and one by Barbirolli for cor anglais and str., *c*.1937.

Schafer, R. Murray (*b* Sarnia, Ontario, 1933). Canadian composer, teacher, and writer. Went to Vienna 1956, then worked in Eng. Returned to Canada 1962 founding '10 Centuries Concerts'. Composer-in-residence Simon Fraser Univ., Vancouver, 1965–75, founding EMS. Works incl. *Loving/Toi*, music th. (1963–6); series

of multimedia th. pieces entitled *Patria*, consisting of: *Prologue, The Princess of the Stars* (1981), 1. *Wolfman* (orig. *The Characteristics Man*) (1974), 2. *Requiems for the Party Girl* (1972), 3. *The Greatest Show* (1987), 4. *The Black Theatre of Hermes* (1989), 5. *The Crown of Ariadne* (1992), 6. *RA* (1983), 7. *Asterion* (? in progress), 8. *The Palace of the Cinnabar Phoenix* (2000), 9. *The Enchanted Forest* (1993), 10. *The Spirit Garden* (1996); also *Gita*, ch., 8 brass tape (1967); *Son of Heldenleben*, orch. tape (1968); *Music for the Morning of the World*, mez., 4-track tape (1970); str. qts. No.1 (1970), No.2 (*Waves*) (1976), No.3 (1989), No.4 (1989), No.5 (1989), No.6 (1993), No.7 (1998), No.8 (2001); *Enchantress*, mez., fl., 8 vc. (1971 rev. 1972); *Arcana*, v., ens. (1972); *East*, chamber orch. (1972); *North White*, orch. (1973); *Adieu Robert Schumann*, alto, orch. (1976); *Hymn to Night*, sop., orch. (1976); *Cortège*, orch. (1977); *Apocalypsis*, music th. (1976–7); fl. conc. (1985); *Minnelieder*, mez., orch. (1986); hp. conc. (1987); gui. conc., chamber orch. (1989); *Gitanjali*, sop., orch. (1991); *Tristan and Iseult*, 6 vv. (1992); *The Falcon's Trumpet*, tpt., sop., orch. (1995); va. conc. (1997); *Imagining Incense*, unacc. ch. (2001); *Thunder: Perfect Mind*, mez., orch. (2003). Books and articles incl. *Ezra Pound and Music* (1977) and *British Composers in Interview* (1963).

Schale(n) (Ger.). *Cymbal(s).

Schalk, Franz (*b* Vienna, 1863; *d* Edlach, 1931). Austrian conductor. Cond. in Liberec 1886, Reichenbach 1888–9, Graz 1889–95, Prague 1895–8, Berlin 1899–1900, Vienna Opera 1900–29 (Joint dir. with R. Strauss 1919–24). CG 1898, 1907, and 1911 (3 *Ring* cycles); NY Met 1898–9, first uncut *Ring* in USA (début *Die Walküre*). Co-founder of Salzburg Fest. Ed. several Bruckner syms., making cuts and, in the deplorable case of No.5, recomposing parts and adding instr. Cond. f.p. of *Die Frau ohne Schatten* (Vienna, 1919). Joint ed. with Krenek of *Adagio* and *Purgatorio* movts. from Mahler's 10th sym. and cond. their f.p., Vienna 1924.

Schallbecken (Ger.). *Cymbals.

Schallplatte (Ger.). Sound plate. Gramophone record.

Schalmey, Schalmei. Another name for the *shawm.

scharf (Ger.). Sharply—in various contexts, such as *scharf betont*, given out with emphatic accent. *Schärfe*, sharpness, definiteness, precision.

Scharrer, Irene (*b* London, 1888; *d* London, 1971). Eng. pianist. London début 1904, last appearance there 1958. First visited USA 1925. Cousin of Myra *Hess.

Scharwenka, (Franz) **Xaver** (*b* Samter, Posen, 1850; *d* Berlin, 1924). Ger. pianist, conductor, and composer. Taught at Kullak Acad., Berlin, 1868–73. Début Berlin 1869. European tours from 1874. Visited London on occasions between 1879 and 1899. Founded cons. in Berlin 1881 (merged with Klindworth Cons. 1893). Lived in USA 1891–8, founding cons. in NY. Returned to Ger. and was co-dir. Klindworth-Scharwenka Cons. 1898–1914. Opened new sch. in Berlin 1914. Comps. incl. opera, sym., 4 pf. concs., 2 pf. sonatas, church mus., chamber mus., and many songs. Ed. Schumann's pf. works.

Schauspieldirektor, Der (Mozart). See *Impresario, The*.

Schech, Marianne (*b* Geitau, 1914; *d* Munich, 1999). Ger. soprano. Début at Coblenz 1937 (Marta in *Tiefland*). From 1937 to 1945 sang in Münster, Munich, Düsseldorf, and Dresden. Member of Bavarian State Opera, Munich, 1945–70, specializing in Wagner and Strauss roles. CG début 1956; NY Met 1957; S. Francisco 1959. Was one of singers of trio from *Der Rosenkavalier* at Strauss's funeral, 1949.

Scheherazade. See *Sheherazade*.

Scheibler, Johann Heinrich (*b* Montjoie, nr. Aix-la-Chapelle, 1777; *d* Crefeld, 1837). Ger. silk manufacturer with interest in acoustics. Experimented in measurement of pitch and in 1834 at Stuttgart proposed 440 vibrations for A at 69° F, adopted as 'Stuttgart pitch'. Invented 'Aura', first mouth harmonica, 1816. Writings on subject pubd. 1838.

Scheidt, Samuel (*b* Halle, 1587; *d* Halle, 1654). Ger. organist and composer. Org., Moritzkirche, Halle, from *c*.1603; org. and choirmaster to Margrave of Brandenburg in Halle from *c*.1609, becoming court cond. 1619. Best known in his day for his vocal works, incl. *cantiones sacrae* for 8 vv. (1620) and 70 *Symphonien auf Concerten-Manier* with 3 vv. and basso continuo (1644). Most important was his book of org. mus., *Tabulatura nova* (1624, 3 vols.) proposing staff notation for org. instead of *tablature.

Schein, Johann Hermann (*b* Grünhain, Saxony, 1586; *d* Leipzig, 1630). Ger. composer. Chorister, Dresden court chapel from 1599. Court Kapellmeister, Weimar, from 1615. Cantor of Thomas Sch., Leipzig, from 1616. One of first Ger. musicians to benefit from It. influence. Wrote nearly 100 chorale melodies and harmonizations, sacred songs in It. style, *villanelles*, madrigals, *Venus Kräntzlein* (new secular songs, 1609), motets, dance suites, wedding-songs, etc.

Schelle(n) (Ger.). Bell(s). Also *Schellenbaum* (belltree), *Jingling Johnny; Schellengeläute* (bell-ringing), sleigh-bells; *Schellentrommel* (bell-drum), *tambourine. *Schallbecken* is Ger. for cymbals.

Schelomo (Hebrew, Solomon; Eng. transliteration is *Shelomo*, but Ger. version more often used). Rhapsody for vc. and orch. by Bloch, based on Book of Ecclesiastes, authorship of which is attrib. to Solomon. Comp. 1916, f.p. NY 1916.

Schemelli Hymn Book. Coll. of 954 hymns and 69 tunes (*Musikalisches Gesangbuch*) pubd. 1736 by

Georg Christian Schemelli (*b* Herzberg, *c*.1676; *d* Zeitz, 1762), cantor of Zeitz castle, and ed. by J. S. Bach, who comp. 3 of the tunes and provided or improved the figured basses.

Schenk, Manfred (*b* Stuttgart, 1930; *d* 1999). Ger. bass. Sang in Frankfurt radio ch. Member Frankfurt Opera 1967–90. Glyndebourne début 1973 (Sarastro in *Die Zauberflöte*); NY Met 1977; CG 1981; Bayreuth Fest. début 1981; Salzburg 1985.

Schenk, Otto (*b* Vienna, 1930). Austrian producer and actor. Began career as actor (Salzburg 1952 in Nestroy's *Die Träume von Schale und Kern*) and was noted for portrayal of the jailer Frosch in *Die Fledermaus*. First opera prod. was *Die Zauberflöte*, Salzburg Landestheater 1957. Moved to forefront with Vienna Fest. prods. of *Dantons Tod* and *Lulu*, 1962. Salzburg début as prod. 1963; Vienna Opera 1964 (resident dir. from 1965); NY Met début 1968; La Scala 1974; CG 1975. Prod. *Der Ring des Nibelungen*, NY Met 1986–91.

Schenker, Heinrich (*b* Wisniowczyki, Galicia, 1868; *d* Vienna, 1935). Austrian pianist, writer, and teacher. Wrote songs and was for a time accomp. to bar. Johannes Messchaert. Thereafter devoted himself to theoretical research. Ed. Beethoven's pf. sonatas, Handel's org. works, and C. P. E. Bach's kbd. music. Wrote several theoretical books. Inventor of famous system of analysis based on theory that one type of mus. structure was basis of all masterpieces from Bach to Brahms.

Scherchen, Hermann (*b* Berlin, 1891; *d* Florence, 1966). Ger. conductor and violist. Violist in Berlin PO 1907–10. Worked with Schoenberg 1910–12 helping to prepare f.p. of *Pierrot Lunaire*, making début as cond. 1911. Cond. Riga SO 1914. Founded Berlin soc. for new mus., 1918. Cond. Frankfurt Museum concerts 1922–4. Dir., Musikkollegium, Winterthur, 1922–47. Mus. dir. at Königsberg 1928–33. Left Ger. 1933, making Switzerland his base. Ardent champion of 20thcent. mus., especially that of Schoenberg and Webern. Cond., Zurich Radio Orch. 1944–50. Opened EMS at Gravesano, 1954. Amer. début, Philadelphia 1964. Cond. f.ps. of operas by Dallapiccola, Henze, and Dessau, and f.ps. of Berg's *Three Fragments from Wozzeck* (1924), *Chamber Concerto* (1927), *Der Wein* (1930), and vn. conc. (1936). Wrote *Handbook of Conducting* (1929) and *The Nature of Music* (1946).

Scherchen-Hsiao, Tona (*b* Neuchâtel, 1938). Swiss composer (later Fr. cit.). Settled in Fr. 1972. Works incl. *Wai*, mez., str. qt., perc. (1966); *Shen*, 6 perc. (1968); *Khouang*, orch. (1966–8); *Tzi*, unacc. ch. (1969–70); *Tao*, alto, orch. (1971); *Tjao-Houen*, chamber orch. (1973); *Lien*, va. (1973); *Vague T'ao*, orch. (1974–5); *L'Invitation au Voyage*, chamber orch. (1976–7); *Œil de chat*, orch. (1976–7); *Lo*, tb., 12 str. (1978–9); *Ziguidor*, wind quintet (1977); *Tzing*, brass quintet (1979); *Tarots*, hpd., 7 instrs. (1981–2); *Lustucru*, variable ens.

(1983); *L'illégitime*, orch., tape. (1985–6); *Space-flight*, tape (1987); *Lude pour Alicelia*, mez., tuba, elecs., tape (1989); *Le jeu du Pogo*, film score (1991). Has won several comp. prizes in Paris. Daughter of H. *Scherchen.

Scherz (Ger.). Fun, joke. *scherzend, scherzhaft*, jocular.

scherzetto, scherzino (It.). A short **scherzo*.

Scherzi, Gli (Haydn). See *Russian Quartets*.

Scherzi musicali (Musical Jokes). 2 sets of madrigal-like songs, influenced by Fr. style, by Monteverdi. 1st set (1607) for 3 vv. contains 15 songs, the 2nd (1632) for 1 or 2 vv. with basso continuo contains 10.

scherzo (It., plural *scherzi*). Jest, joke. Name for a movt. in orch. mus., but the term was first applied in 17th cent. to vocal mus., e.g. Monteverdi's **Scherzi musicali*. Generally it is the 3rd (or 2nd) movt. of a sym. or str. qt., etc., the liveliest movt., usually but not necessarily the most light-hearted. It is the successor to the 18th-cent. minuet and trio, which was developed almost to *scherzo* pitch by Haydn. A movt. in S. Storace's 2nd pf. quintet (1784) is a scherzo. Beethoven was the real creator of the scherzo (as early as the Op.1 pf. trios), investing the movt. with a rough, almost savage humour, with marked rhythm, generally in 3/4 time. The contrasting section is known as the trio, but not all scherzos have trios. Chopin called 4 of his pf. works *Scherzo*, but they are marked more by vigour and intensity than by anything in the nature of a jest.

scherzoso; scherzosamente (It.). Playful; playfully, i.e. like a **scherzo*. Thus *scherzando, scherzante*: joking, playful; *scherzevole, scherzevolmente*: jokingly, playfully.

Schickele, Peter (*b* Ames, Iowa, 1935). Amer. composer. Taught at Juilliard Sch. Wrote film scores, songs for Joan Baez, and formed chamber-rock group, 1967–70. Works incl. *The Civilian Barber*, orch. (1953); *A Zoo Called Earth* (1970); *The Birth of Christ*, ch. (1960); *Bestiary* (1982); 5 str. qts. (1983–98); 3 pf. sonatinas; 4 *Rags* (1972); str. trio (1960); concs for fl. (1990), ob. (1994), chamber orch. (1998), bn. (1999), vc. (2000), ob. & vn. (2001); *Elegy*, str. (1992); *Folk Song Set*, chamber orch. (2002); 2 syms. (1995, 2001). Has written series of humorous works under pseudonym 'P. D. Q. Bach', incl. operas *The Stoned Guest, The Abduction of Figaro* (1984), and *Oedipus Tex* (1990).

Schicksalslied (Song of Destiny). Setting by Brahms, Op.54, for ch. and orch. of part of a poem by Hölderlin. Comp. 1871.

Schiff, András (*b* Budapest, 1953). Hung. pianist. Début aged 9. Professional début Budapest 1972. Prizes in Tchaikovsky comp., Moscow 1974, Leeds (equal 3rd) 1975. NY début with orch. 1978, recital 1989. Settled in West 1979. Salzburg début 1982.

Schiff, Heinrich (*b* Gmunden, 1951). Austrian cellist and conductor who began as pianist. Won prizes at comps. in Geneva, Vienna, and Warsaw, then played concs. with leading orchs. in Vienna, Amsterdam, and London. Had Salzburg début (as cellist) 1972; Amer. début 1981. Took up cond. 1984. Art. dir. Northern Sinfonia 1990–6. Chief cond. Vienna CO from 2004.

Schikaneder, Emanuel (Johann) [Johannes Joseph] (*b* Straubing, 1751; *d* Vienna, 1812). Ger. theatre manager, librettist, singer, and actor. Was singer and actor in troupe of strolling players before becoming manager of Kärntnerthor Th., Vienna, 1783 and later of Theater an der Wieden there. For latter, persuaded Mozart to write mus. for his lib. *Die Zauberflöte* (1791) and himself played Papageno. In 1801 was partner in opening Theater an der Wien, managing it until 1806. Other libs. by him were set by Schack, *Paisiello, *Süssmayr, etc. His *Vestas Feuer*, 1805, was begun by Beethoven, but eventually set by Weigl.

Schillinger, Joseph (*b* Kharkov, 1895; *d* NY, 1943). Russ.-born composer, teacher, and writer (Amer. cit. 1936). Taught comp. Kharkov State Acad. 1918–22; comp. for Leningrad State Acad. Th. 1925–8. Settled in USA 1928, teaching comp., mathematics, and art history at various institutions. Taught *Gershwin, Benny Goodman, Glenn Miller, and Tommy Dorsey. Pubd. manual of new tone progressions. Comp. *Airphonic Suite* for theremin (1929), also vn. sonata, *Symphonic Rhapsody* (1927), *North Russian Symphony*, accordion and orch. Writings incl. *Kaleidophone, New Sources of Melody and Harmony* (NY 1940), *Schillinger System of Musical Composition* (NY 1941–6, 2 vols.), and *Mathematical Basis of the Arts* (NY 1948).

Schillings, Max von (*b* Düren, 1868; *d* Berlin, 1933). Ger. composer, administrator, and conductor. Ass. stage cond. 1892 and from 1902 chorusmaster at Bayreuth Fest. Prof. of mus., Munich Univ. from 1903. Ass. to Intendant, Stuttgart Opera, 1908–11, gen. mus. dir. 1911–18. Intendant Berlin State Opera 1919–25. Gen. mus. dir. Riga Opera 1929–32. Visited USA 1924 and 1931 with Ger. Opera Co. Comp. 4 operas, incl. *Mona Lisa* (1915), several monodramas, vn. conc., choral works, chamber mus., and songs, incl. the *Glockenlieder* with orch. (1908). Second wife was sop. Barbara *Kemp.

Schindler, Anton (*b* Meedl, Moravia, 1795; *d* Bockenheim, Frankfurt, 1864). Austrian violinist and conductor, remembered as friend and biographer of Beethoven. Leader and cond. at Josephstadt Th., Vienna, 1822, Kärntnerthor Th., 1825. Choirmaster, Münster Cath., 1831–5, mus. dir. and choirmaster, Aachen 1835–40. Met Beethoven 1814, becoming kind of secretary 1816, living in his house 1822–4, and caring for him in his last illness 1826–7. Published biography of Beethoven (Münster 1840, many subsequent edns.), but despite its immense value, there are many inaccuracies and scholarship has convicted him of forgeries in the Beethoven conversation-books. Wrote 2 masses and chamber mus.

Schiøtz, Aksel (*b* Roskilde, Denmark, 1906; *d* Copenhagen, 1975). Danish tenor. In 1939 made opera début at Copenhagen (Ferrando in *Così fan tutte*) and in 1942 début as recitalist. Eng. début, Glyndebourne 1946. Toured USA 1948. Noted *Lieder* singer. Illness halted career 1950; later resumed it as bar. Taught at Minnesota Univ. 1955–8, Royal Cons. of Mus., Toronto, 1958–61, Colorado Univ. 1961–8. Returned to teach in Denmark 1968. Danish knighthood 1947.

Schipa, Tito (Raffaele Attilio Amadeo) (*b* Lecce, 1888; *d* Wickersham, NY, 1965). It. tenor. Opera début Vercelli, 1910 (Alfredo in *La traviata*). Rome 1914; La Scala 1915. Created Ruggero in *La *rondine*, Monte Carlo 1917. Member, Chicago Opera 1919–32. NY début 1920. NY Met 1932–5 and 1940–1. Sang in It. until 1952. Last stage appearances Buenos Aires and Lecce 1954. Concert tour of Russia 1957. Taught in Rome and wrote operetta (1929).

Schippers, Thomas (*b* Kalamazoo, Michigan, 1930; *d* NY, 1977). Amer. conductor. Début NY 1948. Closely assoc. with *Menotti and cond. f.p. in NY of *The Consul* 1950 and f.p. in London 1951, also première of *Amahl and the Night Visitors* (TV 1951). Cond. NY City Opera 1952–4; cond. f.p. of Copland's *The Tender Land* (1954) and Menotti's *The Saint of Bleecker Street* (1954). Cond. Cherubini's *Medea* for Callas, Milan 1962. Débuts NY Met and La Scala 1955. Cond. f.p. of Barber's *Antony and Cleopatra* 1966. Mus. dir. Spoleto Fest. 1958–76. Bayreuth Fest. 1963; CG début 1968. Cond. Cincinnati SO from 1970 to his death.

Schirmer, G., Inc. Firm of NY music publishers founded 1861 by Gustav Schirmer (1829–93) and B. Beer. Schirmer gained full control 1866, and later his sons joined him as partners. Publishers of many leading Amer. composers, incl. Creston, Barber, Harris, Schuman, Menotti, and Bernstein. *The Musical Quarterly* was launched by the firm in 1915. Schirmer Music Co. of Boston, founded 1921 by a nephew of G. Schirmer, is a separate firm and publishes many of the *avant-garde* Amer. composers in addition to Copland, Del Tredici, R. Thompson, Piston, and Rorem.

schlagen (Ger.). To strike; hence *Schlägel*, drumstick; *Schlaginstrumente*, perc. instr.

Schlagobers (Whipped cream). 'Gay Viennese ballet' in 2 acts by R. Strauss, Op.70, to his own lib., choreog. Kröller. Comp. 1921–2. Prod. Vienna and Breslau 1924.

Schleifer. (1) *Ländler*.

(2) Old ornament in instr. mus., the essential feature of which was the filling in of an interval between 2 melodic notes with a kind of slide.

schleppend (Ger.). Dragging. Often found in Mahler's scores in the negative, *nicht schleppend*, i.e. don't let the tempo drag.

Schlesinger, Maurice [Moritz] (*b* Berlin, 1798; *d* Baden-Baden, 1871). Fr. music publisher of Ger. descent. Settled in Paris *c*.1820 and started own business 1821. Issued scores by Meyerbeer, Moscheles, Weber, Hummel, complete edns. of pf. works of Beethoven (whom he knew), and pubd. his str. trios, qts., and quintets, and early works by Mendelssohn, Liszt, and Berlioz. Pubd. about 40 of Chopin's works. Established the weekly *Gazette musicale de Paris* 1834 (later *Revue et gazette musicale*, ceased publication 1880). From 1840 to 1842 employed Wagner to make pf. arrs. of scores by Donizetti, Halévy, and others. Sold business 1846 and retired.

Schlumpf, Martin (*b* Aarau, Switz., 1947). Swiss composer and pianist. Works incl. songs with orch., fl. trio, *5 Pieces for Orch.*, str. qt., etc.

Schlusnus, Heinrich (*b* Braubach, 1888; *d* Frankfurt, 1952). Ger. baritone. Concert début Frankfurt 1912, operatic début Hamburg 1914 (Herald in *Lohengrin*). Hamburg Opera 1914–15; Nuremberg 1915–17; Berlin State Opera 1917–45; Chicago 1927–8; Bayreuth 1933. Leading Verdi bar. of his day in Ger., but at his finest in *Lieder* (especially Schubert).

Schlüssel (Ger.). Clef. See *notation*.

Schluß-Satz. (Ger.). Coda. See *Satz*.

Schlußzeichen (Ger.). Close-sign. The double-bar with pause which indicates the end of a repeated section after which the movt. ends.

schmachtend (Ger.). Yearning, longing.

Schmedes, Erik (*b* Gentofte, Copenhagen, 1868; *d* Vienna, 1931). Danish tenor. Sang as bar., Wiesbaden 1891–4 (début as Herald in *Lohengrin*). Début as lyric ten. Nuremberg 1894. Dresden 1894–7. Engaged by Mahler for Vienna Opera, making début as Siegfried 1898 and remaining there until 1924. NY Met 1908–9; Bayreuth 1899–1902. One of great Wagnerian tens. of Mahler régime.

schmetternd (Ger.). In hn.-playing, blared, i.e. notes prod. as stopped (with hand inserted in the bell), combined with hard blowing. Normal Brit. indication is + together with *ff*.

Schmid, Erich (*b* Balsthal, Switz., 1907; *d* Zurich, 2000). Swiss conductor. Mus. dir. Glarus, Switz., 1934–49; cond. Tonhalle Orch., Zurich, 1949–57, Beromünster Radio Orch. 1957–72. Champion of 20th-cent. mus. Made orch. arr. of Debussy's pf. duet *Six Épigraphes antiques*, and comp. chamber works.

Schmidt, Andreas (*b* Düsseldorf, 1960). Ger. baritone. Début Deutsche Oper 1984 (Malatesta in *Don Pasquale*). Created title-role in Rihm's *Oedipus*, Berlin 1987. CG début 1986; Salzburg Fest. début 1989. Created Ryuji in Henze's *Das verratene Meer*, Berlin 1990. Noted *Lieder* singer.

Schmidt, Bernhard. See *Smith, 'Father'*.

Schmidt, Franz (*b* Pressburg (Pozsony; now Bratislava), 1874; *d* Perchtoldsdorf, Vienna, 1939). Austrian composer, pianist, conductor, and cellist. Cellist in Vienna PO 1896–1911. Prof. of pf., Vienna Acad. of Mus., 1914–22, prof. of comp. 1922, dir. 1925–7, rector of Vienna Hochschule für Musik 1927–31. Regarded in Austria as composer in tradition of Bruckner. Works incl.:

OPERAS: **Notre Dame* (1902–4, 1904–6); **Fredigundis* (1916–21).

ORCH.: syms.: No.1 in E major (1896–9), No.2 in E♭ major (1911–13), No.3 in A major (1927–8), No.4 in C major (1932–3); *Zwischenspiel* (Intermezzo) from *Notre Dame* (1902–4); *Variations on a Hussar Song* (1930–1); *Chaconne* in C♯ minor (1931, orch. of 1925 org. work); *Concertante Variations on a Theme of Beethoven*, pf. (left-hand), orch. (1923); pf. conc. in E♭ (left-hand) (1934).

CHORAL: *Das Buch mit sieben Siegeln* (The Book with Seven Seals), oratorio, soloists, ch., org., orch. (1935–7); *Deutsche Auferstehung*, cantata (incomplete), soloists, ch., org., orch. (1938–9).

CHAMBER MUSIC: pf. quintet (1926); cl. quintet No.1 in B major (1932), No.2 in A major (1938), both scored for cl., vn., va., vc., and pf. left-hand; str. qt. No.1 in A major (1925), No.2 in G major (1929); quintet in G, pf. left-hand, 2 vn., va., vc. (1926); *3 Little Fantasy-Pieces* on Hung. nat. melodies, vc. and pf. (1892).

ORGAN: Fantasy and Fugue in D (1924); *Toccata* in C major (1924); Prelude and Fugue in E♭ (1924); *Chaconne* in C♯ minor (1925); *4 Little Choral-Preludes* (1926); *Solemn Fugue* (1937).

Schmidt, Joseph (*b* Bavideni, Bukovina, 1904; *d* Girenbad internment camp, nr. Zurich, 1942). Romanian tenor. Made name as radio singer and on gramophone records. Small stature prevented his operatic career. Settled Switz. 1939.

Schmidt, Ole (*b* Copenhagen, 1928). Danish conductor, composer, and pianist. Début as cond. 1955. Royal Opera and Ballet, Copenhagen, 1958–65. Chief cond. Hamburg SO 1970–1, Danish Radio SO from 1971, Århus SO 1979–85. Début with BBCSO 1977. Amer. début 1980 (Oakland SO). Chief guest cond. RNCM 1986–9 where in 1989 he cond. f. Czech-language p. in Eng. of *From the *House of the Dead*. Comps. incl. 2 syms.; pf. conc.; 2 concs. for accordion; hn. conc.; vn. conc.; tuba conc.; guitar conc.; 6 str. qts.; and ballets.

Schmidt, Trudeliese (*b* Saarbrücken, 1934; *d* Saarbrücken, 2004). Ger. mezzo-soprano. Stage début Saarbrücken 1965 (Hänsel). Joined Deutsche Oper am Rhein, Düsseldorf, 1967. Brit. début Edinburgh Fest. 1972 (with Deutsche

Oper). Vienna début 1974; CG 1974; Salzburg Fest. 1974; Bayreuth 1975; Glyndebourne 1976. Notable as Composer in *Ariadne auf Naxos*.

Schmidt-Isserstedt, Hans (*b* Berlin, 1900; *d* Holm-Holstein, nr. Hamburg, 1973). Ger. conductor and composer. Cond. in Wuppertal, then Rostock 1928–31, Darmstadt 1931–3, and at Hamburg State Opera 1935–42. Dir., Deutsches Oper, Berlin, 1942–5. Founded N. Ger. Radio SO (Hamburg Radio SO) in 1945, remaining cond. until 1971. Toured Eng. with it 1951 (first foreign orch. to play in rebuilt Free Trade Hall, Manchester). From cond. Stockholm PO 1955–64. Cond. Glyndebourne 1958 and CG 1962. Comp. comic opera, orch. mus., and songs.

Schmieder, Wolfgang (*b* Bromberg, 1901; *d* Fürstenfeldbruck, 1990). Ger. musicologist. Archivist, Breitkopf and Härtel, Leipzig; head of mus. div. of Frankfurt State Library 1942–63. Compiled thematic catalogue of Bach's mus. (Leipzig 1950) which provides standard method of numbering his work. See *BWV*.

Schmitt, Florent (*b* Blâmont, Nancy, 1870; *d* Neuilly-sur-Seine, 1958). Fr. composer. Won *Grand Prix de Rome* 1900. Dir., Lyons Cons. 1922–4. Frequent writer on mus. (in *Le Temps*, etc.). Mus. is rich in orch. colouring, often exotically scored. Works incl.:

ORCH.: *Feuillets de Voyage* (1903–13, orch. from pf. duet); *La tragédie de *Salomé*, sym.-poem (1910, rev. of 1907 mimodrama); *Légende*, va. (or vn. or sax.), orch. (1918); *Antony and Cleopatra*, 6 symphonic episodes (1919–20); *Salammbô*, 6 symphonic episodes (1925); *Symphonie concertante*, pf., orch. (1931); sym. (1958).

MIMODRAMA: *La tragédie de *Salomé* (1907, rev. as sym.-poem 1910).

VOICE(S) & ORCH.: *Psalm 47* (46 in Vulgate), sop., ch., orch. (1904); *4 Poèmes de Ronsard* (1940).

CHAMBER MUSIC: pf. quintet (1901–8); vn. sonata (1918–19); sax. qt. (1943); str. trio (1944); fl. qt. (1944); qt., 3 tb., tuba (1946); str. qt. (1947–8); sextet, 6 cl. (1953); *Chants alizés*, wind quintet (1952–5); *Suite*, fl., pf. (1954–8).

Also many pf. pieces and songs.

Schnabel, Artur (*b* Lipnik, 1882; *d* Axenstein, Switz., 1951). Austrian-born pianist, composer, and teacher (Amer. cit. 1944). Public début at age 8. Became one of world's most respected and admired pianists, famous for his Beethoven and Schubert interpretations. Notable recordings. Taught at Berlin Hochschule 1925–33 and later in Switz. Ed. Beethoven pf. sonatas and, with *Flesch, the Mozart and Brahms vn. sonatas. Settled in USA 1939–45, before returning to Switz. Rarely played 20th-cent. mus. but comp. in atonal style: works incl. 3 syms., 5 str. qts., and pf. conc. Wrote 3 books.

Schnabel, Karl Ulrich (*b* Berlin, 1909; *d* Danbury, Conn., 2001). Ger. born pianist (Amer. cit.

1944), son of Artur *Schnabel. Début Berlin 1926. Settled USA 1938, teaching in NY. Wrote *Modern Technique of the Pedal* (1950).

Schnarre (Ger.). Rattle. *Schnarrtrommel*, side-drum. *Schnarrsaite*, rattle-string, i.e. the snare. But the *Schnarrwerk* of an organ is the reed department.

Schnebel, Dieter (*b* Lahr, 1930). Ger. composer. Entered Lutheran church; teacher of religion in Frankfurt 1963–70. Believes in theory that mus. can only be saved through abandonment. Hence works incl. non-mus. sounds and noises, and his *Nostalgie* (*Visible Music II*), 1962, is for cond. only. Other orch. works incl. *Webern-Variationen* (1972); *Canones* (1975–7, 1993–4); *Schubert-Phantasie* (1977–8); *Wagner-Idyll* (1980); *Beethoven-Sinfonie* (1984–5); *Mahler-Moment* (1984–5); *Sinfonie X*, cont., orch., elecs. (1987–92, 2004–5); *Hymnus*, pf. conc. from *Symfonie X*, (1989–92); *Medusa*, accordeon (1989–93); *Languido*, bfl., elec. (1993); *Museumsstücke II (MoMA)*, vv., instr. (1994). *inter*, small orch. (1994); *Totentanz*, 2 spkrs., sop., bass, ch., orch./elec. (1994); *Toccata and Fugue*, org. (1995–6); *Jo*, gui., fl., perc. (1996); *Ekstasis*, sop., narr., 2 children's vv., perc., ch., orch. (1997); *Motetus II*, 2 unacc. ch. (1997–8); *Aschermittwochmusik*, ch., org., perc. (2005). Has written books on K. Stockhausen (1963–71) and Kagel (1970).

Schnéevoigt, Georg (*b* Viipuri, 1872; *d* Malmö, 1947). Finn. conductor and cellist. Cellist in Helsinki PO for 8 years, then toured Europe as soloist. Cond. début Riga 1901. Cond. Kaim Orch., Munich, 1904–8. Formed new sym. orch. in Helsinki 1912 which in 1914 became Helsinki City Orch. Cond. Helsinki City Orch. 1916–41 (jointly with *Kajanus 1916–32). Cond. in Stockholm 1915–24, Oslo PO 1919–27, Riga Opera 1928–32, Los Angeles PO 1927–9, Malmö 1930–47.

Schneider, (Abraham) **Alexander** (*b* Vilnius, 1908; *d* Manhattan, 1993). Russ.-born violinist and conductor (Amer. cit.). Leader, Frankfurt Museum Soc. Orch. 1925–32. 2nd vn. Budapest Qt. 1932–44, and 1955–67 (when it disbanded). Settled USA 1938. Helped *Casals to found Prades Fest. 1950 and Casals Fest., Puerto Rico, 1957. Led his own str. qt. from 1952. Founded Brandenburg Players, 1972. Active as a teacher and director of seminars. Member of several chamber ens. Cond. Chamber Orch. of Europe in London 1991. Wrote autobiography, *Sasha: a Musician's Life* (NY, 1988).

Schneider, (Johann Christian) **Friedrich** (*b* Alt-Waltersdorf, 1786; *d* Dessau, 1853). Ger. composer, conductor, organist, and teacher. Org., St Thomas's, Leipzig, from 1812; court cond. Dessau from 1821. Cond. of many Ger. choral fests. Wrote 16 oratorios, 7 operas, 23 syms., many choruses and songs, 7 pf. concs., much church and chamber mus. His perf. of Beethoven's 5th pf. conc. in Leipzig, in Dec. 1810 is thought to have been work's f.p.

Schneider, Peter (*b* Vienna, 1939). Austrian conductor. Sang in Vienna Boys' Choir. Operatic début Salzburg Landestheater 1959 (*Giulio Cesare*). Prin. cond. Heidelberg Opera 1961–7, Deutsche Oper am Rhein, Düsseldorf, 1968–77, Bremen 1978–85, Mannheim 1985–7, Bavarian State Opera, Munich, 1993–8. Bayreuth début 1981. Cond. *Ring* at Bayreuth 1984. CG début 1986.

Schneiderhan, Wolfgang (*b* Vienna, 1915; *d* Vienna, 2002). Austrian violinist. Toured Eur. at age of 11. Lived in Eng. 1929–32. Leader Vienna SO 1932–6, then played in opera orch. Leader Vienna PO 1937–51. Founded and led Schneiderhan Quartet 1937–51. Prof. of vn. Salzburg Mozarteum 1938–56, and Vienna Acad. of Mus. 1939–50. On staff Lucerne Cons. from 1949. Frequent soloist with leading orchs. With wife Irmgard *Seefried gave f.p. of Henze's *Ariosi*, for sop., vn., and orch. (Edinburgh Fest. 1964).

Schneider-Siemssen, Günther (*b* Augsburg, 1926). Ger.-born Austrian designer. Designed for plays and films in Berlin and Munich 1947–54 and for Salzburg marionette th. 1952–72. Designed his first *Ring* from 1954 in Bremen, and *Ring* cycles at CG (1962–4), Salzburg Easter Fest. (1967–70), and NY Met (1967–72 and 1986–91). Notable collab. with Karajan in Vienna and Salzburg. CG début 1962. Aims for realistic effects with modern methods, incl. subtle use of lighting.

schnell; schneller (Ger.). Quick, Quicker. *Schnelligkeit*, Speed.

Schnittke [Schnitke, Shnitke], **Alfred** (Garriyevich) (*b* Engel's, nr. Saratov, 1934; *d* Hamburg, 1998). Russ. composer. Private pf. lessons in Vienna 1946–8. Teacher of counterpoint and comp. Moscow Cons. 1962–72. Also worked in Moscow Experimental Studio of Elec. Mus. Influenced by 12-note composers, also by Stockhausen, Cage, and Ligeti, but after 1966 gave dramatic, programmatic basis to his works, using quotations and pastiche. Has written articles on aspects of Shostakovich's work. Prin. works:

OPERAS: *The 11th Commandment* (*Odinnadtsataya Zapoved*) (1962, completed in pf. score only); *Life With an Idiot* (*Zhizn's idiotom*) (1990–1); *Historia von D. Johann Fausten* (1989–93); *Gesualdo* (1993–4).

BALLETS: *Labyrinths* (*Labirinti*) (1971); *Yellow Sound* (*Zhyoltiy zvuk*), mime, 9 musicians, tape, lighting (1974); *Othello* (1985); *Sketches* (1985); *Peer Gynt* (1986).

ORCH.: syms. No.1 (1969–72), No.2 (*St Florian*), chamber ch., orch. (1979), No.3 (1981), No.4, SATB soloists, chamber orch. (1984), No.5 (Concerto Grosso No.4) (1987–8), No.6 (1993), No.7 (with vn.) (1993), No.8 (1993), No.9 (1995–7); concs.: pf. (1960), pf., str. (1979), pf. (4 hands), chamber orch. (1989), vn. No.1 (1957, rev. 1962), No.2 (1966), No.3 (1978), No.4 (1981–2), ob., hp., str. (1971), va. (1985), vc. No.1 (1985–6), No.2 (1989–90); *Poem of the Cosmos* (1961); *Music for Chamber Orch.* (1964); *Music for Piano and Chamber Orch.* (1964); *Pianissimo* (1968); *Concerto Grosso*, No.1, 2 vns., hpd., 21 str. (1977), No.2, vn., vc., orch. (1981–2), No.3, 2 vns., chamber orch. (1985), No.4 (sym. No.5) (1988), No.5, vn., pf., orch. (1990–1); *In Memoriam* (orch. of pf. quintet) (1972–8); *Requiem*, soloists, ch., orch. (1975); *Passacaglia* (1979–80); *Gogol Suite* (1980); *Ritual* (1984–5); *(K)ein Sommernachtstraum* (1985); *Epilogue, Peer Gynt*, orch., tape (1987); *Quasi una Sonata* (orch. of 2nd vn. sonata) (1987); *Trio-Sonata* (orch. of str. trio) (1987); *Four Aphorisms* (1988); *Monologue*, va., str. (1989); *Sutartines*, org., perc., str. (1990); *Symphonic Prelude* (1993); *For Liverpool* (1994); Triple Conc., vn., va., vc., orch. (1994); va. conc. (1995–8).

CHORAL: *Nagasaki*, oratorio, mez., ch., orch. (1958); *Songs of War and Peace*, cantata (1959); *Voices of Nature*, women's ch., vib. (1972); *Minnesang*, 52 vv. (1980–1); *'Seid Nüchtern und Wachet . . .' History of Dr Johann Faust*, cantata, counterten., cont., ten., bass, ch., org., orch. (1982); *Concerto*, mixed ch. (1984–5); *Busslieder*, ch. (1988); *Agnus Dei (Mass for Peace)*, 2 sop., women's ch., ch., orch. (1995).

CHAMBER MUSIC: str. qts., No.1 (1966), No.2 (1981), No.3 (1983), No.4 (1989); vn. sonatas, No.1 (1963), No.2 (1968); *Dialogue*, vc., fl., ob., cl., hn., tpt., pf., perc. (1965); *Serenade*, cl., pf., perc., vn., db. (1968); *Canon in memory of Stravinsky*, str. qt. (1971); pf. quintet (1972–6); *Hymns, I-IV*, ens. (1974–9); *Cantus perpetuus*, hpd., perc. (1975); *Prelude in memory of Shostakovich*, 2 vn. (1975); *Moz-Art*, 2 vn. (1976); *Moz-Art à la Haydn*, 2 vn., 11 str. (1977); vc. sonata (1978); *Stille Nacht*, carol arr. vn., pf. (1978); *Stille Musik*, vn., vc. (1979); *Moz-Art*, ob., hpd., hp., vn., vc., db. (1980); septet, fl., 2 cl., str. qt. (1982); *Lebenslauf*, 4 metronomes, 3 perc., pf. (1982); *A Paganini*, vn. (1982); *Schall und Hall*, tb., org. (1983); str. trio (1985); pf. qt. (1988); *Klingende Buchstaben*, vc. (1988); *3 x 7*, cl., hn., tb., hpd., vn., vc., db. (1988); *Moz-Art à la Mozart*, 8 fl. hp. (1990); *3 Fragments*, hpd. (1990).

PIANO: sonatas, No.1 (1987–8), No.2 (1990); *Prelude and Fugue* (1963); *Improvisation and Fugue* (1965).

ORGAN: *2 Short Pieces* (1980).

TAPE: *The Stream* (*Potok*) (1969).

Schnorr von Carolsfeld, Ludwig (*b* Munich, 1836; *d* Dresden, 1865). Ger. tenor. Opera début Karlsruhe 1855. Prin. tenor Karlsruhe 1858–60, Dresden Opera 1860–5. Wagner, having heard him sing Lohengrin, asked him to create role of Tristan at Munich, 1865, with his Danish wife Malvina Schnorr von Carolsfeld (*b* Copenhagen, 1825; *d* Karlsruhe, 1904) as Isolde. Ludwig died 6 weeks after *Tristan* première and Malvina became singing teacher.

Schobert, Johann (*b* c.1735; *d* Paris, 1767). Silesian composer and harpsichordist. Moved to Paris, c.1760, becoming court harpsichordist. Composer of variety of works in so-called Mannheim style, influencing Mozart's early kbd. works. Died with his family after eating poisonous fungi.

Schock, Rudolf (*Johann*) (*b* Duisburg, 1915; *d* Gürzenich, 1986). Ger. tenor. Opera début Duisburg, then sang chiefly in Berlin, Hamburg (1947–56), and Munich, joining Vienna Opera

1953. CG début 1949 (Rodolfo in *La bohème*); Salzburg début 1948; Bayreuth 1959. Created Ercole in Liebermann's *Penelope*, Salzburg 1954. Later sang operetta and for films and TV.

Schoeck, Othmar (Gottfried) (*b* Brunnen, Switz., 1886; *d* Zurich, 1957). Swiss composer and conductor. Choral cond. 1909–17, then cond. St Gallen sym. concerts 1917–44. Noted for lyrical vocal comps. Works incl. 5 operas, incl. *Penthesilea* (1924–5), *Elegie*, v. and chamber orch. (1922–3), *Lebendig begraben*, low v. and orch. (1926), *Notturno*, bar., str. qt. (1931–3), several song-cycles with pf. acc., vc. conc., hn. conc., vn. conc., and chamber mus.

Schoenberg [Schönberg], **Arnold** (*b* Vienna, 1874; *d* Los Angeles, 1951). Austrian-born composer, conductor, and teacher (Amer. cit. 1941). One of most influential figures in history of mus. Learned vn. and vc. as boy. Mainly self-taught in theory, but had lessons in counterpoint from *Zemlinsky, 1894. Began composing when youth; str. qt. and songs perf. 1897. Earned living scoring other composers' operettas and in 1901 became cond. of Wolzogen's *Überbrettl* (satirical cabaret; Wolzogen was librettist of R. Strauss's *Feuersnot*). In 1899 comp. *Verklärte Nacht* and in 1900 began work on *Gurrelieder*, both being in romantic post-Wagnerian style. On strength of Part I of *Gurrelieder*, obtained teaching post and scholarship at Stern Cons., Berlin, on recommendation of Strauss. While there comp. tone-poem *Pelleas und Melisande*. Returned to Vienna in 1903. At rehearsal of his chamber mus. by Rosé Qt., met Mahler. Among his students at this time were men who became lifelong disciples—Webern, Berg, Wellesz, Erwin Stein. In Schoenberg's comps. of 1903–7, chromatic harmony was explored to its limits and tonal structures became ever more elusive until, in 1909, he arrived at *atonality* with the *3 Pieces* for pf., Op.11, and the song-cycle *Das Buch der hängenden Gärten*. Perfs. of these works met with vehement hostility, and with equally vehement acclaim from his supporters. In 1911 he pubd. his masterly book *Harmonielehre*. At this time, also painted in striking 'expressionist' style. In 1912 comp. *Pierrot Lunaire* for actress Albertine Zehme, a work for reciter (in *Sprechstimme*) and chamber ens. Its Vienna perf. was the occasion of further hostility, but the f.p. there of the early-style *Gurrelieder* was a success. The *5 Orchestral Pieces* were first played complete in London, 1912. In 1918 founded in Vienna a Soc. for Private Mus. Perfs. from which critics were excluded, no programme was announced in advance, and applause was forbidden. Wrote little between 1913 and 1921, and when next completed works appeared in 1923—the *5 Piano Pieces*, Op.23 and the *Serenade*, Op.24—they introduced to the world the 'method of comp. with 12 notes', which was Schoenberg's technique for organizing atonal mus. *Suite* for pf., Op.25, was first work wholly in 12-note method. Side-by-side with this revolutionary procedure, Schoenberg also returned to a strict use of traditional forms. In 1925 was invited to Berlin to teach comp. at the Prussian Acad. of Arts, remaining until 1933 when dismissed by Nazis and left Ger. Reconverted to Judaism in Paris in 1933, and emigrated to USA. Settled in Los Angeles and taught at Univ. of Calif. 1936–44. At this time announced his preference for spelling of his name Schoenberg instead of Schönberg. In the next 18 years comp. inconsistently in 12-note or tonal styles, dismaying his followers but not himself, for he said that all composers had varied their styles to suit their creative needs and purposes. Also rev. earlier works, wrote several religious pieces, and returned to two major undertakings he had abandoned in Europe, the oratorio *Die Jakobsleiter*, which remained unfinished, and the opera *Moses und Aron*, of which only two of the 3 acts were completed and which, when prod. after his death, was revealed as a deeply moving experience, although he wrote only a few bars for Act 3 in 1951.

Schoenberg's mus., full of melodic and lyrical interest, is also extremely complex, taking every element (rhythm, texture, form) to its furthest limit and making heavy demands on the listener. But more and more listeners find the effort worth making. His greatness lies not only in his own mus. but in his artistic courage and in his powerful and continuing influence on 20th-cent. mus. He is likely to remain always a controversial, revered, and revolutionary musician. He was also a talented painter. Prin. works:

STAGE: **Erwartung*, Op.17, monodrama (1909); *Die *glückliche Hand*, Op.18, drama with mus. (1910–13); **Von Heute auf Morgen*, Op.32, opera (1928–9); **Moses und Aron* (1930–2, 1951).

ORCH.: *Frühlingstod*, incomplete sym.-poem (1899, f.p. Berlin 1983); **Verklärte Nacht*, Op.4 (orig. str. sextet 1899, arr. for str. orch. 1917, rev. 1943); **Pelleas und Melisande*, Op.5 (1902–3); *Kammersymphonie* (Chamber Symphony) No.1, Op.9, 15 solo instr. (1906, arr. for orch. 1922; new version Op.9b, 1935; arr. by Webern for 5 instr. 1922); *5 *Orchestral Pieces (fünf Orchesterstücke)*, Op.16 (1909, rev. 1922 and 1949; arr. for 2 pf. by Webern); *3 Little Pieces*, chamber orch. (1910); *Variations*, Op.31 (1926–8); **Accompaniment to a Film Scene (Begleitungsmusik zu einer Lichtspielszene)* Op.34 (1929–30); vc. conc. (after conc. for clavicembalo by **Monn*) (1932–3); conc. for str. qt. and orch. (after Handel's Concerto Grosso Op.6 No.7) (1933); *Suite*, str. (1934); vn. conc., Op.36 (1934–6); *Second Chamber Symphony*, Op.38a (1906–16, 1939); pf. conc., Op.42 (1942); *Theme and Variations*, Op.43a, band (1943), Op.43b for orch. (1943).

VOICE(s) & INSTR(s).: **Gurrelieder*, 5 soloists, narrator, ch., orch. (1900–3, 1910–11); *Lied der Waldtaube* (Song of the Wood Dove) from *Gurrelieder*, mez., chamber orch. (1922); *6 Songs with Orchestra*, Op.8 (1903–4, also with pf.); *Herzgewächse*, Op.20, high sop., cel., harmonium, hp. 1911); **Pierrot Lunaire*, Op.21, spkr., chamber ens. (1912); *4 Songs*, Op.22, v., orch. (1913–16); *Die *Jakobsleiter*, oratorio (unfinished), 6 soloists,

speaking ch., ch., orch. (1917–22, scoring completed by W. Zillig); **Kol Nidre*, Op.39, rabbi, ch., orch. (1938); **Ode to Napoleon Buonaparte*, Op.41, str. qt., pf., reciter (1942), Op.41b for str. orch., pf., reciter (1944); *Genesis Prelude*, Op.44, ch., orch. (1945); *A *Survivor from Warsaw*, Op.46, narr., male ch., orch. (1947); *Moderne Psalmen*, Op.50c, mixed ch., spkr., orch. (1950).

UNACC. CHORUS: *Friede auf Erden* (Peace on Earth), Op.13 (1907); *4 Pieces*, Op.27 (No.4 with acc. of mandoline, cl., vn., vc.) (1925); *3 Satires*, Op.28 (No.3, *Der neue Klassizismus* (The new classicism) with va., vc., pf.) (1925); *3 German Folk-Songs* (1928); *6 Pieces*, Op.35, male ch. (1929–30); *Birthday Canons*, 3 vv. (1943); *3 Folk-Songs*, Op.49 (1948); *Dreimal tausend Jahre*, Op.50a (1949); *De Profundis*, Op.50b (1950). Also many other canons, 1905–49.

CHAMBER MUSIC: str. qt. in D (1897); str. qt. No.1 in D minor, Op.7 (1905), No.2 in F♯ minor, with sop. v. in 3rd and 4th movts., text by S. George (1907–8), No.3, Op.30 (1927), No.4, Op.37 (1936); **Verklärte Nacht*, Op.4, str. sextet (1899; str. orch. version 1917; *Serenade*, Op.24, cl., bass cl., mandoline, guitar, vn., va., vc., and bar. in 4th of 7 movts. (1920–3); *Weihnachtsmusik (Christmas Music)*, 2 vn., vc., harmonium, pf. (1921); wind quintet, Op.26 (1923–4); *Suite* (septet), Op.29, pf., picc., cl. (or fl.), bass cl. (or bn.), vn., va., vc. (1924–6); str. trio, Op.45 (1946); *Phantasy*, Op.47, vn.,pf. (1949).

PIANO: *3 Pieces*, Op.11 (1909, rev. 1924; No.2 orch. Busoni 1909); *6 Little Pieces*, Op.19 (1911); *5 Pieces*, Op.23 (1920–3); *Suite*, Op.25 (1921); *2 Piano Pieces*, Op.33a (1928), Op.33b (1931).

ORGAN: *Variations on a Recitative*, Op.40 (1941).

SONGS WITH PIANO: *2 Songs*, Op.1 (1897); *4 Songs*, Op.2 (1899); *6 Songs*, Op.3 (1899–1903); *Cabaret Songs* (1901); *8 Songs*, Op.6 (1903–5); *2 Ballads*, Op.12 (1907); *2 Songs*, Op.14 (1907–8); *2 Songs* (1909, pubd. 1966); *Das *Buch der hängenden Gärten*, Op.15, 15 songs for sop. (1908–9); *German Folk-Songs* (1930); *3 Songs*, Op.48 (1933).

ARRS. OF OTHER COMPOSERS: Bach: *2 Chorale-Preludes* arr. for large orch. (1922) (1. *Komm, Gott, Schöpfer, Heiliger Geist*; 2. *Schmücke dich, O liebe Seele*); *Prelude and Fugue* in E♭ (org.) arr. for large orch. (1928). Brahms: Pf. Qt. No.1 in G minor, Op.25, arr. for orch. (1937). Loewe: *Der Nöck*, ballad, arr. for orch. (?1910). J. Strauss II: *Kaiserwalzer* (Emperor Waltz), arr. for fl., cl., str. qt., pf. (1925).

BOOKS: *Harmonielehre* (Treatise on harmony) (Vienna 1911, 2nd edn. 1922, abridged Eng. trans. by D. Adams, NY 1948; complete Eng. trans. by R. E. Carter 1978); *Style and Idea* (NY 1950, enlarged edn. London 1972); *Structural Functions of Harmony* (NY 1954).

See also *atonal*; *serialism*; *Klangfarbenmelodie*.

Schöffler, Paul (*b* Dresden, 1897; *d* Amersham, 1977). Ger.-born Austrian baritone. Opera début Dresden 1925 (Herald in *Lohengrin*). Member, Dresden Opera 1925–37, then Vienna Opera until early 1970s. CG début 1934 singing there each year to 1939 and 1949–53. Salzburg Fest. début

1938; NY Met 1950–6; Bayreuth 1943, 1944, 1956. Outstanding in Verdi roles, but best known for his Wagner parts (Sachs, Wotan, Dutchman) and as Barak in *Die Frau ohne Schatten*. Created title-role in **Dantons Tod* (Salzburg 1947), and sang Jupiter in *Die *Liebe der Danae* (Salzburg 1952). Settled in Eng.

Scholes, Percy (Alfred) (*b* Leeds, 1877; *d* Vévey, Switz., 1958). Eng. mus. critic, organist, teacher, and lexicographer. Active in 'music appreciation' movt. Founded *Music Student* (1908; now *Music Teacher*). Wrote on mus. for *The Observer*, 1920–7, and *Radio Times* (1923–9). Compiled and ed. *Oxford Companion to Music* (1938 and subsequent edns.), *Concise Oxford Dictionary of Music* (1952 and subsequent edns.), and *The Mirror of Music 1844–1944* (1947, 2 vols.). Wrote books on *God Save the King* (1942), opera, Eng. mus., Puritans and mus., etc. OBE 1957.

Scholl, Andreas (*b* Kiedrich im Rheingau, 1967). Ger. counter-tenor. Joined Kiedricher Chorbuben aged 7. At 13 sang Second Boy in *Zauberflöte* at Wiesbaden. Studied in Basle at Schola Cantorum Basiliensis with Richard Levitt and René Jacobs, later with Evelyn Tubb and Anthony Rooley. Prof. début Paris 1993 (*St John Passion*). Many recordings of baroque mus. Glyndebourne début 1998 (Bertarido in Handel's *Rodelinda*). Title-role in Handel's *Giulio Cesare*, Copenhagen 2002. First counter-tenor to sing solo at Last Night of the Proms, London 2005.

Schonberg, Harold C(harles) (*b* NY, 1915; *d* NY, 2003). Amer. music critic and author. Mus. critic, *NY Sun* 1946–50, *NY Times* 1950 (senior critic 1960–80). Pulitzer Prize for criticism 1971. Author of books on pianists, conds., and composers. Expert on chess.

Schöne Melusine, Die (Mendelssohn). See *Melusina, The Fair*.

Schöne Müllerin, Die (The Fair Maid of the Mill). Song-cycle by Schubert, D795, comp. 1823, for male v. and pf. to 20 poems by Wilhelm Müller (1794–1827) from *Gedichte aus den hinterlassenen Papieren eines reisenden Waldhornisten* (1821). Songs are: *Das Wandern* (Wandering); *Wohin?* (Where to?); *Halt*; *Danksagung an den Bach* (Grateful address to the millstream); *Am Feierabend* (After the day's work); *Der Neugierige* (Curiosity); *Ungeduld* (Impatience); *Morgengruss* (Morning greeting); *Des Müllers Blumen* (The Miller's Flowers); *Tränenregen* (Rain of Tears); *Mein* (Mine); *Pause*; *Mit dem grünen Lautenbande* (With the Lute's green ribbon); *Der Jäger* (The Huntsman); *Eifersucht und Stolz* (Jealousy and Pride); *Die liebe Farbe* (The beloved colour); *Die böse Farbe* (The hated colour); *Trockne Blumen* (Dry flowers); *Der Müller und der Bach* (The Miller and the Millstream); *Des Baches Wiegenlied* (The Millstream's Lullaby).

Schönherr, Max (*b* Marburg, 1903; *d* Mödling, nr. Vienna, 1984). Austrian conductor and composer. Cond. opera at Graz 1924–8, then at Theater an der Wien, Vienna, 1929–33, and Volksoper 1933–8. Cond. Vienna Radio 1931–68. Specialist in Johann Strauss, Lehár.

Schønwandt, Michael (*b* Copenhagen, 1953). Danish conductor. Début Copenhagen 1977, Royal Danish Opera 1979. Prin. cond. Collegium Musicum, Copenhagen, from 1981. Amer. début S. Francisco 1992; CG 1984.

Schönzeler, Hans-Hubert (*b* Leipzig, 1925; *d* London, 1997). Ger.-born conductor and musicologist (Eng. cit. 1947). Cond. 20th-Cent. Ens., London, 1957–61; Western Australian SO 1967. Specialist in Bruckner, on whom he wrote a book (1970). Cond. f.p. of original version (1884–7) of Bruckner's Sym. No.8 in BBC broadcast 1973.

School for Fathers. Eng. title of Dent's trans. of Wolf-Ferrari's I **Quattro rusteghi*.

Schoolmaster, The (Haydn). See *Schulmeister, Der*.

Schools of Music. See under names of individual schools and colleges.

Schöpfung, Die (Haydn). See *Creation, The*.

Schorr, Friedrich (*b* Nagyvarád, 1888; *d* Farmington, Conn., 1953). Hung.-born bass-baritone (Amer. cit.). Sang Steersman in *Tristan und Isolde*, Chicago 1912, later same year sang Wotan in *Die Walküre* at Graz. Sang at Prague Opera 1916–18; Cologne 1918–23; Berlin 1923–31; CG 1924–33; Bayreuth 1925–31; NY Met 1924–43; S. Francisco 1931–8. The outstanding Wagnerian bass of the inter-war years.

Schott, B., und Söhne (Schott and Sons). Firm of Ger. mus. publishers est. at Mainz 1780 by Bernhard Schott (1748–1809), succeeded in 1817 by his sons. London branch founded 1835, also branches in Paris, Leipzig, Rotterdam, and NY. Acquired Eulenburg 1957. Publishes much contemporary music, e.g. Henze, Penderecki, Tippett, Maxwell Davies, Goehr, etc. Publisher of Hoboken's Haydn catalogue.

Schottische (Ger. plural). Scottish. Type of ballroom round dance similar to polka, introduced to Eng. in 1848 and known as 'German polka'. No connection with **Écossaise* and none with Scotland.

Schrammel Quartet. Viennese instr. combination for perf. of light mus.—2 vn., gui., and accordion (replacing the G cl.). Named after Joseph Schrammel (1850–93), leader of a qt. of this kind and composer of waltzes etc. for it. Originally a trio, formed 1878, qt. from 1886.

Schreier, Peter (Max) (*b* Meissen, 1935). Ger. tenor and conductor. One of the 3 Boys in *Die Zauberflöte*, Dresden State Opera 1944. Début Dresden 1961 (1st Prisoner in *Fidelio*) and with co. 1961–3; Berlin Staatsoper from 1963. Bayreuth 1966; London (SW) 1966 (Hamburg co.

visit); Salzburg Fest. 1967; NY Met 1967; La Scala 1968. Specialist in *Lieder* and Mozart roles. Recital début London 1978. Début as cond. 1969; Salzburg Fest. 1988.

Schreierpfeifen (Ger.). Crying fife. Renaissance reed-cap woodwind instr., member of shawm family, made in 4 sizes (bass, 2 ten., alto). Sometimes known as *Schryari*. Were used in military bands outdoors. None extant.

Schreker, Franz (*b* Monaco, 1878; *d* Berlin, 1934). Austrian composer and conductor. Founded and cond. Vienna Phil. Ch. 1908–20. Cond. f.p. of *Gurrelieder*, Vienna 1913. Taught comp. at Vienna Acad. 1912–20. Cond. at Volksoper. Dir., Berlin Hochschule für Musik 1920–32. His mus. is powerful and expressionist, his biggest success being with the opera *Der *ferne Klang* (comp. 1901–10) in 1912 which influenced Berg's *Wozzeck*. Among his other operas were *Das Spielwerk und die Prinzessin* (1909–12, rev. 1920), *Die Gezeichneten* (1913–15), *Der Schatzgräber* (1915–18), *Irrelohe* (1919–23), *Der singende Teufel* (1924–8), *Christophorus* (1925–9), and *Der Schmied von Gent* (1929–32). In 1908 he composed a ballet-pantomime based on Wilde, *Der Geburtstag der Infantin*, for str. orch., producing a *Suite* from it scored for full orch. in 1923. Wrote chamber sym., works for str., and about 50 songs.

Schröder, Jaap (*b* Amsterdam, 1925). Dutch violinist and teacher. Début Holland 1949. Leader, Hilversum Radio Chamber Orch. 1950–63. Member of Netherlands Str. Qt. 1952–69. Founded Quadro Amsterdam, 1962, and Quartetto Esterházy, 1971, which played on period instrs. (disbanded 1981). Leader, Academy of Ancient Mus., London, for a time. Prof. of vn., Amsterdam Cons.

Schröder-Devrient, Wilhelmine (*b* Hamburg, 1804; *d* Coburg, 1860). Ger. soprano. Began career as actress. Opera début Kärntnertorth., Vienna, 1821 (Pamina in *Die Zauberflöte*). In 1822 sang Leonore in *Fidelio* in presence of Beethoven in Vienna. Sang in Dresden 1823–47; Paris 1830–2; London 1832, 1833, 1837. Wagner was so overwhelmed by her singing that he vowed to dedicate his life to creating a new kind of opera. She created 3 Wagner roles: Adriano in *Rienzi* (1842), Senta in *Der fliegende Holländer* (1843), and Venus in *Tannhäuser* (1845), all in Dresden. Retired 1847. Schumann's song *Ich grolle nicht* was dedicated to her. Also sang in Rossini, Bellini, and Gluck. Although her vocal technique was apparently flawed, her dramatic powers made her interpretations unforgettable.

Schubart, Christian Friedrich Daniel (*b* Sontheim, 1739; *d* Stuttgart, 1791). Swabian organist, composer, and poet. Court poet, Stuttgart, from 1787. Spent 10 years in prison 1777–87, ostensibly for insulting a duke's mistress but probably for 'free-thinking' writings. Works incl.

operetta, cantatas, and songs. Wrote words of Schubert's songs *Die Forelle*, *An mein Klavier*, *An den Tod*, and *Grablied auf einen Soldaten*.

Schubert, Franz (*b* Dresden, 1808; *d* Dresden, 1878). Ger. violinist and composer. Played in Dresden court orch. 1823–73 (leader from 1861). Comp. works for vn. and orch. and popular vn. piece *L'Abeille* (The Bee).

Schubert, Franz (Seraph Peter) (*b* Vienna, 1797; *d* Vienna, 1828). Austrian composer. Son of impoverished schoolmaster, who was his first teacher. In 1808 admitted as boy sop. to imperial chapel, living in the Konvikt. Played vn. in sch. orch., for which he wrote his 1st Sym. (1813). Became pupil of *Salieri for theory, 1812. Left Konvikt when v. broke 1813, and worked as ass. schoolmaster to father, but continued to compose prolifically. Frequently attended opera in Vienna and wrote his first opera, *Des Teufels Lustschloss* in 1814, the first of many stage works, none of which was successful. On 19 Oct. 1814 set Goethe's *Gretchen am Spinnrade*, his first masterpiece and the song that, it is inaccurately but understandably said, gave birth to the *Lied*. This released a flood of inspiration. In 1815 Schubert comp. 144 songs, incl. 8 in one day in Oct. In addition, comp. a sym., 2 Masses, and other works. Altogether wrote over 600 songs, of which about 200 are different settings of poems he had already set—he set some poems (particularly those by Goethe and Schiller) up to 6 times.

In 1817 he abandoned teaching and lived in Vienna with one or other of his friends, among whom the poet Mayrhofer was the closest. They talked, drank, discussed the questions of the day, and made mus. in coffee-houses and at their homes. Schubert also met at this time the bar. Michael *Vogl, one of the outstanding opera singers of the day, who became the foremost interpreter of his songs, often acc. by the composer. Apart from church mus., the first public concert of Schubert's mus. was in Mar. 1818, at which were perf. (on 2 pf.) the ovs. he had written in imitation of Rossini, whose operas were all the rage in Vienna from 1816. In 1818 spent summer as teacher to the 2 daughters of Count Johann Esterházy at summer estate at Zseliz, where he heard Slav and gipsy folk-mus. On return to Vienna, Schubert lived with Mayrhofer and Hültenbrenner, latter acting as factotum, assembling Schubert's MSS. His *Singspiel*, *Die Zwillingsbrüder*, received 6 perfs. in Vienna in June 1820, with Vogl singing the roles of the twin brothers; and in Aug. his incidental mus. for *Die Zauberharfe* was used at the Theater an der Wien. Other works comp. in this period were the 'Trout' Quintet, written at Steyr, Upper Austria, during holiday in 1819 with Vogl, the oratorio *Lazarus*, setting of *Psalm 23*, *Wanderer Fantasy*, and the *Quartettsatz*. In 1821 Diabelli pubd. song *Erlkönig*, the first mus. by Schubert to appear in print. Others followed. In 1820–1, the Schubert circle of friends changed as some members left Vienna. Among new associates were painters

Leopold Kupelweiser and Moriz von Schwind, and musician Franz Lachner.

In 1821 sketched his 7th Sym., in E major, but left it unorch. (several musicians have 'completed' it, among them J. F. Barnett, 1884, Felix Weingartner, 1935, and Brian Newbould, 1977). The following year, comp. an 8th Sym. in B minor, but completed only 2 movts. in full and 130 bars of a scherzo. However, the 'Unfinished' Sym. is a complete work of art in itself as it stands. Schubert heard Weber conduct *Der *Freischütz* and *Euryanthe* in Vienna and himself wrote several stage works between 1821 and 1823, the operas *Alfonso und Estrella* and *Der häusliche Krieg*, and incidental mus. for *Rosamunde, Fürstin von Cypern*, a play by Helmina von Chézy (librettist of *Euryanthe*) which ran for 2 perfs.

Ill-health began to trouble Schubert in 1823; while in hospital that year comp. some of the songs of the song-cycle *Die schöne Müllerin*. At Zseliz in 1824 with the Esterházy family, wrote A minor str. qt. and *Grand Duo* for pf. duet. In the summer of 1825, joined Vogl for a 5-month tour of Austria, composing all the time. At Gmunden and Gastein said to have comp. a sym. of which no trace has been found, but modern scholarship tends to take the view that this is the 'Great' C major Sym. (No.9), usually ascribed to 1828 but now thought to date from 1825. Scholarship is equally divided over what personal contact there was between Schubert and Beethoven, but incontrovertibly Schubert was a torchbearer at Beethoven's funeral in 1827 and had earlier visited him on his deathbed.

The last 2 years of Schubert's short life are fully documented in *Schubert: The Final Years* by John Reed (1972). To them belong the song-cycle *Winterreise*, the E♭ pf. trio, *Moments musicaux* and 3 pf. sonatas, many songs, and Str. Quintet in C major. All Schubert's mus., even the happiest, has a tinge of sadness; the works of his last years, when illness increasingly afflicted him, are at an extreme of poignancy. In Mar. 1828 gave a public concert of his works in Vienna. It made a profit for him, but none of the city's mus. critics attended. Died on 19 Nov. 1828 and was buried near to Beethoven at Währing. Both composers were later exhumed and reburied in the Central Cemetery of Vienna.

Many of the works by Schubert which we hold most dear were not perf. until several years after his death. As a composer of songs he has no equal in fertility of melodic invention, but all his work is so graced with melody of the most seraphic kind that there was at one time a tendency to regard him as an 'undisciplined' composer for whom form meant little. How wrong a judgement this was can be realized simply by studying the great chamber works and late pf. sonatas alone. He ranks among the very greatest of composers in all forms except opera, and concs. (of which he wrote none), and the listener has a lifetime of discoveries among his vast output. His works were catalogued by O. E. *Deutsch and are now given Deutsch (D) nos. Prin. comps.:

OPERAS: *Des Teufels Lustschloss* (1813–14, D84); *Die Bürgschaft* (fragment, 1816, D435); **Alfonso und Estrella* (1821–22, D732); *Der häusliche Krieg* (1823, D787; orig. title *Die Verschworenen* (The Conspirators)); **Fierrabras* (1823, D796).

OPERETTAS: *Claudine von Villa Bella* (1815, D239); *Die Freunde von Salamanka* (1815, D326); *Fernando* (1815, D220); *Der vierjährige Posten* (1815, D190); *Die *Zwillingsbrüder* (1818–19, D647).

STAGE MUSIC: *Die *Zauberharfe* (The Magic Harp), melodrama (1820, D644); **Rosamunde, Fürstin von Cypern* (1823, entr'actes, ballet mus., Romanza for sop., Shepherd's Song, and choruses, D797).

ORCH.: syms.: No.1 in D (1813, D82), No.2 in B♭ (1814–15, D125), No.3 in D (1815, D200), No.4 in C minor ('Tragic', 1816, D417), No.5 in B♭ (1816, D485), No.6 in C major (1818, D589), No.7 in E major (1821, unscored by Schubert), No.8 in B minor (**Unfinished', 2 movts. only, 1822, D759), No.9 in C major ('Great', 1825, D944); ovs.: in B♭ (1812, D11), in C major (D591) and D major (D590) (both 'in Italian style', 1817), in D (1817, D556), in E minor (1819, D648); *5 German Dances* (1813, D90); *5 Minuets with 6 Trios* (1813, D89); *Rondo* in A major, vn. and orch. (1816, D438).

CHURCH MUSIC: Masses: F major (1814, D105 with 2nd Dona nobis 1815, D185), G major (1815, D167), C major (1816, D452), A♭ (1819–22, D678), B♭ (1815, D324), E♭ (1828, D950), *Deutsche Messe* (1826–7, D872); **Lazarus*, oratorio (1820, D689); *Hymn to the Holy Spirit*, male vv. and wind (1828, D964); *Kyrie* in D minor (1812, D31), B♭ (1813, D45), D minor (1813, D49), F major (1813, D66); *Salve Regina*, sop., orch., organ (1812, D27); *Psalm 23*, women's vv. (1820, D706); *Tantum ergo* in C (1822, D739), in D (1822, D750).

VOICES & ORCH.: *Cantata in honour of Spendou* (1816, D472); *Prometheus* (1816, lost, D451); *Namensfeier* (1813, D80).

VOICES (unacc. or with pf./gui.): *An die Sonne* (1816, D439); *Die Advokaten* (1812, D37); *Begräbnislied* (1815, D168); *Cantata for Vogl's birthday* (1819, D666); *Cantata for Salieri's jubilee* (1816, D441); *Christ ist erstanden* (1816, D440); *Coronach* (1825, D836); *Das Leben ist ein Traum* (1815, D269); *Der Entfernten* (c.1816, D331); *Der Geistertanz* (1816, D494); *Der Tanz* (1825, D826); *Frühlingsgesang* (1822, D740); *Gebet* (1824, D815); *Geist der Liebe* (1822, D747); *Gesang der Geister über den Wassern* (Song of the Spirit over the Waters) (1817, 2 versions, D538, 1821 with orch. D714); *Gondelfahrer* (1824, D809); *Gott der Weltschöpfer* (c.1815, D986); *Gott im Ungewitter* (c.1815, D985); *Gott in der Natur* (1822, D757); *Grab und Mond* (1826, D893); *Hymne an den heiligen Geist* (1828, D964); *Hymne an den Unendlichen* (1815, D232); *Im Gegenwärtigen Vergangenes* (c.1821, D710); *Jünglingswonne* (?1822, D983); *Lebenslust* (1818, D609); *Mondenschein* (1826, D875); *Nachthelle* (1826, D892); *Nur wer die Sehnsucht kennt* (1819, D877/4); *Punschlied* (1815, D277); *Ständchen* (1827, D920); *Trinklied* (1815, D148); *Verschwunden sind die Schmerzen* (1813, D88).

CHAMBER MUSIC: str. qts.: No.1 in B♭ (1812, D18), No.2 in C (1812, D32), No.3 in B♭ (1813, D36),

No.4 in C (1813, D46), No.5 in B♭ (1813, D68), No.6 in D (1813, D74), No.7 in D (1814, D94), No.8 in B♭ (1814, D112), No.9 in G minor (1815, D173), No.10 in E♭ (1813, D87), No.11 in E (1816, D353), No.12 in C minor (*Quartettsatz*) (1820, D703), No.13 in A minor (1824, D804), No.14 in D minor (*Death and the Maiden, 1824, D810), No.15 in G (1826, D887); String Quintet (2 vn., va., 2 vc.), C major (1828, D956); pf. quintet, A major (*Die Forelle* (*Trout*), 1819, D667); qt. for guitar, fl., va., vc. (arr. of *Notturno* by Matiegka) (1814 D96); pf. trios: No.1 in B♭ (1827, D898), No.2 in E♭ (1827, D929), *Notturno* in E♭ for pf. trio (1825, D897), sonata for pf. trio in B♭ (1812, D28); sonatas: vn. and pf. in A (1817, D574), *arpeggione (or vc.) and pf. in A minor (1824, D821); sonatinas: vn. and pf., No.1 in D (1816, D384), No.2 in A minor (1816, D385), No.3 in G minor (1816, D408); *Octet* in F (2 vn., va., vc., db., cl., bn., hn.) (1824, D803). Miscellaneous: *Adagio and Rondo Concertante*, pf., vn., va., vc. (1816, D487); *Fantasia on Sie mir gegrüsst* in C, vn., pf. (1827, D934); *Rondo brillant* in B minor, vn. and pf. (1826, D895); *Introduction and Variations on Trock'ne Blumen*, fl. and pf. (1824, D802); *Minuet and Finale* in F for wind octet (1813, D72).

2 PIANOS: *Divertissement à la hongroise* (1824?, D818), *Fantasia* in F minor (1828, D940), sonata in B♭ (1818, D617), sonata in C (*Grand Duo* (1824, D813), *Introduction and Variations on an Original Theme* in B♭ (c.1818, D603), 2 *Marches caractéristiques* in C (1826, D886), 3 *Marches militaires* (No.1 in D, No.2 in G, No.3 in E♭, 1822, D733, also for orch.); also polonaises, rondos, ovs., and sets of variations.

PIANO: sonatas: No.1 in E (1815, D157, unfinished), No.2 in C (1815, D279, unfinished), No.3 in E (1816, D459), No.4 in A minor (1817, D537), No.5 in A♭ (1817, D557), No.6 in E minor (1817, D566), No.7 in D♭ (1817, D567), No.8 in B (1817, D575), No.9 in C (1818, D613, unfinished), No.10 in F minor (1818, D625, unfinished), No.11 in A (1819, D664), No.12 in A minor (1823, D784), No.13 in C (1825, D840, unfinished), No.14 in A minor (1825, D845), No.15 in D (1825, D850, rev. of No.7), No.16 in G (1826, D894), No.17 in C minor (1828, D958), No.18 in A (1828, D959), No.19 in B♭ (1828, D960); *Allegretto* in C minor (1827, D915); *Fantasia* in C (*Wanderer, 1822, D760; version for pf. and orch. by Liszt); 11 *Impromptus* (1828): No.1 in C minor, No.2 in E♭, No.3 in G♭, No.4 in A♭ (D899), No.5 in F minor, No.6 in A♭, No.7 in B♭, No.8 in F minor (D935), No.9 in E♭ minor, No.10 in E♭, No.11 in C (D946); *Klavierstück* in A (1818, D604); 12 *Ländler* (1823, D790); 6 *Moments musicaux* (1823–8, D780): No.1 in C, No.2 in A♭, No.3 in F minor, No.4 in C♯ minor, No.5 in F minor, No.6 in A♭; 3 *Klavierstücke* (1828, D946): No.1 in E♭ minor, No.2 in E♭, No.3 in C; *Rondo* in D (1818, D608); 2 *Scherzos* (1817, D593); *Hungarian Melody* (1824, D817); *Valses nobles* (1827, D969); 13 *Variations in A minor on a theme of Anselm Hüttenbrenner* (1817, D576); 12 *Waltzes* (1815–21, D145); 36 *Waltzes* (1816–21, D365).

SONG-CYCLES: *Die *schöne Müllerin* (1823, D795); *Winterreise* (1827, D911); *Schwanengesang* (1827–8, D957, publisher's coll., not conceived as cycle). See individual entries for names of component songs.

SONGS: It is impracticable to list here all Schubert's songs. A selection of the best known is given here, with poet's name:

Abendstern (Mayrhofer, 1824, D806), *Die abgeblühte Linde* (Széchényi, 1817, D514), *Alinde* (Rochlitz, 1827, D904), *Allein, nachdenklich wie gelähmt* (Petrarch, 1818, D629), *Die Allmacht* (Pyrker, 1825, D852), *Am Bach im Frühling* (Schober, 1816, D361), *Am Grabe Anselmos* (Claudius, 1816, D504), *Am See* (Bruchmann, 1823, D746), *An den Frühling* (Schiller, 1815, D245), *An den Mond* (Goethe, 1815, D296), *An die Entfernte* (Goethe, 1822, D765), *An die Freude* (Schiller, 1815, D189), *An mein Klavier* (Schubart, c. 1816, D342), *An die Laute* (Rochlitz, 1827, D905), *An die Leier* (Bruchmann, 1822, D737), *An die Musik* (Schober, 1817, D547), *An die Nachtigall* (Holty, 1815, D196), *An die untergehende Sonne* (Kosegarten, 1816, D457), *An eine Quelle* (Claudius, 1817, D530), *An schwager Kronos* (Goethe, 1816, D369), *An Sylvia* (Shakespeare, 1826, D891), *Auf dem Wasser zu singen* (Stolberg, 1823, D774), *Auf der Bruck* (Schulze, 1825, D853), *Auf der Donau* (Mayrhofer, 1817, D553), *Auflösung* (Mayrhofer, 1824, D807), *Ave Maria* (Ellen's Song, W. Scott, trans. Storck, 1825, D839), *Bei dir Allein* (Seidl, 1826, D866/2), *Beim Winde* (Mayrhofer, 1819, D669), *Berthas Lied in der Nacht* (Grillparzer, 1819, D653), *Der blinde Knabe* (Cibber, 1825, D833, 2nd version), *Die Bürgschaft* (Schiller, 1815, D246), *Cronnan* (Ossian, 1815, D282), *Delphine* (Schütz, 1825, D857), *Des Fischers Liebesglück* (Leitner, 1827, D933), *Du bist die Ruh'* (Rückert, 1823, D776), *Der Einsame* (Lappe, 1825, D800), *Epistel* (Collin, 1822, D749), *Erlkönig* (Goethe, 1815, D328), *Die erste Liebe* (Fellinger, 1815, D182), *Der Fischer* (Goethe, 1815, D225), *Fischerweise* (Schlechta, 1826, D881), *Die Forelle* (Schubart, 1817, D550), *Frühlingsglaube* (Uhland, 1820, D686), *Frühlingslied* (Anon, 1816, D398), *Ganymed* (Goethe, 1817, D544), *Geheimes* (Goethe, 1821, D719), *Geheimnis* (Mayrhofer, 1816, D491), *Die Götter Griechenlands* (Schiller, 1819, D677), *Grablied* (Kenner, 1815, D218), *Gretchen am Spinnrade* (Goethe, 1814, D118), *Gruppe aus dem Tartarus* (Schiller, 1817, D583), *Harfenspieler I—Wer sich der Einsamkeit ergibt* (Goethe, 1816, D478); *II—An die Türen will ich schleichen* (Goethe, 1816, D479); *III—Wer nie sein Brot* (Goethe, 1816, D480), *Heidenröslein* (Goethe, 1815, D257), *Heimliches Lieben* (Klenke, 1827, D922), *Heiss' mich nicht reden* (Goethe, Mignon Song, 1826, 2nd version D877/2), *Hektors Abschied* (Schiller, 1815, D312), *Hermann und Thurnelda* (Klopstock, 1815, D322), *Herrn Josef Spaun* (Collin, 1822, D749), *Der Hirt auf dem Felsen* (The *Shepherd on the Rock) with cl. obbl. (Müller and von Chézy, 1828, D965), *Horch, horch, die Lerch* (Shakespeare, 1826, D889), *Im Abendrot* (Lappe, 1824, D799), *Im Frühling* (Schulze, 1826, D882), *Im Haine* (Bruchmann, 1822, D738), *Iphigenia* (Mayrhofer, 1817, D573), *Jäger, ruhe von der Jagd*

(W. Scott, 1815, D838), *Die junge Nonne* (Craigher, 1825, D828), *Der Jüngling am Bache* (Schiller, 3 versions, 3rd, 1819, D638), *Der Jüngling an der Quelle* (1821, D300), *Der Jüngling und der Tod* (Spaun, 1817, D545), *Kennst du das Land?* (Goethe, 1815, D321), *Der König in Thule* (Goethe, 1816, D367), *Lachen und Weinen* (Rückert, 1823, D777), *Licht und Liebe* (Collin, 1816, D352), *Die Liebende schreibt* (Goethe, 1819, D673), *Liebhaber in allen Gestalten* (Goethe, 1817, D558), *Lied eines Schiffers an die Dioskuren* (Mayrhofer, 1816, D360), *Das Mädchen* (Schlegel, 1819, D652), *Das Mädchen aus der Fremde* (Schiller, 1814, D117), *Meeresstille* (Goethe, 1815, D216), *Mignon und der Harfer* (Goethe, 1826, D877/1), *Minnelied* (Holty, 1816, D429), *Miriams Siegesgesang* for sop. and ch. (Grillparzer, 1828, D942), *Morgenlied* (Werner, 1820, D685), *Der Musensohn* (Goethe, 1822, D764), **Nacht und Träume* (Collin, 1822, D827), *Nachtgesang* (Kosegarten, 1815, D314), *Nachtviolen* (Mayrhofer, 1822, D752), *Nähe des Geliebten* (Goethe, 1816, D162), *Normans Gesang* (W. Scott, trans. Storck, 1825, D846), *Nunmehr, da Himmel, Erde* (Petrarch, 1818, D630), *Nur wer die Sehnsucht Kennt* (Goethe, Mignon song, 5 versions. 5th, 1826, D877/4), *La pastorella* (Goldoni, 1817, D528), *Der Pilgrim* (Schiller, 1823, D794), *Prometheus* (Goethe, 1819, D674), *Rastlose Liebe* (Goethe, 1815, D138), *Raste, Krieger* (Scott, 1825, D837), *Die Rose* (Schlegel, 1822, D745), *Das Rosenband* (Klopstock, 1815, D280), *Der Sänger* (Goethe, 1815, D149), *Schäfers Klagelied* (Goethe, 1814, D121), *Der Schiffer* (Mayrhofer, 1817, D536), *Schlummerlied* (Mayrhofer, 1817, D527), *Der Schmetterling* (Schlegel, 1815, D633), *Schwestergruss* (Bruchmann, 1822, D762), *Sehnsucht* (Schiller, 1813, D52), *Sei mir gegrüsst* (Rückert, 1822, D741), *Seligkeit* (Holty, 1816, D433), *So lasst mich scheinen* (Goethe, Mignon song, 2 versions, 2nd, 1826, D877/3), *Sprache der Liebe* (Schlegel, 1816, D410), *Ständchen* (Horch, horch, die Lerche) (Grillparzer, 1827, D921), *Die Sterne* (Leitner, 1828, D939), *Suleika's Songs I—Was bedeutet die Bewegung* (Willemer, 1821, D720), *II—Ach, um deine feuchten Schwingen* (Willemer, 1821, D717), *Der Tod und das Mädchen* (*Death and the Maiden) (Claudius, 1817, D531), *Totengräbers Heimweh* (Craigher, 1825, D842), *Trost im Liede* (Schober, 1817, D546), *Über Wildemann* (Schulze, 1826, D884), *Dem Unendlichen* (Klopstock, 1815, D291), *Der Vater mit dem Kind* (Bauernfeld, 1827, D906), *Versunken* (Goethe, 1821, D715), *Die Vögel* (Schlegel, 1820, D691), *Der Wanderer* (Lübeck, 1816, D493), *Der Wanderer an den Mond* (Solde, 1826, D870), *Wanderers Nachtlied* (Goethe, 2 settings, 2nd 1822, D768), *Wehmut* (Collin, 1823, D772), *Wiegenlied* (Anon., 1815, D498), *Wiegenlied* (Seidl, 1826, D867), *Der zürnende Barde* (Bruckmann, 1823, D785), *Der Zwerg* (Collin, 1822, D771).

Schuch, Ernst von (*b* Graz, 1846; *d* Kötzschenbroda, nr. Dresden, 1914). Austrian conductor. Début as cond., Breslau 1867. Cond. Dresden Court Opera 1872–1914 (gen. mus. dir. from 1889). Ennobled by Austrian emperor 1898. Made Dresden among world's leading opera houses. During his 42-year régime, Dresden had 51 world premières of operas and 117 other operas were added to the Dresden repertory. Cond. f.ps. of *Feuersnot* (1901), *Salome* (1905), *Elektra* (1909), and *Der Rosenkavalier* (1911). NY Met 1900. Married Clementine Schuch-Proska (orig. Procházka) (1850–1932), leading coloratura sop. at Dresden 1873–1904.

Schuh, Oscar Fritz (*b* Munich, 1904; *d* Salzburg, 1984). Ger. director and administrator. Began career as th. producer in Munich, 1923 (Hauptmann's *Hanneles Himmelfahrt*). After working in several cities, incl. Darmstadt and Prague, became res. prod. at Vienna Opera and then Intendant of Berlin Freie Volksbühne. Intendant, Cologne State Theatres 1959–62, Deutsches Schauspielhaus, Hamburg, 1962–8. Salzburg Fest. début as prod. 1946 (*Le nozze di Figaro*). CG début 1962. Famed prods. of Mozart and Strauss in Munich, Vienna, and Salzburg.

Schuh, Willi (*b* Basle, 1900; *d* Zurich, 1986). Swiss music critic and author. Mus. critic of *Neue Zürcher Zeitung* 1928–65 (mus. ed. from 1944); teacher at Zurich Cons. 1930–44. Ed. Busoni and Wagner letters. Friend of and authority on R. Strauss, who appointed him his official biographer. First vol., *Richard Strauss: Jugend und frühe Meisterjahre 1864–98*, pubd. Zurich 1976 (Cambridge 1982, trans. Mary Whittall). Also ed. Strauss's *Recollections and Reflections* (1949), Strauss–Hofmannsthal letters (1952), Strauss's letters to his parents (1954), to Bülow (1954), to Zweig (1957), and to Schuh (1969).

Schulhoff, Erwin [Ervin] (*b* Prague, 1894; *d* Wülzbourg concentration camp, 1942). Cz. pianist and composer. Worked with A. *Hába on microtones and also influenced by jazz. Wrote 8 syms. (Nos. 7 and 8 unfinished) (1925–42); opera *Flames* (1927–8); 2 ballets (both 1925); cantata *The Communist Manifesto* (1932, f.p. Prague 1962); 2 pf. concs. (1913, 1923); conc. for fl. and pf. (1927); conc. for str. qt. and wind orch. (1930); 2 str. qts. (1924, 1925); str. sextet (1924); 4 pf. sonatas (1918–27).

Schuller, Gunther (Alexander) (*b* NY, 1925). Amer. composer, conductor, and horn-player, son of violinist in NYPO. Prin. hn., Cincinnati SO 1943–5. Joined NY Met orch. in 1945, playing in it until 1959. Taught hn. Manhattan Sch. 1950–63. Assoc. prof. of mus., Yale Univ. 1964–7, president, New England Cons. 1967–77, supervising contemp. mus. concerts at Tanglewood and teaching there 1965–84. Influenced by Webern and Stravinsky but with great interest in jazz, his comps. drawing on jazz elements being among the most successful and convincing yet written. Commissioned by Hamburg Opera to compose *The Visitation* (Hamburg 1966). Joint art. dir., Berkshire Music Center 1970–85. Author of books on jazz and hn. technique. Guest cond. of leading Amer. and Brit. orchs. Prin. comps.:

OPERAS: *The Visitation* (1966); *The Fisherman and his Wife* (1970); *A Question of Taste* (1989).

BALLET: *Variants* (1960, choreog. Balanchine).

ORCH.: hn. conc. No.1 (1944), No.2 (1976); vc. conc. (1945, rev. 1985); *Suite*, chamber orch. (1945); *Vertige d'Eros* (1945); *Symphonic Study* (1947–8); *Recitative and Rondo*, vn., orch. (1953); *Symphonic Tribute to Duke Ellington* (1955); *Little Fantasy* (1957); *Contours*, chamber orch. (1958); *Spectra* (1958); concertino, jazz qt., orch. (1959); *7 Studies on Themes of Paul Klee* (1959); *Capriccio*, tuba, orch. (1960); *Contrasts*, ww. quintet, orch. (1960); *Journey to the Stars* (1962); *Movements*, fl., str. (1962); pf. conc. No.1 (1962), No.2 (1981); *Composition in Three Parts* (1963); *Diptych*, brass quintet and band (1963, and orch. (1964); *Threnos*, ob., orch (1963); sym. (1965); *Concertos for Orchestra (Farbenspiel)* No.1 (1966), No.2 (1976), No.3 (1985); *Triplum I* (1967), *II* (1975); *Colloquy*, 2 pf., orch. (1968); *Shapes and Designs* (1969); *Museum Piece*, Renaissance instrs., orch. (1970); *Concerto da camera* (1971); *4 Soundscapes—Hudson Valley Reminiscences* (1974); vn. conc. (1976); *Symphony for Brass and Percussion* (1950); *Deaï-Encounters*, 7 vv., 3 orch. (1977); contrabassoon conc. (1978); tpt. conc. (1979); *Eine kleine Posaunenmusik*, tb., orch. (1980); *In Praise of Winds*, large wind orch. (1981); alt. sax. conc. (1983); *Concerto quaternio*, vn., fl., ob., tpt., orch. (1984); *Concerto festivo*, brass quintet, orch. (1984); bn. conc. (1985) va. conc. (1985); conc., str. qt., orch. (1988); fl. conc. (1988); *On Winged Flight*, band (1989); *Chamber Sym.* (1989); conc. for pf. 3 hands (1989); *Song and Dance*, vn., band (1990); vn. conc. No.2 (1991); org. conc. (1993); *The Past is in the Present* (1994); *An Arc Ascending* (1996); *Concerto da Camera No. 2*, perc., hp., str. (2002); *Encounters*, 2 sax., tpt., opt. 6 vv., orch. (2003); *Grand Concerto for Perc. and Kbds.*, 8 perc., hp., cel., pf. (2005).

CHAMBER MUSIC: *Romantic Sonata*, cl., hn., pf. (1941, rev. 1983); *Suite*, ww. quintet (1945); *Fantasia Concertante* No.1, 3 obs., pf. (1947), No.2, 3 tbs., pf. (1947), qt., 4 dbs. (1947); trio, ob., hn., va. (1948); *Duo Sonata*, cl., bcl. (1948–9); ob. sonata (1948–51); *Fantasy*, vc. (1951); str. qts. No.1 (1957), No.2 (1965), No.3 (1986), No. 4 (2002); ww. quintet (1958); *Fantasy*, hp. (1959); *Fantasy Qt.*, 4 vas. (1959); *Lines and Contrasts*, 16 hns. (1960); *Music for Brass Quintet* (1961); *Studies for Horn* (1962); *Episodes*, cl. (1964); *Aphorisms*, fl., str. trio (1967); *Sonata serenata*, cl., vn., vc., pf. (1978); octet (1979); pf. trio (1983); *On Light Wings*, pf. qt. (1984); sextet, bn., pf., str. qt. (1986); *Chimeric Images*, chamber group (1988); *A bouquet for collage*, cl., fl., vn., vc., pf., perc. (1988); hn. sonata (1988); *5 Impromptus*, ca., str. qt. (1989); *Paradigm Exchanges*, fl., cl., pf. trio (1991); *Marimbology*, mar. (1993); Sextet, wind quintet, pf. left hand (1994); *Quodlibet*, ob., hn., vn., vc., hp. (2001).

VOCAL: *O Lamb of God*, ch., org. (opt.) (1941); *6 Renaissance Lyrics*, ten., 7 instrs. (1962); *5 Shakespeare Songs*, bar., orch.; *Sacred Cantata*, ch., chamber orch. (1966); *The Power Within Us*, oratorio, bar., narr., ch., orch. (1971); *Poems of Time and Eternity*, ch., 9 instrs. (1972); *Thou Art the Son of God*, ch., chamber ens. (1987); *Magnificat*

and Nunc dimittis, ch. (1994); *Mondrian's Vision*, ch., fl., ob., cl., sax., bn., hn., tpt., 3 perc., pf., str. (1994).

Schulmeister, Der (The Schoolmaster). Nickname for Haydn's Sym. No.55 in E♭ (Hob. I:55) comp. 1774. Dotted figure in slow movt. suggests admonishing finger of schoolmaster, and scholars believe Haydn authorized title.

Schultze, Norbert (*b* Brunswick, 1911; *d* Bad Tölz, nr. Munich, 2002). Ger. composer. Worked in cabaret in Munich 1931–2, cond. opera in Heidelberg 1932–3, Darmstadt 1933–4. Later comp. for films and TV and ran publishing business. Wrote 2 operas and an operetta, but best known for song *Lili Marleen* (1938), words by Hans Leip (1894–1983), which was taken up during the Second World War by Ger. and Allied soldiers and sung by, among others, Marlene Dietrich, Ann Shelton, and Vera Lynn. First recorded 1939 by Lale Andersen. Eng. vers. by Tommy Connor.

Schuman, William (Howard) (*b* NY, 1910; *d* Manhattan, NY, 1992). Amer. composer and administrator. As youth composed jazz arrs. In 1933 enrolled for teacher's course at Columbia Univ., attended Salzburg Mozarteum summer course 1935 where he began work on 1st Sym. This he submitted for advice to Roy Harris, who gave him private lessons. His 3rd Sym. was played in Boston in 1941 under *Koussevitzky, who became his champion. Henceforward composed prolifically, and became prof. at Sarah Lawrence Coll., Larchmont, 1935–45. His cantata *A Free Song* won the first *Pulitzer Prize for mus. (1943). Became president of Juilliard Sch. in 1945, holding this post until 1962; president of Lincoln Center for Performing Arts, 1962–9.

His syms. are a major feature of Amer. mus. His mus. has a firm melodic basis, large in gesture and conception, with strong contrapuntal element and motor rhythms, some derived from jazz. He comp. in most forms, incl. ballets for Antony Tudor and Martha Graham, and was much honoured by Amer. institutions. Prin. works:

OPERAS: *The Mighty Casey* (baseball opera, 1951–3, rev. as cantata *Casey at the Bat*, 1976); *A Question of Time* (1989–91).

BALLETS: *Undertow* (1945); *Night Journey* (1947); *Judith* (1949); *Voyage for a Theater* (1953, withdrawn); *The Witch of Endor* (1965, withdrawn).

ORCH.: syms.: No.1 (1935, withdrawn), No.2 (1937, withdrawn); No.3 (1941), No.4 (1941), No.5 (*Symphony for Strings*) (1943), No.6 (1948), No.7 (1960), No.8 (1962), No.9 (*Le Fosse ardeatine*) (1968), No.10 (*American Muse*) (1975); pf. conc. (1938, rev. 1942); *American Festival Overture* (1939); *William Billings Overture* (1943, withdrawn); *Circus Overture* (1944 for small orch., 1945 for large); vn. conc. (1947, rev. 1954, 1959); *New England Triptych* (1956); *Song of Orpheus*, vc., orch. (1961); *The Orchestra Song* (1963); *To Thee Old Cause* (1968); *In*

Praise of Shahn (1969); *Voyage for Orchestra* (1972); *Prelude for a Great Occasion*, brass, perc. (1974); *3 Colloquies*, hn., orch. (1979); *American Hymn* (1980; also for band and brass quintet).

CHORAL: *Pioneers!* (1937); *This is Our Time* (1940); *A Free Song*, cantata (1942); *Te Deum* (1944); *Carols of Death* (1958); *Mail Order Madrigals* (1971); *The Young Dead Soldiers*, sop., hn., ww., str. (1975); *Perceptions* (1982); *On Freedom's Ground*, bar., ch., orch. (1985).

CHAMBER MUSIC: str. qts.: No.1 (1936, withdrawn), No.2 (1937), No.3 (1939), No.4 (1950), No.5 (1987); *Amaryllis*, str. trio (1964); *25 Opera Snatches*, tpt. (1978); *Dances*, wind quintet, perc. (1984); *Awake, thou wintry earth*, cl., vn. (1986); *Cooperstown Fanfare*, 2 tpt., 2 tb. (1987); *The Lord Has a Child*, ch., brass quintet (1990).

PIANO: *Voyage* (1953, orch. 1972); *3 Piano Moods* (1958); *Chester: Variations* (1988).

Schumann (*née* Wieck), **Clara** (Josephine) (*b* Leipzig, 1819; *d* Frankfurt, 1896). Ger. pianist and composer, wife of Robert *Schumann. Daughter and pupil of F. *Wieck. Début aged 9. Toured Ger. 1831 and elsewhere in Europe from 1832. Overcame fierce parental opposition to marriage to Schumann 1840, becoming his foremost interpreter. Toured Russia 1844. First visit to Eng. 1856, often thereafter to 1888. Lived in Berlin 1856–63. Head of pf. faculty, Hoch Cons., Frankfurt, 1878–92. Championed Brahms in his youth and remained lifelong friend. Last public perf. 1891. Comp. pf. conc. (in A minor) (1836), pf. trio (1847), pf. concertino (1847), many pf. pieces, several songs, and cadenzas for concs. by Mozart and Beethoven. Had distinguished pupils. Was renowned for the breadth and integrity of her playing.

Schumann, Elisabeth (*b* Merseburg, 1888; *d* NY, 1952). Ger.-born soprano (Amer. cit. 1944). Opera début Hamburg 1909 (Shepherd in *Tannhäuser*), remaining member of co. until 1919. NY Met 1914–15 (début as Sophie in *Der Rosenkavalier*, one of her best famous and effective roles). Vienna Opera 1919–37; Salzburg début 1922; CG 1924–31. Toured USA 1921 in recitals with R. Strauss as accompanist. One of best-loved and most admired singers of her day, notable interpreter of Schubert and Strauss *Lieder* and of such Mozart *soubrette* roles as Susanna, Zerlina, Despina, Blonde. Also memorable Adèle in *Die Fledermaus*. Left Austria 1938 and settled in USA, teaching for a brief spell at Curtis Inst.

Schumann, Robert (Alexander) (*b* Zwickau, 1810; *d* Endenich, 1856). Ger. composer, pianist, cond., and critic. Studied law at Leipzig and Heidelberg Univs., but main interests were mus. and Romantic literature, e.g. Jean-Paul Richter. In 1828 met Clara Wieck, to whose father Friedrich he went for pf. lessons in 1829, lodging with him and beginning to compose. In 1832 permanently injured hand by device he had invented to keep 4th finger immobile while practising. Was already contributing mus. criticism to Ger. papers and in 1831 called attention to Chopin's genius.

Depressed by mus. situation in Ger., founded 'David Club' in 1834 to fight artistic philistines, and periodical *Neue Zeitschrift für Musik*, which he ed. for 10 years. In writings and comps., gave himself dual personality: Florestan for his impetuous self and Eusebius for his contemplative side. In 1838 visited Vienna and discovered MS of Schubert's 'Great' C major sym., which he sent to Mendelssohn. Married Clara Wieck 1840 after long opposition from her father, this being followed by outpouring of songs and song-cycles. In 1841 concentrated on syms., in 1842 on chamber mus., and in 1843 choral works. Taught comp. at Leipzig Cons. Toured Russia with Clara, 1844. On return had severe attack of depression. Moved to Dresden in search of quiet, living there until 1850. In 1846 Clara gave f.p. of his pf. conc. and Mendelssohn cond. f.p. of 2nd Sym. In 1850 moved to Düsseldorf in hope of earning more by conducting, but was not a success. Met 20-year-old Brahms in 1853, acclaiming him in article 'New Paths'. The next year his mental health failed and he threw himself into Rhine, but was saved and taken to private asylum where he lived another 2 years.

Schumann was one of the greatest composers for pf., enriching its literature with a series of poetic works in which classical structure and Romantic expression are combined. His vocal and chamber mus. is of comparable quality, with the freshness, vitality, and lyricism which also characterize the orch. works. His orchestration is sometimes criticized for its thickness and lack of fluency, and various attempts have been made to 'improve' the scoring, e.g. by Mahler, but the present-day tendency is to prefer the spontaneity of Schumann's own. His songs, particularly his song-cycles, are among the glories of *Lieder*. His works contain many musical quotations and allusions and a number of his themes have been shown to be musical cryptograms. Prin. comps.:

OPERA: **Genoveva*, Op.81 (1847–9).

INCIDENTAL MUSIC: **Manfred*, Op.115 (Byron) (1848–9).

ORCH.: syms.: No.1 in B♭ (*Frühling*, **Spring*), Op.38 (1841), No.2 in C, Op.61 (1845–6), No.3 in E♭ (**Rhenish*), Op.97 (1850), No.4 in D minor (begun 1841, 2nd in order of comp., rev. 1851), Op.120; *Overture, Scherzo, and Finale*, Op.52 (1841, rev. 1845); *Overture to Shakespeare's Julius Caesar*, Op.128 (1851); *Overture on Goethe's Hermann and Dorothea*, Op.136 (1851).

CONCERTOS, etc.: pf. conc. in A minor, Op.54 (1st movt. written as *Fantasie* 1841, rest added 1845); *Konzertstück*, 4 hns., in F, Op.86 (1849); *Introduction and Allegro appassionato*, pf., Op.92 (1849); vc. conc. in A minor, Op.129 (1850); *Fantasy* in C, vn., Op.131 (1853); *Concert-Allegro and Introduction* in D minor, pf., Op.134 (1853); vn. conc. in D minor, Op.2 posth. (1853).

CHORUS AND ORCH.: *Das Paradies und die Peri* (**Paradise and the Peri*), Op.50 (1843); *Requiem für Mignon*, Op.98b (1849); *Nachtlied*, Op.108 (1849); *Der Rose Pilgerfahrt*, Op.112 (1851); *Der Königssohn*, Op.116 (1851): *Des Sängers Fluch*,

Op.139 (1852); *Mass*, Op.147 (1852); *Requiem*, Op.148 (1852); *Scenes from Goethe's *Faust* (1844–53).

CHAMBER MUSIC: str. qts.: Op.41, No.1 in A minor, No.2 in F, No.3 in A (1842); pf. qts.: in C minor (1829), in Eb, Op.47 (1842); pf. quintet in Eb, Op.44 (1842); pf. trios: No.1 in D minor, Op.63 (1847), No.2 in F, Op.80 (1847), No.3 in G minor, Op.110 (1851); vn. sonata No.1 in A minor, Op.105 (1851), No.2 in D minor, Op. 121 (1851); *Adagio and Allegro* in Ab, hn. (or vn. or vc.), pf., Op.70 (1849); *Fantasiestücke*, cl. (or vn. or vc.), pf., Op.73 (1849); *Fantasiestücke*, pf., vn., vc., Op.88 (1842); 3 *Romanzen*, ob. (or vn. or cl.), pf., Op.94 (1849); *Märchenbilder*, va. (or vn.), pf., Op.113 (1851); 5 *Pieces in Folk Style*, vc. (or vn.), pf., Op.102 (1849); *Märchenerzählungen*, pf., cl. (or vn.), va., Op.132 (1853); pf. accs. to 6 vn. sonatas and partitas by J. S. Bach (1854).

PIANO: *Abegg Theme with Variations*, Op.1 (1830); *Papillons*, Op.2 (1829–31); 12 *Concert Studies on Paganini Caprices*, Set I, Op.3 (1832), Set II, Op.10 (1833); 6 *Intermezzi*, Op.4 (1832); *Impromptus on a Theme by Clara Wieck*, Op.5 (1833, rev. 1850); 18 *Davidsbündlertänze*, Op.6 (1837, rev. 1850); *Toccata* in C, Op.7 (1830); *Allegro* in B minor, Op.8 (1831); *Carnaval: Scènes mignonnes sur 4 notes*, Op.9 (1834–5); sonatas: No.1 in F♯ minor, Op.11 (1833–5), No.2 in G minor, Op.22 (1833–8), No.3 in F minor, Op.14 (1835, rev. 1853); 8 *Fantasiestücke*, Op.12 (1837–8); *Études symphoniques* (Symphonic Studies), Op.13 (1834–7, rev. 1852); *Kinderscenen*, Op.15 (1838); *Kreisleriana*, Op.16 (1838, rev. 1850); *Fantasy* in C, Op.17 (1836); *Arabeske* in C, Op.18 (1839); *Blumenstück* in Db, Op.19 (1839); *Humoreske* in Bb, Op.20 (1839); 8 *Novelletten*, Op.21 (1838); 4 *Nachtstücke*, Op.23 (1839); *Faschingsschwank aus Wien*, Op.26 (1839); 3 *Romanzen*, Op.28 (1839); *Album für die Jugend*, Op.68, Book I containing 18 pieces, Book II, 25 (1848); *Waldscenen*, Op.82 (1848–9); *Bunte Blätter*, Op.99 (1852); 3 *Fantasiestücke*, Op.111 (1851); 3 pf. sonatas 'fur die Jugend', Op.118 (1853); *Albumblätter*, Op.124 (1832–45); 7 *Piano Pieces in the form of fugues*, Op.126 (1853); 5 *Gesänge der Frühe*, Op.133 (1853).

PIANO DUETS: 6 *Impromptus*, Op.66 (1848), *Ball-Scenen*, Op.109 (1851).

ORGAN: 6 *Fugues on the Name of Bach*, Op.60 (1845).

PART-SONGS: mixed: 5 *Lieder*, Op.55 (1846); *Romanzen und Balladen*, 4 vols., Opp. 67, 75, 145, 146 (1846–9); women's: *Romanzen*, 2 vols., Opp. 69, 91 (1849); men's: 6 *Lieder*, Op.33 (1840); 5 *Hunting-Songs*, with 4 optional hn., Op.137 (1849).

SONGS & SONG-CYCLES: *Liederkreis* (Heine), Op.24 (1840); *Myrthen*, cycle of 26 songs, Op.25 (1840); *Lieder und Gesänge*, I, Op.27 (1840), II, Op.51 (1842), III, Op.77 (1840 and 1850), IV, Op.96 (1850); 12 *Gedichte*, Op.35 (1840); 6 *Gedichte*, Op.36 (1840); 12 *Gedichte aus Liebesfrühling*, Op.37 (1840); *Liederkreis* (Eichendorff), Op.39 (1840); *Frauenliebe und -Leben*, song-cycle, Op.42 (1840); *Romanzen und Balladen*, I, Op.45 (1840), II, Op.49 (1840), III, Op.53 (1840), IV, Op.64 (1841 and 1847); *Dichterliebe*, song-cycle, Op.48 (1840); *Liederalbum für die Jugend*, Op.79 (1849); 3 *Gesänge*,

Op.83 (1850); 6 *Gesänge*, Op.89 (1850); 6 *Gedichte*, Op.90 (1850); 3 *Gesänge*, Op.95 (1849); 9 *Lieder und Gesänge aus Wilhelm Meister*, Op.98a (1849); 7 *Lieder*, Op.104 (1851); 6 *Gesänge*, Op.107 (1851–2); 4 *Husarenlieder*, Op.117 (1851); 3 *Gedichte*, Op.119 (1851); 5 *Heitere Gesänge*, Op.125 (1851); 5 *Lieder und Gesänge*, Op.127 (1850–1); *Gedichte der Königin Maria Stuart*, Op.135, (1852); 4 *Gesänge*, Op.142 (1852).

Schumann-Heink (*née* Rössler), **Ernestine** (*b* Lieben, 1861; *d* Hollywood, Calif., 1936). Cz.-born contralto (Amer. cit. 1908). Début Graz 1876 in Beethoven's 9th Sym.; opera début Dresden 1878 (Azucena in *Il trovatore*). Member Hamburg Opera 1883–98. CG début 1892 (Erda in *Das Rheingold*, cond. Mahler). Bayreuth 1896–1914 (excl. 1904). Amer. début (Chicago) 1898; NY Met 1899. Sang mainly in USA until retirement 1932 (her last role at NY Met was as Erda at the age of 70). Created Klytemnästra in *Elektra*, Dresden 1909. Repertory of 150 roles. Voice of power and range allied to exceptional dramatic skill.

Schuppanzigh, Ignaz (*b* Vienna, 1776; *d* Vienna, 1830). Austrian violinist and conductor. Friend of Beethoven, whom he taught vn. and va. Member of Prince *Lichnowsky's qt. 1794–5. Formed his own str. qt. 1804–5. Leader of Count *Rasoumovsky's qt. 1808–14, giving f.p. of several Beethoven qts. Member of Vienna court opera orch. from 1824, conducting there from 1828. Comp. some vn. pieces.

Schuricht, Carl (*b* Danzig, 1880; *d* Corseaux-sur-Vévey, Switz., 1967). Ger. conductor. Cond. posts in Mainz, Dortmund, etc. Chief cond., Wiesbaden 1911–44 where he championed Delius, Ravel, Stravinsky, and Schoenberg. Cond. Dresden PO 1942–4. Settled Switzerland 1944. Salzburg Fest. début 1946. Cond. Vienna PO on its first Amer. tour, 1956.

Schurmann, Gerard (*b* Kertosono, Indonesia, 1924). Indonesian-born Dutch composer and conductor. Settled in Eng. 1941. Cond. Dutch radio, Hilversum. Works incl. 6 *Studies of Francis Bacon*, orch., (1968); *Variants*, orch. (1970); pf. conc. (1972–3); vn. conc. (1975–8); *Songs of Absence*, vc., orch. (1988); *The Gardens of Exile*, orch. (1990); fl. sonatina (1968); *Contrasts*, pf. (1973); wind quintet (1963, rev. 1976); *Chuench'i*, v., pf. (7 songs from Chinese, trans. Waley) (1966, also with orch. 1967); *The Double Heart*, cantata (1976); *Piers Plowman*, SCTB, ch., orch. (1979–80); *Duo*, vn., pf. (1984); qt., pf., str., No.1 (1986), No.2 (1997–8); *Slovak Folk Songs*, high v., pf. (1987); *The Gardens of Exile*, vc., orch. (1989–90); Concerto for Orch. (1994–6); 6 *Songs of Wm. Blake*, v., pf. (1996–7); *Gaudiana* ('Symphonic Studies'), orch. (2000–1); trio, cl., vc., pf. (2002); str. qt. (2003–4); Sonata, str. (2004).

Schütz, Heinrich (*b* Köstritz, 1585; *d* Dresden, 1672). Ger. composer and organist, one of greatest of Bach's predecessors. Studied law, but patron, impressed by his mus. ability, sent him in

1609 to study in Venice with G. Gabrieli until 1612. Court org., Kassel, 1613. Kapellmeister, Dresden electoral court, 1617–57. Spent 3 periods as court cond. in Copenhagen 1633–45. In Dresden with court orch. from 1645. Comp. first Ger. opera, *Dafne*, 1627 (mus. destroyed by fire 1760). Revisited It. 1628–9. His special importance lies in his grafting of It. choral and vocal style on to Ger. polyphonic tradition. Wrote magnificent settings of Passions, Christmas oratorio, *7 Words from Christ on the Cross*, etc. Works pubd. in 16 vols. 1885–94, ed. *Spitta, with suppl. vol. 1927, contents as follows: 1. 4 Passions, *Resurrection* oratorios, and *Sieben Worte Jesu Christi am Kreuz*; 2 and 3. Psalms and Motets, 1619; 4. *Cantiones sacrae*, 4 vv., 1625; 5. *Symphoniae sacrae*, Pt.I, 1629; 6. *Geistliche Concerte*, 1–5 vv., 1636 and 1639; 7. *Symphoniae sacrae*, Pt.II, 1647; 8. *Musicalia ad chorum sacrum*, 1648; 9. It. madrigals, Venice 1611; 10 and 11. *Symphoniae sacrae*, Pt.III, 1630; 12–15. Motets, concs., arias, psalms, etc; 16. Psalms for 4 vv. Suppl.: Christmas oratorio: *Die Historia von der freuden und gnadenreichen Geburt Gottes und Mariens Sohns* (1664, lost until 1908).

Schwanda the Bagpiper (*Švanda Dudák*). Opera in 2 acts by *Weinberger to lib. by Kareš and Max Brod after folk-tale by Tyl. Prod. Prague 1927, NY Met 1931, CG 1934.

Schwanendreher, Der (The Swan-turner). Conc. for va. and small orch. by Hindemith based on Ger. folk-songs, the soloist being (in composer's words) one 'who comes among merry company and performs the music he has brought from afar: songs grave and gay and, to conclude, a dance'. Movts. are entitled: (1) *Zwischen Berg und tiefem Tal* (Between mountain and deep valley); (2) *Nun laube, Lindlein, laube* (Now shed your leaves, little linden); (3) *Seid ihr nicht der Schwanendreher?* (Is it not the swan-turner?). F.p. Amsterdam 1935, Hindemith (soloist), Mengelberg (cond.).

Schwanengesang (Swan Song). Coll. of 14 songsettings by Schubert (D957) issued after his death as a 'cycle' by publisher Haslinger; comp. 1827–8. The poets are Heine, Rellstab, and Seidl. The songs, in pubd. order, are: *Liebesbotschaft* (Love-message), *Kriegers Ahnung* (Warrior's presentiment), *Frühlingssehnsucht* (Longing for Spring), *Ständchen* (Serenade), *Aufenthalt* (Staging-post), *In der Ferne* (In the distance), *Abschied* (Farewell), *Der Atlas* (Atlas), *Ihr Bild* (Her Portrait), *Das Fischermädchen* (The Fisher Girl), *Die Stadt* (The Town), *Am Meer* (By the Sea), *Der Doppelgänger* (The ghostly double), *Die Taubenpost* (The Pigeon-post).

Schwarz, Gerard (Ralph) (*b* Weehawken, NJ, 1947). Amer. conductor and trumpeter. Began tpt. lessons at age of 8. Trumpeter in Amer. Brass Quintet 1965–73 and Amer. SO in NY 1966–72. Co-prin. tpt. NYPO 1972–5. Mus. dir., Waterloo Fest., Stanhope, NJ, 1975–85 (prin. cond. from

1986), NY Chamber Symphony 1977–86, Los Angeles Chamber Orch. 1978–86. Mus. dir. Seattle SO from 1986; cond. RLPO 2001–6.

Schwarz, Hanna (*b* Hamburg, 1943). Ger. mezzo-soprano. Début Hanover 1970 (Maddalena in *Rigoletto*). Hamburg Opera from 1973. Bayreuth début 1975. Amer. début (S. Francisco) 1977; CG 1980. Sang Countess Geschwitz in f. complete p. of *Lulu*, Paris 1979. Salzburg Fest. début 1979.

Schwarz, Rudolf (*b* Vienna, 1905; *d* London, 1994). Austrian-born conductor (Brit. cit. 1952). Violist in Vienna PO. Ass. cond. Düsseldorf Opera 1923, later at Karlsruhe 1927–33. Mus. dir. Jüdischer Kulturbund, Berlin, 1936–9. Prisoner in Belsen concentration camp 1943–5. Settled in Eng. Cond. Bournemouth Municipal Orch. 1946–51. CBSO 1951–7. Chief cond. BBC SO 1957–62. Prin. cond. Northern Sinfonia Orch. 1964–73. CBE 1973.

Schwarz, Vera (*b* Zagreb, 1888; *d* Vienna, 1964). Croatian soprano. Début in operetta at Theater an der Wien 1908. After success as Rosalinde in *Die Fledermaus*, sang in opera in Hamburg, Berlin, and, from 1921, Vienna. Frequently sang with Tauber in Lehár operettas. Salzburg Fest. 1929; Glyndebourne 1938. Went to Hollywood 1939, becoming teacher. Returned to Austria 1948 to teach at Salzburg Mozarteum.

Schwarze Maske, Die ('The Black Mask'). Opera in 3 acts by Penderecki to lib. by H. Kupfer and composer after play by G. Hauptmann. Comp. 1984–6. Prod. Salzburg 1986, Santa Fe 1988.

Schwarzendorf. See *Martini, G. P.*

Schwarzkopf, (Dame) (Olga Maria) **Elisabeth** (Friederike) (*b* Jarocin, nr. Poznań, 1915; *d* Schruns, Austria, 2006). Ger.-born soprano (Brit. cit.). Opera début Berlin 1938 (Flower Maiden in *Parsifal*). Vienna début 1942, remaining there in coloratura roles until 1944. Rejoined Vienna Opera 1946. Salzburg début 1947; CG début (with Vienna Opera) 1947. Settled in Eng. 1948, member of CG co. 1948–52. Milan début 1948; S. Francisco from 1955; NY Met 1964. Created Anne Trulove in *The Rake's Progress*, Venice 1951. Famous in Strauss roles such as the Marschallin, which she sang on her farewell to stage, Brussels 1972. Retired from concert platform 1975 and gave master classes. One of greatest sops. of her generation, superb interpreter of *Lieder*, especially Wolf. Was wife of Walter *Legge, who produced many of her recordings. DBE 1992.

Schwebung (Ger.). Fluctuation. (1) The 'beats' between 2 notes nearly but not quite in tune.

(2) (Org.) The *tremulant.

Schweigen (Ger.). Silence, or to be silent. *schweigt*, *tacet*; *Schweigezeichen* ('silence-sign'), *rest.

Schweigsame Frau, Die ('The Silent Woman'). Opera in 3 acts by R. Strauss to lib. by Stefan

Zweig after Ben Jonson's *Epicoene* (1609). Comp. 1933–4. Prod. Dresden 1935, NY 1958, CG 1961, Glyndebourne 1977, Garsington 2003.

Schweinitz, Wolfgang von (*b* Hamburg, 1953). German composer. Worked at Center for Computer Research in Music and Acoustics, Stanford Univ., Calif., and at Ger. Acad., Rome, 1978–9. Won first Schneider-Schott prize for young Ger. composers, 1986. His 'musical action in seven acts', *Patmos*, a setting of *Revelations* was commissioned by city of Munich, where it was first performed in 1990 in a prod. by Ruth Berghaus.

Schweitzer, Albert (*b* Kaysersberg, Alsace, 1875; *d* Lambaréné, Gabon, 1965). Fr. (Alsatian) organist and Bach scholar (also theologian and medical missionary). Org., Strasbourg Bach concerts from 1896 and Paris Bach concerts from 1906. Ed. Bach's org. works (first 5 vols. (1912–14) with Widor, remainder (1954–67) with Nies-Berger). Biography of Bach (in Fr. 1905, rewritten in Ger. 1908; Eng. trans. by E. Newman, 1911). Wrote book on Fr. and Ger. orgs. 1906. Worked as medical missionary in Fr. Congo, returning 1922 to give org. recitals to raise money for mission. Nobel Peace Prize 1952. Hon. OM 1955.

Schweizerpfeife (Ger.). Swiss pipe. Renaissance name for military fife or *Feldpfeife* (Field pipe).

schwellen (Ger.). To swell, i.e. to increase in vol. of tone (*crescendo). *Schweller*, the *swell of an org., *Schwellwerk*, swell Org.; *Schwellkasten*, swell Box.

schwer (Ger.). (1) Heavy (in style).
(2) Difficult. *schwermütig, schwermutsvoll*. Heavyhearted.

Schwertsik, Kurt (*b* Vienna, 1935). Austrian composer. Played hn. in Lower Austrian Tonkünstler Orch. 1955–9, 1962–8. With *Cerha, founded Viennese new mus. ens., *Die Reihe*, 1958. Studied with *Stockhausen in Cologne and Darmstadt 1959–62 and with Kagel and Cage in 1962. In 1965 pub. manifesto attacking aspects of post-1945 *avant-garde*. Played 2nd hn. in Vienna SO 1968. Taught comp. at Vienna Cons. from 1979. Wrote operas, ballets, orch. works, chamber mus., and many songs and song-cycles.

schwindend (Ger.). Diminishing (in tone, i.e. *diminuendo).

Schwung (Ger.). Swing. Term beloved of critics when describing an idiomatic perf. of, for example, *Die Fledermaus*. Also *schwungvoll*, full of go, vigorous.

Scimone, Claudio (*b* Padua, 1934). It. conductor. Founded chamber ens. I Solisti Veneti, 1959, to specialize in 18th-cent. It. instr. mus. and contemporary works by Bussotti, Donatoni, Malipiero, etc. (Salzburg Fest. début 1966). Teacher at Venice Cons. 1961–7, Verona 1967–74, and dir., Padua Cons., 1974–83.

sciolto, scioltamente (It.). Untied. Loosely, i.e. in a free and easy manner. The noun is *scioltezza*.

Sciutti, Graziella (*b* Turin, 1927; *d* Geneva, 2001). It. soprano. Opera début Aix-en-Provence 1951 (Lucy in *The* *Telephone). Glyndebourne 1954–9 and 1977 when she produced and sang *La* *voix humaine; CG 1956–62; La Scala from 1956; Salzburg Fest. début 1958; Amer. début (S. Francisco) 1961. Outstanding in soubrette roles (Despina, Norina, etc.). Also prod. operas in NY, Chicago, and London.

scivolando (It.). Sliding, i.e. *glissando.

scordatura (It.). Mistuning. Abnormal tuning of a str. instr. in order to obtain special chordal effects and changes of tonal quality. Prevalent in vn. mus. (e.g. of Heinrich Biber), of 17th and 18th cents., possibly originating with them. Paganini and Bériot in 19th cent. tuned G string of vn. up a tone to increase vol. and to make certain passages easier. In *andante* movement of Schumann's Pf. Qt., the C string of the vc. is tuned down to B♭ to increase the compass. Mahler in the scherzo of his 4th sym. has a solo vn. tuned up a tone to represent the 'dance of death'. Other 20th-cent. examples of *scordatura* occur in Kodály's sonata for unacc. vc., Stravinsky's *Firebird*, and Bartók's *Contrasts* (finale).

score. A mus.-copy which shows in ordered form the parts allotted to the various performers, as distinct from 'parts' which show only that of one performer. Thus to speak of *score and parts* means a comprehensive copy, used by the cond., and separate copies for individual instrs. and singers. A *full score* shows all the parts separately displayed. A *vocal score* gives all the v. parts of a choral work or opera with the orch. parts reduced to a pf. part. *Short score* is a stage in comp. where the composer may write out his mus. giving indications (but not full details) of scoring and harmonization. Mahler's 10th Sym. was left mainly in short score. A *piano score* is a reduction to a pf. part of *all* the parts of a work. A *miniature, study,* or *pocket score* is a full score issued in a handy size for study or for following a work at a concert. Conds. who know a work very well (and have good eyesight) sometimes use a miniature score.

scoring. (1) The art and process of orchestrating a comp.
(2) Taking the separate parts of a work and assembling them in a score, e.g. where only the parts have been preserved.

scorrendo, scorrevole (It.). (1) Gliding from note to note, i.e. *glissando.
(2) In a flowing style.

Scotch snap (catch). A rhythmic figuration in which a dotted note is preceded by a note of shorter value. It is a feature of the *Strathspey and is found in some Scottish songs. It seems to be not earlier than 18th-cent., and of unknown origin. Occurs in the mus. of composers, e.g. Rossini, who have never been within hailing distance of Scotland.

Scotch Symphony. Mendelssohn's Sym. No.3 in A minor, Op.56, begun 1830 and completed 1842. Now usually known as the *Scottish* sym. Inspired by visit to Holyrood, Edinburgh, and ded. to Queen Victoria. F.p. Leipzig, March 1842, f. Eng. p. London, June 1842.

Scott, Cyril (Meir) (*b* Oxton, 1879; *d* Eastbourne, 1970). Eng. composer, poet, and pianist. Settled in Liverpool 1898 as pf. teacher. Composed *Heroic Suite*, cond. Richter in Liverpool and Manchester 1900, and First Sym. perf. in Darmstadt same year. Pf. quintet perf. London 1901 and 2nd Sym. (later rev. as *3 Symphonic Dances*) cond. Wood 1903. Through terms of publisher's contract, wrote many short pf. pieces in impressionist style which earned him title of 'English Debussy' and reputation as miniaturist. Other works incl. vn. sonata (1908–10), notable for constant changes of time-signature, *La Belle Dame sans merci* for ch. and orch. (1915–16), opera *The Alchemist* (prod. Essen 1925), 2 other operas, sym. *The Muses*, (1939), 2 pf. concs. (1913–14, 1958), 3 vn. concs. (1927, 1935), 2-vn. conc., vc. conc., *The Ballad of Fair Helen of Kirkconnel*, bar., orch., 4 str. qts., 3 pf. sonatas, and 2 str. trios. Also wrote poetry and philosophical and medical books. Taught *Rubbra comp.

Scott, John (Gavin) (*b* Wakefield, 1956). Eng. organist. Début, London Prom. Concert 1977. Org. and ass. cond., Bach Choir. Org. and mus. dir., St Paul's Cath., London, from 1990. Prof. of org., RAM.

Scott, Marion (Margaret) (*b* London, 1877; *d* London, 1953). Eng. writer on music. Formed str. qt. and led Morley Coll. orch. when Holst was cond. Founded Soc. of Women Musicians, 1911. Wrote mus. criticism for *Christian Science Monitor* 1919–33. Noted for research on Haydn, especially the str. qts. Also wrote books on Beethoven and Mendelssohn.

Scotti, Antonio (*b* Naples, 1866; *d* Naples, 1936). It. baritone. Opera début Naples 1889 (Cinna in *La Vestale*). Sang for 9 seasons in It., Sp., Russia, and S. America. Débuts: La Scala 1898; CG 1899, singing there regularly until 1910; Amer. (Chicago) 1899; NY Met 1899–1933. First Scarpia in London and NY. At Met he sang 832 perfs. of 36 roles, being heard frequently as Scarpia, Sharpless, Falstaff, Iago, and Rigoletto. Managed and financed touring opera co., 1919–23.

Scottish Chamber Orchestra. Chamber orch. with headquarters in Queen's Hall, Edinburgh, and serving all Scotland. Founded 1974 with Roderick *Brydon as art. dir. R. *Leppard prin. guest cond. from 1978. Jukka-Pekka Saraste prin. cond. 1987–94, Ivor Bolton 1994–6; Joseph Swenson 1996–2005. Played for Scottish Opera, when appropriate, up to 1979. Has toured abroad.

Scottish Fantasy. Fantasia on Scottish Folk Tunes for vn. and orch. by Bruch, comp. 1879–80, f.p. Hamburg 1880 (Sarasate). In 4 movts., last being an *Allegro guerriero* (warlike). Scottish tune featured in each movt.: *Auld Rob Morris*, *The Dusty Miller*, *I'm a doun for lack of Johnnie*, and *Scots wha hae wi' Wallace bled*.

Scottish National Orchestra. See *Royal Scottish National Orchestra*.

Scottish Opera. Opera co. based in Glasgow but giving seasons in Edinburgh, Aberdeen, and elsewhere in Scotland, also paying periodic visits to Eng. provinces, particularly Newcastle upon Tyne. Has played in London, at Edinburgh Fest., and made several tours abroad. Founded 1962 by Alexander *Gibson, first season being of 2 operas, *Madama Butterfly* and *Pelléas et Mélisande*, in King's Th., Glasgow. With Peter *Hemmings as administrator from 1963, co. began to build a reputation for striking productions, with excellent sets and lighting; singers were mainly Brit. but with several int. artists who worked with the co. for long spells, e.g. Helga *Dernesch. Contemporary works were perf., notably of Britten, and operas were commissioned from Scottish composers, e.g. Wilson's *Confessions of a Justified Sinner*. In 1969, Berlioz's *Les Troyens* was perf., with Janet Baker as Dido, and in 1966, with *Die Walküre*, the co. began to build a *Ring* cycle, culminating in 1971 in Glasgow with the first Brit. perf. of the *Ring* outside London for about 40 years. In 1975 the co. moved into the re-equipped and refurbished Th. Royal, Glasgow, as its permanent headquarters, setting the seal on the finest and most important operatic development in Britain since the foundation of Glyndebourne. In 1976 Hemmings was appointed dir. of Australian Opera and was succeeded by Peter Ebert, former chief prod. of Scottish Opera. He resigned in 1980. His successor was John *Cox, appointed in 1982, who handed over to Richard Mantle in 1985. Mantle was succeeded by Richard Jarman (1991–7), Ruth Mackenzie (1997–9), Christopher Barron (2000–5), Alex Reedijk from 2006. Formed own orch. 1980, Scottish Nat. Orch. and others having played until then. Scottish Opera is a remarkable example of the flowering of Scottish mus. life since 1945, especially under the aegis of Sir Alexander Gibson. John *Mauceri succeeded Gibson as mus. dir. 1987–93, Richard Armstrong 1993–2005.

Scottish Symphony (Mendelssohn). See *Scotch Symphony*.

Scotto, Renata (*b* Savona, 1933). It. soprano. Opera début Savona 1952 (Violetta in *La traviata*). Member of La Scala co. from 1954; Débuts: London (Stoll) 1957; Edinburgh Fest., 1957 (replaced Callas as Amina in *La Sonnambula* at very short notice); Amer. (Chicago) 1960; CG 1962; NY Met 1965. Specially successful in Puccini and Verdi. Last sang at NY Met 1987 (as Butterfly), having directed *Madama Butterfly* there in 1986. Autobiography *More Than a Diva* (NY 1984).

Scozzese (It.). Scottish.

Scriabin, Alexander (Nikolayevich) (*b* Moscow, 1872; *d* Moscow, 1915). Russ. composer and pianist, son of a lawyer and his wife who was a brilliant pianist. Prodigy pianist; enrolled in Moscow Cadet School but studied pf. with N. S. Zverev. Entered Moscow Cons. 1888, studying pf. with Safonov and comp. with Taneyev and Arensky. While at the cons., attracted notice of the publisher Belayev who issued his early comps. under generous terms and in 1896 sponsored Scriabin's tour of Europe as pianist in his own works. Prof. of pf., Moscow Cons., 1898–1903, an occupation with which he became increasingly bored. Settled in Switz. 1903 when former pupil settled annuity on him. Toured USA 1906–7 and found new publisher and champion in *Koussevitzky. Since 1905 he had been under the influence of Mme. Blavatsky's theosophy and mystical influences; regarded his works from that date as preparation for a 'supreme ecstatic mystery' which would accompany a final cataclysm. Toured Russ. 1910 with Koussevitzky's orch. and in 1911 perf. his works with Mengelberg and Concertgebouw Orch. of Amsterdam. Visited London 1914 for perf. of his *Prometheus* under Wood and to play his pf. conc. and give recitals. Toured Russ. 1914 then became ill, dying from septicaemia from tumour on his lip.

Scriabin's early works are strongly flavoured by Chopin and Liszt. As he developed his personal theories he grew harmonically bolder in his pf. works, using chords built of 4ths and sometimes of 2nds, sometimes achieving what has been called 'impressionist atonality'. In his sym.-poem, *Prometheus*, and 7th pf. sonata, he developed the 'mystic' chord, a series of 4ths—C, F♯, B♭, E, A, and D. This extreme chromaticism was combined with a strong feeling for classical form. His obsession with extra-mus. ideas has tended to divert attention from the undoubted excellent qualities of his mus. Prin. works:

ORCH.: syms.: No.1 in E, with ch. (1899–1900, f.p. 1901), No.2 in C minor (*c.* 1901, f.p. 1902), No.3 in C, *Bozhestvennaya poema* (*Divine Poem*, 1902–4, f.p. 1905); sym.-poems: in D minor (1896–7); *Poema ekstasa* (*Poem of Ecstasy*, 1905–8, f.p. 1908), *Promethei, Poema Ogyna* (*Prometheus, the Poem of Fire*, 1908–10, f.p. 1911); pf. conc. in F♯ minor (1896, f.p. 1897).

PIANO: sonatas: No.1 in F minor (1892), No.2 in G♯ minor (*Fantasy*) (1892–7), No.3 in F♯ minor (1897), No.4 in F♯ (1903), No.5 in F♯ (1907), No.6 in G (1911), No.7 in F♯ (*White Mass*) (1911), No.8 in A (1913), No.9 in F (*Black Mass*) (1913), No.10 in C (1913); 24 *Études*; 85 *Preludes*; *Concert Allegro* in B♭ minor; *Waltzes, Impromptus, Mazurkas*, etc.

Scribe, (Augustin) **Eugène** (*b* Paris, 1791; *d* Paris, 1861). Fr. dramatist and librettist. Most prolific librettist of his day, complete works comprising 76 vols. Among composers for whom he wrote libretti were Adam, Auber (38), Bellini (*La sonnambula*), Boieldieu (*La dame blanche*), Cherubini, Ciléa (*Adriana Lecouvreur*), Donizetti (5, incl. *L'elisir*

d'amore and *La favorite*), Gounod, Halévy (6, incl. *La juive*), Hérold, Macfarren, Meyerbeer (5, incl. *L'Africaine, Les Huguenots*, and *Le prophète*), Offenbach, Rossini (2, incl. *Le Comte Ory*), Suppé, Verdi (*Vêpres siciliennes* and *Un ballo in maschera*), and Zandonai.

Sculthorpe, Peter (Joshua) (*b* Launceston, Tasmania, 1929). Australian composer and pianist. First pf. lesson at age 8. Teacher at Sydney Univ. from 1963. Comp.-in-residence Yale Univ., 1966; visiting prof., Sussex Univ., 1972–3. Set out to be 'Australian' composer in sense that Copland expressed something peculiarly American and Bloch depicted biblical wilderness. Rejected atonality and serialism as inappropriate to his task, and concentrated on rhythmic procedures and orch. sonorities. Influenced also by Balinese melodies and rhythms. OBE 1977. Prin. works:

STAGE: *Ulterior Motifs* (1956); *Sun Music*, ballet (1968); *Rites of Passage* (1972–3); *Quiros* (1982); *Tatea* (1988).

ORCH: *Irkanda IV*, vn., str., perc. (1961); *Small Town from The 5th Continent*, spkr., orch. (1963, rev. 1976); *Sun Music* I (1965), III (1967), IV (1967), V (*Ketjak*) (1969); *From Tabuh Tabuhan*, str., perc. (1968); *Music for Japan* (1970); *Overture for a Happy Occasion* (1970); *Rain* (1970); *Love 200*, rock band, 2 singers, chamber orch. (1970); *Love 201*, rock band, chamber orch. (1971); *Lament for Strings* (1976); *Port Essington*, str. trio, str. orch. (1977); *Mangrove* (1979); gui. conc. (1980); *Little Suite*, str. (1983); pf. conc. (1983); *Sonata for Strings* No.1 (1983), No.2 (1988); *Sun Song* (1984); *Earth Cry* (1986); *At the Grave of Isaac Nathan* (1988); *Kakadu* (1988); *Nourlangie*, gui., perc., str. (1989); *Nangaloar* (1991); *Memento-Mori* (1992–3); *Darwin Marching* (1995); *Cello Dreaming*, vc., perc., str. (1997–8); *Great Sandy Island* (1998).

CHAMBER MUSIC: 16 str. qts. (1947–2005); solo vn. sonata (1954); *The Loneliness of Bunjil*, str. trio (1954, rev. 1960); *Irkanda I*, solo vn. (1955), *II*, str. qt. No.5 (1959), *III*, pf. trio (1961), *IV*, v., str., perc. (1961); va. and perc. sonata (1960); *Tabuh Tabuhan*, wind quintet, perc. (1968); *Dream* (1970); *How the Stars were made*, perc. ens. (1971); *Alone*, vn. (1976); *Sun Song*, recorder qt. (1976); *Little Serenade*, str. qt. (1977); *Landscape II*, pf. qt. (1978); *Requiem*, vc. (1979); *Cantares*, flamenco, classical and jazz guitars, str. qt. (1980); *Tailitnama Song*, fl., perc., vn., vc. (1981), vc., pf. (1989); *Songs of Sea and Sky* (1987); *Sun Song* (1989); *Dream Tracks*, vn., cl., pf. (1992); *Chorale*, 8 vc. (1994); *From the River*, pf., vn., va., vc., db. (2000).

VOCAL & CHORAL: *Sun Music II*, vv., perc. (1966, rev. 1969); *Night Piece*, ch., pf. (1966); *Morning Song for the Christ Child*, unacc. ch. (1966); *Autumn Song*, unacc. ch. (1968); *Ketjak*, 6 male vv. with tape echo (1972); *The Song of Tailitnama*, sop., 6 vc., perc. (1974); *Eliza Fraser Sings*, sop., fl., pf. (1978); *Child of Australia*, sop., narr., ch., orch. (1988); *Maranoa Lullaby*, mez., str. qt. (1996); *Love Thoughts*, sop., 2 spkr., 5 instr. (1998); *Requiem*, ch., orch., didjeridu (2004).

PIANO: *Sonatina* (1954); *Left Bank Waltz* (1957); *3 Haiku* (1966); *5 Night Pieces* (1965–71); *Landscape I*, pf. with tape echo and pre-recorded tape (1971); *Koto Music I and II*, amplified pf. and pre-recorded tape loop (1973–6); *Mountains* (1981); *Djilile* (1986); *Callabona* (1986, rev. 1989); *The Rose Bay Quadrilles* (1989); *Nocturnal* (1989).

Scythian Suite (Ala and Lolly). Work for orch. in 4 movts. by Prokofiev, his Op.20. Comp. 1914–15. F.p. Petrograd 1916 cond. Prokofiev, f. Eng. p. London 1920, cond. Coates.

sdrucciolando (It.). Sliding, i.e. *glissando.

Sea, The. Suite for orch. by Frank Bridge, comp. 1910–11 and pubd. by Carnegie Trust.

Sea Drift. Setting by Delius for bar., ch., and orch. of extract from Whitman's *Out of the cradle endlessly rocking*. Comp. 1903–4. F.p. Essen 1906 (cond. Georg Witte), Sheffield 1908 (cond. Wood), London 1909 (cond. Beecham).

Sea Fever. Setting for v. and pf. by *Ireland, 1913, of poem by John Masefield beginning 'I must down to the seas again', but the song begins 'I must go down . . .'.

Sea Interludes, Four. Concert work Op.33a by Britten of the descriptive mus. in his opera *Peter Grimes* (1945). Comprises *Dawn* (Act I), *Sunday Morning* (Act II), *Moonlight* (Act III), and *Storm* (Act I); the *Passacaglia* (Act II) Op.33b is often added. F.p. Cheltenham, 1945, cond. Britten.

Seaman, Christopher (b Faversham, Kent, 1942). Eng. conductor. Timpanist, Nat. Youth Orch., LPO 1964–7. Ass. cond. BBC Scottish SO 1968–70, prin. cond. 1971–7. Prin. cond. Northern Sinfonia 1973–9. Chief guest cond., Utrecht SO 1979–83. Cond.-in-res., Baltimore SO 1987–98. Chief cond., Robert Mayer children's concerts. Mus. dir. Rochester PO from 1999.

Sea Pictures. Song-cycle, Op.37, for cont. or mez. and orch. (or pf.) by Elgar to 5 poems by Roden Noel (*Sea-Slumber Song*), C. A. Elgar (*In Haven (Capri)*), E. B. Browning (*Sabbath Morning at Sea*), Richard Garnett (*Where Corals Lie*), and Lindsay Gordon (*The Swimmer*). Comp. 1897–9. F.p. Norwich 1899 (with Clara Butt); 4 of the songs were sung in London 2 days later by Butt with Elgar playing pf. acc.

Searle, Humphrey (b Oxford, 1915; d London, 1982). Eng. composer and writer on music. Worked. of BBC mus. dept. 1938–40 and 1946–8. Prof. of comp. RCM 1965–76. Comp.-in-res., Stanford Univ., Calif., 1964–5, Univ. of Calif., Los Angeles, 1976–7. Expert on mus. of Liszt, about which he wrote book (1954, rev. 1967). In own works used version of 12-note technique and showed predilection for unusual forms. Several settings of poems by Edith Sitwell. CBE 1968. Works incl.:

OPERAS: *The Diary of a Madman* (1958); *The Photo of the Colonel* (1963–4); *Hamlet* (1964–8).

BALLETS: *Noctambules* (1956); *The Great Peacock* (1957–8); *Dualities* (1963).

ORCH.: syms.: No.1 (1953), No.2 (1956–8), No.3 (1958–60), No.4 (1961–2), No.5 (1964); pf. concs.: No.1 (1944), No.2 (1955); suites: No.1 for str. (1942), No.2 (1943); *Night Music* (1943); *Poem* for 22 str. (1950); concertante, pf., str., perc. (1954); *Scherzi* (1964); *Hamlet Suite* (1968); *Sinfonietta* (1968–9); *Zodiac Variations* (1970); *Labyrinth* (1971); *Tamesis* (1979).

CHORUS & INSTR(S).: *Gold Coast Customs*, spkrs., male ch., orch. (1947–9); *The River-run* (Joyce), spkr., orch. (1951); *The Shadow of Cain*, spkrs., male ch., orch. (1952); *Jerusalem*, speakers, ten., ch., orch. (1970); *My Beloved Spake*, ch., org. (1976); *Dr Faustus*, solo vv., ch., orch. (1977).

VOICE & ORCH.: *3 Songs of Jocelyn Brooke*, high v., ens. (1954); *Oxus*, ten., orch. (1967); *Contemplations*, mez., orch. (1975); *Kubla Khan*, ten., orch. (1973).

UNACC. CHORUS: *The Canticle of the Rose* (Sitwell) (1965); *Rhyme Rude to My Pride*, male ch. (1974).

CHAMBER MUSIC: bn. quintet (1945); *Intermezzo* for 11 instr. (1946); qt. for cl., bn., vn., va. (1948); *Passacaglietta in nomine Arnold Schoenberg*, str. qt. (1949); *Gondoliera*, ca., pf. (1950); *The *Owl and the Pussy-Cat*, spkr., fl., vc., gui. (1951); *Suite*, cl., pf. (1956); *3 Movements*, str. qt. (1959); vc. fantasia (1972); *Five*, gui. (1974); *Il Penseroso e L'Allegro*, vc., pf. (1975).

SONG-CYCLE: *Les fleurs du mal*, ten., hn., pf. (1972).

SONG: *Counting the Beats*, high v., pf. (1963).

PIANO: Sonata (1951); *Suite* (1955); *Prelude on Theme by Rawsthorne* (1965).

Seasons, The (*Die Jahreszeiten*). (1) Secular oratorio by Joseph Haydn (Hob. XXI:3) to Ger. text by G. van Swieten based on Eng. poem (1726–30) by James Thomson (1700–48). Comp. 1799–1801. F.p. Vienna 1801.

(2) 1-act ballet by Glazunov, Op.67 (1899).

(3) Sub-title of Spohr's Sym. No.9 (1849–50).

Sea Symphony, A. Sym. (his first) by Vaughan Williams for sop., bar., ch., and orch., to text taken from poems by Whitman. Comp. 1903–9, rev. 1910, 1918, and 1924. F.p. Leeds Fest. 1910, cond. composer. F. London p. 1913.

Sebastiani, Johann (b nr. Weimar, 1622; d Königsberg, 1683). Ger. composer. Settled in Königsberg 1650, becoming cantor of cath. 1661. Court Kapellmeister of Brandenburg 1663–79. His major work was a *St Matthew Passion*, comp. *c.*1663, scored for soloists, 5-part ch., and 2 vns., 4 viols, and continuo, and the earliest setting known to incl. chorales. Also comp. *Funeral Songs* for 5 vv. and continuo (1663–80), and many occasional pieces.

sec (Fr.). Dry. Direction for note to be played and released sharply; in perc. playing, indication that the note should be damped, i.e. not allowed to ring on.

secco (It.). Dry. See *recitative*.

Sechter, Simon (b Friedberg, 1788; d Vienna, 1867). Ger.-Bohem. composer, organist, and teacher of theory. Court org., Vienna 1824; prof.

of counterpoint, Vienna Cons. 1851–63. Taught Bruckner. Wrote comic opera, str. qts., org. pieces, etc. Schubert, just before his death in 1828, had one lesson from him. Wrote over 8,000 works, incl. 5 operas, 35 Masses, and 2 Requiems.

Sechzehntel or **Sechzehntelnote** (Ger.). Sixteenth or sixteenth-note (semiquaver).

second. (1) As noun: interval in melody or harmony, being 2 steps in major or minor scale. *Minor second* is a semitone, e.g. C up to D♭; *major second* is 2 semitones, e.g. C up to D; *augmented second* is 3 semitones, e.g. C up to D♯.
(2) As adjective: term denoting perf. of lower-pitched part, such as 2nd vn., 2nd tb.

second inversion. In lay-out of a chord, that in which the 5th becomes the bass.

secondo (It.). Second. Lower of the 2 parts in pf. duet, higher being *primo.*

Second Viennese School. Somewhat imprecise generalization, usually understood to mean the group of composers who worked in Vienna (and Berlin) between 1910 and 1930 under the moral leadership of Schoenberg (e.g. Berg, Webern, Skalkottas); their common ground being adoption of the 12-note method of comp.

Secret, The (*Tajemství*). Opera in 3 acts by *Smetana to lib. by E. Krásnohorská. Comp. 1877–8. Prod. Prague 1878, Oxford 1956.

Secret Marriage, The (Cimarosa). See *Matrimonio segreto, Il.*

Secret of Susanna, The (Wolf-Ferrari). See *Segreto di Susanna, Il.*

Secunde, Nadine (*b* Independence, Ohio, 1953). Amer. soprano. Joined Wiesbaden Opera 1980, moving to Cologne 1985 (début there as Káťa Kabanová). Débuts: Bayreuth 1987; CG 1988; Chicago 1988; Los Angeles 1991.

sedlák. Same as *furiant.*

Seefried, Irmgard (*b* Köngetried, Bavaria, 1919; *d* Vienna, 1988). Austrian soprano of Ger. birth. Début Aachen 1940 (Priestess in *Aida*) where she remained until 1943. Vienna Opera from 1943. Sang Composer in *Ariadne auf Naxos* in Vienna 1944 in honour of Strauss's 80th birthday. Débuts: Salzburg Fest. 1946; CG (with Vienna State Opera) 1947; La Scala 1949; NY Met 1953. Outstanding in Strauss and Mozart, one of most appealing artists of her time. Wife of violinist Wolfgang *Schneiderhan, Henze's *Ariosi* for sop., vn., and orch. (1963) being comp. for them. Also noted for singing of *Lieder.*

Seeger, Charles (Louis) (*b* Mexico City, 1886; *d* Bridgewater, Conn., 1979). Amer. musicologist, teacher, and composer. Cond. at Cologne Opera 1910–11. Chairman, mus. dept., Univ. of Calif., Berkeley, 1912–19. Taught at Inst. of Mus. Art.,

NY, 1921–33 and at New Sch. for Social Research 1931–5, where in 1932 (with *Cowell) he gave first classes in USA in ethnomusicology. Chief, mus. division, Pan-American Union, 1941–53. Research Musicologist, UCLA 1960–70. Taught at Harvard from 1972. Specialist on proletarian mus. Second wife was Ruth Porter *Crawford. His son Pete(r) (*b* NY, 1919) was a folk-singer who wrote *Where have all the flowers gone?*

Seeger, Ruth Crawford. See *Crawford, Ruth.*

Seele (Ger.). Soul. (1) Feeling. *seelenvoll*, soulful.
(2) The soundpost of a bowed instr.

Segal, Uri (*b* Jerusalem, 1944). Israeli conductor. Won 1969 Mitropoulos Comp., NY. Cond. début Copenhagen 1969. Brit. début 1970 (BBC Welsh SO). Amer. début with Chicago SO at Ravinia Park Fest. 1972. Opera début Santa Fe 1973. Prin. cond. Philharmonia Hungarica 1979–84, Bournemouth SO 1980–3.

Segerstam, Leif (*b* Vasa, Finland, 1944). Finn. conductor and composer. Cond. Finnish Nat. Opera 1965–8 (dir. 1973–4), Stockholm Royal Opera 1968–72, Deutsche Oper, Berlin, 1971–3, gen. man., Finn. Nat. Opera 1973–4, chief cond. Austrian Radio SO 1975–82, Finn. Radio SO 1977–87, mus. dir. Rheinland-Pfalz State PO 1983–9, chief cond. Danish Radio SO 1989–95; Helsinki PO from 1996. Salzburg Fest. début 1971. Works incl. 15 syms. (1977–90), 6 vn. concs., 4 vc. concs., 3 pf. concs., 3 2-pf. concs., 28 str. qts., *Pandora* (essay for orch. and 9 dancers), songs, etc.

segno (It.). The 'sign' (see *dal segno, al segno*).

Segovia, Andrés, Marquis of Salobreña (*b* Linares, 1893; *d* Madrid, 1987). Sp. guitarist and composer. Début in Granada 1909. Madrid 1912, Paris 1924, NY 1928. More than any other man responsible for revival of interest in guitar as 'classical' instr. Works specially comp. for him by Castelnuovo-Tedesco, Ponce, etc. Created Marquis of Salobreña by King Juan Carlos, 1981. Segovia int. gui. comp. founded 1981. Transcr. works by Bach and others for guitar. Continued world tours well into his 80s. Wrote pieces for guitar.

Segreto di Susanna, Il (Susanna's Secret). Opera in 1 act by *Wolf-Ferrari to lib. by E. Golisciani. Prod. (as *Susannas Geheimnis*) Munich 1909, NY and CG 1911. The secret is that Susanna smokes: what her jealous husband smells is not a lover's cigarette smoke.

segue (It.). It follows. Direction that next section is to follow without a break.

seguidilla. Andalusian dance, found as early as 16th cent., in simple triple time, similar to the bolero but quicker. The participants interpolate vocal passages called *coplas*, which are in short lines of alternately 5 and 7 syllables, with assonance (agreement of vowels) rather than rhyme. Castanets, and usually guitar, are used for acc. Many regional variants.

Seguidillas Gitanas. See *Playera*.

Sehnsucht (Ger.). Longing, yearning (noun). Adjectives are *sehnsuchtsvoll, sehnsüchtig*. Several *Lieder*, e.g. by Schubert and Strauss, bear the title *Sehnsucht*.

Seiber, Mátyás (György) (*b* Budapest, 1905; *d* Kruger Nat. Park, S. Africa, in car crash, 1960). Hung.-born composer and cellist. Settled in Ger. where he played in th. orchs. and taught jazz at Frankfurt. Went to Eng. 1935, working for publisher. Taught at Morley Coll. from 1942. Co-founder of Committee (now Soc.) for Promotion of New Mus., 1942. Founder and cond., Dorian Singers, 1945. Great influence as teacher. Eclectic in style, his mus. is distinguished by fastidious craftsmanship and imagination. Works incl. opera *Eva spielt mit Puppen* (1934); ballet *The Invitation* (1960); *Missa brevis* (1924); *4 Greek Folk-Songs*, sop., str. (1942); cantata *Ulysses* (1946–7); *Faust*, sop., ten., ch., orch. (1949); *Cantata secularis*, ch., orch. (1949–51); *3 Fragments from Joyce's Portrait of the Artist as a Young Man*, narr., ch., ens. (1956–7); *Fantasia Concertante*, vn., str. (1943–4); *Elegy*, va., str. (1953); cl. concertino (1954); *Tre Pezzi*, vc., orch. (1956); 3 str. qts. (1924, 1934–5, 1948–51); *Concert piece*, vn., pf. (1953–4); *Improvisation*, ob., pf. (1957); *Permutazione a cinque*, wind quintet (1958); vn. sonata (1960); pf. pieces; and film mus. (notably for Orwell's *Animal Farm*).

Seidl, Anton (*b* Pest (now Budapest), 1850; *d* NY, 1898). Hung. conductor. In 1872 went to Bayreuth where he made first copy of score of *Der Ring des Nibelungen* for Wagner and, in 1876, assisted at first fest. Cond., Leipzig Opera 1879–82. Toured Ger., Holland, Eng., and It. 1882 as cond. of Neumann's Wagner co. Cond. first *Ring* cycle in London, 1882 (Her Majesty's Th.). Cond. Bremen Opera 1883–5. Cond. of Ger. opera at NY Met from 1885. Cond. f. Amer. ps. of *Die Meistersinger* (1886), *Tristan und Isolde* (1886), and *Ring* (except *Die Walküre*) (1889). Cond. NYPO 1891–8. Cond. f.p. of Dvořák's *New World* Sym., 1893. CG début 1897.

Seiffert, Peter (*b* Düsseldorf, 1954). Ger. tenor. Sang opera first with Deutsche Oper am Rhein, Düsseldorf; joined Deutsche Oper, Berlin, 1982. Munich début 1983 (Fenton in *Die *lustigen Weiber von Windsor*). CG début 1988, Bayreuth 1996.

Seinemeyer, Meta (*b* Berlin, 1895; *d* Dresden, 1929). Ger. soprano whose early death was tragic loss. Opera début Berlin 1918 (in *Orpheus in the Underworld*). Sang at Berlin Opera 1918–25. NY début (with Hurok's Ger. Opera Co.) 1923; Dresden 1925–9; CG début 1929. Created Duchess of Parma in *Doktor Faust*, 1925. Notable Verdi singer.

Seite (Ger.). Side, e.g. page of book, end of drum, and side of gramophone record.

Selby, Philip (*b* Nuneaton, 1948). Eng. composer and guitarist. Gui. début Birmingham 1966. Comps. incl. suite for gui. (1965–7); *Symphonic Dance*, orch. (1973); *Fantasia*, gui. (1974); *Rhapsody*, pf., orch. (1975); gui. conc. (1976–7); pf. sonatina (1978); *Isa Upanishad*, double ch., orch. (1979–87); timp. sonata (1980); *Siddhartha (Dance Sym.)* (1981–4); *Logos*, tpt. (1982); *Ring Out Ye bells*, carol (1988); songs and gui. pieces.

Sellars, Peter (*b* Pittsburgh, 1957). Amer. theatre and opera director. Formed th. group Explosives B Cabaret whilst at Harvard Univ. Prod. Gogol's *The Inspector General*, Cambridge, Mass., 1980 in modernist style. Prod. Handel's *Orlando*, Cambridge, Mass., 1981–2 and *The Mikado* for Chicago Lyric Opera 1982. Dir., Boston Shakespeare Co. 1983, producing f. Amer. p. of Maxwell Davies's *The Lighthouse*. Dir., Amer. Nat. Th. Co., Washington D.C., 1984. At Purchase, NY, prod. contemp. Amer. settings of *Così fan tutte* (1986), *Don Giovanni* (1987), and *Le nozze di Figaro* (1988). Brit. début GTO 1987 (f.p. of Osborne's *The Electrification of the Soviet Union*). Prod. f.p. of Adams's *Nixon in China*, Houston 1987, f.p. of *The Death of Klinghoffer*, Brussels 1991, and *Dr. Atomic*, San Francisco 2005; *Saint François d'Assise*, Salzburg 1992. CG début 1995, *Mathis der Maler*; *Theodora*, Glyndebourne 1996; *Idomeneo*, Glyndebourne 2003; *Tristan und Isolde*, Paris 2005. Dir. Adelaide Fest. 2002; art. dir. *New Crowned Hope*, Vienna Fest. 2006.

Sellick, Phyllis (Doreen) (*b* Newbury Park, Essex, 1911). Eng. pianist. Début Harrogate 1933 (Grieg conc.). Duettist with husband, Cyril *Smith. OBE 1971.

Sellinger's Round, Variations on an Elizabethan Theme. Composite work for str. orch. comprising 6 variations on Elizabethan tune 'Sellinger's Round' comp. to celebrate Coronation of Elizabeth II 1953 and f.p. at Aldeburgh Fest. that year, cond. Britten. Composers were Oldham, Tippett, L. Berkeley, Britten, Searle, and Walton. Tippett expanded his contribution into his *Divertimento* (1953–4), the tune appearing in all 5 movts.

Sembrich, Marcella [Kochánská, Praskeda Marcelina] (*b* Wiśniewczyk, 1858; *d* NY, 1935). Polish-born soprano (Amer. cit). Child pianist and violinist. Liszt urged her to study singing. Début Athens 1877 (Elvira in *I Puritani*). Dresden Opera 1878–80; CG début 1880, returning each season to 1884 and in 1895. NY Met début 1883 (the night after the th. opened). Member of Met co. 1898–1909. Sang in concerts to 1917. V. of beauty and brilliance, controlled by superb technique. Taught at Curtis Inst. and Juilliard Sch. from 1924.

Semele. (1) Dramatic oratorio in 3 parts by Handel to text adapted from Congreve's lib. for Eccles's opera *Semele* about Semele's love for Jupiter. Comp. 1743. Classified as 'near opera'. F.p. London (concert) 1744. Contains arias *Sleep, why dost thou leave me?* and *Where'er you walk*.

F. modern stage p. Cambridge 1925, London 1954, CG 1982. Amer. stage première Evanston, Ill., 1959.

(2) Opera in 3 acts by *Eccles to lib. by Congreve after Ovid's *Metamorphoses*. Comp. *c*.1706. F.p. Oxford 1964; London 1972.

semibiscroma (It.). 64th note or hemidemisemiquaver.

semibreve (   ). The whole-note, half the time-value of the *breve and double the value of the half-note or minim.

semichorus. Half-chorus. In some choral works, e.g. Elgar's *The Dream of Gerontius* and Vaughan Williams's *A Sea Symphony*, special antiphonal effect is created by contrasting small group of singers (semich.) with full body, or the semich. alone is used for certain passages.

semicroma (It.). 16th note or semiquaver.

semidemisemiquaver (♬) or **hemidemisemiquaver**. The 64th note, i.e. ¼₄ the time-value of the whole-note or semibreve.

semiminima (It.). The quarter-note or crotchet.

semi-opera. Term denoting type of Eng. Restoration drama in which there were extensive mus. episodes, similar to *masques, perf. only by subsidiary characters. Form was developed by Betterton with *The Tempest*, 1674, an adaptation of Shakespeare's play with mus. by Humfrey, Locke, and others. Another example was *King Arthur*, text by Dryden (1684) and mus. by Purcell (1691). Purcell was also involved in *Dioclesian* (1690), *The Fairy Queen* (1692, rev. 1693), and *The Indian Queen* (1695). Only *King Arthur* was specifically devised as a semi-opera, the others being Betterton versions of earlier plays. Daniel Purcell, John Eccles, and D'Urfey also wrote semi-operas, but early in the 18th cent. the form was superseded by It. opera.

semi-perfect cadence. Perfect cadence with 3rd or 5th of tonic in highest part.

semiquaver (♪). The 16th-note, i.e. ¹⁄₁₆ the time-value of the whole-note or semibreve.

Semiramide. Opera in 2 acts by Rossini to lib. by G. Rossi after Voltaire's *Sémiramis* (1748). Comp. 1822. Prod. Venice 1823, London 1824, New Orleans 1837. Also subject of about 40 other operas, incl. those by Porpora, Vivaldi, Hasse, Gluck, Galuppi, Paisiello, Salieri, Meyerbeer, and Respighi. With exception of Respighi's, all were settings of text by *Metastasio.

semitone. Half a tone. Smallest interval in European mus. On pf., interval between any note and the next, up or down. There are three types of semitone: *diatonic* (same as a minor 2nd); *chromatic* (difference between major 2nd and minor 2nd); and *enharmonic* (doubly diminished 3rd). Diatonic semitone has ratio of 16/15, and two chromatic semitone intervals are recognized

('lesser semitone' of 25/24 and 'greater semitone' of 135/128). These intervals occur between values of chromatic-scale notes conventionally accepted as 'just' or 'perfect'.

Semkow, Jerzy (*b* Radomsko, Poland, 1928). Polish conductor. Ass. cond. Leningrad PO 1954–6; cond. Bolshoy Opera and Ballet, 1956–8; prin. cond. Warsaw Opera 1959–62; cond. Royal Opera, Copenhagen, 1965–8. London début 1968 (LPO), CG 1970. Amer. début (Cleveland) 1970–1. Mus. dir. St. Louis SO 1976–9. Art. dir. RAI orch., Rome, 1979–83. Prin. cond. Rochester (NY) PO 1985–9.

semplice; semplicità (It.). Simple, simplicity. *semplicemente*, simply; *semplicissimo*, extremely simple.

sempre (It.). Always; e.g. *sempre legato*, the whole passage or comp. to be played smoothly.

Senaillé [Senaillié], **Jean-Baptiste** (*b* Paris, 1687; *d* Paris, 1730). Fr. violinist and composer. From 1720 member of Louis XV's court orch. (les violons du roi). Introduced It. methods to Fr. sch. of vn.-playing. Comp. numerous vn. sonatas, incl. 50 for solo vn.

Senesino [Bernardi, Francesco] (*b* Siena, *c*.1680; *d* Siena, by 1759). It. alto castrato. Pupil of Bernacchi in Bologna. Sang in Venice 1707–8, Genoa 1709 and 1712, Naples 1715–16, Dresden, 1717–20. Handel heard him and engaged him for London, where he sang with Handel's co. 1720–8 (singing in 32 operas, 13 by Handel) and 1730–3 when he joined Porpora's rival co. until 1736. Returned to Italy after having made fortune. Created leading roles in 17 Handel operas incl. title roles in *Floridante*, *Ottone*, *Giulio Cesare*, *Admeto*, *Riccardo Primo*, *Siroe*, *Tolomeo*, *Ezio*, *Sosarme*, and *Orlando*, and Guido in *Flavio*, Andronicus in *Tamerlano*, Bertarido in *Rodelinda*, and Lucejo in *Scipione*. Voice was considered more beautiful even than Farinelli's.

sennet. Flourish or longer piece for wind instr. Term used in Elizabethan times, e.g. Shakespeare's *Macbeth* Act III, Sc.1 'Sennet sounded. Enter Macbeth as King'. Dekker's *Satiromastix* calls for 'a flourish and then a sennate'. Also found as *synnet* and *cynet*.

sensibile; sensibilità (It.). Sensitive; sensitivity (the *nota sensibile* is the *leading note).

senza (It.). Without, hence *senza sordino*, or *senza sordini*, without mute(s) of str. instr. In pf.-playing, *senza sordini* means without dampers, i.e. use the right pedal, which throws the dampers out of action and leaves the strs. to vibrate freely.

Seow, Yitkin (*b* Singapore, 1955). Malaysian pianist. Début London 1968. Won Rubinstein prize, Tel Aviv, 1977. Toured Russ. 1985. Recorded pf. mus. of Satie and Janáček.

séparé (Fr.). Separated. In Fr. org. mus., uncoupled.

septet (Fr. *septette, septuor*; It. *settimino, septetto*; Ger. *Septett*). Any combination of 7 performers (usually instr.), or any piece of mus. for such, e.g. Beethoven's *Septet* in E♭, Op.20, for vn., va., hn., cl., bn., vc., and db. Famous operatic septets occur in *Les Huguenots* (1836) and *Les Troyens* (1863) ('Tout n'est que paix et charme').

septième (Fr.). Seventh. Org. stop, same as **flat twenty-first.*

septimole, septolet. See *septuplet.*

septuor. See *septet.*

septuplet. Group of 7 notes of equal time-values written where a group of 4 or 6 notes is suggested by time-signature. See *irregular rhythmic groupings.*

sequence. (1) In mus. construction, the more or less exact repetition of a passage at a higher or lower level of pitch. If the repetition is of only the melody it is called a *melodic sequence*; if it is of a series of chords it is a *harmonic sequence*. If the intervals between the notes of the melody are to some extent altered (a major interval becoming a minor one and so forth, as is practically inevitable if the key is unchanged) it is called a *tonal sequence*; if there is no variation in the intervals (usually achieved by altering not merely the pitch of the notes but also the key) it is called a *real sequence*. If there are several repetitions, some of them tonal and some real, the result is a *mixed sequence*. A harmonic real sequence is sometimes called **rosalia* (some authorities, however, require as an additional qualification for this description a rise of one degree of the scale at each repetition).

(2) In ecclesiastical use the term sequence is applied to a type of hymn which began as one of the many forms of interpolation in the original liturgy of the Western Christian Church. As the traditional plainsong did not provide for such interpolations, special melodies were composed. In the Church's service sequences follow (whence the name) the gradual and alleluia. The earliest sequences were in prose, not, as later, in rhymed verse, and the term 'prose' is still sometimes used instead of 'sequence'. The following are examples of the sequence: *Dies Irae* (now a part of the Requiem), *Veni Sancte Spiritus, Lauda Sion*, and *Stabat Mater dolorosa*.

sequencer. Elec. device enabling a succession of several sounds (together with modifications in each) to be pre-set.

Sequenza (Sequence). Title given by **Berio to series of short aleatory virtuoso works for solo instr. e.g. hp., vn., tb., pf., ob., fl., va., perc., and female v. Nos. II, VI, and VII were later arr. with orch. and called *Chemins I, II*, and *IV* respectively.

Serafin, Tullio (*b* Rottanova di Cavarzere, Venice, 1878; *d* Rome, 1968). It. cond. Played vn. in orch. of La Scala. Début as cond. Ferrara 1898. Turin 1903, Rome 1906, then cond. at La Scala

1909–14 and at subsequent intervals to 1946–7. CG 1907, 1931, 1959, 1960. Salzburg Fest. début 1939. NY Met 1924–34 (début *Aida*), cond. f. Amer. ps. of *Turandot* and *Simon Boccanegra*. Chief cond. and art. dir., Rome Opera, 1934–43 and from 1962. NY City Opera début 1952, Chicago Opera 1956–8. Cond f.ps. in Italy of *Der Rosenkavalier, Wozzeck*, and *Peter Grimes*. Furthered career of Rosa **Ponselle and was encourager of **Callas in early years. Coached and cond. Joan **Sutherland in *Lucia di Lammermoor*, CG 1959.

Seraglio, The (Mozart). See *Entführung aus dem Serail, Die.*

Serban, Andrei (*b* Bucharest, 1943). Romanian theatre and opera producer. Went to NY where his prod. of Chekhov's *The Cherry Orchard* was acclaimed. First opera prod. 1980 *Eugene Onegin* for WNO. CG début 1984 (*Turandot*, joint prod. with Los Angeles); NY City Opera 1983. Prod. f.p. of Glass's *The Juniper Tree*, Baltimore Opera 1985. Art. dir., Nat. Th., Bucharest, 1990–3. Dir. arts centre, Columbia Univ., NY, from 1992.

Serebrier, José (*b* Montevideo, 1938). Uruguayan composer, conductor, and teacher. Mus. dir., Amer. Shakespeare Fest. 1962–4. Taught at Eastern Michigan Univ. 1966–8. Ass. cond., Amer. SO 1962–7. Comp.-in-residence, Cleveland Orch., 1968–70. Works incl. sonatas for solo vn. and solo va.; sym. for perc.; sax. qt.; sym.; *Partita* for orch.; *Variations on a Theme from Childhood*, tb. and str. qt. or orch.; *Erotica*, sop., tpt., ww. quintet; *Nueve*, db., orch.

serenade (Fr.). Evening music. Properly, open-air evening mus. (opposite of **aubade*) such as song by lover outside beloved's window (as by Don Giovanni in Mozart's opera), but a term extended to other meanings. The instr. serenade was developed towards the end of 18th cent. as type of work similar to cassation and divertimento, particularly by Mozart (e.g. his *Eine kleine Nachtmusik*). It was scored for small ens. and sometimes for wind instr. alone, and written in several movts. (midway between sym. and suite). Beethoven's serenades were chamber works. Other fine examples are those by Brahms, Dvořák, Tchaikovsky, Elgar, and Strauss. In Ger., *Nachtmusik* implies the instr. form and *Ständchen* the vocal.

Serenade for Tenor, Horn, and Strings. Song-cycle by Britten, Op.31, being prol. and epilogue (for unacc. hn.) enclosing 6 settings of poems on theme of evening: 1. *Pastoral* (Cotton), 2. *Nocturne* (Tennyson), 3. *Elegy* (Blake), 4. *Lyke-Wake Dirge* (Anon.), 5. *Hymn* (Jonson), and 6. *Sonnet* (Keats). F.p. London 1943 (Pears, D. Brain, cond. W. Goehr). A discarded setting of Tennyson's *Now sleeps the crimson petal*, ed. by C. Matthews, was f.p. in 1987 and pubd.

Serenade to Music. Setting by Vaughan Williams for 16 solo vv. (4 sop., 4 cont., 4 ten., 4 bass) and orch. of passage from Shakespeare's *The Merchant of Venice*, comp. for Sir Henry Wood's golden jubilee as a cond., London, Oct. 1938. Orig. singers were *Stiles Allen, Isobel *Baillie, Elsie Suddaby, Eva *Turner, Margaret Balfour, Muriel *Brunskill, Astra *Desmond, Mary *Jarred, Parry Jones, Heddle *Nash, Frank Titterton, Walter *Widdop, Norman *Allin, Robert Easton, Roy *Henderson, and Harold Williams. Also arr. for 4 soloists and orch., for ch. and orch., or for orch. (1940).

serenata (It.). Serenade. (1) Instr. serenade, as Mozart's *Serenata Notturna* (1776, K239).
  (2) 18th-cent. term for dramatic cantatas which might also be called 'semi-operas', such as Handel's *Acis and Galatea*. In 16th cent. meant a satirical polyphonic comp. of the *villanelle* type. Term first appeared in print in 1560 as the title of one of Alessandro Stiggio's 6-part madrigals.

Serenata Notturna (Nocturnal Serenade). Title of Mozart's Serenade No.6 in D (K239) for 2 small orchs., comp. 1776.

seria (It.). Serious; e.g. *opera seria*, serious (or tragic) opera—as distinct from *opera buffa*, comic opera.

serialism, serial technique, serial music. Terms applied to the 20th-cent. revolution in comp. whereby traditional melodic, harmonic, rhythmic, and tonal rules and conventions were replaced. Serial mus. is that in which a structural 'series' of notes governs the total development of the comp. It originated in *Schoenberg's atonality, leading to his system of composing with 12 notes (1923). This system is based on use of a series of intervals (note-row) involving in turn all 12 notes of the chromatic scale in any order selected by the composer. In its strictest application, no note should be repeated until the other 11 have appeared and the order of the *series* remains unaltered throughout the work, with certain permitted modifications. Schoenberg later broke his own rules and other modifications were introduced by *Berg and *Webern. While the *series* in Schoenberg's hands remained comparable with a theme, in Webern's it was more subtly pervasive and often not perceptible as a given sequence of 12 notes. The next stage in *serialism* was foreshadowed in 1944 by *Messiaen in his *Technique de mon langage musical*, in which he wrote about serialization of durations. By the 1950s several components (parameters) of a work were being serialized by, for example, Babbitt, Boulez, and Stockhausen. With the introduction of elec. media, the scope for serial permutations became much enlarged, in relation to time. By the end of the 1960s, many composers renounced serialism as too restrictive; others, incl. Boulez, questioned its continued necessity because *aleatory developments and new sounds available through elec. means achieve by synthesis the ends of serialism. Whatever the future of serialism, it remains a development which radically altered the tenets of mus. comp.

serinette (from Fr. *serin*, canary). Small hand org. reproducing 10–13 high-pitched notes and formerly used to teach canaries to sing.

Serkin, Rudolf (*b* Eger, Bohemia, 1903; *d* Guilford, Vt., 1991). Austrian-born pianist (Amer. cit. 1939). Début Vienna 1915. Salzburg début 1925. Played in chamber mus. and sonata recitals with the violinist Adolf *Busch, whose son-in-law he became. Amer. début with Busch, Washington DC 1933. Settled in USA. Head of pf. dept. at Curtis Inst. from 1939, becoming dir. 1968–76. One of greatest pianists of his time. Art. dir. of Marlboro mus. fests. in Vermont, which he helped to establish 1950.

Sérly, Tibór (*b* Losonc, 1900; *d* London, 1978). Hung.-born composer, conductor, and string player (Amer. cit. 1911). Taken to USA in 1905. Played va. in Cincinnati SO 1926–7, in Philadelphia Orch. 1928–35 (ass. cond. 1933–5), and in NBC SO 1937–8. Settled in NY as teacher, 1937. Comp. va. conc., 2 syms., chamber mus., etc. Completed last 17 bars of Bartók's 3rd pf. conc. and completed Bartók's va. conc. from composer's sketches, 1945.

Sermisy, Claude de (Claudin) (*b* c.1490; *d* Paris, 1562). Fr. composer and priest. Singer at Fr. Chapel Royal from 1508, and attended Field of the Cloth of Gold 1520. Wrote over 200 *chansons*, many Masses, motets, etc.

Serocki, Kazimierz (*b* Torun, Poland, 1922; *d* Warsaw, 1981). Polish composer and pianist. In 1949, with Baird and Krenz, formed 'Group 49'. Concert pianist until 1952. Co-founder, Warsaw fest. of modern mus., 1956. Began in neo-classicist, folk-influenced style of comp., wrote Webern-type serial mus. in 1950s, developing use of aleatory procedures. Works incl. syms. (No.2 with sop., bar., ch., and orch.); tb. conc.; *Segmenti* for 19 instr.; *Symphonic Frescoes: Forte e piano*, 2 pf. and orch.; *Niobe*, 2 narrators, ch., and orch.

serpent. Obsolete bass member of *cornett family, 8′ long and roughly S-shaped, hence the name. Made of wood, sometimes of metal; had 6 fingerholes and sometimes keys. First introduced in Fr. towards end of 16th cent., where it was used in church to double male vv. Became popular military-band instr. and was in use in Eng. church bands to mid-19th cent. (mentioned by Thomas Hardy).

Serra, Luciana (*b* Genoa, 1946). It. soprano. Début Budapest 1966 (Cimarosa's *Il Convito*). Member Teheran Opera 1969–76. Débuts: CG 1980; La Scala 1983; Amer. (Charleston) 1983.

serré (Fr.). Tightened. With increasing tension and speed, as in It. *stringendo*.

Serse (*Xerxes*). Opera in 3 acts by Handel to anonymous text revised from a lib. by S. Stampiglia for Bononcini's *Il Xerse*, Rome 1694, based on Minato's *Il Xerse* written for Cavalli, Venice 1654. Comp. 1737–8. Prod. London 1738, Northampton,

Mass., 1928. Contains in Act I aria *Ombra mai fù* for Serse, male sop., praising a tree that gives him shade. It is marked *larghetto*, but the tune, in countless spurious arrs., has become known as 'Handel's *Largo*'.

Serva padrona, La (The maid as mistress). Intermezzo (to *Il prigionero superbo*) in 2 parts by Pergolesi to lib. by G. A. Federico after J. A. Neelli's play; prod. Naples 1733, Paris 1746, London 1750, Baltimore 1790.

Service. In mus. sense, elaborate and continuous setting of the canticles from the Anglican prayerbook for morning and evening services, or Communion service. The terms *Short Service* and *Great Service* were used in 16th and early 17th cents. to distinguish between normal daily service and that for an elaborate special occasion. Tye, Tallis, Byrd, Gibbons, Tomkins, Weelkes, etc. all comp. fine services. Later examples are by Walmisley, S. S. Wesley, Stanford, Vaughan Williams, Howells, etc.

sesquialtera (Lat.). One and a half. (1) Org. mixture stop properly of 2 ranks (12th and 17th) but sometimes of 3–5 ranks.
(2) Relationship of 3:2 in mensural mus.

Sessions, Roger (Huntington) (*b* Brooklyn, NY, 1896; *d* Princeton, NJ, 1985). Amer. composer and teacher. Began mus. studies early and wrote opera at age of 13. Mus. faculty Smith Coll., Northampton, Mass., 1917–21, studying privately with Bloch. Became ass. to Bloch at Cleveland Inst. of Mus., 1921–5. Lived in Florence, Rome, Berlin 1927–33. His first sym. (1927) perf. Boston 1927 and at ISCM Fest., Geneva, 1929. Taught Boston Univ. 1933–5, Princeton Univ. 1935–45; prof. of mus., Univ. of Calif., Berkeley, 1945–51; prof. of mus., Princeton, 1953–65. Taught at Juilliard Sch. 1965–85. Pupils incl. Babbitt, Imbrie, and Diamond. Sessions's mus. has been described as 'constructively eclectic', drawing on the chief 20th-cent. influences but retaining a serious individual stamp. Author of several books, and tireless champion of contemporary mus. Prin. works:

OPERAS: *Lancelot and Elaine* (1910); *The Trial of Lucullus* (1947); *Montezuma* (1941–63).

ORCH.: syms.: No.1 (1927), No.2 (1944–6), No.3 (1957), No.4 (1958), No.5 (1964), No.6 (1966), No.7 (1967), No.8 (1968), No.9 (1975–8); vn. conc. (1930–5, with orch. without vns. and with 5 cl.); *Idyll of Theocritus*, sop., orch. (1953–4); pf. conc. (1956); *Divertimento* (1959–60); *Rhapsody* (1970); conc. for vn., vc., and orch. (1971); *Concertino* (1972); *Concerto for Orchestra* (1979–81).

CHAMBER MUSIC: str. qts.: No.1 (1936), No.2 (1951); 3 vn. sonatas (1916, 1953, 1981 (unfinished)); pf. trio (1916); solo vn. sonata (1953); str. quintet (1957–8); *6 Pieces* for vc. (1966); *Canons*, str. qt. (1971).

CHORAL: *Turn, O Libertad*, ch. and 2 pf. or orch. (1944); Mass (1955); *When Lilacs Last in the Dooryard Bloom'd*, soloists, ch., orch. (1964–70).

PIANO: 3 sonatas (1927–30, 1946, 1964–5); *From my Diary* (1937–9); *5 Pieces* (1975); *Waltz* (1977–8).

set. Term normally applied to *atonal mus.*, meaning a small group of notes (a cell or a unit) which the composer or the analyst of the work concerned deems to be of structural significance, e.g. the notes B–C–F in the 4th of Webern's *5 Movements* for str. qt. In a serial work the series or part of it may be considered as the set. And so can the opening notes of Beethoven's 5th Sym.!

Ševčík, Otakar (*b* Horaždowitz, Bohemia, 1852; *d* Pisek, 1934). Cz. violinist and teacher. Leader of orch. at Salzburg Mozarteum 1870–3; début Vienna 1873. Settled in Russia. Taught Imperial Russ. Mus. Sch., Kiev, 1875–92. Prof. of vn., Prague Cons. 1892–1906. Dir., vn. master-sch., Vienna Acad. of Mus. 1909–19. Returned to Prague 1919. Developed special intonation and bowing techniques, set out in detail in his pubd. method.

Seven Deadly Sins, The (*Die sieben Todsünden der Kleinbürger*). Ballet with songs, for sop., male ch., and orch., in prol., 7 scenes, and epilogue by *Weill to lib. by Brecht, choreog. Balanchine. Prod. Paris 1933. New Balanchine choreog. NY 1958.

Seven Last Words of our Saviour from the Cross, The (*Die sieben letzten Worte unseres Erlösers am Kreuz*). Work by Haydn commissioned by Cadiz Cath. 1785 as orch. interludes to separate the sermons on Good Friday. Pubd. in Vienna as 7 *sonate, con un' introduzione, ed al fine un terremoto* (7 sonatas, with an introduction, and at the end an earthquake). In 1787 arr. by Haydn for str. qt. as Op.51, Nos. 1–7 (qts. Nos. 50–6), and also arr. by him as cantata with soloists and ch. (1795–6).

Seven Sonnets of Michelangelo. Song-cycle, Op.22, for ten. and pf. by Britten, comp. 1939–40, f. public p. London 1942 (Peter Pears and Britten). It. settings of sonnets 16, 31, 30, 55, 38, 32, and 24.

seventeenth. Org. *mutation stop; length and pitch 1⅗ sounding 2 octaves and a 3rd (i.e. 17th) above normal.

seventh. Interval in melody or harmony when 2 notes, major or minor, are 7 steps apart (counting bottom and top notes). A up to G♯ is *major seventh*; A up to G♮ is *minor seventh*; A up to G♭ is *diminished seventh*.

Sévérac, (Marie-Joseph-Alexandre) **Déodat de** (*b* St Félix de Caraman en Lauragais, 1872; *d* Céret, 1921). Fr. composer. Mus. (esp. his songs) evokes atmosphere of his native Provence. Wrote 4 operas, 4 sym.-poems, chamber works, pf. pieces, and songs.

Severn Suite. 5-movt. suite for brass band, Op.87, by Elgar, comp. 1930 (using sketches from as far back as 1879) for Crystal Palace competitive band fest. (Brass band orch. from Elgar's piano score by H. Geehl. Rev. edn. (restoring orig. key of C major) by G. Brand, 1983.) Ded. to Bernard Shaw. Arr. for orch. by composer 1932. Arr. for org. as sonata No.2, Op.87a, by I. *Atkins, 1933 (this omits a movt. and contains mus. comp. by Atkins).

sevillana. (1) Seville variety of the Sp. *seguidilla* folk-dance.
(2) Orch. work, Op.7, by Elgar, f.p. Worcester 1884, London 1884 (first Elgar work perf. in London).

sextet (Fr. *sextette* or *sextuor*; It. *sestetto*; Ger. *Sextett*). Performing group of 6 instrumentalists or singers, or work written for them to perform, e.g. Brahms's str. sextets. Schoenberg's *Verklärte Nacht* (1899) was orig. a str. sextet. Janáček's *Mládí* (1924) is a wind sextet. Strauss's opera *Capriccio* (1940–1) opens with a str. sextet. The most famous operatic sextet is the Act II *finale* of Donizetti's *Lucia di Lammermoor* (1835), 'Chi mi frena in tal momento'.

sextolet. See *sextuplet*.

sextuor. See *sextet*.

sextuplet. Group of 6 notes of equal time-values written where a group of 4 notes is suggested by time-signature. See *irregular rhythmic groupings*.

Seyfried, Ignaz Xaver, Ritter von (b Vienna, 1776; d Vienna, 1841). Austrian composer. Close friend of Mozart. Cond. at *Schikaneder's ths. 1797–1826. Wrote over 100 stage works, biblical dramas, church mus., and chamber works. Arr. Mozart pf. pieces as *Ahasuerus* (1823) and Haydn themes as *Singspiel Das Ochsenmenuette* (1823).

sf, sfz. Abbreviation for *sforzando, sforzato*.

sfogato (It.). Airy, evaporated. Light and easy in style. *Soprano sfogato* is a light sop. Term used by Chopin indicating need for delicate touch in his mus.

sforzando, sforzato (It.). Reinforced. Direction that a note or chord be strongly accented or played in a 'forced' manner. Usually found in abbreviation *sf.* or *sfz*. Beethoven made much use of it.

sfp. *sforzando* followed immediately by *piano*.

Sgambati, Giovanni (b Rome, 1841; d Rome, 1914). It. composer, conductor, and pianist. Had Eng. mother. Founded orch. and chamber concerts in Rome 1866, introducing Ger. classics to It. audiences. Toured Ger., Eng., It., Fr., and Russia as pianist and cond. Founder Liceo Musicale, Rome, and pf. prof. Wagner persuaded Schott to publish Sgambati's 2 pf. quintets. Rich melodic gift and one of few It. composers of 19th cent. interested in instr. mus. Wrote 2 syms., *Requiem Mass*, pf. conc., str. qt., pf. pieces, and songs.

Shacklock, Constance (b Sherwood, Notts., 1913; d London, 1999). Eng. mez. Professional début 1944. Member CG co. 1946–56. Also sang in oratorio, notably as Angel in Elgar's *The Dream of Gerontius*. Sang in London prod. of *The Sound of Music* 1961–6. Prof of singing, RAM, 1968–78. OBE 1970.

shake. Early Eng. name for *trill*.

Shakers (Shaking Quakers). Name for members of the United Society of Believers in Christ's Second Appearing, a religious celibate community founded in the USA after 1774 by Ann Lee (1736–84), formerly of Manchester in Eng. They developed their own hymnology, incl. spirituals and dance, and in the 1840s two tunebooks were pubd. giving details of Shaker mus. theory, notation, and tunes. When a Shaker had a religious seizure which resulted in a hymn or dance-tune, a scribe wrote down the tune in a primitive littoral notation. The words of the songs were sometimes in Eng., at others were nonsense, or derived from Indian or Negro speech. *Copland quotes the Shaker tune *Simple Gifts* in his *Appalachian Spring*. Shakers are now almost extinct, but their mus. has been collected and is studied.

Shakespeare and Music. The influence of William Shakespeare (b Stratford-upon-Avon, 1564; d Stratford, 1616) upon composers, from his own time until today, is of such magnitude that a short entry is essential. *Morley comp. songs for the f.ps. of some of the plays. Since then nearly every composer of note has set a Shakespeare song—among the greatest being Schubert's *Who is Sylvia?* Incidental mus. to the plays ranges from Mendelssohn's and Orff's for *A Midsummer Night's Dream* to Walton's for *Macbeth*. Walton and Shostakovich are among those who have written mus. for Shakespeare films. In categories of their own are Berlioz's dramatic sym. and Tchaikovsky's fantasy-ov. *Romeo and Juliet*, Elgar's symphonic study *Falstaff*, and Vaughan Williams's *Serenade to Music* (a setting of words from *The Merchant of Venice*). Operas based on Shakespeare are many. Among them are: Adès's *The Tempest*; Barber's *Antony and Cleopatra*; Bloch's *Macbeth*; Britten's *A Midsummer Night's Dream*; Berlioz's *Béatrice et Bénédict* (*Much Ado About Nothing*); Goetz's *Der widerspänstigen Zähmung* (*The Taming of the Shrew*); Hahn's *Le merchand de Venise* (*The Merchant of Venice*); Nicolai's *Die lustigen Weiber von Windsor* (*The Merry Wives of Windsor*); Oliver's *Timon of Athens*; Rossini's *Otello*; Reimann's *Lear*; Searle's *Hamlet*; Storace's *Gli equivoci* (*The Comedy of Errors*); Thomas's *Hamlet*; Vaughan Williams's *Sir John in Love* (*Merry Wives of Windsor*); Verdi's *Falstaff, Otello*, and *Macbeth*; and Wagner's *Das Liebesverbot* (*Measure for Measure*). Purcell's *The Fairy Queen* is a masque based on *A Midsummer Night's Dream* although no word of Shakespeare's text is set. Bellini's *I Capuleti e i Montecchi* is based on *Romeo and Juliet* but not on Shakespeare's version. Walton's *Troilus and Cressida* is also *not* based on Shakespeare's play and Rossini's *Otello* only slightly.

shakuhachi. Japanese end-blown long fl., dating from *c*.14th cent., made in several types, one having 4 fingerholes, another 7.

Shalyapin, Fyodor. See *Chaliapin, Fyodor*.

Shankar, Ravi (*b* Varanasi, Uttar Pradesh, 1920). Indian sitar-player and composer. Dir. of instr. ens., India Radio, 1949–56. Founder-dir., Kinnara Sch. of Mus., Bombay, 1962. Toured Europe and N. Amer. giving sitar recitals which led to awakening of interest in Indian mus. Wrote opera-ballet *Ghanashyam* (A Broken Branch) (1989), ballet scores, 2 concs. for sitar and orch. (1971, 1976), and film and TV mus. incl. *Gandhi* and *Alice in Wonderland*. Hon. KBE 2002.

shanty (chanty). Sailors' work-song, originating in days of sailing ships, sung while pulling together on a rope and helping to secure rhythmic unanimity. 'Shanty man', placed apart, sang the tune, the rest joining in ch. Tune and words are traditional. Famous examples are *Shenandoah, The Rio Grande, What shall we do with the drunken sailor?*, etc.

Shapey, Ralph (*b* Philadelphia, 1921; *d* Chicago, 2002). Amer. composer, conductor, and teacher. Ass. cond. Philadelphia Nat. Youth Admin. SO 1938–47. Founder and mus. dir. Contemporary Chamber Players, Chicago Univ. 1954. Prof. of mus. Chicago Univ. 1964–85 and from 1986. Prof. of mus. Aaron Copland Sch. of Mus., Queen's Coll, City Univ. of NY 1985–6. Works incl sym. (1952); cl. conc. (1954); conc. for vn., vc., orch. (1983); conc. for pf., vc., str. (1986); 7 str. qts. (1946–72); pf. quintet (1946–7); vn. sonata (1949–50); vc. sonata (1953); brass quintet (1963); *2 for 1*, snare drum (1988); *Concerto fantastique*, orch. (1989); *Movts. of Varied Moments for Two*, fl., vib. (1993).

sharp. (1) As noun, the sign (♯) which, placed by a note, raises its pitch by a semitone. A sharp in the key signature affects all notes on corresponding degree of scale. See *inflection of notes*. (In Amer. usage a note is 'sharped'; in Eng. 'sharpened'.)

(2) As adjective, describes singing or playing which departs from correct intonation upwards (opposite of flat, downwards).

Sharp, Cecil (James) (*b* Denmark Hill, London, 1859; *d* Hampstead, 1924). Eng. folk-song and folk-dance collector and editor, organist, and writer. Trained as lawyer and practised as such in Australia. Org., Adelaide Cath., 1889–92. Prin., Hampstead Cons. of Mus. 1896–1905. In 1899 began systematic coll. of Eng. folk-dances and in 1903 began to collect folk-songs. Though not first in the field, his proselytizing and energy inspired others to emulate him. Founded English Folk Dance Soc., 1911. With M. *Karpeles, collected folk-songs in Appalachian mountains of N. Amer., 1916–18. Pubd. many arrs. and colls. of folk-songs and dances (some in collab. with G. Butterworth, Vaughan Williams, C. L. Marson, etc.). Wrote *English Folk Song* and other books. After his death Cecil Sharp House, in London, was built as headquarters of amalgamated *English Folk Dance and Song Society.

sharp mixture. Org. *mixture stop of high-pitched pipes and bright tone.

Shaw, Artie (Arthur Jacob Arshawsky) (*b* NY, 1910; *d* Los Angeles, 2004). Amer. clarinettist, bandleader, and composer. Played alto sax. at 15 in dance band. Took up cl. at 16. Worked as arranger and mus. dir. for Austin Wylie Orch., Cleveland, until 1929. Toured as tenor saxophonist and went to NY, playing in Harlem. Free-lance musician 1931–5. Formed his own band 1936 and swing band in 1937 which had hit with 1938 recording of Cole Porter's *Begin the Beguine*. Other successful recordings were *Frenesi* and *Concerto for Clarinet* (1940). Played concs. with several sym. orchs. and gave recital at Carnegie Hall, NY. Formed and led several 'big bands' and smaller groups, the Gramercy Five (1940–54). His 8 wives incl. the actresses Lana Turner and Ava Gardner.

Shaw, George Bernard (*b* Dublin, 1856; *d* Ayot St Lawrence, 1950). Irish playwright, essayist, and music critic. Wrote mus. criticism—arguably the most brilliant in the language—for London periodicals, the *Star* and the *World*, from 1888 to 1894 having earlier (from *c*.1876) 'ghosted' for music critic of *The Hornet*. Adopted pseudonym 'Corno di Bassetto', until 1890. Early champion of Wagner's mus. and one of first to put political interpretation on *The Ring* (in *The Perfect Wagnerite*, 1898). Criticisms reprinted in *London Music 1888–9*, *Music in London 1890–94* (3 vols.), *How to become a Musical Critic* (ed. Laurence 1960), and *Shaw's Music* (ed. Laurence, 1981). Friend of Elgar, whose *Severn Suite* is ded. to Shaw. His play *Arms and the Man* was basis of operetta *The Chocolate Soldier* (*Der tapfere Soldat*, 1908) by O. Straus, and his *Pygmalion* became Loewe's musical *My Fair Lady* (1956). Composers of music for films based on Shaw plays incl. Honegger (*Pygmalion*, 1938), Walton (*Major Barbara*, 1941), Auric (*Caesar and Cleopatra*, 1945), and Richard Rodney Bennett (*The Devil's Disciple*, 1959).

Shaw, Martin (Edward Fallas) (*b* London, 1875; *d* Southwold, 1958). Eng. composer, organist, and conductor. Org., St Martin-in-the-Fields, 1920–4. Campaigner for better church mus. and for Eng. opera. Co-ed. with Vaughan Williams of hymnbook *Songs of Praise* (1925, rev. 1931) and *Oxford Book of Carols* (1928). Comp. ballad-opera *Mr Pepys* (1926), anthems, hymns, songs, etc. OBE 1955.

Shaw, Robert (Lawson) (*b* Red Bluff, Calif., 1916; *d* New Haven, Conn., 1999). Amer. cond., particularly of choirs. Founder and cond. Collegiate Chorale, NY, 1941–54. Cond., Robert Shaw Chorale 1948–66. Taught at Juilliard Sch. Cond. San Diego SO 1953–7. Ass. cond. Cleveland Orch. 1956–67. Cond. Atlanta SO 1967–88. One of most gifted of choral conductors and trainers. First prof. cond. in USA to perf. Bach's Mass in B minor and Handel's *Messiah* with small forces.

Shaw, (Harold) **Watkins** (*b* Bradford, Yorks., 1911; *d* Worcester, 1996). Eng. writer, teacher, and musicologist. Lect., Worcester Coll. of Education

1949–71. Hon. librarian, St Michael's Coll., Tenbury Wells, from 1948. Keeper, Parry Room Library, RCM 1971–80. Specialist in church mus. and Handel's *Messiah* (of which he made celebrated edn., 1965). Hon. gen. ed., Church Mus. Soc. 1956–70. OBE 1985.

Shawe-Taylor, Desmond (Christopher) (*b* Dublin, 1907; *d* Long Crichel, Dorset, 1995). Irish mus. critic and author. Wrote literary criticism until 1939, then contrib. mus. criticism to *The Times*, *New Statesman* (1945–58) etc. Mus. critic, *Sunday Times*, 1958–83. Specialist in opera. Author of book on CG 1948. Ed. (with E. Sackville-West) of *The Record Guide* (1951, rev. 1955 with A. Porter and W. S. Mann; suppl. 1956). CBE 1965.

shawm (from Lat. *calamus*, 'reed'; Eng. *shawm*, *shalm*; Fr. *chalemie*, Ger. *Schalmei*). Woodwind instr., double-reeded forerunner of the ob., made in 7 sizes from sopranino to great bass, with keys. Some shawms were described as *bombards*. Had piercing brilliance of tone, with great carrying power outdoors. In Middle Ages, had broad cane reed controlled by player's lips. On largest sizes, reed was placed on end of crook (as in bn.); on smaller, it was placed on a staple inside a *pirouette. All shawms had a number of vent-holes, placed between little-finger hole and end of bell. Modern reproductions have been made.

Shchedrin, Rodion (Konstantinovich) (*b* Moscow, 1932). Russ. composer. Taught comp. Moscow Cons. 1964–9. Specialist in Russian folk mus. of the various regions. Some of his later works use Western *avant-garde* processes formerly frowned upon in Soviet Union. Prin. comps. incl. operas *Not Love Alone* (*Nye tol'ko lyubov*) (1961) and *Dead Souls* (1976); ballets *Little Hump-Backed Horse* (*Konyok-gorbunok*) (1959), *Carmen Suite*, transcr. from Bizet (1967), and *Anna Karenina* (1971); 3 syms. (1958, 1965, subtitled *25 Preludes for Orchestra*, 2000); 2 pf. concs.; Conc. for Orch., No.1, *Naughty Limericks* (*Ozornyye chastushki*) (1963); No.2, *Chimes* (*Zvoni*) (1967); *24 Preludes and Fugues* for pf. (1963–70); oratorio *Poetoria*, for poet, woman's v., ch., and orch. (1968); cantata *Lenin Lives* (*Lenin zhiryot*) (1969); 2 str. qts. (1951, 1954); pf. quintet (1952); 6 pf. concs. (1954–2003); 5 Concs. for Orch. (1963–98); *Anna Karenina*, ballet (1971); *Dead Souls*, opera (1976); *Solemn Ov.*, orch. (1982); *Music for Str.*, *2 Hn.*, *2 Ob.*, and *Cel.* (1986); *Russian Tunes*, vc. (1990); *Prayer (Molenie)*, ch., orch. (1991); *Lolita*, opera (1993); tpt. conc. (1993); vc. conc. (*Sotto voce*) (1994); *Glorification*, str. (1995); Sonata, vc., pf. (1996); *Menuhin Sonata*, vn., pf. (1999); *Duo*, vn. (2000); *Dialogues with Shostakovich*, orch. (2001); *The Enchanted Wanderer*, concert opera (2001–2); *Questions*, pf. (2003); *Concerto parlando*, vn., tpt., str. (2003–4); *Hommage à Chopin*, 4 pf. (2005).

Shebalin, Vissarion (*b* Omsk, 1902; *d* Moscow, 1963). Russ. composer. Prof. of comp., Moscow Cons., from 1935, dir. 1942–8. Relieved of post in 1948 when, like Shostakovich and Prokofiev, was

condemned for *formalism. Reinstated 1951. Completed Mussorgsky's opera *Sorochintsy Fair* 1930. Wrote opera *The Taming of the Shrew* (1946–56); 5 syms. (1925–62); choral sym.-poem *Lenin* (1931); vn. conc.; hn. concertino; 9 str. qts. (1923–63); pf. trio; pf. mus.; and songs.

Sheep may safely graze (Bach). See *Schafe können sicher weiden*.

Sheherazade. (1) Symphonic suite for orch., 'after the Thousand and One Nights' by Rimsky-Korsakov, Op.35, comp. 1888, f.p. St Petersburg, 1889.

(2) *Shéhérazade*, ov. for orch. by Ravel, comp. 1898, f.p. Paris 1899, unpubd.

(3) *Shéhérazade*, song-cycle for v. and orch. by Ravel to poems by Tristan Klingsor (pseudonym of Léon Leclère), comp. 1903, f.p. Paris 1904. Songs are: 1. *Asie* (Asia), 2. *La flûte enchantée* (The magic flute), 3. *L'Indifférent* (The indifferent one).

Shelley, Howard (Gordon) (*b* London, 1950). Eng. pianist and conductor. Début London 1971, followed by int. career. Pf. duettist with wife, Hilary Macnamara, and recitalist with Malcolm Messiter (ob.) and Jane Manning (sop.). Has recorded 1-pf. version of Vaughan Williams's conc. Gave f.p. of complete Rachmaninov pf. works, London 1983. Cond. début London (Barbican) 1985 (LSO).

Shepherd Fennel's Dance. Orch. piece by Balfour *Gardiner, 1910, based on Hardy's story *The Three Strangers* (from *Wessex Tales*, 1888).

Shepherd [Sheppard], **John** (*b c.*1515; *d* 1558). Eng. composer and organist. Org., Magdalen Coll., Oxford, 1541–2 and 1544 to *c.*1547. Member of Chapel Royal in Mary's reign from 1552. Wrote 4 Masses, incl. *Western Wynde Mass* and *French Mass*, also *Haec dies*, many motets and anthems.

Shepherd on the Rock, The (*Der Hirt auf dem Felsen*). Song by Schubert (Oct. 1828, D965) for sop. and pf. with cl. obbl., setting of words by Müller and H. von Chézy put together, presumably, by the sop. Anna Milder who commissioned the song.

Shepherds of the Delectable Mountains, The. Pastoral episode in 1 act by Vaughan Williams to his own lib. based on Bunyan's *The Pilgrim's Progress* (1678, 1684). Comp. 1921–2. Prod. London 1922. Incorporated, with final section omitted, into morality *The *Pilgrim's Progress* (1951) as Scene 2 of Act IV.

Sheriff, Noam (*b* Ramat-Gan, Israel, 1935). Israeli composer. Founder and cond. Hebrew Univ. SO 1955–9. Teacher of orchestration, Jerusalem Acad. of Mus. from 1966 and Tel Aviv Nat. Acad. from 1967. Prof. comp. and cond., Rubin Acad. of Mus., Tel Aviv, 1990–2000 (dir. 1998–2000). Mus. dir. Israel SO 1989–96; Israel CO 2002–5; New Haifa SO from 2004. Works incl. *Songs of Degrees*, orch. (1959); pf. sonata (1962); *Metamorphoses on a Galliard*, orch. (1966); *Chaconne*, orch. (1968); *Cain*, choreog. drama with elec. mus. on tape (1969); *Sonata*, chamber orch. (1973); str. qt. (1973); hp. quintet (1975–6); *The Story of Deborah*, choreog. movement for ch., brass, perc., synthesizers (1976); va. sonata (1976); *Prayers*, str. (1983); *La Follia*, vars. for orch. (1984); str. qt. No.1 (1982), No.2 (1996); *Revival of the Dead*, ten., bar., boys' ch., male ch., orch. (1985); vn. conc. (1986); vc. conc. (1987, rev. 1996); *Sephardic Passion*, ten., alto, ch., orch. (1992); pf. conc. (*Scarlattiana*) (1994); *The Sacrifice of Isaac*, orch. (1997); *Genesis*, soloists, children's ch., orch. (1998); *Sonata à 3*, fl., alto fl., picc. (1998); *Golam 13*, opera, 2006.

Sherlaw Johnson, Robert. See *Johnson, Robert Sherlaw*.

Shield, William (*b* Swalwell, Co. Durham, 1748; *d* London, 1829). Eng. composer, pupil of *Avison. Violinist in travelling orchs. and theatre cos. Giardini heard him at Scarborough and advised him to go to London. Played in orch. at King's Th., Haymarket, 1771–89, first as violinist, then as prin. va. Wrote first opera, *The Flitch of Bacon*, in 1778, the forerunner of 35 more. In most of his operas about one-third of the mus. was borrowed or arr. from other sources. In his first opera for CG, *Rosina* (1782), the ov. ends with a tune orchestrated to suggest bagpipes which later became popular as *Auld Lang Syne*. (He may well have heard the tune in Northumbria.) The song *The Plough Boy*, often thought to be a folk-song and popularized in the 20th cent. by *Pears and *Britten, was comp. by Shield for *The Farmer* (1787), with a piccolo solo as part of the acc. Master of the King's Mus. 1817–29, composing in 1818 the last of Eng. court odes. Comp. str. qts., str. trios, vn. duets, and wrote text-books on harmony (1800) and thoroughbass (1815).

Shifrin, Seymour (*b* Brooklyn, NY, 1926; *d* Boston, 1979). Amer. composer. Teacher at Univ. of Calif., Berkeley, 1952–66 (prof. of mus. from 1964); and prof. of mus., Brandeis Univ. 1966–79. Mus., in intensely chromatic style, uses highly contrasted material. Works incl. 5 str. qts., chamber sym., *Satires of Circumstance* (Hardy) for mez. and chamber ens., vc. sonata, etc.

Shilling, Eric (*b* London, 1920; *d* London, 2006). Eng. bass- baritone. Début SW 1945 (Marullo in *Rigoletto*). Toured as prin. bar. and prod. of Intimate Opera in such works as Hopkins's *Three's Company*, 1948–58. Prin. bar. SW (later ENO) from 1959 for over 30 years. Sang Count Rostov in f. Brit. p. of Prokofiev's *War and Peace*, 1972. Prof. of singing RCM 1964–71. Retired 1994.

Shirai, Mitsuko (*b* Japan, 1952). Japanese mezzo-soprano. Made rapid reputation as concert singer and as interpreter of *Lieder* with Hart-

mut Holl as accomp. Salzburg Fest. début 1984. Opera début Frankfurt 1987 (Despina in *Così fan tutte*).

Shirley, George (Irving) (*b* Indianapolis, 1934). Amer. tenor. Opera début with Turnau Opera Players, Woodstock, NY, 1959 (Eisenstein in *Die Fledermaus*). Won Metropolitan Opera Auditions 1960–1. NY Met début 1961, subsequently opera perfs. in Santa Fe 1963; Glyndebourne 1966; CG and Scottish Opera 1967, Netherlands Opera and Monte Carlo 1976. Noted singer of Pelléas in Debussy's opera.

Shirley-Quirk, John (Stanton) (*b* Liverpool, 1931). Eng. baritone. Opera début Glyndebourne, 1962 (Doctor in *Pelléas et Mélisande*). Joined EOG 1964. Created 3 roles in Britten church parables (1964, 1966, 1968), Coyle in *Owen Wingrave* (tv 1971, CG 1973), and all 7 bar. roles in *Death in Venice* (1973). Sang Eugene Onegin with Glyndebourne. NY Met début 1974. Created Lev in *The *Ice Break*, CG 1977. Sang in *Die Meistersinger*, Edinburgh Fest. 2006. Outstanding interpreter of choral works by Elgar, Tippett, Britten, etc. CBE 1975.

Shnitke, Alfred. See *Schnittke, Alfred*.

shofar (Heb.). Wind instr. made of ram's horn, used in Jewish synagogue rituals, sounding only natural scale. Elgar employs it in *The Apostles* (1903), simulated by brass.

Shore, Andrew (*b* Oldham, 1952). Eng. baritone. Studied theology at Bristol Univ., then turned to singing and directing. Started career with Opera for All (1977–9) and Kent Opera (1979–87). Débuts: Opera North 1985 (King Didon in *Le Coq d'or*); ENO 1988 (Don Alfonso); GTO 1989 (Dr Bartolo); Glyndebourne 1990 (Falstaff); WNO 1990 (Bartolo); CG 1992 (Trombonok in *Viaggio a Rheims*); Paris, Bastille, 1995 (Sacristan in *Tosca*); USA, San Diego, 1996 (Dulcamara); Santa Fe 2001 (Falstaff); NY Met 2006 (Dulcamara); Bayreuth 2006 (Alberich). Sang Falstaff in Vaughan Williams's *Sir John in Love* (ENO 2006). Creator of Ulysses S. Grant in Philip Glass's *Appomattox*, San Francisco 2007.

Shore, Bernard (Alexander Royle) (*b* London, 1896; *d* Hereford, 1985). Eng. va.-player. Studies interrupted by war; on return to RCM studied va., hn. and cond. Also had va. tuition from *Tertis. Joined Queen's Hall Orch. 1922; début as soloist 1925. Prin. va. BBC SO 1930–40. Prof. of va., RCM. Mus. dir., Rural Mus. Schools Assoc. Inspector of Schools and Staff Inspector, Ministry of Education 1948–59. Composer of vn. pieces and songs. Author of notable character-studies of conds. in *The Orchestra Speaks* (1938), also of *Sixteen Symphonies* (1949). CBE 1955.

short octave and **broken octave**. Devices for avoiding expenditure on the lowest and biggest (and consequently most costly) pipes of the organ, and as they were adopted also in domestic kbd. instrs. such as virginals, spinet, and clavichord, the economic motive probably operated in their case also.

(1) Where the *short octave* device was adopted the lowest octave incl. only 9 notes instead of 13 (C, D, E, F, G, A, Bb, B, and C) and these were distributed over 6 long finger-keys and 3 short ones, the omitted notes being those which in the days before equal *temperament were not likely to be needed in the bass.

(2) Where the *broken octave* device was adopted the arrangement was generally the following or something like it. The lowest octave was complete from C to C, except that the lowest C♯ was replaced by a more useful note, the A from below. This device was still to be seen in some Eng. organs at the beginning of the 19th cent.

short score. See *score*.

Short Service. See *service*.

Shostakovich, Dmitry (Dmitryevich) (*b* St Petersburg, 1906; *d* Moscow, 1975). Russ. composer and pianist. Had pf. lessons from his mother at age 9 and later at Glasser Sch. of Mus. 1916–18. Entered Petrograd Cons. 1919, encouraged and helped by Glazunov, and studied pf. with Nikolayev and comp. with M. Steinberg. Completed pf. course in 4 years and made several concert appearances. Gained 'honourable mention' in Int. Chopin Comp., Warsaw, 1927. His diploma work, the 1st Sym., was perf. in Leningrad and Moscow in 1926 and earned the composer world fame at the age of 20. As a convinced believer in Russ. socialism, he sought ways in which his mus. could serve the state. Prompted by the cond. Malko, he wrote for the stage and films, in the next decade producing his opera *The Nose*, the ballets *The Age of Gold* and *The Bolt*, and several cinema scores. These works, particularly *The Nose*, reflect the then-permitted influence of Western *avant-garde* music, but *The Nose* was regarded as a sign of 'bourgeois decadence' and withdrawn from the stage. His opera *The Lady Macbeth of the Mtsensk District* and ballet *Bright Stream* had both been successfully prod. when on 28 Jan. 1936 the opera was savagely attacked in the official Soviet newspaper *Pravda* for 'leftist distortion', 'petty-bourgeois sensationalism', and 'formalism' in an article headed 'Chaos instead of Music' (*Sumbur vmesto muzyki*). This article is said to have been written (or at any rate inspired) by Stalin himself, who had hated the opera. Another article attacking the ballet *Bright Stream* appeared in *Pravda* 10 days later. It almost seemed that Shostakovich's career was at an end, and he withdrew his 4th Sym. after initial rehearsals. His response was his 5th Sym. (1937), described by an unidentified commentator as 'A Soviet artist's practical creative reply to just criticism', a work which became and has remained one of his most popular. Significantly he avoided the stage for many years and between 1938 and 1953 wrote 5 more syms. and 4 str. qts. He taught comp. at Leningrad Cons. 1937–41 and was a fire-fighter during Ger. siege of Leningrad in 1941. From these experiences came his 7th Sym. (the Lenin-

grad), which had a tremendous wartime success not only in USSR but in Eng. and USA, although it is now suggested that the barbaric march in the 1st movt. depicts Stalinist brutality rather than the Ger. army's advance. His pf. quintet (1940) won the Stalin Prize. In 1943 he settled in Moscow, becoming prof. of comp. at the Cons. In 1948, with other leading Russ. composers, he was again in disgrace following the notorious Zhdanov decree against *formalism' and 'anti-people art'. He was relieved of his Moscow professorship and did not resume the post until 1960. He made an official recantation, but his published works from 1948 to 1953 (when Stalin died) were chiefly film music and patriotic cantatas, exceptions being the 24 *Preludes and Fugues* for pf. The first Vn. Conc. (1947–8, rev. 1955), the 4th str. qt., and the song-cycle *From Jewish Folk Poetry* were all withheld from performance until after Stalin's death, and the arrival, under Khruschev, of a relatively and temporarily more liberal political and cultural climate.

In 1953 the 10th Sym. appeared, a masterpiece which is one of several highly personal works using the motif DSCH (based on the initials of his name in Ger. notation). This sym. inaugurates the great final period of his career, 22 years in which he comp. some of his finest mus.—the 10th to 15th Syms., the 6th to 15th str. qts., 2 vc. concs., *The Execution of Stepan Razin* to a text by the poet Yevtushenko, the 2nd vn. conc., the vn. and va. sonatas, and the *Suite on Verses of Michelangelo*. He visited England in 1958 and 1974, becoming a close friend and admirer of *Britten. He had heart attacks in 1969 and 1971 and was in fragile health thereafter.

Many consider that Shostakovich is the greatest 20th-cent. composer. In his 15 syms., 15 qts., and in other works he demonstrated mastery of the largest and most challenging forms with mus. of great emotional power and technical invention. Nearly all the significant features of his mus. are present in the 1st Sym.: sectionalized structures, with themes built up into a mosaic, and frequent use of solo instr. in their highest and lowest registers. All his works are marked by emotional extremes—tragic intensity, grotesque and bizarre wit, humour, parody, and savage sarcasm (the *scherzo* of the 10th Sym. is said to be a portrait of Stalin). He frequently uses quotation, of himself and others. After his illness his mus. seemed preoccupied with death, and the great final works have an extraordinary and alarming power and tension. His admiration for, and knowledge of, Mahler is evident in his symphonic works, and he follows the Mahlerian precedent of juxtaposing the banal and the sublime. His student days in the decade following the Revolution were a time of comparative liberalism in Leningrad and it is evident from his 1st Sym. that he had studied the Western *avant-garde* of the time (Berg, Hindemith, and Krenek). The influence of Berg's *Wozzeck*, perf. in Leningrad, 1927, may be discerned in the *Lady Macbeth* opera. It is apparent now that Shostakovich soon became disillusioned with the Soviet system and that the intensifying darkness and bitterness of his work reflect a spiritual misery connected with external events (his attributed memoirs, published in the West in 1979, give convincing proof of his attitude). The tensions within him produced a succession of masterpieces. Prin. works:

OPERAS: The *Nose (Nos), Op.15 (1927–8); *Lady Macbeth of the Mtsensk District (Ledi Makbet Mtsenskovo uyezda), Op.29 (1930–2) rev. 1955–63 as *Katerina Izmaylova, Op.29/114; Moskva, Cheryomushki, musical comedy (ov. and 39 nos.), Op.105 (1958); The *Gamblers (Igroki), Op.63 unfinished (1941; concert perf. Leningrad 1978; completion by K. Meyer perf. Wuppertal 1983).

BALLETS: The *Age of Gold (Zolotoy vek), Op.22 (1927–30); The *Bolt (Bolt), Op.27 (1930–1); Bright Stream (Svetytoly ruchey), Op.39 (1934–5); The Dreamers, mus. drawn chiefly from The Age of Gold and The Bolt, with some new material (1975).

SYMS.: No.1 in F minor, Op.10 (1924–5), f.p. Leningrad, cond. Malko, 1926; No.2 in B major (October) with ch. (text by A. Bezymensky), Op.14 (1927), f.p. Leningrad, cond. Malko, 1927; No.3 in E♭ (First of May) with ch. (text by S. Kirsanov), Op.20 (1929), f.p. Leningrad, cond. A. Gauk, 1930; No.4 in C minor, Op.43 (1935–6) (withdrawn during rehearsal), f.p. Moscow, cond. Kondrashin, 1961; No.5 in D minor (A *Soviet Artist's Practical Creative Reply to Just Criticism), Op.47 (1937), f.p. Leningrad, cond. Mravinsky, 1937; No.6 in B minor, Op.54 (1939), f.p. Leningrad, cond. Mravinsky, 1939; No.7 in C major (*Leningrad), Op.60 (1941), f.p. Kuibyshev, cond. S. Samosud, 1942; No.8 in C minor, Op.65 (1943), f.p. Moscow, cond. Mravinsky, 1943; No.9 in E♭, Op.70 (1945), f.p. Leningrad, cond. Mravinsky, 1945; No.10 in E minor, Op.93 (1953), f.p. Leningrad, cond. Mravinsky, 1953; No.11 in G minor (The Year 1905), Op.103 (1957), f.p. Moscow, cond. N. Rachlin, 1957; No.12 in D minor (1917), Op.112 (1961), f.p. Moscow, cond. Kondrashin, 1961; No.13 in B♭ minor (*Babi-Yar), Op.113, bass, bass ch., orch. (poems by Y. Yevtushenko) (1962), f.p. Moscow, V. Gromadsky (bass), cond. Kondrashin, 1962; No.14, sop., bass, str., perc., Op.135 (11 poems by Lorca, Apollinaire, Küchelbecker, and Rilke) (1969), f.p. Leningrad, G. Vishnevskaya (sop.), M. Reshetin (bass), cond. Barshay, 1969; No.15 in A major, Op.141 (1971), f.p. Moscow, cond. M. Shostakovich, 1972.

CONCS.: pf.: No.1 in C minor, pf., tpt., str., Op.35 (1933), No.2 in F, Op.102 (1957); vn.: No.1 in A minor, Op.77 (1947–8, f.p. 1955 and orig. pubd. as Op.99), No.2 in C♯ minor, Op.129 (1967); vc.: No.1 in E♭, Op.107 (1959), No.2 in G, Op.126 (1966).

ORCH. (except for syms. and concs., listed above): Scherzo in F♯ minor, Op.1 (1919); Theme with Variations, Op.3 (1921–2); Scherzo in E♭, Op.7 (1924); Prelude and Scherzo, str. octet or str. orch., Op.11 (1924–5); Tahiti Trot (*Tea for Two), Op.16 (1928); 2 Scarlatti Pieces, transcr. for wind, Op.17 (1928); Suite, Age of Gold, Op.22a (1929–32); Suite, The Bolt (Ballet Suite No.5), Op.27a (1931); Suite, Golden Mountains, Op.30a (1931); *Hamlet, suite of

13 movts., small orch., Op.32a (1932); Suite for Jazz Orch., No.1 (1934), No.2 (1938); 5 Fragments, small orch., Op.42 (1935); Fragments from Maxim Film-Trilogy (assembled by L. Atovmyan), Op.50a (1938, 1961); Suite from Pirogov (assisted by Atovmyan), Op.76a (1947); Suite from Young Guards (assisted by Atovmyan), Op.75a (1947–8, 1951); Suite from Meeting on the Elbe, Op.80a (c.1948); Ballet Suite No.1 (1949), No.2 (1951), No.3 (1952), No.4 (1953); Fragments from The Memorable Year 1919 (assisted by Atovmyan), Op.89a (1951, ?1955); Festival Overture, Op.96 (1954); Fragments from The Gadfly (assisted by Atovmyan), Op.97a (1955); Suite in 5 scenes from Katerina Izmaylova (1956); Novorossiysk Chimes (1960); Suite from 5 Days, 5 Nights (assisted by Atovmyan), Op.111a (1961); Overture on Russian and Kirghiz Folk Themes, Op.115 (1963); Suite from Hamlet (film mus.) (assisted by Atovmyan), Op.116a (1964); Chamber Symphony (arr. of 8th Str. Qt. for str. by Barshay); Symphony for Strings (arr. of 10th Str. Qt.); Funeral-Triumphal Prelude, Op.130 (1967); October, sym.-poem, Op.131 (1967).

CHORUS & ORCH. (excl. syms.): Poem of the Motherland, cantata, Op.74, mez., ten., 2 bar., bass soloists (1947); The Song of the Forests, oratorio, Op.81, ten., bass soloists, children's ch. (1949); The Sun Shines over our Motherland, cantata, Op.90, with children's ch. (1952); Fragments from the 1st Echelon, Op.99a (1956); The *Execution of Stepan Razin (Kazn' Stepana Razina), cantata, Op.119, bass soloist (1964).

UNACC. CHORUS: 10 Poems on Texts by Revolutionary Poets, SATB, Op.88 (1951); 2 Russian Folksong Adaptations, SATB, Op.104 (1957); Loyalty, 8 ballads for male ch., Op.136 (1970).

SOLO VOICE(S) & ORCH.: 2 Fables of Krylov, Op.4, mez. (also with pf., 1922); Suite, The Nose, Op.15a, ten., bar. (1927–8); 6 Romances on Words by Japanese Poets, Op.21, ten. (1928–32); 8 English and American Folksongs, low v. (1944); From Jewish Folk-Poetry, Op.79, sop., cont., ten. (1963, with pf. 1948); 7 Romances on Poems of Alexander Blok, Op.127, suite, sop., pf. trio (1967); 6 Romances on Verses of English Poets, Op.140, bass (1971, with pf., Op.62, 1942); 6 Poems of Marina Tsvetayeva, Op.143a, cont. (1973, with pf., Op.143, 1973); Suite on Verses of *Michelangelo Buonarroti, Op.145a, bass (1974, with pf., Op.145, 1974).

VOICE & PIANO: 2 Fables of Krilov, Op.4, mez. (1922); 4 Romances on Verses of Pushkin, Op.46, bass (1936); 6 Romances on Verses of English Poets, Op.62, bass (1942); Vow of the People's Commissar, bass, ch. (1942); 2 Songs (texts by Svetlov), Op.72 (1945); Homesickness (1948, arr. by composer 1956); From Jewish Folk-Poetry, Op.79, sop., cont., ten. (1948); 2 Romances on Verses by Lermontov, Op.84, male v. (1950); 4 Songs to words by Dolmatovsky, Op.86 (1951); 4 Monologues on Verses of Pushkin, Op.91, bass (1952); 5 Romances (Songs of our Days), Op.98, bass (1954); 6 Spanish Songs, Op.100, sop. (1956); Satires (Pictures of the Past), 5 Romances, Op.109, sop. (1960); 5 Romances on texts from Krokodil Magazine, Op.121, bass (1965); Preface to the Complete Collection of my Works, and Brief Reflections à propos this Preface, Op.123, bass (1966); Spring, Spring

(Pushkin), Op.128, bass (1967); 6 *Poems of Marina Tsvetayeva*, Op.143, cont. (1973); *Suite on Verses of *Michelangelo Buonarroti, Op.145, bass (1974); 4 Verses of Capitan Lebyadkin*, Op.146, bass (texts by Dostoyevsky) (1974).

CHAMBER MUSIC: str. qts.: No.1 in C, Op.49 (1938), No.2 in A, Op.68 (1944), No.3 in F, Op.73 (1946), No.4 in D, Op.83 (1949. also arr. for 2 pf. by composer), No.5 in B♭, Op.92 (1953), No.6 in G, Op.101 (1956), No.7 in F♯ minor, Op.108 (1960), No.8 in C minor, Op.110 (1960, arr. for str. orch. by Barshay as *Chamber Symphony*), No.9 in E♭, Op.117 (1964), No.10 in A♭, Op.118 (1964, arr. for str. orch. by Barshay as *Symphony for Strings*), No.11 in F minor, Op.122 (1966), No.12 in D♭, Op.133 (1968), No.13 in B♭ minor, Op.138 (1970), No.14 in F♯ major, Op.142 (1972–3), No.15 in E♭ minor, Op.144 (1974); pf. trio No.1, Op.8 (1923), No.2 in E minor, Op.67 (1944); 2 *Pieces (Prelude and Scherzo)* for str. octet, Op.11 (1924–5); pf. quintet in G minor, Op.57 (1940).

PIANO: sonatas: No.1, Op.12 (1926), No.2 in B minor, Op.61 (1942); 8 *Preludes*, Op.2 (1919–20); 5 *Preludes* (1920–1); 3 *Fantastic Dances*, Op.5 (1922); 10 *Aphorisms*, Op.13 (1927); *Polka (Age of Gold)* (1935, arr. for 4 hands 1962); 24 *Preludes*, Op.34 (1932–3) (No.14, orch. Stokowski); *Children's Notebook*, Op.69 (1944–5); 24 *Preludes and Fugues*, Op.87 (1950–1); 7 *Dances of the Dolls* (1952–62).

2 PIANOS: *Suite* in F♯ minor, Op.6 (1922); *Polka (Age of Gold)* (1962); *Prelude and Fugue* No.15 from Op.87 (?1963); *Concertino*, Op.94 (1953); *Tarantella from The Gadfly* (?1963).

INCIDENTAL MUSIC FOR PLAYS: *The Flea (Klop)* (Mayakovsky), Op.19 (1929); *Rule, Britannia! (Pyotrovsky)*, Op.28 (1931); *Conditionally Killed*, Op.31 (1931); *Hamlet* (Shakespeare), Op.32 (1931–2); *The Human Comedy* (Sukotkin, after Balzac), Op.37 (1933–4); *Salute to Spain* (Apinogenov), Op.44 (1936); *King Lear* (Shakespeare), Op.58a (1940); *Native Country*, Op.63 (1942); *Russian River*, Op.66 (1944); *Victorious Spring*, Op.72 (1945).

FILM MUSIC: *New Babylon*, Op.18 (1928, score missing: suite reconstructed by *Rozhdestvensky, 1976); *Alone*, Op.26 (1930–1); *Golden Mountains*, Op.30 (1931, lost, new version 1936); *Encounter*, Op.33 (1932); *Love and Hate*, Op.38 (1934); *Maxim's Youth (The Bolshevik)*, Op.41 (i) (1934–5); *Girl Companions*, Op.41 (ii) (1934–5); *The Tale of the Priest and his worker Balda*, Op.36 (1936, not released); *Maxim's Return*, Op.45 (1936–7); *Volochayev Days*, Op.48 (1936–7); *Vyborg District*, Op.50 (1938); *Friends*, Op.51 (1938); *The Great Citizen (Part I)*, Op.52 (1938); *Man at Arms*, Op.53 (1938); *The Great Citizen (Part II)*, Op.55 (1939); *Zoya*, Op.64 (1944); *Simple Folk*, Op.71 (1945); *Pirogov*, Op.76 (1947); *Young Guards*, Op.75 (1947–8); *Michurin*, Op.78 (1948); *Meeting on the Elbe*, Op.80 (1948); *The Fall of Berlin*, Op.82 (1949); *Belinsky*, Op.85 (1950); *The Memorable Year 1919*, Op.89 (1951); *Song of a Great River*, Op.95 (1954); *The Gadfly*, Op.97 (1955); *The 1st Echelon*, Op.99 (1956); *Five Days—Five Nights*, Op.111 (1960); *Cheryomushki* (1962); *Hamlet*, Op.116

(Shakespeare, trans. Pasternak, 1963–4); *A Year Like a Life*, Op.120 (1965); *Sofya Perovoskaya*, Op.132 (1967); *King Lear*, Op.137 (1970).

ARRS. OF OTHER COMPOSERS: Scarlatti: 2 *Scarlatti Pieces* for wind orch., Op.17 (1928); Mussorgsky: *Boris Godunov*, re-orch., Op.58 (1939–40, f.p. 1959); *Khovanshchina*, ed. and orch., Op.106, (1959, for film version, f. stage p. 1960); *Songs and Dances of Death* (orch. 1962); Davidenko (1899–1934): 2 *Choruses*, arr. for ch. and orch., Op.124 (1962); Schumann: vc. conc., re-orch. (1963); Youmans: *Tea for Two*, orch. as *Tahiti Trot*, Op.16 (1928).

Shostakovich, Maxim (*b* Leningrad, 1938). Russ. conductor and pianist, son of Dmitry *Shostakovich. Ass. cond. Moscow SO 1963–5. Toured Europe, Japan, USA, and Mexico. London concert début 1968 (LPO). Ass. cond., USSR State Orch. 1966–71, prin. cond. 1971–81. Début as opera cond., London 1979 (*The *Nose*). Cond. f.ps. of D. Shostakovich's sym.-poem *October*, 1967, sym. No.15, 1972, and *Suite on Verses of Michelangelo* (orch. version), 1975. Solo pf. in f.p. of pf. conc. No.2, 1957. Cond. of many recordings of his father's works. Settled in USA 1981. Prin. cond. Hongkong PO 1983–5, mus. dir. Hartford (Conn.) SO 1985–6, New Orleans SO, 1986–91. Amer. opera début, Juilliard Amer. Opera Center, NY, 1984 (*Lady Macbeth of the Mtsensk District*).

Shropshire Lad, A. Book of poems by A. E. Housman (1859–1936) pubd. 1896 which had profound influence on many Eng. composers. Settings of the poems (to the poet's dislike) by, among others, Vaughan Williams (*On Wenlock Edge, Along the Field*), John *Ireland (*Land of Lost Content*), Ivor *Gurney, Graham *Peel, *Somervell, Frank Lambert, C. W. Orr, and George *Butterworth. Butterworth's song-cycle retained the name *A Shropshire Lad*, and he later based an orch. rhapsody (1913) of the same title on a theme from the song *Loveliest of trees*.

Shrubsole, William (*b* Canterbury, 1760; *d* London, 1806). Eng. composer and organist. Org., Bangor Cath. 1782–4 and Lady Huntingdon's Chapel, Clerkenwell, 1784–1806. Wrote hymn-tune *Miles Lane* (pubd. anonymously 1799), sung to words 'All hail the power of Jesu's name' by E. Perronet (1762–92), and others. Subject of famous essay (1943) by Vaughan Williams.

Shuard, Amy (*b* London, 1924; *d* London, 1975). Eng. soprano. Opera début Johannesburg 1949 (Aida). Member SW Opera 1949–55. CG 1954 till death. Fine dramatic sop. in roles such as Turandot, Elektra, Santuzza, and Aida. Bayreuth 1968. Sang Brünnhilde at CG, 1964. Sang Kátá Kabanová (SW 1951) and Jenůfa (CG 1956) in first Eng. stage perfs. Vienna 1961, Milan 1962. CBE 1966.

Shudi, Burkat [Tschudi, Burkhardt] (*b* Schwanden, Switz., 1702; *d* London, 1773). Swiss-born harpsichord-maker who settled in Eng. 1718. Founded own business 1742 to which in 1772 his son-in-law John *Broadwood succeeded. Among those who bought his instrs. were Frederick the Great, Maria Theresia, Haydn, Handel, Gainsborough, and Reynolds. From 1769 Shudi hpds. had the 'Venetian swell', which varied volume by means of louvres worked by a foot-pedal.

Shumsky, Oscar (*b* Philadelphia, 1917; *d* NY, 2000). Amer. violinist and conductor. Début with Stokowski and Philadelphia Orch. 1925 (Suk's *Fantasy*). Joined NBC SO under Toscanini 1939–42 and became leader of Primrose Qt. Début as cond. 1959. Mus. dir. Canadian Stratford Fest. 1959–67. On staff of Juilliard Sch. 1953–81, Curtis Inst. 1961–5, Yale Sch. of Mus. 1975–81. After virtually abandoning concert-platform for 30 years, he gave up teaching in 1981 and returned to clamorous critical acclaim.

Shylock. 6 items of incidental mus. by Fauré, Op.57, for a verse-drama (based on Shakespeare's *The Merchant of Venice*) by Edmund Haraucourt. Comp. 1889. F.p. Paris 1889.

si (Fr.). The note B (see *pitch names of the notes). *si bémol*, B♭, *si dièse*, B♯. Also 7th degree of major scale according to d'Arezzo system. In *tonic sol-fa it has been changed to *te.

Sibelius, Jean [Johan Julius Christian] (*b* Hämeenlinna (Tavastehus), 1865; *d* Järvenpää, 1957). Finn. composer, the nat. mus. v. of his country. In boyhood was called Janne by his friends and later adopted first name of an uncle, Jean Sibelius. Comp. as a child before he had technical instruction. Learned pf. and vn., hoping to become virtuoso of latter. Studied comp. in text-books. Entered Helsinki Univ. as law student 1885, taking special courses in mus. at Cons. and abandoning law in 1886. Studied comp. with Wegelius and vn. with Csillag at Helsinki Cons. 1886–9, being encouraged also by *Busoni, in Berlin 1889–90 (comp. with A. Becker), and at Vienna Cons. 1890–1 (comp. with K. Goldmark and R. Fuchs). Taught vn. and theory, Helsinki Mus. Institute 1892–7. Inspired by nationalist feeling sweeping Finland in protest at Russ. domination, comp. choral sym. for soloists, male ch., and orch., *Kullervo*, based on Finn. nat. epic *Kalevala*. This had great success in Helsinki, 1892, but was withdrawn and not perf. again until after composer's death, when it was found to contain, amid immaturities, many indications of the later Sibelius. In the period 1893–7 he wrote the 4 Kalevala *Legends* about the hero Lemminkäinen and in 1892 the highly original tone-poem *En Saga*, a theme of which was taken from a student str. octet. In 1897 the Finnish state voted Sibelius an annual pension (increased in 1926) to enable him to concentrate solely on comp. His tone-poem *Finlandia*, which became almost a nat. emblem, dates from 1899, the year of his first visit to It. He had by then completed his 1st Sym., which blends Sibelian originality with a Slav romanticism derived from Tchaikovsky. The 2nd Sym. (1902), while

still classical in outline, contains more of Sibelius's individual use of short themes gradually building into a larger whole, his fondness for ostinati, and his predilection for long, atmospheric str. passages (often inevitably likened to the Finnish wind) and for unusual and effective grouping of instr., esp. woodwind. The vn. conc. was written in 1903, its warm middle movt. reflecting the It. visit, and rev. 1905 when Strauss cond. it in Berlin. The 3rd Sym., often regarded as traditional but one of the most original of the 7, followed in 1904–7. It is ded. to *Bantock, one of his earliest Eng. champions. Sibelius first visited Eng. in 1905, conducting the 2nd Sym. in Liverpool. In Nov. 1907 *Mahler visited him in Helsinki and they had a famous conversation in which they expressed their contrasted views of the sym. For Mahler it was 'the world—it must embrace everything'; for Sibelius, it was the 'profound logic creating a connection between all the motifs' and the 'severity of style' which were the attractions. His 4th Sym. (1911) is indeed the antithesis of the Mahlerian symphony, epigrammatic, austere (but not lacking passion), economically scored, the whole work severely concentrated. Its introspective character, like that of the str. qt. *Voces Intimae* of 1908–9, is possibly attributable to his fear that a throat ailment from which he suffered at that period might be cancer. In 1914 he visited the USA, conducting at the Norfolk Fest., Conn., and taking a new symphonic poem, *The Oceanides*. On return to Finland he was isolated by World War I but celebrated his 50th birthday by composing the 5th Sym., later much rev. This work, in the heroic key of E♭ major, is among his most popular works, summing up all the familiar Sibelian characteristics and possessing a strong emotional power. After the war he revisited London in 1921 and in 1923 completed his 6th Sym., the most 'pastoral' and elusive of the set, with modal harmonies and a flavour of his admiration for Palestrina. In 1924 he finished the 7th Sym., compressed into one movt. but with the conventional 4 symphonic movts. easily recognizable. This was followed by incid. mus. for *The Tempest*. Another tone-poem, *Tapiola*, commissioned by the NY Sym. Soc., appeared in 1926. He wrote some male chs., and some pieces for vn. and pf., and 2 pieces for org. in 1931. Thereafter, although he wrote and destroyed an 8th Sym., he never pubd. another note in the remaining 26 years of his life. Yet despite this silence he remained a dominating figure, elevated to heroic status in his own country, in Eng., and the USA, but not in Ger. or Fr. In Eng. in the 1930s he was regarded by many composers as almost the only worthwhile figure in contemporary mus. and this effectively closed Eng. ears to Schoenberg, Berg, Webern, and to a large extent Stravinsky, until a rearguard action was fought on their behalf coincident with Sibelius's death. His reputation then suffered an exaggerated relapse, but a more balanced view of his highly original and rewarding style, particularly in the syms., now prevails. His mastery of the orch. has overshadowed the beauty of his choral works and his songs. Like Elgar, he wrote a good deal of lighter music of high worth and his incidental mus. is among the finest in existence. The picture of him as an ascetic, bleak figure is not supported by the facts of his far from austere life, nor is the mus. the 'cold, forbidding' art which some writers have portrayed. His place in symphonic development is assured, particularly if he is regarded as complementary to Mahler and the late romantics rather than as the antithesis. His songs, too, have been belatedly recognized as superlative examples of his art. Prin. works:

OPERAS: *The Building of the Boat (Veenen luominen)* (1893–4, unfinished. Ov. became *The Swan of Tuonela); The Maiden in the Tower (Jungfrun i tornet)* (1896).

ORCH.: syms.: No.1 in E minor, Op.39 (1898–9, f.p. Helsinki 1899, f.p. in England, London 1903), No.2 in D, Op.43 (1901–2, f.p. Helsinki 1902, f.p. in England, Manchester 1905), No.3 in C, Op.52 (1904–7, f.p. Helsinki 1907, f.p. in England, London 1908), No.4 in A minor, Op.63 (1911, f.p. Helsinki 1912, f.p. in England, Birmingham 1912), No.5 in E♭, Op.82 (1914–15, rev. 1916 and 1919, f.p. Helsinki 1915, 1916 version, Helsinki 1916, 1919 version Helsinki 1919, f.p. in England, London 1921), No.6 in D minor, Op.104 (1923, f.p. Helsinki 1923, f.p. in England, Gloucester 1925), No.7 in C, Op.105 (1924, f.p. under title *Fantasia sinfonica*, Stockholm 1924, f.p. in England, London 1927); sym.-poems: *Kullervo*, sop., bar., male ch., and orch., Op.7 (1892, f.p. Helsinki 1892, f.p. in England, Bournemouth 1970), *En Saga*, Op.9 (1892, rev. 1901), *The Wood Nymph (Skogsrået)*, Op.15 (1895), *Spring Song (Vårsång)*, Op.16 (1894), *Tiera*, brass and perc., (1898), *Finlandia*, Op.26 (1899, rev. 1900, orig. 6th tableau of 'Press Celebration' mus. from which *Scènes historiques* were also taken), *Pohjola's Daughter* (symphonic fantasia), Op.49 (1906), *Night Ride and Sunrise*, Op.55 (1907), *Luonnotar*, Op.70, sop., orch. (1910–13), *The Dryad*, Op.45, No.1 (1910), *The *Bard*, Op.64 (1913, rev. 1914), *The *Oceanides*, Op.73 (1914), *Tapiola*, Op.112 (1925–6); suites, etc: *Karelia*, ov., Op.10, suite Op.11 (1893), *Rakastava*, str., triangle, timp., Op.14 (1911, see also UNACC. VOICES); *Lemminkäinen* (4 Legends), Op.22 (1893–7, rev. 1897, 1900, 1939), No.3 is *The *Swan of Tuonela; King Christian II*, Op.27 (1898), *Scènes historiques I*, Op.25 (1899, rev. 1911), *II*, Op.66 (1912), *Romance in C*, str., Op.42 (1903), *Valse triste*, Op.44 (1904, being rev. of item of incidental mus. to *Kuolema), Scene with cranes*, Op.44 (1906, being rev. of Nos. 3 and 4 of *Kuolema), Vn. Conc.*, Op.47 (1903, f.p. Helsinki 1904, rev. 1905, f.p. Berlin 1905, f.p. in England, London 1907), *Autumn Evening*, Op.38 No.1 (1907, orch. of song), *Dance Intermezzo*, Op.45 No.2 (1907, orch. of pf. piece), *Pelléas et Mélisande*, Op.46 (1905), *Belshazzar's Feast*, Op.51 (1906–7), *Pan and Echo*, Op.53 (1906), *Swanwhite*, Op.54 (1908–9), *In Memoriam*, funeral march, Op.59 (1909), *2 Pieces (Canzonetta and Valse romantique)*, Op.62 (1911, for rev. version of *Kuolema), 2 Serenades*, vn., orch., D

major and G minor, Op.69 (1912–13), *2 Pieces*, vn. (or vc.), orch., *Cantique and Devotion*, Op.77 (1914), *2 Humoresques*, vn., orch., Op.87 (1917), *4 Humoresques*, vn., orch., Op.89 (1917, 2 with str. only), *Valse lyrique*, Op.96 No.1 (1920), *Valse chevaleresque*, Op.96 No.3 (1920), *Suite mignonne*, fl., str., Op.98 No.1 (1921), *Suite champêtre*, str., Op.98 No.2 (1921), *Andante festivo*, str. (1922, orig. str. qt.), *Suite caractéristique*, hp., str., Op.100 (1922), *The *Tempest*, Suites I and II, Op.109 (1925).

THEATRE MUSIC: *Karelia* (1893, unpubd.); *King Christian II* (A. Paul) Op.27 (1897–8); *Kuolema (Death)* (A. Järnefelt) Op.44 (1903, 6 'scenes', str., bass drum, church bell); *Pelléas et Mélisande* (Maeterlinck), Op.46 (1905); *Belshazzar's Feast* (H. Procopé), Op.51 (1906); *Swanwhite* (Strindberg), Op.54 (1908); *The Lizard (Ödlan)* (Lybeck), Op.8, vn., str. quintet (1909, unpubd.); *2 Songs for Twelfth Night'* (Shakespeare), Op.60, v., gui. (or pf.)(1909); *Scaramouche* (Knudsen and Bloch), Op.71 (1913); *Everyman* (Hofmannsthal), Op.83 (1916, unpubd.); *The *Tempest* (Shakespeare), Op.109 (1925).

VOICE(S) & INSTR(S).: *Kullervo*, Op.7 (see ORCH.); *The Rapids-Shooter's Brides (Koskenlaskijan morsiamet)*, Op.33, bar. or mez., orch. (1897); *Song of the Athenians (Atenarnes sång)*, Op.31 No.3, boys' and men's vv., wind, perc. (1899); *Impromptu*, Op.19, women's ch., orch. (1902, rev 1910); *The Origin of Fire (Tulen synty)* Op.32, bar., male ch., orch. (1902, rev. 1910); *The Liberated Queen (Vapautettu Kuningatar)*, Op.48, cantata (1906); *Luonnotar* (see ORCH.); *Scout March*, Op.91 No.2, ch., orch. (?1917); *Song of the Earth (Jordens sång)*, Op.93, cantata (1918); *Väinö's song (Väinön virsi)*, Op.110 (1926); *Masonic Ritual Music*, Op.113, male vv., pf., org. (1927); *Karelia's Fate*, male ch., pf. (1930).

UNACC. VOICES: *Rakastava* (The Lover), Op.14, male vv. (1893, see also ORCH.); *Natus in curas*, Op.21 No.2, male vv. (1896); *10 Songs for Mixed Chorus*, Op.23 (1897, from *Cantata for University Ceremonies of 1897)*; *Carminalia* (1899); *Nostalgia (Kotikaipaus)*, 3 women's vv. (1902); *9 Partsongs*, Op.18, male vv. (1893–1904); *2 Partsongs*, Op.65, mixed ch. (1911–12); *3 Songs for American Schools*, children's vv. (1913); *5 Partsongs*, Op.84, male vv. (1914–15); *In the moonlight (Kuntamolla)*, male vv. (1916); *Fridolin's Folly, The roaring of a wave, Jonah's voyage, One hears the storm outside*, male vv. (1917–18); *2 Partsongs*, Op.108, male vv. (1925); *Introductory Antiphons*, mixed ch. (1925); *The way to school*, children's vv. (1925); *You are mighty, O Lord*, mixed ch. (1927).

CHAMBER MUSIC: *2 Pieces*, Op.2, vn., pf. (1888, rev. 1912); *Malinconia*, Op.20, vc., pf. (1901); str. qt. in D minor (*Voces Intimae)*, Op.56 (1908–9); *4 Pieces*, Op.78, vn. (or vc.), pf. (1915–19); *6 Pieces*, Op.79, vn., pf. (1915); sonatina in E, Op.80, vn., pf. (1915); *5 Pieces*, Op.81, vn., pf. (1915); *5 Danses Champêtres*, Op.106, vn., pf. (1925); *4 Pieces*, Op.115, vn., pf. (1929); *3 Pieces*, Op.116, vn., pf. (1929).

PIANO: *6 Impromptus*, Op.5 (1893); sonata in F, Op.12 (1893); *10 pieces*, Op.24 (1894–1903); *6 Finnish Folksongs* (1903); *Kyllikki* (3 Lyric Pieces), Op.41 (1904); *Dance Intermezzo*, Op.45 No.2 (1904); *10 Pieces*, Op.58 (1909); *3 sonatinas*, Op.67, F♯ minor, E major, B♭ minor (1912); *2 Rondinos*,

Op.68 (1912); 10 *Pensés Lyriques*, Op.40 (1912–14); *4 Lyric Pieces*, Op.74 (1914); *5 Pieces*, Op.75 (1914); *13 Pieces*, Op.76 (c.1914); *10 Pieces*, Op.34 (1914–16); *5 Pieces*, Op.85 (1916); *Mandolinato* (1917); *6 Pieces*, Op.94 (1919); *6 Bagatelles*, Op.97 (1920); *8 Pieces*, Op.99 (1922); *5 Romantic Pieces*, Op.101 (1923); *5 Pieces*, Op.103 (1924); *Morceau romantique* (1925); *5 Esquisses*, Op.114 (1929).

ORGAN: *2 Pieces*, Op.111 (1925–31).

SONGS (VOICE & PIANO): *7 Songs of Runeberg*, Op.13 (1891–2); *7 Songs*, Op.17 (1894); *6 Songs*, Op.36 (1899); *5 Songs*, Op.38 (1903–4, No.1, *Autumn Evening*, with orch. 1907); *Extinct (Erloschen)* (1906); *6 Songs*, Op.50 (1906); *2 Songs*, Op.35 (1907–8); *8 Songs*, Op.57 (1909); *8 Songs*, Op.61 (1910); *5 Christmas Songs*, Op.1 (1895–1913); *6 Songs*, Op.72 (1907–15); *6 Songs*, Op.86 (1916); *6 Songs*, Op.88 (1917); *6 Songs*, Op.90 (1917).

siciliano(a) (It.), **sicilienne** (Fr.). Sicilian. Type of dance, song, or instr. piece, presumably of Sicilian origin, in compound duple or quadruple time and with a swaying rhythm, often in minor key. Usually pastoral in character and popular in 18th cent. 'Pastoral symphony' in Handel's *Messiah* is *alla siciliana*. Style uncommon after 18th cent., but Fauré used siciliano as 3rd entr'acte of his incidental music to *Pelléas et Mélisande* (1898), and 3rd movt. of Walton's *Partita* (1957) is *Pastorale siciliana*.

Sicilian Vespers, The (Verdi). See *Vêpres siciliennes, Les*.

side-drum (snare-drum). Small cylindrical drum with parchment at each end, one having str. (snares) across it to add a rattling effect and thus increase brilliance of tone, other end being left for use of 2 drumsticks. Famous passage for side-drum occurs in 1st movt. of *Nielsen's 5th sym., where player is instructed to improvise in order to drown the sound of the rest of the orch.

Sieben letzten Worte, Die (Haydn). See *Seven Last Words, The*.

Siège de Corinthe, Le (The Siege of Corinth). Opera in 3 acts by Rossini to Fr. lib. by L. Balocchi and A. Soumet after C. della Valle's It. lib. for Rossini's *Maometto II*. Prod. Paris 1826, London 1834, NY 1835. Rev. of earlier opera *Maometto II*, prod. Naples 1820.

Siege of Rhodes, The. Opera in 5 acts with mus. (lost) by Locke, H. Lawes, H. Cooke, C. Coleman, and G. Hudson to lib. by W. D'Avenant. Prod. London 1656. Said to be first all-sung Eng. opera.

Siegfried. Mus. drama in 3 acts by Wagner to his own lib., being 3rd part of *Der *Ring des Nibelungen*. Comp. 1856–7 (early sketches 1851), 1864–71. F.p. Bayreuth 1876, London 1882, NY Met 1887.

Siegfried Idyll. Comp. for orch. by Wagner, comp. 1870 as birthday gift for his wife Cosima and f.p. on Christmas morning 1870, her 33rd birthday, and twice later in same day. F.p. by about 15 musicians, incl. Hans *Richter (who learned tpt. specially for the occasion), cond. Wagner, standing outside Cosima's bedroom in their villa at *Tribschen on shore of Lake Lucerne. Orig. scoring was for a few str., fl., ob., 2 cl., tpt., 2 hn., and bn., but Wagner later scored it for larger orch. Material is based on themes from unfinished str. qt., comp. 1864 when Wagner met Cosima, *motifs* from opera *Siegfried*, on Act III of which he was working in 1869 when their son Siegfried was born, and a lullaby he had noted (or comp.) in 1868. MS ded. stated: 'Tribschen Idyll, with Fidi's Bird-Song and Orange Sunrise, presented as a Symphonic Birthday Greeting to his Cosima by her Richard, 1870.' 'Fidi' was domestic name for Siegfried, the 'orange sunrise' referred to memory of how the sunrise lit up the orange wallpaper on the morning of his birth. The Idyll was never intended for public perf., but financial hardship compelled Wagner to sell it in 1877 and it was pubd. 1878.

Siegfrieds Tod (Siegfried's Death). Proposed opera by *Wagner, lib. of which he wrote in 1848. From it developed the scheme for a 4-opera cycle on the legend of Siegfried and the Nibelung's Ring. *Siegfrieds Tod*, much rev., eventually became *Götterdämmerung* (f.p. Bayreuth 1876).

Siegmeister, Elie (*b* NY, 1909; *d* Manhasset, NY, 1991). Amer composer. Worked in NY as cond., pianist, and teacher. Founded Amer. Ballad Singers 1939 and toured with them for 5 years to promote Amer. folk mus. On teaching faculty at Hofstra Coll. (now Univ.) near NY, 1949–76, becoming prof. of mus. and composer-in-residence 1966. Author of several books. Works incl. opera *The Plough and the Stars* (1963–9); 8 syms. (1947–89); 3 vn. sonatas; 3 str. qts.; pf. conc.; vn. conc.; cl. conc.; fl. conc.; cantata *I Have a Dream*, bar., narr., ch., orch. (1967); *Cantata for FDR*, bar., ch., wind ens. (1981); sextet, brass, perc.

Siems, Margarethe (*b* Breslau (now Wrocław), 1879; *d* Dresden, 1952). Ger. soprano. Opera début Prague 1902 (Marguerite de Valois in *Les Huguenots*). Member of Dresden Opera 1908–22. Created roles of Chrysothemis in *Elektra*, Marschallin in *Der Rosenkavalier*, and Zerbinetta in *Ariadne auf Naxos* (first version, 1912). CG début 1913. Taught in Berlin 1920–6, then in Dresden and Wrocław until 1940. Sang in concerts after Second World War and taught in Dresden.

Siepi, Cesare (*b* Milan, 1923). It. bass. Opera début at Schio, near Vicenza, 1941 (Sparafucile in *Rigoletto*). Member of La Scala co. from 1946. CG début 1950; NY Met 1950; Salzburg Fest. 1953–8. Memorable Don Giovanni, singing it with Furtwängler on several occasions. Member of Met co. for 24 years.

Siesta. Comp. for small orch. by Walton, comp. 1926, rev. 1962. F.p. London 1926. Perf. as ballet *pas de deux*, choreog. Ashton, London 1936, and with new choreog. by Ashton 1972.

Sifflöte (Ger.). Whistle-flute. High-pitched org. stop (2′ or 1′).

sight-reading, sight-singing. The reading or singing of mus. at first sight in order to perform it. Various methods of sight-singing have been used through the centuries, from d'Arezzo's *hexachords* in the 11th cent. to *tonic sol-fa. Most Eng.-speaking countries now use systems based on *movable-doh or *fixed-doh.

signal horn. Another name for *bugle.

signature. A 'sign' placed at the opening of a comp. or of a section of a comp., indicating the key (key signature) or the value of the beat and the no. of beats in each measure (time signature). The key signature consists of one or more sharps or flats; the time signature usually of figures resembling a fraction, e.g. 3/4.

signature-tune. A term which gained currency in the 1920s with the growing popularity of dance-bands, especially when broadcasting. As a means of quick identification, each band began and ended its perf. with a tune, known as the 'signature tune'. Most bands used one tune, e.g. Jack Payne's *Say it with music*, but some used one tune at the beginning and another 'to sign off', e.g. Henry Hall played *It's just the time for dancing* at the start and *Here's to the next time* at the end. Individual variety artists introduced their acts with a signature-tune; and if one wished to be facetious, one could say that the *leitmotiv* of characters in Wagner's *Ring* are their 'signature-tunes'.

Signor Bruschino, Il; ossia il figlio per Azzardo. Opera in 1 act by Rossini to lib. by G. M. Foppa after Fr. comedy *Le fils par hasard* by A. de Chazet and E. T. M. Ourry. Comp. 1812. Prod. Venice 1813, NY Met 1932, Orpington 1960.

Sigurd. Opera in 5 acts by *Reyer to lib. by Du Locle and Blau. Comp. 1866–70. Prod. Brussels and CG 1884, New Orleans 1891. Lib. is based on Nibelung legend which supplied basis of Wagner's *Ring* tetralogy.

Sigurd Jorsalfar (Sigurd the Crusader). Play by Bjørnson for which Grieg wrote 5 items of incidental mus., Op.22, for Oslo perf. celebrating dramatist's 70th birthday, 1872. Titles are: 1. *Borghild's Dream* (intermezzo), 2. *Trial of Strength*, 3. Song: *The Northern people will wander*, 4. *Ceremonial March*, 5. *The King's song*. Nos. 1, 2, and 4 arr. for orch. as Op.56 and rev. 1892 (also arr. for pf. 2 hands and 4 hands). No.2 also arr. for vn. and pf., 1874.

Siki, Béla (*b* Budapest, 1923). Hung.-born pianist. Won Liszt comp., Budapest 1942 and 1943. Début Budapest 1945. Settled in USA. Int. concert career. Prof. of pf., Univ. of Washington, Seattle, 1965–79, Univ. of Cincinnati Coll.-Cons. of Mus. from 1980. Much in demand as juror for pf. comps.

Sikorski, Tomasz (*b* Warsaw, 1939; *d* Warsaw, 1988). Polish composer and pianist. Concert pianist, esp. in contemp. works. Comps. incl. *Concerto breve*, pf., 24 winds, 4 percussionists; pf. sonata; *Diafonia*, 2 pf.; radio opera *Sinbad the Sailor* (1971); *Music from afar*, ch., instr. (1974); *Music in Twilight*, pf., orch. (1978); *Self-Portrait*, orch. (1983); *Homage in memory of Borges*, 4 pf., orch. (1987). Possibly first Polish *minimalist.

Silbermann. Ger. firm of org.-builders, hpd. and pf. manufacturers, founded in Strasbourg by Andreas Silbermann (*b* Klein-Bobritzsch, 1678; *d* Strasbourg, 1734) and his brother Gottfried (*b* Klein-Bobritzsch, 1683; *d* Dresden, 1753). Gottfried settled in Freiburg, building cath. org. there in 1714 and 46 other orgs., incl. Dresden court church. Was first Ger. pf.-maker. Andreas built Strasbourg Cath. org. and 29 others. Business carried on by descendants.

Silent Woman, The (R. Strauss). See *Schweigsame Frau, Die*.

Silja, Anja (*b* Berlin, 1935). Ger. soprano. Solo recital in Berlin aged 15. Opera début Brunswick 1955 (Rosina in *Il barbiere di Siviglia*). Notable Wagnerian (Bayreuth from 1960). Débuts: London (SW) 1963 (with Frankfurt co.); CG 1967; Amer. (Chicago) 1968; NY Met 1972; Salzburg 1971. Hamburg Opera 1974–84. Remarkable singer-actress, especially in Wagnerian roles in Wieland Wagner prods., also as Salome and Elektra, and as Marie and Lulu. Glyndebourne début 1989.

Silken Ladder, The (Rossini). See *Scala di seta, La*.

Sills, Beverly [Silverman, Belle] (*b* Brooklyn, NY, 1929). Amer. soprano and opera administrator. Child performer on radio and later in Gilbert and Sullivan operettas. Opera début Philadelphia 1947 (Frasquita in *Carmen*). S. Francisco 1953; NY City Opera 1955; Vienna 1967; Milan 1969; CG 1970; NY Met 1975. Outstanding in coloratura roles. Retired from singing 1980. Dir., NY City Opera 1979–89. Chairman, Lincoln Center, NY, 1994–2002, Chairman NY Met 2002–5. Autobiographies: *Bubbles: A Self-portrait* (NY 1976, rev. 1981 as *Bubbles: An Encore*), and *Beverly: An Autobiography* (NY 1987).

Siloti, Alexander. See *Ziloti, Alexander*.

Silver, Sheila (*b* Seattle, 1946). Amer. composer. Won *Prix de Rome* at Amer. Acad. Teacher of comp. State Univ. of NY, Stony Brook, from 1979. Works incl. opera *The Thief of Love* (1986); *Chariessa*, sop., orch. (1980); *Dance of the Wild Angels*, chamber orch. (1990); str. qt. No. 1 (1977), No. 2 (1997); vc. sonata (1988); *6 Preludes*, pf. (1990); *From Darkness Emerging*, 2 vn., va., vc., hp. (1995); *Transcending*, bar., pf. (1995); pf. conc. (1996); *Winter Tapestry*, chamber ens. (1998); *Moon Prayer*, 2 vn., 2 va., 2 vc. (2002); *Midnight Prayer*, orch. (2003); *Chant*, db., pf. (2000–4).

silver band. Brass band with instr. coated with substance giving impression of silver.

Silveri, Paolo (*b* Ofena, nr. Aquila, 1913; *d* Rome, 2001). It. baritone. Opera début as bass, Rome 1939 (Hans Schwarz in *Die Meistersinger*). Bar. from 1944 and sang Germont *père* in *La traviata* in Rome. CG début 1946, member of CG Opera Co. 1947–9; NY Met 1950–3. Sang ten. role of Verdi's Otello, Dublin 1959. Outstanding as Falstaff, Scarpia, etc. Teacher in Rome from 1970.

Silverstein, Joseph (*b* Detroit, 1932). Amer. violinist and conductor. Violinist in Houston SO and Philadelphia Orch., then leader Denver SO. Joined Boston SO 1955, becoming leader 1962–83 and ass. cond. 1971–83. Frequent soloist and chamber-mus. player. Won Queen Elisabeth of Belgians comp., Brussels 1959. Mus. dir. Toledo SO 1979–80, Utah SO 1983–98.

Silvestri, Constantin (*b* Bucharest, 1913; *d* London, 1969). Romanian-born conductor, pianist, and composer (Brit. cit. 1967). Début as cond. 1930 (Bucharest Radio SO). Career as pianist until 1935, then coach and cond. Bucharest Opera 1935–60 (mus. dir. from 1955). Cond., Bucharest PO 1947–53. Prof. of cond. Bucharest Acad. of Mus. 1949. Went to Paris 1956, settled in London 1957. Cond. Bournemouth SO 1961–9. CG début 1963. Wrote orch. and chamber music.

similar motion. When any 2 vv. or parts of a comp. proceed notationally in the same direction they are in *similar motion*. If the procession is by the same intervals (numerically considered), it is called *parallel motion*.

simile, simili (It.). The same. Composer's direction in score to indicate that phrase, etc., is to be perf. in same manner as parallel preceding phrase, thus avoiding copying expression marks at each repetition.

Simionato, Giulietta (*b* Forlì, 1910). It. mezzo-soprano. Winner of Bel Canto Comp., Florence 1933. Operatic début in Montagnana 1928 (Lola in *Cavalleria rusticana*). Sang in f.p. of Pizzetti's *Orséolo* (Florence 1935). La Scala début 1936, regular member of company 1939–66. Sang at first Edinburgh Fest. 1947. CG début 1953; Amer. début (S. Francisco) 1953; Chicago 1954–61; NY Met 1959–63; Salzburg Fest. début 1957. A wide range and agility enabled her to sing brilliant Rossini, Bellini, and Donizetti roles. Retired 1966.

Simmes, William (*fl.* 1607–16). Eng. composer of viol fantasies, anthems, etc.

Simon, Abbey (*b* NY, 1922). Amer. pianist. Recital début NY 1940. Lived in Europe 1949–59. Int. career as conc. soloist. Taught at Indiana Univ. Sch. of Mus., Bloomington, 1960–74 and Juilliard Sch. and Univ. of Houston from 1977.

Simon Boccanegra. Opera in prol. and 3 acts by Verdi to lib. by Piave and Montanelli, based on play *Simón Boccanegra* by Gutiérrez. Comp.

1856–7. Prod. Venice 1857. Lib. rev. by Boito 1880, Verdi revising the score and composing new council chamber scene (Act I, Sc. 2). Prod. Milan 1881, NY Met 1932, London (SW) 1948.

Simoneau, Léopold (*b* Saint-Flavien, Quebec, 1916; *d* Victoria, BC, 2006). Canadian tenor. Opera début Montreal 1941 (Hadji in *Lakmé*). Début, Opéra Comique, Paris, and Opéra, 1949. Glyndebourne début 1951; Chicago Opera 1954; Salzburg Fest. 1956; NY Met 1963. Noted Mozartian. Art. dir. L'Opéra du Quebec 1971–2. Trans. Reynaldo Hahn's *Du chant* (*On Singers and Singing*, 1990) and from 1990 wrote opera surtitles in Eng. and Fr.

Simonov, Yury (Ivanovich) (*b* Saratov, 1941). Russ. conductor. Won 5th int. cond. competition, Rome, 1969. Cond. Kislovodsk Phil. Soc. 1967–9, ass. cond. Leningrad PO 1968–9, Bolshoy Opera, Moscow, 1969 (début in *Aida*), chief cond. 1970–85. Prof. of cond., Moscow Cons. 1978–91. NY Met 1975 (with Bolshoy co.); CG début 1982. Chief. cond. Bulgarian Nat. Orch. 1994–2002, Moscow PO from 1998.

Simple Gifts (or The Gift to be Simple). *Shaker hymn, probably comp. 1848 in Shaker community in Alfred, Maine, by Joseph Brackett (1797–1882). Quoted by Copland in *Appalachian Spring*; he also arr. it in his first set of *Old American Songs* (1950).

Simple Symphony. 4-movt. work for str. orch. (or str. qt.), Op.4, by Britten, based on themes he wrote in 1923, 1924, 1925, and 1926 and re-scored in 1933–4. Movts. are named: *Boisterous Bourrée, Playful Pizzicato, Sentimental Saraband, Frolicsome Finale*. F.p. Norwich, 1934, cond. Britten.

simple time (duple, triple, quadruple, etc.). Time in which each beat in a measure has a simple note value, e.g. 3/4 means 3 quarter-note (crotchet) beats in a measure, 4/2 means four half-notes (minims) in a measure. Each beat has two equal subdivisions. See also *compound time* and *time signature*.

Simpson, Robert (Wilfred Levick) (*b* Leamington, 1921; *d* Tralee, Co. Kerry, 1997). Eng. composer, musicologist, and author. On BBC mus. staff 1951–80. Author of *Carl Nielsen, Symphonist* (1952), *Bruckner and the Symphony* (1960), *Sibelius and Nielsen* (1965), *The Essence of Bruckner* (1966, rev. 1978), *The Beethoven Symphonies* (1970), *The Proms and Natural Justice* (1981). Awarded Nielsen Medal (1956) and Bruckner Medal (1962). Works firmly based in tonality, with Beethoven as model for organic unity. Prin. works:

ORCH.: syms.: No.1 (1951), No.2 (1956), No.3 (1962), No.4 (1972), No.5 (1972), No.6 and No.7 (1977), No.8 (1981), No.9 (1985–7), No.10 (1988), No.11 (1990); vn. conc. (1959); pf. conc. (1967); fl. conc. (1989); vc. conc. (1991); *Allegro deciso*, str. (1954); *Variations on a Theme of Carl Nielsen* (1983); *Variations and Fugue on a Theme of Bach*, str. (1991); vc. conc. (1991).

INCIDENTAL MUSIC: *The Pretenders* (Ibsen) (1965); *Samson Agonistes* (Milton) (1974).

BRASS BAND: *Canzona*, brass (1958); *Energy*, symphonic study (1971); *Volcano* (1979); *The Four Temperaments* (1983); *Introduction and Allegro on a Bass by Max Reger* (1987); *Vortex* (1989); quintet (1989).

CHAMBER MUSIC: str. qts.: No.1 (1952), No.2 (1953), No.3 (1954), No.4 (1973), No.5 (1974), No.6 (1975), No.7 (1977), No.8 (1982), No.9 (*Variations on a Theme of Haydn*) (1982), No.10 (1983), No.11 (1984), No.12 (1987), No.13 (1989), No.14 (1990), No.15 (1991); *Variations and Fugue*, recorder, str. qt. (1959); trio, cl., vc., pf. (1967); cl. quintet (1968); qt., hn., vn., vc., pf. (1975); quintet, cl., bcl., str. trio (1981); hn. trio (1984); vn. sonata (1984); str. trio (1987); str. quintet No. 1 (1987), No. 2 (1995); pf. trio (1988-9).

CHORAL: *Media morte in vita sumus* (1975); *Tempi*, unacc. mixed ch. (1985).

PIANO: sonata (1946); *Variations and Finale on a Theme of Haydn* (1948); 2-pf. sonata (1979); *Variations and Finale on a Theme of Beethoven* (1990).

ORGAN: *Eppur si muove* (*Ricercar e Passacaglia*) (1985).

Simrock, Nikolaus (*b* Mainz, 1751; *d* Bonn, 1832). Ger. publisher. Played hn. in Bonn court orch. with Beethoven. Founded publishing firm 1793 in Bonn, issuing many of Beethoven's works. Business continued by son and grandson. Firm moved to Berlin 1870. Publishers of Brahms's mus. Branches opened in London and Paris. Sold to Benjamin, of Hamburg, 1929.

Sin' (It.). Abbreviation of **sino*, until, e.g. *sin' al segno*, until the sign.

Sinatra, Frank [Francis] (Albert) (*b* Hoboken, NJ, 1915; *d* Los Angeles, 1998). Amer. singer (light baritone) and actor. Radio début 1938. Sang with Harry James Band (1939) and Tommy Dorsey Band (1940-2). Solo career from 1942, with radio shows. Inspired excitement among 'bobbysoxers' of 1940s unequalled until advent of Elvis Presley and Beatles. Had successful career as 'straight' film actor, e.g. *From Here to Eternity* (1952), *Von Ryan's Express* (1965), and *The Detective* (1968). Resumed vocal career and made international tours in 1970s. Secret of his artistry was his emphasis on a song's lyrics.

Sinclair, George (Robertson) (*b* Croydon, 1863; *d* Birmingham, 1917). Eng. organist and conductor. Ass. organist, Gloucester Cath. 1879. Org. and choirmaster, Truro Cath., 1880-9. Org., Hereford Cath., 1889-1917, cond. at 3 Choirs Fest. 1891-1912. Cond. Birmingham Choral Union 1899-1917. Friend and champion of Elgar, who incl. him as the 11th (G.R.S.) of **Enigma Variations* (though the mus. is really about Sinclair's bulldog Dan).

Sinding, Christian (August) (*b* Kongsberg, Norway, 1856; *d* Oslo, 1941). Norweg. composer and pianist. Lived in Oslo from 1884 apart from spell as teacher at Eastman Sch. 1921-2. Life pension from Norweg. Govt. 1910. Works incl. operas; 4 syms. (1880-1936); 3 vn. concs.; pf. conc.; pf. quintet; 2 str. qts.; 4 vn. sonatas; 3 pf. trios; over 200 songs; and many pf. pieces, incl. famous **Rustle of Spring* (*Frühlingsrauschen*), No.3 of 6 *Pieces*, Op.32 (1896).

sinfonia (It.). Symphony. (1) Symphony.

(2) Bach's term for his 3-part inventions.

(3) Name given in Baroque period to orch. piece which served as 3-movt. introduction to opera, suite, or cantata, i.e. an early form of ov. Operatic *sinfonia* standardized *c.*1690 by A. Scarlatti into so-called 'Italian overture'.

(4) In 20th cent., often means a chamber orch., e.g. Northern Sinfonia, English Sinfonia.

Sinfonia Antartica (Antarctic Symphony). Title given by **Vaughan Williams to his 7th sym. for orch., sop. solo, and women's ch. Comp. 1949-52. F.p. Manchester 1953 (Hallé Orch. cond. Barbirolli). Work based on mus. composed 1947-8 for film *Scott of the Antarctic*, about Capt. Scott's last expedition to S. Pole, 1910-12. Score contains parts for wind-machine and organ.

Sinfonia concertante. Term preferred to conc. by Haydn, Mozart, and others, for comp. for more than one solo instr. and orch., e.g. Mozart's for vn. and va. In 20th cent. Walton, Williamson, and others have used the term even where only one solo instr. is employed, to imply that solo part is more closely integrated with orch. than in a 'display' conc.

Sinfonia da Requiem. Orch. work in 3 movts., Op.20, by Britten, comp. 1940 in memory of his parents. F.p. NY 1941, London 1942. Commissioned by Japanese Govt. to celebrate (spurious) 2,600th anniversary of Mikado's dynasty in 1940, and rejected because of work's reference to terms from RC liturgy. Autograph score discovered in Japan in 1987. Britten revised *finale* in providing new full score for NY première. F.p. orig. vers., Birmingham 1989, cond. Rattle.

Sinfonia eroica (Beethoven). See *Eroica Symphony*.

Sinfonia Espansiva (Expansive Symphony). Sub-title of Nielsen's 3rd Sym., Op.27, comp. 1910-11. F.p. Copenhagen 1912, cond. Nielsen; f. Eng. p. 1937 (broadcast), London (public) 1962. Sop. and bar. solo vv. used.

Sinfonia Sacra. Sym. (No. 3) by **Panufnik, comp. 1963, f.p. Monte Carlo, cond. Frémaux 1964.

Sinfonia Semplice (Simple Symphony). Sub-title of Nielsen's 6th sym., Op. posth., comp. 1924-5. F.p. Copenhagen 1925, cond. Nielsen; f.p. in England 1954.

sinfonietta (It.). Little symphony. (1) Short, and perhaps light, sym., e.g. those by Moeran, Roussel, and Janáček, whose *Sinfonietta* (1926) has a special brass ens. of 9 tpts., 2 ten. tubas, and 2 bass tpts., with 2 pairs of timpani. In finale 12 tpts. are used.

(2) Small sym. orch., such as Bournemouth Sinfonietta, London Sinfonietta, etc.

Singakademie (Ger.). Singing-school. Choir founded in Berlin 1791 by *Fasch. Mendelssohn cond. it in 1829 revival of Bach's *St Matthew Passion*. Name has been appropriated by other choirs.

singing. Mus.-making by the human v. either solo or with others. Styles of singing and methods of v. prod. have varied over the centuries. In 14th and 15th cents., use of *falsetto* was favoured, hence high range of much mus. of that era; in 17th and 18th cents., the *castrati* imparted special brilliance, purity, and flexibility to operatic roles, qualities inherited by the *bel canto* singers of early 19th cent. opera (Bellini, Donizetti, Rossini, etc.). In the 19th cent. the growing expressive and dramatic nature of mus., e.g. the works of Beethoven, Berlioz, Verdi, Wagner, led to a new style of singing in which vocal characterization was regarded as of more importance than mere technical agility. In 20th cent., with jazz, *Sprechstimme*, and a host of effects required by *avant-garde* composers, the demands on singers' virtuosity and versatility became even heavier. At the same time, revival of interest in early and baroque mus. restored styles of earlier centuries.

singing saw. Ordinary handsaw held between player's knees and played on by a vn. bow (or, more rarely, struck with a drumstick); its blade is meanwhile bent, under a lesser or greater tension, by the player's left hand, so producing different pitches.

Singspiel (Ger.). Song-play. Type of opera, Ger. equivalent of *dramma per musica*, which developed *c*.1700, term orig. being applied to all operas. From *c*.1750, *Singspiel* implied an opera with spoken dialogue, comparable to Eng. ballad-opera and Fr. *opéra-comique*, e.g. those by Hiller and Benda. Zenith was reached with Mozart's *Die Entführung aus dem Serail*, 1782 and *Die Zauberflöte*, 1791. Beethoven's *Fidelio* is technically a *Singspiel*, but term generally implies a comic or light subject.

Sinigaglia, Leone (*b* Turin, 1868; *d* Turin, 1944). It. composer. Rare among It. composers of his day in writing no opera. Wrote mainly instr. works, incl. orch. variations, *Romanza e umoresca* for vc. and orch., chamber mus., choral pieces, and songs.

sinistra (It.). Left (hand).

Sink-a-Pace (from Fr. *cinque-pace*). Name by which orig. 5-step form of *galliard* was known.

sino (It.). Until. *sin' al fine*, until the end; *sin' al segno*, until the sign, etc.

Sinopoli, Giuseppe (*b* Venice, 1946; *d* Berlin, 2001). It. composer and conductor. Attended Darmstadt summer courses 1968. Founded Bruno

Maderna Ens., Venice, 1975, to play contemp. mus. Début Royan Fest. 1975. Opera début La Fenice, Venice, 1978 (*Aida*). CG début 1983; NY Met début 1985; Bayreuth début 1985. Prin. cond. and mus. dir. Philharmonia Orch. 1984–94 (Salzburg concert début 1990); mus. dir. Deutsche Oper, Berlin, from 1990. Works incl. opera *Lou Salomé* (1981); pf. conc. (1974–5); *Symphonic Imaginaire* for 3 solo vv., 10 children's vv., 3 ch., 3 orch. (1972–3); pf. sonata (1973–5); str. qt. (1977).

Sir John in Love. Opera in 4 acts by Vaughan Williams to his own lib. based on Shakespeare's *The Merry Wives of Windsor* (1600–1), with interpolations from other Elizabethan dramatists. Comp. 1924–8. Score quotes several folk-songs, incl. *Greensleeves*, which is sung by Mrs. Ford in Act III. Prod. London (RCM) 1929, NY (Columbia Univ.) 1949, London (SW) 1946, ENO 2006. See also *In Windsor Forest*.

Sir Roger de Coverley. Eng. country dance to tune of uncertain orig. (being variant of *The Maltman*, a Scottish tune sometimes called *Roger the Cavalier*). First printed by Playford, 1685. Arrs. by Grainger, Bridge, etc.

sistrum. Ancient type of rattle used in worship of goddess Isis, comprising rings or bells which jingled on a metal frame when shaken by handle. Sometimes called for by 19th-cent. composers.

sitar. Indian long-necked lute, with 18 movable frets and wooden body. Orig. had 3 str., but 4 to 7 now common (5 melody and 2 drone if the latter). Nine to 13 or more sympathetic under-str. increase resonance. Played with plectrum worn on right forefinger or with finger-nails. Popularized outside India in 1950s by virtuosity of Ravi *Shankar.

Sitkovetsky, Dmitry (*b* Baku, 1954). Russ.-born Amer. violinist. Son of Julian Sitkovetsky, violinist, and Bella Davidovich, pianist. Won Kreisler comp. Vienna 1979. Début 1980 (Berlin PO). Amer. début 1983; Salzburg Fest. 1985; London 1986 (Proms).

Six, Les (Fr.). The Six. Name applied by Fr. mus. critic Henri Collet in 1920 to group of young Fr. composers who, under influence of *Satie and Cocteau, had achieved notoriety for their advanced ideas. They were Auric, Durey, Honegger, Milhaud, Poulenc, and Tailleferre. However, they soon went their separate ways and did not long operate as a group.

Six Épigraphes Antiques (6 Ancient Inscriptions). Set of pf. duets by Debussy, comp. 1914. 1. *Pour invoquer Pan, dieu du vent d'été* (To invoke Pan, god of the summer wind); 2. *Pour un tombeau sans nom* (For a nameless tomb); 3. *Pour que la nuit soit propice* (That night may be propitious); 4. *Pour la danseuse aux crotales* (For the dancing girl with castanets); 5. *Pour l'Égyptienne* (For the Egyptian girl); 6. *Pour remercier la pluie du matin* (To thank the morning rain). Orch. versions by Rudolf Escher (1976–7) and Erich Schmid.

six-four chord. 2nd *inversion of a chord, e.g. C major chord with G in bass.

sixteenth note. The note ♪ (semiquaver). Its rest is notated ♪.

sixth. Interval in melody or harmony, encompassing 6 degrees of the major or minor scale, counting bottom and top notes. *Major 6th* is distance, for instance, from C up to A, *minor 6th* (semitone less) from C up to A♭, *augmented 6th* (semitone more) from C up to A♯. See *Neapolitan 6th*.

sixty-fourth note. The note ♪ (hemidemisemiquaver). Rest is notated ♪.

sizzle cymbal. Cymbal with 5 or 6 small jingles (sizzlers) loosely attached to its upper surface. Played with special type of side-drumstick.

Skalkottas, Nikolaos [Nikos] (*b* Chalkis, 1904; *d* Athens, 1949). Greek composer and violinist. Studied in Athens and then in Berlin. Returned to Gr. 1933, where his mus. attracted little attention and he comp. mainly in secret, working as back-desk orch. violinist. Collected Greek folk mus. After his death, committee was formed to promote interest in and publication of his mus., much of which was written in the 12-note system, but after 1938 was often freely atonal. Works incl.:

ORCH.: *Symphonic Suite* No.1 (1929, rev. 1935), No.2 (1944, orch. 1946–9); conc. for wind (1929); conc., pf., vn. (1929–30); pf. concs.: No.1 (1931), No.2 (1937–8), No.3, 10 winds, perc. (1939); *36 Greek Dances* (1933–6); *9 Greek Dances*, large wind orch. (transcr. from *36 Greek Dances*, 1936); vc. conc. (1937–8); *The Maid and Death*, ballet suite (1938); vn. conc. (1937–8); conc., vn., va., large wind orch. (1939–40); *10 Sketches*, orch. (1940); db. conc. (1942–3); *Little Suite*, str. (1942); *The Return of Ulysses* (1942–3); conc., 2 vn. (1944–5); *5 Short Greek Dances* (1946); *Classical Symphony in A*, wind (1947); *Sinfonietta in B♭* (1948); *Ballet Suite* (1948); *The Sea*, ballet (1949); Pf. Concertino in C (1949).

CHORAL, etc.: *The Unknown Soldier* (1949); *The Mayday Spell*, narrator, sop., dancers, orch. (1944–9).

CHAMBER MUSIC: str. qt. (1923–24); str. qts.: No.1 (1928), No.2 (1929), No.3 (1935), No.4 (1940); *Easy Str. Qt.* (1929); str. trio (1923–4); sonata, solo vn. (1925); vn. sonatinas, No.1 (1928), No.2 (1929), Nos. 3 and 4 (1935); vn. sonata No.1 (1928), No.2 (1940); octet, 4 ww., str. qt. (1931); *Piece*, 8 ww. or double str. qt. (1931); pf. trio (1936); *March of the Little Soldiers*, vn., pf. (1937–8); *Rondo*, vn., pf. (1936); *Little Chorale and Fugue*, vn., pf. (1936); *8 Variations on a Greek Theme*, pf. trio (1938); *Suite*, vc., pf. (1938); vc. sonata (1938); concertino, ob., pf. (1939); *Duo*, vn., pf. (1938); *Largo*, vc., pf. (1941–2); Qt., pf., winds, No.1 (1941–3), No.2 (1941–3); concertino, tpt., pf. (1940–2); *Sonate concertante*, bn., pf. (1943); *Little Suite*, vn., pf., No.1 (1946), No.2 (1949); *Echo*, hp. (1947); *Duo*, vn., vc.

(1947); *Bolero*, vc., pf. (1945); *Little Serenade*, vc., pf. (1945); vc. sonatina (1949); *Tender Melody*, vc., pf. (1949).

VOICE(S) & PIANO: *Sometime* (1939); *The Moon* (1942); *16 Songs* (poems by Evelpidis) (1941).

PIANO: *Greek Suite* (1924); *Suite*, 2 pf. (1924); *Sonatina* (1927); *15 Little Variations* (1927); *10 Canons* (1936); *32 Pieces* (1940); *Piano Suites*, No.1 (1936), Nos. 2, 3, and 4 (1940); *4 Études* (1940).

sketch (Ger. *Skizze*; Fr. *esquisse*). (1) Short piece, usually for pf. and often pictorial in intention, e.g. 'Woodland Sketch'.
(2) Composer's preliminary jottings, out of which work is built, of great fascination to mus. scholars as showing workings of composer's mind (e.g. Beethoven's sketchbooks show how a comp. went through many stages over several years).

Skrowaczewski, Stanisław (*b* Lwów, 1923). Polish-born conductor and composer (Amer. cit. 1963). Early career as pianist until injury, then concentrated on cond.: Wrocław PO 1946–7, Katowice Nat. PO 1949–54, Kraków PO 1955–6, Warsaw Nat. PO 1957–9. Amer. début Cleveland Orch. 1958. Salzburg Fest. 1968. Mus. dir. Minneapolis (later Minnesota) SO 1960–79. Prin. cond. Hallé Orch. 1984–92. Comps. incl. 5 syms. (1936–54); ca. conc. (1969); cl. conc. (1981); vn. conc. (1985); *Fantasia for 6*, ob., vn., va., vc., db., pf. (1988); *Fantasia for 3*, fl., ob., vc. (1992); Chamber Conc. (1993); *Passacaglia immaginaria*, orch. (1995); Conc. for Orch. (1999); pf. conc. (2002); 4 str. qts.; cl. trio; str. trio; film scores; and songs.

Skryabin, Alexander. See *Scriabin, Alexander.*

slancio (It.). Dash. Impetuosity, outburst, thus *con slancio*, with impetuosity.

slargando, slargandosi (It.). Slowing, broadening, widening. Same as *rallentando.*

Slatkin, Leonard (Edward) (*b* Los Angeles, 1944). Amer. conductor and pianist. Début with Youth SO of NY, 1966. Ass. cond. to Susskind, St Louis SO 1968, assoc. cond. 1971, assoc. prin. cond. 1974, and prin. guest cond. 1975. Mus. dir. New Orleans PO 1977–8, St Louis SO 1979–95, Nat. SO of Washington from 1996. London début 1974 (RPO). Chief cond. BBCSO 2000–5.

Slavonic Dances. 2 sets of dances by *Dvořák in folk-mus. style but 'original' in melody. Written for pf. duet, Nos. 1–8, Op.46, in 1878, Nos. 9–16, Op.72, in 1886. All orch. by Dvořák, in which form they are now usually heard.

Slavonic Rhapsodies. 3 comps. for orch. by Dvořák, Op.45, comp. 1878, in vein of folk-mus. but all 'original': No.1 in D, No.2 in G minor, No.3 in A♭.

Sleeping Beauty, The (*Spyashchaya krasavitsa*). Ballet in prol. and 3 acts with mus. by *Tchaikovsky to lib. by Petipa and Vsevolojsky, based on Perrault's fairy-tale, choreog. Petipa. Comp. 1888–9. Prod. St Petersburg 1890, London 1921 (under title *The Sleeping Princess*). Last act sometimes perf. separately as *Aurora's Wedding*. Additions to orig. choreog. by Ashton, 1968, and MacMillan 1973.

slentando (It.). Becoming slower; same as *rallentando*.

Slezak, Leo (*b* Krásná Hora, 1873; *d* Egern am Tegernsee, 1946). Austro-Cz. tenor. Sang in ch. of Brno Opera, making début there 1896 as Lohengrin. Berlin Royal Opera 1898–9. Engaged by Mahler for Vienna Opera 1901, remaining until 1927. Débuts: CG 1900; La Scala 1905; NY Met 1909. Sang Herman in Amer. première of *Queen of Spades* under Mahler, 1910. Fine *Lieder* singer. On retirement wrote several books (incl. autobiography *Songs of Motley*, NY 1938) and appeared in Austrian films as comedian.

slide. (1) In vn.-playing, expressive means of passing from one note to another, usually at distance of a 3rd or 4th. Paganini introduced virtuoso slide by executing chromatic passages, singly or in 3rds, with the same fingers.
(2) Device fitted to wind instr. to adjust the pitch by altering length of vibrating air-column. Mainly used on tb.
(3) An ornament; when 2 or more notes approach main note by conjunct *motion.

slide trumpet. Mechanism, as in the tb., was fitted to tpts. as early as 15th cent. Bach probably meant this instr. when he scored for *tromba da tirarsi*. At beginning of 19th cent. new device was invented with springs to bring back slide to normal position. This lacked agility and became obsolete on invention of valve tpt.

Slobodskaya, Oda (*b* Vilna, 1888; *d* London, 1970). Russ. soprano. Opera début St. Petersburg 1918 (Lisa in *Queen of Spades*). Left Russia for Paris 1922. London début 1931, CG 1932. Appeared in operetta in London 1930–2 as Odali Careno.

Slonimsky, Nicolas [Nikolai] (Leonidovich) (*b* St Petersburg, 1894; *d* Los Angeles, 1995). Russ.-born Amer. conductor, composer, and lexicographer (Amer. cit. 1931). Had first pf. lesson at age of 6 from his aunt, Isabella Vengerova. Became rehearsal pianist at Kiev Opera and taught at Yalta Cons. 1920. Went to Paris as secretary to Koussevitzky. Settled in USA 1923. Cond. concerts of Amer. mus. in Europe 1931–2, incl. *Ives's Three Places in New England*, and cond. f.ps. in USA of works by Varèse (world premières), Riegger, Cowell, and Chávez. Comps. used atonal, polytonal, and quarter-tone effects. Founder and cond., Boston Chamber Orch., 1927–34. Ed. of complete rev. of *Baker's Biographical Dictionary of Musicians* (5th, 6th, 7th, and 8th edns. 1958, 1978, 1984, 1991). Author of *Music Since 1900* (chronological list of major mus. events throughout world, 1937, 4th edn. 1971, supp. 1986, 1993), *Lexicon of Musical Invective* (1952), *Lectionary of Music* (1988), and autobiography *Perfect Pitch* (1988).

slur. Curved line used in musical notation to group together notes. Most common indication

is that notes concerned are to be played or sung smoothly (*legato*). For a str.-player, this signifies that the notes should be taken in one stroke of the bow, for a wind-player or singer that they should be taken in one breath. If notes within slur have dots above or below, this means they are to be played slightly detached. Slur also used in vocal mus. to indicate that one syllable is to be sung to several notes. See also *tie* and *curved lines*.

Smallens, Alexander (*b* St Petersburg, 1889; *d* Tucson, Arizona, 1972). Russ.-born conductor (Amer. cit. 1919). Taken to USA 1890. Ass. cond., Boston Opera House 1911–14; cond. Chicago Opera 1919–23, mus. dir. Philadelphia Civic Opera 1924–31. Ass. cond., Philadelphia Orch. 1927–34. Mus. dir. Radio City Music Hall, NY, 1947–50. Long assoc. with contemp. mus. Cond. f.p. Gershwin's *Porgy and Bess* (1935; also cond. revival 1942 and int. tour 1956).

Smalley, Roger (*b* Swinton, Manchester, 1943). Eng. composer and pianist. Specialized as pianist in contemp. mus. First composer-in-residence, King's Coll., Cambridge, 1967. Co-founder, 1969, of Intermodulation, instr. ens. for scores involving live elecs. (disbanded 1976). Uses elec. and aleatory techniques in comps. On staff Univ. of W. Australia from 1976. Author of articles on contemporary mus.

smanioso (from It. *smania*, 'frenzy'). With furious excitement; also *smaniato* and *smaniante*.

Smart, (Sir) **George** (Thomas) (*b* London, 1776; *d* London, 1867). Eng. conductor, composer, organist, violinist, and teacher. Chorister in Chapel Royal. Violinist, *Salomon's concerts. Org., Chapel Royal from 1822, composer to Chapel Royal from 1838. One of founders of Phil. Soc., London, 1813, and one of its conds. 1813–44. Cond. f.p. in England of Beethoven's 9th Sym., 1826. Weber died while staying at Smart's London home, 1826. Cond. many Eng. choral fests. Cond. f.ps. in England of Beethoven's *Christus am Ölberge* (London 1814) and Mendelssohn's *St Paul* (Liverpool, 1836). Was cond. at Manchester Fest. 1836 on occasion of *Malibran's fatal collapse. Dir. of mus. for coronations of William IV (1830) and Victoria (1837). Notable singing teacher. Wrote church mus., ed. O. Gibbons's madrigals and Handel's *Dettingen Te Deum*. Knighted 1811.

Smetana, Bedřich (*b* Litomyšl, 1824; *d* Prague, 1884). Bohem. composer, pianist, and conductor, regarded as the founder of Czech music. Played in str. qt. at age 5, pf. recital at 6, and wrote first comp. at 8. Settled in Prague in 1843, working as teacher to aristocratic family while having lessons from J. Proksch. Heard Liszt play and became close friend. Took part in fighting at barricades during abortive 1848 nationalist uprising. Set up mus. sch. but in 1856 went to Sweden as dir. of Göteborg Phil. Soc. Visited Liszt in Weimar and comp. 3 symphonic poems on Lisztian lines, incl. *Wallenstein's Camp* (1858–9).

Returned to Prague 1861 but, through financial instability, toured Europe as concert pianist until 1863, coinciding with reawakening of Cz. nationalist fervour after Austria's defeat by Hungary. Became cond. of a Prague choral soc. and critic for daily newspaper. His patriotic opera *The Brandenburgers in Bohemia*, was prod., after much controversy, at Prague Provisional Th. (est. 1862) in 1866 and won him public success. Smetana was appointed cond. of the th. and dir. f.p. of *The Bartered Bride* (1866), which was a failure. For laying of foundation-stone of permanent Prague Nat. Th. in 1868 he comp. the opera *Dalibor*. This, too, was a failure and was criticized as insufficiently nationalist because of Wagnerian influences on score, but his comic opera *The Two Widows* was a success in March 1874. Resigned conductorship of Provisional Th. in 1874 because of total deafness, the result of venereal disease. Over next 5 years comp. his cycle of 6 symphonic poems *Má Vlast* (My Country) and in 1876 wrote his E minor str. qt. subtitled 'From My Life', in which the high-pitched note heard in finale represents the noise in his head which he experienced continually during onset of deafness. Living in isolation in the country, he comp. choral pieces and two operas, *The Kiss* and *The Secret*. During 1880s nat. celebrations marked his achievement and his opera *Libuše* was chosen to inaugurate Prague Nat. Th. in 1881. Encouraged, comp. last opera, *The Devil's Wall*, but this was a failure in 1882, though it contains some of his best mus. He worked on *Viola*, an adaptation of Shakespeare's *Twelfth Night* which had occupied him for many years, but wrote only 363 bars before he became insane and died in asylum.

Smetana was buried as a nat. hero. With *The Bartered Bride* he wrote the incomparable masterpiece of folk-opera. His other operas had to wait until many years after his death for a proper appreciation of their virtues. Inevitably there was a Germanic influence on his work, since he grew up under Austrian domination of Czech culture, but although Janáček and later composers are more truly 'Czech', the ground was furrowed by Smetana, and his mus. has freshness and strength which ensure its popularity. Prin. works:

OPERAS: *The Brandenburgers in Bohemia (Braníbori u Čechách)* (1863); *The *Bartered Bride (Prodaná Nevěstá)* (1863–6, rev. 1869 and 1869–70); **Dalibor* (1865–7, rev. 1870); *Libuše* (1869–72); *The *Two Widows (Dvě vdovy)* (1873–4, rev. 1877, 1882); *The *Kiss (Hubička)* (1875–6); *The *Secret (Tajemství)* (1877–8); *The Devil's Wall (Čertova Stěna)* (1879–82); *Viola* (unfinished, 1874, 1883–4).

ORCH.: *Triumph Symphony* in E (1854); sym.-poems: *Richard III* (1858), *Wallenstein's Camp* (1858–9), *Hakon Jarl* (1861); *Festival Overture* (1868); **Má Vlast* (1872–9); *Carnival in Prague* (1883).

CHAMBER MUSIC: pf. trio in G minor (1855, rev. 1857); str. qts.: No.1 in E minor (*Z mého života*, Eng. **From my Life*, Ger. *Aus meinem Leben*) (1876); No.2 in D minor (1882–3); *From my Home*, duets, vn., pf. (1880).

VOCAL: Male vv.: *The Three Horsemen* (1882), *The Renegade* (1864), *The Farmer, Peasant Song* (1868), *Sea Song* (1877), *The Dower*, Prayer (1880). Female vv.: *3 Choruses* (1878). Mixed vv.: *Song of the Czechs*, cantata with orch. (1878), *Our Song* (1883).

PIANO: *6 Characteristic Pieces* (1848), *Album Leaves* (1851), *Sketches* (1856–7), *3 Polkas, 3 Poetical Polkas* (1855), *Memories of Bohemia* (1859–60), *At the Seashore* (1862), *Dreams* (1874–5), *14 Czech Dances* (1877–9, orch. by others).

Smetana Quartet. Cz. string quartet formed in 1945 by students of J. Micka at Prague Cons. Début Prague, Nov. 1945. First va. player was Václav *Neumann, who left in 1946 to pursue cond. career. First tour abroad (Poland) 1950. London début 1955, Salzburg 1955, NY 1957. Quartets by Dvořák, Janáček and Smetana were basis of repertory. Many recordings. Disbanded 1989.

Smirnov, Dmitri (Alexeievich) (*b* Minsk, 1948). Russian composer. Editor in publishing-house Sovetsky Kompozitor, 1973–80. Several of his works are inspired by poetry and painting of Blake. Married to composer Elena *Firsova. Settled in Eng. 1991. Joint composer-in-residence (with Firsova), Keele Univ. from 1992. Comps. incl. 2 operas; Sym. No.1 (*The Seasons*) (1980), No.2 (1982), No.3 (1995); 2 pf. concs. (1971, 1978); cl. conc. (1974/1977); vc. conc. (1992); *Conc.-Piccolo*, vc., orch. (2001); many choral and vocal works; 6 str. qts. (1973–98); 3 vn. sonatas (1969, rev. 1971, 1979, 1998); 4 pf. sonatas (1967, rev. 1977, 1980, 1992, 2000); *Magic Music Box*, 50 pf. pieces for children (1993); *The Music of the Spheres*, pf. (1995); *Set me as a seal*, chamber ens., 3 tpt., 3 tb. (1997); *Mass*, unacc. ch. (1998); *Chaconne*, vn., va., hp. (2001); *The Stony Path*, v., pf., vc. (2002).

Smit, Leo (*b* Philadelphia, 1921; *d* Encinitas, Calif., 1999). Amer. composer and pianist. Worked as pianist with Balanchine ballet 1936–7 and NY City Sym. 1947–8. Taught at various colleges and univs. Prof. Fred Hoyle, Eng. astronomer, wrote lib. for his opera *The Alchemy of Love* (1969). Works incl. ballet *Virginia Sampler* (1947), 3 syms., pf. conc., *Academic Graffiti* for v. and chamber ens. (text by Auden), chamber mus., etc.

Smith, Cyril (James) (*b* Middlesbrough, 1909; *d* East Sheen, 1974). Eng. pianist. Début Birmingham 1929 (Brahms 2nd conc.). Prom. début 1929. Prof. of pf. RCM 1934–74. Well-known as pf. duettist with wife, Phyllis *Sellick. They gave f.p. of Vaughan Williams's conc. in 2-pf. vers., 1946. Fine interpreter of Rachmaninov. On their visit to USSR 1956, had stroke which deprived him of use of one hand, but continued to play duets for 3 hands, several works being specially comp. for them (by Bliss, Arnold, Jacob, etc.). OBE 1971.

Smith, 'Father' [Schmidt, Bernhard] (*b c*.1630; *d* London, 1708). Ger.-born organ-builder. Went to Eng. 1666 after Restoration, when use of org. was renewed in churches. With 2 nephews, built orgs. for St Margaret's, Westminster (1675), St Paul's Cath. (1697), Temple Church (1684), Banqueting Hall, Whitehall (1699), Durham Cath. (1683), Sheldonian Th., Oxford, etc. Organist, St Margaret's, Westminster, from 1676.

Smith, John Christopher [Schmidt, Johann Christoph] (*b* Anspach, 1712; *d* Bath, 1795). Ger.-born composer and keyboard player. Went to Eng. as child. In Europe 1745–8. Org., Foundling Hospital Chapel from 1754; played org. and hpd. at Handel oratorio perfs. Wrote 10 operas (incl. *The Tempest*), oratorio *Paradise Lost* and others, songs, hpd. suites, and ovs. for Garrick productions at Drury Lane.

Smith, Julia (*b* Denton, Texas, 1911; *d* NY, 1989). Amer. composer and pianist. Taught at various colleges of mus., then devoted herself from 1946 to comp. and playing. Works incl. 6 operas, pf. conc., str. qt., etc.

Smith, Patrick J(ohn) (*b* NY, 1932). Amer. critic, author, and editor. Mus. critic for *High Fidelity*, *Musical America*, *Musical Quarterly*, and *Musical Times*. NY mus. correspondent of London *Times*. Ed.-in-chief *Opera News* 1985–98. Wrote *The Tenth Muse, a Historical Study of the Opera Libretto* (1970) and *A Year at the Met* (1983).

Smith, Russell (*b* Tuscaloosa, Alabama, 1927; *d* Munich, 1998). Amer. composer. Teacher at various colleges. Ed. for Ricordi in NY 1961–5 and H. W. Gray 1965–66. Comp.-in-residence Cleveland Orch. 1966–7, New Orleans PO 1969–70. Also writer on mus. Comps. incl. opera, 2 pf. concs., ballet *Antigone*, *Anglican Mass*, chamber mus., etc.

Smith Brindle, Reginald (*b* Bamber Bridge, Lancs., 1917; *d* Caterham, Surrey, 2003). Eng. composer and author. Worked for It. radio 1956–61. Taught at Univ. Coll., Bangor, 1967–70. Prof. of mus., Surrey Univ., 1970–85. Mus. influenced by It. *avant-garde* sch. of Berio, Maderna, Nono, etc. Books incl. *Serial Composition* (1966), *Contemporary Percussion* (1970), *The New Music* (1975). Comps. incl. *Antigone*, opera (1969); 2 syms. (1954, 1990); cl. conc. (1960); choral and vocal works; chamber mus.; pieces for guitar; and some comps. using elec./tape.

smorzando (It., abbreviation *smorz.*, past participle *smorzato*). Extinguishing. Gradually dying away.

Smyth, (Dame) **Ethel** (Mary) (*b* Footscray, Kent, 1858; *d* Hook Heath, Woking, 1944). Eng. composer and conductor. Studied Leipzig Cons. and in Berlin. Came into prominence with Mass in D, perf. London 1893. First 3 operas were prod. in Ger. Active in militant campaign for women's suffrage and was jailed 1911. Comp. *March of the Women* as their battle-song and cond. it in Holloway Jail with tooth-brush. Music was Ger.-influenced but with breezy Eng. quality typical of her personality. Her operas *The Wreckers* and *The*

Boatswain's Mate contain mus. of considerable quality. Wrote highly entertaining autobiography. DBE 1922. Prin. works:

OPERAS: *Fantasio* (1892–4); *The Forest* (*Der Wald*) (1899–1901); *The* *Wreckers* (1903–4); *The* *Boatswain's Mate* (1913–14); *Fête galante* (1923); *Entente Cordiale* (1925).

ORCH.: *Serenade* in D (1890); Ov., *Antony and Cleopatra* (1890); *On the Cliffs of Cornwall* (prelude, Act II, *The Wreckers*) (1928); conc., vn., hn., orch. (1927); 2 *Interlinked French Melodies* (1929).

CHORAL: Mass in D (1891, rev. 1925); *March of the Women* (1911); *Hey Nonny No*, ch., orch. (1911); *Sleepless Dreams*, ch., orch. (1912); *A Spring Canticle*, ch., orch. (1926); *The Prison*, sop, bass, ch., orch. (1930).

CHAMBER MUSIC: str. quintet (1884); str. qt. No.1 (1894), No.2 (1902–12); vc. sonata (1887); vn. sonata (1887); pf. sonatas; organ preludes; songs (some with orch.).

snare-drum. See *side-drum*.

Snegurochka (Rimsky-Korsakov). See *Snow Maiden, The*.

Snow Maiden, The (*Snegurochka*). Opera in prol. and 4 acts by Rimsky-Korsakov to his own lib. based on Ostrovsky's play (1873). Comp. 1880–1, rev. *c*.1895. Prod. St Petersburg 1882, Seattle and NY Met 1922, London 1933.

Snowman, Nicholas (*b* London, 1944). Eng. administrator. Founder and administrator Cambridge Univ. Opera Soc. 1965–7. Ass. to Head of Mus. Staff, Glyndebourne, 1967–9. Co-founder and gen. man. London Sinfonietta 1967–72. Dir., artistic dept., IRCAM, Paris, 1972–86. Gen. dir. (arts) South Bank Centre 1987–99. Gen. dir. Glyndebourne 1998–2003, Opéra du Rhin, Strasbourg, from 2003.

soap opera. Nothing to do with opera. Term to describe long-running, often daily or several-times-weekly serial on TV and radio, e.g. (in Britain) *Coronation Street*, *EastEnders*, *The Archers*. Genre originated in USA on commercial radio and was sponsored by a firm—soap manufacturer, for instance—wishing to advertise its product. Irreverently, one could claim *The Ring* as the biggest soap opera in the world.

soave; soavità (It.). Suave; suavity (or gentle; gentleness). *soavemente*, suavely.

Sociable Songs. Title given by *Warlock to 3 settings of anonymous poems for male vv. and pf., comp. 1924–5, pubd. 1926. Titles are: 1. *The Toper's Song*, 2. *One more river*, 3. *The Lady's Birthday*.

Society for the Private Performance of Music (*Verein für Musikalische Privataufführungen*). Society founded in Vienna in Nov. 1918 by *Schoenberg, with Berg, Ratz, and Paul A. Pisk. Aim was presentation of 'all modern mus. from that of Mahler and Strauss to the newest' under best possible conditions. Subscribers only admitted; critics were excluded. Comps. frequently perf. twice. Much organizational work undertaken by Berg. Dissolved 1922. Among composers whose mus. was played were Schoenberg, Berg, Webern, Mahler, Stravinsky, Scriabin, Debussy, Marx, Wellesz, Bartók, Ravel, and Suk. The pianist several times was Rudolf Serkin. Prague branch under presidency of *Zemlinsky 1921–4.

Society for the Promotion of New Music (SPNM). Organization founded as Committee for the Promotion of New Music in Jan. 1943 by Francis *Chagrin, with Mátyás Seiber and Roy Douglas. Hon. pres. was Vaughan Williams, chairman Bliss, with Britten and Tippett on the committee. Aim was 'to encourage works that show promise in whatever style'. In its first 50 years, over 850 composers were represented in its concerts and over 9,000 scores were submitted to it.

Socrate (Socrates). Symphonic drama in 3 parts for 4 sop. and orch. by *Satie to lib. by Plato (trans. by V. Cousin). Parts are entitled 1. *Portrait de Socrate*, 2. *Les bords de l'Ilussus*, 3. *Mort de Socrate*. Comp. 1918. F.p. Paris 1920; f.p. in England BBC broadcast 1949; f. Amer. p. NY (concert) 1965.

Söderström(-Olow), (Anna) **Elisabeth** (*b* Stockholm, 1927). Swed. soprano. Opera début Drottningholm 1947 (Bastienne in *Bastien und Bastienne*), while still student. Joined Stockholm Royal Opera 1950. Salzburg début 1955; Glyndebourne 1957; NY Met 1959; CG 1960 (with Royal Swed. Opera). Notable Strauss singer, but wide repertory of roles, including Janáček roles of Emilia Marty, Káťa Kabanová, and Jenůfa. Created Juliana Bordereau in Argento's *The Aspern Papers*, Dallas 1988. Accomplished singer of Britten's vocal music in addition to his operatic roles. Art. dir. Drottningholm Court Th. 1993–6. Hon. CBE 1985.

soft pedal. Pf. pedal, operated by left foot, which reduces vol. by causing fewer than normal number of str. to be struck or by bringing the hammers nearer the str. before they start to move.

soggetto (It.). Subject, meaning, in a mus. sense, the subject of a fugue.

soh. See *sol*.

Soirées musicales (Musical Evenings). Coll. of songs and duets by *Rossini, pubd. 1835. *Britten orch. 5 of these (1936) under same title, others were orch. by *Respighi in ballet *La *Boutique fantasque*. 12 were transcr. for pf. by Liszt, 1837.

Soir (et la Tempête), Le (The Evening (and the Storm)). Nickname of Haydn's Sym. No.8 (Hob. I:8) *c*.1761, Nos. 6 and 7 being known respectively as *Le *Matin* (Morning) and *Le Midi* (Noon) (Hob. I:6 and 7).

sol. The 5th degree (dominant) of major scale and so used (spelt *soh*) in *Tonic Sol-fa. In many countries, where *fixed-doh principles apply, it means the note G in any key, thus *sol dièse* is G♯ in Fr.

Soldaten, Die (The Soldiers). Opera in 4 acts by B. A. *Zimmermann to lib. by composer after J. M. Reinhold Lenz's play. Comp. 1958–60, rev. 1963–4. For orch., singing and speaking vv., elecs., and *musique concrète*, with ballet, mime, film, and lighting effects. Cologne Opera, which commissioned the work, rejected 1st vers. as technically impossible. Prod. Cologne 1965, Edinburgh 1972, Boston 1982, NY City Opera 1991, Paris (Bastille), 1994, London (ENO) 1996. Also orch. suite.

Soldier's Tale, The (Stravinsky). See *Histoire du Soldat, L'*.

Soleil des eaux, Le (The sun of the waters). Music by Boulez orig. comp. for radio play by René Char (1948). Rev. 1950 as cantata for sop., ten., bass, chamber orch. Rev. 1958 for sop., ten., bass. ch., and orch. Rev. 1965 for sop. and ch. F.p. 1965 version, Berlin 1965.

Solemn Melody. Comp. for org. and str. by Walford *Davies, 1908.

solenne, solennemente, solennita (It.); **solennel(le), solennellemente** (Fr.); **solemnis, solennis** (Lat.). Solemn, solemnly, solemnity.

Soler, Antonio (*b* Olot, nr. Gerona, 1729; *d* El Escorial, 1783). Sp. composer, organist, and friar. Choirmaster at Lérida. Became monk 1752, entering Escorial monastery as organist 1753. Wrote theoretical treatise 1762. Disciple of D. Scarlatti and wrote 120 keyboard sonatas. Also comp. several quintets for org. and str. qt., church mus., etc.

Solesmes. Fr. village near Le Mans where the monks of the Benedictine monastery became famous for their work on restoration of liturgical mus. Order founded 1833 by Dom Prosper Gueranger. Important publications on nature of plainsong issued in 1883, 1891, and 1896. When Pope Pius X in 1904 est. commission to prepare new official edn. of plainchant, the Solesmes Benedictines were appointed eds. This edn. was known as Vatican Edn. (but some authorities on the subject strongly criticize its interpretation of Gregorian rhythm). In 1901, because of their non-compliance with Law of Associations, the monks were expelled from Solesmes and moved to I.o.W. and later to Quarr Abbey, near Ryde. Returned to Solesmes 1922.

solfeggio (It., plural *solfeggi*; Fr. *solfège*). Term for method of sight-reading or vocal exercise in which names of the notes are used as in *fixed-doh system, e.g. *do* for C, *sol* for G, etc. Fr. term *solfège* is also used to cover all rudimentary mus. instruction.

soli (It.). Alone; plural of *solo, but 'solos' in general usage today.

solmization. System of designating notes by the sol-fa syllables in any of the various methods used since Guido d'Arezzo in 11th cent., as in the It. *do, re, mi, fa*, etc. and Tonic sol-fa *doh, ray, me, fah*, etc.

solo (It.). Alone. A vocal or instr. piece or passage perf. by one performer, i.e. a solo song is for one singer, with or without acc. The solo instr. in a conc. might also be acc. by a solo passage for one of the orch. players. The word *soloistic* is sometimes regrettably used to denote a composer's use of the individual qualities of an instr.

Solomon. Oratorio by Handel to text adapted from Bible by unknown author. F.p. London 1749 (comp. 1748).

Solomon [Cutner, Solomon] (*b* London, 1902; *d* London, 1988). Eng. pianist. Début at 8, playing Tchaikovsky's 1st conc. at Queen's Hall, London, 1911. Studied in Paris with Lazare Lévy and Marcel Dupré. Returned to London with dislike of pf. and was advised by Sir Henry Wood to retire for a while. Resumed career 1923. Amer. début 1926. Gave f.p. of Bliss's pf. conc., NY World Fair 1939. Brilliant career as conc. soloist, recitalist, and chamber-mus. player of exceptional sensitivity cut short by illness 1965. CBE 1946.

Solomon, Yonty (*b* Cape Town, 1938). Brit. pianist of S. African birth. Moved to London 1963 to study with Myra *Hess. Has given f.ps. of works by Richard Rodney Bennett, W. Josephs, and Merilaainen. Wide repertory from Bach to Ives (*Concord Sonata*). Prof. of pf. RCM from 1978 and TCL from 2002.

solo organ. Manual on some orgs., with solo stops such as cl., tuba, fl., etc.

solo pitch. Tuning of instrs. rather higher than normal pitch in order to obtain greater brilliance of tone.

solo stop. Any org. stop used solo against acc. of softer stops played on a different kbd. Some stops are more suitable than others for solo use.

Solti, (Sir) **Georg** [György] [Stern, Gyuri] (*b* Budapest, 1912; *d* Antibes, France, 1997). Hung.-born conductor and pianist (Brit. cit. 1972). Ass. at Budapest Opera 1930. Début as cond. Budapest 1938 (*Le nozze di Figaro*). Assisted Toscanini at Salzburg Fest. 1936 and 1937, not making his début until 1951 (*Idomeneo*). Left Hungary for Switz. 1939, earning living as pianist. Mus. dir. Munich Opera 1946–52, Frankfurt Opera 1952–61, CG 1961–71 (his tenure there being a decade of particular distinction). London concert début 1949 (LPO). Mus. dir. Dallas SO 1960–1, Chicago SO 1969–91, LPO 1979–83. Cond., Orchestre de Paris 1971–5. Débuts: Amer. (S. Francisco Opera) 1953; Glyndebourne 1954; CG 1959; NY Met 1960; Bayreuth 1983 (*Der Ring des Nibelungen*); art. dir. Salzburg Easter Fest. 1992–3. Fine cond. of Wagner, Strauss, Mahler, Elgar, etc. Cond. first complete studio recording of *Der Ring*. Hon. CBE 1968. Hon. KBE 1971.

Sombrero de tres picos, El (Falla). See *Three-cornered Hat, The*.

Somers, Harry (Stewart) (*b* Toronto, 1925; *d* Toronto, 1999). Canadian composer, pianist, and guitarist. Worked as taxi-driver, copyist, radio commentator, and later as teacher. In some works tonal and atonal materials are juxtaposed in the manner of Ives. Works incl. operas, notably *Louis Riel* (1967), ballets, syms., 2 pf. conc., sonatas, str. qts., and *Voiceplay* (for singer-actor, male or female, any range).

Somervell, (Sir) **Arthur** (*b* Windermere, 1863; *d* London, 1937). Eng. composer. Teacher at RCM 1894–1901. From 1901, inspector of mus. to Board of Education and Scottish Education Dept. (chief inspector 1920–8). Prolific composer, his song-cycle *Maud* being of high quality. Possibly first to set Housman *Shropshire Lad* poems (1904). Knighted 1929. Works incl. sym., *Normandy* (symphonic variations for pf. and orch., 1912), *Highland Concerto* (pf. and orch., 1921), vn. conc. (1932), cl. quintet, 2 Masses, *Ode on the Intimations of Immortality* (Leeds Fest. 1907), song-cycles *Maud* and *A Shropshire Lad*, and solo songs.

Sommer, Raphael (*b* Prague, 1937; *d* Israel, 2001). Cz. cellist. Won Casals Int. Comp. 1961 and other prizes. Prof. of vc., RMCM 1967–71, RNCM 1972–89. Dir. of 1st chamber orch. RCM 1974–9. Prof. of vc., GSMD 1989–2001. Soloist with leading orchs.

Son and Stranger (*Die Heimkehr aus der Fremde*, The Homecoming from Abroad). Operetta in 1 act by *Mendelssohn, Op.89, to lib. by K. Klingemann, comp. 1829 for family perf. in celebration of his parents' silver wedding, Dec. 1829. F. public p. Leipzig 1851, f. Eng. p. (in trans. by H. F. *Chorley) 1851.

sonata (It., sounded, from *suonare*, to sound; Fr., Ger. *Sonate*). Instr. comp. for pf., or for other instr(s). with pf. acc., e.g. vc. sonata, fl. sonata, in several movts. (sometimes in one, as in Liszt's B minor pf. sonata). Formal features of the sonata are found in other instr. comps., such as sym., qt., trio, but the term sonata is usually reserved for works involving not more than 2 performers. The sonata originated in the 16th cent., when it meant anything not sung but played. During early part of 17th cent., comps. for instr. ens., which were div. into 5 or more contrasting sections were known as sonatas. From these the baroque sonata developed, having 3–6 movts. like a suite, and taking 2 forms, the *sonata da camera* ('chamber sonata', often for 2 or more players with kbd. acc., in dance rhythms) and *sonata da chiesa* ('church sonata', of more serious character). The earliest sonatas for kbd. alone are by Salvatore and Kuhnau, and these reached their apogee with D. Scarlatti and C. P. E. Bach. Later in that century, the Viennese classical sonata of Haydn, Mozart, and Beethoven, usually but not invariably in 3 movts., marked the greatest period in the development of the form, leading to the superb romantic era. Like the orch. sym., the sonata remains the most important form for 1 or 2 instr., and the majority of important 20th-cent. composers have written them. Most sonatas are written in *sonata-form or a version of it. The Haydn/Mozart sonata is usually in 3 movts., allegro–andante–allegro. Beethoven introduced the minuet (later scherzo), as 3rd movt., but in his Op.111 pf. sonata he anticipated the 1-movt. sectional structure adopted by later composers. The last movt. of a 3- or 4-movt. sonata is often in sonata or *rondo form, or is sometimes a set of variations. Some 20th-cent. composers have revived 18th-cent. application of term to works for several instr., e.g. Walton's *Sonata for Strings* and C. Matthews's *Sonata* for orch. The fact is that a sym. is a sonata for orch., a str. qt. a sonata for 4 str. instr., etc.

sonata da camera (It.). Chamber sonata. Baroque type of sonata, the term originally indicating place (i.e. court, chamber), rather than type, of perf. Had several dance-like movts. for 2 or 3 str. players with kbd. acc. Corelli standardized the form as a suite consisting of introduction, followed by 3 or 4 dances.

sonata da chiesa (It.). Church sonata. Like the *sonata da camera, but of a more serious character appropriate to ecclesiastical surroundings. The standard Corelli *sonata da chiesa* is in 4 movts., slow–fast–slow–fast.

sonata form. Type of mus. construction (sometimes known as compound binary form) normally used in 1st movt. of a *sonata, sym., or conc. (and in other types of work). Used also in other movts. Regular sonata form implies 3 sections: 1. *exposition* (containing first subject, in tonic key, and 2nd subject, in dominant, and sometimes further subjects), often repeated and followed by 2. *development* (in which the material of the exposition is worked out in a kind of free fantasia), and 3. *recapitulation* (in which the exposition is repeated, though often with modification, and with the 2nd subject now in the tonic). The recapitulation has a coda, a peroration of moderate length though some composers, incl. Beethoven, extend it into what amounts to a 2nd development section. The basis of sonata form is key relationships.

sonata rondo. Movt. designed as combination of sonata and rondo form (e.g. finale of Beethoven's 8th Sym.). Outline is: *exposition* (ABA, i.e. first subject in tonic: rondo theme; 2nd subject in dominant or another key; first subject in tonic), *development* (C), *recapitulation* (ABA, i.e. rondo first subject in tonic; 3rd episode, with 2nd subject now in tonic; rondo theme leading to coda). There are many variants.

sonatina (It.; Fr. *sonatine*). Little sonata. A short sonata, usually lighter and easier (but several 20th-cent. sonatinas, e.g. by Ravel, Milhaud, Busoni, etc. are technically difficult).

Sondheim, Stephen (Joshua) (*b* NY, 1930). Amer. composer and lyric-writer. Wrote words for *Bernstein's *West Side Story* (1957), Jule Styne's *Gypsy* (1959), Shevelove and Gelbart's *A Funny Thing Happened on the Way to the Forum* (1962), and Rodgers's *Do I Hear a Waltz?* (1965). Comp. successful musicals incl. *Company* (1970), *Follies* (1971), *A Little Night Music* (1973), *Pacific Overtures* (1976), *Sweeney Todd* (1979), *Merrily We Roll Along* (1981), *Sunday in the Park with George* (1985), *Into the Woods* (1987), *Assassins* (1990), *Passion* (1994), *Bounce* (2003); *The Frogs* (1974, rev. 2004).

Sonetti di Petrarca, Tre (3 Petrarch Sonnets). 3 songs by Liszt (1839) which he later transcr. for pf. as *Sonetti del Petrarca*, Nos. 4–6 of the *Seconde Année (Italie)* of *Années de pèlerinage* (1837–49).

song. Short vocal comp., acc. or solo. Song is the natural human means of mus. self-expression (as it is for most birds). There are various types of song—the individual folk-song, the part-song for a group of vv., the art-song for the trained performer. Today a 'song recital' generally means an evening of Eng. songs (mus. settings of poems), Ger. *Lieder, or Fr. *mélodies*. In opera the term *aria* or air is preferred to 'song' for a solo vocal item. Many composers—Berlioz, Mahler, Strauss, Elgar, Britten, Shostakovich, etc.—have written songs with orch., and the term is sometimes applied to a large-scale piece, e.g. *Song of the Earth* (Mahler) and *Song of Destiny* (Brahms).

Probably prehistoric man uttered some sort of song, and the origins of folk-songs are beyond discovery (though not beyond speculation!). Synagogue and church were among the official institutions where song developed, through chants and hymns, some of the latter being adaptations of folk and popular songs. With 12th-cent. minstrels and troubadours, the love-song and ballad developed, to be followed in the 14th and 15th cents. by songs of the Ger. *Minnesinger and *Meistersinger. By the end of the 15th cent., following the revolution of *ars nova, song colls., many of them polyphonic settings, were pubd. in several countries. In Eng. in the 16th and 17th cents. the lute-songs, exemplified by Dowland and the madrigals of Weelkes and Byrd, in Sp. the lute-songs of Milán, and in It. the madrigals of Monteverdi and others all played a significant role in the growth of elaborate song-writing. Ger. developed the *Lied*, beginning with Hassler and Abert, and continuing through Mozart and Beethoven to the great flowering of Schubert who, with more than any composer made the song a mus. form into which as much emotional and dramatic expression could be poured as into a sym. Some of his songs are *strophic*, i.e. repeating the tune in successive stanzas, others are 'through-composed' (*durchkomponiert*), i.e. developing freely from start to finish. Schubert was followed by Schumann, Brahms, Wolf, Loewe, Marx, Mahler, Strauss, Pfitzner, and others. In Fr., Duparc, Debussy, and especially Fauré developed the *mélodie* in as distinctive and complex a fashion as the great Germans developed the *Lied*. Indeed, in the 19th and 20th cents., composers in Eng., Sp., USA, Russia, Hungary, etc. have added masterpieces to the world's treasury of song. Nor should the immense world of 'popular song', from 19th-cent. mus.-hall songs to today's 'pop' songs, be forgotten, ignored, or under-rated. Brave the man who will make a didactic value-judgement between *Dives and Lazarus, Gretchen am Spinnrade*, and *Smoke gets in your eyes*.

song-cycle (Ger. *Liederkreis*). Set of songs grouped into an artistic unity by the composer in a particular order and referring to a particular theme—love, death, jealousy, nature, etc.—or telling a story, or both. Examples are Beethoven's *An die ferne Geliebte*, Schubert's *Winterreise*, Schumann's *Frauenliebe und -Leben*, Mahler's *Kindertotenlieder*, Berlioz's Les *Nuits d'Été*, Elgar's *Sea Pictures*, Vaughan Williams's *On Wenlock Edge*, Britten's *Nocturne*, etc. Some of the above are with pf. acc., some with chamber ens., and some with orch. Coprario's *Funeral Teares* (1606) is one of the earliest, if not the earliest, of song-cycles.

song-form. Another, if misleading, name for ordinary *ternary* form as generally applied in an instr. slow movt.

Song for the Lord Mayor's Table, A. Cycle of 6 songs for sop. and pf. by *Walton to words collected by Christopher Hassall from poems by Blake, Thomas Jordan, Charles Morris, Wordsworth, and 2 anon. 18th-cent. poets. Written for City of London Fest. 1962. F.p. Schwarzkopf 1962. Re-scored for sop. and orch. 1970. F.p. City of London Fest. 1970 with Janet Baker.

Songmakers' Almanac, The. Eng. ensemble who give song-recital programmes devoted to a particular theme, often literary, in which songs are perf. with complementary readings (e.g. Scott's influence on composers; Schubert in 1827, etc.). Founded 1976 (début London, August) with art. dir. Graham *Johnson and Felicity *Lott (sop.), Ann *Murray (mez.), Anthony Rolfe Johnson (ten.), and Richard Jackson (bar.). Fest. appearances Aldeburgh, King's Lynn, Buxton, Edinburgh, etc.

Song of Destiny (Brahms). See *Schicksalslied*.

Song of the Earth, The (Mahler). See *Lied von der Erde, Das*.

Song of the Flea. Song for v. and pf. by Mussorgsky, 1879, setting of Mephistopheles's song in Goethe's *Faust*. Also set by Beethoven, in 6 *Lieder*, Op.75, No.3.

Song of the High Hills, The. For orch. and ch. (wordless) by Delius, with solo parts for sop. and ten. from ch. Comp. 1911, f.p. London 1920, cond. Coates.

Songs and Dances of Death (*Pesni i plyaski smerti*). Cycle of 4 songs for v. and pf. by Mussorgsky, 1875–7, to poems by Golenischev-Gutuzov. Titles are: 1. *Trepak, Death and the Peasant*. 2.

Cradle Song, the Child breathes gently. 3. *Death the Serenader, Soft is the Night*. 4. *Field Marshal Death, War Rumbles*. Orch. by Shostakovich, 1962.

Songs for a Mad King, Eight. Th. piece by *Maxwell Davies for male actor-singer and chamber ens. (incl. railway whistle, dijeridu, chains). Text by Randolph Stow and King George III. Has 8 movements. F.p. London 1969.

Songs for Dov. Cycle of songs for ten. and small orch. (with 6 perc. players) by *Tippett, 1970, the texts written by himself. Based on songs for the character Dov in Tippett's 3rd opera The *Knot Garden*. F.p. Cardiff 1970, Gerald English and London Sinfonietta, cond. Tippett.

Songs my Mother Taught Me. Song for high v. and pf. by Dvořák, to words by Heyduk, being No.4 of his *Gipsy Songs*, Op.55 (1880).

Songs of a Wayfarer (Mahler). See *Lieder eines fahrenden Gesellen*.

Songs of Farewell. (1) 6 unacc. secular motets by *Parry, comp. 1916–18 to texts from the Bible, Donne, Vaughan, J. Davies, and Campion, and Lockhart. Nos. 1–5 f.p. London 1916, No.6 f.p. Oxford 1918, f. complete p. Oxford 1919 (cond. Hugh *Allen in each case).
(2) 5 settings of Whitman for double ch. and orch. by Delius, comp. 1930, f.p. London 1932 cond. Sargent. One of works written with help of E. *Fenby.

Songs of Gurra (Schoenberg). See *Gurrelieder*.

Songs of Sunset. Delius's settings of poems by Ernest Dowson for mez., bar., ch., and orch. 1906–8. F.p. London 1911, cond. Beecham.

Songs of the Fleet. Five settings of poems by Henry Newbolt (1862–1938) for bar., ch., and orch. by *Stanford, Op.117, f.p. Leeds Fest. 1910. No.3 is *The Middle Watch*.

Songs of the Sea. Five settings of poems by Henry Newbolt (1862–1938) for bar., male ch., and orch. by *Stanford, Op.91, f.p. Leeds Fest. 1904.

Songs of Travel. Song-cycle for v. and pf. by Vaughan Williams to 9 poems by Robert Louis Stevenson from his *Songs of Travel*. F.p. London 1904. 1. *The Vagabond*, 2. *Let Beauty Awake*, 3. *The Roadside Fire*, 4. *Youth and Love*, 5. *In Dreams*, 6. *The infinite shining heavens*, 7. *Whither must I wander?*, 8. *Bright is the Ring of Words*, 9. *I have trod the upward and the downward slope*. All often sung separately. 9th song not perf. until 1960. F.p. as cycle, May 1960 (BBC).

Songs on the Death of Children (Mahler). See *Kindertotenlieder*.

Songs without Words (Mendelssohn). See *Lieder ohne Worte*.

Sonnambula, La (The Sleepwalking Girl). Opera in 2 acts by Bellini to lib. by Romani. Comp. 1831. Prod. Milan and London 1831, NY 1835.

Sonnleithner, Joseph (*b* Vienna, 1766; *d* Vienna, 1835). Austrian art-collector and impresario. Manager of Vienna court ths. 1804–14 and of Theater an der Wien until 1807. Trans. opera libs., incl. Beethoven's *Fidelio*. Friend of Grillparzer and Schubert. One of founders of Gesellschaft der Musikfreunde (1812).

Sonnleithner, Leopold Edler von (*b* Vienna, 1797; *d* Vienna, 1873). Austrian connoisseur. Friend of Schubert, preserving many of his songs and, with others, pubd. *Erlkönig*, etc. Aided *Jahn with material for life of Mozart.

sonore (Fr.), **sonoro** (It.). Sonorous; so *sonorité* (Fr.) and *sonorità* (It.), sonority; *sonoramente* (It.), sonorously.

sons bouchés (Fr.). Stopped notes in hn. playing.

Sontag, Henriette [Walburgis, Gertrude] (*b* Koblenz, 1806; *d* Mexico City, 1854). Ger. soprano. First public appearance at age 6. Opera début Prague Cons. 1821 (Princess in Boieldieu's *Jean de Paris*). Sang in Vienna from 1822. At Weber's request created title-role in *Euryanthe*, 1823. Sang sop. part in f.p. of Beethoven's 9th Sym. (Vienna 1824) and f. Vienna p. of *Missa solemnis* (1824). Berlin début 1825; Paris 1826; London 1828. Her voice was exceptionally clear and reached E *in alt* with ease. Retired from stage on marriage to Count Rossi, but continued concert work. Returned to opera 1849. Died of cholera in Mexico.

Sonzogno, Edoardo (*b* Milan, 1836; *d* Milan, 1920). It. publisher. Firm founded at end of 18th cent.; began publication of Fr. and It. mus. in 1874. Est. series of competitions for new operas 1883, 2nd contest in 1889 being won by Mascagni with *Cavalleria Rusticana*. Last contest 1903.

sopra (It.). On, above. *sopra una corda*, on one str. (of vn., etc.); for pf. application see *corda*; *come* (*di*) *sopra*, as above.

sopranino (It.). Little soprano. Name given to size of instr. higher than sop., e.g. sopranino recorder, sopranino sax., sopranino flügelhorn, etc.

soprano (from It. *sopra*, 'above'). (1) The highest register of female (or artificial male) v. A boy sop. is known as a *treble. Normal female range is from middle C upwards for 2 octaves. The male sop. was a *castrato, used in opera and church mus. in 17th and 18th cents. In the opera house, many sub-divisions of the term *soprano* exist, e.g. dramatic, lyric, coloratura, soubrette, character, etc.

(2) Sop. clef is obsolete clef, with middle C on bottom line of staff.

(3) The term is also used for high instr. register, e.g. soprano cornet, soprano sax. (See also *sopranino*.)

See also *mezzo-soprano*.

Sor [Sors], **Fernando** [Ferdinando] (*b* Barcelona, 1778; *d* Paris, 1839). Sp. guitarist and composer. Virtuoso of guitar, teaching in Paris, London, and elsewhere. Played his 'concertante' for guitar and vn., va., and vc. at Phil. Soc. concert in London, 1817. Wrote many pieces for guitar, an opera, ballet *Cendrillon*, perf. in London 1822, syms., and str. qts.

Sorabji, Kaikhosru Shapurji [Sorabji, Leon Dudley] (*b* Chingford, Essex, 1892; *d* Winfrith, Dorset, 1988). Eng.-born composer, pianist, and writer. Son of Parsi father and Sp.-Sicilian mother. Played his pf. works in London and Paris 1921 and Vienna 1922, but thereafter discouraged public perf. of his mus. until relenting in mid-1970s, though he remained something of a cult figure. Wrote music criticism notable for acerbity and wit, also for championship of then unfashionable composers, e.g. Mahler and Szymanowski. Works are of great complexity, the *Opus clavicembalisticum* for pf. (1930) being in 3 parts with 12 sub-divisions, incl. a theme with 49 variations, a passacaglia with 81 variations, and lasting nearly 4 hours. Other works, demanding elaborate forces, incl. syms., 3 organ syms., 8 pf. concs., pf. sonatas, etc.

Sorcerer, The. Operetta in 2 acts by Sullivan to lib. by Gilbert. Comp. 1877, rev. 1884. Prod. London 1877, NY 1879.

Sorcerer's Apprentice, The (Dukas). See *Apprenti sorcier, L'*.

sordino, sordina (It., plural *sordini*). A mute for an instr. Thus, *con sordini*, with mutes, means put the mutes on. Other phrases are *sordini alzati* or *sordini levati*, mutes raised (taken off). On the pf., *sordini* means the dampers; *senza sordini* is without dampers, meaning that the sustaining pedal is to be depressed.

Sordun (Ger.). (1) See *sourdine*.
(2) Org. stop of muffled tone (8′ and 16′).

Sorochintsy Fair (*Sorochintskaya Yarmarka*). 3-act unfinished opera by Mussorgsky to composer's lib. based on Gogol's story (1831–2). Comp. 1876–81. Mussorgsky completed only the prelude, the market scene and part of the next, most of Act 2, a scene based on his *Night on the Bare Mountain*, an instr. episode, and 2 songs. Ed. 1904 and 1912 by Lyadov and Karatygin: version from these edns. prod. Moscow 1913. Completion by *Cui prod. Petrograd 1917; by *Tcherepnin prod. Monte Carlo 1923, NY Met 1930, London 1934. Completion by Shebalin pubd. 1933. Sometimes spelt *Sorochints Fair* or called *The Fair at Sorochintsi*.

sospirando, sospirante, sospirevole, sospiroso (It.). Sighing, i.e. plaintive in style.

Sospiri (Sighs). Comp. for str., hp., and org., Op.70, by Elgar. Comp. 1914, f.p. London 1914. Also arr. for vn. and pf.

sostenuto (It.), **soutenu** (Fr.). Sustained. Direction that notes must be sustained to their full value in a smooth flow; it can also be interpreted as meaning that a passage is to be played at a slower but uniform speed. Also *sostenendo*, sustaining.

sotto voce (It.). Below the voice. In an undertone or barely audible (as in an aside). Applied to vocal and instr. perf.

soubasse (Fr.). Contra-bourdon org. stop (32′).

soubrette (Fr.). Light sop. taking rather pert roles in opera and operetta such as Despina in *Così fan tutte*, Blonde in *Die Entführung aus dem Serail*, Adèle in *Die Fledermaus*, etc.

Souliotis [Suliotis], **Elena** (*b* Athens, 1943; *d* Florence, 2004). Greek soprano. Début Naples 1964 (Santuzza in *Cavalleria rusticana*). La Scala 1966; Amer. début (Chicago) 1966; London 1968; CG and NY Met 1969.

sound-board. (1) Wooden board on pf. (and other kbd. instr.) placed behind the str. in an upright instr., below them in a grand, to amplify the vol. of sound.
  (2) In an org., the upper portion of wind chest on which pipes sound.

sound-holes. The holes, shaped like an f, cut in the belly of a vn. and related instr. to assist resonance. In lutes, guitars, etc., the holes are more ornamental and are called 'roses'.

soundpost. Piece of wood fixed inside a vn. and other str. instr., vertically connecting upper and lower surfaces and helping to support pressure of str. on the bridge. Thus the vibrations of the str. are distributed over the body of the instr.

sourdine (Fr.). Mute. (1) Mute, used in same sense as *sordino*. *Mettez* (put on), *ôtez* (take off) *les sourdines*.
  (2) Fr. name for early form of bn. (Ger. *Sordun*, It. *sordone*), also known as *courtaut*. Appeared first in 16th cent. and was made in several sizes from bass to descant. Had no bell, the sound coming from lateral hole at top near the crook. Had 12 finger-holes, some also having 2 keys.

Sousa, John Philip (*b* Washington D.C., 1854; *d* Reading, Penn., 1932). Amer. composer and bandmaster. As youth played vn. in th. orchs. Cond., US Marine Corps band 1880–92. Formed own military band 1892 which became very popular and toured Europe 4 times between 1900 and 1905 and the world in 1910–11. It was a victim of the 1931 Depression. Best known for his superb marches, of which he comp. nearly 100, among them *Semper Fidelis* (1888), *The Washington Post* (1889), *Liberty Bell* (1893), *King Cotton* (1895), *The Stars and Stripes Forever* (1896), *El *Capitán* (1896), *Hands across the Sea* (1899), and many more. Also wrote several operettas, incl. *The Queen of Hearts* (1885) and *El *Capitán* (1895).

sousaphone. Amer. helical form of bass tuba made to circle the player's body, with a large

bell turned up through 2 right angles to face forward and terminating in a flange 2′ wide. Made first in 1898 for Sousa's band, the earliest model having bell which opened directly upward. New version dates from 1908. Also used in jazz.

Souster, Tim(othy Andrew James) (*b* Bletchley, 1943; *d* Cambridge, 1994). Eng. composer. BBC mus. producer 1965–7. Comp.-in-residence, King's Coll., Cambridge, 1969–71. Teaching ass. to *Stockhausen, Cologne, 1971–3. Co-founder, 1969, of elec. group Intermodulation. Research fellow in elec. mus., Keele Univ. 1975–7. Also writer on mus. Works incl. *Songs of 3 Seasons*, sop., va. (1965); *Metropolitan Games*, pf. duet (1969); *Song of an Average City*, orch., tape (1974); Sonata, chamber ens. (1979); *Curtain of Light*, metal perc., tape (1984); tpt. conc. (1988); *La Marche*, brass quintet (1992).

Soustrot, Marc (*b* Lyons, 1949). French conductor. Won Rupert Foundation cond. comp., London 1974, Besançon int. comp. 1975. Ass. cond. to André Previn with LSO 1974–6. Deputy cond., then mus. dir., Loire PO 1976–86. Art. dir. Nantes Opera 1986–90. Cond. f.ps. of Ohana's 1st pf. conc. 1981 and Louvier's Conc. for Orch. 1987.

soutenu (Fr.). See *sostenuto*.

Souvenirs de Bayreuth (Memories of Bayreuth). 'Fantaisie en forme de quadrille sur les thèmes favoris de l'Anneau du Nibelung de Richard Wagner', for pf. duet (4 hands) by Fauré and Messager. Comp. probably 1888. Pubd. 1930. Arr. for pf. solo by Samazeuilh.

Souzay, Gérard [Tisserand, Gérard Marcel] (*b* Angers, 1918; *d* Antibes, 2004). Fr. baritone. Recital début Paris 1945. NY début 1950. Occasional appearances in opera, début 1957 at Aix Fest. (Count Robinson in *Il *matrimonio segreto*). Salzburg Fest. début 1959; NY Met début 1965; Glyndebourne 1965. Best known for fine singing of Fr. songs and Ger. *Lieder*. Accompanist from 1954, Dalton Baldwin. Joined faculty of Indiana Univ. Sch. of Mus., Bloomington, 1985, Univ. of Texas in Austin 1986.

Soviet Artist's Practical Creative Reply to Just Criticism, A. Sub-title of Shostakovich's 5th Sym., provided by an anonymous commentator in 1937 after the Soviet hierarchy had criticized 'formalist' tendencies in the composer's opera *Lady Macbeth of the Mtsensk District* and ballet *Bright Stream*.

Sowerby, Leo (*b* Grand Rapids, Mich., 1895; *d* Fort Clinton, Ohio, 1968). Amer. composer and organist. *Prix de Rome* fellow for mus., 1921–4. Taught comp., Amer. Univ., Chicago, 1925–62. Founded College of Church Musicians, Washington, 1962. Prolific composer of org. mus. but wrote in most genres except opera. Works incl. 5 syms., 2 pf. concs., choral works, vn. conc., 2 vc. concs., org. sym., 2 org. concs., *Symphonia Brevis* for org., several cantatas, chamber mus., and over 300 songs.

spagnoletto, spagnoletta, spagniletta, spagnicoletta. Old round dance, probably related to the **pavan*.

Spanisches Liederbuch (Spanish Songbook). 44 songs for v. and pf. by *Wolf, comp. 1889–90, being Ger. trans. by Paul von Heyse (1830–1914) and Emanuel Geibel (1815–84) of Sp. poems pubd. 1852 as *Spanisches Liederbuch*.

Spanish Caprice. Orch. work by Rimsky-Korsakov, Op.34, comp. 1887, often known by mixed It.-Fr. title *Capriccio espagnol*.

Spanish Hour, The (Ravel). See *Heure espagnole, L'*.

Spanish Lady, The. Title of projected opera in 2 acts by Elgar, Op.89, to lib. by Barry Jackson based on Jonson's *The Devil is an Ass* (1616). Begun 1932. 2 songs, ed. P. M. Young, pubd. 1955, and suite for str., ed. Young, 1956. Perf. vers. of opera ed. Young prod. Cambridge 1994.

Spanish Rhapsody (Ravel). See *Rapsodie espagnole*.

Spanish Symphony (Lalo). See *Symphonie espagnole*.

sparta, sparto; spartita, spartito (It.). *Score.

Spartacus (*Spartak*). Ballet in 4 acts, mus. by *Khachaturian, lib. by Volkov, choreog. Jacobson. Comp. 1954, rev. 1968. Four suites, Nos.1–3 (1955–7), No.4 (1967). Prod. Leningrad 1956, Moscow 1958. Extract from mus. used as theme mus. for Brit. TV series *The Onedin Line*.

speaker-keys. Keys fitted to reed wind instr. to facilitate production of harmonics. They open hole(s) which break continuity of air column. Obs. have two and cls. one.

Speaks, Oley (*b* Canal Winchester, Ohio, 1874; *d* NY, 1948). Amer. baritone and composer. Of his 200 songs, best-known are *The Road to Mandalay* and *When the Boys Come Home*.

species. Name given to each of 5 types of process in strict counterpoint. The species are: 1. Added voice (i.e. the counterpoint melody) proceeds at same pace as *cantus firmus (a note to a measure). 2. Added voice proceeds at 2 or 3 times pace of *cantus firmus*. 3. Added voice proceeds at 4 or 6 times pace of *cantus firmus*. 4. Added voice proceeds (as in 2) at rate of 2:1, but 2nd note is tied over to 1st note of following measure (syncopation). 5. Added voice uses mixture of processes of other 4 species and also introduces shorter notes (florid counterpoint).

Spectre de la rose, Le. 1-act ballet, choreog. Fokine, set to mus. of Weber's *Aufforderung zum Tanz* (**Invitation to the Dance*), Op.65, 1819, and danced by Karsavina and Nijinsky, Monte Carlo 1911. Also poem by T. Gautier set by Berlioz as No.2 of song-cycle *Les *Nuits d'été* (1840–1).

Spectre's Bride, The (*Svatebni košile*, The Wedding Shift). Cantata by Dvořák, Op.69, comp.

1884, to text by K. J. Erben, f.p. Pilsen, 1885; (in Eng.) Birmingham Fest. 1885. Same text set by Novák 1913, as his Op.48.

Spells. Setting of poems by Kathleen Raine for sop., ch., and orch. by Richard Rodney *Bennett, comp. 1974, f.p. Worcester Fest. 1975. (2nd and 5th movts. arr. as *Love Spells* for sop. and orch. (1974).) F. p. London 1978.

Spem in alium nunquam habui (In no other is my hope). Motet by *Tallis in 40 parts for eight 5-v. choirs. Commissioned by Thomas Howard, 4th Duke of Norfolk (1538–72) as rival to Alessandro Striggio's 40-part motet *Ecce beatam lucem* (1561). F.p. in Long Gallery of Arundel House, the Duke's London residence on bank of Thames, in 1568 or 1569. Duke is said to have taken gold chain from his neck and placed it round Tallis's in honour of achievement. (Eng. setting entitled 'Sing and Glorify Heaven's High Majesty' was made for banquet after Prince Henry's investiture as Prince of Wales, 1610.) First pubd. (in inaccurate edn.) 1888, then in *Tudor Church Music* 1928 (rev. 1966 by P. Brett).

spianato, spianata (from It. *spiana*, carpenter's plane). Planed, levelled, smoothed.

spiccato (It.). Separated. In playing of bowed str. instr., form of staccato bowing in which the bow is allowed to bounce on the str.; prod. by rapid movements with restricted (central) portion of the bow. Same as *saltando. See also *sautillé*.

Spider's Feast, The (Roussel). See *Festin de l'araignée, Le*.

Spiegl, Fritz (*b* Zurndorf, 1926; *d* Liverpool, 2003). Austrian-born flautist, writer, and broadcaster. Prin. flautist RLPO 1948–63. Expert on mus. curiosities, also on misuse of Eng. language.

spiel; spielen (Ger.). Play; To play. So *spielend*, playing, playful; *Volles Spiel*, Full Org.; *Spieler*, player.

Spieloper (Ger.). A 19th cent. comic opera with spoken dialogue, virtually the same as *Singspiel. Examples are Lortzing's *Der Wildschütz* (1842), Nicolai's *Die lustigen Weiber von Windsor* (1849), and Berlioz's *Béatrice et Bénédict* (1862). Term has also been used, confusingly, to indicate an all-sung opera.

spinet (Fr. *Épinette*; It. *spinetta*). Small type of early kbd. instr. of hpd. family in which str. ran diagonally in front of player or more or less parallel to kbd. as on virginals. Often made in uneven 6-sided shape with kbd. on longest side. Normally one set of str. and 4-octave compass. The name 'spinet' is indiscriminately applied to a no. of plucked kbd. instr. First mentioned 1496. A theory is that it was named after Giovanni Spina, an instr.-maker active in late 15th cent., another that the name derives from its thorn-like plectra, *spinetta* being diminutive of *spina*, a thorn. The 19th-cent. square pf. is often incorrectly called a spinet.

Spink, Ian (*b* London, 1932). Eng. teacher and authority on Eng. lute-songs. Lect. in mus. Sydney Univ., NSW, 1962–9. Head of mus. dept., Royal Holloway Coll., London Univ. 1969–92 (prof. of mus. 1974–97), dean, Faculty of Arts 1973–5, dean, Faculty of Mus., London Univ. 1974–8. Ed. Stainer and Bell edn. of *English Lute-Songs* vols. 17, 18, and 19, *English Song 1625–60* in *Musica Britannica*, xxxiii (1971). Wrote *English Song: Dowland to Purcell* (1974); *Vocal Music from 1660* (1992); *Restoration Cathedral Music, 1660–1714* (1995); *Henry Lawes: Cavalier Songwriter* (2000).

Spinner, Leopold (*b* Lwów, 1906; *d* London, 1980). Austrian composer and teacher. Settled in London 1938. Though influenced by Webern, his works are on a larger scale. They incl.: Sym. (1933), *Passacaglia* for chamber orch. (1934), pf. conc. with chamber orch. (1948), vn. conc. (1955), *Concerto for Orchestra* (1957), *Ricercata*, orch. (1965), *Chamber Sym.* (1979); 3 str. qts. (1935, 1941, 1952), vn. sonata (1936), pf. quintet (1937), pf. sonata (1943), pf. trio (1950), quintet for cl., bn., hn., guitar, db. (1961), cl. sonata (1961), vc. sonatina (1973), cantata *Lebenslauf* (Hölderlin), sop., ch., orch. (1955), and songs.

Spinnerlied (Ger.). Spinning song.

spinto (It.). Pushed, urged on. Term used of certain variety of v., particularly sop. or ten., e.g. *soprano lirico spinto*, meaning a v. which has been 'pushed' into more forceful singing. Butterfly is an example of a *spinto* sop. role.

spirito; spiritoso (It.). Spirit, spirited.

Spirit of England, The. Settings by Elgar, Op.80, for sop. or ten. soloist, ch., and orch. of 3 poems by Binyon, (1) *The 4th of August*, (2) *To Women*, (3) *For the Fallen*. Comp. 1915–17. F.p. of (1) Birmingham 1917, of (2) and (3) Leeds 1916, of complete work London 1917.

spiritual. Folk-hymn which developed during Amer. religious revival of *c.*1740 and took its name from 'spiritual song', the term by which publishers distinguished it from hymns and metrical psalms. Negroes attended revivalist meetings and their characteristic adaptations of spirituals became the religious folk-songs of the Amer. Negro, e.g. *Swing low, sweet chariot, Go down Moses, Deep River*, etc. Became prominent *c.*1871 in concerts by Fisk Jubilee Singers, but even better known in 20th cent. through singing of Paul Robeson and Marian Anderson. Dvořák was deeply touched by Negro spirituals, though their influence on his Amer. works is arguable, and Tippett used some very effectively as chorales in his oratorio *A *Child of Our Time*.

Spitfire Prelude and Fugue. 2 items from film mus. for *The First of the Few* by Walton (1942) rearr. for full orch. F.p. Liverpool 1943. Title refers to Spitfire fighter aircraft used by RAF in Battle of Britain, 1940 (the film told story of its designer, R. J. Mitchell).

Spitta, (Julius August) **Philipp** (*b* Wechold, Hoya, 1841; *d* Berlin, 1894). Ger. music scholar and writer. Taught in various towns incl. Leipzig. Prof. of mus. history, Berlin, 1875–94 and permanent secretary to Berlin Acad. of Arts. Dir., Berlin Hochschule für Musik, 1875–94. Contrib. to several dictionaries, histories, etc. Wrote 2-vol. life of Bach (1873, 1880, Eng. trans. 1884–5) and history of Ger. romantic opera. Ed. organ works of Buxtehude, (1876–7), complete works of Schütz (1885–94), and selected works of Frederick the Great (1889).

Spitze (Ger.). Point. Hence, in str. playing, *an der Spitze*, at the point (of the bow).

Spitzflöte (Ger.). Point-flute. Metal org. stop of slightly conical shape; 8′, 4′, or 2′ length and pitch.

Spivakovsky, Tossy (*b* Odessa, 1907; *d* Westport, Conn., 1998). Russ.-born violinist (later Amer. cit.). Début Berlin 1917. Toured Europe 1920–33, settled in Australia 1933–9. Went to USA 1940. NY recital début 1940. Developed new techniques of bowing in the solo works of Bach.

Spleen. Poem by Verlaine set for v. and pf. by Debussy, 1887–8, as No.6 of *Ariettes oubliées* and by Fauré, 1889, as No.3 of his Op.51.

Spohr, Ludwig (Louis) (*b* Brunswick, 1784; *d* Kassel, 1859). Ger. composer, violinist, and conductor. Child prodigy as violinist and composer. At 14 member of Duke of Brunswick's court orch. Toured Russ. 1802, meeting Clementi and Field. From 1805 toured Ger. as violinist and cond., composing operas and oratorios. Leader of ducal orch. at Gotha from 1805. Vienna début 1812, becoming leader of orch. at Theater an der Wien until 1815. London début at Philharmonic Soc. concert 1820 as solo violinist in his own 8th conc., thereby inaugurating Spohr vogue in Eng. Visited Eng. five more times. Was one of first conds. to use baton. Appointed court cond. for life at Hesse-Kassel 1822 (gen. mus. dir. from 1847). Completed vn. method 1831. Early champion of Wagner, conducting *Der fliegende Holländer* at Kassel 1843 and *Tannhäuser* 1853. Spohr's operas were successful in their day (and *Faust* was successfully revived in London, 1984), but it is the melodic charm of his chamber mus. and his vn. concs. which has principally led to a moderate revival of interest in his work. Prin. comps.:

OPERAS: *Die Prüfung* (1806); *Alruna, die Eulenkönigin* (1808); *Der Zweikampf mit der Geliebten* (1811); *Faust* (1813, rev. 1852); *Zemire und Azor* (1818–19); *Jessonda* (1822–3); *Der Berggeist* (1825); *Pietro von Abano* (1827); *Der Alchymist* (1830); *Die Kreuzfahrer* (1845).

ORATORIOS: *Das jüngste Gericht* (1812); *Die letzten Dinge* (1825–6); *Des Heilands letzte Stunden* (1835); *Der Fall Babylons* (1842).

ORCH.: syms.: No.1 in E♭ (1811), No.2 in D minor (1820), No.3 in C minor (1828), No.4 (*Die Weihe der Töne*, The Power of Sound) (1835), No.5 in C minor (1838), No.6 in G (*Historical Symphony*) (1840), No.7 in C (Double Symphony, *Irdisches und Göttliches im Menschenleben*) (1842), No.8 in G minor (1847), No.9 in B minor (*The Seasons*) (1850), No.10 (1857); 6 ovs.; Waltzes.

CONCERTOS: 18 for vn. (c.1799–1844), No.8 in A minor being sub-titled *Gesangszene*, 'in the form of a vocal scena'; 4 for cl.; potpourris for vn., vc., and orch.; conc. for str. qt. (1845)

CHAMBER MUSIC: 34 str. qts.; 4 double str. qts.; 7 str. quintets; octet in E major (str. and wind); septet for pf. and wind; nonet in F for str. qt., fl., ob., cl., bn., hn.; pf. and wind quintet; 3 pf. trios; str. sextet; sonatas, etc.

Spontini, Gaspare (Luigi Pacifico) (*b* Majolati, Ancona, 1774; *d* Majolati, 1851). It. composer. Some church mus. earned him opera commission for Rome, 1796. 5 other operas followed. Went to Paris 1803, meeting with barely moderate success until the triumph of *La Vestale* in 1807. Became composer to Empress Joséphine 1805, and won favour with Napoléon. Became cond. of It. Opera in Paris 1810, improving standards and giving f. Paris p. of Mozart's *Don Giovanni* in its orig. form. Dismissed 1812, but reinstated 1814. Cond., Berlin Court Opera 1820. There, too, his tenure was stormy and controversial, partly because his quick temper and pompous manner made him hard to work with, and partly because he continued to promote his own Italianate works in the face of the new enthusiasm for Ger. romantic opera engendered by the success of Weber's *Der Freischütz*. When his royal patron died in 1840, Spontini was dismissed in 1841 and sentenced to 9 months imprisonment for *lèse majesté*, but the new king lifted the sentence. Thereafter he lived chiefly in Paris until returning to his native village, to whose poor he left all his property. Operas incl.: *Li puntigli delle donne* (1796), *L'eroismo ridicolo* (1798), *Il finto pittore* (1800), *La fuga in maschera* (1800), *La finta filosofa* (1799), *Milton* (1804), *La *Vestale* (1807), *Fernand Cortez* (1809), *Olympie* (1819), *Nurmahal* (1822), *Alcidor* (1825), *Agnes von Hohenstaufen* (1829). Fest. pageant: *Lalla Rookh* (1821). Most of Spontini's operas were rev. several times. Some have been perf. in It. since 1945 and *La Vestale* was also revived at Wexford, 1979, and later by ENO.

Sprechgesang, Sprechstimme (Ger.). Spoken song, speech-song. Type of vocal perf. between speech and song. First used by *Humperdinck in first version of his opera *Königskinder* (1897), where singers were told to approximate the pitches but were doubled by instr. playing exact pitches. *Schoenberg used the idea in his *Gurrelieder* (1900–11), in *Die *glückliche Hand* (1910–13), and especially in *Pierrot Lunaire* (1912) and in his opera *Moses und Aron* (1930–2). Berg used the device in *Wozzeck*, and many others have used it since. Schoenberg was liberal in his attitude to

manner of perf., as his recording of *Pierrot Lunaire* shows. In general usage, *Sprechgesang* is the term for the vocal technique, *Sprechstimme* for the v.-part employing it. A well-known example of *Sprechgesang* is that of Rex Harrison (and his successors) as Prof. Higgins in *My Fair Lady*.

springer. (1) (Ger. *Nachschlag*). Ornament in which an extra note, indicated in smaller mus.-type, takes part of the preceding note's time-value, i.e. the opposite of *appoggiatura.
(2) Norweg. folk-dance (*springar*) in 3/4 time, used in their mus. by Grieg and Svendsen.

Spring Sonata (*Frühlingssonate*). Nickname given by someone other than Beethoven to his Sonata in F, Op.24, for vn. and pf. (1801)—the name is not inappropriate.

Spring Song (*Frühlingslied*). Unauthorized name for Mendelssohn's *Lied ohne Worte*, No.30 in A, Op.62, No.6.

Spring Symphony. Choral work, Op.44, by Britten for sop., cont., and ten. soloists, ch., boys' choir, and orch. Setting of poems by Herrick, Auden, Barnefield, Peele, Blake, Beaumont, Fletcher, Nashe, Vaughan, Spenser, Clare, Milton and Anon. Comp. 1948–9. F.p. Amsterdam 1949, f. London p. 1950.

'Spring' Symphony. Title given to Schumann's Sym. No.1 in B♭ major (1841).

spugna, bacchetta di (It.). Sponge-headed drumstick.

square piano. Rectangular form of *piano invented in London in 18th cent. and later made by the firm of Broadwood. Several restored instr. are now used to play mus. of the period.

squillante, squillanti (It.). Clanging. (Applied to cymbals, it means that they should be suspended and struck with drumsticks.)

Staatskapelle (Ger.). Literally 'State chapel', but any est. mus. institution such as an orch., deriving from the time of princely courts. Thus, the 400-year-old Dresden orch. is known still as *Staatskapelle Dresden*.

Staatsoper (Ger.). State or municipal opera company in Ger. and Austria. Best known are Berlin, Munich, Dresden, and Vienna. See also *Städtische Oper*.

Stabat Mater Dolorosa (Lat.). 'A grief-stricken mother was standing'. Devotional poem about Virgin Mary's vigil by Christ's Cross, used as sequence in RC liturgy since 1727 to plainchant melody. Text once attrib. Jacopo de Benedetti, Among the many comp. settings are those by Palestrina, Pergolesi, Haydn, Rossini, Verdi, Dvořák, Stanford, Szymanowski, Berkeley, Howells, and others.

Stäbchen (Ger.). Little staff. *Triangle beater.

Stabile, Mariano (*b* Palermo, 1888; *d* Milan, 1968). It. baritone. Opera début Palermo 1911

(Marcello in *La bohème*). Sang title-role in *Falstaff* at La Scala in 1921 under Toscanini; he sang it nearly 1,200 times until 1960 and his perf. is regarded as unsurpassed. Sang at CG 1926–31; Salzburg Fest. 1931–9; Glyndebourne 1936–9. Returned to London at Cambridge and Stoll Th.s' opera seasons 1946–8. Repertory of over 60 parts, incl. Iago, Figaro, Don Giovanni, and Scarpia.

staccato (It.). Detached. Method of playing a note (shown by a dot over the note) so that it is shortened—and thus 'detached' from its successor—by being held for less than its full value. Superlative is *staccatissimo*. For signs used to indicate degrees of staccato see diagram below.

Stade, Frederica von (*b* Somerville, NJ, 1945). Amer. mezzo-soprano. Opera début with NY Met 1970 (3rd Boy in *Die Zauberflöte*) and sang small roles there for three seasons. Glyndebourne début 1973; Salzburg Fest. début 1974; CG début 1975. Sang Mélisande at Santa Fe 1972 and Penelope in *Il *Ritorno d'Ulisse in patria* at NY City Opera 1976, roles she later sang often elsewhere. Exceptional Oktavian in *Der Rosenkavalier*. Successful in Broadway musical recordings, e.g. Bernstein's *On the Town*.

Stader(-Erismann), **Maria** (*b* Budapest, 1911; *d* Zurich, 1999). Hung.-born Swiss sop. Won Geneva int. comp. 1939. Salzburg Fest. début (concert) 1947. Celebrated singer of Mozart and Strauss. Teacher at Zurich Mus. Acad. Retired 1969.

Stadlen, Peter (*b* Vienna, 1910; *d* London, 1996). Austrian-born pianist, conductor, and music critic (Brit. cit. 1946). Career as pianist from 1934, specializing in Viennese classics and 2nd Viennese Sch. Gave f.ps. of Webern's Pf. Variations (1937), Krenek's *Bagatelles* for pf. duet, with composer (1936). Settled in Eng. 1939. Master classes

in modern pf. works, Darmstadt 1948–51. Soloist in f. Ger. p. of Schoenberg conc. (Darmstadt 1948). Schoenberg Medal 1952. Mus. lect., Reading Univ., 1965–9. Mus. critic, *Daily Telegraph*, from 1960 (chief critic 1977–86). Author of monographs on Beethoven's metronome marks, decline of serialism, Schoenberg and *Sprechgesang*, and Schindler's Beethoven forgeries.

Stadler, Anton (Paul) (*b* Bruck an der Leitha, 1753; *d* Vienna, 1812). Austrian clarinettist and basset-horn player. Member of Vienna court orch. 1787–99. Friend of Mozart, who greatly admired his playing of the 'basset clarinet' (a cl. with a downward extension of 4 semitones) and wrote for him the Cl. Trio in E♭ (K498, 1786), the Cl. Quintet in A (K581, 1789), and the Cl. Conc. in A (K622, 1791), as well as other pieces such as the cl. and basset-horn obbligati in *La Clemenza di Tito* which Stadler played at the f.p. in Prague, 1791. The quintet and conc. were pubd. in altered form to suit a normal cl., but in the 20th cent. Alan *Hacker has played the orig. versions to good effect. Stadler and Mozart played together in f.p. of Mozart's E♭ quintet (K452), Vienna 1784. Also comp. many pieces for cl. and 18 trios for 3 basset-horns.

Städtische Oper (Ger.). City or municipal opera house. The company working there is the *Staats-oper*.

Stadtpfeifer (Ger.). Town piper. Musician(s) in employ of town council. Term used since late 14th cent. in European cities. Duties of these musicians incl. perf. at official festivities, weddings, baptisms, royal visits, etc. They had exclusive right to provide mus. in the city boundaries.

staff (stave, plural staves). The system of parallel lines on and between which the notes are written, from which mus. is played, the pitch being

Mezzo-staccato (shorten the note by about $^1/_4$)	**Staccato** (shorten the notes by about $^1/_2$)	**Staccatissimo** (shorten the notes by about $^3/_4$)
Written or		
Played (approximately)		

The sign ⸗ ⸗ ⸗ (i.e. a combination of accent marks and staccato marks) indicates a combination of pressure with a slight detachment.

determined by the *clef written at the beginning of the staff. Normally of 5 lines, but plainsong uses a staff of 4 lines. In medieval tablature a 6- or even 7-line staff was used. 'Staff notation' means ordinary notation as distinct from Tonic Sol-fa, etc. See also *great staff*.

Staggins, Nicholas (*d* Windsor, 1700). Eng. composer and violinist. Appointed Master of the King's Band (i.e. Master of the King's Musick) by Charles II in 1674. First prof. of mus. Cambridge Univ., 1684. Wrote songs.

stagione (It.). Season. Term used with reference to opera. *Stagione lirica* is the opera season at It. ths.; a *stagione* th. is one in which each opera in its repertory is perf. for a short season of perfs.

Stainer, (Sir) **John** (*b* London, 1840; *d* Verona, 1901). Eng. composer, organist, teacher, and scholar. Chorister, St Paul's Cath., 1849–54. Org., St Paul's 1872–88. Prof. of org. and harmony, Nat. Training Sch. of Mus., and prin. 1881–9. Prof. of mus., Oxford Univ., 1889–1901. Wrote books on harmony and about *Du Fay. His *Early Bodleian Music* (1901) is one of first serious studies of medieval music. Comp. much church mus., incl. *Sevenfold Amen*, and oratorios and cantatas of which the best-known is The *Crucifixion* (1887). Knighted 1888.

Stainer and Bell. Eng. firm of mus. publishers, founded 1907 by group of composers to publish Brit. music (there was no Mr Stainer nor Mr Bell). Publisher of Carnegie coll. of modern Brit. works from 1917. Also pubd. Eng. madrigalists, lute-song writers, works of Byrd, etc.

Stamitz [Stamic], **Anton** (Johann) [Jan Antonín] (*b* Nĕmecký Brod, 1750; *d* ?Paris, after 1789). Member of Cz. family of musicians who settled in Ger. and adopted Ger. form of surname. Son of Johann Wenzel *Stamitz. Went with brother Karl to Paris in 1770 and settled there as comp., violinist, and viola player. Wrote 12 syms., various concs., str. qts., etc.

Stamitz [Stamic], **Johann Wenzel** [Jan Václav Antonín] (*b* Nĕmecký Brod, Bohemia, 1717; *d* Mannheim, 1757). Bohem.-born violinist and composer. Played vn. at coronation of Karl VII 1742 and was heard by Elector of Mannheim who made him court violinist and mus. dir. in 1743. Raised the orch. there to standards which became famous throughout Europe and influenced composers such as Haydn and Mozart. Visited Paris 1754–5, playing at Concert Spirituel. As composer, greatly developed sonata-form principles in the sym., giving new importance to development section. Wrote 58 syms., 15 vn. concs., vn. sonatas, and much else.

Stamitz [Stamic], **Karl** [Karel] (*b* Mannheim, 1745; *d* Jena, 1801). Ger. composer and violinist, son of Johann Wenzel *Stamitz. Violinist in Mannheim orch. 1762–70. Went to Paris with brother in 1770 and to London 1777–9. Returned to Ger. as cond. at Jena. Also visited Russ. Wrote

operas, over 50 syms., 38 sinfonie concertanti (for vn. and va., etc.), concs. for various instr. (incl. vn., vc., va. d'amore, bn., cl., fl., hpd.), and chamber mus.

Standage, Simon (*b* High Wycombe, 1941). Eng. violinist and conductor. Member of LSO, later deputy leader ECO. Leader Eng. Concert 1973, and of City of London Sinfonia. Founded Salomon Qt. 1981. Teacher of baroque vn., RAM, from 1983. Founded Collegium Musicum 90, 1990. Assoc. dir., Acad. of Ancient Mus. from 1991.

Ständchen (Ger.). Serenade. Songs by Schubert, R. Strauss, etc., carry this title.

Standford, Patric (John) (*b* Barnsley, 1939). Eng. composer. Awarded Mendelssohn Schol. 1964 and went to It. to study with *Malipiero and *Lutosławski, 1964–5. Prof. of comp. GSMD 1967–80; also taught at Goldsmiths' Coll and Chetham's Sch. of Mus., Manchester. Dir. of Mus. Sch., Bretton Hall Coll. (Univ. of Leeds), Wakefield, 1980–93. Awarded City of Geneva's Ansermet Prize 1983 for his 3rd Sym. Works incl. *Villon*, opera (1972–84); 5 syms. (1971–84); concs.: vc. (1974), vn. (1975); pf. (1979); *Stabat Mater* (1966); 3 str. qts. (1964, 1973, 1992); pf. qt. (1988); *3 Nocturnes*, pf. (1991); *A Jersey Suite*, orch. (1994); *A Prayer of St Francis*, ch., orch. (1997); *Concertino*, hpd., small orch. (1999); *The Winged Messenger*, ob. (2001); *Symphonic Scherzo 'Mozartiana'*, orch. (2005); *Serenata*, 2 gui., cl., vn., va. (2006).

Stanford, (Sir) **Charles Villiers** (*b* Dublin, 1852; *d* London, 1924). Irish composer, conductor, organist, and teacher. Org., Trinity College, Cambridge, 1873–92. Cond., Cambridge Univ. Mus. Soc. from 1873, winning it high reputation and giving f. Eng. ps. of works by Brahms. Tennyson asked him to write incidental mus. for his play *Queen Mary*, 1876. Prof. of comp., RCM, 1883–1924, pupils incl. Vaughan Williams, Bliss, Howells, Ireland, Holst, Gurney, etc. Prof. of mus., Cambridge Univ., 1887–1924. Cond., Bach Choir 1885–1902, also cond. of orch. concerts and opera at RCM. Cond. of several Leeds Fests. after 1901. Prolific composer, whose best work is to be found in his operas, choral mus., and songs rather than in his orch. and chamber mus., where his admiration for Brahms tended to become paramount. One of prin. figures in late 19th-cent. 'renaissance' of Brit. mus. Ed. and arr. colls. of Irish traditional tunes. Knighted 1901. Prin. works:

OPERAS: *The Veiled Prophet of Khorassan* (1877); *Savonarola* (1884); *The *Canterbury Pilgrims* (1884); *Lorenza* (unpubd.); *Shamus O'Brien* (1896); *Much Ado About Nothing* (1900); *The *Critic* (1915); *The *Travelling Companion* (1919).

ORCH.: syms.: No.1 in B♭ (1875), No.2 in D minor (*Elegiac*) (1882), No.3 in F minor (*Irish*) (1887), No.4 in F (1888), No.5 in D (*L'Allegro ed il Penserioso*) (1894), No.6 in E♭ (1905), No.7 in D minor (1911); *Overture in the Style of A Tragedy*

(1904); 6 *Irish Rhapsodies*; cl. conc. (1902); 3 pf. concs. (1895, 1915, 1919); 2 vn. concs. (1904, 1918); *Irish Concerto*, vn., vc., orch. (1919).

CHORAL: oratorios: *The Three Holy Children* (1885), *Eden* (1891); *Requiem* (1897); *Te Deum* (1898); *Stabat Mater* (1907); *Magnificat in G*; *The *Revenge*, choral ballad (1886); *Phaudrig Crohoore* (1896); *The Last Post* (1900); 5 **Songs of the Sea*, bar., male ch., orch. (1904); 5 **Songs of the Fleet*, bar., ch. (1910).

CHAMBER MUSIC: 8 str. qts., 2 str. quintets, 2 pf. trios, 2 pf. qts., pf. quintet, 2 vn. sonatas, 2 vc. sonatas, cl. sonata.

Also organ preludes, songs, partsongs (incl. *The *Blue Bird*), anthems, and church services (notably that in B♭, Op.10, 1879 with additions 1910).

Stanley, (Charles) **John** (*b* London, 1712; *d* London, 1786). Eng. composer and organist, blinded at age 2. Org. of various London churches, incl. the Temple, from 1734. Wrote 6 cantatas, 1748, oratorio *Jephtha* 1751-2. The 6 concs. for str., with org. or hpd., Op.10, have considerable appeal, influenced by Handel, and he also wrote 30 org. voluntaries, fl. solos, etc. Succeeded Boyce as Master of the King's Musick, 1779.

Star Clusters, Nebulae, and Places in Devon. Work for mixed double ch. and brass by David *Bedford, comp. 1971; arr. Bram Wiggins, 1974, for mixed double ch. and brass band.

stark (Ger.). Strong, loud; so *stärker*, stronger, louder. **stark anblasen, stark blasend**. Strongly blown (wind instr.).

Starker, János (*b* Budapest, 1924). Hung.-born cellist (Amer. cit. 1954). Début age of 11. Prin. cellist Budapest Opera and PO, 1945-6. Settled in USA 1948. Prin. cellist Dallas SO 1948-9, NY Met opera orch. 1949-53, Chicago SO 1953-8. Prof. of vc., Indiana Univ. Sch. of Mus., Bloomington, from 1958. Invented a vc. bridge.

Starlight Express, The. Incidental mus. by Elgar, Op.78, to play by Violet Pearn based on Algernon Blackwood's *Prisoner in Fairyland*. Prod. London 1915. Contains songs for sop. and bass soloists. Quotes themes from **Wand of Youth*. Cowbells and wind-machine used in score. Not to be confused with A. Lloyd Webber's *Starlight Express* (1984).

Star-Spangled Banner, The. Nat. anthem of USA, officially adopted under Senate Bill in 1931 but long used as such before that. Words written by Francis Scott Key (1779-1843) of Baltimore on 15 Sept. 1814, after he had seen defence of Fort McHenry, near Baltimore, against Brit. bombardment. First appeared in *Baltimore Patriot*, 20 Sept. 1814. Metre of poem indicates it was written to tune of *To Anacreon in Heaven* by Eng. composer J. Stafford Smith which was then popular in Amer. as official song of Anacreontic socs. there.

Stasov [Stassov], **Vladimir** (Vasilyevich) (*b* St Petersburg, 1824; *d* St Petersburg, 1906). Russ. critic. Worked in art div. of Imperial Public Library, St Petersburg, from 1856. Champion of Russ. nationalism in arts, esp. mus. Wrote monographs on Mussorgsky, Borodin, Cui, Rimsky-Korsakov, Dargomizhsky, Glinka, and others. In 1867, in newspaper article, coined phrase 'mighty handful' (*moguchaya kuchka*) later applied to Russ. nationalist composers known as 'The *Five'.

stave. Same as **staff*.

Steane, J(ohn) **B**(arry) (*b* Coventry, 1928). Eng. writer and broadcaster. Reviewer for *Gramophone* from 1972. Author of *The Grand Tradition: 70 Years of Singing on Record* (1974), *Voices, Singers and Critics* (1992), and *Singers of the Century* (1996-8). Contributor to many operatic periodicals and dictionaries.

Steber, Eleanor (*b* Wheeling, W. Virginia, 1916; *d* Langhorne, Penn., 1990). Amer. soprano. Gave recitals and became church soloist in NY. Opera début Boston 1936 (Senta in *Der fliegende Holländer*). Won Metropolitan Auditions of the Air 1940, making début at Met in Dec. 1940 and then member of Met co. until 1963, highly successful in Mozart and Strauss, also in Puccini and as Marie (*Wozzeck*). S. Francisco début 1945; Bayreuth 1953. Created title-role in Barber's *Vanessa*, her Salzburg début (1958). Sang with Glyndebourne at Edinburgh Fest. 1947. Sang title-role in f. Amer. p. of *Arabella* (NY Met 1955) and gave f.p. of Barber's *Knoxville: Summer of 1915* (1948) which she commissioned. After retirement from stage, gave *Lieder* recitals and was head of voice dept., Cleveland Inst. of Mus. 1963-72. Taught at New England Cons. and Juilliard Sch. (both from 1971) and at Amer. Inst. of Mus. Studies, Graz., 1978-80 and 1988.

steel band. Type of instr. ens. in the Caribbean, 'instruments' being old oil drums whose heads are indented, etc., so that each head will produce several notes. Used extensively in calypso mus.

Steel, (Charles) **Christopher** (*b* London, 1939; *d* Cheltenham, 1991). Eng. composer. Taught mus. at Cheltenham College, 1963-6, ass. dir. of mus. Bradfield College 1966-8, dir. 1966-81. Wrote several works for amateur enjoyment in addition to orch. mus. and choral pieces. Chief comps.: 7 syms. (3rd being *A Shakespeare Symphony* for bar., ch., orch., 1965); conc., str. qt., orch. (1966); org. conc.; *Odyssey* (suite for brass band, 1973); *Mass* in 5 movts., sop., ten., ch., orch. (1964); *Gethsemane*, cantata (1964); *Mary Magdalene*, cantata (1966); **Paradise Lost*, cantata, sop., ten., bass, ch., orch. (1966); *Passion and Resurrection according to St Mark*, sop., ten., bass, ch., orch. (1979); pf. sonatinas; cl. sonatina; *Divertimento*, wind quintet; pf. trio; str. qt.; 6 *Pieces*, org.; org. sonata; fl. trio, etc., and chamber opera *Angry River* (f.p. Cheltenham 1990).

Steel-Perkins, Crispian (*b* Exeter, 1944). Eng. trumpeter. Specialist in baroque tpt., having taken part in over 700 recordings. Frequent soloist and performer with City of London Sinfonia, ECO, King's Consort, Parley of Instruments, and Eng. Baroque Soloists. Prof. of tpt., GSMD, from 1980. Toured USA 1988, Japan 1990.

Stefano, Giuseppe di. See *Di Stefano, Giuseppe*.

Steg (Ger.). Bridge (of vn., etc.). *am Steg*, same as **sul ponticello*, i.e. bow on (near) the bridge.

Steibelt, Daniel (Gottlieb) (*b* Berlin, 1765; *d* St Petersburg, 1823). Ger. pianist and composer. Deserted from Prussian army in 1784 and travelled through Eur. as pianist. From 1790 to 1797 was fashionable teacher and pianist in Paris, where his opera *Romeo and Juliet* was prod. 1793. From 1797 to 1808 he was often in London, as well as in Vienna, 1799, where he was involved in an improvisation contest with Beethoven and came off much the worse. In Paris, 1800, he cond. Haydn's *The Creation* with additions and alterations of his own. Wrote ballets for London, 1804–5. Court cond. to Emperor Alexander in St Petersburg 1810, succeeding Boieldieu as cond. of Fr. opera there. Wrote 8 pf. concs., over 160 vn. sonatas, and a pf. method.

Steiger, Anna (*b* Los Angeles, 1960). Amer. soprano. Won Sir Peter Pears Award 1982, Richard Tauber Prize 1984, John Christie Award 1985. In Glyndebourne chorus 1983. Opera début 1984, with Opera 80 (Dorabella in *Così fan tutte*). Débuts: GTO 1985; Glyndebourne 1986; CG 1987; ENO 1988; Los Angeles 1989; NY City Opera 1990.

Stein, Erwin (*b* Vienna, 1885; *d* London, 1958). Austrian-born conductor, editor, and critic (later Eng. cit.). Pupil of Schoenberg 1906–10 and active as opera cond. Ed. for Universal Edition in Vienna 1924–38. Settled in London 1938, joining Boosey and Hawkes. Ed. Schoenberg's letters. Associate and friend of Britten. Book of essays, *Orpheus in New Guises*, 1953.

Stein, Fritz (Friedrich Wilhelm) (*b* Gerlachsheim, Baden, 1879; *d* Berlin, 1961). Ger. musicologist and cond. Mus. dir., later prof., Jena Univ. 1906–14, 1915–18, court cond., Meiningen 1914–15. Taught musicology at Kiel Univ. 1920–33 (prof. from 1928). Dir., Berlin Hochschule für Musik 1933–45. While at Jena found in library parts of sym. which he pubd. in 1911 as 'an unknown sym. of Beethoven's youth'. This became known as **Jena' Symphony*. In 1957 Robbins **Landon discovered it was the work of Friedrich Witt.

Stein, Horst (Walter) (*b* Elberfeld, 1928). Ger. conductor. Cond. at Hamburg Opera 1951–5, Berlin State Opera 1955–61, Mannheim 1963–70, Vienna 1970–2. Gen. mus. dir. Hamburg State Opera 1972–7. Cond., Orchestre de la Suisse Romande 1980–5, Bamberg SO 1986–96. Bayreuth début 1969 (*Parsifal*), subsequently cond. *Der Ring des Nibelungen* 1970–5. Salzburg Fest. début 1973 (Vienna PO concert), opera 1985 (*Capriccio*).

Stein, Peter (*b* Berlin, 1937). Ger. theatre and opera producer. Joined Munich Kammerspiele 1964. Co-founder and art. dir. Schaubühne Co., Berlin, 1970–85. First opera prod. Paris 1976 (*Das Rheingold*). For WNO has prod. *Otello* (1986), *Falstaff* (1988), and *Pelléas et Mélisande* (1992). Drama dir., Salzburg Fest. 1992–4.

Steinbach, Fritz (*b* Grünsfeld, Baden, 1855; *d* Munich, 1916). Ger. conductor and composer. Second cond. at Mainz 1880–6. Taught in Frankfurt 1883–6. Cond. Meiningen Orch. 1886–1902, taking it on tour (incl. England) 1902. Guest cond. NYPO 1906. Cond. Gürzenich concerts, Cologne (succeeding Wüllner) and dir., Cologne Cons. from 1902. Famous as Brahms interpreter, also cond. several Elgar works in Ger. Wrote chamber mus. and songs. Retired 1914.

Steinberg, Maximilian (*b* Vilna, 1883; *d* Leningrad, 1946). Russ. composer and teacher. Son-in-law of Rimsky-Korsakov from 1908. Prof. of comp. St Petersburg Cons. from 1908, becoming dir. 1934. Pupils incl. **Shostakovich. Comps. incl. 4 syms. (1907, 1909, 1928, 1933), ballets, vn. conc., choral works, 2 str. qts., pf. pieces, and songs.

Steinberg, Pinchas (*b* NY, 1945). Amer. conductor. Ass. cond. Chicago Lyric Opera 1967 (début *Don Giovanni*). Guest cond. Eur. sym. orchs. from 1972 and cond. opera in Berlin, Frankfurt, London, Paris, and S. Francisco. Gen. mus. dir. Bremen 1985–9. Chief cond. Austrian Radio SO 1989–96; art. & mus. dir. Orch. de la Suisse Romande 2002–5. Salzburg début 1990.

Steinberg, William [Wilhelm Hans] (*b* Cologne, 1899; *d* NY, 1978). Ger.-born conductor (Amer. cit. 1944). Ass. cond. to Klemperer at Cologne Opera 1920. Cond., German Th. in Prague 1925–9. Mus. dir. Frankfurt Opera 1929–33 (cond. f.p. of Schoenberg's *Von Heute auf Morgen* 1930); mus. dir. Jewish Culture League, Ger., 1933–6. In Palestine 1936–8. Settled in USA 1938. Ass. cond. NBC SO 1938–41. Cond. Buffalo PO 1945–52, Pittsburgh SO 1952–76. Salzburg Fest. début 1962. Prin. cond. LPO 1958–62, Boston SO 1969–72, prin. guest cond. NYPO 1964–8.

Steiner, Max(imilian Raoul) (*b* Vienna, 1888; *d* Hollywood, Calif., 1971). Austrian-born composer (Amer. cit.). Cond. musical comedies in London 1905–11. Settled in USA 1914. Worked in NY as orchestrator and cond. of musicals. Went to Hollywood 1929 and wrote mus. for many successful films, incl. *King Kong*, *The Informer*, *Now, Voyager*, *Gone With the Wind*, *Since You Went Away*, and *The Treasure of Sierra Madre*.

Steinitz, (Charles) **Paul** (Joseph) (*b* Chichester, 1909; *d* Oxted, 1988). Eng. organist and choral conductor. On teaching staff RAM. Org., St Bartholomew the Great, Smithfield, 1949–61. Founder and cond., London Bach Soc. from 1946. Prof., RAM, from 1945 and taught at Goldsmiths' Coll., Univ. of London, 1948–76. Famous for perfs. of Bach's *St Matthew Passion* in Ger. with forces near to Leipzig orig. Wrote *Bach's Passions* (London, 1979). OBE 1985.

Steinspiel (Ger.). Stone-play. Perc. instr. specially made for *Orff's operas *Antigone* and *Oedipus Tyrannus*. Shaped like a kbd., it is an arr. of stone bars, struck by beaters held in player's hand.

Steinway and Sons. NY firm of pf. manufacturers founded 1853 by Heinrich Engelhard Steinway (orig. Steinweg) (*b* Wolfshagen, 1797; *d* NY, 1871) and his sons Charles and Henry, who in 1851 had gone to NY from Hamburg where they were involved in the Steinweg firm which eventually became Grotrian-Steinweg. At 1855 NY World Fair, Steinway prod. iron-framed pf. of much greater sonority than had hitherto been heard. A 3rd son, Theodore, joined the firm in the 1860s and developed the concert-grands which made the firm world-famous. Branch opened in London 1875 by 4th son, William, and factories est. in Hamburg 1880. Amer. factory moved to Long Island to site which became known as Steinway. Firm sold to CBS in 1972.

Stemme, Nina (*b* Stockholm, 1967). Swed. soprano. Studied at Adolf Fredrik Sch. of Mus. Played va. before taking up singing. Studied business administration and economics at Stockholm Univ. parallel with 2-year course at Stockholm Opera Studio. Début Cortona 1989 (Cherubino), then studied at Nat. Coll. of Opera, Stockholm, until 1994. Won Domingo comp. 1993. Bayreuth Fest. 1994 (Freia in *Das Rheingold*). Joined Cologne Opera 1996, singing roles such as Pamina, *Figaro* Countess, Mimì, and Agathe. NY Met début 2000 (Senta), Glyndebourne 2003 (Isolde), CG 2005 (Amelia in *Ballo in maschera*). Wigmore Hall début 2006.

stendendo (It.). Extending, i.e. spacing out the notes (same as *rallentando*).

Stenhammar, (Karl) **Wilhelm** (Eugen) (*b* Stockholm, 1871; *d* Stockholm, 1927). Swedish pianist, composer, and conductor. Mus. dir., Stockholm Phil. 1897–1900, 2nd cond. Royal Th., Stockholm, 1900–1 and chief cond. 1924–5. Cond. Göteborg SO 1906–22. Wrote 2 operas; 2 syms. (1902–3, 1911–15); 2 pf. concs. (1893, 1904–7); *2 Sentimental Romances*, vn., orch. (1910); *Serenade* (1911–13, rev. 1919); 6 str. qts. (1894–1916); vn. sonata; 2 pf. sonatas; songs.

Stenz, Markus (*b* Bad Neuenahr, 1965). Ger. conductor. Cond. f.p. of *Das *verratene Meer*, Berlin 1990. Los Angeles Opera début 1993. Mus. dir. Montepulciano Fest. 1989–94. Prin. cond. London Sinfonietta 1994–8. ENO début 1995. Chief cond. and art. dir. Melbourne SO 1998–2004; mus. dir Cologne Opera from 2004.

Stephan, Rudi (*b* Worms, 1887; *d* Tarnopol, Galicia, 1915). Ger. composer. After success of *Music for 7 String Instruments* (2 vn., va., vc., db., hp., pf.) at Danzig Fest. 1912, was regarded as one of leaders of new *Jungdeutsch* school. His style re-

sembled *Zemlinsky and he was influenced by Strauss, Debussy, and Delius. Killed in action. Works incl. opera *Die ersten Menschen* (1911–14, prod. Frankfurt 1920); *Liebeszauber*, 1st vers. ten., orch. (1909–10) withdrawn, 2nd vers. bar., orch. (1913); *Music for 7 String Instruments* (1911); *Music for Orchestra* (1912); *Music for Violin and Orchestra* (1913); 18 songs (1908–14).

Steppes of Central Asia, In the (Borodin). See *In the Steppes of Central Asia*.

sterbend (Ger.). Dying away.

Stern, Isaac (*b* Kremenets, 1920; *d* NY, 2001). Russ.-born Amer. violinist, taken as infant to San Francisco. Début 1935 (recital), and 1936 with S. Francisco SO (Saint-Saëns 3rd vn. conc.). NY début 1937. Int. career as conc. soloist, also fine chamber-mus. player, esp. in assoc. with Eugene Istomin (pf.) and Leonard Rose (vc.).

steso (It., 'spread out'). Slow.

stesso, stessa, stessi, stesse (It.). Same.

Steuermann, Eduard (*b* Sambor, nr. Lwów, 1892; *d* NY, 1964). Polish-born pianist and composer (Amer. cit.). Pianist in f.ps. of Schoenberg's *Pierrot Lunaire* 1912 and of most other Schoenberg works with pf. part. Also gave f.p. of Berg's sonata. Pianist for Schoenberg's Society for Private Musical Performances. Taught pf. at Lwów and at Kraków Cons. (1932–6). Settled in USA 1936, teaching and playing in NY. Taught at Philadelphia Cons. 1948–63 and at Juilliard Sch. 1952–64. Gave summer classes at Salzburg Mozarteum 1953–63. Tireless champion of 12-note mus., especially Schoenberg's, several of whose orch. works he transcr. for pf. Gave series of concerts of contemporary mus. in NY. Works incl. cantata to text by Kafka, *Variations* for orch., *Suite* for chamber orch., song-cycles, str. qts., etc.

Stevens, Bernard (George) (*b* London, 1916; *d* Great Maplestead, Essex, 1983). Eng. composer. Prof. of comp., RCM, from 1948. Works incl. *Symphony of Liberation* (1945); 2nd Sym. (1964); vn. conc. (1943); vc. conc. (1952); pf. conc. (1955); chamber mus.; songs; film mus.

Stevens, Denis (William) (*b* High Wycombe, 1922; *d* London, 2004). Eng. musicologist, critic, violinist, and conductor. Worked as mus. critic in Calcutta and Oxford. Played vn. and va. in Philharmonia Orch. 1946–9. On BBC mus. staff as producer specializing in Renaissance and Baroque mus. 1949–54. Cond., Ambrosian Singers 1956–60. Prof., RAM 1956–61, prof. of musicology, Columbia Univ., NY, 1964–74. Ed. of Monteverdi's *Vespers* (1961, rev. 1993) and *Orfeo* (1967). Salzburg Fest. 1967; cond. first Monteverdi at Proms, 1967. Author of books on Tudor church mus. and Thomas Tomkins, ed. of Eng. madrigals, Tudor org. mus., etc. Trans. letters of Monteverdi (1980). CBE 1984.

Stevens, Halsey (*b* Scott, NY, 1908; *d* Long Beach, Calif., 1989). Amer. composer and writer.

Held various univ. teaching posts from 1935, becoming prof. and chairman of mus. dept. at Univ. of S. California, Los Angeles, Sch. of Mus. 1948–76. Author of *Life and Music of Béla Bartók* (NY 1953, rev. 1964). Prolific composer, works incl. 3 syms.; vc. conc.; cl. conc.; double conc.; va. conc.; choral pieces (many unacc.); songs; and much chamber mus., incl. 3 str. qts.

Stevens [Steenberg], **Risë** (*b* NY, 1913). Amer. mezzo-soprano. Début Little Th. Opera, NY, 1931 in *The Bartered Bride*. Sang in Prague 1936–8, also in Vienna and Buenos Aires. NY Met début 1938; Glyndebourne début 1939. Member of Met co. until 1961. Outstanding Carmen, Oktavian, Delilah, and Orlofsky. Appeared in films (e.g *Going My Way* with Bing *Crosby). Retired 1965. Gen. man., Met Nat. Touring Co. 1965–7. Pres., Mannes Coll. 1975–8. Taught at Juilliard Sch. from 1975.

Stevenson, Robert (Murrell) (*b* Melrose, New Mexico, 1916). Amer. musicologist, composer, and pianist. Début pf. recital NY 1942, London 1953. Joined faculty of UCLA 1949 (prof. from 1961, faculty research lect. 1981). Retired in 1990s. Authority on Sp., Portuguese, and Latin-Amer. music.

Stevenson, Ronald (*b* Blackburn, 1928). Scottish pianist and composer. Taught comp. at Cape Town Univ. 1963–5. London Prom début 1972 (his 2nd pf. conc.). Mus. influenced by Busoni and Scottish folk mus. Self-confessed aim is for an 'epic music . . . absorbing elements from East and from Africa, as well as from Western culture'. Works incl. *Prelude, Fugue, and Fantasy on Busoni's Faust*, pf. (1949–59); *Passacaglia on DSCH*, pf. (1961–2); *Jamboree for Grainger*, orch. (1961); *Weyvers o' Blegburn* (Weavers of Blackburn), boy's broken v., weak amateur ten., amateur ch., pf. (to Lancashire dialect) (1961); hpd. sonata (1968); pf. conc. No.1 (*Faust Triptych*) (1960), No.2 (*The Continents*) (1972); *Peter Grimes Fantasy*, pf. (1970); *Border Boyhood*, song-cycle, ten., pf. (1970); *9 Haiku*, sop., ten., pf./hp. (1971); *Ben Dorain*, choral sym. (1973); vn. conc. (*The Gipsy*) (1973); *Corroboree for Grainger*, pf., wind band (1987); *St Mary's May Songs*, sop., str. (1988); *Voces Vagabundae*, str. qt. (1990); *Choral Recitative and Psalm 23*, ch., org. (1990–2); vc. conc. (1992); *A Carlyle Suite*, pf. (1995); *Pan-Celtic Wind Quintet*, fl., cl., ob., bn., hn. (2000).

Stewart, Thomas (James) (*b* San Saba, Texas, 1928; *d* Rockville, Md., 2006). Amer. baritone. Opera début as student NY 1954 (La Roche in *Capriccio*). NY City Opera 1954 (Commendatore in *Don Giovanni*). Berlin State Opera 1957–64; CG 1960–78; Bayreuth 1960–72; NY Met 1966–80; S. Francisco 1971. Particularly impressive in Wagner. Sang title-role in Amer. première of Reimann's *Lear*, S. Francisco 1981.

Stich, Johann Wenzel. See *Punto, Giovanni*.

Stich-Randall, Teresa (*b* New Hartford, Conn., 1927). Amer. soprano. While at Columbia Univ.

created Henrietta M in Amer. premières of Thomson's *The Mother of us all* and sang in Bloch's *Macbeth*. In 1949 chosen by Toscanini to sing in NBC perfs. of *Aida* (Priestess) and *Falstaff* (Nannetta). Won Lausanne int. competition for opera singers. Débuts: Eur. (Florence) 1951; Salzburg Fest. 1952; Vienna Opera 1952; Aix Fest. 1955 (and until 1971); Chicago Opera 1955; NY Met 1961. First American to be made an Austrian *Kammersängerin*, 1962.

sticker. Light wooden rod in org. which operates the pallet.

Stiedry, Fritz (*b* Vienna, 1883; *d* Zurich, 1968). Austrian-born conductor (Amer. cit.). Recommended by Mahler to *Schuch, who engaged him at Dresden Opera 1907–8. 2nd cond. Kassel court opera 1913; 1st cond. Berlin Opera 1916–23; cond. Vienna Volksoper 1924–5 (f.p. of *Die *glückliche Hand*, 1924); Berlin Städtische Oper 1928–33. Mus. dir., Leningrad PO 1934–7. Went to USA 1938. Cond. f.p. of Schoenberg's 2nd Chamber Sym. 1940. Cond., New Opera Co., NY, 1941, Chicago 1945–6, NY Met 1946–58, being prin. Wagner cond. but, as in Berlin, cond. major Verdi prods. Cond. Glyndebourne 1947; CG 1953–4. Retired to Zurich.

Stierhorn (Ger., 'Bull horn'). Giant medieval bugle horn used in war. Straight tubes with exact conical bore and no bell flare. Wagner requires them offstage in *Die Walküre*, Act 2, and in *Götterdämmerung*, Acts 2 and 3. Three special instrs. were made, in C, D♭, and D, played by trombonists.

Stiffelio. Opera in 3 acts by Verdi to lib. by Piave after play *Le Pasteur* (1849) by E. Souvestre and E. Bourgeois. Comp. 1850. Prod. Trieste 1850 and later staged, because of censorship problems, under title *Guglielmo Wellingrode*. Revived at Parma 1968; London (Collegiate Th.) 1973, CG 1993; Boston 1978, NY Met 1993. Rev. as *Aroldo*, 1856–7, with new lib. by Piave and newly composed 4th act. Prod. Rimini 1857, NY 1863.

Stignani, Ebe (*b* Naples, 1904; *d* Imola, 1974). It. mezzo-soprano. Début Naples (San Carlo) 1925 (Amneris in *Aida*). Engaged by Toscanini for La Scala 1925–6, where her mez. roles were considered the finest of the day. CG début 1937; San Francisco 1938. V. of immense range in top register. Last appearance 1958, Drury Lane, London (Azucena in *Il trovatore*).

stile antico (It.). Old style. Term to describe church mus. written after *c*.1600 in an archaic style, in imitation of Palestrina, by Soriano, Anerio, and Allegri. Its antithesis was *stile moderno*.

stile concertante (It.). In concerto-like style. Style of baroque mus. in which instr. are treated as rivals in conc.-like fashion.

stile concitato (It.). In excited style. Style of baroque mus. in which dramatic expression and excitement were paramount, e.g. in Monteverdi's *Il combattimento di Tancredi e Clorinda*, 1624.

stile rappresentativo (It.). In representational style. Term used by early It. composers of opera and oratorio to describe their new device of recit., in which human speech was represented dramatically as in Peri's *Euridice* (1600) and Monteverdi's *Arianna* (1608).

Stiles Allen, Lilian (b London, 1896; d Tunbridge Wells, 1982). Eng. soprano. Noted for oratorio perfs. but also sang Brünnhilde and other dramatic sop. roles. One of orig. 16 singers in Vaughan Williams's *Serenade to Music* 1938. Teacher after retirement, pupils incl. Julie Andrews, popular mus. comedy and film actress (*My Fair Lady, The Sound of Music*, etc.).

Still, William Grant (b Woodville, Miss., 1895; d Los Angeles, 1978). Amer. composer and conductor. Played vn., vc., and ob. in orchs. and worked in 1920s as orchestrator for Paul Whiteman's band and for Broadway musicals and radio shows. Worked for CBS from 1935. Works incl. 9 operas, 4 ballets, 5 syms., first being *Afro-American Symphony* (1930), *Pages from Negro History* for orch. (1943), chamber mus.

Stimme (Ger., plural *Stimmen*). Voice. (1) The human v.

(2) Instr. part and org. stop. Part-writing or v.-leading in Ger. is *Stimmführung*.

Stimmung (Ger.). Mood. (1) Atmosphere or mood, hence *Stimmungsbild*, mood picture, title given to short comp. evoking particular mood, e.g. Strauss's *5 Stimmungsbilder*, Op.9, for pf., 1883–4.

(2) Tuning.

Stimmung (Tuning). Comp. by K. *Stockhausen, 1968, for 6 unacc. singers (2 sop., 1 alto, 2 ten., 1 bass) vocalizing without words for 75 mins.

stinguendo (It.). Extinguishing, i.e. fading out.

stirando, stirato; stiracchiando, stiracchiato (It.). Stretching, stretched, i.e. making the mus. last out. Same as *ritardando*.

stochastic (from Gr., 'point of aim' or 'target'). Term first used by Swiss 18th-cent. mathematician Bernoulli regarding mathematical laws of probability. Applied by *Xenakis to mus. procedures whereby overall sound contours are determined but inner details are left to chance or worked out mathematically by composer or by computer, i.e. *chance* in stochastic works is restricted to the comp. process, the result being fully notated for the performer.

Stock, Frederick (August) (b Jülich, Prussia, 1872; d Chicago, 1942). Ger.-born conductor, violinist, and composer (Amer. cit. 1919). Violinist in Cologne orch. 1891–5. Went to USA as violist in Theodore Thomas Orch., 1895. Became ass. cond. to Thomas 1901, succeeding him 1905 and remaining cond. until his death (orch. became Chicago SO 1912). Gave f.p. of several Amer. works and introduced many modern works to Amer. audiences. Commissioned Walton's *Scapino* ov., 1940. Wrote 2 syms., vn. conc., chamber mus., etc.

Stockhausen, Julius (Christian) (b Paris, 1826; d Frankfurt, 1906). Fr.-born Ger. baritone, son of harpist-composer and his singer wife. As child learned several instr. Sang in *Elijah* at Basle, 1848, and joined Paris Opéra-Comique 1857. Gave f. public p. of Schubert's *Die schöne Müllerin*, Vienna, May 1856. Dir., Hamburg Phil. Concerts and Choir 1863–7. Many recital tours. Cond., Sternscher Gesangverein, Berlin, 1874–8 (see *Stern, Julius*); teacher at Hoch Cons., Frankfurt, 1878–80 and 1883–4. Wrote 2-vol. singing method, 1886–7. Regarded as one of finest interpreters of Schubert's *Winterreise* and other *Lieder*. Brahms ded. songs to him.

Stockhausen, Karlheinz (b Mödrath, nr. Cologne, 1928). Ger. composer, regarded as leader of electronic *avant-garde*. Son of village schoolmaster. Began to learn pf. at 5, also vn. and ob. Worked after 1945 as farmhand, also played pf. in dance-bands. Studied at Cologne Musik-Hochschule 1947–51 (pf. and theory) and Cologne Univ. 1952. Studied comp. 1950 with Frank *Martin and began his own analytical studies of Schoenberg, Bartók, and Webern. At Darmstadt int. summer school 1951 met Messiaen and Boulez. At this time he wrote his *Kreuzspiel* for pf., ob., bass cl., and perc. Lived in Paris 1952–3, studying with Messiaen. Worked in *musique concrète* studios of Fr. Radio and experimented with use of elec. tone generators. In 1953 returned to Cologne, becoming assistant to Herbert *Eimert in elec. mus. studio of W. Ger. Radio. Became dir. of the studio in 1963. From 1954 to 1956 studied phonetics and acoustics with W. Meyer-Eppler at Bonn Univ., this enabling him to have a complete understanding of his mus. material through ability to produce an infinite number of sounds and their permutations and to analyse them scientifically. In 1954 became ed. of new magazine for serial mus., *Die Reihe*, founded by Eimert. Gave first lecture- concerts in USA 1958 and since then has toured frequently as lecturer and cond. of small ens. Pupils from all over the world went to study with him and in 1957 he was appointed head of comp. courses at Darmstadt. Visiting prof. at several Amer. univs. Founded, 1963, Cologne Course for New Mus., teaching comp. until 1968. Prof. of comp., Cologne Musik-Hochschule 1971–7. Collected writings pubd. in several vols.

Few composers of the 20th-cent. 'New Music' can approach Stockhausen in the length and extent of his studies for his task. The first and strongest influence on his development was the mus. of Webern. Through detailed and profound analysis of Webern's mus., he realized how much further he could take Webern's techniques. He evolved the theory of 'parameters' or dimensions of sound: pitch, intensity, duration, timbre, and position in space. As Webern had serialized pitches, so Stockhausen in his early works serialized each parameter. Webern's method of composing with small 'cells' of *motifs* was developed by Stockhausen into what he called 'group composition', a group being a slice of mus. time (the larger groups are called 'moments'). How various groups are inter-related decides the formal design of a work. The culmination of this period came in 1961–4 with *Momente*. The next step was a new attitude to mus. mobility, whereby the order of self-contained groups could be varied so that mus. continuity could be altered. The 11th (1956) of his series of pf. works *Klavierstücke* is in mobile form, the groups being playable in any order the performer selects. In *Zyklus* (1959) for solo percussionist, the performer may start at any of its 17 pages and go on until he returns to his starting-point (he may read from left to right or turn over the score and go from right to left). The element of *chance* in these works means that no 2 perfs. are ever likely to be identical. In elec. mus., Stockhausen explored the spatial parameter (and transferred the same procedures to live mus. in his *Gruppen* for 3 orchs.). He began to specify the procedures—placing and use of microphones, etc.—for producing sounds, sometimes, as in *Carré*, calculating beforehand the basic materials and forms but leaving realization of details to someone else. In *Prozession* (1967), the mus. events are taken from various of his earlier comps.

The whole concept of elec. mus. is still so strange to ears accustomed to the disciplines of instr. comp. that the majority of audiences find it beyond their ken. But Stockhausen has an enormous following. He is constantly re-examining his theories, restructuring his comps., and exploring new media, in contrast to Boulez who seems to have remained where he was 20 years earlier. He has reached a wide audience with such works as *Gesang der Jünglinge*, which combines elec. sounds with the v. of a boy sop. altered by echo-effects, filters, etc., and the Orient-inspired *Stimmung*, in which for 75 minutes 6 singers take up elec. tones coming from concealed speakers and create a trance-like but ever-shifting vocalization. Prin. works:

OPERAS: *Licht* (1977–2003), series of 7 operas, 1 for each day of the week (e.g. *Donnerstag aus Licht*), of which many of the acts and scenes can be perf. separately.

ORCH.: *Formel* (1951); *Punkte* (1952, rev. 1962; rev. as *Kontra-Punkte*, 10 instr. 1952–3); *Spiel* (1952, rev. 1973); *Gruppen*, 3 orch. (1955–7); *Carré*, 4 orch., 4 choirs (1959–60); *Stop* (1965; Paris version 1969 for 18 players in 6 groups; London version 19 instrs., 1973); *Fresco*, 4 orch. groups (1969); *Trans* (1971); *Inori* (*Adorations*), soloist, orch. (1973–4); *Jubiläum* (1977); Scenes from *Licht* (Part I, *Der Jahreslauf*, dancers, orch. 1977; Part 2 *Michaels Reise um die Erde*, tpt., ens. 1978; Part 3, *Michaels Jugend*, sop., ten., bass, tpt., basset horn, tb., modulated pf., 3 dancers, tape, 1978–9; Part 4, *Michaels Heimkehr*, as Part 3 except that ch. and orch. replace tape, 1979).

CHAMBER ENSEMBLE: *3 Lieder*, high v., chamber orch. (1950); *Kreuzspiel*, ob., bass cl., pf., perc. (1951); *Percussion trio*, pf., perc. (1952, rev. 1974); *Kontra-punkte*, 10 instr. (1952–3, rev. of *Punkte* for orch.); *Zeitmasze*, 5 winds (1955–6); *Refrain*, pf., cel., perc. (1959); *Momente*, sop., 4 ch. groups, 13 instr. (1961–4, another version 1972); *Adieu*, wind quintet (1966); *Aus den sieben Tagen*, 15 comps. for ens. (1968); *Für Dr. K*, sextet (1969); *Für Kommende Zeiten*, 17 texts for intuitive mus. (1968–70); *Ylem*, 19 players or singers (1972); *Tierkreis* (*Zodiac*) (1975–7); *In Freundschaft*, fl., cl., ob., tpt., vn., va. (1977).

ELECTRONIC: *Electronic Study I* (1953), *II* (1954); *Gesang der Jünglinge*, on tape (boy's v.) (1955–6); *Kontakte*, pf., perc., elec. sounds (1959–60), also for elec. sounds (1959–60), and *Originale* (1961), mus. th. piece with *Kontakte*; *Mikrophonie I*, tam-tam and elecs. (1964), *II*, ch., Hammond org., elecs. (1965); *Mixtur*, 5 orch., elecs. (1964), reduced scoring (1967); *Solo*, melody instr. with feedback (1965–6); *Telemusik*, on tape (1966); *Hymnen*, tape and concrete mus. (1966–7), tape and concrete mus. with 4 soloists (1966–7), with orch. (1969, much shorter version); *Prozession*, tam-tam, pf., elecs. (1967); *Kurzwellen* (*Short-wave*), tam-tam, pf., elecs. (1968); *Spiral*, soloist with short-wave receiver (1969); *Sirius*, elecs., 4 soloists (1975).

VOICES: *Chöre für Doris*, unacc. mixed ch. (1950); *Choral*, unacc. ch. (1950); *Stimmung*, 6 singers (1968); 'Am Himmel wandre Ich . . .', 12 Indian songs (1972); *Atmen gibt das Leben . . .*, mixed ch. (1974, rev. as 'choral opera' 1977).

PIANO(S): *Klavierstücke*: I–IV (1952–3), V (1954–5), VI (1954–5), VII (1954–5), VIII (1954–5), IX (1954–5, rev. 1961), X (1954–5, rev. 1961), XI (1956); *Pole*, 2 pf., 2 short-wave receivers (1969–70); *Expo*, 3 pf. (1969–70); *Mantra*, 2 pianists, elecs. (1969–70); *Klavierstücke XIII* (part of *Samstag aus Licht* (1984)).

SOLO PERCUSSION: *Zyklus* for 1 percussionist (1959).

CHAMBER MUSIC: sonatina, vn., pf. (1951); *Laub und Regen*, cl., va. (1974); *Harlekin*, cl. (1975); *Der kleine Harlekin*, cl. (1975); *Amour*, 5 pieces, cl. (1976).

Stokowski, Leopold (Anthony) (*b* London, 1882; *d* Nether Wallop, Hants., 1977). Eng.-born conductor and organist (Amer. cit. 1915), son of Polish father and Irish mother. Org., St James's, Piccadilly, 1900, then St Bartholomew's NY, 1905–8. Returned to London and cond. orch. concerts, but settled in USA shortly afterwards. Cond. Cincinnati SO 1909–12, Philadelphia Orch. 1912–38 (mus. dir. from 1931 and last 2 years jointly with *Ormandy). Made Philadelphia one of world's finest orchs. and introduced many major works to USA, e.g. Mahler's 8th Sym., Berg's *Wozzeck*, Stravinsky's *Rite of Spring*, Schoenberg's *Gurrelieder*, Varèse's *Amériques*, etc. Also championed new Amer. mus., incl. that of Ives. Cond. f.ps. of 3 Rachmaninov works, Sym. No. 3, Pf. Conc. No.4, and *Rhapsody on a Theme of Paganini*. Appeared in films and cond. mus. for Disney's

Fantasia, 1940, in which mus. and cartoons were allied. Founder and cond. All-American Youth Orch. 1939–41; chief guest cond. NBC Orch. 1941–4; founder and cond. NY City SO 1944–5; chief guest cond. NYPO 1946–50; cond. Houston SO 1955–61, Amer. SO of NY 1962–72. NY Met début 1961; Salzburg Fest. 1951 (Vienna PO). Returned to Eng. 1972, frequently conducting LSO. Made transcrs. of Bach (for large sym. orch.). Was a master of sound and put his stamp on every orch. he cond. Opinions differed on quality of that stamp, for he took unusual liberties (which included alterations to the composer's scoring) in order to obtain effects he required, but that he was a superb cond. can scarcely be denied. He was active to the day of his death.

Stolzman, Richard (Leslie) (*b* Omaha, 1942). Amer. clarinettist. Started lessons aged 8 and played in jazz bands. Taught at Calif. Inst. of Arts 1970–5. NY solo recital 1974 and at Carnegie Hall 1982. Soloist with int. orchs.

Stolz, Robert (Elisabeth) (*b* Graz, 1880; *d* Berlin, 1975). Austrian composer, pianist, and conductor. Son of mus. teacher and pianist, and greatnephew of Teresa *Stolz. Toured Europe as pianist, playing Mozart at age 7. First comp. pubd. in Berlin, 1891. Répétiteur at Graz 1897, 1st cond. Salzburg 1902–3, and Ger. Th., Brno, 1903–5. Succeeded Bodanzky as chief cond., Theater an der Wien, Vienna, 1905–17. Cond. f.p. of Straus's *Der tapfere Soldat* (1908). Lived in Paris 1938–40 and in USA 1940–6, returning to Austria 1946–50. Wrote music for ice revues 1952–71. While in USA, composed scores for Hollywood films, winning 2 'Oscars'. The most successful of his many operettas were *Der Tanz ins Glück* (Waltz into Happiness) 1921 and *Wo die kleinen Veilchen blühen* (Wild Violets) 1932; wrote extra mus. for *Im Weissen Rössl* (White Horse Inn). Active as cond. in his 90s. Wrote over 60 operettas, over 100 film scores, and nearly 2,000 songs (incl. *Im Prater blüh'n wieder die Bäume*).

Stolz, Teresa [Stolzová, Terezie] (*b* Elbekosteletz, 1834; *d* Milan, 1902). Bohem. soprano. Opera début at Tiflis 1857. It. début at Turin 1863. Became mistress of cond. Mariani and later of Verdi. Milan début 1865. Sang Elisabeth in *Don Carlos*, Milan 1868, first It. Aida, 1872; created sop. role in Verdi's *Requiem*, 1874. Retired from opera 1877, concerts 1879. Voice of great range, dramatic expression, and flexibility.

Stolze, Gerhard (*b* Dessau, 1926; *d* Garmisch-Partenkirchen, 1979). Ger. tenor. Début Dresden 1949 (Moser in *Die Meistersinger*). Bayreuth Fest. 1951–69; Berlin Staatsoper 1953–61; Vienna début 1957; CG 1960; NY Met 1968. Splendid character-ten. e.g. as Mime in *The Ring* (recorded with Solti), Herod in *Salome*.

Stone Flower, The (*Kamenny tsvetok*). Ballet in prol. and 3 acts by Prokofiev, Op.118, lib. by

M. Mendelson and Lavrovsky, choreog. Lavrovsky, comp. 1948–53. Prod. Moscow 1954. New choreog. by Grigorovich, Leningrad 1957.

Stone Guest, The (*Kamenny Gost*). Opera in 3 acts by Dargomyzhsky, a setting of Pushkin's drama (1830) on same story as *Don Giovanni*. Comp. 1860–9 and left almost finished. Orch. by Rimsky-Korsakov, ov. by Cui. Prod. St Petersburg 1872. Rev. vers. (re-orch. by Rimsky-Korsakov 1898–1902 and with prelude added 1903), prod. Moscow 1906, Florence 1954, NY 1986, London 1987.

Stone Litany. 'Runes from a House of the Dead' for mez. and orch. by *Maxwell Davies. F.p. Glasgow 1973 by Jan de Gaetani (mez.), SNO, cond. *Gibson.

stop (as noun). (1) Row of pipes on org. (registers), all operated by handles or draw-stops placed near the player. Both the pipes and the handles are called *stops*.

(2) Hpd. mechanism for similar purpose as org. stop, i.e. to vary tone-colour, simulate sounds of other instr., etc.

stop (verb). (1) on str. instr., 'stopping' means the placing of the fingers on a str., thereby determining length of portion of str. which is to vibrate. Thus double-stopping, triple stopping, means this action on 2, 3 str. at once.

(2) In hn.-playing, the insertion of a hand into the bell of the hn. to alter pitch and tone-quality of a note.

(3) In orgs.: to block passage of air through one end of pipe (i.e. end-stopped pipe), thereby producing note an octave lower than would otherwise be sounded.

Storace, Anna (Selina) [Nancy] (*b* London, 1765; *d* Dulwich, 1817). Eng. soprano, daughter of It. father. Début as singer, Haymarket Th., London, 1774. Sang in Florence 1780, Parma 1781, and Milan, Venice, and Rome 1782. Engaged as prin. sop. at Imperial Th., Vienna, 1784. Operas written for her by Paisiello and Soler. Created Susanna in *Le nozze di Figaro*, 1786. Returned to Eng., 1787, singing in It. comic operas. For her farewell perf. in Vienna, Mozart comp. concert aria *Ch'io mi scordi di te* (K505) for sop., pf., and orch., and played kbd. part himself. She sang in her brother Stephen *Storace's *The Haunted Tower*, 1789, thereafter confining herself to comic roles in Eng. works. Sang at Handel Fest. 1791. Became mistress of ten. *Braham, bearing him a son, and touring Europe with him. CG 1801–8. Died very wealthy.

Storace, Stephen (*b* London, 1762; *d* London, 1796). Eng. composer, brother of Anna *Storace. Child violinist. Joined his sister in It. when she arrived in 1778 and went with her to Vienna, where 2 of his operas, *Gli sposi malcontenti* (1785) and *Gli equivoci* (1786, with lib. by da Ponte), were prod. Friend of Mozart. Returned to Eng. 1787. Wrote series of dialogue-operas in which he incorporated popular airs and adapted other composers' mus. Among them were *The Haunted Tower* (1789),

No Song, No Supper (1790), *The Siege of Belgrade* (1791), *The Pirates* (1792), *The Prize* (1793), *Cherokee* (1794), etc. His last full-scale opera, *Dido, Queen of Carthage*, was prod. at King's Th. in May 1792. Many of his scores were lost in the Drury Lane fire of 1809, but *The Pirates* was reconstructed in 1975 by Richard Vardigans from vocal score and MS lib. *Gli equivoci*, based on Shakespeare's *Comedy of Errors*, was revived in London in 1974 and showed that Storace's contemporary reputation was deserved. Also revived at Wexford 1992.

Storchio, Rosina (*b* Venice, 1876; *d* Milan, 1945). It. soprano. Début Milan 1892 (Micaëla in *Carmen*); La Scala 1895. Created Musetta in Leoncavallo's *La bohème*, Venice 1897, and title-role in his *Zazà*, Milan 1900. Created title-role in *Madama Butterfly*, Milan 1904. Sang in Barcelona 1898–1923 and in Buenos Aires 1904–14. Amer. début Chicago 1921; NY 1921.

stornello (It., plural *stornelli*). A traditional type of Tuscan folk-song often improvised by a *stornellatore* (masc.) or *stornellatrice* (fem.). The stanza has 3 lines each of 11 syllables.

Story of a Real Man, The (Russ. *Povest' o nastoyashchem cheloveke*). Opera in 4 acts, Op.117, by Prokofiev to lib. by composer and Mira Mendelson after B. Polevoy's novella (1946). Comp. 1947–8. F.p. Leningrad 1948 (run-through, without sets and costumes), Moscow 1960 (in 3 acts with cuts and omissions).

Stott, Kathryn (Linda) (*b* Nelson, Lancs., 1958). Eng. pianist. Début London 1978. Specialist in Fauré. Art. dir., Fauré fest., Manchester 1995.

straccinato (It.). Stretched out, i.e. *ritardando*.

Stradella, Alessandro (*b* Nepi, nr. Viterbo, 1639; *d* Genoa, 1682). It. composer. Taught singing in Venice and Rome. Page to Roman aristocrat 1653–60. From 1667 wrote oratorios, prologues, and intermezzi for operas in Rome. Went to Genoa 1677 where he became impresario and wrote 4 operas there. Was murdered, supposedly after involvement in adulterous affair. Flotow's opera *Alessandro Stradella* (Hamburg 1844) is a romanticized and inaccurate account of events leading to his death.

Stradivari [Stradivarius]. Family of vn.-makers of Cremona, N. Italy. The greatest of them was Antonio Stradivari (*b* 1644; *d* Cremona, 1737), apprenticed as youth to Nicola *Amati, continuing connection with Amati's workshop to 1684. Inserted his own label into vn. 1666 (signing himself, as always afterwards, by Maltese cross and initials A. S. enclosed within double circle). After 1684, his work developed experimentally towards perfection of design and balance, leading in 1690 to invention of the 'Long Strad'. 1700–20 was Stradivari's 'golden period' during which he prod. a series of magnificent instr., inc. vcs. and vas., and those made in the last 17 years of his life show no decline in craftsmanship. He made his last vn. in 1737 at age 92. It is calcu-

lated in the standard work on Stradivari by the Hill brothers (1902, rev. 1909) that he made 1,116 instruments after 1666 of which over 600 are still in existence. Many are known by names e.g. La Pucelle, Viotti, Alard, Messie, Rode, etc. He paid vigilant attention to detail and personally designed pegs, fingerboards, tailpieces, inlaid patterns, and bridges; he designed the cases and also made bows. His application of the varnish was unsurpassed, soft in texture and shading from orange to red. The tone of the instrs. varies, of course, but is generally a sop. tone compared with the more cont. *Guarneri. Stradivari was assisted by his sons Francesco (*b* Cremona, 1671; *d* 1743) and Omobono (*b* Cremona, 1679; *d* 1742) and by Carlo Bergonzi. These instruments bore the label 'sotto la disciplina d'Antonio Stradivari' but in many cases these were later unscrupulously removed and a label substituted attributing the instr. to Stradivari himself. Hence the controversies over the authenticity of certain 'Strads', important in view of the high prices the genuine instr. can fetch.

strambotto (It.). 'Rustic Song'. It. Renaissance poetical form, often set to mus. on the lines of the *frottola. Poem had 8 lines, rhyming abababcc; and the mus. setting was usually strophic, with only 2 lines set to mus. and repeated for each remaining pair. See also *rispetto*.

Straniera, La (The Foreigner). Opera in 2 acts by Bellini to lib. by Romani after V.-C. Prévôt's novel *L'etrangère*. Comp. 1828. Prod. Milan 1829, London 1832, NY 1834.

Stransky, Josef (*b* Humpolec, Bohemia, 1872; *d* NY, 1936). Bohemian conductor. Prin. cond., Landestheater, Prague, 1898, Hamburg 1903–10. Also cond. in Berlin, Dresden, London, Amsterdam, etc. Succeeded Mahler as cond. NYPO 1911, holding post until 1923. Retired 1924, going into art-dealing business. Wrote operas and other works, and adapted Berlioz's *Béatrice et Bénédict*. Figures in R. Strauss's opera *Intermezzo* as Stroh; he was the cond. for whom Strauss was mistaken by an importunate lady, thereby nearly precipitating Strauss's divorce.

strascicando; strascinando; strascinato (It.). Dragging; dragged (e.g. heavily slurring notes in bowing, singing *portamento*, etc.).

Stratas, Teresa [Strataki, Anastasia] (*b* Toronto, 1938). Canadian soprano of Gr. parentage. As a child sang in father's restaurant. Opera début Toronto 1958 (Mimì in *La bohème*). Won NY Met opera auditions 1959, making her début at Met in Oct. 1959; CG début 1961; Salzburg Fest. début 1969. Excellent Mozart singer in roles such as Despina. Sang Lulu in f. complete p. of opera, Paris 1979. Also an impressive Salome and specialist in mus. of Weill. Created Marie Antoinette in *The *Ghosts of Versailles*, NY Met 1991.

Strathspey. Lively Scottish dance. Mus. is in simple quadruple time, with many dotted notes and some use of the *Scotch snap. Appeared in mid-18th cent. See *reel*.

Straube, (Montgomery Rufus) **Karl** (Siegfried) (*b* Berlin, 1873; *d* Leipzig, 1950). Ger. organist, conductor, and teacher. Had Eng. mother. Toured Ger. giving org. recitals 1894–7, winning high reputation. Org., Wesel Cath. 1897–1902, Thomaskirche, Leipzig (Bach's post) from 1902 and cond. of Leipzig Bach Soc. Prof. of org., Leipzig Cons., from 1907. Cantor of Thomasschule from 1918. Cond. several Bach Fests. 1904–23 and 1925 Handel Fest. which led to formation of Handel Soc. Friend of Reger and champion of his mus., as of that of other 20th-cent. composers, incl. Vaughan Williams and Holst. Ed. choral works of Bach and Handel, and organ works by Bach and Liszt.

Straus, Oscar (*b* Vienna, 1870; *d* Bad Ischl, 1954). Austrian-born composer (Fr. cit. 1939). Cond. th. orchs. in Ger. 1893–9, his first opera being perf. in Bratislava 1894. Pianist 1900 for Wolzogen's *Überbrettl* in Berlin, for which he comp. many songs. Returned to Vienna 1904, composing operettas yearly and achieving major success in 1907 with *Ein Walzertraum*. In 1908 wrote *Der tapfere Soldat*, based on Shaw's *Arms and the Man* (1894). This was f.p. Vienna 1908, and in NY 1909 and London 1910 as *The *Chocolate Soldier*. Many other operettas followed, but none had much success until *Der letzte Walzer* (*The Last Waltz*), Vienna 1920, comp. for Fritzi Massary, who sang in several of his works. Left Europe 1937, living in Paris until 1940 and Hollywood until settling in Bad Ischl 1948. His last success was with theme-tune for the film *La Ronde*, 1950. Also comp. 2 ballets, chamber mus., many film scores, and nearly 500 songs. Name spelt Strauss on birth certificate, but he deleted one of final 's' to differentiate himself from other composers with the name.

Strauss, Eduard I (*b* Vienna, 1835; *d* Vienna, 1916). Austrian composer and conductor, youngest son of Johann *Strauss I. Played hp. in brother Johann Strauss II's orch. Début as cond. 1862, succeeding brother at St Petersburg 1865. In 1872 took over conductorship of court balls which Johann had held since 1863. Took Strauss orch. to London 1885, disbanded it 1901. Wrote over 300 dances, many of them polkas. In 1907 burned all original MSS of Strauss family because he believed world no longer deserved to possess them. Thus many waltzes have been preserved only in pf. reductions.

Strauss, Eduard (Leopold Maria) **II** (*b* Vienna, 1910; *d* Vienna, 1969). Austrian conductor, nephew of J. Strauss III. Début 1949. Cond. Vienna SO in recordings and toured with Vienna Johann Strauss Orch.

Strauss, Franz Joseph (*b* Parkstein, 1822; *d* Munich, 1905). Ger. horn-player and composer.

Prin. hn., Munich Court opera orch. 1847–89. Taught at Munich Acad. until 1896. Cond. semi-professional orch. (Wilde Gungl) 1875–96. Although he disliked Wagner's mus., played in several Wagner premières and was consulted by composer on Siegfried's hn.-call. Wrote hn. conc., works for hn. and pf., etc. The composer Richard *Strauss was his son by his 2nd wife.

Strauss, Johann I (*b* Vienna, 1804; *d* Vienna, 1849). Austrian composer, conductor, and violinist, founder of the 'Strauss Waltz Dynasty', and known as Johann Strauss I to distinguish him from his son. Studied vn. and played va. in 1819 in *Lanner's qt. With Lanner until 1825, when he began to compose his own waltzes. In 1826 appeared with 14-piece orch. at the 'Swan' in the Rossau suburb of Vienna and captivated public. With larger orch. engaged for 6 years at the 'Sperl', in the Leopoldstadt. Among those who heard him there were Chopin, Wagner, and Hans Christian Andersen. Also appointed Kapellmeister of first Bürger-regiment, responsible for mus. at court fêtes and dances. Toured Ger. and other parts of Europe from 1833. Visited London 1838, giving 72 concerts and playing at festivities in honour of Victoria's coronation. In 1840 introduced the quadrille to replace the galop. Successive tours were triumphal processions for Strauss. Visited Eng. again 1849, and died of scarlet fever shortly after return to Vienna. Comp. 251 works, 152 of which were waltzes, but his fame in this respect was eclipsed by his eldest son and his *Radetzky March* (1848) is by far the strongest survivor of his life's work.

Strauss, Johann II (*b* Vienna, 1825; *d* Vienna, 1899). Austrian composer, conductor, and violinist, eldest son of Johann *Strauss, and deservedly known as 'the Waltz King'. Because his father did not want his sons to choose mus. as career, worked as bank clerk but learned vn. secretly and studied comp. with Drechsler. In 1844 formed own orch. of 24 and appeared as cond. of his own and his father's waltzes in rivalry to his father (they also supported opposing sides in the 1848 revolution). When his father died, amalgamated both orchs. and toured Austria, Poland, and Ger. In 1855 engaged to direct summer concerts in Petropaulovsky Park, St Petersburg, for 10 years. Cond. of Austrian court balls 1863–72. Comp. nearly 400 waltzes which have come to epitomize Viennese gaiety and sentiment. Visited Paris 1867, London 1867, USA 1872. Turned to stage 1871, when first of a series of successful operettas was produced at the Theater an der Wien, the most famous being *Die Fledermaus* (1874). Of his waltzes, the *Blue Danube* (1867), *Roses from the South* (1880), the great *Emperor Waltz* (1888), and *Tales from the Vienna Woods* (1868) are beloved wherever mus. is played, as are his polkas and other dances. Was friend and admirer of Wagner, who, like Brahms and other composers incl. Schoenberg, were what we should now call 'fans' of Strauss, recognizing a supreme master of a genre who comp. with style, elegance, taste, and wit. Prin. works:

OPERETTAS: *Indigo und die vierzig Räuber* (1871); *Der Karneval in Rom* (1873); *Die *Fledermaus* (1873–4); *Cagliostro in Wien* (1875); *Prinz Methusalem* (1877); *Blindekuh* (1878); *Das Spitzentuch der Königin* (1880); *Der lustige Krieg* (1881); *Eine *Nacht in Venedig* (1883); *Der *Zigeunerbaron* (1885); *Simplicius* (1887); *Ritter Pazman* (1892); *Fürstin Ninetta* (1893); *Jauka* (1894); *Waldmeister* (1895); *Die Götten der Vernunft* (1897).

BALLET: *Cinderella* (1899; completed as *Aschenbrödel* by J. Bayer, f.p. Berlin 1901, f. Eng. p. Manchester 1979).

WALTZES: *Abschied von St Petersburg*, Op.210; *Accelerationen*, Op.234; *An der schönen blauen Donau* (On the beautiful *Blue Danube*), Op.314; *Architektenball-Tänze*, Op.36; *Cagliostro*, Op.370; *Erinnerung an Covent Garden*, Op.139; *Freuet euch des Lebens*, Op.340; *Frühlingsstimmen* (Voices of Spring), Op.410; *Geschichten aus dem Wienerwald* (*Tales From the Vienna Woods), Op.325; *Grossfürstin Alexandra*, Op.181; *Hofballtänze*, Op.298; *Juristenballtänze*, Op.177; **Kaiser-Walzer* (Emperor Waltz) Op.437; *Kronungslieder*, Op.184; *Künstlerleben*, Op.316; *Der Kuss*, Op.400; *Lagunen*, Op.411; *Liebesliederwalzer*, Op.114; **Morgenblätter* (Morning Papers), Op.279; *Nordseebilder*, Op.380; *O schöner Mai*, Op.365; *Rathausballtänze*, Op.438; *Rosen aus dem Süden* (*Roses from the South), Op.388; *Schneeglockchen*, Op.143; *Seid umschlungen Millionen*, Op.443; *Wein, Weib und Gesang* (Wine, Woman and Song), Op.333; *Wiener Blut* (Vienna Blood), Op.354; *Wiener Bonbons*, Op.307; *Wo die Zitronen blüh'n*, Op.364.

POLKAS: *Aesculap*, Op.130; *Annen*, Op.117; *Armenball*, Op.176; *Aurora*, Op.165; *Bürgerball*, Op.145; *Champagne*, Op.211; *Damenspende*, Op.305; *Demolierer*, Op.269; *Electropher*, Op.297; *Explosionen*, Op.43; *Figaro*, Op.320; *Juristenball*, Op.280; *Lagerlust*, Op.431; *Leichtes Blut*, Op.319; *Pizzicato Polka* (with Josef Strauss); *Tritsch, Tratsch*, Op.214; *Unter Donner und Blitz* (Thunder and Lightning), Op.324.

Also, marches, galops, and *Perpetuum Mobile*, Op. 257.

Strauss, Josef (*b* Vienna, 1827; *d* Vienna, 1870). Austrian composer, 2nd son of Johann *Strauss I. Became architect, but studied mus. secretly and cond. in place of his brother Johann in 1853. Formed own orch. and comp. waltzes, etc., for it, writing 283 pieces. Polkas more often played today than his waltzes, but the latter incl. *Dynamiden*, Op.173 (1865), borrowed by R. Strauss for one of waltz-themes in opera *Der Rosenkavalier*, and *Dorfschwalben aus Österreich* (Village Swallows), Op.164.

Strauss, Richard (Georg) (*b* Munich, 1864; *d* Garmisch-Partenkirchen, 1949). Ger.-born composer, conductor, and pianist (Austrian cit. 1947). Son of Franz *Strauss, hn.-player in Munich court orch. Had pf. lessons at 4 and began

composing at 6. Vn. lessons at 8. Studied theory with F. Meyer 1875, but went to no mus. acad., having normal education, ending at Munich Univ. At 16 wrote first sym. and str. qt., both being perf. in Munich, 1881. In 1882 *Serenade* for wind perf. in Dresden, leading to commission from *Bülow for Meiningen Orch. 2nd Sym. perf. NY 1884. Ass. cond. to Bülow at Meiningen 1885, succeeding him after a month. Left Meiningen 1886, visited It., and became 3rd cond. at Munich Opera. His *Aus Italien* perf. Munich 1887. Mus. ass. to Levi at Bayreuth 1889. 3rd cond. Weimar Opera 1889. Success of symphonic poem *Don Juan* est. him as most important young composer in Ger. and natural successor to Wagner, whose widow took great interest in his career. Bayreuth Fest. début as cond. 1894 (*Tannhäuser*). Married sop. Pauline de *Ahna 1894 and wrote many songs for her, appearing as her accompanist. First opera *Guntram* failure at Weimar 1894. Ass. cond., Munich Opera 1894, chief cond. 1896–8. Cond. Berlin PO 1894–5. Series of tone-poems— *Till Eulenspiegel*, *Also sprach Zarathustra*, *Don Quixote*, and *Ein Heldenleben*—between 1895 and 1899 confirmed his stature as master of the orch. 2nd opera *Feuersnot* success in Dresden and Vienna, 1901 and 1902. Visited Eng. 1903, USA 1904. F.p. of *Symphonia Domestica* in NY. Operas *Salome* (1905) and *Elektra* (1909) caused sensations through their supposedly 'obscene' treatment of biblical and classical subjects. In latter Strauss first collab. with Austrian poet Hugo von *Hofmannsthal, who was to be librettist of 5 more of his operas, beginning in 1911 with the 18th-cent. comedy *Der Rosenkavalier*. This work was a triumph at its Dresden première, went straight into the repertory of world's leading opera houses, and has stayed there. Since 1898 Strauss had been cond. of Berlin Royal Opera, living in the capital, but after 1908 lived in villa at Garmisch and was in constant demand as cond. of his own works. Completed his last full-scale orch. work, *Eine Alpensinfonie*, in 1915. Resigned Berlin post 1918 and became joint dir., Vienna Opera, 1919–24. With Max Reinhardt, Hofmannsthal and others, founded Salzburg Fest. 1920 and cond. *Don Giovanni* and *Così fan tutte* there 1922. His opera *Die Frau ohne Schatten* and ballet *Schlagobers* were prod. in Vienna 1919 and 1924. Opera *Intermezzo*, to his own lib. representing incident in his own marriage, prod. Dresden 1924. During comp. of *Arabella*, Hofmannsthal died, 1929. In 1933 new Nazi régime in Ger. appointed Strauss pres. of Reichsmusikkammer, but removed him in 1935 because of disapproval of his collab. with Jewish librettist Stefan *Zweig on opera *Die schweigsame Frau*, which was banned after 4 perfs. Thereafter Strauss was tolerated by régime but kept under surveillance because of Jewish daughter-in-law. Visited London 1936, receiving Gold Medal of Royal Phil. Soc. and conducting at CG. 1-act operas *Friedenstag* and *Daphne* prod. 1938. During World War II lived mostly in Vienna and comp. operas *Die Liebe der Danae* and *Capriccio*. In 1943 reverted to instr. comps., writing 2nd hn. conc., wind sonatinas, ob. conc., and 'study for 23 strings' *Metamorphosen*, partly inspired by destruction of Ger. opera houses in bombing raids. Moved to Switzerland 1945–9, where in 1947–8 he wrote his last masterpiece, the *Vier letzte Lieder (Four Last Songs)* for sop. and orch. Officially cleared in 1948 of complicity in Nazi régime. Visited London 1947, conducting own works and attending perfs. cond. by Beecham. His last work, completed 23 Nov. 1948, was a song *Malven* (Knobel), ded. to Maria *Jeritza. After operation in Lausanne in Dec. 1948, returned to Garmisch May 1949, dying there on 8 Sept.

Strauss, like his friend and contemporary Mahler, had immense dual reputation as composer and cond. He was a master of several mus. forms. No sym. orch. can reasonably exist without having in its repertory his series of magnificent tone-poems, in which brilliance of scoring and vividness of representational detail are matched by satisfying mus. construction. Of his 15 operas at least half are regularly in the repertories of the major opera houses. They provide superb singing roles, particularly for women's vv., of which, through his marriage to a sop., he had a profound understanding. In *Der Rosenkavalier* alone, he wrote parts for 3 sop. in which many a 20th-cent. reputation has been made and which have contributed to making it the most popular opera written in the 20th cent., with the probable exception of *Madama Butterfly*. In *Elektra* he approached the atonal and neuro-psychological world of Schoenberg and Berg, but turned aside to what Stravinsky called the 'time-travelling' of *Der Rosenkavalier* and *Ariadne auf Naxos*, the latter being one of several operas in which Strauss treated subjects from classical mythology, investing them with 20th-cent. traits e.g. *Die ägyptische Helena*, *Daphne*, and *Die Liebe der Danae*. His last opera, a 'conversation piece', *Capriccio*, has become more frequently perf. in recent years. Strauss's mus. is in the Ger. 19th-cent. tradition deriving from Mendelssohn, Liszt, and especially Wagner. However, his love for Mozart, of whose mus. he was a fine cond., is also reflected in many works, leading to a curious but satisfying blend of 18th-cent. elegance and Wagnerian richness as in *Rosenkavalier*, *Ariadne*, and *Capriccio*, and particularly in the superb instr. works of his last years. His natural gift for counterpoint leads to complex and interweaving textures in all his works, which has led his critics to complain of 'note-spinning' for its own sake (a charge that has some justification), but the former tendency to 'write off' Strauss operas comp. between 1919 and 1940 is gradually being reversed as their virtues become apparent. Though he wrote some concs., his big display pieces are for full orch. and for vv. His unacc. choral works are in a class of their own, and he wrote many first-rate *Lieder*, some with orch. A song such as *Morgen!*, for example, is a perfect blend of melody and expression of the text, while its style epitomizes the highly-developed melodic conversational-recit. which was Strauss's lifelong preoccupation in his operas and which even forms part of the subject-matter of *Capriccio*. The *Vier letzte Lieder* is a remarkable and moving

summing-up of his life's work as well as a testament to all that the late-romantic style had meant to the art of mus. Prin. works:

OPERAS (with dates of comp., f.p., and cond.): *Guntram*, Op.25, comp. 1887–93, rev. 1934–9 (Weimar 1894, Strauss; rev. vers. Weimar 1940, Heger); *Feuersnot*, Op.50, comp. 1900–1 (Dresden 1901, Schuch); *Salome*, Op.54, comp. 1903–5 (Dresden 1905, Schuch); *Elektra*, Op.58, comp. 1906–8 (Dresden 1909, Schuch); *Der *Rosenkavalier*, Op.59, comp. 1909–10 (Dresden 1911, Schuch); *Ariadne auf Naxos*, Op.60, comp. 1911–12 (Stuttgart 1912, Strauss), rev. version, Prologue comp 1916 (Vienna 1916, Schalk); *Die *Frau ohne Schatten*, Op.65, comp. 1914–17 (Vienna 1919, Schalk); *Intermezzo*, Op.72, comp. 1917–23 (Dresden 1924, Busch); *Die *ägyptische Helena*, Op.75, comp. 1923–7 (Dresden 1928, Busch), rev. vers. 1933 (Salzburg, Krauss); *Arabella*, Op.79, comp. 1930–2 (Dresden 1933, Krauss); *Die *schweigsame Frau*, Op.80, comp. 1933–4 (Dresden 1935, Böhm); *Friedenstag*, Op.81, comp. 1935–6 (Munich 1938, Krauss); *Daphne*, Op.82, comp. 1936–7 (Dresden 1938, Böhm); *Die *Liebe der Danae*, Op.83, comp. 1938–40 (dress rehearsal only, Salzburg 1944, Krauss; Salzburg 1952, Krauss); *Capriccio*, Op.85, comp. 1940–1 (Munich 1942, Krauss).

BALLETS & OTHER STAGE WORKS: *Josephslegende*, Op.63 (1913–14); *Der Bürger als Edelmann (Le *Bourgeois Gentilhomme)*, incidental mus. for Molière-Hofmannsthal play, Op.60 (1912–17); *Schlagobers*, Op.70 (1921–2); *Des Esels Schatten*, children's mus. play (1947–8, completed from sketches by K. Haussner), Ettal 1964, London 1970.

ORCH.: *Serenade* in E♭, for 13 wind instr., Op.7 (1881–2); *Suite* in B♭, for 13 wind instr., Op.4 (1883–4); syms.: No.1 in D minor (1880, unpubd.), No.2 in F minor, Op.12 (1883–4); *Symphonia Domestica*, Op.53 (1902–3), *Eine *Alpensinfonie*, Op.64 (1911–15); *Aus Italien*, symphonic fantasy, Op.16 (1886); sym.-poems: *Macbeth*, Op.23 (1887–8, rev. 1889–90), *Don Juan*, Op.20 (1888), *Tod und Verklärung*, Op.24 (1888–9), *Till Eulenspiegels lustige Streiche*, Op.28, (1894–5), *Also sprach Zarathustra*, Op.30 (1895–6), *Don Quixote*, Op.35 (1896–7), Ein *Heldenleben*, Op.40 (1897–8); *Festliches Präludium*, orch., org., Op.61 (1913); *Suite, Le *Bourgeois Gentilhomme*, Op.60, (1918); *Dance Suite* (after Couperin) (1922); Waltz, *München*, 1st vers. (1930), 2nd vers. (1945); Sonatina No.1 in F, 16 wind instr. (1943), No.2 in E♭, 16 wind instr. (1944–5); *Metamorphosen*, 23 solo str. (1944–5).

CONCERTOS etc: hn. conc. No.1 in E♭, Op.11 (1882–3), No.2 in E♭ (1942); vn. conc. in D minor, Op.8 (1881–2); *Burleske* in D minor, pf., orch. (1885–6, rev. 1890); *Parergon zur Symphonia Domestica*, pf. (left hand), orch., Op.73 (1925); *Panathenäenzug*, pf. (left hand), orch., Op.74 (1927); oboe conc. (1945–6); *Duett-Concertino*, cl., bn., str., hp. (1947).

CHORAL: *Wandrers Sturmlied*, Op.14, ch., orch. (1884); *Der Abend* and *Hymne*, Op.34, unacc. ch. (1897);

Taillefer, Op.52, sop., ten., bar., ch., orch. (1903); *Deutsche Motette, Op.62, sop., cont., ten., bass, unacc. ch. (1913, rev. 1943); *Die Tageszeiten*, Op.76, 4 songs, male ch., orch. (1928); *Die Göttin im Putzzimmer*, unacc. ch. (1935); *An den Baum Daphne, unacc. ch. (1943).

CHAMBER MUSIC: Str. Qt. in A, Op.2 (1880); Vc. Sonata, Op.6 (1883); Pf. Qt. in C minor, Op.13 (1883–4); Vn. Sonata in E♭, Op.18 (1887).

PIANO: Sonata in B minor, Op.5 (1881); *5 Stimmungsbilder*, Op.9 (1883–4).

SONG-CYCLES: *Krämerspiegel, Op.66, v., pf. (1918); *Vier letzte Lieder (4 Last Songs), high v., orch. (1948).

SONGS (with pf. and/or orch.): Strauss wrote over 200 songs, publishing them in groups. Listed below alphabetically is a selective group of the best-known, with opus numbers where applicable. The sign † means that an orch. acc. (not necessarily by Strauss) exists: *Allerseelen*, Op.10 No.9 (1885), *All' mein Gedanken*, Op.21 No.1 (1888), †Das Bächlein (1933), †Befreit, Op.39 No.4 (1898), †Cäcilie, Op.27 No.2 (1894), *Du meines Herzens Krönelein*, Op.21 No.2 (1888), *Einerlei*, Op.69 No.3 (1918), *Einkehr*, Op.47 No.4 (1900), †Freundliche Vision, Op.48 No.1 (1900), *Gefunden*, Op.56 No.1 (1903–6), *Hat gesagt*, Op.36 No.3 (1897), †Die Heiligen drei Königen, Op.56 No.6 (1906), †Heimkehr, Op.15 No.5 (1886), †Heimliche Aufforderung, Op.27 No.3 (1894), †Ich wollt' ein Sträusslein binden, Op.68 No.2 (1918), †Liebeshymnus, Op.32 No.3 (1896), †Mein Auge, Op.37 No.4 (1897), †Meinem Kinde, Op.37 No.3 (1897), †Morgen!, Op.27 No.4 (1894), †Muttertanderlei, Op.43 No.2 (1899), *Die Nacht*, Op.10 No.3 (1885), *Nachtgang*, Op.29 No.3 (1895), *Nichts*, Op.10 No.2 (1885), †Das Rosenband, Op.36 No.1 (1897), †Ruhe, meine Seele, Op.27 No.1 (1894), †Säusle, Liebe Myrthe, Op.68 No.3 (1918), *Schlechtes Wetter*, Op.69 No.5 (1918), †Ständchen, Op.17 No.2 (1887), *Der Stern*, Op.69 No.1 (1918), †Traum durch die Dämmerung, Op.29 No.1 (1895), †Waldseligkeit, Op.49 No.1 (1901), †Wiegenlied, Op.41 No.1 (1899), *Wozu noch, Mädchen*, Op.19 No.1 (1887–8), †Zueignung, Op.10 No.1 (1885).

Stravaganza, La (The Extraordinary). Title of Vivaldi's Op.4, 12 vn. concs., pubd. Amsterdam c.1714.

Stravinsky, Fyodor (Ignat'yevich) (*b* Rechitskiy, Minsk, 1843; *d* St Petersburg, 1902). Russ. bass, father of Igor *Stravinsky. Sang Don Basilio in *Il barbiere di Siviglia* in student prod. 1873. Kiev 1873 (début as Rodolfo in *La sonnambula*). Prin. bass Mariinsky Th., St Petersburg, 1876–1902, making over 1,200 appearances in 64 roles. Created Tchaikovsky roles of His Highness in *Vakula the Smith* (1876), Dunois in *The Maid of Orleans* (1881), and Mamïrov in *The Enchantress* (1887); also created Headman in *May Night (1880) and Grandfather Frost in *The *Snow Maiden* (1882).

Stravinsky, Igor (Fyodorovich) (*b* Oranienbaum, 1882; *d* NY, 1971). Russ.-born composer, conductor, pianist, and writer (Fr. cit. 1934, Amer. cit. 1945). Son of Fyodor *Stravinsky. Went to St Petersburg Univ. 1901 to study law but increas-

ingly spent time in mus. pursuits. Spent much time at Rimsky-Korsakov's house, becoming his pupil in 1903. Began 1st sym., 1905, also pf. sonata. When his short orch. pieces *Fireworks* and *Scherzo fantastique* were played in St Petersburg in 1909, they were heard by *Diaghilev, who had by then formed the famous Ballets Russes in Paris. He invited Stravinsky to compose a ballet on the legend of *The Firebird*, Lyadov having failed to meet his deadline, for 1910 season. Its success made Stravinsky world-famous, and was followed by *Petrushka* (1911) and by *The Rite of Spring* (1913), the f.p. of the latter causing a riot. By then, Stravinsky was regarded as the leader of the mus. *avant-garde*. With the Russ. Revolution of 1917, resulting in confiscation of his property, and the financial troubles of the Diaghilev co., Stravinsky thought of forming a small touring th. co. to present inexpensively mounted productions. The result was *The Soldier's Tale* (*L'Histoire du Soldat*), for chamber ens.; it also enabled him to combine 2 of his main interests, Russ. folk-rhythms and Amer. jazz. His ballet *Pulcinella*, composed for Diaghilev in 1919–20, was a 're-composition' of mus. attrib. to Pergolesi and initiated the 'neo-classical' phase in Stravinsky's career. His last overtly Russ. works of this period were the ballet *Les Noces* and the opera *Mavra*. Settling in Fr., he wrote a series of works in which the spirit of the 18th cent. is invoked but with unmistakably 20th-cent. harmonic and rhythmic flavouring. The pf. conc., in which he played the solo part, the *Capriccio* for pf. and orch., the vn. conc., the ballet *Apollo Musagetes*, the Sym. in C major and, most of all the Hogarthian opera *The Rake's Progress* (1951), are the finest flowers of this facet of Stravinsky's art. On the other hand, the opera-oratorio *Oedipus Rex* (1926–7), for which Cocteau wrote the text, is 19th cent. and Verdian in its heroic melodies. In 1939 he settled in the USA, moving eventually to Los Angeles where the climate suited one who had contracted tuberculosis in 1936–7. His first major 'American' work was the *Symphony in 3 Movements* of 1945. Yet another turning-point was the ballet *Orpheus* (1947), which had led Stravinsky to study of Monteverdi, and a meeting with the young Amer. cond. Robert *Craft, who (besides an enthusiasm for Stravinsky) combined interest in the Baroque period with intense sympathy for the 2nd Viennese Sch. of Schoenberg, etc. Stravinsky had lately shown awareness of serialism, particularly as practised by Webern, and, spurred by Craft, his work now began to reflect these new interests, as in the *Canticum Sacrum* of 1955, the *Threni* of 1958, the ballet *Agon*, and *Movements* for pf. and orch. In 1962 he was invited to return to Russ., a triumphant tour ending in his reception by the then Soviet leader Khruschev at the Kremlin. In his final years he wrote short, bare works, many of them religious in feeling and form, at the opposite pole from the opulence of his early successes. He is buried in the island cemetery of San Michele, Venice, near to Diaghilev, as he wished.

Stravinsky's place as a seminal figure in 20th-cent. mus. and individually as a great composer seems assured. Though it used to be said he 'changed his skin' every few years, and though he did, superficially at any rate, alter his style more than once, he remained fundamentally himself throughout his life. Like his antithesis Strauss, he was a time-traveller, at home in centuries other than his own. Yet when he touched Pergolesi, Gesualdo, and Tchaikovsky, they became Stravinskyan re-creations. Where the prin. features of Strauss's mus. are complex harmonic and contrapuntal textures, the overriding feature of Stravinsky from first to last is rhythm. It is rhythm, in many wonderful forms from the primitive (*Les Noces*) to the sophisticated (*Rite of Spring*), which is the mainspring of his work. With the great Diaghilev ballets he took part in a golden age in assoc. with some of the most extraordinary talents of the century, not only Diaghilev but Nijinsky, Picasso, Bakst, Fokine, and others. Later Cocteau, Auden, and Dylan Thomas came within his orbit. The sense of th. and of the dance is never wholly absent from even his most austere works, such as the *Mass* of 1948, nor his delight in childlike fun (the *Circus Polka, Jeu de cartes*, etc.), and his sardonic humour. It seems appropriate that almost his last work was a setting of Lear's *The Owl and the Pussycat*. His critics once wrote of a 'soulless' mus., bare of expression and emotion. As he recedes from us and his mus. comes into perspective, the wrongheadedness of this judgement provokes either mirth or anger. Prin. works:

OPERAS: *The *Nightingale* (1908-9, 1913-14); **Mavra* (1921-2); **Oedipus Rex* (1926-7, also can be perf. as oratorio); *The *Rake's Progress* (1947-51).

THEATRE PIECES: **Renard*, burlesque (1915-16); *L'*histoire du soldat* (*The Soldier's Tale*) (1918); **Perséphone*, melodrama, ten., ch., orch. (1933-4); *The *Flood*, mus. play (1961-2).

BALLETS: *The *Firebird* (*Zhar-Ptitsa*) (1909-10); **Petrushka* (1910-11); *The *Rite of Spring* (*Vesna Svyashchennaya*) (1911-13); *Les *Noces* (1914-17, and revisions); **Pulcinella* (after Pergolesi) (1919-20); **Apollo Musagetes* (1927-8); *The Fairy's Kiss* (*Le *baiser de la fée*) (after Tchaikovsky) (1928, rev. 1950); **Jeu de cartes* (1936); **Circus Polka* (1942); **Orpheus* (1947); **Agon* (1953, 1956-7).

ORCH.: syms.: No.1 in E♭ (1905-7), Sym. in C (1938-40), **Symphony in 3 Movements* (1942-5); *Scherzo Fantastique* (1907-8); **Fireworks* (1908); *Suite, The Firebird* (first version 1911, 2nd version 1919, 3rd version 1945); *Song of the Nightingale*, sym.-poem from mus. of the opera (1917), *Ragtime*, 11 instr. (1918); *Suites*, small orch., No.1 (1917-25), No.2 (1921); **Symphonies of Wind Instruments* (1918-20, rev. 1945-7); *Suite from Pulcinella*, chamber orch. (c.1922, rev. 1947); *Divertimento* (arr. from *The Fairy's Kiss*) (1934, rev. 1949); *Preludium* (orig. for jazz band 1936-7, orch. 1953); Conc., chamber orch. **Dumbarton Oaks* (1937-8); *Danses Concertantes* (1941-2); *4 Norwegian Moods* (1942); *Ode* (1943); *Scherzo à la Russe* (1943-4, version for Paul Whiteman Band 1944); **Circus Polka* (1944, orch. of pf. piece 1942); Conc. in D, str. (1946); *Tango*, 19 instr. (1953, orch. of pf. piece 1940); *Greetings Prelude* (1955); *Monumentum pro Gesualdo di Venosa ad CD annum*, 3 Gesualdo madrigals recomposed for instr. (1960); *Variations* (in memoriam Aldous Huxley) (1963-4).

SOLO INSTR. & ORCH.: conc., pf., wind instrs. (1923-4); *Capriccio*, pf., orch. (1928-9); vn. conc. (1931); **Ebony Concerto*, cl., chamber orch. (1945); **Movements*, pf., orch. (1958-9).

VOICES & INSTR(S).: *The King of the Stars*, cantata, male ch., orch. (1911-12); **Symphony of Psalms*, ch., orch. (1930); *Babel*, cantata, narr., male ch., orch. (1944); *Mass*, mixed ch., double wind quintet (1944-8); **Cantata*, sop., ten., female ch., chamber ens. (1951-2); **Canticum Sacrum ad honorem Sancti Marci Nominis*, ten., bar., ch., orch. (1955); **Threni*, sop., cont., 2 tens., bass, basso profundo, ch., orch. (1957-8); *A Sermon, A Narrative, and a Prayer*, cantata, alto, ten., spkr., ch., orch. (1960-1); **Abraham and Isaac*, bar., chamber orch. (1962-3); *Introitus* (T. S. Eliot in memoriam), tens., basses, chamber ens. (1965); *Requiem Canticles*, alto, bass, ch., orch. (1965-6).

UNACC. VOICES: *Saucers: 4 Russian Peasant Songs*, unacc. female vv. (1914-17, rev. for equal vv., 4 hn., 1954); *Pater Noster*, mixed ch. (1926); *Credo*, mixed ch. (1932, 1949, 1964); *Ave Maria*, mixed ch. (1934, 1949); *Little Canon*, 2 tens. (1947); *The Dove Descending*, mixed ch. (1962).

CHAMBER MUSIC: *3 Pieces*, cl. (1919); *Concertino*, str. qt. (1920), arr. for 12 instr. (1952); *Octet*, fl., cl., 2 bn., 2 tpt., ten. tb., bass tb. (1922-3, rev. 1952); *Duo Concertant*, vn., pf. (1931-2); *Suite Italienne* (arr. from *Pulcinella*), vn. or vc., pf. (1932); *Elegy*, vn. con sordini (1944); *Septet*, cl., hn., bn., pf., vn., va., vc. (1952-3); *Epitaphium*, fl., cl., hp. (1959).

PIANO: Sonata in F♯ minor (1903-4); *4 Studies* (1908); *3 Easy Pieces*, duet (1914-15); *5 Easy Pieces*, duet (1916-17); *Piano Rag-Music* (1919); *Sonata* (1924); *Serenade* in A (1925); Conc., 2 solo pf. (1931, 1934-5); *Tango* (1940, arr. for 19 instr. 1953); **Circus Polka* (1942, arr. for orch. 1944); Sonata, 2 pf. (1943-4).

SONGS WITH PIANO OR OTHER INSTR.: *Faun and Shepherdess*, song suite, mez., orch. (1906); *Pastorale*, sop., pf. (1907); *2 Melodies*, mez., pf. (1907-8); *2 Verlaine Poems*, bar., pf. (1910, with orch. 1951); *2 Balmont Poems*, high v., pf. (1911, with chamber orch. 1954); *3 Japanese Lyrics*, sop., pf. (1912-13); **Pribaoutki*, v., instr. (1914); *Cat's Cradle Songs*, alto, 3 cls. (1915-16); *Berceuse*, v., pf. (1917); *3 Shakespeare Songs*, mez., fl., cl., va. (1953); *In Memoriam Dylan Thomas*, ten., str. qt., 4 tbs. (1954); *Elegy for J.F.K.* [J. F. Kennedy, President of USA], bar., 3 cls. (1964); *The *Owl and the Pussycat*, v., pf. (1966).

ARRANGEMENTS: Chopin: *Nocturne* in A♭ and *Valse brillante* in E♭, orch. for *Les Sylphides* (1909); Bach: *Vom Himmel hoch*, mixed ch., orch. (1955-6); *2 Preludes and Fugues* from the '48', str., ww. (c.1969); Gesualdo: *Tres sacrae cantiones*, reconstructed parts (1957 and 1959); Sibelius: *Canzonetta*, Op.62a (orig. for str., 1911), arr. for 4 hns., 2 cls., hp., db. (1963); Wolf: *2 Sacred Songs* from *Spanisches Liederbuch*, mez., 9 instr. (1968). Other works: *Song of the Volga Boatmen*, orch. (1917); *La Marseillaise*, solo vn. (1919); *The Star-Spangled Banner*, orch., optional ch. (1941).

Stravinsky, (Svyatoslav) **Soulima** (*b* Lausanne, 1910; *d* Sarasota, 1994). Swiss-born pianist, son of Igor *Stravinsky. Stravinsky wrote the Conc. for 2 solo pf. (1931–5) for Soulima and himself to play and they gave f.p. in Paris, 1935. Settled in USA.

Streatfield, Simon (*b* Windsor, 1929). Eng. violist and conductor. Prin. va., SW orch 1953–5, 1956–65, Vancouver SO 1965, ass. cond. 1967, assoc. cond. 1972–7. Mus. dir. and cond. Vancouver Bach Choir 1969–81. Visiting prof., faculty of mus., Univ. of W. Ontario 1977–81. Cond. Regina SO 1981–4, Quebec SO 1984–91; Manitoba CO 1982–2000.

Streetcar Named Desire, A (Previn). Opera in 3 acts to a lib. by the composer based on the play by Tennessee Williams. Comp. 1997. F.p. San Francisco 1998, cond. Previn; f. Brit. p. London (Barbican, semi-staged) 2003, cond. Previn.

Street Corner. Ov. for orch. by Rawsthorne, f.p. 1944. Version for wind band by R. O'Brien.

street piano. Instr. used by vagrant musicians, being a mechanical type of pf. By turning a handle to operate a barrel-and-pin mechanism, a selection of tunes is available. Sometimes called *piano-organ*.

Street Scene. Opera in 2 acts by Weill to lib. by Elmer Rice after his own play with lyrics by Langston Hughes and Rice. Comp. 1946. Prod. Philadelphia 1946, NY 1947, London 1983 (semi-staged), London 1987, ENO 1989.

Strehler, Giorgio (*b* Barcola, Trieste, 1921; *d* Lugano, 1997). It. theatre producer. Began career as actor 1940. Dir. first th. prod. 1943. Co-founder Piccolo Teatro, Milan, 1947, winning reputation for radical direction and beautiful settings. Prod. first opera La Scala 1947 (*La traviata*). Prod. It. premières of *Love for Three Oranges*, *Lulu*, and *Aufstieg und Fall der Stadt Mahagonny*. Salzburg Fest. début 1965.

Streich (Ger.). Stroke (of bow). *Streichquartett*, string quartet, *Streichstimmen*, string-toned stops (org.), etc.

Streich, Rita (*b* Barnaul, 1920; *d* Vienna, 1987). Ger. soprano. Opera début Aussig (now Ústí nad Labem) 1943 (Zerbinetta in *Ariadne auf Naxos*). Berlin State Opera 1946–50; Berlin City Opera 1950–3. Débuts: Bayreuth Fest. 1952; Vienna State Opera 1953; Salzburg Fest. 1954; London (RFH) 1954 (with Vienna Opera); S. Francisco 1957; Glyndebourne 1958. Outstanding in Mozart (Queen of the Night, Constanze, Pamina) and Strauss (Zerbinetta, Sophie), Verdi's Gilda.

Streit, Kurt (*b* Itazuke, Japan, 1959). Amer. tenor. Sang with Milwaukee Skylight comic opera and in Dallas. Eur. début with Hamburg Opera. Salzburg Fest. début 1989; Glyndebourne 1990; CG 1993.

strepitoso (It.). 'Noisy', 'loud'. Direction to play forcefully, with the implication of headlong excitement. Elgar used it as an expression mark. Liszt's *Tasso* begins *allegro strepitoso*.

Strepponi, Giuseppina (Clelia Maria Josepha) (*b* Lodi, 1815; *d* Sant'Agata, nr. Busseto, 1897). It. soprano and 2nd wife of Giuseppe *Verdi. Concert début Lodi 1834. Opera début Adria 1834 in Ricci's *Chiara di Rosembergh*. At Trieste 1835 sang in *Matilde di Shabran*. Sang in Vienna, Rome, Venice, before La Scala début 1839. Instrumental in getting Verdi's first opera *Oberto* staged at Milan, 1839. Created Abigaille in *Nabucco*, Milan, 1842. Retired from stage 1846 to live with Verdi. Married him 1859.

stretta (It.). Drawn together, tightening (feminine of *stretto*). Passage at end of It. operatic aria, ens., or act where tempo is quickened for final climax.

stretto (It.). Drawn together. (1) Quicker tempo. (2) In fugue: when entry of the answer occurs before subject is completed, overlapping with it. This is a way of increasing excitement, as in a 4-part fugue when all 4 vv. enter in *stretto*.

Strich or **Bogenstrich** or **Anstrich** (Ger.). A stroke (with a bow); hence *mit breitem Strich*, with the breadth of the whole bow, and so forth. So also *Strichart*, manner of bowing; *Aufstrich*, up-bow; *Niederstrich*, down-bow.

strict canon. *Canon in which intervals of the imitating v. are same as those of v. imitated.

strict counterpoint. See *counterpoint*.

Striggio, Alessandro (*b* Mantua, 1535; *d* Mantua, 1592). It. composer. Prin. composer at court of Medicis in Florence in 1560s, writing *intermedi* for ceremonial occasions. Visited Eng. as political emissary 1567. Wrote madrigals for Ferrara 1584. Returned to Mantua 1584. Skilled instrumentalist, playing lira da gamba and descant viol. Unusual for his time in composing little sacred mus. His son Alessandro Striggio (*b* Mantua, *c*.1573; *d* Venice, *c*.1630) was a diplomat, viol player, and author of the libretto for Monteverdi's *Orfeo*, Mantua 1607.

string(s). The sound-producing agent of certain instr., i.e. thin strands of wire or gut vibrated on vn., va., vc., db., etc. by bow, on pf. by hammers, and on hpd., harp, guitar, etc. by plucking. But *strings*, meaning str. instr., is taken as referring in an orch. to the vns., vas., vcs., and dbs. A *string orchestra* comprises these only. A *string quartet* is 2 vn., va., vc.; *string trio*, vn., va., vc.

stringendo (It.). Squeezing. Direction that intensity of the mus. is to be increased, by quickening the tempo (as when approaching a climax).

string quartet. Group of 4 players (almost always 2 vn., va., vc.) or comp. written for them to play. Like the sym. in orch. mus., the str. qt. in chamber mus. has become the highest medium for a composer's thought. Form first developed at beginning of 18th cent. with A. Scarlatti, Tartini, etc., but achieved its flowering with Haydn, Mozart, Beethoven, and Schubert. Since then most composers have written str. qts., and the 19th and 20th cent. produced many superb qts. of performers, e.g. the Joachim, Brodsky, Bohemian, Léner, Griller, Amadeus, Gabrieli, Vermeer, Vegh, Chilingirian, Beethoven, Borodin, Endellion, Alban Berg, Takács, Kronos, Emerson, Arditti, Belcea, Sorrel, and the new Brodsky.

string quintet. Group of performers (2 vn., 2 va., vc.; or 2 vn., va., 2 vc.; or 2 vn., va., vc., db.) or work written for them. Great examples are those by Mozart and Schubert.

string-toned stops. Org. stops whose tone quality resembles that of str. instr., e.g. *gamba.

string trio. Group of 3 players (usually 2 vn. and vc., or vn., va., vc.) or comp. written for them to perf. Trios for 2 vn. and vc. were derived from baroque trio sonata. Haydn seems to have been the first to write for vn., va., and vc. and was emulated by Boccherini. Mozart's *Divertimento* (K563) is a notable example and there are others by Beethoven. An unusual combination of instr. is Dvořák's *Terzetto* for 2 vn. and va. (1887). In the 20th cent. trios for vn., va., and vc. have been written by Webern (1927), Schoenberg (1945), Dohnányi, Hindemith, Roussel, Moeran, and L. Berkeley. In 1938 Vaughan Williams wrote a double str. trio (2 vn., 2 va., 2 vc.), revised it in 1942, and rewrote it 1946–8 as *Partita* for str.

strisciando (It.). Trailing. Smooth, correct It. term for what is usually called *glissando.

Strohfiedel (Ger.). Xylophone. (*Stroh* = straw, on ropes of which the wooden blocks of the instr. formerly rested).

stromento (It., old form of *strumento*). Instrument, *stromento a corde*, str. instr.; *stromenti d'arco*, bowed instr.; *stromenti di legno*, woodwind instr.; *stromenti d'ottone*, brass instr.; *stromenti a percossa*, perc. instr.; *stromenti a fiato*, wind instr.; *stromenti da tasto*, kbd. instr. Also, *recitativo stromentato*, acc. recit.

strophic (from Gk. *strophe*). Term applied to song in which the same mus. is repeated, perhaps with very minor change, for each successive stanza of setting of a poem, in manner of folksong. The opposite, where the mus. progresses, is called 'through-composed' (Ger. *Durchkomponiert*). In general, the strophic song is simple and lyrical, the through-composed more dramatic or complex.

Stuart, Leslie [Thomas Augustine Barrett] (*b* Southport, 1864; *d* Richmond, Surrey, 1928). Eng. composer and organist. Org., Salford Cath. 1879–86, and Church of the Holy Name, Manchester, 1886–93. Went to London 1895 where he became composer of such popular songs as *Soldiers of the Queen* (1895), *Little Dolly Daydream*

(1897), *Lily of Laguna* (1898) (the last two being made famous by the Amer. 'coon' singer Eugene Stratton), and operettas *Florodora* (1899) (which contains the sextet 'Tell me, pretty maiden'), *The Belles of Mayfair* (1906), etc.

Stück (Ger.). Piece, as in *Konzertstück, concert piece.

Stuckenschmidt, Hans Heinz (*b* Strasbourg, 1901; *d* Berlin, 1988). Ger. critic, author, and composer. Cond. concerts of new mus. in Hamburg, 1923–4. Mus. critic in Berlin 1929–34, when removed by Nazis, and in Prague 1937–41. Head of new mus. dept., Berlin radio, 1946. Returned to Berlin mus. criticism 1947. Prof. of mus. history, Berlin Tech. Univ. from 1948 (emeritus from 1967). Author of books on Busoni, Stravinsky, Ravel, Blacher, and David. His major biography of Schoenberg appeared in 1974 (Eng. trans. 1978).

Studer, Cheryl (*b* Midland, Mich., 1955). Amer. soprano. After singing in concerts in USA, joined Bavarian State Opera, Munich, 1980 (début as Mařenka in *The Bartered Bride*). Darmstadt Opera 1983–5; Deutsche Oper, Berlin, from 1985. Débuts: Chicago Opera 1984; Bayreuth 1985; Paris 1986; CG 1987; Vienna and Salzburg Fest. 1989. Notable Strauss singer.

study. See *étude*.

Sturm und Drang (Ger., 'Storm and stress'). Term applied to period, roughly 1760–80, in Ger. literature and mus. when emotionalism was at height. Specially applied to works comp. by Joseph *Haydn at that time, particularly syms. (roughly Nos. 40–59), and str. qts. These works are marked by new and audacious formal and harmonic features. Also used to describe much kbd. mus. by C. P. E. Bach.

Stuttgart Chamber Orchestra. Founded by Karl *Münchinger, first concert 18 Sept. 1945. Tours to France, Britain, and Spain 1949, Central and S. Amer. 1952, USA 1954, Far East 1955, and Russia 1959. Made many recordings, notably of Bach's Brandenburg Concs. and his choral works. Orch. augmented in 1966 to 45 players to form Stuttgart Klassische Philharmonie. Chief cond. Martin Sieghart 1990–5; Dennis Russell Davies from 1995.

style galant (Fr.). **Galanter Stil** (Ger.). See *galant*.

su (It., other forms incl. *sul, sull', sulla, sulle*, etc.).
(1) On, near. *sul G* (in vn. playing), on the G str.
(2) Up, e.g. *arcata in su*, up-bowed.

sub-bourdon. Org. pedal end-plugged stop of 16′ length and 32′ pitch.

subdominant. 4th degree of major or minor scale, e.g. F in key of C. So called because it is the same distance below the tonic as the *dominant is above it (not because it is the note below the dominant or less important).

subito (It.). Suddenly. Quickly, immediately, as in *volti subito* (abbreviated to *V.S.*), turn over at once; *attacco subito*, go on without a break. Sometimes *subitamente* is used.

subject. (1) Term in mus. analysis meaning a motif, phrase, or melody which forms a basic element in the construction of a comp. Thus, in sonata-form, one has the 1st and 2nd subjects, sometimes more. These are introduced in the exposition, then developed and recapitulated.

(2) In *fugue, the melodic theme which is stated at the beginning, reappearing at various places and pitches during the comp. The answer is the imitation of the subject.

submediant. 6th degree of major or minor scale, e.g. A in key of C major, A♭ in key of C minor, lies midway between tonic and subdominant in the same way as the *mediant is midway between tonic and dominant.

sub-octave coupler. Coupler on pedal organ which duplicates notes played an octave lower on same stop.

Subotnick, Morton (*b* Los Angeles, 1933). Amer. composer and clarinettist. Played cl. in orchs., then became mus. dir. Lincoln Center Repertory Th., 1967. Fellow of Inst. for Advanced Mus. Studies, Princeton Univ., 1959–60. Founder and Dir., S. Francisco Tape Music Center 1961–6. Taught at Mills Coll. 1959–66, NY Univ. 1966–9. On staff Calif. Inst. of the Arts, from 1969. Mainly concerned with elec. mus., using synthesizer designed for him by D. Buchla. His *Silver Apples of the Moon* (1967) was first elec. mus. comp. for records. At NY toyshop, devised panels of buttons for shoppers to push which enabled instant creation of elec. works.

Suchoň, Eugen (*b* Pezinok, Slovakia, 1908; *d* Bratislava, 1993). Slovak composer. Prof. of theory, Bratislava Acad. 1933–48, prof. and head of dept. of mus. education, Bratislava Teacher Training Coll., 1948–59, prof. of mus. theory, Bratislava Univ. 1959–74. Author of textbooks on harmony. Works incl. operas *Krútňava* (Whirlpool) (1941–9) and *Svätopluk* (1951–9); *Serenade*, wind quintet; cl. concertino; *Rhapsodic Suite*, pf., orch.; str. qt.; pf. qt.; and songs. Evolved his own branch of serialism from 1959.

Suggia, Guilhermina (*b* Oporto, 1888; *d* Oporto, 1950). Portuguese cellist. Taught as child by father. Public début at age 7. Prin. cellist of Oporto orch. at age 12. In 1904 went to Leipzig to study under Klengel. Début at Gewandhaus cond. Nikisch, followed by tours. Studied in 1906 with Casals. Resumed int. career 1912 and settled in London. Subject of highly dramatic portrait by Augustus John, 1923. Came out of retirement to play at Edinburgh Fest. 1949.

Suisse Romande, Orchestre de la. See *Orchestre de la Suisse Romande*.

suite (Fr., Eng.; Old Fr. *ordre*; Old Eng. *lesson*; Old Ger. *Partita* or *Partia*; Old It. *sonata da camera*). A following. Orig. a piece of instr. mus. in several movts., usually in dance-style. During 17th and 18th cents. was one of most important forms of instr. mus. During Baroque period, typical *suite* would have framework of allemande, courante, sarabande, and gigue, with frequent interpolations of minuet, gavotte, passepied, bourrée, musette, and rigaudon. The various movts. were usually based on one key, though modulations occurred within individual movts. Nearly all movts. were in simple binary form. Fr. kbd. suites sometimes contained up to 18 movts., but these were not necessarily all intended to be perf. at once: the composer left it to the player to make a selection. In importance the suite was superseded by the sonata and the sym., and the title was given to works of a lighter type, e.g. Grieg's *Holberg* and Elgar's *Wand of Youth* Suites, and assemblages of movts. from opera or ballet scores, e.g. Ravel's *Daphnis et Chloé* suites. 20th-cent. neo-classic composers revived the term (Stravinsky for example).

Suite Bergamasque (Bergomask suite). Pf. suite by Debussy containing 4 movts., *Prélude, Menuet, *Clair de Lune*, and *Passepied*. Comp. 1890, rev. 1905. Orch. version of Nos. 1, 2, and 4 by G. Cloez, No.3 by *Caplet.

Suite on Verses of Michelangelo (Shostakovich). See *Michelangelo Buonarroti, Suite on Verses of*.

Suitner, Otmar (*b* Innsbruck, 1922). Austrian conductor. Début Innsbruck 1942. Mus. dir. Remscheid 1952–7, gen. mus. dir. Ludwigshafen 1957–60. Chief cond. Dresden Opera and State Orch. 1960–4. Cond., Deutsche Staatsoper, Berlin, 1964–71, gen. mus. dir. 1974–9. Bayreuth 1964–7.

Suk, Josef (*b* Křečovice, 1874; *d* Benešov, nr. Prague, 1935). Cz. composer and violinist. 2nd vn. in Bohemian Str. Qt. 1892–1933. Married Dvořák's daughter (*d* 1905). Prof. of comp., Prague Cons. 1922–35. Early works influenced by Dvořák, but later developed a more complex harmonic and polyphonic style, sometimes near to atonality. Works incl.:

ORCH.: *Serenade* in E♭, str. (1892); sym. No.1 in E (1897–9), No.2 *Asrael* (1905–6); *Pohádka (Fairy Tales)*, suite (1899–1900); *Fantastic Scherzo* (1903); *Praga* (Prague), sym.-poem (1904); *Pohádka léta* (A Summer's Tale) (1907–9); *Zrání* (Harvest Time), sym.-poem (1912–17); *War Triptych*, Op.35, No.1 *Svatý Václave* (Oh, St Wenceslas), *Meditation on an old Bohemian Chorale* (1914), No.2 *Legend of the Dead Victors* (1919), No.3 *Sokol ceremonial march*, *V nový život* (Towards a New Life, 1919–20); *Fantasia* in G minor, vn., orch. (1902).

CHORAL: *10 Songs*, women's ch. (1899); *4 Songs*, male ch. (1900).

VOICE(S) & PIANO/ORCH.: *Chant d'Amour*, v., pf. (1892); *O matince* (About Mother), 5 songs, v., pf. (1907); *Životem a snem* (Life and Dreams), v., pf. (1909); *Epilogue*, sop., bar., bass, ch., orch. (1920–9).

CHAMBER MUSIC: 2 str. qts. (1896, 1911); pf. qt., pf. quintet, pf. trio; *4 Pieces*, vn., pf.; *Ballad*, vn., pf.; *Meditation on old Bohemian Chorale* Op.35a (1914), arr. for str. qt. from orch. work.

PIANO: Sonata (1883); *6 Pieces* (1891–3); *Spanish Joke* (1909).

Suk, Josef (*b* Prague, 1929). Cz. violinist, grandson of Josef *Suk. Début Prague 1940. Played in Prague Nat. Th. orch. and in Prague Qt. 1951–2. Won Cz. State Prize 1964. Soloist in concs. with world's leading orchs. Salzburg début 1963. Amer. début and London début (Proms) 1964.

sul, sull', sulla, sui, sugli, sulle (It.). See *su*.

Šulek, Stjepan (*b* Zagreb, 1914; *d* Zagreb, 1986). Croatian composer, conductor, and violinist. Teacher of comp., Zagreb Acad. from 1945. Works incl. 7 syms., 3 pf. concs., vn. conc., va. conc., cantata, pf. sonata, and incidental mus. for Shakespeare's *The Tempest* and *Coriolanus*.

sul G (sul IV) (It.). Term used in vn. mus. meaning on the G (4th) str.

Suliotis, Elena. See *Souliotis, Elena*.

Sullivan, (Sir) **Arthur** (Seymour) (*b* Lambeth, 1842; *d* Westminster, 1900). Eng. composer, conductor, and organist. Son of Irish bandmaster at Sandhurst. Chorister, Chapel Royal, 1854. First comp., an anthem, pubd. 1855. First holder of Mendelssohn Scholarship, RAM, 1856, becoming pupil of Goss and Sterndale Bennett. Went to Leipzig Cons. where his teachers incl. Rietz, David, and Moscheles. Returned to Eng. 1861 and became organist, St Michael, Chester Sq. In 1862 his mus. for Shakespeare's *The Tempest* was played under Manns at Crystal Palace and made Sullivan's name. Ballet *L'Île enchantée* prod. CG 1864 and cantata *Kenilworth* Birmingham Fest. later same year. To 1864 also belongs comp. of *Irish Symphony*. Prof. of comp. RAM 1866, in which year he wrote vc. conc. for Piatti. Went with *Grove to Vienna in 1867 to recover Schubert's *Rosamunde* mus. and to examine MS of 'Great' C major Sym. In 1866 wrote light opera *Cox and Box*, first of works in genre which was to ensure Sullivan's lasting fame.

For a time, however, Sullivan persisted with oratorio (*The Prodigal Son*, Worcester 1869) and incidental mus. to Shakespeare. In 1871 met playwright William Schwenck Gilbert (1836–1911) and collaborated in unsuccessful light opera *Thespis*, following it in 1872 with tune for hymn 'Onward, Christian Soldiers'. *Festival Te Deum* followed, then another Birmingham oratorio, *The Light of the World* (1873). By now much in demand as cond. and administrator, and was also friend of royalty. In 1875 another collaboration with Gilbert, engineered by Richard D'Oyly Carte, resulted in successful curtain-raiser *Trial by Jury*. This led to D'Oyly Carte's leasing of Opéra-Comique Th. especially to produce operas by Gilbert and Sullivan. *The Sorcerer* (1877) justified the risk, running for 175 nights, but this was eclipsed by the 700-night run of *H.M.S. Pinafore* (1878). Despite copyright pirates, these works were in demand throughout the Western world, particularly in USA. *The Pirates of Penzance* (1879) continued run of success, followed by *Patience* (1881). During run of *Patience*, D'Oyly Carte opened his new th., the Savoy, and the operas became known as the Savoy operas and the cast 'Savoyards'. Sullivan was knighted 1883. It is a tragic irony that Sullivan and some of his friends felt that the success of the operettas was beneath the dignity of the dir. of the Nat. Training Sch. for Mus., 1876–81; they were happier with *The Martyr of Antioch* (Leeds 1880) and *The Golden Legend* (Leeds 1886) than with *Iolanthe* (1882), *Princess Ida* (1883), and *The Mikado* (1885). These were followed by further 'hits': *Ruddigore* (1886), *The Yeomen of the Guard* (1888), and *The Gondoliers* (1889). During run of the last-named, the 2 partners quarrelled (supposedly over a new carpet at the Savoy Th.). *Haddon Hall* (1892) was comp. to a lib. by S. Grundy. Reconciliation with Gilbert led to *Utopia Limited* (1893) and *The Grand Duke* (1896). During quarrel, Sullivan's only 'grand opera', *Ivanhoe*, to a lib. by Julian Sturgis, was prod. in 1891 at new Eng. Opera House built by D'Oyly Carte. Had 160 perfs., but costly venture failed and th. became a mus.-hall. By then, Sullivan's health was beginning to rebel against the strain he put on it. He was cond. of the Phil. Soc. 1885–7, frequently cond. at the Hallé Concerts in Manchester, was cond. of the Leeds Fest. from 1883, and continued to write th. mus., anthems, etc. In his last years his path crossed that of the rising Elgar. He died on St Cecilia's Day 1900 at comparatively early age of 58.

Sullivan's 'serious' work, by which he set such store, survives in the occasional ch. from *The Golden Legend* and the infrequent revivals of his sym. and incidental mus. and of *Ivanhoe*. These show talent, not quite as much, it could be argued, as in his hymn-tunes and in his popular ballads, such as *My dearest heart* and *The *Lost Chord* (written in 1877 on the death of his brother and given a further lease of fame by the Amer. comedian Jimmy 'Schnozzle' Durante in his song 'The guy who found the Lost Chord'). But in the Savoy operettas there is genius. In them Sullivan's melodic felicity, light-fingered orchestration, and truly astonishing gift for pastiche and parody (Handel, Verdi, Donizetti, Wagner—all are paid the compliment of witty imitation) found their proper outlet and gave England a unique type of mus. entertainment and cult. Sometimes parody seems to have taken over completely and one longs to call out 'Will the real Sullivan stand up?' At other times, Gilbert's cruelties and facetiousness become oppressive; also the stylized, unchanging ritual of the D'Oyly Carte prods. became wearisome except to devotees, of whom there are millions, seemingly versed in every phrase of both mus. and lib. With such a following, Sullivan's fame seems secure for as long as one dares to foretell. Prin. works:

OPERA: *Ivanhoe* (1890).

OPERETTAS (where no librettist is given, Gilbert is implied): *Cox and Box* (Burnand, 1866);

Contrabandista (Burnand, 1867); **Thespis* (1871, lost); **Trial by Jury* (1875); *The Zoo* (Stevenson, 1875); *The *Sorcerer* (1877, rev. 1884); **H.M.S. Pinafore* (1878); *The *Pirates of Penzance* (1879); **Patience* (1880–1); **Iolanthe* (1882); **Princess Ida* (1883–4); *The *Mikado* (1884–5); **Ruddigore* (1886–7); *The *Yeomen of the Guard* (1888); *The *Gondoliers* (1889); *Haddon Hall* (Grundy, 1892); **Utopia Limited* (1893); *The Chieftain* (Burnand, 1894); *The *Grand Duke* (1895–6); *The Beauty Stone* (Pinero and Comyns Carr, 1897–8); *The Rose of Persia* (Hood, 1899); *The *Emerald Isle* (Hood, 1900, mus. completed by *German).

INCIDENTAL MUSIC: Shakespeare: *The Tempest* (1862); *The Merchant of Venice* (1871); *The Merry Wives of Windsor* (1874); *King Henry VIII* (1877); *Macbeth* (1888); *The Foresters* (Tennyson, 1892); *King Arthur* (Comyns Carr, 1894).

ORCH.: sym. in E (*Irish*) (1864–6); Ov., *In Memoriam* (1866); *Overture Di Ballo* (1870); *Imperial March* (1893); vc. conc. (1866).

CHORAL: Oratorios: *The *Prodigal Son* (1869); *The Light of the World* (1873, rev. 1890); *The Martyr of Antioch* (1880, rev. as opera 1898); Cantatas: *Kenilworth* (1864); *On Shore and Sea* (1871); *The *Golden Legend* (1886).

Also songs, chamber mus., ballads, hymns, anthems.

sul ponticello (It.). On the bridge. Instruction to the player of the vn., va., vc., and db. that he is to take the bow as near as possible to the bridge to produce a rather metallic but mysterious sound-effect.

sul tasto (It.). On the touch. Direction to player of vn., etc., to take the bow over the fingerboard, giving a rich, mellow sound. *Sulla tastiera* (on the fingerboard) means the same.

Sumer is Icumen In (Old Eng.). Summer is coming in. Eng. comp., dating supposedly from *c.*1240, sometimes known as the Reading Rota because the MS originated at Reading Abbey. The conjectural author was a monk of Reading, *John of Fornsete. An infinite canon at the unison for 4 ten. vv., with 2 basses repeating a ground bass or *pes*, also in canon at the unison. Can claim to be the earliest extant canon, 6-part comp., example of ground bass, and mus. setting of both sacred (Latin) and secular words.

summation tone. Acoustical phenomenon whereby, when 2 loud notes are sounded, another note, higher than orig. 2, may also be heard, corresponding to sum of their vibrations.

Summer Night on the River. Title of 2nd of 2 *Mood Pictures* for small orch. by Delius, comp. 1911 and f.p. in Leipzig 1913, London 1914. First piece is **On hearing the first cuckoo in Spring* (1912). Not to be confused with Delius's 2 chs. *To be sung of a summer night on the water*, 1917.

Summers, Jonathan (*b* Melbourne, 1946). Australian baritone. Début Kent Opera 1975 (Rigoletto). GTO 1976; CG début 1977. Many roles with ENO, Opera North, and Scottish Opera. Australian Opera 1981; NY Met 1988; Chicago 1990.

Summer's Last Will and Testament. Work by C. *Lambert for solo bar., ch., and orch., comp. 1935, f.p. London 1936. Setting of 5 lyrics from play of same name (1593) by Thomas Nashe, movements being entitled *Intrata, Drinking Chorus, King Pest* (rondo burlesca for orch.), *Madrigal, Sarabande*.

Sumsion, Herbert (Whitton) (*b* Gloucester, 1899; *d* Frampton-on-Severn, 1995). Eng. organist, conductor, and composer. Ass. org. to *Brewer, Gloucester Cath. 1916–17 and again 1919–22. Org., Christ Church, Lancaster Gate, London, 1922–6. Prof. of harmony and counterpoint, Curtis Inst. 1926–8. Org. and choirmaster Gloucester Cath. 1928–67, cond. at 3 Choirs Fests. within that period. Dir. of mus., Cheltenham Ladies College, 1935–68. Wrote org. mus., church services, etc. CBE 1961.

suo (It.). Its own, e.g. *suo loco*, indicating a return to 'its own place' after transposition of vocal or instr. part up or down an octave, etc.

Suor Angelica (Sister Angelica). Opera in 1 act by Puccini to lib. by Forzano. Part 2 of *Il *Trittico*. Comp. 1917. Prod. NY Met 1918, Rome and Chicago 1919, London 1920.

super-octave coupler. Coupler on an org. which duplicates notes played an octave higher on same stop.

supertonic. 2nd degree of the scale, lying whole tone above tonic, e.g. in key of C (major or minor), the D lying immediately above the tonic C (1st degree).

Supervia, Conchita (*b* Barcelona, 1895; *d* in childbirth London, 1936). Sp. mezzo-soprano and mezzo-contralto. Début at 14 in Buenos Aires (in Stiattesi's *Blanca de Beaulieu*). Chicago Opera 1915–16 and 1932–3; La Scala début 1926; CG 1934–5. Created title-role in Lehár's *Frasquita* (1922). Singer of vivacious originality, with distinctive timbre.

Suppé, Franz von (*b* Split (Spalato), 1819; *d* Vienna, 1895). Austrian composer and conductor, born in Dalmatia, of Belg. descent. Name is Ger. form of Francesco Ezechiele Ermenegildo, Cavaliere Suppé-Demelli. Relative of Donizetti, who helped him. Became cond. at Josephstadt Th., Vienna, 1841, later in Pressburg and Baden. Sang in opera, making début at Ödenburg 1842 (Dulcamara in *L'elisir d'amore*). Cond. in Vienna at Theater an der Wien 1845–62, and at Carltheater (formerly Leopoldstadt Th.) 1865–82. Comp. serious works, incl. *Requiem* (1855), but fame rests on series of tuneful operettas (about 30 in number). These incl. **Pique Dame (Die Kartenschlägerin)* (1862); *Die schöne Galatea* (The *Beautiful Galathea) (1865), *Leichte Cavallerie* (*Light Cavalry)

(1866), *Banditenstreiche* (The Jolly Robbers) (1867), and **Boccaccio* (1879). The famous *Poet and Peasant* ov. (1846) is part of the incidental mus. to Elmar's play *Dichter und Bauer*.

supprimez (Fr.). Suppress. In Fr. org. mus. it means 'put out of use' the stop in question.

sur la touche (Fr.). On the fingerboard. Direction in str. playing to bow over the fingerboard.

sur le chevalet (Fr.). On the bridge. Direction in str. playing to bow on or near the bridge, same as **sul ponticello*.

Surprise Symphony. Nickname of Haydn's Sym. in G major, No.94 (Hob. I:94)., comp. London 1791, so called because of sudden *forte* drumbeat in slow movt. In Ger., sym. is known as *mit dem Paukenschlag* (with the drumstroke).

Sursum Corda (Lift up your hearts). (1) Work for str., brass, and org., Op.11, by Elgar, f.p. Worcester Cath. 1894. Comp. for visit of Duke of York (later King George V) to Worcester.
    (2) No.7 of Liszt's *Troisième année* (pubd. 1883) of the *Années de pèlerinage* for solo pf.

surtitles. Translations, usually specially prepared, of extracts from opera libretto, projected on screen above stage (or, at Santa Fe and NY Met, on the backs of seats) during performance to enable members of audience who do not speak language in which opera is set to follow the action. Standard format is 2 lines of text per title with maximum of 40 letters per line. Some operas use up to 600 titles. Introduced by Canadian Opera Co., Toronto, for *Elektra*, 21 Jan. 1983, on initiative of Lotfi Mansouri, dir. of co. at that time. First used in Brit. at CG school perfs. of *La bohème* and *Falstaff*, 1984. Introduced by GTO, Oct. 1984, and at Glyndebourne 1985. CG's regular use began 1986. Florence used them 1986 and Salzburg 1993 (*L'incoronazione di Poppea*, in Ger. and Eng.). Controversy rages over their use. James Levine said they would be used at NY Met 'over my dead body', but the Met introduced them. Eng. surtitles have been used in Eng. language operas, e.g. *The Electrification of the Soviet Union*, Glyndebourne 1987, and *Gawain*, CG 1991. ENO adopted surtitles in 2005.

Survivor from Warsaw, A. For narr., male ch., and orch. by Schoenberg, Op.46, comp. Aug. 1947. Eng. text by Schoenberg, Fr. version by R. Leibowitz, Ger. by Maquet Peter. F.p. Albuquerque, New Mexico, 1948, f.p. in England 1951.

Susa, Conrad (Stephen) (*b* Springdale, Pa., 1935). Amer. pianist and composer of Slovak parentage. Studied at Carnegie Inst. of Technology and at Juilliard School with William Bergsma and Vincent Persichetti. Was pianist for Pittsburgh SO. Teacher in comp. dept. of San Francisco Cons. from 1988 (chairman from 2000). Comp.-in-res. Old Globe Th., San Diego, 1959–94; mus. dir. APA-Phoenix Repertory Company, NY, 1961–8, Amer. Shakespeare Fest., Stratford, Conn., 1969–71. His main interest has always been in dramatic works. Has

written several operas, incl. *Transformations* (1973), *The Love of Don Perlimplin* (1984), and *The Dangerous Liaisons* (1994, rev. 1996–7); the choral work *Dirge from Cymbeline* for male ch. and off-stage tpt. (1991); many scores for documentary films and TV prods.; instrumental works and songs.

Susanna's Secret (Wolf-Ferrari). See *Segreto di Susanna, Il*.

suspended cadence. Delay before final cadence of a comp. so that performer in conc. (or, formerly, aria) may insert cadenza.

suspension. Opposite of **anticipation: a note in a chord is held over (sounded slightly late) as a momentary discordant part of the combination which follows; it is then resolved by falling a degree to a note which forms a real part of the 2nd chord. When 2 notes are held over it is called a double suspension. In many 20th-cent. works suspensions are often left unresolved.

Susskind [Süsskind], (Jan) **Walter** (*b* Prague, 1913; *d* Berkeley, Calif., 1980). Cz.-born conductor and pianist (Eng. cit. 1946). Début (*La traviata*) as cond., Ger. Opera, Prague, 1934–8. Pianist in Czech Trio 1933–8. Went to London 1938, playing in Czech Trio in exile until 1942. Prin. cond. Carl Rosa Opera, 1943–5. Cond., Scottish Orch. 1946–52, Victorian SO of Melbourne, 1953–5, Toronto SO 1956–65, Aspen Mus. Fest. 1962–8, St Louis SO 1968–75. Taught at Univ. of S. Ill., 1968–75. Mus. adviser and prin. guest cond., Cincinnati SO 1975–80. Comp. str. qt. and songs.

Süssmayr, Franz Xaver (*b* Schwanenstadt, 1766; *d* Vienna, 1803). Austrian composer. Cond. at Nat. Th., Vienna, 1792–4, 2nd cond., court th. 1794. Wrote several operas incl. *Die liebe für den König* (1785), *Moses* (1792), *Il turco in Italia* (1794), *Der Spiegel von Arkadien* (1794), *Soliman der Zweite* (1799), *Das Hausgesinde* (1802), oratorios, masses, etc. Comp. secco recitatives for Mozart's *La clemenza di Tito*, 1791. Assisted in completion of Mozart's *Requiem* (K626).

sustaining pedal. Pf. pedal, often erroneously called 'loud pedal', operated by right foot to prolong sound by holding off the dampers. Beethoven, as a player, was said to make teʬing use of this pedal, which is much exploite⸍ by Romantic composers.

susurrando, susurrante (Ɪ. Whispering.

Sutcliffe, Tom (*b* Norwi͜ 1943). Eng. critic and countertenor. Eng. tu⸜͜ Central Tutorial Sch. for Young Musiciansⵎw Purcell Sch.). Counterten. in Westmiᵣvata 1965–71. Counterten. in Westmiᵣn ed., *Music and Musicians* manager, Musica ͡Cath. Choir 1966–70. Advert. manage͡era, and drama critic, *Vogue*, 1968–73; mͥuritic, *The Guardian*, 1973–96. Evening Stand᷈ 1975–87. O⸍96–2002. Wrote *Believing in Opera* (1996) a᷈ *Faber Book of Opera* (2000).

Sute᷈er, Heinrich (*b* Feuerthalen, 1910; *d* ᷈ 1995). Swiss composer. Worked as *répétiteur* at Berne Stadttheater. Taught comp. at Hanover Hochschule für Musik 1963–75. Influenced by Verdi's last works and by *Orff, determined to write melodic 20th-cent mus. Works incl.:

OPERAS: *Die schwarze Spinne* (The Black Spider), radio opera (1936, rev. for stage 1948); *Romeo und Julia* (after Shakespeare, 1939); *Die Zauberinsel* (The Magic Island, after Shakespeare's Tempest, 1942); *Niobe* (1946); *Raskolnikoff* (after Dostoyevsky, 1945–7); *Der rote Stiefel* (The Red Shoe) (1951); *Titus Feuerfuchs* (1957–8); *Seraphine* (after Rabelais, 1959); *Das Gespenst von Canterville* (The Canterville Ghost (after Wilde), TV, 1962–3); *Madame Bovary* (after Flaubert, 1966–7); *Das Flaschenteufel* (TV, 1971); *Le roi Bérenger* (after Ionesco, 1985).

ORCH.: suite, *Romeo und Julia* (1940); *Die Alpen* (1948); Divertimento No.1 for str. (1936), No.2 for orch. (1959–60); *Serenade* (1970); 3 pf. concs. (1944, 1954, 1961–2); vc. conc. (1954–5).

CHORAL: 8 Cantatas (1938–1966); *Requiem*, sop., bar., ch., orch. (1952); *Te Deum* (1975).

Also songs with pf./orch., pf. pieces, etc.

Suthaus, (Heinrich) **Ludwig** (*b* Cologne, 1906; *d* Berlin, 1971). Ger. tenor. Opera début Aachen 1928 (Walther in *Die Meistersinger*). Essen Opera 1931–3; Stuttgart 1933–41; Berlin Staatsoper 1941–9; Berlin Städtische (later Deutsche) Oper 1948–65; Vienna 1948–71. CG début 1953; Bayreuth début 1943; Amer. début (S. Francisco) 1953. Besides Wagner, roles incl. Otello. Recorded Tristan with Flagstad, cond. Furtwängler, 1952.

Sutherland, (Dame) **Joan** (*b* Sydney, NSW, 1926). Australian soprano. Début Sydney 1947 in concert perf. of *Dido and Aeneas*. Created title-role in Goossens's *Judith*, NSW Cons., 1951. CG début 1952. Created Jenifer in *The Midsummer Marriage*, 1955. Glyndebourne début 1956 (in Liverpool); at Glyndebourne 1957. Sang New Prioress in f. Eng. p. of *Les dialogues des Carmélites*, 1958. Under guidance of Richard Bonynge, whom she married 1954, developed dramatic coloratura possibilities of *bel canto* roles. Had enormous success as Lucia di Lammermoor, CG 1959. Amer. début (Dallas) 1960; débuts La Scala and NY Met 1961. Revived many Donizetti and Bellini roles. Took own opera co. to Australia 1965 and 1974. Retired 1990. CBE 1961. DBE 1979. OM 1991.

Suzuki, Shin-ichi (*b* Nagoya, 1898; *d* Matsumoto, 1998). Japanese vn. teacher. Son of maker of violins. Founded Suzuki Qt. 1928 with 3 of his brothers. Founded Tokyo Str. Orch. which introduced baroque mus. to Japanese listeners. Pres. of Teikoku Mus. Sch. from 1930 and put into practice his belief that a child could reach a high standard of ability with external stimuli. Taught violinist by adapting Kyōiku Kenkyū-kai, Matsumoto 1950 at Sainō. Visited USA 1964, Eng. 1973.

Svanholm, Set (Karl Viktor) (*b* Saltsjö-Duvnäs, nr. Stockholm, 1904; *d* Saltsjö-Duvnäs, nr. Stockholm, 1964). Swed. tenor, orig. baritone. Taught at Stockholm Cons. Opera Sch. 1929 after spell as chorister. ...ganist.

Début as bar., Stockholm 1930 (Silvio in *Pagliacci*). Resumed training, then made ten. début in 1936 (Radames in *Aïda*). Sang first Wagner roles 1937; Salzburg Fest. 1938; Bayreuth 1942; NY Met 1946–56; S. Francisco 1946–51; CG 1948–57. In 1940s and 1950s was world's leading Wagnerian ten., in demand as Siegfried and Tristan and frequently singing with *Flagstad. First Peter Grimes in Stockholm, 1945. Intendant, Stockholm Opera 1956–63.

svegliando; svegliato (It.). Awakening; awakened, i.e. brisk, alert.

Svendsen, Johan (Severin) (*b* Christiania, 1840; *d* Copenhagen, 1911). Norweg. composer, conductor, and violinist. Went to Paris 1868, playing in orch. there. Sym. played at Leipzig, 1871. Became close friend of Wagner and played in orch. at laying of Bayreuth foundation-stone, 1872. Returned to Norway as cond. and teacher, 1872–7. First visit to London 1878. Prin. cond. Danish Royal Opera, Copenhagen, 1883–1908. Works incl. 2 syms.; vc. conc.; vn. conc.; *Carnaval à Paris; 4 Norwegian Rhapsodies; Romance* for vn. and orch.; and chamber mus. and songs.

Svetlanov, Yevgeny (Fyodorovich) (*b* Moscow, 1928; *d* Moscow, 2002). Russ. conductor and composer. Cond. Moscow Radio 1953. Cond., Bolshoy Th., Moscow, 1954–62, chief cond. 1962–4. Cond. USSR State SO 1965–2002. Comp. sym.-poems, cantata, sonatas, songs.

Svoboda, Josef (*b* Čáslav, 1920; *d* Prague, 2002). Cz. stage designer. Chief designer and tech. dir., Prague Nat. Th. 1951–6. Influenced by Appia and Craig, developed concept of 'psychoplastic stage', concentrating on 'inner meaning' of work. Has made inspired use of modern lighting techniques, incl. laser beams in his 1970 *Die Zauberflöte* in Munich. Other celebrated opera designs were seen at Venice 1961 (*Intolleranza*); La Scala 1971 (*Wozzeck*); CG 1966 (*Die Frau ohne Schatten*) and *The Ring* (1974–6); NY Met 1972 (*Carmen*); at Deutsche Oper, Berlin, 1991 (*Salome*).

Swan Lake (*Lebedinoye ozero*; Fr. *Le lac des cygnes*). Ballet in 4 acts, mus. by Tchaikovsky, comp. 1875–6, to lib. by Begitchev and Geltser, choreog. Reisinger, prod. Moscow 1877. Later choreog. Petipa and Ivanov (St Petersburg 1895).

Swann, Donald (Ibrahim) (*b* Llanelli, 1923; *d* London, 1994). Eng. composer and pianist. Accompanist and composer for revues 1948–56. Wrote mus. for Henry Reed satirical features, BBC Third Prog. 1950s. Successful partnership with Michael Flanders in revues *At the Drop of a Hat* and *At the Drop of Another Hat* (1957–67). Comps. incl. 4 operas; carols; children's songs; and pf. pieces.

Swan of Tuonela, The. 'Symphonic legend' by *Sibelius, orig. comp. as prelude to unfinished opera *The Building of the Boat*, 1893, but pubd. as Op.22, No.3, one of the 4 *Lemminkäinen Legends* for orch. Rev. 1897 and 1900. F.p. Helsinki 1896, f.p. in England 1905. Tuonela is Finnish Hades. Cor anglais solo depicts swan.

Swan Song (Schubert). See *Schwanengesang*.

Swarowsky, Hans (*b* Budapest, 1899; *d* Salzburg, 1975). Hung. conductor. Cond. posts in Stuttgart, Berlin, Hamburg, and Zurich (1937–40). Cond. Polish PO in Kraków, 1944–6. Salzburg Fest. 1946 (*Der Rosenkavalier*). Dir. Graz Opera 1947–9. Cond. Vienna Opera 1957. Cond. SNO 1957–9. Head of cond. class at Vienna Acad. of Mus. from 1946, pupils incl. *Abbado and *Mehta. Ed. Fr. versions of Gluck's *Alceste* and *Orphée*. Wrote parts of lib. of Strauss's *Capriccio* (incl. the Sonnet) but his part in this was suppressed by C. Krauss, the official librettist.

Swayne, Giles (Oliver Cairnes) (*b* Stevenage, 1946). Eng. composer and conductor. Opera *répétiteur* at Wexford Fest. 1972 and 1973, and Glyndebourne 1973–4. Teacher at Bryanston Sch. 1974–6 and St Paul's Girls' Sch. 1976. Won Lancaster Univ. composer's prize, 1974. Studied with Messiaen 1976–7. Visited The Gambia 1981–2 to study and record mus. of Jola people. Works incl. *Le nozze di Cherubino*, opera (1983–4); ballet; Sym. (1983); *Naaotwa Lala*, orch. (1984); many vocal works, incl. *Cry*, 28 amp. solo vv. (1978); *The Song of the Tortoise*, narr., vv., orch. (1992); *Goodnight Sweet Ladies*, sop., pf. (1994–5); *Tombeau*, pf. (1997); *Chinese Whispers*, org., chamber orch. (1997); *The Silent Land*, ch., vc. (1998); *HAVOC*, counterten., 2 sop., mez., ch., ens. (1999); also 3 str. qts. (1971–93) and kbd. pieces.

Sweelinck [Swybbertszoon], **Jan Pieterszoon** (*b* Deventer or Amsterdam, 1562; *d* Amsterdam, 1621). Dutch composer, organist, harpsichordist, and teacher. Succeeded father as organist of Old Church, Amsterdam, *c*.1580, remaining in post until death. First composer to give independent part to the pedal and to write fully worked-out fugues, thus pioneering and establishing form to be used by Bach. Taught most of great N. Ger. school of organists and was of immense influence. Wrote over 250 vocal works and 70 for keyboard. Set the entire psalter. Keyboard works show Eng. and It. influences.

swell. Mechanical device on org. and certain other kbd. instr., e.g. hpd., for increasing (and lessening) the vol. of sound.

swell organ (Swell). Section of organ in which the pipes are enclosed in a *swell box*. Player can increase or diminish vol. of sound by means of *swell pedal* which opens and closes a Venetian shutter. Manual controlling this is placed above *great org. and is known as *swell manual*. On some modern orgs. 'swell' effect may be obtained also on choir and solo manuals.

Swieten, Gottfried, Baron van (*b* Leiden, 1733; *d* Vienna, 1803). Dutch-born Austrian patron of music. Went to Vienna 1745 when his father became empress's physician. Held diplomatic posts in Brussels, Paris, and London, and was ambassador to Berlin 1770–7. Prefect of Imperial Lib., Vienna, 1778–1803. Wrote light operas and syms., but remembered for commissioning works from C. P. E. Bach, Haydn, and Mozart. Introduced Mozart to mus. of Bach and Handel 1782–3. Mozart made his arrs. of Handel oratorios and other vocal works for private concerts van Swieten founded. Wrote or adapted texts of Haydn's *Seven Last Words* (ch. version 1796), *The Creation* (1798), and *The Seasons* (1801). Helped the young Beethoven, who dedicated his 1st Sym. to him.

swing. See *jazz*.

Swingle, Ward (*b* Mobile, Ala., 1927). Amer. conductor and arranger. Career as solo pianist and accomp. 1953–5. Cond. Ballets de Paris 1955–9. Founded Swingle Singers 1963, giving about 2,000 concerts throughout world 1963–91 and taking part in works by Berio, some of which were comp. for them. Made over 100 arrs. for Swingle Singers.

Sydney Symphony Orchestra. Orch. based in Sydney, NSW. Began in 1932 as broadcasting orch. (ABC) also giving public and schools concerts. Title of Sydney SO adopted permanently in 1945. First cond. Joseph Post. Prin. conds. since have incl. Joseph Post; Sir Eugene Goossens (1947–56); Nikolay Malko (1957–61); Dean Dixon (1963–7); Moshe Atzmon (1969–71); Willem van Otterloo (1973–8); Louis Frémaux (1979–81); Sir Charles Mackerras (1982–5); Zdeněk Mácal (1986); Stuart Challender (1987–91); Edo de Waart 1993–2003; Gianluigi Gelmetti from 2004. Gives over 160 concerts a year, mainly in Sydney Opera House Concert Hall.

Sylphides, Les (The Sylphs). Ballet in 1 act, orig. called *Chopiniana*, arr. to mus. of Chopin, choreog. Fokine. Prod. St Petersburg 1907 (Pavlova among dancers). This first version used 5 pieces orch. by Glazunov: *Polonaise* in A, Op.40 No.1, *Nocturne* in F, Op.15 No.1, *Mazurka* in C♯ minor, Op.50 No.3, *Waltz* in C♯ minor, Op.64 No.2, and *Tarantella* in A♭, Op.43. Rev. version by Fokine prod. St Petersburg 1908 with additional pieces orch. by Maurice Keller. This comprised *Polonaise* in A, Op.40 No.1 (in most Western versions *Prelude* in A, Op.28 No.7), *Nocturne* in A♭, Op.32 No.2, *Waltz* in G♭, Op.70 No.1, *Mazurka* in D, Op.33 No.2, *Mazurka* in C, Op.67 No.3, *Prelude* in A, Op.28 No.7, *Mazurka* in C♯ minor, Op.50 No.3, *Grand Waltz* in E♭, Op.18 No.1. Later Fokine choreographed *Mazurka* in C, Op.33 No.3 as alternative to Op.67 No.3. Revived by Diaghilev, Paris 1909. Extra items were scored by Tcherepnin and Lyadov, and Stravinsky rescored the *Nocturne* in A♭, Op.32 No.2 and the *Grand Waltz* in E♭, Op.18 No.1. One of most popular ballets in repertory. Eng. versions have used Chopin arrs. by Roy Douglas, Gordon Jacob, and Malcolm Sargent.

Sylvia, ou La Nymphe de Diane. Ballet in 3 acts, mus. by Delibes, lib. by Barbier and de Reinach, choreog. Mérante. Prod. Paris 1876, London 1911. New choreog. by Ashton CG 1952.

sympathetic strings. Those str. on a bowed, plucked, or hammered instr. which vibrate (and thereby sound a note) in sympathetic resonance with the note sounded near them by some other agent. Certain instr., e.g. viola d'amore, were strung with sympathetic str., tuned to certain pitches, which vibrated because of proximity to bowed str. above them and thus enriched the tone.

symphonia. (1) Gr. word taken into Lat. and sometimes used by composers instead of 'symphony'. Thus R. Strauss's *Symphonia Domestica* is correct title given by composer, not *Sinfonia Domestica* (It.).
(2) Name given in medieval period to hurdy-gurdy, first str. instr. to which kbd. principle was applied. Perhaps so called because it was used in polyphonic mus., a master of polyphony being then sometimes called a *symphoneta* (Gr.).

Symphonia Domestica (Domestic Symphony). Orch. tone-poem by R. Strauss, Op.53, comp. 1902–3, f.p. NY 1904, f. Eng. p. London 1905. Depicts a day in the life of the Strausses, with themes representing wife Pauline, their baby son, and himself, but is also a sectional sym. in 1 movt. not solely dependent on programme for mus. effectiveness.

Symphonic Dances. Orch. work in 3 movts. by Rachmaninov, Op.45, comp. 1940, f.p. Philadelphia 1941.

Symphonic Metamorphosis of Themes by Carl Maria von Weber. Orch. work by Hindemith, comp. 1940–3, f.p. NY 1944. Originated in sketches (1940) for ballet for Massine on Weber themes, using *Turandot* ov. The Weber themes used are: 1st movt. (*Allegro*), No.4 (*All'Ongarese*) of *Eight Pieces* for pf. duet, 1818–19; 2nd movt. (*Turandot Scherzo*), theme from ov. to incid. mus. for Schiller's trans. of Gozzi's *Turandot, Prinzessin von China*, 1809; 3rd movt. (*Andantino*), No.2 of 6 *Petites Pièces faciles*, pf. duet, 1801; 4th movt. (*Marsch*), No.7 of *Eight Pieces* for pf. duet, 1818–19.

symphonic poem (Ger. *sinfonische Dichtung*). Descriptive term applied by *Liszt to his 13 one-movt. orch. works which, while on a symphonic scale, were not 'pure' syms. because they dealt with descriptive subjects taken from classical mythology, Romantic literature, recent history, or imaginative fantasy, e.g. *Prometheus, Mazeppa, Les Préludes*, etc. In other words, they were 'programmatic'. Other composers followed his line, e.g. Smetana (*Wallenstein's Camp*, etc.), Tchaikovsky (*Francesca da Rimini*, etc.), Saint-Saëns (*Le Rouet d'Omphale*, etc.), Franck (*Le chasseur maudit*, etc.), and many others. Richard Strauss, who carried pictorialism a stage further, preferred the term *Tondichtung* for his works in this form (*Don Juan*, etc.). This is usually translated as 'tone-poem', but it has been well suggested that 'sound-poem' comes nearer to the intention. Most late 19th- and early 20th-cent. composers wrote symphonic poems though they did not always so describe them, e.g. Delius's *In a Summer Garden*. Elgar used designation 'concert-ov.' for what are in effect 3 symphonic poems, *Froissart, Cockaigne*, and *In the South*, and he called *Falstaff* a *symphonic study. Later 20th-cent. composers have shown less interest in the form, but it still survives in such works as Birtwistle's *The Triumph of Time* (1972) and Tippett's *The Rose Lake* (1991–3).

symphonic study. Term used by various composers in different ways. Schumann called his 1837 set of pf. variations *Études symphoniques*; Elgar applied the term to his sym.-poem *Falstaff*, presumably to show that it was an 'in depth' character-study; Rawsthorne described an orch. set of variations as *Symphonic Studies*.

Symphonie espagnole (Spanish Symphony). Orch. work for vn. and orch. by Lalo, Op.21, comp. 1874, written for and first played by *Sarasate in 1875.

Symphonie fantastique (Fantastic Symphony). Orch. work, Op.14, in C major by Berlioz, comp. 1830 when he was 26, although some of the 3rd movt. was adapted from the *Messe Solennelle* of 1824. F.p. Paris, 5 Dec. 1830. F. Eng. p. Manchester, cond. Hallé, 9 Jan. 1879. F. complete London p., cond. W. Ganz, April 1881. One of most remarkable Romantic comps. and forerunner of the programme-syms. and sym.-poems of Liszt, Mahler, Strauss, Tchaikovsky, and others. Subtitled 'Episode in the Life of an artist', it was inspired by Berlioz's then unrequited love for the Irish actress Harriet Smithson, whom he later married. This is symbolized in the mus. by a melody (*idée fixe*) which acts as a motto-theme recurring in various guises, like a Wagnerian leitmotiv, in each of the 5 movts. A theme in the 1st movt. was taken from a song Berlioz wrote when he was 12 and the *March to the Scaffold* was taken from his unfinished opera *Les Francs Juges* (1826). Berlioz rev. the *Symphonie Fantastique* in Rome, 1831–2, and made other re-touchings before publication 1846. Titles of the movts. are: 1. *Rêveries, passions* (Dreams, Passions). 2. *Un bal* (a ball). 3. *Scène aux champs* (Scene in the fields). 4. *Marche au supplice* (March to the Scaffold). 5. *Songe d'une nuit du Sabbat* (Dream of a Witches' Sabbath). Arr. for pf. by Liszt, 1833. See also *Lélio*.

Symphonie funèbre et triomphale ('Funereal and triumphal symphony'). Work by Berlioz, sometimes known as *Grande Symphonie funèbre et triomphale*, composed 1840 to commission by French Government to mark 10th anniversary of 1830 Revolution. Originally scored for large military band and perf. out of doors. Berlioz in 1842 added parts for optional str. orch. and later also for chorus to patriotic text by A. Deschamps. In 3 movts.: 1. *Marche funèbre* in F minor; 2. *Oraison funèbre* in G; 3. *L'Apothéose* in B♭. Probably comp. from earlier sketches.

Symphonie Liturgique. Honegger's Sym. No.3, comp. 1945–6. F.p. Zurich 1946.

Symphonies of Wind Instruments. Work by Stravinsky comp. 1918–20, in memory of Debussy. F.p. London June 1921 (cond, Koussevitzky),

Philadelphia 1923 (cond. Stokowski). Pf. vers. of chorale section f.p. Paris January 1921. Rev. 1945–7, with re-orch. of chorale and considerable changes in orch. of whole work so that 1947 vers. is virtually a different piece.

Symphonie sur un chant montagnard français

(Symphony on a French mountain song). D'Indy's Op.25, sub-titled *Symphonie Cévenole* because the theme comes from the Cévennes region. Specified as 'for orch. and pf.'. Comp. 1886, f.p. Paris, Lamoureux concert 1887.

symphony (from Gk., 'a sounding together'; Ger. *Sinfonie*, Fr. *symphonie*, It. *sinfonia*, Gk.-Lat. *symphonia*). A term which has had several meanings over the centuries: (1) In 17th and 18th cents., *sinfonia* meant what we should now call an 'overture' to an opera, etc., i.e. a short instr. piece often consisting of 3 short sections or movts. in quick-slow-quick form.

(2) It was also used of an orch. interlude, e.g. the 'Pastoral' sym. in Handel's *Messiah*, in a vocal work. Some 20th-cent. composers have revived this archaic usage of the term, e.g. Stravinsky in his *Symphonies of Wind Instruments* (1920).

(3) As the word is now generally used, it means a large-scale orch. comp. (usually in 4 movts. but often in 1, 3, or 5, occasionally in 2), a *sonata for orch., the 1st movt. and others being in sonata-form. It is reserved by composers for their most weighty and profound orch. thoughts, but of course there are many light-hearted, witty, and entertaining syms. The movts. of the Classical and early Romantic sym. were usually an opening allegro, followed by a slow movt., then a minuet or scherzo, finally another allegro or rondo. Frequently the slow movt. is placed 3rd, sometimes last. Early composers of the 18th-cent. 4-movt. sym. were Sammartini, Wagenseil, Gossec, J. C. and C. P. E. Bach, Boyce, and especially the composers of the Mannheim School, Stamitz, Cannabich, Richter, and others, who made innovations in dynamics, expanded the development of themes, and broadened the harmonic idiom. The average 18th-cent. sym. orch. comprised str., double woodwind (cls. later), hns., and a continuo instr., usually hpd. The sym. was brought to a new peak by Joseph Haydn, who wrote 107, and was the first composer to demonstrate what later composers also seized upon, namely that the word 'symphony' should not imply rigidity of form or material. Some of Haydn's syms. have 6 movts.; some utilize mus. he wrote for plays; some themes are based on folk-songs; most have slow introductions; many movts. are mono-thematic; rondos, variations, and minuets are used; wit and humour are deployed; rare keys are explored; deep emotions are aroused. Haydn's example was followed and improved upon by Mozart, especially in his 3 last syms. of 1788, and these in turn led to even further marvels from Haydn in his last 12 syms. written for his 2 visits to Eng.

Taking over from Haydn and Mozart, Beethoven raised the sym. to a new plane of emotional expression, his 3rd Symphony (*Eroica*, 1803–4) ending the 18th cent. at a stroke and striding forward into an age when democracy, revolution, and ethics were to become influential factors in art, while at the same time effecting a mus. revolution by its enlarged dimensions, boldness of harmony, subtlety of key relationships, and general scope. In the *Pastoral Symphony*, No.6 (1807–8), Beethoven reconciled perfectly the claims of 'absolute' and 'descriptive' mus., and in the 9th (1817–23) he introduced human vv. into the finale in a setting of Schiller's *Ode to Joy*. The floodgates were now open. Schubert's syms. bridged the way to the Romantic period. The syms. of Mendelssohn and Schumann combine classical outlines with romantic feeling and some pictorialism, as in the former's *Scotch* and *Italian* syms. and the latter's *Spring* and *Rhenish*. Brahms's 4 syms. eschew pictorial associations and uphold the virtues of classical design (though they are deeply romantic in essence and also formally unusual in places) as an antidote to the growing craze for Lisztian symphonic poems and the operas of Wagner (who wrote only one early sym. but was contemplating others when he died). Berlioz's *Symphonie Fantastique* (1830) is one of the most remarkable works in the genre, frankly programmatic, brilliantly orchestrated, and opening up horizons which were not further explored until the picturesque late-19th-cent. syms. of Tchaikovsky. Yet the epitome of the Romantic sym., imbued still with classical principles while on a huge architectural scale, is to be found in the 9 syms. of Bruckner. Berlioz's pioneering was taken a stage further by Mahler, whose 10 syms. not only bridge the 19th and 20th cents. but also form a 'transition passage' of their own between 19th-cent. mus. idioms and the new 20th-cent. preoccupation with the dissolution of tonality. The crisis of the sym. in the early years of the 20th cent. is exemplified by the contrasting approaches of Sibelius and Mahler. The former expressed his faith in compression, concentration, and 'absolute' mus. whereas Mahler said that 'the symphony must embrace everything'. In Sibelius, especially in the 4th and 7th syms., symphonic thought and processes are elliptical and pared to essentials. In Mahler, vv. are used in 4 of the syms., philosophical and religious theories are at the root of their inspiration, and wildly juxtaposed thematic material is brought into cohesive unity by sheer force of conviction, the instrumentation being exotic and multiple. The two attitudes, regarded as mutually exclusive, are in fact not incompatible and a compromise has governed the development of the 20th-cent. sym., often within the works of the same composer, e.g., compare the severe 'classicism' of Vaughan Williams's 4th Sym. with the programmatic 7th, *Sinfonia Antartica*; compare Shostakovich's 5th Sym. with his 13th and 14th.

From time to time throughout the 20th cent. composers and pundits have pronounced the sym. dead but it shows an encouraging refusal to lie down. Nielsen (6), Vaughan Williams (9),

Bax (7), Shostakovich (15), Ives (4), W. Schuman (10), Rubbra (11), Arnold (9), Maxwell Davies (8), Henze (8), not to mention Hovhaness (well over 60), and many others show that the sym. has lost neither its attraction nor its challenge for composers. Argument frequently occurs over whether certain works designated 'symphony' really merit the description, e.g. Stravinsky's *Symphony in 3 Movements* (1945), Messiaen's *Turangalîla* (1946–8), etc. An answer to this is that no mus. form can be regarded as immutable. The 18th-cent. composer (with the likely exception of Haydn) would scarcely recognize some 20th-cent. syms. in form, but there is more to a sym. than its title. It implies an attitude of mind, a certain mental approach by the composer, and in this respect the 4 syms. of Tippett and those by Maxwell Davies, as well as many others comp. since 1960, suggest that, for some time to come, reports of the demise of the sym. will prove to have been exaggerated.

(4) In the USA 'symphony' also means 'symphony orchestra').

(5) Sym. concert means, pedantically, a concert at which a sym. is played, but it is generally used to mean a concert by a sym. orch., whatever it is playing.

Symphony in 3 Movements. Orch. work by *Stravinsky comp. 1942–5 and f.p. NYPO cond. Stravinsky 1946. F. Eng. p. 1946, cond. Ansermet (broadcast). Work's genesis is of special interest; 1st movt. began, in 1942, as pf. conc. or conc. for orch. with *concertante* pf. part, inspired by film on China's 'scorched earth' tactics. 2nd movt. was written as acc. for apparition of Virgin Mary in film *Song of Bernadette*, an abortive project where Stravinsky was concerned. 3rd movt. influenced by wartime newsreels.

Symphony of a Thousand. Nickname, not wholly approved by the composer, for Mahler's Sym. No.8 in E♭ major, comp. 1906–7, f.p. Munich 1910 (cond. Mahler), because of the huge forces employed to perf. it. It is, however, not necessary to use 1,000 people, although at the f.p. more than that number were on the platform. F. Eng. p. London 1930 (Wood).

Symphony of Psalms. Work for mixed ch. and orch. in 3 movts. by *Stravinsky, Lat. text being drawn from the Psalms 39, 40, and 150. Comp. 1930 to commission from Boston SO for 50th anniversary. F.p. Brussels 1930, cond. Ansermet; f.p. in USA 6 days later, Boston, cond. Koussevitzky; f.p. in England London 1931, cond. Stravinsky.

syncopation. Device used by composers in order to vary position of the stress on notes so as to avoid regular rhythm. Syncopation is achieved by accenting a weak instead of a strong beat, by putting rests on strong beats, by holding on over strong beats, and by introducing a sudden change of time-signature. First used at time of *ars nova*, and exploited to fullest capabilities

by jazz musicians, often in improvisation. Stravinsky, Bartók, etc. also employ syncopation with dramatic effect.

synthesizer. Term for system of elec. apparatus which can be used to control or produce sounds (usually from a kbd.). Used by composers of elec. mus. Its invention, by Robert Moog in 1965, revolutionized elec. comp. by speeding up the process and doing away with drudgery of assembling and splicing small sections of tape. The first synthesizer was built from voltage-controlled and selected non-voltage-controlled components. It could play itself in mobile sound patterns which might be recurrent or non-repetitive and could also, by use of a device called a 'sequencer', memorize long and complex mus. structures and play them live without recording or tape editing. (It is possible to reproduce instr. mus. on a synthesizer, as was convincingly demonstrated in 1969 by the success of Walter Carlos's commercial recording 'Switched-on Bach'.) Its numerous functions are controlled by punched paper tape. A means of producing mobility is by an 'envelope shaper', a device to control the shape of a sound or other parameter. It has controls which est. the time of attack, sustain, delay, and end of a sound. An initial drawback was that most synthesizers could perform only one note at a time. Since 1976, however, polyphonic synthesizers have been developed. See also *electronic music*.

Syrinx. For solo fl., by Debussy, comp. 1913 for Louis Fleury who gave f.p. Paris 1913. Syrinx was the Gr. term for the *pan-pipes, instr. played by the mythical god Pan (half-goat, half-man).

Szabó, Ferenc (*b* Budapest, 1902; *d* Budapest, 1969). Hung. composer. Lived in Russia and Ger. 1932–45. Prof. of comp. Liszt Acad. 1945–67 (dir. from 1958). Works incl. opera, ballet, oratorio, sym., 2 str. qts., solo vn. sonatas, etc.

Szántó, Theodor (*b* Vienna, 1877; *d* Budapest, 1934). Austrian-born Hung. pianist and composer. Rev. vers. of Delius's pf. conc. (1906–7) is ded. to him; gave f.p. at Promenade Concert in London 1907. Wrote opera *Typhoon* (1924), orch. works, and chamber music.

Székely, Zoltán (*b* Kocs, 1903; *d* Banff, 2001). Hung.-born violinist (Amer. cit. 1960). Founded Hungarian Str. Qt., 1935. Gave f.p. in Amsterdam, 1938, of Bartók's Vn. Conc. No.2, which is ded. to him. Settled in USA 1949. Taught at Amer. univ.

Szell, Georg (*b* Budapest, 1897; *d* Cleveland, Ohio, 1970). Hung.-born conductor, pianist, and composer (Amer. cit. 1946). Solo pianist in Mozart conc. at age 10 with Vienna SO and at 17 cond. Berlin PO in one of his own comps. Cond., Strasbourg Stadttheater 1917–18, on recommendation of R. Strauss. Cond., Deutsches Landtheater, Prague, 1919–21, Darmstadt 1921–2, Düsseldorf 1922–4, Berlin 1924–9. Returned to Prague 1930–6. Cond., Scottish Orch. 1936–9.

Amer. début 1930, St Louis SO. Settled in USA 1939, teaching at Mannes Sch. Cond. NY Met 1942–6 (début with *Salome*). Cond. Cleveland Orch. 1946–70, making it one of the finest in world and taking it on int. tours. Salzburg Fest. début 1949. Last Salzburg appearance 1969 (Vienna PO). Noted for his Wagner, Strauss, Mahler, and the classics but outstanding in modern scores. Many stories are told of his amazing memory for mus. and mus. detail and of his caustic wit. Hon. CBE 1963.

Szenkar, Eugen (Jenö) (*b* Budapest, 1891; *d* Düsseldorf, 1977). Hung. conductor. Cond. Deutsches Landestheater, Prague, 1911–13, Budapest Volksoper 1913–15, Salzburg Mozarteum 1915–16, Altenburg 1916–20, Frankfurt Opera 1920–3, Berlin Volksoper 1923–4, Cologne Opera 1924–33. Left Ger. for Russia 1933. Cond., Brazilian SO, Rio, from 1944. Returned to Mannheim Opera 1950–1, Düsseldorf Opera 1952–6.

Szeryng, Henryk (*b* Warsaw, 1918; *d* Cassel, 1988). Polish-born violinist (Mexican cit. 1946). Début Warsaw 1933 (Brahms conc.). In 1939 was official translator for Sikorski's Polish Government in exile in London. Went to S. Amer. 1941 to find homes for 4,000 Polish refugees. Settled in Mexico. Gave over 300 concerts for Allied servicemen in Second World War. Salzburg Fest. début 1965 (recital). Int. career as virtuoso violinist.

Szidon, Roberto (*b* Porto Alegre, Brazil, 1941). Brazilian pianist. Début Porto Alegre at age 9. Int. career as soloist. Settled in Ger.

Szigeti, Josef (*b* Budapest, 1892; *d* Lucerne, 1973). Hung.-born violinist (Amer. cit. 1951). Début Berlin 1905. London début 1907, living there until 1913 and giving f.p. of Harty's vn. conc. 1909. Taught at Geneva Cons. 1917–24. Salzburg Fest. 1922 (Mozart conc. K218, cond. R. Strauss). Settled in USA 1926 after NY début with Philadelphia Orch. 1925 (Beethoven conc.). Wide repertory from Bach to modern composers such as Prokofiev, Bartók, and Bloch, whose conc. he championed. Retired to Switz. 1960. Wrote cadenzas and made many transcriptions for vn. and pf., including one of Elgar's *Serenade* for pf. (1932).

Szokolay, Sándor (*b* Kúnágota, 1931). Hung. composer. Worked for Hung. radio 1957–61. Teacher at Budapest Acad. from 1966. Works incl. operas *Hamlet* (1966–8), *Vérnász* (Blood Wedding, after Lorca, 1962–4); Passion-opera *Ecce homo* (1987); vn. conc. (1956–7); pf. conc. (1958); tpt. conc. (1968); *Déploration*, in memoriam Poulenc, ch. and orch. (1964); 2 str. qts. (1976, 1984); *Bagatelles*, hpd., hp., or 2 pf. (1978); *Conc. for Orch.* (1982); *Aeternitas temporis*, sop., str. qt. (1988); *On the Year '56*, unacc. ch. (1996); 3 syms. (1997, 1998, 1999).

Szymanowski, Karol (*b* Tymoshovka, Ukraine, 1882; *d* Lausanne, 1937). Polish composer. Boyhood spent in Ukraine, where many Poles owned land. Showed early mus. promise and because of leg injury which compelled a sedentary life, stu-

died much mus. and conceived lifelong enthusiasm for Chopin. Studied theory with Neuhaus and wrote 9 pf. preludes in 1900. In 1901 went to Warsaw to study comp. with Noskowski. Moved to Berlin 1905, attracted by brilliance of Strauss and others, and wrote first sym. there. With 3 compatriots (Fitelberg, Rózycki, and Szeluta) formed 'Young Poland in Music' soc., the Berlin PO giving a concert of their works. Left Berlin 1908, returning to Tymoshovka, his mus. being championed by other Polish musicians, e.g. the pianist Arthur Rubinstein, the cond. Fitelberg, and his sister Stanislawa, for whose sop. v. he wrote many of his songs. Another Polish virtuoso, the violinist Paul Kochánsky, was inspiration of the 1st vn. conc. and other works. Family home was destroyed in 1917 and for four years Szymanowski abandoned music while he wrote a long novel *Efebos* (the manuscript was destroyed in Warsaw in 1939). Left Russia 1920 for Warsaw, but visited Paris, London, and NY, taking part in concerts of modern mus. Back in Poland, wrote several works inspired by folklore. Became dir., Warsaw Cons. 1927–9, revolutionizing teaching methods. F.p. in 1928 of his *Stabat Mater* was his first big Polish triumph. Resigned directorship 1929 because of tuberculosis but became rector of Warsaw Acad. (which replaced Cons.) in 1930, resigning in 1932 after a dispute. Completed 2nd vn. conc. 1933, f.p. being given by Kochánsky shortly before he died. In 1933–4, Szymanowski toured Europe as solo pianist in his *Symphonie Concertante*, but continued ill-health weakened him and he died in a sanatorium.

Szymanowski is typical of many 20th-cent. composers who searched for some key to the liberation of what they felt to be their individual characteristics. Through his works can be traced the influence of the Ger. school of Strauss, etc., from which he was released by admiration for Debussy and the Fr. 'impressionist' composers. From them he took what he needed, experimenting further with atonality, polytonality, microtones, elaborate rhythms, and declamatory passages. The return to Poland awakened his latent nationalism—inspired by Chopin—as he studied his native mus., particularly the songs and dances of the Tatra mountaineers, which led to the *Mazurek* for pf. and the colourful, exotic ballet *Harnasie*. His opera *King Roger* is among his best works, a notable example of modern romanticism, and the vn. concs. are particularly rewarding. The *Stabat Mater* is an especially beautiful setting. Prin. comps.:

OPERAS: *Hagith*, Op.25 (1912–13); *King Roger (*Król Roger*), Op.46 (1918–24).

BALLETS: *Mandragora*, Op.43 (1920); *Harnasie*, Op.55 (1923–31).

ORCH.: syms.: No.1 in F minor, Op.15 (1906–7), No.2 in B♭, Op.19 (1909–10, re-orch. 1936, rev. by Skrowaczewski 1967), No.3, ten. (or sop.), male ch., orch. (*Song in the Night* to Cz. trans. of 13th-cent. Persian text), Op.27 (1914–16), No.4, *Symphonie Concertante*, Op.60, pf., orch. (1931–2);

vn. concs.: No.1, Op.35 (1916), No.2, Op.61 (1932–3); Concert Ov. in E, Op.12 (1904–5, rev. 1912, 1913).

VOICE(S) & ORCH.: *Penthesilea*, sop., orch., Op.18 (1908, reorch. 1912); *Love Songs of Hafiz*, Op.26, v., orch. (1914, incl. orch. of Nos. 1, 4, and 5 of Op.24, 1911, v., pf.); *Demeter*, alto, women's ch., orch., Op.38 (1917, reorch. 1924); *Agawa*, sop., ch., orch., Op.39 (1917); *Stabat Mater*, sop., cont., bar., women's ch., orch., Op.53 (1925–6); *Veni Creator*, sop., ch., org., orch., Op.57 (1930); *Litany of the Virgin Mary* (*Litania do Marii Panny*), sop., women's ch., orch. (1930–3).

CHAMBER MUSIC: vn. sonata in D minor, Op.9 (1904); str. qts.: No.1, Op.37 (1917), No.2, Op.56 (1927).

VIOLIN & PIANO: *Romance*, Op.23 (1910); *Notturno e Tarantella*, Op.28 (1915); 3 *Myths* (*Mity*) (The **Fountain of Arethusa, Narcissus, Dryads and Pan*), Op.30 (1915); 3 *Paganini Caprices*, transcr., Op.40 (1918); *Berceuse d'Aitacho Enia*, Op.52 (1925).

PIANO: *9 Preludes*, Op.1 (1900); *Variations in B♭ minor*, Op.3 (1903); *4 Studies*, Op.4 (1902); sonatas: No.1 in C minor, Op.8 (1904), No.2 in A minor, Op.21 (1911), No.3, Op.36 (1917); *Variations on a Polish Theme*, Op.10 (1904); *Fantasy in F minor*, Op.14 (1905); *Métopes*, 3 poems (The *Sirens' Isle, Calypso, Nausicaa*), Op.29 (1915); *12 Studies*, Op.33 (1916); *3 Masques* (*Maski*), Op.34 (*Shéhérazade, Tantris the clown, Don Juan's Serenade*) (1916); *Mazurek* (1925); *4 Polish Dances*, Op.47 (1926); *20 Mazurkas*, Op.50 (1924–5); *2 Mazurkas*, Op.62 (1934).

VOICE & PIANO: *12 Songs*, Op.17 (1907); *6 Songs*, Op.20 (1909); *Love Songs of Hafiz*, 1st cycle of 6, Op.24 (1911); *6 Songs of the Fairy Princess*, Op.31 (1915); *4 Songs* to poems by Tagore, Op.41 (1918), *6 Songs of the Infatuated Muezzin*, Op.42 (1918); *2 Basque Songs*, Op.44 (1921); *Slopiewnie*, 5 songs, Op.45 (1921); *3 Lullabies*, Op.48 (1922); *20 Children's Rhymes* (*Rymy dzieciece*), Op.49 (1923); *4 Songs* to words by Joyce, Op.54 (1926); *12 Kurpian Songs*, Op.58 (1930–3).

T

t. Tonic sol-fa symbol for 7th degree of scale, pronounced *te*.

Tabachnik, Michel (*b* Geneva, 1942). Swiss cond. and composer. Ass. cond. to Boulez 1967–71. Début Royan Fest. Guest cond. with European and Brit. orchs. Cond., Gulbenkian Orch., Lisbon, 1973–5. Art. dir. Ensemble Inter-Contemporain, Fr., 1976–7. Cond. Lorraine PO 1975–81. Cond. North Netherlands Orch. from 2005.

Tabarro, Il (The Cloak). Opera in 1 act by Puccini to lib. by Adami, after Didier Gold's play *La Houppelande* (1910). Part 1 of *Il *trittico*. Comp. 1913–16. Prod. NY Met 1918, Rome and Chicago 1919, London 1920.

tabla. Indian small hand-drum with single head but double body of 2 truncated cones. Played with fingers. Usually wedged in crook of right knee of seated player. Some Western composers have scored for it, e.g. Berio and Cowell.

tablature. System of writing down mus. to be perf. other than by use of notes. Instead figures, letters, and similar signs were used. There were systems of org. and lute tablature in which the symbols represented the position of the player's fingers, not the pitch. Diagrammatic notation used today in popular mus. for guitar, ukelele, etc. is type of tablature.

tabor. Small drum used in medieval times to accompany folk-dancing, usually played in conjunction with end-blown pipe. Performer struck drum with one hand, holding pipe in the other.

tacet (Lat.). It is silent. Indication that particular performer or instr. has no part to play for considerable time. *Tacet al fine* means he has no more to play.

tactus (Lat.). Term used in 15th and 16th cents. to designate a specified 'beat', either a unit of time, or the cond.'s beat. For a considerable period, the *tactus* was the equivalent of the whole-note.

Taddei, Giuseppe (*b* Genoa, 1916). It. baritone. Opera début Rome Opera 1936 (Herald in *Lohengrin*). Vienna Opera 1946–7. London début (Cambridge Th.) 1947; Salzburg 1948; S. Francisco 1957; Chicago 1959; CG 1960; NY Met 1985. Famous as Scarpia and in buffo roles.

Tafelmusik (Ger.). Table-music. Mus. to be sung or played during or after a meal. Telemann wrote a fine example of *Tafelmusik* 1733, in 3 sections, each with 6 movts., for various groups of instr. In *Der Rosenkavalier*, the off-stage band in Act III is described to Baron Ochs as *Tafelmusik*.

Tagliabue, Carlo (*b* Mariano Comense, 1898; *d* Monza, 1978). It. baritone. Opera début Lodi

1922 (Amonasro in *Aida*). Sang at La Scala 1930–53. CG 1938 and 1946; NY Met 1937–9. Noted Verdi bar., also sang Wagner parts in It.

Tagliavini, Ferruccio (*b* Reggio Emilia, 1913; *d* Reggio Emilia, 1995). It. tenor. Opera début Florence 1939 (Rodolfo in *La bohème*). Leading It. lyric ten. during Second World War (La Scala 1942–53), then Buenos Aires 1946–7. Amer. début (Chicago) 1946; NY Met 1947–54; CG 1950 (with visiting La Scala co.). Excelled in *bel canto* roles.

Tahiti Trot (Shostakovich). See *Tea for Two*.

taille (Fr.). Old name for middle v., particularly ten., and for instr. of similar register, e.g. *taille de basson*, ten. ob., or *taille*, va. In Bach's cantatas, *taille* is taken to mean ten. ob. (*oboe da caccia*).

Tailleferre [Taillefesse], **Germaine** (Marcelle) (*b* Parc St Maur, nr. Paris, 1892; *d* Paris, 1983). Fr. composer and pianist, one of *Les *Six*. Visited USA 1926 as pianist. Was discouraged from composing by both her husbands. Comps. incl.:

OPERAS: *Zoulaina* (1930–1); *Le marin du Bolivar* (1937); *Dolorès* (1950); *Il était un petit navire* (1950); *Parfums* (1950); *La fille d'opera* (1955); *Le bel ambitieux* (1955); *Parisiana* (1955); *M. Petitpois achète un château* (1955); *La pauvre Eugénie* (1955); *La petite sirène* (1957); *Mémoires d'une bergère* (1959); *Le maître* (1959).

BALLETS: *Le marchand d'oiseaux* (1922–3); *Paris-Magie* (1949).

ORCH.: pf. conc. (1919); hp. concertino (1926); *Overture* (1932); conc., 2 pf., v., orch. (1933); *La guirlande de Campra* (1952); *Petite Suite* (1957).

CHAMBER MUSIC: str. qt. (1918); *Image*, pf., fl., cl., str. qt., cel. (1918); vn. sonatas No.1 (1921), No.2 (1951); *Pastorale*, vn., pf. (1921); *Pastorale*, fl., pf. (1939); *Hommage à Rameau*, 4 perc., 2 pf. (1964); *Sonatine*, vn., pf. (1973).

VOICE(S) & INSTRS.: *Nocturno-Fox*, 2 bar., ens. (1928–58); *Chansons françaises*, v., instr. (1930); *Cantate de Narcissus*, v., orch. (1937); *9 Chansons du Folklore de France*, v., ens. (1952–5); *Concerto des vaines paroles*, bar., orch. (1956).

PIANO: *Jeux de plein air*, 2 pf. (1918); *Seule dans la forêt* (1951).

Tajo, Italo (*b* Pinerolo, 1915; *d* Cincinnati, 1993). It. bass. Opera début Turin 1935 (Fafner in *Das Rheingold*). Sang in Rome 1939–41. Sang Doctor in It. première of *Wozzeck*, 1942. La Scala 1946–56. Sang at first Edinburgh Fest., 1947, with Glyndebourne Co.; S. Francisco 1948–56; CG 1950 (with visiting La Scala co.); NY Met 1948–50. Outstanding in Donizetti buffo roles. Taught at Cincinnati Coll.-Cons. of Mus. 1966. Salzburg Fest. début 1989 (Sacristan).

Takács, Klara (*b* Hungary, 1945). Hung. mezzo-soprano. Hung. State Opera from 1973. Won

Erkel int. comp., Budapest, 1975. Toured Japan with Vienna Opera 1986. Buenos Aires 1987 (Charlotte in *Werther*). Concert work in Haydn, Mozart, Liszt, and Mahler.

Takács Quartet. String quartet founded 1975 by G. Takács-Nagy. Won Evian int. comp. 1977, Portsmouth int. comp. 1979. Toured Far East, Eur., and USA. Mozart cycle, London 1991. Bartók cycle Paris 1991, Beethoven cycles Zurich, Dublin, London, and Paris 1991–2. Quartet-in-residence Barbican 1988–91, with master classes at GSMD. Salzburg Fest. 1987. Many recordings.

Takemitsu, Toru (*b* Tokyo, 1930; *d* Tokyo, 1996). Japanese composer. Organized experimental workshop for painters and composers in Tokyo, 1951. Designed Space Theatre at Osaka Exposition 1970. Visiting prof., Yale Univ. 1975. Comp.-in-residence Aldeburgh Fest. 1984, Huddersfield Fest. 1990. His mus. uses *avant-garde* procedures and much of it is on tape. Influenced at first by Schoenberg, Messiaen, and Schaeffer's *musique concrète*. Much concerned, like Ligeti, with timbre. Works incl.:

ORCH.: *Requiem*, str. (1957); *Solitude Sonore* (1958); *Tableau noir*, narr., chamber orch. (1958); *Scene*, vc., str. (1959); *Coral Island*, sop., orch. (1959); *Music of Trees* (1961); *Arc*, Part I, pf., orch. (1963–6/1976), Part II, pf., orch. (1964–6/1976); *Dorian Horizon*, 17 str. (1966); *Green* (1967); *November Steps*, shakuhachi, biwa, orch. (1967); *Asterism*, pf., orch. (1967); *Crossing*, 4 instr. soloists, women's vv., 2 orchs. (1970); *Eucalypts I*, fl., ob., hp., str. (1970); *Winter* (1971); *Cassiopeia*, perc. solo, orch. (1971); *Gemeaux*, ob., tb., 2 orch, 2 cond. (1971–86); *Autumn*, biwa, shakuhachi, orch. (1973); *Gitimalya* (*Bouquet of Songs*), marimba, orch. (1974); *Quatrain*, vn., vc., cl., pf., orch. (1975); *Marginalia* (1976); *A Flock descends into the pentagonal garden* (1977); *Far Calls, Coming, far!*, vn., orch. (1980); *Dreamtime* (1981); *A Way a Lone II* (vers. of str. qt.), str. (1981); *Toward the Sea II* (vers. of work for alt. fl., gui.), alt. fl., hp., orch. (1981); *Star-Isle* (1982); *Rain Coming*, chamber orch. (1982); *To the Edge of Dream*, gui., orch. (1983); *Orion and Pleiades*, vc., orch. (1984); *Vers, l'arc-en-ciel, Palma*, gui., ob. d'amore, orch. (1984); *riverrun*, pf., orch. (1984); *Dream/Window* (1985); *I hear the water dreaming*, fl., orch. (1987); *Nostalghia (in memory of Andrey Tarkovsky)*, vn., str. (1987); *Twill by Twilight (in memory of Morton Feldman)* (1988); *Tree Line*, chamber orch. (1988); *A String Around Autumn*, va., orch. (1989); *Visions* (1990); *My Way of Life (in memory of Michael Vyner)*, bar., ch., orch. (1990); *From me flows what you call Time*, 5 perc., orch. (1990).

CHORAL: *Wind Horse*, ch. (1961–6); *Grass*, male ch. (1982); *Handmade Proverbs (4 Pop Songs)*, 6 male vv. (1987)

CHAMBER MUSIC: *Distance de fée*, vn., pf. (1951, rev. 1989); *Le son calligraphié* I and II, 4 vv., 2 va., 2 vc. (1958–60); *Masque*, 2 fl. (1959–60); *Landscape*, str. qt. (1960); *Ring*, fl., gui., lute (1961); *Sacrifice*, alt. fl., lute, vib. (1962); *Valeria*, vn., vc., gui., elec. org. (1965); *Hika*, vn., pf. (1966); *Munari by Munari*,

perc. solo (1967–72); *Stanza I*, gui., pf., hp., vib., female v. (1969); *Eucalypts II*, fl., ob., hp. (1971); *Voice*, fl. (1971); *Stanza II*, hp., tape (1971); *Distance*, ob. (1972); *Folios*, gui. (1974); *Garden Rain*, brass (1974); *Bryce*, fl., 2 hp., 2 perc. (1976); *Waves*, solo cl., hn., 2 tb., bass drum (1976); *Quatrain II*, cl., vn., vc., pf. (1977); *Waterways*, cl., vn., vc., pf., 2 hp., 2 vib. (1978); *A Way a Lone*, str. qt. (1981); *Toward the Sea*, alt. fl., gui. (1981); *Rain Spell*, fl., cl., hp., pf., vib. (1982); *Rocking Mirror Daybreak*, 2 vn. (1983); *From far beyond Chrysanthemums and November Fog*, vn., pf. (1983); *Orion*, vc., pf. (1984); *Entre-Temps*, ob., str. qt. (1986); *Rain Dreaming*, hpd. (1986); *All in Twilight*, gui. (1987); *Itinerant*, fl. (1989); *Toward the Sea III*, alt. fl., hp. (1989).

ELEC. MUS. & THEATRE PIECES: *Static Relief*, magnetic tape (1955); *Vocalism A.I.*, magnetic tape (1956); *Sky, Horse and Death*, tape (1958); *Water Music*, tape (1960); *Kwaidan*, tape (1964); *Toward*, tape (1970); *A Minneapolis Garden*, tape (1986); *The Sea is Still*, tape (1986).

PIANO: *Lento in due movimenti* (1950); *Uninterrupted Rest* (1952–9); *Piano Distance* (1961); *Crossing* (1962); *For away* (1973); *Les yeux clos I* (1979), II (1988); *Rain Tree Sketch* (1982).

Takt (Ger.). (a) 'Time' (b) 'Beat' (c) 'Measure' (i.e. bar). So **im Takt**, 'in time' (= 'A tempo'); **ein Takt wie vorher zwei**, 'one beat as previously two' (one beat allowed as much time as two beats previously).

Among compounds and derivatives of Takt, are: Taktart, 'time-species'—duple, triple, etc.; taktfest ('time-firm'), 'in steady time'; Takt halten, 'to hold (keep) time'; taktieren, 'to beat time'; Taktschlag ('time-stroke'), 'beat'; Taktzeichen ('time-sign'), 'signature'; Taktwechsel, 'time-change'; taktmässig ('time moderated'), generally meaning the same as *'tempo comodo'; Taktmesser (time-measure), 'metronome'; Taktnote ('bar-note'), 'semibreve'; Taktpause, 'measure-rest' (i.e. bar-rest); Taktstock ('time-stick'), 'baton'; Taktstrich ('bar-stroke'), 'bar-line'; taktig, 'bar-ish', in such connection as 3-taktig, 'three-bar-ish', i.e. having 3-bar (3-measure) phrases.

Tal [Gruenthal], **Josef** (*b* Pinne, 1910). Ger.-born Israeli composer and pianist. Settled in Palestine 1934. Prof. of pf. and comp., Jerusalem Cons. 1937. Dir., Israel Acad. of Mus. 1948–52. Chairman, musicology dept., Hebrew Univ. 1965–70, prof. from 1971. Dir., Israel EMS from 1961. Works incl. 7 operas (incl. *Ashmedai*, *Die Versuchung*, 1973–4, and *Der Garten*, 1988); elec. ballets; several choral works to Heb. texts; 5 syms.; 6 pf. concs. (Nos. 4, 5, and 6 with tape); va. conc.; hpd. conc. with tape; ww. quintet; ob. sonata; and 5 *Instructive Compositions in Dodecaphonic Technique* for pf.

tala. Indian term for rhythm, being a fixed time-span for mus., repeated in cycles, and articulated by hand-beats, drum-beats, or by a percussive *idiophone.

Tale of Two Cities, A. Opera in 6 scenes by A. Benjamin to lib. by Cedric Cliffe after Dickens. Comp. 1949–50 and awarded a Fest. of Britain prize (1951), broadcast 3 times by BBC in 1953 and on Canadian radio 1954, but not prod. until 1957 (London, SW). S. Francisco 1960.

Tales from the Vienna Woods (*Geschichten aus dem Wienerwald*). Waltz, Op.325, by Johann Strauss II. Comp. 1868.

Tales of Hoffmann, The (*contes d'Hoffmann, Les*). Opera in prol., 3 acts, and epilogue by *Offenbach to lib. by J. Barbier and M. Carré based on stories *Der Sandmann, Geschichte von verlorenen Spiegelbilde*, and *Rat Krespel* by E. T. A. *Hoffmann. Comp. 1877–80, but left incomplete at Offenbach's death (many numbers unfinished, sketches only of others). At f.p. the Giulietta act was omitted and Guiraud provided revisions, recitatives (in place of the correct spoken dialogue), and some of the orchestration. In 1893, Giulietta act was restored as Act 2, where it is placed in the largely corrupt Choudens edn. of 1907. New edn. by Fritz Oeser (1980) attempts to interpret Offenbach's final intentions, with acts in the order: 1. Olympia, 2. Antonia, 3. Giulietta. F.p. Paris 1881, NY 1882, London 1907. Famous *Barcarolle*, orig. written for *Die Rheinnixen* (1864), occurs in Giulietta act as orch. intermezzo before epilogue.

Talich, Václav (*b* Kroměříž, Moravia, 1883; *d* Beroun, 1961). Cz. conductor and violinist. Leader, Berlin PO 1903–4. Taught vn. in Tiflis 1905–7. Cond. Ljubljana PO 1908, then opera at Plzeň (Pilsen) 1912–15. Chief cond., Cz. PO 1919–31, 1933–41, during which the orch. became world-famous through tours and records. Cond., Stockholm PO 1931–3. Re-orch. substantial parts of Janáček's operas, *Káťa Kabanová* and *The Cunning Little Vixen*. Art. dir. and cond. Prague Nat. Opera 1935–44; dismissed 1945, restored to post 1947, again removed by Communist régime 1948 and restored 1954. Founded Slovak PO of Bratislava 1949–52. Guest cond. Cz. PO 1952–4. Retired 1956. Taught cond. in Prague and Bratislava.

Tallis, Thomas (*b c.*1505; *d* Greenwich, 1585). Eng. composer and organist. Org., Waltham Abbey from *c.*1538 to 1540. Lay clerk, Canterbury Cath. 1540–2. Gentleman of the Chapel Royal 1540–85, serving under Henry VIII, Edward VI, Mary, and Elizabeth I, and organist jointly with *Byrd. In 1575 Elizabeth granted Tallis and Byrd letters patent giving them 21-year monopoly for printing mus. and mus. paper. In that year they pubd. 34 *Cantiones sacrae* in 5 and 6 parts (16 by Tallis and 18 by Byrd). Tallis wrote some pieces for kbd. and viols, but is mainly known for church mus. of great contrapuntal ingenuity and technical dexterity. In this respect his masterpiece is perhaps the 40-part motet *Spem in alium*, in the opening section of which 20 vv. enter successively with theme in imitation. The other 20 then enter with new material and, after passages for varying numbers of vv., all 40 combine for the ending. Of special interest, too, is the use of modulation in the 2 *Lamentations* from near the end of his long career. The tune known as *Tallis's Canon* was one of 9 which Tallis comp. for Archbishop Parker's metrical *Whole Psalter*, 1567, where it is attached to Ps. 67. In 1732 it was linked with Bishop Ken's Winchester evening hymn, 'Glory to thee, my God, this night'. Another tune written for this psalter was that used by Vaughan Williams in 1910 as the basis of his *Fantasia on a Theme by Thomas Tallis* for str.

Talma, Louise (*b* Arcachon, 1906; *d* Saratoga Springs, NY, 1996). Fr.-born Amer. composer. Teacher from 1928 at Hunter Coll., NY, 1928–79 (prof. from 1952). Taught at Fontainebleau Sch. of Mus. 1936–9, 1978, 1981–2. Winner of several prizes and scholarships. Works incl. opera *The Alcestiad*, 1955–8 (Frankfurt 1962); oratorio *The Divine Flame; Dialogues*, pf., orch.; vn. sonata; str. qt.; *All the days of my life*, ten., cl., vc., pf., perc. (1965); *Voices of Peace*, ch., str. (1973); *Summer Sounds*, cl., str. qt. (1973); *Textures*, pf. (1978); *Ambient Air*, fl., vn., vc., pf. (1983); *Full Circle*, orch. (1985); *Ave atque vale*, pf. (1989); *Psalm 115*, unacc. ch. (1992); *Spacings*, va., pf. (1994).

talon (Fr.). Heel. The nut end of the bow of a str. instr.

Talvela, Martti (Olavi) (*b* Hiitola, 1935; *d* Juva, 1989). Finn. bass. Début Stockholm 1961 (Sparafucile in *Rigoletto*). Royal Opera, Stockholm, 1961–2; Bayreuth 1962; CG début 1970; Salzburg Fest. from 1968; NY Met début 1968. Art. dir. Savonlinna Opera Fest., Finland, 1972–9. Appointed gen. dir., Nat. Opera, Helsinki, but died before taking office.

Tamagno, Francesco (*b* Turin, 1850; *d* Varese, 1905). It. tenor. Sang in ch. of Turin Opera, 1870. Opera début 1870 (Nearco in Donizetti's *Poliuto*). La Scala from 1877. Toured S. Amer. 1880, then sang in Lisbon and Madrid. Chosen by Verdi to create title-role in *Otello* in Milan 1887, his famous 'trumpet tone' being ideally suited. London début 1889 at Lyceum; CG 1895; Chicago 1889–90; NY Met 1891. Retired 1904.

Tamberlik, Enrico (*b* Rome, 1820; *d* Paris, 1889). It. tenor. Opera début Naples 1841 (Tebaldo in *I Capuleti e i Montecchi*). CG début 1850, then regularly until 1864. Created Alvaro in *La *forza del destino*, St Petersburg 1862. Noted as Rossini's Otello and as Florestan in *Fidelio*. Some authorities say he was Romanian, orig. Nikita Torna.

tambour (Fr.). Drum. Hence, *tambour de Basque*, tambourine; *tambour militaire*, side-drum.

tambourin (Fr.). (1) Small 2-headed medieval drum, i.e. the tabor.
(2) Old Provençal dance, orig. acc. by pipe and tabor. Rameau's operas contain several *tambourins*, and he wrote kbd. pieces in the style of the dance.

tambourine. Type of perc. instr. of Arab orig. but known in Europe before 1300. Small, shallow, single-headed drum; 'jingles' (circular metal discs) are inserted into its wooden frame. It can be played by (a) hitting the head with knuckles, clenched fist, or back of the hand, or by striking it on the player's knee; (b) shaking it so that the jingles rattle; (c) rubbing a thumb along the edge to cause a tremolo from the jingles; (d) playing near rim with fingers or sticks. Mozart used the tambourine in his *German Dances* (K571, 1787) and it was also used by Weber and Berlioz, and often since then, especially in scenes of revelry, etc.

tambura (also *tanbura, tanpura*). Long-necked Indian lute, unfretted and round-bodied. 4 wire str. all played open and together as drone acc. Plucked with fingers.

Tamburin (Ger.), **tamburino** (It.). Usually the *tambourine, but sometimes the tabor.

Tamburini, Antonio (*b* Faenza, 1800; *d* Nice, 1876). It. baritone. Sang in Faenza opera ch. at 12. Opera début Cento 1818 (in Generali's *Contessa di Colle*). Sang in main It. opera houses 1824–32. London début 1832; Paris 1832–43 during period of Rubini, Lablache, Grisi, and Viardot. Created Ernesto in *Il Pirata* 1827, Riccardo in *I Puritani* 1835, and Malatesta in *Don Pasquale* 1843 (in addition to creating several other Donizetti roles). Was noted Don Giovanni. Retired 1855, but five years later in Nice sang Figaro in *Il barbiere di Siviglia*.

tamburo (It.). Drum. Thus *tamburo Basco*, tambourine; *tamburo grande* or *grosso* (or *gran tamburo*), bass drum; *tamburo militare* and *tamburo piccolo*, side drum; *tamburo rullante*, ten. drum.

tamburone (It.). Bass drum.

Tamerlano ('Tamerlane'). Opera in 3 acts by Handel to lib. by N. F. Haym adapted from Piovene's *Tamerlano* (1711) and from *Bajazet* (1719), rev. vers. of lib. by Zanelli and Borosini after Pradon's play *Tamerlan* (1675). Comp. 1724, rev. 1731. Prod. London 1724. F. modern ps. Karlsruhe 1924, Birmingham 1962, Bloomington, Ind., 1985.

Taming of the Shrew, The (*Der widerspenstigen Zähmung*). Opera in 4 acts by *Goetz to lib. by J. V. Widmann based on Shakespeare's play. Comp. 1868–72. Prod. Mannheim 1874; London 1879; NY 1886; Wexford 1991.

Tamir, Alexander. See *Eden and Tamir*.

Tam O'Shanter. (1) Concert-ov. by Malcolm *Arnold, Op.51 (1955) based on the poem by Burns.
(2) Symphonic ballad for orch. by George *Chadwick (1911).
(3) Mackenzie's *Scottish Rhapsody* No.3 for orch. (1911).

tampon (Fr.). Drumstick. *tampon double* is 2-headed stick used to produce roll on bass drum (imitating thunder, etc.).

tam-tam. The gong, especially one of indefinite pitch. Nothing to do with *tom-tom.

Tancredi. Opera (*melodramma eroico*) in 2 acts by Rossini to lib. by Rossi after Tasso's *Gerusalemme liberata* (1575) and Voltaire's *Tancrède* (1760). Comp. 1812. Prod. Venice 1813, London 1820, NY 1825.

Tan, Melvyn (*b* Singapore, 1956). Malayan-born Eng. keyboard player. Made special study of performing practice. Played pf. to 1980, then hpd. and fortepiano. Toured USA 1985.

Tan Dun (*b* Si Mao, Central Hunan, 1957). Chinese composer. While working as rice-planter, collected folk-songs. In 1975 became fiddle-player and arranger with provincial opera troupe. Entered Central Cons., Beijing, 1978. Wrote 1st Sym., *Li Sao*, at age of 22 and became leader of 'new wave' in Chinese mus. His str. qt. won Weber prize in Dresden 1983 (first Chinese composer since 1949 to win int. prize), but his mus. was criticized in China for its Western inclination and was banned for 6 months. Went to Columbia Univ., NY, 1986, and his mus. was featured in Glasgow, 1988, in BBC festival of new mus. from China. Awarded Suntory prize commission 1992. His later mus., combining Chinese and Western methods, is influenced by Cage. Comps. incl.:

OPERAS: *Nine Songs* (ritual opera) (1989); *Marco Polo* (1993–4); *Peony Pavilion* (1998); *Tea: a Mirror of Soul* (2002).

ORCH.: *Li Sao* (sym.) (1979–80); pf. conc. (1983); *Self-Portrait* (from *Death and Fire*), str. (1983/92); Sym. in 2 movts. (1985); *On Taoism*, v., orch. (1985); *Out of Peking Opera*, vn., orch. (1987); *Orchestral Theatre O* (1990), I: *Xun* (1990), II: *Re* (1992), III: *Red* (1993–4), IV: *The Gate* (1999); *Death and Fire: Dialogue with Paul Klee* (1992); *Yi*, vc. conc. (1993–4); *Heaven Earth Mankind*, sym. (1997); *2000 Today: a World Symphony for the Millennium* (1999); *Crouching Tiger Concerto*, vc., orch. (2000); Conc. for Orch., gui., orch. (2002); *Paper Concerto for Paper Perc. & Orch.*, orch. (2003).

ENS. (& VOICE): *Fu*, sops., bass, ens. (1982); *Silk Road*, sop., perc. (1989); *Circle with 4 Trios, Conductor, and Audience* (1992); *Lament: Autumn Wind*, any 6 instrs., any v., cond. (1993); *Memorial 19 Fucks*, v., pf., db. (1993); *A Sinking Love*, v., ens. (1998).

CHAMBER MUSIC: Str. Qt.: *Feng Ya Song* (1982); *8 Colours*, str. qt. (1986–8); *In Distance*, picc., hp., bass drum (1987); *Elegy: Snow in June*, vc., 4 perc. (1991); *Music for Pipa and Str. Qt.* (1999); *Secret Land*, 12 solo vc. (2004).

PIANO: *A Child's Diary* (1978); *5 Pieces in Hunan Accent* (1978); *Traces* (1989–92); *R: Beatles* (1990); *CAGE* (1993).

EXPERIMENTAL: *The Silk Road*, poet's v., 5 performers (1989); *Soundshape*, ceramics, v., movement (1990); *Silent Earth*, ceramics, 7 performers (1991); *Jo-Ha-Kyu*, acoustic mus. (1992); *The Pink*, acoustic mus. for paper (1993).

Taneyev, Sergey (Ivanovich) (*b* Govt. of Vladimir, 1856; *d* Dyudkovo, 1915). Russ. composer and pianist. Début as pianist 1875. Gave f.

Moscow p. of Tchaikovsky's B♭ minor conc. Dec. 1875. Toured with violinist Auer 1876. Prof. of instrumentation Moscow Cons. 1878, then of pf. and later of comp. 1881–7, dir., 1885–9, prof. of counterpoint 1889–1905. Opponent of nationalist sch. in Russia. Student of works of Ockeghem, Desprès, and Lassus. Wrote books on theory. Completed vocal version of Tchaikovsky's *Romeo and Juliet*. Wrote opera *Oresteya* (1887–94); 4 syms. (No.1 in E minor, 1874; No.2 in B♭, 1877–8, orch. Blok 1974; No.3 in D minor, 1884; No.4 in C minor, 1898); *Overture on Russian Themes*; choral works; 10 str. qts.; much other chamber mus.; songs.

tangent (from Lat. *tangere*, to touch). Part of *clavichord, a small metal 'tongue', which touches a str. when key is struck and produces sound. Remains in contact with str. while note sounds.

Tanglewood. Estate near Lenox, Mass., which in 1937 was offered to the Boston SO so that it could establish the Berkshire (now Tanglewood) Music Center for instruction in conducting, opera and instrumental perf., and composition at a summer school founded by *Koussevitzky in 1940. The summertime Berkshire Fest., directed by the incumbent cond. of the Boston SO and his guests, has over the years accommodated thousands of students and enthusiasists. Among operas which have received their Amer. premières there are *Idomeneo*, *La clemenza di Tito*, *Zaide*, *Peter Grimes*, *Down by the Greenwood Side*, Maderna's *Satyricon*, and the 1806 vers. of *Fidelio*.

tango. Argentinian dance, possibly imported into America by African slaves, perf. by couples at slow walking pace to mus. in simple duple time and with dotted rhythm like *habanera*. Became popular ballroom dance after 1907. Some composers have used the tango in their works, e.g. Walton, in his suite *Façade*, and Stravinsky.

Tannhäuser und der Sängerkrieg auf Wartburg (Tannhäuser and the Singing Contest on the Wartburg, usually abbreviated to *Tannhäuser*). Opera (*Handlung*) in 3 acts by Wagner to his own lib. Comp. 1843–5, rev. 1847–51 and 1861–75. Prod. Dresden 1845, NY 1859, CG 1876. First rev. vers., known as 'Paris version', prod. Paris 1861 (occasion of Jockey Club riot), NY 1889, CG 1896. Paris version is now usually perf., but Dresden version was used at CG 1984.

Tansman, Aleksander (*b* Lódź, 1897; *d* Paris, 1986). Polish-born Fr. composer and pianist (Fr. cit. 1938). Settled in Paris 1919, where he was encouraged by Ravel. Amer. début 1927. World tour 1933. Settled in USA 1940–6, when he wrote film mus. in Hollywood. Returned to Paris 1946. Works incl. 6 operas; 7 syms. (1925–44); 2 pf. concs.; va. conc.; vn. conc.; vc. conc.; cl. conc.; gui. concertino; oratorio *Isaiah the Prophet*; Conc. for Orch.; *Resurrection*, orch.; ob. concertino; fl. concertino; 8 str. qts. (1917–56); vc. sonata, etc. Wrote book on Stravinsky.

tanto (It.). So much, as much, too much. *non tanto*, not too much, don't overdo it! (e.g. allegro non tanto). *tantino* means a very little.

Tantum ergo (Lat., 'Therefore we before Him bending, this great sacrament revere', in Eng. version). Opening words of last section of St Thomas Aquinas's Corpus Christi hymn *Pange lingua*. Used in services other than that of Corpus Christi and especially in that of Benediction. Has own plainsong, but has often been set by composers.

Tanz, Tänze (Ger.). Dance, dances. *Tänzchen*, little dances.

tap box. See *Chinese wood block*.

Tapfere Soldat, Der (Straus). See *Chocolate Soldier, The*.

Tapiola. Tone-poem for orch., Op.112, by *Sibelius, comp. 1925–6 to commission by NY Sym. Soc. who gave f.p. in NY 1926, cond. W. Damrosch. F.p. in England London 1928. Tapio was god of Finnish forests.

tarantella (It.), **tarantelle** (Fr.). Neapolitan dance in 6/8 time which probably takes its name from Taranto, in the heel of Italy, or from a spider common there, the tarantula, whose bite is mildly poisonous. The music is of great rapidity with an approach to the *perpetuum mobile*. The *saltarello is a similar type. Chopin, Rossini, Liszt, and Mendelssohn are among composers who have used the *tarantella* in their works.

Taras Bulba. (1) Rhapsody for orch. by Janáček, comp. 1915–18, f.p. Brno 1921, f. Eng. p. 1928. Bulba was historical Ukrainian Cossack leader; Janáček based this work on story about him by Gogol. The 3 movts. are: 1. *Death of Andrea* (*Smrt Andrijova*). 2. *Death of Ostap* (*Smrt Ostapova*). 3. *Capture and Death of Taras Bulba* (*Proroctví a smrt Tarase Bulby*).

(2) Opera by Argentinian composer Berutti (1895).

tarbouka. Flower-pot-shaped drum from N. Africa, used by Berlioz in the Slave Dance in *Les Troyens*.

tardo, tarda (It.). Slow. So *tardamente*, slowly; *tardando*, *tardantemente*, slowing (gradually); *tardato*, slowed (gradually).

tarógató. Hung. single-reed, conical-bore woodwind instr. similar to sax., with cl. mouth-piece, which is sometimes used for 2nd of the shepherd's tunes in Act 3 of Wagner's *Tristan und Isolde*. Wagner specifies a *Holztrompete* (wooden tpt.), but while at Budapest Opera (1888–91) Mahler used the tarógató and this was also adopted at Bayreuth by Richter. Orig. tarógató was a wooden cornett, sounding only natural notes, used for military signals.

Tarr, Edward (Hankins) (*b* Norwich, Conn., 1936). Amer. trumpeter and musicologist.

Specialist in revival of early tpt. works on modern and old instr. Works written for him by Kagel and Stockhausen. Founded Edward Tarr Brass Ensemble 1967. Taught in Cologne 1968–70 and in Basle from 1972. Dir., tpt. museum, Bad Säckingen from 1985. Edited many baroque works for modern perf., notably tpt. works of Torelli.

Tárrega, Francisco (*b* Villarreal, 1852; *d* Barcelona, 1909). Sp. guitarist and composer. Gave recitals in Paris and London 1880, being acclaimed as 'Sarasate of the guitar'. Prof. of guitar, Madrid Cons. Wrote many guitar preludes, and transcr. works by Granados, Albéniz, Beethoven, and Chopin.

Tartini, Giuseppe (*b* Pirano, Istria, 1692; *d* Padua, 1770). It. violinist, composer, teacher, and inventor. Fled from Padua 1710 because of disapproval of his marriage. Took refuge in monastery at Assisi where he studied comp. and acoustics, invented new vn. bow, and gave vn. recitals. Returned to Padua, forgiven, 1715. Played as orch. violinist; became first vn. at Cappella del Santo, Padua, 1721–3. Kapellmeister of Count Kinsky's band, Prague, 1723–5, playing also in Vienna. On return to Padua founded, 1728, school of vn.-playing , becoming known as 'Master of Nations' and numbering many subsequently celebrated violinists among his pupils. Was teaching up to 1768. Discovered *resultant tones, which he then called *terzo suono* (3rd sound), though it was left to *Helmholtz to explain them years later. Wrote several treatises and comp. some religious vocal mus. and *canzone* in addition to 42 vn. sonatas, 12 sonatas for vn. and vc., 135 vn. concs., vc. concs., and concs. for other instr. incl. cls., obs., and tpt. Celebrated *'Devil's Trill' sonata was almost certainly composed after 1745, but no autograph exists.

Taruskin, Richard (Filler) (*b* NY, 1945). Amer. critic and musicologist. Taught at Columbia Univ. 1973–87. Prof. of mus., Univ. of Calif., Berkeley, from 1987. Authority on 15th-cent. *chanson* and especially on Russ. mus. from 18th cent. to today. Strong critic of 'early music' movt. Wrote *Oxford History of Western Music* (2005, 6 vols., 4272pp.).

Taste(n) (Ger.). Key(s) of kbd. instr., etc.

tastiera (It.). Same meanings as *tasto*, below. Thus *sulla tastiera = sul tasto*.

tasto, tasti (It.). (1) Key(s) (i.e. of kbd. instr.). In early mus. with figured bass, *tasto solo* means 'Play the key alone', i.e. only the bass line, without adding chords.

(2) The fingerboard of a bowed str. instr. *Sul tasto* (on the fingerboard) means 'bow over the fingerboard'. See also *tastiera*.

Tate, Jeffrey (*b* Salisbury, 1943). Eng. conductor. Worked at London Opera Centre 1970–1. Répétiteur CG 1971–7. Ass. to Boulez on 1976 Bayreuth prod. of *The Ring*. Ass. to cond. Cologne Opera

1978–80. Cond. début Göteborg Opera 1978 (*Carmen*). NY Met 1980 (*Lulu*, having been ass. to Boulez for Paris 3-act première, 1979). CG 1982; S. Francisco 1984; Salzburg Fest. 1985. Prin. cond. ECO 1985–2000, CG 1986–91. Prin. cond. and mus. dir. Rotterdam PO 1991–5. Mus. dir. Th. San Carlo, Naples, from 2005. CBE 1990.

Tate, Nahum (*b* ?Dublin, 1652; *d* London, 1715). Irish-born poet and playwright, poet laureate from 1692. Wrote lib. of Purcell's *Dido and Aeneas* and collab. with Nicholas Brady (*b* Bandon, Co. Cork, 1659; *d* Richmond, Surrey, 1726) in metrical version of Psalms (pubd. 1696).

Tate, Phyllis (Margaret Duncan) (*b* Gerrards Cross, 1911; *d* Hampstead, 1987). Eng. composer. Held no official posts, devoting herself to comp. Imaginative and skilled composer, who wrote especially well for vv. and small ens. Works incl.:

OPERAS: *The *Lodger* (1959–60); *Dark Pilgrimage* (TV) (1963).

ORCH.: Sax. conc. (1944); *Panorama*, str. (1977).

BRASS BAND: *Illustrations* (1969).

VOICE(S) & INSTR(S).: *Nocturne*, SATB soloists, str. qt., db., bcl., cel. (1946); *The *Lady of Shalott*, ten., chamber ens. (1956); *A Victorian Garland*, sop., cont., hn., pf. (1965); *Gravestones*, for Cleo Laine (1966); *Apparitions*, ten., harmonica, pf. quintet (1968); *Coastal Ballads*, bar., instr. (1969); *Creatures Great and Small*, mez., gui., db., perc. (1973); *2 Ballads*, mez., gui. (1974); *Songs of Sundrie Kinds*, ten., lute (1975); *Scenes from Kipling*, bar., pf. (1976); *Scenes from Tyneside*, mez., cl., pf. (1978); *The Ballad of Reading Gaol*, bar., org., vc. (1980).

CHORAL: *Choral Scene from The Bacchae*, mixed ch., opt. org. (1953); *Witches and Spells*, ch. (1959); *7 Lincolnshire Folk Songs*, ch., ens. (1966); *A Secular Requiem*, ch., org., orch. (1967); *To Words by Joseph Beaumont*, women's ch. (1970); *Serenade to Christmas*, mez., ch., orch. (1972); *St Martha and the Dragon*, narr., soloists, ch., orch. (1976); *All the World's a Stage*, ch., orch. (1977); *Compassion*, ch., orch. (or org.) (1978).

CHAMBER MUSIC: sonata, cl., vc. (1947); str. qt. (1952, rev. 1982); *Air and Variations*, vn., cl., pf. (1958); *Variegations*, va. (1970); *The Rainbow and the Cuckoo*, ob., str. trio (1974); *Sonatina pastorale*, harmonica, hpd. (1974); *Seasonal Sequence*, va., pf. (1977); *3 Pieces*, cl. (1979); *Prelude, Aria, Interlude, Finale*, cl., pf. (1981).

PIANO: *Explorations around a Troubadour Song* (1973); *Lyric Suite*, 2 pf. (1973).

Tátrai, Vilmos (*b* Kispest, 1912). Hung. violinist. Played in various orchs. 1931–3, Budapest Municipal Orch. 1933–6, Buenos Aires Radio Orch. 1936–7. Leader, Hungarian State SO 1940–78. Founded Tátrai Qt. 1946. Taught vn. and chamber mus. Bartók Cons. 1947–54. Founder-leader Hung. CO 1957. Prof. at Liszt Acad., Budapest, 1965.

Tátrai Quartet. Hung. string quartet formed by Vilmos *Tátrai in 1946 from soloists of Budapest Municipal Orch. Won 1948 Bartók Comp. Toured Europe 1952. Salzburg Fest. 1966. Recorded complete cycles of Beethoven and Bartók qts. Had repertoire of 360 compositions and gave 64 f.ps. of Hung. composers and 54 of foreign composers.

tattoo. The mus. of bugles and drums, recalling soldiers to their barracks at night. In the Brit. Army it begins with the *First Post*, lasts about 30 minutes, and ends with the **Last Post*. Another meaning is a display by the army, involving mock battles, etc., as at the Aldershot Tattoo.

Tauber [Seiffert], **Richard** (*b* Linz, 1892; *d* London, 1948). Austrian-born tenor, conductor, and composer (Brit. cit. 1940). Début Chemnitz 1913 (Tamino in *Die Zauberflöte*). Dresden Opera 1913–22; Berlin Opera 1915; Vienna Opera 1922–8, 1932–8; Salzburg Fest. début 1922; Berlin State Opera 1923–33; CG 1938–9 (but had often sung in Eng. before then in operettas); Amer. début (NY recital) 1931. Superb Mozart and *Lieder* singer, also known for his perfs. in operetta, especially those of Lehár, whose work he first sang in Vienna 1922 (*Frasquita*). Wrote musicals, e.g. *Old Chelsea*. Made last appearances in NY March 1947 and at CG autumn 1947, singing Ottavio in *Don Giovanni* with colleagues of Vienna Opera on their visit to London although he had serious lung trouble which led to his death a few months later.

Taubman, Howard (*b* NY, 1907; *d* Sarasota, Fla., 1996). Amer. music critic and author. Ass. mus. critic, *New York Times* 1930–55, chief mus. critic 1955–60, drama critic 1960–6 and 'critic-at-large' 1966–72. Wrote biography of Toscanini (1951).

Tauriello, Antonio (*b* Buenos Aires, 1931). Argentine composer, pianist, and conductor. Cond. ballet at Teatro Colón, Buenos Aires. Cond. of 'Ritmus' perc. ens. Opera coach and répétiteur, Chicago Lyric Opera, NY City Opera, etc. Works incl. Rabelais opera *Les Guerres Picrocholines*, 2 pf. concs., *Canti* for vn. and orch., *Serenade* for orch., *Aria* for fl. and ens.

Tausky, Vilem (*b* Prerov, Cz., 1910; *d* London, 2004). Cz.-born conductor and composer (Eng. cit.). Cond. Brno Opera 1929–39. Settled in Eng. Mus. dir., Carl Rosa Opera 1945–9. Art. dir. Phoenix Opera from 1967. Dir. of opera GSMD from 1966. Cond. f. Eng. p. (BBC) of Janáček's *Osud*, 1972. Works incl. ob. conc., harmonica concertino, *Divertimento* for str., str. qt. CBE 1981.

Tavener, (Sir) **John** (Kenneth) (*b* London, 1944). Eng. composer and organist. Org., St John's, Kensington, 1960. Prof. of mus., TCL, 1969–74. Mus. of rich imaginative and eclectic resource and of profound religious spirit, as in *Ultimos ritos* and *Celtic Requiem*, in which children's games are linked to the idea of death. Convert to Gr. Orthodox Church. Knighted 2000. Prin. works:

OPERAS & MUSIC THEATRE: *The Cappemakers* (1965, rev. of 1964 choral work, see below); *Thérèse* (1973–6); *A Gentle Spirit* (after Dostoyevsky), sop., ten., small ens. (1976–7); *Eis Thanaton* (1986); *Mary of Egypt* (1991).

ORCH.: pf. conc. (1962–3); chamber conc. (1965, rev. 1968); *Grandma's Footsteps*, 5 mus. boxes, chamber

ens. (1967–8); *Variations on 3 Blind Mice* (1972); *Palintropos*, pf., orch. (1978–9); *Towards the Son: Ritual Procession*, tb., 4 gongs, 4 bowed psalteries, perc., str. (1982); *The Protecting Veil*, vc., str. (1987); *The Repentant Thief*, cl., perc., timp., str. (1990); *Eternal Memory*, vc., ens. (1992); *Theophany*, str., ww., alto fl., brass, perc. (1994); *Tears of the Angels*, vn., str. (1995); *Petra*, str. (1996); *Ekstasis*, sop., tpt., vn., orch. (2000); *Hymn of Dawn*, sop., bar., vn., fl., orch. (2002); *Pratirūpa*, pf., str. (2005).

SOLOIST(S), CHORUS, & ORCH.: *The Cappemakers*, 2 narr., 10 soloists, male ch., orch. (1964, rev. for stage 1965); *The *Whale*, mez., bar., ch., children's ch., speaker, 6 actors, org., orch., tape (1965–6); *Introit for March 27, the Feast of St John Damascene*, sop., alto, ch., orch. (1967–8); *Nomine Jesu*, mez., ch., ens., 5 speaking vv. (1970); *Responsorium in memory of Annon Lee Silver*, 2 sop., ch., 2 fl. (opt.) (1971); **Ultimos Ritos*, SATB soloists, ch., 5 spkrs., orch. (1972); *Kyklike Kinēsis*, sop., vc., ch., pf., str. (1977); *Akhmatova: Requiem*, sop., bar., orch. (1979–80); *Akathist of Thanksgiving*, soloists, ch., bells, str. (1986–7); *Ikon of St Seraphim*, bar., 4 bass, ch., orch. (1988); *Resurrection*, soloists and actors, ch., male ch., orch. (1989); *We Shall See Him As He Is*, sop., ten., ch., org., 2 tpt., timp., str. (1991–2); *Hymns of Paradise*, bass, ch., str. (1992–3); *The Apocalypse*, sop., mez., ten., counterten., treble, bass, ch., children's ch., orch. (1993–4); *Eternity's Sunrise*, sop., baroque orch. (1998); *Lamentations and Praises*, ch., orch. (2000); *Song of the Cosmos*, sop., bar., ch., orch. (2000); *Lament for Jerusalem*, sop., counterten., ch., orch. (2002); *The Veil of the Temple*, soloists, 4 ch., orchs. (2003).

SOLO VOICE(S) & INSTR(S).: *3 Holy Sonnets* (*John Donne*), bar., small orch., tape (1962); *Cain and Abel*, SATB soloists, orch. (1965); *3 Surrealist Songs*, mez., tape, pf. (1967–8); *In Alium*, sop., org., pf., str. (1968); **Celtic Requiem*, sop., ch., children's ch., ens. (1969); *Canciones españolas*, 2 sop. or counterten., 2 fl., org., hpd. (1972); *Requiem for Father Malachy*, 2 counterten., ten., 2 bar., bass, ens., org., str. qt. (1973, rev. 1979); *6 Russian Folk Songs*, v., ens. (1978); *The Immurement of Antigone*, sop., orch. (1978); *6 Abbasid Songs*, ten., 3 fl., alto fl. (1979); *Sappho: Lyrical Fragments*, 2 sop., str. (1980); *To a Child Dancing in the Wind*, sop., fl., hp., va. (1983); *16 Haiku of Seferis*, sop., ten., handbells, str. (1984); *Meditation on the Light*, counterten., gui., handbells (1986); *The Child Lived*, sop., ens. (1992); *Akhmatova Songs* (new vers.), sop., ens. (1995).

CHORUS (unacc. except where indicated): *Coplas*, SATB soloists, ch., tape (1970); *Ma fin est mon commencement*, 4-part ten. ch., 4 tb., 4 vc. (1972); *Canticle of the Mother of God*, sop., ch. (1976); *The Liturgy of St John Chrysostom* (1978); *Risen!* ch., pf., org., str. (1981); *Prayer for the World* (1981); *Funeral Ikos* (1981); *The Great Canon of St Andrew of Crete* (1981); *Doxa* (1982); *Lord's Prayer* (1982); *The Lamb* (1982); *He hath entered the Heven*, trebles, opt. handbells (1982); *Ikon of Light*, ch., str. trio (1984); *Orthodox Vigil Service*, ch., handbells (1984); *A Nativity*, women's ch. (1984); *Angels*, ch., org. (1985); *Love bade me welcome* (1985); *2 Hymns to the Mother of God* (1985); *Panikhida* (1986); *Ikon of St*

Cuthbert of Lindisfarne (1986); Magnificat and Nunc Dimittis (1986); Wedding Prayer (1987); Many Years (1987); Acclamation (1987); God is with us, ch., org. (1987); Hymn to the Holy Spirit (1987); The Tyger (1987); Apolytikion for St Nicholas (1988); The Call (1988); Let not the Prince be silent, 2 ch. (1988); The Uncreated Eros (1988); Lament of the Mother of God, sop., ch. (1988); Today the Virgin (1989); Eonia (1989); Psalm 121 (1989); Thunder entered her, ch., org., male ch., handbells (1990); Ikon of the Trinity (1990); Do not move on (1990); A Christmas Round (1990); Ikon of the Nativity (1991); A Village Wedding (1992); Wedding Greeting, ten., ch. (1992); Prayer to the Holy Trinity (1995); As one who has slept (1996); Feast of Feasts (1996); Apolytikon of St Martin (1997); Awed by the Beauty, male ch. (2001); Butterfly Dreams (2002); Maha Maya, double ch., org. (2003); Invocations and Last Word, ch., semich. (2005).

CHAMBER MUSIC: In memoriam Igor Stravinsky, 2 alt. fl., org., handbells (1971); Greek Interlude, fl., pf. (1979); Trisagion, brass quintet (1981); Little Missenden Calm, ob., cl., bn., hn. (1984); Chant, gui. (1984); The Hidden Treasure, str. qt. (1989); Thrinos, vc. (1990); The Last Sleep of the Virgin, str. qt., handbells (1991); Diodia, str. qt. (1997); The World, sop., str. qt. (1999); The Bridegroom, chamber orch. (2000); Cantus mysticus, sop., cl., str. (2004).

VOICE & PIANO: 3 Sections from T. S. Eliot's 'The Four Quartets', v. (1963-4); Lamentation, Last Prayer, and Exaltation, sop., handbells or pf. (1977); Mini-Song Cycle for Gina, sop. (1984); Prayer (for Szymanowski), bass (1987); Epistle of Love, sop., pf. (2002).

PIANO: Palin (1977; expanded as Palintropos with orch.); My Grandfather's Waltz, pf. duet (1980); Mandoodles (1982); In memory of Cats (1986); Ypakoë (1997); Pratrirúpa (2003).

ORGAN: Mandelion (1981).

Taverner. Opera in 2 acts by *Maxwell Davies to his own lib. drawn from 16th-cent. letters and documents concerning life of composer John *Taverner, with 14 singing roles, ch., and boys' ch. Comp. 1962-8, rev. 1970, 1983. Prod. CG 1972, cond. E. Downes; Boston 1986.

Taverner, John (b c.1490; d Boston, Lincs., 1545). Eng. composer and organist. Org. of Cardinal Coll. (now Ch. Ch.), Oxford, 1526-30. One of great polyphonic masters of 16th-cent. Eng. mus. Wrote 8 Masses, incl. one based on secular song The Western Wynde (36 variations, 9 in each of 4 movts.). His Mass Gloria tibi Trinitas was fount of the *In nomine form for str.; this came about because the instr. comps. by Taverner called In nomine are transcrs. of the passage in the Benedictus of his Mass which sets the words In nomine Domini. Other composers followed his example and used the same title. Also wrote 3 Magnificats and several motets. Taverner was link between medieval mus. and Renaissance. Maxwell Davies's opera *Taverner is based on legend about his life.

Taylor, (Joseph) **Deems** (b NY, 1885; d NY, 1966). Amer. composer, critic, and author. Mus. critic, New York World 1921-5. Orch. works well received; commissioned by NY Met to write opera

The King's Henchman (1926-7), this being followed by Peter Ibbetson (1930-1). Became mus. adviser to CBS 1936 and well-known for narrations of NY Met broadcasts and NYPO concerts. Spoke narration in Disney's Fantasia. Popular orch. works incl. Through the Looking Glass (1922) and Marco Takes a Walk (1942).

Taylor, Samuel Coleridge-. See Coleridge-Taylor, Samuel.

Tchaikovsky [Chaykovsky], **Boris** (Alexandrovich) (b Moscow, 1925; d Moscow, 1996). Russ. composer and pianist. Works, several based on folk mus., incl. syms.; opera The Star (1949); Fantasia on Russian Folk Themes, orch. (1950); Capriccio on English Themes, orch. (1954); cl. concertino (1957); Sinfonietta; str. qts.; pf. trio; vn. sonata; pf. quintet; and film scores.

Tchaikovsky [Chaykovsky], **Pyotr** (Ilyich) (b Votkinsk, 1840; d St Petersburg, 1893). Russ. composer and conductor. Studied law in St Petersburg. Worked as civil servant and studied 1863-5 at mus. coll. instituted by A. Rubinstein which became St Petersburg Cons. Went to Moscow 1866, becoming prof. of harmony at new Cons. under directorship of N. Rubinstein. During first 2 years there wrote 1st Sym. and opera Voyevoda. In 1868 met nationalist group of young Russ. composers headed by Rimsky-Korsakov and was stirred by their enthusiasm, as is shown by his 2nd Sym., but later came to be regarded by them as cosmopolitan rather than truly Russ. From 1869 to 1875 wrote 3 more operas and played pf. conc. and was mus. critic of Russkiye vedomosti 1872-6, going to first Bayreuth Fest. 1876. In 1877 married one of his pupils, separating from her 9 weeks later, attempting suicide, and coming near to mental collapse, psychological result of fatal step for a man of homosexual tendencies. At this time was taken under patronage of wealthy widow, Nadezhda von Meck, who out of admiration gave him yearly allowance which enabled him to abandon teaching and devote himself wholly to comp. She and Tchaikovsky never spoke to each other, though they corresponded voluminously. Fourth Sym. is ded. to her. Went to Switz. and It., composing opera Eugene Onegin, prod. by students of Moscow Cons. 1879, with moderate success. By 1880, his works were popular in Russia (thanks to advocacy of N. Rubinstein), and in Brit. and USA but still met with hostility in Paris and Vienna. In 1885 bought country house, first of several, at Klin, living in hermit-like isolation. There, wrote Manfred and in 1887 made début in Moscow as cond. of rev. version of opera Vakula the Smith under title Cherevichki (The Slippers). In 1888 toured Ger., Fr., and London as cond., returning to Ger. and Eng. in 1889. Ballet Sleeping Beauty prod. 1890, after which Tchaikovsky went to Florence to work on opera Queen of Spades, prod. St Petersburg 1890. Year ended with sudden rupture of relationship with Mme von Meck; illness (or the disapproval by her family of her patronage of Tchaikovsky) had dictated her decision, which wounded

Tchaikovsky deeply. Visited USA with great success 1891, and in Jan. 1892 heard Mahler conduct *Eugene Onegin* at Hamburg. Ballet *Nutcracker* comp. 1891–2, as double bill with opera *Yolanta*, and work started on a 6th Sym. In that year, again visited Vienna and in 1893 went to Eng., where hon. doctorate of mus. was conferred on him by Cambridge Univ. During 1893 wrote 6th Sym., having abandoned sym. begun in 1891–2 and re-worked it as a 3rd pf. conc., eventually retaining only one movt. (2nd and 3rd orch. from the surviving sketches by Taneyev after Tchaikovsky's death). F.p. of the sym. was only moderately successful, though Tchaikovsky was con- vinced it was his best work. It is usually stated that 4 days later he felt ill and drank a large glassful of unboiled water (possibly with deliberate intent) and developed cholera, which led to his death. But in 1979 the Russian scholar Alexandra Orlova published a theory that the composer's death was suicide by poison, ordered by a private court of his former law-student colleagues to prevent revelation of a homosexual scandal involving the aristocracy. This theory is violently opposed by some scholars and the matter remains controversial and unresolved.

Few composers are more popular with audiences than Tchaikovsky; the reasons are several and understandable. His music is extremely tuneful, luxuriously and colourfully scored, and filled with emotional fervour directed to the heart rather than to the head (though the notion that Tchaikovsky's syms. are lacking in symphonic thinking and structure does not bear serious consideration). Undoubtedly the emotional temperature of the mus. reflected the man's nature. He was doubly afflicted: by repressed homosexuality (hence his disastrous attempt at marriage) and by the tendency to extreme fluctuations between elation and depression, each success being followed by a period of introspective gloom and melancholy which stemmed from psychological defects rather than from 'typical Russian melancholy'. This showed itself also in his attitude to his visits abroad. As soon as he left Russia he was ill with homesickness; once back, he was restlessly planning to be off again.

In 19th-cent. Russ. mus., Tchaikovsky stands alone. His *Romeo and Juliet* was ded. to Balakirev, one of the 'Five', but he never identified himself with out-and-out nationalism. He succumbed to the influence of neither Brahms nor Wagner, but greatly admired the Fr. mus. of Bizet and Saint-Saëns. This can be linked with his lifelong passion for Mozart, and many passages in Tchaikovsky's mus. are as delicately detailed and coloured as works by Bizet and Mozart. The other element of his nature, the fate-laden, Byronic, emotional impact of the last 3 syms., is traceable in many episodes in the operas, notably *Eugene Onegin*. None of his operas was a success on its first appearance, but *Onegin* and *Queen of Spades* are now widely perf. and admired, and adventurous cos. have explored the others. The true theatrical Tchaikovsky is to be found in the ballets, a supreme combination of melodic inventiveness,

grand sweep, and constant freshness. Nor should the superb songs be forgotten: in them, in miniature, the soul of Tchaikovsky is enshrined as surely as in the great syms., concs., and orch. masterpieces. Prin. works:

OPERAS: syms.: *Voyevoda*, Op.3 (*Dream on the Volga*) (1867–8); *Undine* (destroyed) (1869); *Oprichnik* (*The Life Guardsman*) (1870–2); **Vakula the Smith*, Op.14 (*Kuznets Vakula*) (1874, rev. 1885 and 1886 as **Cherevichki* (The Slippers) or *Oxana's Caprice*); **Eugene Onegin* (*Evgeny Onyegin*), Op.24 (1877–8); The **Maid of Orleans* (*Orleanskaya Deva*) (1878–9, rev. 1882); **Mazeppa* (1881–3); The *Sorceress* (*Charodeyka*) (1885–7); **Queen of Spades* (*Pikovaya Dama*), Op.68 (1890); **Yolanta*, Op.69 (1891).

BALLETS: **Swan Lake* (*Lebedinoye ozero*), Op.20 (1875–6); The **Sleeping Beauty* (*Spyashchaya krasavitsa*), Op.66 (1888–9); **Nutcracker* (*Shchelkunchik*), Op.71 (1891–2).

ORCH.: syms.: No.1 in G minor, Op.13 (*Winter Daydreams*) (1866, rev. 1874), No.2 in C minor, Op.17 (**Ukrainian* or **Little Russian*) (1872, rev. 1879–80), No.3 in D, Op.29 (**Polish*) (1875), No.4 in F minor, Op.36 (1877–8), No.5 in E minor, Op.64 (1888), No.6 in B minor, Op.74 (**Pathetic*) (1893); concertos, etc.: pf.: No.1 in B♭ minor, Op.23 (1874–5), No.2 in G, Op.44 (1879–80, rev. 1893 Ziloti), *Concert Fantasy*, Op.56 (1884); vn. conc. in D, Op.35 (1878), *Sérénade mélancolique*, vn., Op.26 (1875), *Valse-Scherzo*, vn., Op.34 (1877); *Variations on a Rococo Theme*, vc., Op.33 (1876), *Pezzo capriccioso*, vc., Op.62 (1887); symphonic fantasies: The **Tempest*, Op.18 (1873), **Francesca da Rimini*, Op.32 (1876); *Slavonic March*, Op.31 (1876); *Serenade*, str., Op.48 (1880); *1812*, *Ceremonial Overture*, Op.49 (1880); **Manfred Symphony*, Op.58 (1885); ov., The *Storm*, Op.76 (1864); sym.-poem *Fate*, Op.77 (1868); fantasy ovs.: **Hamlet*, Op.67a (1888), **Romeo and Juliet* (1869, rev. 1870 and 1880); **Italian Caprice*, Op.45 (1880); symphonic ballad, *Voyevoda*, Op.78 (1891); Suites: No.1 in D, Op.43 (1878–9), No.2 in C, Op.53 (1883), No.3 in G, Op.55 (1884, *Theme and Variations* movt. often perf. separately), No.4 **Mozartiana*, Op.61 (1887), *Nutcracker*, Op.71a (1892). (N.B. The 'Sym. No.7 in E♭' and the 'Pf. Conc. No.3 in E♭' are compilations by other hands. The sym. was begun by Tchaikovsky in 1891–2, but abandoned. He scored 1st movt. as pf. conc., Taneyev later adding *andante* and *finale* from sketches of the sym. S. Bogatyryov (1890–1960) prod. perf. version of orig. sym. from same sketches. Taneyev also completed vocal duet version (1893) of part of *Romeo and Juliet* ov. for sop., ten., and orch.)

CHAMBER MUSIC: str. qts.: No.1 in D, Op.11 (contains *Andante cantabile* often played separately) (1871), No.2 in F, Op.22 (1874), No.3 in E♭ minor, Op.30 (1876); pf. trio in A minor (in memory of a great artist), Op.50 (1881–2); *Souvenir de Florence*, str. sextet, Op.70 (1887–90, rev. 1891–2).

PIANO: *Valse Caprice*, Op.4 (1868); *Capriccio*, Op.8 (1870); *3 Pieces*, Op.9 (1870); *Nocturne* and *Humoreske*, Op.10 (1871); *6 Pieces*, Op.19 (1873); *6 Pieces on One Theme*, Op.21 (1873); sonata in G, Op.37 (1878); The *Seasons*, 12 characteristic pieces

(1875–6); *Children's Album: 24 Pieces*, Op.39 (1878); *12 Pieces*, Op.40 (1878); *6 Pieces*, Op.51 (1882); *Dumka*, Op.59 (1886); *18 Pieces*, Op.72 (1893; the 10th of these, *Scherzo-Fantaisie* in E♭ minor, exists in orch. sketch of 1891–2 and is presumed to have been intended as scherzo of projected sym. Incorporated by Bogatyryov in '7th Sym.', see above); Sonata in C♯ minor (posth.).

CHORAL: *Liturgy of St John Chrysostom*, Op.41 (1878); *Russian Vesper Service*, unacc., Op.52 (1881–2).

SONGS: Tchaikovsky's songs were pubd. in the following groups (no. of songs, Op.no. and date): 6, Op.6, 1869; 6, Op.16, 1872; 6, Op.25, 1874; 6, Op.27, 1874; 6, Op.28, 1874; 6, Op.38, 1877; 7, Op.47, 1879; 16 for children, Op.54, 1883; 6, Op.57, 1883; 12, Op.60, 1886; 6, Op.63, 1888; 6, Op.65, 1888; 6, Op.73, 1893. Among the best-known are: *Again as before*; *As they kept on saying*; *At the ball*; *Behind the window*; *Cradle Song*; *Deception*; *Don Juan's Serenade*; *Evening*; *Exploit*; *In the early Spring*; *My spoiled darling*; *Night*; *No, only he who has known* (*None but the lonely heart*) (Op.6 No.6); *Not a word, my friend*; *Over the golden cornfields*; *Reconciliation*; *To forget so soon*; *Wait*; *Why did I dream of you?*

Tchaikowsky, André (*b* Warsaw, 1935; *d* Oxford, 1982). Polish-born pianist and composer. Début Paris 1948. Leading recitalist. Settled in Eng. Comps. incl. opera *The Merchant of Venice* (1960–82), vn. conc., 2 pf. concs., fl. conc., cl. conc., sym., cl. sonata, 2 str. qts., and pf. pieces. Bequeathed skull to Royal Shakespeare Co. for use in perfs. of *Hamlet* (début 1984).

Tcherepnin, Alexander (Nikolayevich) (*b* St Petersburg, 1899; *d* Paris, 1977). Russ.-born composer and pianist (Amer. cit. 1958), son of Nikolay *Tcherepnin. Went to Paris 1921. Earned int. reputation as pianist and in 1923 wrote ballet, *Ajanta's Frescoes*, for Pavlova, who prod. it at CG. His first sym. (Paris 1927) caused protests because of its dissonance. Wrote several more ballets and scored Mussorgsky's unfinished opera, *The Marriage*. Visited USA 1926. Prof. of pf. and comp. at DePaul Univ., Chicago, 1949–64. In tours of Far East 1934–7 taught young Chinese and Japanese composers. Mus. influenced by Georgian and Oriental folk-mus. and by his formulation of 9-note scale, leading to complex chords. Comp. 3 operas (one to libretto by Hofmannsthal); 4 syms. (1927–57); 6 pf. concs. (1919–65); harmonica conc.; *The Story of Ivan the Fool* (cantata after Tolstoy, using elec. devices, 1968); 2 str. qts.; 2 pf. sonatas; and many smaller works.

Tcherepnin, Nikolay (*b* St Petersburg, 1873; *d* Issy-les-Moulineaux, nr. Paris, 1945). Russ. composer. Cond. of Belyayev concerts 1901 and at Mariinsky Th. Cond. for Diaghilev Ballet 1909–14. Dir., Tiflis Cons. 1918–21. Settled in Paris 1921, with son Alexander *Tcherepnin. Dir., Russ. Cons., Paris, 1925–9, 1938–45. Wrote 2 operas, 6 ballets, orch. works, and pf. conc. Completed *Mussorgsky's *Sorochintsy Fair* (prod. Monte Carlo 1923).

TCL, TCM. *Trinity College of Music, London.

te. In *tonic sol-fa, spoken name for 7th degree of scale, written *t*.

Tea for Two. Song by *Youmans, comp. for musical *No, No, Nanette* (1925). In 1928 orch. version was made by Shostakovich in, it is said, 45 mins. at the request of the cond. *Malko who wanted something extra to perf. at a concert of Shostakovich's mus. at Moscow Cons. on 25 Nov. 1928. The cond. Aleksandr Gauk included it as an entr'acte in Shostakovich's ballet *The Age of Gold*. Shostakovich gave the arrangement the title *Tahiti Trot (Taiti trot)* because this was the Russ. name for the song.

Tear, Robert (*b* Barry, Glamorgan, 1939). Welsh tenor. In 1960 appointed lay vicar, St Paul's Cath., and worked with Ambrosian Singers. International chair of vocal studies, RAM, from 1986. Opera début with EOG 1963 (Quint in The *Turn of the Screw*) and was member of Group 1964–70. CG début 1970. Created Dov in The *Knot Garden*, CG 1970. Has sung with Scottish Opera in Verdi and Mozart. Sang The Painter in f.p. of complete *Lulu*, Paris 1979. Salzburg Fest. début 1985; GTO 1989; Glyndebourne 1992. Took up conducting. Autobiography *Tear Here* (1990). CBE 1984.

Tebaldi, Renata (*b* Pesaro, 1922; *d* San Marino, 2004). It. soprano. Opera début Rovigo 1944 (Elena in Boito's *Mefistofele*). Chosen by Toscanini for re-opening concert at La Scala 1946, and sang there 1946–7 (début as Mimì in *La bohème*), 1949–54, and 1959. San Carlo, Naples, 1948–9; Florence 1948–53; CG début 1950 (with Scala co.); Royal Opera début 1955; Amer. début (S. Francisco) 1950; NY Met 1955–73; Chicago 1955–69. V. of power and beauty, esp. in Verdi and Puccini roles. Retired from opera 1973, concerts 1976.

tedesco, tedesca (It., plural *tedeschi, tedesche*). German. Found in the term *alla tedesca*, 'in the Ger. style', which has had several meanings. Beethoven indicated a Ger. waltz by it, others mean a Ger. dance of any kind. In his tuba conc., 1954, Vaughan Williams's *Rondo alla tedesca* means a rondo as in a Ger. comp.

Te Deum Laudamus (We praise thee, O God). Ecclesiastical canticle, or hymn of thanksgiving, the words of which were probably written in 5th cent. Adopted by both RC and Anglican churches. Has traditional plainsong melody, but has been set by innumerable composers, incl. Purcell, Handel, Berlioz, Verdi, Dvořák, Bruckner, Vaughan Williams, Britten, Walton, often on highly elaborate scale for soloists, ch., and orch. as well as more simply.

Teil or **Theil** (Ger.). Part, in the sense of portion or section. So *teilen* or *theilen*, to divide.

Te Kanawa, (Dame) **Kiri** (*b* Gisborne, Auckland, NZ, 1944). NZ soprano. Opera début as Elena in Rossini's *La donna del lago*, Camden Fest.

1969, then CG début 1970. First major CG role was Countess in *Le nozze di Figaro* 1971. Amer. début (Santa Fe) 1971; Glyndebourne 1973; NY Met début 1974; Salzburg Fest. 1979. Chosen by bridegroom to sing at wedding of Prince of Wales and Lady Diana Spencer in St Paul's Cath., 1981. Fine lyric sop., especially in Mozart, Verdi, and Strauss. Recorded *West Side Story*, cond. Bernstein. OBE 1973. DBE 1982.

Tel Aviv Quartet. Israeli str. qt. founded in 1962, making an international tour every year. Strong modern representation in repertory. 2nd vn. has changed three times, otherwise personnel remains the same as at first concert.

Telemann, Georg Philipp (*b* Magdeburg, 1681; *d* Hamburg, 1767). Ger. composer and organist. Self-taught by study of scores (esp. those of Lully and Campra). Org., Neuekirche, Leipzig, 1704, having already written several operas. Kapellmeister at Eisenach 1708–12, moving then to Frankfurt. In 1721 he went to Hamburg as Kantor of the Johanneum and mus. dir. of the 5 main churches. When in 1722 an attempt was made to prevent his taking part in operatic performances, he retaliated by applying for the vacant post of Kantor at the Thomaskirche, Leipzig. He was appointed, in preference to J. S. Bach, but Hamburg retained him by increasing his salary and appointing him mus. dir. of the Opera. Extremely prolific composer, skilled in counterpoint and of great facility, but his mus. has surface charm rather than depth. The best of it, however, is delightful. Among his voluminous output, which incl. 600 ovs. in the It. style, 44 Passions, 12 complete services, and 40 operas, are the following:

OPERAS: *Pimpinone* (1725); *Der geduldige Sokrates* (1721).

ORATORIOS: *Der Tag des Gerichts* (The Day of Judgement); *Die Tageszeiten* (The Times of Day); *Der Tod Jesu* (The Death of Jesus); *Die Auferstehung Christi* (The Resurrection of Christ); *St Luke Passion* (1728, 1744); *St Mark Passion* (1759); *St Matthew Passion* (1730).

CANTATAS: *Cantata oder Trauer-Musik eines kunsterfahrenen Kanarien-Vogels* (Funeral Music for a sweet-singing canary); *Der Schulmeister* (The Schoolmaster); *Die Landlust* (The Joy of Country Life); *In dulci jubilo*.

ORCH.: *Tafelmusik* (Table Music) I, II, and III; Suite, *Don Quichotte*, str. and b.c.; *La Lyra*, suite in E♭, str. and b.c.; concertos: 3 tpt., drums, 2 ob., str., b.c.; in G for vn., str., b.c.; A minor for concertino vn., str., b.c.; C major, 2 vn., str.; E minor, fl., str.; E minor, 2 fl., vn., str.; E minor, ob., str.; A major, ob. d'amore, str.; A minor, treble recorder, viola da gamba, str.; D major for D tpt., str.; D major, hn., str.; C major, 4 vn.; G major, 4 vn.; 12 12-part qts.

Also many trio sonatas, suites, fl. qts., etc.

Telephone, The. Opera in 1 act by *Menotti to his own lib. Comp. 1946. Prod. NY 1947, London 1948.

Tel jour telle nuit (Such a day, such a night). Song-cycle by Poulenc to 9 poems by Paul Eluard. Comp. 1936–7, f.p. by Pierre Bernac acc. Poulenc. Titles are: *Bonne Journée, Une Ruine coquille vide, Le Front comme un drapeau perdu, Une Roulotte couverte en tuile, À toutes brides, Une Herbe pauvre, Je n'ai envie que de t'aimer, Figure de force brûlante et farouche, Nous avons fait la nuit*.

Tellefsen, Arve (*b* Trondheim, 1948). Norweg. violinist. Prof. of vn., Oslo Acad. of Mus. from 1973. Won Harriet Cohen Award 1962. Soloist with int. orchs. Founded Oslo chamber mus. fest. 1989.

Teller (Ger.). Plate (e.g. of cymbal).

Telmányi, Emil (*b* Arad, Hung. (now Romania), 1892; *d* Holte, Denmark, 1988). Hung. violinist and conductor. Début, with Berlin PO 1911, when he gave f.p. on Continent of Elgar conc. Thereafter leading soloist and chamber-mus. player. London début 1923 on visit with *Nielsen, whose works he played and conducted (and whose daughter was his first wife). Founded own str. quintet. Cond. concerts in Europe, opera in Budapest. Supervised invention of special Vega (arched) bow (1954) for perf. of Bach's vn. works. Transcr. and arr. works by Handel, Beethoven, Brahms, etc. Settled in Copenhagen 1919. On staff Århus Cons. 1940–69.

tema (It.). Theme, as in *Tema con variazioni*, Theme and Variations.

Temirkanov, Yuri (*b* Nalchik, 1938). Russ. conductor. Cond. début Leningrad Opera 1965. Won USSR All-Union conductors' comp. 1966. Cond. Leningrad SO 1968–76, Kirov Opera and Ballet 1977. Salzburg Fest. 1971. Amer. tour 1978. Prin. guest cond. RPO 1979, prin. cond. 1992–5. Chief cond. Leningrad (now St Petersburg) PO from 1988, mus. dir. Baltimore SO 1999–2006.

temperament. Adjustment in tuning (i.e. 'tempering') of mus. intervals away from 'natural' scale so that such pairs of notes as B♯ and C, or C♯ and D♭, are combined instead of being treated individually. This leaves neither note accurate but sufficiently so for the ear to accept it. In kbd. instr. this avoids unmanageable number of finger-keys. The pf., organ, and other fixed-pitch modern instr., are tuned to *equal temperament*, in which each semitone is made an equal interval, making it easy to play in any key and to modulate. Before equal temperament (which was introduced for pfs. in Eng. in 1846 and for organs a little later), the commonest system was *mean-tone temperament*, which left certain keys tolerable, others less so, and some unusable. The untempered scale is known as *just intonation*. Instr. such as the vn. family can have no system of temperament, the player determining the pitch and checking it by ear. Some 20th-cent. composers have restored 12-note scale to *just* *intonation*. Others have used microtonal scales in just relationship. Still more have used 'prepared' instr. producing unexpected pitches, or elec. systems, or computers.

Temperley, Nicholas (*b* Beaconsfield, 1932). Eng.-born musicologist, composer, and pianist (Amer. cit. 1977). Ass. lect. in mus., Cambridge Univ. 1961–6. Ass. prof., Yale Univ. 1966–7; assoc. prof. Univ. of Illinois 1967 (prof. and chairman of musicology dept. 1972–5). Has written organ pieces. Ed. of *Pinto's pf. sonatas. Author of *The Music of the English Parish Church* (1979, 2 vols.). Ed. *Loder's opera *Raymond and Agnes* (prod. Cambridge 1966) and Berlioz's *Symphonie Fantastique* (new Berlioz edn., xvii, Kassel 1972, a collation of 14 versions). His realization of *The Beggar's Opera* perf. Illinois 1986. Completed and orch. one act of Mozart's *L'oca del Cairo*, prod. Illinois 1991.

Tempest, The. Play by Shakespeare (his last, 1612–13) for which various composers have written songs and incidental mus. Among works connected with the play are:

(1) *The Tempest*, incidental mus. Op.109, by *Sibelius, comp. 1925, in 34 parts for soloists, ch., harmonium, and orch. F.p. Copenhagen 1926. 2 orch. suites, with Prelude, No.1 of 9 items, No.2 of 9; f. Eng. p. of *Prelude*, Hastings 1930, of Suite 1, Leeds 1934.

(2) Symphonic-fantasy for orch., Op.18 by Tchaikovsky, 1873.

(3) Opera in 3 acts, *Der Sturm* (1952–5) by Frank *Martin, prod. Vienna 1956.

(4) Opera in 2 acts by *Sutermeister *Die Zauberinsel* (The Magic Island), prod. Dresden 1942.

(5) Incidental mus. by John *Weldon for Restoration version of play, *c*.1712.

(6) Symphonic prelude *The Magic Island* by *Alwyn, 1953.

(7) Opera in 3 acts by John C. Eaton, *The Tempest*, to lib. by Andrew Porter, prod. Santa Fe 1985.

(8) Opera in 3 acts by *Adès, lib. by M. Oakes, prod. CG 2004, Santa Fe 2006.

temple block. See *Korean temple block*.

Templeton, Alec (Andrew) (*b* Cardiff, 1909; *d* Greenwich, Conn., 1963). Welsh-born pianist and composer (Amer. cit. 1941). Blind from birth. After career in London as radio entertainer, settled in USA 1936. Wrote orch. and pf. works, but best-known for his witty 'skit', *Mr Bach Goes to Town*, a jazzed-up pastiche of Bach.

tempo, tempi (It.). Time(s). The speed at which a piece of mus. is perf. The anglicized 'tempos' is an acceptable plural, like 'concertos'. Among the many mus. terms containing the word are the following: *a tempo*, resume orig. speed; *tempo a piacere*, please yourself what speed; *tempo comodo*, at a comfortable or moderate speed; *tempo di ballo*, in dance time, or a movt. in dance style; *tempo di gavotta*, in gavotte tempo; *tempo di minuetto*, in minuet time; *tempo giusto*, in exact time, or at speed the style of the mus. demands; *tempo*

maggiore, same as *alla breve* (take the half-note as your beat unit); *tempo minore, tempo ordinario*, ordinary time, moderate speed, same speed as before; *tempo primo*, resume orig. speed; *tempo rubato*, see *rubato*; *tempo wie vorher* (Ger.), same as *tempo primo*.

temps (Fr.). Time, same as *tempo but also used in the sense of 'beat'.

ten. Short for (1) *tenor.

(2) *tenuto.

Tender Land, The. Opera in 2 acts by *Copland to lib. by H. Everett. Comp. 1952–4, rev. 1955. Prod. NY 1954, Cambridge 1962.

Tenducci, Giusto Ferdinando (*b* Siena, *c*.1736; *d* Genoa, 1790). It. male soprano. Went to London 1758, being hailed as Guadagni's successor. Sang in f.p. of Arne's *Artaxerxes*, 1762. Sang at King's Th., 1763–6 and in Dublin 1765–8. Sang at Handel Fests. 1784 and 1791. Mozart wrote song for him (lost). Wrote hpd. sonatas and treatise on singing. Last appearance 1785 as Orfeo (Gluck).

tenebroso (It.). Dark. Gloomy.

tenendo (It.). Sustaining, e.g. *tenendo il canto*, sustaining the melody.

tenero (It.). Tender. So *teneroso, teneramente*, tenderly; *tenerezza*, tenderness.

Tennstedt, Klaus (*b* Merseburg, 1926; *d* Kiel, 1998). Ger. conductor and violinist. Leader of theatre orch. at Halle 1948, becoming prin. cond. there 1953. Opera début 1952 (Wagner-Régeny's *Der Günstling*). On cond. staff, Dresden Opera, 1958–62; cond. Schwerin State Orch. 1962–71. Worked in Scandinavia from 1971, then in W. Ger. as mus. dir. Kiel Opera. Canada début 1974 (Toronto SO), Boston SO 1974, London 1976 (LSO). Prin. guest cond. Minnesota Orch. 1979–83. Prin. cond. N. Ger. Radio SO 1979–82. Salzburg Fest. 1982. Prin. cond. LPO 1983–7. NY Met début 1983 (*Fidelio*). Fine interpreter of Mahler. Retired 1994.

tenor (from It. *tenore*, 'holding'). (1) Highest normal male v., its name deriving from medieval times when it was the v. which carried the plainsong or other *cantus firmus* while other vv. sang a counterpoint. Range from C below middle C, upwards for 2 octaves. There are various categories of ten., e.g. *tenor di forza*, heroic ten., as for Verdi's Otello; *tenor di grazia*, lyrical ten., as Nemorino in *L'elisir d'amore*; *tenor robusto*, powerful ten., as Manrico in *Il trovatore*; *tenor spinto*, forceful lyric ten., as Rodolfo in *La bohème*; see also *counter-tenor* and *Heldentenor*.

(2) Name given to certain instr. deemed to be equivalent in range, etc., of ten. v., e.g. ten. sax., ten. tuba, etc.

(3) The va.

tenor clef. Type of clef, almost obsolete but still sometimes used for vc., ten. tb., bn., in which middle C is indicated on 2nd line down of staff.

tenor cor. The mellophone, instr. of hn.-like character but easier to play, used in some bands as substitute for hns.

tenuto (It.). Held. Direction to hold note to its full value, sometimes even longer.

Terfel [Jones], **Bryn** (*b* Pantglas, N. Wales, 1965). Welsh bass-baritone. Won Ferrier memorial schol. 1988, Cardiff Singer of the World *Lieder* prize 1989. Opera début Cardiff (WNO) 1990 (Guglielmo in *Così fan tutte*). Débuts: Amer. (Santa Fe) 1991; London (ENO) 1991; CG 1992; Salzburg Fest. 1992; Chicago 1993; Vienna 1993; NY Met 1994. Sang his first (stage) Wotan, CG 2004–5. Concert repertoire incl. Elgar, Britten, Vaughan Williams, Handel, Monteverdi, Schubert. CBE 2003. Queen's Medal for Music, 2006.

ternary. In 3 parts or sections. *ternary form* is the form of a movt. in 3 sections, the 3rd being an exact or near-exact repetition of first. Term still applies if first section is stated twice, making 4 sections but only 3 where subject-matter is concerned.

Ternina [Trnina], **Milka** (*b* Vesišće, 1863; *d* Zagreb, 1941). Croatian soprano. Opera début while student at Zagreb, 1882 (Amelia in *Un ballo in maschera*). Sang opera at Leipzig 1883–4; Graz 1884–6; Bremen 1886–9; Munich 1890–9. London début 1895; CG début 1898 singing regularly to 1906; Amer. début (Boston) 1896 (with Damrosch's German Opera Co.); NY Met 1900–4; Bayreuth 1899, but banned from Bayreuth after 1903 when she sang in 'pirate' *Parsifal* in NY. One of greatest singers of her day and type who excelled in Wagnerian roles. Forced by illness to retire, 1906. Taught at Inst. of Mus. Art, NY.

Terry, Charles Sanford (*b* Newport Pagnell, 1864; *d* Westerton of Pitfodels, Aberdeen, 1936). Eng. historian and music scholar. Chorister, St Paul's Cath. Prof. of history, Aberdeen Univ. 1903–30. Became interested in life and time of Bach, becoming leading authority of day on subject. Wrote life of Bach (1928, rev. 1933, 6th edn. 1967) and of J. C. Bach (1929), ed. Bach's chorales in 3 vols. (1915–21), also Mass in B minor, and arr. *Coffee Cantata* for stage under title *Coffee and Cupid* (1924; perf. by BNOC).

Terry, (Sir) **Richard** (Runciman) (*b* Ellington, Northumberland, 1865; *d* London, 1938). Eng. organist, conductor, composer, and scholar. Org. and choirmaster St John's Cath., Antigua, 1892–6, Downside Abbey 1896–1901. While at Downside revived church mus. by early Eng. composers, reviving Byrd's Masses for 5 and 3 vv. and works by Tallis, Taverner, etc. Org. and dir. of mus., Westminster Cath. 1901–24, where he raised standard of choral singing to new height, continued to revive Tudor mus., Palestrina, and others. Works specially written for Westminster Cath. choir by Howells, Stanford, Holst, Bax, and Vaughan Williams. Wrote 5 masses, *Requiem*, motets, etc. Ed. *Westminster Hymnal* 1912, and 2 vols. of Shanties. Knighted 1922.

Tertis, Lionel (*b* West Hartlepool, 1876; *d* Wimbledon, 1975). Eng. violist, son of Russ. father and Polish mother, both naturalized Britons. Took up va. at 19 to play in str. qt. Prof. of va. RAM from 1901. Prin. va. Queen's Hall Orch. 1900–4. Prin. va. Beecham Orch. 1909. Gave f.ps. of many works for va. written for him or as a result of his artistry. Devoted life to cause of va., then the 'Cinderella' of str. instr. Played in several str. qts. Dir. of ens. class, RAM 1924–9. Designed Tertis Model viola, 16¾″ long. Arr. and ed. many works for va., incl. Elgar vc. conc., Delius vn. sonatas, Brahms cl. sonatas. Many distinguished pupils. Last played in public at age of 87. CBE 1950.

terzetto (It.). Generally applied to a comp. for any combination of 3 vv., but also used sometimes (instead of trio) for instr. comps., e.g. Dvořák's *Terzetto* for 2 vn. and va., Op.74 (1887) and Holst's *Terzetto* for fl., ob., and va. (1925).

Teschemacher, Margarete (*b* Cologne, 1903; *d* Bad Wiessee, 1959). Ger. soprano. Opera début Cologne 1923 (Ruth in d'**Albert's *Die toten Augen*). Sang at Aachen 1925–7; Mannheim Opera 1928–31; Stuttgart 1931–4; Dresden 1935–46. Salzburg Fest. 1941. Created title-role in *Daphne* and was first Dresden *Capriccio* Countess. Joined Düsseldorf Opera 1947–52. CG début 1931. Admired in Strauss and as Jenůfa.

Teseo (Theseus). Opera in 5 acts by Handel to lib. by N. F. Haym after P. Quinault's lib. set by Lully as *Thésée* (1675). Comp. 1712. Prod. London 1713. Modern revivals Göttingen 1947, Manchester (RNCM) 1984, Boston 1985.

Tess. Opera in 4 acts by F. d'Erlanger to lib. by Illica, based on Hardy's novel *Tess of the d'Urbervilles* (1891). Prod. Naples 1906 and CG 1909 (with *Destinn as Tess).

tessitura (It.). Texture. Term which indicates prevailing or average position of a comp.'s notes in relation to compass of v. or instr. for which it was written, high, low, or medium.

testa, voce di. See *head voice*.

Testore, Carlo Giuseppe (*b*. Novara, *c*.1660; *d c*.1720). It. violin-maker, pupil of Grancino. Worked in Milan 1690–1715. Sometimes criticized for hasty construction. Instr. often branded with emblem of an eagle. His two sons, Carlo Antonio and Paolo Antonio, also made vns.

tetrachord (Gr. 'four string'). Succession of four notes contained within compass of a perfect fourth. In Ancient Gr. mus. a tetrachord consisted of 4 notes descending through a perfect fourth in the order tone-tone-semitone (A–G–F–E) and joined together to form a series of eight-note modes. The modern diatonic scale is divisible into two tetrachords (C–D–E–F, and G–A–B–C).

Tetrazzini, Eva (*b* Milan, 1862; *d* Salsomaggiore, 1938). It. soprano, sister of Luisa *Tetrazzini.

Opera début Florence 1882 (Marguérite in *Faust*). First NY Desdemona in *Otello* (1888). CG début 1890. Sang with Manhattan Opera, NY, 1908.

Tetrazzini, Luisa [Luigia] (*b* Florence, 1871; *d* Milan, 1940). It. soprano. Opera début Florence 1890 (Inez in *L'*Africaine*). Sang for several years in Argentina. Major success on Amer. début at S. Francisco 1904. CG début 1907 (to sensational acclaim); NY début Manhattan 1908; Met 1911; Chicago Grand Opera 1911–13. Concert appearances only after 1918 until 1934. Brilliant coloratura technique.

Teutsch. Mozart's (and Old Ger.) way of spelling *Deutsch* (Ger.) as in *Teutsche Tänze* (Ger. Dances).

Teyte, (Dame) **Maggie** [Margaret Tate] (*b* Wolverhampton, 1888; *d* London, 1976). Eng. soprano. Début Monte Carlo 1907 (Tyrcis in Offenbach's *Myriam et Daphné*). Sang Debussy's Mélisande, Paris, 1908, having studied role with composer. Paris Opéra-Comique 1908–10. London opera début 1910. Chicago Opera 1911–14; Boston 1914–17. BNOC from 1922. In inter-war years appeared also in mus. plays (*Monsieur Beaucaire*, *Tantivy Towers*, etc.). Last operatic role, Belinda in *Dido and Aeneas*, London 1951 (with *Flagstad). Superb interpreter of songs by Debussy, Fauré, Hahn, etc. DBE 1958. Annual prize in her memory.

Thaïs. Opera in 3 acts by Massenet to lib. by L. Gallet after the novel by Anatole France (1890). Comp. 1892–3, rev. 1897. Prod. Paris 1894, rev. vers. 1898; NY (Manhattan Op. Co.) 1907, Met 1917; CG 1911.

Thalben-Ball, (Sir) **George** (Thomas) (*b* Sydney, NSW, 1896; *d* Wimbledon, 1987). Australian-born organist and composer. Settled in Eng. Org., Temple Church, London, 1923–81, City of Birmingham, 1949. Mus. adviser to BBC religious broadcasting dept. 1941–69, and cond. BBC Singers. CBE 1967. Knighted 1982.

Thalberg, Sigismond (Fortuné François) (*b* Geneva, 1812; *d* Posillipo, 1871). Swiss-born Austrian pianist and composer. Public début 1826. London début 1830, followed by tour of Ger., playing his own conc. and other works. Paris 1835; London 1836, after which he and Liszt were regarded as two greatest rival virtuosi. Toured USA 1856 with Vieuxtemps, entering opera management. Wrote 2 operas, pf. conc., and many pf. works and songs. Contrib. to *Hexaméron*, 1837.

Thamos, König in Ägypten (Thamos, King of Egypt). Play by Tobias von Gebler for which Mozart comp. incidental mus. (K345) for prod. by Schikaneder's co. in Salzburg, 1780. Mozart had written 2 chs. for this play in Vienna in 1773 and these were rev. 1776 and 1779–80.

Thayer, Alexander Wheelock (*b* South Natick, Mass., 1817; *d* Trieste, 1897). Amer. writer. the biographer of Beethoven. While student, determined to write life of Beethoven and went to Ger., Austria, and Bohemia 1849–52 to begin coll. of material. Over next decade spent much

time interviewing people who had known Beethoven and examining documents. Book, entitled *Ludwig van Beethovens Leben*, was written in Eng., trans. into Ger. by H. Deiters of Bonn, and pubd. in Berlin, Vol. I (1770–96) in 1866, Vol. II (1797–1806) in 1872, Vol. III (1807–16) in 1879. Vol. IV was unfinished when he died and was completed by *Riemann and pubd. in 1907. Riemann pubd. Vol. V in 1908 and rev. of Vols. II and III in 1910–11. Eng. edn. in 3 vols. by H. E. Krehbiel was pubd. in NY, 1921, and by E. Forbes, pubd. in Princeton 1964, rev. 1967.

Theater an der Wien. Vienna th. built by *Schikaneder and opened 1801. Held 1,230 people. F.ps. of *Fidelio* (1805), *Die Fledermaus* (1874), and *Die *lustige Witwe* (1905) given there, also Viennese premières of several Rossini operas. Home of Vienna State Opera 1945–54 while Staatsoper was being rebuilt. Bought by city of Vienna 1961, renovated, and reopened 1962. Now used mainly for staging of musicals.

theatre organ. Org., also called cinema org., installed in cinemas in 1920s and 1930s to provide mus. during breaks in the programme. Usually a *unit org., with special effects. In 17th and 18th cents., the term applied to organs used in theatrical entertainments, operas, and concerts.

Thebom, Blanche (*b* Monessen, Penn., 1918). Amer. mezzo-soprano of Swed. parents. Concert début NY 1941. Opera début Philadelphia (Brangäne in *Tristan und Isolde*, with NY Met on tour). NY Met début 1944, singing with this company until 1967. Glyndebourne 1950; CG 1957. Later sang in operetta. Art. dir., Atlanta Opera co. 1967–8.

Theil (Ger.). See *Teil*.

thematic material. The themes, subjects, motifs, rhythmic figures, from which a comp. is constructed.

theme. Succession of notes which play important part in construction of a comp. Same as *subject*, but also refers to part of a subject. In *Theme and Variations*, means the mus. statement on which variations are built. *Theme-song* is an unspecific term with several meanings, e.g. in a mus. play or film, a theme-song is a song which recurs several times, or has a special significance in a plot, or is the song from which the play takes its title. Also, tune assoc. with a variety artist and played when he or she comes on to the stage to perform is called his or her 'theme song', like *signature-tune*.

Theodora. Oratorio by Handel to lib. by T. Morell. F.p. London 1750. Staged as opera, Glyndebourne 1996.

Theodorakis, Mikis (*b* Chios, Gr., 1925). Gr. composer. Lived in Paris 1953–61. Arrested as Communist after Greek military coup and imprisoned 1967–70. Works incl. 5 operas; ballets;

oratorios; 7 syms.; pf. conc.; *7 Songs of Lorca*; *Requiem*; and mus. for films *Zorba the Greek* (1964) and *The Man with the Carnation* (1980).

theorbo (Fr. *théorbe*, Ger. *Theorb*, It. *tiorba*; possibly from Arabic *tarab*). Renaissance instr., a larger type of *lute (but not so large as *chittarone). Used as accompanying instr., but solo repertory exists. Resonant lower register, caused by longer fingerboard and greater str. length. Probably developed in It.; first mentioned 1544. Had between 14 and 16 courses, plus extra bass str. Gut str. Often used for continuo instead of organ and hpd. in Eng. 17th-cent. songs. Handel scored for it in *Esther* (1732) and *Athalia* (1733). Modern revivals for early mus. perf.

theremin. 'Space-controlled' elec. instr. developed by the Russian, Lev Theremin (*b* St Petersburg, 1896; *d* Moscow, 1993), and first publicly demonstrated in the Soviet Union 1920. Introduced to USA 1927. 'Space-controlled' means that it is played by movts. of the hands, which do not touch the instr. The theremin is built like a radio receiver, with an antenna protruding from the right and a metal loop on the left. The mus. is prod. by 2 high-frequency circuits, employing oscillating (thermionic) valves, one being at constant frequency while that of the other is altered when the player moves his hand through the air in front of the antenna. The resultant oscillation is called 'heterodyning' ('beating together'), and the heterodyne frequency can be made audible by amplification through a loud-speaker. Vol. is controlled by a switch and by the movt. of the player's left hand over the metal loop. Sounds similar to the human v. or to those of about 7 instr. can be prod. Plays only one note at a time; range of 5 octaves. First comp. to use instr. was Pashchenko's *Symphonic Mystery*, for theremin and orch., Leningrad, 1924. Martinů wrote a *Fantasy* for theremin, str. qt., ob., and pf. Instr. was further developed by *Moog and was used by the Beach Boys in 'hit' *Good Vibrations*, 1966.

Theresienmesse (Theresa Mass). Nickname of Haydn's Mass No.10 in B♭, comp. 1799, referring to consort of Emperor Francis II of Austria.

These Things Shall Be. Cantata for bar. (or ten.) solo, ch., and orch. by *Ireland, text taken from *A Vista* by J. A. Symonds (1840–93). Comp. 1936–7, f.p. 1937. Originally quoted the *Internationale*, but this reference was later removed by Ireland.

Thespis, or The Gods Grown Old. 'Grotesque opera' by Sullivan to lib. by Gilbert (their first collab.). Score now lost. Prod. London 1871.

Thibaud, Jacques (*b* Bordeaux, 1880; *d* in air crash near Mt. Cemet, Fr. Alps, 1953). Fr. violinist. Début Paris 1898. Soloist many times in 1898 with Colonne Orch., Paris. Thereafter world tours. Salzburg Fest. 1932. Member of pf. trio

with Cortot and Casals. Taught at École Normale de Musique, Paris. With Marguerite Long, founded Long-Thibaud comp., 1943.

Thibaudet, Jean-Yves (*b* Lyons, 1961). Fr. pianist. Entered Lyons Cons. at age of 5, winning gold medal 1974. Paris Cons. 1974–81, winning *premier prix* in pf. and chamber mus. NY recital 1989. Fine exponent of Fr. music.

Thielemann, Christian (*b* Berlin, 1959). Ger. conductor. Studied va., pf., and cond. at Berlin High Sch. for Mus. Staff cond. Düsseldorf Opera 1985. Gen. dir. Nuremberg Opera 1988–92. Vienna Opera début 1987 (*Così fan tutte*), CG 1988 (*Jenůfa*), Bayreuth Fest. 2000 (*Meistersinger*). Vienna PO début 2000. Salzburg Easter Fest. 2002 (Berlin PO), Salzburg Fest. 2002 (Vienna PO). Gen. mus. dir. Deutsche Oper, Berlin, 1997–2004. Cond. Munich PO from 2004. Bayreuth Fest. *Ring* 2006.

Thieving Magpie, The (Rossini). See *Gazza ladra, La*.

Things to Come. Korda film (1935) based on H. G. Wells's futuristic novel *Shape of Things to Come* (1933) for which Bliss wrote the mus. and from which he later arr. an orch. suite, the March being especially well known.

third (noun). Melodic and harmonic interval, reckoned as taking 3 steps in scale (major or minor) counting bottom and top notes, thus, *major third* (C up to E) or *minor third* (C up to E♭) or *diminished third* (C♯ up to E♭).

third inversion. In harmony, when determining lay-out of a chord, that inversion in a 4-note chord in which 4th note becomes the bass is the *third inversion*, e.g. in chord G–B–D–F, the form F–G–B–D or F–B–G–D, etc.

third stream. Term coined in 1950s by Gunther *Schuller to describe mus. in which the styles of both jazz and concert works are combined.

thirty-second note. Demisemiquaver, notated ♪, with rest notated as ♪.

This Day (Vaughan Williams). See *Hodie*.

This Have I Done for my True Love. Work for unacc. ch., Op.34, by Holst, comp. 1916. Setting of traditional carol.

Thomas, (Charles Louis) **Ambroise** (*b* Metz, 1811; *d* Paris, 1896). Fr. composer. *Prix de Rome* 1832. Wrote some ballets for Paris Opéra, but from 1840 concentrated on operas for Opéra-Comique, achieving greatest success with *Mignon (1866) and *Hamlet (1868). Prof. of comp. Paris Cons. from 1856, dir. from 1871. Other stage works incl. *Le songe d'une nuit d'été* (1850), *Raymond* (1851), *Le *Carnaval de Venise* (1857), and *Françoise de Rimini* (1882). Also wrote choral works, *Fantasia* for pf. and orch., chamber mus., and songs.

Thomas, David (*b* Orpington, 1943). Eng. bass. Came to prominence as soloist with A. Rooley's

Consort of Musicke, C. Hogwood's Academy of Ancient Music, and other early music groups. Opera début 1981, Kent Opera (Pluto in Monteverdi's *Il Ballo delle ingrate*). Amer. début (Hollywood Bowl) 1984; Los Angeles 1988.

Thomas, Jess (Floyd) (*b* Hot Springs, S. Dakota, 1927; *d* Tiburon, Calif., 1993). Amer. tenor. Opera début S. Francisco 1957 (Malcolm in *Macbeth*). Career then mainly in Ger., singing at Karlsruhe for 3 years. Débuts: Bayreuth 1961; NY Met 1962; Munich 1963; Salzburg Fest. 1964; CG 1969. Created Caesar in Barber's *Antony and Cleopatra* (1966), but best known for his singing of Strauss and Wagner (Walther).

Thomas, Michael Tilson (*b* Hollywood, Calif., 1944). Amer. conductor and pianist. Ass. cond. to Boulez at Ojai Fest., 1967. Ass. cond. Boston SO 1969, assoc. cond. 1970. Mus. dir. Buffalo PO 1971–9. London début with LSO 1970, prin. cond. LSO 1988–95. Cond. f. Amer. p. 3-act *Lulu* (Santa Fe 1979). Salzburg Fest. début 1988. Prin. cond. S. Francisco SO from 1995. Also many comps., incl. *From the Diary of Anne Frank*, narr., orch. (1990); *Shówa/Shoáh*, orch. (1995); *3 Whitman Songs*, bar., orch. (1999); *Poems of Emily Dickinson*, sop., orch. (2002).

Thomas, Mansel (Treharne) (*b* Tylorstown, Rhondda Valley, 1909; *d* Abergavenny, 1986). Welsh composer and conductor. Mus. ass. BBC Welsh Region 1936–40. Cond. BBC Revue Orch. 1941–3. Cond. BBC Welsh Orch. 1946–50. Head of Mus., BBC Wales 1950–65. Comp. operetta, *Breton Suite*, religious and secular choral works, str. qt., songs. OBE 1970.

Thomas, Theodore (*b* Esens, Hanover, 1835; *d* Chicago, 1905). Ger.-born conductor (Amer. cit.). Taken to USA in 1845. Played vn. and hn. Played vn. in *Jullien's orch. 1853, in NYPO 1854. Leader of NY Acad. of Mus. Orch., 1856, taking over at short notice as cond. for perf. of *La Juive* in 1858. Formed own orch. 1862 and gave concerts in many inland cities which had never before heard an orch., always incl. some unfamiliar work. Dir., Philadelphia Centennial Concerts 1876. Cond., Brooklyn PO 1862–3, 1866–8, 1873–8. Cond., NYPO 1877–8, 1879–91; dir., Cincinnati Coll. of Mus. 1878–9; First cond. Chicago SO 1891–1905. Always progressive in his taste, introduced many modern works to USA, e.g. f.p. of R. Strauss's F minor Sym. in NY 1884.

Thompson, Oscar (*b* Crawfordsville, Ind., 1887; *d* NY, 1945). Amer. critic, author, and editor. Critic for *Musical America* 1919, becoming ed. 1936–43. Mus. critic *NY Evening Post* 1928–34, *NY Sun* from 1937. Taught at Curtis Inst. and Columbia Univ. Wrote book on Debussy. Ed.-in-chief, *International Cyclopedia of Music and Musicians* (1st–3rd edns.).

Thompson, Randall (*b* NY, 1899; *d* Boston, Mass., 1984). Amer. composer and teacher. Various teaching posts, then prof. of mus., Univ. of Calif. at Berkeley, 1937–9. Dir., Curtis Inst. 1938–

40. Head of mus. dept., Virginia Univ., 1941–6. Prof. of mus., Princeton Univ. 1946–8, Harvard Univ. 1948–65. Comp. 2 operas; ballet; 3 syms. (1929–49); many choral works, incl. *St Luke Passion* (1965); unacc. *Requiem* and *Americana*, and str. qt. *The Wind in the Willows*.

Thomson, Bryden (*b* Ayr, 1928; *d* Dublin, 1991). Scottish conductor. Ass. to Ian *Whyte with BBC Scottish Orch. 1958–62. Cond. opera at Oslo and Stockholm. Prin. cond. BBC Northern SO 1968–73; mus. dir. Ulster Orch. 1977–85; chief guest cond. Trondheim SO; prin. cond. BBC Welsh SO 1978–82, Radio Telefis Eireann SO, Dublin, 1984–7, SNO from 1988 to his death.

Thomson, George (*b* Limekilns, Dunfermline, 1757; *d* Leith, 1851). Scot. publisher and educationist. Secretary, board of trustees for encouragement of arts and manufactures in Scotland 1780–1830. Collected folk-songs. Commissioned Haydn, Pleyel, and Beethoven to compose accs. for Scottish and Welsh songs. Haydn made 187 Scots settings for Thomson (and a further 221 for another Edinburgh publisher) and Beethoven 126. Those by Haydn pubd. in Vols. 3 and 4 of Scottish Songs (1802, 1805), 4 in Vol. 5 (1818), 12 in Vol. 6 (1841) and some in 2nd edn. of Vol. 2 (1803). Of those by Beethoven, 26 were in Vol. 5 and 13 in Vol. 6. Of Haydn's Welsh songs, 20 were in Vol. 1 (1809), 17 in Vol. 2 (1811), and 4 in Vol. 3 (1814); of Beethoven's, 26 in Vol. 3. In 1818–20, Beethoven wrote variations on a dozen Scot. melodies, pubd. by Thomson, and in 1825 Weber arr. 10 Scots songs for him. In view of Haydn's age, some scholars believe many of his arrs. must have been done by pupils or associates.

Thomson, Virgil (Garnett) (*b* Kansas City, 1896; *d* NY, 1989). Amer. composer, critic, and organist. Mus. child prodigy. Wrote criticism for *Vanity Fair*. Lived in Paris 1925–32, associating with *Les Six* and Gertrude Stein. Returned to NY permanently 1940, becoming mus. critic of *Herald-Tribune* until 1954. Had considerable success with comic opera *Four Saints in Three Acts*, lib. by Stein, prod. 1934, followed in 1947 by *The Mother of Us All*, also to a Stein lib. Wrote several successful film scores (incl. *Louisiana Story*, 1948) and much incidental mus., esp. for Shakespeare plays. Influenced by Debussy and Satie. Inveterate champion of 20th-cent. mus. A waspish, occasionally percipient, critic. Works incl.:

OPERAS: *Four Saints in Three Acts* (1927–8, orch. 1933); *The Mother of Us All* (1947); *Lord Byron* (1961–8).

ORCH.: 3 syms. (1928, 1931 rev. 1941, 1972, 3rd being transcr. of 2nd str. qt., 1932); *Suite* (*Portraits*) Nos. 1 and 2 (1944); vc. conc. (1949); *Ode to the Wonders of Nature*, brass, perc. (1965); *A Love Scene* (1982).

CHAMBER MUSIC: 2 str. qts. (1931, rev. 1957, 1932, rev. 1957); *5 Portraits*, 4 cl. (1929); *4 Portraits*, vn., pf. (1931); *7 Portraits*, vn. (1928).

VOCAL: *Capital, Capitals*, 4 male vv., pf. (1927). Also 4 pf. sonatas and other works, songs, etc.

Thorborg, Kerstin (*b* Venjan, 1896; *d* Falun, Dalarna, 1970). Swed. mezzo-soprano. Début Royal Opera Stockholm 1924 as Ortrud (*Lohengrin*). Stockholm Opera 1924–30; Prague 1932–3; Berlin 1933–5; Vienna 1935–8. Salzburg Fest. 1935–7; CG début 1936; NY Met 1936–50. Mainly Wagner and Strauss operatic roles. Soloist in famous 1936 Bruno Walter recording in Vienna of *Das *Lied von der Erde*.

thoroughbass. See *basso continuo*.

Three Choirs Festival. Name for the annual meeting of the 3 (Cath.) Choirs of Gloucester, Hereford, and Worcester, held by rotation in these cities. First was held probably in 1715 with aim of alleviating poverty of widows and orphans of clergy in the 3 dioceses. Early meetings lasted 2 days, and in 18th cent. mus. of Handel was frequently perf. In 1737 William Boyce was engaged for Worcester as chief cond. of fest. *Messiah* was first oratorio to be perf. complete in the caths. (Hereford 1759, Worcester 1761, Gloucester 1769). In 19th cent., 'star' singers became chief attractions and the mus. of Mendelssohn the staple fare. In 1875 the church authorities at Worcester refused use of the cath. because the perfs. could not be equated with the idea of worship. In the 2nd half of the 19th cent. the fests. became a leading forum for Eng. oratorios etc., from Sullivan's *The Prodigal Son* (1869) to Parry's *Job* in 1892. In 1878 one of the orch. violinists was a local man, Edward Elgar (a Catholic), who was to become the prin. figure at the fests. from 1902 to 1933, although few of his works were specially written for the 3 Choirs. Exceptions were *Froissart* (1890), *Lux Christi* (1896), and the *Te Deum and Benedictus* (1897). The organists at this period, Ivor Atkins (Worcester), G. R. Sinclair (Hereford), and Herbert Brewer (Gloucester) were Elgar's friends, Sinclair being immortalized by G.R.S. in the *Enigma Variations*. Elgar cond. *Gerontius* at Worcester, 1902; thereafter his conducting of his own major works was the foundation of the programmes each year. Other composers who came to be assoc. with the 20th-cent. fests. were Coleridge-Taylor, Walford Davies, Vaughan Williams (several of whose works had f.ps. at the fests., e.g. *Tallis Fantasia, 5 Mystical Songs* and *Hodie*), Holst (*Choral Fantasia*), Bliss, Howells, Finzi, etc. Sibelius's *Luonnotar* had f.p. at Gloucester in 1913, and Kodály's *Psalmus Hungaricus* was cond. by the composer there in 1928. There were no fests. 1914–19 but they resumed at Worcester in 1920. A similar break occurred 1939–45. Since 1945 the programmes, both sacred and secular, have been much expanded and a more adventurous policy has been followed. For many years the LSO led by W. H. Reed provided the chief orch. support, but the RPO, CBSO, RLPO and BBC Philharmonic have lately been engaged. Works by John McCabe, Geoffrey Burgon, Philip Cannon, Malcolm Williamson, Jonathan Harvey, Gordon Crosse, Maxwell Davies, Christopher Steel, Paul Patterson, William Mathias, Howard

Blake, and others have been commissioned or performed, and the programmes have been broadened to include Mahler's 8th Sym., David Fanshawe's *African Sanctus*, and Walton's *Belshazzar's Feast* (for many years regarded as too 'barbaric' for these surroundings).

Three-Cornered Hat, The (*El sombrero de tres picos*; Fr. *Le Tricorne*). 1-act ballet with mus. by Falla, choreog. by Massine, and scenario by Martinez Sierra based on P. A. de Alarcon's story *El sombrero de tres picos* (1874). F.p. London 1919 (Diaghilev Ballets Russes). Rev. version of pantomime by Sierra and Falla, *El corregidor y la molinera*, Madrid 1917. Same plot as *Wolf's opera *Der *Corregidor*.

Threepenny Opera, The (Weill). See *Dreigroschenoper, Die*.

Three Places in New England. Orch. work (with optional org.) by *Ives, also known as *Orchestral Set No.1*. Comp. 1908–14. Movts. are 1. *Boston Common: Colonel Shaw and his Colored Regiment*. 2. *Putnam's Camp*. 3. *The Housatonic at Stockbridge*. F.p. NY 1931, f.p. in England, London 1960.

Three Screaming Popes. Orch. work by Mark-Anthony Turnage based on painting by Francis Bacon. Comp. 1988–9. F.p. Birmingham (CBSO cond. Rattle), 1989.

Three Tenors, The. Collaboration, inaugurated by It. manager Mario Dradi, between tenors José *Carreras, Plácido *Domingo, and Luciano *Pavarotti. Début Baths of Caracalla, Rome, 7 July 1990 (eve of World Cup football final), with orch. cond. by Zubin *Mehta, to raise money for Carreras's foundation for leukaemia research. Great commercial success. Further concerts, produced by Tibor Rudas, usually in large outdoor venues, in Los Angeles 1994 (Mehta), Paris 1998 (Mehta), and Yokohama 2002 (James *Levine), as well as in other cities. Huge sales of CDs and DVDs.

Threni (id est Lamentationes Jeremiae Prophetae) (That is to say, the lamentations of the Prophet Jeremiah). Setting of biblical words for 6 soloists (sop., cont., 2 ten., bass, basso profundo), mixed ch., and orch. by *Stravinsky. Comp. 1957–8. F.p. Venice 1958, f.p. in England, London 1959.

threnody. Dirge.

through-composed (Ger. *Durchkomponiert*). See *Durch* and *Strophic*.

Thuille, Ludwig (Wilhelm Andreas Mario) (*b* Bozen, Tyrol, 1861; *d* Munich, 1907). Ger. composer. Prof., Munich Sch. of Mus. from 1883. Friend of R. Strauss, who cond. several of his early works. Wrote 3 operas: *Theuerdank* (1893–5), *Lobetanz* (1896), and *Gugeline* (1898–1900), also sym. (1886), pf. quintet (1897–1901), sextet for wind and pf., vc. sonata, vn. sonata, org. sonata, 78 songs, and pf. pieces.

Thule, the Period of Cosmography. Madrigal for 6 vv. by *Weelkes pubd. 1600; one of most remarkable examples of mus. settings of ostensibly unmus. words.

thunder machine. Theatrical contraption for imitating sound of thunder, required by some composers in their scores, e.g. Strauss for *Eine Alpensinfonie*.

thunder stick, bull roarer, whizzer (Ger. *Schwirrholz*, 'whirlingwood'; Fr. *planchette ronflante*, 'roaring board'). Instr. in use among Amer. Indians, Australian aborigines, natives of Central Africa, etc. A thin, flat piece of wood, swung to produce a whirring noise, rising or falling in pitch with changing speed of motion.

Thurston, Frederick (John) (*b* Lichfield, 1901; *d* London, 1953). Eng. clarinettist. Prin. cl. BBC SO 1930–46 and other orchs. Prof. of cl., RCM. Several Eng. composers (e.g. Bliss, Howells, Finzi, Bax) wrote works for him. CBE 1952.

Thus Spake Zoroaster (Strauss). See *Also sprach Zarathustra*.

Tibbett [Tibbet], **Lawrence** (Mervil) (*b* Bakersfield, Calif., 1896; *d* NY, 1960). Amer. baritone. Began career as actor, then sang in light opera. Opera début Los Angeles 1923 (Amonasro in *Aida*). NY Met 1923. Made name as Ford in *Falstaff*, NY Met 1925. S. Francisco Opera 1927–49; Chicago 1936–46. CG début 1937. Sang at Met until 1950. Outstanding as Iago and in other Verdi roles, and Puccini roles. Sang in early recording of extracts from *Porgy and Bess*. Made several films. Equally popular as concert singer. Autobiography *The Glory Road* (NY 1933).

tibia. Org. stop, not brilliant but full-toned. Varieties are: *tibia major* (8' or 16' length and pitch); *tibia minor* (4' or 8'); *tibia plena* (8', loud); *tibia profunda* (16'); *tibia dura* (4', hard in tone); *tibia clausa* (4').

tie (or bind). Curved line placed over note and its repetition to indicate that the 2 shall be perf. as one unbroken note of their combined timevalue. Thus *tied note*. See also *slur* and *curved lines*.

tief (Ger.). Deep, low, thus *tiefgespannt*, deepstretched, i.e. of a drum, so as to give a low sound.

Tiefland (Lowland). Opera in prol. and 3 acts by d'*Albert, to text by R. Lothar (Rudolph Spitzer) after Catalan play *Terra baixa* by A. Guimerá. Prod. Prague 1903, NY (revised version) 1908, CG 1910.

tierce (Fr. noun). Third. (1) Interval of a 3rd, major or minor.
(2) 4th of series of natural harmonics.
(3) Org. stop of same pitch as similarly-named harmonic.

tierce de Picardie (Fr.). Picardy third. Term applied to major 3rd used at end of a comp. which

is otherwise in a minor key, thus converting expected minor chord into major, e.g. in key of C minor the expected chord C–E♭–G becomes C–E–G. Commonly used up to end of 18th cent. Reason for name unknown.

Tietjen, Heinz (*b* Tangier, 1881; *d* Baden-Baden, 1967). Ger. conductor, producer, and opera director. Cond. and producer at Trier 1904–7, intendant 1907–22. Intendant at Breslau 1922–4, Berlin City Opera 1925–30, Berlin City Opera 1927–45. Art. dir., Bayreuth Fest. 1931–44; Intendant Berlin City Opera 1948–54, Hamburg 1954–9. Prod. CG 1950 and 1951. Last conducted at Bayreuth 1959.

Tietjens, Thérèse (Carolina Johanna Alexandra) (*b* Hamburg, 1831; *d* London, 1877). Ger. soprano. Opera début Altona 1849 (title-role in *Lucrezia Borgia*). Frankfurt Opera 1850–6; Vienna 1856–9. London début 1858, thereafter settling in Eng. CG début 1868. Sang in NY 1874 and 1876. One of great opera and oratorio singers of her day, famous as Norma and Donna Anna. Was first to sing Marguerite in *Faust* in London (1863), also created several Verdi roles for London.

Till Eulenspiegel. Tone-poem for orch., Op.28, by R. Strauss, full title being *Till Eulenspiegels lustige Streiche, nach alter Schelmenweise–in Rondeauform–für grosses Orchester gestetzt* (Till Eulenspiegel's merry pranks, in the manner of an old rogue–in rondo form–set for full orchestra). Comp. 1894–5, f.p. Cologne 1895 cond. Wüllner. Strauss abandoned idea of opera on the subject 1893–4. Till's adventures were first told in a 15th-cent. book and remain part of Ger. folklore. Other composers who have treated the subject incl. Alpaerts (symphonic poem), Blockx (opera, 1900), Jeremiáš (opera, 1949), Rezniček (opera, 1902), and M. Steinberg (ballet). Strauss's score has been basis of several ballets, incl. one by Nijinsky (1916).

Tilney, Colin (*b* London, 1933). Eng. harpsichordist. Soloist and ens. performer since 1960s. Amer. début 1971. Plays kbd. works on most appropriate instr., using clavichords and early pianos (historical and modern replica). Ed. of Forqueray's hpd. mus. Has recorded *Parthenia* and complete kbd. works of Locke.

Tilson Thomas, Michael. See *Thomas, Michael Tilson*.

timbales. Pair of single-headed cylindrical drums, usually assoc. with Latin-Amer. dance orch. but also used by composers of modern orch. mus., e.g. Lipkin in *Interplay* (1975), who uses six instead of timpani.

timbre (Fr.; Ger. *Klangfarbe*). Tone-colour; that which distinguishes the quality of tone or v. of one instr. or singer from another, e.g. fl. from cl., sop. from mez., etc.

timbrel. Medieval tambourine. Also Hebrew instr. in biblical times, thought to be similar to tambourine.

time. Fundamental rhythmical patterns of mus., e.g. 3/8 time = three 8th-notes to the measure. One speaks of waltz time (3/4) and march time (usually 2/4), and more generally of 'quick time'.

time signature. Sign placed after the clef and *key-signature at the beginning of a piece of music, or during the course of it, to indicate the time or metre of the music. Normally it comprises two numbers, one above the other, the lower defining the unit of measurement in relation to the whole-note, the upper indicating the number of those units in each measure (bar). Thus the time signature 3/4 indicates three quarter-notes (crotchets) to the measure, one of 6/8 that there are six eighth-notes (quavers) in the measure. But see also *compound time* and *simple time*.

timpani (It.). See *drum*.

Tinctoris, Johannes (*b* Braine l'Allend, *c*.1435; *d* ?1511). Franco-Flemish theorist and composer. Entered service of King of Naples *c*.1472 as tutor to King's daughter. His treatise *Terminorum musicae diffinitorium* (Treviso, 1495) was probably written in 1472. It contains 299 definitions of terms then in use. His *Liber de arte contrapuncti* (1477) contains principles of consonance and dissonance and discussions on counterpoint. Comp. several masses and secular songs. Was also painter, lawyer, and mathematician.

Tinsley, Pauline (Cecilia) (*b* Wigan, 1928). Eng. soprano. Opera début London 1961 (Desdemona in Rossini's *Otello*). Sang with WNO 1962–72; SW 1963–74; CG début 1965. Returned to WNO 1975–81. Amer. début Santa Fe 1969. Well known for Verdi roles such as Lady Macbeth, also for Janáček and Strauss.

Tintagel. Orchestral tone-poem by Bax, comp. 1917–19. F.p. London, 1920. Quotes motif from Wagner's *Tristan und Isolde*.

tin-whistle. 6-holed keyless wind instr. made of metal. Also called penny-whistle.

Tiomkin, Dimitri (*b* St Petersburg, 1894; *d* London, 1979). Russ.-born composer and pianist (Amer. cit. 1937). Toured Europe as pianist. Amer. cond. début 1928. Settled in USA 1929 and wrote over 150 film scores 1930–70, incl. those for *Mr Smith Goes to Washington* (1939), *Duel in the Sun* (1946), *High Noon* (1952), *Dial M for Murder* (1954), *The Alamo* (1960), *The Guns of Navarone* (1961), and many more. Autobiography *Please Don't Hate Me* (1959).

tiple (Sp.). Soprano or upper v. Also means a small guitar.

Tippett, (Sir) **Michael** (Kemp) (*b* London, 1905; *d* London, 1998). Eng. composer. Studied RCM 1923–8 (comp. with Charles Wood, cond. with Boult and Sargent). Became schoolmaster and cond. choral soc.; in 1930 studied counterpoint and fugue privately with R. O. Morris. Cond. S. London Orch. (of unemployed) at Morley Coll., 1933–40. Mus. dir., Morley Coll. 1940–51, dir. of Bath Fest. 1969–74. Imprisoned during 1943 for failure to comply with conditions of his conscientious exemption from military service. Autobiography *Those Twentieth Century Blues* (1991). CBE 1959. Knighted 1966. CH 1979. OM 1983.

Tippett's life was his mus. A late developer, he did not achieve any kind of recognition until 1935 with his first str. qt. The work which made his name more familiar was the Conc. for Double Str. Orch. (1938–9). His oratorio *A Child of Our Time*, comp. 1939–41, was among the first of his works which reconcile personal vision with expression of 'collective' feeling. After 6 years of work he completed his first opera, *The Midsummer Marriage*, in 1952. Though not successful until its revival over 20 years later, this opera marks the culmination of Tippett's early lyrical style, a style that is complex in its madrigalian, contrapuntal, inter-weaving but which repays close study. He entered a tougher middle phase in 1962 with the opera *King Priam* and the 2nd pf. sonata, works of rhetoric and drama. This period culminated in the *Concerto for Orchestra* and the elaborate choral work *The Vision of St Augustine*. With the opera *The Knot Garden* (1969) Tippett entered a 3rd period in which he fused his 2 earlier periods, the 'lyrical' and the 'disjunct', as they have been called, and also extended his bounds by reference to popular and serious mus., past and present, e.g. 'blues', quotations from Monteverdi, and a tighter control of form as shown in the 3rd pf. sonata and the 4th sym. Yet, like all great composers, Tippett remained essentially himself, and the flowing lines of the Double Conc. are still discernible in *King Priam*, just as the exuberant, life-enhancing lyricism of *The Midsummer Marriage* spills over into the pf. conc., the *Corelli Fantasia*, the 4th sym., the Triple Conc., and the last of his operas, the 'space-age' *New Year*. But perhaps the most comprehensive synthesis of his work is the huge oratorio *The Mask of Time*, while in his 5th str. qt. he achieved an ethereal epigrammatic serenity. Some of his determinedly popular passages in recent years, as in the opera *The Ice Break*, may come to sound increasingly self-conscious, but this is part of the price to be paid for Tippett's open-eyed, even naive outlook on the world expressed in mus. of exceptional technical sophistication. Prin. works:

OPERAS: *The *Midsummer Marriage* (1946–52); *King Priam* (1958–61); *The *Knot Garden* (1966–70); *The *Ice Break* (1973–6); *New Year* (1986–8).

ORCH.: syms.: No.1 (1944–5, f.p. 1945), No.2 (1956–7, f.p. 1958), No.3, sop., orch. (1970–2, f.p. 1972), No.4 (1976–7, f.p. 1977); conc. for double str. orch. (1938–9); *Fantasia on a Theme of Handel*, pf., orch. (1939–41); *Little Music*, str. (1946); *Ritual Dances from The Midsummer Marriage* (1947–52); *Suite in D for the Birthday of Prince Charles* (1948); *Fantasia Concertante on a Theme of Corelli*, str. (1953); *Divertimento on Sellinger's Round* (1953–4); pf. conc. (1953–5); *Concerto for Orchestra* (1962–3); conc. for str. trio and orch. (1978–9); *Water Out of*

Sunlight (arr. for str. by M. Bowen of 4th str. qt.) (1988); *New Year Suite* (1989); *The Rose Lake* (1991–3).

CHORAL: *A *Child of Our Time*, SATB soloists, ch., orch. (1939–41); *The Source* and *The Windhover*, unacc. ch. (1942); *Plebs angelica*, unacc. double ch. (1943); *The Weeping Babe*, sop., ch. (1944); *Dance, Clarion Air*, 5 vv. (1952); *4 Songs from the British Isles*, ch. (1956); *Wadhurst*, ch. (1958); *Crown of the Year*, women's ch., chamber ens. (1958); *Music*, vv., str., pf. or vv., pf. (1960); *Magnificat and Nunc Dimittis* (1961); *The *Vision of St Augustine*, bar., ch., orch. (1963–5); *The Shires Suite*, ch., orch. (1965–70); *The *Mask of Time*, sop., mez., ten., bar., ch., orch. (1980–2).

VOICE & ORCH./INSTR.: **Boyhood's End*, ten., pf. (1943); *The *Heart's Assurance*, v., pf. (1950–1, vers. for v. and orch., arr. M. Bowen 1990); *'Words for Music, Perhaps'*, narr., ens. (1960); *Songs for Achilles*, ten., gui. (1961); *Songs for Ariel*, v., pf. (or v., hpd. or v., ens.) (1962); **Songs for Dov*, ten., small orch. (1970); *Byzantium*, sop., orch. (1989–90).

CHAMBER MUSIC: str. qts.: No.1 (1934–5, rev. 1943), No.2 (1941–2), No.3 (1945–6), No.4 (1977–8), No.5 (1990–1); *4 Inventions*, descant and treble recorders (1954); *Sonata for 4 Horns* (1955); *In memoriam magistri*, fl., cl., str. qt. (1971); *The Blue Guitar*, gui., (1982–3); *Prelude: Autumn*, ob., pf. (1991).

PIANO: *sonatas*: No.1 (1936–7, rev. 1942, 1954), No.2 (1962), No.3 (1972–3), No.4 (1984).

ORGAN: *Preludio al Vespro di Monteverdi* (1946).

BRASS: fanfare No.1 (1943), No.2 (1953), No.3 (1953), No.4 (*Wolf Trap*) (1980), No.5 (1987); *Festal Brass with Blues* (1983); *Suite in D for the Birthday of Prince Charles* (arr. Brian Bowen, 1983); *Triumph*, concert band (1992).

EDITIONS (in collab. with W. Bergmann): J. S. Bach: songs, *Amore traditore*, cantata for bass, *If thou art near*, *Come sweet death*, and *Jesu, in thy love*; Handel: *Lucretia*, cantata for sop.; Humfrey: *A Hymne to God the Father*; Purcell: *Come ye sons of art*, sop., 2 altos, bass, ch., orch., *Ode for St Cecilia's Day* (1692), sop., 2 altos, ten., bar., bass, ch., orch., *Golden Sonata*, 2 vns., basso continuo; and songs and duets.

tirana. Sp. song-dance popular in Andalusia, usually with rhythmic guitar acc. in 6/8 time.

tirasse (Fr.). Coupler of organ—generally a pedal coupler. So *tirasse du positif, du récit, du grande orgue*, mean respectively Choir to Pedal, Swell to Pedal, Great to Pedal. These may be abbreviated to *Tir. P.*, *Tir. R.*, and *Tir. G.O. Tirasse G.P.R.* means that all 3 couplers are to be used.

Tiresias. Ballet in 3 scenes, lib. and mus. by *Lambert, choreog. Ashton. Comp. 1950–1. Prod. London 1951.

Tirésias, Les mamelles de (Poulenc). See *Mamelles de Tirésias, Les.*

Tirimo, Martino (*b* Larnaca, Cyprus, 1942). Gr. pianist and conductor. Début Cyprus 1949, London 1965. Cond. *La traviata* at Cyprus Fest. 1955.

Won Geneva int. pf. comp. 1972. Specialist in Schubert sonatas (played complete set, London 1975, 1985).

Tishchenko, Boris (Ivanovich) (*b* Leningrad, 1939). Russ. composer. Teacher at Leningrad Cons. from 1965. Works incl. opera; ballets; 7 syms. (1960–94); pf. conc.; 2 vc. concs. (No.1 orch. by Shostakovich 1969, No.2 for soloist with 48 vc. and 2 db.); conc., fl., pf.; hp. conc.; 2 vn. concs.; chamber mus.; songs; film mus.

Titus, Alan (Wilkowski) (*b* NY, 1945). Amer. baritone. As student at Juilliard Sch., sang Figaro in *Il barbiere di Siviglia*. Prof. opera début Washington 1969 (Marcello in *La bohème*). Eur. début Amsterdam 1973; S. Francisco 1975; NY Met 1976; Glyndebourne 1979; Santa Fe 1985; Salzburg Fest. début 1990; CG 1995.

ti tzu. Chinese fl., played transversely. 6 fingerholes and extra hole covered with membrane which vibrates to give characteristic reedy tone.

toccata (It.). Touched. One of oldest names for kbd. piece (org., hpd., etc.), orig. a short movt., often merely a prelude, in which the player's 'touch' was displayed through rapidity and delicacy. But note that Monteverdi's first opera *Orfeo*, 1607, begins with a *Toccata* for baroque tpts. Later the toccata form was combined with a ricercare, and Bach wrote several toccatas and fugues. Bach also comp. hpd. toccatas in several movts. Several 20th-cent. composers have used the term *toccata* for movts. of orch. works, e.g. Vaughan Williams for 1st movt of pf. conc. and 4th movt. of 8th Sym. First printed source for use of word is G. A. Casteliono's *Intabolatura de leuto de diversi autori* (1536). Earliest printed keyboard toccatas were by S. Bertoldo (1591).

Toch, Ernst (*b* Vienna, 1887; *d* Santa Monica, Calif., 1964). Austrian-born composer and pianist (Amer. cit. 1940). Taught comp. at Mannheim 1913–29, privately in Berlin 1929–32. Went to Eng. 1933, writing mus. for BBC 1934; then to USA 1934, teaching in NY 1934–6. Went to Hollywood, composed some film scores, and became prof. of comp., UCLA, 1940–8. Wrote 3 operas; 7 syms. (1950–64); choral sym. *To My Fatherland*; *The Chinese Flute*, sop., chamber orch. (1922, rev. 1949); *Big Ben*, variations for orch. (1934); vc. conc.; 2 pf. concs.; pf. sonata; pf. quintet; 13 str. qts. (1902–53).

Tod Jesu, Der (The Death of Jesus). Passion-cantata by *Graun to text by Ramler. Berlin 1755, London 1877. Annually perf. in Berlin far into 20th cent.

Tod und das Mädchen, Der (Death and the Maiden). Song by Schubert (1817, D531), to poem by Claudius, which is also used as theme for variations in 2nd movt. of Str. Qt. No.14 in D minor (1824, D810). Arr. for str. orch. by Mahler *c*.1894. F.p. (slow movt. only) Hamburg 1894 cond. Mahler; f. complete p. NY 1984 cond. Atzmon, London 1985 cond. Tate.

Tod und Verklärung (Death and Transfiguration). Orch. tone-poem, Op.24, by R. Strauss depicting a man's death-bed visions. Comp. 1888–9; f.p. Eisenach 1889, cond. Strauss.

togli (It.). Take away, used in org. mus. for the shutting off of any stop, etc.

Tomasini, Luigi (*b* Pesaro, 1741; *d* Eisenstadt, 1808). It. violinist. Member of Haydn's orch. for Prince Esterházy from 1757 at Eisenstadt, becoming leader 1761. Later dir. of chamber mus., Haydn composing qts. with his playing in mind. Wrote vn. concs., qts., and 24 divertimenti for *baryton.

tombeau (Fr.). Tomb, tombstone. Fr. 17th-cent. composers' term for memorial works, revived by several 20th-cent. composers, notably by Ravel in *Le *Tombeau de Couperin* (1914–17).

Tombeau de Couperin, Le (The Tomb of Couperin). Suite for solo pf. by Ravel of 6 movts. each ded. to memory of friends who died in World War I, comp. 1914–17: 1. *Prélude*, 2. *Fugue*, 3. *Forlane*, 4. *Rigaudon*, 5. *Menuet*, 6. *Toccata*. F.p. Paris 1919. Nos. 1, 3, 5, and 4 (in that order) orch. by Ravel 1919, f.p. 1920. Prod. as ballet, Paris 1920, choreog. Berlin, later choreog. Balanchine, NY 1975.

Tom Jones. (1) Comic opera in 3 acts by *German, lib. by A. M. Thompson and R. Courtneidge based on Fielding. Prod. Manchester and London 1907.

(2) Opera in 3 acts by Stephen *Oliver to his own lib. based on Fielding's novel (1749). Comp. 1974–5. Prod. Snape 1976 (EMT), Nottingham and London 1976.

(3) Comic opera in 3 acts by Philidor, to lib. by A. A. H. Poinsinet and B. Davesne based on Fielding. Prod. Paris 1765, rev. with lib. altered by M. J. Sedaine, Paris 1766. Modern revivals: Cambridge 1971, London (Fr. Inst.) 1978, Los Angeles 1980.

Tomkins, Thomas (*b* St David's, Pembroke, 1572; *d* Martin Hussingtree, Worcs., 1656). Welsh composer, grandson of organist of Worcester Cath. and one of large family of musicians. Org., Worcester Cath. 1596–1646, Chapel Royal from 1621. Comp. mus. for Charles I's coronation 1625. Wrote mus. for consorts, pavans and galliards (incl. *Sad Pavan for these distracted times*), 95 anthems, and services, but his finest work is in his polyphonic madrigals *Songs of 3, 4, 5, and 6 parts*, pubd. 1622. These incl. *Above the stars, Music divine, Oft did I marle, See, see, the shepherd's queen, When David heard that Absalom was slain*, and *When I observe*. His sacred works were pubd. posthumously in *Musica Deo sacra* (1668).

Tomlinson, (Sir) **John** (*b* Oswaldtwistle, 1946). Eng. bass. In Scottish Opera ch. 1968. Opera début 1972, GTO (Colline in *La bohème*) and Kent Opera (Leporello in *Don Giovanni*). Sang Reade in f. Eng. p. of Goehr's *Arden Must Die*, London 1974 (New Opera Co.). ENO début 1974, then prin. bass ENO 1975–81. CG début 1979; S. Francisco 1983;

Opera North 1986; Scottish Opera 1987; Bayreuth 1988 (Wotan in *Der Ring*); Salzburg Fest. début 1988. Created Green Knight in *Gawain*, London (CG) 1991. Prod. *Oberto* for Opera North, 1994. CBE 1997. Knighted 2005.

Tommasini, Vincenzo (*b* Rome, 1878; *d* Rome, 1950). It. composer. Wrote operas, orch. works, and 4 str. qts., but is remembered for his arr. of mus. by D. Scarlatti for Diaghilev ballet *The *Good-humoured Ladies* (*Le donne di buon umore*) (comp. 1916, prod. Rome 1917, suite 1920).

Tomowa-Sintow, Anna (*b* Stara Zagora, 1941). Bulgarian soprano. Appeared on stage as Butterfly's child. Début Stara Zagora 1965 (Tatyana in *Eugene Onegin*). Sang in Leipzig from 1967. Won Sofia int. comp. 1970, Rio de Janeiro int. comp. 1971. Berlin Staatsoper 1972–6; Salzburg Fest. début 1973; Amer. début (S. Francisco) 1974; CG 1975; Vienna 1977; NY Met 1978. Sang Mozart and Strauss roles at Salzburg Fest., cond. Karajan, who admired her greatly.

tom-tom. Type of drum, imitative of African small hand-played drums, used in Western dance-bands from 1920s and sometimes in orch. works. May or may not be tuned. Not the same as *tam-tam.

ton (Fr.). Pitch, key, mode, tone, crook, sound, note; e.g. *donner le ton*, to give the pitch; *ton de cor*, horn crook.

Ton (Ger.). Pitch, key, mode, note, sound, mus., e.g. *Tonfarbe*, tone-colour; *Tonkunst*, tonal art (i.e. mus.), *Tondichtung*, tone-poem.

tonada (Sp.). Tune or air; used as title of works by some Sp. composers.

tonadilla (Sp.). (1) Diminutive of *tonada.

(2) Cantata with vocal solos, usually incl. choral and instr. movts. Such works were used as satirical intermezzi in the th.; their popularity was est. by Luìs Misón, Sp. fl. virtuoso and cond. (who from *c*.1757 wrote over 100), and others. Form revived by Granados. Originally a topical solo song, with guitar acc., added to Sp. theatrical interludes.

tonal. (1) Opposite to *real* in such technicalities as *answer* and *sequence*. See *fugue*.

(2) Of keys, as in *tonal* basis.

(3) Of *tonality, i.e. the opposite of *atonal, as in *tonal* comp.

tonality. Key, meaning particularly observance of a single tonic key as basis of comp., thus, *bitonality*, use of 2 keys at once; *polytonality*, use of several keys at once; *atonality*, loyalty to no key.

Tonart (Ger.). Mode, scale, or key.

Tondichter (Ger.). Sound-poet, i.e. composer.

Tondichtung (Ger.). Tone-poem; term preferred to *symphonic poem by R. Strauss.

tone. (1) Mus. sound, as in analysis to show that a vn. note has several different *tones*.

(2) Interval of major 2nd, e.g. C–D, E–F♯.

(3) Quality of sound, as in 'sweet *tone*', 'harsh *tone*', 'dry *tone*'.

(4) Plainsong melody, as in Gregorian tone.

(5) Amer. usage for 'note', hence *12-tone mus.* and *tone-row* instead of 12-note and note-row.

tone-cluster. Amer. term for **cluster*, i.e. group of notes on pf. played by placing the forearm flat on the keys.

tone-colour. See *timbre*.

tone-poem. See *symphonic poem*.

Tone Roads. Name of 2 works by **Ives. No.1 for small orch., comp. 1911; No.3 for chamber orch., comp. 1915.

tonguing. Use of the tongue to articulate certain notes in playing of wind instr. Thus, single-, double-, and triple-tonguing refer to increasingly fast playing. *flutter-tonguing* (Ger. *Flatterzunge*) is used chiefly by flautists, but occasionally by clarinettists and trumpeters, for a trilling effect required by composers from R. Strauss and Mahler to the present day.

tonic. First degree of the major or minor scale. The 'key-note' from which the key takes its name, as Key of A etc.

tonic sol-fa. Eng. system of sight-singing and notation first mooted by D. Sower in 1832, developed by Sarah Ann Glover (1785–1867) as *Norwich Sol-fa*, and pioneered by John Curwen (1816–80) in the 1840s. Based on *movable-doh* system of **solmization. Notes of major scale are named (in ascending order) *doh, ray, me, fah, soh, lah, te*, where *doh* is the tonic, other notes being thus related to tonic of the moment, not fixed in pitch. Minor is treated as mode of the major, first note being *lah*, 2nd *te*, 3rd *doh*, etc. In notation notes are written as d, r, m, f, s, l, t. Sharps and flats are indicated by change of vowel, sharps to 'e', flats to 'a' (pronounced 'aw'). E.g. *doh* sharpened is *de*; *me* flattened is *ma*. Double dots (:) separate beat from beat; single dots are used when a beat has to be divided into a half-beat, commas to divide half-beats into quarters. Horizontal lines show that notes are held; blanks indicate rests.

Tonkunst (Ger.). 'Sound art'. Music.

tono (It., plural *toni*). Tone—in all the various senses of the English word (see *tone*). Also mode, key.

tono (Sp.). Type of part-song or madrigal, of 2 or 3 stanzas, sung before play in 17th cent.

Tonreihe (Ger.). **Note-row*.

Tonus Peregrinus (Lat.). Foreign tone. (1) Medieval term for minor scale.

(2) Plainsong for Psalm 114 (*When Israel went out of Egypt*).

Tooley, (Sir) **John** (*b* Rochester, 1924). Eng. administrator. Secretary, GSMD 1952–5. Ass. to

gen. admin., Royal Opera House, CG, 1955–60; ass. gen. admin. 1960–70; gen. admin. 1970–80; gen. dir. 1980–7. Knighted 1979.

Toovey, Andrew (*b* London, 1962). Eng. composer. Dir. of Ixim, contemp. mus. ens., from 1987. Comps. incl.:

OPERAS & MUSIC THEATRE: *The Spurt of Blood*, 3 singers, 4 players (1988–90); *Ubu*, opera (1991–2); *The Juniper Tree*, opera (1993).

ORCH.: *Āté*, chamber ens. (1986); *Black Light*, chamber ens. (1989); *Mozart*, str. (1991); *Acrobats*, ww., brass, str. (1995); ob. conc., str. (1997); va. conc. (2004).

VOICE(S) & ENS.: *Winter Solstice*, v., 7 players (1984, rev. 1988); *An die Musik*, mez., vib. (1989); *Adam Adamah*, sop., ens. (1991); *Ja ja ja ja ja, nee nee nee nee nee*, vv., ens. (1991); *Irish Settings*, ten., mez., va. (1994); *I'll be there for you*, sop., mez., ten., bar., pf. (2000).

ENS.: *White Fire*, cl., opt. dbn., pf., vn., vc. (1988); *Adam*, ob., cl., 2 tb., vc., db. (1989); *Splice (for Bridget Riley)*, bcl., hn., pf., vn., vc. (1991).

CHAMBER MUSIC.: *Untitled String Quartet* (1985); *Veiled Wave I*, fl. (with picc. and alt. fl.), *II*, cl. or bcl. (1985); *Cântec*, va., pf. (1986); *Shining*, vn., vc. (1987); *Shining Forth*, pf., vn., vc. (1987); *String Quartet Music* (1987); *(nobody'll know)*, vc., pf. (1988); *Shimmer Bright*, str. trio (1988); *Lament, Strathspey, Reel*, vn. (1988); *Whisper(ingly) Crumbling (into) Silence*, perc. trio (1988); *Snow Flowers*, picc., va., hp. (1988); *Whirling*, pf., perc. trio (1989); *Still Far Off*, fl., ob., pf. (1990); *Fallen*, v., vn. (1991); *Your Mouth*, va., perc. (1993); *Fast Net*, vn. (1994); *Transparencies*, vn. (2000); *Going Home*, str. qt. (2003).

PIANO: *Artaud* (1986); *Fragments after Artuad* (1988); *Out Jumps Jack Death!* (1989); *Down there by the sea* (1989); *Embrace*, 2 pf. (1990); *Cantus firmus* (1992); *Techno Stomp* (1997); *Red Bird* (2003); *Dear Judith* (2004).

Torelli, Giuseppe (*b* Verona, 1658; *d* Bologna, 1709). It. violinist and composer. Brother of painter Felice Torelli. Attached to Church of San Petronio, Bologna, 1686–95. Visited Vienna. Leader of band at court of Margrave of Brandenburg-Anspach, 1697–99. Returned to Bologna 1701. Comp. mus. for str. and continuo, incl. 12 concerti grossi, Op.8 (1708), gui. conc., tpt. concs., suites for tpt., str., and continuo, etc.

Torke, Michael (*b* Milwaukee, 1961). Amer. composer. Won *Prix de Rome*. Mus. incl. elements of minimalism, jazz, and rock. Prin. comps.:

OPERAS: *The Directions* (1986); *King of Hearts* (1994); *Strawberry Fields* (1999); *The Listener*, musical (2005).

BALLET: *Black and White* (1988); *The Contract* (2002).

ORCH.: *Vanada* (1984); *Bright Blue Music* (1985, arr. for pf. trio as *The Harlequins are Looking at you*, 1985); *Ecstatic Orange* (1985–7); *Green* (1986); *Verdant Music* (1986); *Purple* (1987); *Copper*, brass quintet, orch. (1988); *Ash* (1989); *Slate*, concertante group, orch. (1989); *Bronze* (1990); pf. conc. (1991); *Red* (1991); *Run* (1992); *Javelin*

(1994); *Brick Symphony* (1997); *Corner in Manhattan*, orch. (2000), see also under CHAMBER MUSIC; perc. conc. (*Rapture*) (2001); *An Italian Straw Hat* (2004).

ENS.: *Ceremony of Innocence*, fl., cl., vn., vc., pf. (1983); *The Yellow Pages*, fl., cl., vn., vc., pf. (1984); *Adjustable Wrench*, chamber ens. (1987); *Rust*, pf., winds (1989); *Music on the Floor* (1991); *Monday and Tuesday* (1992); *Overnight Mail* (1997).

CHAMBER MUSIC: *Chalk*, str. qt. (1992); *Corner in Manhattan*, str. qt. (2000), see also under ORCH.; *August*, brass quintet (2002); *After the Forest Fire*, mar., fl., vc. (2005).

CHORAL: *Mass*, bar., ch., chamber orch. (1990); *Book of Proverbs*, sop., bar., ch., orch. (1996); *Four Seasons*, SATB soloists, children's ch., ch., orch. (1999).

VOICE & ENS.: *4 Proverbs*, female v., pf., synth., str. (1993); *Song of Isaiah*, sop., ens. (2002).

PIANO: *Laetus* (1982); *Two Drinks* (2000); *Bay of Huatulco* (2006).

tornada (Sp.). Type of refrain in many of the folk-songs of Catalonia.

Toronto. Principal city of English-speaking Canada and capital of Ontario. Rich musical life dates from 1820s. Toronto Mus. Soc. founded 1836, Phil. Soc. 1845, neither surviving for long. Mendelssohn Choir, founded 1894 by A. S. Voigt, rapidly became famous throughout N. Amer. and from 1902 sang with leading Amer. orchs. visiting Canada. First toured USA 1905 and sings regularly with Toronto SO since 1935. Toronto SO founded 1906 by Frank Welsman, performing mainstream repertory with distinguished soloists. Disbanded 1914 but in 1926 New SO (founded 1922 with Luigi von Kunits as cond.) acquired its charter and assets and became Toronto SO. Conds. were Kunits (1926–31); Ernest *MacMillan (1931–56, under whom it became a major orch.); Walter Susskind (1956–65); Seiji Ozawa (1965–9); Karel Ančerl (1969–73); Andrew Davis (1975–88); Gunther Herbig (1989–94); Jukka-Pekka Saraste (1994–2001); Peter Oundjian (from 2003). Performed in Massey Hall (capacity 2,765) 1923–82, then moved to Roy Thomson Hall (capacity 2,812). Gives 160 concerts a year. Canadian Broadcasting Corp. has studios in Toronto and had its own orch. (CBCSO) 1952–64 which made recordings with Stravinsky, among others. Opera was first perf. in Toronto 1825 by co. from Rochester, NY. Various local opera cos. gave seasons until Royal Cons. Opera Sch. was founded 1946, its first prod. being *The Bartered Bride* (1947). From this grew the Canadian Opera Co. (1958) which perf. about six operas a season at O'Keefe Centre or the smaller Elgin Th. until the opening in 2006 (with a *Ring* cycle) of a new opera house, the Four Seasons Centre for the Performing Arts. Has given f.ps. of several Canadian operas, f. Canadian p. of Berg's *Lulu* and prods. of Wagner, Strauss, and Britten. Gen. dirs. have incl. Hermann Geiger-Torel (1958–76); Lotfi Mansouri (1976–89); Bryan Dickie (1989–93); Richard Bradshaw (from 1994, gen. dir. from 1998). *Surtitles were introduced for the first time anywhere by Mansouri, 1983.

Tórroba, Federico Moreno (*b* Madrid, 1891; *d* Madrid, 1982). Sp. composer of zarzuelas, guitar works, flamenco conc., etc. Dir., Royal Acad. des Beaux Arts de Madrid.

Tortelier, Paul (*b* Paris, 1914; *d* Villarçeaux, 1990). Fr. cellist, conductor, and composer. Studied Paris Cons., winning first vc. prize 1930 (playing Elgar conc.). Prof. début 1931 with Lamoureux Orch. Prin. vc., Monte Carlo Orch. 1935–7; 3rd cellist, Boston SO 1937–40; prin. cellist Société des Concerts du Conservatoire, Paris, 1946–7, then solo career with world's leading orchs. Eng. début (in Strauss's *Don Quixote*), London 1947. Lived in Israel 1955–6. Prof. of vc., Paris Cons., 1956–9, Nice Cons. 1978–80. Works incl. 2 vc. concs., conc. for 2 vc., *Israel Symphony*, vc. sonata, *Suite* for unacc. vc. Also chamber-mus. player with wife Maud Martin Tortelier (*b* 1926) cellist, daughter Maria de la Pau (*b* 1950) pianist, and son Yan Pascal *Tortelier, violinist and cond.

Tortelier, Yan Pascal (*b* Paris, 1947). Fr. conductor and violinist, son of Paul *Tortelier. Début as soloist London 1962 (Brahms Double Conc.). Assoc. cond. Orch. du Capitole, Toulouse, 1974–83. Brit. début as cond., London 1978 (RPO). Amer. début 1985 (Seattle SO). Prin. cond., Ulster Orch. 1989–92, BBC Philharmonic 1992–2002.

Tosca. Opera in 3 acts by Puccini to lib. by Giacosa and Illica based on Sardou's play *La Tosca* (1887). Comp. 1898–9. Prod. Rome and London 1900; NY Met 1901.

Toscanini, Arturo (*b* Parma, 1867; *d* NY, 1957). It. conductor and cellist. Entered Parma Cons. 1876, studying vc. and comp. Engaged as cellist in opera orch. for S. American tour, 1886 and in Rio de Janeiro replaced regular cond., conducting *Aida* from memory. In It. later that year cond. Catalani's *Edmea* in Turin. Played vc. in f.p. of *Otello*, Milan 1887. Cond. opera in various It. cities. Cond. f.p. of *Pagliacci* in Milan (Teatro dal Verme), 1892, f.p. of *La bohème*, Turin 1896. Cond. f.ps. in Italy of *Götterdämmerung*, Turin 1895, and of *Siegfried*, Milan 1899. Début as sym. cond. Turin 1896 with municipal orch.; opera début at La Scala 1898 in *Die Meistersinger* as prin. cond. under management of *Gatti-Casazza. Stayed till 1903, resigning after demonstration when he refused to allow ten. an encore in a Verdi opera. Returned 1906–8. Went to NY Met with Gatti-Casazza 1908, making début in *Aida*. Cond. f.p. of *La *fanciulla del West* 1910, and f.ps. in USA of several operas, incl. *Boris Godunov* (1913). Cond. Verdi's *Requiem* at Met 1909 and Beethoven's 9th Sym. there 1913. Returned to It. 1915 and again became chief cond. at La Scala 1921–9, one of its golden periods. Cond. f.p. *Turandot*, 1926. Friction with Fascists led to his departure. Cond. part of NYPO seasons 1926–8 (orch. becoming Phil.-Sym. Orch. of NY, 1928), prin. cond. 1928–36. Took orch. on European tour 1930. Cond. at Bayreuth 1930 and 1931, at Salzburg 1934–7 (famous perfs. of *Falstaff*, *Fidelio*, and *Die Meistersinger*). Début with Vienna PO 1933. Refused to cond. in Ger., It., and Austria under Nazi and Fascist régimes. Cond. inaugural concerts of Palestine SO (now Israel PO), 1936. NBC formed new orch. in NY for him which he cond. 1937–54, giving public concerts and many famous concert perfs. of operas. Guest cond. in London of BBC SO 1935 and 1937–9, with whom he recorded Beethoven's *Pastoral Symphony*, 1938, and of Philharmonia Orch. 1952 in Brahms series. Returned to La Scala 1946, conducting a concert of It. operatic music and, in subsequent years, several other concerts. Last appearance as cond. NY June 1954. Encouraged Amer. composers, especially Barber and Hanson. Always cond. from memory, but not only because he was extremely shortsighted. Tyrannized orchs., but drilled them to remarkable standards. Regarded by many Amer. critics as beyond criticism, but, like all conds., had his limitations, far outweighed in his case by virtues of clarity, expressiveness, and ens. Outstanding in It. opera, but also in Wagner and in a limited range of composers of symphonic mus. from Haydn to his own day.

Toselli, Enrico (*b* Florence, 1883; *d* Florence, 1926). It. pianist and composer. Wrote operetta, sym.-poem, chamber mus., and songs, incl. the well-known *Serenata* (1900).

Tosti, (Sir) (Francesco) Paolo (*b* Ortano sul Mare, Abruzzi, 1846; *d* Rome, 1916). It.-born composer and singing-teacher. Became singing-teacher to future Queen of It. Visited Eng. 1875, appointed royal singing-master 1880. Took Eng. nationality 1906 and was knighted (KCVO) 1908. Wrote songs and duets to It., Fr., and Eng. texts. His *Good-bye* extremely popular.

tosto (It.). (1) Rapid, quick; (2) sooner, at once; *piuttosto*, sooner or rather; *più tosto*, or *piùt-tosto*, as ordinary It. expressions, mean rather, or more quickly, faster. Superlative is *tostissimo*, very rapid, *tostissamamente*, very rapidly.

Tost Quartets. Name given to 12 str. qts. by Haydn, 1788–90 (Hob. III:57–68; or Op.54, Nos. 1–3, Op.55 Nos. 1–3, Op.64 Nos. 1–6). So-called because of ded. to Viennese violinist Johann Tost.

total serialism. Comp. which treats all mus. parameters serially, not only pitch but time-values, vol., etc.

Totenberg, Roman (*b* Lódź, 1911). Polish-born violinist and teacher (Amer. cit. 1943). Toured Eur. with Szymanowski 1935–6, giving recitals. Settled in USA. Head of vn. dept., Aspen Sch. of Mus., 1950–60. Taught at Mannes Coll. 1951–7. Prof. of mus. and chairman of str. dept., Boston Univ., 1961–78. Dir., Longy Sch. of Mus., Cambridge, Mass., 1978–85.

Totentanz (Dance of Death). Work by Liszt for pf. and orch., being variations on *Dies Irae*. Comp. 1849, rev. 1853, 1859. Also arr. Busoni (1918).

Tote Stadt, Die (The Dead City). Opera in 3 acts by Erich *Korngold to lib. by 'Paul Schott' (himself and his father) based on Ger. trans. by S. Trebitsch of G. Rodenbach's play *Le Mirage*, itself adapted from his novella *Bruges la Morte* (1892). Prod. Hamburg and Cologne (joint premières) 1920; Vienna and NY 1921; London (concert) 1996.

To the Children (*K detyam*). Song for v. and pf. by Rachmaninov, Op.26, No.7 (1906), a setting of poem by Khomyakov. F.p. Moscow 1907 by Ivan Grizunov.

touch (Ger. *Anschlag*). (1) Applied to kbd. instr., the weight required to bring keys into effect. Applied to performers it means the manner of pressing or striking the keys and is one of the most subtle and indefinable facets of the art of pf.-playing.
(2) (Old Eng.). Sound. Also used in 16th and 17th cents. to mean *toccata, e.g. a *touch* by Byrd.

touche (Fr.). Fingerboard—of vn., etc., e.g. *sur la touche*, bow over the fingerboard. Also used in Fr. for the keys of a pf. as in Debussy's *Étude pour les touches blanches*.

Tourel [Davidovich], **Jennie** (*b* Vitebsk, 1900; *d* NY, 1973). Russian-born mezzo-soprano (Amer. cit. 1946). Left Russ. with family 1918, settling in Danzig and Paris. Opera début Chicago 1930 (2nd Scholar in Moret's *Lorenzaccio*). NY Met début 1937. Sang in Paris until 1940, when she settled in USA. NY Met 1943–5, 1946–7. Created Baba the Turk in *The Rake's Progress*, Venice 1951. Taught at Juilliard Sch. and Aspen Sch. of Mus. Last stage appearance Chicago 1973.

Tournemire, Charles (Arnould) (*b* Bordeaux, 1870; *d* Arcachon, 1939). Fr. organist and composer. At age of 11, org. of St Pierre, Bordeaux, later of St Seurin. Went to Paris Cons., studying pf. with Bériot and winning *premier prix* for org. in Widor's class. Org. of Ste Clotilde, Paris, from 1898. Prof. at Paris Cons. from 1919. Deeply influenced by Franck and Widor. Comp. 4 operas (3 unpubd.), 8 syms. (last 3 unpubd.), songs, choral works, chamber mus., and many works for org., incl. *L'Orgue mystique* (1927–32), which lasts as long as the entire org. mus. of J. S. Bach.

Tours, Berthold (*b* Rotterdam, 1838; *d* London, 1897). Dutch-born violinist, teacher, organist, and music editor. Spent 2 years in Russia. Settled in London 1861, as orch. violinist, writer, and teacher. Org., Swiss Church, Holborn, 1862. Mus. adv. and ed. to Novello from 1878. Made pf. reduction of Beethoven's Mass in C, Mendelssohn's *Elijah*, etc. Wrote hymns and anthems, pf. pieces, and songs. Author of vn. primer.

Tourte, François (Xavier) (*b* Paris, 1747; *d* Paris, 1835). Fr. maker of violin bows, one of a family, and known as 'the Stradivari of the bow'. Developed between 1782 and 1790 the modern bow, known as 'Tourte bow'. Selected Pernambuco wood which he set in permanent curvature by subjection to moderate heat. Determined true length and curvature, tapered it towards point, and determined height of point and nut. Invented method of fixing hairs on face of nut by means of movable metal band.

Tovey, (Sir) **Donald** (Francis) (*b* Eton, 1875; *d* Edinburgh, 1940). Eng. pianist, composer, conductor, teacher, and writer. Began to compose at 8. Pianist with Joachim 1894. Played own works at London chamber concerts 1900–1. Prof. of Mus., Edinburgh Univ. from 1914. Est. Reid orch. concerts 1917, for which he wrote celebrated programme-notes (pubd. in 6 vols. as *Essays in Musical Analysis*, 1935–8). Amer. début as pianist 1925. Wrote opera *The Bride of Dionysus* (1918), pf. conc. (1903), sym. (1913), vc. conc. (for Casals, 1934), much chamber mus. Made conjectural completion of unfinished fugue in Bach's *Die* *Kunst der Fuge*. Many books and articles on mus. subjects. Knighted 1935.

Toward the Unknown Region. Song for mixed ch. and orch. by Vaughan Williams to words by Whitman from *Whispers of Heavenly Death* (1870). Comp. 1905–7. F.p. Leeds Fest. 1907. Set simultaneously in friendly competition by Holst, whose setting was judged (by the composers themselves) as inferior, and suppressed.

toye. Light 16th- and early 17th-cent. comp. for virginals or lute.

Toye, Francis (John) (*b* Winchester, 1883; *d* Florence, 1964). Eng. music critic and author. Wrote for various Eng. papers and journals, incl. *Morning Post* 1925–37. Author of books on Verdi (1931) and Rossini (1934). Lived in Rio de Janeiro 1939–46 and from 1946 in Florence. Comp. songs. Dir., Brit. Inst., Florence 1936–9. CBE 1954.

Toye, (Edward) **Geoffrey** (*b* Winchester, 1889; *d* London, 1942). Eng. conductor and composer, brother of Francis *Toye. Cond. f.p. of orig. version of Vaughan Williams's *A London Symphony*, 1914. Cond., Beecham Opera Co. and D'Oyly Carte Opera Co., 1919–24. Cond. Old Vic and SW 1925–35; man. dir., CG 1935. Wrote operetta *The Red Pen* (1926), sym., songs, and popular ballet *The *Haunted Ballroom* (1934).

Toy Symphony (Ger. *Kindersymphonie*). Simple sym. in which toy instr. are used, in addition to str. and pf. Most popular example, formerly attrib. to Joseph Haydn, is by Leopold Mozart, with toy instr. probably added by M. Haydn. Several others exist, e.g. by A. Romberg, and by Malcolm Arnold (1957).

tr. Abbreviation for (1) trill or *tremolo, tremolando*, (2) trumpet.

tracker. Rod (thin flat strip of wood) in mechanism of org. which connects kbd. to pallets. *tracker action* is the operating of this linking-system, later succeeded by pneumatic or electric action, or by tracker-pneumatic action, a combination of both.

tradotto (It.), **traduit** (Fr.). (1) Translated.
(2) Arranged (see *arrangement*).
(3) Transposed.

traduzione (It.), **traduction** (Fr.). (1) Translation.
(2) *Arrangement.
(3) Transposition.

Traetta, Tommaso (Michele Francesco Saverio) (*b* Bitonto, 1727; *d* Venice, 1779). It. composer. Opera *Il Farnace* prod. with success at Naples 1751. Wrote 43 operas in all, 2 of them for Vienna. Worked in Venice 1765–8. Succeeded Galuppi as Russ. Empress Catherine II's court composer 1768–75. Visited London without success. Returned to Venice 1777. Also wrote choral works and instr. divertimenti. His *Buova d'Antona*, to a lib. by Goldoni, prod. Venice 1758, was revived at La Fenice, Venice, 1993 in edn. by A. *Curtis.

Tragic Overture (*Tragische-ouvertüre*). Concert-ov. by Brahms, Op.81, comp. 1880–1 and f.p. Breslau 1881. No particular tragedy is depicted.

Tragic Symphony. Schubert's own title for his Sym. No.4 in C minor (D417), comp. 1816. Mahler orig. intended to call his 6th Sym. (1903–5) the 'Tragic', but changed his mind.

traîné (Fr.). Dragged, slurred, lingering.

Trampler, Walter (*b* Munich, 1915; *d* Port Joli, Nova Scotia, 1997). Ger.-born violist (Amer. cit. 1944). Member Strub Qt., violist in Ger. Radio SO. Went to USA 1939. Founding member of New Mus. Qt. 1947–56. Prof. of va. and chamber mus., Juilliard Sch. 1962–71, prof. of mus., Yale Univ. Mus. Sch. from 1971. Soloist and chamber-mus. player. Commissioned and gave f.ps. of Berio's *Chemins* II and III (1969). Gave f.p. of va. conc. by Bainbridge (1978).

Tranchell, Peter (Andrew) (*b* Cuddalore, India, 1922; *d* Southampton, 1993). Eng. composer. Music lect. Cambridge Univ. from 1950; dir. of mus. Gonville and Caius Coll. from 1960. Comp. opera *The Mayor of Casterbridge* (1951); mus. comedy *Zuleika* (1954); ballets *Fate's Revenge* (Ballet Rambert 1951) and *Images of Love* (CG 1964); several 'concert entertainments', incl. *The Mating Season* (based on P. G. Wodehouse, 1962, rev. 1969); anthems, etc.

tranquillo (It.). Tranquil. So *tranquillamente*, tranquilly; *tranquillità, tranquillezza*, tranquillity.

Transcendental Studies (Liszt). See *Études d'exécution transcendante*.

transcription. (1) Arr. of mus. comp. for a performing medium other than orig. or for same medium but in more elaborate style.
(2) Conversion of comp. from one system of notation to another.

Transfiguration de Notre Seigneur Jésus-Christ, La. Work in 14 movts. to texts from the

Bible, the Missal, and St Thomas Aquinas by *Messiaen for ten., bar., ch., pf., and orch. Comp. 1965–9. F.p. Lisbon, 1969, cond. Baudo.

Transfigured Night (Schoenberg). See *Verklärte Nacht*.

transition. (1) Modulation from one key to another, particularly of a sudden and abrupt nature.

(2) Transition passage is one which acts as link between 2 more substantial passages (in sym., conc., etc.).

transposing instruments. Instruments which are not notated at their true pitch but (mechanically and without any effort on the player's part) produce the effect of that pitch. For example, the cl. is made in several sizes, the B♭ and A being the most often used because these keys reduce the difficulty of playing in the flat and sharp keys, respectively, by reducing the number of flats or sharps with which the player has to cope. In the B♭ instr., that key is to its player the 'natural key' (as C is to the pianist): the player faced with music in (say) the key of E♭ finds the music written in the key of F, i.e. there are 2 flats fewer to consider. Similarly with the A instrument a piece written in the key of B is notated in the key of D, i.e. there are 3 sharps fewer to consider. Thus music for the B♭ cl. is notated a tone higher than it is to sound and music for the A cl. a minor 3rd higher. Many players, with improved mechanism and developed technique, use the B♭ instrument for all keys, making the transposition mentally. On the rare C cl. the note sounded is the note written; the E♭ cl. transposes 1½ tones higher than written note; the bass clarinet in B♭ an octave and a tone lower.

The transposing instruments are as follows: (a) bass fl.; (b) cor anglais, ob. d'amore, ob. in E♭, heckelphone, sarrusophone; (c) cl. in B♭ and A, bass cl., high cl. in E♭ and D, alto cl. in E♭ and F, basset hn., pedal cl.; (d) saxophones; (e) cornets; (f) French hns.; (g) tpts.; (h) saxhorns; (i) kettledrums (up to Mozart's period, but excluding Handel).

transposition. Changing of the pitch of a comp. without other change, e.g. the raising of the pitch of a piece in the key of C to that of key D, or its lowering to the key of B or A.

transverse flute. Side-blown fl., distinguished from recorder, which is end-blown and therefore held pointing downwards.

trascinado (It.). Dragging. Holding back, same as *rallentando*.

trattenuto (It.). (1) held back. (2) sustained.

tratto (It.). Dragged (used in the negative, *non tratto*, not dragged).

Traubel, Helen (Francesca) (*b* St Louis, 1899; *d* Santa Monica, Calif., 1972). Amer. soprano. Début with St Louis SO 1926. NY Met début 1937. Chicago Opera 1937–46. Notable Met success as Sieglinde, 1939. Leading Wagnerian sop. at Met after Flagstad left, 1941–53. Left over disagreement about singing in night clubs. Appeared on Broadway, in films, and on TV. Wrote detective stories, incl. *The Metropolitan Opera Murders* (1951). Autobiography, *St Louis Woman* (1959).

Trauer (Ger.). Mourning, grief. Hence, *Trauermarsch*, funeral march; *Trauermusik*, funeral mus.; *traurig*, heavily, mournfully.

Träumerei (Reverie). Pf. piece by Schumann, No.7 of his *Kinderscenen*, Op.15, 1838.

Trauermusik (Mourning Music). Work for va. (or vn. or vc.) and str. by Hindemith comp. (1936) in a few hours on death of King George V for perf. at concert the next day. Last of 4 short movts. uses chorale *Vor deinen Thron tret ich hiermit* (The Old Hundredth).

trautonium. Elec. instr. first exhibited in Berlin in 1930 by Friedrich Trautwein (*b* Würzburg, 1888; *d* Düsseldorf, 1956). Similar to *theremin, but with extra devices enabling the player to obtain the correct notes of the tempered scale and a variety of tone-colour. Hindemith wrote conc. for it in 1931.

Travelling Companion, The. Opera in 4 acts by Stanford to lib. by Henry Newbolt, based on story by Hans Andersen, comp. 1919, prod. Liverpool 1925, Bristol, 1926.

travesti (It. 'disguised'.; Eng. 'trousers-role', 'breeches-part', Ger. *Hosenrolle*). Term to describe operatic roles which, though male characters, are sung by women, e.g. Romeo in *I Capuleti e i Montecchi*, Cherubino in *Le nozze di Figaro*, Prince Orlofsky in *Die Fledermaus*, Oktavian in *Der Rosenkavalier*, and the Composer in *Ariadne auf Naxos*.

Can also be applied to men who play female roles (e.g. pantomime dames or in early Victorian operas and baroque operas, e.g the Nurse in *L'incoronazione di Poppea*). Also the Madwoman in *Curlew River*.

Traviata, La (The Fallen Woman, or The Woman Gone Astray). Opera in 3 acts by Verdi to lib. by Piave based on Dumas *fils*'s play *La Dame aux camélias* (1852), based in turn on his partly autobiographical novel of the same name (1848). Comp. 1852–3, rev. 1854. Prod. Venice 1853, London and NY 1856.

Travis, Roy (Elihu) (*b* NY, 1922). Amer. composer. Teacher at Mannes Coll. 1952–7, then at UCLA from 1957 (prof. 1968), working since 1969 in EMS. Comps. incl. opera *The Passion of Oedipus* (1965), *African Sonata* for pf., *Collage* for orch., pf. conc., septet, conc. for fl., pre-recorded African instr., and synthesizer.

Treatise on Orchestration (*Grande traité de l'instrumentation et d'orchestration modernes*). Berlioz's historic book on orch. scoring pubd. in Paris in 1843 as his Op.10. 2nd edn. (1855) incl. suppl.: *Le *chef d'orchestre, théorie de son art.* Trans. into several languages. (Eng. 1855). Ed. and enlarged by R. Strauss 1904–5, in Ger.

treble. (1) Highest v. in choral singing, term today usually being applied to children, adult equivalent being *soprano.

(2) Upper part of comp., opposite in pitch of bass.

(3) Applied as adjective to certain high-pitched instr. e.g. treble recorder, treble viol.

treble clef. The sign 𝄞 (derived from old letter G) which indicates that the line on which it is placed is the G a 5th above middle C. Used for high-pitched instr., for high vv., and for right-hand pf. parts. For ten. v., treble clef is modified to indicate that notes are sounded octave lower than written.

Tremblay, Gilles (*b* Arvida, Quebec, 1932). Fr.-Canadian composer. His mus. concentrates on wind and perc. and incl. *Sonorization* (elec. sounds on 24 tape channels); *Cantique de durées*, orch.; *Kékoba*, ondes Martenot; *Champs* I, II, and III (I, pf., 2 perc., II, wind, brass, perc., pf., db., III, wind, brass, perc., str.); *Solstices*, ww., perc., db.; *Fleuves*, orch.; *Les Vêpres de la Vierge*, sop., ch., 13 instrs.; *Cèdres en voiles*, vc.; and pf. works.

tremolando (It.). Trembling. With *tremolo effect.

tremolo (It.). Shaking, trembling. In playing of str. instr., the rapid reiteration of a note or chord by back-and-forth strokes of the bow; also, on other instr. as well as str., the very rapid alternation between 2 notes. Note that *tremolo* is the rapid iteration or alternation of *notes*, whereas *vibrato* is fluctuation of *pitch*.

tremulant. Mechanical org. device, operated by a stop-knob, which varies the wind-pressure and thus imparts a 'wobbling' effect to the note being sounded.

trepak. Lively Russ. popular dance in 2/4 time, introduced by some Russ. composers, e.g. Mussorgsky, into their works. Famous example is in Tchaikovsky's *Nutcracker*.

triad. Chord of 3 notes, basically a 'root' and the notes a third and a fifth above it, forming two superimposed thirds, e.g. C–E–G ('common chord' of C major). If lower third is major and the upper minor, the triad is major. If lower third is minor and the upper major, the triad is minor. If both are major the triad is *augmented*. If both are minor, the triad is *diminished*.

trial. Term applied at Paris Opéra-Comique to ten. of dramatic rather than vocal powers (thin, nasal voice) who specializes in comedy or peasants' and simpletons' roles. Named after Antoine Trial (*b* Avignon, 1737; *d* Paris, 1795).

Trial by Jury. Operetta in 1 act (styled 'dramatic cantata') by Sullivan, lib. by Gilbert, the only one

of their works sung throughout (i.e. no spoken dialogue). Its success led to a continuation of the partnership. Comp. 1875. Prod. London 1875.

triangle. Perc. instr. of indefinite pitch, made of metal shaped into a triangle and struck with metal stick to give tinkling sound. Much used by composers to intensify excitement, e.g. in 3rd movt. of Brahms's 4th sym. Liszt's pf. conc. No.1 in E♭ has important part for triangle.

Tribschen [Triebschen]. Villa near Lucerne, Switz., on Vierwaldstätter lake, where Wagner lived from 1866 until 1872 when he moved to Bayreuth. On its staircase on Christmas Day 1870, *Siegfried Idyll* was f.p. (orig. title *Tribschen Idyll*). (The spelling *Triebschen*, although incorrect, was Wagner's own.)

Tricorne, Le (Falla). See *Three-Cornered Hat, The*.

trill (shake). Ornament comprising rapid alternation of main note and note above, normally slurred, and assoc. with cadences. Occurs instrumentally and vocally. Is indicated by *tr* ∿∿ and ✚. Wavy line often indicates length of trill.

Trillo del Diavolo (Tartini). See *Devil's Trill*.

Trinity College of Music, London. Mus. coll. incorporated as Trinity Coll., London, 1875, developed from mus. soc. founded 1872. In 1874 complete system of testing by examination, both of teachers and their pupils, was organized at centres throughout Brit. and Ireland and, from 1876, at centres in S. Africa and other places then under Brit. rule. Today TCL examiners visit nearly 40 countries. Now part of Univ. of London. Awards graduate diploma (GTCL).

Trinklied (Ger.). Drinking song.

trio (It.). Three. (1) Any body of 3 performers together, or piece of mus. written for them to perform, e.g. *string trio*, usually vn., va., vc., *piano trio*, usually pf., vn., vc. The comp. called a trio is usually in sonata form and in 3 movts.

(2) The central section of a minuet, scherzo, or march, usually in gentler contrast to the first section and its repeat. So called because formerly it was written in 3-part harmony, as for a trio.

(3) A vocal trio may be acc. or unacc. In the 16th cent. the minor-key sections of the mass were often written for 3 vv.; there were also 3-part canzonets. In opera, the simultaneous combination of 3 vv. is a *trio*, a famous example being that for 3 sop. in Act 3 of Strauss's *Der Rosenkavalier*, but there are of course many examples of trios for 3 different types of v.

(4) For the org. a *trio* is intended for manuals and the pedals, each in a different registration for contrast (and, of course, played by one performer).

Trionfi–Trittico Teatrale (It.). Triumphs. Theatrical triptych by *Orff comprising *Carmina Burana*, *Catulli Carmina*, *Trionfo di Afrodite*.

Trionfo di Afrodite (Triumph of Aphrodite). Scenic conc. by *Orff, the 3rd part of his trilogy

*Trionfi. Comp. 1950–1, to Lat. and Gr. texts by Catullus, Sappho, and Euripides. For soloists, ch., and orch. Prod. Milan 1953.

trio sonata. Comp. prevalent in late 17th and early 18th cents. (Baroque period), usually for 2 vn. and vc. or bass viol, with kbd. continuo. The most important genre of Baroque chamber mus. Towards the end of the 17th cent. the form diverged into the *sonata da chiesa* and the *sonata da camera*. Among the most celebrated examples of the trio sonata are the 48 by Corelli, 12 by Purcell, 28 by Handel, 14 by François Couperin, and 12 by Vivaldi.

triple concerto. Conc. for 3 solo instr. and orch. or ens. Beethoven's is for pf., vn., and vc., but there are other combinations, e.g. Tippett's for vn., va., and vc.

triple counterpoint. That concerning 3 vv. or parts which are capable of changing places with one another, so making 6 positions of the parts possible.

triple-croche (Fr.). Triple-hook. 32nd note, or demisemiquaver.

triplet. Group of 3 notes, or notes and rests, equal in time-value, written where a group of 2 notes is suggested by time signature. Usually indicated by adding numeral 3 above each group.

triple time. Where the primary division is into 3 beats. Usually indicated by figure 3 (in simple time) or 9 (in *compound time*) as upper digit of a *time signature, e.g. 3/4 or 9/8.

Tristan. Preludes for pf., orch., and tape by *Henze. Comp. 1973. F.p. London, 1974 (Homero Francesch, pf., cond. C. Davis).

Tristan und Isolde. Mus. drama (*Handlung*, action) in 3 acts by Wagner to his own lib., based on G. von Strassburg's *Tristan, c.*1210, and ultimately on Arthurian legend. Comp. 1857–9. Prod. Munich 1865, London 1882, NY Met 1886. The Prelude to Act I and Isolde's *Liebestod* (Love Death) are often perf. as concert item.

tritone. Interval of augmented 4th which comprises 3 whole tones, e.g. from F up or down to B. Difficult to sing, and in medieval times its use was prohibited. There was saying, involving the Hexachord names for the notes, *Mi contra fa diabolus est in musica*, 'Mi against fa is the devil in music', hence the frequent use of the tritone in comps. to suggest evil.

Trittico, Il (The Triptych). Set of three 1-act operas for perf. on one evening by Puccini, comprising *Il *tabarro (The Cloak) (1913–16), *Suor Angelica (Sister Angelica) (1917), *Gianni Schicchi (1917–18). Prod. NY Met 1918, Rome and Chicago 1919, London 1920.

Triumphlied (Song of Triumph). Setting by Brahms, his Op.55, for ch. and orch. of text from *Revelation*. Comp. 1871, f.p. 1872, to celebrate Prussia's defeat of Fr.

Triumph of Neptune, The. Eng. pantomime in 10 scenes, mus. by *Berners, lib. by S. Sitwell, choreog. Balanchine. Prod. London 1926. Some of this was scored by *Walton. Orch. suite (1926–7), arr. Berners, longer suite arr. R. Douglas.

Triumphs of Oriana, The. Coll. of Eng. madrigals in 5 and 6 parts by various composers, ed. by *Morley in honour of Elizabeth I and dated 1601 but issued only after her death in 1603. Modelled on It. *Trionfo di Dori* 1592. In first edn. 24 composers were incl., as follows: Michael East (*Hence Stars*); Daniel Norcome (*With Angel's Face*); John Mundy (*Lightly she Tripped*); Ellis Gibbons (*Long live fair Oriana*); John Benet (*All Creatures now are Merry-minded*); John Hilton (*Fair Oriana, beauty's Queen*); George Marson (*The Nymphs and Shepherds danced*); Richard Carlton (*Calm was the Air*); John Holmes (*Thus Bonny-boots*); Richard Nicholson (*Sing shepherds all*); Thomas Tomkins (*The Fauns and Satyrs*); Michael Cavendish (*Come gentle Swains*); William Cobbold (*With Wreaths of Rose and Laurel*); Thomas Morley (*Arise, awake*); John Farmer (*Fair Nymphs*); John Wilbye (*The Lady Oriana*); Thomas Hunt (*Hark, did ye ever Hear so Sweet a Singing?*); Thomas Weelkes (*As Vesta was from Latmos Hill descending*); John Milton (*Fair Orian*); Ellis Gibbons (*Round about her Chariot*); G. Kirbye (*Bright Phoebus*) (*With Angel's Face*); Robert Jones (*Fair Oriana*); John Lisley (*Fair Cytherea*); Thomas Morley (*Hard by a Crystal Fountain*); Edward Johnson (*Come blessed Bird*); Giovanni Croce (*Hard by a Crystal Fountain*). To these in later edns. were added: Thomas Bateson (*When Oriana walked to Take the Air* and *Hark, hear you not?*) and Francis Pilkington (*When Oriana walked to Take the Air*). There were 2 issues of first edn.: in the first Kirbye's madrigal has the words *With Angel's Face*, already set by Norcome, and in the 2nd the same mus. is set to *Bright Phoebus*.

For 20th-cent. Eng. composers' similar tribute to Elizabeth II, 1953, see *Garland for the Queen*.

Troilus and Cressida. Opera in 3 acts by *Walton to lib. by Christopher Hassall based on Chaucer and other sources (but not Shakespeare). Comp. 1947–54. Prod. CG 1954, S. Francisco and NY 1955, Milan 1956; rev. and prod. CG 1963; further rev., with Cressida's role altered to mez., 1972–6, prod. CG 1976, Leeds (Opera North) 1995.

tromba. (1) (It.). Trumpet.
(2) 8′ organ stop.

tromba da tirarsi (It.). Drawing-out trumpet. Slide tpt., probably invented in 14th cent., and required by Bach in 7 of his cantatas.

tromba marina (It.). Marine trumpet. Not a tpt., but a type of *monochord, developed in 12th cent. Had 3-sided body about 4′ long, tapering towards pegbox. Single str. (2 after 15th cent.) and played with bow. Produced only natural harmonics (hence assoc. with tpt. tone): player's left thumb lightly touched str(s)., his right hand drawing bow across str(s). Reason for 'marine' in title remains obscure (possibly corruption of Marian).

tromba spezzata (It.). Broken trumpet, i.e. *trombone.

Tromboncino, Bartolomeo (*b* Verona, *c.*1470; *d* ?Venice, after 1535). It. composer, prolific composer of *frottole. Active in Mantua until 1489, in Florence 1489–94. Returned to Mantua. In 1499 he murdered his wife and her lover. He was pardoned, but fled from Mantua in 1501 and for the next 6 years was in service of Lucrezia Borgia in Ferrara. In 1521 he settled in Venice.

trombone (from It., large trumpet). (1) Non-transposing brass instr., derived from *sackbut, of semi-cylindrical bore and cup-mouthpiece, generally equipped with slide which serves to extend length of the tube. In any one of the 7 recognized slide positions, the 7 fundamental notes of harmonic series can be prod. a semitone apart. A few pedal notes can also be prod.: the first tones of the harmonic series in various positions. Tbs. make a noble sound and have been used by composers for dramatic effect, e.g. by Mozart in *Don Giovanni* and by Beethoven in his 5th sym. (their first use in sym.). Many tb. concs. have been written. In baroque times they were confined to church mus. but are now standard in military and brass bands, and have been effectively used in jazz (several brilliant solo players incl. Tommy Dorsey and Glenn Miller). Members of the tb. family are: *treble*: required in scores by Purcell and Bach; *alto*: much used in baroque mus. but later replaced by ten. Britten uses one in *The Burning Fiery Furnace*; *tenor*: the most generally used, notated in either ten. or bass clef, with chromatic range from E below bass stave upwards for about 2½ octaves; *bass*: compass is a 4th below that of ten.; *tenor-bass*: ten. with a mechanism which allows for extra length of tubing for conversion to bass; *double-bass* or *contrabass*: octave in pitch below ten., sometimes required by Wagner; *valve*: with valves in place of a slide. made in ten. and bass sizes.

(2) Org. stop, type of *tuba* or *tromba*, 16' pitch, generally on pedal.

trombonino (It.). Alto trombone.

Trommel (Ger.). Drum, thus *kleine Trommel*, side-drum; *grosse Trommel*, bass drum; *Trommelschlägel*, drumstick.

Trompete (Ger.). *Trumpet.

trompette (Fr.). *Trumpet, hence *trompette à coulisse*, slide tpt.; *trompette à pistons*, normal tpt.; *trompette basse*, bass tpt.; *trompette cromatique*, valve tpt.

tronco, tronca (It.). Broken off short, truncated (used of a note, especially in singing).

trope. (1) Interpolations in plainsong words, resulting either in mus. melisma on one note or a fragment of new melody. Practice flourished from 9th to 15th cent., was abused, and finally banned by Tridentine reform. Survived only as the *sequence (trope set to final melisma of Alleluia).

(2) Term used by *Hauer to describe 44 pairs of unordered hexachords which are basis of his version of 12-note technique.

troppo (It.). Too much. Found usually in such directions as *allegro ma non troppo*, fast but not too fast.

Trotter, Thomas (Andrew) (*b* Birkenhead, 1957). Eng. organist. Won St Albans int. org. comp. 1979. Début London (RFH) 1980. Org., St Margaret's, Westminster, from 1982, City of Birmingham from 1983.

troubadours. See *minstrels*.

Trouble in Tahiti. Opera in 1 act by Leonard Bernstein, to own lib. Prod. Brandeis Univ. June 1952, cond. Bernstein; NY 1958. In 1984 was incorporated into rev. of *A Quiet Place*.

Troutbeck, John (*b* Blencowe, Cumberland, 1832; *d* Westminster, 1899). Eng. translator and clergyman. Precentor, Manchester Cath. 1865–9, minor canon, Westminster Abbey from 1869. For Novello's, trans. Bach *Passions*, *Christmas Oratorio*, *Magnificat*, etc., Beethoven *Mount of Olives*, Brahms *Song of Destiny*, Dvořák *Spectre's Bride*, *St Ludmilla*, Gounod *Redemption*, Weber *Jubilee Cantata*. His opera trans. incl. Mozart's *Così fan tutte* and *Die Entführung aus dem Serail*, Wagner's *Der fliegende Holländer*, and Gluck's *Orfeo*, *Iphigénie en Tauride*, and *Iphigénie en Aulide*.

Trout, The (*Die Forelle*). Song for v. and pf. by Schubert comp. 1817 (D550) to words by *Schubart. Exists in 4 versions, differing in only minor ways; last version (1821) has 5-measure pf. prelude. See also *'Trout' Quintet*.

'Trout' Quintet. Nickname of pf. quintet in A major by Schubert (D667), so called because 4th of 5 movts. is set of variations on his song *Die Forelle* (The *Trout, 1817, D550). Comp. 1819.

trouvères. See *minstrels*.

Trovatore, Il (The Troubadour). Opera in 4 acts by Verdi to lib. by Cammarano (with part of 3rd act and all 4th act completed after Cammarano's death by L. E. Bardare). Based on play *El trovador* by Gutiérrez. Comp. 1851–2, rev. 1856. Prod. Rome 1853, NY and London 1855.

Trowell, Brian (Lewis) (*b* Wokingham, 1931). Eng. musicologist. Lect. in mus. at Birmingham Univ., 1957–62, and King's Coll., London, 1964–5. Dir. of operas, GSMD 1963–7. Head of radio opera, BBC, 1967–70. Returned to King's Coll. 1970 as reader, becoming prof. 1974. Prof. of mus. Oxford Univ. 1988–96. Authority on 15th-cent. Eng. mus. and on opera of all periods.

Troyanos, Tatiana (*b* NY, 1938; *d* NY, 1993). Amer. mezzo-soprano. Joined NY City Opera 1963 (début as Hippolyta in *A Midsummer Night's Dream*). Hamburg Opera 1965–75. Aix-en-Provence Fest., 1966; Salzburg Fest. début 1969; CG 1969; NY Met 1976; La Scala 1977.

Troyens, Les (The Trojans). Opera in 5 acts by Berlioz to his own lib. from Virgil's *Aeneid*. Comp. 1856–8. To achieve a staging, Berlioz in 1863 divided it into two operas: Acts I and II became *La Prise de Troie* (The Capture of Troy) in 3 acts; Acts III, IV, and V became *Les Troyens à Carthage* (The Trojans at Carthage) in 5 acts with prelude not in orig. score, this part being perf. in Paris 4 Nov. 1863. First prod. of whole work but with the 2 parts on successive evenings, Karlsruhe, 6–7 Dec. 1890, cond. F. Mottl, likewise in Glasgow 18–19 March 1935, cond. E. Chisholm. F.p. on one evening, London, CG 1957, cond. Kubelik (but cut by 20 mins), f.p. complete on one evening, sung in Eng., Glasgow (Scottish Opera) May 1969, cond. Gibson, f.p. complete on one evening, sung in Fr., London CG Sept. 1969, cond. C. Davis. In Amer., f.p. of condensed vers. Boston March 1955, complete NY Met Sept. 1973.

trumpet. (1) Metal wind instr. of cylindrical bore, which in last quarter of its length widens into a moderate-sized bell. Cup-shaped mouthpiece. Since mid-19th cent. fitted with 3 valves which admit air to additional lengths of tubing, making available harmonic series at 6 pitches. Either a transposing instr. in B♭ (which may be switched to A) with compass from e upwards for nearly 3 octaves, or non-transposing in C (a tone higher). Used in orch. and jazz bands, also in military and brass bands (though sometimes replaced by cornet). Medieval tpts. without slides, valves, or finger-holes, were restricted to 'natural' notes of harmonic series. Straight tpt. of that time was over 6′ long, made in jointed metal sections, often with flared bell. Known as buisine. Shorter tpts. were called *claro* or *clarion*. In Renaissance, new methods of metalworking greatly improved sound quality, and the brilliant, high-pitched effects required from the baroque tpt. by Monteverdi and others were obtained from the *clarino*. Mutes in that day were inserted so far into the bell that they raised pitch by whole tone. Members of tpt. family are: *bass trumpet*: rare, sounding in C an octave lower than normal valved tpt.; *piccolo trumpet*; pitched octave higher, and sometimes has 4 valves; *Bach trumpet*: 19th-cent instr., in D, specially made (with valves) to play high tpt. parts in works of Baroque period. Ravel, Stravinsky, and Britten have included it in certain scores, and Maxwell Davies wrote a sonata for it. See also under *crook*.

(2) Org. reed stop, 8′ pitch.

trumpet marine (marine trumpet). See *tromba marina*.

trumpet tune or **voluntary**. Piece which, while not comp. for a tpt., imitates its sound, as on

tpt.-like org. stop. Title *Trumpet Voluntary* was given by Henry Wood to his transcr. of a kbd. piece for organ, brass, and kettledrums. This piece was mistakenly attrib. to Purcell, but is now known to be by Jeremiah *Clarke.

Truscott, Harold (*b* Ilford, 1914; *d* 1992). Eng. writer and composer. Worked for Royal Mail until 1948. Contrib. to various mus. periodicals, championing Brian, Schmidt, Medtner, Pfitzner, and other unfashionable composers. Wrote book on Beethoven's late str. qts. (1968). Taught pf. and comp. Blackheath Cons. and lect. at Huddersfield Tech. Coll. Comp. sym., 3 vn. sonatas, and 17 pf. sonatas.

Tsar's Bride, The (*Tsarskaya nevesta*). Opera in 4 acts by Rimsky-Korsakov to lib. adapted from L. A. Mey's play (1849) with extra scene by I. F. Tumenev. Comp. 1898. Prod. Moscow 1899, Seattle 1922, London 1931.

Tschaikowsky, Pyotr (Ger.). See *Tchaikovsky, Pyotr*.

Tschudi, Burkhardt. See *Shudi, Burkat*.

tuba. (1) Type of bass brass instr. played in vertical position in contrast to horizontal position of tpt., tb., etc. Term covers several kinds of brass-band instr., e.g. *euphonium, but term tuba usually means the standard orch. *bass tuba* in F (invented 1835) with compass from f an octave below bass clef upwards for about 3 octaves. Vaughan Williams comp. a conc. for bass tuba, 1954. There is a French 6-valve tuba which can cover four octaves and play Wagner contrabass parts. The *contrabass tuba* has become standard in orchestras since the 1940s, where it is known as the 'double C' (CC) tuba. This is a whole tone higher than the 'double B♭' (BB♭), with either 3 or 4 valves, which is generally used in bands. Most of tuba family are of semi-conical bore, with from 3 to 5 valves, and cup mouthpiece. The *tenor tuba* is rare, but is required by Strauss in *Don Quixote*, and in Brit. is identical with *euphonium*. Brass and military band tubas, sometimes called 'basses', are in E♭ (same as double-bass tuba). See also *sousaphone* and *Wagner tuba*.

(2) Sonorous organ stop, like *trumpet*, 8′, 16′, or 4′ pitch.

Tuba mirum (Hark, the trumpet). Part of the Requiem Mass, being a section of the *Dies Irae*. Verdi's setting is especially fine.

Tubb, Carrie [Caroline] (Elizabeth) (*b* London, 1876; *d* London, 1976). Eng. soprano. Principally known for work in oratorio, etc., but sang in opera (*Elektra, Hänsel und Gretel* etc.) at CG 1910 and later in Beecham co. Taught at GSMD from 1930 for over 30 years.

Tubin, Eduard (*b* Kallaste, 1905; *d* Stockholm, 1982). Estonian-born composer and conductor (Swed. cit. 1961). Cond. Vanemuine Th. Orch., Tartu, 1930–44. Keen interpreter of Stravinsky,

Bartók, and Kodály. Settled in Swed. 1944. His mus. is strongly melodic and attractively scored. Comps. incl.:

OPERAS: *Barbara von Tisenhusen* (1969); *Prosten från reigi (The Pastor of Reigi)* (1971).

ORCH.: syms., No.1 (1934), No.2 (1937), No.3 (1942), No.4 (1943), No.5 (1946), No.6 (1954), No.7 (1958), No.8 (1966), No.9 (1970), No.10 (1973); vn. conc. No.1 (1941), No.2 (1945); *Concertino*, pf., orch. (1944-6); db. conc. (1948); conc. for chamber orch. (1963); balalaika conc. (1964).

VOCAL: *Ylermi*, bar., orch. (1935, rev. 1977); *5 Kosjalaulud Songs*, bar., orch. (1975).

CHAMBER MUSIC: vn. sonata No.1 (1936), No.2 (1949), No.3 (1963); pf. sonata (1950); sax. sonata (1951); va. sonata (1965); *Capriccio*, vn., pf. (1971); fl. sonata (1979); *Quartet on Estonian Motifs*, str. qt. (1979).

PIANO: *10 Preludes* (1928-76); sonata (1950).

tubular bells. Orch. instr. in form of suspended tubes, tuned to the diatonic scale, struck by hammer held by player. Set of tubular bells sometimes spans an octave. Vaughan Williams wrote for them in finale of his 8th Sym., 1953-5.

Tucker, Norman (*b* Wembley, 1910; *d* Ruislip, 1978). Eng. pianist, opera administrator, and translator. Promising career as Mozart pianist cut short by manual disability. Co-dir., SW Th., 1947-54, dir. 1954-66. Under his aegis Janáček operas were brought into the Eng. repertory and (at that time) rare Verdi operas such as *Simon Boccanegra* (f. Brit. p. 1948), *Don Carlos*, and *Luisa Miller*. Nurtured Eng. singers such as Peter Glossop and Amy Shuard and conds. Colin Davis, Charles Mackerras, and Alexander Gibson. Trans. *Simon Boccanegra*, *Luisa Miller*, *Káťa Kabanová*, *Excursions of Mr Brouček*, *Visit of the Old Lady*, and other works. CBE 1956.

Tucker, Richard [Ticker, Reuben] (*b* Brooklyn, NY, 1913; *d* Kalamazoo, 1975). Amer. tenor. Sang in synagogues as cantor. Opera début NY 1943 (Alfredo in *La traviata*). Débuts: NY Met 1945, becoming prin. ten. there in It. and Fr. operas; Eur. (Verona) 1947 (with Callas on her It. début); CG 1958; La Scala 1969. Sang in Toscanini concert-opera perf. (*Aida*). His brother-in-law was Jan *Peerce. Only singer whose funeral service took place on the stage of the Met.

tucket. Old Eng. term for fanfare or flourish.

Tuckwell, Barry (Emmanuel) (*b* Melbourne, 1931). Australian horn-player and conductor. Hn.-player in Sydney SO 1947-50. Settled in Brit. 1951. Hallé 1951-3, SNO 1953-4, Bournemouth SO 1954-5, LSO 1955-68. Prof. of hn., RAM 1963-74. Salzburg Fest. 1975. Formed Tuckwell Wind Quintet. Soloist in concs. and chamber works. Cond. Tasmanian SO 1980-3. OBE 1965.

Tudor, Antony [William Cook] (*b* London, 1908; *d* NY, 1987). Eng. choreographer, dancer, and teacher. Joined Ballet Rambert 1930. Founded Dance Th. with A. de Mille 1937. Formed London Ballet 1938. Worked in NY 1940-50 as dancer and choreog. Royal Swed. Ballet 1949-50, NY City Ballet 1951-2. Dir. NY Met Opera Ballet Sch. 1950. Joined teaching staff, Juilliard Sch. Dir., Royal Swed. Ballet 1963-4. Ass. dir., Amer. Ballet Th. 1974. One of foremost and most perceptive 20th-cent. choreogs. Ballets (composers in parentheses) incl. *Dark Elegies* (Mahler) 1937, *Judgement of Paris* (Weill) 1938, *Gala Performance* (Prokofiev) 1938, *Romeo and Juliet* (Delius) 1943, *Lady of the Camellias* (Verdi) 1951, *Shadowplay* (Koechlin) 1967, *Knight Errant* (R. Strauss) 1968.

Tudor, David (Eugene) (*b* Philadelphia, 1926; *d* Tomkins Cove, NY, 1996). Amer. pianist, organist, and composer. Org., St Mark's, Philadelphia 1938-43, Swarthmore Coll. 1944-8. Taught pf. in NY 1948. Musician with Merce Cunningham Dance Co. from 1953. Began assoc. with *Feldman and *Cage 1948-9. Member 1951-3 of Cage's elec. studio project. Helped Cage in 1960s to pioneer 'live' elec. mus., as distinct from pre-recorded. Took part as pianist in f.p. of several Cage works, incl. *Music of Changes*, pf. conc., and *Atlas Eclipticalis with Winter Music*. Gave f.p.o. of *Bussotti's *5 Piano Pieces for David Tudor* and f. Amer. p. of Boulez's 2nd pf. sonata. Also player of bandoneon, performing works written for it by Kagel. Expertise in elec. works pioneered many techniques for composers. His own works use visual forces, e.g. light systems, laser projections, dance, TV, etc. They incl.: *Fluorescent Sound*, *Rain Forest*, *Assemblage*, *Video/Laser* I, II, and III, *4 Pepsi Pieces*, and many 'collaborative realizations' of mus. by Cage, Oliveros, etc.

Tudor Church Music. Name of famous critical edn. of mus. by Eng. composers of 16th and 17th cents. pubd. in 10 vols., 1929, with appendix 1948, under editorship of Percy Buck, E. H. Fellowes, Sylvia Townsend Warner, and A. Ramsbotham. Vols. contain: 1. Taverner Masses. 2. Byrd Services, etc. 3. Taverner motets. 4. Gibbons services and anthems. 5. Whyte. 6. Tallis. 7. Byrd Graduals. 8. Tomkins services, etc. 9. Byrd masses, etc. 10. Merbecke, Aston, and Parsley.

Tudway, Thomas (*b* c.1650; *d* Cambridge, 1726). Eng. composer and organist. Chorister, Chapel Royal, under Blow, 1660. Org., King's Coll., Cambridge, 1670-1726. Prof. of mus., Cambridge Univ., from 1705 (he was suspended from his university posts from July 1706 to Mar. 1707 for making uncomplimentary puns about Queen Anne). Wrote church mus. and compiled (1714-20) 6 MS vols. of Eng. church mus. from Reformation to Restoration.

tune. (1) As noun. Melody.

(2) Upper part of any simple comp.

(3) As verb. To est. correct intonation of an instr., e.g. to *tune* a pf. so that it is 'in tune'.

tuning. Adjustment of pitch in any instr. so that it corresponds to accepted norm. Str. players tune their instrs. just before playing by simple adjustments to the str., but kbd. instr. need lengthy professional attention.

tuning-fork. 2-pronged metal instr., invented 1711 by the trumpeter John Shore (*b* c.1662; *d* London, 1752; noted for his playing of Purcell and Handel). When set in vibration, it produces a sound wherewith to check the pitch of instr. and to give the pitch to singers. Gives a 'pure' tone, without upper harmonics.

Tunley, David (Evatt) (*b* Sydney, NSW, 1930). Australian composer and musicologist. Joined mus. faculty of Univ. of W. Australia 1958 (prof. from 1979, head of mus. dept. from 1985). Authority on 18th-cent. Fr. cantatas, Couperin, and Australian mus. in 20th cent. Comps. incl. cl. conc. (1966). Order of Australia 1987.

Turandot. (1) Opera in 3 acts by Puccini to lib. by Adami and Simoni after Gozzi's play (1762). Comp. 1920–6. His last work, the final scene being completed by *Alfano. Prod. Milan 1926, NY Met 1926, London 1927.

(2) Opera in 2 acts by Busoni to his own lib. after Gozzi, prod. Zurich 1917. Based on incidental mus. to the play, comp. 1911.

(3) Incidental music by Weber, comprising an ov. and 6 instr. items, to Schiller's trans. of Gozzi's play, prod. Stuttgart, Sept. 1809. Hindemith used a theme from it in his *Symphonic Metamorphosis of Themes by Weber*.

Turangalîla-symphonie (Sanskrit, *turanga*, 'the passage of time, movement, rhythm', and *lîla*, 'play in the sense of divine action on the cosmos, also the play of creation, destruction, life and death, also love'). Sym. in 10 movts. by *Messiaen for large orch. incl. Martenot, pf., and section of pitched and unpitched perc. Largest of 3 works inspired by Tristan and Isolde legend (the others being 5 *Rechants and *Harawi). Commissioned by *Koussevitzky, comp. between July 1946 and Nov. 1948. F.p. Boston SO cond. Bernstein, 1949. F.p. in England BBC broadcast, cond. W. Goehr, 1953; public, 1954. Movements entitled: *Introduction, Chant d'amour 1, Turangalîla 1, Chant d'amour 2, Joie du sang des étoiles, Jardin du sommeil d'amour, Turangalîla 2, Développement de l'amour, Turangalîla 3, Final*. Basis of complete ballet, choreog. Petit, Paris 1968, and choreog. Vesak, S. Francisco 1971. In 1960 at Hamburg 3 movts. were used for ballet, choreog. Van Dyk.

turbae (Lat.). Crowds. Name given to the chs. in oratorios and Passions in which the crowd participate in the action, e.g. in Bach's *St Matthew Passion*.

Turca, alla (It.). In the *Turkish style.

Turco in Italia, Il (The Turk in Italy). Opera in 2 acts by Rossini to lib. by Romani after C. Mazzola's *Il Turco in Italia* set by F. Seydelmann (1788). Prod. Milan 1814, London 1821, NY 1826.

Tureck, Rosalyn (*b* Chicago, 1914; *d* NY, 2003). Amer. pianist and conductor. Début Chicago 1923, NY 1935. Toured Europe from 1947, specializing in playing Bach on the modern pf. Formed Tureck Bach Players, London, 1959. First

woman to cond. NYPO, 1958. Taught at Philadelphia Cons. 1935–42, Juilliard Sch. 1943–55, and Univ. of Calif., San Diego, 1966–72. Prof. of mus., Univ. of Maryland 1982–4. Author of several books.

Turina (y Perez), **Joaquin** (*b* Seville, 1882; *d* Madrid, 1949). Sp. composer, conductor, and pianist. Cond. ballet in Sp.; prof. of comp., Madrid Cons., from 1931. Wrote mus. criticism. Works, nationalist in style, incl.:

OPERAS: *La sulamita* (c.1900); *Margot* (1914); *Jardin de oriente* (1923).

ORCH.: *La *procesión del Rocio* (1913); *Danzas fantásticas* (1920); *Sinfonia Sevillana* (1920); *Ritmos* (1928); *Rapsodia sinfónia*, pf., str. (1931).

CHAMBER MUSIC: pf. quintet (1907); str. qt. (1911); *La oración del torero*, str. qt. (also str. orch.) (1925); 2 vn. sonatas (1929, 1934); pf. qt. (1931); *Circulo*, pf. trio (1942).

PIANO: *Sonata romántica* (1909); *3 Andalusian Dances* (1912); *Mujeres españoles* (2 sets, 1917, 1932); *Jardines de Andalucia* (1924); *5 Tarjetas postales* (1930); *5 Siluetas* (1932).

VOICE & PIANO: *Poema en forma de canciones* (1918); *Saeta en forma de salve*; *Triptico* (1929).

GUITAR: sonata (1931); sonatina; *Fandanguillo* (1926); *Hommage a Tárrega* (1932); *Sevillana* (1923).

Turkish Music. Name given in 18th cent. to mus. for cymbals, triangles, and bass drum, the typical perc. instr. of Turkish military bands, several of which visited Austria. Thus Mozart introduced 'Turkish' effects into his opera *Die Entführung aus dem Serail*, K384 (1782) and called the finale of his pf. sonata No.11 in A, K331 (1778) a *rondo alla turca*.

turn. See *gruppetto*.

Turnage, Mark-Anthony (*b* Grays, Essex, 1960). Eng. composer. Comp.-in-association with CBSO 1989–93. Distinctive if eclectic style deriving from many sources incl. rock and jazz. Prin. comps.:

OPERAS: *Greek (1986–8); *Killing Time* (TV) (1991); *The Country of the Blind* (1996–7); *The Silver Tassie* (1997–9).

ORCH.: *Let us sleep now*, chamber orch. (1979, rev. 1982); *Night Dances* (1980–1); *Kind of Blue* (1981–2); *Ekaya* (1984); *Gross Intrusion*, amp. str. qt., str., 14 players (1987); *Three Screaming Popes* (1988–9); *Momentum* (1990–1); *Drowned Out* (1992–3); *Your Rockaby*, sax. conc. (1993); *Dispelling the Fears*, 2 tpt., orch. (1994–5); *Still Sleeping* (1997); *Bass Inventions*, db., orch. (2000); *Dark Crossing* (2001); *Scorched*, jazz trio, orch. (2002); *Eulogy* (2002–3); *On Opened Ground*, va. conc. (2003); *Scherzoid* (2003–4); *Crying Out Loud* (2004); *Yet Another Set To*, tb. conc. (2005); *Hidden Love Song*, sax. conc. (2005).

VOICE(S) & ENS.: *Lament for a Hanging Man*, sop., ens. (1983); *One Hand in Brooklyn Heights*, 16 vv., perc. (1986); *Greek Suite*, mez., ten., ens. (1989); *Some Days*, mez., orch. (1989); *Leaving*, sop., ten., ch., ens. (1990, rev. 1992); *Her Anxiety*, sop., ens.

(1991); *Twice Through the Heart*, scena, mez., 16 instr. (1994–6); *2 Baudelaire Songs*, sop., ens. (2003–4); *When I Woke*, sop., ens. (2005).

CHAMBER ENS.: *And Still a Softer Morning*, fl., vib., hp., vc. (1978, rev. 1983); *After Dark*, wind quintet, str. quintet (1982–3); *On All Fours*, chamber ens. (1985); *Sarabande*, sop. sax., pf. (1985); *Release*, 8 players (1987); *Kai*, vc., ens. (1989–90); *3 Farewells*, fl., cl., hp., str. qt. (1990); *Are You Sure?*, str. qt. (1990, rev. 1991); *3 Lullabies*, vc., pf. (1992); *This Silence*, cl., hn., bn., str. qt. (1992–3); *Set To*, brass ens. (1992–3); *Blood on the Floor*, large ens. (1993–4); *Two Elegies Framing a Shout*, sop. sax., pf. (1994); *An Invention on Solitude*, cl. quintet (1997); *A Fast Stomp*, pf. trio (2004); pf. quintet (2005); *Bleak Moments*, hn., str. quintet (2005).

PIANO: *Entranced* (1982); *Tune for Toru* (1996).

Turner, (Dame) **Eva** (*b* Oldham, 1892; *d* London, 1990). Eng. soprano. Joined ch., Carl Rosa Opera, 1916, singing with them to 1924 (solo début as Page in *Tannhäuser*, 1916). CG début 1920 (with Carl Rosa co.). Went to Milan 1924 for audition with Toscanini. La Scala début 1924. Thereafter est. as leading dramatic sop. in It. and Wagnerian repertory, particularly as Brünnhilde and as Turandot (although she did not create the role). Sang with BNOC, then CG 1928–30, 1933, 1935–9, 1947–8. Member of Chicago Opera 1928–9, 1938. Prof. of singing, Oklahoma Univ. 1950–9. Taught at RAM in London from 1959. One of orig. 16 soloists in Vaughan Williams's *Serenade to Music* 1938. DBE 1962.

Turn of the Screw, The. Opera in prol. and 2 acts, Op.54, by Britten to lib. by Myfanwy Piper based on Henry James's story (1898). Comp. 1954. Prod. Venice and London 1954, NY 1958. The 'screw' is represented by a theme and 15 variations, interludes between the 16 scenes. Scored for chamber orch.

Turnovský, Martin (*b* Prague, 1928). Cz. conductor. Début 1952, Prague SO. Cond. Czech Army SO 1955–60. Won Besançon int. comp. 1958. Cond., Brno State PO 1960–3, Pilsen Radio Orch. 1963–7, Dresden Staatskapelle 1967–8. Mus. dir. Norwegian Opera, Oslo 1975–80, Bonn Opera 1979–83. Amer. début 1968. Brit. début 1968. Chief cond. Prague SO 1992–2000.

tutti (plural of It. *tutto*, other forms *tutta, tutte*). All. (1) *tutti*, meaning 'everybody', is loosely used. A *tutti* is a passage, e.g. in conc., where the orch. (but not necessarily or even usually the whole orch.) plays without the soloist. 'The opening tutti' is a phrase often used in this connection.

(2) *tutte le corde*, 'all the str.': in pf. mus., means 'cease to play *una *corda'. tutto il cembalo* means the same.

Tuxen, Erik (Oluf) (*b* Mannheim, 1902; *d* Copenhagen, 1957). Ger.-born Danish conductor (Danish parentage; settled in Denmark 1916). Cond. Danish State Radio Orch. 1936–41. Guest cond. of leading orchs. in USA and Europe.

twelfth. Org. stop of the *mutation kind. Length and pitch 2⅔′ sounding an octave and a 5th (i.e. a 12th) above normal.

twelve-note composition (Ger. *Zwölftonmusik*). System of comp. in which all 12 notes within octave (7 white and 5 black notes of pf.) are treated as 'equal', in an ordered relationship where no group of notes predominates as in major/minor key system. One of first, if not the first, to devise such a system was J. M. *Hauer, but it is generally assoc. with *Schoenberg, whose 'method of composing with 12 notes which are related only to one another' was developed gradually 1920–5 and first used by him partially in his Op.23 and Op.24 (the *5 Piano Pieces* and *Serenade*) and throughout his Op.25 (the *Suite* for pf.). In the Schoenberg method, all pitches are related to a fixed order of the 12 chromatic notes, this order providing the work's basic shape. The fixed order is called a note-row (or series or set). No note is repeated within a row, which therefore comprises 12 different notes and no other. The note-row is not a theme but a source from which the comp. is made. It can be transposed to begin on any of the 12 pitches, and it may appear in retrograde, inversion, and retrograde-inversion. Since each of these transformations may also be transposed, each note-row can have 48 related pitch successions. Schoenberg's foremost contemporary disciples were *Berg and *Webern, but it should be noted that their application of his theory differs considerably from his own, particularly in the case of Webern, who explored the possibility of 'cellular' comp., i.e. self-contained structures within the note-row. From his type of serialism, later composers progressed to *total serialism.

Certain composers, e.g. Dallapiccola, Frank Martin, and Stravinsky, have used 12-note technique but have retained not only their marked individuality of style but a relationship in their work to the major/minor system of tonality. Other composers who do not subscribe to Schoenbergian tenets have used all 12 notes without repeating any one note. Examples of this are to be found in Walton, Britten, Hindemith, and Shostakovich.

Argument will no doubt continue about which composer was the first to use 12-note technique. Medieval candidates may be found, and Scriabin's 'mystic chord' is a pointer. Hauer's system pre-dated Schoenberg's; and the Ger. critic Herbert Eimert has written that Jef Golyscheff comp. 'the first unequivocal 12-note music' in 1914.

Twilight of the Gods (Wagner). See *Götterdämmerung*.

Two Widows, The (*Dvě vdovy*). Comic opera in 2 acts by Smetana to lib. by Emanuel Züngel adapted from *Les Deux Veuves* by Félicien Mallefille. Comp. 1873–4, rev. 1877 and 1882, prod. Prague 1874 (with spoken dialogue), 1878 (with recitatives and extra numbers); NY 1949; London 1963 (GSMD), 1993 (ENO); Wexford 1978.

Tye, Christopher (*b* c.1505; *d* Doddington-cum-Marche, 1573). Eng. composer. Lay clerk at King's College, Cambridge, 1537, having taken Mus.B. in 1536 after 10 years' study and teaching. Choirmaster, Ely Cath. 1543–61; Mus.D., Cambridge, 1545. Thought to have been teacher of Edward VI. In 1553 pubd. *The Acts of the Apostles*, trans. into Eng. metre, for 4 vv., with lute. Ordained 1560 and in 1561 became rector of Doddington-cum-Marche, Isle of Ely. Wrote anthems in popular and tuneful style, several motets, services, and masses, incl. a 'Western Wynde' mass, and the *Euge bone* mass. Also instr. *In nomines*.

tympanon. Medieval name for **dulcimer*.

tympanum, tympana. The kettledrum(s) as spelt in medieval documents (sometimes *tymbal*), but the modern spelling *timpani* is now standard.

Tyrrell, John (*b* Salisbury (now Harawe), S. Rhodesia (Zimbabwe), 1942). Rhodesian-born musicologist. Lect. in mus., Nottingham Univ. 1976, reader in opera studies 1989–2000. Prof. of mus. Cardiff. Univ. from 2000. Authority on Janáček. Author of *Káťa Kabanová* (Cambridge Opera Handbook, 1982); *Janáček's Operas: a Documentary Account* (1992); *Intimate Letters: Janáček's correspondence with Kamila Stösslová* (1994); and *Czech Opera* (1988). Executive ed. *New Grove Dictionary of Music and Musicians* (2nd edn., 2001).

Tyson, Alan (Walter) (*b* Glasgow, 1926; *d* 2000). Scottish musicologist. Fellow of All Souls Coll., Oxford, 1952–94. Visiting prof. of mus., Columbia Univ., NY, 1969 and Univ. of Calif. at Berkeley 1977–8. Authority on Beethoven. Ed. of *Beethoven Studies* Vol.I (1973), II (1977), III (1982). Pubd. Clementi thematic catalogue 1967 and (with A. Rosenthal) *Mozart's Thematic Catalogue* (facsimile) (1990). Wrote (with Douglas Johnson and Robert Winter) *The Beethoven Sketchbooks* (1985); *Mozart: Studies of the Autograph Scores* (1987). CBE 1989.

Tzigane (Gipsy). Concert rhapsody for vn. and pf. by Ravel, comp. 1924; also orch. version, 1924.

U

Überbrettl. Type of cabaret est. in Berlin on 18 Jan. 1901 until 1902 by the writer Ernst von Wolzogen (librettist of Strauss's *Feuersnot*), in assoc. with the poets Bierbaum and Wedekind. Their aim was to raise standard of variety theatre by mimes, poems recited with mus., etc. Mus. contributions from such composers as Oscar Straus, Zemlinsky, and Schoenberg (whose *Pierrot Lunaire* of 1912 demonstrates the surviving influence of the cabaret).

Uccelli, Gli (Respighi). See *Birds, The*.

Uchida, Mitsuko (*b* Tokyo, 1948). Japanese pianist. Début Vienna 1963. Won Beethoven comp. 1968, 2nd prize in Chopin comp., Warsaw, 1970, 2nd prize Leeds comp. 1975. Played all Mozart sonatas, London and Tokyo, 1982, and all Mozart concs. as soloist-cond. with ECO, London 1985–6. NY début 1987. Salzburg Fest. 1989.

Uhde, Hermann (*b* Bremen, 1914; *d* Copenhagen, 1965). Ger. bass-baritone. Opera début Bremen 1936 (Titurel in *Parsifal*). Freiburg Opera 1938–40; Munich 1940–2; Hamburg 1949–50; Munich again after 1951. Débuts: Salzburg Fest. 1949; Bayreuth 1951; CG 1953; NY Met 1955. First Met Wozzeck. Particularly fine as Wagner's Dutchman. Died during perf. of Bentzon's *Faust III*.

Uhl, Fritz (*b* Matzleinsdorf, nr. Vienna, 1928; *d* Munich, 2001). Austrian tenor. Opera début Graz 1952. Munich Opera 1958; Vienna from 1961. Débuts: Bayreuth 1957; CG 1963; Salzburg Fest. 1968. A fine Florestan and Walther. Prof., Vienna Cons. from 1981.

Uilleann pipes (*uilleann*, 'elbow'). Irish bagpipes, played by wind supplied by bellows held under player's arm.

ukelele [ukulele] (from Hawaiian 'leaping flea'). Small 4-str. instr. like a guitar, of Portuguese orig. and introduced by the Portuguese to Sandwich Island *c*.1877. Patented in Hawaii 1917, where it became very common, its popularity spreading to USA and Europe. Easy to learn, with special notation. Played by strumming with fingers. Eng. popularity much aided by its assoc. with the Lancashire comedian George Formby (1905–61).

Ukrainian Symphony. One of nicknames for Tchaikovsky's Sym. No.2 in C minor, Op.17 (the other being 'Little Russian') owing to use of Ukrainian folk-tunes in 1st and 4th movts. Comp. 1872, rev. 1879–80.

Ullmann, Viktor (*b* Teschen, 1898; *d* Auschwitz concentration camp, 1944). Austrian composer. Ass. cond. to Zemlinsky at New Ger. Th., Prague, 1920–7. Prin. cond. Aussig Opera 1927–8. As follower of Rudolf Steiner, worked in bookstore in Stuttgart before returning to Prague in 1933 to teach, write, and lecture. In Sept. 1942 was deported to Theresienstadt (Terezin) concentration camp where he organized concerts, lectured, and comp. until his removal to Auschwitz. His opera *Der Kaiser von Atlantis* was written in Theresienstadt and reached dress-rehearsal stage when the Nazi guards recognized its satirical portrait of Hitler. Works incl.:

OPERAS: *Peer Gynt* (1928, lost); *Der Sturz des Antichrist* (1935); *Der zerbrockene Krug* (1940); *Der *Kaiser von Atlantis* (1943).

ORCH.: *5 Variations and Double Fugue on a Piano Piece of Arnold Schoenberg* (1929); *Concerto for Orchestra* (1940); pf. conc. (1940); ov., *Don Quixote* (1943, pf. score only); *Sinfonie 'Von meiner Jugend'* (reconstructed by B. Wulff) (1943).

CHAMBER MUSIC: 3 str. qts. (No.3 written in Theresienstadt); Octet, pf., winds, str.; vn. sonata.

PIANO: 7 sonatas.

Ulster Orchestra, The. Sym. orch. of N. Ireland. Founded 1966 to give regular concert series in Belfast and in other towns in province. First recording 1979 (music by Harty to mark his centenary). Prin. conds.: M. Miles 1966–7; S. Comissiona 1967–9; E. Cosma 1969–74; A. Francis (ass. cond. from 1969) 1974–7; B. Thomson 1977–85; V. Handley 1985–9; Y. P. Tortelier 1989–92; En Shao 1992–5; Dmitry Sitkovetsky 1996–2001; Thierry Fischer from 2001. Orch. has toured England and has added works by Harty and Bax to its list of recordings.

Ultimos Ritos (Last Rites). Oratorio by *Tavener for sop., alto, ten., and bass soloists, 5 priests (speakers), ch., org., large orch. Comp. 1972. F.p. Haarlem 1974, f.p. in England, Winchester and London 1975.

Ulysses. (1) Cantata by *Seiber, 1946–7, based on text from Joyce's novel of same name (1922).

(2) Opera (*Ulisse*) by *Dallapiccola, 1959–68, in prologue, 2 acts, and epilogue, to his own lib. based on Homer. Prod. Berlin 1968, London 1969 (BBC studio perf.).

(3) Opera (*Ulysse*) in 5 acts by Rebel to lib. by H. Guichard based on Homer. Prod. Paris 1703.

(4) Opera (*Ulysses*) in 3 acts by Keiser to lib. by F. M. Lersner after Guichard's lib. *Ulysse*. Prod. Copenhagen 1722.

(5) Opera (*Ulysses*) in 3 acts by J. C. Smith to lib. by S. Humphreys based on Homer. Prod. London 1733.

See also *Il *ritorno d'Ulisse in patria*.

umstimmen (Ger.). To tune in some special way (see *scordatura*). So the noun *Umstimmung*.

Unanswered Question, The (or *A Contemplation of a Serious Matter*). Orch. work by *Ives, comp. 1906, rev. *c*.1932, for tpt., 4 fl. (or 2 fl., ob., cl.), str., and pf.

unda maris (Wave of the sea). Org. stop much like *voix céleste*.

Undine [Ondine]. Ballet in 3 acts and 5 scenes by Henze, choreog. Ashton. Prod. London 1958, Munich, Berlin, 1959. Also opera by *Lortzing (1845).

unessential note. A passing note, suspension, appoggiatura, etc., whereas an essential note is an actual note of a chord.

'Unfinished' Symphony. There are many unfinished syms. (e.g. by Tchaikovsky, Mahler, Elgar, Shostakovich) but this title is generally taken to refer only to Schubert's No.8 in B minor (1822, D759). His 7th in E was also left incomplete. No one knows why the 8th was left unfinished—2 movts. were completed and sketches exist for the scherzo. Romantic solutions have been invented, but the truth seems to be that Schubert either forgot about it or abandoned it because he could not find comparable inspiration for the 3rd and 4th movts. F.p. Vienna, Dec. 1865, cond. Herbeck. Among 'completions' of the sym. are those by G. Abraham (1971) and B. Newbould.

Ungar, Ungarisch (Ger.). Hungarian.

Unger [Ungher], **Caroline** (*b* Stuhlweissenburg, 1803; *d* Florence, 1877). Austrian contralto. Opera début Vienna 1821 as Rossini's Tancredi. In 1824 in Vienna sang in f.p. of Beethoven's 9th Sym. (it was she who turned the deaf Beethoven to face the audience after the 9th so that he could see applause). Sang for several years in It., creating roles in Donizetti operas and Bellini's *La straniera*. Paris début 1833, winning high praise from Rossini. Retired on marriage 1843.

Unger, Georg (*b* Leipzig, 1837; *d* Leipzig, 1887). Ger. tenor. Has claim to be the first Wagner *Heldentenor*. Opera début Leipzig 1867. At Hans Richter's suggestion, created role of Siegfried at first Bayreuth Fest. 1876. Sang in London 1877 at Wagner's concerts in Royal Albert Hall, although he frequently failed to appear. Sang at Leipzig Opera until 1881.

Unger, Gerhard (*b* Bad Salzungen, Thuringia, 1916). Ger. tenor. Opera début Weimar 1947. Berlin Deutsche Staatsoper 1949–61; Stuttgart 1961–3; Hamburg 1963–6; Vienna 1966–70. Salzburg Fest. début 1962. Wide repertory of character parts, e.g. Pedrillo (which he sang over 300 times), the Captain in *Wozzeck*, Skuratov in *From the House of the Dead*, and Mime (*Der Ring*).

ungherese (It.). Hungarian.

unison. Sounding of the same note by all perf., e.g. *unison singing*, everyone singing the same tune but not in harmony.

uniti (It.). United. Term used to revoke a direction such as *divisi*.

unit organ. Type of org., sometimes called extension org., which, to save space, has various stops which 'borrow' pipes from each other, e.g. pipes of 8′ stop may also be used for 4′ stop by a connection which draws on them an octave higher throughout. Cinema orgs. are unit orgs.

Universal Edition. Publishing house formed in Vienna 1901 by amalgamation of several privately-owned businesses. In 1904 bought Munich firm of Aibl which brought in many R. Strauss works. Other firms were absorbed and after Alfred Kalmus joined the firm in 1909 the catalogue was extended to include a large number of contemporary composers (Delius, Bartók, Mahler, Schoenberg, Webern, Zemlinsky, Szymanowski, and Janáček among them). Since the Second World War the firm has published works by Berio, Birtwistle, Boulez, Dallapiccola, Einem, Kagel, Kurtag, Ligeti, Shostakovich, and Stockhausen. Universal Edn. was founded by Kalmus in 1937 and is an independent house.

Universal Prayer. Cantata by *Panufnik to poem by Pope for sop., cont., ten., and bass soloists, 3 harps, org., and mixed ch. Comp. 1968–9. F.p. NY (Cath. of St John the Divine) cond. Stokowski, 1970.

un poco (It., sometimes shortened to *un po'*; Fr. *un peu*). A little (often in the sense of 'rather').

unprepared suspension. Effect similar to *suspension* but without *preparation, i.e. the sounding in a chord of a concordant note which is to remain (in the same 'part') in next chord as a discordant note.

Unsuk Chin (*b* Seoul, 1961). S. Korean composer and pianist. She settled in Berlin, working at Technical Univ. EMS. Works incl. *Trojan Women*, 13 female singers, women's ch., orch. (1986, rev. 1990); *Acrostic-Wordplay*, sop., ens. (1991–3); *Santika Ekatala*, orch. (1993); *Fantaisie mécanique*, 5 instr. (1994); pf. conc. (1996–7); *Kalá*, sop., bass, ch., orch. (2000); vn. conc. (2001); Double Conc., pf., perc., ens. (2002); *snagS 7 Snarls*, sop., orch. (2003–4).

Unterwerk (Ger.). Under work. *choir organ.

up-beat. Upward movement of cond.'s baton or hand, especially to indicate beat preceding barline. See also *Anacrusis*.

upper mordent. See *mordent*.

upper partials. 2nd, 3rd, 4th, and higher tones in harmonic series which are at fixed intervals above fundamental.

Uppman, Theodor (*b* Pao Alto, San Jose, Calif., 1920; *d* NY, 2005). Amer. baritone. Opera début Stanford Univ., 1946 (Papageno in *Die Zauberflöte*). Sang Pelléas (with Maggie Teyte as Mélisande) in concert perf. cond. Monteux, S. Francisco SO, 1947. S. Francisco Opera 1948; NY City Opera 1948. Created Billy Budd in Britten's opera, CG 1951. NY Met 1953–77 (début as Pelléas).

upright piano. Pf. in which str. are upright (vertical), not, as in grand pf., horizontal. First built by Hawkins of Philadelphia, 1800.

Upshaw, Dawn (b Nashville, Tenn., 1960). Amer. soprano. Sang title-role in f. Amer. p. of Hindemith's *Sancta Susanna* at Manhattan Sch., 1983. Spoleto Fest. (USA) 1984 (Echo in *Ariadne auf Naxos*). Débuts: NY Met 1985; Salzburg Fest. 1986; London 1990 (Prom.). Created Clemence in Saariaho's *L'amour de loin*, Salzburg 2000. Soloist in celebrated recording of Gorécki's 3rd Sym.

Urhan, Chrétien (b Montjoie, 1790; d Paris, 1845). Fr. violinist and composer. Played in Paris Opéra orch. 1816–27. Leader Orch. de Société des Concerts du Conservatoire from 1828. Used a 5-string vn. Comp. str. qts., pf. pieces, etc.

Ursuleac, Viorica (b Cernăuti, Romania, 1894; d Ehrwald, Tyrol, 1985). Romanian soprano. Opera début Agram 1922 (Charlotte in *Werther*); Vienna Volksoper 1924–6; Frankfurt Opera 1926–30; Vienna 1930–4; Berlin 1935–7; Munich 1937–44. Salzburg Fest. 1930–4 (début as Marschallin in *Der Rosenkavalier*), 1942, 1944, 1952. R. Strauss's favourite sop. in 1930s. Created Arabella (1933), Maria in *Friedenstag* (1938), and Countess in *Capriccio* (1942). Also sang Danae at Salzburg dress rehearsal of *Die Liebe der Danae* 1944. Married to cond. Clemens *Krauss. CG début 1934. Had 83 roles in her repertory and sang 506 perfs. of 12 Strauss roles during her career.

Urtext (Ger.). Orig. text, meaning an edn. of a score giving, or purporting to give, composer's intentions without later editorial additions—much needed in case of *Bruckner, for example.

Ussachevsky, Vladimir (Alexis) (b Hailar, Manchuria, 1911; d NY, 1990). Manchurian-born composer of Russ. parentage (Amer. cit.). Settled in USA 1930. Taught at Columbia Univ. 1947–80 (prof. from 1964). Co-dir., Columbia-Princeton elec. mus. centre from 1959. Up to 1951 wrote mus. with Russ. romantic flavour, then experimented with tape-recorder comp. in collab. with Otto Luening. After that comp. mainly elec. mus., incl. scores for theatre, radio, TV, and films.

Ustvolskaya, Galina (Ivanovna) (b Petrograd, 1919). Russ. composer. Taught comp. at coll. attached to Leningrad Cons. 1948–77. Her mus. was little played during Stalin régime, being regarded as 'narrow-minded'. Shostakovich defended her and sent her his works in MS for comment. He quotes from the finale of her cl. trio (1949) in his 5th str. qt. and in his *Suite on Verses of Michelangelo*. Some of her works are on a vast scale and she used serialism in some. Prin. comps.:

ORCH.: syms.: No.1, 2 boys' vv., orch. (1955), No.2 (*True and Eternal Bliss*), v., orch. (1979), No.3 (*Jesus Messiah, Save Us!*), soloist, orch. (1983), No.4 (*Prayer*), tpt., tom-tom, pf., alt. (1985–7), No.5 (*Amen*), ob., tpt., tuba, vn., perc. (1989–90); conc., pf., str., timp. (1946).

INSTR. ENS.: *Composition No.1 (Dona nobis pacem)*, picc., tuba, pf. (1970–1), *No.2 (Dies Irae)*, 8 db., perc., pf. (1972–3), *No.3 (Benedictus qui venit)*, 4 fl., 4 bn., pf. (1974–5).

CHAMBER MUSIC: cl. trio (1949); Octet, 2 ob., 4 vn., timp., pf. (1949–50); vn. sonata (1952); *Grand Duo*, vc., pf. (1959); *Duet*, vn., pf. (1964).

PIANO: sonatas: No.1 (1947), No.2 (1949), No.3 (1952), No.4 (1957), No.5 (1986), No.6 (1988).

ut. Keynote of major scale, according to system of vocal syllables derived from d'Arezzo, now generally replaced by *do* (*doh* in *Tonic Sol-fa). In many countries, incl. France, *ut* and *doh* have become attached to C in whatever key this may occur.

utility music. See *Gebrauchsmusik*.

Utopia Limited, or The Flowers of Progress. Operetta by Sullivan to lib. by Gilbert. Comp. 1893. Prod. London 1893, NY 1894.

Utrecht Te Deum and Jubilate. Setting by Handel, 1712–13, to celebrate Peace of Utrecht and f.p. in St Paul's Cath., London, 7 July 1713.

Utrenja. Choral work by *Penderecki (1969–71) in 2 parts, both commissioned by W. Ger. Radio (Cologne). Part I, *The Entombment of Christ*, sop., cont., ten., bass, and basso profundo soloists, 2 mixed ch., and orch. F.p. Altenberg Cath. 1970. Part II, *The Resurrection of Christ*, for same forces plus boys' ch. F.p. Münster Cath. 1971. 'Utrenja' is the Russ. Orthodox matins.

V

va. Short for viola.

Vactor, David van. See *Van Vactor, David*.

Vaduva, Leontina (*b* Romania, 1964). Romanian soprano. Opera début Toulouse 1987 (Massenet's *Manon*). Paris 1988; CG début 1988.

Vakula the Smith (*Kuznets Vakula*). Opera in 3 acts by Tchaikovsky to lib. by Y. Polonsky after Gogol's story *Christmas Eve*. Comp. 1874. Prod. St Petersburg 1876, BBC (studio prod.) 1990. Rev. 1885 and 1886 as *Cherevichki.

Valdengo, Giuseppe (*b* Turin, 1914). It. baritone. Opera début Parma 1936 (Figaro in *Il barbiere di Siviglia*). Débuts: La Scala 1941; NY City Opera 1946; NY Met 1947; Glyndebourne 1955. Sang Iago (*Otello*), Amonasro (*Aida*), and Falstaff in Toscanini's NBC opera broadcasts.

Válek, Jiří (*b* Prague, 1923). Cz. composer. Ed.-in-chief of publishers of Guild of Czech Composers 1959–73. Works incl. 2 operas (incl. *Hamlet Our Contemporary*, 1979–84); 16 programmatic syms. (No.5 is *Guernica*, 1968); vn. conc.; vc. conc.; ca conc.; 4 str. qts.; 3 pf. sonatas; songs.

Valen, Fartein (Olav) (*b* Stavanger, 1887; *d* Haugesund, 1952). Norweg. composer. Spent early years in Madagascar. Mus. librarian Oslo Univ. 1927–36. Came under influence of Schoenberg in 1913, and evolved own system of atonal polyphony. Wrote 5 syms. (5th unfinished); vn. conc.; pf. conc.; 2 str. qts.; *Sonette di Michelangelo* for orch.; 2 str. qts.; vn. sonata; pf. trio; 2 pf. sonatas; organ works; songs.

Valentini-Terrani, Lucia (*b* Padua, 1946; *d* Seattle, 1998). It. mezzo-soprano. Début Padua 1969 (title-role in *La Cenerentola*). Sang Rossini roles at La Scala from 1973 and at Pesaro from 1984. NY Met début 1974; Los Angeles 1979; CG 1987.

Välkki, Anita (*b* Sääksmäki, 1926). Finn. soprano. Began career as actress and in operetta. Opera début Helsinki 1955. Royal Opera, Stockholm, from 1960. Débuts: CG 1961; NY Met 1962; Bayreuth 1963. Fine Brünnhilde, Kundry, Turandot, and Aida.

Valkyrie, The (Wagner). See *Walküre, Die*.

Vallée d'Obermann (Obermann Valley). Pf. work by Liszt, No.6 of *Première Année (Suisse)* of *Années de pèlerinage* (1848–54).

Vallin, Ninon [Vallin-Pardo, Eugénie] (*b* Montalieu-Veraieu, 1886; *d* Lyons, 1961). Fr. soprano. Début Paris Opéra-Comique 1912 (Micaela in *Carmen*). Sang at Opéra-Comique for rest of her career in roles such as Mimi, Mignon, Louise, Manon, and Carmen. La Scala 1916–17; Buenos Aires 1916–36; Paris Opéra début 1920.

Valois, (Dame) **Ninette de** [Stannus, Edris] (*b* Baltiboys, Ireland, 1898; *d* London, 2001). Irish dancer, choreographer, and administrator. Danced at CG in opera ballet 1919 and with Ballets Russes 1923–6. Opened London Acad. of Choreog. Art 1926 (closed 1931) and began collab. with Lilian Baylis at Old Vic. First choreog. for Mozart's *Les Petits Riens*, 1928. Dir., Vic-Wells Ballet (later SW Ballet) 1931, running SW Ballet sch. at same time. Founded SW Opera Ballet (later SW Theatre Ballet) 1946 (became Royal Ballet 1956). Resigned as dir., Royal Ballet, 1963. Among ballets she choreog. are *La Création du monde* (Milhaud, 1931), *Job* (Vaughan Williams, 1931), *The Haunted Ballroom* (Toye, 1934), *The Rake's Progress* (Gordon, 1935), *The Gods go a-begging* (Handel-Beecham, 1936), *Checkmate* (Bliss, 1937), *The Prospect before us* (Boyce-Lambert, 1940), and *Don Quixote* (Gerhard, 1950). CBE 1947, DBE 1951, CH 1982, OM 1992.

valse. See *waltz*.

Valse, La (The Waltz). *Poème choréographique* for orch. by Ravel. Begun 1906–14, completed 1919–20. F.p. Paris 1920. Also prod. as 1-act ballet, Paris 1928, Monte Carlo 1929, choreog. by Nijinskaya for Ida Rubinstein. Other versions by Balanchine 1951, Ashton 1958. Versions for solo pf. and 2 pf. by Ravel, for 4 hands by L. Garban.

Valses Nobles et Sentimentales (Noble and Sentimental Waltzes). Work for solo pf. by Ravel, comp. and f.p. 1911 (arr. for 4 hands by L. Garban). Orch. by Ravel 1912 for ballet *Adélaïde, ou Le Langage des fleurs* to lib. by Ravel, choreog. Clustine, prod. Paris 1912 (later lib. and choreog. Lifar 1938, Ashton 1947, MacMillan 1966, Hynd 1975).

Valse Triste (Sad Waltz). Waltz by *Sibelius, Op.44, orig. comp. for str. 1903 as one of 6 items of incidental mus. to play *Kuolema* (Death) by Arvid Järnefelt, in Helsinki. Rev. for orch. 1904.

valve (Fr. *piston*; Ger. *Ventil*; It. *pistone*). Mechanism invented *c.*1813 by the horn-player Heinrich Stölzel and improved in 1818 in collaboration with Friedrich Blühmel, whereby all the notes of the chromatic scale were made available to brass instr. Pitch altered by increasing or decreasing length of tube through which wind must go to produce sound (except normal *trombones, for which slide is sufficient). 2 types in use, *piston*, in which piston works up and down in casing, and *rotary*, a 4-way stop-cock turning in cylindrical case and governed by a spring. Credit for the first type of valve must go to Charles Clagget, an

Irishman, who patented an invention in 1788 which enabled pitch to be altered by means of a lever.

valve instruments. Brass instrs. which have *valves, i.e. all except certain *trombones.

Valverde, Joaquin (*b* Badajoz, 1846; *d* Madrid, 1910). Sp. composer, conductor, and flautist. Played fl. in th. orchs. 1859–71, then cond. 1871–91. Wrote over 30 *zarzuelas* and songs, incl. the popular *Clavelitos* (Carnations), and over 200 instr. works.

vamping. Improvised acc. to a song or instr. solo, often by pianist who cannot read notation but 'plays by ear'.

Vampyr, Der (The Vampire). Opera in 2 acts by Marschner to lib. by W. A. Wohlbrück after H. L. Ritter's play based on story *The Vampyre* (1819) by Byron's doctor J. W. Polidori, who worked on sketches abandoned by Byron. Comp. 1827–8. Prod. Leipzig 1828, London 1829. Usually perf. in edn. by Pfitzner, 1925.

Van Allan, Richard [Jones, Alan Philip] (*b* Clipstone, Notts., 1935). Eng. bass. Glyndebourne ch. 1964 (John Christie Award 1966). Glyndebourne début 1966 (2nd Priest, 2nd Armed Man in *Die Zauberflöte*). CG début 1971. Has sung with ENO, WNO, Paris Opéra, Wexford Fest. Ochs in *Der Rosenkavalier* for first time at San Diego 1976. Dir., Nat. Opera Studio, 1986–2002. CBE 2002.

Van Beinum, Eduard (*b* Arnhem, Holland, 1900; *d* Amsterdam, 1959). Dutch conductor. Began career in Haarlem 1926–31; 2nd cond., Concertgebouw Orch. of Amsterdam 1931–8, then associate to *Mengelberg whom he succeeded as chief cond. 1945. London début, LPO 1946. Took Concertgebouw Orch. on Amer. tour 1954. Prin. cond. LPO 1949–51. Cond. Los Angeles PO 1956–9. Salzburg Fest. 1957 (Berlin PO).

van Biene, August. See *Biene, August van*.

Van Dam, José [Van Damme, Joseph] (*b* Brussels, 1940). Belg. bass. Opera début Liège 1960 (Don Basilio in *Il barbiere di Siviglia*). Sang minor roles at Paris Opéra and Opéra-Comique 1961–5. Geneva Opera 1965–7; Deutsche Oper, Berlin, from 1967. Salzburg Fest. début 1968. CG début 1973 as Escamillo, a role he has sung with much success in all leading opera houses, e.g. NY Met 1965. Created title-role in Messiaen's *Saint François d'Assise*, Paris 1983. Wide concert repertory.

Vandernoot, André (*b* Brussels, 1927; *d* Brussels, 1991). Belg. conductor. Cond. Royal Flemish Opera, Antwerp, 1958. Mus. dir. Brussels Théâtre Royal de la Monnaie 1959–73, Belg. Nat. Orch. 1974–5, Brabants Orch. 1979–89.

van der Stucken, Frank V. See *Stucken, Frank V. van der*.

van Dieren, Bernard. See *Dieren, Bernard van*.

Vaness, Carol (Theresa) (*b* San Diego, 1952). Amer. soprano. Won S. Francisco Opera audi-

tions 1976. Début S. Francisco 1977 (Vitellia in *La clemenza di Tito*). Débuts: NY City Opera 1979; Eur. (Bordeaux) 1981; CG 1982; Glyndebourne 1982; NY Met 1984; Salzburg Fest. 1988; La Scala 1990. Frequent soloist in Verdi's *Requiem*, Beethoven's 9th Sym., etc.

Vanessa. Opera in 4 acts by Barber, Op.32, to lib. by Menotti based on I. Dinesen's *Seven Gothic Tales* (1934). Comp. 1956–7, rev. 1964. Prod. NY Met 1958, Salzburg Fest. 1958.

Van Kampen, Christopher (Francis Royle) (*b* Pinner, 1945; *d* Pinner, 1997). Eng. cellist. Début with Bournemouth SO 1967 in Elgar conc. Prin. vc., RPO 1970–3, London Sinfonietta. Soloist with leading orchs.

Van Rooy, Anton(ius Maria Josephus) (*b* Rotterdam, 1870; *d* Munich, 1932). Dutch bass-baritone. Sang Wotan at Bayreuth 1897 and thereafter at every fest. until 1902. Sang Wagner roles at CG 1898–1908, 1912–13, and NY Met 1898–1908 (except one season). Sang Amfortas in unauthorized *Parsifal*, NY 1903, and was banned from Bayreuth. Finest male Wagnerian of his generation, and equally good in *Lieder*. Retired 1913.

Vänskä, Osmo (*b* Sääminki, Finland, 1953). Finn. conductor and clarinettist. Prin. cl. Turku PO 1971–6, co-prin. cl. Helsinki PO 1977–82. Studied cond. with Jorma Panula at Sibelius Acad. 1st prize Besançon int. cond. comp. 1982. Chief cond. Lahti SO from 1988. Cond. Iceland SO 1993–6. Chief cond. BBC Scottish SO 1995–2002. Boston SO début 2002, NYPO 2003, Berlin PO 2004. Mus. dir. Minnesota Orch. from 2003.

van Wyk, Arnold. See *Wyk, Arnold van*.

Várady, Julia (*b* Oradea, 1941). Hungarian-born soprano. Cluj State Opera 1960–70; Frankfurt 1970–2; Munich from 1972. Débuts: Brit. (Edinburgh Fest.) 1974 (with Scottish Opera as Gluck's Alcestis); Salzburg Fest. 1976; NY Met 1978; CG 1992. Outstanding Vitellia in *La clemenza di Tito* and other dramatic roles. Created Cordelia in Reimann's *Lear* (Munich 1978). Sings sop. role in Britten's *War Requiem*.

Varèse, Edgard (Victor Achille Charles) (*b* Paris, 1883; *d* NY, 1965). Fr.-born composer and conductor (Amer. cit. 1926). Studied in Turin, Schola Cantorum, Paris, 1904–5 (comp. with d'Indy, theory with Roussel), and Paris Cons. with Widor 1905. Lived mainly in Berlin 1907–15, active as cond. Went to NY 1915. Founder-cond. New SO 1919 to perform modern mus.; resigned because of pressure to popularize programmes. With Salzedo, founded International Composers' Guild 1921, devoted to new mus., which lasted until 1927, when (with Slonimsky, Ives, Cowell, and Chávez) founded Pan-American Assoc. of Composers. Returned to Paris 1928–32, then taught at Amer. colleges. Founded ch. to perform early mus. in NY 1940. Began to experiment with tape and elecs. 1953. Tireless experimenter with unusual sounds and instr. combinations, many of his works being patterns of rhythm and accents. Was championed by Stokowski in Philadelphia where *Amériques* and *Arcana* provoked hostile reactions. Most of his early works, in a romantic idiom, are lost or destroyed. Prin. comps.:

ORCH.: **Amériques* (1918–21); *Hyperprism*, small orch. and perc. (1923); **Octandre*, small orch. (1923); **Intégrales*, woodwind, brass, perc. (1924–5); *Arcana* (1925–7); **Ionisation*, perc. (1929–31); *Déserts* (with optional tapes) (1950–4).

VOICE & ORCH.: *Offrandes*, sop., small orch. (1921); *Ecuatorial*, bass v. and orch. (1933–4); *Nocturnal*, sop., bass ch., orch. (1961, unfinished; ed. and completed 1973 by Chou Wen-chung).

INSTRUMENTAL: *Density 21.5*, solo fl. (1936).

ELECTRONIC: *Good Friday Procession in Verges* (1955–6); *Poème electronique* (1957–8).

Varga, Tibór (*b* Győr, 1921; *d* Sion, Switz., 2003). Brit. violinist of Hung. birth. Début 1931. Prof. of vn., Detmold Acad. 1949–55. Founded chamber orch. 1954 (cond. until 1988). Settled in Switzerland 1955. Founder of Sion Fest. 1964.

variant. (1) Name for differing versions of same piece of mus.
(2) Sudden changes from major to minor.
(3) Differing versions of folk-songs, the tune often slightly altering from region to region.

variation. Piece of mus. which is a varied version of a well-known tune or of an orig. theme specially comp. as basis for variations. Some variations follow the orig. tune closely, others make the briefest reference to it, sometimes harmonically rather than thematically. Popular form with composers from 16th cent., as in 'divisions on a ground'. In some comps., one movement takes the form of a theme with variations, e.g. the finale of Beethoven's *Eroica* sym., and movements of several Haydn syms. Among famous sets of variations are Beethoven's on a waltz by Diabelli, Brahms's on a theme by Haydn, Schumann's *Études symphoniques*, Strauss's *Don Quixote*, Elgar's *Enigma*, Rachmaninov's *Rhapsody on a theme of Paganini*, and Britten's *Variations on a Theme of Frank Bridge*.

Variations. 6 works comp. between 1958 and 1966 in which *Cage took *indeterminacy to remarkable limits. Some of them consist of transparent plastic sheets inscribed with lines and circles, and instructions explaining how these can be 'performed' by any number of players using any means. In Var. V the performer is merely supplied with a description of previous perfs., involving actions as well as sounds.

Variations and Fugue on a Theme by Purcell (Britten). See *Young Person's Guide to the Orchestra*.

Variations on 'America' (*Variations on a National Hymn, 'America'*). Orig. work for organ by *Ives comp. 1891 or 1892. Arr. for orch. by William Schuman 1964 and for concert band by Schuman and W. Rhoads.

Variations on a Rococo Theme. Work for vc. and orch. by Tchaikovsky. Op.33. Comp. 1876 as introduction, theme, and 8 vars. for Ger. cellist Wilhelm Fitzenhagen (1848–90), a colleague at Moscow Cons., who gave f.p. in Moscow Nov. 1877 with pf. accomp. (N. Rubinstein). Fitzenhagen ed. vc. part and after f.p. made changes which he claimed were authorized by composer, e.g. he altered dynamics and phrasing, transferred cadenza and 3rd and 4th vars. to end of work, and omitted final var. Score pubd. in this vers., in which it is still usually heard, 1889. F.p. of Tchaikovsky's orig. score was given by Daniel Shafran in 1941. Pubd. 1956. Among cellists who have recorded orig. vers. are Julian Lloyd Webber and Steven Isserlis.

Variations on a Theme by Haydn. Orch. comp., 1873, by Brahms, Op.56a, or in version for 2 pf., Op.56b. Often called the 'St Anthony' Variations, because the theme is called the 'St Anthony Chorale'. Brahms took the theme from a suite in B♭ for military band (*Feld-partita*) by Haydn but research has shown that the theme was borrowed by Haydn. However, since Brahms named the work 'Variations on a Theme by Haydn' there seems no good reason to discard this title for a musicological nicety.

Variations on a Theme of Frank Bridge. Work for str. orch. Op.10 by Britten comp. 1937 for Salzburg Fest. but f.p. two days earlier in Radio Hilversum studio concert. Theme is taken from *Bridge's *Idyll* No.2 for str. qt. Arr. for 2 pfs., 1942, by Colin McPhee for ballet *Jinx*.

Varnay, Astrid (Ibolyka Maria) (*b* Stockholm, 1918; *d* Munich, 2006). Swed.-born soprano of Austro-Hung. parentage, resident in USA from childhood. Opera début NY Met 1941 as last-minute deputy for Lotte *Lehmann as Sieglinde in *Die Walküre*. Stayed at Met until 1956, becoming leading Wagnerian and Strauss sop. Débuts: CG 1948; Bayreuth 1951; Salzburg Fest. 1964. Exciting Wagnerian singer. Late in career sang mez. roles, e.g. Klytemnästra, and made deep impression as Kostelnička.

varsoviana, varsovienne. A dance originating in France during 1850s, a slow, genteel type of *mazurka. Popular at balls in the Tuileries. Named from Fr. form of 'Warsaw'.

Varviso, Silvio (*b* Zurich, 1924; *d* Antwerp, 2006). Swiss conductor. Début St Gall 1944 (*Die Zauberflöte*). 1st cond., Basle Opera 1950–62 (mus. dir. from 1956). Leading opera cond. at int. fests. Amer. début (S. Francisco 1959). Cond. f. Amer. p. of *A Midsummer Night's Dream*, S. Francisco 1960. NY Met début 1961; Brit. début Glyndebourne 1962; CG 1962. Prin. cond. Stockholm Royal Opera 1965–71. Mus. dir., Württemberg Opera, Stuttgart, 1972–8. Bayreuth Fest. 1969–74. Salzburg Fest. 1979. Mus. dir. Paris Opéra 1980–5.

Vásáry, Tamás (*b* Debrecen, 1933). Hung. pianist and conductor. Début at age 8. Learned theory, Liszt Acad. Won Queen Elisabeth of Belgians comp. 1956, Rio de Janeiro int. comp. 1956. Swiss resident from 1958. London début 1961, NY 1962. Salzburg Fest. 1970. Specialist in Liszt. Début as cond. 1970. Joint cond., Northern Sinfonia 1979–82; prin. cond. Bournemouth Sinfonietta 1989–91; mus. dir. and prin. cond. Budapest SO from 1993.

Vasilenko, Sergey (*b* Moscow, 1872; *d* Moscow, 1956). Russ. composer. Prof. of comp., Moscow Cons. 1906–41, 1943–56. Wrote 5 operas (incl. *Christopher Columbus*, 1933); ballets; 5 syms.; symphonic poems; vn. conc.; balalaika conc.; 3 str. qts.; songs, etc.

vaudeville (Fr., either from *vaux de vire* or *voix de ville*). (1) In late 16th cent., song with amorous words as sung in the valleys (*vaux*) near Vire or catches sung in the streets of towns.

(2) In 18th cent., the term came to mean a song with different verses sung in turn by different singers, and this meaning was incorporated into operatic terminology, e.g. a 'vaudeville finale', as in Mozart's *Die Entführung aus dem Serail*.

(3) In 19th cent., meant short comedies interspersed with popular songs, as in Fr. revues.

(4) In late 19th and 20th cents., a synonym for a variety show or mus.-hall, particularly in USA.

Vaughan, Denis (Edward) (*b* Melbourne, Victoria, 1926). Australian conductor, organist, and musicologist. Org. and kbd. recitalist in Europe and USA 1948–56. Ass. cond. to Beecham 1954–7. Made special study of Verdi's and Puccini's autographs, noting discrepancies in printed scores, etc. Adviser on copyright to UNESCO 1962–7. Mus. dir. State Opera of S. Australia 1981–4. Amer. opera début, Juilliard Opera Center, NY, 1984. Moved to the UK in 1987 and became instrumental in creation of the National Lottery to increase access to culture and sport for the young.

Vaughan, Elizabeth (*b* Llanfyllin, Montgomery, 1937). Welsh soprano. Won 1959 Ferrier schol. Sang Abigaille (*Nabucco*) with WNO 1960. CG début 1962; NY Met début 1972. Toured USA with ENO 1984. A particularly fine Butterfly. Later sang mezzo roles, e.g. Herodias and Kabanicha. Prof. of singing, GSMD.

Vaughan Williams, Ralph (*b* Down Ampney, Glos., 1872; *d* London, 1958). Eng. composer, conductor, and organist. Studied at Cambridge Univ. 1892–5 and RCM 1890–2, 1895, teachers incl. Parry, Charles Wood, Alan Gray, and Stanford; later in Ger. with Bruch and in Paris 1908 with Ravel. Org., St Barnabas, S. Lambeth, 1897. Began collecting Eng. folk-songs 1902. Mus. ed., *English Hymnal*, 1906. Cond. Leith Hill (Dorking) Fest., 1905–53. Prof. of comp. RCM 1919–39. Cond., Bach Choir, London, 1920–7. OM 1935.

One of leaders, with Holst and others, of 20th-cent. revival of Eng. mus. in wake of Elgar. Early works mainly songs, such as the famous *Linden Lea* and *Silent Noon*, and chamber mus. Deeply influenced by revival of interest in Eng. 16th-cent. composers and by his own folk-song collecting. Studied for 3 months with Ravel when 36 and thereafter produced series of major works, incl. *Fantasia on a Theme by Thomas Tallis* for str., *On Wenlock Edge*, song-cycle on Housman's 'Shropshire Lad' poems, and *A London Symphony* (1913). Served in 1914–18 war although over military age and after war was active in every phase of Eng. mus. life as cond. of amateur choral fests., teacher, writer, and of course composer. Lived at Dorking, Surrey, 1929–53, then returned to London. Gave constant encouragement to young musicians; had strong prejudices, about which he wrote entertainingly in various essays.

Vaughan Williams's mus. is strongly individual, with the modal harmonies characteristic of folk-song composers, yet owing something to Fr. influence of Ravel and Debussy. He wrote works in almost every genre, from operas and syms. to choral works for amateurs as well as for highly professional choirs, concs. for neglected instrs. such as harmonica and tuba, a suite for pipes, etc. He believed that a composer should 'make his art an expression of the whole life of the community', but he was paradoxically a very personal composer rather than a state laureate. His operas have not so far held the stage, except for *Riders to the Sea*, but all are spasmodically revived, for they contain fine mus. His 9 syms. range from the choral *Sea Symphony* (Whitman text) and the picturesque *London* to the programmatic *Antartica* and the sternly 'absolute' Nos. 4, 5, 6, and 9. A wide range of orch. colour is deployed in these works and in his large-scale choral works such as *Sancta Civitas*. The basis of his work is melody, rhythm sometimes being unsubtle, but its visionary quality, as in the masque *Job* and the 5th and 9th syms., its broad humanity, and its appeal at several levels make it a remarkable expression of the nat. spirit in mus. just as the man himself personified all that was best in the liberal 19th-cent. tradition of which he was a scion. Prin. works:

OPERAS: *Hugh the Drover (1910–14, rev. 1924 and 1956); *The* **Shepherds of the Delectable Mountains* (1921–2); *Sir John in Love (1924–8); **Riders to the Sea* (1925–32); *The* *Poisoned Kiss (1927–9, rev. 1934–7, 1956–7); *The* **Pilgrim's Progress* (1925–36, 1944–51, 1951–2).

BALLETS, etc: *Old King Cole, with optional ch. (1923, also suite); *On Christmas Night*, masque (1925–6); **Job, a Masque for Dancing* (1927–30); *The Bridal Day*, masque (1938–9, rev. 1952–3); *The First Nowell*, nativity play for soloists, ch., orch. (1958).

ORCH.: syms.: *A* *Sea Symphony, sop., bar., ch., orch. (1903–9, rev. 1910, 1918, 1924), *A* *London Symphony (1911–13, rev. 1918, 1920, 1933), *A* **Pastoral Symphony* (1916–21, rev. 1950–1), No.4 in F minor (1931–4), No.5 in D (1938–43), No.6 in E minor (1944–7), **Sinfonia Antartica* (1949–52), No.8 in D minor (1953–5), No.9 in E minor (1956–7, rev. 1958); *In the Fen Country* (1904, rev. 1905, 1907, 1908, 1935); *Norfolk Rhapsody (1906, rev. *c*.1921); Aristophanic Suite, *The* *Wasps (1909, orig. incidental mus.); **Fantasia on a Theme* by Thomas Tallis, str. qt., double str. orch. (1910, rev. 1913, 1919); Charterhouse Suite (1923, orch. of 6 pf. pieces); English Folk Songs, suite, military band (1923, arr. full orch. Jacob 1942, brass band Jacob 1956; Sea Songs (1942, version of march for bands 1923); The Running Set (1933); *Fantasia on 'Greensleeves' (arr. from Sir John in Love by Greaves, 1934); 2 Hymn-Tune Preludes (1936); *Serenade to Music (1940, orch. version of ch. work); Partita, double str. orch. (1946–8); 5 Variants of *Dives and Lazarus, str., hps. (1939); Suite, Story of a Flemish Farm (1945; see Film Music); Concerto grosso, str. (1950); Prelude on an Old Carol Tune (1953); Prelude on 3 Welsh Hymn Tunes, brass band (1954); Variations, brass band (1957; arr. for orch. Jacob 1959); Flourish for Glorious John (1957, 'Glorious John' being affectionate name for *Barbirolli).

CONCERTOS, etc: The *Lark Ascending, Romance, vn., orch. (1914, rev. 1920); *Flos Campi, suite for va., ch., orch. (1925); vn. conc. in D minor, with str. (1924–5); pf. conc. in C (1926–31, rev. 1946 for 2 pf. with some new material); Suite for va., small orch. (1934); ob. conc. in A minor, with str. (1943–4); Fantasia on Old 104th Psalm Tune, pf., ch., orch. (1949); Romance in Db, harmonica, str., pf. (1951); tuba conc. in F minor (1954).

CHORUS & ORCH.: *Toward the Unknown Region (1905–7); A *Sea Symphony; 5 Mystical Songs, bar., optional ch., orch. (1911); *Fantasia on Christmas Carols, bar., ch., orch. (1912); Lord, Thou hast been our refuge (1921); *Sancta Civitas, ten., bar., ch., orch. (1923–5); *In Windsor Forest (cantata from *Sir John in Love) (1931); *Benedicite, sop., ch., orch. (1929); The 100th Psalm (1929); Magnificat, cont., fl., women's ch., orch. (1932); *Five Tudor Portraits, choral suite, mez., bar., ch., orch. (1935); *Dona nobis pacem, sop., bar., ch., orch. (1936); Festival Te Deum (1937); *Serenade to Music (1938); Epithalamion, bar., ch., orch. (1957, based on Bridal Day); Thanksgiving for Victory, sop., spkr., ch., orch. (1944); An *Oxford Elegy, spkr., ch., orch. (1949); Folk Songs of the 4 Seasons, women's ch., orch. (1949); The Sons of Light (1950); The Old 100th Psalm Tune (1953); *Hodie (This Day), Christmas Cantata, sop., ten., bar., ch. (1953–4).

VOCAL: 3 Elizabethan Songs (1890–1902); 5 English Folk Songs (1913); O clap your hands (1920); O vos omnes (1922); Mass in G minor, unacc. double ch. (1920–1); Services in D minor (1939); 6 Choral Songs in time of War (1940); Valiant for Truth (1940); The Souls of the Righteous (1947); Prayer to the Father of Heaven (1948); 3 Shakespeare Songs (1951); O taste and see (1952); Silence and Music (1953); Heart's Music (1954); A *Vision of Aeroplanes (1956); and many folk-song arrs.

VOICE & ENS.: *On Wenlock Edge, ten., str. qt., pf. (1908–9); 4 Hymns, ten., pf., va. (or str. and va.) (1914); Merciless Beauty, v., str. trio or pf. (1921).

SONGS (excluding above): Linden Lea (1901); Silent Noon (1903); Orpheus with his lute (1901 and new setting 1925); The House of Life, 6 Rossetti sonnets, v., pf. (1903); *Songs of Travel, 9 Stevenson poems for v., pf. (1904, 3 orch. by composer 1905, rest by R. Douglas 1960); Dreamland (1905); Buonaparty (1908); 2 Poems by Seumas O'Sullivan (1925); 3 Songs

from Shakespeare (1925); 4 Poems by Fredegond Shove (1925); 3 Poems by Whitman (1925); Along the Field, 8 Housman songs, v., vn. (1926); 7 Songs from 'The Pilgrim's Progress' (1952); In the Spring (1952); 10 Blake Songs, v., ob. (1957); 3 Vocalises, sop., cl. (1958); 4 Last Songs, v., pf. (1954–8); and many folk-song arrs.

CHAMBER MUSIC: str. qts.: No.1 in G minor (1908, rev. 1921), No.2 in A minor ('For Jean on her Birthday') (1942–4); Phantasy Quintet (1912); Suite de Ballet, fl., pf. (1920); 6 Studies in English Folk-Song, vc. (or vn., va., cl.), pf. (1926); Suite for Pipes (1938–9); Household Music, str. qt. or alternatives (1940–1); vn. sonata in A minor (1954).

PIANO: Suite of 6 short Pieces (1920, arr. for str. as Charterhouse Suite); Hymn-Tune Prelude on 'Song 13' by O. Gibbons (1928); 6 Teaching Pieces (1934); Introduction and Fugue (2 pf.) (1946); The lake in the mountains (1947).

ORGAN: 3 Preludes on Welsh Hymn-Tunes (1920); Prelude and Fugue in C minor (1930); Wedding Tune for Ann (1943); 2 Organ Preludes (1956).

FILM MUSIC: 49th Parallel (1940–1); Coastal Command (1942); The People's Land (1941–2); The Flemish Farm (1943); Stricken Peninsula (1944); The Loves of Joanna Godden (1946); Scott of the Antarctic (1947–8); Dim Little Island (1949); Bitter Springs (1950); The England of Elizabeth (1955); The Vision of William Blake (1957).

Vaughan Williams, Ursula (b Valletta, 1911). Eng. poet and librettist. Married composer Ralph *Vaughan Williams 1953. For him wrote many texts incl. that for The Bridal Day (1938), verses for The Pilgrim's Progress (1951), and Four Last Songs (1954–8). Wrote RVW: a Biography (1964). Also wrote texts for other composers, 3 novels and 5 vols. of poetry.

Vautor, Thomas (b c.1580). Eng. composer, one of last of madrigal school. Pubd. madrigal coll., 1619, for vv. and viols., incl. Sweet Suffolk Owl.

Vazsonyi, Bálint (b Budapest, 1936; d Washington, DC, 2003). Hung. pianist and writer. Début Budapest 1948. Taught at Indiana Univ. Sch. of Mus., Bloomington, 1978–84. Perf. Beethoven's 32 sonatas in chronological order, NY 1976, London 1977. Author of books on Dohnányi and Schumann's pf. mus.

vc. Short for violoncello.

Veasey, Josephine (b Peckham, London, 1930). Eng. mezzo-soprano. CG début as soloist 1955 (Shepherd Boy in Tannhäuser). Member of CG co. 1955–82, singing 780 perfs. of 60 roles. Her many roles at CG under Solti régime included Wagner. Glyndebourne 1957–69; NY Met 1968. Created the Emperor in Henze's We Come to the River (CG 1976). Successful career on concert-platform in Verdi Requiem, Berlioz's Nuits d'Été, etc. Retired from opera 1982. Taught at RAM 1983–4. Vocal consultant ENO from 1984. CBE 1970.

Vecchi, Orazio (b Modena, 1550; d Modena, 1605). It. composer and priest. Choirmaster,

Modena Cath., 1584–6 and 1593–1605, and court choirmaster there from 1598. Wrote madrigals, masses, motets. His *L'*Amfiparnaso*, comp. 1594 and prod. Modena 1594, is the first known example of a madrigal-comedy.

Végh, Sándor (Alexandre) (*b* Kolozsvár (now Cluj, Rom.), 1905; *d* Paris, 1997). Hung. violinist and conductor. Played in concert cond. Strauss, 1927. Founded Hungarian Trio 1931, leader then 2nd vn. Hungarian Qt. 1935–40. Gave f. Eur. p. of Bartók's 5th str. qt., Barcelona 1936. Prof. of vn., Budapest Hochschule 1940; founder and leader Végh Qt. 1940–80. Left Hung. 1946, teaching in Zermatt 1952–62, Basle Cons. 1953–63, Fribourg 1954–62, Düsseldorf 1962–79, Salzburg from 1971. Dir., Vegh Chamber Orch. 1968–71, Orch. of Marlboro Fest. 1974–7, Salzburg Mozarteum Camerata from 1979. Salzburg Fest. début 1973 (chamber concert). Worked with Casals at Prades Fest. 1953–69. Has given some of the most successful televised *master classes. Founded int. seminar, Prussia Cove, Cornwall, 1972. CBE 1989.

veloce, velocemente (It., superlatives *velocissimo, velocissimamente*). With speed, very fast.

Venetian Games (*Gry weneckie; Jeux venétiens*). Work for orch. by *Lutosławski, comp. 1960–1. First in which he used *aleatory procedures.

Vengerov, Maxim (*b* Novosibirsk, 1974). Russ. violinist. Began lessons at age 5 with Galina Turtschaninova and later studied at junior dept. RAM and with Zakhar Bron. Won Junior Wieniawski Comp. 1984 and Carl Flesch Comp. 1990. Brit. début 1991. NY début 1991. London (Proms) début 1992. Has recorded concs. with Rostropovich as cond. Occasionally conducts.

Vengerova, Isabelle (*b* Minsk, 1877; *d* NY, 1956). Russ.-born pianist and teacher. Taught at St Petersburg Cons. 1906–20 (prof. from 1910). Toured Russ. and Eur. 1920–3. Went to USA 1923. Amer. début Detroit SO 1925. Prof. of pf., Curtis Inst. 1924–56. Aunt of Nicholas *Slonimsky.

Venice. Italian city, capital of region of Veneto. Its importance as a musical centre dates from 1527 when the Netherlands composer *Willaert was appointed choirmaster of S. Marco Cath. Through his influence, Venice became centre of madrigal composition in private houses and academies. Under Zarlino, choirmaster from 1564, an instr. ens. was formed (1568) which, augmented, performed at large fests. Use of choral and instr. forces by dividing them into groups placed in different galleries of the cath. (*cori spezzati*) led to the dominating splendour of Venetian church mus. 1575–1610, notably under G. *Gabrieli and A. *Gabrieli. In 1612 *Monteverdi was appointed choirmaster and remained for 30 years. He revivified the city's musical life, introducing younger composers, e.g. Cavalli and Grandi. The plague of 1630 ended the dominance of S. Marco in Venetian music-making and the balance was

tipped towards operas, of which Monteverdi provided several masterly examples and was followed by Cavalli. Refusal of the authorities after 1642 to raise the salary of the choirmaster led to a decline in standard, halted only by Legrenzi, who achieved an increase in the size of the choir and orch. (to 36 and 34 respectively).

After 1700 Venetian musicians made their living in the *ospedali*, charitable institutions for the sick and orphaned where mus. was taught and perf. in the chapels. From this milieu arose the next great sch. of Venetian composers, Vivaldi, Porpora, Sarti, Galuppi, Traetta, Jommelli, and Albinoni. Visitors to Venice included Gasparini, A. Scarlatti, and Handel.

Galuppi excelled in *opera buffa* and collab. with the playwright Goldoni from 1749. Opera thrived again after the opening of the Teatro La *Fenice in 1792 with a work by Paisiello. No Venetian sch. now existed, but f.ps. were given at La Fenice of operas by Cimarosa, Rossini (*Tancredi*, 1813), Meyerbeer (*Il Crociato in Egitto*, 1824), Bellini (*I Capuleti e i Montecchi*, 1830), and Donizetti (*Maria di Rudenz*, 1838). Several Verdi operas were commissioned for La Fenice, notably *La traviata*, 1853.

In the 20th cent. La Fenice was the birthplace of Dallapiccola's ballet *Marsia* (1948), Stravinsky's *The Rake's Progress* (1951), Britten's *The Turn of the Screw* (1954), Prokofiev's *The Fiery Angel* (1955), Nono's *Intolleranza* (1960), and Bussotti's *Lorenzaccio* (1973). It also staged the Venetian Malipiero's operas. These operas were given at the annual fest. of contemporary mus. held between 1948 and 1973. Stravinsky also comp. several choral and instr. works for Venice 1956–60 and was buried there near *Diaghilev. The fascination of Venice for composers is epitomized by Britten's opera *Death in Venice* (1973) and it was in Venice that the dying composer wrote some of his 3rd str. qt. (1975). And not the least of Venice's claims to musical fame is that Richard Wagner died there on 13 Feb. 1883.

Veni creator spiritus (Come Holy Ghost). Whitsuntide hymn generally attrib. Hrabanus Maurus, 9th-cent. Archbishop of Mainz, and sung liturgically to harmonized adaptation of plainsong melody. Set by several composers. Mahler's setting for soloists, ch., and orch. forms Part I of his 8th Sym. (1906–7).

Veni sancte spiritus (Come Holy Spirit). *Sequence of RC liturgy for Whitsunday sung to traditional plainsong. Text ascribed to Pope Innocent III and Stephen Langton. Settings include those by Du Fay, Després, Willaert, Palestrina, and Victoria.

Venite (Come). Ps.95 (Ps.94 in Vulgate) chanted as canticle at Anglican matins to words 'O come, let us sing unto the Lord'. Settings by several composers, incl. Mendelssohn.

vent (Fr.). Wind. *instruments à vent*, wind instruments.

Ventil (Ger.), **ventile** (It.). Valve. *Ventilhorn* (Ger.), *corno ventile* (It.), valve horn.

Venus and Adonis. (1) Opera in prol. and 3 acts by *Blow to lib. by unknown author. Prod. London *c*.1683. Revived Glastonbury 1920, Cambridge, Mass., 1941.

(2) Opera in 1 act by Henze (comp. 1983–5) to lib. by H.-U. Treichel. F.p. Munich 1997, London (concert) 1997, Santa Fe 2000.

Vêpres siciliennes, Les (The Sicilian Vespers). Opera in 5 acts by Verdi to Fr. lib. (*Le duc d'Albe*) by Scribe and Duveyrier. Comp. 1854, prod. Paris 1855, London and NY 1859. Trans. into It. as *I vespri siciliani*. Lib. *Le duc d'Albe* was orig. written 1839 for Halévy, who did not set it. Donizetti partly set it (prod. 1882).

Vera costanza, La ('True constancy'). Opera in 3 acts by Haydn, Hob. XXVIII:8, to lib. by F. Puttini. Comp. 1777–8. Rev. 1785 after score was burnt in fire at Eszterháza opera th. Prod. Eszterháza 1779, rev. vers. 1785; Cleveland 1967, NY (Katonah) 1980; London (Opera Viva) 1976 (Abbey Opera, in edn. by Robbins Landon); Garsington 1992.

Verbrugghen, Henri (*b* Brussels, 1873; *d* Northfield, Minn., 1934). Belg. violinist and conductor. Member, Scottish Orch. 1893, Lamoureux Orch., Paris, 1894–5. Leader, Queen's Hall Orch., 1902–5, Scottish Orch. from 1903. Cond., summer concerts Llandudno 1895–7, Colwyn Bay 1898–1902. Cond., Glasgow Choral Union 1911. Dir., State Cons. of NSW, Sydney, 1915–22. Cond. Minneapolis SO 1923–31. Soloist in f. Eng. p. of Sibelius's vn. conc., London, 1907.

verbunkos. Hung. soldiers' dance, used from *c*.1775 to attract recruits for the army. Danced, to gipsy mus., by uniformed hussars. Survived after introduction of conscription in 1849 as ceremonial dance with two or more sections, similar to those of *csárdás. Used by Liszt in his *Hungarian Rhapsody No.2*, and by Bartók and Kodály.

Verdi, Giuseppe (Fortunino Francesco) (*b* Le Roncole, nr. Busseto, Parma, 1813; *d* Milan, 1901). It. composer. Son of innkeeper. Taught by local organist, Antonio Barezzi, a wholesale grocer and merchant, who liked mus., recognized his mus. ability and offered to pay for him to go to Milan Cons., but authorities would not admit him, partly because of poor pf.-playing. Studied in Milan privately for 2 years. Returned to Busseto, where he continued studies, directed town's mus. activities, and married his patron Barezzi's daughter. Completed opera *Rocester* (now lost) in 1836, but *Oberto* was prod. at La Scala 1839 with some success, followed by comic opera, *Un giorno di regno* (1840), a failure. Between 1838 and 1840, Verdi's wife and 2 children died. Prostrate with grief, vowed to abandon comp., but was persuaded to compose *Nabucco* (1841); its triumphant success made him most prominent of young It. composers. Thereafter wrote series of operas, some more successful than others at their premières, but each

eagerly sought by impresarios. In 1847 he comp. *I masnadieri* for Her Majesty's, London, with Jenny Lind and Lablache heading the cast. In 1849 he bought a farming estate at Sant'Agata, near Busseto, to which he returned whenever possible. In the sensitive political climate of 19th-cent. It., Verdi's libs. (e.g. for *Rigoletto*, *Un ballo in maschera*, etc.) frequently caused trouble with the censors, especially when they dealt with historical events which could be interpreted as referring to contemporary political events, Verdi's sympathies for It. independence from Austria being well known. In 1860, after the It. war of independence, he was elected a Deputy in first It. nat. parliament, resigning 5 years later. His next 3 operas were written for perf. outside It., *La forza del destino* for St Petersburg, 1862, *Don Carlos* for Paris, 1867, and *Aida* for Cairo, 1871. 16 years were to pass before the next opera, but in 1874 the great *Requiem*, comp. in memory of the poet Manzoni, was perf. in Milan. It was an immediate success. Verdi cond. 15 perfs. of it in Paris in 1874 and 1875, 4 in Vienna, and 3 in London. In 1879, his publisher Ricordi suggested Shakespeare's *Othello* as an operatic subject, and *Boito, with whom Verdi's relations had hitherto been cool, submitted a draft lib. The work (*Otello*) was f.p. in Milan in 1887 and was acclaimed as the supreme achievement not only of its composer but of It. opera. In 1889 Boito suggested a further collaboration, on *Falstaff*. Its prod. at Milan in 1893, though a personal triumph, was not such a success as that of *Otello* and it has taken until recent times for this masterpiece of comic opera to become a popular favourite. In 1859 Verdi had married the sop. Giuseppina Strepponi, with whom he had lived for a decade before that. Her death in 1897 marked the end of Verdi's composing career. He died at the Hotel Milano, a short distance from La Scala, leaving most of his money to a home for elderly musicians which he had founded in Milan.

Verdi's stature as one of the 2 or 3 greatest opera composers is unchallengeable. Though his technical mastery continually developed and was refined, and his powers of characterization became more subtle and expressive, the essential Verdi—direct, noble, and intense—remained unchanging from *Nabucco* to *Falstaff*. There was no 'change of style' in *Otello*: the lib. drew from Verdi his greatest mus., but it is still recognizably the work of the composer of *Il trovatore* and *Simon Boccanegra*. In recent years the earlier works have been revived and have revealed their considerable merits—the comic *Un giorno di regno*, for example, is particularly fine. In operas like *Rigoletto*, *La traviata*, and *Aida*, Verdi put on to the stage operatic characters who are as real as the characters in Shakespeare. His 3 Shakespeare operas are major achievements and his failure to compose *King Lear*, though he toyed with the idea for many years, must ever be regretted. Prin. works:

OPERAS: *Oberto, Conte di San Bonifacio* (1835–9, rev. 1840–1); *Un *giorno di regno* (1840); *Nabucco* (1841, rev. 1842); I *Lombardi alla prima crociata* (1842–3, rev. 1843), adapted to Fr. lib. as

Jérusalem, with rev. and some new mus., 1847; **Ernani* (1843–4); *I *due Foscari* (1844, rev. 1845–6); **Giovanna d'Arco* (1844–5, rev. 1845); *Alzira* (1845); **Attila* (1845–6); **Macbeth* (1846–7, rev. 1864–5); *I *masnadieri* (1846–7); *Il *corsaro* (1847–8); *La *battaglia di Legnano* (1848–9); **Luisa Miller* (1849); **Stiffelio* (1850), adapted to new lib., with some new mus., as **Aroldo* (1856–7); **Rigoletto* (1850–1); *Il *trovatore* (1851–2, rev. 1856); *La *traviata* (1852–3, rev. 1854); *Les *Vêpres siciliennes* (1854); **Simon Boccanegra* (1856–7, lib. and mus. rev. 1880–1); *Un *ballo in maschera* (1857–8); *La *forza del destino* (1861–2, rev. 1868–9); **Don Carlos* (1866–7, rev. as 4-act work, with some new music, 1882–3); **Aida* (1870); **Otello* (1884–6, rev. 1887); **Falstaff* (1889–92, rev. 1893 and 1894).

CHORAL: *Inno delli nazioni* (Hymn of the Nations), ten., ch., orch. (1862); *Libera me*, sop., ch., orch. (1868–9, incorp. into *Requiem*, 1874); *Pater Noster*, unacc. ch.; *Ave Maria*, sop., str. (1879–80); *Requiem* (1873–4); **Quattro pezzi sacri: Ave Maria*, unacc. ch. (1888–9), *Stabat Mater*, ch., orch. (1895–7), *Laudi alla Vergine Maria*, women's ch. (1888–9), *Te Deum*, sop., ch., orch. (1895–7).

CHAMBER MUSIC: str. qt. in E minor (1873).

SONGS: *6 Romances* (1838); *L'esule* (The Exile); *La seduzione*; *Notturno: Guarda che bianca luna* (Nocturne: See the pale moon) (1839); *Chi i bei di m'adduce ancora* (Who will bring back the beautiful days?) (1842); *6 Romances* (1845); *Il poveretto* (The beggar) (1847); *Suona la tromba* (Sound the trumpet) (1848); *L'Abandonnée* (The forsaken woman) (1849); *Fiorellin che sorge appena* (The little flower that rises) (1850); *La preghiera del poeta* (The poet's prayer) (1858); *Il brigidin* (The rosette) (1863); *Tu dici che non m'ami* (You say you do not love me) (1869).

verdoppeln (Ger.). To double. *verdoppelt*, doubled; *verdoppelung*, doubling.

Verein (Ger.). Society, as in *Musikverein*, mus. soc.

Veress, Sándor (*b* Kolozsvár, 1907; *d* Berne, 1992). Swiss composer of Hung. birth. Helped Bartók on folk mus. research at Budapest Acad. of Sciences 1937–40. Taught at Budapest State Acad. 1943–8. Teacher of comp., Berne Cons. 1950–77, prof. of musicology, Berne Univ. 1968–77 (dir. of dept. from 1971). Taught in USA and Australia and was a regular juror at Llangollen int. eisteddfod. Works incl. ballet *The Miraculous Pipe* (1937); vn. conc. (1937–9); *Threnody in memoriam Béla Bartók* (1945); *Homage to Paul Klee*, 2 pf., str. (1952); pf. conc. (1952); 2 syms. (1940, 1952); conc. for str. qt. and orch. (1960–1); cl. conc. (1981–2); fl. conc. (1988–9); conc. for 2 tb. (1989); 2 str. qts.; 2 vn. sonatas; cl. trio (1972); songs; and *Fingermarks*, 88 pieces for pf. based on his teaching methods (1946).

verhallend (Ger.). Dying away.

verismo (It.). Realism. Term applied to 'realistic' sch. of It. opera in which (following Zola in literature) subjects treated were usually contemporary and often sordid or down-to-earth, e.g.

Cavalleria rusticana, *Fedora*, *Il tabarro*, etc. But, like all such terms, it is imprecise and has acquired a slight pejorative tinge. Also, some *verismo* operas are not truly *verismo*, and where does one draw the line—is *La traviata* not *verismo*? But the opera-lover understands the Mascagni type of work by this term. Composers in other countries also wrote *verismo* operas, e.g. *La Navarraise* (1894) and *Jenůfa* (1904). And what about *Peter Grimes* (1945)?

Verklärte Nacht (Transfigured Night). Str. sextet (2 vn., 2 va., 2 vc.) Op.4, by Schoenberg, based on poem by Richard Dehmel (from *Weib und Welt*). Comp. 1899. F.p. Vienna 1902, f.p. in England 1914. Version for str. orch. by Schoenberg 1917, rev. 1943. Used as mus. for 1-act ballet *Pillar of Fire*, choreog. A. Tudor, prod. NY Met 1942.

verlierend (Ger.). Losing itself, i.e. dying away.

verlöschend (Ger.). Extinguished, i.e. dying away.

Vermeer Quartet. Amer. str. qt. founded 1969 by its 1st vn., Shmuel Ashkenasi, with 3 colleagues from professorial staff N. Illinois Univ. Orig. members were Pierre Menard (2nd vn., succeeded by Mathias Tacke), Nobuko Imai (va., succeeded by Jerry Horner, Bernard Zaslav, and Richard Young), and Marc Johnson (vc.). First European tour 1972–3. London début 1974.

Verne [Wurm], **Mathilde** (*b* Southampton, 1865; *d* London, 1936). Eng. pianist, pupil of Clara Schumann. Organized chamber concerts in London. Founded sch. of pf.-playing in Kensington, pupils incl. **Solomon.

Véronique. Operetta in 3 acts by Messager to lib. by Vanloo and Duval. Prod. Paris 1898, New Orleans 1900, London 1903, NY 1905.

Verrall, John (Weedon) (*b* Britt, Iowa, 1908; *d* Laurelhurst, WA, 2001). Amer. composer. Teacher at Washington Univ. from 1948. Works incl. operas, 4 syms., pf. conc., va. conc., 7 str. qts., fl. sonata, songs.

Verratene Meer, Das (The Sea betrayed). Opera in 2 acts by Henze to lib. by H.-U. Treichel based on Mishima's novel *Gogo no eiko*. Comp. 1986–9. Prod. Berlin 1990, S. Francisco 1991.

Verrett, Shirley (*b* New Orleans, 1931). Amer. mezzo-soprano, capable of singing soprano roles (e.g. Norma and Lady Macbeth). Début Yellow Springs, Ohio, 1957 (Lucretia in *The Rape of Lucretia*), then NY City Opera 1958 under name Shirley Carter. Recital début NY 1958. Eur. début (Cologne) 1959; CG début 1966; NY Met début 1968. Sang Carmen throughout the world. Recital repertory incl. Schubert, Brahms, Mahler, and Rorem.

verschiebung (Ger.). Shoving away. Soft pedal.

verschwindend (Ger.). Disappearing, i.e. dying away.

verse. (1) Term used in Anglican church mus. meaning a passage for solo v. (or several solo vv.)

as contrasted with full ch., thus *verse anthem*, an anthem in which solo v. and full ch. are contrasted.

(2) Biblical verse in Gregorian chant.

verset (Fr.). Verse. Short org. piece, replacing sung verse of psalm in RC service.

Versetzung (Ger.). Transposition. *Versetzungszeichen*, accidental.

versicle. In the Roman or Anglican service a short verse spoken or chanted by the priest and responded to by the congregation (or ch.).

Verzierungen (Ger.). Embellishments.

Vesalii Icones (Images of Vesalius). Th. piece by *Maxwell Davies for dancer, solo vc., and ens. (incl. motor horn, anvil, saucepan, knife-grinder, out-of-tune pf.). Comp. 1969. F.p. London 1969, cond. composer. Its 14 dances are based on the anatomical drawings by the physician Vesalius in his *De humani corporis fabrica* (1543), with the 14 Stations of the Cross superimposed on the Vesalian images.

Vesperae Solennes de Confessore (Solemn Vespers of the Confessor). Work for 4 vv., ch., orch., and org. by Mozart (K339) comp. 1780.

vespers. 7th of Canonical Hours of RC Church, also known as Evensong. Famous large-scale setting by *Monteverdi (1610).

Vespers of 1610 (Monteverdi). See *Vespro della Beata Vergine*.

Vespro della Beata Vergine (Vespers of the Holy Virgin). A collection of Masses (Psalms and Hymns) by Monteverdi comp. 1610 for perf. in small surroundings at Mantua and comprising *Audi coelum, verba mea*, solo v. and 6 vv.; *Ave, Maris stella*, 8 vv.; *Dixit Dominus Domino meo*, 6 vv.; *Domine ad adjuvandum*, 6 vv.; *Duo Seraphim*, 3 vv.; *In illo tempore*, 6 vv.; *Laetatus sum*, 6 vv.; *Lauda Jerusalem*, 7 vv.; *Laudate pueri*, 8 vv.; *Magnificat*, 6 vv.; *Magnificat*, 7 vv.; *Nigra sum*, solo v.; *Nisi Dominus*, 10 vv.; *Pulchra es*, 2 vv. (all with basso continuo); *Sancta Maria, ora pro nobis* (sonata) for solo v. with 8 instr. (2 cornets, 2 vn., 2 tb., one of which can be replaced with viola da braccio, and double tb.). This last item can be perf. separately. There are several modern eds. of the *Vespers*, e.g. by Harnoncourt, W. Goehr, Redlich, Norrington, etc.

Vestale, La. Opera by Spontini in 3 acts, comp. 1807, to lib. by E. de Jouy (originally written for Boieldieu and later refused by Méhul). Comp. 1805 and much rev. F.p. Paris 1807. Milan 1824, London 1826, New Orleans 1828. Revived for *Ponselle (NY Met 1925) and *Callas (La Scala 1954).

Vestris (*née* Bartolozzi), **Lucia Elizabeth** (*b* London, 1797; *d* London, 1856). Eng. cont. Opera début London 1815. Sang at It. Opera, Paris, and King's Th., London, 1821–5. Wife of Auguste Armand Vestris, one of celebrated ballet family,

who was ballet master at King's Th. 1809–17. Sang in Eng. f.ps. of several Rossini operas at King's Th. 1821–4. Frequently sang in Dublin, 1824–47. Created Fatima in Weber's *Oberon*, 1826. Became manager of CG 1839–42, having previously managed Olympic Th. 1831–8 and subsequently the Lyceum 1847–55, with her 2nd husband Charles Matthews. Sang male roles, incl. Don Giovanni.

Viaggio a Reims, Il, ossia L'albergo del giglio d'oro (The Journey to Rheims or The Inn of the Golden Lily). Opera in 1 act by Rossini to lib. by L. Balocchi after novel *Corinne, ou l'Italie* by Mme. de Staël (1807). Comp. 1825 for Coronation of Charles X. About half of mus. used again in *Le Comte Ory* (1828). MS sources of *Viaggio* lost until located in 1970s in Rome, Paris, and Vienna, enabling work to be reconstructed. Prod. Paris 1825, Pesaro 1984, St Louis 1986, London (GSMD) 1987, CG 1992.

Viardot-García, Pauline (*b* Paris, 1821; *d* Paris, 1910). Fr. mezzo-soprano of Sp. parentage. Daughter of Manuel *García and sister of Maria *Malibran and Manuel *García. Concert début Brussels 1837, opera début London 1839 (Desdemona in Rossini's *Otello*). Paris 1839. Married writer Louis Viardot, Paris, 1840. Toured Russ. 1843 and thereafter championed Russ. mus. CG 1849–55. Famous in Mozart roles and as Gluck's Orphée and Alceste. Retired from stage 1863 and wrote plays, painted, and comp. operettas and songs. Taught singing at Paris Cons. 1871–5.

vibraharp. Same as *vibraphone*.

vibraphone (colloquial, 'vibes'). Perc. instr. similar to *marimba. Tuned metal bars, laid out like pf. kbd., are struck by the player holding small padded hammer in each hand. Beneath bars are resonators fitted with lids which constantly open and close electrically, giving pulsating sound to any of the metal bars when struck by the player. Compass f–f'''. Used first in jazz (Lionel Hampton a celebrated player), then frequently in symphonic and operatic works, e.g. by Berg in *Lulu*, Vaughan Williams, McCabe, Britten, Milhaud, Henze, Messiaen, Tippett, and Boulez.

vibrato (It.). Vibrated. Undulation of pitch of a note, prod. in str. instr. by controlled vibration of player's finger stopping the str. and in wind instr. by breath-control. Not the same as *tremolo. In singing the greatest skill is needed in use of *vibrato* or it can become an uncontrolled wobble.

Vicentino, Nicolà (*b* Vicenza, *c*.1511; *d* Rome, 1575 or 1576). It. composer. Ded. to revival of ancient Gr. modes; built 6-kbd. 'archiorgano' to illustrate his system and wrote madrigals. Pubd. *The Ancient Music reduced to Modern Practice*, Rome 1555.

Vick, Graham (*b* Liverpool, 1953). Eng. opera producer. Worked at Glyndebourne and with EMT. Dir. of prod., Scottish Opera 1984–7; art. dir. CBTO (now Birmingham Opera Company) from 1987, producing touring versions with reduced orch. of *Falstaff* (1987), *Die Zauberflöte* (1988), and *The Ring* (1990, presented on 2 evenings as *The Ring Saga*, re-orch. J. Dove). Also Rameau's *Les Boréades* (1993). ENO début 1984; CG 1989; Amer. début (St Louis) 1986; Berlin 1991; Kirov Opera 1991; Glyndebourne 1992. Dir. of prods., Glyndebourne, 1993–2000.

Vickers, Jon(athan Stewart) (*b* Prince Albert, Saskatchewan, 1926). Canadian tenor. Sang with Toronto SO. Opera début Toronto, 1952 (Duke in *Rigoletto*). Débuts: CG 1957; Bayreuth 1958; S. Francisco 1959; NY Met 1960; La Scala 1961; Salzburg Fest. 1966. Outstanding Tristan, Peter Grimes, Florestan, Siegmund, etc.

Victoria, Tomás Luis de (*b* Avila, *c*.1548; *d* Madrid, 1611). Sp. composer. Went to Rome 1565 as student for priesthood (ordained 1575) and was possibly a pupil of Palestrina. Org. and choirmaster S. Maria di Monserrato, Rome, 1569–71; choirmaster Collegium Romanum 1571–3, Collegium Germanicum 1573–8. Chaplain at Church of S. Girolamo della Carità 1578–85, working with St Philip Neri, founder of oratorio. Returned to Spain 1595. (Because of long residence in It., name is often spelt in It. form, *Vittoria*.) Organist and choirmaster, convent of Descalzas Reales, Madrid, 1596–1611. With Palestrina, regarded as one of supreme contrapuntists of his age, his mus. having a dramatic vigour and colour which reflect his nationality. Wrote only church mus., incl. settings of all hymns of RC liturgical year. Works pubd. in complete modern edn. by Pedrell (Leipzig 1902–13). The 8 vols. comprise: I, 44 motets; II, 10 Masses; III, 18 Magnificats and a Nunc Dimittis; IV, 5 Masses; V, 34 hymns and *Officium Hebdomadae Sanctae*; VI, 5 Masses; VII, 10 psalms, 10 settings of Marian antiphons, 3 other works; VIII, Biography, bibliography, and 5 other works. Among greatest works are motets *Vexilla regis*, *O magnum mysterium*, *O quam gloriosum*, *O vos omnes*; *Requiem* (1583 and 1603).

Victory. Opera in 3 acts by Richard Rodney Bennett to lib. by Beverley Cross based on novel by Joseph Conrad. Comp. 1968–9. Prod. London (CG) 1970.

Victory, Gerard [Alan Loraine] (*b* Dublin, 1921; *d* Dublin, 1995). Irish composer and conductor. Mus. producer, Radio Telefis Eireann 1948–67, dir. of mus. 1967–82. Works incl. 15 operas and operettas (incl. *Eloise and Abelard*, 1973); *Jonathan Swift*, orch.; *Homage to Petrarch*, str.; 4 syms. (1961–88); hp. conc.; vc. conc.; *Miroirs*, orch.; str. qt.; pf. quintet, etc.

Vida breve, La (Short Life). Opera in 2 acts by *Falla to lib. by Carlos Fernández Shaw. Comp. 1904–5. Prod. Nice (in Fr.) 1913; Madrid (in Sp.) 1914; NY Met 1926; Edinburgh 1958.

vide (Fr.). Empty. Thus *corde à vide* means open string.

vielle (Fr.). Medieval name for various instr., e.g. hurdy-gurdy and fiddle.

vielle à roue (Fr.). Wheel fiddle, i.e. the *hurdy-gurdy.

Vienna Boys' Choir (Ger. *Wiener Sängerknaben*). Choir of Vienna Seminary Sch., founded 1498, formerly providing mus. for chapel of Austrian imperial court. Present-day ch. gives secular concerts. First appearance at Salzburg Fest. 1929, and perf. there regularly to present day.

Vienna Philharmonic Orchestra (Ger. *Wiener Philharmoniker*). Austrian orch. founded in Vienna 1842, first cond. being Otto *Nicolai 1842–8. The concerts were interrupted by the 1848 revolution. A few were given under Karl Eckert between 1854 and 1857, but a regular season of 8 concerts did not occur until 1860. Orch. soon recognized as one of world's greatest, a reputation it has maintained. Among prin. conds. after Nicolai were Dessov (1860–75), *Richter (1875–98), Mahler (1898–1901), Hellmesberger (1901–3), Weingartner (1907–27), Furtwängler (1927–8), Krauss (1929–33), Furtwängler and Walter (1933–8), Furtwängler (1938–54), Karajan (1957–64), Abbado (1971–82), Lorin Maazel (1982–4). Orch. is self-governing and plays for *Vienna State Opera. Gave its first concert at Salzburg Fest. 1926 and perfs. there regularly to present day, both in the concert-halls and the opera theatres. Many other conds., notably Karl *Böhm, have been assoc. with it and have made recordings with it.

Vienna State Opera (Ger. *Wiener Staatsoper*). Prin. Austrian opera house and co., one of leading opera organizations of world. Orig. Vienna Court Opera (*Wiener Hofoper*). The first opera was perf. in Vienna in 1633 (Bartolaia's *Il Sidonio*). Opera then became est. as regular court entertainment and special th. built. Theater bei der Hofburg was opened 1748. Gluck was court Kapellmeister 1754–70, 10 of his operas being written for Vienna. Towards end of 18th cent., Burgtheater lost ground to Theater am Kärntnerthor (built 1708), where *Salieri became cond. Mozart's *Die Entführung aus dem Serail* (1782), *Le nozze di Figaro* (1786), and *Così fan tutte* (1790) all had f.ps. at Burgtheater, while *Don Giovanni* had its first Vienna perf. there (with additions) in 1788. In 1842 Donizetti was both court composer and cond. Court opera's first permanent cond. was Karl Eckert (1854–60) who introduced Wagner's operas to the city. New theatre, Die Oper am Ring, opened 1869. *Richter became cond. in 1875 and shared directorship with Jahn from 1880 to 1896, the co. in this period having singers of the quality of Materna, Reichmann, Winkelmann, and van Dyck. In 1897 Mahler became dir. and initiated the most glorious decade in the history of the th., with a great singing-acting co. incl. Gutheil-Schoder, Mildenburg, Selma Kurz, Schmedes, Mayr, and Slezak, and *Roller as designer. Mahler was succeeded by Weingartner 1907–11 and Hans Gregor

1911–18. In 1918 Court Opera became State Opera, with Schalk and R. Strauss as joint dirs. 1919–24, Schalk continuing alone until 1929. The singers now included Lotte Lehmann, Elisabeth Schumann, Jerger, Piccaver, and Jeritza, who were joined in the 1930s by Tauber, Kern, Ursuleac, Kiepura, Schorr, Olszewska, Dermota, etc. Krauss was cond. 1929–34, Weingartner 1934–6, Walter 1936–8. After an interregnum, Karl Böhm became dir. in 1943 until the th. was bombed in March 1945. For 10 years, with Böhm, Josef Krips, and Krauss as conds. the State Opera played in the Theater an der Wien and the Volksoper, and visited London in 1948. Böhm again became dir. 1955 and the rebuilt th. (capacity 2,200) opened in 1955 with *Fidelio*. Böhm resigned 1956, being succeeded by Karajan 1956–64. The post-war vocal galaxy incl. Gueden, Schwarzkopf, Reining, Seefried, Welitsch, Hotter, Patzak, Schöffler, and Weber. In the 1970s Bernstein, Böhm, Karajan, and Mehta cond. famous perfs. In 1982 Lorin *Maazel, an American, was appointed dir., with a contract until 1986, but he left in 1984 after a controversial period of musical politics which his predecessors Mahler and Strauss would have recognized as characteristically Viennese. Claudio *Abbado was appointed in 1986 but—politics again!—resigned in 1991. No successor was appointed until Seiji Ozawa, 2002. It may be fairly said that the history of the Vienna Opera is one of spectacular triumphs, petty politics, a fairly conservative policy towards new mus., and glorious singing.

Vienna Symphony Orchestra (Ger. *Wiener Symphoniker*). Orch. founded in 1900 as Wiener Konzertverein Orchester. In 1921 it merged with Verein Wiener Tonkünstler (formed 1907 under Oskar Nedbal) and became Wiener Sinfonie-Orchester. It assumed present name in 1933, with over 120 players. Administered by Gesellschaft der Musikfreunde, Wiener Konzerthausgesellschaft, Bregenz Fest., and Austrian Radio. First cond. was Ferdinand *Löwe, 1900–24. In 1934 became Vienna's main broadcasting orch. and in 1938 was taken over by city as its municipal orch. Made many recordings.

Vie parisienne, La (Parisian Life). *Opéra-bouffe* in 5 (later 4) acts by Offenbach to lib. by Meilhac and Halévy. Comp. 1866, rev. 1873. Prod. Paris 1866; NY 1869, London 1872. Rev. vers. Paris 1873. See *Gaîté parisienne*.

Vier ernste Gesänge (Four Serious Songs). Songcycle for low v. and pf., Op.121, by Brahms, comp. 1896 to biblical texts. 1. *Denn es gehet dem Menschen*; 2. *Ich wandte mich und sahe an alle*; 3. *O Tod, O Tod, wie bitter bist du*; 4. *Wenn ich mit Engelszungen redete*. Inspired by his emotion over Clara *Schumann's final illness. Orch. version by Malcolm *Sargent.

Vier letzte Lieder (Four Last Songs). Songs for high v. and orch. by R. Strauss, comp. 1948. 5th song left unfinished. In order of comp.: 1. *Im Abendrot* (In the Sunset) (Eichendorff), 2. *Frühling* (Spring), 3. *Beim schlafengehen* (Falling asleep), 4. *September*. (Poems of 2, 3, and 4 by Hesse). Title of cycle given by publisher after Strauss's death. Strauss is said to have favoured order 3, 4, 2, 1. Some authorities believe that orch. vers. (1948) of *Ruhe, meine Seele!* (1894) was intended as part of the cycle. F.p. London 1950, Flagstad and Philharmonia Orch., cond. Furtwängler.

Vierne, Louis (Victor Jules) (*b* Poitiers, 1870; *d* Paris, 1937). Fr. organist and composer, born blind, but had limited sight after operation in 1877. Org., Nôtre Dame de Paris 1900–37. Taught org., Paris Cons. 1894–1911; prof. of org., Schola Cantorum, Paris, from 1912. Toured Europe and USA as org. recitalist. Wrote 6 org. syms. (1898–1930) and shorter pieces for org., also mass, str. qt., vn. sonata, vc. sonata, pf. quintet, and an orch. sym. (1907–8). Died playing org. at Notre Dame.

Viertel(note) (Ger.). Quarter-note (the crotchet).

Vierundsechzigstel(note) (Ger.). 64th note (the hemidemisemiquaver).

Vieuxtemps, Henri (Joseph François) (*b* Verviers, 1820; *d* Mustapha-lez-Alger, Algeria, 1881). Belg. violinist and composer. Played conc. with orch. in Verviers at age of 6. Toured Ger. 1833. Revived interest (1834) in Beethoven's vn. conc. Visited Russia 1838, USA 1844. Court violinist and prof. of vn., St Petersburg 1846–52. Prof. of vn., Brussels Cons. 1871–3. Regarded as one of greatest violinists of his day. Wrote 7 vn. concs., vn. sonata, 3 str. qts., many vn. pieces, and cadenzas for Beethoven conc.

Vignoles, Roger (Hutton) (*b* Cheltenham, 1945). Eng. pianist. Début London 1967. Répétiteur CG 1969–71, EOG 1968–74. Accompanist to many singers. Salzburg Fest. début 1984 (recital with Heinrich *Schiff). Prof. of accomp., RCM 1974–81. Début as opera cond., Buxton Fest. 1992.

vihuela. Sp. Renaissance instr. of guitar type. Word was used generically for all str. instrs., so further identification was necessary, e.g. *vihuela de arco*, bowed vihuela; *vihuela de penole*, plectrum-plucked vihuela; *vihuela de mano*, finger-plucked vihuela. Main period of popularity 1530–80. Luis de Milán's book on the *vihuela de mano* (1536) is a teaching manual containing first solo songs printed in Sp. Larger than guitar, usually with 6 courses, and up to 10 frets. Superseded by guitar *c*.1700. Mus. notated in tablature.

Village Romeo and Juliet, A (*Romeo und Julia auf dem Dorfe*). Opera in 6 *tableaux* by Delius to Ger. lib. by composer based on short story *Romeo und Julia auf dem Dorfe* from coll. of *Novellen* entitled *Die Leute von Seldwyla* (1856) by Gottfried Keller (1819–90). Comp. 1899–1901. Prod. Berlin 1907, cond. Cassirer, London CG 1910, cond. Beecham, Washington DC 1972. The intermezzo between scenes 5 and 6 was rewritten and extended in 1906 to cover the scene-change and became known in the concert-hall as the 'Walk to the Paradise Garden'. Suite for orch. arr. Fenby (1948).

Villa-Lobos, Heitor (*b* Rio de Janeiro, 1887; *d* Rio de Janeiro, 1959). Brazilian composer. First mus. lessons from father, who taught him vc. Had harmony lessons 1907, otherwise self-taught, earning living by playing in cafés, etc. Played vc. in Rio opera and sym. orchs., absorbing influences from Russ. nationalists, Stravinsky, and Strauss, under whose baton he played in 1920. Befriended by *Milhaud when latter was Claudel's secretary at Fr. embassy, and by Arthur Rubinstein, 1921, who played his pf. mus. Spent 1923–4 in Europe and 1927–30 in Paris where he was influenced by Satie and Milhaud and by fashionable neoclassicism. Result was series of works called *Bachianas Brasileiras* in which Baroque forms were re-created with Brazilian 'local colour'. Returning to Brazil 1930, held series of official teaching posts. Founded Conservatório Nacional de Canto Orfeónico 1942 and Brazilian Acad. of Mus., 1945 (pres. 1945–59). Visited USA 1944 as cond. of own mus. Extremely prolific composer, with expected sharp variations in quality. Though his mus. suggests the folk idiom, he rarely, if ever, quoted a folksong, relying instead on colour and rhythm to give Brazilian flavour. Melodist and romantic, he used the popular *chôro* form as a basis for series of works for various combinations of instr. and vv. with specific nationalist intent. Prin. works incl.:

OPERAS: *Izaht* (1912–14); *Yerma* (1955–6).
*CHÔROS: No.1, gui, (1920); No.2, fl., cl. (1924); No.3, 7 winds, male ch. (1925); No.4, 2 hn., tb. (1926); No.5, pf. (1926); No.6, orch. (1926); No.7, 5 winds, vn., vc. (1924); No.8, 2 pf., orch. (1925); No.9, orch. (1929); No.10, orch., ch. (1925); No.11, pf., orch. (1928); No.12, orch. (1929); No.13, 2 orchs., band (1929); No.14, orch., band, ch. (1928). Also *Chôros bis*, vn., vc. (1928)
*BACHIANAS BRASILEIRAS: 1. 8 vc. (1930); 2. *The Little Train of the Caipira*, chambér orch. (1934); 3. pf., orch. (1934); 4. pf. (1930–40) or orch. (1941); 5. v., 8 vcs. (1938); 6. fl., bn. (1938); 7. orch. (1942); 8. orch. (1944); 9. unacc. ch. or str. (1944).
ORCH.: syms.: No.1 (1916), No.2 (1917), Nos. 3 and 4 (1919), No.5 (1920)—Nos. 3, 4, and 5 are a World War I trilogy, subtitled respectively 'Guerra', 'Vitória', and 'Paz'—No.6 (*Montanhas do Brasil*) (1944), No.7 (*Odisséia da paz*) (1945), No.8 (1950), No.9 (1951), No.10 (*Sume pater patrium*), soloists, ch., orch. (1952), No.11 (1955), No.12 (1957); *Suite Suggestive* No.1 (1929); 4 *Suites, Descrobimento di Brasil* (Discovery of Brazil) (1936–7, 1942); *New York Skyline* (1940); vc. concs., No.1 (1915), No.2 (1953); 5 pf. concs. (1945–54); gui. conc. (1951); hp. conc. (1953); harmonica conc. (1955).
CHAMBER MUSIC: 17 str. qts. (1915–58); 3 pf. trios (1911–18); 4 vn. sonatas (1912–23); *Berceuse* (1915); 2 vc. sonatas (1915, 1916); Nonet (1923); *Sextetto místico* (1945).

PIANO: *Suite Infantil* Nos. 1 and 2 (1912, 1913); *A Prole do Bebê* Nos. 1 and 2 (The Baby's Family) (1918, 1921); *Rudepoema* (1921–6, also for pf. and orch.); *Saudades das Selvas Brasileiras* (1927).
GUITAR: 12 *Études* (1928); 5 *Preludes* (1940)

villancico (from Sp. *villano*, rustic). (1) 16th-cent. choral comp., like cantata, generally on subject of Christmas, for soloists, ch., and str. and/or org.
(2) Madrigalian setting for 3 to 5 vv. of Sp. verse-form called *villancico*.

villanella (It.; Fr. *villanelle*). Street song popular in 16th cent., also a type of part-song less complicated than madrigal. The first song in Berlioz's cycle *Les Nuits d'été* is entitled *Villanelle*.

Villazón, Rolando (*b* Mexico City, 1972). Mexican tenor. Joined Espacios Acad. for Perf. Arts 1983. Taught by Arturo Nieto 1990. Entered Mex. Nat. Cons. of Mus. 1992 to study with Enrique Jaso. Sang as student in *La scala di seta*, *Il Signor Bruschino*, and *Il re pastore*, then was taught by Gabriel Mijares. Prof. début Mexico City 1996 (Parpignol in *La bohème*). Member of Pittsburgh Opera young artists' programme 1998, singing in *Lucia di Lammermoor* and *Vanessa*. Eur. début Genoa 1999 (Des Grieux in *Manon*). Paris début 2000 (Alfredo in *La traviata*), Glyndebourne 2003 (Rodolfo), CG 2004 (Hoffmann), NY Met 2004 (Alfredo), Salzburg Fest. 2005 (Alfredo).

Villi, Le (The Willis). Opera in 1 act, revised to 2 acts, by Puccini to lib. by F. Fontana after A. Karr's story *Les Wilis* (1852). Comp. 1883. Prod. Milan 1884. Rev. version in 2 acts prod. Turin 1884, Manchester (in Eng.) 1897, NY Met 1908.

villotta (It.). Plebeian 16th-cent. song, later known as *villanella.

Vinay, Ramón (*b* Chillán, Chile, 1912; *d* Puebla, Mex., 1996). Chilean tenor (also baritone). Opera début (as bar.) Mexico City 1931 (Alphonse in *La Favorite*). Tenor début Mexico City 1943 (Don José in *Carmen*). Débuts: NY City Opera 1945; NY Met 1946; La Scala 1947; CG 1950; Salzburg 1951; Bayreuth 1952. Superb Otello, coached in role by Toscanini with whom he made famous recording. Resumed bar. roles 1962, singing Telramund (*Lohengrin*, at Bayreuth 1962), Iago, Falstaff, and Scarpia. Producer until 1972.

Vincent, John (*b* Birmingham, Alabama, 1902; *d* Santa Monica, Calif., 1977). Amer. composer and teacher. Head of mus. dept. W. Kentucky State Univ. 1937–45 and succeeded Schoenberg as prof. of comp. UCLA 1946–69. Employed 'paratonality' in his mus., i.e. diatonic element predominating in polytonal or atonal passages. Wrote comic opera *Primeval Void* (1969–71), prod. Vienna 1973; Sym. in D (1954); *Nude Descending the Staircase*, xyl., str. (1972); *Stabat Mater*, sop., male vv. (1969); *Mary at Calvary*, sop., ch., org. (1976); 2 str. qts. (1936, 1967); and songs.

Viñes, Ricardo (*b* Lérida, 1875; *d* Barcelona, 1943). Sp. pianist. Champion of contemp. composers, being among first pianists to play works of Debussy, Ravel, and others. Introduced much Russ. pf. music to France (incl. Mussorgsky's *Pictures at an Exhibition*). In 1936 gave f.ps. of works by *Messiaen.

viol. Type of bowed str. instr., made in various sizes. Developed in Renaissance period, then superseded by vn. family, now revived for perf. of early mus. Origins obscure, but probably developed from efforts to apply bow to plucked instr. during 2nd half of 15th cent. in Spain. Term 'viol' was used generically, like *vihuela in Sp. Consort of viols mentioned in Eng. records of King's Musick for 1540. Shape of viol varied much during first century of existence. Documentation of 1556 says that Fr. viols had 5 str. tuned in 4ths, whereas It. viols had 6. All viols were played held downwards, larger sizes between the legs, smaller resting on knees. Eng. composers from Byrd to Purcell wrote superb series of works for viols, a consort (or chest) normally comprising 2 trebles, 2 tenors, and 2 basses. Viol had flat back, frets, and C-shaped sound-holes. Bow held in underhand grip with fingers controlling tension of horse-hair. Prin. types of viol. are: *division viol*: smaller version of bass viol suitable for agile playing of *divisions (variations); *lyra-viol*: instr. specially built for virtuoso viol players who practised double- and triple-stopping, pizzicato, etc.; mus. written in tablature. Tobias Hume's *First Part of Ayres*, 1605, is lyra-viol mus. See also *baryton, viola d'amore, viola da braccio, viola da gamba*.

viola (Fr. *alto* or *taille*; Ger. *Bratsche*). (1) Bowed 4-str. instr., sometimes known as *alto* or *tenor* because of its lower pitch compared with vn., to which it is closely related. Tuned to c, g, d′, a′. Va. section standard in all orchs.; one va. is standard component of str. qt. Also used as solo instr., several concs. and conc.-type works having been written for it. *viola pomposa* was rare 18th-cent. type with a higher 5th str. See also *Tertis, Lionel*.
(2) Org. stop of 8′ length and pitch.
(3) Generic It. term for str. instrs. in Renaissance and baroque periods, incl. *viole da gamba* (leg viols), i.e. members of the *viol family; and *viole da braccio* (arm viols), the forerunners of the vn. family.

viola alta (It.; Ger. *Altgeige*). High viola, i.e. large va. with 5 str. introduced by H. Ritter in 1876 and used by Wagner at Bayreuth. Cumbersome to play.

viola bastarda. Continental equivalent of Eng. *division *viol.

viola da braccio (It.). Arm-viol. First known use of term in 1543 as generic description of str. instr. played on the arm (e.g. *rebec, Renaissance fiddle, and *lira da braccio*) but later meaning members of *violin family.

viola da gamba (It.). Leg-viol. (1) Strictly, every *viol was a *viola da gamba* because of the way it was held for perf., but term applies mainly to

bass viol because it was held between the knees like the modern vc.
(2) Org. stop. See *gamba*.

viola d'amore (It.). Love-viol. Bowed str. instr. of the *viol family but without frets and played under the chin. Larger than modern *viola, with 7 bowed gut str. and 7 sympathetic str. (which give the instr. its name) which vibrate to the sound of the stopped strs. Particularly beautiful sound.

viola pomposa. Instr. of vn. family with 5 str. used in Baroque works for high vc. passages. Larger than va.

viole (Fr.). (1) *Viol.
(2) *Viola.

violin (Fr. *violon*; It. *violino*; Ger. *Geige* or *Violine*). Bowed 4-str. instr., prin. and treble member of its family (va., vc., and db. being the others). Tuned g d′ a′ e″; compass of over 3½ octaves. Standard feature of every orch., where vns. are divided into '1sts' and '2nds', corresponding to higher- and lower-pitched parts. Str. qt. has 2 vn. (1st and 2nd). Emerged independently of the *viol, to which it is not related. A 3-str. vn. is represented in paintings at Ferrara 1508–9. At some time in It. before 1550 the 4-str. instr. was invented and was regarded as the instr. for dancing whereas the viol was the courtly instr. Earliest printed vn. mus. is 2 dances incl. in the *Balet comique de la royne* of 1581. Undoubtedly the vn. was perfected by one man, Andrea *Amati of Cremona, from whom the king of Fr. ordered 38 str. instrs. in 1560. For account of later development of instr., see *Stradivari*. Vn. is made from wood, with 2 f-shaped sound holes. Str., made of gut or metal, are stretched along upper surface (belly). Sound from the str. when touched by *bow is transmitted by upright bridge which supports the str. and which they cross at fractionally less than a right angle. Str. are held in place by tailpiece, cross bridge, and continue over ebony fingerboard attached to upper surface of neck. At extreme end they cross nut, or saddle, and enter a pegbox where they are attached to, and tuned by, 4 pegs. Among the most expressive of instr., the vn. has inspired a treasury of great mus. and great performers. The *violino piccolo* (It., little violin) was a small, higher-pitched instr. used in Baroque period in such works as Bach's Brandenburg Conc. No.1. The vn. bow used to be convex, but since late 18th cent. has been concave, with increased tension.

Violinbogen (Ger.). Vn. bow.

violino. (1) (It.). *Violin.
(2) Org. stop of 4′ (sometimes 8′) length and pitch.

Violins of Saint-Jacques, The. Opera in 3 acts by *Williamson to lib. by William Chappell after novel by Patrick Leigh Fermor. Comp. 1966. Prod. London (SW) 1966.

Violin-Steg (Ger.). Vn. bridge.

violoncello (It., usually abbreviated to 'cello'; Ger. *Violoncell*; Fr. *violoncelle*). Bowed 4-str. instr., one of *violin family, originating in early 16th cent. Played between performer's knees. Tuned to C G d a; compass of over 3 octaves. All sym. orchs. contain vc. section, and one vc. is part of every str. qt. Noble sound of instr. has been well catered for in concs., those by Dvořák and Elgar in particular exploiting its expressive capabilities to the full.

violone. Imprecise term. In 16th and 17th cent. It., *violone* meant a *viol and later a bass viol, especially the larger and deeper types of instr. such as the viola da gamba. During the Baroque period in Ger., *violone* meant a double bass, whereas in It. during the same period it meant an early type of *violoncello.

Viotti, Giovanni Battista (*b* Fontanetto, Piedmont, 1755; *d* London, 1824). It. composer and violinist. Son of blacksmith who played hn. and taught him mus. Toured Ger. and Russia with *Pugnani, 1780. Played in Concert Spirituel, Paris, 1782, becoming accompanist to Marie Antoinette. Visited London 1792, making début in 1793 at Salomon concert and playing in Haydn's benefit concerts 1794 and 1795, and at It. opera at King's Th., 1795–8. Returned to London 1801, becoming wine merchant. Active in formation of Phil. Soc. 1813. Dir., It. Opera in Paris 1819–22. Died impoverished after commercial misfortunes. Reckoned as greatest classical player of his day and founder of modern sch. of classical playing. Wrote 29 vn. concs., of which No.22 in A minor is especially important, 21 str. qts., 21 str. trios, many vn. duets, 18 vn. sonatas with bass, pf. concs., fl. qts., and other pieces.

Viotti, Marcello (*b* Vollorbe, Switzerland, 1954; *d* Munich, 2005). Swiss-born conductor of It. parentage. Studied pf., vc., and singing at Geneva and Lausanne Cons. Cond. début Geneva 1979, with wind ens. which he founded. 1st prize in Gino Marinuzzi Cond. Comp. 1982 launched his career. Prin. cond. Turin Opera 1986–9; mus. dir. Lucerne Opera 1987–91; gen. mus. dir. Bremen 1990–3; mus. dir. Saarbrücken Radio SO 1991–5. Début Vienna PO 1997. Worked mainly in opera, at all major int. opera houses, but from 1998 was mus. dir. Munich Radio Orch. (disbanded 2006) and directed *Paradisi Gloria*, series of concerts of 20th-cent. choral mus. Début NY Met 2000 (*Madama Butterfly*). Mus. dir. La Fenice, Venice, from 2002.

virelai (*chanson balladée*). Medieval Fr. song, probably of Sp. origin, consisting of refrain alternating with (usually) 3 stanzas. Est. as common Fr. poetic and mus. form by Machaut; continued in use throughout 15th cent. (by Du Fay, Ockeghem, and Busnois). The word derives from old Fr. *virer*, to turn or twist, thus suggesting a dance origin.

virginal(s). This word (not of Eng. origin) was used in Eng. as generic term for all types of plucked kbd. instr., but also had specific mean-

ing. First mentioned *c*.1460, name being used in Fr. and Ger. Typical virginals of oblong shape with one set of strs., parallel to kbd. (Differed from hpd. in shape of soundbox, placing of strs.—at right angles on hpd.—and existence of 2 bridges.) Kbd. on Flemish virginals was set to right or left, in others it was centrally placed. Double virginals had 2 kbds. Much fine mus. written for virginals by Byrd, Bull, Morley, Farnaby, etc. See *Fitzwilliam Virginal Book*. Origin of name obscure, but probably comes from instrument's association with female performers or possibly from its tone (like a young girl's voice).

virtuoso (It.). (1) As noun: a performer of exceptional skill with particular reference to technical ability.

(2) As adjective: a performance of exceptional technical accomplishment. There is sometimes an implication that a virtuoso performance excludes emotional and expressive artistry, or subdues it to technical display, but a true virtuoso is both technician and artist.

Visconti (di Modrone), (Count) **Luchino** (*b* Milan, 1906; *d* Rome, 1976). It. producer, designer, and writer. Came of family with long assoc. with La Scala. Began career as stage and film dir. and went into opera because of admiration for Maria *Callas, for whom he prod. *La Vestale* in 1954. Later he staged, for Callas, *La sonnambula*, *La traviata*, *Anna Bolena*, and *Iphigénie en Tauride*, all at La Scala. His first opera prod. outside It. was the memorable *Don Carlos* at CG (1958). His last opera prod. was *Manon Lescaut* at Spoleto, 1972. Among his protégés were the designers Sanjust and Zeffirelli. Wrote lib. for Mannino's opera *Il Diavolo in giardino* (Palermo 1963) and scenario of Henze's ballet *Maratona* (1956). Directed film of Thomas Mann's *Death in Venice* (1971) in which he made use of Mahler's mus. His productions were notable for their authentic period style, attention to detail and characterization, and visual taste.

Vishnevskaya, Galina (Pavlovna) (*b* Leningrad, 1926). Russ. soprano. Sang at Leningrad Operetta Th. 1944–8, then opera début, Leningrad 1950 in Strelnikov's *Kholopka*. Joined Bolshoy Opera 1952. Débuts: NY Met 1961; CG 1962; La Scala 1964; Salzburg Fest. 1975. Fine dramatic singer. Wife of *Rostropovich, whom she married 1955 and with whom she left USSR. Sop. part of Britten's *War Requiem*, 1962, written for her, but she did not sing at f.p. in Coventry. Gave f.p. of Britten's *The Poet's Echo*, Moscow 1965. Shostakovich dedicated his *7 Romances*, Op.127, to her (f.p. Moscow 1967) and she sang soprano part in f.p. of his 14th Sym., Leningrad 1969. Sang title-role in first recording of orig. version of Shostakovich's *The Lady Macbeth of the Mtsensk District*. Retired from opera 1982. Autobiography *Galina* (1984).

Vision of Aeroplanes, A. Motet for mixed ch. and org. by Vaughan Williams on text from Ezekiel, Ch.1. F.p. Cornhill, London, 1956.

Vision of Judgement, The. Oratorio by *Fricker, his Op.29, to text compiled by him from 8th-cent. poem by Cynewulf. For sop. and ten. soloists, ch., and orch. Comp. for 1958 Leeds Fest., where its f.p. was cond. by John Pritchard.

Vision of St Augustine, The. Setting of Lat. text for bar., ch., and orch. by *Tippett, comp. 1963-5. F.p. London 1966 by Dietrich Fischer-Dieskau, LSO and LSO Ch. cond. Tippett.

Visions de l'Amen. Suite in 7 movements for 2 pf. by *Messiaen, comp. 1943. F.p. Paris, 1943 (Loriod and Messiaen).

Visions fugitives (Fleeting Visions). 20 pieces for solo pf. by Prokofiev, Op.22, comp. 1915-17. F.p. Petrograd, 1918 (Prokofiev).

Visit of the Old Lady, The (*Der Besuch der alten Dame*). Opera in 3 acts by G. von *Einem to lib. by Dürrenmatt based on his own play. Comp. 1970. Prod. Vienna 1971, S. Francisco 1972, Glyndebourne, 1973.

Vitali, Giovanni Battista (*b* Bologna, 1632; *d* Modena, 1692). It. composer and violinist. Held court post at Modena from 1674. One of pioneers of sonata. Wrote *sonate da chiesa*, sonatas for 2 vn. with bass, etc.

Vitali, Tomaso Antonio (*b* Bologna, 1663; *d* Modena, 1745). It. violinist and composer, son of G. B. *Vitali. Chamber musician in Modena. Wrote sonatas (1693-5) and famous Chaconne for vn. with figured bass (though this is of doubtful attrib.).

Vittoria. See *Victoria, Tomás Luis de*.

vivace, vivacemente (It.). Vivacious, from *vivacità, vivacezza*, vivacity. Fast and lively. *vivacissimo*, very fast. Composers (e.g. Schubert) often use *vivace* as an indication of mood rather than tempo. In 18th cent. it often meant something between *allegro* and *largo*.

Vivaldi, Antonio (*b* Venice, 1678; *d* Vienna, 1741). It. composer and violinist. Son of violinist in orch. of St Mark's, Venice, under *Legrenzi. Taught by father. Entered church, becoming priest 1703, though after 2 years never said Mass because of congenital chest complaint. Taught vn. at orphanage (Ospedale della Pietà) from 1703 and gave recitals. Pubd. trio sonatas, Op.1, 1705 and vn. sonatas, Op.2, 1709. First opera, *Ottone in villa*, prod. Vicenza 1713; first Venetian opera, *Orlando finto pazzo*, 1714. Was also operatic impresario in Venice and cond. and played vn. in opera perfs. Spent 3 years in service of Landgrave of Hesse-Darmstadt in Mantua, probably 1719-21. Between 1722 and 1725, wrote operas for Mantua, Vicenza, Milan, and Rome. His famous Op.8, incl. *Le quattro stagioni* (The Four Seasons), was pubd. 1725. By this time, Vivaldi was known and admired throughout Europe. In 1734 first collaborated with librettist Goldoni (1709-93). In 1737 prod. of a new Vivaldi opera at Ferrara was forbidden by papal authorities on ground that Vivaldi was a priest who did not say Mass and had a relationship with a woman singer. In 1738, visited Amsterdam, where his mus. had been pubd. since 1711, for royal th. centenary celebrations—his reputation stood higher in Fr., Holland, and Eng. in his lifetime than it did in Venice. Despite intermittent disputes over the years, Vivaldi was still maestro at the Pietà and was still writing cantatas for perf. there in 1740. In 1741 he decided to leave Venice for Vienna, presumably in search of some court appointment, but died there, being buried in a pauper's grave.

Among contemporaries who appreciated Vivaldi was J. S. Bach, who transcr. 10 Vivaldi concs. as hpd. or org. concs. Like Bach's, Vivaldi's mus. fell out of favour for many years, but the 20th cent., in particular since the revival of interest in authentic methods of performing baroque mus., has seen it re-est. Once regarded merely as the composer of works for str., his genius as an opera composer is now recognized (he said he wrote 94, but fewer than 50 are extant) as well as the Venetian splendour of his church mus. No composer did more to establish the vc. as a solo instr., and he displayed a keen interest in the use of unusual instr.: it is the infinite variety and invention of his work that has made it so beloved 300 years after his birth. There have been several catalogues of his work, the most recent (Leipzig 1974) by Peter Ryom (works are numbered with the prefix RV = *Ryom-Verzeichnis*). Prin. works:

OPERAS: *Bajazet (Tamerlano)* (1735); *Catone in Utica* (1737); *Dorilla in Tempe* (1726); *Ercole sul Termodonte* (1723); *Farnace* (1727); *La fida ninfa* (1732); *Il Giustino* (1724); *Griselda* (1735); *L'incoronazione di Dario* (1716); *L'Olimpiade* (1734); *Orlando finto pazzo* (1714); *Orlando furioso* (1727); *Ottone in villa* (1713); *Rosilena ed Oronta* (1728); *Rosmira* (1738); *Il Teuzzone* (1719); *Tito Manlio* (1719); *La verità in cimento* (1720).

PUBLISHED WORKS IN HIS LIFETIME: Op.1, 12 sonatas for 2 vn. and basso continuo (1705); Op.2, 12 sonatas for vn. and basso continuo (1709); Op.3, *L'*estro armonico* (Harmonic inspiration), 12 concs. for various combinations (4 vn., 4 vn. and vc., etc.) (1711); Op.4, *La *stravaganza* (The extraordinary), 12 vn. concs. (c.1714); Op.5 (2nd part of Op.2), 4 sonatas for vn. and 2 sonatas for 2 vn. and basso continuo (1716); Op.6, 6 vn. concs. (1716-21); Op.7, 2 ob. concs. and 10 vn. concs. (1716-21); Op.8, *Il cimento dell' armonia e dell' inventione* (The Contest between Harmony and Invention), 12 vn. concs., the first 4, in E, G minor, F, and F minor being known as *The *Four Seasons* (*Le quattro stagioni*) (1725); Op.9, *La cetra* (The lyre), 11 vn. concs. and 1 for 2 vn. (1727); Op.10, 6 fl. concs. (c.1728); Op.11, 5 vn. concs., 1 ob. conc. (1729); Op.12, 5 vn. concs. and 1 without solo (1729); Op.13, *Il pastor fido* (The Faithful Shepherd), 6 sonatas for musette, viella, recorder, ob. or vn., and basso continuo (1737, doubtful authenticity).

The rest of Vivaldi's instr. output is so vast that it can only be summarized:

10 sonatas, vc., basso continuo; 28 sonatas, vn., basso continuo; 4 sonatas, fl., basso

continuo; sonatas, 2 vns., basso continuo; concs. for various instr. (fl., ob., recorders, vns., bn., etc.) and basso continuo; over 60 concs., sinfonias, and sonatas for str. and basso continuo; 170 concs. and sinfonias for vn., orch., and basso continuo; 7 concs. for viola d'amore; 28 vc. concs.; mandolin conc.; 9 fl. concs.; 2 recorder concs.; 14 ob. concs.; over 40 bn. concs.; many concs. for 2 vns., 2 vc., 2 mandolins, 2 ob., 2 hn., 2 tpt., etc.

SACRED MUSIC: Mass; *Kyrie* for double ch.; 3 *Glorias*; 2 *Dixit Dominus*; 3 *Laudate pueri*; 2 *Magnificat*; 3 *Salve Regina*; *Stabat Mater*; **Juditha triumphans* (oratorio, Venice 1716); also many secular cantatas, etc.

vivo (It.). Lively; *vivissimo* is the superlative.

vl. Short for violin in orch. scores. In this and other dictionaries, vn. is used.

Vlad, Roman (*b* Cernăuti, 1919). Romanian composer and writer. Comp. in 12-note idiom from 1943. Taught at Dartington summer sch., 1954 and 1955. Art. dir., Accademia Filarmonica Romana 1955–8, Maggio Musicale, Florence, 1964, and Teatro Comunale, Florence, 1968–72. Art. dir. Ravello Mus. Fest. from 1975, RIA Orch. 1976–80, La Scala, Milan, 1994–7. Prof. of comp., Perugia Cons. from 1968. Contributor to several periodicals; author of book on Stravinsky (Eng. trans. 1967). Works incl. opera *Storia di una mamma* (1950–1), ballets *La strada sul caffé* (1944), *La dama delle camelie* (1945), *Sinfonia all' antica*, orch. (1947–8), *Variazioni concertanti*, pf. and orch., based on series of 12 notes in Mozart's *Don Giovanni*, *Serenata* for str., *De Profundis*, sop., ch., and orch. (1949); *Cantata No.3*, ch., orch. (1952–3); *Music for Str.* No.1 (1955–7), No.2 (1988); *Divertimento sinfonico*, orch. (1965–7); *The Seagull*, ballet after Chekhov (1968); *The Magic Flute of Severino*, fl., pf. (1971); *The Dream*, opera after Strindberg (1973); *Meditations on an Old Russian Tune*, orch. (1982); *Sestupla melodia*, 11 str. (1993); *The Japanese Seasons*, 70 haiku (1994); *Mutations*, gui. (1996). Has written biographies of Stravinsky and Dallapiccola and *A History of Twelve-Tone Music* (1958).

Vltava (Smetana). See *Má Vlast*.

vn. Abbreviation for violin.

vocalise. A wordless vocal exercise or concert piece sung to one or more vowels. One of first concert pieces was Ravel's *Vocalise en forme d'habanera*. There are also *Vocalise*, for v. and pf. by Rachmaninov, Op.34, No.14, comp. 1912, rev. 1915, and *3 Vocalises* for sop. and cl. by Vaughan Williams (1958).

vocal score (abbreviated to V.S.). Score of a comp. which gives all the v.-parts of a work but with the orch. parts reduced to a pf. acc. In USA is called *piano-vocal score*.

voce, voci (It.). Voice, voices. *colla voce*, with the voice, i.e. direction to the accompanist closely to follow the singer's fluctuations of tempo, etc.

voce di petto (It.). See *chest voice*.

voce di testa (It.). See *head voice*.

Voces Intimae (Friendly Voices). Sibelius's subtitle for his str. qt. in D minor, Op.56, comp. 1908–9. F.p. Helsinki Cons. 1910.

Vogel, Jaroslav (*b* Pizeň, 1894; *d* Prague, 1970). Cz. conductor, composer, and writer. Opera cond. in Pizeň 1914–15 and in Ostrava 1919–23, returning as chief cond. 1927–43. Cond. in Prague 1923–7. Cond., Prague Nat. Th. 1949–58, chief cond. Brno State PO 1959–62. In Ostrava his perfs. of operas by Janáček, Smetana, and Novák were renowned. Wrote 4 operas. Also notable for his extensive study of Janáček's life and works (Prague 1958, abridged Eng. trans. 1962; rev. by K. Janovický, Eng. trans. 1981). Cond. first complete recording of a Janáček opera (*Jenůfa*, 1952).

Vogel, Vladimir (*b* Moscow, 1896; *d* Zurich, 1984). Russo-Ger.-born composer (Swiss cit. 1954). Taught at Klindworth-Scharwenka Cons. 1929–33, then settled in Switzerland. Several large-scale works using speaking ch. and *Sprechstimme*. Style a compound of Berg's 12-note technique and Busoni neo-classicism. Works incl.: 4 *Études* for orch. (1930–2); *Tripartita* for orch. (1934); vn. conc. (1937); vc. conc. (1954); *Epitaph for Alban Berg*, pf. (1936); *Thyl Claes*, sop., 2 speakers, speaking ch., orch. (1938–42); *Flucht*, oratorio for soloists (1963–4); 4 *Sprechstimmen*, speaking ch., orch. (1963–4); *Goethe Aphorisms*, sop., str. (1955); chamber mus., etc.

Vogelweide, Walther von der (*b* c.1170; *d* ?Würzburg, c.1230). Ger. singer and composer, one of greatest of Ger. **Minnesinger*. About 8 of his melodies have survived. Mentioned by Wagner in *Die Meistersinger von Nürnberg*, Act I, when the hero, Walther, tells the Masters that he is a pupil of Vogelweide. 'A good Master', says Sachs.

Vogl, Heinrich (*b* Au, nr. Munich, 1845; *d* Munich, 1900). Ger. tenor, outstanding in Wagnerian parts. Opera début Munich 1865 (Max in *Der Freischütz*). Took over role of Tristan after death of Schnorr von Carolsfeld. Created Loge in *Das Rheingold* 1869 and Siegmund in *Die Walküre* 1870. Sang at Bayreuth 1876–97, incl. Loge in first *Ring* cycle. London début 1882 (1st London Loge and Siegfried). NY Met 1890. Wrote opera, 1899. Wife was sop. Therese Thoma (*b* Tutzing, 1845; *d* Munich, 1921), who made début in Munich 1866, singing there until 1892. Created Sieglinde 1870. London 1882 (first London Brünnhilde). For some years was only Ger. Isolde.

Vogl, (Johann**) Michael** (*b* Ennsdorf, nr. Steyr, Austria, 1768; *d* Vienna, 1840). Austrian baritone. While at school sang in *Singspiel* by **Süssmayr*, a fellow-pupil. Studied law at Vienna Univ. but was persuaded to join Süssmayr's opera co. Sang at Vienna Court Opera 1795–1822. Met Schubert *c.1817* through Schober and became first singer of many of his *Lieder*. Sang twins (who never appear on stage together) in Schubert's *Singspiel, Die Zwillingsbrüder*, 1820. Travelled with Schubert, 1819, to Upper Austria, and again in 1823 and 1825. First to sing *Winterreise* cycle, 1827. Created Pizarro in *Fidelio* in the 1814 revision.

Vogler, Georg Joseph (Abbé Vogler) (*b* Pleichach, nr. Würzburg, 1749; *d* Darmstadt, 1814). Ger. composer, theorist, organist, and teacher. Ordained priest in Rome 1773. Returned to Mannheim 1775 and founded mus. sch. Became 2nd Kapellmeister and wrote operas. After visits to Paris (1780) and London (1783) to propagate his theories of musical performance, he became court cond. at Munich 1784–6. Travelled widely from 1786. Court mus. dir. Stockholm 1786, founding mus. sch. there. Travelled again from 1799. Taught in Vienna 1803–4. Court cond., Darmstadt 1807. Invented 'simplifications system' for org., demonstrating it in Eng., Denmark, and Holland on portable 'orchestrion'. Famous for his 'storm' effects in org. recitals. Wrote 10 operas, cantata, much church mus., pf. concs., many theoretical works, 32 org. preludes in every key (with analysis), arr. 12 Chorales by J. S. Bach. Pupils incl. Aloysia Weber (singing), Meyerbeer, Weber, Danzi, etc. (comp.). Subject of poem *Abt Vogler* by Robert Browning (1812–89) containing line 'The rest may reason and welcome; 'tis we musicians know'.

voice. (1) Means of producing sounds in humans and animals using 2 vibrating agents called vocal cords. The various kinds of human v., e.g. *soprano, *tenor, *bass, etc., are described under their individual entries.

(2) Separate strand of mus. in counterpoint or harmony, also known as 'part' or, more confusingly, 'voice-part' (e.g. a Mass for 5 voices is not a work for 5 singers but for 5 different *vocal ranges*, each of which could contain *any number* of singers). A fugue is in several vv. or parts, whether these are sung or played.

(3) As verb, meaning to adjust org.-pipe at construction stage so that it meets required standards of pitch, etc.

Voice of Ariadne, The. Opera in 3 acts by Musgrave, to lib. by A. Elguera based on James's *The Last of the Valerii* (1874). Comp. 1972–3. F.p. Snape Maltings, 1974, NY 1977.

voix (Fr.). Voice or voices.

voix céleste (Fr.). Heavenly voice. Org. stop, 8′ pitch, with 2 pipes to each note, tuned slightly apart and producing effect not unlike str. of orch.

Voix humaine, La (The Human Voice). Lyric tragedy in 1 act by Poulenc to text by Cocteau after his play. Monodrama for sop. and orch. Comp. 1958 for Denise Duval. Prod. Paris 1959, NY (concert) 1960, Edinburgh (concert) 1960, Glyndebourne (stage) 1976.

Volans, Kevin (*b* Pietermaritzburg, 1949). S. African composer (later Irish cit.). Worked for

W. Ger. Radio. Taught at Natal Univ., Durban, 1982–4. Comp.-in-res. Queen's Univ., Belfast, 1986–9, Princeton, NJ, 1992. Prin. comps.:

OPERAS: *The Man with Footsoles of Wind* (1993); *Zeno at 4 am* (2000–1); *Confessions of Zeno* (2002).

DANCE: *Wanting to Tell Stories* (1993); *Things I Don't Know* (1997–9).

ORCH.: *Into Darkness* (1987); *Chevron* (1989); *One Hundred Frames* (1991); Conc. for Pf. and Wind (1995); vc. conc. (1997, rev. 1998); *Conc. for Double Orch.* (2001); *Strip-Weave* (2002, rev. 2003).

CHAMBER MUSIC: str. qts. No.1 (*White Man Sleeps*) (1986), No.2 (*Hunting: Gathering*) (1987), No.3 (*The Songlines*) (1988), No.4 (*The Ramanujan Notebooks*) (1990), No.5 (*Dancers on a Plane*) (1994), No.6 (2000), No.7 (2002), No.8 (2004), No.10 (2005); *Movement*, str. qt. (*Notes d'un peintre*) (1987); *White Man Sleeps*, 2 hpd., va. de gamba, perc. (1982); *Walking Song*, fl., hpd., 2 hand-clappers (1984); *She who sleeps with a small blanket*, perc. (1985–6); *Into Darkness*, 2 cl., pf., mar., vib., vn., vc. (1987); *Wanting to Tell Stories*, cl., va., db., pf. (1992); *Wild Air*, 2 amp. gui., 2 amp. vc. (1998); Tpt. and Str. Qt., Nos. 1 and 2 (2002); pf. trio (2002); *Chakra*, 3 perc. (2003); *Double Take*, cl., pf. (2004).

KEYBOARD: 9 *Beginnings*, 2 pf. (1979); *Mbira*, 2 hpd., rattles (1980); *Matepe*, 2 hpd., rattles (1980); *Leaping Dance*, 2 pf. (1984) *Kneeling Dance*, 2 pf. (1985), 6 pf. (1992); *Cicada*, 2 pf. (1993–4); *Wrist Rock*, pf. (1999); 6 *Piano Études*, pf. (2004).

TAPE: *Studies in Zulu History* (1980); *Kwazulu Summer Landscape* (1980); *Cover him with grass* (1982).

volante (It.). Flying. Swift, light. In vn. playing, a certain bow-stroke in which the bow has to bounce from the str. in a slurred staccato.

Volkonsky, Andrey (Mikhaylovich) (*b* Geneva, 1933). Swiss-born Russ. composer, pianist, conductor, and harpsichordist. Co-founder with *Barshay of Moscow Chamber Orch. Influenced by Schoenberg, Boulez, Berio, etc. and encountered difficulties from Soviet authorities because of modern trend of his works. Founded *Madrigal*, early mus. ens. of Moscow Phil. Emigrated to Israel 1972. Works incl. Conc. for Orch., cantata *Dead Souls*, *Serenade to an Insect* for chamber orch., str. qts., pf. sonata, and music-theatre pieces.

Volkslied (Ger.). Folk-song, but often extended to incl. nat. and popular song which is properly covered by term *volkstümliches Lied*.

volles Werk (Ger.). Full Org.

volonté (Fr.). Will. *à volonté*, at one's own pleasure, i.e. *ad libitum*.

volta (It.). (1) 'Time', in sense of *prima volta*, 1st time.

(2) Quick dance in triple time, also known as 'Lavolta', resembling galliard. A Lavolta is danced in Britten's *Gloriana*.

volti (It.). Turn, as in *volti subito* (abbreviated to V.S.), turn over page quickly (found in orch. parts).

voluntary. (1) Org. solo at beginning and end of Anglican church service, sometimes but not necessarily extemporized.

(2) In 16th cent., applied to extemporized instr. comp. See also *trumpet tune* or *voluntary*.

Von Heute auf Morgen (From One Day to the Next). Comic opera in 1 act, Op.32, by *Schoenberg to lib. by Max Blonda (Gertrud Schoenberg). Comp. 1928–9. Prod. Frankfurt 1930, London (concert) 1963. Orch. score requires saxs., mandoline, guitar, banjo, and flexatone.

Vonk, Hans (*b* Amsterdam, 1942; *d* Amsterdam, 2004). Dutch conductor. Ass. cond. Dutch Nat. Ballet 1966–73. Ass. cond. Concertgebouw Orch., Amsterdam, 1969–72. Début with Netherlands Opera 1971 (mus. dir. 1976–85). London début 1974, assoc. cond., RPO 1977. Amer. début 1974. La Scala début 1980. Cond. Hague Residentie Orch. 1980–5, Dresden State Opera 1985–91, Dresden Staatskapelle 1985–91 (Salzburg Fest. 1987). Chief cond. Cologne Radio SO 1991–7.

Von Stade, Frederica. See *Stade, Frederica von*.

vorbereiten (Ger.). To prepare (applied to the registration of org. mus., often in the form of *bereite vor*, mentioning a stop). *Vorbereitung*, preparation.

Vorhalt (Ger.). (1) Suspension.
(2) Retardation.
(3) Long appoggiatura.
(4) Syncopation.

Vorschlag (Ger.). Forestroke. *kurzer Vorschlag* (short forestroke), *acciaccatura; langer Vorschlag* (long forestroke), *appoggiatura.

Vorspiel (Ger.). Foreplay. Ov. or prelude, used by Wagner in relation to his operas.

vox (Lat.). Voice. Thus *vox humana* (human voice), org. reed stop of 8′ pitch, supposedly but not actually like human v.

Vranický, Anton. See *Wranitzky, Anton*.

Vronsky, Vitya (*b* Evpatoria, Crimea, 1909; *d* Cleveland, 1992). Russ.-born pianist (Amer. cit.). Married Victor *Babin 1933, forming celebrated pf. duo and settling in USA.

V.S. (1) *vocal score.
(2) *volti subito, turn over quickly.

Vuillaume, Jean Baptiste (*b* Mirecourt, 1798; *d* Paris, 1875). Fr. maker of string instruments. Went to Paris 1818, where est. own business 1828. Made fine vns. and vcs.

Vulpius, Melchior (*b* Wasungen, Henneberg, *c*.1570; *d* Weimar, 1615). Ger. composer and cantor. Comp. chorales, *cantiones sacrae, St Matthew Passion* (1613), and ed. mus. compendium.

vuoto, vuota (It., 'empty'). Applied musically (1) to indicate a general pause, i.e. measure in which all parts have 'rest'; or (2) as indication to violinist to play on open str. (*corda vuota*).

Vyšehrad (Smetana). See *Má Vlast*.

Vyvyan, Jennifer (Brigit) (*b* Broadstairs, 1925; *d* London, 1974). Eng. soprano. Joined Glyndebourne ch. Opera début 1948 (Jenny Diver in EOG prod. of Britten's vers. of *The Beggar's Opera*). Won Geneva int. comp. 1951. Joined SW Opera 1952. Created Penelope Rich in *Gloriana* (CG 1953), Governess in *The Turn of the Screw* (Venice 1954), Tytania in *A Midsummer Night's Dream* (Aldeburgh 1960), and Mrs Julian in *Owen Wingrave* (TV 1971, CG 1973). Also successful career in concert works.

W

W. Abbreviation for *Werk(e)* (Ger., work(s)), the same as Opus. In Kinsky's Beethoven catalogue, *WoO signifies *Werk ohne Opuszahl*, 'work without opus number'.

Waart, Edo (Eduard) **de** (*b* Amsterdam, 1941). Dutch conductor and oboist. Prin. oboe, Concertgebouw Orch. of Amsterdam, 1962–3. Winner, Mitropoulos Comp., NY 1964. Ass. cond., Concertgebouw Orch. 1966. Prin. cond., Rotterdam PO 1973–7; S. Francisco SO 1977–85. Cond. Minnesota Orch. 1986–95. Chief cond., Sydney SO 1994–2003. British début Folkestone (RPO) 1969; CG 1976. Amer. opera début (Santa Fe) 1971. Art. dir. and chief cond. Hong Kong PO from 2004.

Wachet auf (Wake up!, often trans. as 'Sleepers, awake'). Church cantata No.140 by J. S. Bach, 1731, based on Lutheran chorale. Also choral-prelude for organ (BWV 645) by J. S. Bach. 'Wach' auf' is ch. in Act 3 of Wagner's *Die Meistersinger*, sung to words by orig. Hans Sachs.

Wachtelpfeife (Ger.). Quail-pipe. Instr. imitative of quail used in Toy Sym. attrib. Leopold Mozart. Beethoven, in ob. part in 2nd movt. of *Pastoral* Sym., uses this term where imitation of quail is required.

Wächter, Eberhard (*b* Vienna, 1929; *d* Vienna, 1992). Austrian baritone. Opera début Vienna Volksoper 1953 (Silvio in *Pagliacci*). Member of Vienna State Opera from 1955. Débuts: CG 1956; Salzburg Fest. 1956; Bayreuth 1958; La Scala 1960; NY Met 1961. Dir., Vienna Volksoper 1987–92, art. co-dir. Vienna State Opera 1991–2.

Wagenaar, Bernard (*b* Arnhem, 1894; *d* York, Maine, 1971). Dutch-born composer (Amer. cit. 1927). Went to USA 1920, joining NYPO as violinist 1921–3. Taught at Juilliard Sch. 1925–68. Works incl. 4 syms. (1926, 1931, 1935, 1949); triple conc., fl., hp., vc. (1937); *Sinfonietta* (1929); *Song of Mourning*, orch. (1944); *5 Tableaux*, vc., orch. (1952); vn. conc. (1940); 4 str. qts.; vn. sonata; song-cycle, etc.

Wagenseil, Georg Christoph (*b* Vienna, 1715; *d* Vienna, 1777). Austrian composer and pianist. Court composer, Vienna, from 1739, becoming mus.-master to Empress Maria Theresia. Wrote 16 operas (incl. *La clemenza di Tito*, 1746), at least 30 syms., hpd. concs., hp. concs., chamber mus.

Wagner, Cosima (*née* Liszt) (*b* Bellaggio, Lake Como, 1837; *d* Bayreuth, 1930). Of Franco-Hungarian birth, daughter of *Liszt and Countess Marie d'Agoult. Went to Ger. and in 1857 married Hans von Bülow, pianist and cond., by whom she had 2 children. First met Richard Wagner in Paris 1853; declared love for each other in Berlin 1863. Went to Munich 1864 to be near Wagner. Daughter, Isolde, born to them 1865. Lived with Wagner at Tribschen, Lucerne, from 1868. Another daughter, Eva, born 1867. Divorced from von Bülow 1869. Son, Siegfried, born to her and Wagner 1869. Married Wagner 1870. Moved with him to Bayreuth 1872 and was active in preparations for 1876 festival. After Wagner's death in 1883, became mus. dir. of Bayreuth Fest., handing over to her son Siegfried in 1908. Became blind 1920. Her diaries, covering years 1869–83, are invaluable source of information on Wagner's life and thought.

Wagner, Johanna (*b* Seelze, nr. Hanover, 1826; *d* Würzburg, 1894). Ger. soprano. Illegitimate child of army officer and singer, adopted by R. Wagner's brother. Engaged at Dresden, where Wagner was cond., 1843. Created role of Elisabeth in *Tannhäuser* 1845. Sang in Berlin 1850–62, then lost v. but became actress. London début 1856. Resumed singing in 1870s. Sang alto part in Beethoven's 9th Sym. at Bayreuth stone-laying ceremony 1872. Created Schwertleite in *Die Walküre* and First Norn in *Götterdämmerung*, 1876. Taught in Munich 1882–4.

Wagner, (Wilhelm) **Richard** (*b* Leipzig, 1813; *d* Venice, 1883). Ger. composer, conductor, poet, and author. One of the handful of composers who changed the course of mus. Went to sch. in Dresden and attended Thomasschule, Leipzig, 1830–1. Deeply interested in literature as youth. Mus. inclination intensified by hearing *Schröder-Devrient in Bellini. Wrote sym. 1832 and later that year made first attempt at opera, *Die Hochzeit*, which he destroyed. Choral cond. at Würzburg 1833 and in 1834 completed opera *Die Feen*. Became cond. of orch. at th. in Lauchstädt and later in 1834 mus. dir. of th. at Magdeburg. His 2nd opera *Das Liebesverbot*, based on Shakespeare's *Measure for Measure*, prod. there 1836. Married actress Minna Planer. Ass. cond. at Riga 1837–9. Went to Paris 1839. Wrote *Rienzi* 1838–40 and *Der fliegende Holländer* 1841. Lived in poverty in Paris, doing mus. hack-work and writing articles. In 1842 returned to Dresden, where *Rienzi* was prod. with great success. *Der fliegende Holländer* equal success in 1843, leading to Wagner's appointment as court opera cond. Cond. legendary perfs. of Beethoven's 9th Sym. and works by Mozart, Weber, and Gluck. *Tannhäuser* prod. at Dresden 1845. Began project for series of operas based on Nibelungen sagas, completing lib. of *Siegfrieds Tod*, 1848. Sided with revolutionaries in 1849 uprising in Dresden. Fled to Liszt at Weimar after police issued warrant for his arrest, eventually settling in Zurich where he wrote series of essays, incl. the important *Oper und Drama* in which he expounded his theory of *music drama, the unification of mus. and drama superseding all other considerations (such as singers' special requirements in the way of display arias). Also continued to write text of his Nibelung operas and comp. mus. of *Das Rheingold* and *Die Walküre*. In permanent financial straits, was helped by Julie Ritter and by Ger. merchant Otto Wesendonck, with whose wife Mathilde Wesendonck he had affair. Under the influence of this emotional experience he wrote lib. and mus. of *Tristan und Isolde* (1857–9), interrupting *Siegfried* after completing Act 2. In 1855 visited London as cond. of Phil. Soc. concerts. Wife Minna left him (not for first time) in 1858 because of Wesendonck affair but rejoined him in 1859. Cond. in Paris 1860 and rev. *Tannhäuser* for perf. at Opéra in 1861; but tried to withdraw it after riots instigated by Jockey Club. Allowed to re-enter Ger., except Saxony. Heard *Lohengrin* (comp. 1846–8) in Vienna and hoped for prod. there of *Tristan*, but it was abandoned after 77 rehearsals as 'unperformable'. Amnesty granted from Saxony 1862. At work on *Die Meistersinger von Nürnberg* from 1862. Fled Vienna 1864 because of pressing debts, but while in Stuttgart was 'rescued' by young King Ludwig of Bavaria, a passionate admirer of Wagner's mus., who became his patron and invited him to Munich, where *Tristan* was prod. 1865, cond. by Hans von Bülow, with whose wife, Cosima, Wagner had been in love since 1863. Work resumed on Nibelung operas under stimulus of Ludwig's enthusiasm. Opposition to Wagner in Munich political circles led to his departure from Munich and his settling at the villa of *Tribschen, Lucerne, where Cosima, having borne him 2 daughters, joined him in 1868. Minna having died in 1866 and Cosima's marriage being annulled in 1869 (the year in which she gave birth to Wagner's son Siegfried), Wagner and Cosima were married in 1870. *Das Rheingold* and *Die Walküre* prod. in Munich 1869 and 1870, *Die Meistersinger* in 1868. In 1871 persuaded *Bayreuth municipal authority to grant land for erection of th. specially designed for staging of *Der Ring des Nibelungen*; foundation-stone laid 1872. Toured Ger. to seek artists and raise funds for first Bayreuth Fest. Settled into new home, *Wahnfried, at Bayreuth 1874, where he completed *Götterdämmerung*, 4th opera in *Ring* project begun in 1848. Bayreuth th. opened August 1876 and *Ring* perf. complete under Hans *Richter, supervised in every detail by Wagner. In 1877 cond. series of concerts at Royal Albert Hall, London, to raise funds to cover Bayreuth deficit, and then began work on *Parsifal*, which he had first contemplated in 1857 (completed 1882, perf. in July at Bayreuth). From 1878, suffered series of heart attacks, fatal one occurring in Venice on 13 Feb. 1883. Buried at Wahnfried.

Wagner's mus., richly expressive, intensely illustrative, and on the grandest scale, dominated the 19th cent. and split the mus. world into opposing factions. His influence, good and bad, on countless other composers is still a prime factor a century after his death. He wrote the texts of all his operas, reading copiously in the sources of the legends he selected as subjects and writing a prose sketch, then the poem (lib.) before he comp. any of the mus., though it is clear that certain ideas came to him ready-clothed in mus. He was inspired by the Ger. Romantic spirit of Weber's operas, and to some extent by the grandiose operatic aims of Meyerbeer, whom he despised. In Liszt he found a fellow-spirit from whom he learned much, as he did from Berlioz. But he surpassed them all in the single-mindedness with which he pursued his dream of an art form in which mus. and drama should be one and indivisible, his *Zukunftsmusik* (mus. of the future). With the chromaticism of *Tristan* he took tonality to its limits and beyond, and opened the way for the Schoenbergian revolution. Philosophical and psychological undertones contribute immensely to the spell of the *Tristan* mus. Wagner brought to a fine art the use of *Leitmotiv* to depict not only characters but their emotions, and wove them into an orch. texture of such richness that the orch. assumed an extra dimension in operatic terms. His operas also required a new technique of singing and a new breed of singers with the intelligence to convey the subtleties of his art. The idea that 'bawling' was all that Wagner needed has long been disproved by generations of singers by whom his music has been shown to be as singable as *bel canto*. In a sense Wagner was a dead-end, since he was a unique genius. The sheer mastery of *The Ring*, the sustaining of such an imposing achievement at a white-heat of inspiration for something like 15 hours of mus., is among the most amazing artistic achievements of the human spirit. But opera could never be the same after him: he made it the vehicle for the expression of the most complex emotional and psychological issues, but, being first and foremost a musician, these are still secondary to the hypnotic power of the mus., at least for those (and they number millions) who fall under its sway. Prin. works:

OPERAS AND MUSIC DRAMAS: *Die *Feen* (The Fairies) (1833–4); *Das *Liebesverbot* (Forbidden Love) (1835–6); *Rienzi* (1838–40); *Der *fliegende Holländer* (The Flying Dutchman) (1840–1, various rev.); *Tannhäuser* (1843–5, rev. 1847–51, 1861–75); *Lohengrin* (1846–8); *Der *Ring des Nibelungen* (The Nibelung's Ring): *Das *Rheingold* (The Rhine Gold) (1853–4), *Die *Walküre* (The Valkyrie) (1854–6), *Siegfried* (1856–7 and 1864–71), *Götterdämmerung* (Twilight of the Gods) (1869–74, some ideas composed as *Siegfrieds Tod* many years earlier); *Tristan und Isolde* (1857–9); *Die *Meistersinger von Nürnberg* (The Mastersingers of Nuremberg) (1862–7); *Parsifal* (1877–82).

ORCH.: Concert Ov. in D minor (1831), in C (1832); Ov. in E minor (to E. Raupach's play *König Enzio*) (1831–2); sym. in C (1832); *Christopher Columbus, ov. (1834–5); *Polonia, ov. (1836); *Rule, Britannia, ov. (1837); *Faust, ov. (1839–40, rev. 1843–4, 1855); *Trauermusik* (after motifs from Weber's *Euryanthe*), wind instr. (1844); *Träume*, vn., small orch. (1857); *Huldigungsmarsch, military band

(1864; orch. vers. 1865, completed by Raff, 1871);
Siegfried Idyll (1870); *Kaisermarsch* (1871);
Centennial March (1876).

CHORAL: *Weihegruss* (1843); *Das *Liebesmahl der
Apostel* (The Love Feast of the Apostles), orch.
with male ch. (1843); *An Webers Grabe* (1844);
Kinder-Katechismus, children's vv., pf (1873), rev.
with orch. (1874).

PIANO: sonata in B♭ (1831); *Lied ohne Worte* (1840);
Album Sonata in A♭ (1853); *Albumblätter* in A♭
and C (1861).

SONGS: *7 Songs from Goethe's Faust* (1832); *Der
Tannenbaum* (1838); *Les deux grenadiers* (1839–40);
Les adieux de Marie Stuart (1840); *5 Gedichte von
Mathilde Wesendonck* (5 *Wesendonck Songs), v.
and pf. (1857–8; orch. Mottl; arr. Henze for high
v. and chamber orch., 1979).

WRITINGS: *My Life* (1865–80); *German Opera* (1851);
Art and Revolution (1849); *Judaism in Music* (1850);
Opera and Drama (1850–1); *The Music of the Future*
(1860); *Religion and Art* (1880); *On Conducting*
(1869).

Wagner, Roger (Francis) (*b* Le Puy, 1914; *d* Dijon, 1992). Fr.-born choral conductor (Amer. cit.).
Son of org. of Dijon Cath. Taken to USA at age of
7. Org. and choirmaster, Church of St Ambroise,
Los Angeles, at 12. Mus. dir., St Joseph's Church,
Los Angeles, 1937. Founded Roger Wagner Chorale 1946, which toured widely and won high reputation as one of the finest Amer. choirs. Head
of mus. dept., Marymount Coll., Los Angeles,
1951–66. Dir., choral mus., UCLA 1959–81.
Authority on Desprès. Papal Knight 1966.

Wagner, (Helferich) **Siegfried** (Richard) (*b*
Tribschen, Lucerne, 1869; *d* Bayreuth, 1930). Ger.
composer and conductor. Only son of Richard
*Wagner and Cosima *Wagner (then von Bülow).
Educated as architect, but turned to mus. Ass.
cond. Bayreuth 1894, cond. (left-handed) *Der Ring
des Nibelungen* perfs. there 1896, 1897, 1899,
1901, 1902, 1906, 1911, 1912, and 1928. Succeeded mother as art. dir., Bayreuth Fest. from
1908, producer from 1901. Married English-
woman Winifred Williams (1894–1980) who dir.
Bayreuth 1931–44. Wrote 13 operas, incl. *Der
Bärenhäuter (1898), *Der Kobold* (1903), *An allem ist
Hütchen schuld* (1914), and *Der Schmied von Marien-
burg* (1920), sym.-poems, vn. conc. (1915), and
sym. (1925).

Wagner, Sieglinde (*b* Linz, 1921). Austrian
mezzo-soprano. Début Linz 1942 (Erda in *Das
Rheingold*). Vienna Volksoper 1947–52; Berlin
Stadtische Oper 1952–86. Salzburg Fest. début
1949. Created Leda in *Die Liebe der Danae* (Salzburg [official première] 1952). Bayreuth 1962–73.

Wagner, Wieland (Adolf Gottfried) (*b* Bayreuth,
1917; *d* Munich, 1966). Ger. opera producer and
designer. Son of Siegfried *Wagner. Worked
among stage staff at pre–1939 Bayreuth Fests.
and designed scenery for *Parsifal* (1937), and *Die
Meistersinger* (1943). With his brother Wolfgang
*Wagner became art. dir. of Bayreuth Fest.
1951 and revolutionized Wagner prods., causing

intense controversy. Scrapped representational
productions, substituting settings with little
scenery, emphasis on lighting, and all-purpose
circular platform. Many of Wagner's stage directions were ignored. Also prod. operas by other
composers at Hamburg, Stuttgart, etc., notably
Fidelio (1954), from which he removed spoken
dialogue, and *Salome* (1962).

Wagner, Wolfgang (Manfred Martin) (*b* Bayreuth, 1919). Ger. opera impresario and producer.
Son of Siegfried *Wagner. With his brother Wieland *Wagner was co-dir. of Bayreuth Fest. 1951–
66, mainly concerned with administration but
prod. *Lohengrin* 1953. Succeeded brother as art.
dir., 1966. Though less controversial a producer
than Wieland, caused controversy by choice of
other producers, e.g. Patrice Chéreau for centenary *Ring*, 1976.

Wagner-Régeny, Rudolf (*b* Szász-Régen, Romania, 1903; *d* E. Berlin, 1969). Romanian-born
composer, conductor, and pianist (Ger. cit.
1933). Chorusmaster, Berlin Volksoper 1923–5,
worked with Laban's dance co. 1927–30. Dir. Rostock Hochschule für Musik, 1947–50, prof. of
comp. East Berlin Acad. of Arts 1950–68. Influenced by Weill-Brecht works, later by 12-note
procedures. Comp. 12 operas (incl. *Die Bürger von
Calais* 1936–8, *Johanna Balk* 1938–40, and *Das Bergwerk zu Falun* 1958–60); 3 ballets (incl. *Tristan*,
1958); pf. conc.; ch. works; etc.

Wagner tuba. Brass instr. invented by Wagner
as compromise between hn. and tb. to give special tone-colour in orchestration of *Der Ring des
Nibelungen* (for Hunding in *Die Walküre*, for example). Look more like hns. than tubas. The 4 used
in the *Ring* are 2 tenors in B♭, with 3 valves plus
extra for correcting intonation of lowest octave
and 2 basses in F. Played by 5th–8th hns. Wagner
had the idea for the tubas after seeing some instruments in Sax's workshops in 1853 which
may have been saxhorns. Possibly the tubas used
at Bayreuth in 1876 were made in Berlin. They
did not survive after 1939. In any case they were
replaced in 1890 by a set made in Mainz. CG
used brass band instruments until 1935 when
Beecham obtained a set from Mainz. Wagner
tubas were used also by Bruckner, R. Strauss, and
by Stravinsky in *The Rite of Spring*.

Wahnfried. Name of villa at Bayreuth into
which Wagner and his wife moved in April
1874 and where they are buried. Now a museum
housing valuable archives. Name chosen by
Wagner (orig. Wahnfriedheim) from Hesse town
of Wahnfried because he liked its mysticism, the
word meaning 'Peace from Wahn' (*Wahn* = madness, illusion, etc.). Above portal he engraved:
*Hier, wo mein Wähnen Frieden fand—Wahnfried sei
dieses Haus von mir benannt* (Here where my illusion found peace, be this house named by me
Peace from Illusion).

wait(s) (Old Eng.). Watchman. (1) Musicians in
medieval Eng. who acted as town watchmen,

marking the hours of the night by sounding instr. By 16th cent. they formed town bands, each having its *'signature-tune', thus *London Waits, Chester Waits*, etc. Some waits were renowned for singing, and this originated application of term to groups who sang hymns and carols in the streets at Christmas.

(2) Old Eng. name for *shawm, much used by waits. Other name for shawm was *wayte-pipe*.

Wakasugi, Hiroshi (*b* Tokyo, 1935). Japanese conductor. Cond. Kyoto SO 1975–7, Cologne Radio SO 1977–83, gen. mus. dir. Düsseldorf 1981–6. Amer. début 1981. Chief cond., Tonhalle Orch., Zurich, 1987–91, cond. Dresden Opera 1982–91. Tokyo Metropolitan SO 1987–95, cond. NHKSO from 1995. Cond. f. Japanese ps. of *Gurrelieder, Parsifal,* and *Capriccio*.

Walcha, Helmut (*b* Leipzig, 1907; *d* Frankfurt am Main, 1991). Ger. organist, blind since age of 16. Ass. org. Thomaskirche, Leipzig, 1926–9. Org., Frankfurt Friedenskirche 1929, teacher of org. Hoch Cons. 1933 (prof. 1938–72), and at State Mus. Sch. 1938–72. Org., Dreikönigskirche from 1946. Famous Bach interpreter, preferring to play on orgs. resembling those of Bach's day. Ed. of Handel org. concs. Comp. 25 chorale preludes for org. Author of book on Reger.

Waldflöte (Ger.). Woodland Flute. Org. stop like *clarabel, but often of 4′ length and pitch, and with inverted mouth.

Waldhorn (Ger.). Forest horn. The hunting hn., i.e. 'natural' hn. without valves.

Waldscenen (Woodland Scenes). 9 pieces for solo pf. by R. Schumann, Op.82, comp. 1848–9.

Waldstein Sonata. Beethoven's pf. sonata No.21 in C major, Op.53, comp. 1804 and so called because of ded. to his patron Count Ferdinand Waldstein (*b* Dux, Bohemia, 1762; *d* Vienna, 1823). Orig. slow movement, replaced by present *adagio*, was pubd. separately as *Andante favori* (WoO 57).

Waldteufel [Lévy], **Emil** (*b* Strasbourg, 1837; *d* Paris, 1915). Fr. (Alsatian) composer and pianist. Court pianist and dir. of court balls from 1865. Cond. at CG promenade concerts 1885. Wrote over 250 dances, especially waltzes, incl. *España* (1886, after Chabrier), *Estudiantina* (1883), and *Les Patineurs* (Skaters) (1882).

Walker, Alan (*b* Scunthorpe, 1930). Eng. musicologist and writer. Prof. of harmony, GSMD, 1958–60. BBC mus. prod. 1961–71. Prof. of mus., McMaster Univ., Hamilton, Ontario, 1971–80. Author of *Liszt: the Virtuoso Years* (1983) and *Liszt: the Weimar Years* (1989). Has also written extensively on Schumann, and musical criticism.

Walker, Edyth (*b* Hopewell, NY, 1867; *d* NY, 1950). Amer. mezzo-soprano. Opera début Berlin 1894 (Fidès in *Le Prophète*). Member of Vienna Opera 1895–1903. CG début 1900; NY Met 1903–6;

Hamburg 1906–12, singing sop. and mez. parts; Munich 1912–17. First London Elektra (1910). Bayreuth début 1908. Taught at Amer. Cons., Fontainebleau, 1933–6, then privately in NY.

Walker, Ernest (*b* Bombay, 1870; *d* Oxford, 1949). Eng. composer and scholar. Mus. dir., Balliol College, Oxford, 1900–25, running series of chamber concerts. Wrote *Stabat Mater*, chamber mus., and songs. Author of several books, incl. *A History of Music in England* (1907, 1924, and 1952, with Westrup).

Walker, Frank (*b* Gosport, 1907; *d* Tring, 1962). Eng. musicologist and author. Worked for General Post Office, but devoted all spare time to meticulous biographical research from orig. sources. Wrote superb biographies of Hugo Wolf (1951, 2nd edn. 1968 with new material suppressed in 1st edn.; Ger. trans. 1953), and Verdi (1962, It. trans. 1964).

Walker, Norman (*b* Shaw, Lancs., 1907; *d* London, 1963). Eng. bass. CG 1935–9 and from 1946; Glyndebourne début 1937. Created Collatinus in *The Rape of Lucretia* (Glyndebourne 1946) and Evangelist in *The Pilgrim's Progress* (CG 1951). Taught at GSMD 1951–5.

Walker, Penelope (*b* Manchester, 1956). Eng. mezzo-soprano. Concert début London 1976. Won Kathleen Ferrier memorial schol. 1980. Opera début Paris, Opéra-Comique, 1982. London opera début 1983; ENO 1985; WNO 1986. Prin. mez. Zurich Opera from 1991.

Walker, Robert (Matthew) (*b* Northampton, 1946). Eng. composer. Chorister at St Matthew's, Northampton. Org. and schoolmaster for 5 years in Grimsby, then freelance composer. Lived in Elgar's Sussex cottage 'Brinkwells'. Works incl. sym. (1987); *Pavan*, vn., str. (1975); *Requiem*, ten., ch., orch. (1976); *Canticle of the Rose*, sop., bar., ch., orch. (1980); Chamber Sym. (1981); *Variations on a Theme of Elgar*, orch. (1982); str. qt. (1982); *The Sun Used to Shine*, ten., hp., str. (1983); pf. quintet (1984); *Missa brevis* (1985); *Jubilate* (1987); *English Parody Mass*, ch., org. (1988); *Secret Rooms*, org. (1990); *De profundis*, bar., ch., orch. (1990). Made a perf. edn. of Elgar's unfinished pf. conc., Op.90 (sketches 1909), f.p. 1997.

Walker, Sarah (*b* Cheltenham, 1943). Eng. mezzo-soprano. Opera début 1969 (Ottavia in *The Coronation of Poppea* for Kent Opera). Glyndebourne début 1970. Many roles with ENO. Chicago début 1977; CG début 1979; Vienna 1981; NY Met 1986. Created Agave in Buller's *Bakxai* (ENO 1992). Also noted recitalist. CBE 1991.

Walk to the Paradise Garden, The. Intermezzo for orch. before last scene of Delius's opera *A *Village Romeo and Juliet* and frequently played as concert item. The 'Paradise Garden' was the village inn. Orig. intermezzo, comp. 1900–1, was re-written and extended in 1906 to cover scene-change in projected Berlin f.p., and it is this version that is now so well-known.

Walküre, Die (The Valkyrie). Opera (mus. drama) in 3 acts by *Wagner to his own lib., being 2nd opera of *Der Ring des Nibelungen*. Comp. 1854–6 (first sketches 1852). F.p. Munich 1870, NY 1877 (incomplete), London 1882; f.p. as part of complete cycle, Bayreuth 1876. The Valkyrie of the title is Brünnhilde.

Wallace, Ian (Bryce) (*b* London, 1919). Eng. bass-baritone. Opera début London 1946 (Schaunard in *La bohème*). New London Opera Co. 1946–9. Sang with Glyndebourne co. at Edinburgh Fest. 1948 and at Glyndebourne 1949–50, 1952–6, 1959–61. Scottish Opera 1966–75. Successful buffo singer, also in Gilbert and Sullivan. Many appearances in popular musicals and as member of radio panel games. OBE 1983.

Wallace, Lucille (*b* Chicago, 1898; *d* London, 1977). Amer. harpsichordist and pianist. Did much to revive interest in kbd. mus. of D. Scarlatti and Couperin. Wife of Clifford *Curzon from 1931.

Wallace, (William) **Vincent** (*b* Waterford, 1812; *d* Château de Haget, nr. Vieuzos, 1865). Irish composer. Played org. and vn. as boy. Led orch. in Dublin th. Emigrated to Australia 1835, opening music coll. in Sydney (which failed) and then touring as violinist and pianist in Chile, Argentina, Cuba, and USA, where he was lionized. Returned to London 1845 where he composed successful opera *Maritana* (1845). Operas *Lurline* (1847) and *The Amber Witch* (1861) were successful, as was his pf. mus.

Wallace, William (*b* Greenock, 1860; *d* Malmesbury, 1940). Scottish composer and writer. Entered RAM 1889 after practising as surgeon. Hon. Sec., Phil. Soc. 1911–13. Wrote 6 sym.-poems, *The Passing of Beatrice* (1892) being said to be first Brit. work in the genre. Others included *William Wallace* (1905) and *François Villon* (1909). Also comp. sym., suites *The Lady from the Sea* (after Ibsen, 1892) and *Pelléas et Mélisande* (1900), songs, etc. Prof. at RAM. Wrote *Richard Wagner as he lived* (1925).

Wallenstein, Alfred (*b* Chicago, 1898; *d* NY, 1983). Amer. cellist and conductor. Début as cellist, Los Angeles 1912. Later played in S. Francisco SO 1916–17 and Los Angeles PO. Prin. cellist, Chicago SO 1922–9, NYPO 1929–36 (under Toscanini). Became radio cond. Cond. Los Angeles PO 1943–56. Taught at Juilliard Sch. 1968–79.

Waller, 'Fats' (Thomas Wright) (*b* NY, 1904; *d* Kansas City, 1943). Amer. jazz pianist, organist, and composer. Studied pf. with Carl Bohm and later with Leopold Godowsky, while working from age of 14 as organist in Harlem film th. Encouraged by jazz pianist James P. Johnson. Made nearly 500 records, wrote about 400 copyright works, and many more without copyright. Comp. mus. comedy *Hot Chocolates*, 1929 (which contained song *Ain't Misbehavin'*), and the song *Honeysuckle Rose*, c.1928. After working with Ted

Lewis and Jack Teagarden, formed his own band, Fats Waller and his Rhythm, 1934. His amusing vocal style masked the serious and influential qualities of his piano-playing. Appeared in films.

Wallerstein, Lothar (*b* Prague, 1882; *d* New Orleans, 1949). Cz.-born composer, pianist, and opera producer (Amer. cit. 1945). Taught pf., Geneva Cons. Cond., Poznań opera 1910–14. Chief producer, Breslau opera 1918–22, Frankfurt 1924–6, Vienna 1927–38 (in which period prod. 65 operas), Salzburg Fest. 1926–37. Guest producer Milan, Buenos Aires. Went to USA, 1941, working at Met until 1946. Collab. with R. Strauss in Vienna 1930 in 're-working' of Mozart's *Idomeneo* (f.p. Vienna 1931).

Wallfisch, Peter (*b* Breslau, 1924; *d* London, 1993). Ger.-born pianist. Settled in Eng. Prof. of pf., RCM. Worldwide tours as recitalist. Bartók Prize 1948.

Wallfisch, Raphael (*b* London, 1953). Eng. cellist. Son of Peter *Wallfisch. Won Cassado int. comp., Florence 1977. Début London 1974. Played in chamber mus. with Heifetz, Amadeus Qt., and his father. Has recorded most Eng. vc. concs. Prof. of vc., GSMD from 1980.

Wally, La. Opera in 4 acts by *Catalani to lib. by Illica after W. von Hillern's novel *Die Geyer-Wally* (1875). Comp. 1890–1. Prod. Milan 1892, NY Met 1909, Manchester 1919.

Walmisley, Thomas Attwood (*b* London, 1814; *d* Hastings, 1856). Eng. organist and composer. Org., Croydon church 1830, Trinity and St John's Colleges, Cambridge, 1833. Prof. of mus., Cambridge Univ. from 1836. Also brilliant mathematician. Comp. anthems, installation odes, and famous Services in B♭ (1834) and D minor (c.1855). One of first to give mus. lectures with practical examples. Pioneer in Eng. appreciation of J. S. Bach.

Walsh, John (*b* ?1665 or 6; *d* London, 1736). Eng. music publisher, established off the Strand, London, by c.1690. Appointed instrument maker to king, 1692. Pubd. Handel's works from 1711 (*Rinaldo*). Succeeded by son John (1709–66).

Walsh, Stephen (*b* Chipping Norton, 1942). Eng. music critic. Ass. mus. critic, *Observer*, 1966–85. Mus. critic, *The Listener*, 1965–7. Senior lect. in music, Cardiff Univ., from 1976. Author of *Bartók Chamber Music* (1982), *The Music of Stravinsky* (1988/1993), and *Stravinsky* (Vol.1, *A Creative Spring*, 1999; Vol. 2, *The Second Exile*, 2006).

Walsh, Thomas (Joseph) (*b* Wexford, 1911; *d* Wexford, 1988). Irish writer on music and anaesthetist. Founded Wexford Fest. 1951, when Balfe's *Rose of Castille* was prod. Art. dir. 1951–66. Author *Opera in Old Dublin 1819–38* (1952), *Opera in Dublin 1705–97* (1973), *Monte Carlo Opera 1879–1909* (1975), *Second Empire Opera: the Théâtre Lyrique,*

Paris, 1851–70 (1981), *Monte Carlo Opera 1910–51* (1985), *Opera in Dublin 1798–1820: Frederick Jones and the Crow Street Theatre* (1993, posth.).

Walter [Schlesinger], **Bruno** (*b* Berlin, 1876; *d* Beverly Hills, Calif., 1962). Ger.-born conductor and pianist (Amer. cit.). Coach and ass. cond., Cologne Opera, 1893–4, Hamburg 1894–8 as ass. to Mahler, Riga 1898–1900, Berlin 1900–1, Vienna 1901 (with Mahler till 1907)–1912, Munich Opera 1913–22. Disciple of Mahler and cond. f.ps. of *Das Lied von der Erde*, Munich 1911, and 9th Sym., Vienna 1912. Cond. f.p. of Pfitzner's *Palestrina* 1917. Amer. début 1923. Cond. Berlin Municipal Opera 1925–9, Leipzig Gewandhaus Orch. 1929–33. Mus. dir., Vienna Opera 1936–8. Assoc. with Salzburg Fest. 1925–37, and 1949, 1950, 1953, and 1956. Emigrated to Fr., and became Fr. cit. 1938, and then moving to USA, where he became Amer. cit. London début 1909, Phil. Soc. concerts, CG 1910. From 1924 to 1931, cond. regularly at CG, incl. memorable perfs. of *Der Rosenkavalier*, *Die Fledermaus*, and *Le nozze di Figaro*. After Second World War returned to London to cond. LPO 1946. At first Edinburgh Fest., 1947, cond. legendary perf. of *Das Lied von der Erde* with Kathleen Ferrier and Peter Pears. Accompanied (pf.) Ferrier at recitals in Edinburgh and Salzburg and ?twb> recorded *Das Lied von der Erde* with her in Vienna, 1952. Cond. at NY Met 1941–6, 1950–1, and 1955–6. Prin. cond. NYPO 1947–9. Last visit to Eng., 1955. One of greatest conds., especially of Beethoven, Bruckner, Schubert, and Mahler. His warm, expansive approach was at opposite pole to Toscanini's precision and brilliance. Comp. 2 syms., str. qt., pf. quintet, pf. trio, and songs. Wrote biography of Mahler (1936, Eng. edns. 1937 and 1958) and autobiography *Theme and Variations* (1946).

Walton, (Sir) **William** (Turner) (*b* Oldham, 1902; *d* Forio d'Ischia, 1983). Eng. composer. Son of choirmaster and singing-teacher. Chorister at Christ Church Cath. Sch., Oxford, 1912–18, during which time wrote anthems and songs. Wrote pf. qt. 1918–21. 'Adopted' as a brother by Osbert, Sacheverell, and Edith Sitwell, 1919, living with them in London and It. Comp. first version of *Façade*, instr. accs. to recited poems by Edith Sitwell, in 1921, f.p. London (privately) 1922. Str. qt. played at Salzburg 1923. Made jazz arrs. for Savoy Orpheans, 1923. Public perf. of *Façade* 1923 caused furore. Ov. *Portsmouth Point* perf. at Zurich 1926. Came into wider prominence in 1929 with va. conc., f.p. at Promenade concert with Hindemith as soloist. This was followed at 1931 Leeds Fest. by dramatic cantata *Belshazzar's Feast*. In 1934 1st Sym. was perf. without finale, which was added 1935. Next large-scale work was vn. conc. commissioned by Heifetz, 1939. Wrote mus. for film of Shaw's *Major Barbara*, 1940, followed by several other wartime film scores, best-known being that for *The First of the Few* (1942), story of building of Spitfire fighter aircraft, and Olivier's *Henry V* (1944). Next major work was str. qt., 1947. From 1948 to 1954 was engaged on

large-scale opera, *Troilus and Cressida*, prod. CG 1954. Followed by vc. conc. for *Piatigorsky, 2nd Sym., *Variations on a Theme of Hindemith*, a 1-act 'extravaganza' *The Bear*, based on Chekhov, and shorter works. From 1948 lived in Ischia, Bay of Naples. Knighted 1951. OM 1967.

Walton's mus., although it was at first regarded in Eng. as that of an *enfant terrible* because of *Façade* and the 'jazz-age' influence on his early works, remained remarkably consistent. It is fundamentally lyrical and romantic, with two basic ingredients: a pungent, spiky rhythmic impetus, with wide intervals and tangy harmonies, and a brooding melancholy. It is as if two influences were perpetually at war in his nature: the 20th-cent. Stravinsky-Prokofiev strain and the 19th-cent. Elgar. His true qualities can be discerned in *Façade*, a masterpiece which never 'dates', because it is musically so good and true. Almost alone among later Eng. composers, he successfully wore the Elgarian pomp-and-circumstance mantle, as in his two Coronation Marches, much of the film mus., and parts of *Belshazzar's Feast*, but the finest of his works—the 3 concs., the 1st Sym., the *Hindemith Variations, Belshazzar, The Bear*, and parts of *Troilus and Cressida*—have a powerful individuality in which the opposing strains are successfully reconciled. All his mus. is fastidiously fashioned and it has a Mediterranean luxuriousness which is reconciled to the robust qualities of a composer whose place in the history of 20th-cent. Eng. mus. is high and important. Prin. works:

OPERAS: *Troilus and Cressida* (1947–54, rev. 1963, 1972–6); The *Bear* (1965–7).

BALLETS: *The First Shoot* (1935); The *Wise Virgins* (transcr. of J. S. Bach) (1939–40); *The Quest* (1943); *Façade* (1929, 1931, 1935, 1940, 1972).

ENTERTAINMENT: *Façade*, reciter and instr. ens. (1921, rev. 1926, 1928, 1942, 1951, 1978); *Façade 2* (1979, after rev.).

ORCH.: syms.: No.1 in B♭ minor (1931–5), No.2 (1957–60); concs.: va. in A minor (1928–9, rev. 1936, 1961), vn. in B minor (1938–9, rev. 1943), vc. (1955–6), Sinfonia Concertante for orch. with pf. (1926–7, rev. 1943); *Portsmouth Point* (1924–5); *Siesta* (1926); *Façade*, Suite No.1 (1926), No.2 (1938); Coronation March, *Crown Imperial* (1937, rev. 1963); Suite, The *Wise Virgins* (1940); *Music for Children* (1940, orch. of *Duets for Children*); Comedy Ov., *Scapino* (1940, rev. 1950); *Spitfire Prelude and Fugue* (1942); *2 Pieces for Strings from Henry V* (1943–4); Coronation March, *Orb and Sceptre* (1952–3); Finale, *presto giocoso*, of *Variations on an Elizabethan Theme* (*Sellinger's Round*) (1953); *Johannesburg Festival Overture* (1956); Partita (1957); *Variations on a Theme of *Hindemith* (1962–3); *Capriccio Burlesco* (1968); *Improvisations on an Impromptu of Benjamin *Britten* (1968–9); *Sonata for Strings* (1971, transcr. of str. qt. 1945–7); *Varii Capricci* (1975–6, orch. of 5 Bagatelles for guitar); *Prologo e Fantasia* (1981–2).

CHORUS & ORCH.: *Belshazzar's Feast*, bar., ch., orch. (1930–1, rev. 1931, 1948, 1957); *In Honour of the City of London*, ch., orch (1937); *Coronation Te Deum*,

2 ch., 2 semi ch., boys' ch., org., orch., military brass (1952–3); *Gloria*, cont., ten., bass, ch., orch. (1960).

SONG-CYCLES: *Anon in Love, 6 songs, ten., gui. (1959; ten., small orch. 1971); A *Song for the Lord Mayor's Table, 6 songs, sop., pf. (1962; sop., orch. 1970).

VOCAL (unacc. except where stated): *A Litany* (Drop, drop, slow tears) (1916, rev. 1930); *Make we Joy now in this Fest* (1931); *Set me as a Seal upon thine Heart* (1938); *Where does the Uttered Music Go?* (1946); *What Cheer?* (1960); *The Twelve*, with org. (1964–5); *Missa brevis*, double ch., org. (in *Gloria* only) (1965–6); *All This time* (1970); *Jubilate Deo*, with org. (1972); *Cantico del Sole* (Song of the Sun) (1973–4); *Magnificat and Nunc Dimittis*, with org. (1974, rev. 1975); *Antiphon*, ch., org. (1977).

CHAMBER MUSIC: pf. qt. (1918–21, rev. 1974–5); str. qt. (2 movts. 1919, rev. and central scherzo added 1921–2); *Toccata in A minor*, vn., pf. (1922–3); str. qt. (1945–7; version for str. orch. entitled *Sonata* 1971); vn. sonata (1947–8, rev. 1949–50); 2 *Pieces*, vn., pf. (1948, 1950); 5 *Bagatelles*, gui. (1970–1; transcr. for orch. as *Varii Capricci* 1975–6); *Passacaglia*, vc. (1979–80); *Duettino*, ob., vn. (1982).

SONGS: *The Winds* (1918); *Tritons* (1920); *3 Songs* by E. Sitwell (1931–2, rev. of songs written in 1923).

PIANO: *Duets for Children* (duet 1940; orch. as *Music for Children*).

ORGAN: *3 Pieces* from *Richard III* (1955).

BRASS BAND: *The First Shoot* (1979–80, re-scoring of ballet written for revue, 1935).

FILMS: *Escape Me Never* (1934), *As You Like It* (1936), *Dreaming Lips* (1937), *Stolen Life* (1938), *Major Barbara* (1940), *Next of Kin* (1941), *The Foreman Went to France* (1941–2), *The First of the Few* (1942), *Went the Day Well?* (1942), *Henry V* (1943–4), *Hamlet* (1947), *Richard III* (1955), *The Battle of Britain* (1969), *Three Sisters* (1969).

THEATRE & RADIO INCID. MUS.; *A Son of Heaven* (L. Strachey) (1924–5), *The Boy David* (Barrie) (1935), *Macbeth* (1941–2), *Christopher Columbus* (1942).

waltz (Ger. *Walzer*; Fr. *valse*). Dance in 3/4 time probably deriving from Ger. *Ländler* which came into prominence in last quarter of 18th cent. both among composers and in the ballroom. Where the latter was concerned, the waltzes of the Viennese composers Johann *Strauss I and *Lanner were popular throughout Europe. Beethoven, Schubert, and Hummel wrote waltzes. Weber's *Invitation to the Dance* is in waltz rhythm and is the first 'sophisticated' treatment of the waltz. Chopin's waltzes are fine examples. In symphonic mus. the 2nd movt. of Berlioz's *Symphonie fantastique* and 3rd movt. of Tchaikovsky's 5th sym. are outstanding. Tchaikovsky also wrote great waltzes in his operas and ballets; and those by Johann Strauss II, Richard Strauss (*Der Rosenkavalier*), Ravel, and others are deservedly cherished.

Waltz, Gustavus (*fl.* 1732–59; *d* London, *c*.1759). Eng. bass of Ger. birth. Sang in Arne's Eng. opera season at Little Haymarket Th., 1732 in Lampe's *Amelia*. Went with Handel to Oxford in July 1733, singing in 4 of his oratorios and in anthems. Member of Handel's opera co. 1733–6, creating the King of Scotland in *Ariodante* (1735) and Melisso in *Alcina* (1736). Rejoined Handel for oratorio season 1738–9. In later part of career sang mainly in lighter works by Lampe and Arne. Sang in chorus at Foundling Hospital perfs. of *Messiah* 1759. Story that he was once Handel's cook is unverified, as is Handel's alleged remark in 1745 that 'Gluck knew no more of counterpoint than my cook Waltz'.

Wälzel, Camillo (pseudonym F. Zell) (*b* Magdeburg, 1829; *d* Vienna, 1895). Ger. librettist. Trans. Fr. comedies. Wrote texts, often collab. Richard Genée, for operettas by Suppé, Johann Strauss II, Millöcker, and others.

Wand, Günter (*b* Elberfeld, 1912; *d* Ulmitz, 2002). Ger. conductor and composer. Held cond. posts at Wuppertal and Detmold. Cond., Cologne Opera 1938–44, Salzburg Mozarteum Orch. 1944–5. Mus. dir. Cologne Opera 1945–8, cond. Cologne Gürzenich concerts 1946–74. London début 1951. Cond. Berne SO 1974–82. Prin. cond. North German Radio SO (Hamburg) from 1982. In 1980s worked frequently with BBCSO. Noted for Bruckner interpretations. Comps. incl. cantata, ballet, and songs.

'Wanderer' Fantasy. Nickname for Schubert's Fantasia in C for pf. (1822, D760), so called because the adagio section, or movement, has variations on a passage from his song *Der Wanderer* (1816, D493). Liszt arranged it for pf. and orch. some time before 1852 and for 2 pfs. after 1851.

Wandering Scholar, The. Chamber opera in 1 act, Op.50, by Holst to lib. by Clifford Bax founded on incident in Helen Waddell's *The Wandering Scholars* (1927). Comp. 1929–30. Prod. Liverpool 1934.

Wand of Youth, The. 2 orch. suites by Elgar, Opp. 1a and 1b, arr. and orch. in 1907 and 1908 respectively from material written by Elgar as a child of 12 for a family play. Some themes used again in mus. for the *Starlight Express*.

Wangenheim, Volker (*b* Berlin, 1928). Ger. conductor and composer. Chief cond. Berlin Mozart Orch. 1950–9, mus. dir., city of Bonn 1957–63, gen. mus. dir. 1963–78. Chief cond. Ger. Nat. Youth Orch. 1969–84. Cond., Bournemouth Sinfonietta 1977. Prof. of cond., Cologne Hochschule für Musik from 1972. Works incl. sym., *Mass*, and *Stabat Mater*.

War and Peace (*Voyna i Mir*). Opera in 5 acts (13 scenes and epigraph) by Prokofiev, Op.91, to lib. by composer and Mira Mendelson based on Tolstoy's novel (1869). Comp. 1941–3, rev. 1946–7, 1948–53. F.p. (8 scenes, concert perf. with pf.) Moscow 1944; 9 scenes, concert with orch., Moscow 1945; 2-evening vers., Leningrad 1946, 1947; new 1-evening vers., Florence 1953; 11 scenes,

Leningrad 1955; 13 scenes, cut, Moscow 1957; NBC TV, NY 1957; relatively complete, Moscow 1959; Leeds (concert) 1967; London (ENO) 1972; Boston 1974.

Ward, David (*b* Dumbarton, 1922; *d* Dunedin, NZ, 1983). Scottish bass. SW ch. 1952. Sang Count Walter in Verdi's *Luisa Miller*, SW 1953. Prin. bass, SW 1952–9; Glyndebourne 1960; CG from 1960; Bayreuth Fest. 1960–2; NY Met 1963. Many appearances as Wotan with Scottish Opera, with CG in the 1964 *Ring*, and in 6 *Ring* cycles at Buenos Aires, 1967. The nobility and dignity of his performance were impressive. Also outstanding concert singer. CBE 1972.

Ward, Joseph (*b* Preston, 1932). Eng. tenor, singing teacher, and producer. Created Starveling in *A Midsummer Night's Dream*, 1960. As bar., sang Billy Budd in f.p. rev. vers. of opera in BBC broadcast 1960. CG début 1962. Tutor in Sch. of Vocal Studies, RNCM, 1972–92 (Head from 1986, dir. of opera from 1989). At RNCM prod. several operas. incl. *The *Pilgrim's Progress*. OBE 1992.

Ward, Robert (*b* Cleveland, 1917). Amer. composer and conductor. Taught at Juilliard Sch. 1946–56 and Columbia Univ. 1946–8. Managing ed. Galaxy Music (Publishers) 1956–67. Won Pulitzer Prize 1962 with opera *The Crucible*. Pres., N. Carolina Sch. of Arts, 1967–75, prof. of comp. 1975–9. Prof. of mus. Duke Univ., N. Carolina, 1979–87. Works incl. operas *He Who Gets Slapped* (1956) and *The Crucible*, 6 syms., pf. conc., sax. conc., *Yankee Overture*, choral mus., vn. sonata, str. qt., and songs.

Warlock, Peter [Heseltine, Philip Arnold] (*b* London, 1894; *d* London, 1930). Eng. composer, critic, and author. Pubd. his mus. under pseudonym Peter Warlock. Studied mus. at Eton, then helped by van *Dieren and Delius. Founded and co-ed. periodical *The Sackbut* 1920 and wrote book on Delius 1923. Friend of Cecil Gray, E. J. Moeran, and Constant Lambert. Edited much 16th- and 17th-cent. music in collab. with *Mangeot. His songs alternate between lyricism of Delius and roistering spirit reminiscent of first Elizabethan age. His personality veered between extrovert, heavy-drinking joviality and neurotic introspection. Eventually (it may be presumed, despite the open verdict at the inquest) took his own life. Sensitive critic and writer. His mus., especially his songs and part-songs, is of high merit. Prin. works:

ORCH.: *An Old Song* (1917); *Serenade for Delius on his 60th birthday*, str. (1921–2); *Capriol*, suite for str. (1926: for full orch. 1928).

CHORUS & ORCH.: *3 Carols* (1923).

VOICE & ENS.: *The *Curlew*, song-cycle, ten., fl., cor anglais, str. qt. (1920–1, rev. 1922); *Corpus Christi*, sop., bar., str. qt. (1919–23); *Sorrow's Lullaby*, sop., bar., str. qt. (1927).

CHORUS & KEYBOARD: *Sociable Songs*, male vv., pf., (1924–5); *What Cheer? Good cheer!*; *Where Riches is everlastingly*, ch., org. (1927); *The bailey beareth the bell away*, 2 vv., pf. (1918–28); *Lullaby*, women's

trio, pf. (1918–28); *The First Mercy*, 3 vv. and pf. (1927–8); *The Five Lesser Joys of Mary*, ch., org. (1929).

UNACC. VOICES: *Cornish Christmas Carol* (1918); *As dewe in Aprylle* (1918); *Corpus Christi*, cont., ten., ch. (1919); *The Full Heart* (1917–22); *3 Dirges of Webster* (1923–5, No.3 is *The Shrouding of the Duchess of Malfi*, male vv.); *The Spring of the Year* (1925); *Bethlehem Down* (1927).

SOLO SONGS: *3 Saudades* (1916–17), *The bailey beareth the bell away* (1918), *There is a lady* (1919), *Balulalow* (1919), *Captain Stratton's Fancy* (1920), *Mr Belloc's Fancy* (1921–30), *Piggesnie* (1922), *6 Peterisms*, sets 1 and 2 (1922), *Sleep* (1922), *Tyrley Tyrlow* (1922), *Milkmaids* (1923), *Candlelight* (12 nursery rhymes) (1923), *Peter Warlock's Fancy* (1924), *Twelve Oxen* (1924), *Yarmouth Fair* (1924), *3 Belloc Songs* (1926), *Sigh no more, ladies* (1927), *Passing by* (1928), *The Passionate Shepherd* (1928), *The Cricketers of Hambledon* (1928), *The Frostbound Wood* (1929), *Bethlehem Down* (1927–30), *The Fox* (1930), and others.

Warner, H. Waldo (*b* Northampton, 1874; *d* London, 1945). Eng. violinist, violist, and composer. Prof. of va., GSMD, 1893–1920. Violist of London Str. Qt. from its foundation 1907 until 1928. Prin. va. leading London orchs. Wrote opera and over 100 songs, but best mus. is for chamber groups, e.g. pf. trio (won *Cobbett Prize), str. qt., va. sonata.

Warrack, Guy (Douglas Hamilton) (*b* Edinburgh, 1900; *d* Englefield Green, 1986). Scottish conductor and composer. On staff RCM 1925–35, conducting class at RCM from 1945. Cond. BBC Scottish Orch. 1935–45, SW Ballet 1948–51. Wrote film mus. and works for orch., incl. *Variations* (1924) and sym. (1932).

Warrack, John (Hamilton) (*b* London, 1928). Eng. critic and author, son of Guy *Warrack. Freelance oboist 1951–4. Mus. critic *Daily Telegraph* 1954–61, *Sunday Telegraph* 1961–72. Art dir. Leeds Fest. 1978–83. Lect. in mus., Oxford Univ. 1984–93. Author of books on Weber and Tchaikovsky. Co-author (with Harold Rosenthal), *The Concise Oxford Dictionary of Opera* (1964, 2nd edn. 1979, 3rd edn. 1996, with E. West); (with Ewan West), *The Oxford Dictionary of Opera* (1992); *German Opera: From the Beginnings to Wagner* (2001).

Warren [Warenoff], **Leonard** (*b* NY, 1911; *d* NY, 1960). Amer. baritone of Russ. parentage. Won NY Met Auditions of Air 1938. Opera début NY Met 1939 (Paolo in *Simon Boccanegra*, though he had sung excerpts from operas there in 1938). S. Francisco 1943–56; Chicago 1944–6. La Scala début 1953. Became leading bar. at Met (and elsewhere) in such roles as Iago, Rigoletto, etc. Died on stage of NY Met while singing Don Carlo in *La forza del destino*.

War Requiem. Choral work, Op.66, by Britten, interpolating 9 poems by Wilfred Owen (1893–1918) into liturgical Mass. Comp. 1961 and f.p. in new Coventry Cath. May 1962. Sop., ten., and bar. soloists, ch., boys' ch., org., and orch. Owen poems are acc. by chamber orch., sometimes, but not necessarily, under 2nd cond. F.p. was cond. by Meredith Davies, with Britten cond. of chamber orch. F. London p., Westminster Abbey, Nov. 1962.

Wasps, The. Incidental mus. for ten. and bar., male ch., and orch. comp. by Vaughan Williams for Cambridge Univ. prod., 1909, of Aristophanes's play. Orch. suite of 5 movts. (1912), incl. frequently-played ov.

wassail. Old Eng. term for jovial and convivial song which often occurs in Christmas carols.

Watanabe, Akeo (*b* Tokyo, 1919; *d* Tokyo, 1990). Japanese conductor. Début 1945 (Tokyo SO). Cond., Tokyo PO 1948–54; founder and cond. Japan P.-SO 1956–68, 1978–83; mus. dir. Kyoto SO 1970–2, Tokyo Metropolitan SO 1972–8, Hiroshima SO 1988–90. Prof. of cond. Tokyo Univ. of Arts 1962–7. Guest cond. of European and Amer. orchs.

Watanabe, Yoko (*b* Fukuoka, 1953; *d* Milan, 2004). Japanese soprano. Début Treviso 1978 (Nedda in *Pagliacci*). Celebrated exponent of Madama Butterfly, which she sang with the Royal Opera in Manchester 1983; Chicago and Tokyo 1986; NY Met 1987; CG 1989 (début there). La Scala début 1985.

Water Carrier, The (Cherubini). See *Deux Journées, Les*.

Waterhouse, William (*b* London, 1931). Eng. bassoonist. In CG orch. 1953–5, prin. bn. Italian-Swiss Radio Orch., Lugano, 1955–8. Prin. bn. LSO 1958–64, BBC SO from 1964. Joined Melos Ensemble 1959. Prof. of bn. RMCM 1966–72, later at RNCM.

Waterman, (Dame) Fanny (*b* Leeds, 1920). Eng. pianist and piano teacher. Co-founder and joint chairman, Leeds Int. Pf. Competition from 1963. OBE 1971. CBE 1999. DBE 2005.

Water Music. Instr. suite by Handel, the origin of which is unknown. The legend that Handel wrote it for a royal water party in 1715 to restore himself to favour with King George I is attractive but unsubstantiated. (The King had been Elector of Hanover when Handel had effectively deserted his post as Kapellmeister at Hanover in order to visit Eng., where he settled.) However, it is documented that Handel provided mus. for a royal journey on the Thames on 17 July 1717. No complete autograph score of the mus. exists and contemporary edns. differ in several respects. Some of the movements in autograph exist in earlier versions, so dating the mus. is impossible. About 20 numbers were written, scored for tpts., hns., obs., bns., fls., recorders, and str. Best-known of modern orchestrations is that by *Harty.

Water Music. Work by *Cage (1952) in which pianist has to make the visual element a major feature of the perf., being provided with radio, whistles, water containers, a pack of cards, and a score mounted like a poster.

water organ. See *Hydraulis*.

Watkins, Michael Blake (*b* Ilford, 1948). Eng. composer. Fellow in television comp. with London Weekend TV 1981–3. His double conc. won Menuhin comp. prize 1975. Works incl.:

ORCH.: *Proem* (1972); *Double Conc. (After Psallein)*, ob., gui., orch. (1972); *Concertante*, 11 players (1973); *Clouds and Eclipses*, gui., str. (1973); hn. conc., str., opt. hp. (1974); *Dreams* (1975); vn. conc. (1977); *Étalage* (1979); *Sinfonietta* (1982); tpt. conc. (1988); vc. conc. (1991–2).

ENS.: *Psallein*, gui., with gui. ens. of 6 players, clavichord, perc. (1971); *The Magic Shadow-Show*, vc., ens. (1980).

VOICE(S) & INSTR(S).: *Those Dancing Days Are Gone*, ten., vn., cl., gui. (1969); *Invocation*, ten., lute (1972); *Before the Beginning of Years*, sop., ten., pf. (1972); *Youth's Dream and Time's Truth*, ten., tpt., hp., str. (1973); *Solarium*, school ch., orch. (1974); *All That We Read in Their Smiles* (5 Songs), ten., hn., pf. (1977); *The Spirit of the Universe*, sop., ens. (1978); *The Bird of Time*, ten., ob. (1979); *The Spirit of Night*, ten., gui. (1980).

CHAMBER MUSIC: *Synthesis*, pf. (1969); *Cavatina*, vc. (1972); gui. qt. (4 guitars) (1972); *Solus*, gui. (1975); *The Wings of Night*, vn. (1975); *The Spirit of the Earth*, gui. (1978); str. qt. (1979); quintet, cl., vn., va., vc., pf. (1981); ob. qt. (1984).

BRASS: *Aubade*, brass band (1973); *From the High Towers*, 2 tpts., hn., ten. tb., tuba (1976).

Watson (*née* McLamore), **Claire** (*b* NY, 1927; *d* Utting am Ammersee, 1986). Amer. soprano. Opera début Graz 1951 (Desdemona in *Otello*). Member of Frankfurt Opera 1956–8; Bavarian State Opera, Munich, 1958–76. Débuts: CG 1958; Glyndebourne 1960; Salzburg 1966. Roles incl. Ellen Orford (*Peter Grimes*), which she recorded with Britten.

Watson, Henry (*b* Burnley, 1846; *d* Salford, 1911). Eng. organist, teacher, composer, and collector. Org., Congregational Church, Withington, Manchester. Founded and cond. Manchester Vocal Union. On orig. teaching staff of RMCM 1893 as choirmaster. Collected over 5,000 mus. books and scores with intention of founding free reference library. Gave them in 1899 to Manchester Corporation and they form nucleus of Henry Watson Mus. Library, part of Manchester Central Reference Library. Gave coll. of rare instr. to RMCM (now at RNCM).

Watson, Janice (*b* London, 1964). Eng. soprano. Won Kathleen Ferrier memorial schol. 1987. Début London (Opera London) 1988 (Drusilla in *L'incoronazione di Poppea*). Débuts: WNO 1989; CG 1990; ENO 1991; Santa Fe 1996. Sang title-role in *Daphne*, S. Francisco (concert) and London (concert) 1993. Concert repertory incl. Britten, Berlioz, Brahms, Elgar, and Strauss.

Watson, Lillian (b London, 1947). Eng. soprano. Prof. début Wexford Fest. 1970 (Cis in *Albert Herring*). Prin. sop. WNO 1971–5. Débuts: CG 1971; GTO 1975; Glyndebourne 1976; ENO 1978; Opera North 1980; Salzburg Fest. 1982; Vienna 1983. Sang title-role in *The Cunning Little Vixen*, CG 1990. Sang Fairy Godmother in f. Brit. p. of *Cendrillon*, Cardiff (WNO) 1993.

Watts, André (b Nuremberg, 1946). Amer. pianist. Début 1955 with Philadelphia Orch. Soloist with NYPO cond. Bernstein 1963. Eur. début (London) 1966. NY recital début 1966. Salzburg Fest. début 1976. World tours after 1967. Superb player of Liszt and Brahms.

Watts, Helen (Josephine) (b Milford Haven, 1927). Welsh contralto. Joined Glyndebourne and BBC choruses. London concert début 1955 (Prom). Opera début London 1958 (Didymus in Handel's *Theodora*) with Handel Opera Soc., later singing other Handel roles. Toured USSR with EOG 1964. Salzburg Fest. début 1964; CG 1965–71; WNO 1969–83; Amer. début (NY) 1967. Specialist in oratorio, e.g. Elgar, Bach, Beethoven, Handel. CBE 1978.

Wat Tyler. Opera in prol. and 2 acts by Alan Bush to lib. by Nancy Bush. Comp. 1948–50. Awarded prize in Fest. of Britain 1951 but not prod. in Eng. until 1974 (SW). F.p. East German Radio 1952, stage Leipzig 1953.

wayte. See *wait*. Also an old name for the hautboy.

Weber, (Maria) **Aloysia** (Louise) (b Zell or Mannheim, c.1760; d Salzburg, 1839). Ger. soprano. Lessons from Mozart 1777–8, who fell in love with her and took her, with her father (also a singer), on concert tours. Later that year, in Munich, she rejected him. Vienna début 1779, remaining there until 1792, having married actor Joseph Lange in 1780. Mozart wrote several arias for her and the part of Mme. Herz in *Der Schauspieldirektor*. Sang Donna Anna in f. Vienna p. of *Don Giovanni*, 1788. Her younger sister Constanze (1762–1842) became Mozart's wife in 1782.

Weber, Ben (b St Louis, 1916; d NY, 1979). Amer. composer. On staff NY College of Mus. from 1966. Works incl. *Symphony on Poems of William Blake*, bar., chamber ens., vn. conc., pf. conc., chamber mus., songs, etc. One of first Amer. composers to use 12-note technique, but generally with strong tonal associations.

Weber, Carl Maria (Friedrich Ernst) **von** (b Eutin in Oldenburg, 1786; d London, 1826). Ger. composer, conductor, and pianist. Son of town musician and theatrical impresario and his 2nd wife, a singer and actress. Taught as boy by Michael *Haydn in Salzburg, then by court organist, Kalcher, in Munich 1798–1800. By 1800 had already composed opera, mass, and pf. works. Went to Vienna in 1803 as pupil of *Vogler, through whose influence became Kapellmeister at Breslau municipal th. 1804–6. Worked in

Karlsruhe 1806–7, where he wrote 2 syms. Court secretarial post Stuttgart 1807–10, where he was encouraged by Kapellmeister, *Danzi. While there wrote incidental mus. to *Turandot*, opera *Silvana*, and other works. Banished from Stuttgart because of false suspicion of embezzlement, went to Mannheim, where he was befriended by Gottfried *Weber (no relation), then to Darmstadt, where he met Vogler again and took lessons from him in company with *Meyerbeer. At this time wrote comic opera *Abu Hassan*, pf. conc., and vn. sonatas. Travelled to Munich 1811, where he wrote bn. conc. for court windplayer, and to Prague, where his pf. improvisations were acclaimed. Appointed dir., Prague Opera, 1813–16. Court Kapellmeister, Dresden, 1817, with commission to est. Ger. opera alongside It. variety. Wrote Mass in E♭ 1818 and worked on opera *Der Freischütz*. Work continually frustrated by opposition from It. opera dir., Morlacchi. Weber rehearsed operas exhaustively, making himself responsible for every aspect of prods., and, in his operatic theories, anticipating those of his disciple Wagner. *Der Freischütz* was prod. in Berlin, to tumultuous acclaim, in 1821 and was taken up throughout Ger., making Weber the most popular composer of the day. At the same time, he was at work on a comic opera *Die drei Pintos*, which he never finished and which was subsequently prepared for perf. by Mahler. He interrupted work on it to compose an opera commissioned by the Vienna Kärntnerthor Th. for 1822–3 season. This was *Euryanthe*, prod. Vienna, Oct. 1823. While in Vienna, Weber met Beethoven, with whom he had been in correspondence. By now, Weber's health was seriously undermined by tuberculosis. In 1824, the manager of CG, Kemble, commissioned an opera from Weber, who agreed to set Planché's Eng. lib. *Oberon*. Went to London 1826, staying with Sir George *Smart in Great Portland St., supervising rehearsals at CG and conducting several concerts. After *Oberon* première, became increasingly ill and died 7 weeks later in Smart's house. Body taken to Moorfields Chapel. In 1844, on instigation of the Dresden Kapellmeister Richard Wagner, coffin was shipped back to Ger. and buried in Dresden Catholic cemetery on 15 Dec. after funeral oration by Wagner and the perf. of Wagner's *Hebt an den Sang* (*An Webers Grabe*) for unacc. male ch.

Weber's place in history of Ger. mus. is that of a liberator, setting it free from It. influences and showing how the shape of folk tunes could be adapted for operatic and other purposes. Marschner and Lortzing were his immediate successors, Wagner his culmination. In his instr. and vocal works, his virtuosity, startling effects achieved without use of unusual instrs., and formal and technical innovations stimulated Chopin, Liszt, Berlioz, and in due course Mahler. According to Debussy, the sound of the Weber orch. was achieved by 'scrutiny of the soul of each instrument'. Though handicapped by the weakest of libs. (by the eccentric poetess Helmina von Chézy), *Euryanthe* contains mus. of outstanding subtlety and strength; while the powerful atmospheric spell of the 'nature' mus. in *Freischütz* is created by the poetic establishment of a mood. For some time Weber was regarded as more important as an influence on others than for his own achievement. Today his rightful place as a master is acknowledged. Prin. works:

OPERAS: *Das Waldmädchen* (1800); **Peter Schmoll und seine Nachbarn* (1801–2); *Rübezahl* (1804–5); *Silvana* (1808–10); **Abu Hassan* (1810–11); *Der *Freischütz* (1817–21); **Euryanthe* (1822–3); *Die *drei Pintos* (begun 1820); **Oberon* (1825–6).

THEATRE MUSIC: Ov. and 6 nos. for **Turandot* (1809); Ov. and 11 nos. for **Preciosa* (1820); and many other items for plays.

CHURCH MUSIC: Mass in E♭ (*Grosse Jugendmesse*) (1802); Mass in E♭ (1818); Mass in G (1819).

CHORAL: *Der erste Ton*, reciter, ch., orch. (1808); *Kampf und Sieg*, SATB soloists, ch., orch. (1815); *Jubel-Kantate*, SATB soloists, ch., orch. (1818).

ORCH.: syms: No.1 in C (1807), No.2 in C (1807); ov., *The *Ruler of the Spirits* (*Der Beherrscher der Geister*) (1811); *Jubel-Ouvertüre* (Jubilee Overture) (1818); *Andante und Rondo Ungarese*, va., orch. (1809, rev. for bn. 1813); pf. concs: No.1 in C (1810), No.2 in E♭ (1812); *Konzertstück* in F minor, pf. (1821); cl. concertino (1811); cl. concs.: No.1 in F minor (1811), No.2 in E♭ (1811); bn. conc. in F (1811, rev. 1822); hn. concertino (1815); *Romanza Siciliana*, fl., orch. (1805); *Grand Potpourri*, vc., orch. (1808).

CHAMBER MUSIC: pf. qt. (1809); cl. quintet (1815); trio, fl., vc., pf. (1819); *6 Progressive Sonatas*, vn., pf. (1810); *Grand Duo Concertant* in E♭, pf., cl. (1816); *Divertimento*, gui., pf. (1816).

PIANO: *6 Variations on Original Theme* (1800); *12 Allemandes* (1801); *Écossaises* (1802); *7 Variations on Original Theme* (1808); *Momento capriccioso* (1808); *Grande Polonaise* (1808); sonatas: No.1 in C (1812), No.2 in A♭ (1816), No.3 in D minor (1816), No.4 in E minor (1822); *7 Variations on a Theme from Méhul's Joseph* (1812); *7 Variations on a Gipsy Song* (1817); *Rondo brillante* (1819); **Invitation to the Dance* (*Aufforderung zum Tanz*) (1819); *Polacca brillante* (1819).

PIANO DUETS: *6 Petites pièces faciles* (1801); *6 Pieces* (1809); *8 Pieces* (1818–19).

SONGS (a selection of Weber's many songs): *Wiedersehn* (1804); *Serenade* (1809); *Trinklied* (1809); *Wiegenlied* (1810); *Leyer und Schwerdt* (Lyre and Sword) Vol. I, 4 songs (1814), Vol. II, 6 songs for 4 male vv. (1814), Vol. III (1816); *Die Temperamente beim Verluste der Geliebten* (1816); *Elfenlied* (1819); *Das Licht im Thale* (1822); also many canons and part-songs.

ARRS.: *God Save the King*, 3 versions, for male vv. (?1818), male vv. (?1818), and SATB and wind (1819); *10 Scottish National Songs*, v. with fl., vn., vc., pf.

Weber, (Jacob) **Gottfried** (*b* Freinsheim, 1779; *d* Kreuznach, 1839). Ger. composer and theorist. Friend of C. M. von *Weber. Comp. songs, church mus., and chamber works. Wrote several textbooks, incl. a study of the authenticity of Mozart's *Requiem* (1826). His most important theoretical work was the *Versuch einer geordneten Theorie der Tonsetzkunst* (Mainz, 1817–21, 1832, Eng. trans. 1851) in which he proposed a new and easier system of terminology and figuration.

Weber, Ludwig (*b* Vienna, 1899; *d* Vienna, 1974). Austrian bass. Opera début Vienna Volksoper 1920. Sang in opera at Elberfeld 1925–7; Düsseldorf 1927–30; Cologne 1930–3; Munich 1933–45; Vienna from 1945. CG début 1936, appearing there to 1939, then 1947, 1950–1; Salzburg Fest. 1939–47; Bayreuth Fest. 1951–60. One of greatest 20th-cent. basses in Mozart, Wagner, and Strauss roles. Created Holsteiner in *Friedenstag* (Munich 1938).

Webern, Anton (Friedrich Wilhelm von) (*b* Vienna, 1883; *d* Mittersill, 1945). Austrian composer and conductor. Early tuition from his mother, a pianist. (Most of his works were written in her memory.) Studied at Klagenfurt with Edwin Komauer, composing first works in 1899. Entered Vienna Univ. 1902, studying musicology with Guido *Adler. Studied comp. with Pfitzner but became pupil of *Schoenberg 1904–8. Ed. works of 15th-cent. Dutch composer Heinrich Isaak. Became close friend of *Berg. Was operetta cond. at Bad Ischl (1908), Teplitz (1910), Danzig (1910–11), Stettin (1911–12), and Prague 1917. In Vienna 1918–22 was active in Schoenberg's Soc. for Private Perfs., and cond. Vienna workers' sym. concerts 1922–34. Cond. and mus. adviser, Austrian Radio 1927–38. Visited London 5 times to conduct for BBC (1929, 1932, 1933, 1935, 1936). Music proscribed by Nazis as 'cultural Bolshevism' although Webern was sympathetic to their cause (as is reflected in texts of his cantatas). Worked as publisher's proof-reader during war. Accidentally shot by Amer. sentry, 1945. (See *The Death of Anton Webern: a drama in documents* by Hans Moldenhauer, NY 1961.)

Largely ignored except by the BBC in his lifetime, Webern's mus. became a rallying-point for the post–1945 generation of European composers, such as Stockhausen, Boulez, and Maderna (and for some of the older generation, e.g. *Stravinsky and Eimert). They were attracted by the way in which his mus., through its sheer concentration, opened up a new and more complete *serialism based on the est. of the relationship between a particular note and a particular quality of sound. Even in the earliest works to which he gave an opus no. there is preoccupation with the inter-relationship of symmetrical structures. From 1908 until the late 1920s Webern wrote in a free atonal style. A characteristic of many of the works of this period is their epigrammatic brevity. The 4th of his *6 Pieces* for orch. has only 6 bars. Timbre plays an important role, also str. effects such as *col legno and *sul ponticello. In his vocal mus., the extremes of range are contrasted, with fragmented instr. accs. In this period he wrote his last atonal work, the *5 Canons*, Op.16, and adopted 12-note technique from his Op.18, *3 Songs*. His last group of works, 1928–45, is marked on the one hand by a simplification of the contrapuntal texture and on the other by an increasingly complex use of the note-row. The row is often broken down to 3 or 6 notes, and the resulting structures are related by imitation, inversion, retrograde-inversion, palindromic devices, etc. The sym. of 1928 has a theme and variations as its 2nd of 2 movts., the theme and each variation being symmetrical. He comp. an important set of pf. variations, and 3 cantatas in which the beauty of the vocal writing is a reminder of how much Webern derived from the medieval masters whose work he had studied. Although the post-war *avant-garde* admired his mus. for its technical innovations, such as serialization of durations and dynamic levels, it should not be forgotten that Webern's place is in the romantic tradition, as his choice of texts implies, and that his homage to classical forms, such as the passacaglia and the canon, is an unwavering feature of his work. He remained, too, a lifelong admirer of Wagner's operas and he was apparently a superb cond. of Schubert, Mahler, and Brahms. Prin. works:

ORCH.: *Im Sommerwind*, idyll (1904); *3 Studies on a Ground* (1908; f.p. 1978); *Passacaglia*, Op.1 (1908); *5 Movements*, Op.5 (orig. for str. qt., arr. for str. 1929); *6 Stücke* (6 Pieces), Op.6 (1909–10, rev. for smaller orch. 1928); *5 Stücke*, Op.10 (1911–13); *5 Stücke* (1911–13, f.p. 1969, pubd. 1971); *Sym.*, Op.21, cl., bcl., 2 hn., hp., vns., vas., vcs. (1928); *Concerto for 9 instruments*, Op.24, fl., ob., cl., hn., tpt., tb., vn., va., pf. (1931–4); *Variations*, Op.30 (1940). Also *5 Stücke*, 1913, related to Op.6 and Op.10; *8 Fragmente*, 1911–13, related to Op.10.

CHORAL: *Entflieht auf Leichten Kähnen* (Flight to Light boats), Op.2, double canon, unacc. ch. (1908); *2 Goethe Lieder*, Op.19, ch., gui., cel., vn., cl., bcl. (1926); *Das *Augenlicht* (Eyesight), Op.26, ch., orch. (1935); *Erste Kantate* (1st Cantata), Op.29, sop., ch., orch. (1938–9); *Zweite Kantate* (2nd Cantata), Op.31, sop., bass, ch., orch. (1941–3).

VOICE(S) & INSTR(S).: *Siegfrieds Schwert* (Siegfried's Sword), ballad, ten., orch. (1903, f.p. 1978); *2 Lieder* (Rilke), Op.8, v., cl., hn., tpt., cel., hp., vn., va., vc. (1910); *3 Lieder*, sop., small orch. (1913–14); *4 Lieder*, Op.13, sop., orch. (1914–18); *6 Lieder* (Trakl), Op.14, high v., cl., bcl., vn., vc. (1917–21); *5 Geistliche Lieder* (5 Spiritual Songs), Op.15, high sop., fl., cl., bcl., tpt., hp., vn., va. (1917–22); *5 Canons* (Latin texts), Op.16, high sop., cl., bcl. (1923–4); *3 Folk-Songs*, Op.17, v., cl., bcl., vn. or va. (1924); *3 Lieder*, Op.18, v., E♭ cl., gui. (1925).

VOICE & PIANO: *2 Songs* (Avenarius) (1900–1); *3 Gedichte* (1899–1903); *8 frühe Lieder* (1901–4); *3 Lieder* (Avenarius) (1903–4); *5 Dehmel Lieder* (1906–8); *5 Lieder aus der siebente Ring* (George), Op.3 (1907–8); *5 Stefan George Lieder*, Op.4 (1908–9); *4 Lieder*, Op.12 (1915–17); *3 Gesänge* (Jone), Op.23 (1934); *3 Lieder* (Jone), Op.25 (1934–5).

CHAMBER MUSIC: str. qt. in 1 movt. (1905); *Langsamer Satz*, str. qt. (1905); pf. quintet in 1 movt. (1906); *5 Movements*, str. qt., Op.5 (1909, scored for str. orch. 1929); *4 Pieces*, Op.7, vn., pf. (1910); *6 Bagatelles*, Op.9, str. qt. (1913); *3 Little Pieces*, Op.11, vc., pf. (1914); vc. sonata (1914); *Movement*,

str. trio (1925); str. trio, Op.20 (1926–7); qt., Op.22, vn., cl., ten. sax., pf. (1930); str. qt., Op.28 (1936–8).

PIANO: *Kinderstück* (1924); *Variations*, Op.27 (1935–6).

ARRS. OF OTHER COMPOSERS: Bach: *Ricercare* from *The Musical Offering* for chamber orch. Schoenberg: Nos. 2 and 6 of *6 Orchester-Lieder*, Op.8, arr. for v. and pf.; *Kammersymphonie*, Op.9, arr. for fl. (or 2 vn), cl. (or va.), vn., vc., pf. (1922); *5 Orchestral Pieces*, Op.16, arr. for 2 pf.; Prelude and Interludes from *Gurrelieder*, arr. 2 pf., 8 hands (1910). Schubert: *Deutsche Tänze vom Oktober 1824*, arr. for orch.; *Rosamunde Romanze, Ihr Bild, Der Wegweiser, Du bist die Ruh'*, and *Tränenregen*, arr. for v. and small orch. Wolf: *Lebe wohl, Der Knabe und das Immelein*, and *Denk es, O Seele*, arr. for v. and full orch.

Webster, (Sir) **David** (Lumsden) (*b* Dundee, 1903; *d* London, 1971). Scots-born impresario and opera administrator. Began career as department store gen. manager in Liverpool, taking major part in city's cultural activities, and becoming chairman, Liverpool Phil. Soc. 1940–5. Gen. administrator, Royal Opera House, CG 1944–70, presiding over post-war development of opera at CG, finding and encouraging many Brit. singers. Knighted 1960, KCVO 1970.

wechseln (Ger.). To change. **Wechselnote**, *Changing Note.

We Come to the River (*Wir erreichen den Fluss*). Opera (actions for music) in 2 parts and 11 scenes by Henze to lib. by Edward Bond (Ger. version by Henze). Comp. 1974–6. Prod. London 1976, Berlin 1976, Santa Fe 1984.

Wedding, The (Stravinsky). See *Noces, Les*.

Wedding Day at Troldhaugen. Pf. piece by Grieg, No.6 of his *Lyric Pieces* (Book 8), Op.65 (1897), later orch. Grieg's villa, built in 1885 outside Bergen, was called Troldhaugen.

Wedding March. Many court composers have written marches for the weddings of royal and aristocratic brides, but Brit. brides have for long favoured entry into the church to the strains of the bridal ch. from Wagner's *Lohengrin* and exit to the wedding march which is the 6th no. of Mendelssohn's incidental mus. to Shakespeare's *A Midsummer Night's Dream*. The vogue for the Mendelssohn began in 1847 and received a boost in 1858 when Queen Victoria's daughter, the Princess Royal, used it at her wedding. Its supremacy was dented in 1961 by the Duchess of Kent, who left York Minster to the *Toccata* from Widor's 5th Sym. for org., her example being widely followed. Various more bizarre mus. selections are occasionally reported.

Wedekind, (Benjamin) **Frank**(lin) (*b* Hanover, 1864; *d* Munich, 1918). Ger. playwright and musician. Two of his plays, *Der Erdgeist* (Earth Spirit) 1895 and *Die Büchse der Pandora* (Pandora's Box) 1902, were adapted by *Berg as lib. for his opera

Lulu. Wrote songs with lute acc. His sister Erika (1869–1944) was leading sop. at Dresden Opera 1894–1909.

'Wedge' Fugue. Nickname of Bach's org. fugue in E minor (BWV 548), comp. between 1727 and 1736. So called because of shape of subject, which proceeds in gradually widening intervals.

Weelkes, Thomas (*b* ?Elstead, Sussex, *c*.1576; *d* London, 1623). Eng. composer and organist. Book of madrigals in 3, 4, 5, and 6 vv. pubd. 1597, followed in 1600 by 2 further books, one of 5-part madrigals, the other of 6-part. Organist, Winchester College, 1598. Wrote 6-part madrigal *As Vesta was from Latmos hill descending* for The **Triumphs of Oriana*, 1601. Took Mus.B., Oxford Univ., 1602. Organist, Chichester Cath. from *c*.1601–2. His *Ayres or Phantasticke Spirites* for 3 vv. was pubd. 1608, and shows a lighter, satirical side to his art. One of greatest of Eng. madrigalists, with daring harmonies and imaginative expression. *O Care, wilt though despatch me*, **Thule, the period of cosmography*, and *Like two proud armies* are among the finest examples of their kind. Wrote much church mus., incl. many anthems (notably *Hosanna to the Son of David*), and instr. pieces for viols, In Nomines, pavans, etc. Wrote 3-part song, *Death hath Deprived me of my Dearest Friend*, in memory of *Morley. Buried in St Bride's, Fleet Street.

Weerbeke, Gaspar van (*b* Oudenaarde, *c*.1445; *d* after 1517). Flemish composer. Spent his time in service of ducal chapel in Milan, papal chapel in Rome, and at Burgundian court. Wrote cycles of motets to replace normal movts. of the Mass (e.g. *Kyrie* and *Gloria*). Was connected with Du Fay and his circle.

Weidt, Lucie (*b* Troppau, *c*.1880; *d* Vienna, 1940). Austrian soprano, later mez., whose father was a conductor and composer. Member of Vienna Opera 1902–27, taking over *Mildenburg's roles under Mahler régime. Celebrated Leonore in *Fidelio*. First Vienna Marschallin. Sang Brünnhilde (*Der Ring*) at NY Met 1910–11 season and in Buenos Aires 1912. Created Nurse in *Die Frau ohne Schatten*, Vienna 1919.

Weigl, Karl (*b* Vienna, 1881; *d* NY, 1949). Austrian-born composer, conductor, and teacher (Amer. cit. 1943). Singing coach at Vienna Opera under Mahler, 1904–7. Taught theory and comp. at New Vienna Cons. 1918–28. Prof. of music theory, Vienna Univ. 1931–8. Many of his works, written in a tonal and conservative idiom, were perf. in Vienna by Furtwängler, Szell, the Rosé Qt., and Elisabeth Schumann. Succeeded Gál at Vienna Univ. Inst. of Musicology. Went to USA 1938. Worked in NY public library, then taught at Hartt Sch. of Mus., Hartford, Conn., 1941–2, Brooklyn Coll. 1943–5, was head of mus. theory dept., New Eng. Cons., Boston, 1945–8, and taught at Philadelphia Acad. of Mus. 1948–9. Wrote memories of Mahler (1947, 1948). Works incl. opera *The Pied Piper of Hamelin* (*Der Rattenfänger von Hameln*) (*c*.1922); 6 syms. (1908–47); concs.:

pf. (left hand) (1925), vn. (1928), pf. (1929–30), vc. (1934); 8 str. qts. (1905–49); 2 vn. sonatas (1922–3, 1937); choral and vocal comps.; many songs; pieces for kbd.

Weihe des Hauses, Die (Beethoven). See *Consecration of the House, The*.

Weihnachtslied (Ger.). Christmas carol.

Weihnachts Oratorium (Bach). See *Christmas Oratorio*.

Weikl, Bernd (*b* Vienna, 1942). Austrian baritone. Sang with Hanover Opera 1968–70 (début as Ottakar in *Der Freischütz*); Düsseldorf 1970–2; Salzburg Easter Fest. 1971; Bayreuth from 1972; CG début 1975; NY Met 1977; Salzburg Fest. début 1984. Outstanding Mandryka and Sachs.

Weil, Bruno (*b* Hahnstatten, 1949). Ger. conductor. Won 2nd prize in Karajan comp. 1979. Gen. mus. dir. Augsburg Opera 1979–89. Débuts: Vienna Opera 1985; Salzburg Fest. 1987; Amer. (NY) 1988; Los Angeles 1989; Glyndebourne 1992. Toured Ger. with ECO 1990–1. Mus. dir. Carmel Bach Fest., Calif., from 1991.

Weill, Kurt (Julian) (*b* Dessau, 1900; *d* NY, 1950). Ger.-born composer (Amer. cit. 1943). Opera coach at Dessau 1918–21 and th. cond. at Lüdenscheid. Founded new sch. of popular opera which attracted wide attention in Ger. and also attracted implacable hostility of Nazi régime when it achieved power. First opera *Der Protagonist*, Dresden 1926. In 1927 collab. with Bertolt *Brecht in radio cantata about Lindbergh's flight across the Atlantic and in 'Songspiel' *Mahagonny* which in 1929 they reworked into 3-act opera *Rise and Fall of the City of Mahagonny*, a satire on Amer. life. His outstanding success came in Berlin in 1928 with updated version of *The *Beggar's Opera* called *Die Dreigroschenoper* (The Threepenny Opera) containing satirical topical references to Ger. life at the time and evoking by its jazzy and harsh but brilliant scoring the atmosphere of that particular period even for those who did not experience it. Brecht's lyrics and the singing of Lotte *Lenya, who became Weill's wife, were significant factors in its success. Its 'hit' number was *Mack the Knife*. Driven from Ger. in 1933, Weill went to Paris, then to London, and finally to NY in 1935. In America he wrote several successful Broadway musicals, lacking the pungency of his Ger. operas but of high merit nonetheless. The evocative melody 'September Song' was written for *Knickerbocker Holiday* (1938) and *Street Scene* is a vivid picture of NY tenement life. After his death, *The Threepenny Opera* was given an Eng. lib. by Marc *Blitzstein and ran successfully in NY. Weill's music, like Coward's on another level, captures the flavour of an era and also successfully fuses jazz with classical elements. Prin. works:

OPERAS, MUSICALS, etc. (librettist in parentheses):
   Der Protagonist (Kaiser) (1925); *Die*
   *Dreigroschenoper (Hauptmann, Brecht) (1928);

Rise and Fall of the City of Mahagonny (Aufstieg und Fall der Stadt Mahagonny) (Brecht) (1927–9); *Der Zar lässt sich photographiern* (The Tsar has his photograph taken) (Kaiser) (1927); *Happy End* (Hauptmann, Brecht) (1929); *Der Jasager* (Brecht) (1930); *Die Bürgschaft* (Neher) (1930–1); *Der Silbersee* (Kaiser) (1932–3); *Marie galante* (Deval) Paris (1933); *Der Kuhhandel* (Vamberg) (1934), rev. as *A Kingdom for a Cow*, (Arkell) London (1935); *Der Weg der Verheissung* (Werfel) (1935), rev. as *The Eternal Road* (Mayer) (1936); *Johnny Johnson* (Green) NY (1936); *Knickerbocker Holiday* (Maxwell Anderson) NY (1938); *Davy Crockett* (Hays) NY (1938); *The Railroads on Parade* (Hungerford) NY (1939); *Ulysses Africanus* (Anderson) NY (1939); *Lady in the Dark* (M. Hart, I. Gershwin) NY (1940); *One Touch of Venus* (Perelman, O. Nash) NY (1943); *The Firebrand of Florence* (Mayers, I. Gershwin) NY (1945); *Down in the Valley* (Sundgaard) NY (1945–8); **Street Scene* (Rice) NY (1946); *Love Life* (Lerner) NY (1948); *Lost in the Stars* (Anderson) NY (1949).

BALLET: *Zaubernacht* (1922); **Seven Deadly Sins (Die sieben Todsünden)*, sop., male ch., orch. (1933).

ORCH.: syms.: No.1 (1921, unperf. until 1958), No.2 (1933–4); *Quodlibet*, Op.9 (1923); vn. conc., wind ens., Op.12 (1924); *Der neue Orpheus*, Op.16, sop., vn., orch. (1925); *Vom Tod in Wald*, bass, 10 wind instr. (1927); *3 Walt Whitman Songs*, bar., orch. (1940); *Kleine Dreigroschenmusik* (suite from *Threepenny Opera*).

CHORAL: *Recordare*, unacc. ch. (1923); *Das Berliner Requiem*, ten., bar., bass, ch., ens. (1928); *Der Lindberghflug*, radio cantata (with Hindemith), ten., bar., bass, ch., orch. (1929, re-scored by Weill 1929, rev. 1930 as *Der Flug des Lindberghs*); *The Ballad of the Magna Carta*, soloists, ch., orch. (1939); *Kiddush*, ten., ch., org. (1946).

CHAMBER MUSIC: str. qt. in B minor (1919); vc. sonata (1920); str. qt. No.1 (1923).

SONGS: *September Song; Ballade vom ertrunken Mädchen; Happy End; Bilbao Song; Surabaya Johnny; Matrosen Tango; Havanalied; Alabama Song; Der Silbersee; Lied der Fennimore*; etc.

14 MSS of Weill compositions were discovered in NY in 1983. All date from before 1921 and are available for study at the Weill/Lenya Research Center, NY. They include an orch. suite in E, an *Intermezzo* for pf., a song-cycle to 12th-cent. Jewish texts, and 3 *Lieder* to Ger. Romantic texts.

Wein, Der (The Wine). Concert aria for sop. and very large orch. by Berg, comp. 1929. Text poem by Baudelaire in Ger. trans. by S. George. F.p. Königsberg 1930 cond. Scherchen.

Weinberger, Jaromír (*b* Prague, 1896; *d* St Petersburg, Florida, 1967). Cz.-born composer (Amer. cit.). Taught at Ithaca Cons., NY, in 1922, then worked in Prague, Vienna, etc. Fled to USA 1939 at the time of the *Anschluss*. Prolific composer of operas, operettas, orch. works, religious mus., songs, etc., but achieved success with 2 works, the opera *Švanda Dudák* (*Schwanda the Bagpiper) (1927) and the *Variations and Fugue on Under the Spreading Chestnut Tree* for orch. (1939, rev. 1941).

Weiner, Leó (*b* Budapest, 1885; *d* Budapest, 1960). Hung. composer and teacher. On faculty Budapest State Acad. from 1908 (prof. of comp. from 1912, of chamber mus. from 1920, prof. emeritus 1949–60). Famous teacher of chamber mus. Ed. Beethoven's pf. and vn. sonatas. Wrote sym.-poem, 2 vn. concs., 3 str. qts., 2 vn. sonatas, th. mus., and *Suite on Hung. Folk Dances* (1931) for orch.

Weingartner, (Paul) **Felix, Edler von Münzberg** (*b* Zara, Dalmatia, 1863; *d* Winterthur, Switz., 1942). Austrian conductor, composer, and writer. Pupil of Liszt 1883 at Weimar, who recommended his opera *Sakuntala* for production in Weimar in 1884. Opera cond., Königsberg 1884–5, Danzig 1885–7, Hamburg 1887–9, Mannheim 1889–91, Berlin 1891–8, Vienna (after Mahler) 1907–11, Hamburg 1912–14, Darmstadt 1914–19, Vienna Volksoper 1919–24, Boston 1912–13. His orch. appointments included Berlin royal concerts 1891–1907, Kaim Orch., Munich, 1898–1905, Vienna PO 1907–27, Basle 1927–33. Dir., Basle Cons. 1927–35, dir. Vienna Opera 1935–6. Guest cond., London orchs. from 1898. CG début 1939. NY concert début 1904. Amer. opera début (Boston) 1912. Salzburg Fest. début 1934. Comp. several operas, 7 syms. (1899–1937), sym.-poems, concs. (vn., vc.), choral works, 5 str. qts., etc. Wrote autobiography and several other books, incl. treatise on cond. and on interpretation of Beethoven syms.

Weinzweig, John (Jacob) (*b* Toronto, 1913; *d* Toronto, 2006). Canadian composer. Prof. of comp., Toronto Royal Cons. 1939–43, 1945–60, and at Toronto Univ. 1952–78. Co-founder, Canadian League of Composers, 1951. First Canadian to use 12-note procedures. Wrote mus. for films and radio in addition to sym. (1940); vn. conc. (1955); 4 *Divertimenti*; hp. conc.; pf. conc.; vn. sonata; vc. sonata; pf. suites; 3 str. qts.; *Around the stage in 25 minutes during which a number of instruments are struck*, for 1 percussionist (1970); *12 Divertimenti*, orch. (1945–89); *Cadenza*, cl. (1986); *What's That?* ch. (1986); *Belaria*, vn., va., vc. (1992); *Parodies and Travesties*, mus. th. for sop., mez., pf. (1995); *Netscapes*, pf. (2000); and *Prologue to a Tango*, mez., 4 vn. (2002).

Weir, (Dame) **Gillian** (Constance) (*b* Martinborough, NZ, 1941). NZ organist and harpsichordist. Début London 1965 (RFH) and was soloist in Poulenc's conc. at 1965 Proms. Gave f. Eng. p. of Messiaen's *Méditations sur le mystère de la Ste. Trinité*, London 1973. Amer. début NY 1967. Worldwide reputation as recitalist in org. mus. of several periods. CBE 1989. DBE 1996.

Weir, Judith (*b* Aberdeen, 1954). Scottish composer. Played in Nat. Youth Orch. of Great Britain. Worked on computer mus., Mass. Inst. of Technology 1973. On staff of Glasgow Univ. 1979–82. Creative arts fellowship, Trinity Coll., Cambridge, 1983–5. Comp.-in-residence RSAMD 1988–91. CBE 1995. Works incl.:

OPERAS: *The Black Spider* (1984); *A *Night at the Chinese Opera* (1986–7); *The Vanishing Bridegroom* (1990); *Blond Eckbert* (1993–4); *Armida* (2005).

ORCH.: *Wunderhorn* (1978); *Isti Mirant Stella* (1981); *Ballad*, with bar. solo (1981); *The Ride Over Lake Constance* (1983–4); *Variations on 'Sumer is icumen in'* (1987); *Sederunt principes* (1987); *Music Untangled* (1991–2); *Heroische Bogenstriche (Heroic Strokes of the Bow)* (1992); *Forest* (1995); pf. conc. (1997); *The welcome arrival of rain* (2001); *Bright Cecilia* (2002).

CHORAL: *Ascending into Heaven*, ch., org. (1983); *Illuminare, Jerusalem*, ch., org. (1985); *Lovers, Learners and Libations*, early mus. consort (1987); *Missa del Cid*, ch., spkr. (1988); *Heaven Ablaze in His Breast*, ch., 2 pf., 8 dancers (1989); *Our revels now are ended*, ch., wind (1995); *Moon and Star*, ch., orch. (1995); *Sanctus*, ch., orch. (1995); *Storm*, youth ch., orch. (1997); *All the ends of the earth*, ch., orch. (1999); *We are shadows*, ch., orch. (1999); *a blue true dream of sky*, sop., ch. (2003); *Vertue*, unacc. ch. (2005).

ENS. (also with VOICE(S)): *25 Variations*, sop., 6 players (1976); *Black Birdsong*, bar., fl., ob., vn., vc. (1977); *Between Ourselves*, 7 players (1978); *Hans the Hedgehog*, spkr., 2 ob., bn., hpd. (1978); *King Harald's Saga*, sop. (1979); *King Harald sails to Byzantium*, 6 players (1979); *Thread!*, narr., 8 players (1981); *The Consolations of Scholarship*, sop., 9 players (1985); *Airs from Another Planet*, fl., ob., cl., bn., hn., pf. (1986); *The Romance of Count Arnaldos*, sop., 2 cl., va., vc., db. (1989); *Ox Mountain Was Covered by Trees*, sop, counterten., bar., orch. (1990); *Scipio's Dream* (re-composition of Mozart's *Il sogno di Scipione*), sop., mez., ten. or high bar., bass, opt. ch., ens. (1991); *The Alps*, sop., cl., va. (1992); *Broken Branches*, sop., pf., db. (1992); *Combattimento II* (re-composition of Monteverdi's *Il Combattimento di Tancredi e Clorinda*), 12 singers, 2 vn., va., vc., db. (1992); *Musicians Wrestle Everywhere*, chamber ens. (1994); *Waltraute's Narration*, large ens. (1996); *Tiger under the table*, small ens. (2002); *Psyche*, narr., 6 instr. (2005).

VOICE & SOLO INSTR.: *Scotch Minstrels*, ten. (or sop.), pf. (1982); *Songs from the Exotic*, low v., pf. (1987); *A Spanish Liederbooklet*, sop., pf. (1988); *Don't Let That Horse*, sop., hn. (1990); *On Buying a Horse*, medium v., pf. (1991); *Ständchen*, bar., pf. (1997); *The Voice of Desire*, mez., pf. (2003).

CHAMBER MUSIC: *Out of the Air*, wind quintet (1975); *Harmony and Invention*, hp. (1978, rev. 1980); *Pas de Deux*, vn., ob. (1980); *Several Concertos*, fl., vc., pf. (1980); vc. sonata (1980); *Music for 247 Strings*, vn., pf. (1981); *Pleasant Dreams*, db., tape (1983); *A Serbian Cabaret*, pf. qt. (1983–4); *Sketches from a Bagpiper's Album*, cl., pf. (1984); *The Bagpiper's String Trio*, vn., va., vc. (1985); *Gentle Violence*, picc., gui. (1987); *Mountain Airs*, fl., ob., cl. (1988); *Distance and Enchantment*, pf. qt. (1989); str. qt. (1990); *I broke off a golden branch*, vn., va., vc., db., pf. (1991); *El Rey de Francia*, vn., va., vc., pf. (1993); pf. trio No.1 (1998), No.2 (2004); *Arise! Arise! you slumbering sleepers*, pf. qt. (1998); pf. qt. (2000); *Rain and Mist are on the mountain, I'd better buy some shoes*, 2 vns. (2005); *St Agnes*, va., vc. (2006); *What sound will chase elephants away?*, 2 db. (2006).

KEYBOARD: *An mein Klavier*, pf. (1980); *Wild Mossy Mountains*, org. (1982); *The Art of Touching the Keyboard*, pf. (1983); *Ettrick Banks*, org. (1983); *Michael's Strathspey*, pf. (or org.) (1985); *Ardnamurchan Point*, 2 pf. (1990); *Roll off the Ragged Rocks of Sin*, pf. (1992); *The King of France*, pf. (1993).

Weisgall, Hugo (David) (*b* Eibenschütz (now Ivançice), 1912; *d* NY, 1997). Cz.-born comp. and cond. (Amer. cit. 1926). Settled in USA 1920. Cond., Baltimore Str. Sym. 1937–9, and other Baltimore organizations 1949–60. Chairman of faculty, Cantors' Inst., NY, from 1952. Teacher at Juilliard Sch. 1957–70, prof. Queens Coll., NY from 1961. Works incl. 9 operas (9 *Rivers from Jordan*, 6 *Characters in Search of an Author*, *Purgatory*, etc.), cantata *A Garden Eastward*, ballet, songs, radio music.

Weissenberg, Alexis (Sigismond) (*b* Sofia, 1929). Fr. pianist of Bulgarian birth. First prize Leventritt int. competition 1948. Début with NYPO, cond. Szell 1947. Salzburg Fest. début 1968. London début 1974. World-wide tours and appearances with leading orchs.

Weldon, George (*b* Chichester, 1906; *d* Cape Town, 1963). Eng. conductor. Prin. cond. CBSO 1943–51; assoc. cond. (to Barbirolli) Hallé Orch. from 1952. Cond. SW Ballet 1955–6.

Weldon, John (*b* Chichester, 1676; *d* London, 1736). Eng. composer and organist. Pupil of Purcell. Org., New Coll., Oxford, 1694, Chapel Royal 1708, St Martin-in-the-Fields 1714. Wrote 4 operas incl. *The Judgment of Paris* (1701), masque, anthems, songs, and mus. for *The Tempest*. (Scholars believe that the music for *The Tempest* usually attrib. Purcell may be by Weldon.)

Welitsch [Veličkova], **Ljuba** (*b* Borissovo, 1913; *d* Vienna, 1996). Bulgarian-born Austrian soprano. Opera début Sofia 1934 (in *Louise*). Sang in opera at Graz 1936–40; Hamburg 1941–3; Munich 1943–6; Vienna 1946–58. Salzburg Fest. début 1946; CG début 1947; sang with Glyndebourne co. at Edinburgh Fest. (1949); NY Met début 1948. Exciting singer-actress, memorable as Salome, which she sang in Vienna 1944 for Strauss's 80th birthday, and in Eng. at CG 1949. Also a fine Tosca, Aida, and capricious Musetta.

Weller, Walter (*b* Vienna, 1939). Austrian conductor and violinist. Violinist in Vienna PO from 1956, becoming leader 1961–9. Founder and leader Weller Str. Qt. from 1958, touring Europe and USA. Prof. cond. début 1968, Vienna Opera 1969. Salzburg Fest. début as violinist 1966, as cond. 1971. Gen. mus. dir. Detmold Opera 1971. Prin. cond. RLPO 1977–80; RPO 1980–5. Guest cond. various opera cos. Mus. dir. RSNO 1991–7.

Welles Raises Kane. Mus. 'portrait of Orson Welles' (actor and film producer) by *Herrmann, based on mus. he wrote for Welles's films 'Citizen Kane' and 'The Magnificent Ambersons'. Comp. 1942, f.p. NY cond. composer, 1942.

Wellesz, Egon (Joseph) (*b* Vienna, 1885; *d* Oxford, 1974). Austrian-born composer, conductor, scholar, and teacher (Brit. cit.). Lessons from Schoenberg 1905–6; attended Mahler rehearsals at Vienna Opera. Taught at Vienna Univ. 1913–38 (prof. of history of mus. from 1929). Went to Eng. 1938, joining faculty of mus. at Oxford Univ. as lect. Reader in Byzantine Mus. 1948–56. Pupils incl. *Rubbra. Authority on Byzantine mus. and Gregorian chant. Several books on these and other subjects. First biographer of Schoenberg, 1921. CBE 1957. Works, some in idiom of Schoenberg and medieval mus., but in later years reverting to diatonicism, incl.:

OPERAS: *Die Prinzessin Girnara*, Op.27 (1921, rev. 1928); *Alkestis*, Op.35 to Hofmannsthal lib. (1922–3); *Die Opferung des Gefangenen* (The Prisoner's Sacrifice), Op.40 (1924–5); *Scherz, List, und Rache* (Joke, Cunning, and Revenge), Op.41 (1926–7); *Die Bakchantinnen* (The Bacchantes), Op.44 (1929–30); *Incognita* (1951).

BALLETS: *Persisches Ballett* (Persian Ballet), Op.30 (1920); *Achilles auf Skyros*, Op.32 (1921); *Die Nächtlichen* (The Night People), Op.37 (1923); *Das Wunder der Diana*, Op.18 (1924).

ORCH.: syms.: No.1, Op.62 (1945), No.2, Op.65 (1948), No.3, Op.68 (1951), No.4 (*Symphonia austriaca*), Op.70 (1952), No.5, Op.75 (1956), No.6, Op.95 (1965), No.7, Op.102 (1967–8), No.8, Op.110 (1970), No.9, Op.111 (1971); *Vorfrühling*, Op.12 (1912); *Suite*, vn., chamber orch., Op.38 (1924); pf. conc., Op.49 (1934); *Prosperos Beschwörungen*, Op.53 (1936); vn. conc., Op.84 (1961); *Symphonischer Epílog*, Op.108 (1969–70).

VOICE & INSTR(S).: *Gebete der Mädchen zu Maria*, sop., women's ch., orch., Op.5 (1910); *6 George Lieder*, mez., pf., Op.22 (1917); *Amor Timido*, sop., orch., Op.50 (1933); *Sonnets of E. B. Browning* (in Rilke trans.), sop., str., Op.52 (1934); *The Leaden Echo and the Golden Echo*, sop., vn., vc., pf. (1944); *5 Lieder aus Wien*, bar., pf., Op.82 (1959); *4 Songs of Return*, sop., chamber orch., Op.85 (1961); *Duineser Elegie*, sop., ch., chamber ens., Op.90 (1963).

CHORAL: *Mitten im Leben*, Op.45, sop., ch., orch. (1932); Mass in F minor (1934), in C (1937); *Missa brevis* (1936); *Mirabile mysterium*, Christmas cantata, sop., bar., ch., orch., Op.101 (1967); *Canticum sapientiae*, bar., ch., orch., Op.104 (1968).

CHAMBER MUSIC: str. qts. 1–9 (1912–66); Octet, cl., bn., hn., str. quintet, Op.67 (1948–9); cl. quintet (1959); str. trio, Op.86 (1962); str. quintet, Op.109 (1970).

PIANO: *3 Sketches*, Op.6 (1911); *4 Eclogues*, Op.11 (1912); *5 Epigrams*, Op.17 (1914); *5 Idylls*, Op.21 (1916); *5 Dance Pieces*, Op.42 (1926); *5 Studies in Grey*, Op.106 (1969).

ORGAN: *Partita* (1966).

Wellington's Victory (Beethoven). See *Battle Symphony*.

Well-Tempered Klavier (Bach). See *Wohltemperierte Klavier, Das*.

Welser-Möst [Möst], **Franz** (*b* Linz, 1960). Austrian conductor. Finalist in Karajan comp. 1979. Prin. cond. Austrian Youth Orch. 1979–85. Mus. dir. Winterthur and Norrköping Orchs. 1985. Salzburg Fest. début 1985. Cond. LPO on Eur. tour in Amsterdam, Berlin, and Vienna 1986. Opera début Vienna 1987. Amer. début 1989 (St Louis SO). Prin. cond. LPO 1990–6. Glyndebourne début RFH 1993, Sussex 1994. Mus. dir. Zurich Opera 1996–2002, prin. cond. 2002–5, gen. mus. dir. from 2005; Mus. dir. Cleveland Orch. from 2002.

Welsh, Moray (Meston) (*b* Haddington, 1947). Scottish cellist. London début 1972. Cello tutor at RNCM 1973–93. Co-prin. vc. LSO from 1993. Soloist with leading orchs. and member of pf. trio with Anthony Goldstone (pf.) and Ralph Holmes (vn.) until 1984.

Welsh National Opera. Opera co. based in Cardiff and founded on amateur basis in 1943, becoming fully professional 1950. First stage prod. Cardiff 1946 (*Cav.* and *Pag.*). Soon built fine reputation for its perfs. of such rare Verdi operas as *Nabucco*, *I Lombardi*, and *Les Vêpres siciliennes*. Professional ch. (WNO Chorale) from 1968 and professional orch. (Welsh Philharmonia, renamed Orch. of WNO 1979) from 1970 (début in *Aida*, Llandudno, cond. James *Levine). Tours widely, giving seasons in Birmingham, Liverpool, Swansea, Bristol, and Southampton. In joint venture with *Scottish Opera, embarked on cycle of Janáček operas, first in Brit. Its Britten prods. have won great admiration, especially *Billy Budd* and *A Midsummer Night's Dream*. Has visited London and perf. at the Proms, and toured abroad (e.g. Barcelona and Frankfurt). Its prod. of *Tristan und Isolde* was perf. at CG 1993. Mus. dirs.: Idloes Owen (1944–52), Leo Quayle (1952–3), Frederick Berend (1953–5), Vilem Tausky (1955), Warwick Braithwaite (1956–61), Charles Groves (1961–3), Bryan Balkwill (1963–6), James Lockhart (1968–73), Richard Armstrong (1973–86), Charles Mackerras (1987–92), Carlo Rizzi (1992–2001); Tugan Sokhiev (2003–4); Rizzi from 2004. Gave early opportunities to sops. Gwyneth Jones, Elizabeth Vaughan, and Margaret Price. First Brit. opera co. to stage *Lulu* (1971, before 3rd act completion). Gave f.ps. of Grace Williams's *The Parlour* (1966), Hoddinott's *The Beach of Falesá* (1974), Mathias's *The Servants* (1980), Metcalf's *The Journey* (1981), *Tornrak* (1990), and Maxwell Davies's *The Doctor of Myddfai* (1996), and f. Brit. p. of Martinů's *The Greek Passion* (1981). Moved to its first permanent home in Cardiff, at newly opened arts complex, the Welsh Millennium Centre, 2004.

Welte-Mignon Reproducing Piano. Type of *pianola using photo-electric cell, developed by Edwin Welte, 1904. His uncle, Emil Welte (1841–1923), est. branch of Freiburg family business of making pneumatic mus. instrs. in NY in 1865 and developed paper roll used with pneumatic action. On these rolls are preserved historic perfs. of pf.-playing by Mahler and others.

Wenkoff, Spas (*b* Tírnovo, 1928). Bulgarian tenor. Début Tírnova 1954 (in Dolidse's *Keto and Kote*). Sang in E. Ger. from 1965; Dresden 1975; Bayreuth 1976–83; NY Met 1981; Vienna 1982. Specialist in Wagner roles (Tristan, etc.).

Wenzinger, August (*b* Basle, 1905; *d* Basle, 1996). Swiss cellist, conductor, and teacher. Prin. vc. Bremen SO 1929–34, Basle orch. 1934–70. Cellist in Basle Qt. 1933–47. Teacher of viola da gamba and ornamentation at Basle Schola Cantorum from 1934. Prof. of mus., Basle Acad.*, from 1936. Expert in perf. of early music.

Werba, Erik (*b* Baden, nr. Vienna, 1918). Austrian pianist. Worked as mus. critic 1945–65. From 1949 toured Eur. as accomp. to leading singers. Salzburg Fest. début 1954. Prof. of song and oratorio, Vienna Acad. of Mus. from 1949. Comp. chamber mus. and songs and author of books on Joseph Marx and Hugo Wolf.

Wert, Giaches de (Jakab von) (*b* ?Weert, nr. Antwerp, 1535; *d* Mantua, 1596). Flemish composer. Boy chorister in It., becoming choirmaster Mantua 1565 and holding ducal court post. Pubd. several books of madrigals, 1558–95, canzonets, and motets.

Werther. Opera in 4 acts by Massenet to lib. by Edouard Blau, Paul Milliet, and Georges Hartmann based on Goethe's novel *The Sorrows of Young Werther* (*Die Leiden des jungen Werthers*, 1774). Comp. 1885–7. Prod. (in Ger.) Vienna 1892, Paris 1893, Chicago (NY Met tour), NY Met, and London 1894. Massenet arr. title-role for bar. Battistini in 1902.

Wesendonck (*née* Luckemeyer), **Mathilde** (*b* Elberfeld, 1828; *d* Villa Traunblick, Altmünster, 1902). Ger. amateur poet and wife of Otto Wesendonck (*b* Elberfeld, 1815; *d* Berlin, 1896), a wealthy merchant. They befriended *Wagner and put house at his disposal in Zurich 1857 where he wrote part of *Tristan und Isolde* and set 5 of Mathilde's poems to mus. as the *Wesendonck Songs*. She was assumed to be Wagner's mistress at this time, the inspiration of Isolde and Sieglinde. Spelling Wesendonk was adopted by her son some years later.

Wesendonck Songs, 5 (*Fünf Gedichte von Mathilde Wesendonck*). Set of 5 songs for v. and pf. by Wagner to poems written by his mistress Mathilde *Wesendonck. Comp. Zurich 1857–8. Orch. by Mottl under Wagner's supervision. Arr. for vn. and pf. 1872 by H. Léonard (1819–90). Arr. Henze for high v. and chamber orch. (1979). *Träume* arr. by Wagner for vn. and orch. Titles of songs are 1. *Der Engel* (The Angel) 1857, 2. *Stehe still!* (Stand still!) 1858, 3. *Im Treibhaus* (In the greenhouse) 1858, 4. *Schmerzen* (Agonies) 1857, 5. *Träume* (Dreams) 1857. Themes from *Tristan* occur in Nos. 3 and 5, which are designated 'studies for Tristan'. Often called *Wesendonck-Lieder*.

Spelling Wesendonck is accurate; form Wesendonk was not adopted by family until some years after the songs were written.

Wesley, Charles (*b* Bristol, 1757; *d* London, 1834). Eng. organist, harpsichordist, and composer. Son of the Methodist Charles Wesley who wrote hymns *Jesu, Lover of my Soul* and *Hark, the herald angels sing*. Child prodigy, pupil of Boyce; held church org. posts in London and wrote kbd. concs., etc. in his teens. Did not fulfil youthful promise.

Wesley, Samuel (*b* Bristol, 1766; *d* London, 1837). Eng. composer and organist, brother of Charles *Wesley. Child prodigy; wrote part of oratorio at 8 and pubd. hpd. tutor at 11. Became RC 1784. One of earliest Eng. Bach enthusiasts, playing important part in *Bach revival. Cond., Birmingham Fest. 1811. Regarded as greatest org. of his day, but career interrupted by recurring illness stemming from injury to skull after fall in 1787. Wrote oratorios *Ruth* (1774) and *The Death of Abel* (1779); cantatas *Ode to St Cecilia* (1794) and *Confitebor tibi, Domine* (1799); 5 Masses; motets (*In exitu Israel* the best-known); services; anthems; songs; glees; 4 syms. (1784–1802); 4 org. concs. (one based on *Rule, Britannia!*) (1787–1815); 2 hpd. concs. (both 1774); 8 vn. conc. (1779–1812); 3 str. qts. (1779–1800); other chamber mus.; and many kbd. pieces.

Wesley, Samuel Sebastian (*b* London, 1810; *d* Gloucester, 1876). Eng. composer, organist, and conductor, illegitimate son of Samuel *Wesley. Chorister, Chapel Royal, 1820. Org. of several London and suburban churches 1826–32, also th. cond. Org., Hereford Cath. 1832–5, Exeter Cath. 1835–41, where est. as country's leading org. and church musician. Org., Leeds Parish Church 1842–9, Winchester Cath. 1849–65, Gloucester Cath. from 1865. Prof. of org., RAM from 1850. Advocate of and tireless fighter for improvements in standards of Anglican church mus., publishing tract on need for reform, 1849. Comp. splendid anthems (notably *Thou wilt keep him in perfect peace*), 5 Services (that in E major, 1845, being the finest), hymns (incl. the famous *Aurelia*), glees, songs, and pf. mus. Cond. f.p. of Bach's *St. Matthew Passion* at a Three Choirs Fest. (Gloucester 1871). His genius as an org. was such that church authorities overlooked his often questionable conduct in personal and professional affairs.

Wesley-Smith, Martin (*b* Adelaide, 1945). Australian composer. Senior lect. in comp. and elec. mus., NSW State Cons., Sydney. In 1986 est. first computer mus. studio in Beijing Central Cons. of Mus. Works incl. *Interval Piece*, orch. (1970); *Who Killed Cock Robin* (1979); *White Knight and Bearer* (1984); *Songs for Snark-Hunters* (1985); *Snark-Huntingdon* (1986); *Café Concertino*, fl., cl., vn., va., vc., pf. (1991); *Stroke*, pf. (1994); *Charisma*, cl., vc., pf. (2002); *Electric Cello*, vc. (2005).

Westergaard, Peter (*b* Champaign, Ill., 1931). Amer. composer. Taught in Ger. 1957–8. Taught at Columbia Univ. 1958–66, assoc. prof. of mus. Princeton Univ. 1968, prof. 1971, chairman, mus. dept. 1974–8, 1983–6. Works incl. 2 chamber operas, cantata to text by Dylan Thomas (1958), *5 Movements* for orch., chamber works.

Western Wynde. Eng. 16th-cent. secular tune used as *cantus firmus* in Masses by *Taverner, *Tye, and John *Shepherd which are therefore known as 'Western Wynde' Masses. The use of secular tunes in sacred mus. was eventually banned by the RC church, not surprisingly when one considers that the anonymous and beautiful words to which congregations were accustomed to hearing this tune sung were:

> Western wynde, when wilt thou blow,
> The small raine down can raine.
> Christ, if my love were in my armes
> And I in my bedde again!

Westrup, (Sir) **Jack Allan** (*b* London, 1904; *d* Headley, Hants., 1975). Eng. teacher, scholar, writer, and conductor. Founder-member, Oxford Univ. Opera Club. Ed. Monteverdi's *Orfeo* for perf. while undergraduate (1925) and *L'incoronazione di Poppea* (1927). Also ed. Locke's *Cupid and Death*. Taught classics, Dulwich College, 1928–34. Ass. mus. critic, *Daily Telegraph*, 1934–40, lect. in history of mus., RAM 1938–40. Lect. in mus. King's College, Newcastle upon Tyne, 1941–4, prof. of mus., Birmingham Univ., 1944–6, Oxford Univ. 1947–71. Ed., *Monthly Musical Record*, 1933–45; ed., *Music and Letters* from 1959. Pres. RMA, 1958–63. Cond. Oxford Univ. Orch. 1954–63, Oxford Bach Ch. and Orch. Soc. 1970–1. Contrib. to many mus. dictionaries, ed. of encyclopaedias. Author of books on Purcell, Handel, Liszt, Bach cantatas, and Schubert chamber mus. While at Oxford after 1947 cond. many opera perfs., incl. f. Brit. ps. of *Hans Heiling* (1953), The *Secret* (1956), *L'*enfant et les sortilèges* (1958). One of most practical of scholars. Knighted 1960.

West Side Story. Amer. musical in 2 acts on modernized version of Romeo and Juliet story with mus. by Leonard Bernstein, lib. by Arthur Laurents, and words of songs by Stephen Sondheim. Comp. 1956–7. Prod. Washington and NY 1957, London 1958. In 1960 Bernstein wrote the orch. work *Symphonic Dances from West Side Story*.

Wexford. Town in south-eastern part of Republic of Ireland where autumn opera fest. has been held in highly convivial atmosphere since 1951. Has made speciality of reviving It. operas of *bel canto* sch. or once-popular operas such as *Tiefland*, but has also prod. operas by Britten, Janáček, and Maw. Good record of discovering rising star singers, conductors, and producers. Founded by Dr T. J. *Walsh (art. dir. 1951–66). Other dirs. Brian Dickie 1966–74, Thomson Smillie 1974–8, Adrian Slack 1979–81, Elaine Padmore 1982–94, Luigi Ferrari 1995–2004, David Agler from 2005.

Whale, The. Cantata by *Tavener for mez. and bar., speaker, ch., organ, tape, orch., on text assembled from various sources by composer. Comp. 1965–6 and f.p. 1968 at inaugural concert of London Sinfonietta.

When Lilacs last in the Dooryard Bloom'd. (1) 'Requiem for those we love' for mez., bar., ch., and orch. by *Hindemith to text by Whitman (Ger. trans. by Hindemith). Comp. April 1946 in memory of F. D. Roosevelt and Americans killed in World War II. F.p. NY 1946.

(2) Cantata for sop., bar., ch., and orch. by *Sessions, f.p. at Univ. of Calif., Berkeley, 1971.

Where the Wild Things Are. Fantasy opera in 1 act (9 scenes), Op.20, by Oliver Knussen to lib. by Maurice Sendak and composer, based on children's book by Sendak. Comp. 1979–83. Orig. vers. f.p. Brussels 1980. F. concert p. of rev. vers. London 1982 (both incomplete); f. stage p. (complete) London 1984 (by GTO), Glyndebourne 1985; f. Amer. p. St Paul, Minn., 1985.

Whettam, Graham (Dudley) (*b* Swindon, 1927). Eng. composer. First professional perf. of his work 1950; ob. conc. at Proms 1953. Chairman, Composers' Guild 1971, being specially concerned with matters of copyright. Gregynog Arts Fellowship 1978. Chairman, Composers' Guild of GB 1971 and 1983–6. Pubd. own comps. from 1970s. Several early works withdrawn and disowned. Many works f.p. abroad.

whip (slapstick) (Fr. *fouet*; Ger. *Holzklapper*; It. *frusta*). Instr. in form of wooden clapper, comprising two pieces of wood hinged at base to form handle. The pieces are struck together rapidly. Used by Mahler (7th sym.), Ravel (pf. conc. in G), and Britten (several works).

whistle. (1) As verb. Sound produced by emitting breath through small aperture in pursed lips, pitch being controlled by shaping of the mouth as resonating chamber. Some people can whistle through their teeth. Some professional whistlers have appeared on concert platform. Bing Crosby was a mellifluous whistler. Harty, at rehearsal, did not sing or hum phrases to the orch. to indicate how he wished them to be played but whistled in perfect pitch and tune.

(2) As noun. Term for various primitive wind instr., e.g. tin-whistle.

White, Eric Walter (*b* Bristol, 1905; *d* London, 1985). Eng. writer on music and arts administrator. Worked as translator for League of Nations 1929–33. From 1942 to 1971 worked for CEMA and its successor (1946), the Arts Council. Author of books on Stravinsky and Britten (1948, rev. 1970, 1983) and of *A History of English Opera* (1983).

White, Maude Valérie (*b* Dieppe, 1855; *d* London, 1937). Eng. composer. First woman to win Mendelssohn Schol. 1879. Studied in Vienna with R. Fuchs. Wrote 200 songs to Eng., Fr., and Ger. texts, also ballet *The Enchanted Heart* (1912).

White [Whyte], **Robert** (*b c.*1538; *d* Westminster, 1574). Eng. composer and organist. Possibly pupil of *Tye, since the Ellen Tye he married was the older composer's daughter. Mus.B., Cambridge, 1560. Choirmaster, Ely Cath., 1562–6. Org., Chester Cath. 1567 then, from 1569, org. and choirmaster, Westminster Abbey. Died of plague, as did wife and 3 children. One of finest Eng. composers of his time. Wrote mainly church mus., making brilliant use of imitation. Works incl. *Magnificat*, 2 *Lamentations*, 20 motets, and 4 anthems.

White, (Sir) **Willard** (*b* St Catherine, Jamaica, 1946). West Indian bass-baritone. Won schol. to Juilliard Sch. 1968 and took part in *Callas masterclasses. Début Washington DC 1974 (Trulove in *The Rake's Progress*). Débuts: NY City Opera 1974; Eur. (Cardiff, WNO) 1974; ENO 1976; Glyndebourne 1978; CG 1978; Salzburg Fest. 1990. Sang Porgy in Gershwin's opera at Glyndebourne 1986, and Wotan in Scottish Opera's *Das Rheingold* (1989) and *Die Walküre* (1991). Concert career incl. bass parts in Elgar's *Dream of Gerontius* and Shostakovich's 13th Sym. CBE 1995. Knighted 2004.

Whitehead, Gillian (*b* Whangarei, NZ, 1941). NZ composer. Lived in Brit. and Eur. 1967–81. Northern Arts comp.-in-residence, Newcastle upon Tyne, 1978–81. Lect. in comp., NSW Cons. of Mus., Sydney, from 1982. Works incl. chamber operas *Tristan and Iseult* (1977–8), *The Tinker's Curse* (1979), *Eleanor of Aquitaine* (1982), *The King of the Other Country* (1984), *The Pirate Moon* (1986), *Bride of Fortune* (1988), *The Art of Pizza* (1995), *Outrageous Fortune* (1998); *Missa Brevis* (1963); *Requiem*, sop., org. (1981); *Voices of Tane*, pf. (1976); *Bright Forms Return*, mez., str. qt. (1980); *Tongues, Swords, Keys*, SATB (2 of each), 4 perc. (1985); *4 Pieces*, pf. (1988); *Resurgences*, orch. (1989); *Moon, Tides and Shoreline*, str. qt. (1990); *NGA Haerenga*, 2 sop., 2 mez., male narr., perc. (2000); . . . *The Improbable Ordered Dance* . . . , orch. (2000).

Whiteman, Paul (*b* Denver, 1890; *d* Doylestown, Penn., 1967). Amer. jazz band director, known as 'king of jazz'. Violist in Denver SO from 1912 and S. Francisco SO 1917–18. Formed Paul Whiteman Orch. 1920, larger than usual jazz band, which bridged gap between jazz and other forms of mus. by what he called 'symphonic jazz'. Orch. contained several great jazz musicians, e.g. Bix Beiderbecke (trumpet), Joe Venuti (vn.), Tommy Dorsey (tb.), Eddie Lang (guitar). Commissioned Gershwin's *Rhapsody in Blue*, giving f.p. in NY on 12 Feb. 1924. Toured Eur. 1926. One of Paul Whiteman Rhythm Boys vocal group was Bing *Crosby. Most Whiteman orchestrations were by *Grofé.

White Peacock, The. Work by *Griffes, being orch. version (1919) of No.1 of his 4 *Roman Sketches*, Op.7, for pf. after poems of William Sharp, comp. 1915–16.

Whittaker, W(illiam) **G**(illies) (*b* Newcastle upon Tyne, 1876; *d* Orkney Isles, 1944). Eng. composer,

conductor, organist, and scholar. Studied Armstrong College, Newcastle upon Tyne, joining its staff as, successively, instructor, lect., and reader in mus. Devoted most of his life to promoting mus. activities, particularly choral singing, in NE of Eng. Specialist in cantatas of J. S. Bach (his 2-vol. book on them was pubd. posthumously, 1959). Championed mus. of his friends Holst and Vaughan Williams, also of Debussy, Satie, and Poulenc. Founder and cond., Newcastle Bach Ch. 1915. Cond. Newcastle and Gateshead Choral Union 1919–29. With Newcastle Bach Ch., gave first complete perf. for 3 centuries of Byrd's *Great Service*, 1924 (Newcastle Cath. and St Margaret's, Westminster). First Gardiner Prof. of Mus., Glasgow Univ., 1929–41; Prin., Scottish Nat. Acad. of Mus. (now RSAMD) 1929–38, 1939–41. ENSA mus. adviser to Scottish Command, 1942–4. In 1930 rediscovered at Uppsala Univ., Sweden, sonatas of Eng. composer, William *Young (*d* 1671) and gave their f.p. in Brit.

Whittaker's work as cond. and scholar overshadowed his creative work, but perf. of several of his works in his centenary year revealed an orig. and compelling composer, ahead of his time, whose mus. deserves further and widespread exploration. In addition, his many arrs. of North Country folk-songs, pipe-tunes, and ballads, and of works by Bach, Purcell, Gluck, etc., have their own high value. Prin. works:

BALLET: *The Boy who didn't like fairies*, fl., str., pf., perc.

ORCH.: Prelude, *The Coephori of Aeschylus* (1921); 3 *Mood Pictures* (orig. for pf.) (1923); pf. conc., with str.

CHORUS & ORCH.: *A Lyke-Wake Dirge* (1924); *The Coelestial Sphere* (1923); *A Festal Psalm* (1932); Choruses (women's) from *The Coephori*; *Southward Bound*; *Ode*, male ch.

VOICE & ORCH.: *To the Beloved*, sop.

CHORAL: Psalm 139 (1925); *Candle Gate* (1929); *The Concertina* (1929); *I said in the noontide of my days* (1930); *Chorus of Spirits from Prometheus* (1931); *Where neither moth nor rust* (1931); *4 Poems by Bridges*; *The wind and the rain*; *Jocelyn*; *The Ship of Rio*; and other works still in MS.

CHAMBER MUSIC: *Among the Northumbrian Hills*, pf., str. qt. (1921); *Phantasie*, qt. (1929); *Phantasie*, qt., pf., str. (1929); *Phantasie*, str. trio (1930); wind quintet (1930); va. suite (1932); vn. sonatina (1928); fl. suite (1925); *Suite of North Country Folk-Tunes*, pf., str. qt.; *Swedish Impressions*, sextet, pf., wind.

PIANO: *A Day in the Country* (1916); 3 *Mood Pictures* (1918, orch. 1923); 4 *Short Pieces* (1924); 5 *Short Sketches* (1926); *A Short Suite* (1930); *By Running Water*.

SONGS: *The Ship of Rio* (1919); *Dream Song* (1919); 4 *Songs of the Northern Roads* (1919); 2 *Song Carols* (1921); *Bog Love* (1924); *Stay in Town* (1924); 2 *Lyrics from the Chinese* (1925); *Michael's Song* (1926); *Gay Robin is seen no more* (1936).

Whittall, Arnold (Morgan) (*b* Shrewsbury, 1935). Eng. musicologist. Univ. posts at Nottingham 1964–9, Cardiff 1969–75; reader at King's Coll., London, from 1975, prof. of mus. theory

1982–96. Expert in analysis of works by Schoenberg, Britten, Webern, and other 20th cent. composers. Author of study of Britten and Tippett and *Musical Composition in the Twentieth Century* (2000).

Whitworth-Jones, Anthony (*b* Gerrards Cross, 1945). Eng. opera administrator. Admin. dir., London Sinfonietta 1972–81. Administrator, GTO 1981–8. Gen. dir. Glyndebourne Fest. Opera 1989–98, Dallas Opera 2000–2, Porto from 2002, Garsington Opera from 2006.

whole consort. See *consort*.

whole-note. The semibreve.

whole-tone. Interval of 2 semitones, e.g. from C up to adjacent D. *whole-tone scale* progresses entirely in whole-tones instead of partly in whole-tones and partly in semitones as in major and minor scales and modes. The scale is obtained by taking every other note of the 12-semitone chromatic (or equal-tempered) scale, thus only 2 whole-tone scales are possible, one beginning on C, the other on C♯ (but since there is no keynote each scale can begin on any note). Used by Debussy, Vaughan Williams, Glinka, and others for chords and short passages.

Whyte, Ian (*b* Dunfermline, 1901; *d* Glasgow, 1960). Scottish conductor and composer. Mus. dir., BBC (Scotland) 1931–46. Formed BBC Scottish Orch. 1935, conducting it after 1945 in adventurous programmes. Wrote operas, 2 syms., sym.-poems *Edinburgh* and *Tam o'Shanter*, ballet *Donald of the Burthens*, concs. (pf., vn., va.), choral works, and songs. OBE 1952.

Whythorne [Whithorne], **Thomas** (*b* Ilminster, 1528; *d* London, 1596). Eng. composer. Employed by Duchess of Northumberland. Left Eng. on accession of Queen Mary. Travelled in It. Returned to Eng. 1555 as mus. tutor to various aristocratic households. Pubd. secular songs in 3, 4, and 5 parts, 1571, also duos, with option for vv. or instrs., and works for viols. Wrote autobiography, rediscovered 1955 and pubd. 1961.

Wicks, (Edward) **Allan** (*b* Harden, Yorks., 1923). Eng. organist and conductor. Sub-org. York Minster, 1947–54; org. and choirmaster Manchester Cath. 1954–61, Canterbury Cath. 1961–88. One of first brilliant Eng. players of Messiaen's org. mus. CBE 1988.

Widdop, Walter (*b* Norland, Halifax, 1892; *d* London, 1949). Eng. tenor. Opera début BNOC (Leeds) 1923 (Radames in *Aida*). CG 1924, 1928–33, 1935, 1937–8. Fine oratorio singer, but better known for Wagner roles such as Siegmund and Lohengrin. Sang Tristan to *Leider's and *Flagstad's Isolde. Sang in Barcelona (1927), Amsterdam, and Ger. Sang title-role in f. Eng. p. of *Oedipus Rex* (1936, cond. Ansermet).

Widerspenstigen Zähmung, Der (Goetz). See *Taming of the Shrew, The*.

Widor, Charles-Marie (Jean Albert) (*b* Lyons, 1844; *d* Paris, 1937). Fr. organist and composer. Org., St Sulpice, Paris 1870–1933. Succeeded Franck as prof. of org., Paris Cons., 1890, prof. of comp. from 1896. Mus. critic of *L'Estafette* for many years. Famous as improviser. Ed. complete org. works of Bach (with *Schweitzer). Wrote treatise on modern orchestration, 1904. Comp. 5 operas; ballet; 2 syms. with org.; sym.-poems; 2 pf. concs.; vc. conc.; 10 org. syms.; shorter org. pieces; choral works; and chamber music.

Wieck, (Johann Gottlob) **Friedrich** (*b* Pretzsch, nr. Torgau, 1785; *d* Loschwitz, nr. Dresden, 1873). Ger. music teacher. Settled in Leipzig where he gave lessons, est. a piano factory, and founded a lending library. Moved to Dresden 1844, where he became one of most famous of piano teachers. Pupils inc. *Bülow, Robert *Schumann, and his daughter (by his first wife) Clara, who married Schumann. Wrote book *Klavier und Gesang* (1853, rev. 1878).

Wiegenlied (Ger.). Cradle song. Lullaby or *berceuse*. Title given to songs by Wolf, R. Strauss, and many others.

Wieniawski, Henryk (*b* Lublin, 1835; *d* Moscow, 1880). Polish violinist and composer. Entered Paris Cons. at age 8. Gave first concert 1848, toured Poland and Russia, returned to Cons. Appointed solo violinist to Tsar, 1860; taught at St Petersburg Cons. 1862–9. Toured USA with A. Rubinstein 1872. Prof. of vn., Brussels Cons. 1875–7. Wrote 2 vn. concs., mazurkas, études, caprices, and other pieces. Regarded by many good judges as one of the greatest violinists after Paganini.

Wigglesworth, Mark (*b* Sussex, 1964). Eng. conductor. Début 1989 (Dutch Radio PO). Opera début London (Opera Factory) 1990 (*Don Giovanni*). Mus. dir. Opera Factory from 1991. Scottish Opera 1991 (*Le nozze di Figaro*). Début Berlin PO 1994, Los Angeles PO 1885. Cond., BBC Nat. Orch. of Wales 1996–9. NY Met début 2006 (*Figaro*). Mus. dir. Th. de la Monnaie, Brussels, from 2008.

Wigmore Hall. London concert hall in Wigmore Street, opened 1901 as Bechstein Hall (architect, Collcutt). Capacity 543. Used often for recitals by artists making their débuts or London débuts.

Wihan, Hanuš (*b* Politz, 1855; *d* Prague, 1920). Bohem. cellist. Played in several Eur. orchs. Prin. cellist Munich court orch. from 1880 and cellist in King Ludwig's qt., which played at Wagner's Bayreuth home. Prof. of vc., Prague Cons. 1888–91, 1919–20. Est. Bohemian Str. Qt. 1892, becoming its cellist 1897–1914. Gave f.p. of R. Strauss's vc. sonata 1883 and was dedicatee of Dvořák's vc. conc. 1895, although he did not give the first performance, when the soloist was Leo Stern.

Wilbraham, John (*b* Bournemouth, 1944; *d* Wells, 1998). Eng. trumpeter. Trumpeter in New Philharmonia Orch. 1966–8, RPO 1968–72, BBC SO 1972–90. Brilliant player of Baroque mus.

Wilby, Philip (*b* Pontefract, 1949). Eng. composer and violinist. Violinist in Nat. Youth Orch. of GB. Violinist in CG orch. and CBSO. Senior lect. Leeds Univ. 1972–2004. Has reconstructed several Mozart fragments. Comps. incl. syms.; perc. conc. (1993); *Trinity Service*, ch., org. (1992); *Laudibus in Sanctus*, wind orch. (1993); '... *The Night and All the Stars*', hn. quintet (1985); *Capricorn Suite*, 4 tb. (1987); works for kbd.

Wilbye, John (*b* Diss, 1574; *d* Colchester, 1638). Eng. composer. Took post at Hengrave Hall, near Bury St Edmunds, 1593, remaining there for rest of his life and becoming wealthy landowner after 1613. Wrote some sacred motets but chiefly known as among greatest of Eng. madrigal sch. Absorbed It. influence of Marenzio, and incorporated solo-song features into his madrigals similar to lute air. Pubd. 2 books of madrigals, 1598 and 1609. Seems to have written nothing after 1614. Among best-known of his madrigals are: *Adieu, sweet Amaryllis*; *All Pleasure is of this Condition*; *Down in a Valley*; *Draw on, Sweet Night*; *Flora gave me Fairest Flowers*; *Lady, your Words do Spite Me*; *Softly, softly*; *Stay, Corydon*; *Sweet Honey-Sucking Bees*; *Unkind, O Stay thy Flying*; *Weep, Weep mine Eyes*.

Wild, Earl (*b* Pittsburgh, Penn., 1915). Amer. pianist. Pianist with KDKA Radio, Pittsburgh, 1930–5. Pianist in NBC SO under Toscanini 1937–44. NY recital début 1944. On mus. staff ABC TV in NY, 1944–68. Renowned Liszt player. London début 1973. Taught at Penn. State Univ. 1965–8. Juilliard Sch. 1977–87, Manhattan Sch. of Mus. 1982–4, Ohio State Univ. 1986–98. Some comps., incl. ballet and oratorio.

Wilde, David (Clark) (*b* Stretford, Lancs., 1935). Eng. pianist and conductor. BBC staff accompanist, Glasgow, 1959–62. Won Liszt–Bartók comp., Budapest 1961. Prof. of pf., RAM 1965–7, RMCM 1967–9. Prof. of pf. Hanover Mus. Acad. 1981–2000; Edinburgh Univ. from 2001. Recitals throughout Europe and USA. Liszt and Bartók specialist. Some comps, incl. *The Cellist of Sarajevo* (1992) and opera *London under Siege* (1998).

Wildschütz, Der, oder Die Stimme der Natur (The Poacher or The Voice of Nature). Opera in 3 acts by Lortzing to his own lib. after Kotzebue's comedy *Der Rehbock*. Comp. 1842. Prod. Leipzig 1842, Brooklyn 1856, London 1895.

Wilhelmj, August (*b* Usingen, 1845; *d* London, 1908). Ger. violinist and teacher. Début 1854. Leipzig Cons. 1861–4 with Ferdinand *David. World tour 1878–82. Led orch. at first Bayreuth Fest. 1876 and for Wagner's concerts in London 1877. Taught at Blasewitz, Dresden, 1886–94. works for vn. and orch. Wrote cadenzas for classical vn. concs. Arr. Bach melody as *Air on the G string* and Wagner's *Träume* for vn. and small orch.

Wilhem [Bocquillon], **Guillaume-Louis** (*b* Paris, 1781; *d* Paris, 1842). Fr. teacher. Organized teaching of sight-singing in Paris schs. from 1835 and instituted male-v. choirs throughout Fr. Wrote textbooks on *fixed-doh. System was later adapted by *Hullah for Eng. usage.

Wilkinson [Wylkynson], **Robert** (*b* c.1450; *d* ?Eton, 1515 or later). Eng. composer. Some church mus. survives in MS at Eton College Library, 2 *Salve Regina* settings, a 13-part creed, and *O Virgo prudentissima*.

Wilkomirska, Wanda (*b* Warsaw, 1929). Polish violinist. Début at age 7. Won int. comp. 1946. Soloist after 1946 with leading orchs., making speciality of modern concs., esp. those by Szymanowski and Britten. Has toured internationally since 1955. Salzburg Fest. début 1962. Gave f.p. of Penderecki's *Capriccio*, 1967. Settled in West, 1983. On staff Sydney Cons. of Mus. from 1999, Melbourne Nat. Acad. of Mus. from 2001.

Willaert, Adriaan (*b* Bruges or Roulaers, c.1490; *d* Venice, 1562). Flemish composer. Went to Rome 1515 and was then in service of cardinal at Ferrara until 1520, having visited Hungary 1517–19 with his employer. Appointed choirmaster, St Mark's, Venice, 1527. Founded singing sch. there and established the foundations of the 'Venetian School' of which he was a major figure. One of first madrigal composers. Wrote much church mus., some of it for double ch. (because of 2 orgs. and 2 choirs at St Mark's), his motets being his finest works.

Willcocks, (Sir) **David** (Valentine) (*b* Newquay, 1919). Eng. conductor, organist, composer, and teacher. Org., Salisbury Cath., 1947–50, Worcester Cath. 1950–7. Cond. City of Birmingham Ch. 1950–7, Bradford Festival Choral Soc. 1955–74. Dir. of mus., King's College, Cambridge, 1957–73, univ. org., 1958–74, cond. Cambridge Univ. Mus. Soc. 1958–73, lect. Cambridge Univ. 1957–74. Mus. dir., Bach Ch. 1960–96. Cond. f.p. in Italy of Britten's *War Requiem*, Milan 1963. Dir., RCM 1974–84. Expert cond. of Eng. mus. of which he has made many recordings. Comp. church mus., arr. carols. CBE 1971. Knighted 1977.

Willi, Herbert (*b* Vorarlberg, 1956). Austrian composer. Won Austrian state schol. 1985. Comp.-in-res. Salzburg Fest. 1992. Works incl. *Stück für Flöte* (1985–6); *Für 16* (Little Chamber Concerto) (1990); *Räume*, orch. (1991); *Concerto for Orchestra* (1992–3); *Schlafes Bruder*, opera (1994–5); *Begegnung* (*Meeting*), orch. (1997–8); tpt. conc. (2002); conc. (... *geraume Zeit*), fl., ob., orch. (2003); cl. conc. (2006).

Williams, Grace (Mary) (*b* Barry, S. Wales, 1906; *d* Barry, 1977). Welsh composer. Taught in London and after 1946 worked on BBC educational programmes in Wales. Works incl. *Fantasia on Welsh Nursery Tunes, Sea Sketches*, str. (1944); vn. conc. (1950); *Penillion*, orch. (1955); tpt. conc.; opera *The Parlour* (1961); 2 syms.; *Fairest of Stars*, sop., orch., etc.

Williams, John (*b* Melbourne, Victoria, 1941). Australian guitarist. Moved to London 1952. Début, London 1958. Duo with Julian *Bream. Founder of ens. 'Sky' which plays jazz and pop in addition to works in classical style. Concs. written for him. Prof. of gui., RCM, 1960–73. OBE 1980.

Williams, John (Towner) (*b* NY, 1932). Amer. composer. As boy, played pf., tb., tpt., and cl. Moved to Los Angeles 1948. Cond. Boston Pops Orch. 1980–93. Wrote mus. for film and TV. Pianist, arranger, and cond. for Columbia Records. In films, assoc. with the director Steven Spielberg. Scores incl. *The Towering Inferno* (1974); *Jaws* (1975); *Close Encounters of the Third Kind* (1977); *Star Wars* (1977); *Superman* (1978); *The Empire Strikes Back* (1980); *Raiders of the Lost Ark* (1982); *E.T.* (1982); *Return of the Jedi* (1983); *Home Alone* (1990); *Schindler's List* (1993); *Saving Private Ryan* (1998); *Angela's Ashes* (1999); *Harry Potter and the Chamber of Secrets* (2002); *Harry Potter and the Prisoner of Azkaban* (2004); *War of the Worlds* (2005); *Memoirs of a Geisha* (2005). Also comp. 2 syms., vn. conc., fl. conc., *Essay*, str., *Olympic Fanfare* (1984), cl. conc. (1991), vc. conc. (1994), bn. conc. (1995), tpt. conc. (1996), *Seven for Luck*, song-cycle, sop., orch. (1998).

Williams, Peter (Fredric) (*b* Wolverhampton, 1937). Eng. musicologist and organist. His research on 18th- and 19th-cent. Eng. org. mus. was supervised by T. *Dart. Lect. in mus. Edinburgh Univ. 1962–72, reader 1972–82, prof. 1982–5. Prof. of mus. and univ. org., Duke Univ., Durham, N. Car., from 1985. Author of *New History of the Organ* (1980), *The Organ Music of J. S. Bach*, 3 vols. (1980–4), and *The Organ in Western Culture, 750–1250* (1993), besides many papers on org. mus. and technique.

Williams, Ralph Vaughan. See *Vaughan Williams, Ralph*.

Williamson, Malcolm (Benjamin Graham Christopher) (*b* Sydney, NSW, 1931; *d* Cambridge, 2003). Australian composer, pianist, organist, and conductor. Entered Sydney Cons. at 11 to study pf., hn., and comp. (with Eugène Goossens). London 1953 to study with *Lutyens and Erwin *Stein. Played org. at church and pf. in nightclub to support himself. Lecturer in mus., Central Sch. of Speech and Drama, London, 1961–2. Bax Memorial Prize 1963. Org. work commissioned for opening of Coventry Cath., 1962. Perf. as soloist in his own org. and pf. concs. Emulated Britten in writing works for children. Comp.-in-residence, Westminster Choir Coll., Princeton, 1970–1. Visiting Prof. Strathclyde Univ. 1983–6. His style, influenced by Messiaen, Britten, jazz, and popular mus., is individualistic, essentially melodic, versatile in approach, and technically accomplished. Succeeded *Bliss as Master of the Queen's Music, 1975. CBE 1976. Prin. works:

OPERAS: *Our Man in Havana* (1962–3); *The English Eccentrics* (1963–4); *The *Happy Prince* (1964–5); *Julius Caesar Jones* (1965); *The *Violins of Saint-Jacques* (1966); *Dunstan and the Devil* (1967); *The *Growing Castle* (1968); *Lucky-Peter's Journey* (1969); *Genesis* (1971); *The Red Sea* (1971–2); *The Death of Cuchulain* (1972); *The Musicians of Bremen* (1971–2); *The Winter Star* (1972).

BALLETS: *The Display* (1963–4); *Sun into Darkness* (1965–6); *BigfellaTootsSquoodge and Nora* (1967); *Perisynthyon* (1974); *Heritage* (1985); *Have Steps Will Travel* (3rd pf. conc.) (1988).

ORCH.: syms., No.1 (*Elevamini*) (1956–7), No.2 (*Pilgrim på havet*) (1968), No.3 (*The Icy Mirror*), sop., mez., 2 bar., ch., orch. (1972); No.4 (1977), No.5 (*Aquerò*) (1979–80); No.6 (1982); No.7, str. (1984); *Santiago de Espada*, ov. (1957); *Sinfonia Concertante*, 3 tpt., pf., str. (1958–62); Suite, *Our Man in Havana* (1963); suite, *The Display* (1964); *Sinfonietta* (1965–7); *Concerto Grosso* (1964–5); *Symphonic Variations* (1965); *Epitaphs for Edith Sitwell*, str. (also org.) (1966); *A Word from Our Founder* (1969); *2 Pieces* for str. from *The Bridge That Van Gogh Painted* (1975); *The Bridge That Van Gogh Painted*, str. (1975, orig. pf.); suite, *The House of Windsor* (1977); *Fiesta* (1978); *Ochre* (1978, also for org. and str.); *Fanfarade* (1979); *Ode for Queen Elizabeth*, str. (1980); *In Thanksgiving—Sir Bernard Heinze* (1982); *Cortège for a Warrior* (1984); *Lento for Strings* (1985); *Bicentennial Anthem* (1988).

CONCERTOS: pf., No.1 (1957–8), No.2, with str. (1960), No.3 (1962), No.4 (1993–4); org. (1961); vn. (1964–5); 2 pf., str. (1972); hp., str. (*Au Tombeau du Martyr Juif Inconnu*) (1973–6); *Lament* (in memory of Lord Mountbatten) (1979–80).

SOLO VOICE & ORCH.: *Hasselbacher's Scena* (*Our Man in Havana*), bass (1963); *6 English Lyrics*, low v., str. or pf. (or ch. and pf.) (1966); *Hammarskjöld Portrait*, sop., str. (1974); *Les Olympiques*, mez., str. (1976); *Tribute to a Hero*, bar., orch. (or pf.) (1981); *Next Year in Jerusalem*, sop., orch. (1985).

CHORUS & ORCH.: Concert Suite, *Our Man in Havana*, sop., ten., bass, ch., orch. (1963); *The Brilliant and the Dark*, women's ch., orch. (1966); Sym. No.3 (*The Icy Mirror*), sop., mez., 2 bar., ch., orch. (1972); *Ode to Music*, ch., echo ch., orch. (or pf.) (1972–3); *Jubilee Hymn*, ch., orch. (or pf.) (1977); *Mass of Christ the King*, 2 sop., ten., bar., ch., echo ch., orch. (1975–8); *Songs for a Royal Baby*, vocal qt. (SATB) or ch., str. (1979); *A Pilgrim Liturgy*, mez., bar., ch., orch. (1984); *The True Endeavour*, narr., ch., orch. (1988); *The Dawn is at Hand*, sop., alt., ten., bar., ch., orch. (1989).

CHORUS & ORGAN OR PIANO: *Adoremus*, Christmas cantata, alto, ten., ch., org. (1959); *Dawn Carol* (1960); *Ascendit Deus* (1961); *Tu es Petrus*, spkr., ch., org. (1961); *Agnus Dei*, sop., ch., org. (1961); *Dignus est Agnus*, sop., ch., org. (1961); *Procession of Psalms*, ch., org. or pf. (1961); *Easter Carol* (1962); *Jesu, Lover of My Soul*, solo qt., double ch., org. (1962); *12 New Hymn Tunes* (1962); *Harvest Thanksgiving*, ch., org. (1962); *Wrestling Jacob*, sop., ch., org. (1962); *The Morning of the Day of Days*, sop., ten., ch., org. (1962); *Te Deum*, vv., pf. or org. (1963); *An Australian Carol*, ch., org. (1963); *Epiphany Carol* (1963); *6 Christmas Songs for the Young*, vv., pf., with opt. perc. (1963); *Mass of St Andrew*, vv., pf. or org. (1964); *6 Evening Hymns*, vv., pf., or org. (1964); *A Psalm of Praise* (Psalm 148), vv., org.

(1965); *I will lift up mine eyes* (Psalm 121), ch., echo ch., org. (1970); *Cantate Domino* (Psalm 98), ch., org. (1970); *In Place of Belief*, ch., pf. duet (1970); *Te Deum*, ch., org., opt. brass (1970–1); *6 Wesley Songs for the Young*, vv., pf. (1971); *O Jerusalem, The King of Love, Who is the King of Glory*, and *Together in Unity*, ch., congregation, org. (1972); *Canticle of Fire*, ch., org. (1973); *The World at the Manger*, sop., bar., ch., org. or pf. duet (1973); *Communion Hallelujahs*, children's ch., male ch., org. (1974–5); *16 Hymns and Processionals*, vv., pf. or org. (1975); *This is My Father's World*, ch., org. (1975); *Love Chorales*, vv., pf. or org. or gui. (1975); *Dove Chorales*, vv., pf. or org. (1975); *Above Chorales*, vv., pf. or org. (1975); *Mass of St James*, vv., pf. or org. (1975); *20 Psalms of the Elements*, ch., congregation, org. (1975); *This Christmas Night*, ch., pf. (1977); *Kerygma*, ch., org. (1979); *Little Mass of St Bernadette*, unbroken vv., org. or instr. (1980); *Mass of St Margaret of Scotland*, congregation, opt. ch., org. (1977–80); *Mass of the People of God*, vv., org. (1980–1); *Now is the Singing Day*, bar., mez., ch., str., pf. (4 hands), perc. (1981); *Our Church Lives*, ch., org. (1989); *Mass of St Etheldreda (on Themes of Lennox Berkeley)*, ch., org. (1990).

UNACC. CHORUS: *2 Motets* (1954); *Dawn Carol* (1960); *Symphony for Voices*, cont., ch. (1960–2); *Planctus*, male vv. (1962); *English Eccentrics*, choral suite (1964); *A Young Girl* (1964); *A Canon for Stravinsky* (1967); *Sonnet* (1969); *Love, the Sentinel* (1972); *The Musicians of Bremen*, 2 counterten., ten., 2 bar., bass (1971–2); *3 Choric Hymns* (No.2, 1980, Nos. 1 and 3, 1947); *Galilee* (1987); *Easter in St Mary's Church* (1987); *Requiem for a Tribe Brother* (1992).

VOICE(S) & INSTR(S).: *A Vision of Beasts and Gods*, high v., pf. (1958); *Celebration of Divine Love*, high v., pf. (1963); *3 Shakespeare Songs*, high v., gui. or pf. (1964); *A Christmas Carol*, low v., pf. (1964); *North Country Songs*, low v., orch. or pf., opt. ch. (1965); *6 English Lyrics*, low v., pf. or str. or for ch., pf. (1966); *From a Child's Garden* (R. L. Stevenson), song-cycle, high v., pf. (1967–8); *The Death of Cuchulain* (Yeats), 5 male vv., perc. (1968–71); *Vocalise in G minor*, mez., pf. (1973); *Pietà*, sop., ob., bn., pf. (1973); *White Dawns*, low v., pf. (1985); *Vocalise in G*, mez., pf. (1985); *The Mower to the Glowworms*, low v., pf. (1986); *The White Island*, low v., pf. (1986); *Day that I have Loved*, low v., pf. (1986); *The Feast of Eurydice*, song-cycle, female v., fl., perc., pf. (1986).

CHAMBER MUSIC: str. qts.: No.1 (*Winterset*) (1947–8), No.2 (1954), No.3 (1993); incid. mus. to *The Merry Wives of Windsor*, chamber ens. (1964); *Variations*, vc., pf. (1964); conc., wind quintet, 2 pf. (8 hands) (1964–5); *Serenade*, fl., pf., vn., va., vc. (1967); *Pas de Quatre*, fl., ob., cl., bn., pf. (1967); pf. quintet (1968); *Partita on Themes of Walton*, va. (1972); pf. trio (1975–6); *Day that I have loved*, hp. (1993–4).

BRASS: *Canberra Fanfare*, brass, perc. (1973); *Adelaide Fanfare*, brass, org. (1973); *Konstanz Fanfare*, brass, perc., org. (1980); *Richmond Fanfare*, brass, perc., org. (1980); *Fontainebleau Fanfare*, brass, perc., org. (1981); *Concertino for Charles*, sax., band (1987); *Fanfare of Homage*, military band (1988); *Ceremony for Oodgeroo*, brass quintet (1988); *Fanfares and Chorales*, brass quintet (1991).

PIANO(S): sonatas, No.1 (1955–6), No.2 (1957, rev. 1970–1), No.3 (fortepiano) (1958), No.4 (1963); *Travel Diaries* (1960–1); *5 Preludes* (1966); sonata for 2 pf. (1967); *Haifa Watercolours* (1974); *The Bridge That Van Gogh Painted and the French Camargue* (1975); *Ritual of Admiration* (1976); *Himna Titu* (1984); *Springtime on the River Moskva* (1987).

ORGAN: *Fons Amoris* (1955–6); *Résurgence du Feu (Pâques 1959)* (1959); sym. (1960); *Vision of Christ Phoenix* (1961, rev. 1978); *Elegy—J.F.K.* (1964); *Epitaphs for Edith Sitwell* (1966, or str.); *Peace Pieces (2 Books)* (1970–1); *Little Carols of the Saints* (1971–2); *Mass of a Medieval Saint* (1973); *Fantasy on 'This is My Father's World'* (1975); *Fantasy on 'O Paradise!'* (1976); *The Lion of Suffolk (for Benjamin Britten)* (1977); *Offertoire* from *Mass of the People of God* (1980–1).

FILM & TV SCORES: *The Timber Getters* (1948); *Arid Lands* (1960); *The Brides of Dracula* (1960); *North Sea Strike* (1964); *September Spring* (1964); *Rio Tinto Zinc* (1965); *Crescendo* (1969); *The Horror of Frankenstein* (1969); *Churchill's People* (TV) (1974–5); *The House of Windsor* (TV) (1977); *Watership Down* (1978); *The Masks of Death* (1984).

William Tell (Rossini). See *Guillaume Tell*.

Willis, Henry (*b* London, 1821; *d* London, 1901). Eng. organ builder. Invented special manual and pedal couplers. Founded own business, London 1848. Built or renewed many cath. orgs. incl. those in St Paul's Cath., London (1872), and Gloucester Cath. (1874); also those in St George's Hall, Liverpool (1854), and the Royal Albert Hall, London (1871).

Wilson, Catherine (*b* Glasgow, 1936). Scottish soprano. Opera début as mez. London (SW) 1960 (Angelina in *La Cenerentola*). Glyndebourne début 1960; WNO 1960; Wexford 1976. Created Jenny in *The *Mines of Sulphur*, SW 1965 and title-role in Musgrave's *Mary, Queen of Scots*, Scottish Opera 1977. Taught at RNCM 1980–91.

Wilson, John (*b* Faversham, Kent, 1595; *d* Westminster, 1674). Eng. composer, singer, lutenist, and viol-player. Set some of Shakespeare's songs, and is thought to be the 'Jack Wilson' who acted and sang in Shakespeare's co. Court musician to Charles I 1635; prof. of mus., Oxford Univ., 1656–61; court musician to Charles II 1660; Gentleman of Chapel Royal 1662. Wrote catches, church mus., and fantasies for lute.

Wilson, Robert (*b* Waco, Texas, 1941). Amer. director, playwright, and designer. Collab. and designer of Glass's *Einstein on the Beach (Avignon 1974, NY Met 1976). Designed Charpentier's *Médée* (Lyons 1984) and sections of Glass's *The Civil WarS*, which he wrote with Glass and Bryars (1984, 1985, 1987, Rome and NY). Also designed *Salome* (La Scala 1987). Prod. *Die Zauberflöte* (Paris Bastille 1991) and *Madama Butterfly* (Paris Bastille 1993). Work is often highly controversial and on an epic scale.

Wilson, (Sir) (James) **Steuart** (*b* Bristol, 1889; *d* Petersfield, 1966). Eng. tenor and administrator.

Came into prominence singing Tamino in *Die Zauberflöte*, Cambridge 1910, and Vaughan Williams's *On Wenlock Edge* 1911. Lung damaged in 1914–18 war but resumed career. Involved in Glastonbury Fest. opera ventures. Founder-member of English Singers (specialists in Elizabethan and folk-songs), sang with BNOC, and famous as Evangelist in Bach's *St Matthew Passion* and as Elgar's Gerontius. Taught at Curtis Inst. 1939–42; overseas mus. dir. BBC 1942–5, mus. dir., Arts Council, 1945–8; head of mus., BBC 1948–9; deputy gen. administrator, CG 1949–55. Prin., Birmingham Sch. of Mus., 1957–60. With A. H. Fox Strangways, made singing trans. of Schubert *Lieder*. Knighted 1948.

Wilson, Thomas (Brendan) (*b* Trinidad, Colorado, 1927; *d* Glasgow, 2001). Scottish composer. Lect., Glasgow Univ. 1957–72, Reader from 1972, Prof. from 1977. CBE 1990. Works incl.:

OPERAS: *The Charcoal Burners* (1968); **Confessions of a Justified Sinner* (1974).

BALLET: *Embers of Glencoe* (1973).

ORCH.: syms.: No.1 (1956), No.2 (1965), No.3 (1979), No.4 (*Passeleth Tapestry*) (1988), No. 5 (1998); *Toccata* (1959); *Variations* (1960); *Pas de Quoi*, str. (1964); *Touchstone, a Portrait* (1967); *Concerto for Orchestra* (1967); *Threnody* (1970); *Ritornelli*, str. (1972); *Mosaics*, chamber orch. (1981); pf. conc. (1985); *Chamber Conc.* (1986); *St Kentigern Suite*, 11 solo str. (1986); va. conc. (1987); *Chamber Sym.* (1990); *Carillon* (1990); vn. conc. (1993); gui. conc. (1996).

CHORAL: *Missa pro mundo conturbato*, ch., perc., hp., str. (1970); *Sequentiae passionis*, ch., orch., tape (1971); *Te Deum*, ch., orch. (1971); *Songs of Hope and Expectation*, ch., pf., elec. org., hpd. (1977); *Amor Christi*, chamber ch., perc., hp., str. (1989); *Cantigas para Semana Santa*, chamber ch. (1992); *Confitemini domino*, ch., brass quintet, org. (1993).

CHAMBER MUSIC: str. qts. No.3 (1958), No.4 (1978); vn. sonata (1961); cl. sonatina (1962); *Fantasia*, vc. (1964); *Concerto da camera* (1965); pf. trio (1966); *Sinfonia*, 7 instr. (1968); *Soliloquy*, gui. (1969); *3 Pieces*, gui. (1971); vc. sonata (1971); *Canti notturni*, fl., cl., vn., va., vc., pf. (1972); *Coplas del Ruisenor*, gui. (1972); *Complementi*, cl., vn., vc., pf. (1973); *Cancion*, gui. (1982); *Dream Music*, gui. (1983); *Chanson de geste*, hn. (1991); *Threads*, bcl., mar., vib. (1996).

VOICE & INSTR(S).: *3 Orkney Songs*, sop., bar., fl., ob., vn., vc., pf. (1961); *6 Scots Songs*, v., pf. (1962); *Carmina sacra*, high v., hp., str. (1964); *One foot in Eden*, mez. (1977); *The Willow Branches*, v., ens. (1983).

CHURCH MUSIC: *Mass* in D minor, unacc. (1955); *Missa brevis*, unacc. (1955); *Night Songs*, unacc. (1967); *Ave Maria* and *Pater Noster*, unacc. (1967); *A Babe is born*, ch., org. (1967); *My Soul longs for Thee*, unacc. women's vv. (1967); *There is no rose*, unacc. (1974); *Ubi caritas et amor*, male ch., perc. (1976).

BRASS: *Sinfonietta* (1967); *Cartoon*, cornet (1969); *Refrains and Cadenzas* (1973).

KEYBOARD: *Sonatina*, pf. (1956); sonata, pf. (1964); *3 Pieces*, pf. (1964); *Incunabula*, pf. (1983); *Toccata festevole*, org. (1990).

Wilson-Johnson, David (*b* Northampton, 1950). Eng. bass-baritone. Career as soloist in Elgar oratorios, *Belshazzar's Feast*, *8 *Songs for a Mad King*, Beethoven's 9th Sym., and recitalist in *Winterreise*, etc. Opera début CG 1976 (in *We Come to the River*). Created Arthur in *The Lighthouse*, Edinburgh 1980. WNO 1978; GTO 1980. Sang title-role in f. Brit. p. (concert) of Messiaen's *St François d'Assise*, London 1988. Salzburg Fest. début 1989.

Winbergh, Gösta (*b* Stockholm, 1943; *d* Vienna, 2002). Swedish tenor. Début Göteborg 1971 (Rodolfo in *La bohème*). Prin. tenor, Royal Opera, Stockholm, 1973–80. Débuts: Glyndebourne 1980; Salzburg Fest. 1982; CG 1982; NY Met 1983; La Scala 1985; Houston 1988. Sang Walther in *Die Meistersinger*, CG 1993.

wind-band. In medieval times, bands of roving pipers who later received official recognition as 'town pipers', providing mus. for civic occasions. In modern usage, the term denotes a band of mixed wind instr., often with perc., and is more often called a 'military band' to distinguish it from the 'brass band' in which no woodwind is used. In USA 'wind band' denotes a military band. Haydn's *Wind-band Mass* (*Harmoniemesse*), 1802, is named because the wind instr. are prominent in the scoring, not because they are the only instr. used.

wind chest. Box-like construction which receives the wind from an org.'s bellows and supplies it to the pipes when the pallets are opened. See *organ*.

Windgassen, Wolfgang (Fritz Hermann) (*b* Andemasse, 1914; *d* Stuttgart, 1974). Ger. tenor. Opera début Pforzheim 1941 (Alvaro in *La forza del destino*). Stuttgart Opera 1945–73; Vienna Opera from 1953. Débuts: Bayreuth Fest. 1951; La Scala 1952; CG 1954; NY Met 1957. Outstanding singer of Parsifal, Tristan, Siegfried, and other Wagner roles, though not a *Heldentenor* of traditional kind. Art. dir. Stuttgart Opera 1972–4.

wind instruments. Those mus. instrs. in which sound is produced by vibrations of a column of air set in motion by the perf.'s blowing. Two main categories are woodwind (not all made of wood) and brass (not all made of brass), e.g. fl., picc., ob., cl., bn., among former; hn., tpt., tb., tuba, among latter. An org. is not a wind instr. in the sense defined here, since the air is mechanically impelled.

wind machine. Device to simulate sound of wind, a barrel-shaped framework being covered with silk or other fabric and rotated by a handle. Friction with wood or cardboard produces sound which can be varied in pitch by pace at which handle is turned. Used by several composers, e.g. by Strauss in *Don Quixote* and *Eine Alpensinfonie* and by Vaughan Williams in *Sinfonia Antartica*.

wind quintet. Composition for five wind instr., or the performers who play it. Usual combination is fl., ob., cl., bn., and hn., but there are several exceptions (Elgar's were written for 2 fl. and no hn.). Among composers of wind quintets are Reicha, Danzi, Schmitt, Françaix, Carter, Milhaud, Nielsen, Fricker, Henze, Gerhard, Stockhausen, and Schoenberg.

Winkelmann [Winckelmann], **Hermann** (*b* Brunswick, 1849; *d* Vienna, 1912). Ger. tenor. Began career as piano maker. Opera début Sondershausen 1875 (Manrico in *Il trovatore*). Sang Wagner roles in Vienna and created Parsifal at Bayreuth 1882. London début Drury Lane 1882 cond. Richter. Was first London Tristan and Walther. Concert début USA 1884. Vienna Opera 1883–1906. Sang in Theodore Thomas's Wagner fests., NY 1884.

Winter, Louise (*b* Preston, 1959). Eng. mezzosoprano. Opera début 1983, GTO (Tisbe in *La Cenerentola*). Sang Zerlina (*Don Giovanni*) with Glyndebourne co. at Hong Kong Fest. 1986. Débuts: Glyndebourne 1986; CG 1988; ENO 1990.

Winter Journey (Schubert). See *Winterreise*.

Winterreise (Winter Journey). Song-cycle for male v. and pf. by Schubert (D911), settings of 24 poems by Wilhelm Müller (pubd. 1823 and 1824). Comp. (1827) and pubd. (1828) in 2 instalments, each of 12 songs. The titles of the individual songs, in Schubert's (not Müller's) selected order are: I. *Gute Nacht* (Good Night), *Die Wetterfahne* (The Weathervane), *Gefrorne Tränen* (Frozen Tears), *Erstarrung* (Frozen Rigidity), *Der Lindenbaum* (The Lime-Tree), *Wasserflut* (Flood), *Auf dem Flusse* (On the River), *Rückblick* (Backward Glance), *Irrlicht* (Will-o'-the-Wisp), *Rast* (Rest), *Frühlingstraum* (Dream of Spring), *Einsamkeit* (Loneliness); II. *Die Post* (The Post), *Der greise Kopf* (The hoary head), *Die Krähe* (The Crow), *Letzte Hoffnung* (Last Hope), *Im Dorfe* (In the Village), *Der stürmische Morgen* (The Stormy Morning), *Täuschung* (Delusion), *Der Wegweiser* (The Sign-post), *Das Wirtshaus* (The Inn), *Mut* (Courage), *Die Nebensonnen* (Phantom Suns), *Der Leiermann* (The Hurdy-Gurdy Man).

Winter Words. Song-cycle of 8 poems by Thomas Hardy set for high v. and pf., Op.52, by Britten. F.p. Leeds Fest. 1953 (in Harewood House). Title taken from Hardy's last pubd. vol. of poetry, 1928. The songs are: 1. *At day-close in November*, 2. *Midnight on the Great Western*, or *The journeying boy*, 3. *Wagtail and Baby*, 4. *The little old table*, 5. *The Choirmaster's burial*, or *The tenor man's story*, 6. *Proud songsters, thrushes, finches, and nightingales*, 7. *At the railway station, Upway*, or *The convict and boy with the violin*, 8. *Before life and after*. Discarded settings *The Children and Sir Nameless* and *If it's ever Spring again* f.p. 1985.

Wirbel (Ger.). Whirl. Drum roll.

Wirbeltrommel (Ger.). Ten. drum.

wire brush. Variety of drumstick with head consisting of several stiff wires. Produces 'brushing' or 'swishing' sound from side-drum or cymbals. Used mainly in jazz, but also by many 20th-cent. composers.

Wirén, Dag (Ivar) (*b* Striberg, 1905; *d* Danderyd, 1986). Swed. composer. Mus. critic, *Svenska Morgonbladet* 1938–46. From 1944 used 'Metamorphosis technique', i.e. construction of a work from a single 'cell' or set of cells. Works incl. 5 syms. (1938–64); vn. conc. (1946); pf. conc. (1950); vc. conc. (1936); *Serenade for Strings*, Op.11 (1937); Sinfonietta; 5 str. qts.; and radio opera, *Blått, gult, rott* (1940), inspired by Churchill's 'blood, tears, sweat' speech.

Wise, Michael (*b* ?Salisbury, *c*.1648; *d* Salisbury, 1687). Eng. singer, organist, and composer. Org. and choirmaster, Salisbury Cath., 1668–85, choirmaster St Paul's Cath., 1687. Killed in quarrel with night watchman after argument with his wife. Wrote anthems, services, and catches.

Wise Virgins, The. Ballet in 1 act by Walton, music being his arr. of 9 items from the church cantatas of J. S. Bach selected by Constant Lambert. Scenario based on parable of Wise and Foolish Virgins in *St Matthew XXV*. Comp. 1939–40. Choreog. by Frederick Ashton, designs by Rex Whistler. Prod. London (SW) 1940 with Fonteyn as the Bride. Orch. suite 1940, of 6 movts.: 1. What God hath done is rightly done (*Was Gott thut, das ist wohlgetan*, BWV 99); 2. Lord, hear my longing (*Herzlich thut mich verlangen*, BWV 727); 3. See what His love can do (*Seht was die Liebe tut*, from BWV 85); 4. Ah! how ephemeral (*Ach wie flüchtig, ach wie nichtig*, BWV 26); 5. Sheep may safely graze (*Schafe können siche weiden*, from BWV 208); 6. Praise be to God (*Gelobet sei der Herr, mein Gott*, from BWV 129).

Wishart, Peter (Charles Arthur) (*b* Crowborough, 1921; *d* Frome, Som., 1984). Eng. composer. Lect. in mus., Birmingham Univ. 1950–9, prof., GSMD 1961–77, King's Coll., London, 1972–7, prof. of music, Reading Univ. 1977–84. Works incl. operas *The Clandestine Marriage, Klytemnestra, Two in the Bush*, and *The Captive*; 2 syms.; 2 vn. concs.; *Te Deum*; 5 *Pieces*, str.; and choral works.

Wit, Antoni (*b* Cracow, 1944). Polish conductor. 2nd prize, Karajan comp. 1971. Ass. cond. Warsaw Nat. PO 1967–70; cond. Poznań State PO 1970–2, Pomeranian PO, Bydgoszcz, 1974–7. Art. dir. Polish Radio and TV SO, Cracow, 1977–83, Katowice from 1983. Salzburg Fest. début 1972.

Witt, (Jeremias) **Friedrich** (*b* Niederstetten, 1770; *d* Würzburg, 1836). Ger. composer and cellist. Court cond., Würzburg, from 1802. Wrote operas, oratorios, and much instr. mus. Comp. so-called **Jena' Symphony*, at one time erroneously attrib. to Beethoven.

Wittgenstein, Paul (*b* Vienna, 1887; *d* Manhasset, NY, 1961). Austrian-born pianist (Amer. cit. 1946). Début Vienna 1913. Lost right arm in First World War, so developed remarkable left-hand technique. Commissioned concs. or similar works for left-hand pianist from several composers, incl. Korngold (conc.), Ravel (conc.), R. Strauss (*Parergon zur Symphonia Domestica* and

Panathenäenzug), Prokofiev (4th conc.), Schmidt (*Conc. Vars.*), Weigl (conc.), and Britten (*Diversions*). Salzburg Fest. début 1936. Settled in NY 1938 and taught privately there 1938–60. Brother of Ludwig Wittgenstein, the philosopher.

Wittich, Marie (*b* Giessen, 1868; *d* Dresden, 1931). Ger. soprano. Début Magdeburg 1882 (Azucena in *Il trovatore*). Sang in Düsseldorf etc., then joined Dresden Opera 1889–1914. Bayreuth 1901–9; CG 1905–6. In Dresden 1905 created title-role in *Salome*, though not without protest about its 'indecency'.

Wixell, Ingvar (*b* Luleå, 1931). Swedish baritone. Concert début Gävle 1952. Opera début Stockholm 1955 (Papageno in *Die Zauberflöte*). Member of Royal Opera, Stockholm, from 1956, Deutsche Oper, Berlin, from 1967. Sang in Verdi and Handel operas at CG 1960 with Swedish co. Débuts: Glyndebourne 1962; Salzburg Fest. 1966; Amer. (Chicago) 1967; Bayreuth 1971; CG 1972; NY Met 1973.

Wlaschiha, Ekkerhard (*b* Pirna, 1938). Ger. baritone. Début Gera 1961 (Don Fernando in *Fidelio*). Sang in Dresden and Weimar 1964–70, Leipzig Opera from 1970. Bayreuth début 1986; CG début 1990. Outstanding as Alberich, which he has sung in *Ring* prods. worldwide.

Wohltemperierte Klavier, Das (The Well-tempered Klavier). Title given by Bach to his 24 Preludes and Fugues for kbd., Cöthen 1722, in all the major and minor keys, and also applied to 2nd set of 24 composed in Leipzig, 1744, the 2 sets often being known simply as 'the 48'. Bach's object was to demonstrate the advantages of the then new equal *temperament. Pubd. 1800–1.

wolf. (1) Jarring sound which sometimes occurs from bowed str. instrs. when body of instr. resonates to a particular note.
   (2) Out-of-tune effect on old orgs. (before equal *temperament) when playing in certain extreme keys.

Wolf, Hugo (Filipp Jakob) (*b* Windischgraz, 1860; *d* Vienna, 1903). Austrian composer. Taught rudiments of mus. by his father, a leather-dealer. Entered Vienna Cons. 1875 (fellow-pupil of Mahler). Expelled 1877 (unjustly) and made bare living by teaching pf. 2nd cond. at Salzburg 1881, but gave up after 3 months. Mus. critic. in Vienna 1883–7, making enemies by his fanatical praise of Wagner and dislike of Brahms. From 1888, when he discovered the poetry of Mörike, poured out dozens of songs, incl. the *Spanish Songbook*, in which the art of the *Lied* reached one of its most sophisticated and intricately-wrought stages, with the pf. part no longer simple acc. but an integral part of the song. The concentrated characterization of each song is unequalled in *Lieder*, demanding the utmost artistry from the performers, psychological as well as vocal and instr. For 3 years from 1892 to 1894, Wolf wrote nothing except the orch. arr. of the *Italian Serenade*, but his fame gradually

spread and in Berlin a 'Hugo Wolf Society' was founded. Even Vienna began to capitulate late in 1894. In 1895 he wrote an opera based on *The Three-Cornered Hat* which he called *Der Corregidor*. In the spring of 1896, he wrote the 24 songs of the *Italian Songbook* (Vol. II). In 1897 he began his Michelangelo settings and a 2nd opera, *Manuel Venegas*. But in the autumn his mind gave way, the outcome of venereal disease, and he was taken to an asylum. Though he seemed to be 'cured' in 1898 he tried to drown himself in Oct. of that year and spent his last years insane in a mental hospital. Prin. works:

OPERAS: *Der *Corregidor* (1895); *Manuel Venegas* (1897, incomplete).

ORCH.: *Penthesilea*, sym.-poem (1883); *Italienische Serenade* (1892, orch. of work for str. qt. 1887).

CHAMBER MUSIC: str. qt. in D minor (1878); *Serenade in G* for str. qt. (1887; arr. for str. orch. 1892 as *Italienische Serenade* (*Italian Serenade*)).

CHORAL: 6 Eichendorff chs., unacc. (1881), *Christ-Nacht*, soloists, ch., orch. (1886–9); *Elfenlied* ('You spotted snakes', from *A Midsummer Night's Dream*), sop., ch., orch. (*c*.1890, arr. from song for v. and pf., 1888, but not same as *Elfenlied* in *Mörike-Lieder*); *Der Feuerreiter* (The Fire-rider) (Mörike song 1888 arr. ch and orch. 1892); *Dem Vaterland* (song for v. and pf. 1888, arr. for male ch. and orch. 1888–91).

SONGS (mostly with pf. acc., but some with orch.): *12 Lieder aus der Jugendzeit* (1877–8); *6 Songs for Woman's Voice*; *6 Poems of Scheffel, Mörike, Goethe, and Kerner*; *4 Poems of Heine, Shakespeare, and Byron*; *6 Poems by Gottfried Keller*; *3 Ibsen Songs*; *3 Poems by Reinick* (1877–87); *53 *Mörike-Lieder* (1888); *20 Eichendorff-Lieder* (1880–8); *51 Goethe-Lieder* (incl. *Mignon Lieder*) (1888–9); **Spanisches Liederbuch* (44 songs) (1889–90); *Italienisches Liederbuch*, Vol. I (22 songs) (1890–1); *Italienisches Liederbuch*, Vol. II (24 songs) (1896); *3 Poems by Michelangelo* (1897). Among the best-loved Wolf songs (selectively chosen) are: *An die Geliebte*; *Abschied*; *Anakreons Grab*; *Begegnung*; *Denk es, O Seele*; *Einsame*; *Elfenlied*; *Der Feuerreiter*; *Gebet*; *Gesang Weylas*; *Heimweh*; *Im Frühling*; *In dem Schatten meiner Locken*; *Jägerlied*; *Kennst du das Land?*; *Lebewohl*; *Schlafendes Jesuskind*; *Der Tambour*; *Verborgenheit*; *Das verlassene Mägdlein*.

Wolff, Albert (Louis) (*b* Paris, 1884; *d* Paris, 1970). Fr. conductor and composer. Chorusmaster Opéra-Comique, Paris, 1908, cond. from 1911, mus. dir. 1921–4, th. dir. 1945–6. Cond. first Paris perf. of Ravel's *L'Enfant et les sortilèges*, 1926, and f.p. of Poulenc's *Les *mamelles de Tirésias*, Paris 1947. Cond. Fr. repertoire at NY Met 1919–21. CG début 1937. Cond., Concerts Lamoureux 1928–34, then Concerts Pasdeloup 1934–40. Fine interpreter of Roussel. Wrote opera *L'Oiseau bleu* (NY 1919).

Wolff, Hugh (MacPherson) (*b* Paris, 1953). Amer. conductor. Taken to USA aged 10. Selected as Exxon/Arts endowment cond. with National SO of Washington, DC, as ass. to Rostropovich, and became ass. cond. 1982–5. Eur. début 1982 (LPO). Cond. New Jersey SO 1985–92, prin. cond., St

Paul's Chamber Orch. 1988–92, mus. dir. 1992–2000; cond. Frankfurt Radio SO 1997–2006. NY City Opera début 1986. Specialist in 17th- and 18th-cent. repertoire.

Wolf-Ferrari, Ermanno (b Venice, 1876; d Venice, 1948). It. composer, son of Ger. father and It. mother. Dir., Liceo Benedetto Marcello 1903–9. Prof. of comp. Salzburg Mozarteum 1939–45. Wrote mainly operas, being adept at light works based on Goldoni comedies, elegantly scored and immediately appealing. Some were produced in Ger. before It. Prin. works:

OPERAS: *Irene* (1896); *Cenerentola* (1897–1900, rev. 1902); *Le donne curiose* (1903); I **quatro rusteghi* (c.1904–5); Il **segreto di Susanna* (1909); I **gioielli della Madonna* (1911); *L'amore medico* (1913); *Gli amanti sposi* (1914–16, 1925); *La veste di cielo* (c.1917–25, 1927); *Sly* (1927); *La vedova scaltra* (1931); *Il Campiello* (c.1934); *La dama boba* (1939); *Gli dei a Tebe* (1943); modern edn. of *Idomeneo* (Mozart), Munich 1931.

Also wrote oratorios, chamber sym., vn. conc., vc. conc., chamber mus., *Suite* for bn., 2 hn., and str., etc.

Wolpe, Stefan (b Berlin, 1902; d NY, 1972). Ger.-born composer (Amer. cit. 1944). Wrote th. mus. for Brecht in 1920s and was ardent radical socialist, writing works on political themes. Went to Austria 1933, then to Palestine 1934–8 (prof. of comp. at Cons.), finally to USA. Taught at various colls. in NY 1938–52. Head of mus. dept., Long Island Univ., 1957–68, prof. of comp. Mannes College, 1968. Most of his later works employ serial technique based on small pitch cells rather than on 12-note rows. Also influenced by Jewish mus. traditions and harmonies. Works incl. 2 operas, ballet *The Man from Midian* (1942), incid. music for plays by G. von Wangenheim and Brecht, sym., several cantatas, tpt. conc., chamber mus. for various combinations, and songs.

Woman without a Shadow, The (Strauss). See *Frau ohne Schatten, Die.*

Women's Love and Life (Schumann). See *Frauenliebe und -Leben.*

WoO. Werk ohne Opuszahl (Work without opus number). Applied, for example, to Beethoven's works in Kinsky's catalogue and to those of Richard Strauss in Asow's catalogue.

Wood, Charles (b Armagh, 1866; d Cambridge, 1926). Irish composer and teacher. Taught harmony at RCM from 1888, later becoming prof. Cond. Cambridge Univ. Mus. Soc. 1888–94. Org. scholar Gonville and Caius, Cambridge, 1889–94. Lect. in harmony and counterpoint, Cambridge Univ., 1897–1924, prof. of mus. from 1924. Pupils incl. **Vaughan Williams. Wrote mus. for Gr. plays; 2 chamber operas, *A Scene from Pickwick* (1921) and *The Family Party* (1923); *Ode to the West Wind* (1894); *Dirge for Two Veterans* (1901); 3 str. qts.; partsongs; solo songs incl. *Ethiopia Saluting the Col-*

ours (Whitman); and much church mus. incl. over 30 anthems and several services. Wrote the chimes for the clock of Gonville and Caius Coll.

Wood, Haydn (b Slaithwaite, Yorks., 1882; d London, 1959). Eng. composer and violinist. Won Cobbett Prize with Phantasy Qt., also wrote pf. conc., vn. conc., 9 orch. rhapsodies, 7 song-cycles, and about 200 songs. It is on these last that his fame chiefly depends, for they incl. *Love's Garden of Roses* (1914), *A Brown Bird Singing* (1922), and *Roses of Picardy* (1916) which gained poignancy from its associations with First World War. (He pronounced Haydn with the 'Hay' as in hay- making, not as in the composer after whom he was named).

Wood, (Sir) **Henry** (Joseph) (b London, 1869; d Hitchin, 1944). Eng. conductor and organist. Taught by his mother, and was deputy church organist at age of 10. Org., St John's Fulham, 1887. Studied RAM under Prout and García, intending to be composer. Obtained post as cond. with Rousbey touring opera co., 1889. Helped Sullivan to rehearse *Ivanhoe* 1890. Cond. for Carl Rosa, 1891. Cond. f.p. in England of *Eugene Onegin*, 1892. Taught singing until 1894, when he was mus. adviser to Mottl's Wagner concerts at new Queen's Hall. In 1895 engaged by Robert Newman as cond. of his new series of **Promenade concerts in London. These he built to be a premier feature of Eng. mus. life, retaining conductorship until year of his death. After 1896 cond. no more opera but devoted himself to concert work in London and in many provincial cities and at all the leading fests. (Birmingham, Leeds, Sheffield, Norwich, etc.). Waged war on 'deputy' system, whereby orch. players could send deputy to a concert while they took a more remunerative engagement, and did as much as any Eng. cond. to raise standards of playing. Amer. début NYPO 1904. Declined conductorship of Boston SO, 1918. Tireless champion of contemp. mus. List of works of which he gave f.ps. and f.ps. in England is long and honourable. Tchaikovsky, Sibelius, Strauss, Scriabin, Bartók, and Debussy were championed by him before their present popularity. Cond. first complete perf. of Schoenberg's *5 Orchestral Pieces* in 1912, the f.ps. in England of Mahler's 1st, 4th, 7th, and 8th syms. and *Das Lied von der Erde*, and introduced the mus. of Janáček to Eng. Every major Eng. composer of his lifetime was perf. at the Proms, and he helped the careers of many Brit. singers and instrumentalists. At his golden jubilee concert, 1938, 16 leading Brit. singers took part in Vaughan Williams's **Serenade to Music*, ded. to Wood. Made several orch. transcriptions, incl. Mussorgsky's *Pictures at an Exhibition* and Bach's *Toccata and Fugue* in D minor (under the name P. **Klenovsky) and arr. **Fantasia on British Sea Songs* perf. on last night of every Prom season, with audience participation (orig. written for Trafalgar centenary concert 1905). Knighted 1911. CH 1944.

Wood, Hugh (Bradshaw) (b Parbold, Lancs., 1932). Eng. composer. Prof. of harmony RAM

1962–5, teacher at Morley Coll., London, 1958–67. Research fellow in comp., Glasgow Univ., 1966–70; lect. in mus., Liverpool Univ., 1971–3, Cambridge Univ. 1977–99. His mus., while reflecting a variety of influences from Tippett and Messiaen to *avant-garde* techniques, is consistent in its shapeliness, lyricism, and expressive concentration. Prin. works:

ORCH.: vc. conc., Op.12 (1965–9); chamber conc., Op.15 (1971, rev. 1978); vn. conc., Op.17 (1970–2); sym., Op.21 (1979–82); *Comus Quadrilles*, small orch. (1988); pf. conc., Op.32 (1990–1); *Variations*, Op.39 (1998); *Serenade and Elegy*, Op.42, str. (1999).

VOICE(S) & ORCH.: *Scenes from Comus*, Op.6, sop., ten., orch. (1962–5); *Laurie Lee Songs*, Op.28, high v., orch. (1986–7); *Cantata*, Op.30, ch., orch. (1989).

UNACC. CHORUS: *3 Choruses*, Op.7 (1965–6); *To a friend whose work has come to nothing* (1973–89); *A Christmas Poem*, Op.27 (1984); *The Kingdom of God*, Op.38 (1994).

CHAMBER MUSIC: str. qts.: str. qt. in B♭ (1959); No.1, Op.4 (1960–2), No.2, Op.13 (1969–70), No.3, Op.20 (1976–8), No.4, Op.34 (1992–3), No.5, Op. 45 (2001); pf. trio (1984); *Variations*, Op.1, va., pf. (1958); trio, Op.3, fl., va., pf. (1961); quintet, Op.9, cl., hn., vn., vc., pf. (1967); pf. trio, Op.24 (1984); *Paraphrase on Bird of Paradise*, Op.26, cl., pf. (1985); hn. trio, Op.29 (1987–9); *Funeral Music*, Op.33, brass quintet (1992); *Poem*, Op.35, vn., pf. (1993); cl. trio, Op.40, cl., pf., vc. (1997); *Serenade and Elegy*, Op.42, str. qt., orch. (1999); *Cantilena and Fugue*, tpt., org. (2004); *Overture*, pf., vn., vc. (2005).

PIANO: *3 Pieces*, Op.5 (1961); *50 Chords for David Matthews*, 2 pf. (1993).

ORGAN: *Capriccio*, Op.8 (1968).

SONGS: *Laurie Lee Songs*, high v., pf. (1959, with orch., Op.28, 1986–7); *Logue Songs*, Op.2 (1961, rev. 1963); *D. H. Lawrence Songs*, Op.14, high v., pf. (1966–74); *Graves Songs Set I*, Op.18, high v., pf. (1966–77), *Set II*, Op.22, high v., pf. (1977–82), *Set III*, Op.25, high v., pf. (1966–83); *The Horses* (Ted Hughes), Op.10 (1967, rev. 1968); *The Rider Victory* (Edwin Muir), Op.11 (1968); *Song-Cycle to Poems of Neruda*, Op.19, high v., chamber ens. (1973–4); *Songs*, Op.23, high v., pf. (1983); *Lines to Mr Hodgson*, sop., pf. (1988); *Marina*, Op.31, high v., alt. fl., hn., hp. va. (1988–9); *D. H. Lawrence Songs*, Op.14, high v., pf. (1998); *Robert Graves Songs*, Op.49, ten., pf. (2006).

wood block. See *Chinese wood block*.

Wood Dove, The (*Holoubek*). Sym.-poem for orch., Op.110, by Dvořák, comp. 1896.

Wooden Prince, The (*A fából faragott Királyfi*). Ballet in 1 act by Bartók to scenario by Béla Balázs comp. 1914–17 and f.p. Budapest 12 May, 1917. Orch. suite f.p. Budapest 1931.

Woodforde-Finden, Amy (*b* Valparaiso, Chile, 1860; *d* London, 1919). Eng. composer of songs. Remembered for the *Indian Love Lyrics* (poems by 'Laurence Hope', Adela Florence Nicolson, 1865–1904), incl. *Pale hands I loved beside the Shalimar*, which were pubd. privately in 1902.

Woodward, Roger (Robert) (*b* Sydney, NSW, 1942). Australian pianist. Débuts Warsaw and London 1967. Won 23rd Int. Chopin Comp., Warsaw, 1968. Rapid rise to leading place among exponents of *avant-garde* mus. of Boulez, Stockhausen, etc. Perf. complete works of Chopin in 16 recitals, 1985. OBE 1980.

woodwind. Name for wind instrs. orig. and usually made of wood, either blown directly by mouth (fl. and recorder) or by means of a reed (cl. and ob.). Saxs. are classified as woodwind. *double woodwind*, in descriptions of a composer's scoring for orch., means 2 players of each standard type of woodwind instr., e.g. fl., ob., cl., bn. (this being usual Beethoven or Schubert orch.). *triple woodwind* means 3 of each, one player normally taking an extra member of the family of his instrument, e.g. picc. with fl., cor anglais with ob., bcl. with cl., double bn. with bn. *quadruple woodwind* means 4 of each, as in Strauss, Mahler, and other composers for very large orch.

Wooldridge, David (Humphry Michael) (*b* Deal, 1927). Eng. conductor, composer, and writer. Staff cond., Bavarian State Opera, 1954–5, guest cond. Amer. orchs. 1957–68, mus. dir. Beirut SO 1961–5, cond. Cape Town Orch. 1965–7. Works incl. va. conc., *Partita* for orch., and film mus. Author of *Conductors' World* (1970) and biography of Charles Ives (1974).

Woolrich, John (*b* Cirencester, 1954). Eng. composer. Northern Arts Fellow in comp., Durham Univ. 1982–5, comp.-in-residence, Nat. Centre for Orch. Studies 1985–6. Ass. art. dir. Aldeburgh Fest. from 2004. Comps. incl.:

OPERAS: *In the House of Crossed Desires* (1996); *Bitter Fruit* (2000).

ORCH.: *The Barber's Timepiece* (1986); *The Ghost in the Machine* (1990); *The Theatre Represents a Garden: Night* (1991); ob. conc. (1996); va. conc. (1996); vc. conc. (1998); *Conc. for Orch.* (1998–9); *A Capriccio to Calliope Herself* (2000); *Double Mercury* (2003); *The Elephant from Celebes* (2005).

ENS.: *Stone Dances*, 8 players (1980); *Spalanzani's Daughter*, 8 players (1983); *Dartington Doubles*, 9 players (1988); *Barcarolle*, 6 players (1989); *Lending Wings*, 14 players (1989); *Ulysses Awakes* (after Monteverdi), str. (1989); *It is Midnight, Dr Schweitzer*, str. (1992); *Si va facendo notte*, 12 players (1992); *Caprichos*, ens. (1997); *Cutting a Caper*, ob., cl., tpt., vn., vc., ens. (2001); *After the Clock*, ens. (2005).

VOICE(S) & ENS.: *Cascades*, sop. (1983); *Harlequinade*, sop. (1983); *Black Riddle*, sop. (1984); *3 Macedonian Songs*, sop. (1984); *Serbian Songs*, sop. (1984); *The Turkish Mouse*, sop. (1988), v., pf. (1990); *Poor Mr Snail*, sop. (1992); *Ariadne Laments*, sop., 2 vn., va., vc., db. (or str. orch.) (1994); *Good Morning – Midnight*, sop., pf. (2000); *Farewel adieu*, mez., triple hp., viol (2004).

CHAMBER MUSIC: *Quick Steps*, wind octet (1990); *Contredanse*, str. octet (1991); *The Death of King Renaud*, str. quintet (1992); *A Farewell*, cl., va., pf.

(1992); *That is the Night*, vn., pf. (1995); *Adagissimo*, pf., vn., va., vc. (1997); *Arcangelo*, chamber orch. (2002); *Elegy*, vc., pf. (2001).

Wordsworth, Barry (*b* Worcester Park, Surrey, 1949). Eng. conductor. Freelance cond. of ballet in Amer. and Canada. Cond. BBC Concert Orch. from 1989. Mus. dir. Royal Ballet and Birmingham Royal Ballet 1991–5; chief cond. BBC Concert Orch. 1989–2006. CG opera début 1991.

Wordsworth, William (Brocklesby) (*b* London, 1908; *d* Kingussie, Inverness-shire, 1988). Eng. composer. His 2nd sym. won Edinburgh Fest. Int. Comp. 1950. Mus. in idiom unfashionable in 1960s and 1970s but of expressive emotional range, melodic attraction, fine craftsmanship, and consistent integrity. Lived many years in Surrey, then moved in 1960s to Scottish Highlands (in which he anticipated Maxwell Davies) and helped to form Scottish branch of Composers' Guild. Prin. works:

ORCH.: syms.: No.1 in F minor (1944), No.2 in D (1947–8), No.3 in C (1951), No.4 in E♭ (1953), No.5 in A minor (1959–60), No.6 (1976–7), No.7 (1981), No.8 (1986); concs.: pf. in D minor (1946), vn. in A (1955); vc. (1963); *Divertimento* in D (1954); *Sinfonietta* (1957); *Variations on a Scottish Theme* (1962); *Highland Overture* (1964); *Jubilation* (1965); *Valediction* (1969), sym. vars. (1975); *Elegy for Frieda*, str. (1982).

CHORAL: *The Houseless Dead*, bar., ch., orch. (1939); *Dies Domini*, oratorio (1942–4); *In No Strange Land* (1951); *A Song of Praise* (1956); *2 Seasonal Songs* (1971).

CHAMBER MUSIC: str. qts.: No.1 (1941), No.2 (1944), No.3 (1947), No.4 (1950), No.5 (1957), No.6 (1964); *4 Lyrics*, ten., str. qt. (1941); str. trio (1945); pf. qt. (1948); pf. trio (1949); ob. qt. (1949); cl. quintet (1952); pf. quintet (1959); *The Solitary Reaper*, sop., cl., pf. (1973); vc. sonata (1937); vn. sonata (1944); *Theme and Variations*, ob., pf. (1954); va. sonatina (1961); *Prelude and Scherzo*, ob., pf. (1974).

PIANO: sonata in D minor (1939); *Cheesecombe Suite* (1945–6); *Ballade* (1949); *Valediction* (1967).

VOICE & PIANO: *4 Songs*, high v. (1936); *3 Songs*, medium v. (1938); *4 Sacred Sonnets* (Donne), low v. (1944); *4 Blake Songs*, high v. (1948); *Ariel's Songs*, medium v. (1968).

working-out. The development section in *sonata form*.

Worshipful Company of Musicians. Ancient London guild. Royal charter 1604, revoked 1632, renewed 1950. Offers prizes for chamber mus. comps. and awards Collard Fellowship and other scholarships.

Wotquenne, Alfred (*b* Lobbes, 1867; *d* Antibes, 1939). Belg. musicologist. Librarian, Brussels Cons. 1894–1918. Among his works are a bibliographical study of *Galuppi* (1899, enlarged 1902), catalogue of 17th-cent. It. opera and oratorio libs. (1901–14), thematic catalogue of works of Gluck (1904) and of C. P. E. Bach (1905). See *Wq*.

Wozzeck. (1) Opera in 3 acts of 5 scenes each by Berg, Op.7, to lib. by Berg based on play *Wozzeck* by Georg Büchner (1836). Comp. 1914–22. Prod. Berlin 1925 (cond. Kleiber), Philadelphia and NY 1931, London (concert) 1934 (cond. Boult), stage CG 1952 (cond. Kleiber). Play is often named as 'Woyzeck' since contemporary (1830s) newspaper account of the original incident came to light giving this spelling (Büchner's MS was presumed to read 'Wozzeck'). Important feature of the opera is that each scene is in a strict mus. form e.g. Act I Sc. 1–5, suite, rhapsody and hunting song, march and lullaby, passacaglia (21 variations on a note-row), rondo; Act II Sc. 6–10, sym. in 5 movts.: sonata-allegro, fantasia and fugue on 3 themes, largo, scherzo, rondo; Act III Sc. 11–15, theme and variations, pedal-point, a rhythm, 6-note chord, key (D minor), equal movement in 8ths *quasi toccata* (this act being 6 'inventions').

(2) Opera by Gurlitt (1920–5).

Wq. Abbreviated prefix to numbers in the *Wotquenne catalogue of C. P. E. Bach's works.

Wranitzky [Vranický], **Anton** (Antonín) (*b* Neureisch, now Nová Říše, 1761; *d* Vienna, 1820). Moravian composer and violinist, brother of P. *Wranitzky. Court cond. for Prince Lobkowitz in Vienna from 1797, becoming orch. dir. of court theatre 1807–20. Wrote 14 syms., 15 vn. concs., and much church and chamber mus.

Wranitzky [Vranický], **Paul** (Pavel) (*b* Neureisch, now Nová Říše, 1756; *d* Vienna, 1808). Moravian composer and violinist. Violinist in Eszterháza orch. under Haydn. Leader of Vienna court opera orch., 1790–1808. Comp. operas (incl. *Oberon*, 1789), ballets, 51 syms., 60 str. qts., 25 str. quintets, and many other works. Cond. f.p. of Beethoven's 1st sym., Vienna, 2 Apr. 1800.

Wreckers, The. Opera in 3 acts by Ethel Smyth to lib. in Fr. by 'H. B. Laforestier' (Harry Brewster) and composer. Comp. 1903–4. Prod. Leipzig, 1906; London 1909.

Wührer, Friedrich (*b* Vienna, 1900; *d* Mannheim, 1975). Austrian pianist and teacher. Toured Eur. and USA as pianist 1923. Salzburg Fest. début 1938. Taught pf. at Vienna Acad. 1922–32, 1939–45, Mannheim 1934–6, 1952–7, Kiel 1936–9, Salzburg Mozarteum 1948–51, Munich 1957–68. One of best and most influential of teachers. Gave many perfs. of pf. works by Schoenberg, Berg, Webern, Bartók, and Stravinsky. Comp. str. qts., pf. pieces, and songs.

Wüllner, Franz (*b* Münster, 1832; *d* Braunfels, 1902). Ger. conductor, composer, and pianist. Prof. of pf., Munich Cons. 1856–8. Mus. dir., Aix-la-Chapelle 1858–64. Court ch. cond., Munich, 1864, succeeding Bülow 1871 as cond. of Munich Opera. Cond. premières of *Das *Rheingold*, Munich 1869, and *Die *Walküre*, Munich 1870. Court cond. and dir. of Cons., Dresden, 1877–82. Dir., Cologne Cons. from 1884 and cond. of Gürzenich concerts there. Cond. f.ps. of

R. Strauss's *Till Eulenspiegel* (1895) and *Don Quixote* (1898). Cond. early Ger. perfs. of works by Elgar. Wrote choral and chamber mus.

Wüllner, Ludwig (*b* Münster, 1858; *d* Kiel, 1938). Ger. tenor, also baritone, and actor, son of Franz *Wüllner. Career as teacher and actor, then studied mus. *Lieder* singer from 1895. Sang Elgar's Gerontius in Düsseldorf 1901 and 1902 and at f.p. in London 1903. Toured USA 1908 and 1909–10. Gave f.p. in NY of Mahler's *Kindertotenlieder*, cond. Mahler, 1910.

Wulstan, David (*b* Birmingham, 1937). Eng. conductor and teacher. Founder and cond., The Clerkes of Oxenford, specialists in Early and Tudor Eng. mus., from 1961. Prof. of mus., Univ. Coll., Cork 1980–3, Univ. Coll., Aberystwyth from 1983. Comp. carols. Authority on early Eng. church music.

Wunderhorn, Des Knaben. See *Knaben Wunderhorn, Des*.

Wunderlich, Fritz (*b* Kusel, 1930; *d* Heidelberg, 1966). Ger. tenor. Début as soloist with Freiburg Bach Choir, *c*.1951. Opera début Freiburg 1954 in sch. perf. (Tamino in *Die Zauberflöte*). Sang with Stuttgart Opera 1955–8 (prof. début as Eislinger in *Die Meistersinger*). Frankfurt 1958–60; Bavarian State Opera, Munich, from 1960; Vienna from 1962. Recognized as fine Mozart ten. Débuts: Aix-en-Provence Fest. 1958; Salzburg Fest. 1959; CG 1965; Edinburgh Fest. 1966. Recorded ten. songs of Mahler's *Das Lied von der Erde* with Klemperer. Superb singer of operetta. Died in fall (3 weeks before making his NY Met début as Don Ottavio) at height of recognition as one of greatest of Ger. lyric tens. for many years.

Wunsch (Ger.). Wish. So *nach Wunsch*, according to one's wish, same as *ad libitum*.

Wuorinen, Charles (*b* NY, 1938). Amer. composer, conductor, and pianist. Taught at Columbia 1964–71 and Mannes Coll. from 1971. Co-founder Group for Contemp. Mus., 1962. Prolific composer of works in many genres, incl. elec. Tonal up to *c*.1960, then 12-note technique as propounded by Babbitt. Works incl. 8 syms. (1950–2006); *Symphonia sacra*; *Evolutio transcripta*, chamber orch. (1961); Octet; 4 pf. concs. (1966, 1971 (amp.), 1983, 2003); 4 chamber concs.; str. trio; *Time's Encomium* (elec., 1969); *Contrafactum*, orch. (1969); cantata *A Message to Denmark Hill* (1970); 4 str. qts. (1971, 1979, 1987, 2000); tuba conc.; masque *The Politics of Harmony* (1968), conc., amplified vn.; *The W. of Babylon* (1975), baroque burlesque, 8 soloists, narr., orch.; sym., 24 perc. (1976); pf. sonata No.2 (1976); *Rhapsody*, vn., orch. (1985); Sonata, vn., pf. (1988); *Genesis*, ch., orch. (1989); *Missa brevis* (1991); pf. quintet (1994); brass quintet (1999); *Haroun and the Sea of Stories*, opera (2001); *Fifty-Fifty*, 2 pf. (2002); *Duo Sonata*, fl., pf., No.1 (1960), No.2 (2004); *Flying to Kahani*, pf., orch. (2005); *Theologoumena*, orch. (2005).

Wurlitzer. Amer. firm of org.-builders founded 1856, particularly assoc. with th. and cinema orgs. of period 1920–40. After the period of the cinema and th. org., the firm prod. electric pfs. and jukeboxes. The business eventually closed, the NY building now housing factory units and apartments.

Wuthering Heights. Opera (lyric drama) in prol. and 4 acts by *Herrmann to lib. by Lucille Fletcher adapted from Emily Brontë's novel (1847). Comp. 1943–51. F.p. Portland, Oregon, 1982. Also opera by Carlisle *Floyd (1958).

Wyner [Weiner], **Yehudi** (*b* Calgary, 1929). Canadian-born Amer. composer, pianist, conductor, and teacher. Mus. dir., Turnau Opera Co., Woodstock, NY, 1962–4. Taught in NY before joining Yale mus. faculty 1964–77 (chairman, mus. dept. 1969–73). Prof. of Mus., State Univ. of NY at Purchase, 1978–90 (dean of mus. division 1978–82), prof. of comp. Brandeis Univ. from 1989. Wrote liturgical mus. for Jewish synagogue; *Partita* for pf.; pf. sonata; *Serenade*, 7 instr.; *Passover Offering*, *Torah Service*, ch., 4 brass, db.; *Da camera* (pf. conc.); *Cadenza!* cl., hpd.; and *Leonardo Vincitore*, 2 sop., db., pf., for Bernstein's 70th birthday (1988); *Trapunto Junction*, 3 brass, perc. (1991); *Brandeis Sunday*, str. qt (1994); *Praise ye the Lord*, sop., ens. (1996); *Madrigal*, str. qt. (1999); *Voices of Women* (1999); *Tuscan Triptych*, str. (2002); *Commedia*, cl., pf. (2002); *Chiavi in mano*, pf. conc. (2004); vn. conc. (2005).

Wynne, David (*b* Hirwaun, Glam., 1900; *d* Pencoed, Mid-Glamorgan, 1983). Welsh composer. Worked for 6 years in the coal mines, then studied mus. Became schoolteacher until 1961, then taught comp. at Welsh Coll. of Mus. and Drama and Univ. Coll., Cardiff. Works incl. 3 one-act operas; 5 syms.; 2 pf. concs.; vn. conc.; va. conc.; str. qts.; sonatas; song-cycles, etc.

Wyss, Sophie (*b* Neuveville, 1897; *d* Bognor Regis, 1983). Swiss soprano. Settled in Eng. 1925. Gave f.ps. of several works by Brit. composers, incl. Britten's *Our Hunting Fathers* (1936) and *Les Illuminations* (1940).

Wyttenbach, Jürg (*b* Berne, 1935). Swiss pianist, conductor, and composer. Taught Biel Mus. Sch., 1958–67, Berne Cons. 1960–7, and Basle Acad. of Mus. from 1967. Specialist in contemp. mus. as cond. and pianist. Comps., some in aleatory and serial techniques, incl. *Divisions* for pf. and 9 str., *Nachspiel* for 2 pf., *Contests* for musicians, *Exécution ajournée* (Jokes for musicians).

X

Xenakis, Iannis (*b* Braila, Romania, 1922; *d* Paris, 2001). Romanian-born Gr. composer (Fr. cit. 1965). Parents moved back to Gr. in 1932. Began mus. study 1934 with Kundurov. Fought in Gr. Resistance during Second World War and was condemned to death. Went to Paris 1947, studying with Honegger and Milhaud, later with Messiaen 1950–1. Worked as architect with Le Corbusier 1947–60; designed Philips pavilion for 1958 Brussels Exhibition. Est. School of Mathematical and Automated Music, Paris 1966 and at Indiana Univ. where he also taught 1967–72. Prof. of mus., Sorbonne, 1972–89. Although he used elecs., most of Xenakis's works employ traditional human forces, but embody his concept of *stochastic music. This mathematical term, as applied to mus., is a theory of probability: that the results of chance will reach a determinate end. In contrast to the *aleatory processes of *Cage and others, Xenakis worked to retain the composer's domination of his material, and calculated the events in his mus. himself or by means of a computer, e.g. speeds of glissandi, density of sonorities, etc. Xenakis converted the printout from the computer either into a score for conventional instr. or into an elec. comp. In 2 works, *Duel* and *Stratégie*, he used his 'theory of games' to introduce an aleatory element into perf., but the rules of the games are strictly pre-determined. Prin. works:

BALLETS: *Kraanerg*, orch., tape (1968–9); *Antíkhthon* (1971).

THEATRE MUSIC: *Oresteia*, bar., ch., chamber ens. (1965–6); *The Bacchae* (1992–3).

ORCH.: *Metastasis* (After-standstill), 61 players (1953–4); *Pithoprakta*, 50 players (1955–6); *Achorripsis*, 21 players (1956–7); *ST/10*, 10 players (1956–62); *Atrées*, 10 instr. (1958–62); *Analogiques A and B*, str., tape (1959); *Duel*, 2 orch. (1959); *Syrmos*, 18 str. (1959); *ST/48*, 48 instr. (1959–62); *Stratégie*, 2 orch. and 2 cond. (1959–62); *Akrata*, 16 wind instr. (1964–5); *Terrêtektorh*, orch. deployed among audience (1966); *Polytope de Montréal*, 4 small orch. (1967); *Nomos gamma*, orch. deployed among audience (1967–8); *Synaphaï*, pf., orch. (1969); *Aroura*, str. (1971); *Eridanos*, 68 players (1973); *Erikhthon*, pf., orch. (1974); *Noomena* (1975); *Empreintes* (1975); *Ionchaies* (1977); *Pour les Baleines*, str. (1982); *Palimpsest*, pf., ens. (1982); *Shaar* (1983); *Lichens* (1983); *Alax* (1985); *Horos* (1986); *Keqrops*, pf., orch. (1986); *Tracées* (1987); *Ata* (1987); *Tuorakemsu* (1990); *Kyania* (1990); *Krinoïdi* (1991); *Roáï* (1991).

TAPE: *Diamorphoses*, 2-track (1957–8); *Conret PH*, 2-track (1958); *Analogique B*, 2-track (1958–9); *Orient-Occident*, 2-track (1960); *The Thessaloníki World Fair*, 1-track (1961); *Bohor*, 4-track (1962); *Hibiki-hanama*, 12-track (1969–70); *Persepolis*, 8-track (1971); *Polytope de Cluny*, 8-track, lighting (1972); *Polytope II*, tape, lighting (1974); *Bohor II*, 4-track (1975);

Diatope, 4 or 8-track (1977); *Mycènes Alpha*, 2-track (1978); *Pour la paix*, vers. for 4-track (1981); *Taurtriphanie*, 2-track (1987); *Voyage absolu des Unari vers Andromède*, 2-track (1989); *Gendy3*, 2-track (1991).

CHAMBER & ENS.: *ST/4*, str. qt. (1956–62); *ST/10*, cl., bcl., 2 hn., hp., perc., str. qt. (1956–62); *Morsima-Amorsima*, pf., vn., vc., db. (1956–62); *Amorsima-Morsima*, cl., bcl., 2 hn., hp., tpt., tb., 2 perc., vn., vc. (1962); *Eonta*, 2 tpt., 3 tb., pf. (1963–4); *Anaktoria*, cl., bn., hn., str. qt., db. (1969); *Persephassa*, 6 perc. (1969); *Aroura*, 12 str. (1971); *Linaia-Agon*, hn., tb., tuba (1972); *N'shima*, 2 mez., 2 hn., 2 tb., vc. (1975); *Phlegra*, 11 instr. (1975); *Epeï*, ca., cl., tpt., 2 tb., db. (1976); *Retours-Windungen*, 12 vc. (1976); *Akanthos*, sop., 8 players (1977); *Pleiades*, 6 perc. (1978); *Ikhoor*, str. trio (1978); *Aïs*, bar., perc., orch. (1979); *Khal Perr*, 5 hn., perc. (1983); *Tetras*, str. qt. (1983); *Thalleïn*, 14 players (1984); *Jalons*, 15 players (1986); *À l'Île de Gorée*, amp. hpd., 12 players (1986); *Akea*, pf. qt. (1986); *XAS*, sax. qt. (1987); *Waarg*, 13 players (1988); *Échange*, bcl., 13 players (1989); *Okho*, 3 players (1989); *Epicycle*, vc., 12 players (1989); *Dox-Orkh*, vn., 89 players (1991); *Troorkh*, tb., 89 players (1991); *Ergma*, str. qt. (1994); *Paille in the Wind* (1994).

SOLO & DUO INSTR(S).: *Nomos Alpha*, vc. (1966); *Charisma*, cl., vc. (1971); *Mikka*, vn. (1971); *Psappha*, perc. (1975); *Theraps*, db. (1975–6); *Mikka "S"*, vn. (1976); *Dmaathen*, ob., perc. (1976); *Kottos*, vc. (1977); *Dikhthas*, vn., pf. (1979); *Embellie*, va. (1981); *Keren*, tb. (1986); *Rebonds*, perc. (1988).

CHORAL: *Polla ta dhina*, children's vv., wind, perc. (1962); *Hiketides*, 50 women's vv., 10 instr. or orch. (1964); *Oresteia*, ch., ens. (1965–6); *Medea*, male vv., orch. (1967); *Nuits*, unacc. (1967–8); *Cendrées*, ch., orch. (1973–4); *À Hélène*, mez., women's vv., 2 cl. (1977); *Akanthos*, sop., ens. (1977); *À Colone*, male (or female) vv., ens. (1977); *Anemoessa*, ch., ens. (1979); *Nekuïa*, ch., orch. (1981); *Serment-Orkos*, unacc. (1981); *Pour la Paix*, tape, unacc. ch., 4 vers. (1981); *Chant des Soleils*, ch., children's ch., ens. (1983); *Idmen A*, ch., 4 perc. (1985); *Idmen B*, ch., 6 perc. (1985); *Knephas*, unacc. (1990).

KEYBOARD: *Herma*, pf. (1960–1); *Evryali*, pf. (1973); *Gmeeoorh*, org. (1974); *Khoaï*, hpd. (1976); *Komboï*, hpd., perc. (1981); *Mists*, pf. (1981); *Naama*, hpd. (1984); *A r. (Hommage à Ravel)*, pf. (1987); *Oophaa*, hpd., perc. (1989).

xylophone (Gr.). Wood sound. (1) Perc. instr. consisting of graduated tuned wooden bars, arr. as on pf. kbd., and played by being struck with small hard or soft hammers held in the hands. Compass from middle C upwards for 4 octaves. Orig. found in Africa and in Javanese orch. in 14th cent. First mentioned in Eur. in 1511 as 'wooden clatter', later being known as straw-fiddle (*Strohfiedel*) because the bars lay on straw. First used in orch. 1874, by Saint-Saëns in *Danse* *macabre*, its sound being particularly apt for representation of rattling skeletons. Since then regular feature of perc. section, most 20th-cent. composers making use of it, e.g. Mahler in 6th Sym., Puccini in *Madama Butterfly*, Strauss in *Salome*, Walton in *Belshazzar's Feast*, Stravinsky, Vaughan Williams, etc.

(2) Perc. organ stop of 8′ pitch, played electrically to duplicate sound of xylophone.

xylorimba. Perc. instr.—combination of xylophone and *marimba—with compass of about 5 octaves. Used in scores by Berg, Stravinsky, Messiaen, Dallapiccola, and Gerhard.

Y

Yakar, Rachel (*b* Lyons, 1938). Fr. soprano. Début Strasbourg 1963. Sang with Deutsche Oper am Rhein, Düsseldorf, for over 20 years from 1964. Débuts: Bayreuth 1976; Glyndebourne 1977; Salzburg Fest. 1978; CG 1978. Sang Angel in concert perf. of *Saint François d'Assise*, Salzburg 1985. Specialist also in baroque roles. Teacher at Paris Conservatoire until 1997.

Yamaha. Brand name of mus. instrs. manufactured by firm of Nippon Gakki, Hamamatsu, Japan, founded 1887 by Torakusu Yamaha (1851–1916). Makes pfs., elec. orgs., harmoniums, brass and ww. instrs. Yamaha Mus. Sch. founded in Tokyo 1954, Yamaha Foundation for Mus. Education 1966.

Yamash'ta, Stomu [Yamashita, Tsutomu] (*b* Kyoto, 1947). Japanese percussionist and composer. Percussionist in Kyoto PO and Osaka PO 1961. Début as soloist in Milhaud conc. with Osaka PO 1963. Played with jazz quintet in USA. Aldeburgh Fest. 1970 when he scored success in Henze's *El Cimarrón*. Remarkable virtuoso perf. Founder-member of Red Buddha Th. 1970 Composer of scores for nearly 100 Japanese films and of works for own perf.

Yaniewicz, Feliks. See *Janiewicz, Feliks*.

Yankee Doodle. Popular Amer. tune with confused history of both words and mus., the 2 words of the title being still unexplained as to orig. Earliest printed version of tune, under this title, in Vol. I of Aird's *Selection of Scotch, English, Irish, and Foreign Airs for the Fife, Violin, or German Flute* (Glasgow, *c*.1775). Many sets of humorous or nonsense words fitted to it since. Anton Rubinstein wrote pf. variations on tune, and Vieuxtemps's *Caprice burlesque*, vn. and pf., is based on it. It is used, altered, in theme in finale of Dvořák's *New World* Sym.

Yansons, Arvid (*b* Liepaya, Latvia, 1914; *d* Manchester, 1984). Latvian conductor. Début as cond., Riga 1944 in ballet. Assoc. cond., Leningrad PO from 1948, became joint prin. cond. with Mravinsky. Chief guest cond., Hallé Orch. from 1965. See *Jansons, Mariss*.

Yan Tan Tethera. 'Mechanical pastoral' by Birtwistle to lib. by T. Harrison after a northern folktale. Comp. 1983–4. Prod. London 1986.

Yardumian, Richard (*b* Philadelphia, 1917; *d* Bryn Athyn, Pa., 1985). Amer. composer, of Armenian parentage. Works incl. syms., vn. conc., pf. conc., str. qt., *Armenian Suite, Cantus animus et Cordis* for str., *Chorale Prelude*, etc.

Yeomen of the Guard, The, or The Merryman and his Maid. Operetta by Sullivan to lib. by Gilbert. Comp. 1888. Prod. London and NY 1888.

Yepes, Narciso (*b* Lorca, 1927; *d* Lorca, 1997). Sp. guitarist. Début Madrid 1947. Used (from 1961) 10-str. guitar of his own creation. Specialist in Sp. mus. from 15th to 20th cents. Recorded complete lute works of Bach.

Yevgeny Onyegin (Tchaikovsky). See *Eugene Onegin*.

yodel. Eng. spelling of *jodel*. See *jodelling*.

Yolanta (Iolanta). Lyric opera in one act by Tchaikovsky to lib. by M. Tchaikovsky after V. Zotov's trans. of H. Hertz's *King René's Daughter*. Comp. 1891. F.p. St Petersburg 1892 in double-bill with ballet *The Nutcracker*. F. Amer. p. Scarborough-on-Hudson 1933; f. Brit. p. London 1968, Leeds, double bill with *The Nutcracker* (Opera North, and Adventures in Motion Pictures) 1992.

Yonge, Nicholas (*b* Lewes, Sussex; *d* London, 1619). Eng. musician, possibly a singer in choir of St Paul's Cath., London. Introduced It. madrigal into Eng. when he published *Musica transalpina* (2 vols., 1588 and 1597), coll. of It. madrigals, by Marenzio, Palestrina, Lassus, and others, in Eng. trans. 1st vol. contained 57, 2nd had 24.

Youmans, Vincent (Millie) (*b* NY, 1898; *d* Denver, 1946). Amer. composer. Worked as mus. publisher 1918. Wrote successful musical comedies from 1921, having enormous success on both sides of Atlantic with *No, No, Nanette* (1924), which incl. song 'Tea for Two'. Illness forced retirement 1933. Among his other songs are 'I want to be happy', 'Hallelujah', 'Sometimes I'm happy', 'Carioca', 'Without a Song', and 'More than you know'.

Young [Youngs], (Basil) **Alexander** (*b* London, 1920; *d* Macclesfield, 2000). Eng. tenor. Opera début with Glyndebourne co. at Edinburgh Fest. 1950 (Scaramuccio in *Ariadne auf Naxos*, 1st vers.). Wide repertory in opera, *Lieder*, and songs. Chosen by Stravinsky to sing Tom Rakewell in recording of *The Rake's Progress*, 1964 (which he had sung 1953 in f. Eng. p. (BBC studio perf.). CG 1955–70. Head of Sch. of Vocal Studies, RNCM, 1973–86. Fine singer of Handel, Ferrando. Founder and cond., Jubilate Choir, Manchester, 1977.

Young, Douglas (*b* London, 1947). Eng. composer and pianist. Début as pianist, London 1970. Wrote 2 ballets for Royal Ballet and a third for Munich Staatsoper Ballet. Has also written works for schools and amateurs. Formed his own ensemble, Dreamtiger, 1973. Influenced by Carter and Boulez. Comps. incl. ballets, *Pasiphae* (1969); *Charlotte Brontë* (1973–4); *Ludwig, Fragmente eines Rätsels* (1986); *Sinfonietta*, orch. (1968–70); *William Booth Enters Heaven (after Ives)*, orch. (1980); *The*

Hunting of the Snark, narrator, ch., pf., small orch. (1981–2); *Landscapes and Absences*, sop., fl. (1972–3); *Essay*, str. qt. (1971); *Arabesque brève*, vc. (1982); *Lament*, sitar (1984); *The Tailor of Gloucester*, opera (1989); *Cada canción*, v., pf. (1987); *Sir Edward at Garmisch*, vn. (1992–6); *The Excursions of M. Jannequin*, pf. (1997); *The Eternal Waterfall*, vc., pf. (1998).

Young, La Monte (*b* Bern, Idaho, 1935). Amer. composer. Founded Theatre of Eternal Music, 1962. Method of composition may be deduced from his directions for perf. of certain of his works: *Composition 1960 #2* is building a fire in front of the audience; #5 is releasing butterflies; *Composition 1961* is 'draw a straight line and follow it'. Has also 'written' *The Tortoise, his Dreams and Journeys*, a continuing perf. (since 1964) for vv., mixers, amplifiers, drones, and loudspeakers (but no tortoise). *The Well Tuned Piano* (1964), written for prepared pf., can be considered his most important work. He has perf. it on many occasions, the perf. lasting over 6 hours.

Young, Percy (Marshall) (*b* Northwich, 1912; *d* York, 2004). Eng. author, teacher, organist, and composer. Adv., Stoke-on-Trent, 1937–44; dir. of mus., Wolverhampton Coll. of Technology, 1944–66. Author of over 50 books, subjects incl. Handel, Schumann, Kodály, Elgar, Sullivan, Sir George Grove, and Vaughan Williams. Ed. various letters of Elgar. Arr. suite from Elgar's unfinished opera *The Spanish Lady* and made perf. vers. of opera (Cambridge 1994). Wrote va. conc., pf. conc., and choral works.

Young, Simone (*b* Sydney, NSW, 1961). Australian conductor. Début with Australian Opera. Cologne Opera 1987. Berlin début 1992 (Komische Oper). First woman to cond. at a Vienna opera house (*Les contes d'Hoffmann* at Volksoper 1992) and to cond. Vienna PO. Vienna State Opera début 1993; Paris début 1993; CG début 1994. Prin. cond. Bergen PO 1998–2002; mus. dir. Australian Opera 2001–3; gen. dir. Hamburg State Opera and chief cond. Hamburg PO from 2005.

Young, Victor (*b* Chicago, 1900; *d* Palm Springs, 1956). Amer. composer, conductor, and violinist. Début with Warsaw PO 1917. Returned to Chicago 1920, Amer. début (Chicago) 1921. After radio career, went to Hollywood 1935 to comp. film mus. Songs incl. *Sweet Sue*, *Love Letters*, and *Indian Summer*. Wrote score for film *Around the World in 80 Days*, 1956.

Young, William (*d* Innsbruck, 1662). Eng. composer, viol player, and flautist. Worked on Continent, in Italy and Austria. At Innsbruck his playing enchanted Queen Christina of Sweden in 1655. There in 1653 he pubd. earliest set of (21) sonatas for 3, 4, and 5 parts (for 3 vns., va., bass viol, and continuo, the Purcell type of *trio-sonata*). Returned to Eng. 1661 and became member of King's band.

Young Lord, The (Henze). See *Junge Lord, Der*.

Young Person's Guide to the Orchestra, The. Orch. work (or for speaker and orch.), Op.34, by Britten which is sometimes known (against the composer's wishes) only by its sub-title *Variations and Fugue on a Theme of Purcell*. Written for documentary film (1946), *The Instruments of the Orchestra* (commentary written by Eric *Crozier), in which narr. described the uses and characteristics of various sections of the orch., these being illustrated by Britten's variations. Theme is from Purcell's incid. mus. to the play *Abdelazer* (1695). F.p. of orch. version, Liverpool 1946.

Youth's Magic Horn, The. See *Knaben Wunderhorn, Des*.

Yradier [Iradier], **Sebastián** (*b* Sauciego, Álava, 1809; *d* Vitoria, 1865). Sp. composer and singing teacher. Taught at Madrid Cons. then went to Paris where he was singing teacher to Empress Eugénie. Also collected Creole songs in Cuba. Wrote many popular songs, which were sung by Viardot, Patti, and other celebrities, best known being *La paloma* (The Dove). His *El Arreglito: chanson havanaise* was adapted by Bizet as the Habanera in Act 1 of *Carmen* (1875) under mistaken impression it was a folk-song.

Ysaÿe, Eugène(-Auguste) (*b* Liège, 1858; *d* Brussels, 1931). Belg. violinist, conductor, and composer. Leader of Bilse's orch., Berlin, 1879–81. Toured Russia and Scandinavia with Anton Rubinstein 1882. Lived in Paris 1883–6, forming close ties with Franck, Chausson, Fauré, Saint-Saëns, and Debussy. Prof. of vn., Brussels Cons., 1886–98. Formed Ysaÿe Qt. 1886, giving f.p. of Debussy's str. qt. 1893. Founded and cond. Ysaÿe concerts, Brussels. London début 1889. Amer. début 1894. Played many new works, incl. Franck vn. sonata (ded. to him) and Elgar conc. (but never in Eng.). Cond. Cincinnati SO 1918–22. One of most remarkable virtuosi of his day, with powerful tone. Wrote 6 vn. concs., several solo vn. sonatas, *Variations on a Theme of Paganini*, and other pieces. Also wrote opera in Walloon dialect.

Ysaÿe, Théophile (*b* Verviers, 1865; *d* Nice, 1918). Belg. pianist and composer, brother of Eugène *Ysaÿe. Prof. of pf., Geneva Acad. of Music 1889–1900. Wrote sym., *Fantasy on Walloon Songs* for orch., 2 pf. conc., *Requiem*, etc.

Yu, Julian (Jing-Jun) (*b* Beijing, 1957). Chinese composer. Settled in Australia 1985. At Tanglewood 1988 studied with Henze and Knussen. Works incl. puppet opera *The White Snake* (1990); *Reclaimed Prefu II* (1991); *Wu-Yu*, orch. (1987); *Great Ornamental Fuga Canonica*, orch. (1988); *Medium Ornamental Fuga Canonica*, wind quintet (1988); *Scintillation II*, pf., 2 vib., glock. (1987); *3 Haiku*, mez., vc. (1987); *Impromptu*, pf. (1982); *Scintillation I*, pf. (1987); *4 Haiku*, sop., pf. (1988–92); *Philopentatonia*, chamber orch. (1994); *Pentatonicophilia*, fl., db., perc., hp., vn., va., vc. (1995); *mar. conc.* (1996); *Lyrical Conc.*, fl., chamber orch. (1997); *Not a Stream, but an Ocean*, orch. (2000).

Yun, Isang (*b* Tongyong, S. Korea, 1917; *d* Berlin, 1995). Korean-born composer (Ger. cit. 1971). Settled in Berlin 1963–7. Abducted from Berlin 1967 by S. Korean agents and taken with his wife to Seoul to be tried for sedition. He was sentenced to life imprisonment, but international outcry obtained his release after 2 years. Taught in Hanover 1969–70 and at Berlin Hochschule für Musik 1970–85 (prof. from 1973). Scrapped early works up to 1959 when he began to use Darmstadt total serial procedures into which he injected sounds and rhythms of Korean mus. Works incl. operas *The Dream of Liu-Tung* (1965), *Butterfly Widow* (1967), *Geisterliebe* (1969–70), and *Sim Tjong* (1972); syms.: *I* (1982–3), *II* (1984), *III* (1985), *IV* (*Singing in the dark*) (1986), *V*, bar., orch. (1987); *Colloides sonores*, str. orch.; *Loyang*, chamber ens.; *Fluctuations*, orch. (1964); vc. conc. (1976); fl. conc. (1977); conc., ob., hp., small orch. (1977); cl. conc. (1981); conc., ob., vc., str. (1987); 4 str. qts.; fl. quintet (1985); fl. qt. (1989); octet; and many pf. pieces.

Yurisich, Gregory (*b* Mount Lawley, W. Australia, 1951). Australian baritone. Début Sydney (Australian Opera) 1974 (Paolo in *Simon Boccanegra*). Member of Australian Opera 1974–87. Prin. bar. Frankfurt Opera 1988–90. Débuts: NY (Lincoln Centre Trust) 1985; ENO 1988; CG 1990; Glyndebourne 1991. Created Alcibiades in Oliver's *Timon of Athens* (ENO 1991), and Cadmus in Buller's *Bakxai* (ENO 1992).

Z

Z. Abbreviated prefix to numbers in the Zimmerman catalogue of Henry *Purcell's works.

Zabaleta, Nicanor (*b* San Sebastián, 1907; *d* San Juan, Puerto Rico, 1993). Sp. harpist. Début Paris 1925, NY 1934. Soloist with world's orchs. Revived much forgotten hp. mus. and commissioned works from Krenek, Milhaud, Tailleferre, Villa-Lobos, Ginastera, and Tal. *Rodrigo arr. his *Concierto de Aranjuez*, for hp. for Zabaleta.

Zaccaria, Nicola (*b* Piraeus, 1923). Gr. bass. Début Athens 1949 (Raimondo in *Lucia di Lammermoor*). Opera appearances at Milan, Genoa, and many fests. La Scala 1953–74; CG début 1957 (Oroveso in *Norma* with Callas); Salzburg Fest. 1957; Sang King Mark (*Tristan und Isolde*) at Dallas, 1976.

Zacharewitsch, Michael (*b* Ostrov, 1879; *d* London, 1953). Russ.-born violinist (Brit. cit. 1915). Début Odessa 1894 in Tchaikovsky conc., cond. by composer. Later studied in Prague with Ševčík and with Ysaÿe in Brussels. Eng. début 1903; settled in Eng. 1909. Wrote treatise on violin playing, 1934. Wrote vn. conc. *Dunkirk 1940* (1945).

Zacharias, Christian (*b* Tamshedpur, India, 1950). Ger. pianist and conductor. Broadcasting Union Ravel prize 1975. London début 1976, Amer. début 1979 (Boston SO), Salzburg Fest. 1981. Cond. début 1992 (Orch. de la Suisse Romande); Amer. cond. début 2000 (Los Angeles PO). Art. dir. and prin. cond. Lausanne CO from 2000. Opera début Geneva 2006 (*La clemenza di Tito*).

Zacher, Gerd (*b* Meppen, 1929). Ger. composer and organist. Cantor and org. in Santiago, Chile, 1954–7; org. and mus. dir., Luther Church, Hamburg, 1957–70; prof. Inst. of Church Music, Essen, from 1970. Has given f.ps. of org. works by Kagel, Ligeti, and Yun. Works incl. *The Prayers of Jonah in the Fish's Belly*, sop., org. (1963); *Text*, org.; *St Luke Passion*, ch.; *Ré*, org.; etc.

Zadek, Hilde (*b* Bromberg, Austria, 1917). Ger. soprano. Left Ger. for Palestine 1934 and worked as nurse in Jerusalem. Début Vienna Opera 1947 (Aida). Salzburg Fest. début 1948; Salzburg 1949; Brit. début 1950 (Glyndebourne co. at Edinburgh Fest.) Sang at NY Met and in S. Francisco. Teacher at Vienna Acad. from 1967.

Zadok the Priest. No.1 of 4 anthems comp. Handel for coronation of George II, 1727, and perf. at every Eng. coronation since then. Henry *Lawes had set the same text for the coronation of Charles II, 1660.

Zádor, Jenö (Eugene) (*b* Bátaszék, 1894; *d* Hollywood, 1977). Hung.-born composer (Amer. cit.). Taught at New Vienna Cons. 1922–8. Settled in USA 1939, working in Hollywood as orch. of over 120 film scores. Composed 12 operas (incl. *The Island of the Dead*, 1925, and *Christopher Columbus*, 1939), ballet *The Machine-Man* (1934), orch. works, wind quintet, and songs.

Zagrosek, Lothar (*b* Waging, 1942). Ger. conductor. Cond. opera in Salzburg, Kiel, and Darmstadt 1967–73. Salzburg Fest. début 1973 (Mozarteum Orch.). Specialist in contemp. mus. and worked with London Sinfonietta from 1978. Chief cond. Austrian Radio SO 1982–5, mus. dir. Paris Opéra 1986–8. Brit. opera début GTO 1984; Glyndebourne début 1987; ENO 1989. Cond. concert perf. of Messiaen's *Saint François d'Assise*, Salzburg 1985. Gen. mus. dir., Leipzig City Opera 1990–2. Prin. cond. Württemberg Opera, Stuttgart, 1997–2006; Berlin SO from 2006.

Zaide. Unfinished opera in 2 acts (K344, 1779–80) by Mozart to lib. in Ger. by A. Schachtner after F. J. Sebastiani's *Das Serail*. Prod. in 1838 vers. with extra mus. by J. A. André, Frankfurt 1866, London 1953, Tanglewood 1955. Mozart completed only 15 numbers and did not give the work a title. Plot is similar to *Die Entführung aus dem Serail* and lib. was probably based on Friebert's operetta *Das Serail*.

zamba (Sp.). Argentinian scarf dance in 6/8 time, with guitar introduction to vocal section. Originated in Peru.

Zambello, Francesca (*b* NY, 1956). Amer. opera director. Collab. with Ponnelle on his prod. of Rossini's *L'occasione fa il ladro*, Pesaro 1987. Ass. dir. Chicago Lyric Opera 1981–2, S. Francisco Opera 1983–4. Co-art. dir. Skylight Opera Th., Milwaukee, 1985–90. Works in many Eur. and Amer. opera houses. At Wexford Fest. prod. Dvořák's *The Devil and Kate* (1988), Marschner's *Der Templer und die Jüdin* (1989), Donizetti's *L'assedio di Calais* (1991), and Tchaikovsky's *Cherevichki* (1993). NY Met début 1992. First Amer. to direct at Bolshoy, Moscow, 1991 (*Turandot*). Prod. f.p. Glass's *Orphié* (NY 1993), Amer. première of Weir's *Blond Eckbert* (Santa Fe 1994), world première of Picker's *Thérèse Raquin* (Dallas 2001) and his *An American Tragedy* (NY Met 2005).

zambra (Sp.). Moorish dance, perf. with clasped hands to woodwind mus.

Zampa, ou la fiancée de marbre (Zampa, or the Marble Bride). Opera in 3 acts by *Hérold to lib. by Mélesville (A. H. J. Duveyrier). Comp. 1831. Prod. Paris 1831, London and Boston, Mass., 1833.

Zampieri, Mara (*b* Padua, 1941). It. soprano. Début Pavia 1972 (Nedda in *Pagliacci*). Débuts: La Scala 1978; Brit. (Newcastle upon Tyne) 1983; CG 1984. Sang Salome in Vienna 1991.

Zancanaro, Giorgio (*b* Verona, 1939). It. baritone. Won Vociu Verdiane comp. 1970. Début Milan 1970 (Riccardo in *I Puritani*). Salzburg Fest. début 1971; NY Met début 1982; CG 1985.

Zander, Benjamin (*b* Gerrards Cross, 1939). Eng.-born conductor and cellist. Began to comp. at age of 9. Lessons from Britten and Imogen Holst. At 10 took up cello and at 12 was youngest member of Nat. Youth Orch. of Great Britain. Pupil of Herbert Withers, then of Cassadó in Florence 1954–9. Completed cello studies at Cologne Cons. In 1965 went to USA for graduate work at Brandeis and Harvard Univs. On faculty of New England Cons. from 1967. Cond. Boston PO from 1979, specializing in Mahler and Romantics. Regular guest cond. of Philharmonia Orch., with whom he has recorded Mahler syms.

Zandonai, Riccardo (*b* Sacco di Rovereto, Trentino, 1883; *d* Pesaro, 1944). It. composer. Dir., Pesaro Cons. 1940–3. Wrote operas in *verismo* style successful at time. Works incl.:

OPERAS: *Il grillo del Focolare* (1905–8); *Conchita* (1909–10); *Melenis* (1911); **Francesca da Rimini* (1912–13); *La via della finestra* (1919, rev. in 2 acts 1923); *Giulietta e Romeo* (1920–1); *I Cavalieri di Ekebu* (1923–4); *Giuliano* (1926–7); *Una partita* (1930); *La farsa amorosa* (1931–2); *Il bacio* (1940–4).

ORCH.: *Il ritorno di Ulisse*, sym.-poem; vn. conc.; *Serenata medievale*.

CHORAL: *Ave Maria*; *Alla patria*.

Zanelli [Morales], **Renato** (*b* Valparaiso, 1892; *d* Santiago, 1935). Chilean baritone, later tenor. Début Santiago 1916 (Valentin in *Faust*). NY Met 1919–20. In It., 1923, was adv. to change to ten. and made début at Naples 1924 (Raoul in *Les Huguenots*). CG début 1928. Later sang Tristan and Siegmund in It. Regarded as best Otello since **Tamagno*.

Zapateado (Sp.). Sp. solo dance, in triple time, in which rhythm is marked by stamping of the heels, frequently in syncopation.

Zareska, Eugenia (*b* Rava Ruska, nr. Lwów, 1922; *d* Paris, 1979). Ukrainian-born mezzo-soprano (Brit. cit.). Début Milan 1941 (Dorabella in *Così fan tutte*). London début 1947; CG 1948; Glyndebourne 1948. Fine *Lieder* singer. Taught singing in Paris.

Zarewitsch, Der ('The Tsarevich'). Operetta in 3 acts by Lehár to lib. by H. Reichart and B. Jenbach after the play by G. Zapolska. Comp. 1926. Prod. Berlin 1927, Vienna 1928.

Zar und Zimmermann (Tsar and Carpenter). Opera in 3 acts by **Lortzing to his own lib. after play *Le bourgeois de Sardam* by Mélesville (A. H. J. Duveyrier), Merle, and De Boirie (1818). Prod. Leipzig 1837, NY 1851, London 1871 (as *Peter the Shipwright*).

zarzuela (Sp. from *zarza*, 'bramble bush'). Idiomatic Sp. form of opera in which mus. is intermingled with spoken dialogue. Name comes from entertainments perf. in 17th cent. at royal palace of La Zarzuela, near Madrid, for Philip IV and court. First known composer of zarzuelas was Juan Hidalgo, *c.*1644. In 18th cent., popularity of the form was challenged by **tonadillas*, which were racier and more satirical. Despite brief revival, the zarzuela languished until nat. movement of 19th cent. when desire to create a Sp. nat. opera led to comp. of numerous zarzuelas by such composers as Barbieri, Arieta, Bretón, and Vives. Some were in 3 acts, with serious subjects. In the 20th cent., Alonso and Tórroba have written large-scale zarzuelas, and the form, always flexible, has been expanded to embrace features from operetta and jazz.

Zaslaw, Neal (Alexander) (*b* NY, 1939). Amer. musicologist. Taught at City Coll. of City Univ. of NY 1968–70. Prof. of mus. Cornell Univ. from 1970. Ed.-in-chief *Current Musicology* 1967–70. Wrote biography of Edward MacDowell (1964) and *Mozart's Symphonies: Context, Performance, Practice, Reception* (1989); co-ed. (with W. Cowdery) *The Compleat Mozart* (1990). Wrote *Mozart's Piano Concertos* (1996) and *The New Köchel* (2000).

Zauberflöte. Metal organ stop, 8′ pitch, with stopped pipes and hole pierced in such a place that note heard is 3rd harmonic, not the 2nd (octave).

Zauberflöte, Die (The Magic Flute). Opera in 2 acts by Mozart (K620) to lib. by E. Schikaneder after the story *Lulu* by Liebeskind in Wieland's collection of Oriental fairy-tales *Dschinnistan* (1786). Comp. 1790–1. Prod. Vienna 1791, London 1811, NY 1833.

Zauberharfe, Die (The Magic Harp). Melodrama by G. E. Hoffmann for which Schubert comp. ov. and other items in 1820 (D644). Prod. Vienna 1820. Ov. now known as **Rosamunde*.

Zazà. Opera in 4 acts by Leoncavallo to his lib. after play by C. Simon and P. Berton (1898). Comp. 1899–1900. Prod. Milan (cond. Toscanini) 1900, S. Francisco 1903, London 1909, Wexford 1990.

Zecchi, Carlo (*b* Rome, 1903; *d* Salzburg, 1984). It. pianist and conductor. Début as pianist, Berlin 1920. Career as solo pianist ended 1939 when he formed duo with cellist Mainardi (Salzburg Fest. début as duo, 1955). From 1938 studied cond. and launched new career 1947. Taught in Rome and Salzburg. Ed. D. Scarlatti kbd. works.

Zedda, Alberto (*b* Milan, 1928). It. conductor and musicologist. Début Milan 1956. Taught at Cincinnati Coll. of Mus. 1957–9. Cond. at Deutsche Oper, Berlin, 1961–3, then NY City Opera. Prod. critical edn. of Rossini's *Il barbiere di Siviglia* (Milan 1969) which he cond. at CG 1975. Co-ed. with Philip Gossett of complete edn. of Rossini's works.

Zednik, Heinz (*b* Vienna, 1940). Austrian tenor. Début Graz 1963 (Trabuco in *La forza del destino*). Has appeared in Paris, Montreal, Moscow, and

Munich. Débuts: Vienna Opera 1965; Bayreuth 1970 (and sang Loge and Mime in centenary *Ring* 1976); NY 1981; Salzburg Fest. 1981. Created Regisseur in *Un re in ascolto* (Salzburg 1984) and Hadank in Penderecki's *Die schwarze Maske* (Salzburg 1986). One of most admired of contemp. character tenors.

Zeffirelli [Corsi], **Franco** (*b* Florence, 1923). It. producer and designer. Began as actor, but became ass. to *Visconti. Turned to opera 1948. Prod., *La Cenerentola*, La Scala 1953. CG début 1959 (*Lucia di Lammermoor*). Other CG prods. incl. *Falstaff* (1961), *Don Giovanni* and *Alcina* (1962), and *Tosca* (1964). Glyndebourne 1961 (*L'elisir d'amore*). Amer. début, Dallas 1958 (*La traviata* for *Callas). NY Met début 1964 (*Falstaff*). Prod. and designed Barber's *Antony and Cleopatra* (1966), first opera at new Met. Prods. notable for extravagant Romantic realism. Made films of *La traviata* (1983) and *Otello* (1986), both operas being cut. Hon. KBE 2004.

Zeitlin, Zvi (*b* Dubrovna, USSR, 1923). Russ.-born Amer. violinist. Début with Palestine SO 1940. Amer. début NY 1951, London 1961. Authority on concs. of Nardini. Prof. of vn., Eastman Sch., from 1976. Head of vn. dept., Mus. Acad. of West, Santa Barbara, Calif., from 1973; teacher at RNCM from 1992.

Zeitmass (Ger.). Time-measure, i.e. tempo. *Zeitmesser*, metronome. Stockhausen comp. *Zeitmasze* for 5 wind instr., 1955–6.

Zell, F. See *Wälzel, Camillo*.

Zeller, Carl (*b* St Peter-in-der-Au, Austria, 1842; *d* Baden, Vienna, 1898). Austrian composer. Wrote chiefly operettas incl. *Joconde* (1876), *Capitän Nicoll* (1880), *Der Vagabund* (1886), *Der Vogelhändler* (1891), *Der Obersteiger* (1894), and *Der Kellermeister* (prod. 1901 completed by J. Brandl).

Zelter, Carl Friedrich (*b* Berlin, 1758; *d* Berlin, 1832). Ger. composer, conductor, and teacher. Dir., Berlin Singakademie from 1800. Founded *Liedertafel*, Berlin, 1809, and Royal Inst. for Church Mus. 1820. Friend and teacher of Mendelssohn, allied with him in Bach revival. Wrote oratorio, operas, cantatas, and *Lieder*.

Zémire et Azor. *Comédie-ballet* in 4 acts by Grétry to lib. by J. F. Marmontel after the story *Beauty and the Beast* by J. M. Le Prince de Beaumont and after La Chaussée's play *Amour pour Amour* (1742). Prod. Fontainebleau 1771, London 1776 (revived by Beecham, Bath 1955). Other operas on this subject by Tozzi, Spohr, and García.

Zemlinsky, Alexander (von) (*b* Vienna, 1871; *d* Larchmont, NY, 1942). Austrian composer and conductor. Studied at Vienna Cons. with A. Door for pf. 1887–90, and J. Fuchs for comp. 1890–2. Joined Vienna Society of Musicians 1893, having several chamber works played, some of which pleased Brahms. Met Schoenberg 1893, and gave him lessons in counterpoint and introduced him

to Wagner's mus. Cond. amateur orch. Polyhymnia in which Schoenberg played vc. Schoenberg said that Zemlinsky was the man he had to thank 'for practically all my knowledge of technique and the problems of composition'. Zemlinsky's sister Mathilde became Schoenberg's first wife in 1901. Cond. at Carltheater, Vienna, 1900–3, Theater an der Wien 1903–4, Volksoper 1904–11 (at Court Opera 1907–8). Encouraged by Mahler, who helped to revise and conducted the opera *Es war einmal* in 1900. Gave comp. lessons to Alma Schindler, who became Mahler's wife. Arr. Mahler's 6th sym. for pf. (4 hands), pubd. 1906. Cond. of opera at Deutsches Landestheater, Prague, 1911–27, where he cond. f.ps. of 3 of Schoenberg's *6 Songs with Orchestra*, Op.8, in 1914, and the monodrama *Erwartung* in 1924, also many other important new works. Pres. of Prague branch of *Society for Private Performance, 1921–4. Taught comp. at Ger. Acad. of Mus., Prague, from 1920. Ass. cond. to Klemperer at Kroll Opera 1927–31. Taught at Berlin Hochschule für Musik 1927–33. Fled to Vienna 1933, to USA via Prague 1938.

Zemlinsky's mus. was greatly admired by Schoenberg and it had a high reputation generally in the early years of the cent. In later years it was almost forgotten, but since *c*.1975 has enjoyed a gradual and accelerating climb back to favour. It has a flavour of Wagner–Strauss and remains determinedly tonal. Zemlinsky did not follow Schoenberg into atonality and his mus. offers much to those who enjoy Mahler. The *Lyrische Symphonie* is avowedly inspired by *Das *Lied von der Erde* and is none the worse for it, while the 2nd str. qt. owes much to early Schoenberg and repays the debt with interest. His Maeterlinck settings are very attractive and the Wilde-based opera *Der Zwerg* is a masterpiece of concentrated lyric drama. Prin. works:

OPERAS: *Sarema* (1894–6, prod. Munich 1897); *Es war einmal* (1897–9, prod. Vienna 1900); *Der Traumgörge* (1903–6, prod. Nuremberg 1980); *Kleider machen Leute* (1907–10, rev. 1922, prod. Vienna 1910, rev. vers. Prague 1922); *Eine florentinische Tragödie* (Wilde, trans. Meyerfeld) (1915–16, prod. Stuttgart 1917); *Der *Zwerg* (Klaren, after Wilde's *The Birthday of the Infanta*) (1920–1, prod. Cologne 1922); *Der Kreidekreis* (1930–2, prod. Zurich 1933); *Der König Kandaules* (1935–6, complete in short score, completed by Antony Beaumont, 1989). Also 5 unfinished operas.

BALLET: *Das gläserne Herz* (after Hofmannsthal's *Der Triumph der Zeit*) (1900–1).

INCID. MUSIC: *Cymbeline* (1914).

ORCH.: syms., No.1 in D minor (1892), No.2 in B♭ (1897); *Suite* (*c*.1894); ov., *Der Ring des Ofterdingen* (1894–5); *Die Seejungfrau* (1902–3); *Sinfonietta* (1934).

CHURCH MUS.: *Psalm 83*, ch., orch. (1900); *Psalm 23*, vv., orch. (1910); *Psalm 13*, vv., orch. (1935).

VOICE(S) & INSTR(S).: *Waldgespräch* (Eichendorff), sop., 2 hns., hp., str. (1895–6); *Der alte Garten* (Eichendorff), v., orch. (1895); *Die Riesen*

(Eichendorff), v., orch. (1895); *Orientalisches Sonett*, v., pf. (1895); *Nun schwillt der See so bang*, v., pf. (1896); *Süsse Sommernacht*, v., pf. (1896); *Frühlingsglaube* (Uhland), vv., str. (1896); *Frühlingsbegräbnis* (Heyse), sop., alto, ten., bass. ch., orch. (1896); *Lieder* (Heyse, Liliencron), 2 books, v., pf. (1894–6); *Gesänge* (Heyse, Liliencron), 2 books, v., pf. (*c.* 1896); *Walzer-Gesänge nach toskanischen Volksliedern* (Gregorovius), v., pf. (1898); *Irmelin Rose und andere Gesänge* (Dehmel, Jacobsen), v., pf. (1898); *Turmwächterlied und andere Gesänge* (Jacobsen, Liliencron), v., pf. (1898–9); *Ehetanzlied und andere Gesänge* (Bierbaum, Morgenstern), v., pf. (*c.* 1900); *Es war ein alter König* (Heine), v., pf. (1903); *Schmetterlinge* (Liliencron), v., pf. (1904); *Ansturm* (Dehmel), v., pf. (1907); *Auf See* (Dehmel), v., pf. (1907); *Jane Grey* (Ammann), v., pf. (1907); *6 Gesänge* (Maeterlinck), mez. or bar., pf. (1910–13, and with orch.); *Lyrische Symphonie* (Tagore), sop., bar., orch. (1929); *6 Lieder* (Morgenstern, Goethe), v., pf. (1934); *12 Lieder* (George, Kalidasa, Goethe), v., pf. (1937).

CHAMBER MUSIC: *Serenade* in A, vn., pf. (1892); *Suite* in A, vn., pf. (*c.* 1893); str. quintet in D minor (2 vn., 2 va., vc.) (*c.* 1895); trio for cl. or va., vc., pf. (1895); str. qts., No.1 in A (*c.* 1895, f.p. 1896), No.2 (1913–15), No.3 (1924), No.4 (*Suite*) (1936).

PIANO: *Ländliche Tänze* (1892); *Fantasien über Gedichte von Richard Dehmel* (1898).

Zenatello, Giovanni (*b* Verona, 1876; *d* NY, 1949). It. tenor, orig. baritone. Opera début Belluno 1898 (Silvio in *Pagliacci*); as ten., Naples 1899 (Canio in *Pagliacci*). La Scala 1903–7. Created role of Pinkerton in *Madama Butterfly* 1904. CG 1905–6, 1908–9, 1926; NY (Manhattan Opera) 1907; Boston Opera 1909–14; Chicago 1912–13. Famous singer of title-role in Verdi's *Otello*. Helped to launch Verona open-air opera 1913, singing Radames (*Aida*) at opening perf. and later becoming its manager. Retired 1928 and taught.

Zender, (Johannes Wolfgang) **Hans** (*b* Wiesbaden, 1936). Ger. conductor and composer. Ass. cond., Freiburg Opera 1959. Prin. cond., Bonn Opera 1964–8; gen. mus. dir. Kiel 1969–71; prin. cond. Saar Radio SO 1971–84. Salzburg Fest. début 1983. Gen. mus.-dir. Hamburg Opera 1984–7. Cond. Netherlands Radio Chamber Orch. 1987–90. Cond. at Bayreuth 1975. London début 1977. Comps. incl. opera *Stephen Climax* (1986); *Zeitströme* (Time Stream) (1974); *Cantos I–VI*, vv., instr.; *5 Haiku*, fl., str. (1982); *Don Quixote of La Mancha*, opera (1989–91); *Shir Hashirim*, oratorio, soloists., ch., orch., elec. (1992–6); *Schumann*, orch. (1997); *Chief Joseph*, mus. th. (2005); elec. works.

Zeugheer, Jakob [J. Z. Herrmann] (*b* Zurich, 1803; *d* Liverpool, 1865). Swiss-born violinist and conductor. Formed str. qt. in Munich after hearing Schuppanzigh Qt. in Vienna, 1823. Toured Europe and settled in Liverpool 1830. Cond.,

*Gentlemen's Concerts, Manchester, 1831–8, Liverpool Phil. Soc. 1843–65. Wrote 2 syms., vn. conc., str. qt., songs, etc.

Zich, Jaroslav (*b* Prague, 1912). Cz. composer, son of Otakar *Zich. Teacher in Prague. Wrote mainly chamber mus. and songs.

Zich, Otakar (*b* Králové Městec, 1879; *d* Oubénice, 1934). Cz. composer and scholar. Prof. at Prague Univ. from 1924. Expert on Slavonic folk-song. Wrote operas and choral ballads. Author of books on Berlioz, Smetana, aesthetics, the dance, and Cz. folk-songs.

Zichy, Géza (Count Vazöny-Keö) (*b* Sztára, Hung., 1849; *d* Budapest, 1924). Hung. pianist, composer, opera intendant, and lawyer. Lost right arm as boy but studied with Liszt and became proficient left-hand player. Pres., Hung. Nat. Acad. of Mus. until 1892. Intendant, Budapest Nat. Opera 1891–4, dir. Nat. Cons. of Mus. 1895–1918. One of his first acts at Budapest Opera 1891 was to dismiss Mahler, who retaliated some years later by successfully defying royal wish for a Zichy opera to be staged in Vienna. Wrote 5 operas (incl. *Rákóczy* trilogy), pf. conc., pf. studies for left hand, and songs.

Žídek, Ivo (*b* Kravaře, 1926; *d* Prague, 2003). Cz. tenor. Début Ostrava 1945 (Werther). Joined Prague Nat. Th. 1948, specializing in Janáček roles. Débuts: Vienna Opera 1957; NY 1966; Brit. (Edinburgh Fest.) 1964 (with Prague co.); Wexford Fest. 1972. Intendant, Prague Nat. Opera 1989–91.

Ziegler, Delores (*b* Atlanta, Ga., 1951). Amer. mezzo-soprano. Concert career, then stage début Oxfield, Tenn., 1978 (Flora in *La traviata*). Took part in Santa Fe apprentice scheme 1978–9. St Louis 1979 (Maddalena in *Rigoletto*). Débuts: Eur. début (Bonn) 1981; Cologne Opera 1982; La Scala 1984; Glyndebourne 1984; Salzburg Fest. 1985; NY Met 1990.

ziehen (Ger.). To draw out.

Ziehharmonika (Ger.). *accordion.

Ziesak, Ruth (*b* Hofheim, 1963). Ger. soprano. Début Heidelberg 1988 (Valencienne in *Die lustige Witwe*). Débuts: Düsseldorf 1989; Salzburg Fest. 1989; Berlin (Deutsche Oper) 1993; Paris (Bastille) 1993; CG 1997; Glyndebourne 2003.

Zigeunerbaron, Der (The Gipsy Baron). Operetta in 3 acts by Johann Strauss II to lib. by I. Schnitzer, altered from Jokai's libretto on his story *Saffi*. Prod. Vienna 1885, NY 1886, London (amateur) 1935, SW 1964.

Zigeunerlieder (Gipsy Songs). 11 songs by Brahms, his Op.103 (1887) for vv. and pf. Texts are verses by Hugo Conrat adapted from prose versions of Hung. folk poems by a Fräulein Witzl. 8 also pubd. as solo songs with pf. (1889).

Zilcher, Hermann (*b* Frankfurt, 1881; *d* Würzburg, 1948). Ger. composer and pianist. Toured as accompanist to singers. Prof. of pf. and comp., Munich Acad. 1908–20; dir., Würzburg Cons. 1920–44. Wrote 2 operas; 5 syms.; 3 vn. concs.; 2 pf. concs.; several song-cycles; incidental mus.; chamber works.

Zillig, Winfried (*b* Würzburg, 1905; *d* Hamburg, 1963). Ger. composer, conductor, and writer. Répétiteur Oldenburg 1928–32. Cond. at Düsseldorf 1932–7, 1946–7; chief cond. Essen Opera 1937–40. Mus. dir. Poznán Opera 1940–3. Chief cond. Hesse Radio, Frankfurt, 1947–51, where he promoted 20th cent. mus., incl. f. European p. of Schoenberg's vn. conc. Freelance cond. 1951–9. Dir. of mus., Hamburg Radio, 1959–63. His mus. is nearer to Berg than Schoenberg. Wrote 7 operas, incl. *Troilus and Cressida* (1949, rev. 1963), vn. conc., 2 str. qts., and choral mus. Completed scoring of Schoenberg's oratorio *Die Jakobsleiter* (f.p. in Zillig version, Vienna 1961), and prepared vocal score of *Moses und Aron*.

Ziloti [Siloty], **Alexander** (*b* nr. Kharkov, 1863; *d* NY, 1945). Russ. pianist and conductor. Pupil of Liszt at Weimar 1883–6. Début Moscow 1880, Leipzig 1883. Prof. of pf., Moscow Cons. 1887–90. Extensive tours, incl. Eng. and USA 1898–9. Cond., Moscow PO 1901–2; formed own orch. in St Petersburg. Left Russia 1919, settled in NY. Taught at Juilliard Sch. 1925–42. Arr. concs. by Bach and Vivaldi.

Zimbalist, Efrem (Alexandrovich) (*b* Rostov, 1889; *d* Reno, Nevada, 1985). Russ.-born violinist and violist (Amer. cit.). Début Berlin 1907 in Brahms conc. Tours of Eur. London début 1907. Amer. début, Boston 1911. Settled in USA 1911. Dir., Curtis Inst. 1941–68, having taught there from 1928. Retired as player 1949, but returned to give f.p. of Menotti conc., NY 1952, and played Beethoven conc. in Philadelphia 1955. On jury Tchaikovsky comp., Moscow, 1962 and 1966. Wrote *American Rhapsody*, vn. conc., etc. From 1914 was married to the soprano Alma *Gluck, who died in 1938.

zimbalon. See *cimbalom*.

Zimbelstern (Ger.). A toy organ-stop, prevalent in N. Eur. *c*.1500–1800. It comprised a revolving star near the top of the organ-case with a set of tuned or untuned bells attached to a wind-blown driving-wheel behind the case. It was an effect often used on feast days. There is a Zimbelstern on the org. of the chapel of St John's Coll., Cambridge.

Zimerman, Krystian (*b* Zabrze, 1956). Polish pianist. Won Chopin int. comp., Warsaw 1975. Soloist with Berlin PO cond. Karajan 1976. Salzburg Fest. début 1977; Amer. début 1979 (NYPO). Gave f. Brit. p. of Lutosławski's pf. conc., London (Proms) 1989.

Zimmermann, Franklin Bershir (*b* Wauneta, Kansas, 1923). Amer. musicologist. Taught at Univ. of S. Calif. 1959–64; prof. of mus. Dartmouth Coll. 1964–7, Kentucky Univ. 1967–8,

Pennsylvania Univ. from 1968. Specialist in Eng. baroque mus., especially Purcell. Has pubd. analytical catalogue of Purcell's mus. (London 1963), *Henry Purcell, His Life and Times* (London 1967), and other works.

Zimmermann, Agnes (Marie Jacobina) (*b* Cologne, 1845; *d* London, 1925). Ger.-born pianist and composer, taken to Eng. as child. Début London 1863, Leipzig 1864. Eur. tours. Comp. pf. sonatas, vn. sonatas, and songs. Ed. pf. works of Mozart, Beethoven, and Schumann. Gave f. Eng. p. of Beethoven's transcr. of his vn. conc. for pf., 1872.

Zimmermann, Bernd Alois (*b* Bliesheim, nr. Cologne, 1918; *d* Königsdorf, 1970). Ger. composer. Studied at Bonn, Königsdorf, and Berlin Univs. while earning living as labourer and dance-band player. Studied comp. with Jarnach, and with Fortner and Leibowitz at Darmstadt. Taught history of mus. theory, Cologne Univ., 1950–2, comp. at Cologne Hochschule from 1958. Works covered whole field of mid-20th cent. comp. techniques from serialism to elecs. Opera *Die Soldaten* a 'pluralistic' work, because it uses mixed-media resources and combines conventional orch. with elecs. Made much use of quotations, referring to this method as 'collage'. Prin. works:

OPERAS: *Die *Soldaten* (The Soldiers) (1958–60, rev. 1963–4); *Funkoper* (radio) (1952).

BALLETS: *Alagoana* (1950–5); *Kontraste* (1953); *Perspektiven* (1955–6); *Présence* (1961); *Musique pour les soupers du Roi Ubu* (1962–6).

ORCH.: sym. in 1 movement (1947, rev. 1953); conc. for orch. (1948); conc. for str. (1948); *Symphonic Variations and Fugue on In dulci jubilo* (1940); vn. conc. (1950); ob. conc. (1952); *Canto di Speranza* (1952, rev. 1957); *Contrasts* (1953); tpt. conc. (1954); *Impromptu* (1958); *Dialogues*, 2 pf., orch. (1960, rev. 1965); vc. conc. (1965–6); *Photoptosis* (1968); *Stille und Umkehr* (1970).

CHORAL: *Lob der Torheit*, burlesque cantata (1948); *Die Soldaten*, vocal sym. from opera, 6 solo vv., orch. (1959); *Requiem for a young poet*, speaking and singing ch., elecs., orch. (1967–9).

CHAMBER MUSIC: str. trio (1944); vn. sonata (1950); solo vn. sonata (1951); solo va. sonata (1955); solo vc. sonata (1960); *Tempus loquendi*, 3 fl. (1963).

PIANO: *Extemporale* (1939–46); *Capriccio* (1946); *Configurations* (1956); *Monologue*, 2 pf. (1964).

Zimmermann, Frank Peter (*b* Duisburg, 1965). Ger. violinist. Public début with Duisburg SO 1975 (Mozart conc. K216). Amer. début 1984 (Pittsburgh SO). Salzburg Fest. début 1986.

Zimmermann, Louis (*b* Groningen, 1873; *d* Amsterdam, 1954). Dutch violinist and composer. Member, Concertgebouw Orch., 1899–1904. Taught vn. at RAM 1904–11. Leader, Concertgebouw Orch. from 1911. Soloist in modern concs. Wrote vn. conc., chamber mus., and cadenzas for Beethoven, Brahms, and Mozart concs.

Zimmermann, Udo (*b* Dresden, 1943). Ger. composer and conductor. Three times explorer of E. Germany's Mendelssohn schol. Prod. at Dresden Opera 1970. Prof. of comp., Dresden Hochschule für Mus., 1978; prof. of experimental mus. th., Dresden, 1982. Intendant Leipzig State Opera 1990–2001; Deutsche Oper, Berlin, 2001–3. Works incl. 5 operas; timpani conc. (1965); *Dramatic Impression of the Death of J. F. Kennedy*, vc., orch. (1963); *Sinfonia come un grande lamento* (1970); str. qt. (1974); settings of Neruda and Rózewicz for v. and pf.; and operas *The Schuhu and the Flying Princess* (1976), *The Wondrous Shoemaker Woman* (1982), and *The White Rose* (1986).

Zingarelli, Niccolò Antonio (*b* Naples, 1752; *d* Torre del Greco, 1837). It. composer and violinist. Held court posts in Naples, then went to Milan, writing operas for La Scala from 1785. Haydn produced 2 of his operas at Eszterháza. In Paris 1790. Choirmaster Milan Cath. 1792, Loreto 1794, St Peter's, Rome, 1804–11. Dir., Naples RCM from 1813, choirmaster Naples Cath. 1816. Prolific composer, writing over 30 operas up to 1811 when he concentrated on church mus. Best-known opera *Giulietta e Romeo*, 1796, a favourite with *Malibran.

zingaro, zingara (It.). Gipsy. *alla zingarese*, in gipsy style; *zingaresca*, gipsy song.

Zinman, David (Joel) (*b* NY, 1936). Amer. conductor. Ass. to Monteux at Me. summer sch. 1961–3. Début Holland Fest. 1963. Mus. dir. Netherlands Chamber Orch. 1965–77, Rochester PO 1974–85. Chief cond., Rotterdam PO 1979–82. Mus. dir. Baltimore SO 1985–98; Tonhalle Orch. from 1995.

zither. Folk instr., descendant of medieval psaltery, prevalent in Austrian Tyrol and Bavaria. Consists of flat wooden soundbox over which are stretched 4 or 5 melody str. and up to 37 acc. str. Melody str., nearest to player, are stopped on fretted fingerboard with fingers of left hand and plucked by plectrum on right thumb. Acc. str. are plucked by fingers of either hand. Used for 'local colour' in operetta scores. Gained great popularity in Eng. after World War II when film *The Third Man* had as theme mus. a zither tune written and played by Anton Karas.

zitternd (Ger.). Trembling. Same as *tremolando.

Zivoni, Yossi (*b* Tel Aviv, 1939). Israeli violinist. Won Paganini int. comp. 1960, Queen Elisabeth int. comp., Brussels, 1963. Début Amsterdam 1964. World tours as soloist and chamber music player. Prof. of vn. RMCM, 1968–72, then teacher at RNCM from 1973. Leader Gabrieli Str. Qt. from 1995.

znamenny. Russ. liturgical chant as used from 11th to 17th cents. Name derived from *znamya* (sign or neum). Underwent many changes. System included over 90 different signs for single notes.

zögernd (Ger.). Delaying, i.e. *rallentando*.

zoppa, alla (It. *zoppo, zoppa*, lame, limping). Mus. application is in the sense of *syncopation, or with a *Scotch snap.

zortziko (zortzico). Basque folk dance in 5/4 time, like the *rueda* except that the 2nd and 4th beats are almost always dotted notes. Formed 3rd figure in *aurresku* communal dance.

zu 2 (Ger.). (1) 2 instr. to play the same part.
(2) All the instr. in question (e.g. first vns.) to divide into 2 parts.

zug (Ger.). The action of pulling; thus org. stop knob, or pf. pedal (which pulls down some mechanism). *Zugposaune*, slide tb., *Zugtrompete*, slide tpt.

Zukerman, Pinchas (*b* Tel Aviv, 1948). Israeli violinist and conductor. Leventritt Award 1967, sharing 1st prize with Kyung-Wha Chung. Début with NYPO 1969. Eng. début 1969 Brighton Fest. but he had appeared on TV and made a recording in 1968. Salzburg Fest. début 1970. World-wide reputation as soloist and as chamber mus. player with Barenboim, Perlman, etc. Superb exponent of Elgar conc. Also plays va. Began to be soloist/dir. in baroque music 1971. Debut as cond., London 1974 (New Philharmonia), later guest cond. of NYPO, Boston SO, Los Angeles PO. Mus. dir. St Paul Chamber Orch., Minn., 1980–7.

Zukofsky, Paul (*b* Brooklyn, NY, 1943). Amer. violinist, conductor, composer, and teacher. Began to play vn. age 4, and made public début at 6. Début as soloist with orch., New Haven SO 1953. First NY recital 1956. London début 1969. Specialist in 20th-cent. mus., particularly that demanding new techniques. Has given f.ps. of concs. and similar works by Sessions, Wuorinen, Cage, I. Hamilton, Babbitt, and Crumb. Dir. of chamber mus., Juilliard Sch. 1987–9.

Zumpe, Johannes (*fl.* 1735–83). Ger. employed by Shudi, London hpd. maker, who in 1761 began manufacture of *square pianos, though it is not known certainly if he invented them.

Zurich. Swiss city with long musical tradition. Main orch. is the Tonhalle, founded 1868. Its cond. have incl. Friedrich Hegar (1868–1906), Volkmar Andreae (1906–49), and Erich Schmid (1949–57) jointly with Hans Rosbaud (1950–62), Rudolf Kempe (1965–72), and Charles Dutoit (1967–71). Among smaller ensembles the Collegium Musicum was cond. by Paul *Sacher from 1941. At the opera house, *Parsifal* had its first authorized stage perf. outside Bayreuth in 1913. Operas given f. stage p. in Zurich incl. *Lulu* (1937), *Mathis der Maler* (1938), *Moses und Aron* (1957 cond. Rosbaud), *The Greek Passion* (1961), and Sutermeister's *Madame Bovary* (1967).

zurück (Ger.). Back again. *zurückgehend*, going back (i.e. to orig. tempo); *zurückhaltend*, holding back (i.e. *rallentando*).

Zweig, Stefan (*b* Vienna, 1881; *d* Petrópolis, Brazil, 1942). Austrian novelist and playwright.

Wrote lib. of *Die schweigsame Frau* for Richard Strauss and supervised libs. of *Friedenstag* and *Daphne*. Further collaboration with Strauss forbidden by Nazis because he was Jewish. Correspondence with Strauss pubd. (Frankfurt 1957, Eng. trans., Univ. of Calif., 1977). Died in suicide pact with his second wife.

Zweiunddreissigstel, Zweiunddreissigstelnote (Ger.). 32nd, 32nd note (the demisemiquaver).

Zwerg, Der (The Dwarf). Opera in 1 act by *Zemlinsky to lib. by G. C. Klaren based on Wilde's *The Birthday of the Infanta*. Comp. 1920–1. F.p. Cologne 1922 (cond. Klemperer), f. Brit. p. Edinburgh Fest. 1983 (by Hamburg Opera in double bill with Zemlinsky's *Eine florentinische Tragödie*, also based on Wilde, f.p. Stuttgart, 1917), CG (in same double-bill) 1985. In the 1983 Hamburg prod. and subsequent recording of *Der Zwerg*, a new lib. by Adolf Dresen is sung.

Zwilich, Ellen Taaffe (*b* Miami, 1939). Amer. composer. Played in American SO 1965–72. Won Pulitzer Prize with sym. 1983. Teacher at Florida State Univ. Works incl.:

BALLET: *Tanzspiel* (1987).

ORCH.: syms.: No.1 (1982), No.2 (*Cello Symphony*) (1985), No.3 (1992), No.4 (*The Gardens*), ch., orch. (1999); *Symposium* (1973); *Passages*, sop., orch. (1982); *Prologue and Variations*, str. (1983); *Celebrations* (1984); *Concerto grosso 1985* (1985); pf. conc. (1986); *Images*, 2 pf., orch. (1987); *Symbolon* (1988); tb. conc. (1988); sym. for winds (1989); fl. conc. (1990); ob. conc. (1991); vn. & vc. conc. (1991); bn. conc. (1992); hn. & str. qt. conc. (1993); *Fantasy* (1993); *Romance*, vn., orch. (1993); *Amer. Conc.*, tpt., orch. (1994); conc. for pf., vn., vc. (1995); *Jubilation* (1996); *Peanuts Gallery*, pf., orch. (1996); vn. conc. (1997); *Upbeat!* (1998); *Millennium Fantasy*, pf., orch. (2000); *Partita*, vn., str. (2000); *Openings* (2001); cl. conc. (2002); *Rituals*, 5 percs., orch. (2003).

VOCAL: *Einsame Nacht*, bar., pf. (1971); *Im Nebel*, cont., pf. (1972); *Trumpets*, sop., pf. (1974); *Emlékezet*, sop., pf. (1978); *Passages*, sop., fl., cl., vn., va., vc., pf., perc. (1981, orch. vers. 1982); *One Nation*, ch., orch., (1991).

CHAMBER MUSIC: vn. sonata (1973–4); str. qt. No.1 (1974), No.2 (1998); clarino qt. (1977); *Chamber Sym.*, fl., cl., vn., va., vc., pf. (1979); str. trio (1982); *Divertimento*, fl., cl., vn., vc. (1983); *Intrada*, fl., cl., vn., vc., pf. (1983); *Double Quartet*, str. (1984); *Chamber Conc.*, tpt., 5 players (1984); pf. trio (1987); cl. quintet (1990); *Romance*, vn., pf. (1993); *Lament for Linus*, pf. (1996); *Episodes*, vn., pf. (2003); ob. qt. (2004).

Zwillingsbrüder, Die (The Twin Brothers). Operetta (Singspiel) in 1 act by Schubert (D647, 1819) to lib. by G. von Hofmann, adapted from Fr. vaudeville *Les deux Valentins*. Comp. 1818–19. Prod. Vienna 1820, Leipzig 1938, Bethlehem, Pa., 1957.

Zwischenspiel (Ger.). Between-play. Any comp. having the character of an interlude or intermezzo, e.g. (1) Org.-playing between the stanzas of a hymn.

(2) Episodes of a fugue.

(3) Solo portions between the *tuttis* of a conc.

Zwölftonmusik (Ger.). 12-note music.

Zyklus (Cycle). Work for solo percussionist by *Stockhausen, 1959, involving random choice and improvisation, and notated in graphics, dynamics of notes being indicated by their size.

Zylis-Gara, Teresa (*b* Landvarov, 1935). Polish soprano. Début Kraków 1957 (title-role in Moniuszko's *Halka*). Sang in Dortmund and Düsseldorf 1960–70. Won Munich int. comp. 1960. Débuts: Glyndebourne 1965; CG 1968; Salzburg Fest. 1968; NY Met 1968; Vienna Opera from 1972.

Oxford Paperback Reference

The Concise Oxford Dictionary of Art & Artists
Ian Chilvers

Based on the highly praised *Oxford Dictionary of Art*, over 2,500 up-to-date entries on painting, sculpture, and the graphic arts.

'the best and most inclusive single volume available, immensely useful and very well written'

Marina Vaizey, *Sunday Times*

The Concise Oxford Dictionary of Art Terms
Michael Clarke

Written by the Director of the National Gallery of Scotland, over 1,800 entries cover periods, styles, materials, techniques, and foreign terms.

A Dictionary of Architecture
James Stevens Curl

Over 5,000 entries and 250 illustrations cover all periods of Western architectural history.

'splendid ... you can't have a more concise, entertaining, and informative guide to the words of architecture'

Architectural Review

'excellent, and amazing value for money ... by far the best thing of its kind'

Professor David Walker

OXFORD

More Art Reference from Oxford

The Grove Dictionary of Art

The 34 volumes of *The Grove Dictionary of Art* provide unrivalled coverage of the visual arts from Asia, Africa, the Americas, Europe, and the Pacific, from prehistory to the present day.

'succeeds in performing the most difficult of balancing acts, satisfying specialists while … remaining accessible to the general reader'

The Times

The Grove Dictionary of Art – Online
www.groveart.com

This immense cultural resource is now available online. Updated regularly, it includes recent developments in the art world as well as the latest art scholarship.

'a mammoth one-stop site for art-related information'

Antiques Magazine

The Oxford History of Western Art
Edited by Martin Kemp

From Classical Greece to postmodernism, *The Oxford History of Western Art* is an authoritative and stimulating overview of the development of visual culture in the West over the last 2,700 years.

'here is a work that will permanently alter the face of art history … a hugely ambitious project successfully achieved'

The Times

The Oxford Dictionary of Art
Edited by Ian Chilvers

The Oxford Dictionary of Art is an authoritative guide to the art of the western world, ranging across painting, sculpture, drawing, and the applied arts.

'the best and most inclusive single-volume available'

Marina Vaizey, *Sunday Times*

OXFORD

Oxford Paperback Reference

The Oxford Dictionary of Dance
Debra Craine and Judith Mackrell

Over 2,500 entries on everything from hip-hop to classical ballet, covering dancers, dance styles, choreographers and composers, techniques, companies, and productions.

'A must-have volume ... impressively thorough'

Margaret Reynolds, *The Times*

Who's Who in Opera
Joyce Bourne

Covering operas, operettas, roles, perfomances, and well-known personalities.

'a generally scrupulous and scholarly book'

Opera

The Concise Oxford Dictionary of Music
Michael Kennedy

The most comprehensive, authoritative, and up-to-date dictionary of music available in paperback.

'clearly the best around ... the dictionary that everyone should have'

Literary Review

OXFORD

Oxford Paperback Reference

The Concise Oxford Companion to English Literature
Margaret Drabble and Jenny Stringer

Based on the best-selling *Oxford Companion to English Literature*, this is an indispensable guide to all aspects of English literature.

Review of the parent volume
'a magisterial and monumental achievement'

Literary Review

The Concise Oxford Companion to Irish Literature
Robert Welch

From the ogam alphabet developed in the 4th century to Roddy Doyle, this is a comprehensive guide to writers, works, topics, folklore, and historical and cultural events.

Review of the parent volume
'Heroic volume ... It surpasses previous exercises of similar nature in the richness of its detail and the ecumenism of its approach.'

Times Literary Supplement

A Dictionary of Shakespeare
Stanley Wells

Compiled by one of the best-known international authorities on the playwright's works, this dictionary offers up-to-date information on all aspects of Shakespeare, both in his own time and in later ages.

OXFORD

Oxford Paperback Reference

The Concise Oxford Dictionary of Quotations
Edited by Elizabeth Knowles

Based on the highly acclaimed *Oxford Dictionary of Quotations*, this paperback edition maintains its extensive coverage of literary and historical quotations, and contains completely up-to-date material. A fascinating read and an essential reference tool.

The Oxford Dictionary of Humorous Quotations
Edited by Ned Sherrin

From the sharply witty to the downright hilarious, this sparkling collection will appeal to all senses of humour.

Quotations by Subject
Edited by Susan Ratcliffe

A collection of over 7,000 quotations, arranged thematically for easy look-up. Covers an enormous range of nearly 600 themes from 'The Internet' to 'Parliament'.

The Concise Oxford Dictionary of Phrase and Fable
Edited by Elizabeth Knowles

Provides a wealth of fascinating and informative detail for over 10,000 phrases and allusions used in English today. Find out about anything from the 'Trojan horse' to 'ground zero'.

OXFORD

Oxford Paperback Reference

The Concise Oxford Dictionary of World Religions
Edited by John Bowker

Over 8,200 entries containing unrivalled coverage of all the major world religions, past and present.

'covers a vast range of topics ... is both comprehensive and reliable'
The Times

The Oxford Dictionary of Saints
David Farmer

From the famous to the obscure, over 1,400 saints are covered in this acclaimed dictionary.

'an essential reference work'
Daily Telegraph

The Concise Oxford Dictionary of the Christian Church
E. A. Livingstone

This indispensable guide contains over 5,000 entries and provides full coverage of theology, denominations, the church calendar, and the Bible.

'opens up the whole of Christian history, now with a wider vision than ever'
Robert Runcie, former Archbishop of Canterbury

OXFORD

Oxford Paperback Reference

The Kings of Queens of Britain
John Cannon and Anne Hargreaves

A detailed, fully-illustrated history ranging from mythical and pre-conquest rulers to the present House of Windsor, featuring regional maps and genealogies.

A Dictionary of Dates
Cyril Leslie Beeching

Births and deaths of the famous, significant and unusual dates in history – this is an entertaining guide to each day of the year.

'a dipper's blissful paradise ... Every single day of the year, plus an index of birthdays and chronologies of scientific developments and world events.'

Observer

A Dictionary of British History
Edited by John Cannon

An invaluable source of information covering the history of Britain over the past two millennia. Over 3,600 entries written by more than 100 specialist contributors.

Review of the parent volume
'the range is impressive ... truly (almost) all of human life is here'

Kenneth Morgan, *Observer*

OXFORD

Oxford Paperback Reference

The Concise Oxford Dictionary of English Etymology
T. F. Hoad

A wealth of information about our language and its history, this
reference source provides over 17,000 entries on word origins.

'A model of its kind'

Daily Telegraph

A Dictionary of Euphemisms
R. W. Holder

This hugely entertaining collection draws together euphemisms from all
aspects of life: work, sexuality, age, money, and politics.

Review of the previous edition
'This ingenious collection is not only very funny but extremely
instructive too'

Iris Murdoch

The Oxford Dictionary of Slang
John Ayto

Containing over 10,000 words and phrases, this is the ideal reference for
those interested in the more quirky and unofficial words used in the
English language.

'hours of happy browsing for language lovers'

Observer

OXFORD

Oxford Paperback Reference

Concise Medical Dictionary

Over 10,000 clear entries covering all the major medical and surgical specialities make this one of our best-selling dictionaries.

'"No home should be without one" certainly applies to this splendid medical dictionary'

Journal of the Institute of Health Education

'An extraordinary bargain'

New Scientist

'Excellent layout and jargon-free style'

Nursing Times

A Dictionary of Nursing

Comprehensive coverage of the ever-expanding vocabulary of the nursing professions. Features over 10,000 entries written by medical and nursing specialists.

An A-Z of Medicinal Drugs

Over 4,000 entries cover the full range of over-the-counter and prescription medicines available today. An ideal reference source for both the patient and the medical professional.

OXFORD

Oxford Paperback Reference

A Dictionary of Psychology
Andrew M. Colman

Over 10,500 authoritative entries make up the most wide-ranging dictionary of psychology available.

'impressive ... certainly to be recommended'
Times Higher Educational Supplement

'Comprehensive, sound, readable, and up-to-date, this is probably the best single-volume dictionary of its kind.'
Library Journal

A Dictionary of Economics
John Black

Fully up-to-date and jargon-free coverage of economics. Over 2,500 terms on all aspects of economic theory and practice.

A Dictionary of Law

An ideal source of legal terminology for systems based on English law. Over 4,000 clear and concise entries.

'The entries are clearly drafted and succinctly written ... Precision for the professional is combined with a layman's enlightenment.'
Times Literary Supplement

OXFORD

Oxford Companions

'Opening such books is like sitting down with a knowledgeable friend. Not a bore or a know-all, but a genuinely well-informed chum ... So far so splendid.'

Sunday Times [of *The Oxford Companion to Shakespeare*]

For well over 60 years Oxford University Press has been publishing Companions that are of lasting value and interest, each one not only a comprehensive source of reference, but also a stimulating guide, mentor, and friend. There are between 40 and 60 Oxford Companions available at any one time, ranging from music, art, and literature to history, warfare, religion, and wine.

Titles include:

The Oxford Companion to English Literature
Edited by Margaret Drabble
'No guide could come more classic.'

Malcolm Bradbury, *The Times*

The Oxford Companion to Music
Edited by Alison Latham
'probably the best one-volume music reference book going'

Times Educational Supplement

The Oxford Companion to Western Art
Edited by Hugh Brigstocke
'more than meets the high standard set by the growing number of Oxford Companions'

Contemporary Review

The Oxford Companion to Food
Alan Davidson
'the best food reference work ever to appear in the English language'

New Statesman

The Oxford Companion to Wine
Edited by Jancis Robinson
'the greatest wine book ever published'

Washington Post

OXFORD